August 9-13, 2015
Santiago, Chile

Association for
Computing Machinery

Advancing Computing as a Science & Profession

SIGIR 2015

Proceedings of the 38th International ACM SIGIR Conference on

Research and Development in Information Retrieval

Sponsored by:

ACM SIGIR

Supported by:

Baidu, Google, Microsoft Research, Yahoo Labs, eBay, Facebook, IBM, Yandex, Universidad de Chile, Universidad de Santiago de Chile, Universidad Técnica Federico Santa María, Pontificia Universidad Católica de Chile, Yahoo Labs-Latin America, Morgan & Claypool, NOW, and Springer

Association for
Computing Machinery

Advancing Computing as a Science & Profession

The Association for Computing Machinery
2 Penn Plaza, Suite 701
New York, New York 10121-0701

ISBN: 978-1-4503-3621-5 (Digital)

ISBN: 978-1-4503-3888-2 (Print)

Additional copies may be ordered prepaid from:

ACM Order Department
PO Box 30777
New York, NY 10087-0777, USA

Phone: 1-800-342-6626 (USA and Canada)
+1-212-626-0500 (Global)
Fax: +1-212-944-1318
E-mail: acmhelp@acm.org
Hours of Operation: 8:30 am – 4:30 pm ET

Printed in the USA

SIGIR 2015 General Chair's Welcome

It is my great pleasure to welcome you to Santiago de Chile, my hometown, and to the *38th International SIGIR Conference on Research and Development in Information Retrieval*, the premier annual forum for presentations of research in information retrieval (IR) and related topics. This five-day event has a broad technical program that we hope you find interesting, useful, and insightful.

Amazingly, *SIGIR 2015* is not only held in my hometown, but also where I did my high school studies. Could I ever imagine that? No way! So in this venue where I have plenty of mixed memories, we start the conference on Sunday with nine great tutorials, thanks to Yoelle Maarek; the Doctoral Consortium, organized by J. Shane Culpepper and Brian Davidson; and we finish the day with the opening reception in the central patio.

The next three days we have the core of the conference, highlighted with the keynotes by Nick Belkin (*Salton Award)* on how we interact with information, and ChengXiang Zhai on game theory applied to IR. We also have 70 technical papers selected by the program committee chaired by Mounia Lalmas, Alistair Moffat and Berthier Ribeiro-Neto. Thanks for your great and hard work! We also have 79 short papers and 12 demos presented in a special session before the banquet on Tuesday that will be held at a nearby palace on Cerro Santa Lucía. Thanks to Maarten de Rijke, Ee-Peng Lim and Ryen White for handling the short papers and Djoerd Hiemstra and Mirella Moro for arranging the demonstrations.

On Wednesday we also have the industry track, SIRIP, organized by Hang Li and Jaime Teevan. This track combines eight invited talks and four refereed papers. This day we have been able to keep the number of parallel tracks to just three, and also have the final panel on industry impact from academia, as a single track event. Finally, on Thursday we have seven interesting workshops, thanks to the committee chaired by Fernando Diaz and Diane Kelly.

None of this would be possible without the support of the local organizers from four universities and Yahoo Labs Latin America, all in Santiago. They are Universidad Católica de Chile, Universidad de Chile, Universidad de Santiago de Chile and Universidad Técnica Federico Santa María. They are represented by the local arrangements chair, Diego Arroyuelo, the finance chair, Mauricio Marín, and the website chair, Marcelo Mendoza. Thanks to all of them!

Without financial support, this conference would have been more austere. Thanks to our supporters, Baidu (platinum); Google, Microsoft Research and Yahoo Labs (gold); eBay (silver); Facebook, IBM and Yandex (bronze); and Morgan & Claypool, Now and Springer (associated publishers); we were able to provide many student scholarships, include lunches, and upgrade the social program. Thanks to Vanessa Murdock and Sergei Vassilvitskii for their great help on this.

Finally, we hope that you share your ideas with other researchers and practitioners, enjoy the social program, and have time to visit Santiago and other interesting places in this long and amazing country that is Chile, from the Atacama Desert to the Lake District and the Patagonia glaciers, always between the Andes Mountains and the Pacific Ocean, without forgetting the navel of the world, Rapa Nui or Easter Island. Thanks for coming, without you there would be no SIGIR!

Ricardo Baeza-Yates
SIGIR 2015 General Chair
Yahoo Labs, USA

Program Chairs' Preface

Welcome to SIGIR 2015, the 38th Annual International ACM-SIGIR Conference on Research and Development in Information Retrieval, the premier conference in the area. We acknowledge all those who submitted papers to the conference and gave the Program Committee an opportunity to evaluate their work for potential inclusion in the program. Huge thanks are owed to the 66 Senior Program Committee Members, 235 Program Committee Members, and the 41 additional referees, for their dedicated work in evaluating the submissions. That pool of people spans 32 countries and of the order of 200 institutions.

The conference received 361 submissions in to the full-paper track, a 7% decrease compared to 2014. Of these, 10 papers were subsequently withdrawn by the authors after having been noted in an initial vetting process as being unready for review. A number of other submissions were revised during the same filtering pass to ensure that they were sufficiently anonymized for the review process. A total of 351 papers then went to review.

As has been customary for many years, SIGIR 2015 employed a two-tier double-blind review process. Two Senior Program Committee Members (SPCMs) and three Program Committee Members (reviewers) were assigned to each paper. Once the three reviewers had completed their evaluations, the Primary SPCM for the paper led a discussion, based on which they wrote a meta-review that synthesized the range of opinions, and gave an overall evaluation, including (if required) further commentary based on their own evaluation of the work. The Secondary SPCM assigned to each paper double-checked the reviews and discussion, and in some cases provided an additional review. The PC Chairs ranked the submitted papers by the meta-review scores assigned by the Primary SPCM and Secondary SPCM, and then by the average score of the three reviewer scores. A Program Meeting was held in San Francisco on 9–10 April, with all of the Senior Program Committee invited to attend; fourteen of them were able to participate, plus the three Program Committee Chairs. All papers that could not be categorized as "clear accepts" or "clear rejects" based on the three first-tier reviews and the Primary SPCM's meta-review were discussed at the meeting, and in some cases re-read; and for many of them, further reviews or commentaries were added to the package of information that was eventually returned to authors. Reviews and acceptance notifications were emailed to all authors on April 16, four days ahead of schedule.

This process led to the selection of 70 papers for oral presentation at the conference, a 20% acceptance ratio, and consistent with the last several years.

A few statistics about the authorship of the 351 papers that were refereed: there were 1,188 author-paper combinations (an average of 3.4 authors per submitted paper) and a total of 944 distinct authors that submitted to the conference (an average of 1.3 submitted papers per author). One paper had nine coauthors, and two others had eight; only 29 of the submitted papers had a single author. There were 14 people who were each authors of five or more submissions, and between them those 14 people accounted for 85 (7%) of the author-paper combinations. Across the accepted papers, there were 257 author-paper combinations, and 222 distinct authors who have had papers accepted for presentation at SIGIR 2015.

In terms of country of origin, over the 351 refereed papers there were 261 author-paper combinations from the USA, 239 from China, 62 from Great Britain, 45 from Australia, and 42 from Singapore. Germany, the Netherlands, Spain, Brazil, and Canada completed the top ten countries, with a total of 37 different countries represented in the author pool. Amongst the 70 accepted papers, 21 different countries are represented, with the top 10 countries (by author-paper combinations) being the USA (77), China (38), Great Britain (17), the Netherlands (15), Spain and Italy (13), Australia, Brazil, Canada and Russia (9). Of the counties listed, Italy, the Netherlands, Russia, and Spain (in that order) had the highest ratios of successful authors to submitting authors. Denmark also scored well in this metric, off a smaller number of submitted author-paper combinations.

Breaking the 351 papers in to seven bands by paper number, which corresponds to forming groups of 50 papers defined by when the submission process was initiated for each paper, the numbers of accepted papers in the bands are 9, 9, 7, 6, 12, 11, and 16. Submitting the abstract close to the deadline seems to help the odds of being accepted; whether this is a significant outcome we leave for future work.

To summarize the themes of the oral presentations, we made a tag cloud from the 70 full paper titles using the tool provided at `https://www.jasondavies.com/wordcloud/`.

We hope that you enjoy the result, and the papers that it represents.

Alistair Moffat, Mounia Lalmas, Berthier Ribeiro-Neto
June 2015.

Short Papers

The Short Papers Track received 252 submissions, of which 79 were accepted (31% acceptance). Each submitted paper received three reviews in a double-blind process, together with an overall meta-review from one of the three Chairs. Short papers are four pages in length, and will be presented at the conference during what can be expected to be a highly engaging Poster Session. We thank the many referees who contributed to the reviewing process, and are particularly grateful to John Tait, who managed a separate Short Paper conflict of interest track for submissions co-authored by any of the three Chairs. We look forward to the lively discussions that always accompany the SIGIR Poster Session

Maarten de Rijke, Ee-Peng Lim, Ryen White
June 2015.

Demonstrations

The Demonstrations Track received 24 submissions of which 12 were accepted. We thank the pool of expert referees who assisted with the task of selecting the final set of demos. The results of their work will provide a stimulating complement to the conference's Poster Session; and we are confident that, as always, the successful presentations will generate extensive discussion and lead to further new ideas.

Djoerd Hiemstra, Mirella Moro
June 2015.

Doctoral Consortium

The Doctoral Consortium received 14 submissions this year, of which 10 were recommended for acceptance, with almost equal representation across Asia, Europe, and America. Having facilitated the review process, we are now looking forward to chairing the Consortium on the first day of the conference, and welcoming and working with these new members of our community. We are especially grateful to the 17 referees that assisted with our candidate selections, many of whom will also be mentors on the day.

Shane Culpepper, Brian Davison
June 2015.

Table of Contents

SIGIR 2015 Conference Organization xxi

SIGIR 2015 Sponsor & Supporters xxxv

Salton Award
Session Chair: Charlie Clarke *(University of Waterloo)*

- **Salton Award Lecture: People, Interacting with Information** 1
  Nicholas J. Belkin *(Rutgers University)*

Session 1A: Assisting the Search
Session Chair: Ellen Voorhes *(NIST)*

- **Exploring Session Context using Distributed Representations of Queries and Reformulations** 3
  Bhaskar Mitra *(Microsoft)*
- **An Eye-Tracking Study of Query Reformulation** 13
  Carsten Eickhoff *(ETH Zurich)*, Sebastian Dungs, Vu Tran *(University of Duisburg-Essen)*
- **Differences in the Use of Search Assistance for Tasks of Varying Complexity** 23
  Robert Capra, Jaime Arguello, Anita Crescenzi, Emily Vardell *(University of North Carolina at Chapel Hill)*

Session 1B: Multimedia
Session Chair: Doug Oard *(University of Maryland)*

- **Dynamic Query Modeling for Related Content Finding** 33
  Daan Odijk *(University of Amsterdam)*, Edgar Meij *(Yahoo Labs)*,
  Isaac Sijaranamual, Maarten de Rijke *(University of Amsterdam)*
- **Image-based Recommendations on Styles and Substitutes** 43
  Julian McAuley *(University of California, San Diego)*,
  Christopher Targett, Qinfeng ('Javen') Shi, Anton van den Hengel *(University of Adelaide)*
- **Semi-supervised Hashing with Semantic Confidence for Large Scale Visual Search** 53
  Yingwei Pan *(University of Science and Technology of China)*, Ting Yao *(Microsoft Research)*,
  Houqiang Li *(University of Science and Technology of China)*, Chong-Wah Ngo *(City University of Hong Kong)*,
  Tao Mei *(Microsoft Research)*

Session 1C: Efficient Algorithms
Session Chair: Andrew Trotman *(Ebay)*

- **Optimal Aggregation Policy for Reducing Tail Latency of Web Search** 63
  Jeong-Min Yun *(Pohang University of Science and Technology)*,
  Yuxiong He, Sameh Elnikety *(Microsoft Research)*, Shaolei Ren *(Florida International University)*
- **QuickScorer: A Fast Algorithm to Rank Documents with Additive Ensembles of Regression Trees** 73
  Claudio Lucchese, Franco Maria Nardini *(ISTI-CNR)*, Salvatore Orlando *(Università di Venezia)*,
  Raffaele Perego, Nicola Tonellotto *(ISTI-CNR)*, Rossano Venturini *(Università di Pisa)*
- **High Quality Graph-Based Similarity Search** 83
  Weiren Yu, Julie A. McCann *(Imperial College London)*

Session 2A: Diversity and Bias
Session Chair: Gareth Jones *(Dublin City University)*

- **Summarizing Contrastive Themes via Hierarchical Non-Parametric Processes** 93
  Zhaochun Ren, Maarten de Rijke *(University of Amsterdam)*

- **Splitting Water: Precision and Anti-Precision to Reduce Pool Bias** 103
  Aldo Lipani, Mihai Lupu, Allan Hanbury *(Vienna University of Technology)*
- **Learning Maximal Marginal Relevance Model via Directly Optimizing Diversity Evaluation Measures** 113
  Long Xia, Jun Xu, Yanyan Lan, Jiafeng Guo, Xueqi Cheng *(Chinese Academy of Sciences)*

Session 1B: Queries

Session Chair: Milad Shokouhi *(Microsoft Research)*

- **Analyzing User's Sequential Behavior in Query Auto-Completion via Markov Processes** 123
  Liangda Li *(East China Normal University & Georgia Institute of Technology)*,
  Hongbo Deng, Anlei Dong, Yi Chang *(Yahoo Labs)*,
  Hongyuan Zha *(East China Normal University & Georgia Institute of Technology)*,
  Ricardo Baeza-Yates *(Yahoo Labs)*
- **Learning by Example: Training Users with High-quality Query Suggestions** 133
  Morgan Harvey *(Northumbria University)*, Claudia Hauff *(TU Delft)*, David Elsweiler *(University of Regensburg)*
- **adaQAC: Adaptive Query Auto-Completion via Implicit Negative Feedback** 143
  Aston Zhang *(University of Illinois at Urbana-Champaign)*, Amit Goyal *(Yahoo Labs)*,
  Weize Kong *(University of Massachusetts, Amherst)*, Hongbo Deng, Anlei Dong, Yi Chang *(Yahoo Labs)*,
  Carl A. Gunter, Jiawei Han *(University of Illinois at Urbana-Champaign)*

Session 2C: Graphs

Session Chair: Jaap Kamps *(University of Amsterdam)*

- **A Random Walk Model for Optimization of Search Impact in Web Frontier Ranking** 153
  Giang Tran *(University of Hannover)*, Ata Turk *(Boston University)*,
  B. Barla Cambazoglu *(Yahoo Labs)*,Wolfgang Nejdl *(University of Hannover)*
- **A Similarity Measure for Weaving Patterns in Textiles** 163
  Sven Helmer *(Free University of Bozen-Bolzano)*, Vuong M. Ngo *(Ho Chi Minh City Open University)*
- **Local Ranking Problem on the BrowseGraph** 173
  Michele Trevisiol *(Universitat Pompeu Fabra & Yahoo Labs)*, Luca Maria Aiello *(Yahoo Labs)*,
  Paolo Boldi *(Universita' degli Studi di Milano)*, Roi Blanco *(Yahoo Labs)*

Session 3A: Search Experience

Session Chair: Birger Larsen *(Aalborg University)*

- **How Many Results Per Page? A Study of SERP Size, Search Behavior and User Experience** 183
  Diane Kelly *(University of North Carolina)*, Leif Azzopardi *(University of Glasgow)*
- **Influence of Vertical Result in Web Search Examination** 193
  Zeyang Liu, Yiqun Liu *(Tsinghua University)*, Ke Zhou *(Yahoo Labs)*,
  Min Zhang, Shaoping Ma *(Tsinghua University)*
- **Unconscious Physiological Effects of Search Latency on Users and Their Click Behaviour** 203
  Miguel Barreda-Ángeles *(Barcelona Media)*, Ioannis Arapakis, Xiao Bai, B. Barla Cambazoglu *(Yahoo Labs)*,
  Alexandre Pereda-Baños *(Barcelona Media)*

Session 3B: Social Media

Session Chair: Claudia Hauff *(TU Delft)*

- **Multiple Social Network Learning and Its Application in Volunteerism Tendency Prediction** 213
  Xuemeng Song, Liqiang Nie, Luming Zhang, Mohammad Akbari, Tat-Seng Chua *(National University of Singapore)*

- **HSpam14: A Collection of 14 Million Tweets for Hashtag-Oriented Spam Research** 223
  Surendra Sedhai, Aixin Sun *(Nanyang Technological University)*
- **Uncovering Crowdsourced Manipulation of Online Reviews** 233
  Amir Fayazi *(Texas A&M University)*, Kyumin Lee *(Utah State University)*,
  James Caverlee *(Texas A&M University)*, Anna Squicciarini *(The Pennsylvania State University)*

Session 3C: Entities

Session Chair: Krisztian Balog *(University of Stavanger)*

- **Relevance Scores for Triples from Type-Like Relations** 243
  Hannah Bast, Björn Buchhold, Elmar Haussmann *(University of Freiburg)*
- **Fielded Sequential Dependence Model for Ad-Hoc Entity Retrieval in the Web of Data** ...253
  Nikita Zhiltsov *(Kazan Federal University & Textocat)*,
  Alexander Kotov, Fedor Nikolaev *(Wayne State University)*
- **Mining, Ranking and Recommending Entity Aspects** 263
  Ridho Reinanda *(University of Amsterdam)*, Edgar Meij *(Yahoo Labs)*, Maarten de Rijke *(University of Amsterdam)*

Session 4A: User Models

Session Chair: Diane Kelly *(University of North Carolina)*

- **Bayesian Ranker Comparison Based on Historical User Interactions** 273
  Artem Grotov, Shimon Whiteson, Maarten de Rijke *(University of Amsterdam)*
- **Incorporating Non-sequential Behavior into Click Models** 283
  Chao Wang, Yiqun Liu *(Tsinghua University)*, Meng Wang *(HeFei University of Technology)*,
  Ke Zhou *(Yahoo Labs)*, Jian-yun Nie *(Université de Montréal)*, Shaoping Ma *(Tsinghua University)*
- **Untangling Result List Refinement and Ranking Quality: A Framework for Evaluation and Prediction** 293
  Jiyin He *(Centrum Wiskunde & Informatica)*, Marc Bron *(Yahoo Labs)*,
  Arjen de Vries *(Centrum Wiskunde & Informatica)*, Leif Azzopardi *(University of Glasgow)*,
  Maarten de Rijke *(University of Amsterdam)*

Session 4B: Recommending

Session Chair: Paul Benett *(Microsoft Research)*

- **WEMAREC: Accurate and Scalable Recommendation through Weighted and Ensemble Matrix Approximation** 303
  Chao Chen *(Tongji University)*, Dongsheng Li *(IBM Research - China)*, Yingying Zhao *(Tongji University)*,
  Qin Lv, Li Shang *(University of Colorado Boulder)*
- **Effective Latent Models for Binary Feedback in Recommender Systems** 313
  Maksims N. Volkovs, Guang Wei Yu *(Milq Inc)*
- **Personalized Recommendation via Parameter-Free Contextual Bandits** 323
  Liang Tang, Yexi Jiang, Lei Li, Chunqiu Zeng, Tao Li *(Florida International University)*

Session 4C: Classifying & Ranking

Session Chair: Yi Chang *(Yahoo Labs)*

- **An Efficient and Scalable MetaFeature-based Document Classification using Massively Parallel Computing** 333
  Sérgio Canuto, Marcos André Goncálves *(Federal University of Minas Gerais)*,
  Wisllay Santos, Thierson Rosa, Wellington Martins *(Universidade Federal de Goiás)*
- **Listwise Collaborative Filtering** 343
  Shanshan Huang *(Shandong University)*, Shuaiqiang Wang *(University of Jyväskylä)*,
  Tie-Yan Liu *(Microsoft Research Asia)*, Jun Ma, Zhumin Chen *(Shandong University)*,
  Jari Veijalainen *(University of Jyväskylä)*
- **BROOF: Exploiting Out-of-Bag Errors, Boosting and Random Forests for Effective Automated Classification** 353
  Thiago Salles, Marcos Gonçalves, Victor Rodrigues *(Federal University of Minas Gerais)*,
  Leonardo Rocha *(Federal University of São João Del-Rei)*

Session 5A: Deep Learning

Session Chair: Berthier Ribeiro-Neto *(Google Brazil)*

- **Monolingual and Cross-Lingual Information Retrieval Models Based on (Bilingual) Word Embeddings** 363
  Ivan Vulić, Marie-Francine Moens *(KU Leuven)*
- **Learning to Rank Short Text Pairs with Convolutional Deep Neural Networks** 373
  Aliaksei Severyn *(Google Inc.)*, Alessandro Moschitti *(Qatar Computing Research Institute)*
- **Context- and Content-aware Embeddings for Query Rewriting in Sponsored Search** 383
  Mihajlo Grbovic, Nemanja Djuric, Vladan Radosavljevic, Fabrizio Silvestri, Narayan Bhamidipati *(Yahoo Labs)*

Session 5B: Products

Session Chair: Grace Hui Yang *(Georgetown University)*

- **Retrieval of Relevant Opinion Sentences for New Products** 393
  Dae Hoon Park *(University of Illinois at Urbana-Champaign)*, Hyun Duk Kim *(Twitter Inc.)*, ChengXiang Zhai *(University of Illinois at Urbana-Champaign)*, Lifan Guo *(TCL Research America)*
- **Learning Hierarchical Representation Model for Next Basket Recommendation** 403
  Pengfei Wang, Jiafeng Guo, Yanyan Lan, Jun Xu, Shengxian Wan, Xueqi Cheng *(Chinese Academy of Sciences)*
- **Parametric and Non-parametric User-aware Sentiment Topic Models** 413
  Zaihan Yang, Alexander Kotov, Aravind Mohan, Shiyong Lu *(Wayne State University)*

Session 5C: Locations

Session Chair: Craig Macdonald *(University of Glasgow)*

- **Learning to Extract Local Events from the Web** 423
  John Foley *(University of Massachusetts)*, Michael Bendersky *(Google)*, Vanja Josifovski *(Pinterest)*
- **Rank-GeoFM: A Ranking based Geographical Factorization Method for Point of Interest Recommendation** 433
  Xutao Li, Gao Cong *(Nanyang Technological University)*, Xiao-Li Li *(A*STAR)*, Tuan-Anh Nguyen Pham *(Nanyang Technological University)*, Shonali Krishnaswamy *(A*STAR)*
- **GeoSoCa: Exploiting Geographical, Social and Categorical Correlations for Point-of-Interest Recommendations** 443
  Jia-Dong Zhang, Chi-Yin Chow *(City University of Hong Kong)*

Session 6A: Experiment Design

Session Chair: Alistair Moffat *(University of Melbourne)*

- **Optimised Scheduling of Online Experiments** 453
  Eugene Kharitonov *(Yandex & University of Glasgow)*, Craig Macdonald *(University of Glasgow)*, Pavel Serdyukov *(Yandex)*, Iadh Ounis *(University of Glasgow)*
- **Predicting Search Satisfaction Metrics with Interleaved Comparisons** 463
  Anne Schuth *(University of Amsterdam)*, Katja Hofmann, Filip Radlinski *(Microsoft)*
- **Sequential Testing for Early Stopping of Online Experiments** 473
  Eugene Kharitonov *(Yandex & University of Glasgow)*, Aleksandr Vorobev *(Yandex)*, Craig Macdonald *(University of Glasgow)*, Pavel Serdyukov *(Yandex)*, Iadh Ounis *(University of Glasgow)*

Session 6B: Predicting

Session Chair: Djoerd Hiemstra *(University of Twente)*

- **Inferring Searcher Attention by Jointly Modeling User Interactions and Content Salience** 483
  Dmitry Lagun *(Google)*, Eugene Agichtein *(Emory University & Yahoo Labs)*

- **Different Users, Different Opinions: Predicting Search Satisfaction with Mouse Movement Information** 493
  Yiqun Liu, Ye Chen *(Tsinghua University)*, Jinhui Tang *(Nanjing University of Science and Technology)*, Jiashen Sun *(Samsung R&D Institute China - Beijing)*, Min Zhang, Shaoping Ma *(Tsinghua University)*, Xuan Zhu *(Samsung R&D Institute China - Beijing)*
- **Predicting Search Intent Based on Pre-Search Context** 503
  Weize Kong *(University of Massachusetts, Amherst)*, Rui Li, Jie Luo *(Yahoo Labs)*, Aston Zhang *(University of Illinois at Urbana-Champaign)*, Yi Chang *(Yahoo Labs)*, James Allan *(University of Massachusetts, Amherst)*

Session 6C: Tasks and Devices
Session Chair: Emine Yilmaz *(University College London)*

- **Leveraging Procedural Knowledge for Task-oriented Search** 513
  Zi Yang, Eric Nyberg *(Carnegie Mellon University)*
- **Personalizing Search on Shared Devices** 523
  Ryen W. White, Ahmed Hassan Awadallah *(Microsoft Research)*
- **Leveraging User Reviews to Improve Accuracy for Mobile App Retrieval** 533
  Dae Hoon Park *(University of Illinois at Urbana-Champaign)*, Mengwen Liu *(Drexel University)*, ChengXiang Zhai *(University of Illinois at Urbana-Champaign)*, Haohong Wang *(TCL Research America)*

Keynote
Session Chair: Ricardo Baeza-Yates *(Yahoo Labs)*

- **Towards a Game-Theoretic Framework for Information Retrieval** 543
  ChengXiang Zhai *(University of Illinois at Urbana-Champaign)*

Session 7A: Assessing
Session Chair: Justin Zobel *(University of Melbourne)*

- **Representative & Informative Query Selection for Learning to Rank using Submodular Functions** 545
  Rishabh Mehrotra, Emine Yilmaz *(University College London)*
- **Impact of Surrogate Assessments on High-Recall Retrieval** 555
  Adam Roegiest, Gordon V. Cormack, Charles L. A. Clarke *(University of Waterloo)*, Maura R. Grossman *(Wachtell, Lipton, Rosen & Katz)*
- **The Benefits of Magnitude Estimation Relevance Assessments for Information Retrieval Evaluation** 565
  Andrew Turpin *(University of Melbourne)*, Falk Scholer *(RMIT University)*, Stefano Mizzaro, Eddy Maddalena *(University of Udine)*

Session 7B: Terms
Session Chair: Arjen de Vries *(CWI)*

- **Learning to Reweight Terms with Distributed Representations** 575
  Guoqing Zheng, Jamie Callan *(Carnegie Mellon University)*
- **A Probabilistic Model for Information Retrieval Based on Maximum Value Distribution** 585
  Jiaul H. Paik *(University of Maryland, College Park)*
- **Non-Compositional Term Dependence for Information Retrieval** 595
  Christina Lioma, Jakob Grue Simonsen, Birger Larsen, Niels Dalum Hansen *(University of Copenhagen)*

Session 8A: Variability in Test Collections

Session Chair: Mark Smucker *(University of Waterloo)*

- **On the Relation Between Assessor's Agreement and Accuracy in Gamified Relevance Assessment** 605
  Olga Megorskaya, Vladimir Kukushkin, Pavel Serdyukov *(Yandex)*
- **Assessor Differences and User Preferences in Tweet Timeline Generation** 615
  Yulu Wang *(University of Maryland)*, Garrick Sherman *(University of Illinois, Urbana-Champaign)*, Jimmy Lin *(University of Maryland)*, Miles Efron *(University of Illinois, Urbana-Champaign)*
- **User Variability and IR System Evaluation** 625
  Peter Bailey *(Microsoft)*, Alistair Moffat *(The University of Melbourne)*, Falk Scholer *(RMIT University)*, Paul Thomas *(CSIRO)*

Session 8B: Citations

Session Chair: Mark Sanderson *(RMIT)*

- **An Entity Class-Dependent Discriminative Mixture Model for Cumulative Citation Recommendation** 635
  Jingang Wang, Dandan Song *(Beijing Institute of Technology)*, Qifan Wang, Zhiwei Zhang, Luo Si *(Purdue University)*, Lejian Liao *(Beijing institute of Technology)*, Chin-Yew Lin *(Microsoft Research)*
- **Scientific Information Understanding via Open Educational Resources (OER)** 645
  Xiaozhong Liu *(Indiana University Bloomington)*, Zhuoren Jiang *(Dalian Maritime University)*, Liangcai Gao *(Peking University)*
- **In Situ Insights** 655
  Yuanhua Lv *(Microsoft Research)*, Ariel Fuxman *(Google Inc.)*

Session 9A: Streams

Session Chair: Fernando Diaz *(Microsoft Research)*

- **Islands in the Stream: A Study of Item Recommendation within an Enterprise Social Stream** 665
  Ido Guy *(Yahoo Labs)*, Roy Levin, Tal Daniel *(IBM Research)*, Ella Bolshinsky *(Technion)*
- **Evaluating Streams of Evolving News Events** 675
  Gaurav Baruah, Mark D. Smucker, Charles L. A. Clarke *(University of Waterloo)*

Session 9B: Cards

Session Chair: Eugene Agichtein *(Emory University)*

- **Information Retrieval as Card Playing: A Formal Model for Optimizing Interactive Retrieval Interface** 685
  Yinan Zhang, Chengxiang Zhai *(University of Illinois at Urbana-Champaign)*
- **From Queries to Cards: Re-ranking Proactive Card Recommendations Based on Reactive Search History** 695
  Milad Shokouhi, Qi Guo *(Microsoft)*

Short Papers

- **Using Sensor Metadata Streams to Identify Topics of Local Events in the City** 711
  M-Dyaa Albakour, Craig Macdonald, Iadh Ounis *(University of Glasgow)*
- **StarSum: A Simple Star Graph for Multi-document Summarization** 715
  Mohammed Al-Dhelaan *(King Saud University)*
- **When Relevance Judgement is Happening? An EEG-based Study** 719
  Marco Allegretti *(Mitech Srl)*, Yashar Moshfeghi, Maria Hadjigeorgieva, Frank E. Pollick, Joemon M. Jose *(University of Glasgow)*, Gabriella Pasi *(University of Milano-Bicocca)*
- **Search Engine Evaluation based on Search Engine Switching Prediction** 723
  Olga Arkhipova, Lidia Grauer, Igor Kuralenok, Pavel Serdyukov *(Yandex LLC)*

- **Time-Aware Authorship Attribution for Short Text Streams** 727
  Hosein Azarbonyad, Mostafa Dehghani, Maarten Marx, Jaap Kamps *(University of Amsterdam)*
- **A Priori Relevance Based on Quality and Diversity of Social Signals** 731
  Ismail Badache, Mohand Boughanem *(Toulouse Institute of Computer Science Research)*
- **Document Comprehensiveness and User Preferences in Novelty Search Tasks** 735
  Ashraf Bah, Praveen Chandar, Ben Carterette *(University of Delaware)*
- **Cost-Aware Result Caching for Meta-Search Engines** 739
  Emre Bakkal, Ismail Sengor Altingovde, Ismail Hakki Toroslu *(Middle East Technical University)*
- **From Unlabelled Tweets to Twitter-specific Opinion Words** 743
  Felipe Bravo-Marquez, Eibe Frank, Bernhard Pfahringer *(University of Waikato)*
- **The Best Published Result is Random: Sequential Testing and its Effect on Reported Effectiveness** 747
  Ben Carterette *(University of Delaware)*
- **Load-sensitive CPU Power Management for Web Search Engines** 751
  Matteo Catena *(Gran Sasso Science Institute & National Research Council of Italy)*,
  Craig Macdonald *(University of Glasgow)*, Nicola Tonellotto *(National Research Council of Italy)*
- **Retrieval from Noisy E-Discovery Corpus in the Absence of Training Data** 755
  Anirban Chakraborty, Kripabandhu Ghosh, Swapan Kumar Parui *(Indian Statistical Institute, Kolkata)*
- **Opinion Spammer Detection in Web Forum** 759
  Yu-Ren Chen, Hsin-Hsi Chen *(National Taiwan University)*
- **Multi-Faceted Recall of Continuous Active Learning for Technology-Assisted Review** 763
  Gordon V. Cormack *(University of Waterloo)*, Maura R. Grossman *(Wachtell, Lipton, Rosen & Katz)*
- **Time Pressure and System Delays in Information Search** 767
  Anita Crescenzi, Diane Kelly *(University of North Carolina)*, Leif Azzopardi *(University of Glasgow)*
- **How Random Decisions Affect Selective Distributed Search** 771
  Zhuyun Dai, Yubin Kim, Jamie Callan *(Carnegie Mellon University)*
- **Comparing Approaches for Query Autocompletion** 775
  Giovanni Di Santo *(Universita degli studi dell'Aquila)*,
  Richard McCreadie, Craig Macdonald, Iadh Ounis *(University of Glasgow)*
- **Sign-Aware Periodicity Metrics of User Engagement for Online Search Quality Evaluation** 779
  Alexey Drutsa *(Yandex)*
- **Modelling Term Dependence with Copulas** 783
  Carsten Eickhoff *(ETH Zurich)*, Arjen P. de Vries *(CWI Amsterdam)*, Thomas Hofmann *(ETH Zurich)*
- **Modeling Website Topic Cohesion at Scale to Improve Webpage Classification** 787
  Dhivya Eswaran *(Indian Institute of Technology, Madras)*, Paul N. Bennett *(Microsoft Research)*,
  Joseph J. Pfeiffer III *(Purdue University)*
- **Topic-centric Classification of Twitter User's Political Orientation** 791
  Anjie Fang, Iadh Ounis, Philip Habel, Craig Macdonald, Nut Limsopatham *(University of Glasgow)*
- **Word Embedding based Generalized Language Model for Information Retrieval** 795
  Debasis Ganguly *(Dublin City University)*, Dwaipayan Roy, Mandar Mitra *(Indian Statistical Institute)*,
  Gareth J. F. Jones *(Dublin City University)*
- **A Head-Weighted Gap-Sensitive Correlation Coefficient** 799
  Ning Gao, Douglas W. Oard *(University of Maryland, College Park)*
- **On Term Selection Techniques for Patent Prior Art Search** 803
  Mona Golestan Far, Scott Sanne *(NICTA & ANU)*, Mohamed Reda Bouadjenek *(INRIA & LIRMM)*,
  Gabriela Ferraro *(NICTA & ANU)*, David Hawking *(Microsoft (Bing) & ANU)*
- **Automatic Feature Generation on Heterogeneous Graph for Music Recommendation** 807
  Chun Guo, Xiaozhong Liu *(Indiana University Bloomington)*

- **Differences in Eye-tracking Measures Between Visits and Revisits to Relevant and Irrelevant Web Pages** 811
  Jacek Gwizdka, Yinglong Zhang *(University of Texas at Austin)*
- **Reducing Hubness: A Cause of Vulnerability in Recommender Systems** 815
  Kazuo Hara *(National Institute of Genetics)*,
  Ikumi Suzuki, Kei Kobayashi, Kenji Fukumizu *(The Institute of Statistical Mathematics)*
- **Modularity-Based Query Clustering for Identifying Users Sharing a Common Condition** 819
  Maayan Harel *(Technion - Israel Institute of Technology)*, Elad Yom-Tov *(Microsoft Research)*
- **Understanding Temporal Query Intent** 823
  Mohammed Hasanuzzaman *(Normandie University)*, Sriparna Saha *(IIT-Patna)*,
  Gaël Dias, Stéphane Ferrari *(Normandie University)*
- **On the Reusability of Open Test Collections** 827
  Seyyed Hadi Hashemi *(University of Amsterdam)*,
  Charles L. A. Clarke, Adriel Dean-Hall *(University of Waterloo)*, Jaap Kamps *(University of Amsterdam)*,
  Julia Kiseleva *(Eindhoven University of Technology)*
- **Towards Vandalism Detection in Knowledge Bases: Corpus Construction and Analysis** 831
  Stefan Heindorf *(University of Paderborn)*, Martin Potthast, Benno Stein *(Bauhaus-Universität Weimar)*,
  Gregor Engels *(University of Paderborn)*
- **About the 'Compromised Information Need' and Optimal Interaction as Quality Measure for Search Interfaces** 835
  Eduard Hoenkamp *(Queensland University of Technology & Radboud University)*
- **I See You: Person-of-Interest Search in Social Networks** 839
  Hsun-Ping Hsieh *(National Taiwan University)*, Cheng-Te Li *(Academia Sinica)*, Rui Yan *(Baidu Inc.)*
- **Towards Quantifying the Impact of Non-Uniform Information Access in Collaborative Information Retrieval** 843
  Nyi Nyi Htun *(Glasgow Caledonian University)*, Martin Halvey *(University of Strathclyde)*,
  Lynne Baillie *(Heriot-Watt University)*
- **Features of Disagreement Between Retrieval Effectiveness Measures** 847
  Timothy Jones *(RMIT University)*, Paul Thomas *(CSIRO)*, Falk Scholer, Mark Sanderson *(RMIT University)*,
- **Subsequence Search in Event-Interval Sequences** 851
  Orestis Kostakis, Aristides Gionis *(Aalto University)*
- **Searcher in a Strange Land: Understanding Web Search from Familiar and Unfamiliar Locations** 855
  Elad Kravi *(Technion & Yahoo Labs)*, Eugene Agichtein *(Yahoo Labs & Emery University)*,
  Ido Guy *(Yahoo Labs)*, Yaron Kanza *(Cornell Tech)*, Avihai Mejer, Dan Pelleg *(Yahoo Labs)*
- **Evaluating Retrieval Models through Histogram Analysis** 859
  Kriste Krstovski *(University of Massachusetts, Amherst & Harvard-Smithsonian Center for Astrophysics)*,
  David A. Smith *(Northeastern University)*, Michael J. Kurtz *(Harvard-Smithsonian Center for Astrophysics)*
- **Inter-Category Variation in Location Search** 863
  Chia-Jung Lee *(University of Massachusetts, Amherst)*, Nick Craswell, Vanessa Murdock *(Microsoft)*
- **Reachability based Ranking in Interactive Image Retrieval** 867
  Jiyi Li *(Kyoto University)*
- **Modeling Multi-query Retrieval Tasks Using Density Matrix Transformation** 871
  Qiuchi Li *(Tianjin University & Tsinghua University)*, Jingfei Li, Peng Zhang *(Tianjin University)*,
  Dawei Song *(Tianjin University & The Open University)*
- **Predicting User Behavior in Display Advertising via Dynamic Collective Matrix Factorization** 875
  Sheng Li *(Northeastern University)*, Jaya Kawale *(Adobe Research)*, Yun Fu *(Northeastern University)*
- **Zero-shot Image Tagging by Hierarchical Semantic Embedding** 879
  Xirong Li, Shuai Liao, Weiyu Lan, Xiaoyong Du, Gang Yang *(Renmin University of China)*

- **Using Term Location Information to Enhance Probabilistic Information Retrieval** 883
  Baiyan Liu, Xiangdong An, Jimmy Xiangji Huang *(York University)*
- **Learning Context-aware Latent Representations for Context-aware Collaborative Filtering** 887
  Xin Liu, Wei Wu *(Institute for Infocomm Research)*
- **Exploiting User and Business Attributes for Personalized Business Recommendation** 891
  Kai Lu, Yi Zhang, Lanbo Zhang *(University of California, Santa Cruz)*, Shuxin Wang *(Chinese Academy of Sciences)*
- **Speeding up Document Ranking with Rank-based Features** 895
  Claudio Lucchese, Franco Maria Nardini *(ISTI-CNR)*, Salvatore Orlando *(Università di Venezia)*, Raffaele Perego, Nicola Tonellotto *(ISTI-CNR)*
- **Mining Measured Information from Text** 899
  Arun S. Maiya, Dale Visser, Andrew Wan *(Institute for Defense Analyses)*
- **An Initial Investigation into Fixed and Adaptive Stopping Strategies** 903
  David Maxwell, Leif Azzopardi *(University of Glasgow)*, Kalervo Järvelin, Heikki Keskustalo *(University of Tampere)*
- **Regularised Cross-Modal Hashing** 907
  Sean Moran, Victor Lavrenko *(The University of Edinburgh)*
- **Adapted B-CUBED Metrics to Unbalanced Datasets** 911
  Jose G. Moreno, Gaël Dias *(Normandie University)*
- **A Time-aware Random Walk Model for Finding Important Documents in Web Archives** 915
  Tu Ngoc Nguyen, Nattiya Kanhabua, Claudia Niederée, Xiaofei Zhu *(Leibniz Universität Hannover)*
- **A Test Collection for Spoken Gujarati Queries** 919
  Douglas W. Oard, Rashmi Sankepally *(University of Maryland)*, Jerome White *(New York University)*, Aren Jansen, Craig Harman *(Johns Hopkins University)*
- **Discovering Experts across Multiple Domains** 923
  Aditya Pal *(IBM Almaden Research)*
- **Using Key Concepts in a Translation Model for Retrieval** 927
  Jae Hyun Park, W. Bruce Croft *(University of Massachusetts, Amherst)*
- **On the Cost of Phrase-Based Ranking** 931
  Matthias Petri, Alistair Moffat *(The University of Melbourne)*
- **Location-Aware Model for News Events in Social Media** 935
  Mauricio Quezada, Vanessa Peña-Araya, Barbara Poblete *(University of Chile)*
- **Exploring Opportunities to Facilitate Serendipity in Search** 939
  M. Ataur Rahman, Max L. Wilson *(University of Nottingham)*
- **Combining Orthogonal Information in Large-Scale Cross-Language Information Retrieval** 943
  Shigehiko Schamoni, Stefan Riezler *(Heidelberg University)*
- **Tailoring Music Recommendations to Users by Considering Diversity, Mainstreaminess, and Novelty** 947
  Markus Schedl, David Hauger *(Johannes Kepler University)*
- **Challenges of Mathematical Information Retrieval in the NTCIR-11 Math Wikipedia Task** 951
  Moritz Schubotz *(Technische Universität Berlin)*, Abdou Youssef *(The George Washington University)*, Volker Markl *(Technische Universität Berlin)*, Howard S. Cohl *(National Institute of Standards and Technology)*
- **Probabilistic Multileave for Online Retrieval Evaluation** 955
  Anne Schuth, Robert-Jan Bruintjes, Fritjof Büttner, Joost van Doorn, Carla Groenland, Harrie Oosterhuis, Cong-Nguyen Tran, Bas Veeling, Jos van der Velde, Roger Wechsler, David Woudenberg, Maarten de Rijke *(University of Amsterdam)*

- **Twitter Sentiment Analysis with Deep Convolutional Neural Networks** 959
  Aliaksei Severyn *(Google Inc.)*, Alessandro Moschitti *(Qatar Computing Research Institute)*
- **Anchoring and Adjustment in Relevance Estimation** 963
  Milad Shokouhi, Ryen White *(Microsoft)*, Emine Yilmaz *(University College London)*
- **Cognitive Activity during Web Search** 967
  Md. Hedayetul Islam Shovon, D (Nanda) Nandagopal, Jia Tina Du *(University of South Australia)*,
  Ramasamy Vijayalakshmi *(PSG College of Technology)*, Bernadine Cocks *(University of South Australia)*
- **Personalized Semantic Ranking for Collaborative Recommendation** 971
  Song Xu, Shu Wu, Liang Wang *(Chinese Academy of Sciences)*
- **Active Learning for Entity Filtering in Microblog Streams** 975
  Damiano Spina *(RMIT University)*, Maria-Hendrike Peetz, Maarten de Rijke *(University of Amsterdam)*
- **Relevance-aware Filtering of Tuples Sorted by an Attribute Value via Direct Optimization of Search Quality Metrics** 979
  Nikita Spirin *(University of Illinois at Urbana-Champaign)*,
  Mikhail Kuznetsov *(Moscow Institute of Physics and Technology)*,
  Julia Kiseleva *(Eindhoven University of Technology)*, Yaroslav V. Spirin *(Datastars)*,
  Pavel Izhutov *(Stanford University)*
- **Multi-source Information Fusion for Personalized Restaurant Recommendation** 983
  Jing Sun, Yun Xiong, Yangyong Zhu *(Fudan University)*, Junming Liu *(Rutgers University)*,
  Chu Guan *(University of Science and Technology of China)*, Hui Xiong *(Rutgers University)*
- **Joint Matrix Factorization and Manifold-Ranking for Topic-Focused Multi-Document Summarization** 987
  Jiwei Tan, Xiaojun Wan, Jianguo Xiao *(Peking University)*
- **Towards Understanding the Impact of Length in Web Search Result Summaries over a Speech-only Communication Channel** 991
  Johanne R. Trippas, Damiano Spina, Mark Sanderson, Lawrence Cavedon *(RMIT University)*
- **Early Detection of Topical Expertise in Community Question Answering** 995
  David van Dijk *(Amsterdam University of Applied Sciences & University of Amsterdam)*,
  Manos Tsagkias *(904Labs)*, Maarten de Rijke *(University of Amsterdam)*
- **LBMCH: Learning Bridging Mapping for Cross-modal Hashing** 999
  Yang Wang *(The University of New South Wales & Australian E-Health Research Centre)*,
  Xuemin Lin *(The University of New South Wales)*, Lin Wu *(The University of Adelaide)*,
  Wenjie Zhang *(The University of New South Wales)*, Qing Zhang *(Australian E-Health Research Centre)*
- **Gibberish, Assistant, or Master? Using Tweets Linking to News for Extractive Single-Document Summarization** 1003
  Zhongyu Wei *(University of Texas at Dallas)*, Wei Gao *(Qatar Computing Research Institute)*
- **Context-aware Point-of-Interest Recommendation Using Tensor Factorization with Social Regularization** 1007
  Lina Yao, Quan Z. Sheng, Yongrui Qin, Xianzhi Wang, Ali Shemshadi, Qi He *(The University of Adelaide)*
- **Adaptive User Engagement Evaluation via Multi-task Learning** 1011
  Hamed Zamani, Pooya Moradi, Azadeh Shakery *(University of Tehran)*
- **Compact Snippet Caching for Flash-based Search Engines** 1015
  Rui Zhang *(Nankai University)*, Pengyu Sun, Jiancong Tong *(Nankai University & Baidu, Inc.)*,
  Rebecca J. Stones, Gang Wang, Xiaoguang Liu *(Nankai University)*
- **When Personalization Meets Conformity: Collective Similarity based Multi-Domain Recommendation** 1019
  Xi Zhang, Jian Cheng, Shuang Qiu *(Chinese Academy of Sciences)*, Zhenfeng Zhu *(Beijing Jiaotong University)*,
  Hanqing Lu *(Chinese Academy of Sciences)*
- **Sub-document Timestamping of Web Documents** 1023
  Yue Zhao, Claudia Hauff *(Delft University of Technology)*

Demonstrations

- **DINFRA: A One Stop Shop for Computing Multilingual Semantic Relatedness** 1027
  Siamak Barzegar, Juliano Efson Sales *(NUI Galway)*, Andre Freitas, Siegfried Handschuh *(University of Passau)*, Brian Davis *(NUI Galway)*
- **VenueMusic: A Venue-Aware Music Recommender System** 1029
  Zhiyong Cheng, Jialie Shen *(Singapore Management University)*
- **Shiny on Your Crazy Diagonal** 1031
  Giorgio Maria Di Nunzio *(University of Padua)*
- **CricketLinking: Linking Event Mentions from Cricket Match Reports to Ball Entities in Commentaries** 1033
  Manish Gupta *(Microsoft)*
- **An Aspect-driven Social Media Explorer** 1035
  Nedim Lipka *(Adobe Research)*, W. Bruce Croft *(University of Massachusetts)*
- **ERICA: Expert Guidance in Validating Crowd Answers** 1037
  Nguyen Quoc Viet Hung, Duong Chi Thang *(École Polytechnique Fédérale de Lausanne)*, Matthias Weidlich *(Humboldt-Universität zu Berlin)*, Karl Aberer *(École Polytechnique Fédérale de Lausanne)*
- **Large-scale Image Retrieval using Neural Net Descriptors** 1039
  David Novak, Michal Batko, Pavel Zezula *(Masaryk University)*
- **Galean: Visualization of Geolocated News Events from Social Media** 1041
  Vanessa Peña-Araya, Mauricio Quezada, Barbara Poblete *(University of Chile)*
- **SciNet: Interactive Intent Modeling for Information Discovery** 1043
  Tuukka Ruotsalo *(Aalto University)*, Jaakko Peltonen *(University of Tampere & Aalto University)*, Manuel J. A. Eugster *(Aalto University)*, Dorota Głowacka, Aki Reijonen, Giulio Jacucci, Petri Myllymäki *(University of Helsinki)*, Samuel Kaski *(Aalto University & University of Helsinki)*
- **Linse: A Distributional Semantics Entity Search Engine** 1045
  Juliano Efson Sales *(NUI Galway)*, André Freitas, Siegfried Handschuh *(University of Passau)*, Brian Davis *(NUI Galway)*
- **Online News Tracking for Ad-Hoc Queries** 1047
  Jeroen B. P. Vuurens *(Delft University of Technology)*, Arjen P. de Vries *(CWI & Delft University of Technology)*, Roi Blanco, Peter Mika *(Yahoo Research)*
- **DUMPLING: A Novel Dynamic Search Engine** 1049
  Andrew Jie Zhou, Jiyun Luo, Hui Yang *(Georgetown University)*

Doctoral Consortium

- **Promoting User Engagement and Learning in Amorphous Search Tasks** 1051
  Piyush Arora *(Dublin City University)*
- **Cross-Platform Question Routing for Better Question Answering** 1053
  Mossaab Bagdouri *(University of Maryland)*
- **Time Pressure in Information Search** 1055
  Anita Crescenzi *(University of North Carolina at Chapel Hill)*
- **Controversy Detection and Stance Analysis** 1057
  Shiri Dori-Hacohen *(University of Massachusetts, Amherst)*
- **Using Contextual Information to Understand Searching and Browsing Behavior** 1059
  Julia Kiseleva *(Eindhoven University of Technology)*
- **Transfer Learning for Information Retrieval** 1061
  Pengfei Li *(RMIT University)*
- **Enhancing Mathematics Information Retrieval** 1063
  Martin Líška *(Faculty of Informatics, Masaryk University)*
- **Improving Search using Proximity-Based Statistics** 1065
  Xiaolu Lu *(RMIT University)*

- **Spoken Conversational Search: Information Retrieval over a Speech-only Communication Channel** 1067
  Johanne R. Trippas *(RMIT)*
- **Finding Answers in Web Search** 1069
  Evi Yulianti *(RMIT)*

Industry Track Preface

- **SIRIP 2015 Chairs' Welcome** 1071
  Hang Li *(Huawei Technologies)*, Jaime Teevan *(Microsoft Research)*

Industry Track Invited Talks

- **From Web Search Relevance to Vertical Search Relevance** 1073
  Yi Chang *(Yahoo Labs)*
- **Finding Money in the Haystack: Information Retrieval at Bloomberg** 1075
  Jonathan J. Dorando, Konstantine Arkoudas, Parth Vasa, Gary Kazantsev, Gideon Mann *(Bloomberg L.P.)*
- **If SIGIR Had an Academic Track, What Would Be In It?** 1077
  David Hawking *(Microsoft)*
- **WeChat Search & Headline: Sogou Joins Force with Tencent on Mobile Search** 1079
  Chao Liu *(Sogou Inc.)*
- **Structure, Personalization, Scale: A Deep Dive into LinkedIn Search** 1081
  Asif Makhani *(LinkedIn Corporation)*
- **Location in Search** 1083
  Vanessa Murdock *(Microsoft)*
- **Challenges and Opportunities in Online Evaluation of Search Engines** 1085
  Pavel Serdyukov *(Yandex)*
- **Lower Search Cost** 1087
  Dou Shen *(Baidu Inc.)*

Industry Track Refereed Papers

- **Practical Lessons for Gathering Quality Labels at Scale** 1089
  Omar Alonso *(Microsoft Corporation)*
- **Incremental Sampling of Query Logs** 1093
  Ricardo Baeza-Yates *(Yahoo Labs)*
- **Where to Go on Your Next Trip? Optimizing Travel Destinations Based on User Preferences** 1097
  Julia Kiseleva *(Eindhoven University of Technology)*, Melanie J.I. Mueller, Lucas Bernardi, Chad Davis, Ivan Kovacek, Mats Stafseng Einarsen *(Booking.com)*, Jaap Kamps *(University of Amsterdam)*, Alexander Tuzhilin *(New York University)*, Djoerd Hiemstra *(University of Twente)*
- **Bringing Order to the Job Market: Efficient Job Offer Categorization in E-Recruitment** 1101
  Emmanuel Malherbe *(Multiposting)*, Mario Cataldi *(Université Paris 8)*, Andrea Ballatore *(University of California, Santa Barbara)*

Tutorials

- **SIGIR 2015 Tutorials Chair's Welcome** 1105
  Yoelle Maarek *(Yahoo Labs)*
- **Building and Using Models of Information Seeking, Search and Retrieval: Full Day Tutorial** 1107
  Leif Azzopardi *(University of Glasgow)*, Guido Zuccon *(Queensland University of Technology)*

- **Advanced Click Models and Their Applications to IR: SIGIR 2015 Tutorial** 1111
  Aleksandr Chuklin *(Google Switzerland & University of Amsterdam)*,
  Ilya Markov, Maarten de Rijke *(University of Amsterdam)*
- **An Introduction to Click Models for Web Search: SIGIR 2015 Tutorial** 1113
  Aleksandr Chuklin *(Google Switzerland & University of Amsterdam)*,
  Ilya Markov, Maarten de Rijke *(University of Amsterdam)*
- **IR Evaluation: Modeling User Behavior for Measuring Effectiveness** 1117
  Charles L. A. Clarke, Mark D. Smucker *(University of Waterloo)*, Emine Yilmaz *(University College London)*
- **Information Retrieval with Verbose Queries** 1121
  Manish Gupta *(Microsoft)*, Michael Bendersky *(Google)*
- **Revisiting the Foundations of IR: Timeless, Yet Timely** 1125
  Paul B. Kantor *(Rutgers University & CCICADA)*
- **IR Evaluation: Designing an End-to-End Offline Evaluation Pipeline** 1129
  Jin Young Kim *(Microsoft)*, Emine Yilmaz *(University College London)*
- **Music Retrieval and Recommendation: A Tutorial Overview** 1133
  Peter Knees, Markus Schedl *(Johannes Kepler University)*
- **Exploiting Wikipedia for Information Retrieval Tasks** 1137
  Bracha Shapira, Nir Ofek, Victor Makarenkov *(Ben-Gurion University of the Negev)*

Workshops

- **Workshop Chairs' Welcome** 1141
  Fernando Diaz *(Microsoft Research)*, Diane Kelly *(University of North Carolina at Chapel Hill)*
- **Web Question Answering: Beyond Factoids: SIGIR 2015 Workshop** 1143
  Eugene Agichtein *(Emory University & Yahoo Labs)*, David Carmel *(Yahoo Labs)*,
  Charles L. A. Clarke *(University of Waterloo)*, Praveen Paritosh *(Google inc.)*,
  Dan Pelleg, Idan Szpektor *(Yahoo Labs)*
- **Graph Search and Beyond: SIGIR 2015 Workshop Summary** 1145
  Omar Alonso *(Microsoft)*, Marti A. Hearst *(University of California, Berkeley)*,
  Jaap Kamps *(University of Amsterdam)*
- **SIGIR 2015 Workshop on Reproducibility, Inexplicability, and Generalizability of Results (RIGOR)** 1147
  Jaime Arguello *(University of North Carolina at Chapel Hill)*, Fernando Diaz *(Microsoft Research)*,
  Jimmy Lin *(University of Maryland)*, Andrew Trotman *(eBay Inc.)*
- **SIGIR 2015 Workshop on Temporal, Social and Spatially-aware Information Access (#TAIA2015)** 1149
  Klaus Berberich *(Max Planck Institute for Informatics)*, James Caverlee *(Texas A&M University)*,
  Miles Efron *(University of Illinois)*, Claudia Hauff *(Delft University of Technology)*,
  Vanessa Murdock, Milad Shokouhi *(Microsoft Corporation)*, Bart Thomee *(Yahoo Labs)*
- **NeuroIR 2015 – Neuro-Physiological Methods in IR Research** 1151
  Jacek Gwizdka *(University of Texas at Austin)*, Joemon Jose *(University of Glasgow)*,
  Javed Mostafa *(University of North Carolina at Chapel Hill)*, Max L. A. Wilson *(University of Nottingham)*
- **SPS'15 – 2015 International Workshop on Social Personalization & Search** 1155
  Christoph Trattner *(NTNU)*, Denis Parra *(PUC)*, Peter Brusilovsky *(University of Pittsburgh)*,
  Leandro Marinho *(UFCG)*
- **Privacy-Preserving IR 2015: When Information Retrieval Meets Privacy and Security** ... 1157
  Hui Yang *(Georgetown University)*, Ian Soboroff *(National Institute of Standards and Technology)*

Author Index 1159

SIGIR 2015 Conference Organization

Conference Chair:	Ricardo Baeza-Yates, Yahoo Labs, USA
Program Committee Chairs:	Mounia Lalmas, Yahoo Labs, UK Alistair Moffat, University of Melbourne, Australia Berthier Ribeiro-Neto, Google, Brazil, and UFMG, Brazil
Short Papers Chairs:	Maarten de Rijke, University of Amsterdam, The Netherlands Ee-Peng Lim, Singapore Management University, Singapore Ryen White, Microsoft Research, USA
Demonstrations Chairs:	Djoerd Hiemstra, University of Twente, The Netherlands Mirella Moro, Universidade Federal de Minas Gerais, Brazil
Tutorial Chair:	Yoelle Maarek, Yahoo Labs, Israel
Workshop Chairs:	Fernando Diaz, Microsoft Research, USA Diane Kelly, University of North Carolina at Chapel Hill, USA
Doctoral Consortium Chairs:	Shane Culpepper, RMIT University, Australia Brian Davison, Lehigh University, USA
Industry Day Chairs:	Hang Li, Huawei, China Jaime Teevan, Microsoft Research, USA
Best Paper Chair:	Susan Dumais, Microsoft Research, USA
Sponsorship Chairs:	Vanessa Murdock, Microsoft Research, USA Sergei Vassilvitskii, Google, USA
Local Arrangements Chair:	Diego Arroyuelo, UTFSM & Yahoo Labs, Chile
Finance Chair:	Mauricio Marín, Universidad de Santiago de Chile & Yahoo Labs, Chile
Publications Chairs:	Roberto González-Ibáñez, Universidad de Santiago de Chile, Chile Nicolás Hidalgo, Universidad de Santiago de Chile, Chile
Website Chair:	Marcelo Mendoza, UTFSM, Chile
Social Events Chairs:	Erika Rosas, Universidad de Santiago de Chile, Chile Carolina Bonacic, Universidad de Santiago de Chile & Yahoo Labs, Chile

Publicity Chair: Bárbara Poblete, Universidad de Chile, Chile

Venue Chair: Valeria Herskovic, Pontificia Universidad Católica de Chile, Chile

Local Organization Committee:
Sara Quiñones, Yahoo Labs, Chile
Rodrigo Scheihing, Yahoo Labs, Chile
Roberto Solar, Universidad de Santiago de Chile, Chile
Javier Velasco, Universidad de Santiago de Chile, Chile

Senior Program Committee:
Eugene Agichtein, Emory University, USA
James Allan, University of Massachusetts Amherst, USA
Javed A. Aslam, Northeastern University, USA
Leif Azzopardi, University of Glasgow, UK
Krisztian Balog, University of Stavanger, Norway
Nicholas J. Belkin, Rutgers University, USA
Paul Bennett, Microsoft Research, USA
Jamie Callan, Carnegie Mellon University, USA
David Carmel, Yahoo Labs, Israel
Ben Carterette, University of Delaware, USA
Carlos Castillo, Qatar Computing Research Institute, Qatar
Yi Chang, Yahoo Labs, USA
Charles L. A. Clarke, University of Waterloo, Canada
Kevyn Collins-Thompson, University of Michigan, USA
Nick Craswell, Microsoft, USA
Fabio Crestani, University of Lugano (USI) , Switzerland
Bruce Croft, University of Massachusetts Amherst, USA
Ronan Cummins, University of Cambridge, UK
Arjen P. de Vries, Centrum Wiskunde & Informatica, The Netherlands
Fernando Diaz, Microsoft Research, USA
David Elsweiler, University of Regensburg, Germany
Hui Fang, University of Delaware, USA
Jianfeng Gao, Microsoft Research, USA
Shlomo Geva, Queensland University of Technology, Australia
Marcos Goncalves, Universidade Federal de Minas Gerais, Brazil
Julio Gonzalo, UNED, Spain
Claudia Hauff, TU Delft, The Netherlands
Djoerd Hiemstra, University of Twente, The Netherlands
Xian-Sheng Hua, Microsoft Research, USA
Jimmy Huang, York University, Canada
Gareth Jones, Dublin City University, Ireland
Jaap Kamps, University of Amsterdam, The Netherlands
Gabriella Kazai, Lumi.do, UK
Diane Kelly, University of North Carolina at Chapel Hill, USA
Wessel Kraaij, Radboud University Nijmegen, The Netherlands
Oren Kurland, Technion, Israel

Senior Program Committee (continued):

Birger Larsen, Aalborg University Copenhagen, Denmark
Jimmy Lin, University of Maryland, USA
Wei-Ying Ma, Microsoft Research Asia, China
Craig Macdonald, University of Glasgow, UK
Stephane Marchand-Maillet, University of Geneva, Switzerland
Massimo Melucci, University of Padua, Italy
Donald Metzler, Google, USA
Stefano Mizzaro, University of Udine, Italy
Isabelle Moulinier, Thomson Reuters, France
Edleno S. Moura, Universidade Federal de Amazonas, Brazil
Jian-Yun Nie, Université de Montréal, Canada
Douglas W. Oard, University of Maryland, USA
Dan Pelleg, Yahoo Labs, Israel
Benjamin Piwowarski, Université Pierre et Marie Curie, France
Ian Ruthven, University of Strathclyde, UK
Tetsuya Sakai, Waseda University, Japan
Mark Sanderson, RMIT University, Australia
Falk Scholer, RMIT University, Australia
Milad Shokouhi, Microsoft, UK
Fabrizio Silvestri, Yahoo Labs, UK
Mark D. Smucker, University of Waterloo, Canada
Dawei Song, Tianjin University, China, and The Open University, UK
Andrew Trotman, eBay, USA
Ellen M. Voorhees, NIST, USA
Jun Wang, University College London, UK
Grace Hui Yang, Georgetown University, USA
Yiming Yang, Carnegie Mellon University, USA
Emine Yilmaz, University College London, UK
ChengXiang Zhai, University of Illinois at Urbana-Champaign, USA
Justin Zobel, The University of Melbourne, Australia

Program Committee:

Mikhail Ageev, Moscow State University, Russia
Elif Aktolga, University of Massachusetts Amherst, USA
Omar Alonso, Microsoft, USA
Ismail S. Altingovde, Middle East Technical University, Turkey
Robin Aly, University of Twente, The Netherlands
Gianni Amati, Fondazione Ugo Bordoni, Italy
Enrique Amigó, UNED, Spain
Avi Arampatzis, Democritus University of Thrace, Greece
Ioannis Arapakis, Yahoo Labs, Spain
Jaime Arguello, University of North Carolina at Chapel Hill, USA
Azin Ashkan, Technicolor Labs, USA
Xiao Bai, Yahoo Labs, Spain
Peter Bailey, Microsoft, Australia

Program Committee (continued):

Niranjan Balasubramanian, Stony Brook University, USA
Steve Beitzel, Applied Communication Sciences, USA
Michael Bendersky, Google, USA
Fabricio Benevenuto, Universidade Federal de Minas Gerais, Brazil
Klaus Berberich, Max Planck Institute for Informatics, Germany
Bodo Billerbeck, Microsoft, Australia
Roi Blanco, Yahoo Labs, UK
Toine Bogers, Aalborg University Copenhagen, Denmark
Edward Bortnikov, Yahoo Labs, Israel
Mohand Boughanem, IRIT-University of Toulouse, France
Martin Braschler, Zurich University of Applied Sciences, Switzerland
Nieves R. Brisaboa, Universidade da Coruña, Spain
George Buchanan, City University London, UK
Ivan Cantador, Universidad Autónoma de Madrid, Spain
Rob Capra, University of North Carolina at Chapel Hill, USA
Mark Carman, Monash University, Australia
Claudio Carpineto, Fondazione Ugo Bordoni, Italy
Marc-Allen Cartright, Google, USA
James Caverlee, Texas A&M University, USA
Soumen Chakrabarti, IIT Bombay, India
Raman Chandrasekar, Independent consultant, USA
Kevin C. Chang, University of Illinois at Urbana-Champaign, USA
Edgar Chavez, National University of Mexico (UNAM), Mexico
Yi Chen, NJIT, USA
Tat Seng Chua, National University of Singapore, Singapore
Francisco Claude, Universidad Diego Portales, Chile
Stephane Clinchant, Xerox Research Center Europe, France
Paul Clough, University of Sheffield, UK
Jack G. Conrad, Thomson Reuters, USA
Gordon V. Cormack, University of Waterloo, Canada
Shane Culpepper, University, Australia
Tonya Custis, Honeywell Labs, USA
Van Dang, Google, USA
Kareem Darwish, Qatar Computing Research Institute, Qatar
Altigran S. da Silva, Universidade Federal do Amazonas, Brazil
Gianluca Demartini, University of Sheffield, UK
Thomas Demeester, Ghent University, Belgium
Laura Dietz, University of Massachusetts Amherst, USA
Shuai Ding, Google, USA
Zhicheng Dou, Renmin University of China, China
Miles Efron, University of Illinois, USA
Carsten Eickhoff, ETH Zurich, Switzerland
Yi Fang, Santa Clara University, USA
Henry Feild, Endicott College, USA
Nicola Ferro, University of Padua, Italy

Program Committee (continued):

Marcus C. Fontoura, Microsoft, USA
Dayne Freitag, SRI International, USA
Ingo Frommholz, University of Bedfordshire, UK
Atsushi Fujii, Tokyo Institute of Technology, Japan
Patrick Gallinari, Université Pierre et Marie Curie, France
Debasis Ganguly, Dublin City University, Ireland
Bin Gao, Microsoft Research Asia, China
Eric Gaussier, Université Joseph Fourier, France
Fredric Gey, University of California at Berkeley, USA
Nazli Goharian, Georgetown University, USA
Peter B. Golbus, Wayfair LLC, USA
Siddharth Gopal, Carnegie Mellon University, USA
Brigitte Grau, LIMSI-CNRS, France
Qi Guo, Microsoft, USA
Maxim Gurevich, Bento Labs, USA
Cathal Gurrin, Dublin City University, Ireland
Ido Guy, Yahoo Labs, Israel
Jacek Gwizdka, University of Texas at Austin, USA
Martin Halvey, University of Strathclyde, UK
Sanda M. Harabagiu, University of Texas, Dallas
Donna Harman, NIST, USA
Morgan Harvey, Northumbria University, UK
Ahmed Hassan, Microsoft Research, USA
David Hawking, Microsoft, Australia
Ben He, Chinese Academy of Sciences, China
Daqing He, University of Pittsburgh, USA
Jiyin He, CWI, The Netherlands
Qi He, LinkedIn, USA
Katja Hofmann, Microsoft Research, UK
Liangjie Hong, Yahoo Labs, USA
Winston H. Hsu, National Taiwan University, Taiwan
Xuanjing Huang, Fudan University, China
Samuel Huston, Google, USA
Hervé Jégou, INRIA, France
Jing Jiang, Singapore Management University, Singapore
Hideo Joho, University of Tsukuba, Japan
Joemon M. Jose, University of Glasgow, UK
Min-Yen Kan, National University of Singapore, Singapore
Noriko Kando, National Institute of Informatics, Japan
Evangelos Kanoulas, University of Amsterdam, The Netherlands
David Karger, MIT, USA
Jussi Karlgren, Gavagai & KTH, Sweden
Makoto Kato, Kyoto University, Japan
Enver Kayaaslan, INRIA, France
Jaana Kekalainen, University of Tampere, Finland

Program Committee (continued):

Heikki Keskustalo, University of Tampere, Finland
Jin Young Kim, Microsoft, USA
Weize Kong, University of Massachusets Amherst, USA
Marijn Koolen, University of Amsterdam, The Netherlands
Alexander Kotov, Wayne State University, USA
Udo Kruschwitz, University of Essex, UK
Anagha Kulkarni, San Francisco State University, USA
Susana Ladra, Universidade da Coruña, Spain
Dmitry Lagun, Google, USA
Wai Lam, The Chinese University of Hong Kong, China
Martha Larson, Delft University of Technology, The Netherlands
Ray R. Larson, University of California at Berkeley, USA
Dawn Lawrie, Loyola University Maryland, USA
Matthew Lease, University of Texas at Austin, USA
Chia-Jung Lee, University of Massachusetts Amherst, USA
Gary Geunbae Lee, Postech, South Korea
Jochen L. Leidner, Thomson Reuters, UK
Daniel Lemire, Université du Québec, Canada
Lei Li, Samsung Digital Media Solutions Lab, USA
Kewen Liao, University of Melbourne, Australia
Christina Lioma, University of Copenhagen, Denmark
Jialu Liu, University of Illinois at Urbana-Champaign, USA
Qiaoling Liu, Emory University, USA
Tie-Yan Liu, Microsoft Research Asia, China
Xingjie Liu, Square Inc., USA
Yiqun Liu, Tsinghua University, China
Robert W.P. Luk, The Hong Kong Polytechnic University , China
Yuanhua Lv, Microsoft Research Asia, China
Hao Ma, Microsoft Research, USA
Andrew MacFarlane, City University London, UK
Prasenjit Majumder, DAIICT Gandhinagar, India
Ilya Markov, University of Amsterdam, The Netherlands
Yosi Mass, IBM Research, Israel
James Mayfield, Johns Hopkins University, USA
Richard McCreadie, University of Glasgow, UK
Paul McNamee, Johns Hopkins University, USA
Qiaozhu Mei, University of Michigan, USA
Edgar Meij, Yahoo Labs, UK
Thomas Mensink, University of Amsterdam, The Netherlands
Lupu Mihai, Vienna University of Technology, Austria
Marie-Francine Moens, Katholieke Universiteit Leuven, Belgium
Alessandro Moschitti, Qatar Computing Research Institute, Qatar
Yashar Moshfeghi, University of Glasgow, UK
Josiane Mothe, IRIT-University of Toulouse, France
Sung Hyon Myaeng, KAIST, South Korea

Program Committee (continued):

Gonzalo Navarro, University of Chile, Chile
Michael L. Nelson, Old Dominion University, USA
Chong-Wah Ngo, City University of Hong Kong, China
Dong Nguyen, University of Twente, The Netherlands
Alexandros Ntoulas, Zynga, USA
Heather O'Brien, University of British Columbia, Canada
Iadh Ounis, University of Glasgow, UK
Paul Over, NIST, USA
Jiaul Paik, University of Maryland, USA
Laurence Park, University of Western Sydney, Australia
Gabriella Pasi, University of Milano-Bicocca, Italy
Virgil Pavlu, Northeastern University, USA
Jan Pedersen, Microsoft, USA
Jian Pei, Simon Fraser University, Canada
Raffaele Perego, Consiglio Nazionale delle Ricerche (CNR), Italy
Vassilis Plachouras, Thomson Reuters, UK
Barbara Poblete, Universidad de Chile, Chile
Martin Potthast, University of Weimar, Germany
Kunal Punera, Bento Labs, USA
Filip Radlinski, Microsoft, UK
Fiana Raiber, Technion, Israel
Karthik Raman, Cornell University, USA
Edie Rasmussen, University of British Columbia, Canada
Yongli Ren, RMIT University, Australia
Soo Young Rieh, University of Michigan, USA
Haggai Roitman, IBM Research, Israel
Dmitri Roussinov, University of Strathclyde, UK
Rodrygo Santos, Universidade Federal de Minas Gerais, Brazil
Shin'ichi Satoh, National Institute of Informatics, Japan
Jacques Savoy, University of Neuchatel, Switzerland
Ralf Schenkel, University of Passau, Germany
Pavel Serdyukov, Yandex, Russia
Chirag Shah, Rutgers University, USA
Jialie Shen, Singapore Management University, Singapore
Anna Shtok, Technion, Israel
Laurianne Sitbon, Queensland University of Technology, Australia
Catherine L. Smith, Kent State University, USA
Ian Soboroff, NIST, USA
Aya Soffer, IBM Research, Israel
Oren Somekh, Yahoo Labs, Israel
Alessandro Sordoni, Université de Montréal, Canada
Alessandro Sperduti, University of Padova, Italy
Torsten Suel, New York University, USA
Jian-Tao Sun, Microsoft, USA
Le Sun, Chinese Academy of Sciences, China

Program Committee (continued):

Mingxuan Sun, Louisiana State University, USA
Idan Szpektor, Yahoo Labs, Israel
S. M. M. Tahaghoghi, Microsoft, USA
Jiliang Tang, Arizona State University, USA
Paul Thomas, CSIRO, Australia
Anastasios Tombros, Queen Mary University of London, UK
Manos Tsagkias, 904Labs, The Netherlands
Theodora Tsikrika, Centre for Research and Technology Hellas, Greece
David Vallet, Google, Australia
Emre Velipasaoglu, OpsClarity, USA
Adriano Veloso, Universidade Federal de Minas Gerais, Brazil
Rossano Venturini, University of Pisa, Italy
Robert Villa, University of Sheffield, UK
Bin Wang, Chinese Academy of Sciences, China
Jian Wang, LinkedIn, USA
Lidan Wang, IBM Research, USA
Lidan Wang, University of Illinois, USA
Meng Wang, Hefei University of Technology, China
Quan Wang, Chinese Academy of Sciences, China
Xin-Jing Wang, Microsoft Research Asia, China
William Webber, University of Melbourne, Australia
Ingmar Weber, Qatar Computing Research Institute, Qatar
Wouter Weerkamp, 904Labs, The Netherlands
Gerhard Weikum, Max Planck Institute for Informatics, Germany
Ji-Rong Wen, Renmin University of China, China
Max L. Wilson, University of Nottingham, UK
Wei Wu, Microsoft Research Asia, China
Xiaobing Xue, Twitter, USA
Zheng Ye, York University, Canada
Xing Yi, Yahoo Labs, USA
Dawei Yin, Yahoo Labs, USA
Minoru Yoshida, University of Tokushima, Japan
Xiaojun Yuan, State University of New York at Albany, USA
Dell Zhang, University of London Birkbeck, UK
Lanbo Zhang, Twitter, USA
Min Zhang, Tsinghua University, China
Yi Zhang, Unversity of California at Santa Cruz, USA
Le Zhao, Google, USA
Ke Zhou, Yahoo Labs, UK
Mianwei Zhou, Yahoo Labs, USA
Nivio Ziviani, Universidade Federal de Minas Gerais, Brazil
Guido Zuccon, Queensland University of Technology, Australia

Short Papers Committee:

Mikhail Ageev, Moscow State University, Russia
Eugene Agichtein, Emory University, USA
M-Dyaa Albakour, University of Glasgow, UK
Omar Alonso, Microsoft, USA
Javed A. Aslam, Northeastern University, USA
Krisztian Balog, University of Stavanger, Norway
Klaus Berberich, Max Planck Institute for Informatics, Germany
Bodo Billerbeck, Microsoft, Australia
Roi Blanco, Yahoo Labs, UK
Paolo Boldi, University of Milan, Italy
Gloria Bordogna, Consiglio Nazionale delle Ricerche (CNR), Italy
Mohand Boughanem, IRIT-University of Tolouse, France
Andrei Broder, Google, USA
Hendra Bunyamin, University of Amsterdam, The Netherlands
Rui Cai, Microsoft, USA
B. Barla Cambazoglu, Yahoo Labs, Spain
Mark Carman, Monash University, Australia
Ben Carterette, University of Delaware, USA
Marc-Allen Cartright, Google, USA
Francine Chen, FX Palo Alto Laboratory, USA
Hsin-His Chen, National Taiwan University, Taiwan
Kevyn Collins-Thompson, University of Michigan, USA
Bin Cui, Peking University, China
Shane Culpepper, RMIT University, Australia
Saly Jo Cunningham, University of Waikato, New Zealand
Kareem Darwish, Qatar Computing Research Institute, Qatar
Emanuele Di Buccio, University of Padova, Italy
Giorgio Maria Di Nunzio, University of Padua, Italy
Debora Donato, StumbleUpon, USA
Miles Efron, University of Illinois at Urbana-Champaign, USA
Carsten Eickhoff, ETH Zurich, Switzerland
Yi Fang, Santa Clara University, USA
Nicola Ferro, University of Padova, Italy
Luanne Freund, University of British Columbia, Canada
Ingo Frommholz, University of Bedfordshire, UK
Patrick Gallinari, Université Pierre-et-Marie-Curie, France
Bin Gao, Microsoft, China
Wei Gao, Qatar Computing Research Institute, Qatar
Susan Gauch, University of Arkansas, USA
Ayse Goker, Robert Gordon University, UK
Brigitte Grau, Université Paris-Sud, France
David Graus, University of Amsterdam, The Netherlands
Artem Grotov, University of Amsterdam, The Netherlands
Jacek Gwizdka, University of Texas at Austin, USA
Claudia Hauff, TU Delft, The Netherlands

Short Papers Committee (continued):

Ben He, University of Chinese Academy of Sciences, China
Daqing He, University of Pittsburgh, USA
Jiyin He, CWI, The Netherlands
Katja Hofmann, Microsoft, UK
Frank Hopfgartner, University of Glasgow, UK
Jimmy Huang, York University, Canada
Adam Jatowt, Kyoto University, Japan
Jiepu Jiang, University of Massachusetts Amherst, USA
Hideo Joho, University of Tsukuba, Japan
Joemon Jose, University of Glasgow, UK
Jaap Kamps, University of Amsterdam, The Netherlands
Noriko Kando, National Institute of Informatics, Japan
Nattiya Kanhabua, L3S Research Center, Germany
Evangelos Kanoulas, University of Amsterdam, The Netherlands
Diane Kelly, University of North Carolina at Chapel Hill, USA
Liadh Kelly, Trinity College Dublin, Ireland
Irwin King, Chinese University of Hong Kong, China
Julia Kiseleva, Technical University of Eindhoven, The Netherlands
Alexander Kotov, Wayne State University, USA
Udo Kruschwitz, University of Essex, UK
Giridhar Kumaran, eBay, USA
Sanna Kumpulainen, University of Amsterdam, The Netherlands
Wai Lam, Chinese University of Hong Kong, China
Martha Larson, Delft University of Technology
Victor Lavrenko, University of Edinburgh, UK
Jochen Leidner, Thomson Reuters, UK
Chenglian Li, Wuhan University, China
Hui Li, University of Hong Kong, China
Shangsong Liang, University of Amsterdam, The Netherlands
Christina Lioma, University of Copenhagen, Denmark
Suzanne Little, Dublin City University, Ireland
Carla Teixeira Lopes, University of Porto, Portugal
Hao Ma, Microsoft, USA
Andrew MacFarlane, City University London, UK
Takuya Maekawa, Osaka University, Japan
Walid Magdy, Qatar Computing Research Institute, Qatar
Prasenjit Majumder, Dhirubhai Ambani Institute of ICT, India
Stephane Marchand-Maillet, University of Geneva, Switzerland
Ilya Markov, University of Amsterdam, The Netherlands
Paul McNamee, Johns Hopkins University, USA
Edgar Meij, Yahoo Labs, UK
Marie-Francine Moens, Katholieke Universiteit Leuven, Belgium
Michael L. Nelson, Microsoft, UK
Dong Nguyen, Twente University, The Netherlands

Short Papers Committee (continued):

Jian-Yun Nie, Université de Montréal, Canada
Daan Odijk, University of Amsterdam, The Netherlands
Neil O'Hare, Yahoo Labs, USA
Iadh Ounis, University of Glasgow, UK
Virgil Pavlu, Northeastern University, USA
Tamara Polajnar, University of Cambridge, UK
Filip Radlinski, Microsoft, UK
Edie Rasmussen, University of British Columbia, Canada
Zhaochun Ren, University of Amsterdam, The Netherlands
Haggai Roitman, IBM Research, Israel
Stefan Rüger, Open University, UK
Anne Schuth, University of Amsterdam, The Netherlands
Jangwon Seo, Google, USA
Chirag Shah, Rutgers University, USA
Jialie Shen, Singapore Management University, Singapore
Milad Shokouhi, Microsoft, UK
Fabrizio Silvestri, Yahoo Labs, UK
Mark D. Smucker, University of Waterloo, Canada
Laure Soulier, IRIT-University of Toulouse, France
Damiano Spina, RMIT University, Australia
Aixin Sun, Nanyang Technological University, Singapore
Mingxuan Sun, Pandora, USA
S.M.M. Tahaghoghi, Microsoft, USA
Lynda Tamine, IRIT-University of Toulouse, France
Michael Taylor, Old Dominion University, USA
Martin Theobald, University of Ulm, Germany
James A. Thom, RMIT University, Australia
Bart Thomee, Yahoo Labs, USA
Qi Tian, University of Texas at San Antonio, USA
Anastasios Tombros, Queen Mary University of London, UK
Ricardo Torres, University of Campinas, Brazil
Andrew Trotman, eBay, USA
Manos Tsagkias, 904Labs, The Netherlands
Howard Turtle, Syracuse University, USA
Christophe Van Gysel, University of Amsterdam, The Netherlands
Suzan Verberne, Radboud University, The Netherlands
Stephen Wan, CSIRO, Australia
Changchu Wang, Microsoft, China
Hongning Wang, University of Illinois at Urbana-Champaign, USA
Lidan Wang, University of Illinois at Urbana-Champaign, USA
Wouter Weerkamp, 904Labs, The Netherlands
Xing Wei, Google, USA
Max L. Wilson, University of Nottingham, UK
Zheng Ye, Maluuba, Canada

Short Papers Committee (continued):
Emine Yilmaz, University College London, UK
Elad Yom-Tov, Microsoft, Israel
Xiaojun Yuan, State University of New York at Albany, USA
Dong Zhou, Hunan University of Science and Technology, China
Ke Zhou, Yahoo Labs, UK
Guido Zuccon, Queensland University of Technology, Australia

Demonstrations Committee:
B. Barla Cambazoglu, Yahoo Labs, Spain
Laura Dietz, University of Massachusetts Amherst, USA
Bin Gao, Microsoft Research Asia, China
Marcos Gonçalves, Federal University of Minas Gerais, Brazil
Manish Gupta, Microsoft Bing, India
Elizabeth León Guzmán, National University of Colombia, Colombia
Vanessa Lopez, IBM Research, Ireland
Alessandro Moschitti, University of Trento, Italy
Liqiang Nie, National University of Singapore, Singapore
Barbara Poblete, University of Chile, Chile
Rodrygo Santos, Federal University of Minas Gerais, Brazil
Heiko Schuldt, University of Basel, Switzerland
Ricardo da Silva Torres, University of Campinas, Brazil
Altigran Soares da Silva, Universidade Federal de Amazonas, Brazil
Andrew Trotman, eBay, USA
Leandro Wives, Federal University of Rio Grande do Sul, Brazil

Workshops Committee:
Eytan Adar, University of Michigan, USA
Ioannis Arapakis, Yahoo Labs, Spain
Michael Bendersky, Google, USA
Norbert Fuhr, University of Duisburg-Essen, Germany
Katja Hofmann, Microsoft Research, UK
Kalervo Jarvelin, University of Tampere, Finland
Hideo Joho, University of Tsukuba, Japan
Josiane Mothe, IRIT-University of Toulouse, France
Filip Radlinski, Microsoft Research, UK
Ian Soboroff, NIST, USA
Paul Thomas, CSIRO, Australia
Guido Zuccon, Queensland University of Technology, Australia

Doctoral Consortium Committee:

Eugene Agichtein, Emory University, USA
Leif Azzopardi, University of Glasgow, UK
Krisztian Balog, University of Stavanger, Norway
Charles L. A. Clarke, University of Waterloo, Canada
Kevyn Collins-Thompson, University of Michigan, USA
Claudia Hauff, TU Delft, The Netherlands
Gareth Jones, Dublin City University, Ireland
Diane Kelly, University of North Carolina at Chapel Hill, USA
Oren Kurland, Technion, Israel
Dave Lewis, Independent consultant, USA
Doug Oard, University of Maryland, USA
Iadh Ounis, University of Glasgow, UK
Denis Parra, Pontificia Universidad Católica de Chile, Chile
Mark Sanderson, RMIT University, Australia
Falk Scholer, RMIT University, Australia
Jaime Teevan, Microsoft Research, USA
Emine Yilmaz, University College London, UK

Doctoral Consortium Mentors:

Eugene Agichtein, Emory University, USA
Krisztian Balog, University of Stavanger, Norway
Charles L. A. Clarke, University of Waterloo, Canada
Kevyn Collins-Thompson, University of Michigan, USA
Claudia Hauff, TU Delft, The Netherlands
Gareth Jones, Dublin City University, Ireland
Diane Kelly, University of North Carolina at Chapel Hill, USA
Dave Lewis, Independent consultant, USA
Doug Oard, University of Maryland, USA
Iadh Ounis, University of Glasgow, UK
Denis Parra, Pontificia Universidad Católica de Chile, Chile
Mark Sanderson, RMIT University, Australia
Jaime Teevan, Microsoft Research, USA

SIGIR 2015 Sponsors & Supporters

SPONSORS

SIGIR
Special Interest Group
on Information Retrieval

acm Association for Computing Machinery

PLATINUM SUPPORTER

Baidu 百度

GOLD SUPPORTERS

Google

Microsoft Research

YAHOO! LABS

SILVER SUPPORTERS

ebay

BRONZE SUPPORTERS

facebook

IBM

Yandex

LOCAL SUPPORTERS

Pontificia Universidad Católica de Chile

Universidad de Chile

UdeSantiago de Chile

Universidad Tecnica Federico Santa Maria

Yahoo! Labs Latin America

Affiliated Publishers

Morgan & Claypool Publishers

now the essence of knowledge

Springer

Salton Award Lecture
People, Interacting with Information

Nicholas J. Belkin
Rutgers, The State University of New Jersey
New Brunswick, NJ, USA
belkin@rutgers.edu

ACM Classification
H.3.3 [**Information Search and Retrieval**] -- *Retrieval models, Search*

General Terms
Design; Human Factors; Theory

Keywords
Interactive information retrieval; Information behavior

Abstract

Colleagues, friends, let me begin by expressing how pleased, and humbly honored I am to be a recipient of the Gerard Salton Award. Gerry was a great man, and to receive the award named for him is very special. For me personally, it is especially meaningful, given the sometime disputatious nature of our professional interactions, and what seemed, on the surface, to be quite different ideas about information retrieval. I say, on the surface, because in the end, I believe that he and I both shared the same goal for the field, although we approached it from quite different positions. In this presentation, I will speak at some length on that goal, and on how I think it might be best addressed.

I am humbled also by the honor of having joined the ranks of the previous recipients of this award; the founders, leaders and innovators in information retrieval (IR), from the earliest beginnings of the field to today. It has been my distinct good fortune to have known all of the previous recipients, to have collaborated with many of them, to have argued with all of them, to have learned from them, and, I hope, to have been able to appropriately incorporate their insights into my own work.

Today, following the example of many of my predecessors, I'd like to take this opportunity to, in Sue Dumais's words of 2009, "present a personal reflection on information retrieval." This will include an overview of my history in IR, a discussion of my personal take on its proper goals, and on how those might be best achieved, and saying something about the challenges that IR theory, experiment and practice face both now, and in the future, and how we might best address those challenges.

I came to the field of IR from a starting point in information science; specifically, with the concern of addressing general problems of information in society. I initially thought that the best way to do this would be to establish a firm framework for a science of information. Acting on my then understanding of what a science constituted, I began the project of defining information. Fortunately for me, I did this at University College, London, with B.C. Brookes as my Ph.D. supervisor, and Steve Robertson my office mate. It didn't take long for me to be disabused of a) the idea that information could be defined; and b) that defining its phenomena of interest was a necessary precondition to a "real" science. Instead, perhaps under the influence of the great pragmatist, Jeremy Bentham, founder of University College, I turned to attempting to develop a concept of information which would lead to being able to predict its effect on a person's state of knowledge, which I took at that time as what IR systems should be attempting to do.

The confluence of all these factors resulted in my attempting to understand what led people to engage in information seeking, which led in turn to the Anomalous State of Knowledge (ASK) hypothesis. Collaboration with Bob Oddy then led to a general model of IR as a series of interactions between a person (in particular, that person's changing ASK) and information objects, mediated by the IR systems and its representations of the person's ASK and of the underlying structure of the information objects which it would propose to the person.

Thus began what I now understand as the unifying theme and goal of my research throughout my career, understanding and supporting people's interactions with information. The operationalization of this goal has changed over time, beginning with attempts to represent an information seeker's ASK, going on to designing ASK-based IR systems, to understanding the ASK as an aspect of a person's problematic situation (thanks to Gernot Wersig and Alfred Schutz), to my current stance concerning the goal of IR: supporting people in accomplishing the task or goal which led them to engage in information seeking, by supporting appropriate interaction with information objects. In all these somewhat different modes, there have been two constants: emphasis on the person (often called the "user") as the central actor in the IR situation; and, understanding interaction as its central process. This position, for perhaps the first 2/3 of my career, has been in quite distinct contrast, not to say conflict, with "mainstream" IR research, which, until quite recently, focused almost exclusively on information object representation and retrieval techniques, and on models of IR which included the "user" as merely an input and feedback device, if at all, and which had no room for interaction as a process at all.

In her Salton Award Lecture in 1988, Karen Spärck Jones, one of the foremost contributors to our understanding of information object representation, and to the development of retrieval techniques and models, and arch experimenter, said the following, referring to IR research at least through the 1970s:

> But these concerns, though worthy, had unfortunate consequences. One was that, in spite of references to

SIGIR '15, August 09-13, 2015, Santiago, Chile.
ACM 978-1-4503-3621-5/15/08.
http://dx.doi.org/10.1145/2766462.2767854

> environmental parameters and so forth, it tested information systems in an abstract, reductionist way which was not only felt to be disagreeably arid but was judged to neglect not only important operational matters but, more importantly, much of the vital business of establishing the user's need.

And, referring to her own research in relevance feedback:

> More importantly, I felt that the required next step in this line of work was to carry out real, rather than simulated, interactive searching ...

Karen's example demonstrates that there has been, for some time, recognition that IR research would be wise to more directly address the user, as a significant actor in the IR system, and the interaction of the user with the system and with the information objects, as research foci. Why then have the terms and concepts of users and people and interaction only so recently appeared in any significant number in venues such as SIGIR?

Clearly, the inertia associated with reluctance to give up what seem to have been successful methods and practices has played a significant part in this state of affairs. But more important, I think, have been other factors, two especially. One has been the reluctance, or inability of IR researchers to accept a broader and more realistic goal of their enterprise; that is, to go beyond identification of relevant, or even authoritative, information objects, to the support of people in achievement of the goal or task which led them to engage in information seeking. The other is more technical, but perhaps equally important. That is, that the theories, and research methods and techniques necessary for addressing the issues of users and interaction in IR, and the related evaluation methods and measures, are so very different from what we are familiar with, and also, so very difficult to both develop and implement.

I think that there's no question that the actual practice and performance of IR in contemporary systems demonstrates that its goal needs to be expanded to at least that which I propose, and that, therefore, evaluation of performance of IR systems needs to be radically changed. The recent emergence of a move toward evaluation of performance of IR systems over an entire search session is evidence of recognition of this need; the not un-related disappearance of the TREC Session Track of the difficulty of the enterprise. The emergence of the term, interactive information retrieval, the amount of research conducted under that rubric, and the lack of agreement about how to conduct, and to evaluate, such research, are further testimony to both the significance and the difficulty of the task.

So, IR faces daunting challenges, including: understanding why people engage in information seeking; identifying the aspects of that condition that need to be considered in supporting them in achieving their goals; how to design support for evolving user goals and knowledge; how best to support people's interactions with information objects and the other components of the IR system with respect to different and dynamic intentions; and, perhaps most daunting of all, how to evaluate, in ways as rigorous and successful as IR evaluation has been to date, IR systems which attempt to address this broader goal.

I, and others, have proposed that moving from relevance to usefulness as the main criterion for evaluation of IR system performance, could provide a basis for addressing many of these challenges. For instance, evaluating an IR system's usefulness in helping people to achieve a motivating task/goal necessarily entails the development of an empirically-based taxonomy of such tasks/goals, which in turn requires the development of methods for investigation of the behaviors and intentions of people prior to, during, and after engagement in an IR system. Adapting methods of information behavior research to the specific requirements of IR system design is a likely path to such outcomes. This, in turn, could lead to the ability to accurately simulate whole search sessions, which might enable TREC-style evaluation of interactive IR systems. Furthermore, evaluation according to usefulness allows considering search sessions both as whole entities, and as coherent sequences of different types of interactions with information and system, each with its own specific support techniques and usefulness-based performance measures.

The recent Dagstuhl Interactive IR and NII-Shonan Whole Session Evaluation seminars, and the new SIGIR Conference on Information Interaction and Retrieval (CHIIR), and its immediate predecessors, IIiX and HCIR, are explicit demonstration of our field's newly found commitment to accepting and addressing these challenges. I can't help but feel that my being a recipient of the Salton Award is further evidence of information retrieval's acceptance of including people, interacting with information, as a major concern, and for this I sincerely thank you all.

BIO

Nicholas J. Belkin is a Distinguished Professor at the School of Communication and Information at Rutgers University. Among the main themes of his research are understanding human information behavior, interactive information retrieval, personalization of interaction with information systems, and evaluation of information retrieval systems. Belkin is best known for his work on human-centered Information Retrieval and the hypothesis of Anomalous State of Knowledge (ASK). Belkin realized that in many cases, users of search systems are unable to precisely formulate what they need. They miss some vital knowledge to formulate their queries. In such cases it is more suitable to attempt to describe a user's anomalous state of knowledge than to ask the user to specify her/his need as a request to the system. Dr. Belkin was the chair of SIGIR in 1995-99, and the president of American Society (now Association) for Information Science and Technology in 2005.

Exploring Session Context using Distributed Representations of Queries and Reformulations

Bhaskar Mitra
Microsoft
Cambridge, UK
bmitra@microsoft.com

ABSTRACT

Search logs contain examples of frequently occurring patterns of user reformulations of queries. Intuitively, the reformulation "san francisco" → "san francisco 49ers" is semantically similar to "detroit" → "detroit lions". Likewise, "london" → "things to do in london" and "new york" → "new york tourist attractions" can also be considered similar transitions in intent. The reformulation "movies" → "new movies" and "york" → "new york", however, are clearly different despite the lexical similarities in the two reformulations. In this paper, we study the distributed representation of queries learnt by deep neural network models, such as the *Convolutional Latent Semantic Model*, and show that they can be used to represent *query reformulations* as vectors. These reformulation vectors exhibit favourable properties such as mapping semantically and syntactically similar query changes closer in the embedding space. Our work is motivated by the success of continuous space language models in capturing relationships between words and their meanings using offset vectors. We demonstrate a way to extend the same intuition to represent query reformulations.

Furthermore, we show that the distributed representations of queries and reformulations are both useful for modelling session context for query prediction tasks, such as for query auto-completion (QAC) ranking. Our empirical study demonstrates that short-term (session) history context features based on these two representations improves the mean reciprocal rank (MRR) for the QAC ranking task by more than 10% over a supervised ranker baseline. Our results also show that by using features based on both these representations together we achieve a better performance, than either of them individually.

Categories and Subject Descriptors

H.3 [**Information Storage and Retrieval**]: H.3.3 Information Search and Retrieval

Keywords

Query auto-completion; Deep learning; Contextual search

SIGIR'15, August 09 - 13, 2015, Santiago, Chile.
© 2015 ACM. ISBN 978-1-4503-3621-5/15/08 ...$15.00. .
DOI: http://dx.doi.org/10.1145/2766462.2767702

1. INTRODUCTION

Latent semantic models, such as Latent Semantic Analysis (LSA) [10], Latent Dirichlet Allocation (LDA) [3], Bi-Lingual Topic Model (BLTM) [12] and more recently neural network based models such as Semantic Hashing [34] and Convolutional Latent Semantic Model (CLSM) [36], have been successfully applied to various information retrieval (IR) tasks. By representing queries and documents as low-dimensional vectors in a semantic space these models provide a mechanism to study higher order relationships between these query and document entities. In this paper, we explore ways to model short-term (session) history of Web search users for retrieving contextually more relevant query suggestions using the vector space framework.

As users type their query into the search box, search engines provide ranked lists of query suggestions based on the current prefix at the given point in time. When only a few characters have been entered the search engine has little understanding of the actual user intent and the generic suggestions provided by a non-contextual *query auto-completion* (QAC) system typically perform poorly [1]. The high ambiguity associated with short prefixes makes QAC a particularly interesting candidate for leveraging any additional information available about the user's current task. The same study also showed that 49% of Web searches are preceded by a different search which can be used to gain additional insights into the user's current information need.

The majority of previous work [7, 35] on using short-term user history for search personalization has been focused on modelling the topical relevance of the candidate results (documents or query suggestions) to the previous queries and viewed documents in the same search session. Using such *implicit feedback* has been shown to be a very attractive strategy for improving retrieval performance when the user intent is ambiguous. For example, knowing that the user's previous query was "guardians of the galaxy" can help to inform a QAC system to promote the query "imdb" in ranking over "instagram" when the user has just typed "i" in the search box. Query reformulation behaviours within search sessions have also been studied but are mostly limited to taxonomy based classifications [20, 28] and models based on syntactic changes [14]. A quick study of a sample of Bing's search engine logs reveal that users frequently search for "san francisco 49ers" and "san francisco weather" immediately after searching for "san francisco". Similarly, the query "detroit" is often followed by the queries "detroit lions" and "detroit weather". Intuitively, "san francisco" → "san francisco 49ers" represents a similar shift in user's intent as "detroit" → "detroit lions". We can see many such frequently occurring patterns of reformulations in large scale search logs. Modelling these reformulations using lexical matching alone is difficult. For example, we understand that "movies" → "new movies" is not the same intent shift as "york" → "new york" even though in both cases the same term was added to both the queries by the user. On the other hand, "london" $\rightarrow$ "things to do in london" and "new york" $\rightarrow$ "new york tourist attractions" are semantically similar although the two reformulations involve the addition of completely disjoint sets of new terms to the queries.

In text processing, Mikolov et al. [31] demonstrated that the distributed representation of words learnt by continuous space language models are surprisingly good at capturing syntactic and semantic relationships between the words. Simple algebraic operations on the word vectors have been shown to produce intuitive results. For example, $vector(\text{"king"}) - vector(\text{"man"}) + vector(\text{"woman"})$ results in a vector that is in close proximity to the $vector(\text{"queen"})$. In Section 3, we will show that the embeddings learnt by the *Convolutional Latent Semantic Model* (CLSM) [36] exhibit similar favourable properties and hence provide an intuitive mechanism to represent *query reformulations* as the offsets between the query vectors.

Our empirical study, described in Section 4, demonstrate that the vector representations of queries and reformulations can be useful for capturing session context for the retrieval of query suggestions. The CLSM models are trained to map queries (and documents) with similar intents to the same neighbourhood in the semantic space. Therefore they are suitable for measuring the topical similarity between candidate suggestions and the user's recent queries. In addition, our experiments show that the vector representation of the reformulation, from the user's previous query to the candidate suggestion, can also be a useful signal for predicting the relevance of the suggestion. We present our results in Section 5 that demonstrate that session context features based on these vector representations can significantly improve the QAC ranking over the supervised ranking baseline proposed by Shokouhi [37].

The main contributions of this paper are,

- Demonstrating that *query reformulations* can be represented as low-dimensional vectors which map syntactically and semantically similar query changes close together in the embedding space. We believe that this is the first time that a distributed representation for query reformulations has been proposed and studied in the literature.
- Using features based on the distributed representations of queries and reformulations to improve upon a supervised ranking baseline for session context-aware QAC ranking. Our experiments on the large-scale query logs of the Bing search engine and the publicly available AOL query logs [33] show that these features can improve the *Mean Reciprocal Rank* (MRR) by more than 10% on these testbeds.
- Demonstrating that convolutional latent semantic models trained on *session query pairs* perform significantly better for the contextual QAC ranking task compared to the CLSM model trained on clicked query-document pairs.

Next, we review related work that are relevant to this study.

2. RELATED WORK

Latent semantic models for Web search. Latent semantic models have received significant attention in IR. Latent Semantic Analysis (LSA) [10], Probabilistic LSA (PLSA) [18] and Latent Dirichlet Allocation (LDA) [3] are some of the well-known models proposed to represent queries and documents in low-dimensional space for semantic matching. Unlike these models, which commonly use unsupervised learning, Gao et al. [12] trained Bi-Lingual Topic Models (BLTM) and linear Discriminative Projection Models (DPM) on *clickthrough* data, consisting of query and clicked documents. Salakhutdinov and Hinton [34] used auto-encoders to show that deep learning can be useful for extracting hierarchical semantic structures from queries and documents.

More recently, Huang et al. [21] discriminatively trained a Deep Structured Semantic Model (DSSM) on clickthrough data to maximize the conditional likelihood of the clicked documents for the corresponding queries. By training on query-document pairs they generate a pair of models for projecting the queries and the documents, respectively, to the same embedding space. Their experiments demonstrated better retrieval performance over other existing semantic models by directly optimizing for the document ranking task. They also proposed a *word hashing* technique for dealing with large vocabularies that are commonly associated with Web corpora. The first layer of their model maps the high-dimensional term vectors corresponding to the input queries and documents into a lower-dimensional letter based n-gram vectors, while the subsequent layers learn a non-linear projection of this n-gram vectors to a low-dimensional semantic space. The cosine similarity between the vectors of a query and a document represents their mutual relevance.

While the DSSM treats an input query as a raw term vector or a *bag-of-words*, Shen et al. [36] added a convolutional-pooling structure to the network architecture in the *Convolutional Latent Semantic Model* (CLSM) to capture richer contextual structures in the input text. The CLSM model has been shown to perform better than DSSM and many other existing state-of-the-art techniques on various information retrieval tasks such as Web document ranking and contextual entity search [13].

An examination of the CLSM model outputs reveals syntactic and semantic regularities in the distributed representation of queries. The regularities are akin to the ones reported by Mikolov et al. [31] about the embeddings learnt by continuous space language models, where simple vector offsets between words were found to capture semantic and syntactic inter-word relationships. Mikolov et al. [29] further proposed models that can be trained on large scale datasets and extended the vector representations to phrases [30]. Unlike these continuous space language models [30, 31], CLSM can project multi-word variable length queries into the embedding space. In this paper, we study the vector offset technique in the context of the CLSM outputs.

Query auto-completion. Most modern browsers, search engines, text editors and command shells implement some form of an auto-completion feature to aid users in faster text entry. In Web search, *pre-computed auto-completion* systems are popular, where the suggestions are typically filtered by exact prefix matching from a pre-selected set of candidates and ranked according to past popularity. Ranking suggestions by past frequency is commonly referred to as the *MostPopularCompletion* (MPC) model and can be regarded as a maximum likelihood approximator [1]. Given a prefix $\mathcal{P}$ and all queries $\mathcal{Q}$ from the search logs,

$$MPC(\mathcal{P}) = \underset{\bar{q} \in completions(\mathcal{P})}{\arg\max} P(\bar{q}), \quad P(\bar{q}) = \frac{Freq(\bar{q})}{\sum_{q_i \in \mathcal{Q}} Freq(q_i)} \tag{1}$$

Weber and Castillo [39] and Shokouhi [37] showed how query distributions change across different user demographics and argued that QAC systems based on personalization features can significantly outperform popularity-based baselines. Ranking suggestions based on temporal context has also been explored [38, 41].

The two QAC related studies most relevant to our work have been done by Shokouhi [37] and Kharitonov et al. [24]. To capture short-term context, Shokouhi [37] relied on letter n-gram matches between the previous queries and the candidates, and trained a supervised ranking model for combining them with MPC and other non-contextual and user demographic features. Kharitonov et al. [24] proposed a unified framework for contextualizing and diversifying the ranking of QAC suggestions. Their empirical evaluations show that by considering the user's previous query alone more than 96% of the improvements can be achieved, as compared to additionally considering the document examination history and diversification context. Given the previous query, their proposed model computes the expected probability of a given completion as follows,

$$P(q_1|q_0) = P(c = 0|q_0)P(q_1) + P(c = 1|q_0)P(q_1|c = 1, q_0) \tag{2}$$

Where c is an indicator variable whose value is 1 if the user continues the current task, and 0 otherwise. The two primary components of the above equation are $P(q_1)$ and $P(q_1|c = 1, q_0)$, which correspond to the probability of observing the query q_1 globally and in the context of the query q_0, respectively, in the query logs.

For our evaluation, we implement the supervised ranking framework proposed by Shokouhi and include the n-gram similarity, the query frequency and the query pairwise frequency features among others as described in Section 4. We believe that the baseline used in our experiment is comparable with any state-of-the-art baselines described in the literature for QAC ranking.

Session context. In Web search, Bennett et al. [2] investigated the impact of short-term and long-term user behaviour on relevance prediction, and showed that short-term user history becomes more important as the session progresses. Li et al. [25] evaluated DSSM and convolutional-DSSM for modelling session context for Web search. Besides the primary IR task, QAC as opposed to Web ranking, our work differs from this study by going beyond computing the topical similarity using the existing models and explicitly modelling query reformulations as vectors. We also show the benefits of optimizing a CLSM model directly for capturing session context by training on session query pairs.

Yan et al. [44] proposed an approach that maps queries and clicks to latent search intents represented using Open Directory Project[1] categories for making context-aware query recommendations. Cao et al. [7] and Liao et al. [27] have explored session context using latent concept clusters from click-through bipartite graphs, while Guo et al. [15] represented the user's previous queries using a regularized topic model. Zhang et al. [45] proposed a task-centric click model for characterizing user behaviour within a single search session. Cao et al. [8] learnt a variable length *Hidden Markov Model* from large scale search logs, whereas Boldi et al. [4] studied *random walks* on query-flow graphs for improved recommendations.

Lastly, previous studies on the relationships between neighbouring queries from a search session have been mostly focused on categorizing the reformulations based on broad manually defined taxonomies (e.g., *generalization*, *specialization*, *error correction* and *parallel move*) [5] or understanding the user goals behind common actions (e.g., *addition*, *removal* or *substitution* of terms) [19]. Motivated by the broad manually identified reformulation categories Xiang et al. [43] and Jiang et al. [23] designed simple features for supervised retrieval models. Finally, Guan et al. [14] use reinforcement learning for modifying term weights in response to the observed modifications made to the query by the user.

While clearly using session context for Web search is a well-studied topic, context-sensitive query auto-completion has been discussed less thoroughly in the literature. Also, to the best of our knowledge this is the first time that an explicit vector representation of query reformulations has been proposed and studied.

[1] http://www.dmoz.org/

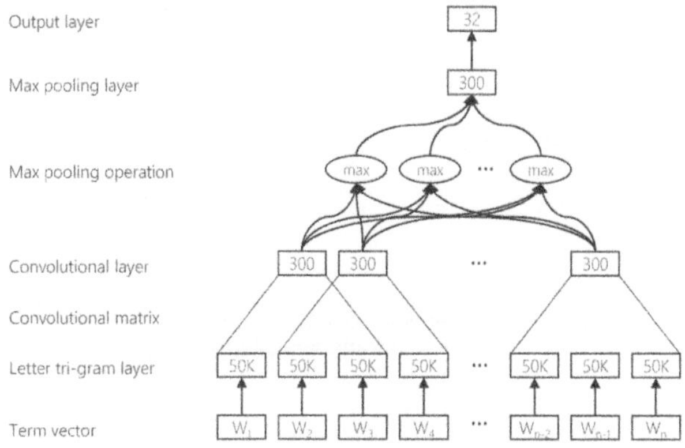

Figure 1: Architecture of the convolutional latent semantic model (CLSM). The model has an input layer that performs the *word hashing*, a convolutional layer, a max pooling layer, and an output layer that produces the final semantic vector representation of the query.

3. MODELS

Architecture. We adopt the CLSM architecture proposed by Shen et al. [36] for our study. As illustrated in Figure 1, the CLSM model is a deep neural network with a convolutional-pooling structure that projects a variable-length text into a fixed-length real-valued vector.

Each word in the input text (e.g., query) is first *hashed* to a letter trigram vector as described by Huang et al. [21]. The *word hashing* step, for example, maps the word "top" to a feature vector with non-zero values corresponding to the trigrams "#to", "top" and "op#", where "#" denotes the word boundary. It has been pointed out in previous work [21] that the trigram hashing technique is a robust strategy for dealing with misspellings and morphological variants of words in the data. It also scales much better for large vocabularies compared to the *one-hot*[2] representation where each unique word is associated with a separate identifier. The number of unique words in a Web corpus can be extremely large, whereas the number of distinct letter trigrams tends to be much more manageable (limited to the top 50K for this study). These factors makes the trigram hashing strategy particularly useful for Web search.

Next, for each word the convolutional layer extracts contextual features based on its immediate neighbours as defined by a pre-determined window size. A max pooling layer combines the output of the convolutional layer into a fixed-length feature vector. The max pooling layer in turn is connected to the output layer which produces the final vector representation of the whole query. Unless specified otherwise, for all models in this paper the window size for the convolutional layer is set to three and the dimensions of the output vector to 32.

Training. The training data for the CLSM models consists of source-target text pairs. The original DSSM [21] and CLSM [36] models were trained on *clickthrough data* which consists of pairs of queries and document titles, corresponding to clicked results.

In addition to clickthrough data, we also train the CLSM models on sampled pairs of queries from search logs that were observed in succession during user sessions. In the rest of this paper, we refer to this as the *session pairs* dataset. For a pair of observed queries $\{q_1, q_2\}$, if the dataset includes both the ordering $\{q_1, q_2\}$ and $\{q_2, q_1\}$

[2] http://en.wikipedia.org/wiki/One-hot

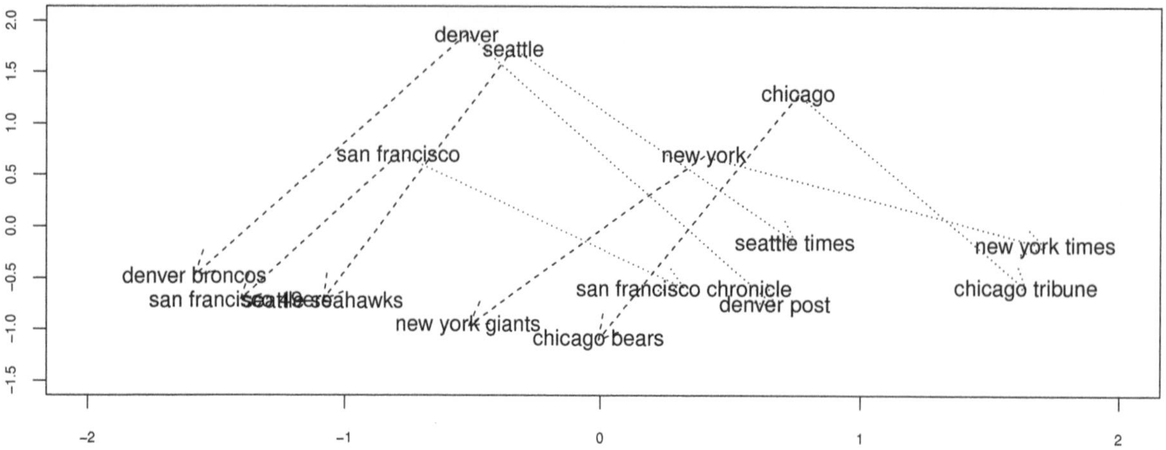

Figure 2: A two-dimensional PCA projection of the 32 dimensional CLSM output vectors shows how intuitively similar intent transitions, represented by the directed edges, are automatically modelled in the embedding space. The CLSM model used for this illustration is trained on the symmetric session pairs dataset.

then we refer to it as the *symmetric* session pairs dataset, otherwise as *asymmetric*. The symmetric session pairs data is further randomly sub-sampled by half to keep the count of the training pairs in both the datasets comparable.

The *session pairs* datasets are extracted from the exact same user sessions from which the *clickthrough* data is generated. While this does not imply that the actual count of training pairs in these two types of datasets are equal, it does make the comparison more meaningful as it assumes the same amount of raw log data is examined for training both the types of models. In practice, however, we did observe the data sizes to be comparable across all three datasets during this study.

All the CLSM models in this study are trained using mini-batch based stochastic gradient descent, as described by Shen et al. [36]. Each mini-batch consists of 1024 training samples (source-target pairs) and for each positive pair 100 negative targets are randomly sampled from the data for that source that were not originally paired.

Distributed Representations. The CLSM models project the queries to an embedding space with fixed number of dimensions. The semantic similarity between two queries q_1 and q_2 in this semantic space is defined by,

$$Sim(q_1, q_2) = cosine(y_1, y_2) = \frac{y_1^T y_2}{\|y_1\| \|y_2\|} \tag{3}$$

where y_1 and y_2 are the CLSM vector outputs corresponding to the two queries, respectively. A close examination of the CLSM output vectors reveal that the learnt distributed representations hold useful information about inter-query relationships. Figure 2 illustrates how the offset vectors between pairs of queries, represented by the directed edges, are directionally similar in the embedding space for similar intent transitions. This matches the observations made by Mikolov et al. [29] on continuous space language models for text processing, and gives us an intuitively understandable representation of query reformulations as their offset vectors in the embedding space. More specifically, we define the *reformulation* from query q_1 to q_2 as,

$$Ref(q_1, q_2) = \hat{y_2} - \hat{y_1} = \frac{y_2}{\|y_2\|} - \frac{y_1}{\|y_1\|} \tag{4}$$

where y_1 and y_2 are the CLSM vector embeddings of the two queries, respectively. This explicit vector representation provides a framework for studying frequently occurring query reformulation patterns. To illustrate this, we randomly sample approximately 65K pairs of queries that were observed in succession in Bing's logs. For each pair, we compute the offset vector using a CLSM model. We then run a simple k-means clustering (k = 100) and examine the top clusters. Example reformulations from five of the biggest clusters are shown in Table 1.

A further study of these reformulation vectors can reveal important insights about user behaviour, such as the popularity of certain reformulation patterns. For example, we randomly sampled 100,000 adjacent pairs of queries from Bing's logs that were observed in search sessions. Our analysis show that there are more pairs similar to the *narrowing* reformulation "new york" $\rightarrow$ "things to do in new york" in the sampled set, than its inverse. Similarly, the misspelling "fcebook" followed by "facebook" is a more commonly observed pattern than the other way around, as illustrated in Figure 3.

Next, we list qualitative examples in Table 2 to demonstrate the predictive aspect of these reformulation vectors. Similar to the analogy based test proposed by Mikolov et al. [29], these examples show that we can obtain intuitively understandable results by performing simple algebraic operations in the embedding space. For example, we compute the vector sum of the projections (normalized to their unit norm) of the queries "new york" and "newspaper".

$$y_{target} = \hat{y}_{newyork} + \hat{y}_{newspaper} = \frac{y_{newyork}}{\|y_{newyork}\|} + \frac{y_{newspaper}}{\|y_{newspaper}\|} \tag{5}$$

Then from a fixed set of candidates we find the query whose embedding has the highest cosine similarity with y_{target}. For our analysis we picked the top one million most popular queries from one day of Bing's logs as the candidate set. In this query set, the closest query vector to y_{target} corresponds to the query "new york times". Similarly, the nearest neighbour search for $vector$("how old is gwen stefani") $-$ $vector$("gwen stefani") $+$ $vector$("meghan trainor") yields a vector close to $vector$("how old is meghan trainor"). These examples show that the vector representation captures simple syntactic as well as semantic relationships. We intentionally also include some examples where the nearest neighbour search yields unex-

Table 2: **Examples of simple syntactic and semantic relationships in the query embedding space. The nearest neighbour search is performed on a candidate set of one million most popular queries from one day of Bing's logs.**

Query vector	Nearest neighbour
$vector$("chicago") + $vector$("newspaper")	$vector$("chicago suntimes")
$vector$("new york") + $vector$("newspaper")	$vector$("new york times")
$vector$("san francisco") + $vector$("newspaper")	$vector$("la times")
$vector$("beyonce") + $vector$("pictures")	$vector$("beyonce images")
$vector$("beyonce") + $vector$("videos")	$vector$("beyonce videos")
$vector$("beyonce") + $vector$("net worth")	$vector$("jaden smith net worth")
$vector$("www.facebook.com") − $vector$("facebook") + $vector$("twitter")	$vector$("www.twitter.com")
$vector$("www.facebook.com") − $vector$("facebook") + $vector$("gmail")	$vector$("www.googlemail.com")
$vector$("www.facebook.com") − $vector$("facebook") + $vector$("hotmail")	$vector$("www.hotmail.xom")
$vector$("how tall is tom cruise") − $vector$("tom cruise") + $vector$("tom selleck")	$vector$("how tall is tom selleck")
$vector$("how old is gwen stefani") − $vector$("gwen stefani") + $vector$("meghan trainor")	$vector$("how old is meghan trainor")
$vector$("how old is gwen stefani") − $vector$("gwen stefani") + $vector$("ariana grande")	$vector$("how old is ariana grande 2014")
$vector$("university of washington") − $vector$("seattle") + $vector$("chicago")	$vector$("chicago state university")
$vector$("university of washington") − $vector$("seattle") + $vector$("denver")	$vector$("university of colorado")
$vector$("university of washington") − $vector$("seattle") + $vector$("detroit")	$vector$("northern illinois university")

pected results (e.g., $vector$("beyonce") + $vector$("net worth")) to highlight that these predictions are often noisy.

4. EXPERIMENT SETUP

Our empirical evaluations are based on the learning to rank framework proposed by Shokouhi [37] for personalized query auto-completions. In this setup, we learn a supervised ranking model based on training data generated from implicit user feedback. The output of the CLSM models, described in the previous section, are used to generate additional features for this supervised ranking model. The baseline ranking model (henceforth referred to simply as the *baseline model*) contains both the non-contextual and the (non-CLSM based) contextual features. We compare all models using the mean reciprocal rank (MRR) metric, and the study is repeated on two different testbeds to further confirm the validity of the results.

4.1 Testbeds

We conduct our experiments on a large scale search query dataset sampled from the logs of the Bing search engine. We also reproduce our results using the publicly available AOL query logs [33]. In the rest of this paper we refer to these two datasets as the *Bing testbed* and the *AOL testbed*, respectively.

Bing testbed. Bing's logs contain a record of all the queries submitted by its users associated with the corresponding anonymized user IDs, timestamps and any clicked Web results[3] (the URL and the displayed title). We sampled queries from these logs for the duration of the last week of October, 2014 and use this as the *background data*, for computing the feature values and training the CLSM models. From the first week of November, we sampled 175,392 queries from two consecutive days for training the supervised ranking models, and from the following two individual days we sampled 79,000 queries for validation and 74,663 queries for testing, respectively.

AOL testbed. This dataset contains queries sampled between 1 March, 2006 and 31 May, 2006. For each query, the data includes an anonymized user ID and a timestamp. If a result was clicked then the rank of the clicked item and the domain portion of its URL are also included. In aggregate, the data contains 16,946,938 query submissions and 36,389,567 document clicks by 657,426 users.

We consider all queries before 1 May, 2006 as the *background data.* All queries from the next two weeks of data are used for training the supervised ranking models, and the remaining two sets, consisting of one week of data each, is used for validation and testing, respectively.

To have a separation of users in training and test datasets, on both the testbeds we use only the users with even user IDs for training and validation, and those with odd numbered user IDs for testing. Also, in all the datasets the queries are lower-cased and the punctuations are removed.

4.2 Learning to rank

To generate the training, the validation and the test sets we sample query impressions from the corresponding portions of the logs. For each query impression, a prefix is generated by splitting the query at a randomly selected position[4]. For each prefix a positive relevance judgment is assigned to the suggestion candidate that matches the final submitted query and all the others are labelled as irrelevant.

The training data collected in the above process consists of labelled *prefix-query* pairs. With respect to the choice of learning-to-rank algorithms, we chose LambdaMART [42], a boosted tree version of LambdaRank [6], that won the Yahoo! Learning to Rank Challenge (2010) [9] and is considered as one of the state-of-the-art learning algorithms. We train 500 trees across all our experiments with the same set of fixed parameters tuned using standard training and validation on separate sets.

We consider the top 10 million most popular queries in the background data as the pre-computed list of suggestion candidates and filter out all the impressions where the final submitted query is not present in this list. For each impression in the training, the validation and the test sets we retain a maximum of 20 suggestion candidates - the submitted query as the positive candidate and 19 other most frequently observed queries from the background data that starts with the same prefix, as the negative examples. Furthermore, for each impression up to 10 previous queries from the same session are

[3]For impressions with multiple clicked results we consider only the last clicked document.

[4]The prefixes in our study are strictly shorter than the original query and limited to no more than 30 characters in length.

Table 1: k-means clustering of 65K in-session query pairs observed in search logs. Examples from five of the top ten biggest clusters shown here. The first and the second clusters contain examples where the follow up query is a different formulation of the exact same intent. The third and the fourth clusters contain examples of *narrowing* intent, in particular the fourth cluster contains reformulations where the additional specification is based on location disambiguation. Finally, the last cluster contains examples of intent jumps across tasks.

soundcloud	→	www.soundcloud.com
coasthills coop	→	www.coasthills.coop
american express	→	www.barclaycardus.com login
duke energy bill pay	→	www.duke-energy.com pay my bill
cool math games	→	www.coolmath.com
majesty shih tzu	→	what is a majesty shih tzu
hard drive dock	→	what is a hard drive dock
lugia in leaf green	→	where is lugia in leaf green
red river log jam	→	what is th red river log jam
prowl	→	what does prowl mean
rottweiler	→	rottweiler facebook
sundry	→	sundry expense
elections	→	florida governor race 2014
pleurisy	→	pleurisy shoulder pain
elections	→	2014 rowan county election results
cna classes	→	cna classes in lexington tennessee
container services inc	→	container services ringgold ga
enclosed trailers for sale	→	enclosed trailers for sale north carolina
firewood for sale	→	firewood for sale in asheboro nc
us senate race in colorado	→	us senate race in georgia
siol	→	facebook
cowboy bebop	→	facebook
mr doob	→	google
great west 100 west 29th	→	facebook
avatar dragons	→	youtube

made available for computing the session context features. Similar to other previous work [11, 22] we define the end of a session by a 30 minute window of user inactivity.

For our final evaluation we report the Mean Reciprocal Rank of the submitted query averaged over all sampled impressions on each of the two testbeds.

4.3 Features

The baseline contextual and non-contextual features, as well as the features based on the CLSM outputs are described in this section.

Non-contextual features. The *MostPopularCompletion* (MPC) model is one of the baselines for our study. We also use the output of this model as a feature for the supervised ranking model. Other non-contextual features include the *prefix length* (in characters), the *suggestion length* (in both characters and words), the *vowels to alphabets* ratio in the suggestion and a boolean feature indicating whether the *suggestion contains numeric* characters.

N-gram similarity features. We compute the character n-gram similarity (n=3) between the suggestion candidate and the previous queries from the same user session. This is an implementation of the *short history* features described by Shokouhi [37]. A maximum of 10 previous queries are considered.

Pairwise frequency feature. From the background data, we generate the top 10 million most popular adjacent pairs of queries observed in search sessions. For a given impression, the previous

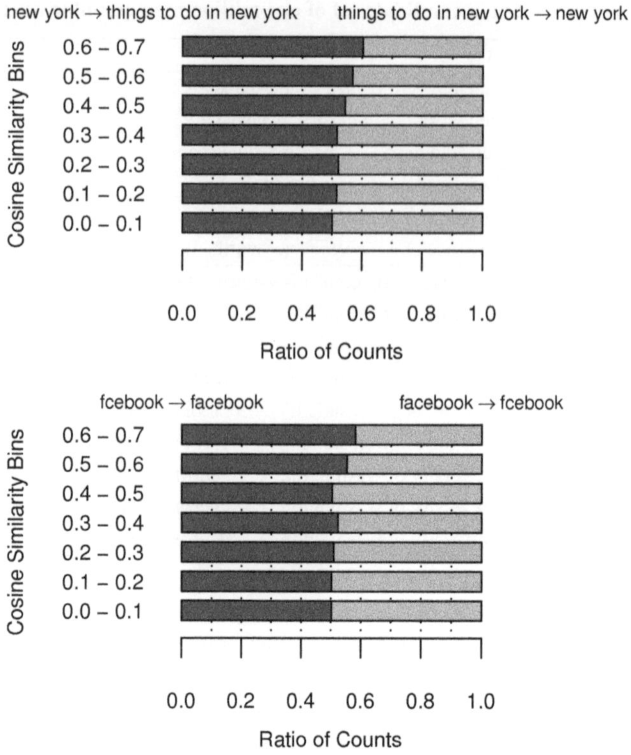

Figure 3: Visualization of the cosine similarity scores of a given reformulation with respect to a set of 100,000 other reformulations randomly sampled from Bing's logs. The similarity scores are binned and the ratio of the counts are shown above. The counts corresponding to bins with cosine similarity greater than 0.7 were too small, hence excluded.

query and the suggestion candidate pair is matched against this dataset and the corresponding frequency count is used as the feature value. If no matches are found, then the feature value is set to zero.

CLSM topical similarity features. The CLSM models are trained as described in Section 3 using the background portion of the data on each testbed. The cosine similarity between the CLSM vectors corresponding to the suggestion candidate and a maximum of previous 10 queries from the same session are computed and used as 10 distinct features in the QAC ranking model.

Training on the session query pairs data produces a pair of *pre-post* CLSM models. When trained on the asymmetric data, the *pre*-model is used for projecting the user's previous queries and the *post*-model is used for projecting the suggestion candidates for the cosine similarity computation. For the symmetric data however, both the *pre-* and the *post-* models are equivalent, and hence we use only the *pre-* model in our experiments.

The AOL logs contains only the domain portion of the clicked results. Hence we are unable to get the corresponding document titles. Therefore we only train the session pairs based CLSM models on this testbed and report those results in this paper.

CLSM reformulation features. We compute the n-dimensional (n=32) vector representation of the reformulation from the previous query to the suggestion candidate. The raw values from this vector are used as n distinct features into the supervised ranking model.

Table 3: Comparison of QAC ranking models trained with CLSM based features against the MPC model and the supervised baseline ranker model. All the reported MRR improvements are statistically significant by the t-test ($p < 0.01$) over the MPC baseline and the baseline model. Additionally, corresponding to each of the different CLSM models, the ranking model containing both the *similarity* and the *reformulation* features shows statistically significant ($p < 0.01$) improvements in MRR over the model containing only the *similarity* features on both the testbeds. The three highest MRR improvements per testbed are shown in bold below.

Models	Bing	AOL	
	% Improv.	MRR	% Improv.
Baselines			
MostPopularCompletion	-	0.5110	-
Baseline Model	+48.6	0.7983	+56.2
CLSM (query-document pairs)			
All features	+55.9	-	-
Reformulation features	+54.3	-	-
Similarity features	+55.3	-	-
CLSM (Asymmetric session query pairs)			
All features	**+58.0**	0.8775	**+71.7**
Reformulation features	**+57.4**	0.8747	**+71.2**
Similarity features	+54.2	0.8580	+67.9
CLSM (Symmetric session query pairs)			
All features	**+59.0**	0.8801	**+72.2**
Reformulation features	+57.2	0.8744	+71.1
Similarity features	+55.8	0.8636	+69.0

For both the session pair based models, the *pre-* model is used for projecting the suggestion candidates, as well as the previous query.

5. RESULTS

Table 3 compares the results of training the supervised QAC ranking model with the different CLSM based session context features. Due to the proprietary nature of Bing's data, we report only relative improvements of each of the models over the MPC baseline for this testbed. On the AOL testbed, however, we report both the absolute MRR values and the relative improvements for all the models.

On both the testbeds, the *baseline model* which also contains session context features (the n-gram similarity and the pairwise frequency) shows a large improvement over the *MPC* baseline, which is expected. All the models trained with the CLSM based contextual features show further statistically significant improvements over the baseline model. Both the CLSM models trained on *session pairs* perform better than the models trained on *clickthrough* data, with the model trained on the *symmetric* session pairs performing slightly better overall. Table 5 lists examples of cases from one of the test sets where the ranking model with the CLSM based contextual features perform better compared to both the baselines.

The supervised ranking models trained with both the CLSM based similarity features and the CLSM based reformulation features perform better than the corresponding models trained with the similarity features alone. The improvements are statistically significant and demonstrate the additional information provided by the reformulation features to the ranking model over the CLSM based similarity features. The reformulation features perform particularly superior when the CLSM model has been trained on the *session pairs* dataset.

Table 4: Comparison of QAC ranking models with CLSM similarity features computed considering different maximum number of previous queries in the same session. The results show that most of the improvements from short-term history similarity features can be achieved by considering just the immediately previous query.

Models	Bing	AOL	
	% Improv.	MRR	% Improv.
Baselines			
MostPopularCompletion	-	0.5110	-
Baseline Model	+48.6	0.7983	+56.2
CLSM (Symmetric session query pairs)			
Previous 1 query	+55.2	0.8631	+68.9
Previous 3 queries	+56.1	0.8639	+69.1
Previous 5 queries	+56.1	0.8642	+69.1
Previous 10 queries	+55.8	0.8636	+69.0

Table 4 shows the impact of considering different number of previous queries in the session for computing the CLSM based similarity features. The results indicate that considering the previous query alone achieves most of the improvements observed from these similarity features.

We also compare the improvements from the different models based on the length of the input prefixes. Bar-Yossef and Kraus [1] have previously reported that non-contextual QAC systems generally perform poorly when the user has typed only a few characters due to the obvious ambiguity in user intent. Figure 4 illustrates this behaviour on the AOL testbed. Both the supervised ranking models, the baseline and the model with the CLSM features, show significantly large improvements over the MPC baseline on short prefixes. After the user has typed a few more characters in the search box, the set of suggestion candidates reduce significantly and the performance of the MPC model improves. Therefore the improvements on the longer prefixes are smaller for both the supervised ranking models. The supervised ranking model with the CLSM features, however, show statistically significant better MRR compared to both the MPC baseline and the supervised baseline ranking model on all the prefix length based segments. Finally, Figure 5 shows that better MRR can be achieved by training the CLSM model with a higher number of output dimensions.

6. DISCUSSION

In the previous section we demonstrated significant improvements in the query auto-completion ranking task using the CLSM based session context features. We now discuss potential implications of these vector representations on session modelling and list some of the assumptions and limitations of the evaluation framework used in this study.

Implications for session modelling. The distributed representation of queries and query reformulations provides an interesting framework for thinking about sessions and task context. The sequence of queries (and documents) in a search session can be considered as a directed path in the embedding space. What are the common attributes shared by these *session paths*? What properties of these paths vary depending on the type of the user task or information need? These are examples of research questions that may be interesting to study under the distributed representation framework. Hassan et al. [16], for example, studied long search sessions and compared user behaviours when the user is *struggling* in their

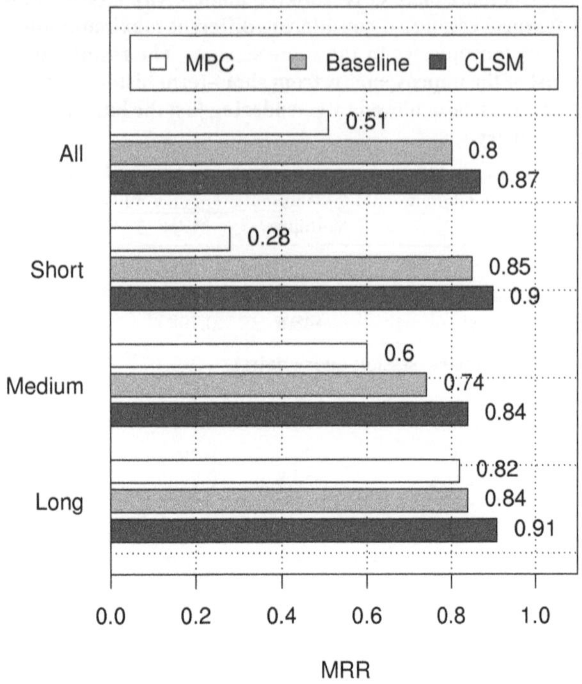

Figure 4: Comparison of the MPC model, the baseline ranker model and the experimental ranker model with the CLSM based features (the CLSM model considered here is trained on *symmetric session pairs* with *all features*) across different prefix lengths on the AOL testbed. Prefixes less than 4 characters are considered as *short*, 4 to 10 characters as *medium*, and greater than 10 characters as *long*. Both the supervised ranking models contain contextual features (CLSM based or otherwise) and hence show large improvements on the short prefixes where the ambiguity is maximum. Across all prefix lengths the model with CLSM based features out-perform the baseline ranking model. All reported differences in MRR are statistically significant by the t-test ($p < 0.01$).

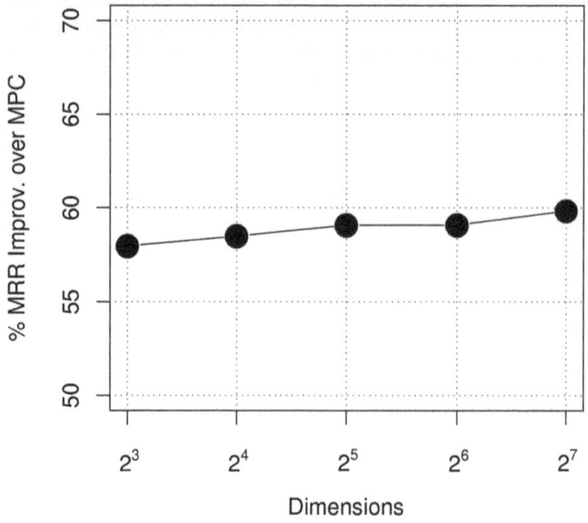

Figure 5: Evaluation of the impact of training the CLSM models with different number of dimensions. Except for the pair of CLSM models trained with 32 and 64 dimensions, all other reported differences in MRR are statistically significant by the t-test ($p < 0.01$).

information task to when they are *exploring*. Features based on the CLSM projections of queries and documents, such as the types of user reformulations in the session and the similarity between submitted queries and viewed documents, can be explored to improve the prediction accuracy for such session classification tasks.

In this paper we have examined individual query reformulations. Studying reformulation chains may teach us further about how user intents evolve during a session and support the design of future models for *session search*. For example, White and Huang [40] have explored the value of *search trails*, over the origins and the destinations. While we have only examined the representation of queries and reformulations in this paper, CLSM also allows for documents to be represented in the same embedding space. A unified study of queries, reformulations and viewed (searched or browsed) documents using the vector representation framework is an area for future work.

In the query change retrieval model (QCM) proposed by Guan et al. [14], we can explore using the reformulation vectors for representing the user agent's actions. Similarly, we may be able to gain further insights by conducting a similar study as Hollink et al. [19] by examining query changes under the vector representation framework.

Generating a distributed representation of users based on their search and other online activities is also an interesting problem. Other potential directions for future studies using the vector framework includes examining how query reformulations differ based on the search expertise of the user and the kind of device the search is performed on.

Assumptions and limitations. We have based our empirical study on the supervised ranking framework proposed by Shokouhi [37]. In doing so, we inherit some of the assumptions in the designs of that framework. Firstly, we assume that the user has a predetermined query in mind for input and would be satisfied if it appears in the QAC suggestions list. However Hofmann et al. [17] have shown that due to the high examination bias towards top-ranked results, sub-optimal QAC ranking can negatively affect the quality of the query submitted by the user. As most popular Web search engines implement some form of an auto-completion feature, it is likely that those QAC systems influenced the actual query observed in the logs. We ignore this effect in the generation of our training and test sets.

The generation of the prefixes also assumes that each query was typed *completely* by the user in a strictly left-to-right progression and the user is equally likely to examine and engage with the QAC system after each character is typed. In practice, however, users are often aided in the query formulation process (partially or completely) by various features of the search engine, such as QAC or related query recommendations. Users also often correct already entered text during the query formulation process. In these cases the generation of all possible prefixes from the submitted query does not accurately reflect the actual prefixes typed by the user.

Li et al. [26] and Mitra et al. [32] have also shown that user engagement with QAC varies with different factors such as whether the user is at a word boundary or the distance of the next character to be typed on the keyboard. This suggests that prefixes should be sampled with different importance depending on the likelihood that the user would examine the QAC suggestions for that prefix. Li et al. [26] proposed a two-dimensional click model for QAC, demonstrating that in the presence of keystroke level logging of QAC sessions the click model can be used to filter out prefix impressions

Table 5: Examples from the win-loss analysis on one of the test sets. For a given prefix and the previous query from the same user session, the top ranked suggestion by the different models are shown below. The actual submitted query is denoted by the checkmark (✓). The CLSM features include both the similarity and the reformulation features and the CLSM model is trained on the symmetric session pairs dataset.

Previous query	the fighter	airline tickets	pace university
Prefix	amer	amer	amer
MPC model	american express	american express	american express
Supervised Baseline model	american express	american express	american girl
Supervised Model with CLSM Features	american psycho movie ✓	american airlines ✓	american university ✓
Previous query	usairways	2007 toyota yaris	master of philosophy jobs
Prefix	us	us	us
MPC model	us elections 2014 predictions	us elections 2014 predictions	us elections 2014 predictions
Supervised Baseline model	usps.com	usaa	usps.com
Supervised Model with CLSM Features	usairways.com ✓	used cars ✓	usa jobs ✓

with low expected probability of examination. However, as the testbeds we consider for this study do not all have the keystroke level granularity of records, we do not pursue this line of experimentation.

Lastly, Shokouhi [37] generates all the possible prefixes of each query in the log data. This results in an obvious over-representation of long prefixes in the generated datasets. To avoid this issue we extract a single prefix per query by splitting at a random position within the query.

Despite the different underlying assumptions, the framework proposed by Shokouhi [37] provides a reasonable setup to learn a baseline context-aware ranking model for QAC, and hence we adopt it for this study.

7. CONCLUSION

We have demonstrated that the distributed representation of queries by the convolutional latent semantic models holds useful information about inter-query relationships. The reformulation vectors exhibit regularities that makes them interesting for modelling session context for query suggestion tasks. Our experiments show that using features based on the reformulation vectors improves MRR for QAC ranking over using features based on the query vectors alone. The best improvements, however, are achieved by the combination of features based on both these vector representations. We have also demonstrated that training the latent semantic models on session query pairs produces further improvements over the model trained on query-document pairs. While the biggest improvements are observed on short prefixes, the ranking model containing the CLSM based features perform better than the supervised ranking baseline on all the prefix length based segments. We have also studied the effects of considering different number of previous queries within the session for context and the number of dimensions used to represent the query and reformulation vectors on the model performance. While we evaluate these models on the query auto-completion ranking task, the features we described in this paper may also be useful for generating context sensitive related query recommendations and query rewriting. Furthermore, by projecting documents to this same embedding space, future studies may be able to extend these contextual features to document ranking in Web search.

Lastly, the reformulation vectors provide an interesting framework for studying sessions and intent progressions. We anticipate that these distributed representations of queries, documents and reformulations will become more frequently used as tools for future studies on search personalization and session search.

Acknowledgements. The author is grateful to Nick Craswell, Milad Shokouhi, Filip Radlinski, Vanessa Murdock, Xiaodong He, Jianfeng Gao, Piotr Mirowski, Peter Bailey, David Hawking, Katja Hofmann, Panagiotis Tigkas and Daniel Voinea for their insightful feedback, questions and discussions around related areas.

References

[1] Z. Bar-Yossef and N. Kraus. Context-sensitive query auto-completion. In *Proc. WWW*, pages 107–116, 2011.

[2] P. N. Bennett, R. W. White, W. Chu, S. T. Dumais, P. Bailey, F. Borisyuk, and X. Cui. Modeling the impact of short- and long-term behavior on search personalization. In *Proc. SIGIR*, pages 185–194, 2012.

[3] D. M. Blei, A. Y. Ng, and M. I. Jordan. Latent dirichlet allocation. *the Journal of machine Learning research*, 3: 993–1022, 2003.

[4] P. Boldi, F. Bonchi, C. Castillo, D. Donato, and S. Vigna. Query suggestions using query-flow graphs. In *Proceedings of the 2009 workshop on Web Search Click Data*, pages 56–63. ACM, 2009.

[5] P. Boldi, F. Bonchi, C. Castillo, and S. Vigna. Query reformulation mining: models, patterns, and applications. *Information retrieval*, 14(3):257–289, 2011.

[6] C. Burges, R. Ragno, and Q. Le. Learning to rank with non-smooth cost functions. In *Proc. NIPS*, 2006.

[7] H. Cao, D. Jiang, J. Pei, Q. He, Z. Liao, E. Chen, and H. Li. Context-aware query suggestion by mining click-through and session data. In *Proc. SIGKDD*, pages 875–883, 2008.

[8] H. Cao, D. Jiang, J. Pei, E. Chen, and H. Li. Towards context-aware search by learning a very large variable length hidden markov model from search logs. In *Proc. WWW*, pages 191–200. ACM, 2009.

[9] O. Chapelle, Y. Chang, and T.-Y. Liu. The yahoo! learning to rank challenge, 2010. *URL http://learningtorankchallenge. yahoo. com.*

[10] S. C. Deerwester, S. T. Dumais, T. K. Landauer, G. W. Furnas, and R. A. Harshman. Indexing by latent semantic analysis. *JASIS*, 41(6):391–407, 1990.

[11] D. Downey, S. Dumais, D. Liebling, and E. Horvitz. Understanding the relationship between searchers' queries and information goals. In *Proc. CIKM*, pages 449–458. ACM, 2008.

[12] J. Gao, K. Toutanova, and W.-t. Yih. Clickthrough-based latent semantic models for web search. In *Proc. SIGIR*, pages 675–684. ACM, 2011.

[13] J. Gao, P. Pantel, M. Gamon, X. He, L. Deng, and Y. Shen. Modeling interestingness with deep neural networks. In *Proceedings of the 2013 Conference on Empirical Methods in Natural Language Processing*, 2014.

[14] D. Guan, S. Zhang, and H. Yang. Utilizing query change for session search. In *Proc. SIGIR*, pages 453–462. ACM, 2013.

[15] J. Guo, X. Cheng, G. Xu, and X. Zhu. Intent-aware query similarity. In *Proc. CIKM*, pages 259–268, 2011.

[16] A. Hassan, R. W. White, S. T. Dumais, and Y.-M. Wang. Struggling or exploring?: disambiguating long search sessions. In *Proc. WSDM*, pages 53–62. ACM, 2014.

[17] K. Hofmann, B. Mitra, F. Radlinski, and M. Shokouhi. An eye-tracking study of user interactions with query auto completion. In *Proc. CIKM*, pages 549–558. ACM, 2014.

[18] T. Hofmann. Probabilistic latent semantic indexing. In *Proc. SIGIR*, pages 50–57. ACM, 1999.

[19] V. Hollink, J. He, and A. de Vries. Explaining query modifications. In *Advances in Information Retrieval*, pages 1–12. Springer, 2012.

[20] J. Huang and E. N. Efthimiadis. Analyzing and evaluating query reformulation strategies in web search logs. In *Proc. CIKM*, pages 77–86. ACM, 2009.

[21] P.-S. Huang, X. He, J. Gao, L. Deng, A. Acero, and L. Heck. Learning deep structured semantic models for web search using clickthrough data. In *Proc. CIKM*, pages 2333–2338. ACM, 2013.

[22] B. J. Jansen, A. H. Spink, C. Blakely, and S. Koshman. Defining a session on web search engines. *Journal of the American Society for Information Science and Technology*, 58 (6):862–871, 2007.

[23] J.-Y. Jiang, Y.-Y. Ke, P.-Y. Chien, and P.-J. Cheng. Learning user reformulation behavior for query auto-completion. In *Proc. SIGIR*, pages 445–454. ACM, 2014.

[24] E. Kharitonov, C. Macdonald, P. Serdyukov, and I. Ounis. Intent models for contextualising and diversifying query suggestions. In *Proc. CIKM*, pages 2303–2308. ACM, 2013.

[25] X. Li, C. Guo, W. Chu, Y.-Y. Wang, and J. Shavlik. Deep learning powered in-session contextual ranking using clickthrough data. In *Proc. NIPS*, 2014.

[26] Y. Li, A. Dong, H. Wang, H. Deng, Y. Chang, and C. Zhai. A two-dimensional click model for query auto-completion. In *Proc. SIGIR*, pages 455–464. ACM, 2014.

[27] Z. Liao, D. Jiang, E. Chen, J. Pei, H. Cao, and H. Li. Mining concept sequences from large-scale search logs for context-aware query suggestion. *ACM Trans. on Intelligent Systems and Technology*, 3(1):17:1–17:40, Oct. 2011.

[28] C. Liu, J. Gwizdka, J. Liu, T. Xu, and N. J. Belkin. Analysis and evaluation of query reformulations in different task types. *Proceedings of the American Society for Information Science and Technology*, 47(1):1–9, 2010.

[29] T. Mikolov, K. Chen, G. Corrado, and J. Dean. Efficient estimation of word representations in vector space. *arXiv preprint arXiv:1301.3781*, 2013.

[30] T. Mikolov, I. Sutskever, K. Chen, G. S. Corrado, and J. Dean. Distributed representations of words and phrases and their compositionality. In *Proc. NIPS*, pages 3111–3119, 2013.

[31] T. Mikolov, W.-t. Yih, and G. Zweig. Linguistic regularities in continuous space word representations. In *HLT-NAACL*, pages 746–751. Citeseer, 2013.

[32] B. Mitra, M. Shokouhi, F. Radlinski, and K. Hofmann. On user interactions with query auto-completion. In *Proc. SIGIR*, pages 1055–1058, 2014.

[33] G. Pass, A. Chowdhury, and C. Torgeson. A picture of search. In *Proc. InfoScale*. ACM, 2006. ISBN 1-59593-428-6.

[34] R. Salakhutdinov and G. Hinton. Semantic hashing. *International Journal of Approximate Reasoning*, 50(7): 969–978, 2009.

[35] X. Shen, B. Tan, and C. Zhai. Context-sensitive information retrieval using implicit feedback. In *Proc. SIGIR*, pages 43–50. ACM, 2005.

[36] Y. Shen, X. He, J. Gao, L. Deng, and G. Mesnil. Learning semantic representations using convolutional neural networks for web search. In *Proc. WWW*, pages 373–374. International World Wide Web Conferences Steering Committee, 2014.

[37] M. Shokouhi. Learning to personalize query auto-completion. In *Proc. SIGIR*, pages 103–112, 2013.

[38] M. Shokouhi and K. Radinsky. Time-sensitive query auto-completion. In *Proc. SIGIR*, pages 601–610, 2012.

[39] I. Weber and C. Castillo. The demographics of web search. In *Proc. SIGIR*, pages 523–530, 2010.

[40] R. W. White and J. Huang. Assessing the scenic route: measuring the value of search trails in web logs. In *Proc. SIGIR*, pages 587–594. ACM, 2010.

[41] S. Whiting and J. M. Jose. Recent and robust query auto-completion. In *Proc. WWW*, pages 971–982. International World Wide Web Conferences Steering Committee, 2014.

[42] Q. Wu, C. Burges, K. Svore, and J. Gao. Adapting boosting for information retrieval measures. *Journal of Information Retrieval*, 13:254–270, 2009.

[43] B. Xiang, D. Jiang, J. Pei, X. Sun, E. Chen, and H. Li. Context-aware ranking in web search. In *Proc. SIGIR*, pages 451–458, 2010.

[44] X. Yan, J. Guo, and X. Cheng. Context-aware query recommendation by learning high-order relation in query logs. In *Proc. CIKM*, pages 2073–2076. ACM, 2011.

[45] Y. Zhang, W. Chen, D. Wang, and Q. Yang. User-click modeling for understanding and predicting search-behavior. In *Proc. SIGKDD*, pages 1388–1396. ACM, 2011.

An Eye-Tracking Study of Query Reformulation

Carsten Eickhoff
Dept. of Computer Science
ETH Zurich, Switzerland
ecarsten@inf.ethz.ch

Sebastian Dungs
University of Duisburg-Essen
Duisburg, Germany
dungs@is.inf.uni-due.de

Vu Tran
University of Duisburg-Essen
Duisburg, Germany
vtran@is.inf.uni-due.de

ABSTRACT

Information about a user's domain knowledge and interest can be important signals for many information retrieval tasks such as query suggestion or result ranking. State-of-the-art user models rely on coarse-grained representations of the user's previous knowledge about a topic or domain. In this paper, we study query refinement using eye-tracking in order to gain precise and detailed insight into which terms the user was exposed to in a search session and which ones they showed a particular interest in. We measure fixations on the term level, allowing for a detailed model of user attention. To allow for a wide-spread exploitation of our findings, we generalize from the restrictive eye-gaze tracking to using more accessible signals: mouse cursor traces. Based on the public API of a popular search engine, we demonstrate how query suggestion candidates can be ranked according to traces of user attention and interest, resulting in significantly better performance than achieved by an attention-oblivious industry solution. Our experiments suggest that modelling term-level user attention can be achieved with great reliability and holds significant potential for supporting a range of traditional IR tasks.

Categories and Subject Descriptors

Information Systems [**Information Retrieval**]:
Query Reformulation

Keywords

Eye-gaze Tracking; Knowledge Acquisition; Domain Expertise; Query Reformulation; Query Refinement; Query Suggestion; Mouse Cursor Tracking.

1. INTRODUCTION

Users of information retrieval systems have been shown to struggle with forming an accurate mental image of their information needs and the resources to satisfy them. Belkin et al. describe this observation as an *Anomalous State of Knowledge* (ASK), hindering users' query formulation and search success [4]. To mitigate this effect, Web search engines offer query suggestions and recommendations that guide the searcher towards popular queries, frequently issued by other users. It is, however, often unclear how relevant such suggestions are for the individual user, especially for non-transactional information needs. Ideally, we would like to promote those suggestions, that lead the user to relevant, novel and understandable documents rather than just generally popular ones. Personalized generation of query suggestions based on the user's previous search and interaction history has been found as one way to address this problem [10]. The proposed models, however, are coarse-grained and represent only high-level notions of the user's active query vocabulary. They consider, for example, all previously encountered terms (e.g., all terms present on recently visited Web sites) to be known and understandable. While this family of approaches makes a valuable first step towards integrating an understanding of the user's state of knowledge into the query suggestion process, one would require a system that can account for the user's vocabulary at a significantly finer granularity, ideally on the term level.

The same issue plays up at other points of the search process, for example during result ranking. State-of-the-art relevance models often include representations of the user and their specific context such as previous search history [48], preferences in terms of high-level topics [26], or content readability [11]. While such notions of text complexity have been demonstrated to significantly increase retrieval performance by providing users with resources of appropriate reading level, the readability metrics themselves are not personalized and rely on general complexity estimates based on a very diverse audience of users. Instead, it would be strongly desirable to know which exact terms the searcher is able to recognize, understand and actively use.

In this paper, we use eye-gaze fixations and cursor movement information in order to study which concrete terms the user is exposed to on Web pages and search engine result pages (SERPs) and how they are subsequently re-used as query terms. In this way, we make three novel contributions over the state of the art in user modelling. **(1)** For the first time, we inspect the evolution of users' active query vocabulary during Web search on the term-level in a qualitative user study. **(2)** Based on the eye-gaze signal, we model the likelihood of the searcher using a given term for query reformulation. **(3)** Eye-gaze tracking requires expensive hardware that would greatly restrict the exploitation and adaptation of our method. In order to make our in-

SIGIR'15, August 09 - 13, 2015, Santiago, Chile.
© 2015 ACM. ISBN 978-1-4503-3621-5/15/08 ...$15.00.
DOI: http://dx.doi.org/10.1145/2766462.2767703.

sights flexibly applicable in most Web search settings, we substitute fixation information with traces of cursor movement.

2. RELATED WORK

Our investigation of related work will be guided by a number of topics that have been pursued in recent years. **(1)** First of all, we will revisit the body of work dedicated to measuring and tracking domain expertise, both statically as well as over time. **(2)** Secondly, there is an extensive line of work with the goal of query suggestion, reformulation and expansion. **(3)** And finally, we will give an overview of those eye-gaze or cursor-trace based studies that investigated user behaviour during the various stages of the search process.

Modern retrieval models rely on a diverse set of features in order to produce the final result ranking. One family of such features is concerned with measuring how familiar the searchers are with the topic of their information need. White et al. [49] investigated the behavior of domain experts and novices during Web search. They report higher likelihoods of search success for experts. Additionally, the authors observed gradual developments in domain expertise over the course of several weeks of search activity. Liu et al. [36] further find characteristic differences in user behaviour depending on the search task at hand. Wildemuth [50] studied concrete strategies and strategy types that domain experts and novices follow during information search. They find that over time, novices "learn" to use the same search patterns as experts if they are exposed to in-domain information for longer periods. This transition was studied in detail by Liu et al. [35], who investigated changes in domain expertise when searchers were following the same overarching tasks across multiple sessions. Eickhoff et al. [15] further showed session-level evidence of domain expertise increases in response to in-domain searches. The authors put a particular focus on the acquisition of new query terms which is explained by previous page visits. Zhang et al. [53] proposed an automatic prediction framework that was able to identify domain experts and novices based on a range of behavioral features. Kim et al. [29] cast the expertise problem as a combination of preferred reading level per topic. In this way, they tracked the notion of topic-normalized resource complexity for different users.

Query formulation can represent one of the cognitively most challenging steps in the information search process [13]. Building on the early investigations of Spink [47] and Saracevic [46], query suggestion functionality aims to aid the user at this initial stage. Chirita et al. [10] rely on information gathered on the user's local desktop in order to expand Web search queries. Kelly et al. [27] investigated query reformulation behaviour by offering query and term suggestions based on clustering and pseudo relevance feedback. They report a clear user preference for query suggestions over term suggestions. Gao et al. [16] rely on information mined from large-scale query log files to provide suggestions. Independently, Song and He [45], as well as Ma et al. [38], propose personalized query suggestions by analysing the user's previous click behaviour within the session in order to mine suggestion terms from skipped and visited documents.

Eye-gaze tracking has been used for unobtrusive tracking of user attention and interest for several decades [24, 43]. In the information retrieval community, a wide array of studies and applications have been proposed in recent years. Cutrell and Guan [12] compare various degrees of SERP verbosity for different task types, finding that inherently navigational tasks require less information per item than informational ones. Granka et al. [17, 23] conducted an eye-tracking study of users' interaction with search result lists. They confirm several established notions such as the well-known position bias of user attention and note significant potential for using eye gaze signals as implicit relevance indicators. In a number of small-scale (5-8 participants) qualitative studies, Kunze et al. use head-mounted eye gaze tracking devices for inferring language expertise [30] and document types [31] based on reading styles and eye movement patterns. Williams and Morris [51] contrast the fixation duration of familiar and unknown words during silent reading. They find that unfamiliar words receive significantly longer attention windows than known ones. We will revisit this finding in Section 6 of this paper.

Salojärvi et al. [44], as well as Brooks et al. [6] investigate a range of low-level eye-gaze features for inferring passage-level relevance labels for information retrieval and collaborative filtering[42]. Loboda et al. [37] investigated eye-gaze indicators of sentence-level relevance. They found the overall number of fixations, the number of first pass fixations as well as the total viewing time to carry most indicative power. Interestingly, and somewhat conflicting with the findings of both this paper as well as [8], the authors could not find any clues of term-level relevance. Buscher et al. [8, 7] use fixation length and frequency as relevance indicators for query expansion and search result personalization. Their work is closely related to the application scenario presented in Section 6 of this paper. While their approach relied on shallow term-level feedback mechanisms, we leverage semantic information via related or synonymous terms as well as using a wider array of eye-gaze signals. Ajanki et al. [2, 41] use eye tracking hardware to infer document-level relevance across a manually curated document corpus and, subsequently, generate alternate queries based on salient terms. There is some evidence of the origin of previously encountered Terms being reused in active vocabulary [51, 15], but there has not yet been a dedicated study to further investigate and understand this vocabulary acquisition process.

Independently, Guo and Agichtein [19] as well as Huang et al. [22] propose to infer user eye gaze and, implicitly, user interest, from mouse cursor position and movement. The authors show a substantial overlap between both sources that motivates further exploitation as for example presented later in this work. In a follow-up publication [18], the authors exploit a similar range of signals in order to infer post-click document relevance. Finally, Huang et al. [21] predict click-through on the basis of cursor position and movement signals.

Our work differs from the above body of research in that: **(1)** it measures user vocabulary knowledge and its development over time at a much finer granularity than previous efforts, which mainly concentrate on broad topic verticals. **(2)** Our model is based on actual observations of user attention to individual terms as evidenced by eye-gaze and mouse-cursor traces. Previous work on domain expertise is based mainly on the posterior analysis of search engine log files in which the mere presence or absence of a term on a page or SERP is regarded as a signal. Information about whether the user actually saw the term, and if so, how long the engagement lasted, are not available. **(3)** The breadth of existing eye-gaze and mouse cursor movement studies has investigated many aspects of the search process. However, an in-depth study of query reformulation behaviour at the term level, as we propose in this paper, has not yet been attempted. The timeliness and relevance of this study is further evidenced by several pieces of prior related work that explicitly state the need for a more qualitative understanding of query reformulation and term acquisition on the Web (e.g., [15]).

3. METHODOLOGY

The user study took place in a controlled lab environment at a university campus. Participants were recruited through advertisements (flyers and Internet ads) and public announcements. Overall, 17 persons (8 female and 9 male) participated in our study. All participants were students majoring in a range of different, often IT-related, subjects. All participants were between 19 and 27 year old (average 22.7). On average, each participant had 9.8 years of active Internet usage. All participants had experience with Web search engines as well as searching in digital libraries. Experiments lasted for about 60 minutes and participants were compensated by a payment of € 10. 7 (3 female, 4 male) of the participants were part of an initial pilot study while the remaining 10 persons contributed to the final experiments that will be analysed in the further course of this paper. Due to incremental changes to the experimental setup as well as occasional technical glitches during the pilot study, we report only the outcomes of the final experiment.

At the beginning of each experiment, a short introduction to the study, including the eye tracking hardware, was given. Participants were not informed about the concrete research questions and hypotheses of the study. Subsequently, the eye tracking hardware was calibrated and participants were told to maintain a firm yet comfortable seating position for the duration of the experiment.

All sessions were conducted on a Windows 7 system with 22" (1680 × 1150) display, running a Firefox 25.0.1 Web browser. Eye-gaze traces were recorded with an SMI RED remote eye tracking system that is integrated into the monitor. This setup is considered to be less intrusive than head-mounted alternatives. The system captures gaze positions at an update frequency of 60Hz and an accuracy of 0.4°. The recordings and analysis were made using iViewX, Experiment Center, and Begaze 3.4. We rely on a number of essential smoothing techniques such as fixation grouping, e.g., described in [5]. Our instrumented Web browser saves screenshots of each accessed page and the final mapping between fixation coordinates and terms rendered on screen is established via OCR technology. This approach has the advantage of making **all** rendered text accessible, regardless whether it was expressed in plain HTML, or encapsulated in AJAX or JS containers. Previous work [14] found that the inability to parse text contained in such elements can significantly limit the performance of analytical and inference methods.

After the calibration, the Web browser was used to present the questionnaires and tasks to the users. The same tab was used for the questionnaires as well as the input boxes for task completion. Participants were asked to leave the instruction tab open at all times and to use other tabs to their liking. Task presentation and questionnaires were structured as follows:

To ensure task diversity yet obtain a reasonable amount of overlap between tasks, we hand-picked 6 topics (ids 31, 38, 41, 42, 55, 69) from the 2006 and 2007 editions of the TREC Question Answering Track's complex interactive QA task [28]. In the initial pilot study, we found that scientific and biomedical tasks resulted in more frequent query reformulations per session as users gradually acquired the relevant domain vocabulary. Many of the politically and societally motivated tasks have been comprehensively investigated and summarized, due to the time that has passed since the original formulation of the tasks. This resulted in socio-political tasks being mostly answerable with a single page visit. As a consequence, we expanded our pool by several additional topics (ids 53, 70, 72, 73). Our final selection consists of 10 tasks, originating mainly from the bio-medical domain.

Each participant was asked to complete three search tasks. For each task, they were offered two options and were told to choose a task according to their personal preference. As a result, we obtain a total of 30 search sessions (10 participants each choosing 3 tasks). We decided to offer this choice to allow participants to focus on tasks that they found personally interesting, which in turn is expected to spark better engagement and richer interactions during the session. A Web application scheduled the tasks, ensuring that each of the 10 topics was offered for selection equally often and in non-repeating pairings (in our case each topic was shown exactly 6 times to offer 10 participants each 3 choices of two of the 10 available topics). After the task selection, a demographic questionnaire was given to the participants. Subsequently, each of the actual tasks was presented in the browser and accompanied by short pre-task and post-task questionnaires. Pre-task questionnaires covered topic specific aspects like familiarity and confidence as well as perceived difficulty. Post-task questionnaires again covered the aspects of perceived task difficulty as well as perceived completeness and quality of the answers given by the users. We allocated up to 20 minutes time per search task, resulting in an overall duration of up to 60 minutes per participant across all tasks. After all three working tasks had been completed, the searcher's general opinion of the experiment was elicited in a post-experiment questionnaire.

Table 1 discusses some of the salient characteristics in anticipated and actual task difficulty according to the pre- and post session questionnaires. Since we offered the participants to choose their tasks, we can note interesting differences in task frequency. We report averages across all participants that selected and completed a given task. Answers were given on a 5-point scale ranging between settings of 1 (not at all [easy, familiar, ...]) to 5 (very [easy, familiar, ...]). We can note distinct task-specific levels of difficulty originating from different coverage of the topic on the Web. Due to the mostly bio-medical nature of the tasks and the lack of a relevant formal background knowledge among the participants, we see relatively low scores of prior familiarity. This can be further seen by the fact that our bio-medical laypeople generally overestimated the difficulty of the task (with the exception of Task 31, which also showed the lowest overall participant satisfaction with the results of their search activity).

Table 1: Lab-study task characteristics.

Task Id	Frequency	familiar (pre)	interesting (pre)	easy (pre)	easy (post)	understandable (post)	found good results (post)
31	4	2.25	3.75	2.50	1.25	3.50	1.75
38	4	2.75	3.50	3.00	2.75	4.50	2.75
41	1	4.00	4.00	2.00	5.00	5.00	5.00
42	4	1.00	2.75	2.50	4.00	4.50	3.25
53	3	2.33	3.67	2.67	3.33	4.00	3.33
55	5	1.20	2.80	3.40	3.20	4.60	3.40
69	1	1.00	4.00	4.00	5.00	5.00	4.00
70	6	1.17	2.5	2.5	2.33	3.5	2.67
72	0	-	-	-	-	-	-
73	2	1.50	4.50	3.50	4.00	4.50	4.50
Overall	30	1.73	3.23	2.83	3.00	4.17	3.06

4. EYE-TRACKING EXPERIMENTS

In this section, we present the outcome of the previously described eye-tracking study. Following previous work [43], our experiments centrally consider eye-gaze *fixations*, brief periods of time when the reader focuses on a single location, during which no significant eye movement can be noted. The frequency and duration for which the gaze is kept steady are established signals of user attention.

4.1 Literal Term Acquisition

As a starting point to our investigation, let us revisit the findings of Eickhoff et al. [15] who conducted a log-based analysis of query term acquisition. They report that a significant share of all subsequently added query terms in a search session were present on SERPs and previously visited pages earlier in the same session. The authors interpret this observation as evidence of query term acquisition, but already state that, based solely on log files, there is no reliable way of determining which of these co-occurrences are genuine (i.e., the user actually sees and reuses a new term). Intuition suggests that many such cases are due to chance and are never really seen, processed and acquired by the user, e.g., because they were outside of the visible screen area displayed to the reader. To correct for these inaccuracies we reproduce their log-based approach for the search sessions collected in the previous section and contrast it with actual eye-gaze fixations. Similar to previous research, we find a share of 43% of all added query terms to have occurred on previously visited pages and SERPs. The number of actually fixated terms that later on are being used as query terms, however, is much lower (21%). As surmised originally, mere term presence is too coarse an estimator of query vocabulary evolution. The attention-based subset that we capture via eye-gaze tracking, instead, describes what the user has actually seen and potentially adopted from SERPs and Web pages.

To begin our in-depth investigation of term-level user attention and its effect on query reformulation behaviour, let us briefly introduce some necessary notation. Each search session comprises a number of SERPs and visited pages. We break these pages down into white space-separated tokens t. We distinguish between those tokens that appear in any of the session's queries T_q and the much larger remaining set of non-query terms T_n. The overall set of all tokens displayed in the session is given by the union $T = T_q \cup T_n$. Besides the displayed tokens, we also collect F, the set of all eye gaze fixations that were measured in the session. Each fixation $f \in F$ is described in terms of its duration $dur(f)$ and screen coordinate $loc(f)$. Using the previously described mapping between screen coordinates and display terms, we can now associate fixations with the terms that were rendered at the respective coordinates on the screen. As for display tokens, we can now subdivide fixations into those that rest on query terms (F_q) and those that focus any other terms (F_n). For this study, we disregard any fixations that, after application of a tolerance threshold of 5 pixels, do not coincide with the bounding box coordinates of a display token. This step removes all fixations that fall on browser control elements, images or page margins.

Table 2: Term-level fixation statistics show higher-than-average user attention on query terms.

	Non-query terms	Query terms
Relative frequency on page	0.83	0.17
Share of overall fixations	0.68	0.32
Rel. number of fixations per token	0.25	**0.57***
Share of overall fixation duration	0.61	0.39
Avg. fixation duration per token	58ms	**218ms***

$$att_{rel}(T_q) = \frac{|F_q|}{|T_q|} \tag{1}$$

$$dur_{rel}(F_q) = \frac{\sum_{f \in F_q} dur(f)}{\sum_{f \in F} dur(f)} \tag{2}$$

Let us now compare the way in which users interact with query terms and non-query terms. Table 2 shows an overview of several eye-gaze fixation statistics. We note that the general distribution of tokens in T is heavily biased towards non-query terms. Unsurprisingly, as a consequence of this skewed distribution, T_n also receives the largest share of the session's fixations. If we, however, discount those absolute fixation frequencies by the overall distribution of query terms and non-query terms (see Equation 1), it becomes apparent that tokens in T_q receive a significantly higher relative number of fixations per token than their non-query counterparts T_n. Similarly, we notice that the duration of individual fixations, both in terms of the absolute per-fixation duration $dur(f)$ as well as the relative share of the overall fixation duration $dur_{rel}(F_q)$, are biased towards giving significantly more attention to T_q. The statistical significance of the differences between query and non-query terms was determined by means of a Wilcoxon signed-rank test at $\alpha = 0.05$ level.

In practice, these effects result in situations as observed for example in Session 001, during which a participant with-

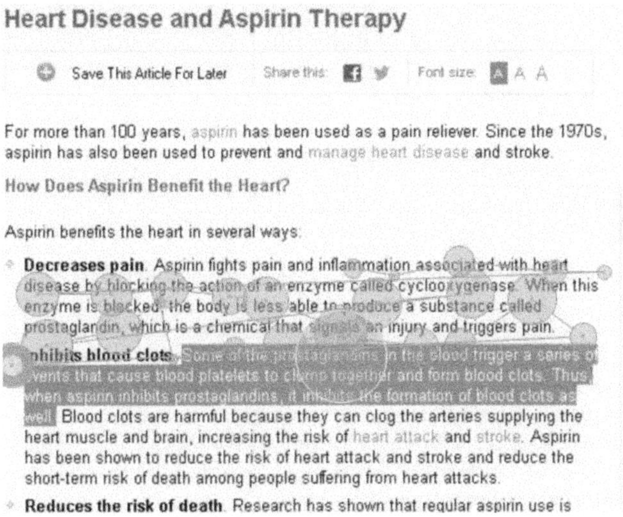

Figure 1: Eye-gaze patterns of Session 001 prior to query reformulation show strong evidence for acquisition of the medical term "prostaglandin" occurring in a paragraph of user-highlighted text.

out formal medical background was solving Task 42: "What effect does Aspirin have on coronary heart diseases?". The participant started with a query that consisted of all nouns taken from the original task descriptor and studied a number of high-ranked results. On one of the visited pages, the participant encountered a text passage discussing the interplay between Aspirin and a particular kind of lipid compounds, so-called *prostaglandins*. After having read the paragraph, the participant reformulated the query, adding prostaglandin as a new query term. Figure 1 shows a visual representation of the eye-tracker output for this acquisition of medical jargon. The orange lines display gaze patterns and the size of circles depicts the duration of each fixation. This session, as well as many similar examples that we encountered in our experiments, motivate the use of term-level eye-gaze tracking output for modelling user attention. In Section 6, we will demonstrate that exact scenario at the example of re-ranking query suggestion candidates.

4.2 Semantic Proximity of Reformulations

Up to this point, we studied fixated words on SERPs and visited pages that were subsequently picked up as query terms for reformulation. While those literal term acquisitions occur frequently, the majority of reformulations cannot be explained in this way. We will now, instead, inspect the semantic relatedness between reformulation terms and previously fixated ones. The updated hypothesis being that even though eye-gaze fixations do not literally forecast all newly added terms, they describe the user's interest accurately enough to allow for us to infer which semantic cluster of terms will indeed be used. This scenario includes cases such as synonyms or antonyms of fixated terms being employed for reformulation. To measure semantic proximity, we rely on WordNet and the well-known Leacock-Chodorow similarity [34]. The LCH metric is based on the *length* of the shortest path between the synsets containing the two terms and the maximum taxonomy depth D_t. We used the WS4J implementation of LCH (`https://code.google.com/p/ws4j/`).

Table 3: Per-term fixation likelihood and duration show a general upwards trend as the semantic proximity to query terms increases.

	fixation duration	fixation likelihood
$LCH < 0.25$	30ms	0.09
$0.25 \leq LCH < 0.5$	36ms	0.15
$0.5 \leq LCH < 0.75$	39ms	0.23
$0.75 \leq LCH < 1.0$	34ms	0.18
$1.0 \leq LCH < 1.25$	32ms	0.13
$1.25 \leq LCH < 1.5$	38ms	0.27
$1.5 \leq LCH < 1.75$	**45ms***	**0.35***
$1.75 \leq LCH < 2.0$	**53ms***	**0.43***
$LCH \geq 2.0$	**86ms***	**0.49***

$$LCH = -log(\frac{length}{2 \times D_t}) \quad (3)$$

To test our hypothesis, we will inspect the distribution of user attention across the spectrum of LCH similarity scores between query terms and fixated terms. Please note that for this experiment, we exclude all direct query term occurrences from the comparison to allow for an exclusive and unperturbed study of semantically related terms. Table 3 shows the per-term likelihood and duration of fixation as functions of semantic proximity in terms of LCH scores. Also note that the LCH scale, in this case, does not reach its full extent (normally around scores of 3.0) because we pruned away all literal query term occurrences for this experiment. We can observe an initial local attention peak at an early point of the scale (LCH scores between 0.5 and 0.75) which is due to the highly frequent, but at the same time hardly related, stop words. As we, however, approach the far end of the LCH scale, we note a significant increase in user attention, bearing evidence of the importance of semantic proximity, even if literal term overlap is not given. For the highest proximity ranges ($LCH \geq 1.5$), we note a statistically significant increase in both fixation duration and likelihood as compared to each of the lower ranges ($LCH < 1.5$). Statistical significance of improvements was measured by means of a Wilcoxon signed rank test at $\alpha < 0.05$-level. Later on, in Section 6 of this paper, we will make use of this observation for model smoothing purposes.

We experimented with a number of alternative measures of semantic proximity including HSO [20], LESK [3], or WUP [52]. All considered metrics show the same initial rise of fixation frequency and duration followed by a monotonic rise as semantic proximity scores increased. There did not seem to be a systematically beneficial choice of metrics. Finally, LCH was chosen due to its low computational complexity.

4.3 Term Length and Complexity

In the previous sections, we showed how future query terms as well as semantically related terms received significantly higher-than-average amounts of user attention. In order to verify that this conclusion is indeed valid and not just due to hidden correlations with other unobserved effects, the

Table 4: Query terms receive significantly longer fixations than unrelated terms of comparable length.

	all terms		stop words removed	
Length	query terms	non-query terms	query terms	non-query terms
< 4	30ms	29ms	32ms	30ms
4-7	**38ms***	30ms	**39ms***	32ms
8-11	**49ms***	33ms	**49ms***	33ms
12-15	**55ms***	38ms	**55ms***	38ms
16-19	**69ms***	41ms	**69ms***	41ms
≥ 20	**82ms***	51ms	**82ms***	51ms

Table 5: Query terms receive significantly longer per-term fixations than unrelated terms of comparable complexity.

	all terms		stop words removed	
AOA	query terms	non-query terms	query terms	non-query terms
< 4	30ms	31ms	31ms	32ms
4-6	35ms	32ms	35ms	33ms
6-8	**49ms***	32ms	**49ms***	34ms
8-10	**72ms***	36ms	**72ms***	36ms
10-12	**112ms***	41ms	**112ms***	41ms
12-14	**173ms***	48ms	**173ms***	48ms
14-16	**228ms***	59ms	**228ms***	59ms
16-18	**287ms***	64ms	**287ms***	64ms
≥ 18	**384ms***	89ms	**384ms***	89ms

following paragraphs will discuss the effects of term length, complexity and stop words on user attention.

It is intuitively plausible that term length should play a role in the division of user attention. Longer terms take longer to read and have a greater likelihood of capturing chance fixations. Table 4 shows an overview of fixation duration on terms of various lengths. We note a monotonic, yet mild increase in fixation duration as terms grow longer. This applies to both query terms and non-query terms alike. However, for all but the very shortest length category, we see significantly longer durations for query terms than for arbitrary ones. Statistical significance of improvements was measured by means of a Wilcoxon signed rank test at $\alpha < 0.05$-level.

Previous work established how complex or unknown terms generally captivate the reader's attention longer than easy or well-known ones. Given the mainly scientific domain of our tasks, it is possible that the increase in attention, that we observed previously, is explained by the terms inherent complexity rather than their relevance. To investigate this hypothesis, we rely on previous work by Kuperman et al. [32], who compiled a list of 50,000 English terms along with their average age of acquisition (AOA). Common words such as *"the"*, *"a"*, or *"house"* show low ages of acquisition, usually between 1.6 and 4.0. Higher ages of acquisition, on the other hand, indicate greater term specificity and complexity, such as *"epithalamium"* with an average AOA of 17.67. Table 5 shows the distribution of attention received by query terms and non-query terms of given AOA grades. For both classes, we can note a mild upwards trend as AOA ranks increase. A much greater margin, however, separates the two classes from each other. We can therefore safely assume, that while term complexity plays a role in the distribution of user attention among terms on the screen, the governing factor is indeed topical relevance, as assumed in Sections 4.1 and 4.2.

As a conclusion to our overview of potential hidden factors correlated with user attention, we would like to draw special attention to stop words. This class of highly frequent but individually uninformative terms form the "syntactic glue" that ties together the content terms that carry actual meaning. Using the popular *Snowball* list of stop words [40], we observe that stop words receive much less attention (on average 30 ms per term) than non stop words (65 ms). In order to control for the influence of stop words on the previous investigations of term complexity and length, both Tables 4 and 5 show the respective measurements after stop words were removed. Following intuition, stop words are short (average length of 3.9 characters) and non-complex (average AOA of 5.09). Accordingly, we exclusively observe changes in the early rows that list short and of low complexity. Even in those categories, the changes are only marginal, supporting the conclusion that stop words do not play a special role with respect to user attention but rather follow the general trend dictated by their individual lengths and complexities.

Table 6: The effect of individual query reformulation strategies on LCH proximity between queries and user attention.

Strategy	Observed Frequency	Avg. change in $LCH(t)$
Specification	48%	+24%
Generalization	16%	+18%
Reformulation	36%	+37%

4.4 Alternative Reformulation Strategies

Throughout this section, we investigate various ways of explaining query reformulation in which users add new terms to an existing query. Lau and Horvitz [33] refer to this case as *specialization* since the focus of the conjunctive query is narrowed down with the addition of each new query term. They introduce 2 additional types of modifications, *generalization*, during which terms are removed which results in a broader, more diverse set of results, and *reformulation*, the exchange of one query term for another. This final case can effectively result in a radical topic shift depending on how semantically similar the terms are. To investigate the effect of all three major reformulation strategies, we group all instances of query reformulations depending on whether terms were added (specialization), removed (generalization) or exchanged (reformulation) and measure the average semantic similarity between the terms fixated by the user and the query, before and after the reformulation took place and report the relative difference. Table 6 shows the results of this experiment. As we can see, all three reformulation strategies result in a net gain in LCH scores, increasing the similarity between fixated terms and produced query vocabulary. The highest individual gains were noted for reformulations. Here, typically, mildly related terms are exchanged for highly related ones. Generalizations introduce the least dramatic increase in similarity. Mostly, this strategy corrects for previously added terms that drove the result set in an undesired topical direction.

5. CURSOR-TRACKING EXPERIMENTS

Based on the previously studied eye-gaze signals, we were able to show various forms of evidence of term acquisition during Web search. The main shortcoming of this approach (e.g., for improving the ranking quality) is the need for expensive, non-portable hardware to collect the required eye-gaze traces. As a consequence, the number of observations is very limited. Previous work has found a strong correlation

Table 7: Term-level cursor hover statistics.

	Non-query terms	Query terms
Relative frequency	0.79	0.21
Share of overall hovers	0.74	0.26
Rel. number of hovers per token	0.045	**0.059***
Share of overall hover duration	0.78	0.22
Avg. hover duration per token	130ms	**135ms***

between eye gaze and cursor movements [19, 22]. In this section, we roll out the previously described experimental setup, identically, to a large and diverse audience of crowdsourcing workers on Amazon Mechanical Turk (AMT). Since the availability of eye tracking hardware cannot be ensured in this altered setup, we will instead rely on traces of cursor movement to infer user attention. Where, previously, we investigated duration and frequency of fixations, we will now replace them with the duration and frequency of mouse cursor hovers over terms on the screen. Aside from this substitution, all previously introduced formulas and notations remain the same.

We conducted an initial experiment comprising 500 search sessions. 137 individual workers were presented with a randomly selected topic out of the previously introduced pool of 10 and were redirected to a custom-built Web search engine based on the public API of a popular search engine provider. Each search session was remunerated with $ 0.25. The crowd demographics are more diverse in terms of age, level of education, field of study, and language background. The gender split is comparable to the situation described earlier for the lab study. Table 7 shows cursor hover statistics across 500 individual search sessions. Again, the majority of tokens on the page does not fall into the query term category T_q. Despite this heavily skewed prior distribution, the relative number of hovers per token as well as the time for which the cursor rests on query terms is significantly greater than for non-query terms.

Let us now move on from literal query term occurrences to a final inspection of semantic relatedness. Table 8 compares per-term hover duration and likelihood for varying ranges of LCH proximity scores. While the middle ground of the distribution is less indicative than in the fixation case earlier, we still note a significant increase in hover likelihood and duration between terms of low to moderate semantic proximity ($LCH < 1.0$) and those of high semantic proximity ($LCH > 1.75$). Statistical significance of improvements was measured by means of a Wilcoxon signed rank test at $\alpha < 0.05$-level. Short hovers are much more likely to be caused by unrelated terms while very long hovers occur more frequently for related terms. This finding is supported by recent work by Ageev et al. [1], who investigate the connection between mouse cursor hover durations over relevant document passages to the results of user generated document summaries. Especially, their Figure 3 is in line with our findings here as well as earlier in Table 3.

When comparing our findings to the ones presented earlier in Section 4, it becomes obvious, that fixations are richer and more accurate predictors of user attention than cursor traces. The majority of users only occasionally use the mouse cursor in order to highlight text, mark their current reading position or follow textual hyper links. The result are the previously discussed correlations with topically relevant terms. For a share of 13.6% of the 500 search sessions, however, we observed a stronger connection between eye gaze and mouse movement. Here, users employed the cursor to trace every line of text as they read, creating a pattern that closely mimics the shape of eye gaze traces. Informal discussion with industry researchers from Google revealed that they as well noted this behaviour for 12 - 15% of their user base during an earlier, yet unpublished, large-scale experiment. Having shown that in settings where eye gaze traces are not available, substantial insight into topical relevance of terms can be gained from mouse cursor movements, the next section of this paper will demonstrate the use of this source of evidence for the task of query suggestion.

Table 8: Per-term cursor hover frequency and duration show a general upwards trend as the semantic proximity to query terms increases.

	hover duration	hover likelihood
$LCH < 0.25$	116ms	0.041
$0.25 \leq LCH < 0.5$	121ms	0.041
$0.5 \leq LCH < 0.75$	119ms	0.039
$0.75 \leq LCH < 1.0$	123ms	0.043
$1.0 \leq LCH < 1.25$	127ms	0.047
$1.25 \leq LCH < 1.5$	126ms	0.048
$1.5 \leq LCH < 1.75$	129ms	0.050
$1.75 \leq LCH < 2.0$	**133ms***	**0.053***
$LCH \geq 2.0$	**135ms***	**0.055***

6. MODELLING QUERY TERM USAGE

In the past, various successful applications integrated attention and interest information in the form of document display times [25, 23], clickthrough features [9, 45], hitting time [39], or the contents of personal data collections [10]. Most notably, Buscher et al. [8] use fixations on different document parts to reorder query expansion candidates. Their work proposed 4 different interest metrics, the best-performing one of which we will include as a baseline for comparison to our own method. Several advances in eye-tracking technology allow us to infer even more fine-grained signals than those studied by previous work. Concretely, **(1)** we map fixation durations and frequencies to individual terms while Buscher et al. rely on paragraph-level information. **(2)** In the previous sections, we saw that many reformulations are inspired by fixated terms, but often use related terms rather than the literal fixation term. In order to account for this effect, we include a model of semantic relatedness between candidate terms and fixation terms. Essentially, this broadens the coverage of our method and accounts for reformulations that include previously unseen terms in a fashion similar to language model smoothing.

6.1 Methodology

Buscher et al. [8] report best query expansion performance for their *Gaze-Length-Filter* (GLF). The method expands the well-known tf-idf formula by a user interest model based on the number of fixations on text segments shorter than 230 characters that contain a word w ($SA(w)$) and the frequency of longer text segments $LA(w)$ containing that same term. Their approach modifies the standard tf-idf formula in such a way, that only the frequency of w in those segments of the document that were gazed at (c_A) is considered. We include

Table 9: Query suggestion performance.

Method	MRR	σ_{RR}
API Output	0.76	0.28
Gaze-Length-Filter (GLF)	0.79*	0.26
Term-Attention-Model (TAM)	0.80*	0.24
Term-Attention-Model + Relatedness (TAM-R)	0.86▼*	0.29

their model as a performance baseline. Please note that, in the following, we speak about words w rather than the previously discussed tokens t. While tokens are the atomic unit that receives measurable user attention, words represent general concepts. As a consequence, we add up the cumulative attention measured for each occurrence (token) t_w of a word w in order to estimate the word's relevancy to the user's information need.

$$GLF(w) = tf(w, c_A) \times idf(w, C) \times \frac{LA(w)}{LA(w) + SA(w)} \quad (4)$$

Additionally, we propose two novel, term-level attention models. $TAM_\lambda(w)$ combines $F(w)$, the frequency of attention to term w with the cumulative length for which the attention lasted $D(w) = \sum dur(t_w)$. The mixture parameter λ balances the relative contribution of the two terms, biasing the score towards attention frequency, as λ increases.

$$TAM_\lambda(w) = \lambda F(w) + (1 - \lambda) D(w) \quad (5)$$

At this point, neither the GLF baseline nor the TAM score can account for the addition of previously unseen terms w. In Sections 4 and 5, however, we observed significant shares of added query terms to not have been explicitly present or fixated before the reformulation. To remedy this, $TAM\text{-}R_\Lambda(w)$ expands TAM by a semantic similarity metric $LCH(w)$ between candidate term w and the set F of all terms that previously received user attention (fixation or cursor hover, respectively). In this way, we can ensure that the overall model score does not default to zero for unseen terms. The weight vector Λ defines the concrete relative contributions of semantic relatedness, attention frequency and attention duration.

$$TAM\text{-}R_\Lambda(w) = \lambda_l LCH(w) + \lambda_f F(w) + \lambda_d D(w)s \quad (6)$$

6.2 Experiments

Our experiments are based on another series of crowdsourcing tasks on our custom search engine interface. The experimental setup is identical to the one described earlier in Section 5. In this case, however, we included the top 7 query suggestions delivered by a commercial search engine API and measured the reciprocal rank (RR) of accepted (clicked) suggestions. We compare the original order of query suggestions with 3 alternative variants, each re-ranked by decreasing averaged scores in the three attention metrics (GLF, TAM, TAM-R) that were computed based on cursor hover information. Table 9 compares the query suggestion performance of the unmodified commercial API output with that of the various, previously introduced user attention-based models in terms of mean RR (MRR) across all accepted suggestions. Additionally, we inspect the stability of the methods in terms of their RR score variance.

For of all models that employ traces of user attention, we can observe consistently and significantly higher ranking performance with respect to the original API output. The mild performance gap, favouring TAM over the passage-based GLF could not be confirmed significant. As we, however, include the proximity-based smoothing functionality of TAM-R, query suggestion performance improves. Statistical significance of improvements was measured by means of a Wilcoxon signed rank test at $\alpha < 0.05$-level. Significant improvements over the baseline API output are denoted by an asterisk, while significant improvements over the GLF baseline are indicated by the ▼ symbol. Manual analysis of the re-orderings introduced by the various models confirms that GLF and TAM incorporate knowledge about literal term acquisitions from previously consumed material. TAM-R, indeed, accounts for the addition of terms that relate to the same topic that the user is interested in, but that did not directly occur in the explored document segments. The best-performing combination of mixture weights ($\lambda_l = 0.3$, $\lambda_f = 0.5$, $\lambda_d = 0.2$) was determined by means of a greedy parameter sweep in the range $[0, 1]$ with step size 0.1, ensuring $\sum \lambda_i = 1$ at all times.

6.3 Qualitative Performance Analysis

Besides the mere quantitative performance overview, we manually inspected those cases in which the various systems performed especially well (or badly) in order to give qualitative insight into the respective strengths and weaknesses of the presented methods. As reflected by the solid baseline performance, the raw API output in many cases returns the correct suggestion candidate on the highest ranks. Exceptions to this rule were broad queries that cover many potential aspects of a topic. As one out of several examples that we encountered, take Topic 38, that deals with psychological and emotional consequences of obesity. While our test subjects were mainly interested in mental problems that accompany this medical condition, top ranking query suggestions were concerned with vascular conditions as well as damage to the joints caused by dramatically increased weight.

All three user attention based models successfully placed such off-focus suggestions at the bottom of the candidate list, thereby increasing ranking performance. Both GLF and TAM struggled with previously unseen terms. Users that only briefly explored the available information before reformulating their query saw worst performance issues since their sparse observation vectors were not indicative towards the correct choice of suggestion.

TAM-R, finally, showed significant improvements in such situations. The use of the semantic proximity component served to assign probability mass to previously unseen terms. In practice, this resulted in promoting suggestion candidates that named concrete anabolic steroid substances such as the legally sold Prostanozol rather than the overall class. The remaining performance gap can mostly be accounted to pairwise candidate swaps between the top ranks of our list and the clicked suggestion. In many cases, this happened for near-duplicate candidates such as "*steroid consequences*" and "*steroid substance consequences*" in which the added term "*substance*" does not significantly modify the query semantics.

7. CONCLUSION

In this paper, we studied query reformulation by means of an eye-gaze tracking system. Inspired by topics drawn from the TREC QA track, we conduct a series of lab-based user studies. Tracking user attention at the term level, a finer granularity than was previously used in the IR literature, we make a range of interesting observations: **(1)** A significant share of newly added query terms were previously present on SERPs and visited pages in the same session. Previous work on the log-based recognition of query term acquisition [15] overestimated this effect. With the help of eye tracking hardware, we were able to gain a more realistic impression of how many such term occurrences were indeed seen by the user. **(2)** We find that literal query term acquisition is often indicated by significantly higher-than-average amounts of prior user attention in the form of frequency and duration of fixations to the prospective query terms. **(3)** Often, query expansion does not literally re-use previously encountered terms but highly related ones, instead. In a series of experiments we highlighted the importance of semantic proximity between query expansion terms and the center of user attention. **(4)** To ensure the broad applicability of our results, we replicated our lab-based eye-tracking experiments in a distributed fashion at much larger scale by measuring mouse cursor movements instead of eye gaze fixations. We note that our high-level findings generalize well between the two signals and the conclusions drawn from the lab-based study are confirmed by mouse cursor traces. **(5)** Finally, we demonstrate the usefulness of our findings for established IR tasks by comparing a passage-level attention model proposed by previous work to two variants of our term-level attention model, finding that term-level models including information about semantic proximity between candidate terms and user interest can deliver significantly better ranking performance of query suggestions than an industrial baseline.

The insights presented in this paper inspire many interesting directions for future work. First of all, the significant performance gains achieved by incorporating estimates of user attention into the query reformulation process motivate an evaluation of other related tasks. User attention models empowered by eye-gaze or cursor movement signals hold potential gains for ranking results to subsequent queries in a session, diversifying result sets, estimating domain expertise or personalized textual complexity. In this work, we used a very short-lived attention model based exclusively on the contents of the current search session. This was mainly due to limited availability of resources of users. Assuming an industrial setting, long-term attention models that include the searcher's general interest in addition to the current session context can be expected to become powerful tools for a wide number of inference tasks. In this way, one could estimate a general user vocabulary model, that describes the searcher's active and passive language use in more than just term frequencies. Such a model could for example describe the ease with which a user generates and consumes a given term, the speed at which they expand their vocabulary of new domains, or gradual shifts in interest. Wide-coverage models like that are especially interesting in query-free environments in which the system pro-actively pushes information about standing queries or upcoming events to the user.

In this work, we showed how models of knowledge acquisition in terms of previously unknown terms can benefit IR tasks. There are many other types of knowledge acquisition, e.g., factual or procedural knowledge, that can greatly benefit retrieval performance. Gaining an understanding of these learning processes holds significant potential for delivering smarter, more user-aware retrieval facilities. Finally, while the focus of this work lies on fixations, there are multiple other signals that can be captured by means of eye-tracking hardware. In our experiments, we additionally measured pupil dilation and saccade patterns. These signals turned out to be rather noisy and inconclusive when broken down on term level. For reasons of space, we omitted the respective results from the paper. In the future, we plan to conduct a dedicated investigation of these adjunct signals.

8. REFERENCES

[1] M. Ageev, D. Lagun, and E. Agichtein. Improving search result summaries by using searcher behavior data. In *SIGIR 2013*.

[2] A. Ajanki, D. Hardoon, S. Kaski, K. Puolamäki, and J. Shawe-Taylor. Can eyes reveal interest? implicit queries from gaze patterns. *User Modeling and User-Adapted Interaction*, 2009.

[3] S. Banerjee and T. Pedersen. An adapted lesk algorithm for word sense disambiguation using wordnet. In *Computational linguistics and intelligent text processing*. Springer, 2002.

[4] N. Belkin, R. Oddy, and H. Brooks. Ask for information retrieval: Part i. background and theory. *Journal of documentation*, 1982.

[5] D. Beymer and D. Russell. Webgazeanalyzer: a system for capturing and analyzing web reading behavior using eye gaze. In *CHI 2005*. ACM.

[6] P. Brooks, K. Phang, R. Bradley, D. Oard, R. White, and F. Guimbretire. Measuring the utility of gaze detection for task modeling: A preliminary study. In *Workshop on Intelligent Interfaces for Intelligent Analysis*, 2006.

[7] G. Buscher, A. Dengel, and L. van Elst. Eye movements as implicit relevance feedback. In *CHI 2008*. ACM.

[8] G. Buscher, A. Dengel, and L. van Elst. Query expansion using gaze-based feedback on the subdocument level. In *SIGIR 2008*. ACM.

[9] H. Cao, D. Jiang, J. Pei, Q. He, Z. Liao, E. Chen, and H. Li. Context-aware query suggestion by mining click-through and session data. In *KDD 2008*. ACM.

[10] P. Chirita, C. Firan, and W. Nejdl. Personalized query expansion for the web. In *SIGIR 2007*. ACM.

[11] K. Collins-Thompson, P. Bennett, R. White, S. de la Chica, and D. Sontag. Personalizing web search results by reading level. In *CIKM 2011*. ACM.

[12] E. Cutrell and Z. Guan. What are you looking for?: an eye-tracking study of information usage in web search. In *CHI 2007*. ACM.

[13] E. Efthimiadis. Query expansion. *Annual review of information science and technology*, 1996.

[14] C. Eickhoff, P. Serdyukov, and A. P. De Vries. A combined topical/non-topical approach to identifying web sites for children. In *WSDM 2011*.

[15] C. Eickhoff, J. Teevan, R. White, and S. Dumais. Lessons from the journey: A query log analysis of within-session learning. In *WSDM 2014*. ACM.

[16] W. Gao, C. Niu, J. Nie, M. Zhou, J. Hu, K. Wong, and H. Hon. Cross-lingual query suggestion using query logs of different languages. In *SIGIR 2007*. ACM.

[17] L. Granka, T. Joachims, and G. Gay. Eye-tracking analysis of user behavior in www search. In *SIGIR 2004*. ACM.

[18] Q. Guo and E. Agichtein. Beyond dwell time: estimating document relevance from cursor movements and other post-click searcher behavior. In *WWW 2012*. ACM.

[19] Q. Guo and E. Agichtein. Towards predicting web searcher gaze position from mouse movements. In *CHI 2010*. ACM.

[20] G. Hirst and D. St-Onge. Lexical chains as representations of context for the detection and correction of malapropisms. *WordNet: An electronic lexical database*, 1998.

[21] J. Huang, R. White, G. Buscher, and K. Wang. Improving searcher models using mouse cursor activity. In *SIGIR 2012*. ACM.

[22] J. Huang, R. White, and S. Dumais. No clicks, no problem: using cursor movements to understand and improve search. In *CHI 2011*. ACM.

[23] T. Joachims, L. Granka, B. Pan, H. Hembrooke, and G. Gay. Accurately interpreting clickthrough data as implicit feedback. In *SIGIR 2005*. ACM.

[24] M. Just and P. Carpenter. A theory of reading: From eye fixations to comprehension. *Psychological review*, 1980.

[25] D. Kelly and N. Belkin. Display time as implicit feedback: understanding task effects. In *SIGIR 2004*. ACM.

[26] D. Kelly and C. Cool. The effects of topic familiarity on information search behavior. In *JCDL 2002*. ACM.

[27] D. Kelly, K. Gyllstrom, and E. Bailey. A comparison of query and term suggestion features for interactive searching. In *SIGIR 2009*. ACM.

[28] D. Kelly and J. Lin. Overview of the trec 2006 ciqa task. In *SIGIR Forum 2007*. ACM.

[29] J. Kim, K. Collins-Thompson, P. Bennett, and S. Dumais. Characterizing web content, user interests, and search behavior by reading level and topic. In *WSDM 2012*. ACM.

[30] K. Kunze, H. Kawaichi, K. Yoshimura, and K. Kise. Towards inferring language expertise using eye tracking. In *CHI 2013*.

[31] K. Kunze, Y. Utsumi, Y. Shiga, K. Kise, and A. Bulling. I know what you are reading: recognition of document types using mobile eye tracking. In *Proceedings of the 17th annual international symposium on wearable computers*. ACM, 2013.

[32] V. Kuperman, H. Stadthagen-Gonzalez, and M. Brysbaert. Age-of-acquisition ratings for 30,000 english words. *Behavior Research Methods*, 2012.

[33] T. Lau and E. Horvitz. Patterns of search: Analyzing and modeling web query refinement. *Courses and lectures-International Centre for Mechanical Sciences*, 1999.

[34] C. Leacock and M. Chodorow. Combining local context and wordnet similarity for word sense identification. *WordNet: An electronic lexical database*, 1998.

[35] J. Liu, N. Belkin, X. Zhang, and X. Yuan. Examining users' knowledge change in the task completion process. *IPM 2012*.

[36] J. Liu, M. J. Cole, C. Liu, R. Bierig, J. Gwizdka, N. J. Belkin, J. Zhang, and X. Zhang. Search behaviors in different task types. In *JCDL 2010*. ACM.

[37] T. Loboda, P. Brusilovsky, and J. Brunstein. Inferring word relevance from eye-movements of readers. In *Proceedings of the 16th international conference on Intelligent user interfaces*. ACM, 2011.

[38] H. Ma, H. Yang, I. King, and M. Lyu. Learning latent semantic relations from clickthrough data for query suggestion. In *CIKM 2008*. ACM.

[39] Q. Mei, D. Zhou, and K. Church. Query suggestion using hitting time. In *CIKM 2008*. ACM.

[40] M. Porter. Snowball: A language for stemming algorithms, 2001.

[41] K. Puolamäki, A. Ajanki, and S. Kaski. Learning to learn implicit queries from gaze patterns. In *ICML 2008*. ACM.

[42] K. Puolamäki, J. Salojärvi, E. Savia, J. Simola, and S. Kaski. Combining eye movements and collaborative filtering for proactive information retrieval. In *SIGIR 2005*. ACM.

[43] K Rayner. Eye movements in reading and information processing: 20 years of research. *Psychological bulletin*, 1998.

[44] J. Salojärvi, I. Kojo, J. Simola, and S. Kaski. Can relevance be inferred from eye movements in information retrieval. In *WSOM 2003*.

[45] Y. Song and L. He. Optimal rare query suggestion with implicit user feedback. In *WWW 2010*. ACM.

[46] A. Spink and T. Saracevic. Interaction in information retrieval: selection and effectiveness of search terms. *JASIS*, 1997.

[47] Amanda Spink. Term relevance feedback and query expansion: relation to design. In *SIGIR 1994*. Springer.

[48] J. Teevan, S. Dumais, and E. Horvitz. Personalizing search via automated analysis of interests and activities. In *SIGIR 2005*. ACM.

[49] R. White, S. Dumais, and J. Teevan. Characterizing the influence of domain expertise on web search behavior. In *WSDM 2009*. ACM.

[50] B. Wildemuth. The effects of domain knowledge on search tactic formulation. *JASIST 2004*.

[51] R. Williams and R. Morris. Eye movements, word familiarity, and vocabulary acquisition. *European Journal of Cognitive Psychology*, 2004.

[52] Z. Wu and M. Palmer. Verbs semantics and lexical selection. In *ACL 1994*.

[53] X. Zhang, M. Cole, and N. Belkin. Predicting users' domain knowledge from search behaviors. In *SIGIR 2011*. ACM.

Differences in the Use of Search Assistance for Tasks of Varying Complexity

Robert Capra, Jaime Arguello, Anita Crescenzi, Emily Vardell

School of Information & Library Science
University of North Carolina at Chapel Hill
Chapel Hill, NC, USA
[rcapra,jarguell,amcc,evardell]@email.unc.edu

ABSTRACT

In this paper, we study how users interact with a search assistance tool while completing tasks of varying complexity. We designed a novel tool referred to as the *search guide* (SG) that displays the search trails (queries issued, results clicked, pages bookmarked) from three previous users who completed the task. We report on a laboratory study with 48 participants that investigates different factors that may influence user interaction with the SG and the effects of the SG on different outcome measures. Participants were asked to find and bookmark pages for four tasks of varying complexity and the SG was made available to half the participants. We collected log data and conducted retrospective stimulated recall interviews to learn about participants' use of the SG. Our results suggest the following trends. First, interaction with the SG was greater for more complex tasks. Second, the *a priori* determinability of the task (i.e., whether the task was perceived to be well-defined) helped predict whether participants gained a bookmark from the SG. Third, participants who interacted with the SG, but did not gain a bookmark, felt less system support than those who gained a bookmark and those who did not interact. Finally, a qualitative analysis of our interviews suggests differences in motivation and benefits from SG use for different levels of task complexity. Our findings extend prior research on search assistance tools and provide insights for the design of systems to help users with complex search tasks.

Categories and Subject Descriptors

H.3 [**Information Storage and Retrieval**]: Information Storage and Retrieval

Keywords

Search assistance, search trails, search behavior

SIGIR'15, August 09 - 13, 2015, Santiago, Chile.

ACM 978-1-4503-3621-5/15/08 ...$15.00.
DOI: http://dx.doi.org/10.1145/2766462.2767741.

1. INTRODUCTION

Current search engines are effective in helping users complete simple search tasks such as homepage-finding and fact-finding. However, they provide less support in helping users with complex tasks that may involve exploration, analysis, comparison, and evaluation. Prior work has sought to address this limitation by exploring different types of interactive tools to support and assist search engine users. These include tools to help users formulate better queries [9, 15, 18], to communicate system features [17], to assist with note-taking [8], and tools that display the "search trails" followed by other users who completed a related task [20, 23, 26].

Our focus in this work is on search trails. The idea underlying search trails is simple and intuitive—search engine users may benefit from seeing how someone else approached the same or a similar task. To support this, search trails provide an interactive display with information about how another person searched, and may include the queries issued, results clicked, pages viewed, pages bookmarked, and annotations made by the original searcher. Trails can be created manually, or algorithmically from search log or toolbar data.

Prior research on search trails has focused on measuring the information content of search trails [23], understanding the differences between trails generated by domain experts versus novices [26], developing algorithms for predicting search trails for a given search session [19], and evaluating the usefulness of trail-end point pages for different types of search tasks [21]. While this prior work suggests the usefulness of search trails and their feasibility as a form of search assistance, there have been few controlled laboratory studies to directly evaluate their benefits and use. This is the main focus of our work. We investigate how users engage with an interactive search trail, when they use it (i.e., for which types of tasks), and what benefits they report.

We study user interaction with a search assistance tool we refer to as the *search guide* (SG). Our search guide tool displays the search trails from three users who completed the same task. Each trail shows the sequence of queries that were issued, the results that were clicked, and the pages that were bookmarked. We report on a user study with 48 participants. Participants were given search tasks and asked to use a search engine to find and bookmark pages that would help in constructing a response for the task. Access to the SG was a between subjects variable—24 participants had access to the SG and 24 participants used a control system without the SG. To gain insight into factors affecting user interaction with the SG, the study used a concurrent think-aloud protocol followed by a stimulated recall interview.

In this paper, we investigate five main research questions. In our first research question (RQ1), we study the effects of task complexity on user interaction with the SG. Participants completed four tasks of varying levels of *cognitive* complexity, which refers to the amount of learning and cognitive effort required to complete the task [1]. Prior studies found that more cognitively complex tasks are perceived to be more difficult and require more search effort [2, 3, 12, 24]. We suspected that these characteristics may lead people to seek search assistance more frequently for complex tasks.

Our second research question (RQ2) investigates combined factors of the user and the task that may influence user interaction with the SG. For this question, we consider *pre-task* factors such as the participant's level of interest in the task, prior knowledge and search experience in the task domain, and expectations about the task difficulty.

In our third research question (RQ3), we study whether having access to the SG influences outcome measures that reflect the user's experience during the search task. We consider *post-task* measures such as the level of enjoyment, acquired interest and knowledge, satisfaction with the solution and search strategy, experienced difficulty, and perceived level of system support. Seeking search assistance incurs a cost to the user in terms of time and effort. In this respect, outcome measures such as satisfaction and perceived level of system support are likely to depend on whether the user was successful in seeking search assistance. In our fourth research question (RQ4), we investigate whether post-task outcome measures differed among searches where participants: (1) used the SG and gained from it, (2) used the SG but did not gain from it, and (3) did not use the SG at all. In our final research question (RQ5), we examine the effects of task complexity on *why* and *how* users interact (or choose not to interact) with the SG. This question differs from RQ1 in that qualitative data from our stimulated recall interviews was used to characterize SG use and non-use along three dimensions: (1) motivations for use, (2) benefits gained from use, and (3) reasons for non-use.

2. RELATED WORK

This work is informed by three branches of prior research: (1) studies of task complexity and its effects on users' perceptions, behaviors, and outcomes; (2) studies of help-seeking in information retrieval; and (3) studies of search assistance.

Task Complexity. A large body of prior work has focused on characterizing tasks along different dimensions (see Li and Belkin [16]). One such dimension is task complexity, which is an inherent property of the task, and is independent of the task doer [16]. Different characterizations of task complexity have been proposed. Early work by Campbell [7] characterized task complexity in terms of the number of required outcomes, the number of alternative paths to the outcomes, the level of uncertainty regarding the paths, and the degree of interdependence between paths. Byström and Järvelin [6] defined task complexity based on the *a priori* determinability of the task, a measure of the extent to which a searcher can read the task description and deduce the required outcomes, the information needed to produce the outcomes, and the processes associated with finding the required information. Bell and Ruthven [4] defined task complexity in terms of the *a priori* determinability of the information required to complete the task, the search strategy, and the ability to recognize relevant content. Finally, Jansen *et al.* [12] (and later Arguello *et al.* [3, 2] and Wu *et al.* [24]) characterized task complexity in terms of the amount of learning and cognitive effort required to complete the task. To this end, they adopted a taxonomy of learning outcomes proposed by Anderson and Krathwohl [1] for designing educational materials. In this work, we use this *cognitive* view of task complexity. Prior studies have shown that more cognitively complex tasks are associated with higher levels of expected (pre-task) difficulty [24], higher levels of experienced (post-task) difficulty [2, 24], and higher levels of search activity as indicated by measures derived from queries, clicks, bookmarks, and task completion time [2, 3, 12, 24]. We contribute to this body of literature by investigating whether and how task complexity affects use of search assistance.

Help-Seeking in Information Retrieval. Searchers encounter difficulty in different ways and for different reasons. In a large-scale user study, Xie and Cool [25] found that searchers encounter difficulty with seven general processes: (1) getting started, (2) identifying relevant resources, (3) navigating a resource, (4) constructing queries, (5) constraining the search results, (6) recognizing useful information, and (7) monitoring the task process. They also identified factors that give rise to help-seeking situations including: the user's domain knowledge and search experience, properties of the task (e.g., its complexity), and characteristics of the interface and the quality of the search results.

Search assistance tools provide an opportunity to support users who encounter difficulty. However, there are challenges in creating successful assistance tools. Prior work points to several reasons for why users do not use help systems, including the cost of cognitively disengaging from the main task, the fear of unproductive help-seeking, and the refusal to admit defeat [10]. Prior studies also found that users may not notice the help when they are cognitively engaged in the main task [10, 13] or may prefer to attempt the task on their own before seeking assistance [13].

Search Assistance Tools. Search assistance tools are aimed to help users with different aspects of the search process. In this review, we focus on prior work on search trails.

White *et al.* [21] experimented with a search assistant tool called *popular destinations*. Given a query, the search system presented a set of trail-endpoint webpages for trails originating from similar queries. Results from a user study found that popular destinations were better suited for exploratory tasks, while query suggestions were better suited for known-item tasks. For exploratory tasks, popular destinations were associated with improved perceptions about the search experience, the quality of the information found, and the level of system support. In a follow-up study, White and Chandrasekar [22] proposed a modification to the popular destinations tool to help users with difficult known-item tasks. The proposed tool surfaces 'labels' associated with the probable target page. Labels were generated from anchor text, queries with clicks on the target, and social bookmarks. A query-log analysis suggests that surfacing labels might help users find target webpages faster.

White and Huang [23] analyzed search trails captured using a browser toolbar and compared the usefulness of the first trail page, the last page, and the full trail, which includes visited pages in between. Using different heuristics, full trails were associated with more coverage, diversity, novelty, and utility, suggesting that users have something to gain from seeing the full trail versus only the endpoints.

Yuan and White [26] compared the quality of search trails produced by experts and novices in the medical domain. Study participants were explicitly asked to produce search trails to be used by others. Experts produced trails with more relevant pages, more objective information, and a more logical transition from general to specific information.

An important step in using trails to support searchers is to predict which trail to display for a particular search session. Singla *et al.* [19] formulated the task as predicting the best trail in response to an input query-click pair. They developed different trail-finding algorithms and evaluated their performance retrospectively using toolbar data. Results suggest that different algorithms perform well for different metrics based on coverage, diversity, utility, and relevance, and that based on a particular metric, the best-found trail often outperformed the one followed by the actual user.

Finally, Fisher *et al.* [11] evaluated the usefulness of *knowledge maps* constructed by a single user or different users over several iterations. Knowledge maps are different from trails and consist of bookmarked pages that are organized and annotated to convey the *schema* of the solution. Interestingly, knowledge maps that were iterated upon were found to be more useful precisely because the schema of the solution was easier to understand and intrinsically valuable. This suggests that search trails may become more valuable if they can be extended and curated by users over time.

3. METHODS AND MATERIALS

3.1 User Study

A laboratory study with 48 participants was conducted to investigate our five main research questions (RQ1-RQ5). Participants were undergraduate university students (75% female). The study used a concurrent think-aloud protocol with a retrospective stimulated recall interview. Each participant completed four search tasks of varying levels of cognitive complexity (Section 3.3). Participants were asked to use a live search system to find and bookmark webpages that would be useful in constructing a response for the task. The system used the Bing Web Search API to retrieve results from the open web and allowed participants to issue queries, click and view results, navigate away from a landing page, and bookmark pages. Participants were asked to provide a brief justification when bookmarking each page.

Access to the SG was a between-subjects variable—24 participants were given access to the SG and 24 participants were not. Task complexity was a within-subjects variable—participants completed four tasks associated with four different levels of cognitive complexity (remember, understand, analyze, and evaluate) and all four tasks were from the same domain (Section 3.3). Cognitive complexity was rotated across participants using a Latin square.

The study protocol proceeded as follows. First, participants were asked to complete a consent form and a demographic questionnaire. Next, participants were shown a video describing the bookmarking features of the system. For the 24 participants who were given access to the SG, the video contained an additional section describing its basic functionality. Participants were told that the SG conveyed information about how three other searchers completed a similar task. The video described how each of the three search trails or "paths" showed the queries that were issued and the results that were clicked and bookmarked.

Our study protocol involved having participants think-aloud while they searched. Participants were instructed to narrate their searches by describing their thought processes and actions. To familiarize participants with the system and to help them become comfortable with thinking aloud, we asked them to spend a few minutes exploring the system and trying an example task before starting the main tasks.

All four tasks followed the same procedure. First, participants were asked to read the task carefully and then complete a pre-task questionnaire (Section 3.4). Next, participants were directed to the search interface. During the search, participants were gently prompted to continue thinking aloud if they fell silent. Participants were given 12 minutes to complete each task. A pop-up message notified participants when they had three minutes remaining. After completing the task, participants were directed to a post-task questionnaire (Section 3.4). All four search sessions and think-aloud comments were recorded using Morae screen recording software. After completing all four tasks, participants started the retrospective portion of the study.

During the search sessions where participants had access to the SG, the study moderator used Morae Observer to view the participant's search and mark the points where the participant moused or clicked in the SG. These points were later used in the stimulated recall interview (Section 3.5).

3.2 Search Interface and Search Guide

Search Interface. The search interface used in the study is shown in Figure 1. The interface in the experimental and control conditions looked identical except that the SG was only present in the experimental condition. The system allowed participants to issue queries, click results, bookmark pages, delete bookmarks, and (in the experimental condition) to interact with the SG. The search task description (A) was always displayed directly above the query input box (B). Results were returned using the Bing Web Search API, which produces 50 results per query. The top 10 results were displayed directly below the query input box (C) and pagination controls were shown below the results. Participants used a Chrome web browser with four buttons integrated into the browser bookmark bar (D). These buttons allowed participants to: (1) return to the search page, (2) bookmark the current page, (3) show the current set of bookmarks, and (4) terminate the task. Clicking the "bookmark this page" button displayed a pop-up window (not shown) that prompted participants to: "Briefly describe why you are bookmarking this page." Participants could bookmark any page including pages linked directly and indirectly from the SERP or the SG. Clicking the "show bookmarks" button displayed a pop-up window (not shown) that listed the current set of bookmarks, with justifications included. From the bookmark view page, participants could delete a bookmark if desired. In the experimental condition, the search guide was displayed to the right of the search results (E). We used Javascript and AJAX to log all user interactions on the SERP including scroll and mouse-enter events.

Search Guide. As shown in Figure 1(E), the SG displayed three "paths" taken by three different users who completed the same search task. Participants could explore the paths using tabs (Path 1-3). Each path included the list of queries that were issued by another user and, for each query, the sequence of search results that were clicked and bookmarked. Participants could use an accordion control

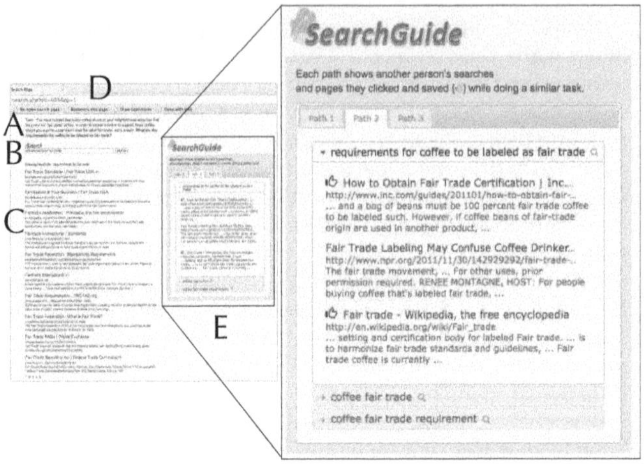

Figure 1: Search Interface and Search Guide

to expand a query to see the sequence of results that were clicked and bookmarked for that query. Clicked and bookmarked pages were displayed using the page title, URL, and summary snippet, and bookmarked pages were distinguished using a thumbs-up icon displayed to the left of the result title. Participants could hover their mouse over a bookmarked page to trigger a tooltip that displayed the justification provided when the page was bookmarked. Clicking on an SG result took the participant to the landing page. Finally, clicking on the magnifying glass icon to the right of an SG query re-issued the query and displayed the results in the main SERP region. Again, we used Javascript and AJAX to record all user interactions with the search guide, including mouse-enter events, clicks on an SG result or query, clicks to expand the accordion control, and tooltip display events.

Two decisions regarding the search guide had to be made—When to display the SG and which paths to display? In regard to the first question, the SG was displayed to participants after issuing the first query and was present on all SERPs for the rest of the search session. In practice, a system might need to predict when to display the SG. We decided against displaying the SG dynamically in order to control how participants experienced the SG and to learn about SG use at *all* points in the search process, including early in the search session. In regard to the second question, as explained in more detail below, we decided to show paths for the *same* search task. In practice, a system might need to predict which paths to show. We were interested in exploring the best-case scenario where the system finds paths that match the user's current search task. However, to avoid biasing participants to use the SG, they were told that the paths corresponded to searches for a *similar* task.

Search Paths. We used a total of 12 search tasks in our study (Section 3.3). Each search task was associated with its own unique set of SG paths. For a given task, participants in the SG condition saw the same SG paths. Paths were selected from a previous user study that included the same search tasks [2]. For each task, we selected three paths that had at least three queries, at least one click per query, and a total of at least three bookmarks.

3.3 Search Tasks

Participants completed four tasks of varying levels of *cognitive* complexity. Cognitive complexity refers to the amount of learning and cognitive effort required to complete the task. We used a subset of 12 tasks from the original 20 tasks developed by Wu *et al.* [24]. The tasks varied across three domains (commerce, health, science) and across four levels of cognitive complexity from Anderson and Krathwohl's Taxonomy of Learning [1]: (1) *remember*: recalling relevant knowledge from long-term memory, (2) *understand*: constructing meaning through summarizing and explaining, (3) *analyze*: breaking material into constituent parts and determining how the parts relate to each other, and (4) *evaluate*: making judgements through checking and critiquing. The tasks were situated in scenarios geared towards our participant population (undergraduate students) [5].

Table 1 shows the four tasks associated with the health domain. Higher-complexity tasks required more information and more mental processing: remember tasks required finding a fact; understand tasks required compiling a list of items; analyze tasks required compiling a list of items and understanding their differences; and evaluate tasks required compiling a list of items, understanding their differences, and making a recommendation.

Remember—You recently watched a documentary about people living with HIV in the United States. You thought the disease was nearly eradicated, and are now curious to know more about the prevalence of the disease. **Specifically, how many people in the US are currently living with HIV?**
Understand — Your nephew is considering trying out for a football team. Most of your relatives are supportive of the idea, but you think the sport is dangerous and are worried about the potential health risks. **Specifically, what are some long-term health risks faced by football players?**
Analyze—Having heard some of the recent reports on risks of natural tanning, it seems like a better idea to sport an artificial tan this summer. **What are some of the different types of artificial tanning methods? What are the health risks associated with each method?**
Evaluate—One of your siblings got a spur of the moment tattoo, and now regrets it. **What are the current available methods for tattoo removal, and how effective are they? Which method do you think is best? Why?**

Table 1: Example Search Tasks from Health Domain

3.4 Pre- and Post-Task Questionnaires

The pre-task questionnaire asked about five measures: (1) level of interest, (2) prior knowledge, (3) prior search experience, (4) *a priori* determinability, and (5) expected difficulty. Questions were asked using five-point scales with labeled endpoints, except level of interest, which used a 7-point scale, and prior search experience, which had 4 choices. We asked participants one question each about their level of interest in the task, prior knowledge about the task, and prior search experience in the task domain. We included three questions about *a priori* determinability. Participants were asked how defined the task was in terms of the (i) expected solution, (ii) the information needed to solve the task, and (iii) the steps required to find the necessary information. These three questions were combined into a single *a priori* determinability scale (Cronbach's α = .777). We included five questions about expected difficulty. Participants were asked about their expected level of difficulty in (i) constructing queries for the task, (ii) understanding the search results, (iii) determining the usefulness of the results, (iv) deciding when to stop gathering information, as well as their (v) expected level of overall difficulty. These five questions were combined into a single expected difficulty scale (Cronbach's α = .848).

The post-task questionnaire asked about nine measures: (1) level of enjoyment, (2) engagement, (3) concentration, (4) acquired interest, (5) acquired knowledge, (6) experienced difficulty, (7) satisfaction, (8) time pressure, and (9) system support. All questions were asked using five-point scales with labeled endpoints. We asked participants one question each about their experienced level of enjoyment, engagement, concentration, and time pressure during the task. Similarly, we asked one question each about their level of acquired interest and knowledge. Consistent with the pre-task questionnaire, we included five questions about experienced difficulty that were combined into a single experienced difficulty scale (Cronbach's $\alpha = .853$). We asked two questions about satisfaction: (i) satisfaction with the information found and (ii) the satisfaction with the chosen search strategy. These two questions were combined into a single satisfaction scale (Cronbach's α=.792). Finally, we included three questions about system support. Participants were asked whether the system (i) helped them get started, (ii) helped them find resources with useful information, and (iii) provided overall support in completing the task. Again, these three questions were combined into a single system support scale (Cronbach's α=.808).

3.5 Stimulated Recall Interview

After completing the post-task questionnaire for the final search task, a stimulated recall interview was conducted with the 24 participants in the SG condition. For each search task, the study moderator used the Morae markers to identify the first and last use of the SG (if any). For each of these SG uses, the moderator played back a portion of the recording around the point of use and asked a series of structured questions. In order to stimulate the participant's memory of the context, the playback included their think-aloud comments, and started about 10 seconds before the SG use started and continued until the SG use ended. After each playback, the moderator asked questions to elicit: (1) motivations for using the SG and (2) benefits gained from using the SG. At the end of each task, we asked about (3) the times and reasons when the participant purposely avoided using the SG. Participants gave verbal free-form responses to all the questions, which were recorded for later analysis.

Interview Analysis. We used qualitative techniques to analyze participants' responses from the interviews. This analysis involved three rounds of qualitative coding. In the first round, two of the researchers independently coded interviews from four participants (16 interviews) using open coding and then resolved their codes to form an initial set of closed codes for each interview question. In a second round, two researchers used the closed codes on interviews from four additional participants and made refinements to the coding scheme. Then, using the final coding scheme, two researchers each coded half of all interviews and reviewed the codes for the other researcher's half. Any points of disagreement were discussed and resolved by both researchers.

4. RESULTS

In this section we present results from our study. First, we present results of a manipulation check to see whether more cognitively complex tasks were found to be more difficult and required more effort (Section 4.1). Then we present results for each of our main research questions (RQ1-RQ5) in Sections 4.2-4.6, respectively.

4.1 Task Complexity Check

Participants completed four tasks of varying levels of cognitive complexity. As a manipulation check, we first examine whether more complex tasks were found to be more difficult by participants. We focus on four aspects of difficulty: (1) expected difficulty, (2) *a priori* determinability, (3) level of search activity, and (4) experienced difficulty. Expected difficulty and *a priori* determinability were measured using responses to the pre-task questionnaire; level of search activity was measured using behavioral signals captured by the system; and experienced difficulty was measured using responses to the post-task questionnaire. In terms of search activity, we derived behavioral signals from queries, clicks, bookmarks, mouse-overs, scrolls, and elapsed time.

We used ANOVAs to measure the effects of task complexity on all measures. Results are presented in Table 2.[1] Overall, more complex tasks were found to be more difficult in terms of the four aspects of difficulty considered. More complex tasks were associated with higher levels of expected and experienced difficulty, and lower levels of *a priori* determinability. That is, more complex tasks were perceived to be less well-defined in terms of the expected solution, required information, and steps to follow. Finally, more complex tasks were associated with more search activity: more queries, clicks, and bookmarks; lower-ranked clicks and bookmarks; more queries without a click or bookmark; more mouse-enter and scroll events; and required more time to complete. Post-hoc tests found that, in most cases, remember tasks were significantly different from understand, analyze, and evaluate tasks. However, understand, analyze, and evaluate tasks were often indistinguishable. This distinction will be important as we discuss the main results.

4.2 Effect of Task Complexity on SG Use

Our first research question (RQ1) investigates whether task complexity affects user interaction with the search guide. To explore this question, for each of the 96 task sessions where participants had access to the SG (24 participants x 4 tasks), we computed three binary measures that indicate different levels of interaction with the SG:

SGclicked: Represents if the participant clicked somewhere in the SG during the task (1), or not (0). This considered all clicks in the SG, including clicks on the accordion and tab controls to explore the SG queries and paths. This measure is an indication of whether the participant was receptive to search assistance for the task.

SGclickedRQ: Represents whether the participant clicked on at least one SG *result* or *query* during the task (1), or not (0). This measure indicates not only the desire for assistance, but whether the participant found something of interest in the SG.

SGbookmarked: Represents whether the participant bookmarked a page that was discovered by clicking on an SG result (1), or not (0).[2] This measure is an indication of whether the participant gained a direct benefit from interacting with the SG.

Figure 2 shows the number of participants that reached each level of SG interaction, organized by task complexity level (max of 24).

[1]TotalScrollDistance was measured in units equal to the height of the SERP.

[2]Includes bookmarks made directly on an SG result as well as bookmarks found by navigating links from an SG result.

Table 2: **Effects of task complexity on expected and experienced difficulty, *a priori* determinability, and search activity.**

	Remember	Understand	Analyze	Evaluate	F(3,188); p-value	post-hoc
A Priori Det.	4.59 (0.55)	3.90 (0.86)	3.62 (0.82)	3.87 (0.79)	14.14; p=.000	R<U,A,E
Expected Diff.	1.65 (0.64)	2.25 (0.66)	2.50 (0.83)	2.31 (0.73)	12.40; p=.000	R<U,A,E
NumQueries	1.92 (1.44)	3.42 (1.80)	4.81 (3.09)	5.15 (3.09)	17.10; p=.000	R<U<A,E;
NumClicks	3.90 (2.32)	5.71 (2.91)	6.98 (3.66)	7.27 (3.07)	12.36; p=.000	R<U,A,E
ClicksPerQuery	2.43 (1.27)	2.08 (1.69)	1.79 (1.03)	1.78 (0.92)	2.79; p=.042	R<E
AvgClickRank	2.91 (1.36)	4.19 (2.21)	3.62 (1.98)	3.81 (2.18)	3.59; p=.015	R<U
AvgTimeToFirstClick	23.59 (9.10)	26.08 (13.29)	31.34 (20.94)	31.60 (19.45)	2.80; p=.041	-
NumAbandonedQueries	0.38 (0.82)	0.77 (1.02)	1.37 (1.93)	1.25 (1.45)	5.38; p=.001	R<A,E
PctAbandonedQueries	0.11 (0.19)	0.17 (0.19)	0.21 (0.22)	0.20 (0.18)	2.60; p=.054	-
NumBooks	2.02 (1.02)	3.46 (1.24)	4.29 (1.99)	4.67 (2.38)	21.66; p=.000	R<U,A,E;U<E
NumBooksPerQuery	1.37 (0.67)	1.35 (0.98)	1.20 (0.88)	1.10 (0.58)	1.23; p=.301	-
AvgBookRank	2.73 (1.80)	4.03 (2.49)	3.60 (2.33)	3.35 (2.58)	2.62; p=.052	R<U
QueriesWOBooks	0.60 (1.18)	1.23 (1.36)	1.96 (2.26)	1.88 (1.86)	6.50; p=.000	R<A,E
PctQueriesWOBooks	0.17 (0.27)	0.28 (0.25)	0.30 (0.26)	0.31 (0.21)	3.08; p=.029	R<E
NumMouseovers	43.90 (43.25)	79.71 (65.72)	80.42 (64.46)	91.58 (66.13)	5.61; p=.001	R<U,A,E
TotalScrollDistance	1.77 (2.09)	4.81 (5.51)	4.26 (5.27)	5.01 (4.69)	5.07; p=.002	R<U,A,E
TimeToComplete	287.39 (368.46)	461.26 (207.37)	507.50 (194.85)	540.72 (169.04)	9.94; p=.000	R<U,A,E
Experienced Diff.	1.73 (0.90)	2.22 (0.92)	2.24 (0.79)	2.23 (0.80)	4.14; p=.007	R<A,E

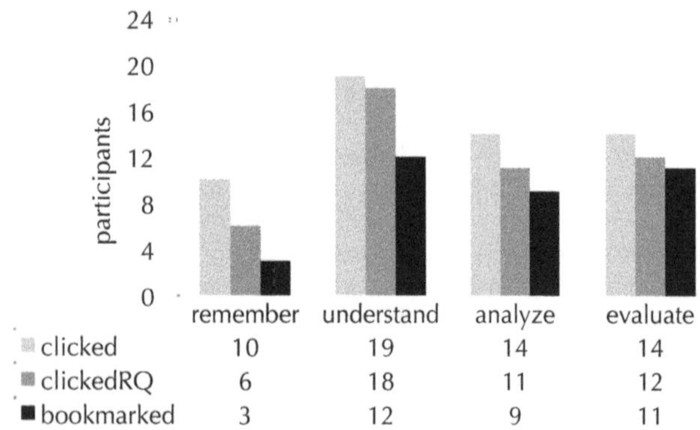

Figure 2: Number of participants (out of 24) who reached each level of SG interaction for different task complexity levels.

As Figure 2 shows, SG interaction was different based on task complexity level. For *SGclicked*, there was a significant effect of task complexity (Cochran's Q test, $Q(3) = 11.372$, $p = .01$). Post-hoc McNemar tests[3] showed that fewer participants interacted with the SG during the remember-level tasks as compared to the understand tasks.

For *SGclickedRQ*, task complexity also had a significant effect ($Q(3) = 15.316$, $p = .002$). Post-hoc tests showed that more participants clicked on SG results and queries during the understand-level tasks as compared to the remember and analyze ones (evaluate was marginally significant).

There was also a significant effect of task complexity on *SGbookmarked* ($Q(3) = 11.038$, $p = .012$). Post-hoc tests showed that fewer participants gained a bookmark from interacting with the SG during the remember tasks as compared to the understand and evaluate ones.

These results show that task complexity had an effect on SG use. As indicated by *SGclicked*, there was an interest in using the SG across all task complexity levels. The effect of task complexity was stronger for measures of interaction that indicate more benefit from the SG use (*SGclicked* and *SGbookmarked*). Finally, the differences in SG interaction were the most pronounced between the remember and understand tasks, with remember tasks having less SG interaction. In Section 4.6, we examine differences in the motivations and benefits that participants described when using the SG during tasks of different complexity levels.

[3]Throughout our analysis, for non-parametric post-hoc tests we use the modified Bonferroni correction outlined by Keppel [14]. For ANOVAs, we use the Tukey correction.

4.3 Effect of Pre-task Factors on SG Use

Our second research question (RQ2) investigates whether the factors measured in our pre-task questionnaire (interest, prior knowledge, search experience, *a priori* determinability, and expected difficulty) influenced interaction with the SG. To investigate this question, we ran three logistic regressions to predict the binary measures of SG interaction defined in Section 4.2. Again, this analysis was conducted on the 96 task sessions where participants had access to the SG (24 participants x 4 tasks). Since task complexity was a known source of variance (from RQ1), we also included it as a factor in our model using three indicator variables to distinguish understand (U), analyze (A), and evaluate (E) tasks from remember tasks (treated as the baseline).

Figures 3(a)-3(c) show the mean values of each pre-task factor for each SG interaction measure. For *SGclicked*, the regression model was not statistically significant ($\chi^2(8) = 10.865$, $p = .209$), meaning that the pre-task factors did not significantly predict whether or not a participant clicked on the SG during a task.

For *SGclickedRQ*, the regression model was statistically significant ($\chi^2(8) = 19.907$, $p = .011$). The model explained 25.0% of the variance (Nagelkerke R^2) and correctly classified 66.7% of the cases. Only task complexity was a significant predictor ($p = .01$). *A priori* determinability was marginally significant ($p = .058$).

For *SGbookmarked*, the regression model was statistically significant, ($\chi^2(8) = 17.895$, $p = .022$). Table 3 shows the results. The model explained 23.3% of the variance (Nagelkerke R^2) and correctly classified 70.8% of the cases (an increase of 11% from the 63.5% baseline of always predicting *SGbookmarked* to be zero). Using the Wald criteria, two variables were significant: task complexity ($p = .01$) and *a priori* determinability ($p = .035$). Based on the odds ratio ($\text{Exp}(\mathcal{B})$), participants were 2.581 times more likely to gain a bookmark from the SG for every unit increase in the *a priori* determinability of the task.

Overall, results for RQ2 show that none of the pre-task factors were significant predictors of clicked-based interaction with the SG. However, the *a priori* determinability of the task (along with task complexity) was a significant predictor of whether a participant gained a bookmark from the

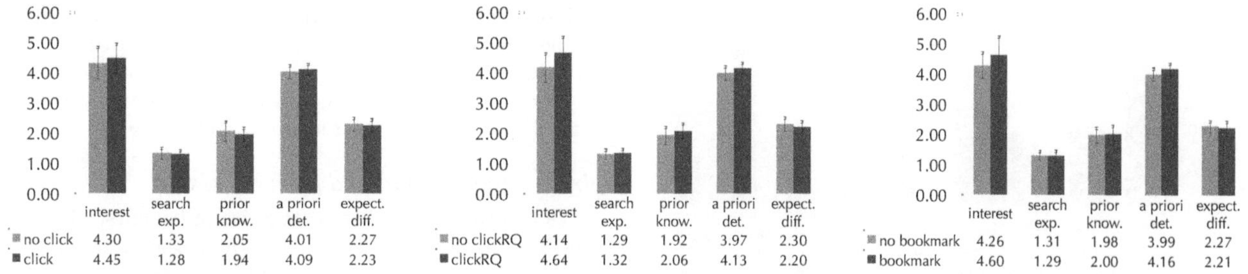

(a) SGclicked (b) SGclickedRQ (c) SGbookmarked

Figure 3: Mean pre-task factor rating from participants who achieved each level of SG interaction.

SG. In other words, participants were more likely to gain a bookmark from the SG when they perceived the task to be well-defined in terms of the expected solution, required information, and associated steps.

Table 3: Logistic Regression for SGbookmark, $\chi^2(8) = 17.895$, $p = .022$

	$\mathcal{B}$	S.E.	df	p-value	Exp($\mathcal{B}$)
interest	0.14	0.14	1	0.309	1.152
search exp.	-0.31	0.48	1	0.516	0.732
prior know.	-0.12	0.30	1	0.679	0.885
a priori det.	**0.95**	**0.45**	**1**	**0.035**	**2.581**
expect. diff.	0.05	0.44	1	0.914	1.048
complexity			**3**	**0.010**	
complexity(U)	**2.65**	**0.83**	**1**	**0.001**	**14.166**
complexity(A)	**2.31**	**0.87**	**1**	**0.008**	**10.116**
complexity(E)	**2.63**	**0.86**	**1**	**0.002**	**13.869**
constant	**-6.52**	**2.76**	**1**	**0.018**	**0.001**

4.4 Effect of SG Access on Post-task Factors

Our third research question (RQ3) investigates whether access to the search guide had an effect on the factors measured in our post-task questionnaire. To address this, we compare post-task measures of the 24 participants who had access to the SG to the 24 in the control condition.

Figure 4 shows the means and 95% confidence intervals for each post-task measure. We conducted ANOVAs to see if access to the SG influenced the post-task scores on enjoyment, engagement, concentration, interest and knowledge increase, task difficulty, time pressure, satisfaction, and the perceived level of system support. Of these, none were significant except for system support ($F(1, 189) = 10.587$, $p < .001$). Interestingly, participants who had access to the SG reported *lower* levels of system support ($M = 3.80$, $SD = .89$) than participants who did not ($M = 4.27$, $SD = .78$). This result surprised us. Analysis of the effects of SG *use* presented in the next section helps shed light on this result.

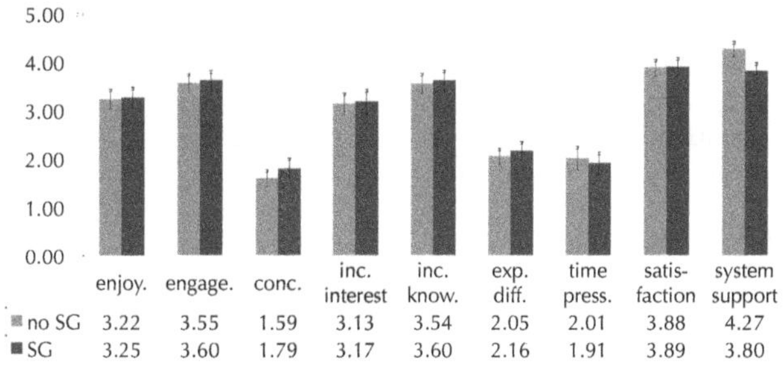

Figure 4: Mean post-task factor ratings the control (no SG) and experimental (SG) group.

4.5 Effect of SG Use on Post-task Factors

Seeking assistance from the SG required time and cognitive effort from users. For this investment, users may expect to benefit. For RQ4, we investigate whether participants' post-task outcome ratings differed among searches where they used the SG and gained a clear benefit, those where they used the SG but did not gain, and those where they did not use the SG at all. To examine this, we categorized each of the 96 SG task sessions into one of three categories: (1) the participant did not click on the SG ($n = 38$), (2) the participant clicked on the SG, but did not gain a bookmark from using it ($n = 22$), and (3) the participant clicked on the SG and gained a bookmark ($n = 35$).

Figure 5 shows the means for each post-task factor, grouped by category. Results of ANOVAs found a significant effect of category on level of engagement ($F(2, 92) = 3.93$, $p < .023$) and level of experienced difficulty ($F(2, 92) = 3.18$, $p < .046$), and a marginally significant effect on level of system support ($F(2, 92) = 2.76$, $p < .07$). No other post-task factors were significant.

Post-hoc tests showed the following differences. With regard to engagement, when participants gained a bookmark from using the SG, they reported signicantly higher levels of engagement ($M = 3.97$, $SD = .82$, $p = .02$) than when they did not click on the SG at all ($M = 3.29$, $SD = 1.21$). For experienced difficulty, when participants clicked but did not gain, they reported higher levels of experienced difficulty ($M = 2.54$, $SD = 1.12$, $p = .036$) than when they did not click ($M = 1.92$, $SD = .92$). In terms of system support, when participants gained a bookmark, they reported higher levels of system support ($M = 4.04$, $SD = .80$, $p = .058$) than when they clicked but did not gain ($M = 3.48$, $SD = .94$). Interestingly, when participants clicked but did not gain, they reported less system support than when they did not click at all ($M = 3.76$, $SD = .91$), but this difference was not significant ($p = .487$).

Together, the above results suggest that outcome measures that relate to the user experience (e.g., engagement, experienced difficulty, and perceptions of system support) may depend not only on the use of search assistance, but on whether the use is productive and results in a tangible benefit (e.g., a bookmark). These results underscore the importance of providing relevant, high-quality trails.

Finally, these results also provide insight into the surprising result from Section 4.4. Comparing the results for system support in Figures 4 and 5, we see that even participants who gained a bookmark from the SG reported lower levels of system support ($M = 4.04$, $SD = .80$) than the participants in the control condition, who did not have ac-

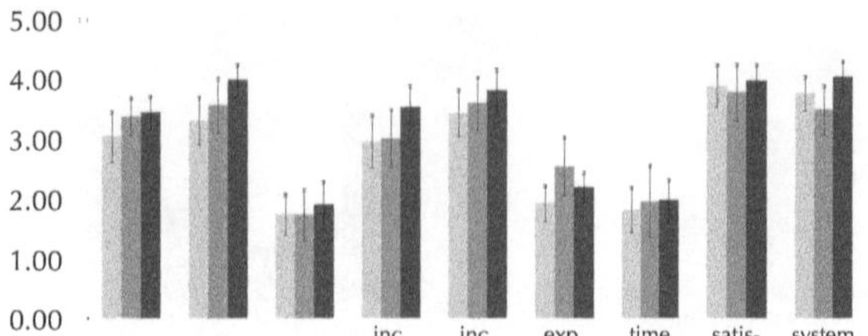

	enjoy.	engage.	conc.	inc. interest	inc. know.	exp. diff.	time press.	satis-faction	system support
no click	3.03	3.29	1.74	2.95	3.42	1.92	1.82	3.88	3.75
click/no-book	3.36	3.55	1.73	3.00	3.59	2.54	1.95	3.77	3.48
bookmark	3.43	3.97	1.89	3.51	3.80	2.19	1.97	3.97	4.04

Figure 5: Mean post-task factor rating from participants in different SG use groups: (1) did not click, (2) clicked, but did not gain a bookmark, (3) clicked and gained a bookmark.

cess to the SG (M = 4.27, SD = .78). This suggests that participants in the experimental and control groups had different expectations (or used different grounds for comparison) when responding to our questions about system support. This highlights an important risk in providing search assistance—users' expectations may also increase.

4.6 Differences in SG Use by Task Complexity

Our final research question (RQ5) investigates how SG use and non-use varies for different task complexity levels by evaluating participants' responses during the retrospective stimulated recall interviews. Data from the interviews was used to characterize SG use along three dimensions: (1) motivations for use, (2) benefits from use, and (3) reasons for non-use. We report on participants' free-form responses to our questions using the coding scheme developed.

4.6.1 Motivations for Use

We identified three main categories of motivations for using the SG: (1) to find new information, (2) to confirm previously found information or to confirm the search approach, and (3) to change the search approach. Figure 6(a) shows the number of participants who described each motivation category at least once during the interview (max of 24 for each bar). We elaborate on each category below.

Find new information. Participants described wanting to find new or better information than they had already found, wanting to get closer to an "answer", and wanting to explore what others had found. As Figure 6(a) shows, "find new information" was cited by more participants for the higher complexity level tasks (U=11, A=10, E=12) than for the remember tasks (R=5).

Confirm information already found. As opposed to finding new information, participants also used the SG to confirm information they had already found. This category included motivations to confirm a specific fact, to confirm their search approach, and to confirm the completeness of their findings. This type of motivation was described by more participants for the lower complexity tasks (R=9, U=10) than for the higher complexity tasks (A=4, E=4). This illustrates a theme that we will see again later in this section—for the lower complexity tasks, the SG was used more to confirm information, but for the higher complexity tasks it was used to find new information.

Change approach. Another motivation for using the SG was to help change a participant's search approach. This included using the SG to help get started with the search, to get new ideas for query terms, and to look for divergent or contradictory information. Again this motivation was cited by more participants for the higher complexity levels (U=5, A=5, E=8) than for the remember tasks (R=1).

4.6.2 Benefits Gained from SG Use

We identified four main categories of benefits: (1) gained specific information, (2) gained a new search strategy, (3) reassurance, and (4) no gain. Figure 6(b) shows the number of participants who described each gain category at least once during the interview.

Gained specific information. Participants described a variety of ways that they gained specific information from using the search guide. Responses in this category included: finding relevant web pages in the SG results, directly finding an answer as part of an SG result snippet, finding information that contributed to their knowledge of the task domain, and identifying new dimensions of an answer that they had not considered. Following the same trend as the "find new info" motivation, this benefit was cited by more participants for the higher complexity tasks (U=13, A=9, E=9) than for remember tasks (R=2). Interestingly, the highest number of participants cited this for the understand-level (U=13) tasks, suggesting that there may be characteristics of these tasks that make them well-suited to SG use.

Gained a new search strategy. Participants also described gaining new search strategies through their use of the SG. This category included gaining new query terms to use and getting ideas for search strategies from the paths in the SG. This category followed a similar trend to the "gained specific information" benefit: more participants cited it for the higher complexity tasks (U=7, A=10, E=7) than for the remember tasks (R=1).

Reassurance. Participants described gaining reassurance about a specific source of data, about their search approach, about a specific answer, and reassurance that they had found enough information and not missed anything. Reassurance followed a pattern somewhat opposite to "gained specific info" and "gained a new strategy"; it was mentioned more for the lower-complexity tasks (R=8, U=10) than for the higher ones (A=6, E=3). These results are consistent with the overall trends for the motivation categories—when participants used the SG for lower-complexity tasks, they mainly did so to confirm information they had already found, and the benefits they gained were reassurance that the information they found was good.

No gain. In some instances where the participants interacted with the SG, they reported no gain or benefit. These cases are important to consider because they represent situations where the participant sought help, but the SG failed to provide it. Reports of "no gain" were most prevalent for the lowest (R=5) and highest levels of complexity (E=7), suggesting that the SG was more helpful for tasks at the middle levels of complexity (U=4, A=2).

4.6.3 Non-Use

We identified three main reasons for non-use of the SG: (1) the task was straightforward, (2) the participant preferred to search on their own (at least in the beginning), and (3) reasons related to the novelty and unfamiliarity of the SG. Figure 6(c) shows the number of participants who described each non-use reason at least once during the interview.

Straightforward. One of the most frequent reasons for not using the SG was that the task was straightforward and the participant did not think they needed help for the task. This reason was cited by more participants for the remember tasks (R=12) than for the higher complexity tasks (U=4, A=4, E=4).

Wanted to start the search on their own. In many cases, participants mentioned that they did not use the SG at first, but intended to use it later to verify the quality or completeness of information they found. Participants said that they preferred to start searching on their own more frequently for the higher complexity tasks (U=6, A=8, E=7) than for the remember tasks (R=3).

Novelty/Unfamiliarity. Another reason participants reported for not using the SG was the novelty of the tool or the participant's unfamiliarity with it. We did not notice any trend for this reason across levels of task complexity.

5. DISCUSSION

Our findings provide insights about when, why, and how searchers engaged with search assistance, and about the effects of task complexity on use and benefits of the search guide. Next, we discuss our main findings and implications.

Task complexity influenced help-seeking (RQ1). We found a significant effect of task complexity on user interaction with the SG. Users were more likely to interact with the SG (and to gain a bookmark) for the more complex tasks (understand, analyze, evaluate) than for the least complex (remember). Our manipulation check (Section 4.1) found a similar grouping of task complexity levels with respect to difficulty and search effort. Post-hoc tests showed that remember tasks were consistently different than understand, analyze, and/or evaluate tasks. Together, these findings suggest that more complex tasks were more difficult and led users to seek and benefit more from search assistance. Previously, Xie and Cool [25] suggested that task complexity might influence help-seeking and our findings support this hypothesis. In addition, our results extend work by White *et al.* [21] who found differences in help-seeking behaviors for fact-finding versus exploratory tasks.

Well-defined tasks were more likely to lead to SG interaction and gains (RQ2). In addition to task complexity, the *a priori* determinability of the task also influenced SG interaction and gain. This result suggests that users are more likely to navigate and gain information from someone else's search trail when they perceive the task to be well-defined in terms of the expected solution and the steps required. One possible explanation is that when the task is well-defined, the searcher is better able to understand how another person's search trail may be accessible and beneficial.

An interesting area for future work is to explore ways to improve the accessibility and utility of search trails, especially for less well-defined tasks. In the context of distributed sensemaking applications, Fisher *et al.* [11] found that knowledge maps created by one person were not as easy to understand and as helpful as ones that had been iteratively refined by a sequence of users. Search trails may benefit from a similar approach. Rather than showing the exact trail from a single individual, trails could be iteratively refined and organized. Through this process, the accessibility and usefulness of search trails for more open-ended tasks could be improved by moving the trail toward the most common interpretations and approaches to the task.

Interest, prior knowledge, and search experience did not influence SG use (RQ2). Our results did not find pre-task factors such as level of interest, prior knowledge, and search experience to be significant predictors of SG use. Prior work by Jansen and McNeese [13] considered whether users' self-rated problem solving abilities influenced whether they sought search assistance, but also found no effect. These results suggest that other properties of the system and task (such as task complexity) play a larger role in determining whether assistance is sought.

Presenting search assistance can lower impressions of support (RQ3). Participants with access to the SG reported lower levels of system support than participants in the control group. A possible explanation for this is that by adding the search guide, participants' expectations were raised but not fully met, resulting in lower support scores. Another factor may be that having the SG available throughout the task (even at times it was not needed or desired) may have created negative perceptions. This result suggests the importance of showing search assistance dynamically when it is needed. Future work should explore this difference and investigate methods to confidently predict points during the search when assistance is likely to be beneficial.

Users' experience is worse when assistance fails to deliver (RQ4). When our participants interacted with the SG, but did not gain a bookmark from it, they reported experiencing the lowest levels of system support and the highest levels of experienced difficulty. In contrast, when users gained a bookmark from interacting with the SG, they reported the highest levels of system support and engagement within the SG group. These results show that users' perceptions of the search experience can depend on whether or not the use of search assistance was productive. These findings illustrate the importance of predicting the best search trail to display and ensuring that the trail quality is high. Work by Singla *et al.* [19] has reported on techniques to predict the best trails.

Verify and confirm for simple tasks; provide new ideas for complex tasks; allow users to start searches on their own (RQ5). Analysis from our retrospective interviews shows that for the least complex (remember) tasks, when participants used the SG, it was mainly to confirm and verify information. In contrast, for the more complex tasks they used it to find new sources of information and new search strategies. In general, participants did not use the SG to get started, instead preferring to attempt the search on their own before seeking assistance. These results have implications for the design and implementation of search assistance tools. First, since users did not use the SG to get started, search trails do not need to be shown immediately. This represents an opportunity for the system to accumulate evidence about the current task before predicting which search trail(s) to display. Second, the trail selection criteria should consider task type. For simple tasks, the trails could be geared towards verification and confirmation, for example, by showing only the trail endpoints. For complex tasks, the trails could convey more information about the search process or the system could select trails with more divergent information.

6. CONCLUSION

We reported on a user study that investigated five research questions about user interaction with our search guide (SG) tool. Our findings show that users engaged with the SG and benefited more for complex tasks compared to simpler

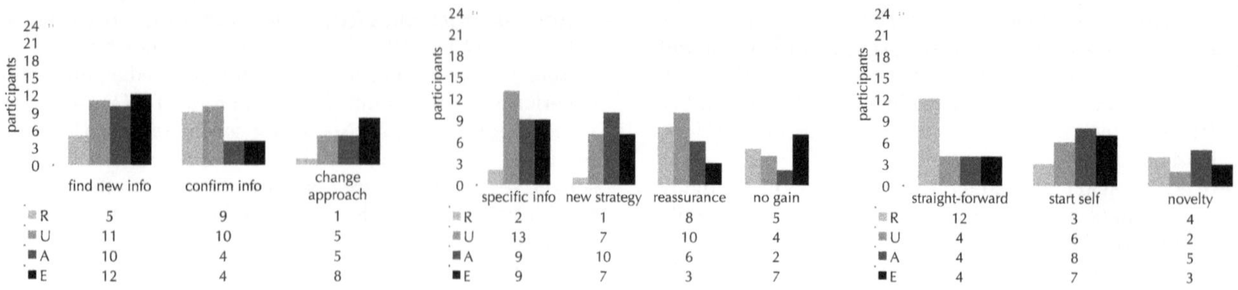

(a) Motivation for SG use (b) Benefits from SG use (c) Reasons for non-use

Figure 6: Differences in SG use for different levels of task complexity.

ones (RQ1). Tasks that were perceived as well-defined were more likely to lead to benefits from using the SG, but other pre-task factors such as level of interest and prior knowledge did not influence SG use or gain (RQ2). Having access to the SG was not found to impact outcome measures such as enjoyment, engagement, and satisfaction (RQ3). However, system support ratings were lower for participants who had access to the SG, suggesting that expectations differed when the SG was shown. When participants interacted with the SG but did not gain a bookmark, they reported higher levels of difficulty and lower levels of system support compared to searches where they did gain or did not use the SG (RQ4).

Analysis of our qualitative results shows that task complexity had an effect on participants' motivations for SG use, benefits from SG use, and reasons for non-use. For the least complex tasks, participants mostly relied on the SG for confirmation and reassurance, and when they did not use it, it was because the task was straightforward. For the more complex tasks, participants relied on the SG to find new information or search strategies, and when they did not use it, it was because they preferred to start on their own.

Our findings point to several directions for future work. Behavioral measures that vary with task complexity may be useful features for predicting when to offer search assistance. Another challenge is how to make search trails more accessible for tasks that are not well-defined and for which users are likely to diverge widely in their approaches. Finally, depending on the task complexity, users are likely to have different motivations for interacting with search trails. Future work might consider customizing the trail display or the trail-finding algorithm to fit different goals (e.g., confirmation vs. finding new information).

7. REFERENCES

[1] L. W. Anderson and D. R. Krathwohl. *A taxonomy for learning, teaching, and assessing: A revision of Bloom's taxonomy of educational objectives*. New York: Longman, 2001.

[2] J. Arguello. Predicting search task difficulty. In *ECIR*. Springer-Verlag, 2014.

[3] J. Arguello, W.-C. Wu, D. Kelly, and A. Edwards. Task complexity, vertical display and user interaction in aggregated search. In *SIGIR*, pages 435–444. ACM, 2012.

[4] D. J. Bell and I. Ruthven. Searchers' assessments of task complexity for web searching. In *ECIR*, pages 57–71. Springer-Verlag, 2004.

[5] P. Borlund. Experimental components for the evaluation of interactive information retrieval systems. *Journal of Documentation*, 56(1):71–90, 2000.

[6] K. Byström and K. Järvelin. Task complexity affects information seeking and use. *Inf. Process. Manage.*, 31(2):191–213, 1995.

[7] D. J. Campbell. Task complexity: A review and analysis. *The Academy of Management Review*, 13(1):40–52, 1988.

[8] D. Donato, F. Bonchi, T. Chi, and Y. Maarek. Do you want to take notes?: Identifying research missions in yahoo! search pad. In *WWW*, pages 321–330. ACM, 2010.

[9] H. Duan, Y. Li, C. Zhai, and D. Roth. A discriminative model for query spelling correction with latent structural svm. In *EMNLP-CoNLL*, pages 1511–1521. Association for Computational Linguistics, 2012.

[10] G. Dworman and S. Rosenbaum. Helping users to use help: Improving interaction with help systems. In *CHI*, pages 1717–1718. ACM, 2004.

[11] K. Fisher, S. Counts, and A. Kittur. Distributed sensemaking: Improving sensemaking by leveraging the efforts of previous users. In *CHI*, pages 247–256. ACM, 2012.

[12] B. J. Jansen, D. Booth, and B. Smith. Using the taxonomy of cognitive learning to model online searching. *Inf. Process. Manage.*, 45(6):643–663, Nov. 2009.

[13] B. J. Jansen and M. D. Mcneese. Evaluating the effectiveness of and patterns of interactions with automated searching assistance. *JASIST*, 56:1480–1503, 2005.

[14] G. Keppel and T. D. Wickens. *Design and Analysis: A Researcher's Handbook*. Prentice Hall, 3rd edition, 1991.

[15] Y. Kim and W. B. Croft. Diversifying query suggestions based on query documents. In *SIGIR*, pages 891–894. ACM, 2014.

[16] Y. Li and N. J. Belkin. A faceted approach to conceptualizing tasks in information seeking. *Information Processing and Management*, 44(6):1822 – 1837, 2008.

[17] N. Moraveji, D. Russell, J. Bien, and D. Mease. Measuring improvement in user search performance resulting from optimal search tips. In *SIGIR*, pages 355–364. ACM, 2011.

[18] M. Shokouhi. Learning to personalize query auto-completion. In *SIGIR*, pages 103–112. ACM, 2013.

[19] A. Singla, R. White, and J. Huang. Studying trailfinding algorithms for enhanced web search. In *SIGIR*, pages 443–450. ACM, 2010.

[20] A. Wexelblat and P. Maes. Footprints: History-rich tools for information foraging. In *CHI*, pages 270–277. ACM, 1999.

[21] R. W. White, M. Bilenko, and S. Cucerzan. Studying the use of popular destinations to enhance web search interaction. In *SIGIR*, pages 159–166. ACM, 2007.

[22] R. W. White and R. Chandrasekar. Exploring the use of labels to shortcut search trails. In *SIGIR*, pages 811–812. ACM, 2010.

[23] R. W. White and J. Huang. Assessing the scenic route: Measuring the value of search trails in web logs. In *SIGIR*, pages 587–594. ACM, 2010.

[24] W.-C. Wu, D. Kelly, A. Edwards, and J. Arguello. Grannies, tanning beds, tattoos and nascar: evaluation of search tasks with varying levels of cognitive complexity. In *IIIX*, pages 254–257. ACM, 2012.

[25] I. Xie and C. Cool. Understanding help seeking within the context of searching digital libraries. *JASIST*, 60(3):477–494, 2009.

[26] X. Yuan and R. White. Building the trail best traveled: Effects of domain knowledge on web search trailblazing. In *CHI*, pages 1795–1804. ACM, 2012.

Dynamic Query Modeling for Related Content Finding

Daan Odijk[†] d.odijk@uva.nl
Edgar Meij[‡] emeij@yahoo-inc.com
Isaac Sijaranamual[†] i.b.sijaranamual@uva.nl
Maarten de Rijke[†] derijke@uva.nl

[†] University of Amsterdam, Amsterdam, The Netherlands
[‡] Yahoo Labs, London, United Kingdom

ABSTRACT

While watching television, people increasingly consume additional content related to what they are watching. We consider the task of finding video content related to a live television broadcast for which we leverage the textual stream of subtitles associated with the broadcast. We model this task as a Markov decision process and propose a method that uses reinforcement learning to directly optimize the retrieval effectiveness of queries generated from the stream of subtitles. Our dynamic query modeling approach significantly outperforms state-of-the-art baselines for stationary query modeling and for text-based retrieval in a television setting. In particular we find that carefully weighting terms and decaying these weights based on recency significantly improves effectiveness. Moreover, our method is highly efficient and can be used in a live television setting, i.e., in near real time.

Categories and Subject Descriptors

H.3.1 [**Information Storage and Retrieval**]: Content Analysis and Indexing

Keywords

Information retrieval; Query representation; Text streams

1. INTRODUCTION

The way we watch television is changing: a growing number of people do so either on an interactive device or with such a device nearby [31]. Razorfish [36] found that 38% of "mobile multitaskers" access content that is related to the TV program they are watching. The consumption of TV programs can trigger searches for related information or content, e.g., for a broader perspective or to dive deeper into a topic. Thus, we require effective methods to support these emerging information needs. Since people increasingly expect to have related content directly available instead of having to search for it—especially in a TV watching setting—we need to minimize the disruption of having to manually search for related content. An ideal system would therefore present related content in an automatic and timely fashion.

SIGIR'15, August 09–13, 2015, Santiago, Chile.

ACM 978-1-4503-3621-5/15/08 ... $15.00.
DOI: http://dx.doi.org/10.1145/2766462.2767715.

This new and emerging television landscape is beginning to generate new and interesting information retrieval problems. For instance, Blanco et al. [8] perform text-based retrieval in a TV setting and Odijk et al. [32] consider the problem of linking encyclopedic content to a live television stream. Given the highly diverse set of information sources to be retrieved, including web pages, social media, and other video content, we focus in this paper on information needs stemming from live television news broadcasts and provide an approach for retrieving archived video content.

Consider watching a news bulletin as motivation for our retrieval task. As a news item is being covered, users may find themselves interested in watching background video material on one or more of the main entities or themes of the item, either to view at that very moment or to bookmark for later consumption. In order to present users with related video items that provide relevant background information, we require an algorithm that is able to automatically select video items for each news item as it is being broadcast. The output of a system implementing such an algorithm is depicted in Figure 1. Up to four related video items are suggested in an overlay on top of the news broadcast, each consisting of a keyframe and title; in the screenshot the left-most suggestion is highlighted (indicated by the red rectangle). The scenario that we cover in this paper is one in which a user interrupts or pauses the newscast to find videos relevant to the current news item to learn more about the topic. The content retrieved to complement the ongoing broadcast is not personalized but should be related to the broadcast and interesting for a wide audience.

Figure 1: Screenshot of a smart TV application showing related items as an overlay on top of a live TV news broadcast.

In the setting of live television news, a constant stream of subtitles is typically available, generated with only a very slight delay as an aid for the hearing-impaired. To be able to retrieve related content, we analyze these subtitles and generate search queries from the stream that we subsequently use to search a video news archive.

As a news item is being broadcast, additional textual information capturing the content of the news item becomes available. Thus, the challenge that we face is to iteratively incorporate this new information as it appears in the stream to generate and maintain an effective query model, and to do so in near real time.

In this paper we propose our solution: a *dynamic* query modeling approach that explicitly considers the dynamics of streaming sources and is suited for the near real-time setting of live TV. We cast the task of finding video content related to a live television broadcast as a Markov decision process (MDP) and use reinforcement learning to optimize the retrieval effectiveness of queries based on a stream of live television subtitles [4, 38, 39]. We significantly outperform state-of-the-art baselines for stationary query modeling [26] and for text-based retrieval in a television setting [8]. Thus, in this paper, we make the following contributions:

(1) We formalize the task of related content finding to a live television broadcast as a Markov decision process.

(2) We propose a dynamic query modeling approach, using reinforcement learning to optimize a retrieval model that is sufficiently efficient to be run in near real time in a live television setting and that significantly improves retrieval effectiveness over state-of-the-art baselines for stationary query modeling and for text-based retrieval in a television setting.

(3) We provide a thorough evaluation and an analysis of when and why our approach works. We find that adding more weighted query terms and decaying term weights based on their recency significantly improve the effectiveness. Static term features derived from the target collection and background corpora are more important for selecting effective query terms than dynamic features that are dependent on the stream of subtitles.

The remainder of the paper is organized as follows. Related work is discussed in Section 2. Section 3 describes our approach to dynamic query modeling. Our experimental setup is detailed in Section 4. Results are presented and analyzed in Section 5 and discussed further in Section 6. We conclude in Section 7.

2. RELATED WORK

Dynamic query modeling is related to a number of tasks in information retrieval. We discuss related work on search in a streaming setting, on query modeling, on temporal relevance feedback, and on reinforcement learning and MDPs in information retrieval.

Search in a streaming setting. We use dynamic query modeling to find related content based on a textual stream. Similarly, keyword modeling has been studied in a streaming setting, e.g., analyzing transcripts of automatic speech recognition (ASR) [11] and meetings [37]. In this setting, the subsequent task of searching based on the stream is not considered.

VideoCLEF [24] features a linking task aimed at linking video content to related resources across languages. Noisy ASR for Dutch is used to produce links to target English Wikipedia articles. Odijk et al. [32] study the task of finding relevant background information for a second screen in a live TV setting. They approach this as an entity linking problem and propose a graph-based context model. Although both deal with streaming textual content, neither studies the task of search. The MediaEval Search and Hyperlinking task considers two related tasks: finding a known item in broadcast video and providing video hyperlinks for specific anchors. The first is a video retrieval task and for the second task participants focused on the multimedia aspect, e.g., by using image-based retrieval approaches. Our work differs because we model the entire textual stream and base our approach on modeling effective queries.

Henzinger et al. [18] propose an approach to find relevant news articles during broadcast news. Every 15 seconds, they produce a two term query, using a "history feature," consisting of the last three blocks of text. Recent work by Blanco et al. [8] on Yahoo! IntoNews builds and improves on the work of Henzinger et al. [18]. Their focus is on the problem of detecting a change of topic, for which they propose several segmentation approaches. After segmentation, queries are generated using a bag-of-word approach with TF.IDF scores for each term. We include the query modeling approach of Blanco et al. [8] as our first baseline.

Generic methods to automatically segment (e.g., TextTiling [17]) have been extensively studied and shown to perform well in the streaming settings of new event detection [1] and story segmentation, a subtask of topic detection and tracking (TDT). Specific segmentation approaches have been proposed for streaming settings similar to ours (such as [8, 18]). Our dynamic query modeling approach can be applied after using these segmentation methods, instead of the relatively simple TF.IDF approaches used in [8, 18]. This would improve retrieval effectiveness, as we will see below in the comparison with Blanco et al. [8]'s baseline. Furthermore, our approach of decaying term weights based on their recency might provide a combined solution for the segmentation and query modeling problems. In future work, we plan to further investigate the use of decaying term weights in a setting where we need to address segmentation. However, the subtitles that we work with are generated from an auto-cue and thus contain markings indicating the start and finish of an item. Segmenting items or switching from one news item to the next will therefore not be covered in this paper.

Query modeling. A natural way of looking at search in streaming settings is to view it as a query modeling task, where the aim is to model an effective query based on a larger volume of text. This task has two distinct aspects: (i) query reduction and (ii) content-based query suggestion. The former deals with reformulating long or descriptive queries to shorter and more effective queries. Driving this research is that shorter queries are not only more likely to retrieve more focused results, they are also more efficient to process [5]. The latter task is to generate queries and the methods used here are similar to those used for query reduction. Content-based query suggestion has been used for linking news archives across modalities [10] and for generating phrasal-concept queries in literature search with pseudo-relevant feedback [22]. It differs from content-based recommendation, where a user profile or user interactions are also available. Bendersky et al. [7] propose a hybrid approach using content-based heuristics and signals from user interactions to retrieve video suggestions for related YouTube videos. Such a hybrid approach is not feasible in our scenario, as we have no user interactions that relate to the live TV content.

The state of the art in query modeling is formed by a family of related methods, e.g., [23, 26]. The typical approach is to produce query terms, score each, and generate one or more queries. Term scoring is often based on term features taken from large background corpora. Queries are selected based on query difficulty prediction features; these require an initial retrieval round, and as such are not feasible in real time. Lee and Croft [27] generate queries from textual passages by extracting noun phrases or named entities; a conditional random field is used to find selections that optimize retrieval effectiveness. In a web search setting, Kumaran and Carvalho [23] cast query reduction as a sub-query ranking problem. Given a long query, they generate all possible sub-queries for which they subsequently predict query quality and use learning to rank to select the best. Balasubramanian et al. [2] improve web search results by dropping query terms and estimating reductions in query difficulty.

Methods to improve the retrieval effectiveness of descriptive queries are proposed in [6, 25, 26]. Lease et al. [25, 26] generate queries of up to six terms by sampling term weights and then computing a metric to learn query term weights. Bendersky and Croft [5] extract key concepts from verbose queries to improve retrieval. An extended approach with parameterized query expansion is particularly effective for verbose queries [6]. Similar features are used in [6, 26, 27]; the first two obtain comparable scores on descriptive queries. We propose a dynamic query modeling approach that is tailored for use in a streaming setting and outperforms the stationary baseline based on Lease et al. [26]. Our work differs in that we explicitly model the dynamic nature of streaming sources and in that we generate more complex queries (e.g., using field weights).

The dynamic nature of a document collection is studied in temporal information retrieval (IR), that specifically deals with modeling temporal patterns to improve information retrieval. Efron [14] uses linear time series models for weighting terms, where the time series are computed on the target document collections. Similarly, Peetz et al. [34] use temporal bursts in a microblog collection to reweigh query terms for improved retrieval. Our work differs in that we model temporal dynamics in the stream of subtitles from which we generate queries. We discuss experiments in which we also model temporal dynamics on the collection side in Section 6.

Reinforcement learning and MDPs. We model the task of finding video content related to a live television broadcast as a Markov decision process (MDP) [15] and base our approach on methods from reinforcement learning (RL) [38]. RL intertwines the concepts of optimal control and learning by trial and error. Central is the concept of an "agent" optimizing its actions by interacting with the environment. This is achieved by learning a *policy* that maps *states* to *actions*. An MDP is a specific type of reinforcement learning problem that was proposed before the field was known as reinforcement learning. In an MDP, we decide on the optimal action in a Markov process [4]. The Markov property holds when the policy for a state is independent on the previous states. A Markov state thus has to represent the entire history of previous states as far as this is relevant for the value of the policy.

MDPs have been used to model diverse IR problems, e.g., to explicitly model user behavior in session search [16, 28, 29]. Jin et al. [21] utilize reinforcement learning and MDPs to improve ranking over multiple search result pages. Guan et al. [16] decrease weights of new terms based on past rewards, whereas Luo et al. [28] model session search as a dual-agent stochastic game. Investigating the design choices for MDPs, they find that technology selection and explicit feedback are most effective in session search [29].

In our setting, new subtitles keep coming in, hence we are dealing with a non-stationary MDP. More specifically, because the decision of what action to choose does not influence the states that emerge from the environment, this is considered an associative search task [3]. Perhaps the best studied application of reinforcement learning in IR is such an associative search task, online learning to rank [19, 35, 40]. Here, a retrieval system is optimized based on noisy feedback from user interactions. Our work differs from the work listed above in that we are not just optimizing ranking, but we focus primarily on query generation.

3. DYNAMIC QUERY MODELING

The search task we address is to find relevant content for a dynamic textual stream. We analyze the stream of subtitles that comes with television broadcasts and generate search queries from this stream. We subsequently use these to search a news video archive. Our dynamic query modeling (DQM) approach is designed to take streaming textual data as input and combines a retrieval model that defines a set of hyperparameters w with a learning approach that optimizes these hyperparameters w based on feedback. For learning, we regard the retrieval model as a black box with hyperparameters that affect the retrieval process and we obtain feedback based on the retrieval results. Our learning approach is therefore able to directly optimize for retrieval effectiveness. Figure 2 depicts the retrieval model and Figure 3 summarizes the learning approach. We discuss the learning approach in more detail in Section 3.3. The retrieval model and its hyperparameters will be further detailed below in Section 3.2, after we describe the terminology we will use.

3.1 Terminology

In the context of using subtitles for content linking, Odijk et al. [32] define dynamic textual streams as sources that continually produce "chunks" of text. A chunk is the amount of subtitle text that can be displayed on a single screen. Hence, chunks do not necessarily form a grammatical sentence. However, as these chunks are produced to be read in sequence, syntactic phrases generally do not cross chunk boundaries. Chunks are relatively short, containing about seven terms on average. Chunks form a growing sequence $S = \langle s_1, s_2, \ldots \rangle$, where each s_i is a chunk. The task we address in this paper is to generate, in real time, a query q_i for chunk s_i (having observed chunks $s_1, \ldots, s_{i-1}$) that is able to retrieve relevant video content at that point in the broadcast.

3.2 Retrieval model

The retrieval model we employ consists of four major parts, which are depicted in Figure 2 and described in Algorithm 1. Our retrieval model consists of four steps. First, we incrementally update a list of candidate query terms that we obtain from the textual stream of subtitles. We then compute a score for each term with a weighted sum of term features. Next, we generate a query from the scored query term candidates. The generated queries are complex, consisting of many weighted query terms, and they are selected from the highest scoring query term candidates. Finally, we retrieve the results. The retrieval model defines a set of hyperparameters $w = w_d \cup w_s \cup w_f \cup w_n \cup w_e$ that each alter the retrieval process. The hyperparameters w_d and w_s can be construed as feature weights and w_f as field weights, while hyperparameters w_n and w_e alter the number of selected query terms and the decay of query term candidate scores respectively. We provide more details with respect to these hyperparameters later in this section.

For the first step, *generating query term candidates*, we employ a bag-of-words approach which has proven to be effective in most retrieval settings, including settings similar to ours [26]. We generate a list of query term candidates by tokenizing the subtitles (line 2 in Algorithm 1). All terms from the subtitles in the video segment are considered as query term candidates. For each query term can-

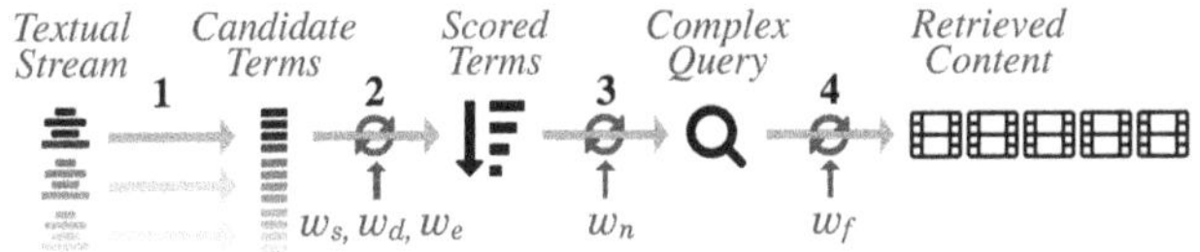

Figure 2: DQM retrieval model for textual streams, consisting of four steps: (1) query term candidate generation; (2) query term candidate scoring; (3) query generation; (4) retrieval.

Table 1: Dynamic term features for stream S.

$TF(t)$	Frequency of the term t in S
$TF.IDF(t)$	$TF(t)$, multiplied by $IDF(t)$ in the target collection
$AugmentedTF(t)$	$0.5 + \frac{0.5*TF(t)}{max\{TF(t'):t' \in C\}}$
$Capitalized(t)$	Binary feature to indicate whether t has appeared capitalized in S

Table 2: Static term features and their per corpus availability.

		Target collection	Google Web1T	Wikipedia title	Wikipedia body	Wikipedia anchors
$P(t,c)$	Probability of term t appearing in c		✓			
$TF(t,c)$	Frequency of term t in c	✓	✓			✓
$DF(t,c)$	Number of docs in c where t occurs	✓		✓	✓	✓
$IDF(t,c)$	$\log \frac{\lvert c \rvert}{DF(t,c)}$, where $\lvert c \rvert$ is number of docs	✓		✓	✓	✓
$RIDF(t,c)$	Residual IDF [13]	✓				✓

Algorithm 1: Dynamic query modeling

Input: Textual stream $S = \langle s_1, \ldots \rangle$.
Output: Stream of complex queries $Q = \langle q_1, \ldots \rangle$, where each query q_i is a set of (term, field, weight) tuples.
Data: Set of hyperparameters:
- w_d weights of dynamic features,
- w_s weights of static features,
- w_e decay rate for a query term candidate weight,
- w_n number of query terms for complex query,
- w_f weight for each document *field*.

```
1  foreach new chunk in S do
       Step 1: Generate query term candidates
2      Tokenize the new chunk.
3      Update term candidates with new terms and last seen index.
       Step 2: Assign score to each query term candidate
4      Compute static features for new candidates.
5      foreach query term candidate do
6          Compute dynamic features for each candidate term.
7          Compute query term candidate score as the weighted
           sum of feature values, using weights w_d and w_s.
8          Decay query term candidate score with e^(-w_e·i), where i
           is the relative age of term t in the stream thus far (0 for
           the current chunk and 1 for the first chunk).
       Step 3: Generate complex query
9      Select top w_n query term candidates with highest score.
10     Generate complex query with individual field weights w_f.
```

The next step in the DQM retrieval model is to *assign a score* to each of the candidate query terms. A score for a query term candidate is initially computed as a weighted sum of the term's features. The feature weights are hyperparameters w_s and w_d for the retrieval model. We use a set of term features that are either static for the term or updated dynamically with the stream of text. The static features are computed once for each new query term candidate in the stream (line 4). The dynamic features are updated in each new state for all query term candidates (line 6). The dynamic and static features are listed in Tables 1 and 2 respectively.

The dynamic features are computed with information from the textual stream S. They include the term frequency $TF(t)$ and augmented term frequency, intended to prevent a bias towards longer documents. $TF.IDF(t)$ is computed using the target collection. The $Capitalized(t)$ feature indicates whether a term appeared capitalized in the stream, ignoring the beginning of a sentence. The intuition behind this is that a person or location is likely to appear capitalized and might be an effective query term.

We also compute five static features over three corpora (see Table 2). The first corpus we compute static features for is the target collection, where the features indicate whether the candidate query term will be effective in searching that collection. The two other corpora provide an indication of how common a term is across the web and in different document fields of an encyclopedic source. Both our subtitle source and the descriptions for the video items in our target collection are in Dutch. We therefore use the Dutch unigrams of the Google Web1T [9] corpus as counts of how common a term is on web pages. The counts were generated from approximately one hundred billion tokens. We use Wikipedia, with articles separated into title, body and anchor, as a source to indicate how common a term is in an encyclopedic text. Each should provide different clues about a term. A term appearing in the title might be more important than one appearing in the body. Likewise, if a term is used as anchor text, it might describe well what it refers to. Our five static features include the frequency of a term t, the number of documents it appears in and the probability of observing term t in the corpus c. From the document frequency we derive the inverse document frequency (IDF) and the residual IDF. This is the difference between the observed IDF and the value predicted by a Poisson model [13]: $RIDF(t,c) = IDF(t,c) - \log_2 \frac{1}{1-e^{TF(t,c)/|c|}}$, where $|c|$ is the number of documents in c. Not all features can be computed for each corpus, e.g., the Google Web1T collection lacks document counts. The sets of dynamic and static features are extended with logarithmically transformed values. All 38 resulting features are min-max normalized.

For each query term candidate we compute a score as the weighted sum of all 38 features multiplied by an exponential term decay factor (lines 7 and 8 in Algorithm 1). This term decay factor is computed separately for each term candidate, based on how recently the term was observed in the stream S. The intuition behind this is that a more recently mentioned term might be more relevant than one that has not recently been mentioned. Hyperparameter w_e governs the decay rate. Concretely, we multiply the weighted sum of features with $e^{-w_e \cdot i}$, where i is the relative age of term t in the stream thus far. This relative age ranges from 0 to 1 and is 0 for the current chunk and 1 for the first chunk in the stream. The number of steps between 0 and 1 is equal to and increases with the number of chunks between the current and the first chunk in the stream.

The third step in the DQM retrieval model is to *generate a complex query* (lines 9 and 10 in Algorithm 1). From the ranked query term candidates we generate complex queries for the top n terms, where n is based on a hyperparameter w_n. The weights for each term in the resulting query are set to the score produced in the query term candidate scoring stage. We explicitly allow for negative weights for term features which may cause negative term candidate scores. In this case we omit the term, resulting in a query with fewer query terms. We extend the query with learned field weights, allowing the model to learn to attribute more importance to specific fields, such as the title of a video. The field weights w_f are also exposed as hyperparameters.

The final step in the DQM retrieval model is to *retrieve* the results. For this we use a state-of-the-art search engine that uses language modeling for retrieval and is described further in Section 4.

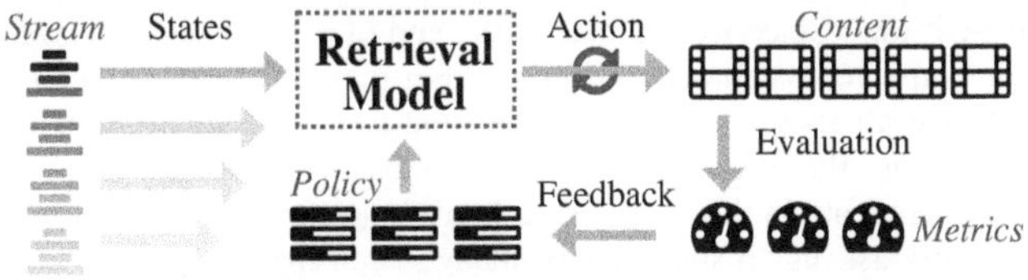

Figure 3: DQM learning approach. A textual stream is processed using a retrieval model that defines a set of hyperparameters. Feedback on the retrieval results is used to optimize the hyperparameters.

Algorithm 2: Our implementation of the Dueling Bandits Gradient Descent algorithm [40].

Input: step size δ, learning rate α, initial weights w_1, retrieval function *retrieve*, a *metric*, *maxIterations*

$w = w_1$
for $i \in \{1, .., maxIterations\}$ **do**
  Sample small step ε of maximally length δ.
  $w' = \frac{w+\varepsilon}{|w+\varepsilon|}$
  $a = retrieve(f * w)$
  $b = retrieve(f * w')$
  $d = metric(b) - metric(a)$
  if $d > 0$ **then** $w = \frac{w+\alpha*\varepsilon}{|w+\alpha*\varepsilon|}$

3.3 Learning

The learning approach (depicted in Figure 3) considers the retrieval model as a black box that defines a set of hyperparameters, altering the retrieval process in a complex manner (cf. Section 3.2). We regard this learning problem as an MDP. A new *state* occurs when a new chunk of subtitles presents itself. In our setting we optimize the *action* of generating a query based on *feedback* in terms of retrieval effectiveness. We obtain this feedback by generating search results through our retrieval model that is governed by a set of hyperparameters. In reinforcement learning (RL) terms, we regard these hyperparameters as the *policy* that we are optimizing.

RL differs from supervised machine learning in that it explicitly deals with optimizing actions for the whole problem space based on goals within an uncertain environment. RL's trial and error type of learning fits well with the nature of our problem. We do not just optimize a single problem dimension, i.e., a combination of ranking features, but we optimize the entire process, from selecting and scoring candidate terms to generating a complex query.

We learn an optimal policy using the Dueling Bandits Gradient Descent (DBGD) algorithm [40], detailed in Algorithm 2. This algorithm iteratively tries a new policy w' that is a small change from the current best policy w. Based on feedback on the effects of both policies w' and w, it finds a winning policy. From this comparison it decides to keep the current policy w or to move the current best policy in the direction of w'. By iteratively updating the current best policy w, DBGD performs hill climbing to obtain an optimal policy based on the feedback. It thus obtains hyperparameter settings that optimize retrieval effectiveness for our DQM retrieval model.

DBGD has two parameters: step size δ for generating a new w' and learning rate α. Here, δ controls how big a change in weights we compare the current best to. The learning rate α controls how large a step is taken towards a better weight vector once it is found. We initially set the weights w_1 randomly for the feature weights w_d and w_s and the number of terms w_n to 10. We initialize the retrieval model, with equal field weights w_f and a decay term w_d of 0.

To compare the effects of two policies w and w', we retrieve results produced by the DQM retrieval model for both policies. We are not in a position to experiment with actual users from whom we could obtain online feedback, e.g., using interleaved comparison methods [35]. We therefore use offline relevance assessments. For both retrieval results (obtained through w and w'), we compute a retrieval performance metric. This can be any metric; see Sections 4 and 5.3. Based on the outcomes, we decide whether the new policy w' is better than the current best policy w. In case of a draw, the current best is kept. If we were to use feedback from live user interactions, the feedback would be more noisy; we explore how noisy feedback affects learning in the analysis in Section 5.3.

Since the items of a news broadcast are segmented, our task can be performed naturally on subsequences, which we call "video segments" (i.e., *episodes* in RL terminology). The last chunk of a video segment produces a special state, the terminal state. It is followed by a reset to the start state. DQM is *episodic* with an *indefinite horizon*, i.e., episodes are finite, but without a predefined length. The policy we optimize is generic across episodes, i.e., it does not consider any episode-specific information and will not be reset after a terminal state. Our view of this learning problem as an episodic MDP fits well with the segmented nature of TV news.

A typical issue for any RL problem is deciding when to learn: should we explore new policy options or exploit the current policy. We assume that users are interested in related content near the end of an episode, as this is where they will have learned most about a topic. We therefore chose to only do an explorative learning action in the terminal state of an episode. In the other states, we exploit the current best policy. This way, we obtain less feedback but optimize the policy at the states where it is most important to perform optimal.

4. EXPERIMENTAL SETUP

We seek to answer the following research questions regarding our proposed model:

RQ1 Does dynamic query modeling improve retrieval effectiveness over state-of-the-art stationary query modeling baselines?

RQ2 What do the components of the DQM retrieval model contribute to effectiveness?

We ask the following research question regarding our reinforcement learning approach:

RQ3 How do the reinforcement learning parameters, choice of optimization metric and noisy feedback influence the speed of the learning process and the resulting retrieval effectiveness?

To answer these research questions, we create an annotated dataset and set up experiments. Below, we describe the dataset, experimental set-up and detail our evaluation.

Subtitles. We obtain a dataset of subtitles for the hearing impaired from the Dutch eight o'clock evening news broadcast of the Nederlandse Omroep Stichting (NOS), the Dutch public news broadcaster. We selected this as our source because its content is diverse and volatile; it may cover items broadly and for minutes, or just very briefly. A news broadcast typically lasts about 25 minutes and contains around ten items, which we refer to as *video segments* or *episodes* in RL terms. A typical video segment consists of 44 chunks of on average seven terms per chunk and 306 terms per video segment. For evaluation purposes, seven news broadcasts are randomly selected from broadcasts dated May 2013, containing 50 video segments in total. The video segments do not overlap in main topic. The subtitles are prepared based on the text for the teleprompter or auto-cue. It therefore contains markings to indicate when a new video segment starts.

Collection. As our target collection we use the video archive of the same news broadcaster, NOS, which contains individual news item videos. The video items are often taken from news broadcasts, but can also be longer versions of interviews or aimed to provide further background. This collection is publicly available and can be crawled via their website.[1] Our index covers the years 2011–2013 and contains 37,884 video items, with an average of 40 video items per day. For our experiments, we limit the queries to only the video items that were published before the news broadcast. We consider the title, description and tags as different textual fields. Note that we do not use any video specific information and thus regard the video items simply as textual metadata records.

Ground truth. To establish ground truth for our evaluation,[2] we ask assessors to read the subtitles of a video segment and then rate videos for relevance. These items are obtained by pooling the top rankings for each baseline to on average 79 videos per segment. The video items in the pool are presented in random order. We train two assessors and each one annotated half of the video segments. Our instructions to the assessors were: *Imagine that you interrupted the news broadcast after the segment because you're interested in watching related video content. How would you rate each video?* We use a five-point scale to capture the level of relevance of each video [12] (with the usual labels *perfect*, *excellent*, *good*, *fair* and *bad*). The distribution of the ratings over the respective labels from perfect to bad is 5%, 5%, 8%, 16% and 66%. This suggests that the task is not an easy task, but there are plenty of good videos to rank. For each video item, the assessors are provided with all metadata (title, date, description, keywords) and can watch and explore the original video to make a better judgement.[3]

Evaluation. In our setting, a viewer is searching for related video content for a news broadcast item, most likely at the end of an item or just after it has finished. We therefore evaluate the retrieval effectiveness at the end of a video segment or in RL terms, the terminal state of an episode. In the DQM setting, it is important to provide the most relevant video and to provide them as high in the ranking as possible. In a live TV setting, a user would not examine a full result list, but only a limited number of video items. As our main evaluation metric we choose normalized discounted cumulative gain (nDCG) [20], as it can handle graded relevance assessments and takes positional importance into account. We compute nDCG for the entire result list and for the first five positions as nDCG@5, skipping video items that were not annotated. We perform leave-one-out cross validation to evaluate our approach. For each video segment we train an individual model where all other video segments serve as training material. We then evaluate the effectiveness on the video segment that was left out of the training set. We consider nDCG@5 more relevant for our setting but optimize for nDCG as it is smoother than nDCG@5 and already gives high importance to the retrieved documents at the top of the ranking. We assume that taking the improvements in ranking below the fifth position into account will benefit learning in the long run. We revisit this decision in the analysis of our approach (Section 5).

Retrieval engine. For all experiments we use the language modeling and inference network-based Indri retrieval model [30], with stopword removal and without stemming. We use Dirichlet smoothing with smoothing parameter μ set to the default 2500.

[1] http://nos.nl [2] http://ilps.science.uva.nl/resources/sigir2015-dqm

[3] We evaluate assessor-agreement over a set of 25 videos from five doubly annotated segments; Spearman's rank correlation measures 0.8636, signaling good agreement.

Baselines. Since we evaluate at the end of a video segment, we can compare to stationary *baselines*. For these baselines, we concatenate all subtitles of a video segment to form a single pseudo document. Based on this pseudo document we search for related video content. In this way, the task becomes similar to the more-like-this task, that is supported by many search engines. We include two stationary approaches, that we label "Baseline" and "Modified Lease." The first, "Baseline", uses the top-10 terms from a bag-of-words model of the pseudo document, ranked by TF.IDF score (where the document frequency is computed on the target collection). This baseline is how Blanco et al. [8] perform query modeling in their text-based retrieval approach for TV. The second stationary approach ("Modified Lease") is comparable to the state-of-the-art model of Lease et al. [26]. The retrieval model is based on regression to learn queries that consist of no more than six terms. The terms are selected and weighted based on supervised machine learning (regularized linear regression) using a bag-of-words representation of the pseudo document. The features we use for the Modified Lease baseline are the same as for our DQM approach, excluding the features based on Wikipedia (not used in [26]). Furthermore, we choose not to include the simple part-of-speech features and the lexical context features (the word before and word after) from their model. These features get relatively low weights in [26] and are less applicable in our setting than in their descriptive queries setting (hence, we dub this approach "Modified Lease").

5. RESULTS & ANALYSIS

We describe the results of our experiments and investigate the effectiveness of our DQM approach, following the three research questions listed in the previous section.

5.1 Retrieval effectiveness

To answer RQ1, we compare the effectiveness of DQM to that of the stationary baselines. Table 3 shows the performance in terms of retrieval effectiveness. Both baselines show a decent performance with an nDCG score of around 0.7. We cannot directly compare the performance of the baselines to that of Lease et al. [26], as they report on different collections and use shorter descriptive queries. Surprisingly, the modified Lease approach is not able to significantly improve on the less complex baseline. A plausible explanation for this is the limited number of query terms in the modified Lease approach; see the analysis in Section 5.2 below.

Rows 3–8 of Table 3 show the retrieval effectiveness of our DQM approach, building up from a basic approach (labeled DQM$^-$) to

Table 3: Retrieval effectiveness of the dynamic query modeling (DQM) approach vs the two baselines. Significant differences, tested using a two-tailed paired t-test, are indicated with $^-$ (none), $^\triangle$ ($p < 0.05$) and $^\blacktriangle$ ($p < 0.01$); the position of the symbol indicates whether the comparison is against row 1 (left most), row 2 (center) or row 3 (right most).

Method	nDCG@5	nDCG
1. Baseline [8]	0.6486 $^{\ -\blacktriangledown}$	0.6113 $^{\ -\blacktriangledown}$
2. Modified Lease [26]	0.6994$^{-\ -}$	0.6484$^{-\ \blacktriangledown}$
3. DQM$^-$	0.7570$^{\blacktriangle -}$	0.7393$^{\blacktriangle\blacktriangle}$
4. DQM$^-$ + field weights	0.7651$^{\blacktriangle\triangle -}$	0.7566$^{\blacktriangle\blacktriangle\triangle}$
5. DQM$^-$ + term weighting	0.7814$^{\blacktriangle\blacktriangle -}$	0.7845$^{\blacktriangle\blacktriangle\blacktriangle}$
6. DQM$^-$ + term and field weighting	0.7781$^{\blacktriangle\blacktriangle -}$	0.7945$^{\blacktriangle\blacktriangle\blacktriangle}$
7. DQM$^-$ + decayed term weighting	0.7940$^{\blacktriangle\blacktriangle\blacktriangle}$	0.7897$^{\blacktriangle\blacktriangle\blacktriangle}$
8. DQM	0.8005$^{\blacktriangle\blacktriangle\blacktriangle}$	0.8072$^{\blacktriangle\blacktriangle\blacktriangle}$

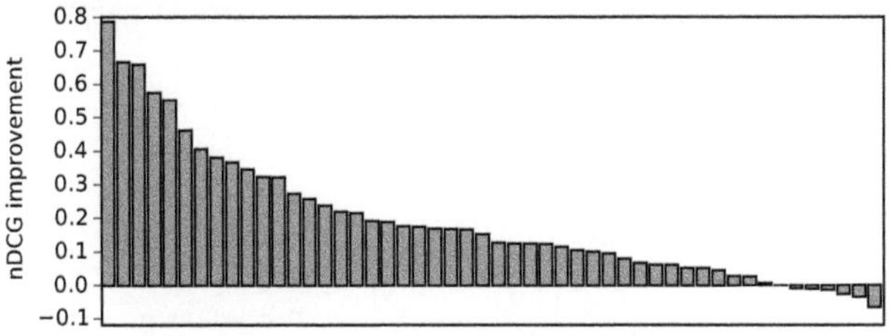

Figure 4: Improvement in terms of nDCG for DQM over the baseline, where each bar represents a video segment.

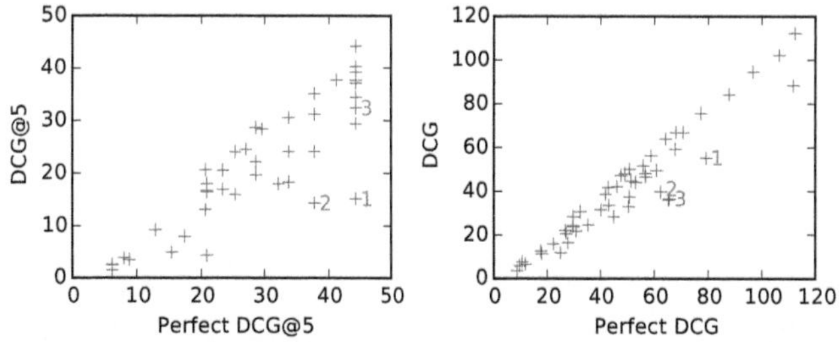

Figure 5: DCG for DQM versus perfect DCG for each video segment for the top five (left) and for the full result list (right).

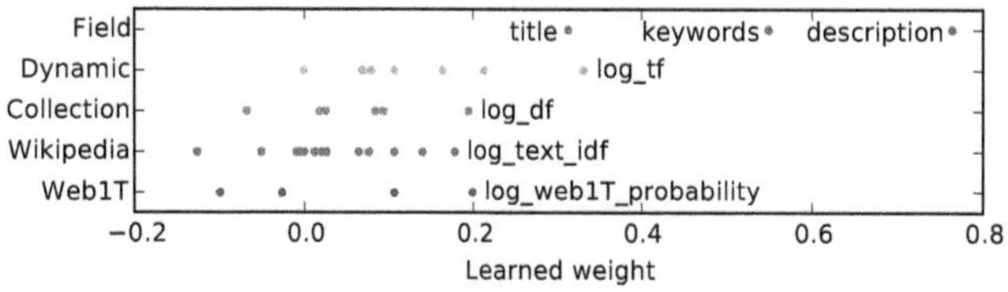

Figure 6: Feature and field weights for the DQM approach. The field weights and top weights for each group are annotated.

the full DQM approach. DQM$^-$ uses only the dynamic and static term features to select query terms. It is, however, already able to significantly improve nDCG over both baselines (row 3). Next, we look at the weighting in DQM. Enabling field weighting gives a small boost in retrieval effectiveness (row 4). If we enable term weighting based on the machine learned scores, the model performs significantly better on the full result list, although the effect is not significantly present on nDCG@5 (row 5). Interestingly, adding field weights to the term weighting approach results in a drop of retrieval effectiveness for the top five, but improved effectiveness for the full rank list (row 6). Enabling term weight decay without field weights gives an additional boost towards a significantly better approach than the base approach, both on the top five and the full result list (row 7). Finally, our full DQM approach in row 8 significantly improves over the stationary baselines and the base DQM$^-$ approach. The effects are similar in nDCG and nDCG@5, although they are more clear for nDCG, i.e., the full ranked list.

To investigate where our approach works, we look at the effectiveness per video segment compared to the baseline. We plot the difference in nDCG in Figure 4. Our approach is able to substantially improve retrieval effectiveness for the bulk of the video segments. There are seven segments where our approach hurts performance. A closer look at these reveals that they mostly already have a high nDCG score for the baseline. There does not seem to be an influence of the length of the segments.

We further study the effectiveness across video segments by separating the nDCG scores into their components: the DCG score and the perfect DCG score. *Perfect DCG* is the DCG score obtained when the documents are ideally ranked according to the ground truth. If a ranking is ideal, the DCG score is equal to the perfect DCG score and nDCG is equal to 1. We plot the DCG scores versus the perfect DCG scores in Figure 5, for the top five and the full result list. A perfect nDCG score would be on the diagonal. The closer a result is to the bottom, the lower the nDCG score. We see a similar pattern for the full ranked list as for the top five, although more distinctly for the top five. DQM is able to obtain perfect scores for video segments with both high and low perfect DCG scores. However, we also perform below perfect; this does not seem to be related to the perfect score that can be obtained.

We look in more detail at three video segments that are far from the diagonal (and thus have a low nDCG score), marked in Figure 5 as 1, 2 and 3. Interestingly, segments 1 and 3 are in the top five most improved by our approach and segment 2 is one of the few that is hurt by DQM (respectively the 4th and the 5th bar from the left and the 4th from the right in Figure 4). Segment 1 is broad, linking French protests against a new law on gay marriage to a movie at the Cannes film festival. Segment 3 is a short item about the increase in ATM robberies and segment 2 is a broad item about the relationship between the Netherlands and Germany, on the occasion of a trade summit. From this we can see that, although DQM gets substantial improvements for broad items, there is still something to be gained.

5.2 Analysis of components

To answer RQ2, we investigate the contribution of the components of our approach. The learned values of the DQM retrieval model hyperparameters are plotted in Figure 6. Looking at field weights w_f, we observe that different values are learned, the highest weight is twice the value of the lowest weight. The highest weight is given to the longer description field. The keywords get a higher weight than the title field.

Number of weighted query terms. Next, we turn to the number of weighted query terms that DQM generates. In our experiments, this parameter was set through RL to a value close to 100 terms. This can include terms with very small weights or even negative weights (and thus not included in the final query). This is a substantially larger number than the fixed number of 6 query terms in the Lease approach. We investigate the impact on the retrieval effectiveness of DQM and the baselines; see Figure 7. From this figure we observe that both baselines clearly benefit from adding more terms to the query. The modified Lease approach consistently outperforms the baseline approach. Interestingly, for the baseline approach, adding more query terms than around 30 does not further improve the effectiveness on the top five results, but does steadily improve the effectiveness on the entire ranked list. The modified Lease approach actually shows a drop in effectiveness on the top five when using more than around 50 query terms. For any number of query terms, DQM consistently outperforms both the baseline and Modified Lease on both metrics. For DQM, the retrieval effectiveness in terms of nDCG for the top five results and the entire result list show a qualitatively similar pattern. The effectiveness of DQM increases with the number of query terms, until it reaches a plateau at around 40 query terms.

Term decay. In our experiments the term decay factor w_e was set through RL to a value of 0.5601. Our retrieval model thus has a mild preference for more recent terms. With this decay factor query term candidates from the first chunk are given a score that is 57% lower than the most recent terms. In Table 3, we observed a small boost in retrieval effectiveness when enabling decayed term weights for our full DQM approach. Interestingly, adding term decay to our baseline gives an nDCG improvement of 11.90% for the top 5 and 16.29% for the full ranked list. This suggests that term decay does indeed contribute to improving retrieval effectiveness.

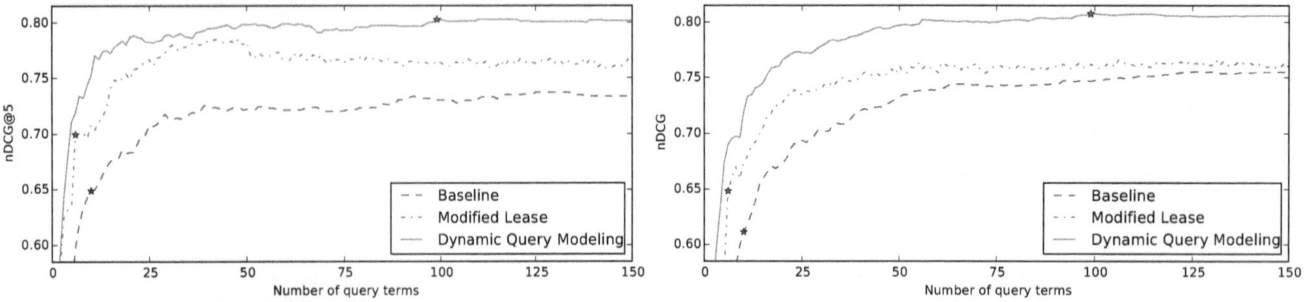

Figure 7: Baseline retrieval effectiveness with different number of query terms as measured on the top five (nDCG@5, left) and on the entire result list (nDCG, right). The settings used in our main experiments are marked with a star.

Term feature weights. Next, we turn to the term feature weights w_d and w_s, plotted in Figure 6. We observe that a diverse set of features receive high weights; there is no single most important feature. The highest weights are assigned to the dynamic features. Of the static features, the collection features receive the highest weights, specifically the logarithm of the document frequency. For Wikipedia-based features, the log IDF in text receives the highest weight. The weights for features derived from the title and anchor text are substantially smaller than for the all Wikipedia text. For Web1T, the log term probability receives the highest weight. Five features receive negative weights, most notably the document frequency in Wikipedia text and the frequency in Web1T. These weights indicate a natural negative bias for common terms.

Contributions of components. We perform an ablation study and disable parts of DQM to investigate the effects on the retrieval effectiveness; see Table 4. We evaluate the effectiveness of our DQM approach with specific sets of term features disabled. These results are presented in rows 2–6 of Table 4. On rows 2 and 3, we see the effects of disabling respectively the entire set of dynamic and of static term features. Both result in a significant drop of performance. In fact, if we disable all static term features, the performance on the top five drops below the modified Lease baseline. Clearly, the static term features are essential for the performance of DQM. This makes it surprising that the dynamic term features obtain the highest weights. To further investigate this, we disable specific subsets of static term features. We observe from rows 4–6 in Table 4 that disabling any of the subsets significantly degrades the performance of DQM. For Web1T, this effect is not significant in the top five and not as significant as for the Wikipedia and collection features. Lastly, we investigate whether our strong static term features are strong enough by themselves, without the other features. The results in rows 7–9 of Table 4 show a qualitatively similar pattern to rows 4–6. Using only one subset of the static term features and no dynamic features significantly degrades the performance, although all variants still outperform our baselines. Using only Wikipedia for term features comes closest to our full DQM model, but it still performs significantly worse.

5.3 Learning

To answer the reinforcement learning related research question RQ3, we investigate how DQM learns by looking at learning curves. These curves are generated by evaluating the DQM model at each iteration on the left-out video segments. The curves are averaged over five runs for each of the 50 video segments and are thus comparable to the numbers in Tables 3 and 4.

Reinforcement learning parameters. First, we turn to the two parameters of the DBGD algorithm: the step size δ and the learning rate α. δ determines the distance between the current best weights and the new weights. The learning rate α is the size of the step taken towards the best scoring weight vector. We explore different values for δ and α and plot the results in Figure 8a.

Table 4: Ablation analysis of the contributions of DQM term feature sets to retrieval effectiveness. Significant differences, tested using a two-tailed paired t-test against row 1, are indicated for rows 2–9 with $^{-}$ (none), $^{\triangledown}$ ($p < 0.05$) and $^{\blacktriangledown}$ ($p < 0.01$).

Method	nDCG@5	nDCG
1. Full Dynamic Query Modeling (DQM)	0.8005	0.8072
2. without static features	$0.6884^{\blacktriangledown}$	$0.6721^{\blacktriangledown}$
3. without dynamic features	0.7823^{-}	$0.7698^{\blacktriangledown}$
4. without Web1T features	0.8012^{-}	$0.7967^{\triangledown}$
5. without Wikipedia features	$0.7459^{\blacktriangledown}$	$0.7485^{\blacktriangledown}$
6. without Collection features	$0.7421^{\blacktriangledown}$	$0.7267^{\blacktriangledown}$
7. with only Web1T features	$0.7387^{\blacktriangledown}$	$0.7377^{\blacktriangledown}$
8. with only Wikipedia features	$0.7633^{\triangledown}$	$0.7617^{\blacktriangledown}$
9. with only Collection features	$0.7571^{\triangledown}$	$0.7583^{\blacktriangledown}$

We can observe from Figure 8a that for the same step size δ, a larger learning rate means that we reach higher effectiveness in fewer iterations. A larger step size δ will also result in faster learning, although there appears to be a risk in setting the δ to high. Despite early gains when using $\delta = 0.5$ and $\alpha = 0.2$, at around 75 iterations, it gets taken over by the run with the much smaller step size of $\delta = 0.1$ and higher learning rate of $\alpha = 0.5$. At $\alpha = 0.5$ the medium step size $\delta = 0.25$ appears to be able to better learn the subtleties when the effectiveness reaches a plateau, in comparison with the higher learning rate $\alpha = 0.5$.

Next, we investigate how optimizing for nDCG influences the performance as measured by nDCG@5. In Figure 8b we plot nDCG and nDCG@5 for runs in which we optimize either the nDCG or the nDCG@5 metric. We observe a consistently higher nDCG value when optimizing nDCG versus optimizing nDCG@5. Interestingly, we also see a consistently higher nDCG@5 value, confirming our idea that optimizing nDCG will also optimize nDCG@5.

Noisy feedback. DQM is also suited for use in a setting where feedback comes from user interaction and thus is not always perfect. We study how well it can deal with noisy feedback. For this we run a variant of DQM where we replace the comparison in the DBGD algorithm with a noisy comparison. This noisy comparison randomly returns a random comparison outcome. The noise level controls how often this occurs, where a noise level of zero is equal to our regular setting and a noise level of one results in completely random feedback. The results of this analysis are presented in Figure 8c. We observe that given completely random feedback, DQM will not improve in terms of effectiveness. However, it will also not degrade in performance. Adding more noise to the feedback for DQM will increase the number of iterations it takes to learn an

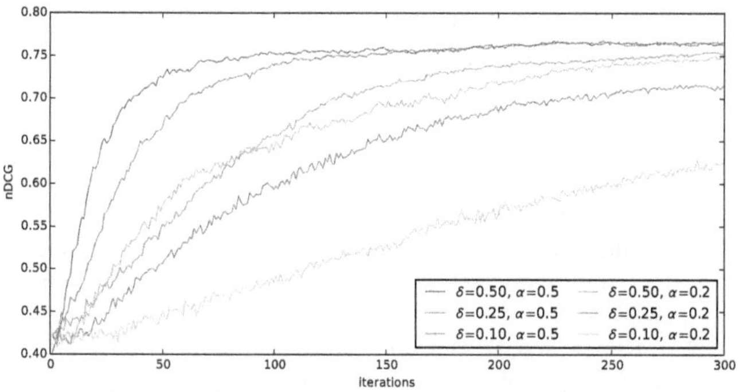

(a) Learning curves for different values of DBGD parameters δ and α.

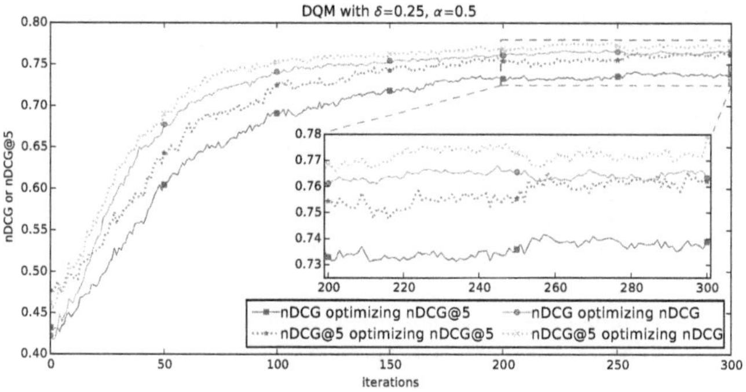

(b) Development nDCG(@5) when optimizing for nDCG or nDCG@5.

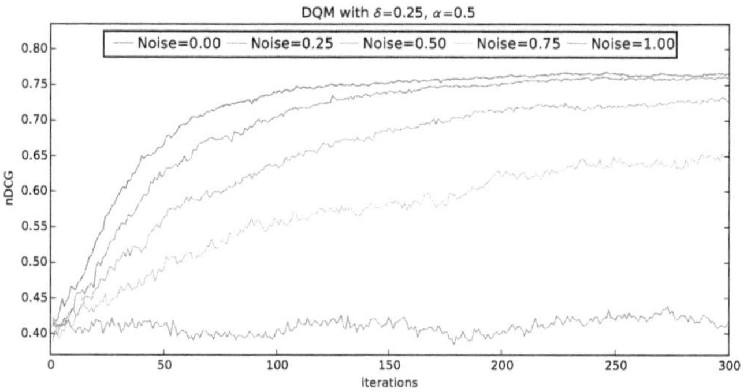

(c) Influence of noise on the convergence rate of effectiveness.

Figure 8: Learning curves showing the development in terms of effectiveness for the DQM approach across learning iterations. Metrics are computed using leave-one-out cross validation and averaged over five runs and 50 video segments at each iteration.

optimal value, but an optimal value will be found even with highly noisy feedback. This suggests that DQM is also suited for use in a setting where feedback comes from user interaction.

6. DISCUSSION

We see two obvious improvements to retrieval effectiveness for our DQM approach, which we will discuss here. First, we could use pseudo-relevance feedback (PRF) to do query expansion, an approach shown to be effective for generating phrasal-concept queries in literature search [22]. To increase recall, the original query is expanded with pseudo-relevant terms taken from the top retrieved documents. We experimented with enabling pseudo-relevant feedback. For the baseline, this increases nDCG with 3.5% for the top five and 7.3% for the full ranked list. We observed no improvement in retrieval effectiveness for DQM when enabling PRF. A possible explanation is that DQM's retrieval model uses many query terms, selected partly based on term statistics for the target collection. Instead of Indri's out-of-the-box PRF approach, a PRF approach that is tailored to our DQM retrieval model and the complex queries that it produces might be able to improve retrieval effectiveness.

Second, a plausible assumption is that more recent videos might be more relevant. We therefore also explored using temporal document priors, specifically ones inspired by human memory [33]. The DQM learning approach found no preference for recent documents and we observed no improvements in retrieval effectiveness with a temporal document prior compared to without one. An analysis of our ground truth confirmed that more recent documents were not found to be more relevant. This might be due to our retrospective annotation of the ground truth. In a live TV setting, with feedback from actual user interactions, more experimentation with a temporal document prior (e.g., a Weibull decay) would be advised.

So far, the discussion of our results has focused on effectiveness. However, our target setting is live TV, where efficiency is of great importance. To verify that we can efficiently perform DQM in near real time, we compute the average number of chunks we process per second on a single core machine, averaged over ten passes over all 50 video segments. DQM is able to process 23.9 chunks per second. Odijk et al. [32] report that they observe an average of 0.24 chunks per second in a live TV setting similar to ours, two orders of magnitude less than what we are able to achieve.

7. CONCLUSION

We formalized the task of finding video content related to a live television broadcast as a Markov decision process and proposed a reinforcement learning approach to directly optimize retrieval effectiveness. We showed that our approach significantly improves retrieval effectiveness over state-of-the-art stationary baselines, while remaining sufficiently efficient to be used in near real time in a live television setting. We have shown that each DQM retrieval model component contributes to the overall effectiveness. A larger number of weighted query terms significantly improve effectiveness. Static term features that are dependent on the target collection and background corpora are more important for selecting effective query terms than dynamic features derived from the stream of subtitles. Decaying term weights based on their recency further improves retrieval effectiveness.

Regarding our reinforcement learning approach we have found that a medium explorative step size and a larger learning rate are the best choice in our setting. We have shown that optimizing nDCG also yields the best nDCG@5 scores. Lastly, we showed that our reinforcement learning based approach to DQM still learns effectively when feedback becomes noisy. This suggests that our DQM approach is also suited for use in a setting where feedback comes from user interaction.

To understand the broader applicability of our work, it helps to point out that DQM is a task that combines two traditional basic information retrieval tasks: search and filtering. In a typical search task the query changes and the collection remains static. In a typical document filtering task, a standing query is used to filter a stream of documents. Our task concerns both. Similar tasks exist, such as summarizing social media in real time and finding replications of news articles while they appear. We believe that our DQM approach is applicable to those tasks too.

As to future work, we plan to explore learning from noisy feedback from actual user interactions. DQM generates a single query in each state. It may be useful to generate multiple queries and merge either queries or results. Similarly, an extension that explicitly generates temporally or topically diverse results may enhance the user experience. We could model this as a slot filling problem, where we have four video slots for which we select the most interesting video to show a user.

Acknowledgements. We thank NOS, NPO, and TWC for cooperating on the smart TV application that formed the setting for this research. This research was supported by the European Community's Seventh Framework Programme (FP7/2007-2013) under grant agreement nr 312827 (VOX-Pol), the Netherlands Organisation for Scientific Research (NWO) under project nrs 727.011.005, 612.001.116, HOR-11-10, 640.006.013, 612.066.930, CI-14-25, SH-322-15, Amsterdam Data Science, the Dutch national program COMMIT, the ESF Research Network Program ELIAS, the Elite Network Shifts project funded by the Royal Dutch Academy of Sciences (KNAW), the Netherlands eScience Center under project number 027.012.105, the Yahoo! Faculty Research and Engagement Program, the Microsoft Research PhD program, and the HPC Fund.

REFERENCES

[1] J. Allan, J. Carbonell, G. Doddington, J. Yamron, and Y. Yang. Topic detection and tracking pilot study final report. Computer Science Department Paper 341, CMU, 1998.

[2] N. Balasubramanian, G. Kumaran, and V. R. Carvalho. Exploring reductions for long web queries. In *SIGIR '10*, pages 571–578. ACM, 2010.

[3] A. G. Barto, R. S. Sutton, and P. S. Brouwer. Associative search network: A reinforcement learning associative memory. *Biological cybernetics*, 40(3):201–211, 1981.

[4] R. E. Bellman. A markovian decision process. *J. Math. Mech.*, 6:679–684, 1957.

[5] M. Bendersky and W. B. Croft. Discovering key concepts in verbose queries. In *SIGIR '08*, pages 491–498. ACM, 2008.

[6] M. Bendersky, D. Metzler, and W. B. Croft. Parameterized concept weighting in verbose queries. In *SIGIR '11*, pages 605–614. ACM, 2011.

[7] M. Bendersky, L. Garcia-Pueyo, J. Harmsen, V. Josifovski, and D. Lepikhin. Up next. In *KDD '14*, pages 1769–1778, New York, New York, USA, Aug. 2014. ACM Press.

[8] R. Blanco, G. D. F. Morales, and F. Silvestri. Intonews: Online news retrieval using closed captions. *Inf. Proc. & Man.*, 51(1):148–162, 2015.

[9] T. Brants and A. Franz. Web 1T 5-gram 10 european languages version 1 LDC2009T25. Philadelphia: Linguistic Data Consortium, 2009.

[10] M. Bron, B. Huurnink, and M. de Rijke. Linking archives using document enrichment and term selection. In *TPDL '11*, pages 360–371. Springer, 2011.

[11] E. Brown, S. Srinivasan, A. Coden, D. Ponceleon, J. Cooper, A. Amir, and J. Pieper. Towards speech as a knowledge resource. In *CIKM '01*, pages 526–528. ACM, 2001.

[12] B. Carterette and R. Jones. Evaluating search engines by modeling the relationship between relevance and clicks. In *NIPS*, volume 7, pages 217–224, 2007.

[13] K. W. Church and W. A. Gale. Poisson mixtures. *Nat. Lang. Eng.*, 1:163–190, 1995.

[14] M. Efron. Linear time series models for term weighting in information retrieval. *J. American Society for Information Science and Technology*, 61(7):1299–1312, 2010.

[15] E. Feinberg and A. Shwartz. *Handbook of Markov Decision Processes.* Kluwer, 2002.

[16] D. Guan, S. Zhang, and H. Yang. Utilizing query change for session search. In *SIGIR '13*, pages 453–462. ACM, 2013.

[17] M. A. Hearst. TextTiling: Segmenting text into multi-paragraph subtopic passages. *Comput. Linguist.*, 23 (1):33–64, March 1997.

[18] M. Henzinger, B.-W. Chang, B. Milch, and S. Brin. Query-free news search. *WWW '05*, 8(2):101–126, 2005.

[19] K. Hofmann, S. Whiteson, and M. de Rijke. Balancing exploration and exploitation in listwise and pairwise online learning to rank for information retrieval. *Information Retrieval*, 16(1):63–90, 2013.

[20] K. Järvelin and J. Kekäläinen. Cumulated gain-based evaluation of IR techniques. *ACM Trans. Inf. Syst.*, 20(4): 422–446, Oct. 2002.

[21] X. Jin, M. Sloan, and J. Wang. Interactive exploratory search for multi page search results. In *WWW '13*, pages 655–666. ACM, 2013.

[22] Y. Kim, J. Seo, W. B. Croft, and D. A. Smith. Automatic suggestion of phrasal-concept queries for literature search. *Inf. Proc. & Man.*, 50(4):568–583, 2014.

[23] G. Kumaran and V. R. Carvalho. Reducing long queries using query quality predictors. In *SIGIR '09*, pages 564–571. ACM, 2009.

[24] M. Larson, E. Newman, and G. Jones. Overview of VideoCLEF 2009. In *CLEF '09*. Springer, 2010.

[25] M. Lease. An improved markov random field model for supporting verbose queries. In *SIGIR '09*, pages 476–483, New York, NY, USA, 2009. ACM.

[26] M. Lease, J. Allan, and W. B. Croft. Regression rank: Learning to meet the opportunity of descriptive queries. In *ECIR '09*, pages 90–101. Springer, 2009.

[27] C.-J. Lee and W. B. Croft. Generating queries from user-selected text. In *Proc. of the 4th Information Interaction in Context Symposium*, pages 100–109. ACM, 2012.

[28] J. Luo, S. Zhang, and H. Yang. Win-win search: Dual-agent stochastic game in session search. In *SIGIR '14*, pages 587–596, New York, NY, USA, 2014. ACM.

[29] J. Luo, S. Zhang, X. Dong, and H. Yang. Designing states, actions, and rewards for using pomdp in session search. *ECIR '15*, 2015.

[30] D. Metzler and W. B. Croft. Combining the language model and inference network approaches to retrieval. *Inf. Proc. & Man.*, 40(5):735–750, 2004.

[31] Nielsen. State of the media: The cross-platform report. http://bit.ly/1hNXs4m, 2013.

[32] D. Odijk, E. Meij, and M. de Rijke. Feeding the second screen: Semantic linking based on subtitles. In *OAIR '13*, 2013.

[33] M.-H. Peetz and M. de Rijke. Cognitive temporal document priors. In *ECIR '13*, pages 318–330. Springer, 2013.

[34] M.-H. Peetz, E. Meij, M. de Rijke, and W. Weerkamp. Adaptive temporal query modeling. In *ECIR '12*, pages 455–458. Springer, 2012.

[35] F. Radlinski, M. Kurup, and T. Joachims. How does clickthrough data reflect retrieval quality? In *CIKM '08*, pages 43–52. ACM, 2008.

[36] Razorfish. Forget mobile, think multiscreen. http://razorfish-outlook.razorfish.com/articles/forgetmobile.aspx, 2011.

[37] H.-J. Song, J. Go, S.-B. Park, and S.-Y. Park. A just-in-time keyword extraction from meeting transcripts. In *NAACL-HLT '13*, pages 888–896, 2013.

[38] R. S. Sutton and A. G. Barto. *Introduction to Reinforcement Learning.* MIT Press, 1998.

[39] C. J. C. H. Watkins. *Learning from delayed rewards.* PhD thesis, U. Cambridge, 1989.

[40] Y. Yue and T. Joachims. Interactively optimizing information retrieval systems as a dueling bandits problem. In *ICML '09*, pages 1201–1208. ACM, 2009.

Image-based Recommendations on Styles and Substitutes

Julian McAuley
UC San Diego
jmcauley@ucsd.edu

Christopher Targett
University of Adelaide
christopher.targett@student.adelaide.edu.au

Qinfeng ('Javen') Shi
University of Adelaide
javen.shi@adelaide.edu.au

Anton van den Hengel
Australian Centre for Robot Vision;
University of Adelaide
anton.vandenhengel@adelaide.edu.au

ABSTRACT

Humans inevitably develop a sense of the relationships between objects, some of which are based on their appearance. Some pairs of objects might be seen as being alternatives to each other (such as two pairs of jeans), while others may be seen as being complementary (such as a pair of jeans and a matching shirt). This information guides many of the choices that people make, from buying clothes to their interactions with each other. We seek here to model this human sense of the relationships between objects based on their appearance. Our approach is not based on fine-grained modeling of user annotations but rather on capturing the largest dataset possible and developing a scalable method for uncovering human notions of the visual relationships within. We cast this as a network inference problem defined on graphs of related images, and provide a large-scale dataset for the training and evaluation of the same. The system we develop is capable of recommending which clothes and accessories will go well together (and which will not), amongst a host of other applications.

1. INTRODUCTION

We are interested here in uncovering relationships between the appearances of pairs of objects, and particularly in modeling the human notion of which objects complement each other and which might be seen as acceptable alternatives. We thus seek to model what is a fundamentally human notion of the visual relationship between a pair of objects, rather than merely modeling the visual similarity between them. There has been some interest of late in modeling the visual style of places [6, 27], and objects [39]. We, in contrast, are not seeking to model the individual appearances of objects, but rather how the appearance of one object might influence the desirable visual attributes of another.

There are a range of situations in which the appearance of an object might have an impact on the desired appearance of another. Questions such as 'Which frame goes with this picture', 'Where is the lid to this', and 'Which shirt matches these shoes' (see Figure 1) inherently involve a calculation of more than just visual similarity, but rather a model of the higher-level relationships between objects. The primary commercial application for such technology is in recommending items to a user based on other items they have already showed interest in. Such systems are of considerable economic value, and are typically built by analysing meta-data, reviews, and previous purchasing patterns. By introducing into these systems the ability to examine the appearance of the objects in question we aim to overcome some of their limitations, including the 'cold start' problem [28, 41].

SIGIR '15 August 09 - 13, 2015, Santiago, Chile

ACM 978-1-4503-3621-5/15/08 ...$15.00.
http://dx.doi.org/10.1145/2766462.2767755.

Figure 1: A query image and a matching accessory, pants, and a shirt.

The problem we pose inherently requires modeling human visual preferences. In most cases there is no intrinsic connection between a pair of objects, only a human notion that they are more suited to each other than are other potential partners. The most common approach to modeling such human notions exploits a set of hand-labeled images created for the task. The labeling effort required means that most such datasets are typically relatively small, although there are a few notable exceptions. A small dataset means that complex procedures are required to extract as much information as possible without over-fitting (see [2, 5, 22] for example). It also means that the results are unlikely to be transferable to related problems. Creating a labeled dataset is particularly onerous when modeling pairwise distances because the number of annotations required scales with the square of the number of elements.

We propose here instead that one might operate over a much larger dataset, even if it is only tangentially related to the ultimate goal. Thus, rather than devising a process (or budget) for manually annotating images, we instead seek a freely available source of a large amount of data which may be more loosely related to the information we seek. Large-scale databases have been collected from the web (without other annotation) previously [7, 34]. What distinguishes the approach we propose here, however, is the fact that it succeeds despite the indirectness of the connection between the dataset and the quantity we hope to model.

1.1 A visual dataset of styles and substitutes

We have developed a dataset suitable for the purposes described above based on the Amazon web store. The dataset contains over 180 million relationships between a pool of almost 6 million objects. These relationships are a result of visiting Amazon and recording the product recommendations that it provides given our (apparent) interest in the subject of a particular web page. The statistics of the dataset are shown in Table 1. An image and a category label are available for each object, as is the set of users who reviewed it. We have made this dataset available for academic use, along with all code used in this paper to ensure that our results are reproducible and extensible.[1] We label this the *Styles and Substitutes* dataset.

The recorded relationships describe two specific notions of 'compatibility' that are of interest, namely those of *substitute* and *complement* goods. Substitute goods are those that can be interchanged (such as one pair of pants for another), while complements are those that might be purchased together (such as a pair of pants and a matching shirt) [23]. Specifically, there are 4 categories of relationship represented in the dataset: 1) 'users who viewed X also viewed Y' (65M edges); 2) 'users who viewed X eventually bought Y' (7.3M edges); 3) 'users who bought X also bought Y' (104M edges); and 4) 'users bought X and Y simultaneously' (3.4M edges). Critically, categories 1 and 2 indicate (up to some noise) that two products may be substitutable, while 3 and 4 indicate that two products may be complementary. According to Amazon's own tech report [19] the above relationships are collected simply by ranking products according to the cosine similarity of the sets of users who purchased/viewed them.

Note that the dataset does not document users' preferences for pairs of images, but rather Amazon's estimate of the set of relationships between pairs objects. The human notion of the visual compatibility of these images is only one factor amongst many which give rise to these estimated relationships, and it is not a factor used by Amazon in creating them. We thus do not wish to summarize the Amazon data, but rather to use what it tells us about the images of related products to develop a sense of which objects a human might feel are visually compatible. This is significant because many of the relationships between objects present in the data are not based on their appearance. People co-purchase hammers and nails due to their functions, for example, not their appearances. Our hope is that the non-visual decision factors will appear as uniformly distributed noise to a method which considers only appearance, and that the visual decision factors might reinforce each other to overcome the effect of this noise.

1.2 Related work

The closest systems to what we propose above are content-based recommender systems [18] which attempt to model each user's preference toward particular types of goods. This is typically achieved by analyzing metadata from the user's previous activities. This is as compared to collaborative recommendation approaches which match the user to profiles generated based on the purchases/behavior of other users (see [1, 16] for surveys). Combinations of the two [3, 24] have been shown to help address the sparsity of the review data available, and the cold-start problem (where new products don't have reviews and are thus invisible to the recommender system) [28, 41]. The approach we propose here could also help address these problems.

There are a range of services such as Jinni[2] which promise content-based recommendations for TV shows and similar media, but the features they expoit are based on reviews and meta-data (such as cast, director etc.), and their ontology is hand-crafted. The Netflix prize was a well publicized competition to build a better personalized video recommender system, but there again no actual image analysis is taking place [17]. Hu et al. [9] describe a system for identifying a user's style, and then making clothing recommendations, but this is achieved through analysis of 'likes' rather than visual features.

Content-based image retrieval gives rise to the problem of bridging the 'semantic-gap' [32], which requires returning results which have similar semantic content to a search image, even when the pixels bear no relationship to each other. It thus bears some similarity to the visual recommendation problem, as both require modeling a human preference which is not satisfied by mere visual similarity. There are a variety of approaches to this problem, many of which seek a set of results which are visually similar to the query and then separately find images depicting objects of the same class as those in the query image; see [2, 15, 22, 38], for example. Within the Information Retrieval community there has been considerable interest of late in incorporating user data into image retrieval systems [37], for example through browsing [36] and click-through behavior [26], or by making use of social tags [29]. Also worth mentioning with respect to image retrieval is [12], which also considered using images crawled from Amazon, albeit for a different task (similar-image search) than the one considered here.

There have been a variety of approaches to modeling human notions of similarity between different types of images [30], forms of music [31], or even tweets [33], amongst other data types. Beyond measuring similarity, there has also been work on measuring more general notions of compatibility. Murillo et al. [25], for instance, analyze photos of groups of people collected from social media to identify which groups might be more likely to socialize with each other, thus implying a distance measure between images. This is achieved by estimating which of a manually-specified set of 'urban tribes' each group belongs to, possibly because only 340 images were available.

Yamaguchi et al. [40] capture a notion of visual style when parsing clothing, but do so by retrieving visually similar items from a database. This idea was extended by Kiapour et al. [14] to identify discriminating characteristics between different styles (hipster vs. goth for example). Di et al. [5] also identify aspects of style using a bag-of-words approach and manual annotations.

A few other works that consider visual features specifically for the task of clothing recommendation include [10, 13, 20]. In [10] and [13] the authors build methods to parse complete outfits from single images, in [10] by building a carefully labeled dataset of street images annotated by 'fashionistas', and in [13] by building algorithms to automatically detect and segment items from clothing images. In [13] the authors propose an approach to learn relationships between

[1] http://cseweb.ucsd.edu/~jmcauley/

[2] http://jinni.com

Category	Users	Items	Ratings	Edges
Books	8,201,127	1,606,219	25,875,237	51,276,522
Cell Phones & Accessories	2,296,534	223,680	5,929,668	4,485,570
Clothing, Shoes & Jewelry	3,260,278	773,465	25,361,968	16,508,162
Digital Music	490,058	91,236	950,621	1,615,473
Electronics	4,248,431	305,029	11,355,142	7,500,100
Grocery & Gourmet Food	774,095	120,774	1,997,599	4,452,989
Home & Kitchen	2,541,693	282,779	6,543,736	9,240,125
Movies & TV	2,114,748	150,334	6,174,098	5,474,976
Musical Instruments	353,983	65,588	596,095	1,719,204
Office Products	919,512	94,820	1,514,235	3,257,651
Toys & Games	1,352,110	259,290	2,386,102	13,921,925
Total	20,980,320	5,933,184	143,663,229	180,827,502

Table 1: The types of objects from a few categories in our dataset and the number of relationships between them.

clothing items and events (e.g. birthday parties, funerals) in order to recommend event-appropriate items. Although related to our approach, these methods are designed for the specific task of clothing recommendation, requiring hand-crafted methods and carefully annotated data; in contrast our goal is to build a general-purpose method to understand relationships between objects from large volumes of *unlabeled* data. Although our setting is perhaps most natural for categories like clothing images, we obtain surprisingly accurate performance when predicting relationships in a variety of categories, from recommending outfits to predicting which books will be co-purchased based on their cover art.

In summary, our approach is distinct from the above in that we aim to generalize the idea of a visual distance measure beyond measuring only similarity. Doing so demands a very large amount of training data, and our reluctance for manual annotation necessitates a more opportunistic data collection strategy. The scale of the data, and the fact that we don't have control over its acquisition, demands a suitably scalable and robust modeling approach. The novelty in what we propose is thus in the quantity we choose to model, the data we gather to do so, and the method for extracting one from the other.

1.3 A visual and relational recommender system

We label the process we develop for exploiting this data a *visual and relational recommender system* as we aim to model human visual preferences, and the system might be used to recommend one object on the basis of a user's apparent interest in another. The system shares these characteristics with more common forms of recommender system, but does so on the basis of the appearance of the object, rather than metadata, reviews, or similar.

2. THE MODEL

Our notation is defined in Table 2.

We seek a method for representing the preferences of users for the visual appearance of one object given that of another. A number of suitable models might be devised for this purpose, but very few of them will scale to the volume of data available.

For every object in the dataset we calculate an F-dimensional feature vector $\mathbf{x} \in \mathbb{R}^F$ using a convolutional neural network as described in Section 2.3. The dataset contains

notation	explanation
$\mathbf{x}_i$	feature vector calculated from object image i
F	feature dimension (i.e., $\mathbf{x}_i \in \mathbb{R}^F$)
r_{ij}	a relationship between objects i and j
$\mathcal{R}$	the set of relationships between all objects
$d_\theta(\mathbf{x}_i,\mathbf{x}_j)$	parameterized distance between $\mathbf{x}_i$ and $\mathbf{x}_j$
$\mathbf{M}$	$F \times F$ Mahalanobis transform matrix
$\mathbf{Y}$	an $F \times K$ matrix, such that $\mathbf{Y}\mathbf{Y}^T = \mathbf{M}$
$\mathbf{D}^{(u)}$	diagonal user-personalization matrix for user u
$\sigma_c(\cdot)$	shifted sigmoid function with parameter c
$\mathcal{R}^*$	$\mathcal{R}$ plus a random sample of non-relationships
$\mathcal{U}, \mathcal{V}, \mathcal{T}$	training, validation, and test subsets of $\mathcal{R}^*$
$\mathbf{s}_i$	K-dimension embedding of $\mathbf{x}_i$ into 'style-space'

Table 2: Notation.

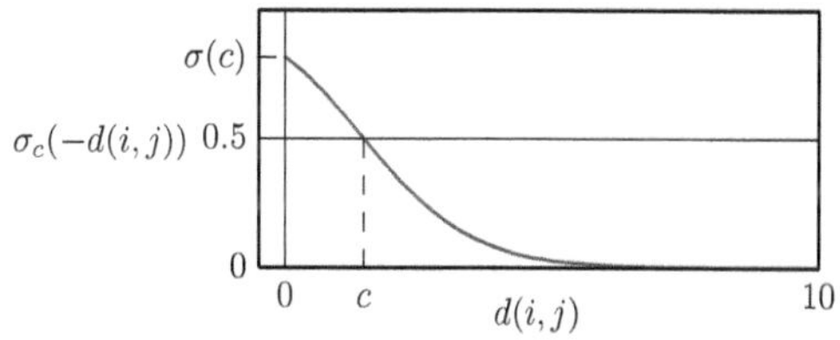

Figure 2: Shifted (and inverted) sigmoid with parameter $c = 2$.

a set $\mathcal{R}$ of relationships where $r_{ij} \in \mathcal{R}$ relates objects i and j. Each relationship is of one of the four classes listed above. Our goal is to learn a parameterized distance transform $d(\mathbf{x}_i,\mathbf{x}_j)$ such that feature vectors $\{\mathbf{x}_i,\mathbf{x}_j\}$ for objects that are related ($r_{ij} \in \mathcal{R}$) are assigned a lower distance than those that are not ($r_{ij} \notin \mathcal{R}$). Specifically, we seek $d(\cdot,\cdot)$ such that $P(r_{ij} \in \mathcal{R})$ grows monotonically with $-d(\mathbf{x}_i,\mathbf{x}_j)$.

Distances and probabilities: We use a shifted sigmoid function to relate distance to probability thus

$$P(r_{ij} \in \mathcal{R}) = \sigma_c(-d(\mathbf{x}_i,\mathbf{x}_j)) = \frac{1}{1+e^{d(\mathbf{x}_i,\mathbf{x}_j)-c}}. \quad (1)$$

This is depicted in Figure 2. This decision allows us to cast the problem as logistic regression, which we do for reasons of scalability. Intuitively, if two items i and j have distance $d(\mathbf{x}_i,\mathbf{x}_j) = c$, then they have probability 0.5 of being related; the probability increases above 0.5 for $d(\mathbf{x}_i,\mathbf{x}_j) < c$, and decreases as $d(\mathbf{x}_i,\mathbf{x}_j) > c$. Note that we do not specify c in advance, but rather c is chosen to maximize prediction accuracy.

We now describe a set of potential distance functions.

Weighted nearest neighbor: Given that different feature dimensions are likely to be more important to different relationships, the simplest method we consider is to learn which feature dimensions are relevant for a particular relationship. We thus fit a distance function of the form

$$d_{\mathbf{w}}(\mathbf{x}_i,\mathbf{x}_j) = \|\mathbf{w} \circ (\mathbf{x}_i - \mathbf{x}_j)\|_2^2, \quad (2)$$

where $\circ$ is the Hadamard product.

Mahalanobis transform: (eq. 2) is limited to modeling the visual similarity between objects, albeit with varying emphasis per feature dimension. It is not expressive enough to model subtler notions, such as which pairs of pants and shoes belong to the same 'style', despite having different appearances. For this we need to learn how different feature dimensions *relate* to each other, i.e., how the features of a pair of pants might be transformed to help identify a compatible pair of shoes.

To identify such a transformation, we relate image features via a *Mahalanobis distance*, which essentially generalizes (eq. 2) so that weights are defined at the level of pairs of features. Specifically we fit

$$d_{\mathbf{M}}(\mathbf{x}_i,\mathbf{x}_j) = (\mathbf{x}_i - \mathbf{x}_j)\mathbf{M}(\mathbf{x}_i - \mathbf{x}_j)^T. \quad (3)$$

A full rank p.s.d. matrix $\mathbf{M}$ has too many parameters to fit tractably given the size of the dataset. For example, using features with dimension $F = 2^{12}$, learning a transform as in (eq. 3) requires us to fit approximately 8 million parameters; not only would this be prone to overfitting, it is simply not practical for existing solvers.

To address these issues, and given the fact that $\mathbf{M}$ parameterises a Mahanalobis distance, we approximate $\mathbf{M}$ such that $\mathbf{M} \simeq \mathbf{Y}\mathbf{Y}^T$ where $\mathbf{Y}$ is a matrix of dimension $F \times K$. We therefore define

$$\begin{aligned} d_{\mathbf{Y}}(\mathbf{x}_i,\mathbf{x}_j) &= (\mathbf{x}_i - \mathbf{x}_j)\mathbf{Y}\mathbf{Y}^T(\mathbf{x}_i - \mathbf{x}_j)^T \\ &= \|(\mathbf{x}_i - \mathbf{x}_j)\mathbf{Y}\|_2^2. \end{aligned} \quad (4)$$

Note that all distances (as well as their derivatives) can be computed in $O(FK)$, which is significant for the scalability of the method. Similar ideas appear in [4, 35], which also consider the problem of metric learning via low-rank embeddings, albeit using a different objective than the one we consider here.

2.1 Style space

In addition to being computationally useful, the low-rank transform in (eq. 4) has a convenient interpretation. Specifically, if we consider the K-dimensional vector $\mathbf{s}_i = \mathbf{x}_i\mathbf{Y}$, then (eq. 4) can be rewritten as

$$d_{\mathbf{Y}}(\mathbf{x}_i,\mathbf{x}_j) = \|\mathbf{s}_i - \mathbf{s}_j\|_2^2. \quad (5)$$

In other words, (eq. 4) yields a low-dimensional embedding of the features $\mathbf{x}_i$ and $\mathbf{x}_j$. We refer to this low-dimensional representation as the product's embedding into 'style-space', in the hope that we might identify $\mathbf{Y}$ such that related objects fall close to each other despite being visually dissimilar. The notion of 'style' is learned automatically by training the model on pairs of objects which Amazon considers to be related.

2.2 Personalizing styles to individual users

So far we have developed a model to learn a *global* notion of which products go together, by learning a notion of 'style' such that related products should have similar styles. As an addition to this model we can personalize this notion by learning for each individual user which dimensions of style they consider to be important.

To do so, we shall learn personalized distance functions $d_{\mathbf{Y},u}(\mathbf{x}_i,\mathbf{x}_j)$ that measure the distance between the items i and j *according to the user* u. We choose the distance function

$$d_{\mathbf{Y},u}(\mathbf{x}_i,\mathbf{x}_j) = (\mathbf{x}_i - \mathbf{x}_j)\mathbf{Y}\mathbf{D}^{(u)}\mathbf{Y}^T(\mathbf{x}_i - \mathbf{x}_j)^T \quad (6)$$

where $\mathbf{D}^{(u)}$ is a $K \times K$ diagonal (positive semidefinite) matrix. In this way the entry $\mathbf{D}_{kk}^{(u)}$ indicates the extent to which the user u 'cares about' the kth style dimension.

In practice we fit a $U \times K$ matrix $\mathbf{X}$ such that $D_{kk}^{(u)} = \mathbf{X}_{uk}$. Much like the simplification in (eq. 5), the distance $d_{\mathbf{Y},u}(\mathbf{x}_i,\mathbf{x}_j)$ can be conveniently written as

$$d_{\mathbf{Y},u}(\mathbf{x}_i,\mathbf{x}_j) = \|(\mathbf{s}_i - \mathbf{s}_j) \circ X_u\|_2^2. \quad (7)$$

In other words, X_u is a personalized *weighting* of the projected style-space dimensions.

The construction in (eq. 6 and 7) only makes sense if there are *users* associated with each edge in our dataset, which is not true of the four graph types we have presented so far. Thus to study the issue of user personalization we make use of our rating and review data (see Table 1). From this we sample a dataset of triples (i,j,u) of products i and j that were both purchased by user u (i.e., u reviewed them both). We describe this further when we outline our experimental protocol in Section 4.1.

2.3 Features

Features are calculated from the original images using the Caffe deep learning framework [11]. In particular, we used a Caffe reference model[3] with 5 convolutional layers followed by 3 fully-connected layers, which has been pre-trained on 1.2 million ImageNet (ILSVRC2010) images. We use the output of FC7, the second fully-connected layer, which results in a feature vector of length $F = 4096$.

3. TRAINING

Since we have defined a probability associated with the presence (or absence) of each relationship, we can proceed by maximizing the likelihood of an observed relationship set $\mathcal{R}$. In order to do so we randomly select a negative set $\mathcal{Q} = \{r_{ij} | r_{ij} \notin \mathcal{R}\}$ such that $|\mathcal{Q}| = |\mathcal{R}|$ and optimize the log likelihood

$$l(\mathbf{Y},c|\mathcal{R},\mathcal{Q}) = \sum_{r_{ij}\in\mathcal{R}} \log(\sigma_c(-d_{\mathbf{Y}}(\mathbf{x}_i,\mathbf{x}_j))) + \sum_{r_{ij}\in\mathcal{Q}} \log(1 - \sigma_c(-d_{\mathbf{Y}}(\mathbf{x}_i,\mathbf{x}_j))). \quad (8)$$

Learning then proceeds by optimizing $l(\mathbf{Y},c|\mathcal{R},\mathcal{Q})$ over both $\mathbf{Y}$ and c which we achieve by gradient ascent. We use (hybrid) L-BFGS, a quasi-Newton method for non-linear optimization of problems with many variables [21]. Likelihood

[3]bvlc_reference_caffenet from caffe.berkeleyvision.org

(eq. 8) and derivative computations can be naïvely parallelized over all pairs $r_{ij} \in \mathcal{R} \cup \mathcal{Q}$. Training on our largest dataset (Amazon books) with a rank $K = 100$ transform required around one day on a 12 core machine.

4. EXPERIMENTS

We compare our model against the following baselines:

We compare against *Weighted Nearest Neighbor (WNN)* classification, as is described in Section 1.3. We also compare against a method we label *Category Tree (CT)*; CT is based on using Amazon's detailed category tree directly (which we have collected for Clothing data, and use for later experiments), which allows us to assess how effective an image-based classification approach *could* be, if it were perfect. We then compute a matrix of coocurrences between categories from the training data, and label two products (a,b) as 'related' if the category of b belongs to one of the top 50% of most commonly linked categories for products of category a.[4] Nearest neighbor results (calculated by optimizing a threshold on the ℓ_2 distance using the training data) were not significantly better than random, and have been suppressed for brevity.

Comparison against non-visual baselines As a non-visual comparison, we trained topic models on the reviews of each product (i.e., each document d_i is the set of reviews of the product i) and fit weighted nearest neighbor classifiers of the form

$$d_{\mathbf{w}}(\theta_i, \theta_j) = \|\mathbf{w} \circ (\theta_i - \theta_j)\|_2^2, \quad (9)$$

where θ_i and θ_j are topic vectors derived from the reviews of the products i and j. In other words, we simply adapted our WNN baseline to make use of topic vectors rather than image features.[5] We used a 100-dimensional topic model trained using Vowpal Wabbit [8].

However, this baseline proved not to be competitive against the alternatives described above (e.g. only 60% accuracy on our largest dataset, 'Books'). One explanation may simply be that is is difficult to effectively train topic models at the 1M+ document scale; another explanation is simply that the vast majority of products have few reviews. Not surprisingly, the number of reviews per product follows a power-law, e.g. for Men's Clothing:

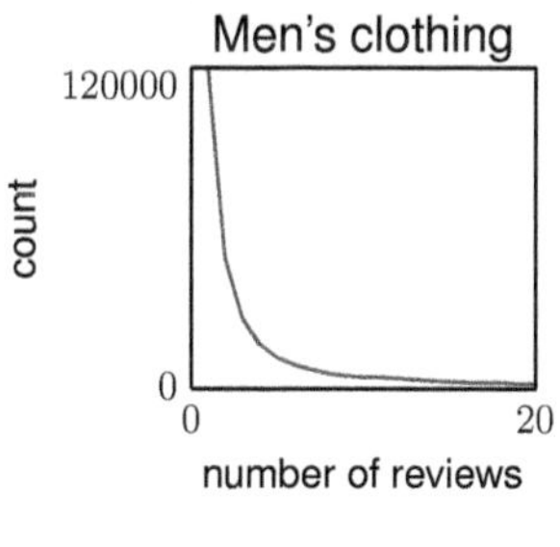

This issue is in fact exacerbated in our setting, as to predict a relationship between products we require both to have reliable feature representations, which will be true only if *both* products have several reviews.

Although we believe that predicting such relationships using text is a promising direction of future research (and one we are exploring), we simply wish to highlight the fact that there appears to be no 'silver bullet' to predict such relationships using text, primarily due to the 'cold start' issue that arises due to the long tail of obscure products with little text associated with them. Indeed, this is a strong argument in favor of building predictors based on visual features, since images are available even for brand new products which are yet to receive even a single review.

[4]We experimented with several variations on this theme, and this approach yielded the best performance.

[5]We tried the same approach at the word (rather than the topic) level, though this led to slightly worse results.

Category	method	substitutes: buy after viewing	substitutes: also viewed	complements: also bought	complements: bought together
Books	WNN	66.5%	62.8%	63.3%	65.4%
	$K = 10$	70.1%	68.6%	69.3%	68.1%
	$K = 100$	71.2%	69.8%	71.2%	68.6%
Cell Phones and Accessories	WNN	73.4%	66.4%	69.1%	79.3%
	$K = 10$	84.3%	78.9%	78.7%	83.1%
	$K = 100$	85.9%	83.1%	83.2%	87.7%
Clothing, Shoes, and Jewelry	WNN	·	77.2%	74.2%	78.3%
	$K = 10$	·	87.5%	84.7%	89.7%
	$K = 100$	·	88.8%	88.7%	92.5%
Digital Music	WNN	60.2%	56.7%	62.2%	53.3%
	$K = 10$	68.7%	60.9%	74.7%	56.0%
	$K = 100$	72.3%	63.8%	76.2%	59.0%
Electronics	WNN	76.5%	73.8%	67.6%	73.5%
	$K = 10$	83.6%	80.3%	77.8%	79.6%
	$K = 100$	86.4%	84.0%	82.6%	83.2%
Grocery and Gourmet Food	WNN	·	69.2%	70.7%	68.5%
	$K = 10$	·	77.8%	81.2%	79.6%
	$K = 100$	·	82.5%	85.2%	84.5%
Home and Kitchen	WNN	75.1%	68.3%	70.4%	76.6%
	$K = 10$	78.5%	80.5%	78.8%	79.3%
	$K = 100$	81.6%	83.8%	83.4%	83.2%
Movies and TV	WNN	66.8%	65.6%	61.6%	59.6%
	$K = 10$	71.9%	69.6%	72.8%	67.6%
	$K = 100$	72.3%	70.0%	77.3%	70.7%
Musical Instruments	WNN	79.0%	76.0%	75.0%	77.2%
	$K = 10$	84.7%	87.0%	85.3%	82.3%
	$K = 100$	89.5%	87.2%	84.4%	84.7%
Office Products	WNN	72.8%	75.0%	74.4%	73.7%
	$K = 10$	81.2%	84.0%	84.1%	78.6%
	$K = 100$	85.9%	87.2%	85.8%	80.9%
Toys and Games	WNN	67.0%	72.8%	71.7%	77.6%
	$K = 10$	75.8%	78.3%	78.4%	80.3%
	$K = 100$	77.1%	81.9%	82.4%	82.6%

Table 3: Accuracy of link prediction on top-level categories for each edge type with increasing model rank K. Random classification is 50% accurate across all experiments.

4.1 Experimental protocol

We split the dataset into its top-level categories (Books, Movies, Music, etc.) and further split the Clothing category into second-level categories (Men's, Women's, Boys, Girls, etc.). We focus on results from a few representative subcategories. Complete code for all experiments and all baselines is available online.[6]

For each category, we consider the subset of relationships

[6]http://cseweb.ucsd.edu/~jmcauley/

Category	method	substitutes also viewed	complements also bought	bought together
Baby	CT	77.1%	70.5%	80.1%
	WNN	83.0%	87.7%	81.7%
	$K = 10$	92.2%	92.7%	91.5%
	$K = 100$	94.6%	94.3%	93.3%
Boots	CT	75.0%	72.7%	74.2%
	WNN	83.9%	85.6%	84.7%
	$K = 10$	93.0%	94.9%	95.4%
	$K = 100$	94.6%	96.8%	96.4%
Boys	CT	81.9%	77.3%	83.1%
	WNN	85.0%	87.2%	87.9%
	$K = 10$	94.4%	94.1%	93.8%
	$K = 100$	96.5%	95.8%	95.1%
Girls	CT	83.0%	76.2%	78.7%
	WNN	83.3%	86.0%	84.8%
	$K = 10$	94.5%	93.6%	93.0%
	$K = 100$	96.1%	95.3%	94.5%
Jewelry	CT	50.1%	49.5%	51.1%
	WNN	81.2%	81.6%	75.8%
	$K = 10$	89.6%	89.3%	82.8%
	$K = 100$	89.1%	91.6%	86.4%
Men	CT	88.2%	78.4%	83.6%
	WNN	86.9%	78.4%	82.3%
	$K = 10$	91.6%	89.8%	92.1%
	$K = 100$	92.6%	93.3%	95.1%
Novelty Costumes	CT	79.1%	76.3%	81.5%
	WNN	80.1%	74.1%	76.0%
	$K = 10$	86.3%	86.6%	85.0%
	$K = 100$	89.2%	90.0%	89.1%
Shoes and Accessories	CT	81.3%	78.1%	90.4%
	WNN	75.4%	80.2%	77.9%
	$K = 10$	89.7%	90.4%	93.5%
	$K = 100$	92.3%	94.7%	96.2%
Women	CT	86.8%	79.1%	84.3%
	WNN	78.8%	76.1%	80.0%
	$K = 10$	88.9%	87.8%	91.5%
	$K = 100$	90.4%	91.2%	94.3%

Table 4: Accuracy of link prediction on subcategories of 'Clothing, Shoes, and Jewelry' with increasing rank K. Note that 'buy after viewing' links are not surfaced for clothing data on Amazon.

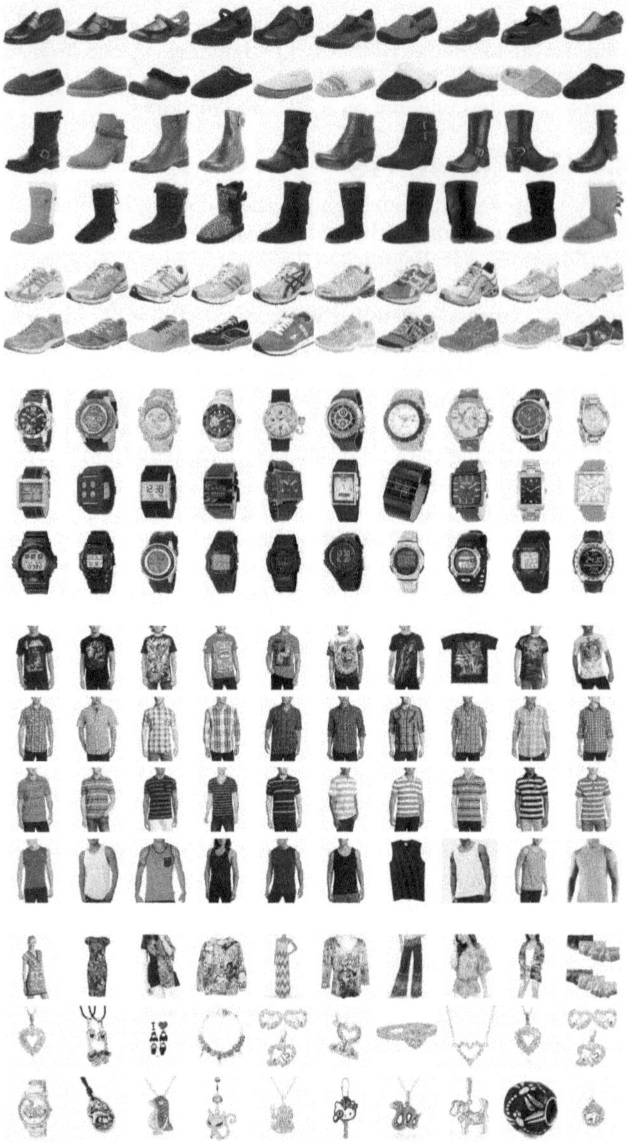

Figure 3: Examples of closely-clustered items in style space (Men's and Women's clothing 'also viewed' data).

from $\mathcal{R}$ that connect products within that category. After generating random samples of non-relationships, we separate $\mathcal{R}$ and $\mathcal{Q}$ into training, validation, and test sets (80/10/10%, up to a maximum of two million training relationships). Although we do not fit hyperparameters (and therefore do not make use of the validation set), we maintain this split in case it proves useful to those wishing to benchmark their algorithms on this data. While we did experiment with simple ℓ_2 regularizers, we found ourselves blessed with a sufficient overabundance of data that overfitting never presented an issue (i.e., the validation error was rarely significantly higher than the training error).

To be completely clear, our protocol consists of the following:

1. Each category and graph type forms a single experiment (e.g. predict 'bought together' relationships for Women's clothing).
2. Our goal is to distinguish relationships from non-relationships (i.e., link prediction). Relationships are identified when our predictor (eq. 1) outputs $P(r_{ij} \in \mathcal{R}) > 0.5$.
3. We consider *all* positive relationships and a random sample of non-relationships (i.e., 'distractors') of equal size. Thus the performance of a random classifier is 50% for all experiments.
4. All results are reported on the test set.

Results on a selection of top-level categories are shown in Table 3, with further results for clothing data shown in Table 4. Recall when interpreting these results that the learned model has reference to the object images only. It is thus estimating the existence of a specified form of relationship purely on the basis of appearance.

In every case the proposed method outperforms both the category-based method and weighted nearest neighbor, and

Figure 4: A selection of widely separated members of a single K-means cluster, demonstrating an apparent stylistic coherence.

Figure 5: Examples of K-means clusters in style space (Books 'also viewed' and 'also bought' data). Although 'styles' for categories like books are not so readily interpretable as they are for clothes, visual features are nevertheless able to uncover meaningful distinctions between different product categories, e.g. the first four rows above above appear to be children's books, self-help books, romance novels, and graphic novels.

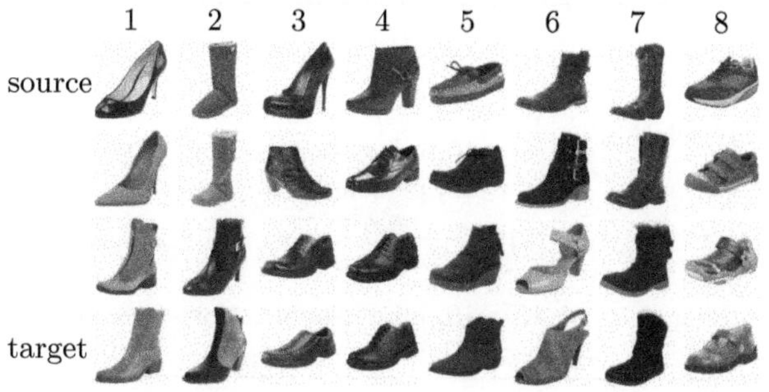

Figure 6: Navigating to distant products: each *column* shows a low-cost path between two objects such that adjacent products in the path are visually consistent, even when the end points are not.

Figure 7: A 2-dimensional embedding of a small sample of Boys clothing images ('also viewed' data).

the increase from $K = 10$ to $K = 100$ uniformly improves performance. Interestingly, the performance on compliments vs. substitutes is approximately the same. The extent to which the $K = 100$ results improve upon the WNN results may be seen as an indication of the degree to which visual similarity between images fails to capture a more complex human visual notion of which objects might be seen as being substitutes or compliments for each other. This distinction is smallest for 'Books' and greatest for 'Clothing Shoes and Jewelery' as might be expected.

We have no ground truth relating the true human visual preference for pairs of objects, of course, and thus evaluate above against our dataset. This has the disadvantage that the dataset contains all of the Amazon recommendations, rather than just those based on decisions made by humans on the basis of object appearance. This means that in addition to documenting the performance of the proposed method, the results may also be taken to indicate the extent to which visual factors impact upon the decisions of Amazon customers. The comparison across categories is particularly interesting. It is to be expected that appearance would be a significant factor in Clothing decisions, but it was not expected that they would be a factor in the purchase of Books. One possible interpretation of this effect might be that customers have preferences for particular genres of books and that individual genres have characteristic styles of covers.

4.2 Personalized recommendations

Finally we evaluate the ability of our model to personalize co-purchasing recommendations to individual users, that is we examine the effect of the user personalization term in (eqs. 6 and 7). Here we do not use the graphs from Tables 3 and 4, since those are 'population level' graphs which are not annotated in terms of the individual users who co-purchased and co-browsed each pair of products. Instead for this task we build a dataset of co-purchases from products that users have *reviewed*. That is, we build a dataset of tuples of the form (i,j,u) for pairs of products i and j that were purchased by user u. We train on users with at least 20 purchases, and randomly sample 50 co-purchases and 50 non-co-purchases from each user in order to build a balanced dataset. Results are shown in Table 5; here we see that the addition of a user personalization term yields a small but significant improvement when predicting co-purchases (similar results on other categories withheld for brevity).

5. VISUALIZING STYLE SPACE

Recall that each image is projected into 'style-space' by the transformation $\mathbf{s}_i = \mathbf{x}_i\mathbf{Y}$, and note that the fact that it is based on pairwise distances alone means that the embedding is invariant under isomorphism. That is, applying rotations, translations, or reflections to $\mathbf{s}_i$ and $\mathbf{s}_j$ will preserve their distance in (eq. 5). In light of these factors we perform k-means clustering on the K dimensional embedded coordinates of the data in order to visualize the effect of the embedding.

Figure 3 shows images whose projections are close to the centers of a set of selected representative clusters for Men's

Category	method	accuracy
Men's clothing	CT	84.8%
	WNN	84.3%
	$K = 10$, no personalization	90.9%
	$K = 10$, personalized	93.2%
Women's clothing	CT	80.5%
	WNN	80.8%
	$K = 10$, no personalization	87.6%
	$K = 10$, personalized	89.1%

Table 5: Performance of our model at predicting copurchases with a user personalization term (eqs. 6 and 7).

and Women's clothing (using a model trained on the 'also viewed' graph with $K = 100$). Naturally items cluster around colors and shapes (e.g. shoes, t-shirts, tank tops, watches, jewelery), but more subtle characterizations exist as well. For instance, leather boots are separated from ugg (that is sheep skin) boots, despite the fact that the visual differences are subtle. This is presumably because these items are preferred by different sets of Amazon users. Watches cluster into different color profiles, face shapes, and digital versus analogue. Other clusters cross multiple categories, for instance we find clusters of highly-colorful items, items containing love hearts, and items containing animals. Figure 4 shows a set of images which project to locations that span a cluster.

Although performance is admittedly not outstanding for a category such as books, it is somewhat surprising that an accuracy of even 70% can be achieved when predicting book co-purchases. Figure 5 visualizes a few examples of style-space clusters derived from Books data. Here it seems that there is at least some meaningful information in the cover of a book to predict which products might be purchased together—children's books, self-help books, romance novels, and comics (for example) all seem to have characteristic visual features which are identified by our model.

In Figure 6 we show how our model can be used to navigate between related items—here we randomly select two items that are unlikely to be co-browsed, and find a low cost path between them as measured by our learned distance measure. Subjectively, the model identifies visually smooth transitions between the source and the target items.

Figure 7 provides a visualization of the embedding of Boys clothing achieved by setting $K = 2$ (on co-browsing data). Sporting shoes drift smoothly toward slippers and sandals, and underwear drifts gradually toward shirts and coats.

6. GENERATING RECOMMENDATIONS

We here demonstrate that the proposed model can be used to generate recommendations that might be useful to a user of a web store. Given a query item (e.g. a product a user is currently browsing, or has just purchased), our goal is to recommend a selection of other items that might complement it. For example, if a user is browsing pants, we might want to recommend a shirt, shoes, or accessories that belong to the same style.

Here, Amazon's rich and detailed category hierarchy can help us. For categories such as women's or men's clothing, we might define an 'outfit' as a combination of pants, a top, shoes, and an accessory (we do this for the sake of demonstration, though far more complex combinations are possible—our category tree for clothing alone has hundreds of nodes). Then, given a query item our goal is simply to select items from each of these categories that are most likely to be connected based on their visual style.

Figure 8: Outfits generated by our algorithm (Women's outfits at left; Men's outfits at right). The first column shows a 'query' item that is randomly selected from the product catalogue. The right three columns match the query item with a top, pants, shoes, and an accessory, (minus whichever category contains the query item).

Specifically, given a query item $\mathbf{x}_q$, for each category $\mathcal{C}$ (represented as a set of item indices), we generate recommendations according to

$$\underset{j \in \mathcal{C}}{\text{argmax}}\, P_{\mathbf{Y}}(r_{qj} \in \mathcal{R}), \tag{10}$$

i.e., the minimum distance according to our measure (eq. 4) amongst objects belonging to the desired category. Examples of such recommendations are shown in Figures 1 and 8, with randomly chosen queries from women's and men's clothing. Generally speaking the model produces apparently reasonable recommendations, with clothes in each category usually being of a consistent style.

7. OUTFITS IN THE WILD

An alternate application of the model is to make assessments about outfits (or otherwise combinations of items) that we observe 'in the wild'. That is, to the extent that the tastes and preferences of Amazon customers reflect the zeitgeist of society at large, this can be seen as a measurement of whether a candidate outfit is well coordinated visually.

To assess this possibility, we have built two small datasets of real outfits, one consisting of twenty-five outfits worn by the hosts of *Top Gear* (Jeremy Clarkson, Richard Hammond, and James May), and another consisting of seventeen 'before' and 'after' pairs of outfits from participants on the television show *What Not to Wear* (US seasons 9 and 10). For each outfit, we cropped each clothing item from the image, and then used *Google*'s reverse image search to identify images of similar items (examples are shown in Figure 9).

Figure 9: Least (top) and most (bottom) coordinated outfits from our Top Gear dataset. Richard Hammond's outfits typically have low coordination, James May's have high coordination, and Jeremy Clarkson straddles both ends of the coordination spectrum. Pairwise distances are normalized by the number of components in the outfit so that there is no bias towards outfits with fewer/more components.

Next we rank outfits according to the average log-likelihood of their pairs of components being related using a model trained on Men's/Women's co-purchases (we take the average so that there is no bias toward outfits with more or fewer components). All outfits have at least two items.[7] Figure 9 shows the most and least coordinated outfits on *Top Gear*; here we find considerable separation between the level of coordination for each presenter; Richard Hammond is typically the least coordinated, James May the most, while Jeremy Clarkson wears a combination of highly coordinated and highly uncoordinated outfits.

A slightly more quantitative evaluation comes from the television show *What Not to Wear*: here participants receive an 'outfit makeover', hopefully meaning that their made-over outfit is more coordinated than the original. Examples of participants before and after their makeover, along with the change in log likelihood are shown in Figure 10. Indeed we find that made-over outfits have a higher log likelihood in 12 of the 17 cases we observed ($p \simeq 7\%$; log-likelihoods are normalized to correct any potential bias due to the number of components in the outfit). This is an important result, as it provides external (albeit small) validation of the learned model which is independent of our dataset.

8. CONCLUSION

We have shown that it is possible to model the human notion of what is visually related by investigation of a suitably large dataset, even where that information is somewhat tangentially contained therein. We have also demonstrated that the proposed method is capable of modeling a variety of visual relationships beyond simple visual similarity. Perhaps what distinguishes our method most is thus its ability to model what makes items *complementary*. To our knowledge this is the first attempt to model human preference for the appearance of one object given that of another in terms of more than just the visual similarity between the two. It is almost certainly the first time that it has been attempted directly and at this scale.

We also proposed visual and relational recommender systems as a potential problem of interest to the information retrieval community, and provided a large dataset for their training and evaluation. In the process we managed to figure out what not to wear, how to judge a book by its cover, and to show that James May is more fashionable than Richard Hammond.

Acknowledgements. This research was supported by the Data 2 Decisions Cooperative Research Centre, and the Australian Research Council Discovery Projects funding scheme DP140102270.

[7]Our measure of coordination is thus undefined for a subject wearing only a single item, though in general such an outfit would be a poor fashion choice in the opinion of the authors.

References

[1] G. Adomavicius and A. Tuzhilin. Toward the next generation of recommender systems: A survey of the state-of-the-art and possible extensions. *TKDD*, 2005.

[2] G. Carneiro, A. B. Chan, P. J. Moreno, and N. Vasconcelos. Supervised learning of semantic classes for image annotation and retrieval. *IEEE Trans. on PAMI*, 2007.

[3] W. Chu and S.-T. Park. Personalized recommendation on dynamic content using predictive bilinear models. In *WWW*, 2009.

[4] M. Der and L. Saul. Latent coincidence analysis: A hidden variable model for distance metric learning. In *NIPS*, 2012.

[5] W. Di, C. Wah, A. Bhardwaj, R. Piramuthu, and N. Sundaresan. Style finder: Fine-grained clothing style detection and retrieval. In *CVPR Workshops*, 2013.

[6] C. Doersch, S. Singh, A. Gupta, J. Sivic, and A. A. Efros. What makes paris look like paris? *SIGGRAPH*, 2012.

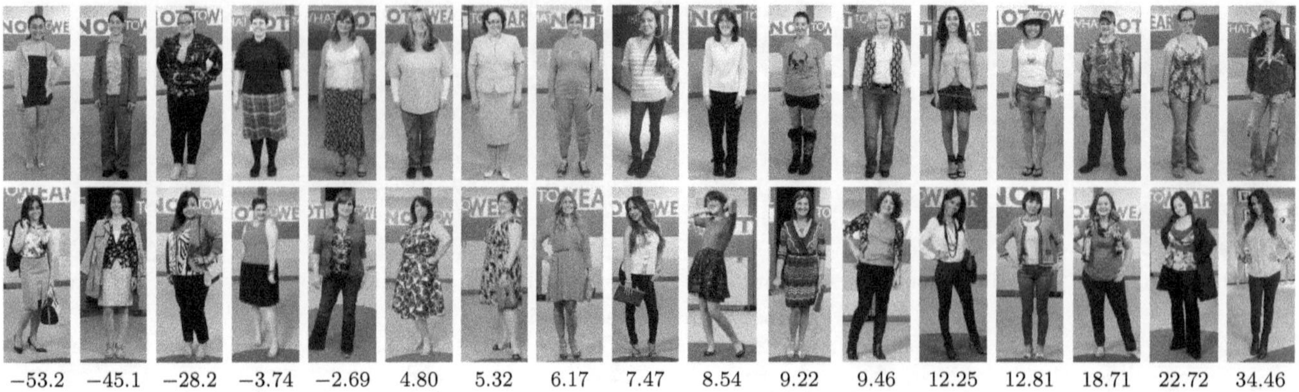

Figure 10: Contestants in *What Not to Wear*. Original outfits (top), 'made-over' outfits (bottom), and the change in log-likelihood (δ) between the components of the old and the new outfits (positive δ denotes an increase in coordination).

[7] J. Hays and A. A. Efros. Im2gps: estimating geographic information from a single image. In *CVPR*, 2008.

[8] M. D. Hoffman, D. M. Blei, and F. Bach. Online learning for latent dirichlet allocation. In *In NIPS*, 2010.

[9] D. J. Hu, R. Hall, and J. Attenberg. Style in the long tail: Discovering unique interests with latent variable models in large scale social e-commerce. In *KDD*, 2014.

[10] V. Jagadeesh, R. Piramuthu, A. Bhardwaj, W. Di, and N. Sundaresan. Large scale visual recommendations from street fashion images. *arXiv:1401.1778*, 2014.

[11] Y. Jia, E. Shelhamer, J. Donahue, S. Karayev, J. Long, R. Girshick, S. Guadarrama, and T. Darrell. Caffe: Convolutional architecture for fast feature embedding. *arXiv:1408.5093*, 2014.

[12] X. Jin, J. Luo, J. Yu, G. Wang, D. Joshi, and J. Han. Reinforced similarity integration in image-rich information networks. *IEEE Trans. on KDE*, 2013.

[13] Y. Kalantidis, L. Kennedy, and L.-J. Li. Getting the look: Clothing recognition and segmentation for automatic product suggestions in everyday photos. In *ICMR*, 2013.

[14] M. H. Kiapour, K. Yamaguchi, A. C. Berg, and T. L. Berg. Hipster wars: Discovering elements of fashion styles. In *ECCV*. 2014.

[15] W. Kong, W.-J. Li, and M. Guo. Manhattan hashing for large-scale image retrieval. In *SIGIR*, 2012.

[16] Y. Koren and R. Bell. Advances in collaborative filtering. In *Recommender Systems Handbook*. Springer, 2011.

[17] Y. Koren, R. Bell, and C. Volinsky. Matrix factorization techniques for recommender systems. *Computer*, 2009.

[18] M. S. Lew, N. Sebe, C. Djeraba, and R. Jain. Content-based multimedia information retrieval: State of the art and challenges. *ACM TOMCCAP*, 2006.

[19] G. Linden, B. Smith, and J. York. Amazon.com recommendations: Item-to-item collaborative filtering. *IEEE Internet Computing*, 2003.

[20] S. Liu, J. Feng, Z. Song, T. Zhang, H. Lu, C. Xu, and S. Yan. Hi, magic closet, tell me what to wear! In *ACM Conference on Multimedia*, 2012.

[21] Y. Liu, W. Wang, B. Lévy, F. Sun, D.-M. Yan, L. Lu, and C. Yang. On centroidal Voronoi tessellation – energy smoothness and fast computation. *ACM Trans. on Graphics*, 2009.

[22] A. Makadia, V. Pavlovic, and S. Kumar. A new baseline for image annotation. In *ECCV*. 2008.

[23] A. Mas-Colell, M. Whinston, and J. Green. *Microeconomic Theory*. Oxford University Press, 1995.

[24] P. Melville, R. J. Mooney, and R. Nagarajan. Content-boosted collaborative filtering for improved recommendations. In *AAAI*, 2002.

[25] A. C. Murillo, I. S. Kwak, L. Bourdev, D. Kriegman, and S. Belongie. Urban tribes: Analyzing group photos from a social perspective. In *CVPR Workshops*, 2012.

[26] Y. Pan, T. Yao, T. Mei, L. Houqiang, C.-W. Ngo, and Y. Rui. Click-through-based cross-view learning for image search. In *SIGIR*, 2014.

[27] P. Peng, L. Shou, K. Chen, G. Chen, and S. Wu. The knowing camera 2: Recognizing and annotating places-of-interest in smartphone photos. In *SIGIR*, 2014.

[28] A. Schein, A. Popescul, L. Ungar, and D. Pennock. Methods and metrics for cold-start recommendations. In *SIGIR*, 2002.

[29] B.-S. Seah, S. Bhowmick, and A. Sun. Prism: Concept-preserving social image search results summarization. In *SIGIR*, 2014.

[30] A. Shrivastava, T. Malisiewicz, A. Gupta, and A. A. Efros. Data-driven visual similarity for cross-domain image matching. *ACM Trans. on Graphics*, 2011.

[31] M. Slaney, K. Weinberger, and W. White. Learning a metric for music similarity. In *International Conference of Music Information Retrieval*, 2008.

[32] A. W. Smeulders, M. Worring, S. Santini, A. Gupta, and R. Jain. Content-based image retrieval at the end of the early years. *IEEE Trans. on PAMI*, 2000.

[33] D. Spina and J. Gonzalo. Learning similarity functions for topic detection in online reputation monitoring. In *SIGIR*, 2014.

[34] A. Torralba, R. Fergus, and W. T. Freeman. 80 million tiny images: A large data set for nonparametric object and scene recognition. *IEEE Trans. on PAMI*, 2008.

[35] L. Torresani and K. chih Lee. Large margin component analysis. In *NIPS*, 2007.

[36] M. Trevisiol, L. Chiarandini, L. Maria Aiello, and A. Jaimes. Image ranking based on user browsing behavior. In *SIGIR*, 2012.

[37] C.-C. Wu, T. Mei, W. Hsu, and Y. Rui. Learning to personalize trending image search suggestion. In *SIGIR*, 2014.

[38] H. Xia, P. Wu, S. Hoi, and R. Jin. Boosting multi-kernel locality-sensitive hashing for scalable image retrieval. In *SIGIR*, 2012.

[39] K. Xu, H. Li, H. Zhang, D. Cohen-Or, Y. Xiong, and Z.-Q. Cheng. Style-content separation by anisotropic part scales. *ACM Trans. on Graphics*, 2010.

[40] K. Yamaguchi, M. H. Kiapour, and T. L. Berg. Paper doll parsing: Retrieving similar styles to parse clothing items. In *ICCV*, 2013.

[41] K. Zhou, S.-H. Yang, and H. Zha. Functional matrix factorizations for cold-start recommendation. In *SIGIR*, 2011.

Semi-supervised Hashing with Semantic Confidence for Large Scale Visual Search*

Yingwei Pan †, Ting Yao ‡, Houqiang Li †, Chong-Wah Ngo #, Tao Mei ‡
† University of Science and Technology of China, Hefei, China
‡ Microsoft Research, Beijing, China
# City University of Hong Kong, Kowloon, Hong Kong
panyw.ustc@gmail.com, {tiyao, tmei}@microsoft.com;
lihq@ustc.edu.cn; cscwngo@cityu.edu.hk

ABSTRACT

Similarity search is one of the fundamental problems for large scale multimedia applications. Hashing techniques, as one popular strategy, have been intensively investigated owing to the speed and memory efficiency. Recent research has shown that leveraging supervised information can lead to high quality hashing. However, most existing supervised methods learn hashing function by treating each training example equally while ignoring the different semantic degree related to the label, i.e. semantic confidence, of different examples.

In this paper, we propose a novel semi-supervised hashing framework by leveraging semantic confidence. Specifically, a confidence factor is first assigned to each example by neighbor voting and click count in the scenarios with label and click-through data, respectively. Then, the factor is incorporated into the pairwise and triplet relationship learning for hashing. Furthermore, the two learnt relationships are seamlessly encoded into semi-supervised hashing methods with pairwise and listwise supervision respectively, which are formulated as minimizing empirical error on the labeled data while maximizing the variance of hash bits or minimizing quantization loss over both the labeled and unlabeled data. In addition, the kernelized variant of semi-supervised hashing is also presented. We have conducted experiments on both CIFAR-10 (with label) and Clickture (with click data) image benchmarks (up to one million image examples), demonstrating that our approaches outperform the state-of-the-art hashing techniques.

Categories and Subject Descriptors

H.3.3 [**Information Storage and Retrieval**]: Information Search and Retrieval—*Retrieval models*

* This work was performed when Yingwei Pan was visiting Microsoft Research as a research intern.

SIGIR'15, August 09 - 13, 2015, Santiago, Chile.

DOI: http://dx.doi.org/10.1145/2766462.2767725.

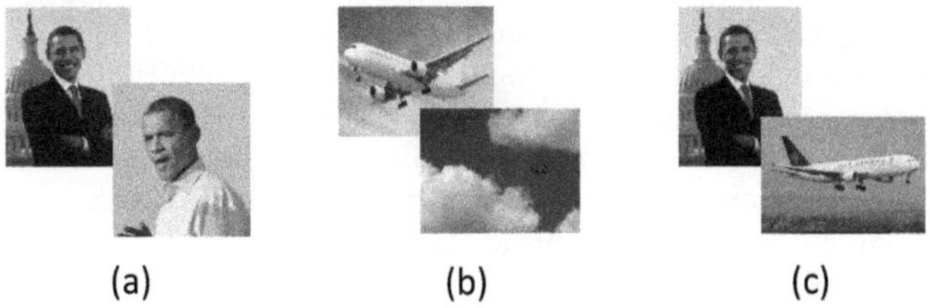

Figure 1: Three exemplary image pairs. (a) Both images are highly relevant to the common label "Barack Obama;" (b) One is highly relevant and the other is weakly relevant to the label "Airplane;" (c) One is highly relevant to the label "Barack Obama," and the other is highly relevant to the label "Airplane."

General Terms

Algorithms, Performance, Experimentation.

Keywords

Hashing; similarity learning; neighbor voting; semi-supervised hashing; click-through data

1. INTRODUCTION

The rapid development of Web 2.0 technologies has led to the surge of research activities in large scale visual search. One fundamental research problem is similarity search, i.e., nearest neighbor search, which attempts to identify similar instances according to a query example. The need to search for millions of visual examples in a high-dimensional feature space, however, makes the task computationally expensive and thus challenging.

Hashing techniques [23][26][29], one direction of the most well-known Approximate Nearest Neighbor (ANN) search methods, have received intensive research attention for its great efficiency in gigantic data. The basic idea of hashing is to design a compact binary code in a low-dimensional space for each example, making the Hamming distances on similar examples minimized and simultaneously maximized on dissimilar examples. In the similarity search process, the query example is usually first transformed to its hashing code. Then, the Hamming distances between the hash codes of instances in the retrieved database and the query example are computed. The instances within small Hamming distances are returned. Through hashing, the storage is substantially reduced as the representations of examples are highly compressed with a low-dimensional binary space and the Hamming distance between two hash codes can be implemented by bitwise XOR operation, leading to a very efficient searching process.

While existing hashing approaches are promising to retrieve neighbors, each example is treated equally during the learning of hash function. Importantly, we argue that hashing would obtain higher search accuracy if the semantic degree to the label of each example, i.e., semantic confidence, is taken into account. Figure 1 shows three exemplary image pairs. Conventional supervised hashing methods use to learn hash function to make the corresponding binary codes similar for images annotated by the common label while dissimilar for those with different labels. However, take the two pairs in Figure 1 (a) and (b) as examples, although each pair is relevant to an individual label, the two images in (a) are all highly relevant and thus their hashing code should be closer in proximity than the image pair in (b). Meanwhile, for images that share different labels in Figure 1 (c), their hash codes should be made as dissimilar as possible, especially when they are highly relevant to their respective labels.

By encoding the semantic confidence into hash function learning, this paper presents a novel and principled semi-supervised hashing framework for large scale image search, as illustrated in Figure 2. The semantic confidence is formulated by devising a confidence factor that evaluates the semantic relatedness of an example to a label. We consider two kinds of confidence factors computed based upon image neighbor voting and click count respectively. By assuming the availability of labeled examples, the former first builds a similarity graph over all images of a given label followed by assigning each image a confidence score based on the number of its out-link neighbors. The latter considers click-through data and relates the confidence score directly to the number of click counts an image receives. Based on the semantic confidence, the pairwise and triplet relationships among image examples are further developed and incorporated into the hash function learning in standard (with pairwise supervision) and ranking (with listwise supervision) semi-supervised hashing framework, respectively. In addition, to accommodate linearly inseparable data, a kernel formulation is employed on ranking semi-supervised hashing. After the hash function learning, each image is mapped to compact binary codes. For any query image, the image search list will be returned by sorting their Hamming distances with the query.

In summary, this paper makes the following contributions:

- Instead of assuming each image contributes equally to learning, we explore the learning of a hash function by taking into account the semantic degree to which an image is associated with a label, on the basis that the degree can be quantified as a numeric score (or semantic confidence factor). To the best of knowledge, this paper represents the first effort towards this target.

- By considering two different ways of devising semantic confidences, we propose a general hashing framework that facilitates the exploration of pairwise and triplet image relationships for semi-supervised hashing, ranking-based semi-supervised hashing, and its kernelized variant respectively.

- An extensive set of experiments on two real world image datasets, i.e., CIFAR-10 sampled from 80-million tiny images collection with labels and Clickture collected from one-year click log from a commercial image search engine, to demonstrate the advantages of the proposed methods over several state-of-the-art hashing techniques.

The remaining sections are organized as follows. Section 2 briefly surveys several popular hashing methods. Section 3 presents the semantic confidence, the pairwise and triplet relationships with semantic confidence, while Section 4 further details the utilization of the two relationships in semi-supervised hashing framework. Section 5 provides empirical evaluations, followed by the discussion and conclusions in Section 6.

2. RELATED WORK

We briefly group the related works into three categories: unsupervised, supervised, and semi-supervised hashing.

2.1 Unsupervised Hashing

Unsupervised hashing refers to the setting when the label information is not available. Locality Sensitive Hashing (LSH) [3] is one of the most popular unsupervised hashing methods, which simply uses random linear projections to construct hash functions. This method was continuously expanded to Kernelized and Multi-Kernel Locality Sensitive Hashing [11][31]. Another effective method called Iterative Quantization (ITQ) [4] was suggested for better quantization rather than random projections. The Spectral Hashing (SH) in [30] was proposed to design compact binary codes by preserving the similarity between samples, which can be viewed as an extension of spectral clustering [33]. Recently, the graph based hashing technique namely Anchor Graph Hashing (AGH) was proposed by Liu *et al.* in [14], which can leverage low-dimensional manifold structure of data to design efficient hash codes. Later in [12], Discrete Graph Hashing (DGH) was proposed to generate high-quality codes by preserving the neighborhood structure of massive data in a discrete code space.

2.2 Supervised Hashing

In contrast, when the label information is available, we refer to the problem as supervised hashing. For example, Linear Discriminant Analysis Hashing (LDAH) [24] can tackle supervision via easy optimization. The deep neural network stacked with Restricted Boltzman Machine (RBM) [6] was applied to learn binary hash codes in [23]. To utilize the pairwise supervision information in the hash function learning, Kernel-Based Supervised Hashing (KSH) proposed in [13] used pairwise relationship between samples to achieve high quality hashing. Binary Reconstructive Embedding (BRE) [10] was proposed to learn hash functions by minimizing the reconstructed error between the metric space and Hamming space. Minimal Loss Hashing (MLH) was proposed in [16] which aims to learn similarity-preserving binary codes by using the pairwise relationship. Moreover, there are also several works using the ranking order information to design hash functions. Ranking-based Supervised Hashing (RSH) [27] was proposed to leverage listwise supervision into the hash function learning framework. Besides RSH, the tree-based method [20] and a hamming metric learning framework presented in [17] also aim to preserve the ranking orders.

In addition, several cross-view hashing methods have been proposed as well. The Canonical Correlation Analysis with

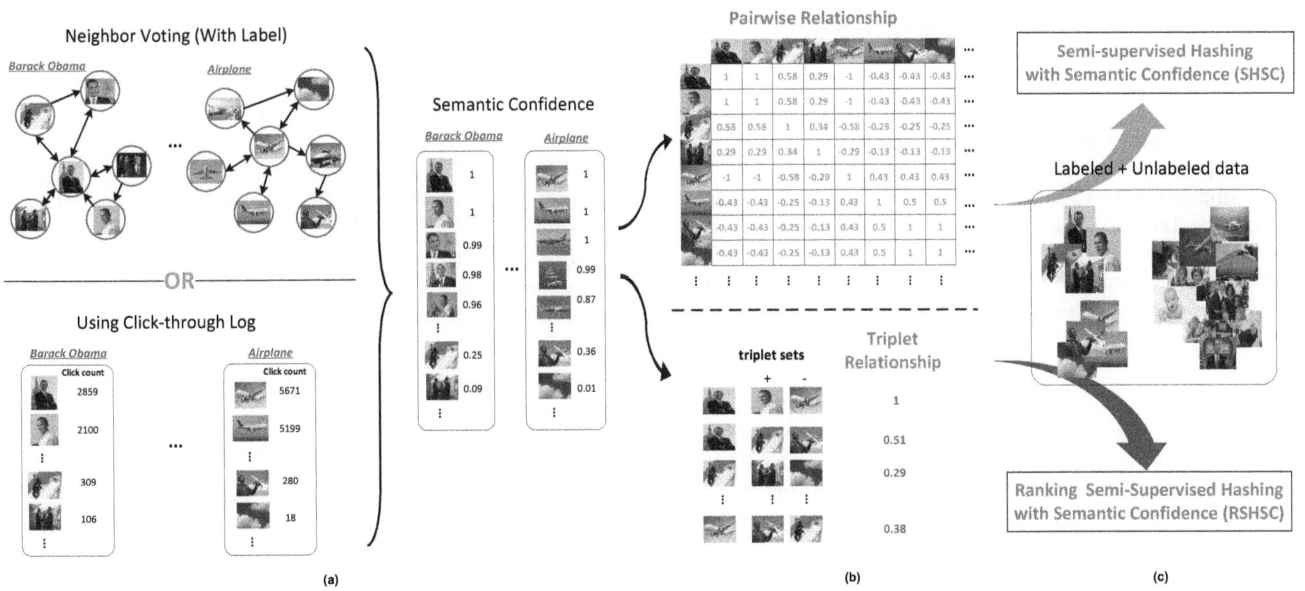

Figure 2: Semi-supervised hashing with semantic confidence. (a) Semantic confidence measurement of each image example: on the labeled data, the semantic confidence is based on the number of out-link neighbors of each image in the similarity graph built on all images of each label. With the click-through data, click count of an image is considered as an indicator of its semantic confidence in answering the query. (b) Pairwise and Triplet Relationship with semantic confidence: pairwise and triplet relationship is derived by exploiting semantic confidence of each example for hashing with pairwise and listwise supervision, respectively. (c) Semi-supervised hashing: the learnt pairwise and triplet relationship is further incorporated into the hash function learning in standard and ranking semi-supervised hashing framework, respectively. For better viewing, please see original color pdf file.

Iterative Quantization (CCA-ITQ) was proposed in [4] to learn the hash codes from the content features and tags. In [21], Rastegari *et al.* proposed Predictable Dual-View Hashing (PDH) to create a cross-view hamming space by embedding proximity of data samples in the original spaces.

2.3 Semi-supervised Hashing

Semi-supervised hashing methods have also been proposed. One representative work is Semi-Supervised Hashing (SSH) [26] which utilizes pairwise information on labeled samples to preserve semantic similarity while remaining robust to overfitting. Semi-Supervised Discriminant Hashing (SSDH) can learn hash codes based on Fisher's discriminant analysis to maximize the separability between labeled data in different classes while the unlabeled data are used for regularization [8]. In another work [15], the label-regularized maximum margin partition (LAMP) method was proposed to enhance hashing quality by using kernel-based similarity and additional pairwise constraints as side information. Semi-Supervised Tag Hashing (SSTH) proposed in [28] can fully incorporate tag information into hash function learning by exploring the correlation between tags and hashing bits.

In short, our approach belongs to semi-supervised hashing. While these aforementioned semi-supervised hashing methods focus on the regularization of both labeled and unlabeled examples from different means, they treat each image equally and hence the role that each image should play and contribute in learning is overlooked. Our work in this paper contributes by exploring this issue through not only devising the rigorous ways of measuring semantic confidences, but also how the hash function can be more reliably learnt by exploring the semantic confidence.

3. LEARNING RELATIONSHIP WITH SEMANTIC CONFIDENCE

In this section, we first define the semantic confidence measurement for each image example, i.e. confidence factor, in the context of scenarios with label and click-through data, respectively. Then, pairwise and triplet relationships with semantic confidence is further devised to be encoded into hash function learning in semi-supervised hashing.

3.1 Confidence Factor

Given a label t, let $X = \{x_1, x_2, \cdots, x_L\}$ be the set of all images annotated by the label t, where x_i represents the ith image in X and its image feature vector is denoted as $\mathbf{v}_i$. Let $N_k(i)$ be the k-nearest neighbor set of the ith image. A directed graph is then built where nodes are all images in X and there is an edge between the ith and j^{th} image if and only if the ith image appears in $N_k(j)$. Deriving from the idea of neighbor voting [34], the semantic confidence of the ith image is reflected by the number of the image appearing in the neighbors of other images in the graph, i.e., the number of out-link neighbors. Specifically, the confidence factor is generally formulated as

$$s_i = \frac{(o_i^+)^\gamma}{\max_j (o_j^+)^\gamma}, \tag{1}$$

where (o_i^+) is the number of out-link neighbors of the ith image and it is normalized by the maximum number of out-link neighbors of all images in the graph. γ is used to control the impact of the number of out-link neighbors. The rationale underlying this formula is that, if the ith image always appears in the k-nearest neighbors of other images, the ith

image is similar to the other images of the category and thus should be more semantically related to this category.

In the scenario with click-through data, we view the click count of an image in response to a query (category) as an indicator of their relevance [19]. As most image search engines display results as thumbnails, the users can view the entire image before clicking on it. As such, the users predominantly tend to click on images that are relevant to the query. Therefore, click count can be served as a reliable connection between queries and images. Then, the confidence factor can be re-expressed as

$$s_i = \frac{(c_i)^\gamma}{\max_j (c_j)^\gamma}, \tag{2}$$

where c_i is the click count of the ith image in response to the query and $\max_j(c_j)$ is the maximum click count of the returned images for the query. Particularly, the higher the click count, the more the relevance between the image and the query.

3.2 Pairwise Relationship with Semantic Confidence

Most of the existing learning to hash methods are to generate hashing code to satisfy pairwise supervision, i.e., making the Hamming distance minimized on similar pairs while maximized on dissimilar pairs. As a result, pairwise relationship is first developed with semantic confidence of each example. Let $\mathcal{M}$ and $\mathcal{C}$ be the set of neighbor pairs and non-neighbor pairs, respectively. Specifically, a pair $(\mathbf{v}_i, \mathbf{v}_j) \in \mathcal{M}$ is denoted as a neighbor pair in which $\mathbf{v}_i$ and $\mathbf{v}_j$ are from the same category or in answering the common query. Similarly, a pair $(\mathbf{v}_i, \mathbf{v}_j) \in \mathcal{C}$ is called as a non-neighbor pair if $\mathbf{v}_i$ and $\mathbf{v}_j$ are from the different category or in response to the different query. By incorporating the semantic confidence, the pairwise relationship is defined as

$$S_P(\mathbf{v}_i, \mathbf{v}_j) = \begin{cases} \sqrt{s_i s_j} e^{-|s_i - s_j|}, & \text{if } (\mathbf{v}_i, \mathbf{v}_j) \in \mathcal{M} \\ -\sqrt{s_i s_j} e^{-|s_i + s_j - 2|}, & \text{if } (\mathbf{v}_i, \mathbf{v}_j) \in \mathcal{C} \end{cases}, \tag{3}$$

where s_i and s_j are the confidence factor for the ith and j^{th} image, respectively.

The spirit of pairwise relationship with semantic confidence is to make the neighbor pair in close proximity if the two examples of the pair both have high confidence factors, while weakening the relationship of the neighbor pair if any one in the pair has a low confidence. On the other hand, if the two examples in a non-neighbor pair are both with high confidence to each category, the pair will receive a very dissimilar relationship strengthened by their semantic confidences.

3.3 Triplet Relationship with Semantic Confidence

To further leverage the listwise supervision [27] which has been employed to design more effective hash functions in search tasks, semantic confidence is then encoded into triplet relationship learning. Denote $\mathcal{T}$ as the set of triplets, and each triplet as $(\mathbf{v}_i, \mathbf{v}_j^+, \mathbf{v}_k^-)$. In the case when labels are available, $\mathbf{v}_i$ refers to a query image, $\mathbf{v}_j^+$ $(\mathbf{v}_k^-)$ as the image with the same (different) category as $\mathbf{v}_i$. For click data, $\mathbf{v}_j^+$ refers to the clicked image of the same query on image $\mathbf{v}_i$, and $\mathbf{v}_k^-$ is a clicked image of another query different from that of $\mathbf{v}_i$. For any triplet, we can derive the relationship with semantic confidence as

$$S_T(\mathbf{v}_i, \mathbf{v}_j^+, \mathbf{v}_k^-) = \frac{1}{2}\left(S_P(\mathbf{v}_i, \mathbf{v}_j^+) - S_P(\mathbf{v}_i, \mathbf{v}_k^-)\right), \tag{4}$$

where $S_P(\mathbf{v}_i, \mathbf{v}_j^+)$ and $S_P(\mathbf{v}_i, \mathbf{v}_k^-)$ are the pairwise relationship defined in Section 3.2. It is straightforward to see that the triplet $(\mathbf{v}_i, \mathbf{v}_j^+, \mathbf{v}_k^-)$ will be associated with a strong relationship when the image $\mathbf{v}_j^+$ is close to the query image $\mathbf{v}_i$, and simultaneously the image $\mathbf{v}_k^-$ holds a quite dissimilar relationship with the image $\mathbf{v}_i$.

4. SEMI-SUPERVISED HASHING

In this section, we will present our semi-supervised hashing framework under the umbrella of encoding the learnt relationships with semantic confidence to three primary aspects: semi-supervised hashing by exploiting pairwise relationship with semantic confidence, ranking semi-supervised hashing by leveraging triplet relationship with semantic confidence and its kernelized variant.

Suppose there are n images in the whole set, represented as: $V = \{\mathbf{v}_i | i = 1, \cdots, n\}$, where $\mathbf{v}_i \in \mathbb{R}^D$ represents the image feature vector and $\mathbf{V} = \{\mathbf{v}_1, \mathbf{v}_2, \ldots, \mathbf{v}_n\} \in \mathbb{R}^{D \times n}$ is the feature matrix of the image set. Similarly, assume there are L $(L < n)$ labeled images and the feature matrix of the labeled images are denoted as $\mathbf{V}_l \in \mathbb{R}^{D \times L}$. Note that the feature matrices are normalized to zero-centered. Our goal is to map $\mathbf{V} \in \mathbb{R}^{D \times n}$ to a compact binary code representation $\mathbf{B} \in \{-1, 1\}^{K \times n}$ in a low-dimensional Hamming space, where K is the code length.

4.1 Semi-supervised Hashing with Semantic Confidence (SHSC)

Here we use the linear formulation to design the hashing functions. For each bit $k = 1, \ldots, K$, its hash function is defined as

$$h_k(\mathbf{v}_i) = sgn(\mathbf{w}_k \cdot \mathbf{v}_i), \tag{5}$$

where $\mathbf{w}_k \in \mathbb{R}^D$ is the coefficient vector and $sgn(\bullet)$ is the signum function. Let $\mathbf{W} = \{\mathbf{w}_1, \mathbf{w}_2, \ldots, \mathbf{w}_K\}^\top \in \mathbb{R}^{K \times D}$ be the projection matrix, we can get the K-bit binary code representation $\mathbf{B}$ of an image set $\mathbf{V}$ as

$$\mathbf{B} = sgn(\mathbf{WV}). \tag{6}$$

Inspired by the idea of semi-supervised hashing [26], we propose the semi-supervised hashing with semantic confidence. The problem is formulated as simultaneously maximizing empirical accuracy on the labeled images and the variance of hash bits over both the labeled and unlabeled images, in which pairwise relationship with semantic confidence is encoded into the computation of empirical accuracy. Specifically, the empirical accuracy on the label images is defined as

$$\begin{aligned} J_1(\mathbf{W}) = \sum_k \Big(& \sum_{(\mathbf{v}_i, \mathbf{v}_j) \in \mathcal{M}} S_P(\mathbf{v}_i, \mathbf{v}_j) h_k(\mathbf{v}_i) h_k(\mathbf{v}_j) \\ & + \sum_{(\mathbf{v}_i, \mathbf{v}_j) \in \mathcal{C}} S_P(\mathbf{v}_i, \mathbf{v}_j) h_k(\mathbf{v}_i) h_k(\mathbf{v}_j) \Big), \end{aligned} \tag{7}$$

where $S_P(\mathbf{v}_i, \mathbf{v}_j)$ is the pairwise relationship with semantic confidence for pair $(\mathbf{v}_i, \mathbf{v}_j)$. By defining the pairwise relationship matrix $\mathbf{S} \in \mathbb{R}^{L \times L}$ on the labeled images $\mathbf{V}_l$ with its element $\mathbf{S}_{i,j} = S_p(\mathbf{v}_i, \mathbf{v}_j)$, the empirical accuracy $J_1(\mathbf{W})$ can be represented as

$$J_1(\mathbf{W}) = \frac{1}{2}\mathrm{tr}\left(sgn(\mathbf{W}\mathbf{V}_l)\ \mathbf{S}\ sgn(\mathbf{W}\mathbf{V}_l)^\top\right). \quad (8)$$

Through maximizing empirical accuracy on the labeled images, the hash codes will be in close proximity for neighboring pairs with high pairwise relationship, while very different for non-neighboring pairs especially when both samples are with high confidence to different category.

On the other hand, to generate hash codes in which each bit maximizes the information by generating a balanced partition of the data, the variance of hash bits should be also maximized. Here, the variance of hash bits over the labeled and unlabeled images is measured as

$$J_2(\mathbf{W}) = \frac{1}{2}\mathrm{tr}\left(\mathbf{W}\mathbf{V}(\mathbf{W}\mathbf{V})^\top\right). \quad (9)$$

The overall objective function integrates the empirical accuracy on the labeled images and the variance of hash bits over the labeled and unlabeled images. Hence we get the following optimization problem

$$\max_{\mathbf{W}} J_1(\mathbf{W}) + \mu J_2(\mathbf{W}) \quad s.t.\ \mathbf{W}\mathbf{W}^\top = \mathbf{I}, \quad (10)$$

where μ is the tradeoff parameter and the constraint $\mathbf{W}\mathbf{W}^\top = \mathbf{I}$ limits the hashing projection matrix to be orthogonal.

We use non-orthogonal projection learning [26] for the optimization, which relaxes the orthogonality constraint and solves the non-convex problem with matrix decomposition.

4.2 Ranking SHSC

To design more effective hash functions, we further incorporate the triplet relationship with semantic confidence into ranking semi-supervised hashing which represents the ranking information by a set of ranking triplets. The training of Ranking SHSC (RSHSC) is performed by minimizing both the triplet loss based on the labeled images and the quantization loss on the whole image set.

Formulation. For Ranking SHSC, we still use the linear form of hash functions as defined in Eq.(5). Formally, given an image pair $(\mathbf{v}_i, \mathbf{v}_j)$, we revise a distance function to measure the degree of hash code difference as

$$d(\mathbf{v}_i, \mathbf{v}_j) =$$
$$(sgn(\mathbf{W}\mathbf{v}_i) - sgn(\mathbf{W}\mathbf{v}_j))^\top (sgn(\mathbf{W}\mathbf{v}_i) - sgn(\mathbf{W}\mathbf{v}_j)). \quad (11)$$

The triplet loss on the labeled images $\mathbf{V}_l$ is defined as

$$J_1(\mathbf{W}) = \sum_{(\mathbf{v}_i, \mathbf{v}_j^+, \mathbf{v}_k^-) \in \mathcal{T}} S_T(\mathbf{v}_i, \mathbf{v}_j^+, \mathbf{v}_k^-) L(\mathbf{v}_i, \mathbf{v}_j^+, \mathbf{v}_k^-), \quad (12)$$
$$L(\mathbf{v}_i, \mathbf{v}_j^+, \mathbf{v}_k^-) = \max\left(0, d(\mathbf{v}_i, \mathbf{v}_j^+) - d(\mathbf{v}_i, \mathbf{v}_k^-) + 1\right),$$

where $S_T(\mathbf{v}_i, {\mathbf{v}_j}^+, {\mathbf{v}_k}^-)$ is the triplet relationship with semantic confidence consisting of the query image $\mathbf{v}_i$, an image ${\mathbf{v}_j}^+$ from the same category and an image ${\mathbf{v}_k}^-$ from a different category. Note that all the triplets in Eq.(12) are from the triplet sets $\mathcal{T}$ generated on labeled images $\mathbf{V}_l$. The triplet loss exploits the margin ranking loss [5][32] that is widely used in information retrieval weighted by the triplet relationship. By minimizing the triplet loss on the labeled images, the relative distance relationship for hash codes in hamming space is preserved under the listwise supervision. Specifically, for the triplet $(\mathbf{v}_i, {\mathbf{v}_j}^+, {\mathbf{v}_k}^-)$ with strong relationship, we aim to make the hash codes in close proximity for $\mathbf{v}_i$ and ${\mathbf{v}_j}^+$, and simultaneously get the very different bits for $\mathbf{v}_i$ and ${\mathbf{v}_k}^-$.

To better generate hash codes and avoid overfitting, we additionally incorporate another term by using all the labeled and unlabeled images, leading to a semi-supervised framework. Motivated by iterative quantization [4], the quantization loss is defined on the whole image set $\mathbf{V}$ as

$$J_2(\mathbf{W}) = \|\mathbf{B} - \mathbf{W}\mathbf{V}\|_F^2, \quad (13)$$

where $\mathbf{B} = sgn(\mathbf{W}\mathbf{V})$ and $\|\bullet\|_F$ denotes the Frobenius norm. Minimization of the quantization loss will preserve the original locality structure better in the generated hash codes.

The overall objective function for Ranking SHSC is comprised of the triplet loss in Eq.(12) and the quantization loss in Eq.(13). Hence we get the following optimization problem for our RSHSC:

$$\min_{\mathbf{W}} \sum_{(\mathbf{v}_i, \mathbf{v}_j^+, \mathbf{v}_k^-) \in \mathcal{T}} S_T(\mathbf{v}_i, \mathbf{v}_j^+, \mathbf{v}_k^-) L(\mathbf{v}_i, \mathbf{v}_j^+, \mathbf{v}_k^-)$$
$$+\alpha \|\mathbf{B} - \mathbf{W}\mathbf{V}\|_F^2 \quad s.t.\ \mathbf{W}\mathbf{W}^\top = \mathbf{I}, \quad (14)$$

where α is the tradeoff parameter and the constraint $\mathbf{W}\mathbf{W}^\top = \mathbf{I}$ forces the hashing projection matrix $\mathbf{W}$ to be orthogonal, making the bits of the generated hash codes uncorrelated to each other.

Optimization. The orthogonal constraints and the non-differentiable terms (i.e., $sgn(\bullet)$) in Eq.(14) make the optimization difficult to be solved. To address this problem, we first relax the overall objective function by replacing the signum function in Eq.(11) with its signed magnitude as suggested in [26][28]. With this relaxation, the distance function in Eq.(11) can be rewritten as

$$d(\mathbf{v}_i, \mathbf{v}_j) = (\mathbf{W}(\mathbf{v}_i - \mathbf{v}_j))^\top \mathbf{W}(\mathbf{v}_i - \mathbf{v}_j). \quad (15)$$

Thus, the triplet loss in Eq.(12) becomes differentiable.

Next, the orthogonal constraint $\mathbf{W}\mathbf{W}^\top = \mathbf{I}$ can be relaxed by appending the converted soft penalty term to the objective function. The penalty term is defined as

$$J_3(\mathbf{W}) = \left\|\mathbf{W}\mathbf{W}^\top - \mathbf{I}\right\|_F^2. \quad (16)$$

After the two relaxations, the overall objective function becomes

$$\min_{\mathbf{W}} \sum_{(\mathbf{v}_i, \mathbf{v}_j^+, \mathbf{v}_k^-) \in \mathcal{T}} S_T(\mathbf{v}_i, \mathbf{v}_j^+, \mathbf{v}_k^-) L(\mathbf{v}_i, \mathbf{v}_j^+, \mathbf{v}_k^-)$$
$$+\alpha \|\mathbf{B} - \mathbf{W}\mathbf{V}\|_F^2 + \beta \left\|\mathbf{W}\mathbf{W}^\top - \mathbf{I}\right\|_F^2, \quad (17)$$

where α and β are the tradeoff parameters.

To address the relaxed optimization problem in Eq.(17), the stochastic gradient descent is used for its efficiency and capability in dealing with highly scalable problems. Note that the quantization loss term in Eq.(13) cannot be relaxed by its signed magnitude directly, otherwise this quantization loss will go to 0, which is meaningless in practice. Similar to the common solution used in [4][28], in each iteration of the gradient descent procedure, we split the optimization process into two steps: 1) fix $\mathbf{W}$ and update $\mathbf{B} = sgn(\mathbf{W}\mathbf{V})$; 2) fix $\mathbf{B}$ and update $\mathbf{W}$ according to the gradient descent for the objective function. We alternate the process of updating $\mathbf{B}$ and $\mathbf{W}$ to find a locally optimal solution. The whole RSHSC algorithm is given in Algorithm 1.

Algorithm 1 Ranking Semi-supervised Hashing with Semantic Confidence (RSHSC)

```
Input: Training images V and labeled images V_l.
Generate a set of triplets T consisting of (v_i, v_j^+, v_k^-)
from the labeled images V_l.
Initialize the projection matrix W using a normal distribution with mean zero and standard deviation one.
Initialize the learning rate η, and two tradeoff parameters α and β.
for iter = 1 to T_max do
  Select a random triplet (v_i, v_j^+, v_k^-) from T.
  B = sgn(WV)
  W = W − η(−2α(B − WV)V^T + 2β(WW^T − I)W)
  L(v_i, v_j^+, v_k^-) = max(0, d(v_i, v_j^+) − d(v_i, v_k^-) + 1)
  if L(v_i, v_j^+, v_k^-) ≻ 0 then
    ∇L = 2W(v_i − v_j^+)(v_i − v_j^+)^T
         −2W(v_i − v_k^-)(v_i − v_k^-)^T
    Compute S_T(v_i, v_j^+, v_k^-) via Eq.(4).
    W = W − η S_T(v_i, v_j^+, v_k^-) ∇L
  end if
end for
Output:
  The optimized hashing projection matrix W.
```

4.3 Kernel-based Ranking SHSC

Our Ranking SHSC method can be easily kernelized (Kernel-based Ranking SHSC) through the kernel trick which has been proven to be able to tackle linearly inseparable data. To kernelize Ranking SHSC, we use a kernel function $\kappa : \mathbb{R}^D \times \mathbb{R}^D \mapsto \mathbb{R}$ to construct the hash functions. Following the kernel-based hashing algorithms [11][13], we define the kernelized hash function with the kernel κ plugged in as

$$\tilde{h}(\mathbf{v}_i) = sgn\left(\sum_{j=1}^{m} \kappa(\mathbf{v}_{(j)}, \mathbf{v}_i)w_j - b\right), \tag{18}$$

where $\mathbf{v}_{(1)}, \dots, \mathbf{v}_{(m)}$ are m samples randomly selected from $\mathbf{V}$, $w_j \in \mathbb{R}$ is the coefficient and $b \in \mathbb{R}$ is the bias. It is worth noting that in order to make this kernel-based hashing fast, m is set to be much smaller than the image dataset size n. Following the balancing criterion [4][13] in hash function that the generated hash bit should take as much information as possible, the bias b is set as

$$b = \sum_{i=1}^{n}\sum_{j=1}^{m} \kappa(\mathbf{v}_{(j)}, \mathbf{v}_i)w_j/n. \tag{19}$$

Therefore, the kernelized hash function is rewritten as

$$\begin{aligned}\tilde{h}(\mathbf{v}_i) &= sgn\left(\sum_{j=1}^{m} (\kappa(\mathbf{v}_{(j)}, \mathbf{v}_i) - \frac{1}{n}\sum_{i=1}^{n} \kappa(\mathbf{v}_{(j)}, \mathbf{v}_i))w_j\right) \\ &= \mathrm{sgn}\left(\mathbf{w}\overline{\kappa}(\mathbf{v}_i)\right),\end{aligned} \tag{20}$$

where $\mathbf{w} = [w_1, \dots, w_m]$ is the coefficient vector and $\overline{\kappa} : R^D \mapsto R^m$ is the vectorial map, which is defined as

$$\begin{aligned}\overline{\kappa}(\mathbf{v_i}) &= [\kappa(\mathbf{v}_{(1)}, \mathbf{v}_i) - b_1, \dots, \kappa(\mathbf{v}_{(m)}, \mathbf{v}_i) - b_m]^\top, \\ b_j &= \frac{1}{n}\sum_{i=1}^{n} \kappa(\mathbf{v}_{(j)}, \mathbf{v}_i).\end{aligned} \tag{21}$$

With the vectorial map $\overline{\kappa}$, we can obtain the kernelized feature matrix $\mathbf{V}_\kappa \in \mathbb{R}^{m\times n}$. The K-bit kernel-based binary code representation $\mathbf{B}_\kappa$ of the image set $\mathbf{V}$ is then given as

$$\mathbf{B}_\kappa = sgn(\mathbf{W}\mathbf{V}_\kappa), \tag{22}$$

where $\mathbf{W}$ is learnt by using the proposed Ranking SHSC method.

Figure 3: Ten example images randomly selected from each class in CIFAR-10 dataset. The class label is given in the first column.

5. EXPERIMENTS

We conducted large-scale image retrieval experiments on two image datasets, i.e., CIFAR-10[1], a tiny image collection in 10 classes and Clickture [7], a click-based image dataset.

5.1 Datasets

The **CIFAR-10** dataset contains 60,000 real world tiny images (32×32 pixels), which is a labeled subset of the 80 million tiny images dataset [25]. It consists of 10 object classes and each class contains 6K samples. Every image in this dataset is assigned to a mutually exclusive class label and represented by a 512-dimensional GIST feature vector [18]. Figure 3 shows 10 randomly selected images from each class in CIFAR-10.

The dataset is partitioned into two parts: a training set with 59K images and a test set with 1K images evenly sampled from ten classes. We additionally sample 100 images from each class in the training set and constitute 1K labeled subset for training. For each test image, the ground-truth similar images are derived from class label, i.e., images from the same class are deemed to be similar.

Clickture is a large-scale click based image dataset [7]. It was collected from one year click-through data of one commercial image search engine. The dataset comprises two parts, i.e., the training and development (dev) sets. The training set consists of 23.1 million {*query*, *image*, *click*} triads of 11.7 millions distinct queries and 1.0 million unique images. Figure 4 shows a few exemplary queries with their clicked images and click counts in the Clickture. For example, users clicked the first image 25 times in the search results

[1]http://www.cs.toronto.edu/~kriz/cifar.html

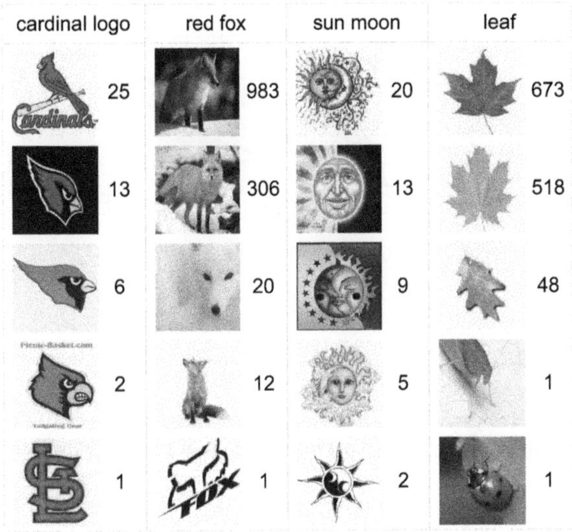

Figure 4: Examples in Clickture dataset (upper row: search queries; lower row: images with click times in response to the upper query).

when submitting query "cardinal logo" in total. In the dev dataset, there are 79,926 $\langle query, image \rangle$ pairs generated from 1,000 queries, where each image to the corresponding query was manually annotated on a three point ordinal scale: Excellent, Good, and Bad. Inspired by the success of deep convolutional neural networks (DCNN) [1][9], we take the output of 1000-way fc8 classification layer by using DeCAF [2] as the image representation for Clickture dataset, which constitutes a 1000-dimensional feature vector.

In the experiment, we adopt 1.0 million unique images in the training set as our training data and randomly sampled 10K images as labeled subset. Moreover, 1K unique images that are annotated as "Excellent" to the query in the dev set are randomly selected as the test images. To ensure objective as well as effective evaluation, the ground truth data are carefully generated on the click-through. Specifically, for each test image, the set of images clicked by the same query in the training set are taken as the semantically similar images. In addition, for training queries that share more than one common noun phrase with the query of the test image, their clicked images are also regarded as the similar ones. The other images in the training set are all used as dissimilar ones to the test image.

5.2 Protocols and Baseline Methods

We follow three evaluation protocols, i.e., hash lookup, recall and mean average precision (MAP), which are widely used in [4][13][26]. Hash lookup takes constant search time over a lookup table. We carry out hash lookup within a Hamming radius 2 of the query and report the search precision. Following [26], query failing in finding any hash bucket receives zero score in precision. Given the number of the retrieved images, the fraction of relevant ones, i.e., recall, is given as well. MAP is further exploited to evaluate the ranking quality in Hamming space for each query image.

We compare the following approaches for performance evaluation:

- Locality Sensitive Hashing [3] (*LSH*). *LSH* aims to map similar examples to the same bucket with high probability by using a Gaussian random projection matrix. The property of locality in the original space will be largely preserved in the Hamming space.
- PCA Hashing (*PCAH*). *PCAH* simply uses the matrix of top-k PCA directions as projection matrix.
- Spectral Hashing [30] (*SH*). *SH* is based on quantizing the values of analytical eigenfunctions computed along PCA directions of the data.
- Semi-supervised Hashing [26] (*SSH*). *SSH* formulates the hashing problem as minimizing empirical error on the labeled data while maximizing variance of hash bits over both the labeled and unlabeled data.
- Semi-supervised Hashing with Semantic Confidence (*SHSC*) based on our proposal presented in Section 4.1.
- Ranking SHSC (*RSHSC*) based on Algorithm 1.
- Kernel-based Supervised Hashing [13] (*KSH*). *KSH* employs a kernel formulation for learning the hash functions to handle linearly inseparable data. We name this run as *KSH* in short.
- Kernel-based Ranking SHSC (*KRSHSC*) based on our proposal in Section 4.3. A slightly different of this run is name as $KRSHSC^-$, which measures the quantization loss only on the labeled data.

5.3 Parameter Settings

To ensure that all the methods are comparable under the same setting, as in [13], we use the same Gaussian RBF kernel $\kappa(\mathbf{v}_i, \mathbf{v}_j) = exp(-\|\mathbf{v}_i - \mathbf{v}_j\|/2\sigma^2)$ and $m = 300$ support samples in all kernel-based methods. The parameter σ is tuned on each dataset. The parameters α and β are selected from $\{0.2, 0.4, 0.6, 0.8, 1.0\}$ and the optimal values are determined by using a validation set. Finally, α and β are both set to 0.8.

5.4 Results on CIFAR-10 Dataset

Performance Comparison. Figure 5(a) shows the MAP performances of nine runs on CIFAR-10 dataset. Overall, the results on MAP across different lengths of hash code consistently indicate that hashing with semantic confidence leads to a performance boost. There is a significant performance gap between the kernel-based and linear runs. It is not very surprising to see that *LSH* provides the worst MAP performance since the random hash functions lack discrimination power for small bit lengths. On the other hand, *PCAH* and *SH* work relatively well for small bit sizes, but getting worse as the number of bits increases, indicating that PCA is effective in preserving semantic consistency for small hash code lengths. Furthermore, by additionally incorporating semantic confidence, *SHSC* exhibits better performance than *SSH*. Similar is spirit, $KRSHSC^-$ improves *KSH*, but the performance is still lower than that of *KRSHSC*, demonstrating the advantage of exploiting the unlabeled data in semi-supervised hashing approaches. The improvement can also be observed of *RSHSC* compared to *SHSC*.

In the evaluation of hash lookup within Hamming radius 2 as shown in Figure 5(b), the precisions for most of the

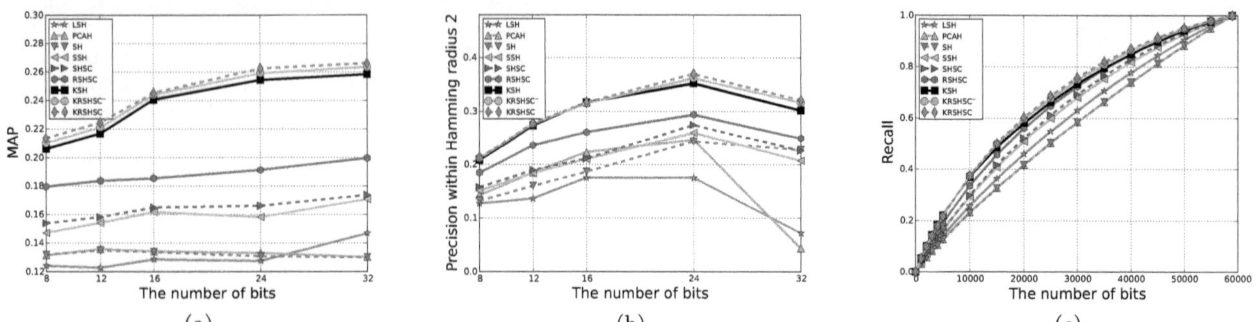

(a) (b) (c)

Figure 5: Comparisons with state-of-the-art approaches on CIFAR-10 dataset. (a) Mean average precision (MAP) performance. (b) Precision within Hamming radius 2 using hash lookup. (c) Recall curves with 32 bits. For better viewing, please see original color pdf file.

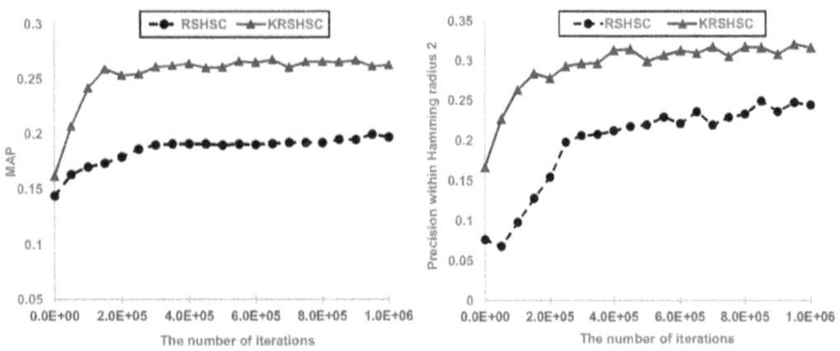

Figure 6: MAP performances and Precisions within Hamming radius 2 using hash lookup with the increase of the number of iterations on CIFAR-10 dataset with 32 bits.

compared methods drop when a longer size of hash code is used (32 bits in our case). This is because the number of samples falling into a bucket decreases exponentially for longer sizes of hash code. Therefore, for some query images, there are even no any neighbor in a Hamming ball of radius 2. Even in this case, our proposed *KRSHSC* provides the best performance and the drop in precision for long size of hash code is less than others.

We further details the recall at different numbers of returned examples in Figure 5(c). The results confirm the trends seen in Figure 5(a) and demonstrate performance improvement using the proposed semi-supervised hashing with semantic confidence approaches, especially *KRSHSC*, over other runs. In addition, to verify that the performance of different approaches is not by chance, we conducted significance test using the randomization test [22]. The number of iterations used in the randomization is 100,000 and at 0.05 significance level. *KRSHSC* is found to be significantly better than others.

Varying the number of iterations. In our *RSHSC* and *KRSHSC* algorithms, the learning of hash function is an iterative process. Next, we conducted experiments to evaluate the performances of our proposed approaches by varying the number of iterations from 1 to 1.0 million on CIFAR-10 dataset. Note that the training time grows linearly with the number of iterations.

MAP performances and precisions within Hamming radius 2 hash lookup with 32 hashing bits are reported in Figure 6. Not surprisingly, we can observe that the performances of *RSHSC* and *KRSHSC* are both improved with the increase of iterations. Furthermore, after a number of iterations (600K in our case), the performances of *RSHSC* and *KRSHSC* change very smoothly, as the algorithms have already received sufficient knowledge to learn a good hash function.

5.5 Results on Clickture Dataset

Figure 7 shows the experimental results on Clickture dataset. As for some queries in Clickture dataset, there are only tens of or even less than ten clicked (relevant) images, making the search task very challenging. MAP performance and precision with Hamming radius 2 using hash lookup are given in Figure 7(a) and (b), respectively. Our *KRSHSC* approach consistently outperforms other runs. In particular, the MAP performance and precision with Hamming radius 2 using hash lookup of *KRSHSC* can achieve 0.0818 and 0.1735 with 48 hash bits, which make the improvement over the best competitor *KSH* by 3.5% and 12.8%. Methods that learn hash functions with semantic confidence, e.g. $KRSHSC^-$ and *SHSC*, are generally better than *KSH* and *SSH*, respectively. Similar to the observations on CIFAR-10 dataset, *LSH* performs poorly especially for small bit sizes and *SH* leads to better performance gain than *PCAH* for longer hash code. Figure 8 showcases some exemplar query images and their retrieved neighbors with 48 bits. *KRSHSC* still exhibits the best search quality in terms of visual relevance.

5.6 Complexity Analysis

The time complexities for training *RSHSC* and *KRSHSC* are $T_{max} \times \mathcal{O}(nKD + DK^2 + D)$ and $T_{max} \times \mathcal{O}(nKm + mK^2 + m)$, respectively, which scales linearly with n given $n \gg D \succ m \succ K$. In practice, take the training on 1 million triplets for example, *KRSHSC* takes about 30 minutes on a server with 2.40GHz CPU and 128GB RAM. For each query, the hashing time of *RSHSC* and *KRSHSC* are $\mathcal{O}(KD)$ and $\mathcal{O}(Dm + Km)$, respectively.

6. DISCUSSION AND CONCLUSION

In this paper, we have presented an important concept, i.e. semantic confidence, for the learning of hash function. Particularly, we propose two ways of measuring the

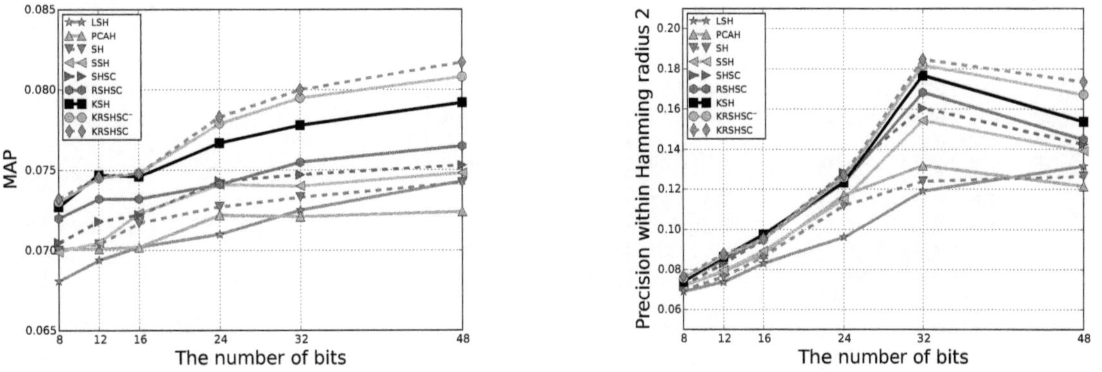

(a) (b)

Figure 7: Comparisons with state-of-the-art approaches on Clickture dataset (Better viewed in color). (a) Mean average precision (MAP) performance. (b) Precision within Hamming radius 2 using hash lookup.

semantic confidence, by neighbor voting and click counts, where the former is for general purpose and the latter exploits the click-through data which is largely available by search engine. With the semantic confidence, pairwise and triplet relationships are deployed and further incorporated into semi-supervised hashing learning framework with pairwise and listwise supervision, respectively. Finally, a kernel-based version is proposed to handle the linearly inseparable data.

We performed extensive experiments on two image datasets and compared with the state-of-the-art hashing techniques. Experimental results demonstrated that the proposed semi-supervised hashing with semantic confidence yields superior performance. The current work can be extended with the design of multiple listwise supervised hash tables, which is expected to show even better performance.

Acknowledgments

This work was supported in part by the 973 Programme under Grant 2015CB351803, the 863 Programme under Grant 2014AA015102, and National Natural Science Foundation of China (No. 61272290, No. 61325009).

7. REFERENCES

[1] C. F. Cadieu, H. Hong, D. Yamins, N. Pinto, N. J. Majaj, and J. J. DiCarlo. The neural representation benchmark and its evaluation on brain and machine. In *ICLR*, 2013.

[2] J. Donahue, Y. Jia, O. Vinyals, J. Hoffman, N. Zhang, E. Tzeng, and T. Darrell. Decaf: A deep convolutional activation feature for generic visual recognition. *arXiv preprint arXiv:1310.1531*, 2013.

[3] A. Gionis, P. Indyk, and R. Motwani. Similarity search in high dimensions via hashing. In *VLDB*, 1999.

[4] Y. Gong, S. Lazebnik, A. Gordo, and F. Perronnin. Iterative quantization: A procrustean approach to learning binary codes for large-scale image retrieval. *IEEE Trans. PAMI*, 35(12):2916–2929, 2013.

[5] R. Herbrich, T. Graepel, and K. Obermayer. *Large Margin Rank Boundaries for Ordinal Regression.* MIT Press, January 2000.

[6] G. E. Hinton and R. R. Salakhutdinov. Reducing the dimensionality of data with neural networks. *Science*, 313(5786):504–507, 2006.

[7] X.-S. Hua, L. Yang, J. Wang, J. Wang, M. Ye, K. Wang, Y. Rui, and J. Li. Clickage: Towards bridging semantic and intent gaps via mining click logs of search engines. In *ACM MM*, 2013.

[8] S. Kim and S. Choi. Semi-supervised discriminant hashing. In *ICDM*, 2011.

[9] A. Krizhevsky, I. Sutskever, and G. E. Hinton. Imagenet classification with deep convolutional neural networks. In *NIPS*, 2012.

[10] B. Kulis and T. Darrell. Learning to hash with binary reconstructive embeddings. In *NIPS*, 2009.

[11] B. Kulis and K. Grauman. Kernelized locality-sensitive hashing. *IEEE Trans. PAMI*, 34(6):1092–1104, 2012.

[12] W. Liu, C. Mu, S. Kumar, and S.-F. Chang. Discrete graph hashing. In *NIPS*. 2014.

[13] W. Liu, J. Wang, R. Ji, Y.-G. Jiang, and S.-F. Chang. Supervised hashing with kernels. In *CVPR*, 2012.

[14] W. Liu, J. Wang, S. Kumar, and S.-F. Chang. Hashing with graphs. In *ICML*, 2011.

[15] Y. Mu, J. Shen, and S. Yan. Weakly-supervised hashing in kernel space. In *CVPR*, 2010.

[16] M. Norouzi and D. M. Blei. Minimal loss hashing for compact binary codes. In *ICML*, 2011.

[17] M. Norouzi, D. M. Blei, and R. Salakhutdinov. Hamming distance metric learning. In *NIPS*, 2012.

[18] A. Oliva and A. Torralba. Modeling the shape of the scene: A holistic representation of the spatial envelope. *IJCV*, 42(3):145–175, 2001.

[19] Y. Pan, T. Yao, T. Mei, H. Li, C. W. Ngo, and Y. Rui. Click-through-based cross-view learning for image search. In *SIGIR*, 2014.

[20] P. Ram, D. Lee, H. Ouyang, and A. G. Gray. Rank-approximate nearest neighbor search: Retaining meaning and speed in high dimensions. In *NIPS*, 2009.

[21] M. Rastegari, J. Choi, S. Fakhraei, D. Hal, and L. Davis. Predictable dual-view hashing. In *ICML*, 2013.

Figure 8: Examples showing the top 20 image search results by different methods in response to two query images on Clickture dataset (better viewed in color). In each row, the first image with a red bounding box is the query image and the relevant images in the retrieved list are enclosed in a blue bounding box.

[22] J. P. Romano. On the behavior of randomization tests without a group invariance assumption. *Journal of the American Statistical Association*, 85(411):686–692, 1990.

[23] R. Salakhutdinov and G. Hinton. Semantic hashing. *International Journal of Approximate Reasoning*, 50(7):969–978, 2006.

[24] C. Strecha, A. M. Bronstein, M. M. Bronstein, and P. Fua. Ldahash: Improved matching with smaller descriptors. *IEEE Trans. PAMI*, 34(1):66–78, 2012.

[25] A. Torralba, R. Fergus, and W. Freeman. 80 million tiny images: A large data set for nonparametric object and scene recognition. *IEEE Trans. PAMI*, 30(11):1958–1970, 2008.

[26] J. Wang, S. Kumar, and S.-F. Chang. Semi-supervised hashing for large-scale search. *IEEE Trans. PAMI*, 34(12):2393–2406, 2012.

[27] J. Wang, W. Liu, A. X. Sun, and Y.-G. Jiang. Learning hash codes with listwise supervision. In *ICCV*, 2013.

[28] Q. Wang, L. Si, and D. Zhang. Learning to hash with partial tags: Exploring correlation between tags and hashing bits for large scale image retrieval. In *ECCV*. 2014.

[29] Q. Wang, D. Zhang, and L. Si. Semantic hashing using tags and topic modeling. In *SIGIR*, 2013.

[30] Y. Weiss, A. Torralba, and R. Fergus. Spectral hashing. In *NIPS*, 2008.

[31] H. Xia, P. Wu, S. C. Hoi, and R. Jin. Boosting multi-kernel locality-sensitive hashing for scalable image retrieval. In *SIGIR*, 2012.

[32] T. Yao, T. Mei, C.-W. Ngo, and S. Li. Annotation for free: Video tagging by mining user search behavior. In *ACM MM*, 2013.

[33] L. Zelnik-Manor and P. Perona. Self-tuning spectral clustering. In *NIPS*, 2004.

[34] X. Zhu, W. Nejdl, and M. Georgescu. An adaptive teleportation random walk model for learning social tag relevance. In *SIGIR*, 2014.

Optimal Aggregation Policy for Reducing Tail Latency of Web Search

Jeong-Min Yun[1], Yuxiong He[2], Sameh Elnikety[2], Shaolei Ren[3]

[1]POSTECH [2]Microsoft Research [3]Florida International University

ABSTRACT

A web search engine often employs partition-aggregate architecture, where an aggregator propagates a user query to all index serving nodes (ISNs) and collects the responses from them. An aggregation policy determines how long the aggregators wait for the ISNs before returning aggregated results to users, crucially affecting both query latency and quality. Designing an aggregation policy is, however, challenging: Response latency among queries and among ISNs varies significantly, and aggregators lack of knowledge about when ISNs will respond. In this paper, we propose aggregation policies that minimize tail latency of search queries subject to search quality service level agreements (SLAs), combining data-driven offline analysis with online processing. Beginning with a single aggregator, we formally prove the optimality of our policy: It achieves the offline optimal result without knowing future responses of ISNs. We extend our policy for commonly-used hierarchical levels of aggregators and prove its optimality when messaging times between aggregators are known. We also present an empirically-effective policy to address unknown messaging time. We use production traces from a commercial search engine, a commercial advertisement engine, and synthetic workloads to evaluate the aggregation policy. The results show that compared to prior work, the policy reduces tail latency by up to 40% while satisfying same quality SLAs.

Categories and Subject Descriptors

H.3.3 [**Information Storage and Retrieval**]: Information Search and Retrieval—*Search process*

Keywords

Aggregation; Scheduling; Tail Latency; Web Search

1. INTRODUCTION

A web search engine often employs partition-aggregate architecture, forming a distributed system with aggregators and index serving nodes (ISNs). The web index is large, containing information on billions of web documents, and is typically document-sharded among hundreds of ISNs [7, 12]. Such a system includes aggregators that merge results collected from ISNs (e.g., a single aggregator (Figure 1(a))).

An *aggregation policy* determines how long the aggregator waits for its ISNs before sending the results back. Designing a good aggregation policy is crucial: It directly impacts quality and responsiveness, which are among the most important metrics in web search. For example, the aggregator can choose to wait for responses from all ISNs, returning complete results, or it may wait for only a fixed time duration, returning partial results from a subset of ISNs. There is a clear trade-off: The longer the aggregator waits, the more results it collects, improving quality but degrading responsiveness. The objective of the aggregation policy can be expressed as reducing a high latency percentile while meeting one or more quality constraints. Reducing a high latency percentile, i.e., tail latency, is more suitable than average latency to ensure *consistently* low latency, which is important to attract and retain users [4, 17, 25, 27, 34].

Designing an effective online aggregation policy is challenging: Aggregators do not know when ISNs will return their results and their response times vary significantly. For example, different web search queries exhibit highly variable demand: the 99-th percentile query execution time is often a factor of 10 larger than the average [13, 22]. Even for the same query, the response times of different ISNs could vary widely [5]: It may take only 10 ms to collect responses from a majority of ISNs but require another 200 ms to receive the remaining few.

Prior work provides aggregation heuristics that reduce the tail latency compared to simply waiting for all responses, but they miss significant potential latency improvement. Instead of using heuristics, we take a different approach: Imagine if the aggregator knows the future, in particular when each ISN will respond. We study this case to derive an offline policy, which decides when to return the results on a per-query basis. We further show that this offline policy is optimal, forming a clear latency target that an online policy strives to achieve.

However, in practice, the aggregator must make online decisions without knowing the future information (e.g., when ISNs will respond), which invalidates offline policies and makes the problem challenging. When an online aggregation policy decides to terminate a query and returns its partial results, it makes a bet that waiting for the remaining responses to arrive will take too much time. However, all the remain-

SIGIR'15, August 09 - 13, 2015, Santiago, Chile.

ACM 978-1-4503-3621-5/15/08:.$15.00.
DOI: http://dx.doi.org/10.1145/2766462.2767708.

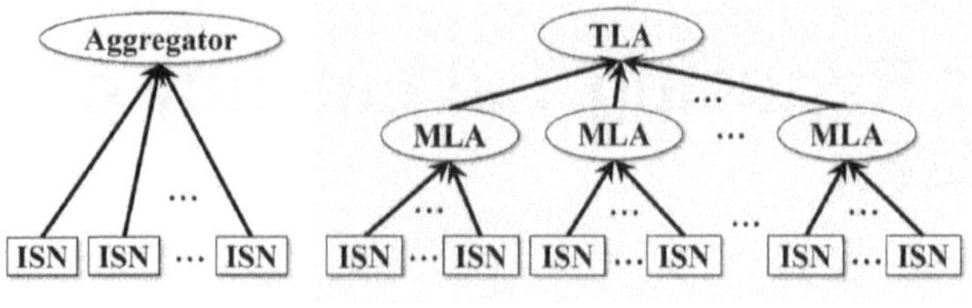

Figure 1: Web search engine architecture: (a) single-level aggregation, (b) two-level aggregation.

ing responses might arrive immediately afterwards. In this situation, search quality is degraded with only a marginal latency reduction.

Inspired by the offline policy, we develop an online policy that uses two thresholds, one for query quality and the other is a time threshold. Only if a query meets or exceeds the quality threshold at the time threshold, the aggregator terminates the query. We employ offline analysis of the query logs to compute the quality and time thresholds.

We prove a surprising result: The aggregation policy is optimal, providing the same results as the offline optimal policy. It minimizes the tail latency of queries while meeting their quality service level agreements (SLAs). In contrast, prior work does not identify the optimal structure of the online policy, or compare to the offline optimal solution. They employ heuristics to reduce tail latency indirectly, for example, by minimizing latency variance [20].

Next, we study multiple levels of aggregators, which is an important practical case yet largely unaddressed in prior work. There is no heuristic specifically designed for multiple aggregators. Figure 1(b) shows a cluster with two-level aggregation, containing a single top-level aggregator, called TLA, and several mid-level aggregators, called MLAs. Microsoft Bing search employs the two-level aggregation architecture [1]. This architecture fits naturally with the hierarchy of data center networks, where MLAs collect responses from ISNs located in the same rack and TLA collects responses from the MLAs, reducing inter-rack communication. Moreover, MLAs can reduce the processing load of the top aggregator, for example by re-ranking results and removing near duplicates [35].

Multilevel aggregation is significantly more challenging than single-level aggregation because the aggregator's decisions at the different levels are coupled and cannot be optimized independently. For example, an aggressive TLA policy (e.g., terminating queries based on a lower time or quality threshold) needs to be combined with a more conservative MLA policy to meet the quality SLAs. Finding a good policy requires exploring various combinations of aggregation decisions at different levels and deciding the parameters used at each level jointly, which significantly increases the design space and computation complexity. Further, messaging time between aggregators (including both processing and transmission time) may or may not be known online.

We extend our policy to address the challenges for multilevel aggregation and prove its optimality when messaging times between aggregators are known. For unknown messaging times, we show that the policy performs very close to the offline optimal using empirical evaluation. To the best of our knowledge, this policy is the first one to solve the multilevel aggregation problem.

We assess our techniques using query logs from a production cluster of a commercial search engine, a commercial advertisement engine, as well as using synthetic workloads derived from well-known distributions. We evaluate the policy extensively in both single-level and two-level aggregation clusters with different quality and latency targets, varying the number of ISNs, latency distributions. We conclude our policy consistently outperforms the state-of-the-art techniques. In particular, the results show, to meet the target quality constraints, on a 44-ISN search cluster with a single aggregator, we reduce the 95-th tail latency by 36% (from 59 ms to 38 ms) compared with the best existing work. The results also show similar savings for two-level aggregation.

The key contributions of this work are the following: (1) We characterize the workload to outline how a good aggregation policy should behave. (2) We develop an optimal aggregation policy, combining both data-driven offline analysis with online processing, to minimize a crucial metric — tail latency of search queries — subject to quality constraints. (3) We generalize our policy to address multilevel aggregation, which has practical importance but has not been addressed in prior research. (4) We conduct extensive evaluation using production traces as well as various synthetic workloads to assess the benefits of the proposed aggregation policy and show that it outperforms existing solutions.

2. PROBLEM FORMULATION

Aggregation policy assigns an online algorithm for each aggregator to decide when it returns its response.

Latency. Web search requires *consistently* low latency to attract and retain users [4, 17, 25, 27, 34], for which average latency is not a suitable metric due to potentially very large variation in latency. Thus, service providers often target to reduce high percentile latency of web search queries, which is also called *tail latency* [13, 19, 31]. We define *query latency* as the latency measured at top aggregator.

Quality. To quantify search quality, we define the *utility* of a query as the fraction of ISNs from which the TLA receives results and returns to the user. This definition is also used in prior work [20]. Lower utility indicates the query is more likely to miss important answers, thus resulting in a lower quality. A utility of 1 is the best baseline case: The aggregators receive responses from all ISNs.

We use both average utility and tail utility, which are two important metrics for web search SLAs [2, 19]. The average utility is the mean utility of all queries, and tail utility is high-percentile utility of queries, ensuring consistently high quality results for the search queries.

Optimization Objective. The objective of an aggregation policy is to minimize query tail latency of a large-scale web search engine, while satisfying average and tail utility constraints. This is a common objective in many prior studies [11, 20, 22] as well as in real systems. For example, the optimization criteria of Bing search is to minimize the 95-th tail latency subject to an average utility of 0.99 and 95-th tail utility of 0.95.

Given an aggregation policy $\mathcal{A}$ and a set of n queries, we denote the latency and utility of query i by t_i and u_i, respectively, for $i = 1, 2, \cdots, n$. Note that both latency and utility are affected by the aggregation policy $\mathcal{A}$. The k-th percentile latency for the set of n queries, denoted by $t_{k\%}$, is the $\lceil kn \rceil$-th largest latency among these n queries. Likewise, the h-th percentile utility, denoted by $u_{h\%}$, is the

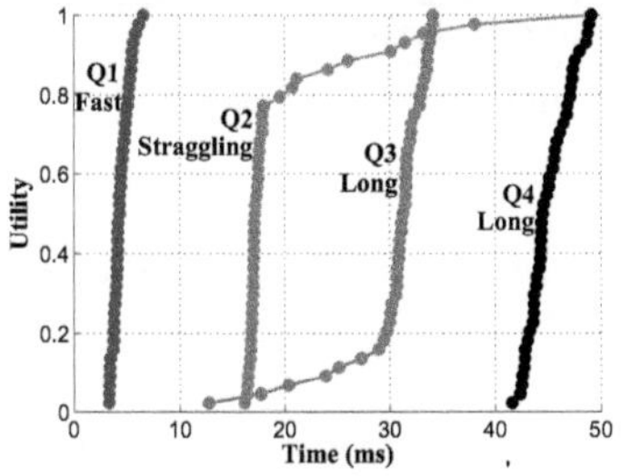

Figure 2: Progress of 4 sample queries.

Table 1: Aggregation Policy Comparison.

	Complete Fast	Terminate Straggling	Complete Long	Inputs		Multi level
				Time	Utility	
Wait-All	✓	✗	✓	✗	✗	✗
Time-Only	✓	✓	✗	✓	✗	✗
Utility-Only	✗	✓	✗	✗	✓	✗
Time-Utility	✓	✓	✗	✓	✓	✗
Kwiken	✓	✓	✗	✓	✓	✗
FSL	✓	✓	✓	✓	✓	✓

$\lceil hn \rceil$-th lowest utility. Thus, we formulate the tail latency minimization problem (called TLM) as follows:

$$\text{TLM}: \quad \text{minimize}_{\mathcal{A}} \ t_{k\%} \qquad (1)$$

$$s.t., \quad \frac{1}{n}\sum_{i=1}^{n} u_i \geq \bar{u}_{\text{avg}} \text{ and } u_{h\%} \geq \bar{u}_{h\%} \qquad (2)$$

Constraint (2) specifies the average and tail utility.

Production Deployment Environment. When an aggregator decides to return partial results, there is an implementation choice to either abort query execution on the ISNs that have not yet responded or to let them complete. The later is more common in practice as observed in both commercial search engines, e.g., Bing [20], and the well-known open source search software Apache Lucene [18]. Supporting query abort has a cost and comes with limited benefits.

Supporting abort messages and interrupting running queries increases search engine implementation complexity, making logging, testing, debugging more difficult in addition to the message processing overhead of the abort messages. Also, the computational resource savings from aborting a late query are often negligible. More specifically, as query processing on ISNs has a timeout limit (e.g., $\leq$ 200 ms in Bing search [19]), no query takes longer processing time than the timeout limit. Moreover, to meet an average utility of 0.99, at most 1% of ISNs could terminate processing earlier using an abort message, making the overall computational resource savings limited. Finally, aborting late messages also has little impact on the waiting time (and thus the latency) of other concurrent queries, because commercial search engines are provisioned with additional capacity to ensure that ISNs operate at low to modest loads with a very small query waiting time [21].

Therefore, we present and evaluate our aggregation policies based on systems without abort messages. However, as the performance impact of abort messages is small, these policies are also well applicable to systems with aborts.

3. INTUITIONS

We derive the key intuitions of our aggregation policy using query workload characteristics. Then, we discuss what a good policy should do and what existing policies miss.

Workload Characterization. The execution time distribution of web search queries has a high variability: Prior work shows that the 99-th percentile query execution time is a factor of 10x larger than the average, and even 100x larger than the median [13, 22]. In addition, for processing a single query, some ISNs may take much longer than others even if they all use the same hardware due to several well-known factors, such as document partitioning scheme, correlation between query term frequencies and inverted list sizes [5].

Figure 2 shows utility progress for a few examples from Bing. We categorize queries into three types: (1) *Fast* query for which the responses from all ISNs arrive quickly, e.g., Q1 in Figure 2. (2) *Straggling* query for which most of the responses arrive quickly but a few ISNs take much longer to respond, e.g., Q2 in Figure 2. (3) *Long* query for which most responses take a long time, e.g., Q3 and Q4.

Key Intuition. Our policy identifies query type and decides which queries among the three types to complete or terminate by considering the tradeoff of latency and utility:

Complete fast queries. Since they do not impact tail latency even if we wait for all responses, we complete them with full utility.

Terminate straggling queries. We reduce latency with little utility loss. For any given utility target, we can only tolerate a limited utility loss. For example, for an average utility of 0.99, only 0.01 utility loss is allowed. We allocate the allowed utility loss to straggling queries to maximize latency reduction.

Complete long queries. As their responses from ISNs arrive late but altogether at TLA, terminating them early can cause major utility loss. Thus, we let long queries complete without affecting the tail latency, because a latency percentile target allows for a few slow queries without penalty (e.g., for 95-th latency, 5% slow queries are allowed), which we call *tail latency slackness.*

The distinction among fast, straggling and long queries is relative, depending on the selection of time and utility thresholds obtained by offline analysis of query workloads.

Existing Policies. Table 1 compares six aggregation policies with respect to their actions on the three types of queries, inputs, and support for multilevel aggregations.

Wait-All waits for every ISN before returning the results. The query latency is dominated by the slowest ISN, resulting in a high latency. *Time-Only* terminates a query upon a timeout threshold [22]. It terminates both long and straggling queries without differentiation. *Utility-Only* terminates a query if it already received a given percentage of responses, even including fast queries whose full completion does not affect tail latency. These three policies miss either time or utility to differentiate among query types.

Time-Utility terminates a query when its timeout threshold is triggered and the query utility reaches a threshold. It is better than Time-Only, but it still early terminates long queries after they receive the threshold percentage of responses. *Kwiken* [20] terminates a query if it runs a fixed time interval either after a utility threshold or exceeding a time threshold. It selects these thresholds by minimizing latency variance among all responses. Although minimizing latency variance may indirectly reduce tail latency, it can degrade utility significantly. For example, in Figure 2, Q2 and Q3 have similar variances in terms of latency from their ISNs. However, terminating the straggling query Q2 causes little utility loss, while terminating a long query Q3 results in a large utility loss. Although Time-Utility and Kwiken use both time and utility for aggregation, neither of them directly optimizes for tail latency by exploiting tail latency slackness to obtain high utility for long queries.

Furthermore, none of the existing policies address multi-level aggregation, which is common in practice, and is much more challenging than a single level. In comparison, our policy takes effective actions for Fast, Straggling and Long queries, so we name it FSL. FSL exploits time and utility, and addresses single and multiple aggregation levels.

4. SINGLE-LEVEL AGGREGATION

This section presents the design and analysis of our policy FSL (for fast, straggling and long queries) for a single aggregator. FSL decides when to terminate a query by combining both online processing and offline analysis. For online processing, FSL jointly considers the time and utility of a query. In particular, we define a time threshold t^* and a utility threshold u^*. Based on whether a query is completed by t^*, and its utility at time t^*, we categorize the running query as fast, straggling or long, and take actions accordingly. The offline processing calculates the optimal values of t^* and u^* according to the workload information, utility target, and type of tail latency we seek to minimize. As response time distributions of interactive services vary slowly over time [20, 24], we trigger offline processing periodically to update the parameters for online processing. The latency can also be monitored online to trigger offline analysis whenever needed. To adapt to varying system load, we can construct a table that maps each load (e.g., query arrival rate) to its time and utility threshold values through offline analysis of the corresponding query logs. Then, online processing simply applies the proper parameters for the current load. FSL is *not* another heuristic: We derive an offline optimal algorithm with complete future information in Section 4.3 and prove that the online algorithm FSL is optimal, performing as well as offline optimal without knowing future responses of queries.

4.1 Online Processing

Online processing of FSL takes two runtime properties of a query — time and utility — as inputs, and it decides when to terminate query under execution. In particular, as described in Algorithm 1, if the aggregator does not receive all query responses after the query has been sent to the ISNs for time t^*, FSL checks the progress of the query: if the utility of the current query is higher than or equal to u^*, then terminate the query at time t^* (for reducing tail latency with a small utility loss); otherwise, let the query run till completion (to avoid significant utility loss).

Intuitively, FSL uses t^* and u^* to differentiate the three types of queries and take actions accordingly. (1) If a query completes by t^*, the query is fast: FSL executes fast queries till completion. (2) If a query has received most of the responses by t^*, the remaining utility of the query is marginal and the query is straggling: FSL early terminates straggling queries. (3) If responses are only received from no or a few ISNs at time t^*, the query is long: FSL executes long queries till completion, avoiding a significant utility degradation. Moreover, to optimize a tail latency target, e.g., 95%, the longest 5% of queries have no effect. Thus, by carefully choosing the values of t^* and u^* through offline analysis (as shown in Section 4.2), FSL allows long queries to complete, avoiding utility degradation without affecting the desired target tail latency.

Algorithm 1 FSL: Online processing

Input: time threshold t^* and utility threshold u^*
for each query **do**
  if all the responses are returned within t^* **then**
    Do nothing
  else if utility $u \geq u^*$ after the aggregator waits for t^* **then**
    Early terminate this query
  else
    Run query until completion (or system failure timeout)
  end if
end for

In practice, system failure timeouts are set at the aggregators to prevent them from waiting forever in the case of server/network failures. Upon this timeout, FSL returns the collected results, just like all other aggregation policies. In addition, when there is only a tail utility constraint without average utility constraints, FSL can return the results of long queries after reaching the target tail utility rather than query completion.

4.2 Offline Processing

Offline processing includes a search algorithm to find the optimal time and utility thresholds. Algorithm 2 presents its formal description.

Inputs and outputs. FSL takes the workload data, utility constraints and tail latency objective as inputs. The workload data includes receiving time of each ISN responses for every query in the training set, which is the duration from aggregator sending the query to receiving its response. The output of FSL is the optimal time and utility threshold (t^*, q^*) that minimizes the k-th percentile latency subject to all utility constraints.

High-level description. The search algorithm iterates over all possible values of time thresholds. For each time threshold t, it calculates the optimal value of utility threshold u to maximize query utility (average and/or tail) while producing k-th percentile latency of t. Then among all the t values, we select the smallest one which meets the utility constraints, producing the optimal k-th latency subject to utility constraints. The corresponding (t, q) values are the optimal time and utility thresholds (t^*, q^*).

Step 1. Given a step size δ, there are a set of candidate time thresholds $\{\delta, 2\delta, ..., m\delta\}$, where m is decided by the maximum latency t_{max} of all responses. The tail latency of FSL can exceed the (theoretically) true optimal by at most δ. By reducing δ, our result approaches arbitrarily close to the theoretically optimal, while the search complexity increases, trading off algorithm complexity for accuracy. For web search, δ =1 ms is sufficiently accurate.

Step 2. For any possible time threshold t, we compute the corresponding utility of each query. We sort the queries according to a descending order of the utility values. Figure 3(a) shows an example for a set of queries with sorted utility. The queries at the top of the list are fast queries: they complete before time threshold t and each gets a full utility of 1. At the very bottom are long queries, whose utility is affected significantly by early termination at t. Between fast and long queries are straggling queries, which, if

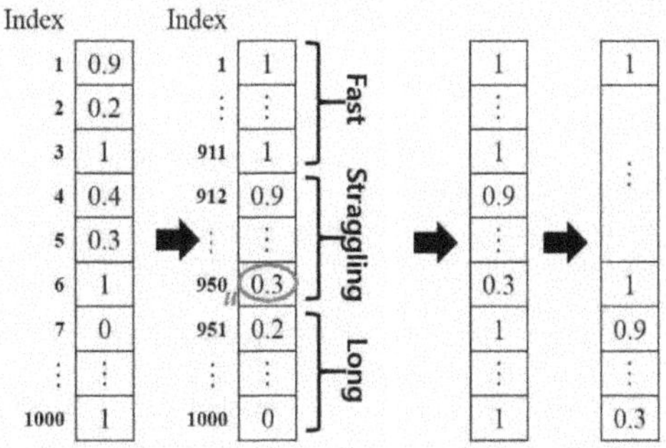

(a) Construct B (b) Construct C

Figure 3: Example of the matrix construction of B and C at time threshold t, where $k = 95$ and $n = 1000$.

early terminated, incur smaller utility loss than long queries would. Such a list of utility values for a given time threshold t corresponds to column t/δ of matrix B in Algorithm 2.

A research question here is how we differentiate straggling versus long queries, which also relates to how we compute the utility threshold u. Given a latency objective k, (e.g., k=95 for optimizing 95-th latency), we know that we can disregard the latency of less than $(100 - k) = 5$ percent of queries (i.e., classify these queries as long queries). We choose the long queries to be those with the highest loss in utility if we early terminate them, i.e., the bottom $(100-k)$ percent of queries in the list. The remaining queries are straggling queries to be early terminated, losing less utility in total. Here, the utility threshold u is equal to the utility value of the $(100 - k)$-th percent query from the bottom. As shown in Figure 3(a), suppose that there are $n = 1000$ queries in total, u corresponds to the utility value of the $n * k/100 = 950$-th query from the top. The beauty of differentiating straggling and long queries in this way is that (1) it allows us to obtain the highest utility gain for any given latency target, and (2) during online processing, it does not require future response times of ISNs to differentiate straggling versus long queries.

Step 3. We update the resulting utilities of queries according to online processing: the utility values of fast and straggling queries remain unchanged, while the utility values of the long queries become 1 since these queries will run till completion. An example is shown in Figure 3(b).

In the case where long queries are returned due to system failure timeout, their utility values are set to the utility of the query at the timeout instead of a full utility of 1.

Step 4. We find the smallest termination time threshold t value that meets all quality SLAs.

Time complexity. Let r represent the number of ISNs, m the number of time threshold candidates, and n the number of queries. Step 1 takes time $n * r$ to compute t_{max}. Step 2 takes $O(rnm)$ for the matrix construction of A, and takes $O(n\log(n)m)$ for the sorting to compute B. Step 3 take $O(n\log(n)m)$ for sorting, and other operations have lower asymptotical order. Step 4 performs a search over all entries of the table with cost of $O(nm)$. Therefore, the overall time complexity of the offline processing of FSL is $O((rn + n\log(n))(t_{max}/\delta)$. The offline processing is an efficient polynomial time algorithm for any given value of δ. For 10,000 queries, 1,000 ISNs, $t_{max} = 350$ ms, and $\delta = 1$ ms, we compute this in 43 seconds on a desktop PC.

Algorithm 2 FSL: Offline Processing

Input:
- time step size δ and log data $X = [X_{i,r}]$ for n queries: $X_{i,r}$ is the response time for r-th ISN and i- th query
- constraints: average utility u_A, k_T-percentile utility u_T
- optimization objective: latency percentile k

Procedure:

Step 1. $t_{max} = \max_{i,r} X_{ir}$; $m = \lceil \frac{t_{max}}{\delta} \rceil$

Step 2. Construct $A = [A_{i,j}] \in \mathbb{R}^{n \times m}$: $A_{i,j}$ represents the utility of i-th query when terminating it at time $j \times \delta$; construct $B = [B_{i,j}] \in \mathbb{R}^{n \times m}$: The j-th column of B is sorted results (in descending order of the utility) of j-th column of A.

Step 3. Construct $C = [C_{i,j}] \in \mathbb{R}^{n \times m}$: set $C_{i,j} = B_{i,j}$ for $i \le \lfloor \frac{k \cdot n}{100} \rfloor$ and $C_{i,j} = 1$ otherwise; construct $C' \in \mathbb{R}^{n \times m}$ by resorting each column of C in descending order of the utility.

Step 4. Find time threshold.

// *For the k_T-percentile utility constraint u_T*

Set $t_T = j_T \times \delta$, where $j_T = \min\{j | C_{\lfloor \frac{k_T n}{100} \rfloor, j} \ge u_T\}$

// *For the average utility constraint u_A*

Set $t_A = j_A \times \delta$, where $j_A = \min\{j | \frac{\sum_i C'_{i,j}}{n} \ge u_A\}$

Output: time threshold $t^* = \max\{t_T, t_A\}$ and utility threshold $u^* = B_{\lceil \frac{kn}{100} \rceil, t^*/\delta}$

4.3 Optimality Proof

FSL is an online policy without future information: it does not know when the remaining responses will be returned by ISNs. In Theorem 1, we compare FSL with an optimal offline policy, which assumes complete information. We show that FSL performs as well as the optimal offline policy — FSL is an optimal online policy achieving the minimum tail latency subject to utility constraints.

We first define an *optimal offline policy*, which decides termination time of each query by assuming full knowledge of the query as well as the entire query set. Each query may have its own termination time. A simple brute-force algorithm to compute such an optimal solution is as follows. For each query i, its candidate termination time t_i is one of the response times of all ISNs, and hence there are r choices (assuming that there are r ISN). For a set of n queries, the search space is r^n. The brute-force algorithm finds the set of $\{t_i\}$, which produces the smallest tail latency while satisfying all utility constraints.

THEOREM 1. *For a cluster with a single aggregator, FSL achieves an arbitrarily close-to-minimum tail latency while meeting average and tail utility constraints.*

PROOF. We show the equivalency of FSL and the optimal offline policy.

First, we perform a transformation from the optimal solution to FSL. Suppose that the offline optimal finishes query i at t_i. Without loss of generality, we assume that $t_1 \le t_2 \le \cdots \le t_n$ among a total of n queries. Then, k-th tail latency of the optimal offline policy is $t' = t_{(k*n/100)}$, and we have two observations.

- For queries whose finish time is smaller than t', finishing them at t' does not change the k-th tail latency.
- For queries whose finish time is bigger than t', waiting for all ISNs does not change the k-th tail latency.

This observation indicates, in the optimal offline policy, each query can have three possible cases: finish before t' (i.e., fast query), finish exactly at t' (i.e., straggling query) or wait until receiving all ISNs' results (i.e., long query). Hence, this is the same as our policy. Algorithm 2 of FSL is a constructive proof of finding the minimum t', which is equivalent to the minimum time threshold t^* (with a deviation smaller than the step size δ). Thus, when the search time step size $\delta \to 0$, the tail latency produced by FSL can be made arbitrarily close to offline optimal. □

5. MULTILEVEL AGGREGATION

This section extends FSL for multiple levels of aggregators, which are common in practice but are much more challenging than a single level. First, the aggregators' decisions on different levels are coupled and must be coordinated to reduce tail latency subject to quality SLAs. Second, the number of communication messages between different levels of aggregators must be small, e.g., an MLA cannot simply forward the results to TLA whenever it receives an ISN response, which further magnifies the design challenge.

At runtime, an MLA may or may not know the messaging time between itself and its higher-level aggregators in advance. Here the messaging time primarily includes network latency plus some lightly-weighted processing such as reranking and removing near duplicates. We consider three different scenarios of the messaging time: (a) known messaging time, (b) unknown but varying in a small bounded range, (c) general case of unknown messaging time with potentially large variations. In this section, we first focus on two-level aggregation, and generalize our results to arbitrary levels in Section 5.4.

5.1 Known Messaging Times

Inspired by FSL and its analysis in Theorem 1, we develop an optimal online policy for two (or multiple) levels of aggregators when messaging times between aggregators are known. We call this FSL-K, where 'K' stands for Known messaging time. The key idea of FSL-K is as follows: A TLA returns the results of each query in one of the three ways: (1) return full results before/at time threshold t^*; (2) based on the query utility progress at t^*, return partial results at a time threshold t^*, or (3) wait until receiving all responses from MLAs. We show that FSL-K at TLA is optimal, performing as well as an optimal offline policy. Once the top-level aggregation policy is known, we derive the time threshold for MLA by considering both t^* and the messaging time between TLA and MLAs.

Online Processing of FSL-K. Online processing of FSL-K takes as inputs time threshold t^* and utility threshold q^*, as decided by offline analysis.

TLA policy. For each query, if TLA receives responses from all MLAs and their ISNs prior to the time threshold t^*, this query is fast and TLA returns complete results. Otherwise, TLA has two choices: (1) If the utility of the current query is no less than q^*, then return the query results at t^*; Or (2) Complete the query and collect the results from all MLAs and their ISNs. In practice, system failure timeouts are set at TLA/MLA to stop waiting in case of server/network failure.

MLA policy. Suppose the messaging time between an MLA i and its TLA is d_i. For each query, MLA i responds to TLA in one of the two cases.

- If MLA i received all ISN responses before time $t^* - d_i$, it sends back the responses to TLA. This is a common case, where an MLA only sends one message to TLA.
- Otherwise, the MLA sends its results to TLA twice, because it cannot tell if a query is straggling or long (without global information from TLA). First, at time $t^* - d_i$, it sends back all the responses it received so far to TLA, in order to catch the checkpoint time of TLA at t^*. Second, the MLA sends the additional results to TLA after it received the responses from all of its ISNs, which is to obtain full results for the long queries that do not finish prior to $t^* - d_i$.

Algorithm 3 FSL-K: Offline processing

Input:
- time step size δ and log data $X = [X_{i,r}]$ for n queries: $X_{i,r}$ is the response time for r-th ISN and i- th query
- log data $Y = [Y_{i,q}]$: $Y_{i,q}$ is the messaging time from q-th MLA to TLA for i-th query
- utility constraints and latency percentile k from inputs of Algorithm 2

Procedure:

Step 1. $t_{max} = \max_{i,r} X_{i,r} + \max_{i,q} Y_{i,q}$; $m = \lceil \frac{t_{max}}{\delta} \rceil$

Step 2. Construct $A = [A_{i,j}] \in \mathbb{R}^{n \times m}$: $A_{i,j}$ represents the utility of i-th query when its finish time at TLA is $j \times \delta$; construct $B = [B_{i,j}] \in \mathbb{R}^{n \times m}$: The j-th column of B is sorted results (in descending order) of j-th column of A.

// *To compute A_{ij}, we first compute the utility of each q-th MLA at $(j \times \delta - Y_{i,q})$, and compute the sum of them.*

Step 3. Do Steps 3 & 4 in Algorithm 2

Output: time threshold $t^* = \max\{t_T, t_A\}$ and utility threshold $u^* = B_{\lceil \frac{kn}{100} \rceil, t^*/\delta}$

Alternatively, a TLA can inform its MLAs of not sending the second message when it decides to early return. The benefits of this alternative are arguable since (1) This does not decrease the overall number of messages (i.e., reducing one MLA message for straggling queries by adding a TLA message); (2) MLAs still send two messages for the long queries; (3) Search engines usually do not abort execution of straggling queries at ISNs (Section 2).

FSL-K is efficient at runtime in terms of both computation and communication. Its computation cost at both TLA and MLAs is negligible, requiring a simple counting on the number of responses. For communication cost, each MLA sends at most two messages to TLA. The average number of messages is even smaller: in most of the cases, queries are fast, requiring one message per MLA only; even if queries are straggling or long, only the MLAs with slow ISNs send two messages. For example, MLAs send 2 messages only 5.58% of the time on our evaluation using commercial advertisement search workloads (Section 6.2).

Offline Processing of FSL-K. Algorithm 3 presents offline processing of FSL-K, which has a similar flow as FSL with two differences. (1) FSL-K requires messaging times from MLAs to TLA as additional inputs. (2) At Step 2, to compute the utility of a query i at a time threshold t at TLA, we sum over its utilities obtained at the q-th MLA at time threshold $t - d_q$. Its time complexity is still $O((rn + n\log(n))(t_{max}/\delta))$.

Optimality Proof. Theorem 2 shows the optimality of FSL-K. Its proof is analogous to Theorem 1, which we skip for interest of space.

THEOREM 2. *For two-level aggregation with known messaging time, FSL-K achieves an arbitrarily close-to-minimum tail latency while meeting utility constraints.*

5.2 Bounded Messaging Times

We extend FSL-K to FSL-B for the case when messaging times between aggregators are unknown but bounded within a small range, where 'B' of FSL-B stands for Bounded messaging time. Suppose that the messaging time from the q-th MLA to TLA for the i-th query is bounded in the range $[Y_{i,q}^-, Y_{i,q}^+]$. To meet the utility constraints, FSL-B considers the (worst-case) upper bound $Y_{i,q}^+$ as messaging time, and then uses the same offline and online processing as FSL-K. *Thus, FSL-B is guaranteed to satisfy all utility constraints, and the resulting tail latency is at most* $\max_{i,q}(Y_{i,q}^+ - Y_{i,q}^-)$ *higher than theoretically optimal in the worst case.*

5.3 Unknown Messaging Times

Now, we consider a general case where the messaging times between aggregators are unknown with potentially large variations. It models the cases such as with poor network condition or with aggregators sharing processing with other workloads. In this case, even if we find the optimal time threshold t^* at TLA, it is still difficult for MLAs to decide when to respond to TLA to meet the checkpoint t^*. While it is challenging to provide a performance guarantee, we develop an effective heuristic policy, which shows very good empirical performance (Section 6). We call this FSL-U, where 'U' stands for Unknown messaging time.

FSL-U defines three parameters: besides time and utility thresholds t^* and q^*, respectively, FSL-U includes the third parameter, i.e., MLA threshold t_m^*, which indicates the time threshold when MLAs shall return their results to TLA. Note that we choose to use the same t_m^* for all MLAs, because without knowing how much it may take each MLA to respond, there is no reason to differentiate MLAs in terms of the time thresholds for returning their responses. For search engine in practice, each MLA is often associated with the same number of ISNs and running on the same hardware.

Online Processing of FSL-U. TLA still takes t^* and u^* as inputs, working in the same way as FSL-K. MLA also works similarly as FSL-K, but it applies an additional MLA time threshold of t_m^*, obtained by offline processing. Under FSL-U, each type of queries behaves as follows.

• Fast queries: TLA receives complete results before t^*. To achieve this, every MLA must have received all its ISNs' responses before t_m^*, and all messaging times between MLAs and TLA are smaller than $t^* - t_m^*$.

• Straggling queries: The utility at TLA is not equal to 1, but bigger than or equal to u^* at t^*. This can happen if any one of the above conditions for fast queries does not satisfy.

• Long queries: The utility at TLA is smaller than u^* at t^*. In this case, TLA waits for the responses from all MLAs and their associated ISNs (within timeouts).

Offline Processing of FSL-U. Algorithm 4 uses both ISN latencies and inter-aggregator messaging times to search for the optimal values of the three parameters. Compared with FSL-K, the main difference is that FSL-U needs to search over one more dimension — the time threshold t_m^* for MLA (Step 2 of Algorithm 4). The time complexity of Algorithm 4 is $O((rn + n\log(n))(t_{max}/\delta)^2)$, which is higher than FSL-K by a multiplicative factor $O(t_{max}/\delta)$ due to the enlarged search space of t_m^*.

Note that, although offline processing of FSL-U still finds the best aggregation policy parameters (t^*, u^*, t_m^*) based on log data to minimize the tail latency, we cannot claim that FSL-U is optimal when applied online. The offline optimal solution may give different MLA time threshold values to each MLA, because it has the offline information on the inter-aggregator messaging times for each query while this information cannot be obtained online (unlike FSL-K where the messaging time is assumed to be known online). However, our empirical results in Section 6 show FSL-U performs close to offline optimal.

Algorithm 4 FSL-U: Offline processing

Input: take the same input as Algorithm 3
Procedure:
Step 1. Set $t_{max}^m = \max_{i,r} X_{i,r}$ and $t_{max} = t_{max}^m + \max_{i,q} Y_{i,q}$
Step 2. Given each candidate t_m^*, find t^* and u^* for TLA
Set $v = 1$
// *Denote the number of MLAs as p*
for $v \leq \lceil t_{max}^m/\delta \rceil$ **do**
  Construct $D = [D_{i,q}] \in \mathbb{R}^{n \times p}$: $D_{i,q}$ is the utility of q-th mid-level aggregator for i-th query if we finish it at $v \times \delta$.
  Construct $E = [E_{i,q}] \in \mathbb{R}^{n \times p}$: $E_{i,q}$ is the finish time of the q-th mid-level aggregator for i-th query
  // $E_{i,q} = \min\{v'\delta, v\delta\}$, *where* $v'\delta$ *is the time the q-th aggregator receives all the responses*
  Construct $A = [A_{i,j}] \in \mathbb{R}^{n \times m'}$, where $m' = \lceil \frac{t_{max}}{\delta} \rceil$: $A_{i,j}$ represents the utility of i-th query when its finish time at the top-level aggregator is $j \times \delta$
  // *For each query i, the utility at* $j \times \delta$ *is determined by adding up all entries of* $D_{i,q}$ *whose corresponding value of* $E_{i,q} + Y_{i,q}$ *(i.e., the receiving time of q-th mid-level aggregator's response at the top-level) is smaller than* $j \times \delta$
  Construct $B = [B_{i,j}] \in \mathbb{R}^{n \times m}$: The j-th column of B is sorted results (in descending order of the utility) of j-th column of A.
  Do Steps 3 & 4 in Algorithm 2.
  Set $t_v^* = \max\{t_T, t_A\}$ and $u_v^* = B_{\lceil \frac{kn}{100} \rceil, t_v^*/\delta}$
  $v = v + 1$
end for
Step 3. Find $v^* = \arg\min_v\{t_v^*\}$ and set $(t^*, u^*, t_m^*) = (t_v^*, u_v^*, v^* \times \delta)$
Output: time threshold at the top-level t^*, utility threshold u^*, and time threshold at the mid-level t_m^*

5.4 Generalization to Multilevel Aggregation

We can easily extend FSL-K, FSL-B, and FSL-U to more than two levels of aggregators. Here, we still call the top-level aggregator as TLA, but there may be more than one level of MLAs. For FSL-K (known messaging time), TLA still has one time threshold t^* and utility threshold q^*. All levels of MLAs send their responses in advance such that TLA receives the responses prior to or at t^*. The optimality of FSL-K still holds, and the time complexity is $O((srn + n\log(n))(t_{max}/\delta))$ with s levels of aggregators. The extension of FSL-B to multilevel aggregation is also straightforward, following that of FSL-K. The performance bound of FSL-B becomes the summation of the upper bounds on messaging times over all levels. To extend FSL-U to multiple levels, we use a different time threshold t_m^* for each level of MLA. The resulting complexity of offline processing increases with the increased level of MLAs, due to enlarged search space, the time complexity is $O((rn+n\log(n))(t_{max}/\delta)^s)$, since each level of MLA has a search complexity of $O(t_{max}/\delta)$.

6. EVALUATION

We evaluate FSL for single-level aggregation by comparing it to alternative policies using a production trace of a 44-ISN cluster from a commercial web search engine, and we use several latency objectives and utility constraints. We also study several distributions forming synthetic workloads. For two-level aggregation, we create eight aggregation policies and compare FSL-K and FSL-U to them using a trace from a two-level commercial advertisement engine, in addition to a synthetic workload to model a large system with 1936 ISNs.

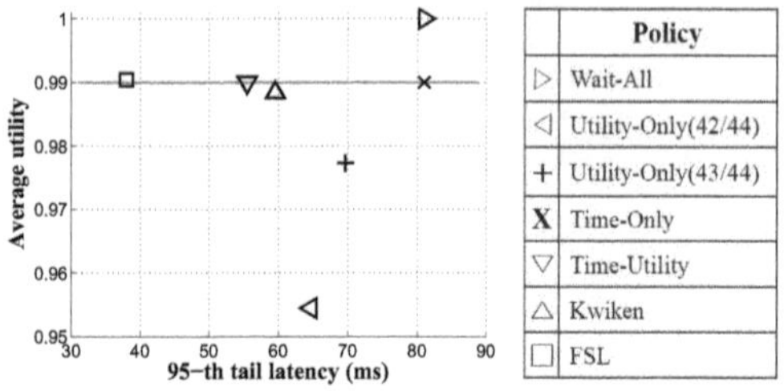

Figure 4: Tail latency comparison for single aggregator with Bing production traces.

6.1 Single Aggregator

Bing Production traces. We use a query log from a production cluster of Microsoft Bing search engine. The log records the latency of 44 ISNs over 66,922 queries. These queries missed the result cache and were sent to ISNs for processing. We use a subset of 10,000 queries for training, and the remaining 56,922 queries for evaluation. As Bing search does not abort processing of late responses at ISNs (Section 2), the recorded query execution times of ISNs remain unaffected by aggregation policy and hence we replay in our simulation to compare the alternative aggregation policies. We set the system failure timeout as 500 ms. A response that does not arrive by 500 ms is ignored by all policies.

Evaluation with production traces. Our target is to minimize the 95-th tail latency under the constraint that average utility is greater than or equal to 0.99. We implement all policies in Table 1 and compute the best parameters for each policy using the same training dataset. We show their results in Figure 4 that depicts the 95-th tail latency on the x-axis and the average utility on the y-axis. Wait-All is the baseline with *utility* = 1 and it has the highest 95-th tail latency. For Utility-Only we use two configurations because when the utility threshold is 0.99, the aggregator must wait for responses from all ISNs because $(43/44) < 0.99$. We, therefore, set utility threshold to $(43/44) = 0.977$ and to $(42/44) = 0.955$, and report both settings in the figure. FSL provides the shortest tail latency compared to all other schemes: (FSL: 38 ms, Time-Utility: 65 ms, and Kwiken: 59 ms). In particular, FSL reduces the tail latency by 53% over Wait-All and by 36% over the best alternative. All policies have similar average latencies (between 15 and 17 ms) because the average response latency is determined mainly by fast queries which constitute majority queries.

To see why FSL achieves lower tail latency, we study the utility of all queries according to their length (measured as the maximum latency of all ISN responses) quantized into bins of 20 ms as depicted in Figure 5. The first point on each curve shows the average utility for the queries with length $\in [0, 20]$, and second point for $\in [20, 40]$. Notice that the first two points represent over 92% of queries. We do not show a curve for Utility-Only because it is a horizontal line across all queries regardless of their length. Time-only terminates all queries after a threshold and we see a similar behaviour for Time-Utility: All relatively slow queries are terminated

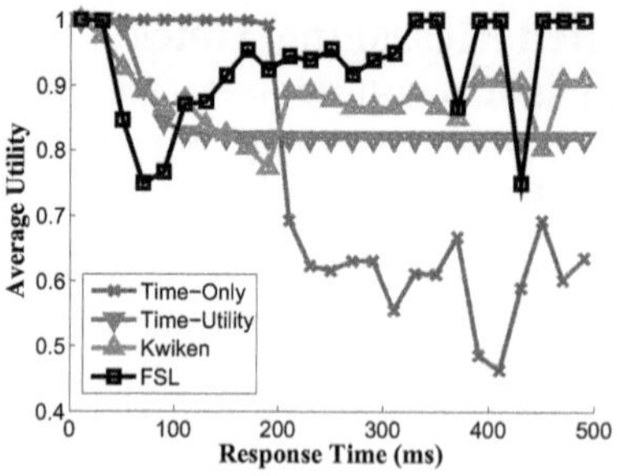

Figure 5: Average utility for quantized query length (single aggregator & Bing production traces).

early regardless of being long or straggling. Next, Kwiken terminates queries starting from the second point which impacts many fast queries, and again, all relatively slow queries are terminated early. In contrast, FSL exploits the (5%) latency slackness to obtain high utility for long queries, which allows it to terminate straggling queries more aggressively, reducing tail latency further while meeting utility targets.

Sensitivity study. Using the production traces, we study the two tail latency optimization targets (95-th and 99-th) under several utility constraints as depicted in Table 2. The values of the first row show the 95-th tail latency corresponding to data in Figure 4. The stricter the utility constraint, the fewer the chances to reduce the tail latency (compared with Wait-All) while meeting the constraint. This behaviour applies both for average and tail utility constraints as well as across the two tail latency objectives. The last row shows that we can enforce two utility constraints, one on average and another on the 95-th tail utility. Under all configurations FSL reduces the tail latencies the most: It provides the minimum tail latency while meeting the utility constraints, consistently outperforming heuristic policies.

Synthetic datasets. We evaluate the policies using several synthetic datasets with average utility constraints (AVG ≥ 0.99) assuming a single aggregator with 44 ISNs. For each dataset, we generate 66,922 queries and use 10,000 as a training set and the remaining 56,922 for evaluation. We use two methods to generate synthetic datasets: (1) In one-phase sampling, query latency at each ISN is sampled independently from a distribution. (2) In two-phase sampling, we first sample the query mean from a distribution, and then sample its latency at each ISN from a second distribution parametrized by the query mean. While one-phase sampling generates latencies from all ISNs of all queries assuming independence, two-phase sampling models the scenarios where long (short) queries tend to have overall higher (lower) latencies from many of its ISN responses. We report the average of Pearson's correlation coefficient (PCC) between ISNs for all pairs of ISNs, as well as the average of coefficient of variation (σ/μ) for all queries. As a reference, for the production traces: $PCC = 0.9920$ which is a high value showing significant correlation among ISN latencies for a particular query, and $CV = 0.1777$, a small value as workload is dominated by many fast queries.

Evaluation with synthetic datasets. Table 3 reports the results. The first two rows show one-phase sampling with log-normal and exponential distributions. PCC is small indicating little correlation among ISN latencies per query: each query has similar utility at any time point, which does not produce the straggling and long query behaviours. The policies Time-Only, Time-Utility, Kwiken reduce the tail la-

Table 2: Percentage of tail latency reduction over Wait-All policy for different utility constraints with Bing production traces and single aggregator. A higher value is better, i.e., bigger latency reduction.

Utility constraint	95-th tail latency reduction (%)				99-th tail latency reduction (%)			
	Time-Only	Time-Utility	Kwiken	FSL	Time-Only	Time-Utility	Kwiken	FSL
AVG ≥ 0.99	0	31.57	26.63	53.11	15.48	15.48	15.48	18.05
AVG ≥ 0.999	0	0	8.91	34.60	9.90	10.09	9.90	12.90
95-th tail ≥ 0.95	19.79	19.79	27.93	70.38	72.11	19.45	72.11	80.26
95-th tail ≥ 0.99	3.75	3.75	17.31	64.21	66.53	19.45	66.53	75.54
99-th tail ≥ 0.99	0	0	3.42	29.66	6.04	6.04	2.29	10.76
AVG ≥ 0.99&95-th tail ≥ 0.95	0	19.79	26.63	53.11	15.48	15.48	15.48	18.05

tency compared to the baseline, and FSL provides bigger tail latency reduction. We observe similar behaviour under all the distributions we employed (not reported due to space).

Next, we study the two-phase sampling, which has higher correlation and is more realistic for search workloads. We use both Exponential and Bounded Pareto distributions for the first sampling phase. We use log-normal distribution for the second-phase sampling because sampling from normal distribution may result in negative values for latency. FSL clearly outperforms the other policies and the improvement of FSL over other polices increases as PCC increases.

6.2 Two-Level Aggregation

Symbol	▷	◁	◀	X	▽	▼	△	▲	□	■
Policy: MLA	Wait-All	Wait-All	Utility-Only	Time-Only	Time-Utility	Wait-All	Kwiken	Wait-All	FSL-K	FSL-U
Policy: TLA	Wait-All	Utility-Only	Utility-Only	Time-Only	Wait-All	Time-Utility	Wait-All	Kwiken		

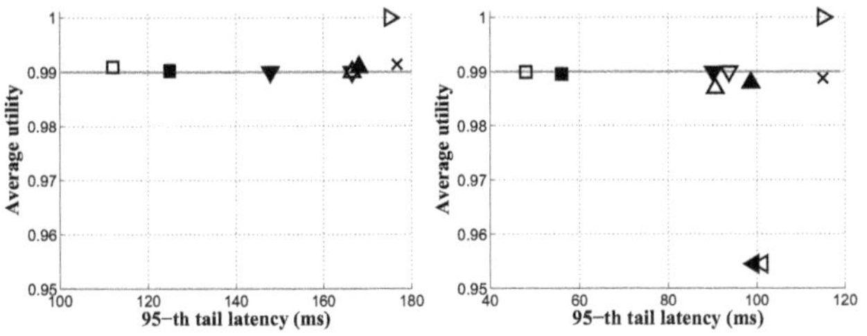

(a) Advertisement Engine (b) Synthetic

Figure 6: Policy comparison for cluster with two-level aggregators on (1) production traces of advertisement engine and (2) synthetic datasets.

We evaluate two-level aggregation using a production trace of Bing Advertisement Engine as well as a synthetic dataset modelling a large-scale system with a few thousand ISNs.

Advertisement engine production traces. We use a query log from a production cluster with two-level aggregation of Bing advertisement engine. The log records the latencies of 1 TLA, 16 MLAs and 4 ISNs per MLA (total ISNs is 64) over 16,311 queries. We use a subset of 10,000 queries for training and the remaining 6,311 for evaluation.

There is no policy that targets two-level aggregation in prior work. So we develop the following eight policies for the MLA&TLA policies. (1) Wait-All & Wait-All (baseline), (2) Wait-All & Utility-Only (0.95), (3) Utility-Only (0.95) & Utility-Only (0.95), (4) Time-Only & Time-Only, (5) Time-Utility & Wait-All, (6) Wait-All & Time-Utility,(7) Kwiken & Wait-All, (8) Wait-All & Kwiken. We make the MLA delay known to FSL-K (which obtains the optimal solution) and unknown to FSL-U (which is heuristic) and study how they compare to each other as well as to other polices.

Figure 6(a) compares the 95-th tail latencies for average utility target of 0.99. FSL-K offers the shortest tail latency (112 ms). FSL-U is close (125 ms), within 12% of the optimal, lower by 30% over the baseline and lower by 15% over the best alternative policy. (Wait-All & Utility-Only and Utility-Only & Utility-Only produce same tail latency and average utility as baseline, so are not plotted in the figure.)

Evaluation with synthetic datasets. We also evaluate FSL using a synthetic dataset modelling a large-scale system with two levels of aggregation containing 1 TLA, 44 MLA and 44 ISNs per MLA (total ISNs is 1,936). The synthetic dataset has the same mean and variance as Bing queries. In addition, the MLA messaging delay is sampled from an exponential distribution with parameter $\mu = 7.5$ ms, which is the measured average messaging time between aggregators. Figure 6(b) shows that FSL-K provides the shortest tail latency (49 ms), and FSL-U is close (54 ms) and is substantially better than the other polices; the tail latency of FSL-U is within 16% of the optimal, and lower by 51% over the baseline and by 38% over the best alternative. A thorough sensitivity study is presented in a technical report [32].

7. RELATED WORK

Complementary latency reduction techniques on web search. ISNs of web search often employ dynamic pruning to early terminate the post-list processing of a query and to avoid scoring the postings for the documents that unlikely make the top-k retrieved set [3, 33]. Early termination is an example that web search trades completeness of query response for latency. Prior work [19] quantifies the relationship of quality and latency at ISNs, and trades quality for latency under heavy loads. Multicores [15, 22] and graphics processors [14] have also been used to parallelize query processing and reduce query latency. All the above techniques improve ISN latency, complementary to our study where we take ISN latency as inputs and focus on aggregation policy.

Beyond ISN-level improvement, there are studies on reducing the latency for search queries across different system components, e.g., optimizing caching [6, 9, 10, 16, 26] and prefetching [23] to mitigate I/O costs, and improving network protocols between ISNs and aggregators [28]. These studies are also complementary to our work. Only queries that are not cached are sent to ISNs for processing. We take transmission time between ISNs and aggregators as inputs, working (orthogonally) for any transmission protocols.

Request reissue is a standard technique to reduce latency tail in distributed systems at the cost of increased resource usage [13, 20, 29, 34]. When web indices are replicated, reissuing a query at another cluster or server may improve latency by using responses that finishes first. Reissuing consumes extra resources to replicate indexes and to process a query more than once. Therefore, it is more preferable to have an effective aggregation policy to reduce latency and meet quality SLAs without reissuing many queries.

Table 3: 95-th tail latency reduction (%) of policies over Wait-All policy for single aggregator and synthetic distributions.

ISN latency (X) distribution	PCC	CV	Time-Only	Time-Utility	Kwiken	FSL
Log-normal distribution ($X_{i,r} \sim \ln\mathcal{N}(1,1)$)	0.0030	1.1574	50.28	50.28	50.28	53.83
Exponential distribution ($X_{i,r} \sim \exp(0.1)$)	0.0031	0.9793	30.31	31.79	30.31	34.76
$m_i \sim \exp(0.1), X_{i,r} \sim \ln\mathcal{N}(\log(m_i), \log(1+m_i)/5)$	0.4724	0.4205	39.27	49.05	39.27	60.21
$m_i \sim \exp(0.1), X_{i,r} \sim \ln\mathcal{N}(\log(m_i), \log(1+m_i)/10)$	0.8108	0.2035	12.60	29.47	22.17	41.73
$m_i \sim \exp(0.1), X_{i,r} \sim \ln\mathcal{N}(\log(m_i), \log(1+m_i)/100)$	0.9978	0.0200	0	3.20	3.92	12.57
$m_i \sim$ BoundedPareto($\alpha = 0.5, lo = 1, hi = 300$), $X_{i,r} \sim \ln\mathcal{N}(\log(m_i), \log(1+m_i)/100)$	0.9963	0.0213	4.51	6.06	4.81	25.36

Aggregation policies. We will not repeat the discussions of existing aggregation policies and performance in Sections 3 and 6. Broder and Mitzenmarcher [8] study a related problem on maximizing reward as a function of time and utility, but they assume the responses of ISNs are i.i.d (independent and identically distributed), which Section 6.1 shows that ISN responses are highly correlated in practice. Moreover, they do not consider multilevel aggregations. Finally, we note that aggregation problem also exists in other domains (e.g., aggregate data sources in wireless sensor networks for energy minimization [30]), which requires domain-specific techniques and differs from our work.

8. CONCLUSION

We develop an aggregation policy, combining data-driven offline analysis with online processing, to reduce tail latency of web search queries subject to search quality SLAs. We first focus on a single aggregator and prove the optimality of our policy. We then extend our policy for multilevel aggregation and prove its optimality when messaging times between aggregators are known. We also introduce an empirically-effective policy to address unknown messaging time. We conduct experiments using production logs from a commercial web search engine, a commercial advertisement engine and synthetic workloads. Compared with prior work, the proposed policy reduces tail latency by up to 40%.

Acknowledgements

This work was partially done while J.-M. Yun was an intern at Microsoft Research. S. Ren was supported in part by the U.S. NSF CNS-1423137 and CNS-1453491.

References

[1] M. Alizadeh, A. Greenberg, D. A. Maltz, J. Padhye, P. Patel, B. Prabhakar, S. Sengupta, and M. Sridharan. Data center tcp (dctcp). *SIGCOMM Comput. Commun. Rev.*, 41(4):–, Aug. 2010.

[2] I. S. Altingovde, R. Blanco, B. B. Cambazoglu, R. Ozcan, E. Sarigil, and O. Ulusoy. Characterizing web search queries that match very few or no results. In *CIKM*, 2012.

[3] V. N. Anh, O. de Kretser, and A. Moffat. Vector-space ranking with effective early termination. In *SIGIR*, 2001.

[4] I. Arapakis, X. Bai, and B. B. Cambazoglu. Impact of response latency on user behavior in web search. In *SIGIR*, 2014.

[5] C. S. Badue, R. Baeza-Yates, B. Ribeiro-Neto, A. Ziviani, and N. Ziviani. Analyzing imbalance among homogeneous index servers in a web search system. *Inf. Process. Manage.*, 43(3), 2007.

[6] R. Baeza-Yates, A. Gionis, F. Junqueira, V. Murdock, V. Plachouras, and F. Silvestri. The impact of caching on search engines. In *SIGIR*, 2007.

[7] L. A. Barroso, J. Dean, and U. Hölzle. Web search for a planet: The google cluster architecture. *IEEE Micro*, 23(2):22–28, 2003.

[8] A. Broder and M. Mitzenmacher. Optimal plans for aggregation. In *PODC*, 2002.

[9] B. B. Cambazoglu, I. S. Altingovde, R. Ozcan, and Ö. Ulusoy. Cache-based query processing for search engines. *ACM Transactions on the Web*, 6(4):14, 2012.

[10] B. B. Cambazoglu, F. P. Junqueira, V. Plachouras, S. Banachowski, B. Cui, S. Lim, and B. Bridge. A refreshing perspective of search engine caching. In *WWW*, 2010.

[11] B. B. Cambazoglu, V. Plachouras, and R. Baeza-Yates. Quantifying performance and quality gains in distributed web search engines. In *SIGIR*, 2009.

[12] J. Dean. Challenges in building large-scale information retrieval systems (Invited talk). In *WSDM*, 2009.

[13] J. Dean and L. A. Barroso. The tail at scale. *Commun. ACM*, 56(2):74–80, Feb. 2013.

[14] S. Ding, J. He, H. Yan, and T. Suel. Using graphics processors for high performance ir query processing. In *WWW*, 2009.

[15] E. Frachtenberg. Reducing query latencies in web search using fine-grained parallelism. In *WWW*, 2009.

[16] Q. Gan and T. Suel. Improved techniques for result caching in web search engines. In *WWW*, 2009.

[17] J. Hamilton. The cost of latency. `http://perspectives.mvdirona.com/2009/10/31/TheCostOfLatency.aspx`, 2009.

[18] E. Hatcher and O. Gospodnetic. *Lucene in Action*. Manning Publications Co., 2004.

[19] Y. He, S. Elnikety, J. Larus, and C. Yan. Zeta: Scheduling interactive services with partial execution. In *SOCC*, 2012.

[20] V. Jalaparti, P. Bodik, S. Kandula, I. Menache, M. Rybalkin, and C. Yan. Speeding up distributed request-response workflows. In *SIGCOMM '13*, 2013.

[21] M. Jeon, Y. He, S. Elnikety, A. L. Cox, and S. Rixner. Adaptive parallelism for web search. In *EuroSys*, 2013.

[22] M. Jeon, S. Kim, S.-W. Hwang, Y. He, A. L. Cox, and S. Rixner. Taming tail latencies in web search. In *SIGIR*, 2014.

[23] S. Jonassen, B. B. Cambazoglu, and F. Silvestri. Prefetching query results and its impact on search engines. In *SIGIR*, 2012.

[24] J. R. Lorch and A. J. Smith. Improving dynamic voltage scaling algorithms with PACE. In *SIGMETRICS*, 2001.

[25] C. Macdonald, N. Tonellotto, and I. Ounis. Learning to predict response times for online query scheduling. In *SIGIR*, 2012.

[26] R. Ozcan, I. S. Altingovde, and Ö. Ulusoy. Cost-aware strategies for query result caching in web search engines. *ACM Transactions on the Web*, 5(2):9, 2011.

[27] E. Schurman and J. Brutlag. The user and business impact of server delays, additional bytes, and http chunking in web search. In *Velocity*, 2009.

[28] G. Upadhyaya, V. S. Pai, and S. P. Midkiff. Expressing and exploiting concurrency in networked applications with aspen. In *PPoPP*, 2007.

[29] A. Vulimiri, O. Michel, P. B. Godfrey, and S. Shenker. More is less: Reducing latency via redundancy. In *HotNets*, 2012.

[30] Z. Ye, A. A. Abouzeid, and J. Ai. Optimal stochastic policies for distributed data aggregation in wireless sensor networks. *IEEE/ACM Trans. Netw.*, 17(5):1494–1507, Oct. 2009.

[31] J. Yi, F. Maghoul, and J. Pedersen. Deciphering mobile search patterns: A study of Yahoo! mobile search queries. In *WWW*, 2008.

[32] J.-M. Yun, Y. He, S. Elnikety, and S. Ren. Optimal aggregation policy for reducing tail latency of web search. Technical Report MSR-TR-2015-39, Microsoft Research, 2015. `http://research.microsoft.com/apps/pubs/?id=246273`.

[33] F. Zhang, S. Shi, H. Yan, and J.-R. Wen. Revisiting globally sorted indexes for efficient document retrieval. In *WSDM*, 2010.

[34] J. Zhang, X. Long, and T. Suel. Performance of compressed inverted list caching in search engines. In *WWW*, 2008.

[35] S. Zhu, A. Potapova, M. Alabduljalil, X. Liu, and T. Yang. Clustering and load balancing optimization for redundant content removal. In *WWW*, 2012.

QuickScorer: A Fast Algorithm to Rank Documents with Additive Ensembles of Regression Trees

Claudio Lucchese
ISTI–CNR, Pisa, Italy
c.lucchese@isti.cnr.it

Franco Maria Nardini
ISTI–CNR, Pisa, Italy
f.nardini@isti.cnr.it

Salvatore Orlando
Univ. di Venezia, Italy
orlando@unive.it

Raffaele Perego
ISTI–CNR, Pisa, Italy
r.perego@isti.cnr.it

Nicola Tonellotto
ISTI–CNR, Pisa, Italy
n.tonellotto@isti.cnr.it

Rossano Venturini
Univ. di Pisa, Italy
rossano@di.unipi.it

ABSTRACT

Learning-to-Rank models based on additive ensembles of regression trees have proven to be very effective for ranking query results returned by Web search engines, a scenario where quality and efficiency requirements are very demanding. Unfortunately, the computational cost of these ranking models is high. Thus, several works already proposed solutions aiming at improving the efficiency of the scoring process by dealing with features and peculiarities of modern CPUs and memory hierarchies. In this paper, we present QuickScorer, a new algorithm that adopts a novel bitvector representation of the tree-based ranking model, and performs an interleaved traversal of the ensemble by means of simple logical bitwise operations. The performance of the proposed algorithm are unprecedented, due to its cache-aware approach, both in terms of data layout and access patterns, and to a control flow that entails very low branch mis-prediction rates. The experiments on real Learning-to-Rank datasets show that QuickScorer is able to achieve speedups over the best state-of-the-art baseline ranging from 2x to 6.5x.

Categories and Subject Descriptors

H.3.3 [**Information Storage and Retrieval**]: Information Search and Retrieval—*Search process*

Keywords

Learning to Rank, Efficiency, Cache-aware Algorithms

1. INTRODUCTION

Ranking query results according to a relevance criterion is a fundamental problem in Information Retrieval (IR). Nowadays, an emerging research area named Learning-to-Rank (LtR) [7, 2] has shown that effective solutions to the ranking problem can leverage machine learning techniques. A LtR-based function, which *scores* a set of candidate documents according to their relevance to a given user query, is learned from a *ground-truth* composed of many training examples. The examples are basically a collection of queries $\mathcal{Q}$, where each query $q \in \mathcal{Q}$ is associated with a set of assessed documents $\mathcal{D} = \{d_0, d_1, \ldots\}$. Each pair (q, d_i) is in turn labeled by a *relevance judgment* y_i, usually a positive integer in a fixed range, stating the degree of relevance of the document for the query. These labels induce a partial ordering over the assessed documents, thus defining their *ideal ranking* [6]. The scoring function learned by a LtR algorithm aims to approximate the *ideal ranking* from the examples observed in the training set.

The ranking process is particularly challenging for Web search engines, which, besides the demanding requirements for result pages of high quality in response to user queries, have also to deal with efficiency constraints, which are not so common in other ranking-based applications. Indeed, two of the most effective LtR-based rankers are based on additive ensembles of regression trees, namely Gradient-Boosted Regression Trees (GBRT) [4], and Lambda-MART (λ-MART) [18]. Due to the thousands of trees to be traversed at scoring time for each document, these rankers are also the most expensive in terms of computational time, thus impacting on response time and throughput of query processing. Therefore, devising techniques and strategies to speed-up document ranking without losing in quality is definitely an urgent research topic in Web search [14, 3, 10, 5, 19].

Usually, LtR-based scorers are embedded in complex two-stage ranking architectures [3, 16], which avoid applying them to all the documents possibly matching a user query. The first stage retrieves from the inverted index a sufficiently large set of possibly relevant documents matching the user query. This phase is aimed at optimizing the recall and is usually carried out by using a simple and fast ranking function, e.g., BM25 combined with some document-level scores [9]. LtR-based scorers are used in the second stage to *re-rank* the candidate documents coming from the first stage, and are optimized for high precision. In this two-stage architecture, the time budget available to re-rank the candidate documents is limited, due to the incoming rate of queries and the users' expectations in terms of quality-of-service. Strongly motivated by time budget considerations, the IR community has started to investigate low-level optimizations to reduce the scoring time of the most effective LtR

SIGIR '15, August 09 - 13, 2015, Santiago, Chile

ACM 978-1-4503-3621-5/15/08 $15.00
DOI: http://dx.doi.org/10.1145/2766462.2767733.

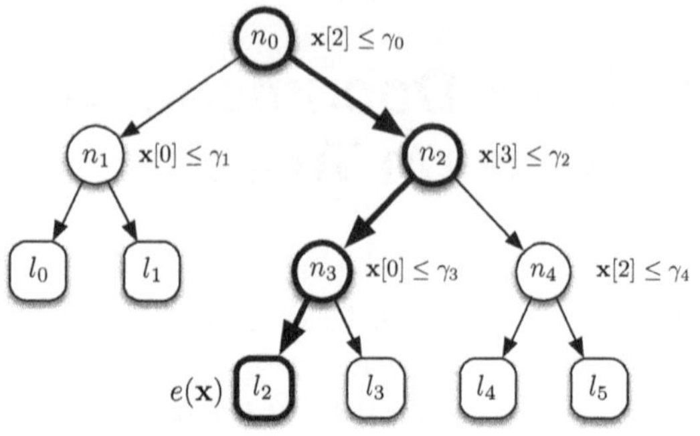

Figure 1: A decision tree.

rankers based on ensembles of regression trees, by dealing with features and peculiarities of modern CPUs and memory hierarchies [1, 12]. In this work we advance the state of the art in this field, and propose QUICKSCORER (QS), a new algorithm to score documents with an ensemble of regression trees. The main contributions of our proposal are:

- a novel representation of an ensemble of binary regression trees based on bitvectors, allowing QS to perform a fast interleaved traversal of the trees by using efficient logical bitwise operations. The performance benefits of the resulting traversal are unprecedented, due to a cache-aware approach, both in terms of data layout and access patterns, and to a program control flow that entails very low branch mis-prediction rates;
- an extensive experimental assessment conducted on publicly available LtR datasets with various λ-MART models, differing for both the size of the ensemble and the number of tree leaves. The results of the experiments show that QS achieves impressive speedups over the best state-of-the-art competitor, ranging from 2x up to 6.5x. Moreover, to motivate the very good performance of QS over competitors, we evaluate in-depth some CPU counters that measure important performance events, such as number of instructions executed, cache-misses suffered, or branches mis-predicted;
- a block-wise version of QS for scoring large tree ensembles and large sets of documents. BLOCKWISE-QS (BWQS) splits the set of documents and the tree ensemble in disjoint groups that can be processed separately. Our experiments show that BWQS performs up to 1.55 times better than the original QS, thanks to cache reuse which reduces cache misses.

The rest of the paper is structured as follows: Section 2 provides background information and discusses the related work, while Section 3 details the QS algorithm and its features. Then, Section 4 reports on the results of our comprehensive evaluation. Finally, we conclude our investigation in Section 5 by reporting some conclusions and suggestions for future research.

2. BACKGROUND AND RELATED WORK

GRADIENT-BOOSTED REGRESSION TREES (GBRT) [4] and LAMBDA-MART (λ-MART) [18] are two of the most effective Learning-to-Rank (LtR) algorithms. They both generate additive ensembles of regression trees aiming at predicting the relevance labels y_i of a query document pair (q, d_i). The GBRT algorithm builds a model by approximating the root mean squared error on a given training set. This loss function makes GBRT a point-wise LtR algorithm, i.e., query-document pairs are exploited independently. The λ-MART algorithm improves over GBRT by directly optimizing list-wise information retrieval measures such as NDCG [6]. Thus, λ-MART aims at finding a scoring function that generates an ordering of documents as close as possible to the ideal ranking. In terms of scoring process there is thus no difference between λ-MART and GBRT, since they both generate a set of weighted regression trees.

In this work, we discuss algorithms and optimizations for scoring efficiently documents by means of regression tree ensembles. Indeed, the findings of this work apply beyond LtR, and in any application where large ensembles of regression trees are used for classification or regression tasks.

Each query-document pair (q, d_i) is represented by a real-valued vector $\mathbf{x}$ of *features*, namely $\mathbf{x} \in \mathbb{R}^{|\mathcal{F}|}$ where $\mathcal{F} = \{f_0, f_1, \ldots\}$ is the set of features characterizing the candidate document d_i and the user query q, and $\mathbf{x}[i]$ stores feature f_i. Let $\mathcal{T}$ be an ensemble of trees representing the ranking model. Each tree $T = (N, L)$ in $\mathcal{T}$ is a decision tree composed of a set of internal nodes $N = \{n_0, n_1, \ldots\}$, and a set of leaves $L = \{l_0, l_1, \ldots\}$. Each $n \in N$ is associated with a *Boolean test* over a specific feature with id ϕ, i.e., $f_\phi \in \mathcal{F}$, and a constant threshold $\gamma \in \mathbb{R}$. This test is in the form $\mathbf{x}[\phi] \leq \gamma$. Each leaf $l \in L$ stores the *prediction* $l.\mathtt{val} \in \mathbb{R}$, representing the potential contribution of tree T to the final score of the document.

All the nodes whose Boolean conditions evaluate to FALSE are called *false nodes*, and *true nodes* otherwise. The scoring of a document represented by a feature vector $\mathbf{x}$ requires the traversing of all the trees in the ensemble, starting at their root nodes. If a visited node in N is a false one, then the *right* branch is taken, and the *left* branch otherwise. The visit continues recursively until a leaf node is reached, where the value of the *prediction* is returned. Such leaf node is named *exit leaf* and denoted by $e(\mathbf{x}) \in L$. We omit $\mathbf{x}$ when it is clear from the context.

Hereinafter, we assume that nodes of T are numbered in breadth-first order and leaves from left to right, and let ϕ_i and γ_i be the feature id and threshold associated with i-th internal node, respectively. It is worth noting that the same feature can be involved in multiple nodes of the same tree. For example, in the tree shown in Figure 1, the features f_0 and f_2 are used twice. Assuming that $\mathbf{x}$ is such that $\mathbf{x}[2] > \gamma_0$, $\mathbf{x}[3] \leq \gamma_2$, and $\mathbf{x}[0] \leq \gamma_3$, the exit leaf e of the tree in the Figure 1 is the leaf l_2.

The tree traversal process is repeated for all the trees of the ensemble $\mathcal{T}$, denoted by $\mathcal{T} = \{T_0, T_1, \ldots\}$. The score $s(\mathbf{x})$ of the whole ensemble is finally computed as a *weighted sum* over the contributions of each tree $T_h = (N_h, L_h)$ in $\mathcal{T}$ as:

$$s(\mathbf{x}) = \sum_{h=0}^{|\mathcal{T}|-1} w_h \cdot e_h(\mathbf{x}).\mathtt{val}$$

where $e_h(\mathbf{x}).\mathtt{val}$ is the predicted value of tree T_h, having weight $w_h \in \mathbb{R}$.

In the following we review state-of-the-art optimization techniques for the implementation of additive ensemble of regression trees and their use in document scoring.

Tree traversal optimization. A naïve implementation of a tree traversal may exploit a node data structure that stores the feature id, the threshold and the pointers to the left and right children nodes. The traversal starts from the root and moves down to the leaves accordingly to the results of the Boolean conditions on the traversed nodes. This method can be enhanced by using the optimized data layout in [1]. The resulting algorithm is named STRUCT+. This simple approach entails a number of issues. First, the next node to be processed is known only after the test is evaluated. As the next instruction to be executed is not known, this induces frequent *control hazards*, i.e., instruction dependencies introduced by conditional branches. As a consequence, the efficiency of a code strongly depends on the *branch misprediction rate* [8]. Finally, due to the unpredictability of the path visited by a given document, the traversal has low temporal and spatial locality, generating low *cache hit ratio*. This is apparent when processing a large number of documents with a large ensemble of trees, since neither the documents nor the trees may fit in cache.

Another basic, but well performing approach is IF-THEN-ELSE. Each decision tree is translated into a sequence of if-then-else blocks, e.g., in C++ language. The resulting code is compiled to generate an efficient document scorer. IF-THEN-ELSE aims at taking advantage of compiler optimization strategies, which can potentially re-arrange the tree ensemble traversal into a more efficient procedure. The size of the resulting code is proportional to the total number of nodes in the ensemble. This makes it impossible to exploit successfully the instruction cache. IF-THEN-ELSE was proven to be efficient with small feature sets [1], but it still suffers from *control hazards*.

Asadi *et al.* [1] proposed to rearrange the computation to transform *control hazards* into *data hazards*, i.e., data dependencies introduced when one instruction requires the result of another. To this end, node n_s of a tree stores, in addition to a feature id ϕ_s and a threshold γ_s, an array `idx` of two positions holding the addresses of the left and right children nodes data structures. Then, the output of the test $\mathbf{x}[\phi_s] > \gamma_s$ is directly used as an index of such array in order to retrieve the next node to be processed. The visit of a tree of depth d is then statically "un-rolled" in d operations, starting from the root node n_0, as follows:

$$d \text{ steps} \begin{cases} i \leftarrow n_0.\mathtt{idx}\,[\mathbf{x}[\phi_0] > \gamma_0] \\ i \leftarrow n_i.\mathtt{idx}\,[\mathbf{x}[\phi_i] > \gamma_i] \\ \vdots \qquad\qquad \vdots \\ i \leftarrow n_i.\mathtt{idx}\,[\mathbf{x}[\phi_i] > \gamma_i] \end{cases}$$

Leaf nodes are encoded so that the indexes in `idx` generate self loops, with dummy ϕ_s and γ_s. At the end of the visit, the exit leaf is identified by variable i, and a look-up table is used to retrieve the prediction of the tree.

This approach, named PRED, removes control hazards as the next instruction to be executed is always known. On the other hand, data dependencies are not solved as the output of one instruction is required to execute the subsequent. Memory access patterns are not improved either, as they depend on the path along the tree traversed by a document. Finally, PRED introduces a new source of overhead: for a tree of depth d, even if document reaches a leaf early, the above d steps are executed anyway.

To reduce *data hazards* the same authors proposed a *vectorized* version of the scoring algorithm, named VPRED, by interleaving the evaluation of a small set of documents (16 was the best setting). VPRED was shown to be 25% to 70% faster than PRED on synthetic data, and to outperform other approaches. The same approach of PRED was also adopted in some previous works exploiting GPUs [11], and a more recent survey evaluates the trade-off among multi-core CPUs, GPUs and FPGA [13].

In this work we compare against VPRED which can be considered the best performing algorithm at the state of the art. In the experimental section, we show that the proposed QS algorithm has reduced *control hazard*, smaller *branch mis-prediction* rate and better *memory access patterns*.

Memory latency issues of scoring algorithms are tackled in Tang *et al.* [12]. In most cases, the cache memory may be insufficient to store the candidate documents to be scored and/or the set of regression trees. The authors proposed a cache-conscious optimization by splitting documents and regression trees in *blocks*, such that one block of documents and one block of trees can both be stored in cache at the same time. Computing the score of all documents requires to evaluate all the tree blocks against all the document blocks. Authors applied this computational scheme on top of both IF-THEN-ELSE and PRED, with an average improvement of about 28% and 24% respectively. The blocking technique is indeed very general and can be used by all algorithms. The same computational schema is applied to QS in order to improve the *cache hit ratio* when large ensembles are used.

Other approaches and optimizations. Unlike our method that aims to devise an efficient strategy for fully evaluating the ensemble of trees, other approaches tries to approximate the computation over the ensemble for reducing the scoring time. Cambazoglu *et al.* [3] proposed to early terminate the scoring of documents that are unlikely to be ranked within the top-k results. Their work applies to an ensemble of additive trees like ours, but the authors aims to save scoring time by reducing the number of tree traversals, and trades better efficiency for little loss in raking quality. Although our method is thought for globally optimizing the traversal of thousands of trees, the idea of early termination can be applied as well along with our method, by evaluating some proper exit strategy after the evaluation of some subsets of the regression trees.

Wang *et al.* [15, 17, 16] deeply investigated different efficiency aspects of the ranking pipeline. In particular, in [16] they propose a novel cascade ranking model, which unlike previous approaches, can simultaneously improve both top-k ranked effectiveness and retrieval efficiency. Their work is mainly related to the tuning of a two-stage ranking pipeline.

3. QUICKSCORER: AN EFFICIENT TREE ENSEMBLE TRAVERSAL ALGORITHM

In order to efficiently exploit memory hierarchies and to reduce the branch mis-prediction rate, we propose an algorithm based on a totally novel traversal of the trees ensemble, called QUICKSCORER (QS). The building block of our approach is an alternative method for tree traversal based on bitvector computations, which is presented in Subsection 3.1. Given a tree and a vector of document features, our traversal processes all its nodes and produces a bitvector which encodes the exit leaf for the given document. In isolation this traversal is not particularly advantageous over the others, since in principle it requires to evaluate all the nodes of a tree. However, it has the nice property of being insensitive to the order in which the nodes are processed. This makes it possible to interleave the evaluation of the trees in the ensemble in a *cache-aware* fashion. In addition, the proposed bitvector encoding allows to save the computation of many test conditions.

The interleaved evaluation of a trees ensemble is discussed in Subsection 3.2. Intuitively, rather than traversing the ensemble tree after tree, our algorithm performs a global visit of the ensemble by traversing portions of all the trees together, feature by feature. For each feature, we store all the associated thresholds occurring anywhere in the ensemble in a sorted array, to easily to compute the result of all the test conditions involved. A bitvector for each tree is updated after each test, in such a way to encode, at the end of the process, the exit leaves in each tree for a given document. These bitvector are eventually used to lookup the predicted value of each tree.

3.1 Tree traversal using bitvectors

We start by presenting a simpler version of our tree traversal and, then, we introduce two crucial refinements for the performance of this algorithm when used in the interleaved evaluation of all the trees as described in Subsection 3.2.

Given an input feature vector $\mathbf{x}$ and a tree $T_h = (N_h, L_h)$, our tree traversal algorithm processes the internal nodes of T_h with the goal of identifying a set of *candidate exit leaves*, denoted by C_h with $C_h \subseteq L_h$, which includes the actual exit leaf e_h. Initially C_h contains all the leaves in L_h, i.e., $C_h = L_h$. Then, the algorithm evaluates one after the other in an arbitrary order the test conditions of all the internal nodes of T_h. Considering the result of the test for a certain internal node $n \in N_h$, the algorithm is able to infer that some leaves cannot be the exit leaf and, thus, it can safely remove them from C_h. Indeed, if n is a *false node* (i.e., its test condition is false), the leaves in the left subtree of n cannot be the exit leaf and they can be safely removed from C_h. Similarly, if n is a *true node*, the leaves in the right subtree of n can be removed from C_h. It is easy to see that, once all the nodes have been processed, the only leaf left in C_h is the exit leaf e_h.

The first refinement turns the above algorithm into a lazy one. This lazy algorithm uses an oracle, called **FindFalse**, that, given T_h and $\mathbf{x}$, returns the false nodes in N_h without the need of evaluating all the associated test conditions. Then, the algorithm removes from C_h the leaves in the left subtrees of all the false nodes returned by the oracle. For the moment we concentrate on the set C_h obtained at the end of the algorithm and we defer the materialization of the above oracle to Subsection 3.2 where the interleaved evaluation of all the trees makes its implementation possible. Observe that C_h may now contain several leaves. As an extreme example, the set C_h, in absence of false nodes, will contain all the leaves in L_h. Interestingly, we can prove (see Theorem 1 below) that the *exit leaf* e_h is always the one associated with the smallest identifier in C_h, i.e., the leftmost leaf in the tree. A running example is reported in Figure 2 which shows the actual traversal (bold arrows) for a vector $\mathbf{x}$, and also the true and false nodes. The figure shows also the set C_h after the removal of the leaves of the left subtrees of false nodes: C_h is $\{l_2, l_3, l_5\}$ and, indeed, the exit leaf is the leftmost leaf in C_h, i.e., $e_h = l_2$.

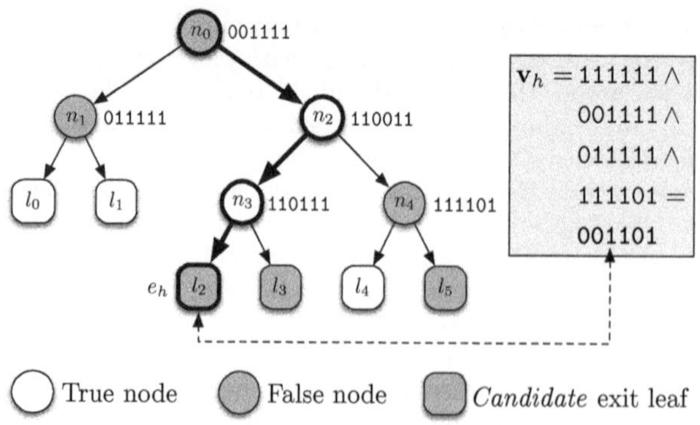

Figure 2: Tree traversal example.

The second refinement implements the operations on C_h with fast operations on compact bitvectors. The idea is to represent C_h with a bitvector $\mathbf{v}_h$, where each bit corresponds to a distinct leaf in L_h, i.e., $\mathbf{v}_h$ is the characteristic vector of C_h. Every internal node n is associated with a *node bitvector* (of the same length), acting as a bitmask that encodes (with 0's) the set of leaves to be removed from C_h whenever n is a false node. This way, the bitwise logical AND between $\mathbf{v}_h$ and the node bitvector of a false node n corresponds to the removal of the leaves in the left subtree of n from C_h. We finally observe that the exit leaf corresponds to the leftmost bit set to 1 in $\mathbf{v}_h$. Figure 2 shows how the initial bitvector $\mathbf{v}_h$ is updated by using bitwise logical AND operations.

The full approach is described in Algorithm 1. Given a binary tree $T_h = (N_h, L_h)$ and an input feature vector $\mathbf{x}$, let u.**bitvector** be the precomputed bitwise mask associated with a generic $n \in N_h$. First the result bitvector $\mathbf{v}_h$ is initialized with all bits set to 1. Then, **FindFalse**$(\mathbf{x}, T_h)$ returns all the false nodes in N_h. For each of such nodes, $\mathbf{v}_h$ is masked with the corresponding node bitvector. Finally, the position of the leftmost bit of $\mathbf{v}_h$ identifies the exit leaf e_h, whose output value is returned. The correctness of this approach is stated by the following theorem.

THEOREM 1. *Algorithm 1 is correct.*

PROOF. We prove that for each binary decision tree T_h and input feature vector $\mathbf{x}$, Algorithm 1 always computes

Algorithm 1: Scoring a feature vector $\mathbf{x}$ using a binary decision tree T_h

Input :
- $\mathbf{x}$: input feature vector
- $T_h = (N_h, L_h)$: binary decision tree, with
  - $N_h = \{n_0, n_1, \ldots\}$: internal nodes of T_h
  - $L_h = \{l_0, l_1, \ldots\}$: leaves of T_h
  - n.**bitvector**: node bitvector associated with $n \in N_h$
  - l_j.**val**: output value associated with $l_j \in L_h$

Output:
- tree traversal output value

```
Score(x,T_h):
  v_h ← 11...11
  U ← FindFalse(x, T_h)
  foreach node u ∈ U do
    v_h ← v_h ∧ u.bitvector
  j ← index of leftmost bit set to 1 of v_h
  return l_j.val
```

a result bitvector $\mathbf{v}_h$, where the leftmost bit set to 1 corresponds to the exit leaf e_h.

First, we prove that the bit corresponding to the exit leaf e_h in the result bitvector $\mathbf{v}_h$ is always set to 1. Consider the internal nodes along the path from the root to e_h, and observe that only the bitvectors applied for those nodes may change the e_h's bit to 0. Since e_h is the exit leaf, it belongs to the left subtree of any true node and to the right subtree of any false node in this path. Thus, since the bitvectors are used to set to 0 leaves in the left subtrees of false nodes, the bit corresponding to e_h remains unmodified, and, thus, will be 1 at the end of Algorithm 1.

Second, we prove that the leftmost bit equal to 1 in $\mathbf{v}_h$ corresponds to the exit leaf e_h. Let $l_{\leftarrow}$ be the leaf corresponding to the leftmost bit set to 1 in $\mathbf{v}_h$. Assume by contradiction that e_h is not the leftmost bit set to 1 in $\mathbf{v}_h$, namely, $l_{\leftarrow} \neq e_h$. Let u be their lowest common ancestor node in the tree. Since $l_{\leftarrow}$ is smaller than e_h, the leaf $l_{\leftarrow}$ belongs to u's left subtree while the leaf e_h belongs to u's right subtree. This leads to a contradiction. Indeed, on one hand, the node u should be a true node otherwise its bitvector would have been applied setting $l_{\leftarrow}$'s bit to 0. On the other hand, the node u should be a false node since e_h is in its right subtree. Thus, we conclude that $l_{\leftarrow} = e_h$ proving the correctness of Algorithm 1. □

Algorithm 1 represents a general technique to compute the output value of a single binary decision tree stored as a set of precomputed bitvectors. Given an additive ensemble of binary decision trees, to score a document $\mathbf{x}$ we have to loop over all the trees $T_h \in \mathcal{T}$ by repeatedly applying Algorithm 1. Unfortunately, this naïve algorithm is inefficient, since this method does not permit us to implement efficiently `FindFalse`$(\mathbf{x}, T_h)$.

In the following section we present QS, which overcomes this issue by performing a global visit of the whole tree ensemble $\mathcal{T}$. The QS algorithm realizes the goal of identifying efficiently the false nodes of all the tree ensemble by exploiting an *interleaved* evaluation of all the trees in the ensemble.

3.2 The QS Algorithm

Our QS algorithm scores a feature vector $\mathbf{x}$ with an interleaved execution of several tree traversals, one for each tree in the ensemble. The algorithm does not loop over all the trees in $\mathcal{T}$ one at the time, as one would expect, but does loop instead over all the features in $\mathcal{F}$, hence incrementally discovering for each $f_k \in \mathcal{F}$ the false nodes involving f_k in any tree of the ensemble. This is a very convenient order for two reasons: i) we are able to identify all the false nodes for all the trees without even considering their true nodes, thus effectively implementing the oracle introduced in the previous section; ii) we are able to operate in a cache-aware fashion with a small number of Boolean comparisons and branch mis-predictions.

During its execution, QS has to maintain the bitvectors $\mathbf{v}_h$'s, encoding the set C_h's for all the tree T_h in the ensemble. The bitvector $\mathbf{v}_h$ of a certain tree is updated as soon as a false node for that tree is identified. Once the algorithm has processed all the features in $\mathcal{F}$, each of these $\mathbf{v}_h$ is guaranteed to encode the exit leaf in the corresponding tree. Now the algorithm can compute the overall score of $\mathbf{x}$ by summing up (and, possibly, weighting) the scores of all these exit leaves.

Let us concentrate on the processing of a feature f_k and describe the portion of the data structure of interest for this feature. The overall algorithm simply iterates this process over all features in $\mathcal{F}$. Each node involving f_k in any tree $T_h \in \mathcal{T}$ is represented by a *triple* containing: (i) the feature threshold involved in the Boolean test; (ii) the id of the tree that contains the node, where the id is used to identify the bitvector $\mathbf{v}_h$ to update; (iii) the node bitvector used to possibly update $\mathbf{v}_h$. We sort these triples in *ascending order* of their feature thresholds.

This sorting is crucial for obtaining a fast implementation of our oracle. Recall that all the conditions occurring in the internal nodes of the trees are of the form $\mathbf{x}[k] \leq \gamma_s^h$. Hence, given the sorted list of all the thresholds involving $f_k \in \mathcal{F}$, the feature value $\mathbf{x}[k]$ splits the list in two, possibly empty, sublists. The first sublist contains all the thresholds γ_s^h for which the test condition $\mathbf{x}[k] \leq \gamma_s^h$ evaluates to FALSE, while the second sublists contains all thresholds for which the test condition evaluates to TRUE. Thus, if we sequentially scan the sorted list of the thresholds associated with f_k, all the values in the first sublist will cause negative tests. Associated with these thresholds entailing false tests, we have false nodes belonging to the trees in $\mathcal{T}$. Therefore, for all these false nodes we can take in sequence the corresponding bitvector, and perform a bitwise logical AND with the appropriate result bitvector $\mathbf{v}_h$.

This large sequence of tests that evaluates to FALSE corresponds to the repeated execution of conditional branch instructions, whose behavior is indeed very predictable. This

Algorithm 2: The QUICKSCORER Algorithm

Input :
- $\mathbf{x}$: input feature vector
- $\mathcal{T}$: ensemble of binary decision trees, with
  - $w_0, \ldots, w_{|\mathcal{T}|-1}$: weights, one per tree
  - `thresholds`: sorted sublists of thresholds, one sublist per feature
  - `tree_ids`: tree's ids, one per threshold
  - `bitvectors`: node bitvectors, one per threshold
  - `offsets`: offsets of the blocks of triples
  - `v`: result bitvectors, one per each tree
  - `leaves`: output values, one per each tree leaf

Output:
- Final score of $\mathbf{x}$

```
QuickScorer(x,T):
  foreach h ∈ 0, 1, ..., |T| − 1 do
      v[h] ← 11...11
  foreach k ∈ 0, 1, ..., |F| − 1 do                    // Step ①
      i ← offsets[k]
      end ← offsets[k + 1]
      while x[k] > thresholds[i] do
          h ← tree_ids[i]
          v[h] ← v[h] ∧ bitvectors[i]
          i ← i + 1
          if i ≥ end then
              break
  score ← 0
  foreach h ∈ 0, 1, ..., |T| − 1 do                    // Step ②
      j ← index of leftmost bit set to 1 of v[h]
      l ← h · |L_h| + j
      score ← score + w_h · leaves[l]
  return score
```

is confirmed by our experimental results, showing that our code incurs in very few branch mis-predictions.

We now present the layout in memory of the required data structure since it is crucial for the efficiency of our algorithm. The triples of each feature are stored in three separate arrays, one for each component: **thresholds**, **tree_ids**, and **bitvectors**. The use of three distinct arrays solves some data alignment issues arising when tuples of heterogeneous data types are stored contiguously in memory. The arrays of the different features are then juxtaposed one after the other as illustrated in Figure 3. Since arrays of different features may have different lengths, we use an auxiliary array **offsets** which marks the starting position of each array in the global array. We also juxtapose the bitvectors $\mathbf{v}_h$ into a global array **v**. Finally, we use an array **leaves** which stores the output values of the leaves of each tree (ordered from left to right) grouped by their tree id.

Algorithm 2 reports the steps of QS as informally described above. After the initialization of the result bitvectors of each tree (loop starting al line 1), we have the first step of QS that exactly corresponds to what we discussed above (loop starting at line 3). The algorithm iterates over all features, and inspects the sorted lists of thresholds to update the result bitvectors. Upon completion of the first step, we have the second step of the algorithm (loop starting at line 13), which simply inspects all the result bitvectors, and for each of them identifies the position of the leftmost bit set to 1, and uses this position to access the value associated with the corresponding leaf stored array **leaves**. The value of the leaf is finally used to update the final score.

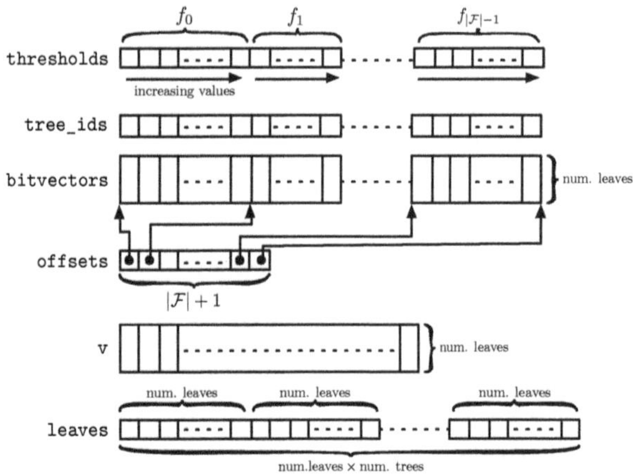

Figure 3: Arrays used by algorithm QS.

Implementation details. In the following we discuss some details about our data structures, their size and access modes.

A few important remarks concern the bitvectors stored in **v** and **bitvectors**. The learning algorithm controls the accuracy of each single tree with a parameter Λ, which determines the maximal number of leaves for each $T_h = (N_h, L_h)$ in $\mathcal{T}$, namely $|L_h| \leq \Lambda$. Usually, the value of Λ is kept small (≤ 64). Thus, the length of bitvectors, which have to encode tree leaves, is equal to (or less than) a typical machine word of modern CPUs (64 bits). As a consequence, the bitwise operations performed by Algorithm 2 on them can be realized very efficiently, because they involve machine words (or halfwords, etc).

We avoid any possible performance overhead due to shifting operations to align the operands of bitwise logical ANDs by forcing the bitvectors to have uniform length of B bytes. To this end, we pad each bitvector on its right side with a string of 0 bits, if necessary. We always select the minimum number of bytes $B \in \{1, 2, 4, 8\}$ fitting Λ.

Let us now consider Table 1, which shows an upper bound for the size of each linear array used by our algorithm. The array **offsets** has $|\mathcal{F}|$ entries, one entry for each distinct feature. The array **v**, instead, has an entry for each tree in $\mathcal{T}$, thus, $|\mathcal{T}|$ entries overall. The sizes of the other data structures depends on the number of total internal nodes or leaves in the ensemble $\mathcal{T}$, besides the datatype sizes. Any internal node of some tree of $\mathcal{T}$ contributes with an entry in each array **thresholds**, **bitvectors** and **tree_ids**. Therefore the total number of entries of each of these arrays, i.e., $\sum_0^{|\mathcal{T}|-1} |N_h|$, can be upper bounded by $|\mathcal{T}| \cdot \Lambda$, because for every tree T_h we have $|N_h| < |N_h| + 1 = |L_h| \leq \Lambda$. Finally, the array **leaves** has an entry for each leaf in a tree of $\mathcal{T}$, hence, no more than $|\mathcal{T}| \cdot \Lambda$ in total.

Table 1: Data structures used by QS, the corresponding maximum sizes, and the access modes.

Data structure	*Maximum Size (bytes)*	*Data access modes*
thresholds	$\lvert\mathcal{T}\rvert \cdot \Lambda \cdot$ sizeof(float)	1. *Sequential (R)*
tree_ids	$\lvert\mathcal{T}\rvert \cdot \Lambda \cdot$ sizeof(uint)	
bitvectors	$\lvert\mathcal{T}\rvert \cdot \Lambda \cdot B$	
offsets	$\lvert\mathcal{F}\rvert \cdot$ sizeof(uint)	
v	$\lvert\mathcal{T}\rvert \cdot B$	1. *Random (R/W)* 2. *Sequential (R)*
leaves	$\lvert\mathcal{T}\rvert \cdot \Lambda \cdot$ sizeof(double)	2. *Seq. Sparse (R)*

The last column of Table 1 reports the *data access modes* to the arrays, where the leading number, either 1 or 2, corresponds to the step of the algorithm during which the data structures are read/written. Recall that the first step of QS starts at line 3 of Algorithm 2, while the second at line 13. We first note that **v** is the only array used in both phases of function QUICKSCORER($\mathbf{x}, \mathcal{T}$). During the first step **v** is accessed randomly in reading/writing to update the $\mathbf{v}_h$'s. During the second step the same array is accessed sequentially in reading mode to identify the exit leafs l_h of each tree T_h, and then to access the array **leaves** to read the contribution of tree T_h to the output of the regression function. Even if the trees and their leaves are accessed sequentially during the second step of QS, the reading access to array **leaves** is sequential, but very sparse: only one leaf of each block of $|L_h|$ elements is actually read.

Finally, note that the arrays storing the triples, i.e., **thresholds**, **tree_ids**, and **bitvectors**, are all sequentially read during the first step, though not completely, since for each feature we stop its inspection at the first test condition that evaluates to TRUE. The cache usage can greatly benefit from the layout and access modes of our data structures, thanks to the increased references locality.

We finally describe an optimization which aims at reducing the number of comparisons performed at line 6 of Algorithm 2. The (inner) while loop in line 6 iterates over the list of threshold values associated with a certain feature $f_k \in \mathcal{F}$ until we find the first index j where the test fails, namely, the value of the kth feature of vector $\mathbf{x}$ is greater than **thresholds**[j]. Thus, a test on the feature value and the current threshold is carried out at each iteration. Instead of testing each threshold in a prefix of **thresholds**[i : end], our optimized implementation tests only one every Δ thresholds, where Δ is a parameter. Since the subvector **thresholds**[i : end] is sorted in ascending order, if a test succeed the same necessarily holds for all the preceding $\Delta - 1$ thresholds. Therefore, we can go directly to update the result bitvector $\mathbf{v}_h$ of the corresponding trees, saving $\Delta - 1$ comparisons. Instead, if the test fails, we scan the preceding $\Delta - 1$ thresholds to identify the target index j and we conclude. In our implementation we set Δ equal to 4, which is the value giving the best results in our experiments. We remark that in principle one could identify j by binary searching the subvector **thresholds**[i : end]. Experiments have shown that the use of binary search is not profitable because in general the subvector is not sufficiently long.

4. EXPERIMENTS

In this section we provide an extensive experimental evaluation that compares our QS algorithm with other state-of-the-art competitors and baselines over standard datasets.

Datasets and experimental settings. Experiments are conducted by using publicly available LtR datasets: the MSN[1] and the Yahoo! LETOR[2] challenge datasets. The first one is split into five folds, consisting of vectors of 136 features extracted from query-document pairs, while the second one consists of two distinct datasets (Y!S1 and Y!S2), made up of vectors of 700 features. In this work, we focus on MSN-1, the first MSN fold, and Y!S1 datasets. The features vectors of the two selected datasets are labeled with relevance judgments ranging from 0 (irrelevant) to 4 (perfectly relevant). Each dataset is split in training, validation and test sets. The MSN-1 dataset consists of 6,000, 2,000, and 2,000 queries for training, validation and testing respectively. The Y!S1 dataset consists of 19,944 training queries, 2,994 validation queries and 6,983 test queries.

We exploit the following experimental methodology. We use training and validation sets from MSN-1 and Y!S1 to train λ-MART [18] models with 8, 16, 32 and 64 leaves. We use QuickRank[3] an open-source parallel implementation of λ-MART written in C++11 for performing the training phase. During this step we optimize NDCG@10. The results of the paper can be also applied to analogous tree-based models generated by different state-of-the-art learning algorithms, e.g., GBRT [4].

In our experiments we compare the scoring efficiency of QS[4] with the following competitors:

- IF-THEN-ELSE is a baseline that translates each tree of the forest as a nested block of if-then-else.
- VPRED and STRUCT+ [1] kindly made available by the authors[5].

Given a trained model and a test set, all the above scoring methods achieve the same result in terms of effectiveness. Hence, we do not report quality measures.

[1]`http://research.microsoft.com/en-us/projects/mslr/`
[2]`http://learningtorankchallenge.yahoo.com`
[3]`http://quickrank.isti.cnr.it`
[4]The C++11 implementation of QS is available at `http://github.com/hpclab/quickscorer`.
[5]`http://nasadi.github.io/OptTrees/`

All the algorithms are compiled with GCC 4.9.2 with the highest optimization settings. The tests are performed by using a single core on a machine equipped with an Intel Core i7-4770K clocked at 3.50Ghz, with 32GiB RAM, running Ubuntu Linux 3.13.0. The Intel Core i7-4770K CPU has three levels of cache. Level 1 cache has size 32 KB, one for each of the four cores, level 2 cache has size 256 KB for each core, and at level 3 there is a shared cache of 8 MB.

To measure the efficiency of each of the above methods, we run 10 times the scoring code on the test sets of the MSN-1 and Y!S1 datasets. We then compute the average per-document scoring cost. Moreover, to deeply profile the behavior of each method above we employ `perf`[6], a performance analysis tool available under Ubuntu Linux distributions. We analyze each method by monitoring several CPU counters that measure the total number of instructions executed, number of branches, number of branch mis-predictions, cache references, and cache misses.

Scoring time analysis. The average time (in μs) needed by the different algorithms to score each document of the two datasets MSN-1 and Y!S1 are reported in Table 2. In particular, the table reports the per-document scoring time by varying the number of trees and the leaves of the ensemble employed. For each test the table also reports between parentheses the gain factor of QS over its competitors. At a first glance, these gains are impressive, with speedups that in many cases are above one order of magnitude. Depending on the number of trees and of leaves, QS outperforms VPRED, the most efficient solution so far, of factors ranging from 2.0x up to 6.5x. For example, the average time required by QS and VPRED to score a document in the MSN-1 test set with a model composed of 1,000 trees and 64 leaves, are 9.5 and 62.2 μs, respectively. The comparison between QS and IF-THEN-ELSE is even more one-sided, with improvements of up to 23.4x for the model with 10,000 trees and 32 leaves trained on the MSN-1 dataset. In this case the QS average per-document scoring time is 59.6 μs with respect to the 1396.8 μs of IF-THEN-ELSE. The last baseline reported, i.e., STRUCT+, behaves worst in all the tests conducted. Its performance is very low when compared not only to QS (up to 38.2x times faster), but even with respect to the other two algorithms VPRED and IF-THEN-ELSE. The reasons of the superior performance of QS over competitor algorithms are manyfold. We analyse the most relevant in the following.

Instruction level analysis. We used the `perf` tool to measure the total number of instructions, number of branches, number of branch mis-predictions, L3 cache references, and L3 cache misses of the different algorithms by considering only their scoring phase. Table 3 reports the results we obtained by scoring the MSN-1 test set by varying the number of trees and by fixing the number of leaves to 64. Experiments on Y!S1 are not reported here, but they exhibited similar behavior. As a clarification, L3 cache references accounts for those references which are not found in any of the previous level of cache, while L3 cache misses are the ones among them which miss in L3 as well. Table 3 also reports the number of visited nodes. All measurements are per-document and per-tree normalized.

[6]`https://perf.wiki.kernel.org`

Table 2: **Per-document scoring time in μs of QS, VPRED, IF-THEN-ELSE and STRUCT+ on MSN-1 and Y!S1 datasets. Gain factors are reported in parentheses.**

Method	Λ	Number of trees/dataset							
		1,000		5,000		10,000		20,000	
		MSN-1	Y!S1	MSN-1	Y!S1	MSN-1	Y!S1	MSN-1	Y!S1
QS	8	**2.2** (–)	**4.3** (–)	**10.5** (–)	**14.3** (–)	**20.0** (–)	**25.4** (–)	**40.5** (–)	**48.1** (–)
VPRED		7.9 (3.6x)	8.5 (2.0x)	40.2 (3.8x)	41.6 (2.9x)	80.5 (4.0x)	82.7 (3.3)	161.4 (4.0x)	164.8 (3.4x)
IF-THEN-ELSE		8.2 (3.7x)	10.3 (2.4x)	81.0 (7.7x)	85.8 (6.0x)	185.1 (9.3x)	185.8 (7.3x)	709.0 (17.5x)	772.2 (16.0x)
STRUCT+		21.2 (9.6x)	23.1 (5.4x)	107.7 (10.3x)	112.6 (7.9x)	373.7 (18.7x)	390.8 (15.4x)	1150.4 (28.4x)	1141.6 (23.7x)
QS	16	**2.9** (–)	**6.1** (–)	**16.2** (–)	**22.2** (–)	**32.4** (–)	**41.2** (–)	**67.8** (–)	**81.0** (–)
VPRED		16.0 (5.5x)	16.5 (2.7x)	82.4 (5.0x)	82.8 (3.7x)	165.5 (5.1x)	165.2 (4.0x)	336.4 (4.9x)	336.1 (4.1x)
IF-THEN-ELSE		18.0 (6.2x)	21.8 (3.6x)	126.9 (7.8x)	130.0 (5.8x)	617.8 (19.0x)	406.6 (9.9x)	1767.3 (26.0x)	1711.4 (21.1x)
STRUCT+		42.6 (14.7x)	41.0 (6.7x)	424.3 (26.2x)	403.9 (18.2x)	1218.6 (37.6x)	1191.3 (28.9x)	2590.8 (38.2x)	2621.2 (32.4x)
QS	32	**5.2** (–)	**9.7** (–)	**27.1** (–)	**34.3** (–)	**59.6** (–)	**70.3** (–)	**155.8** (–)	**160.1** (–)
VPRED		31.9 (6.1x)	31.6 (3.2x)	165.2 (6.0x)	162.2 (4.7x)	343.4 (5.7x)	336.6 (4.8x)	711.9 (4.5x)	694.8 (4.3x)
IF-THEN-ELSE		34.5 (6.6x)	36.2 (3.7x)	300.9 (11.1x)	277.7 (8.0x)	1396.8 (23.4x)	1389.8 (19.8x)	3179.4 (20.4x)	3105.2 (19.4x)
STRUCT+		69.1 (13.3x)	67.4 (6.9x)	928.6 (34.2x)	834.6 (24.3x)	1806.7 (30.3x)	1774.3 (25.2x)	4610.8 (29.6x)	4332.3 (27.0x)
QS	64	**9.5** (–)	**15.1** (–)	**56.3** (–)	**66.9** (–)	**157.5** (–)	**159.4** (–)	**425.1** (–)	**343.7** (–)
VPRED		62.2 (6.5x)	57.6 (3.8x)	355.2 (6.3x)	334.9 (5.0x)	734.4 (4.7x)	706.8 (4.4x)	1309.7 (3.0x)	1420.7 (4.1x)
IF-THEN-ELSE		55.9 (5.9x)	55.1 (3.6x)	933.1 (16.6x)	935.3 (14.0x)	2496.5 (15.9x)	2428.6 (15.2x)	4662.0 (11.0x)	4809.6 (14.0x)
STRUCT+		109.8 (11.6x)	116.8 (7.7x)	1661.7 (29.5x)	1554.6 (23.2x)	3040.7 (19.3x)	2937.3 (18.4x)	5437.0 (12.8x)	5456.4 (15.9x)

We first observe that VPRED executes the largest number of instructions. This is because VPRED always runs d steps if d is the depth of a tree, even if a document might reach an exit leaf earlier. IF-THEN-ELSE executes much less instructions as it follows the document traversal path. STRUCT+ introduces some data structures overhead w.r.t. IF-THEN-ELSE. QS executes the smallest number instructions. This is due to the different traversal strategy of the ensemble, as QS needs to process the *false nodes* only. Indeed, QS always visits less than 18 nodes on average, out of the 64 present in each tree of the ensemble. Note that IF-THEN-ELSE traverses between 31 and 40 nodes per tree, and the same trivially holds for STRUCT+. This means that the interleaved traversal strategy of QS needs to process less nodes than in a traditional root-to-leaf visit. This mostly explains the results achieved by QS.

As far as number of branches is concerned, we note that, not surprisingly, QS and VPRED are much more efficient than IF-THEN-ELSE and STRUCT+ with this respect. QS has a larger total number of branches than VPRED, which uses scoring functions that are branch-free. However, those branches are highly predictable, so that the mis-prediction rate is very low, thus, confirming our claims in Section 3.

Observing again the timings in Table 2 we notice that, by fixing the number of leaves, we have a super-linear growth of QS's timings when increasing the number of trees. For example, since on MSN-1 with $\Lambda = 64$ and 1,000 trees QS scores a document in 9.5 μs, one would expect to score a document 20 times slower, i.e., 190 μs, when the ensemble size increases to 20,000 trees. However, the reported timing of QS in this setting is 425.1 μs, i.e., roughly 44 times slower than with 1000 trees. This effect is observable only when the number of leaves $\Lambda = \{32, 64\}$ and the number of trees is larger than 5,000. Table 3 relates this super-linear growth to the numbers of L3 cache misses.

Considering the sizes of the arrays as reported in Table 1 in Section 3, we can estimate the minimum number of trees that let the size of the QS's data structure to exceed the cache capacity, and, thus, the algorithm starts to have more cache misses. This number is estimated in 6,000 trees when the number of leaves is 64. Thus, we expect that the number of L3 cache miss starts increasing around this number of trees. Possibly, this number is slightly larger, because portions of the data structure may be infrequently accessed at scoring time, due the the small fraction of false nodes and associated bitvectors accessed by QS.

These considerations are further confirmed by Figure 4, which shows the average per-tree per-document scoring time (μs) and percentage of cache misses QS when scoring the MSN-1 and the Y!S1 with $\Lambda = 64$ by varying the number of trees. First, there exists a strong correlation between QS's timings and its number of L3 cache misses. Second, the number of L3 cache misses starts increasing when dealing with 9,000 trees on MSN and 8,000 trees on Y!S1.

BWQS: a block-wise variant of QS

The previous experiments suggest that improving the cache efficiency of QS may result in significant benefits. As in Tang *et al.* [12], we can split the tree ensemble in disjoint blocks of size τ that are processed separately in order to let the corresponding data structures fit into the faster levels of the memory hierarchy. This way, we are essentially scoring each document over each tree blocks that partition the original ensemble, thus inheriting the efficiency of QS on smaller ensembles. Indeed, the size of the arrays required to score the documents over a block of trees depends now on τ instead of $|\mathcal{T}|$ (see Table 1 in Section 3). We have, however, to keep an array that stores the partial scoring computed so far for each document.

The temporal locality of this approach can be improved by allowing the algorithm to score blocks of documents together over the same block of trees before moving to the next block of documents. To allow the algorithm to score a block of δ documents in a single run we have to replicate in δ copies the array v. Obviously, this increases the space occupancy and may result in a worse use of the cache. Therefore, we need to find the best balance between the number of documents δ and the number of trees τ to process in the body of a nested loop that first runs over the blocks of trees (outer loop) and then over the blocks of documents to score (inner loop).

This algorithm is called BLOCKWISE-QS (BWQS) and its efficiency is discussed in the remaining part of this section.

Table 3: **Per-tree per-document low-level statistics on MSN-1 with 64-leaves λ-MART models.**

Method	Number of Trees				
	1,000	5,000	10,000	15,000	20,000
Instruction Count					
QS	**58**	**75**	**86**	**91**	**97**
VPRED	580	599	594	588	516
IF-THEN-ELSE	142	139	133	130	116
STRUCT+	341	332	315	308	272
Num. branch mis-predictions (above) / Num. branches (below)					
QS	0.162	**0.035**	**0.017**	**0.011**	**0.009**
	6.04	7.13	8.23	8.63	9.3
VPRED	**0.013**	0.042	0.045	0.049	0.049
	0.2	**0.21**	**0.18**	**0.21**	**0.21**
IF-THEN-ELSE	1.541	1.608	1.615	1.627	1.748
	42.61	41.31	39.16	38.04	33.65
STRUCT+	4.498	5.082	5.864	6.339	5.535
	89.9	88.91	85.55	83.83	74.69
L3 cache misses (above) / L3 cache references (below)					
QS	0.004	**0.001**	**0.121**	**0.323**	0.51
	1.78	**1.47**	**1.52**	**2.14**	**2.33**
VPRED	0.005	0.166	0.326	0.363	**0.356**
	12.55	12.6	13.74	15.04	12.77
IF-THEN-ELSE	**0.001**	17.772	30.331	29.615	29.577
	27.66	38.14	40.25	40.76	36.47
STRUCT+	0.039	12.791	17.147	15.923	13.971
	7.37	18.64	20.52	19.87	18.38
Num. Visited Nodes (above) / Visited Nodes/Total Nodes (below)					
QS	**9.71**	**13.40**	**15.79**	**16.65**	**18.00**
	15%	**21%**	**25%**	**26%**	**29%**
VPRED	54.38	56.23	55.79	55.23	48.45
	86%	89%	89%	88%	77%
STRUCT+	40.61	39.29	37.16	36.15	31.75
IF-THEN-ELSE	64%	62%	59%	57%	50%

Table 4 reports average per-document scoring time in μs of algorithms QS, VPRED, and BWQS. The experiments were conducted on both the MSN-1 and Y!S1 datasets by varying Λ and by fixing the number of trees to 20,000. It is worth noting that our QS algorithm can be thought as a limit case of BWQS, where the blocks are trivially composed of 1 document and the whole ensemble of trees. VPRED instead vectorizes the process and scores 16 documents at the time over the entire ensemble. With BWQS the sizes of document and tree blocks can be instead flexibly optimized according to the cache parameters. Table 4 reports the best execution times, along with the values of δ and τ for which BWQS obtained such results.

The blocking strategy can improve the performance of QS when large tree ensembles are involved. Indeed, the largest improvements are measured in the tests conducted on models having 64 leaves. For example, to score a document of MSN-1, BWQS with blocks of 3,000 trees and a single document takes 274.7 μs in average, against the 425.1 μs required by QS with an improvement of 1.55x.

Table 4: Per-document scoring time in μs of BWQS, QS and VPRED algorithms on MSN-1.

Λ	Method	MSN-1 Block δ	MSN-1 Block τ	MSN-1 Time	Y!S1 Block δ	Y!S1 Block τ	Y!S1 Time
8	BWQS	8	20,000	**33.5** (–)	8	20,000	**40.5** (–)
	QS	1	20,000	40.5 (1.21x)	1	20,000	48.1 (1.19x)
	VPRED	16	20,000	161.4 (4.82x)	16	20,000	164.8 (4.07x)
16	BWQS	8	5,000	**59.6** (–)	8	10,000	**72.34** (–)
	QS	1	20,000	67.8 (1.14x)	1	20,000	81.0 (1.12x)
	VPRED	16	20,000	336.4 (5.64x)	16	20,000	336.1 (4.65x)
32	BWQS	2	5,000	**135.5** (–)	8	5,000	**141.2** (–)
	QS	1	20,000	155.8 (1.15x)	1	20,000	160.1 (1.13x)
	VPRED	16	20,000	711.9 (5.25x)	16	20,000	694.8 (4.92x)
64	BWQS	1	3,000	**274.7** (–)	1	4,000	**236.0** (–)
	QS	1	20,000	425.1 (1.55x)	1	20,000	343.7 (1.46x)
	VPRED	16	20,000	1309.7 (4.77x)	16	20,000	1420.7 (6.02x)

The reason of the improvements highlighted in the table are apparent from the two plots reported in Figure 4. These plots report for MSN-1 and Y!S1 the per-document and per-tree average scoring time of BWQS and its cache misses ratio. As already mentioned, the plot shows that the average per-document per-tree scoring time of QS is strongly correlated to the cache misses measured. The more the cache misses, the larger the per-tree per-document time needed to apply the model. On the other hand, the BWQS cache misses curve shows that the block-wise implementation incurs in a negligible number of cache misses. This cache-friendliness is directly reflected in the per-document per-tree scoring time, which is only slightly influenced by the number of trees of the ensemble.

5. CONCLUSIONS

We presented a novel algorithm to efficiently score documents by using a machine-learned ranking function modeled by an additive ensemble of regression trees. Our main contribution is a new representation of the tree ensemble based on bitvectors, where the tree traversal, aimed to detect the leaves that contribute to the final scoring of a document, is performed through efficient logical bitwise operations. In addition, the traversal is not performed one tree after another, as one would expect, but it is interleaved, feature by feature, over the whole tree ensemble. Our tests conducted on publicly available LtR datasets confirm unprecedented speedups (up to 6.5x) over the best state-of-the-art competitor. The motivations of the very good performance figures of our QS algorithm are diverse. First, linear arrays are used to store the tree ensemble, while the algorithm exploits cache-friendly access patterns (mainly sequential patterns) to these data structures. Second, the interleaved tree traversal counts on an effective oracle that, with a few branch mis-predictions, is able to detect and return only the internal node in the tree whose conditions evaluate to FALSE. Third, the number of internal nodes visited by QS is in most cases consistently lower than in traditional methods, which recursively visits the small and unbalanced trees of the ensemble from the root to the exit leaf. All these remarks are confirmed by the deep performance assessment conducted by also analyzing low-level CPU hardware counters. This analysis shows that QS exhibits very low cache misses and branch mis-prediction rates, while the instruction count is

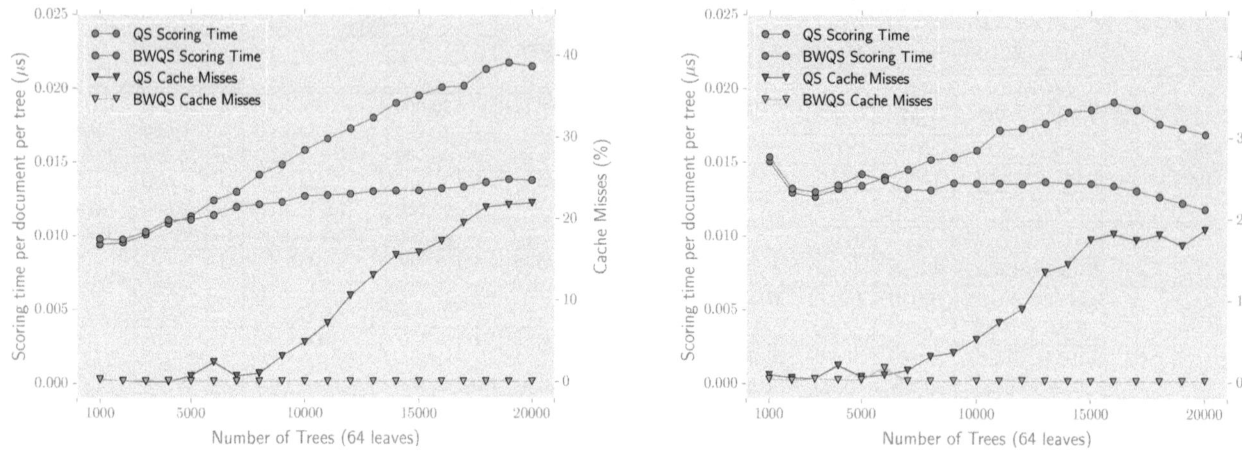

(a) MSN-1 (b) Y!S1

Figure 4: Per-tree per-document scoring time in μs and percentage of cache misses of QS and BWQS on MSN-1 (left) and Y!S1 (right) with 64-leaves λ-MART models.

consistently smaller than the counterparts. When the size of the data structures implementing the tree ensemble becomes larger the last level of the cache (L3 in our experimental setting), we observed a slight degradation of performance. To show that our method can be made scalable, we also present BWQS, a block-wise version of QS that splits the sets of feature vectors and trees in disjoint blocks that entirely fit in the cache and can be processed separately. Our experiments show that BWQS performs up to 1.55 times better than the original QS on large tree ensembles.

As future work, we plan to apply the same devised algorithm to other contexts, when a tree-based machine learned model must be applied to big data for classification/prediction purposes. Moreover, we aim at investigating whether we can introduce further optimizations in the algorithms, considering that the same tree-based model is applied to a multitude of feature vectors, and thus we could have the chance of partially reusing some work. Finally, we plan to investigate the parallelization of our method, which can involve various dimensions, i.e., the parallelization of the scoring task of each single feature vector, or the parallelization of the simultaneous scoring of many feature vectors.

Acknowledgements

We acknowledge the support of Tiscali S.p.A. In particular, we wish to warmly thank Domenico Dato and Monica Mori (Istella) for fruitful discussions and valuable feedbacks helping us in concretizing this paper.

6. REFERENCES

[1] N. Asadi, J. Lin, and A. P. de Vries. Runtime optimizations for tree-based machine learning models. *IEEE Trans. Knowl. Data Eng.*, 26(9):2281–2292, 2014.

[2] C. J. Burges. From ranknet to lambdarank to lambdamart: An overview. Technical Report MSR-TR-2010-82, 2010.

[3] B. B. Cambazoglu, H. Zaragoza, O. Chapelle, J. Chen, C. Liao, Z. Zheng, and J. Degenhardt. Early exit optimizations for additive machine learned ranking systems. In *Proc. ACM WSDM*, pages 411–420. ACM, 2010.

[4] J. H. Friedman. Greedy function approximation: a gradient boosting machine. *Annals of Statistics*, pages 1189–1232, 2001.

[5] Y. Ganjisaffar, R. Caruana, and C. V. Lopes. Bagging gradient-boosted trees for high precision, low variance ranking models. In *Proc. ACM SIGIR*, pages 85–94, New York, NY, USA, 2011. ACM.

[6] K. Järvelin and J. Kekäläinen. Cumulated gain-based evaluation of ir techniques. *ACM Trans. Inf. Syst.*, 20(4):422–446, 2002.

[7] T.-Y. Liu. Learning to rank for information retrieval. *Foundations and Trends in Information Retrieval*, 3(3):225–331, 2009.

[8] D. Patterson and J. Hennessy. *Computer Organization and Design (4th ed.)*. Morgan Kaufmann, 2009.

[9] S. Robertson and H. Zaragoza. The probabilistic relevance framework: Bm25 and beyond. *Found. Trends Inf. Retr.*, 3(4):333–389, 2009.

[10] I. Segalovich. Machine learning in search quality at yandex. ACM SIGIR, Industry track, 2010.

[11] T. Sharp. Implementing decision trees and forests on a gpu. In *Proc. Computer Vision*, pages 595–608. Springer, 2008.

[12] X. Tang, X. Jin, and T. Yang. Cache-conscious runtime optimization for ranking ensembles. In *Proc. ACM SIGIR*, pages 1123–1126, 2014.

[13] B. Van Essen, C. Macaraeg, M. Gokhale, and R. Prenger. Accelerating a random forest classifier: Multi-core, gp-gpu, or fpga? In *Proc. IEEE FCCM*, pages 232–239. IEEE, 2012.

[14] P. Viola and M. J. Jones. Robust real-time face detection. *Int. J. Comput. Vision*, 57(2):137–154, 2004.

[15] L. Wang, J. J. Lin, and D. Metzler. Learning to efficiently rank. In *Proc. ACM SIGIR*, pages 138–145, 2010.

[16] L. Wang, J. J. Lin, and D. Metzler. A cascade ranking model for efficient ranked retrieval. In *Proc. ACM SIGIR*, pages 105–114, 2011.

[17] L. Wang, D. Metzler, and J. J. Lin. Ranking under temporal constraints. In *Proc. ACM CIKM*, pages 79–88, 2010.

[18] Q. Wu, C. Burges, K. Svore, and J. Gao. Adapting boosting for information retrieval measures. *Information Retrieval*, 2010.

[19] Z. Xu, K. Weinberger, and O. Chapelle. The greedy miser: Learning under test-time budgets. In *Proc. ICML*, pages 1175–1182, New York, NY, USA, 2012. ACM.

High Quality Graph-Based Similarity Search

Weiren Yu[†], Julie A. McCann[†]
[†]Imperial College London, United Kingdom
{weiren.yu, j.mccann}@imperial.ac.uk

ABSTRACT

SimRank is an influential link-based similarity measure that has been used in many fields of Web search and sociometry. The best-of-breed method by Kusumoto *et al.* [7], however, does not always deliver high-quality results, since it fails to accurately obtain its diagonal correction matrix D. Besides, SimRank is also limited by an unwanted "connectivity trait": increasing the number of paths between nodes a and b often incurs a decrease in score $s(a,b)$. The best-known solution, SimRank++ [1], cannot resolve this problem, since a revised score will be zero if a and b have no common in-neighbors.

In this paper, we consider high-quality similarity search. Our scheme, $\mathsf{SR}^{\#}$, is efficient and semantically meaningful: (1) We first formulate the exact D, and devise a "varied-D" method to accurately compute SimRank in linear memory. Moreover, by grouping computation, we also reduce the time of [7] from quadratic to linear in the number of iterations. (2) We design a "kernel-based" model to improve the quality of SimRank, and circumvent the "connectivity trait" issue. (3) We give mathematical insights to the semantic difference between SimRank and its variant, and correct an argument in [7]: "if D is replaced by a scaled identity matrix $(1-\gamma)I$, top-K rankings will not be affected much". The experiments confirm that $\mathsf{SR}^{\#}$ can accurately extract high-quality scores, and is much faster than the state-of-the-art competitors.

Categories and Subject Descriptors

H.3.3 [**Information Search and Retrieval**]: Information Storage and Retrieval

Keywords

Link Analysis; Graph-Based Similarity; High Quality Search

1. INTRODUCTION

The Web today is a huge, self-organized, and hyperlinked network. These salient features bring striking challenges to data management, and call for new search abilities to extract meaningful knowledge automatically from the gigantic Web. Link-based similarity search is a modern means to quantify node-to-node relationships based on graph topologies, with a wide range of successful applications, *e.g.,* link prediction, collaborative filtering, and co-citation analysis.

SIGIR'15, August 09 - 13, 2015, Santiago, Chile.
© 2015 ACM. ISBN 978-1-4503-3621-5/15/08 ...$15.00.
DOI: http://dx.doi.org/10.1145/2766462.2767720.

SimRank, conceived by Jeh and Widom [5], is one of the most influential similarity measures. The central idea underpinning SimRank is a simple recursion that "two nodes are assessed as similar if they are in-linked from similar nodes". For a digraph $G = (V, E)$ with $|V|$ nodes and $|E|$ edges, let $N_a = \{x \in V | (x, a) \in E\}$ be the in-neighbor set of node a. Then, SimRank score between nodes a and b is defined by[1]

$$s(a,b) = \begin{cases} 1 & (a = b) \\ \gamma \cdot \frac{\sum_{(i,j)\in N_a \times N_b} s(i,j)}{|N_a||N_b|} & (a \neq b) \end{cases} \quad (1)$$

where $\gamma \in (0,1)$ is a decay factor. Generally, $\gamma = 0.6$ [12] or 0.8 [5], which penalizes long paths relative to short ones.

In contrast with other similarity measures, SimRank has the following prominent features: (a) It takes a concise form that captures both direct and indirect neighbors recursively, unlike Bibliographic Coupling and Co-citation that focus only on direct neighbors. (b) It considers structural equivalence of two nodes, whereas Personalized PageRank focuses on reachability from every node to a query. Therefore, SimRank has attracted increasing attention in recent years [3,4,12].

1.1 The Quality of SimRank Search

Despite much effort devoted to fast SimRank computation (*e.g.,* [2,7,8,12,13]), the quality of SimRank search is still less desirable, due to the following two reasons:

(1) Superfluous Diagonal Correction Error ϵ_{diag}. The best-of-breed SimRank method by Kusumoto *et al.* [7] is based on the following "linearized SimRank formula":

$$s(a,b) = e_a^\top D e_b + \gamma (Pe_a)^\top D (Pe_b) + \gamma^2 (P^2 e_a)^\top D (P^2 e_b) + \cdots \quad (2)$$

where D is a precomputed diagonal correction matrix, e_a is a unit vector with a 1 in the a-th entry, and P is the column normalized adjacency matrix, with $P_{a,b} = \begin{cases} 1/|N_b|, & \text{if } (a,b)\in E; \\ 0, & \text{if } (a,b)\notin E. \end{cases}$

According to [7], before Eq.(2) is computed, D requires to be determined in advance. However, it is too difficult to compute the exact D (not to mention within linear memory) since SimRank results have a recursive impact on D. Note that even Kusumoto *et al.* [7] have not obtained the exact D, but simply approximated D by $\tilde{D} := (1-\gamma)I$. Consequently, *the diagonal correction error* is produced:

$$\epsilon_{\text{diag}} := |s(a,b) - s_{\tilde{D}}(a,b)|, \quad (3)$$

[1]To avoid division by 0 in Eq.(1), $s(a,b) = 0$ if $|N_a||N_b| = 0$.

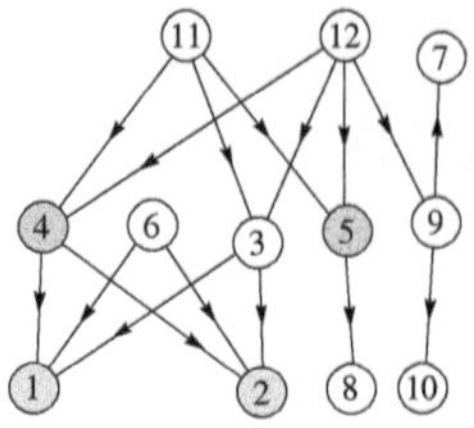

	$s(1,2)$	$s(4,5)$	$s(2,8)$	$s(8,10)$	$s(3,9)$
SR	0.24	0.30	0.12	0.18	0.30
SR^{++}	0.20	0.23	0	0	0.15
RS	0.34	0.24	0.05	0.07	0.12
SR$^{\#}$	0.38	0.24	0.14	0.10	0.17

	SR	SR^{++}	RS	SR$^{\#}$
$s(1,2) > s(4,5)$	✗	✗	✓	✓
$s(2,8) > s(8,10)$	✗	✗	✗	✓
$s(4,5) > s(3,9)$	✗	✓	✓	✓

Figure 1: SimRank++ (SR^{++}) and RoleSim (RS) may not resolve the "connectivity trait" problem of SimRank (SR)

where $s_{\tilde{D}}(a,b)$ is the estimated similarity when D is replaced by $\tilde{D}$ in Eq.(2). After D is estimated, [7] uses an iterative method that sums up only the first k terms of series $s_{\tilde{D}}(a,b)$, denoted as $s_{\tilde{D}}^{(k)}(a,b)$. This yields *the iterative error*:

$$\epsilon_{\text{iter}} := |s_{\tilde{D}}(a,b) - s_{\tilde{D}}^{(k)}(a,b)| \leq \tfrac{\gamma^{k+1}}{1-\gamma}.$$

Hence, the total error for approximating $s(a,b)$ by $s_{\tilde{D}}^{(k)}(a,b)$, in a nutshell, consists of two ingredients: ϵ_{diag} and ϵ_{iter}.

We argue ϵ_{diag} is far more serious than ϵ_{iter}, because ϵ_{iter} is guaranteed to converge by [7], and can be minimized by increasing the number of iterations. This increase, however, cannot minimize ϵ_{diag}. Worse still, there is no bound on ϵ_{diag} for Eq.(3). The only argument about ϵ_{diag} in [7] is that *"estimating D as $\tilde{D} := (1-\gamma)I$ does not much affect the top-K rankings of $s_{\tilde{D}}(*,*)$ and $s(*,*)$"*, but this, as will be shown in Section 4.1, bears a blemish.

This motivates us to design an accurate and fast approach that has no ϵ_{diag} and can avoid computing the exact D.

(2) "Connectivity Trait" Problem. Another factor that plagues the quality of SimRank is the "connectivity trait": increasing the number of *paths* between nodes a and b often incurs a contrary decrease in $s(a,b)$. However, a paucity of existing works [1, 2, 11] only noticed a special case (1-hop neighbor) of the above phenomenon: "increasing the number of *common in-neighbors* between nodes a and b will decrease $s(a,b)$." The best-known treatment is due to Antonellis *et al.* who proposed SimRank++ [1] that replaces γ in Eq.(1) with the following "evidence factor":

$$\tilde{\gamma} := \gamma(1 - e^{-|N_a \cap N_b|}) \quad \text{or} \quad \tilde{\gamma} := \gamma \textstyle\sum_{i=1}^{|N_a \cap N_b|} \frac{1}{2^i} \tag{4}$$

These revised "evidence factors" have a good property: $\tilde{\gamma}$ is increasing with respect to $|N_a \cap N_b|$. Hence, a larger $\tilde{\gamma}$ means that there are more common *direct* in-neighbors (*i.e.*, more paths of length 2) between a and b.

However, we observe a weakness of SimRank++ [1]: *SimRank++ score $\tilde{s}(a,b)$ is always zero if nodes a and b have no common (direct) in-neighbors.* This is because, by the definition in Eq.(4), if $N_a \cap N_b = \varnothing$, then $\tilde{\gamma} = 0$. Thus, $\tilde{s}(a,b) = 0$, regardless of how many common l-hop in-neighbors ($l > 2$) exist between a and b.

Other pioneering works (*e.g.*, RoleSim [6], PSimRank [2], and MatchSim [11]) to quantify $s(a,b)$ also resort to common *direct* in-neighbors between a and b, all of which can resolve the special case (1-hop) of the SimRank "connectivity trait" problem (see related work in Section 1.3.2 for more details). However, increasing the number of paths with length > 2 between a and b may still lead to a decrease in $s(a,b)$.

Example 1. *Consider a real Web graph G in Figure 1. We evaluate the similarity of each node-pair by 4 measures: (a) SR (Jeh and Widom's SimRank [5]); (b) SR^{++} (SimRank++ [1]); (c) RS (RoleSim [6]); (d) SR$^{\#}$ (our method). The results are partly depicted in the table. We notice that SR^{++} and RS do not well resolve the SR "connectivity trait".*

For example, most people may agree $s(1,2) > s(4,5)$ since node-pair $(1,2)$ has 3 common in-neighbors $\{4,6,3\}$ whereas $(4,5)$ has only 2 in common $\{11,12\}$. However, although SR^{++} narrows the gap between $s(1,2)$ and $s(4,5)$, it gives the same counter-intuitive answer $s(1,2) < s(4,5)$ as SR.

Another example is the comparison of $s(2,8)$ and $s(8,10)$. For SR^{++}, $s(2,8) = s(8,10) = 0$. This is because $(2,8)$ has no common direct *in-neighbors, $N_2 \cap N_8 = \varnothing$; neither has $(8,10)$. Thereby, their "evidence factors" $\tilde{\gamma} = 0$. However, there are 4* indirect *path-pairs in-linked from $(2,8)$:*

$$2 \leftarrow 4 \leftarrow \boxed{11} \rightarrow 5 \rightarrow 8, \quad 2 \leftarrow 3 \leftarrow \boxed{11} \rightarrow 5 \rightarrow 8$$

$$2 \leftarrow 4 \leftarrow \boxed{12} \rightarrow 5 \rightarrow 8, \quad 2 \leftarrow 3 \leftarrow \boxed{12} \rightarrow 5 \rightarrow 8$$

as opposed to only 1 from $(8,10)$: $8 \leftarrow 5 \leftarrow \boxed{12} \rightarrow 9 \rightarrow 10$. Thus, node-pair $(2,8)$ has a higher connectivity than $(8,10)$, but this connectivity trait is ignored by SR^{++}. Regarding RS, since it is a "role" similarity measure, it emphasizes more on similar node degrees than high connectivities. Thus, RS can only partially resolve the SR "connectivity trait" problem. □

Example 1 suggests that the state-of-the-art methods (*e.g.*, SimRank++ [1] and RoleSim [6]) cannot solidly circumvent the "connectivity trait" problem of SimRank. Unfortunately, as illustrated by our statistical experiments in Section 5.2, there are many node-pairs suffering from this problem (*e.g.*, 62.3% in social networks, 82.7% in Web graphs, and 56.4% in citation graphs), which has adversely affected the quality of similarity search. This highlights our need for a high-quality model to resolve the "connectivity trait" problem.

1.2 Our Contributions

Our main contributions are summarized as follows:

- We formulate the exact diagonal correction matrix D, and propose a "varied-D" method to accurately compute SimRank with no ϵ_{diag} and in linear memory. Moreover, by grouping computation, we also optimize the algorithm [7] from quadratic to linear time *w.r.t.* k. (Section 2)
- We observe a "connectivity trait" problem for SimRank, which SimRank++ [1] cannot resolve in a recursive style. To circumvent this problem, we design a "kernel-based" model and improve the search quality. (Section 3)
- We give mathematical insights to the semantic difference between Jeh and Widom's model [5] and its variant [9], and correct an argument [7]: if D is replaced by $(1-\gamma)I$, top-K rankings will not be affected much. (Section 4)

The comprehensive experiments verify that our methods (1) improve an accuracy of average NDCG$_{200}$ by ~30% over SimRank on various real networks, and (2) are ~10x faster than the state-of-the-art competitors on large datasets with 65.8M links for 1000 queries.

1.3 Related Work

1.3.1 SimRank Computation

Recent years have witnessed a surge of efficient methods to compute SimRank. They can be categorized as follows:

- *Single-source SimRank* [3,7,8]. Compute all $s(i,*)$.
- *All-pairs SimRank* [9,12,13,16]. Compute all $s(*,*)$.
- *Single-pair SimRank* [2,7,10]. Compute $s(i,j)$.

Type	Algorithm	Error	Time	Memory
single source	Proposed	γ^{k+1}	$O(k\|E\|)$	$O(\|E\|+k\|V\|)$
	Kusumoto *et al.* [7]	$(\frac{\gamma^{k+1}}{1-\gamma})+\epsilon_{\text{diag}}$	$O(k^2\|E\|)$	$O(\|E\|+\|V\|)$
	Fujiwara *et al.* [3]	$\epsilon_{\text{rank-}r}+\epsilon_{\text{diag}}$	$O(r\|V\|^2)$	$O(r\|V\|^2)$
	Lee *et al.* [8]	γ^{k+1}	$O(d^{2k})$	$O(d^{2k}+\|V\|)$
all pairs	Proposed	γ^{k+1}	$O(k\|V\|\|E\|)$	$O(\|E\|+k\|V\|)$
	Kusumoto *et al.* [7]	$(\frac{\gamma^{k+1}}{1-\gamma})+\epsilon_{\text{diag}}$	$O(k^2\|V\|\|E\|)$	$O(\|E\|+\|V\|)$
	Yu *et al.* [13]	γ^{k+1}	$O(kd'\|V\|^2)$	$O(\|V\|^2)$
	Lizorkin *et al.* [12]	γ^{k+1}	$O(k\|V\|\|E\|)$	$O(\|V\|^2)$
	Yu *et al.* [16]	$\epsilon_{\text{rank-}r}+\epsilon_{\text{diag}}$	$O(r\|V\|^2)$	$O(\|V\|^2)$
	Li *et al.* [9]	$\epsilon_{\text{rank-}r}+\epsilon_{\text{diag}}$	$O(r^4\|V\|^2)$	$O(r^2\|V\|^2)$
	Jeh *et al.* [5]	γ^{k+1}	$O(k\|E\|^2)$	$O(\|V\|^2)$

Table 1: A comparison with previous deterministic methods (with low-rank $r \le |V|$, degree $d = \frac{|E|}{|V|}$, and $d' \le d$)

In Table 1, we briefly summarize the accuracy, time, and memory of previous works for each type of SimRank search.

Compared with the best-known method [7], our techniques not only well preserve the scalability of [7], but also achieve high accuracy and fast computational time. Furthermore, for high accuracy, our methods not only remove superfluous error ϵ_{diag} but also attain a better bound on ϵ_{iter} than [7].

1.3.2 SimRank "Connectivity Trait"

Fogaras *et al.* [2] is the first to notice one special case of the SimRank "connectivity trait" problem: "if two nodes a and b have β common (direct) in-neighbors, then $s(a,b) \le 1/\beta$." To address this problem, they employed an unwieldy method that divides the entire search space into three probabilities: $\frac{|N_a \cap N_b|}{|N_a \cup N_b|}$, $\frac{|N_a - N_b|}{|N_a \cup N_b|}$, and $\frac{|N_b - N_a|}{|N_a \cup N_b|}$. However, this complicates the revised SimRank equation, which is rather tedious.

Recently, Antonellis *et al.* [1] gave an excellent revision, called SimRank++, by introducing the "evidence factor" $\tilde{\gamma}$. Unfortunately, $\tilde{\gamma}$ can only, in part, alleviate a special case of the "connectivity trait" problem, since, if $|N_a \cap N_b| = 0$, then $\tilde{\gamma} = 0$ has no recursive impact on SimRank any more.

Jin *et al.* [6] also gave an excellent exposition on "role similarity". Their proposed model, namely RoleSim, has the advantage of utilizing "automorphic equivalence" to improve the quality of similarity search in "role" based applications. Their initial intention, however, was not to deal with the SimRank "connectivity trait" problem.

There is also a SimRank-like "connectivity trait" problem in other SimRank variant models, such as MatchSim, SimRank*, SimFusion+ [15]. Our proposed methods for SimRank are also extensible to SimRank*. Due to space limitation, we omit it in this paper.

1.3.3 Semantics between SimRank and Its Variant

There are some interesting works (*e.g.*, [3, 4, 9, 14, 17]), based on the following model, to evaluate similarity $\tilde{S}$:

$$\tilde{S} = \gamma P^\top \tilde{S} P + (1-\gamma) I. \tag{5}$$

[7] argued that "the top-K rankings of $\tilde{S}$ in Eq.(5) and S in Eq.(1) are not affected much". However, we correct this argument, and provide new mathematical insights into the subtle difference of $\tilde{S}$ and S from a semantic perspective.

2. ACCURATE AND FAST SIMRANK

We first show the sensitivity of diagonal correction matrix D to SimRank matrix S, and formulate the exact D. Then, we devise an accurate fast "varied-D" model to compute S.

2.1 Sensitivity of Diagonal Correction Matrix

In matrix forms, SimRank in Eq.(1) can be rewritten as

$$S = \max\{\gamma P^\top S P,\ I\}, \tag{6}$$

where $\max\{*\}$ denotes the matrix entry-wise maximum, *i.e.*, $(\max\{A, B\})_{i,j} = \max\{A_{i,j}, B_{i,j}\}$.

Kusumoto *et al.* [7] have showed that there exists a unique diagonal matrix D such that Eq.(6) can be converted to

$$S = \gamma P^\top S P + D, \tag{7}$$

where D is called *the diagonal correction matrix*, which needs to be determined beforehand.

However, [7] did not mention how to accurately compute the exact D, but simply approximated D by $\tilde{D} = (1-\gamma)I$.

In fact, D is very sensitive to the resulting S. Even small errors in D may lead to large changes in SimRank scores S by a factor of up to $\frac{1}{1-\gamma}$, as shown in Lemma 1.

LEMMA 1. *Let S be the solution to Eq.(7), and $S_{\tilde{D}}$ be the solution to the equation:*

$$S_{\tilde{D}} = \gamma P^\top S_{\tilde{D}} P + \tilde{D}, \tag{8}$$

and let $\Delta D := D - \tilde{D}$ and $\Delta S := S - S_{\tilde{D}}$. Then,

$$\|\Delta S\|_{\max} \le \tfrac{1}{1-\gamma} \|\Delta D\|_{\max}.^{2} \tag{9}$$

PROOF. The recursion of $S_{\tilde{D}}$ in Eq.(8) naturally leads to the following series:

$$S_{\tilde{D}} = \tilde{D} + \gamma P^\top \tilde{D} P + \gamma^2 (P^\top)^2 \tilde{D} P^2 + \cdots, \tag{10}$$

We subtract Eq.(10) from Eq.(2), and then take $\|*\|_{\max}$ norms on both sides:

$$\|\Delta S\|_{\max} \le \|\Delta D\|_{\max} + \textstyle\sum_{i=1}^{\infty} \gamma^i \overbrace{\|(P^\top)^i \Delta D (P^i)\|_{\max}}^{\le \|\Delta D\|_{\max}}$$
$$\le (1 + \gamma + \gamma^2 + \cdots)\|\Delta D\|_{\max} = \tfrac{1}{1-\gamma}\|\Delta D\|_{\max}. \quad \square$$

2.2 Formulating Diagonal Correction Matrix

We next derive an exact explicit formulation of D in Eq.(7). For ease of exposition, the following notations are adopted.

DEFINITION 1 (ENTRY-WISE PRODUCT). *For matrices X and Y, their entry-wise product $X \circ Y$ is defined as*

$$(X \circ Y)_{i,j} = X_{i,j} Y_{i,j}.$$

Let $diag(Z)$ be a diagonal matrix whose diagonal entries are those of Z, *i.e.*, $(diag(Z))_{i,i} = Z_{i,i}$.

Using this notation, Eq.(6) can be represented as

$$S = \gamma P^\top S P + I - \gamma diag(P^\top S P). \tag{11}$$

Due to D uniqueness, Eqs.(7) and (11) imply that

$$D = I - \gamma diag(P^\top S P). \tag{12}$$

To formulate the exact D in Eq.(12) only in terms of P, we introduce the following lemma.

LEMMA 2. *Let $\overrightarrow{diag}(Z)$ be a column vector of the diagonal entries of Z, i.e., $(\overrightarrow{diag}(Z))_i = Z_{i,i}$. For two $n \times n$ matrices X and Y, and an $n \times n$ diagonal matrix Z, we have*

$$\overrightarrow{diag}(X^\top Z Y) = (X \circ Y)^\top \overrightarrow{diag}(Z).$$

[2] $\|*\|_{\max}$ returns the maximum element of a matrix.

Combining Lemma 2 with Eq.(12), we next formulate D.

THEOREM 1. *The diagonal correction matrix D in Eq.(7) can be explicitly formulated as*

$$\overrightarrow{diag}(D) = \left(\sum_{k=0}^{+\infty} \gamma^k (P^k \circ P^k)\right)^{-\top} \vec{1}, \tag{13}$$

where $\vec{1}$ is a $|V| \times 1$ vector of all 1s, and $(*)^{-\top} := ((*)^\top)^{-1}$.

PROOF. Taking $\overrightarrow{diag}(*)$ on both sides of Eq.(2) produces

$$\overrightarrow{diag}(S) = \overrightarrow{diag}(D) + \gamma \overrightarrow{diag}(P^\top D P) + \gamma^2 \overrightarrow{diag}((P^\top)^2 D P^2) + \cdots \tag{14}$$

By SimRank definition Eq.(6), we have $S_{i,i} = 1$ $(\forall i \in V)$, which implies that $\overrightarrow{diag}(S) = \vec{1}$.

Applying Lemma 2 to the right-hand side of Eq.(14) yields

$$\vec{1} = \left(I + \gamma (P \circ P) + \gamma^2 (P^2 \circ P^2) + \cdots\right)^\top \overrightarrow{diag}(D), \tag{15}$$

Since $0 \le (P \circ P)_{i,j} \le P_{i,j} \le 1$, one can readily show that $\left(I + \gamma (P \circ P) + \gamma^2 (P^2 \circ P^2) + \cdots\right)^\top$ is diagonally dominant. Multiplying both sides by its inverse produces Eq.(13). □

Theorem 1 characterizes the exact D as an *infinite* series. Hence, prior to computing S, it is too difficult to obtain the *exact* D in only a *finite* number of iterations. This tells us that using the method of [7] will innately produce ϵ_{diag}.

Theorem 1 also implies that the estimation $D \approx (1-\gamma)I$ in [7] is not appropriate for accurately computing S in Eq.(7). This is because replacing $(P^k \circ P^k)$ by P^k in Eq.(13) yields

$$\overrightarrow{diag}(D) \approx \left(\sum_{k=0}^{+\infty} \gamma^k P^k\right)^{-\top} \vec{1} = (I - \gamma P)^\top \vec{1} = (1-\gamma)\vec{1},$$

which suggests that the approximation $D \approx (1-\gamma)I$ in [7] is equivalent to the approximation $P^k \circ P^k \approx P^k$. Clearly, most people will not agree that $\left((P^k)_{i,j}\right)^2 \approx (P^k)_{i,j}$ is reasonable. In Section 4.2, we will further discuss $D \approx (1-\gamma)I$ from the viewpoint of semantics.

One benefit of Theorem 1 is that it narrows the boundaries for the range of D in [7], based on the following corollary.

COROLLARY 1. $(1-\gamma)I \le D \le I - \gamma diag(P^\top P)$ [3]

PROOF. Since $0 \le P_{i,j} \le 1$, we can readily show that

$$(P \circ P)^k \le (P^k \circ P^k) \le P^k.$$

Applying this to Eq.(13) yields

$$\left(\sum_{k=0}^{+\infty} \gamma^k P^k\right)^{-\top} \vec{1} \le \overrightarrow{diag}(D) \le \left(\sum_{k=0}^{+\infty} \gamma^k (P \circ P)^k\right)^{-\top} \vec{1}.$$

Since $\sum_{k=0}^{+\infty} X^k = (I - X)^{-1}$, it follows that $(I - \gamma P)^\top \vec{1} \le \overrightarrow{diag}(D) \le \left(I - \gamma (P \circ P)\right)^\top \vec{1}$. Then, applying Lemma 2 on both sides, we obtain the results. □

In comparison, the best-known bounds for the range of D in Proposition 2 of [7] (*i.e.*, $(1-\gamma)I \le D \le I$) are loose, and independent of P, which is isolated from graph structures.

2.3 A "Varied-D" Iterative Model

Another important consequence of Theorem 1 is to derive an accurate SimRank algorithm without ϵ_{diag}.

Instead of determining the exact D in advance, our method is to iteratively update D and S at the same time. Precisely, we leverage *the "varied-D" SimRank model* as follows:

$$S^{(k)} := D_k + \gamma P^\top D_{k-1} P + \cdots + \gamma^k (P^\top)^k D_0 P^k, \tag{16}$$

[3]For matrices A and B, $A \le B$ refers to $A_{i,j} \le B_{i,j}$, $\forall i, j$.

where $\{D_k\}$ is a diagonal matrix sequence (convergent to D), which can be iteratively obtained while S is being iterated.

Different from the model Eq.(2) by Kusumoto *et al.* [7], our "varied-D" model Eq.(16) replaces all Ds by a convergent sequence $\{D_k\}$. The main advantage of our replacement is that Eq.(16) can avoid determining the *exact* D beforehand, and thereby, will not produce the superfluous error ϵ_{diag}.

The correctness of our "varied-D" model can be verified by taking limits $k \to \infty$ on both sides of Eq.(16). As $k \to \infty$, $D_k \to D$ and $S^{(k)} \to S$.[4] Thus, Eq.(16) converges to Eq.(2).

2.3.1 Finding D_k in "Varied-D" Model

The challenging problem in our "varied-D" Eq.(16) is to determine the diagonal matrix D_k. Our main idea is based on two observations: (a) $S^{(k)}$ in Eq.(16) can be iterated as

$$S^{(l)} = \gamma P^\top S^{(l-1)} P + D_l \quad \text{with} \quad S^{(0)} = D_0. \tag{17}$$

(b) To ensure $diag(S^{(l)}) = I$, D_l in Eq.(17) must satisfy

$$D_l = I - \gamma diag(P^\top S^{(l-1)} P). \tag{18}$$

Coupling these observations, we can compute D_k in Eq.(16).

THEOREM 2. *The diagonal correction matrices in Eq.(16) can be iteratively obtained as follows:*

$$(D_k)_{i,i} = 1 - \sum_{l=1}^{k} (h_l \circ h_l)^\top \overrightarrow{diag}(D_{k-l}) \quad \textit{with} \quad D_0 = I, \tag{19}$$

where the auxiliary vectors $h_1, \cdots, h_k$ are derived from

$$\begin{cases} h_0 = e_i \\ h_l = \sqrt{\gamma} P h_{l-1} \quad (l = 1, 2, \cdots, k) \end{cases} \tag{20}$$

PROOF. First, we derive a complete matrix formula of D_k. By Lemma 2, Eq.(19) can be converted to

$$(D_k)_{i,i} = 1 - \sum_{l=1}^{k} {h_l}^\top D_{k-l} h_l \tag{21}$$

Successive substitution applied to Eq.(20) yields $h_l = \sqrt{\gamma^l} P^l e_i$. Then, substituting this back into Eq.(21) produces

$$D_k = I - \sum_{l=1}^{k} \gamma^l diag\left((P^l)^\top D_{k-l} (P^l)\right) \tag{22}$$

Next, we show that D_k in Eq.(22) satisfies Eqs.(16)–(18). It follows from Eq.(16) that

$$\begin{aligned} diag(\gamma P^\top S^{(k-1)} P) &= diag\left(\sum_{l=0}^{k-1} \gamma^{l+1} (P^{l+1})^\top D_{k-1-l} P^{l+1}\right) \\ &= diag\left(\sum_{l=1}^{k} \gamma^l (P^l)^\top D_{k-l} P^l\right). \end{aligned}$$

Thus, the above equation implies that

$$I - diag(\gamma P^\top S^{(k-1)} P) = I - \sum_{l=1}^{k} \gamma^l diag\left((P^l)^\top D_{k-l} (P^l)\right)$$

Applying Eq.(22) to the right-hand side yields Eq.(18). □

Theorem 2 provides a simple efficient way to compute D_k.

Algorithm 1: Compute Diagonal Matrix D_k

initialize $t := 0,\ h_0 := e_i,\ D_0 := I$;
for $l := 1, 2, \cdots, k$ **do**
  compute $h_l := \sqrt{\gamma} P h_{l-1}$;
  update $t := t + (h_l \circ h_l)^\top \overrightarrow{diag}(D_{k-l})$;
return $(D_k)_{i,i} := 1 - t$;

The correctness of Algorithm 1 is verified by Theorem 2. Regarding complexity, we have the following result.

[4]The convergence of $S^{(k)}$ will be proved in Section 2.3.2.

THEOREM 3. *Given the total iteration number $k = 1, 2, \cdots$, Algorithm 1 is in $O(k|V|)$ memory and $O(k(|E|+|V|))$ time.*

In contrast to the linear-memory SimRank method in [7], Theorem 3 implies that our "varied-D" method to compute D_k will not compromise the scalability of [7] for high quality search, since D_k can be computed in linear memory as well.

2.3.2 Fast Convergence of "Varied-D" Model

Besides no ϵ_{diag} and no need to precompute the exact D, our "varied-D" model Eq.(16) also converges faster than [7].

THEOREM 4. *Let $S^{(k)}$ and S be the k-th iterative and the exact SimRank in Eqs.(16) and (7), respectively. Then,*

$$\|S^{(k)} - S\|_{\max} \leq \gamma^{k+1}. \tag{23}$$

PROOF. We subtract Eq.(7) from Eq.(17) to obtain, $\forall k$,

$$S^{(k)} - S = \gamma P^\top (S^{(k-1)} - S)P + (D^{(k)} - D). \tag{24}$$

We notice from Eq.(18) that $(S^{(k)})_{i,i} = S_{i,i} = 1,\ \forall i \in V$. Thus, when $i \neq j$, it follows from Eq.(24) that, $\forall i, j \in V$,

$$\begin{aligned}(S^{(k)} - S)_{i,j} &= \gamma (P^\top)_{i,*} (S^{(k-1)} - S) P_{*,j}. \\ &\leq \gamma \|S^{(k-1)} - S\|_{\max} \leq \cdots \leq \gamma^k \|I - S\|_{\max}\end{aligned} \tag{25}$$

By Eq.(1), $\|I - S\|_{\max} \leq \gamma$. Thus, Eq.(23) holds. □

In comparison to the bound $\left(\frac{\gamma^{k+1}}{1-\gamma}\right)$ (see Eq.(10) of [7]), Theorem 4 shows that our "varied-D" model not only eliminates ϵ_{diag}, but also has a better bound on ϵ_{iter} than [7]. Thus, our "varied-D" model achieves both high-quality and fast convergence rate at the same time.

2.4 Efficiently Computing $S^{(k)}$

Having determined D_k in our "varied-D" model Eq.(16), we next propose our method to efficiently compute $S^{(k)}$.

The method [7] requires $O(k^2|E|)$ and $O(k^2|V||E|)$ time, respectively, to compute single-source and all-pairs SimRank. If we merely apply the method [7] and replace D with D_k, then our "varied-D" Eq.(16) to compute $S^{(k)}$ will retain the same complexity as [7] except with no ϵ_{diag}, as follows:

Procedure 2: Single-Source "Varied-D" SimRank(i)

1 initialize $h := \vec{0},\ x := e_i$;
2 **for** $l := 0, 1, \cdots, k$ **do**
3 update $h := h + \gamma^l (P^\top)^l (D_{k-l}) x,\quad x := Px$;
4 **return** $(S^{(k)})_{i,*} := h$;

However, we observe that there exist many duplicate products in [7]. Precisely, to obtain the result of the sums

$$(S^{(k)})_{i,*} = D_k x_0 + \gamma P^\top D_{k-1} x_1 + \cdots + \gamma^k (P^\top)^k D_0 x_k, \tag{26}$$

the method [7] *separately* computes every $\left(\gamma^l (P^\top)^l (D_{k-l}) x_l\right)$ and then adds them together. Its main limitation is that, to compute any power of $(P^\top)$, [7] has to go through all of the previous powers from scratch. As a result, there are l matrix-vector products to compute each h in Line 3, leading to $\sum_{l=1}^k l = O(k^2)$ products for k iterations in total.

We now propose an efficient method for Procedure 2, which reduces $O(k^2|E|)$ to $O(k|E|)$ time, with no loss of accuracy. Our key observation is that "doing each matrix-vector multiplication separately is equivalent to multiplying a matrix by a group of the resulting vectors added together". Hence, we rearrange the computation of Eq.(26) as follows:

$$\begin{aligned}(S^{(k)})_{i,*} = D_k x_0 + \gamma P^\top (D_{k-1} x_1 + \gamma P^\top (D_{k-2} x_2 + \cdots \\ \cdots + \gamma P^\top (D_1 x_{k-1} + \gamma P^\top (D_0 x_k))))\end{aligned} \tag{27}$$

and obtain the result by starting with the innermost brackets and working outwards. In contrast with the method [7], Eq.(27) has only $O(k)$ matrix-vector products in k brackets, as opposed to $O(k^2)$ products in Procedure 2.

Based on Eq.(27), we give an efficient way of Procedure 2.

Algorithm 3: Optimized Single-Source SimRank(i)

initialize $x_0 := e_i$;
for $l := 1, 2, \cdots, k$ **do**
update $x_l := P x_{l-1}$;
initialize $y_0 := \overrightarrow{diag}(D_0) \circ x_k$;
for $l := 1, 2, \cdots, k$ **do**
update $y_l := \overrightarrow{diag}(D_l) \circ x_{k-l} + \gamma P^\top y_{l-1}$;
return $(S^{(k)})_{i,*} := y_k$;

Algorithm 3 can reduce not only the time of single-source SimRank from $O(k^2|E|)$ [7] to $O(k|E|)$, but also the time of all-pairs SimRank from $O(k^2|V||E|)$ [7] to $O(k|V||E|)$, since all-pairs SimRank runs $|V|$ times of single-source SimRank.

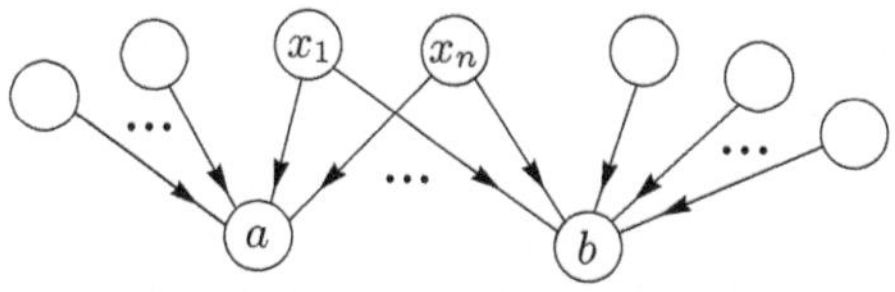

Figure 2: SimRank "Connectivity Trait" Problem

3. ENHANCING SIMRANK QUALITY

After the superfluous ϵ_{diag} is avoided, we next focus on the "connectivity trait" problem of SimRank.

3.1 The "Connectivity Trait" Problem

We observe that the root cause of the "connectivity trait" problem is that the order of the normalized factor $\frac{1}{|N_a||N_b|}$ in the SimRank definition Eq.(1) is too high. To clarify this, let us consider the following situation in Figure 2:

Let δ be the number of paths $\{a \leftarrow x \rightarrow b\}$ to be inserted between nodes a and b. By SimRank definition Eq.(1), after insertions, $s(a, b)$ will become a function of δ:

$$s_\delta(a, b) = \gamma \cdot \frac{|N_a \cap N_b| + \delta}{(|N_a| + \delta)(|N_b| + \delta)} \sim \gamma \cdot \frac{\delta}{\delta^2} \to 0. \quad (\delta \to \infty) \tag{28}$$

This suggests that, for large δ, $s_\delta(a, b)$ behaves like $(\gamma \cdot \frac{1}{\delta})$, which is eventually decreasing *w.r.t.* δ.

3.2 Our Kernel-Based SimRank Model

To avoid the order inconsistency between denominator and numerator in Eq.(28), our goal is to judiciously adjust the order of $\frac{1}{|N_a||N_b|}$ while normalizing $s(a, b)$ correctly.

DEFINITION 2. *Let A be an adjacency matrix. The "cosine-based" SimRank $\hat{S}_{a,b}$ between a and b is defined by*

$$\hat{S}_{a,b} = (1 - \gamma) \sum_{k=0}^{\infty} \gamma^k \frac{e_a^\top (A^k)^\top A^k e_b}{\|A^k e_a\|_2 \|A^k e_b\|_2}, \tag{29}$$

where $\|x\|_2 := \sqrt{\sum_i |x_i|^2}$ denotes the L_2-norm of vector x.

To prevent division by zero in Eq.(29), we define the k-th term of the sums to be 0 if $(A^k)_{*,a}$ or $(A^k)_{*,b} = \vec{0}$.

Our cosine-based SimRank $\hat{S}_{a,b}$ integrates weighted cosine similarities between a's and b's multi-hop in-neighbor sets. This can be seen more clearly when we rewrite Eq.(29) as

$$\hat{S}_{a,b} = (1-\gamma)\sum_{k=0}^{\infty}\gamma^k\phi(A^k e_a, A^k e_b) \text{ with } \phi(x,y) := \tfrac{x^\top y}{\|x\|_2\|y\|_2}. \quad (30)$$

We call $\phi(x,y)$ *a kernel similarity function.* In Definition 2, we take $\phi(x,y)$ as the well-known cosine similarity function. The vector $A^k e_a$ (*resp.* $A^k e_b$) in Eq.(30) collects the information about k-hop in-neighbors of node a (*resp.* b). Hence, the term $\phi(A^k e_a, A^k e_b)$ in Eq.(30) evaluates how similar node a's and b's k-hop in-neighbor sets are likely to be in terms of the number of length-k paths in-linked from both a and b. The factor γ^k penalizes connections made with distant k-hop in-neighbors, and $(1-\gamma)$ normalizes $\hat{S}_{a,b}$ into $[0,1]$. Thus, $\hat{S}_{a,b}$ not only distills the self-referentiality of SimRank, but also extends a one-step cosine similarity to a multi-step one.

THEOREM 5. *The cosine-based SimRank model in Eq.(29) can circumvent the SimRank "connectivity trait" problem.*

PROOF. Let $\mathsf{hop}_k(x) = \{i \in V | (A^k e_x)_i > 0\}$ be the k-hop in-neighbor set of node x. Then, we have

$$e_a^\top (A^k)^\top A^k e_b = |\mathsf{hop}_k(a) \cap \mathsf{hop}_k(b)|,$$
$$\|A^k e_a\|_2 = \sqrt{e_a^\top (A^k)^\top A^k e_a} = \sqrt{|\mathsf{hop}_k(a)|}.$$

Plugging these into Eq.(29) produces

$$\hat{S}_{a,b} = (1-\gamma)\sum_{k=0}^{\infty}\gamma^k \frac{|\mathsf{hop}_k(a) \cap \mathsf{hop}_k(b)|}{\sqrt{|\mathsf{hop}_k(a)| \cdot |\mathsf{hop}_k(b)|}}. \quad (31)$$

When inserting the following δ paths between a and b:

$$\underbrace{a \leftarrow \circ \leftarrow \cdots \leftarrow \circ \leftarrow}_{k_1 \text{ edges}} \boxed{\circ} \underbrace{\rightarrow \circ \rightarrow \cdots \rightarrow \circ \rightarrow b}_{k_2 \text{ edges}} \quad (32)$$

we notice that, only for $k_1 = k_2$, the k_1-th term of the series Eq.(31) will be changed to a function of δ:

$$f(\delta) = \gamma^{k_1}\frac{|\mathsf{hop}_{k_1}(a) \cap \mathsf{hop}_{k_1}(b)| + \delta}{\sqrt{(|\mathsf{hop}_{k_1}(a)|+\delta)\cdot(|\mathsf{hop}_{k_1}(b)|+\delta)}}. \quad (\delta > 0)$$

To show $f(\delta)$ increases *w.r.t.* δ, we take $\log(*)$ on both sides, and then use implicit differentiation *w.r.t.* δ on both sides:

$$f'(\delta) = f(\delta)\Big(\tfrac{1}{|\mathsf{hop}_{k_1}(a)\cap\mathsf{hop}_{k_1}(b)|+\delta} - \tfrac{1}{2(|\mathsf{hop}_{k_1}(a)|+\delta)} - \tfrac{1}{2(|\mathsf{hop}_{k_1}(b)|+\delta)}\Big).$$

Since $f(\delta) > 0$ and $|\mathsf{hop}_{k_1}(a)| \geq |\mathsf{hop}_{k_1}(a) \cap \mathsf{hop}_{k_1}(b)|$ and $|\mathsf{hop}_{k_1}(b)| \geq |\mathsf{hop}_{k_1}(a) \cap \mathsf{hop}_{k_1}(b)|$, we can obtain $f'(\delta) > 0$. Thus, $f(\delta)$ increases *w.r.t.* δ, which implies that paths (32) insertion will not decrease $\hat{S}_{a,b}$. □

Indeed, by using $Pe_b = Ae_b/\|Ae_b\|_1$ [5] to the original SimRank Eq.(2), we notice that both Eqs.(2) and (29) tally the same paths in-linked from a and b. The difference is norms $\|*\|_2$ and $\|*\|_1$ used by Eq.(29) and Eq.(2)[6], respectively. Since the SimRank "connectivity trait" problem is due to the high order of $\frac{1}{|N_a||N_b|}$ in Eq.(1), it is reasonable for us to prevent its high order by replacing $\|*\|_1$ with $\|*\|_2$ since $\|x\|_2 \leq \|x\|_1$. Moreover, by using $\|*\|_2$, $\hat{S}_{a,b}$ can be correctly normalized into $[0,1]$. This is because $\phi(*,*) \in [0,1]$, which indicates that $0 \leq \hat{S}_{a,b} \leq (1-\gamma)\sum_{k=0}^{\infty}\gamma^k \leq 1$ in Eq.(30).

[5] $\|x\|_1 := \sum_i |x_i|$ denotes the L_1-norm of vector x.

[6] P is associated with $\frac{1}{|N_a||N_b|}$ $(= \frac{1}{\|Pe_a\|_1\|Pe_b\|_1})$ in Eq.(1).

EXAMPLE 2. *Recall the δ paths $\{a \leftarrow x \rightarrow b\}$ to be added into G in Figure 2. After insertion, $\hat{S}_{a,b}(\delta)$ in Eq.(29) can circumvent the "connectivity trait" problem. This is because*

$$Ae_a = (\underbrace{1,1,\cdots,1}_{|N_a|},\underbrace{0,0,\cdots 0}_{|N_b-N_a|},\underbrace{1,1,\cdots,1}_{\delta})^\top$$
$$Ae_b = (\underbrace{0,0,\cdots 0}_{|N_a-N_b|},\underbrace{1,1,\cdots,1}_{|N_b|},\underbrace{1,1,\cdots,1}_{\delta})^\top$$

Then, we have $(Ae_a)^\top Ae_b = |N_a \cap N_b| + \delta$ *and*

$$\|Ae_a\|_2 = \sqrt{\underbrace{1^2+\cdots+1^2}_{|N_a|}+\underbrace{1^2+\cdots+1^2}_{\delta}} = \sqrt{|N_a|+\delta}, \quad \|Ae_b\|_2 = \sqrt{|N_b|+\delta}$$

Therefore, it follows from Eq.(29) that

$$\hat{S}_{a,b}(\delta) = (1-\gamma)\gamma \cdot \tfrac{|N_a \cap N_b|+\delta}{\sqrt{|N_a|+\delta}\sqrt{|N_b|+\delta}} \rightarrow (1-\gamma)\gamma \quad (\delta \rightarrow \infty) \quad (33)$$

Comparing this with Eq.(28), $\hat{S}_{a,b}(\delta)$ is not eventually decreasing w.r.t. δ, which is due to norm $\|*\|_2$ used in Eq.(29). □

In contrast to SimRank++ [1] and PSimRank [2] whose revised weight factors rely only on common N_a and N_b, our method Eq.(29), even if $N_a \cap N_b = \varnothing$, can evaluate $s(a,b)$ from common multi-hops neighbors $\mathsf{hop}_k(a) \cap \mathsf{hop}_k(b)$.

To compute the cosine-based SimRank score $\hat{S}_{a,b}$, if $a = b$, Eq.(29) implies $\hat{S}_{a,b} = 1$. If $a \neq b$, we compute $\hat{S}_{a,b}$ as

$$\hat{S}_{a,b}^{(k)} = \hat{S}_{a,b}^{(k-1)} + (1-\gamma)\gamma^k (u^{(k)})^\top v^{(k)} \quad \text{with } \hat{S}_{a,b}^{(0)} = 0 \quad (34)$$

where the auxiliary vectors $u^{(k)}$ and $v^{(k)}$ are obtained by

$$\begin{cases} u^{(0)} = e_a \\ u^{(k)} = \frac{Au^{(k-1)}}{\|Au^{(k-1)}\|_2} \end{cases} \quad \begin{cases} v^{(0)} = e_b \\ v^{(k)} = \frac{Av^{(k-1)}}{\|Av^{(k-1)}\|_2} \end{cases} \quad (35)$$

Eqs.(34)–(35) provide an algorithm to compute $\hat{S}_{a,b}^{(k)}$, which is in $O(k|E|)$ time and $O(|E|+k|V|)$ memory for k iterations.

4. SEMANTIC DIFFERENCE

Apart from Jeh and Widom's SimRank model [5]:

$$S = \max\{\gamma P^\top S P,\ I\}, \quad (36)$$

recent years have witnessed many studies (*e.g.*, [3,4,9,14]) to compute similarity, based on Li *et al.*'s model [9]:

$$\tilde{S} = \gamma P^\top \tilde{S} P + (1-\gamma) I. \quad (37)$$

In this section, we explore their relationship from a semantic perspective, and correct two arguments in [9] and [7].

4.1 A Fly in the Ointment of [7,9]

There are only two works [7,9] that have mentioned the relationship between $\tilde{S}$ and S. (a) Li *et al.* [9] argued that *"$\tilde{S}$ affects only the absolute similarity value of S, but not the relative similarity ranking of S."* (b) The recent work by Kusumoto *et al.* [7] states that "*$\tilde{S}$ does not much affect the top-K ranking of S.* [7]" However, either of them implies a limitation, as disproved by the following counterexample.

EXAMPLE 3. *Consider graph G in Figure 3, for $\gamma = 0.6$, the top-10 similarity rankings by S and $\tilde{S}$ are shown in part:*

node pairs	(3,3)	(6,6)	...	(1,2)	(7,8)
rank by S	*1*	*1*	...	*9*	*9*
rank by $\tilde{S}$	*4*	*3*	...	*10*	*9*

[7] In essence, $S \approx \tilde{S}$ is equivalent to $D \approx (1-\gamma)I$.

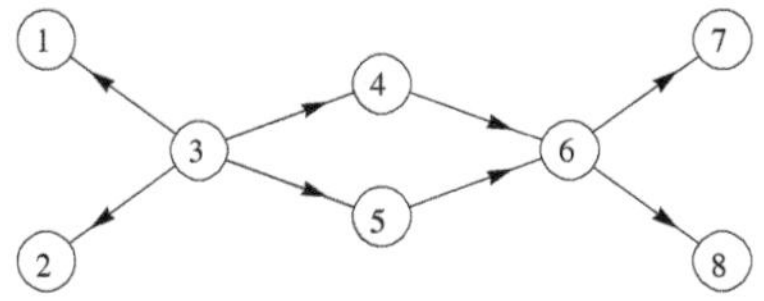

Figure 3: A Citation Graph (A Counterexample)

From the table, we can discern the following:
(a) $\tilde{S}$ does not preserve the relative similarity rankings of S;
(b) At least 4 out of top-10 rankings of S are affected by $\tilde{S}$.
Thus, neither of the statements by [7, 9] is correct. □

4.2 Semantic Relationship Between S and $\tilde{S}$

To "rekindle" the semantic relationship between S and $\tilde{S}$, let us first introduce the following notation:

DEFINITION 3 (OFF-DIAGONAL OPERATOR). *For square matrix X, let $(*)_{\mathit{off}}$ be a matrix operator defined by*

$$(X)_{\mathit{off}} := X - \mathit{diag}(X).$$

This notation is introduced to bring new insights into S.

THEOREM 6. *The similarity S in Jeh and Widom's model Eq.(36) can be characterized as follows:*

$$S = I + \gamma (P^\top P)_{\mathit{off}} + \gamma^2 (P^\top (P^\top P)_{\mathit{off}} P)_{\mathit{off}} + \cdots + \gamma^k \underbrace{(P^\top \cdots (P^\top (P^\top P)_{\mathit{off}} P)_{\mathit{off}} \cdots P)_{\mathit{off}}}_{k \text{ nested } (*)_{\mathit{off}}} + \cdots \quad (38)$$

PROOF. Applying $(*)_{\mathit{off}}$, Eq.(36) can be iterated as

$$S_k = \gamma (P^\top S_{k-1} P)_{\mathit{off}} + I. \quad (39)$$

We now construct the iterations: starting with $R_0 = I$,

$$R_k = \gamma^k \underbrace{(P^\top \cdots (P^\top (P^\top P)_{\mathit{off}} P)_{\mathit{off}} \cdots P)_{\mathit{off}}}_{k \text{ nested } (*)_{\mathit{off}}} + R_{k-1}. \quad (40)$$

Using induction on k, we next show that $S_k = R_k$ $(\forall k)$. Clearly, $S_0 = I = R_0$. Assume $S_k = R_k$ holds, we consider

$$\begin{aligned} S_{k+1} &= \gamma (P^\top S_k P)_{\mathit{off}} + I \qquad \text{(using the hypothsis } S_k = R_k) \\ &= \gamma^{k+1} (P^\top \underbrace{(P^\top \cdots (P^\top P)_{\mathit{off}} \cdots P)_{\mathit{off}}}_{k \text{ nested } (*)_{\mathit{off}}} P)_{\mathit{off}} + \underbrace{\gamma (P^\top R_{k-1} P)_{\mathit{off}} + I}_{=\{\text{using Eq.(39)}\}} \\ &= \gamma^{k+1} \underbrace{(P^\top (P^\top \cdots (P^\top P)_{\mathit{off}} \cdots P)_{\mathit{off}} P)_{\mathit{off}}}_{(k+1) \text{ nested } (*)_{\mathit{off}}} + R_k = R_{k+1}. \end{aligned}$$ □

By Theorem 6, S in Eq.(36) is the weighted sums of

$$\underbrace{(P^\top \cdots (P^\top (P^\top P)_{\mathit{off}} P)_{\mathit{off}} \cdots P)_{\mathit{off}}}_{k \text{ nested } (*)_{\mathit{off}}} \qquad \forall k = 1, 2, \cdots \quad (41)$$

In contrast, $\tilde{S}$ in Eq.(37) is the weighted sums of the terms

$$\underbrace{(P^\top \cdots (P^\top (P^\top P) P) \cdots P)}_{k \text{ nested brackets}} \qquad \forall k = 1, 2, \cdots \quad (42)$$

To find out the semantic difference between S and $\tilde{S}$, we merely need to compare the paths tallied by (41) and (42):

THEOREM 7. *Given a graph G, the terms in Eq.(41) tally the following paths in G:*

$$\underbrace{x_0 \leftarrow x_1 \leftarrow \cdots \leftarrow x_{k-1} \leftarrow}_{k \text{ edges}} \boxed{x_k} \underbrace{\rightarrow x_{k+1} \rightarrow \cdots \rightarrow x_{2k-1} \rightarrow x_{2k}}_{k \text{ edges}} \quad (43)$$

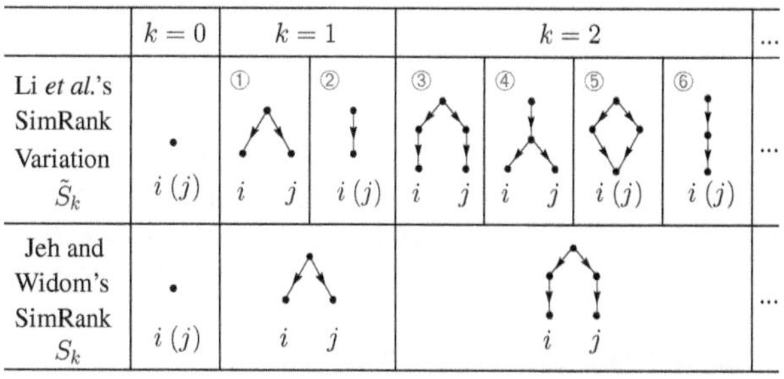

Figure 4: Different Paths Tallied by S and $\tilde{S}$

where $x_0, \cdots, x_{2k}$ can be any nodes, but with no repetition of nodes x_i and x_{2k-i} allowed, $\forall i \in \{0, 1, \cdots, 2k\} - \{k\}$.

In comparison, the terms in Eq.(42) tally the paths of (43) in G without having such a constraint on nodes x_i and x_{2k-i}.

PROOF. By the power property of the adjacency matrix, $((P^k)^\top P^k)_{i,j}$ tallies the paths of (43) between i and j.

To show the terms in Eq.(41) tally the paths of (43) with the additional constraint, we use induction on k as follows.

When $k = 1$, $((P^\top P)_{\mathit{off}})_{i,j} = (P^\top P)_{i,j}$ for $i \neq j$, and 0 for $i = j$. Thus, $((P^\top P)_{\mathit{off}})_{i,j}$ tallies $i \leftarrow x \rightarrow j$ with $i \neq j$.

Assume that, for the fixed k, the term

$$E_k := \underbrace{(P^\top \cdots (P^\top (P^\top P)_{\mathit{off}} P)_{\mathit{off}} \cdots P)_{\mathit{off}}}_{k \text{ nested } (*)_{\mathit{off}}}$$

tallies the length-$2k$ paths (43) with no repetition of nodes x_l and x_{2k-l} $(\forall l)$. We now consider the term E_{k+1} for $k+1$. Due to $(E_{k+1})_{i,j} = (P^\top)_{i,*} E_k (P)_{*,j}$ if $i \neq j$, and 0 if $i = j$, $(E_{k+1})_{i,j}$ tallies the length-$(2k+2)$ paths concatenated by $i \leftarrow x_0$, paths (43), and $x_{2k} \rightarrow j$, which is

$$i \leftarrow \underbrace{x_0 \leftarrow x_1 \leftarrow \cdots \leftarrow x_{k-1} \leftarrow}_{k \text{ edges}} \boxed{x_k} \underbrace{\rightarrow x_{k+1} \rightarrow \cdots \rightarrow x_{2k-1} \rightarrow x_{2k}}_{k \text{ edges}} \rightarrow j$$

with no repetition of nodes x_i and x_{2k-i} and $i \neq j$. □

EXAMPLE 4. *Recall the graph in Figure 3. By Theorem 7, the path $7 \leftarrow 6 \leftarrow 5 \leftarrow \boxed{3} \rightarrow 4 \rightarrow 6 \rightarrow 8$ is tallied by the term $((P^3)^\top P^3)$, but not by $(P^\top (P^\top (P^\top P)_{\mathit{off}} P)_{\mathit{off}} P)_{\mathit{off}}$.*

Indeed, regarding the term $(P^\top (P^\top (P^\top P)_{\mathit{off}} P)_{\mathit{off}} P)_{\mathit{off}}$, the innermost $(*)_{\mathit{off}}$ disallows paths with repetition of nodes 5 and 4; the second nested $(*)_{\mathit{off}}$ disallows the repetition of nodes 6 and 6 (which the considered path violates); the outermost $(*)_{\mathit{off}}$ disallows the repetition of nodes 7 and 8. □

In light of Theorem 7, the semantic relationship between S and $\tilde{S}$ is evident: $\tilde{S}$ often aggregates more paths than S, and S excludes the paths with self-intersecting nodes that are considered by $\tilde{S}$. Figure 4 depicts an illustrative comparison of the paths tallied by $(S_k)_{i,j}$ and $(\tilde{S}_k)_{i,j}$ for $k = 0, 1, 2$.

For verification, let us apply $(*)_{\mathit{off}}$ definition to expand, e.g., the term $(P^\top (P^\top P)_{\mathit{off}} P)_{\mathit{off}}$ as follows:

$$\underbrace{((P^\top (P^\top P)_{\mathit{off}} P)_{\mathit{off}})_{i,j}}_{③} = \underbrace{((P^2)^\top P^2)_{i,j}}_{③④⑤⑥} - \underbrace{(P^\top \mathit{diag}(P^\top P) P)_{i,j}}_{④⑥} - \underbrace{(\mathit{diag}((P^2)^\top P^2))_{i,j}}_{⑤⑥} + \underbrace{(\mathit{diag}(P^\top \mathit{diag}(P^\top P) P))_{i,j}}_{⑥}$$

where a circled number beneath each term is associated with a path numbered in the upper-left corner of Figure 4.

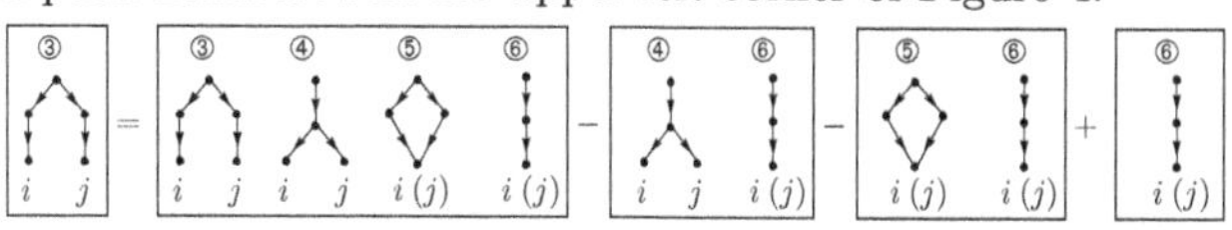

The following result shows the specific types of paths that are tallied by $\tilde{S}$ but not by S.

COROLLARY 2. *Let $\mathcal{P}(S)$ and $\mathcal{P}(\tilde{S})$ be the sets of paths tallied by S and $\tilde{S}$, respectively. Then, $\mathcal{P}(\tilde{S}) \supseteq \mathcal{P}(S)$, and $\mathcal{P}(\tilde{S}) - \mathcal{P}(S)$ is the set of "special" cycles of length $2k$ ($k = 1, 2, \cdots$), with first k contiguous edges oriented in one direction, and next k contiguous edges in the opposite direction.*

5. EXPERIMENTAL STUDIES

5.1 Experimental Setting

(1) Real Data. The details are described below:

Dataset	$\|V\|$	$\|E\|$	$\|E\|/\|V\|$	Type
WikiV	7,115	103,689	14.57	Directed
CaD	15,683	55,064	5.31	Undirected
CitH	34,546	421,578	12.20	Directed
WebN	325,729	1,497,134	4.59	Directed
ComY	1,134,890	2,987,624	2.63	Undirected
SocL	4,847,571	68,993,773	14.23	Directed

(a) WikiV, a Wikipedia who-votes-on-whom graph[8], where nodes are users, and an edge $i \to j$ means user i voted on j.

(b) CaD, a collaboration graph, where each node is an author, and edges co-authorships. The graph is derived from 6-year publications (2006–2011) in seven major conferences.

(c) CitH, a citation graph from arXiv high energy physics theory, where each node is a paper labeled with meta information (*e.g.*, title, authors, abstract) and an edge a citation.

(d) WebN, a web graph from University of Notre Dame, where a node is a page (from `nd.edu`) and an edge a link.

(e) ComY, an undirected Youtube social graph, where a node is a user and an edge a friendship.

(f) SocL, a friendship graph of a LiveJournal community, where $i \to j$ is a recommendation of user j from user i.

(2) Synthetic Data. To produce SYN, we adopt a scale-free graph generator based on the Barabasi-Albert model[9]. This generator takes as input two parameters: $(|V|, |E|)$.

(3) Query Generator. (i) To evaluate all-pairs $s(*, *)$, we generate the query-pair set (A, B), by using two criteria:

(a) *Importance coverage* is to ensure the selected (A, B) to comprehensively contain a broad range of any possible pairs. To this end, we first sort all nodes in V in descending order by PageRank (PR), and split them into 10 buckets: nodes with PR $\in [0.9, 1]$ are in the first bucket; nodes with PR $\in [0.8, 0.9)$ the second, etc. We next randomly select $\lceil \frac{1}{10}|A| \rceil$ (*resp.* $\lceil \frac{1}{10}|B| \rceil$) nodes from each bucket to A (*resp.* B). Thus, (A, B) has both important and non-important pairs.

(b) *Overlapping coverage* is to ensure that (A, B) contains node-pairs with many multi-hop in-neighbors overlapped. To achieve this, we first sort node-pair (a, b) in descending order via a scoring function:[10] $f_{a,b} := \sum_{k=1}^{5} \frac{|\mathsf{hop}_k(a) \cap \mathsf{hop}_k(b)|}{|\mathsf{hop}_k(a) \cup \mathsf{hop}_k(b)|}$. We then split all pairs into 5 buckets: pairs with $f_{a,b} \in [4, 5]$ are in the first bucket; pairs with $f_{a,b} \in [3, 4)$ the second, etc. For each bucket, we next sort node-pair (a, b) in descending order based on the value of $g_{a,b} := \sum_{k=1}^{5} |\mathsf{hop}_k(a) \cap \mathsf{hop}_k(b)|$, and select top $\lceil \frac{1}{5}|A||B| \rceil$ node-pairs from each bucket. Hence, (A, B) covers node-pairs with many multi-hop in-neighbors in common. (ii) Similarly, to evaluate single-source $s(\star, q)$, the query set for q can be sampled as "importance coverage".

[8] http://snap.stanford.edu/data/index.html

[9] http://graphstream-project.org/doc/Generators/

[10] All paths of length up to 10 between a and b can be tallied by our queries, ensuring results accurate to 2 decimal places.

(4) Algorithms. We implement the following, all in VC++.

Name	Description
SR$^{\#}$	our scheme ("cosine" kernel + computation sharing)
MSR	the state-of-the-art SimRank [7]
OIP	all-pairs SimRank (fine-grained clustering) [13]
PSUM	all-pairs SimRank (partial sums memoization) [12]
SMAT	single-source SimRank (matrix decomposition) [3]
JSR	Jeh and Widom's SimRank [5]
LSR	Li *et al.*'s SimRank [9]
SR^{++}	SimRank++ (revised "evidence factor") [1]
RS	RoleSim (automorphism equivalence) [6]
RWR	Random Walk with Restart
COS	classic cosine similarity

(5) Parameters. We set (a) $\gamma = 0.6$, as suggested in [12]. (b) $k = 10$, guaranteeing $S^{(k)}$ accurate to 2 decimal places.

(6) Evaluation Metrics. To evaluate the semantic quality of the similarity search, we consider four metrics:

(a) *Normalized Discounted Cumulative Gain at position p*: $\text{NDCG}_p := \frac{1}{\text{IDCG}_p} \sum_{i=1}^{p} \frac{2^{\mathsf{rel}_i} - 1}{\log_2(1+i)}$, where rel_i is the graded relevance at position i, and IDCG_p is the ideal DCG ranking.

(b) *Spearman's* $\rho := 1 - \frac{6 \sum_{i=1}^{n} d_i^2}{n(n^2-1)}$, where d_i is the difference of two ranks at position i, and n is the number of elements.

(c) *Kendall's* τ: $= \frac{(\#\text{ of concordant pairs}) - (\#\text{ of discordant pairs})}{0.5n(n-1)}$.

(d) *Query coverage* is the queries from our query sample.

(7) Ground Truth. (a) To label ground truth for similar users on WikiV, a manual evaluation is carried out by 50 professional members who have accumulated a long history of activity on Wikipedia. Each pair of users is considered by an evaluator, and is assigned a score on a scale from 1 to 4, with 1 meaning irrelevant, 4 meaning completely relevant, and 2 and 3 meaning "somewhere in between". The judgement is based on evaluator's knowledge and public votes on promotion of individuals to adminship. (b) To mark ground truth labels for similar authors on CaD, 30 members from 5 database groups are invited. Each pair of authors is given a score based on the collaboration distance between authors. The judgement relies on evaluator's knowledge and "separations" of Co-Author Path in Microsoft Academic Search.[11] (c) To establish the ground truth of similar articles on CitH, 28 research associates from the School of Physics are hired. Each pair of articles is assigned a score based on evaluator's knowledge on paper abstracts and citation relations.

All experiments are run with an Intel Core(TM) i7-4700MQ CPU @ 2.40GHz CPU and 32GB RAM, on Windows 7.

5.2 Experimental Results

5.2.1 Semantic Quality

We first evaluate the high semantic quality of SR$^{\#}$ against SR^{++}, JSR, LSR[12], RS, COS, RWR on real WikiV, CitH, CaD. For each dataset, we randomly issue 300 queries for $s(*, q)$ and $s(*, *)$ via *importance coverage* criterion, and use 3 metrics (NDCG, Kendall, Spearman) to evaluate each method, respectively. Fig. 5a shows the average quantitative results. (1) In all cases, SR$^{\#}$ exhibits higher semantic quality than the other methods. This is because SR$^{\#}$ can avoid "connectivity trait" issue by utilizing a "cosine" kernel *recursively* in a SimRank-like style, whereas COS considers only *direct* overlapped in-neighbors, and JSR and LSR both have a "connectivity trait" problem. (2) In several cases, the NDCG_{200} of SR^{++} (on CitH) and RS (on CaD) may even worse than that of JSR and LSR. This is because, for SR^{++}, its evi-

[11] http://academic.research.microsoft.com/VisualExplorer

[12] For semantics evaluation, MSR produces the same similarity values as LSR, since [7] approximates D by $(1-\gamma)I$.

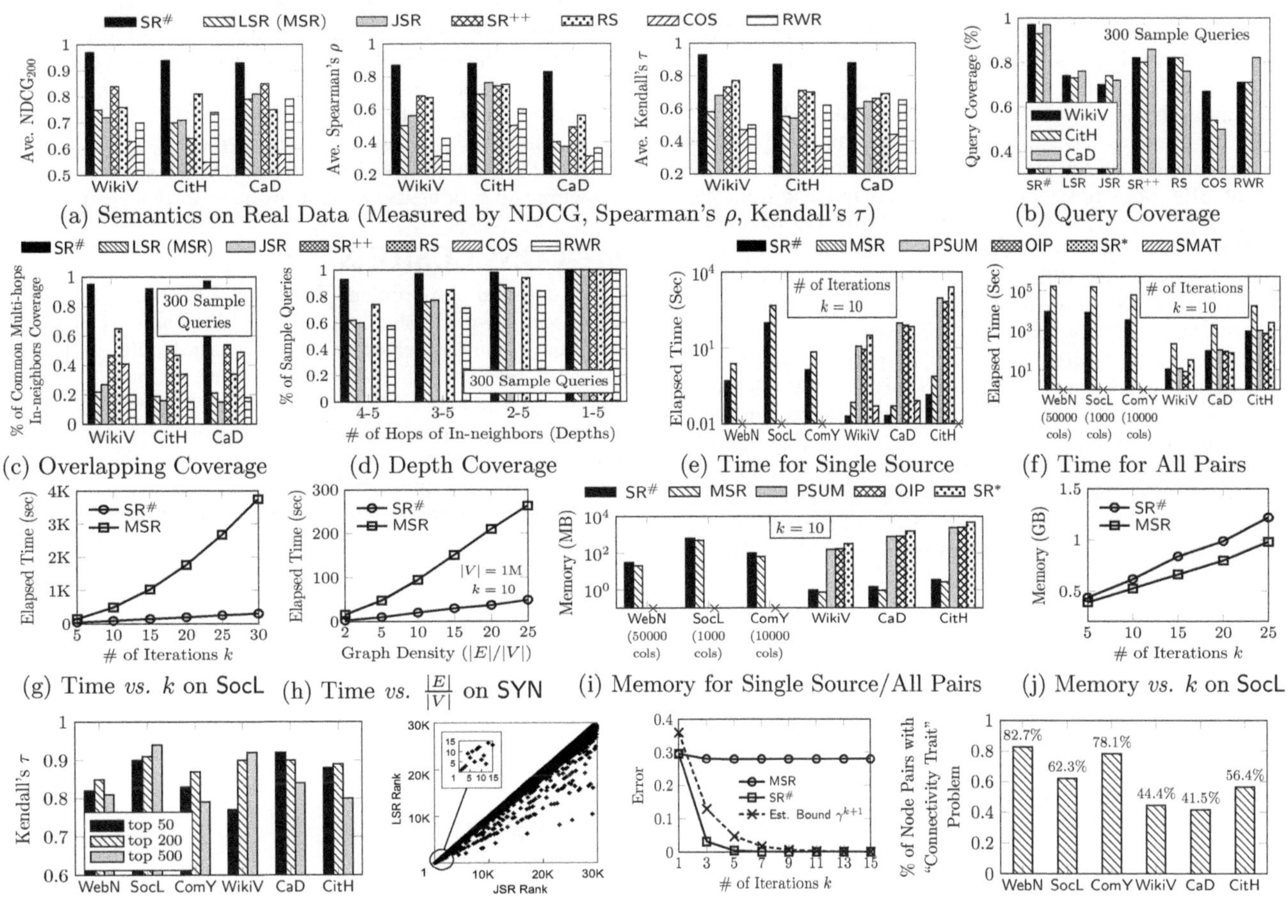

(a) Semantics on Real Data (Measured by NDCG, Spearman's ρ, Kendall's τ) (b) Query Coverage

(c) Overlapping Coverage (d) Depth Coverage (e) Time for Single Source (f) Time for All Pairs

(g) Time *vs.* k on SocL (h) Time *vs.* $\frac{|E|}{|V|}$ on SYN (i) Memory for Single Source/All Pairs (j) Memory *vs.* k on SocL

(k) LSR and JSR Relative Ordering (l) Ranking on WikiV (m) $(\epsilon_{\text{diag}} + \epsilon_{\text{iter}})$ *vs.* k (n) % of "Connectivity Trait" Issues

Figure 5: Performance Evaluations on Real and Synthetic Datasets

dence factor will be 0 whenever there are no common *direct* in-neighbors; for RS, automorphism equivalence has priority over connectivity in similarity assessment. Thereby, SR^{++} and RS may not resolve the "connectivity trait" problem.

Fig. 5b compares the percentage of queries from the 300 queries sample (based on *importance coverage* criterion) that SR$^{\#}$, SR^{++}, JSR, LSR, RS, COS, RWR provide similarities for on real WikiV, CitH, CaD, respectively. For each dataset, SR$^{\#}$ substantially improves the coverage of JSR/LSR ($\sim$0.73) and SR^{++}/RS ($\sim$0.81) to $\sim$0.95. This can be considered as expected, since (a) the "connectivity trait" problem of JSR and LSR will downgrade similarities of node-pairs with high connectivity, and (b) SR^{++} can only partially fix the "connectivity trait" issue within 1-hop in-neighborhood.

Fig. 5c depicts the percentage of queries with overlapped multi-hop in-neighbors from the 300 queries sample (via *overlapping coverage* criterion) that SR$^{\#}$, SR^{++}, JSR, LSR, RS, COS, RWR are able to identify on real WikiV, CitH, CaD, respectively. (1) For each dataset, SR$^{\#}$ significantly achieves $\sim$0.95 coverage of common multi-hop in-neighbors, much superior to JSR/LSR ($\sim$0.20), SR^{++}($\sim$0.51) and COS($\sim$0.41). The reason is that our "cosine" kernel provides an appropriate normalization factor $\| * \|_2$ that can recursively fix the "connectivity trait" problem. In contrast, the $\| * \|_1$ normalization factor of JSR/LSR excessively squeezes the range of similarity $[0, 1]$. (2) Under *overlapping coverage* criterion, COS ($\sim$0.41) outperforms JSR/LSR ($\sim$0.20) since COS is not limited by the "connectivity trait" problem.

To further evaluate the search depth of SR$^{\#}$, SR^{++}, JSR, LSR, RS, COS, RWR, we first apply *overlapping coverage* criterion to generate 2,000 queries, and then generate 300 queries via *importance coverage* criterion, and classify them into 4 groups, *e.g.*, "4-5" collects queries (a, b) whose path length between a and b is 8–10. Fig. 5d depicts the search depth of all the methods on WikiV. (1) For each group, SR^{++} and COS have the lowest quality of depth search among all the methods, since they cannot capture the paths of length > 2 between nodes. (2) SR$^{\#}$ achieves the highest quality, and its superiority is more pronounced in the groups that have longer paths. This tells us that the "connectivity trait" issue has a large influence on node-pairs with long paths.

5.2.2 Time Efficiency

Fig. 5e illustrates the running time of SR$^{\#}$, MSR, PSUM, OIP, SR*, SMAT for single-source $s(*, q)$ on 6 real datasets. (1) In all cases, SR$^{\#}$ always substantially outperforms the other methods. This is because SR$^{\#}$ can eliminate duplicate computations for maximal sharing, whereas MSR computes each term separately. (2) PSUM, OIP, SR*, SMAT will crash on large WebN, SocL, ComY, due to the memory allocation. On WikiV and CaD, they are 3-4 orders of magnitude slower than SR$^{\#}$, since their iterative models to compute $s(*, q)$ rely on all-pairs outputs of the previous iteration.

Fig. 5f shows the time of SR$^{\#}$, MSR, PSUM, OIP, SR* for all-pairs $s(*, *)$ on 6 real datasets. (1) Only SR$^{\#}$, MSR survive on all datasets, whereas PSUM, OIP, SR* fail on large

WebN, SocL, ComY, due to the memory allocation. (2) MSR is slower than others as it sacrifices speed for scalability. In contrast, SR$^{\#}$ not only scales well on large graphs, but also has comparable speed to those of PSUM, OIP, SR*.

Fig. 5g presents the impact of the iteration number k on the time of SR$^{\#}$ and MSR. When k grows from 5 to 30, the time of SR$^{\#}$ does not increase significantly (just from 42s to 301s), as opposed to the time of MSR growing from 152s to 3744s. The reason is that MSR contains many duplicate computations among different iterations, whereas SR$^{\#}$ can merge these results after rearranging the computation order. It is consistent with our analysis in Subsection 2.4.

Fig. 5h demonstrates the impact of network density on the computational time of SR$^{\#}$ and MSR on synthetic data. Fixing $|V| = 1,000,000$ and $k = 10$, we generate a synthetic dataset by increasing the graph density from 2 to 25. (1) When the density increases, the time of both algorithms will increase. (2) For dense graphs, the speedup for SR$^{\#}$ is significantly higher than MSR, due to the number of iterations with a huge influence on MSR compared with SR$^{\#}$. This is in agreement with the complexity of SR$^{\#}$ and MSR.

5.2.3 Memory Efficiency

Fig. 5i shows the memory of SR$^{\#}$, MSR, PSUM, OIP, SR* on six real datasets. (1) For large WebN, SocL and ComY, only SR$^{\#}$ and MSR survive, highlighting their scalability. (2) For each dataset, SR$^{\#}$ requires slightly more memory than MSR because it requires to store D_k.

Fig. 5j reports the impact of the iteration number k on the memory of SR$^{\#}$ and MSR on SocL. (1) When k varies from 5 to 25, the memory requirements of SR$^{\#}$ and MSR increase, since they need to memorize the k intermediate vectors from previous iterations, as expected. (2) The disparity in the memory between SR$^{\#}$ and MSR is due to storing D_k.

5.2.4 Relative Order

Fig. 5k compares the relative order between LSR and JSR for the top K results on 6 real datasets ($K = 50, 200, 500$). The order gap is measured by Kendall's τ. (1) For different graphs, the quality of the relative order is irrelevant to top K size. For instance, on SocL, top 500 (0.94) is better preserved than top 200 (0.91) and top 50 (0.9), whereas on CaD, top 500 (0.84) is worse than both top 200 (0.9) and top 50 (0.92). (2) On each dataset, the average Kendall's τ for top 50 is 0.77–0.92, which indicates that LSR does not maintain the relative rank of JSR, even for top 50. Thus, approximating D by $(1 - \gamma)I$ would adversely affect the top K ranking.

Further, a qualitative result on WikiV is depicted in Fig. 5l, where x (y) axis is the ranking by JSR (LSR). Other datasets also statistically exhibit similar phenomena. (1) Many points below the diagonal imply that low-ranked node-pairs by JSR have greater likelihood to get promoted to a high rank of LSR. This association does not imply a (near) linear relationship between the rankings of JSR and LSR. (2) For high top-K ranking (*e.g.*, $K = 15$), the top 15 of JSR may be inconsistent with those of LSR. Hence, the relative order preservation of JSR and LSR hinges on network structure.

Fig. 5m tests ($\epsilon_{\text{diag}} + \epsilon_{\text{iter}}$) of MSR and SR$^{\#}$ *w.r.t.* k. (1) When k increases from 1 to 15, the error of each algorithm decreases. While the error of SR$^{\#}$ approaches 0, MSR levels off at 0.28. The large disparity between their convergent solutions is due to the approximation of D by $(1 - \gamma)I$ in MSR; our "varied-D" iterative model can guarantee the error to be 0 when k increases. (2) The SR$^{\#}$ curve is always below the Est. Bound curve, showing the correctness of Theorem 4.

Fig. 5n statistically shows the percentage of node-pairs with the "connectivity trait" problem over all real datasets. From the results, we see that the percentages are all high (*e.g.*, 82.7% on WebN, 62.3% on SocL, 78.1% on ComY), showing the seriousness of this problem in real scenarios.

6. CONCLUSIONS

We consider the problem of high-quality similarity search. Observing that (1) the best-of-breed SimRank [7] produces diagonal correction error ϵ_{diag} and (2) SimRank++ [1] does not well resolve the "connectivity trait" problem, we proposed our scheme, SR$^{\#}$. First, we characterize the exact D, and devise a "varied-D" model to compute SimRank with no ϵ_{diag} in linear memory. We also speed up the computational time from quadric [7] to linear in terms of k. Next, we devise a "kernel-based" model to circumvent the "connectivity trait" problem. Finally, we give new insights into the semantic difference between Jeh and Widom's SimRank and its variant, and correct an argument in [7]. We empirically show that SR$^{\#}$ (1) improves an accuracy of average NDCG_{200} by ~30% on real graphs, and (2) can be ~10x faster than [7] on SocL with 65.8M links for 1000 queries.

Acknowledgment. This work forms part of the Big Data Technology for Smart Water Network research project funded by NEC Corporation, Japan.

7. REFERENCES

[1] I. Antonellis, H. G. Molina, and C. Chang. SimRank++: Query rewriting through link analysis of the click graph. *PVLDB*, 1(1), 2008.

[2] D. Fogaras and B. Rácz. Scaling link-based similarity search. In *WWW*, 2005.

[3] Y. Fujiwara, M. Nakatsuji, H. Shiokawa, and M. Onizuka. Efficient search algorithm for SimRank. In *ICDE*, 2013.

[4] G. He, H. Feng, C. Li, and H. Chen. Parallel SimRank computation on large graphs with iterative aggregation. In *KDD*, 2010.

[5] G. Jeh and J. Widom. SimRank: A measure of structural-context similarity. In *KDD*, 2002.

[6] R. Jin, V. E. Lee, and H. Hong. Axiomatic ranking of network role similarity. In *KDD*, 2011.

[7] M. Kusumoto, T. Maehara, and K. Kawarabayashi. Scalable similarity search for SimRank. In *SIGMOD*, 2014.

[8] P. Lee, L. V. S. Lakshmanan, and J. X. Yu. On top-k structural similarity search. In *ICDE*, 2012.

[9] C. Li, J. Han, G. He, X. Jin, Y. Sun, Y. Yu, and T. Wu. Fast computation of SimRank for static and dynamic information networks. In *EDBT*, 2010.

[10] P. Li, H. Liu, J. X. Yu, J. He, and X. Du. Fast single-pair SimRank computation. In *SDM*, 2010.

[11] Z. Lin, M. R. Lyu, and I. King. MatchSim: A novel similarity measure based on maximum neighborhood matching. *Knowl. Inf. Syst.*, 32(1), 2012.

[12] D. Lizorkin, P. Velikhov, M. N. Grinev, and D. Turdakov. Accuracy estimate and optimization techniques for SimRank computation. *VLDB J.*, 19(1), 2010.

[13] W. Yu, X. Lin, and W. Zhang. Towards efficient SimRank computation on large networks. In *ICDE*, 2013.

[14] W. Yu, X. Lin, and W. Zhang. Fast incremental simrank on link-evolving graphs. In *ICDE*, pages 304–315, 2014.

[15] W. Yu, X. Lin, W. Zhang, Y. Zhang, and J. Le. SimFusion+: Extending SimFusion towards efficient estimation on large and dynamic networks. In *SIGIR*, 2012.

[16] W. Yu and J. A. McCann. Sig-SR: SimRank search over singular graphs. In *SIGIR*, 2014.

[17] W. Yu and J. A. McCann. Efficient partial-pairs SimRank search for large networks. *PVLDB*, 8(5):569–580, 2015.

Summarizing Contrastive Themes via Hierarchical Non-Parametric Processes

Zhaochun Ren
z.ren@uva.nl

Maarten de Rijke
derijke@uva.nl

University of Amsterdam, Amsterdam, The Netherlands

ABSTRACT

Given a topic of interest, a contrastive theme is a group of opposing pairs of viewpoints. We address the task of summarizing contrastive themes: given a set of opinionated documents, select meaningful sentences to represent contrastive themes present in those documents. Several factors make this a challenging problem: unknown numbers of topics, unknown relationships among topics, and the extraction of comparative sentences. Our approach has three core ingredients: contrastive theme modeling, diverse theme extraction, and contrastive theme summarization. Specifically, we present a hierarchical non-parametric model to describe hierarchical relations among topics; this model is used to infer threads of topics as themes from the nested Chinese restaurant process. We enhance the diversity of themes by using structured determinantal point processes for selecting a set of diverse themes with high quality. Finally, we pair contrastive themes and employ an iterative optimization algorithm to select sentences, explicitly considering contrast, relevance, and diversity. Experiments on three datasets demonstrate the effectiveness of our method.

Categories and Subject Descriptors

H.3.3 [**Information Search and Retrieval**]: Information filtering

Keywords

Contrastive theme summarization; Structured determinantal point processes; Hierarchical sentiment-LDA; Topic modeling

1. INTRODUCTION

In recent years multi-document summarization has become a well studied task for helping users understanding a set of documents. Typically, the focus has been on relatively long, factual and grammatically correct documents [6, 17, 25, 41, 44, 48]. However, the web now holds a large number of opinionated documents, especially in opinion pieces, microblogs, question answering platforms and web forum threads. The growth in volume of such opinionated documents on the web motivates the development of methods to facilitate the understanding of subjective viewpoints present in sets of documents.

Given a set of opinionated documents, we define a *viewpoint* to be a topic with a specific sentiment label, following [37]. A *theme* is a set of viewpoints around a specific set of topics and an explicit sentiment opinion. Given a set of specific topics, two themes are *contrastive* if they are related to the topics, but opposite in terms of sentiment. The phenomenon of contrastive themes is widespread in opinionated web documents [8]. In Fig. 1 we show an example of three contrastive themes about the "Palestine and Israel relationship." Here, each pair of contrastive themes includes two sentences representing two relevant but opposing themes. In this paper, our focus is on developing methods for automatically detecting and describing contrastive themes.

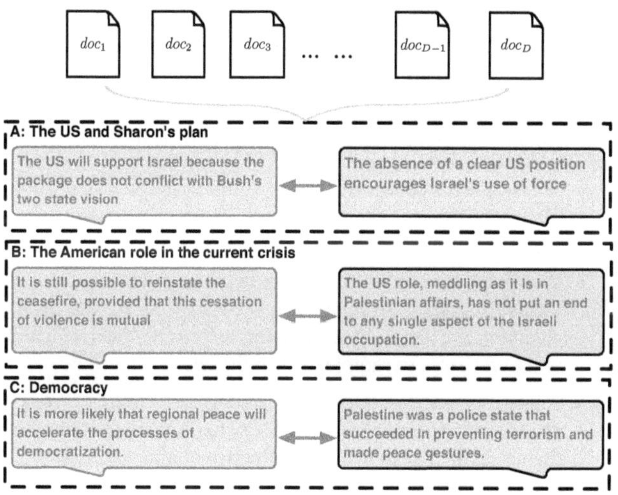

Figure 1: Three example contrastive themes related to "Palestine and Israel." Each contrastive theme shows a pair of opposing sentences.

The task on which we focus is *contrastive summarization* [18, 37] of multiple themes. The task is similar to *opinion summarization*, in which opinionated documents are summarized into structured or semi-structured summaries [12, 13, 15, 19]. However, most existing opinion summarization strategies are not adequate for summarizing contrastive themes from a set of unstructured documents. To our knowledge, the most similar task in the literature is the *contrastive viewpoint summarization* task [37], in which the authors extract contrastive but relevant sentences to reflect contrastive topic aspects, which are derived from a latent topic-aspect model [36]. However, their proposed method for *contrastive viewpoint sum-*

SIGIR'15, August 09 - 13, 2015, Santiago, Chile.

ACM 978-1-4503-3621-5/15/08 ...$15.00.
DOI: http://dx.doi.org/10.1145/2766462.2767713.

marization neglects to explicitly model the number of topics and the relations among topics in contrastive topic modeling—these are two key features in contrastive theme modeling.

The specific contrastive summarization task that we address in this paper is *contrastive theme summarization of multiple opinionated documents*. In our case, the output consists of contrastive sentence pairs that highlight every contrastive theme in the given documents. To address this task, we employ a non-parametric strategy based on the nested Chinese restaurant process (nCRP) [4]. Previous work has proved the effectiveness of non-parametric models in topic modeling [1, 39]. But none of them considers the task of contrastive theme summarization. We introduce a topic model that aims to extract contrastive themes and describe hierarchical relations among the underlying topics. Each document in our model is represented by hierarchical threads of topics, whereas a word in each document is assigned a finite mixture of topic paths. We apply collapsed Gibbs sampling to infer approximate posterior distributions of themes.

To enhance the diversity of the contrastive theme modeling, we then proceed as follows. Structured determinantal point processes (SDPPs) [21] are a novel probabilistic strategy to extract diverse and salient threads from large data collections. Given theme distributions obtained via hierarchical sentiment topic modeling, we employ SDPPs to extract a set of diverse and salient themes. Finally, based on themes extracted in the first two steps, we develop an iterative optimization algorithm to generate the final contrastive theme summary. During this process, *relevance*, *diversity* and *contrast* are considered.

Our experimental results, obtained using three publicly available opinionated document datasets, show that contrastive themes can be successfully extracted from a given corpus of opinionated documents. Our proposed method for multiple contrastive themes summarization outperforms state-of-the-art baselines, as measured using ROUGE metrics.

To sum up, our contributions in this paper are as follows:

- We focus on a contrastive theme summarization task to summarize contrastive themes from a set of opinionated documents.
- We apply a hierarchical non-parametric model to extract contrastive themes for opinionated texts. We tackle the diversification challenge by employing structured determinantal point processes to sample diverse themes.
- Jointly considering relevance, diversity and contrast, we apply an iterative optimization strategy to summarize contrastive themes, which is shown to be effective in our experiments.

We introduce related work in §2. We formulate our research problem in §3 and describe our approach in §4. Then, §5 details our experimental setup and §6 presents the experimental results. Finally, §7 concludes the paper.

2. RELATED WORK

2.1 Multi-document summarization

Multi-document summarization (MDS) is useful since it is able to provide a brief digest of large numbers of relevant documents on the same topic [34]. Most existing work on MDS is based on the extractive format, where the target is to extract salient sentences to construct a summary. Both unsupervised and supervised based learning strategies have received lots of attention. One of the most widely used unsupervised strategies is clustering with respect to the centroid of the sentences within a given set of documents; this idea has been applied by NeATS [28] and MEAD [38]. Many other recent publications on MDS employ graph-based ranking methods [10]. Wan and Yang [48] propose a theme-cluster strategy based on conditional Markov random walks. Similar methods are also applied in [49] for a query-based MDS task. Celikyilmaz and Hakkani-Tur [6] consider the summarization task as a supervised prediction problem based on a two-step hybrid generative model, whereas the Pythy summarization system [47] learns a log-linear sentence ranking model by combining a set of semantic features. As to discriminative models, CRF-based algorithms [44] and structured SVM-based classifiers [25] have proved to be effective in extractive document summarization. Learning to rank models have also been employed to query-based MDS [43] and to topic-focused MDS [50]. In recent years, with the development of social media, multi-document summarization is being applied to social documents, e.g., tweets, weibos, and Facebook posts [7, 9, 35, 40, 41]. Temporal and update summarization [2] is becoming a popular task in MDS research [34]; for this task one follows a stream of documents over time and summarizes information on what is new compared to what has been summarized previously [31, 35, 45].

2.2 Opinion summarization

In recent years, *opinion* summarization has received extensive attention. Opinion summarization generates structured [15, 24, 30, 32] or semi-structured summaries [13, 16, 20] given opinionated documents as input. Opinosis [12] generates a summary from redundant data sources. Similarly, a graph-based multi-sentence compression approach has been proposed in [11]. Meng et al. [33] propose an entity-centric topic-based opinion summarization framework, which is aimed at generating summaries with respect to topics and opinions.

Other relevant work for our contrastive summarization has been published by Lerman and McDonald [23] and Paul et al. [37]. Lerman and McDonald [23] propose an approach to extract representative contrastive descriptions from product reviews. A joint model between sentiment mining and topic modeling is applied in [37].

2.3 Non-parametric topic modeling

Non-parametric topic models are aimed at handling infinitely many topics; they have received much attention. For instance, hierarchical Latent Dirichlet Allocation (hLDA) [4] describes latent topics over nested Chinese restaurant processes. To capture the relationship between latent topics, nested Chinese restaurant processes generate tree-like topical structures over documents. Traditional non-parametric topic models do not explicitly address diversification among latent variables during clustering. To tackle this issue, Kulesza and Taskar [21, 22] propose a stochastic process named structured determinantal point process (SDPP), where diversity is explicitly considered. As an application in text mining, Gillenwater et al. [14] propose a method for topic modeling based on SDPPs. As far as we know, the determinantal point process has not been integrated with other non-parametric models yet.

To the best of our knowledge, there is little previous work on summarizing contrastive themes. In this paper, by optimizing the number of topics, building relations among topics and enhancing the diversity among themes, we propose a hierarchical topic modeling strategy to summarize contrastive themes in the given documents.

3. PRELIMINARIES

3.1 Problem formulation

Before introducing our method for contrastive theme summarization, we introduce our notation and key concepts. Table 1 lists the notation we use in this paper.

Table 1: Glossary.

Symbol	Description
$\mathcal{D}$	candidate documents
$\mathcal{W}$	vocabulary in corpus $\mathcal{D}$
$\mathcal{K}$	themes set in $\mathcal{D}$
$\mathcal{T}$	themes tuples from $\mathcal{K}$
d	a document, $d \in \mathcal{D}$
s_d	a sentence in document d, i.e., $s_d \in d$
w	a word present in a sentence, $w \in \mathcal{W}$
x	a sentiment label, $x \in \{neg, neu, pos\}$
o_s	sentiment distribution of sentence s
c^x	a topic path under label x
b	a topic node on a topic path
z^x	a topic level under x label
ϕ^x	topic distribution of words, under label x
$k_{c,x}$	a theme corresponding to topic path c, under label x
t	a contrastive theme tuple
θ_d	probability distribution of topic levels over d
$\mathcal{S}_t$	contrastive summary for theme tuple t

Given a corpus $\mathcal{D}$, we begin by defining the notions of topic, sentiment and theme in our work. Following topic modeling customs [3], we define a *topic* in a document d to be a probability distribution over words. Unlike "flat" topic models [3], we assume that each document d can be represented by multiple topics that are organized in an infinite tree-like hierarchy $c = \{(z_0, c), (z_1, c), \ldots\}$, $z_0 \prec z_1 \prec \ldots$, i.e., c indicates a path from the root topic level z_0 on the infinite tree to more specialized topics that appear at the leaves of the tree, and for each topic level z we define a topic node $b = (z, c)$ on the topic path c.

Sentiment is defined as a probability distribution over sentiment labels *positive*, *negative*, and *neutral*. A *sentiment label* x is attached with each word w. Considering the *sentiment*, we divide topics into three classes: positive topics (2), neutral topics (1) and negative topics (0).

Given all hierarchical topics and sentiment labels, we define a *theme* $k_{c,x}$ as a threaded topic path c from the root level to the leaf level for the given sentiment label x. Let $\mathcal{K}$ be the set of themes, and let $\mathcal{K}^{pos}$, $\mathcal{K}^{neg}$, $\mathcal{K}^{neu}$ indicate the set of positive, negative and neutral themes, respectively, i.e., $\mathcal{K} = \mathcal{K}^{pos} \cup \mathcal{K}^{neg} \cup \mathcal{K}^{neu}$. Furthermore, we define a *contrastive theme* to be a theme tuple $t = (c^{pos}, c^{neg}, c^{neu})$ by extracting themes fromis contained in $\mathcal{K}^{pos} \times \mathcal{K}^{neg} \times \mathcal{K}^{neu}$. Themes c^{pos}, c^{neg} and c^{neu} in each tuple t are relevant in topic but opposite in sentiment labels.

Finally, we define contrastive theme summarization. Given a set of documents $\mathcal{D} = \{d_1, d_2, ..., d_D\}$, the purpose of the contrastive theme summarization task (CTS) is to select a set of meaningful sentences $\mathcal{S}_t = \{S_{c^{pos}}, S_{c^{neg}}, S_{c^{neu}}\}$ to reflect the representative information in each possible theme tuple $t = (c^{pos}, c^{neg}, c^{neu})$.

3.2 Determinantal point process

A point process $\mathcal{P}$ on a discrete set $\mathcal{Y} = \{y_1, y_2, \ldots, y_N\}$ is a probability measure on the power set $2^{\mathcal{Y}}$ of $\mathcal{Y}$. We follow the definitions from [21]. A determinantal point process (DPP) $\mathcal{P}$ is a point process with a positive semidefinite matrix M indexed by the elements of $\mathcal{Y}$, such that if $\mathcal{Y} \sim \mathcal{P}$, then for each $\mathcal{A} \subseteq \mathcal{Y}$, there is $\mathcal{P}(\mathcal{A} \subseteq \mathcal{Y}) = \det(M_{\mathcal{A}})$. Here, $M_{\mathcal{A}} = [M_{i,j}]_{y_i, y_j \in \mathcal{A}}$ is the restriction of M to the entries indexed by elements of $\mathcal{A}$. Matrix M is defined as the marginal kernel, where it contains all information to compute the probability of $\mathcal{A} \subseteq \mathcal{Y}$. For the purpose of modeling data, the construction of DPP is via *L-ensemble* [5]. Using L-ensemble, we have

$$\mathcal{P}(\mathcal{Y}) = \frac{\det(L_{\mathcal{Y}})}{\sum_{\mathcal{Y}' \subset \mathcal{Y}} \det(L_{\mathcal{Y}'})} = \frac{\det(L_{\mathcal{Y}})}{\det(L + I)}, \tag{1}$$

where I is the $N \times N$ identity matrix, L is a positive semidefinite matrix; $L_{\mathcal{Y}} = [L_{i,j}]_{y_i, y_j \in \mathcal{Y}}$ refers to the restriction of L to the entries indexed by elements of $\mathcal{Y}$, and $\det(L_\emptyset) = 1$. For each entry of L, we have

$$L_{ij} = q(y_i)\varphi(y_i)^{\mathrm{T}}\varphi(y_j)q(y_j), \tag{2}$$

where $q(y_i) \in \mathbb{R}^+$ is considered as the "quality" of an item y_i; $\varphi(y_i)^{\mathrm{T}}\varphi(y_j) \in [-1, 1]$ measures the similarity between item y_i and y_j. Here, for each $\varphi(y_i)$ we set $\varphi(y_i) \in \mathbb{R}^D$ as a normalized D-dimensional feature vector, i.e., $\|\varphi(y_i)\|_2 = 1$. Because the value of a determinant of vectors is equivalent to the volume of the polyhedron spanned by those vectors, $\mathcal{P}(\mathcal{Y})$ is proportional to the volumes spanned by $q(y_i)\varphi(y_i)$. Thus, sets with high-quality, diverse items will get the highest probability in DPP.

Building on the DPP, *structured* determinantal point processes (SDPPs) have been proposed to efficiently handle the problem containing exponentially many structures [14, 21, 22]. In the setting of SDPPs, items set $\mathcal{Y}$ contains a set of threads of length T. Thus in SDPPs, each item y_i has the form $y_i = \{y_i^{(1)}, y_i^{(2)}, \ldots, y_i^{(T)}\}$, where $y_i^{(t)}$ indicates the document at the t-th position of thread y_i. To make the normalization and sampling efficient, SDPPs assume a factorization of $q(y_i)$ and $\varphi(y_i)^{\mathrm{T}}\varphi(y_j)$ into parts, decomposing quality multiplicatively and similarity additively, as follows:

$$q(y_i) = \prod_{t=1}^{T} q(y_i^{(t)}); \quad \varphi(y_i) = \sum_{t=1}^{T} \varphi(y_i^{(t)}); \tag{3}$$

the quality function $q(y_i)$ has a simple log-linear model setting $q(y_i) = \exp(\lambda w(y_i))$, where λ is set as a hyperparameter that balances between quality and diversity. An efficient sampling algorithm for SDPPs has been proposed by Kulesza and Taskar [21].

Since SDPPs specifically address "diversification" and "saliency," we apply them to identify diversified and salient themes from themes sets $\mathcal{K}$. We will detail this step in §4.

4. METHOD

4.1 Overview

We provide a general overview of our method for performing contrastive theme summarization (CTS) in Fig. 2. There are three main phases: (A) contrastive theme modeling; (B) diverse theme extraction; and (C) contrastive theme summarization. To summarize, we are given a set of documents $\mathcal{D} = \{d_1, d_2, \ldots, d_D\}$ as input. For each document $d \in \mathcal{D}$, in phase (A) (see §4.2), we obtain a structured themes set $\mathcal{K}$ with a root node r, topic distributions ϕ and opinion distributions o_s.

In (B) (see §4.3), given the structured output themes $\mathcal{K}$, we employ a structured determinantal point process to obtain a subset $\mathcal{K}' \subseteq \mathcal{K}$ to enhance the saliency and diversity among themes.

Based on themes $\mathcal{K}'$ and their corresponding topic distributions and opinion distributions, in (C) (see §4.4) we generate the final contrastive theme summary $\mathcal{S}$. We develop an iterative optimization algorithm for this process: the first part in §4.4 is to generate the contrastive theme tuples $\mathcal{T}$, each of which includes relevant themes for a topic but contrastive in sentiment; the second part in §4.4 is meant to generate the final contrastive summary $\mathcal{S} = \{S_t\}$ for each theme tuple.

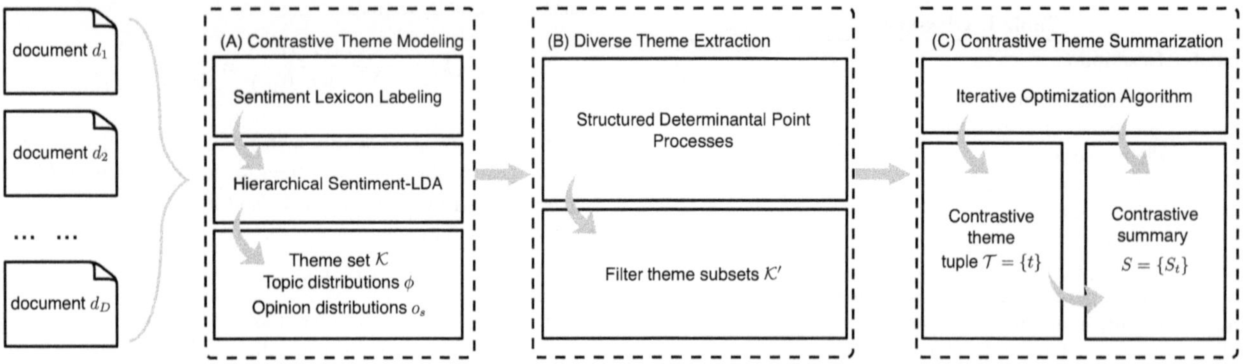

Figure 2: Overview of our approach to contrastive theme summarization. (A) indicates contrastive theme modeling; (B) indicates a structured determinantal point process to diversify topics; and (C) refers to the contrastive summary generation algorithm. Crooked arrows indicate the output in each step; while straight arrows indicate processing directions.

4.2 (A) Contrastive theme modeling

We start by proposing a hierarchical sentiment-LDA model to jointly extract topics and opinions from our input corpus. Unlike previous work on traditional "flat" topic models [37], our method can adaptively generate topics organized in a tree-like hierarchy.

Briefly, each document $d \in \mathcal{D}$ can be represented as a collection of sentences, whereas each sentence $s \in d$ is composed of a collection of words. By using a state-of-the-art sentiment analysis method [46], for each word w in each document d we extract its sentiment label x_w, where $x_w \in \{pos, neu, neg\}$. Generally, for document d we select three threaded topic paths $\{c^x\}$, with $x = pos, neu, neg$, each of which is generated by a nested Chinese restaurant process (nCRP) [4]. After deriving the sentiment label x, each word $w \in d$ is assigned to a specific topic level z by traversing from the root to the leave on the path c^x.

Next, we give a more detailed technical account of our model. Following the nested Chinese restaurant process [4], our topic model identifies documents with threaded topic paths generated by nCRP. Given level z, we consider each node (z, c) on a threaded topic path c as a specific topic. To select the exact topic level $z \in [1, L]$, we draw a variable θ_d from a Dirichlet distribution derived from hyperparameter m, to define a probability distribution on topic levels along the topic path c. Given a draw from a Dirichlet distribution, document d is generated by repeatedly selecting a topic level. We assume that each document $d \in \mathcal{D}$ is represented by three classes of topics: positive, negative and neutral topics.

In document d, for each sentence $s \in d$ we define a sentiment distribution o_s from a Dirichlet distribution over a hyper parameter γ. For each word $w \in \mathcal{W}$, we select three topic levels z^{pos}, z^{neg} and z^{neu} from a discrete distribution over θ_d, respectively. While the sentiment label is derived from a multinomial distribution over o_s, w is derived from a discrete distribution over topic levels $\{z^{pos}, z^{neg}, z^{neu}\}$. The generation process of our proposed model is shown in Fig. 3.

Since exact posterior inference in hierarchical sentiment-LDA is intractable, we employ a collapsed Gibbs sampler to approximate the posterior distributions of topic level z_w for each word w and topic path c_d for each document d. In our model, two sets of variables are observed: the sentiment labels x_w for each word w, and the words set $\mathcal{W}$. Our sampling procedure is divided into two steps for each iteration: (1) sampling a topic path for each document; (2) sampling level allocation for each word.

For the sampling procedure of thread c_d, given current other variables on document d, we have:

$$p(c_d^x | c_{-d}^x, z, o) \propto p(c_d^x | c_{-d}^x) \cdot p(W_d | W_{-d}, c, x, o, z) \quad (4)$$

1. For each topic level $z^x \in \mathcal{Z}^x$ in infinite tree:
   - Draw $\phi^x \sim Dirichlet(\beta^x)$;
2. For each document $d \in \mathcal{D}$:
   - Draw $c_d^x \sim nCRP(p)$;
   - Draw $\theta_d \sim Dirichlet(m)$;
   - For each sentence $s \in d$:
     - Draw opinion $o_s \sim Dirichlet(\gamma)$;
     - For each word $w \in N$:
       * Draw sentiment $x \sim Multinomial(o_s)$;
       * Draw topics $z^x \sim Discrete(\theta_d)$:
       * Draw word $w \sim Discrete(\phi_{z^x, c_d^x})$;

Figure 3: Generative process in hierarchical sentiment-LDA.

where $p(c_d^x | c_{-d}^x)$ in (4) is the prior distribution implied by the nested Chinese restaurant process, whereas for each topic node (z, c_d) on path c_d, we have:

$$\begin{cases} P((z, c_d) = b_i) = \frac{n_i}{n+p-1} \\ P((z, c_d) = b_{new}) = \frac{p}{n+p-1} \end{cases} \quad (5)$$

where b_i indicates a node that has been taken before, b_{new} indicates a new node that has not been considered yet; n_i refers to the number of times that topic node (z, c_d) is assigned to a document. To infer $p(W_d | W_{-d}, c, x, o, z)$, we integrate over multinomial parameters and have:

$$p(W_d | W_{-d}, c, x, o, z) \propto \prod_{z=1}^{L} \left(\frac{\Gamma(n_{-d}^{z,c} + W\beta)}{\prod_{w \in W} \Gamma(n_{w,-d}^{z,c} + \beta)} \frac{\prod_{w \in W} \Gamma(n_{w,-d}^{z,c} + n_{w,d}^{z,c} + \beta)}{\Gamma(n_{-d}^{z,c} + n_d^{z,c} + W\beta)} \prod_{s \in S_d} \frac{\prod_{x \in X} \Gamma(n_{s,x} + \gamma_x)}{\Gamma(n_s + \gamma)} \right), \quad (6)$$

where $n_{-d}^{z,c}$ indicates the number of times that documents have been assigned to topic node (z, c) leaving out document d; $n_{w,-d}^{z,c}$ denotes the number of times that word w has been assigned to the topic node (z, c) leaving out document d.

To sample topic level $z_{d,n}$ for each word w_n in document d, we find its joint probabilistic distribution of terms, sentiment labels and topics as follows:

$$p(z^x_{d,n} = \eta | z^x_{-(d,n)}, c^x, x, o, w) \propto$$
$$\frac{n^{\eta,c}_{w_n,-n} + \beta}{n^{\eta,c}_{-n} + W\beta} \frac{n^{\eta}_{d} + m}{n^{\eta}_{d,-n} + Lm} \frac{\prod_{x \in X} \Gamma(n_{s,x} + \gamma_x)}{\Gamma(n_s + \gamma)} \quad (7)$$

where $z^x_{-(d,n)}$ denotes the vectors of level allocations leaving out $z^x_{d,n}$ in document d. Further, $n^{\eta,c}_{w_n,-n}$ denotes the number of times that words have been assigned to topic node (η, c) that are the same as word w_n; $n^{\eta}_{d,-n}$ denotes the number of times that document d have been assigned to level k leaving out word w_n.

After Gibbs sampling, we get a set of topic paths $\{c^x\}$ that can be represented as themes $\mathcal{K} = \{k_{c,x}\}$; for each word w in d, we have hybrid parametric distributions ϕ^x that reflect the topic distribution given a specific level z on path c, i.e., $P(w, x|c, z) = \phi^x_{z,c,w}$. For each sentence s, we have a probability distribution o_s over sentiment labels, i.e., $P(x|s) = o_{s,x}$.

4.3 (B) Diverse theme extraction

Given a set of themes $\mathcal{K} = \{k_{c,x}\}$ resulting from step (A), some further issues need to be tackled before we arrive at our desired summary. On the one hand, many themes in $\mathcal{K}$ share common topics; on the other hand, many words' topic probabilities ϕ are similar, which makes it difficult to distinguish the importance of the themes.

To address this dual problem, we employ the structured determinantal point process (SDPP) [22] to select a subset of salient and diverse themes from $\mathcal{K}$. Following [21], we define a structured determinantal point process $\mathcal{P}$ as a type of probability distribution over a subset of themes belonging to $\mathcal{K}$. Two main factors are considered in SDPPs: the *quality* q_i and the *similarity* ${\varphi_i}^T \varphi_j$. A subset with high quality and highly diverse themes will be assigned the highest probability $\mathcal{P}$ by the SDPPs.

Given themes $\mathcal{K}$ sampled from (A), we proceed as follows. Firstly, for each theme $k \in \mathcal{K}$ we use $q((z_i, c))$ to indicate the "quality" of topic $(z_i, c) \in k$ and we use $\varphi((z_i, c))^T \varphi((z_j, c')) \in [0, 1]$ to refer to a measure of similarity between two topics (z_i, c) and (z_j, c'):

$$q((z_i, c)) = \sum_{w \in \mathcal{W}_H} \phi_{z_i,c,w};$$
$$\varphi((z_i, c))^T \varphi((z_j, c')) = \exp\left(-\frac{\left\|\Phi_{z_i,c} - \Phi_{z_j,c'}\right\|_2^2}{2\sigma^2}\right), \quad (8)$$

where $\Phi_{z_i,c}$ indicates the vector $\{\phi_{z,c,w}\}_{w \in \mathcal{W}}$; $\left\|\Phi_{z_i,c} - \Phi_{z_j,c'}\right\|_2^2$ is the squared Euclidean distance between $\Phi_{z_i,c}$ and $\Phi_{z_j,c'}$; $\mathcal{W}_H$ indicates the top-n salient words; σ is a free parameter. Based on (1) and (2), we construct the semidefinite matrix $\mathcal{M}$ for SDPPs.

For two topic paths $c_i = \{(z_1, c_i), \ldots, (z_L, c_i)\}$ and $c_j = \{(z'_1, c_j), \ldots, (z_L, c_j)\}$, $c_i, c_j \in \mathcal{K}$, we assume a factorization of the quality $q(c)$ and similarity score $\varphi(c_i, c_j)$ into parts, decomposing quality multiplicatively and similarity additively, i.e., for topic paths c_i and c_j, $q(c_i)$ and $\varphi(c_i, c_j)$ are calculated by (3), respectively.

To infer the posterior results of SDPPs over themes, we adapt an efficient sampling algorithm as described in Algorithm 1. Following [21], we let $\mathcal{M} = \sum_{k=1}^{K} \lambda_k v_k v_k^T$ be an orthonormal eigendecomposition, and let e_i be the ith standard basis K-vector. The sampling algorithm of SDPPs outputs a subset of themes, i.e., $\mathcal{K}' = \{k'_{c,x}\}$, which reflect a trade-off between high quality and high diversity.

Algorithm 1: Sampling process for SDPPs

Input : Eigenvector/values pairs $\{(v_k, \lambda_k)\}$; Themes set $\mathcal{K}$;
Output: Filtered themes set $\mathcal{K}'$ from SDPPs;
$\mathcal{J} \leftarrow 0$; $\mathcal{K}' \leftarrow 0$;
for $k \in \mathcal{K}$ **do**
  $\mathcal{J} \leftarrow \mathcal{J} \cup \{k\}$ with probability $\frac{\lambda_k}{1+\lambda_k}$;
end
$V \leftarrow \{v_k\}_{k \in \mathcal{J}}$;
while $|V| > 0$ **do**
  Select k_i from $\mathcal{K}$ with $P(k_i) = \frac{1}{|V|} \sum_{v \in V} (v^T e_i)^2$;
  $\mathcal{K}' \leftarrow \mathcal{K}' \cup k_i$;
  $V \leftarrow V_{\perp}$ as an orthonormal basis for the subspace of V orthonormal to e_i;
end
return $\mathcal{K}'$.

4.4 (C) Contrastive theme summarization

In this section, we specify the sentence selection procedure for contrastive themes. Considering the diversity among topics, we only consider leaf topics in each theme $k'_{c,x} \in \mathcal{K}'$. Thus, each theme $k'_{c,x}$ can be represented by a leaf topic (z^x_L, c^x) exclusively. For simplicity, we abbreviate leaf topics sets $\{(z^x_L, c^x)\}$ as $\{c^x\}$.

Given $\{c^x\}$, we need to connect topics in various classes to a set of contrastive theme tuples of the form $t = (c^{pos}_i, c^{neg}_{ii}, c^{(neu)}_{iii})$. To assess the correlation between two topics (c^x_i) and (c^y_{ii}) in different classes, we define a *correlation* based on topic distributions $\Phi_{z,c}$ as follows:

$$1 - \frac{1}{N} \sum_{d \in \mathcal{D}} \left| \sum_{w \in d} \phi_{z_L, c^x_i, w} - \sum_{w' \in d} \phi_{z_L, c^y_{ii}, w'} \right|. \quad (9)$$

We sample three leaf topics from the three classes mentioned earlier (positive, negative and neutral), so that the total *correlation* values for all three topic pairs has maximal values.

Next, we extract representative sentences for each contrastive theme tuple $t = (c^{pos}_i, c^{neu}_{ii}, c^{neg}_{iii})$. An intuitive way for generating the contrastive theme summary is to extract the most salient sentences as a summary. However, high-degree topical relevance cannot be taken as the only criterion for sentence selection. To extract a contrastive theme summary $\mathcal{S}_t = \{S_{c^{pos}_i}, S_{c^{neu}_{ii}}, S_{c^{neg}_{iii}}\}$ for tuple $t = (c^{pos}_i, c^{neu}_{ii}, c^{neg}_{iii})$, in addition to *relevance* we consider two more key requirements *contrast* and *diversity*. Given selected sentences $\mathcal{S}'_t$, we define a salient score $F(s_i|\mathcal{S}'_c, t)$:

$$F(s_i|\mathcal{S}'_t, t) = ctr(s_i|\mathcal{S}'_t, t) + div(s_i, \mathcal{S}'_t) + rel(s_i|t) \quad (10)$$

where $ctr(s_i|\mathcal{S}'_t, t)$ indicates the contrast between s_i and $\mathcal{S}'_t$ for t; $div(s_i, \mathcal{S}'_t)$ indicates the divergence between s_i and $\mathcal{S}'_t$; $rel(s_i|t)$ indicates the relevance of s_i given t.

Contrast calculates the sentiment divergence between the currently selected sentence s_i and the results of extracted sentences set $\mathcal{S}'_t$, under the given theme t. Our intention is to make the current sentence as contrastive as possible from extracted sentences as much as possible. Therefore, we have:

$$ctr(s_i|\mathcal{S}'_t, t) = \max_{\{s \in \mathcal{S}'_t, x\}} \left| (o_{s_i,x} - o_{s,x}) \cdot (\phi^x_{z_L,c,w} - \phi^x_{z_L,c,w}) \right|. \quad (11)$$

Diversity calculates the information divergence among all sentences within the current candidate result set. Ideally, the contrastive summary results have the largest possible difference in theme distribu-

Algorithm 2: Iterative process for generating the summary $\mathcal{S}$.

Input : $\mathcal{T} = \{(c_i^{pos}, c_{ii}^{neg}, c_{iii}^{neu})\}$, μ,π,S,N;
Output: $\mathcal{S} = \left\{\{S_{c_i^{pos}}, S_{c_{ii}^{neg}}, S_{c_{iii}^{neu}}\}_{(t)}\right\}$;

for *each* $t = (c_i^{pos}, c_{ii}^{neg}, c_{iii}^{neu})$ **do**
  Rank and extract relevant sentences to $\mathcal{C}$ by $rel(s|t)$;
  Initialize: Extract $\frac{N}{|\mathcal{T}|}$ sentences from $\mathcal{C}$ to $\mathcal{S}_t$;
  repeat
    Extract $\mathcal{X} = \{s_x \in \mathcal{C} \cap s_x \notin \mathcal{S}_t\}$;
    for $s_x \in \mathcal{X}, \forall s_y \in \mathcal{S}_t$ **do**
      Calculate $\mathcal{L} = \sum_{s_i \in \mathcal{S}_t} F(s_i|\mathcal{S}_t, t)$;
      Calculate
      $\Delta\mathcal{L}_{s_x,s_y} = \mathcal{L}((\mathcal{S}_t - s_y) \cup s_x) - \mathcal{L}(\mathcal{S}_t)$;
    end
    Get $\langle \hat{s_x}, \hat{s_y} \rangle$ that $\langle \hat{s_x}, \hat{s_y} \rangle = \arg\max_{s_x,s_y} \Delta\mathcal{L}_{s_x,s_y}$;
    $\mathcal{S}_t = (\mathcal{S}_t - \hat{s_y}) \cup \hat{s_x}$;
  until $\forall \Delta S_{s_x,s_y} < \varepsilon$;
  $\mathcal{S} = \mathcal{S} \cup \mathcal{S}_t$;
end
return $\mathcal{S}$.

tions with each other. The equation is as follows:

$$div(s_i|\mathcal{S}'_t) = \max_{s \in \mathcal{S}'_t} |rel(s_i|t) - rel(s|t)|\,. \tag{12}$$

Furthermore, a contrastive summary should contain relevant sentences for each theme t, and minimize the information loss with the set of all candidate sentences. Thus, given $\phi^x_{z_L,c,w}$, the *relevance* of sentence s_i given theme t is calculated as follows:

$$rel(s_i|t) = \frac{1}{N_{s_i}} \sum_x \sum_{w \in s_i} \phi^x_{z_L,c,w}. \tag{13}$$

Algorithm 2 shows the details of our sentence extraction procedure.

5. EXPERIMENTAL SETUP

5.1 Research questions

We list the research questions **RQ1–RQ4** that guide the remainder of the paper.

RQ1 Is hierarchical sentiment-LDA effective for extracting contrastive themes from documents? (See §6.1.) Is hierarchical sentiment-LDA helpful for optimizing the number of topics during contrastive theme modeling? (See §6.2.)

RQ2 Is the structured determinantal point process helpful for compressing the themes into a diverse and salient subset of themes? (See §6.2 and §6.3.) What is the effect of SDPP in contrastive theme modeling? (See §6.3).

RQ3 How does our iterative optimization algorithm perform on contrastive theme summarization? Does it outperform baselines? (See §6.4.)

RQ4 What is the effect of *contrast*, *diversity* and *relevance* for contrastive theme summarization in our method? (See §6.5.)

5.2 Datasets

We employ three datasets in our experiments. Two of them have been used in previous work [36, 37], and another one is extracted from news articles of the New York Times.[1] All documents in our datasets are written in English. All three datasets include human-made summaries, which are considered as ground-truth in our experiments. As an example, Table 2 shows statistics of 15 themes from the three datasets that include the largest number of articles in our dataset. In total, 15,736 articles are used in our experiments.

Table 2: Top 15 topics in our three datasets. Column 1 shows the name of topic; column 2 shows the number of articles included in the topic; column 3 shows the publication period of those articles, and column 4 indicates to which dataset the topic belongs.

General description	# articles	Period	Dataset
U.S. International Relations	3121	2004–2007	3
Terrorism	2709	2004–2007	3
Presidential Election of 2004	1686	2004	3
U.S. Healthcare Bill	940	2010	1
Budgets & Budgeting	852	2004–2007	3
Israel-Palestine conflict	594	2001–2005	2
Airlines & Airplanes	540	2004–2007	3
Colleges and Universities	490	2004–2007	3
Freedom and Human Rights	442	2004–2007	3
Children and Youth	424	2004–2007	3
Computers and the Internet	395	2004–2007	3
Atomic Weapons	362	2004–2005	3
Books and Literature	274	2004–2007	3
Abortion	170	2004–2007	3
Biological and Chemical Warfare	152	2004–2006	3

The first dataset ("dataset 1" in Table 2) consists of documents from a Gallup[2] phone survey about the 2010 U.S. healthcare bill. It contains 948 verbatim responses, collected March 4–7, 2010. Respondents indicate if they are "for" or "against" the bill, and there is a roughly even mix of the two opinions (45% for and 48% against). Each document in this dataset only includes 1–2 sentences.

Our second dataset ("dataset 2") is extracted from the Bitterlemons corpus, which is a collection of 594 opinionated articles about the Israel-Palestine conflict. The Bitterlemons corpus consists of the articles published on the Bitterlemons website[3] from late 2001 to early 2005. This dataset has also been applied in previous work [29, 36]. Unlike the first dataset, this dataset contains long opinionated articles with well-formed sentences. It too contains a fairly even mixture of two different perspectives: 312 articles from Israeli authors and 282 articles from Palestinian authors.

Our third dataset ("dataset 3") is a set of articles from the New York Times. The New York Times Corpus contains over 1.8 million articles written and published between January 1, 1987 and June 19, 2007. Over 650,000 articles have manually written article summaries. In our experiments, we only use *Opinion* column articles that were published during 2004–2007.

5.3 Baselines and comparisons

We list the methods and baselines that we consider in Table 3. We write HSDPP for the overall process as described in Section 4, which includes steps (A) contrastive theme modeling, (B) diverse theme extraction and (C) contrastive theme summarization. We write HSLDA for the model that only considers steps (A) and (C), so skipping the structured determinantal point processes in (B). To evaluate the effect of *contrast*, *relevance* and *diversity*, we consider HSDPPC, the method that only considers *contrast* in contrastive

[1] http://ilps.science.uva.nl/resources/nyt_cts

[2] http://www.gallup.com/home.aspx
[3] http://www.bitterlemons.org

Table 3: Our methods and baselines used for comparison.

Acronym	Gloss	Reference
HSDPPC	HSDPP only considering *contrast* in (C) contrastive theme summarization	This paper
HSDPPR	HSDPP only considering *relevance* in (C) contrastive theme summarization	This paper
HSDPPD	HSDPP only considering *diversity* in (C) contrastive theme summarization	This paper
HSLDA	Contrastive theme summarization method in (C) with HSLDA, without SDPPs	This paper
HSDPP	Contrastive theme summarization method in (C) with HSLDA and SDPPs	This paper
Topic models		
TAM	Topic-aspect model based contrastive summarization	[36]
Sen-TM	Sentiment LDA based contrastive summarization	[24]
LDA	LDA based document summarization	[3]
HLDA	Hierarchical LDA based document summarization	[4]
Summarization		
LexRank	LexRank algorithm for summarization	[10]
DFS	Depth-first search for sentence extraction	[13]
ClusterCMRW	Clustering-based sentence ranking strategy	[48]

theme summarization. We write HSDPPR for the method that only considers *relevance* and HSDPPD for the method that only considers *diversity* in the summarization.

To assess the contribution of our proposed methods, our baselines include recent related work. For contrastive theme modeling, we use the Topic-aspect model (TAM, [36]) and the Sentiment-topic model (Sen-TM, [24]) as baselines for topic models. Both focus on the joint process between topics and opinions. Other topic models, such as Latent dirichlet allocation (LDA) [3] and hierarchical latent dirichlet allocation (HLDA) [4], are also considered in our experiments. For the above "flat" topic models, we evaluate their performance using varying numbers of topics (10, 30 and 50 respectively). The number of topics used will be shown as a suffix to the model's name, e.g., TAM-10.

We also consider previous document summarization work as baselines: (1) A depth-first search strategy (DFS, [13]) based on our topic model. (2) The LexRank algorithm [10] that ranks sentences via a Markov random walk strategy. (3) ClusterCMRW [48] that ranks sentences via a clustering-based method. (4) Random, which extracts sentences randomly.

5.4 Experimental setup

Following existing models, we set pre-defined values for some parameters in our proposed method. In our proposed hierarchical sentiment-LDA model, we set m as 0.1 and γ as 0.33 as default values in our experiments.

Optimizing the number of topics is a problem shared between all topic modeling approaches. In our hierarchical sentiment-LDA model, we set the default length of L to 10, and we discuss it in our experiments. As same as other non-parametric topic models, our HSLDA model optimizes the number of themes automatically. Under the default settings in our topic modeling, we find that for the Gallup investigation data, the optimal number of topics is 23; the Bitterlemons corpus, it is 67; for the New York Times dataset, it is 282.

5.5 Evaluation metrics

To assess the saliency of contrastive theme modeling in our experiments, we adapt the *purity* and *accuracy* in our experiments to measure performance. To evaluate the diversity among topics we calculate the *diversity* as follows:

$$diversity = \frac{1}{|\mathcal{W}|}\sum_{w\in\mathcal{W}} \max\left|\phi^{x}_{z,c,w} - \phi^{x}_{z',c',w}\right| \quad (14)$$

We adopt the ROUGE evaluation metrics [27], a widely-used recall-oriented metric for document summarization that evaluates the overlap between a gold standard and candidate selections. We use ROUGE-1 (R-1, *unigram based method*), ROUGE-2 (R-2, *bigram based method*) and ROUGE-W (R-W, *weighted longest common sequence*) in our experiments.

Statistical significance of observed differences between the performance of two runs is tested using a two-tailed paired t-test and is denoted using $^{\blacktriangle}$ (or $^{\blacktriangledown}$) for strong significance for $\alpha = 0.01$; or $^{\vartriangle}$ (or $^{\triangledown}$) for weak significance for $\alpha = 0.05$. In our experiments, significant difference are with regard to TAM and TAM-Lex for contrastive theme modeling and contrastive theme summarization, respectively.

6. RESULTS AND DISCUSSION

6.1 Contrastive theme modeling

We start by addressing **RQ1** and test whether HSLDA and HSDPP are effective for the contrastive theme modeling task. First, Table 4 shows an example topic path of our hierarchical sentiment-LDA model. Column 1 shows the topic levels, columns 2, 3 and 4 show the 7 most representative words with positive, neutral and negative sentiment labels, respectively. For each sentiment label, we find semantic dependencies between adjacent levels.

Table 5 compares the *accuracy* and *purity* of our proposed methods to four baselines. We find that HSDPP and HSLDA tend to outperform the baselines. For the *Bitterlemons* and *New York Times* corpora, HSDPP exhibits the best performance both in terms of *accuracy* and *purity*. Compared to TAM, HSDPP shows a 9.5% increase in terms of *accuracy*. TAM achieves the best performance on the *Healthcare Corpus* when we set its number of topics to 10. However, the performance differences between HSDPP and TAM on this corpus are not statistically significant. This shows that our proposed contrastive topic modeling strategy is effective in contrastive topic extraction.

6.2 Number of themes

To start, for research question **RQ1**, to evaluate the effect of the length of each topic path to the performance of contrastive theme modeling, we examine the performance of HSDPP with different values of topic level L, in terms of *accuracy*. In Figure 4, we find that the performance of HSDPP in terms of *accuracy* peaks when the length of L equals 12; with fewer than 12, performance keeps increasing but if the number exceeds 12, due to the redundancy of topics in contrastive summarization, performance decreases.

Unlike TAM and Sen-LDA, HSDPP and HSLDA determine the optimal number of topics automatically. In Table 5 we find that the results for TAM change with various number of topics. However, for HSDPP we find that it remains competitive for all three corpora while automatically determining the number of topics.

6.3 Effect of structured determinantal point processes

Turning to **RQ2**, Table 5 shows that performance of HSDPP and HSLDA on contrastive theme modeling in terms of *accuracy* and *purity*, for all three datasets. We find that HSDPP outperforms HSLDA in terms of both *accuracy* and *purity*. Table 5 also contrasts the evaluation results for HSDPP with TAM and Sen-TM in

Table 4: **Part of an example topic path of hierarchical sentiment-LDA result about "College and University." Columns 2, 3 and 4 list popular positive, neutral and negative terms for each topic level, respectively.**

Topic level	Positive	Neutral	Negative
1	favor, agree, accept, character paid, interest, encourage	college, university, university school, editor, year	lost, suffer, fish, wrong, ignore drawn, negative
2	education, grant, financial, benefit save, recent, lend, group	Harvard, president, summer, Lawrence university, faculty, term, elite	foreign, hard, low global, trouble lose, difficulty
3	attract, meaningful, eligible, proud essence, quarrel,qualify	summers, Boston, greek, season seamlessly, opinion, donation	short, pity, unaware, disprove disappoint, idiocy, disaster
4	practical, essay, prospect respect, piously, behoove	write, march, paragraph, analogy analogy, Princeton, english	dark, huge, hassle, poverty depression, inaction, catastrophe
5	grievance, democratic, dignity, elite interest, frippery, youthful	June, volunteer, community, Texas classmate, liberal, egger	cumbersome, inhumane, idiocy, cry mug, humble, hysteria

Table 5: RQ1 and RQ2: *Accuracy*, *purity* and *diversity* values for contrastive theme modeling. Significant differences are with respect to TAM-10 (row with shaded background).

	Healthcare Corpus			Bitterlemons Corpus			New York Times		
	accuracy	*purity*	*diversity*	*accuracy*	*purity*	*diversity*	*accuracy*	*purity*	*diversity*
LDA-10	0.336$^{\blacktriangledown}$	0.337$^{\blacktriangledown}$	0.156$^{\triangledown}$	0.346$^{\blacktriangledown}$	0.350$^{\blacktriangledown}$	0.167$^{\triangledown}$	0.321$^{\blacktriangledown}$	0.322$^{\blacktriangledown}$	0.172$^{\blacktriangledown}$
LDA-30	0.313$^{\blacktriangledown}$	0.315$^{\blacktriangledown}$	0.134$^{\blacktriangledown}$	0.324$^{\blacktriangledown}$	0.332$^{\blacktriangledown}$	0.137$^{\blacktriangledown}$	0.317$^{\blacktriangledown}$	0.317$^{\blacktriangledown}$	0.144$^{\blacktriangledown}$
LDA-50	0.294$^{\blacktriangledown}$	0.298$^{\blacktriangledown}$	0.115$^{\blacktriangledown}$	0.304$^{\blacktriangledown}$	0.309$^{\blacktriangledown}$	0.121$^{\blacktriangledown}$	0.295$^{\blacktriangledown}$	0.301$^{\blacktriangledown}$	0.134$^{\blacktriangledown}$
TAM-10	**0.605**	0.602	0.222	0.645	0.646	0.241	0.551	0.560	0.271
TAM-30	0.532$^{\triangledown}$	0.534$^{\triangledown}$	0.194	0.623	0.626	0.224	0.564	0.564	0.242
TAM-50	0.522$^{\triangledown}$	0.525$^{\triangledown}$	0.152	0.596$^{\triangledown}$	0.596$^{\triangledown}$	0.174	0.576	0.582	0.195$^{\blacktriangledown}$
Sen-TM-10	0.530$^{\triangledown}$	0.531	0.194	0.537$^{\blacktriangledown}$	0.539$^{\blacktriangledown}$	0.209	0.514	0.518	0.255
Sen-TM-30	0.484$^{\blacktriangledown}$	0.488$^{\blacktriangledown}$	0.184	0.492$^{\blacktriangledown}$	0.502$^{\blacktriangledown}$	0.163$^{\triangledown}$	0.473	0.478	0.195$^{\blacktriangledown}$
Sen-TM-50	0.471$^{\blacktriangledown}$	0.481$^{\blacktriangledown}$	0.164	0.479$^{\blacktriangledown}$	0.482$^{\blacktriangledown}$	0.152$^{\triangledown}$	0.454$^{\blacktriangledown}$	0.456$^{\blacktriangledown}$	0.182$^{\blacktriangledown}$
HLDA	0.324$^{\blacktriangledown}$	0.326$^{\blacktriangledown}$	0.223	0.346$^{\blacktriangledown}$	0.342$^{\blacktriangledown}$	0.263	0.329$^{\blacktriangledown}$	0.330$^{\blacktriangledown}$	0.291
HSLDA	0.591	0.598	0.225	0.658	0.660	0.269	0.573	0.578	0.292
HSDPP	0.603	**0.604**	**0.244**	**0.692**	**0.696**	**0.292**$^{\blacktriangle}$	**0.609**$^{\blacktriangle}$	**0.610**$^{\blacktriangle}$	**0.326**$^{\blacktriangle}$

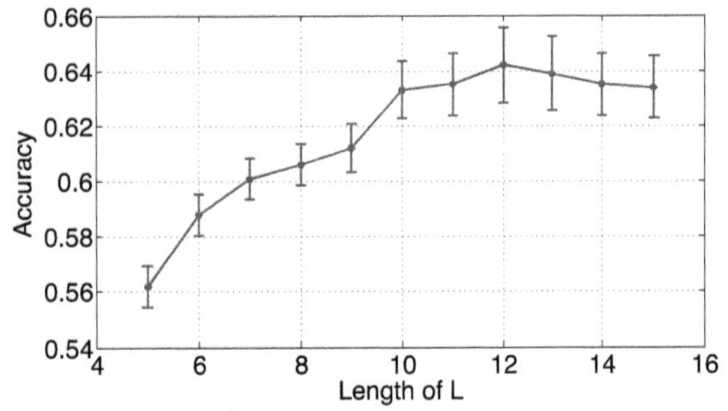

Figure 4: RQ1: Performance with different values of hierarchical topic level L, in terms of accuracy

terms of diversity (columns 4, 7, 10). We evaluate the performance of TAM and Sen-TM by varying the number of topics. HSDPP achieves the highest diversity scores. The diversity scores for TAM and Sen-TM decrease as the number of topics increases. In Table 6, we see that HSDPP outperforms HSLDA for all top 15 topics in our dataset in terms of diversity. In terms of diversity, HSDPP offers a significant increase over HSLDA of up to 18.2%.

To evaluate the performance before and after structured determinantal point processes in terms of *accuracy*, Table 6 contrasts the evaluation results for HSDPP with those of HSLDA, which excludes structured determinantal point processes, in terms of *accuracy*. We find that HSDPP outperforms HSLDA for each topic listed in Table 6. In terms of *accuracy*, HSDPP offers a significant increase over HSLDA of up to 14.6%. Overall, HSDPP outperforms HSLDA with a 5.6% increase in terms of accuracy. Hence, we conclude that the structured determinantal point processes helps to enhance the performance of contrastive theme extraction.

6.4 Overall performance

To help us answer **RQ3**, Table 7 lists the ROUGE performance for all summarization methods. As expected, Random performs worst. Using a depth-first search-based summary method (DFS) does not perform well in our experiments. Our proposed method HSDPP significantly outperforms the baselines on two datasets, whereas on the *healthcare corpus* the LexRank-based method performs better than HSDPP, but not significantly. A manual inspection of the outcomes indicates that the contrastive summarizer in HSDPP (i.e., step (C) in Fig. 2) is being outperformed by the LexRank summarizer in HSDPP-Lex on the *Healthcare* dataset because of the small vocabulary and the relative shortness of the documents in this dataset (at most two sentences per document). The summarizer in HSDPP prefers longer documents and a larger vocabulary. We can see this phenomenon on the *Bitterlemons Corpus*, which has 20–40 sentences per document, where HSDPP achieves a 10.3% (13.4%) increase over TAM-Lex in terms of ROUGE-1 (ROUGE-2), whereas the ROUGE-1 (ROUGE-2) score increases 2.2% (4.8%) over HSDPP-Lex. On the *New York Times*, HSDPP offers a significant improvement over TAM-Lex of up to 13.2% and 18.2% in terms of ROUGE-1 and ROUGE-2, respectively.

6.5 Contrastive summarization

Several factors play a role in our proposed summarization method, HSDPP. To determine the contribution of *contrast*, *relevance* and *diversity*, Table 8 shows the performance of HSDPPD, HSDPPR,

Table 7: RQ3: ROUGE performance of all approaches to contrastive document summarization. Significant differences are with respect to TAM-Lex (row with shaded background).

	Healthcare Corpus			Bitterlemons Corpus			New York Times		
	ROUGE-1	ROUGE-2	ROUGE-W	ROUGE-1	ROUGE-2	ROUGE-W	ROUGE-1	ROUGE-2	ROUGE-W
Random	0.132▼	0.022▼	0.045▼	0.105▼	0.019▼	0.038▼	0.102▼	0.015▼	0.033▼
ClusterCMRW	0.292▼	0.071▼	0.155▼	0.263▼	0.065▼	0.106	0.252▼	0.066▼	0.098▼
DSF	0.264▼	0.064▼	0.125▼	0.235▼	0.054▼	0.091▼	0.211▼	0.047▼	0.088▼
Sen-TM-Lex	0.312▼	0.077▽	0.141	0.296▼	0.062▼	0.129	0.284▼	0.057▼	0.122
TAM-Lex	0.397	0.085	**0.147**	0.362	0.071	0.135	0.341	0.068	0.125
HSDPP	**0.398**	**0.089**	0.142	**0.404**▲	**0.082**▲	**0.159**▲	**0.393**▲	**0.082**▲	**0.149**▲

Table 6: RQ2: Effect of structured determinantal point processes in topic modeling for the top 15 topics in our datasets. Acc. abbreviates accuracy, Div. abbreviates diversity.

	HSLDA		HSDPP	
Descriptions	Acc.	Div.	Acc.	Div.
U.S. Inter. Relations	0.532	0.294	**0.583**△	**0.312**
Terrorism	0.569	0.301	**0.621**▲	**0.341**▲
2004 Election	0.591	0.266	**0.641**▲	**0.281**
US. Healthcare	0.591	0.225	**0.603**	**0.244**
Budget	0.506	0.248	**0.551**▲	**0.299**△
Israel-Palestine	**0.658**	0.269	0.652	**0.292**
Airlines	0.602	0.325	0.602	**0.384**▲
Universities	**0.596**	0.207	0.562	**0.219**
Human Rights	0.571	0.199	**0.624**△	**0.206**△
Children	**0.712**	0.352	0.622	**0.394**▲
Internet	0.547	0.277	**0.601**▲	**0.298**
Atomic Weapons	0.614	0.292	**0.662**△	**0.306**△
Literature	0.555	0.212	**0.611**△	**0.255**△
Abortions	0.594	0.301	**0.608**	**0.322**△
Bio.&Chemi. warfare	0.596	0.275	**0.597**	**0.302**△
Overall	0.581	0.296	**0.614**△	**0.317**△

and HSDPPC in terms of the ROUGE metrics. We find that HSDPP, which combines *contrast*, *relevance* and *diversity*, outperforms the other approaches on all corpora. After HSDPP, HSDPPR, which includes *relevance* during the summarization process, performs best. Thus, from Table 8 we conclude that *relevance* is the most important part during the summarization process.

7. CONCLUSION

We have considered the task of contrastive theme summarization of multiple opinionated documents. We have identified two main challenges: unknown number of topics and unknown relationships among topics. We have tackled these challenges by combining the nested Chinese restaurant process with contrastive theme modeling, which outputs a set of threaded topic paths as themes. To enhance the diversity of contrastive theme modeling, we have presented the structured determinantal point process to extract a subset of diverse and salient themes. Based on the probabilistic distributions of themes, we generate contrastive summaries subject to three key criteria: contrast, diversity and relevance. In our experiments, we have demonstrated the effectiveness of our proposed method, finding significant improvements over state-of-the-art baselines tested with three manually annotated datasets. Contrastive theme modeling is helpful for extracting contrastive themes and optimizing the number of topics. We have also shown that structured determinantal point processes are effective for diverse theme extraction.

Although we focused mostly on news articles or news-relate articles, our methods are more broadly applicable to other settings with opinionated and conflicted content, such as comment sites or product reviews. Limitations of our work include its ignorance of word dependencies and, being based on hierarchical LDA, the documents that our methods work with should be sufficiently large.

As to future work, parallel processing methods may enhance the efficiency of our topic model on large-scale opinionated documents. Also, the transfer of our approach to streaming corpora should give new insights. It is interesting to consider recent studies such as [26] on search result diversification for selecting salient and diverse themes. Finally, supervised and semi-supervised learning can be used to improve the accuracy in contrastive theme summarization [42].

Acknowledgments. This research was supported by the European Community's Seventh Framework Programme (FP7/2007-2013) under grant agreement nr 312827 (VOX-Pol), the Netherlands Organisation for Scientific Research (NWO) under project nrs 727.011.005, 612.001.116, HOR-11-10, 640.006.013, 612.066.930, CI-14-25, SH-322-15, Amsterdam Data Science, the Dutch national program COMMIT, the ESF Research Network Program ELIAS, the Elite Network Shifts project funded by the Royal Dutch Academy of Sciences (KNAW), the Netherlands eScience Center under project number 027.012.105, the Yahoo! Faculty Research and Engagement Program, the Microsoft Research PhD program, and the HPC Fund.

8. REFERENCES

[1] A. Ahmed, L. Hong, and A. Smola. Nested chinese restaurant franchise process: Applications to user tracking and document modeling. In *ICML*, 2013.

[2] J. Allan, C. Wade, and A. Bolivar. Retrieval and novelty detection at the sentence level. In *SIGIR*, 2003.

[3] D. M. Blei, A. Y. Ng, and M. I. Jordan. Latent dirichlet allocation. *J. Machine Learning research*, 3:993–1022, 2003.

[4] D. M. Blei, T. L. Griffiths, and M. I. Jordan. The nested chinese restaurant process and bayesian nonparametric inference of topic hierarchies. *J. ACM*, 57(2), 2010.

[5] A. Borodin. Determinantal point processes. In *The Oxford Handbook of Random Matrix Theory*. Oxford University Press, 2009.

[6] A. Celikyilmaz and D. Hakkani-Tur. A hybrid hierarchical model for multi-document summarization. In *ACL*, 2010.

[7] D. Chakrabarti and K. Punera. Event summarization using tweets. In *ICWSM*, 2011.

[8] S. Dori-Hacohen and J. Allan. Detecting controversy on the web. In *CIKM*, 2013.

[9] Y. Duan, F. Wei, C. Zhumin, Z. Ming, and Y. Shum. Twitter topic summarization by ranking tweets using social influence and content quality. In *Coling*, 2012.

[10] G. Erkan and D. Radev. Lexrank: Graph-based lexical centrality as salience in text summarization. *J. Artificial Intelligence Research*, 22:457–479, 2004.

Table 8: RQ4: ROUGE performance of all our proposed methods in contrastive document summarization. Significant differences are with respect to the row labeled HSDPPD, with shaded background.

	Healthcare Corpus			Bitterlemons Corpus			New York Times		
	ROUGE-1	ROUGE-2	ROUGE-W	ROUGE-1	ROUGE-2	ROUGE-W	ROUGE-1	ROUGE-2	ROUGE-W
HSDPPD	0.291	0.054	0.133	0.301	0.045	0.136	0.284	0.042	0.132
HSDPPR	0.392▲	0.082▲	0.138	0.394▲	0.079▲	0.146▲	0.376▲	0.072▲	0.147▲
HSDPPC	0.362	0.078	0.136	0.319	0.059	0.136	0.308	0.067	0.141
HSDPP	**0.398▲**	**0.089▲**	**0.142△**	**0.404▲**	**0.082▲**	**0.159▲**	**0.393▲**	**0.082▲**	**0.149▲**

[11] K. Filippova. Multi-sentence compression: Finding shortest paths in word graphs. In *Coling*, 2010.

[12] K. Ganesan, C. Zhai, and J. Han. Opinosis: a graph-based approach to abstractive summarization of highly redundant opinions. In *Coling*, 2010.

[13] K. Ganesan, C. Zhai, and E. Viegas. Micropinion generation: an unsupervised approach to generating ultra-concise summaries of opinions. In *WWW*, 2012.

[14] J. Gillenwater, A. Kulesza, and B. Taskar. Discovering diverse and salient threads in document collections. In *EMNLP-CoNLL*, 2012.

[15] M. Hu and B. Liu. Mining opinion features in customer reviews. In *AAAI*, 2004.

[16] M. Hu and B. Liu. Opinion extraction and summarization on the web. In *AAAI*, 2006.

[17] X. Huang, X. Wan, and J. Xiao. Comparative news summarization using concept-based optimization. *Knowledge and Information Systems*, 38(3):691–716, 2013.

[18] H. D. Kim and C. Zhai. Generating comparative summaries of contradictory opinions in text. In *CIKM*, 2009.

[19] H. D. Kim, K. Ganesan, P. Sondhi, and C. Zhai. Comprehensive review of opinion summarization. *Tech. Rep*, 2011.

[20] H. D. Kim, M. G. Castellanos, M. Hsu, C. Zhai, U. Dayal, and R. Ghosh. Ranking explanatory sentences for opinion summarization. In *SIGIR*, 2013.

[21] A. Kulesza and B. Taskar. Structured determinantal point processes. In *NIPS*, 2010.

[22] A. Kulesza and B. Taskar. Determinantal point processes for machine learning. *Found. & Tr. Machine Learning*, 5(2–3): 123–286, 2012.

[23] K. Lerman and R. McDonald. Contrastive summarization: an experiment with consumer reviews. In *NAACL*, 2009.

[24] F. Li, C. Han, M. Huang, X. Zhu, Y.-J. Xia, S. Zhang, and H. Yu. Structure-aware review mining and summarization. In *Coling*, 2010.

[25] L. Li, K. Zhou, G. Xue, H. Zha, and Y. Yu. Enhancing diversity, coverage and balance for summarization through structure learning. In *WWW*, 2009.

[26] S. Liang, Z. Ren, and M. de Rijke. Fusion helps diversification. In *SIGIR*, 2014.

[27] C.-Y. Lin. Rouge: A package for automatic evaluation of summaries. In *ACL*, 2004.

[28] C.-Y. Lin and E. Hovy. From single to multi-document summarization: A prototype system and its evaluation. In *ACL*, 2002.

[29] W.-H. Lin, T. Wilson, J. Wiebe, and A. Hauptmann. Which side are you on? Identifying perspectives at the document and sentence levels. In *CoNLL*, 2006.

[30] Y. Lu, C. Zhai, and N. Sundaresan. Rated aspect summarization of short comments. In *WWW*, 2009.

[31] R. McCreadie, C. Macdonald, and I. Ounis. Incremental update summarization: Adaptive sentence selection based on prevalence and novelty. In *CIKM*, 2014.

[32] Q. Mei, X. Ling, M. Wondra, H. Su, and C. Zhai. Topic sentiment mixture: modeling facets and opinions in weblogs. In *WWW*, 2007.

[33] X. Meng, F. Wei, X. Liu, M. Zhou, S. Li, and H. Wang. Entity-centric topic-oriented opinion summarization in twitter. In *KDD*, 2012.

[34] A. Nenkova and K. McKeown. Automatic summarization. *Found. & Tr. Information Retrieval*, 5(2-3):103–233, 2012.

[35] J. Nichols, J. Mahmud, and C. Drews. Summarizing sporting events using twitter. In *IUI*, 2012.

[36] M. Paul and R. Girju. A two-dimensional topic-aspect model for discovering multi-faceted topics. *AAAI*, 2010.

[37] M. J. Paul, C. Zhai, and R. Girju. Summarizing contrastive viewpoints in opinionated text. In *EMNLP*, 2010.

[38] D. Radev et al. MEAD–A platform for multidocument multilingual text summarization. In *LREC*, 2004.

[39] L. Ren, D. B. Dunson, and L. Carin. The dynamic hierarchical dirichlet process. In *ICML*, 2008.

[40] Z. Ren, J. Ma, S. Wang, and Y. Liu. Summarizing web forum threads based on a latent topic propagation process. In *CIKM*, 2011.

[41] Z. Ren, S. Liang, E. Meij, and M. de Rijke. Personalized time-aware tweets summarization. In *SIGIR*, 2013.

[42] Z. Ren, M.-H. Peetz, S. Liang, W. van Dolen, and M. de Rijke. Hierarchical multi-label classification of social text streams. In *SIGIR*, 2014.

[43] C. Shen and T. Li. Learning to rank for query-focused multi-document summarization. In *ICDM*, 2011.

[44] D. Shen, J. Sun, H. Li, Q. Yang, and Z. Chen. Document summarization using conditional random fields. In *IJCAI*, 2007.

[45] L. Shou, Z. Wang, K. Chen, and G. Chen. Sumblr: continuous summarization of evolving tweet streams. In *SIGIR*, 2013.

[46] R. Socher et al. Recursive deep models for semantic compositionality over a sentiment treebank. In *EMNLP*, 2013.

[47] K. Toutanova, C. Brockett, M. Gamon, J. Jagarlamudi, H. Suzuki, and L. Vanderwende. The pythy summarization system: Microsoft research at DUC 2007. In *DUC*, 2007.

[48] X. Wan and J. Yang. Multi-document summarization using cluster-based link analysis. In *SIGIR*, 2008.

[49] F. Wei, W. Li, Q. Lu, and Y. He. Query-sensitive mutual reinforcement chain and its application in query-oriented multi-document summarization. In *SIGIR*, 2008.

[50] Y. Zhu, Y. Lan, J. Guo, P. Du, and X. Cheng. A novel relational learning-to-rank approach for topic-focused multi-document summarization. In *ICDM*, 2013.

Splitting Water: Precision and Anti-Precision to Reduce Pool Bias

Aldo Lipani
Inst. of Software Technology & Interactive Systems
Vienna University of Technology
Vienna, Austria
lipani@ifs.tuwien.ac.at

Mihai Lupu
Inst. of Software Technology & Interactive Systems
Vienna University of Technology
Vienna, Austria
lupu@ifs.tuwien.ac.at

Allan Hanbury
Inst. of Software Technology & Interactive Systems
Vienna University of Technology
Vienna, Austria
hanbury@ifs.tuwien.ac.at

ABSTRACT

For many tasks in evaluation campaigns, especially those modeling narrow domain-specific challenges, lack of participation leads to a potential pooling bias due to the scarce number of pooled runs. It is well known that the reliability of a test collection is proportional to the number of topics and relevance assessments provided for each topic, but also to same extent to the diversity in participation in the challenges. Hence, in this paper we present a new perspective in reducing the pool bias by studying the effect of merging an unpooled run with the pooled runs. We also introduce an indicator used by the bias correction method to decide whether the correction needs to be applied or not. This indicator gives strong clues about the potential of a "good" run tested on an "unfriendly" test collection (i.e. a collection where the pool was contributed to by runs very different from the one at hand). We demonstrate the correctness of our method on a set of fifteen test collections from the Text REtrieval Conference (TREC). We observe a reduction in system ranking error and absolute score difference error.

Categories and Subject Descriptors

H.3.4 [**Information Storage and Retrieval**]: Systems and Software—*Performance evaluation*

General Terms

Experimentation, measurement, performance

Keywords

Evaluation, bias, pool, test collection, TREC

1. INTRODUCTION

A test collection is a valuable resource for Information Retrieval (IR) researchers because it gives the IR community a common ground to facilitate the development of search models. Numerous test collections have been developed in the field since the first Cranfield experiments in the 1960s. Since the start of TREC in the 1990s, this creation happens at a rate of approximately 25 test collections per year. A test collection is composed of: a set of documents, a set of topics and a set of relevance assessments for each topic, derived from the collection of documents. The number of documents in the collection generally makes the full judgment of the document set for every topic infeasible. Therefore, the relevance assessment process is generally optimized by pooling the top N documents for each run. The pool is constructed from systems taking part in the challenge for which the collection was made, at a specific point in time, after which the collection is generally frozen in terms of relevance judgments. The pooling technique aims to identify an unbiased sample of relevant documents. Nevertheless, pool bias negatively affects the score of unpooled runs—those of systems not present at the time of test collection creation. This is a drawback that ultimately affects the reliability of the test collection. The variables controlling this reliability are [14]: the number of topics and their representativeness of the information needs of the target user, the number of documents assessed per run, and, last but not least, the diversity of the pooled systems (often however only assessed as the cardinality of the set of runs).

In the last decades the IR community has branched out significantly in a variety of domains and applications, with the creation of specific IR test collections focusing on specific problems. At the same time, benchmarking techniques developed in the IR community are being implemented in industry. Information aware companies request measures to quantify the quality of their information access systems in general, and search systems in particular. With a narrower focus however, the effort to successfully solve the challenges facing the creators of test collections takes on new significance. Most notably, it is often difficult to acquire a sufficient number of participants and diverse systems in order to fulfill the required run diversity to guarantee a reliable test collection.

In this paper, we estimate the pool bias by studying the effect of an unpooled run on the set of pooled runs, when a fixed-depth pooling strategy is used. We do this through the estimation of an *average unjudged rate*, which we then normalize with its potential growth interval, in order to adjust the pool bias. Additionally, we introduce an indicator that

SIGIR'15, August 09 - 13, 2015, Santiago, Chile.

ACM 978-1-4503-3621-5/15/08 ...$15.00.
DOI: http://dx.doi.org/10.1145/2766462.2767749 .

provides strong clues about the quality of a new, unpooled run.

We do this based for Precision at cut-off $P@n$. There are two reasons to consider such a "simple" metric. First, it is a cornerstone for many other metrics developed for the most popular of user models these days: the web user [12]. Second, it is easy to understand by all users. This "understandability" of the IR metrics has drawn moderate attention from our community recently [10]. Our own experience in the industry leads us to believe that, when results are not presented as simply precision and recall, any numbers are just *assumed* to be precision or recall. Decision makers at lower or higher levels, trying to make sense of MAP, or any other commonly used metric in our community, will most often read 0.12 as 12% and simply assume that either 12% of documents are relevant or 12% of relevant documents have been returned on average. Of course, we do not forget why all the other metrics have been invented to replace, or complement, precision at cut-off: 1) for an ideal run, if the topic has less relevant documents then n, $P@n$ does not reach 1; it is not normalized by the number of relevant documents, therefore it is difficult to average over topics, 2) it partially neglects the position of the documents. Nevertheless, there are many cases where $P@n$ is useful (most often, but not only, for the user modeled as considering blocks of 10 documents at a time on the web). This is also demonstrated by its continued use and reporting throughout a majority of evaluation tracks at TREC, CLEF, or NTCIR.

We propose a new bias correction method and demonstrate its effectiveness through leave-one-out experiments, at different levels and combinations, organizations and systems, all the pooled runs, or only the 75% of the top runs as done in previous papers [22, 19, 2, 21, 20]. We then evaluate the results using the mean absolute error (MAE) and the system rank error (SRE), comparing it against the results obtained with the reduced pool, and with the method of correcting pool bias introduced by Webber and Park [23]. We do this on fifteen test collections from TREC, five of which are domain specific test collections.

In short, the contributions of this study are as follows:

1. a new perspective on $P@n$, based on the effect of a new run on the set of runs which contributed to the creation of the pool;
2. an indicator to trigger bias correction only when it is indeed necessary;
3. a bias correction method for $P@n$, including extensive experimental results to show that it outperforms existing bias correction methods,

The remainder of the paper is structured as follows: in Section 2 we provide a brief summary of the extensive work already done to assess and correct pool bias. Section 3 provides the intuition of our method and introduces the required concepts, followed in Section 4 by the method itself. In Section 5 we present and discuss our experimental results. We conclude in Section 6.

2. RELATED WORK

Work related to pool bias can be grouped in three categories: first, that aiming to fundamentally change the way assessment is done, by, instead of pooling, choosing assessment documents in order to maximize some evaluation goal. For instance, Cormack et al. [11] suggest to boost the proportional of relevant documents, Moffat et al. [15] to focus on the score accuracy of the best-performing systems, Carterette et al [7, 6] to maximize confidence that one system has or has not a better score then another one, using different models of probability of relevancy. While important, this is not the focus of the current paper, which instead addresses the problem of evaluating against existing test collections built using pooling.

Second, there are those studies aiming to assess the reliability of a test collection. This reliability (or lack thereof) can be often traced back to the pooling procedure. Most recently Urbano et al. [20] proposed an estimation of reliability of a test collection using Generalization Theory. We shall use this in our study to better understand the observations made in our experiments.

Finally, and most related to this study, are those works that address the problem of pool bias directly. Here, three different strategies have been studied: removing the bias from the onset, at test collection creation time; creating new metrics to better handle unjudged documents; or estimating the score error to make an adjustment in the metric.

The first strategy is the most desirable: enforcing a diverse set of runs through the efforts of the test collection creators themselves. Especially early test collections have, for instance, created manual runs to increase the likelihood of relevant documents appearing in the pool. The benefit of such efforts has been demonstrated, among others by Kuriyama et al. [13]. Nevertheless, not all test collections have this advantage, and adding such runs a posteriori, after an initial set of systems have been evaluated, is not done because it breaks the comparability of the runs evaluated across the years.

A lot more can be done and has been done for the second strategy: new metrics. In 2004, Buckley and Voorhees [4] introduced BPref as a metric specifically designed to handle incomplete information, which, as pointed out by Sakai in 2007 [17], is a restricted form of Average Precision (AP) on a so called 'condensed list'. These are condensed versions of the runs where unjudged documents are filtered out. Sakai introduces a new metric (the Q-measure) and shows that it is possible to obtain better performance then BPref even applying already well-known metrics to the condensed list. The concept of condensed list, first denoted as such by Sakai, was however already explored in relation to AP with the measure Induced AP, introduced by Yilmaz and Aslam [24] the year before, in 2006. Induced AP is Average Precision calculated on condensed lists. The methods explored by these three contributions do not simulate the effect of shallow pooling or of comparing unpooled runs against pooled ones, because they remove the effect of bias sampling from the query relevance (qrel) set, ending up with an unrealistic use case. This was later addressed by Sakai [18], who demonstrated that the condensed list approach leads in favor of new systems, the effect of these metrics instead creating incomplete relevance information by playing with the depth of the pool. Also in their 2006 report, Yilmaz and Aslam [24] introduce the Inferred AP, a more complex metric which is a closer approximation of AP but requires knowledge about the documents down to depth 100. Inferred AP adjusts the score sampling uniformly from the pooled documents and then estimates the true mean of the sample to adjust AP.

Later, Aslam and colleagues address the issue of the uniform sampling used in the 2006 version of Inferred AP [25]. In this later version they use a stratified sampling scheme.

However, their finding that the method is not subject to pooling bias is not confirmed in practice by Carterette et al. in 2008 [8]. As they write, this is possibly because aggregating probability of inclusion across multiple runs by taking the mean of the per run probabilities may not properly account for reinforcement by similar systems.

The problem of incomplete judgments leads to the definition of a completely new metric, defined by Moffat and Zobel [16]—called Rank-Biased Precision—expressed by a single value and a residual. The Residual quantifies the uncertainty introduced by the unjudged documents. Its value is computable thanks to the fact that it is not normalized by the number of relevant documents. This implies that the computation of the metric defines a lower bound for the given run. Moffat and Zobel attempted to make a measure that is naturally convergent, where the contribution of each rank has a fixed weight. This would have both benefits of a normalized metric and those of a metric averageable over topics with different numbers of relevant documents. This attempt was unsuccessful, as pointed out by Sakai [18], who proved this to be inferior with respect to the condensed list.

At this point we have the transition to the third category of approaches to solve the pool bias: metric error estimation and correction.

In their presentation of Rank-Biased Precision (RBP), Moffat and Zobel had already introduced the discussion concerning the fact that the residual can be used to estimate and correct pool bias. Webber and Park [23] continue their work on RBP by adding to the score the average residual calculated against the pool proceeding with a leave-one-run-out approach. To estimate it they span two dimensions: the topics and the systems. They used Rank-Biased Precision at ten (RBP@10) and Precision at ten (P@10) although the results for this last metric were not reported in the 2009 paper, the authors only mentioned that they were similar to RBP. In the present study we return to precision at cut-off and look not only at coefficients to correct pool bias, but also at whether there is something to correct in the first place.

3. PRECISION AND ANTI-PRECISION

The intuition at the base of the proposed method is that we can observe how a new, unpooled run impacts the existing, pooled runs. Given such an existing run, we can imagine reranking it based on the ranks of its documents in the unpooled run. A "bad" new run will tend to bring down known relevant documents and push up non-relevant ones. Quantifying these changes we create a measure of the potential quality of the new run.

In the following we describe theoretically the measures later used to reduce the pool bias. In evaluating IR systems, Precision (P) is one of the two fundamental measures. We recall its definition: given D a set of documents, D_r a subset of D (the documents in a run r), q a topic, and σ a function of relevancy returning the level of relevancy of the document d for the topic q, P is defined as:

$$P = \frac{|d \in D_r : \sigma(d,q) > 0|}{|D_r|}$$

Precision represents the proportion of relevant and retrieved documents against the retrieved ones. From P we derive the definition of Precision at cut-off n ($P@n$), used to better handle ranked retrieval systems: given ρ a function that returns the rank of a document d in a run r, we have:

$$P@n = \frac{|d \in D_r : \sigma(d,q) > 0, \rho(d,r) \leq n|}{n}$$

The measure takes into account only the relevant documents because it is supposed to be used when there is a complete knowledge of the relevance function over the documents in the run. When we consider the problem of missing relevance assessments this assumption is not true, ending up considering unjudged documents as non-relevant. To overcome this problem and take into account the missing information about the run, we define the complement of Precision, called Anti-Precision ($\overline{P}$). Anti-Precision measures the proportion of non-relevant and retrieved documents against the retrieved documents. In statistics, a similarly defined quantity is referred to as the False Discovery Rate (FDR) [1]. It is used in quantifying the results of multiple hypothesis testing experiments. However, given the very different use of it here, we continue to refer to it as Anti-Precision in this study, and define it as:

$$\overline{P} = \frac{|d \in D_r : \sigma(d,q) = 0|}{|D_r|}$$

As well as for Precision, we define also the cut-off version ($\overline{P}@n$):

$$\overline{P}@n = \frac{|d \in D_r : \sigma(d,q) = 0, \rho(d,r) \leq n|}{n}$$

Indeed, when a run is fully judged the following equation holds:

$$P + \overline{P} = 1$$

When it is not, and unjudged documents are present in the run, the sum of P and $\overline{P}$ is lower than 1, reduced by a quantity that represents the proportion of retrieved and unjudged documents against the retrieved documents. We refer to this as k bar ($\bar{k}$).

$$P + \overline{P} = 1 - \bar{k}$$

This quantity represents the uncertainty of the measurement. Just as P and $\overline{P}$, $\bar{k}$ can be also defined at cut-off ($\bar{k}$@n).

3.1 Analysis of a run shuffle

Before going on to the details of our proposed method, let us perform an imagination exercise in order to better understand the information content of a partially judged run. We want to analyze which kind of information precision and anti-precision expose if a given run r gets shuffled. As in a deck of cards a shuffling changes the order of the documents of a run and produces a new run that we will indicate as r'. This run has the same set of documents as before. We want to observe the variation in score the run obtains in the two states, original and shuffled. If we would use P, since there is no information about the position of the documents in the formula, we would measure a change of 0. Therefore, let us observe $P@n$. Given a run r and its shuffled version r' we define:

$$\delta P@n(r') = P@n(r') - P@n(r)$$

$\delta P@n$ has domain $[-1, 1]$ and is the variation in precision of the run after a shuffle. Its increase in value is the result of the combination of the following two related effects: the shuffle moved up relevant documents, placing them in the top n, or moved down non-relevant or unjudged documents with the consequential moving up of potential relevant documents in the run. It decreases if the opposite happens. We also define $\delta\overline{P}@n$ as following:

$$\delta\overline{P}@n(r') = \overline{P}@n(r') - \overline{P}@n(r)$$

$\delta\overline{P}@n$ has domain $[-1, 1]$ and is the variation in anti-precision of the run after a shuffle. Its increase in value is the result of the combination of the following two related effects: the shuffle moved up non-relevant documents, placing them in the top n, or moved down relevant or unjudged documents with the consequential moving up of potential non-relevant documents in the run. It decreases if the opposite happens.

Finally, $\delta\bar{k}@n$ that is derived as following:

$$\begin{aligned} \delta\bar{k}@n(r') &= \bar{k}@n(r') - \bar{k}@n(r) \\ &= 1 - (P@n(r') + \overline{P}@n(r')) \\ &\quad - [1 - (P@n(r) + \overline{P}@n(r))] \\ &= -\delta P@n(r') - \delta P@n(r) \end{aligned} \tag{1}$$

$\delta\bar{k}@n$ has domain $[-1, 1]$ and is the variation of *unjudged* documents on a given run. Its increase in value is the result of the combination of the following effects: the shuffle moved up unjudged documents or moved down relevant and non-relevant documents with the consequential moving up of potential unjudged documents in the run. An interesting property of this function, which is possible to prove, is that if r has been judged to depth $d : d \geq n$, then the domain of the function $\delta\bar{k}@n$ is $[0, 1]$. This property always holds for pooled runs because they verify the condition (provided of course that no mistakes occurred in the pooling process).

In summary, when a run changes the order of its documents, δP, $\delta\overline{P}$, and $\delta\bar{k}$ are indicators of the direction of the judged relevant, judged non-relevant, and unjudged documents in the list.

3.2 Effect of a run on a pooled run

Now let us make a step further and consider not the relationship between a run and a random shuffle of itself, but between a run and another run. In the particular case where each run ranks completely the entire collection, this is the same as above. In general however, the systems only provide runs down to a certain limit (say 1000). To study this effect, we need to define a merging function between the two runs. The unpooled run will have an effect on the pooled run, measured by the quantities described above.

Such a merging function can simply be based on the rank of the documents in the run. The aim here is not to add or remove documents from a run, so although the word "merging" could imply the transfer of documents between the two runs to make a new one, we must keep in mind that all we need to do here is transfer only the information about the rank of the documents. We do this by linearly combining the ranks if the two runs share the same document.

In the following formula, by r_u we denote the new, previously unseen and unpooled run, whose effect on r_p an existing run, we want to study. This effect we represent as a new, synthetic run r', which consists exclusively of documents present in r_p, potentially re-ordered.

$$r' = r_p \circ r_u = \{d \in r_p : \rho(d, r') = \mu(d, r_p, r_u)\} \tag{2}$$

where

$$\mu(d, r_p, r_u) = \begin{cases} \rho(d, r_p)(1-\alpha) + \rho(d, r_u)\alpha & \text{if } d \in r_u \\ \rho(d, r_p) & \text{if } else \end{cases}$$

μ is the weighted arithmetic mean between the rank of the document in r_p and the rank of the document in r_u, with $0 \leq \alpha \leq 1$. When the same rank is assigned by μ to two different documents, which can happen in some cases for a pair of documents of which one is also in r_u and the other one is not, the common document is inserted after the r_p-exclusive document. In other words, the original run rank has priority.

As any functional composition operator, our merging operator $\circ$ is not commutative and always represents the effect of its right member on its left member.

In this context, $\delta P@n$ and $\delta\overline{P}@n$ can be used to analyze the quality of an unpooled run against the pooled one. An increase in $\delta P@n$ is the result of two forces, one direct and one indirect: 1) direct, if the relevant documents in the top n of r_u are the same documents found at the bottom of r_p, they will be pushed up; 2) indirect, if the r_u has non-relevant or unjudged documents in the bottom that are in the top n documents of r_p, they will be pushed down. The contribution decreases if the contrary happens. As well for $\delta\overline{P}@n$ the contribution is: 1) direct, if the non-relevant documents in the top n of r_u are shared with documents in the bottom of r_p; 2) indirect, if the r_u has relevant or unjudged documents in the bottom that are in the top n documents of r_p. If the run r_p would be judged in its totality, these two effects would be perfectly correlated and it would be possible to calculate one just knowing the other from the following equation:

$$\delta P@n + \delta\overline{P}@n = 0$$

However, when r_p contains unjudged documents at ranks below n, their sum becomes $-\delta\bar{k}@n$, as shown in Eq. 1.

As explained above, $\delta\bar{k}@n$ represents the ratio of unjudged documents brought to the top n of the run r_p by the run r_u. Moreover, it is possible to prove that $\delta P = 0$ and $\delta\overline{P} = 0$ if and only if one of the following two conditions occurs: 1) the two runs r_p and r_u do not share any documents with each other in their top n documents, or 2) the two runs are identical in the top n. These are the two cases where our method will not say anything about the new run r_u just by using the existing run r_p (but we might based on other pooled runs).

Let us now take an example to illustrate how this indicator could be useful to understand the behavior of a run and predict its quality. We use the test collection Robust 2005 and in particular we focus our attention on a special run that presents an unusual effect, the routing run `sab05ror1`. It has the peculiarity of being strongly discounted when it is not in the pool. Buckley et al. [3] studied it at length, pointing out that the reason for its behavior was related to the size of the test collection. For this run let us calculate $P@10$ and $\bar{k}@10$. Let us also consider the average of $\delta P@10$ and $\delta\overline{P}@10$, which we denote as follows:

$$\Delta P@10 = \frac{1}{|R_p|} \sum_{r \in R_p} \delta P@10(r_p \circ r_u)$$

$$\Delta\overline{P}@10 = \frac{1}{|R_p|} \sum_{r \in R_p} \delta\overline{P}@10(r_p \circ r_u)$$

where R_p is the set of runs used in the creation of the test collection.

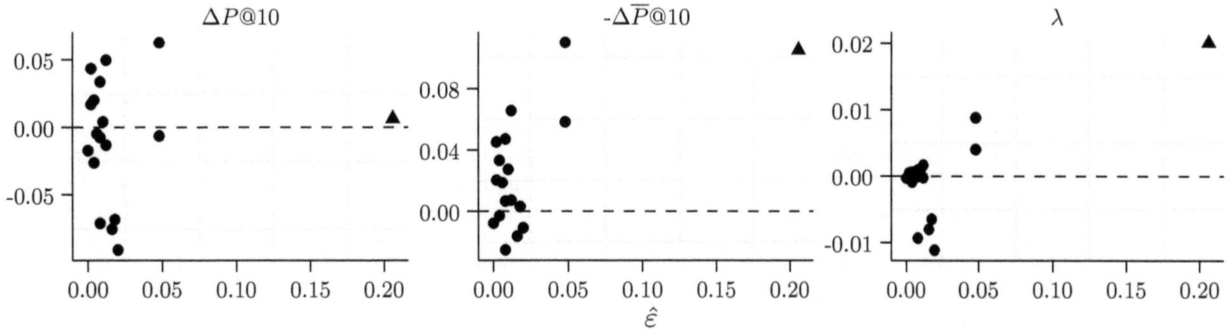

Figure 1: Plot of ΔP@10, $\Delta \overline{P}$@10 and λ against the residual ($\hat{\varepsilon}$) in a leave-one-organization-out experiment, for the Robust 2005 test collection. The run indicated as ▲ is the unusual run `sab05ror1`.

Table 1: Measures computed for the run `sab05ror1` when it is not part of the pool

P@10	$\bar{k}$@10	ΔP@10	$\Delta \overline{P}$@10
0.4220	0.444	0.0065	-0.1053

Table 1 shows these values for this particular run.

When the run is not part of the pool, P@10 assigns it the 11th position in 18th runs. $\bar{k}$@10 says that there are many documents that are unjudged and that therefore there is a high potential to grow. ΔP@10 indicates a low average positive contribution to the pooled runs, and shows that among the relevant documents there is little intersection. $\Delta \overline{P}$@10 instead is negative which suggests that many non-relevant documents have been ranked lower than before, therefore suggesting a good ability of this special run to discriminate relevant documents from non-relevant ones.

In Figure 1 we show the resulted ΔP@10, $\Delta \overline{P}$@10 against the residual error ($\hat{\varepsilon}$, the difference between the true score and the unpooled score), generated with a leave-one-organization-out approach. Here we can observe that just using ΔP@10 is not enough because it takes into account only one of the two positive contributions of the run, the other one being the reduction in $\Delta \overline{P}$@10.

Let us now return to the general case. When the average negative contribution of the unpooled run to other runs is reduced (i.e. $\Delta \overline{P} < 0$) and the run has a positive contribution (i.e. $\Delta P > 0$), the run suffers from pool bias and its score should be adjusted. More problematic is the case when $\Delta \overline{P}$ and ΔP have the same sign (i.e. the run has both a negative and a positive contribution, on average). Indeed, if we have $\Delta \overline{P} > 0$ and $\Delta P > 0$ we would improve the P@n score of the run only if their ratio is greater then the ratio of P to $\overline{P}$, because it means that there is a chance to improve the existing score. On the other hand, if we have $\Delta \overline{P} < 0$ and $\Delta P < 0$ we would improve only if their ratio is lower then the ratio of P to $\overline{P}$ because it means that the contribution of the run is more able to discriminate the non-relevant documents.

From these observations we derive a single value indicator that merges the information of all the indicators defined:

$$\lambda = \bar{k}@n(\Delta P@n \cdot \overline{P}@n - \Delta \overline{P}@n \cdot P@n) \quad (3)$$

For all runs where $\lambda > 0$ we apply our correction method.

The sign of the difference in the brackets is equivalent to the ratios discussion above. The $\bar{k}$ factor has no impact on the sign (as $\bar{k} \geq 0$), but removes those special cases where $\bar{k} = 0$, since in these cases there is no possibility to improve the score of the run (i.e. to get it closer to what we would have obtained if the run had been contributing to the pool).

Algorithm 1 Adjustment based on pooled runs

$r_u \leftarrow$ unpooled run
$R_p \leftarrow$ set of pooled runs
$T \leftarrow$ set of topics
$Q \leftarrow$ qrels on T derived from R_p
$s_{r_u} \leftarrow P@n(r_u)$
$\overline{s}_{r_u} \leftarrow \overline{P}@n(r_u)$
$\bar{k}_{r_u} \leftarrow 1 - (s_{r_u} + \overline{s}_{r_u})$
for all $r_p \in R_p$ **do**
  $r'_p \leftarrow r_p \circ r_u$
  $\delta P_{r_p} \leftarrow (P@n(r'_p)$ - $P@n(r_p))$
  $\delta \overline{P}_{r_p} \leftarrow (\overline{P}@n(r'_p)$ - $\overline{P}@n(r_p))$
  $\delta \bar{k}_{r_p} \leftarrow (-\delta P r_p - \delta \overline{P} r_p)$
end for
$\Delta P_{r_u} \leftarrow \frac{1}{|R_p|} \sum_{r_p \in R_p} \delta P_{r_p}$
$\Delta \overline{P}_{r_u} \leftarrow \frac{1}{|R_p|} \sum_{r_p \in R_p} \delta \overline{P}_{r_p}$
$\lambda \leftarrow \bar{k}_{r_u} (\Delta P_{r_u} \overline{s}_{r_u} - \Delta \overline{P}_{r_u} s_{r_u})$
if $\lambda > 0$ **then**
  $\Delta \bar{k}_{r_u} \leftarrow \frac{1}{|R_p|} \sum_{r_p \in R_p} \delta \bar{k}_{r_p}$
  $a \leftarrow \bar{k}_{r_u} \max(\Delta \bar{k}_{r_u}, 0)$
else
  $a \leftarrow 0$
end if
return $s_{r_u} + a$

Returning briefly to the example of the `sab05ror1` run, we can now see in Figure 1 that λ clearly distinguishes this run from the rest.

4. ADJUSTING SCORE FOR BIAS

Now that we have an understanding of which runs are suffering from pool bias, with respect to precision at cut-off, we proceed by presenting our method to adjust the score (Algorithm 1). As hinted at before, the method is to adjust the pool bias suffered by a system that has not been pooled by measuring the effect of the system on the pooled runs. The only information that is needed is the relevance assessments for each topic and the pooled runs, normally available for most existing test collections. As we presented earlier, P@n as calculated with the incomplete pool is a lower bound for the score of r_u. To correct the pool bias we want to add a quantity that stays within its uncertainty limit $\bar{k}_{r_u}$. In other words, our growth potential in terms of $P@n$ is bounded by $\bar{k}_{r_u}$. We are interested in estimating the missing precision of the unjudged documents in the run r_u.

The question is then: Where in this interval do we find our correction value? In the absence of any other external information, we will take the average effect of this run r_u on the existing runs, in terms of $\bar{k}$.

We do this by computing the $\delta\bar{k}_{r_p}$ produced by r_u on a pooled run r_p via the run composition function defined in Eq. 2. This measures the aggregated change in precision and anti-precision, as described by Eq. 1. We do this for each run in the pool, and average these values. This average, denoted $\Delta\bar{k}_{r_u}$, when positive, acts as a maximum likelihood estimator for our position in $[0,\bar{k}_{r_u}]$. Therefore, the correction quantity is the product between $\Delta\bar{k}_{r_u}$ and $\bar{k}_{r_u}$. The following section will therefore add $\bar{k}_{r_u}\max(\Delta\bar{k}_{r_u}, 0)$ to the $P@n$ for those runs with $\lambda > 0$, as shown in the last seven lines of Algorithm 1.

5. EXPERIMENTS

To test the pool bias adjustment developed in the previous section we used 15 test collections sampled from TREC: 7 test collections from the Ad Hoc track, 3 from the Web track, and 5 from more domain specific IR tracks: Genomics, Robust, Legal, Medical and Microblog. We tested the algorithm[1] through a leave-one-out approach comparing our method with that of Webber and Park [23]. As the baseline we consider the traditional evaluation against the reduced pool. We call this the *reduced* pool to distinguish it from the ground truth pool—the one also containing documents exclusively contributed by the removed runs or organizations. We performed the leave-one-out at two different levels: 1) *leave-one-run-out*: as firstly described by Zobel [26], one run at a time is exited from the pool. This is done by removing all the documents uniquely introduced by it from the relevance assessments; 2) *leave-one-organization-out*: as introduced by Büttcher [5], it is similar to the *leave-one-run-out*, with the difference that not only is one run removed from the pool, but also all the runs generated by the same organization. This is done by removing all the documents uniquely introduced by the organization's runs from the relevance assessments. This second approach simulates better the testing of a new run, since in most cases it has been observed that the runs produced by the same organization come from the same system, with only some parameter variation. Therefore, they often bring to the pool the same relevant documents. Finally, as in previous studies [2, 19, 20, 21, 22], to avoid buggy implementations of some of the systems that took part in the challenges, we tested again with only the top 75% of runs of each test collection.

The results for the *leave-one-run-out*, in addition to being less realistic as a model of real life, are also more conservative than those for *leave-one-organization-out*, such that in the following we shall discuss only the latter.

5.1 Correction results

In these settings, we explored the different value of the weight of the merging function α. In which we observe that as expected, as α goes from 1 to 0, the role of the new run on the runs in the pool decreases, to the point where, for $\alpha = 0$, the method no longer makes any change to the existing runs. This degree of change in α also affects the variability of ΔP and $\Delta\overline{P}$ which decreases as well due to the lower variation between the synthetic and the pooled runs. This effect grows linearly with α and in the following we shall report the maximum effects, obtained for $\alpha = 1$. Moreover, we tested the algorithm with different bias indicators (i.e. replacing λ with ΔP or $\Delta\overline{P}$, as discussed in Section 3.2), thus testing the presence and absence of information about relevant or non-relevant documents in the relevance assessment as potential flags to trigger bias correction. We consistently observe lower performance compared with λ.

Figure 3 shows the comparison, per test collection, of the three different approaches in the *leave-one-organization-out* experiment as a function of the Mean Absolute Error (MAE). As defined before in [23], the Mean Absolute Error is computed as the absolute difference between the scores of two runs, averaged over the set of topics. In addition to observing the error in the scores, it is also of interest to see how many rank reversals occur. The System Rank Error (SRE) is the sum of all the variation on rank of the system given the true rank. Figure 4 shows the SRE. For the experiments with the 75% top runs, actual values are reported in Table 2. In addition to these two measures, in Table 2, we also reported the SRE*, which only counts the variation on system rank when the difference among them is statistically significant in the ground truth (Tukey's test, $p < 0.05$ [9]).

In the table and plots we observe that our method, in a majority of cases outperforms the reduced pool and the Webber method. The last lines of Table 2 show how often each method outperformed both other methods (ties are not counted). It also shows how often it obtained the absolute worst score. It can be observed that, of the 675 tests summarized in Table 2, the proposed method obtains the worst performer mark exactly three times. On the other hand, the competing method is significantly more aggressive in its bias correction. In the majority of the cases it obtains worse system scores and rankings when compared to the simpler method of not doing anything (i.e. the reduced pool). This happens in particular in Ad Hoc 6, 7, 8 and Robust 2005. The proposed method is shown to be stable. Particularly important, it gets worse scores exactly once on SRE*, the metric measuring reversals among systems identified to be statistically significantly different. And, it happens with Medical 2011 and $P@100$, increasing the SRE* from 0 (for reduced pool) to 10, which reason should be found in the used shallow pool depth of 10.

5.2 Relation to test collection stability

The results observed in Figures 3 and 4, as well as in Table 2 lead us to question whether or not there is a connection between the effect of our method and the quality of the test collection. We therefore compare the percentage MAE change for each test collection and for each n of $P@n$, with the two coefficients of stability recently adapted by Urbano et al. [20] from Generalizability Theory: the Generalizability Coefficient ($E\rho^2$) and Dependability (Φ). $E\rho^2$ measures the stability based on system variance and the relative differences between systems; Φ measures the stability based on system variance and the absolute effectiveness scores. To infer that a test collection is reliable, both measures must tend to 1. Figure 2 shows the relation between these two factors and the change in MAE for $P@10$ and $P@100$ for

[1]The software is available on the website of the first author.

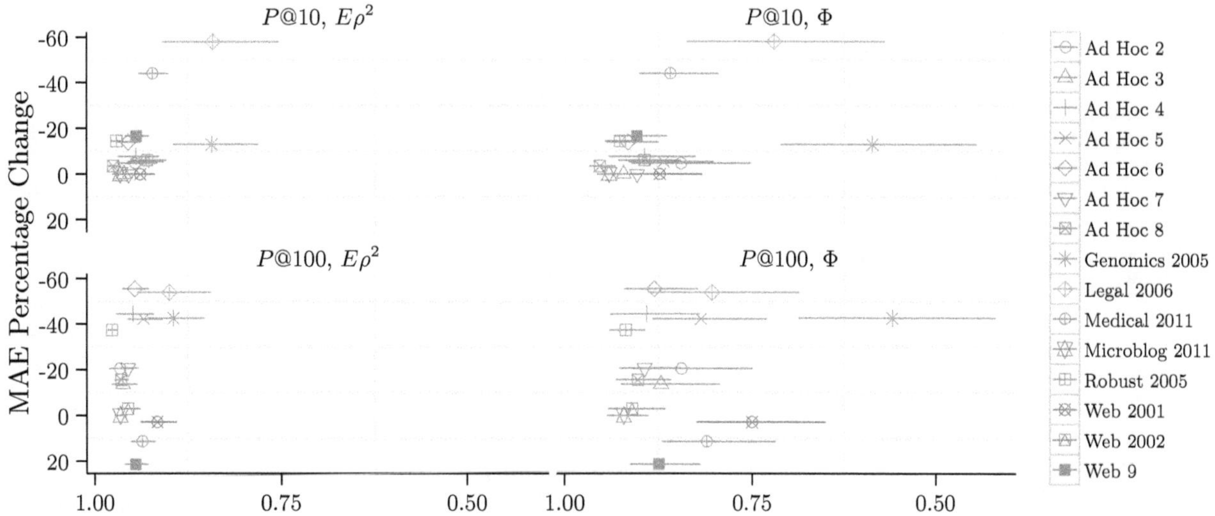

Figure 2: Plots of the percentage change of Mean Absolute Error for $P@10$ and $P@100$ against the coefficients of stability, Generalizability Coefficient ($E\rho^2$) and Dependability (Φ). Spearman's rank correlation for P@10: $E\rho^2$ is 0.48 (p>0.07) and for Φ is 0.36 (p>0.18). For P@100: $E\rho^2$ is 0.17 (p>0.54) and for Φ is 0.09 (p>0.74).

the 15 test collections studied here. This change in MAE is calculated between our method and the traditional, reduced pool method. In general, we observe a weak correlation with $E\rho^2$ and Φ (i.e. less error for more unstable test collections). With $P@10$ our method has a stronger effect with more unstable test collections. An interesting case happens at $P@100$, where for some test collection the MAE percentage change is positive, that is resulting in a lack of correlation, with which we get more ambiguous results.

To understand this, it is needed to understand that when the cut-off of $P@n$ is greater then the depth of the pool, we are essentially comparing with an uncertain ground truth, since also the large pool (the one with the runs of the organization we removed for testing) is affected by the presence of unjudged documents. This uncertainty in comparing the result when the depth of the pool is less then the considered $P@n$ needs to be considered when looking at these results, as well as those of all other proposed methods. The *depth* of each test collection is available for reference in Table 2.

6. CONCLUSION

The primary focus of this paper is an insight that information about the quality of an unpooled run can be obtained by observing its effect on existing, pooled runs. Such an effect is modeled by the creation of a synthetic run, obtained by merging the two runs—the pooled and the unpooled—in a very simple way, by linearly combining the ranks of each document in the old run (i.e. we do not want to add new documents to the old run, just observed how its own documents shift as a function of the information provided by the new run). The effect is measured with essentially three quantities: the change in the position of the judged relevant documents (measured via precision), the change in the position of the judged non-relevant documents (measured via anti-precision), and the change in the position of the unjudged documents (measured via a measure $\bar{k}$ we define). Observing these changes across the set of pooled runs—the effect of the new run on the existing runs—we identify a coefficient λ whose sign allows us to decide whether a bias correction should be made or not. We then proceed with the provision of a bias correction procedure based on the above three quantities, which we show to be conservative in the sense that it never damages significant rank orders, and only very rarely affects changes in system rankings. This is opposed to previous methods which are too aggressive in the bias correction, and in so being, add another level of uncertainty to the system rankings.

The proposed method addresses a significant concern coming from research but also from practice: the necessity to have a reliable, yet understandable metric, which we can communicate to partners outside of our community. This last condition significantly restricts our possible choices. Precision at cut-off is by far the most easily understood quantity to communicate and with this study we have shown that we can correct pool bias when considering a run that has not participated in the creation of the pool.

Acknowledgements

This research was supported by the Austrian Science Fund (FWF) project number P25905-N23 (ADmIRE).

7. REFERENCES

[1] Y. Benjamini and Y. Hochberg. Controlling the false discovery rate: a practical and powerful approach to multiple testing. *Journal of the Royal Statistical Society*, B57(1), 1995.

[2] D. Bodoff and P. Li. Test theory for assessing ir test collections. In *Proc. of SIGIR*, 2007.

[3] C. Buckley, D. Dimmick, I. Soboroff, and E. Voorhees. Bias and the limits of pooling for large collections. *Inf. Ret.*, 10(6), 2007.

[4] C. Buckley and E. M. Voorhees. Retrieval evaluation with incomplete information. In *Proc. of SIGIR*, 2004.

[5] S. Büttcher, C. L. A. Clarke, P. C. K. Yeung, and I. Soboroff. Reliable information retrieval evaluation

Table 2: Summary of the results per test collection generate trough a leave-one-organization-out using the top 75% of the pooled runs. With: $|R|$ number of runs submitted, $|O|$ number of organizations involved, $|R_p|$ number of pooled runs, d depth of the pool and $|T|$ number of topics.

Track		P@n	Ours			Webber			Reduced Pool		
			MAE	SRE	SRE*	MAE	SRE	SRE*	MAE	SRE	SRE*
Ad Hoc 2	$\|R\|$: 38	5	0.0063	19	0	0.0069	18	0	0.0065	19	0
	$\|O\|$: 22	10	0.0082	32	0	0.0084	27	0	0.0085	32	0
	$\|R_p\|$: 36	20	0.0132	50	0	0.0119	48	0	0.0138	52	0
	d : 100	30	0.0149	51	0	0.0129	42	0	0.0164	56	0
	$\|T\|$: 50	100	0.0216	88	2	0.0169	61	2	0.0293	122	4
Ad Hoc 3	$\|R\|$: 40	5	0.0025	3	0	0.0038	3	0	0.0025	3	0
	$\|O\|$: 22	10	0.0024	5	0	0.0029	0	0	0.0025	5	0
	$\|R_p\|$: 26	20	0.0042	5	0	0.0041	6	0	0.0042	5	0
	d : 200	30	0.0049	13	0	0.0051	12	0	0.0051	13	0
	$\|T\|$: 50	100	0.0067	21	0	0.0071	28	0	0.0085	25	0
Ad Hoc 4	$\|R\|$: 33	5	0.0065	17	0	0.0069	20	0	0.0073	18	0
	$\|O\|$: 19	10	0.0081	23	0	0.0081	22	0	0.0093	25	0
	$\|R_p\|$: 32	20	0.0089	29	0	0.0096	33	0	0.0107	33	0
	d : 100	30	0.0089	27	0	0.0098	31	0	0.0117	32	0
	$\|T\|$: 50	100	0.0084	26	0	0.0115	35	0	0.0161	52	0
Ad Hoc 5	$\|R\|$: 61	5	0.0067	39	0	0.0073	39	0	0.0069	39	0
	$\|O\|$: 21	10	0.0070	50	0	0.0072	50	0	0.0074	50	0
	$\|R_p\|$: 61	20	0.0071	59	0	0.0077	61	0	0.0080	66	0
	d : 100	30	0.0068	61	0	0.0080	73	0	0.0085	77	0
	$\|T\|$: 50	100	0.0048	66	0	0.0086	116	0	0.0104	136	0
Ad Hoc 6	$\|R\|$: 74	5	0.0179	16	3	0.0308	28	5	0.0234	20	5
	$\|O\|$: 17	10	0.0224	15	6	0.0354	29	8	0.0283	22	11
	$\|R_p\|$: 19	20	0.0253	18	6	0.0355	35	12	0.0336	31	12
	d : 55	30	0.0263	20	6	0.0365	38	11	0.0389	31	11
	$\|T\|$: 50	100	0.0136	25	0	0.0186	34	4	0.0288	41	4
Ad Hoc 7	$\|R\|$: 103	5	0.0011	4	0	0.0018	4	0	0.0012	4	0
	$\|O\|$: 42	10	0.0017	8	0	0.0022	8	0	0.0017	8	0
	$\|R_p\|$: 79	20	0.0021	13	0	0.0027	18	0	0.0022	13	0
	d : 100	30	0.0022	24	0	0.0029	28	0	0.0025	27	0
	$\|T\|$: 50	100	0.0025	40	0	0.0038	58	0	0.0038	53	0
Ad Hoc 8	$\|R\|$: 129	5	0.0036	11	8	0.0042	11	8	0.0038	11	8
	$\|O\|$: 41	10	0.0036	7	5	0.0043	9	7	0.0038	9	7
	$\|R_p\|$: 80	20	0.0035	6	1	0.0042	14	2	0.0038	7	2
	d : 100	30	0.0035	7	1	0.0042	10	1	0.0038	8	2
	$\|T\|$: 50	100	0.0030	26	6	0.0049	42	8	0.0043	38	7
Web 9	$\|R\|$: 104	5	0.0023	15	0	0.0031	15	0	0.0023	15	0
	$\|O\|$: 23	10	0.0022	17	0	0.0027	19	0	0.0025	19	0
	$\|R_p\|$: 64	20	0.0027	25	0	0.0027	21	0	0.0030	26	0
	d : 100	30	0.0027	41	0	0.0026	34	0	0.0034	43	0
	$\|T\|$: 50	100	0.0043	105	0	0.0036	109	1	0.0052	147	3
Web 2001	$\|R\|$: 97	5	0.0010	5	0	0.0015	5	0	0.0010	5	0
	$\|O\|$: 29	10	0.0016	9	0	0.0021	9	0	0.0016	9	0
	$\|R_p\|$: 61	20	0.0017	14	0	0.0021	17	0	0.0019	14	0
	d : 100	30	0.0018	26	0	0.0021	15	0	0.0022	27	0
	$\|T\|$: 50	100	0.0040	96	0	0.0026	63	0	0.0041	87	0
Web 2002	$\|R\|$: 69	5	0.0038	54	0	0.0038	54	0	0.0038	54	0
	$\|O\|$: 16	10	0.0045	76	0	0.0040	80	0	0.0049	80	0
	$\|R_p\|$: 69	20	0.0041	78	0	0.0039	78	0	0.0051	95	0
	d : 50	30	0.0044	106	0	0.0036	87	0	0.0052	120	0
	$\|T\|$: 50	100	0.0039	138	0	0.0024	92	0	0.0038	136	0
Genomics 2005	$\|R\|$: 62	5	0.0052	64	0	0.0054	69	0	0.0057	69	0
	$\|O\|$: 32	10	0.0063	111	0	0.0061	110	0	0.0073	117	0
	$\|R_p\|$: 58	20	0.0077	89	0	0.0066	80	0	0.0088	106	0
	d : 60	30	0.0084	106	0	0.0069	81	0	0.0100	139	0
	$\|T\|$: 49	100	0.0055	93	0	0.0049	93	0	0.0091	197	0
Robust 2005	$\|R\|$: 74	5	0.0179	16	3	0.0308	28	5	0.0234	20	5
	$\|O\|$: 17	10	0.0224	15	6	0.0354	29	8	0.0283	22	11
	$\|R_p\|$: 19	20	0.0253	18	6	0.0355	35	12	0.0336	31	12
	d : 55	30	0.0263	20	6	0.0365	38	11	0.0389	31	11
	$\|T\|$: 50	100	0.0136	25	0	0.0186	34	4	0.0288	41	4
Legal 2006	$\|R\|$: 34	5	0.0593	80	0	0.1146	135	11	0.1327	136	11
	$\|O\|$: 8	10	0.0572	94	15	0.1097	138	25	0.1440	139	25
	$\|R_p\|$: 23	20	0.0306	64	12	0.0813	128	24	0.0984	139	33
	d : 10	30	0.0219	63	1	0.0636	117	17	0.0750	130	30
	$\|T\|$: 39	100	0.0063	54	17	0.0224	101	33	0.0250	107	39
Medical 2011	$\|R\|$: 127	5	0.0267	142	0	0.0309	159	0	0.0464	261	0
	$\|O\|$: 29	10	0.0265	157	0	0.0377	219	1	0.0586	336	5
	$\|R_p\|$: 56	20	0.0224	152	0	0.0209	142	0	0.0326	206	2
	d : 10	30	0.0201	153	0	0.0153	121	0	0.0229	174	0
	$\|T\|$: 34	100	0.0092	176	8	0.0054	97	0	0.0078	149	0
Microblog 2011	$\|R\|$: 184	5	0.0053	101	14	0.0056	101	14	0.0053	101	14
	$\|O\|$: 58	10	0.0060	183	57	0.0063	183	57	0.0062	183	57
	$\|R_p\|$: 119	20	0.0065	217	68	0.0065	217	64	0.0067	217	68
	d : 30	30	0.0069	272	77	0.0070	256	76	0.0076	294	95
	$\|T\|$: 49	100	0.0022	156	12	0.0022	143	13	0.0024	159	14
	top performer		46	35	20	18	23	2	0	0	0
	worst performer		2	3	1	26	18	1	44	33	12

with incomplete and biased judgements. In *Proc. of SIGIR*, 2007.

[6] B. Carterette. Robust test collections for retrieval evaluation. In *Proc. of SIGIR*, 2007.

[7] B. Carterette, J. Allan, and R. Sitaraman. Minimal test collections for retrieval evaluation. In *Proc. of SIGIR*, 2006.

[8] B. Carterette, V. Pavlu, E. Kanoulas, J. A. Aslam, and J. Allan. Evaluation over thousands of queries. In *Proc. of SIGIR*, 2008.

[9] B. A. Carterette. Multiple testing in statistical analysis of systems-based information retrieval experiments. *ACM Trans. Inf. Syst.*, 30(1), Mar. 2012.

[10] C. L. A. Clarke and M. D. Smucker. Time well spent. In *Proc. of IIiX*, 2014.

[11] G. V. Cormack, C. R. Palmer, and C. L. A. Clarke. Efficient construction of large test collections. In *Proc. of SIGIR*, 1998.

[12] C. Hauff and F. de Jong. Retrieval system evaluation: Automatic evaluation versus incomplete judgments. In *Proc. of SIGIR*, 2010.

[13] K. Kuriyama, N. Kando, T. Nozue, and K. Eguchi. Pooling for a large-scale test collection: An analysis of the search results from the first NTCIR workshop. *Inf. Ret.*, 5(1), 2002.

[14] W.-H. Lin and A. Hauptmann. Revisiting the Effect of Topic Set Size on Retrieval Error. In *Proc. of SIGIR*, 2005.

[15] A. Moffat, W. Webber, and J. Zobel. Strategic system comparisons via targeted relevance judgments. In *Proc. of SIGIR*, 2007.

[16] A. Moffat and J. Zobel. Rank-biased precision for measurement of retrieval effectiveness. *ACM Trans. Inf. Syst.*, 27(1), Dec. 2008.

[17] T. Sakai. Alternatives to bpref. In *Proc. of SIGIR*, 2007.

[18] T. Sakai and N. Kando. On information retrieval metrics designed for evaluation with incomplete relevance assessments. *Inf. Ret.*, 11(5), 2008.

[19] M. Sanderson and J. Zobel. Information retrieval system evaluation: Effort, sensitivity, and reliability. In *Proc. of SIGIR*, 2005.

[20] J. Urbano, M. Marrero, and D. Martín. On the measurement of test collection reliability. In *Proc. of SIGIR*, 2013.

[21] E. M. Voorhees. Topic set size redux. In *Proc. of SIGIR*, 2009.

[22] E. M. Voorhees and C. Buckley. The effect of topic set size on retrieval experiment error. In *Proc. of SIGIR*, 2002.

[23] W. Webber and L. A. F. Park. Score adjustment for correction of pooling bias. In *Proc. of SIGIR*, 2009.

[24] E. Yilmaz and J. A. Aslam. Estimating average precision with incomplete and imperfect judgments. In *Proc. of SIGIR*, 2006.

[25] E. Yilmaz, E. Kanoulas, and J. A. Aslam. A simple and efficient sampling method for estimating AP and NDCG. In *Proc. of SIGIR*, 2008.

[26] J. Zobel. How reliable are the results of large-scale information retrieval experiments? In *Proc. of SIGIR*, 1998.

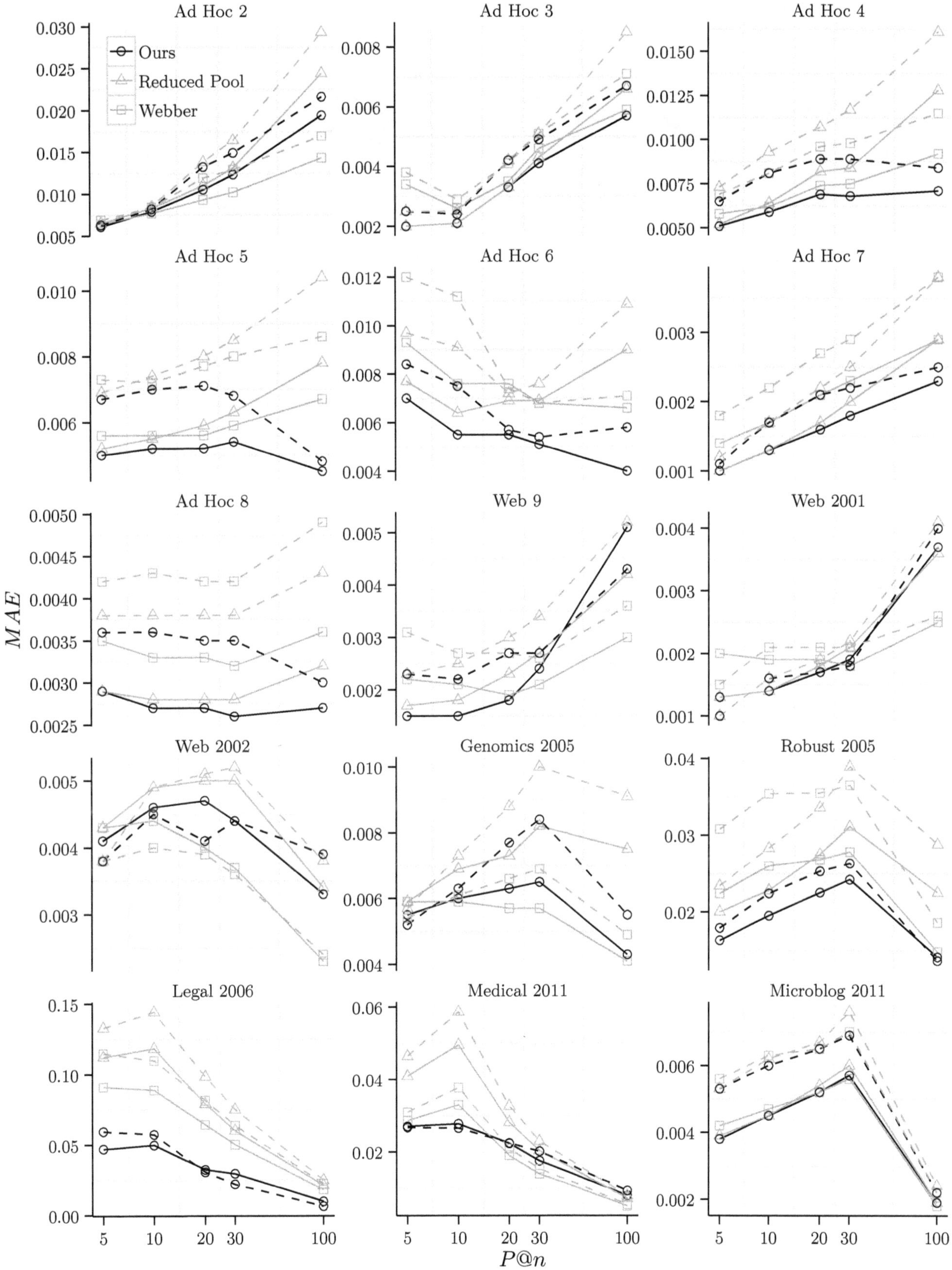

Figure 3: Plots per test collection of the Mean Absolute Error against the $P@n$ of the Reduced Pool and the two approaches, Ours and Webber, to correct pool bias. Generated using a leave-one-organization-out, using all the runs for the continuous lines and only the top 75% for the dashed lines. Our approach uses as indicator λ and $\alpha = 1$.

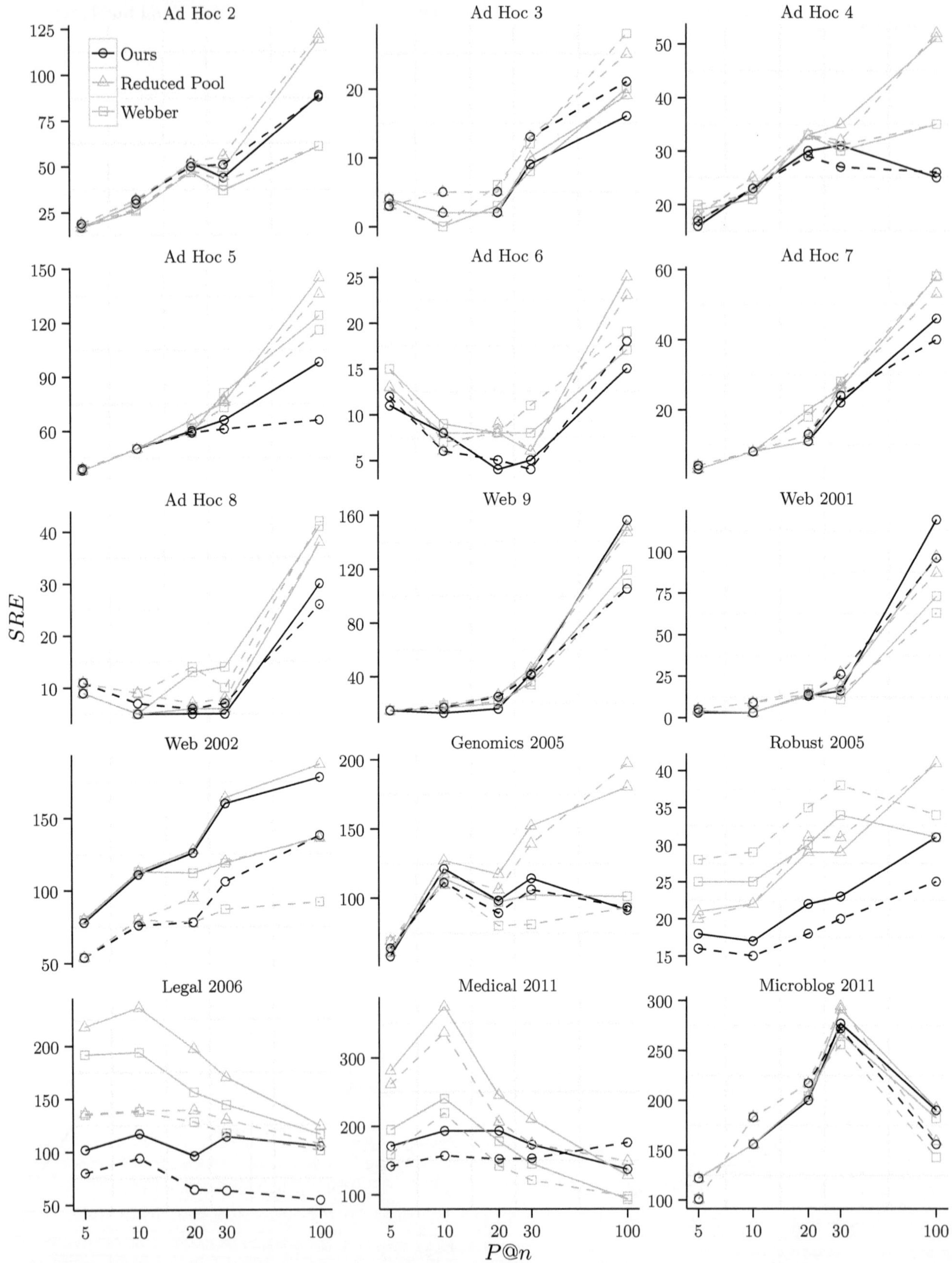

Figure 4: Plots per test collection of the System Rank Error against the $P@n$ of the Reduced Pool and the two approaches, Ours and Webber, to correct pool bias. Generated using a leave-one-organization-out, using all the runs for the continuous lines and only the top 75% for the dashed lines. Our approach uses as indicator λ and $\alpha = 1$.

Learning Maximal Marginal Relevance Model via Directly Optimizing Diversity Evaluation Measures

Long Xia Jun Xu Yanyan Lan Jiafeng Guo Xueqi Cheng
CAS Key Lab of Network Data Science and Technology,
Institute of Computing Technology, Chinese Academy of Sciences
xialong@software.ict.ac.cn, {junxu, lanyanyan, guojiafeng, cxq}@ict.ac.cn

ABSTRACT

In this paper we address the issue of learning a ranking model for search result diversification. In the task, a model concerns with both query-document relevance and document diversity is automatically created with training data. Ideally a diverse ranking model would be designed to meet the criterion of maximal marginal relevance, for selecting documents that have the least similarity to previously selected documents. Also, an ideal learning algorithm for diverse ranking would train a ranking model that could directly optimize the diversity evaluation measures with respect to the training data. Existing methods, however, either fail to model the marginal relevance, or train ranking models by minimizing loss functions that loosely related to the evaluation measures. To deal with the problem, we propose a novel learning algorithm under the framework of Perceptron, which adopts the ranking model that *maximizes marginal relevance at ranking and can optimize any diversity evaluation measure in training.* The algorithm, referred to as PAMM (Perceptron Algorithm using Measures as Margins), first constructs positive and negative diverse rankings for each training query, and then repeatedly adjusts the model parameters so that the margins between the positive and negative rankings are maximized. Experimental results on three benchmark datasets show that PAMM significantly outperforms the state-of-the-art baseline methods.

Categories and Subject Descriptors

H.3.3 [**Information Search and Retrieval**]: Information Search and Retrieval – *Retrieval Models*

General Terms

Algorithms

Keywords

search result diversification; maximal marginal relevance; directly optimizing evaluation measures

SIGIR'15, August 09 - 13, 2015, Santiago, Chile.
© 2015 ACM. ISBN 978-1-4503-3621-5/15/08 ...$15.00.
DOI: http://dx.doi.org/10.1145/2766462.2767710.

1. INTRODUCTION

It has been widely observed that users' information needs, described by keyword based queries, are often ambiguous or multi-faceted. It is important for commercial search engines to provide search results which balance query-document relevance and document diversity, called search result diversification [1, 30]. One of the key problems in search result diversification is ranking, specifically, how to develop a ranking model that can sort documents based on their relevance to the given query as well as the novelty of the information in the documents.

Methods for search result diversification can be categorized into heuristic approaches and learning approaches. The heuristic approaches construct diverse rankings with handcrafted ranking rules. As a representative method in the category, Carbonell and Goldstein [2] propose the maximal marginal relevance (MMR) criterion for guiding the construction ranking models. In MMR, constructing of a diverse ranking is formulated as a process of sequential document selection. At each iteration, the document with the highest marginal relevance is selected. The marginal relevance can be defined as, for example, a linear combination of the query-document relevance and the maximum distance of the document to the selected document set. A number of approaches have been proposed [8, 23, 24, 25] on the basis of the criterion and promising results have been achieved. User studies also shows that the user browsing behavior matches very well with the maximal marginal relevance criterion: usually users browse the web search results in a top-down manner, and perceive diverse information from each individual document based on what they have obtained in the preceding results [5]. Therefore, in a certain sense, we can say that maximal marginal relevance has been widely accepted as a criterion for guiding the construction of diverse ranking models.

Recently, machine learning approaches have been proposed for the task of search result diversification [14, 20, 22, 29, 31], especially the methods that can directly optimize evaluation measures on training data [16, 28]. Yue and Joachims [28] propose SVM-DIV which formulates the task as a problem of structured output prediction. In the model, the measure of subtopic diversity is directly optimized under the structural SVM framework. Liang et al. [16] propose to conduct personalized search result diversification via directly optimizing the measure of α-NDCG, also under the structural SVM framework. All of these methods try to resolve the mismatch between the objective function used in training and the final evaluation measure used in testing. Experimental results also showed that directly optimizing the diversity evaluation measures can indeed improve the diverse ranking performances [16, 28]. One problem with the direct optimization approaches is that it is hard, if not impossible, to define a ranking model that can meet the maximal marginal relevance criterion under the direct optimization framework.

In this paper, we aim to develop a new learning algorithm that utilizes the maximal marginal relevance model for ranking as well as can directly optimize any diversity evaluation measure in training. Inspired by the work of R-LTR [31] and Perceptron variations [7, 15], we propose a new algorithm for search result diversification, referred to as PAMM (Perceptron Algorithm using Measures as Margins). PAMM utilizes a sequential document selection process as its ranking model. In learning, it first generates positive rankings (ground truth rankings) and negative rankings for the training queries. It then repeats the process of estimating the probabilities for the rankings, calculating the margins between the positive rankings and negative rankings in terms of the ranking probabilities, and updating the model parameters so that the margins are maximized. We show that PAMM algorithm minimizes an upper bound of the loss function that directly defined over the diversity evaluation measures.

PAMM offers several advantages: 1) adopting the ranking model that meets the maximal marginal relevance criterion; 2) ability to directly optimize any diversity evaluation measure in training; 3) ability to use both positive rankings and negative rankings in training.

To evaluate the effectiveness of PAMM, we conducted extensive experiments on three public TREC benchmark datasets. The experimental results showed that our methods significantly outperform the state-of-the-art diverse ranking approaches including MMR, SVM-DIV, and R-LTR. We analyzed the results and showed that PAMM makes a good balance between the relevance and diversity via maximizing marginal relevance in ranking. We also showed that by directly optimizing a measure in training, PAMM can indeed enhance the ranking performances in terms of the measure.

The rest of the paper is organized as follows. After a summary of related work in Section 2, we describe the general framework of learning maximal marginal relevance model in Section 3. In Section 4 we discuss the proposed PAMM algorithm. Experimental results and discussions are given in Section 5. Section 6 concludes this paper and gives future work.

2. RELATED WORK

Methods of search result diversification can be categorized into heuristic approaches and learning approaches.

2.1 Heuristic approaches

It is a common practice to use heuristic rules to construct a diverse ranking list in search. Usually, the rules are created based on the observation that in diverse ranking a document's novelty depends on not only the document itself but also the documents ranked in previous positions. Carbonell and Goldstein [2] propose the maximal marginal relevance criterion to guide the design of diverse ranking models. The criterion is implemented with a process of iteratively selecting the documents from the candidate document set. At each iteration, the document with the highest marginal relevance score is selected, where the score is a linear combination of the query-document relevance and the maximum distance of the document to the documents in current result set. The marginal relevance score is then updated in the next iteration as the number of documents in the result set increases by one. More methods have been developed under the criterion. PM-2 [8] treats the problem of finding a diverse search result as finding a proportional representation for the document ranking. xQuAD [25] directly models different aspects underlying the original query in the form of sub-queries, and estimates the relevance of the retrieved documents to each identified sub-query. See also [3, 9, 10, 11, 21]

Heuristic approaches rely on the utility functions that can only use a limited number of ranking signals. Also, the parameter tuning cost is high, especially in complex search settings. In this paper, we propose a learning approach to construct diverse ranking models that can meet the maximal marginal relevance criterion.

2.2 Learning approaches

Methods of machine learning have been applied to search result diversification. In the approaches, rich features can be utilized and the parameters are automatically estimated from the training data. Some promising results have been obtained. For example, Zhu et al. [31] proposed the relational learning to rank model (R-LTR) in which the diverse ranking is constructed with a process of sequential document selection. The training of R-LTR amounts to optimizing the likelihood of ground truth rankings. More work please refer to [14, 20, 22, 29]. All these methods, however, formulate the learning problem as optimizing loss function that loosely related to diversity evaluation measures.

Recently methods that can directly optimize evaluation measures have been proposed and applied to search result diversification. Yue and Joachims [28] formulate the task of constructing a diverse ranking as a problem of predicting diverse subsets. Structural SVM framework is adopted to perform the training. Liang et al. [16] propose to conduct personalized search result diversification, also under the structural SVM framework. In the model, the loss function is defined based on the diversity evaluation measure of α-NDCG. Thus, the algorithm can be considered as directly optimizing α-NDCG in training. One issue with the approach is that it is hard to learn a maximal marginal relevance model under the structural SVM framework.

In this paper, we propose a Perceptron algorithm that can learn a maximal marginal relevance model, at the same time directly optimizing diversity evaluation measures.

3. LEARNING MAXIMAL MARGINAL RELEVANCE MODEL

We first describe the general framework of learning maximal marginal relevance model for search result diversification.

3.1 Maximal marginal relevance model

Suppose that we are given a query q, which is associated with a set of retrieved documents $X = \{\mathbf{x}_1, \cdots, \mathbf{x}_M\}$, where each document $\mathbf{x}_i$ is represented as a D-dimensional relevance feature vector. Let $R = \mathcal{R}^{M\times M\times K}$ denotes a 3-way tensor representing relationship among the M documents, where R_{ijk} stands for the k-th relationship feature of document $\mathbf{x}_i$ and document $\mathbf{x}_j$.

Algorithm 1 Ranking via maximizing marginal relevance

Input: documents X, document relation R, and ranking model parameters ω_r and ω_d

Output: ranking $\mathbf{y}$

1: $S_0 \leftarrow \phi$

2: **for** $r = 1, \cdots, M$ **do**

3: $\quad y(r) \leftarrow \arg\max_{j:\mathbf{x}_j \in X \backslash S_{r-1}} f_{S_{r-1}}(\mathbf{x}_j, R_j)$

4: $\quad S_r \leftarrow S_{r-1} \cup \{\mathbf{x}_{y(r)}\}$

5: **end for**

6: **return** $\mathbf{y}$

The maximal marginal relevance model creates a diverse ranking over X with a process of sequential document selection. At each step, the document with the highest marginal relevance is selected and added to the tail of the list [31]. Specifically, let $S \subseteq X$ be the set of documents have been selected for query q at one of the document selection step. Given S, the marginal relevance score of each document $\mathbf{x}_i \in X \backslash S$ at current step is defined as a linear combination of the query-document relevance and diversity of the document to the documents in S:

$$f_S(\mathbf{x}_i, R_i) = \omega_r^T \mathbf{x}_i + \omega_d^T h_S(R_i), \tag{1}$$

where $\mathbf{x}_i$ denotes the relevance feature vector of the document, $R_i \in \mathcal{R}^{M \times K}$ is the matrix representation of the relationship between document $\mathbf{x}_i$ and the other documents (note that $R_{ij} \in \mathcal{R}^K$ denotes the relationship feature vector of document pair $(\mathbf{x}_i, \mathbf{x}_j)$), and ω_r and ω_d are the weights for the relevance features and diversity features, respectively. The first term in Equation (1) represents the relevance of document $\mathbf{x}_i$ to the query and the second term represents the diversity of $\mathbf{x}_i$ w.r.t. documents in S. Following the practice in [31], the relational function $h_S(R_i)$ is defined as the minimal distance:

$$h_S(R_i) = \left(\min_{\mathbf{x}_j \in S} R_{ij1}, \cdots, \min_{\mathbf{x}_j \in S} R_{ijK} \right).$$

According to the maximal marginal relevance criterion, sequential document selection process can be used to create a diverse ranking, as shown in Algorithm 1. Specifically, given a query q, the retrieved documents X, and document relationship R, the algorithm initializes S_0 as an empty set. It then iteratively selects the documents from the candidate set. At iteration r ($r = 1, \cdots, M$), the document with the maximal marginal relevance score $f_{S_{r-1}}$ is selected and ranked at position r. At the same time, the selected document is inserted to S_{r-1}.

3.2 Learning the ranking model

Machine learning approaches can be used to learn the maximal marginal relevance model. Suppose we are given N labeled training queries $\{(X^{(n)}, R^{(n)}, J^{(n)})\}_{n=1}^N$, where $J^{(n)}$ denotes the human labels on the documents, in the form of a binary matrix. $J^{(n)}(i, s) = 1$ if document $\mathbf{x}_i^{(n)}$ contains the s-th subtopic of q_n and 0 otherwise[1]. The learning process, thus, amounts to minimize the loss over all of the training queries:

$$\min_{\omega_r, \omega_d} \sum_{n=1}^N L\left(\hat{\mathbf{y}}^{(n)}, J^{(n)}\right), \tag{2}$$

[1]Some datasets also use graded judgements. In this paper, we assume that all labels are binary.

Table 1: Summary of notations.

Notations	Explanations
q	query
$X = \{\mathbf{x}_1, \cdots, \mathbf{x}_M\}$	list of documents for q
$\mathbf{x}_i \in \mathcal{R}^D$	document relevant feature vector
$R \in \mathcal{R}^{M \times M \times K}$	relationship tensor among M documents
$\mathcal{Y}$	set of rankings over documents
$\mathbf{y} \in \mathcal{Y}$	the ranking of documents
$y(t) \in \{1, \cdots, M\}$	index of the document ranked at t
$S_r \subseteq X$	selected documents before iteration r
$f_S(\mathbf{x}_i, R_i)$	the scoring function at each step
$h_S(R_i)$	the relational function on R_i
ω_d	weights for relevance features
ω_r	weights for diversity features
J	human labels on document subtopics
$E(X, \mathbf{y}, J) \in [0, 1]$	diversity evaluation measure

where $\hat{\mathbf{y}}^{(n)}$ is the ranking constructed by the maximal marginal relevance model (Algorithm 1) for documents $X^{(n)}$, and $L(\hat{\mathbf{y}}^{(n)}, J^{(n)})$ is the function for judging the 'loss' of the predicted ranking $\mathbf{y}^{(n)}$ compared with the human labels $J^{(n)}$.

3.3 Diversity evaluation measures

In search result diversification, query level evaluation measures are used to evaluate the 'goodness' of a ranking model. These measures include α-NDCG [5], ERR-IA [4], and NRBP [6] etc. We utilize a general function $E(X, \mathbf{y}, J) \in [0, 1]$ to represent the evaluation measures. The first argument of E is the set of candidate documents, the second argument is a ranking $\mathbf{y}$ over documents in X, and the third argument is the human judgements. E measures the agreement between $\mathbf{y}$ and J.

As an example of diversity evaluation measures, α-NDCG [5] is a variation of NDCG [13] in which the newly found subtopics are rewarded and redundant subtopics are penalized. The α-NDCG score at rank k can be defined by replacing the raw gain values in standard NDCG@k with novelty-baised gains:

$$\alpha\text{-NDCG@}k = \frac{\sum_{r=1}^k NG(r)/\log(r+1)}{\sum_{r=1}^k NG^*(r)/\log(r+1)}, \tag{3}$$

where $NG(r) = \sum_s J(y(r), s)(1-\alpha)^{C_s(r-1)}$ is the novelty-biased gain at rank r in ranking $\mathbf{y}$, $C_s(r-1) = \sum_{k=1}^{r-1} J(y(k), s)$ denotes the number of documents observed within top $r-1$ that contain the s-th subtopic, $NG^*(r)$ is the novelty-biased gain at rank r in a positive ranking, and $y(k)$ denotes the index of the document ranked at k. Usually the parameter α is set to 0.5.

ERR-IA [4] is another popular used diversity evaluation measure. Given a query with several different subtopics s, the probability of each intent $\Pr(s|q)$ can be estimated, where $\sum_s \Pr(s|q) = 1$. The intent-aware ERR at rank k can be computed as:

$$\text{ERR-IA@}k = \sum_s \Pr(s|q)\text{ERR@}k(s), \tag{4}$$

where ERR@$k(s)$ is the expected reciprocal rank score at k in terms of subtopic s.

Table 1 gives a summary of the notations described above.

4. OUR APPROACH: PAMM

4.1 Evaluation measure as loss function

We aim to maximize the diverse ranking accuracy in terms of a diversity evaluation measure on the training data. Thus, the loss function in Equation (2) becomes

$$\sum_{n=1}^{N}\left(1-E(X^{(n)},\hat{\mathbf{y}}^{(n)},J^{(n)})\right). \quad (5)$$

It is difficult to directly optimize the loss as E is a non-convex function.

We resort to optimize the upper bound of the loss function under the framework of structured output prediction. According to Theorem (2) in [27], we know that the loss function defined in Equation (5) can be upper bounded by the function defined over the ranking pairs:

$$\sum_{n=1}^{N}\max_{\substack{\mathbf{y}^{+}\in\mathcal{Y}^{+(n)};\\ \mathbf{y}^{-}\in\mathcal{Y}^{-(n)}}}\left(E(X^{(n)},\mathbf{y}^{+},J^{(n)})-E(X^{(n)},\mathbf{y}^{-},J^{(n)})\right)\cdot$$
$$\left[\!\left[F(\mathbf{y}^{+},X^{(n)},R^{(n)})\leq F(\mathbf{y}^{-},X^{(n)},R^{(n)})\right]\!\right], \quad (6)$$

where $\mathcal{Y}^{+(n)}$ is the set of all possible 'positive' rankings (rankings whose α-NDCG/ERR-IA equals to one) for the n-th query, $\mathcal{Y}^{-(n)}$ is the set of all possible 'negative' rankings (rankings whose α-NDCG/ERR-IA is less than one) for the n-the query, $[\![\cdot]\!]$ is one if the condition is satisfied otherwise zero, and $F(X,R,\mathbf{y})$ is the query level ranking model. F takes the document set X, document relationship R, and ranking over the document $\mathbf{y}$ as inputs. The output of F is the confidence score of the ranking $\mathbf{y}$. The predicted $\hat{\mathbf{y}}^{(n)}$ in Equation (5) can be considered as the ranking that maximizes F:

$$\hat{\mathbf{y}}^{(n)}=\arg\max_{\mathbf{y}\in\mathcal{Y}^{(n)}}F(X^{(n)},R^{(n)},\mathbf{y}), \quad (7)$$

where $\mathcal{Y}^{(n)}$ is the set of all possible rankings over $X^{(n)}$. Here F is defined as the probability of generating the ranking list $\mathbf{y}$ with a process of iteratively selecting the top ranked documents from the remaining documents, and using the marginal relevance function f_S in Equation (1) as the selection criterion:

$$\begin{aligned}F(X,R,\mathbf{y})=&\Pr(\mathbf{y}|X,R)\\=&\Pr(\mathbf{x}_{y(1)}\cdots\mathbf{x}_{y(M)}|X,R)\\=&\prod_{r=1}^{M-1}\Pr(\mathbf{x}_{y(r)}|X,S_{r-1},R)\\=&\prod_{r=1}^{M-1}\frac{\exp\{f_{S_{r-1}}(\mathbf{x}_i,R_{y(r)})\}}{\sum_{k=r}^{M}\exp\{f_{S_{r-1}}(\mathbf{x}_i,R_{y(k)})\}}\end{aligned} \quad (8)$$

where $y(r)$ denotes the index of the document ranked at the r-th position in $\mathbf{y}$, $S_{r-1}=\{\mathbf{x}_{y(k)}\}_{k=1}^{r-1}$ is the documents ranked at the top $r-1$ positions in $\mathbf{y}$, $f_{S_{r-1}}(\mathbf{x}_i,R_i)$ is the marginal relevance score of document $\mathbf{x}_i$ w.r.t. the selected documents in S_{r-1}, and $S_0=\phi$ is an empty set. With the definition of F, it is obvious that the maximal marginal relevance process of Algorithm 1 actually greedily searches the solution for optimizing the problem of Equation (7).

To conduct the optimization under the Perceptron framework, the upper bound of Equation (6) is further relaxed, by replacing the max with sum and moving the term $(E(X^{(n)},\mathbf{y}^{+},J^{(n)})-E(X^{(n)},\mathbf{y}^{-},J^{(n)}))$ into $[\![\cdot]\!]$ as margin. The upper bound of Equation (6) becomes:

$$\sum_{n=1}^{N}\sum_{\mathbf{y}^{+};\mathbf{y}^{-}}\left[\!\left[F(X^{(n)},R^{(n)},\mathbf{y}^{+})-F(X^{(n)},R^{(n)},\mathbf{y}^{-})\leq\right.\right.$$
$$\left.\left.E(X^{(n)},\mathbf{y}^{+},J^{(n)})-E(X^{(n)},\mathbf{y}^{-},J^{(n)})\right]\!\right]. \quad (9)$$

This is because $\sum_i x_i\geq\max_i x_i$ if $x_i\geq 0$ holds for all i, and $[\![x-y\leq z]\!]\geq z\cdot[\![x\leq y]\!]$ holds if $z\in[0,1]$. Please note that we assume $E(X,\mathbf{y}^{+},J)\in[0,1]$ and thus we have $(E(X^{(n)},\mathbf{y}^{+},J^{(n)})-E(X^{(n)},\mathbf{y}^{-},J^{(n)}))\in[0,1]$ because $E(X^{(n)},\mathbf{y}^{+},J^{(n)})>E(X^{(n)},\mathbf{y}^{-},J^{(n)})$.

4.2 Direct optimization with Perceptron

The loss function in Equation (9) can be optimized under the framework of Perceptron. In this paper, inspired by the work of structured Perceptron [7] and Perceptron algorithm with uneven margins [15], we have developed a novel learning algorithm to optimize the loss function in Equation (9). The algorithm is referred to as PAMM and is shown in Algorithm 2.

PAMM takes a training set $\{(X^{(n)},R^{(n)},J^{(n)})\}_{n=1}^{N}$ as input and takes the diversity evaluation measure E, learning rate η, number of positive rankings per query τ^{+}, and number of negative rankings per query τ^{-} as parameters. For each query q_n, PAMM first generates τ^{+} positive rankings $PR^{(n)}$ and τ^{-} negative rankings $NR^{(n)}$ (line (2) and line (3)). $PR^{(n)}$ and $NR^{(n)}$ play as the random samples of $\mathcal{Y}^{+(n)}$ and $\mathcal{Y}^{-(n)}$, respectively. PAMM then optimizes the model parameters ω_r and ω_d iteratively in a stochastic manner over the ranking pairs: at each round, for each pair between a positive ranking and a negative ranking $(\mathbf{y}^{+},\mathbf{y}^{-})$, the gap of these two rankings in terms of the query level ranking model $\Delta F=F(X,R,\mathbf{y}^{+})-F(X,R,\mathbf{y}^{-})$ is calculated based on current parameters ω_r and ω_d (line (9)). If ΔF is smaller than the margin in terms of evaluation measure $\Delta E=E(X,\mathbf{y}^{+},J)-E(X,\mathbf{y}^{-},J)$ (line (10)), the model parameters will be updated so that ΔF will be enlarged (line (11) and line (12)). The iteration continues until convergence. Finally, PAMM outputs the optimized model parameters (ω_r,ω_d).

Next, we will explain the key steps of PAMM in detail.

4.2.1 Generating positive and negative rankings

In PAMM, it is hard to directly conduct the optimization over the sets of positive rankings $\mathcal{Y}^{+(n)}$ and negative rankings $\mathcal{Y}^{-(n)}$, because in total these two sets have $M!$ rankings if the candidate set contains M documents. Thus, PAMM samples the rankings to reduce the training time.

For each training query, PAMM first samples a set of positive rankings. Algorithm 3 illustrates the procedure. Similar to the online ranking algorithm shown in Algorithm 1, the positive rankings are generated with a sequential document selection process and the selection criteria is the diversity evaluation measure E. After generating the first positive ranking $\mathbf{y}^{(1)}$, the algorithm constructs other positive rankings based on $\mathbf{y}^{(1)}$, by randomly swapping the positions of two documents whose subtopic coverage are identical.

For each training query, PAMM also samples a set of negative rankings. Algorithm 4 shows the procedure. The algorithm simply generates random rankings iteratively. If the generated ranking is not a positive ranking and satisfies the

Algorithm 2 The PAMM Algorithm

Input: training data $\{(X^{(n)}, R^{(n)}, J^{(n)})\}_{n=1}^{N}$, learning rate η, diversity evaluation measure E, number of positive rankings per query τ^+, number of negative rankings per query τ^-.
Output: model parameters (ω_r, ω_d)

1: **for** $n = 1$ **to** N **do**
2: $\quad PR^{(n)} \leftarrow$PositiveRankings$(X^{(n)}, J^{(n)}, E, \tau^+)$ {Algorithm 3}
3: $\quad NR^{(n)} \leftarrow$NegativeRankings$(X^{(n)}, J^{(n)}, E, \tau^-)$ {Algorithm 4}
4: **end for**
5: initialize $\{\omega_r, \omega_d\} \leftarrow$ random values in $[0, 1]$
6: **repeat**
7: $\quad$ **for** $n = 1$ **to** N **do**
8: $\quad\quad$ **for all** $\{\mathbf{y}^+, \mathbf{y}^-\} \in PR^{(n)} \times NR^{(n)}$ **do**
9: $\quad\quad\quad \Delta F \leftarrow F(X^{(n)}, R^{(n)}, \mathbf{y}^+) - F(X^{(n)}, R^{(n)}, \mathbf{y}^-)$ {$F(X, R, \mathbf{y})$ is defined in Equation (8)}
10: $\quad\quad\quad$ **if** $\Delta F \leq E(X^{(n)}, \mathbf{y}^+, J^{(n)}) - E(X^{(n)}, \mathbf{y}^-, J^{(n)})$ **then**
11: $\quad\quad\quad\quad$ calculate $\nabla\omega_r^{(n)}$ and $\nabla\omega_d^{(n)}$ {Equation (10) and Equation (11)}
12: $\quad\quad\quad\quad (\omega_r, \omega_d) \leftarrow (\omega_r, \omega_d) + \eta \times (\nabla\omega_r^{(n)}, \nabla\omega_d^{(n)})$
13: $\quad\quad\quad$ **end if**
14: $\quad\quad$ **end for**
15: $\quad$ **end for**
16: **until** convergence
17: **return** (ω_r, ω_d)

Algorithm 3 PositiveRankings

Input: documents X, diversity labels J, evaluation measure E, and the number of positive rankings τ^+
Output: positive rankings PR

for $r = 1$ **to** $|X|$ **do**
$\quad y^{(1)}(r) \leftarrow \arg\max_{j:\mathbf{x}_j \in X \backslash S_{r-1}} E\left(S_{r-1} \cup \{\mathbf{x}_j\}, \left(y^{(1)}(1), \cdots, y^{(1)}(r-1), j\right), J\right)$
$\quad S_r \leftarrow S_{r-1} \cup \{\mathbf{x}_{y^{(1)}(r)}\}$
end for
$PR \leftarrow \{\mathbf{y}^{(1)}\}$
while $|PR| < \tau^+$ **do**
$\quad \mathbf{y} \leftarrow \mathbf{y}^{(1)}$
$\quad (k, l) \leftarrow$ randomly choose two documents whose human labels are identical, i.e., $J(y(k)) = J(y^{(1)}(l))$
$\quad y(k) \leftrightarrow y(l)$ {swap documents at rank k and l}
$\quad$ **if** $\mathbf{y} \notin PR$ **then**
$\quad\quad PR \leftarrow PR \cup \{\mathbf{y}\}$
$\quad$ **end if**
end while
return PR

Algorithm 4 NegativeRankings

Input: documents X, diversity labels J, evaluation measure E, and number of negative rankings τ^-
Output: NR

$NR = \phi$
while $|NR| < \tau^-$ **do**
$\quad \mathbf{y} \leftarrow$ random shuffle $(1, \cdots, |X|)$
$\quad$ **if** $\mathbf{y} \notin NR$ **and** $E(X, \mathbf{y}, J)$ is as expected **then**
$\quad\quad NR \leftarrow NR \cup \{\mathbf{y}\}$
$\quad$ **end if**
end while
return NR

user predefined constraints (e.g, α-NDCG@20 ≤ 0.8), the ranking will be added into the ranking set NR.

Please note that in some extreme cases Algorithm 3 and Algorithm 4 cannot create enough rankings. In our implementations, the algorithms are forced to return after running enough iterations.

4.2.2 *Updating ω_r and ω_d*

Given a ranking pair $(\mathbf{y}^+, \mathbf{y}^-) \in PR^{(n)} \times NR^{(n)}$, PAMM updates ω_r and ω_d as

$$\omega_r \leftarrow \omega_r + \eta \times \nabla\omega_r \text{ and } \omega_d \leftarrow \omega_d + \eta \times \nabla\omega_d,$$

if $F(X, R, \mathbf{y}^+) - F(X, R, \mathbf{y}^-) \leq E(X, \mathbf{y}^+, J) - E(X, \mathbf{y}^-, J)$. The goal of the update is to enlarge the margin between $\mathbf{y}^+$ and $\mathbf{y}^-$ in terms of query level model: $\Delta F = F(X, R, \mathbf{y}^+) - F(X, R, \mathbf{y}^-)$. For convenience of calculation, we resort to the problem of

$$\max_{\omega_r, \omega_d} \log \frac{F(X, R, \mathbf{y}^+)}{F(X, R, \mathbf{y}^-)},$$

because $F(X, R, \mathbf{y}) > 0$ and $\log(\cdot)$ is a monotonous increasing function. Thus, $\nabla\omega_r$ can be calculated as the gradient:

$$\begin{aligned}\nabla\omega_r =& \frac{\partial \log \frac{F(X,R,\mathbf{y}^+)}{F(X,R,\mathbf{y}^-)}}{\partial\omega_r} \\ =& \frac{\partial \log F(X, R, \mathbf{y}^+)}{\partial\omega_r} - \frac{\partial \log F(X, R, \mathbf{y}^-)}{\partial\omega_r},\end{aligned} \quad (10)$$

where

$$\frac{\partial \log F(X, R, \mathbf{y})}{\partial\omega_r} = \frac{\partial \sum_{j=1}^{|X|-1} \log \Pr(\mathbf{x}_{y(j)} | X \backslash S_{j-1}, R)}{\partial\omega_r}$$
$$= \sum_{j=1}^{|X|-1} \left\{ \mathbf{x}_{y(j)} - \frac{\sum_{k=j}^{|X|} \mathbf{x}_{y(k)} \exp\{f_{S_{j-1}}(\mathbf{x}_{y(k)}, R_{y(k)})\}}{\sum_{k=j}^{|X|} \exp\{f_{S_{j-1}}(\mathbf{x}_{y(k)}, R_{y(k)})\}} \right\}.$$

Similarly, $\nabla\omega_d$ can be calculated as

$$\nabla\omega_d = \frac{\partial \log F(X, R, \mathbf{y}^+)}{\partial\omega_d} - \frac{\partial \log F(X, R, \mathbf{y}^-)}{\partial\omega_d}, \quad (11)$$

where

$$\frac{\partial \log F(X, R, \mathbf{y})}{\partial\omega_d} = \sum_{j=1}^{|X|-1} \left\{ h_{S_{j-1}}(R_{y(j)}) - \frac{\sum_{k=j}^{|X|} h_{S_{j-1}}(R_{y(k)}) \exp\{f_{S_{j-1}}(\mathbf{x}_{y(k)}, R_{y(k)})\}}{\sum_{k=j}^{|X|} \exp\{f_{S_{j-1}}(\mathbf{x}_{y(k)}, R_{y(k)})\}} \right\}.$$

Intuitively, the gradients $\nabla\omega_r$ and $\nabla\omega_d$ are calculated so that the line 12 of Algorithm 2 will increase $F(X, R, \mathbf{y}^+)$ and decrease $F(X, R, \mathbf{y}^-)$.

4.3 Analysis

We analyzed time complexity of PAMM. The learning process of PAMM (Algorithm 2) is of order $\mathcal{O}(T \cdot N \cdot \tau^+ \cdot \tau^- \cdot$

Table 2: **Statistics on WT2009, WT2010 and WT2011.**

Dataset	#queries	#labeled docs	#subtopics per query
WT2009	50	5149	$3 \sim 8$
WT2010	48	6554	$3 \sim 7$
WT2011	50	5000	$2 \sim 6$

$M^2 \cdot (D + K))$, where T denotes the number of iterations, N the number of queries in training data, τ^+ the number of positive rankings per query, τ^- the number of negative rankings per query, M the maximum number of documents for queries in training data, D the number of relevance features, and K the number of diversity features. The time complexity of online ranking prediction (Algorithm 1) is of order $\mathcal{O}(M^2(D + K))$.

PAMM is a simple yet powerful learning algorithm for search result diversification. It has several advantages compared with the existing learning methods such as R-LTR [31], SVM-DIV [28], and structural SVM [26].

First, PAMM employs a more reasonable ranking model. The model follows the maximal marginal relevance criterion and can be implemented with a process of sequential document selection. In contrast, structural SVM approaches [26] calculate all of the ranking scores within a single step, as that of in relevance ranking. The marginal relevance of each document cannot be taken into consideration at ranking time.

Second, PAMM can incorporate any diversity evaluation measure in training, which makes the algorithm focus on the specified measure when updating the model parameters. In contrast, R-LTR only minimizes loss function that is loosely related to diversity evaluation measures and SVM-DIV is trained to optimize the subtopic coverage.

Third, PAMM utilizes the pairs between the positive rankings and the negative rankings in training, which makes it possible to leverage more information in training. Specifically, it enables PAMM algorithm to enlarge the margins between the positive rankings and negative rankings when updating the parameters. In contrast, R-LTR only uses the information in the positive rankings and the training is aimed to maximizing the likelihood.

5. EXPERIMENTAL RESULTS

5.1 Experiment setting

We conducted experiments to test the performances of PAMM using three TREC benchmark datasets for diversity tasks: TREC 2009 Web Track (WT2009), TREC 2010 Web Track (WT2010), and TREC 2011 Web Track (WT2011). Each dataset consists of queries, corresponding retrieved documents, and human judged labels. Each query includes several subtopics identified by TREC assessors. The document relevance labels were made at the subtopic level and the labels are binary[2]. Statistics on the datasets are given in Table 2.

All the experiments were carried out on the ClueWeb09 Category B data collection[3], which comprises of 50 million English web documents. Porter stemming, tokenization, and stop-words removal (using the INQUERY list) were applied to the documents as preprocessing. We conducted 5-fold cross-validation experiments on the three datasets. For each dataset, we randomly split the queries into five even subsets. At each fold three subsets were used for training, one was used for validation, and one was used for testing. The results reported were the average over the five trials.

As for evaluation measures, α-NDCG@k (Equation (3)) with $\alpha = 0.5$ and $k = 20$ is used. We also used ERR-IA@k (Equation (4)) with $k = 20$ to evaluate the performances.

We compared PAMM with several types of baselines. The baselines include the conventional relevance ranking models in which document diversity is not taken into consideration.

Query likelihood (QL) [18] language models for information retrieval.

ListMLE [17] a representative learning-to-rank model for information retrieval.

We also compared PAMM with three heuristic approaches to search result diversification in the experiments.

MMR [2] a heuristic approach to search result diversification in which the document ranking is constructed via iteratively selecting the document with the maximal marginal relevance.

xQuAD [25] a representative heuristic approach to search result diversification.

PM-2 [8] another widely used heuristic approach to search result diversification.

Please note that these three baselines require a prior relevance function to implement their diversification steps. In our experiments, ListMLE was chosen as the relevance function.

Learning approaches to search result diversification are also used as baselines in the experiments.

SVM-DIV [28] a representative learning approach to search result diversification. It utilizes structural SVMs to optimize the subtopic coverage. SVM-DIV does not consider relevance. For fair performance comparison, in the baseline, we first apply ListMLE to capture relevance, and then apply SVM-DIV to re-rank the top-K retrieved documents.

Structural SVM [26] Structural SVM can be configured to directly optimize diversity evaluation measures, as shown in [16]. In the paper, we used structural SVM to optimize α-NDCG@20 and ERR-IA@20, denoted as StructSVM(α-NDCG) and StructSVM(ERR-IA), respectively.

R-LTR [31] a state-of-the-art learning approach to search result diversification. The ranking function is a linear combination of the relevance score and diversity score between the current document and those previously selected. Following the practice in [31], in our experiments we used the results of R-LTR$_{min}$ which defines the relation function $h_S(R)$ as the minimal distance.

5.2 Features

As for features, we adopted the features used in the work of R-LTR [31]. There are two types of features: the relevance features which capture the relevance information of a query with respect to a document, and the diversity features which represent the relation information among documents. Table 3 and Table 4 list the relevance features and diversity features used in the experiments, respectively.

[2]WT2011 has graded judgements. In this paper we treat them as binary.
[3]http://boston.lti.cs.cmu.edu/data/clueweb09

[4]http://www.dmoz.org

Table 3: Relevance features used in the experiments. The first 4 lines are query-document matching features, each applied to the fields of body, anchor, title, URL, and the whole documents. The latter 3 lines are document quality features. [31]

Name	Description	# Features
TF-IDF	The tf-idf model	5
BM25	BM25 with default parameters	5
LMIR	LMIR with Dirichlet smoothing	5
MRF[19]	MRF with ordered/unordered phrase	10
PageRank	PageRank score	1
#inlinks	number of inlinks	1
#outlinks	number of outlinks	1

Table 4: The seven diversity features used in the experiments. Each feature is extracted over two documents. [31]

Name	Description
Subtopic Diversity	Euclidean distance based on PLSA[12]
Text Diversity	Cosine-based distance on term vectors
Title Diversity	Text diversity on title
Anchor Text Diversity	Text diversity on anchor
ODP-Based Diversity	ODP[4] taxonomy-based distance
Link-Based Diversity	Link similarity of document pair
URL-Based Diversity	URL similarity of document pair

5.3 Experiments with TREC datasets

In the experiments, we made use of the benchmark datasets of WT2009, WT2010, and WT2011 from the TREC Web Track, to test the performances of PAMM.

PAMM has to tune some parameters. The learning rate parameter η was tuned based on the validation set during each experiment. In all of the experiments in this subsection, we set the number of positive rankings per query $\tau^+ = 5$, and number of negative rankings per query $\tau^- = 20$. As for the parameter E of PAMM, α-NDCG@20 and ERR-IA@20 were utilized. The results for PAMM using α-NDCG@20 in training are denoted as PAMM(α-NDCG). The PAMM results using ERR-IA@20 as measures are denoted as PAMM(ERR-IA).

The experimental results on WT2009, WT2010, and WT2011 are reported in Table 5, Table 6, and Table 7, respectively. Numbers in parentheses are the relative improvements compared with the baseline method of query likelihood (QL). Boldface indicates the highest score among all runs. From the results, we can see that PAMM(α-NDCG) and PAMM(ERR-IA) outperform all of the baselines on all of the three datasets in terms of both α-NDCG@20 and ERR-IA@20. We conducted significant testing (t-test) on the improvements of PAMM(α-NDCG) over the baselines in terms of α-NDCG@20 and ERR-IA@20. The results indicate that all of the improvements are statistically significant ($p\text{-value} < 0.05$). We also conducted t-test on the improvements of PAMM(ERR-IA) over the baselines in terms of α-NDCG@20 and ERR-IA@20. The improvements are also statistically significant. All of the results show that PAMM is effective for the task of search result diversification.

We observed that on all of the three datasets, PAMM(α-NDCG) trained with α-NDCG@20 performed best in terms of α-NDCG@20 while PAMM(ERR-IA) trained with ERR-IA@20 performed best in terms of ERR-IA@20. The results indicate that PAMM can enhance diverse ranking performances in terms of a measure by using the measure in training. We will further discuss the phenomenon in next section.

Table 5: Performance comparison of all methods in official TREC diversity measures for WT2009.

Method	ERR-IA@20	α-NDCG@20
QL	0.164	0.269
ListMLE	0.191(+16.46%)	0.307(+14.13%)
MMR	0.202(+23.17%)	0.308(+14.50%)
xQuAD	0.232(+41.46%)	0.344(+27.88%)
PM-2	0.229(+39.63%)	0.337(+25.28%)
SVM-DIV	0.241(+46.95%)	0.353(+31.23%)
StructSVM(α-NDCG)	0.260(+58.54%)	0.377(+40.15%)
StructSVM(ERR-IA)	0.261(+59.15%)	0.373(+38.66%)
R-LTR	0.271(+65.24%)	0.396(+47.21%)
PAMM(α-NDCG)	0.284(+73.17%)	**0.427**(+58.74%)
PAMM(ERR-IA)	**0.294**(+79.26%)	0.422(+56.88%)

Table 6: Performance comparison of all methods in official TREC diversity measures for WT2010.

Method	ERR-IA@20	α-NDCG@20
QL	0.198	0.302
ListMLE	0.244(+23.23%)	0.376(+24.50%)
MMR	0.274(+38.38%)	0.404(+33.77%)
xQuAD	0.328(+65.66%)	0.445(+47.35%)
PM-2	0.330(+66.67%)	0.448(+48.34%)
SVM-DIV	0.333(+68.18%)	0.459(+51.99%)
StructSVM(α-NDCG)	0.352(+77.78%)	0.476(+57.62%)
StructSVM(ERR-IA)	0.355(+79.29%)	0.472(+56.29%)
R-LTR	0.365(+84.34%)	0.492(+62.91%)
PAMM(α-NDCG)	0.380(+91.92%)	**0.524**(+73.51%)
PAMM(ERR-IA)	**0.387**(+95.45%)	0.511(+69.21%)

Table 7: Performance comparison of all methods in official TREC diversity measures for WT2011.

Method	ERR-IA@20	α-NDCG@20
QL	0.352	0.453
ListMLE	0.417(+18.47%)	0.517(+14.13%)
MMR	0.428(+21.59%)	0.530(+17.00%)
xQuAD	0.475(+34.94%)	0.565(+24.72%)
PM-2	0.487(+38.35%)	0.579(+27.81%)
SVM-DIV	0.490(+39.20%)	0.591(+30.46%)
StructSVM(α-NDCG)	0.512(+45.45%)	0.617(+36.20%)
StructSVM(ERR-IA)	0.513(+45.74%)	0.613(+35.32%)
R-LTR	0.539(+53.13%)	0.630(+39.07%)
PAMM(α-NDCG)	0.541(+53.70%)	**0.643**(+41.94%)
PAMM(ERR-IA)	**0.548**(+55.68%)	0.637(+40.62%)

5.4 Discussions

We conducted experiments to show the reasons that PAMM outperforms the baselines, using the results of the WT2009 dataset as examples.

5.4.1 Effect of maximizing marginal relevance

We found that PAMM makes a good tradeoff between the query-document relevance and document diversity via maximizing marginal relevance. Here we use the result with regard to query number 24 ("diversity" which contains 4 subtopics), to illustrate why our method is superior to the baseline method of Structural SVM trained with α-NDCG@20 (denoted as StructSVM(α-NDCG)). Note that structural

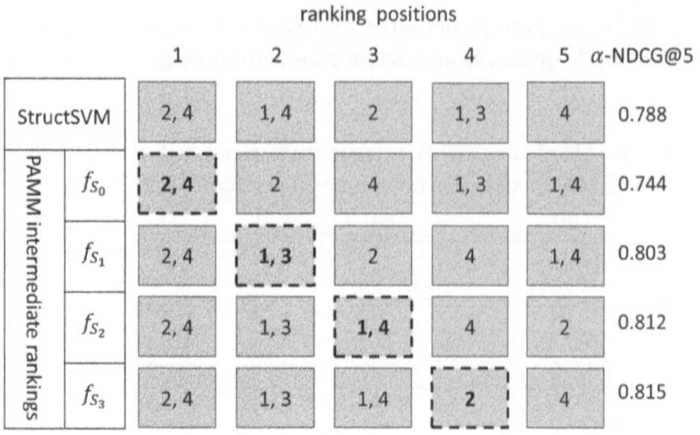

Figure 1: Example rankings from WT2009. Each shaded block represents a document and the number(s) in the block represent the subtopic(s) covered by the document.

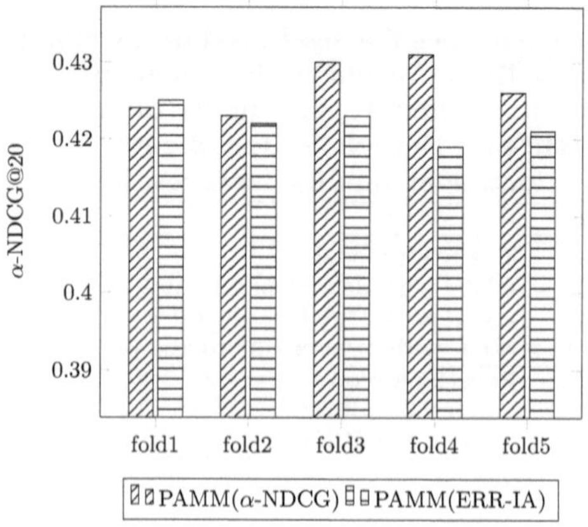

Figure 2: Performance in terms of α-NDCG@20 when model is trained with α-NDCG@20 or ERR-IA@20.

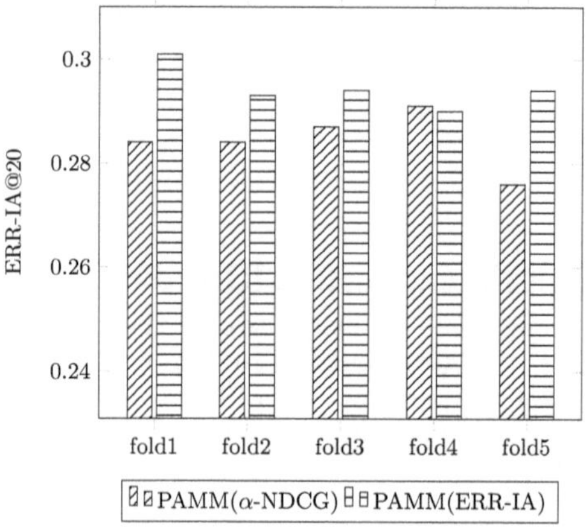

Figure 3: Performance in terms of ERR-IA@20 when model is trained with α-NDCG@20 or ERR-IA@20.

SVM cannot leverage the marginal relevance in its ranking model. Figure 1 shows the top five ranked documents by StructSVM(α-NDCG), as well as four intermediate rankings generated by PAMM(α-NDCG) (denoted as $f_{S_0}, f_{S_1}, f_{S_2}$, and f_{S_3}). The ranking denoted as f_{S_r} is generated as: first sequentially selecting the documents for ranking positions of $1, 2, \cdots, r-1$ with models $f_{S_0}, f_{S_1}, \cdots, f_{S_{r-2}}$, respectively; then ranking the remaining documents with $f_{S_{r-1}}$. For example, the intermediate ranking denoted as f_{S_2} is generated as: selecting one document with f_{S_0} and setting it to rank 1, then selecting one document with f_{S_1} and set it to rank 2, and finally ranking the remaining documents with f_{S_2} and putting them to the tail of the list. Each of the shaded block indicates a document and the number(s) in the block indicates the subtopic(s) assigned to the document by the human annotators. The performances in terms of α-NDCG@5 are also shown in the last column. Here we used α-NDCG@5 because only the top 5 documents are shown.

The results in Figure 1 indicate the effectiveness of the maximal marginal relevance criterion. We can see that the α-NDCG@5 increases steadily with the increasing rounds of document selection iterations. In the first iteration, f_{S_0} selects the most relevant document and puts it to the first position, without considering the diversity. Thus, the α-NDCG@5 of the ranking generated by f_{S_0} is lower than that of by StructSVM(α-NDCG). In the second iteration, the ranking function f_{S_1} selects the document associated with subtopics 1 and 3 and ranks it to the second position, according to the maximal marginal relevance criterion. From the view point of diverse ranking, this is obviously a better choice than StructSVM(α-NDCG) made, which selects the document with subtopics 1 and 4. (Note that both Structural SVM and PAMM select the document with subtopics 2 and 4 for the first position.) In the following steps, f_{S_2} and f_{S_3} select documents for ranking positions of 3 and 4, also following the maximal marginal relevance criterion. As a result, f_{S_1}, f_{S_2}, and f_{S_3} outperforms StructSVM(α-NDCG).

5.4.2 *Ability to improve the evaluation measures*

We conducted experiments to see whether PAMM has the ability to improve the diverse ranking quality in terms of a measure by using the measure in training. Specifically, we trained models using α-NDCG@20 and ERR-IA@20 and evaluated their accuracies on the test dataset in terms of both α-NDCG@20 and ERR-IA@20. The experiments were conducted for each fold of the cross validation and performances on each fold are reported. Figure 2 and Figure 3 show the results in terms of α-NDCG@20 and ERR-IA@20, respectively. From Figure 2, we can see that on all of the 5 folds (except fold 1), PAMM(α-NDCG) trained with α-NDCG@20 performs better in terms of α-NDCG@20. Similarly, from Figure 3, we can see that on all of the 5 folds (except fold 4), PAMM(ERR-IA) trained with ERR-IA@20 performs better in terms of ERR-IA@20. Similar results have also been observed in experiments on other datasets (see the results in Table 5, Table 6, and Table 7). All of the results indicate that PAMM can indeed enhance the diverse ranking quality in terms of a measure by using the measure in training.

5.4.3 *Effects of positive and negative rankings*

We examined the effects of the number of positive rankings generated per query (parameter τ^+). Specifically, we compared the performances of PAMM(α-NDCG) w.r.t. different τ^+ values. Figure 4 shows the performance curve in terms of α-NDCG@20. The performance of R-LTR base-

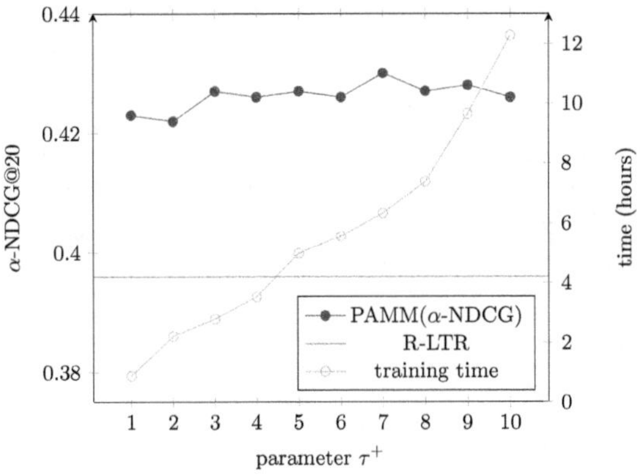

Figure 4: Ranking accuracies and training time w.r.t. τ^+.

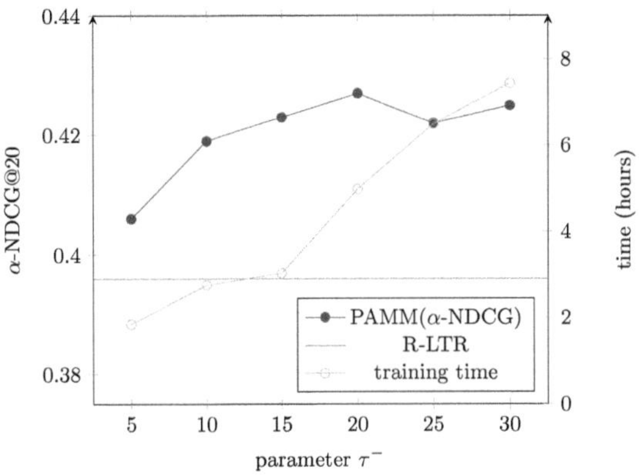

Figure 5: Ranking accuracies and training time w.r.t τ^-.

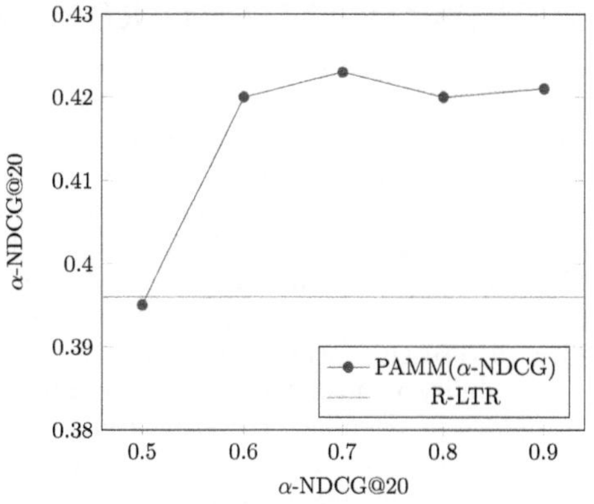

Figure 6: Ranking accuracies w.r.t. different α-NDCG@20 values of the negative rankings.

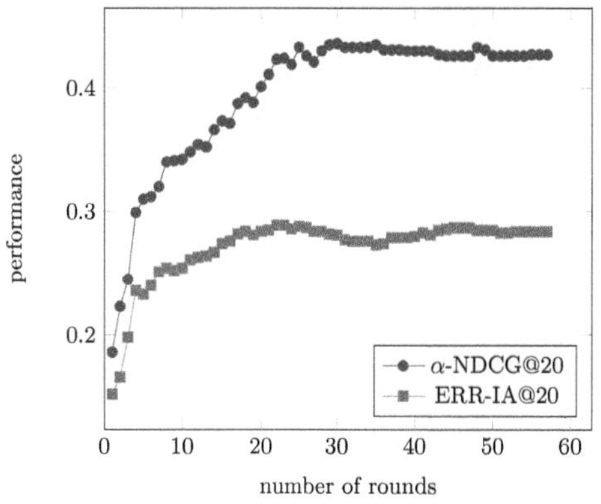

Figure 7: Learning curve of PAMM(α-NDCG).

line is also shown for reference. From the result, we can see that the curve does not change much with different τ^+ values, which indicates the robustness of PAMM. Figure 4 also shows training time (in hours) w.r.t. different τ^+ values. The training time increased dramatically with large τ^+, because more ranking pairs are generated for training. In our experiments τ^+ was set to 5.

We further examined the effect of the number of negative rankings per query (parameter τ^-). Specifically, we compared the performances of PAMM(α-NDCG) w.r.t. different τ^- and the results are shown in Figure 5. From the results, we can see that the performance of PAMM increasing steadily with the increasing τ^- values until $\tau^- = 20$, which indicates that PAMM can achieve better ranking performance with more information from the negative rankings. As the cost, the training time increased dramatically, because more training instances are involved in training. In our experiments, τ^- was set to 20.

We also conducted experiments to show the effect of sampling the negative rankings with different α-NDCG values. Specifically, in each of the experiment, we configured the Algorithm 4 to choose the negative rankings whose α-NDCG@20 values are 0.5, 0.6, 0.7, 0.8, and 0.9, respectively. Figure 6 shows the performances of PAMM(α-NDCG) w.r.t. different α-NDCG@20 values of the sampled negative rankings. From the results, we can see that PAMM performs best when the α-NDCG@20 of the sampled negative rankings ranges from 0.6 to 0.9. The results also indicate that PAMM is robust and not very sensitive to different methods of sampling the negative rankings.

5.4.4 Convergence

Finally we conducted experiments to show whether PAMM can converge in terms of the diversity evaluation measures. Specifically, we showed the learning curve of PAMM(α-NDCG) in terms of α-NDCG@20 and ERR-IA@20 during the training phase. At each training iteration the model parameters are outputted and evaluated on the test data. Figure 7 shows the performance curves w.r.t. the number of training iterations. From the results, we can see that the ranking accuracy of that PAMM(α-NDCG) steadily improves in terms of both α-NDCG@20 and ERR-IA@20, as the training goes on. PAMM converges and returns after running about 60 iterations. We also observed that in all of our experiments, PAMM usually converges and returns after running 50$\sim$100 iterations. Similar phenomenon was also observed from the learning curve of PAMM(ERR-IA). The results indicates that PAMM converges fast and conducts the training efficiently.

6. CONCLUSION AND FUTURE WORK

In this paper we have proposed a novel algorithm for learning ranking models in search result diversification, referred to as PAMM. PAMM makes use of the maximal marginal relevance model for constructing the diverse rankings. In training, PAMM directly optimizes the diversity evaluation measures on training queries under the framework of Perceptron. PAMM offers several advantages: employs a ranking model that follows the maximal marginal relevance criterion, ability to directly optimize any diversity evaluation measure, and ability to utilize both positive rankings and negative rankings in training. Experimental results based on three benchmark datasets show that PAMM significantly outperforms the state-of-the-art baseline methods including SVM-DIV, structural SVM, and R-LTR.

Future work includes theoretical analysis on the convergence, generalization error, and other properties of the PAMM algorithm, and improving the efficiency of PAMM in both offline training and online prediction.

7. ACKNOWLEDGMENTS

This research work was funded by the 973 Program of China under Grants No. 2014CB340401, No. 2012CB316303, the 863 Program of China under Grants No. 2014AA015204, the National Natural Science Foundation of China under Grant No. 61232010, No. 61425016, No. 61173064, No. 61472401, No. 61203298, and No. 61202214.

We would like to express our gratitude to Prof. Chengxiang Zhai who has offered us valuable suggestions in the academic studies.

8. REFERENCES

[1] R. Agrawal, S. Gollapudi, A. Halverson, and S. Ieong. Diversifying search results. In *Proceedings of the 2th ACM WSDM*, pages 5–14, 2009.

[2] J. Carbonell and J. Goldstein. The use of mmr, diversity-based reranking for reordering documents and producing summaries. In *Proceedings of the 21st ACM SIGIR*, pages 335–336, 1998.

[3] B. Carterette and P. Chandar. Probabilistic models of ranking novel documents for faceted topic retrieval. In *Proceedings of the 18th ACM CIKM*, pages 1287–1296, 2009.

[4] O. Chapelle, D. Metlzer, Y. Zhang, and P. Grinspan. Expected reciprocal rank for graded relevance. In *Proceedings of the 18th ACM CIKM*, pages 621–630, 2009.

[5] C. L. Clarke, M. Kolla, G. V. Cormack, O. Vechtomova, A. Ashkan, S. Büttcher, and I. MacKinnon. Novelty and diversity in information retrieval evaluation. In *Proceedings of the 31st ACM SIGIR*, pages 659–666, 2008.

[6] C. L. Clarke, M. Kolla, and O. Vechtomova. An effectiveness measure for ambiguous and underspecified queries. In *Proceedings of the 2nd ICTIR*, pages 188–199, 2009.

[7] M. Collins. Discriminative training methods for hidden markov models: theory and experiments with perceptron algorithms. In *EMNLP '02*, pages 1–8, 2002.

[8] V. Dang and W. B. Croft. Diversity by proportionality: an election-based approach to search result diversification. In *Proceedings of the 35th ACM SIGIR*, pages 65–74, 2012.

[9] S. Gollapudi and A. Sharma. An axiomatic approach for result diversification. In *Proceedings of the 18th WWW*, pages 381–390, 2009.

[10] S. Guo and S. Sanner. Probabilistic latent maximal marginal relevance. In *Proceedings of the 33rd ACM SIGIR*, pages 833–834, 2010.

[11] J. He, V. Hollink, and A. de Vries. Combining implicit and explicit topic representations for result diversification. In *Proceedings of the 35th ACM SIGIR*, pages 851–860, 2012.

[12] T. Hofmann. Probabilistic latent semantic indexing. In *Proceedings of the 22nd ACM SIGIR*, pages 50–57, 1999.

[13] K. Järvelin and J. Kekäläinen. Cumulated gain-based evaluation of ir techniques. *ACM Trans. Inf. Syst.*, 20(4):422–446, Oct. 2002.

[14] L. Li, K. Zhou, G.-R. Xue, H. Zha, and Y. Yu. Enhancing diversity, coverage and balance for summarization through structure learning. In *Proceedings of the 18th WWW*, pages 71–80, 2009.

[15] Y. Li, H. Zaragoza, R. Herbrich, J. Shawe-Taylor, and J. Kandola. The perceptron algorithm with uneven margins. In *Proceedings of the 19th ICML*, pages 379–386, 2002.

[16] S.-S. Liang, Z.-C. Ren, and M. de Rijke. Personalized search result diversification via structured learning. In *Proceedings of the 20th ACM SIGKDD*, pages 751–760, 2014.

[17] T.-Y. Liu. *Learning to Rank for Information Retrieval.* Springer, 2011.

[18] C. D. Manning, P. Raghavan, and H. SchÜtze. *An Introduction to Information Retrieval.* Cambridge University Press, 2009.

[19] D. Metzler and W. B. Croft. A markov random field model for term dependencies. In *Proceedings of the 28th ACM SIGIR*, pages 472–479, 2005.

[20] L. Mihalkova and R. Mooney. Learning to disambiguate search queries from short sessions. In *Machine Learning and Knowledge Discovery in Databases*, volume 5782, pages 111–127, 2009.

[21] F. Radlinski and S. Dumais. Improving personalized web search using result diversification. In *Proceedings of the 29th ACM SIGIR*, pages 691–692, 2006.

[22] F. Radlinski, R. Kleinberg, and T. Joachims. Learning diverse rankings with multi-armed bandits. In *Proceedings of the 25th ICML*, pages 784–791, 2008.

[23] D. Rafiei, K. Bharat, and A. Shukla. Diversifying web search results. In *Proceedings of the 19th WWW*, pages 781–790, 2010.

[24] K. Raman, P. Shivaswamy, and T. Joachims. Online learning to diversify from implicit feedback. In *Proceedings of the 18th ACM SIGKDD*, pages 705–713, 2012.

[25] R. L. Santos, C. Macdonald, and I. Ounis. Exploiting query reformulations for web search result diversification. In *Proceedings of the 19th WWW*, pages 881–890, 2010.

[26] I. Tsochantaridis, T. Joachims, T. Hofmann, and Y. Altun. Large margin methods for structured and interdependent output variables. *J. Mach. Learn. Res.*, 6:1453–1484, Dec. 2005.

[27] J. Xu, T.-Y. Liu, M. Lu, H. Li, and M. Wei-Ying. Directly optimizing evaluation measures in learning to rank. In *Proceedings of the 31th ACM SIGIR*, pages 107–114, 2008.

[28] Y. Yue and T. Joachims. Predicting diverse subsets using structural svms. In *Proceedings of the 25th ICML*, pages 1224–1231, 2008.

[29] Y. Yue and T. Joachims. Interactively optimizing information retrieval systems as a dueling bandits problem. In *Proceedings of the 26th ICML*, pages 1201–1208, 2009.

[30] C. X. Zhai, W. W. Cohen, and J. Lafferty. Beyond independent relevance: methods and evaluation metrics for subtopic retrieval. In *Proceedings of the 26th ACM SIGIR*, pages 10–17, 2003.

[31] Y. Zhu, Y. Lan, J. Guo, X. Cheng, and S. Niu. Learning for search result diversification. In *Proceedings of the 37th ACM SIGIR*, pages 293–302, 2014.

Analyzing User's Sequential Behavior in Query Auto-Completion via Markov Processes

Liangda Li[¶†], Hongbo Deng[‡], Anlei Dong[‡], Yi Chang[‡], Hongyuan Zha[¶†], and Ricardo Baeza-Yates[‡]

[†]College of Computing, Georgia Institute of Technology, Atlanta, GA 30032

[‡]Yahoo Labs, 701 First Avenue, Sunnyvale, CA 94089

[¶]Software Engineering Institute, East China Normal University, Shanghai, China 200062

ldli@cc.gatech.edu, {hbdeng, anlei, yichang}@yahoo-inc.com, zha@cc.gatech.edu, rbaeza@acm.org

ABSTRACT

Query auto-completion (QAC) plays an important role in assisting users typing less while submitting a query. The QAC engine generally offers a list of suggested queries that start with a user's input as a prefix, and the list of suggestions is changed to match the updated input after the user types each keystroke. Therefore rich user interactions can be observed along with each keystroke until a user clicks a suggestion or types the entire query manually. It becomes increasingly important to analyze and understand users' interactions with the QAC engine, to improve its performance. Existing works on QAC either ignored users' interaction data, or assumed that their interactions at each keystroke are independent from others. Our paper pays high attention to users' sequential interactions with a QAC engine in and across QAC sessions, rather than users' interactions at each keystroke of each QAC session separately. Analyzing the dependencies in users' sequential interactions improves our understanding of the following three questions: 1) how is a user's skipping/viewing move at the current keystroke influenced by that at the previous keystroke? 2) how to improve search engines' query suggestions at short keystrokes based on those at latter long keystrokes? and 3) facing a targeted query shown in the suggestion list, why does a user decide to continue typing rather than click the intended suggestion? We propose a probabilistic model that addresses those three questions in a unified way, and illustrate how the model determines users' final click decisions. By comparing with state-of-the-art methods, our proposed model does suggest queries that better satisfy users' intents.

Categories and Subject Descriptors:
I.2.6 [**Artificial Intelligence**]: Learning; H.3.3 [**Information Storage and Retrieval**]: Information Search and Retrieval; J.4 [**Computer Applications**]: Social and Behavioral Sciences

General Terms: Algorithm, Experimentation, Performance

Keywords: hidden Markov model, variational Inference, query auto-completion

SIGIR'15, August 09 - 13, 2015, Santiago, Chile.

DOI: http://dx.doi.org/10.1145/2766462.2767723.

1. INTRODUCTION

Query auto-completion (QAC) has been widely used in modern search engines to reduce users' effort to submit a query by predicting the users' intended queries. The QAC engine generally offers a list of suggested queries that start with a user's input as a prefix, and the list of suggestions is changed to match the updated input after the user types each character. Let us suppose that a user is going to submit a query q to the search engine, and the user types the prefix of the query q of length i as $q[1..i]$ sequentially. The QAC engine will return the corresponding suggestion list after the user types each character, until the user clicks the suggestion q from the list or presses return, ending the interaction with the QAC engine. Usually, even for submitting the same query q, different users may have different interactions with the QAC engine, which are shown from their different sequential behaviors. For example, user u_a chooses the suggestion q at position 5 after typing 3 characters, while user u_b chooses the suggestion q at position 1 after typing 5 characters. In order to better improve users' search experience, it becomes increasingly important to analyze users' sequential behavior with the QAC engine, to understand users' real preferences and then improve the performance of QAC.

Recently, many studies have been proposed to address the QAC problem in different perspectives, including designing more efficient indexes and algorithms [2, 20, 11], leveraging context in long term and short term query history [1], investigating the time-sensitive aspect of QAC [19, 21], learning to combine more personalized signals [18], etc. Despite of those numerous works on QAC, most of them only utilize the information of submitted queries and associated prefixes, thus lose details of how users' interact with the QAC engine, such as the suggested query lists of each prefix before query submission, users' query typing speed, and so on. Recently, a high-resolution QAC dataset was collected from PC (personal computer) and mobile phones [15], where each keystroke of users and clicks were recorded. A two-dimensional click model was trained on this high-resolution QAC dataset, revealing users' behaviors such as horizontal skipping bias and vertical position bias. However, this work assumed that users' behaviors at different keystrokes are independent in order to simplify the model estimation, which results in information loss.

Our work, on the other hand, attempts to capture three types of relationship between users' behaviors at different keystrokes that are ignored or failed to model until now: 1) **State transitions between skipping and viewing.** The study on high-resolution query log data revealed that a user may choose to either view or skip the suggestion list at each keystroke in a QAC session. It already explored how users' interactions with QAC engine at the current keystroke, such as typing speed and whether the end of current prefix is at word boundary, influence users' decisions on skipping or viewing. However, besides those factors, we believe that such decisions should also be influenced by their decisions on skipping or viewing at the previous keystroke. For instance, imagine a user u has 5 sequential skipping moves in one QAC session and 2 sequential skipping moves in another QAC session, the chance becomes higher for the same user to stop and view the suggestion list at the current keystroke after 5 sequential skipping moves. On the other hands, if the same user has already viewed too many keystrokes continuously but finds no intended query, it becomes more likely that he/she may skip the next one; 2) **Users' real preference of suggestions**. For each keystroke, the associated users' real preference is hard to be detected from the current suggested query list alone. On the other hand, we need to utilize the rankings of suggested query lists of latter keystrokes together with users' final click choices to re-rank the suggested queries in the list of the current keystroke. Intuitively, a clicked query, i.e. the user's intended query, should get a higher rank not only at the keystroke he/she makes the click, but also at previous keystrokes where this query appears, despite that it is not clicked at that time; and 3) **User-specific cost between position clicking and typing**. Some users prefer typing than viewing and clicking, while others don't. Consequently, users' click choices are not only affected by their intent, but also by the position where the intended query is shown and their preference of clicking that position over typing the remaining keystrokes. For instance, a user that prefers clicking will probably click an intended query the first time it is shown to him/her, despite that it may be shown in a low position; while another user focuses on typing his/her intended query despite that the query already appears in the suggestion list, until it is ranked at the top position, or even worse, he/she will type the entire query manually without any intent to click the suggestions.

To model these three aspects, we propose a probabilistic model, which is a combination of three parts that address each separately. The hidden Markov model part takes the skipping and viewing choices as two different states, and assumes the transition between keystrokes is influenced by users' interactions with the QAC engine at that keystroke. The logistic regression part weighs a set of our designed user-specific relevance features that imply users' own preference on each prefix-query pair, which is expected to capture users' real preference. The Dirichlet prior part estimates the ratio between position-biased clicking and typing costs. Those three parts together determine the probability that a user clicks a certain suggested query located at a certain position of the suggested query list of a certain keystroke in a QAC session. We develop a mean-field variational inference algorithm to learn the parameters that optimize the data likelihood.

We evaluate our method on high-resolution QAC logs collected from a commercial search engine on both PCs and mobile phones. We compare the performance of our model with some alternative probabilistic models and state-of-the-art QAC algorithms. Experimental results show that the proposed method can predict queries that better satisfy users' search intent. Moreover, the learned model provides us insights into the relationship between users' behaviors at different keystrokes.

In a nutshell, the major contributions of this paper include:

1. We explore the relationship between users' behaviors at different keystrokes in each QAC session, which existing works failed to model;
2. We propose a new probabilistic model that combines three parts to model each aspect of the relationship between users' behaviors at different keystrokes, and make them together effectively predict users' click actions on high-resolution QAC logs; and
3. We propose a generic model whose parameters are shared by all users, instead of using user-specific parameters, which sharply reduces the number of parameters to learn, and is suitable for new users.

The rest of the paper is organized as follows. We first introduce related work in Section 2, after that we formally define our problem and introduce the proposed model in Section 3. In Section 4, we develop a fast mean-field variational inference algorithm to optimize the solution. We then describe and report the experimental evaluations in Section 5, and finally present our conclusions and future work in Section 6.

2. RELATED WORK

Query Auto-Completion (QAC). The main objective of QAC is to predict users' intended queries and assist them formulate a query while typing. The most popular QAC algorithm is to suggest completions according to their past popularity. Generally, a popularity score is assigned to each query based on the frequency of the query in the query log from which the query database was built. This simple QAC algorithm is called MostPopularCompletion (MPC), which can be regarded as an approximate maximum likelihood estimator [1].

Several QAC methods [1, 19, 18, 21] were proposed to extend MPC from various aspects. Bar-Yossef and Kraus [1] introduced the context-sensitive QAC method by treating users' recent queries as context and taking into account the similarity of QAC candidates with this context for ranking. But there is no consensus of how to optimally train the relevance model. Shokouhi [18] employed learning-based strategy to incorporate several global and personal features into the QAC model. However, these methods only exploit the final submitted query or simulate the prefixes of the clicked query, which do not investigate the users' interactions with the QAC engine.

In addition the above models, there are several studies addressing different aspects of QAC. For example, [19, 21] focused on the time-sensitive aspect of QAC. Other methods studied the space efficiency of index for QAC [2, 11]. Duan and Hsu [7] addressed the problem of suggesting query completions when the prefix is misspelled. Kharitonov et al. [13] proposed two new metrics for offline QAC evaluation, and [12] investigated user reformation behavior for QAC.

The QAC is a complex process where a user goes through a series of interactions with the QAC engine before clicking on a suggestion. As can be seen from the related work, little attention has been paid to understand the interactions with the QAC engine. Until recently, Li et al. [15] created a two-dimensional click model to combine users' behaviors with the existing learning-based QAC model. The study assumed users' behaviors at different keystrokes, even for the consecutive two keystrokes, are independent in order to simplify the model estimation, which results in information lose. In this paper, we attempt to directly model and leverage the relationship between users' behaviors, so as to improve the performance of QAC.

Click Models. This work is related to click models. In the field of document retrieval, the main purpose for modeling users' clicks is to infer the intrinsic relevance between the query and document by explaining the positional bias. The position bias assumption was first introduced by Granka et al. [9], stating that a document on higher rank tends to attract more clicks. Richardson et al. [17]

attempted to model the true relevance of documents by imposing a multiplicative factor. Later examination hypothesis is formalized in [5], with a key assumption (Cascade Assumption) that a user will click on a document if and only if that document has been examined and it is relevant to the query. In addition, several extensions were proposed, such as the User Browsing Model (UBM) [8], the Bayesian Browsing Model [16], the General Click Model [23] and the Dynamic Bayesian Network model (DBN) [4]. Despite the abundance of click models, these existing click models cannot be directly applied to QAC without considerable modification. The click model most similar to our work is [22], which models users' clicks on a series of queries in a session. However, because of the main difference between QAC and document retrieval, our model is very different from [22].

3. PROBLEM DEFINITION

In this section, we first introduce the concept of the high-resolution QAC log, and then propose appropriate models to predict how likely a user will click a certain query at a certain location in a QAC session.

3.1 A High-Resolution QAC Log

Traditionally, the search query log only includes the submitted query and its associated search results, while it does not contain the sequential keystrokes (prefixes) users typed in the search box, as well as their corresponding QAC suggestions. In order to better analyze and understand real users' behaviors, a high-resolution QAC log is introduced and analyzed in [15], which records users' interactions with a QAC engine at each keystroke and associated system respond in an entire QAC process. For each submitted query, there is only one record in a traditional search query log. However, in the high-resolution QAC log, each submitted query is associated with a **QAC session**, which is defined to begin with the first keystroke a user typed in the search box towards the final submitted query. The recorded information in each QAC session includes each keystroke a user has entered, the timestamp of a keystroke, the corresponding top 10 suggested queries to a prefix, the anonymous user ID, and the final clicked query.

Let us take a toy example to briefly introduce how a user interacts with a QAC engine and makes the final click in an entire QAC session. As shown in Figure 1, a **QAC session** contains S keystrokes and each keystroke has a suggested query list of length D.[1] A QAC session ends at the keystroke where the user clicks a query in the suggested query list, or when the prefix at that keystroke is exactly the query the user enters into the search engine. Among the $S \times D$ *slots* in each QAC session, where each slot q_{ij} is indexed by the i-th position at the j-th keystroke, a user clicks at most one of them, although the user intended query may appear in many slots. Since users' clicked queries are usually their intended queries, appropriate modeling of users' click actions can be a good solution of the QAC problem. The ideal QAC engine should be able to rank the user intended query higher with less keystrokes or short prefixes. In this work, we leverage such a QAC log data to get a better understanding of user's sequential behavior in the QAC process.

3.2 Assumptions on QAC User Behavior

We view the QAC problem, which predicts a user's intended query, as the problem of predicting the query the user will click. Unlike existing works on query auto-completion, which paid no attention to those non-clicked suggested queries at the keystrokes before users' make clicks, or failed to straightforwardly analyze and reveal the difference between click cases and non-click cases, our paper proposes a model which predicts the most likely slot a user will click in each QAC session by capturing the relationship between users' behaviors at different keystrokes.

To predict how likely a user will click a certain slot, there are mainly three issues we need to solve:

- Whether the user has viewed the slot;
- Whether the query shown on the slot satisfies the user's intent; and
- Whether the user is willing to click the slot.

We use Figure 2 to illustrate how the above three issues together determine users' click choices among all potential slots. Figure 2 shows a QAC session which contains S(=4) columns/keystrokes, and each keystroke contains D(=4) positions, thus makes a total number of 16 potential slots to click. Among those 16 potential slots, the queries in 12 of them do not satisfy the user's intent, thus the user will not click it anyway. On the other hand, the user's intended query appears in the other four slots, where each keystroke contains one appearance. The user viewed the suggested query lists at both the first and second keystrokes, however, the intended query is ranked at a relatively low position, which the user failed to pay attention to, or thought this position costs him/her too much effort to click, thus he/she didn't click it. At the third keystroke, although the intended query is ranked at the top position, the user didn't view this suggestion, thus he/she missed the information and failed to click. Finally, at the last keystroke, the user viewed it, found his/her intended query lies at the top position, and then he/she clicked that query.

3.3 Modeling Clicks in QAC

In the following, we show how to better address the above issues by taking the relationship between users' behaviors at different keystrokes into account. We also introduce some analysis conducted on the real-world high-resolution QAC log, to show why our proposed ideas are reasonable.

Skipping or viewing a keystroke? Existing works [2, 1] mostly failed to address the first (and the third) issue since they lack the information of users' interactions with a QAC engine before making a click, i.e., the high-resolution QAC log. Generally, it is assumed that a user makes a decision to either viewing or skipping at each keystroke, which depends only upon the user's interaction with the QAC engine at that keystroke. Based on its definition that "skipping behavior happens when the final clicked query is ranked within top 3 in the suggestion list of any of the prefixes except the final prefix" as introduced in [15], we count the sequential appearance of skipping and viewing states statistically on a real-world high-resolution QAC log collected from a commercial search engine, and find that 78.4% of the states are followed the same type of states. Thus the transitions between skipping and viewing states are not random, and the error of inferring state type based only upon user behavior at that keystroke can be significant. Thus, our paper, on the other hand, assumes that the user's decision will also be influenced by his/her decision at the previous keystroke besides his/her interaction. As shown in Figure 1, we use a hidden Markov model to capture such influence, and take viewing and skipping as $K = 2$ states. We assume that T state transition rules exist in the observed QAC logs, where each rule is actually a probability matrix corresponding to a certain type of viewing/skipping behavior. Users' interactions with the QAC engine, such as typing speed and reaching word boundary, at the current keystroke influence their choice of transition rules at this keystroke. For instance, for a fast

[1]We experiment with real-world QAC logs where $D = 10$.

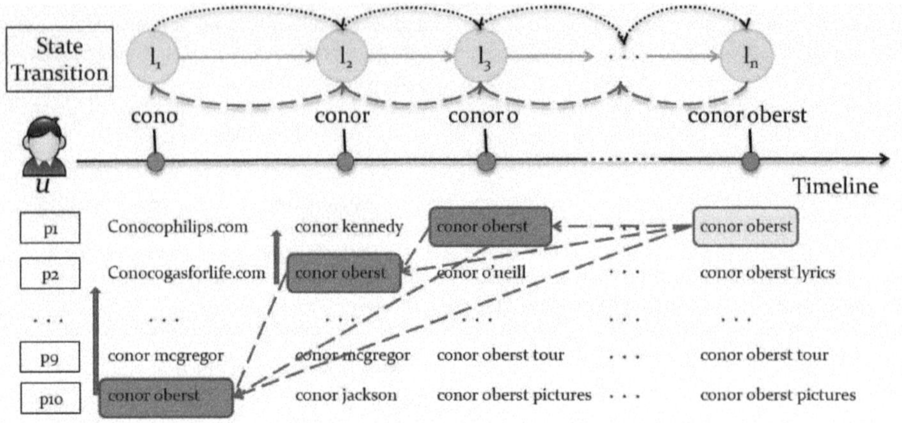

Figure 1: A Toy Example of a QAC Session in High-resolution QAC logs. Yellow tag highlights the query a user finally clicks, red tag highlights the user's intended query he/she doesn't click. Black dot line represents the dependency between users' skipping/viewing states captured by Markov process, and blue line denotes the influence of suggested query lists of latter keystrokes together with users' final click choices to the raise of the ranking of intended queries in the list of the current keystroke.

typing user, the probability of transition from skipping to skipping can be very small. When a user reaches a word boundary, he is very likely to follow the transition rule where the probability of transition from skipping to viewing is significant. Assuming T user interaction patterns lie in the entire QAC log, and each user interaction pattern ω_t' corresponds to one state transition rule δ_t, at each keystroke, we analyze a user's interaction with the QAC engine and find which interaction pattern it belongs to, then choose accordingly the corresponding move transition rules. We use features introduced in [15] to describe users' interactions with the QAC engine, and denote those interaction features as X'.

How to capture users' intent? We adopt logistic regression (LR) to model how likely a query satisfies a user's intent under the current prefix. Existing works [15] already demonstrated a set of relevance features, which characterize the relevance between a certain prefix-query pair, to be effective in predicting the user's intent given certain prefixes. However, we find those features not enough due to two drawbacks: 1) those features mainly reflect the general interest of majority of users, and care little about users' personal history and preference; and 2) those features rarely imply the relationship between different prefixes, which makes them difficult to utilize users' preference of queries in the suggested lists of other keystrokes to improve the ranking at the current keystroke. As shown in Figure 1, a user's intended query, should get a higher rank at previous keystrokes where this query appears, despite that it is not clicked at that time. Actually, the real-world QAC log shows that 29.4% of users' submitted queries (this number counts redundant appearances) have been submitted more than 3 times by a user, while among those queries, only 18.4% of them has been submitted multiple times by more than 25% of users, i.e. different users favorite different query sets. Thus, besides existing features, we also employ a set of user-specific relevance features, which are designed to capture users' personal preference of queries and their corresponding relationship with keystrokes.

We summarize these search behavior features in Table 2. Our features generally originate from statistical counting of users' interactions with the QAC engine in their own historical sessions. For each user, given a certain query, we measure the number of times the same query has been clicked by that user in the past (denoted as Query Clicks). For users who have some queries daily issued, such as "facebook" or "youtube", this feature is capable of predicting his intent at the first few keystrokes. We also measure the average length of queries the user has clicked in the past (denoted as Query Length), the average number of words in queries that a user clicked (denoted as Query Word Number). In addition, we define the ratio between the length of a prefix and that of a query as *Prefix/Query Length Ratio (PQLR)*, and calculate the distribution of the associated PQLR of queries the user clicked in the past. For each new coming query, we estimate the percentage of the appearance of the associated PQLR in the user's history (denoted as Prefix/Query Ratio). PQLR is supposed to capture a user's preference of typing when taking the query length into consideration.

Clicking a position or continue typing? In addressing the third issue, we find it very necessary to take a user's tendency of viewing and clicking a certain position or continuing typing into consid-

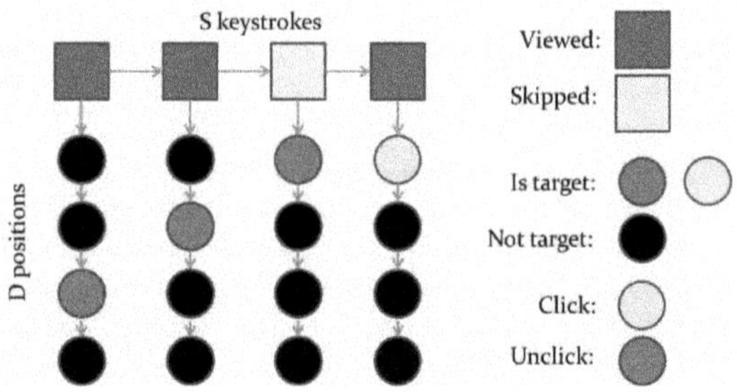

Figure 2: How Users Choose to Click Suggested Queries.

Table 1: User-Specific Relevance Features

Feature x	Description
Query Length	The average length of queries a user clicked.
Query Word Number	The average number of words in queries that a user clicked.
Query Clicks	The number of clicks a user makes on the current query.
Prefix/Query Ratio	The percentage of the appearance of *PQLR* of the current prefix-query pair in the history.

Table 2: Major Notations

Symbol	Description
S	The number of keystrokes in a QAC session.
D	The number of suggested queries at a keystroke.
x	The relevance features.
x'	The interaction features.
β	The bias of viewing and clicking each position.
z	Whether a query is clicked.
ω	Feature weights of the relevance features.
δ_t, ω'_t	The t-th move transition pattern and the associated user interaction pattern.

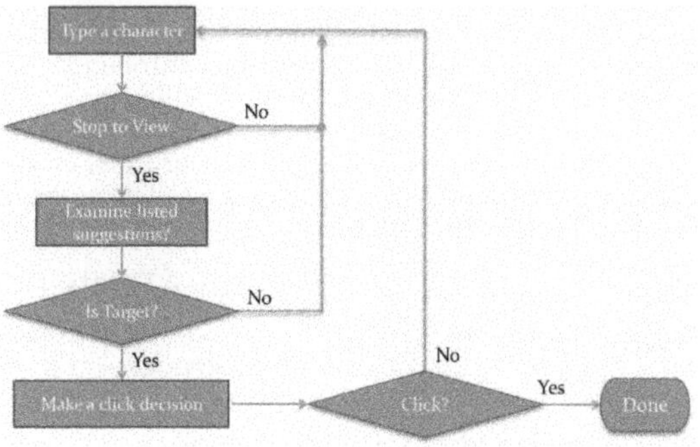

Figure 3: RBCM Flowchart.

eration. On the real-world QAC log, we find that when a user's intended query (the click this user finally clicks in a QAC session) is ranked within the top 2 positions, 37.6% of them will be clicked by users. On the other hand, if this intended query is ranked out of the top 2 positions, only 13.4% of them will be clicked by users. Furthermore, such tendencies can be very different for different groups of users. For mobile users, 42.9% of intended queries will be clicked if they are ranked within the top 2 positions, otherwise, 23.0% of them will be clicked. While for PC users, 35.1% of intended queries will be clicked if they are ranked within the top 2 positions, otherwise, 11.7% of them will be clicked. Here we can clearly find that on mobile, users are more likely to make clicks when their intended queries appear on the suggestion lists, even if they are ranked at low positions, while PC users prefer typing, since typing on PC is much more convenient than on mobile.

We use a D-dimensional Dirichlet prior α to learn the relative cost ratio of viewing and clicking a certain position against typing. Such a prior allows each user m to have distinguished position bias β_m in the preference of viewing and clicking than typing. Users who prefer clicking than typing will have a higher average *clicking/typing cost ratio (CTCR)* than users who prefer typing than clicking. The gaps of CTCR between high position and low position of users who rarely click suggested queries in low positions are generally larger than those of users who tend to click their intended queries the first time they are suggested no matter how lower their positions are.

Let us consider a typical scenario where M users issue M corresponding query sequences, where for each user m, the QAC log records N_m QAC sessions. The n-th QAC session of user m contains $S_{m,n}$ keystrokes, where each keystroke contains D suggested queries. In total, each QAC session has $S \times D$ potential slots where a user can click, and we use $z_{m,n,s,d} = 1$ to denote that a user clicks the slot ranked d at the s-th keystroke, and $z_{m,n,s,d} = 0$ otherwise. We also use $x_{m,n,s,d}$ to denote the relevance feature of a prefix-query pair, where the prefix is at the s-th keystroke and the query is ranked d at that keystroke. Then given the weights ω of those relevance features, we can derive the relevance score of each suggestion as $\omega x_{m,n,s,d}$. In addition, we use $x'_{m,n,s}$ to denote a user's interaction with the QAC engine at the s-th keystroke.

Based on our proposed solution of the listed three issues and above definitions, finally, we present our generative model as follows:

- For each user m, draw a D dimensional membership vector $\beta_m \sim \text{Dirichlet}(\alpha)$.

- For each move transition pattern t, draw a move transition matrix $\delta_t \sim \text{Dirichlet}(\alpha')$, where each pattern is associated with a user interaction pattern ω'_t.

- For the n-th query issued by user m, and for the prefix at step s,
  - Draw the user's move transition pattern membership $\pi_{m,n,s} \sim \text{Multinomial}(\theta)$, where θ is the prior distribution of move transition pattern membership.
  - Draw the user's interaction with the QAC engine through $x'_{m,n,s} \sim \text{Gaussian}(\omega'_{\pi_{m,n,s}}, \sigma)$.
  - Draw the user's next move, which is either type or view, $Y_{m,n,s} \sim \text{Multinomial}(\delta_{\pi_{m,n,s-1}, Y_{m,n,s-1}})$. If we have $Y_{m,n,s} = 1$, continue to type; otherwise, stop and view the results.
  - For each position d in the suggestion list of the current prefix, draw the user's clicked suggestion through $z_{m,n,s,d} \sim \text{Multinomial}(\text{LR}(\beta_{m,d} \omega x_{m,n,s,d}))$. If we have $z_{m,n,s,d} = 1$, select the suggestion in position d to click, then go to the $n+1$-th query; otherwise, continue to type, i.e., go to the next prefix.

Notice that the proposed model is a combination of three parts that address the listed issues respectively. We name this probabilistic model as relationship-based click model (RBCM). To better illustrate the generative process of the proposed RBCM model, we show the flowchart of user behaviors in Figure 3.

Under our RBCM model, the joint probability of the click information $Z = \{\{z_{m,n}\}_{n=1}^{N_m}\}$, the relevance features $X = \{\{x_{m,n}\}_{n=1}^{N_m}\}$, the user interaction features $X' = \{\{x'_{m,n}\}_{n=1}^{N_m}\}$ and latent variables $\{\beta_{1:M}, \pi, Y\}$ can be written as follows:

$$
\begin{aligned}
& p(Z, X, X', \beta_{1:M}, Y, \pi, \delta | \alpha, \alpha', \omega, \omega', \theta) \\
= & \prod_{m,n,s,d} P(z_{m,n,s,d} | x_{m,n,s,d}, \beta_{m,d}, \omega, Y_{m,n,s}) \\
& \times \prod_{m,n,s} P(Y_{m,n,s} | Y_{m,n,s-1}, \delta, \pi_{m,n,s-1}) P(x'_{m,n,s} | \pi_{m,n,s-1}, \omega') \\
& \times \prod_{m,n,s} P(\pi_{m,n,s} | \theta) \prod_{t} P(\delta_t | \alpha'_t) \prod_{m} P(\beta_m | \alpha).
\end{aligned}
$$

4. INFERENCE

In this section, we derive a mean-field variational Bayesian inference algorithm for our proposed RBCM model.

4.1 Variational Inference

Under the RBCM model, given observations of both click information $Z = \{Z_m\} = \{\{z_{m,n}\}_{n=1}^{N_m}\}$, the relevance features X, and the user interaction features X', the log-likelihood for the complete data is given by $\log P(Z, X, X' | \alpha, \alpha', \omega, \omega', \theta)$. Since this true posterior is hard to infer directly, we turn to variational methods [3, 14], whose main idea is to posit a distribution over the latent variables with variational parameters, and find the settings of the parameters so as to make the distribution close to the true posterior in Kullback-Leibler (KL) divergence. Our paper chooses to introduce a distribution of latent variables q specified as the mean-field fully factorized family as follows:

$$q(Y, \pi, \beta_{1:M}, \delta|\rho, \phi, \gamma_{1:M}, \eta) = \prod_m q_2(\beta_m|\gamma_m) \prod_t q_2(\delta_t|\eta_t) \times \prod_m \prod_n \prod_s q_1(Y_{m,n,s}|\rho_{m,n,s}) q_1(\pi_{m,n,s}|\phi_{m,n,s})$$

where q_1 is a multinomial, q_2 is a Dirichlet, and $\{\rho, \phi, \gamma_{1:M}\}$ are the set of variational parameters. We optimize those free parameters to tight the following lower bound $\mathcal{L}'$ for our likelihood:

$$\log p(Z, X, X'|\alpha, \alpha', \omega, \omega', \theta) \geq -E_q\left[\log q(Y, \pi, \beta, \delta|\rho, \phi, \gamma_{1:M}, \eta)\right] + E_q\left[\log p(Z, X, X', \beta, Y, \pi, \delta|\alpha, \alpha', \omega, \omega', \theta)\right]. \quad (1)$$

Under a coordinate descent framework, we optimize the lower bound as in Eqn (1) against each variational latent variable and the model hyper-parameter. For variational latent variables, we have the following process

- update rules for γ's as:

$$\gamma_{m,d} = \alpha_d + \sum_n \sum_s \log\left(1 + \exp\left(z_{m,n,s,d}\omega_m x_{m,n,s,d}\right)\right);$$

- update rules for ρ's as:

$$\rho_{m,n,s,k=1} \propto \exp\left(-\sum_d z_{m,n,s,d} - b_{m,n,s,1}\right);$$

$$\rho_{m,n,s,k=2} \propto \exp\left(b_{m,n,s,2} - \sum_d \log\left(1 + \exp\left(z_{m,n,s,d} - \omega_m x_{m,n,s,d}\left[\Phi(\gamma_{m,d}) - \Phi\left(\sum_d \gamma_{m,d}\right)\right]\right)\right)\right).$$

where

$$b_{m,n,s,k} = \sum_{k'} \sum_t \phi_{m,n,s,t}\left[\Phi(\eta_{t,k',k}) - \Phi\left(\sum_{k''} \eta_{t,k',k''}\right)\right] + \sum_{k'} \sum_t \phi_{m,n,s+1,t}\left[\Phi(\eta_{t,k,k'}) - \Phi\left(\sum_{k''} \eta_{t,k.k''}\right)\right]$$

- update rules for ϕ's as:

$$\phi_{m,n,s,t} \propto \exp\left(\sum_{k,k'} \rho_{m,n,s,k}\rho_{m,n,s+1,k'}\left[\Phi(\eta_{t,k,k'}) - \Phi\left(\sum_{k''} \eta_{t,k,k''}\right)\right] - \frac{1}{2\sigma^2}\left\|x'_{m,n,s} - \omega'_t\right\|_2^2\right)$$

- update rules for η's as:

$$\eta_{t,k,k'} = \alpha'_t + \sum_m \sum_n \sum_s \phi_{m,n,s,t} \sum_{k,k'} \rho_{m,n,s,k}\rho_{m,n,s-1,k'}$$

4.2 Learning

We use a variational expectation-maximization (EM) algorithm [6] to compute the empirical Bayes estimates of the Dirichlet hyper-parameters α and α' in our RBCM model. This variational EM algorithm optimizes the lower bound as in Eqn (1) instead of the real likelihood, and iteratively approximates the posterior by fitting the variational distribution q and optimizes the corresponding bound against the parameters.

In updating α, we use a Newton-Raphson method, since the approximate maximum likelihood estimate of α doesn't have a closed form solution. The Newton-Raphson method is conducted with a gradient and Hessian as follows:

$$\frac{\partial \mathcal{L}'}{\partial \alpha_d} = N\left(\Psi\left(\sum_d \alpha_d\right) - \Psi(\alpha_d)\right) + \sum_m \left(\Psi(\gamma_{m,d}) - \Psi\left(\sum_d \gamma_{m,d}\right)\right),$$

$$\frac{\partial \mathcal{L}'}{\partial \alpha_{d_1}\alpha_{d_2}} = N\left(\mathbb{I}_{(d_1=d_2)}\Psi'(\alpha_{d_1}) - \Psi'\left(\sum_d \alpha_d\right)\right).$$

Similar update rules can be derived for α'.

On the other hand, to obtain the approximate maximum likelihood estimation of ω, we employ the stochastic gradient descent to update ω in each interaction based on the observed click data z, relevance features x, and the inferred latent variables ρ and γ. On the other hand, the approximate maximum likelihood estimation of ω' will lead to the following update rule,

$$\omega'_t = \frac{\sum_m \sum_n \sum_s \phi_{m,n,s,t} x'_{m,n,s}}{\sum_m \sum_n \sum_s \phi_{m,n,s,t}}.$$

Our variational inference algorithm, named RBCM, can be interpreted intuitively in the following way. The CTCR distribution γ of each user is determined by both the topic prior and the accuracy that the learned weights of relevance features predict users' intended queries. Users' viewing/skipping states ρ at each keystroke is determined by the influence from users' states at the previous keystroke and that from users' states at the next keystroke. The state transition at each keystroke is determined by the transition prior, users' interaction patterns at that keystroke, and users' states at that keystroke and the keystroke before that. The probability of the interaction of a user m at the s-th keystroke in the n-th QAC session belonging to interaction pattern k is jointly determined by the state transition between the current and the next keystroke and the user's interaction at the current keystroke.

In our mean-field variation inference algorithm, the computational cost of inferring variational variables is $O(N*\bar{S}*T+M*D)$, where $\bar{S}$ is the average number of keystrokes in a QAC session, and $N = \sum_m N_m$ is the total number of QAC sessions in the entire high-resolution QAC log. The computational cost of the estimation of Dirichlet hyper-parameters is $O(M * D)$. The computational cost of the estimation of weights of relevance features is $O(N * \bar{S} * D)$, while the cost of the estimation of user interaction patterns is $O(N * \bar{S} * T)$. Thus the total computational cost of our algorithm is $O(N * \bar{S} * (T + D))$. Since T and D are both small constants, we can view the computational cost as linear in the total number of keystrokes in all sessions in the QAC log.

5. EXPERIMENTS

We evaluated our RBCM model on real-world data sets, and compared the performance with the following baselines: three alternative probabilistic models that only use two parts of the proposed model and four state-of-the-art QAC algorithms:

Alternative-A: This model does not use the hidden Markov model to capture the state transition of skipping/viewing moves. The state of skipping/viewing is determined by users' interactions with the QAC engine only.

Alternative-B: This model avoids using user-dependent features in the logistic regression part to capture users' real preference of suggested queries. It only utilizes user-independent features in the logistic regression part.

Alternative-C: This model avoids using a Dirichlet prior to model users' CTCR. Instead, it assumes users have no preference in clicking different positions as well as typing, i.e., the probabilities of clicking any positions and typing are all equal, and user's clicked suggestion is drawn via $z_{m,n,s,d} \sim \text{Multinomial}(\text{LR}(\omega x_{m,n,s,d}))$.

MPC [1, 18]: This method, named MostPopularCompletion, is a widely used baseline in Query Auto-Completion, and employed as one main feature in many QAC engines.

UBM [8]: This User Browsing Model proposes a number of assumptions on user browsing behavior that allows the estimation of the probability of observing a document. It depends on statistical counting of prefix-query pairs, thus unable to predict unseen prefix-query pairs.

BSS [10]: This Bayesian Sequential State model uses a probabilistic graphical model to characterize the document content and dependencies among the sequential click events within a query with a set of descriptive features. This is a content-aware model, which is able to predict unobserved prefix-query pairs.

TDCM [15]: This is a two-dimensional click model which emphasizes two kinds of user behaviors. It consists of a horizontal model, which explains the skipping behavior, and a vertical model that depicts the vertical examination behavior.

5.1 Real-world Data

We conducted extensive experiments on two real-world high-resolution QAC logs that collected from a commercial search engine. The first data set, which we name *LargeQAC*, contains high-resolution QAC logs from May 2014 to July 2014. The collection consists of a sample of 7.4 million QAC session from about 40,000 users over a 3-month period. We randomly selected a subset of active users who submitted over 500 QAC sessions during this period, and collected their corresponding search activities, including the anonymized user ID, query string, timestamp, and the clicked URL. As a result, we collected 3,954 users with 2.6 million queries, and their activities span from 22 days to 3 months. According to different platforms (PC or mobile phones), we split the entire dataset into two subsets. One is PC, which contains 1.6 million QAC sessions, while the other is mobile phones, which contains 1.0 million QAC sessions.

The second data set is also collected from a commercial search engine. We name this data *SmallQAC* to distinguish it from the previous one. This data set is constituted of random sampled high-resolution QAC logs dating from Nov 2013 to Jan 2014. The log contains 125 thousand QAC sessions from PCs. Since existing QAC algorithms utilizing high-resolution QAC logs have already shown rich results on the QAC log, we utilize both data sets to evaluate our proposed model and compare with the state-of-the-art methods in the following section.

5.2 Experimental Results

Model Fitness. This section evaluates the fitness of our proposed model on real-world data, and compares our model with probabilistic model based methods. We split the data based on the time information: the QAC sessions occurred in the first 90% of the time period are used as the training data, while the remaining 10% used as the test data. Table 3 shows the log predictive likelihood on sessions falling in the final 10% of the total time of QAC log data. According to Table 3, RBCM fits the real-world data better than the three alternative probabilistic models and TDCM. This illustrates that in the proposed RBCM model, all three parts play an important role in capturing the relationship between users' behaviors at different keystrokes. Alter-A performs the worst among all three alternative probabilistic models, which shows the importance of using the Markov process to model the state transition between skipping and viewing. Alter-B performs the best among three alternative probabilistic models, which shows that user-specific features do not fully utilize the relationship between users' behaviors. The reason may be that, even when the relevance features and their associated weights fail to reflect users' real preference of suggested queries, the other two parts of the proposed model can reduce the harm of those mispredictions by inferring reasonable skipping/viewing states and user-specific CTCR. TDCM performs the worst, since it fails to utilize the relationship between users' behaviors from any aspects.

Query Auto-Completion. To evaluate the effectiveness of the proposed model in suggesting users intended queries in each QAC session, we compare the proposed model with both alternative probabilistic models and state-of-the-art QAC algorithms. All compared methods re-rank the suggested queries at each keystroke and compete to rank the intended query as high as possible. In the proposed RBCM model, we use the relevance model part $\text{LR}(\beta\omega x)$ to re-rank the suggested queries. We employ the Mean Reciprocal Rank (MRR) as the relevance measurement, which is a widely used evaluation metric in measuring QAC performance [1, 18, 15],

$$MRR = \frac{1}{|Q|} \sum_{q \in Q} \frac{1}{\text{rank}_q},$$

where Q is the set of queries a user finally submitted, and rank_q denotes the rank of the query q in the suggested query list.

Notice that among the suggested query lists of all keystrokes, those lists that do not contain users' finally submitted queries are removed from our experimental analysis. Since our experiments are conducted on high-resolution QAC data, we report both the average MRR score of all keystrokes, and the average MRR of the last keystroke only, since this is the keystroke where the user's click occurs. Notice that existing works which didn't make use of high-resolution QAC logs usually used the MRR of the last keystroke to measure their performance. In the following experiments, the whole dataset is divided evenly into a training set and a test set for different settings.

Figure 4 compares the proposed model with alternative probabilistic models and state-of-the-art QAC algorithms by MRR. We can observe that RBCM performs the best among all compared approaches, and outperforms existing QAC algorithms by over 6%, for all the data sets and different settings. The advantage of RBCM over Alter-A illustrates the necessity of modeling the transition between skipping and viewing. The learned transition rules work for both existing users and new coming users, thus can provide better query suggestions for new coming users than TDCM, which models no relationship between users' behaviors at different keystrokes. In addition, the three alternative probabilistic models generally perform better than existing QAC algorithms. Such phenomenon demonstrates the effectiveness of making use of the relationship between users' interactions in different keystrokes in solving the QAC task. Essentially, appropriate modeling of such relationships together makes the proposed model much better than those alternative baselines. In specific, the advantage of Alter-B over TDCM illustrates that for those unseen prefix/query pairs, the proposed model can also achieve a sound performance, which attributes to the skipping/viewing transition and the user-specific preference of position clicking and typing captured by the proposed model. Besides our proposed model and its alternatives, TDCM performs better than the rest of existing QAC algorithms, which we attribute to

Table 3: Log Predictive Likelihood on Real-world Data

Model/Data set	Platform	RBCM	Alter-A	Alter-B	Alter-C	TDCM
LargeQAC	PC	-185.37	-192.83	-189.43	-191.84	-208.65
LargeQAC	Mobile	-177.95	-187.64	-184.91	-185.50	-195.04
SmallQAC	PC	-206.32	-218.14	-214.98	-216.69	-234.83

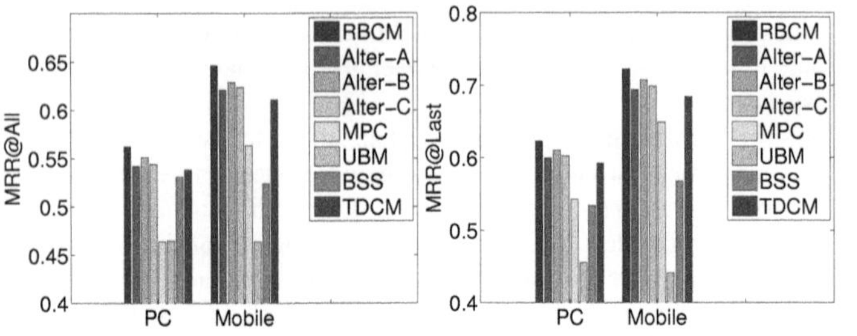

(a) LargeQAC (all keystrokes) (b) LargeQAC (last keystroke)

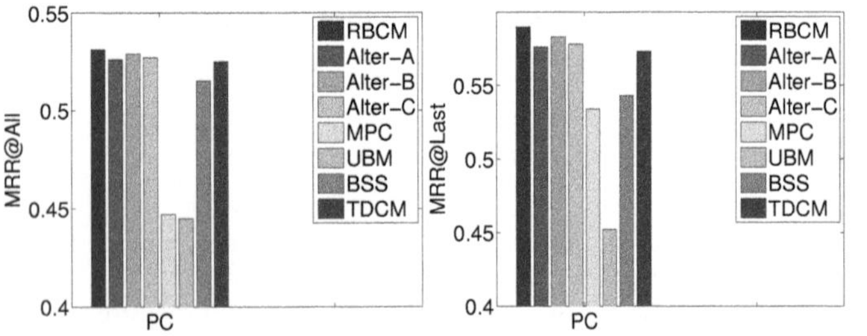

(c) SmallQAC (all keystrokes) (d) SmallQAC (last keystroke)

Figure 4: Performance Comparison of QAC Methods.

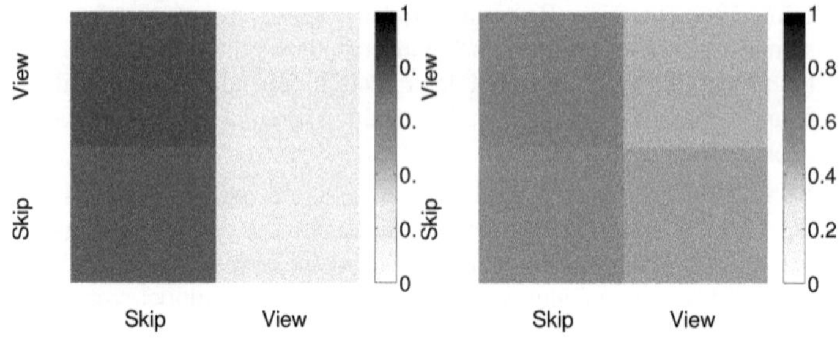

(a) Skipping User (b) Viewing User

Figure 5: State Transition of Skipping/Viewing.

the usage of high-resolution QAC logs. BBS outperforms UBM since it adopts the content-aware relevance model. MPC performs the worse, since it pays little attention to users' behaviors in QAC logs. By comparing with the performance using all the keystrokes and last keystroke only, we find that the advantages of the proposed model are ever more significant when measured by MRR@All. It indicates that the proposed model can recommend user intended queries higher when only a few keystrokes have been typed.

State Transition of Skipping/Viewing. Based on the state transition matrices and the corresponding user interaction patterns that learned by the proposed RBCM model from real world QAC logs, we provide a detailed analysis on the difference of transition rules between skipping/viewing and the associated user interaction patterns. Among all learned state transition rules, we pick two of them which differ the most in probability. Figure 5 shows the state transition rules and their corresponding user interaction patterns, where each block is the transition probability from the previous state (vertical) to the current state (horizontal). Intuitively, we find Figure 5(a) represents *skipping users*, i.e., users who prefer skipping than viewing, as these users have a much higher probability to skip at the current keystroke no matter the previous state is skipping or viewing, while Figure 5(b) represents *viewing users*, i.e., users who prefer viewing than skipping, because these users are more likely to switch to the viewing state from previous skipping or viewing status. Notice that *skipping* and *viewing users* only refer to the tendency of users' at each keystroke. A user who always skips suggested query lists will behave like *skipping user* consistently, while a user who has no habit in querying may alternatively switch between *skipping* and *viewing users* from time to time.

From Figure 5, we find that no matter what the state of the current keystroke is, *skipping users* are more likely to skip the suggested query list of next keystroke than *viewing users*. On the contrary, *viewing users* are more likely to view the suggested query list of next keystroke than *skipping users* under all circumstances. We also find that no matter which type a user belongs to, if he/she already viewed the suggested query list of the current keystroke, he/she will be more likely to skip the next keystroke than that under the situation where he/she skipped the current keystroke. Moreover, the corresponding user interaction patterns of different state transition rules appear quite different. *Skipping users* generally have faster typing speed, and come across less word boundaries, and enter more navigational queries.

Users' Real Preference of Suggested Queries. We use this series of experiments to discuss how our designed user-specific features enable the proposed model to understand users' real preference of suggested queries. We compare the proposed model with Alter-B on the QAC task measured by MRR, so as to illustrate the importance of using user-specific features. From Figure 6, we find that the proposed model performs better than Alter-B in recommending users' queries that satisfy their intent. In addition, we list a subset of learned weights of those designed user-specific features in Figure 7. From here, we can find that the history of queries that a user clicked plays a very important role in predicting the future queries he/she will click, especially when certain prefixes are given. Meanwhile, the length of the queries a user used to click is a significant signal for learning users' real preference of queries in the suggested query lists. The reason can be that such a signal implies users' clicking habit from some aspects. A skipping user who always clicks long queries will probably ignore his/her intended queries shown to him/her, before he/she enters enough number of keystrokes. Under such situation, the signal of query length will be capable of capturing users' real preference at keystrokes with short prefixes, which enables the proposed model to rank the intended queries at higher positions than those shorter queries. On the other hand, when a user has no preference in clicking long queries,

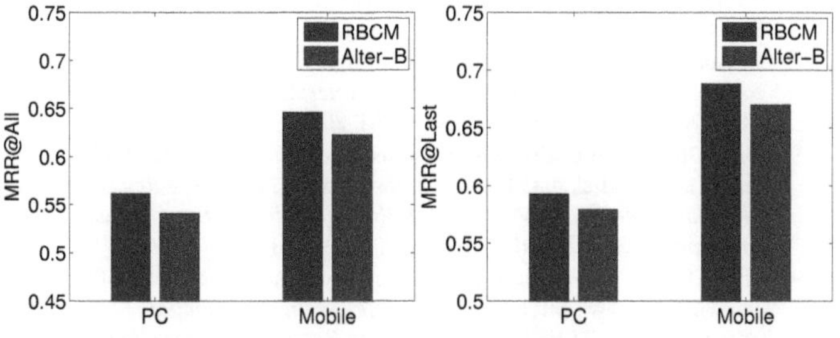

(a) LargeQAC (all keystrokes) (b) LargeQAC (last keystroke)

Figure 6: Comparison of RBCM with Alter-B.

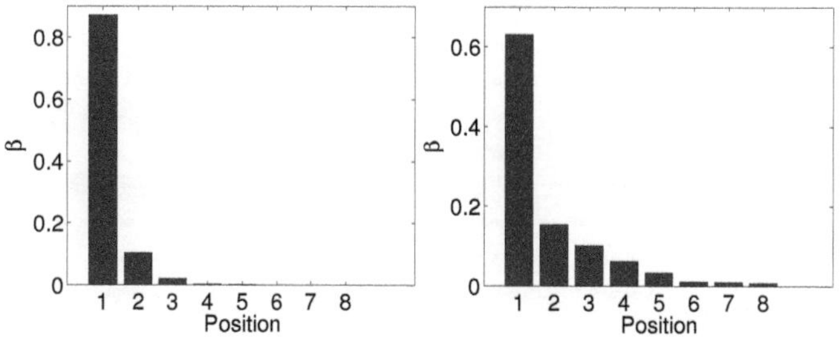

(a) Typing User (b) Clicking User

Figure 8: User-Specific Clicking/Typing Cost Ratio.

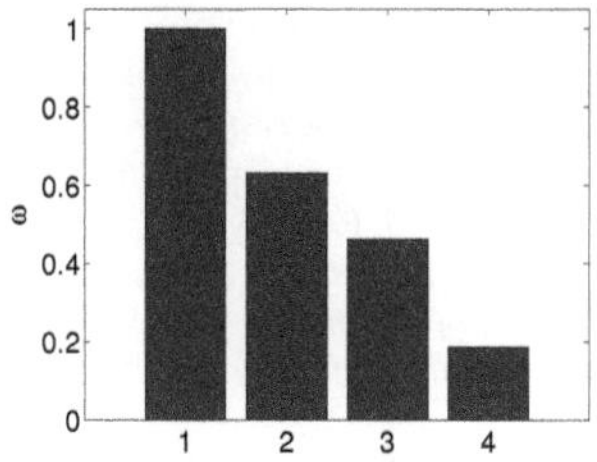

Figure 7: Weights of Relevance Features Learned by RBCM. Indice of selected user-specific relevance features: 1-Query Clicks, 2-Query Length, 3-Prefix/Query Ratio, 4-Query Word Number. The values of weights are scaled to the range of $[0, 1]$ to clarify the comparison of relative importance of different features.

this signal will not take effect, and the proposed model will recommend popular queries according to the frequency of the occurrence of prefix-query pairs. Such suggested queries are usually not that much longer than the given prefixes.

User-specific Cost Between Position Clicking and Typing. Based on the latent variable γ learned by the proposed model, we analyze the specific cost balance between position clicking and typing of different users. We select two subsets of users: one named *typing user*, which is formed by the top 20% users with the highest average click positions, and another, *clicking user*, is formed by the bottom 20% users with the lowest average click positions. We calculate the averaged *CTCR* of both two subsets of users, separately, and plot the results in Figure 8. From here, we find that the learned CTCR γ's of *typing users* and *clicking users* have very different distributions. Although users from both subsets are most likely to click the top query of a suggested query list, *clicking users* also occasionally click queries located at the middle positions of a suggested query list, while *typing users* rarely click those positions.

Furthermore, we try to distinguish the difference between *typing user&clicking user* and *viewing user&skipping user*. We select the top 20% users with the largest percentage of viewing states , and the bottom 20% users with the smallest percentage of skipping states. We compared the selected subsets of *typing users* with *skipping users*, and the selected subset of *clicking users* with *viewing users*. Table 4 shows the overlaps of the two pairs of compared subsets. According to Table 4, we find that there exists overlap between *typing users* and *skipping users*, *clicking users* and *viewing users*. For users sharing the same tendency of skipping/viewing

Table 4: Overlap between *typing user-skipping user* pair and *clicking user-viewing user* pair

Overlap	Percentage
typing user∩*skipping user*	34.2%
clicking user∩*viewing user*	22.7%

state choices, the difference of users in choosing clicking and typing becomes smaller. Skipping and typing are two reasons that a user does not click his/her intended query when it appears. Skipping users are more likely to click upper position queries, but this is not always true. A user who owns a high typing speed may not only prefer skipping than viewing but also prefer typing than clicking. However, he/she may also click the intended query the first time he/she views it.

Case Study of Query Auto-Completion. Now we show a few examples that illustrate how RBCM recommends users queries that better satisfy user intent by capturing the relationship between users' behaviors at different keystrokes. Figure 9 shows a QAC session where a user finally submitted "star wars", which is the user's intended query in this session. From Figure 9, we can find that the proposed model generally ranks users' intended queries higher than TDCM, especially at keystrokes with shorter prefixes. For example, with the prefix "st", RBCM ranks the intended query at the position 3 while TDCM ranks it at the position 10. The reason is that the proposed model utilizes the user's preference of the clicked queries at the last keystroke to improve its ranking at shorter keystrokes in the future by modeling the relationship between users' behaviors at different keystrokes. Our designed relevance features show that the query "star wars" has been issued many times by this user. Thus, although for the entire user collection, the generally frequencies of the appearances of "star wars" are relatively low given short prefixes, such as "st" or "sta", the proposed model ranks this query at the higher position for the specific user than other users who rarely search "star wars". We also notice that queries of similar intent, such as "star wars the old republic" and "star wars episode 7" are also ranked higher by our proposed model than by TDCM, which emphasizes that our model can better capture users' personal interests. Actually, through the analysis of the historical log of this particular user, we can find that he/she is a science fiction fan, which explains why our model also ranks "star trek" higher than TDCM. Thus we can conclude that appropriate modeling of such relationships is critical for predicting users' intended queries given short prefixes.

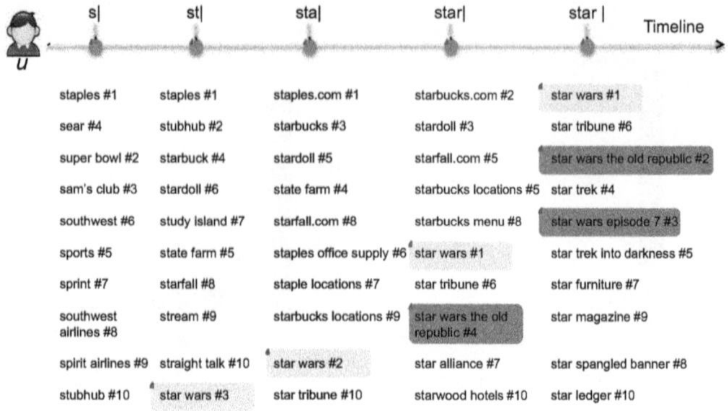

Figure 9: Case Study: The position of list queries from top to down shows the ranking of suggested queries predicted by TDCM, while the number tagged with # behind each query shows its ranking given by the proposed model. The yellow box highlights the user's intended query, and the green box highlights queries satisfy similar user intent. Notice that "|" is the cursor.

6. CONCLUSION AND FUTURE WORK

In this paper, we have presented a probabilistic model to solve the query auto-completion (QAC) task by capturing the relationship between users' behaviors at different keystrokes in high-resolution QAC logs. The proposed model integrates three parts, each addressing a single aspect of the above relationship, and illustrates how the three parts together determine users' final click decisions. We have applied the proposed model to predict users' intended queries on real world high-resolution QAC logs collected from a commercial search engine, and compare it with several alternative approaches. Experimental results show that the improvements of our proposed model are consistent, and our model achieves the best performance. In future work, it would be interesting to consider more complex relationships between users' behaviors at different keystrokes. For instance, we could increase the number of states from simply skipping or viewing to viewing to a certain position d, which enables a more precise modeling of users' behaviors in QAC.

7. ACKNOWLEDGMENT

This work is supported in part by NSF grant IIS-1116886.

8. REFERENCES

[1] Z. Bar-Yossef and N. Kraus. Context-sensitive query auto-completion. In *Proceedings of the 20th international conference on World wide web*, pages 107–116. ACM, 2011.

[2] H. Bast and I. Weber. Type less, find more: fast autocompletion search with a succinct index. In *Proceedings of the 29th annual international ACM SIGIR conference on Research and development in information retrieval*, pages 364–371. ACM, 2006.

[3] D. Blei and M. Jordan. Variational inference for dirichlet process mixtures. In *Bayesian Analysis*, volume 1, pages 121–144, 2005.

[4] O. Chapelle and Y. Zhang. A dynamic bayesian network click model for web search ranking. In *Proceedings of the 18th international conference on World wide web*, pages 1–10. ACM, 2009.

[5] N. Craswell, O. Zoeter, M. Taylor, and B. Ramsey. An experimental comparison of click position-bias models. In *Proceedings of the 2008 International Conference on Web Search and Data Mining*, pages 87–94. ACM, 2008.

[6] A. P. Dempster, N. M. Laird, and D. B. Rubin. Maximum likelihood from incomplete data via the EM algorithm. *Journal of the Royal Statistical Society. Series B (Methodological)*, pages 1–38, 1977.

[7] H. Duan and B.-J. P. Hsu. Online spelling correction for query completion. In *Proceedings of the 20th international conference on World wide web*, pages 117–126. ACM, 2011.

[8] G. E. Dupret and B. Piwowarski. A user browsing model to predict search engine click data from past observations. In *Proceedings of the 31st annual international ACM SIGIR conference on Research and development in information retrieval*, pages 331–338. ACM, 2008.

[9] L. A. Granka, T. Joachims, and G. Gay. Eye-tracking analysis of user behavior in www search. In *Proceedings of the 27th annual international ACM SIGIR conference on Research and development in information retrieval*, pages 478–479. ACM, 2004.

[10] A. D. H. Wang, C. Zhai and Y. Chang. Content-aware click modeling. In *WWW*, 2013.

[11] B.-J. P. Hsu and G. Ottaviano. Space-efficient data structures for top-k completion. In *Proceedings of the 22nd international conference on World Wide Web*, pages 583–594. International World Wide Web Conferences Steering Committee, 2013.

[12] J.-Y. Jiang, Y.-Y. Ke, P.-Y. Chien, and P.-J. Cheng. Learning user reformulation behavior for query auto-completion. In *Proceedings of the 37th international ACM SIGIR conference on Research & development in information retrieval*, pages 445–454. ACM, 2014.

[13] E. Kharitonov, C. Macdonald, P. Serdyukov, and I. Ounis. User model-based metrics for offline query suggestion evaluation. In *Proceedings of the 36th international ACM SIGIR conference on Research and development in information retrieval*, pages 633–642. ACM, 2013.

[14] L. Li, H. Deng, A. Dong, Y. Chang, and H. Zha. Identifying and labeling search tasks via query-based hawkes processes. In *Proceedings of the 20th ACM SIGKDD International Conference on Knowledge Discovery and Data Mining*, KDD '14, pages 731–740, New York, NY, USA, 2014. ACM.

[15] Y. Li, A. Dong, H. Wang, H. Deng, Y. Chang, and C. Zhai. A two-dimensional click model for query auto-completion. In *Proceedings of the 37th International ACM SIGIR Conference on Research and Development in Information Retrieval*, SIGIR '14, pages 455–464, New York, NY, USA, 2014. ACM.

[16] C. Liu, F. Guo, and C. Faloutsos. Bayesian browsing model: Exact inference of document relevance from petabyte-scale data. *ACM Transactions on Knowledge Discovery from Data (TKDD)*, 4(4):19, 2010.

[17] M. Richardson, E. Dominowska, and R. Ragno. Predicting clicks: estimating the click-through rate for new ads. In *Proceedings of the 16th international conference on World Wide Web*, pages 521–530. ACM, 2007.

[18] M. Shokouhi. Learning to personalize query auto-completion. In *Proceedings of the 36th international ACM SIGIR conference on Research and development in information retrieval*, pages 103–112. ACM, 2013.

[19] M. Shokouhi and K. Radinsky. Time-sensitive query auto-completion. In *Proceedings of the 35th international ACM SIGIR conference on Research and development in information retrieval*, pages 601–610. ACM, 2012.

[20] R. W. White and G. Marchionini. Examining the effectiveness of real-time query expansion. *Information Processing & Management*, 43(3):685–704, 2007.

[21] S. Whiting and J. M. Jose. Recent and robust query auto-completion. In *Proceedings of the 23rd international conference on World wide web*, pages 971–982. International World Wide Web Conferences, 2014.

[22] Y. Zhang, W. Chen, D. Wang, and Q. Yang. User-click modeling for understanding and predicting search-behavior. In *Proceedings of the 17th ACM SIGKDD international conference on Knowledge discovery and data mining*, pages 1388–1396. ACM, 2011.

[23] Z. A. Zhu, W. Chen, T. Minka, C. Zhu, and Z. Chen. A novel click model and its applications to online advertising. In *Proceedings of the third ACM international conference on Web search and data mining*, pages 321–330. ACM, 2010.

Learning by Example: Training Users with High-quality Query Suggestions

Morgan Harvey*
MIS Department
Northumbria University
Newcastle, UK
pwhq2@northumbria.ac.uk

Claudia Hauff
Web Information Systems
TU Delft
The Netherlands
c.hauff@tudelft.nl

David Elsweiler
I:IMSK University of Regensburg
Germany
david@elsweiler.co.uk

ABSTRACT

The queries submitted by users to search engines often poorly describe their information needs and represent a potential bottleneck in the system. In this paper we investigate to what extent it is possible to aid users in learning how to formulate better queries by providing examples of high-quality queries interactively during a number of search sessions. By means of several controlled user studies we collect quantitative and qualitative evidence that shows: (1) study participants are able to identify and abstract qualities of queries that make them highly effective, (2) after seeing high-quality example queries participants are able to themselves create queries that are highly effective, and, (3) those queries look similar to expert queries as defined in the literature. We conclude by discussing what the findings mean in the context of the design of interactive search systems.

Categories and Subject Descriptors: H.3.3 Information Search and Retrieval
General Terms: Measurement, Experimentation, Human Factors
Keywords: Search expertise; Reflection; Behavioural Change; User Study

1. INTRODUCTION

Much of the IR research in the last half century has, with great success, focused on developing improved retrieval models to enhance the utility of retrieval systems for the end user [41]. In this line of research search queries submitted to a retrieval system are considered as a given. The focus is placed on what to do systematically to return relevant documents given this limited representation of the user's information need. A complementary approach with potentially more scope for future performance gains is to focus on giving the system more to work with by assisting users in creating better queries for specific search systems [32, 24].

*All three authors contributed equally to this work.

SIGIR'15, August 09 - 13, 2015, Santiago, Chile.

DOI: http://dx.doi.org/10.1145/2766462.2767731.

Considerable evidence exists showing that many users do not know how to generate good queries. Analyses of search transaction logs show that people use short queries, especially on the Web [2] and even in this familiar domain a good proportion of searches fail completely [13]. In many search domains, including Web and Email search (with domain-specific search systems and interfaces), expert users achieve better retrieval effectiveness than novices and demonstrate different querying behaviour [3, 12, 43]. Moreover, despite the fact that most users today have to navigate through a range of search systems in their digital life, it has been reported that many users are inflexible in their approach and tend to use the same querying strategies regardless of task and available search system [29].

Typical solutions to assist users in creating effective search queries are the use of search UI features, such as query suggestions [35], related searches [36] or query autocompletion [5]. Alternatively, systems can employ context and personalisation techniques [11], which involve storing (and learning from) personal search histories and preferences to understand what a user knows and likes [18].

A third approach is to educate users about how to become better searchers [28] or to help users reflect on their own behaviour by comparing it to experts [6]. This method has the advantage that it is complementary to technical solutions. Our research continues along this path by investigating to what extent we can teach users how to pose better search queries to a particular search system. In contrast to existing approaches, we aim to understand if users are able to recognise, compare and contrast the properties of their own queries with good queries (provided by the system) and make changes to the queries they generate based on these insights. This is a new way of thinking about query suggestions; instead of providing automated examples for users to simply click on, we present them in a way that leads the user to reflect on his own behaviour, positively influencing his actions as a result.

The two principle research questions we answer are:

RQ1 Are users able to notice differences between good queries and their own and abstract these differences to change their own behaviour? If so, what are the noticeable differences?

RQ2 How effectively can users learn and abstract from good queries; do users who are "trained" perform better than users who did not receive the training? Which properties of their queries do users adapt after training?

2. RELATED WORK

It is well-recognised that searchers have difficulties communicating their information needs [7, 38, 24]. Taylor writes of a series of stages a user goes through when seeking information. These range from experiencing a visceral need, which is "probably inexpressible in linguistic terms" to a compromised need - a "representation of the inquirer's need within the constraints of the system and its files" [38]. Therefore, in order to generate successful queries, the user must overcome several cognitive challenges: 1) to determine himself what the need is and what kind of document will solve it; 2) to choose terms that describe that document well out of a very large set of possibilities [15] and 3) to communicate using the system's vocabulary and not his own [9].

Many interactive solutions have been designed to help the user overcome these challenges and improve the representations of information needs systems have to work with. The following subsection briefly reviews such work.

2.1 Interactive Query Support

IR systems can attain better descriptions of information needs by explicitly asking for certain details. The I3R system offered a means for users to provide terms and concepts they felt were important and identify relationships between these terms and other concepts in the domain [10]. Similarly, Kelly and Fu [24] used clarification forms to elicit additional information about the search context from users. The forms queried users on what they knew and what they would like to know about the topic and why. These were shown to be helpful in achieving improved retrieval performance.

A second technique is to assist the user to iteratively improve their own queries by adding additional terms suggested by the system, commonly referred to as interactive query expansion (IQE) [17]. This approach gives the user much more control over the search than if the query were to be expanded automatically (i.e. where the system selects expansion terms without user input [31]). Although IQE can offer improved performance [25], it has been shown that users are poor at identifying the terms that will offer the best improvement to their queries [33, 1]. This finding is intriguing with respect to our aims as it begs the question of whether or not users are able to identify qualities of good terms or whether they just assume terms suggested by a system will automatically be of a high quality.

Relevance feedback systems [34] are a further means to expand queries without explicitly choosing terms. Instead, relevance judgements are solicited on the returned documents. In addition to expanding queries, other scholars have investigated the performance of systems suggesting similar or related queries e.g. [36].

Improving user queries need not be achieved via technical solutions. One group in the 2007 SIGIR workshop breakout group identified a spectrum of possible solutions from manually-led approaches (based on improved information literacy and teaching) through to automatic, system-based approaches (based on more intelligent systems) [32]. The following section reviews literature on changing user behaviour via primarily non-technical means.

2.2 Changing Behaviour

Behaviour change support systems are "information systems designed to form, alter, or reinforce attitudes or behaviours or both without using coercion or deception" [30]. Within the context of search, changes can be made to the underlying retrieval engine or to the interface to 'nudge' people towards submitting longer or better queries or to look deeper in the results list [6]. Altering the size [14] and wording [8] of the search box, for example, has been shown to influence the length of queries submitted. Moreover providing a simple "Google-like" search interface as opposed to a complicated multi-field catalogue search can radically alter user behaviour [27]. Training users on how to construct queries can improve search behaviour [26]. For example, providing guidance on the advanced features that can help with specific search tasks can improve performance for these tasks and users are able to preserve and use the knowledge gained weeks later [28]. Moreover, allowing users to reflect on their own behaviour and, importantly, compare their behaviour to other, expert users, enables individuals to improve their own habits. In [6] users, after reflection, spent longer considering search results and issued longer queries. They also used a wider range of techniques and search engine features.

We extend some of the ideas in [6] here. Rather than inviting users to compare their behaviour with that of experts, however, we investigate if they are able to learn by comparing their own queries to examples generated by the system to be near optimal for the task at hand. In doing so we relate the kinds of approaches shown in Section 2.1 with the approaches in this section. We attempt to 'nudge' users to improve their queries via high-quality examples shown via widgets similar to those described above.

3. RESEARCH METHODOLOGY

The aim of our work is to establish whether showing users of an *unfamiliar* search system examples of high-quality queries (for a small number of information needs) enables them to create better-performing queries themselves. We investigate to what extent users learn more successful querying behaviours from those examples.

Based on our two research questions (Section 1) we devised the following research hypotheses:

H1 Users are able to adapt their querying behaviour to pose good queries to an unfamiliar search system.

H2 Users are able to identify characteristics of high-performing queries that allow them to perform so well.

H3 A small number of "training queries" is sufficient to enable a user to learn how to pose good queries themselves.

H4 A user who receives training with queries he can relate to (i.e. that are anticipated to perform well), learns *better* than a user receiving training with queries that are not predicted to perform well.

H5 A user who receives training with queries he can relate to, learns *faster* than a user receiving training with queries that are not predicted to perform well.

We conducted a number of user studies (Figure 1), each requiring the *automatic generation of high-quality queries* for a given information need and search system (described in Section 4.1). To address the issue of predicted performance, we performed an initial user study (Section 4.2) to investigate participants' perceptions of the generated queries. In contrast to the later studies, participants were not given access to our search system, their judgement was solely based on their own past experience.

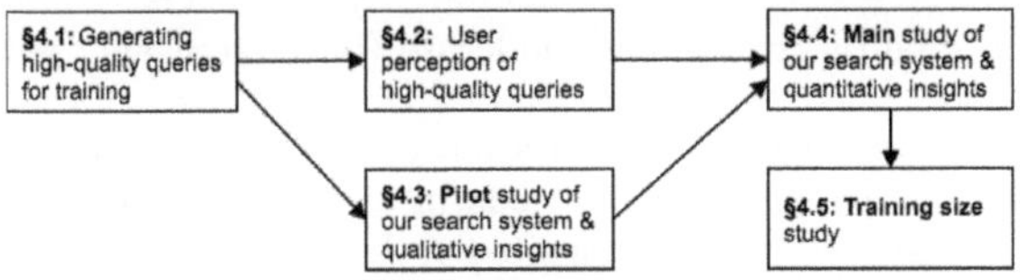

Figure 1: Overview of our experimental design.

Concurrently with the *User Perception Study*, we performed a *Pilot Study* (Section 4.3) which gave us qualitative insights into the characteristics of good queries that users were able to identify. The results of these two studies then allowed us to conduct a larger *Main Study* (Section 4.4) and a follow-up *Variable Training Size Study* (Section 4.5) with a consistent design, but different training parameters. The aim here was to better understand how much training is required to achieve an effect. In each of these studies participants were asked to perform a series of ad-hoc retrieval tasks using our search system.

To maintain maximum control over the experiments and have access to complete statistics of the collection the participants were searching over, we used a standard test collection: AQUAINT[1] together with the 50 TREC 2005 Robust track queries [40]. As our indexing and search engine we chose Apache SOLR[2]. To provide our study participants with a familiar user interface for searching the collection, we developed a web-based front-end in PHP (Figure 3).

4. EXPERIMENTS & RESULTS

In this section, we present an overview of each study and its results in turn.

4.1 Generating High-Performing Queries

In generating the "high-performing" query examples, we make the assumption that a query q_a is better than another query q_b for a given information need if q_a returns a higher Average Precision (AP) score. It is also important that the queries are understandable by humans and are not excessively long. Therefore, we are not interested in queries that happen to return good results because of a statistical anomaly or because they are overly verbose and specific.

Candidate queries were obtained via a recursive, greedy search algorithm. For each topic and its corresponding set of relevant documents, a collection was built consisting of only those relevant documents. The query building process is initiated by first considering only queries of length 1 (i.e. single-term queries) and choosing each of the top 100 terms from the topic-specific document collection (after stop words had been removed). Each initialisation of the recursive method takes in a base query and adds each of the top 100 terms to it. All 100 new potential queries are run against the entire collection using the standard SOLR search system and the AP score of the top 50 returned documents is computed. The list of queries is then ranked by their AP values and the top 10 are added to the candidate query list. Subsequently, the algorithm is initiated again with new base query having the newly-selected term added to the end. This recursive process was continued up to a query length of 4. At the end of the process any duplicate queries were removed and the top 100 queries (according to AP) were selected as the final list of candidates.

Note that this approach differs significantly from previous methods proposed in the literature for generating queries, e.g. [4], as our goal is fundamentally different. Rather than generating queries which appear to be samples from the collection (i.e. stochastically drawn from collection statistics), we are specifically interested in queries which yield high performance, are understandable and would, potentially, be posed by real users. Other related approaches used to find optimal queries in Boolean systems (e.g. [37]) were inappropriate due to differences in the underlying retrieval system. While our greedy approach does not produce globally optimal queries, it quickly produces large numbers of queries with an AP score of around 0.4. Concrete examples of generated queries can be found in the last column of Table 4.

Considering the top 100 queries for each topic, the median AP obtained by the generated queries over the first 20 returned results was 0.389. On a per-topic basis, the median was 0.391, the lowest average achieved was 0.054 and the maximum was 0.948 (IQR=0.31). Overall, 28 out of 50 topics had at least one query with an AP score greater than 0.5 and only 11 topics had any queries in the top 100 with an AP score below 0.2.

4.2 User Perception of Queries

To gain insights into how users perceive our high-quality queries (and as a precursor to answering hypotheses **H4** and **H5**), we conducted a crowd-sourcing experiment on the CrowdFlower[3] platform.

4.2.1 Study Overview

Each crowd-sourced task consisted of one search topic (in natural language form) and one of the queries generated in Section 4.1. Specifically, the workers were instructed as follows:

> *You already know query suggestions from search engines such as Google that present you with suggested queries while you type or show related queries alongside search results.*
>
> *In this task, you will be given an information need (in natural language form) and a query suggestion that has been derived for this information need. You are asked to judge the query suggestion along three dimensions - surprise, usage and relevance.*

Four questions had to be answered on a 5-point Likert scale:

1. How much do you know about the topic of the information need? (1: Very little, 5: A lot)
2. How surprised are you about the generated query suggestion? (1: Not at all surprised, 5: Extremely surprised)
3. Would you use this suggestion in an actual search? (1: No, I would not use it, 5: Yes I would use it)
4. What do you think the search result quality will be if this suggestion is used as query? (1: Very low quality, 5: Very high quality)

[1]We removed duplicate documents in a pre-processing step, to provide a better and more familiar user experience.
[2]`http://lucene.apache.org/solr/`
[3]`http://www.crowdflower.com`

Each job consisted of 10 tasks and workers were paid 12 cents (a standard rate). In this and all following CrowdFlower experiments the participants were restricted to countries where English is a native language.

For each of the Robust track topics, the 15 most effective queries generated were judged by CrowdFlower workers. Each query was judged by 3 workers, and thus, for each topic 45 judgements were collected. Three examples of topics, generated suggestions and worker ratings are shown in Table 4.

4.2.2 Results

Our workers found many of the search topics rather challenging with an average topic knowledge rating of 2.21. The most familiar topics tended to be of broad interest to many different communities; the two with the highest average knowledge ratings (3.00 and 2.89 respectively) were *What factors contributed to the growth of consumer on-line shopping?* (topic 639) and *Identify drugs used in the treatment of mental illness.* (topic 383). In contrast, search topics focusing on very specific themes or entities tended to elicit the lowest familiarity ratings; the topic with the lowest average knowledge rating (1.58) was *What is the status of The Three Gorges Project?* (topic 416).

When considering how unexpected the presented suggestions were (i.e. the "surprise" factor) we found that the vast majority of queries (more than 80%) were at least somewhat expected, receiving a rating between 1 and 3 (top-left of Figure 2). Only a small number of suggestions were considered to be *extremely surprising* and those were mostly found in topics our study participants knew little about. This indicates that our query generation approach is achieving its goal of generating queries understandable to humans.

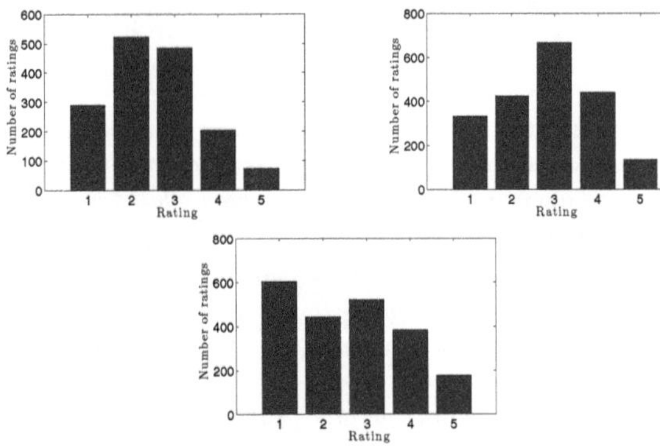

Figure 2: Histograms of "surprise" (top-left), "search quality" (top-right) and "suggestion usage" (bottom) ratings across the 750 different generated query suggestions, each rated by three users.

Of note is that fewer than 7% of judgements estimated the queries to achieve a *very high quality* of search results (top-right of Figure 2), while in contrast nearly 17% of the judgements were rated as likely to return *very low quality* search results. This result indicates that users are not able to judge the quality of query suggestions well, corroborating previous findings that users are unable to differentiate good search terms from bad ones [33, 1]. This result can only be partially explained by their lack of topical domain knowledge as the correlation between knowledge ratings and search quality ratings was moderate (but significant) with $r = 0.35$.

Lastly, we consider the question of to what extent users would use the shown suggestions in an actual search (bottom of Figure 2). Not unexpectedly, the correlation between the estimated search result quality and the potential usage is high ($r = 0.77$). Based on the ratings we have to conclude that many suggestions are not convincing, only a small number would definitely be used (9% of those rated 5) while 30% would definitely not be used (ratings of 1).

In summary, we find that user perception of our high-quality queries varies; many of them are not recognised as being effective. We make use of this result in the *Main Study*: one group of users receives high-quality suggestions recognised as high quality in this study, while another group of users receives high-quality suggestions that were rated as low quality in this study.

4.3 Pilot Study

The pilot study had three goals: (i) to test the validity of our system and task setup, (ii) to learn more about experimental factors such as participant fatigue, and (iii) most importantly, to collect qualitative data in order to establish whether participants are able to notice qualities of example queries that make them so effective as hypothesised in **H2**.

4.3.1 Study overview

The participants (n=22) consisted of university students and staff members recruited via email lists and announcements in lectures from a major European university. Although the participants were not native English speakers, all had advanced English language skills. They were given access to our search system and asked to complete 10 search tasks. As seen in Figure 3 the information need was prominently displayed to the participants. Each time they issued a query *(1)*, its retrieval effectiveness was displayed *(5)* in terms of the number of returned relevant documents within the top 20 results and the average precision (which was referred to as "search performance score"). Any relevant documents returned by the search were highlighted in blue *(4)*.

The participants were instructed to submit queries that they believed would return relevant documents (i.e. useful and containing information pertinent to the task). They were told that the documents had already been evaluated for relevance and that each submitted query would be scored in terms of how many relevant documents were returned in the top 20 results and the positions of those documents within the ranked list. This second score is simply average precision as used during the automatic query generation process and users were encouraged to focus on this to determine how well they were doing in the task. Users could move on to the next topic with a click on the *New topic, please* button *(6)*. Due to the interactive nature of the study, we selected 10 of the 50 Robust TREC topics by first eliminating those that that were either very difficult or very easy for our search system (measured in average precision achieved when using the title of the search topic as query) and then drawing randomly from the remaining topics[4].

The study participants were provided with query suggestions as shown in Figure 3 *(3)* similarly to how Web search

[4]The topics used were 303*, 362, 367*, 375*, 378, 383*, 401, 426*, 638* and 689. * indicates those that were later also used in the *Main Study*.

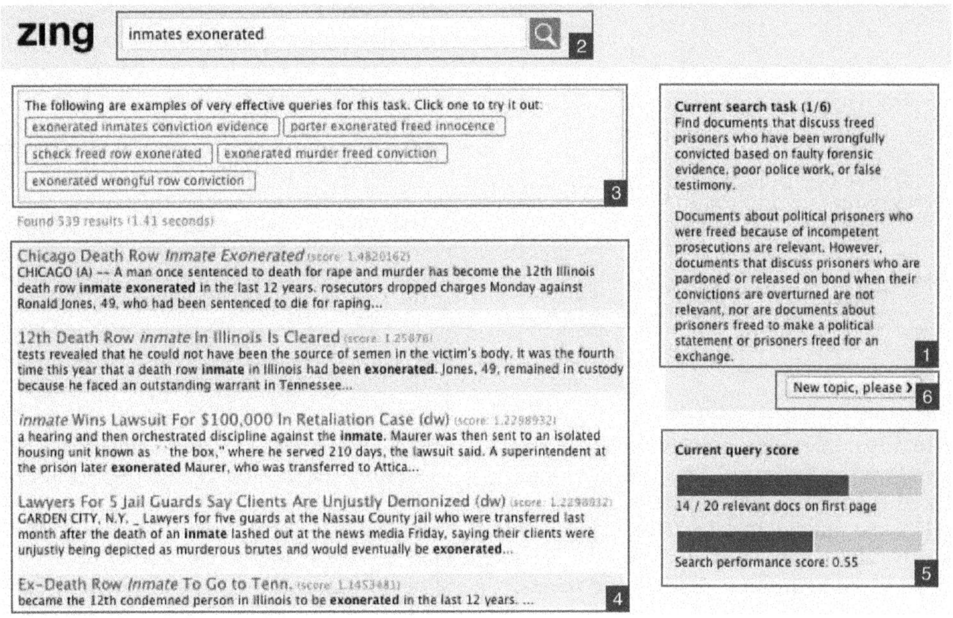

Figure 3: Screenshot of search interface showing a list of search results as well as some query suggestions.

engines often present query suggestions. After participants have posed their first two queries to the system for a particular topic, they are shown a number of our high-quality query suggestions. All displayed suggestions are *more effective* (achieve an AP at least 10% higher) than the participant's previous queries. Thus, different participants receive different suggestions, depending on the quality of their initial queries. The interface conveys to the participant that these are high-quality queries and they are encouraged to use them (Figure 3 *(3)*).

To test hypothesis **H2**, i.e. to establish whether users are able to learn from high quality query examples, after every use of a suggestion participants were prompted to describe in a text box *why* they considered it to be effective: "*You used the suggested query* [query]. *Considering your previous queries for this topic (shown below), what do you think is it about the suggested query that makes it so effective?*".

4.3.2 Results

The pilot findings help fine-tune our setup for the *Main Study*. Overall, the setup worked well, however we did establish fatigue to be a considerable factor. Figure 4 plots for each topic in sequence (recall that study participants receive the 10 topics in random order) the AP achieved by all queries submitted for the nth topic across all study participants. It is evident that over time (i.e. queries submitted for later topics) the retrieval effectiveness degrades. In particular after the 7th topic, the median AP is close to zero.

To investigate hypothesis **H2** we analysed the free-text explanations from participants describing why they believe the example queries performed so well. The responses show that participants were indeed able to identify positive query characteristics. In total 81 descriptions were supplied and out of the 22 participants, 15 gave at least one description of a suggestion. 3 participants gave descriptions for all of the suggested queries they used.

We analysed the responses qualitatively using an affinity diagramming technique, a process allowing the discovery and validation of patterns in qualitative data [16]. 12 codes were generated describing qualities participants assigned to high-performing suggestions. These are shown in Table 1.

Category
C1: Specific query terms (specification)
C2: More general query terms (generalisation)
C3: Queries not in topic description
C4: Unexpected or surprising vocabulary
C5: Surprising non-use of vocabulary
C6: Uses term the user was surprised at the usefulness of (i.e. perhaps not surprising given the topic, but surprising that it was good for performance)
C7: Thinking creatively
C8: Advanced vocabulary (rare but not on a specialist subject relating to the topic)
C9: Specialist vocabulary (rare and to do with a specialist subject relating to the topic)
C10: Good combination of search terms
C11: Using synonyms and related concepts
C12: Query requires specialist or background knowledge

Table 1: Overview of the query categories identified during the pilot study

Not only does the established coding scheme provide evidence that users *are* capable of noticing and abstracting differences between the suggested queries and their own - a prerequisite to learning - but the responses given are similar to those reported in the literature as being useful query reformulation strategies [23] or typical for queries submitted

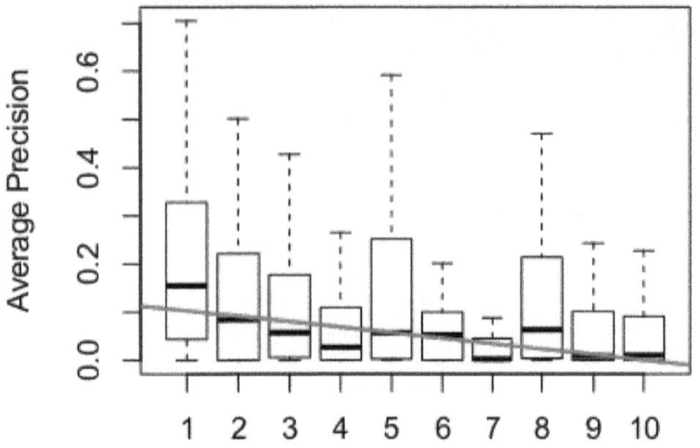

Figure 4: Pilot study: Average precision over sequences of topics showing fatigue. The nth element of the box plot contains the AP achieved over all queries across all users submitted for the nth topic the users worked on (since topics were issued in randomised order, the topic sequence differs per user).

by system and domain experts. For example, a common way to improve queries is to either make them more specfic (C1) or general (C2) [23]. Experts submit queries which are more elaborate [21] (C7, C11, C12), use broader and more varied vocabulary [39] (C1, C2), exploit synonyms and related concepts [22](C11), and include terms not used in topic descriptions [21]. Moreover, domain experts often search with queries containing specialist or domain knowledge [42] (C9, C12).

We take this as evidence to accept hypothesis **H2**. It is important to point out, however, that some of the participants explicitly mentioned in their responses that they would not be able to create some of the examples due to lack of domain knowledge or vocabulary (C10, C13).

We conclude that, despite the fact that participants are not universally able to recognise good queries (Section 4.2.2), our pilot data show that for many queries people can determine a range of properties that explain good performance.

4.4 Main Study

The main study addresses hypotheses **H1**, **H3**, **H4** & **H5** and draws from the outcomes of the two previously discussed user studies.

4.4.1 Study overview

In this study, we use search topics that our workers in the user perception study considered themselves knowledgeable about to reduce the potential influence of domain knowledge on our results. We base our choice of experimental conditions on the reported perceptions of queries to reflect **H2** and we reduced the number of tasks to six in an effort to counteract the fatigue effect observed in the pilot.

We use a between-groups design with participants randomly assigned to one of three experimental conditions:

- Group G_{exp_high}: this experimental group receives high-quality query suggestions in the training phase which were predicted to be effective in the user perceptions study (Section 4.2).
- Group G_{exp_low}: this experimental group receives high-quality query suggestions in the training phase which were predicted to be ineffective in the user perceptions study (Section 4.2).
- Group $G_{control}$: the control group does not receive any query suggestions.

For groups G_{exp_high} and G_{exp_low}, where suggestions are given, we split tasks into two phases: the first four topics are considered the *training phase*, where suggestions are shown, and the final two tasks are referred to as the *test phase*, where no suggestions are presented. Suggestions are provided using the same approach and interface as in the *Pilot Study*, i.e. suggestions were only given after two freely-created queries had been submitted and when there were queries available that would increase the AP score by at least 10%. Again, topics were issued in random order.

The participants (n=91, 29 in G_{exp_high}, 34 in G_{exp_low} and 28 in $G_{control}$) were also recruited via CrowdFlower and were paid 50 cents for the completion of a job. A job consisted of using our search system on six ad-hoc retrieval tasks; the study participants were not informed about the two phases of the study, they simply performed six search tasks (after four of which the query suggestion UI element was removed).

4.4.2 Results

We first compare the effectiveness of the issued queries, before looking at properties of the submitted queries and the fatigue factor.

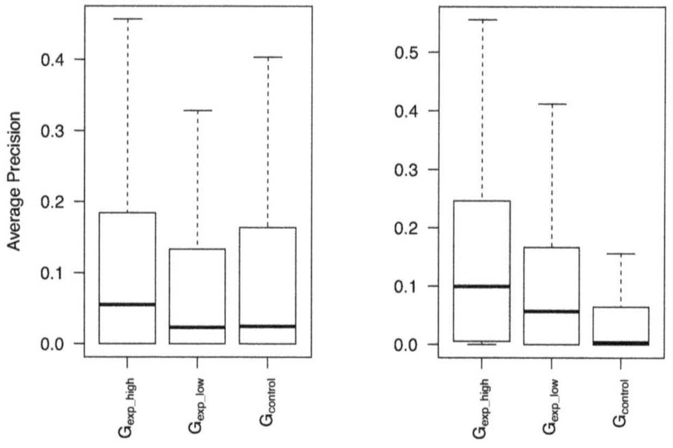

Figure 5: Main study: Querying performance over groups. Left: training topics. Right: test topics.

Effectiveness of Submitted Queries.

The fairest way to compare the performance across groups is to consider only the first 2 queries submitted by each participant for each topic. Doing so means we only consider queries submitted before suggestions are provided for a topic. Kruskal-Wallace rank sum tests show no significant difference between the groups on the training topics (p-value=0.320) but a significant difference for the test topics (p-value=0.002), with both experimental groups (G_{exp_high} and G_{exp_low}) performing significantly better than $G_{control}$.

If we consider all queries submitted for the test topics, not just the first 2 (as now no suggestions are shown to any user group), then these results become even clearer as shown in the top half of Table 2; participants of the G_{exp_high} group issue on average queries achieving an AP of 0.10, while participants of the alternative experimental condition G_{exp_low} achieve an AP of 0.06. The control group $G_{control}$ at this stage submits queries which are an order of a magnitude worse, with a mean AP of 0.004.

Figure 5 presents an alternative view of the submitted queries' effectiveness across groups; the left boxplot shows the retrieval effectiveness for the training topics whereas on the right the effectiveness for the testing topics is shown. It is evident that participants who receive high-quality training suggestions perform better on average, but also that they are able to achieve much higher maximum average precision scores.

Main study	Training 2 Queries	Testing 2 Queries	Testing All Queries
1: G_{exp_high}	0.0560	0.043	0.0998†
2: G_{exp_low}	0.0238	0.041	0.0571†
3: $G_{control}$	0.025	0.024	0.0039
Training-size study	**Training 2 Queries**	**Testing 2 Queries**	**Testing All Queries**
1: G_{exp_high}	0.0922	0.055†	0.0591†
2: G_{exp_low}	0.014	0.0343	0.0666†
3: $G_{control}$	0.04	0.0132	0.0132

Table 2: Average AP values aggregated across the first two queries of the training topics (column II), the first two queries of the test topics (column III) and all queries submitted for the test topics (column IV). † indicates a significant improvement over the $G_{control}$ condition (Kruskal-Wallace rank sum test, p-value $\ll$ 0.01).

If we look at how retrieval effectiveness changes as participants query more on the same topic, we see a strong trend where G_{exp_high} and G_{exp_low} continue to improve while those in $G_{control}$ do not (Figure 6). At query position 1 there is very little difference between the groups; $G_{control}$ is only scoring on average 0.005 worse than G_{exp_high}. However, this pattern changes quickly with the experimental groups able to achieve steadily more effective queries the more they submit, which is not the case for the control group $G_{control}$. By the 4th query the difference between $G_{exp_high}$and $G_{control}$ widens considerably to 0.135.

These findings provide strong evidence of retrieval effectiveness improvements for the experimental groups over the control group. The analyses so far, however, do not evidence a significant difference in performance gain between experimental conditions G_{exp_high} and G_{exp_low}.

Properties of Submitted Queries.

Beyond simply considering the retrieval effectiveness attained by a given query, we can also look at other properties of it that relate to its effectiveness or quality. These properties (shown in Table 3) go some way towards explaining the observed improvements in performance achieved by both experimental groups. We evaluated the submitted queries with metrics reflecting the literature on expert querying behaviour (see Section 4.3.2). On many of these metrics the experimental groups G_{exp_high} and G_{exp_low} significantly outperform the control group $G_{control}$. The trend is generally that group G_{exp_high} scores highest, group G_{exp_low} scores slightly

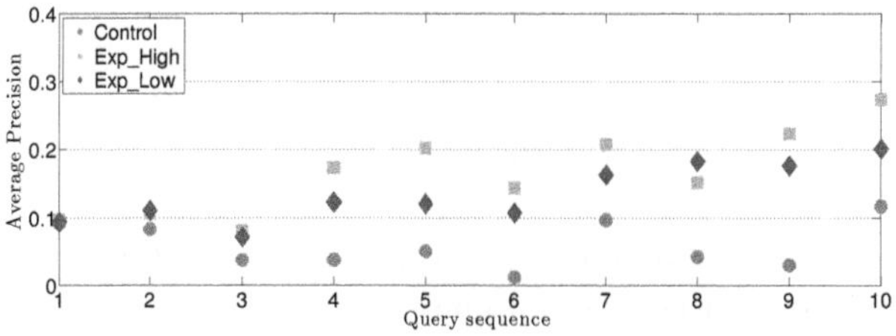

Figure 6: Main study: Average precision over sequences of queries on test topics. Each point in the plot represents the mean AP of all queries submitted as nth query. Truncated at query 10 as later queries have very few data points associated with them.

lower, but often not significantly so, and group $G_{control}$ achieves the poorest scores. Participants in G_{exp_high} and G_{exp_low}, for example, tended to submit longer queries (in both words and characters), which is noteworthy as the example queries they were shown were designed not to be overly long.

Out of all three groups, participants in G_{exp_high} submitted the rarest query terms. We measured this both in terms of the IDF statistics for the collection (i.e. their query terms feature significantly less often in the test corpus as a whole) and in terms of the number of overall participants who submitted those terms (we refer to this as median *UserCount-Term* in Table 3). Comparing the Jaccard-coefficient scores for query and topic description terms across the experimental conditions reveals that participants of G_{exp_high} were also the most likely to take terms from the topic descriptions given to them. These results suggest that a good query creation strategy was to use rare terms and seek inspiration from the topic descriptions, echoing findings from the literature [44]. While this could be negatively construed, since topic descriptions do not exist in real-life and users actually have difficulties in describing what they want [38], this finding does not explain the whole picture as there is no significant correlation (r=0.21) between AP and the overlap of queries with the topic descriptions (Jaccard score).

G_{exp_high} participants also submitted significantly more queries per topic than $G_{control}$ participants. However, this is less likely to explain the performance gains as there is no significant difference in the median number of queries submitted between G_{exp_high} and G_{exp_low} nor between G_{exp_low} and $G_{control}$. From the median time per topics it is also evident that G_{exp_high} and G_{exp_low} spend significantly more time working on each topic than $G_{control}$.

Fatigue.

One factor that could potentially affect the results is that of fatigue; are groups G_{exp_high} and G_{exp_low} doing better because they are feeling less fatigued by the task, perhaps as a result of getting some assistance in the early topics or by being shown that high performance was possible and thus increasing motivation? There are a number of metrics we can consider to try to ascertain if fatigue is present: the amount of time spent per query (query duration) and the amount of time spent per topic (topic duration) and the number of queries submitted. For all 3 groups the median query duration does seem to decrease slightly over the topics - linear models show a significant negative coefficient over the top-

	G_1: G_{exp_high}	G_2: G_{exp_low}	G_3: $G_{control}$	Wilcox (p-value) G_1/G_2	G_1/G_3	G_2/G_3
Median query length (words)	5.4	4.4	4.3	$p < 0.05$	$p < 0.01$	—
Median query length (chars)	29	28	23	—	—	$p < 0.05$
Median #queries per topic	3, IQR=4	2, IQR=4	2, IQR=2	—	$p < 0.05$	—
Median time per topic (seconds)	165	150	97	$p < 0.01$	$p < 0.01$	$p < 0.01$
Median time per query (seconds)	13	11	13	$p < 0.01$	—	—
Median query term IDFs	4.9	5.24	5.15	$p < 0.01$	—	—
Median UserCountTerm	43	45	51	—	$p < 0.01$	—
Jaccard coefficient (query terms, topic descr. terms)	0.3	0.25	0.25	$p < 0.01$	$p < 0.01$	—

Table 3: Main study: Overview of query properties aggregated for each user group across the two topics issued during the test phase.

ics of between -0.6 and -0.99. This is not the case for topic duration, however, as there is no significant trend for any of the 3 groups meaning that they all spend roughly the same amount of time on each topic. The same consistency is also present when looking at the number of queries submitted. There is no significant correlation between topic sequence and number of queries for any of the groups although groups G_{exp_high} and G_{exp_low} do submit more queries overall. These factors do not point strongly to fatigue being a factor, although the subtle changes in query duration do suggest that users are spending less time thinking about each query as time goes on, which may explain the consistent reduction in average precision.

4.5 Variable Training Size Study

An obvious question to ask, given these results, is what impact does the number of training topics given to the test groups have on performance. A final study investigated to what extent the number of training topics (hypothesis **H3**) influences a user's ability to formulate good queries.

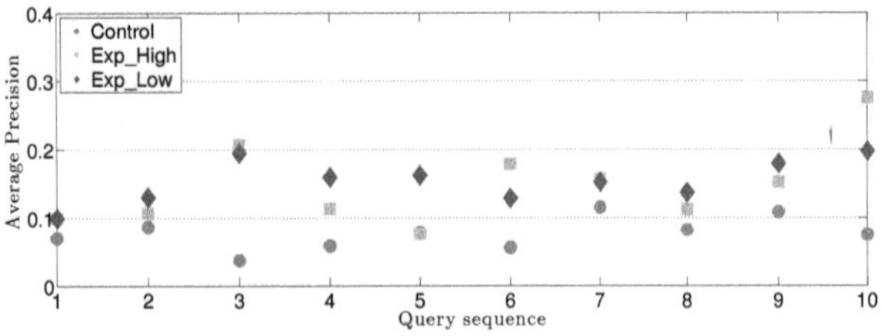

Figure 7: Training-size study: Average precision over sequences of queries on test topics. Each point in the plot represents the mean AP of all queries submitted as nth query. Truncated at query 10 as later queries have very few data points associated with them.

4.5.1 *Study overview*

We used the same setup and experimental design as in the *Main Study* and varied only the ratio between training and test topics: in this study we used two topics for training, and the remaining four topics for testing. As in the *Main Study*, participants (n=57, 19 participants in each condition) were recruited via CrowdFlower.

4.5.2 *Results*

The results from this study were analysed in the same fashion as those from the main study as can be seen in the bottom half of Table 2. The major finding of the *Main Study* holds in this experiment as well: both experimental groups outperform the control group wrt. effectiveness. Thus, even a very small amount of training (2 topics) is useful and aids users in learning to formulate better queries.

In contrast to the *Main Study*, and unsurprising given the lower amount of training, we observe a smaller difference in retrieval effectiveness across the test topics: 0.05 (G_{exp_high}), 0.054 (G_{exp_low}) and 0.024 ($G_{control}$) respectively.

These results suggest that some form of learning is taking place and that the relative improvements are smaller if less training is given. They also serve to further highlight the unexpected finding that there is little difference between G_{exp_high} and G_{exp_low}.

5. SUMMARY AND DISCUSSION

Our findings vs. our research hypotheses.

Hypothesis **H1** has been shown to hold - users are indeed able to adapt their search behaviour to an unfamiliar search system. While $G_{control}$ (which received no training) does not adapt, we clearly see significant changes in querying behaviour in both experimental groups (i.e. those who received training).

Our pilot study served to confirm hypothesis **H2**; the study participants were indeed able to determine a set of characteristics that well-performing queries contain. Recognising such characteristics is a necessary requirement for learning how to create better queries in general and not just for specific topics.

The main study and the follow-up focusing on the training set size provide evidence for hypothesis **H3**. The two experimental groups outperform $G_{control}$ significantly, both when being shown two and four training topics respectively. Thus, even a very small set of training topics is sufficient to improve users' ability to pose good queries.

Our results do not support **H4**. In terms of AP, although Figure 5 hints that G_{exp_high} may have outperformed G_{exp_low},

ID	Information need	av. KNOW	av. SUR	av. QUAL	Query suggestion examples
303	*Identify positive accomplishments of the Hubble telescope since it was launched in 1991*	2.64	2.62	2.98	[*universe astronomer faint hubble*], [*infrared galaxies universe hubble*], [*infrared stars universe hubble*]
383	*Identify drugs used in the treatment of mental illness.*	2.89	2.45	3.36	[*antidepressant risk zoloft prozac*], [*zoloft studies prozac*], [*antidepressant effective zoloft prozac*]
416	*What is the status of The Three Gorges Project?*	1.58	3.09	2.60	[*cofferdams damming generating 2009*], [*dam corporation phase 2009*], [*2009 river construction*]

Table 4: Examples of Robust track search tasks and the generated high-quality query suggestions. Columns 3-5 contain user rating data from our study on user perceptions of queries. Column 3 (KNOW) contains the average knowledge rating of the information need across all users of the study. Columns 4 and 5 contain the average rating users assigned to all query suggestions of the topic with respect to the surprise (SUR) factor and the estimated result quality (QUAL).

the difference is not significant. There were some features of the queries that were statistically distinguishable between these groups, but we feel that the evidence is not strong enough to claim that **H4** holds.

Finally, based on the evidence in Figures 6 and 7, we have to reject **H5** - our participants in both experimental groups had a comparable learning rate (though with different absolute performance scores).

Our findings vs. prior work.

Previous work has presented mixed evidence for people's ability to accurately determine which query terms will have utility. Our findings suggest this is a complex behaviour. Although participants were able to identify positive characteristics of queries shown to be effective (Section 4.3.2), many high-performing queries were not predicted to be such (Section 4.2.2). Perhaps these potentially contradictory findings indicate a potential systems bias, i.e. do users implicitly trust suggestions presented by the system as good? Is it only when doubt is introduced by explicitly questioning users about the queries that they perceive suggestions to be potentially not of good quality? What does this mean for the learning effect? This line of thought opens up many fascinating questions of how query suggestions are presented.

Our work has added to the small base of literature demonstrating means for users to learn how to provide higher-quality queries. One limitation of our work has to do with the time period of learning. Our findings support the claim that being shown good suggestions can lead to users learning how to produce better queries, however this is only demonstrated over the period of a session i.e. the test groups achieved better performance for later queries and for later topics. Ideally, however, what we want to show is learning over longer periods of time, such as weeks [28] and months [6] as previous studies have done. This requires a different mode of evaluation as crowd-sourcing is not suited to such tasks and represents an important next stage in our project.

A further limitation, with respect to how our findings may be used, is that in a real-life scenario a search system would normally not have access to relevance judgements. This means our method of creating queries cannot typically be applied. We argue that there are situations, though, that may be ideally suited to such an approach. For example in web search we have implicit indicators for difficult tasks (i.e. where better queries might be required) [20] and we also have good models for determining search success based on user behaviour [19]. When such instances combine (i.e. when users are successful in tasks they have been struggling with), this might be the perfect time to present a query suggestion, perhaps along the line of "The following query would get this page further up the ranking". Another potential use-case might be to present examples when a user switches context or to a new search-engine where new strategies are required. It has been suggested that users tend not to vary their strategy [29] and our approach might help encourage more diverse or tailored behaviour.

6. CONCLUSIONS

The set of user studies described in this paper have demonstrated that it is possible to use high-quality query examples to influence the queries users submit themselves. We have shown that users can recognise and abstract positive qualities of good queries. Users change the properties of the queries they submit and achieve better retrieval performance after seeing good examples for other tasks. Our findings open up a range of interesting questions relating to how query examples should be presented and how this affects learning and the influence of learning duration, i.e. is user behaviour influenced over the longer term? Finally is domain knowledge an important factor? We hope to address these issues in upcoming work.

7. REFERENCES

[1] P. Anick, *Using terminological feedback for web search refinement: a log-based study*, SIGIR '03, ACM, 2003, pp. 88–95.

[2] A. Arampatzis and J. Kamps, *A study of query length*, SIGIR '08, ACM, 2008, pp. 811–812.

[3] A. Aula, N. Jhaveri, and M. Käki, *Information search and re-access strategies of experienced web users*, WWW '05, ACM, 2005, pp. 583–592.

[4] L. Azzopardi, M. De Rijke, and K. Balog, *Building simulated queries for known-item topics: an analysis using six european languages*, SIGIR '07, ACM, 2007, pp. 455–462.

[5] H. Bast and I. Weber, *Type less, find more: fast autocompletion search with a succinct index*, SIGIR '06, ACM, 2006, pp. 364–371.

[6] S. Bateman, J. Teevan, and R.W. White, *The search dashboard: how reflection and comparison impact search behavior*, SIGCHI, ACM, 2012, pp. 1785–1794.

[7] N.J. Belkin, *Helping people find what they don't know*, Commun. ACM **43** (2000), no. 8, 58–61.

[8] N.J. Belkin, D. Kelly, G Kim, J-Y Kim, H-J Lee, G. Muresan, M-C Tang, X-J Yuan, and C. Cool, *Query length in interactive information retrieval*, SIGIR '03, ACM, 2003, pp. 205–212.

[9] J.L. Bennett, *The user interface in interactive systems*, Annual review of information science and technology **7** (1972), no. 159-196.

[10] W.B. Croft and R.H. Thompson, *I3r: A new approach to the design of document retrieval systems*, JASIST **38** (1987), no. 6, 389–404.

[11] Z. Dou, R. Song, and J. Wen, *A large-scale evaluation and analysis of personalized search strategies*, WWW '07, ACM, 2007, pp. 581–590.

[12] D. Elsweiler, *Supporting human memory in personal information management*, Ph.D. thesis, University of Strathclyde, 2007.

[13] B.M. Evans and E.H. Chi, *An elaborated model of social search*, IP&M **46** (2010), no. 6, 656–678.

[14] K. Franzen and J. Karlgren, *Verbosity and interface design*, SICS Research Report (2000).

[15] G.W. Furnas, T.K. Landauer, L.M. Gomez, and S.T. Dumais, *The vocabulary problem in human-system communication*, Communications of the ACM **30** (1987), no. 11, 964–971.

[16] J. Hackos and J. Redish, *User and task analysis for interface design*, John Wiley & Sons, Inc., 1998.

[17] D. Harman, *Towards interactive query expansion*, SIGIR '88, ACM, 1988, pp. 321–331.

[18] M. Harvey, F. Crestani, and M.J. Carman, *Building user profiles from topic models for personalised search*, CIKM '13, ACM, 2013, pp. 2309–2314.

[19] A. Hassan, R. Jones, and K. L. Klinkner, *Beyond dcg: user behavior as a predictor of a successful search*, WSDM, ACM, 2010, pp. 221–230.

[20] A. Hassan, R. W. White, S. T Dumais, and Y. Wang, *Struggling or exploring?: disambiguating long search sessions*, WSDM, ACM, 2014, pp. 53–62.

[21] H.A. Hembrooke, L.A. Granka, G.K. Gay, and E.D. Liddy, *The effects of expertise and feedback on search term selection and subsequent learning*, JASIST **56** (2005), no. 8, 861–871.

[22] I. Hsieh-yee, *Effects of search experience and subject knowledge on the search tactics of novice and experienced searchers*, JASIST **44** (1993), 161–174.

[23] B.J. Jansen, D.L. Booth, and A. Spink, *Patterns of query reformulation during web searching*, Journal of the American Society for Information Science and Technology **60** (2009), no. 7, 1358–1371.

[24] D. Kelly and X. Fu, *Eliciting better information need descriptions from users of information search systems*, IP&M **43** (2007), no. 1, 30–46.

[25] J. Koenemann and N.J. Belkin, *A case for interaction: a study of interactive information retrieval behavior and effectiveness*, SIGCHI '96, ACM, 1996, pp. 205–212.

[26] W. Lucas and H. Topi, *Training for web search: Will it get you in shape?*, JASIST **55** (2004), no. 13, 1183–1198.

[27] D. McKay and G. Buchanan, *Boxing clever: how searchers use and adapt to a one-box library search*, OzCHIÕ13, ACM, 2013, pp. 497–506.

[28] N. Moraveji, D. Russell, J. Bien, and D. Mease, *Measuring improvement in user search performance resulting from optimal search tips*, SIGIR '11, ACM, 2011, pp. 355–364.

[29] J. Nielsen, *Incompetent research skills curb users' problem solving http://www.useit.com/alertbox/search-skills.html last accessed january, 2015*, Alertbox (2011).

[30] H. Oinas-Kukkonen and M. Harjumaa, *Towards deeper understanding of persuasion in software and information systems*, ACHI '08, IEEE, 2008, pp. 200–205.

[31] S.E. Robertson, *On term selection for query expansion*, Journal of Documentation **46** (1990), no. 4, 359–364.

[32] K. Rodden, I. Ruthven, and R.W. White, *Workshop on web information seeking and interaction*, ACM SIGIR Forum, vol. 41, ACM, 2007, pp. 63–67.

[33] I. Ruthven, *Re-examining the potential effectiveness of interactive query expansion.*

[34] I. Ruthven and M. Lalmas, *A survey on the use of relevance feedback for information access systems*, The Knowledge Engineering Review **18** (2003), no. 02, 95–145.

[35] B. Shneiderman, *Dynamic queries for visual information seeking*, Software, IEEE **11** (1994), no. 6, 70–77.

[36] B. Smyth, E. Balfe, J. Freyne, P. Briggs, M. Coyle, and O. Boydell, *Exploiting query repetition and regularity in an adaptive community-based web search engine*, User Modeling and User-Adapted Interaction **14** (2004), no. 5, 383–423.

[37] E. Sormunen, *A method for measuring wide range performance of boolean queries in full-text databases*, Tampere University Press, 2000.

[38] R.S. Taylor, *Question-negotiation and information seeking in libraries*, College & Research Libraries **29** (1968), no. 3, 178–194.

[39] P. Vakkari, *Changes in search tactics and relevance judgements when preparing a research proposal a summary of the findings of a longitudinal study*, Information Retrieval **4** (2001), no. 3-4, 295–310.

[40] E.M. Voorhees, *The trec 2005 robust track*, SIGIR Forum **40** (2006), no. 1, 41–48.

[41] E.M. Voorhees, D.K. Harman, et al., *Trec: Experiment and evaluation in information retrieval*, vol. 63, MIT press Cambridge, 2005.

[42] R.W. White, S.T. Dumais, and J. Teevan, *Characterizing the influence of domain expertise on web search behavior*, WSDM '09, ACM, 2009, pp. 132–141.

[43] R.W. White and D. Morris, *Investigating the querying and browsing behavior of advanced search engine users*, SIGIR '07, ACM, 2007, pp. 255–262.

[44] P. Willett and I. Ruthven, *Relevance behaviour in trec*, Journal of Documentation **70** (2014), no. 6, 1098–1117.

adaQAC: Adaptive Query Auto-Completion via Implicit Negative Feedback

Aston Zhang*[1], Amit Goyal[2], Weize Kong[3], Hongbo Deng[2]
Anlei Dong[2], Yi Chang[2], Carl A. Gunter[1], Jiawei Han[1]
[1]University of Illinois at Urbana-Champaign, IL, USA, [2]Yahoo! Labs, CA, USA
[3]University of Massachusetts Amherst, MA, USA
{lzhang74, cgunter, hanj}@illinois.edu,
{goyal, hbdeng, anlei, yichang}@yahoo-inc.com, wkong@cs.umass.edu

ABSTRACT

Query auto-completion (QAC) facilitates user query composition by suggesting queries given query prefix inputs. In 2014, global users of Yahoo! Search saved more than 50% keystrokes when submitting English queries by selecting suggestions of QAC.

Users' preference of queries can be inferred during user-QAC interactions, such as dwelling on suggestion lists for a long time without selecting query suggestions ranked at the top. However, the wealth of such implicit negative feedback has not been exploited for designing QAC models. Most existing QAC models rank suggested queries for given prefixes based on certain relevance scores.

We take the initiative towards studying implicit negative feedback during user-QAC interactions. This motivates re-designing QAC in the more general "(static) relevance–(adaptive) implicit negative feedback" framework. We propose a novel adaptive model adaQAC that adapts query auto-completion to users' implicit negative feedback towards unselected query suggestions. We collect user-QAC interaction data and perform large-scale experiments. Empirical results show that implicit negative feedback significantly and consistently boosts the accuracy of the investigated static QAC models that only rely on relevance scores. Our work compellingly makes a key point: QAC should be designed in a more general framework for adapting to implicit negative feedback.

Categories and Subject Descriptors

H.3.3 [**Information Storage and Retrieval**]: Information Search and Retrieval—*Query Formulation*

Keywords

Query Auto-Completion; Implicit Negative Feedback

1. INTRODUCTION

Query auto-completion (QAC) helps user query composition by suggesting queries given prefixes. As illustrated in Fig. 1, upon a user's keystroke, QAC displays a *suggestion list* (or *list*) below the current *prefix*. We refer to queries in a suggestion list as *suggested queries* or *query suggestions*. A user can select to submit a suggested query; a user can also submit a query without selecting query suggestions. In 2014, global users of Yahoo! Search saved more than 50% keystrokes when submitting English queries by selecting suggestions of QAC.

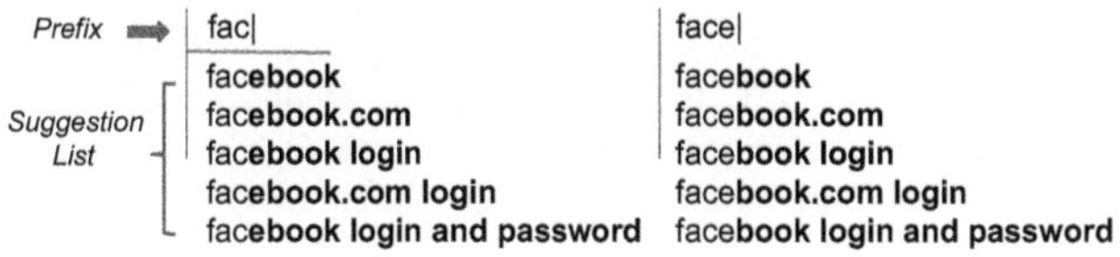

Figure 1: A commercial search engine QAC. Given prefixes "fac" and "face", popular "facebook"-related queries are suggested to users after being ranked by certain relevance scores.

Typically, a user *favors* and submits a query if it reflects the user's query intent in a query composition. However, predicting query intent is challenging. Many of the recently proposed QAC models rank a list of suggested queries for each prefix based on different relevance scores, such as popularity-based QAC (using historical query frequency counts) [2], time-based QAC (using time information) [32, 35], context-based QAC (using previous query information of users) [2], personalized QAC (using user profile information) [31], time-and-context-based QAC (using both time and previous query information of users) [5].

The aforementioned models use different relevance features but do not fully exploit user-QAC interactions, such as users' dwell time on suggestion lists and ranked positions of suggested queries by QAC. When users do not select query suggestions at keystrokes of compositions, users implicitly express negative feedback to these queries. Hence at such keystrokes, the user-QAC interaction information is users' *implicit negative feedback* to unselected queries. We aim at complementing relevance features with implicit negative feedback to improve the existing QAC models.

We start with a motivating example.

Motivating Example: Consider a user who wants to query Apple Inc.'s "facetime" with a popularity-based QAC [2]. When the user types "fac", "facebook" is ranked at the top in the suggestion list because it is most popular in historical query logs. The user dwells for a long time to examine the suggested query "facebook" but does not select it because it is not "facetime". However, in the next keystroke "e", popularity-based QAC still makes "facebook" top in the list because it is still the most popular query that matches

---

*Part of the work was completed at Yahoo! Labs.

SIGIR'15, August 9-13, 2015, Santiago, Chile.
©2015 ACM. ISBN 978-1-4503-3621-5/15/08...$15.00
DOI: http://dx.doi.org/10.1145/2766462.2767697

the prefix "face". Fig. 1 depicts our interactions with a commercial search engine QAC known to depend on relevance scores only.

Here the user implicitly expresses negative feedback to "facebook": "facebook" is the top query suggestion, and the user dwells on the suggestion list for a long time without selecting this query. Hence, based on such implicit negative feedback, the user may not favor this unselected query. Can QAC be more accurate and demote "facebook" properly given the prefix "face"?

Our Approach: To the best of our knowledge, no existing QAC adapts its ranking of query suggestions to implicit negative feedback. We refer to a QAC model as **static QAC**, if its ranking of suggested queries does not adapt to implicit negative feedback in a query composition. Examples include popularity-based QAC, time-based QAC, and context-based QAC.

We go beyond static QAC by designing QAC in the new and more general "(static) relevance–(adaptive) implicit negative feedback" framework. In this framework, we propose a novel adaQAC model that adapts QAC to implicit negative feedback. adaQAC reuses the relevance scores of queries from static QAC to pre-index top-N queries. In a single query composition, adaQAC re-ranks these N queries at every keystroke based on users' implicit negative feedback. Personalized learning for every different user with batch inference is employed by adaQAC, and adaQAC can be extended by un-personalized learning and online inference.

Our Contributions: This work has many distinctions from related research in QAC, negative feedback, and dynamic information retrieval; we present detailed discussions on such distinctions in §5. Our contributions are summarized as follows.

• To the best of our knowledge, this is the first study on implicit negative feedback in user-QAC interactions. We find that the strength of implicit negative feedback to unselected query suggestions can be inferred, and a simple model fails (§2).

• We go beyond static QAC under a general "(static) relevance–(adaptive) implicit negative feedback" framework: we propose a novel adaQAC model that adapts QAC to implicit negative feedback using personalized learning with batch inference, including un-personalized learning and online inference extensions (§3).

• We collect user-QAC interaction data from a commercial search engine and perform large-scale experiments. We show that implicit negative feedback significantly and consistently boosts the accuracy of the investigated static QAC models (§4).

2. IMPLICIT NEGATIVE FEEDBACK IN USER-QAC INTERACTIONS

We study QAC log data from a commercial search engine and discuss several motivational observations on implicit negative feedback in user-QAC interactions.

Terminology: In general, on search engines, queries are *submitted* upon users' *selection* from suggestion lists. Below are the other used terms.

Query composition (Composition): The duration of composing and submitting a single query. It starts from the keystroke of a new query's first character, or from the keystroke starting to edit a previous query. It ends when a query is submitted.

Dwell time: The time dwelled on a suggestion list. It is the time gap between two immediate keystrokes in a query composition.

Position: The ranked position of a query in a suggestion list by QAC. Position 1 means being ranked highest or at the top, while 10 corresponds to being ranked lowest or at the bottom.

QAC log data: Our collected user-QAC interaction data from Yahoo! Search. There are 2,932,035 query compositions via desktops and they are sampled over five months in 2014. A composition has the prefixes, timestamps and suggested queries of every keystroke, and the submitted query. More details of the data are in §4.1. Due to the proprietary nature of the data, some details are omitted in data descriptions and figures.

2.1 Implicit Negative Feedback

Typically, a user favors and submit a query that reflects the user's query intent in a query composition. We make the following assumption.

ASSUMPTION 1. *In a query composition, a user submits a query if and only if the user favors it.*

When a suggestion list is displayed, a user may examine or ignore a suggested query [21]. If a user ignores and does not select a suggested query, whether the user favors this query is unknown. If a user examines a suggested query but does not select it, there are two usual cases: (1) the user does not favor it; (2) the user still favors the suggestion but the user thinks selecting it from the list is less convenient than typing. In spite of possibly complicated cases, under Assumption 1 we make the following assumption.

ASSUMPTION 2. *In a query composition, suppose a user favors a suggested query. For the user, the likelihood of selecting this query is proportional to the likelihood of examining the query.*

Suppose a user examines a suggested query in a composition with a higher likelihood. From Assumption 2, if the user favors the query, the user selects it with a higher likelihood. Otherwise, if the user does not select a suggested query after examining the query, it hints that the user may not favor this query. Under Assumption 1, this user may not submit this unfavored query in the composition. Hence, the examined but unselected query may be demoted at the subsequent keystrokes in the same composition; it allows the user's favored query to rank higher in the composition.

Therefore, in a composition when a user does not select a suggested query, it may be helpful to know whether the user examines the unselected query. In other words, if the user examines an unselected query with a higher likelihood, this query may be demoted more heavily at the subsequent keystrokes of the composition.

For an unselected query suggestion, although whether a user examines it, is not observed, user-QAC interactions can be observed. Such interaction information includes user behavior (dwell time) and settings (position) that are observed during the interactions.

Implicit negative feedback from a user to an unselected query suggestion is observed user-QAC interaction information, when the query is suggested to the user upon keystrokes of a composition. In other words, a user can implicitly express negative feedback to an unselected query "facebook": "facebook" is the top query suggestion, and the user dwells on the list for long without selecting it.

We claim that implicit negative feedback can be strong or weak, and its *strength* cannot be directly observed thus has to be inferred. The properly inferred implicit negative feedback strength may be used to properly demote unselected query suggestions. Recall the discussion that "if the user examines an unselected query with a higher likelihood, this query may be demoted more heavily". Some implicit negative feedback may indicate the likelihood of a user's examination of an unselected query suggestion. Hence, such feedback is of interest. Important examples are dwell time and position.

2.2 Dwell Time

If a user dwells on a suggestion list for a longer time, the user may have more time to carefully examine the suggested queries.

On the other hand, if a user dwells for a shorter time, more likely the suggested queries are ignored; thus, even if these queries are unselected, whether the user favors them is unknown.

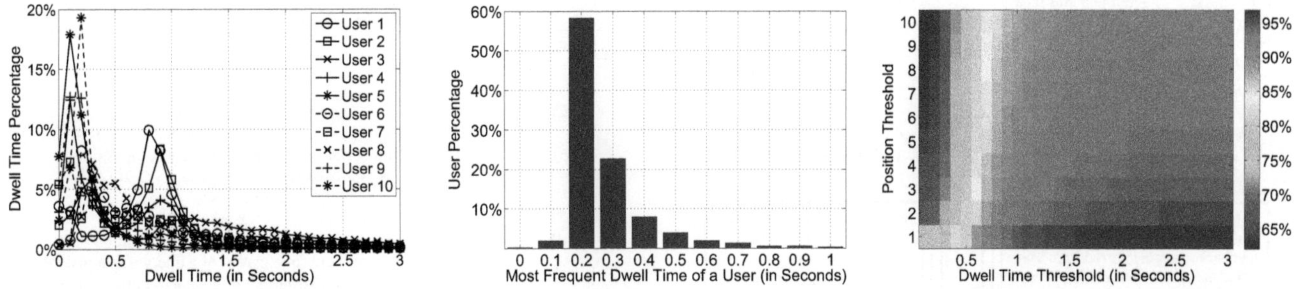

(a) Distributions of dwell time from 10 randomly sampled users from QAC log data.

(b) Histogram of the most frequent dwell time of a user. Bins with a user percentage below 0.25% are omitted.

(c) Percentage of the unselected query suggestions that are not submitted by users.

Figure 2: Dwell time and position study. In (a) and (b), Value t at the horizontal axis corresponds to the dwell time bin $[t, t + 0.1)$.
(a) The two peak clusters imply two broad groups of users in the figure: User 1 and 2 generally type slower than the rest;
(b) The distribution shows that different users may have different typing speed;
(c) The percentage varies with different combinations of dwell time and position thresholds. Red color (wide on the right) corresponds to a higher percentage while blue color (narrow on the left) corresponds to a lower percentage. With a longer dwell time and a higher position, the likelihood that an unselected query suggestion will not be submitted by users at the end of query compositions is higher.

Fig. 2(a) elucidates the distributions of the 0.1-second dwell time bin between 0 and 3.1 seconds of 10 randomly sampled users from QAC log data[1]. Dwell time t (in seconds) falls in the bin $[t, t + 0.1)$. As the peak shows the most frequent dwell time bin of a user, it may suggest the user's comfortable typing speed: if the peak falls in the bin of a longer dwell time, the user's general typing speed is slower. The observed heavy-tails of the distributions manifest that longer dwell time is generally rarer, and the peak can characterize the user's typing speed. Thus, in Fig. 2(a), the two peak clusters may imply two broad groups of users: User 1 and 2 generally type slower than the rest.

Fig. 2(b) zooms out from 10 users' dwell time distributions to all the users' implied comfortable typing speed with a distribution for dwell time of the peaks in Fig. 2(a). It demonstrates that different users may have different typing speed. Hence, inference of implicit negative feedback strength by dwell time should be personalized.

2.3 Dwell Time and Position as Implicit Negative Feedback

We study dwell time and position of unselected query suggestions that are not submitted by users.

The suggested queries at all the keystrokes in query compositions are collected. Then, suggested queries at the final keystrokes in query compositions are excluded because users may select a suggested query at the final keystroke: only the percentage of unselected queries that are not submitted by users is of interest.

Suppose a dwell time threshold T_{DT} and a position threshold T_P are set up. Consider all the suggested queries $\mathbf{Q}(T_{DT}, T_P)$ that are, both in the list that is dwelled for no shorter than T_{DT}, and, ranked at positions no lower than T_P (dwell time $\geq T_{DT}$ and position $\leq T_P$). Given T_{DT} and T_P, $\forall q \in \mathbf{Q}(T_{DT}, T_P)$, the percentage of occurrences of q that are not submitted by users at the end of query compositions is recorded. The recorded results are illustrated in Fig. 2(c), with 300 different combinations of T_{DT} and T_P values, where $T_{DT} \in \{0.1, 0.2, \ldots, 3.0\}$ and $T_P \in \{1, 2, \ldots, 10\}$.

Recall Assumption 1 that a user submits the favored query in a composition. The percentage of users' unselected query suggestions that are not favored by them, can be interpreted by the corresponding color in Fig. 2(c). As discussed in §2.1, implicit negative feedback strength may indicate how to demote unselected queries. For a more accurate QAC, the demotion should properly reflect the likelihood of not favoring or submitting an unselected query: such likelihood is higher with a longer dwell time and a higher position, as shown in Fig. 2(c). Thus, the results in Fig. 2(c) support the hypothesis that dwell time and position are important to infer the strength of implicit negative feedback.

From Fig. 2(c), when a position threshold T_P is fixed, a dwell time threshold T_{DT} better differentiates the likelihood of not favoring or submitting an unselected query, when $0 < T_{DT} < 1$. This agrees with the results in Fig. 2(a)—2(b) that, longer dwell time is generally rarer.

2.4 Filtering Queries by Thresholds Fails

Following the findings in Fig. 2(c), it is tempting to extend an existing QAC model by filtering out all the suggested queries based on dwell time and position thresholds. Thus, we set up a baseline model **Filtering QAC** to filter out all the suggested queries by using fixed dwell time and position thresholds in the subsequent keystrokes of a query composition. For instance, for $T_{DT} = 2$ and $T_P = 3$, any previously suggested queries with positions higher than or equal to 2 and dwell time longer than or equal to 3 seconds are not suggested anymore in the subsequent keystrokes of the same query composition. To ensure a higher ranking accuracy, the results of Filtering QAC are tuned among $T_{DT} \in \{0.1, 0.2, \ldots, 3.0\}$ and $T_P \in \{1, 2, \ldots, 10\}$.

However, experimental results (§4.2) show this simple model fails to significantly boost the static QAC models.

3. ADAPTIVE QUERY AUTO-COMPLETION

Motivated by the findings from large commercial search engine QAC log data in §2, we propose a novel **adaQAC** model that adapts query auto-completion to implicit negative feedback.

3.1 Method Overview

We describe the system design of adaQAC to rank the suggested queries for a given prefix. A toy example with two queries "face-

[1]Binning masks details of the data for its proprietary nature.

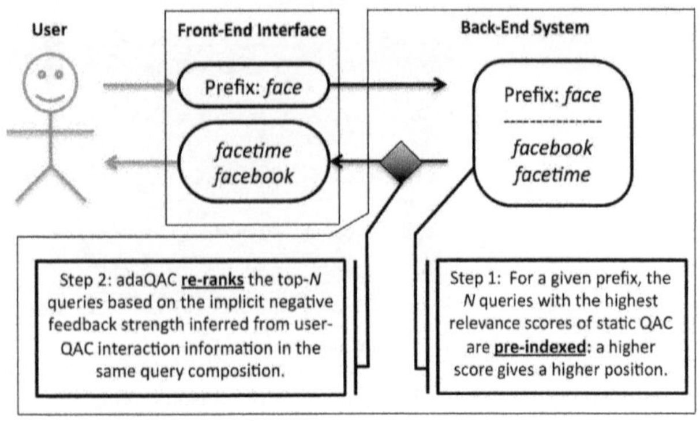

Figure 3: The system design and data flow of adaQAC

book" and "facetime" that match prefixes "fac" and "face" at top positions is used to illustrate the idea. Fig. 3 explains the system design and data flow of adaQAC: it has two stages.

Stage 1 (Pre-indexing): For a given prefix, top-N query suggestions with the highest relevance scores of static QAC are pre-indexed: the higher score, the higher position. In Fig. 3, for the prefix "face", the top-2 ($N = 2$) queries "facebook" and "facetime" are pre-indexed by static QAC based on the historical query frequency counts.

Stage 2 (Re-ranking): adaQAC re-ranks these top-N queries based on the implicit negative feedback strength inferred from user-QAC interaction information in the same composition. To illustrate Stage 2, upon a keystroke "e" following the prefix "fac" from a user, the front-end interface takes the current prefix "face" as an input and immediately fetches the pre-indexed queries "facebook" and "facetime". Suppose when "facebook" was ranked highest in the suggestion list at the prefix "fac", the user dwells for a long time but does not select it. With this observation, suppose adaQAC is able to infer the user's implicit negative feedback strength. Thus, adaQAC updates the ranking score of "facebook" and re-ranks the top 2 ($N = 2$) queries "facebook" and "facetime". With re-ranking, "facetime" is now at Position 1, after "facebook" is demoted to Position 2.

The number of the pre-indexed top queries N can be set to a small positive integer in a production, such as 10 in our experiments. With a small constant value N, sorting N queries based on the updated ranking scores can be achieved in constant time [7].

3.2 "(Static) relevance–(Adaptive) Implicit Negative Feedback" Framework

We highlight that, adaQAC is designed in a more general **"(static) relevance–(adaptive) implicit negative feedback" framework**. The "relevance" component is the relevance score of a query for a user that can be obtained from an existing static QAC model, such as popularity-based QAC; the other "implicit negative feedback" component adapts QAC to implicit negative feedback.

The "(static) relevance–(adaptive) implicit negative feedback" framework is more general for both reusing existing static QAC research and adapting QAC to the newly discovered implicit negative feedback. In this framework, adaQAC is not constrained to employ a certain relevance score: in §4 we investigate several different relevance scores with different parameter values in these scores.

3.3 Problem Formulation

Consider a user $u \in \mathbf{U}$, where $\mathbf{U}$ is the set of all adaQAC users, at the k-th keystroke in a query composition $c \in \mathbf{C}(u)$, where $\mathbf{C}(u)$ is the query composition set of u. adaQAC suggests a ranked list of queries in $\mathbf{Q}$ according to the ranking scores determined by a probabilistic model. The probabilistic model is based on a combination of the relevance score and the inferred strength of implicit negative feedback. For a query q that matches the prefix at the keystroke k in the query composition c, the relevance score of q for the user u is denoted as $r^{(k)}(u, q, c)$.

Implicit negative feedback from the user u to the query q at the k-th keystroke in the query composition c is represented by a feature vector $\mathbf{x}^{(k)}_{l\times 1}(u, q, c)$, where l is the number of features. The strength of implicit negative feedback is based on $\mathbf{x}^{(k)}_{l\times 1}(u, q, c)$ and its associated implicit negative feedback feature weight vector $\boldsymbol{\phi}_{l\times 1}(u)$ for u. $\boldsymbol{\phi}_{l\times 1}(u)$ is a column vector indexed by u from the implicit negative feedback feature weight matrix $\mathbf{\Phi}_{l\times m}(\mathbf{U})$ for all the users in $\mathbf{U}$. Here m is the number of users in $\mathbf{U}$.

In a query composition c, prefixes with the corresponding suggestion lists are referred to by sequential keystroke indices $k \in \{1, 2, \ldots, K(c)\}$, where $K(c)$ is the number of keystrokes in a query composition c. For instance, for a query composition c starting from an empty string with three keystrokes "fac" ($K(c) = 3$), the prefix "fac" with the suggestion list in the left of Fig. 1 can be referred to by $k = 3$ in c or simply $K(c)$ in c. Table 1 briefly summarizes the main notations.

Table 1: Main Notations

Symbol	Description
$\mathbf{U}$	User set.
u	User.
$\mathbf{C}(u)$	Query composition set of a user u.
c	Query composition.
$K(c)$	Number of keystrokes in a query composition c.
k	Keystroke index: $k \in \{1, 2, \ldots, K(c)\}$.
$\mathbf{Q}$	Query set.
q, q'	Query.
$q^*(c)$	Submitted query in a query composition c.
$r^{(k)}(u, q, c)$	Relevance score for a user u of a query q that matches the prefix at a keystroke k in a query composition c.
$\mathbf{Q}^{(k)}(r, u, c, N)$	Set of top N queries ranked by $r^{(k)}(u, q, c)$.
$\mathbf{x}^{(k)}_{l\times 1}(u, q, c)$	Implicit negative feedback feature vector from a user u to a query q at a keystroke k in a query composition c.
$\mathbf{\Phi}_{l\times m}(\mathbf{U})$	Implicit negative feedback feature weight matrix for a user set $\mathbf{U}$.
$\boldsymbol{\phi}_{l\times 1}(u)$	Implicit negative feedback feature weight vector for a user u.
$p^{(k)}(u, q, c)$	Preference for a query q of a user u at a keystroke k in a query composition c.
λ	Regularizer weight parameter.

Table 2: Feature descriptions of the adaQAC model. The implicit negative feedback feature vector $\mathbf{x}^{(k)}(u, q, c)$, from a user u to a query q at a keystroke k in a query composition c, contains the following information collected from the beginning of c to the $(k-1)$-th keystroke in c.

Feature	Description
DwellT-M	The maximum dwell time when q is suggested.
DwellT	Total dwell time where q is suggested.
WordBound	No. of the keystrokes at word boundaries when q is suggested.
SpaceChar	No. of the keystrokes at space characters when q is suggested.
OtherChar	No. of the keystrokes at non-alphanum. char. when q is suggested.
IsPrevQuery	1 if q is the immediately previous query; 0 otherwise.
Pos@i	No. of the keystrokes when q is at Position i of a suggestion list ($i = 1, 2, \ldots, 10$).

*Dwell time greater than 3 seconds at one suggestion list is set to 3 seconds.

3.4 Personalized Learning

Table 2 lists the features used by adaQAC to fit in the "implicit negative feedback" component. Dwell time and positions are studied in §2.3. Likewise, the other features also indicate how likely users examine query suggestions.

Based on §2.2, such as the observation that different users may have different typing speed, personalized learning is used: $\phi(u)$ is to be learned separately for each $u \in \mathbf{U}$ to form $\mathbf{\Phi}(\mathbf{U})$.

3.4.1 Probabilistic Model

We model preference $p^{(k)}(u, q, c)$ for a query q of a user u at a keystroke k in a query composition c, by a generalized additive model [10]:

$$p^{(k)}(u, q, c) = r^{(k)}(u, q, c) + \phi^\top(u)\mathbf{x}^{(k)}(u, q, c). \quad (1)$$

In Equation 1, the preference model $p^{(k)}(u, q, c)$ is able to reflect a user u's preference for a query q after the implicit negative feedback $\mathbf{x}^{(k)}(u, q, c)$ is expressed to q before the k-th keystroke in a query composition c. With the associated feature weights $\phi(u)$ personalized for u, $\phi^\top(u)\mathbf{x}^{(k)}(u, q, c)$ encodes the strength of implicit negative feedback to q from u with personalization.

When a user u submits a query $q^*(c)$ at the final keystroke $K(c)$ in a query composition c, c ends. The likelihood of the observations on the submitted query in a query composition together with implicit negative feedback in Table 2 is to be maximized. Hence, we define a probabilistic model for a submitted query $q^*(c)$ by u at $K(c)$ in c with a softmax function that represents a smoothed version of the "max" function [3, 38]:

$$\mathbb{P}\Big(Q = q^*(c) \mid u, c, K(c)\Big) = \frac{\exp\Big[p^{(K(c))}\Big(u, q^*(c), c\Big)\Big]}{\sum_{q \in \mathbf{Q}^{(k)}(r,u,c,N) \bigcup \{q^*(c)\}} \exp\Big[p^{(K(c))}(u, q, c)\Big]}, \quad (2)$$

where $\mathbf{Q}^{(k)}(r, u, c, N)$ represents the set of top N queries ranked by $r^{(k)}(u, q, c)$. Its union with $\{q^*(c)\}$ ensures proper normalization. Likewise, adaQAC predicts the likelihood that a query $q' \in \mathbf{Q}^{(k)}(r, u, c, N)$ to be submitted by a user u at any k in c by

$$\mathbb{P}\Big(Q = q' \mid u, c, k\Big) = \frac{\exp\Big[p^{(k)}(u, q', c)\Big]}{\sum_{q \in \mathbf{Q}^{(k)}(r,u,c,N)} \exp\Big[p^{(k)}(u, q, c)\Big]} \propto p^{(k)}(u, q', c). \quad (3)$$

In practice, the simpler form $p^{(k)}(u, q', c)$ in Equation 3 is used for re-ranking in Stage 2 of adaQAC (§3.1) after $\phi(u)$ in Equation 1 is inferred. If a query q never appears in any suggestion list before a keystroke k in a query composition c, $\mathbf{x}^{(k)}(u, q, c)$ is a zero vector and the user u's preference for q is the same as the relevance score $r^{(k)}(u, q, c)$. Here k, c are used to refer to the prefix at k in c and suggested queries must match the prefix. However, if u expresses possibly stronger implicit negative feedback to q before k in c, say q is dwelled longer and at a higher position for several times, then the corresponding weights in $\phi(u)$ updates preference for q of u at k in c with a lower $p^{(k)}(u, q, c)$ value; while possibly weaker implicit negative feedback may correspond to shorter dwell time and a lower position. The strength of the expressed implicit negative feedback determines the level of penalizing u's preference for q in $p^{(k)}(u, q, c)$, which affects how to re-rank in Stage 2 of adaQAC. This agrees with the earlier discussions on using proper implicit negative feedback strength to properly demote an unselected query suggestion (§2).

We highlight that, the preference model $p^{(k)}(u, q, c)$ in Equation 1 is designed in the more general framework as discussed in §3.2. The "(static) relevance" component is $r^{(k)}(u, q, c)$, and $\phi^\top(u)\mathbf{x}^{(k)}(u, q, c)$ acts as "(adaptive) implicit negative feedback".

3.4.2 Batch Inference

In Equation 1 $\phi(u)$ is inferred with batch inference. The likelihood for all compositions $C(u)$ of a user u should be maximized.

$$\underset{\phi(u)}{\text{maximize}} \prod_{c \in \mathbf{C}(u)} \mathbb{P}\Big(Q = q^*(c) \mid u, c, K(c)\Big). \quad (4)$$

By Equation 2 and 4, a constrained optimization problem out of minimizing negative log-likelihood with $L2$ regularization (to avoid overfitting) is obtained as

$$\begin{aligned} \underset{\phi(u)}{\text{minimize}} \quad & \sum_{c \in \mathbf{C}(u)} \log \sum_{q \in \mathbf{Q}^{(k)}(r,u,c,N) \bigcup \{q^*(c)\}} \exp\Big[p^{(K(c))}(u, q, c)\Big] \\ & - p^{(K(c))}(u, q^*(c), c) \\ \text{subject to} \quad & \|\phi(u)\|_2^2 \le v, \; v \in \mathbb{R}^+. \end{aligned} \quad (5)$$

There is a one-to-one correspondence between the parameters v in Equation 5 and $\lambda \in \mathbb{R}^+$, and the corresponding un-constrained optimization problem is:

$$\begin{aligned} \underset{\phi(u)}{\text{minimize}} \quad & \sum_{c \in \mathbf{C}(u)} \log \sum_{q \in \mathbf{Q}^{(k)}(r,u,c,N) \bigcup \{q^*(c)\}} \exp\Big[p^{(K(c))}(u, q, c)\Big] \\ & - p^{(K(c))}(u, q^*(c), c) + \frac{\lambda}{2}\|\phi(u)\|_2^2, \end{aligned} \quad (6)$$

where λ is the regularizer weight parameter. As there is no closed-form solution for the optimization problem in Equation 6 due to non-linearity of the softmax function [3], iterative batch inference by gradient descent is used. We refer to an adaQAC model using personalized learning with batch inference as **adaQAC-Batch**. Details for inferring $\phi(u)$ are in Appendix A.

3.4.3 Optimum and Convergence

The objective function of negative log-likelihood for softmax functions with $L2$ regularization in Equation 6 is strongly convex [28]. Hence, the inference is guaranteed to converge to the global optimum [29]: adaQAC-Batch can be inferred precisely. As we know, for a strongly convex objective function $f(x)$ whose optimal value is achieved with $x = x^*$, the number of iterations to get to accuracy $|f(x^*) - f(x)| \le \epsilon$ takes a $\mathcal{O}(\ln(\frac{1}{\epsilon}))$ time [4]. Our experiments in §4.3 reinforce that, adaQAC-Batch converges quickly and reaches the global optimum within a constant number of iterations.

3.4.4 Computational Complexity

Suppose the relevance scores of queries for users, which depend on static QAC, are available. During the training phase for a user u, $\phi(u)$ is inferred with the constructed feature vectors. Assuming the number of queries in a suggestion list and the number of top queries for re-ranking (N in §3.1) are fixed small constants, the feature construction has a time complexity of $\mathcal{O}(lK(c))$, where l is the feature vector size and $K(c)$ is the number of keystrokes in a query composition c. Since the inference algorithm in Appendix A converges within a constant number of steps (§3.4.3), it takes a $\mathcal{O}(l^2 |\mathbf{C}(u)|)$ time with a constant factor corresponding to the number of convergence steps or a predefined value. Here $|\mathbf{C}(u)|$ is the number of query compositions for a user u. Note that the features in Table 2 are all distributive functions: the result derived by applying the function to aggregate values is the same as that derived by applying the function on all the data without partitioning. To explain, let $\mathbf{x}_i^{(k)}(u, q, c)$ be *DwellT-M*$^{(k)}(u, q, c)$;

$DwellT\text{-}M^{(k+1)}(u, q, c)$ can be updated by simply taking the larger value of $DwellT\text{-}M^{(k)}(u, q, c)$ and the dwell time at $k + 1$ in c, if q appears in the suggestion list. With a fixed small constant value N (§3.1), the suggestion at each keystroke takes a $\mathcal{O}(l)$ time.

3.4.5 Scalability on Hadoop MapReduce

A nice property of personalized learning is scalability. As adaQAC-Batch infers $\phi(u)$ for each individual user u, the inference is parallel for different users on big query log data.

In particular, in the Hadoop MapReduce framework, the $\mathbf{\Phi}(\mathbf{U})$ inference phase of our experiments is conducted in parallel for different users by different Reducer nodes.

3.5 Extensions

For a user u, adaQAC-Batch requires training data related to u to infer the feature weight $\phi(u)$. Now we consider a more challenging cold-start scenario where u is a new user without related data for training. Two ways of extensions can address the challenge.

3.5.1 Un-Personalized Learning

The first way is to infer the feature weights from all the existing users excluding the new user. To maintain scalability on Hadoop MapReduce, a gradient descent variant with averaging is used [38]. This un-personalized approach does not differentiate one user from another, and is referred to as **adaQAC-UnP**.

Because only one feature weight vector is stored and shared by all the users, adaQAC-UnP is cheap in storage.

3.5.2 Online Inference

adaQAC-Batch can be extended to an online inference style. For a new user, first, assign the un-personalized learning output to initialize the feature weights; then, keep update the feature weights with more observations of the user's interactions with QAC.

We call this personalized online learning style extension **adaQAC-Online**. Stochastic gradient descent is used for the online inference. It is similar to batch inference with the constrained optimization problem out of minimizing negative log-likelihood with $L2$ regularization in Equation 5 replaced by

$$\begin{aligned} \underset{\phi(u)}{\text{minimize}} \quad & \log \sum_{q \in \mathbf{Q}^{(k)}(r,u,c,N) \bigcup \{q^*(c)\}} \exp\left[p^{(K(c))}(u,q,c)\right] \\ & - p^{(K(c))}(u, q^*(c), c) \\ \text{subject to} \quad & \|\phi(u)\|_2^2 \le v, \; v \in \mathbb{R}^+. \end{aligned}$$

Details for inferring $\phi(u)$ are in Appendix B.

Cost Analysis: adaQAC-Online costs more storage than adaQAC-UnP due to maintaining different weights for all the users. As shown in §4.4, adaQAC-Online trades its storage cost for slightly higher accuracy than adaQAC-UnP. Compared with adaQAC-Batch, the inference of adaQAC-Online takes a $\mathcal{O}(tl^2)$ time, where t is the number of observations and l is the feature vector size. Generally adaQAC-Online takes less time than adaQAC-Batch in inference and has the same storage requirement for maintaining different feature weights for all the users. Comparing with adaQAC-Batch, adaQAC-UnP takes the same order of time with less storage requirement as it maintains only one feature weight vector that is shared by all the users.

4. EVALUATION

We evaluate the proposed adaQAC-Batch and its two extensions adaQAC-UnP and adaQAC-Online on QAC log data.

4.1 Data and Evaluation Measures

Data: We describe important details of our collected QAC log data. Due to the proprietary nature of the data, some details are omitted. The QAC log data are collected from Feb 28 to Jul 28, 2014 and all the queries are submitted via desktops. If a query is submitted by more than two different users, its corresponding query composition is used for evaluation. As adaQAC-Batch requires training data for the feature weight inference, all the users with fewer than 100 query compositions during the given five-month range are filtered out. After the filtering, users are randomly sampled and their 2,932,035 query compositions constitute the evaluation data. There are in total 481,417 unique submitted queries. All the query compositions have their anonymized user IDs and the submitted queries. In one composition, the prefixes, timestamps and suggested queries of every keystroke are collected.

The training, validation and testing data are split with a ratio of 50%/25%/25% in an ascending time order: the first half of a user's query compositions are used for training; the second and third quarters are for validation and testing respectively. The validation data are only used for parameter tuning. As adaQAC infers implicit negative feedback from user-QAC interactions in query compositions, in §4.2—§4.5 we experiment on the prefixes at the last keystroke of query compositions to use more interaction information. The average length of query prefixes is 8.53 characters.

The data standardization procedure is transforming data to zero mean and unit variance. All the feature values in Table 2 and the relevance scores are standardized.

Measures for Accuracy: Mean reciprocal rank (MRR) is the average reciprocal of the submitted query's ranking in a suggestion list. It is a widely-adopted measure to evaluate the ranking accuracy of QAC [2, 21, 15, 31]. Success Rate@top-k (SR@k) denotes the average percentage of the submitted queries that can be found in the top-k suggested queries on the testing data, and was also used to evaluate the QAC ranking accuracy [15]. In general, a higher MRR or SR@k indicates a higher ranking accuracy of QAC [2, 21, 15, 31, 5]. Paired-t test is used to validate the statistical significance of the accuracy improvement ($p < 0.05$).

4.2 Boosting the Accuracy of Static QAC with Implicit Negative Feedback

Following the "(static) relevance–(adaptive) implicit negative feedback" framework (§3.2), we investigate relevance scores from popular static QAC with different parameter settings to compare the accuracy of adaQAC-Batch, Filtering QAC, and static QAC.

The relevance scores reuse the existing research: MPC [2, 15, 21, 31], Personal(-S) [2, 5, 31], and TimeSense(-S) [5, 32, 35, 27].

• **MPC:** Most Popular Completion (MPC) ranks suggested queries for a prefix based on the historical popularity of a query. A more popular query gets a higher rank. Despite its simplicity, it was found competitive by various studies [2, 15, 21, 31].

• **Personal:** Personal QAC for distinguishing different users can achieve better accuracy [2, 5, 31]. Although personal information may take many different forms, the Personal relevance score in this work is an equal-weighted linear combination of the MPC score and the standardized personal historical query frequency counts.

• **Personal-S:** It is the Personal relevance score with an optimal combination with different weights of the MPC score and the standardized personal query frequency counts. The optimal weights achieving the highest accuracy are tuned on validation data. Tuning to the optimal weights makes Personal-S more competitive.

• **TimeSense:** Time is useful in QAC [5, 32, 35]. Hence, TimeSense is the same as Personal except that the personal historical

Table 3: **Accuracy comparison of static QAC, Filtering QAC, and adaQAC-Batch (in percentage). Boldfaced results denote that the accuracy improvement over static QAC is statistically significant ($p < 0.05$) for the same relevance score. adaQAC-Batch significantly and consistently boosts the accuracy of static QAC for each relevance score. For instance, adaQAC-Batch (MPC) significantly boosts static QAC (MPC) by 21.2% in MRR.**

Relevance	MRR			SR@1			SR@2			SR@3		
	Static	Filter	adaQAC-Batch	Static	Filter	adaQAC-Batch	Static	Filter	adaQAC-Batch	Static	Filter	adaQAC-Batch
MPC	50.62	51.83	**61.33 (+21.2%)**	40.74	42.27	**55.86 (+37.1%)**	52.03	53.19	**63.17 (+21.4%)**	58.09	59.21	**66.09 (+13.8%)**
Personal	61.85	62.68	**70.97 (+14.8%)**	51.31	52.45	**64.27 (+25.3%)**	64.02	64.78	**73.71 (+15.1%)**	70.34	71.09	**76.94 (+9.4%)**
Personal-S	66.02	66.52	**74.43 (+12.7%)**	55.30	56.24	**67.09 (+21.3%)**	68.51	68.92	**77.73 (+13.5%)**	74.58	74.97	**80.97 (+8.6%)**
TimeSense	64.32	65.14	**73.70 (+14.6%)**	53.77	54.92	**66.82 (+24.3%)**	66.54	67.45	**76.41 (+14.8%)**	72.39	73.28	**79.81 (+10.3%)**
TimeSense-S	65.56	66.19	**74.69 (+13.9%)**	55.02	56.11	**67.57 (+22.8%)**	67.83	68.27	**77.76 (+14.6%)**	73.68	74.11	**80.97 (+9.9%)**

*Static: Static QAC; Filter: Filtering QAC

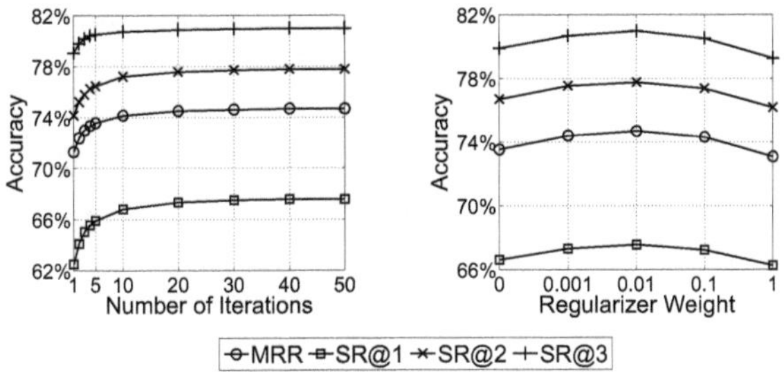

Figure 4: Convergence (left) and regularizer weight (right) study for adaQAC-Batch (TimeSense-S). Plots are similar for the other relevance scores. adaQAC-Batch converges quickly and is not sensitive to the chosen regularizer weight near its optimum.

query frequency counts is replaced by the all-user popularity counts of a query in the 28-day time window before a query composition.

- **TimeSense-S:** It is the same as Personal-S except that Personal is replaced by TimeSense.

For brevity, we denote "static QAC employing the MPC relevance score" as "Static (MPC)". Similar notations are used for QAC models employing any relevance score.

Parameters values are tuned to achieve the highest accuracy on validation data. Unless otherwise stated we set the number of iterations to 40 (adaQAC-Batch and adaQAC-UnP) and the regularizer weight to 0.01. Personal-S and TimeSense-S both combine a MPC score with the optimal weight α and the other score with the weight $1 - \alpha$. The optimal weights in Personal-S ($\alpha = 0.34$) and TimeSense-S ($\alpha = 0.42$) achieve the highest MRR for static QAC.

In §2.4 we set up Filtering QAC with relevance scores, by additionally filtering out all the suggested queries with certain dwell time thresholds (T_{DT}) and position thresholds (T_P) in the subsequent keystrokes in a composition. To ensure higher competitiveness, the model is tuned among the 300 threshold value combinations in §2.4. We set $T_{DT} = 0.9$ and $T_P = 1$.

Table 3 presents the accuracy comparison of static QAC, Filtering QAC, and adaQAC-Batch. The simple Filtering QAC model fails to outperform the corresponding static QAC with the same relevance scores significantly. For each same relevance score, adaQAC-Batch exploiting the added implicit negative feedback information significantly and consistently boosts the accuracy of these static QAC models that only use relevance scores. With more accurate relevance scores such as Personal and TimeSense, adaQAC-Batch is more accurate. Given the relevance scores with different parameter settings (Personal *vs.* Personal-S and TimeSense *vs.* TimeSense-S), the accuracy of adaQAC-Batch slightly varies depending on the accuracy of the relevance scores for the chosen parameter values.

The newly-discovered implicit negative feedback is promising in boosting the accuracy of the existing static QAC models.

4.3 Parameter Study

Here we set the number of iterations and regularizer weight to different values for the parameter study on the validation data. adaQAC-Batch (TimeSense-S) is tested. The results for the other relevance scores are similar.

Convergence: Fig. 4 (left) shows the evaluation measures against the number of iterations. The results reinforce the fact that, adaQAC-Batch converges quickly and the precise global optimum can be reached within a constant number of iterations (§3.4.3).

Regularizer Weight: Fig. 4 (right) plots the evaluation measures of adaQAC-Batch (TimeSense-S) with regularizer weights that are varied around the optimum 0.01. adaQAC-Batch is not sensitive to different regularizer weights near the optimum. This property shows that the accuracy of adaQAC-Batch has less dependence on the chosen regularizer weight value.

4.4 Un-Personalized Learning and Online Inference

Motivated by the more challenging cold-start scenario where there is a lack of training data for new users, we evaluate the two adaQAC extensions adaQAC-UnP (§3.5.1) and adaQAC-Online (§3.5.2).

For a user u, the un-personalized learning is performed by learning from training data related to all the users excluding u, and the learned feature weights are fed into adaQAC-Online for u as the initial feature weights. Neither adaQAC-UnP nor adaQAC-Online uses the training data related to u.

Table 4 shows that, both adaQAC-UnP and adaQAC-Online significantly and consistently boost the accuracy of static QAC for each relevance score. The mean measure values of adaQAC-UnP and adaQAC-Online are slightly lower than those of adaQAC-Batch for the same relevance score. This slight difference can be justified by the added benefits of the more expensive personalized learning with batch inference of adaQAC-Batch.

It was pointed out that (§3.5.2), adaQAC-Online costs more storage than adaQAC-UnP due to maintaining different weights for all the users. The slight difference between the mean of the measure values of adaQAC-Online and adaQAC-UnP in Table 4 shows that, adaQAC-Online trades its storage cost for slightly higher accuracy than adaQAC-UnP. In addition to the benefits for addressing the cold-start challenge, according to the cost analysis in §3.5.2, an important practical implication from the results of Table 4 is, adaQAC-UnP and adaQAC-Online can be good substitutes for the more expensive adaQAC-Batch if time and storage budgets are limited in the real-world productions.

Table 4: Accuracy of adaQAC-UnP and adaQAC-Online in comparison with static QAC (in percentage). Boldfaced results denote that the accuracy improvement over static QAC is statistically significant ($p < 0.05$) for the same relevance score. Both of the adaQAC extension models significantly and consistently boost the accuracy of static QAC for each relevance score. For instance, adaQAC-Online (MPC) significantly boosts static QAC (MPC) by 20.3% in MRR.

Relevance	MRR		SR@1		SR@2		SR@3	
	adaQAC-UnP	adaQAC-Online	adaQAC-UnP	adaQAC-Online	adaQAC-UnP	adaQAC-Online	adaQAC-UnP	adaQAC-Online
MPC	**60.60 (+19.7%)**	**60.92 (+20.3%)**	**54.54 (+33.9%)**	**55.06 (+35.1%)**	**62.75 (+20.6%)**	**62.99 (+21.1%)**	**66.01 (+13.6%)**	**66.11 (+13.8%)**
Personal	**69.80 (+12.9%)**	**70.22 (+13.5%)**	**62.27 (+21.4%)**	**62.98 (+22.7%)**	**72.76 (+13.7%)**	**73.06 (+14.1%)**	**76.64 (+9.0%)**	**76.77(+9.1%)**
Personal-S	**73.16 (+10.8%)**	**73.59 (+11.5%)**	**64.87 (+17.3%)**	**65.59 (+18.6%)**	**76.83 (+12.1%)**	**77.11 (+12.6%)**	**80.65 (+8.1%)**	**80.81 (+8.4%)**
TimeSense	**72.69 (+13.0%)**	**73.05 (+13.6%)**	**65.00 (+20.9%)**	**65.61 (+22.0%)**	**75.69 (+13.8%)**	**75.97 (+14.2%)**	**79.64 (+10.0%)**	**79.74 (+10.2%)**
TimeSense-S	**73.57 (+12.2%)**	**73.96 (+12.8%)**	**65.65 (+19.3%)**	**66.26 (+20.4%)**	**76.78 (+13.2%)**	**77.13 (+13.7%)**	**80.74 (+9.6%)**	**80.91 (+9.8%)**

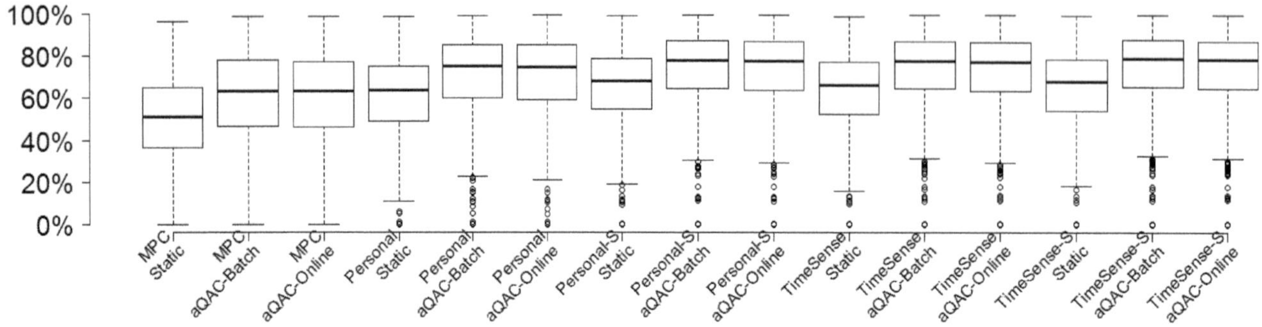

Figure 5: Box-and-Whisker plots of individual users' MRR for static QAC, adaQAC-Batch, and adaQAC-Online with five relevance scores. Each data instance is the corresponding MRR on one user. The minimum (bottom bar), quartiles (box edges), median (middle of the box), and maximum (top bar) after removal of the detected outliers (empty circles) are depicted. adaQAC with more accurate relevance scores are able to detect more outliers with the raised minimum bars.

4.5 Model Accuracy on Different Users

We study the model accuracy on different users using the Box-and-Whisker plots. With each data instance being the MRR on one user, Fig. 5 shows the minimum (bottom bar), quartiles (box edges), median (middle of the box), maximum (top bar) after removal of the detected outlier users (empty circles).

In general, model comparison using medians and quartiles of MRR agrees with the results in Table 3—4 and reaffirms the boosted accuracy by the added implicit negative feedback.

Note that, all the models perform poorly on a few users. Models with the MPC relevance score fail to detect any outlier, and have minimum bars close to 0. The other models still perform poorly on certain users with MRR close to 0. These users are detected as the outliers. The outlier users may behave inconsistently, submit rare queries, or the collected data related to them are noisy or incomplete due to unknown reasons.

To explain, models with the MPC relevance have a larger MRR variance (implied by a longer box in Fig. 5) so outlier users cannot be easily detected. It is easier to see when comparing adaQAC-Online (MPC) with Static (Personal): they have close medians but the lower-variance Static (Personal) is able to detect a few outliers and raise its minimum bar after their removal. When the relevance score is more accurate with a lower variance, adaQAC is able to detect more outliers thus raises the minimum bar by further improving the MRR on the majority of the users.

Hence, even though the implicit negative feedback research is promising, further research on more accurate relevance scores is still required.

4.6 Varying-Length Prefix Study

Now we consider another challenging scenario where testing is based on all possible prefixes in query compositions. Table 5 reports MRR of static QAC, adaQAC-Static and adaQAC-Online for prefixes with varying lengths at every keystroke in query compositions. Both adaQAC-Batch and adaQAC-Online still significantly and consistently boost the accuracy of static QAC under all prefix lengths for each relevance score.

The MRR gap between adaQAC-Batch and adaQAC-Online is subtle and both are more accurate when prefixes are of "middle" lengths. That is, when the prefixes are short, the collected implicit negative feedback features probably contain little useful information to improve the re-ranking in Stage 2 of adaQAC (§3.1). When prefixes get longer, more user-QAC interaction information is obtained to make adaQAC more accurate in the adaptive re-ranking stage. However, when prefixes are longer, the QAC problem becomes less challenging due to a reduction of the matched queries: static QAC employing relevance scores are more accurate and it is harder to further improve the accuracy, even though the implicit negative feedback information may be richer.

4.7 Case Study

adaQAC has advantages over static QAC. We describe the following cases of Yahoo! Search, and hope that this work can inspire ongoing studies in a broader research community.

Disambiguation: When users have clear query intent and prefer disambiguated queries, adaQAC generally outperforms static QAC. Typically, users may prefer queries of the form "entity name + attribute" to "entity name only". Suppose a user wants to know the showtime of lefont sandy springs. When the user composes the query during the keystrokes "lefon", the entity name "lefont sandy springs" is the top suggestion. The user does not select it because an entity name query may result in diverse search results. So, the query "lefont sandy springs" receives implicit negative feedback. When the prefix becomes "lefont", "lefont sandy springs" is de-

Table 5: MRR of static QAC, adaQAC-Batch, and adaQAC-Online under prefixes with varying lengths at every keystroke in query compositions (in percentage). Boldfaced results denote that the accuracy improvement over static QAC is statistically significant ($p < 0.05$) for the same relevance score and prefix length range. Both adaQAC-Batch and adaQAC-Online significantly and consistently boost the accuracy of static QAC under all prefix lengths for each relevance score. For instance, adaQAC-Batch (MPC) significantly boosts static QAC (MPC) by 17.1% in MRR under all prefix lengths.

Relevance	Static	adaQAC-Batch	adaQAC-Online	Static	adaQAC-Batch	adaQAC-Online	Static	adaQAC-Batch	adaQAC-Online
	$1 \leq$ Prefix Length ≤ 3			$4 \leq$ Prefix Length ≤ 6			$7 \leq$ Prefix Length ≤ 9		
MPC	21.76	22.66	22.52	33.64	**38.67 (+15.0%)**	**38.40 (+14.1%)**	41.60	**52.21 (+25.5%)**	**52.13 (+25.3%)**
Personal	29.34	30.31	30.10	45.41	**49.52 (+9.1%)**	**49.38 (+8.7%)**	49.81	**56.34 (+13.1%)**	**56.19 (+12.8%)**
Personal-S	31.60	32.59	32.36	50.14	**53.38 (+6.5%)**	**53.30 (+6.3%)**	53.94	**58.69 (+8.8%)**	**58.57 (+8.6%)**
TimeSense	29.98	**31.94 (+6.5%)**	**31.91 (+6.4%)**	47.75	**52.61 (+10.2%)**	**52.65 (+10.3%)**	52.48	**58.63 (+11.7%)**	**58.46 (+11.4%)**
TimeSense-S	30.93	32.69	32.59	49.27	**53.69 (+9.0%)**	**53.67 (+8.9%)**	53.65	**59.19 (+10.3%)**	**59.14 (+10.2%)**
	$10 \leq$ Prefix Length ≤ 12			Prefix Length ≥ 13			All Prefix Lengths		
MPC	47.28	**55.13 (+16.6%)**	**54.82 (+15.9%)**	55.12	**59.28 (+7.5%)**	**58.94 (+6.9%)**	38.19	**44.72 (+17.1%)**	**44.43 (+16.3%)**
Personal	52.16	**57.79 (+10.8%)**	**57.33 (+9.9%)**	56.59	**59.93 (+5.9%)**	59.32	46.67	**51.75 (+10.9%)**	**51.20 (+9.7%)**
Personal-S	55.21	**59.33 (+7.5%)**	**58.77 (+6.4%)**	58.40	60.85	60.16	49.83	**54.30 (+9.0%)**	**53.66 (+7.7%)**
TimeSense	54.91	**59.43 (+8.2%)**	**59.06 (+7.6%)**	58.49	61.08	60.54	48.59	**53.77 (+10.7%)**	**54.01 (+11.2%)**
TimeSense-S	55.73	**59.83 (+7.4%)**	**59.37 (+6.5%)**	58.97	61.29	60.76	49.48	**54.47 (+10.1%)**	**53.95 (+9.0%)**

*Static: Static QAC

moted by adaQAC and "lefont sandy springs showtime" gets promoted.

Query Reformulation: When users prefer new queries when reformulating older queries, adaQAC generally outperforms static QAC. Suppose a user wants to query "detroit lions" after querying "detroit red wings". When the user reformulates the query from "detroit red wings" to "detroit r" by consecutively hitting Backspace, "detroit red wings" is ranked highest but the user does not select it. So, the query "detroit red wings" receives implicit negative feedback. Hence, when the prefix becomes "detroit" after the user hits two more Backspace, "detroit red wings" is demoted by adaQAC; some other queries, such as "detroit lions", are promoted accordingly.

Smoothing "Over-Sense": Certain relevance scores may be sensitive to specific signals: TimeSense is sensitive to time. Studies showed users may have query intent for new or ongoing events [1, 16, 20]. In Yahoo! Search, we investigate the QAC results responded by the time-sensitive component. When a user wants to query an earlier event "russia attack georgia", the time-sensitive QAC keeps ranking a more recent event "russia attack ukraine" highest during keystrokes "russia att". Instead, adaQAC receives users' implicit negative feedback to 'russia attack ukraine" hence demotes it, and raises "russia attack georgia" up to the top.

5. RELATED WORK

Query Auto-Completion (QAC): Numerous QAC models have been developed in recent years, such as popularity-based QAC using historical frequency counts [2], time-based QAC using time information [32, 35], context-based QAC using previous query information of users [2], personalized QAC learning from user profile information [31]. The relevance scores investigated in our work make use of the existing research, such as MPC [2, 15, 21, 31], Personal(-S) [2, 5, 31], and TimeSense(-S) [5, 32, 35, 27]. More recent QAC methods also predicted the probability that a suggested query would be clicked by users based on user models [18, 21], determined suggestion rankings based on query reformulation patterns [15], or combined information such as time and previous queries from users [5]. Furthermore, user interactions with QAC just began to be explored. Mitra *et al.* discussed user-QAC interactions from perspectives such as word boundaries, fraction of query typed, and keyboard distance [26]. Hofmann *et al.* identified common behavior patterns of user-QAC interactions [11].

Other aspects of QAC have also been studied, such as space efficient indexing [13] and spelling error toleration [6, 14, 8, 36].

However, none of the aforementioned work aimed at inferring implicit negative feedback from user-QAC interactions, or adapting QAC to such feedback. We take these initiatives and show that QAC can adapt to implicit negative feedback and be more accurate.

Negative Feedback: Relevance feedback is useful for improving information retrieval models, but further improving it using negative feedback was considered challenging [30, 25]. Recently, more efforts on negative feedback research was made in document retrieval tasks. Wang *et al.* found negative relevance feedback useful to improve vector-space models and language models [34]. Hong *et al.* proposed a hierarchical distance-based measure to differentiate the opposite intent from the true query intent [12]. Zhang and Wang studied language models with negative feedback through positive and negative document proportion on query classification [39]. New models using negative relevance feedback were also developed in TREC [22]. In particular, negative feedback was also found useful to retrieve documents for difficult queries [33, 17, 24].

However, these negative feedback studies focus only on document retrieval tasks. The richer interaction information, presented in the QAC settings, such as dwell time and positions, is not available in general document retrieval settings.

Dynamic IR: Recent work have gone beyond existing IR techniques to incorporate dynamics in session search [9, 23]. In this task, added or removed terms compared with the other queries of the same search session will update term weights to retrieve documents for the completed query [9, 23]. There are important differences between such research and ours. First, search and QAC are different problems. Second, adaQAC emphasizes adapting dynamics over a single query composition rather than multiple queries over a search session. Third, adaQAC does not assign weights to characters, prefixes or terms of a query. Other dynamic IR work was surveyed in a tutorial by Yang *et al.* [37].

6. CONCLUSIONS

We studied interactions between users and QAC where users implicitly express negative feedback to suggested queries. Under the more general "(static) relevance–(adaptive) implicit negative feedback" framework, our proposed adaQAC model can reuse the existing static QAC research and adapt QAC to implicit negative feedback using personalized learning with batch inference. Extensions with un-personalized learning and online inference were also presented. We collected user-QAC interaction data from a commercial search engine. Large-scale empirical results showed that implicit negative feedback significantly and consistently boosts the accuracy of the investigated static QAC models.

Acknowledgment: Research was sponsored in part by National Science Foundation CNS 09-64392, IIS-1017362, IIS-1320617, and IIS-1354329, and by the U.S. Army Research Lab under Cooperative Agreement No. W911NF-09-2-0053 (NSCTA).

7. REFERENCES

[1] E. Adar, D. S. Weld, B. N. Bershad, and S. S. Gribble. Why we search: visualizing and predicting user behavior. In *WWW*, 2007.

[2] Z. Bar-Yossef and N. Kraus. Context-sensitive query auto-completion. In *WWW*, 2011.

[3] C. M. Bishop. *Pattern recognition and machine learning*, volume 1. 2006.

[4] S. Boyd and L. Vandenberghe. *Convex optimization*. 2009.

[5] F. Cai, S. Liang, and M. de Rijke. Time-sensitive personalized query auto-completion. In *CIKM*, 2014.

[6] S. Chaudhuri and R. Kaushik. Extending autocompletion to tolerate errors. In *SIGMOD*, 2009.

[7] T. H. Cormen, C. E. Leiserson, R. L. Rivest, and C. Stein. *Introduction to algorithms*, volume 2. 2001.

[8] H. Duan and B.-J. P. Hsu. Online spelling correction for query completion. In *WWW*, 2011.

[9] D. Guan, S. Zhang, and H. Yang. Utilizing query change for session search. In *SIGIR*, 2013.

[10] T. Hastie, R. Tibshirani, and J. Friedman. *The elements of statistical learning*, volume 2. 2009.

[11] K. Hofmann, B. Mitra, F. Radlinski, and M. Shokouhi. An eye-tracking study of user interactions with query auto completion. In *CIKM*, 2014.

[12] Y. Hong, Q. Cai, S. Hua, J. Yao, and Q. Zhu. Negative feedback: the forsaken nature available for re-ranking. In *COLING*, 2010.

[13] B.-J. P. Hsu and G. Ottaviano. Space-efficient data structures for top-k completion. In *WWW*, 2013.

[14] S. Ji, G. Li, C. Li, and J. Feng. Efficient interactive fuzzy keyword search. In *WWW*, 2009.

[15] J.-Y. Jiang, Y.-Y. Ke, P.-Y. Chien, and P.-J. Cheng. Learning user reformulation behavior for query auto-completion. In *SIGIR*, 2014.

[16] S. R. Kairam, M. R. Morris, J. Teevan, D. J. Liebling, and S. T. Dumais. Towards supporting search over trending events with social media. In *ICWSM*, 2013.

[17] M. Karimzadehgan and C. Zhai. Improving retrieval accuracy of difficult queries through generalizing negative document language models. In *CIKM*, 2011.

[18] E. Kharitonov, C. Macdonald, P. Serdyukov, and I. Ounis. User model-based metrics for offline query suggestion evaluation. In *SIGIR*, 2013.

[19] Y. Koren, R. Bell, and C. Volinsky. Matrix factorization techniques for recommender systems. *Computer*, 42(8), 2009.

[20] A. Kulkarni, J. Teevan, K. M. Svore, and S. T. Dumais. Understanding temporal query dynamics. In *WSDM*, 2011.

[21] Y. Li, A. Dong, H. Wang, H. Deng, Y. Chang, and C. Zhai. A two-dimensional click model for query auto-completion. In *SIGIR*, 2014.

[22] Y. Li, X. Tao, A. Algarni, and S.-T. Wu. Mining specific and general features in both positive and negative relevance feedback. In *TREC*, 2009.

[23] J. Luo, S. Zhang, and H. Yang. Win-win search: Dual-agent stochastic game in session search. In *SIGIR*, 2014.

[24] Y. Ma and H. Lin. A multiple relevance feedback strategy with positive and negative models. *PloS ONE*, 9(8), 2014.

[25] C. D. Manning, P. Raghavan, and H. Schütze. *Introduction to information retrieval*, volume 1. 2008.

[26] B. Mitra, M. Shokouhi, F. Radlinski, and K. Hofmann. On user interactions with query auto-completion. In *SIGIR*, 2014.

[27] T. Miyanishi and T. Sakai. Time-aware structured query suggestion. In *SIGIR*, 2013.

[28] K. P. Murphy. *Machine learning: a probabilistic perspective*. 2012.

[29] A. Nedić. *Optimization*. Technical Report, UIUC, 2011.

[30] J. J. Rocchio. Relevance feedback in information retrieval. *The SMART Retrieval System Experiments in Automatic Document Processing*, 1971.

[31] M. Shokouhi. Learning to personalize query auto-completion. In *SIGIR*, 2013.

[32] M. Shokouhi and K. Radinsky. Time-sensitive query auto-completion. In *SIGIR*, 2012.

[33] X. Wang, H. Fang, and C. Zhai. Improve retrieval accuracy for difficult queries using negative feedback. In *CIKM*, 2007.

[34] X. Wang, H. Fang, and C. Zhai. A study of methods for negative relevance feedback. In *SIGIR*, 2008.

[35] S. Whiting and J. M. Jose. Recent and robust query auto-completion. In *WWW*, 2014.

[36] C. Xiao, J. Qin, W. Wang, Y. Ishikawa, K. Tsuda, and K. Sadakane. Efficient error-tolerant query autocompletion. *VLDB*, 6(6), 2013.

[37] H. Yang, M. Sloan, and J. Wang. Dynamic information retrieval modeling. In *SIGIR*, 2014.

[38] S.-H. Yang, B. Long, A. J. Smola, H. Zha, and Z. Zheng. Collaborative competitive filtering: learning recommender using context of user choice. In *SIGIR*, 2011.

[39] W. Zhang and J. Wang. The study of methods for language model based positive and negative relevance feedback in information retrieval. In *ISISE*, 2012.

APPENDIX

A. INFERENCE FOR ADAQAC-BATCH

Let $f\left[\boldsymbol{\phi}^{(t)}(u)\right]$ be the objective function in Equation 6, where $\boldsymbol{\phi}^{(t)}(u)$ is the value of $\boldsymbol{\phi}(u)$ at the t-th iteration,

$$\boldsymbol{\phi}^{(t+1)}(u) = \boldsymbol{\phi}^{(t)}(u) - \eta \nabla f\left[\boldsymbol{\phi}^{(t)}(u)\right], \tag{7}$$

where

$$\nabla f\left[\boldsymbol{\phi}(u)\right] = \left[\frac{\partial f\left[\boldsymbol{\phi}(u)\right]}{\partial \phi_1(u)}, \frac{\partial f\left[\boldsymbol{\phi}(u)\right]}{\partial \phi_2(u)}, \ldots, \frac{\partial f\left[\boldsymbol{\phi}(u)\right]}{\partial \phi_l(u)}\right]^\top, \tag{8}$$

and $\forall i = 1, 2, \ldots, l$,

$$\frac{\partial f\left[\boldsymbol{\phi}(u)\right]}{\partial \phi_i(u)} = \sum_{c \in \mathbf{C}(u)} \frac{S_1}{S_2} - \mathbf{x}_i^{\left(K(c)\right)}(u, q^*(c), c) + \lambda \phi_i(u), \tag{9}$$

where by denoting $\exp\left[r^{(k)}(u,q,c) + \boldsymbol{\phi}^\top(u)\mathbf{x}^{\left(K(c)\right)}(u,q,c)\right]$ as $E(q)$,

$$\begin{aligned} S_1 &= \sum_{q \in \mathbf{Q}^{(k)}(r,u,c,N) \bigcup \{q^*(c)\}} E(q)\mathbf{x}_i^{\left(K(c)\right)}(u,q,c), \\ S_2 &= \sum_{q \in \mathbf{Q}^{(k)}(r,u,c,N) \bigcup \{q^*(c)\}} E(q). \end{aligned} \tag{10}$$

In the experiments, $\boldsymbol{\phi}^{(0)}(u)$ in Equation 7 is randomly sampled from:

$$\boldsymbol{\phi}^{(0)}(u) \sim \mathrm{Uniform}(0, 0.01).$$

B. INFERENCE FOR ADAQAC-ONLINE

The feature weight $\boldsymbol{\phi}^{(0)}(u)$ is initialized as the un-personalized learning weight (§3.5.1). After each query composition c, the feature weight is updated as in Equation 7—10 with Equation 9 replaced by

$$\frac{\partial f\left[\boldsymbol{\phi}(u)\right]}{\partial \phi_i(u)} = \frac{S_1}{S_2} - \mathbf{x}_i^{\left(K(c)\right)}(u, q^*(c), c) + \lambda \phi_i(u),$$

and η is discounted by a factor of 0.9 after each update as an annealing procedure [19].

A Random Walk Model for Optimization of Search Impact in Web Frontier Ranking

Giang Tran*
L3S Research Center / University of Hannover
Hannover, Germany
gtran@l3s.de

Ata Turk
Boston University
Boston, United States
ataturk@bu.edu

B. Barla Cambazoglu
Yahoo Labs
Barcelona, Spain
barla@yahoo-inc.com

Wolfgang Nejdl
L3S Research Center / University of Hannover
Hannover, Germany
nejdl@l3s.de

ABSTRACT

Large-scale web search engines need to crawl the Web continuously to discover and download newly created web content. The speed at which the new content is discovered and the quality of the discovered content can have a big impact on the coverage and quality of the results provided by the search engine. In this paper, we propose a search-centric solution to the problem of prioritizing the pages in the frontier of a crawler for download. Our approach essentially orders the web pages in the frontier through a random walk model that takes into account the pages' potential impact on user-perceived search quality. In addition, we propose a link graph enrichment technique that extends this solution. Finally, we explore a machine learning approach that combines different frontier prioritization approaches. We conduct experiments using two very large, real-life web datasets to observe various search quality metrics. Comparisons with several baseline techniques indicate that the proposed approaches have the potential to improve the user-perceived quality of web search results considerably.

Categories and Subject Descriptors

H.3.3 [**Information Storage and Retrieval**]: Information Search and Retrieval

Keywords

Web search engine; web crawling; URL prioritization; web frontier; discovery; frontier ranking; result relevance; random walks.

*This work is conducted during the author's internship at Yahoo Labs Barcelona.

SIGIR'15, August 09 - 13, 2015, Santiago, Chile.
© 2015 ACM. ISBN 978-1-4503-3621-5/15/08 ...$15.00.
DOI: http://dx.doi.org/10.1145/2766462.2767737.

1. INTRODUCTION

Large-scale search engines need to crawl the web content continuously to be able to cope with the constant growth and the content-wise dynamic nature of the Web [25]. In commercial search engines, web pages are downloaded through two independent crawling processes: refreshing and discovery [5]. The objective of the first process is to selectively refetch pages whose content was already downloaded and stored in the web repository of the search engine. This way, potential modifications in the online content can be detected and reflected to the index of the search engine, reducing the staleness of search results presented to the users. The objective of the second process is to discover previously unseen pages and fetch their content for the first time. This lets the search engine grow its web frontier[1] and increase its coverage of the Web. While discovery may be seen primarily as a mechanism to increase the recall of the search engine (with respect to the content available on the Web), it can also affect the quality of search results presented to the users.

In this work, we are mainly interested in the discovery process, which essentially requires maintaining a priority queue for the web pages in the frontier. The download decisions of the crawler are guided by this queue such that highly ranked (important) web pages in the queue are tried to be fetched earlier than the rest. Besides the scalability and efficiency challenges in maintaining a web-scale priority queue [17, 21], the main issue here is to decide how the pages should be ordered in the queue for download. This is because, in practice, delaying the download of important pages may have direct implications on the overall quality of the search engine's web repository and, consequently, on the user experience with the retrieved search results.

The discovery process requires a metric to quantify web page importance and prioritizing pages accordingly. The early work on this issue relied on page importance metrics that exploit the connectivity of a page in the web graph. A commonly adopted approach was to attribute higher importance to pages that have larger PageRank values (computed over a partially complete web graph). Although the connectivity-based metrics performed fairly well in model-

[1]The web frontier refers to the set of web pages that were discovered by the crawler but whose content is not yet fetched.

ing page importance, they were indirect in the way they captured the impact of crawling a web page on the search engine's result quality. Based on this observation, the latter work adopted a more direct approach where the discovery process is guided by the actual impact on search quality. For example, the technique proposed in [29] prioritized pages in decreasing order of their likelihood of being retrieved in search result pages, increasing the utility of web crawling for many search queries and users. The main difficulty in search-centric approaches is the need to estimate the impact of a web page that is not yet exposed to any user in search results. That is, estimating the impact of a page requires using only auxiliary signals without exploiting any explicit user feedback (e.g., clicks or dwell time) about the page.

The main contribution of this work is a hybrid frontier prioritization approach that combines the two lines of work mentioned above. In particular, we propose a novel random walk model that incorporates the inferred search impact of pages into the standard connectivity-based page importance computation. We measure the actual search impact of a web page in terms of two different metrics: the number of times the page is clicked and the number of times it is viewed in search results. To infer these two measures for a newly discovered web page, we exploit the observed click and view counts of its referring pages which were previously shown in search results. Moreover, we enhance our random walk model by a novel teleportation approach which lets us go beyond the original web graph by connecting pages that have a good chance of being influential for each other in terms of their search impact. Finally, we combine the proposed technique and various baselines under a machine learning model to show further improvements.

We evaluate the performance of the proposed frontier prioritization approach over two large-scale, real-life web collections. As the ground truth for search quality, we use a web search query log obtained from Yahoo. Comparisons with several frontier prioritization approaches taken from the literature indicate that the proposed approach can lead to considerable improvement in search quality. In particular, we observe that our approach obtains up to 60%–70% of the search quality attainable by an ideal web crawler while outperforming the best baseline by a margin of 5%–10%.

The rest of the paper is organized as follows. We present some preliminary information about our problem in Section 2. In Section 3, we describe the data and baselines used in our work. The proposed frontier prioritization approach is presented in Section 4. We report the results of our experiments in Section 5. In Section 6, we present a machine learning solution for the problem. In Section 7, we survey the related work. Section 8 concludes the paper.

2. PRELIMINARIES

Search engines continuously crawl the Web to discover and download newly created content. It is practically impossible to crawl all the pages in the Web within a time frame that will enable meaningful use of the crawled collection. Thus, crawlers aim to download and maintain a reasonably representative and high-quality snapshot of the Web by (i) keeping important pages in the collection fresh, (ii) expanding the collection with new important pages, and (iii) removing unimportant pages from the collection. Herein, we focus on (ii), which requires prioritizing the pages in the crawler's frontier according to a page importance metric.

2.1 Page Importance Measures

As discussed in Section 1, previously proposed page importance metrics can be grouped under two headings as connectivity-based [1, 23, 27] and search-centric [28, 29] page importance metrics. Herein, we are only interested in search-centric page importance metrics as they provide a more direct measure of the crawled web collection's utility for the search engine. For a given web page p, we measure the search impact in two different ways:

- *Click impact*: The click impact, $I_C(p,t)$, of page p indicates the number of times the page's link was clicked in search results during a period of t units of time since the page was last crawled. This definition is the same as the measure used in [14], which compares the effect of various crawling policies on web search effectiveness.
- *View impact*: The view impact, $I_V(p,t)$, of page p indicates the number of times the page's link was displayed in the top 10 search results during a period of t units of time since the page was last crawled. This definition is similar to (but simpler than) the measure in [29], where the view count of a page is normalized by taking into account the rank of the page in search results. In our work, we prefer not to use this sort of normalization as we want to have query-independent impact definitions that can be computed efficiently during crawling.

Without loss of generality, these two impact measures can be extended to a set of pages. For a set S of web pages, the click impact is denoted by $I_C(S,t)$ and is equal to the sum of the click impacts of all pages in S. The view impact of S is denoted by $I_V(S,t)$ and is computed similarly.

In the rest of the paper, we use the above-mentioned two measures although the proposed techniques are not tied to a particular measure. In our analyses, we focus on the short-term search impact of the crawled collection (e.g., within a few days) rather than the long-term impact, which largely depends on the recrawling policy as addressed in [7, 26, 28].

2.2 Problem Definition

We formally define the frontier prioritization problem in the expected case as follows.

DEFINITION 1 (FRONTIER PRIORITIZATION PROBLEM). *Given a set D of already crawled URLs, a set F of URLs in the frontier, a time period t, and a limit ℓ indicating the number of new URLs to be added to the collection,*[2] *find a subset $S \subset F$, such that $|S| \leq \ell$, and depending on the impact definition, either $\mathbb{E}_C(S) = \sum_{p \in S} I_C(p,t)$ or $\mathbb{E}_V(S) = \sum_{p \in S} I_V(p,t)$ is maximized, where $\mathbb{E}_C$ and $\mathbb{E}_V$ are two potential objective functions in the expected case.*

We note that the described frontier prioritization problem is NP-hard in the worst case and cannot admit the fully polynomial-time approximation scheme [29]. Hence, we opt for an expected-case optimization, where the time complexity of the algorithm depends on the time complexity of the computation of rank distribution.

3. EXPERIMENTAL SETUP

In this section, we first introduce the datasets we used to evaluate the proposed techniques. We then provide a brief description of the techniques we used as baselines. Table 1 presents some statistics about the experimental datasets.

[2]We assume a system crawling the web pages in batches.

Table 1: Dataset statistics

Dataset	total # of pages		# of clicked pages		# of viewed pages		# of links		frontier impact ratio	
	D	F	D_C	F_C	D_V	F_V	$D \to D$	$D \to F$	$\lvert F_C\rvert/\lvert F\rvert$	$\lvert F_V\rvert/\lvert F\rvert$
`Wikipedia`	476,805	127,411	98,709	34,926	148,812	45,213	1,532,121	347,071	27.4%	35.5%
`WebCrawl`	74,270,857	23,613,846	105,495	94,902	245,092	194,512	876,871,434	304,709,842	0.4%	0.8%

3.1 Datasets

3.1.1 *Wikipedia*

Wikipedia is an Internet encyclopedia with 18 billion page views and nearly 500 million unique visitors each month [9]. With 34 million pages,[3] dense linking among its articles, constant revisions on existing articles, and few article removals, Wikipedia stands as a small-scale representative of the informative portion of the Web. Wikipedia regularly provides database dumps of all of its available content.[4]

Our `Wikipedia` dataset contains the pages in the English Wikipedia dumps provided for the January 1, 2013 – April 30, 2014 period.[5] In the dumps, each Wikipedia page can have multiple revisions that are available in the Web in different time periods. Fortunately, the dumps also provide the revision time of each page. Hence, we can clearly identify the time period that each revision was online.

In our experiments, we assumed that the revisions of Wikipedia pages that were online from January 1, 2013 to December 31, 2013 were already downloaded by the crawling system, i.e., these revisions constituted set D. We placed in the frontier (set F) the revisions that were (i) linked by the revisions in set D, (ii) online from January 1, 2014 to April 30, 2014, and (iii) not present in D. For each revision in D and F, we counted the number of times it was shown in a search result page and the number of times it was clicked, during a short time period after the revision was created.

3.1.2 *Web Crawl*

The `WebCrawl` dataset is obtained by sampling pages from a large-scale web crawl performed by Yahoo during June 2014. In this case, set D contained pages that were crawled before June 15, 2014, while set F contained pages linked by the pages in set D and crawled before the end of June 2014. We filtered both sets D and F to ensure that $D \cap F = \emptyset$. As in the case of the previous dataset, for each page in D and F, we counted the number of times it was shown in a search result page and the number of times it was clicked during a limited time period after the page was crawled.

3.2 Existing Solutions

As the baseline frontier prioritization techniques, we evaluate the following five approaches:

- `Random`: Frontier pages are crawled in a random order.
- `InDegree`: For each page in the frontier, we maintain an in-degree value (i.e., the total number of links from the set of downloaded pages). The frontier page with the highest in-degree value is crawled first.
- `PageRank`: This is similar to `InDegree`, but instead of in-degree values, we use the PageRank scores [27] to prioritize the pages.
- `Q-Overlap` (query overlap): The impact of a page is estimated by the overlap between the set of page's referring anchor text and a set of search queries issued in the past [29].
- `Q-Hybrid` (query hybrid): The impact of a page is computed as a linear combination of a PageRank-based impact estimate and the `Q-Overlap` score [29]. As suggested in [29], we use decision tree regression[6] to map the `PageRank` scores to impact estimates.

[3] `http://en.wikipedia.org/wiki/Wikipedia:Size_of_Wikipedia.`

[4] `http://en.wikipedia.org/wiki/Wikipedia:Database_download.`

[5] `http://dumps.wikimedia.org/enwiki/.`

4. IMPACT-AWARE FRONTIER PRIORITIZATION

In this section, we describe the proposed web frontier-prioritization approach. The heart of our approach lies in the propositions that (i) high impact pages in F are more likely to be discovered by following the outbound links of high impact pages in D, and (ii) the current web browsing trend is such that a user is more likely to "teleport" to a related page by going through a search engine instead of jumping to a random page within a browsing session. Based on these two propositions, we propose a random walk model that subsumes the impact of pages into the traditional link-based computation (proposition (i)). We then enhance the model with a novel teleportation mechanism (proposition (ii)) by virtually connecting similar pages based on their link structure. Finally, we elaborate on the convergence property of our model.

4.1 Impact-Based Linkage Analysis

We argue that high impact pages in D are more likely to link other high impact pages in F. We assume that, for each page $p \in D$, we already have the $I_C(p, \Delta t)$ and/or $I_V(p, \Delta t)$ scores. Let D_C, D_V, D_{NC}, and D_{NV} denote the set of clicked, viewed, not clicked, and not viewed pages in D, respectively. Similarly, let F_C, F_V, F_{NC}, and F_{NV} denote the set of clicked, viewed, not clicked, and not viewed pages in F, respectively. We note that $D = D_C \cup D_{NC} = D_V \cup D_{NV}$ and $F = F_C \cup F_{NC} = F_V \cup F_{NV}$. As an example, based on the click impact metric, Figs. 1(b) and 1(c) illustrate the partition of a sample D set into D_C and D_{NC} sets and the partition of a sample F set into F_C and F_{NC} sets, respectively.

4.1.1 *Frontier Impact Ratio*

Given a set $X \subset D$, let the set of pages in F linked from the pages in X be denoted as $L(X \to F)$. Then, we define the average *frontier click-impact ratio*, $r_c(X \to F)$, of pages in X as follows:

$$r_c(X \to F) = \frac{\sum_{p_i \in L(X \to F)} I_C(p_i)}{|X|} = \frac{I_C(L(X \to F))}{|X|}. \quad (1)$$

Similarly, we define the average *frontier view-impact ratio*, $r_v(X \to F)$, of pages in X as follows:

$$r_v(X \to F) = \frac{\sum_{p_i \in L(X \to F)} I_V(p_i)}{|X|} = \frac{I_V(L(X \to F))}{|X|}. \quad (2)$$

[6] We use the implementation in the scikit-learn toolkit [30].

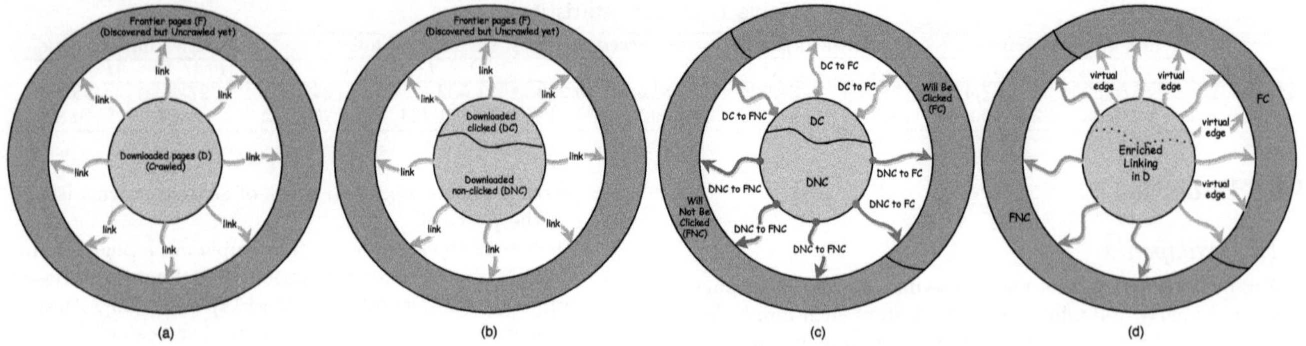

Figure 1: (a) The set of downloaded (D) and frontier (F) pages. (b) Partition of D into search impacting (clicked pages in D_{C}) and non-impacting (not clicked pages in D_{NC}) page sets. (c) Partition of F into search impacting (clicked pages in F_{C}) and non-impacting (not clicked pages in F_{NC}) page sets. We also separate the links from D to F into categories based on their source and destination (e.g., from D_{NC} to F_{NC}). (d) After link graph enrichment: A set of pages in D that had no link to F_{C} before enrichment now have links to F_{C}. The linking structure in D is enriched as well, improving impact propagation.

Table 2: Analysis of how pages in the downloaded set are linked with search impacting pages in the frontier set

Dataset		Clicks	r_{c}	Views	r_{v}
Wikipedia	$L(D_{\mathrm{C}} \rightarrow F)$	0.6M	5.76	–	–
	$L(D_{\mathrm{NC}} \rightarrow F)$	0.4M	1.07	–	–
	$L(D_{\mathrm{V}} \rightarrow F)$	–	–	2.0M	13.68
	$L(D_{\mathrm{NV}} \rightarrow F)$	–	–	1.0M	3.15
WebCrawl	$L(D_{\mathrm{C}} \rightarrow F)$	15.4M	162.17	–	–
	$L(D_{\mathrm{NC}} \rightarrow F)$	27.3M	0.03	–	–
	$L(D_{\mathrm{V}} \rightarrow F)$	–	–	26.8M	137.99
	$L(D_{\mathrm{NV}} \rightarrow F)$	–	–	50.5M	0.06

Intuitively, r_{c} and r_{v} provide a measure of how important X is in suggesting good candidate pages for crawling. Table 2 shows the frontier impact ratio values for the pages in D_{C}, D_{V}, D_{NC}, and D_{NV}. We observe that pages in D_{C} and D_{V} have significantly higher impact ratio values than the pages in D_{NC} and D_{NV}. In other words, despite the fact that clicked and viewed pages in the downloaded page set constitute a small fraction of this set, these pages are promising sources for discovering new pages (frontier) with high search impact.

4.2 Random Walk Model

We have observed in Table 2 that the relatively small set of clicked or viewed pages in D are more likely to directly link clicked or viewed pages in F. Generally speaking, the high-impact pages in the frontier are likely to be discovered through the outbound links of the high-impact pages in the downloaded set. Furthermore, in our analyses, we also observed that there is a significant number of high-impact pages in D that do not directly link pages in F, but are at two- or three-hop distance to the high-impact pages in F. These observations pointed us in the direction of a random walk model where the impact of pages can trickle down to the pages that are reachable via following outbound links.

A random walk on a given graph is a Markov process, where each node represents a state and a walk transiting from one state to another state based on a transition probability matrix. One of the well-known random walk algorithms is PageRank [27], and variants of it are used for frontier prioritization [1] in state-of-the-art web crawlers.[7] PageRank determines the importance of pages by modeling the web surfing behavior of users. The random surfer model of PageRank assumes that a user visiting a given page can either follow one of the outbound links of that page or arbitrarily jumps to another page. Formally, the random walk process of PageRank can be defined as

$$x_t(j) = \alpha \sum_{i \in L_j^-} M_{ij} x_{t-1}(i) + (1-\alpha) v_j, \qquad (3)$$

where M_{ij} is the transition probability from page p_i to p_j, $x_t(j)$ is the importance score of page p_j at step t, α is a damping factor that controls how often the walker jumps to an arbitrary node, v_j is the initial probabilistic importance score (generally set to $1/n$, where n is the number of nodes in the graph), and L_i^- is the set of inbound links of page p_i, respectively. When t is iterated enough, the importance scores reach a stationary distribution that can be used as a source of information for ranking pages.

The main drawback of the traditional PageRank process in Eq. (3) is that it captures only the observed linking characteristics of pages and ignores other sources of information which can also be indicators of their importance. To overcome this drawback, we introduce an *impact factor* for every page and use this to augment the traditional PageRank process to make use of other sources of information. The proposed random walk model (RW) allows the random walker to take into account multiple sources of information and perform the voting adaptively and more effectively.

To define our model formally, let $G = \{\mathcal{V}, \mathcal{E}\}$ denote the link graph, where vertices in $\mathcal{V} = D \cup F$ with $|\mathcal{V}| = n$ represent pages and edges in $\mathcal{E}$ represent the links among pages. We compute the transition probability for $p_i \rightarrow p_j$ as $M_{ij}{=}1/|L_i^+|$, where L_i^+ denotes the set of outbound links of page p_i (obviously, $p_j \in L_i^+$). We define the impact factor $\mathcal{F}_i$ of a page p_i used in embedding the search-centric impact of a page as

$$\mathcal{F}_i = \frac{\mathcal{I}_i}{\max_j \mathcal{I}_j} \times (d_i^+)^\gamma. \qquad (4)$$

Here, the term $\mathcal{I}_i / \max_j \mathcal{I}_j$ represents the normalized search-centric impact of p_i.[8] $d_i^+ \in [0,1]$ is the normalized out-degree

[7] https://wiki.apache.org/nutch/NewScoring.

[8] We note that, in the implementation, we use $\mathcal{I}_i = I_{\mathrm{C}}(i, \Delta t) + \epsilon$ or $\mathcal{I}_i = I_{\mathrm{V}}(i, \Delta t) + \epsilon$, depending on the optimization objective. $\mathcal{I}_i$ is smoothed by adding a small ϵ value

of p_i, i.e., $d_i^+ = |L_i^+|/\max_k |L_k^+|$. The $(d_i^+)^\gamma$ multiplier is added to enable a fine-tuning capability for favoring pages with high out-degrees. As γ gets larger than zero, the model increases the effect of impactful pages with high out-degree. Our observation is that the set of pages with non-zero impact in D are rather small, and among such pages, the ones that have a high out-degree can be considered as hubs linking authoritative pages [19]. We set $\gamma = 1$ for the `Wikipedia` dataset and $\gamma = 0$ for the `WebCrawl` dataset because of this characteristic.

The impact factor is embedded into Eq. (3) to iteratively compute the importance score $x_t(j)$ of a page p_j as

$$x_t(j) = \alpha \sum_{i \in L_j^-} \mathcal{F}_i M_{ij} x_{t-1}(i) + (1-\alpha) v_j. \tag{5}$$

Intuitively, our random walk process can be explained as follows. When following the outbound links of a node, the random walker is likely to contribute the voting impact of the node to its neighbors with a high rate when this node has a good impact (i.e., more clicks or views in our case). Otherwise, its neighbors will receive its voting impact with a low rate. Here, we should note that, the importance score computations of the pages in the frontier according to Eq. (5) can be done in a separate iteration as the outbound links of those pages are not known. Hence, their contributions to other pages' importance scores are practically zero. In other words, it is possible to compute the accumulated score contribution of the pages in D to pages in F first and reflect that onto pages in F in one iteration later. For further computational efficiency, it is possible to compute the scores of pages in D offline and update them incrementally adopting techniques similar to those defined for incremental PageRank computation [11].

It is worth mentioning that `RW` converges to a stationary distribution. Let Λ be the diagonal matrix with diagonal elements $(\mathcal{F}_1, \mathcal{F}_2, .., \mathcal{F}_n)$, I be the $n \times n$ identity matrix, $\mathbf{v}$ be the transpose of $1 \times n$ uniform stochastic vector, and M denote the transition matrix for G.

PROPOSITION 1. $(\mathbf{I} - \alpha\mathbf{M}^T\Lambda)$ *is invertible for all* $\mathbf{M}, \Lambda, \alpha$.

PROOF. Let $\mathbf{P} = \mathbf{M}^T\Lambda$, we need to prove that $\mathbf{I} - \alpha\mathbf{P}$ is invertible. Equivalently, we prove its transpose $\mathbf{I} - \alpha\mathbf{P}^T$ is invertible, which can be proved by showing that $(\mathbf{I} - \alpha\mathbf{P}^T)\mathbf{y} = 0$ only has the trivial solution $\mathbf{y} = 0$.

$$\begin{aligned}(\mathbf{I} - \alpha\mathbf{P}^T)\mathbf{y} &= 0 \\ \mathbf{y} &= \alpha\mathbf{P}^T\mathbf{y} \\ y_i &= \alpha \sum_j P_{ji} y_j \\ &= \alpha \sum_j (\mathcal{F}_i M_{ij} y_j).\end{aligned} \tag{6}$$

Let $u = \text{argmax}_j\, y_j$. Eq. (6) infers

$$\begin{aligned} y_u &\le \alpha\mathcal{F}_u \sum_j (\mathcal{F}_i M_{ij} y_u) \\ y_u &\le \alpha\mathcal{F}_u y_u \\ y_u(1 - \alpha\mathcal{F}_u) &\le 0.\end{aligned} \tag{7}$$

(empirically set to 0.001) to its absolute count to avoid random ranking in the case all inbound links to a page have zero impact value.

Since $\alpha < 1$ and $\mathcal{F}_u \le 1$, we have $(1 - \alpha\mathcal{F}_u) > 0$ and hence $y_u \le 0$. Similarly, let $v = \text{argmin}_j\, y_j$. We have $y_v \ge 0$. As $y_v \le y_u$, this implies $y_u = y_v = 0$ to satisfy all inequalities. Consequently, $y_i = 0$ for all i, or $\mathbf{y} = 0$. Thus, $\mathbf{I} - \alpha\mathbf{P}^T$ is invertible. Equivalently, $(\mathbf{I} - \alpha\mathbf{M}^T\Lambda)$ is invertible. □

PROPOSITION 2. *The iteration in Eq. (5) converges to* $(1-\alpha)(I - \alpha\mathbf{M}^T\Lambda)^{-1}\mathbf{v}$.

PROOF. Let $\mathbf{P} = \mathbf{M}^T\Lambda$. We can rewrite Eq. (5) in matrix form as

$$\begin{aligned}\mathbf{x}_t &= \alpha\mathbf{M}^T\Lambda\mathbf{x}_{t-1} + (1-\alpha)\mathbf{v} \\ &= \alpha\mathbf{P}\mathbf{x}_{t-1} + (1-\alpha)\mathbf{v} \\ &= (\alpha\mathbf{P})^t\mathbf{x}_0 + (1-\alpha)(\sum_{i=1}^{t}(\alpha\mathbf{P})^{i-1})\mathbf{v}.\end{aligned} \tag{8}$$

We will show that $\lim_{t\to\infty} \mathbf{x}_t = (1-\alpha)(I - \alpha\mathbf{P})^{-1}\mathbf{v}$. We have

$$\begin{aligned}\sum_i (\alpha P)_{ij}^t &= \sum_i \sum_k (\alpha P)_{ik} (\alpha P)_{kj}^{t-1} \\ &= \sum_k (\alpha P)_{kj}^{t-1} \sum_i (\alpha P)_{ik} \\ &= \sum_k (\alpha P)_{kj}^{t-1} \alpha \sum_i (\mathcal{F}_k M_{ki}) \\ &= \sum_k (\alpha P)_{kj}^{t-1} \alpha\mathcal{F}_k \\ &\le \sum_k (\alpha P)_{kj}^{t-1} \alpha \\ &\le (\alpha)^t.\end{aligned} \tag{9}$$

Because $\alpha < 1$, this column sum converges to zero when $t \to \infty$. We then derive $\lim_{t\to\infty} (\alpha\mathbf{P})^t\mathbf{x}_0 = 0$. When $t \to \infty$, given Proposition 1, by applying Neumann series, Eq. (8) becomes:

$$\mathbf{x}_t = (\alpha\mathbf{P})^t\mathbf{x}_0 + (1-\alpha)(I - \alpha\mathbf{P})^{-1}\mathbf{v}.$$

Hence,

$$\lim_{t\to\infty} \mathbf{x}_t = (1-\alpha)(I - \alpha\mathbf{P})^{-1}\mathbf{v}.$$

Convergence proved. □

4.3 Random Walk with Graph Enrichment

In the previous section, we have sketched our random walk model, which presumes that when a random walker is at some page p, it can either visit the outbound links of p or teleport to a random page with a certain probability and these visit probabilities provide some voting impact to the rank of the candidate pages. In this model, the teleportation probability to other pages is fixed.

We hypothesize that the user browsing experiences generally start with a query issued to a search engine and by clicking on a search result, possibly followed by a number of page visits performed by tracking the outbound links of the encountered pages. Then, if the search task did not end, it is followed by another (possibly related/refined) query to the search engine. In this scenario, teleportation is also generally performed via visits to a search engine and a user is more likely to "teleport" to a related or similar page instead of a random page in a search session. Following this hypothesis, in our random walk model, when a page p is visited,

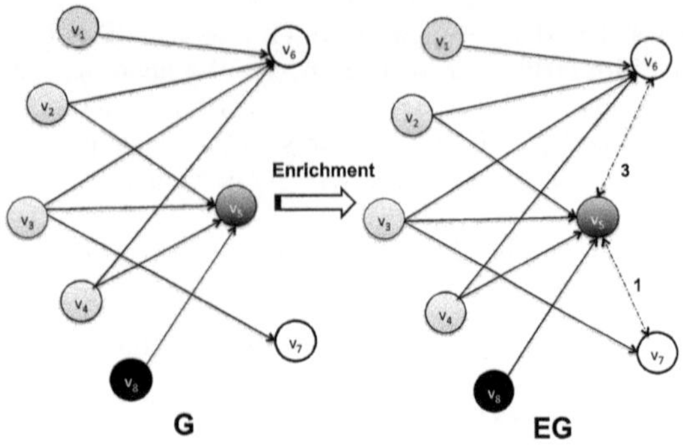

Figure 2: Illustration of graph enrichment technique.

Table 3: Analysis on the search impact of pages in F linked via enriched edges from D_C and D_V

Dataset		Clicks	r_C	Views	r_V
Wikipedia	$EG(D_C \to F)$	0.6M	6.17	–	–
	$EG(D_V \to F)$	–	–	2.2M	14.67
WebCrawl	$EG(D_C \to F)$	21.9M	207.63	–	–
	$EG(D_V \to F)$	–	–	36.9M	150.59

even if the outbound links of p are not followed, pages that are similar to p should have a higher chance of being visited next.

The implication of the above discussion for prioritizing frontier pages is that pages in F that are similar to high impact pages in D are more likely to be teleported to. There are a number of ways for performing this special form of teleportation. Herein, we opted to enhance the link graph via virtual edges that link similar pages. Since one of the best information we have about the pages in the frontier is their in-link structure, we define a similarity metric based on the in-link structure of pages. We refer to the set of virtual edges as $\mathcal{E}'$. Extending the original graph G via virtual edges in $\mathcal{E}'$ forms the enriched graph $EG = \{\mathcal{V}, \mathcal{E} \cup \mathcal{E}'\}$. Applying our random walk model on EG yields a random walk model with a graph enrichment solution (RW-EG) for the frontier prioritization problem.

In this enhanced model, we consider pages linked by the same pages as similar. We create a virtual edge between a page p_i and another page p_j if and only if they have at least one page p_x that has links to both of them. The weight w_{ij} of the virtual edge between p_i and p_j is computed as $w_{ij} = |L_i^- \cap L_j^-|$.

Fig. 2 provides an example for our link graph enrichment technique. The regular link graph G is shown on the left while the enriched graph EG is shown on the right. Shaded vertices in the figure indicate already crawled pages, and white vertices indicate URLs in the frontier. The darker a crawled vertex is, the higher the search-impact of the corresponding page. As seen in the figure, two virtual edges are added to G after the enrichment process. The edge between v_5 and v_7 is added as both of them have a common inbound link from v_3. The weight of the (v_5, v_7) edge is 1 since the number of common link providers of these two vertices is one. The edge (v_5, v_6) is added as both of them have common inbound links from v_2, v_3, and v_4. The weight of (v_5, v_6) edge is 3 since the number of common link providers is three.

Table 3 shows the frontier impact ratio values for the pages in D_C and D_V after enrichment. We observe that, via enrichment, the impact of the set of pages in the frontier that are linked by D_C and D_V has increased. Fig. 1(d) demonstrates how the link graph changes after enrichment.

To formally define our random walk model with graph enrichment, let M' be an $n \times n$ matrix, such that M'_{ij} indicates the virtual transition probability among pages p_i and p_j based on virtual edges in $\mathcal{E}'$. M'_{ij} is computed as $M'_{ij} = \frac{w_{ij}}{\sum_k w_{ik}}$. We also define $L_j^{-\prime}$ as the list of inbound links based on virtual edges and $\mathcal{F}'_j$ as the influence impact of a page p_j based on virtual edges. We propose to compute the impact-based importance score $x_t(j)$ of a page p_j using the enriched graph EG as

$$x_t(j) = \alpha\omega \sum_{i \in L_j^-} \mathcal{F}_i M_{ij} x_{t-1}(i) + \alpha(1-\omega) \sum_{i \in L_j^{-\prime}} \mathcal{F}'_i M'_{ij} x_{t-1}(i) \quad + (1-\alpha)v_j. \tag{10}$$

Here, $0 \leq \omega \leq 1$ is the hyper-parameter to control the proportion of the impact a page distributes to its neighbors via its original links. When $\omega = 1$, no virtual link is taken into account in the importance calculation, and when $\omega = 0$ only the virtual links are used. The proposed random walk process can be interpreted as follows. At every node, the random walker can either follow the original outbound links with a probability $\alpha\omega$ or teleport to a similar node with a probability $\alpha(1-\omega)$. Otherwise, it teleports to an arbitrary node with probability $1-\alpha$.

Similar to the RW model, the RW-EG model converges to a stationary distribution. Let Λ and Λ' be diagonal matrices with diagonals $(\mathcal{F}_1, \mathcal{F}_2, .., \mathcal{F}_n)$ and $(\mathcal{F}'_1, \mathcal{F}'_2, .., \mathcal{F}'_n)$, respectively.

PROPOSITION 3 (INVERTIBLE). *$(\mathbf{I} - \alpha(\omega\mathbf{M}^T\Lambda + (1-\omega)\mathbf{M}'^T\Lambda'))$ is invertible for all $\mathbf{M}, \mathbf{M}', \Lambda, \Lambda', \alpha, \omega$.*

PROPOSITION 4 (CONVERGENCE). *The iteration in Eq. (10) converges to $(1-\alpha)(\mathbf{I} - \alpha(\omega\mathbf{M}^T\Lambda + (1-\omega)\mathbf{M}'^T\Lambda'))^{-1}\mathbf{v}$.*

PROOF. Let $\mathbf{P} = \omega\mathbf{M}^T\Lambda + (1-\omega)\mathbf{M}'^T\Lambda'$. The proof is similar to those of Propositions 1 and 2. □

5. EXPERIMENTAL RESULTS

5.1 Parameter Tuning

We randomly split the frontier of each dataset into training and test sets. The training set is used to train and tune the parameters of the algorithms, while the test set is used for evaluation. In both datasets, we use roughly 65% of the pages for training.

RW-EG is parametrized by ω, which linearly combines the votes based on original links and the votes based on virtual links, and α, which determines the probability that the surfer chooses to follow one of the outbound of the current page. We set, $\alpha = 0.85$ as suggested by [27] and tune ω on the training data before applying the model on the test data. Our tuning strategy is straightforward: We vary ω to identify the ω value maximizing the objective function. For higher confidence and to avoid data randomness, we apply the 0.632+ bootstrapping technique [12] to generate multiple samples from the tuning data and measure the average performance on these samples while tuning.

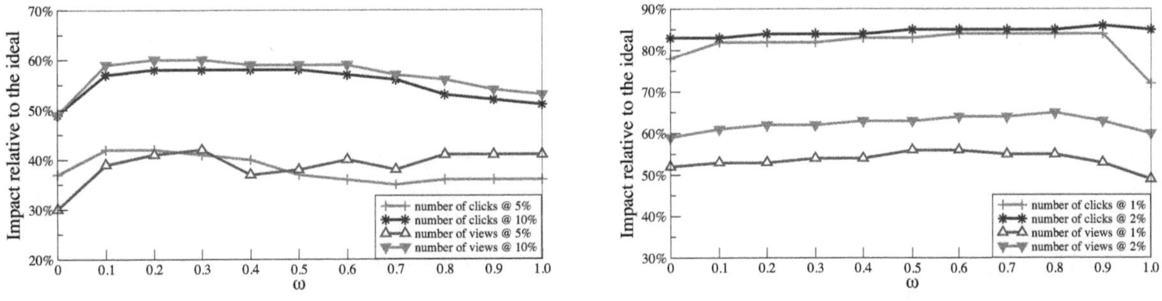

(a) Wikipedia. (b) WebCrawl.

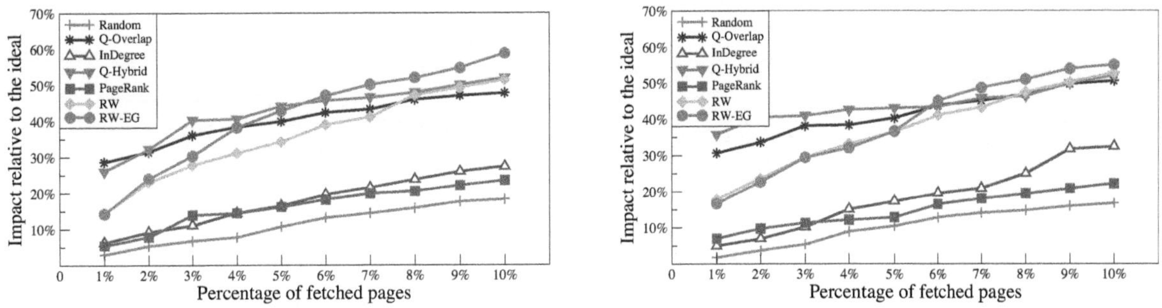

(a) Click impact. (b) View impact.

Figure 4: Performance comparison on the WebCrawl dataset.

Figs. 3a and 3b show the performance of RW-EG on the tuning data as we increase the value of ω from 0 to 1 in steps of 0.1. For each ω value on the x axis, we present the percentage of search impact of RW-EG with respect to that of an ideal ranking, which orders the pages in the frontier according to their actual search impacts. We select the highest ranked 5% and 10% frontier pages according to RW-EG for the Wikipedia dataset. Similarly, we select the highest ranked 1% and 2% frontier pages according to RW-EG for the WebCrawl dataset. The summed impact of pages selected by RW-EG are divided against that of the ideal ranking to obtain the provided figures. We observe that the best combination for Wikipedia is at $\omega = 0.1$ and $\omega = 0.2$ for the click impact and view impact metrics, respectively. For WebCrawl, the best combination is found at $\omega = 0.9$ for the click impact metric and $\omega = 0.8$ for the view impact metric.

5.2 Performance Analysis

Figs. 4a, 4b, 5a, and 5b present the performance of all approaches on the two datasets and in terms of the two impact metrics. The performance values are provided as a percentage of the click impact and view impact measures attained by the ideal ranking (observed within the first week following the crawling). We note that similar results are observed when the observation period is limited up to a day. For Wikipedia, similar to [29], we aim to maximize the search impact while selecting 10% of the frontier. This is a reasonable assumption considering the size of the Wikipedia frontier. For WebCrawl, we aim to maximize the impact while selecting up to 2% (approximately 160K pages) of the frontier. In practice, it may be more effective to crawl a few hundred thousand pages in a crawling iteration and rerun the ranking algorithm with additional discovered pages.

5.2.1 Performance on the Wikipedia Dataset

Figs. 4a and 4b present the performance of the investigated approaches on the Wikipedia dataset. As seen in the figures, when the fraction of the downloaded pages exceeds 6% of the frontier, RW-EG provides the best results. However, when the fraction of downloaded pages is below 5%, Q-Overlap and Q-Hybrid outperforms RW and RW-EG. This is due to the fact that the query overlap score used in Q-Overlap and Q-Hybrid is very effective in informative pages such as those in Wikipedia.

RW and RW-EG provide considerably better performance compared to PageRank, showing the positive influence of incorporating click and view impact in predicting high-impact frontier pages. The difference in the performance of RW and RW-EG indicates the effectiveness of the proposed link graph enrichment technique. We note that, even though Random provides the worst ordering among all approaches, it still obtains approximately 20% of the impact attained by the ideal ranking, both in click and view impact metrics. This shows that the Wikipedia dataset, by its nature, contains high-impact pages.

5.2.2 Performance on the WebCrawl Dataset

Figs. 5a and 5b show the performance of all approaches on the WebCrawl dataset. As mentioned before, we evaluate the search impact up to top 2% of the frontier. Unlike the Wikipedia dataset, WebCrawl has a highly skewed distribution in terms of impact, with a tiny fraction (0.4%–0.8%) of pages receiving the majority of clicks and views.

In the figures, we first observe that Random provides nearly zero impact frontier selection. This is another indicator for the difference between Wikipedia and WebCrawl. Second, we observe that Q-Overlap and Q-Hybrid both perform better

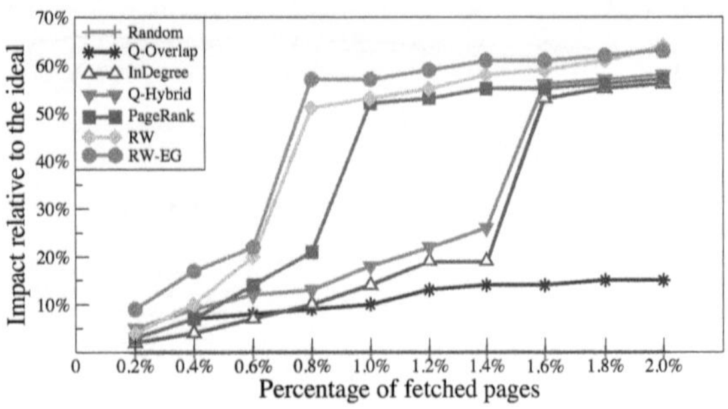

(a) Click impact.

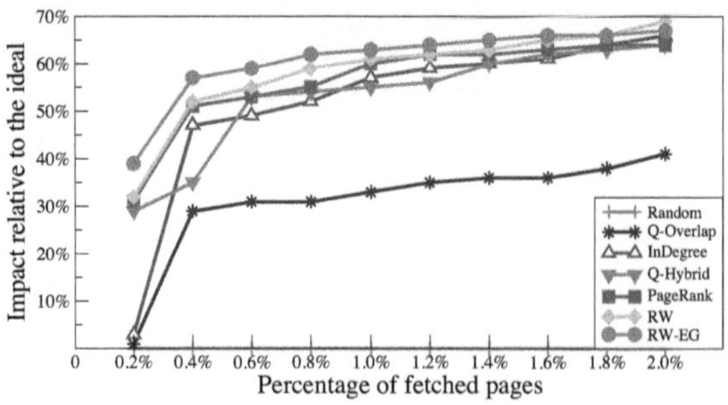

(b) View impact.

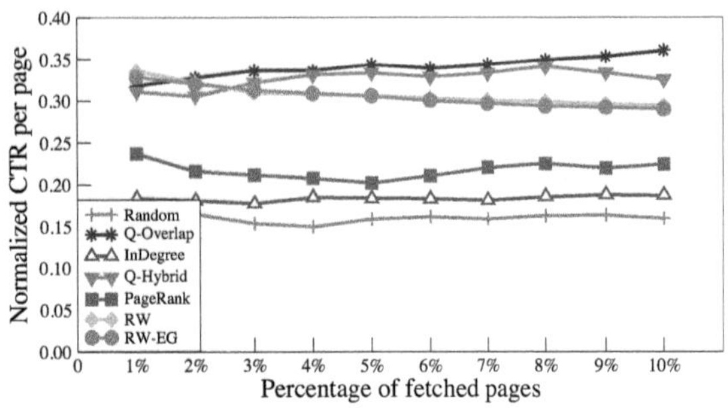

(a) `Wikipedia`.

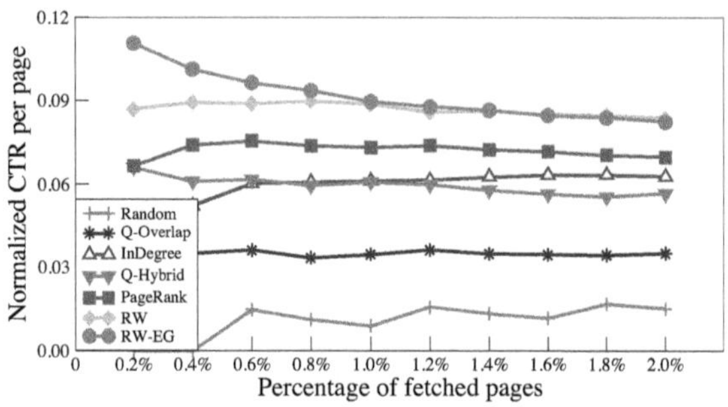

(b) `WebCrawl`.

Figure 6: Average CTR values for different approaches.

than **PageRank** and **InDegree** in identifying the top fraction (0.2%) of pages with high click impact. However, as they download a larger fraction of frontier pages, they perform rather poorly. As suggested in [29], a very rapid "drying up" trend is observed for **Q-Overlap**. **WebCrawl** possesses a very low fraction of high-impact pages, and selecting the set of pages that match previously observed queries in and itself is not enough in tackling the complex problem of identifying these small number of high-impact frontier pages and may even lead to the selection of low-impact pages. Finally, Figs. 5a and 5b show that **RW** and **RW-EG** are superior when compared to the other algorithms. This proves the effectiveness of the proposed approaches that incorporate the search impact into a random walk model. Once again, we observe that **RW-EG** improves over **RW** by selecting higher impact pages in the early stages.

5.3 Analysis of Other Quality Metrics

We investigate the quality of highly ranked frontier pages in terms of two other quality metrics: click-through rate (CTR) and PageRank score. Fig. 6 presents the normalized CTR values per page for the investigated algorithms. As seen in the figure, for the **Wikipedia** dataset, **Q-Overlap** and **Q-Hybrid** lead to higher average CTR while, for the **WebCrawl** dataset, **RW** and **RW-EG** lead to higher average CTR.

Fig. 7 presents the average PageRank scores for each approach. As expected, **PageRank** performs the best in this metric. As **RW** and **RW-EG** employ random walk models, they also tend to select pages with relatively high PageRank scores. Similarly, as **Q-Hybrid** incorporates PageRank, it performs relatively well in this metric. We observe that pages selected by **Q-Overlap** tend to have low PageRank scores.

Table 4: Features used in the machine learning model

Feature	Description
InDegree	Number of inbound links of the page
PageRank	PageRank score of the page
Q-Overlap	Q-Overlap score of the page
Q-Hybrid	Q-Hybrid score of the page
RW	RW scores of the page (click/view-impact)
RW-EG	RW-EG scores of the page (click/view-impact)
RW (virtual)	RW scores on virtual edges (click/view-impact)

6. MACHINE-LEARNED APPROACH

The analyses in the previous section show that **RW** and **RW-EG** both perform better than the baseline frontier prioritization approaches. However, the information provided by the baseline approaches may still be useful. Hence, in this section, we describe a machine learning approach (**ML**) that exploits the ranking scores of all available approaches. Our aim is to show that by combining approaches that make use of different information wells (e.g., links, search impact, query neediness), it is possible to perform better than the individual approaches.

In **ML**, for every page in the frontier, we compute the features given in Table 4. Then, a model is learned using the set of training pages, where the (ground-truth) search impact scores obtained by using the query logs are used as prediction targets. In practice, there exists a wide range of machine learning algorithms that can be used to train our model. In our experiments, we use the decision tree regression technique[9] and the online gradient-descent-based regression technique[10] with the **Wikipedia** and **WebCrawl** datasets, respectively.

[9] We use the implementation in the scikit-learn toolkit [30].
[10] We use the implementation in the Vowpal Wabbit toolkit.

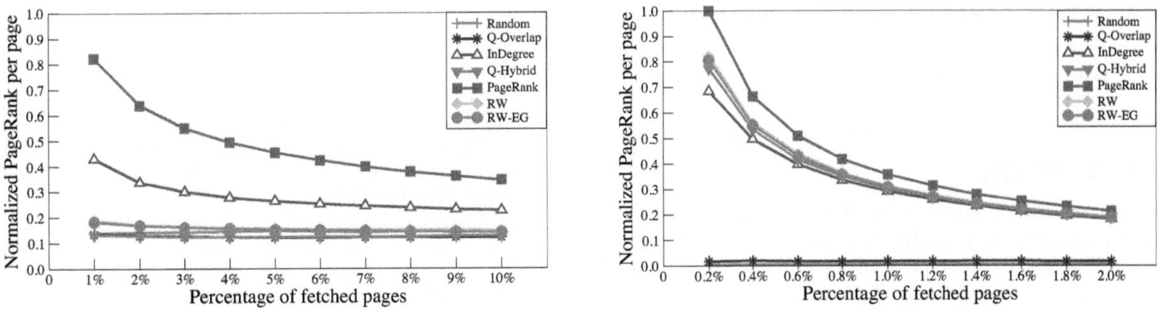

(a) `Wikipedia`. (b) `WebCrawl`.

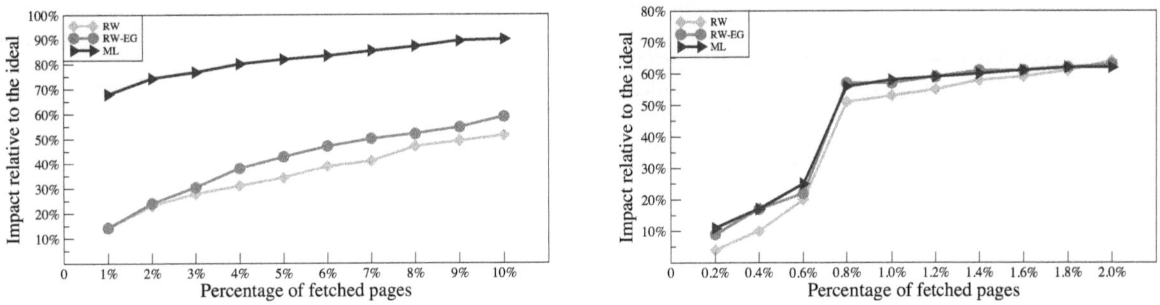

(a) `Wikipedia`. (b) `WebCrawl`.

Figure 8: Comparison of the `ML`, `RW`, and `RW-EG` approaches in terms of the click-impact metric.

Figs. 8a and 8b compare the performance of `ML` with those of `RW` and `RW-EG` in terms of the click impact metric, using the `Wikipedia` and WebCrawl datasets, respectively. We do not report the results for the view impact metric as the findings are similar. In Fig. 8a, we observe that `ML` outperforms `RW` and `RW-EG` for the `Wikipedia` dataset. This finding encourages the idea that information coming from different prioritization approaches, when combined in the right way, can provide additional benefits. In Fig. 8b, however, we observe that `ML` does not show the same relative performance for `WebCrawl`. We hypothesize that, as `WebCrawl` is highly skewed in terms of impact distribution, the task of combining the features in the right way becomes much more difficult. There are techniques to cope with this issue, such as supervising a random walk model [3] or stratified sampling via weighted random walks [20].

7. RELATED WORK

Some recent work investigated passive content discovery techniques [4, 18], such as those that rely on bookmarking or toolbar data, as complementary techniques to web crawling. We limit our attention here only to conventional crawling strategies where the Web is actively crawled by following hyperlinks [25]. We also do not cover the scalability and efficiency issues encountered in crawling [21]. Interested reader may refer to [5] for a more detailed coverage of practical issues involved in web crawling. Below we cover the two main lines of research on crawling: recrawling [7, 26, 28] and frontier prioritization [8, 13, 15, 16, 22, 23, 25, 29].

Recrawling. Evolution of the Web has been investigated in several research work [2, 24]. These work pointed out the rapid change in both content and link structure of the Web, demonstrating the importance of recrawling. An early study of the recrawling problem is available in [31]. The work in [7] investigated different page refresh policies. The authors of [7] defined two metrics to estimate the freshness of a web repository, and the refresh policies proposed therein were shown to improve the freshness over simpler refresh policies. The work in [28] proposed guiding the recrawling process based on the potential impact on the search experience of users. The authors empirically demonstrated that the same user experience can be attained by allocating much fewer resources to the recrawling process, enabling the use of freed resources in the discovery process. In [26], the authors argued that ephemeral and persistent web content should be distinguished when deciding which pages should be refreshed. Based on this observation, they designed a recrawling policy that takes the longevity of web pages into account. This approach was shown to lead to better freshness in the web repository also reducing the crawling cost.

Frontier prioritization. The discoverability of the content in the Web was investigated in [10]. The early work in [8] defined different page importance metrics and proposed crawling the Web according to page importance. The authors showed that importance-based prioritization of pages can significantly improve the quality of a web repository. In [23], the relatively simple breadth-first crawling strategy was shown to discover high-quality pages early. In [13], the authors tried to prioritize the pages in the crawler's frontier by exploiting the hierarchical structure of the Web and showed that this is more efficient than the PageRank-based prioritization approach proposed in [8]. The work in [16] focused on the discovery of good pages, specifically focusing on filtering out spam content during the crawling process. The authors of [29] proposed ordering the pages in the frontier according to their estimated impact on search results. They showed that their technique enables crawling of tail web content that is of interest to some users, not only popular content. In two concurrent work [14] and [6], the authors investigated the impact of well-known crawling strategies on web search effectiveness.

8. CONCLUSION

We formalized the frontier prioritization problem as a search-centric optimization problem, where the objective is to maximize the impact of the crawled collection on the result quality of the search engine. To tackle the problem, we presented a novel random walk model that incorporates the inferred search impact of pages into the standard connectivity-based page importance computation. We also proposed a link graph enrichment technique that approximates user's searching and browsing behavior and improves the voting process in the proposed random walk model. Finally, we combined different solutions for the frontier prioritization problem under a common machine learning model. To evaluate the proposed approaches, we conducted experiments over two large-scale web collections. The results of our experiments indicated that the proposed approaches perform considerably better than the state-of-the-art frontier prioritization approaches in improving search quality.

Acknowledgement

This work was supported by the ERC Advanced Grant ALEXANDRIA (339233) and the LEADS project (ICT-318809), funded by the European Community.

9. REFERENCES

[1] S. Abiteboul, M. Preda, and G. Cobena. Adaptive on-line page importance computation. In *Proc. 12th Int'l Conf. World Wide Web*, pages 280–290, 2003.

[2] E. Adar, J. Teevan, S. T. Dumais, and J. L. Elsas. The Web changes everything: Understanding the dynamics of web content. In *Proc. 2nd ACM Int'l Conf. Web Search and Data Mining*, pages 282–291, 2009.

[3] L. Backstrom and J. Leskovec. Supervised random walks: Predicting and recommending links in social networks. In *Proc. 4th ACM Int'l Conf. Web Search and Data Mining*, pages 635–644, 2011.

[4] X. Bai, B. B. Cambazoglu, and F. P. Junqueira. Discovering URLs through user feedback. In *Proc. 20th ACM Int'l Conf. Information and Knowledge Management*, pages 77–86, 2011.

[5] B. B. Cambazoglu and R. Baeza-Yates. Scalability challenges in web search engines. In M. Melucci and R. Baeza-Yates, editors, *Advanced Topics in Information Retrieval*, volume 33 of *The Information Retrieval Series*, pages 27–50. Springer Berlin Heidelberg, 2011.

[6] B. B. Cambazoglu, V. Plachouras, and R. Baeza-Yates. Quantifying performance and quality gains in distributed web search engines. In *Proc. 32nd Int'l ACM SIGIR Conf. Research and Development in Information Retrieval*, pages 411–418, 2009.

[7] J. Cho and H. Garcia-Molina. Effective page refresh policies for web crawlers. *ACM Transactions on Database Systems*, 28(4):390–426, 2003.

[8] J. Cho, H. Garcia-Molina, and L. Page. Efficient crawling through URL ordering. *Computer Networks and ISDN Systems*, 30(1-7):161–172, 1998.

[9] N. Cohen. Wikipedia vs. the small screen, 2014.

[10] A. Dasgupta, A. Ghosh, R. Kumar, C. Olston, S. Pandey, and A. Tomkins. The discoverability of the Web. In *Proc. 16th Int'l Conf. World Wide Web*, pages 421–430, 2007.

[11] P. Desikan, N. Pathak, J. Srivastava, and V. Kumar. Incremental page rank computation on evolving graphs. In *Special Interest Tracks and Posters of the 14th Int'l Conf. World Wide Web*, pages 1094–1095, 2005.

[12] B. Efron and R. Tibshirani. Improvements on cross-validation: The .632+ bootstrap method. *Journal of the American Statistical Association*, 92(438), 1997.

[13] N. Eiron, K. S. McCurley, and J. A. Tomlin. Ranking the web frontier. In *Proc. 13th Int'l Conf. World Wide Web*, pages 309–318, 2004.

[14] D. Fetterly, N. Craswell, and V. Vinay. The impact of crawl policy on web search effectiveness. In *Proc. 32nd Int'l ACM SIGIR Conf. Research and Development in Information Retrieval*, pages 580–587, 2009.

[15] Z. Guan, C. Wang, C. Chen, J. Bu, and J. Wang. Guide focused crawler efficiently and effectively using on-line topical importance estimation. In *Proc. 31st Annual Int'l ACM SIGIR Conf. Research and Development in Information Retrieval*, pages 757–758, 2008.

[16] Z. Gyöngyi, H. Garcia-Molina, and J. Pedersen. Combating web spam with Trustrank. In *Proc. 38th Int'l Conf. Very Large Data Bases*, pages 576–587, 2004.

[17] A. Heydon and M. Najork. Mercator: A scalable, extensible web crawler. *World Wide Web*, 2(4):219–229, 1999.

[18] P. Heymann, G. Koutrika, and H. Garcia-Molina. Can social bookmarking improve web search? In *Proc. 1st Int'l Conf. Web Search and Data Mining*, pages 195–206, 2008.

[19] J. M. Kleinberg. Hubs, authorities, and communities. *ACM Computing Surveys*, 31(4es), 1999.

[20] M. Kurant, M. Gjoka, C. T. Butts, and A. Markopoulou. Walking on a graph with a magnifying glass: Stratified sampling via weighted random walks. In *Proc. ACM SIGMETRICS Joint Int'l Conf. Measurement and Modeling of Computer Systems*, pages 281–292, 2011.

[21] H.-T. Lee, D. Leonard, X. Wang, and D. Loguinov. IRLbot: Scaling to 6 billion pages and beyond. In *Proc. 17th Int'l Conf. World Wide Web*, pages 427–436, 2008.

[22] F. Menczer, G. Pant, P. Srinivasan, and M. E. Ruiz. Evaluating topic-driven web crawlers. In *Proc. 24th Annual Int'l ACM SIGIR Conf. Research and Development in Information Retrieval*, pages 241–249, 2001.

[23] M. Najork and J. L. Wiener. Breadth-first crawling yields high-quality pages. In *Proc. 10th Int'l Conf. World Wide Web*, pages 114–118, 2001.

[24] A. Ntoulas, J. Cho, and C. Olston. What's new on the Web?: The evolution of the Web from a search engine perspective. In *Proc. 13th Int'l Conf. World Wide Web*, pages 1–12, 2004.

[25] C. Olston and M. Najork. Web crawling. *Foundations and Trends in Information Retrieval*, 4(3):175–246, 2010.

[26] C. Olston and S. Pandey. Recrawl scheduling based on information longevity. In *Proc. 17th Int'l Conf. World Wide Web*, pages 437–446, 2008.

[27] L. Page, S. Brin, R. Motwani, and T. Winograd. The PageRank citation ranking: Bringing order to the web. Technical Report 1999-66, Stanford InfoLab, 1999.

[28] S. Pandey and C. Olston. User-centric web crawling. In *Proc. 14th Int'l Conf. World Wide Web*, pages 401–411, 2005.

[29] S. Pandey and C. Olston. Crawl ordering by search impact. In *Proc. 1st Int'l Conf. Web Search and Data Mining*, pages 3–14, 2008.

[30] F. Pedregosa, G. Varoquaux, A. Gramfort, V. Michel, B. Thirion, O. Grisel, M. Blondel, P. Prettenhofer, R. Weiss, V. Dubourg, J. Vanderplas, A. Passos, D. Cournapeau, M. Brucher, M. Perrot, and E. Duchesnay. Scikit-learn: Machine learning in Python. *Journal of Machine Learning Research*, 12:2825–2830, 2011.

[31] J. L. Wolf, M. S. Squillante, P. S. Yu, J. Sethuraman, and L. Ozsen. Optimal crawling strategies for web search engines. In *Proc. 11th Int'l Conf. World Wide Web*, pages 136–147, 2002.

A Similarity Measure for Weaving Patterns in Textiles

Sven Helmer
Free University of Bozen-Bolzano
Piazza Domenicani 3
Bolzano BZ, Italy
shelmer@inf.unibz.it

Vuong M. Ngo
Ho Chi Minh City Open University
Vo Van Tan 97
Ho Chi Minh City, Vietnam
vuong.nm@ou.edu.vn

ABSTRACT

We propose a novel approach for measuring the similarity between weaving patterns that can provide similarity-based search functionality for textile archives. We represent textile structures using hypergraphs and extract multisets of k-neighborhoods from these graphs. The resulting multisets are then compared using Jaccard coefficients, Hamming distances, and cosine measures. We evaluate the different variants of our similarity measure experimentally, showing that it can be implemented efficiently and illustrating its quality using it to cluster and query a data set containing more than a thousand textile samples.

1. INTRODUCTION

Textiles and their creation play an important part in studying history and prehistory. In fact, some cultures, such as the pre-Columbian civilizations found in the Andes, documented and communicated complex information via textiles [28]. Although today many fabrics are produced using fully automated mechanical looms, traditional methods of weaving are still kept alive in communities around the world, including countries as diverse as the United Arab Emirates, China, and Peru. Compared to industrially produced textiles, archaeological specimens and artifacts created manually by traditional craftsmen exhibit a significantly more complex structure, which makes it much harder to represent, compare, and retrieve them in an information system.

In the humanities, the digitization of cultural heritage and cultural practices plays an ever more important role [32]. When looking at publicly accessible digital archives for textiles, we encounter the following situation. The American Textile History Museum (`http://www.athm.org/`) and the TEXMEDIN digital library (`http://www.texmedindigitallibrary.eu/`) offer keyword search over their collections, while the Textile Museum of Canada (`http://www.textilemuseum.ca/`) also supports browsing facilities according to different categories, such as textile type, region, materials, techniques, and period, and the University of Leeds International Textile Archive (ULITA) (`http://ulita.leeds.ac.uk/`) organizes their collection by region. In an earlier project [5, 25], "Weaving Communities of Practice", we provided additional search functionality by applying an ontological approach to building a knowledge base for Andean textiles. However, this system, like the other archives mentioned above, does not offer a facility to search and compare textiles according to their internal structure.

Providing techniques to represent and compare textiles according to their structure would help researchers investigating them (such as archaeologists, ethnographers, and anthropologists) to search for variations of specific patterns. In turn this facilitates the process of identifying fabrics and the methods used to create them. Moreover, this can help domain experts gain deeper insights into how textiles evolved over time and spread across different regions. With our work, we contribute to this effort in the following ways.

- We propose a novel approach for modeling textiles using hypergraphs that can represent many different structures, such as woven, knitted, or braided textiles. Orientation invariance is an important feature of our representation.
- Based on this representation we develop similarity measures to compare textiles at the structural level.
- We illustrate the effectiveness of our technique in an experimental evaluation clustering a data set containing over a thousand textiles, showing that our clustering comes close to the correct categorization. Additionally, we ran experiments querying our text collection and achieved very good results in terms of retrieval performance, e.g., a mean average precision (MAP) of around 0.93.

The remainder of the paper is organized as follows. In the next section we review the related work and Section 3 covers existing methods for modeling textile structures in more detail and discusses their merits and drawbacks. We introduce our approach in Section 4 and its implementation in Section 5. An experimental evaluation and its results are presented in Section 6. A summary and outlook concludes the paper.

2. RELATED WORK

One of the most comprehensive and systematic expositions on classifying the structures of textiles according to basic patterns was compiled by Emery [10], who was a curator at the Textile Museum in Washington D.C. Although Emery's terminology is widely used, the use of terms is not always consistent, even among domain experts [4]. This is especially true for textiles produced in different cultural contexts such as the South American Andes [1, 9, 33], specimens of which we were confronted with in our earlier project [5, 25]. Additionally, due to the huge diversity of textile structures, it is impractical to come up with a complete natural language

SIGIR'15, August 09 - 13, 2015, Santiago, Chile.
 ISBN 978-1-4503-3621-5/15/08 ...$15.00.
DOI: http://dx.doi.org/10.1145/2766462.2767735.

classification of every possible structure. Consequently, there have been several attempts to define textile structures in a formal and mathematical way [13, 14].

Textiles created by mechanical looms exhibit a very regular pattern and can be described using a grid structure, which can be mapped to a binary matrix representation [18, 26]. Since we set out to also describe structures originating from manual techniques, whose shape may be much more irregular, this is not an option for us. A more general approach for textile modeling is based on topology, i.e., representing fabrics with the help of elements taken from knot theory. Early research in this area specialized on specific techniques, such as knitting [21, 22] and is therefore not generally applicable. Grishanov et al. [13, 14] developed a more general method relying on tangles, which are knot fragments embedding arcs into a sphere [7].[1] While this approach is more expressive compared to previous topological models, it is only applicable to structures that are periodical in two perpendicular directions. Also, certain structures that can only be created manually and multi-layered disjoint fabrics are not considered. Furthermore, the main purpose of the topological techniques described above are the enumeration and classification of textile structures, not their fast retrieval. For instance, the problem of determining whether two given structures described by knots, links, or tangles are equivalent is intractable in the general case [8].

Another way to represent textiles consists of specifying structures based on image-processing techniques. Most of these techniques, e.g. those described in [27, 34], can only be applied to specific textile structures, such as regular rectangular grids or knitting. Moreover, while image processing has the advantage that most of the preprocessing can be automated, textiles, especially complex ones, are three-dimensional objects and some of the structure may be hidden. Ma et al. introduce a special binary encoding to retain some of this information [23], however, their approach is also only applicable to regular grid-like structures. From our point of view Zheng et al. come closest to what we have in mind by developing a method for indexing and retrieving textiles based on their structure [37]. Their technique, though, is only applicable to plain, twill, and satin weave patterns and also shares most of the drawbacks of the other image-processing approaches.

3. TEXTILE MODELING

Before going into details about existing techniques for modeling textiles we have to define the term *textile structure*, by which we mean the spatial relationships between elements such as yarns, threads, strands, or other similar long and continuous spun pieces of fiber. Basically, given (part of) a textile structure we want to be able to find other structures in which the elements are arranged in a similar manner. In her book [10], Emery distinguishes three broad types of textile structures: interworked elements, interlaced elements, and felted fibers. The last one, felted fiber, is not of interest to us, as it is created by compressing, matting, and condensing fibers. This results in the fibers getting entangled with each other in a very irregular and dense pattern, which makes it virtually impossible, not to mention irrelevant, to identify all of the relationships between individual fibers. In interworked elements, threads are connected by means of knotting, linking, stitching, looping, or twining, whereas in interlaced elements, they pass over and under each other without connecting in any other way. Providing all the details of Emery's full classification scheme goes beyond the scope of this paper, due to the fact that our goal is to develop a formal mathematical model of textile structures rather than establishing natural language descriptions. Nevertheless, we show some typical examples of textile structures in Figure 1 (Fig. 1(a) and (b) illustrate interworked elements, Fig. 1(c) and (d) interlaced ones).

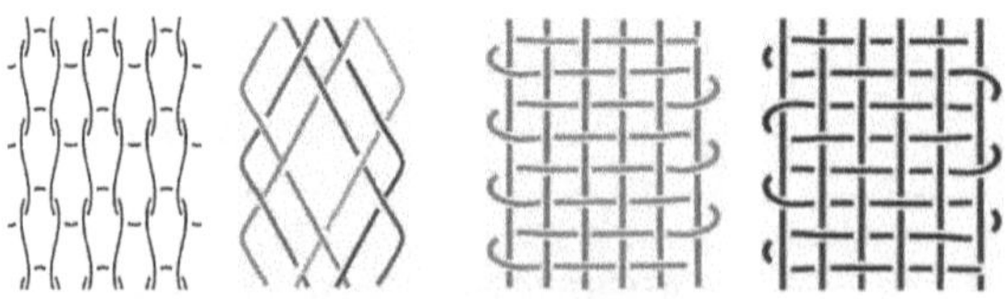

(a) Knitting (b) Braid (c) Plain weave (d) Twill (2/1)
Interworked elements Interlaced elements

Figure 1: Examples of textile structures

In the following we give a brief informal summary of topological concepts that have been used to model textile structures, in particular *knots*, *links*, *tangles*, and their two-dimensional projections. Detailed, formal definitions can be found in [8, 13].

3.1 Knots

A *knot* is a one-dimensional subset of points $K \subset \mathbb{R}^3$ homeomorphic to a circle. Figure 2(a) shows a trivial knot, a circle, while Figure 2(b) depicts a so-called trefoil. We want to be able to distinguish the different types of knots, i.e., determine whether two knots are equivalent. Intuitively, two knots are of the same type if we can continuously deform one knot into the other without breaking it or intersecting it with itself. Figure 2(c) and (d) shows an example of two knots that can be transformed into each other.

(a) Trivial knot (b) Non-trivial knot (c) Knot A (d) Knot B
Types Transformations

Figure 2: Examples of knots and transformations

3.2 Links

A knot is an embedding of a single circle into $\mathbb{R}^3$, this can be generalized to a collection of knots, which is called a *link*. Figure 3 shows two link examples, a trivial link in (a) and Borromean rings in (b). Similar to knots, two links are equivalent if we can transform one into the other by deforming it without cutting it.

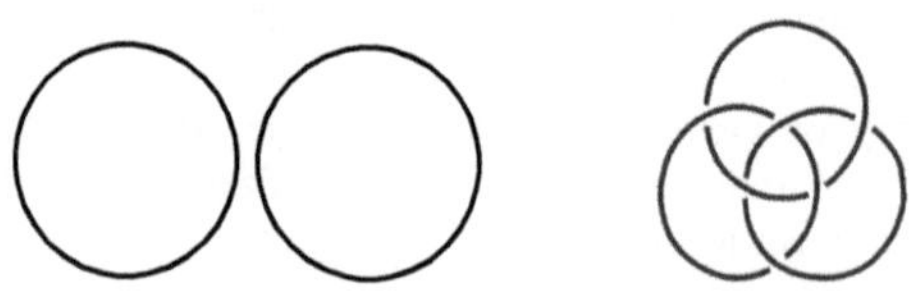

(a) Trivial link (b) Borromean rings

Figure 3: Examples of links

3.3 Tangles

While the theory of knots and links provides a well-established foundation and mathematical tools, it cannot be directly applied to textile structures. Rarely are textiles made up of a collection of

[1]We provide more background on knots, links, and tangles in Section 3.

intertwined and deformed circles. Conway introduced knot fragments called *tangles* [7], which can be used to describe knots and links as well as textile structures. Conway's original intention was to develop a simpler notation for systematically enumerating and classifying knots and links. Grishanov et al. first applied this concept to describing textile structures [12].

Figure 4: Examples of tangles

In his original definition, Conway described a tangle as a knot fragment with two arcs protruding into the four corners of the tangle. The corners are labeled NW, NE, SW, and SE after a compass rose (see Figure 4 for examples). Conway's definition of tangles has also been generalized to n*-tangles* containing n arcs instead of just two.

3.4 Two-dimensional Projections

As the main interest is usually in the type of a structure and not its exact three-dimensional form, often a planar representation is applied, projecting knots and links from $\mathbb{R}^3$ to $\mathbb{R}^2$. While this loses knowledge of the exact height of a point, enough information is retained to be able to identify types of links. A link is placed in general position with respect to the projection, i.e., no edge of the link is parallel to the projection direction and the projection $\pi : \mathbb{R}^3 \mapsto \mathbb{R}^2$ is regular. π is regular if it is injective except for a finite number of points c_i (these are crossings in a link) and only two points in the link are projected onto each c_i. Last but not least for each crossing c_i the arc that is on top needs to be distinguished from the one below. The arc passing underneath is usually indicated by a break in the line (so far we have used this convention implicitly).

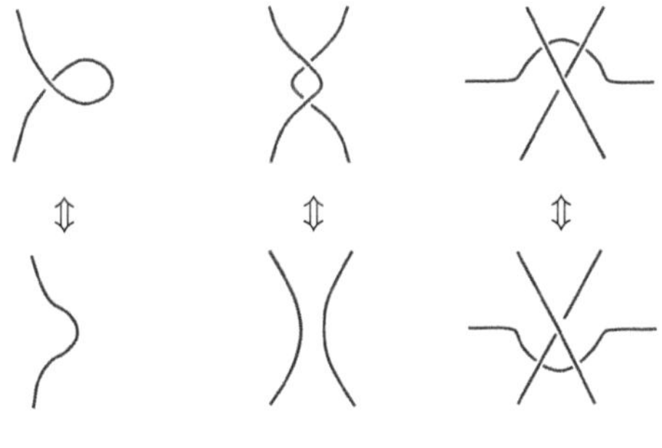

Figure 5: Reidemeister moves

Gradually deforming a link that has been projected to two dimensions may lead to a violation of the regularity of the projection π at certain steps during the transformation. In order to prevent this from happening Reidemeister introduced three types of moves, allowing the arcs of a link to "jump" across critical sections of the transformation [31]; Figure 5 depicts the *Reidemeister moves*. Equivalence of links is then defined as a (finite) sequence of deformations and Reidemeister moves to transform one link into another.

3.5 Discussion

The main problem that Grishanov et al. attack with topological methods is the classification of textile structures, i.e., deciding whether two given structures are equivalent [14]. Applying knot theory allows them to re-use results for determining knot equivalence. However, there is a catch: one of the first algorithms by Haken for doing so is extremely complex and was never implemented [16]. Hass et al. review a number of knot algorithms and conclude that they are impractical and that the exact complexity of several general problems in this area is not even clear [17]. Hotz claims to have found an efficient algorithm for the knot equivalence problem [19], but it turns out that the complexity of his algorithm is $O(2^{\frac{n}{3}})$.

Due to the challenge of finding efficient algorithms, the development of *knot invariants* is pursued as well. Invariants are functions mapping the set of knots to some other set (e.g. integers, polynomials, or matrices). Knots from the same equivalence class get mapped to the same element in the codomain of the function. A considerable number of knot and link invariants exist, dividing knots and links into various equivalence classes. One of the simplest invariants for links is the multiplicity $\mu(L)$ of a link L, i.e., the number of its components. Some invariants, such as the *unknotting number*, i.e., the minimum number of times a link has to cross itself to be transformed into a trivial link, are simple to formulate, but hard to compute.

In summary, this leaves us with inefficient algorithms of knot equivalence and a comprehensive overview by Grishanov et al. of invariants that can be used to classify doubly-periodic textile structures [14]. However, it is not clear how these techniques can be used for textile pattern retrieval, as no similarity measures between textile structures or invariants are defined. Moreover, the methods often rely on deforming or unknotting an object, which in the context of textile structures would in some cases decompose a fabric into individual strands, unraveling (parts of) the structure. This would make it very difficult to compare the relative location of crossings to each other in two different textiles. Our work, which we start describing in the following section, is inspired by knot theory and especially the concept of tangles, but we follow a different approach taking into account efficiency and performance aspects.

4. OUR APPROACH

In the following we first define a hypergraph representation of textile structures, then show how we can extract features, called neighborhoods, from hypergraphs that we can use for measuring the similarity of these graphs.

4.1 Textile Graphs

The basic unit we use is a *crossing* of two threads with four links to neighboring crossings. In principle, this is a 2-tangle, but we have exactly one crossing within this structure, breaking down a fabric into its most basic elements. We formalize the representation of textile structures using hypergraphs, which we have chosen due to their better suitability (compared to traditional graphs) to represent objects, their spatial relationships, and contexts [35].

Definition 1. A *textile graph* is defined as a hypergraph $H(C, T, \Xi, \Pi, \Omega)$, where C is a set of vertices that belong to crossings, T a set of terminal nodes that end threads, Ξ a set of hyperedges (of degree four) that connect vertices from C, Π a set of regular edges (of degree two) that indicate which thread is on top in each crossing, and Ω a set of edges connecting vertices to vertices from other crossings or to terminal nodes.

A textile graph has the following characteristics. $|C|$ is a multiple of four and every $c_i \in C$ belongs to exactly one $x_j \in \Xi$. Every x_j in turn contains only one $p_j \in \Pi$, that is only two c_i in each crossing are connected via a so-called top edge. In addition to this, we connect every node c_i to either one node from another crossing or one terminal node, i.e., each c_i and each t_i appear in only one $o \in \Omega$. Terminal nodes end threads, so every $t_i \in T$ has a degree of one. If T is empty, then the structure modeled in the hypergraph represents a knot or link. We can even represent non-textile structures such as chain mail with our approach. Here we focus on textile applications, though.

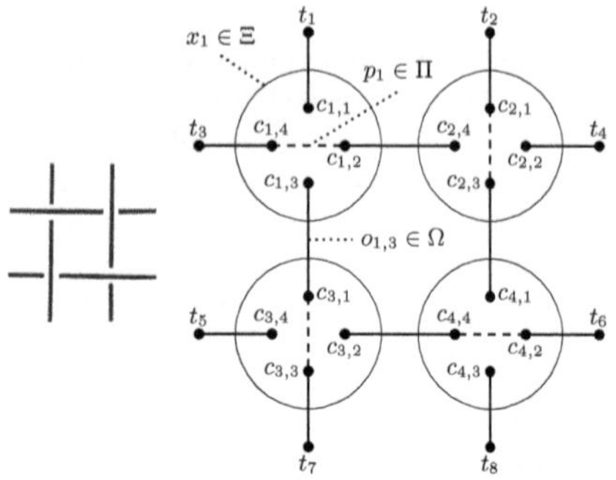

Figure 6: A textile structure and its hypergraph H_1

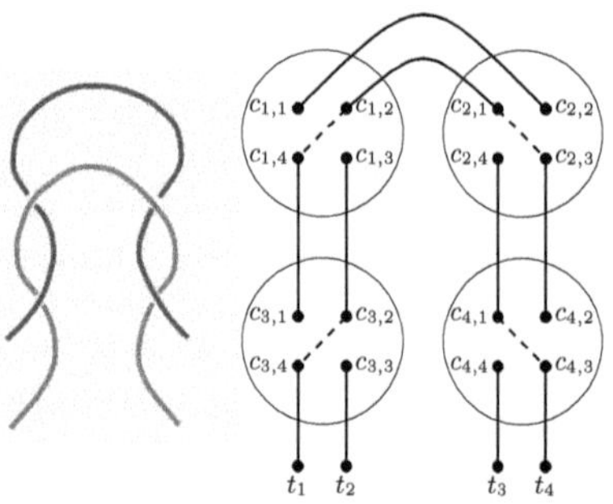

Figure 7: Another example: hypergraph H_2

Figures 6 and 7 show two examples of simple textile structures and their hypergraph representation. The nodes $c_{i,j}$ belong to C, the t_i to T. The solid lines are the edges in Ω, the dashed lines those in Π, while the hyperedges in Ξ are represented by circles.

4.2 Comparing Textile Graphs

Now that we have defined textile graphs, we have to formalize the notion of what it means to compare these graphs. One approach is to look for subgraph isomorphisms, which, in the general case, is a hard problem when applied to hypergraphs [2]. While it is interesting to know whether two textile graphs are isomorphic, we have a different goal: we want to measure the similarity of two structures, which means we need a hypergraph similarity measure. While different similarity measures have been proposed for traditional graphs [30], among them graph edit distances (GED) [11], the picture looks different for hypergraphs. There are a few approaches based on mathematical morphology [3] and error-tolerant hypergraph matching, including edit distance [6]. However, common to these approaches is their high computational cost.

We follow an efficient two-phase approach in approximating the similarity of two textile graphs. In a first phase we extract information about the structure of a textile in the form of subgraphs, which we cover in Section 4.3, and in a second phase we measure the similarity based on the extracted information, which is the topic of Section 4.4

4.3 Extracting Structural Information

Star structures, which are small subgraphs, have been used to describe the internal structure of graphs [36]: every vertex in the graph is interpreted as the root of a tree with depth 2, meaning it includes the vertex itself and all its neighbors. However, this method does not consider any order among the neighbors. While in principle our textile hypergraph is also unordered, we exploit the constraints imposed by the application domain, in particular the fact that we know the relative position of threads in a crossing. (Later on, we also generalize this concept to arbitrary depths, something that Zeng et al. do not do [36].) Before defining the extracted subgraph structure we formalize the positional information of threads, though.

Definition 2. Given a node c_i belonging to crossing $x_i \in \Xi$ and a node c_j belonging to crossing $x_j \in \Xi$ $(x_i \neq x_j)$ connected by an edge $o_{i,j} = (c_i, c_j) \in \Omega$, we say that $o_{i,j}$ is

- *alternating*, if one of its endpoints is found in Π (i.e., it is connected via a top edge) and the other is not. More formally, either $(\exists \gamma_i \in x_i : (c_i, \gamma_i) \in \Pi) \wedge (\forall \gamma_j \in x_j : (c_j, \gamma_j) \notin \Pi)$ or $(\forall \gamma_i \in x_i : (c_i, \gamma_i) \notin \Pi) \wedge (\exists \gamma_j \in x_j : (c_j, \gamma_j) \in \Pi)$.
- *non-alternating*, if both of its endpoints are either connected via a top edge or both are not. Formally, $\exists \gamma_i \in x_i, \gamma_j \in x_j : (c_i, \gamma_i) \in \Pi \wedge (c_j, \gamma_j) \in \Pi$ or $\forall \gamma_i \in x_i, \gamma_j \in x_j : (c_i, \gamma_i) \notin \Pi \wedge (c_j, \gamma_j) \notin \Pi$.
- *terminated*, if one of its endpoints is a terminator: $\exists t_j \in T : (c_i, t_j) \in \Omega$

Basically, an alternating thread changes from top to bottom or vice versa from one crossing to the next. For example, the edge from $c_{1,4}$ to $c_{3,1}$ in Figure 7 is alternating, the edge from $c_{1,1}$ to $c_{2,2}$ is not, while $c_{3,4}$ to t_1 is terminated.

4.3.1 Neighborhoods

The *neighborhood* of a crossing is defined by a 2-tuple containing two sets of labels. The first set specifies whether the outgoing edges from the top edge vertices are alternating ('a'), non-alternating ('n'), or connect to a terminal ('t'). The second set specifies the same for the vertices on the bottom.

Definition 3. Given a crossing defined by $x_i \in \Xi$, let $c_{i,1}$ and $c_{i,2}$ stand for the top thread, i.e. $(c_{i,1}, c_{i,2}) \in \Pi$ and $c_{i,3}$ and $c_{i,4}$ for the bottom thread, i.e. $(c_{i,3}, c_{i,4}) \notin \Pi$. $B(x_i) = [\{z_1, z_2\}, \{z_3, z_4\}]$ is the *neighborhood* of crossing x_i where

$$z_j = \begin{cases} \text{'a'} & \text{if } (c_{i,j}, \gamma_{l,j}) \in \Omega \text{ alternating} \\ \text{'n'} & \text{if } (c_{i,j}, \gamma_{l,j}) \in \Omega \text{ non-alternating} \\ \text{'t'} & \text{if } (c_{i,j}, t_l) \in \Omega \text{ terminated} \end{cases}$$

and the $\gamma_{l,j}$ are nodes from the other crossings that the $c_{i,j}$ connect to or terminators, such as t_l.

For example the neighborhood of crossing 1 in Figure 6 is described by the tuple $[\{\text{'t'}, \text{'a'}\}, \{\text{'t'}, \text{'a'}\}]$. Hence, one of the main advantages of this approach becomes evident: the representation retains all the relative spatial relationships, but at the same time is orientation invariant. Rotating the textile pattern by 90 or 180 degrees or mirroring the structure has no effect on the textile graph and its crossing neighborhoods.

We describe a textile graph by computing the neighborhood of every crossing in the hypergraph and storing this information as a multiset of tuples.

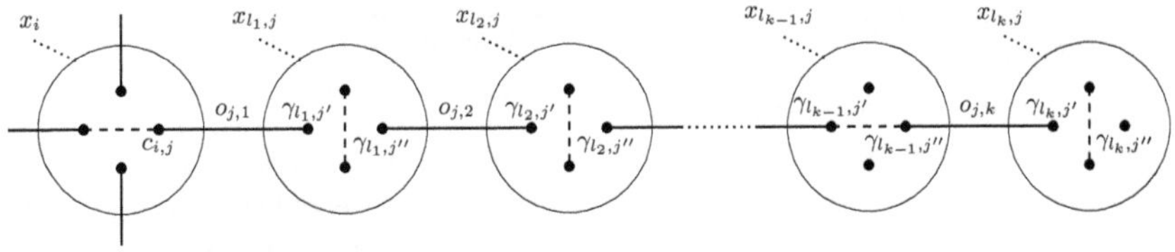

Figure 8: Illustration of one branch of a k-neighborhood

Definition 4. The *fingerprint* $F(H)$ of a textile graph $H(C, T, \Xi, \Pi, \Omega)$ is the multiset of the neighborhoods of its crossings: $F(H) = \{B(x_i) | x_i \in \Xi\}$

For example, the fingerprint of the textile graph shown in Figure 6 is $F(H_1) = \{[\{\text{'a'}, \text{'t'}\}, \{\text{'a'}, \text{'t'}\}], [\{\text{'a'}, \text{'t'}\}, \{\text{'a'}, \text{'t'}\}], [\{\text{'a'}, \text{'t'}\}, \{\text{'a'}, \text{'t'}\}], [\{\text{'a'}, \text{'t'}\}, \{\text{'a'}, \text{'t'}\}]\}$, which means that all the nodes of the crossings are connected to terminals or are part of alternating edges. This makes sense, as the textile shown in Figure 6 is a plain weave, which is characteristically defined by alternating threads. The fingerprint of the textile in Figure 7, on the other hand, looks different: $F(H_2) = \{[\{\text{'a'}, \text{'n'}\}, \{\text{'a'}, \text{'n'}\}], [\{\text{'a'}, \text{'n'}\}, \{\text{'a'}, \text{'n'}\}], [\{\text{'a'}, \text{'t'}\}, \{\text{'a'}, \text{'t'}\}], [\{\text{'a'}, \text{'t'}\}, \{\text{'a'}, \text{'t'}\}]\}$.

4.3.2 k-Neighborhoods

The concept of a neighborhood can be generalized by not just looking at the immediate neighbors of a crossing, but by following a thread to further crossings and checking for each connection whether it is alternating or not. Clearly, we stop tracing a thread as soon as we hit a terminator node. This schema specifies a *k-neighborhood*, in which we follow each of the four emerging threads to the next k neighbors:

Definition 5. Given a crossing defined by $x_i \in \Xi$, again let $c_{i,1}$ and $c_{i,2}$ stand for the top thread, i.e. $(c_{i,1}, c_{i,2}) \in \Pi$ and $c_{i,3}$ and $c_{i,4}$ for the bottom thread, i.e. $(c_{i,3}, c_{i,4}) \notin \Pi$. Furthermore, let $x_{l_1,j}, x_{l_2,j}, \ldots, x_{l_k,j}$ be the sequence of k crossings we encounter when following the thread leaving x_i via $c_{i,j}$ and let $\gamma_{l_h,j'}, \gamma_{l_h,j''} \in x_{l_h,j}$ be the nodes in each crossing along this thread, i.e., either $\gamma_{l_h,j'}, \gamma_{l_h,j''} \in \Pi$ or $\gamma_{l_h,j'}, \gamma_{l_h,j''} \notin \Pi$. The edges $o_{j,h} \in \Omega$ connect nodes from different crossings, so $o_{j,1}$ connects $c_{i,j}$ and $\gamma_{l_1,j'}$, and for $h \geq 2$ $o_{j,h}$ connects $\gamma_{l_{h-1},j''}$ and $\gamma_{l_h,j'}$. Figure 8 illustrates this situation. Then $B_k(x_i) = [\{y_1, y_2\}, \{y_3, y_4\}]$ is the *k-neighborhood* of crossing x_i with $y_j = [y_{j,1}, y_{j,2}, \ldots, y_{j,k}]$ where each

$$y_{j,m} = \begin{cases} \text{'a'} & \text{if } o_{j,m} \in \Omega \text{ alternating} \\ \text{'n'} & \text{if } o_{j,m} \in \Omega \text{ non-alternating} \\ \text{'t'} & \text{if } o_{j,m} \in \Omega \text{ terminated} \end{cases}$$

If $o_{j,m}$ is a terminated edge for $m < k$, we only have m elements in tuple y_j. For the example in Figure 8 the tuple y_j is equal to $[\text{'a'}, \text{'n'}, \ldots, \text{'a'}]$.

This makes the neighborhood described in Definition 3 a special case of a k-neighborhood with $k = 1$. The 2-neighborhood of crossing x_1 in Figure 7, for example, is $[\{[\text{'n'}, \text{'a'}], [\text{'a'}, \text{'t'}]\}, \{[\text{'n'}, \text{'a'}], [\text{'a'}, \text{'t'}]\}]$. The fingerprints of hypergraphs using k-neighborhoods are computed accordingly, we just have to replace $B(x_i)$ with $B_k(x_i)$ in Definition 4.

Having defined fingerprints of textile patterns, we now have to specify how to actually measure their similarity or distance.

4.4 Measuring Similarity

Typical distance metrics used for measuring the similarity of objects in non-Euclidean spaces include the Jaccard distance, the Hamming distance, and the cosine measure [20], all of which we cover in the following sections.

4.4.1 Jaccard Coefficient

Since the fingerprints of our textile graphs are multisets rather than sets, we need to use the Jaccard coefficient for multisets. For every element in a multiset we store the number of occurrences of the element, so, for example, the multiset $\{a, a, a, b, c, c\}$ becomes $\{a : 3, b : 1, c : 2\}$ or just $(3, 1, 2)$ if we assign fixed positions to each element, position 1 representing the frequency of a, position 2 the frequency of b, and position 3 the frequency of c. Given two multisets $R = (r_1, r_2, \ldots, r_n)$ and $S = (s_1, s_2, \ldots, s_n)$ in a vector representation, $R \cap S$ is computed as $\sum_{i=1}^{n} \min(r_i, s_i)$ and $R \cup S = \sum_{i=1}^{n} \max(r_i, s_i)$. Consequently, we get the following distance measure:

$$D_J(R, S) = 1 - \frac{\sum_{i=1}^{n} \min(r_i, s_i)}{\sum_{i=1}^{n} \max(r_i, s_i)} = \frac{\sum_{i=1}^{n} |r_i - s_i|}{\sum_{i=1}^{n} \max(r_i, s_i)} \quad (1)$$

Computing $D_J(F(H_1), F(H_2))$ gives us the distance between two textile graphs H_1 and H_2. For example, the fingerprint of H_1 (Figure 6) is made up of four times the tuple $[\{\text{'a'}, \text{'t'}\}, \{\text{'a'}, \text{'t'}\}]$ and does not contain $[\{\text{'a'}, \text{'n'}\}, \{\text{'a'}, \text{'n'}\}]$, while the fingerprint of H_2 contains both of these tuples two times each, i.e., we can represent H_1 by $(0, 4)^\mathsf{T}$ and H_2 by $(2, 2)^\mathsf{T}$. Applying Formula (1), we obtain $^{2+2}/_{2+4} = {}^2/_3$.

4.4.2 Hamming Distance

Fixing the positions of the elements within the multisets allows us to interpret them as vectors. Using a vector representation, we can apply the Hamming distance, which computes the number of components that differ in two vectors. Let $f_H(r_i, s_i)$ be a function that compares two components, such that

$$f_H(r_i, s_i) = \delta_{r_i, s_i} = \begin{cases} 0 & \text{if } r_i = s_i \\ 1 & \text{if } r_i \neq s_i \end{cases}$$

Then a formal definition of the Hamming distance yields

$$D_H(R, S) = \sum_{i=1}^{n} f_H(r_i, s_i) \quad (2)$$

Applying Formula (2) to the frequency vectors of the fingerprints of $H_1 = (0, 4)^\mathsf{T}$ and $H_2 = (2, 2)^\mathsf{T}$ gives us $1 + 1 = 2$.

There are a few issues with the Hamming distance. First, it is not normalized, the distance between two vectors ranges from 0 to n, which even varies depending on the size of the vectors. Second, if the elements of the domain used for the vector components are comparable, e.g. in the case of integers, intuitively the vector $(1,0,3)^\mathsf{T}$ is closer to $(1,0,2)^\mathsf{T}$ than $(1,0,7)^\mathsf{T}$. However, applying the original definition would give us a distance of 1 in both cases. We can redefine the function f_H to consider this fact: $f_{\tilde{H}}(r_i, s_i) = |r_i - s_i|$. Consequently, the distance measure becomes

$$D_{\tilde{H}}(R,S) = \sum_{i=1}^{n} f_{\tilde{H}}(r_i, s_i) = \sum_{i=1}^{n} |r_i - s_i| \qquad (3)$$

Applying Formula (3) to the frequency vectors of the fingerprints of $H_1 = (0,4)^\mathsf{T}$ and $H_2 = (2,2)^\mathsf{T}$ gives us $2 + 2 = 4$.

4.4.3 Cosine Measure

Formally, the cosine distance measure is defined via an inner vector product:

$$D_c(R,S) \;=\; 1 - \frac{\sum_{i=1}^{n} r_i \cdot s_i}{\sqrt{\sum_{i=1}^{n} r_i^2} \cdot \sqrt{\sum_{i=1}^{n} s_i^2}} \qquad (4)$$

$D_c(F(H_1), F(H_2))$ gives us the cosine measure distance between two textile graphs H_1 and H_2. For example, applying Formula (4) to the frequency vectors of the fingerprints of $H_1 = (0,4)^\mathsf{T}$ and $H_2 = (2,2)^\mathsf{T}$ yields $1 - {}^{0+8}/_{4\sqrt{8}} = 1 - \sqrt{2}/2$.

Often term frequency (TF) and inverse document frequency (IDF) are applied to the vectors when using the cosine measure. This is done to consider the fact that an increase in term frequency within an individual document has less and less impact and that terms appearing less often in a document collection tend to be more important. In our case we also compare textiles using logarithmic TF-IDF factors: $\text{TF}_{p,t} = 1 + \log(f_{p,t})$ and $\text{IDF}_p = \log \frac{N}{f_p}$ where $f_{p,t}$ is the frequency of fingerprint p in textile t, N is the overall number of textiles in the collection, and f_p is the number of textiles in the collection in which fingerprint p occurs.

5. IMPLEMENTATION DETAILS

Algorithm 1 shows a description of the fingerprint computation in pseudo-code. We iterate through all crossings and select all four nodes of a crossing in turn to follow a thread to the next k crossings, noting any change of position on the way. Let the first two nodes, $c_{i,1}$ and $c_{i,2}$, denote those of the top-level thread, i.e., $(c_{i,1}, c_{i,2}) \in \Pi$, while the other two nodes, $c_{i,3}$ and $c_{i,4}$, belong to the bottom-level thread, i.e., $(c_{i,3}, c_{i,4}) \notin \Pi$. We use the function NEIGHBOR to find the connecting node in a neighboring crossing, the function FINDLABEL to determine the label of an edge, and the function OPPOSITE to find a node's counterpart within a crossing. If we reach the end of a thread before encountering k crossings, we fill up the labels with NULL values.

We have implemented our algorithm efficiently by storing the crossing nodes of a hypergraph in an array. Every node has the following structure:

```
struct node {
  int nextNode;
  bool onTop;
  int oppositeNode; }
```

The four nodes of a crossing are stored in neighboring cells of the array, i.e., the nodes at positions $4i$ to $4i+3$ belong to crossing i (for $0 \le i \le n-1$, assuming we have n crossings). The component `nextNode` connects a node to the node of a neighboring crossing by storing the index of this node. If a node connects to a terminal, `nextNode` is equal to -1, which means that we do not

Algorithm 1: FINGERPRINT(H,k)

Input : hypergraph $H(C, T, \Xi, \Pi, \Omega)$ with
C: set of vertices belonging to crossings
T: set of terminals
Ξ: set of hyperedges connecting vertices
Π: set of edges indicating top thread
Ω: set of edges connecting crossings/terminals
k: size of the neighborhood

Output: fingerprint for hypergraph H

FP := $\emptyset$;
for *every* $x_i \in \Xi$ **do**
  for $j := 1$ *to* 4 **do**
    let $c_{i,j}$ be the j-th node of crossing x_i;
    (* $j = 1, 2$ for top-level thread *)
    l := 0, current = $c_{i,j}$;
    repeat
      l++;
      $\gamma_{l,j'}$:= NEIGHBOR(current);
      $\text{label}_{j,l}$:= FINDLABEL(current, $\gamma_{l,j'}$);
      if $label_{j,l} \neq$ 't' **then**
        $\gamma_{l,j''}$:= OPPOSITE($\gamma_{l,j'}$);
        current := $\gamma_{l,j''}$;
      end
    until $k = l$ *or* $label_{j,l}$ = 't';
    for $s := l + 1$ *to* k **do**
      $\text{label}_{j,s}$:= NULL;
    end
  end
  fp_i := [{[$\text{label}_{1,1}, \text{label}_{1,2}, \ldots, \text{label}_{1,k}$],
    [$\text{label}_{2,1}, \text{label}_{2,2}, \ldots, \text{label}_{2,k}$]},
    {[$\text{label}_{3,1}, \text{label}_{3,2}, \ldots, \text{label}_{3,k}$],
    [$\text{label}_{4,1}, \text{label}_{4,2}, \ldots, \text{label}_{4,k}$]}];
  FP := FP $\cup$ fp_i;
end
return FP;

have to store the terminal nodes explicitly. In order to determine whether a node belongs to a top thread, we have added the Boolean variable `onTop`. The component `oppositeNode` is not strictly necessary, as we could determine the opposite node by looking at all other nodes of a crossing and then selecting the one with the same value for `onTop`; it was added for efficiency reasons.

In summary this means that the k-neighborhoods of all n crossings of a textile can be computed in $O(nk)$.

6. EXPERIMENTAL EVALUATION

We evaluated the variants of our similarity measure experimentally, clustering a data set containing over a thousand different textiles and comparing the outcome to the correct classification. Additionally, we also run queries over our data set, measuring the retrieval performance. We also look at the efficiency, presenting numbers on the run time of the algorithm.

6.1 Experimental Setup

The algorithm was implemented using Java JDK 1.7.0_60 running under Windows 7. All experiments were run on a computer with an Intel Core i5 CPU (2.60 GHz) and 2 GB memory.

In order to test the effectiveness of our textile similarity measures, we partition a collection of n textile structures represented as hypergraphs $S = \{H_1, H_2, \ldots, H_n\}$ into m clusters $L = \{\lambda_1, \lambda_2,$

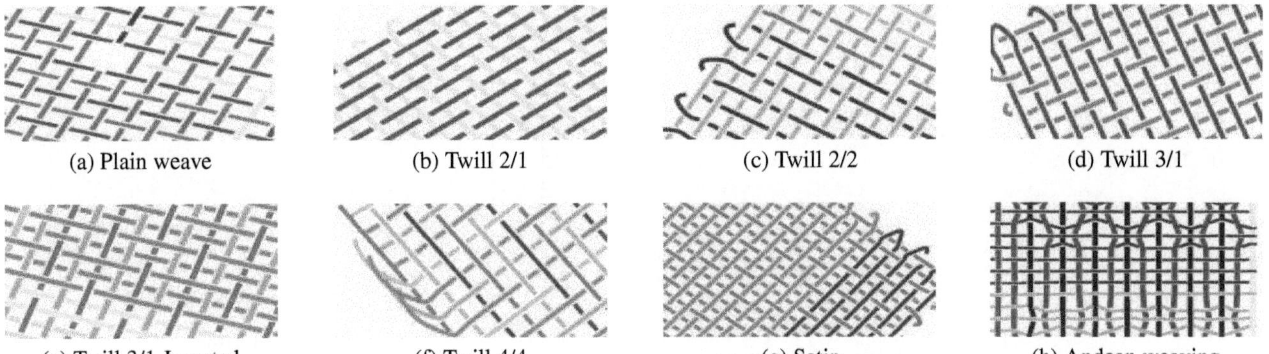

(a) Plain weave (b) Twill 2/1 (c) Twill 2/2 (d) Twill 3/1

(e) Twill 3/1-Inverted (f) Twill 4/4 (g) Satin (h) Andean weaving

Figure 9: Examples of weaving patterns

$\ldots, \lambda_m\}$ and compare the outcome to the m categories of the correct classification $A = \{\alpha_1, \alpha_2, \ldots, \alpha_m\}$.

For clustering, we use hierarchical agglomerative clustering, in which each textile H_i starts out in its own cluster. In every subsequent step, the two nearest subclusters are merged until m clusters remain. The Unweighted Pair Group Method with Arithmetic Mean (UPGMA) is used to calculate the distance between two subclusters u_i and u_j:

$$D_u(u_i, u_j) = \frac{1}{|u_i||u_j|} \sum_{H_r \in u_i} \sum_{H_s \in u_j} D(F(H_r), F(H_s)) \quad (5)$$

For the purpose of measuring the quality of the clustering L compared to the correct classification A, we apply the Rand index [29]. Every pair of textiles $H_i, H_j \in S, i > j$ is categorized as a true positive (TP), true negative (TN), false positive (FP), or false negative (FN), depending on the following conditions:

TP: H_i and H_j are in the same cluster in L and in the same class in A.

TN: H_i and H_j are in different clusters in L and in different classes in A.

FP: H_i and H_j are in the same cluster in L and in different classes in A.

FN: H_i and H_j are in different clusters in L and in the same class in A.

The Rand index (RI) then measures the ratio of textiles placed correctly within the clustering:

$$RI = \frac{TP + TN}{TP + FP + TN + FN}$$

The Rand index assigns equal weight to false positives and false negatives and also includes true negatives. Usually, it is not very difficult to identify a large number of true negatives correctly, therefore we also use the standard quality measures of precision $P = \frac{TP}{TP+FP}$, recall $R = \frac{TP}{TP+FN}$, and F-measure $F = \frac{2PR}{P+R}$.

We evaluate the retrieval performance by using each of the textile objects as a query $q_j \in Q$ and then ranking all the other textiles according to their similarity to the query. All the textiles $\{h_1, h_2, \ldots, h_{m_j}\}$ that are in the same category α_j as q_j are considered to be relevant, while those from other categories are not relevant. We measure the quality of the resulting ranked lists using mean average precision (MAP), average Precision-Recall (PR), and average F-measure-Recall (FR) curves [24]. MAP provides a single value measuring the quality across all recall levels:

$$MAP(Q) = \frac{1}{|Q|} \sum_{j=1}^{|Q|} \frac{1}{m_j} \sum_{k=1}^{m_j} Precision(R_{jk})$$

where R_{jk} is the ranked list from the first textile object down to h_k and $Precision(R_{jk})$ is the precision of the set R_{jk}.

A PR curve shows the change of precision with increasing recall; we calculate the standard 11-point interpolated average precision. The interpolated precision of query q_j at the standard recall level r_l, $0 \leq l \leq 10$, is defined as the highest precision found for any recall level $r \geq r_l$: $P_j(r_l) = \max_{r \geq r_l} P_j(r)$, where $P(r)$ is the precision at recall level r. Therefore, the average precision of Q at the standard recall level r_l is defined as:

$$\bar{P}(r_l) = \frac{\sum_{j=1}^{|Q|} P_j(r_l)}{|Q|}$$

Similarly, the average F-measure of Q at the standard recall level r_l is equal to:

$$\bar{F}(r_l) = \frac{\sum_{j=1}^{|Q|} F_j(r_l)}{|Q|}$$

where $F_j(r_l) = \frac{2P(r_l)r_l}{P(r_l)+r_l}$ is the interpolated F-measure of query q_j at r_l.

6.2 Data Set

We employ a textile editor called InaSawu [15, 25] to model the textiles in the data set and export their representations into plain text files, which we use to create the corresponding hypergraphs. With the help of a domain expert the 1200 fabrics were divided into twelve categories, each containing 100 items of a particular type of textile. On average, each textile consists of 25,352 vertices, 6,311 crossings (hyperedges) and 12,679 edges connecting crossings with each other or with terminals.

In the following, we give an overview of the different kinds of textiles found in each group. One of the simplest weaving patterns is plain weave, in which a weft thread alternates between going over and under a warp thread.[2] In each row, this pattern is shifted by one position (see Figure 9(a)). The next five groups of patterns consist of twills, in which more than one warp thread is crossed over or under. Figures 9(b) to (f) show example patterns, ranging from 2/1 twill to 4/4 twill. In the satin (also known as sateen) weave

[2]Warp threads are longitudinal threads held in place by a frame, while the weft thread is led through the warp threads.

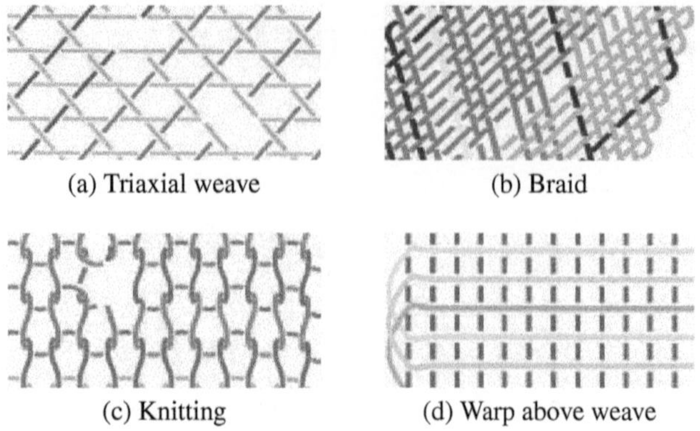

(a) Triaxial weave (b) Braid

(c) Knitting (d) Warp above weave

Figure 10: More examples of textile patterns

structure (see Figure 9(g)), four or even more weft threads float over a warp thread or vice versa. The most complex patterns in our collection are taken from a collection of weavings originating in the Andes. Since they were created manually, they can exhibit a great variety of different styles in a single textile. The pattern depicted in Figure 9(h) indicates this, as the warp and weft threads cross a different number of threads in different parts of the textile. For more examples of Andean textiles, please see `http://www.weavingcommunities.org/`.

For the remaining groups of textiles, shown in Figure 10 we have chosen patterns that are not actually woven. Triaxial weave, although called a weave, is a hybrid structure between weaving and braiding. The resulting structure, an example of which can be seen in Figure 10(a), does not follow a rectilinear pattern. Braids are created by intertwining three or more threads as shown in Figure 10(b). In knitting (see Figure 10(c)), loops are formed by connecting a row of new loops to a row of already existing loops. When done manually, this usually involves needles holding the thread. In the warp above weave pattern all the threads of one type are always located above the other (see Figure 10(d)). We included this group to see how our similarity measure would cope with non-textile patterns.

We have also introduced imperfections into some of the textiles in each group to test the similarity measure's capability to deal with errors in a pattern. Additionally, we also rotated and mirrored some of the textile samples to check that our similarity measure can cope with differently oriented versions of the same weaving pattern.

6.3 Results

Basically, we have two parameters with which we can calibrate our model: the size k of the neighborhoods and the distance metric used for comparing two fingerprints (JaccardDist, HammingBool, HammingFreq, CosineFreq, and CosineTfIdf; see Section 4.4 for details). In the following we investigate the impact of both parameters on the run time and on the cluster and retrieval performance of our algorithms.

6.3.1 Run Time

Figure 11 illustrates how the run time varies with increasing k for the different distance metrics. Every data point in Figure 11 averages the execution time of nine runs each generating a complete distance matrix including the results for the pairwise comparisons of all textiles. In general, the run time of each variant of our algorithm increases linearly with k.

Unsurprisingly, HammingBool, being the simplest formula, is fastest. HammingFreq is slower than HammingBool and slightly faster than JaccardDist, as JaccardDist needs to normalize its result. Slightly surprising is the speed with which the cosine measure

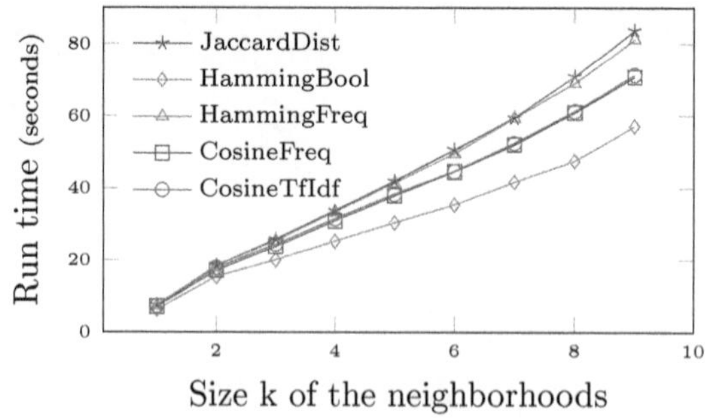

Figure 11: Run Time

variants run, as this involves the most complicated computations compared to the other metrics. This is due to our implementation of the multisets. We refrained from using an explicit vector representation because of the sparsity of the vectors. For instance, although there are 97,871 different (potential) neighborhoods for $k = 9$, on average only 668 appear in a given textile structure. As a consequence we can skip a large part of the inner product calculation.

6.3.2 Cluster Performance

Figure 12 shows the Rand index, while Figure 13 presents the results for precision, recall, and F-measure for the cluster performance. For HammingBool every k-neighborhood has the same influence, regardless of its frequency. This means, that an erroneous neighborhood (due, for example, to imperfections in the textile) will have the same impact as hundreds or thousands of correct identical ones. Additionally, the larger the k, the more neighborhoods will be affected, which leads to the peculiar results seen in Figures 12 and 13: the performance of HammingBool becomes worse with increasing k. To a lesser extent, this is also true for HammingFreq, although storing the frequency of each neighborhood almost compensates for the negative impact of a growing k.

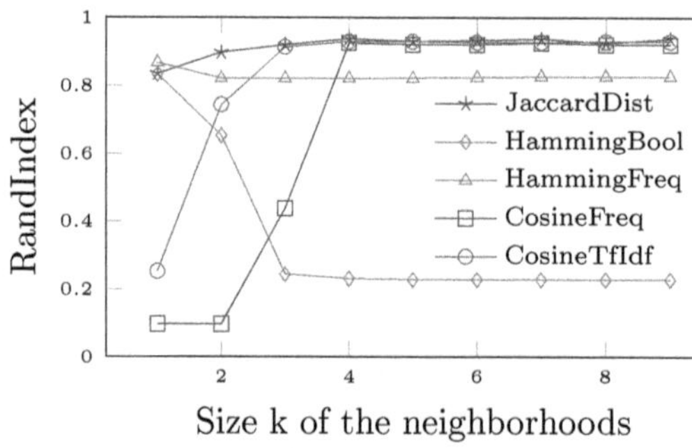

Figure 12: Rand Index

In general, the cosine measure performs in a more expected way. When increasing k, the precision goes up at the price of a slightly decreasing recall. However, the cosine measure variants have a very low precision for small values of k ($k < 4$), making it much worse than JaccardDist for these cases. We found that the cosine measure tends to underestimate the distance between different objects for small values of k, meaning that the wrong patterns are clustered together, leading to more false positives and therefore lower precision. JaccardDist shows the most stable behavior of all the investigated distance metrics, while exhibiting a good cluster performance, so we recommend using it over the others. Also, looking at the results in a general way, we can see that using neighborhoods with $k > 4$ does not bring any substantial improvements,

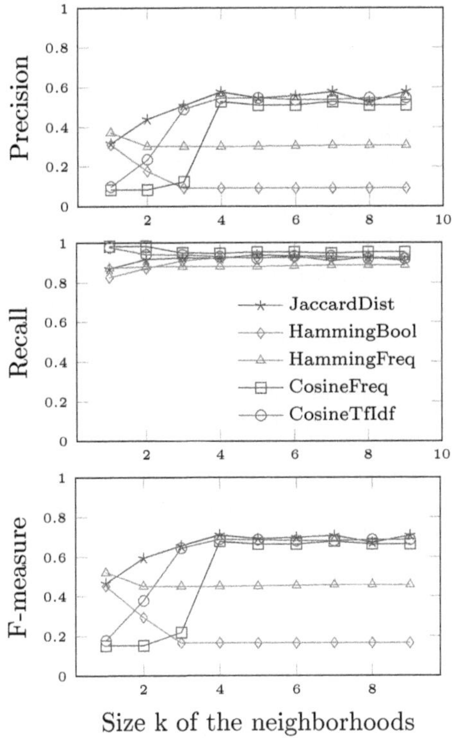

Figure 13: The other measures

on the contrary, sometimes we observed a slightly worse performance.

6.3.3 Retrieval Performance

Figure 14 depicts the mean average precision (MAP) of the different techniques and indicate the overall utility of our textile pattern similarity measure. As for the cluster performance, there is no significant gain in using neighborhoods with a size greater than four, on the contrary, for some techniques the performance even gets worse. The Jaccard distance variant is clearly on top. For the other variants, the situation is not that clear: HammingFreq and CosineTfIdf are roughly comparable (except for very small values of k), while HammingBool and CosineFreq trade places at k equal to four.

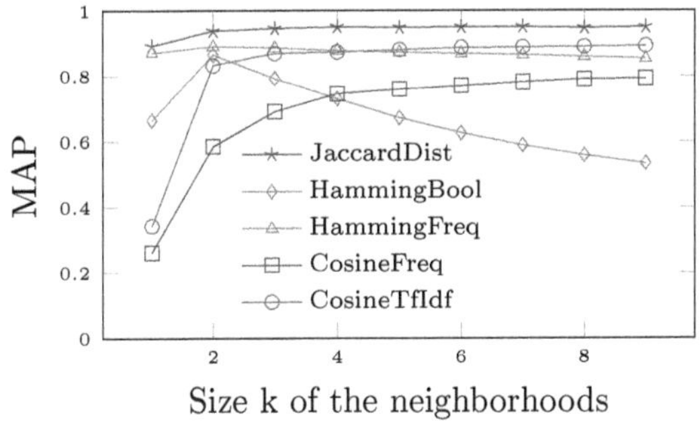

Figure 14: Mean Average Precision

Figure 15 shows the PR and FR curves for neighborhoods of size four. Again, the Jaccard distance shows excellent results, in the PR curve the precision stays above 90% for recall values up to 90% and then drops to around 75%. HammingBool steadily loses ground, while HammingFreq is able to keep up with CosineTfIdf. CosineFreq loses about 20% precision within the first 10% of recall and then is able to keep this level, but is not competitive compared to some of the other techniques. Although the gaps in performance between the different similarity measures are smaller, the FR curve shows a similar picture.

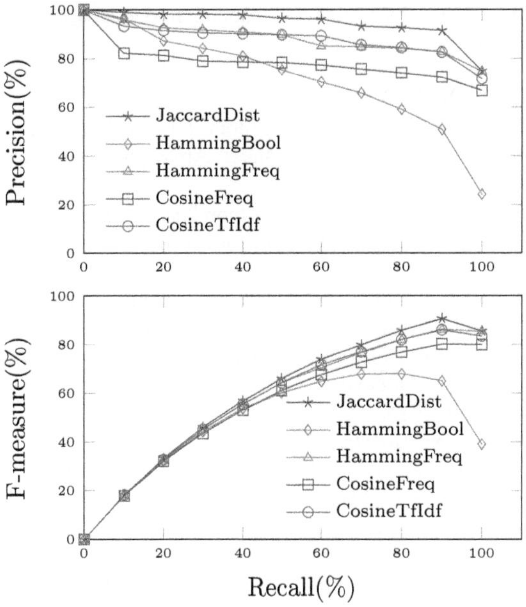

Figure 15: Average PR and FR curves (4-neighborhoods)

7. CONCLUSION AND FUTURE WORK

More and more information is made available in a digitized form, this also includes areas such as the humanities and cultural heritage. A clear advantage of this approach is that digitized material is much easier to access. However, this also brings new challenges with it: users want to be able to search collections in an adequate and fast way. While text search is fairly well understood, other areas still have a lot of catching up to do. For instance, digital archives for textiles offer keyword search and arrange their content taxonomically, but search functionality on the level of thread structure is still missing.

We developed a technique based on hypergraphs to represent textiles using a crossing of two threads as the basic building block. Decomposing such a graph into substructures called k-neighborhoods allows us to determine the similarity of the patterns created by the interwoven threads. In turn, this makes it possible to search a collection of textile patterns given a query pattern. We have experimentally tested several distance metrics for computing the similarity between multisets of k-neighborhoods and found that all of them can be implemented efficiently. Nevertheless, when it comes to actually distinguishing between differently made textiles, there are huge differences. The best variants are Jaccard distance and cosine measure, which are able to cluster textiles taken from a data set of 1200 samples much better than the Hamming distance. We also ran queries over the data set, measuring the retrieval performance. Here, the cosine measure loses some ground compared to the Hamming distance, but Jaccard still comes out on top. Consequently, we recommend using Jaccard, as it shows the best overall performance.

For future work we would like to investigate further distance measures and variations of neighborhoods to see if the technique using k-neighborhoods combined with the Jaccard distance can be further improved upon. Defining a notion of edit distances on hypergraphs for textile structures also looks like a promising direction to take. Finally, evaluating our similarity measure on other data sets to show that it is universally applicable is also an important point to consider. However, at the moment the modeling of the textiles used for the hypergraph representation has to be done manually, in order to automate this process, image-processing techniques for extracting a thread structure and mapping it to graphs would be an interesting topic to look into.

8. REFERENCES

[1] D. Arnold and P. Dransart, editors. *Textiles, Technical Practice and Power in the Andes*. Archetype Books, London, 2014.

[2] L. Babai and P. Codenotti. Isomorphism of hypergraphs of low rank in moderately exponential time. In *FOCS'08*, pages 667–676, 2008.

[3] I. Bloch, A. Bretto, and A. Leborgne. Similarity between hypergraphs based on mathematical morphology. In *Mathematical Morphology and Its Applications to Signal and Image Processing*, volume 7883 of *LNCS*, pages 1–12. Springer, 2013.

[4] C. Brezine. *The Oxford Handbook of the History of Mathematics*, chapter Mathematics and Textiles, pages 468–492. Oxford University Press, Oxford, 2009.

[5] R. Brownlow, S. Capuzzi, S. Helmer, L. Martins, I. Normann, and A. Poulovassilis. An ontological approach to creating an andean weaving knowledge base. *Journal on Computing and Cultural Heritage (JOCCH)*, 4(2), 2015.

[6] H. Bunke, P. Dickinson, M. Kraetzl, M. Neuhaus, and M. Stettler. Matching of hypergraphs – algorithms, applications, and experiments. In *Applied Pattern Recognition*, volume 91 of *Studies in Computational Intelligence*, pages 131–154. Springer, 2008.

[7] J. Conway. *Computational Problems in Abstract Algebra*, chapter An Enumeration of Knots and Links, and Some of Their Algebraic Properties, pages 329–358. Pergamon Press, Oxford, 1970.

[8] P. Cromwell. *Knots and Links*. Cambridge University Press, Cambridge, 2004.

[9] R. D'Harcourt. *Textiles of Ancient Peru and Their Techniques*. Dover Publications, Mineola, NY, 2002.

[10] I. Emery. *The Primary Structures of Fabrics*. Thames and Hudson, London, 2009.

[11] X. Gao, B. Xiao, D. Tao, and X. Li. A survey of graph edit distance. *Pattern Analysis & Applications*, 13(1):113–129, 2010.

[12] S. Grishanov, V. Meshkov, and A. Omel'chenko. Kauffman-type polynomial invariants for doubly periodic structures. *Journal of Knot Theory and Its Ramifications*, 16(6):779–788, 2007.

[13] S. Grishanov, V. Meshkov, and A. Omelchenko. A topological study of textile structures. Part I: An introduction to topological methods. *Textile Research*, 79(8):702–713, 2009.

[14] S. Grishanov, V. Meshkov, and A. Omelchenko. A topological study of textile structures. Part II: Topological invariants in application to textile structures. *Textile Research*, 79(9):822–836, 2009.

[15] G. Gyory. *Advanced Research and Trends in New Technologies, Software, Human-Computer Interaction, and Communicability*, chapter Generic Textile Structure Editor, pages 413–422. IGI Global, 2014.

[16] W. Haken. Theorie der Normalflächen. *Acta Math.*, 105:245–375, 1961.

[17] J. Hass, J. Lagarias, and N. Pippenger. The computational complexity of knot and link problems. *J. ACM*, 46(2):185–211, 1999.

[18] J. Hoskins. *Lecture Notes in Mathematics, Vol. 952*, chapter Factoring Binary Matrices: A Weaver's Approach, pages 300–326. Springer, New York, 1983.

[19] G. Hotz. An efficient algorithm to decide the knot problem. *Bull. of the Georgian National Academy of Sciences*, 2(3):5–16, 2008.

[20] J. Leskovec, A. Rajaraman, and J. D. Ullman. *Mining of Massive Datasets*. Cambridge Univ. Press, 2nd edition, 2014.

[21] U. Liebscher and M. Weber. Topological studies of textiles I. fundamentals. *Textiltechnik*, 30(1):58–61, 1980.

[22] U. Liebscher and M. Weber. Topological studies of textiles II. applications and examples. *Textiltechnik*, 30(3):176–178, 1980.

[23] L. Ma, G. Baciu, J. Hu, and J. Zhang. A novel weave pattern encoding method using neighbor information and its applications. *Textile Research Journal*, 81(6):632–648, 2011.

[24] C. D. Manning, P. Raghavan, and H. Schütze. *Introduction to Information Retrieval*. Cambridge University Press, 2008.

[25] L. Martins, S. Helmer, and D. Y. Arnold. Exploring weaving structures in the andes: Reflections on the creation of a digital archive. *Visual Resources: An International Journal of Documentation*, 29(1-2):59–71, 2013.

[26] V. Milasius and V. Reklaitis. The principles of weave-coding. *The Journal of The Textile Institute*, 79(4), 1988.

[27] T. Miyazaki, Y. Shimajiri, M. Yamada, H. Seki, and H. Itoh. A knitting pattern recognition and stitch symbol generating system for knit designing. *Computers ind. Engineering*, 29(1-4):669–673, 1995.

[28] J. Quilter and G. Urton, editors. *Narrative Threads: Accounting and Recounting in Andean Khipu*. University of Texas Press, Austin, 2002.

[29] W. M. Rand. Objective criteria for the evaluation of clustering methods. *Journal of the American Statistical Association*, 66(336):846–850, 1971.

[30] J. Raymond, E. Gardiner, and P. Willett. Rascal: Calculation of graph similarity using maximum common edge subgraphs. *Computer Journal*, 45(6):631–644, 2002.

[31] K. Reidemeister. Elementare Begründung der Knotentheorie. *Abh. Math. Seminar Univ. Hamburg*, 5(1):24–32, 1927.

[32] D. Rosner, M. Roccetti, and G. Marfia. The digitization of cultural practices. *Communications of the ACM*, 57(6):82–87, 2014.

[33] A. Rowe. *Warp Patterned Weaves of the Andes*. Textile Museum, Washington, 1977.

[34] J. Valiente, F. Albert, C. Carretero, and J. Gomis. Structural description of textile and tile pattern designs using image processing. In *ICPR'04, Vol. 1*, pages 498 – 503, 2004.

[35] A. K. C. Wong, S. W. Lu, and M. Rioux. Recognition and shape synthesis of 3-d objects based on attributed hypergraphs. *IEEE Trans. Pattern Anal. Mach. Intell.*, 11(3):279–290, mar 1989.

[36] Z. Zeng, A. K. H. Tung, J. Wang, J. Feng, and L. Zhou. Comparing stars: on approximating graph edit distance. *PVLDB*, 2(1):25–36, 2009.

[37] D. Zheng, G. Baciu, and J. Hu. Accurate indexing and classification for fabric weave patterns using entropy-based approach. In *The 8th Int. Conf. on Cognitive Informatics (ICCI'09)*, pages 357–364, 2009.

Local Ranking Problem on the BrowseGraph

Michele Trevisiol*† trevisiol@acm.org
Luca Maria Aiello† alucca@yahoo-inc.com
Paolo Boldi§ boldi@di.unimi.it
Roi Blanco† roi@yahoo-inc.com

*Web Research Group, Universitat Pompeu Fabra, Barcelona, Spain
†Yahoo Labs, London, UK
§Dip. di Scienze dell'Informazione, Univ. degli Studi di Milano, Milano, Italy

ABSTRACT

The "Local Ranking Problem" (LRP) is related to the computation of a centrality-like rank on a *local* graph, where the scores of the nodes could significantly differ from the ones computed on the *global* graph. Previous work has studied LRP on the hyperlink graph but never on the *BrowseGraph*, namely a graph where nodes are webpages and edges are browsing transitions. Recently, this graph has received more and more attention in many different tasks such as ranking, prediction and recommendation. However, a web-server has only the browsing traffic performed on its pages (*local BrowseGraph*) and, as a consequence, the local computation can lead to estimation errors, which hinders the increasing number of applications in the state of the art. Also, although the divergence between the local and global ranks has been measured, the possibility of *estimating* such divergence using only local knowledge has been mainly overlooked. These aspects are of great interest for online service providers who want to: *(i)* gauge their ability to correctly assess the importance of their resources only based on their local knowledge, and *(ii)* take into account real user browsing fluxes that better capture the actual user interest than the static hyperlink network. We study the LRP problem on a *BrowseGraph* from a large news provider, considering as subgraphs the aggregations of browsing traces of users coming from different domains. We show that the distance between rankings can be accurately predicted based only on structural information of the local graph, being able to achieve an average rank correlation as high as 0.8.

Categories and Subject Descriptors

H.4 [**Information Systems Applications**]: Miscellaneous; E.1 [**Data Structures**]: Graphs and Networks

Keywords

Local Ranking Problem; BrowseGraph; PageRank; Centrality Algorithms; Domain-specific Browsing Graphs

SIGIR'15, August 09 - 13, 2015, Santiago, Chile.
© 2015 ACM. ISBN 978-1-4503-3621-5/15/08 ...$15.00.
DOI: http://dx.doi.org/10.1145/2766462.2767704.

1. INTRODUCTION

The ability to identify the online resources that are perceived as important by the users of a website is crucial for online service providers. Metrics to estimate the importance of the page from the structure of online links between them are widely used: algorithms that compute the *centrality* of the nodes in a network, such as PageRank [24], HITS [17] and SALSA [19], have been employed extensively in the last two decades in a vast variety of applications. Born and spread in conjunction with the growth of the Web, they can determine a value of importance of a page from the complex network of links that surrounds it. More recently, centrality metrics have been applied to *browsing graphs*, (also referred to as *BrowseGraphs* [22, 28, 27]) where nodes are webpages and edges represent the transitions made by the users who navigate the links between them. Differently from the hyperlink networks, this data source provides the analyst a way of studying directly the dynamics of the navigational patterns of users who consume online content. Also, unlike hyperlinks, browsing traces account for the variation of consumption patterns in time, for instance in the case of online news where articles tend to become rapidly stale. Comparative studies have shown that centrality-based algorithms applied over *BrowseGraphs* provide higher-quality rankings compared to standard hyperlink graphs [23, 22].

Most centrality measures aim at estimating the importance of a node, using information coming from the *global* knowledge of the graph topology. Potentially the addition of new nodes and edges, can have a cascade effect on the centrality values of all other nodes in the network. This fact entails high computational and storage cost for big net-works. More critically, there are some situations in which a global computation on the entire graph is unfeasible, for example when the information about the entire network is unavailable or if only an estimation for specific web pages is required. This is an important limitation in many real-world scenarios, where the graphs at hand are often very large (Web scale) and, most importantly, their topology is not fully known. This practical issue raises the problem of how well one can estimate the actual centrality value of a node by knowing only a local portion of the graph. This is known as the *Local Ranking Problem* (LRP) [10]. One of the questions behind LRP is whether it is possible to estimate efficiently the PageRank score of a web page using only a small subgraph of the entire Web [9]. In other words, if one starts from a small graph around a page of interest and extends it with external nodes and arcs (*i.e.*, those belonging to the whole graph), how fast will one observe the computed scores converging to the real values of PageRank? We extend this line of work in the context of browsing graphs. For the first time we study the LRP on the *BrowseGraph* and shed some light on the bias that PageRank incurs *(i)* when estimating the centrality score of nodes in a *BrowseGraph*, and *(ii)* when only partial information about the graph is available. To achieve that, we monitor the browsing traffic of the news portal and we extract different browsing subgraphs induced by the browsing traces of users coming from different *domains*, such as search engines (*e.g.*, Google, Yahoo, Bing) and social networks (*e.g.*, Facebook, Twitter, Reddit). In this setting, the local *BrowseGraphs* are the subgraphs induced by the different domains, and the global *BrowseGraph* is the one built using indistinctly all the navigation logs of the news portal. We describe and evaluate models that tell apart a subgraph from the others just by looking at the behavior of a random surfer that navigates through their links. The results show how it is possible to recognize the graph using only the very first few nodes visited by the users, because the graphs are very different among them (even if they are extracted from the same big log of the news portal). The implication of this experiment is two-fold: first it highlights how navigation patterns of the users differ among these subgraphs. Second, we learn that it is possible to infer the user domain of origin from the very first browsing steps. This capability enables several types of services, including user profiling [12], web site optimization [31], user engagement estimation [18], and cold-start recommendation [27], even when the referrer URL is not available (*e.g.*when the user comes from mobile social media applications or URL shortening services). Once we show that the subgraphs are different enough, we proceed to perform more involved experiments that we call "Growing Rings". We examine the behavior of the PageRank computed on the local and the global graphs. In order to study how the local PageRank converges to the global one, we apply some strategies of incremental addition ("growing") of external nodes to these subgraphs ("rings"). Finally, we build on these findings by setting up a prediction experiment that, for the first time, tackles the task of estimating the reliability of the PageRank computed locally. We measure *how much* the local PageRank diverges from the global one using only structural features of the local graph, usually available to the local service provider. To sum up, the main contributions of this work are the following:

- We study the *LRP* on a large-scale *BrowseGraph* built from a very popular news website. To the best of our knowledge we are the first to tackle this problem on the increasingly popular *BrowseGraph* [27, 28, 12, 22]. We present an analysis of the convergence of the PageRank on the local graph to the global one, by incrementally expanding the local graph in a snowingreen fashion.

- We tackle the problem of discovering the referrer domain of a user session, when this information is missing or hidden. We show that this is possible using a random surfer model, which is able to tell the referrer domain with high accuracy, just after the very first browsing transitions.

- We show that an accurate estimation of the distance between the local and global PageRank can be obtained looking at the structural properties of the local graph, such as degree distribution or assortativity.

The remainder of the paper is organized as follows. In §2 we overview relevant prior work in the area and in §3 we describe our dataset and the extraction of the browsing graphs. In §4 we analyze the (sub-)graphs and we highlight their differences. In §5 we study the LRP problem on the *BrowseGraph* and compare the approximation accuracy of different graph expansion strategies. In §6 we present the prediction experiment of the PageRank errors of the local graph. Last, in §7 we wrap up and highlight possible extensions to the work.

2. RELATED WORK

This work encompasses two main different research areas that we introduce shortly. Our focus is the *Local Ranking Problem* but our contribution relates also to previous work on browsing log data, especially the ones that investigate or make use of centrality-based algorithms.

Local Ranking Problem

The *Local Ranking Problem* (LRP) was first introduced by Chen *et al.* [10] in 2004, who addressed the problem to approximate/update the PageRank of individual nodes, without performing a large-scale computation on the entire graph. They proposed an approach that can tackle this problem by including a moderate number of nodes in the local neighborhood of the original nodes. Furthermore, Davis and Dhillon [14] estimated the global PageRank values of a local network using a method that scales linearly with the size of the local domain. Their goal was to rank webpages in order to optimize their crawling order, something similar to what was done by Cho *et al.* [13] who instead selected the top-ranked pages first. However, this latter strategy results to be in contrast with Boldi *et al.* [6], as they found that crawling first the pages with highest global PageRank actually perform worse, if the purpose is fast convergence to the real (global) rank values. In this work, we partial expand the local graph with the neighboring nodes with highest (local) PageRank showing an initial improvement on the convergence speed. In 2008 the problem was reconsidered by Bar-Yossef and Mashiach [3], where they simplified the problem calculating a local *Reverse PageRank* proving that it is more feasible and computationally cheaper, as the reverse natural graphs tend to have low in-degree maintaining a fast PageRank convergence. Bressan and Pretto [9] proved that, in the general case, an efficient local ranking algorithm does not exist, and in order to compute a *correct* ranking it is necessary to visit at least a number of nodes linear in the size of the input graph. They also raised some of the research questions tackled in our paper that we discuss in Section 6.1. They reinforce their findings in later work [8], where they summarized two key factors necessary for efficient local PageRank computations: *exploring the graph non-locally* and *accepting a small probability error*. These two constraints are also considered in this paper in order to perform our experiments on the browsing graphs. When one wants to estimate PageRank in a local graph, the problem of the missing information is tackled in various ways. In [3, 9] for example, the authors make use of a model called *link server* (also known as *remote connectivity server* [5]), which responds to any query about a given node with all the in-coming and out-going edges and relative nodes. This approach, with the knowledge about the LRP, allows to estimate the PageRank ranking, or even the score, with the relative costs. A similar problem was studied by Andersen *et al.* [2], where their goal was to compute the PageRank contributions in a local graph motivated by the problem of detecting link-spam: given a page, its PageRank contributors are the pages that contribute most to its rank; contributors are used for spam detection since you can quickly identify the set of pages that contribute significantly to the PageRank of a suspicious page.

The problem we consider here is different and largely unexplored, because we are studying the PageRank of the different subgraphs based on user browsing patterns.

BrowseGraph

In recent years a large number of studies of user browsing traces have been conducted. Specifically, in the last years there was a surge of interest in the *BrowseGraph*, a graph where the nodes are web pages and the edges represent the transitions from one page to another made by the navigation of the users. Characterizing the browsing behavior of users is a valuable source of information for a number of different tasks, ranging from understanding how people's search behaviors differ [32], ranking webpages through search trails [1, 33] or recommending content items using past history [29]. A comparison between the standard hyperlink graph, based on the structure of the network, with the browse graph built by the users' navigation patterns, has been made by Liu *et al.* [22, 23]. They compared centrality-based algorithms like PageRank [24], TrustRank [15], and BrowseRank [22], on both types of graphs. The results agree on the higher quality of ranking based on the browse graph, because it is a more reliable source; they also tried out a combination of the two graphs with very interesting outcomes. The user browsing graph and related PageRank-like algorithms have been exploited to rank different types of items including images [28, 12], photostreams [11], and predicting users demographic [16] or optimizing web crawling [21]. Trevisiol *et al.* [28] made a comparison between different ranking techniques applied to the Flickr *BrowseGraph*. Chiarandini *et al.* [12] found strong correlations between the type of user's navigation and the type of external Referrer URL. Hu *et al.* [16] have shown that demographic information of the users (*e.g.*, age and gender) can be identified from their browsing traces with good accuracy. The *BrowseGraph* has been used also for recommending sequences of photos that users often like to navigate in sequence, following a collaborative filtering approach [11]. In order to implement an efficient news recommender the user's taste have to be considered as they might change over time. Indeed, studying the users browsing patterns, Liu *et al.* [20] showed that more recent clicks have a considerably higher value to predict future actions than the historical browsing record. Finally, Trevisiol *et al.* [27] exploited the *BrowseGraph* in order to build some user models in the news domain, and recommend the next article the user is going to visit. They introduced the concept of *ReferrerGraph*, which is a *BrowseGraph* built with sessions that are generated by the same referrer domain. Even if the purposes of our work are very different, we construct the *ReferrerGraphs* in the same way in order to be in-line with their investigation.

To the best of our knowledge there is no work in the state of the art that tackles the *Local Ranking Problem* on a browsing graphs with the prediction task that we perform and describe in this paper.

3. DATASET

For the purpose of this study, we took a sample of Yahoo News network's[1] user-anonymized log data collected in 2013. The dataset used in this work has been extracted from the data built in [27], that was used with the purpose to study the news consumption with respect to the Referrer URL. In this section we summarize how we built the dataset and the graphs, but the reader may refer to the aforementioned paper for further details. The data is comprised by a large number of pageviews, which are represented as plain text files that contain a line for each HTTP request satisfied by the Web server. For each pageview in the dataset, we gathered the following fields:

$$\langle BCookie, Timestamp, ReferrerURL, URL, UserAgent\rangle$$

The *BCookie* is an anonymized identifier computed from the browser cookie. This information allowed us to re-construct the navigation session of the different users. *URL* and *ReferrerURL* represent, respectively, the current page the user is visiting and the page the user visited before arriving at the destination page. Note that the *Referrer URL* could belong to any domain, *e.g.*, it may be external to the Yahoo News network. The *User-Agent* identifies the user's browser, an information that we used to filter out Web crawlers, and *Timestamp* indicates when the page was visited. All the data were anonymized and aggregated prior to building the browsing graphs. We removed traffic derived from Web crawlers by preserving only the entries whose User-Agent field contains a well-known browser identifier. After applying the filtering steps described above, our sample contains approximately 3.8 million unique pageviews and 1.88 billion user transitions.

3.1 Session Identification and Characteristics

The *BrowseGraph* is a graph whose nodes are web pages, and whose edges are the browsing transitions made by the users. To build it we extract the transitions of users from page to page, and in order to preserve the user behavior (that could vary over time), we group pageviews into *sessions*. We split the activity of a single user, taking the *BCookie* as an identifier, into different sessions when either of these two conditions holds:

- **Timeout:** the inactivity between two pageviews is longer than 25 minutes.
- **External URL:** if a user leaves the news platform and returns from an external domain, the current session ends even if previous visits are within the 25 minute threshold.

Moreover, each news article of the dataset is annotated with a high-level *category* manually assigned by the editors.

3.2 Subgraphs Based on Session Referrer URL

We aim to compare the PageRank scores of the nodes between the full *BrowseGraph*, computed with all the Yahoo News logs, and a subgraph that represents the local graph. This is a way to simulate a real-world scenario in which a service provider knowns only the users navigation logs inside its network (subgraph) while the external navigations

[1]We considered a number of different subdomains like *Yahoo news, finance, sports, movies, travel, celebrity, etc.*

Subgraphs	Nodes	Edges	Density	%GCC
Google	142,646	779,185	$3.8 \cdot 10^{-5}$	0.93
Yahoo	101,116	404,378	$3.9 \cdot 10^{-5}$	0.95
Bing	61,531	255,464	$6.7 \cdot 10^{-5}$	0.91
Homepage	60,287	335,836	$9.2 \cdot 10^{-5}$	0.99
Facebook	21,060	70,266	$1.5 \cdot 10^{-4}$	0.95
Twitter	4,206	7,080	$4.0 \cdot 10^{-4}$	0.87
Reddit	2,445	4,868	$8.1 \cdot 10^{-4}$	0.95

Table 1: Size, density and Giant Connected Component of the extracted subgraphs. Note that there is not a strict relation between the size of the subgraph and the amount of browsing traffic generated in it.

are unknown (full *BrowseGraph*). Since it is not possible to use the full Web browsing log, we perform a simulation using different subgraphs extracted from the same *BrowseGraph* that represent the local graphs of different providers. One possible approach would be to simulate each service provider as a different Yahoo News subdomain (*e.g.*, news, sports, finance). However, news articles are often shared on different Yahoo subdomains and, as a consequence, the users jump among different subdomains in each single session. To avoid such an overlap on the subgraphs, we define a different simulation approach. We extract from the *BrowseGraph* of the Yahoo News dataset various subgraphs built with sessions of users generated by the same Referrer URL. It has been shown [27] that *BrowseGraphs* constructed in this way contain very different users sessions in terms of content consumed (nodes visited). In particular we consider users accessing the news portal directly from the homepage, which is the main entry point for regular news consumption, and in addition from a number of domains that fall outside the Yahoo News network: *search engines* (Google, Yahoo, Bing) and *social networks* (Facebook, Twitter, Reddit). For each source domain we extract a subgraph from the overall *BrowseGraph*, by considering only the browsing sessions whose initial *R*eferrer URL matches that domain. For example, if a user clicks on a link referring to our network that has been posted on Twitter, her *R*eferrer URL will be the Twitter page where she found the link. Next, we consider all the following pageviews belonging to the same session of the user, as being a part of the *twitter-subgraph*, given that all of them have been reached through Twitter. We applied the same procedure for all the sources defined before, and finally, we obtained a weighted graph for each different external URL. The *Weight* accounts for the number of times a user has navigated from the source page to the destination page. On Table 1 a summary with the size of the graphs (in terms of number of nodes and edges) and with their structure is shown. It is interesting to see that all the graphs, even presenting very different size, are very well connected (%GCC between 0.87 and 0.99).

4. REFERRER GRAPHS ANALYSIS

In this section we describe some analysis on these *ReferrerGraphs*, proving that they are consistently different not only in term of nodes and content but also in term of navigation patterns of the users. We also propose an experiment to understand how much the graphs are distinguishable.

4.1 Subgraphs comparison

We consider the seven subgraphs extracted from the main news portal graph with the procedure discussed in §3. Browsing patterns generated by different types of audience, can lead to different pieces of news pages to emerge as the most central ones in the *BrowseGraph*. To check that we ran the PageRank algorithm on each of the (weighted) subgraphs, and for every pair of subgraphs we compared the scores obtained on their common nodes using Kendall's τ distance. The intersection between the node sets of the networks is always large enough to allow us to compute the τ on the intersection only (> 1000 nodes in the case with less overlap). Kendall's τ will provide a clear measure of how much the importance of the same set of nodes varies among different subgraphs. When the ranking between two subgraphs differs greatly (*i.e.*, low Kendall's τ), it is an indication that they either show different content (*i.e.*, webpages) or that the collective browsing behaviour in the two graphs privileged different sets of pages.

Table 2 reports on the cross-distance among the subgraphs and also with respect to the full graph using Kendall's τ. Interestingly, most of the similarity values tend to be very low (<0.3), confirming the hypothesis that the user's interests are tightly related to the domain where they come from. Some of these similarities, however, are considerably higher, remarkably the ones between the three subgraphs that are originated from search engines traffic, *i.e.*, Bing, Google and Yahoo, which yield the most similar rankings of pages (>0.5). However, for the purpose of this work we expect to find a difference among the subgraphs in order to use them as local *BrowseGraph* and study the LRP with the full graph (*i.e.*, *BrowseGraph* made with the entire news log).

4.2 Random Surfer

In §4.1 we showed how users coming from different sources (*i.e.*, referrer domains) behave differently in terms of content discovery and, as a consequence, the importance of the news articles vary significantly among the different *BrowseGraphs*. It has been shown how the referrer domain might be extremely useful to characterize user sessions [12], to estimate user engagement [18] or to perform cold-start recommendation [27]. However, the user's referrer URL is not always visible and, in many cases, it is hidden or masked by services or clients. For instance, any Twitter or mail client (*i.e.*, third-party application) shows an empty referrer URL in the web logs. A similar situation happens with the widespread URL-shortening services (*e.g.*, `Bitly.com`), which mask the original Web page the user is coming from. Nonetheless, in all these cases a provider could make use of her knowledge of the user's trail, to identify automatically the source where the user started her navigation in the local graph. As we have shown, the referrer URL might be useful to characterize the interest of the users, especially in the case where the users are unknown (*i.e.*, the user profile is not available). Thus, being able to identify the referrer URL when it is not available, is an advantage for the content provider. In this section we want to understand if it is feasible to detect the referrer URL of a user while he browses and how many browsing steps are required to be able to do so accurately.

Moreover, if the user sessions are easily distinguishable it means that the subgraphs are different enough to be considered, in our experiment, as *local BrowseGraphs* of different service providers.

	Full	Facebook	Google	Bing	Yahoo	Reddit	Homepage	Twitter
Full	1.0000	0.1791	0.3931	0.3278	0.3548	0.0656	0.2797	0.0764
Facebook	0.1791	1.0000	0.3146	0.4111	0.3430	0.2616	0.4070	0.3026
Google	0.3931	0.3146	1.0000	0.5815	0.5860	0.1088	0.4217	0.1297
Bing	0.3278	0.4111	0.5815	1.0000	0.6624	0.1469	0.5238	0.1688
Yahoo	0.3548	0.3430	0.5860	0.6624	1.0000	0.1245	0.4632	0.1386
Reddit	0.0656	0.2616	0.1088	0.1469	0.1245	1.0000	0.1534	0.2309
Homepage	0.2797	0.4070	0.4217	0.5238	0.4632	0.1534	1.0000	0.1523
Twitter	0.0764	0.3026	0.1297	0.1688	0.1386	0.2309	0.1523	1.0000

Table 2: Kendall's τ correlations between PageRank values ($\alpha = 0.85$) between the common nodes of the subgraphs.

Algorithm 1: `RandomSurfer`(k, α, steps, G)

logPr $\leftarrow$ initialize vector with size $G_k.length()$;
n $\leftarrow$ total number of nodes;
$x_j \leftarrow$ choose (random) starting node $\in G_k$;
/ For each step, compute a random walk in G_k, and compare the probability to be in all the other G */*
for $s \leftarrow 1$ *to steps* **do**
  / Pick the next node of G_k with random walk */*
  x_k = next_node(G_k, x_j);
  for $i \leftarrow 0$ **to** $G.length()$ **do**
    $\langle k_{out} \rangle \leftarrow$ `get_outdegree`(n_p);
    if $\langle k_{out} \rangle == 0$ **then**
      logPr[i] $\leftarrow$ logPr[i] + $\log(1/n)$;
    else
      $p_i(x) = (1-\alpha)/n$;
      $Pd_{x_j} \leftarrow$ `get_prob_distribution`(G_i, x_j);
      $S_{x_j} \leftarrow$ `get_successors`(G_i, x_j);
      if $x_k \in S_{x_j}$ **then**
        $p_i(x) \leftarrow p_i(x) + \alpha * Pd_{x_j}(x_k)$;
      logPr[i] $\leftarrow$ logPr[i] + $\log(p_i(x))$;
return logPr

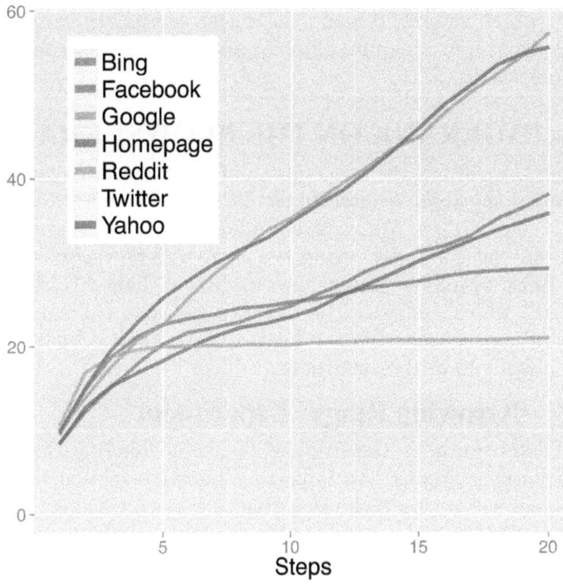

Figure 1: Random Surfer Experiment. Y-axis: log-ratio of the probabilities between the correct graph and the graph with the largest log-probability (as explained in the text). X-axis: number of browsing steps performed by the surfer.

Therefore, we consider the following scenario: a content provider is observing a user surfing the pages of its web service, but it is unaware of the user's referrer URL. In terms of our experimental dataset, this scenario maps into the problem of observing a browsing trace left by a random surfer on one of the referrer-based subgraphs and having to identify which graph it is. Intuitively, the larger the number of page visits (or *steps*) the surfer will make the more distinctive its trace will be, and the easier the identification of the graph. Algorithm 1 shows the pseudocode that describes the process to compute the random surfer experiment.

Formally, observing the sequence of the surfer's visited nodes $\mathbf{x} = (x_1, x_2, \dots, x_s)$ and computing the probability $p_i(\mathbf{x})$ that the surfer has gone through them given that it is surfing G_i, we need to deduce what is G_i (*e.g.*, by maximum log-likelihood). With this goal in mind, we sort the indices of the subgraphs $i_1, i_2, \dots$ so that $p_{i_1}(\mathbf{x}) \geq p_{i_2}(\mathbf{x}) \geq \dots$ and stop as soon as the gap between $\log p_{i_1}(\mathbf{x})$ and $\log p_{i_2}(\mathbf{x})$ is large enough (*e.g.*, $\log p_{i_1}(\mathbf{x}) - \log p_{i_2}(\mathbf{x}) \geq \log 2$), with a maximum of 20 steps that we consider as a representation of a long user session.

In this set of experiments, we considered the seven URL-referral subgraphs $G_1, \dots, G_7$, one at a time. For each subgraph G_i, we simulated a random surfer moving around in G_i (*i.e.*, calling the function **`RandomSurfer`**(i, α, steps, G)), computing at each step (*i.e.*, page visited) the probability of the surfer to navigate in each subgraph $G_1, \dots G_7$: we expect that the probability corresponding to G_i will increase at each step, and will eventually dominate all the others.

To estimate the number of steps required to identify correctly the graph that the surfer is browsing, we measure the difference between log-probabilities for the correct graph G_i and for the graph with the largest log-probability among the other ones. As with PageRank we introduced a certain damping factor ($\alpha = 0.85$); this is necessary to avoid being stuck in terminal components of the graph. Recall that α is the balancing parameter that determines the probability of following in the random walk, instead of teleporting. The results are shown in Figure 1, averaged over 100 executions. The values on the y-axis represent the difference between the log-probabilities (*i.e.*, the logarithm of their ratio): in general, we can observe that the very first steps are enough to understand correctly (and with a huge margin) in which graph the surfer is moving. The inset of Figure 1 displays the first 20 steps and the relative probability to identify the correct graph. Almost all the referrer domains are recognizable at the first step. This translates into a strong advantage for the service provider as it can identify from where the users are coming from, even if they use clients or services that masquerade it. With this information the service provider can personalize the content of the web pages for any users with respect to the referrer.

Interestingly, the plot reveals that some surfers are easier to single out than others; we read this as yet another confirmation that the subgraphs have a distinguished structural difference, or (if you prefer) that users have a markedly different behavior depending on where they come from. This experiment does not only showed that is possible to detect from which referrer domain the surfer is coming from, but that the graphs are quite different and that they can be used for our study.

5. PAGERANK ON THE BROWSEGRAPH

Next, we study the convergence of the PageRank ranking between the *local BrowseGraphs* (*ReferrerGraphs*) and the full *BrowseGraph*. We want to understand how different are the ranking computed using less or more knowledge about the full graph. We present an experiment, called "Growing Rings", which compute the distance between the rankings expanding at each step the known nodes (and edges) with the neighbors of the subgraphs.

5.1 "Growing Rings" Experiment

We first focus on the study of the *Local Ranking Problem* on browsing graphs. An important question related to this problem is how much the PageRank node values vary, when new nodes and edges are added to the local graph. A natural way to determine this is to expand incrementally the graph by adding new nodes and edges in a Breadth-First Search (BFS) fashion, and comparing the PageRank computed on the expanded graph with the one on the global graph.

More formally, given a graph H which is a subgraph of the full graph G, we simulate a growth sequence $H_0, H_1 \ldots H_n$ in the following way:

- $H_0 \longleftarrow H$;
- $V_{H_{k+1}} \longleftarrow \{\ \Gamma_{out}(V_{H_k}) \cup V_{H_k}\}$, with V_x being the set of vertices of a graph, and Γ being the vertex neighborhood function;
- $E_{H_{k+1}} \longleftarrow \{\ (v_1, v_2) | v_1 \in V_{H_{k+1}} \wedge v_2 \in V_{H_{k+1}}\}$, with E_x being the set of edges of a graph.

We refer to the various steps of this expansion as *"rings"*, where the ring H_0 is the initial subgraph and subsequent rings are obtained by adding all the outgoing arcs that depart from the nodes in the current ring and end in nodes that are not in the ring. Observe that, depending on how it is built, H_0 may not be an induced subgraph of G, but $H_1, \cdots, H_n$ are always induced subgraphs, by definition of the expansion algorithm.

Using the Kendall's τ function, we measure the difference between the local PageRank computed for each ring H_i and the global PageRank computed on G. The main objective is to understand how much the ranking gets close the global one at each consecutive step, and whether the ranking values are able to converge even if we just consider a piece of the information contained in the whole graph.

To check the dependency of results from the initial graph selected, we consider three different sets of initial subgraphs, which we will study separately. We describe them next.

- **Referrer-based (RB)**. The seven browsing subgraphs built by referrer URL: Facebook, Twitter, Reddit, Homepage, Yahoo, Google and Bing;
- **Same size referrer-based (SRB)**. To measure how much the different sizes of the graphs impact on the observed behavior, we fix a number of nodes and extract a portion of each subgraph in order to obtain exactly the same size for all networks. The selection is performed with several attempts of BFS expansion, starting from a random node in each graph, until the resulting graphs have very similar size ($\pm 9.4\%$): other ways of selecting subgraphs would end up with disconnected samples, which of course would void the purpose of this experiment. With this procedure instead, we are able to compare the graphs on equal grounds and at the same time control for the effect of size (about $3K$ nodes and $20K$ edges).
- **Random (R)**. To check whether the observed behavior has to do with the user behavior underlying the graph under examination (*e.g.*, the particular structure of the graph determined by the sessions of users coming from Twitter), we take a set of seven *random* graphs each of them reflecting the size of each of the referrer-based subgraphs. Thus, we can explore the behavior of browsing graphs, which preserve the size of the graphs originated by specific types of users, but that are "artificial" in the sense that destroy any connection with the behavior connected to a particular user class. To make sure that the size is the same, we start from a BFS exploration and we prune the last level to match exactly the size we need.

The results related to the **RB** case are shown in Figure 2 (left). The convergence happens relatively quickly, as the value τ approaches 1 in the first 3 iterations. The curves related to different subgraphs are shifted with respect to each other, apparently mainly due to their different size, the biggest networks starting from higher τ values and converging faster than the smaller ones. To determine the dependency on the graph size, we repeat the same experiment for the **SRB** case. The results for this case are shown in Figure 2 (center). Even if the curves resulted to be more flattened (confirming that the initial size has indeed a role in the convergence), we still observe noticeable differences between the curves for the first two expansion levels. This means that different subgraphs are substantially different from one another in terms of their structure: even after forcing them to have the same size, the convergence rates observed on the different graphs varies. At the first iteration, for instance, all the subgraphs in **SRB** have Kendall's τ between 0.3 and 0.5, whereas the ones in **RB** are between 0.4 and 0.6. Moreover in **SRB** the biggest networks starting from higher τ values are not converging faster. This intuition is confirmed by repeating the experiment on graphs selected with the **R** strategy. Results, displayed in Figure 2 (right), show that convergence in this case is much slower and the difference between the curves is less prominent.

Summarizing, with the previous experiment we show that the Growing Rings on random subgraphs behave differen-

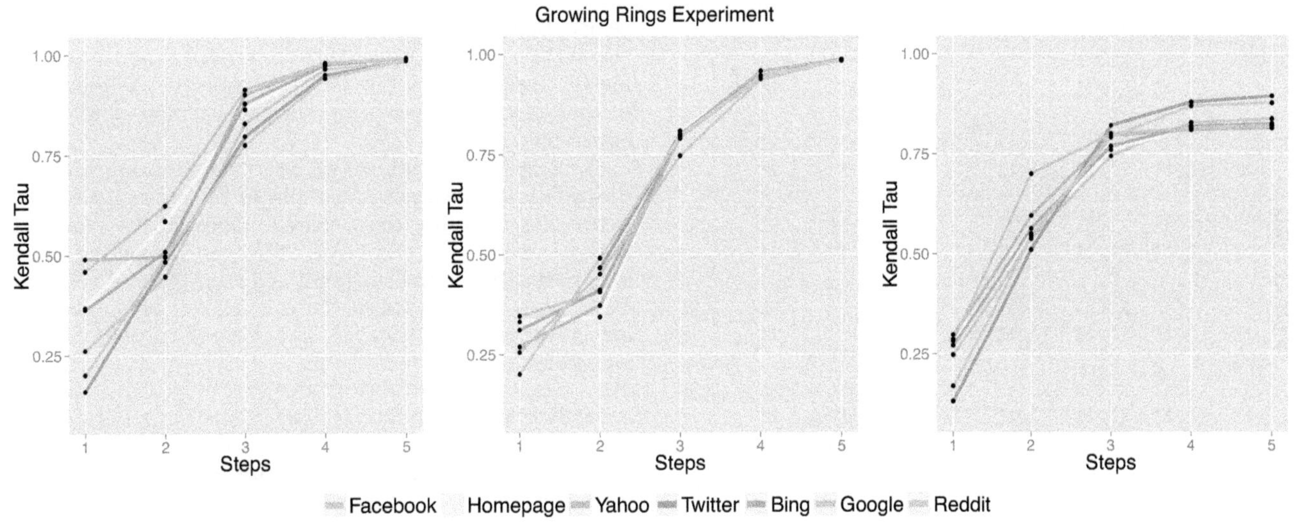

Figure 2: Growing Rings experiment on: (left) original subgraphs built based on the referrer URL, (center) seven subsubgraphs with very similar size, (right) seven subgraphs random selected from the full graph, where each of them has the same size of one of the original.

tly, especially when considering the number of iterations required in order to converge.

5.2 Growing Rings with Selection of Nodes

Besides the selection of the initial graph, the rank convergence depends also on the way the growing rings are built at each iteration. How does the expansion influence convergence if only few more representative nodes are selected? To what extent a higher *volume* of selected nodes helps a quicker convergence or adds more *noise*? At a first glance, one may argue that using all the nodes is equivalent to injecting all the available information, so the convergence to the values of PageRank computed on the full graph G should be faster. On the other hand, instead, one may observe that we are introducing a huge number of nodes in each iteration (as the growth is at each step larger), adding also the ones that are less important and this can induce an incorrect PageRank for some time, until all the graph becomes known. In order to shed light on this aspect, we introduce a variant in the growing-rings expansion algorithm and we select only the nodes with highest PageRank.

More formally, considering H_k as the subgraph at iteration k and V_{H_k} its set of nodes, we select all the external nodes in $Y = \{V_G \backslash V_{H_k}\}$, which are connected through outgoing arcs from the nodes in V_{H_k}. We then compute the PageRank values on the subgraph H_k extended with the nodes Y and obtain a ranked list of nodes. Among all the nodes in Y we select the top $n\%$ with largest PageRank value, and only those ones will be added to H_k in order to build H_{k+1} and advance to the next iteration.

We conducted experiments with this partial expansion at different percentages: 5%, 10%, 30%, 50%, and 100%, and then we computed the average Kendall's τ value for each one of the percentages. The results are shown in Figure 3. Remarkably, the figure highlights how expanding the graph by adding fewer nodes, although the most representative ones, leads to PageRank values that are closer to the *global* ones in the first iterations. Since we are expanding the local graph with a small (highly-central) number of nodes, we could argue that they initially help to boost the local PageRank scores. However, given that we keep on expanding using a few nodes at each iteration, the nodes that have not been added before exclude a large number of nodes among which there might also be highly central ones. This might explain why in the first iteration(s) the convergence rate is high, but on the limit the final convergence values result in a low Kendall's τ. Contrarily, in the long run, expansions that include the highest number of nodes present convergence values closer to 1. This is somehow expected, given that at each iteration any subgraph H closer in size to the full graph G will include almost every node and arc.

Nonetheless, the main significant outcome of this experiment is that it is possible to obtain a yet satisfactory PageRank convergence, with few but very representative nodes. For situations in which including additional pieces of information (in terms of node/arc insertions) implies a non-negligible cost, requesting just a little amount of well-selected information allows to obtain good approximations while minimizing the costs.

6. PAGERANK PREDICTION

In the previous section we have shown how the approximation to the global PageRank varies with the expansion of the initial subgraph. The ranking of the nodes converges quite fast on all the subgraphs: they differ in terms of their content, although they are similar in terms of structure in that all of them are built based on users' navigational patterns. Building upon the findings about how local and global PageRank computed on the *BrowseGraphs* relate to each other, we designed an experiment to assess how well a learned model could perform in predicting this relationship.

We address the problem of predicting the Kendall's τ between the local and the global PageRank, only considering information available on the local graph such as topological features. This is an extremely common situation given that, in general, the information pertaining the local graph is the only one that is readily available and usually of a limited size.

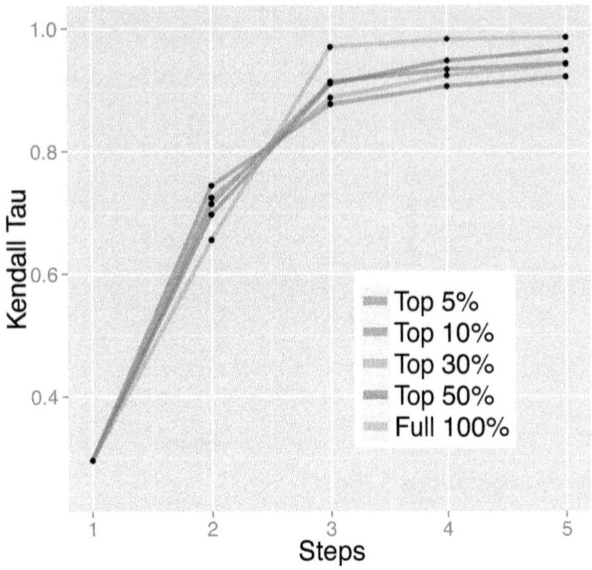

Figure 3: Growing Rings using only the nodes with highest PageRank. The plot shows the average values of the Kendall-τ at each step computed for all the subgraph.

Computing this distance accurately has a high value for service providers, since it translates directly into an estimation of the reliability of the PageRank scores computed on their local subgraphs. As a direct consequence one can apply, with different levels of confidence, methods for optimizing web sites [31], studying user engagement [18], characterizing user's session [12] or content recommendation [27].

6.1 Prediction of Kendall τ Distance

We have seen that the deviation of the local PageRank with respect to the global one can be relevant, depending on factors such as the size of the local graph and the different behavior of the users who browse it (see §5.1 and particularly Figure 2). Recall that we compute the distance comparing the rankings with Kendall's τ, since we are interested in obtaining a ranking as close as possible to the one computed on the entire graph. Although we have previously shown how to expand the view on the local graphs with nodes residing at the border, this practice might not always be possible in a real-world scenario, since service providers often can have access only to the browsing data *within* their domain.

Previous work on local ranking on graphs raised several questions related to this scenario, highlighting practical applications of the local rank estimation non only for web pages but also in social networks [9]. Critically, so far it is not clear whether there are some topological properties of the local graph that make the local ranking problem easier or harder, and if these properties can be exploited by local algorithms to improve the quality of the local ranking. We explore this research direction by studying a fundamental aspect that is at the base of the open questions in this area, namely the possibility of estimating the deviation of the local PageRank from the global one, using the structural information of the local network. The intuition is that, some structural properties of the graph could be good proxies for the τ value difference, computed between local and global ranks. Being able to estimate the Kendall's τ distance between the subgraph available to the service provider and the global graph, implies the ability to estimate the reliability of the current ranking using only information of the local subgraph.

To verify this hypothesis we resort to regression analysis. Starting from the seven subgraphs in the dataset, we build a training set using the jackknife approach, by removing nodes in bulks (1%, 5%, 10%, 20%) and computing the τ value between the full subgraph and their reduced versions. Then, for each instance in the training set we compute 62 structural graph metrics [30, 4] belonging to the following categories:

- **Size and connectivity (S)**. Statistics on the size and basic wiring properties, such as number of nodes and edges, graph density, reciprocity, number of connected components, relative size of the biggest component.
- **Assortativity (A)**. The tendency of node with a certain degree, to be linked with nodes with similar degree. We computed different combinations that take into account the in/out/full degree of the target node vs. the in/out/full degree of the nodes that are connected with it.
- **Degree (D)**. Statistics (average, median, standard deviation, *etc.*) on the degree distribution of nodes.
- **Weighted degree (W)**. Same as **degree**, but considering the weight on edges, which usually referred as node strength. As the edges are the transitions made by the users during the navigation, the weight stand for the number of times the users have navigated the transition.
- **Local Pagerank (P)**. Statistics on the distribution of the PageRank values computed on the local graph.
- **Closeness centralization (C)**. Statistics on the distances (number of hops), which separate a node to the others in the graph, in the spirit of the closeness centralization [30].

We employed different regression algorithms, although we report the performance using random forests [7], which performed better in this scenario than other approaches like support vector regression [25]. We computed the mean square error (MSE) across all examples in all sampled subgraphs. The random forest regression has been computed over a five-fold cross validation averaged over 10 iterations. The mean square residuals that we obtained is very low, around $2.4 \cdot 10^{-6}$. Results, computed for the full set of features and for each category separately, are given in Table 3. The most predictive feature category is the *weighted degree*, which yields a performance that is better (or comparable) than the model using all the features. The *assortativity* features instead, seem to be the ones that have the less predictive power on their own. This might be due to the fact the model with 62 features is too complex for the amount of training data available. On the other hand, the *weighted degree* that is the best performing class of features, contains the statistics of the degree distribution on the weighted edges. In Figure 4 the features included in *weighted degree* are ranked by their discriminative power in predicting the Kendall τ

Feature Class	No. Features	MSE
weighted degree	15	$2.2 \cdot 10^{-6}$
degree	15	$2.9 \cdot 10^{-6}$
local PageRank	10	$3.3 \cdot 10^{-6}$
size and connectivity	9	$3.4 \cdot 10^{-6}$
closeness	5	$4.1 \cdot 10^{-6}$
assortativity	8	$9.3 \cdot 10^{-6}$
ALL features	62	$2.4 \cdot 10^{-6}$

Table 3: MSE of cross validation. Average differences are statistically significant with respect to *weighted degree* and *ALL features* (t-test, p<0.01).

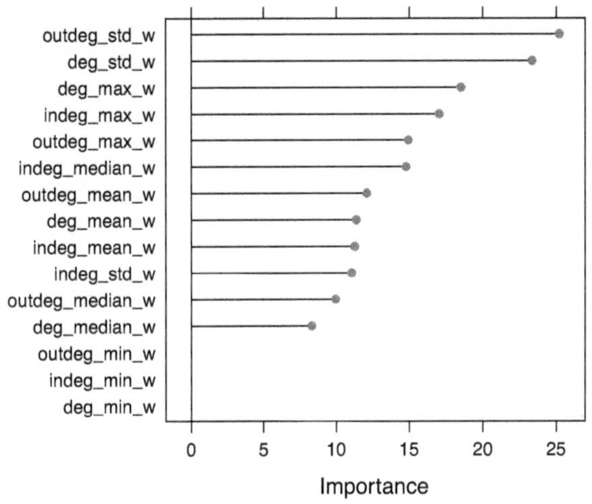

Figure 4: The 15 features of *weighted degree*, the most predictive class, sorted by importance. Note that some of them do not have any contribution to the Kendall-τ prediction, therefore just few features are necessary in order to estimate the distance.

distance using the permutation test proposed by Strobl *et al.* [26]. These features, which are based on the distribution of the out- and in-degree of the nodes, are straightforward to compute from the local graph—a very affordable task for service providers.

We then use the learned model to predict the τ values of the seven subgraphs. When we applied the predictive models learned in the subsamples to regressing the full graphs, the MSE, is less than 0.026 on average, which, even if relatively low, it is higher than the cross-validated performance in the sub-samples. However, the model was able to rank the seven different subgraphs by their Kendall's τ almost perfectly. When using all the features the Spearman's correlation coefficient between the true order and the predicted one is 0.85 (high correlation), and when we used the most predictive features (weighted degree) the correlation was as high as 0.80 (moderate high correlation). Overall, the final rankings are just one swap away (Kendall's τ is over 0.70 in this case). This kind of information can be very helpful when comparing different local sub-domains to determine which one has pages that better estimate the global PageRank.

7. CONCLUSION

In this paper we tackled the *Local Ranking Problem*, *i.e.*, how to estimate the PageRank values of nodes when a portion of the graph is not available, which arises commonly in real use cases of PageRank. We investigated this problem for a novel environment, namely estimating PageRank on a large user-generated browsing graph from Yahoo News. The peculiar characteristic of this graph is that it is built from user's navigation patterns, where nodes represent web pages and edges are the transitions made by the users themselves. Moreover, the information about the domain of origin of the users (namely the referrer URL of their sessions), is also available.

We built a set of *ReferrerGraphs* including the browsing subgraphs based on different referrer URLs, and then we studied their difference in terms of user navigation patterns. We found that all of the browsing patterns initiated from different domains exhibit remarkable differences in terms of which pages users visited next. The referrer URL (or domain) has been found to be extremely useful for characterizing the user behavior [12] or for recommendation of content [27]. With this observation in mind and motivated by the cases where the domain from where the user is coming is not available, such as Facebook and Twitter clients or URL shortening services, we performed a series of experiments with the aim of predicting from which referrer URL the user joined the network, *i.e.*, if a model can predict reliably where the user is entering our network. In general, just a few steps (*i.e.*, visited pages) suffice to recognize the referrer URL correctly because the surfing behavior is very distinctive of the domain the user is coming from.

Then, using the *ReferrerGraphs*, we performed several experiments using a very large network of sites (with almost two billions of user transitions) to assess to what extent the browsing patterns information can be generalized, if one is only provided with information from smaller subgraphs. First, we computed the PageRank of the subgraphs and on their step-by-step BFS expansion, measuring the distance in terms of Kendall's τ with the PageRank computed on the full graph. To control for the subgraph size and type, and to study the impact of the expansion strategy on the PageRank convergence, we used two flavors of BFS and three different sets of initial subgraphs. We found that expanding the local graph with few nodes of largest value of PageRank leads to a faster (74% at the first expansion step), although less accurate convergence in the long run. On the other hand, adding more nodes lead to a slower converge rate in the first steps (65%). Therefore, in all the cases where a strong convergence with the values of the global PageRank is not required, selecting few specific nodes is enough to significantly improve the PageRank values of the local nodes, without having to request and process a larger amount of data. Finally, we considered the case of a service provider that wants to estimate the reliability of the scores of PageRank computed on its local *BrowseGraph*, with respect to the ones computed on the global graph. Therefore, we performed another experiment trying to predict the value of the Kendall's τ between the local and the global PageRank, only considering information available on the local graph. We explored six different sets of topological and structural features of the browse graph, namely size and connectivity, assortativity, degree, weighted degree, local PageRank and closeness. Then we computed those features on a training set that we obtained by applying a jackknife sampling of our subgraphs, and we ran a regression on the Kendall's τ of the PageRank of the full subgraph and the various samplings. We found that a random forest ensemble built on *weighted degree*, outperforms all the other in terms of mean square error. When applying the regression to the task of predicting the τ value of the global graph with the seven subgraphs at hand, we were able to reproduce quite well the ranking of their estimated τ values with their actual ranking, up to a Spearman's coefficient of 0.8.

Future Work. We envision different routes worth being taken into consideration for future work. One line of research we plan to investigate deals with the problem of user browsing prediction. In other words, what extent it may be possible to identify what are the most common patterns of topical behavior in the network and also, to build per-user browsing models to predict what would be the page to be visited next. Further, motivated by real use case scenarios, we considered subgraphs determined by the referrer URL of user sessions; we believe that interesting analytical results could be found, when considering other types of subgraphs, such as networks induced by nodes that belong to the same topical area.

8. ACKNOWLEDGMENTS

This work was partially funded by Grant TIN2009-14560-C03-01 of the Ministry of Science and Innovation of Spain, by the EU-FET grant NADINE (GA 288956) and by a Yahoo Faculty Research Engagement Program.

9. REFERENCES

[1] E. Agichtein, E. Brill, and S. Dumais. Improving web search ranking by incorporating user behavior information. In *SIGIR*, pages 19–26, New York, NY, USA, 2006. ACM.

[2] R. Andersen, C. Borgs, J. Chayes, J. Hopcraft, V. S. Mirrokni, and S.-H. Teng. Local computation of pagerank contributions. In *WAW*, pages 150–165, San Diego, CA, USA, 2007. Springer-Verlag.

[3] Z. Bar-Yossef and L.-T. Mashiach. Local approximation of pagerank and reverse pagerank. In *CIKM*, pages 279–288, Napa Valley, California, USA, 2008. ACM Press.

[4] A. Barrat, M. Barthlemy, and A. Vespignani. *Dynamical Processes on Complex Networks*. Cambridge University Press, New York, NY, USA, 2008.

[5] K. Bharat, A. Broder, M. Henzinger, P. Kumar, and S. Venkatasubramanian. The connectivity server: fast access to linkage information on the web. In *WWW*, volume 30, pages 469–477, Brisbane, Australia, 4 1998. Elsevier Science Publ B. V.

[6] P. Boldi, M. Santini, and S. Vigna. Do your worst to make the best : Paradoxical effects in pagerank incremental computations. In *WAW*, pages 168–180. Springer, 2004.

[7] L. Breiman. Random forests. *Machine Learning*, 45(1):5–32, oct 2001.

[8] M. Bressan, E. Peserico, U. Padova, and L. Pretto. The power of local information in pagerank. In *WWW Companion*, pages 179–180, Rio de Janeiro, Brazil, 2013.

[9] M. Bressan and L. Pretto. Local computation of pagerank: the ranking side. In *CIKM*, pages 631–640. ACM, 2011.

[10] Y.-Y. Chen, Q. Gan, and T. Suel. Local methods for estimating pagerank values. In *CIKM*, pages 381–389, New York, NY, USA, 2004. ACM.

[11] L. Chiarandini, P. Grabowicz, M. Trevisiol, and A. Jaimes. Leveraging browsing patterns for topic discovery and photostream recommendation. In *ICWSM*, Cambridge, MA, USA, 2013. AAAI.

[12] L. Chiarandini, M. Trevisiol, and A. Jaimes. Discovering social photo navigation patterns. In *ICME*, pages 31–36. IEEE, 2012.

[13] J. Cho, H. Garcia-Molina, and L. Page. Efficient crawling through url ordering. In *WWW*, volume 30, pages 161–172, Brisbane, Australia, 4 1998. Elsevier Science Publ B. V.

[14] J. V. Davis and I. S. Dhillon. Large scale analysis of web revisitation patterns. In *KDD*, volume 08, pages 116–125, Philadelphia, PA, USA, 2006. ACM Press.

[15] Z. Gyöngyi, H. Garcia-Molina, and J. Pedersen. Combating web spam with trustrank. In *VLDB*, pages 576–587, Toronto, ON, Canada, 2004.

[16] J. Hu, H.-J. Zeng, H. Li, C. Niu, and Z. Chen. Demographic prediction based on user's browsing behavior. In *WWW*, pages 151–160, New York, NY, USA, 2007. ACM.

[17] J. Kleinberg. Authoritative sources in a hyperlinked environment. *Journal of the ACM*, 46(5):604–632, 1999.

[18] J. Lehmann, M. Lalmas, and R. Baeza-Yates. Measuring inter-site engagement. In *Big Data, 2013 IEEE International Conference on*, pages 228–236. IEEE, 2014.

[19] R. Lempel and S. Moran. Salsa : The stochastic approach for link- structure analysis. *Challenge*, 19(2):131–160, 2001.

[20] J. Liu, P. Dolan, and E. R. Pedersen. Personalized news recommendation based on click behavior. In *IUI*, pages 31–40, New York, NY, USA, 2010. ACM.

[21] M. Liu, R. Cai, M. Zhang, and L. Zhang. User browsing behavior-driven web crawling. In *CIKM*, pages 87–92, New York, NY, USA, 2011. ACM.

[22] Y. Liu, B. Gao, T.-Y. Liu, Y. Zhang, Z. Ma, S. He, and H. Li. Browserank: letting web users vote for page importance. *SIGIR*, 31:451–458, 2008.

[23] Y. Liu, T.-Y. Liu, B. Gao, Z. Ma, and H. Li. A framework to compute page importance based on user behaviors. *Information Retrieval*, 13(1):22–45, 6 2009.

[24] L. Page, S. Brin, R. Motwani, and T. Winograd. The pagerank citation ranking: Bringing order to the web. *World Wide Web Internet And Web Information Systems*, 54(2):1–17, 1998.

[25] A. J. Smola and B. Schölkopf. A tutorial on support vector regression. Technical report, Statistics and Computing, 2003.

[26] C. Strobl, A.-L. Boulesteix, T. Kneib, T. Augustin, and A. Zeileis. Conditional variable importance for random forests. *BMC Bioinformatics*, 9(1):307, 2008.

[27] M. Trevisiol, L. M. Aiello, R. Schifanella, and A. Jaimes. Cold-start news recommendation with domain-dependent browse graph. In *RecSys*, Foster City, CA, 2014. ACM.

[28] M. Trevisiol, L. Chiarandini, L. M. Aiello, and A. Jaimes. Image ranking based on user browsing behavior. In *SIGIR*, pages 445–454, New York, NY, USA, 2012. ACM.

[29] M. Tsagkias and R. Blanco. Language intent models for inferring user browsing behavior. In *SIGIR*, pages 335–344, New York, NY, USA, 2012. ACM.

[30] S. Wasserman and K. Faust. *Social Network Analysis: Methods and Applications*. Cambridge Univ. Press, 1994.

[31] B. Weischedel and E. K. R. E. Huizingh. Website optimization with web metrics: A case study. In *ICEC*, pages 463–470, New York, NY, USA, 2006. ACM.

[32] R. W. White. Investigating behavioral variability in web search. In *In Proc. WWW*, pages 21–30, 2007.

[33] R. W. White and J. Huang. Assessing the scenic route: measuring the value of search trails in web logs. In *SIGIR*, pages 587–594, New York, USA, 2010. ACM.

How Many Results Per Page? A Study of SERP Size, Search Behavior and User Experience

Diane Kelly
School of Information and Library Science, University of North Carolina
Chapel Hill, NC, USA
dianek@email.unc.edu

Leif Azzopardi
School of Computing Science, University of Glasgow
Glasgow, United Kingdom
leif.azzopardi@glasgow.ac.uk

ABSTRACT

The provision of "ten blue links" has emerged as the standard for the design of search engine result pages (SERPs). While numerous aspects of SERPs have been examined, little attention has been paid to the number of results displayed per page. This paper investigates the relationships among the number of results shown on a SERP, search behavior and user experience. We performed a laboratory experiment with 36 subjects, who were randomly assigned to use one of three search interfaces that varied according to the number of results per SERP (three, six or ten). We found subjects' click distributions differed significantly depending on SERP size. We also found those who interacted with three results per page viewed significantly more SERPs per query; interestingly, the number of SERPs they viewed per query corresponded to about 10 search results. Subjects who interacted with ten results per page viewed and saved significantly more documents. They also reported the greatest difficulty finding relevant documents, rated their skills the lowest and reported greater workload, even though these differences were not significant. This work shows that behavior changes with SERP size, such that more time is spent focused on earlier results when SERP size decreases.

Categories and Subject Descriptors

H.3.3 [**Information Storage and Retrieval**]: Information Search and Retrieval:Search Process; H.5.2 [**Information Interfaces and Presentation**]: User Interfaces:Screen Design

Keywords

Search behavior; user studies; search interface; search result page

SIGIR'15, August 09 - 13, 2015, Santiago, Chile

ACM 978-1-4503-3621-5/15/08 ...$15.00
DOI: http://dx.doi.org/10.1145/2766462.2767732.

1. INTRODUCTION

Over the years, the standard design for a search engine results pages (SERPs) has converged on a textual listing of ten results per page; this presentation style is often referred to as 'ten blue links.' Despite many scholars and designers questioning this convention, this standard persists. While the literature contains many examples of alternatives to this design including variable snippet styles e.g., [31] and layout methods e.g., [15], few works have questioned or considered how the number of results presented per page (SERP Size), impacts search behavior and if a different size might lead to a better user experience. Although many experimental search interfaces, in particular pre-Web interfaces, have presented more than ten results per page, and many current search interfaces allow users to configure the number of results per page, to our knowledge, the size of the SERP has only been systematically investigated in a few studies [19, 23, 25].

Understanding how SERP size influences user behavior is important for several reasons. First, users are now accessing search results via a multitude of devices, including desktop computers, mobile phones, tablets, smart watches and smart glasses. Each device displays varying numbers of results above-the-fold and research has shown that this can impact click behavior [12, 18]. Thus understanding how the behaviors and performance of users changes with respect to SERP size can potentially help guide and inform researchers and practitioners who are interested in designing effective interfaces. Second, many IR evaluations measures [11, 22, 28] make assumptions about the number of results presented to the user and how the user will evaluate these results; specifically, that the user examines results linearly and the likelihood of the user examining a result decreases exponentially with rank. This underlying user model might be insufficient if variable SERP sizes are considered. Finally, little is known about how SERP size impacts the user experience; it might be the case that presenting fewer results per page has positive psychological consequences as found by Oulasvirta et al. [23] who examined user preferences for mocked-up search result sets of varying lengths. On the other hand, fewer results may lead to increased browsing costs and increased mental load as users need to flip between result pages detracting from their search experience.

Thus, the purpose of this paper is to investigate the impact of SERP size on search behavior and user experiences. To do so, we create three search interfaces that vary according to the number of results per SERP (three, six or ten) and conduct a between-subjects laboratory experiment.

2. BACKGROUND

Numerous aspects of search engine result pages (SERPs) have been investigated including layout (e.g., ranked list, grid), ordering (ranking of results), components (e.g., aggregated search pages, query suggestion), length and content of snippet summaries (e.g., query-biased), snippet style (e.g., thumbnails) and SERP size. Below we provide a brief overview of some of the research focused on SERP design and SERP size. We also present research on screen size and position effects, which are relevant to this work.

2.1 SERP Design

A range of experiments have been conducted investigating different snippet types, sizes and features, as well as layouts and result combinations. Perhaps the most researched aspect of SERP design has been on the potential advantages of visual snippets (e.g., thumbnails) over textual snippets [2, 13, 24, 31, 34]. For example, Woodruff et al. [34] examined the usefulness of enhanced thumbnail images to represent webpages. The enhanced thumbnail representation magnified salient features of webpages so that searchers could more readily identify whether a page contained relevant material. In comparison with textual summaries and standard thumbnails, it was found that the enhanced thumbnails reduced search time. In more recent work, Teevan et al. [31] explored a variation on generating enhanced thumbnails, referred to as visual snippets, and also found that such an approach decreased the time required to identify relevant documents. TileBars [10] is another example of how researchers have used visual information on the results page to help users make better decisions about the relevance of the result represented by the snippet.

There have also been many studies on the content and size of snippets [6, 8, 32]. For example, Tombros and Sanderson [32] investigated the potential usefulness of query-biased summaries for snippets and found they improved both user accuracy and speed of relevance judgements. Clarke et al. [6] studied different aspects of result snippets which users found attractive and desirable as determined by the number of clicks the snippet received. Clarke et al.'s [6] study showed that well formed snippets with title, summary and URLs that were more readable, contained query terms and query phrases were seen as more desirable.

Cutrell and Guan [8] explored the effect of different snippet lengths (short: 1 line, medium: 2-3 lines and long: 6-7 lines) using eye tracking data. For navigational queries, they found that users examined more results as snippet length increased, but performed slightly worse. They attributed the differences to snippets being a distractor; specifically, as snippets grew longer, users would often ignore the URL. For informational queries, users performed somewhat better as snippet length increased and looked at more results when snippets were medium length.

Alternatives to the linear result list have also been explored, in particular, grid-based layouts [5, 15, 26]. For example, Krammerer and Beinhauer [15] examined differences in user behavior when interacting with a standard list interface (single column of title, URL and snippet stacked vertically), a tabular interface (title, snippet and URL stacked horizontally in 3 columns for each search result) and a grid layout (search results placed in 3 columns). They found users of the grid layout scrutinized the snippets more, and speculated the interface had promise in overcoming the position bias observed in [12] (see Subsection 2.4).

Finally, researchers investigating aggregated search have studied SERP design [29, 1, 36]. Both Sushmita et al. [29] and Arguello et al. [1] studied the differences between blended and tabbed search result pages. Even these more complicated SERP pages, which blend results from multiple sources, still tend to present about 10 results per page, primarily in list format. However, for specific verticals such as images, the number of results shown per page is often larger and grid formats are more common [20].

2.2 SERP Size

With regard to SERP size, or the number of results presented per page, there has been very little systematic research [23, 25, 19]. Although many experimental search interfaces, in particular pre-Web interfaces, have presented more than ten results per page, and many current search interfaces allow users to configure the number of results per page, to our knowledge, the size of the SERP has only been explicitly studied as a variable in a few of studies. For example, Oulasvirta et al. [23] explored the idea that showing fewer results may be preferable to showing more. In their experiment, they showed participants result lists with 6 results or 24 results, as a way to investigate the so called, "paradox of choice." They found that participants rated their satisfaction, carefulness and confidence higher for the six results per page condition. However, the study was performed using paper based mock-ups of screens, where there was no pagination (i.e., 6 or 24 results were shown on one page), so it is unclear how these findings generalize to on-screen desktop conditions, where typically only about 6-7 results are viewed at one time. Also, it is not clear whether the effect would be significantly different between 6 results per page, and the standard 10 results per page, and how the results would differ in an interactive search context.

In an industry report from Google, Linden [19] stated feedback from Google users indicated they desired more than ten results per page. However, it was observed that when the number of results were increased to 30 per page, traffic dropped by 20%. The drop in traffic was attributed to the increase in time to dispatch the page, since a page with 10 results took approximately 0.4 seconds to generate, while a page with 30 results took approximately 0.9 seconds. This report is nearly ten years old so it is unclear if the results regarding user preference are still applicable to today's searchers and search environments.

2.3 Screen Sizes

While few studies have explicitly examined the impact of SERP size on user interaction, this has been indirectly examined in the context of screen size, since screen size impacts the number of results that are viewable. Jones et al. [14] investigated the differences in search performance when searchers used WAP based mobile phones which displayed 5 title snippets per page, PDA devices with 5 snippets per page and desktop search with 10 snippets per page. They found participants using the devices showing 5 results per page would on average examine 2-3 pages of results.

A similar experiment using more modern mobile phones and PDAs was conducted by Sweeney and Crestani [30], but the focus was on what length snippet to present to searchers on the different devices. They note that because transmission costs were high (at the time), SERPs often contained fewer results per page, thus increasing page to page navigation costs [14]. They varied the length of the snippet summary, but kept the number of results per page on each device constant and set to 10. They hypothesized participants using the larger screen would examine more documents, but found participants examined approximately the same number of documents regardless of the condition.

Jaewon et al. [18] compared the differences in people's interaction styles with two screen sizes (desktop vs mobile) where SERP size was set to 10; on one interface all ten could be seen, while on the other, only 3 could be seen. This latter condition simulated the screen size of a mobile phone. Jaewon et al. [18] found for both informational and navigational tasks, participants using the small screen took longer to click on a link and had longer task completion times (though only the task completion times were significantly different). They also found participants scanned slightly fewer documents on the small screen, but scrutinized each link for a longer duration, especially the first three links. On the smaller screen, links 1-3 attracted more clicks for both informational and navigational tasks: 88% and 91% versus 83% and 90%, respectively. This suggests when interacting with restricted screen space, searchers focus more on the visible set of results and make more clicks on these results.

2.4 Position Bias and Click-through Rates

How users interact with the standard baseline SERP has been informed by studies examining where users click on the SERP [4, 7, 12, 16, 35]. In one of the first studies of click bias, Joachims et al. [12] found users inspected 70% down to 20% of result snippets in the top 6 (above the fold), and then 10% down to 5% of results snippets at positions 7-10 (below-the-fold). Essentially, the probability of a click decayed exponentially, while the probability of examining a snippet decreased linearly (above-the-fold, and the flattened out). Similar findings have been reported by others [4, 16, 21]. Joachims et al. [12] wondered whether the distribution of clicks could be used as an absolute indicator of relevance. However, they pointed out two problems in interpreting click data stemming from (i) *trust bias*, where users trust the search engine to deliver the most relevant item first, i.e., following the probability ranking principle [27], and (ii) *quality bias*, where the behavior depends on the quality of the retrieval system. They concluded users are more likely to click on highly ranked documents and that quality influences click behavior, such that if the relevance of the items retrieved decreases, users click on items that are less relevant, on average.

Craswell et al. [7] noted this as a fundamental problem with click data, and referred to the problem as *position bias*, where in the top 10 result lists, the probability of a click decreases with the rank of the document. They put forward several hypotheses for why position bias is observed. From their analysis, they showed a cascade model, which assumed the user would click a result snippet with some probability (p_s) or skip it ($1 - p_s$), fit click behavior at earlier ranks, and a baseline model, which assumed the probability a user would click a result snippet was proportional to its relevance, fitted click behavior at later ranks. Of note is that the click distributions that have been observed are based on interaction with SERPs that display ten results per page. An open question is if these findings generalize to situations where the screen and page sizes vary.

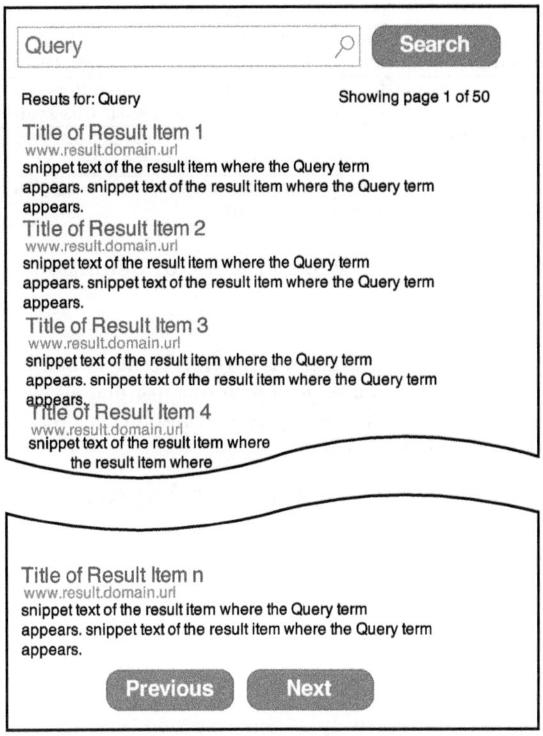

Figure 1: A standard search interface that has a query box and search button, houses n results per page along with pagination buttons. The number of results returned is also shown.

3. METHOD

We conducted a between-subject experiment where subjects were randomly assigned to one of three interfaces that differed according to how many results were displayed per search result page. Figure 1 displays the basic design of the interfaces. One interface functioned as the baseline and displayed 10 results per page (10RPP). The other two interfaces displayed 3 and 6 results per page (3RPP and 6RPP, respectively). For the 3RPP and 6RPP interfaces, all search results were displayed above-the-fold (i.e., no scrolling was required). For the interface displaying 10RPP, the first six results were visible above-the-fold. Our decision to use 6RPP was to make our work more comparable to past research. Specifically, to Oulasvirta et al.'s [23] study where 6RPP were evaluated through a simulation and to Joachims et al. [12] who described click distributions for results above-the-fold (those at ranks 1-6). Although we restrict our investigation to desktop search, we choose 3RPP as another comparison point similar to Jaewon et al. [18].

As shown in Figure 1 all three interfaces had a query box at the top and a search button. Below the search button was information displaying the number of retrieved results and the result surrogates. The surrogates displayed the title of the result, metadata about the result and a short summary. At the bottom of the SERP were buttons that allowed subjects to move forward and backward through the set of result pages. All subjects used the same desktop computer when

Factors	System	Navigate Results	Assess Results
Mental Demand	How mentally demanding was it to use this system to complete the search tasks?	navigate through the search results?	assess and judge documents for relevance?
Physical Demand	How physically demanding was it to use this system to complete the search tasks?	navigate through the search results?	assess and judge documents for relevance?
Temporal Demand	How hurried or rushed did you feel when using this system to complete the search tasks?	navigating through the search results?	assessing and judging documents for relevance?
Effort	How hard did you have to work to accomplish your level of performance with this system?	navigate through the search results?	assess and judge documents for relevance?
Performance	How successful were you using this system to complete the search tasks?	was your navigation through the search results?	were you at assessing and judging documents for relevance?
Frustration Level	How insecure, discouraged, etc. were you while using this system?	navigating through the search results?	assessing and judging documents for relevance?

Table 1: Modified NASA TLX factor definitions for overall system load, navigation load and assessment load.

completing the study, which was in our laboratory and under our control. Subjects used a 19 inch monitor and all aspects of the display, including font size and resolution, were held constant during the study.

3.1 Corpus, Search Topics and System

The Aquaint TREC test collection of over one million newspaper articles was used [33]. We selected three search topics from this collection: 344 (Abuses of E-mail); 347 (Wildlife Extinction) and 435 (Curbing Population Growth). We selected topics that had some contemporary relevance, we thought would be of interest to our target subjects and had a similar number of relevant documents available (123, 165 and 152, respectively). Our selection was also based on evidence from previous user studies with a similar system setup [17] where it was shown that the difficulty of these topics did not significantly differ. Subjects searched all three topics and topics were rotated with a Latin-square.

To situate the search tasks, subjects were instructed to imagine they were newspaper reporters and needed to gather documents to write stories about the provided topics. Subjects were told that there were over 100 relevant documents in the collection for each topic and they should try to find as many of these as possible during the allotted time (10 minutes per topic). While recall-oriented searches are not as common in the general Web population as searches where users are looking for one or a small number of items, these types of searches are still performed by many people, in particular, professionals such as newspaper reporters, patent searchers and business analysts. Because we were interested in examining traditional performance measures, we choose to use a test collection. Since the collection contained newspaper articles, we created a work task situation representing one type of user model (i.e., journalist) and one type of task model (i.e., find as many relevant documents as you can to write a story) that was appropriate given the collection and to which we thought our target participants (i.e., undergraduate students) could relate.

The Whoosh IR Toolkit was used as the core of the retrieval system, with BM25 as the retrieval algorithm, using standard parameters, but with an implicit ANDing of query terms to restrict the set of retrieved documents to only those that contain all the query terms (similar to BM25A used in [3]). This was chosen because most systems, such as web search engines and library catalog systems, implicitly AND terms together. However, subjects could also explicitly use OR, AND, or NOT in their queries. Subjects were not provided with a tutorial of the system.

3.2 Search Behaviors

Search behavior was operationalized with three types of measures: (1) interaction; (2) performance and (3) time spent doing different search activities. All of these measures were computed from log data and TREC q-rels. Interaction measures included: number of queries issued, number of SERPs viewed per query, number of documents viewed, number of documents viewed per query and deepest SERP click. Performance measures included: number of documents marked relevant, number of TREC-relevant documents marked relevant and precision at 3, 5 and 10 documents. Time-based measures included: time spent issuing queries, time spent examining SERPs per query and time spent viewing documents.

3.3 User Experience

To capture user experience, subjects evaluated the search tasks before each search, the system after each search and their experienced workload after completing all search tasks.

Task evaluations were elicited via pre-search questionnaire, which contained five items: (1) How much do you know about this topic? (1=nothing; 5=I know details); (2) How relevant is this topic to your life? (1=not at all; 5=very much); (3) How interested are you to learn more about this topic? (1=not at all; 5=very much); (4) How often have you searched for information related to this topic? (1=never; 5=very often) and (5) How difficult do you think it will be to search for information about this topic? (1=very easy; 5=very difficult).

System evaluations were elicited via post-search questionnaire, which also contained five items: (1) How difficult was it to find relevant documents? (1=very easy; 5=very difficult); (2) How would you rate your skill and ability at finding relevant documents? (1=not good; 5=very good); (3) How would you rate the system's abilities at retrieving relevant documents? (1=not good; 5=very good); (4) How successful was your search? (1=unsuccessful; 5=successful) and (5) How many of the relevant documents do you think you found? (1=a few of them; 5=all of them).

Experienced workload was elicited using a modified version of the NASA Task Load Index (TLX). This instrument elicited ratings of the following: Mental Demand, Physical Demand, Temporal Demand, Performance, Effort and Frustration (Table 1). We modified the TLX statements so they matched the target task (search) and asked subjects to make their evaluations with a 7-point scale. Subjects also completed two other workload questionnaires, which were fo-

	Interface 3RPP	6RPP	10RPP	F	Topic 344	347	435	F
Queries	10.86 (8.89)	10.53 (6.04)	9.58 (6.89)	0.38	15.44 (8.44)	7.64 (5.85)	7.89 (4.24)	16.78**
SERP views	3.56 (2.35)	2.66 (3.52)	1.92 (0.98)	4.24*	1.80 (0.86)	3.79 (3.75)	2.55 (1.83)	6.34*
Doc views	20.06 (9.09)	15.67 (7.12)	24.64 (13.25)	8.18**	14.92 (7.63)	25.11 (13.07)	20.33 (8.23)	10.58**
Docs/query	3.67 (3.44)	3.36 (5.91)	5.66 (7.08)	1.95	1.67 (2.02)	6.53 (6.70)	4.50 (6.24)	7.42**
SERP depth	7.43 (7.34)	10.40 (22.24)	10.23 (8.78)	0.54	3.84 (3.72)	15.76 (22.14)	8.45 (7.26)	7.06**

Table 2: Mean (sd) search interactions & F-statistics for interface & topic (df=2, 107) *p<0.01; **p<0.001

	Interface 3RPP	6RPP	10RPP	F	Topic 344	347	435	F
Marked rel	11.08 (8.27)	8.28 (5.88)	16.08 (12.05)	7.70**	7.44 (6.25)	16.03 (12.12)	11.97 (7.51)	9.08**
TREC rel	4.25 (4.00)	3.92 (3.21)	6.17 (4.48)	3.45	3.67 (4.23)	5.14 (4.38)	5.53 (3.23)	2.25
P@3	0.184 (0.180)	0.200 (0.161)	0.216 (0.198)	0.28	0.148 (0.173)	0.220 (0.193)	0.234 (0.164)	2.36
P@5	0.160 (0.155)	0.156 (0.129)	0.194 (0.143)	0.80	0.112 (0.126)	0.193 (0.168)	0.206 (0.113)	4.87*
P@10	0.140 (0.130)	0.142 (0.128)	0.163 (0.116)	0.41	0.095 (0.108)	0.156 (0.140)	0.193 (1.03)	6.15*

Table 3: Mean (sd) performance & F-statistics for to interface & topic (df=2, 107) *p<0.01; **p<0.001

Time	Interface 3RPP	6RPP	10RPP	F	Topic 344	347	435	F
Query	12.21 (10.72)	15.25 (1.24)	12.93 (1.08)	2.35	13.74 (1.08)	14.01 (1.08)	12.64 (1.08)	0.49
SERP	40.20 (27.17)	44.28 (57.19)	56.77 (72.92)	0.88	33.11 (55.79)	60.86 (59.64)	47.29 (49.14)	2.27
Page	300.97 (117.69)	259.81 (73.01)	261.42 (97.91)	2.10	236.22 (97.94)	291.31 (100.21)	294.67 (89.65)	4.16

Table 4: Mean (sd) time and F-statistics according to interface and topic (df=2, 107). Query Time is the time per query, SERP time is the time spent on the SERP per query, and Page time is the total amount of time spent viewing and assessing documents across the session.

cused on the workloads associated with navigating the search results and assessing the relevance of results. We included these two additional scales to isolate any difficulties arising from the varying number of results shown per page.

3.4 Subjects

Subjects were recruited by sending an email solicitation to undergraduate students at a large research university. Thirty-six undergraduate students participated (12 per interface). Twenty-six subjects were female and ten were male. Their average age was 20.4 (SD=2.6). Sixty-seven percent were science majors, 14% were social science majors and 19% were humanities majors. Each subject was compensated with $15 USD and could earn an extra $5 USD per topic for being one of the top three performers in his/her interface condition.

Subjects' search experience was measured using a modified version of the Search Self-Efficacy scale [9]. This instrument contains 14-items describing different search-related activities. Subjects respond to each item by indicating their confidence in completing each activity on a 10-point scale (1=totally unconfident; 10=totally confident). Reliability analysis of these items demonstrated a high Cronbach's alpha (0.934), so responses were averaged. Overall, subjects reported fairly high search self-efficacy (M=7.51, SD=0.97).

4. RESULTS

Both the search behavior and user experience measures were analyzed according to interface and topic. To evaluate these data, ANOVAs were conducted using interface and topic as factors; both main effects and interaction effects were examined with alpha=0.01. Bonferroni tests were used for post-hoc analysis.

4.1 Search Behaviors

Interactions. Table 2 displays the average number of queries submitted by subjects, SERP pages viewed per query, total number of documents viewed, documents viewed per query, and average SERP depth of the last document viewed per query. Participants entered similar numbers of queries in each interface, but they viewed significantly different numbers of SERP pages and documents. Specifically, those who interacted with 3RPP viewed significantly more SERPs than those who interacted with 10RPP and those who interacted with 6RPP viewed significantly less documents than those who interacted with 10RPP. Interestingly, the average number of SERPs viewed per query for those interacting with 3RPP (3.56) corresponded to about 10 results. Table 2 also displays search interactions according to topic. Significant differences were detected for all measures; in all cases the means for Topic 344 significantly differed from those for Topic 347, as well as from Topic 435 for queries and documents viewed. There were no significant interaction effects between interface and topic.

Performance. Table 3 displays the number of documents subjects marked relevant, the number of documents marked relevant that were also TREC relevant and several precision scores that were calculated using the TREC-relevant documents. Subjects who interacted with 10RPP performed the best according to all performance measures, but only significantly so with respect to number marked relevant. Subjects' performances differed significantly according to topic for three measures: number marked relevant, P@5 and P@10. Subjects marked significantly fewer documents as relevant when completing Topic 344 than Topic 347. Their P@5 scores were significantly worse for Topic 344 than the other two topics and their P@10 scores were significantly worse for Topic 344 than Topic 435. There were no significant interaction effects between interface and topic.

Time-Based Measures. Table 4 displays the amount of time subjects spent performing different search activities: issuing queries, viewing SERP pages per query and viewing documents. Subjects who interacted with 3RPP spent the most time viewing documents, those who interacted with 6RPP spent the most time issuing queries and those who interacted with 10RPP spent the most time on SERPs per query, none of these differences were statistically significant. There were also no significant differences in the amount of time spent engaged in different search activities according to topic. Finally, there were no significant interaction effects between interface and topic.

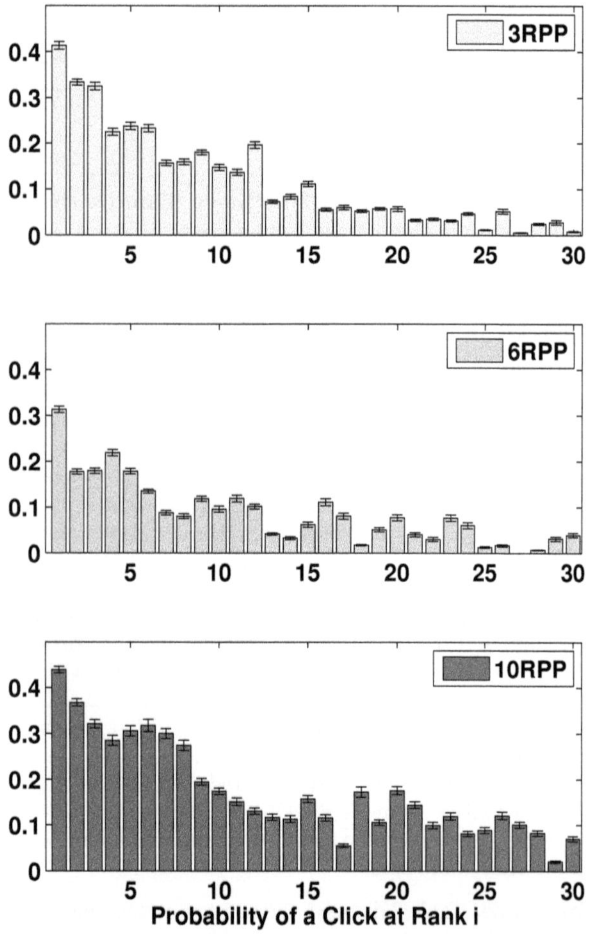

Figure 2: The probability of clicking on a snippet (y-axis) for each rank i ($x-axis$). Top: 3RPP, Middle: 6RPP and Bottom: 10 RPP. The distributions for 3RPP and 6RPP were significantly different to the distribution on the 10RPP interface.

Click Distributions. Figure 2 shows the distribution of clicks on each of the three interfaces (3RPP, 6RPP and 10RPP, Top, Middle and Bottom, respectively). The graphs show the average probability of a user clicking on a result snippet at rank position **i**. Subjects who interacted with 3RPP mainly clicked on the first 3 results (0.41 down to 0.33). A noticeable drop in the probability of a click is observed when subjects went to page 2. Interestingly, the probability stays around 0.22-0.23 for results at ranks 4-6, before another step down in the probability of a click on documents at ranks 7-12. After result 12, i.e., page 5 and onwards, the probability becomes increasingly smaller. Subjects who interacted with 6RPP appeared to be less likely to click on documents overall, but again we observe a small step change after the first page (i.e., 6-12), and again after the second page (i.e., 13-18). In contrast, subjects interacting with 10RPP, clicked with higher probability across most of the ranks, and even after the first page of results (i.e., 11-20), there is no noticeable drop in click probability. To determine if the click distributions were drawn from the same underlying distribution a two-sample Kolmogorov-Smirnov test was used. For 3RPP and 6RPP the distributions were not significantly different (p=0.3420, k=0.2333), indicating that they were drawn from the same underlying distribution. However, the click distributions for 3RPP and 6RPP were found to be significantly different from 10RPP (p=0.0046, k=0.4333, and p=0.0006, k=0.5, respectively).

4.2 User Experience

Task Evaluations. Table 5 displays subjects' task evaluations. With the exception of interest in the topic, subjects' responses to these items differed significantly according to topic. Subjects indicated they had significantly more topic knowledge about Topic 435 (Curbing Population Growth) than Topics 344 (Abuses of E-mail) and 347 (Wildlife Extinction), F(2, 107)=6.53, p=0.002 and had searched more often in the past for information about this topic, F(2,107)= 13.44, p<0.0001. They expected it to be significantly more difficult to search for information about Topic 344, than the other two topics, F(2, 107)=8.79, p=0.0003. An analysis was also conducted to see if subjects' responses differed according to interface condition. Since subjects were randomly assigned to condition, we did not expect differences and none were found. There were also no significant interaction effects.

Topic ID	344	347	435
knowledge*	2.17 (1.03)	2.00 (0.93)	2.81 (1.04)
relevance	2.92 (1.27)	2.14 (0.99)	2.61 (1.15)
interesting	2.86 (1.10)	3.14 (0.93)	3.44 (1.05)
searched**	1.31 (0.67)	1.56 (0.74)	2.31 (1.09)
difficulty**	3.58 (0.77)	2.94 (0.75)	2.94 (0.72)

Table 5: Mean (sd) responses to task evaluation items. *p<0.01; **p<0.0001

System Evaluations. Table 6 displays subjects' system evaluations. For all items, subjects' responses to the items for Topic 344 were significantly different than their responses to the items for the other two topics (note: one subject skipped this questionnaire for Topic 344). This topic was rated as significantly more difficult, F(2, 106)=20.01, p<0.0001, and subjects rated their own skill at finding rele-

Topic ID	344	347	435
difficulty*	4.03 (0.92)	2.50 (0.97)	3.03 (1.18)
skill*	2.43 (0.95)	3.42 (0.81)	3.08 (0.77)
system*	2.40 (1.14)	3.56 (0.81)	3.33 (0.76)
success*	2.46 (1.12)	3.64 (0.68)	3.39 (0.87)
number found*	2.09 (1.04)	3.00 (0.89)	2.67 (0.79)

Table 6: Mean (sd) responses to system evaluation items according to topic. *p<0.0001

Topic ID	3RPP	6RPP	10RPP
difficulty	2.92 (1.25)	3.14 (1.24)	3.47 (1.08)
skill	3.08 (0.98)	3.03 (0.89)	2.83 (0.94)
system	3.25 (0.91)	3.03 (1.20)	3.03 (1.00)
success	3.33 (1.04)	2.91 (1.04)	3.25 (1.00)
number found	2.69 (1.04)	2.51 (1.01)	2.56 (0.91)

Table 7: Mean (sd) responses to system evaluation items according to interface.

vant documents significantly lower, F(2,106)=12.56, p<0.0001, as well as the system's ability at retrieving relevant documents, F(2,106)=12.29, p<0.0001. They also felt they were less successful, F(2,106)=13.71, p<0.0001, and found fewer of the relevant documents, F(2,106)=7.58, p<0.0002.

An analysis was also conducted to see if subjects' responses differed according to interface condition (Table 7). Interestingly, subjects who interacted with 10RPP reported the greatest difficulty finding relevant documents and rated their skills lowest; while those who interacted with 3RPP reported the least difficulty. Those who interacted with 6RPP reported less successful searches. However, no significant differences were found according to interface condition. There were also no significant interaction effects between condition and topic. Taken together, these results suggest subjects had a different search experience with Topic 344 regardless of interface condition, and interface condition did not uniformly impact their system evaluations.

Workload. Figure 3 displays the system, navigation and assessment workloads reported by subjects. With respect to system load, subjects who interacted with 10RPP reported the highest values for all items, with the exception of physical demand. The difference between 10RPP and 3 and 6 RPPs is especially pronounced for mental demand. The same general trends were observed for the navigation and assessment loads, with the exception of performance. Despite these differences, no significant differences were detected.

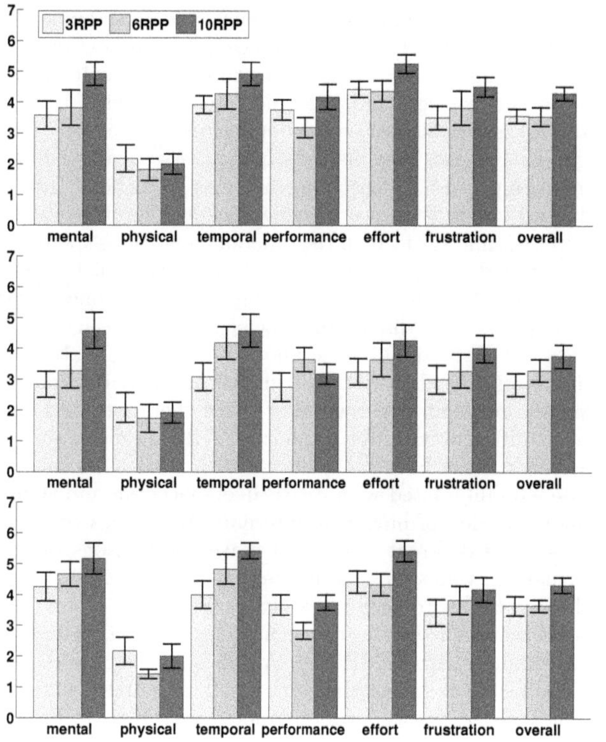

Figure 3: Top: System Load, Middle: Navigation Load, Bottom: Assessment Load

5. DISCUSSION

This purpose of this paper was to investigate the impact of SERP size on search behavior and user experience. We found that subjects who interacted with 3RPP viewed significantly more SERPs per query, which is perhaps to be expected, as subjects needed to paginate more to see more results. Interestingly, the average number of SERPs they examined per query corresponded to about ten results, so perhaps people have been conditioned to view ten results, even if viewing ten results requires expending a bit more effort through pagination. This finding is consistent with the findings of Jones et al. [14] who found that participants who used a device that displayed five results per page examined about 2-3 pages of results. However, in our study, those who interacted with 6RPP and 10RPP viewed 2.66 and 1.92 SERPs per query, respectively, which corresponds to about 20 results per query, so there might be an interaction between the number of results subjects desire to see (whether consciously or subconsciously) and the effort required for pagination.

Subjects who interacted with 3RPP examined fewer documents, but seemed to compensate by spending more time on each document they examined. This is interesting because it suggests that the additional cost and effort of paging through results led to deeper inspection of the documents, which is consistent with Jaewon et al.'s [18] results. From the click distributions, it is interesting to note that the results on the first page were treated more or less equally, but for each subsequent page, fewer and fewer subjects visited them. It might be that with smaller sets of results, subjects treat them more independently or treat them as a batch. Subjects who interacted with 6RPP examined significantly fewer documents, but spent more time formulating queries (although not significantly so). This suggests that subjects might have seen enough results to determine their queries were unsuccessful, and thus spent more time querying. It is interesting to consider how the SERP functions as feedback to the user about the quality of his or her query and how the provision of a smaller SERP size might disrupt or change this function.

We found those who interacted with 10RPP viewed significantly more documents than those who interacted with

6RPP. This is in contrast to Sweeney and Crestani's [30] findings where there was no difference in the number of documents examined according to the number of results viewable on the device. Subjects who interacted with 10RPP also marked significantly more documents as relevant. This might be because they had cheaper access to more documents compared to subjects in the other conditions. Interestingly though, there were no significant differences in the amount of time subjects in the different conditions spent examining SERP pages or documents. Given that each SERP in the 10RPP condition displayed more snippets, one would have expected this difference to be significant. Seeing more results per page might have allowed those in the 10RPP to more quickly identify or distinguish relevant documents from non-relevant documents, or since there were no significant differences in the number of TREC relevant saved, they might have been more liberal with their assessments. Those who interacted with 3RPP likely faced an additional memory burden of having to internally keep track of what they saw on different pages and make comparisons of the information, while those who interacted with 10RPP likely had fewer things to keep track of internally.

A key finding from this research is that the distribution of clicks changes with SERP size. Specifically, the click distributions for those interacting with 3RPP and 6RPP differed significantly from those who interacted with 10RPP. Essentially these participants gave more time and attention to the top results, which may have been a way to reduce the potential memory load described above. When the SERP size was small, fewer snippets were inspected and more time was spent on the top documents. These findings suggest that precision-oriented search algorithms will be of increasing importance as the page size decreases. While we did not test interfaces that display one or two results per page, our findings suggest that users are likely to be even more focused on the top documents in these situations. Further work is need to examine how screen size (i.e. the number of results viewable) and the page size (the number of results per page) interact with one another and how this is related to the user's task and search goals.

Results regarding user experience were not as revealing, but some interesting, although not significant, trends were observed. Most notably, subjects who interacted with 10RPP reported the greatest difficulty finding relevant documents, rated their skills the lowest and reported greater workload. When considered in light of Oulasvirta et al.'s [23] work these findings suggest that smaller SERP sizes might have positive psychological consequences for users since results are chunked in smaller sets. Oulasvirta et al. [23] work was motivated by the idea of the "paradox of choice" and participants in their study rated their satisfaction, carefulness and confidence higher when interacting with 6 results as opposed to 10. The potential psychological benefits of alternative SERP sizes is an interesting avenue for future research.

Although we tried to select search topics that would not differ according to difficulty, we found that one topic (344) was much more difficult than the other two. Not only did subjects expect this topic to be more difficult, they also described it as more difficult after they searched. They exhibited significantly different search behaviors for this topic and performed significantly worse according to most measures. This topic was about abuses of email at the workplace. Our subjects were likely familiar with the general topic of email, but since they were all undergraduates, their knowledge and familiarity with the workplace was likely impoverished which might explain why this topic was rated differently in the pre-search task evaluations. The differences in the system evaluations for this topic might be a result of the challenges of searching for information about email, which can be expressed in a variety of ways (e.g., email, e-mail, electronic mail). While we did not find a significant interaction effect between topic and interface condition, future studies might explore this more systematically with a greater range of topics from different points along the difficulty spectrum. The additional clicking required by the interface with 3RPP might intensify people's feelings of stress if they are experiencing difficulty. Alternatively, fewer results per page might help the person stay more focused and in control.

6. CONCLUSION

In this paper, we have studied how the number of results per page impacts search behavior and search experience in the context of ad-hoc topic retrieval. We created three search interfaces that varied according to the number of results per SERP (three, six or ten) and conducted a between-subjects user-centered evaluation. Our major finding was that subjects' click distributions differed significantly depending on SERP size. Specifically, those interacting with 3RPP and 6RPP spent more time focused on top-ranked results and those interacting with 10RPP. This result has implications for evaluation. Many evaluation measures assume click distributions that neatly decay following an exponential distribution [11, 22, 28]. However, this might be an artifact of the SERP size modeled, and prompts a question as to whether such measures generalize well to SERPs of different sizes. Further work will need to be conducted to determine the impact of different SERP sizes on the distribution of clicks. This is of particular interest as the types of devices used for search are changing from desktop to mobile and wearables devices (such as tablets, mobiles, watches and glasses), where the number of results displayed and the number of results viewable vary.

Furthermore, while we have empirically approached the problem, it would be of interest to formally model how users interact with different screen and page configurations, in order to find optimal or ideal settings for these parameters. Creating a formal model would provide researchers and practitioners with a compact representation of how interaction costs, behaviors and performance are affected when SERP size and display size changes. Such an analytical tool would help in reasoning about the optimal SERP size for different devices and display sizes, as well as other aspects of search context such as type of task and user.

Finally, we noted that different SERP sizes appear to have different psychological effects which may lead to a positive or negative search experience. While none of our user experience measures were significant, the number of users in our study was quite low. Nor did we ask the right questions or study the right constructs to really get at this issue in detail, so further work on this front is also required.

7. ACKNOWLEDGEMENT

We would like to thank to Kathy Brennan from UNC for help with data collection.

8. REFERENCES

[1] J. Arguello, W.-C. Wu, D. Kelly, and A. Edwards. Task complexity, vertical display and user interaction in aggregated search. In *Proceedings of the 35th International ACM SIGIR Conference*, SIGIR '12, pages 435–444, 2012.

[2] A. Aula, R. M. Khan, Z. Guan, P. Fontes, and P. Hong. A comparison of visual and textual page previews in judging the helpfulness of web pages. In *Proceedings of the 19th International WWW Conference*, pages 51–60, 2010.

[3] L. Azzopardi, D. Kelly, and K. Brennan. How query cost affects search behavior. In *Proc. of the 36th International ACM SIGIR Conference*, pages 23–32, 2013.

[4] J. Bar-Ilan, K. Keenoy, M. Levene, and E. Yaari. Presentation bias is significant in determining user preference for search results: A user study. *J. of the Am. Soc. for Info. Sci. and Tech.*, 60(1):135–149, 2009.

[5] F. Chierichetti, R. Kumar, and P. Raghavan. Optimizing two-dimensional search results presentation. In *Proc. of the 4th Int. ACM WSDM Conference*, pages 257–266, 2011.

[6] C. L. A. Clarke, E. Agichtein, S. Dumais, and R. W. White. The influence of caption features on clickthrough patterns in web search. In *Proc. of the 30th Annual International ACM SIGIR Conference*, pages 135–142, 2007.

[7] N. Craswell, O. Zoeter, M. Taylor, and B. Ramsey. An experimental comparison of click position-bias models. In *Proceedings of the 2008 International Conference on Web Search and Data Mining*, WSDM '08, pages 87–94, 2008.

[8] E. Cutrell and Z. Guan. What are you looking for?: an eye-tracking study of information usage in web search. In *Proc. of the SIGCHI conference*, pages 407–416, 2007.

[9] S. Debowski, R. Wood, and A. Bandura. The impact of guided exploration & enactive exploration on self-regulatory mechanisms & information acquisition through electronic enquiry. *J. of Applied Psych.*, 86:1129–1141, 2001.

[10] M. A. Hearst. Tilebars: Visualization of term distribution information in full text information access. In *Proceedings of the SIGCHI Conference*, pages 59–66, 1995.

[11] K. Järvelin and J. Kekäläinen. Cumulated gain-based evaluation of ir techniques. *ACM Trans. Inf. Syst.*, 20(4):422–446, Oct. 2002.

[12] T. Joachims, L. Granka, B. Pan, H. Hembrooke, and G. Gay. Accurately interpreting clickthrough data as implicit feedback. In *Proceedings of the 28th International ACM SIGIR Conference*, pages 154–161, 2005.

[13] H. Joho and J. M. Jose. A comparative study of the effectiveness of search result presentation on the web. In *Proceedings of the 28th European Conference on Information Retrieval*, pages 302–313, 2006.

[14] M. Jones, G. Marsden, N. Mohd-Nasir, K. Boone, and G. Buchanan. Improving web interaction on small displays. In *Proceedings of the Eighth International Conference on World Wide Web*, WWW '99, pages 1129–1137, New York, NY, USA, 1999. Elsevier North-Holland, Inc.

[15] Y. Kammerer and P. Gerjets. How the interface design influences users' spontaneous trustworthiness evaluations of web search results: comparing a list and a grid interface. In *Proc. of the Symp. on Eye-Tracking Research & Applications*, pages 299–306, 2010.

[16] M. T. Keane, M. O'Brien, and B. Smyth. Are people biased in their use of search engines? *Communications of the ACM*, 51(2):49–52, 2008.

[17] D. Kelly, K. Gyllstrom, and E. W. Bailey. A comparison of query and term suggestion features for interactive searching. In *Proceedings of the 32nd ACM SIGIR conference*, pages 371–378, 2009.

[18] J. Kim, P. Thomas, R. Sankaranarayana, T. Gedeon, and H.-J. Yoon. Eye-tracking analysis of user behavior and performance in web search on large and small screens. *J. of the Assoc. for Information Science and Technology*, 2014.

[19] G. Linden. *Marissa mayer at web 2.0*, November 2006. `http://glinden.blogspot.com/2006/11/marissa-mayer-at-web-20.html`.

[20] H. Liu, X. Xie, X. Tang, Z.-W. Li, and W.-Y. Ma. Effective browsing of web image search results. In *Proceedings of the 6th ACM SIGMM International Workshop on Multimedia Information Retrieval*, pages 84–90, 2004.

[21] L. Lorigo, B. Pan, H. Hembrooke, T. Joachims, L. Granka, and G. Gay. The influence of task and gender on search and evaluation behavior using google. *Information Processing & Management*, 42(4):1123–1131, 2006.

[22] A. Moffat and J. Zobel. Rank-biased precision for measurement of retrieval effectiveness. *ACM Trans. on Information Systems*, 27(1):2:1–2:27, 2008.

[23] A. Oulasvirta, J. P. Hukkinen, and B. Schwartz. When more is less: The paradox of choice in search engine use. In *Proceedings of the 32nd International ACM SIGIR Conference*, pages 516–523, 2009.

[24] T. Paek, S. Dumais, and R. Logan. Wavelens: A new view onto internet search results. In *Proceedings of the SIGCHI Conference*, pages 727–734, 2004.

[25] H. Reiterer, G. Tullius, and T. M. Mann. Insyder: a content-based visual-information-seeking system for the web. *Int. Journal on Digital Libraries*, 5(1):25–41, 2005.

[26] M. L. Resnick, C. Maldonado, J. M. Santos, and R. Lergier. Modeling on-line search behavior using alternative output structures. In *Proc. of the Human Factors and Ergonomics Soc. Annual Meeting*, volume 45, pages 1166–1170, 2001.

[27] S. E. Robertson. The probability ranking principle in ir. *Journal of documentation*, 33(4):294–304, 1977.

[28] M. D. Smucker and C. L. Clarke. Time-based calibration of effectiveness measures. In *Proceedings of the 35th ACM SIGIR conference*, pages 95–104, 2012.

[29] S. Sushmita, H. Joho, M. Lalmas, and R. Villa. Factors affecting click-through behavior in aggregated search interfaces. In *Proceedings of the 19th International ACM CIKM Conference*, CIKM '10, pages 519–528, 2010.

[30] S. Sweeney and F. Crestani. Effective search results summary size and device screen size: Is there a relationship? *IPM*, 42(4):1056–1074, 2006.

[31] J. Teevan, E. Cutrell, D. Fisher, S. M. Drucker, G. Ramos, P. André, and C. Hu. Visual snippets: Summarizing web pages for search and revisitation. In *Proceedings of the SIGCHI Conference*, pages 2023–2032, 2009.

[32] A. Tombros and M. Sanderson. Advantages of query biased summaries in information retrieval. In *Proc. of the 21st International ACM SIGIR Conference*, pages 2–10, 1998.

[33] E. M. Voorhees. Overview of the trec 2005 robust retrieval track. In *Proceedings of TREC-14*, 2006.

[34] A. Woodruff, R. Rosenholtz, J. B. Morrison, A. Faulring, and P. Pirolli. A comparison of the use of text summaries, plain thumbnails, and enhanced thumbnails for web search tasks. *J. Am. Soc. Inf. Sci. Technol.*, 53(2):172–185, 2002.

[35] Y. Yue, R. Patel, and H. Roehrig. Beyond position bias: Examining result attractiveness as a source of presentation bias in clickthrough data. In *Proc. of the 19th Int. Conference on World Wide Web*, pages 1011–1018, 2010.

[36] K. Zhou, R. Cummins, M. Lalmas, and J. M. Jose. Evaluating aggregated search pages. In *Proceedings of the 35th International ACM SIGIR Conference*, SIGIR '12, pages 115–124, 2012.

Influence of Vertical Result in Web Search Examination

Zeyang Liu[†], Yiqun Liu[†*], Ke Zhou[‡], Min Zhang[†], Shaoping Ma[†]
[†]Tsinghua National Laboratory for Information Science and Technology, Department of Computer Science & Technology, Tsinghua University, Beijing, China
[‡]Yahoo Labs, London, U.K.
yiqunliu@tsinghua.edu.cn

ABSTRACT

Research in how users examine results on search engine result pages (SERPs) helps improve result ranking, advertisement placement, performance evaluation and search UI design. Although examination behavior on organic search results (also known as "ten blue links") has been well studied in existing works, there lacks a thorough investigation on how users examine SERPs with verticals. Considering the fact that a large fraction of SERPs are served with one or more verticals in the practical Web search scenario, it is of vital importance to understand the influence of vertical results on search examination behaviors. In this paper, we focus on five popular vertical types and try to study their influences on users' examination processes in both cases when they are relevant or irrelevant to the search queries. With examination behavior data collected with an eye-tracking device, we show the existence of vertical-aware user behavior effects including vertical *attraction* effect, examination *cut-off* effect in the presence of a relevant vertical, and examination *spill-over* effect in the presence of an irrelevant vertical. Furthermore, we are also among the first to systematically investigate the internal examination behavior within the vertical results. We believe that this work will promote our understanding of user interactions with federated search engines and bring benefit to the construction of search performance evaluations.

Categories and Subject Descriptors

H.3.3 [**Information Storage and Retrieval**]: Information Search and Retrieval

Keywords

Federated search; User behavior analysis; Eye tracking

1. INTRODUCTION

With the rapid evolvement of Web search engines, traditional search engine result pages (SERPs), which consist of ten web documents (known as ten "blue links" or "organic results"), might become not so effective when users issue their queries to search engines. To advance the efficiency of information search behaviors, it is popular for commercial search portals such as Google, Yahoo! to blend some specific vertical results, whose contents are assembled from other data sources, into the ranked list of standard results. Since users could instantly obtain the information that they expected from relevant verticals, search behavior might be inevitably affected by these "special results". A good example of this is attractiveness bias [5, 9, 28], which shows that users may adopt their visual attention to verticals more quickly, ignoring the other documents on SERPs. It is, therefore, important to gain a good understanding of the influences of vertical results on search behaviors in designing federated search system.

Because of the special design of vertical documents, the embedment of verticals has revolutionized the way users find information on SERPs. Many prior studies have revealed this phenomenon. Chen et al [9] are among the first to propose a federated click model and demonstrate the difference in users' click behaviors in federated search. Wang et al. [28] further found the existence of presentation bias that may lead to different examination behavior on both verticals and other surrounding results, with the help of eye-tracking equipments. Lagun et al. [20] and Arguello et al. [1] indicated that the relevance of verticals could affect search behaviors, including gaze activity and cursor movements.

Although these previous works have revealed the difference in user behavior between federated and traditional search, it is still not sufficient to draw a complete picture of the process of user examination in practical web search scenario. Firstly, compared to the homogeneous presentation style of the organic results, verticals have a wide variety of presentation styles, which might lead to different examination behaviors on the SERPs. Most prior studies, such as [5, 9, 28, 29], commonly divided the vertical type into two categories: textual and multimedia. And the effects of these two types were measured and analyzed independently. However, with the increasing diversity of verticals, the content of vertical documents does not only contain one single type of items. Rather, the vertical blocks that contain both multimedia and textual snippets (e.g., news) exist widely in commercial search engines. *The examination behavior might vary on this "mixed type verticals"*. For example, Figure 1 shows an example of the attention heatmaps for news and image verticals. Interestingly, while users are more likely to be attracted by multimedia verticals [9, 28], our findings indicate that news vertical, which also contained image element in their snippets, do not attract more visual attention on the image (i.e. the users examine carefully on

---
*Corresponding author

SIGIR'15, August 09 - 13, 2015, Santiago, Chile.
© 2015 ACM. ISBN 978-1-4503-3621-5/15/08 ...$15.00.
DOI: http://dx.doi.org/10.1145/2766462.2767714.

the textual snippets without much attention on the image snippet). Secondly, previous works [1, 18, 19] pointed out that vertical quality leads to different user interaction patterns and satisfactions. However, these studies only focus on the page level effect, such as the spill-over effect [1], which means that users might prefer to interact with the web results when the vertical corresponds to the users' intention. To some extent, *this limits the in-depth analysis of user decision process at result level within verticals of different quality.* Essentially, as we demonstrate in our experiments in Section 4.1, the spill-over effect may contribute to different examination distributions on organic results, especially those close to the verticals. In addition, very little is known about *the internal examination of different items presented in the vertical block* from the previous studies. A better understanding of the internal examination will help us take a step further to comprehend the cognitive mechanisms in federated search and design better vertical user interfaces.

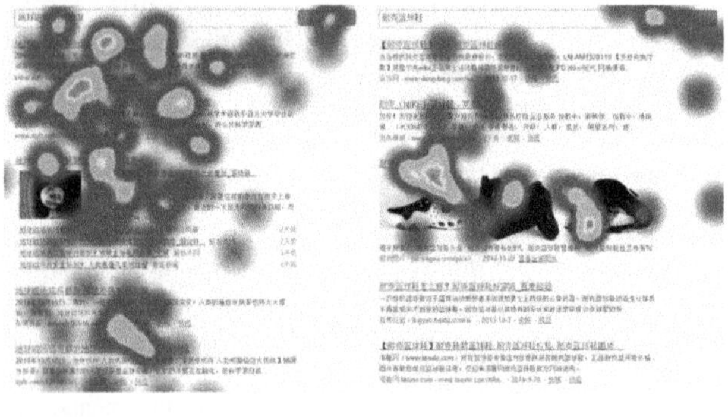

Figure 1: Users' attention heatmaps for news and image vertical on two SERPs (Left: news; Right: image.)

The contribution of the paper is two fold:

- We study the influence of vertical type, embedding position and vertical relevance on users' search examination process;
- We investigate the examination process among different sub-components within the vertical block.

The rest of the paper is organized as follows. Section 2 presents an overview of the related work. Then we thoroughly describe the experimental design for collecting user behavior data. In section 4, we provide the analysis of user examination behavior on SERPs. A summary of this paper is presented in Section 5.

2. RELATED WORK

2.1 Federated Search

How to federate search results from vertical sources into organic web search results has been extensively studied in recent years [1, 9, 11, 28, 3, 2, 21]. Most of the current researches focus on how to select the most relevant verticals [3, 2, 21], how to appropriately embed vertical results into organic web results [3, 2] and how to measure the effectiveness of the federated search pages [9, 28, 29]. Federation on the web can be also referred as aggregated search [1, 9, 28, 29].

With the introduction of verticals, the user behavior has become more and more complex. Recently, several work aim to better understand users' search behavior by either conducting user studies or performing large-scale log analysis. Sushmita et al. [27] conducted a user study and found that users click more on video results than the image and news results. Zhou et al. [30] performed a crowd-sourcing study with explicit user assessments and found similar visual saliency biases. Diaz et al. [11] mined users' mouse movement interactions and found that different result appearances might lead to different bias strengths. Arguello et al. [1] focused on studying aggregated search coherence, which means the extent to which results from different verticals focus on similar senses of an ambiguous or underspecified query. They found that users are more likely to interact with the web results when the vertical results are consistent with the user's intended query sense. By exploiting a commercial search engine log, Chen et al. [9] found that users are more likely to end his/her search sessions immediately after clicking the vertical results.

Most of the work mentioned above focus on implicit signals such as clicks and mouse movements, or explicit user assessments while we move one step forward, towards further understanding of user behavior (especially users' attention) through eye-tracking devices. We revisit some of the biases such as visual saliency, vertical relevance and vertical ranked position, and also obtain several new findings.

2.2 Eye-tracking Studies in Web Search

Eye-tracking device has been widely utilized in understanding user behavior on both sponsored search [8, 24, 12] and organic search results [14, 18, 19]. Since the eye tracker can record users' real-time eye movement information on SERPs, it helps researchers better understand how users examine results. Granka et al. [14], and Joachims et al. [18, 19] are among the first works that start this line of research on organic SERPs and they all found that there exists position bias during users' examination processes. [10] revealed the connection between the length of contextual snippet and user performance by using eye tracking techniques. Recently, Liu et al. [22] indicated that the examination process of search results might have two steps (skim and read) and proposed a two-stage examination model based on the eye-tracking analysis. Eye-tracking experiments also help analyze the users' evaluation on search results. For example, [4] showed that the personal style (economic or exhaustive) and the result relevance can affect search result evaluation. [7] predict the relevance of documents by using the gaze data. Besides, eye-tracking devices are used to investigate the relationship between eye movements and mouse movements, such as [25, 26, 15, 17]

Researchers also conducted eye-tracking experiments in the context of federated search. Wang et al. [28] found that different verticals might create examination biases on the eye movement behavior for both vertical and other results on SERPs. Lagun et al. [20] performed a similar study on mobile devices and found that both vertical relevance and positions have impacts on users' attentions. [13] investigated the influence of social annotations, which present social signals or information, on users' performance in web search. Navalpakkam et al. [23] found that the flow of user attention on non-linear page layouts (e.g., with the existence of knowledge graph components) is different from the widely believed top-down linear examination order of the search results.

Compared to previous work, our work performs a more extensive eye-tracking study that examines a variety of vertical biases and their impacts in organic results on the SERP. We also provide insights for verticals (with five different presentation styles). Another contribution is that we study in-depth users' examination behaviors on different items shown within vertical blocks, which has not been studied before. The insights provided can be helpful in assisting vertical-aware click models [9, 28] by better estimating item-level examination probability.

3. METHODS AND MATERIALS

3.1 Experimental Design

To gain good insights into users' search strategies and processes on SERPs with verticals, we designed an eye-tracking experiment in which participants were asked to complete 30 search tasks. Considering that different layouts and presentation styles of the SERPs may affect users' behavior, we implemented a controlled search engine system to collect users' interaction data. With the system, we present different SERPs to users and track their interaction, such as the gaze duration or movement patterns on the different results of the SERPs.

The SERPs we present to the users vary in three aspects that might have effects in users' examination behavior (i.e. the three independent variables we manipulated in the study):

- Vertical type (see Figure 4(b) for examples): textual, encyclopedia, image-only, application-download, news or none (i.e. organic results). Due to the existence of presentation bias in federated search [9, 28], vertical type plays an important role in affecting users' search behavior. In our experimentation, we selected five different types, which are among the most popular types in commercial search engines, and embedded them into the organic result list respectively.
- Vertical position. Since position bias affects user attention in federated search engine [9, 28], this factor was also taken into account in our experimentation. Vertical results are randomly placed at position 1, 3 and 5 of result lists, respectively.
- Vertical quality. Users' interaction on SERPs may also be influenced by the relevance of results, not only in traditional "ten blue links" but also in sponsored [8] and federated searches [1]. Therefore, both "on topic" (relevant) and "off-topic" (irrelevant) results are also included in result lists.

The *dependent variables* we aim to track in terms of users' examination are:

- Vertical block itself. This again is to study the presentation bias of vertical results under different conditions as an extension of previous work [14, 28].
- Organic results around the vertical. This is to study the users' interaction of the organic results from the perspective of eye fixation under different conditions, which is different from previous works that focus only on implicit interaction signals [1, 11] (e.g. clicks, mouse movements).
- Items within vertical blocks. This is to investigate the examination patterns and the interaction of different elements in the vertical block, which is novel and not studied in previous work.

3.2 Experimental Protocol

Our experimental study is processed in the following steps. Firstly, to ensure that each participant was familiar with the operation of our experimental system and the experiment procedure, they were asked to finish two warm-up tasks. During this step, participants only perceived that their interactions with the search system, including eye activities and mouse movements, will be recorded and were unaware of the real purpose of our study. Then, participants were asked to go through calibration processes before they start the main search tasks so as to collect accurate and reliable eye movement data. Next, every participant performed the same set of 30 search tasks, followed by an exit questionnaire. To eliminate the influence of the different levels of task difficulty [17], we verified that the corresponding results list without verticals, namely organic results list, contained the answers to these tasks, and each task was moderately easy for most participants. At the end of the experiment, participants were required to give some feedback about their search experience and compensated with approximately US$10.

Before each task, participants were directed to a task description page and given an initial query for this task. In order to eliminate the possible ambiguities of the queries, the corresponding description of each query was also displayed on this page. It is worth noting that all of these 30 queries were selected from real-world commercial search logs so that they contain the practical users' search intention. Once participants had read the task description and confirmed what they should look for, they could click the search button and begin the search processes on the SERPs. To make sure that all participants see the same SERPs while performing a certaining search tasks, we crawled the SERPs from search engines and stored them in our web servers. This allowed us to have a consistent initial SERP for each query and to strictly control the experimental variables, which may lead to differences in users' behavior. After these initial SERPs were displayed, there were no restrictions on users' behavior on the search result pages. In other words, participants could be free to behave on the SERP as usual in all ways, such as click links or scroll the screen. The aim of this design is to create a realistic scenario for federated search in a laboratory environment. Furthermore, during the search process, participants' eye movements were recorded by the eye-tracker and their cursor activities, such as click, hover and scroll, were also simultaneously logged by the embedded JavaScript code. Once users are satisfied or too frustrated to continue, they could finish browsing the SERP and click the "finished" button to move on to the next search task. It took about 40 to 60 minutes for each participant to complete the whole experimentation.

3.2.1 SERP Generation

In this paper, we focus on the influence of five major types of vertical results, which were widely applied in current search engines. We modelled the layout of the SERPs based on a commercial search engine, which ensure the realistic and natural appearance of result lists. A federated SERP in our experimentation mainly consist of one specific vertical and nine organic links. All of these results, including vertical and organic results, were crawled from the same search engine, and the presentation order of these organic results remained the same. When a participant searched a query, the vertical result (if any) was randomly selected from a pool of verticals of different quality (relevant or irrelevant) and integrated into the SERP at Position 1 (the top of the first viewport), Position 3 (the middle of the first viewport) or Position 5 (the bottom of the first viewport). It is worth noting that all the organic result lists contained the answers (see Section 3.1) to the tasks so that the difficulty of the federated SERPs was similar regardless of the relevance of the vertical. Following the pre-procedure steps above, we implemented 180 initially fixed SERPs with verticals and 30 organic-only SERPs in total.

3.2.2 Apparatus

We deployed a Tobii X2-30 eye tracker to capture participants' eye movements and deploy the search system on a 17" LCD monitor whose resolution is 1360*768. The Internet Explorer 11 browser was used to display the pages of search system, including the description pages and search result pages. As the vertical may occupy more space of the SERP, the page fold was commonly between the results at the positions 5 and 6. For identifying user examination behavior, we detect fixations using built-in algorithms from Tobii Studio. In these algorithms, the gaze whose duration was above 60ms around a specific location would be collected and treated as a fixation.

3.2.3 Participants

Altogether 35 participants (aged 18 to 25, mean = 18.8) with informed consent were recruited in our experimentation. Because subjects were expected to have a variety of backgrounds, all of these participants were selected from a wide range of majors (e.g., biology, economics, engineering etc.) of a university. Because of the calibration problems with the eye tracker, not all of their eye movement data were available. As a result, data from 32 of these participants was finally taken into account. Particularly, most of the participants had normal vision and were able to browse the on-screen web pages without wearing glasses. Additionally, all the participants self-reported that they were familiar with the operation of search engines and were confident that the SERPs that we provided come from the original search engine without modifications.

3.3 Search Tasks

Each of participants was instructed to perform 30 search tasks using our search system. As described in Section 3.1, to generate appropriate initial queries, we sample a set of "medium frequency" queries from raw search logs, which come from a major commercial search engine. And then, the original SERPs related to these queries were examined one by one, and the SERPs that contained less than three specific verticals could be selected into the initial SERP set. This setup was chosen to reduce the influence of excessive modification of SERPs and be consistent with the realistic scenario as far as possible. Finally, 30 eligible queries were selected and regarded as the initial task queries in our study.

Table 1 shows a set of example search tasks. For each task, the presented verticals on the initial SERP were either relevant or irrelevant. In order to generate the irrelevant vertical results, we use reformulated queries which are modified from the initial task queries collected from practical search logs [1, 8, 28] to retrieve the vertical. Most of the reformulated queries are generalization or specification as shown in Table 1 while the selection criteria is similar to [1] as to reflect the different facets of the query. Since the irrelevant verticals also contained terms from the original queries, the appearance of the irrelevant vertical hyperlinks was similar to the relevant ones. The aim of this is to make the occurrence of irrelevant verticals more natural and reasonable. Base on the interview of the participants, none of them noticed the SERPs with irrelevant verticals had been modified.

In our experimentation, the participants experienced one of the thirty-one experimental conditions (5 vertical types × 3 position × 2 quality conditions of vertical + 1 organic-only result page) for each task. To make sure that all tasks would be completed with equal opportunities in each condition, we used a Graeco-Latin square design [8, 16] of tasks and conditions. Based on this design, we were able to strictly control the effects of tasks and conditions. The task conditions were divided into six groups. Each group consisted of five vertical types, including textual, encyclopedia, image-only, application-download and news. For each specific type, there were six initial pages, which were split by three positions and two levels of quality, corresponding to the tasks. Thus, each participant who performed in one of these six groups would fairly complete all conditions in the

Table 1: Search Tasks and Manipulated Off-target Queries to Retrieve Verticals

Original Query	Off-target Query	Vertical
Ancient Greek Architectural style	Ancient Greek	Textual
Poems on spring rains	Poems on rains	
The 9th zone (movie)	The 9th zone (novel)	Encyclopedia
Covering the Sky (novel)	Covering the Sky (game)	
Nike basketball shoes	Nike football shoes	Image-only
How to cook spiced egg	How to cook omelet	
iTunes download	iTools download	Application
Renren desktop app download	Weibo desktop app download	
Ebola virus mutation	Ebola virus	News
Shanghai 3rd airport	Shanghai flight	

experimentation. Furthermore, to eliminate the effects of task order or other possible learning biases [18, 19, 20], the tasks in each group were presented in a random order. After asking the participants whether they had noticed any variations in search performance among those tasks, none of them detected any differences among these conditions.

4. EXAMINATION BEHAVIOR ANALYSIS

In the following section, we describe the main findings of the users' examination patterns on the SERP with the presence of the vertical results, compared to the ones with only organic results. Especially, we want to know how users' attention are distributed across different page elements (embedded vertical, surrounding organic results). Specifically, we aim to answer the following research questions (RQs):

- **(RQ1)** Are there any attraction biases in the presence of vertical results? How do the vertical type, embedded position and relevance affect these biases?
- **(RQ2)** Are there any effects in users' attention to organic results around verticals? How do the vertical type, embedded position and relevance affect these biases?
- **(RQ3)** Given different verticals and their presentation styles, what are the examination probabilities of different items within the internal vertical block? What are the common browsing patterns among these items?

Since the SERPs in our experiment are organized in a blended fashion [1, 28], i.e. the results (either organic or vertical) are formed into blocks and ranked from top to bottom, we can simply track users' interactions on different ranked positions. In this work, it is assumed that the SERP generally consists of nine organic results and one vertical result block that is embedded within the organic results. In the following sections, we first investigate user attention in terms of gaze duration on different results (ranked positions) in Section 4.1, followed by a detailed analysis of the gaze duration and movement patterns within vertical blocks in Section 4.2.

4.1 Examination Behavior on SERPs with Verticals

First, we present in Table 2 the overall results of how users allocate their attentions on the SERPs based on the different independent variables that we manipulated. The user attention is measured by the fixation distribution we obtained from the eye-tracker. The top part of Table 2 shows the attention distribution of the pure organic result lists and is treated as our baseline for comparison. Note that due to the small fraction of users' attention on the results ranked below position 5 (e.g. 6.81% for organic only SERPs), we present the results of position 6-10 as

Table 2: The user attention (eye fixation distribution) of each ranked position on the SERP when different types and quality of verticals are embedded at various positions on the SERPs. Two-tailed t-test is performed to detect any significant changes against the user attention on organic results only SERPs. Significant results are bold while * and ** represent p < 0.05 and 0.01, respectively. The block color represents the user attention's change of direction compared with organic only SERPs (red denotes increment and blue represents decrement) while the brightness of the color indicates the (normalized) change magnitude.

Position	1	2	3	4	5	6~10	Position	1	2	3	4	5	6~10
No Vertical							No Vertical						
	46.03%	27.92%	9.80%	5.43%	4.01%	6.81%		46.03%	27.92%	9.80%	5.43%	4.01%	6.81%
Relevant							Irrelevant						
Textual							Textual						
1	61.93%*	17.79%	9.36%	5.53%	3.68%	1.71%*	1	35.32%	30.07%	9.44%	11.22%**	6.55%	7.39%
3	43.39%	24.90%	16.13%*	3.05%	8.30%	4.24%	3	41.24%	27.35%	9.99%	6.73%	3.48%	11.20%
5	41.15%	20.96%	10.25%	14.93%**	4.42%	8.29%	5	43.26%	22.07%	8.77%	11.61%*	7.79%	6.49%
Encyclopedia							Encyclopedia						
1	61.6%*	24.90%	6.63%	1.25%*	2.21%	3.41%	1	33.09%	31.59%	14.56%	6.66%	4.75%	9.35%
3	45.15%	20.88%	24.97%**	2.49%	4.00%	2.51%	3	43.06%	18.20%	11.68%	10.46%*	6.15%	10.46%
5	51.61%	17.1%*	9.45%	7.49%	10.89%**	3.47%	5	54.15%	17.27%*	7.03%	6.16%	7.04%	8.35%
Image-only							Image-only						
1	78.37%**	10.48%**	8.12%	1.22%*	1.15%	0.66%*	1	42.36%	32.85%	10.31%	6.17%	4.09%	4.22%
3	38.36%	15.88%*	40.5%**	3.70%	0.91%	0.65%*	3	37.13%	18.22%	21.89%**	8.14%	5.34%	9.28%
5	20.47%**	16.41%*	12.88%	10.91%*	34.4%**	4.92%	5	27.67%**	12.66%**	15.34%	11.43%*	23.42%**	9.48%
Application-download							Application-download						
1	81.36%**	5.7%**	2.57%**	2.49%	5.52%	2.36%	1	41.99%	28.48%	12.98%	5.25%	3.85%	7.45%
3	21.62%**	19.49%	50.12%**	2.10%	4.18%	2.48%	3	35.86%	17.2%*	35.28%**	6.59%	2.85%	2.22%
5	43.62%	17.83%	4.64%	7.34%	25.06%**	1.5%*	5	46.48%	20.91%	13.27%	4.37%	11.03%**	3.95%
News							News						
1	50.55%	10.99%**	10.48%	10.28%*	3.73%	13.97%**	1	42.85%	24.88%	14.15%	3.88%	3.66%	10.59%
3	33.19%	18.94%	29.37%**	5.40%	6.80%	6.29%	3	34.28%	33.01%	17.35%*	6.20%	2.75%	6.40%
5	44.17%	19.09%	10.22%	9.47%	7.97%	9.08%	5	34.91%	30.12%	14.61%	5.78%	4.49%	10.08%

an aggregation. Not surprisingly, aligned with previous eye-tracking results [9, 28], the users' attention on the organic-only results decreases as the ranked position increased on the SERP.

We then present the attention distributions of various verticals that are embedded in different positions (1, 3, 5). In Table 2, the left and right side of the table respectively present the results of when the vertical is relevant and irrelevant. In Table 2, we can observe that when there is no vertical (organic-only SERP), 46.03% and 27.92% of users' fixations are focused on position 1 and 2, respectively. If there is a relevant textual vertical embedded at position 1 on the SERP, the fixation on position 1 (vertical) increases to 61.93%, meanwhile the one of the position 2 (web) decreases to 17.79%. This demonstrates that the vertical embedded in the first result of the SERP significantly (*p-value*=0.05) attracts more user attention compared to a presented organic web result. Similarly, by examining and comparing the attention distribution in Table 2, we can observe a number of interesting findings, as discussed below.

4.1.1 Attraction Effect

Firstly, we focus on users' attention allocation on the vertical results themselves (to answer RQ1), i.e. tracking solely the user attention on the corresponding vertical embedded position: 1, 3, 5. As shown in Table 2, we find a strong attraction bias towards vertical results once it is presented (compared to the corresponding one on the organic-only SERP). This attraction effect is strong for almost all different types of verticals at all embedded positions (1, 3, 5) when the vertical results are relevant (left side of Table 2). We can observe that there are significant increases over the organic-only SERP except for positions 1 and 5 of news vertical. This attraction bias is highly significant (*p-value*<0.01) for image-only and application-download verticals for all positions, position 3 and 5 for encyclopedia and position 3 for news verticals. From the perspective of vertical embedding positions, the attraction bias is strongest in the 3rd ranking position where all verticals obtain statistically significant increases over the organic-only SERP in terms of attention.

When the vertical is irrelevant (right side of Table 2), we can observe that there is still a strong bias towards verticals on positions 3 and 5, especially for image-only and application-download verticals. Although as expected, all the attraction bias is diminished compared to the cases where verticals are relevant. The results above are interesting but not surprising, as users can easily distinguish a vertical result block from organic results (e.g. image-only, application-download). When the vertical is relevant (potentially the vertical results are what the users are looking for), the users tend to pay more attention to the vertical results. Note that although this attraction bias effect has also been noticed in previous eye-tracking based studies [28], we investigate more verticals with various presentation styles. We also study how the vertical relevance (or namely orientation in [27, 29]) affects

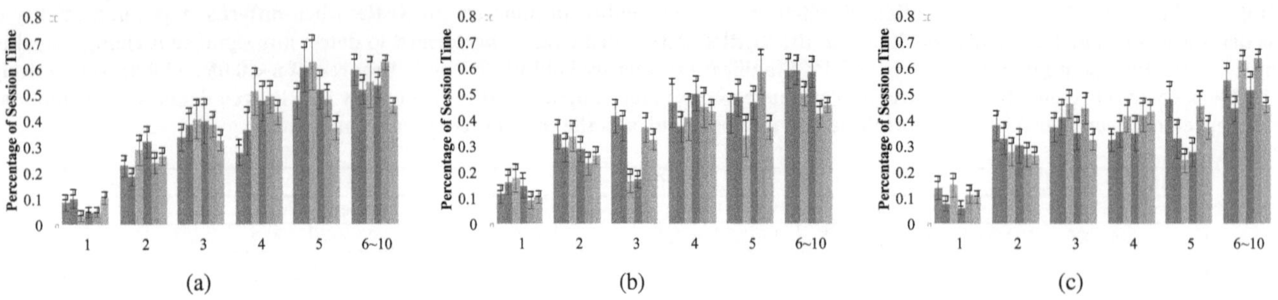

Figure 2: Mean time of arrival at each position when different verticals are placed at position 1, 3, 5 respectively.

the user's interaction and reaffirms previous results through eye-tracking (rather than the click-through analysis).

To further analyze this effect in terms of whether users are attracted by the vertical results and tend to examine them first (with respect to the temporal sequence), we analyze the arrival time distribution of different ranked positions when the various vertical results are embedded in different positions. The results are shown in Figure 2. The x-axis is the ranked positions while the y-axis is the first arrival of eye fixation for a given position (normalized by the whole session length due to user variabilities [27]). We can observe from Figure 2(a) that when there is a vertical shown at position 1 with a strong visual bias in the snippets (e.g. image-only, application and news verticals), users' arrival time to the vertical hugely decreases, i.e. the users recognize the vertical immediately. Due to this visual bias, users also tend to delay their reading of the organic results presented at the other positions compared to organic-only SERP. From Figure 3(b), we can see that users are still attracted to image-only and application-download vertical presented at position 3, but this is not the case for news, encyclopedia and textual verticals. Interestingly, for the news vertical, the users' first arrival time at position 3 is quite different from when shown in the first position (weaker attraction bias). This can be explained by the fact that information in the news vertical may be already covered in organic results with similar content. Therefore, there is no need for users to pay so much attention to news verticals. Figure 3(c) shows similar results while image-only and application-download verticals attract much attention on position 5.

4.1.2 *Cut-off and Spill-over Effect*

We are also interested in users' attention changes in the organic results after users' examination of the vertical results (to answer **RQ2**).

To study this, firstly, we plot in Figure 3 the mean percentages of eye fixation durations on organic results after users have examined the verticals. We present both cases when the vertical presented is relevant or irrelevant. From this figure, we can see that after users examine the vertical results, the users tend to pay less attention to organic results if the vertical is relevant and allocate more attention to organic ones if the vertical is irrelevant. It is interesting that the user behavior has changed when the relevance of the vertical varies.

Now we look into these two different cases in more details. When the vertical is relevant, we can observe in Table 2 that compared to the organic only results, the user attention on the results ranked below the vertical in general decreased. This is especially true for the image-only and application-download

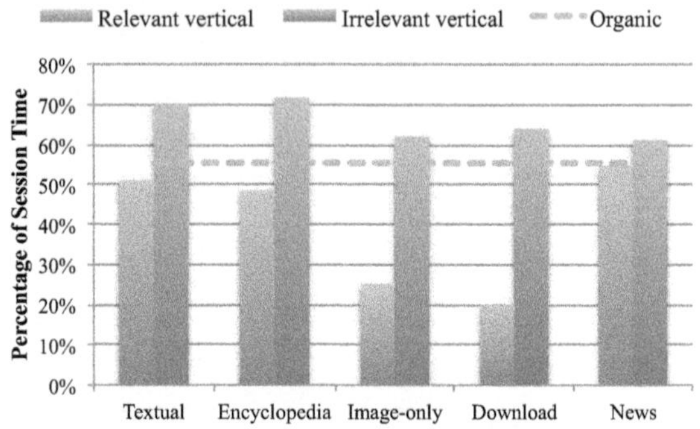

Figure 3: Mean percentage of fixation durations on other surrounding organic results after the users have examined vertical results with different types and qualities (relevance or not). For the organic case (baseline), it is after the user have examined the organic results shown at the corresponding position as same as the vertical position (at Position 1).

verticals, although not all of the engagement differences are significant.

To study how users pay attention to the organic results ranked below the vertical results after they have examined the relevant vertical results, we present the percentage of fixation duration on these lowly ranked organic results and their normalized differences with the organic-only SERPs in Table 3. We can see that after users have viewed the vertical results, they tend to decrease their visual attention on the organic results which are below these verticals, especially when the image-only and application-download verticals was embedded at position 3. Overall, we refer to this effect of paying less attention to the organic results ranked below the relevant vertical as the *cut-off effect*. From Table 3, we can observe that the *cut-off effect* not only depends on the types of verticals, but is also influenced by the verticals' positions. For example, when the verticals are at position 5, the decrease of attention on organic results ranked below the verticals is relatively limited, even for image-only and application-download verticals.

However, when the vertical is irrelevant, we can see in Table 2 that compared to organic only SERP, the users consistently pay more attention to the results after the vertical's presence but less to the results prior to the vertical embedded position. This is *spill-over effect* and it has also been observed in previous work [1] although our results indicate that the spill-over effect happens more often to those documents posterior to the irrelevant verticals.

Table 3: The percentage of fixation duration on organic results ranked below the vertical (the same position for the organic case). This is after the users have examined the relevant vertical results that vary in different embedded position (3 or 5). The difference (Diff) is calculated as (Vertical-Organic)/Organic and two-tailed t-test is performed for significance.

Relevant Vertical	Textual	Encyclo-pedia	Image-only	Application -download	News
	Position = 3				
Organic	34.61%				
Vertical	30.13%	16.70%	8.44%	13.04%	22.61%
Diff	-12.95%	**-51.74%***	**-75.62%****	**-62.32%****	-34.68%
	Position = 5				
Organic	25.27%				
Vertical	26.30%	19.27%	10.33%	6.21%	38.69%
Diff	4.09%	-23.76%	**-59.10%***	**-75.44%***	53.09%

Table 4: The percentage of fixation duration on organic results surrounding the vertical. This is after the users have examined the vertical results that vary in different embedded position (3 or 5) and vertical relevance (relevant or irrelevant). The difference (Diff) is calculated as (Irrelevant-Relevant)/Relevant and two-tailed t-test is performed for significance.

	Textual	Encyclo-pedia	Image-only	Application -download	News
	Position = 3				
Relevant	61.49%	59.90%	45.14%	52.37%	54.86%
Irrelevant	86.72%	87.74%	76.81%	63.14%	64.07%
Diff	**41.04%***	**46.47%****	**70.18%****	20.57%	16.80%
	Position = 5				
Relevant	80.97%	59.56%	46.58%	49.64%	69.81%
Irrelevant	79.92%	91.57%	68.93%	80.01%	85.93%
Diff	-1.30%	**53.75%****	47.99%	**61.16%****	**23.09%***

To further examine this spill-over effect, we also present the user attention of organic results with the relevant and irrelevant vertical results after the users have examined the verticals in Table 4. By comparing this organic result examination distribution for both relevant and irrelevant verticals, we found that it is the case that the users pay more attention to the organic results for irrelevant vertical and there are significantly differences found in encyclopedia and image-only vertical (*p-value*<0.01) between the relevant and irrelevant verticals. We also observe significant differences at position 5 when the types of verticals are encyclopedia and application-download (*p-value*<0.01). This demonstrates that this spill-over effect varies according to the relevance of verticals and can cause more visual attention on the surrounding organic results, especially when the vertical is irrelevant.

4.1.3 Summary

So far, we have extensively analyzed how users examine the vertical and the surrounding organic results on verticals of different types, embedded positions and relevance. To conclude, the findings (for RQ1 and RQ2) of user attention (measured by the gaze duration) on SERPs with verticals in the previous two subsections can be summarized as below:

- *attraction bias*: there is a strong bias towards more attention on the vertical results when the vertical results are relevant or even irrelevant but visually appealing;
- *cut-off effect*: when the vertical results are relevant, there is a strong bias towards paying less attention to the organic results posterior to the relevant vertical;
- *spill-over effect*: irrelevant verticals would increase the attention for organic results.

4.2 Examination Behavior within Vertical Blocks

Although we have gained lots of insights on how users examine results on the SERP with vertical results, however, little is known about how users examine the various items (components) within vertical blocks.

In this section, we aim to understand further the user examination patterns within different vertical blocks (to answer **RQ3**). Specifically we study: (a). the examination probabilities of viewing the various components within the verticals with various presentation styles; (b). the most common examination patterns, especially those reflect how users start and end their vertical examination. We focus on these two research questions for the following reasons:

- A good understanding of the examination probability can help better estimate the relevance of the item within the vertical, which could be useful in vertical-aware click models [9]. So far most of the research only considers using click/skip on the vertical level while utilizing the examination and click of the items within the vertical can be a more fine-grained feedback.
- Understanding better on the browsing patterns under different presentation styles could be useful in studying the decision process of how user percieve the relevance of the vertical. The sequencial information could also help in deciding how to best present the ranked items in order to fit the most relevant one to the first user examined zone.

With the assistance of eye-tracking devices, Figure 4 presents the results of the internal examination process of users. Figure 4(a) shows the examination distributions (measured by fixation) of different components (items, vertical title, etc.) within the vertical block, while (b) shows the vertical block presentation style for the five verticals. Figure 4(c) shows the detailed information on how users examine within the vertical block, specifically on the top 5 most common examination patterns and their corresponding distributions of how they start the examination and where they end their examination. For example, in Figure 4(c) (textual vertical), we can observe that the most popular examination pattern is "(1, END)" which means that the users directly examined zone 1 (i.e. item1) and then end their vertical block examination. Similarly, the second popular examination pattern "(0, 1, END)" indicates the users first examined zone 0 (vertical title) and then zone 1 (item1) before ending their examination.

With respect to Figure 4(a), we can observe several interesting trends among different vertical types. Firstly, we find that a substantial amount of attention (around 30%) has been paid to the vertical title (besides news vertical), which suggests that users pay attention to the vertical type when examining/judging the relevance of the vertical block. Secondly, the users may pay more attention to the items that contain substantial information (e.g. detailed textual snippets) while the examination probabilities for different items within the vertical generally follow the trend that the higher ranked items receive higher attention. Additionally, it is interesting to observe that users tend to allocate their visual attention almost equally on these similar components and the position of these vertical components do not affect users' internal

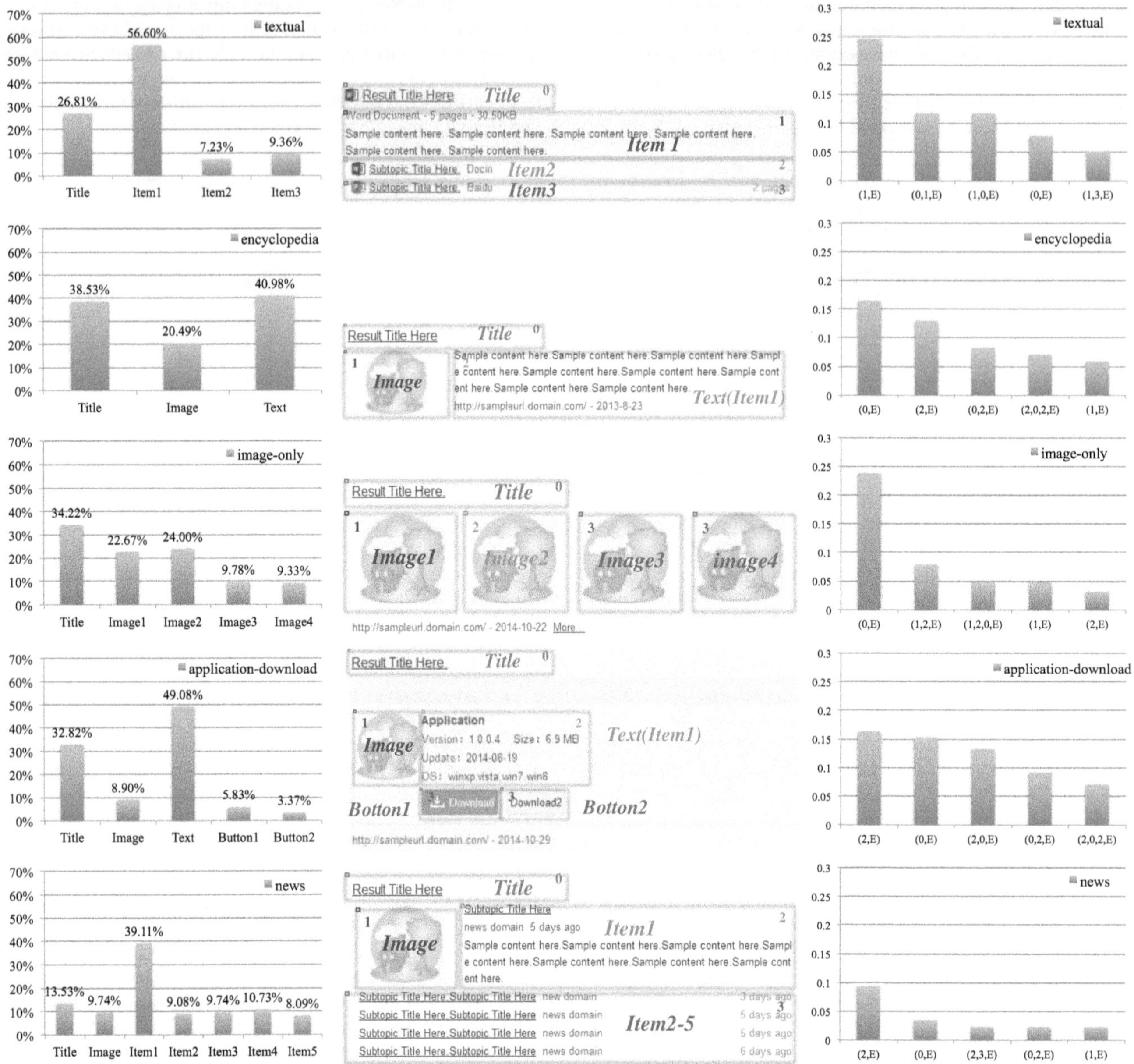

(a) Examination probability distribution of various components within the vertical block

(b) Vertical block style and its component/zone categorization;

(c) The top 5 most common browsing pattern distribution, showing the zone to start the browsing and the zone to end the browsing.

Figure 4: Examination of various vertical blocks: textual, encyclopedia, image, application download and news. Note that the different border color represents different zones in the browsing pattern distribution (red, blue, orange, green denotes zone 0, 1, 2, 3, respectively) for the ease of presentation. These borders of the zones are not displayed during our experimentation.

examination. For example, the percentages of fixation durations are almost similar (around 9%) from item 2 to item 5 in the news vertical.

We also find different attraction effects between text and image in the vertical blocks. By comparing the eye fixations on the text and image of encyclopedia, application-download and news verticals, although image sometimes (e.g. 20% for image-only) is examined, interestingly, the bias of this when examining in the vertical block is not as high as we expected. This suggests that although image in the vertical is visually appealing and could trigger strong attraction bias when the users examine the SERP, the impact of this visual attractiveness is not high after the users has decided to further examine the vertical block. Besides this, the influence of component size on the users' internal examination is also shown in Figure 4(a). We can see that, not surprisingly, the larger components might receive more visual attention and users tend to examine the components which contain substantial information (e.g. detailed textual snippets) in the vertical.

Now we discuss the examination pattern for each vertical. For the textual vertical, we found that most of the attention is paid to the first item while generally the users start or end their vertical examination using the vertical title or the first item (item1). For the encyclopedia vertical, we found that the users, similarly, tend to start and end their sessions by looking at the vertical title or the textual document while seldom using the images as the starting/ending point to examine these vertical blocks. For the image-only vertical, it is interesting to find that the second image item receives more attention (see Figure 4(a)) and is examined more often at the end of the session than the first image item. That suggests that users tend to end their internal examination within image-only vertical after they viewed the second image items. For the application and news vertical, we found similar results to the encyclopedia vertical that users mainly examines item1 and vertical title to decide vertical relevance and the image visual bias is also not high in the vertical block examination stage.

To summarize, in this section, we study the examination patterns within the vertical block and found the following findings:

- The users tend to examine the vertical type (title) and the detailed snippets of the first item to judge the relevance of the vertical and tend to skip the further results if they expect it to be irrelevant.
- After the users decide to examine the vertical block, the image shown within the vertical has relatively weak effect towards users' examination.
- The position of homogeneous components in verticals might weakly affect users' visual attention. Users tend to treat the similar components equally when they examine these items within the vertical blocks.
- The component size has a strong effect on users' internal examination. When the components occupy more area of vertical block and contain detailed information, users are more likely to examine this components and allocate more visual attention on it.

4.3 Summary

In this section, we summarize the main findings and limitations of our study.

4.3.1 Behavior on SERPs

Our first research question (RQ1) investigates whether attraction biases exist in the presence of vertical result. Focusing on the fixation distribution (see Section 4.1), we observe that not all verticals maintain strong attraction biases when the SERPs contain verticals. Essentially, the attraction effect is influenced by the types of verticals, while the vertical quality (relevant or not) does not have a huge impact. Table 5 presents the overview of different effects according to vertical type and quality. From Table 5, it is clear that users are more likely to be attracted by the image-only and application-download verticals than the news ones. Interestingly, news verticals, whose user performance differs much from the others, appear not to capture more visual attention than the organic results (even news contain image in the vertical block). Based on our eye-tracking analysis, we find that users may ignore the image within the news vertical block and treat the news items equally with the other organic results.

We are also interested in whether verticals affect users' attention on organic results (RQ2). Based on the analysis of user interactions after examining the vertical results, we find users may significantly change their behavior on organic results when they notice the presence of vertical. It is interesting to show that users tend to reduce their attention on the organic results ranked below

Table 5: The overview of three user behavior effect on the SERPs. "•" represents the significant results with the corresponding effect, and "○" represents the weak effect (exists but is not significant) of the corresponding vertical type. "–" means the corresponding effect did not perform in this vertical.

	Attraction Effect		Cut-off Effect		Spill-over Effect
	Relevant	Irrelevant	Relevant	Irrelevant	
Textual	•	-	-	-	○
Encyclo-pedia	•	○	○	-	•
Image-only	•	•	•	-	•
Application -download	•	•	•	-	•
News	○	○	-	-	○

the relevant vertical, especially for image-only and application-download. The results of our study reveal that this *cut-off effect* widely exists in the federated search behavior. However, as shown in Table 5, we can observe that this is not the case when the irrelevant vertical results are presented. Besides this, we also focus on the spill-over effect, which has been observed in prior work. We further demonstrate that users would pay more attention on organic results when the irrelevant vertical is placed on the SERPs.

4.3.2 Internal Examination within Vertical

Our third research question (RQ3) focus on the internal examination process within the vertical blocks. In our experiment, it is interesting to observe that different vertical types would also lead to a wide variety of internal examination behavior. We find that users perfer to examine the vertical title and the detail snippets of the first item to judge the relevance and skip the further results. Another interesting finding is that images do not perform a strong attraction effect when users has decided to examine the vertical blocks. In our experiment, we also find the size of components may also affect users' visual attention.

4.3.3 Limitations

There are several potential limitations in our study. Firstly, we mainly focused on informational and transactional search tasks and did not explore tasks with navigational search intent [6, 20]. Because the first result for the navigational search is often the destination site, it is difficult to distinguish the effects of verticals from the task type bias. Secondly, to concentrate on the influence of verticals and create a controlled lab experiment, we did not take multiple verticals into account. In real life, more than one vertical might be presented on SERPs. This might also affect different user behavior.

5. CONCLUSIONS AND FUTURE WORK

As more vertical results are adopted in the Web search, it is necessary to better understand the influence of vertical results on user decision strategies. In this paper, we present an in-depth study using eye-tracking techniques to explore user examination behavior on federated search. Based on the data collected from a controlled experimentation, we systematically analyze user attention both at page level and result level. Our results suggest three interesting effect in federated search. Firstly, we find attraction effect of verticals, which has been observed in existing studies [9, 28], is affected by vertical types and users' search intention. While image-only and application-download verticals has the strongest attraction effect, it is interesting to note that news verticals seem not to attract more users attention than organic results. Secondly, we demonstrate, for the first time, that user may drastically reduce their visual attention on organic results, after examining the relevant verticals. In other words, users' examination on organic may be "cut off" by the placement of vertical results. In our experimentation, the SERPs with application-download verticals perform the most significant *cut-off effect*, followed by the image-only. Then, we confirm the *spill-over effect* also has an influence on users' examination behavior. To take it a step further, we find that the spill-over effect has some special "orientations" in federated search, which means that users prefer to pay more attention on the organic results, when the verticals are irrelevant or off topic.

The internal examination of verticals is another key concern in our study. As most of prior work focused on the vertical effect at page level, this is, to our knowledge, the first quantitative investigation on the internal examination of verticals. Interestingly, our findings show there is a shrap difference in users' attention for the different types of vertical. Interesting directions for future work involve extending this work and developing the popular adopted evaluation metrics based our findings so that they can better correlate with the user preferences on the SERPs with verticals. Moreover, predicting and modeling the users behavior with these three effects on federated search is another interesting challenge in our future work.

6. ACKNOWLEDGMENTS

This work was supported by National Key Basic Research Program (2015CB358700), Tsinghua-Samsung Joint Lab, Tsinghua University Initiative Scientific Research Program (2014Z21032), and Natural Science Foundation (61472206) of China. Part of the work has been done at the Tsinghua-NUS NExT Search Centre, which is supported by the Singapore National Research Foundation & Interactive Digital Media R&D Program Office, MDA under research grant (WBS:R-252-300-001-490).

7. REFERENCES

[1] J. Arguello and R. Capra. The effects of vertical rank and border on aggregated search coherence and search behavior. In *Proceedings of the 23rd ACM International Conference on Conference on Information and Knowledge Management*, pages 539–548. ACM, 2014.

[2] J. Arguello, F. Diaz, and J. Callan. Learning to aggregate vertical results into web search results. In *Proceedings of the 20th ACM international conference on Information and knowledge management*, pages 201–210. ACM, 2011.

[3] J. Arguello, F. Diaz, J. Callan, and J.-F. Crespo. Sources of evidence for vertical selection. In *Proceedings of the 32nd international ACM SIGIR conference on Research and development in information retrieval*, pages 315–322. ACM, 2009.

[4] A. Aula, P. Majaranta, and K.-J. Räihä. Eye-tracking reveals the personal styles for search result evaluation. In *Human-Computer Interaction-INTERACT 2005*, pages 1058–1061. Springer, 2005.

[5] J. Bar-Ilan, K. Keenoy, M. Levene, and E. Yaari. Presentation bias is significant in determining user preference for search results - a user study. *Journal of the American Society for Information Science and Technology*, 60(1):135–149, 2009.

[6] A. Broder. A taxonomy of web search. In *ACM Sigir forum*, volume 36, pages 3–10. ACM, 2002.

[7] G. Buscher, A. Dengel, and L. van Elst. Eye movements as implicit relevance feedback. In *CHI'08 extended abstracts on Human factors in computing systems*, pages 2991–2996. ACM, 2008.

[8] G. Buscher, S. T. Dumais, and E. Cutrell. The good, the bad, and the random: an eye-tracking study of ad quality in web search. In *Proceedings of the 33rd international ACM SIGIR conference on Research and development in information retrieval*, pages 42–49. ACM, 2010.

[9] D. Chen, W. Chen, H. Wang, Z. Chen, and Q. Yang. Beyond ten blue links: enabling user click modeling in federated web search. In *Proceedings of the fifth ACM international conference on Web search and data mining*, pages 463–472. ACM, 2012.

[10] E. Cutrell and Z. Guan. What are you looking for?: an eye-tracking study of information usage in web search. In *Proceedings of the SIGCHI conference on Human factors in computing systems*, pages 407–416. ACM, 2007.

[11] F. Diaz, R. White, G. Buscher, and D. Liebling. Robust models of mouse movement on dynamic web search results pages. In *Proceedings of the 22nd ACM international conference on Conference on information & knowledge management*, pages 1451–1460. ACM, 2013.

[12] S. T. Dumais, G. Buscher, and E. Cutrell. Individual differences in gaze patterns for web search. In *Proceedings of the third symposium on Information interaction in context*, pages 185–194. ACM, 2010.

[13] J. Fernquist and E. H. Chi. Perception and understanding of social annotations in web search. In *Proceedings of the 22nd international conference on World Wide Web*, pages 403–412. International World Wide Web Conferences Steering Committee, 2013.

[14] L. A. Granka, T. Joachims, and G. Gay. Eye-tracking analysis of user behavior in www search. In *Proceedings of the 27th annual international ACM SIGIR conference on Research and development in information retrieval*, pages 478–479. ACM, 2004.

[15] Q. Guo and E. Agichtein. Towards predicting web searcher gaze position from mouse movements. In *CHI'10 Extended Abstracts on Human Factors in Computing Systems*, pages 3601–3606. ACM, 2010.

[16] K. Hofmann, B. Mitra, F. Radlinski, and M. Shokouhi. An eye-tracking study of user interactions with query auto completion. In *Proceedings of the 23rd ACM International Conference on Conference on Information and Knowledge Management*, pages 549–558. ACM, 2014.

[17] J. Huang, R. White, and G. Buscher. User see, user point: gaze and cursor alignment in web search. In *Proceedings of the SIGCHI Conference on Human Factors in Computing Systems*, pages 1341–1350. ACM, 2012.

[18] T. Joachims, L. Granka, B. Pan, H. Hembrooke, and G. Gay. Accurately interpreting clickthrough data as implicit feedback. In *Proceedings of the 28th annual international ACM SIGIR conference on Research and development in information retrieval*, pages 154–161. ACM, 2005.

[19] T. Joachims, L. Granka, B. Pan, H. Hembrooke, F. Radlinski, and G. Gay. Evaluating the accuracy of implicit feedback from clicks and query reformulations in web search. *ACM Transactions on Information Systems (TOIS)*, 25(2):7, 2007.

[20] D. Lagun, C.-H. Hsieh, D. Webster, and V. Navalpakkam. Towards better measurement of attention and satisfaction in mobile search. In *Proceedings of the 37th international ACM SIGIR conference on Research & development in information retrieval*, pages 113–122. ACM, 2014.

[21] X. Li, Y.-Y. Wang, and A. Acero. Learning query intent from regularized click graphs. In *Proceedings of the 31st annual international ACM SIGIR conference on Research and development in information retrieval*, pages 339–346. ACM, 2008.

[22] Y. Liu, C. Wang, K. Zhou, J. Nie, M. Zhang, and S. Ma. From skimming to reading: A two-stage examination model for web search. In *Proceedings of the 23rd ACM International Conference on Conference on Information and Knowledge Management*, pages 849–858. ACM, 2014.

[23] V. Navalpakkam, L. Jentzsch, R. Sayres, S. Ravi, A. Ahmed, and A. Smola. Measurement and modeling of eye-mouse behavior in the presence of nonlinear page layouts. In *Proceedings of the 22nd international conference on World Wide Web*, pages 953–964. International World Wide Web Conferences Steering Committee, 2013.

[24] M. Richardson, E. Dominowska, and R. Ragno. Predicting clicks: estimating the click-through rate for new ads. In *Proceedings of the 16th international conference on World Wide Web*, pages 521–530. ACM, 2007.

[25] K. Rodden and X. Fu. Exploring how mouse movements relate to eye movements on web search results pages. *Web Information Seeking and Interaction*, pages 29–32, 2007.

[26] K. Rodden, X. Fu, A. Aula, and I. Spiro. Eye-mouse coordination patterns on web search results pages. In *CHI'08 Extended Abstracts on Human Factors in Computing Systems*, pages 2997–3002. ACM, 2008.

[27] S. Sushmita, H. Joho, M. Lalmas, and R. Villa. Factors affecting click-through behavior in aggregated search interfaces. In *Proceedings of the 19th ACM international conference on Information and knowledge management*, pages 519–528. ACM, 2010.

[28] C. Wang, Y. Liu, M. Zhang, S. Ma, M. Zheng, J. Qian, and K. Zhang. Incorporating vertical results into search click models. In *Proceedings of the 36th international ACM SIGIR conference on Research and development in information retrieval*, pages 503–512. ACM, 2013.

[29] K. Zhou, R. Cummins, M. Lalmas, and J. M. Jose. Evaluating aggregated search pages. In *Proceedings of the 35th international ACM SIGIR conference on Research and development in information retrieval*, pages 115–124. ACM, 2012.

[30] K. Zhou, R. Cummins, M. Lalmas, and J. M. Jose. Which vertical search engines are relevant? In *Proceedings of the 22nd international conference on World Wide Web*, pages 1557–1568. International World Wide Web Conferences Steering Committee, 2013.

Unconscious Physiological Effects of Search Latency on Users and Their Click Behaviour

Miguel Barreda-Ángeles
Barcelona Media
Barcelona, Spain
miguel.barreda@barcelonamedia.org

Ioannis Arapakis
Yahoo Labs
Barcelona, Spain
arapakis@yahoo-inc.com

Xiao Bai
Yahoo Labs
Barcelona, Spain
xbai@yahoo-inc.com

B. Barla Cambazoglu
Yahoo Labs
Barcelona, Spain
barla@yahoo-inc.com

Alexandre Pereda-Baños
Barcelona Media
Barcelona, Spain
alexandre.pereda@barcelonamedia.org

ABSTRACT

Understanding the impact of a search system's response latency on its users' searching behaviour has been recently an active research topic in the information retrieval and human-computer interaction areas. Along the same line, this paper focuses on the user impact of search latency and makes the following two contributions. First, through a controlled experiment, we reveal the physiological effects of response latency on users and show that these effects are present even at small increases in response latency. We compare these effects with the information gathered from self-reports and show that they capture the nuanced attentional and emotional reactions to latency much better. Second, we carry out a large-scale analysis using a web search query log obtained from Yahoo to understand the change in the way users engage with a web search engine under varying levels of increasing response latency. In particular, we analyse the change in the click behaviour of users when they are subject to increasing response latency and reveal significant behavioural differences.

Categories and Subject Descriptors

H.1.2 [**Models and Principles**]: User/Machine Systems—*Human factors*; H.3.3 [**Information Storage and Retrieval**]: Information Search and Retrieval

Keywords

Web search engine; response latency; user study; physiological signals; user behaviour; query log analysis; click behaviour

SIGIR'15, August 09 - 13, 2015, Santiago, Chile.

DOI: http://dx.doi.org/10.1145/2766462.2767719.

1. INTRODUCTION

Improving the efficiency of search systems has been an active research area in the last few decades. So far, most research in this direction had a very system-oriented viewpoint, specifically focusing on reducing the financial costs involved in the search process. Until recently, the impact of efficiency improvements on users' searching behaviour and experience were left unexplored. However, with the ever-growing competition in online search systems for attracting users and the increasing emphasis on both short- and long-term user engagement, this has started to change. In particular, a new line of research was born to investigate the impact of search response latency on user behaviour and engagement. Our work is an addition to this line of research. Herein, we specifically focus on the physiological effects of latency increase on users and are especially interested in the cases where the latency increase is not very large.

Research on human information processing has consistently demonstrated that human beings are not consciously aware of the mental processes determining their behaviour [21, 23]. Such unconscious influences do not need to be restricted to basic or low-level mental processes, but can also reach high-level psychological processes like motivations, preferences, or complex behaviours [5]. This has obvious implications when it comes to the assessment of user experience in human-computer interaction (HCI) contexts. For example, previous research in the context of web search has shown that response latency values lower than a certain threshold are unnoticeable by the users and, therefore, inconsequential in terms of user experience [1]. However, the conclusions drawn in earlier studies are based on self-reported methods (i.e., methods in which the users are explicitly asked to assess their experience), which are inherently limited as, obviously, the users cannot verbally report information that is not consciously available to them. Therefore, the possibility that even small latency increases, not consciously perceived by users, could affect the experience of using search engines cannot be completely dismissed.

Psychophysiological methods can be very helpful in unveiling attentional and emotional reactions that are not consciously available to us. During the last years, the use of this kind of methods has spread over different fields such as psychology, marketing, and HCI. Besides the fact that they provide information on unconscious processes, other advantages of these methods include their high temporal and spacial resolution, and their robustness against cognitive biases (e.g., social desirability bias). Hence, they always provide "honest" responses. Nevertheless, when using psychophysiological methods, since there is not a direct question to the subject, there is not a direct answer either. The information on the research questions has to be inferred from the variations on the physiological signals and the way they are related to more or less complex psychological constructs. Therefore, physiological data is often used to draw a picture of the cognitive or emotional state of the user.

In this study, we are interested in the impact of response latency increase on user behaviour in web search and, more specifically, in smaller latency increases that may not be consciously perceived by the users. To this end, we employ two different approaches: a small-scale controlled user study and a large-scale query log analysis. In our controlled study, we use physiological methods (electro-dermal activity, electromyography) to get information on the subtle emotional reactions of the users and how they are affected by increasing response latency. We follow the standard approach to research with physiological methods. This approach relies on the bifactorial model of emotions [7], involving two factors: arousal (the intensity of the emotion) and valence (how positive or negative the emotion is). Although this approach requires the use of physical sensors, the sensors do not invade user's privacy and can capture short-term changes not measurable by other means. In our query log analysis, we focus on the variation in the click behaviour of users. The large size of the query log we deal with enables us to observe effects, which were not easy to observe through a small-scale user study. In general, the two approaches are complementary and allow for a more accurate and holistic investigation of the effects of response latency in web search.

The following summarizes our contributions and findings.

- We perform a small-scale controlled experiment and demonstrate the effects of small increases in response latency, using physiological measures of arousal and valence. We compare and contrast these physiological signals with information gathered from self-reports and show that the former are more effective in capturing the attentional and emotional reactions to increasing response latency. We show that there are sizeable effects on users' physiological reactions, even though such effects are not observed in self-reported measures.
- We conduct a large-scale analysis using query logs obtained from Yahoo Web Search and gain insights about the change in the click behaviour of users. In particular, we analyze how a user's click behaviour is affected when the response latency differs upon submission of the same query by the user at different times (under the constraint that retrieved results are identical). This analysis shows that, on average, even small increases in response latency leads to a statistically significant decrease in click likelihood.

The rest of the paper is organised as follows. Section 2 provides a brief summary of the related work on the user impact of search latency. The details of our controlled user study and query log analysis, together with the experimental results, are presented in Sections 3 and 4, respectively. We conclude the paper in Section 5.

2. RELATED WORK

A recent line of work focused on modelling the effort users spent in searching and the corresponding gains in interactive information retrieval [2, 3, 28]. However, in these studies, the response latency was not the main subject under investigation. A relatively older line of research looked into the impact of page load time on the web browsing behaviour of users [9, 11, 12, 13, 20, 24, 30]. A more relevant line of research studied the impact of response latency on user behaviour in the web search context [1, 8, 18, 26, 31]. Herein, we survey only this latter line of research as it has a much higher overlap with the scope of our work.

Schurman and Brutlag [26] conducted a bucket test with live search engine traffic, exposing web search users to different response latency levels. Their study revealed that users who were exposed to higher response latency issued fewer search queries compared to a control group with no added latency. In particular, the authors observed that increasing the response latency by 400ms led to a drop of 0.59% in the daily search volume of affected users. They also observed that the negative effect on the search volume was persistent for a certain period of time even after the latency had returned to the original levels. The study of [26] relied on server-side delays, essentially modelling only the additional server processing time. In our user study, we use client-side delays allowing us to have a greater control on the end-to-end latency actually experienced by the users. Moreover, in our query log analysis, we analyse the impact of latency on click behaviour of users, instead of their querying behaviour.

Arapakis et al. [1] conducted a controlled user study, where participants were exposed to different response latency levels while querying two web search engine front-ends. The study revealed interesting differences in the way users perceived the latency. For example, the users of a fast search engine were found to be more likely to notice the added delays than the users of a slow search engine. In most cases, the users could not notice added latency delays below 500ms. However, when the added delays were above 1,000ms, the users were very likely to notice them. Significant differences were also observed in the reported positive and negative affect scores at post-task, between the fast and slow search engines. The authors also reported a noticeable decrease in the perceived system usability as latency values increased. Hence, the tendency to overestimate or underestimate system performance biased users' interpretations of search interactions and system usability. The work of Arapakis et al. [1] also involved a large-scale query log analysis that shows the change in the click behaviour of users due to increasing latency. The authors showed that, when the response latency is too high, people prefer to browse the returned results on the search engine result page instead of issuing new queries to the search engine. In our query log analysis, we adopt a slightly different experimental methodology than the one used in [1] and also focus on the effects at much lower increases in latency.

A study conducted by Teevan et al. [31] involved a query log analysis on the impact of increasing response latency on user engagement. Similar to the finding in Arapakis et al. [1], with increasing response latency, the authors observed a decrease in the likelihood that the user will click on the search results. Moreover, the authors observed an increase in the time the users issue the first click on the search result page as the response latency increases. Both findings point out the negative consequences of slow response on user engagement.

Brutlag et al. [8] conducted a user study where the participants interacted with two search interfaces serving their results at controlled latency values (one with low latency and one with high latency). The users stated their preferences between the two interfaces through a questionnaire. The findings of the study were mostly inconclusive regarding the impact of response latency on user preferences. Our work complements the work of Brutlag et al. by showing that self-reported studies are not adequate to demonstrate the effects of increasing latency, but physiological effects on users do exist and can be measured by other means.

Maxwell and Azzopardi [18] verified the validity of five different hypotheses (taken from information foraging and search economic theories) about how users' search behaviour should change when faced with delays. The study involved 48 participants who interacted with four different search interfaces with different types of delays (no delay, only query response delay, only document download delay, and both query response and document download delays). The study found strong support for the three of the hypotheses.

With respect to the above-mentioned bucket test [26], user studies [1, 8, 18], and query log analyses [1, 31], the main novelty of our work is in the reported psychophysiological measurements that aim to reveal the unconscious effects of small response latency increases on users. Our work shows that there are sizeable effects on users' physiological reactions to increasing response latency and physiological measurements are more effective in capturing these reactions than the information gathered by self-reported studies. To the best of our knowledge, no such measurements were reported in literature before.

3. CONTROLLED USER STUDY

To understand the impact of increasing response latency on users' search behaviour, we carried out a controlled experiment in which we examined users' interactions with Yahoo Web Search. The goal of the study was to demonstrate the effects on users' experience (more specifically, on their engagement with the search engine and satisfaction with the provided service). We note that most of the response latency values used in this study were lower than what the literature has claimed as the threshold for conscious detection of the delay [1]. The reason for that is because we want to show that, even if these small latencies are unnoticeable, they produce observable reactions in the users. Applied to our object of interest, it seemed logical to expect that if high response latency produces a worse emotional experience in the users, we would find a more negative (in the valence domain) and more intense (in the arousal domain) emotional reaction. Moreover, we combined the measurement of physiological aspects of emotions with self-reported measures of affect, attention, and usability of the system, all known constituent of engagement [19, 22]. This approach allowed us to explore both conscious and "not-necessarily" conscious aspects of the user experience and obtain an accurate picture of how lower or higher latency values affect it.

3.1 Experimental Design

The experiment used a repeated-measures design with one independent variable: search latency (with four levels in milliseconds: "0", "500", "750", and "1,000"). The search latency was controlled using a client-side script that adjusted the latency by a desired amount of delay. The dependent variables were (i) experienced positive and negative affect, (ii) level of focused attention, (iii) perceived system usability, and (iv) participants' physiological responses.

Each of the participants carried out four search tasks, one for each of the four latency conditions. To control for order effects, we randomised the task assignment. The search tasks involved submitting as many navigational queries as possible, selected out of a list of 200 web domains, and retrieving the associated URL within eight minutes.[1] Compared to other types of queries (e.g., informational or commercial), navigational queries introduce a smaller cognitive load to the searcher and promote a convergence in the search intent across all users. An additional advantage is that they do not require native-level knowledge of the language used. Therefore, by mitigating the effort of query formulation, our participants were able to experience the latency effect more effectively. Other types of search queries and levels of task complexity may interact differently with the impact of search latency. However, we leave this investigation for future work. The web domains for constructing the navigational queries were selected from Alexa.[2]

3.2 Apparatus

We used a desktop computer equipped with an LCD monitor, a keyboard, and a mouse. In the background, we ran a custom-made JavaScript code that allowed us to control the search latency. Moreover, the script captured a series of browser events (e.g., mouseover, click), and recorded the timestamps of every submitted query and search result page rendered in response to a query. The script was deployed using the Greasemonkey extension[3] in a Mozilla Firefox web browser. The physiological data were recorded using a Biopac MP-150 Data Acquisition System,[4] using a sampling rate of 1000Hz. The AcqKnowledge 4.2 software was used for the storage and processing of the data while an in-house application, written in Python, was used to synchronise the physiological data with the query submission times.

3.3 Psychophysiological Measures of Engagement

To analyse the emotional reactions of participants, we recorded two types of physiological measures: (i) electrodermal activity (EDA) and (ii) electromyography (EMG). EDA, which refers to the conductivity of the skin, varies according to the activation of the sympathetic branch of the autonomous nervous systems and has been commonly used as an index of emotional arousal [10, 25]. Given this, different aspects of the EDA signal such as the general level of skin conductance or the amplitude or latency of momentary skin conductance responses (SCRs) can be used [10]. In our study, we examined the SCRs elicited in an interval of up to 10 seconds after each query submission. Considering that the SCRs associated to a certain stimulus can take up to 6 seconds from stimulus onset to the point where it reaches the peak of the response, this 10-second time window was considered enough to capture the SCRs related to queries.

[1]We define navigational queries as those that seek a single website or the web page of a single entity.

[2]`http://www.alexa.com/topsites`

[3]`http://www.greasespot.net`

[4]`http://www.biopac.com/`

Table 1: I-PANAS-SF [32]

Positive Affect items	Negative Affect items
active	afraid
alert	ashamed
attentive	hostile
determined	nervous
inspired	upset

Another physiological method commonly used to quantify the valence of the stimuli is the activity of facial muscles, measured through EMG techniques. More specifically, the activity over the *corrugator supercilii* (EMG-CS), a muscle on the eyebrow responsible for frowning, was used as a proxy for the negative valence of the experienced emotions [25]. Since the muscular response appears to be immediate after the stimuli onset, we considered a time window of 3 seconds after each query submission as good enough to capture the possible changes in the EMG activity. As we anticipated that higher latency values would lead to an emotionally negative experience for the users, and this would manifest itself as higher levels of arousal and as negative valence, we also predicted higher levels of SCR and more intense EMG-CS activity in response to higher latency values.

3.4 Self-Reported Measures of Engagement

In our study, we used two types of questionnaires. The first questionnaire was introduced at the beginning and inquired about demographic information. The second questionnaire was administered at post-task and included the User Engagement Scale (UES) and the Computer System Usability Questionnaire (CSUQ). UES [22] is a multi-dimensional survey instrument that measures user engagement with technology. More specifically, it examines the cognitive (felt involvement, focused attention, perceived usability) and affective (positive and negative affect) aspects of interactions. Affect accounts for the hedonic experiences, as well as the motivations that influence and sustain our engagement during computer-mediated activities. The Felt Involvement items gauge users' feelings of being drawn into the experience, while the Focused Attention (FA) scale pertains to being absorbed or losing the track of time. CSUQ [17] is a multi-dimensional user satisfaction questionnaire, designed for use in scenario-based usability evaluations. Out of the four scales it contains, we considered only the scores from system usefulness (SYSUSE). Combined together, UES and CSUQ probe users' perceptions of the pragmatic and hedonic qualities of their interactions, as well as their perceptions of the search engine, all of which are considered key aspects of the user experience [15]. The questions were all forced-choice type and appeared in a random sequence to reduce potential ordering effects.

I-PANAS-SF. The International Positive and Negative Affect Schedule Short Form (I-PANAS-SF) [32] was used to measure the affect at pre-task and post-task (Table 1). I-PANAS-SF is a 10-item version of PANAS [33] that measures affect changes. It includes 5 items measuring positive affect (PAS) and 5 items measuring negative affect (NAS). Participants were asked to respond on a 7-point Likert scale (1: very slightly or not at all, ..., 7: extremely) their agreement to the statement: "You feel this way right now, that is, at the present moment", for each item. Although I-PANAS-SF may not be as efficient and accurate for capturing temporal micro-resolutions of emotional responses, there are several examples of studies from the domain of library and information science [14, 22], where PANAS has been successfully applied for measuring searchers' affect between search tasks. Given that the duration of our search tasks is comparable to those in the aforementioned studies, and considering the effectiveness of self-report methods in general, we believe that our experimental approach for measuring emotions was reasonably accurate.

Table 2: Focused attention scale [22]

1. I forgot my immediate surroundings while performing the search task.
2. I was so involved in my search task that I ignored everything around me.
3. I lost myself in this search experience.
4. I was so involved in my search task that I lost track of time.
5. I blocked out things around me when I was completing the search task.
6. When I was performing this search task, I lost track of the world around.
7. The time I spent performing the search task just slipped away.
8. I was absorbed in my search task.
9. During this search task experience I let myself go.

Focused attention. FA is a 9-item subscale, part of a larger scale for measuring user engagement [22]. FA has been used in past studies [19, 22] to evaluate users' perceptions of time passing and their degree of awareness about what took place outside of their interaction with the given task. Herein, it is adapted to the context of our search tasks. Given the context of our work, FA was a more meaningful dimension, at least compared to other subscales of engagement (e.g., aesthetics, novelty) that were not relevant enough or were addressed by the other questionnaires employed in our study (I-PANAS-SF, CSUQ). To measure FA, the participants were instructed to report on a 7-point Likert scale (1: strongly disagree, ..., 7: strongly agree) their agreement to each item shown in Table 2.

System usability. CSUQ [17] was developed by IBM to measure the perceived usability of systems in realistic scenarios. A 7-point Likert scale of agreement (1: strongly disagree, ..., 7: strongly agree) that quantifies system usefulness is used for each of the eight statements in the SYSUSE subscale. Two example statements are "I am able to complete my work quickly using this search site" and "I am able to efficiently complete my work using this search site".

3.5 Participants

There were 19 participants (female=2, male=17) aged from 18 to 41 and free from any obvious physical or sensory impairment. The participants were of mixed nationality (e.g., Spanish, Turkish, Russian), came from a variety of educational backgrounds (10.5% had a high school diploma, 31.5% had a BSc or college degree, 34.8% had an MSc degree and 21.0% had a PhD degree), and were all proficient with the English language (10.5% intermediate level, 84.2% advanced level, 5.2% native speakers).

3.6 Procedure

The user study was carried out in a laboratory setting. At the beginning of each session, the participants were informed about the conditions of the experiment and were asked to complete a demographics questionnaire. Upon completing the demographics questionnaire and the pre-task I-PANAS, the electrodes for the measurement of the physiological sig-

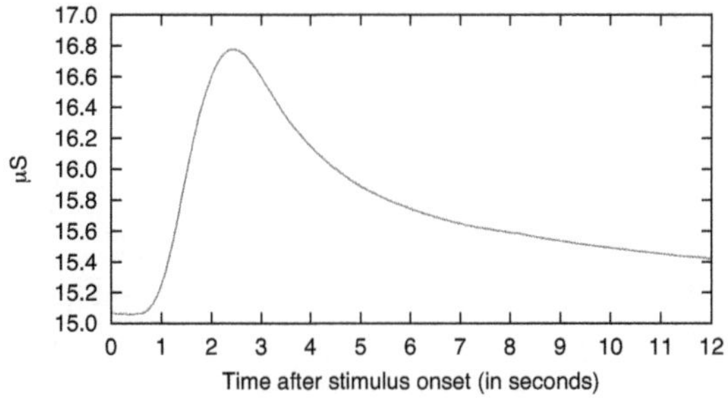

Figure 1: A typical SCR (taken from a participant).

nals were fitted. Two electrodes were placed on two fingers of the non-dominant hand in order to record the EDA signal, while two more electrodes were placed over the eyebrow in the non-dominant side, at the positions described in [29].

Each participant performed four search tasks, one for each latency condition. During the search tasks, the participants were presented with two web browser windows: the first window displayed the search engine used for the search task while the second window displayed the questionnaire. For each navigational query, participants were instructed to locate the associated URL among the first ten results of the search result page and copy-paste it in the corresponding box of the questionnaire. The queries were submitted to the search site the same way as in a realistic search scenario, i.e., by typing and clicking. 1-minute breaks were introduced at the end of each search task, after completing the I-PANAS, CSUQ, and FA scales. At the end of the session, the electrodes were removed, and the participants were debriefed. To motivate the participants, they were informed that they would receive a gift card whose value ranges from 5€ to 10€ depending on the number of queries they manage to submit. In the end, all participants received a 10€ gift card.

3.7 Physiological Data Filtering, Reduction and Analysis

3.7.1 EDA Signal

A smoothing filter with a time window of 200ms was applied to the EDA signal, and a visual inspection was performed to confirm that no artifacts were present in the EDA recordings. With the remaining data, a temporal series was constructed for every physiological signal by averaging the recorded data of every 1-second period, thus producing a temporal series of 480 points for each physiological signal, per participant and per condition. Then, each 10-second period of the EDA signal following a query submission was visually inspected to determine whether an SCR was produced. For determining the presence of an SCR, we examined the data for spikes on the EDA levels. Such spikes would need to begin at the first seconds following a query submission and match the typical form of an SCR, which is characterised by a sharp increase during a time window of length 1 to 3 seconds [10] with a much softer decrease in subsequent seconds (Fig. 1).

A total of 132 SCRs were identified. Participants presented between 1 to 20 SCRs ($M = 7.76, SD = 5.71$) with a mean of 1.94 SCRs by task ($SD = 1.84$). A repeated measures ANOVA showed no significant difference in the number of SCRs by latency condition, ($F(3, 48) = 0.63, p = .6, \eta_p^2 = .04$). Data not related to an SCR following a query submission were excluded from the analysis. Hence, the remaining signal contains ten observations (one observation per second, from seconds 1 to 10) for each of the 132 SCR instances. Next, the EDA value for the timestamp for which the SCR is rendered was used as a baseline and compared with each of the seconds following the query submission to inspect the amplitude of the SCR and to make different SCRs comparable. Thus, the EDA value at second 0 (the moment at which the query is submitted) was subtracted from the EDA values of each posterior second (1 to 10) of the query.

In our data analysis, we applied mixed multilevel models. This type of models present several advantages over other traditional statistical methods (e.g., ANOVA). One such advantage is that they can deal with nested and highly autocorrelated data, such as physiological data [16]. Moreover, the structure in different levels and the possibility of adding random terms allows us to deal with the large variability observed in psychophysiological data. Our model construction approach was similar to the so-called growth modelling [6], in which first null models without predictors are fitted and then both random and fixed factors are progressively introduced to the model. After adding each predictor, a likelihood test is conducted to check whether the new predictor has increased the model fitting [6]. If the model fitting has increased significantly, then the predictor is kept. If the increase is not significant, it is removed. This process is repeated for every factor that can act as a predictor until the model that best fits the data is constructed.

In the case of the EDA data, a visual inspection suggested that, apart from the latency condition, other factors such as the individual differences in participants' mean EDA, the order of presentation of the tasks, as well as the time spent within the tasks could have effects on the EDA signal. Moreover, since the SCR implies an increase followed by a decrease on the EDA levels, the time within each SCR is also likely to have had a significant effect. Thus, all these factors were considered in the construction of EDA models. The final EDA model included a random intercept for participants' means, as well as a random slope for the effects of task presentation order and time within the tasks, indicating that those factors had randomly varying effects between participants. The random intercept suggests that the mean levels of EDA varied among participants. The random slopes for time and order of presentation indicate that the effect of these factors is different (random) among participants. The fixed factors of the model, those that had a fixed effect on the participants, were the latency condition as well as the time within each SCR. The fixed effects are shown in Table 3.

3.7.2 EMG-CS Signal

A band-pass filter between 30–500Hz was applied to the EMG signal [29], and then it was integrated. Visual inspection confirmed the presence of artifacts due to electrode movement or bad adherence to the skin. For those cases, the data of one participant were removed along with the data of another participant, for a specific condition. Then, the EMG-CS signal was averaged for every 1-second window, as in the case of the EDA signal. However, since there is not a particularly defined EMG response, as it is in the case of SCR, we directly included in the analysis the EMG-CS data for the entire 3-second period after each query submission. EMG-CS data were analysed using mixed multilevel models, as in the case of the EDA data.

Table 3: Fixed effects for the EDA and EMG models

EDA model		EMG model	
Fixed factors	Coefficients	Fixed factors	Coefficients
Intercept	−.31*	Intercept	.0188***
Latency 500ms	.50***	Latency 500ms	.0019***
Latency 750ms	.42**	Latency 750ms	.0034***
Latency 1000ms	.60***	Latency 1000ms	.0010*
Seg 2	.11***	Seg 1	.0000393
Seg 3	.36***	Seg 2	.0002397***
Seg 4	.68***	Seg 3	.0003163***
Seg 5	.88***		
Seg 6	.90***		
Seg 7	.80***		
Seg 8	.74***		
Seg 9	.72***		
Seg 10	.69***		

* Correlation is significant at the .05 level (two-tailed).
** Correlation is significant at the .01 level (two-tailed).
*** Correlation is significant at the .001 level (two-tailed).

A random intercept for participants' means, as well as random slopes for the order of presentation and the effect of the time within the task were computed, similar to the analysis of the EDA model. The significant fixed factors for the EMG-CS models were the latency conditions, as well as the effect of time within the first 3 seconds after the query submission. During the model construction, one of the assumptions of our analysis, the homoscedasticity of residuals, was violated. This was confirmed by a visual inspection of the residuals. More specifically, the data of three participants showed clear patterns that deviated from the homoscedastic residuals. Those cases were excluded, and our model was fitted again. Table 3 summarises the final EMG-CS model.

3.7.3 Entropy Analysis

We also investigated the entropy feature for its performance in discriminating participants' physiological responses to web search results served at different latencies. Entropy has been extensively used in signal processing and pattern recognition. In information theory, entropy measures the disorder or uncertainty associated with a discrete, random variable, i.e., the expected value of the information in a message. The application of the entropy concept for the classification of our data is based on the assumption that the physiological signals' spectrum is more organised during signal segments where the user is carrying out their task without any significant "break-downs" or delays compared to signal segments where the user is experiencing stress or discomfort due to experienced latency increase. Thus, a signal segment of the former type would be characterised by low entropy. More specifically, we compute two entropy-based features for the EDA and EMG-CS data: Shannon entropy and permutation entropy.

Shannon entropy: Shannon entropy [27] allows to estimate the average minimum number of bits needed to encode a string of symbols in binary form (if *log* base is 2) based on the alphabet size and the frequency of symbols. Given a finite time series $X(t) = (x_t : 1 \leq t \leq T)$, the Shannon entropy can be expressed as

$$H(X) = \sum_i P(x_i) I(x_i) = -\sum_i P(x_i) \log_b P(x_i), \quad (1)$$

where I is the information content of X, $I(x)$ is the random variable, and b is the base of the logarithm used.

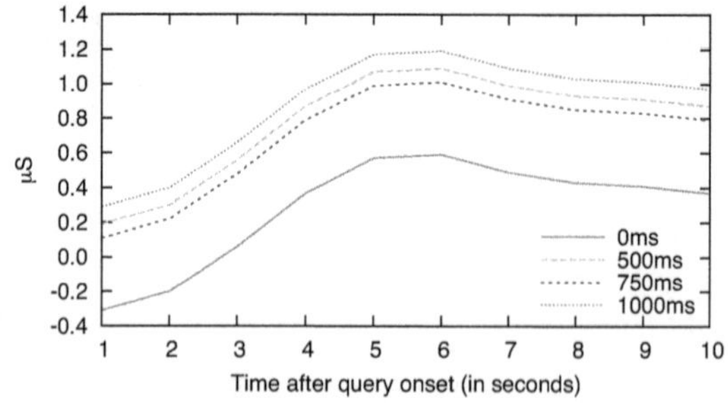

Figure 2: Graphical representation of the values of the fixed coefficients for the EDA model.

Permutation entropy: Permutation entropy [4] provides a fast and robust method for estimating the complexity of time series, by considering the temporal order of the values. More specifically, it calculates the variety of different permutations appearing at the components of a time series.

Let us consider a time series $X(t) = (x_t : 1 \leq t \leq T)$. S_n is the set of all possible $n!$ permutations π of order n. For each $\pi \in S_n$ we determine the relative frequency

$$p(\pi) = \frac{|\{t \mid 0 \leq t \leq T-n, (x_{t+1}, \ldots, x_{t+n}) \text{ has type } \pi\}|}{T-n+1}, \quad (2)$$

which estimates the frequency of π as good as possible for a finite time series. The permutation entropy of order $n \geq 2$ is defined as

$$H(n) = -\sum_{\pi \in S_n} P(\pi) \log p(\pi) \quad (3)$$

The permutation entropy can be calculated for arbitrary real-world time series, and particularly in the presence of dynamical and observational noise. We compute the entropy for all permutations of order $n \in \{2, 3, 4, 5\}$.

3.8 Results

3.8.1 Physiological Data

As we can see in the EDA model (Table 3), the fixed coefficients of the model for the effect of the time after the query describe a curve that approximately fits the form of a typical SCR (Fig. 2). This is not surprising since, during data filtering, queries that are not followed by an SCR were removed, while the remaining data that was analysed contained an SCR after each query submission. What is of interest is that the model can also predict significant increases in the EDA levels associated with the increased latency conditions compared to the no-latency (0ms) condition. The coefficients showed increases of 0.5μS and 0.42μS for the 500ms and 750ms latency conditions, respectively, while a higher increase of 0.60μS was observed in the 1,000ms latency condition. These increases were statistically significant compared to the 0ms condition, which was taken as the baseline in the model for the calculation of the coefficients. Nevertheless, even if the increase associated with the 1,000ms condition seemed to be higher than the increases associated with the 500ms and 750ms conditions, recalculations of the model using different levels of latency as a baseline condition showed that the difference between the coefficients for the three latency conditions (500ms, 750ms, 1,000ms) did not reach statistical significance ($p > .05$), i.e., while the three

Table 4: Means (M) and standard errors (SE) for the post-PAS, post-NAS, FA, CSUQ scales

	Latency condition			
Scale	0ms	500ms	750ms	1,000ms
post-PAS	17.21 ± 1.46	18.21 ± 1.57	18.68 ± 1.51	17.53 ± 1.79
post-NAS	6.42 ± 0.41	6.32 ± 0.54	6.47 ± 0.48	5.95 ± 0.36
FA	29.32 ± 1.71	28.26 ± 2.29	27.95 ± 2.18	26.32 ± 2.00
CSUQ	28.16 ± 1.91	29.37 ± 2.09	27.63 ± 1.81	29.05 ± 1.86

latency conditions are significantly different from the 0ms condition, there is no significant difference between them.

In the case of the EMG-CS data, the model showed that the three higher latency conditions (500ms, 750ms, 1,000ms) resulted in a significant increase in the EMG-CS activity. The largest increase was observed for the 750ms latency condition, while more moderate increases were associated with the 500ms and 1,000ms latency conditions. Recalculations of the model, by changing the condition taken as baseline, showed that the increase in EMG-CS activity related to the 750ms condition was significantly different from the increases associated with the 500ms ($p < .01$) and 1,000ms conditions ($p < .001$), and that there was no significant difference between these two conditions ($p > .05$). Here, we observe that all three latency conditions are associated with emotional experiences that are characterised by a more negative valence. Surprisingly, the 750ms latency condition was found to be associated with the most intense activation of the EMG-CS (i.e., negative emotional valence) compared to the 1,000ms latency condition. However, the EDA and EMG-CS data provide support for the hypothesis that even latencies at low ranges can have a significant effect on the user experience, resulting in intensified, negative emotions.

Finally, we applied the Friedman's ANOVA test to the Shannon entropy and weighted permutation entropy scores computed for the EDA and EMG-CS data ($n \in \{2, 3, 4, 5\}$). With respect to the EDA data, the obtained Shannon entropy scores did not change significantly across the latency conditions ($\chi^2(3) = 3.40, p > .05$). Similarly, the weighted permutation entropy scores did not exhibit a significant difference over the latency conditions, for permutations of order $n = 2$ ($\chi^2(3) = 2.20, p > .05$), $n = 3$ ($\chi^2(3) = 0.33, p > .05$), $n = 4$ ($\chi^2(3) = 0.80, p > .05$), or $n = 5$ ($\chi^2(3) = 0.80, p > .05$). When examining the EMG-CS data, the obtained Shannon entropy scores did not significantly change across the latency conditions ($\chi^2(3) = 0.46, p > .05$). Finally, the weighted permutation entropy scores did not differ significantly across the latency conditions for any of the permutations of order $n = 2$ ($\chi^2(3) = 5.06, p > .05$), $n = 3$ ($\chi^2(3) = 2.86, p > .05$), $n = 4$ ($\chi^2(3) = 0.20, p > .05$), or $n = 5$ ($\chi^2(3) = 0.26, p > .05$). These preliminary findings suggest that the computed entropy features did not contribute significantly to the accurate discrimination of the EDA and EMG-CS data, for the latency conditions we examined. This could be due to the lack of sensitivity towards subtle changes in the data, perhaps measurable more accurately by other means or being affected by additive noise.

3.8.2 *Self-Reported Data*

Participants' responses to the 5-item PAS, 5-item NAS, 9-item FA, and 8-item CSUQ-SYSUSE scales were summed to obtain the final scores (Table 4). Results are reported at a statistical significance level of .05. To take an appropriate control of Type I errors in multiple pair-wise comparisons,

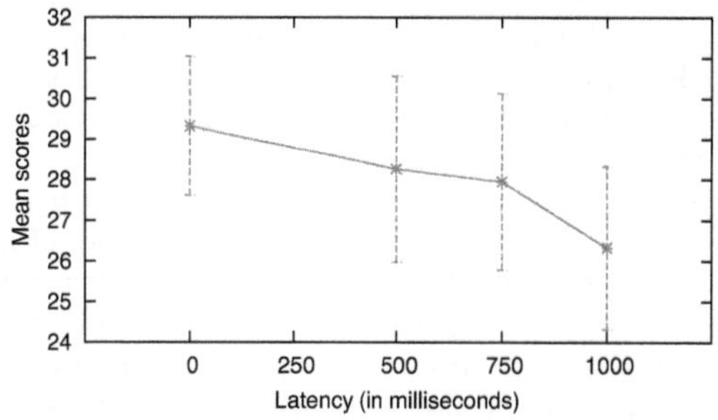

Figure 3: FA levels across all latency conditions.

we applied the Bonferroni correction. The ANOVA test was applied to determine if there were statistically significant differences between the scores assigned to different latency conditions. The results showed no significant differences in the CSUQ ($F(3, 54) = .76, p = .52, \eta_p^2 = .1$) or the FA scores ($F(3, 54) = .79, p = .5, \eta_p^2 = .04$). Similarly, no significant effect was observed for post-NAS ($F(3, 54) = .93, p = .43, \eta_p^2 = .05$) or post-PAS ($F(3, 54) = 1.23, p = .33, \eta_p^2 = .19$). These results suggest that, contrary to the clear effects found in the physiological data, the users did not consciously perceive the experience as better or worse, depending on the latency of the search engine response. However, the absence of significant effects in the users' responses to the self-reports should not be considered as a definite proof of the absence of latency effects on the user experience, as clearly indicated by the physiological data findings. In addition, the data from the FA scale reveals a pattern (Fig. 3) that suggests, although not statistically significant, a reduced engagement as the latency increases to higher values. But, given a larger sample, it is possible that a weak effect of the search latency on the reported FA scores may become more evident.

4. QUERY LOG ANALYSIS

By exploiting physiological measures, the previous study has demonstrated the presence of certain latency effects that are unconsciously experienced by the users. In this section, we investigate the effects of similar small latency increases on the engagement of users with search engine result pages. In particular, we observe the change in users' likelihood of clicking a search result when presented with a fast or slow response. Unlike the previous study, which involved a small number of participants, this analysis is performed using prerecorded search click data obtained from Yahoo Web Search. Hence, it allows us to demonstrate, at large scale, that even small latency increases can lead to a statistically significant decrease in the engagement of a user with a search engine.

4.1 Setup

Click data. We randomly sampled a large number of queries from the web search query log (all queries were submitted on the same day). From this sample, we further selected queries that were (i) issued from desktop computers located in the US and (ii) processed in a specific search data centre in the US. The motivation behind the first filtering was to eliminate a potential bias due to device differences (e.g., desktop, mobile, or tablet) while the second filtering aimed to reduce the bias due to variation in geolocation of users. No other filtering or normalization (e.g., case conversion or stemming) was applied on queries. The resulting set after the filtering had about 30 million queries. For every query in this final set, we also extracted the associated click data. Here, we limited ourselves to clicks issued on algorithmic search results as the only sign of engagement with the search engine result page (e.g., we have not included clicks on vertical search results or advertisements).

User data. The sampled queries were issued by about 6 million users, all located in the US. The number of males and females in the sample was quite similar, whereas there was some skew in the age distribution towards older users. However, each age group involved at least 100K users. The age and gender information were self-reported by the users in their account settings and were available in the query log.

Latency measurement. The latency values used in our analysis correspond to the time difference between the submission of the query by a user and the display of the search result page in the user's browser. This value is measured by a client-side JavaScript code running on the web browser and is communicated to a logging server in the search engine, letting us record the exact user-perceived latency value for every query. This end-to-end latency measurement includes the query processing time in the search engine, the network latency due to transfer of the query and results, and the time spent by rendering retrieved results in the user's browser. Since the rendering time is included in the measurement, we do not have a hidden bias arising from client's processing power, memory, or workload. Hence, we do not expect to have a hidden bias due to potentially uneven distribution of computational capacity by user demographics either.

4.2 Methodology and Metrics

Methodology. A naive method to quantify the effect of increasing latency on click behaviour would be to compute the click-through rate at different latency intervals and to show a negative correlation between the click-through rate and latency. Unfortunately, this method is not feasible because there are external factors that affect both the click-through rate and latency at the same time, most important being the quality of retrieved results [1]. For example, some search result pages may attract more clicks because they contain relevant results, and it may be the case that such pages are more likely to be cached and thus served with low response latency. The methodology we adopted in our analysis is specifically designed to eliminate this kind of potential bias due to the differences in search quality. Our methodology is based on measuring the impact of latency by observing the differences in click behaviour for pairs of "identical" query instances. More specifically, we compare the presence of clicks for two given query instances that are (i) submitted by the same user, (ii) having the same query string, and (iii) matching the same search results. That is, the same user submits the same query at two different times and is exposed to identical search results (but, potentially with different response latency values).[5] Therefore, the quality of presented results is identical, and the differences in click behaviour are more likely to stem from the differences in perceived response latency. We note that our methodology differs from the methodology adopted in [1] in that we also require the user to be identical. This way, our analysis becomes compatible with our controlled user study since the slower instance in a pair corresponds to the case where the user is exposed to an increased latency.

[5]Two search result pages are said to be identical if their top 10 results have the same URLs, ranked in the same order.

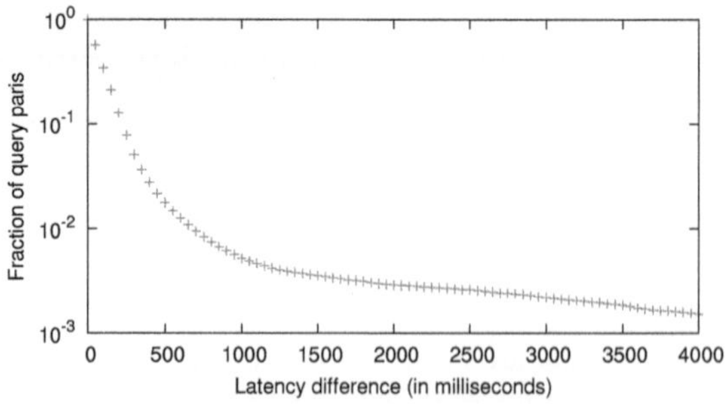

Figure 4: Complementary cumulative distribution of latency differences associated with query pairs.

Metrics. Let us assume a query pair $(q_{\text{fast}}, q_{\text{slow}})$, such that $\ell(q_{\text{fast}}) \leq \ell(q_{\text{slow}})$, where $\ell(q)$ denotes the response latency for query q. Our hypothesis is that, on average, users are more likely to engage with the search result page corresponding to q_{fast} than that of q_{slow} since the latter query is served with higher response latency. To verify this hypothesis, we place query instance pairs in coarse-grain buckets according to the latency difference $\ell(q_{\text{slow}}) - \ell(q_{\text{fast}})$ and, for each bucket, observe two different metrics, which indicate whether the users were engaged more with the results of the fast or slow query, using users' clicks on search results as a proxy for engagement:

Click presence: We compute the fraction of query instance pairs where at least one fast query result was clicked while no slow query result was clicked. We also compute the fraction of query instance pairs where at least one slow query result was clicked while no fast query result was clicked. We refer to these two fractions as *click-on-fast* and *click-on-slow*, respectively. For each latency difference bucket, we then compute the ratio between *click-on-fast* and *click-on-slow*, higher ratios (larger than 1) indicating a user preference towards faster query response.

Click count: We compute the fraction of query instance pairs in which the users have issued a larger number of clicks on the fast query results than the slow query results. We also compute the fraction of query instance pairs in which the users have issued a larger number of clicks on the slow query results than the fast query results. We refer to these two fractions as *click-more-on-fast* and *click-more-on-slow*, respectively.[6] As in the previous metric, we then compute the ratio between *click-more-on-fast* and *click-more-on-slow*, higher ratios (larger than 1) indicating a user preference towards faster query response.

4.3 Results

Fig. 4 shows the complementary cumulative distribution of latency differences across all query instance pairs. We observe that, for more than 99% of the pairs, the latency difference associated with the queries in the pair is less than

[6]In this metric, we consider only the query pairs where at least one result was clicked for each query in the pair.

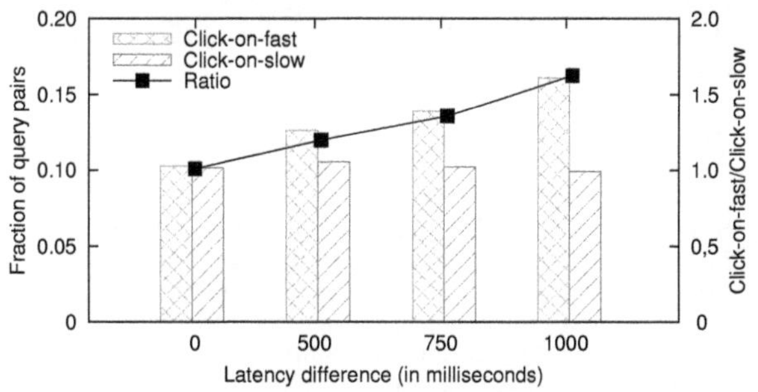

Figure 5: Fast or slow query response preference according to the click presence metric.

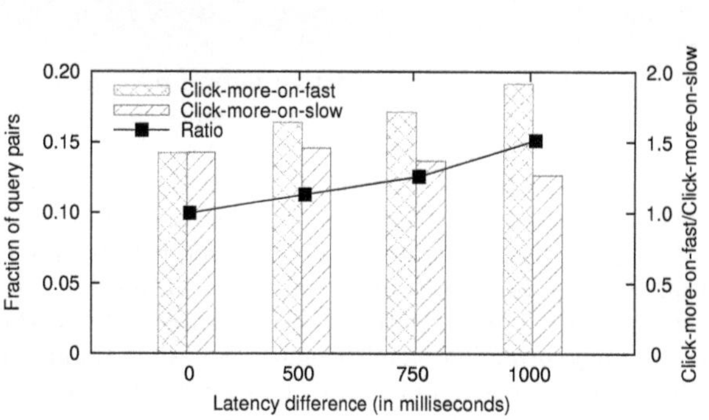

Figure 6: Fast or slow query response preference according to the click count metric.

1,000ms. This is due to two reasons. First, the queries in a pair were issued from a desktop computer and processed in the same search data centre. Hence, the associated network overheads are similar. Second, the submitted query string and retrieved search results were identical for both query instances. Hence, the response times of the search engine are similar, and the differences in latency potentially stem from the differences in the rendering of results in user's web browser. In any case, the range of latency differences we explore is consistent with the latency increments used in the controlled user study presented in Section 3.

In Fig. 5, we show the fraction of query pairs falling under the *click-on-fast* and *click-on-slow* sets, as well as the ratio between the two fractions. Each latency bucket contains the query pairs in which the latency difference between the queries is not less than a certain threshold latency value (the values shown on the x axis: 0ms, 500ms, 750ms, and 1,000ms). According to this figure, when the latency difference increases, the *click-on-fast* set grows quickly while the *click-on-slow* set remains relatively stable. The ratio between the *click-on-fast* and *click-on-slow* sets is always larger than 1, and it keeps increasing as the latency difference increases. To test the statistical significance of the results reported in Fig. 5, we apply the McNemar test to determine whether the marginal frequencies of the binary outcomes are equal. More specifically, we compute a 2×2 contingency table for each latency difference shown in Fig. 5, using the raw counts of query pairs that fall in each possible outcome (*click-on-fast*, *click-on-slow*, *click-on-both*, *click-on-neither*). As expected, the McNemar test does not reveal a statistically significant difference for the 0ms latency difference (the control group). However, the test indicates a significant difference in the proportion of query pairs allocated in the possible outcomes for the 500ms ($\chi^2(1) = 22.41, p < .001$), 750ms ($\chi^2(1) = 31.13, p < .001$), and 1,000ms ($\chi^2(1) = 51.40, p < .001$) latency differences. Hence, we reject the null hypothesis of marginal homogeneity, i.e., the marginal probabilities for each outcome are the same. In other words, given a pair of identical queries and search result pages, users show a clear preference to engage with the search results that are served with lower latency.

Fig. 6 shows the fraction of query pairs falling under the *click-more-on-fast* and *click-more-on-slow* sets, as well as the ratio between the two fractions. We observe that, as the latency difference increases, the size of the *click-more-on-fast* set increases while the size of the *click-more-on-slow* set decreases. As before, the ratio between the size of the *click-more-on-fast* and *click-more-on-slow* sets is always larger than 1 and it keeps increasing as the latency difference increases. We applied the McNemar test to measure the statistical significance of the results reported in Fig. 6. In this case, the outcomes of the 2×2 contingency table are *click-more-on-fast*, *click-more-on-slow*, *click-same-on-both-at-least-one-click*, and *click-same-on-both-zero-click*. As in the previous experiment, we do not observe any statistically significant difference for the 0ms latency difference (the control group). When applying the McNemar test to the remaining latency differences, we note a significant difference in the proportion of users allocated in the possible outcomes for the 500ms ($\chi^2(1) = 13.09, p < .001$), 750ms ($\chi^2(1) = 22.06, p < .001$), and 1,000ms ($\chi^2(1) = 46.37, p < .001$) latency differences. This leads us to reject the null hypothesis of marginal homogeneity in favour of the alternative hypothesis, i.e., the marginal proportions are significantly different from each other. Hence, this experiment shows that the users tend to click on a larger number of result links if they are served with lower latency.

5. CONCLUDING REMARKS

The results of our controlled study revealed that, as the response latency of the search engine reaches higher values, the arousal and the negative valence of the experienced emotions increase as well. Although those effects did not produce changes on the self-reported data, their impact on users' physiological responses was evident. Thus, even if such short latency increases of under 500ms are not consciously perceived, they have sizeable physiological effects that can contribute to the overall user experience. This highlights the need for a more inter-disciplinary approach to the evaluation of human information processing in HCI research, as there are plenty of relevant effects that we might be missing if we rely solely on self-report measures. The fact that latency conditions tested here presented effects with little conscious awareness cannot be taken as a proof that they do not affect user's online behaviour, preferences, or choices. Research in psychology has indicated that our motivations and preferences are not always determined by conscious objectives or reasons. Moreover, it leads to the question of what is the actual effect that such delays might have on the engagement of users. With a large-scale query log analysis, we ascertained the effect on the clicking behaviour of users. As a result of this analysis, we revealed a significant decrease in users' engagement with the search result page, even at small increases in latency.

We believe that the users show high variation in the way they perceive the response latency of a web service as the effect depends on demographics, context, and potentially many other factors. This subjective nature may create an opportunity for search engines. Search results can be served to each user at custom latencies depending on the estimated behavioural impact of latency on the user. For example, if no degradation is expected in user experience, the priority of the user query may be reduced or the search results may be computed using less hardware resources, eventually serving the query with a higher latency. Serving results at higher latencies may bring financial benefits to search engines in the form of decreased hardware investments and reduced energy consumption, also saving time and resources for time-critical queries. To this end, we need to devise mechanisms for accurate prediction of user-perceived response latency as well as the impact of latency on user experience. We can then come up with proper models for personalising response latency on a per-user basis, eventually aiming to achieve financial cost savings for the search engine company without hurting users' engagement and satisfaction.

6. REFERENCES

[1] I. Arapakis, X. Bai, and B. B. Cambazoglu. Impact of response latency on user behavior in web search. In *Proc. 37th Int'l ACM SIGIR Conf. Research and Development in Information Retrieval*, pages 103–112, 2014.

[2] L. Azzopardi. Modelling interaction with economic models of search. In *Proc. 37th Int'l ACM SIGIR Conf. Research and Development in Information Retrieval*, pages 3–12, 2014.

[3] L. Azzopardi, D. Kelly, and K. Brennan. How query cost affects search behavior. In *Proc. 36th Int'l ACM SIGIR Conf. Research and Development in Information Retrieval*, pages 23–32, 2013.

[4] C. Bandt and B. Pompe. Permutation entropy: A natural complexity measure for time series. *Physical Review Letters*, 88, 2002.

[5] J. A. Bargh and T. L. Chartrand. The unbearable automaticity of being. *American Psychologist*, 54(7):462–479, 1999.

[6] P. Bliese. Multilevel modeling in R (2.5): A brief introduction to R, the multilevel package and the NMLE package. `http://cran.r-project.org/doc/contrib/Bliese_Multilevel.pdf`, 2013.

[7] M. Bradley and P. J. Lang. *Emotion and motivation*, pages 581–607. Handbook of psychophysiology. New York: Cambridge University Press, 2007.

[8] J. D. Brutlag, H. Hutchinson, and M. Stone. User preference and search engine latency. In *Proc. ASA Joint Statistical Meetings*, 2008.

[9] E. S. Davis and D. A. Hantula. The effects of download delay on performance and end-user satisfaction in an Internet tutorial. *Computers in Human Behavior*, 17(3):249–268, 2001.

[10] M. E. Dawson, A. M. Schell, and D. L. Fillion. *The electrodermal system*, pages 159–181. Handbook of psychophysiology. New York: Cambridge University Press, 2007.

[11] B. G. C. Dellaert and B. E. Kahn. How tolerable is delay: Consumers' evaluations of Internet web sites after waiting. *Journal of Interactive Marketing*, 13(1):41–54, 1999.

[12] A. R. Dennis and N. J. Taylor. Information foraging on the Web: The effects of "acceptable" Internet delays on multi-page information search behavior. *Decision Support Systems*, 42(2):810–824, 2006.

[13] D. F. Galletta, R. Henry, S. McCoy, and P. Polak. Web site delays: How tolerant are users? *Journal of the Association for Information Systems*, 5:1–28, 2003.

[14] J. Gwizdka and I. Lopatovska. The role of subjective factors in the information search process. *Journal of the American Society for Information Science and Technology*, 60(12):2452–2464, 2009.

[15] M. Hassenzahl. Funology. In M. A. Blythe, K. Overbeeke, A. F. Monk, and P. C. Wright, editors, *The Thing and I: Understanding the Relationship Between User and Product*, pages 31–42. Kluwer Academic Publishers, 2004.

[16] S. D. Kristjansson, J. C. Kircher, and A. K. Webb. Multilevel models for repeated measures research designs in psychophysiology: An introduction to growth curve modeling. *Psychophysiology*, 44(5):728–736, 2007.

[17] J. R. Lewis. IBM computer usability satisfaction questionnaires: Psychometric evaluation and instructions for use. *International Journal of Human-Computer Interaction*, 7(1):57–78, 1995.

[18] D. Maxwell and L. Azzopardi. Stuck in traffic: How temporal delays affect search behaviour. In *Proc. 5th Information Interaction in Context Symp.*, pages 155–164, 2014.

[19] L. McCay-Peet, M. Lalmas, and V. Navalpakkam. On saliency, affect and focused attention. In *ACM SIGCHI Conf. Human Factors in Computing Systems*, pages 541–550, 2012.

[20] F. F.-H. Nah. A study on tolerable waiting time: How long are web users willing to wait? *Behaviour and Information Technology*, 23(3):153–163, 2004.

[21] R. E. Nisbett and T. D. Wilson. Telling more than we can know: Verbal reports on mental processes. *Psychological Review*, 84(3):231–259, 1977.

[22] H. L. O'Brien and E. G. Toms. The development and evaluation of a survey to measure user engagement. *Journal of the American Society for Information Science and Technology*, 61(1):50–69, 2010.

[23] W. Prinz. Why don't we perceive our brain states? *European Journal of Cognitive Psychology*, 4(1):1–20, 1992.

[24] J. Ramsay, A. Barbesi, and J. Preece. A psychological investigation of long retrieval times on the World Wide Web. *Interacting with Computers*, 10(1):77–86, 1998.

[25] N. Ravaja. Contributions of psychophysiology to media research: Review and recommendations. *Media Psychology*, 6(2):193–235, 2004.

[26] E. Schurman and J. Brutlag. Performance related changes and their user impact. In *Velocity – Web Performance and Operations Conf.*, 2009.

[27] C. Shannon. A mathematical theory of communication. *The Bell System Technical Journal*, 27(3):379–423, 1948.

[28] M. D. Smucker. Towards timed predictions of human performance for interactive information retrieval evaluation. In *Proc. Symp. Human-Computer Information Retrieval*, 2009.

[29] L. Tassinary, J. T. Cacioppo, and E. J. Vanman. *The skeletomotor system: Surface electromyography*, pages 267–299. Handbook of psychophysiology. New York: Cambridge University Press, 2007.

[30] N. J. Taylor, A. R. Dennis, and J. W. Cummings. Situation normality and the shape of search: The effects of time delays and information presentation on search behavior. *Journal of the American Society for Information Science and Technology*, 64(5):909–928, 2013.

[31] J. Teevan, K. Collins-Thompson, R. W. White, S. T. Dumais, and Y. Kim. Slow search: Information retrieval without time constraints. In *Proc. Symp. Human-Computer Interaction and Information Retrieval*, pages 1:1–1:10, 2013.

[32] E. R. Thompson. Development and validation of an internationally reliable short-form of the positive and negative affect schedule (PANAS). *Journal of Cross-Cultural Psychology*, 38(2):227–242, 2007.

[33] D. Watson, L. A. Clark, and A. Tellegen. Development and validation of brief measures of positive and negative affect: The PANAS scales. *Journal of Personality and Social Psychology*, 54(6):1063–1070, 1988.

Multiple Social Network Learning and Its Application in Volunteerism Tendency Prediction

Xuemeng Song, Liqiang Nie, Luming Zhang, Mohammad Akbari, Tat-Seng Chua
National University of Singapore
{sxmustc, nieliqiang, zglumg}@gmail.com, akbari@nus.edu.sg,
chuats@comp.nus.edu.sg

ABSTRACT

We are living in the era of social networks, where people throughout the world are connected and organized by multiple social networks. The views revealed by different social networks may vary according to the different services they offer. They are complimentary to each other and comprehensively characterize a specific user from different perspectives. As compared to the scare knowledge conveyed by a single source, appropriate aggregation of multiple social networks offers us a better opportunity for deep user understanding. The challenges, however, co-exist with opportunities. The first challenge lies in the existence of block-wise missing data, caused by the fact that some users may be very active in certain social networks while inactive in others. The second challenge is how to collaboratively integrate multiple social networks. Towards this end, we first proposed a novel model for data missing completion by seamlessly exploring the knowledge from multiple sources. We then developed a robust multiple social network learning model, and applied it to the application of volunteerism tendency prediction. Extensive experiments on real world dataset verify the effectiveness of our scheme. The proposed scheme is applicable to many other domains, such as demographic inference and interest prediction.

Categories and Subject Descriptors

H.3.1 [**Information Storage and Retrieval**]: Content Analysis and Indexing

Keywords

Multiple Social Network Learning; Missing Data Completion; Volunteerism Tendency Prediction

1. INTRODUCTION

With the explosion of social network services, more and more people are involved in multiple social networks for various purposes at the same time. It is reported that 52% of online adults concurrently use multiple social media services[1]. Different aspects of users are disclosed on different social networks due to their different emphasis. In fact, these views are complementary to each other and essentially characterize the same user from different perspectives. As compared with single social network, appropriate aggregation of multiple social networks provides us a potential to comprehensively understand the given users [1, 29]. For example, we can learn descriptive user representation, build predictive models for user profiles, and recommend prescriptive actions based on complete historical behaviors. Hence, an effective technique for multiple social network learning (MSNL) is highly desired. Distinguished from multi-view learning which maximizes the agreement between views using unlabeled data, MSNL works towards supervised learning.

However, integration of multiple sources is non-trivial [27]. The first tough challenge lies in how to fuse users' heterogeneous distributed data from multiple social networks effectively. One naive approach is to concatenate the feature spaces generated from different sources into a unified feature space. Thereby, traditional machine learning models can be further applied. However, this method simply treats the confidence of all data sources equally and may also lead to the curse of dimensionality. Moreover, it ignores two important facts: 1) different aspects of users are revealed in different social networks and are thus distributed in different feature spaces; and 2) all these aspects tend to characterize the same users. In particular, data from multi-sources describes the same user and thus the results predicted by different sources should be similar. Therefore, it is expected to take the source confidence and source consistency into consideration. Another challenge we are facing is the data missing problem. Although some users have social accounts on multiple social networks, generally they are active on only a few of them. One simple approach to address this challenge is to discard all incomplete subjects. It is apparent that this method will dramatically reduce the training size, thereby result in overfitting in the model learning stage. Therefore, accurately completing missing data by jointly utilizing multiple sources is a necessity to enhance the learning performance.

To address these problems, we present a scheme for MSNL, which co-regulates the source confidence and source consistency. Figure 1 shows our proposed scheme comprising of three components. Given a set of users, we first crawl

[1]According Paw Research Internet Project's Social Media Update 2014: http://www.pewinternet.org/

SIGIR'15, August 09 - 13, 2015, Santiago, Chile.

DOI: http://dx.doi.org/10.1145/2766462.2767726.

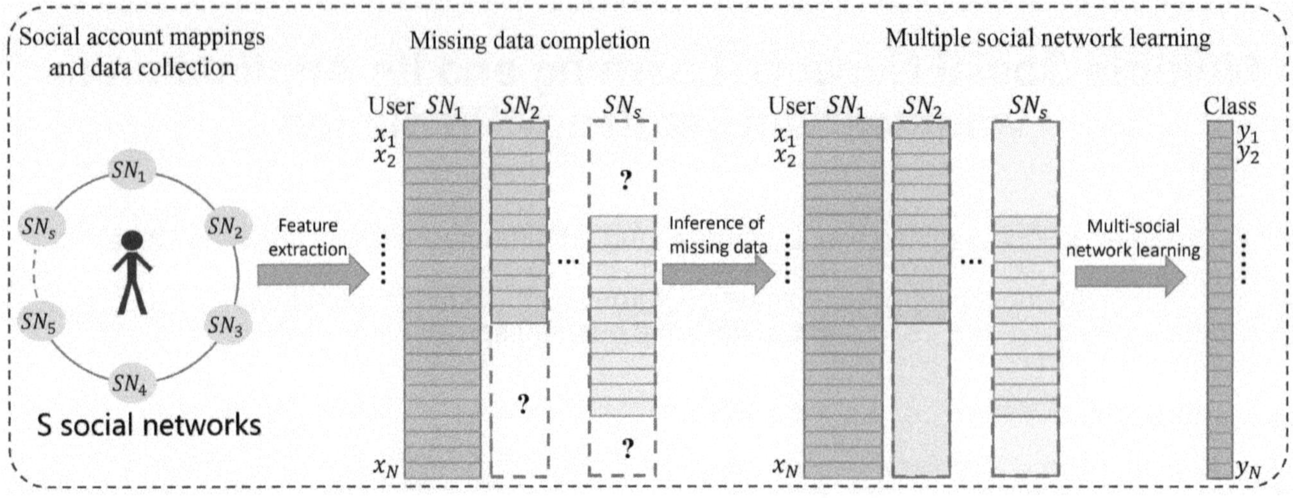

Figure 1: Illustration of our proposed scheme. We first collect and align users' distributed data from multiple social networks. We then jointly infer the block-wise missing data based on the available data. We finally apply MSNL on the complete data. SN_i, x_j, and y_l refer to the i-th social network, j-th user sample, and the l-th corresponding label, respectively.

their historical contents and all social connections. The first component extracts the multi-faceted information cues to describe a given user, including demographic information, practical behaviors, historical posts, and profiles of social connections. To deal with the block-wise missing data, the second component attempts to infer the block-wise missing data by learning a latent space shared by different social networks, achieving a complete input to the next component. We finally use the last component to conduct MSNL on the complete data. Particularly, we model the confidence of different data sources and the consistency among them by unifying two regularization terms into our model.

Based upon our proposed scheme, we introduce one application scenario: volunteerism tendency prediction. Volunteerism was defined in [18] as long-term, planned, prosocial behaviors that occur within organizational settings and can benefit strangers. Persons exhibiting volunteerism are the so-called volunteers, who serve as an important work force in modern society. Traditionally, it is intractable for nonprofit organizations (NPOs) to aimlessly recruit volunteers from the huge crowd. It is thus necessary to develop an automatic volunteerism tendency prediction system to alleviate the dilemma that NPOs are facing. In particular, we take the advantage of users' casually distributed online data, especially from multiple social networks, which can comprehensively reveal users' personal concerns, interests [5, 22] and even personality traits [20, 21]. On the other hand, the real word dataset may contain block-wise missing data due to some users' inactivity in social networks. Moreover, the specific task also brings us another issue in terms of data collection and ground truth construction. Therefore, the proposed scheme naturally fits this application scenario.

Our main contributions can be summarized in threefold:

- We propose a novel MSNL model, which is able to model both the source confidence and source consistency. Specifically, we can obtain a closed-form solution by taking the inverse of a linear system, which has been mathematically proven to be invertible.
- We propose an approach to deal with missing data in multiple social networks, which first learns a common latent subpace shared by different sources [12] and the original missing data can then be derived in turn.
- We empirically evaluate our proposed scheme on the application of volunteerism tendency prediction. In addition, we develop a set of volunteer-oriented features to characterize users' volunteerism tendency. We have released our compiled dataset[2] to facilitate other researchers to repeat our experiments and verify their proposed approaches.

The remainder of this paper is structured as follows, Section 2 briefly reviews the related work. Section 3 describes the proposed MSNL model. Missing data completion is introduced in Section 4. Section 5 presents the set of volunteer-oriented features we developed. Section 6 details the experimental results and analysis, followed by our concluding remarks in Section 7.

2. RELATED WORK

Although our work is distinguished from multi-view learning, we can still benefit from their efforts. Zhang et al. [28] proposed an inductive multi-view multi-task learning model (regMVMT). regMVMT penalizes the disagreement of models learned from different sources over the unlabeled samples. Besides, the authors also studied the structured missing data, which is completely missing for a source in terms of a task. In other words, if a source is available for a task, then all samples will have data from this source. However, they overlooked the source weights and did not pay attention to the partially structured missing data, which are both what we are concerned with. Yuan et al. [25] introduced an incomplete multi-source feature learning method, avoiding the direct inference of block-wise missing data. Particularly, the authors split the incomplete data into disjoint groups, where they conducted feature learning independently. However, such a mechanism constrains us to conduct source level analysis. Later, Xiang et al. [24] investigated multi-source learning with block-wise missing

[2]The compiled dataset is currently publicly accessible via: http://multiplesocialnetworklearning.azurewebsites.net/

data with an application of Alzheimer's Disease prediction and proposed the iSFS model. Apart from feature-level analysis, the authors also conducted source-level analysis by introducing the weights of models obtained from different sources. However, ignoring the consistency relationships among different models seems inappropriate. In addition, the authors also adapted the model to handle cases where block-wise missing data exists. Different from their work, we infer the missing data by making full use of the available data before applying MSNL, which is more generalizable to other applications.

3. MULTIPLE SOCIAL NETWORK LEARNING

This section details our proposed MSNL model and derives an analytic solution by solving the inverse of a linear system, whose invertibility is proved rigorously.

3.1 Notation

We first declare some notations. In particular, we use bold capital letters (e.g. $\mathbf{X}$) and bold lowercase letters (e.g. $\mathbf{x}$) to denote matrices and vectors, respectively. We employ non-bold letters (e.g. x) to represent scalars, and Greek letters (e.g. λ) as parameters. If not clarified, all vectors are in column forms.

Suppose we have a set of N labeled data samples and $S \geq 2$ social networks. We compile the S social networks with an index set $\mathcal{C} = \{1, 2, \cdots, S\}$. Let D_s and N_s denote the number of features and samples in the s-th social network, $s \in \mathcal{C}$, respectively. Let $\mathbf{X}_s \in \mathbb{R}^{N \times D_s}$ denote the feature matrix extracted from the s-th social network. Each row represents a user sample. Then the dimension of features extracted from all these social networks is $D = \sum_{s=1}^{S} D_s$. The whole feature matrix can be written as $\mathbf{X} = \{\mathbf{X}_1, \mathbf{X}_2, \cdots, \mathbf{X}_S\} \in \mathbb{R}^{N \times D}$ and $\mathbf{y} = \{y_1, y_2, \cdots, y_N\}^T \in \{1, -1\}^{N \times 1}$ is the corresponding label vector.

3.2 Problem Formulations

Based on a set of data samples with S social networks, we can learn S predictive models, where each model is individually and independently trained on a social network. The final predictive model can be strengthened via linear combination of these S models. Mathematically, we learn one linear mapping function $\mathbf{f}_s$ for the s-th social network. In addition, we assume that the mapping functions learned from all social networks agree with one another as much as possible. Particularly, we can formalize this assumption using regularization function. Using the least square loss function, we have the following objective function,

$$\min_{\mathbf{f}_s} \frac{1}{2N} \|\mathbf{y} - \mathbf{f}(\mathbf{X})\|^2 + \frac{\mu}{2N} \sum_{s=1}^{S} \sum_{s' \neq s} \|\mathbf{f}_s(\mathbf{X}_s) - \mathbf{f}_{s'}(\mathbf{X}_{s'})\|^2 + \frac{\lambda}{2} \|\mathbf{f}\|^2, \quad (1)$$

where $\mathbf{f}(\mathbf{X})$ is the final predictive model. $\mathbf{f}_s(\mathbf{X}_s)$ is the prediction results generated from data $\mathbf{X}_s$. λ and μ are the nonnegative regularization parameters that regulate the sparsity of the solution regarding $\mathbf{f}_s$ and the disagreement among models learned from different social networks, respectively. If we just treat the confidence of different social networks equally, the final predictive model can be formalized as follows,

$$\mathbf{f}(\mathbf{X}) = \frac{1}{S} \sum_{s=1}^{S} \mathbf{f}_s(\mathbf{X}_s). \quad (2)$$

However, in reality, different social networks always have different confidence to the final prediction, and we consider modeling the weights of multiple sources instead of treating all sources equally by introducing the weight vector: $\boldsymbol{\alpha} = [\alpha_1, \alpha_2, \cdots, \alpha_S]^T \in \mathbb{R}^{S \times 1}$, where α_s controls the weight of model learned from s-th social network. Then the final model is defined as follows,

$$\mathbf{f}(\mathbf{X}) = \sum_{s=1}^{S} \alpha_s \mathbf{f}_s(\mathbf{X}_s) \quad \text{subject to} \quad \mathbf{e}^T \boldsymbol{\alpha} = 1, \quad (3)$$

where $\mathbf{e} = [1, 1, \cdots, 1]^T \in \mathbb{R}^{S \times 1}$. It is worth mentioning that we do not impose the constraint of $\alpha_s \geq 0$, as we want to keep both positive and negative weights. Positive weights indicate the positive correlations of social networks with the final results, while negative weights reflect negative correlations between the given task and different sources, which may contain unreliable and noisy data.

For the s-th social network, we learn a linear mapping function indexed by a model $\mathbf{w}_s \in \mathbb{R}^{D_s \times 1}$. Then the objective function can be rewritten as follows,

$$\min_{\mathbf{w}_s, \boldsymbol{\alpha}} \frac{1}{2N} \left\| \mathbf{y} - \sum_{s=1}^{S} \alpha_s \mathbf{X}_s \mathbf{w}_s \right\|^2 + \frac{\mu}{2N} \sum_{s=1}^{S} \sum_{s' \neq s} \|\mathbf{X}_s \mathbf{w}_s - \mathbf{X}_{s'} \mathbf{w}_{s'}\|^2 + \frac{\lambda}{2} \sum_{s=1}^{S} \|\mathbf{w}_s\|^2 + \frac{\beta}{2} \|\boldsymbol{\alpha}\|^2, \quad (4)$$

where $\mathbf{e}^T \boldsymbol{\alpha} = 1$ and β is the regularization parameter, controlling the sparsity of the solution regarding $\boldsymbol{\alpha}$.

3.3 Optimization

We adopt the alternating optimization strategy to solve the two variables $\boldsymbol{\alpha}$ and $\mathbf{w}_s$ in Eqn. (4). In particular, we optimize one variable while fixing the other one in each iteration. We keep this iterative procedure until the objective function converges.

3.3.1 *Computing $\boldsymbol{\alpha}$ with $\mathbf{w}_s$ fixed*

We denote the objective function as $\boldsymbol{\Gamma}$. For simplicity, we replace $\mathbf{y}$ in Eqn. (4) by $\mathbf{y}\mathbf{e}^T \boldsymbol{\alpha}$, as $\mathbf{e}^T \boldsymbol{\alpha} = 1$. With the help of Lagrangian, $\boldsymbol{\Gamma}$ can be rewritten as follows,

$$\min_{\boldsymbol{\alpha}} \frac{1}{2N} \|\mathbf{y}\mathbf{e}^T \boldsymbol{\alpha} - \mathbf{X}\mathbf{W}\boldsymbol{\alpha}\|^2 + \frac{\beta}{2} \|\boldsymbol{\alpha}\|^2 + \delta(1 - \mathbf{e}^T \boldsymbol{\alpha}), \quad (5)$$

where δ is the nonnegative Lagrange multiplier and $\mathbf{W} = diag(\mathbf{w}_1, \mathbf{w}_2, \cdots, \mathbf{w}_S) \in \mathbb{R}^{D \times S}$. Taking derivative of $\boldsymbol{\Gamma}$ with respect to $\boldsymbol{\alpha}$, we have,

$$\frac{\partial \boldsymbol{\Gamma}}{\partial \boldsymbol{\alpha}} = \frac{1}{N} (\mathbf{y}\mathbf{e}^T - \mathbf{X}\mathbf{W})^T (\mathbf{y}\mathbf{e}^T - \mathbf{X}\mathbf{W}) \boldsymbol{\alpha} + \beta \boldsymbol{\alpha} - \delta \mathbf{e}. \quad (6)$$

Setting Eqn. (6) to zero, it can be derived that,

$$\boldsymbol{\alpha} = \delta \mathbf{M}^{-1} \mathbf{e}, \quad (7)$$

where

$$\mathbf{M} = \frac{1}{N} (\mathbf{y}\mathbf{e}^T - \mathbf{X}\mathbf{W})^T (\mathbf{y}\mathbf{e}^T - \mathbf{X}\mathbf{W}) + \beta \mathbf{I}. \quad (8)$$

Since $\mathbf{e}^T\boldsymbol{\alpha} = 1$, we can obtain that,

$$\delta = \frac{1}{\mathbf{e}^T\mathbf{M}^{-1}\mathbf{e}}, \qquad \boldsymbol{\alpha} = \frac{\mathbf{M}^{-1}\mathbf{e}}{\mathbf{e}^T\mathbf{M}^{-1}\mathbf{e}}. \tag{9}$$

Obviously, $\mathbf{M} \in \mathbb{R}^{S\times S}$ is positive definite and invertible, according to the definition. We thus can obtain the analytic solution of $\boldsymbol{\alpha}$ as Eqn. (9). Moreover, we note that when the prediction results learned from all social networks are equal, where $\mathbf{X}_1\mathbf{w}_1 = \mathbf{X}_2\mathbf{w}_2 = \cdots = \mathbf{X}_S\mathbf{w}_S$, then same weights will be assigned, i.e., $\alpha_1 = \alpha_2 = \cdots = \alpha_S$. In addition, Eqn. (9) tends to assign higher weight α_s, if smaller difference exists between $\mathbf{y}$ and $\mathbf{X}_s\mathbf{w}_s$.

3.3.2 *Computing* $\mathbf{w}_s$ *with* $\boldsymbol{\alpha}$ *fixed*

When $\boldsymbol{\alpha}$ is fixed, we compute the derivative of $\boldsymbol{\Gamma}$ regarding $\mathbf{w}_s$ as follows,

$$\begin{aligned}\frac{\partial\boldsymbol{\Gamma}}{\partial\mathbf{w}_s} &= \frac{1}{N}\alpha_s\mathbf{X}_s^T(\sum_{s=1}^{S}\alpha_s\mathbf{X}_s\mathbf{w}_s - \mathbf{y}) \\ &+ \frac{\mu}{N}\mathbf{X}_s^T\sum_{s=1}^{S}\sum_{s'\neq s}(\mathbf{X}_s\mathbf{w}_s - \mathbf{X}_{s'}\mathbf{w}_{s'}) + \lambda\mathbf{w}_s \\ &= \Big[\lambda\mathbf{I} + \frac{\alpha_s^2}{N}\mathbf{X}_s^T\mathbf{X}_s + \frac{\mu(S-1)}{N}\mathbf{X}_s^T\mathbf{X}_s\Big]\mathbf{w}_s \\ &+ \sum_{s=1}^{S}\sum_{s'\neq s}\frac{1}{N}(\alpha_s\alpha_{s'} - \mu)\mathbf{X}_s^T\mathbf{X}_{s'}\mathbf{w}_{s'} - \frac{\alpha_s}{N}\mathbf{X}_s^T\mathbf{y},\end{aligned} \tag{10}$$

where $\mathbf{I}$ is a $D_s \times D_s$ identity matrix. Setting Eqn. (10) to zero and rearranging the terms, all $\mathbf{w}_s$'s can be learned jointly by the following linear system,

$$\mathbf{L}\mathbf{w} = \mathbf{t}$$

$$\begin{bmatrix}\mathbf{L}_{11} & \mathbf{L}_{12} & \mathbf{L}_{13} & \cdots & \mathbf{L}_{1S}\\ \mathbf{L}_{21} & \mathbf{L}_{22} & \mathbf{L}_{23} & \cdots & \mathbf{L}_{2S}\\ \mathbf{L}_{31} & \mathbf{L}_{32} & \mathbf{L}_{33} & \cdots & \mathbf{L}_{3S}\\ \vdots & \vdots & \vdots & \ddots & \vdots\\ \mathbf{L}_{S1} & \mathbf{L}_{S2} & \mathbf{L}_{S3} & \cdots & \mathbf{L}_{SS}\end{bmatrix}\begin{bmatrix}\mathbf{w}_1\\ \mathbf{w}_2\\ \mathbf{w}_3\\ \vdots\\ \mathbf{w}_S\end{bmatrix} = \begin{bmatrix}\mathbf{t}_1\\ \mathbf{t}_2\\ \mathbf{t}_3\\ \vdots\\ \mathbf{t}_S\end{bmatrix}, \tag{11}$$

where $\mathbf{L} \in \mathbb{R}^{D\times D}$ is a sparse block matrix with $S \times S$ blocks, $\mathbf{w} = [\mathbf{w}_1^T, \mathbf{w}_2^T, \cdots, \mathbf{w}_S^T]^T \in \mathbb{R}^{D\times 1}$ and $\mathbf{t} = [\mathbf{t}_1^T, \mathbf{t}_2^T, \cdots, \mathbf{t}_S^T]^T \in \mathbb{R}^{D\times 1}$ are both sparse block vectors with $S \times 1$ blocks. $\mathbf{t}_s$, $\mathbf{L}_{ss}$ and $\mathbf{L}_{ss'}$ are defined as follows,

$$\begin{cases}\mathbf{t}_s &= \frac{\alpha_s}{N}\mathbf{X}_s^T\mathbf{y},\\ \mathbf{L}_{ss} &= \lambda\mathbf{I} + \frac{\alpha_s^2-\mu}{N}\mathbf{X}_s^T\mathbf{X}_s + \frac{\mu S}{N}\mathbf{X}_s^T\mathbf{X}_s,\\ \mathbf{L}_{ss'} &= \frac{\alpha_s\alpha_{s'}-\mu}{N}\mathbf{X}_s^T\mathbf{X}_{s'}.\end{cases} \tag{12}$$

Technically, $\mathbf{t}$ can be treated as a constant matrix as $\boldsymbol{\alpha}$ is fixed. It is worth noting that $\mathbf{L}$ is symmetric as $\mathbf{L}_{ss'} = \mathbf{L}_{s's}^T$. If we can prove that $\mathbf{L}$ is invertible, then we can derive the closed-form solution of $\mathbf{w}$ as follows,

$$\mathbf{w} = \mathbf{L}^{-1}\mathbf{t}. \tag{13}$$

We now show $\mathbf{L}$ is invertible by proving that $\mathbf{L}$ is a positive-definite matrix. Let $\mathbf{h} = [\mathbf{h}_1^T, \mathbf{h}_2^T, \cdots, \mathbf{h}_S^T]^T \in \mathbb{R}^{D\times 1} \neq \mathbf{0}$ be an arbitrary block vector, where $\mathbf{h}_i \in \mathbb{R}^{D_i\times 1}, i \in \mathcal{C}$. Then

Algorithm 1 Alternative optimization for solving Eqn. (4)

Input: $\mathbf{X}$, $\mathbf{y}$, λ, β, μ
Output: $\boldsymbol{\alpha}$, $\mathbf{w}$

Initialize $(\mathbf{w})^0$ by fitting each source individually on the available data. Initialize $(\boldsymbol{\alpha})^0 = [\frac{1}{S}, \frac{1}{S}, \cdots, \frac{1}{S}]$.
for $k = 1, 2, \cdots$ **do**
  Compute each $(\boldsymbol{\alpha})^k$ according to Eqn. (9).
  Update $(\mathbf{w})^k$ according to Eqn. (13).
  if the objective value stops decreasing **then**
    return $\boldsymbol{\alpha} = (\boldsymbol{\alpha})^k$ and $\mathbf{w} = (\mathbf{w})^k$
  end if
end for

we need to prove that $\mathbf{h}^T\mathbf{L}\mathbf{h}$

$$\begin{aligned}&= \sum_{i=1}^{S}\sum_{j=1}^{S}\mathbf{h}_i^T\mathbf{L}_{ij}\mathbf{h}_j\\ &= \lambda\left\|\mathbf{h}\right\|^2 + \frac{1}{N}\Big[\sum_{i=1}^{S}\left\|\alpha_i\mathbf{X}_i\mathbf{h}_i\right\|^2 + \mu(S-1)\sum_{i=1}^{S}\left\|\mathbf{X}_i\mathbf{h}_i\right\|^2\\ &+ \sum_{i=1}^{S}\sum_{j\neq i}\alpha_i\mathbf{h}_i^T\mathbf{X}_i^T\alpha_j\mathbf{X}_j\mathbf{h}_j - \mu\sum_{i=1}^{S}\sum_{j\neq i}\mathbf{h}_i^T\mathbf{X}_i^T\mathbf{X}_j\mathbf{h}_j\Big],\end{aligned} \tag{14}$$

is always larger than zero. In fact, given an arbitrary vector $\mathbf{b}_i$, we have,

$$\begin{aligned}&\left\|\mathbf{b}_1 - \mathbf{b}_2\right\|^2 + \cdots + \left\|\mathbf{b}_{(S-1)} - \mathbf{b}_S\right\|^2 + \left\|\mathbf{b}_S - \mathbf{b}_1\right\|^2 \geq 0\\ &\sum_{i=1}^{S}\left\|\mathbf{b}_i\right\|^2 \geq \sum_{i=1}^{S}\sum_{j\neq i}\mathbf{b}_i^T\mathbf{b}_j.\end{aligned} \tag{15}$$

Therefore, as $S \geq 2$, we have the following inequality,

$$\begin{aligned}\mu(S-1)\sum_{i=1}^{S}\left\|\mathbf{X}_i\mathbf{h}_i\right\|^2 &\geq \mu\sum_{i=1}^{S}\left\|\mathbf{X}_i\mathbf{h}_i\right\|^2\\ &\geq \mu\sum_{i=1}^{S}\sum_{j\neq i}(\mathbf{X}_i\mathbf{h}_i)^T\mathbf{X}_j\mathbf{h}_j.\end{aligned} \tag{16}$$

Besides, we know that,

$$\begin{aligned}&\sum_{i=1}^{S}\left\|\alpha_i\mathbf{X}_i\mathbf{h}_i\right\|^2 + \sum_{i=1}^{S}\sum_{j\neq i}\alpha_i\mathbf{h}_i^T\mathbf{X}_i^T\alpha_j\mathbf{X}_j\mathbf{h}_j\\ &= \frac{1}{2}\sum_{i=1}^{S}\left\|\alpha_i\mathbf{X}_i\mathbf{h}_i\right\|^2 + \frac{1}{2}\left\|\sum_{i=1}^{S}\alpha_i\mathbf{X}_i\mathbf{h}_i\right\|^2 \geq 0.\end{aligned} \tag{17}$$

Based upon Eqn. (16) and Eqn. (17), we have that,

$$\mathbf{h}^T\mathbf{L}\mathbf{h} \geq \lambda\left\|\mathbf{h}\right\|^2. \tag{18}$$

As $\mathbf{h} \neq \mathbf{0}$, $\mathbf{h}^T\mathbf{L}\mathbf{h}$ is always larger than zero. Consequently, $\mathbf{L}$ is invertible. The overall procedures for alternating optimization are summarized in Algorithm 1. As each iteration can decrease $\boldsymbol{\Gamma}$, whose lower bound is zero, we can guarantee the convergence of Algorithm 1 [7, 16].

4. MISSING DATA COMPLETION

In this section, we deal with a more challenging and realistic situation, where block-wise missing data exists, and propose an approach for multiple social network data completion (MSNDC). In such situations, user samples may not be active in all social networks, which leads to the block-wise data missing.

Suppose we have S data sources in total and each sample has at least one data source available. We employ the subset $\mathcal{C}_i \subseteq \mathcal{C}$ to indicate the presence of each source and the signature of a specific social network combination. Based on these combinations, all the data samples can be split into multiple exclusive sets, where each set corresponds to a combination. Figure 2 illustrates the incomplete data in our dataset. As can be seen, all users have complete features from SN_1, while some users miss data in SN_2 or SN_3. Therefore, our dataset can be split by four exclusive social network combinations: $\mathcal{C}_1 = \{1, 2\}$, $\mathcal{C}_2 = \{1, 2, 3\}$, $\mathcal{C}_3 = \{1, 3\}$, $\mathcal{C}_4 = \{1\}$.

Inspired by [10], we use Non-negative Matrix Factorization (NMF) to explore the latent spaces that are shared by different social networks, and further infer the missing data based upon these latent spaces. It is reasonable to assume that the data from different social networks about the same user shares certain latent features. We employ $\mathbf{X}_s^{\mathcal{C}_i} \in \mathbb{R}^{N_{\mathcal{C}_i} \times D_s}$ to denote the samples generated from the s-th social network. It only contains samples that are available in the set of social networks $\mathcal{C}_i$, where $N_{\mathcal{C}_i}$ stands for the number of these samples. We use $\mathbf{U}_s \in \mathbb{R}^{z \times D_s}$ to represent the latent basis matrix for the s-th social network, and $\mathbf{P}_s^{\mathcal{C}_i} \in \mathbb{R}^{N_{\mathcal{C}_i} \times z}$ to denote the corresponding latent representation of feature matrix $\mathbf{X}_s^{\mathcal{C}_i}$. z is the dimension of the shared latent space of different social networks. The intuitive assumption is that for the samples available in both the s-th and s'-th social networks, their corresponding latent representations should also be quite similar. In particular, we impose this constraint to NMF as follows,

$$\mathbf{P}_s^{\mathcal{C}_i} = \mathbf{P}_{s'}^{\mathcal{C}_i} = \mathbf{P}^{\mathcal{C}_i}, \tag{19}$$

where $s \neq s'$, $s \in \mathcal{C}_i$, and $s' \in \mathcal{C}_i$. We thus learn the shared subspaces by the following objective function,

$$\begin{aligned} \min_{\substack{\mathbf{U}_s \geq \mathbf{0} \\ \mathbf{P}_s \geq \mathbf{0}}} & \left\| \begin{bmatrix} \mathbf{X}_1^{\{1\}} \\ \mathbf{X}_1^{\{1,2\}} \\ \mathbf{X}_1^{\{1,3\}} \\ \mathbf{X}_1^{\{1,2,3\}} \end{bmatrix} - \begin{bmatrix} \mathbf{P}^{\{1\}} \\ \mathbf{P}^{\{1,2\}} \\ \mathbf{P}^{\{1,3\}} \\ \mathbf{P}^{\{1,2,3\}} \end{bmatrix} \mathbf{U}_1 \right\|^2 + \nu \left\|\mathbf{P}_1\right\|_1 + \eta \left\|\mathbf{U}_1\right\|_1 \\ & + \left\| \begin{bmatrix} \mathbf{X}_2^{\{1,2\}} \\ \mathbf{X}_2^{\{1,2,3\}} \end{bmatrix} - \begin{bmatrix} \mathbf{P}^{\{1,2\}} \\ \mathbf{P}^{\{1,2,3\}} \end{bmatrix} \mathbf{U}_2 \right\|^2 + \nu \left\|\mathbf{P}_2\right\|_1 + \eta \left\|\mathbf{U}_2\right\|_1 \\ & + \left\| \begin{bmatrix} \mathbf{X}_3^{\{1,3\}} \\ \mathbf{X}_3^{\{1,2,3\}} \end{bmatrix} - \begin{bmatrix} \mathbf{P}^{\{1,3\}} \\ \mathbf{P}^{\{1,2,3\}} \end{bmatrix} \mathbf{U}_3 \right\|^2 + \nu \left\|\mathbf{P}_3\right\|_1 + \eta \left\|\mathbf{U}_3\right\|_1, \end{aligned} \tag{20}$$

where ν and η are the nonnegative tradeoff parameters for the regularizations. Similarly, we employ the alternating optimization strategy to solve the optimization in Eqn. (20). To be more specific, we first initialize $\mathbf{U}_s$ and compute the optimal $\mathbf{P}_s$. Afterwards, $\mathbf{P}_s$ is updated based on the computed $\mathbf{U}_s$. We keep this iterative procedure until the objective function converges.

The proposed approach differs from [10] in the following three aspects. First, MSNDC is generalized to handle the more challenging scenario where data samples are extracted from more than two social networks. Second, apart from regulating the latent representation matrix, we also incorporate the regularization on the latent basis matrix. Third, we further derive the original missing data from the latent representation, where the authors in [10] just apply cluster algorithms directly to the latent representation of data instead of the original data. This is due to two considerations. One is that we believe the value of original known data is higher than the latent representation. The other one is that we need to preserve the heterogeneity among data from different sources to fit the MSNL model.

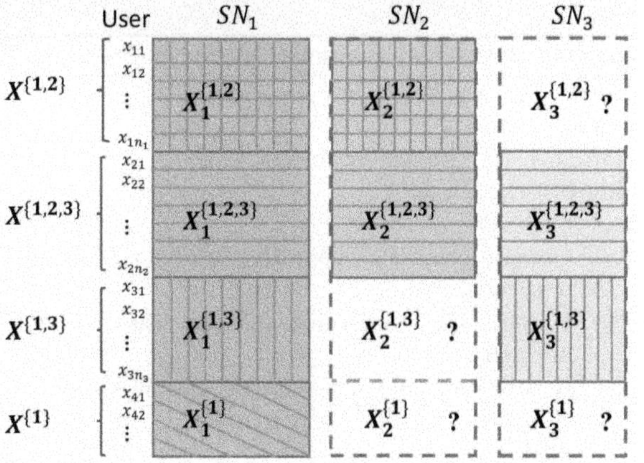

Figure 2: Illustration of the incomplete data from three sources. $\mathbf{X}_s^{\mathcal{C}_i}$ denotes the samples generated from social network s that are only available in the social network combination of $\mathcal{C}_i$.

4.1 Optimization

In order to increase the efficiency of the iterative procedure, we initialize $\mathbf{U}_s$ by optimizing the following objective function,

$$\begin{aligned} \min_{\mathbf{U}_s \geq \mathbf{0}} & \left\|\mathbf{X}_1^{\{1,2,3\}} - \mathbf{P}^{\{1,2,3\}}\mathbf{U}_1\right\|^2 + \nu \left\|\mathbf{P}^{\{1,2,3\}}\right\|_1 + \eta \left\|\mathbf{U}_1\right\|_1 \\ & + \left\|\mathbf{X}_2^{\{1,2,3\}} - \mathbf{P}^{\{1,2,3\}}\mathbf{U}_2\right\|^2 + \eta \left\|\mathbf{U}_2\right\|_1 \\ & + \left\|\mathbf{X}_3^{\{1,2,3\}} - \mathbf{P}^{\{1,2,3\}}\mathbf{U}_3\right\|^2 + \eta \left\|\mathbf{U}_3\right\|_1. \end{aligned} \tag{21}$$

We then alternatively optimize $\mathbf{U}_s$ and $\mathbf{P}_s$ until the objective function converges. Specifically, we employ the greedy coordinate descent (GCD) approach [9], which has been proven to be tremendously fast to solve NMF decomposition with L1-norm regularization. Finally, we obtain $\mathbf{P}_s, \mathbf{U}_s, s \in \mathcal{C}$, based on which we can infer the missing data as follows,

$$\hat{\mathbf{X}}_s^{\mathcal{C}_i} = \mathbf{P}^{\mathcal{C}_i}\mathbf{U}_s, \quad \forall s \notin \mathcal{C}_i. \tag{22}$$

Algorithm 2 summarizes the overall procedures for alternating optimization.

5. APPLICATION: VOLUNTEERISM TENDENCY PREDICTION

In this work, we apply the proposed scheme to an application scenario: volunteerism tendency prediction. In modern society, volunteers are extremely crucial to NPOs to sustain their continuing operations. The discovery of users' volunteerism tendency can significantly facilitate the recruitment of volunteers for NPOs, which can save considerable cost to find the potential volunteers. In particular, we cast the problem of volunteerism tendency prediction as a user binary classification. If the predicted tendency score of a given user is larger than a pre-defined

Algorithm 2 Alternative optimization for solving Eqn. (20)

Input: $\mathbf{X}_1, \mathbf{X}_2, \mathbf{X}_3, \nu, \eta$
Output: $\hat{\mathbf{X}}$

Initialize $\mathbf{U}_s^{(0)}$ according to Eqn. (21).
for $k = 1, 2, \cdots$ **do**
  for $s = 1, 2, \cdots, S$ **do**
    Compute each $\mathbf{P}_s^{(k)}$ according to Eqn. (20) via GCD approach.
    Update $\mathbf{U}_s^{(k)}$ according to Eqn. (20) via GCD approach.
    if the objective value stops decreasing **then**
      return $\mathbf{U}_s = \mathbf{U}_s^{(k)}$ and $\mathbf{P}_s = \mathbf{P}_s^{(k)}$
    end if
  end for
end for
for $j = 1, 2, \cdots, S$ **do**
  for $\mathcal{C}_q \subseteq \mathcal{C}$ **do**
    if $j \in \mathcal{C}_q$ **then**
      $\hat{\mathbf{X}}_j^{\mathcal{C}_q} = \mathbf{X}_j^{\mathcal{C}_q}$.
    else
      Infer $\hat{\mathbf{X}}_j^{\mathcal{C}_q}$ according to Eqn. (22).
    end if
  end for
end for

threshold γ, we regard this user as a volunteer. In this work, we explore three popular social networks: Twitter, Facebook and LinkedIn, as they are representative of a public, private, and professional social network, respectively. Besides, it is known that users exhibit different aspects on different social networks [1], and the combination of these three social networks would help to better characterize user behaviors on social platforms.

5.1 Multiple Social Accounts Mappings

To represent the same users with multiple sources, we need to first tackle the problem of "Social Account Mapping", which aims to align the same users across different social networks by linking their multiple social accounts [1]. To accurately establish this mapping, we employ the emerging social services such as About.me[3] and Quora[4], where they encourage users to explicitly list their multiple social accounts on one profile.

We proposed two strategies to collect data from About.me.

- **Keyword search**: We searched About.me with the keyword "volunteer" and obtained 4,151 volunteer candidates.
- **Random select**: We employed Random API[5], provided by About.me, to collect non-volunteers. This API returns a specified number of random user profiles. Finally, we harvested 1,867 non-volunteer candidates. It is worth mentioning that volunteers may be present in these random users.

To enlarge our dataset, we also collected candidates from Quora by the breadth-first-search method. Particularly, we took advantage of both the follower and followee[6] relations provided by Quora. Initially, we selected two popular users as the seed users and then explored all their neighboring connected users. We applied similar exploration approach to all other non-seed users. In the end, we collected 172,235 users' profiles and only retained those who have accounts in Facebook, Twitter and LinkedIn.

[3]https://about.me/
[4]http://quora.com/
[5]http://about.me/developer/api/docs/
[6]If A follows B, then A is B's follower and B is A's followee.

5.2 Ground Truth Construction

Based on these candidates, we launched a crawler to collect their historical social contents, including their basic profiles, social posts and relations. However, the traditional web-based crawler is not applicable to Facebook due to its dynamic loading mechanism. We thus resorted to the Selenium[7] to simulate users' click and scroll operations on a FireFox browser and load users' publicly available information. We limited the access rate to one request per second to avoid being blocked by the robot checkers. It is worth mentioning that the data we collected is all publicly available. On the other hand, due to the privacy constraint, we could not access uses' social relations in Facebook and LinkedIn. We hence only collected users' followee relations in Twitter.

In order to improve the quality of our dataset, we employed three annotators to finalize our ground truth. As users tend to provide more complete and reliable profiles in LinkedIn, we guided the annotators to study the LinkedIn profiles of candidate users, and determine whether they are "volunteers" by majority votes. To ensure a uniformly labeling procedure, we provided them a piece of guideline. Given a user's LinkedIn profile, we classified the user as a volunteer if and only if this user lists his/her volunteer experiences in the section "Volunteer experience & Causes" or section "Experience". Candidates who do not satisfy the above two criteria were tagged as non-volunteers. We focused on LinkedIn to determine whether users are volunteers because the volunteer experiences in LinkedIn are the most straightforward evidence to identify volunteers. It should be noted that those who do not mention their volunteer experiences in LinkedIn are not necessarily classified as "non-volunteers". However, the absence of these mentions, at least, reveals their limited interests and low enthusiasm in volunteerism. Therefore, in our work, we broadly defined users as "non-volunteers" if they do not mention their relevant volunteerism experiences in LinkedIn.

Table 1 lists the statistics of our dataset. We obtained the data for 1,425 volunteers and 4,011 non-volunteers according to the aforementioned strategies. The crawling was conducted between 22nd August to 11th September, 2013. Here we only selected a subset of non-volunteer data and made the dataset balanced to avoid the training bias. To facilitate this line of research, this dataset has been released after certain privacy preservation processing.

However, in reality, not all users are active enough on all social networks. To ensure the data quality, we treated those inactive users as missing with respect to a specific social network. Therefore, there exists block-wise missing data in our dataset. In particular, we treated a user as missing in Twitter or Facebook, if this user has less than 10 historical social posts. In addition, due to the absence of social post

[7]http://docs.seleniumhq.org/download/

Table 1: Statistics of our dataset.

Data	Volunteer	Non-volunteer
Twitter profiles	~1.5k	~4k
Twitter posts	~559k	~1m
Twitter followees' profiles	~902k	~3m
Facebook profiles	~1.5k	~4k
Facebook posts	~83k	~338k
LinkedIn profiles	~1.5k	~4k

mechanism in LinkedIn, we treated a user as missing[8] in LinkedIn if the word count of this user's profile is less than 50. Figure 3 shows the statistics of our incomplete data. As can be seen, about 50% of users have complete data from all three social networks. 1% and 47% of users only miss the data either from Facebook and LinkedIn, while 2% of users miss the data from both of them.

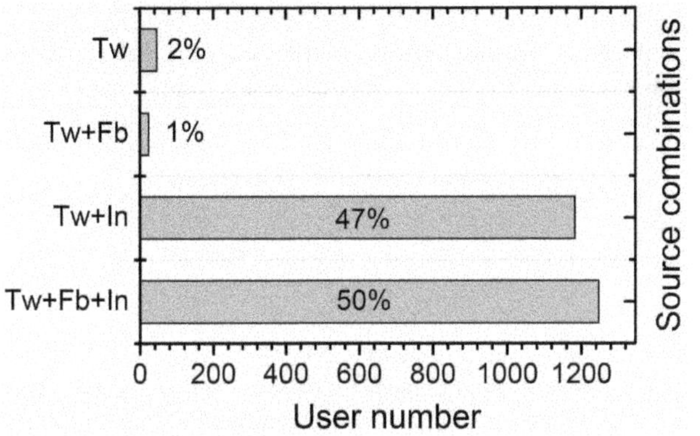

Figure 3: Statistics of the incomplete data. Tw: Users with Twitter data only; Tw+Fb: Users with Twitter and Facebook data only; Tw+In: Users with Twitter and Linkedin data only; Tw+Fb+In: Users without missing data.

5.3 Features

To capture users' volunteerism tendency, we extracted a rich set of volunteer-oriented features.

5.3.1 *Demographic Characteristics*

The study in [19] reported that some demographic characteristics, such as education and income level, are strong indicators for volunteerism. This study inspires us to extract demographic characteristics from users' profiles, especially the Facebook and LinkedIn profiles. In our work, we explored users' demographic characteristics, including *Gender*, *Relationship status*, *Education level*, and *Number of social connections*.

5.3.2 *Linguistic Features*

We also extracted linguistic features, including Linguistic Inquiry and Word Count (LIWC) features, user topics and contextual topics.

LIWC features. LIWC is widely-used to analyze the psycho-linguistic transparent lexicon. It plays an important role in predicting users' personality [2, 15]. The main component of LIWC is a directory which contains the mapping from words to 72 categories[9]. Given a document, LIWC computes the percentage of words in each category and represents it as a vector of 72 dimensions.

To capture the key aspects of LIWC features, we selected the top 5 dimensions as the representative LIWC features according to the information gain ratio. Considering that the emotions for individuals may also affect users' volunteerism tendency, we additionally selected two categories from LIWC: positive emotion and negative emotion. Besides, we also utilized the positive-negative emotion ratio to further reflect users' emotional states. Let $L(\bullet)$ represent the percentage of users' words in certain LIWC category. The positive-negative emotion ratio is defined as,

$$PN_{emo} = L(pos)log\frac{L(pos)+\xi_p}{L(neg)+\xi_n}, \tag{23}$$

where ξ_p and ξ_n are introduced to avoid the situation: individuals have no positive or negative emotional word. They are both set as 0.0001. In total, we have 16 dimension LIWC features, extracted from Twitter and Facebook.

User topics. According to our observation, volunteers may have, on average, a higher probability of talking about topics such as social caring or giving back, while the non-volunteers may mention other topics more often. This motivates us to explore the topic distributions of users' social posts to identify volunteers. We generated topic distributions using Latent Dirichlet Allocation (LDA) [4], which has been widely found to be useful in latent topic modeling [8, 23]. Based on perplexity [14] metric frequently utilized to find the optimal number of hidden topics, we ultimately obtained 52, 26, 42 dimensional topic-level features over users' Twitter, Facebook and LinkedIn data, respectively.

Contextual topics. We define users' contextual topics as the topics of users' connections. We believe that the contextual topics intuitively reflect the contexts of users. "He that lies down with dogs must rise up with fleas" tells us that the context significantly affects a user's tendency. Particularly, we studied followees and retweeting[10] connections on Twitter because of their intuitive reflection of topics that users concern. As the bio descriptions are usually provided by users to briefly introduce themselves and may indicate users' summarized interests, we integrated the bios of a user's followees or those whose tweets are retweeted by this user into two kinds of bio documents, on which we further applied LDA model. We utilized the perplexity to fix the dimensions of topic-level features over followees' bio documents and retweetings' bio documents as 40 and 20, respectively. In this work, we only explored the contextual topics in Twitter, since we were unable to crawl the connections' profiles in LinkedIn and the bio descriptions are usually missing in Facebook.

5.3.3 *Behavior-based features*

This kind of features is characterized by users' posting behavior patterns and networking behavior patterns. The former focuses on the written style of users' social posts, while the latter captures their egocentric network features.

Posting behavior patterns. Posting behavior patterns have been investigated in many scenarios, spanning from

[8]Here we exclude the contents of section "Volunteer experience & Causes" and section "Experience".

[9]http://www.liwc.net/

[10]If A broadcasts a tweet posted by B, then B is A's a retweeting user.

age estimation to social spammers discovery [3, 13]. These patterns can be used to depict users' participation in information diffusion, which correlates with volunteerism tendency much.

On one hand, we employed the fraction of users' posts containing certain behaviors, including emoticons, slang words, acronyms, hashtags, URLs, and user mentions, to intuitively reflect users' engagement in topic discussion and social interaction. On the other hand, we observed that users' posting behaviors in social networks can be classified into a few categories. For example, posts in Twitter can be classified into two categories, $C_{tw} = \{tweets, retweets\}$, while posts in Facebook can roughly be split into eight types: $C_{fb} = \{share\_link, share\_sideo, share\_status, share\_photo, change\_photo, repost, post, tagged\}$. The distributions over users' posts on these categories also reflect their participation in information diffusion, revealing whether a given user tend to share information in social networks. When it comes to Linkedin, we utilized the profile completeness to characterize users' behaviors. Based on our observation, we found that volunteers tend to provide more information for all the sections. This not only reflects volunteers' active participation in LinkedIn but also signals their self-confidence and openness to public. Profile completeness is defined as a boolean vector over six dimensions to denote the presence of the six common sections in LinkedIn profiles: `summary`, `interest`, `language`, `education`, `skill` and `honor`. We excluded the sections on `experience` and `volunteer experience & causes`, because the ground truth is built on these two sections.

Egocentric network patterns. We also studied users' social behaviors from their egocentric networks. Intuitively, we believe that users belong to certain class tend to be connected with several class-specific accounts, as it goes for that "birds of a feather flock together". Therefore, volunteers should interact with some typical accounts in social media. The set of typical accounts is denoted as FV. Inspired by [17], we measured the degree of a user's correlation with volunteerism by three features: the frequency and fraction of a user's "friends" that belong to FV as well as the total number of "friends". In particular, we treated both the followees and retweetings as the "friends" of users in Twitter.

To construct the FV, we utilized the Twitter profile repository Wefollow[11], which allows us to find the most prominent people given a particular category. By crawling prominent users falling into categories of *Nonprofit, Charity, Volunteer, NGO, Community Service, Social Welfare* and *Christian* from Wefollow, we obtained 23,285 accounts.

6. EXPERIMENTS

We conducted extensive experiments to comparatively verify our proposed scheme from various angles over a system equipped with Intel i72.60 GHz CPU, and 8 GB memory. In particular, we launched 10-fold cross validation for each experiment, and reported the average performance. Each fold involves 2,249 training and 250 testing samples.

6.1 On Model Comparison

We compared **MSNL** with four baselines. Before that, the data was completed by **MSNDC**. We also performed significant test to validate the effectiveness of **MSNL**.

[11]http://wefollow.com/

SVM: We chose the learning formulation with the kernel of radial-basis function. We implemented this method based on LIBSVM [6].

RLS: Regularized least squares model [11] aims to minimize the objective function of $\frac{1}{2N}\left\|\mathbf{y}-\mathbf{X}\mathbf{w}\right\|^2+\frac{\lambda}{2}\left\|\mathbf{w}\right\|^2$. In fact, the **RLS** model can be deduced from **MSNL** via the settings of $\alpha=[\frac{1}{S},\frac{1}{S},\cdots,\frac{1}{S}]^T$, $\mu=0$ and $\beta=0$.

iSFS: The third baseline is the incomplete source-feature selection model proposed in [24]. This model only assigns weights to models learned from different social networks but ignores the relationships among them. We can derive **iSFS** from **MSNL** by making $\mu=0$.

regMVMT: The fourth baseline is the regularized multi-view multi-task learning model [28]. This model only regulates the relationships among different views but fails to take the source confidence into account. We can derive **regMVMT** from **MSNL** by making $\alpha=[\frac{1}{S},\frac{1}{S},\cdots,\frac{1}{S}]^T$.

Table 2: Performance of different models(%).

Approaches	F1-measure	P-value
SVM	83.11	0.038
RLS	82.82	0.025
regMVMT	84.07	0.173
iSFS	84.72	0.281
MSNL	**85.59**	-

Table 2 shows the performance comparison between baselines and our proposed **MSNL**. We noticed that **MSNL** significantly outperforms the **SVM** and **RLS**. This implies that the information on multiple social networks are complementary and characterize users' volunteerism tendency consistently. This also proves that the correlations of different social networks with the task of volunteerism tendency prediction cannot be treated equally. In addition, **MSNL** achieves better performance, as compared with **iSFS** and **regMVMT**, which are the derivations of **MSNL**. This demonstrates that both the source confidence and the source consistency deserve particular attention.

6.2 On Data Completion Comparison

We further evaluated the component for missing data completion with the following three baseline methods.

Remove: This method eliminates all data samples that are not complete.

Average: This method imputes the missing features with the average values of the corresponding feature items.

KNN: The missing data is inferred by averaging its K-nearest neighbors. K is experimentally set as 1.

Table 3: Performance of different models over different data completion strategies.

Approaches	SVM	RLS	MSNL
Remove	74.91	74.66	81.81
Average	82.09	81.99	85.43
KNN	82.60	82.22	85.55
MSNDC	83.11	82.82	**85.59**

Table 3 shows the performance of different models over different data completion strategies. It can be seen that **MSNDC** outperforms the other strategies. Additionally, removing all incomplete data samples achieves the worst performance, which may be caused by the fact that it introduces training bias, making the dataset unbalanced and reduces the size of training dataset. We found that the percentage of volunteer samples decreases from 50% to 40% after filtering out all incomplete data samples.

6.3 On Feature Comparison

To examine the discriminative features we extracted, we conducted experiments over different kinds of features using **MSNL**. We also performed significant test to validate the advantage of combining multiple social networks. Table 4 comparatively shows the performance of **MSNL** in terms of different feature configurations. It can be seen that the linguistic features achieves the best performance, as compared against demographic characteristics and behavior-based features. This reveals that volunteerism tendency is better reflected by their social contents, including their own social posts and the self-descriptions of their social connections. This also implies that users with volunteerism tendency may talk about related topics and follow or retweet related social accounts. In addition, we found that contextual topics are more discriminative as compared to users' own topics. This may be due to the fact that users' self-descriptions are of more value and contain less noise than users' tweets. Some hot topics discussed by volunteers are given in Table 5. Besides, the egocentric network patterns also play a dominant role in our task. This implies that one's social connections indeed reflect the user's personal concerns to a large extent.

Table 4: Performance of different features(%).

Features	F1-measure
Demographic characteristics	**68.43**
Linguistic features	**80.06**
User topics	75.04
Contextual topics	78.14
LIWC	68.48
Behavior-based features	**78.52**
Posting behavior patterns	69.83
Egocentric network patterns	75.91

6.4 On Source Comparison

To demonstrate the descriptiveness of multiple social network integration, we conducted experiments over various source combinations. Notably, data from Facebook and LinkedIn is incomplete and we need to infer the block-wise missing data first taking advantage of the complete data samples from Twitter.

Table 6 shows the performance of **MSNL** over different social network combinations. We noted that the more sources we incorporate, the better the performance can be achieved. This implies the complementary relationships rather than mutual conflicting relationships among the sources. Moreover, we found that aggregating data from all these three social networks can achieve significantly better performance as compared to each of the single source. Additionally, as the performance obtained from different single social networks are not the same, this validates that incorporating the confidence of different social networks to **MSNL** is reasonable. Interestingly, we observed that **MSNL** over Twitter alone achieves the much better performance, as compared to that over LinkedIn or Facebook alone. This may be caused by the fact that the most discriminative features evaluated by Section 6.3 are all extracted from Twitter.

Table 5: Hot topics discussed by volunteers. Followee and retweeting: contextual topics; Self: user topics.

Data source	Topic words
Followee	• public, politics, rights, development
	• editor, global, journalist, university
Retweeting	• global, nonprofit, change, community
	• health, education, learning, university
Self	• woman, help, education, child
	• volunteer, nonprofit, support

Table 6: Performance of different social network combinations(%). Facebook* and LinkedIn* both refer to the complete data, whose missing data is pre-inferred. F1: F1-measure.

Social network combinations	F1	p-value
Twitter	82.35	4.2e-2
Facebook*	73.53	5.0e-7
LinkedIn*	74.49	3.1e-7
Twitter+Facebook*	83.67	1.1e-1
Twitter+LinkedIn*	83.84	1.4e-1
Facebook*+LinkedIn*	76.29	6.0e-6
Twitter+Facebook*+LinkedIn*	**85.59**	-

6.5 Size Varying of Positive Samples

In order to verify the usefulness of our model on real world dataset, where the volunteers should account for a minority portion of user population, we tuned the fraction of volunteer samples in our dataset. In particular, we fed x%, $x \in [5, 50]$, of volunteer samples to our model with stepsize 5%. Figure 4 shows the F1-measure with respect to different fraction of volunteer samples of different models. As can be seen, our model can achieve satisfactory performance even when volunteer samples only accounts for 5% of the whole samples. This demonstrates that the proposed **MSNL** model is not sensitive to the percentage of positive samples. Whereas, **SVM** and **RLS** are relatively more sensitive to the fraction of volunteer samples in dataset.

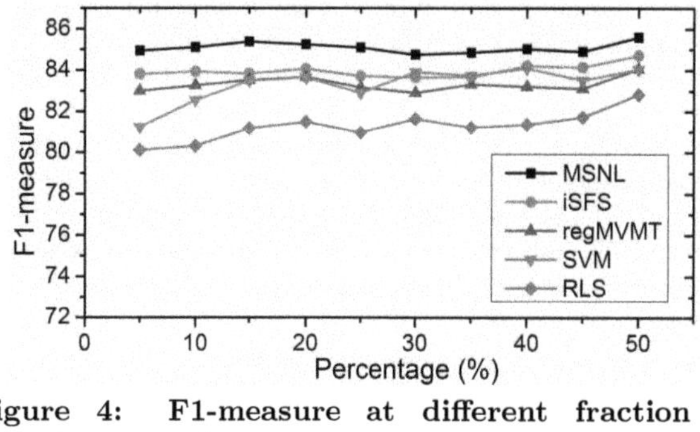

Figure 4: F1-measure at different fraction of volunteer samples.

6.6 Complexity Discussion

In order to analyze the complexity of **MSNL**, we need to solve the time complexity in terms of constructing $\mathbf{M}$, $\mathbf{L}$ and $\mathbf{t}$ as defined in Eqn. (8) and Eqn. (12), and computing the inverse of $\mathbf{M}$ and $\mathbf{L}$. Assume $D \gg S$, the construction of matrix $\mathbf{M}$ has a time complexity of

$\mathbf{O}(NDS)$, and the construction of matrix $\mathbf{L}$ has a time complexity of $\mathbf{O}(ND^2)$. Due to the fact that the cost of matrix multiplications ($\mathbf{X}_s^T\mathbf{X}_{s'}$) and that of constructing $\mathbf{t}$ involved in Eqn. (12) remain the same for all iterations and $\mathbf{L}$ is symmetric, we can save much practical time cost. Also, using the standard method, computing the inverse of two core matrices, $\mathbf{M}$ and $\mathbf{L}$, has the complexity of $\mathbf{O}(S^3)$ and $\mathbf{O}(D^3)$, respectively. Furthermore, using the method of Coppersmith and Winogard, the time cost can be bounded by $\mathbf{O}(S^{2.376})$ and $\mathbf{O}(D^{2.376})$ [26], respectively. We note that the speed bottleneck lies in the number of features and the number of social networks instead of the number of data samples. As S and D are usually small, especially S, **MSNL** should be efficient in time complexity.

To validate the practical efficiency of the proposed **MSNL** model, we conducted a set of experiments. The comparison of average time consumption of different models is shown in Table 7. As can be seen, **MSNL** shows superiority over **SVM** in terms of the time cost, which takes only 19% of the time that **SVM** uses. By careful observation, we observed that **MSNL** converges very fast, which on average takes about 20 iterations. Even though **MSNL** takes more time than **RLS** and **regMVMT** due to the consideration of source consistency and source confidence, it improves the performance in terms of F1-measure.

Table 7: Time cost of different models (%).

Approach	Total (s)	Train (s)	Test (s)
SVM	2.0550	1.8211	0.2339
RLS	0.0639	0.0631	0.0008
regMVMT	0.0605	0.0595	0.0006
iSFS	0.5565	0.5557	0.0008
MSNL	0.3936	0.3929	0.0007

7. CONCLUSIONS AND FUTURE WORK

This paper presented a novel scheme for multiple social network learning. This scheme takes the source confidence and source consistency into consideration by introducing regularization to the objective function. We further demonstrated that the proposed scheme, designed for complete data, is also able to handle the real and more challenging cases where there exists block-wise missing data. In particular, before feeding the data into the proposed MSNL model, we inferred the missing data via NMF technique. Furthermore, we practically evaluated the proposed scheme in an interesting scenario of volunteerism tendency prediction. We developed a set of volunteer-oriented features to characterize users' volunteerism tendency. Experimental results demonstrated the effectiveness of our proposed scheme and verified the advantages of utilizing multiple social network over a single source. Currently, we only consider solving a single task in the proposed scheme. In the future, we will extend our work to the context of multiple task learning.

Acknowledgments

This research is supported by the Singapore National Research Foundation under its International Research Centre @ Singapore Funding Initiative and administered by the IDM Programme Office.

8. REFERENCES

[1] F. Abel, E. Herder, G.-J. Houben, N. Henze, and D. Krause. Cross-system user modeling and personalization on the social web. *UMUAI*, 2013.

[2] B. Bazelli, A. Hindle, and E. Stroulia. On the personality traits of stackoverflow users. In *ICSM*, 2013.

[3] F. Benevenuto, T. Rodrigues, V. Almeida, J. Almeida, and M. Gonçalves. Detecting spammers and content promoters in online video social networks. In *SIGIR*, 2009.

[4] D. M. Blei, A. Y. Ng, and M. I. Jordan. Latent dirichlet allocation. *JMLR*, 2003.

[5] D. Carmel, N. Zwerdling, I. Guy, S. Ofek-Koifman, N. Har'El, I. Ronen, E. Uziel, S. Yogev, and S. Chernov. Personalized social search based on the user's social network. In *CIKM*, 2009.

[6] C.-C. Chang and C.-J. Lin. Libsvm: a library for support vector machines. *TIST*, 2011.

[7] Y. Gao, M. Wang, Z.-J. Zha, J. Shen, X. Li, and X. Wu. Visual-textual joint relevance learning for tag-based social image search. *TIP*, 2013.

[8] J. Guo, G. Xu, X. Cheng, and H. Li. Named entity recognition in query. In *SIGIR*, 2009.

[9] C.-J. Hsieh and I. S. Dhillon. Fast coordinate descent methods with variable selection for non-negative matrix factorization. In *SIGKDD*, 2011.

[10] S.-Y. L. Y. Jiang and Z.-H. Zhou. Partial multi-view clustering. In *AAAI*, 2014.

[11] S. Kim, K. Koh, M. Lustig, S. Boyd, and D. Gorinevsky. A method for large-scale l1-regularized least squares problems with applications in signal processing and statistics. *J-STSP*, 2007.

[12] D. D. Lee and H. S. Seung. Learning the parts of objects by non-negative matrix factorization. *Nature*.

[13] K. Lee, J. Caverlee, and S. Webb. Uncovering social spammers: social honeypots+ machine learning. In *SIGIR*, 2010.

[14] D. Li, B. He, Y. Ding, J. Tang, C. Sugimoto, Z. Qin, E. Yan, J. Li, and T. Dong. Community-based topic modeling for social tagging. In *CIKM*, 2010.

[15] D. Markovikj, S. Gievska, M. Kosinski, and D. Stillwell. Mining facebook data for predictive personality modeling. In *ICWSM*, 2013.

[16] L. Nie, Y.-L. Zhao, X. Wang, J. Shen, and T.-S. Chua. Learning to recommend descriptive tags for questions in social forums. *TOIS*, 2014.

[17] M. Pennacchiotti and A.-M. Popescu. Democrats, republicans and starbucks afficionados: user classification in twitter. In *SIGKDD*, 2011.

[18] L. A. Penner. Dispositional and organizational influences on sustained volunteerism: An interactionist perspective. *JSI*, 2002.

[19] L. A. Penner. Volunteerism and social problems: Making things better or worse? *JSI*, 2004.

[20] D. Quercia, M. Kosinski, D. Stillwell, and J. Crowcroft. Our twitter profiles, our selves: predicting personality with twitter. In *SocialCom*, 2011.

[21] D. Quercia, R. Lambiotte, D. Stillwell, M. Kosinski, and J. Crowcroft. The personality of popular facebook users. In *CSCW*, 2012.

[22] X. Shen, B. Tan, and C. Zhai. Implicit user modeling for personalized search. In *CIKM*, 2005.

[23] X. Wei and W. B. Croft. Lda-based document models for ad-hoc retrieval. In *SIGIR*, 2006.

[24] S. Xiang, L. Yuan, W. Fan, Y. Wang, P. M. Thompson, and J. Ye. Multi-source learning with block-wise missing data for alzheimer's disease prediction. In *SIGKDD*, 2013.

[25] L. Yuan, Y. Wang, P. M. Thompson, V. A. Narayan, and J. Ye. Multi-source learning for joint analysis of incomplete multi-modality neuroimaging data. In *SIGKDD*, 2012.

[26] D. Zhai, H. Chang, S. Shan, X. Chen, and W. Gao. Multiview metric learning with global consistency and local smoothness. *TIST*, 2012.

[27] D. Zhang, F. Wang, and L. Si. Composite hashing with multiple information sources. In *SIGIR*, 2011.

[28] J. Zhang and J. Huan. Inductive multi-task learning with multiple view data. In *SIGKDD*, 2012.

[29] X. Zhu, Z.-Y. Ming, X. Zhu, and T.-S. Chua. Topic hierarchy construction for the organization of multi-source user generated contents. In *SIGIR*, 2013.

HSpam14: A Collection of 14 Million Tweets for Hashtag-Oriented Spam Research

Surendra Sedhai
School of Computer Engineering
Nanyang Technological University, Singapore
surendra001@e.ntu.edu.sg

Aixin Sun
School of Computer Engineering
Nanyang Technological University, Singapore
axsun@ntu.edu.sg

ABSTRACT

Hashtag facilitates information diffusion in Twitter by creating dynamic and virtual communities for information aggregation from all Twitter users. Because hashtags serve as additional channels for one's tweets to be potentially accessed by other users than her own followers, hashtags are targeted for spamming purposes (*e.g.,* hashtag hijacking), particularly the popular and trending hashtags. Although much effort has been devoted to fighting against email/web spam, limited studies are on *hashtag-oriented spam* in tweets. In this paper, we collected 14 million tweets that matched some trending hashtags in two months' time and then conducted systematic annotation of the tweets being spam and ham (*i.e.,* non-spam). We name the annotated dataset **HSpam14**. Our annotation process includes four major steps: (i) heuristic-based selection to search for tweets that are more likely to be spam, (ii) near-duplicate cluster based annotation to firstly group similar tweets into clusters and then label the clusters, (iii) reliable ham tweets detection to label tweets that are non-spam, and (iv) Expectation-Maximization (EM)-based label prediction to predict the labels of remaining unlabeled tweets. One major contribution of this work is the creation of HSpam14 dataset, which can be used for hashtag-oriented spam research in tweets. Another contribution is the observations made from the preliminary analysis of the HSpam14 dataset.

Categories and Subject Descriptors

H.3.1 [**Information Storage and Retrieval**]: Content Analysis and Indexing

Keywords

Twitter; tweets; hashtag; spam

1. INTRODUCTION

Popularity of micro-blogging sites such as Twitter and Weibo has drawn attention of not only legitimate users but also spammers. Spammers create accounts to promote their products and/or services or even steal accounts of legitimate users for the same. The issues become more complicated when third-party applications post to Twitter on behalf of the legitimate users with the permission granted by the users. As the result, tweets posted on one's timeline may not be solely composed by the account owner. The tweets from third-party applications may contain spam information. Grier *et al.* reported that 0.13% of message advertised on Twitter are clicked which is two orders of magnitude higher than email spam [13]. Due to the growing interest of spammers in micro-blogging sites, spam becomes a pervasive problem on Twitter. In their recent study, Thomas *et al.* reported that 17% of spam users exploit hashtags to make their tweets visible in search and trending topics [35]. Hijacking trending topics and popular search terms for spamming has also been observed in web spam and blog spam [14, 40].

Most existing studies on Twitter spam focus on identification of spammers for account blocking. This approach is less effective for spammers who may act as legitimate users by posting non-spam content regularly. This approach may even hurt a legitimate user who happens to grant permission to a third-party application which posts spammy tweets under her username. This legitimate account may be blocked because of the spam tweets posted by the third-party application. While identifying and blocking spammer accounts remain a crucial and challenging task, *tweet-level spam detection* is essential to fight against spamming in a more fine-grained level. In this paper, we take the first step to create a large scale tweet collection for hashtag-oriented spam research. Among all different types of spamming, we mainly focus on the identification and annotation of tweets with hashtags, because hashtags serve as channels to increase the visibility of spam tweets. The cost of hijacking hashtags is very low with the availability of trending hashtags published on many web sites including Twitter.

We make two major contributions in this research. The first contribution is the creation of **HSpam14**, a collection of 14 million annotated tweets in English for hashtag-oriented spam research. We collected trending hashtags on daily basis from `hashtags.org` and used the collected hashtags as query keywords to collect tweets through Twitter streaming API, for two months' time. We then annotated the 14 million tweets with four major steps:

(i) *Heuristic-based tweets selection* to search for tweets that are likely to be spam. The selection was based on popular hashtags, and keywords related to adult content, money gain and others.

(ii) *Near-duplicate cluster based annotation* to group similar tweets into clusters and then label the clusters. Tweets are clustered by using MinHash based algorithm. The assumption is that spam tweets are likely to be posted many times with minor changes for more visibility. The annotation process includes both manual annotation and confident k-nearest neighbor based annotation with human intervention in the process. Tweets posted by the same users and tweets containing links from the same domains are also clustered and annotated in this step.

SIGIR'15, August 09 - 13, 2015, Santiago, Chile.

ACM 978-1-4503-3621-5/15/08 ...$15.00.
DOI: http://dx.doi.org/10.1145/2766462.2767701.

(iii) *Reliable ham tweets detection* to label tweets that are non-spam (also known as ham). Using the labeled tweets in the last step, we have a reasonably large number of examples which are utilized to build a classifier to detect reliable ham tweets. A reliable ham tweet does not contain any word that appears with higher probability in spam tweets than other tweets (*i.e.,* the labeled ham tweets and unlabeled tweets).

(iv) *EM-based label prediction* to predict the labels of the remaining unlabeled tweets using an Expectation-Maximization (EM) algorithm. At this step, we have 2.387 million spam tweets and 4.897 million ham tweets already labeled. We then utilize EM-based label prediction algorithm to label the remaining tweets.

Through manual inspections after each annotation step, the precision of the labels is above 0.94. We believe such quality of labeling is good enough for analyzing hashtag-oriented spam tweets for tweet-level spam detection.

The second contribution made in this paper is the preliminary analysis of the HSpam14 dataset. In our analysis, we made the following observations. First, spam and ham tweets do not differ much in the usage of mentions, but the usage of hashtags is significantly different. More specifically, 76% of ham tweets have no hashtags, and 97% of them have at most 2 hashtags. For spam tweets, only 37% of them have no hashtags, and 40% of them have 3 or more hashtags. Second, spam tweets are likely to contain hashtags in capital letters and with the word "follow" as part of the hashtag. The hashtags mainly present in ham tweets are usually in lower case letters or mixture of lower and upper cases, and the hashtags are more topic specific. We also propose a measure named *Spammy Index* to quantify the extent a hashtag is being used in spam tweets. Last, we observe that spammy hashtags are more likely to co-occur with spammy hashtags.

2. RELATED WORK

Spam is prevalent in all types of online communication medium. There are different types of spam: email spam [9], web spam [33], video spam [2], micro-blog spam [1], comment spam [28], and review spam [17], to name a few. Spammers have used different strategies in different platforms, and they also keep changing their strategies to hide themselves from spam detection systems [5]. Recently, crowdsourcing systems have also been exploited for posting malicious content [21, 37]. Spam detection systems use a wide range of information such as content, link, user behavior, as well as HTTP session information to tackle spam problem [33]. Next, we brief the spam on other platforms (*e.g.,* email, web, comment, and product review), and then review the spam on Twitter.

Spam on Email, Web, Comment, and Product Review. Email spam delivers unwanted advertisement, fraud scheme, promotion, or computer malwares designed to hijack the recipient's computer. To identify such emails, machine learning techniques as well as whitelisting and blacklisting of senders, domains or IP addresses have been used [9]. Various techniques such as language model, content duplication, link-based trust and distrust propagation, graph based techniques, and user behavior modeling have been applied to fight against web spamming which can be in the form of content spamming, link spamming, cloaking and click spamming, and comment spamming [5, 28, 33].

Online product reviews are valuable source of information for potential customers to find the opinions of other users about products before purchase. Due to the importance of product review, spammers are attracted to promote their products and defame the competitors' products. Review content and reviewers' behavior are utilized to detect spam reviews [17, 24, 29]. For example, a topic model based approach was proposed for spam detection in product reviews in [23]. Features derived from part-of-speech tag, n-gram, and sentiment of the reviews, have been used to detect such spams [22, 31]. As spammers are likely to post many pieces of similar content, near duplicate detection techniques have been exploited to identify such similar content and also the spammers [3, 6, 38]. Duplicate detection and classification technique have also been used for spam review detection [17, 18]. They considered all the duplicate reviews as spam reviews. However, it is not valid to consider all duplicate micro-blog posts as spam posts.

Spam on Twitter. Thomas *et al.* reported that there is an underground market in Twitter network which provides spam-as-service in a recent study [35]. In their study, they also reported that 77% of spam accounts are identified by Twitter within the first day of creation, and 92% of spam accounts within first three days of creation. The authors also made the observations that 89% of spam accounts have fewer than 10 followers and 17% of spam users exploit hashtags to make their tweets visible in search and trending topics [35]. This is similar phenomena as in web spam and blog spam, where trending topics and popular search terms are hijacked for spamming [14, 40]. However, there is no existing study specifically on hashtag-oriented spam detection.

The reflexive reciprocity indicates that many users simply follow back when they are followed by someone for the sake of courtesy [39]. It is not difficult for spammers to gain a relatively large number of followers in Twitter. Realizing this fact, social honeypot are deployed to harvest deceptive spam profiles by Lee *et al.* [19]. The profiles that are captured by social honeypot are classified using standard classification technique. Other features derived from user demographics, follower/following social graph, tweet content and temporal aspect of user behavior have also been analyzed and used to identify content polluter [20]. Castillo *et al.* analyzed the credibility of tweets on trending topics based on users' tweeting and retweeting behaviors, tweet content and link present in the tweets [4]. We believe that many of these features can be used for hashtag-oriented spam detection. However, before such research can be conducted, a benchmark dataset needs to be constructed.

User experience in Twitter is adversely affected by spam social bots. Social bots are programs that automatically produce content and interact with humans on social media. Social bots post tweets about popular and focused topics and follow back the users who follow the bots [27]. Using such simple strategies bots could get high influence in Twitter and may pollute timeline of users. These spam bots can be detected by social honeypot traps [19] and also based on features derived from temporal behavior, tweet content, and user profile [7, 10]. In our data collection, we also observe that many tweets share very similar format and are posted by bots. However, not all Twitter users are equally vulnerable to social bots, and the behaviors that make users more susceptible to social bots have been studied in [36].

Other studies on Twitter spam include the studies on the link structure of the users and the links to external resources. As in Web, spammers have also used link farming technique to promote content in Twitter [12, 34]. Tan *et al.* [34] reported that spammers and non-spammers belong to different communities in user graph. Spammers may also include unrelated links with trending words (*e.g.,* hashtags) in tweets [1]. To detect such spam tweets, matrix factorization model was proposed by Hu *et al.* [15] to learn lexical information from external spam resources. The authors further proposed online learning algorithms to cope with the fast evolution of social spammer in [16].

3. DATA COLLECTION AND STATISTICS

3.1 Data Crawling

To collect data for hashtag-oriented spam tweet research, one key issue is to identify candidate hashtags. The tweets containing these candidate hashtags are then collected and labeled. Without the luxury of accessing all tweets or all hashtags, we rely on the trending topics (*i.e.,* hashtags) reported on Hashtags.org.[1] Hashtags.org reports trending hashtags in three categories: *trending up*, *trending down*, and *most popular hashtags*. As expected, we observe that the hashtags in *most popular hashtags* category do not change much for many days. To cover more varieties of hashtags in our data collection, we used the hashtags in *trending up* and *trending down* categories as query keywords to search for tweets on daily basis. On each day, we collect the trending hashtags in these two categories and we then use each collected hashtag as a query keyword to collect tweets using Twitter's streaming API for that day.[2] A tweet is collected through the API if it contains the query keyword as a *hashtag*, *word*, or *link* in its content. On average 135 hashtags were used as query keywords on each day. The data collection process last for two months, May and June 2013.

In total, we collected 24.36 million tweets, which were published by 11.97 million users. The collected tweets contain 20.21 million hashtags and 6.97 million hyperlinks. After resolving the short URLs, there are 3.43 million distinct URLs. Ignoring the deadlinks and the links that require authentication, 2.05 million web pages were successfully downloaded. However, we have not fully utilized these web pages for this labeling process.

Among the collected tweets and web pages, 14.07 million tweets and 1.37 web pages are in English.[3] In our following discussion, we mainly focus on the 14.07 million (or simply 14 million in approximation) tweets in English. The same set of tweets will be annotated with spam and ham labels in the next section.

3.2 Data Statistics

User Distribution. The 14 million English tweets were posted by 7.25 million users and the distribution of the number of tweets per user is plotted in Figure 1(a). Shown in the figure, the data demonstrates a typical power-law distribution that is widely observable in many social related studies. While more than 4.83 million users each contributed only one tweet, the most active user contributed 754 tweets to this collection. Recall that this collection covers two-month period and the tweets were collected by using trending hashtags as queries (*i.e.,* biased sampling). The few extremely active users may post a larger number of tweets regularly or post many tweets targeting on some trending hashtags. Because we do not have the full profiles of the users in this data collection, the underlying reasons cannot be verified. In our following analysis, we mainly focus on the content of the tweets, particularly the usages of hashtags and mentions.

Usages of Hashtags and Mentions. Figure 1(b) plots the frequency distributions of hashtags and mentions. This figure shows that the usages of both hashtags and mentions follow power-law distributions with slightly different slopes in the log-log plot. On the one hand, this figure suggests that hashtags are more commonly used than mentions in tweets, particularly the extremely popular ones. On the other hand, a small set of usernames are frequently

Table 1: The top-20 most popular hashtags. All these 20 hashtags appeared as trending up/down hashtags which were used for sampling the tweets.

Hashtag (#)	Freq.	Hashtag (#)	Freq.
TEAMFOLLOWBACK	666,328	SougoFollow	197,525
TFBJP	527,176	ipad	195,375
gameinsight	510,504	FOLLOWBACK	177,109
android	341,240	THF	165,762
OPENFOLLOW	332,857	FOLLOWNGAIN	149,916
FF	293,748	500aday	146,005
androidgames	286,706	AUTOFOLLOW	141,214
RETWEET	250,992	MUSTFOLLOW	138,040
RT	235,137	TEAMHITFOLLOW	136,043
IPADGAMES	232,335	MUSIC	129,852

being mentioned in tweets. A mention in a tweet is also a form of hyperlink, and clicking a mention leads to the user profile page where much more information about this user is displayed (*e.g.,* user description and recent tweets). For this reason, mention can be intentionally used for spamming purposes, similar to hashtags[4].

Table 1 lists the top-20 most popular hashtags in the 14 million tweets. Observe that the most popular hashtag #TEAMFOLLOWBACK appears in more than half million tweets out of the 14 million. Moreover, 40% of the top-20 most popular hashtags contain the word "follow". Many of the usernames among the popular mentions contain the word "follow". In fact, a quick check of the top-20 most mentioned usernames shows that 11 usernames[5] have been suspended by Twitter. Among the suspended usernames, nearly half contain the word "follow".

Figure 1(c) plots the per-tweet distribution of hashtags and mentions. Note that the y-axis is in log-scale. Both distributions show the same interesting pattern: (i) the number of tweets having 1 to 4 hashtags/mentions drops significantly along the increase of the number of hashtags/mentions; (ii) the rate of dropping becomes much smaller for tweets containing 4 to 10 hashtags/mentions; and (iii) the number of tweets again drop significantly with the increase of contained hashtags/mentions from 10 onwards. As expected, very few tweets contain more than 14 mentions or more than 18 hashtags, given the 140-character length limit of tweets.

4. TWEET ANNOTATION

There are three major challenges in manually labeling millions of tweets: (i) *large number of instances, i.e.,* it is infeasible to manually check every single tweet to determine its label as in many other labeling efforts [8], (ii) *limited amount of information carried by each tweet* because of its shortness, and (iii) *lack of standard criteria* for the classification of spam and ham tweets.

To address the first two challenges, we propose to group the near-duplicate tweets into clusters. Spammers keep changing their behavioral patterns to avoid detection; however, they keep on posting similar promotional tweets exploiting popular keywords. Hence, clustering of near-duplicate tweets captures promotional tweets effectively despite change in behavioral patterns of spammers. Because the tweets in each near-duplicate cluster are nearly identical to each other, the same label applies to all the tweets in the same cluster. The near-duplicate clustering also helps in partially addressing the second challenge. One of the major characteristics

[1] https://www.hashtags.org/trending-on-twitter/ Note that the trending hashtags identified by Hashtags.org are based on the site's proprietary algorithm.

[2] We used Twitter database server code available at http://140dev.com/.

[3] We used language detection library for Java available at http://code.google.com/p/language-detection/

[4] https://blog.twitter.com/2012/shutting-down-spammers

[5] In Twitter, a user may change her username at any time. Mentioning the same username at different time points may refer to different users.

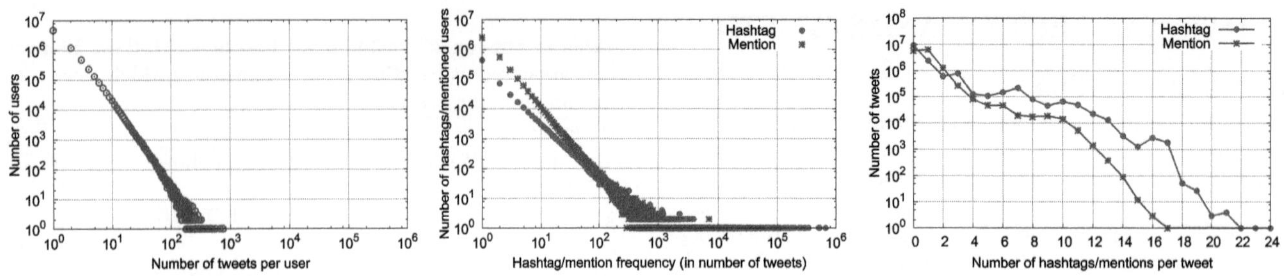

(a) User frequency distribution (b) Hashtag/mention frequency distribution (c) No. of hashtags/mentions per tweet

Figure 1: Distributions of users and hashtag/mention usages in the 14 million English tweets

of spammers is to post near-duplicate content in repetitive manner. If a larger number of near-duplicate tweets are from very few users, then it is relatively easier for us to label spam tweets even if each tweet contain very limited semantics. During the labeling process, we may also access all tweets by a particular user in our data collection to get more contextual information. Regarding the last challenge, we reference to the existing studies on spam detection (*e.g.,* tweets about quick money gain, adult content are considered spammy). In the context of hashtag-oriented spam detection, we also consider tweets containing semantically unrelated hashtags and quick followership gain as spam tweets.

Figure 2 illustrates the four main steps in the annotation process. We now brief the four major steps. More details of the steps and the labeling criteria are described in the next sub-sections.

Heuristics-based Tweet Selection. It is reasonable to assume that majority of tweets are ham. To minimize human labeling effort, it is necessary to label only the tweets that are more likely to be spams. To this end, we selected the tweets that contain most popular hashtags (our assumption is that these hashtags are likely to be hijacked for spamming). We also select the tweets that contain money gain, adult content related keywords, and promoting purposes.

Cluster-based Manual Annotation. Selected tweets are grouped into near-duplicate clusters. A subset of clusters are then labeled with spam or ham, and all the tweets in the same cluster share the same label. The near-duplicate clusters are obtained by *MinHash* algorithm [3]. With an initial set of clusters labeled, we adopt k nearest-neighbor approach to "grow" the labels as in [8]. A cluster is labeled by kNN if the prediction of the label is very confident (based on the percentage of the nearest neighbors in the same class), and manually labeled otherwise. Spam tweets may be posted by some spam user accounts. For the top 10,000 users who posted the largest number of tweets in our dataset, we conduct user-based tweet clustering (*i.e.,* all tweets in each cluster are posted by the same user) and label the clusters. Similarly, based on the domain names of the links embedded in tweets, we cluster the tweets that contain links from the same domain, and label the clusters. The top 10,000 most frequent domains in our dataset are considered.

Reliable Ham Tweet Prediction. By the assumption that majority tweets are ham, a large number of tweets, particularly the unselected tweets left by the heuristics based selection, remain unlabeled. Here, we adopt the approach in *learning from positive examples only* in classification [25] to determine reliable ham tweets.

Label Prediction by EM Algorithm. After getting a reasonably large number of reliable labels of both spam and ham tweets, the EM algorithm by Nigam *et al.* [30] for learning from labeled and unlabeled data is adopted to predict the labels of the remaining tweets.

4.1 Heuristics-based Tweet Selection

We heuristically target on the tweets that are most likely to be spam, with the assumption that most tweets are ham. More specifically, we select three sets of tweets: (i) tweets containing any of the top-100 most popular hashtags in our collection, (ii) tweets containing adult content related keywords, and (iii) tweets containing keywords related to quick money gain, lucky draw, free gift *etc.*.

The first set of tweets is selected based on the heuristic that spammers are likely to exploit popular hashtags to make their content visible to broader audience. Table 1 lists the top-20 most popular hashtags, which is a subset of the 100 selected hashtags. The second set of the selected tweets aligns with most other spam detection tasks in email and web domains. A list of keywords related to adult content is used for this purpose.[6] For the third set of tweets selection, we used the following 23 keywords to capture the tweets related to quick money gain, lucky draw, and free gift: awesome, business, hurray, earn, bargain, deal, adventure, money, click, facebook, want, incredible, gift, money, amazon, ebay, amazing, prize, lucky, check out, shopping, sale, giveaway. Note that, there are tweets repeatedly posted by users with similar content, for promoting purposes related to major websites like Facebook, Amazon, and eBay. Therefore, these website names are included as keywords.

As the result, 7.10 million tweets posted by 3.93 million users were selected by keyword match. A tweet is selected if the tweet contains any of the selected hashtags or keywords in its content.

4.2 Cluster-based Manual Annotation

4.2.1 Near-Duplicate Clustering

To label the tweets more effectively, we group the near-duplicate tweets into clusters using MinHash algorithm [3]. The preprocessing of the tweets includes removal of links, removal of mentions (*i.e.,* @username), removal of the '#' symbols but keep the words in the hashtags, and removal of stop-words using the stop-word list provided in Lucene[7].

Both MinHash and SimHash are widely used for detecting near-duplicate documents [32]. Here, we adopt the MinHash algorithm on tweet's shinglings for duplicate detection [26]. We consider two tweets t_1 and t_2 are (near-)duplicates if minimum hash values of their *uni-gram, bi-gram,* and *tri-gram* representations are the same. More specifically, let $h(\cdot)$ be a hash function, and let tweet t be a n-word sequence $\langle w_1, w_2, \dots w_n \rangle$. The minimum hash value of uni-gram representation of t is $h(w_i)$ iff $h(w_i) \leq h(w_j)$ for any $1 \leq i, j \leq n$ and $i \neq j$. The minimum hash value of bi-gram

[6] We used the stem version of the keywords under pornographic category listed at `http://nymphs.org/RevealDirtyWordList.txt` In total there are 80 keywords in the list, and after stemming, there are 65 word stems.

[7] `http://lucene.apache.org/core/`

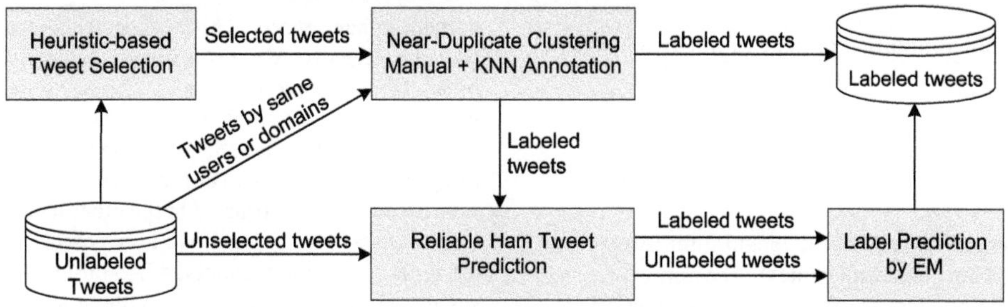

Figure 2: Overview of the four major steps in labeling spam/ham tweets

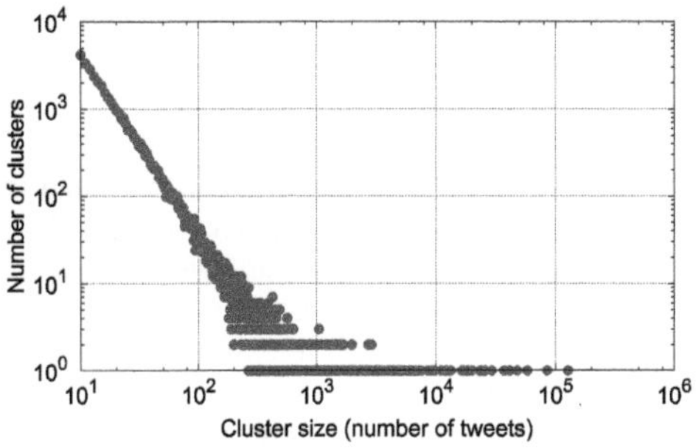

Figure 3: Size distribution of the near-duplicate clusters

representation of t is $h(w_i w_{i+1})$ iff $h(w_i w_{i+1}) \leq h(w_j w_{j+1})$ for any $1 \leq i, j \leq n-1$ and $i \neq j$. The minimum hash value of tri-gram representation is computed in a similar manner. For simplicity, let $h_1(t)$, $h_2(t)$, and $h_3(t)$ be the minimum hash values of uni-gram, bi-gram, and tri-gram representations of tweet t. Then t_1 and t_2 are near-duplicates iff $h_1(t_1) = h_1(t_2)$, $h_2(t_1) = h_2(t_2)$ and $h_3(t_1) = h_3(t_2)$. In our Java implementation, we used the hashCode() method in String class to get the hash value of a n-gram (*i.e.,* a word or a shingling). The clustering process is computationally effective, and can be achieved in one scan of the tweets.

Result and Evaluation. Because our purpose is to label tweets more effectively, the clusters containing fewer than 10 tweets are ignored from manual annotation. The remaining 40,549 clusters contain 3.13 million tweets posted by 1.52 million users. Figure 3 plots the size distribution of these 40,549 clusters. Again, the plot demonstrates a power-law distribution with many clusters each contains 10 or slightly more tweets and very few extremely large clusters. The largest cluster contains 127,559 near-duplicate tweets, mainly due to hashtags #gameinsight, #android, and #androidgames. An example tweet is "RT @username: I've collected 103,501 gold coins! LINK1 #android #androidgames #gameinsight".[8]

In manual annotation, all the tweets in the same near-duplicate cluster will be annotated with the same label (*i.e.,* spam or ham). For this purpose, we must ensure that the tweets in the same cluster are indeed similar to each other, or in other words, are near-duplicate. Table 2 shows two randomly selected near-duplicate clusters containing 4 and 2 example tweets respectively, from each cluster. The examples show that tweets in the same clusters are indeed very similar to each other. However, there is a need to quantitatively evaluate the quality of the clusters in terms of tweet similarity. To this end, we randomly selected 4000 clusters (*i.e.,* about 10% all clusters) and measured the intra-cluster and inter-cluster tweet similarities. For intra-cluster tweet similarity, two tweets are randomly selected from each cluster; for inter-cluster tweet similarity, two tweets are randomly selected from two different clusters without replacement.

Table 2: Example tweets from two near-duplicate clusters

1.
   - RT @username: #Money SEC chief White remains mum on money market fund reforms LINK1 #TonyRocha
   - #Forex: SEC chief White remains mum on money market fund reforms LINK1 LINK2
   - UPDATE 1-U.S. SEC chief White remains mum on money market fund rules LINK1 #news
   - SEC Chief White Remains Mum On Money Market Fund Rules: The top securities regulator remained tight-lipped on ... LINK1
2.
   - RT @username: [Retweet Only If You Want New Follower] #TEAMFAIRYROSE #OpenFollow #Follow #TFBJP #500aday #RT #R_Family #MaxVIP
   - RT @username: [Retweet Only If You Want New Followers] #TEAMFAIRYROSE #FOLLOWNGAIN #Follow #TFBJP #500aday #RT #R_Family #THF

Table 3: Measures of intra-/inter-cluster samples of tweets

Measure	Intra-cluster	Inter-cluster
Jaccard coefficient	0.9169 ± 0.0026	0.0187 ± 0.0006
Cosine similarity	0.9510 ± 0.0017	0.0350 ± 0.0012
Length difference	0.3933 ± 0.0196	5.5895 ± 0.0673

Table 3 reports tweet similarity in terms of Jaccard coefficient and cosine similarity. Cosine similarity is computed based on the bag-of-words model with *TFIDF* weighting. The length differences between the randomly selected pairs of tweets in number of words are also reported. Shown in Table 3, tweets from the same cluster show high similarity in terms of both Jaccard coefficient and cosine similarity with values above 0.91 and 0.95 respectively. On the other hand, inter-cluster similarity of tweets is dramatically lower at 0.019 and 0.035 respectively for Jaccard coefficient and cosine similarity. In terms of length difference, tweets from the same cluster are nearly identical with length difference of 0.39 word, while a pair of tweets from different clusters differ on average 5.59 words.

In summary, the clustering process is able to produce clusters with high intra-cluster similarity and low inter-cluster similarity. Tweets in the same cluster are of very similar length.

4.2.2 Manual Annotation of Near-Duplicate Clusters

Labeling tweets to be spam or ham is non-trivial for two reasons. First, there is no very specific definition of "spam". However, many definitions, including the description in Wikipedia[9], contain the phrase "unsolicited message", and the words "advertisement"

[8] We mask the usernames and links in all example tweets in this paper.

[9] http://en.wikipedia.org/wiki/Spamming

Table 4: Initial manual annotation of near-duplicate clusters

Label	No. of clusters	No. of tweets	No. of users
Spam	1,104	1.63 million	0.61 million
Ham	1,000	0.19 million	0.17 million

and "repeatedly". Second, because of the length limit, tweets are very short, and often do not come with context. The notion of near-duplicate clusters partially addresses these two challenges. Each near-duplicate cluster lists the near-"repeated" tweets and it is easy to identify whether the repeated tweets are from very few users or from some specific apps. Because of the grouping of similar tweets, it is also relatively easy to identify whether these similar tweets were posted because of some important events/topics (*e.g.*, the 4 tweets in the first cluster in Table 2) or were posted for advertisement purposes (*e.g.*, the 2 tweets in the second cluster in Table 2). In other words, we are able to infer the context of the tweets in a collective manner. By considering the tweets in each near-duplicate cluster, the users who posted these tweets, and also the usage of hashtags and links, we are able to label the near-duplicate clusters.

We label ***tweets in a duplicate-cluster to be spam*** if the tweets in this cluster satisfy ***one of the five conditions***: (i) for quick money gain or quick gain of followers; (ii) repeatedly posted for advertisement, promoting products/services, and request for retweet or offering benefits; (iii) about adult content; (iv) contain many unrelated but popular hashtags; (v) automatically posted by bots/apps for multiple times with near identical content. Note that, many bots/apps post legitimate tweets. For example, by linking Twitter and Foursqaure accounts, users have the option to share check-ins made in Foursqaure to Twitter. Such tweets will not be labeled as spam because these tweets are informative (*i.e.*, reporting location information of users). On the other hand, recall that in Section 4.2.1, we report that the largest cluster contains 127,559 near-duplicate tweets in the form of "RT @username: I've collected 103,501 gold coins! LINK1 #android #androidgames #gameinsight". The only difference between any two tweets is the number of gold coins and the links. Moreover, we observe that many users post only tweets in this form in his/her full user profile in Twitter. We consider such tweets less informative and label them as spam.

With the above criteria, we *selectively* label the near-duplicate clusters, because labeling more than 40 thousand near-duplicate clusters is infeasible. The labeling is conducted in two phases. In the first phase, the top-1000 largest clusters ranked by number of tweets in each cluster are labeled. Because of the power-law distribution (see Figure 3), the labeling of the 1000 largest clusters cover a large number of tweets. In the second phase, we aim to cover more diverse tweets by considering the keywords we used in Section 4.1. For each of the keywords used for tweet selection, we label around 10 largest clusters containing this keyword if the keyword is not covered in the top-1000 clusters labeled earlier. As examples, most clusters containing keywords "love" and "news" are ham clusters while clusters containing "gameinsight" and "iphonegame" are mostly spam. In the labeling process, we also encounter some cases where we cannot confidently label the tweets to be ham or spam even after manual inspection. In this case, we assign an "unknown" label to this cluster.

Result and Analysis. After the two phase labeling, 1.82 million tweets in 2,104 near-duplicate clusters are manually labeled, reported in Table 4. Observe that, although the number of spam clusters is similar as the number of ham clusters, the number of spam tweets contained in these clusters is significantly larger than the number of ham tweets. This is expected as spam tweets are mostly posted repeatedly. More specifically, the median number of tweets in the labeled spam clusters is 437 while the median number of tweets in ham clusters is 26. The median number of users in the two sets of clusters are 383 and 25 respectively. It is also observed that 84% of labeled spam clusters have at least one user posting the same tweet multiple times. On the other hand, only 25% of labeled ham clusters have at least one user posting the same tweet multiple times. More interestingly, 47,454 users who posted at least one spam tweet have 0 followers. Without any followers, these users do not pollute the timelines of other users. However, their tweets may have adverse effect on keyword-based or hashtag-based tweet search. The number of users who posted at least one ham tweet and have 0 followers is 4,822, about 10% of those who posted at least one spam tweet.

4.2.3 *k*NN Annotation

Using the 2,104 manually labeled clusters as ground truth, we are able to "grow" labels in a more effective manner with the help of *k*NN classifier. A similar approach has been adopted in creating benchmark dataset for a web image dataset [8].

The most important issue here is to ensure the quality of labels predicted by the *k*NN classifier. We address this issue by assigning a label to a cluster only if 80% of its k-nearest neighbors are from the same class (*i.e.*, spam or ham). Moreover, if this newly labeled cluster c_k causes misclassification of a manually labeled cluster c_m if the same *k*NN rule were applied to c_m, then we consider this newly labeled cluster c_k to be a *difficult cluster*. The *difficult clusters* are then manually inspected and labeled. If a newly labeled cluster does not cause misclassification of any existing manually labeled cluster, then the label of this cluster assigned by *k*NN is considered as a *confident* label. The labeling process is conducted in batch mode and thus confidently labeled clusters in each batch are added as labeled examples for the next batch.

Algorithm 1 summarizes the main steps in *k*NN-based near duplicate cluster labeling. The algorithm takes the set of manually labeled cluster C_ℓ and unlabeled clusters C_u as input, and returns clusters with confident labels C_k as output, in four main steps.

Step 1. A subset of clusters $C_{mk} \subset C_\ell$ is obtained such that within C_{mk} each cluster's label is consistent with the label predicted based on the *k*NN rule (Lines 2 - 5). More specifically, for each cluster c, its k nearest neighbors are obtained from the labeled set C_ℓ using function $C_{NN} = kNN(c, k, C_\ell)$, where C_{NN} denotes the set of c's nearest neighbors, $kNN(c, k, C_\ell)$ finds the k nearest neighbors of c within the set C_ℓ. In Line 4, the function $majorityLabel(C_{NN})$ returns the *number of neighbors* from the majority class in C_{NN} (*e.g.*, either spam or ham). The clusters in C_{mk} will be used to identify the difficult clusters labeled by *k*NN in later steps.

Step 2. The algorithm classifies unlabeled clusters in a batch mode (Lines 10 - 13). Each batch is set to be 20% of the size of the manually labeled examples (Line 10). For the first batch, the set of training examples is initialized to be the set of manually labeled clusters C_ℓ (Line 7). In the subsequent batches, the training examples will include the newly labeled examples (Lines 22 - 23).

Step 3. The algorithm verifies whether the newly labeled examples cause misclassification of some clusters in C_{mk} (Lines 15 - 21). More specifically, the k nearest neighbors of each cluster in C_{mk} is now searched from the set of training examples C_t and the newly labeled batch C_b using the function $kNN(c, k, C_t \cup C_b)$. If the number of neighbors from majority class is smaller than 80% of k, then we consider that the neighbors which are from the newly labeled batch cause the misclassification. These clusters will then

Algorithm 1: kNN Annotation

Input : Set of manually labeled clusters C_ℓ
Set unlabeled near-duplicate clusters C_u
Number of nearest neighbors k
Output: Set of labeled near-duplicate clusters C_k

1 $C_{mk} = \{\}$ `// clusters consistent with kNN result`
2 **foreach** *cluster* $c \in C_\ell$ **do**
3     $C_{NN} = kNN(c, k, C_\ell)$ `// find nearest neighbors`
4   **if** $majorityLabel(C_{NN}) \geq 0.8 \times k$ **then**
5         $C_{mk} = C_{mk} \cup \{c\}$
6 $C_d = \{\}$
7 $C_t = C_\ell$ `// set of training examples`
8 $C_b = \{\}$ `// a batch of labeled clusters`
9 **for** *unlabeled cluster* $c \in C_u$ **do**
10   **if** $|C_b| < 0.2 \times |C_\ell|$ **then**
11         $C_{NN} = kNN(c, k, C_t)$
12   **if** $majorityLabel(C_{NN}) \geq 0.8 \times k$ **then**
13             $C_b = C_b \cup \{c\}$
14   **else** `// verify the current batch`
15   **foreach** *cluster* $c \in C_{mk}$ **do**
16             $C_{NN} = kNN(c, k, C_t \cup C_b)$
17   **if** $majorityLabel(C_{NN}) < 0.8 \times k$ **then**
18   **foreach** *neighbor cluster* $c_n \in C_{NN}$ **do**
19   **if** $c_n \in C_b$ **then**
20                         $C_b = C_b - \{c_n\}$
21                         $C_d = C_d \cup \{c_n\}$
22         $C_t = C_t \cup C_b$ `// add as training examples`
23         $C_b = \{\}$`// start a new batch`
24 Manually label clusters in C_d and add to C_t in Line 7
25 Repeat the labeling process (Lines 9 - 24) till no more clusters can be labeled
26 Return $C_k = C_t - C_\ell$;

be removed from the batch and considered as *difficult clusters*. The difficult clusters are then manually labeled in the next step. The remaining confidently labeled clusters in C_b will be added to C_t for the next batch labeling (Line 22).

Step 4. Observe that the predicted labels of unlabeled clusters in C_u are dependent on the order of labeling because the training examples C_t are updated after each batch of labeling. For this reason, we run the labeling process (Lines 9 - 23) multiple times. Before each run, we manually label the difficult clusters resulted from the last run (Line 24) and add them to C_t in Line 7 because these labels are manually assigned. Note that, for concise presentation, we do not explicitly add this "outer loop" in Algorithm 1. Instead, this step is stated in Line 25 and the iteration continues until there is no unlabeled cluster which has 80% of neighbors from same class. Note that some detailed control structures in the algorithm are ignored, for example, the last batch in each run may not reach the size of $0.2 \times |C_\ell|$.

For nearest neighbor search, the similarity between two clusters is the cosine similarity with *TFIDF* weighting of the word feature vectors for the two clusters, by aggregating all the tweets in each cluster. The value of k is set to 19 empirically in our kNN based annotation process. The size of each batch is about 420.

Annotation Result. As the result of kNN-based annotation, 15,571 spam clusters and 15,913 ham clusters are labeled. In the labeling process, 1,178 clusters were identified to be difficult clusters and were then manually labeled. Among the latter, 826 clusters were labeled ham and 275 were labeled spam clusters; the remaining 77 clusters were difficult to label even after manual inspection. These 77 clusters are labeled "unknown" in our data collection.

After manual and kNN-based annotation, we have labeled more spam tweets than ham tweets. Because spam clusters often contain much repeated tweets, the number of spam tweets is significantly larger than the number of ham tweets. The reason is that, the manual annotation process was targeted on spam tweets by using the most suspicious keywords and most popular hashtags. The kNN-based annotation was guided by the then labeled clusters. In other words, most ham tweets are left untouched in the dataset.

4.2.4 User- and Domain-based Cluster Annotation

We now label repeated tweets posted by spammers and tweets promoting specific links. Instead of restricting to the tweets that match keywords (Section 4.1), we consider all tweets in this step.

User-based Cluster Annotation. In this step, tweets posted by the same user are grouped into near-duplicate clusters. Then the clusters with more than 10 tweets are labeled. The top 10,000 users who posted the largest number of tweets in our dataset are considered. We observe that most user-based clusters are small clusters with fewer than 10 tweets. That is, most of users do not post many similar tweets. As the result, 980 user-based clusters each has more than 10 tweets need to be labeled, consisting of about 25 thousand tweets in total. Among these 980 clusters, 723 are labeled spam (containing about 20 thousand tweets) and 120 clusters are labeled ham (about 2 thousand tweets). Note that, highly similar ham tweets may be posted by the same user repeatedly (*e.g.*, updates of bus services and weather reports). The remaining 137 are labeled unknown, after looking into the content of the tweets and user profiles (*e.g.*, number of followers/followees, number of tweets) .

Because we consider all tweets in this step, some of the tweets in user-based cluster may have already have been labeled in the earlier steps. If the labels are all from manual annotation, then the cluster is considered labeled. If the labels are given in the kNN annotation, these labels are considered as reference and may be corrected during this manual annotation process.

Domain-based Cluster Annotation. Recall that a tweet may embed links to external sources. Here we aim to label the spam tweets that promote links from specific domains. To this end, the tweets that contain links from any of the top 10,000 most frequent domains in our collection are selected and then grouped into near-duplicate clusters based on domains (all the tweets in the same cluster contain links from the same domain). There are 9,038 such clusters each contains at least 10 tweets. Out of these 9,038 clusters, 4,398 are spam clusters (containing about 221 thousand tweets), and 3,785 are ham clusters (about 121 thousand tweets). The remaining 855 clusters could not be labeled even after manual inspection. Similar to that in user-based cluster annotation, the labels from earlier steps are utilized in this annotation process.

During the annotation process, we observe that domain-based cluster annotation is effective in capturing distributed spam activities in promoting online resources. Examples include links related to topics of working from home, best deals, and coupon codes. Note that, in our labeling process, clusters with tweet content that is clearly ham and links that are from major trustworthy sites (*e.g.*, BBC, CNN, NBA) are labeled ham without looking the content of the web pages. Clusters containing links from less popular domains are labeled by looking into the user profiles and the content of the linked pages. However, it is found that in most cases, tweets provide good descriptions of the links. It is uncommon to have similar tweets linking to very different web pages.

Until this step most ham tweets are left untouched in the dataset. In the next section, we aim to detect the ham tweets from the remaining unlabeled data.

4.3 Reliable Ham Tweet Detection

The remaining unlabeled tweets in our tweet collection may contain a large number of ham tweets, but also contain many spam tweets yet to be identified. Given the large number of remaining unlabeled tweets, this problem can be formulated as a *PU Learning problem, i.e.,* learning from Positive and Unlabeled examples [25].

Inspired by the approach for building text classifiers from positive and unlabeled examples proposed in [25], we utilized the *positive words* in spam tweets to identify reliable ham tweets. Positive words are the words that appear more frequently in spam tweets than other tweets. Example positive words are 'followers', 'gain', 'gameinsight', 'please', 'win', 'iphone' etc. More specifically, let $rdf(w, D_s) = \frac{df(w,D_s)}{|D_s|}$ be the relative document frequency of word w in the set of spam tweets D_s labeled so far, where $df(w, D_s)$ denotes the number of tweets containing word w in set D_s. Let $rdf(w, D_h \cup D_u)$ be the relative document frequency of word w in the set of labeled ham tweets D_h and the set of unlabeled tweets D_u. Then w is a positive word if $rdf(w, D_s) > rdf(w, D_h \cup D_u)$. Reliable ham tweets are those tweets that do not contain any positive words. In our implementation, words that are shorter than 3 characters in length are ignored. Note that, number of characters in a hashtag does not include the '#' symbol.

Result and Evaluation. This method is simple but found to be very effective in identifying ham tweets. In total 4.093 million tweets are identified as reliable ham tweets. We evaluated the quality of the labeled tweets by manually inspecting a randomly selected sample of 1000 reliable ham tweets. Among them, 32 tweets are incorrectly labeled as ham, hence the precision of the labels in reliable ham detection is 0.968. Following are three examples of reliable ham tweets detected in this step.

- Why can't I sleep
- The first thunder sound scared me
- @username hey :)) do u know what channel is CNN on???? Lol i forgot it...

4.4 Annotation by EM-Algorithm

Out of the 14 million tweets in our data collection, more than 7 million tweets are now labeled in the earlier steps. With the 2.387 million spam tweets and 4.897 million ham tweets, we have a sizable collection of labeled examples to build a reliable classifier for the prediction of labels of the remaining unlabeled tweets. To this end, we adopt the Expectation-Maximization (EM) algorithm proposed for text classification using labeled and unlabeled documents [30]. EM has also been used to reduce human effort in evaluating IR systems [11]. A Naïve Bayes classifier is firstly constructed by utilizing the existing labeled tweets. In the E-Step, this classifier is used to predict the labels of the remaining unlabeled tweets. In the M-Step, the probabilities of the word features are re-estimated based on the predicted labels. Then the classifier in the E-Step is updated accordingly and is used to re-classify the tweets in the M-Step. This process continues till the number of changes in the predicted labels is below 0.01% of the total unlabeled tweets.

As the result, 5.790 million ham tweets and 0.951 million spam tweets are labeled in this step. To evaluate the quality of the labeling, we randomly selected 500 ham and 500 spam tweets labeled by EM for manual inspection. The precisions for spam and ham labels are 0.94 and 0.96 respectively.

Table 5: Statistics of the labeled tweets in HSpam14 dataset

Annotation step	Spam (million)	Ham (million)
Manual annotation	1.644	0.226
*k*NN-based annotation	0.502	0.455
User-based annotation	0.020	0.002
Domain-based annotation	0.221	0.121
Reliable ham tweet detection	-	4.093
EM-based annotation	0.951	5.790
Total	3.338	10.688

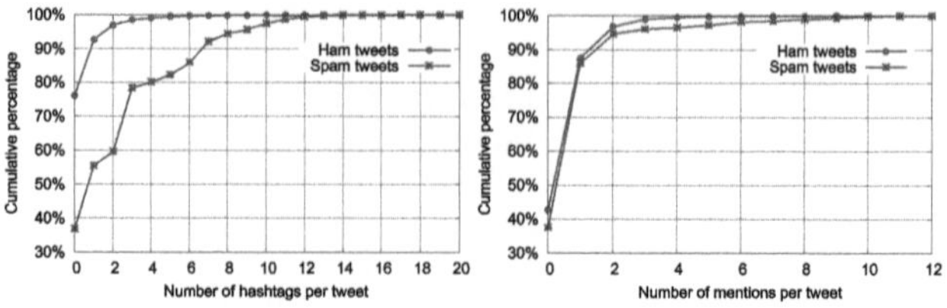

(a) Hashtags per tweet (b) Mentions per tweet

Figure 4: Cumulative percentage of hashtags and mentions per tweet, in spam tweets and ham tweets, respectively.

4.5 Summary

After all these steps, we have labeled almost all the 14 million English tweets. Table 5 reports the number of tweets labeled as ham and spam in each step. Note that, the numbers reported under manual annotation are slightly larger than that reported in Table 4 because the numbers here include the manual annotations conducted in *k*NN-based annotation step as well as the annotations made during the evaluation of subsequent steps. In summary, 3.338 million spam tweets and 10.688 million ham tweets are labeled in the HSpam14 dataset. There are two possible reasons for the relatively large number of spam tweets. First, the tweets in our collection were collected based on trending hashtags, which are more likely to be hijacked for spamming purpose. Second, many of the spam tweets are repetition of similar content, *e.g.,* 127,559 near-duplicate tweets are due to the hashtag #gameinsight.

5. ANALYSIS OF HSPAM14

We believe the quality of the labels are reasonably high based on the manual inspection after each step, if no manual annotation is involved during that step. In this section, we provide a preliminary analysis of the HSpam14 dataset. We mainly focus on the usage of hashtags in spam and ham tweets. Because of the way the tweets were collected, our collection does not contain full user profiles, which limit the user-based analysis.

Per-tweet Hashtag/Mention. Figures 4(a) and 4(b) plot the per-tweet usage distributions of hashtags and mentions in spam and ham tweets respectively. Observe that the mention distributions of spam and ham tweets are very similar to each other with ham tweets use slightly fewer number of mentions. For instance, 43% of ham tweets and 38% of spam tweets do not use mention. The hashtag per-tweet distributions are much more interesting. For ham tweets, 76% of tweets have no hashtags, and 97% of tweets have at most 2 hashtags. However, for spam tweets only 37% of them have no hashtags, and the cumulative percentage of tweets having 2 or fewer hashtags is 60%. The remaining 40% of tweets have 3 or

Table 6: The hashtags with the highest and lowest spammy-index. All hashtags listed in these two tables have frequency larger than 5000, and the hashtags are case-sensitive.

(a) Top-20 hashtags with highest spammy-index

Hashtag	$df(t, D_s)$	$df(t, D)$	$si(t)$
TEAMFOLLOWBACK	661,058	666,328	19.18
TFBJP	526,709	527,176	18.99
gameinsight	509,760	510,504	18.93
OPENFOLLOW	331,643	332,857	18.27
androidgames	286,101	286,706	18.09
android	335,699	341,240	18.06
IPADGAMES	231,725	232,335	17.78
SougoFollow	197,421	197,525	17.58
FOLLOWBACK	176,269	177,109	17.34
ipad	192,706	195,375	17.32
THF	165,407	165,762	17.30
FOLLOWNGAIN	149,708	149,916	17.17
500aday	145,696	146,005	17.12
RETWEET	240,128	250,992	17.10
TEAMHITFOLLOW	136,039	136,043	17.05
AUTOFOLLOW	140,686	141,214	17.04
MUSTFOLLOW	137,502	138,040	17.00
RT	224,640	235,137	16.98
HITFOLLOWSTEAM	127,262	127,264	16.96
Follow	122,575	126,720	16.35

(b) Top-20 hashtags with lowest spammy index

Hashtag	$df(t, D_s)$	$df(t, D)$	$si(t)$
musicjournals	4	6408	0.00
QnA	32	11868	0.01
occupygezi	21	13521	0.01
iCanAdmit	12	6714	0.01
thankyousiralex	25	5788	0.02
Aquarius	43	7270	0.03
blessed	42	6206	0.04
job	80	9786	0.05
BELIEVEtour	206	22758	0.07
Pisces	82	8011	0.07
nbaplayoffs	66	5596	0.07
Capricorn	104	7636	0.09
CFC	125	9271	0.09
jobs	333	26402	0.11
Sagittarius	202	9706	0.16
tbt	382	18157	0.18
TCOT	207	8553	0.19
MUFC	410	17791	0.20
Gemini	283	11156	0.21
Libra	160	5425	0.22

more hashtags. That is, the spam tweets use hashtags much more aggressively than ham tweets, probably aiming for more visibility.

Hashtag Spammy Index. We propose a measure named *Spammy Index* to quantify the extent a hashtag is being used in spam tweets. Given a hashtag t, its spammy index, denoted by $si(t)$, is defined in the following equation.

$$si(t) = \log_2(df(t, D)) \times \frac{df(t, D_s)}{df(t, D)} \qquad (1)$$

In this equation, $df(t, D)$ denotes document frequency, or the number of tweets containing hashtag t in tweets collection D; D_s is the set of spam tweets where $D_s \subset D$. A hashtag is considered to be more spammy if (i) its document frequency is high, and (ii) the probability of being used in spam tweets is high.

The top-20 hashtags with the highest spammy indexes are reported in Table 6(a). For comparison, Table 6(b) lists the 20 hashtags with the lowest spammy indexes among all hashtags with frequency more than 5,000. The two tables show that spammy hashtags are more likely to use capital letters, probably to draw attention. Frequent words appear in spammy hashtags are "follow", "fb"(follow back) and "game". Hashtags with low spammy indexes are less likely to contain all capital letters and many of them are topic specific on music, sports, or functional tags like #job and #jobs. Comparing Table 6(a) and Table 1, most extremely popular hashtags are hijacked for spamming purpose. Popular hashtags such as #android, #ipad are hijacked for spamming purpose so they appeared as top 20 spammy hashtags. The popularity of these hashtags may attribute to the large number of near-duplicate tweets automatically generated by bot like #gameinsight.

For the completeness of the analysis, we also computed the Odds Ratio (OR) of the words (including both case-insensitive hashtags after removing the # symbol and words appear in the content of tweets) in distinguishing spam tweets from ham tweets. The top-20 words with highest OR values are reported in Table 7. The words identified by high OR values are consistent with the hashtags of high spammy indexes, with the dominating word "follow".

Hashtag Co-occurrence Network. The co-occurrence graph for popular hashtags with frequency larger than 25,000 in HSpam14 is plotted in Figure 5. The size of node is proportional to the hashtag frequency (in $\log_2$ scale). The color of node is proportional to the hashtag's spammy index (most spammy hashtags are in red, least spammy hashtags are in green, intermediate ones are in blue). We make two observations from this co-occurrence network. First, the spammy hashtags are more likely to co-occur with each other. Second, the less spammy hashtags are less likely to co-occur with other hashtags. This can be partially explained by the observation that 97% of ham tweets have at most 2 hashtags.

Table 7: Top-20 most spammy words by Odds Ratio

Rank	Word	Rank	Word
1	hitfollowsteam	11	followers
2	tribez	12	ifollowngain
3	maxvip	13	followbacksegur
4	r_family	14	teamfollowwacky
5	follow2befollowe	15	smurfberries
6	teamhitfollow	16	myretweets
7	extraretweets	17	reignd
8	onlyifyouare	18	mesiguestesigo
9	rt2club	19	90sbabyf
10	rt2supergain	20	harvested

6. CONCLUSION AND LIMITATION

In this paper, we make the first step for tweet-level spam detection focusing on hashtag-oriented tweet spam. The main contribution of this work is the creation of HSpam14 data collection, which contains 3.338 million spam tweets and 10.688 million ham tweets, collected in two months' time guided by trending hashtags. While the annotation was not made per tweet basis, the overall quality of the labels are good enough to perform analyses and studies on hashtag-oriented tweet spam detection. Our analysis on this dataset also shows different usage patterns of mentions and hashtags in spam and ham tweets, and shows that spammy hashtags are likely to co-occur with spammy hashtags.

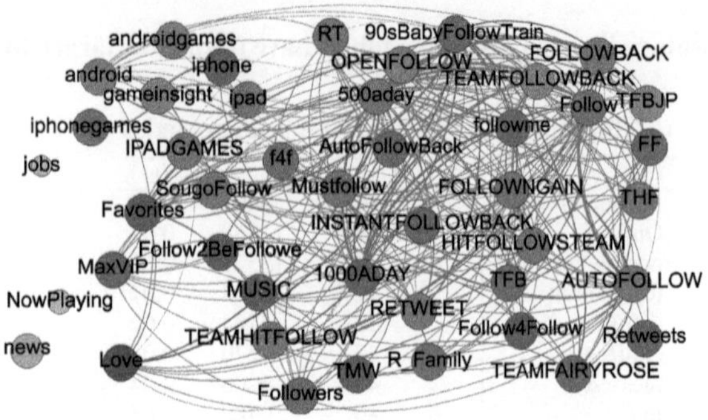

Figure 5: Co-occurrence of the most popular hashtags.

A limitation of this data collection is the lack of full profiles of the users. As the tweets in this collection were collected with the guide of trending hashtags, we do not have full user profiles (*e.g.,* all tweets published by each user, list of her followers/followees) in HSpam14 due to the restriction of Twitter steaming APIs. This may limit the study on user-level spam detection with this dataset. For the same reason, we only utilize very limited user-level features during the annotation process although many other user-level features (*e.g.,* temporal patterns, social connections) have demonstrated their effectiveness in identifying spammers. Another limitation could be the limited keywords used in heuristic-based tweet selection. The existing keywords may not catch spam in specific domains (*e.g.,* healthcare and medical). Part of our future work is to improve the recall of the spam tweets in specific domains.

Acknowledgements: This work was partially supported by Singapore MOE AcRF Tier-1 Grant RG142/14.

7. REFERENCES

[1] F. Benevenuto, G. Magno, T. Rodrigues, and V. Almeida. Detecting spammers on twitter. In *CEAS*, 2010.

[2] F. Benevenuto, T. Rodrigues, V. Almeida, J. Almeida, and M. Gonçalves. Detecting spammers and content promoters in online video social networks. In *SIGIR*, pages 620–627, 2009.

[3] A. Broder. On the resemblance and containment of documents. In *Proc. Compression and Complexity of Sequences*, pages 21–29, 1997.

[4] C. Castillo, M. Mendoza, and B. Poblete. Information credibility on twitter. In *WWW*, pages 675–684, 2011.

[5] D. Chinavle, P. Kolari, T. Oates, and T. Finin. Ensembles in adversarial classification for spam. In *CIKM*, pages 2015–2018, 2009.

[6] A. Chowdhury, O. Frieder, D. Grossman, and M. C. McCabe. Collection statistics for fast duplicate document detection. *ACM Trans. on Info. Sys.*, pages 171–191, 2002.

[7] Z. Chu, S. Gianvecchio, H. Wang, and S. Jajodia. Who is tweeting on twitter: Human, bot, or cyborg? In *Proc. Annual Computer Security Appln Conf.*, pages 21–30, 2010.

[8] T.-S. Chua, J. Tang, R. Hong, H. Li, Z. Luo, and Y. Zheng. Nus-wide: A real-world web image database from national university of singapore. In *CIVR*, pages 48:1–48:9, 2009.

[9] G. V. Cormack. Email spam filtering: A systematic review. *Foundations and Trends in Inf. Ret.*, pages 335–455, 2008.

[10] E. Ferrara, O. Varol, C. Davis, F. Menczer, and A. Flammini. The rise of social bots, 2014. arXiv:1407.5225.

[11] N. Gao, W. Webber, and D. W. Oard. Reducing reliance on relevance judgments for system comparison by using expectation-maximization. In *ECIR*, pages 1–12, 2014.

[12] S. Ghosh, B. Viswanath, F. Kooti, N. K. Sharma, G. Korlam, F. Benevenuto, N. Ganguly, and K. P. Gummadi. Understanding and combating link farming in the twitter social network. In *WWW*, pages 61–70, 2012.

[13] C. Grier, K. Thomas, V. Paxson, and M. Zhang. @spam: The underground on 140 characters or less. In *Proc. ACM Conf. on Computer and Communications Security*, pages 27–37, 2010.

[14] P. Heymann, G. Koutrika, and H. Garcia-Molina. Fighting spam on social web sites: A survey of approaches and future challenges. *IEEE Internet Computing*, 11:36–45, 2007.

[15] X. Hu, J. Tang, and H. Liu. Leveraging knowledge across media for spammer detection in microblogging. In *SIGIR*, pages 547–556, 2014.

[16] X. Hu, J. Tang, and H. Liu. Online social spammer detection. In *AAAI*, pages 59–65, 2014.

[17] N. Jindal and B. Liu. Review spam detection. In *WWW*, pages 1189–1190, 2007.

[18] N. Jindal and B. Liu. Opinion spam and analysis. In *WSDM*, pages 219–230, 2008.

[19] K. Lee, J. Caverlee, and S. Webb. The social honeypot project: Protecting online communities from spammers. In *WWW*, pages 1139–1140, 2010.

[20] K. Lee, B. D. Eoff, and J. Caverlee. Seven months with the devils: A long-term study of content polluters on twitter. In *ICWSM*, 2011.

[21] K. Lee, S. Webb, and H. Ge. The dark side of micro-task marketplaces: Characterizing fiverr and automatically detecting crowdturfing. In *ICWSM*, 2014.

[22] F. Li, M. Huang, Y. Yang, and X. Zhu. Learning to identify review spam. In *IJCAI*, pages 2488–2493, 2011.

[23] J. Li, C. Cardie, and S. Li. Topicspam: a topic-model based approach for spam detection. In *ACL*, pages 217–221, 2013.

[24] E.-P. Lim, V.-A. Nguyen, N. Jindal, B. Liu, and H. W. Lauw. Detecting product review spammers using rating behaviors. In *CIKM*, pages 939–948, 2010.

[25] B. Liu, Y. Dai, X. Li, W. S. Lee, and P. S. Yu. Building text classifiers using positive and unlabeled examples. In *ICDM*, pages 179–186, 2003.

[26] C. D. Manning, P. Raghavan, and H. Schütze. *Introduction to information retrieval*, volume 1. Cambridge University Press, 2008.

[27] J. Messias, L. Schmidt, R. Oliveira, and F. Benevenuto. You followed my bot! transforming robots into influential users in twitter. *First Monday*, 18, 2013.

[28] G. Mishne, D. Carmel, and R. Lempel. Blocking blog spam with language model disagreement. In *AIRWeb*, 2005.

[29] A. Mukherjee, B. Liu, J. Wang, N. Glance, and N. Jindal. Detecting group review spam. In *WWW*, pages 93–94, 2011.

[30] K. Nigam, A. K. McCallum, S. Thrun, and T. Mitchell. Text classification from labeled and unlabeled documents using EM. *Mach. Learn.*, pages 103–134, 2000.

[31] M. Ott, Y. Choi, C. Cardie, and J. T. Hancock. Finding deceptive opinion spam by any stretch of the imagination. In *HLT*, pages 309–319, 2011.

[32] A. Shrivastava and P. Li. In defense of minhash over simhash. In *AISTATS*, pages 886–894, 2014.

[33] N. Spirin and J. Han. Survey on web spam detection: Principles and algorithms. *SIGKDD Explor. Newsl.*, 13(2):50–64, 2012.

[34] E. Tan, L. Guo, S. Chen, X. Zhang, and Y. Zhao. Unik: Unsupervised social network spam detection. In *CIKM*, pages 479–488, 2013.

[35] K. Thomas, C. Grier, D. Song, and V. Paxson. Suspended accounts in retrospect: An analysis of twitter spam. In *IMC*, pages 243–258, 2011.

[36] C. Wagner, S. Mitter, C. Körner, and M. Strohmaier. When social bots attack: Modeling susceptibility of users in online social networks. In *Workshop on Making Sense of Microposts*, 2012.

[37] G. Wang, C. Wilson, X. Zhao, Y. Zhu, M. Mohanlal, H. Zheng, and B. Y. Zhao. Serf and turf: Crowdturfing for fun and profit. In *WWW*, pages 679–688, 2012.

[38] Z. Wang, W. Josephson, Q. Lv, M. Charikar, and K. Li. Filtering image spam with near-duplicate detection. In *Proc. Conf. on Email and AntiSpam*, pages 600–603, 2007.

[39] J. Weng, E.-P. Lim, J. Jiang, and Q. He. Twitterrank: Finding topic-sensitive influential twitterers. In *WSDM*, pages 261–270, 2010.

[40] L. Zhu, A. Sun, and B. Choi. Detecting spam blogs from blog search results. *Inf. Process. Manage.*, 47(2):246–262, 2011.

Uncovering Crowdsourced Manipulation of Online Reviews

Amir Fayazi
Texas A&M University
College Station, TX 77843
afayazi@tamu.edu

Kyumin Lee
Utah State University
Logan, UT 84322
kyumin.lee@usu.edu

James Caverlee
Texas A&M University
College Station, TX 77843
caverlee@cse.tamu.edu

Anna Squicciarini
Pennsylvania State University
University Park, PA 16801
asquicciarini@ist.psu.edu

ABSTRACT

Online reviews are a cornerstone of consumer decision making. However, their authenticity and quality has proven hard to control, especially as polluters target these reviews toward promoting products or in degrading competitors. In a troubling direction, the widespread growth of crowdsourcing platforms like Mechanical Turk has created a large-scale, potentially difficult-to-detect workforce of malicious review writers. Hence, this paper tackles the challenge of uncovering crowdsourced manipulation of online reviews through a three-part effort: (i) First, we propose a novel sampling method for identifying products that have been targeted for manipulation and a seed set of deceptive reviewers who have been enlisted through crowdsourcing platforms. (ii) Second, we augment this base set of deceptive reviewers through a reviewer-reviewer graph clustering approach based on a Markov Random Field where we define individual potentials (of single reviewers) and pair potentials (between two reviewers). (iii) Finally, we embed the results of this probabilistic model into a classification framework for detecting crowd-manipulated reviews. We find that the proposed approach achieves up to 0.96 AUC, outperforming both traditional detection methods and a SimRank-based alternative clustering approach.

Categories and Subject Descriptors: H.3.5 [Online Information Services]: Web-based services

Keywords: crowdsourced manipulation; deceptive review; amazon; crowdsourcing site; review site

1. INTRODUCTION

Reviews are a ubiquitous component of online commerce – from hotel and travel booking sites (e.g., Expedia, Trip Advisor and hotels.com) to e-commerce sites (e.g., Amazon and eBay) to app stores (e.g., Google Play and Apple's App Store). Online reviews provide a voice for customers to praise or criticize a product or service, often in conjunction with a star rating, providing helpful information to future potential customers. Unsurprisingly, research has shown that product review ratings are, indeed, correlated with sales [4, 10].

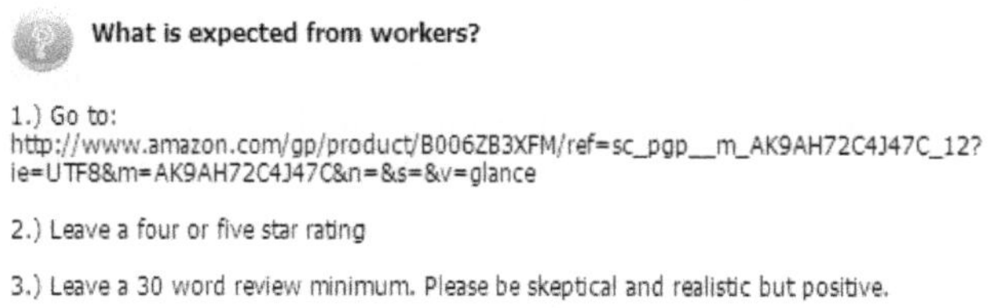

Figure 1: An example deceptive review task posted to a crowdsourcing platform.

Naturally, there is an incentive to pollute these reviews toward promoting one's products or in degrading one's competitors. This pollution has been identified as a growing threat to the trustworthiness of online reviews by major media and by the research literature [7, 20, 22, 25, 26]. Recently, Ott et al. suggested that up to 6% of reviews on sites like Yelp and TripAdvisor may be deceptive [22]. These reviews can have serious consequences: a deceptively promoted weight loss supplement identified as part of this project led one customer to write: *...these pills made me really sick, palpitations, increased heart rate and troubled breathing. I requested a return, and the response I got from the company selling these horrible pills was very rude....*

In a troubling direction, the widespread growth of crowdsourcing platforms has created a new attack vector for polluting online reviews. Crowdsourcing platforms like Amazon Mechanical Turk have been hailed for their effectiveness in intelligently organizing large numbers of people [3, 11]. These platforms however also enable a large-scale, potentially difficult-to-detect workforce of deceptive review writers [17, 28]. To illustrate, Figure 1 shows an example task that asks each worker to leave a high product rating and a "skeptical and realistic but positive" review. Figure 2 shows a sample of two deceptive reviews written in response to this type of crowdsourced task. Compared to traditional spam bots that typically leave identifiable footprints [15, 16, 18], these human-powered deceptive reviews are inherently distinct, linked only by their common theme and not in common keywords, phrases, or other easily identifiable signals. And since crowdsourced deceptive reviews are generated by humans rather than bots, their ongoing detection is even

SIGIR'15, August 09 - 13, 2015, Santiago, Chile.

DOI: http://dx.doi.org/10.1145/2766462.2767742.

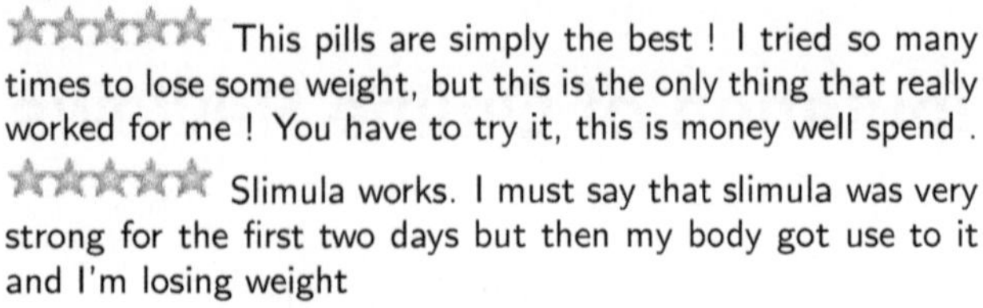

Figure 2: Two crowdsourced reviews for a weight-loss product sold by Amazon.

more challenging since crowds can actively circumvent detection methods.

Unfortunately, there is a significant gap in our understanding of crowdsourced manipulation of online reviews and effective methods for uncovering such manipulation, due to a number of challenges. One critical challenge is a lack of clear ground truth for analyzing deceptive reviews and in building countermeasures; it is difficult to ascertain which reviews are deceptive and which ones are legitimate. A second important challenge is that polluters may rely on multiple communication channels to coordinate their activities – including private methods such as email and instant messenger which are difficult to observe – and so deceptive intent may be further obscured. To tackle these issues, we propose a three-part effort:

- First, we propose a novel sampling method for identifying products that have been targeted for manipulation and a seed set of deceptive reviewers who have been enlisted through the command-and-control of crowdsourcing platforms. To our knowledge, this is the first effort toward "pulling back the curtain" to uncover clear evidence linking deceptive intent with actual reviews.
- Second, we augment the seed set of sampled deceptive reviewers to identify additional deceptive reviewers who participate as part of hidden groups of coordinated manipulation. To capture the hidden infrastructure underlying deceptive reviews, we exploit connections between reviewers through a reviewer-reviewer graph clustering approach based on a conditional random field that models individual potentials (of single reviewers) in combination with pair potentials (between two reviewers).
- Finally, we embed the results of this probabilistic model into a classification framework for detecting crowd manipulated reviews. We find that the proposed approach achieves up to 0.96 AUC, outperforming both traditional detection methods and an alternative SimRank-based clustering approach.

2. RELATED WORK

In this section, we summarize previous research work related to deceptive reviews and crowdsourced manipulation.

First of all, in the deceptive or spam review research field, researchers have analyzed the growth of deceptive reviews over time and have studied how to detect these reviews. For example, Ott el al. [22] have reported that the number of deceptive reviews has grown across multiple consumer-oriented review sites. Danescu-Niculescu-Mizil et al. [5] suggested an underlying model for measuring review quality. They reported that when controversy of a product was high, some of the reviews whose ratings were different from the average rating of the product often got higher helpfulness scores. Other researchers discovered distinguishing patterns between spam and legitimate reviews from product review ratings [9] and temporal distribution of spam reviews [29].

A related line of research has studied coordinated groups of review spammers. Lu et al. [19] found that the social context of reviews was useful to find groups of review spammers. They showed that one can assess the quality of reviews with higher accuracy when one assumed the quality of a reviewer depended on the quality of her peers in the social network. Mukherjee et al. [21] found that analyzing groups of review spammers revealed clearer evidence of spam reviews than analyzing an individual spam review. Ott et al. [23] showed that linguistic features were not reliable for humans to distinguish between deceptive reviews and legitimate reviews. The proposed sampling method, reviewer clustering, and deceptive review classifier in this paper complement these existing approaches.

Next, researchers have begun to study the crowdsourced manipulation problem of spreading manipulated contents to target sites such as social networking sites, review sites, and search engines [17, 27, 28]. Wang et al. [28] analyzed the use of two Chinese crowdsourcing platforms, and estimated that 90% of all tasks were malicious tasks. Lee et al. [17] analyzed tasks in Western crowdsourcing platforms, and found that the primary targeted systems were online social networks including review sites (56%) and search engines (33%). But, the previous research work did not specifically focus on a crowdsourced deceptive review problem. Researchers expressed that labeling fake reviews by human is sometimes hard [13]. Our research is the first work to link crowdsourced deceptive review tasks to target products, and analyze these deceptive reviews and behaviors of deceptive reviewers toward building a deceptive review classifier.

3. OVERALL FRAMEWORK

Our ultimate goal is to identify deceptive online reviews. We formulate this problem as a classification problem, where the goal is to assign a class label of *deceptive* or *legitimate* to a candidate review r based on a classifier c:

$$c : r \rightarrow \{deceptive, legitimate\}$$

The first critical challenge to building an effective classifier is in identifying valid ground truth training data. Typical methods include: (i) rule-based heuristics – like labeling as deceptive all reviews containing a particular keyword or some other intuitive signal – however, such methods are brittle to changes in the strategies of deceptive reviewers; and (ii) asking human labelers to assess reviews, however these labelers typically do not know the intent of the original review writer, and so the labels may be in error. In contrast, we propose instead to sample directly from crowdsourcing platforms that publicly advertise review tasks.

3.1 Sampling Crowdsourcing Platforms for Deceptive Reviews

Our sampling strategy is first to collect tasks from crowdsourcing platforms that require workers to post a review on a target site (e.g., Amazon, Yelp) akin to the example task in Figure 1. By linking these tasks to products in a target site, we can then sample the products targeted, the reviews associated with the product, as well as the reviewers who contributed the reviews. The overall sampling framework is illustrated in Figure 3.

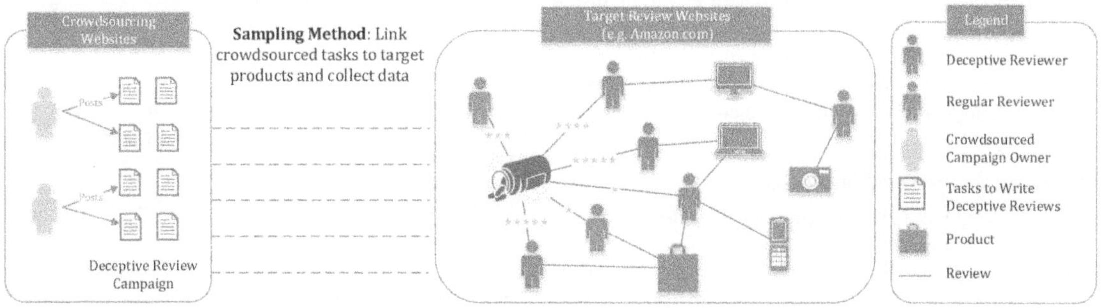

Figure 3: Overall Sampling Framework.

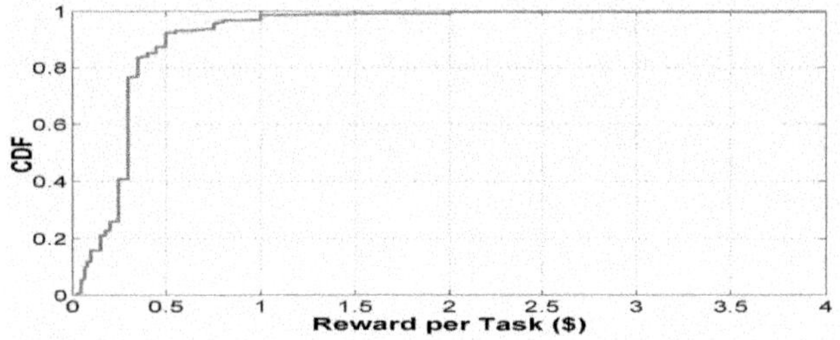

Figure 4: Cumulative Distribution Function of reward per task targeting Amazon.

In particular, we sampled tasks posted to three crowdsourcing platforms over a span of several weeks in 2013: RapidWorkers.com, ShortTask.com, and Microworkers.com. Each of these platforms supports a variety of tasks, typically offering on the order of \$0.25 per task completion. We sampled all tasks on these platforms that target Amazon. Figure 4 presents a cumulative distribution function (CDF) of reward per task targeting Amazon. The average reward per task was \$0.31, and the biggest reward per task was \$3.99. There were various tasks targeting Amazon such as manipulating the number of clicks of a product page and the helpfulness of a review, downloading/purchasing a product and writing deceptive reviews. Among these tasks targeting Amazon, the majority tasks were to write deceptive reviews.

To study crowdsourced manipulation of reviews on Amazon, we extracted the Amazon URL from each task which links to a product page on Amazon, collected the product page, all reviews associated with the product, and all reviewers' information. In total, we identified 1,000 products on Amazon that had been the target of deceptive reviews. We call this the *root dataset*.

We augmented this base set of products, reviews, and reviewers via a breadth-first search crawling method. Specifically, we collected the previous Amazon reviews of each reviewer in the root dataset and the Amazon product pages those reviews were associated with. We subsequently collected all of the new reviews and new reviewer profiles from these product pages. In total, we crawled out three hops from the root dataset to identify a larger candidate set of potential deceptive reviews, reviewers, and targeted products. In total, this *expanded dataset* includes 71.1k reviews, 14.5k reviewers, and 48.9k products.

3.2 Clustering Deceptive Reviewers

Given the expanded dataset consisting of reviewers and products, our next goal is to reveal hidden linkages among the reviewers towards uncovering previously unknown deceptive reviewers who participate as part of hidden groups of coordinated manipulation. The original sampling method identifies products (in the root set) for which we are certain reviewers have targeted for manipulation. However, many efforts to pollute reviews may rely on private command and control (and so be out of reach of our sampling method) [28]. Can we exploit the linkages among reviewers and products to identify these hidden deceptive reviewers? This section presents a Reviewer-Reviewer graph clustering approach based on a pairwise Markov Random Field (MRF) that defines individual potentials (of single reviewers) and pair potentials (between two reviewers). In addition to providing evidence of coordinated manipulation, the output of this clustering approach can be integrated as an additional feature for building the deceptive review classifier.

3.2.1 Building the Reviewer-Reviewer Graph

Our root dataset indicates that the payoff for a single favorable review is generally less than a US dollar, so users are likely to write multiple reviews (about 5 each, in our dataset). As we assume that some reviewers cooperate with one another in targeting certain products, we build a reviewer-reviewer graph to capture these subtle dependencies, and detect "non-crowdsourcing" deviant reviewers.

Our expanded dataset can naturally be represented as a Reviewer-Product graph $G_{R,P}$. The Reviewer-Product graph is a bipartite graph of consumer products connecting reviewers with products, with edges representing reviews.

Using this information, we can construct the Reviewer-Reviewer graph $G_{R,R} := (R, E, W)$ where the vertex set R denotes the reviewers who wrote reviews on Amazon and the weighted edges (arcs) in E indicate how many pairs of reviewers have reviewed the same item during a short time window. Finally, W is the set of edge weights. Edge weights are calculated according to the weighting function $w : E \rightarrow W$, as follows.

$$w_{R,R}(a,b) := \frac{|\{p | p \in N_{R,P}(a) \wedge p \in N_{R,P}(b) \wedge |t(a,p) - t(b,p)| < T\}|}{\min(|N_{R,P}(a)|, |N_{R,P}(b)|)}$$

where $N_{R,P}(a)$ is the set of products rated favorably by a, $t(a,p)$ is the time when a reviewed p, and finally T is a constant time window size which was set to three days in our case. In essence, the numerator captures reviewer similarity by counting the number of products both a and b rated favorably in the same time window.

Following the projection of $G_{R,P}$ onto $G_{R,R}$ we prune edges whose weight denominator is 1.0 and then vertices with degree zero from $G_{R,R}$. The former is to avoid creating a strong ($w = 1.0$) collaboration edge between two reviewers due to a single review co-occurrence.

3.2.2 *Modeling Reviewer Potentials*

Given this Reviewer-Reviewer graph, we now describe a probabilistic approach for clustering reviewers (nodes) toward identifying groups of similar reviewers. We formulate this approach using a MRF defined over the Reviewer-Reviewer graph $G_{R,R}$. Each node in the random field corresponds to a reviewer and is a discrete random variable whose value is the cluster the corresponding reviewer belongs to.

The proposed approach captures the following intuition:

- If two reviewers have collaborated heavily, they should be assigned to the same cluster. This allows for a clustering where connectedness is the criterion, and clusters can expand in a non-convex fashion similar to a spatial clustering. This kind of clustering does not require a precisely pre-determined number of clusters. Instead, it requires assigning a reasonably large number of clusters, and the clustering process will eventually choose the best number of clusters by merging initial clusters (e.g., initially assign 50 clusters, but finally end up with four large clusters).
- Toward creating cohesive clusters, we additionally require that all the reviewers of a cluster display similar features. For instance, reviewers who have actually purchased a product they reviewed and reviewers who did not purchase the product they have reviewed should belong to different clusters.

We model reviewers using two potential functions, capturing the intuitions above. The first is a *singleton potential*, as it is defined per each reviewer ϕ_j. The other type of function is per pair of reviewers ϕ_{pair}, and hence called *pair potential.* The singleton potentials have higher value when the reviewer features are close to that of the mean cluster features in the feature space. The pair potentials are higher when two connected reviewers in the graph are assigned to the same cluster. We aim to determine the most likely cluster assignments given the Reviewer-Reviewer graph and these potential functions are used to factorize the probability distribution:

$$P(\boldsymbol{Z}|\boldsymbol{\theta},\boldsymbol{D}) \propto \prod_j \phi_j(Z_j) \prod_{j,k} \phi_{\text{pair}}(Z_j, Z_k)$$

where D stands for observations from the data, and is bolded to signify a set of random variables; Z represents cluster assignments which is not observed (hidden data); θ represents the parameters of the model; $\phi_j(Z_j)$ is the potential function over the labeling of reviewer j and ϕ_{pair} is over pairs of labels. Since the MRF is wholly conditioned on the observation data D, it is an instance of a Conditional Random Field (CRF). Next we will describe the factors (potentials) in our model.

Singleton Potentials. The singleton potential function is designed to capture how well an individual labeled reviewer corresponds to the cluster in which it belongs. Formally, we define the singleton potential as:

$$\phi_j(Z_j) = \Pr(Z_j, \overbrace{\boldsymbol{F_j}, \boldsymbol{P_j}}^{\text{Observations}} |\boldsymbol{\theta}) = \Pr(\boldsymbol{F_j}, \boldsymbol{P_j}|Z_j, \boldsymbol{\theta}) \Pr(Z_j|\boldsymbol{\theta})$$

where the variables $\boldsymbol{F_j}$ and $\boldsymbol{P_j}$ are the observed data and Z_j is the hidden variable (cluster of reviewer j). $\boldsymbol{\theta}$ represents the model parameters. $\boldsymbol{F_j}$s are the features of a reviewer j. $\boldsymbol{P_j}$s are the products reviewed by reviewer j. In practice, we can adopt any of a number of features that may be good candidates for distinguishing between deceptive and legitimate reviewers. In this paper, we adopt the following six features $\boldsymbol{F_j}$s in the singleton potential function:

- Real Name: Does a reviewer have a real name verified by Amazon? – *Binary*
- Helpfulness of reviews: Are the majority of a reviewer's reviews helpful? – *Binary*
- Verified Purchase: The majority of a reviewer's reviews are based on a verified purchase – *Binary*
- Length of the reviews written – *Log normal*
- Are favorable reviews (4, 5 star) more helpful than other reviews (1 through 3 stars)? – *Binary*
- Whether reviewer has more verified purchases for favorable reviews – *Binary*

We additionally make the assumption that feature values are conditionally independent given the cluster (as illustrated in Figure 5, which shows a graphical model of our independence assumption). As a result, the conditional probability of the observed data is:

$$\Pr(\boldsymbol{F_j}, \boldsymbol{P_j}|\theta, Z_j) = \prod_{F_{jk} \in F_j} \Pr(F_{jk}|Z_j, \theta) \prod_{j \sim k} \Pr(P_{jk}|Z_j, \theta)$$

where the symbol $\sim$ stands for adjacency in the graph.

We can model the binary variables (e.g., *Real Name*, *Helpfulness*) as Bernoulli random variables:

$$\Pr(F = f|Z = c) = \begin{cases} p_c & f = 1 \\ 1 - p_c & f = 0 \end{cases}$$

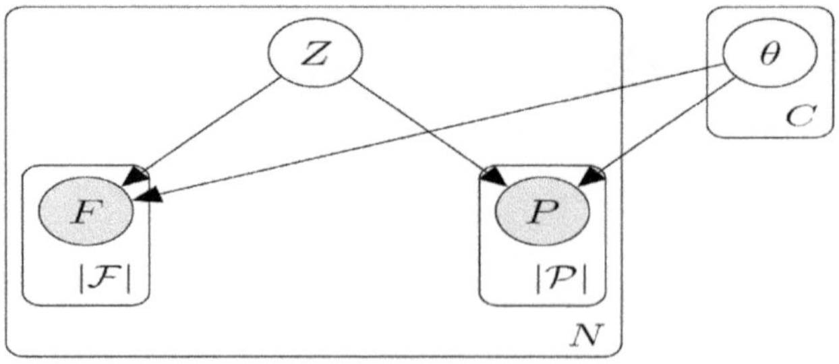

Figure 5: The independence assumption of the variables during calculation of singleton potentials ϕ. The indicator variables P correspond to each product and indicates whether that product was reviewed favorably. We assume the probability of that only depends on which cluster Z the author belongs to and the preference of that cluster θ. F represents various features of the authors in the cluster.

Since we find that the length of reviews has a log-normal distribution, the average log-length of reviews of a reviewer follows a Gaussian distribution which is denoted by L in the following:

$$\Pr(L = \log l | Z = c) = \mathcal{N}(\log l; \mu_c, \sigma)$$

Note that we do not require that each cluster of coordinated reviewers be equally likely to review all the products. Rather, we assume that each reviewer has concentrated on writing reviews for a subset of the products in the cluster. This is modeled by the second part of the singleton potential function. Given the cluster, there is a probability distribution over products π_c where product i has the chance $\pi_{c,i}$ of being reviewed by a reviewer in a cluster c. This part of the singleton potential tends to push dissimilar set of reviewers into separate clusters.

$$\Pr(P_i | Z_j = c) = \pi_{c,i}$$
$$\text{Subject to} \sum_i \pi_{c,i} = 1$$

Pair Potentials. The second potential function of the MRF likelihood formulation is the one between pairs of reviewers. The role of this function is to force that reviewers who have collaborated on writing favorable reviews, end up in the same cluster. In addition, if the number of clusters is larger than the actual underlying number of hidden groups, this potential function will regulate the resulting clustering where too many distinct clusters with edges between them are punished. The likelihood of two adjacent reviewers to be in the same cluster in the graph depends on a tunable parameter τ and on the weight of collaboration between the two reviewers $w_{R,R}(j,k)$.

$$\phi_{\text{pair}}(Z_j, Z_k) = \begin{cases} \tau^{w_{R,R}(j,k)} & Z_j = Z_k \\ (1-\tau)^{w_{R,R}(j,k)} & Z_j \neq Z_k \end{cases}$$

By increasing the value of τ, connected reviewers are more likely to be in the same cluster.

3.2.3 Learning Parameters and Clusters

Based on the probabilistic modeling part described in the previous section, we now have the following:

- Model parameters θ: including μ_c, p_cs, and $\pi_{c,i}$
- Hidden data Z_j: cluster assignments
- Observations: including F_k, P_m, and $w_{R,R}$

We aim to maximize the likelihood $\mathcal{L}(\boldsymbol{Z}, \boldsymbol{\theta}; D)$. That is, we need to see what sort of cluster parameters θ and cluster membership Z fit our evidence (i.e., our reviewer-reviewer graph) D the most. A common way to deal with maximizing likelihood functions which depend on hidden data (Z) is to use a local optimization method like Expectation Maximization (EM). EM is a popular method for missing data problems and has been successfully applied to similar MRF models in other domains [2]. EM iterates over two steps to increase the likelihood [6]. However it might get trapped in a local maximum. Therefore, we use a variant of EM, called *hard EM* with random restarts, which consists of the following steps:

1. Initialize parameters θ^0 to random values
2. While parameters have not converged:

   E-Step Calculate maximum a posteriori (MAP) values for $Z^{(t)}$ given $\theta^{(t)}$. That is, find the best cluster assignment given current parameters

   M-Step Calculate maximum likelihood estimate (MLE) $\theta^{(t+1)}$ given the $Z^{(t)}$. That is, find better parameter estimates given current cluster assignments

In the following, we present our parameter initialization and EM steps.

Parameter Initialization. The p_c parameters for binary features are sampled from a Dirichlet distribution $\text{Dir}([\alpha, \alpha])$. α in this case is a hyper-parameter for the p_c parameters. We pick α values relatively large so the sampled p_c's don't end up being close to the extremes (0 or 1). Instead they will be (in this case) close to 0.5 with a little perturbation. The initialization distribution for $\pi_{c,i}$ is similarly $\text{Dir}([\alpha_1, \cdots, \alpha_P])$ where P is the number of all products and α_is have the same value. For large α the resulting $\pi_{c,i}$ is close to uniform distribution with a little perturbation which is what we desired. The μ_cs of review lengths are initialized uniformly in the range of $[0, \max\{\log(\text{review length})\}]$. The parameter σ for review lengths is fixed at 1.

E-Step. In this step we should assign cluster labels so the following log likelihood function is maximized.

$$\log \mathcal{L}(Z, \boldsymbol{\theta}) = \sum_j \log \phi_j(Z_j) + \sum_{j,k} \log \phi_{\text{pair}}(Z_j, Z_k)$$

We adopt an Integer Program formulation of this problem by Kleinberg and Tardos called *Uniform Metric Labeling* [14]. For each node j (reviewer in the graph) we define an indicator variable $x_{j,c}$. If $x_{j,c} = 1$, it indicates node j is assigned to cluster c. In the pair potentials part of the summation, for each edge (j,k) the variable $d_{jk} = \frac{1}{2}\sum_{c \in C} |x_{j,c} - x_{k,c}|$ is the binary distance between the assigned clusters of j and k, where 0 means identical clusters and 1 is different clusters. For each edge of the reviewer-reviewer graph, we then have the potential:
$\log \phi_{\text{pair}}(Z_j, Z_k) = w_{R,R}(j,k)\,(d_{jk} \log(1-\tau) + (1-d_{jk}) \log \tau)$.
The Integer Program formulation can be relaxed to a Linear Program:

Minimize

$$\sum_{j \in R, c \in C} -\log \phi_j(Z_j = c) x_{jc} + \sum_{(j,k) \in E_{R,R}} -w_{R,R}\left(\log \frac{1-\tau}{\tau}\right) d_{jk}$$

Subject to

$$\sum_{c \in C} x_{j,c} = 1$$
$$d_{jk} = \frac{1}{2} \sum_{c \in C} d_{jkc}$$
$$d_{jkc} \geq x_{jc} - x_{kc}$$
$$d_{jkc} \geq x_{kc} - x_{jc}$$
$$x_{kc} \geq 0$$

Once the optimum x_{jc} are calculated, we pick the c with the highest x_{jc} as the cluster assignment for reviewer j.

M-Step. In the M-Step we update model parameters θ with their maximum likelihood estimate (MLE) given the cluster assignments. The MLE estimates can be simply determined using frequency counts.

$$\Pr(Z = c) = \frac{|\{j \in R \mid Z_j = c\}|}{|R|}$$

$$\pi_{ci} = \frac{|\{(j,i) \in E_(R,P) \mid j \in R, i \in P, Z_j = c\}|}{S}$$

In the denominator, S is the normalizing factor so $\sum_{i \in P} \pi_{ci} = 1$. Similarly, the value of μ_c is updated as follows.

$$\mu_c = \frac{\sum_{a \in C} l_a}{|c|}$$

Similarly, the values for p_cs for various binary features of clusters can be determined with frequency counts.

3.3 Summary

To summarize, our goal toward identifying deceptive reviews (and reviewers) is based on the following logic. First, we sample known products that have been the target of deceptive reviews by crawling several crowdsourcing platforms. We call this the *root dataset*. We augment this base set of products, reviews, and reviewers via a breadth-first search crawling method to identify the *expanded dataset*. Given this expanded dataset, we aim to reveal hidden linkages among reviewers via a probabilistic clustering approach. The output of this clustering are groups of reviewers who often posted reviews to same products. In addition to providing additional evidence of coordinated manipulation, the output of this clustering approach can be integrated as an additional feature for building the deceptive review classifier.

4. EXPERIMENTS

In this section, we evaluate two main sets of experiments. First, we evaluate the reviewer clustering method over: (i) a synthetic dataset to validate the method's capacity to uncover groups of coordinating reviewers; and (ii) the expanded dataset to determine if meaningful groups of deceptive reviewers can be discovered from a real Amazon dataset. Second, we build a deceptive review classifier by using the output of the clustering algorithm as an additional feature and evaluate its performance versus a baseline without knowledge of the clustering output. We then compare this cluster-aware deceptive review classifier versus one based on an alternate clustering method (SimRank + k-medoids) to further validate the design choices in our reviewer-reviewer clustering method.

4.1 Identifying Reviewer Clusters

Our first goal is to understand how well the proposed clustering method performs. This is an important step for connecting known deceptive reviewers to potentially unknown ones. We first consider a synthetic dataset designed to contain natural groupings; does the proposed clustering method recover these underlying groups? Based on these observations, we then apply the clustering method over the *expanded dataset* based on 71.1k reviews, 14.5k reviewers, and 48.9k products. Do we discover groups engaged in coordinated manipulation?

4.1.1 With Synthetic Data

We begin by considering a synthetic dataset that is generated according to the same process the model in Section 3.2 assumes as detailed in Algorithm 1. The data generation procedure takes as input the number of clusters (K) and a total number of reviewers (N), and outputs a synthetic collaboration graph of reviewers. The relative sizes of each of K clusters is sampled from a Dirichlet distribution which is commonly used as a prior distribution for a multinomial. The parameter α determines how variant/uniform the clusters sizes will be. This allows for generating various proportions of cluster sizes. Then for each cluster, all its parameters are sampled.

Algorithm 1 Synthetic data generation procedure

Input: K (no. clusters), N (no. reviewers)
Input: Dirichlet params $(\alpha_1, ..., \alpha_K)$, τ
    ▷ Sample cluster parameters
  Sample cluster sizes $\sim \mathrm{Dir}(\alpha, ..., \alpha)$
  for each cluster c **do**
    Sample μ_c (mean) of review log-length $\sim$ Gaussian
    Sample $p_{c,\mathrm{feature}}$ for features {Helpfulness, RealName, VerifiedPurchase} $\sim$ Uniform $0-1$
    Sample cluster product preferences $\pi_c \sim \mathrm{Dir}(\beta, ..., \beta)$
  end for
    ▷ Sample reviewers' features and edges between them
  Assign reviewers to clusters
  for each cluster c in K clusters **do**
    for each reviewer n in cluster c **do**
      Sample reviewer features RealName, Helpfulness, VerifiedPurchase $\sim$ Bernoulli$(p_{c,\mathrm{feature}})$
    end for
  end for
  for each reviewer a, b pairs **do**
    if cluster(a) = cluster(b) **then**
      add an edge if Bernoulli$(\tau) = 1$
    else
      add an edge if Bernoulli$(1-\tau) = 1$
    end if
  end for

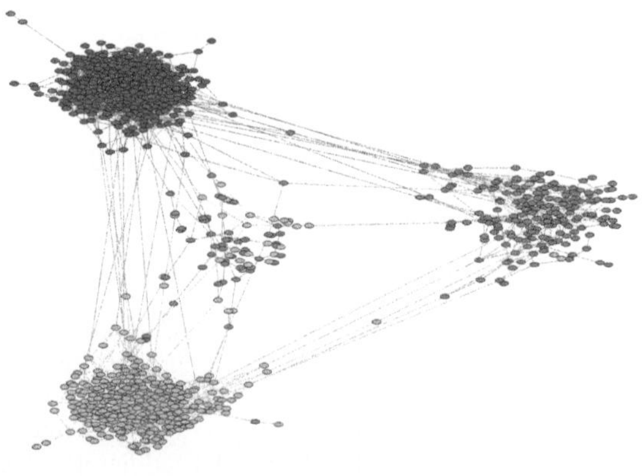

Figure 6: The proposed clustering method identifies four clusters from a synthetic graph consisting of 950 nodes and 2,150 edges. Members of each cluster are colored differently.

Once all cluster parameters are sampled, for each cluster, $|C_i|$ nodes are generated where $|C_i|$ is the cluster size of cluster i. The node values are sampled from the cluster parameter as illustrated in Figure 5. Finally, the edges are sampled. The average degree is kept constant (30 in our

Table 1: Rand Index results of our reviewer clustering approach on synthetic data.

No. Clusters	4	6	10	15
Avg. Rand Index	0.87	0.85	0.85	0.91

case). So for each possible edge, if it is between two nodes of the same cluster, it occurs with probability τ and if the edge is between two dissimilar clusters, it occurs with probability $1-\tau$. An example resulting graph of such a process with 4 clusters is shown in Figure 6. We run our method by over-estimating the number of clusters as 10 and use the same τ that was used by the generation process. Using higher values for τ mostly resulted in two of the detected clusters being labeled as the same cluster.

As shown in Figure 6, our clustering method successfully recovered most of the clusters as long as the intra-cluster edges occurred more frequently than inter cluster edges. Most mistakes happened in the central cluster where the density was low. The clustering method recovered 4 clusters which matched the true number of clusters, and 94.3% of the nodes were clustered correctly.

As another evaluation metric, we used *Rand Index*, a well-known metric for evaluating the quality of clustering when the ground truth is known. Graphs of size 1.2K nodes and 2.6K edges with 4 clusters were generated using the process described earlier. Given different numbers of predetermined clusters to the clustering algorithm, we list the average Rand Index of 10 runs in Table 1. One noticeable point in Table 1 is the improved clustering performance when the number of predetermined clusters over-estimates the actual number. The reason is that the clustering method is based on EM which is a local optimizer of the likelihood. More clusters with random initial parameters spread out in the parameter space mean a better chance of finding a more optimum final likelihood, so we observe better clustering results.

These results suggest that the proposed clustering method works well; but does it uncover meaningful groups over the expanded dataset?

4.1.2 With Real Data

Based on the expanded dataset of products, reviews, and reviewers, we formed the Reviewer-Reviewer graph as described in Section 3.2.1. In the graph, nodes are reviewers, and edges appear when a pair of reviewers write favorable reviews for the same products in a short time frame. The higher number of same products a pair of reviewers posts reviews to, the larger the edge weight of the reviewers is. This graph is shown in Figure 7. As a cleaning step, we discarded small connected components of this graph; we kept reviewers who belonged to a connected component of size 10 or more. We modeled reviewers using the six features described in Singleton Potentials in Section 3.2.2.

Next, we applied the described clustering method on the resulting reviewer graph. The EM algorithm was run with 16 random restarts. The predetermined number of clusters was set to 10. The value of τ determines how likely connected nodes belong to the same cluster. One of the strengths of this clustering method is that connected nodes with dissimilar clusters are punished regardless of the number of predetermined clusters. Hence, the eventual number of emerged clusters can be less than what is predetermined. For a high value of τ like 0.99 we ended up with almost one cluster for

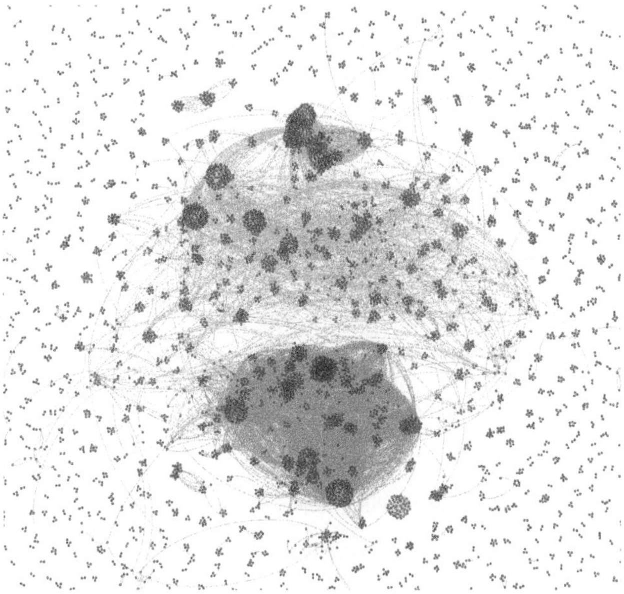

Figure 7: Detected clusters in the Amazon reviewer-reviewer graph. Nodes and edges are colored based on the cluster to which they were assigned. Two out of the three largest clusters are deceptive reviewer clusters.

all the nodes. For lower value of $\tau = 0.7$ we ended up with 6 clusters, 3 of which had higher densities. Since we got a reasonable result returning clusters with high densities when we set $\tau = 0.7$, we used this value for experiments.

Specifically, all listed and detected clusters were dense as shown in Table 2. The three largest clusters had high densities. By inspecting reviewers in the three clusters, we found that the workers, who posted deceptive reviews on products advertised on crowdsourcing websites, belonged to the first two clusters. This indicates this clustering method worked well with the extended dataset. The last cluster contained legitimate reviewers who joined *Amazon Vine* program [1]. Users, who had posted high quality reviews and had gotten high helpfulness from other Amazon users, were invited by Amazon for the Vine program. We analyzed why these reviewers in the third cluster had high density, and found that they posted reviews of similar sets of products in a short time window. Interestingly, these reviewers posted many favorable reviews. The biggest difference between the first two clusters (deceptive reviewers) and the third cluster (legitimate reviewers) is that the legitimate reviewers in the third cluster posted lengthier reviews so that they can share detailed opinions regarding products that they had used.

Finally, we list a number of products associated with deceptive reviews written by the deceptive reviewers in the first two clusters. Table 3 shows the top-15 products favorably reviewed by the deceptive reviewers. Popular target products were health and beauty products, and books.

In summary, we evaluated our clustering method over both a synthetic dataset and a the extended (real) dataset. Our experimental result showed that the clustering method successfully found clusters of deceptive reviewers.

4.2 Detecting Deceptive Reviews

Given these encouraging results, we now turn to the challenge of detecting deceptive reviews. We adopt a standard

Table 2: Statistics and characteristics of detected reviewer clusters.

Cluster	Size	Avg. Weighted Degree	Characteristics
C1	1,079	14.5	Posted deceptive reviews for the same set of mostly health and beauty products
C2	285	31.1	Posted deceptive reviews for a set of meditation books
C3	1,273	13.0	Users of Amazon Vine program who do not write deceptive reviews
Everything Else	5,217	2.3	

Table 3: Titles of top 15 products which were favorably reviewed by deceptive reviewers.

Product Title	Product Category
maXreduce - Guaranteed Weight Loss	Health and Beauty
Krill Oil	Health and Beauty
Best Eye Cream	Misc.
Teeth Whitening	Health and Beauty
Tao II: The Way of Healing, Rejuvenation, Longevity, and Immortality	Hardcover
Omega 3 Fish Oil	Health and Beauty
Meditation: How to Reduce Stress, Get Healthy, and Find Your Happiness...	Paperback
Vitamin D3	Health and Beauty
Tao Song and Tao Dance: Sacred Sound, Movement, and Power...	Hardcover
Tao Song and Tao Dance (Soul Power)	Kindle Edition
Memory Loss	Health and Beauty
Green Tea	Health and Beauty
Soul Wisdom: Practical Treasures to Transform Your Life	Hardcover
Tao II: The Way of Healing, Rejuvenation, Longevity, and Immortality	Kindle Edition
Tao II: The Way of Healing, Rejuvenation, Longevity, and Immortality	Audible Audio Edition

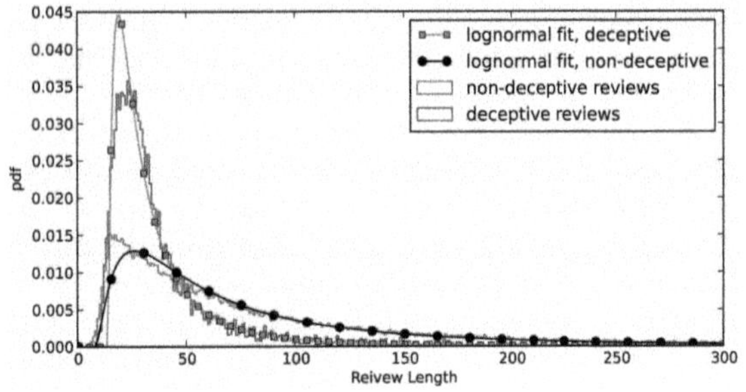

Figure 8: Length distributions of deceptive reviews and legitimate reviews fit log-normal distributions.

Support Vector Machine (SVM) with RBF kernel. We compare a deceptive review classifier using a standard set of features versus one that additionally incorporates the output of the proposed clustering method. We then compare the cluster-aware deceptive review classifier versus one based on an alternate clustering method (SimRank + k-medoids).

Ground Truth. To get the ground-truth (i.e., which review is deceptive or not), we labeled a review as deceptive if (i) the review was associated with a product which was targeted by a crowdsourced malicious task (that is, it was identified in the original *root dataset*); and (ii) the review with a high rating was posted within a few days after the task was posted. Otherwise, it is labeled as a legitimate review. Note that this labeling choice is conservative, in that there may be deceptive reviews that are labeled as legitimate. If a user posted at least one deceptive review, we considered the user as a deceptive reviewer.

Table 4 shows our collected dataset which contains 5.5K deceptive reviews and 65.6K legitimate reviews with a number of corresponding reviewers and products.

Table 4: Dataset.

	|Reviews|	|Reviewers|	|Products|
Deceptive	5.5 K	1.5 K	1 K
Legitimate	65.6 K	13 K	47.9 K

Features. To train and test a classifier, first we converted each review to a set of feature values. In this study, we used seven standard features plus one additional feature based on the output of our reviewer clustering method (see Table 5). The seven standard features are: *1. Verified purchase* feature is a binary feature. If a reviewer actually purchased a product that he reviewed, the feature value would be true. *2. Star rating* is the number of stars given to the product in the review. *3. Review length* is the logarithm of the length of the review in characters. We hypothesize that deceptive reviewers (crowd workers) would not want to spend a long time to write a review. In order to verify this, we compared length of deceptive reviews with length of legitimate reviews. Figure 8 shows length distributions of deceptive reviews and legitimate reviews, which follow log-normal distributions.

The log-normal distributions were also observed in other user generated text [24]. These distributions suggest that length of deceptive reviews are shorter than length of legitimate reviews. *4. Helpfulness ratio* is the number of helpful votes divided by all votes. On Amazon.com, a review has a star rating (1 through 5), and other users can rate the review as either "helpful" or "not helpful". We measured *helpfulness ratio* of each review in our dataset as follows: $\frac{\text{helpful votes}}{\text{helpful + not helpful}}$. Then, we grouped reviews with the same star rating for deceptive reviewers and legitimate reviewers. Figure 9 depicts helpfulness ratios with error bars of deceptive and legitimate reviews under star ratings. A circle and rectangle indicate a median helpfulness ratio of reviews. In star ratings 1 $\sim$ 3, deceptive and legitimate reviewers had

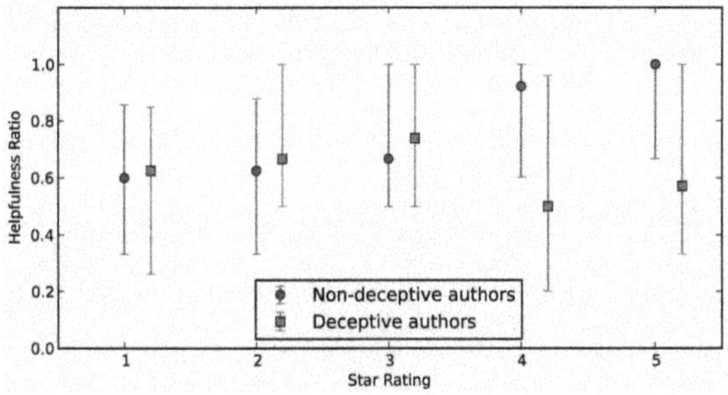

Figure 9: Helpfulness ratio of deceptive reviews and legitimate reviews under different star ratings.

similar helpfulness ratios. But, in $4 \sim 5$, deceptive reviewers' reviews got lower helpfulness ratios compared with ones of legitimate reviewers. This analysis reveals that even though legitimate users were able to punish some of these deceptive reviews with lower helpfulness ratings, many deceptive reviews were not so identified. *5. Total votes* is the denominator of *helpfulness ratio*, and captures the number of votes a review has accumulated. *6. Reviewer got more helpfulness for favorable reviews* is a binary feature that is true when favorable reviews (i.e., star rating is 4 or 5) of a reviewer are more helpful than his unfavorable (i.e., $1 \sim 3$)reviews. *7. Reviewer has more verified purchases for favorable reviews* is another binary feature.

We evaluate the quality of a deceptive review classifier based on these seven features alone versus a classifier based on these seven features plus the output of the proposed reviewer clustering method (from Section 3.2). This eighth feature is: *8. Cluster assignment:* the $K+1$-dimensional feature vector of indicator variables for whether the review author belongs to each of the clusters. The extra cluster is for when the reviewer is missing from the Reviewer-Reviewer Graph. By considering this feature separately, we can evaluate the importance of uncovering "hidden" connections among reviewers.

Unbalanced and Balanced Training and Testing Sets: From our dataset presented in Table 4, we created two pairs of training and testing sets: (i) unbalanced training and testing sets; and (ii) balanced training and testing sets. In the unbalanced training and testing sets, each set contains the half of the original dataset, following the same class ratio. But, to create balanced training and testing sets, first we performed undersampling of legitimate reviews so that the balanced dataset contains the same number of deceptive and legitimate reviews (i.e., 5.5K deceptive and 5.5K legitimate reviews). Then, we split the balanced dataset to the balanced training and testing sets each of which contains the half of the balanced dataset.

Evaluation Metrics and Setup: To evaluate prediction accuracy of our approach, we use three metrics: Area under the ROC Curve (AUC), precision and recall. Especially, we use AUC as our primary evaluation metric, since a higher AUC means that a model is good at correctly predicting both class instances regardless of class imbalance [8].

We developed two SVM classifiers: (i) a basic SVM classifier based on the first seven features in Table 5; and (ii) an advanced SVM classifier based on all eight features including the output of our clustering method. The basic classifier was used as a baseline. Each classifier (e.g., basic and advanced) was trained by each of training sets.

Table 5: Features of our deceptive review classifier.

1. Verified purchase
2. Star rating
3. Review length
4. Helpfulness ratio
5. |helpful + unhelpful votes|
6. Reviewer got more helpfulness for favorable reviews
7. Reviewer has more verified purchases for favorable reviews
8. **Cluster assignment**

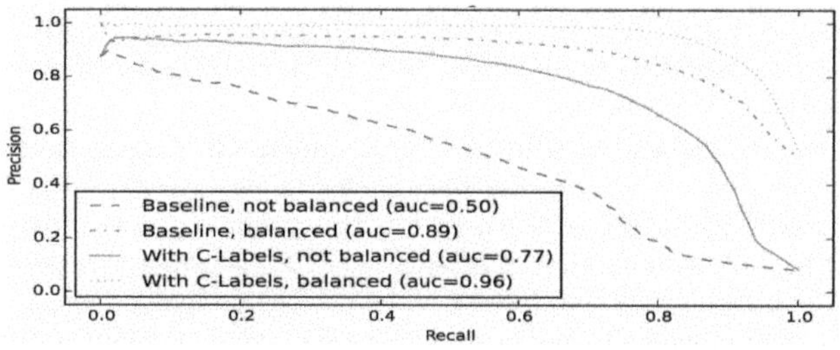

Figure 10: Precision and recall curves of review classification results under four cases (2 different datasets and 2 different classification approaches).

Results: Figure 10 shows experimental results of two classifiers with unbalanced and balanced training and testing sets. In case of using unbalanced training and testing set, while the basic SVM classifier achieved 0.50 AUC, the advanced SVM classifier achieved 0.77 AUC. In case of using balanced training and testing set, AUC has been increased in both basic and advanced SVM classifiers. Specifically, while the basic SVM classifier achieved 0.89 AUC, the advanced SVM classifier achieved 0.96 AUC. Overall, adding the output of our clustering method to feature set significantly improved AUC by 54% and 8% in both unbalanced and balanced data sets. Such performance improvement indicates the effectiveness of incorporating the social context of reviewers (i.e., the output of the clustering method) into deciding whether a review is deceptive or legitimate.

Versus an Alternative Clustering Method: Finally, we investigate the quality of deceptive reviewer classification if the proposed clustering method is swapped out in favor of an alternate one. Concretely, we consider a clustering method based on SimRank [12] and K-medoids. First, SimRank measures similarity between nodes of a graph. Then, k-medoids clustering algorithm is performed based on the similarities of nodes in the graph. Specifically, we calculated SimRank score in two graphs – (i) a bipartite graph containing both reviewers and products; and (ii) the Reviewer-Reviewer collaboration graph $G_{R,R}$. After a similarity matrix of each graph is calculated, we use k-medoids to cluster the reviewers for each graph. Finally, a cluster membership of each reviewer is used as a feature for a SVM based deceptive review classifier. In this experiment, we used the unbalanced training and testing set.

Since we had two different similarity matrices, we built two classifiers. The first clustering method based on the bipartite graph performed poorly enough to be almost identical to the performance of the seven features based SVM classifier without using any clustering output. The second clustering algorithm based on the Reviewer-Reviewer graph achieved 0.71 AUC which was lower than performance (0.77 AUC) of our proposed approach as shown in Figure 11.

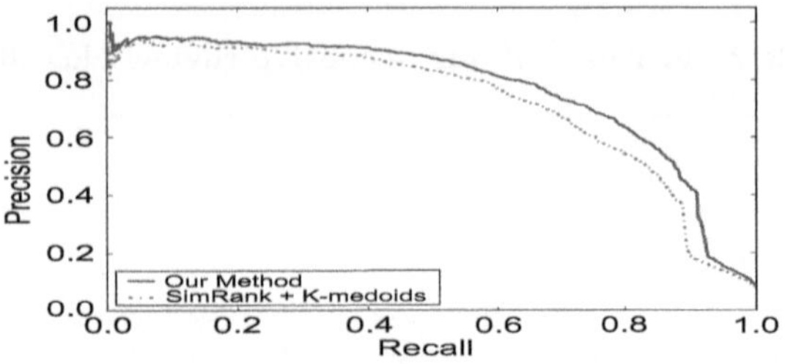

Figure 11: Our classification approach with the cluster assignment (0.77 AUC) outperformed SimRank and k-medoids based classifier (0.71 AUC) under unbalanced dataset.

With respect to efficiency, SimRank took a long time $O(\text{hours})$ for a large graph since time complexity of the original SimRank is $O(n^4)$ where n is the number of the nodes in a graph compared to our pairwise MRF parameterization which has $O(n^2)$ parameters and took $O(\text{minutes})$.

In summary, our proposed clustering based classifier outperformed SimRank and k-medoids based classifier in terms of both effectiveness and efficiency.

5. CONCLUSION

In this paper, we presented a novel sampling method for identifying products that have been targeted for manipulation and a seed set of deceptive reviewers who have been enlisted through the command-and-control of crowdsourcing platforms. Specifically, we have sampled tasks targeting Amazon via the crowd marketplaces RapidWorkers.com, ShortTask.com, and Microworkers.com. We have augmented this seed set to identify additional deceptive reviewers who participate as part of hidden groups of coordinated manipulation through a reviewer-reviewer graph clustering approach. Finally, we have embedded the results of this probabilistic model into a classification framework for detecting crowd-manipulated reviews. Our classification approach using the reviewer clustering results as a feature significantly outperformed a classification approach not using the reviewer clustering results. Specifically, our approach with clustering results have achieved 0.77 AUC in unbalanced testing set and 0.96 AUC in balanced testing set, improving 54% AUC in unbalanced testing set and 8% AUC in balanced testing set respectively compared with the classification approach without using reviewer clustering results. Additionally, the proposed approach has outperformed a SimRank and K-medoids based approach in terms of effectiveness and efficiency.

6. ACKNOWLEDGEMENTS

This work was supported in part by AFOSR Grant FA9550-12-1-0363 and Google Faculty Research Award. Portions of Dr. Squicciarini's work was supported by the Army Research Office under grant W911NF-13-1-0271. Any opinions, findings and conclusions or recommendations expressed in this material are the author(s) and do not necessarily reflect those of the sponsor.

7. REFERENCES

[1] Amazon. Amazon vine program. http://www.amazon.com/gp/vine/help, August 2014.

[2] D. Anguelov, D. Koller, H.-C. Pang, P. Srinivasan, and S. Thrun. Recovering articulated object models from 3d range data. In *UAI*, 2004.

[3] M. S. Bernstein, G. Little, R. C. Miller, B. Hartmann, M. S. Ackerman, D. R. Karger, D. Crowell, and K. Panovich. Soylent: A word processor with a crowd inside. In *UIST*, 2010.

[4] J. A. Chevalier and D. Mayzlin. The effect of word of mouth on sales: Online book reviews. Technical report, National Bureau of Economic Research, 2003, http://www.nber.org/papers/w10148.

[5] C. Danescu-Niculescu-Mizil, G. Kossinets, J. Kleinberg, and L. Lee. How opinions are received by online communities: A case study on Amazon. com helpfulness votes. In *WWW*, 2009.

[6] A. P. Dempster, N. M. Laird, and D. B. Rubin. Maximum likelihood from incomplete data via the EM algorithm. *Journal of the Royal Statistical Society. Series B (Methodological)*, 39:1–38, 1977.

[7] C. Elliott. Hotel reviews online: In bed with hope, half-truths and hype. http://www.nytimes.com/2006/02/07/business/07guides.html, Feb, 2006.

[8] T. Fawcett. An introduction to roc analysis. *Pattern Recogn. Lett.*, 27(8):861–874, June 2006.

[9] S. Feng, L. Xing, A. Gogar, and Y. Choi. Distributional footprints of deceptive product reviews. In *ICWSM*, 2012.

[10] C. Forman, A. Ghose, and B. Wiesenfeld. Examining the relationship between reviews and sales: The role of reviewer identity disclosure in electronic markets. *Information Systems Research*, 19(3):291–313, 2008.

[11] M. J. Franklin, D. Kossmann, T. Kraska, S. Ramesh, and R. Xin. Crowddb: Answering queries with crowdsourcing. In *SIGMOD*, 2011.

[12] G. Jeh and J. Widom. Simrank: A measure of structural-context similarity. In *KDD*, 2002.

[13] N. Jindal and B. Liu. Opinion spam and analysis. In *WSDM*, 2008.

[14] J. Kleinberg and E. Tardos. Approximation algorithms for classification problems with pairwise relationships: Metric labeling and markov random fields. *Journal of the ACM (JACM)*, 49(5):616–639, 2002.

[15] K. Lee, J. Caverlee, Z. Cheng, and D. Z. Sui. Campaign extraction from social media. *ACM Trans. Intell. Syst. Technol.*, 5(1):9:1–9:28, Jan. 2014.

[16] K. Lee, B. D. Eoff, and J. Caverlee. Seven months with the devils: A long-term study of content polluters on twitter. In *ICWSM*, 2011.

[17] K. Lee, P. Tamilarasan, and J. Caverlee. Crowdturfers, campaigns, and social media: Tracking and revealing crowdsourced manipulation of social media. In *ICWSM*, 2013.

[18] S. Lee and J. Kim. Warningbird: Detecting suspicious urls in twitter stream. In *NDSS*, 2012.

[19] Y. Lu, P. Tsaparas, A. Ntoulas, and L. Polanyi. Exploiting social context for review quality prediction. In *WWW*, 2010.

[20] C. C. Miller. Company settles case of reviews it faked. http://www.nytimes.com/2009/07/15/technology/internet/15lift.html, Jul, 2009.

[21] A. Mukherjee, B. Liu, and N. Glance. Spotting fake reviewer groups in consumer reviews. In *WWW*, 2012.

[22] M. Ott, C. Cardie, and J. Hancock. Estimating the prevalence of deception in online review communities. In *WWW*, 2012.

[23] M. Ott, Y. Choi, C. Cardie, and J. T. Hancock. Finding deceptive opinion spam by any stretch of the imagination. In *HLT*, 2011.

[24] P. Sobkowicz, M. Thelwall, K. Buckley, G. Paltoglou, and A. Sobkowicz. Lognormal distributions of user post lengths in internet discussions-a consequence of the weber-fechner law? *EPJ Data Science*, 2(1):1–20, 2013.

[25] D. Streitfeld. In a race to out-rave, 5-star web reviews go for $5. http://www.nytimes.com/2011/08/20/technology/finding-fake-reviews-online.html, Aug, 2011.

[26] VIP deals rebate letter. https://www.documentcloud.org/documents/286364-vip-deals.html, Dec, 2011.

[27] G. Wang, T. Wang, H. Zheng, and B. Y. Zhao. Man vs. machine: Practical adversarial detection of malicious crowdsourcing workers. In *USENIX Security*, 2014.

[28] G. Wang, C. Wilson, X. Zhao, Y. Zhu, M. Mohanlal, H. Zheng, and B. Y. Zhao. Serf and turf: Crowdturfing for fun and profit. In *WWW*, 2012.

[29] S. Xie, G. Wang, S. Lin, and P. S. Yu. Review spam detection via temporal pattern discovery. In *KDD*, 2012.

Relevance Scores for Triples from Type-Like Relations

Hannah Bast, Björn Buchhold, Elmar Haussmann
Department of Computer Science
University of Freiburg
79110 Freiburg, Germany
{bast, buchhold, haussmann}@cs.uni-freiburg.de

ABSTRACT

We compute and evaluate relevance scores for knowledge-base triples from type-like relations. Such a score measures the degree to which an entity "belongs" to a type. For example, Quentin Tarantino has various professions, including Film Director, Screenwriter, and Actor. The first two would get a high score in our setting, because those are his main professions. The third would get a low score, because he mostly had cameo appearances in his own movies. Such scores are essential in the ranking for entity queries, e.g. "american actors" or "quentin tarantino professions". These scores are different from scores for "correctness" or "accuracy" (all three professions above are correct and accurate).

We propose a variety of algorithms to compute these scores. For our evaluation we designed a new benchmark, which includes a ground truth based on about 14K human judgments obtained via crowdsourcing. Inter-judge agreement is slightly over 90%. Existing approaches from the literature give results far from the optimum. Our best algorithms achieve an agreement of about 80% with the ground truth.

1. INTRODUCTION

Knowledge bases allow queries with a well-defined result set. For example, we can easily formulate a precise query that gives us a list of all *american actors* in a knowledge base. Note the fundamental difference to full-text search, where keyword queries are only approximations of the actual search intent, and thus result lists are typically a mix of relevant and irrelevant hits.

But even for well-defined result sets, a ranking of the results is often desirable. One reason is similar as in full-text search: when the set of relevant hits is very large, we want the most "interesting" results first. But even if the result set is small, an ordering often makes sense. We give two examples. The numbers refer to Freebase [7], the largest general-purpose knowledge base to date.

Example 1 (american actors): Consider the query that returns all entities that have *Actor* as their profession and *American* as their nationality. On our Freebase dataset, this query has 64,757 matches. A straightforward ranking would be by popularity, as measured, e.g., by counting the number of occurrences of each entity in a reference text corpus. Doing that, the top-5 results for our query look as follows (the first item means the younger Bush):

George Bush,Hillary Clinton,Tim Burton,Lady Gaga,Johnny Depp

All five of these are indeed listed as actors in Freebase. This is correct in the sense that each of them appeared in a number of movies, and be it only in documentary movies as themselves or in short cameo roles. However, Bush and Clinton are known as politicians, Burton is known as a film director, and Lady Gaga as a musician. Only Johnny Depp, number five in the list above, is primarily an actor. He should definitely be ranked before the other four.

Example 2 (professions of a single person): Consider all professions by Arnold Schwarzenegger. Our version of Freebase lists 10 entries:

Actor, Athlete, Bodybuilder, Businessperson, Entrepreneur, Film Producer, Investor, Politician, Television Director, Writer

Again, all of them are correct in a sense. For this query, ranking by "popularity" (of the professions) makes even less sense than for the query from Example 1. Rather, we would like to have the "main" professions of that particular person at the top. For Arnold Schwarzenegger that would be: *Actor, Politician, Bodybuilder*. Note how we have a very-ill defined task here. It is debatable whether Arnold Schwarzenegger is more of an actor or more of a politician. But he is certainly more of an actor than a writer.

1.1 Problem definition

In this paper, we address the following problem, which addresses the issues behind both of the examples above.

Definition: Given a type-like relation from a knowledge base, for each triple from that relation compute a score from $[0, 1]$ that measures the degree to which the subject belongs to the respective type (expressed by the predicate and object). In the remainder of this paper we often refer to these scores simply as *triple scores*.

Here are four example scores, related to the queries above:

Tim Burton has-profession Actor	0.3
Tim Burton has-profession Director	1.0
Johnny Depp has-profession Actor	1.0
Arnold Schwarzenegger has-profession Actor	0.6

An alternative, more intuitive way of expressing this notion of "degree" is: how "surprised" would we be to see *Actor* in a list of professions of Johnny Depp. We use this formulation in our crowdsourcing task when acquiring human judgments.

Note that the "degree" in the definition above is inherently ill-defined, much like "relevance" in full-text search. In particular, different users might have different opinions on the correct "degree" (for example, on the four scores from above). However, it is one of the results of our crowdsourcing-based experiments that there is

SIGIR'15, August 09 - 13, 2015, Santiago, Chile.
 ISBN 978-1-4503-3621-5/15/08 ...$15.00.
DOI: http://dx.doi.org/10.1145/2766462.2767734.

broad general consensus. Note that we do not take user preferences into account in this paper; we consider this an interesting topic on its own.

1.2 Variants and related problems

The reader may wonder about variants of the problem definition above, and related problems from the literature. We briefly discuss these here.

Degree of Belonging vs. Correctness vs. Accuracy

Our scores are different from correctness or confidence scores. For example, in knowledge fusion, multiple sources might provide conflicting information on the birth date of a person. In those situations we need assessments on the confidence of a particular information and which information is probably correct [12].

Our scores are also different from scores that measure the accuracy. For example, an estimate for the population of a country might be off by a certain margin but not completely wrong, or only a range for the value is given.

We consider a single knowledge base with non-conflicting and precise information. Indeed, for a knowledge base like Freebase, over 99% of all triples are reported to be correct [7]. Even if there are incorrect triples, it is a pleasant side effect of our framework that they would get low scores.

Graded scores vs. Binary scores

We started our research on this topic with binary scores, which we called *primary* and *secondary*, in accordance with existing research on graded relevance in full-text search.[1] We later found that both our crowdsourcing experiments and our algorithms naturally provide finer grades that also make sense in practice. We hence use a continuous score in our definition above. The range $[0, 1]$ is merely a matter of convention.

In our crowdsourcing tasks in Section 3 we still ask each judge for only a binary judgment. However, aggregation of multiple judgments for each triple leads again to a graded score.

Which kind of relations

In principle, our algorithms work for all relations. However, we found that for relations other than type-like, the kind of scores we are interested in are either trivial or can be obtained using other, simpler methods. We distinguish three types of relations.

- Functional relations like *birth date* or *weight*, where each subject has exactly one object. Since we assume a single knowledge base where (almost) all triples are correct, we could simply assign a score of 1.0 to all such triples.

- Non-functional relations between two concrete entities, like *acquired* (between two companies) or *acted in* (between an actor and a movie). For such triples there are two simpler options for a good relevance score, which we do not explore further in this paper. The first option is to take the value from another relation of the knowledge base, like the date of the acquisition or the rank of the actor in the cast listing. This relation could be assigned manually (the number of relations in a knowledge base is relatively small). Or it could be determined heuristically (interesting, but technically completely different from the methods we present). The second option is to adapt our method for type-like relations algorithms also for these relations. The main challenge for finding witnesses in the full text is then to recognize variations of the (fixed) predicate name and not of the (varying) object name. This makes our problem much easier; see Section 4.

- Non-functional relations between an entity and an abstract group or type, like *profession* (between a person and a profession) or *nationality* (between a person and a nationality). We know of no knowledge base with explicit values for the "degree" to which an entity belongs to a certain type. In particular, this is true for *profession* and *nationality*. As we will see in Section 4, such relations are also the hardest for our approaches, because they require a separate classifier for each distinct type (e.g., each distinct profession and nationality), instead of just one for the whole relation. This is why we selected only type-like relations for our benchmark.

We further remark that type information is central to many entity queries. For example, all three tasks from the TREC 2011 Entity Track [2] ask for lists of entities of a particular type. Also, most of the entity queries currently supported by Google are for entities of a certain type, like in the two use cases from our introduction; presumably because of their popularity amongst users.

Triple Scores vs. Full Ranking

The reader may ask why we study scores for individual triples when the motivation is the ranking of results for entity queries. We give two main reasons.

First, the triple scores we consider are a crucial component of any such ranking, and the problem by itself is hard enough to warrant separate study. In fact, in Section 2 we discuss related works on ranking for entity queries that require such scores as input.

Second, for many popular entity queries (like our two use cases from the introduction), our triple scores are basically all that is needed to obtain a good ranking. For the first use case ("american actors"), ranking is a simple matter of combining our triple scores with a popularity measure for each entity. Popularity measures are easily obtained, e.g., by counting the number of mentions in a reference corpus. For the second use case ("professions of a single person"), triple scores are exactly what is needed. Note that for the second use case, a proper ranking is still missing on Google.

1.3 Basic Idea and Challenges

Our basic idea is to find "witnesses" for each triple in a given large text corpus. The more witnesses we find and the more significant they are, the larger the score for that triple.

For example, consider the *profession* relation. In a "learning" step, we compute words that are associated with each profession. For example, for the profession *Actor* these could be: actor, actress, film, cast. For each entity (e.g., *Johnny Depp*) we identify occurrences of these words semantically related to that entity in the text (e.g., *Paramount decided to cast Depp ...*). Then we compute weighted sums of the number of such occurrences for each possible profession. In a final step, we normalize these sums to obtain our scores. This sounds simple, but there are a number of challenges:

- Learning must be unsupervised, given that we have to learn different words for every different possible "type". For example, there are more than 3,552 different professions in Freebase.

- When is a word "semantically related" to an entity in a text? It turns out that considering co-occurrence in the same sentence works, but that a deeper natural language processing helps.

- How much weight to give to each occurrence of a word? It turns out that results can be boosted by graded scores for different words.

- How to get from weighted sums to normalized scores? It turns out that a simple linear mapping works but is often not optimal.

- Why use text and not the knowledge base? For a long time, we also experimented with other facts from the knowledge base as complementary or even as the sole information source. For example, the fact that someone is or once was president of the U.S.

[1] We assume that all triples in our knowledge base are correct, so there are no triples expressing a relationship that is *not relevant*.

implies a high score for the profession Politician. However, we found this knowledge to be consistently less available (especially for less popular entities) and nowhere more reliable than full text. More details about this from our experiments in Section 5.4.

1.4 Contributions and Overview

We consider the following as our main contributions:

- We identify the computation of relevance scores for triples from type-like relations as an interesting research problem, which so far has not achieved much attention. These scores are essential for properly ranking many popular kinds of entity queries.
- We designed and make available a first benchmark for this problem. The required large number of relevance judgments (over 14K) were obtained via crowdsourcing. Given the hard-to-define nature of our scores, designing the task such that untrained human judges provide proper and consistent judgments was a challenging task on its own. Inter-judge agreement is about 90%, which confirms the soundness of our problem definition. See Section 3.
- We introduce a variety of methods (partly new, partly adapted) to compute these scores. All our methods work with an arbitrary knowledge base and text corpus. See Section 4.
- We implemented and evaluated all methods against three baselines, using Freebase as knowledge base and Wikipedia as text corpus. Our best methods achieve an agreement of about 80% with the ground truth. We considered many variants and ideas for improvement, none of which gave better results. See Section 5.
- We make our evaluation benchmark as well as all our code publicly available (see Section 5). In particular, this allows full reproduction of our results.

2. RELATED WORK

There exists a large amount of work about ranking and other problems based on the kind of relevance scores we study here. However, in all these works such scores are assumed to be given. We know of no work that addresses how to compute these scores in the first place. We give a short overview of the various approaches.

Triple Scores for Ranking Structured Queries Several pieces of work deal with integrating scores in a framework for ranking structured queries. For example, in [8], the authors propose an extension to RDF they call Ranked RDF, [13] proposes a ranking model for SPARQL queries with possible text extensions based on Language Models, and [11] discusses how to combine several kinds of scores associated with triples into a meaningful ranking. In all these frameworks, scores that are similar to our triple scores are assumed to be given.

Fuzzy Databases / Knowledge bases This is an old and well-established research area, considering all kinds of "fuzziness" in an information system, including: uncertainty, imprecision, and fractional degrees of membership in sets; see [20] for a survey. However, this body of work is almost entirely about modeling this fuzziness, and how to solve standard tasks (like queries or reasoning) based on fuzzy information. The fuzzy information itself is, again, assumed to be given. We know of no work in this area, where fuzzy scores of the kind we consider are actually computed.

Ranking for Relational Databases SQL allows explicit ordering of the query results (using the *order by* keyword). Still, there are many meaningful queries to databases that return a huge number of results. When confronting users with those results, ranking plays an important role. This problem is tackled in [9]. Apart from the many-answers problem, ranking for databases becomes important when adding a keyword-search component. BANKS [5] has the goal of ranking possible interpretations of a keyword query. Similarly, ObjectRank [1] also takes keyword queries, but ranks "database objects" (e.g., a paper, an author, etc.) according to a query. These approaches share the fact that they work exclusively on the data (or knowledge) base. Going from there, they try to use the structure induced by foreign keys to provide a ranking. For our specialized use case, this is not well suited. Even in a perfect world, where such an approach is able to find the perfect connections to influence the ranking (a hard task in itself), it is restricted to data in the knowledge base. However, as discussed in Section 1.3, we have found structured knowledge to be less available than that from full text for computing our relevance scores.

Ranking Semantic Web Resources In the Semantic Web, one is confronted with data from many differences sources, and of highly varying quality. This gives rise to the problem of ranking these data sources with respect to a given query or topic. For example, TripleRank [16] achieves this by representing the Semantic Web as a 3D tensor and then performs a tensor decomposition. Despite the related-sounding name, this is very different from our scenario, which is about ranking of entities from a single knowledge base.

Topic Models On a technical level, some of our methods are related to *topic models*. These derive high-level topics of documents by inferring important words for each topic and the topic distribution for each document. In our setting, a document could be seen as a subject (e.g., person) and topics as different types (e.g., her professions). One state-of-the-art unsupervised topic model is Latent Dirichlet Allocation (LDA) [6]. LDA (and related methods) infer topics given only the text as input. In a supervised extension called Labeled LDA (L-LDA) [21], topic labels (e.g., our professions) can be provided for each document as part of the input. We compare our methods against L-LDA in Section 5.

3. ESTABLISHING A BENCHMARK

Ranking problems and the notion of relevance are inherently subjective and vague. Human relevance judgments are not only necessary to evaluate algorithms that attempt to solve the problem, but also help understanding it. This has happened for keyword search, where ranking became an established problem with a universally shared understanding.

We decided to use crowdsourcing to create a suitable benchmark for our triple scores for exactly these two reasons: evaluation and problem refinement. Since this helps to understand the problem at hand, we discuss our benchmark before we describe our algorithms to solve the problem.

Recall our use case example from Section 1. We want humans to judge to what extent a person has a certain profession. In this section, we discuss how we select a representative sample of entities, present two ways to set up the task, and explain why one is superior. We then analyze the result of the crowdsourcing experiment. The ground truth files are available for download together with all reproducibility material under the URL given in Section 5.

3.1 Selecting Persons for Evaluation

Our benchmark should feature a representative sample of persons that contains all levels of popularity. This is important for two reasons. First, it can be expected that more information is available for popular persons, so that some approaches might work better (or even only) for those. Second, as discussed in the motivation, while the ranking problem we address also exists for less popular persons, it is more pronounced for popular persons.

Selecting persons from Freebase with more than one profession leaves us with about 240K persons. We use the number of times a person is mentioned in Wikipedia to approximate popularity and restrict our choice to persons having Wikipedia articles. This has practical reasons. In principle, any text collection could be used, but Wikipedia is easy to obtain and, due to hyperlinks, no hard Entity Linking problem has to be solved. Apart from that, we can point human judges directly to the Wikipedia article and hence enable them to make an informed decision without much effort. We observe that (as could be expected) there are lots of people with none or very few mentions and few people with lots of mentions (up to almost 100K mentions). Therefore, a random sampling would almost exclusively contain unpopular entities.

We define buckets of popularity and take a uniform random sample from each bucket. The buckets used were for a popularity (number of mentions) $< 2^4$, between 2^i and 2^{i+1} for $4 \leq i \leq 13$, and $\geq 2^{14}$. In total, we took about 25 samples from each of the 12 buckets. This left us with 298 persons or a total of 1225 person-profession tuples that nicely cover different levels of popularity.

3.2 Evaluate a Single Profession of a Person

An obvious approach is to present a person and his or her profession to a judge and ask whether the profession is primary or secondary for that person. For example:

Arnold Schwarzenegger and the profession *Bodybuilder*. Is the profession primary or secondary for this person?

The task was enriched with instructions, including definitions of the factors listed above. However, this definition is extremely hard to communicate precisely. Also, there is a lot of subjectivity involved: what "feels" primary to one judge does not to another.

Eventually, it turned out that judges mostly resorted to the following strategy: label the profession that is first mentioned in Wikipedia as primary, and all others as secondary. Indeed this is one of our simple baselines in Section 5. Obviously, this cannot work for persons with more than one primary profession.

3.3 Evaluate All Professions of a Person

An improved version that turned out to work well is the following. Instead of labeling a single profession of a person, we ask to label all professions of a person. Additionally, we provide simpler instructions but enrich them with a set of diverse examples of labeled persons. An example is depicted in Figure 1. All professions of *Barack Obama* must be dragged into the box for primary or secondary professions.

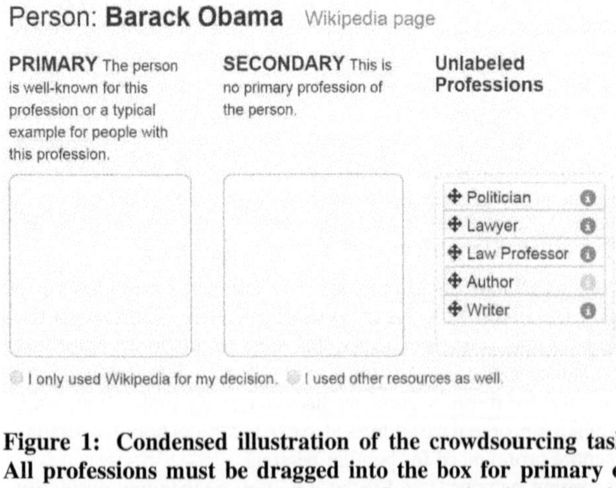

Figure 1: Condensed illustration of the crowdsourcing task. All professions must be dragged into the box for primary or secondary professions. For the complete version including instructions and examples see, go the URL from Section 5.

Below that, we show four examples illustrating a diverse set of possible labelings: Michael Jackson (many professions, some primary some secondary), Ronald Reagan (many professions, two of them primary), Mike Tyson (three professions, only one primary), James Cook (two professions, both primary).

This worked well, and we assume this is mainly due to two reasons:

(1) People could do research on the person, and thus judge all the professions of that person in relation to each other.

(2) The diverse examples helped to form an intuitive theory of what we expected.

3.4 Crowdsourcing Results

We had the professions of each person labeled by seven different judges. As final score for each triple we sum up the number of primary labels, which is then in the range of 0 (all judges label secondary) to 7 (all judges label primary).

On the 298 persons (1225 person-profession tuples) the inter-annotator agreement according to Fleiss' Kappa [15] is 0.47 for the binary judgments. This can be considered moderate agreement. However, what our experiment actually does is to determine a hidden probability p with which a human judge finds a person's profession to be primary. In fact, we use a binary experiment to get gradual scores. Note that, for certain triples, the desired result may actually be a probability around 0.5. Measuring inter-annotator agreement does such a scenario no justice. Instead, we want to make sure that (1) all judges base their decision on the task and the data, and (2) the obtained probabilities are significantly different from random decisions.

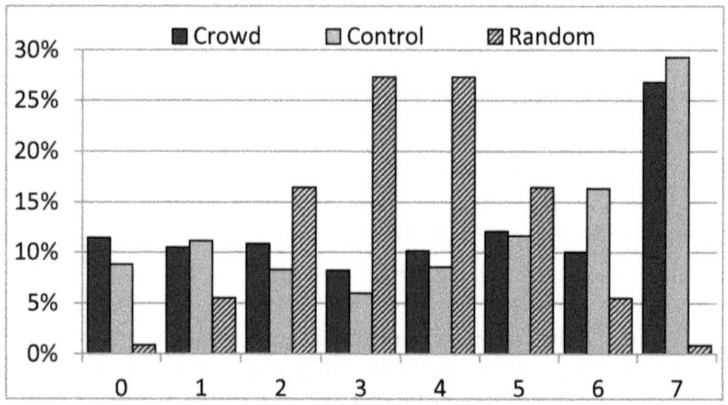

Figure 2: Histogram of score distribution of our crowdsourcing task, the control run, and expected results for randomly (with $p = 0.5$) guessing judges (rounded).

For (1), we have run the same task again (with different annotators) on a subset of every third person (386 person-profession tuples) from our initial sample. Figure 2 depicts how much the scores differ between this control run (*control*) and the full run (*crowd*).

For (2), looking at the distribution of scores shows that they are very far from a random decision. Figure 2 shows a distribution that prefers border cases (especially primary professions) and contains only reasonably few triples with average score (3 or 4). In contrast, a random or unclear task would lead to a distribution with mostly average scores and rare border cases.

In Section 5, we report more details on the results of the control run. The human judges based 95% of their decisions only on the Wikipedia page of the respective person. As we report in Section 5.4, our automatic methods perform much worse when we restrict them in this way. This shows how hard the judgment task is: the relative relevance of the various professions mentioned on a person's Wikipedia page is often highly implicit in the text.

4. COMPUTING TRIPLE SCORES

We propose a variety of algorithms to compute triple scores. For illustration purposes we describe the algorithms using the *profession* relation of a person, but the algorithms are not specific to that relation and should work with any type-like relation. In Section 5 we show that they are equally effective to derive scores for nationalities of persons. Likewise, we use Wikipedia as our source of text and Freebase as knowledge base, but the approaches are not specific to that data. None of our algorithms requires manually labeled data. Instead, we make use of existing facts in an unsupervised or distantly supervised fashion. The crowdsourcing judgments are only used for evaluation.

The different algorithms provide different output: binary classifications, weighted sums and probabilities. In Section 4.6, we describe how we map their output to the range $[0, 1]$.

4.1 Training Data

We want to avoid manually labeled training data. Instead, we use the following definition to obtain positive and negative training examples for each profession:

Positive: people with only the given profession or any specialization of it, i.e. those for which the profession has to be primary.
Negative: people that do not have that profession at all

Thus, Humphrey Bogart is a positive example for the profession *Actor* (because this is his only profession according to Freebase) and Barack Obama, who is listed as politician, lawyer and more (but not as actor), is a negative example for that profession.

We also experimented with other criteria (e.g., allowing the persons used as *positive* examples to also have other professions) but found this selection to work best across all approaches.

4.2 Selecting Text for each Person

All approaches analyze text about a person to derive triple scores. As text we use the English Wikipedia[2], utilizing the fact that persons in Freebase often have a link to their Wikipedia article. We have pre-processed Wikipedia and performed Entity Recognition and Linking, as well as anaphora resolution as described in [3]. With each person we associate all words that co-occur with a linked mention of the person in the same *semantic context*, as provided by the pre-processing. Each semantic context is a sub-sequence of the containing sentence that expresses one fact from the sentence. This yields slight improvements over using full sentences (where numerous facts can be mixed) as contexts. Further, we have found that stemming has almost no effect. These and other variations are discussed in more detail in Section 5.4.

4.3 Binary Classifier per Profession

We train a binary classifier to decide whether a profession is primary or secondary for a given person. For each person we extract features from her associated text. We use word counts as features, which we normalize by the total number of word occurrences in the person's associated text. Thus, feature values are between 0 and 1 (much closer to 0). Weighting feature values by their tf-idf score (instead of the normalization) had no positive effect.

Before training the classifier, we balance positive and negative training examples by randomly selecting an appropriate subset of the negative training examples (there are always more negative than positive training examples).

A logistic regression classifier with L2-regularization is then trained on the balanced training data. As a linear model, logistic regression has the benefit of an intuitive interpretation of features weights. Table 1 lists the features with top weights learned for profession *Actor*.

1. cast	28.21	5. directed	-6.64	9. university	-5.16
2. actor	12.46	6. starring	6.22	10. written	-4.97
3. actress	11.50	7. role	5.62	11. voiced	4.50
4. played	7.19	8. stars	5.26	12. actors	4.48

Table 1: Top features (positive and negative) and their weight learned by the logistic regression classifier for the profession *Actor*.

The learned feature weights form a model for each profession. These models can then be used for persons with multiple professions to make a binary decision if each of his or her professions is primary or not (secondary).

4.4 Count Profession Words

We want to mimic the behavior of humans that want to solve our problem. Therefore, we look at the text associated with an entity and find out how big the portion of text is that discusses profession matters. In the simplest way, we could count how often a profession is mentioned in text associated with the person.

We cannot count exact occurrences, however, because of professions that consist of more than one word, e.g., Film Score Composer. Looking for mentions of such professions already puts them at a disadvantage (or advantage depending on full vs. partial match counting) compared to one-word professions like Composer. Additionally, often slight variations of a profession are mentioned, e.g., actor and actress.

To overcome this issue, we define a suitable prefix for each profession. We can do this automatically (using an off-the-shelf stemmer and the longest common prefix of the stem and the original word) or manually once for each profession. In our experiments (Section 5), we compare manually chosen prefixes as a strong baseline.

Besides the profession names themselves (or their prefixes), we have found that there are many other words that indicate, that some part of the text is about a given profession. For example, consider the positive features learned by the binary classifier as presented in Table 1. We extend our counting based approach by automatically computing indicator words in the following way: For each profession, take all words in the associated text for persons in the *positive* training data (see Section 4.1), compute their tf-idf value and rank the words by that value. During prediction, we set the weight of an indicator mention to 1/rank and build the sum over the weights of all indicator mentions.

1. cast	1.00	5. role	0.20	9. television	0.11
2. actor	0.50	6. starring	0.16	10. appeared	0.10
3. actress	0.30	7. played	0.14	11. born	0.09
4. film	0.25	8. best	0.13	12. series	0.08

Table 2: Top words (by tf-idf) and their weight ($1/$rank) for the profession *Actor*.

Table 2 shows the top words and their weights for the profession *Actor*. There is high overlap with the top features learned by the binary classifier shown in Table 1. Note, that the word weights were computed only from the text associated with *positive* training examples and idf values based on the whole corpus. The *negative* examples were not needed.

[2]downloaded in August 2013

4.5 Generative model

We formulate a generative model where each person is associated with text that can be generated as follows. For a person with k professions and n word occurrences in the associated text: Pick one of the k professions with probability $P(p_i)$; generate word w_j with $P(w_j|p_i)$; repeat until all n words are generated. The joint probability for word w and profession p is then $P(w,p) = P(w|p)P(p)$.

Note that for a given text, the professions selected in the first step above are unobserved. We would like to infer those, because, intuitively, they represent the amount of text that can be associated with a certain profession. We derive these using a maximum likelihood estimate.

Let tf_j be the term frequency of word j, $P(p_i)$ be the probability of profession i and let $P(w_j|p_i)$ be the probability for word j under profession i. The log-likelihood of producing text consisting of n words for k professions is:

$$\log \mathcal{L} = \sum_{j=1}^{N} [tf_j \cdot \log \sum_{i=1}^{k} (P(w_j|p_i)P(p_i))]$$

Training We use the *positive* training examples to derive word probabilities $P(w|p)$. We distinguish two ways. (1) use the term frequency of terms in the text associated with all training examples and assign probabilities accordingly. (2) use the tf-idf values as term frequencies to avoid common, unspecific terms with high probabilities. When using tf-idf values, we use them for both: $P(w|p)$ and as new tf_j when calculating LP. For efficiency reasons, we only keep the probabilities for the top 30K words. We have found that tf-idf values work better and restrict our examples to this setup for the remainder of the paper.

Text that is associated with a person often contains information that is not related to professions, e.g., family and personal life. Therefore, we add a pseudo profession to each person in order to account for these words. We use all text in the English Wikipedia to calculate $P(w|p)$ for the pseudo profession.

1. cast	0.023	5. role	0.007	9. appeared	0.004
2. actor	0.009	6. starring	0.005	10. television	0.004
3. actress	0.008	7. played	0.005	11. born	0.004
4. film	0.008	8. best	0.004	12. roles	0.004

Table 3: Top word probabilities for the profession *Actor*.

Naturally, the top word probabilities depicted in Table 3 are in line with the top word weights presented in Table 2. This is not surprising, since both values are based on the tf-idf scores of words in text associated with the *positive* training samples. The probabilities, however, do not differ as much as the weights we have assigned for the counting approach.

Prediction To derive profession probabilities $\vec{p}$, which have to sum to 1, we maximize the log-likelihood:

$$\vec{p} = \arg\max_{\vec{p}} \sum_{j=1}^{N} [tf_j \cdot \log \sum_{i=1}^{k} (P(w_j|p_i)P(p_i))], \text{s.t.} \sum_{i=1}^{k} p_i = 1$$

To find the maximum likelihood estimate we use Expectation Maximization [10]. Similar to the generative model for pLSI [17] we treat the topic (profession) assignments to word-occurrences as hidden variables. EM iteratively computes posterior probabilities given the hidden variables in the expectation step (E) and then maximizes parameters for the previously computed probabilities in the maximization step (M). The E and M steps are identical to the steps in [17], with the difference that we treat $P(w|p)$ as fixed, because we already computed those from the *positive* examples as described above.

4.6 Mapping to Triple Scores

The above approaches yield a variety of results. Binary classifications, weighted sums and probabilities. However, we actually want to compute scores for triples. While this is trivial for binary classifications (assign minimum and maximum), we distinguish two approaches for sums and probabilities. Keep in mind that we assume there is at least one primary profession for each person. For comparison with the crowdsourcing judgments, we want scores from 0 to 7 but the methods apply for any desired magnitude and, without rounding, naturally allow continuous scores as well.

Maplin Linearly scale computed values to the range 0 to 7. In practice, just divide all sums or probabilities by the highest one. Then multiply by 7 and round to the nearest integer.

Maplog Scale computed values to the range 0 to 7 such that the next highest score corresponds to twice the sum or probability. In practice, divide all sums or probabilities by the highest one. Then multiply by 2^7, take the logarithm to base 2, and finally take the integer portion of the result.

We have found that the intuitive *Maplin* works much better with the sums of weights obtained by counting triples. *Maplog*, however, is stronger when mapping probabilities to triples scores. This is true for both, our generative model, and the topic model, Labeled LDA, we compare against. The probabilistic models tend to assign high probabilities to the top professions, leaving small probabilities to all others. Differences between debatable professions and definite secondary are small in total probability difference value but still observable when comparing magnitudes.

5. EVALUATION

We first discuss the experimental setup: data + ground truth, algorithms compared and quality measures. In Section 5.2, we present and discuss our main results. In Section 5.4, we discuss many variants (algorithms and quality measures) that we also experimented with but which did not turn out to work well.

All of the data and code needed to reproduce our experiments are available under `http://ad.informatik.uni-freiburg.de/publications`.

5.1 Experimental Setup

Data We extracted all triples from the Freebase relations *Profession* and *Country of nationality*. In all experiments we only consider persons with at least two different profession or nationalities, i.e., we only consider the non-trivial cases. Files with all these triples are available under the above URL.

Ground truth For the *profession* relation, we randomly selected a total of 1225 triples pertaining to 298 different people entities, as described in Section 3.1. Each of these triples was then labeled independently by 7 human judges, using crowdsourcing, as described in Section 3.1. This gives a total of 8.575 labels. We repeated the task for all 386 triples of a random subset of 98 from the 298 people. This gives us another 2.702 labels. We used these as control labels to assess the quality of our main set above; see Section 5.2 below. We have presented the distribution of the scores in the ground truth in Section 3.4 in Figure 2. For the *nationaliy* relation, we randomly selected a total of 162 triples pertaining to 77 different people entities and ran the same experiment. This gives us another 1134 judgments.

Algorithms Compared We compare the following: three baselines, six algorithms, and the output of two control experiments.

We normalized all approaches to yield an integer score from the range 0..7 for each triple.

First For each person, take the entity's description from Freebase[3] Look for the first literal mention of one of that person's profession. That profession gets a score of 7, all other professions get a score of 0. This may look overly simplistic, but actually this is what most of the judges did in the previous version of our task as presented in Section 3.2.

Random Make 7 independent judgments for each triple, where for each judgment primary and secondary are equally likely. That is, pick the score at random from a binomial distribution with $n = 7$ and $p = 0.5$. This simulates human judges that guess randomly.

Prefixes For each triple, count the number of occurrences of a hand-picked prefix of the profession (same for all professions) in the Wikipedia article of the person. Map these counts to scores (per person) using *Maplin*, as described in Section 4.6.

Labeled LDA (LLDA) The closest approach from previous work, as described in Section 2. We use a topic label for each profession and label each person with all of her professions. The Dirichlet prior, α, is set to 2.0 and we run Gibbs sampling for 100 iterations. Other parameter settings for α gave much worse results and more iterations showed no improvement. We map the probabilities to scores using *Maplog*.

Words Classification For each triple, make a binary decision (score 0 or 7) using the logistic-regression classifier (see Section 4.3).

Words Counting For each profession, learn a weighted list of words, as described in Section 4.4. For each triple, add the weights of all profession words in all contexts containing the entity. Map these weight sums to scores using *Maplin*.

Words MLE For each triple, we derive a score using the generative model described in Section 4.5 and the *Maplog* mapping.

Counting Combined For each triple, use the *Words Counting* method. Additionally look at the decision of the *Words Classification* method. If the binary classification is positive (score 7), increase the score to the average of the two. The intuition behind this is, that for strongly related professions (e.g., Poet and Playwright), it is hard to attribute a text passage to one of the two. The binary decisions made by the *Words Classification* method do not have this problem.

MLE Combined Similar to *Counting Combined* but starting with the *Words MLE* method instead of the counting.

Control Judges Take the labels from the human control judges, as described above.

Control Expected The expected values when comparing two scorings, where in each scoring each of the seven judgments for a triple is primary with probability p, where p is chosen from the posterior distribution given score s, where s is the score given by the crowdsourcing judges.[4]

Evaluation measures We use two kinds of measures: score-based and rank-based.

Score-based The score-based measures directly compare the scores of two sequences s and s' of triple scores for the same sequence of n triples. We consider two measures: *accuracy* and *average score deviation*. The accuracy has an integer parameter δ and measures the percentage of triple scores that deviate by at most δ. That is, Acc-$\delta = |\{i : |s_i - s'_i| \leq \delta\}|$. The average score deviation is simply the average over all absolute score differences. That is, ASD $= \sum_i |s_i - s'_i|/n$. We will see that the relative performance of the various methods shows in both measures, but that the Acc figures are more intuitive and insightful.

Rank-based The rank-based measures compare two rankings of the same sequence of triples. We will use them to compare two rankings of all professions / nationalities of a single person, and the average over all persons. We consider three standard ranking measures: Kendall's Tau, the footrule distance, and nDCG.

Because scores in the gold standard are discrete, items often share a rank. Such a ranking with ties constitutes a *partial ranking* [14]. To compare partial rankings we use adapted versions of Kendall's τ from [14]: $\tau_p = \frac{1}{Z}(n_d + p \cdot n_t)$, where n_d is the number of *discordant* (inverted) pairs, n_t is the number of pairs that are tied in the gold standard but not in the predicted ranking or vice versa, p is a penalization factor for these pairs which we set to 0.5, and the normalization factor Z (the number of ordered pairs plus p times the number of tied pairs in the gold standard).

The Spearman footrule distance counts the displacements of all elements. It is $f = \frac{1}{Z} \sum |\sigma_p(i) - \sigma_g(i)|$, where i ranges over the items of the list, and $\sigma_p(i)$ and $\sigma_g(i)$ is the rank of item i in the predicted partial ranking and gold standard partial ranking, respectively. The normalization factor Z corresponds to the maximum possible distance and causes f to be in the interval $[0, 1]$.

For nDCG, we remark that it also takes the exact scores into account: ranking a triple lower than it should be is punished more, the higher the score of that triple is.

5.2 Main results

Score-based evaluation of the *profession* triples We first discuss the results for our score-based measures for the *profession* relation, shown in Table 4.

Method	Accuracy (Acc)			Average Score Diff
	$\delta = 1$	$\delta = 2$	$\delta = 4$	
First	41%	**53%**	71%	2.71
Random	31%	**55%**	91%	2.39
Words Classification	47%	**61%**	78%	2.09
Prefixes	50%	**64%**	83%	2.07
LLDA	50%	**68%**	89%	1.86
Words Counting	57%	**75%**	94%	1.61
Words MLE	57%	**77%**	95%	1.61
Count Combined	58%	**77%**	95%	1.52
MLE Combined	63%	**80%**	96%	1.57
Control Expected	75%	**91%**	99%	0.93
Control Judges	76%	**94%**	99%	0.92

Table 4: Accuracies and ASD for the *profession* relation, best methods last.

The last line (Control Judges) shows that the human judges rarely disagree by more than 2 on the 0-7 scale. The Acc-4 measure shows that there are almost no stark disagreements, that is, by more than 4.[5] A disagreement up to 1 is not unusual though. The average score deviation is 0.92. As the next to last line (Control Expected) shows, this is essentially what would be expected from random

[3]For most entities, this is just the abstract of the corresponding Wikipedia page.

[4]That is, $Pr(p = k/7) \propto \Pr(X = k)$, for $k = 0..7$, where X is from the binomial distribution $B(7, s/7)$.

[5]Note that such disagreements can only happen for scores 0-2 and 5-7.

fluctuation. Acc-2 hence seems to be the single most intuitive measure (for integer scores on a scale 0-7). We therefore emphasized the results for that measure in Table 4.

Our binary classification algorithm achieves an Acc-2 of 61%, which gradually improves to 80% for our most sophisticated algorithm. There is hardly a difference between the MLE approach and word counting with proper normalization. Our best approach makes glaring mistakes (Acc-4) for only 4% of all triples. For the Acc-2 measure, our best approach is still more than 10% away from the ideal. In Section 5.4, we discuss various options for improvement, none of which actually gives a significant further improvement though. We conclude that our problem is what could be called "NLP-hard". Under that condition, we consider an Acc-2 of 80% a very good result.

The simple "First" baseline performs similarly bad as the "Random" baseline, which simulates a random guess for each judge. Note that the "Random" baseline makes glaring mistakes (Acc-4) only for 9% of the triples. This is because the scores of this baseline follow a binomial distribution, with a probability of 0.55 that the score is 3 or 4. For these two scores, the deviation from the "true" value cannot be larger than 4. For the more extreme scores, the probability of being off by more than 4 is also low. Acc-2, however, is only about 55% for "Random". Note that a more extreme version of "Random", which picks only one of the scores 3 or 4 at random for each triple, would achieve an Acc-4 of 100%, but an Acc-2 of only 52%.

The relative performance of the various approaches is reflected by the average score difference (ASD), shown in the last column of Table 4. The various Acc measures provide a more refined picture though.

Rank-based results for the *profession* triples We next discuss the results for our rank-based measures for the *profession* relation, shown in Table 5.

Method	Kendall	Footrule	nDCG
Random	**0.51**	0.58	0.80
First	**0.40**	0.47	0.92
LLDA	**0.32**	0.38	0.88
Words Classification	**0.32**	0.35	0.88
Prefixes	**0.31**	0.35	0.88
Words MLE	**0.23**	0.28	0.94
Words Counting	**0.24**	0.29	0.94
Counting Combined	**0.24**	0.28	0.94
MLE Combined	**0.22**	0.27	0.94
Control Judges	**0.18**	0.21	0.97

Table 5: Average rank differences for the *profession* relation, best methods last.

We observe that the relative quality of the various baselines and algorithms is about the same in all three measures. Since Kendall is the simplest and perhaps most intuitive measure, we have highlighted the results for that measure in Table 5.

Footrule is always slightly larger than Kendall. The nDCG values are relative large already for the simple Random baseline. This is an artifact of the short lists we are comparing here (for each person, his or her professions, which are often only two or three). Indeed, for a list with only two items, there are only two possible values for nDCG: 1 and $1/\log_2 3 \approx 0.63$. The average of the two is ≈ 0.82.

The relative order of the methods is similar as for the score-based evaluation of Table 4. The only notable exception is that in the rank-based evaluation, the simple "First" baseline is significantly better than "Random", while in the score-based evaluation, it was the other way round. The reason is simple: "First" almost always gets the first item in the list right (the first profession listed in Wikipedia, is almost always the most obvious profession of the person in question). For persons with only two professions, this already gives the perfect ranking. For persons with three professions, this already gets 2 of the 3 possibly transpositions right. In the score-based evaluation, the score for the triple with this "first" profession is just one out of k, when the person has k professions. Apart from that, "First" (and "Words Classification") make binary decisions for one of the most extreme scores. This is punished by the Accuracy measures. Random, on the other hand, tends to select the middle ground scores 3 and 4 which are not punished as strongly.

Note that the compared rankings are invariant under score mapping (*Maplin* or *Maplog*, see Section 4.6). Hence, score mapping affects neither Kendall nor Footrule. It does, in principle, affect nDCG, since that measure also takes the actual scores into account. We found the effect to be insignificant though (at most 0.02 difference for affected approaches).

Score- and ranked-based evaluation of the *nationality* triples We repeated the experiments above for the triples from the *nationality* relation. We focused on the baselines and the best-performing methods.

Method	Accuracy (Acc) $\delta = 1$	Accuracy (Acc) $\delta = 2$	Accuracy (Acc) $\delta = 4$	Average Score Diff
First	28%	**36%**	51%	3.89
Random	31%	**55%**	91%	2.83
Prefixes	41%	**52%**	71%	2.21
Words MLE	58%	**78%**	95%	1.71
Words Counting	63%	**78%**	96%	1.34
Control Expected	76%	**92%**	99%	0.82

Method	Kendall	Footrule	nDCG
Random	**0.51**	0.58	0.80
First	**0.41**	0.42	0.90
Prefixes	**0.51**	0.53	0.88
Words MLE	**0.44**	0.45	0.92
Words Counting	**0.36**	0.37	0.94

Table 6: Score-based and ranked-based results for the *nationality* relation, best methods last.

Table 6 shows the results for our experiments with triples from the *nationality* relation. Sophisticated approaches have performance similar to the run on triples of the *profession* relation (see Tables 4 and 5). This is good news, because it was not guaranteed that Wikipedia texts provided a sufficiently strong signal for our algorithms to perform well. Interestingly, baselines "First" and "Prefixes" are weaker on this task. Apparently, direct mentions of a nationality in the Wikipedia article are not as useful as they are for professions. A typical example could be the term "German-American" to describe (primary) Americans with German roots. Not only is the secondary nationality mentioned first, the article may also discuss the person's ancestry further, frequently mentioning that country. Statistical signals for the primary nationality, like mentions of the place of residence or typical institutions are only considered by our more advanced approaches.

5.3 Refined analysis

We also conducted an analysis of the "clear cases", that is, the triples, where the score from the crowdsourcing judges were either 6 or 7 or 1 or 0 (all judges, except at most one, agree). We analyzed the percentage of triples, which got the "reverse" scores for these triples, that is 0-1 for 6-7 and 6-7 for 0-1. The figures were very similar to those already captured by the Acc-4 figure in Table 4. Recall that a score deviation of more than 4 can only happen for the extreme scores. Thus, no new insights were provided by this analysis.

We also analyzed the dependency between accuracy and popularity of a person.

Method	Popularity Bucket					
	1	2	3	4	5	6
Words Counting	**58%**	76%	71%	71%	76%	81%
Count Combined	**63%**	81%	72%	68%	76%	81%
Words MLE	**68%**	84%	76%	79%	84%	76%
MLE Combined	**74%**	84%	75%	79%	84%	79%

Method	Popularity Bucket					
	7	8	9	10	11	12
Words Counting	77%	75%	70%	72%	82%	83%
Count Combined	86%	78%	76%	76%	78%	78%
Words MLE	76%	74%	69%	77%	79%	82%
MLE Combined	82%	75%	76%	80%	80%	82%

Table 7: Accuracy-2 for the *profession* relation, breakdown by person popularity. Popularity Bucket i contains persons with a number of occurrences between 2^{i+2} and 2^{i+3}. Buckets 1 and 12 are special cases and contain persons with less than 2^4, resp. more than 2^{14}, occurrences.

The buckets of popularity used in Table 7 pertain to the buckets from our selection for the crowdsourcing task (see Section 3.1). The breakdown shows that approaches function well on all persons with more than 16 occurrences in the text. This corresponds to buckets 2 and above. While more text is always better for our statistical models, we observe that the minimum required to work reasonably well, is already very low. The persons in bucket 1 with very little associated text are harder to get correct. We can observe two things: *Words Counting* has more problems than *Words MLE*. Further, the combination with the classifier specifically helps to even out the problems with entities in this bucket.

5.4 Variants

Our main results show a gap of 11-14% between our best method, and what human judges can achieve. We have experimented with numerous variations of the methods described in Section 4 and 5.1. None of these variations turned out to give an improvement.

Stemming. All approaches from Section 4 can be used with and without stemming. We tried both the Porter [22] and the Lancaster stemmer [19]. For all methods, stemming (in either variant) did more harm than good.

Word pairs instead of just words. One significant source of errors in the methods from Section 4 is that *single* words are ambiguous indicators for certain triples. For example, the word *film* is a strong indicator for both *Actor* and *Film Director*. Some persons have both professions. To distinguish between the two, the context of the word *film* is important. One obvious approach to address this is to consider pairs of words as features, instead of just single words. For the *profession* relation, the influence on both the score-based and the rank-based measure was insignificant though. For the *nationality* relation, results became significantly worse when using word pairs. This is understandable, since for the majority of nationalities single words are perfectly suited to uniquely identify them (e.g., *Canadian*, *Italian*, *German*).

TF versus TF-IDF In our evaluation, we used tf-idf for all our features. We also experimented with tf features, as well as with variations of tf-idf that give more emphasis to the idf part or that dampened the tf factor like in BM25. Results were either unaffected or became slightly worse.

Non-linear score mappings. In Section 3, we discussed two score mappings: Maplin and Maplog. The latter uses the mapping $x \mapsto \log_2 x$. The rationale was that the MLE approach produces raw scores (the probabilities) that grow super-linearly with the actual score. We experimented with a variety of other non-linear score mappings to capture this behavior, in particular, $x \mapsto x^\alpha$, for various value of α. The results were similar but never significantly better than for our Maplog.

Sentences vs. contexts In our methods in Section 4, we consider only those words that occur "in the same context" as the entity in question. We experimented with two realizations of this context: co-occurrence in the same *sentence* and co-occurrence in the same *context*, as described in Section 4. Contexts consistently outperformed sentences by a few percent. The improvement was more pronounced for popular entities, where we have many occurrences of the indicator words. This is in accordance with the theory from [4]. Co-occurrence in the same sentences does not necessarily mean that the two entities / words that co-occur have something to do with each other. When they co-occur in the same context, they have, by the definition of context from [4].

Whole corpus vs. only the Wikipedia article Almost all human judges indicated that they only used the Wikipedia article of a person to make their decision (95% of all decisions). For our methods from Section 4, we considered co-occurrences anywhere in the text corpus. When restricting to only the Wikipedia page of the respective person, like the human judges did, results consistently became much worse. This is easy to understand, since all our methods are statistics-based, and the whole corpus simply provides more information, and hence also more certainty to make a good decision.

Treating hierarchy / specialization In Freebase, a person's professions may include generalizations of another profession that is listed. For example, for John Lennon there are (among other professions) singer-songwriter, keyboard player, guitarist and also musician. Like for Hierarchical Classification [18] problems, two obvious approaches are to (1) ignore the hierarchy and classify each triple and to (2) only classify specializations and infer a score for parent professions. We have experimented with both approaches and found that there is only little difference. If the same inference rules from (2) are used on both, our scores and the human judgments (human judgments are corrected towards a higher score if the human judges have given that higher score to a specialization of the profession), this increases the final scores by a few percent (e.g., 82% for *MLE Combined*). Otherwise, there is not much difference.

Knowledge-base facts An obvious alternative to using text for computing triple scores is to use information from the knowledge base. However, we have made the experience that 1) only few properties are reflected by other facts in the knowledge base and 2) even in cases where they are, they are typically only available for popular instances. For example, an indication for the relevance of an actor may be in how many movies he acted, or how many awards he won for them. But there are no such facts in the knowledge base for a geologist, a surgeon, or a firefighter. Furthermore, in Freebase, out of 612K persons with more than one profession, 400K have less than 10 and 243K less than 6 other facts (besides type and profession information).

5.5 Manual Error Analysis

For all our methods from Section 4, as well as for all the variants discussed in Section 5.4, we conducted a manual error analysis. We discovered two main sources of errors.

Wrong reference An indicator word sometimes co-occurs with the person in question, but is actually relating to another person. For example, Michael Jackson is listed as a Film Director, which is certainly not one of his main professions. The Wikipedia article about him contains many mentions of the word *directed* or *director* though. But most of them relate not to him but to a person directing one of his shows.

Wrong meaning An indicator word is sometimes used with another meaning. For example. John F. Kennedy is listed as a Military Officer, which is certainly not one of his main professions. The Wikipedia article contains many mentions of variants of the word *military* though. But most of them relate to political actions during his presidency with respect to the military.

Some of the variants discussed in Section 5.4 mitigate the effect of these problems somewhat. For example, restricting co-occurrence to semantic contexts instead of full sentences helps the wrong-reference problem in several instances. Or, considering word pairs instead of single words helps with the wrong-meaning problem in several instances. However, a significant number of instances remain, where deep natural language understanding appears to be required. Consider the sentences "<Screenwriter X> was very happy with how his script was visualized" vs "<Film Director Y> was praised a lot for how he visualized the script". It is hard to understand the roles of the persons in these sentences. But it is necessary to correctly decide if the sentence is evidence for a profession *Screenwriter* or *Film Producer*.

6. CONCLUSION

We have studied the problem of computing relevance scores for knowledge-base triples from type-like relations. We have shown that we can compute good such scores in an unsupervised manner from a text corpus with an accuracy of about 80%.

We have described various attempts to further improve the accuracy of our triple scores, towards the over 90% accuracy achieved by human judges. These attempts, together with a manual error analysis, suggest that deep natural language understanding is required to close this gap. In particular, we identified two main error sources: *wrong reference* and *wrong meaning* of indicator words. We consider these a hard but worthwhile task for future work.

The focus of this work is on scores for individual triples. This problem is practically relevant on its own and also hard enough on its own. Still, it would be interesting to follow up on previous work about integrating such triple scores into a meaningful ranking for complex knowledge-base queries.

7. REFERENCES

[1] A. Balmin, V. Hristidis, and Y. Papakonstantinou. ObjectRank: Authority-based keyword search in databases. In *VLDB*, pages 564–575, 2004.

[2] K. Balog, P. Serdyukov, and A. P. de Vries. Overview of the TREC 2011 Entity Track. In *TREC*, 2011.

[3] H. Bast, F. Bäurle, B. Buchhold, and E. Haussmann. Broccoli: Semantic full-text search at your fingertips. *CoRR*, abs/1207.2615, 2012.

[4] H. Bast and E. Haussmann. Open information extraction via contextual sentence decomposition. In *ICSC*, pages 154–159, 2013.

[5] G. Bhalotia, A. Hulgeri, C. Nakhe, S. Chakrabarti, and S. Sudarshan. Keyword searching and browsing in databases using BANKS. In *ICDE*, pages 431–440, 2002.

[6] D. M. Blei, A. Y. Ng, and M. I. Jordan. Latent dirichlet allocation. In *NIPS*, pages 601–608, 2001.

[7] K. D. Bollacker, C. Evans, P. Paritosh, T. Sturge, and J. Taylor. Freebase: a collaboratively created graph database for structuring human knowledge. In *SIGMOD*, pages 1247–1250, 2008.

[8] J. P. Cedeño and K. S. Candan. R^2DF framework for ranked path queries over weighted RDF graphs. In *WIMS*, page 40, 2011.

[9] S. Chaudhuri, G. Das, V. Hristidis, and G. Weikum. Probabilistic ranking of database query results. In *VLDB*, pages 888–899, 2004.

[10] A. P. Dempster, N. M. Laird, and D. B. Rubin. Maximum likelihood from incomplete data via the EM algorithm. *J. R. Stat. Soc.*, pages 1–38, 1977.

[11] R. Q. Dividino, G. Gröner, S. Scheglmann, and M. Thimm. Ranking RDF with provenance via preference aggregation. In *EKAW*, pages 154–163, 2012.

[12] X. L. Dong, E. Gabrilovich, G. Heitz, W. Horn, K. Murphy, S. Sun, and W. Zhang. From data fusion to knowledge fusion. *PVLDB*, 7(10):881–892, 2014.

[13] S. Elbassuoni, M. Ramanath, R. Schenkel, M. Sydow, and G. Weikum. Language-model-based ranking for queries on RDF-graphs. In *CIKM*, pages 977–986, 2009.

[14] R. Fagin, R. Kumar, M. Mahdian, D. Sivakumar, and E. Vee. Comparing and aggregating rankings with ties. In *PODS*, pages 47–58, 2004.

[15] J. L. Fleiss. Measuring nominal scale agreement among many raters. *Psychological bulletin*, 76(5):378, 1971.

[16] T. Franz, A. Schultz, S. Sizov, and S. Staab. TripleRank: Ranking semantic web data by tensor decomposition. In *ISWC*, pages 213–228, 2009.

[17] T. Hofmann. Probabilistic latent semantic indexing. In *SIGIR*, pages 50–57, 1999.

[18] C. N. S. Jr. and A. A. Freitas. A survey of hierarchical classification across different application domains. *Data Min. Knowl. Discov.*, 22(1-2):31–72, 2011.

[19] C. D. Paice. Another stemmer. *SIGIR Forum*, 24(3):56–61, 1990.

[20] S. Parsons. Current approaches to handling imperfect information in data and knowledge bases. *IEEE Trans. Knowl. Data Eng.*, 8(3):353–372, 1996.

[21] D. Ramage, D. L. W. Hall, R. Nallapati, and C. D. Manning. Labeled LDA: A supervised topic model for credit attribution in multi-labeled corpora. In *EMNLP*, pages 248–256, 2009.

[22] C. J. Van Rijsbergen, S. E. Robertson, and M. F. Porter. *New models in probabilistic information retrieval.* Computer Laboratory, University of Cambridge, 1980.

Fielded Sequential Dependence Model for Ad-Hoc Entity Retrieval in the Web of Data

Nikita Zhiltsov*

Kazan Federal University
Kazan, 18 Kremlyovskaya Str, 420008, Russia
nzhilcov@kpfu.ru

Textocat
Kazan, 52 Peterburgskaya Str, 420074, Russia
nzhiltsov@textocat.com

Alexander Kotov
Department of Computer Science
Wayne State University
Detroit, MI 48202, USA
kotov@wayne.edu

Fedor Nikolaev
Department of Computer Science
Wayne State University
Detroit, MI 48202, USA
fedor@wayne.edu

ABSTRACT

Previously proposed approaches to ad-hoc entity retrieval in the Web of Data (ERWD) used multi-fielded representation of entities and relied on standard unigram bag-of-words retrieval models. Although retrieval models incorporating term dependencies have been shown to be significantly more effective than the unigram bag-of-words ones for ad hoc document retrieval, it is not known whether accounting for term dependencies can improve retrieval from the Web of Data. In this work, we propose a novel retrieval model that incorporates term dependencies into structured document retrieval and apply it to the task of ERWD. In the proposed model, the document field weights and the relative importance of unigrams and bigrams are optimized with respect to the target retrieval metric using a learning-to-rank method. Experiments on a publicly available benchmark indicate significant improvement of the accuracy of retrieval results by the proposed model over state-of-the-art retrieval models for ERWD.

Categories and Subject Descriptors

H.3.3 [**Information Storage and Retrieval**]: Information Search and Retrieval

Keywords

Term Dependence; Entity Retrieval; Knowledge Graphs

1. INTRODUCTION

The past decade has witnessed the emergence of numerous large-scale publicly available knowledge bases, such as Freebase[1], DBpedia[2], Wikidata[3] and YAGO[4]. Open source knowledge bases typically adopt Resource Description Framework (RDF) data model and are published as part of the Linked Open Data (LOD)[5] cloud commonly referred to as the Web of Data. A similar trend exists in the industry as well (e.g. Google's Knowledge Graph, Facebook's Open Graph and Microsoft's Satori). Individual RDF datasets in the Web of Data can be considered as massive graphs, in which the nodes are the entities (resources) and the edges are semantic relations between the entities. Each resource describes an object in the Web of Data, which can either be a real entity (e.g. *Albert Einstein* or *Apple, Inc.*) or an abstract concept (*special relativity*). The relations between the entities are represented as subject-predicate-object triples (e.g. <Albert Einstein, *knownFor*, special relativity>).

Graph structured knowledge in general and RDF graphs in particular are well-suited for addressing the information needs that aim at finding specific entities, for which the top results returned by the search systems should consist of structured objects rather than individual documents. The analysis of Web search engine logs reported in [26] revealed that such information needs constitute more than half of search engine queries. They also proposed to classify entity-oriented queries into five classes, each of which requires different treatment by the search systems. The demand for efficient access to knowledge graphs gives rise to the task of Ad-hoc Entity Retrieval from the Web of Data (ERWD). As opposed to the traditional information retrieval task, in which search systems return documents in response to keyword queries, the goal of ERWD is to return an entity or a list of entities based on their unconstrained (and often fairly long) keyword descriptions. This task is focused on retrieval from knowledge bases, as opposed to utilization of knowledge bases in retrieval [7, 15]. Although entities have been studied in textual data mining (e.g. [16]), ERWD is a fairly recent trend in IR. It is related to entity retrieval in the context of expert finding, for which different unigram language model based approaches have been proposed (e.g. [1]). ERWD,

*work performed while the first author was visiting the Textual Data Analytics laboratory at Wayne State University

SIGIR'15, August 09 - 13, 2015, Santiago, Chile.

ACM 978-1-4503-3621-5/15/08 ...$15.00.
DOI: http://dx.doi.org/10.1145/2766462.2767756 .

[1]`http://freebase.com`
[2]`http://dbpedia.org`
[3]`http://wikidata.org`
[4]`http://www.mpi-inf.mpg.de/yago-naga/yago/`
[5]`http://lod-cloud.net/`

however, provides its own unique set of challenges, such as designing effective entity representation methods and novel retrieval models.

While several methods [4, 21, 24] to address the first challenge have been previously proposed, only standard bag-of-words retrieval models, such as BM25 [2, 31] and language modeling (LM) based ones [8, 9, 22], as well as their multi-fielded extensions [4, 5, 20, 21, 24] have been applied to the task of entity retrieval from the Web of Data. It is known, however, that retrieval models incorporating term dependencies (in the form of ordered and unordered n-grams) are substantially more accurate than standard bag-of-words models in case of ad-hoc *document* retrieval [12], particularly for longer, verbose queries [3]. Markov Random Field (MRF) retrieval model [18, 19] provided a theoretical foundation to account for bigrams, as well as ordered and unordered phrases in IR, by representing a query as a graph of dependencies between the query terms. MRF calculates the score of each document with respect to a query as a linear combination of potential functions, each of which is computed based on a document and a clique in the query graph. Sequential Dependence Model (SDM) is a variant of the Markov Random Field model that assumes sequential dependence for the query terms and uses three potential functions: one that is based on unigrams and the other two that are based on bigrams, either as ordered sequences of terms or as terms co-occurring within a window of the pre-defined size.

To address the second challenge, the problem of designing effective retrieval models for ERWD, we propose Fielded Sequential Dependence Model (FSDM), which unifies and generalizes sequential dependence [18] and the mixture of language models (MLM) [23] retrieval models and allows to account for term dependencies in structured document retrieval. Although, in this work, we only experimented with entity retrieval from the knowledge graphs, our proposed model can be utilized for retrieval from collections of any structured documents.

The key contributions of this work are two-fold:

1. novel retrieval model for collections of structured documents and the algorithm to learn its parameters with respect to the target retrieval metric. Retrieval performance of the proposed model has been comprehensively evaluated with respect to the state-of-the-art baselines for ERWD using a publicly available benchmark covering different types of information needs;
2. novel multi-fielded entity representation scheme for ERWD that better captures the semantics of both the entities and relations between them.

The remainder of the paper is organized as follows. Section 2 provides a brief overview of previous related work. In Section 3, we present FSDM, an algorithm to optimize its parameters, and a method to construct multi-fielded entity representations. Experimental results are reported in Section 4 and Section 5 concludes the paper.

2. RELATED WORK

The retrieval model proposed in this paper builds upon the previous work along the following research directions.

Entity retrieval. The task of ERWD as answering arbitrary information needs expressed as keyword queries that aim at finding nodes or aspects of nodes in RDF graphs was first introduced by Pound et al. [26]. They also proposed to classify such queries into five categories: entity queries, type queries (i.e. list search queries or telegraphic queries), attribute queries, relation queries, and other queries. Although multiple open entity retrieval evaluation campaigns providing test collections and query sets covering a variety of information needs and relevance judgments have been conducted [10], most of the previous work along this direction focused on one particular query type. For example, the SemSearch Entity Search challenge[6] focused on finding one particular entity described by a keyword query. Previous successful retrieval approaches for queries of this type involved construction of multi-fielded entity representations by grouping entity attributes together by type [24], into title and content [21], according to manually determined importance [4] or into a two-level hierarchy [20]. Several methods adopted a two-stage approach, in which the initial retrieval results obtained using standard bag-of-words retrieval models were first expanded using relations in the knowledge graph and then the expanded results were re-ranked based on entity similarity. Tonon et al. [31] used Jaro-Winkler similarity between the entity names, while Herzig et al. [11] used Jenson-Shannon divergence between the language models of entities. Zhiltsov and Agichtein [33] proposed a learning-to-rank based approach, which combines explicit entity information with semantic similarity between the entities in latent space determined using a modified algorithm for tensor factorization.

The INEX 2009 Entity Ranking (INEX-XER)[7] track introduced an entity list completion task and provided an evaluation platform for type queries. The TREC 2009 Entity track focused on two related retrieval tasks "related entity finding" (i.e. finding all entities related to a given entity query) and "entity list completion" (i.e. finding entities with common properties given some examples). The List Search track from the SemSearch challenge targets a group of entities that match a keyword query. Bron et al. [5] proposed a hybrid approach that linearly combines the scores of the mixture of language models and a structure-based method, which captures the statistics of predicate-object pairs in triples shared by entity candidates. Elbassouni et al. [9] focused on the case of structured queries consisting of RDF triples and proposed a method that constructs LMs (as multinomial distributions over RDF triples) for both the queries and each possible result sub-graph. The ranking is based on the Kullback-Leibler divergence between the query LM and the LMs of each result sub-graph. The SemSets model [6] utilizes the relevance of entities to automatically constructed categories (semantic sets, SemSets) measured according to structural and textual similarity. Their approach combines a retrieval model with the methods for spreading activation over the link structure of a knowledge graph and evaluation of membership in semantic sets.

Question Answering over Linked Data (QALD)[8] evaluation campaigns aim at developing retrieval methods to answer sophisticated question-like queries. The majority of queries are natural language questions that are focused on finding one particular entity (or several entities) as exact answers to these questions. A method based on integer linear

[6]http://km.aifb.kit.edu/ws/semsearch\{10|11\}
[7]http://www.l3s.de/~demartini/XER09/
[8]http://www.sc.cit-ec.uni-bielefeld.de/qald/

programming for joint segmentation and disambiguation of question-like queries was proposed in [32]. Shekarpour et al. [29] applied the Hidden Markov Model to map question terms into entities and relations in the knowledge graph and translated keyword queries into structured SPARQL queries. For comprehensive overview of approaches to entity retrieval, we refer an interested reader to the recent surveys [17] [27].

Multi-fielded retrieval models. Multi-fielded extensions of different bag-of-words retrieval models have been proposed for structured document retrieval. BM25F [28] allows to either combine the BM25 retrieval scores of individual document fields with different weights into the final document retrieval score or calculate the aggregated basic retrieval statistics, such as TF and field lengths across multiple fields and use them in the original retrieval formula. Mixture of Language Models (MLM) [23] is a multi-fielded extension of the query likelihood retrieval model [25], a standard language modeling based retrieval model. In MLM, the retrieval score of a structured document is a linear combination of probabilities of query terms in the language models calculated for each document field. Although individual field weights in BM25F and MLM can be tuned for a particular collection, they are fixed across different query terms. To overcome this limitation, Probabilistic Retrieval Model for Semistructured Data (PRMS) [14] maps each query term into document fields using probabilistic classification based on collection statistics. Although PRMS was originally proposed for XML retrieval, it was later applied to ERWD [2]. Field Relevance Model (FRM) [13] is an extension of PRMS to the case of relevance feedback.

Incorporating term dependencies into retrieval models. Metzler and Croft proposed the MRF retrieval model, which based on the assumption about the dependencies between the query terms, has three variants: full independence (FI), sequential dependence (SD) and full dependence (FD) models. Bendersky et al. [3] extended SDM to allow learning optimal weights for unigrams and bigrams as a linear combination of features that are based on internal and external collection statistics. Huston and Croft [12] systematically evaluated a large number of bigram dependence models across short and long queries and concluded that retrieval models incorporating term dependencies consistently improve retrieval accuracy over the standard bag-of-words retrieval models. They also experimentally demonstrated that the performance of term dependence models can be significantly improved through parameter tuning.

3. APPROACH

In this section, we introduce the Fielded Sequential Dependence Model (FSDM), a novel model for structured document retrieval, and describe our strategy for building multi-fielded entity description documents.

3.1 FSDM

One of the limitations of standard SDM for structured document retrieval is that it considers term matches in different parts of a document as equally important (i.e. having the same contribution to the final retrieval score of a document), thus disregarding the document structure. For example, in case of unigrams, the potential function looks as follows:

$$f_T(q_i, D) = \log P(q_i|\theta_D) = \log \frac{tf_{q_i,D} + \mu\frac{cf_{q_i}}{|C|}}{|D| + \mu}$$

where q_i is a query term, D is a document, $tf_{q_i,D}$ is the frequency of q_i in D, $|D|$ is the document length, μ is a Dirichlet prior, that is usually set to the average document length in the collection, cf_{q_i} is the collection frequency of q_i and $|C|$ is the total number of terms in the collection. To adapt the MRF framework to multi-fielded entity descriptions, we propose to replace a single document language model $P(q_i|\theta_D)$ with a mixture of language models (MLM) for each document field. Hence, our model is an extension of sequential dependence model, although the same transformation can be applied to the full dependence model.

Consequently, the potential function for unigrams in case of FSDM is:

$$\tilde{f}_T(q_i, D) = \log \sum_j w_j^T P(q_i|\theta_D^j) = \log \sum_j w_j^T \frac{tf_{q_i,D^j} + \mu_j \frac{cf_{q_i}^j}{|C_j|}}{|D^j| + \mu_j}$$

where $j = \overline{1, F}$, F is the number of fields, θ_D^j is a language model of field j smoothed using its own Dirichlet prior μ_j and w_j are the field weights with the following constraints: $\sum_j w_j = 1, w_j \geqslant 0$; tf_{q_i,D^j} is the term frequency of q_i in field j of document D; $cf_{q_i}^j$ is the collection frequency of q_i in field j; $|C_j|$ is the total number of terms in field j across all the documents in the collection and $|D^j|$ is the length of field j in D.

The potential functions for ordered and unordered bigrams $q_{i,i+1} = (q_i, q_{i+1})$ in the query are defined as follows:

$$\tilde{f}_O(q_{i,i+1}, D) = \log \sum_j w_j^O \frac{tf_{\#1(q_{i,i+1}),D^j} + \mu_j \frac{cf^j_{\#1(q_{i,i+1})}}{|C_j|}}{|D^j| + \mu_j}$$

$$\tilde{f}_U(q_{i,i+1}, D) = \log \sum_j w_j^U \frac{tf_{\#uw8(q_{i,i+1}),D^j} + \mu_j \frac{cf^j_{\#uw8(q_{i,i+1})}}{|C_j|}}{|D^j| + \mu_j}$$

where $tf_{\#1(q_{i,i+1}),D^j}$ is the frequency of exact phrase $q_i q_{i+1}$ in field j of document D, $cf^j_{\#1(q_{i,i+1})}$ is the collection frequency of exact phrase $q_i q_{i+1}$ in field j, $tf_{\#uw8(q_{i,i+1}),D^j}$ is the number of times terms q_i and q_{i+1} occur together within a window of 8 word positions in field j of document D, regardless of the order of these terms.

Having separate mixtures of language models with different weights for unigrams as well as ordered and unordered bigrams gives FSDM the flexibility to adjust the multi-fielded document scoring strategy for matching query terms and phrases depending on the query type (entity, type, relation, etc.). Intuitively, an FSDM field weighting scheme, in which unordered bigram matches in the descriptive fields of entity documents are given higher weight than the matches in the name field, should be more effective for informational queries, while giving higher weight to ordered bigram matches in the name field can be beneficial for navigational queries. For example, precision of retrieval results for an informational query SemSearch_LS-1 *"apollo astronauts who walked on the moon"* is likely to increase when more importance is given to the matches of unordered bigrams *apollo astronauts* and *walked moon* within a window inside the descriptive fields of entity documents, rather than the name field, while giving higher weights to the matches of the same unordered bigrams in the name field is likely to have the opposite effect.

Substituting the potential functions $\psi(q_i, D; \Lambda)$ and $\psi(q_i, q_{i+1}, D; \Lambda)$ in the formula for the joint distribution over the document and query terms in the MRF model completes the transformation of SDM into FSDM:

$$\begin{aligned} P_{G,\Lambda}(Q,D) &= \frac{1}{Z_\Lambda} \prod_{c \in Cliques(G)} \psi(c;\lambda_c) \\ &= \frac{1}{Z_\Lambda} \times exp[\lambda_T \tilde{f}_T(q_i,D)] \times \\ & \quad exp[\lambda_O \tilde{f}_O(q_i,q_{i+1},D) + \lambda_U \tilde{f}_U(q_i,q_{i+1},D)] \end{aligned}$$

Note that for the purpose of ranking, it is sufficient to compute the following posterior probability:

$$P_\Lambda(D|Q) = \frac{P_{G,\Lambda}(Q,D)}{P_\Lambda(Q)}$$

Consequently, FSDM is a term dependence retrieval model with the following ranking function:

$$\begin{aligned} P_\Lambda(D|Q) \stackrel{rank}{=} & \lambda_T \sum_{q \in Q} \tilde{f}_T(q_i,D) + \\ & \lambda_O \sum_{q \in Q} \tilde{f}_O(q_i,q_{i+1},D) + \\ & \lambda_U \sum_{q \in Q} \tilde{f}_U(q_i,q_{i+1},D) \end{aligned} \quad (1)$$

It is easy to see from Equation 1 that MLM is a special case of FSDM, when $\lambda_T = 1, \lambda_O = 0, \lambda_U = 0$.

3.2 Parameter Estimation

Overall, FSDM has $3 * F + 3$ free parameters: $\langle \boldsymbol{w}^T, \boldsymbol{w}^O, \boldsymbol{w}^U, \boldsymbol{\lambda} \rangle$. Before introducing the parameter estimation procedure, we would like to emphasize two properties of the ranking function of FSDM. The first property is linearity with respect to $\boldsymbol{\lambda}$. We therefore can apply any linear learning-to-rank algorithm to optimize the ranking function with respect to $\boldsymbol{\lambda}$. The second property is linearity with respect to $\boldsymbol{w}$ of the arguments of monotonic $\tilde{f}(\cdot)$ functions. Therefore, optimization of the arguments as linear functions with respect to $\boldsymbol{w}$, leads to optimization of each function $\tilde{f}(\cdot)$.

Based on the above properties, we propose a two-stage Algorithm 1 to optimize the free parameters of FSDM with respect to the target retrieval metric, which in our case is Mean Average Precision (MAP).

Algorithm 1 An algorithm for training FSDM parameters.

1: $Q \leftarrow$ Train queries
2: **for** $s \in \{T, O, U\}$ **do**
3: $\quad \boldsymbol{\lambda} = \boldsymbol{e}_s$
4: $\quad \hat{\boldsymbol{w}}^s \leftarrow CA(Q, \boldsymbol{\lambda})$
5: **end for**
6: $\hat{\boldsymbol{\lambda}} \leftarrow CA(Q, \hat{\boldsymbol{w}}_T, \hat{\boldsymbol{w}}_O, \hat{\boldsymbol{w}}_U)$

In the first stage (lines 2-5), the algorithm independently estimates the optimal values of MLM parameters for unigrams, ordered and unordered bigrams. The unit vectors $\boldsymbol{e}_T = (1,0,0)$, $\boldsymbol{e}_O = (0,1,0)$, $\boldsymbol{e}_U = (0,0,1)$ are the corresponding settings of the parameters $\boldsymbol{\lambda}$ in the formula of FSDM ranking function (Equation 1). Because of linearity of MLM ranking function with respect to $\boldsymbol{w}$, we make use of the coordinate ascent (CA) algorithm, proposed in [19], to directly optimize MAP. The starting values for each $\boldsymbol{w}_s$ are uniform, i.e., equal to $\frac{1}{F}$ each. Therefore, CA iteratively optimizes MAP by performing a series of line searches along one coordinate direction under the constraint of non-negativity of $\boldsymbol{w}_s$. It repeatedly optimizes each of the parameters $w_1^s, \ldots, w_F^s$, while holding all other parameters fixed. Since MLMs are optimized independently, this stage can be easily parallelized to speed-up the training process.

In the second stage (line 6), the algorithm optimizes the parameters $\boldsymbol{\lambda}$ in Equation 1 on the same query set, given the optimal values of $\hat{\boldsymbol{w}}_T$, $\hat{\boldsymbol{w}}_O$, $\hat{\boldsymbol{w}}_U$. Again, since the right-hand side of Equation 1 is a linear function with respect to $\boldsymbol{\lambda}$, the CA algorithm can be applied to maximize the target metric directly. It starts with $\boldsymbol{\lambda} = (1,0,0)$, which is equivalent to MLM ranking model, and iterates until the gain in MAP is less than a given threshold. To avoid the changes of signs of the document ranking scores that may distort the ranking, non-negativity constraints on $\boldsymbol{\lambda}$ are enforced during CA.

Table 1: **Proposed scheme for multi-fielded representation of entity** e.

Field	Condition
names	$o : \exists(e,p,o) \& p \in P_{names} = regex(*[name\|label]\$)$
attributes	$o : \exists(e,p,o) \& p \in P_{datatypes} \& p \notin P_{names}$
categories	$o : \exists(e_1,p_1,e_2) \& (e_2,p_2,o) \& \& p \in P_{categories} \& p_2 \in P_{names}$
similar entity names	$o : \exists(e_1,p_1,e_2) \& (e_2,p_2,o) \& e_2 \in E_{sim}(e_1) \& p_2 \in P_{names}$
related entity names	$o : \exists(e_1,p_1,e_2) \& (e_2,p_2,o) \& e_2 \notin E_{sim}(e_1) \& p_2 \in P_{names}$

3.3 Modeling Entity Descriptions

Since multi-fielded entity representation proved to be beneficial for ERWD [21, 24], we propose a novel five-field entity representation scheme (Table 1). Attribute values, that satisfy the provided condition, are aggregated into the corresponding field.

The first two fields are the properties of the entities themselves. Other fields capture information from different entities that are related to the given entity. The *names* field contains conventional names of the entities, such as the name of a person or the name of an organization. Some of the predicates that can be used for this purpose are *label* from RDF Schema[9], *name* from FOAF Ontology[10], or */type/object/name* from Freebase[11]. The *attributes* field includes all datatype properties, other than names. The examples are values of *abstract* and *foundingDate* predicates from DBpedia. We found it to be helpful to include predicate names along with the predicate values, e.g. "founding date 1964".

The next three fields are extracted from the *names* field of related entities. The *categories* field combines classes or groups, to which the entity can be assigned. In DBpedia, the membership of entities in classes is represented using the *subject* property, which corresponds to the categories of a Wikipedia article. The *profession* and *ethnicity* attributes for people or the *industry* attribute for companies in Freebase have close semantics. The *similar entity names* field aggregates the names of the entities that are very similar or identical to a given entity, since it is often the case that

[9] `http://www.w3.org/TR/rdf-schema/`
[10] `http://www.foaf-project.org/`
[11] `http://freebase.com`

Table 2: **Multi-fielded entity document for the U.S. president *Barack Obama* (the terms are preprocessed).**

Field	Content
names	barack obama barack hussein obama ii
attributes	44th current president united states birth place honolulu hawaii
categories	democratic party united states senator nobel peace prize laureate christian
similar entity names	barack obama jr barak hussein obama barack h obama ii
related entity names	spouse michelle obama illinois state predecessor george walker bush

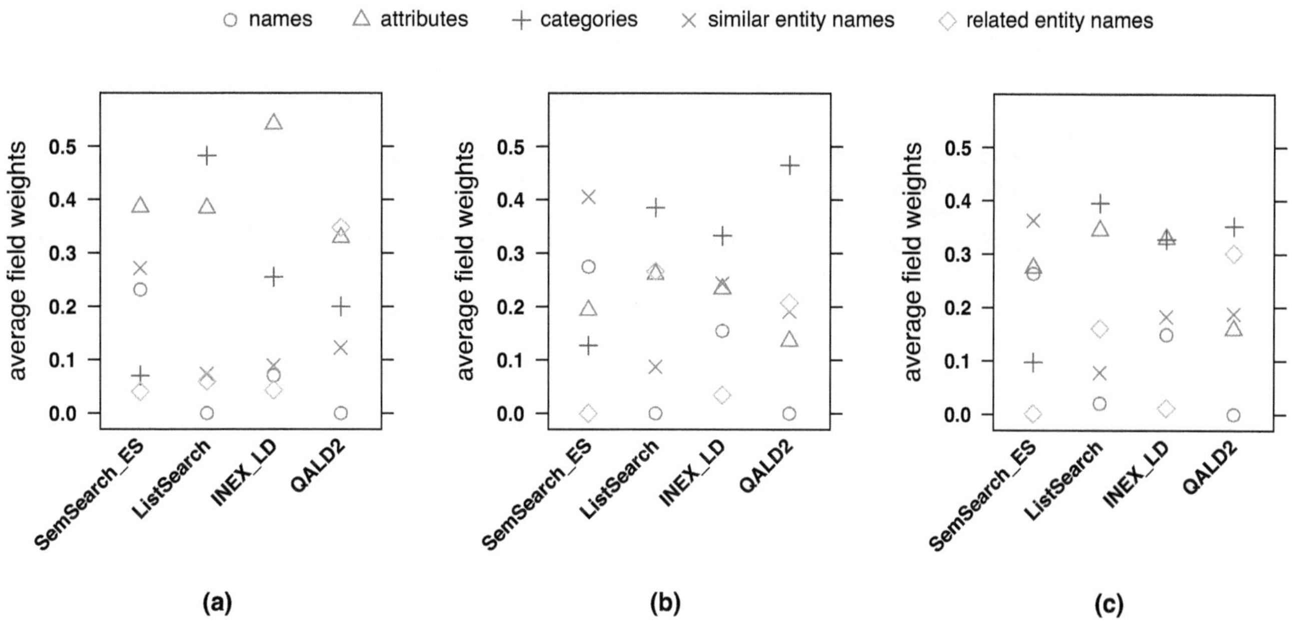

Figure 1: **Field weights in mixtures of language models for (a) unigrams (b) ordered bigrams and (c) unordered bigrams averaged over 5 folds for each query set.**

different knowledge bases (or even the same one) can refer to the same entity with different resource identifiers or describe it according to different schemata. In DBpedia, these values can be obtained with $S1\_1$ SPARQL query from [31] that takes into account *sameAs* property from OWL schema along with *redirect* and *disambiguates* from DBpedia. Finally, the *related entity names* field includes the names of the entities that are part of the same RDF triple with a given entity along with the predicate names, e.g. "spouse michelle obama". Table 2 provides an example of the entity document created using the above approach.

4. EXPERIMENTS

4.1 Experimental setup

We compare the effectiveness of FSDM with existing entity retrieval models based on a publicly available benchmark[12] [2], which combines 485 queries and the corresponding relevance judgments from the past entity retrieval evaluation campaigns. The knowledge graph used in our evaluation is DBPedia 3.7[13]. DBPedia is a structured version of on-line encyclopedia Wikipedia, which provides the descriptions of over 3.5 million entities belonging to 320 classes.

[12] `http://bit.ly/dbpedia-entity`

[13] `http://wiki.dbpedia.org/Downloads37`

Table 3: **Statistics of the query sets used for evaluation.**

Query set	Amount	Query types
SemSearch ES	130	Entity
ListSearch	115	Type
INEX-LD	100	Entity, Type, Attribute, Relation
QALD-2	140	Entity, Type, Attribute, Relation

We report the retrieval results obtained on the query sets in Table 3:

- **SemSearch ES**: this query set primarily contains named entity queries (e.g. *"charles darwin"*, *"orlando florida"*);
- **ListSearch**: this query set combines three query sets (INEX-XER, SemSearch LS, TREC Entity) from [2], since each one of them primarily consists of type queries (e.g. *"continents in the world"*, *"products of medimmune, inc."*);
- **INEX-LD**: this query set covers different types of queries – named entity queries, type queries, relation queries, and attribute queries (e.g. *"einstein relativ-*

ity theory", "tango music composers", "prima ballerina bolshoi theatre 1960");

- **QALD-2**: the Question Answering over Linked Data query set contains natural language questions of 4 different types: e.g., *"who created wikipedia?"* (entity); *"give me all soccer clubs in Spain"* (type); *"what is the currency of the czech republic"* (attribute); *"which books by kerouac were published by viking press?"* (relation).

In total, there are 13,090 available positive relevance judgments. Although some query sets (e.g. SemSearch) contain graded relevance judgments, for the purpose of consistency, we treat all relevance judgments as binary and report only the corresponding retrieval metrics.

For all experiments in this work, we used the multi-fielded entity descriptions constructed from DBpedia RDF graph according to the method presented in Section 3.3. Indexed terms were lower-cased, filtered using the INQUERY stoplist, and stemmed using the Krovetz stemmer. All retrieval models used in the experiments reported in this work were implemented using the Galago Search Engine[14][15]. Parameters of retrieval models were optimized with respect to the Mean Average Precision (MAP) using the Galago's implementation of the coordinate ascent learner based on 5-fold cross validation. All reported evaluation metrics were macro-averaged over 5 folds.

4.2 Parameter tuning

In this section, we discuss the details of optimization procedure for the field weights $\boldsymbol{w}$ and SDM/FSDM parameters $\boldsymbol{\lambda}$, and provide our interpretation of the learned values.

To optimize the field weights in FSDM, we uniformly initialize them and run the CA algorithm under the sum normalization and non-negativity constraints with 5 random restarts. We do not optimize the Dirichlet priors μ_j in language models and set them equal to the average (document or field) lengths, respectively. For optimizing the vectors of SDM parameters $\lambda_T, \lambda_O, \lambda_U$, we initialize them to $(1, 0, 0)$ and run the CA algorithm with 3 random restarts. The unordered window size was set to 8 in all cases, as suggested in previous work [3, 18].

We begin our analysis with the weights for unigram MLMs. Figure 1a depicts the distribution of the learned field weights averaged over all folds for each query set. Interestingly, while fields have similar relative importance across most query sets, some query sets (i.e. query types) are clear outliers. We observe that, compared to other query types, the optimized model strongly favors *names* and *similar entity names* fields for named entity queries (SemSearch ES query set). The *categories* field is important for type queries (ListSearch), while on QALD-2 query set, FSDM puts particularly strong emphasis on *related entity names*, which can be explained by the fact that this query set mostly consists of relation queries, which require capturing the related entity context. INEX-LD query set includes a large number of attribute queries that aim at finding entities primarily through their attributes instead of names. Thus, we observe that the model assigns higher weights to the *attributes* field.

[14]`http://www.lemurproject.org/galago.php`

[15]source code for all retrieval models used in this work as well as run files is available at `https://github.com/teanalab/FieldedSDM`

Since FSDM includes bigram language models, next we investigate the field weights in MLMs for ordered (Figure 1b) and unordered (Figure 1c) bigrams. In particular, we observe that higher weights are assigned to *names* and *similar entity names* fields for entity queries, for which the ordered bigram matchings in these fields is an important relevance factor. Another difference of bigram from unigram MLMs is the increased importance of *categories* field for other (non-entity) types of queries. This can be explained by the fact that bigrams are more effective in matching class names of entities than unigrams. For example, for the query QALD2_tr-89 *"give me all soccer clubs in the premier league"*, an English football club *Bolton Wanderers F.C.*, which is a relevant entity, is assigned to a few DBpedia categories, including *Premier League clubs.* Given this query intent, scoring entities based on matching bigrams *club premier* and *premier league* in the *categories* field is much more effective than scoring based on matching unigrams, since *premier league* is an important specification for the concept *soccer club* and should be considered holistically, as a phrase.

From the perspective of modeling entity descriptions, we can conclude that the *attributes* field is consistently considered to be a very valuable context for queries of any type. The *names* field as well as the *similar entity names* field are highly important for queries aiming at finding named entities, while distinguishing *categories* from *related entity names* is particularly important for type queries.

Overall, these findings support our initial hypothesis that the field weights are dependent on query types. Next, we focus on the analysis of the learned weights $\boldsymbol{\lambda}$ for SDM and FSDM, the distribution of which is depicted in Figures 2a and 2b. The optimal weights of SDM on all query sets, except SemSearch ES, are close to the standard scheme of (0.8, 0.1, 0.1), which was shown to be optimal in several previous works [3, 12, 18]. This discrepancy with SemSearch ES illustrates the significance of bigram matches for named entity queries. The optimal weights of FSDM indicate increased importance of bigram matches on every query set, especially on QALD-2. It follows that transformation of SDM into FSDM increases the importance of bigram matches, which ultimately improves the retrieval performance, as we will demonstrate next.

4.3 Comparison with the baselines

In this section, we present the results of comparing FSDM with the state-of-the-art models for ERWD. In particular, we use MLM-CA (unigram MLM optimized with respect to the field weights w_j by CA) and SDM-CA (SDM optimized with respect to the λ_T, λ_O, λ_U weights by CA) as the baselines. We also used MLM as a baseline to test whether incorporating term dependencies leads to improvement of entity retrieval. SDM leverages only unstructured entity descriptions, in which all fields are merged into a single document. The difference with SDM is measured to show the importance of fielded document representation for ERWD. Additionally, we report the results of the PRMS model using our entity descriptions, since it has been previously shown to have good performance in case of two-fielded entity representations. Finally, we include the results recomputed from the run files of the methods used for evaluation in [2].

Table 4 summarizes the retrieval results of all models on SemSearch ES, ListSearch, INEX-LD, QALD-2 query sets, and the entire query set. MAP and a preference-based mea-

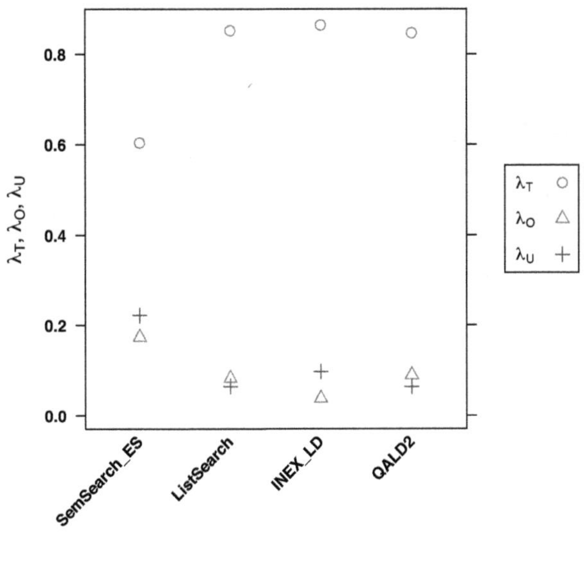

(a)

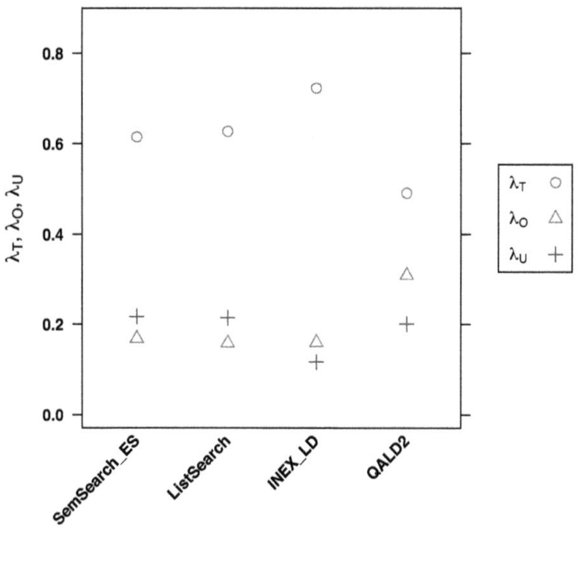

(b)

Figure 2: **Values of λ in (a) SDM; (b) FSDM averaged over 5 folds for each query set.**

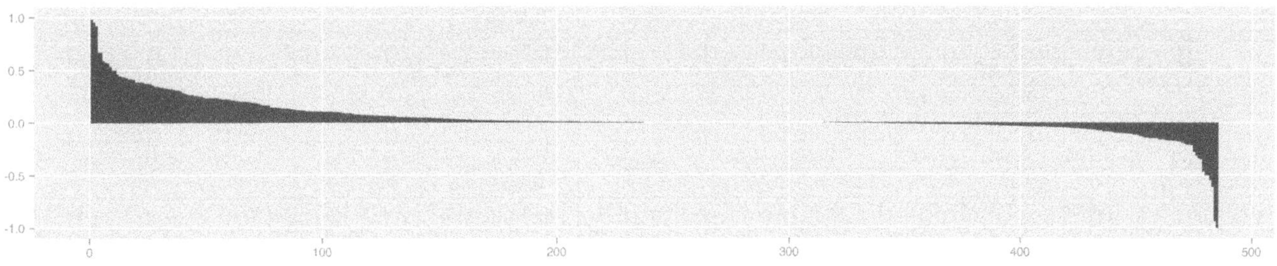

(a) All queries

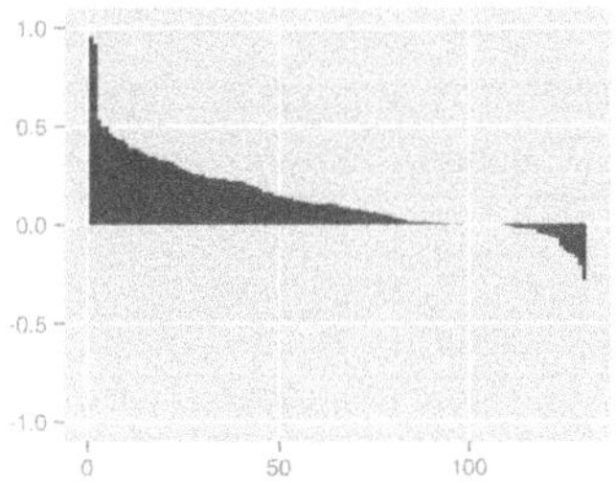

(b) SemSearch ES

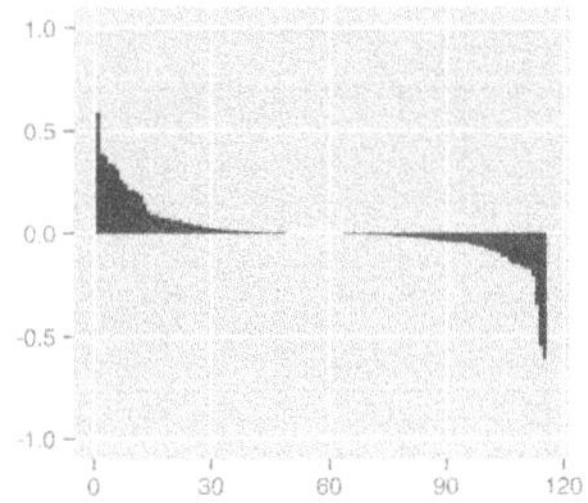

(c) ListSearch

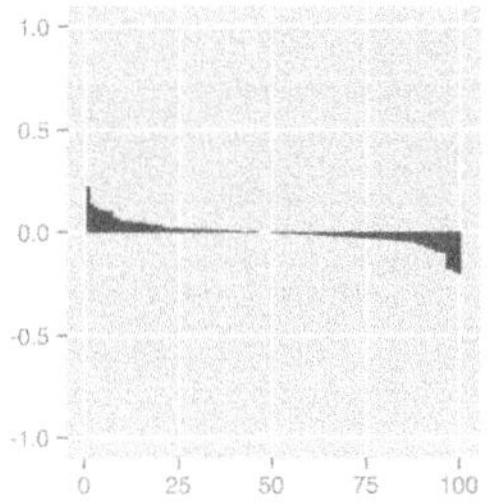

(d) INEX-LD

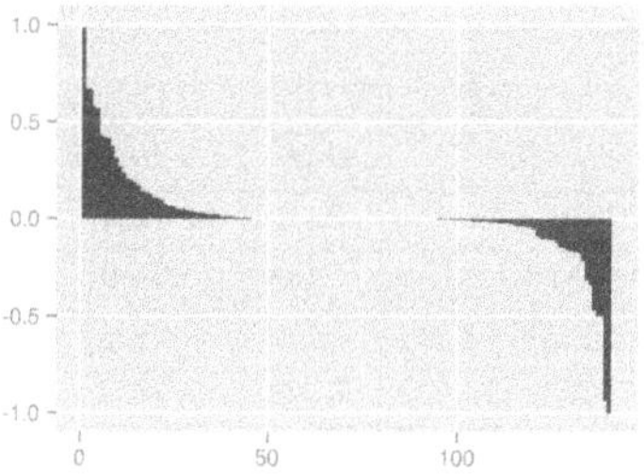

(e) QALD-2

Figure 3: **Topic-level differences in average precision between FSDM and SDM. over a) All queries; b) SemSearch ES; c) ListSearch; d) INEX-LD; e) QALD-2 query sets. Positive values indicate FSDM is better.**

sure (b-pref) are calculated at the top 100 results. As follows from Table 4, the SDM-CA and MLM-CA baselines (optimized SDM and MLM) both outperform previously proposed models on the entire query set, most significantly on QALD-2 and ListSearch query sets. However, the performance of SDM remarkably drops on SemSearch ES query set. To make sure that SDM-CA is not overfit, we run SDM using a standard weighting scheme (0.8, 0.1, 0.1) and got very close results with respect to MAP – 0.258 on SemSearch ES, 0.196 on ListSearch, 0.114 on INEX-LD, 0.186 on QALD-2, and 0.193 on the query set including all queries.

The results of PRMS are significantly worse compared to MLM in our settings, which indicates that the performance of this model degrades in case of a large number of fields in entity descriptions. Bag-of-words models, such as BM25 and LM, achieve comparable results with structured document retrieval models on the more heterogeneous INEX-LD query set, which includes the queries of different types.

Table 4: **Comparison of retrieval models on SemSearch ES, ListSearch, INEX-LD, QALD-2 query sets using the benchmark in [2]. "*" and "†" indicate statistically significant improvement over MLM-CA and SDM-CA baselines, respectively, as measured by the Fisher's randomization test ($\alpha = 0.05$) [30]. Relative improvement over MLM-CA/SDM-CA is shown in parenthesis.**

	SemSearch ES			
	MAP	**P@10**	**P@20**	**b-pref**
LM [2]	$0.314_{\dagger}$ (−1.9%/+23.6%)	$0.251_{\dagger}$ (+0.4%/+24.3%)	$0.179_{\dagger}$ (0.0%/+20.1%)	0.655 (−2.8%/−2.4%)
BM25 [2]	$0.326_{\dagger}$ (+1.9%/+28.3%)	$0.256_{\dagger}$ (+2.4%/+26.7%)	$0.177_{\dagger}$ (−1.1%/+18.8%)	0.658 (−2.4%/−1.9%)
MLM-tc [2]	$0.354_{\dagger}$ (+10.6%/+39.4%)	$0.284^{*}_{\dagger}$ (+13.6%/+40.6%)	$0.200^{*}_{\dagger}$ (+11.7%/+34.2%)	0.694 (+3.0%/+3.4%)
BM25F-tc [2]	$0.334_{\dagger}$ (+4.4%/+31.5%)	$0.263_{\dagger}$ (+5.2%/+30.2%)	$0.180_{\dagger}$ (+0.6%/+20.8%)	0.666 (−1.2%/−0.7%)
PRMS [2]	$0.323_{\dagger}$ (+0.9%/+27.2%)	$0.251_{\dagger}$ (+0.4%/+24.3%)	$0.175_{\dagger}$ (−2.2%/+17.4%)	0.657 (−2.5%/−2.1%)
PRMS	0.230^{*} (−28.1%/−9.4%)	$0.177^{*}_{\dagger}$ (−29.2%/−12.4%)	$0.125^{*}_{\dagger}$ (−30.2%/−16.1%)	$0.569^{*}_{\dagger}$ (−15.6%/−15.2%)
MLM-CA	0.320	0.250	0.179	0.674
SDM-CA	0.254^{*} (−20.6%)	0.202^{*} (−19.2%)	0.149^{*} (−16.8%)	0.671 (−0.4%)
FSDM	**$0.386^{*}_{\dagger}$** (+20.6%/+52.0%)	**$0.286^{*}_{\dagger}$** (+14.4%/+41.6%)	**$0.204^{*}_{\dagger}$** (+14.0%/+36.9%)	**$0.750^{*}_{\dagger}$** (+11.3%/+11.8%)
	ListSearch			
	MAP	**P@10**	**P@20**	**b-pref**
LM [2]	$0.161_{\dagger}$ (−15.3%/−18.3%)	$0.216^{*}_{\dagger}$ (−14.3%/−14.3%)	$0.170^{*}_{\dagger}$ (−11.5%/−15.8%)	$0.403_{\dagger}$ (−5.8%/−14.4%)
BM25 [2]	$0.167_{\dagger}$ (−12.1%/−15.2%)	0.232 (−7.9%/−7.9%)	0.186 (−3.1%/−7.9%)	$0.414_{\dagger}$ (−3.3%/−12.1%)
MLM-tc [2]	$0.153^{*}_{\dagger}$ (−19.5%/−22.3%)	$0.195^{*}_{\dagger}$ (−22.6%/−22.6%)	$0.16^{*}_{\dagger}$ (−16.7%/−20.8%)	$0.398_{\dagger}$ (−7.0%/−15.5%)
BM25F-tc [2]	$0.159^{*}_{\dagger}$ (−16.3%/−19.3%)	$0.221^{*}_{\dagger}$ (−12.3%/−12.3%)	$0.174_{\dagger}$ (−9.4%/−13.9%)	$0.402_{\dagger}$ (−6.1%/−14.6%)
PRMS [2]	0.178 (−6.3%/−9.6%)	0.240 (−4.8%/−4.8%)	0.200 (+4.2%/−1.0%)	$0.407_{\dagger}$ (−4.9%/−13.6%)
PRMS	$0.111^{*}_{\dagger}$ (−41.6%/−43.7%)	$0.154^{*}_{\dagger}$ (−38.9%/−38.9%)	$0.121^{*}_{\dagger}$ (−37.0%/−40.1%)	$0.310^{*}_{\dagger}$ (−27.6%/−34.2%)
MLM-CA	0.190	0.252	0.192	0.428
SDM-CA	0.197 (+3.7%)	0.252 (0.0%)	0.202 (+5.2%)	**0.471^{*}** (+10.0%)
FSDM	**0.203** (+6.8%/+3.0%)	**0.256** (+1.6%/+1.6%)	**0.203** (+5.7%/+0.5%)	0.466^{*} (+8.9%/−1.1%)
	INEX-LD			
	MAP	**P@10**	**P@20**	**b-pref**
LM [2]	0.106 (+3.9%/−9.4%)	0.236 (−0.8%/−8.5%)	0.188 (−1.1%/−5.5%)	$0.290_{\dagger}$ (−8.8%/−13.4%)
BM25 [2]	**0.118** (+15.7%/+0.9%)	0.247 (+3.8%/−4.3%)	0.204 (+7.4%/+2.5%)	$0.309_{\dagger}$ (−2.8%/−7.8%)
MLM-tc [2]	$0.104_{\dagger}$ (+2.0%/−11.1%)	$0.232_{\dagger}$ (−2.5%/−10.1%)	$0.197_{\dagger}$ (+3.7%/−1.0%)	$0.288_{\dagger}$ (−9.4%/−14.0%)
BM25F-tc [2]	0.117 (+14.7%/0.0%)	0.249 (+4.6%/−3.5%)	0.200 (+5.3%/+0.5%)	$0.304_{\dagger}$ (−4.4%/−9.3%)
PRMS [2]	$0.084^{*}_{\dagger}$ (−17.6%/−28.2%)	$0.203^{*}_{\dagger}$ (−14.7%/−21.3%)	$0.163^{*}_{\dagger}$ (−14.2%/−18.1%)	$0.256^{*}_{\dagger}$ (−19.5%/−23.6%)
PRMS	$0.064^{*}_{\dagger}$ (−37.3%/−45.3%)	$0.145^{*}_{\dagger}$ (−39.1%/−43.8%)	$0.123^{*}_{\dagger}$ (−35.3%/−38.2%)	$0.216^{*}_{\dagger}$ (−32.1%/−35.5%)
MLM-CA	0.102	0.238	0.190	0.318
SDM-CA	0.117^{*} (+14.7%)	0.258 (+8.4%)	0.199 (+4.7%)	0.335 (+5.3%)
FSDM	0.111^{*} (+8.8%/−5.1%)	**0.263^{*}** (+10.5%/+1.9%)	**$0.215^{*}_{\dagger}$** (+13.2%/+8.0%)	**0.341^{*}** (+7.2%/+1.8%)
	QALD-2			
	MAP	**P@10**	**P@20**	**b-pref**
LM [2]	$0.107^{*}_{\dagger}$ (−29.6%/−41.8%)	$0.051^{*}_{\dagger}$ (−50.5%/−51.9%)	$0.042^{*}_{\dagger}$ (−50.0%/−53.3%)	$0.233^{*}_{\dagger}$ (−37.5%/−49.9%)
BM25 [2]	$0.118_{\dagger}$ (−22.4%/−35.9%)	$0.066^{*}_{\dagger}$ (−35.9%/−37.7%)	$0.053^{*}_{\dagger}$ (−36.9%/−41.1%)	$0.311^{*}_{\dagger}$ (−16.6%/−33.1%)
MLM-tc [2]	$0.099^{*}_{\dagger}$ (−34.9%/−46.2%)	$0.051^{*}_{\dagger}$ (−50.5%/−51.9%)	$0.037^{*}_{\dagger}$ (−56.0%/−58.9%)	$0.239^{*}_{\dagger}$ (−35.9%/−48.6%)
BM25F-tc [2]	$0.107^{*}_{\dagger}$ (−29.6%/−41.8%)	$0.062^{*}_{\dagger}$ (−39.8%/−41.5%)	$0.049^{*}_{\dagger}$ (−41.7%/−45.6%)	$0.292^{*}_{\dagger}$ (−21.7%/−37.2%)
PRMS [2]	$0.105^{*}_{\dagger}$ (−30.9%/−42.9%)	$0.069^{*}_{\dagger}$ (−33.0%/−34.9%)	$0.051^{*}_{\dagger}$ (−39.3%/−43.3%)	$0.260^{*}_{\dagger}$ (−30.3%/−44.1%)
PRMS	$0.120^{*}_{\dagger}$ (−21.1%/−34.8%)	$0.079^{*}_{\dagger}$ (−23.3%/−25.5%)	$0.067^{*}_{\dagger}$ (−20.2%/−25.6%)	$0.328_{\dagger}$ (−12.1%/−29.5%)
MLM-CA	0.152	0.103	0.084	0.373
SDM-CA	0.184 (+21.1%)	0.106 (+2.9%)	0.090 (+7.1%)	0.465^{*} (+24.7%)
FSDM	**0.195^{*}** (+28.3%/+6.0%)	**$0.136^{*}_{\dagger}$** (+32.0%/+28.3%)	**0.111^{*}** (+32.1%/+23.3%)	**0.466^{*}** (+24.9%/+0.2%)
	All queries			
	MAP	**P@10**	**P@20**	**b-pref**
LM [2]	$0.175^{*}_{\dagger}$ (−10.7%/−8.9%)	$0.182^{*}_{\dagger}$ (−11.7%/−8.1%)	$0.139^{*}_{\dagger}$ (−11.5%/−10.3%)	$0.398^{*}_{\dagger}$ (−12.5%/−19.6%)
BM25 [2]	0.186 (−5.1%/−3.1%)	0.194 (−5.8%/−2.0%)	0.149 (−5.1%/−3.9%)	$0.428^{*}_{\dagger}$ (−5.9%/−13.5%)
MLM-tc [2]	0.181 (−7.7%/−5.7%)	$0.185^{*}_{\dagger}$ (−10.2%/−6.6%)	$0.143^{*}_{\dagger}$ (−8.9%/−7.7%)	$0.409^{*}_{\dagger}$ (−10.1%/−17.4%)
BM25F-tc [2]	0.182 (−7.1%/−5.2%)	0.192^{*} (−6.8%/−3.0%)	$0.145^{*}_{\dagger}$ (−7.6%/−6.5%)	$0.421^{*}_{\dagger}$ (−7.5%/−14.9%)
PRMS [2]	$0.176^{*}_{\dagger}$ (−10.2%/−8.3%)	0.186^{*} (−9.7%/−6.1%)	$0.143^{*}_{\dagger}$ (−8.9%/−7.7%)	$0.400^{*}_{\dagger}$ (−12.1%/−19.2%)
PRMS	$0.136^{*}_{\dagger}$ (−30.6%/−29.2%)	$0.136^{*}_{\dagger}$ (−34.0%/−31.3%)	$0.107^{*}_{\dagger}$ (−31.8%/−31.0%)	$0.365^{*}_{\dagger}$ (−19.8%/−26.3%)
MLM-CA	0.196	0.206	0.157	0.455
SDM-CA	0.192 (−2.0%)	0.198 (−3.9%)	0.155 (−1.3%)	0.495^{*} (+8.8%)
FSDM	**$0.231^{*}_{\dagger}$** (+17.9%/+20.3%)	**$0.231^{*}_{\dagger}$** (+12.1%/+16.7%)	**$0.179^{*}_{\dagger}$** (+14.0%/+15.5%)	**$0.517^{*}_{\dagger}$** (+13.6%/+4.4%)

We also observe that FSDM significantly outperforms the MLM-CA baseline on all query sets and all metrics, except ListSearch. FSDM also significantly outperforms SDM-CA on SemSearch ES and the entire query set with respect to all evaluation metrics. On the remaining query sets, FSDM is more effective than SDM in all but two cases (on INEX-LD with respect of MAP and on ListSearch with respect to b-pref; however, the difference in both cases is not significant), including statistically significant improvement on INEX-LD with respect to P@20 and on QALD-2 with respect to P@10.

4.4 Success/Failure Analysis

In this section, we present the results of quantitative and qualitative analysis of errors in the search results. First, Figure 3 illustrates the per-topic differences in average precision between FSDM and SDM. From Figure 3, it follows that, on the entire query set, FSDM performs better than SDM on a larger number of topics than vice versa, with the most significant difference on SemSearch ES query set. QALD-2 has the largest number of queries with no performance differences, since both FSDM and SDM fail to find any relevant results for 28 out of 140 queries from this fairly difficult query set.

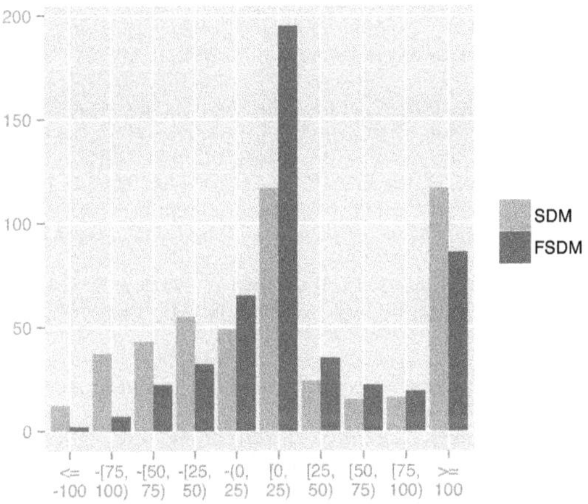

Figure 4: **Robustness of SDM and FSDM methods with respect to the MLM-CA baseline over the entire query set.**

As the next experiment, we analyze the robustness of SDM and FSDM compared to the MLM-CA baseline on the entire query set. Figure 4 shows the histogram for various ranges of relative decreases and increases in MAP with respect to MLM-CA and indicates that FSDM is more robust compared to SDM. In particular, it improves the performance of 50% of the queries with respect to MLM-CA, compared to 45% of the queries improved by SDM. At the same time, FSDM decreases the performance of only 26% of the queries, while SDM degrades the performance of 40% of the queries.

Next, we focus on a more detailed qualitative analysis of queries showing the highest relative gain in terms of MAP. In particular, we observe that a common mistake of SDM on named entity queries is overestimation of importance of matches in the fields other than *names*. For example, for the query SemSearch_ES-22 *"city of charlotte"*, SDM mistakenly promotes the entities, such as *Anthony Foxx*, a former mayor of Charlotte, or *Clayton Heafner*, an American golfer, who lived in this city. Therefore, using SDM for type queries may result in a topic drift and decreased precision. For example, for the query QALD2_tr-89 *"give me all soccer clubs in the premier league"*, SDM ranks higher the soccer clubs from the premier leagues in Tasmania (Northern Rangers) and New Zealand (Metro F.C.). Similar effect is observed for the query INEX_XER-121 *"us presidents since 1960"*, for which SDM promotes the entities with matched bigrams and unigrams in the fields of minor importance, such as *List of people on stamps of Liberia*, whereas FSDM correctly emphasizes term matches in categories and ranks the correct results, such as *Gerald Ford*, *Theodore Roosevelt*, and *Ronald Reagan* at the top.

We also observed that a common cause of many FSDM failures is neglecting the important query terms. For example, for the TREC_Entity-9 query *"members of the beaux arts trio"*, FSDM mistakenly promotes the entities *Emmanuel Pontremoli* and *Pierre Carron*, the members of the Académie des Beaux Arts, which is caused by matching bigrams *members beaux* and *beaux arts* in the *categories* field. However, the query term *trio* provides an important clue that the query intent is about Beaux Arts Trio, a famous piano trio, which FSDM is unable to pick up. Similar reasoning applies to the QALD2_tr-15 query *"who created goofy"*, for which FSDM drifts to cartoons rather than information about the actual character creator, and the QALD2_te-90 query *"where is the residence of the prime minister of spain?"*, for which FSDM promotes the Spanish prime ministers in retrieval results, instead of the exact answer to the question.

The reason of FSDM failure on another difficult query SemSearch_LS-10 *"did nicole kidman have any siblings"* is slightly different. The most precise answer, *Antonia Kidman*, who is the younger sister of the actress Nicole Kidman, does not contain any occurrences of the query term *sibling*. In this case, SDM ranks higher a DBpedia disambiguation page that mentions the right entity. At the same time, FSDM tends to return the movies starring Nicole Kidman as the top results. We hypothesize that query expansion with synonyms can potentially resolve these issues, however we leave verification of this hypothesis to future work.

Table 5: **Comparison of SDM and FSDM on queries of various difficulty (according to the number of positive relevance judgments). "†" indicates statistical significance with respect to the Fisher's randomization test ($\alpha = 0.05$) [30].**

	Difficult queries			
	MAP	**P@10**	**P@20**	**b-pref**
SDM	0.213	**0.067**	0.042	0.599
FSDM	**0.239**	0.065	**0.043**	**0.621**
	Medium queries			
	MAP	**P@10**	**P@20**	**b-pref**
SDM	0.209	0.224	0.165	0.532
FSDM	**0.264**$_†$	**0.272**$_†$	**0.191**$_†$	**0.559**$_†$
	Easy queries			
	MAP	**P@10**	**P@20**	**b-pref**
SDM	0.139	0.298	0.262	0.316
FSDM	**0.166**$_†$	**0.345**$_†$	**0.309**$_†$	**0.330**

To complete the analysis of retrieval performance of FSDM, Table 5 compares the performance of SDM and FSDM on queries of various levels of difficulty. To obtain the results in Table 5, we grouped all the queries into three categories: difficult queries (that have 3 or less positive relevance judgments), medium queries (with 4 to 20, i.e., potential first two SERPs) and easy queries (that have more than 20 positive relevance judgments associated with them). As a result, we obtained 141, 216, and 128 queries in each category, respectively. From Table 5 it follows that FSDM outperforms SDM in each query category with respect to all metrics in all the cases but one (P@10 for difficult queries), with the most significant difference in performance on medium and easy queries. We, therefore, conclude that creating sophisticated entity descriptions is not sufficient for answering *difficult queries* in entity retrieval scenario and better capturing the semantics of query terms is required to further improve the precision of FSDM for difficult queries.

5. CONCLUSION

This paper proposed Fielded Sequential Dependence Model, a novel retrieval model, which incorporates term dependencies into structured document retrieval, and a two-stage algorithm to directly optimize the parameters of this model with respect to the target retrieval metric. Although we only experimented with ERWD, FSDM can be applied to retrieval from collections of structured documents of any type.

We demonstrated that having different field weighting schemes for unigrams and bigrams is effective for different types of queries in ad-hoc entity retrieval scenario. Experimental evaluation of FSDM on a standard publicly available benchmark showed that it consistently and, in most cases, statistically significantly outperforms state-of-the-art structured and unstructured retrieval models for ERWD.

Acknowledgments

This work was partially supported by the subsidy from the government of the Russian Federation to support the program of competitive growth of Kazan Federal University among world class academic centers and universities and by the Russian Foundation for Basic Research (grants # 15-07-08522, 15-47-02472).

6. REFERENCES

[1] K. Balog, M. Bron, and M. D. Rijke. Query Modeling for Entity Search based on Terms, Categories, and Examples. *ACM TOIS*, 29:22, 2011.

[2] K. Balog and R. Neumayer. A Test Collection for Entity Search in DBpedia. In *Proceedings of the 36th ACM SIGIR*, pages 737–740, 2013.

[3] M. Bendersky, D. Metzler, and W. B. Croft. Learning Concept Importance Using a Weighted Dependence Model. In *Proceedings of the 3rd ACM WSDM*, pages 31–40, 2010.

[4] R. Blanco, P. Mika, and S. Vigna. Effective and Efficient Entity Search in RDF Data. In *Proceedings of the 10th ISWC*, pages 83–97, 2011.

[5] M. Bron, K. Balog, and M. de Rijke. Example Based Entity Search in the Web of Data. In *Proceedings of the 35th ECIR*, pages 392–403, 2013.

[6] M. Ciglan, K. Nørvåg, and L. Hluchý. The SemSets Model for Ad-hoc Semantic List Search. In *Proceedings of the 21st WWW*, pages 131–140, 2012.

[7] J. Dalton, L. Dietz, and J. Allan. Entity Query Feature Expansion Using Knowledge Base Links. In *Proceedings of the 37th ACM SIGIR*, pages 365–374, 2014.

[8] S. Elbassuoni and R. Blanco. Keyword Search over RDF Graphs. In *Proceedings of the 20th ACM CIKM*, pages 237–242, 2011.

[9] S. Elbassuoni, M. Ramanath, R. Schenkel, M. Sydow, and G. Weikum. Language-model-based Ranking for Queries on RDF-graphs. In *Proceedings of the 18th ACM CIKM*, pages 977–986, 2009.

[10] K. M. Elbedweihy, S. N. Wrigley, P. Clough, and F. Ciravegna. An Overview of Semantic Search Evaluation Initiatives. *Web Semantics: Science, Services and Agents on the World Wide Web*, 2014.

[11] D. M. Herzig, P. Mika, R. Blanco, and T. Tran. Federated Entity Search Using On-the-Fly Consolidation. In *Proceedings of the 12th ISWC*, pages 167–183. 2013.

[12] S. Huston and W. B. Croft. A Comparison of Retrieval Models using Term Dependencies. In *Proceedings of the 23rd ACM CIKM*, pages 111–120, 2014.

[13] J. Y. Kim and W. B. Croft. A Field Relevance Model for Structured Document Retrieval. In *Proceedings of the 34th ECIR*, pages 97–108, 2012.

[14] J. Y. Kim, X. Xue, and W. B. Croft. A Probabilistic Retrieval Model for Semistructured Data. In *Proceedings of the 31st ECIR*, pages 228–239, 2009.

[15] A. Kotov and C. Zhai. Tapping into Knowledge Base for Concept Feedback: Leveraging ConceptNet to Improve Search Results for Difficult Queries. In *Proceedings of the 5th WSDM*, pages 403–412, 2012.

[16] A. Kotov, C. Zhai, and R. Sproat. Mining Named Entities with Temporally Correlated Bursts from Multilingual Web News Streams. In *Proceedings of the 4th ACM WSDM*, pages 237–246, 2011.

[17] C. L. Koumenides and N. R. Shadbolt. Ranking Methods for Entity-Oriented Semantic Web Search. *JASIST*, 65(6):1091–1106, 2014.

[18] D. Metzler and W. B. Croft. A Markov Random Field Model for Term Dependencies. In *Proceedings of the 28th ACM SIGIR*, pages 472–479, 2005.

[19] D. Metzler and W. B. Croft. Linear Feature-based Models for Information Retrieval. *Information Retrieval*, 10:257–274, 2007.

[20] R. Neumayer, K. Balog, and K. Nørvåg. On the Modeling of Entities for Ad-hoc Entity Search in the Web of Data. In *Proceedings of the 34th ECIR*, pages 133–145, 2012.

[21] R. Neumayer, K. Balog, and K. Nørvåg. When Simple is (more than) Good Enough: Effective Semantic Search with (almost) no Semantics. In *Proceedings of the 34th ECIR*, pages 540–543, 2012.

[22] Z. Nie, Y. Ma, S. Shi, J.-R. Wen, and W.-Y. Ma. Web Object Retrieval. In *Proceedings of the 16th WWW*, pages 81–90, 2007.

[23] P. Ogilvie and J. Callan. Combining Document Representations for Known-item Search. In *Proceedings of the 26th ACM SIGIR*, pages 143–150, 2003.

[24] J. R. Pérez-Aguera, J. Arroyo, J. Greenberg, J. P. Iglesias, and V. Fresno. Using BM25F for Semantic Search. In *Proceedings of the 3rd SemSearch Workshop*, 2010.

[25] J. M. Ponte and W. B. Croft. A Language Modeling Approach to Information Retrieval. In *Proceedings of the 21st ACM SIGIR*, pages 275–281, 1998.

[26] J. Pound, P. Mika, and H. Zaragoza. Ad-hoc Object Retrieval in the Web of Data. In *Proceedings of the 19th WWW*, pages 771–780, 2010.

[27] A. J. Roa-Valverde and S. Miguel-Angel. A Survey of Approaches for Ranking on the Web of Data. *Information Retrieval*, 17(4):295–325, 2014.

[28] S. Robertson, H. Zaragoza, and M. Taylor. Simple BM25 Extension to Multiple Weighted Fields. In *Proceedings of the 13th ACM CIKM*, pages 42–49, 2004.

[29] S. Shakarpour, A.-C. N. Ngomo, and S. Auer. Question Answering on Interlinked Data. In *Proceedings of the 22nd WWW*, pages 1145–1156, 2013.

[30] M. D. Smucker, J. Allan, and B. Carterette. A Comparison of Statistical Significance Tests for Information Retrieval Evaluation. In *Proceedings of the 16th ACM CIKM*, pages 623–632, 2007.

[31] A. Tonon, G. Demartini, and P. Cudré-Mauroux. Combining Inverted Indices and Structured Search for Ad-hoc Object Retrieval. In *Proceedings of the 35th ACM SIGIR*, pages 125–134, 2012.

[32] M. Yahya, K. Berberich, S. Elbassuoni, and G. Weikum. Robust Question Answering over the Web of Linked Data. In *Proceedings of the 22nd ACM CIKM*, pages 1107–1116, 2013.

[33] N. Zhiltsov and E. Agichtein. Improving Entity Search over Linked Data by Modeling Latent Semantics. In *Proceedings of the 22nd ACM CIKM*, pages 1253–1256, 2013.

Mining, Ranking and Recommending Entity Aspects

Ridho Reinanda† r.reinanda@uva.nl
Edgar Meij‡ emeij@yahoo-inc.com
Maarten de Rijke† derijke@uva.nl

† University of Amsterdam, Amsterdam, The Netherlands
‡ Yahoo Labs, London, United Kingdom

ABSTRACT

Entity queries constitute a large fraction of web search queries and most of these queries are in the form of an entity mention plus some context terms that represent an intent in the context of that entity. We refer to these entity-oriented search intents as *entity aspects*. Recognizing entity aspects in a query can improve various search applications such as providing direct answers, diversifying search results, and recommending queries. In this paper we focus on the tasks of identifying, ranking, and recommending entity aspects, and propose an approach that mines, clusters, and ranks such aspects from query logs.

We perform large-scale experiments based on users' search sessions from actual query logs to evaluate the aspect ranking and recommendation tasks. In the aspect ranking task, we aim to satisfy most users' entity queries, and evaluate this task in a query-independent fashion. We find that entropy-based methods achieve the best performance compared to maximum likelihood and language modeling approaches. In the aspect recommendation task, we recommend other aspects related to the aspect currently being queried. We propose two approaches based on semantic relatedness and aspect transitions within user sessions and find that a combined approach gives the best performance. As an additional experiment, we utilize entity aspects for actual query recommendation and find that our approach improves the effectiveness of query recommendations built on top of the query-flow graph.

Categories and Subject Descriptors

H.3.3 [**Information Storage and Retrieval**]: Information Search and Retrieval

Keywords

Entity aspects; Query intent; Semantic search

1. INTRODUCTION

With the proliferation of mobile devices, an increasing amount of available structured data, and the development of advanced search result pages, modern-day web search is increasingly geared towards entity-oriented search [2, 26, 29]. A first step and common strategy to address such information needs is to identify entities within queries, commonly known as *entity linking* [24]. Semantic information that is gleaned from the linked entities (such as entity types, attributes, or related entities) is used in various ways by modern search engines, e.g., for presenting an entity card, showing actionable links, and/or recommending related entities [3, 12, 19].

Entities are not typically searched for on their own, however, but often combined with other entities, types, attributes/properties, relationships, or keywords [29]. Such query completions in the context of an entity are commonly referred to as entity-oriented intents or entity aspects [27, 38]. In this paper we study the problem of mining and ranking entity aspects in the context of web search. In particular, we study four related tasks in this paper: (1) identifying entity aspects, (2) estimating the importance of aspects with respect to an entity, (3) ranking entity aspects with respect to a current query and/or user session, and (4) leveraging entity aspects for query recommendation.

The first step in identifying entity aspects involves extracting common queries in the context of an entity and grouping them based on their similarity. We perform this process offline and investigate three matching strategies for clustering queries into entity aspects: *lexical*, *semantic*, and *click-based*. Gathering such entity aspects can already be valuable on its own since they can be used to, e.g., discover bursty or consistent entity intents or to determine entity type-specific aspects [27].

In the next step we rank the obtained entity aspects for each entity in a query-independent fashion using three distinct strategies. This provides us with a mechanism to retrieve the most relevant aspects for a given entity on its own, which, in turn, can be used to, e.g., summarize the most pertinent information needs around an entity or to help the presentation of entity-oriented search results such as customized entity cards on SERPs [2].

The third task that we consider is aspect recommendation. Given an entity and a certain aspect as input, recommend related aspects. This task is motivated by the increasing proliferation of entity-oriented interface elements for web search that can be improved by, e.g., (re)ranking particular items on these elements. Recommending aspects for an entity can also help users discover new and serendipitous information with respect to an entity. We consider two approaches to recommend aspects: *semantic* and *behavioral*. In the semantic approach, relatedness is estimated from a semantic representation of aspects. The behavioral approach is based on the "flow" of aspect transitions in actual user sessions, modeled using an adapted version of the query-flow graph [5, 6, 34].

In our final task we leverage entity aspects for actual query recommendation, i.e., helping users refine their query and/or to help users accomplish a complex search task [11, 22]. Most methods for query recommendation are similar to the behavioral approach men-

SIGIR '15 August 09–13, 2015, Santiago, Chile.

ACM 978-1-4503-3621-5/15/08 ...$15.00.
DOI: http://dx.doi.org/10.1145/2766462.2767724.

tioned above and based on query transitions within sessions. They do not commonly utilize semantic information, however, which may cause distinct but semantically equivalent suggestions. We aim to ameliorate this problem by utilizing the semantic information captured through the entity aspects for query recommendation.

We perform large-scale experiments on both a publicly available and a commercial search engine's query log to evaluate our proposed methods for mining, ranking, and recommending entity aspects, as well as for recommending queries. We perform contrastive experiments using various similarity measures and ranking strategies. We find that entropy-based methods achieve the best performance compared to maximum likelihood and language modeling on the task of entity aspect ranking. Concerning aspect recommendation we find that combining aspect transitions within a session and semantic relatedness give the best performance. Furthermore, we show that the entity aspects can be effectively utilized for query recommendation.

Our main contributions can be summarized as follows:

- We introduce the task of mining, ranking, and recommending entity aspects.
- We provide an in-depth analysis of the mined aspects.
- We propose two approaches to represent aspect relatedness, and utilize them for recommendation.
- We propose a query recommendation method built on top of the query-flow graph.

After a discussion of related work in Section 2, we formalize our task in Section 3. We then detail our approaches to mining, ranking, and recommending entity aspects in Section 4. A detailed account of experiments and data is given in Section 5. We discuss the results of our experiments in Section 6 and conclude in Section 7.

2. RELATED WORK

In this section we review related work around three main topics: query intent mining, leveraging entity aspects for search, and search task identification.

Intent mining deals with identifying clusters of synonymous or strongly related queries based on *intents*, which are typically defined as "the need behind a query." An intent (sometimes also referred to as an *aspect*) is commonly defined as a set of search queries that together represent a distinct information need relevant to the original search query. Methods for identifying intents are typically based on the query itself, results returned by a retrieval algorithm, clicked results, or any other actions by the user. Hu et al. [13] leverage two kinds of user behavior for identifying query "subtopics" (which can be interpreted as intents): one subtopic per search and subtopic clarification by keyword. They propose a clustering algorithm that can effectively leverage the two phenomena to automatically mine the major subtopics of queries. They represent each subtopic as a cluster containing a number of URLs and keywords. Cheung and Li [8] present an unsupervised method for clustering queries with similar intent and producing patterns consisting of a sequence of semantic concepts or lexical items for each intent. They refer to this step of identifying patterns as *intent summarization*. They then use the discovered patterns to automatically annotate queries.

Other related work focuses on extracting attributes from queries, either unsupervised or in the context of entities from a knowledge base. For instance, Li et al. [16] propose a clustering framework with similarity kernels to identify synonymous query intent "templates" for a set of canonical templates. They integrate signals from multiple sources of information and tune the weights in an unsupervised manner. Li et al. [17] on the other hand, solely aim to discover alternative surface forms of attribute values. They propose a compact clustering framework to jointly identify synonyms for a set of attribute values. In a similar vein, Pasca and Van Durme [28] describe a method for extracting relevant attributes or quantifiable properties for various *classes of objects*. They utilize query logs as a source for these. Yin and Shah [38] propose an approach for building a hierarchical taxonomy of generic search intents for a class of named entities. Their proposed approach finds phrases representing generic intents from user queries and organize these phrases into a tree. They propose three methods for tree building: maximum spanning tree, hierarchical agglomerative clustering, and pachinko allocation model. These approaches are based on search logs only. Moving beyond entity types, Lin et al. [19] introduce the notion of active objects in which entity-bearing queries are paired with actions that can be performed on entities. They pose the problem of finding actions that can be performed on entities as the problem of probabilistic inference in a graphical model that captures how an entity-bearing query is generated.

Another body of related work deals with alternative presentations of search results, e.g., based on intents [9]. For instance, Balasubramanian and Cucerzan [2] propose a method to generate entity-specific topic pages as an alternative to regular search results. Similarly, Song et al. [32] present a model to summarize a query's results using distinct aspects. For this they propose "composite queries" that are used for providing additional information for the original query and its aspects. This works by comparatively mining the search results of different component queries. Wu et al. [37] mine latent query aspects based on users' query reformulation behavior and present a system that computes aspects for any new query. Their system combines different sources of information to compute aspects. They first discover candidate aspects for queries by analyzing query logs. They then use a knowledge base to compute aspects for queries that occur less frequently and to group aspects that are semantically related. Finally, Spina et al. [33] explore the task of identifying aspects of an entity given a stream of microblog posts. They compare different IR techniques and opinion target identification methods for automatically identifying aspects.

Search task identification deals with determining the specific task a user is aiming to solve. Such information enables a search engine to, e.g., suggest relevant queries and/or results. Jones and Klinkner [14] formalize the notion of a *search goal* as an atomic information need which results in one or more queries. They propose a method for the automated segmentation of a users' query stream into hierarchical units. While a search goal is atomic, a series of search goals then form a *search missions* (or *complex search tasks*). Lucchese et al. [20] also aim to identify user search tasks within query sessions. They cluster queries in order to find *user tasks*, defined as a set of queries that is aimed towards the same information need. Later they expand user task detection across user sessions [21], similar to so-called task trails and long-term search tasks [18, 36]. Li et al. [15] model the temporal influence of queries within a search session and then use this temporal influence across multiple sessions to identify and label search tasks.

There exists a large body of work on query recommendation, i.e., suggesting follow-up queries to a user, either in an ad hoc fashion or in the context of a user's session or task. Boldi et al. [5] introduces the notion of query-flow graph for query suggestion and Szpektor et al. [34] later expand this model to increase coverage for long tail queries. Bonchi et al. [6] expand it even further to improve coverage. Feild and Allan [10] show that using contextual information can improve query recommendation, as

Table 1: Glossary of the main notation used in this paper.

t	a term
q	a query
e	an entity
s	a query segment, i.e., a sequence of terms
a	an entity aspect, consisting of zero or more query segments
A_e	the set of entity aspects for e
d	time span

long as the previous queries in the context involve a similar or related task. Hassan Awadallah et al. [11] capitalizes on this idea and propose grouping together similar queries and then using them for query recommendation for complex search tasks, similar to task-specific recommendations [22]. Finally, Verma and Yilmaz [35] extract common tasks in the context of an entity to improve retrieval through query expansion and query term prediction. They extract terms frequently appearing with an entity and aggregate this type of information to an entity type level to obtain a dictionary of entity tasks. They evaluate their work through query term prediction and query expansion.

Our work is different in the following major ways. First, we extract entity aspects from query logs specifically. Second, we weight these aspects and assign their importance with respect to an entity on its own in an ad hoc fashion, i.e., without any user, session or query-based information. Third, we learn their relatedness using semantic and behavioral approaches. Finally, we propose an entity aspect-based query recommendation algorithm building upon the query-flow graph.

3. PROBLEM DEFINITION

In this paper, we study three related entity-oriented tasks that are elemental in modern-day entity-oriented web search: *identifying*, *ranking*, and *recommending* entity aspects. Although they build on one another, we propose effective methods for each of them separately since they are essential building blocks for information access applications on their own as well.

In our methods and experiments we employ user interaction log data in the form of queries and clicks. Formally, such logs can be represented as a sequence of events where each event is an action taken by a user. For each event we store a timestamp, a user ID, and the type of action; these are limited to queries and clicks in our current case. Furthermore, the logs are divided into time-ordered sessions, $h \in H$, for each user where we use a common segmentation method and begin a new session after a predefined period of inactivity (30 minutes unless indicated otherwise).

We formulate the first task of *identifying entity aspects* as follows. Given an annotation function $\lambda_e : Q \rightarrow E$ that assigns entities from the set of all entities E to queries, we detect "entity-bearing queries," i.e., queries Q_e containing an entity e. Then, for each entity, we mine a set of entity aspects: $A_e = \{a_1, \ldots, a_m\}$ from Q_e representing the key search tasks in the context of that entity. Table 1 details the main notation we use in this paper. We employ the following definition of search tasks and entity aspects.

> *Given a "search task," defined as an atomic information need resulting in one or more queries, an "entity aspect" is an entity-oriented search task, i.e., a set of queries that represent a common task in the context of an entity, grouped together if they have the same intent.*

Once entity aspects have been identified we turn to ranking them. That is, we estimate the importance of each aspect with respect to the entity in a query-independent fashion and rank them accordingly. The obtained ranking can be interpreted as a distribution of prior probabilities over users' information needs on the entity and can be used on its own to, e.g., prioritize an entity display. For entity aspect recommendation, we recommend related aspects in the context of the entity given an entity-bearing query. We also study this problem in a context-aware setting, incorporating previous queries within the search session. Finally, for query recommendation we drop this restriction and include all queries in a session.

4. METHOD

In this section, we introduce our methods for each of the tasks introduced in the previous section.

4.1 Identifying entity aspects

To mine aspects for an entity, we first need to identify all queries Q_e that contain entity e from the query log using an annotation function λ_e. Since an entity may be referred to in various ways, we need an effective method for identifying entity mentions in web search queries. Since web search queries are typically short and not grammatically correct [31], we rely on a fairly simple method for entity linking that has been shown to obtain strong performance on such texts [23, 24]. In particular, for each query we generate all possible segmentations and link them to Wikipedia articles. Following [24], we use the CMNS method to generate a link for query segment s:

$$CMNS(e, s) = \frac{|H_{s,e}|}{\sum_{e'} |H_{s,e'}|},$$

where $H_{s,e}$ denotes the set of all links with anchor text s which points to target e in Wikipedia. We start with the longest possible query segments and recurse to smaller n-grams in case no entity mention is detected. In case a segment matches multiple entities, we take the most "common" sense, i.e., the one with the highest CMNS score. We do not specifically evaluate the performance of our linking method for queries in this paper. However, in a recent comprehensive comparison on entity linking for queries, CMNS proved to be a very strong unsupervised baseline for this task [4].

Now that we have the set of all queries containing entity e, we remove the mentions of e from the queries and use the remaining segments as *query contexts*. If the query contains more than one entity, we simply consider each entity on its own with the remainder of the query as its context. In this manner we obtain S_e, the set of all context segments which appear with entity e. We then cluster the contexts $s \in S_e$ such that context segments which have the same intent are grouped together. We consider the following features for clustering: *lexical*, *semantic*, and *click* similarity, covering spelling differences/errors, related words/synonyms, and behavioral information. Below we detail the specific methods for each.

Lexical similarity. We compute the lexical similarity between two query contexts using the Jaro-Winkler distance, computed as follows:

$$lex(s_i, s_j) = \begin{cases} 0 & \text{if } m = 0 \\ \frac{1}{3}\left(\frac{m}{|s_i|} + \frac{m}{|s_j|} + \frac{m-m'}{m}\right) & \text{otherwise,} \end{cases}$$

where m is the number of matching characters, and m' is half the number of transpositions between the two query context segments.

Semantic similarity. To compute the semantic similarity between two query contexts s_i and s_j, we use *word2vec* [25], sum the vectors of each term within the queries, and determine the cosine distance of the resulting vectors:

$$sem(s_i, s_j) = \frac{z(s_i) \cdot z(s_j)}{|z(s_i)| \cdot |z(s_j)|}, \quad (1)$$

where $z(s)$ is a function that calculates the semantic vector of s.

Click similarity. Beside lexical and semantic similarity, we also utilize click similarity. In particular, for each query context $s \in S_e$ we obtain all clicked hostnames for all queries containing e and s and combine them into a click vector. We then compute the click similarity between two query segments s_i and s_j using their cosine similarity:

$$click(s_i, s_j) = \frac{c_i \cdot c_j}{|c_i| \cdot |c_j|},$$

where c_i and c_j are click vectors of query s_i and s_j, respectively. The final segment similarity score is calculated by taking the maximum value of the similarity scores.

In order to cluster query contexts into entity aspects, we then employ Hierarchical Agglomerative Clustering (HAC) with complete linkage. We flatten the obtained hierarchical clusters so that for every object s_i, s_j belonging to the same cluster, $sim(s_i, s_j) \geq \theta$. By the end of this step, we have obtained the entity aspects A_e in the form of the query context clusters.

4.2 Ranking entity aspects

The main goal of entity aspect ranking is to estimate the importance of each aspect in the context of an entity in a query-independent fashion. Given an entity and its aspects as input, the output of this task is a list of aspects that is ranked according to their pertinence to the entity. We consider three methods for ranking aspects given an entity. The first model is based on maximum likelihood where we reward more frequently occurring aspects:

$$score_{MLE}(a, e) = \frac{\sum_{s \in a} n(s, e)}{\sum_{a'} \sum_{s \in a'} n(s, e)} \quad (2)$$

Here, $n(s, e)$ denotes the number of times query segment s is queried for in the context of e. Note that this method will not simply place clusters with most members at a higher rank, since there might be clusters with few members in which the members occur more frequently than in a large cluster.

The second model uses entropy-based scoring where we reward the most "stable" aspects using different time granularities including months, weeks, and days. For instance, in the case of days we partition the query log into daily chunks and count the number of times completion s is queried for in the context of e on that day. We then determine the entropy:

$$score_{E_d}(a, e) = \sum_{d \in D} P(a|d, e) \log_2 P(a|d, e), \quad (3)$$

where D is the set of all time units and $P(a|d, e)$ the probability of observing any $s \in a$ in the context of e on time interval d (we omit the minus sign in order to make these scores comparable). In another variant we determine the joint entropy, incorporating a factor $p(d|e)$:

$$score_{EJ_d}(a, e) = \sum_{d \in D} P(a, d|e) \log_2 P(a, d|e), \quad (4)$$

where $P(a, d|e)$ is the joint probability of observing any $s \in a$ and time interval d in the context of e.

The third and final model is based on language modeling and aims to rank aspects by how likely they are generated by a statistical language model based on a textual representation of the entity. More formally, we introduce the following three variants:

$$score_{LM}(a, e) = \prod_{s \in a} P(s|\theta_e)$$

$$score_{LM\text{-}avg}(a, e) = \frac{1}{|a|} \sum_{s \in a} P(s|\theta_e)$$

$$score_{LM\text{-}max}(a, e) = \max_{s \in a}(P(s|\theta_e)),$$

where $P(s|\theta_e)$ is determined using maximum likelihood estimation with Dirichlet smoothing:

$$P(s|\theta_e) = \prod_{t \in s} P(t|\theta_e) = \prod_{t \in s} \frac{n(t, r(e)) + \mu P(t)}{\sum_{t'} n(t', r(e)) + \mu}.$$

Here, $r(e)$ is the textual representation of e, for which we consider either the entity's Wikipedia article text, LMW, or the frequency-weighted aggregation of all queries leading to a click on the entity's Wikipedia article, LMC. $P(t)$ is the probability of term t estimated from all textual representations of the type at hand. We set μ to the default value of the average document length. Note that the main difference with the MLE method introduced earlier lies in the fact that the LM approaches are based on unigram term probabilities whereas the MLE estimates operate at the segment level.

4.3 Recommending entity aspects

The goal of this task is to recommend aspects related to the entity and aspect currently being queried. Given such an entity and aspect pair as input, the output of this task is a ranked list of aspects. We consider two methods for recommending entity aspects: a *semantic* and a *behavioral* approach. In the semantic approach, we determine the aspects' relatedness based on semantic similarity. In the behavioral approach, we estimate the relatedness from user sessions, inspired by the query-flow graph [5].

We use a graph-based representation for representing entity aspect relatedness. There are two motivations for this decision. First, having a graph-based representation allows the relatedness of the entity aspects to be computed offline. At retrieval time, we retrieve the candidates and rank them based on previously estimated relatedness. Secondly, having this data encoded as graph allows advanced graph-based compression and recommendation techniques to be applied in the future. We construct a different type of graph for each approach: an *aspect-semantic* graph and an *aspect-flow* graph, respectively.

4.3.1 Semantic approach

For the semantic approach we define the aspect-semantic graph for an entity e as an undirected graph $G_{as} = (V, L, w)$ where:

- The nodes are defined as the set of all aspects for e: $V = A_e$,
- $L \subseteq V \times V$ is the set of undirected edges, and
- $w : L \rightarrow (0, 1)$ is a weighting function that assigns a weight w to edges $l_{ij} \in L$.

We construct G_{as} using Algorithm 1 and compute the relatedness between two aspects a_i, a_j using:

$$sem(a_i, a_j) = \frac{z(a_i) \cdot z(a_j)}{|z(a_i)| \cdot |z(a_j)|}, \quad (5)$$

similar to (1). One main difference with (1) is that z is now computed from the mean of the semantic vectors of all query contexts belonging to a. If the relatedness score is above a threshold ϕ, we construct an edge between aspect a_i, and a_j and assign score as weight w_{ij}.

Algorithm 1 Constructing an aspect-semantic graph for e.

Input: Aspect list: A_e
Output: Aspect-semantic graph: G

$G \leftarrow initializeGraph(A_e)$
for each $a_i \in A$ **do**
  for each $a_j \in A$ **do**
    $w \leftarrow sem(a_i, a_j)$
    if $w > \phi$ **then**
      $e \leftarrow createEdge(a_i, a_j, w)$
      $G \leftarrow G \cup e$
    end if
  end for
end for

Algorithm 2 Constructing an aspect-flow graph for e.

Input: Aspect list: A_e, User sessions: H
Output: Aspect-flow graph: G

$G \leftarrow initializeGraph(A_e)$
for each $a_i \in A$ **do**
  for each $a_j \in A$ **do**
    $w \leftarrow adj(H, a_i, a_j)$
    if $w > \varphi$ **then**
      $e \leftarrow createDirectedEdge(a_i, a_j, w)$
      $G \leftarrow G \cup e$
    end if
  end for
end for

4.3.2 *Behavioral approach*

The second approach is based on the query-flow graph. Formally, we define an aspect-flow graph as a directed graph $G_{af} = (V, L, w)$ where:

- The set of nodes is $V = A_e \cup \{s, t\}$, i.e., the set of all aspects for e plus additional nodes s and t representing a starting state and a terminal state,
- $L \subseteq V \times V$ is the set of directed edges, and
- $w : L \rightarrow (0, 1)$ is a weighting function that assigns a weight w to edges $l_{ij} \in L$.

Here, we estimate the relatedness between query aspects from user sessions. We determine the relatedness from the adjacency of the aspects:

$$adj(H, a_i, a_j) = \sum_{h \in H} countAdjacent(h, a_i, a_j),$$

where $countAdjacent(h, a_i, a_j)$ denotes the frequency of query transitions of any query segment $s \in a_i$ to any segment in a_j found in the user session h, i.e., how often a_j follows a_i. We construct the aspect-flow graph for each entity with Algorithm 2. First, we construct a node for every aspect a that occurs in the user sessions, H. Then, for every pair of aspects (a_i, a_j), we compute their adjacency in H. We create an edge between two aspects a_i and a_j if the adjacency is above a threshold φ. We assign the adjacency count, normalized to transition probability, as the weight w_{ij}.

4.3.3 *Generating aspect recommendations*

We utilize the aspect-semantic graph G_{as} and aspect-flow graph G_{af} to generate recommendations for an input aspect a in the context of entity e. In the first variant, we generate aspect recommendations without a user session's context as detailed in Algorithm 3.

Algorithm 3 Aspect recommendation.

Input: Aspect graph: G, Input aspect: a
Output: Ranked aspects: R

$C \leftarrow getCandidatesFromNeighbors(G, a)$
for each $ca \in C$ **do**
  $score[ca] \leftarrow getWeight(G, a, ca)$
end for
$R \leftarrow rankCandidates(score)$

Algorithm 4 Context-aware aspect recommendation.

Input: Aspect graph: G, Input aspect: a, Search context: S
Output: Ranked aspects: R

$C \leftarrow getCandidatesFromNeighbors(G, a)$
for each $ca \in C$ **do**
  $score[ca] \leftarrow getWeight(G, a, ca)$
end for
for each $p \in S$ **do**
  $score_p \leftarrow decay(a, p) * getWeight(G, p, ca)$
  $score[ca] \leftarrow score[ca] + score_p$
end for
$R \leftarrow rankCandidates(score)$

Here, we retrieve candidate recommendations from all nodes adjacent to a in G. For G_{af}, we only retrieve neighboring nodes connected by the outgoing links from a.

We combine the output of both methods to improve the coverage and effectiveness of our recommendations. First, we combine the outputs with a simple round robin strategy, alternating the retrieval of recommendations from the behavioral and the semantic approach, respectively. The intuition is that the semantic method will be able to complement the behavioral method, since it will have higher coverage if constructed with a relatively low threshold ϕ. We also experiment with another combination method: *convex combination*. We retrieve the scores generated by the behavioral and semantic approaches and combine them with a weight λ:

$$score(a, a') = \lambda \cdot flow(a, a') + (1 - \lambda) \cdot semantic(a, a')$$

Since the scores are on a different scale, we perform *min-max normalization* to each score before combining them. Due to our graph construction process there might be cases where either method can not provide any score; for these we simply assign a zero score.

In a variant of this method, we incorporate context-awareness by looking at the previous queries in a user's search session as detailed in Algorithm 4. First, we retrieve the recommendation candidates from the neighbors of a in G. Then we compute initial recommendation scores for each of them and, lastly, we incorporate scores from any previous aspect a' within the search context S, dampened based on their distance:

$$decay(a, a') = \delta^{|a - a'|},$$

where δ is a decay constant, and $|a - a'|$ indicates the distance between a and a'. The distance is the number of aspects queried by the user between a and a' in the current session S.

4.3.4 *Generating query recommendations*

So far, we have focused on problems and approaches for ranking and recommending aspects involving the same entity. In this section, we detail how we leverage entity aspects for query recommendation in general. That is, recommending other entities, other entity aspects, or regular/non-entity queries for a given query. We

Algorithm 5 Generating query recommendation (QFG+A).

Input: Input query: q, Query graph: G
Output: Ranked recommendations: R

for each $q \in Q$ **do**
  $q* \leftarrow annotateQuery(q)$
  $n_q \leftarrow matchToNode(G, q*)$
  $S \leftarrow getCandidates(G, n)$
  for each $n_{ca} \in S$ **do**
    $score[n_{ca}] \leftarrow getWeight(G, n_q, n_{ca})$
  end for
  $R \leftarrow rankCandidates(score)$
end for

complement a state-of-the-art query recommendation method—the query-flow graph [5]—with information from the entity aspects.

We first apply the information from entity aspects when constructing the query-flow graph. We preserve all other queries that are not entity queries, thus forming the query nodes as in a regular query-flow graph. For an entity-bearing query q_e, we link all mentions of an entity e. Next, if the query contains additional query context, we extract the context segment s from q_e. Then, we match s to an appropriate aspect a in the aspect model A_e of e. We perform this matching by finding a which contains s as its cluster member. We collapse different mentions of the same entity into one entity node and collapse semantically-equivalent queries into one entity aspect node. This way, we obtain a "semanticized" query-flow graph.

Lastly, we introduce our recommendation method, detailed in Algorithm 5. For every input query, we perform entity linking of the query to detect entity bearing queries (the *annotateQuery* function). Next, we match an entity query to a node (the *matchToNode* function) with the similar procedure applied during graph construction. Regular queries will be matched straightforwardly. Lastly, we retrieve recommendation candidates from adjacent nodes, scored by their weights in the graph.

5. EXPERIMENTAL SETUP

In this section we detail our experimental setup, including the data we use, the relevance assessments,[1] and the metrics we employ. Our experiments below address the following research questions:

RQ1 When mining entity aspects, how do different similarity measures compare on the task of clustering queries in the context of an entity?

RQ2 How do different aspect ranking methods compare on the task of ranking entity aspects in a query-independent scenario?

RQ3 How do the semantic and behavioral approaches compare on the task of aspect recommendation?

RQ4 Does incorporating context improve aspect recommendation?

RQ5 Can we leverage the semantic information captured through entity aspects to improve the effectiveness of query recommendation built on top of the query-flow graph?

5.1 Experiments

To answer our research questions we set up 4 experiments, which we describe below. In our experiments we test for statistical significance using a paired t-test, indicating significantly better or worse results at the $p < 0.01$ level with ▲ and ▼ respectively.

[1]Our relevance assessments and editorial guidelines are available at `http://ridhorei.github.io/entity-aspects/`.

Evaluating mining entity aspects. In this experiment, aimed at answering RQ1, we evaluate the quality of the extracted entity aspects by manually evaluating the generated clusters. We use a set of 50 entities sampled from user logs in a stratified fashion. That is, we bias the sample such that more popular entities are more likely to be included. We then extract the query completions for each entity over a period of time from the *dev-contexts* collection (introduced in the next section). To obtain ground truth data we manually cluster the query segments by grouping those that represent the same aspect together. To evaluate the quality of each entity aspect we employ commonly used cluster quality metrics: B-cubed recall (B-recall), precision (B-precision), and F1 (B-F1) [1].

Evaluating ranking entity aspects. The second experiment is aimed at answering RQ2. Since manually evaluating aspect rankings for entities without any explicit query is not straightforward, we resort to automatic evaluation. We propose an automatic evaluation based on what we call "underspecified" entity queries, that is, queries that contain only an entity. We rely on the assumption that a good aspect ranking is one that, on average, best satisfies users that issue such underspecified entity queries. Specifically, we consider sessions that contain an underspecified entity query and aim to predict any subsequent queries that again contain the entity, plus additional query terms.

For this experiment we consider one month of query logs (the *test-aspect-ranking* collection) that is disjoint from any log data used for training). Because of this disjointness there might be aspects that our method is unable to predict, simply because they have not been seen before. This includes spelling variants, reformulations, and new aspects. In our experiments below we do keep them as relevant samples in the evaluation data in order to mimic a real-life setting as closely as possible.

We consider the following setup: we aim to predict the next query a user issues in a session, only considering pairs of adjacent entity-bearing queries in the session where the second query contains the same entity plus additional query terms. We then observe at which position our method ranks this subsequent query and score it accordingly. Since we only have pairs of queries and thus only one relevant suggestion for each, we report on mean reciprocal rank (MRR) and success rate (SR).

Evaluating recommending entity aspects. The third experiment is aimed at answering RQ3 and RQ4. Here, we evaluate the effectiveness of recommending entities and aspects in the context of a user session and constituent queries. We follow a similar evaluation approach to the ranking task above, i.e., we consider the next query in the session as the target to predict. As such we again report on mean reciprocal rank (MRR) and success rate (SR).

Since detecting entity-dominated sessions is not trivial, we simulate them through the following procedure. First, we extend the session demarcation boundary, effectively merging the sessions belonging to the same user within a 3-day timeframe (the *test-aspect-recommendation* collection). Then, we consider the first entity within these extended user sessions as the reference entity and evaluate the recommendation methods by their effectiveness in predicting subsequent aspects of the entity throughout the remainder of the session. This setup reflects recommending related entity aspects for complex search tasks in the context of an entity.

Evaluating query recommendation. Our fourth and final experiment addresses query recommendation and is aimed at answering RQ5. Here we evaluate actual query pair predictions, following the automatic evaluation method from [34]. We sample 1,000,000 query sessions from the query logs of a commercial search engine (the *test-query-recommendation* collection) and extract pairs of adjacent queries from the sessions. Queries belonging to same entity aspect are treated as equivalent queries during evaluation. We evaluate this approach in two configurations: looking at all queries within the sessions (*all-pairs*), and using only the first and last queries (*first-last pairs*). Furthermore, we also differentiate between using all query pair occurrences (allowing possible duplicates of popular queries pairs) and using distinct occurrences only. Our main evaluation metrics for this experiment are again mean reciprocal rank (MRR) and success rate (SR). To gain additional insights, we also look at the fraction of correct predictions at different recommendations cut-off levels: 100 and 10.

5.2 Experimental data and settings

We use two sources of data for training and testing, including user logs of the Yahoo web search engine as well as the AOL query logs. From the former we sample a number of datasets. All the development and test datasets that we use are disjoint, i.e., they are sampled from non-overlapping time periods. The *dev-contexts* dataset is a large, 1-year query log sample containing queries that we use to build the full aspect model for our set of entities. The *dev-clicks* dataset is a 1-month sample used to compute click similarity for the context terms. We build our query-flow graph and the aspect-flow graph on the *dev-flow* dataset (a 1-month sample). The test datasets, *test-aspect-ranking*, *test-aspect-recommendation*, *test-query-recommendation*, are all 1-month samples and unseen query logs that are used in our automatic evaluation methods for our second, third, and fourth experiment, respectively. In addition, we also utilize the publicly available AOL dataset in our second experiment. This last dataset includes queries sampled from March 2006 until May 2006.

We define navigational queries as queries that are in the top-40% in terms of the number of pageviews and that also lead to a click on the top search result in at least 40% of the cases. We detect and subsequently discard navigational queries based on this heuristic.

We perform entity linking and context term extraction using the method described in Section 4.1. Below we focus on Wikipedia entities and we leave using other entity repositories for future work. In order to reduce data sparseness we remove entities that occur in less than 100 queries. This results in a set of about 75k entities of interest.

Our approach involves several parameters. The first parameter, θ is the similarity threshold used for clustering. From a preliminary experiment on held-out data, we obtain the optimal value of $\theta = 0.75$. For the minimum relatedness score in the construction of the aspect-semantic graph, we set $\phi = 0.1$. Following the common practice in constructing a query-flow graph [5, 7], we retain only transitions that appear at least two times, thus $\varphi = 1$. After a preliminary experiment, we set $\lambda = 0.85$ when combining the semantic and flow scores. The decay parameter is set to $\delta = 0.85$.

6. EXPERIMENTAL RESULTS

In this section we answer the research questions presented in the previous section.

6.1 Mining aspects

Our first experiment concerns mining entity aspects. We start by evaluating the quality of each cluster and then zoom in on the aspects generated during the mining process. Table 2 presents the results of using different matching strategies to cluster query context terms into entity aspects. Recall that we perform complete-linkage clustering with a parameter θ as threshold for grouping objects.

Table 2: Entity aspect mining results. Significance is tested against the lexical method (row 1).

Method	B-Recall	B-Precision	B-F1
Lexical	0.9164	0.8258	0.8338
Semantic	0.9452▲	0.7744▼	0.8117▼
Click	0.8977	0.6666▼	0.6880▼
Lexical + semantic	0.9216	0.8629▲	0.8607▲
Lexical + click	0.8480▼	0.8155▼	0.7842▼
Semantic + click	0.8686▼	0.7788▼	0.7680▼
Lexical + semantic + click	0.8558▼	0.8465▲	0.8098▼

Table 3: Entity aspect mining: clustering output for entity *Paris Saint-Germain F.C.*.

Cluster	Context terms
1	*real, real madrid vs, vs real madrid, real madrid*
2	*results*
3	*live, live streaming, live stream*
4	*guingamp*
5	*match*
6	*highlights*
7	*transfert*
8	*2013*
9	*monaco, monaco direct, monaco streaming*
10	*om, regarder om*
11	*streaming, en streaming*
12	*barca, barca vs*
13	*barcelona, barcelone*
14	*barcelona vs*
15	*anderlecht*

First, we look at the results of individual similarity measures. As we can see, using just lexical matching already results in a fairly good B-cubed recall and precision score. This can be explained by the fact that the lexical matching strategy allows minor changes caused by spelling variants or spelling errors, and is successful in performing clustering on these cases. Semantic similarity achieves higher recall at the cost of precision. This means that the clustering method with the current threshold clusters the object aggressively, for example, grouping aspects such as "daughter" and "mother" together. Click similarity has the lowest precision compared to the other two measures for reasons that we will explain below.

Although lexical similarity provides a good start, this strategy fails to group queries that are semantically related. Thus, combining it with semantic similarity improves recall and precision. This combination proves to be the best performing one, compared to using individual measure and all measures.

Adding click similarity with our current strategy does not work well. Upon closer inspection, we find that a lot of unrelated query contexts point to the same host name. For example, contexts related to an entertainer's news are often directed to the same entertainment site. Therefore, combining clicks with other measures tends to brings down the performance, in particular precision.

Table 3 shows sample output generated by our aspect mining method for the entity *Paris Saint-Germain F.C.* (a Parisian soccer club). Our manually created clusters are shown in Table 4. The aspect mining produces more clusters than the ground truth. The method fails to group "barca, barca vs, barcelona, barcelone, barcelona vs." instead making three clusters from them. With such short strings, the pairwise Jaro-Winkler distance between two objects is bigger than the threshold, thus preventing the objects from

Table 4: Entity aspect mining: clustering ground truth for entity *Paris Saint-Germain F.C.*.

Cluster	Context terms
1	*read, real madrid vs, vs real madrid, real madrid*
2	*results*
3	*live, live streaming, live stream, streaming, en streaming*
4	*guingamp*
5	*match*
6	*highlights*
7	*transfert*
8	*2013*
9	*monaco, monaco direct, monaco streaming*
10	*om, regarder om*
11	*barca, barca vs, barcelona, barcelone, barcelona vs*
12	*anderlecht*

being clustered with complete linkage. Also, in some cases the lexical clustering method groups queries that should not be clustered together because they represent different intent/vertical. For instance, two separate clusters ("monaco") and ("monaco direct, monaco streaming") should be created instead of putting them together in a single cluster.

Next, we look at the different types of aspect that occur in the context of our example entity *Paris Saint-Germain F.C.*. Many of the aspects refer to a fairly common *transactional* intent for a football club such as "live streaming". Other sets of intents are *relational*, which concerns the relationship of the topic entity with other entities (in this case, other football clubs). Another set of intents are *categorical*, that is, they deal with type-related intents, e.g., "results," "match" "highlights" and "transfers." The last aspect we observe concerns attempts to find something related to a certain time point, such as "2013".

To conclude this section, we formulate our answer to our first research question RQ1. Combining lexical and semantic similarity measures performs best on the task of clustering query context terms for entity aspect mining and we select this method for the remaining experiments. Integrating click similarity tend to hurt performance, particularly precision.

6.2 Ranking entity aspects

Our second experiment evaluates the importance of each aspect with respect to the entity in a query-independent setting. The results of this experiment is displayed in Tables 5 and 6. From these tables we observe consistent results across the two datasets. First, the simple maximum likelihood approach already performs quite well, thus providing a good baseline. The entropy-based methods, in particular using month as time units, achieve the best performance overall, outperforming maximum likelihood and language modeling approaches. We further observe that the absolute scores on the AOL dataset are lower overall which is mainly due to the disjointness nature of the query logs that we use to mine the aspects with the queries in the AOL logs.

We use different granularities of time-slices, and experiment with two variant of entropy-based methods. For the baseline MLE approach, we simply use the aspect popularity over the whole range of our main query logs that is used for mining (1 year of data). The different granularities do not really show much difference in terms of performance, although computing entropy on the monthly data provides a slight edge.

Table 5: Entity aspect ranking: results on *test-aspect-ranking*. Significance is tested against the MLE baseline (row 1).

	MRR	SR
MLE	0.1931	0.1110
E_{days}	0.2013▲	0.1149▲
E_{weeks}	0.2015▲	0.1139▲
E_{months}	0.2031▲	0.1162▲
EJ_{days}	0.2020▲	0.1208▲
EJ_{weeks}	0.2048▲	0.1259▲
EJ_{months}	0.2052▲	0.1262▲
LMW	0.0431▼	0.0135▼
LMW_{avg}	0.0657▼	0.0200▼
LMW_{max}	0.0583▼	0.0170▼
LMC	0.0488▼	0.0176▼
LMC_{avg}	0.0859▼	0.0313▼
LMC_{max}	0.0755▼	0.0259▼

There are several possible reasons why language modeling does not work well for this task. First, it is the only approach that does not include any query popularity or frequency information. Secondly, what users search for does not always align with what Wikipedia editors may put in a Wikipedia article—which is in line with previous research [37]. This may result in a so-called knowledge base gap where a user is searching for an important fact that is not included on a Wikipedia article yet. In our case, this may result in low scores with the language modeling approach. Lastly, the fact that the language model based approaches are unigram-based, while the other methods are segment-based might also contribute to the lower scores.

We also considered a second experimental variant where we look for entity-bearing query pairs in the whole session. That is, we discard any non-entity bearing queries in between. We find that the scores using this variant are comparable to those reported here.

It is important to note that we compare a different and diverse set of features, with appropriate functions defined for each type of features. However, since the previous step (clustering query contexts into aspects) are kept constant across method, we argue that this comparison is still valuable despite having to compare the combination of features and functions simultaneously. The end-to-end aspect ranking scores should be comparable.

In conclusion, the results show that ranking entity aspects can be done successfully, resulting in sensible absolute MRR and SR scores and we find that entropy-based methods are the best in ranking entity aspects in a query-independent scenario.

6.3 Recommending aspects

Our third experiment evaluates the quality of recommending entity aspects within a session, comparing the semantic and behavioral approaches. The results are shown in Tables 7 and 8. Overall, we see that the behavioral aspect-flow approach outperforms the purely semantic approach. When combined, they give the best performance. In our experiments, we experiment with a round-robin and a convex approach to combine the results.

Upon looking at the graphs created by both methods, we see that the semantic method tends to generate larger graphs, thus attaining more coverage. This is not surprising since the flow graph is only constructed with a single month of data. Despite the sparsity and lack of coverage, the behavioral flow-based approach still manages to outperform the semantic approach, providing better quality rec-

Table 6: **Entity aspect ranking: results on the AOL dataset. Significance is tested against the MLE baseline (row 1).**

	MRR	SR
MLE	0.0647	0.0340
E_{days}	0.0710▲	0.0383▲
E_{weeks}	0.0712▲	0.0376▲
E_{months}	0.0709▲	0.0376▲
EJ_{days}	0.0684▲	0.0383▲
EJ_{weeks}	0.0692▲	0.0394▲
EJ_{month}	0.0692▲	0.0395▲
LMW	0.0328▼	0.0132▼
LMW_{avg}	0.0457▼	0.0190▼
LMW_{max}	0.0426▼	0.0170▼
LMC	0.0341▼	0.0146▼
LMC_{avg}	0.0499▼	0.0219▼
LMC_{max}	0.0466▼	0.0195▼

Table 7: Aspect recommendation: results. Significance is tested against row 1.

Method	MRR	SR
Aspect-semantic	0.0431	0.0244
Aspect-flow	0.0602▲	0.0451▲
Aspect-combined-rr	0.0674▲	0.0486▲
Aspect-combined-convex ($\lambda = 0.85$)	0.0650▲	0.0465▲

ommendations overall. Both combination approaches succesfully improve over the individual approaches.

As for incorporating user session context (Table 8), we observe that the semantic approach gains a small improvement by incorporating previous queries in the search context. However, the flow-based approach performs slightly worse when previous query is taken into account. This is related to the sparsity/lack of transition data on the flow-based approach. The size of the context have little effect in the current adjancency-based recommendation setup. In conclusion, we find that the behavioral approach is better than the semantic approach for recommending entity aspects, and they can be combined to generate better recommendations.

6.4 Recommending queries

In this section we investigate whether our aspect model can help to complement the query-flow graph for generic query recommendation. Table 9 shows the result of predicting all queries within the sampled user sessions (*all-pairs*). Table 10 shows the results of using the first query as input to predict only the last query of a session (which can be considered as yielding the desired results).

In the *all-pairs* prediction setup, we see that the aspect-based query recommendation method (labeled *QFG+A* in the table) successfully improves upon the baseline query-flow graph in terms of predictions coverage and ranking. The improvement is small, but consistent and significant across the two different configurations of our experiment. Overall, we achieve around 1% improvement on the correct prediction's coverage. For ranking, our method achieves slightly better mean reciprocal rank and average position of the target query (averaged for correct predictions at the top-100). Considering the large number of queries, these improvements are quite substantial. The improvements become more pronounced as we look at the unique query occurrences rather than all occurrences.

We notice consistent results in the *first-last* experiment also. Improvements in terms of prediction coverage are around 1%, while the ranking also shows consistent and significant improvements.

Table 8: Aspect recommendation: results of context aware experiment where m denotes the context size, i.e., the number of queries used as context. Significance is tested against row 1 of each group.

Method	MRR	SR
Aspect-semantic	0.0431	0.0244
CA-aspect-semantic ($m = 3$)	0.0436▲	0.0248▲
CA-aspect-semantic ($m = 10$)	0.0436▲	0.0248▲
Aspect-flow	0.0602	0.0451
CA-aspect-flow ($m = 3$)	0.0583▼	0.0438▼
CA-aspect-flow ($m = 10$)	0.0583▼	0.0438▼

Table 9: Query recommendation: results on the *all-pairs* dataset for each configuration.

	all occurrences	
	QFG	QFG+A
% pairs in all	0.111	0.123
% pairs in top-100	0.076	0.084
% pairs in top-10	0.042	0.047
% pairs in top-1 (SR)	0.015	0.016
MRR	0.024	0.026
avg. position	20.38	20.09
	unique occurrences	
	QFG	QFG+A
% pairs in all	0.108	0.130
% pairs in top-100	0.070	0.088
% pairs in top-10	0.039	0.048
% pairs in top-1 (SR)	0.013	0.015
MRR	0.021	0.026
avg. position	20.57	20.01

7. CONCLUSION

In this paper we have considered common information access tasks in the context of entity-oriented web search. In particular, we have developed and evaluated methods for mining entity aspects, ranking their importance, and recommending them directly or leveraging them for query recommendation. We have done so through linking entities within queries, extracting the query context terms, and clustering them together into entity aspects if they refer to the same intent.

The first step, mining entity aspects involves extracting common queries in the context of an entity and grouping them based on their similarity. We find that combining the *lexical* and *semantic* matching strategies performs best for this task. In the next step we rank the obtained entity aspects for each entity in a query-independent fashion using three strategies: *maximum likelihood*, *entropy*, and *language modeling*. In the maximum likelihood method, we reward more frequently occurring aspects. In the entropy-based methods, we aim to reward aspects that are stable over time. With the language modeling methods, we estimate the probability that the aspect is generated from a statistical unigram language model of the entity. We find that the entropy-based methods yield the best performance. The third task that we consider is aspect recommendation. That is, given an entity and a certain aspect as input, recommend related aspects. For this we consider two approaches, *semantic* and *behavioral*, and find that the latter provides superior results. In our final task we leverage entity aspects for actual query recommendation. Here we normalize a query graph into a semantic query graph, and use the entity aspects as an additional source of infor-

Table 10: Query recommendation: results on the *first-last* dataset for each configuration.

	all occurrences	
	QFG	QFG+A
% pairs in all	0.147	0.165
% pairs in top-100	0.097	0.110
% pairs in top-10	0.055	0.062
% pairs in top-1 (SR)	0.019	0.021
MRR	0.031	0.034
avg. position	19.20	18.98
	unique occurrences	
	QFG	QFG+A
% pairs in all	0.104	0.126
% pairs in top-100	0.062	0.079
% pairs in top-10	0.031	0.041
% pairs in top-1 (SR)	0.009	0.011
MRR	0.016	0.021
avg. position	21.84	20.90

mation for query recommendation. We find that resolving entities and grouping queries into aspects helps to improve query recommendation in a semantic way, by addressing the sparsity of queries and improving the diversity of recommendations.

As to future work, we would like to extend the study in the following directions. First, we would like to experiment with more advanced graph-based compression and recommendation methods for query recommendation. Secondly, we would like to incorporate more features and study the performance of aspect mining in an even larger-scale setting. Next, just as some entity relations are known to be fluent [30], we would like to study the temporality of the entity aspects. Finally, we would like to the see whether the different aspect ranking methods perform differently per entity type, or per different query triggers, distinguishing e.g., actual user inputs with auto-completions and related searches.

Acknowledgments. This research was supported by the European Community's Seventh Framework Programme (FP7/2007-2013) under grant agreement nr 312827 (VOX-Pol), the Netherlands Organisation for Scientific Research (NWO) under project nrs 727.011.005, 612.001.116, HOR-11-10, 640.006.013, 612.066.930, CI-14-25, SH-322-15, Amsterdam Data Science, the Dutch national program COMMIT, the ESF Research Network Program ELIAS, the Elite Network Shifts project funded by the Royal Dutch Academy of Sciences (KNAW), the Netherlands eScience Center under project nr 027.012.105, the Yahoo! Faculty Research and Engagement Program, the Microsoft Research PhD program, and the HPC Fund.

8. REFERENCES

[1] E. Amigó, J. Gonzalo, J. Artiles, and F. Verdejo. A comparison of extrinsic clustering evaluation metrics based on formal constraints. *Inf. Retr.*, 12(4):461–486, 2009.

[2] N. Balasubramanian and S. Cucerzan. Topic pages: An alternative to the ten blue links. In *IEEE-ICSC 2010*, 2010.

[3] R. Blanco, B. B. Cambazoglu, P. Mika, and N. Torzec. Entity recommendations in web search. In *ISWC '13*, 2013.

[4] R. Blanco, G. Ottaviano, and E. Meij. Fast and space-efficient entity linking for queries. In *WSDM '15*, 2015.

[5] P. Boldi, F. Bonchi, C. Castillo, D. Donato, A. Gionis, and S. Vigna. The query-flow graph: Model and applications. In *CIKM '08*, 2008.

[6] F. Bonchi, R. Perego, F. Silvestri, H. Vahabi, and R. Venturini. Efficient query recommendations in the long tail via center-piece subgraphs. In *SIGIR '12*, 2012.

[7] I. Bordino, G. De Francisci Morales, I. Weber, and F. Bonchi. From Machu Picchu to rafting the Urubamba River: Anticipating information needs via the entity-query graph. In *WSDM '13*, 2013.

[8] J. C. K. Cheung and X. Li. Sequence clustering and labeling for unsupervised query intent discovery. In *WSDM '12*, 2012.

[9] A. Chuklin, P. Serdyukov, and M. de Rijke. Using intent information to model user behavior in diversified search. In *ECIR '13*, 2013.

[10] H. Feild and J. Allan. Task-aware query recommendation. In *SIGIR '13*, 2013.

[11] A. Hassan Awadallah, R. W. White, P. Pantel, S. T. Dumais, and Y.-M. Wang. Supporting complex search tasks. In *CIKM '14*, 2014.

[12] L. Hollink, P. Mika, and R. Blanco. Web usage mining with semantic analysis. In *WWW '13*, 2013.

[13] Y. Hu, Y. Qian, H. Li, D. Jiang, J. Pei, and Q. Zheng. Mining query subtopics from search log data. In *SIGIR '12*, 2012.

[14] R. Jones and K. L. Klinkner. Beyond the session timeout: Automatic hierarchical segmentation of search topics in query logs. In *CIKM '08*, 2008.

[15] L. Li, H. Deng, A. Dong, Y. Chang, and H. Zha. Identifying and labeling search tasks via query-based hawkes processes. In *SIGKDD '14*, 2014.

[16] Y. Li, B.-J. P. Hsu, and C. Zhai. Unsupervised identification of synonymous query intent templates for attribute intents. In *CIKM '13*, 2013.

[17] Y. Li, B.-J. P. Hsu, C. Zhai, and K. Wang. Mining entity attribute synonyms via compact clustering. In *CIKM '13*, 2013.

[18] Z. Liao, Y. Song, L.-w. He, and Y. Huang. Evaluating the effectiveness of search task trails. In *WWW '12*, 2012.

[19] T. Lin, P. Pantel, M. Gamon, A. Kannan, and A. Fuxman. Active objects: Actions for entity-centric search. In *WWW '12*, 2012.

[20] C. Lucchese, S. Orlando, R. Perego, F. Silvestri, and G. Tolomei. Identifying task-based sessions in search engine query logs. In *WSDM '11*, 2011.

[21] C. Lucchese, S. Orlando, R. Perego, F. Silvestri, and G. Tolomei. Discovering tasks from search engine query logs. *ACM Trans. Inf. Syst.*, 31(3):14:1–14:43, Aug. 2013.

[22] C. Lucchese, S. Orlando, R. Perego, F. Silvestri, and G. Tolomei. Modeling and predicting the task-by-task behavior of search engine users. In *OAIR '13*, 2013.

[23] E. Meij, M. Bron, L. Hollink, B. Huurnink, and M. de Rijke. Mapping queries to the linking open data cloud: A case study using dbpedia. *Web Semantics: Science, Services and Agents on the World Wide Web*, 9(4):418–433, 2011.

[24] E. Meij, W. Weerkamp, and M. de Rijke. Adding semantics to microblog posts. In *WSDM 2012*, 2012.

[25] T. Mikolov, I. Sutskever, K. Chen, G. Corrado, and J. Dean. Distributed representations of words and phrases and their compositionality. *CoRR*, abs/1310.4546, 2013.

[26] P. Pantel and A. Fuxman. Jigs and lures: Associating web queries with structured entities. In *ACL '11*, 2011.

[27] P. Pantel, T. Lin, and M. Gamon. Mining entity types from query logs via user intent modeling. In *ACL'12*, 2012.

[28] M. Pasca and B. Van Durme. What you seek is what you get: Extraction of class attributes from query logs. In *IJCAI'07*, 2007.

[29] J. Pound, P. Mika, and H. Zaragoza. Ad-hoc object retrieval in the web of data. In *WWW '10*, pages 771–780, 2010.

[30] R. Reinanda and M. de Rijke. Prior-informed distant supervision for temporal evidence classification. In *Proceedings of COLING 2014*, 2014.

[31] U. Sawant and S. Chakrabarti. Learning joint query interpretation and response ranking. In *WWW '13*, 2013.

[32] W. Song, Q. Yu, Z. Xu, T. Liu, S. Li, and J.-R. Wen. Multi-aspect query summarization by composite query. In *SIGIR '12*, 2012.

[33] D. Spina, E. Meij, M. de Rijke, A. Oghina, M. T. Bui, and M. Breuss. Identifying entity aspects in microblog posts. In *SIGIR '12*, 2012.

[34] I. Szpektor, A. Gionis, and Y. Maarek. Improving recommendation for long-tail queries via templates. In *WWW '11*, 2011.

[35] M. Verma and E. Yilmaz. Entity oriented task extraction from query logs. In *CIKM '14*, 2014.

[36] H. Wang, Y. Song, M.-W. Chang, X. He, R. W. White, and W. Chu. Learning to extract cross-session search tasks. In *WWW '13*, 2013.

[37] F. Wu, J. Madhavan, and A. Halevy. Identifying aspects for web-search queries. *J. Artif. Int. Res.*, 40(1):677–700, 2011.

[38] X. Yin and S. Shah. Building taxonomy of web search intents for name entity queries. In *WWW '10*, 2010.

Bayesian Ranker Comparison Based on Historical User Interactions

Artem Grotov
a.grotov@uva.nl

Shimon Whiteson
s.a.whiteson@uva.nl

Maarten de Rijke
derijke@uva.nl

University of Amsterdam, Amsterdam, The Netherlands

ABSTRACT

We address the problem of how to safely compare rankers for information retrieval. In particular, we consider how to control the risks associated with switching from an existing *production ranker* to a new *candidate ranker*. Whereas existing online comparison methods require showing potentially suboptimal result lists to users during the comparison process, which can lead to user frustration and abandonment, our approach only requires user interaction data generated through the natural use of the production ranker. Specifically, we propose a Bayesian approach for (1) comparing the production ranker to candidate rankers and (2) estimating the confidence of this comparison. The comparison of rankers is performed using click model-based information retrieval metrics, while the confidence of the comparison is derived from Bayesian estimates of uncertainty in the underlying click model. These confidence estimates are then used to determine whether a risk-averse decision criterion for switching to the candidate ranker has been satisfied. Experimental results on several learning to rank datasets and on a click log show that the proposed approach outperforms an existing ranker comparison method that does not take uncertainty into account.

Categories and Subject Descriptors

H.3.3 [**Information Storage and Retrieval**]: Information Search and Retrieval

Keywords

Ranker evaluation; Learning to rank; Click models

1. INTRODUCTION

Comparing rankers is an essential problem in information retrieval. In an industrial setting, an existing *production ranker* must often be compared to a new *candidate ranker* to determine whether to replace the former with the latter. Practical constraints make it difficult to make such decisions well. Because the performance of the candidate ranker is unknown, trying it out to gather data about its performance is often too risky: if it proves to be substantially inferior to the production ranker, the user experience may degrade, leading to abandonment. However, existing historical data (typically collected using the production ranker) may not be sufficiently informative about the candidate ranker. Hence, decisions about when to switch to the candidate ranker that are based on such data can be erroneous, also leading to a degraded user experience.

Controlling the risks associated with switching to a candidate ranker requires ranker comparison methods that can (1) estimate the performance of the production and candidate rankers using only historical data, and (2) quantify their uncertainty about such estimates. Quantification of uncertainty is essential for controlling risk because it enables system designers to switch to a candidate ranker only when they are highly confident that its performance will not be substantially worse than that of the production ranker.

Existing ranker evaluation methods do not fully meet these requirements. Traditional methods rely on explicit relevance labels provided by human assessors to measure metrics such as Normalized Discounted Cumulative Gain (NDCG) and Mean Average Precision (MAP) [20]. However, such labels are expensive to obtain and may not reflect the preferences of real users. Click-based approaches overcome these limitations by estimating performance from the implicit signals in users' click behavior, using A/B testing or interleaving experiments [5, 6, 12, 13, 15, 16, 18, 19, 21]. Nonetheless, these methods typically require trying out the candidate ranker to gain data about it, which, as mentioned above, may be too risky. While interleaving methods have been developed that use importance sampling to estimate ranker performance given only historical data [14], they have limited generalization properties and require historical data to be gathered stochastically.

Click models [3, 10], i.e., probabilistic models of user behavior, can also estimate ranker performance given only historical data [7] and do not share these limitations. The uncertainty in the resulting estimates depends on the relationship between the historical data and the rankers to be evaluated. E.g., if a candidate ranker differs from the production ranker only in that it swaps a lowly ranked but relevant document with a highly ranked but irrelevant one, then the click model can confidently conclude that the candidate ranker is better so long as the historical data shows which of the two documents is relevant. It can do so even if the result lists containing such a swap do not appear in the historical data. By contrast, if the candidate ranker gives a high rank to a document that does not appear in the historical data, then its relevance cannot be estimated with confidence. A key limitation of existing click models is that they do not distinguish between cases such as these. Because they do not quantify their uncertainty about the comparisons they perform, they cannot judge whether the information in the logs is sufficient to compare rankers. Only methods that can measure the confidence of the performed comparisons can be used to safely decide whether to switch from the production ranker to a candidate one.

SIGIR'15, August 09 - 13, 2015, Santiago, Chile.

ACM 978-1-4503-3621-5/15/08 ...$15.00.
DOI: http://dx.doi.org/10.1145/2766462.2767730.

We present *Bayesian Ranker Comparison* (BARACO), a click model-based approach to ranker evaluation that compares the performance of ranker pairs using only historical data and quantifies the uncertainty in such comparisons. The key novelty lies in maintaining a full posterior distribution over the relevance of documents for queries. This posterior is used to estimate the probability that the candidate ranker's performance is not substantially worse than that of the production ranker. By switching to the candidate ranker only when this probability is sufficiently high, the risks associated with switching can be controlled in a principled way.

BARACO is able to estimate not only the probability of a candidate ranker being as good as the production ranker, but also the expected difference in performance between two rankers. Measuring the expected difference can be useful in practice, e.g., to select a single ranker from a set of candidates, all of which have a high probability of beating the production ranker.

We present the results of an empirical evaluation on several learning to rank datasets and on a real click log published by Yandex that compares BARACO to an existing non-Bayesian click model-based ranker evaluation method that estimates only the expected difference in performance between ranker pairs, without quantifying uncertainty. We addresses the following research questions:

RQ1 Can BARACO determine whether the production ranker should be replaced with a candidate ranker better than the non-Bayesian baseline?

RQ2 Does BARACO produce better estimates of the difference in performance of the rankers than the non-Bayesian baseline?

Our results show that BARACO has better performance than the baseline method and can identify more good rankers in a set of candidates more reliably. In addition, the full Bayesian approach enables the production of more precise estimates of the expected differences between rankers than the baseline method.

2. RELATED WORK

Ranker evaluation has long been a central topic in information retrieval. The classical approach is to perform offline evaluation based on the Cranfield paradigm [8, 20], where a collection of documents is manually annotated by human experts. A representative set of queries together with associated user intents are crafted by a group of experts. Then, for each query, documents in the collection are assigned relevance labels. The documents and their relevance labels can then be used in metrics such as NDCG. This approach is widely used, well understood, and benefits from controlled laboratory settings. But it is expensive and assessors' relevance judgements may not adequately reflect real users' opinions.

Online evaluation is a family of techniques that addresses these difficulties by letting users be the judges. In A/B testing [16], the user population is split into two groups, and pairs of rankers are compared by presenting one group with one ranker and the other group with another ranker. The ranker with the best performance on a selected metric (such as CTR) is typically considered to be the winner [16]. Another approach is interleaved comparison: search engine result pages (SERPs) presented to users are obtained by interleaving SERPs of two competing rankers under consideration. The user feedback in the form of clicks is then interpreted as user preference for one ranker over the other [19]. The key problem of online methods is that they require user feedback to evaluate each pair of rankers, which often requires exposing suboptimal SERPs. Consequently, they may be too risky for many real-world settings.

Interleaving methods that exploit importance sampling [14] provide a way to compare rankers using only historical click data. However, importance sampling requires that the source distribution is non-zero everywhere where the target distribution is non-zero (i.e., every SERP that can result from interleaving has a non-zero probability of occurring in the historical data), a requirement that is often not met in practice. Importance sampling guarantees only that the resulting estimator is unbiased, not that it has low variance: the addition of more historical data is not guaranteed to improve estimates, as new data can actually increase the variance [1]. Additionally, importance sampling has poor generalization properties compared to click-based approaches that infer relevance labels of documents. In particular, the latter can generalize across SERPs that differ in the order of documents, while the former cannot.

In recent years, a number of probabilistic models have been developed to describe, understand, and predict user behavior while interacting with an IR system. In particular, click models such as DBN [3], DCM [10] and UBM [9] infer the relevance of documents for queries and model user clicks on documents in the SERP by analysing search engine log files. These inferred relevance labels can be further used for learning to rank [3] and for ranker comparisons using click model-based metrics [7]. However, to our knowledge, none of these approaches provide a way to quantify the uncertainty in the resulting comparison, which is critical for making informed decisions about when to switch from a production ranker to a candidate ranker. For metrics such as EBU [23], ERR [4] and the utility and effort based metrics in [2, 7], the effect on the comparison of a document seen just once and that of one seen a hundred of times is the same, given that the inferred relevance labels have the same value. Furthermore, these metrics do not take into account the number of previously unseen documents that appear in the SERPs produced by the candidate rankers. Hence, these approaches cannot properly control the risks associated with switching to a candidate ranker, as the uncertainty in the comparison is not measured.

We present a new approach to ranker evaluation that is designed to overcome these limitations. It compares rankers using only the log files collected through natural user interactions with the production ranker. In contrast to importance sampling based interleaving methods [14], our method does not require the data to be obtained stochastically. In contrast to the metrics in [2, 4, 7, 23], our method takes into account the uncertainty associated with the inferred relevance labels and the presence of unseen documents and measures the confidence of the resulting comparison.

3. PROBLEM SETTING

We consider two related problems. The first is the *Switching Problem*: deciding whether or not to switch from a production ranker R_p to a candidate ranker R_c. The second is the *Difference Estimation Problem*: estimating the expected difference in performance between the production ranker R_p and candidate ranker R_c.

The Switching Problem is as follows. System designers must decide whether or not to switch from a production ranker R_p to a candidate ranker R_c. They are willing to do so only if they are highly confident that the candidate ranker is at least almost as good as the production ranker, i.e., if

$$p(M_c + \epsilon \geq M_p) \geq 1 - \delta, \quad (1)$$

where M_p and M_c are the expected performance of the production and candidate ranker, respectively, according to some metric; ϵ is the degree to which the candidate ranker is allowed to be worse than the production ranker; and δ is the probability with which the candidate ranker is allowed to fall outside this threshold. The goal of a ranker comparison method in the Switching Problem is to determine whether (1) holds. Note that this requires explicitly reasoning about the uncertainty of comparisons between R_p and R_c.

By contrast, the goal of a ranker comparison method in the Difference Estimation Problem is to accurately estimate the expected difference of the metric values for the two rankers:

$$\mathbb{E}[M_c - M_p]. \quad (2)$$

Unlike the Switching Problem, the Difference Estimation Problem does not require explicitly reasoning about uncertainty. Nonetheless, it can be useful for, e.g., selecting a single ranker from a set of candidates, all of which satisfy (1).

For both problems, the ranker comparison method is given only a log $L = [l_1, \ldots, l_{|L|}]$ of user interaction sessions gathered using R_p. Each session l_j consists of the following: q, the query the user has submitted; $[d_0, \ldots, d_N]$, the list of N documents returned by R_p that make up the SERP; and $[c_0, \ldots, c_N]$, the clicks produced by the user on those documents.

4. CLICK MODEL-BASED METRIC

In this section, we describe the metric used to define M_p and M_c within BARACO, the Bayesian ranker comparison method we introduce in §5. While BARACO can work with any click model that provides relevance estimates, our implementation uses DBN [3] because it has shown high performance in predicting user clicks [7].

DBN, the Dynamic Bayesian Network click model [3], represents the relevance of a document for a query as a combination of two variables: *attractiveness* and *satisfactoriness*. In DBN, each user interaction session l_j begins with a query q from which the SERP, consisting of titles and snippets of the documents $[d_{q,0}, \ldots, d_{q,N}]$, is generated. By assumption, the user starts by examining the first document's title and snippet. If they find the document *attractive*, they click on and examine the document, or otherwise proceed to examine the following documents' titles and snippets in order. If a clicked document *satisfies* the user, they terminate the session. Otherwise, they may or may not continue to examine the SERP. DBN assumes the user will not click a document prior to examining its snippet and cannot be satisfied by a document before clicking on it.

Specifically, for a query q the document at position i in the SERP is modelled with four binary variables: whether it is attractive ($A_{q,i}$), satisfactory ($S_{q,i}$), examined ($E_{q,i}$), and clicked ($C_{q,i}$). The following relationships hold between variables for a given query:

- $E_{q,0} = 1$: the first document is examined,
- $A_{q,i} = 1, E_{q,i} = 1 \Leftrightarrow C_{q,i} = 1$: a document is clicked if, and only if, it is attractive and examined,
- $C_{q,i} = 0 \implies S_{q,i} = 0$: only clicked documents can be satisfactory,
- $S_{q,i} = 1 \implies E_{q,i+1} = 0$: satisfied users abandon the search, and
- $E_{q,i} = 0 \implies E_{q,i+1} = 0$: users do not skip documents.

In addition, the following stochastic relationships hold:

- $p(E_{q,i+1} = 1 | E_{q,i} = 1, S_{q,i} = 0) = \gamma$: users continue to examine the list after not being satisfied with probability γ,
- $p(A_{q,i} = 1) = a_{q,i}$, and
- $p(S_{q,i} = 1 | C_{q,i} = 1) = s_{q,i}$.

Thus, attractiveness and satisfactoriness are governed by stationary Bernoulli distributions with unknown parameters $a_{q,i}$ and $s_{q,i}$, which must be inferred from clicks, the only observed variables. As in [3, 7], we assume γ is fixed and known. Fig. 1 depicts the relationships between all variables in a given session.

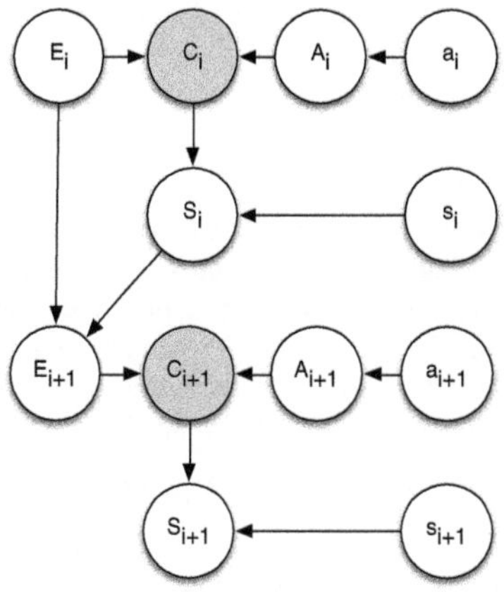

Figure 1: Graphical representation of the DBN click model. The grey circles represent the observed variables.

Once $a_{q,i}$ and $s_{q,i}$ have been inferred, they can be used to compute a metric such as EBU [23], ERR [4], and the utility and effort-based metrics described in [2, 7]. In this paper, we use the expected effort metric defined in [7]. For a query q that yields a document list with N documents, the metric is defined as:

$$rrMetric(q) = \sum_{i=1}^{N} \left(\frac{s_{q,i} a_{q,i}}{i} \prod_{j=1}^{i-1} (1 - s_{q,j} a_{q,j}) \right). \quad (3)$$

For a given ranker R_x, the metric M_x required by (1) can then be defined as the expected value of $rrMetric(q)$ across queries:

$$M_x = \sum_{q \in Q} rrMetric(q) p(q). \quad (4)$$

Comparing the production ranker to a candidate ranker is complicated by the presence of unseen documents in the candidate rankings. In order to compute the values of a metric for rankings with unseen documents, the unseen documents can be either assigned some a priori values of attractiveness and satisfactoriness or excluded from the ranking. The latter strategy is taken in [7] and in the baseline method used in our experiments.

Using an approach based on expectation maximisation (EM), a maximum a posteriori estimate of M_x can be computed [3]. Hence, the Difference Estimation Problem can be addressed by simply estimating M_c and M_p using this EM-based method and then computing the difference between them. However, this approach suffers from a key limitation. Because it is based only on maximum a posteriori estimates, the difference computed by such an EM-based approach is not the true expected difference of the metric values for the two rankers. Instead, it is only the first mode of the posterior distribution of the difference of the metric values, which may not be equal to the expectation if the distribution is multimodal or asymmetric. Because BARACO is a fully Bayesian approach, it can estimate the true expected value of the difference between M_c and M_p, which leads to better quality estimates, as we will see.

Furthermore, the Switching Problem cannot be directly addressed using an EM-based approach because such an approach gives no information about the uncertainty in the resulting estimate. That is, it does not estimate the *distribution* over the metric values of the two rankers. Consequently, it provides no way to estimate the probability that $M_c + \epsilon$ is greater than or equal to M_p. Instead, addressing the Switching Problem using an EM-based method requires resorting to a heuristic approach, e.g., switching only when the estimated difference exceeds some manually tuned threshold. This forms the core of the baseline method we compare against in §7.

Below, we present a method that addresses the shortcomings of an EM-based approach and enables better solutions to both the Switching Problem and the Difference Estimation Problem.

5. BARACO

In this section, we present BARACO. First, §5.1 describes how the posterior distributions over $a_{q,i}$ and $s_{q,i}$ can be inferred from L, the set of user interaction sessions; §5.2 describes how to solve the Switching Problem by evaluating (1) when M_p and M_c are defined according to (4), given posterior distributions over $a_{q,i}$ and $s_{q,i}$; §5.3 describes how to solve the Difference Estimation Problem.

5.1 Inferring click model posteriors

Evaluating (1) and (2) requires knowing the posterior probabilities $p(a_{q,i}|L)$ and $p(s_{q,i}|L)$ for each ranker, query, and document. In this subsection, we describe how to estimate these posteriors.

The algorithm works by iterating over the sessions. To process the first session, the posteriors $p(a_{q,i}|l_1)$ and $p(s_{q,i}|l_1)$ are computed given uniform priors $p(a_{q,i})$ and $p(s_{q,i})$. Then, for each subsequent session l_j, $p(a_{q,i}|L_j)$ and $p(s_{q,i}|L_j)$ are computed given $p(a_{q,i}|L_{j-1})$ and $p(s_{q,i}|L_{j-1})$, where $L_j = [l_1, \ldots, l_j]$. The algorithm terminates when $l = |L|$, yielding $p(a_{q,i}|L)$ and $p(s_{q,i}|L)$.

We now describe how to compute $p(a_{q,i}|L_j)$ and $p(s_{q,i}|L_j)$ given $p(a_{q,i}|L_{j-1})$ and $p(s_{q,i}|L_{j-1})$ and the next session l_j. Because $A_{q,i}$ and $S_{q,i}$ are Bernoulli variables, we can model the distribution over their parameters $a_{q,i}$ and $s_{q,i}$ using a Beta distribution. Focusing on $a_{q,i}$, this yields:

$$p(a_{q,i}|L_j) = Beta(\alpha, \beta) = \frac{{a_{q,i}}^{\alpha-1}(1-a_{q,i})^{\beta-1}}{B(\alpha, \beta)}, \quad (5)$$

where α is the number of observations of $A_{q,i} = 1$ and β is the number of observations of $A_{q,i} = 0$ that have occurred up to and including session j, and $B(\alpha, \beta)$ is a Beta function. $Beta(1, 1)$ corresponds to a uniform distribution, i.e., no prior knowledge about $a_{q,i}$. If $A_{q,i}$ is observed in session l_j, then $p(a_{q,i}|L_j)$ can be updated using Bayes' rule:

$$p(a_{q,i}|L_j) = p(a_{q,i}|A_{q,i}, L_{j-1}) = \frac{p(A_{q,i}|a_{q,i})p(a_{q,i}|L_{j-1})}{p(A_{q,i}|L_{j-1})}, \quad (6)$$

In this case, the update reduces to simply incrementing α or β. Since the Beta distribution is the conjugate prior for the Bernoulli variable, the posterior remains a Beta distribution.

In our setting, $A_{q,i}$ is not directly observed. However, when we know $E_{q,i}$, we can directly infer $A_{q,i}$ from $C_{q,i}$ because the user always clicks on an attractive examined document. Thus, the difficult case is when we do not know $E_{q,i}$, which occurs whenever $i > c$, where c is the index of the last clicked document. The remainder of this subsection describes how to address this case.

There are two steps. Since we do not know $E_{q,i}$ when $i > c$, in the first step we must instead compute a posterior over it: $p(E_{q,i}|L_j)$. Then, in the second step, we use $p(E_{q,i}|L_j)$ to estimate $p(a_{q,i}|L_j)$ and $p(s_{q,i}|L_j)$.

To perform the first step, we use the *sum-product* message passing algorithm [1]. In particular, we extract the subgraph of the graphical model that represents the documents below the last clicked one and remove the nodes representing the satisfactoriness ($S_{q,i}$ and $s_{q,i}$) for documents without clicks. This is because it is not possible to say anything about $s_{q,i}$ for $i > c$ as it is not observed and has no effect on what is observed. Since the resulting graph, shown in Fig. 2, is a polytree, the sum-product algorithm enables us to perform exact inference, which yields $p(E_{q,i}|L_j)$.

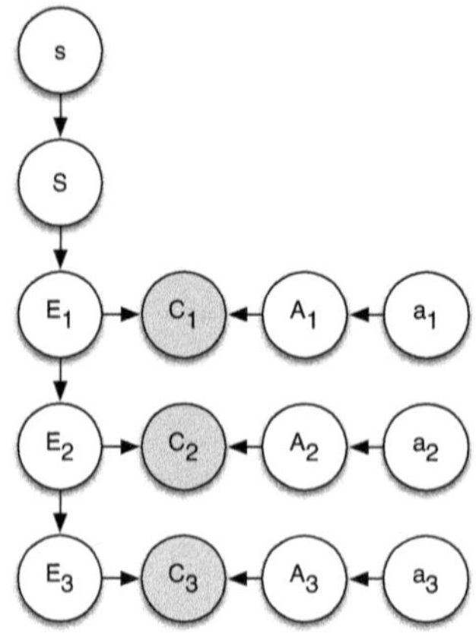

Figure 2: Graphical representation of the DBN click model for the part of the SERP below and including the last clicked document in a session. Grey circles represent observed variables.

For the second step, we compute $p(a_{q,i}|L_j)$ and $p(s_{q,i}|L_j)$ given $p(E_{q,i}|L_j)$. Focusing now on $p(a_{q,i}|L_j)$ and starting from Bayes' rule, we have:

$$p(a_{q,i}|L_j) = p(a_{q,i}|C_{q,i}, L_{j-1}) = \frac{p(C_{q,i}|a_{q,i})p(a_{q,i}|L_{j-1})}{p(C_{q,i}|L_{j-1})}. \quad (7)$$

The likelihood term $p(C_{q,i}|a_{q,i})$ can be computed by marginalizing across A and E:

$$p(C_{q,i}|a_{q,i}) = \sum_{A\in\{0,1\}} \sum_{E\in\{0,1\}} \Big(p(C_{q,i}|E_{q,i} = E, A_{q,i} = A) p(E_{q,i} = E)p(A_{q,i} = A|a_{q,i})\Big). \quad (8)$$

Sticking (8) into (7) and ignoring normalization gives:

$$\begin{aligned} p(a_{q,i}|C_{q,i}, L_{j-1}) \propto & \sum_{A\in\{0,1\}} \sum_{E\in\{0,1\}} \Big(p(C_{q,i}|E_{q,i} = E, A_{q,i} = A) \\ & p(E_{q,i} = E)p(A_{q,i} = A|a_{q,i})p(a_{q,i}|L_{j-1})\Big) \\ \propto \; & p(a_{q,i}|L_{j-1}) \sum_{A\in\{0,1\}} \Big(p(A_{q,i} = A|a_{q,i}) \\ & (p(C_{q,i}|E_{q,i} = 0, A_{q,i} = A)p(E = 0) + \\ & + p(C_{q,i}|E_{q,i} = 1, A_{q,i} = A)p(E_{q,i}))\Big). \end{aligned}$$

Since we are focusing on the case where $i > c$, we know that $C_{q,i} = 0$, i.e., $d_{q,i}$ was not clicked. Furthermore, we know that $p(C_{q,i} = 0|E_{q,i} = 0, A_{q,i} = A) = 1$ and $p(C_{q,i} = 0|E_{q,i} = 1, A_{q,i} = A) = 1 - A$, yielding:

$$\begin{aligned} p(a_{q,i}|C_{q,i} = 0, L_{j-1}) \propto & \\ & p(a_{q,i}|L_{j-1}) \sum_{A\in\{0,1\}} \Big(p(A_{q,i} = A|a_{q,i}) \\ & (1 \cdot p(E_{q,i} = 0) + (1 - A_{q,i}) \cdot p(E_{q,i} = 1))\Big) \\ \propto \; & p(a_{q,i}|L_{j-1}) \sum_{A\in\{0,1\}} \Big(p(A_{q,i} = A|a_{q,i}) \end{aligned}$$

Algorithm 1 ComputePosteriors(L)

InitializePriors()
for l_j in L **do**
  for i in l_j **do**
    $p(E_{q,i}) \leftarrow sumProduct(l_j)$
    if $C_{q,i} = 1$ **then**
      $p(a_{q,i}|C_{q,i} = 1, L_{j-1}) \leftarrow p(a_{q,i}|L_{j-1})a_{q,i}$
      $p(s_{q,i}|C_{q,i+1} = 0, L_{j-1}) \leftarrow p(s_{q,i}|L_{j-1})$ $(p(E_{q,i+1} = 1) + s_{q,i}p(E_{q,i+1} = 0))$
    else
      $p(a_{q,i}|C_{q,i} = 0, L_{j-1}) \leftarrow p(a_{q,i}|L_{j-1})$ $(1 - a_{q,i} \cdot p(E_{q,i} = 1))$
return $p(a|L), p(s|L)$

$$(1 - p(E_{q,i} = 1) + p(E_{q,i} = 1) - A \cdot p(E_{q,i} = 1))\Big)$$

$$\propto \; p(a_{q,i}|L_{j-1}) \sum_{A \in \{0,1\}} \Big(p(A_{q,i} = A|a_{q,i}) \; (1 - A \cdot p(E_{q,i} = 1))\Big). \quad (9)$$

Now we can substitute $p(A_{q,i} = A|a_{q,i})$ for the values of A: $p(A_{q,i} = 1|a_{q,i}) = a_{q,i}$ and $p(A_{q,i} = 0|a_{q,i}) = 1 - a_{q,i}$ yielding:

$$p(a_{q,i}|C_{q,i} = 0, L_{j-1}) \propto p(a_{q,i}|L_{j-1})(1 - a_{q,i} \cdot p(E_{q,i} = 1)). \quad (10)$$

Thus, (10) is the Bayesian update rule for attractiveness. When $p(E_{q,i} = 1) = 1$, e.g., if the document was clicked, the posterior is a Beta distribution because plugging $p(E_{q,i} = 1) = 1$ in (10) yields a term conjugate to the parametrization in (5). Otherwise, we use $p(E_{q,i}|L_j)$, as computed in the first step via a message-passing algorithm that takes into account the satisfactoriness of the last clicked document and the attractivenesses of the unexamined documents. Instead of a Beta distribution, this yields a more general polynomial function. The normalization constant can be found by integration: since the function is a polynomial with known coefficients, it can be integrated analytically and then the definite integral evaluated on the interval $[0, 1]$. The cumulative distribution function is therefore also a polynomial and easy to compute. The same holds for the expectation of the distribution.

Analogously, we can derive an update rule for satisfactoriness:

$$p(s_{q,i}|C_{q,i+1} = 0, L_{j-1}) \propto p(s_{q,i}|L_{j-1})(p(E_{q,i+1} = 1) + s_{q,i}p(E_{q,i+1} = 0)). \quad (11)$$

Algorithm 1 summarizes the steps involved in computing $p(a_{q,i}|L)$ and $p(s_{q,i}|L)$. First, the attractiveness and satisfactoriness of all document query pairs are assigned uniform $Beta(1, 1)$ priors. Then, the log file is processed session by session and the attractiveness and satisfactoriness of all document query pairs in the session are updated using the Bayesian update rules described in this section: (6) and (10) for attractiveness and (11) for satisfactoriness.

5.2 The Switching Problem

To decide whether or not to switch from R_p to R_c, we must determine whether (1) holds. Determining this from L requires evaluating the following double integral:

$$p(M_c + \epsilon \geq M_p \mid L) = \int_{M_c=0}^{M_c=M^*} p(M_c|L) \int_{M_p=0}^{M_p=M_c+\epsilon} p(M_p|L) \, dM_c \, dM_p, \quad (12)$$

Algorithm 2 BARACO-SP($R_p, R_c, L, \epsilon, \delta$)

1: $p(a|L), p(s|L) \leftarrow computePosteriors(L)$ ▷ §5.1
2: **for** k in $1{:}K$ **do** ▷ §5.2
3:   $M_p^k \leftarrow sample(R_p, p(a|L), p(s|L))$
4:   $M_c^k \leftarrow sample(R_c, p(a|L), p(s|L))$
5:   **if** $M_c^k + \epsilon \geq M_p^k$ **then**
6:     $N_{M_c+\epsilon \geq M_p} \leftarrow N_{M_c+\epsilon \geq M_p} + 1$
7: $p(M_c + \epsilon \geq M_p) \leftarrow \frac{N_{M_c+\epsilon \geq M_p}}{K}$
return $p(M_c + \epsilon \geq M_p) \geq 1 - \delta$

where M^* is the maximum possible value of the metric defined in (4). Evaluating this integral requires knowing the posterior probabilities $p(M_p|L)$ and $p(M_c|L)$, which can be computed from (3) and (4) given $p(a_{q,i}|L)$ and $p(s_{q,i}|L)$ for each ranker, query, and document.

Computing (12) analytically is hard, but it can be estimated using a Monte-Carlo sampling scheme. Algorithm 2 describes this scheme, which yields a version of BARACO that solves the Switching Problem.

First, we compute the posteriors $p(a|L)$ and $p(s|L)$ using the approach described in §5.1 (line 1). Then, each sampling iteration k consists of drawing a sample $a_{q,i}$ and $s_{q,i}$ for each ranker, document, and query from $p(a_{q,i}|L)$ and $p(s_{q,i}|L)$. Using these samples, we compute M_c^k and M_p^k, the values of the metrics given the sampled probabilities from the k-th iteration (lines 3–4). Estimating (12) then reduces to computing the fraction of sampling iterations for which $M_c^k + \epsilon \geq M_p^k$ (lines 6–7). If this fraction is greater than $1 - \delta$, we can safely switch to the candidate ranker.

However, sampling $a_{q,i}$ and $s_{q,i}$ from $p(a_{q,i}|L)$ and $p(s_{q,i}|L)$ is itself hard because their cumulative distribution functions are high degree polynomials that are hard to invert. Therefore, we employ the Metropolis-Hastings algorithm [1] with the expected value of the sampled distribution, which can be calculated analytically through integration, as the starting position of the random walk. The proposal distribution is a Gaussian with fixed variance.

5.3 The Difference Estimation Problem

If we are interested only in the expected value of a ranker R_x, and not the uncertainty of this estimate, we can compute it as follows:

$$\mathbb{E}[M_x] = \int_{M_x=0}^{M_x=M^*} M_x p(M_x) \, dM_x.$$

Using the same sampling procedure described above, we can solve the Difference Estimation Problem by estimating this expected value:

$$\mathbb{E}[M_x] \approx \tfrac{1}{K} \textstyle\sum_{k=1}^{K} M_x^k, \quad (13)$$

where K is the number of sampling iterations. We can similarly estimate the expected difference between M_c and M_p:

$$\mathbb{E}[M_c - M_p] \approx \tfrac{1}{K} \textstyle\sum_{k=1}^{K} (M_c^k - M_p^k). \quad (14)$$

Algorithm 3 summarizes the resulting version of BARACO that solves the Difference Estimation Problem. It is essentially the same as Algorithm 2 except that it estimates the expected difference between the production and the candidate rankers' metrics.

6. EXPERIMENTAL SETUP

In this section, we describe the experimental setup used to evaluate BARACO. This evaluation is complicated by the fact that the user's information need, and therefore the true relevance labels, are unknown. We present two evaluations which deal with this problem

Algorithm 3 BARACO-DEP($R_p, R_c, L, \epsilon, \delta$)

$p(a|L), p(s|L) \leftarrow computePosteriors(L)$ ▷ §5.1
$\sum_{\Delta_M} \leftarrow 0$
for k in $1{:}K$ **do** ▷ §5.3
  $M_p^k \leftarrow sample(R_p, p(a|L), p(s|L))$
  $M_c^k \leftarrow sample(R_c, p(a|L), p(s|L))$
  $\sum_{\Delta_M} \leftarrow \sum_{\Delta_M} + M_c^k - M_p^k$
$\mathbb{E}[M_x] \leftarrow \frac{\sum_{\Delta_M}}{K}$
return $\mathbb{E}[M_x]$

in two different ways. The first evaluation, based on the LETOR datasets [17], uses manual relevance assessments as ground-truth labels and synthetic clicks as feedback to BARACO. The second evaluation, based on the WSDM 2014 Web search personalization challenge,[1] uses dwell time as ground-truth labels and real clicks as feedback to BARACO.

Another possibility would be to evaluate BARACO using explicit relevance labels provided by human assessors to measure metrics such as Normalized Discounted Cumulative Gain (NDCG) but this approach is known to have low agreement with metrics based user behavior such as A/B testing or interleaving [4, 6, 19, 24], so it is natural to expect that it would have a low agreement with BARACO as well. It would also be possible to evaluate BARACO using A/B tests or interleavings, but A/B tests have low agreement with interleavings and different metrics collected during A/B tests such as click through rate, clicks@1 and others have low agreement with each other [19]. The only definitive way to evaluate BARACO would be in an industrial setting that measures long-term metrics such as engagement. Such results, however, would be difficult to reproduce. Consequently, the LETOR evaluation is the most reliable and reproducible, as it depends on indisputably unbiased ground truth. In addition, it allows us to explore how the discrepancy between the click model and user behavior affects BARACO's performance. However, the WSDM evaluation, though less reliable, is nonetheless useful because it gives insight into how BARACO performs in a real-world setting with real users.

We compare BARACO to a baseline that, in lieu of our Bayesian approach, uses the EM-based approach described in [3] to compute maximum a posteriori estimates of (4) for M_p and M_c. These estimates can then be directly used in the Difference Estimation Problem. Because this approach does not compute full posteriors, it does not quantify uncertainty in the resulting estimates and therefore cannot be directly used in the Switching Problem. Instead, the baseline method, which we call *Manual Thresholding (MT)*, resorts to a heuristic approach to determine whether (1) holds. In particular, R_c is deemed safe when $\hat{M}_c - \hat{M}_p > \epsilon_m$, where $\hat{M}_c$ and $\hat{M}_p$ are the maximum a posteriori estimates of M_c and M_p produced by the EM-based method and ϵ_m is a threshold parameter whose value must be tuned manually. Because we want to switch whenever $M_c - M_p > -\epsilon$, the quantity $\epsilon + \epsilon_m$ acts as a buffer, i.e., an extra gap that R_c must exceed to be considered safe. Adding this buffer heuristically accounts for the uncertainty in $\hat{M}_c$ and $\hat{M}_p$.

The need to tune ϵ_m for MT poses significant difficulties in practice. To understand the effect of ϵ_m on the behavior of MT would require access to ground truth about a set of candidate rankers, i.e., whether they are in fact no more than ϵ worse than the production ranker. While such ground truth could be obtained using off-line or on-line evaluations, such evaluations pose exactly the difficulties that motivate the need for methods like BARACO: the former is expensive and may not reflect real user preferences. The latter requires showing potentially poor rankers to real users. Furthermore, while such ground truth, even if it could be obtained, would shed light on how ϵ_m affects to which candidate rankers MT switches, it would still not make it possible to select the ϵ_m that is best for a given δ supplied by the system designers. Doing so would require a quantification of the uncertainty about each candidate ranker that is inherent to BARACO but absent in MT.

Importantly, BARACO does *not* require tuning ϵ_m or any analogous parameter. On the contrary, δ and ϵ, which are supplied by the system designers, are simply quantifications of their risk tolerance.

6.1 LETOR Evaluation

The first evaluation is based on the LETOR datasets [17], which include manual relevance assessments. However, they do not include user clicks. In addition, even if they did, these would likely correlate only poorly with the relevance assessments, since the assessors may not interpret the users' information need correctly. To address this difficulty, we instead axiomatically define the relevance assessments to be correct ground-truth labels and use click models to generate the clicks. Since BARACO also relies on click models, we evaluate it in settings where the clicks are generated and interpreted using different click models, to assess BARACO's robustness to errors in its modeling assumptions.

LETOR is split into six sub-datasets: HP2003, HP2004, NP2003, NP2004, TD2003, and TD2004. For each run of each algorithm, we use the data from one sub-dataset. First we train a ranker R_{Ada} using AdaRank [22] on all the data in this sub-dataset. AdaRank, which performs reasonably on all these datasets [22], trains a linear ranking function, i.e., a linear combination of the ranking features for a given query-document pair. The documents are then sorted based on the values produced by this ranking function.

To ensure that some candidate rankers will be better than the production ranker, we craft R_p by "damaging" R_{Ada}, i.e., randomly by adding random vectors to it. These vectors were generated by randomly sampling a normal distribution with mean equal to 0 and standard deviation of 0.2. Finally, to generate a population of candidate rankers R_c, we again perturb R_p 1000 times using the same sampling method. This ranker generation methodology is motivated by the gradient descent algorithm [25]; the standard deviation value was chosen so that some of the rankers would be similar enough to the production ranker and some too different from it for the algorithm to be confident about their performance.

The next step is to generate the log file. To this end, we *generate* user click interaction data using the DBN, sDBN and UBM click models with three user model settings: perfect, navigational and informational. The clicks are then *interpreted* using the DBN click model. The parameters of the click models are summarized in Table 1, where $p(C|R)$ and $p(C|NR)$ denote the probability of a user clicking a relevant document and an irrelevant document, respectively, and $p(s|R)$ and $p(s|NR)$ denote the probability of abandoning the SERP after clicking a relevant document and an irrelevant document, respectively. The closer $p(C|R)$ is to $p(C|NR)$ and $p(s|R)$ to $p(s|NR)$, the more noise there is in the feedback and the more difficult inference becomes. The user interaction data is generated for the production ranker by randomly sampling 500 queries and generating the SERPS and clicks.

The perfect user model setting is used to obtain an upper bound in performance: the user clicks all relevant documents and no irrelevant ones. The navigational and informational user models are based on typical user behavior in web search [11]. The navigational

[1]Personalized Web Search Challenge 2013 https://www.kaggle.com/c/yandex-personalized-web-search-challenge

Table 1: Overview of the user model settings.

Model	$p(C\|R)$	$p(C\|NR)$	$p(s\|R)$	$p(s\|NR)$
Perfect	1.0	0.0	0.0	0.0
Navigational	0.95	0.05	0.9	0.2
Informational	0.9	0.4	0.5	0.1

user model reflects user behavior while searching for an item they know to exist, such as a company's homepage. Because it is easy for users to distinguish between relevant and irrelevant documents, the noise levels are low. The informational user model reflects user behavior while looking for information about a topic, which can be distributed over several pages. Because this task is more difficult, there is more noise in the feedback.

The clicks are generated and interpreted using either the same or different click models. When they are generated and interpreted using the same click model, our findings are not affected by the accuracy of the assumptions in the click model, allowing us to focus on the differences between BARACO and the baseline method. Of course, some assumptions made by DBN, which is used to interpret clicks, may not always hold in practice. For example, DBN assumes that the document that was clicked and led to abandonment is the document that satisfied the user. This assumption typically holds for navigational queries, but may not be valid for informational queries. Therefore, experiments in which the clicks are generated and interpreted using different click models help measure the robustness of BARACO to settings whether the assumptions underlying DBN do not always hold.

In the LETOR Evaluation setup, we compare the performance of BARACO and MT using area under roc curves (AUC), Pearson correlation, and the square root of the mean squared error (RMSE). The rankers are compared using the metric rrMetric (3).

6.2 WSDM Evaluation

We additionally evaluate BARACO using an anonymized click log released by Yandex for the WSDM 2014 Web search personalization challenge. The click log contains sessions with queries submitted by a user. For each query there is a list of search results returned by the engine and the clicks produced by the user. The queries and the clicks have timestamps. However, the units of time are not disclosed. The queries, query terms, documents, and users are represented by IDs in order to protect the privacy of users.

The organizers of the challenge have defined three levels of relevance based on the clicks that the documents receive: documents that receive clicks with dwell time less than 50 time units have relevance 0, clicks with dwell time between 50 and 150 units have relevance 1, and clicks with dwell time of more than 2 time units as well as clicks that are the last clicks for a given query have relevance 2. We use all but the last session for a query for training and use the last session for extracting the relevance labels for query-document pairs.

The candidate rankers are generated by perturbing the result lists observed in the click log in a random way. In order to ensure that some of the candidates are better than the production ranker, the relevant documents have a higher chance to be promoted to top than the irrelevant ones.

In the WSDM Evaluation setup, we compare the performance of BARACO and MT using the following metrics: AUC and Pearson correlation as before. But we do not use RMSE because the graded relevance and the estimated relevance have different scales from 0 to 2, and from 0 to 1 respectively. The candidates are compared using DCG instead of the metric in (3) because (3) requires a mapping from relevance labels to attractiveness and satisfactoriness that is not available for the graded relevance in the click log—it could be computed using, e.g., DBN but then the evaluation would be less sound because the same click model would be used for training the parameters of the documents and for training the metric.[2]

6.3 Parameter Settings

Both BARACO and MT are instantiated with the user persistence parameter $\gamma = 0.9$, as in [3, 7], $\epsilon = 0.01$. For the Metropolis-Hastings sampling procedure described in §5.2, the variance of the proposal distribution was set to 0.1, which was determined experimentally to provide a rejection ratio of around 0.6. For each query/document pair, $N_{samples} = 1000$ samples are drawn and shuffled to reduce autocorrelation in order to evaluate (1). All results are averaged over 30 independent runs for each algorithm. In order to check the significance of observed differences between results, we perform Wilcoxon signed-rank tests; in the result tables, $^{\blacktriangle}$ denotes a significant difference at $p = 0.01$, and $^{\vartriangle}$ at $p = 0.05$.

7. RESULTS

In this section, we present our experimental results aimed at answering RQ1 and RQ2. In §7.1, we analyse the performance of BARACO and MT on the LETOR data; in §7.2, we analyse their performance on the WSDM data.

7.1 LETOR Results

In §7.1.1, we compare BARACO and MT on the Switching Problem; in §7.1.2, we compare BARACO and the EM-based approach [3] that underlies MT on the Difference Estimation Problem.

7.1.1 Switching Problem Results

To address RQ1, we compare the ROC curves of BARACO and MT on the Switching Problem. Such curves show how the true and false positives of both methods change when we fix $\epsilon = 0.01$ and vary across different values of $\delta \in [0, 1]$ for BARACO and $\epsilon_m \in [-4\epsilon, \epsilon]$ for MT. In this context, a true positive occurs when the algorithm recommends switching to R_c and $M_c + \epsilon \geq M_p$, while a false positive occurs when it recommends switching but $M_c + \epsilon < M_p$. We then compare the AUC of both methods for different datasets and user and click models.

Note that this comparison is fundamentally unfair to BARACO because its parameter, δ, does not require tuning but instead is input by the system designers as a quantification of their risk tolerance. By contrast, ϵ_m is a parameter that requires manual tuning and cannot be derived from δ, which MT ignores. As discussed in §6, tuning this parameter is quite difficult in practice. Because the ROC curves show performance across different values of δ and ϵ_m, they allow MT to "cheat" by optimizing its critical parameter, a step that is unnecessary in BARACO. In other words, these ROC curves answer the following question: for each value of δ that a system designer could input to BARACO, how well can MT match the quality of BARACO's decisions about when to switch to R_c *if an oracle provides MT with the best possible value of* ϵ_m? Thus, BARACO can be considered a success if it can match the performance of MT when MT is given this advantage.

Fig. 3 plots the area under the ROC curves for BARACO and MT for all six data sets, three click models, and three user model settings. Fig. 4 shows the ROC curve for the TD2004 dataset, informational user model with the DBN model used for generation. The other ROC curves, omitted for brevity, are qualitatively similar.

[2]In the case of the LETOR evaluation experiments, this mapping is known and can be read from Table 1.

The results in Fig. 3a show that, even at the best value of ϵ_m, BARACO substantially outperforms MT on four of the six datasets (HP2003, HP2004, NP2003, TD2004). On the other two datasets (NP2003 and TD2003), the two methods perform similarly. Analysis of the latter two datasets shows that the production ranker was at a local minimum. Hence, nearly all candidate rankers are better than the production ranker and the best performance is obtained by always switching. As this degenerate policy can be represented just as well by MT as by BARACO, the two perform similarly.

Furthermore, the fact that BARACO performs nearly as well when clicks are generated and interpreted with different models, as shown in Figs. 3b and 3c, shows that BARACO is robust to violations of its modeling assumptions. The baseline substantially outperforms BARACO only for the perfect sDBN user model on the TD2003 and TD2004 datasets. The baseline shows superior performance because there are many more relevant documents in the TD datasets, and many of them are not presented to the user by the production ranker. In the case of the perfect user model, the user only clicks on relevant documents. Therefore, there are many queries for which no clicks are produced because no relevant documents were shown. The baseline essentially removes such queries from consideration through condensing [6], which may be an effective strategy in this case. Overall, these results demonstrate that BARACO can offer a robust and effective means for deciding when to switch rankers: especially in cases where its modeling assumptions hold, it outperforms MT with a tuned ϵ_m parameter for nearly all combinations of dataset and user model.

The values of ϵ_m shown here were chosen because their inflection point lies in the interval $\delta \in [0, 1]$. These are all negative values of ϵ_m because MT has a consistent negative bias: almost all candidate rankers receive a score lower than the production ranker. This bias is a consequence of condensing [6]: almost all candidate rankers have unseen documents that do not contribute to the metric. This further highlights the brittleness of MT: as more data is collected, the relative number of unseen documents may decrease, which would reduce the effect of condensing and therefore the amount of bias, necessitating a retuning of ϵ_m.

7.1.2 Difference Estimation Problem Results

To address RQ2, we compare BARACO to the EM-based method [3] that underlies MT, on the Difference Estimation Problem. BARACO uses (14) to estimate the expected difference while the EM-based method uses $\hat{M}_c - \hat{M}_p$, where $\hat{M}_x$ is the maximum a posteriori estimate of M_x. First, we consider how the RMSE scores of the two approaches differ. Error is defined here to be the difference between the true and estimated value of $M_c - M_p$. The true values are computed from the expert-generated relevance labels in the datasets. Table 2 summarizes the MSE of BARACO and MT. These results show that BARACO consistently outperforms the EM-based approach, in many cases by an order of magnitude. The only exception is the TD2004 dataset for clicks generated using UBM. This exception occurs because there are many unseen relevant documents in the TD2004 dataset and, when the user model assumptions do not hold, the baseline's condensing strategy [6] may be more effective because it does not rely on these assumptions.

However, the fact that BARACO has lower RMSE scores is important only if we are interested in the absolute values of the metric differences. Instead, if we want to be able to rank the candidate rankers by their metric values, we need a different way to compare the methods. To this end, we measure the Pearson's correlation between the ground truth value $M_c - M_p$ and the estimates produced by BARACO or MT. For example, if the correlation with the ground truth was perfect, ordering all the candidate rankers by their ground truth difference with the production ranker would be the same as ordering them by the estimated difference. Thus, the correlation with the ground truth is more informative than RMSE in cases where we care about preserving the ground-truth ranking. This occurs, e.g., when several candidate rankers confidently outperform the production ranker. In such cases, it is desirable to switch to the one that outperforms it by the largest margin, while the exact absolute values of the estimated metrics are not important.

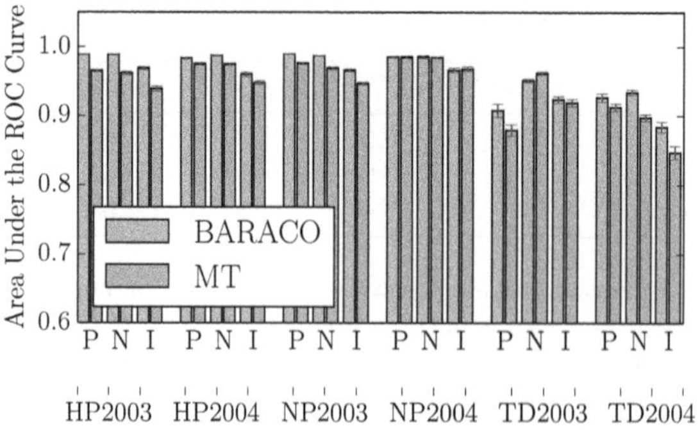

(a) Using DBN for generation and interpretation.

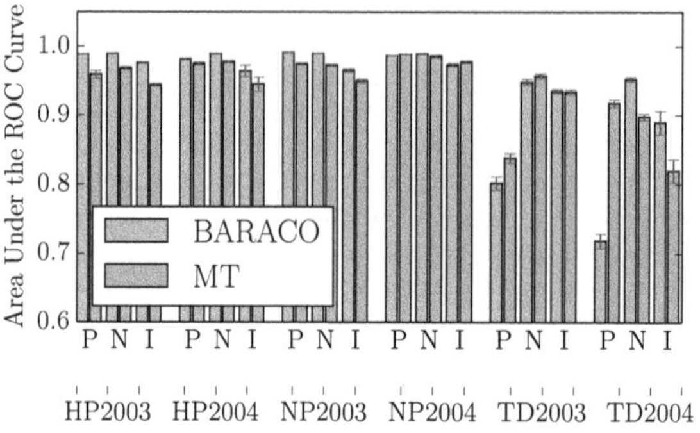

(b) Using sDBN for generation and DBN for interpretation.

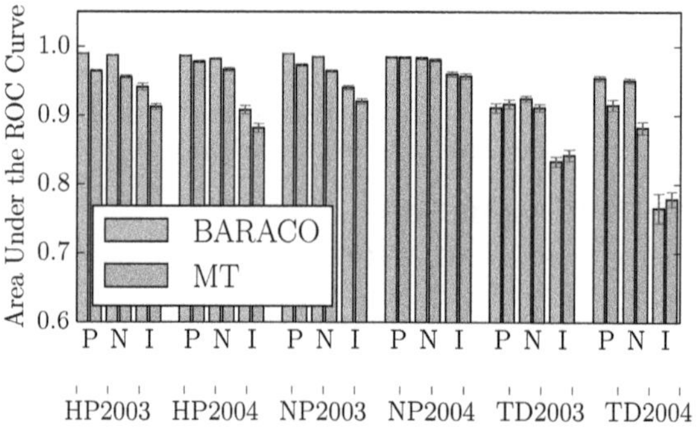

(c) Using UBM for generation and DBN for interpretation.

Figure 3: AUC for all data sets, user and click models. The error bars are standard errors of the means. P - perfect user model setting, I - informational, N - navigational (LETOR evaluation).

Table 3 summarizes the correlations between the ground truth difference of rankers and the difference of rankers computed by BARACO and the EM-based method. Higher correlations with the ground truth mean that the way the rankers are ranked is closer to the ground truth. These results show that BARACO again outperforms the EM-based method. The negative correlation in the informational setting of NP2003 dataset is due to a heavily skewed distribution of candidate rankers when the production ranker is at a

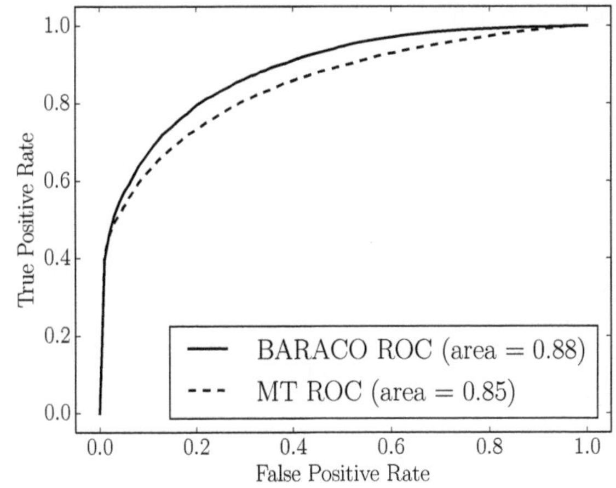

Figure 4: The ROC curves for BARACO and MT, using DBN for generation and interpretation, TD2004 dataset, informational user model (LETOR evaluation).

Table 2: RMSE between the predicted outcome of the comparison and the ground truth, P - perfect user model setting, I - informational, N - navigational (LETOR evaluation).

		DBN		sDBN		UBM	
Dataset	UM	BARACO	EM	BARACO	EM	BARACO	EM
HP2003	P	3.1e−5▲	3.0e−4	3.8e−5▲	3.1e−4	3.5e−5▲	3.2e−4
	N	2.8e−5▲	3.5e−4	2.6e−5▲	3.1e−4	4.7e−5▲	3.0e−4
	I	6.1e−5▲	2.7e−4	4.1e−5▲	2.7e−4	1.1e−4▲	2.6e−4
HP2004	P	2.7e−5▲	2.3e−4	4.3e−5▲	2.0e−4	2.7e−5▲	2.4e−4
	N	1.6e−5▲	2.4e−4	1.9e−5▲	2.3e−4	6.0e−5▲	1.9e−4
	I	6.2e−5▲	2.0e−4	5.3e−5△	1.6e−4	2.2e−4	2.4e−4
NP2003	P	1.3e−5▲	2.9e−4	1.5e−5▲	2.8e−4	1.4e−5▲	2.9e−4
	N	1.4e−5▲	3.0e−4	1.3e−5▲	2.8e−4	3.3e−5▲	2.5e−4
	I	3.7e−5▲	2.8e−4	3.8e−5▲	2.7e−4	1.1e−4▲	2.7e−4
NP2004	P	4.1e−6▲	6.2e−5	6.6e−6▲	5.8e−5	4.3e−6▲	6.6e−5
	N	4.9e−6▲	8.9e−5	3.6e−6▲	7.8e−5	7.9e−6▲	6.4e−5
	I	1.5e−5▲	9.8e−5	1.5e−5▲	1.0e−4	2.5e−5▲	1.2e−4
TD2003	P	7.0e−5▲	1.1e−4	3.7e−4▼	1.2e−4	6.8e−5▲	1.7e−4
	N	8.0e−5▲	3.5e−4	6.2e−5▲	3.8e−4	7.6e−5▲	1.9e−4
	I	6.3e−5▲	2.7e−4	6.9e−5▲	2.7e−4	1.5e−4▲	3.0e−4
TD2004	P	4.0e−4▲	7.8e−4	1.2e−3▼	5.9e−4	5.1e−4▲	9.2e−4
	N	3.2e−4▲	2.3e−3	2.5e−4▲	2.3e−3	6.0e−4▲	1.2e−3
	I	4.7e−4▲	2.0e−3	4.2e−4▲	1.7e−3	1.2e−3▲	1.5e−3

local minimum of the ranker space and almost all candidate rankers are better for the queries in which the production ranker has not presented any relevant documents. This situation is unlikely to occur in the real world since production rankers are typically highly engineered and thus more likely to be local maxima than local minima. As with our earlier results, we see that the performance on the TD2004 dataset using UBM for generation is qualitatively different from the other conditions for the reasons mentioned earlier.

To answer RQ2, we observe that both the RMSE and correlation results show that BARACO outperforms MT: BARACO achieves better estimates in both absolute and relative terms, except on the TD2004 dataset with the UBM click model for generation, whose special nature has been recognized before.

7.2 WSDM Results

In this section, we compare BARACO and MT on the Switching Problem and Difference Estimation Problem, respectively, using the WSDM experimental setup

Table 3: Correlation between the predicted outcome of the comparison and the ground truth, P - perfect user model setting, I - informational, N - navigational (LETOR evaluation)

		DBN		sDBN		UBM	
Dataset	UM	BARACO	EM	BARACO	EM	BARACO	EM
HP2003	P	0.961▲	0.846	0.950▲	0.858	0.963▲	0.857
	N	0.967▲	0.856	0.961▲	0.856	0.950▲	0.808
	I	0.914▲	0.763	0.930▲	0.744	0.510▼	0.664
HP2004	P	0.963▲	0.933	0.946	0.937	0.969▲	0.940
	N	0.980▲	0.926	0.981▲	0.943	0.960▲	0.908
	I	0.931▲	0.825	0.935△	0.825	0.262▼	0.612
NP2003	P	0.979▲	0.890	0.982▲	0.901	0.982▲	0.897
	N	0.973▲	0.878	0.982▲	0.891	0.969▲	0.856
	I	0.902▲	0.777	0.887▲	0.769	0.523▼	0.678
NP2004	P	0.922▲	0.841	0.915▲	0.871	0.925▲	0.861
	N	0.923▲	0.809	0.943▲	0.835	0.864▲	0.751
	I	0.700▲	0.571	0.678▲	0.546	0.464△	0.393
TD2003	P	0.738△	0.678	0.398▼	0.619	0.732	0.723
	N	0.838▲	0.813	0.873△	0.830	0.758▲	0.675
	I	0.777▲	0.689	0.776▲	0.702	0.009 67▼	0.404
TD2004	P	0.846△	0.783	0.434▼	0.817	0.887▲	0.795
	N	0.862▲	0.776	0.890▲	0.753	0.858▲	0.693
	I	0.755▲	0.633	0.829	0.637	−0.156▼	0.464

7.2.1 *Results for the Switching Problem*

To address RQ1, we compare the ROC curves of BARACO and MT on the Switching Problem. The AUC of these curves for both methods are stated in Table 4. The AUCs illustrate that both methods are able to distinguish between strong and weak candidates. Both methods suffer from a weak, systematic bias—they consistently underestimate the quality of the candidates because the relevance labels used in the evaluation are biased towards top results.

Table 4: AUC and Correlation between the predicted outcome of the comparison and the ground truth (WSDM evaluation).

	BARACO	Manual Thresholding
AUC	0.936	0.934
Correlation	0.751	0.735

The real proportion of candidate rankers that are better than the production ranker across different probability levels computed by BARACO is summarized in Table 5. The probabilities output by BARACO are not perfectly calibrated and instead tend to be underestimates. Thus, not all risk prescribed by δ and ϵ can be utilized, making the system somewhat overly conservative.

Unfortunately, a limitation of these WSDM experiments is that there is no way to ascertain how much of this bias is due to discrepancies between the relevance labels and the true information needs of the users who generated the clicks and how much is due to discrepancies between BARACO's click model and those users' behavior. However, because the bias is consistent, correcting for this bias, e.g., by learning a constant offset, is straightforward.

7.2.2 *Results for the Difference Estimation Problem*

The correlations between the true and estimated value of $M_c - M_p$ computed by BARACO and MT are also stated in Table 4. The estimated difference between rankers is strongly correlated with the ground truth in the WSDM dataset, suggesting that both methods can estimate the difference between rankers well given the logged user interactions with the production ranker.

Table 5: Proportion of candidate rankers that beat the production ranker across probability levels computed by BARACO (WSDM evaluation).

Probability Level	0–0.1	0.1–0.2	0.2–0.3	0.3–0.4	0.4–0.5	0.5–0.6	0.6–0.7	0.7–0.8	0.8–0.9	0.9–1
Proportion	0.004	0.037	0.139	0.312	0.546	0.742	0.886	0.971	0.993	1.0

In both experimental setups, i.e., the LETOR and WSDM setup, both BARACO and MT have good performance in most cases and high agreement with the ground truth. In the LETOR setup the performance is often superior to that in the WSDM experiments, especially when there is little noise and no discrepancy between the user behavior and the click model. However, when there is much noise and the clicks are generated and interpreted using different click models, the performance drops to levels lower than in the WSDM experiments. Overall, these results show that, given a reasonable click model, BARACO makes it possible to make informed decisions whether or not to switch to a candidate ranker given historical user interaction data obtained using the production ranker.

8. CONCLUSIONS AND FUTURE WORK

We presented BARACO, a new click model-based method of ranker comparison with two key features: (1) it compares the performance of rankers using only historical data, and (2) it quantifies the uncertainty in such comparisons. Using BARACO, it is possible to decide, using only historical data collected with the current production ranker, whether one can confidently replace the production ranker with a candidate ranker. The algorithm takes as input ϵ, the degree to which the candidate ranker is allowed to be worse than the production ranker; δ, the probability with which the candidate ranker is allowed to fall outside this threshold; and user interaction logs collected with the production system.

Our experiments show that BARACO can correctly and confidently identify candidate rankers that are ϵ as good as the production ranker. BARACO outperforms or has performance comparable to that of the MT baseline that requires manual tuning of the threshold ϵ_m through offline assessments or online user experiments.

A natural application of BARACO is within online learning to rank algorithms, many of which require an evaluation subroutine. For example, in Dueling Bandit Gradient Descent (DBGD) [25], the algorithm randomly picks a candidate ranker from the neighborhood of the current ranker, compares it to the current ranker, and, if the candidate ranker appears to be better, updates the current ranker so that is is closer to the candidate ranker. The evaluation step is usually done using interleaving, which requires showing potentially poor rankings to the user. Using BARACO, DBGD could be performed while restricting the rankings shown to users to those generated by production rankers or candidate rankers in which we have sufficient confidence.

Acknowledgements. This research was supported by the European Community's Seventh Framework Programme (FP7/2007-2013) under grant agreement nr 312827 (VOX-Pol), the Netherlands Organisation for Scientific Research (NWO) under project nrs 727.011.005, 612.001.116, HOR-11-10, 640.006.013, 612.066.930, CI-14-25, SH-322-15, Amsterdam Data Science, the Dutch national program COMMIT, the ESF Research Network Program ELIAS, the Elite Network Shifts project funded by the Royal Dutch Academy of Sciences (KNAW), the Netherlands eScience Center under project number 027.012.105, the Yahoo! Faculty Research and Engagement Program, the Microsoft Research PhD program, and the HPC Fund.

REFERENCES

[1] C. M. Bishop. *Pattern Recognition and Machine Learning*. Springer-Verlag New York, Inc., Secaucus, NJ, USA, 2006.

[2] B. Carterette. System effectiveness, user models, and user utility: a conceptual framework for investigation. In *SIGIR '11*, pages 903–912. ACM, 2011.

[3] O. Chapelle and Y. Zhang. A dynamic bayesian network click model for web search ranking. In *WWW '09*, 2009.

[4] O. Chapelle, D. Metzler, Y. Zhang, and P. Grinspan. Expected reciprocal rank for graded relevance. In *CIKM '09*, pages 621–630. ACM, 2009.

[5] O. Chapelle, T. Joachims, F. Radlinski, and Y. Yue. Large-scale validation and analysis of interleaved search evaluation. *ACM Transactions on Information Systems*, 30(1):6, 2012.

[6] A. Chuklin, A. Schuth, K. Hofmann, P. Serdyukov, and M. de Rijke. Evaluating aggregated search using interleaving. In *CIKM '13*, pages 669–678. ACM, 2013.

[7] A. Chuklin, P. Serdyukov, and M. de Rijke. Click model-based information retrieval metrics. In *SIGIR '13*, page 493. ACM, 2013.

[8] C. W. Cleverdon, J. Mills, and E. Keen. Factors determining the performance of indexing systems (Volume 1: Design). *Cranfield: College of Aeronautics*, 1966.

[9] G. E. Dupret and B. Piwowarski. A user browsing model to predict search engine click data from past observations. In *SIGIR '08*, pages 331–338. ACM, 2008.

[10] F. Guo and Y.-m. Wang. Efficient multiple-click models in web search. In *WSDM '09*. ACM, 2009.

[11] F. Guo, L. Li, and C. Faloutsos. Tailoring click models to user goals. In *Proceedings of the 2009 workshop on Web Search Click Data*, pages 88–92. ACM, 2009.

[12] J. He, C. Zhai, and X. Li. Evaluation of methods for relative comparison of retrieval systems based on clickthroughs. In *CIKM '09*, pages 2029–2032. ACM, 2009.

[13] K. Hofmann, F. Behr, and F. Radlinski. On caption bias in interleaving experiments. In *CIKM '12*, pages 115–124. ACM, 2012.

[14] K. Hofmann, A. Schuth, S. Whiteson, and M. de Rijke. Reusing historical interaction data for faster online learning to rank for IR. In *WSDM '13*, pages 183–192. ACM, 2013.

[15] T. Joachims. Optimizing search engines using clickthrough data. In *KDD '02*, pages 133–142. ACM, 2002.

[16] R. Kohavi, R. Longbotham, D. Sommerfield, and R. Henne. Controlled experiments on the web: survey and practical guide. *Data Mining and Knowledge Discovery*, 18:140–181, 2009.

[17] T. Qin, T.-Y. Liu, J. Xu, and H. Li. LETOR: A benchmark collection for research on learning to rank for information retrieval. *Information Retrieval*, 13(4):346–374, 2010.

[18] F. Radlinski and N. Craswell. Comparing the sensitivity of information retrieval metrics. In *SIGIR '10*, pages 667–674. ACM, 2010.

[19] F. Radlinski, M. Kurup, and T. Joachims. How does clickthrough data reflect retrieval quality? In *CIKM '08*, pages 43–52. ACM, 2008.

[20] M. Sanderson. Test collection based evaluation of information retrieval systems. *Foundations and Trends in Information Retrieval*, 4(4):247–375, 2010.

[21] A. Schuth, F. Sietsma, S. Whiteson, D. Lefortier, and M. de Rijke. Multileaved comparisons for fast online evaluation. In *CIKM '14*, pages 71–80. ACM, 2014.

[22] J. Xu and H. Li. Adarank: A boosting algorithm for information retrieval. In *SIGIR '07*, pages 391–398, New York, NY, USA, 2007. ACM.

[23] E. Yilmaz, M. Shokouhi, N. Craswell, and S. Robertson. Expected browsing utility for web search evaluation. In *CIKM '10*, pages 1561–1564. ACM, 2010.

[24] E. Yilmaz, M. Verma, N. Craswell, F. Radlinski, and P. Bailey. Relevance and effort: an analysis of document utility. In *CIKM '14*, pages 91–100. ACM, 2014.

[25] Y. Yue and T. Joachims. Interactively optimizing information retrieval systems as a dueling bandits problem. In *ICML '09*, pages 1201–1208. ACM, 2009.

Incorporating Non-sequential Behavior into Click Models

Chao Wang[†], Yiqun Liu[†], Meng Wang[‡], Ke Zhou[⋆], Jian-yun Nie[#], Shaoping Ma[†]
[†]Tsinghua National Laboratory for Information Science and Technology, Department of Computer Science & Technology, Tsinghua University, Beijing, China
[‡]School of Computer and Information, HeFei University of Technology
[⋆]Yahoo Labs, London, U.K.
[#]Université de Montréal
yiqunliu@tsinghua.edu.cn

ABSTRACT

Click-through information is considered as a valuable source of users' implicit relevance feedback. As user behavior is usually influenced by a number of factors such as position, presentation style and site reputation, researchers have proposed a variety of assumptions (i.e. click models) to generate a reasonable estimation of result relevance. The construction of click models usually follow some hypotheses. For example, most existing click models follow the *sequential examination hypothesis* in which users examine results from top to bottom in a linear fashion. While these click models have been successful, many recent studies showed that there is a large proportion of non-sequential browsing (both examination and click) behaviors in Web search, which the previous models fail to cope with. In this paper, we investigate the problem of properly incorporating non-sequential behavior into click models. We firstly carry out a laboratory eye-tracking study to analyze user's non-sequential examination behavior and then propose a novel click model named Partially Sequential Click Model (PSCM) that captures the practical behavior of users. We compare PSCM with a number of existing click models using two real-world search engine logs. Experimental results show that PSCM outperforms other click models in terms of both predicting click behavior (perplexity) and estimating result relevance (NDCG and user preference test). We also publicize the implementations of PSCM and related datasets for possible future comparison studies.

Categories and Subject Descriptors

H.3.3 [**Information Storage and Retrieval**]: Information Search and Retrieval

Keywords

click model; non-sequential behavior; eye-tracking

SIGIR'15, August 09 - 13, 2015, Santiago, Chile.
© 2015 ACM. ISBN 978-1-4503-3621-5/15/08 ...$15.00.
DOI: http://dx.doi.org/10.1145/2766462.2767712.

1. INTRODUCTION

Modern search engines record user interactions and use them to improve search quality. In particular, user's click-through has been successfully used to improve click-through rate (CTR), Web search ranking, query recommendation and suggestion, and so on.

Although click-through logs can provide implicit feedback of users' click preferences [1], it is difficult to derive accurate absolute relevance judgments due to the existence of click noises and behavior biases. Joachims et al. [19] worked on extracting reliable implicit feedback from user behaviors, and concluded that click logs are informative yet biased. Previous studies showed that users' clicking behaviors are biased towards many aspects such as "position" [8, 19] (user's attention decreases from top to bottom), "trust" [32] (Web site reputations will affect user's judgment), "presentation" [27] (different search results' display styles will influence users' attention allocation strategies) and so on. To address these problems, researchers have proposed a number of click models to describe user's practical browsing behavior and to obtain an unbiased estimation of result relevance [4, 11, 13].

In [20], users' examination behavior patterns are grouped into two categories according to the findings in eye-tracking studies: the depth-first strategy and the breadth-first strategy. The depth-first model assumes that a user examines result list from top to bottom and decides whether to click immediately after examining a result. The breadth-first strategy, however, draws a different picture: a user will look ahead at a series of results before clicking on the favorite results among them. Since the position bias can be easily incorporated into click models with the depth-first assumption, most existing click models [4, 11, 13] follow this assumption and assume that the user examines search results in a top-to-bottom fashion.

However, recent eye-tracking experiments [22] showed that only 34 % of search users' scan paths are linear while over 50 % of sessions contain revisiting behaviors (i.e. given a search engine result page (SERP), the user first clicks the result at position i and then clicks the one at position $j, j \leq i$) or skipping behaviors. Table 1 shows the non-sequential click proportion of multi-click query sessions (user clicked two or more results on one SERP) from two commercial search engine logs. We can see that nearly one-third of multi-click sessions contain non-sequential click actions. While most existing click models are based on ranking positions rather than action sequences, the click sequence information is usually ignored and non-sequential

Table 1: Non-sequential click proportions of multi-click query sessions in two different search behavior data sets (See data sets' detail in Sec. 5.1.2).

Search Engine	Sogou	Yandex
Percentages	27.9%	30.4%

clicking behaviors are not considered either. [10,14] already showed that the last click in a search session may be more reliable than other clicks. However, the last click performed by a user is not necessarily the one at the lowest position, but the last one in the sequence of clicks. It is thus necessary to take the temporal sequential information into account.

Some existing click models [28–30] have tried to do so. These models relax the restrictions of user's examination sequence (e.g. [28] assumes that examination sequence can be arbitrary) to increase model's descriptive power. However, most of these methods actually abandon the prior knowledge of user browsing preference generated from other user behavior studies, which has been found useful. In practice, these models cannot achieve as good performance as other popular click models according to our experimental results in Section 6.

To better understand user's click and examination sequences, we design a laboratory study to analyze users' practical examination patterns. Our observations confirm clearly that the click behavior of users are non-sequential. On the other hand, the examinations of documents between two clicks usually follow one direction, but with possible skips. This observation shows that some of the assumptions used in the previous position-based models (e.g. the sequential examination assumption) are reasonable in local contexts (i.e. between two clicks). It is thus possible to build a new model upon the existing position-based models by adding new hypotheses. By this means, we not only inherit the framework which has already proved to be effective, but also combine sequential information to better capture user's preference on different search results.

Our contributions in this paper are four-fold:

- An eye-tracking experiment is carried out to analyze user's non-sequential examination and click behavior on search engine result pages (SERPs).
- A novel click model named Partially Sequential Click Model (PSCM) is proposed to incorporate non-sequential behavior.
- We show experimentally that the proposed PSCM model outperforms the existing models on two real-world commercial search engine datasets (one of which is publicly available).
- In addition, we make our implementation of the proposed model available as an open-source project (see Section 5.1).

The paper is organized as follows. Various click models are reviewed in Sec. 2. In Sec. 3, we outline insights of eye-tracking study on non-sequential behavior. In Sec. 4, we formally introduce PSCM. We report the experiments on PSCM and compare it with existing click models in Sec. 5. Finally, conclusions and future work are discussed in Sec. 6.

2. RELATED WORK

In this section, we review a number of important click models and introduce some preliminary assumptions shared by these models and PSCM. As this paper mainly focuses on the influence of click sequence, we separate existing click models into two classes: models following the depth-first assumption (i.e. position-based click models) which cannot take non-sequential click actions into account (Sec. 2.1); other models which are able to consider non-sequential click actions (Sec. 2.2).

Note that most click models follow the examination hypothesis [8]: a document being clicked ($C_i = 1$) should satisfy ($\rightarrow$) two conditions: it is examined ($E_i = 1$) and it is relevant ($R_i = 1$) (most click models assume $P(R_i = 1) = r_u$, which is the probability of the perceived relevance), and these two conditions are independent of each other.

$$C_i = 1 \rightarrow E_i = 1, R_i = 1 \tag{1}$$

$$E_i = 0 \rightarrow C_i = 0 \tag{2}$$

$$R_i = 0 \rightarrow C_i = 0 \tag{3}$$

Following this assumption, the probability of a document being clicked is determined as follows:

$$P(C_i = 1) = P(E_i = 1)P(R_i = 1) \tag{4}$$

2.1 Position-based Click Models

As this class of click models does not take click sequence into account, the click action is simply mapped to each search result's ranking position. Based on the assumption that a user examines from top position to bottom position, this kind of click models naturally takes position bias into account.

Craswell et al. [8] proposed the cascade model, which assumes that while a user examines the results from top to bottom sequentially, he/she immediately decides whether to click on a result. The cascade model is mostly suitable for single-click sessions. A number of succeeding models were proposed to improve both its applicability and performance. Based on the cascade hypothesis, the Dependency Click Model (DCM) [13] extends the cascade model in order to model user interactions within multi-click sessions. DCM assumes that a user may have a certain probability of examining the next document after clicking the current document, and this probability is influenced by the ranking position of the result.

Subsequently, the User Browsing Model (UBM) [11] further refines the examination hypothesis by assuming that the event of a document being examined depends on both the preceding click position and the distance between the preceding click position and the current one.

$$P(E_i = 1 | C_{1...i-1}) = \lambda_{r_i, d_i} \tag{5}$$

where r_i represents the preceding click position and d_i is the distance between the current rank and r_i.

The Dynamic Bayesian Network model (DBN) [4] is the first model to consider presentation bias due to snippet (rather than ranking position). This model distinguishes the actual relevance from the perceived relevance, where the perceived relevance indicates the relevance represented by titles or snippets in SERPs and the actual relevance is the relevance of the landing page.

$$P(R_i = 1) = r_u \quad (6)$$

$$P(S_i = 1|C_i = 1) = s_u \quad (7)$$

$$P(E_{i+1}|E_i = 1, S_i = 0) = \lambda \quad (8)$$

where S_i represents whether the user is satisfied with the i-th document, s_u is the probability of this event, r_u is the probability of the perceived relevance, and λ represents the probability of continuing the examination process.

Although some of these models have achieved great success in interpreting clicks and in predicting relevance, compared to our proposed PSCM, they cannot explain the situation where a user does not follow top-down click sequence and they ignore revisiting or duplicated clicks.

2.2 Click-sequence-based Click Models

To the best of our knowledge, only a few studies [28–30] have tried to take non-sequential behavior into consideration. Xu et al. first proposed a Temporal Click Model (TCM) [30] to model user click behavior for sponsored search. This model can only handle two results/ads in an SERP. The only non-sequential click action in this model is: the user first clicks the second result and then goes back to click the first result. This makes it impossible to cope with the whole ranked result list like other click models.

Wang et al. introduced the partially observable Markov Model (POM) [28] to model arbitrary examination orders. The POM model treats the user examination events as a partially observable stochastic process. Although POM can model non-sequential behaviors, it only considers the examination transition at each position (i.e. different users and different queries share the same examination sequence parameters). Therefore, this model cannot predict the click probability or relevance for a specific query and thus can hardly be used in a practical search environment. Due to this limitation, it cannot be compared with other state-of-the-art click models such as UBM and DBN which need to predict click probability and relevance for a specific query-URL pair. It also makes the first order examination assumption that the current examination behavior only depends on its previous examination step, which might not align with the real user behavior.

Xu et al. proposed a Temporal Hidden Click Model (THCM) [29] to cope with non-sequential click actions. They focused on the revisiting behavior and assumed that after clicking a search result, user has a probability to go back to examine previous results (bottom-up). However, their model is also based on one-order Markov examination assumption and supposes that users examine results one by one in examination process, which does not necessarily correspond to practical user behavior (see Sec. 3).

While the above three click models have the potential to take click sequence information into consideration, compared to our proposed PSCM model, their adopted methodology are less suitable to deal with practical search behavior of modern commercial search engines.[1] In comparison, our PSCM is inspired by the eye-tracking study on real users' non-sequential SERP behavior and therefore corresponds better to real-world user behavior.

[1]We actually adapt TCM and POM in Sec. 5.1 to enable them making click and relevance predictions. They will be used as baselines to compare against our model. In Sec. 5, we empirically demonstrate that these models cannot achieve better performance than the popular position-based click models.

3. NON-SEQUENTIAL USER BEHAVIOR

To investigate user's examination sequence during the search process, we carried out a laboratory study with 37 undergraduate students recruited from a university in China (18 males and 19 females with various self-reported Web search expertise). The number of subjects is similar to other Web search eye-tracking studies such as [9, 12].

Subjects were provided with a list of 25 search tasks. Each task was accompanied by a fixed query (with an explanation of the information need to avoid ambiguity) and a Chinese commercial search engine's first result page. We crawled and stored the corresponding SERP to ensure that all subjects saw the same page for each query. With this setup, each search task (query session) corresponds to one specific SERP. The queries for the search tasks were sampled from the NTCIR IMine task[2]. As different types of information need [2] may also affect the browsing behavior [12], the selected search tasks cover different types of search intent. In the query set, 5 of the queries are "Navigational" (e.g. "Meizu's official website"), 10 are "Informational" (e.g. "What is the sound card") and 10 are "Transactional" (e.g. "Web browser download").

With an eye-tracking device (Tobii X2-30), we recorded each subject's eye movement information on each result for each search task. For quality control purposes, each subject was asked to make an eye-tracking calibration before the experiment. The precision threshold of calibration was less than 1° for both vertical and horizontal directions. Subjects may perform the calibration several times before they meet the precision requriement. Behavior data from several query sessions were removed due to subjects' operation errors or software crashes. After removing data from these sessions, we finally collected 890 (out of 925) valid query sessions. When we look at the click-through behavior in the sessions, we found that there exist many query sessions (22.8%, 203 of 890) that contain non-sequential (revisiting or duplicate) click actions. This number confirms clearly the necessity of incorporating non-sequential behaviors into click models.

With the eye-tracking device, we collected two types of eye movement information: saccades and fixations. Saccade means fast eye movements from point to point in jerks, while fixation means that eyes stop for a short period of time [24]. As for the threshold of fixation, we adopt the one used in most previous works (200-500 ms as in [23, 25]) and set it to 250 ms. Because new information is mainly acquired during fixations, most existing studies [3, 16, 23] assumed that eye fixation is equivalent to user examination sequence. Although some recent study [21] showed that eye fixation does not necessary mean examination in many cases, it would be difficult to collect true examination information because this requires user's explicit feedback. Therefore, we still use the recorded fixation sequences to approximate subjects' examination sequences for simplicity. In this way, both click sequences and examination sequences could be restored.

With the data collected in the experiment, we want to find the answers to the following two questions about users' examination behavior on the SERPs.

[2]http://www.thuir.cn/imine/

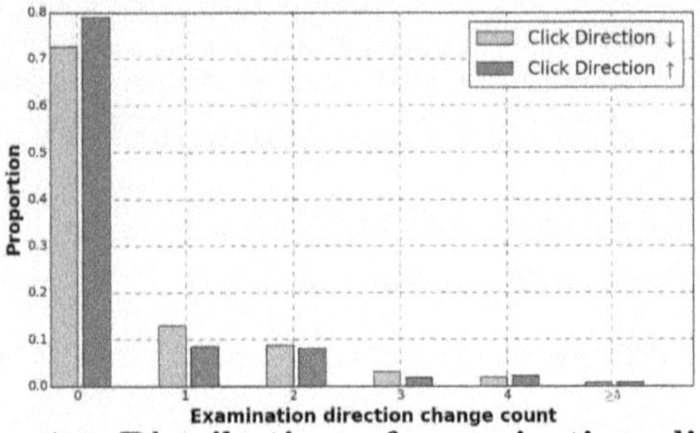

Figure 1: Distribution of examination direction change count for two types of adjacent clicks

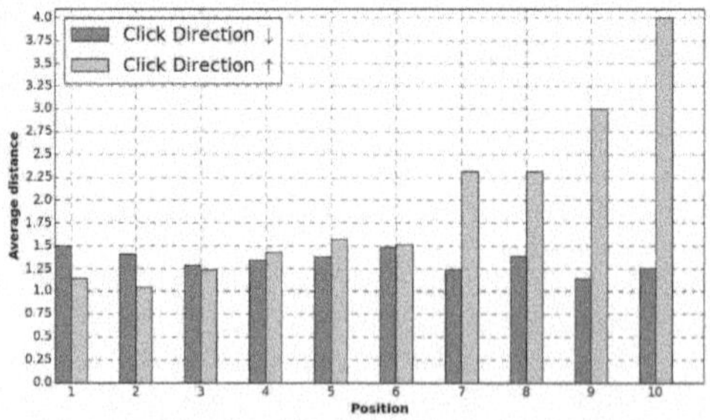

Figure 2: Average examination transition distance according to different examination transition start positions for two types of adjacent clicks.

RQ1: How often do users change the direction of examination between clicks?

RQ2: How far do users' eye gazes jump after examining the current clicked result?

By investigating these two questions, we aim to understand how users behave and to propose corresponding user behavior assumptions in order to model users' examination behavior in a more reasonable way. To simplify the notation, suppose that the first click is at position i and the next click is at position j, if $i < j$, it is a sequential action according to the depth-first assumption (this direction is referred to as "↓"). If $i \geq j$, it is a non-sequential click action according to the definition of revisiting behavior (this direction is referred to as "↑").

To answer the two research questions, we firstly divide all examination sequences into adjacent examination behavior pairs. For a given examination sequence $E =< E_1, E_2, ..., E_t, ..., E_T >$, it will be divided into $T-1$ pairs: $(E_1, E_2), (E_2, E_3), ..., (E_{T-1}, E_T)$. For each pair, similar with the definition of direction in adjacent clicks, we can define its direction as ↑ or ↓ according to whether the sequence of the examination pair follows a depth-first assumption or not.

To investigate ***RQ1***, we consider the examination sequence between ↑ and ↓ adjacent clicks separately. Intuitively, one may believe that the examination sequence between ↓ adjacent clicks should follow the depth-first assumption. In other words, the examination sequence would be consistent with the click sequence.

However, it is also possible that some parts in the examination sequence follow a non-sequential order. Similarly, the examination sequence between ↑ adjacent clicks may also contain ↓ adjacent examination pairs. To find out how often the examination direction change happens between adjacent clicks, we count the number of examination direction changes and the distributions are shown in Figure 1.

From this figure, we can see that no matter whether the click direction is ↑ or ↓, in most cases (72.7% for ↓ and 78.9% for ↑) the whole examination sequences follow the same direction as click direction without any direction changes. The percentage of sequences with direction changes between ↓ clicks is slightly larger than that between ↑ clicks. This phenomenon corresponds well to the behavior pattern in which users re-examine some higher-ranked results before moving to the lower-ranked ones. With this observation, we can formulate the following behavior assumption:

Locally Unidirectional Examination Assumption: Between adjacent clicks, users tend to examine search results in a single direction without changes, and the direction is usually consistent with that of clicks no matter it is ↑ or ↓.

To answer ***RQ2***, we look at the average examination transition distance within adjacent examination pairs. For a given adjacent examination pair (E_{t-1}, E_t), suppose that the first examination E_{t-1} is at position k while the next examination E_t is at position l, the transition distance can be calculated as $|k-l|$. Figure 2 shows the distribution of transition distance in different result positions.

We can see that all transition distances are around 1.25 when user follows top-down (↓) click sequences. While when user follows bottom-up (↑) click sequences, his/her eyes may skip several results to find a specific result.

In particular, we observe larger transition distances for bottom ranking positions, which tend to bring back to the middle positions (positions 5-6) in the list. As all the transition distances are statistically significantly larger than 1 ($p-value < 0.01$ for each position and each click direction based on t-test), we can make the following behavior assumption:

Non First-order Examination Assumption: although the examination behavior between adjacent clicks can be regarded as locally unidirectional, users may skip a few results and examine a result at some distance from the current one following a certain direction.

With the answers to these two research questions, we are able to draw a relatively clear picture of user's examination behavior between adjacent clicks. After a certain user clicks a result i, he/she may start examining results either in a ↑ or a ↓ direction. The user seldom changes the examination direction until he/she clicks another results located at position j (locally unidirectional examination assumption) but he/she may not examine all results on the examination path (non first-order examination assumption).

Compared to existing sequence-based click models such as POM, which assumes that the examination sequence within two clicks can be arbitrary, the actual user behavior shows much simpler patterns. It is thus possible for us to take advantage of the patterns so as to simplify model construction. Compared to THCM that assumes users examine results one by one, the observed user examination behavior demonstrates that user examination may include skips quite frequently. It is necessary for a click model to account for such behaviors.

4. PARTIALLY SEQUENTIAL CLICK MODEL

As we stated in our discussions, the existing click models are unable to correctly cope with the non-sequential behaviors of users we observed. A simple relaxation of the position bias is insufficient for the model to account for the observations we made in the previous section. Therefore, in this paper, we propose to incorporate click sequence information in a different way. At first, click sequence is divided into adjacent click pairs. Considering the two examination behavior assumptions proposed in Sec. 3, the examination process between adjacent clicks could be regarded as both unidirectional and non first-order. With those two assumptions, it is possible for us to employ traditional position-based models in these click sub-sequences. By this means, we can combine the findings in practical user behavior with existing position-based hypotheses consistently.

4.1 Model and Hypotheses

We first introduce some definitions and notations. Suppose that there are N sessions, each of which records certain user interactions with top-M results (M is usually set to 10 in most existing click model resesarches). The result list can be represented as an impression sequence: $D =< d_1, d_2, ..., d_i, ..., d_M >$, where i corresponds to the ranking position (from 1 to M) and d_i is ranked higher than d_j if $i < j$. The relevance of each result is represented by: $R =< R_1, R_2, ..., R_i, ..., R_M >$. With the timestamp information recorded in the logs, we organize the click sequence as $C =< C_1, C_2, ..., C_t, ..., C_T >$, where t is the relative temporal order of a click and C_t records the result position of the t-th click ($1 \leq C_t \leq M$).

The *First-order Click Hypothesis* is usually accepted in most click models such as DBN and UBM. We do the same in this work. It supposes that the click event at time $t + 1$ is only determined by the click event at time t. According to this hypothesis, user's click action $C =< C_1, C_2, ..., C_t, ..., C_T >$ can be independently separated to $T + 1$ adjacent click pairs: $< C_0, C_1 >, ..., < C_{t-1}, C_t >, ..., < C_T, C_{T+1} >$ (C_0 represents the begining of search process and C_{T+1} represents the end of search process). This makes it possible for us to divide a click sequence into sub-sequences (adjacent click pairs).

According to the *Locally Unidirectional Examination Assumption*, given an observation of adjacent clicks at time t: $O = \{< C_{t-1} = m, C_t = n >\}$, users tend to examine the results on the path from m to n without any direction changes. Then the examination and click sequence between C_{t-1} and C_t can be noted as $< \bar{E}_m, ..., \bar{E}_j, ..., \bar{E}_n >$ and $< \bar{C}_m, ..., \bar{C}_j, ..., \bar{C}_n >$, respectively. Note that different from C_t which is used to record the position of click event, $\bar{E}_j$ and $\bar{C}_j$ ($m \leq j \leq n$ *or* $n \leq j \leq m$) are all binary variables representing whether examination or click behavior happens (=1) or not (=0) on the corresponding result position. In addition, we can also deduce that in the click sequence, only $\bar{C}_m$ and $\bar{C}_n$ have value 1 and the other positions on the path have value 0.

The proposed Partially Sequential Click Model (PSCM) adopt these two assumptions. It is then described as follows:

$$P(C_t|C_{t-1}, ..., C_1) = P(C_t|C_{t-1}) \qquad (9)$$

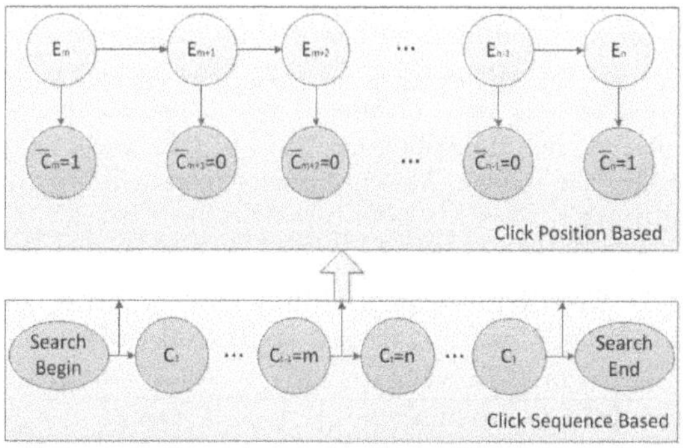

Figure 3: Sketch of Partially Sequential Click Model. Click actions are listed according to their click timestamps. For each adjacent click pair, a position-based framework is constructed based on their click positions.

$$\begin{aligned} &P(C_t = n|C_{t-1} = m) = \\ &P(\bar{C}_m = 1, ..., \bar{C}_i = 0, ..., \bar{C}_n = 1) \end{aligned} \qquad (10)$$

$$\begin{aligned} &P(\bar{E}_i = 1|C_{t-1} = m, C_t = n) = \\ &\begin{cases} \gamma_{imn}, m \leq i \leq n \text{ or } n \leq i \leq m \\ 0, other \end{cases} \end{aligned} \qquad (11)$$

$$\bar{C}_i = 1 \Leftrightarrow \bar{E}_i = 1, R_i = 1 \qquad (12)$$

$$P(R_i = 1) = \alpha_{uq} \qquad (13)$$

Equation (9) encodes the *first-order click hypothesis* while Equation (10) encodes the *locally unidirectional examination assumption* by restricting the examination process to one-way from m to n. We define the examination probability of $\bar{E}_i$ as Equation (11) because according to Figure 2, the examination behavior between adjacent clicks may not follow cascade assumptions (non first-order examination assumption). The probability of examination depends on the positions of the clicks. This is similar to UBM, which also allow skips, but only within sequential behaviors. PSCM also follows examination hypothesis described in Equation (12) as in most existing click models. α_{uq} corresponds to the relevance of the document URL u at position i to the specific query q.

Figure 3 shows the framework of the PSCM model. Unlike previous position-based models (such as UBM or DBN) which suppose user examine results top-down sequentially, PSCM allows non-sequential interactions. A user may click on a lower position (m) and then a higher position ($n > m$), with all the documents between them having some probability to be examined. Such a behavior is modeled by Equation (10) and Equation (11). Compared to the existing click-sequence-based models, PSCM is more flexible than THCM as it no longer makes first-order examination assumption, and is more controlled than POM as it does not allow arbitrary examination. Such a compromised position is justified by the observations we made on user behaviors. A too rigid model such as THCM would be unable to account for the non-sequential behaviors, while a too flexible model such as POM would give the model too much freedom to be correctly parameterized in practice.

Our model uses two groups of parameters: $\{\alpha_{uq}\}$ represents the probability of being relevant for each query-result pair, $\{\gamma_{imn}\}$ represents the examination transition probability in either $\downarrow$ and $\uparrow$ directions. Note that γ are global parameters just as those in UBM. Although setting this parameter according to query (or user) may be helpful, we do not do it in this paper in order to simplify the model. This is a problem we will investigate in the future.

Table 2: Conditional probability for $\bar{C}_i$, $\bar{E}_i$, R_i given parameter $\theta^{(v)}$ and C_t (use Λ as the abbreviation of $(\theta^{(v)}, C_{t-1} = m, C_t = n)$).

Conditional probability	value
$P(\bar{C}_i = 0, R_i = 0, \bar{E}_i = 0\|\Lambda)$	$= (1-\alpha_{uq}^{(v)})(1-\gamma_{imn}^{(v)})$
$P(\bar{C}_i = 0, R_i = 0, \bar{E}_i = 1\|\Lambda)$	$= (1-\alpha_{uq}^{(v)})\gamma_{imn}^{(v)}$
$P(\bar{C}_i = 0, R_i = 1, \bar{E}_i = 0\|\Lambda)$	$= \alpha_{uq}^{(v)}(1-\gamma_{imn}^{(v)})$
$P(\bar{C}_i = 0, R_i = 1, \bar{E}_i = 1\|\Lambda)$	$= 0$
$P(\bar{C}_i = 1, R_i = 0, \bar{E}_i = 0\|\Lambda)$	$= 0$
$P(\bar{C}_i = 1, R_i = 0, \bar{E}_i = 1\|\Lambda)$	$= 0$
$P(\bar{C}_i = 1, R_i = 1, \bar{E}_i = 0\|\Lambda)$	$= 0$
$P(\bar{C}_i = 1, R_i = 1, \bar{E}_i = 1\|\Lambda)$	$= \alpha_{uq}^{(v)}\gamma_{imn}^{(v)}$

As in most existing studies, we assume that the document relevance $\{\alpha_{uq}\}$ and the click events of different sessions are independent of each other. Based on this assumption, we discuss the inference of document relevance.

4.2 Model Inference for PSCM

In our model, two groups of parameters ($\{\alpha_{uq}\}$ and $\{\gamma_{imn}\}$) need to be inferred from click logs. The Expectaction-Maximization (EM) algorithm [15] is used to find the maximum likelihood estimate of the variables $\{\alpha_{uq}\}$ and $\{\gamma_{imn}\}$.

The observation of our model is click sequence ($Y = \{C\}$), the hidden variables are query-result relevance and user examination information ($Z = \{R, E\}$), and the parameters are $\theta = \{\alpha_{uq}, \gamma_{imn}\}$. Therefore, given one specific query-session, the marginal likelihood is:

$$P(Y, Z|\theta) = P(C, E, R|\theta) = \prod_{t=1}^{T} P(C_t, E, R|C_{t-1}, \theta) \quad (14)$$

According to Equation (10) and Equation (12) (omit θ for conciseness):

$$P(C_t = n, E, R|C_{t-1} = m) = \{\prod_{i=m+1}^{n-1} P(\bar{C}_i = 0|\bar{E}_i, R_i)P(R_i)P(\bar{E}_i|C_{t-1} = m, C_t = n)\} \cdot \{P(\bar{C}_n = 1|R_n, \bar{E}_n)P(R_n)P(\bar{E}_n|C_{t-1} = m, C_t = n)\} \quad (15)$$

The conditional expected log-likelihood (Q-function) can be written as (suppose that the parameter at iteration v is $\theta^{(v)}$):

$$Q = E_{E,R|C,\theta^{(v)}}[\log P(C, E, R|\theta)] \quad (16)$$

The values of the required conditional probabilities are given in Table 2. Based on these values, the posterior distributions of $\bar{E}_i$, R_i can be easily calculated. Given N query session and M results for each query, in iteration round v, the formulation of parameter α_{uq} corresponding to a specific query q and result u in Q-function is:

$$Q_{\alpha_{uq}} = \sum_{j=1}^{N}\sum_{\bar{t}}^{T^j}\{I_{mn} \cdot [I_{\neq} \cdot \frac{1-\alpha_{uq}^{(v)}}{1-\alpha_{uq}^{(v)}\gamma_{imn}^{(v)}} \cdot \log(1-\alpha_{uq}) + I_{\neq} \cdot \frac{\alpha_{uq}^{(v)}(1-\gamma_{imn}^{(v)})}{1-\alpha_{uq}^{(v)}\gamma_{imn}^{(v)}} \cdot \log(\alpha_{uq}) + I_{=} \cdot 1 \cdot \log(\alpha_{uq})]\} \quad (17)$$

where j is the j-th session in N, T^j is the click sequence length in this session, $\bar{t}$ corresponds to the t-th adjacent click pair $\{t, C_{t-1} = m, C_t = n\}$, $I(\cdot)$ represents the indicator function, I_{mn} is the abbreviation of $I(m \leq i \leq n \ or \ n \leq i \leq m)$, $I_{=}$ is the abbreviation of $I(d_i^j = u, q^j = q, i = n)$ and $I_{\neq}$ is the abbreviation of $I(d_i^j = u, q^j = q, i \neq n))$.

The formulation of parameter γ_{imn} corresponding to a specific position i (the adjacent clicks are m and n) in Q-function is:

$$Q_{\gamma_{imn}} = \sum_{j=1}^{N}\sum_{\bar{t}}^{T^j}\{I_{mn} \cdot [I_{\neq} \cdot \frac{1-\gamma_{imn}^{(v)}}{1-\alpha_{uq}^{(v)}\gamma_{imn}^{(v)}} \cdot \log(1-\gamma_{imn}) + I_{\neq} \cdot \frac{\gamma_{imn}^{(v)}(1-\alpha_{uq}^{(v)})}{1-\alpha_{uq}^{(v)}\gamma_{imn}^{(v)}} \cdot \log(\gamma_{imn}) + I_{=} \cdot 1 \cdot \log(\gamma_{imn})]\} \quad (18)$$

By separately taking derivation of α_{uq} on Equation (17) and γ_{imn} on Equation (18), we can generate the corresponding updating formulation for $\alpha_{uq}^{(v+1)}$ and $\gamma_{imn}^{(v+1)}$ in iteration round (v):

$$A_1^{(v)} = \sum_{j=1}^{N}\sum_{\bar{t}}^{T^j}\{I_{mn} \cdot I_{\neq} \cdot \frac{1-\alpha_{imn}^{(v)}}{1-\alpha_{uq}^{(v)}\gamma_{imn}^{(v)}}\}$$
$$A_2^{(v)} = \sum_{j=1}^{N}\sum_{\bar{t}}^{T^j}\{I_{mn} \cdot I_{\neq} \cdot \frac{\alpha_{imn}^{(v)}(1-\gamma_{uq}^{(v)})}{1-\alpha_{uq}^{(v)}\gamma_{imn}^{(v)}}\}$$
$$A_3^{(v)} = \sum_{j=1}^{N}\sum_{\bar{t}}^{T^j}\{I_{mn} \cdot I_{=}\} \quad (19)$$
$$\alpha_{uq}^{(v+1)} = \frac{A_2^{(v)} + A_3^{(v)}}{A_1^{(v)} + A_2^{(v)} + A_3^{(v)}}$$

$$G_1^{(v)} = \sum_{j=1}^{N}\sum_{\bar{t}}^{T^j}\{I_{mn} \cdot I_{\neq} \cdot \frac{1-\gamma_{imn}^{(v)}}{1-\alpha_{uq}^{(v)}\gamma_{imn}^{(v)}}\}$$
$$G_2^{(v)} = \sum_{j=1}^{N}\sum_{\bar{t}}^{T^j}\{I_{mn} \cdot I_{\neq} \cdot \frac{\gamma_{imn}^{(v)}(1-\alpha_{uq}^{(v)})}{1-\alpha_{uq}^{(v)}\gamma_{imn}^{(v)}}\}$$
$$G_3^{(v)} = \sum_{j=1}^{N}\sum_{\bar{t}}^{T^j}\{I_{mn} \cdot I_{=}\} \quad (20)$$
$$\gamma_{imn}^{(v+1)} = \frac{G_2^{(v)} + G_3^{(v)}}{G_1^{(v)} + G_2^{(v)} + G_3^{(v)}}$$

5. EXPERIMENTS AND DISCUSSIONS

To test the effectiveness of the proposed PSCM model, we compare its performance with a number of existing click models for click prediction and relevance estimation. We choose two of the most popular position-based click models (UBM [11] and DBN [4]) as our first baselines. As discussed in Section 2.2, there exists a number of sequence-based click models (POM [28], THCM [29] and TCM [30]) which can

Table 3: **Two large-scale commercial search logs (different languages) used to evaluate click models ("#" represents "number of").**

Data	Data-C	Data-Y
Description	Sogou's logs	Yandex's logs
#Distinct Queries	406,345	20,588,928
#Sessions	11,813,260	65,172,853
#Click Sessions	7,951,495	38,288,389
#Multi-click Sessions	2,358,648	11,383,886
Experiments	Click Perplexity NDCG User Preference	Click Perplexity

also take non-sequential behavior into consideration. These models are also used as our baselines.

Three types of experiments are performed to validate our model. First we evaluate the click model in terms of predicting click probabilities (click perplexity) from search logs, which is a widely adopted metric to evaluate click models' performances [4, 11, 29]. After that, we use the predicted relevance as a signal for document ranking and evaluate each click model's ranking performance with traditional IR metrics (in this paper we use NDCG metric [17]). Finally, since professional assessors' relevance annotation may not always agree with users' actual judgments [6], we also conduct a user preference test [26] in which participants are asked to label their preferences on parellaled result lists generated by different models.

5.1 Experimental Setups

As discussed in Sec. 2, TCM and POM are not directly comparable to other click models due to different behavior assumptions. Therefore, we first describe how we address the limitations and adapt them for performance comparison. As for other baseline models, we refer to the implementations from [7]. Our code implementations and evaluation data set are publicly available at https://github.com/THUIR/PSCMModel.

5.1.1 Baseline Model Adaptation

(TCM) As we have mentioned in Sec. 2.2, this model can only handle result lists containing exactly two results. As this model enumerates all possible click sequences for a specific ranking list (5 possible situation for two results [30]), it faces the exponential explosion problem when the number of results becomes large. Therefore, we cannot expand this model to M results in one SERP (M equals to 10 in our data set). In order to compare this model with other existing click models which can handle arbitrary number of results in an SERP, we made an trivial expansion of TCM model: we separate these results into $M/2$ pairs $(< 1,2 >, < 3,4 >, ..., < M-1, M >)$ and implement TCM model for each pair separately. Then, from each pair we can deduce two results' relevance and click probability. We thus combine $M/2$ pairs together to generate click prediction and relevance prediction for the whole result list.

(POM) Although POM can model non-sequential behaviors in user interactions, this model is not designed to predict the click probability or result relevance for a specific query, as we discussed in Sec. 2. It is unfair to compare POM with other models. To make POM more suitable for the click and relevance prediction tasks, we modify the original POM model by setting a relevance score for each specific document-query pair.

According to search logs, clicks can be re-organized as a temporal sequence of behaviors by record timestamps: $E =< E_1, E_2, ..., E_t, ..., E_T >$, where t represents the events' relative order, E_t represents the corresponding ranking of the result being examined at time t and $C =< C_1, C_2, ..., C_t, ..., C_T >$, where C_t represents the corresponding result is clicked or not. From search logs, we can only observe which results are clicked by users. Based on the assumption that user must examine a result before clicking on it (examination hypothesis [8]), we can infer that the clicked results must be examined. Therefore, user may examine some results in his/her browsing process but not click them given a click sequence observation $O = \{(E_1 = e_1, C_1 = 1), ..., (E_T = e_T, C_T = 1)\}$. So an arbitrary $O' = \{(E'_1, C'_1), ..., (E'_k, C'_k), ...(E'_K, C'_K)\}$ can be generated based on the original observation O where $O \subseteq O'$. The POM model assumes that the probability of original observation is the summation of the probabilities of all compatible examination sequences. Furthermore the POM model makes first order assumption that current examining result only depends on previous examination. So the POM model can be represented as follows:

$$P(O) = \sum_{O'} P(O') = \sum_{O'} \prod_{i=1}^{K} P(C_i|E_i)P(E_i|E_{i-1}) \quad (21)$$

$$P(C_i = 1|E_i = m) = c_m \quad (22)$$

$$P(E_i = n|E_{i-1} = m) = e_{mn} \quad (23)$$

where E_0 represents the submitted query received at the begining of a search session, c_m is the click probability of rank m, e_{mn} is the examination transition probability. According to the formulations above, POM model can model arbitrary examination orders. As a matter of fact, it can describe the non-sequential click behavior during search process.

However, in the original POM model, given the examination of a result, the click probability is only dependent on the result position (Equation (22)). Therefore, we simply adopt the examination hypothesis that given the examination of a result, the click probability is dependent on the result's relevance. Therefore, the Equation (22) is revised as:

$$P(C_i = 1|E_i = m) = \alpha_{uq} \quad (24)$$

where α_{uq} is the relevance of query-document pair. So the click probability no longer depends on the rank position but depends on the search query. Once we get α_{uq}, we can compare POM with other click models in terms of click perplexity and NDCG. The parameter estimation formulation is similar to the original model [28] by using Expectation-Maximization (EM) algorithm.

5.1.2 Data Sets

To evaluate the click models, we utilize two real-world large-scale data sets collected by Sogou from China and Yandex[3] from Russia. The detailed statistics of the two

[3]The Yandex dataset is publicly available at https://www.kaggle.com/c/yandex-personalized-web-search-challenge/data.

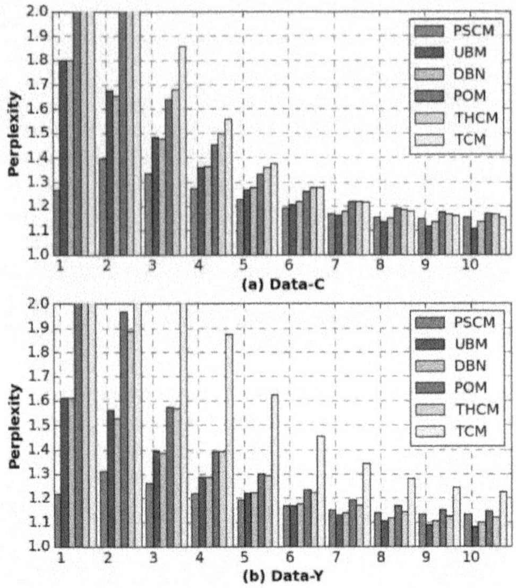

Figure 4: Click perplexities of different positions on Data-C and Data-Y.

Table 4: Overall click perplexity of each model on Data-C and Data-Y (all improvements are statistically significant according to t-test with $p-value < 10^{-5}$).

Model	Data-C	PSCM Impr.	Data-Y	PSCM Impr.
PSCM	1.232	-	1.192	-
UBM	1.332	30.1%	1.265	27.4%
DBN	1.339	31.6%	1.267	27.9%
POM	1.782	70.4%	1.826	76.7%
THCM	1.583	60.3%	1.545	64.7%
TCM	2.435	83.8%	2.691	88.6%

datasets can be found in Table 3. Specifically, we evaluate the click models on click perplexity for both of the whole datasets. Then for evaluating relevance prediction of click models (with respect to either NDCG or user preference), we use a subset of Data-C for testing relevance prediction because relevance annotation is not available for the Yandex set.

5.2 Evaluation of Click Prediction

We use two search logs (see Table 3) to compute the click perplexity of each model. For each dataset, we split all query sessions into the training and testing sets at a ratio of 70% : 30% as previous studies did [5, 27].

Click perplexity [27] measures the probability of the actual click events occurring for each session and each position. It indicates how well a model can predict the clicks. A smaller perplexity value indicates a better modeling performance, and the value reaches 1 in the ideal case. The improvement of click perplexity CP_1 over CP_2 is calculated through $\frac{CP_2 - CP_1}{CP_2 - 1} * 100\%$ [5, 27].

Table 4 illustrates the overall perplexity of each model and Figure 4 shows perplexities in different positions. We can see that PSCM achieves the best overall results among all click models. According to Table 4, existing sequence-based models (POM, THCM and TCM) cannot achieve as good performance as position-based models (UBM and DBN). This suggests that the assumptions on the examination and click sequences are either too strict (e.g. restrict one-by-one examination in THCM) or too flexible (e.g. allowed at any position in POM). As we observed, user behaviors basically follow the same direction, but with occasional changes of direction and jumps. Our model is built on these observations. As we can see in Table 4, our model can better predict clicks than all the other models. This is a strong indication that the sequence of user behaviors is better coped with in our model.

From Figure 4 we can also see that PSCM generates very good results in the top positions (1-5). However, it achieves slightly worse performance than position-based models (UBM and DBN) in the bottom positions (8-10). This phenomenon can be explained by the fact that PSCM has taken more possible examination sequences (compared to position-based models) into account and thus it gives slightly higher click probability in bottom positions. While in most query sessions, a user usually skips results in bottom positions. Therefore, PSCM will receive more penalties in perplexity than UBM and DBN. However, these degradations on bottom positions are much less significant than the improvements on top positions because 1) the scale of the degradations are far less than that of the improvements; and 2) users often care more about the top positions than bottom positions.

5.3 Evaluation of Relevance Estimation

As a click model also provides a prediction on the relevance of a document for a query - α_{uq}, we can rank documents according to this value. The ranking results can be measured using NDCG [17]. This evaluation is performed only on Data-C for which human evaluators can be recruited to judge document relevance. The same evaluation cannot be done on Data-Y because the data has been encoded to unreadable codes, and no relevance information is available.

For a random sample of 1,187 queries in Data-C, several professional assessors (from Sogou.com, without knowing any information about this work) annotated a number of results' relevance scores for each query. The annotation is performed with 5 grades ("Perfect", "Excellent", "Good", "Fair" and "Bad") as in most existing studies such as [31]. Majority voting is adopted to decide the relevance score if there are conflicts (at least 3 assessors were involved in each query-result pair annotation). Due to limited human resources, top five results for 460 queries were annotated while only top 3 results are annotated for the other 727 queries. With the annotation results, we calculated the NDCG@N (N=3,5) scores for different click models and the results are shown in Figure 5.

We can see that PSCM achieves statistically significant improvement over the other click models. We can also see that position-based click models (UBM and DBN) still achieve better relevance prediction than sequence-based click models (POM, THCM and TCM) as in click prediction. This confirms our assumption in Sec. 2 that existing click-sequence-based click models are less suitable to cope with sequences of user interactions.

5.4 User Preference Test

Besides the evaluation in relevance estimation, we also want to find out whether the ranking lists provided by PSCM are preferred by real users than other click models.

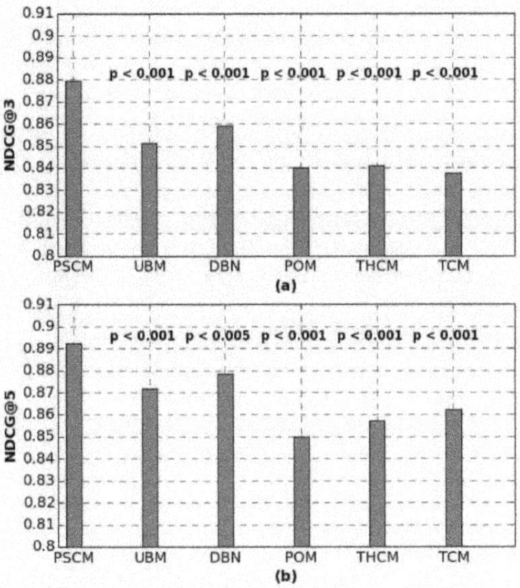

Figure 5: Relevance estimation performances in terms of NDCG@3 (1,187 queries) and NDCG@5 (460 queries) for Data-C. The Improvements of PSCM compared with other models are all significant (paired t-test $p - values$ are also shown in the figure)

Therefore, we conducted a side-by-side user preference test of PSCM against the ranking list provided by DBN (second best performance according to NDCG) as is done in [18].

We randomly sampled 200 queries and recruited 22 human evaluators (all university students with a variety of majors and self-reported search expertise) to label their preferences. For each query, the evaluators were shown two result lists produced by PSCM and DBN respectively. They were required to label a preference degree after reviewing the two lists with 9 levels: "Left results list is better {+4, +3, +2, +1}", "Tie {0}" and "Right results list is better {+1, +2, +3, +4}". The evaluators did not know which list was generated from one specific model as the display side was randomly chosen. Each evaluator annotated at least 50 result list pairs to make sure that each pair was labeled by at least 5 different evaluators.

Figure 6 shows the label distribution of all evaluators. We can see that most of them prefer PSCM (46.5%), and only 27.5% labels prefer DBN. To summarize the user preference for each query, we also use the majority voting method to merge labels from different evaluators. The experimental results are illustrated in Figure 7. We can also see that evaluators show clear preferences to PSCM in nearly half of all queries (47.5%). The proportion of "PSCM better" is statistically significantly larger than the proportion of "Tie" and "DBN better" according to Pearson's chi-squared test ($p - value < 0.001$). This result is consistent with the distribution of labels, which indicates that PSCM can produce better ranking lists than DBN.

With the evaluation results in click perplexity, NDCG and user preference test, we can conclude that our model can better describe user's actual examining and clicking behavior. In addition, this model can also provide more accurate estimations in query-result relevance, and thus generate better result ranking lists.

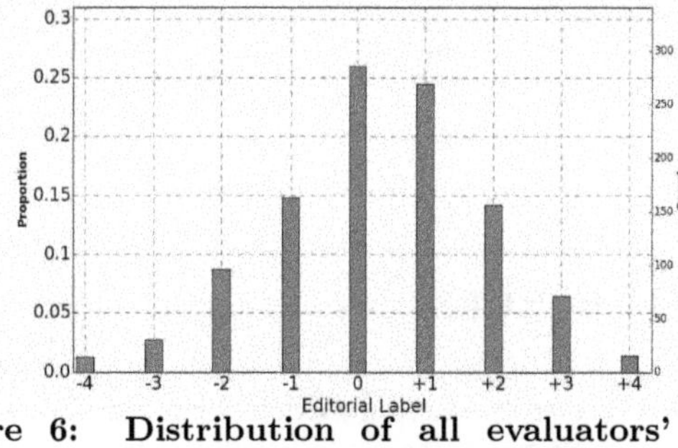

Figure 6: Distribution of all evaluators' labels ("+1 $\sim$ +4" represents user prefers PSCM, "$-1 \sim -4$" represents user prefers DBN and "0" represents tie).

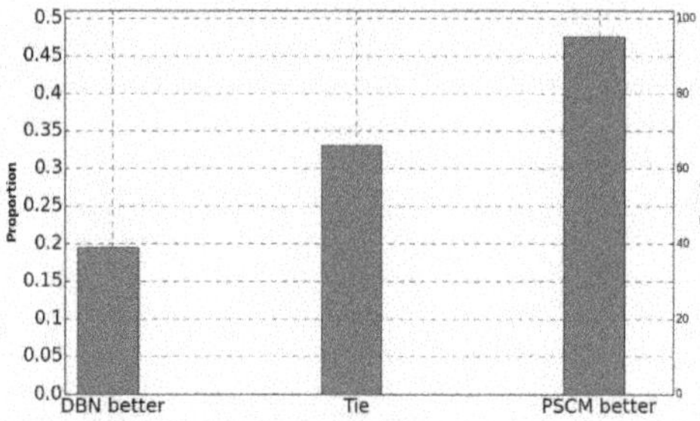

Figure 7: Editorial evaluation for PSCM and DBN in the user preference test.

6. CONCLUSIONS

In this paper, we address the problem of properly incorporating click sequence information into click models. First, we carried out a laboratory eye-tracking experiment to analyze search users' examination behaviors. From the observations, we formulated two assumptions: the locally unidirectional assumption and non-first-order examination assumption. Based on these findings, we proposed a new click model named PSCM, which incorporates non-sequential click behaviors into click models while following the two assumption on examinations between two clicks. The experimental results on large-scale click-through data showed that our model outperforms existing models in click prediction. We also conducted tests on query-result relevance estimation and user preference of ranking lists. The experimental results show that PSCM outperform existing models in both relevance evaluation (NDCG) and user preference test. This study shows the importance for a click model to correct cope with user's interaction sequences. Compared to the previous models, the assumptions made in our model are more realistic and correspond better to the observations in practice. The proposed model can be further improved on several aspects. For example, as click dwell time has been proved to be a very useful signal for relevance prediction, we plan to combine click dwell time information with click sequence information together to better model users' search behaviors in future work.

7. ACKNOWLEDGMENTS

This work was supported by National Key Basic Research Program (2015CB358700), Tsinghua-Samsung Joint Lab, Tsinghua University Initiative Scientific Research Program (2014Z21032), and Natural Science Foundation (61472206) of China. Part of the work has been done at the Tsinghua-NUS NExT Search Centre, which is supported by the Singapore National Research Foundation & Interactive Digital Media R&D Program Office, MDA under research grant (WBS:R-252-300-001-490).

8. REFERENCES

[1] E. Agichtein, E. Brill, S. T. Dumais, and R. Ragno. Learning user interaction models for predicting web search result preferences. *SIGIR'06*, pages 3–10, Aug. 2006.

[2] A. Broder. A taxonomy of web search. In *SIGIR'02*, volume 36, pages 3–10. ACM, 2002.

[3] G. Buscher, S. White, Ryen W, and J. Huang. Large-scale analysis of individual and task differences in search result page examination strategies. In *WSDM'12*, pages 373–382. ACM, 2012.

[4] O. Chapelle and Y. Zhang. A dynamic bayesian network click model for web search ranking. *WWW'09*, pages 1–10, Apr. 2009.

[5] D. Chen, W. Chen, H. Wang, Z. Chen, and Q. Yang. Beyond ten blue links: enabling user click modeling in federated web search. *WSDM'12*, pages 463–472, Feb. 2012.

[6] F. Chen, Y. Liu, Z. Dou, K. Xu, Y. Cao, M. Zhang, and S. Ma. Revisiting the evaluation of diversified search evaluation metrics with user preferences. In *Information Retrieval Technology*, pages 48–59. Springer, 2014.

[7] A. Chuklin, P. Serdyukov, and M. De Rijke. Click model-based information retrieval metrics. In *SIGIR'13*, pages 493–502. ACM, 2013.

[8] N. Craswell, O. Zoeter, M. Taylor, and B. Ramsey. An experimental comparison of click position-bias models. In *WSDM'08*, pages 87–94. ACM, 2008.

[9] E. Cutrell and Z. Guan. What are you looking for?: an eye-tracking study of information usage in web search. In *CHI 07*, pages 407–416. ACM, 2007.

[10] G. Dupret and C. Liao. A model to estimate intrinsic document relevance from the clickthrough logs of a web search engine. In *WSDM'10*, pages 181–190. ACM, 2010.

[11] G. Dupret and B. Piwowarski. A user browsing model to predict search engine click data from past observations. *SIGIR'08*, pages 331–338, July 2008.

[12] L. A. Granka, T. Joachims, and G. Gay. Eye-tracking analysis of user behavior in www search. In *SIGIR 04*, pages 478–479. ACM, 2004.

[13] F. Guo, C. Liu, and Y. M. Wang. Efficient multiple-click models in web search. *WSDM'09*, pages 124–131, Feb. 2009.

[14] Q. Guo, D. Lagun, D. Savenkov, and Q. Liu. Improving relevance prediction by addressing biases and sparsity in web search click data. In *WSCD'12*, pages 71–75, 2012.

[15] M. R. Gupta and Y. Chen. *Theory and use of the EM algorithm*. Now Publishers Inc, 2011.

[16] J. Huang, R. W. White, and S. Dumais. No clicks, no problem: using cursor movements to understand and improve search. In *CHI's 11*, pages 1225–1234. ACM, 2011.

[17] K. Järvelin and J. Kekäläinen. Cumulated gain-based evaluation of ir techniques. *ACM Transactions on Information Systems (TOIS)*, 20(4):422–446, 2002.

[18] L. Jie, S. Lamkhede, R. Sapra, E. Hsu, H. Song, and Y. Chang. A unified search federation system based on online user feedback. In *SIGKDD'13*, pages 1195–1203. ACM, 2013.

[19] T. Joachims, L. A. Granka, B. Pan, H. Hembrooke, and G. Gay. Accurately interpreting click through data as implicit feedback. *SIGIR'05*, pages 154–161, July 2005.

[20] K. Klockner, N. Wirschum, and A. Jameson. Depth- and breadth-first processing of search result lists. *CHI'04*, pages 1539–1539, Apr. 2004.

[21] Y. Liu, C. Wang, K. Zhou, J. Nie, M. Zhang, and S. Ma. From skimming to reading: A two-stage examination model for web search. In *CIKM'14*, pages 849–858. ACM, 2014.

[22] L. Lorigo, B. Pan, H. Hembrooke, T. Joachims, L. A. Granka, and G. Gay. The influence of task and gender on search and evaluation behavior using google. *Information Processing and Management*, 42(4):1123–1131, 2006.

[23] R. Navalpakkam, Vidhya, S. Ravi, A. Ahmed, and A. Smola. Measurement and modeling of eye-mouse behavior in the presence of nonlinear page layouts. In *WWW 13*, pages 953–964, 2013.

[24] K. Rayner. Eye movements and attention in reading, scene perception, and visual search. *The quarterly journal of experimental psychology*, 62(8):1457–1506, 2009.

[25] D. D. Salvucci and J. H. Goldberg. Identifying fixations and saccades in eye-tracking protocols. In *Proceedings of the 2000 symposium on Eye tracking research & applications*, pages 71–78. ACM, 2000.

[26] M. Sanderson, M. L. Paramita, P. Clough, and E. Kanoulas. Do user preferences and evaluation measures line up? In *SIGIR'10*, pages 555–562. ACM, 2010.

[27] C. Wang, Y. Liu, M. Zhang, S. Ma, M. Zheng, J. Qian, and K. Zhang. Incorporating vertical results into search click models. In *SIGIR'13*, pages 503–412. ACM, 2013.

[28] K. Wang, N. Gloy, and X. Li. Inferring search behaviors using partially observable markov(pom) model. *WSDM'10*, pages 211–220, Feb. 2010.

[29] D. Xu, Y. Liu, M. Zhang, S. Ma, and L. Ru. Incorporating revisiting behaviors into click models. In *WSDM'12*, pages 303–312. ACM, 2012.

[30] W. Xu, E. Manavoglu, and E. Cantu-Paz. Temporal click model for sponsored search. In *SIGIR'10*, pages 106–113. ACM, 2010.

[31] H. Yang, A. Mityagin, K. M. Svore, and S. Markov. Collecting high quality overlapping labels at low cost. In *SIGIR'10*, pages 459–466. ACM, 2010.

[32] Y. Yue, R. Patel, and H. Roehrig. Beyond position bias: examining result attractiveness as a source of presentation bias in click through data. *WWW'10*, pages 1011–1018, Apr. 2010.

Untangling Result List Refinement and Ranking Quality: a Framework for Evaluation and Prediction

Jiyin He
CWI
jiyinhe@acm.org

Marc Bron
Yahoo! Labs London
mbron@yahoo-inc.com

Arjen de Vries
CWI
arjen@acm.org

Leif Azzopardi
University of Glasgow
leif.azzopardi@glasgow.ac.uk

Maarten de Rijke
University of Amsterdam
derijke@uva.nl

ABSTRACT

Traditional batch evaluation metrics assume that user interaction with search results is limited to scanning down a ranked list. However, modern search interfaces come with additional elements supporting result list refinement (RLR) through facets and filters, making user search behavior increasingly dynamic. We develop an evaluation framework that takes a step beyond the interaction assumption of traditional evaluation metrics and allows for batch evaluation of systems with and without RLR elements. In our framework we model user interaction as switching between different sublists. This provides a measure of user effort based on the joint effect of user interaction with RLR elements and result quality.

We validate our framework by conducting a user study and comparing model predictions with real user performance. Our model predictions show significant positive correlation with real user effort. Further, in contrast to traditional evaluation metrics, the predictions using our framework, of when users stand to benefit from RLR elements, reflect findings from our user study.

Finally, we use the framework to investigate under what conditions systems with and without RLR elements are likely to be effective. We simulate varying conditions concerning ranking quality, users, task and interface properties demonstrating a cost-effective way to study whole system performance.

Categories and Subject Descriptors

H.5.2 [**User Interfaces**]: Evaluation/methodology

Keywords

Simulation; Search behavior; Faceted search; Evaluation

1. INTRODUCTION

Many of today's enterprises require a dedicated search system, i.e., a particular optimal configuration of both a *ranking algorithm* and *interface*, to effectively support their specific type of user, task, and collection. To select this optimal configuration an evaluation metric–capturing a particular user behavior and interface combination–together with a fixed set of queries, documents, and relevance judgements, is required to determine the quality of various ranking algorithms [33]. Traditional batch evaluation metrics, however, typically assume that after launching a query, user interaction remains limited to scanning down a ranked result list and stops at some rank k [4]. As interfaces of modern search systems are equipped with additional elements, such as result filters, *and* users become more actively involved in the search process, the *whole system* effectiveness no longer solely depends on the quality of the ranking, but also on how the interface elements function, as well as on *how* users operate these elements [3, 14, 16, 26]. Consequently, batch evaluation metrics for traditional search systems no longer accurately reflect system performance when it comes to the combination of a ranking algorithm and interface.

A key problem, then, is how to choose between systems with varying combinations of interface elements and ranking algorithms. As a first step, in this paper, we present a framework for comparing search systems equipped with a particular class of interface elements, i.e., elements supporting *result list refinement* (RLR). We define RLR search systems as those that provide: (i) a fixed set of filter values that remain visible to the user at all times; and (ii) the filter values operate on a fixed initial result set for a particular query. For example, a system with minimal RLR elements has a single filter value, where elements of increasing complexity are a list of multiple filter values (keywords/entities), and filter values grouped in categories (facets). A relation exists between facets and RLR elements, however, we do not require filter values to be mutually exclusive, exhaustive [34], or orthogonal [13].

We limit the initial framework to search systems with RLR elements for two reasons. The first is pragmatic: without loss of generality, user interactions with these elements can be modeled as switching between a limited number of different subsets of a result list. It allows this work to go beyond the standard user interaction model in batch evaluation, cf. [4], while remaining tractable. The second is methodological: we wish to focus on user interactions with a class of elements that require users only to *recognize* a suitable filter value to refine a result list with. This in contrast to, for example, query (re)formulations that require additional mental effort on the part of the user [29], thereby allowing greater variability in user interactions depending on individual user characteristics.

Our evaluation framework for systems with RLR elements has two parts: (i) an evaluation measure specified by a model that characterizes how users interact with systems supporting RLR and a specification of how these interactions are associated with user effort and gain (Section 3); and (ii) a simulation strategy, i.e., an instantiation of the interaction model parameters (Sections 4 and 5).

SIGIR'15, August 09 - 13, 2015, Santiago, Chile.

ACM 978-1-4503-3621-5/15/08$15.00
DOI: http://dx.doi.org/10.1145/2766462.2767740.

The framework has two immediate applications. (i) *Prediction*: by obtaining estimates of the parameters of the interaction models from usage data, e.g., from online systems or user studies, system performance can be predicted and evaluated off-line. This allows optimization of systems by varying the ranking algorithm and interface elements, for a particular application and user group. (ii) *Simulation*: our framework allows us to perform "*what-if*" analyses, i.e., to investigate system performance under varying conditions by simulating different combinations of ranking quality, interface elements, and type of users. Such simulation results can inform decisions about the type of interface, ranking algorithm, and queries to be used when comparing systems in subsequent user studies.

To demonstrate the efficacy of our evaluation framework we apply it to the comparison of two standard snippet-based search systems, one with RLR elements and one without. Here, our first goal is to examine the accuracy of the framework in predicting user effort when interacting with an RLR system. We instantiate the model parameters of the two systems with user data and then compare the model predictions with real usage data. Specifically, we seek answers to the following questions: (i) does the effort predicted by our framework correlate with user effort on a task with the two systems; and (ii) does comparing simulated system performance allow us to accurately predict when RLR elements are beneficial and when they are not?

Having validated its accuracy, our second goal is to investigate system performance under varying conditions, including different ranking quality, filter properties, as well as user behaviors—and how these factors interplay. In short, we study the question: "when does an RLR-enabled system help to improve user performance?"

2. RELATED WORK

User interaction models are closely related to effectiveness metrics developed for batch-evaluation: users invest effort to operate a system in order to gain relevant information. With some abstraction, a batch evaluation metric can be viewed as a function that makes predictions about user effort and gain based on its user interaction model, i.e., assumptions about how users operate the system, cf. [4]. For example, widely used metrics P@K and NDCG@K employ user interaction models of two different types of user search behavior: P@K assumes users examine all top K results in no particular order, and NDCG@K assumes users examine top K results from top-to-bottom and find lower-ranked results of less value. In both cases, we can interpret the number of documents examined as effort, and the number of relevant documents found as gain.

User interaction with a traditional search interface. Modeling user interaction with retrieved results has become a central topic in recent discussions on evaluation methodology [1]. A wide range of stochastic models have been learned from Web search engine click logs [5, 8, 11, 12]. Common to these models are a few assumptions that have been identified as typical user interaction patterns in Web search. For example, the *examination assumption* states that users are less likely to view lower ranked results [21]; and the *cascade model* assumes users browse a ranked result list from top to bottom, and stop once a relevant result is found [9].

Meanwhile, several effectiveness metrics have been proposed in an effort to integrate more realistic user interaction models. For example, the Rank Biased Precision (RBP) [28] models the "persistence" of a user, i.e., how likely a user examines a next result when going down a ranked list; the Expected Reciprocal Rank (ERR) [6] is derived from the cascade model; and Chuklin et al. [7] proposed to turn click models into evaluation measures. Time-biased gain takes into account user variability in terms of the time needed to process information, e.g., reading summaries [31].

An alternative use of user interaction models is to *simulate* user search activities, in order to evaluate system performance under various conditions such as "what if users do X?" which are not likely to be investigated by a user study. For example, Smucker and Clarke [31] presented a method to simulate time-biased gain. A shared assumption in the studies listed so far is the traditional ranked list search interface.

Studies that go beyond the traditional *single* ranked list based user interaction is session-based evaluation [20, 22]. Here, in addition to the examination assumption, an extra user decision—whether to reformulate their query—is modeled (cf. Section 3.1).

Beyond traditional search interfaces. Moving away from the traditional ranked list search interface, Fuhr [14] proposed the interactive probabilistic ranking principle (iPRP) aimed at providing a formal description of user interactions and the corresponding optimization strategy for a system. However, instantiation of this general model for practical use remains an open problem.

More concretely, faceted search is a typical example where user interaction models need to go beyond the assumptions of a ranked list interaction model. Often, simulation based evaluation is employed [23–25, 27, 32]. A key notion shared by these simulation models is "*utility*" [23, 25, 32]—the trade-off between the effort users spend and the benefit gained, e.g., finding a target document.

Various heuristic user interaction models have been proposed for simulation. These models assume different user goals and how users interact with retrieved results and facets. In terms of user goals, Kashyap et al. [23] assumed users examine all filtered results in the context of database queries. Alternatively, in [25, 30, 32] users were assumed to find only one relevant result. In terms of user operation with facets, Koren et al. [25] assumed that users can always recognize the facet that contains relevant document(s), and select facets in one of the following ways: (i) randomly; (ii) facets with least document coverage; (iii) the first facet that contains the target document; or (iv) the optimal facets. Kong and Allan [24] assumed that users sequentially scan facets and skip an entire facet when they find it irrelevant.

Our work. Our goal is to devise a new evaluation method for systems with a search interface enabling RLR elements. What we need is a user interaction model that is able to characterize not only the traditional "examine a result list" interactions, but also interactions with RLR elements.

We evaluate an RLR system under the same notion of utility (user effort and gain) as in the above studies in faceted search. Our work differs in two important ways. First, we model user interactions with RLR elements (including facets) in a more natural way—users scan filtered results without a particular order; and they may and may not recognize a "good" filter value. Second, we do not make explicit assumptions to create categories of users (like in [25]). The variability of users is captured by a probabilistic framework: by varying two model parameters, we are able to simulate a wide range of users. This second property of our model allows us to encompass empirical user interaction models developed for traditional search interfaces, i.e., to fit the model with real usage data and make predictions of system performance with respect to a particular group of users/search tasks.

3. MODELING RLR INTERACTIONS

Our evaluation framework has the following components: (a) a user interaction model that characterizes how users interact with a system that enables result refinement (Section 3.1); (b) associating effort and gain to user interactions for evaluation (Section 3.2); and (c) integration of the above two components (Section 3.3).

We assume that users perform *actions* to make progress on a search task (e.g., inspect results); every action costs *effort*; and the user may *gain* from that action by finding relevant information. With an interaction model, we simulate and predict *action paths* of users during a search task, which vary across users and search tasks, and are influenced by the quality of the result lists. By associating effort and gain with different paths of search actions, we are able to predict user effort given different types of users, tasks and the quality of result lists.

Overall, the effectiveness of a system can be measured by answering questions such as: How much effort is required to achieve x amounts of gain with system A, as compared to system B?

3.1 User interaction at a conceptual level

User interaction with a basic interface. With a basic search interface, the common assumptions are: users browse a result list from top to bottom; and after examining each result, they make a decision—whether to continue to examine another result, or to give up this result list [12, 15].

User interaction with an RLR-enabled interface. With an RLR-enabled interface, apart from examining results in the retrieved ranked list, users may choose to refine the result list by filtering on a particular value. A typical consequence of these RLR interactions is that users switch between different filtered versions of the original result list. We refer to these different versions of the result list, including the original ranked list, as *sublists*.

Without making assumptions about the specific implementation of these elements, at a functional level, we can model the user interactions with RLR elements as *selecting a sublist*.

This leads to at least two additional decisions a user needs to make: (1) continue with the *current* sublist, switch to a different sublist, or quit searching? and (2) if switching, *which* sublist to select next?

Parameterization of user interactions. Each of the decision points introduces uncertainty in computing user effort and gain during a search task: it is at these points users diverge from each other's action paths. Taking these decision points as variables of our interaction model allows us to capture variability in user behavior.

Specifically, to quantify the uncertain nature of user decisions, we model the outcome of the aforementioned decisions as random variables following specific distributions:

- **Continuation decision:** we model the decision of user u at rank r to examine the next result in the *same* result list as a binary variable $s_{r,u} \sim Ber(p_{r,u})$. While it looks similar to the *persistence probability* [28], we do not make the i.i.d. assumption about the continuation behavior at each rank. That is, in [28], a single persistence probability p is shared by results at all ranks; and the probability that a user examines the result at rank r is p^{r-1}. The Bernoulli parameter $p_{r,u}$ in our model, however, is specific to a rank r and a user u, thus leaving more flexibility for setting different hypothesized values for simulation or fitting empirical parameters from log data.
- **Switching decision:** similarly, we model the decision of user u at rank r to switch sublists as a binary variable $l_{r,u} \sim Ber(p^l_{r,u})$ with parameter $p^l_{r,u}$ specific to a user and a rank.
- **Sublist selection decision:** we model user decisions on sublist selection among K candidates as a vector of binary random variables following a categorical distribution $\mathbf{f} \sim Cat(K, \mathbf{c}_u)$. Sublist k is chosen if $f_k = 1$; 0 otherwise; and only one list is chosen at a time. The parameter $\mathbf{c}_u$ determines the likelihood that a list is chosen by a user, e.g., according to his/her perception of the quality of the sublists.

These three probabilities can be set to empirical values estimated from usage logs (Section 4), or based on hypotheses about their values (Section 5). Of course, users may decide to quit searching. However, as quitting is complementary to the continuation and switching decisions, there is no need to explicitly define it.

3.2 User actions, effort, and gain

With the conceptual user interaction model in place, we now specify how we can associate effort and gain to user interactions.

User actions. We consider 3 types of action:

- **Examine result:** Users examine a result to determine its relevance, by inspecting the title, summary, or the document content. While these introduce great variety in the effort needed for an examination, we consider them as a *single* action of constant cost. We wish to focus on factors that change the result list, e.g., pagination or filtering, which may lead to more examination activities. However, it is straightforward to incorporate fine-grained levels of user interactions with our model, which we leave as future work.
- **Pagination:** While not explicitly modeled as a decision, a user will need to paginate if he/she decides to examine a result which is on a next page. Effort required by pagination is directly related to result list quality.
- **Select candidate result list:** This activity involves a series of mental activities such as estimating which sublist is more likely to contain relevant information, e.g., by inspecting the filter names. As with result examination, we abstract away the details and treat the whole process as a single action.

Effort of actions. Each action is associated with an amount of effort. Let A be the possible actions users can perform, and $P_a = a_1, ..., a_t$ be the action path of a user that starts browsing results of q until he/she stops, $a_i \in A$. The user's effort along P_a is

$$\mathcal{E}(q, P_a) = \textstyle\sum_{i=1}^{t} w_i a_i, \quad (1)$$

where w_i is the effort needed for action a_i.

Effort can be implemented in different ways. For example, with NDCG or P@10, the only actions considered are "examine" a document, and each costs a unit effort. With time-biased gain [31], effort is implemented in a more elaborate way, e.g., the effort required for an "examine" may depend on the document length.

Gain of actions. We assume that user gain is determined by the relevant documents they encounter. Let D_{P_a} be the documents a user encounters along action path P_a; its total gain is

$$\mathcal{G}(q, D_{P_a}) = \textstyle\sum_{d \in D_{P_a}} rel(d, q), \quad (2)$$

where $rel(d, q)$ is the relevance judgement of d w.r.t. the query q. This approach to "measuring" effort and gain is of course closely related to the cumulative gain type of evaluation measures [2, 19].

3.3 User action paths

The final ingredient that ties together the above components for measuring user effort/gain when interacting with an RLR system is the user action path P_a. Assuming users examine documents in a ranked list from top to bottom with a basic interface, the order in which users examine documents is deterministic. The only uncertainty is that users may quit, which can easily be handled by computing the gain at a cut-off point, or at an expected search depth [28]. However, with an RLR interface, the possible paths users can take for a query is combinatory given that users can switch between sublists without a particular order. Thus we resort to a Monte Carlo method. The interaction model specified in Section 3.1 allows us to simulate possible user action paths for a given set of parameters, creating a sample of user effort and gain for a particular task and user behavior. System performance can then be compared with these samples using standard statistical tools.

Action path constraints. To further reduce the complexity of the simulation process, we constrain the possible user action paths with the following assumptions.

A1 Users examine results in a ranked list from top to bottom.

A2 When switching between sublists, users *skip and only skip* the results they have already seen. This prevents inflated counts of user gain (e.g., in terms of relevant documents encountered). A similar design choice has been made in the literature for evaluating faceted search systems [30]. In addition, when switching, users always examine the next (unseen) result in the new sublist, preventing an infinite switching loop. If all documents in a sublist are exhausted then its filter value is no longer selected.

A3 Instead of assuming a user quits searching with a certain probability, we assume a deterministic cut-off, leaving two complementary decision points with continuation probability being sufficient. Practically, for gain-based measures, the cut-off is based on a fixed amount of effort, and systems are compared in terms of the amount of gain achieved for a fixed amount of effort (cf., NDCG@K). For effort-based measures, a cut-off can be set to gain and systems are compared in terms of the amount of effort needed to achieve a fixed amount of gain (cf., expected search length).

Steps to simulate a user action path.

1. Specify model parameters (with empirical or hypothesized values), i.e., $p_{r,u}$ for continuation decisions, and $\mathbf{c}_u$ for sublist selection decisions.
2. At each step, draw $s_{r,u} \sim Ber(p_{r,u})$. If $s_{r,u} = 1$, add *examine* to P_a; else draw $\mathbf{f} \sim Cat(K, \mathbf{c}_u)$, add *select sublist* and *examine* to P_a. When encountered, add *pagination* and handle situations specified in A2.
3. Stop when: (1) the total effort/gain meets a predefined cut-off value; or (2) all results are exhausted.

4. VALIDATION OF PREDICTION

The core of our framework consists of a specific mapping $\hat{y} = h(\vec{x})$, where $\hat{y}$ is the estimated user effort, aimed at approximating the actual user effort y, given the input variables $\vec{x}$. In a typical machine learning scenario $h(\cdot)$ would be *selected* from a pool of possible hypotheses by fitting example pairs of y and $\vec{x}$. In contrast, we have *specified* in advance a single hypothesis h^*, i.e., the interaction model motivated in Section 3, and the values of $\vec{x}$ is determined by specific types of user behavior. Here, we validate our hypothesis h^* by examining how well its output, $\hat{y}$, approximates actual user effort y.

In this section, we validate our model using usage data gathered for an RLR interface. Specifically, we calibrate our interaction model parameters ($p_{u,r}$ and $\mathbf{c}_u$) with empirical values derived from the usage log of a particular group of users (i.e., participants of our experiment), and examine whether the model prediction corresponds to the actual user effort as recorded in the log. We aim to answer the following questions:

Q1 Does the predicted effort ($\hat{y}$) correlate to user effort (y) as computed with usage data?

Q2 Can we accurately predict when an RLR interface is beneficial, compared to a basic interface?

4.1 Obtaining usage data

4.1.1 Test collection

We use the TREC Federated Search data [10], for it has two important properties: (1) all document-query pairs in this collection have been assessed. This provides us with a more accurate estimation of system performance; and (2) this collection has been constructed by querying a large number of web search engines all of which are categorized. These categories can be converted to filter values in an RLR system. The complete list contains 24 categories [10, Table 3], including academic, travel, etc.

The collection contains 50 (judged) test topics, their associated web pages, and the summaries (snippets) to represent these pages. We create rankings for each topic based on a standard query likelihood model as implemented in Indri.

We consider two types of system: one with a basic interface, and the other with an RLR interface, where categories are used to construct sublists for each topic. We treat every document as being annotated with the category of its source search engine. Since an engine can be in multiple categories, and documents may have been retrieved by multiple engines, every document is associated via its source(s) to one or more categories.

Relevance judgements for the Federated Search track are graded, 4 levels from highly relevant to non-relevant. We only distinguish between relevant (level 1–3) and non-relevant to ensure more than 10 relevant documents per topic are available (see Section 4.1.3).

4.1.2 Search interfaces

RLR interface. Fig. 1 shows a screenshot of the RLR enabled interface, where numbers 1–6 indicate components of the system. On the left are the filter values (1) as provided by the federated search track [10]. On the right a dashboard (2) is available indicating the number of clicks left for a task and the number of relevant documents found. After 25 clicks a "give up" button (3) would appear providing the option to skip the remainder of the task. The topic description (4) is available at the top of the screen. An additional button allows users to expand the description and review the examples as provided before starting a task. The middle of the screen is devoted to a scrollable result list (5) with 10 snippets. At the bottom of the page a pagination button (6) is available. See [17].

Basic interface. The basic interface is similar to this design except that the filter panel (1) is unavailable. One of the filter values in the RLR interface is "All," which is the unfiltered list as it would be in the basic interface. It is possible for users to ignore the filter values and use the RLR interface exactly as the basic interface.

4.1.3 Setup of user experiment

We investigate the *effort* it takes users to locate relevant documents. While our interaction model can be applied to both effort-based and gain-based measures, in this study design we focus on measuring effort.

User task. Users were asked to find 10 relevant documents for a topic. It is not as trivial as, e.g., finding 1 relevant document, allowing variability between user action paths. Meanwhile, it limits the effort required to a manageable amount.

Specifically, we asked users to locate by clicking on 10 result summaries of relevant documents within 50 clicks, where a click is counted if it is on a result summary, a pagination button, or a filter value. We use the 50-click limit to prevent users from clicking every result and to force users to make conscious choices instead. We require users to only click on summaries to abstract away from actions such as opening and reading documents as well as to keep the

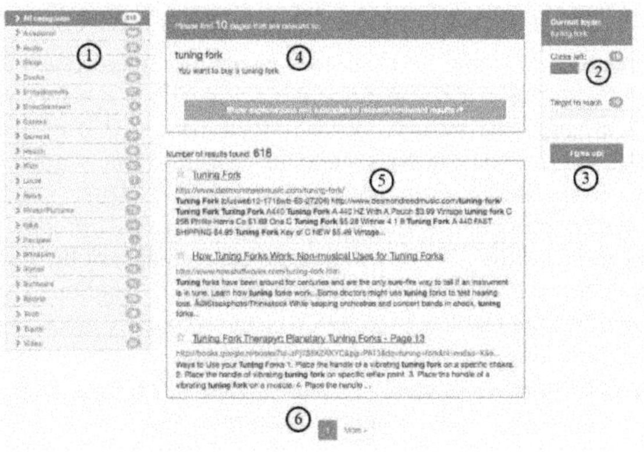

Figure 1: **The RLR interface: (1) filter values; (2) dashboard; (3) give up button; (4) topic description; (5) result list; (6) pagination. The basic interface excludes (1).**

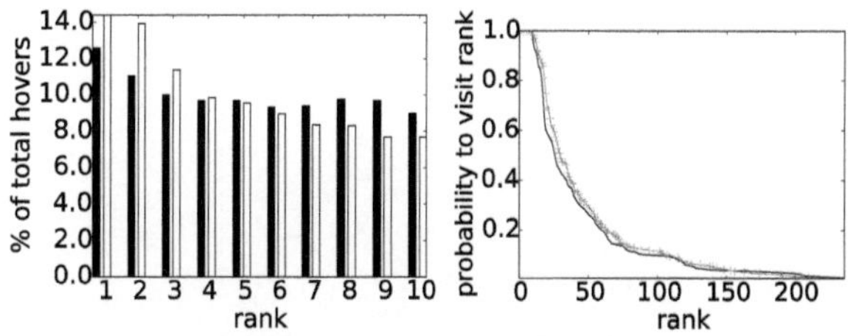

(a) Distribution of hovers over the 10 ranks for basic (black) and RLR (white hatched).

(b) Probability of rank visit for basic (black) and RLR (red hatched) interface.

Figure 2: Users' result page rank visiting behavior.

time necessary to complete a task manageable. To reduce user variability in judgements of relevance, we provide feedback to users whether a clicked result is relevant or not.

Experiment design. We recruited participants via university mailing list and social media. We used a standard between-subject design common to A/B testing, where each new user is randomly assigned to one of the two interfaces and directed to the same interface on subsequent visits. To reduce learning effects, new tasks are randomly assigned to users.

4.1.4 *Obtained usage data*

In total 145 task instances were completed by 49 users for the system with the basic interface, and 255 by 48 users for the RLR interface. The median number of completed task-instances per task is 2 for the basic interface and 3 for the system with an RLR interface. As some tasks have been completed by more participants than others, we consider median values in our analysis.

4.2 Measuring user & predicted effort

To answer Q1 and Q2, we need to compute the following quantities: (i) user effort y (with basic or RLR interface) as derived from the usage data, and (ii) the predicted effort $\hat{y}$, where the model parameters are calibrated with the actual usage data.

4.2.1 *User effort*

For simplicity we assume equal effort for user actions. We measure user effort (y) as the number of result summaries users visited and the clicks they spent on choosing filter values and pagination.

To determine which summaries a user has visited we consider mouse hovers over results, which has been shown to correlate with eye-gaze [18]. Fig. 2(a) shows the percentage of total hovers over the 10 ranks of each result page. We observe that the distribution of hovers over the ranks is relatively uniform, i.e., compared to the distribution of hovers over ranks on Web search engine result pages where differences of 38% between the highest and lowest rank are observed [18]. We observe a difference of 3% between the highest and lowest rank for the basic interface (back bar), and 6% for the RLR interface. That the skew is slightly stronger for the RLR interface is expected as not all filter values return 10 results. The hover data suggests that participants tend to visit all result summaries on a page. This is by design as in our systems we reduced the effort needed to judge a result page (i.e., read summary, open/read the page) to judging the result summary. We are therefore able to focus on user effort as introduced by interaction with RLR elements and not by pages and result summaries.

Given these observations, we approximate the number of result summaries visited as follows. We assume that if a user does pagination, they have seen all the results in the previous page and count all results in SERPs before the last visited page as visited. On the last page, we count the number of results up to the last clicked result.

4.2.2 *Predicted effort*

So far we have obtained user effort y by directly counting the number of actions recorded in the usage log. To compute $\hat{y}$—an approximation of y of our user group—we calibrate our model parameters with empirical values derived from the same log data.

Continuation probability. We compute $p_{r,u}$ using the empirical distributions of the search depths aggregated from all users. The probability that a user will examine the result at rank r is computed as the number of times r has been visited, normalized by the maximum number of times a rank has been visited. In terms of the number of results a user has visited, we take the same approach described above (Section 4.2.1). Fig. 2(b) shows the probability of visiting each rank for the basic and RLR interface. Under the assumption that participants visit all result summaries on a page, ranks 1–10 are visited an equal number of times.

Sublist selection probability. To model user preferences of sublists (filter values), we collect the counts of filter value clicks for each query, and set these as the parameter $\mathbf{c}_u$. That is, the expected value of the probability a filter value will be chosen is proportional to how often it is chosen by the users. Since the original result list, i.e., the filter value "All," is always shown to the users as a starting point, we always add 1 count to it.

4.3 Predicted vs. user effort

We simulated a sample of 1000 $\hat{y}_r$ for an RLR interface. To answer Q1, we perform a correlation analysis between the median of predicted effort ($\hat{y}_r$) and the median of user effort (y_r) over the 50 topics. We see a significant linear correlation between the two (Fig. 3): Pearson $\rho = 0.79$ ($p < 0.001$). This suggests that our proposed model can be used to reliably predict user effort needed in accomplishing a search task in terms of the number of results visited and the number of filter values they need to explore.

4.4 Predicted vs. user benefit

Next, we investigate how the predicted effort can be used to compare system effectiveness, e.g., between a system with a basic interface and with an RLR interface (Q2). To proceed, we investigate whether and on which topics an RLR interface reduces the effort needed to complete the task, as compared to a basic interface.

We compute two quantities for each topic (see Fig. 4):

1. User difference: $\Delta \mathit{effort}_u = y_b - y_r$
2. Predicted difference: $\Delta \mathit{effort}_p = y_b - \hat{y}_r$

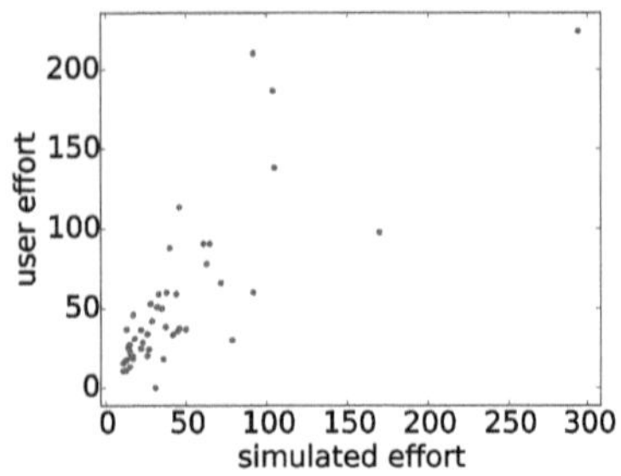

Figure 3: Correlation between estimated effort and user effort.

Note that y_b (effort spent with the basic interface) is fixed as the action path of a user with a basic interface is deterministic.

In terms of user difference, we observe that on 31 out of 50 topics less user effort is needed with the basic interface ($\Delta effort_u < 0$); on 16 topics effort is less with the RLR interface and on 3 there is no difference. Of the 31 topics where $\Delta effort_u < 0$, on 14 a user is able to save more than 10 actions (points of effort), e.g., paginating to a next page and scanning 10 results. Of the 16 topics where $\Delta effort_u > 0$, on 11 a user is able to save more than 10 actions.

On 34 out of 50 topics, $\Delta effort_p$ agrees with $\Delta effort_u$, as in, which interface would reduce user effort in completing a topic. All cases of disagreement are on topics where users of the RLR interface spent more (or the same) amount of effort than users of the basic interface. In these cases participants may have struggled to effectively use filter values or did not use filters at all. If participants did effectively use filters, our interaction model predicted that using filters would save effort.

We observe that our model is able to identify 100% of the cases when an RLR interface is better (i.e., costs less effort) than a basic interface. However, when it predicts that an RLR interface is better, it is only correct in 52% of the cases (0.68 F1-measure). In contrast, it is able to predict when a basic interface is better with 85% precision and 55% recall (0.66 F1-measure). This suggests that if a user would benefit from using the RLR interface, then the model will predict so, and if our model indicates that the basic interface is more beneficial, use of the RLR interface should be avoided.

Further, we find that $\hat{y}_r$ has significant negative correlation with $\Delta effort_u$: $\rho = -0.49$, $p < 0.001$, confirming its predictive power. A negative correlation means that the higher the effort needed with an RLR interface predicted by our model, the more likely that a basic interface is better. The stronger this correlation is, the better the model is at predicting which interface is beneficial.

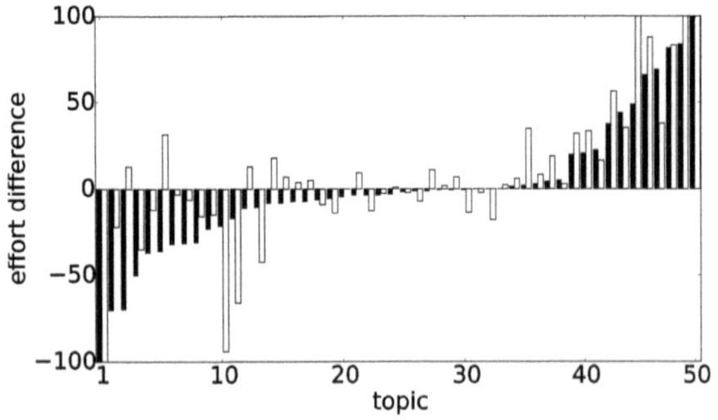

Figure 4: The black bars show $\Delta effort_u$, and the white (hatched) bars show $\Delta effort_p$. A negative value indicates more effort is spent with the RLR interface. Difference values exceeding 100 or less than -100 have been cut-off for legibility.

5. WHOLE SYSTEM PERFORMANCE

In Section 4 we have demonstrated that our user interaction model is simple, tractable, and able to accurately predict user effort with empirical parameter settings. We observed that an RLR interface can be useful for some queries while the basic interface is good for others. Many factors may contribute to this observation, ranging from system properties (backend as well as UI) to user properties. However, it is difficult to investigate the exact impact of these different factors with user studies: a large number of experiments are needed given the number of factors considered and their combination; and it is difficult to control user behavior.

In this section, we discuss how our evaluation framework can be used for studying whole system performance, under strictly controlled and varying conditions that may not be attained in real life studies. We use the same test collection as before, and focus on one question: **Q3.** When does an RLR interface help?

By instantiating our interaction model with parameter values designed to reflect user behavior with desired properties, we generate simulated usage data of large quantity and under strict control. We then study *whether* and *how* various factors (and their interactions) affect the advantage of an RLR interface versus a basic one.

5.1 Simulating user browsing behavior

To start with, we describe how we instantiate the interaction model with parameters that characterize different user behaviors.

Examination depth on a ranked list. Users do not visit all documents in a ranked list. The common *examination assumption* [9] states that the deeper a user investigates a ranked list, the less likely they are to continue examining the list's next document; consistent with the probability ranking principle, deep down the ranked list we expect IR systems to return fewer relevant documents.

In our interaction model, at rank r, users decide either to continue examining another document, or to switch to a different sublist (cf. A3). The assumption that users are more likely to switch when they move deeper down the ranked list can be captured by controlling the parameter $p_{r,u}$ of the Bernoulli distribution with an exponential decay function:

$$p_{r,u} = e^{-\lambda r}, \tag{3}$$

where λ controls the decay rate. That is, a user with a larger λ would decide to switch list at an earlier rank. The resulting exponential decay (Fig. 5(a)) is a good fit for Fig. 2(a).

We simulate the continuation decision of a user with λ_u in the following steps:

1. Compute $p_{u,r}$ with Eq. 3 given λ_u;
2. Draw a decision $s_{u,r} \sim Ber(p_{u,r})$.

Accurate and inaccurate users. When switching between sublists, some users make better choices than others. A good decision leads to a sublist with many (unseen) relevant documents ranked near the top, potentially reducing the total effort the user needs for

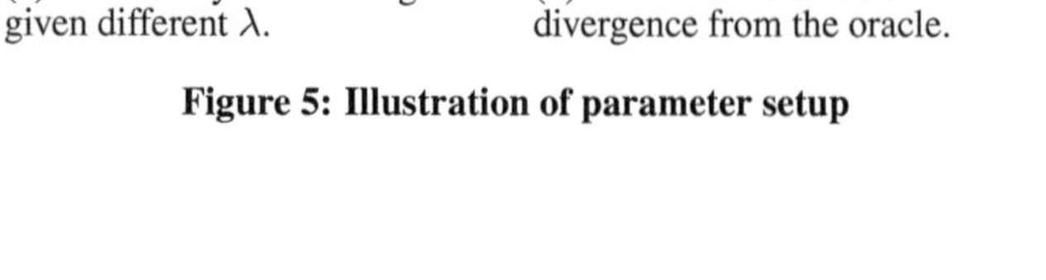

(a) Probability of reaching rank r given different λ. (b) Amounts of smooth vs. KL-divergence from the oracle.

Figure 5: Illustration of parameter setup

his/her search task. We simulate users with different levels of accuracy by varying the *sublist selection probability* (cf. Section 3.1).

Specifically, we sample $\mathbf{c}_u$ from its conjugate prior distribution, i.e., a Dirichlet distribution $Dir(\alpha_u)$, with hyperparameters α_u. By setting α_u to different values we can simulate users with different types of prior knowledge. E.g., users who do not have a clue which sublist to choose can be simulated by setting α_u to a uniform distribution; an "accurate" user can be simulated by setting α_u proportional to the quality of the list, e.g., as measured by NDCG. The properties of the Dirichlet distribution ensure that the expected value of $c_{u,k}$ is $\alpha_k / \sum_j \alpha_j$, i.e., proportional to the performance of the sublists.

In summary, for a given α_u, we simulate a user's choice of sublist with the following procedure:

1. Draw $\mathbf{c}_u \sim Dir(K, \alpha_u)$;
2. Draw the decision vector $(f_1, \ldots, f_K) \sim Cat(K, \mathbf{c}_u)$.

Influence of user behavior on search performance. Before simulating system performance under varying conditions, we conduct a sanity check to examine how the above parameter settings influence estimated user effort given the following setup.

User task We consider an information gathering task where users aim to collect 1, 10, or *all* relevant documents;

Examination depth We set $\lambda \in \{1, .5, .1, .05, .01, .005, .001\}$ to reflect different user examination depths on a ranked list.

User accuracy We consider two cases: a uniform prior $\alpha_{u,k} = 1/K$, and a prior biased on list quality, i.e., α_k is set to the NDCG value of the corresponding result list.

User effort and gain As before, we assume equal effort for all actions and binary relevance to compute gain.

Given the possible settings above, we run the simulation over all combinations of these parameters, each for 1000 times.

Fig. 6 shows the simulation results. We plot the median of simulated user effort with two different user accuracy priors: NDCG vs. Random. With each prior, the continuation probability is set to different values with varying λ. From the figure we observe: (i) in all cases, irrespective of the value of λ and the task type, good prior knowledge about which sublist to choose is beneficial. A uniform prior corresponding to random selection always leads to more effort. (ii) The continuation probability has a limited effect when fewer relevant documents need to be found. When more relevant documents need to be found, e.g., in the Find-all task, it is better to go deeper down a ranked list (i.e., small λ). These observations are intuitive and provide a sanity check on the simulation results using our user interaction model and the proposed simulation strategy.

5.2 Analysis method

Next, we describe the method we employ to analyze conditions when an RLR interface is likely to be beneficial and when it is not.

5.2.1 Factors influencing RLR effectiveness

We identified the following factors that, presumably, determine whether an RLR interface is preferable over a basic one.

Query difficulty for the basic interface (D_q). A priori, if the ranked list in a basic interface is good, i.e., with all relevant documents on top, then users do not need to switch to other sublists for their tasks. We use the effort users need to accomplish a task with the basic interface ($effort_b$) as the indicator of D_q. The higher $effort_b$, the more difficult the query is for a basic interface.

Sublist relevance (R_q). The effectiveness of an RLR element should depend on the quality of the sublists created for result refinement. If the sublists would filter the relevant documents that were buried deep down in the original ranked list, then it is likely to help users to accomplish their tasks faster. We compute R_q as the averaged NDCG scores over the sublists of a query.

Sublist entropy (H_q). A priori, if few sublists cover most of the relevant documents, these could help to effectively filter out irrelevant documents. Meanwhile, if many sublists contain many relevant documents, then it may be easy for users to find them. In short, we believe the effectiveness of an RLR system is related to how the relevant documents are distributed among sublists, but the exact relation is yet to be explored.

We compute $H_q = -\sum_i p_i \log(p_i)$ as the sublist entropy of a query q, where p_i is the probability that the sublist i of query q contains relevant documents, derived from the empirical distribution of the relevant documents among the sublists of q.

User accuracy (U_{level}). As shown in Fig. 6, how users choose the sublists makes a big difference on the effectiveness of using RLR. Following the distribution of NDCG scores of the sublists is a good strategy, while choosing randomly leads to inferior performance.

Here, we aim to investigate the impact of user accuracy at a more refined level, i.e., how accurate should the user be in order to make the RLR work? Recall that user sublist selection behavior is controlled by the parameter α. Assuming user choices following NDCG scores are "oracles," by gradually smoothing out α with respect to this oracle distribution, we can create user accuracies of different levels between the oracle and the complete random choices (i.e., uniform α). Fig. 5(b) shows the relation between amounts of smoothing added and the median of the KL divergence of the "new" user from the "oracle" user over the 50 test topics. We create 4 user levels, with the amount of smoothing set to 0, 0.1, 0.5, and 1.0, corresponding to the oracle user (level 1), and approximately 15% (level 2), 50% (level 3), and 67% (level 4) less accurate users.

User task. Intuitively, the impact of these factors would be different with respect to different user tasks. For example, when the task is to find all relevant documents, it is not important how good the top of the ranked list is, but rather, where the last relevant document is located. We consider finding 1, 10, and *all* relevant documents.

As a final note, in Fig. 6 we have observed the influence of user search depth on the RLR performance. Overall its impact is not as obvious as user accuracy, in terms of the magnitude of changes in efforts it leads to. In this analysis, we focus on the sublist selection aspect of the users and fix λ to 0.01, which seems to be optimal for finding all relevant documents. For the other two tasks it does not seem to make a major difference when set to a different value.

5.2.2 Analyzing the impact of the identified factors

Let $\Delta_{effort} = effort_b - effort_r$ be the difference between the effort needed to complete a search task with a basic interface and that with an RLR interface. We then make $\Delta_{effort} > 0$ a dependent variable (DV), which takes binary values (1 as yes, 0 as no), and the above four factors (D_q, R_q, H_q, and U_{level}) as independent variables (IVs). Our goal is to investigate how each of the IVs, and their interactions, influence the outcome of whether or not an RLR interface improves over a basic interface.

We apply a generalized linear model (GLM) for this purpose, which allows us to analyze how the IVs contribute to explain the variance observed in the DV. Specifically, given that $\Delta_{effort} > 0$ is a binary variable, we take the form of a logistic regression model. We fit the models with the data simulated with parameters set to different user tasks and different U_{levels}. The conditions w.r.t. the rest of the variables D_q, R_q, and H_q are determined at a per-query level, which comes with the test collection.

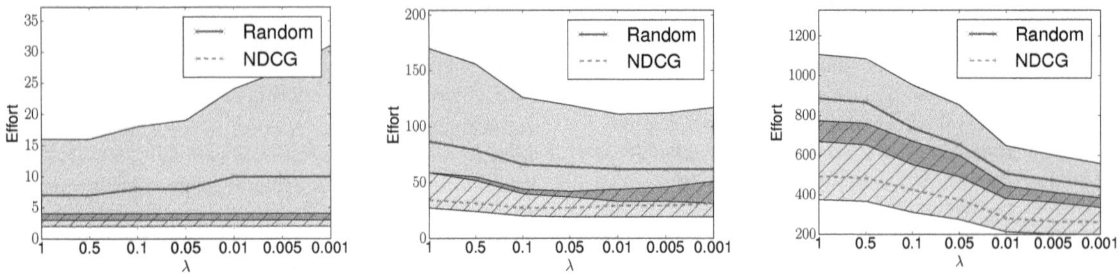

(a) Task: find - 1 (b) Task: find - 10 (c) Task: find - all

Figure 6: Influence of user patience and their accuracy in choosing result lists. The line curves represent the median of the simulation results, and the shades indicate their upper and lower quartiles.

To determine which IVs and interaction terms should be included in the model, we conducted model selection based on the Bayesian information criterion (BIC) using both forward and backward selection. Further, we expect that for different types of tasks (e.g., Find-1 vs. Find-all), the importance of these factors would differ dramatically, and different models would be appropriate. Therefore, we fit a model for each of the user tasks individually.

5.3 When does RLR help?

Table 1 shows the parameters for models best able to predict whether the RLR interface will be effective based on combinations of the four factors for each task.

5.3.1 *Main effect*

We observe that for Find-1 none of the main factors in the model have a significant effect on the dependent variable (RLR effectiveness). However, for Find-10 and Find-all tasks we see that the U_{level} has a significant effect. The negative coefficients for the U_{level} variables indicate that, as users deviate from the "oracle" sublist selection behavior, the log-odds of the RLR interface being effective decrease. Those user level effects for Find-10 and Find-all but not Find-1 suggest that if a user's task is to locate 1 document, then just

Table 1: Estimated coefficients of the selected models and their effects on the odds that an RLR interface helps. The overall effect of user accuracy (ulevel) is tested by Wald test. The model goodness-of-fit (GOF) is tested by Hosmer-Lemeshow test. Significance codes: ≤0.001 (▲); ≤0.01(△); ≤ 0.05(*).

Coefficients	Find-1	Find-10	Find-all
(Intercept)	-7.3401	-10.4365	-0.5337
D_q	0.1058	-0.0686	0.0017
U_{level2}	3.2234	-2.1309▲	-5.1061▲
U_{level3}	1.5590	-5.5278▲	-8.0140▲
U_{level4}	-2.3189	-8.1936▲	-8.0140▲
H_q	-1.0443	3.6347	-1.6492
R_q	–	-49.7916	114.9398▲
$D_q : U_{level2}$	-1.6547	–	–
$D_q : U_{level3}$	-2.0041*	–	–
$D_q : U_{level4}$	-2.0683	–	–
$D_q : H_q$	1.3103▲	-0.0968	–
$D_q : R_q$	–	3.2363△	0.0906*
$H_q : R_q$	–	13.9680	-57.2773▲
$D_q : H_q : R_q$	–	-0.8422*	–
Overall effect of U_{level}	χ^2=1.6 (*df=3*)	$\chi^2 = 16.0^{\triangle}$ (*df=3*)	$\chi^2 = 25.6$▲ (*df=3*)
Model GOF (p-value)	0.9339	0.9928	0.9213

the accuracy with which users select sublists is not enough to predict whether an RLR interface will be beneficial. One explanation is that, since most sublists will have at least one relevant document ranked highly, users do not need to be accurate in their choice of sublist to achieve the task. When collecting more relevant documents however, knowing which sublist to pick *is* important.

Regarding R_q we find that it has a significant effect only for Find-all. As the average relevance of sublists increases the log-odds of the RLR interface being effective increase as well. That is, having sublists with relevant documents ranked high is essential for the RLR interface to be effective for the Find-all task. For the Find-1 and Find-10 tasks sublist relevance alone is not enough to predict RLR effectiveness and the effect depends on the interaction between two or more of the main factors. We look into these interaction terms in more detail next.

5.3.2 *Effect of interaction terms*

To investigate the effect of the interaction terms on the probability of RLR effectiveness, we express the relation visually. Due to space limitation, we focus here on the model for the Find-10 task.

To visualize interaction terms between continuous variables, we plot the predicted value of the DV against one varying IV, and re-center the other IVs to a fixed level. We take the 25% and 75% quantile of the values of a variable as its low and high level, respectively. A model fitting the re-centered data then shows the effect of the varying IV on the DV with respect to the different levels of the re-centered IVs. For Find-10 there are two interactions terms that have significant effect: D_q:R_q and D_q:R_q:H_q. For D_q:R_q, we re-center D_q to its low and high levels, and fix H_q to its median. For D_q:R_q:H_q we re-center both D_q and R_q to a low and high level.

Fig. 7(a) shows the effect of increasing R_q on the probability $P(\Delta_{effort} > 0)$ when D_q is high for varying levels of user accuracy. At relatively low levels (0.15 to 0.25) of R_q there is a steep increase in the probability of RLR being more effective for all user levels. This suggests that when a query is difficult (i.e., the quality of the original ranked list is low), the sublists and the users do not need to be very accurate for an RLR interface to be more effective than a basic interface. In Fig. 7(b) we see that when query difficulty is low, high quality sublists (relevant documents ranked high) and higher user accuracy are necessary for an RLR interface to be helpful.

The relation between D_q, R_q, and H_q in the final interaction term for task Find-10 is shown in Fig. 8. It shows the effect of increasing H_q on $P(\Delta_{effort} > 0)$ under conditions in terms of combinations of different levels of D_q (high/low), R_q (high/low), and varying levels of user accuracy. We see that a high level of D_q combined with low/medium levels of H_q result in a relative high $P(\Delta_{effort} > 0)$ for both high (Fig. 8(c)) and low (Fig. 8(a)) levels of R_q. This interaction aligns with our intuition of when sublists

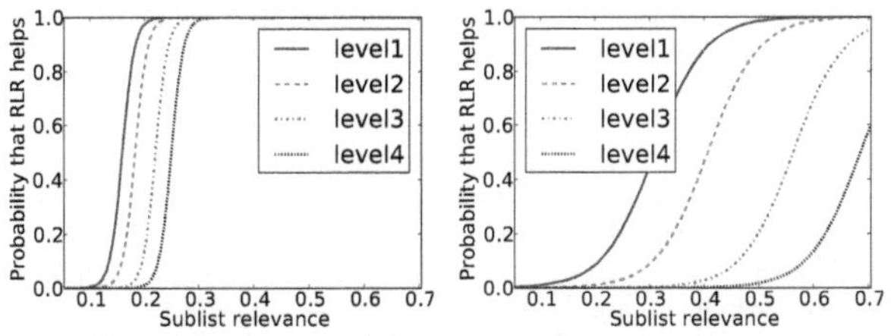

(a) D_q: high; H_q: median (b) D_q: low; H_q: median

Figure 7: Effect of interaction terms query difficulty : sublist relevance for task Find-10.

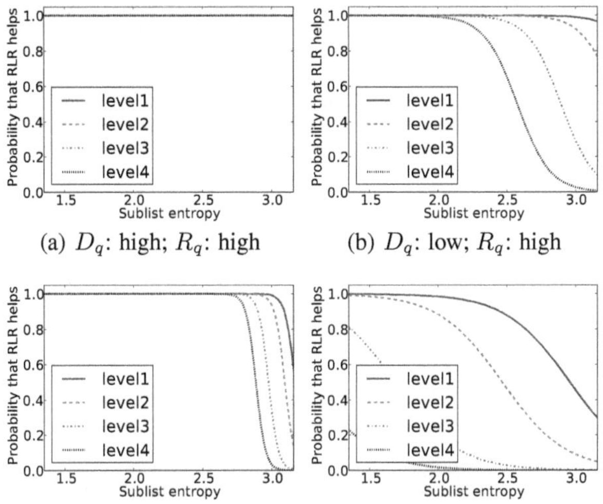

(a) D_q: high; R_q: high (b) D_q: low; R_q: high

(c) D_q: high; R_q: low (d) D_q: low; R_q: low

Figure 8: Effect of interaction terms query difficulty : sublist relevance : sublists entropy for task Find-10.

are beneficial, i.e., having a single high quality sublist when the original ranked list is of low quality. When D_q is low, we observe that $P(\Delta_{\mathit{effort}} > 0)$ decreases at low levels of H_q when R_q is low (Fig. 8(d)) and at medium levels of H_q when R_q is high (Fig. 8(b)). This suggests that at lower levels of query difficulty very specific conditions need to be met for an RLR interface to be beneficial.

H_q plays a role in different interaction terms depending on the task as well (cf. Table 1). For Find-1 we find that as both D_q and H_q increase the log-odds of the RLR interface being beneficial increases. Since the task requires a single relevant document, the ranking within the vertical is less important. Having more sublists with a relevant document allows users to complete the task effectively with the RLR interface even when users select sublists randomly. For Find-all, an increase in both H_q and R_q result in a decrease in the log-odds of the RLR interface being beneficial. As we saw in Fig. 8, for Find-10 high sublist entropy results in low probability of an RLR interface being helpful. Sublist relevance only plays a role when query difficulty is low; however, as the number of relevant documents to be found increases, it is less likely that enough documents are available at the top of the ranking.

5.3.3 Summary

Query difficulty alone is not a good predictor for the probability of an RLR interface being helpful. Depending on the task, different factors determine whether users will be more effective with the basic or RLR interface. In the case of Find-1, sublists do not have to be of high quality for an RLR interface to be helpful; it becomes more likely to be beneficial when the query is difficult and the entropy of the sublists is high. For Find-10, high query difficulty and low entropy are conditions for the RLR interface to be beneficial. The importance of sublist relevance depends on user accuracy; when they are accurate, lower levels of sublist relevance are necessary. For Find-all, the conditions necessary for an effective RLR interface are high query difficulty, high user accuracy, high sublist relevance and low entropy.

6. RELATION TO TRADITIONAL METRICS

We have illustrated how our evaluation framework can be used for simulating and predicting RLR system performance in two ways, and its efficacy has been validated with usage data. Next, we discuss how it relates to metrics for evaluation of traditional search systems, i.e., normalized Discounted Cumulative Gain [19, nDCG], Expected Reciprocal Rank [6, ERR], normalized Rank-biased precision [28], average precision (AP), and precision@10 (P@10).

From a modeling perspective, Carterette [4] has proposed a conceptual framework for analyzing and comparing different effectiveness measures (for traditional systems). Our framework is close to the category of Model 3 under his classification, i.e., computing the effort a user needs to achieve a particular amount of utility. Further, all metrics discussed in [4] compute an expected value (utility, effort or gain). Computing the expected performance directly is rather intractable in our setting, as the order in which sublists are selected and the number of results viewed in each of these lists is non-deterministic. To compute the expected performance, one needs to obtain the distribution of all possible orders in which sublists are selected. Here, simulation provides samples of possible sequences from which performance can be approximated (Section 3.3).

We now move on to an empirical investigation. By examining to what extent metrics for traditional systems are able to predict the performance of an RLR system, we investigate whether our framework offers new insights. Table 2 shows the correlation between traditional measures and actual user effort (column 1, 2; obtained in Section 4), predicted user effort (column 3, 4), and the difference between user effort with the basic and RLR interface ($\Delta \mathit{effort}_u$ in column 5, 6). We observe that nDCG measured at low cut-offs (10) has no significant correlation with user or predicted effort. When all relevant documents are taken into account (nDCG@all), the correlation is significant at $\rho = -.42$ (negative, for gain vs. effort). We observe a similar pattern for binary nDCG (BnDCG); however, in this case the correlation is stronger than for nDCG. When collecting usage data we did not distinguish between highly relevant and relevant documents. Other measures have a negative correlation with user effort and our model in the range between nDCG and BnDCG. We focus on BnDCG here, as it is most strongly correlated.

The correlation between user effort and BnDCG@all is $\rho = -.72$, which indicates that for topics with high BnDCG@all scores, i.e., with many relevant documents at the top of the ranking, user effort is low. The magnitude of the correlation of both BnDCG and our model with actual user effort is high. The negative correlation between BnDCG@all and our model is lower than that of either measure with user effort ($\rho = -0.59$, $p < 0.001$), indicating that these measures disagree on the effort needed for some topics.

We apply BnDCG@all to the task of predicting whether a topic would cost a user more effort with the basic or the RLR interface ($\Delta \mathit{effort}_u$). We compute the correlation between BnDCG@all and $\Delta \mathit{effort}_u$. Results are listed in Table 2 (last two columns). There is no significant correlation ($\rho = 0.04$, $p = 0.776$): BnDCG@all cannot differentiate between topics suitable for a basic or RLR interface. In comparison, the correlation of $\Delta \mathit{effort}_u$ with the pre-

Table 2: Correlation of traditional metrics with user effort, predicted effort, and the $\Delta effort_u$ (cf. Fig. 4).

	user effort		simulated effort		$\Delta effort_u$	
measure	ρ	p-value	ρ	p-value	ρ	p-value
nDCG@10	-0.21	0.142	-0.19	0.185	0.02	0.896
nDCG@all	-0.42	0.002	-0.34	0.016	0.00	0.994
NRBP	-0.41	0.003	-0.33	0.018	0.08	0.568
ERR@10	-0.45	0.001	-0.36	0.010	0.08	0.567
P@10	-0.56	<0.001	-0.46	<0.001	0.00	0.980
AP	-0.63	<0.001	-0.54	<0.001	0.02	0.875
BnDCG@10	-0.54	<0.001	-0.44	0.001	0.02	0.875
BnDCG@all	**-0.72**	**<0.001**	**-0.59**	**<0.001**	0.04	0.776
our model	**0.79**	**<0.001**	–	–	**-0.49**	**<0.001**

dicted effort (by our model) is significant ($\rho = -0.49$, $p < 0.001$). That is, simulated effort tells us which interface is the best.

As a final remark, the lack of correlation between traditional metrics and $\Delta effort_u$ confirms our observation that query difficulty, i.e., the quality of the original ranked list alone, is not sufficient to predict whether an RLR interface is preferable over a basic interface (cf. Section 5.3).

7. CONCLUSION

We have developed a simulation-based evaluation framework that measures the effectiveness of systems enabling result refinement, e.g., facets or filters. Its key component is an interaction model that characterizes the user's search behavior in the presence of result list refinement features. Using this framework, we investigate whole system performance, under various conditions. Instantiating the parameters of the user interaction model, corresponding to properties of search task and user type, allows us to predict system performance for specific groups of users. We validated the predictions made using data collected with two search systems, re-using the TREC Federated Search test collection.

We found that user effort estimated by our model is correlated significantly with actual user effort measured in the user data. We applied our interaction model to the task of predicting when a user should or should not use an RLR interface, and found a significant correlation between the predictions we made and observations in the user data. We did not find such correlations when applying traditional retrieval metrics to this task, demonstrating the value of the proposed user interaction model for search with result refinement.

Our study extends user interaction models beyond the classic "10 blue links." It provides a means to evaluate retrieval systems while considering the interaction effects between non-standard search UI features and search system effectiveness and the variability in how different people use the search UI.

Acknowledgements. This research was partially supported by the European Community's Seventh Framework Programme (FP7/2007-2013) under grant agreement nr 312827 (VOX-Pol), the Netherlands Organisation for Scientific Research (NWO) under project nrs. 727.011.005, 612.001.116, HOR-11-10, 640.006.013, 612.066.930, CI-14-25, SH-322-15, Amsterdam Data Science, the Dutch national program COMMIT, the ESF Research Network Program ELIAS, the Elite Network Shifts project funded by the Royal Dutch Academy of Sciences (KNAW), the Netherlands eScience Center under project nr. 027.012.105, the Yahoo! Faculty Research and Engagement Program, the Microsoft Research PhD program, the HPC Fund, and the Dutch Technology Foundation (STW) under project nr. 13675.

8. REFERENCES

[1] M. Agosti, N. Fuhr, E. Toms, and P. Vakkari. Evaluation methodologies in information retrieval dagstuhl seminar 13441. In *ACM SIGIR Forum*, volume 48, pages 36–41. ACM, 2014.

[2] L. Azzopardi. Modelling interaction with economic models of search. In *SIGIR'14*, pages 3–12, 2014.

[3] M. Bron, J. Van Gorp, F. Nack, L. B. Baltussen, and M. de Rijke. Aggregated search interface preferences in multi-session search tasks. In *SIGIR'13*, pages 123–132. ACM, 2013.

[4] B. Carterette. System effectiveness, user models, and user utility: a conceptual framework for investigation. In *SIGIR'11*, 2011.

[5] O. Chapelle and Y. Zhang. A dynamic bayesian network click model for web search ranking. In *WWW'09*, pages 1–10, 2009.

[6] O. Chapelle, D. Metlzer, Y. Zhang, and P. Grinspan. Expected reciprocal rank for graded relevance. In *CIKM'09*, 2009.

[7] A. Chuklin, P. Serdyukov, and M. de Rijke. Click model-based information retrieval metrics. In *SIGIR '13*, 2013.

[8] A. Chuklin, I. Markov, and M. de Rijke. *Click Models for Web Search*. Morgan & Claypool Publishers, 2015.

[9] N. Craswell, O. Zoeter, M. Taylor, and B. Ramsey. An experimental comparison of click position-bias models. In *WSDM'08*, 2008.

[10] T. Demeester, D. Trieschnigg, D. Nguyen, and D. Hiemstra. Overview of the trec 2013 federated web search track. In *TREC'14*.

[11] D. Downey, S. Dumais, and E. Horvitz. Models of searching and browsing: languages, studies, and applications. In *IJCAI'07*, 2007.

[12] G. Dupret and B. Piwowarski. A user browsing model to predict search engine click data from past observations. In *SIGIR '08*, 2008.

[13] J. English, M. Hearst, R. Sinha, K. Swearingen, and K.-P. Yee. Flexible search and navigation using faceted metadata. In *University of Berkeley*. Citeseer, 2002.

[14] N. Fuhr. A probability ranking principle for interactive information retrieval. *Information Retrieval*, 11(3):251–265, 2008.

[15] F. Guo, C. Liu, and Y. Wang. Efficient multiple-click models in web search. In *WSDM '09*, 2009.

[16] J. He, M. Bron, and A. P. de Vries. Characterizing stages of a multi-session complex search task through direct and indirect query modifications. In *SIGIR'13*, pages 897–900, 2013.

[17] J. He, M. Bron, L. Azzopardi, and A. de Vries. Studying user browsing behavior through gamified search tasks. In *GamifIR'14*, pages 49–52, 2014.

[18] J. Huang, R. W. White, and S. Dumais. No clicks, no problem: using cursor movements to understand and improve search. In *SIGCHI'11*.

[19] K. Järvelin and J. Kekäläinen. Cumulated gain-based evaluation of ir techniques. *ACM Trans. Inf. Syst.*, 20(4):422–446, 2002.

[20] K. Järvelin, S. L. Price, L. M. Delcambre, and M. L. Nielsen. Discounted cumulated gain based evaluation of multiple-query IR sessions. In *ECIR'08*, pages 4–15, 2008.

[21] T. Joachims, L. Granka, B. Pan, H. Hembrooke, and G. Gay. Accurately interpreting clickthrough data as implicit feedback. In *SIGIR'05*, pages 154–161. ACM, 2005.

[22] E. Kanoulas, B. Carterette, P. D. Clough, and M. Sanderson. Evaluating multi-query sessions. In *SIGIR'11*, 2011.

[23] A. Kashyap, V. Hristidis, and M. Petropoulos. Facetor: cost-driven exploration of faceted query results. In *CIKM '10*, 2010.

[24] W. Kong and J. Allan. Extending faceted search to the general web. In *CIKM'14*, 2014.

[25] J. Koren, Y. Zhang, and X. Liu. Personalized interactive faceted search. In *WWW '08*, pages 477–486, 2008.

[26] R. L. Kumar, M. A. Smith, and S. Bannerjee. User interface features influencing overall ease of use and personalization. *Information & Management*, 41(3):289–302, 2004.

[27] C. Li, N. Yan, S. B. Roy, L. Lisham, and G. Das. Facetedpedia: dynamic generation of query-dependent faceted interfaces for wikipedia. In *WWW '10*, pages 651–660. ACM, 2010.

[28] A. Moffat and J. Zobel. Rank-biased precision for measurement of retrieval effectiveness. *ACM Trans. Inf. Syst.*, 27(1):Article 2, 2008.

[29] P. Morville and J. Callender. *Search patterns*. O'Reilly Media, 2010.

[30] A. Schuth and M. Marx. Evaluation methods for rankings of facetvalues for faceted search. In *CLEF'11*, pages 131–136, 2011.

[31] M. D. Smucker and C. L. Clarke. Stochastic simulation of time-biased gain. In *CIKM'12*, pages 2040–2044, 2012.

[32] D. Vandic, F. Frasincar, and U. Kaymak. Facet selection algorithms for web product search. In *CIKM '13*, pages 2327–2332. ACM, 2013.

[33] E. Voorhees, D. K. Harman, et al. *TREC: Experiment and evaluation in information retrieval*. MIT, 2005.

[34] B. S. Wynar, A. G. Taylor, and J. Osborn. *Introduction to cataloging and classification*. Libraries Unlimited, 1985.

WEMAREC: Accurate and Scalable Recommendation through Weighted and Ensemble Matrix Approximation

Chao Chen[§,*], Dongsheng Li[†], Yingying Zhao[§], Qin Lv[‡], Li Shang[‡]
[§]Tongji University, Shanghai, 201804, P.R. China
[†]IBM Research - China, Shanghai, 201203, P.R. China
[‡]University of Colorado Boulder, Boulder, CO 80309, USA
{chench.resch, yyzhao.tj}@gmail.com, ldsli@cn.ibm.com, {qin.lv, li.shang}@colorado.edu

ABSTRACT

Matrix approximation is one of the most effective methods for collaborative filtering-based recommender systems. However, the high computation complexity of matrix factorization on large datasets limits its scalability. Prior solutions have adopted co-clustering methods to partition a large matrix into a set of smaller submatrices, which can then be processed in parallel to improve scalability. The drawback is that the recommendation accuracy is lower as the submatrices only contain subsets of the user-item rating information.

This paper presents WEMAREC, a weighted and ensemble matrix approximation method for accurate and scalable recommendation. It builds upon the intuition that (sub)matrices containing more frequent samples of certain user/item/rating tend to make more reliable rating predictions for these specific user/item/rating. WEMAREC consists of two important components: (1) a *weighting* strategy that is computed based on the rating distribution in each submatrix and applied to approximate a single matrix containing those submatrices; and (2) an *ensemble* strategy that leverages user-specific and item-specific rating distributions to combine the approximation matrices of multiple sets of co-clustering results. Evaluations using real-world datasets demonstrate that WEMAREC outperforms state-of-the-art matrix approximation methods in recommendation accuracy (0.5–11.9% on the MovieLens dataset and 2.2–13.1% on the Netflix dataset) with 3–10X improvement on scalability.

Categories and Subject Descriptors

H.3.4 [**Systems and Software**]: User profiles and alert services

Keywords

R ecommendation; matrix approximation; weighted; ensemble

*Chao Chen and Dongsheng Li contributed equally to this work.

SIGIR'15, August 09 - 13, 2015, Santiago, Chile.
 ISBN 978-1-4503-3621-5/15/08 ...$15.00.
DOI: http://dx.doi.org/10.1145/2766462.2767718 .

1. INTRODUCTION

Collaborative filtering (CF), which predicts users' item ratings based on the ratings of other users with similar taste, has been shown to preform well in many recommender systems [1]. Among existing CF solutions, matrix approximation has become increasingly popular. It formulates the recommendation problem as missing entry prediction using existing entries in a user-item rating matrix, i.e., attempting to predict the missing entries in a partially observed matrix. Given m users and n items, the user-item rating matrix $M \in \mathbb{R}^{m \times n}$ is typically of low-rank, then M can be approximated by a r-rank matrix $\hat{M} = UV^T$, where U $\in \mathbb{R}^{m \times r}$ is the set of user features, V $\in \mathbb{R}^{n \times r}$ is the set of item features, and $r \ll \min(m, n)$. Then, the rating of the i-th user on the j-th item can be predicted by the inner product $U_i V_j^T$. Using matrix approximation, the user/item feature vectors are reduced to lower dimensions, which helps to address the "data sparsity" issue, a challenge to memory-based CF methods [1, 24]. Recent studies have shown that matrix approximation based CF methods outperform many other CF solutions [10, 17, 22, 28].

However, existing matrix approximation based CF methods exhibit poor scalability due to the high computation complexity of matrix factorization on large user-item rating datasets [10, 22, 16, 11, 28]. Recent work adopted co-clustering methods [8, 29, 26] to partition the large user-item rating matrix into a set of smaller submatrices, which can then be processed in parallel to improve system scalability. However, this usually leads to lower recommendation accuracy. Co-clustering tries to find coherent submatrices each of which contains a subset of users who share similar interests on a subset of items. In the ideal case, recommendations based on such submatrices can be as accurate as recommendations based on the original large matrix while requiring much less computation overhead. However, the submatrices obtained by co-clustering methods are not perfect, as a small fraction of user-item ratings may not follow the distribution of majority ratings. As a result, recommendation accuracy on such user-item ratings will degrade, affecting the overall recommendation accuracy. Our study shows that, for the MovieLens dataset with 1 million ratings, the recommendation RMSE (root mean square error) increases from 0.8645 to 0.9 when the co-clustering setting varies from 1×1 to 5×5. Therefore, a better matrix approximation solution that achieves both high accuracy and high scalability for recommendation is needed.

In this work, we have developed WEMAREC, a weighted and ensemble matrix approximation method for accurate and scalable CF-based recommendation. The intuition is that, (sub)matrices only contain partially-sampled information of user/item/rating; if a submatrix contains more samples for a certain user or item or rating, this submatrix can probably make more reliable predictions on the specific user or item or rating. This applies not only to the submatrices generated from a single co-clustering process, but also to the multiple sets of submatrices generated using different co-clustering constraints. Since these submatrices contain different user-item rating information, an intelligent combination of these submatrices can yield better recommendation quality while still enjoy the benefit of high scalability due to parallel processing the co-clustering submatrices.

This work makes the following contributions: (1) identification of the unbalanced predication power on different users/items/ratings due to the partial information that is contained in (sub)matrices; (2) development of a submatrix-based weighting strategy to capture rating-specific prediction power and combine submatrices into the approximation of a single user-item rating matrix; (3) development of an ensemble matrix approximation method that uses different co-clustering constraints to generate and combine multiple sets of submatrices with different rating prediction power for different users and items; and (4) evaluation using two large-scale real-world datasets which demonstrates WEMAREC's improvement in recommendation accuracy and scalability over state-of-the-art matrix approximation techniques.

The rest of this paper is organized as follows. Section 2 formulates the problem. Section 3 describes the proposed WEMAREC method in detail. Section 4 analyzes the error bounds of the proposed method. Section 5 presents the evaluation results. Section 6 discusses the related work, and finally Section 7 concludes this work.

2. PROBLEM FORMULATION

This section provides necessary background for the matrix approximation problem. It then presents case studies to motivate the challenge faced by existing matrix approximation methods. The case studies presented in this section are conducted on the MovieLens (1M) dataset and the standard singular value decomposition (SVD) algorithm is used in matrix approximation.

2.1 Notations and Definitions

In this paper, upper case letters such as M, U, V denote matrices. For matrix $M \in \mathbb{R}^{m \times n}$, we denote M_{i*} as the i-th row vector, M_{*j} as j-th column vector, and M_{ij} as the entry in the i-th row and j-th column. We denote $\mathcal{M}$ as a submatrix of M, i.e., both the rows and columns in $\mathcal{M}$ are subsets of those in M. A r-rank approximation of M is denoted as $\hat{M} = UV^T$, where $U \in \mathbb{R}^{m \times r}, V \in \mathbb{R}^{n \times r}$ and $r \ll \min(m, n)$. In addition, $[n]$ denotes the list of $\{1, \ldots, n\}$, Ω denotes the set of observed entries in the user-item rating matrix M, i.e., $\forall (i,j) \in \Omega$, $M_{i,j} \neq 0$. Then, $|\Omega|$ is denoted as the total number of observed entries in M.

Three matrix norms are used in this paper. The Frobenius norm is denoted as:

$$||M||_F := \sqrt{\sum_{ij} M_{ij}^2}.$$

The nuclear norm is denoted as the sum of singular values:

$$||M||_* := \sum_k \sigma_k.$$

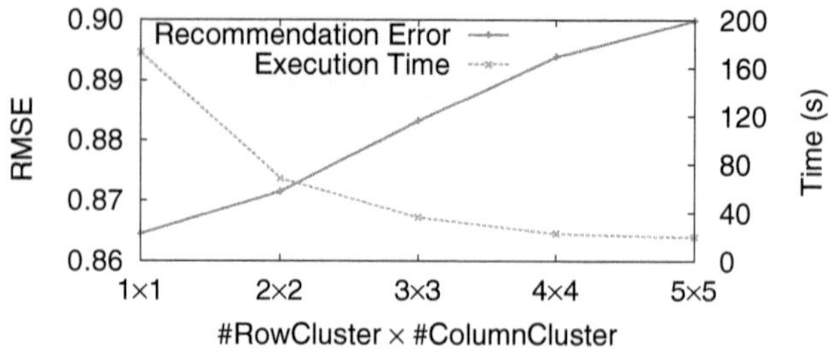

Figure 1: The tradeoff between recommendation accuracy and runtime efficiency when varying the number of co-clusters.

The max norm is denoted as:

$$||M||_\infty = \max\{|M_{ij}|\}.$$

2.2 Existing Low-Rank Matrix Approximation

Two methods have been used for low-rank matrix approximation $\hat{M}$ of M, i.e., SVD and compressed sensing [5, 6]. The SVD method is based on minimizing the sum-squared distance — Frobenius norm:

$$\hat{M} = \arg\min_X \parallel I \otimes (M - X) \parallel_F \quad s.t. \quad rank(X) = r, \quad (1)$$

where each I_{ij} is the indicator function that equals to 1 if M_{ij} is observed and equals to 0 otherwise. The compressed sensing method is based on minimizing the nuclear norm:

$$\hat{M} = \arg\min_X \parallel X \parallel_* \quad s.t. \quad \parallel I \otimes (M - X) \parallel_F < \epsilon. \quad (2)$$

As shown in [22], the problem defined in (1) is a difficult non-convex optimization problem and an iterative method may converge to a local minimum. In contrast to SVD, the problem defined in (2) is convex and can be casted as a semi-definite program [6].

Rating	Distribution	RMSE (w/o weighting)	RMSE (w/ weighting)
1	17.44%	1.2512	1.2533
2	25.39%	0.6750	**0.6651**
3	35.35%	0.5260	**0.5162**
4	18.28%	1.1856	**1.1793**
5	3.50%	2.1477	2.1597
Overall result		0.9517	**0.9479**

Table 1: Rating-specific RMSE when running SVD without (w/o) or with (w/) weighting on a submatrix.

2.3 Motivating Examples

Next, we present case studies to demonstrate the accuracy issue of existing co-clustering based matrix approximation methods, and provide insights on why user-item rating distribution can be leveraged to improve the recommendation accuracy.

2.3.1 *Scalability vs. Accuracy*

Co-clustering is an effective method to improve the scalability of matrix approximation based CF methods [8, 29], because these submatrices can be processed in parallel. In addition, co-clustering tries to find coherent submatrices, each of which containing a subset of users who share similar interests on a subset of items. In the ideal case, users' common interests in each submatrix can be accurately predicted. Unfortunately, the submatrices obtained by co-clustering are not perfect. Within each submatrix, a subset of user-item ratings may not follow the distribution of majority ratings. As a result, the corresponding recommendation accuracy of those minority user-item ratings may be poor, which in turn affects the overall recommendation accuracy.

To evaluate how the recommendation accuracy varies with co-clustering granularity, we apply Bregman co-clustering [2] on the MovieLens dataset. As demonstrated in Figure 1, assuming the co-clustering submatrices are processed in parallel, the scalability of matrix approximation increases when the number of co-clusters increase from 1×1 to 5×5 ($k \times k$). On the other hand, the recommendation error (measured as RMSE) increases from 0.8645 to 0.9 as the number of co-clusters increases. Therefore, in order to utilize co-clustering based scalable matrix approximation methods in recommender systems, one must address the accuracy issue.

2.3.2 *Accuracy vs. Rating Distribution*

Although the submatrices obtained through co-clustering are not informative enough to build accurate recommendation models for all users and all items in each submatrix, they can still be utilized to build "weak" recommendation models which can accurately predict the common interests shared by users in the same submatrix. In this study, we analyze (1) which part of information in each submatrix represents users' common interests and thus can be utilized to build "weak" recommendation models and (2) how we can make these "weak" recommendation models more accurate when predicting users' common interests in a submatrix.

Table 1 shows the distribution of different ratings in a submatrix obtained from Bregman co-clustering, as well as the recommendation quality when applying standard SVD algorithm on the submatrix. As shown in the third column, the RMSE varies by the specific rating and lower RMSEs (i.e., better recommendation accuracy) are achieved for ratings that occur more frequently in the submatrix, such as 3 and 2 ratings. This makes sense because a learning model usually does a better job capturing samples that occur more frequently in the train data. Based on this observation, we can train "weak" recommendation models from the submatrices, which can at least make accurate recommendations on users' common interests, i.e., ratings that occur most frequently in the corresponding submatrix.

Given the biased prediction power of the "weak" models towards ratings that occur more frequently in a submatrix, we could potentially boost the recommendation accuracy by weighting the user-item ratings differently, assigning higher (lower) weights to ratings that occur more frequently (rarely) in the submatrix. The expectation is that we could obtain more accurate recommendations on the majority of the ratings and the overall recommendation accuracy can be improved. The fourth column in Table 1 shows the recommendation quality after adding such weights to differentiate the user-item ratings. Clearly, we can see that the "weak" recommendation model built by SVD with weighting can indeed make more accurate recommendations on the ratings that occur more frequently (i.e., 2, 3 and 4) than the SVD method without weighting. More importantly, the overall recommendation quality also increases after weighting,

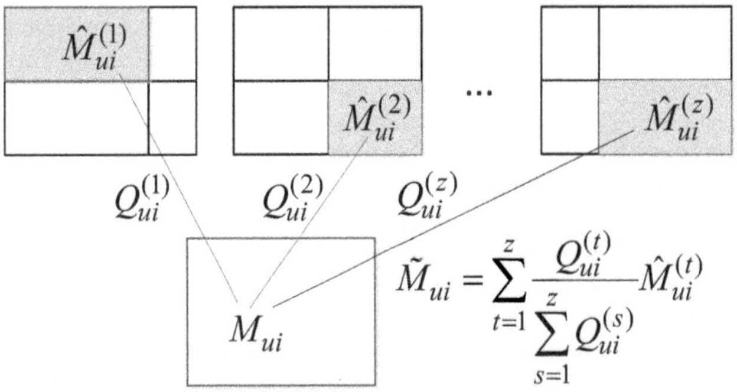

Figure 2: WEMAREC design overview. The original user-item rating matrix M is described by z low-rank matrices, which are based on z different $k \times l$ co-clustering settings. For all pairs $(u,i) \in [m] \times [n]$, the entry M_{ui} is computed based the corresponding entries in the co-cluster-based submatrices (denoted as shaded regions). The equation describes how to compute a unified matrix approximation $\tilde{M}$ from z co-clustering based approximations $\{\hat{M}_1, \hat{M}_2, \ldots, \hat{M}_z\}$.

i.e., RMSE decreases from 0.9517 to 0.9479. These results demonstrate that rating-specific weighting has the potential to boost the accuracy of more frequently-occurring ratings and enhance the overall accuracy as well.

3. WEMAREC ALGORITHM DESIGN

In this section, we present the design details of WEMAREC which can achieve both high recommendation accuracy and high scalability for matrix approximation based CF methods. As illustrated in Figure 2, WEMAREC consists of three key steps:

1. **Co-clustering and submatrices generation.** The original user-item rating matrix is first divided into a set of submatrices by Bregman co-clustering, so that the scalability issue can be addressed by factoring all submatrices in parallel. Also, different co-clusterings can be obtained by varying the constraints in Bregman co-clustering, which naturally offers us the ability to exploit the advantages of different co-clusterings to achieve better recommendation accuracy.
2. **Submatrices-based weighting and matrix approximation.** A new weighting strategy is proposed, which is computed based on each individual submatrix and assigns higher weights to ratings that occur more frequently in a given submatrix. The weighted submatrices from the same co-clustering setting are then used to generate a single matrix approximation.
3. **Ensemble of multiple matrix approximations.** Different co-clustering constraints can lead to different submatrices and thus different matrix approximations. Since each "weak" recommendation model can only make accurate recommendations on some of the user-item ratings, an ensemble strategy is proposed, which utilizes the advantages of different "weak" models to realize a "strong" recommendation model which can achieve high accuracy.

3.1 Co-clustering & Submatrices Generation

Co-clustering is a popular technique which allows simultaneous clustering of both the rows and columns in a given matrix. By applying co-clustering methods on user-item rating matrix in recommender systems, users and items correspond to a co-cluster (submatrix) are highly correlated, i.e., these users will have similar opinions on these items. More formally, let submatrix $\mathcal{M} = \{M_{ui} \mid u \in \mathcal{U}, i \in \mathcal{I}\}$ denote the ratings of a subset of users $\mathcal{U}$ on a subset of items $\mathcal{I}$. If we properly choose a set of very similar users $\mathcal{U}$ and a set of very similar items $\mathcal{I}$, then $\mathcal{M}$ can be reconstructed by fewer number of parameters, i.e., lower rank. Such co-clustering can be beneficial in two aspects: 1) these submatrices can be approximated simultaneously via parallel computing so that high scalability can be achieved and 2) each submatrix will have lower rank than original user-item rating matrix, so that low-rank matrix approximation can be computed more efficiently for each submatrix.

In order to find such coherent submatrices in the user-item rating matrix, we consider to simultaneously partition all users and items into disjoint user clusters $\{\mathcal{U}_1, \ldots, \mathcal{U}_k\}$ and item clusters $\{\mathcal{I}_1, \ldots, \mathcal{I}_l\}$, and a co-cluster $(\mathcal{U}, \mathcal{I})$ corresponds to one desired submatrix. Bregman co-clustering [2] is adopted in this paper to achieve such partitioning. It views the co-clustering as a lossy data compression problem, and attempts to obtain as much information as possible about the original matrix with a few number of critical statistics for co-clusters, such as the row and column averages of each co-cluster. Following common approaches in Bregman co-clustering, we should firstly choose a set of statistics of original matrix that need to be preserved, e.g., the average rating of each user or the average rating of each item, etc., and each statistic can be viewed as a constraint. We denote $\mathcal{C}$ as the constraint set, and six of the most popular non-trivial constraint sets are described as follows:

$$\mathcal{C}_1 = \{\{I_r\}, \{I_c\}\},\ \mathcal{C}_2 = \{\{\hat{I}_r, \hat{I}_c\}\},$$
$$\mathcal{C}_3 = \{\{\hat{I}_r, \hat{I}_c\}, \{I_r\}\},\ \mathcal{C}_4 = \{\{\hat{I}_r, \hat{I}_c\}, \{I_c\}\},$$
$$\mathcal{C}_5 = \{\{\hat{I}_r, \hat{I}_c\}, \{I_r\}, \{I_c\}\},\ \mathcal{C}_6 = \{\{I_r, \hat{I}_c\}, \{\hat{I}_r, I_c\}\},$$

where I_r and I_c are the random variables of row and column indices, which take values over $\{1, \ldots, m\}$ and $\{1, \ldots, n\}$, respectively. $\hat{I}_r$ and $\hat{I}_c$ are the random variables of row and column clusters, which take values over $\{1, \ldots, k\}$ and $\{1, \ldots, l\}$ in a $k \times l$ co-clustering. More specifically, $\mathcal{C}_1$ means that the average values of each row and each column should be preserved, $\mathcal{C}_2$ means the average values of all entries inside each co-cluster should be preserved, and similarly for the other constraint sets. Besides the constraints, we also need to select appropriate Bregman divergence to evaluate a co-clustering, which is defined as follows: for $z_1, z_2 \in \mathbb{R}$, $d_\phi(z_1, z_2) = \phi(z_1) - \phi(z_2) - < z_1 - z_2, \nabla\phi(z_2) >$, where $\nabla\phi$ is the gradient of differential function ϕ. Two popular Bregman divergences are I-divergence and Squared Euclidean distance, defined respectively as follows:

$$d_\phi(z_1, z_2) = z_1 \log(z_1/z_2) - (z_1 - z_2), \phi(z) = z \log z \quad (3)$$
$$d_\phi(z_1, z_2) = (z_1 - z_2)^2, \phi(z) = z^2 \quad (4)$$

Finally, the row and column clustering will be achieved by an iterative meta algorithm, in which the row and column cluster updates can be obtained from the optimal Lagrange multipliers in parallel. The details of the meta algorithms for achieving Bregman co-clustering can be found in [7, 8]. Since the meta algorithms are not the contributions of this paper, details of these algorithms are omitted.

3.2 Submatrices-based Weighting and Matrix Approximation

As described earlier, performing standard matrix approximation on submatrices will not be accurate due to the fact that each submatrix only holds partial information of users/items/ratings. Therefore, we can only learn a "weak" recommendation model from each submatrix, which can make accurate recommendation on a majority of ratings in the corresponding submatrix. As demonstrated in the motivating examples (Section 2.3.2), by associating higher weights to ratings that occur more frequently in a given submatrix, we could potentially improve not only the recommendation accuracy for the frequent ratings, but also the overall recommendation accuracy.

Based on the idea above, we propose a new method for low-rank matrix approximation, which weighs the individual user-item rating differently based on the rating distribution in a submatrix. Specifically, we compute the probabilistic distribution of different ratings in each submatrix and construct a weighted norm by adding the probabilistic information. Since the weight is a function of the rating distribution, we can construct the weighting function $p(x) : \mathbb{F} \to \mathbb{R}$ with Taylor's formula as follows:

$$\begin{aligned} p(x) &= f(\Pr[x]) && (5)\\ &= C_0 + C_1 \Pr[x] + r_p && (6)\\ &\approx 1 + \beta_0 \Pr[x] && (7) \end{aligned}$$

Since $\Pr[x] \in [0, 1]$, the residual term r_p, which is super linear to $\Pr[x]$, can be omitted. Without loss of generality, we can assume that $C_0 = 1$ by scaling all the parameters, then there is only one unknown parameter β_0 in the weighting function. The value of β_0 should be trained such that optimal recommendation accuracy can be achieved. However, this is not straightforward, because recommendation is one-step further after matrix approximation. Therefore, we choose the optimal β_0 by brute force search, in which we check every β_0 value in the linear function $p(x)$. The sensitivity analysis of β_0 is presented in Section 5.2.

After defining the weighting function $p(x)$, we present the extended SVD and compressed sensing matrix approximation methods here, in which weight W_{ij} is $p(M_{ij})$ if the entry is observed and 0 otherwise. It should be noted that the standard low-rank matrix approximation methods, such as SVD, can be regarded as special cases of the proposed method by setting $\beta_0 = 0$.

Extension of SVD :

$$\hat{M} = \arg\min_X \ ||W \otimes (M - X)||_F \ \ s.t. \ \ rank(X) = r. \quad (8)$$

Extension of Compressed Sensing :

$$\hat{M} = \arg\min_X \ ||X||_* \ \ s.t. \ \ ||W \otimes (M - X)||_F < \epsilon. \quad (9)$$

The two optimization problems describe how to estimate $\hat{\mathcal{M}}$ from observed entries in an original submatrix $\mathcal{M}$. Then, missing entries in the original submatrix $\mathcal{M}$ can be obtained from $\hat{\mathcal{M}}$, i.e., user ratings on unrated items can be predicted from $\hat{\mathcal{M}}$ as in other matrix approximation methods.

After applying Bregman co-clustering on the user-item rating matrix M, a $k \times l$ co-clustering (k is the number of user clusters and l is the number of item clusters) can be obtained. Then, we can perform the proposed low-rank matrix approximation on each submatrix. Here, we present a gradient decent learning algorithm for approximating the user-item rating matrix based on the $k \times l$ co-clustering. As described in Algorithm 1, the weight $p(x)$ for each entry in each submatrix is first computed. Then, the proposed low-rank matrix approximation is achieved by a gradient decent method with L_2 regularization. At last, we combine all the resulting submatrix approximations, so that the approximated matrix $\hat{M}$ can be obtained by re-locating each entry in the $k \times l$ submatrices.

Algorithm 1 Co-clustering-based Matrix Approximation

Input: All co-clustering submatrices $\mathcal{M}^{(t)} \subseteq M$ $(t \in [kl])$, rank r, learning rate v, regularization coefficient λ.
Output: Approximated user-item rating matrix $\hat{M}$.

- **for** each $t \in \{1, \ldots, kl\}$ **in parallel do**
  - // Computing weights
  - Compute the rating distribution on $\mathbb{F}$ in $\mathcal{M}^{(t)}$.
  - **for** each observed entry (u, i) in $\mathcal{M}^{(t)}$ **do**
    - $W_{ui} = p(x)$, if $M_{ui} = x$.
  - **end for**
  - // Updating model
  - Initialize $U^{(t)} \in \mathbb{R}^{m \times r}, V^{(t)} \in \mathbb{R}^{n \times r}$ randomly
  - **while** not converged **do**
    - **for** each observed entry (u, i) in $\mathcal{M}^{(t)}$ **do**
      - $\triangle_{ui} = \mathcal{M}^{(t)}_{ui} - U^{(t)}_i (V^{(t)}_j)^T$
      - **for** each $z \in \{1, \ldots, r\}$ **do**
        - $U^{(t)}_{uz} = U^{(t)}_{uz} + v * (\triangle_{ui} * V^{(t)}_{iz} * W_{ui} - \lambda U^{(t)}_{uz})$
        - $V^{(t)}_{iz} = V^{(t)}_{iz} + v * (\triangle_{ui} * U^{(t)}_{uz} * W_{ui} - \lambda V^{(t)}_{iz})$
      - **end for**
    - **end for**
  - **end while**
- **end for**
- **for** each $(u, i) \in [m] \times [n]$ **do**
  - Locate (u, i) in its corresponding submatrix and let the index of the submatrix be ξ.
  - $\hat{M}_{ui} = U^{(\xi)}_u (V^{(\xi)}_i)^T$
- **end for**
- **return** $\hat{M}$

3.3 Ensemble of Multiple Matrix Approximations

As described in Section 3.1, a Bregman co-clustering consists of three components: a constraint set $\mathcal{C}$, a Bregman divergence d_ϕ, and the number of row clusters k and column clusters l. For convenience, we denote a 3-tuple $(\mathcal{C}, d_\phi, k \times l)$ as a co-clustering. It should be noted that different 3-tuples $(\mathcal{C}, d_\phi, k \times l)$ could lead to different matrix approximation results $\hat{M}$ because each entry in $\hat{M}$ is generated based on the corresponding co-cluster. In Section 3.1, we described six constraint sets and two Bregman divergences, which means that we can construct $6 \times 2 = 12$ different $\hat{M}$s by combining different $\mathcal{C}$ and d_ϕ given fixed k and l. Therefore, we propose an ensemble method to intelligently combine the user-item rating predictions obtained from multiple matrix approximations based on different co-clustering settings. Our goal is to further enhance the recommendation accuracy.

To recover a global approximation $\tilde{M}$ from z low-rank approximations $\hat{M}^{(t)}$ $(t \in [z])$, we adopt the weighted mean of $\hat{M}^{(t)}_{ij}$ as $\tilde{M}_{ij}$. The weight for the ensemble method should be determined by the confidences of both users and items. And a predicted rating from a "weak" recommendation model should be considered as more important if 1) the corresponding user frequently gave such rating to items before and 2) the corresponding item was frequently rated by such rating before. More formally, the i-th user (M_{i*}) and the j-th item (M_{*j}) can be viewed as discrete random variables over a finite-field $\mathbb{F}$ with unique distributions $\Pr(x; M_{i*})$ and $\Pr(x; M_{*j})$, $x \in \mathbb{F}$. Furthermore, the prediction of $\mathcal{M}_{ij} = x$ should be considered more confident if user i and item j have (been) rated x many times in M. Therefore, the ensemble weight $q(x) : \mathbb{F} \to \mathbb{R}$ can be regarded as a function of $\Pr(x; M_{i*})$ and $\Pr(x; M_{*j})$ as follows:

$$\begin{aligned} q(x) &= f(\Pr[x; M_{i*}], \Pr[x; M_{*j}]) && (10) \\ &= C_0 + C_1 \Pr[x; M_{i*}] + C_2 \Pr[x; M_{*j}] + r_q && (11) \\ &\approx 1 + \beta_1 \Pr[x; M_{i*}] + \beta_2 \Pr[x; M_{*j}] && (12) \end{aligned}$$

Again, by omit the small residual term r_q and scaling the constant term to 1, we can obtain the final ensemble weight as Equation 12. Then, the proposed ensemble method can be performed as follows:

$$\tilde{M}_{ui} = \sum_{t=1}^{z} \frac{Q^{(t)}_{ui}}{\sum_{s=1}^{z} Q^{(s)}_{ui}} \hat{M}^{(t)}_{ui}, \qquad (13)$$

where $Q^{(t)}_{ui} = q(M_{ui})$. Based on Equation 13, we present Algorithm 2 to describe how to predict missing values in user-item rating matrix for recommendation. We can clearly see that the global matrix approximation $\tilde{M}$ can be efficiently computed because the computation for all entries in $\tilde{M}$ just requires weighted averaging.

Algorithm 2 WEMAREC_Ensemble (u, i)

Input: Resulting matrix approximations $\hat{M}^{(t)}$ $(t \in [z])$ from z different co-clusterings, u and i are the targeted user and item, respectively.
Output: The predicted rating of user u on item i: $\tilde{M}_{ui}$.

- // Computing weights
- **for** $t \in [z]$ **do**
  - $Q^{(t)}_{ui} = q(\hat{M}^{(t)}_{ui})$
- **end for**
- **return** $\tilde{M}_{ui} = \sum_{t=1}^{z} \frac{Q^{(t)}_{ui}}{\sum_{s=1}^{z} Q^{(s)}_{ui}} \hat{M}^{(t)}_{ui}$

3.4 Running Time Analysis

The proposed weighted and ensemble matrix approximation method (WEMAREC) is faster than many state-of-the-art matrix approximation algorithms, although its overall computational complexity is nearly z times larger than solving a regularized SVD problem. The reasons why the proposed WEMAREC method can run faster are as follow: (1) Every co-cluster is independent from each other, and matrix approximation on each co-cluster can be computed in parallel; (2) standard low-rank algorithms have a computation complexity of $\Omega(rmn)$ per-iteration, whereas the proposed WEMAREC method significantly reduces the computation complexity to $\Omega(r|\mathcal{U}||\mathcal{I}|)$ per-iteration because user clusters and item clusters are not overlapping in Bregman co-clustering; and (3) the users inside each co-cluster are highly similar, and so are the items. Therefore, lower rank (r) is required to achieve accurate matrix approximation in the proposed method than other methods, which further reduces its running time. Besides theoretical analysis, we also analyze the scalability of the proposed WEMAREC method in Section 5.

4. ERROR BOUND ANALYSIS

This section analyzes the generalization error bounds of the proposed method. We use the root mean squared error (RMSE), one of the most widely adopted accuracy measures in recommender systems [1], as the evaluation metric:

$$\mathcal{D}(\hat{\mathrm{M}}) = \sqrt{\frac{1}{mn}\sum_{u=1}^{m}\sum_{i=1}^{n}(\hat{\mathrm{M}}_{ui} - \mathrm{M}_{ui})^2}$$

where $M \in \mathbb{F}^{m\times n}$ and $\Pr[\max(\mathbb{F}) \geq \hat{M}_{ui} \geq \min(\mathbb{F})] = 1$. Then, the following proposition establishes the error bound of the proposed weighted matrix approximation method, i.e., the RMSE of the weighted low-rank matrix approximation method on each co-cluster is bounded, so that we can still find optimum submatrix factorization for recommendation by optimizing the extended optimization problems (Equation 8 and 9).

PROPOSITION 1. *For any $M \in \mathbb{F}^{m\times n}$, $m, n > 2$, $\delta > 0$, with probability at least $1 - \delta$ over choosing a subset Ω of entries in M uniformly,*

$$\mathcal{D}(\hat{M}) \leq \mathcal{D}_\Omega(\hat{M}) + \sqrt{\frac{\log\delta}{-2|\Omega|}(\max(\mathbb{F}) - \min(\mathbb{F}))^2}.$$

PROOF. Since the entries of Ω are chosen independently and uniformly, it is reasonable to assume each $loss(\hat{M}_{ui}; M_{ui})$ $= (M_{ui} - \hat{M}_{ui})^2$ is a random variable and satisfies

$$\Pr[\alpha^2 \geq loss(\hat{M}_{ui}; M_{ui}) \geq 0] = 1$$

which $\alpha = \max(\mathbb{F}) - \min(\mathbb{F})$. Hence, based on the Hoeffding Inequality, we have $\Pr[\mathcal{D}(\hat{M}) - \mathcal{D}_\Omega(\hat{M}) \geq \epsilon] \leq e^{\frac{-2|\Omega|\epsilon^2}{\alpha^2}}$. By setting $\epsilon = \sqrt{\frac{\log\delta}{-2|\Omega|}\alpha^2}$, we have

$$\Pr[\mathcal{D}(\hat{\mathrm{M}}) - \mathcal{D}_\Omega(\hat{\mathrm{M}}) \leq \sqrt{\frac{\log\delta}{-2|\Omega|}\alpha^2}] \geq 1 - \delta$$

i.e.,

$$\Pr[\mathcal{D}(\hat{\mathrm{M}}) \leq \mathcal{D}_\Omega(\hat{\mathrm{M}}) + \sqrt{\frac{\log\delta}{-2|\Omega|}(\max(\mathbb{F}) - \min(\mathbb{F}))^2}] \geq 1 - \delta$$

Therefore, the errors of the new problems are bounded. □

Next, we theoretically analyze the generalization error bounds of the proposed co-clustering based matrix approximation algorithm (Algorithm 1) and the ensemble method (Algorithm 2). Since the error bound of SVD based low-rank matrix approximation method has been well analyzed [19, 21], we focus on analyzing the error bound of compressed-sensing based method (defined in Equation 9) by using similar analysis techniques as in [5, 6]. As shown in [5, 6], we can recover a rank r matrix $M \in \mathbb{R}^{m\times n}(n \geq m)$ with probability at least $1 - n^{-3}$, if the number of observed entries is $|\Omega| \geq C\mu^2 nr\log^6 n$, where C is a constant and μ is the strong incoherence parameter. However, this result is not applicable in our case, because the matrix M is approximated by multiple low-rank submatrices. Hence, we develop a new error bound based on a variant of the aforementioned conclusion.

The following analysis makes the following assumptions: (a) every submatrix $\mathcal{M}$ is a rank r matrix that satisfies the strong incoherent properties, and (b) the observed entries are uniformly distributed in submatrices such that the density of the observed entries ϱ in every submatrix is consistent with each other (i.e., $\varrho = \frac{|\Omega|}{mn}$). Without loss of generality, we assume $n \geq m$, and denote $\alpha = \max(\mathbb{F}) - \min(\mathbb{F})$, where $\mathbb{F}$ is the set of ratings. We start by analyzing the error bound of the co-clustering-based model $\hat{M}$ in Proposition 2. Then, based on Proposition 2, we proceed to derive an error bound on the global approximation $\tilde{M}$ in Proposition 3.

PROPOSITION 2. *If the density of the observed entries ϱ is large enough such that $|\Omega| \geq C\mu^2 nr\log^6 n$, then with probability of at leat $1-\delta$, $\hat{M}$ corresponding to a $k\times l$ co-clustering satisfies*

$$\mathcal{D}(\hat{M}) \leq \frac{(1+\beta_0)\alpha}{\sqrt{mn}}(4\sqrt{\frac{(2+\varrho)}{\varrho}(klm)} + 2kl),$$

where $\delta = (2kln)^{-3}$.

PROOF. For every user-item pair (u, i), an observation M_{ui} is equal to $\hat{M}_{ui} + Z$ where Z is a random variable whose absolute error is bounded by

$$\|W \otimes (M - \hat{M})\|_\infty \leq \|(1+\beta_0)(M - \hat{M})\|_\infty \leq (1+\beta_0)\alpha.$$

By applying Theorem 7 in [5] to matrix completion problem with bounded noise, we get with probability greater than $1 - \upsilon^{-3}$ that every co-cluster-based approximation $\hat{\mathcal{M}}$ will satisfy

$$\|\mathcal{W} \otimes (\mathcal{M} - \hat{\mathcal{M}})\|_F \leq (1+\beta_0)\alpha(4\sqrt{\frac{\gamma(2+\varrho)}{\varrho}} + 2) \quad (14)$$

where $\upsilon = \max(|\mathcal{U}|, |\mathcal{I}|)$, $\gamma = \min(|\mathcal{U}|, |\mathcal{I}|)$. For one $k\times l$ co-clustering, there are kl different submatrices $\mathcal{M}_t, \gamma^{(t)}, t \in [kl]$, and obviously $\sum_{t\in[kl]}\gamma^{(t)} \leq m$. Using Cauchy-Schwarz inequality, we get

$$\sum_{t\in[kl]}\sqrt{\gamma^{(t)}} \leq \sqrt{kl\sum_{t\in[kl]}\gamma^{(t)}} \leq \sqrt{klm}. \quad (15)$$

Therefore, we can bound the approximation error as follows:

$$\begin{aligned}\|W \otimes (M - \hat{M})\|_F &\stackrel{(a)}{\leq} \textstyle\sum_{t\in[kl]}\|\mathcal{W}_t \otimes (\mathcal{M}_t - \hat{\mathcal{M}}_t)\|_F\\ &\stackrel{(b)}{\leq} \textstyle\sum_{t\in[kl]}(1+\beta_0)\alpha(4\sqrt{\frac{(2+\varrho)}{\varrho}\gamma^{(t)}} + 2)\\ &\stackrel{(c)}{\leq} (1+\beta_0)\alpha(4\sqrt{\tfrac{2+\varrho}{\varrho}(klm)} + 2kl)\end{aligned} \quad (16)$$

in which (a) holds due to the triangle inequality of Frobenius norm; and (b) holds due to (14); and (c) holds due to (15). Since for all (u, i) pairs, $\mathrm{W}_{ui} \geq 1$. Then, we have

$$\mathcal{D}(\hat{M}) = \frac{\|M - \hat{M}\|_F}{\sqrt{mn}} \leq \frac{\|W \otimes (M - \hat{M})\|_F}{\sqrt{mn}}. \quad (17)$$

Combining (16) and (17), we established the error bound of $\hat{M}$ as stated above. In order to adjust the confidence level, we take a union bound of the events $\|\mathcal{W} \otimes (\mathcal{M} - \hat{\mathcal{M}})\|_F \geq (1+\beta_0)\alpha(4\sqrt{\frac{\gamma(2+\varrho)}{\varrho}} + 2)$ for each submatrix $\mathcal{M}^{(t)}$, then we have

$$\sum_{t\in[kl]}\sqrt[3]{\upsilon^{(t)}} \leq \sqrt[3]{kl\sum_{t\in[kl]}\upsilon^{(t)}} \leq \sqrt[3]{2kln}.$$

i.e., the inequation in Proposition 2 holds with probabilities at least$1 - \delta$ ($\delta = \sqrt[3]{2kln}$). □

PROPOSITION 3. *If Proposition 2 holds, then with probability of at leat $1-\delta$, the $\tilde{M}$ based on z different $k \times l$ co-clustering settings satisfies:*

$$\mathcal{D}(\tilde{M}) \leq \frac{(1+\beta_0)\alpha}{\sqrt{mn}}(4\sqrt{\frac{(2+\varrho)}{\varrho}(klm)}+2kl),$$

where $\delta = z(2kln)^{-3}$.

PROOF. By Proposition 2, we bound the error of $\tilde{M}$ as follows:

$$\begin{aligned}\|\tilde{M}-M\|_F &\overset{(a)}{\leq} \tfrac{1}{z}\|\textstyle\sum_{s\in[z]} Q^{(s)}\otimes(\tilde{M}-M)\|_F \\ &\overset{(b)}{=} \tfrac{1}{z}\|\textstyle\sum_{s\in[z]} Q^{(s)}\otimes(\hat{M}^{(s)}-M)\|_F \\ &\overset{(c)}{\leq} \tfrac{1}{z}\textstyle\sum_{s\in[z]} \|Q^{(s)}\otimes(\hat{M}^{(s)}-M)\|_F \\ &\overset{(d)}{\leq} \tfrac{1}{z}\textstyle\sum_{s}(1+\beta_0)\alpha(4\sqrt{\tfrac{2+p}{p}(klm)}+2kl) \\ &= (1+\beta_0)\alpha(4\sqrt{\tfrac{2+p}{p}(klm)}+2kl)\end{aligned}$$

where (a) holds because every $\sum_{s\in[z]} Q_{ij}^{(s)} \geq \sum_{s\in[z]} 1 = z$; (b) holds due to Equation 13; (c) holds due to the triangle inequality of Frobenius norm; (d) holds due to Equation 16. Finally, by dividing $\sqrt{mn}$ from both sides, we conclude the proof. The confidence level is adjusted to $z(2kln)^{-3}$ using the union bound property as in Proposition 2. □

5. EXPERIMENTAL RESULTS

This section evaluates the proposed method on real-world datasets. The first study conducts sensitivity analysis. The proposed method consists of a set of parameters, i.e., rank of matrices r, and the number of row clusters k and column clusters l. This study evaluates how the recommendation accuracy of the proposed method is affected by these parameters. The second study compares the recommendation accuracy of the proposed method against six state-of-the-art matrix approximation based CF methods using PREA toolkit [13]. The third study evaluates the runtime scalability of the proposed method against standard SVD method.

5.1 Experiment Setup

The experimental study uses three real-world datasets that have been widely used for evaluating recommendation algorithms – 1) MovieLens 1M (10^6 ratings of 6,040 users on 3,706 items); 2) MovieLens 10M (10^7 rating of 69,878 users on 10,677 items); and 3) Netflix (10^8 rating of 480,189 users on 17,770 items). For each dataset, we split it into train and test sets randomly by setting the ratio between train set and test set as $9:1$. The results are presented by averaging the results over five different random train-test splits.

We use learning rate $v = 0.002$ for gradient decent method, $\lambda = 0.01$ for L_2-regularization coefficient, $\epsilon = 0.0001$ for gradient descent convergence threshold, and $T = 100$ for maximum number of iterations. The proposed method (WEMAREC) is compared against six state-of-the-art matrix approximation based CF methods, which are described as follows:

- NMF [Lee et al., NIPS' 01]: assumes the data and components are non-negative and every entry follows the Poisson distribution. Then the approximation is achieved by maximizing the log-likelihood.
- Regularized SVD [Paterek et al., KDD' 07]: is a standard matrix factorization method inspired by the effective methods of natural language processing, in which user/item features are estimated by minimizing the sum-squared error.
- BPMF [Salakhutdinov et al., ICML' 08]: is a Bayesain extension of probabilistic matrix factorization, in which the model is trained using Markov chain Monte Carlo methods.
- APG[1] [Toh et al., PJO 2010]: views the recommendation task as a matrix completion problem, and computes the approximation by solving a nuclear norm regularized linear least squares problem.
- DFC[2] [Mackey et al., NIPS' 11]: divides a large-scale matrix factorization task into smaller subproblems, and uses the techniques from randomized matrix approximation to combine the subproblem solutions.
- LLORMA [Lee et al., ICML' 13]: relaxes the low-rank assumption, and assumes that the original matrix is described using multiple low-rank submatrices, which are constructed using techniques from non-parametric kernel smoothing.

5.2 Sensitivity Analysis

We first show how WEMAREC performs with different combinations of parameters. MovieLens (10M) and Netflix datasets are used in this study with randomly selected 90% of data as training data and the rest 10% as test data.

Figure 3 presents the effects of the weighted function $p(x)$ (Eqn. 5) with β_0 varying in [0, 2.0] on three artificially selected datasets (from MovieLens (10M)) with different rating distributions. The detailed characteristics of the three selected datasets are presented in Table 2. As we can see, the RMSEs on all three datasets first decrease as β_0 increases from 0, and increases after the optimal accuracies are achieved. We also observe that optimal β_0s on more uneven datasets are smaller than those on more even datasets. The reason is that the frequency of different ratings are close on even datasets, so that a greater β_0 is required to make the weights of different ratings more different. Based on the above study, we choose $\beta_0 = 0.4$ for the following experiments because the submatrices generated by Bregman co-clustering are always uneven.

Figure 4 and 5 analyze the effects of Bregman co-clustering by changing the rank r and the numbers of row and column clusters k and l on MovieLens (10M) and Netflix dataset. We can see from the results that recommendation accuracies increase when the rank r increases from 5 to 20 in Figure 4. And the accuracies on the left (I-divergence) and middle (Euclidean-distance) are worse than those on the right (combination of these two distances), which indicates that the combination of different approximations $\hat{M}$ leads to better recommendation accuracy than both original ones. Figure 4 also shows that the recommendation accuracy decreases when k and l increase (from 2×2 to 3×3). This is due to the fact that each co-cluster based submatrix consists of less user-item ratings when k and l increase, resulting in insufficient training data for both model training and prediction. However, the accuracy first increases when k and l increase (from 2×2 to 2×3) in Figure 5, and then decrease when $k\times l = 3\times3$. This implies that larger dataset can be divided into more clusters to further improve the efficiency with improved accuracy. Based on this study, we choose rank $r = 20$ and $k\times l$ as 2×2 or 3×2 in the ensemble method, which offers the best recommendation accuracy for WEMAREC.

[1] http://www.math.nus.edu.sg/~mattohkc/NNLS.html
[2] http://www.cs.ucla.edu/~ameet/dfc/

	Rating = 1	Rating = 2	Rating = 3	Rating = 4	Rating = 5	Entropy
High	0.98%	3.14%	15.42%	40.98%	39.49%	1.174590
Median	3.44%	9.38%	29.25%	37.86%	20.06%	1.387499
Low	18.33%	26.10%	35.27%	16.88%	3.43%	1.445043

Table 2: Characteristics of three artificially selected datasets with different rating distributions (smaller entropy means that the dataset is more uneven).

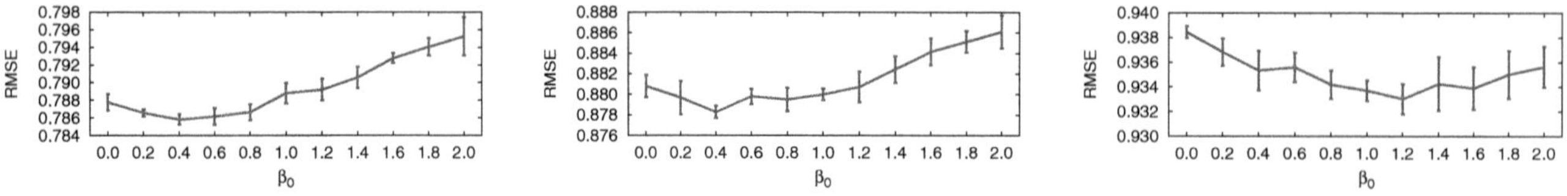

Figure 3: Effects of weighted function $p(x)$ on the performance of cocluster-based model over high-uneven(left), median-uneven(middle), low-uneven(right) datasets, with β_0 varying in $[0,\ 2.0]$.

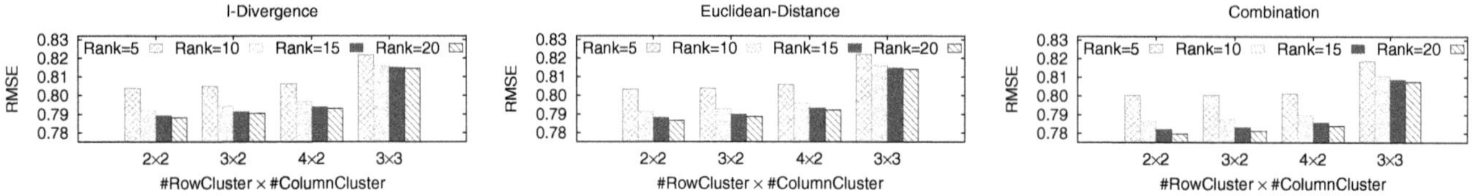

Figure 4: Effects of Bregman co-clustering on the performance of WEMAREC in I-divergence (left), Euclidean-distance (middle), and Combination of both two above distances (right), with the rank of submatrix varying in $\{5, 10, 15, 20\}$, the number of row and column clusters varying in $\{2 \times 2, 3 \times 2, 4 \times 2, 3 \times 3\}$ on MovieLens (10M).

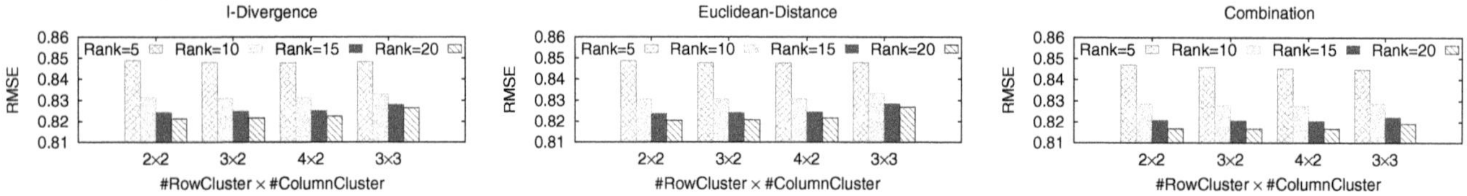

Figure 5: Effects of Bregman co-clustering on the performance of WEMAREC in I-divergence (left), Euclidean-distance (middle), and Combination of both two above distances (right), with the rank of submatrix varying in $\{5, 10, 15, 20\}$, the number of row and column clusters varying in $\{2 \times 2, 3 \times 2, 4 \times 2, 3 \times 3\}$ on Netflix.

Figure 6 analyzes the effect of ensemble weight function $q(x)$ (Eqn. 12) by selecting different β_1 and β_2. And we can see that the accuracies of the proposed weighted average methods always outperform the simple average method without weighting (i.e., $\beta_1 = 0.0, \beta_2 = 0.0$). It seems that larger β_1 will lead to better accuracy, but we also observe that the RMSE becomes stable when $\beta_1 > 40$. Therefore, we adopt $\beta_1 = 3.0$ and $\beta_2 = 40$ in the following experiments.

5.3 Recommendation Accuracy Comparisons

This study evaluates the accuracy of the proposed methods by comparing it with the six state-of-the-art matrix approximation based CF methods summarized in Section 5.1, i.e., NMF [11], Regularized SVD (RSVD) [16], BPMF [18], APG [25], DFC [14], LLORMA [12]. Each of the method is configured using the same parameters provided by the original paper. For the proposed WEMAREC method, we consider $2*2*2 = 8$ resulting matrix approximations, which are constructed by varying $\mathcal{C} \in \{\mathcal{C}_2, \mathcal{C}_5\}$, $d_\phi \in \{$*I-divergence*, *Euclidean-distance*$\}$ and $k \times l \in \{2 \times 2, 3 \times 2\}$. The MovieLens (10M) and Netflix datasets are used in this study.

Table 3 presents the RMSEs of all these matrix approximation based CF methods on the MovieLens (10M) and Netflix datasets. This study shows that the proposed WEMAREC method outperforms all the other six matrix approximation based CF methods on both the datasets. The reason why the proposed method can further improve the recommendation accuracy is due to 1) the new low-rank matrix approximation method can build more accurate models on submatrices because most often appeared ratings (major

	MovieLens (10M)	Netflix
NMF	0.8832 ± 0.0007	0.9396 ± 0.0002
RSVD	0.8253 ± 0.0009	0.8534 ± 0.0001
BPMF	0.8195 ± 0.0006	0.8420 ± 0.0003
APG	0.8098 ± 0.0005	0.8476 ± 0.0028
DFC	0.8064 ± 0.0006	0.8451 ± 0.0005
LLORMA	0.7851 ± 0.0007	0.8275 ± 0.0004
WEMAREC	$\mathbf{0.7769 \pm 0.0004}$	$\mathbf{0.8142 \pm 0.0001}$

Table 3: RMSE on MovieLens (10M) and Netflix of NMF (r=50) [11], Regularized SVD (r=50) [16], BPMF(r=30) [18], APG [25], DFC [14], LLORMA (r=20) [12], WEMAREC (r=20).

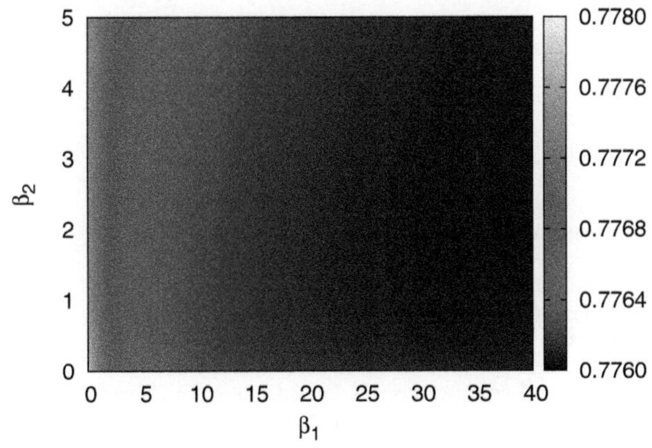

Figure 6: Effects of ensemble weighted function $q(x)$ on the performance of WEMAREC with different β_1 and β_2 on MovieLens 10M.

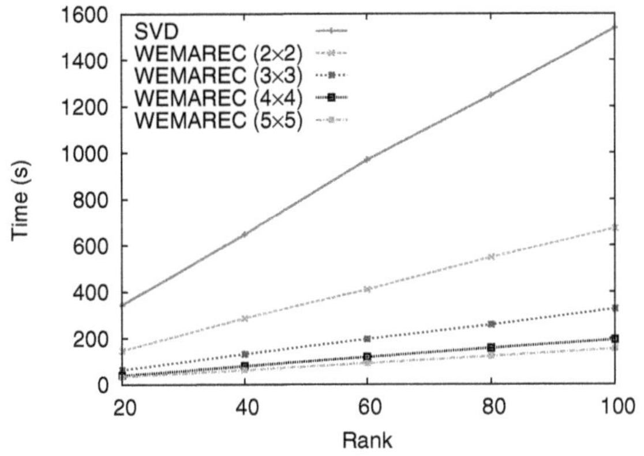

Figure 7: Efficiency comparisons of SVD method and WEMAREC method with different sizes of user-item rating matrix and different numbers of row clusters and column clusters.

interests) of users are treated more importantly; and 2) the ensemble method can effectively take advantage of the high-quality recommendation results from different co-clusterings to further improve the recommendation accuracy.

5.4 Scalability Analysis

This study evaluates how the WEMAREC method can speedup the recommendation process by leveraging parallel computing. The MovieLens (1M) dataset is used in this study. Leveraging parallel computing, all the submatrices are processed in parallel, and the execution time of WEMAREC is determined by that of the largest submatrix.

Figure 7 shows the execution time of WEMAREC by changing the co-clustering settings. The SVD method is included in this study for comparison purpose. This study shows that the execution time of SVD and WEMAREC both increases as the rank increases, and the performance of the WEMAREC method improves as the sizes of the submatrices decrease. WEMAREC outperforms SVD by 3X - 10X when the co-clustering setting varies from 2×2 to 5×5, and the speedup increases as the number of submatrices increases. This study demonstrates that WEMAREC can effectively improve the recommendation system scalability on large datasets.

6. RELATED WORK

Matrix factorization methods have been widely adopted in many applications [27], as well as recommendation systems [10]. Billsus et al. [4] initially introduced SVD to collaborative filtering context. Then, Srebro et al. [23] proposed a maximum-margin matrix factorization (MMMF) method, which can be formulated as a semi-definite programming problem for achieving matrix approximation based CF. Rennie et al. [17] investigated a direct gradient-based optimization method for achieving MMMF based CF, which can effectively improve the efficiency of MMMF method. Singh et al. [20] introduced a collective matrix factorization method based on relational learning to generalize existing matrix factorization methods and yielded new large-scale optimization algorithms for these problems. Yu et al. [28] proposed a non-parametric matrix factorization method, to make matrix approximation based CF methods applicable on large-scale datasets. Salakhutdinov et al. [15] extended matrix factorization to probabilistic algorithms by proposing a Probabilistic Matrix Factorization (PMF) method, which can scale linearly with the number of observations in the matrix. Based on the above work, a fully Bayesian treatment of PMF is present By Salakhutdinov et al. [18], which can train the user-rating matrix in recommender systems using Markov chain Monte Carlo methods.

In addition to single matrix factorization, ensemble methods have also been investigated in the literature. The Netflix Prize winners Bell et al. [3] and Koren et al. [9] utilized the combination of memory-based and matrix factorization methods to improve recommendation accuracy. Different from the above work, Mackey et al. [14] introduced a Divide-Factor-Combine (DFC) framework, in which the expensive task of matrix factorization is randomly divided into smaller subproblems which can be solved in parallel using an arbitrary base matrix factorization algorithms. Lee et al. [12] proposed a local low-rank matrix approximation (LLORMA) method, which generalized the DFC method in a way that a metric structure is used on the original matrix and the matrix partitions are constructed by kernel smoothing.

The DFC method and LLORMA method share similar idea with our method in that ensemble methods are adopted to boost recommendation accuracy. A significant difference between DFC and LLORMA is the construction of submatrices. In DFC, each submatrix is constructed by random sampling, while in LLORMA the submatrix is made of nearest neighbors within certain range. Different from both of them, the submatrices in our method are constructed via partitional co-clustering, so that each submatrix has low-parameter structure with less users and items, i.e., the submatrices in our method are of lower rank. Therefore, matrix approximation on such submatrices can be performed more efficiently. In addition, a submatrix-based weighting strategy is proposed to capture rating-specific prediction power of each submatrix, so that more accurate recommendations can be generated on more frequent samples in each submatrix. Therefore, the overall recommendation accuracy can be improved in each submatrix. Finally, the ensemble strategy in the proposed method can leverage both user-specific and item-specific rating distributions to combine the approximation matrices, which considers much more information compared with simple averaging method in DFC and kernel smoothing method in LLORMA. Moreover, the proposed ensemble method is more efficient than the LLORMA method, because the kernel distance used in LLORMA method is based on the cosine distances between the rows of factor matrices, requiring extra singular value decompositions.

7. CONCLUSIONS

Matrix approximation methods have shown great success in recommender systems. However, tradeoff between scalability and accuracy must be made for most existing matrix approximation based CF methods. In this paper, a weighted and ensemble matrix approximation method (WEMAREC) is proposed to improve both recommendation accuracy and scalability. In WEMAREC, the user-item rating matrix is partitioned into a set of submatrices, which are then processed in parallel to improve system scalability. To optimize recommendation accuracy, a submatrix-based weighting strategy and an ensemble strategy are proposed. The weighting strategy improves the accuracy of the majority ratings of individual submatrices. The ensemble strategy improves the overall recommendation accuracy by combining multiple sets of co-clustering results based on the user-specific and item-specific rating distributions. Experimental study on MovieLens and Netflix datasets demonstrates that the proposed method can outperform state-of-the-art matrix approximation based CF methods on recommendation accuracy and scalability.

8. ACKNOWLEDGMENT

This work was supported in part by the National Natural Science Foundation of China under Grant No. 61233016, and the National Science Foundation of USA under Grant Nos. 1251257, 1334351 and 1442971.

9. REFERENCES

[1] G. Adomavicius and A. Tuzhilin. Toward the next generation of recommender systems: A survey of the state-of-the-art and possible extensions. *IEEE Transactions on Knowledge and Data Engeering*, 17(6):734–749, 2005.

[2] A. Banerjee, I. Dhillon, J. Ghosh, S. Merugu, and D. S. Modha. A generalized maximum entropy approach to bregman co-clustering and matrix approximation. *The Journal of Machine Learning Research*, 8:1919–1986, 2007.

[3] R. Bell, Y. Koren, and C. Volinsky. Modeling relationships at multiple scales to improve accuracy of large recommender systems. In *Proceedings of the 13th ACM SIGKDD international conference on Knowledge discovery and data mining*, pages 95–104. ACM, 2007.

[4] D. Billsus and M. J. Pazzani. Learning collaborative information filters. In *Proceedings of the 15th International Conference on Machine Learning*, pages 46–54, 1998.

[5] E. J. Candès and Y. Plan. Matrix completion with noise. *Proceedings of the IEEE*, 98(6):925–936, 2010.

[6] E. J. Candès and T. Tao. The power of convex relaxation: Near-optimal matrix completion. *IEEE Transactions on Information Theory*, 56(5):2053–2080, 2010.

[7] I. S. Dhillon, S. Mallela, and D. S. Modha. Information-theoretic co-clustering. In *Proceedings of the ninth ACM SIGKDD international conference on Knowledge discovery and data mining*, pages 89–98, 2003.

[8] T. George and S. Merugu. A scalable collaborative filtering framework based on co-clustering. In *The Fifth IEEE Intl. Conference on Data Mining*, pages 625–628. IEEE, 2005.

[9] Y. Koren. Factorization meets the neighborhood: a multifaceted collaborative filtering model. In *Proceedings of the 14th ACM SIGKDD international conference on Knowledge discovery and data mining*, pages 426–434, 2008.

[10] Y. Koren, R. Bell, and C. Volinsky. Matrix factorization techniques for recommender systems. *Computer*, 42(8):30–37, 2009.

[11] D. D. Lee and H. S. Seung. Algorithms for non-negative matrix factorization. In *Advances in neural information processing systems*, pages 556–562, 2001.

[12] J. Lee, S. Kim, G. Lebanon, and Y. Singer. Local low-rank matrix approximation. In *Proceedings of The 30th International Conference on Machine Learning*, pages 82–90, 2013.

[13] J. Lee, M. Sun, and G. Lebanon. Prea: Personalized recommendation algorithms toolkit. *The Journal of Machine Learning Research*, 13(1):2699–2703, 2012.

[14] L. W. Mackey, M. I. Jordan, and A. Talwalkar. Divide-and-conquer matrix factorization. In *Advances in Neural Information Processing Systems*, pages 1134–1142, 2011.

[15] A. Mnih and R. Salakhutdinov. Probabilistic matrix factorization. In *Advances in neural information processing systems*, pages 1257–1264, 2007.

[16] A. Paterek. Improving regularized singular value decomposition for collaborative filtering. In *Proceedings of KDD cup and workshop*, volume 2007, pages 5–8, 2007.

[17] J. D. Rennie and N. Srebro. Fast maximum margin matrix factorization for collaborative prediction. In *Proceedings of the 22nd international conference on Machine learning*, pages 713–719. ACM, 2005.

[18] R. Salakhutdinov and A. Mnih. Bayesian probabilistic matrix factorization using markov chain monte carlo. In *Proceedings of the 25th international conference on Machine learning*, pages 880–887. ACM, 2008.

[19] J. Shawe-Taylor, N. Cristianini, and J. S. Kandola. On the concentration of spectral properties. In *Advances in neural information processing systems*, pages 511–517, 2001.

[20] A. P. Singh and G. J. Gordon. Relational learning via collective matrix factorization. In *Proceedings of the 14th ACM SIGKDD international conference on Knowledge discovery and data mining*, pages 650–658. ACM, 2008.

[21] N. Srebro, N. Alon, and T. S. Jaakkola. Generalization error bounds for collaborative prediction with low-rank matrices. In *Advances In Neural Information Processing Systems*, pages 1321–1328, 2004.

[22] N. Srebro, T. Jaakkola, et al. Weighted low-rank approximations. In *Proceedings of the 20th International Conference on Machine Learning*, pages 720–727, 2003.

[23] N. Srebro, J. Rennie, and T. S. Jaakkola. Maximum-margin matrix factorization. In *Advances in neural information processing systems*, pages 1329–1336, 2004.

[24] X. Su and T. M. Khoshgoftaar. A survey of collaborative filtering techniques. *Advances in Artificial Intelligence*, Jan. 2009. Article ID 421425.

[25] K.-C. Toh and S. Yun. An accelerated proximal gradient algorithm for nuclear norm regularized linear least squares problems. *Pacific Journal of Optimization*, 6(615-640):15, 2010.

[26] B. Xu, J. Bu, C. Chen, and D. Cai. An exploration of improving collaborative recommender systems via user-item subgroups. In *Proceedings of the 21st International Conference on World Wide Web*, pages 21–30, 2012.

[27] J. Yan, M. Zhu, H. Liu, and Y. Liu. Visual saliency detection via sparsity pursuit. *IEEE Signal Processing Letters*, 17(8):739–742, 2010.

[28] K. Yu, S. Zhu, J. Lafferty, and Y. Gong. Fast nonparametric matrix factorization for large-scale collaborative filtering. In *Proceedings of the 32nd international ACM SIGIR conference on Research and development in information retrieval*, pages 211–218, 2009.

[29] Y. Zhang, M. Zhang, Y. Liu, and S. Ma. Improve collaborative filtering through bordered block diagonal form matrices. In *Proceedings of the 36th international ACM SIGIR conference on Research and development in information retrieval*, pages 313–322. ACM, 2013.

Effective Latent Models for Binary Feedback in Recommender Systems

Maksims N. Volkovs
Milq Inc
151 Bloor Street West
Toronto, ON M5S 1S4
maks@milq.com

Guang Wei Yu
Milq Inc
151 Bloor Street West
Toronto, ON M5S 1S4
guangweiyu@milq.com

ABSTRACT

In many collaborative filtering (CF) applications, latent approaches are the preferred model choice due to their ability to generate real-time recommendations efficiently. However, the majority of existing latent models are not designed for implicit binary feedback (views, clicks, plays etc.) and perform poorly on data of this type. Developing accurate models from implicit feedback is becoming increasingly important in CF since implicit feedback can often be collected at lower cost and in much larger quantities than explicit preferences. The need for accurate latent models for implicit data was further emphasized by the recently conducted Million Song Dataset Challenge organized by Kaggle [18]. In this challenge, the results for the best latent model were orders of magnitude worse than neighbor-based approaches, and all the top performing teams exclusively used neighbor-based models. We address this problem and propose a new latent approach for binary feedback in CF. In our model, neighborhood similarity information is used to guide latent factorization and derive accurate latent representations. We show that even with simple factorization methods like SVD, our approach outperforms existing models and produces state-of-the-art results.

Categories and Subject Descriptors

H.4.m [**Information Systems Applications**]: Miscellaneous

Keywords

Collaborative Filtering; Binary Feedback; Latent Models

1. INTRODUCTION

Emerging popularity of e-commerce and social web has highlighted an important challenge of surfacing relevant content to consumers. Recommender systems have proven to be effective tools for this task receiving a lot of attention recently [2, 5, 14]. One approach that is commonly used to build accurate recommender models is collaborative filtering (CF). CF is a method of making predictions about an individual's preferences based on the preference information from many users. CF has been shown to work well across various domains [2], and many successful web-services such as Netflix, Amazon, YouTube and Yahoo! use CF to deliver personalized recommendations to their users.

The majority of the existing approaches in CF can be divided into two categories: neighbor-based approaches and model-based approaches (we review both types in detail in Section 3). Neighbor-based approaches estimate the item preferences for a target user using the similarities from neighboring users and/or items [23, 12]. In contrast, model-based approaches use the observed preferences to create a compact model of the data which is then used to predict the unobserved preferences.

While neighbor-based models can generate accurate and interpretable recommendations when sufficient data is available, they are very inefficient at test time. Most neighbor models require loading large portions of data to estimate user and/or item similarities, and involve several complex operations most of which are difficult to do efficiently in real-time. In many applications where recommendations need to be generated in real-time, model-based approaches are the preferred choice. These methods build compact memory-efficient representations of the data and can be easily scaled to handle millions of users and items. For this reason we primarily concentrate on model-based approaches in this work.

Preference data that is used to learn CF models can be partitioned into two types: *explicit feedback* and *implicit feedback*. Explicit feedback includes all explicit preference actions from users. Data of this type typically comes in the form of ratings (Netflix, Amazon etc.) or thumbs-up/down selection (Youtube, TiVo etc.). While explicit feedback generally provides high quality signal that accurately describes users' preferences, collecting large amounts of this data required to develop accurate recommender models is notoriously difficult and time consuming. For this reason, much of the recent attention have been devoted to implicit feedback where preferences are inferred indirectly by observing user behavior. Implicit feedback can come in many forms that include plays, purchases, browse histories and even mouse clicks and scrolls. Since no additional action is required from users beyond the normal use of the service, large amounts of implicit feedback can often be cheaply collected in a short amount of time. This advantage however, comes at the expense of increased signal noise.

SIGIR'15, August 09 - 13, 2015, Santiago, Chile.

ACM 978-1-4503-3621-5/15/08 ...$15.00.
DOI: http://dx.doi.org/10.1145/2766462.2767716.

Most of the available implicit data is binary where user either conducts the action (purchase, browse, click etc.) on a given item or no data is available. [1] Binary feedback makes the recommendation problem particularly challenging since it is impossible to gauge the degree of preference from such data. Furthermore, the majority of existing model-based approaches are developed for non-binary data and employ objective functions that rely on graded relevance to distinguish positive preferences from negative ones. Such models tend to perform very poorly on binary data. Recently, several model-based approaches have been developed specifically for binary feedback [13, 20], however results on CF challenges have shown that these models don't perform as well as neighbor-based approaches.

The difference in performance between neighbor- and model-based methods on binary data became especially evident during the Million Song Dataset Challenge (MSD) which was recently conducted by Kaggle [18]. In this challenge, song listening histories were made available for 1.2M users and 380K songs, and the goal was to predict the next 500 songs for a subset of 110K users. Full song listening counts were made available but the organizers found these to correlate poorly with user preferences and binarized the data (1 if user listened to a song and 0 otherwise), using Mean Average Precision to evaluate submissions.

From the winners' reports [3] and the challenge forum [2], it became evident that all of the top scoring teams used variations of neighbor-based methods. Moreover, results for the best performing model-based approach were orders of magnitude worse than the best neighbor-based methods. Similar findings were reported by the challenge organizers who found that recommending songs from the same artist outperformed a complex model-based approach by a significant margin [18]. It was also reported that most model-based methods had run-time and/or memory problems on data of this size, and were either too slow to converge or used too much RAM. Given that 150 teams participated in this challenge and its recency, it can be concluded that there currently is no readily-available model-based approach that can perform well on binary data of this size.

Since the majority of implicit feedback is binary, it is highly desirable to develop accurate model-based methods that scale well to large datasets. In this paper we propose one such approach. The main idea behind our approach is to use neighbor similarities to enrich binary preferences and guide latent factor learning for both users and items. We empirically demonstrate that this approach produces latent representations that outperform neighbor-based methods while being considerably more efficient during inference time.

2. BINARY COLLABORATIVE FILTERING FRAMEWORK

In a typical binary collaborative filtering problem we have a set of N users $\mathcal{U} = \{u_1, ..., u_N\}$ and a set of M items $\mathcal{V} = \{v_1, ..., v_M\}$. The users' binary feedback for the items can be represented by an $N \times M$ matrix $\mathbf{R}$ where $\mathbf{R}(u_n, v_m) = 1$ if user u_n expressed preference (played, purchased, clicked etc.) for item v_m and $\mathbf{R}(u_n, v_m) = 0$ otherwise. We use $\mathcal{U}(v_m)$ to denote the set of all users that preferred v_m and $\mathcal{V}(u_n)$ to denote the set of items that u_n has expressed preference for. We use vector notation: $\mathbf{R}(u_n, :)$ denotes the n'th row of $\mathbf{R}$ ($1 \times M$ vector), and $\mathbf{R}(:, v_m)$ denotes the m'th column ($N \times 1$ vector).

Unlike the traditional CF where the goal is to accurately predict ratings for every user-item pair, in binary domain the aim is to produce a top-$\mathcal{T}$ ranking of the items that the user is most likely to prefer next. A ranking of the items $\mathcal{V}$ can be represented as a permutation $\pi : \{1, ..., M\} \rightarrow \{1, ..., M\}$ where $\pi(m) = l$ denotes the rank of the item v_m and $m = \pi^{-1}(l)$. A number of evaluation metrics have been proposed in information retrieval to evaluate the performance of the ranker. Here we concentrate on two of the more commonly used metrics, Normalized Discounted Cumulative Gain (NDCG) [15] and Mean Average Precision (MAP) [4]. For a given user u and ranking π the NDCG is given by:

$$\begin{aligned} \mathrm{NDCG}(u, \pi, \mathbf{R})@\mathcal{T} &= \frac{1}{G_{\mathcal{T}}(u, \mathbf{R})} \sum_{m=1}^{\mathcal{T}} \frac{2^{\wedge}\mathbf{R}(u, v_{\pi^{-1}(m)}) - 1}{\log_2(m+1)} \\ &= \frac{1}{G_{\mathcal{T}}(u, \mathbf{R})} \sum_{m=1}^{\mathcal{T}} \frac{\mathbf{R}(u, v_{\pi^{-1}(m)})}{\log_2(m+1)} \end{aligned}$$

where $\mathcal{T}$ is a truncation constant, $v_{\pi^{-1}(m)}$ is the item in position m in π and $G_{\mathcal{T}}(u, \mathbf{R})$ is a normalizing term which ensures that NDCG $\in [0, 1]$ for all rankings. $\mathcal{T}$ is typically set to a small value to emphasize that the user will only be shown the top-$\mathcal{T}$ ranked items and the items below the top-$\mathcal{T}$ are not evaluated.

MAP is defined in terms of average precision (AP):

$$\mathrm{AP}(u, \pi, \mathbf{R})@\mathcal{T} = \frac{\sum_{m=1}^{\mathcal{T}} \mathrm{P}(u, \pi, \mathbf{R})@m \cdot \mathbf{R}(u, v_{\pi^{-1}(m)})}{\sum_{m=1}^{\mathcal{T}} \mathbf{R}(u, v_{\pi^{-1}(m)})}$$

where P@m is the precision at m:

$$\mathrm{P}(u, \pi, \mathbf{R})@m = \sum_{l=1}^{m} \frac{\mathbf{R}(u, v_{\pi^{-1}(l)})}{m}$$

MAP is then computed by averaging AP over all users. Both NDCG and MAP have similar characteristics and discount relevance of each item by its position in the ranking and are maximized when all relevant items are ranked at the top. In binary CF, all items v with $\mathbf{R}(u, v) = 0$ are assumed to be not relevant to u. This relevance assignment is not entirely accurate since u might not have seen v, however, in the absence of graded relevance most frameworks follow this evaluation scheme.

3. EXISTING WORK

In this section we describe existing neighbor- and model-based approaches developed for binary data.

3.1 Neighbor-Based Approaches

In a binary setting, neighborhood-based CF approaches estimate item scores for a target user using the similarity from neighboring users and/or items. Formally, given an item v and target user u, the *user-user* approach estimates the score for v by comparing u with other users that ex-

[1] Note that some explicit data can also come in binary format e.g., Facebook's "likes".

[2] `www.kaggle.com/c/msdchallenge/forums/t/2365/challenge-retrospective-methods-difficulties`

pressed preference for v:

$$\textbf{user-user:}\ \mathbf{S}(u,v) = \sum_{u' \in \mathcal{U}(v)} \mathbf{R}(u,:)\mathbf{R}(u',:)^T \quad (1)$$

The main idea behind this approach is based on the assumption that if users similar to u prefer v then $\mathbf{S}(u,v)$ should be high and v should be recommended to u. Similarly, in the *item-item* approach v is compared to all items that u has expressed preference for:

$$\textbf{item-item:}\ \mathbf{S}(u,v) = \sum_{v' \in \mathcal{V}(u)} \mathbf{R}(:,v)^T\mathbf{R}(:,v') \quad (2)$$

This method follows a similar idea and aims to recommend items that are similar to items that u has expressed preference for.

After estimating scores for all items either via user-user or item-item method the resulting score vector $\mathbf{S}(u,:)$ is sorted and top-$\mathcal{T}$ items are presented to u. In practice it is often found that the accuracy of each method can be significantly improved if dot product is replaced with a more complex metric like cosine similarity. We found this to be especially true for binary domain, where row and column L^2 normalizations tend to work particularly well [3]:

$$\textbf{row-norm:}\ \mathbf{R}(u,:) = \frac{\mathbf{R}(u,:)}{\sqrt{\sum_{n=1}^{N}\mathbf{R}(u,v_n)^2}} \quad (3)$$

$$\textbf{col-norm:}\ \mathbf{R}(:,v) = \frac{\mathbf{R}(:,v)}{\sqrt{\sum_{m=1}^{M}\mathbf{R}(u_m,v)^2}} \quad (4)$$

We found that for most datasets applying *both* normalizations before computing similarities produced gains of up to 30%; further justification for using normalization can be found in [12]. We also found that the order in which these normalizations are applied is very important and should be validated separately for each dataset. Note that when only row-norm or col-norm normalization is applied, item-item (user-user) scores become the sums of cosine similarities.

3.2 Model-Based Approaches

In contrast to neighbor-based approaches, model-based approaches use the observed preferences to create a compact model of the data which is then used to predict the unobserved preferences. The most popular methods in this category are latent models that derive compact latent factors for both users and items and then use these factors to predict preference. Latent models are often the default choice for many CF problems due to their accuracy and efficiency. Once the factors are estimated, recommendations can be generated very efficiently by computing simple dot products between latent factors, allowing these models to be applied in real-time.

Several model-based approaches have been recently proposed for binary setting, here we review two of the more popular approaches WRMF [13] and BPR-MF [20]. WRMF is a regression method and learns user-item factors by minimizing the weighted reconstruction error:

$$\sum_{n=1}^{N}\sum_{m=1}^{M} c_{nm}(1-\mathbf{U}_r(u_n,:)\mathbf{V}_r(v_m,:)^T)^2+\lambda_{\mathbf{U}}\|\mathbf{U}_r\|^2+\lambda_{\mathbf{V}}\|\mathbf{V}_r\|^2 \quad (5)$$

[3]To avoid introducing extra notation we use self assignment of the form x = f(x) where possible.

where $\mathbf{U}_r$ is an $N \times r$ user factor matrix, $\mathbf{V}_r$ is an $M \times r$ item factor matrix, and c_{nm} is a weight that is set separately for every user-item pair. For binary data c_{nm} is set to:

$$c_{nm} = 1 + \alpha\mathbf{R}(u_n, v_m)$$

This formulation adds an extra α weight to every pair with $\mathbf{R}(u_n, v_m) = 1$ forcing optimization to concentrate on those pairs. Authors of WRMF propose to use alternating least squares to optimize this model with an overall complexity of $O(\mathcal{N}r^2 + (N+M)r^3)$ [13] where $\mathcal{N}$ is the total number of non-zero entries in $\mathbf{R}$. Both $\mathcal{N}r^2$ and $(N+M)r^3$ grow very quickly with r and several teams in the MSD challenge ($\mathcal{N} \approx 50$ million and $N+M \approx 1.6$ million) reported that WRMF took prohibitively long to train even for moderate r sizes.

BPR-MF is a ranking approach and optimizes pairwise objective that attempts to place pairs with observed preference above the unobserved ones:

$$\sum_{(u_n,v_m,v_l)} \log(1+e^{-\mathbf{U}_r(u_n,:)(\mathbf{V}_r(v_m,:)-\mathbf{V}_r(v_l,:))^T}) + \lambda_{\mathbf{U}}\|\mathbf{U}_r\|^2 + \lambda_{\mathbf{V}}\|\mathbf{V}_r\|^2 \quad (6)$$

where triplets (u_n, v_m, v_l) are sampled with a condition that $\mathbf{R}(u_n, v_m) = 1$ and $\mathbf{R}(u_n, v_l) = 0$. Similarly to WRMF, this implies an assumption that all items v_l with $\mathbf{R}(u_n, v_l) = 0$ are not relevant and should be ranked below the relevant items v_m with $\mathbf{R}(u_n, v_m) = 1$. Moreover, all relevant (irrelevant) items are assumed to be *equally* relevant (irrelevant). These assumptions often don't hold in real-life scenarios where noisy implicit signals tend to produce incorrect/outlier preferences that should be discounted.

Due to its pairwise nature BPR-MF is also expensive to optimize with runtime complexity of $O(\mathcal{N}M)$. While authors claim that satisfactory convergence can be achieved significantly faster through sampling, no theoretical guarantees are provided. Another disadvantage of BPR-MF is that when the number of items is large, gradient updates are distributed very unevenly (even with sampling). Popular items with many non-zero entries receive the bulk of updates while the tail-region items receive almost none. This can potentially explain the poor performance of this approach on the MSD dataset where challenge organizers found that it was unable to outperform the simple songs by the same artist baseline [18].

4. OUR APPROACH

We discussed earlier that treating all observed (unobserved) items as equally relevant (irrelevant) is not optimal in the binary CF setting. In this section we further build on this idea and propose a model-based approach that applies neighbor similarities to further distinguish relevant items from irrelevant ones. This information is then used to infer accurate user and item factors.

Before we delve into model description, consider the following simplified example: a fantasy fan purchases "The Lord Of The Rings" trilogy, both "Hobbit" releases and "The Devil Wears Prada" (a present for a friend). If we could request explicit preference data from this user we would immediately know that (s)he does not enjoy movies like "The Devil Wears Prada". However, given that we only have access to purchase history, objectives in WRMF and BPR-MF would treat all purchases as equally relevant. During optimization for this user, both methods would aim to derive latent representations that rank fantasy movies and movies like "The Devil Wears Prada" at the top, which is clearly suboptimal. One way of dealing with this problem is through model regularization and both methods apply strict regularization to penalize user and item factors. However, as the number of outliers increases the problem becomes more severe and might no longer be fixable by heavy regularization.

In contrast, by applying neighbor methods like item-item, we immediately get a lower score for "The Devil Wears Prada" since it's not similar to any other purchase by this user. From this example it is evident that the neighbor approach provides an effective way to resolve ties in the binary preference matrix, and neighbor score matrix **S** reflects user preferences more accurately than the raw binary matrix **R**. Neighbor methods, however, are also not immune to noise. Users/items with very few ratings can heavily skew similarities and result in incorrect rankings. Row and column normalizations can partially alleviate this problem but don't eliminate it completely.

In our model we propose to utilize these advantages of neighbor approaches and factorize the neighbor score matrix **S** instead of the original binary matrix **R**. In addition to producing models that support very efficient inference, applying low-rank factorization to **S** can significantly reduce the noise that is often present when similarities are computed on highly sparse data. One method that readily lends itself for the factorization task is truncated Singular Value Decomposition (SVD). A number of techniques that use truncated SVD such as the Principal Component Analysis and the Latent Semantic Analysis have been found to be very robust to noise and generalize well. Moreover, SVD factorization is a well studied problem and efficient distributed implementations exist that can factorize matrices with hundreds of millions of rows (e.g., Mahout's stochastic SVD [17]), making it applicable to virtually any CF problem.

Encouraged by these results we apply truncated SVD to the neighbor score matrix **S**. We begin by normalizing all rows of **S** to have unit norms:

$$\mathbf{S}(u,:) = \frac{\mathbf{S}(u,:)}{\sqrt{\sum_{m=1}^{M} \mathbf{S}(u, v_m)^2}}$$

The L^2 normalization rescales scores to have comparable ranges across users making factorization more stable. This is especially useful when some users/items have considerably more data than others (common in many CF applications) resulting in highly variable score ranges across users. After row normalization we approximate **S** with a product of three low rank matrices via SVD:

$$\mathbf{S} \approx \mathbf{U}_r \mathbf{\Sigma}_r \mathbf{V}_r^T \tag{7}$$

Here r is SVD rank, $\mathbf{U}_r$ is an $N \times r$ matrix, $\mathbf{\Sigma}_r$ is an $r \times r$ diagonal matrix and $\mathbf{V}_r$ is an $M \times r$ matrix.

Once the factorization is completed $\mathbf{\Sigma}_r$ is absorbed into $\mathbf{U}_r$, $\mathbf{U}_r = \mathbf{U}_r\mathbf{\Sigma}_r$, and the scores for every user-item pair are calculated by computing dot product between the corresponding user and item factors:

$$\textbf{svd:}\;\; \mathbf{S}(u,v) \approx \mathbf{U}_r(u,:)\mathbf{V}_r(v,:)^T \tag{8}$$

Sorting these scores gives top-$\mathcal{T}$ item recommendations for u. Note that for most r this operation is considerably more efficient than computing and summing neighbor similarities (Equations 1 and 2), especially when the number of users or items is large.

While SVD provides an effective way to derive latent representations, current formulation requires computing and storing the full score matrix **S** which is not practical for most large-scale applications. In the following sections we describe several ways of dealing with this problem.

4.1 Block Update

The naive SVD model has runtime complexity of $O(NM\log(r) + (N+M)r^2)$ [4] using the stochastic SVD algorithm [11], and requires $O(NM)$ space. Recently, a number of advances have been made on incremental SVD [7, 1] where factorization is built in stages, allowing to process large amounts of data without explicitly storing it. One of the more efficient algorithms developed by Brand [7] takes as input "current" factorization $\mathbf{U\Sigma V}^T \approx \mathbf{X}$ and matrix $\mathbf{A}$, and produces updated SVD factorization $\mathbf{U}_{new}\mathbf{\Sigma}_{new}\mathbf{V}_{new}^T \approx [\mathbf{X}, \mathbf{A}]$. Note that in this formulation $\mathbf{V}^T$ gets expanded to have the same number of columns as $[\mathbf{X}, \mathbf{A}]$ whereas $\mathbf{U}$ and $\mathbf{\Sigma}$ only get updated but don't change in size. Analogous algorithm can be used to update $\mathbf{U}$: using the fact that $\mathbf{V\Sigma U}^T = \mathbf{X}^T$ we get that $\mathbf{V}_{new}\mathbf{\Sigma}_{new}\mathbf{U}_{new}^T \approx [\mathbf{X}^T, \mathbf{A}^T]$.

We can readily apply these ideas to CF and factorize users incrementally achieving considerable savings in space requirements. Formally, we partition users into blocks of size N_b and for each block we iteratively (1) calculate $N_b \times M$ neighbor score matrix and (2) update SVD factorization to include latent factors for users in the block. The runtime complexity of this block-factorization algorithm is still $O(NM\log(r) + (N+M)r^2)$ for $r < \sqrt{\min(N,M)}$ [11, 7], but the space requirement reduces to $O(N_bM + (N+M)r))$ where $O(N_bM)$ is the block size and $O((N+M)r)$ is the space required to store the final $\mathbf{U}_r$ and $\mathbf{V}_r$ factors. This is a very significant reduction from the original $O(NM)$ and makes the algorithm practical for most CF applications. Moreover, block update provides an effective way to update the SVD model when new users and/or items are added to the system. Finally, note that we concentrated on incrementally processing users here but the same algorithm can be straightforwardly modified to incrementally process items instead. Thus depending on whether $N \gg M$ or $N \ll M$ we can either choose user oriented or item oriented approach (or alternate between the two).

4.2 Sparse Similarity

In the previous section we demonstrated that by using incremental block updates we can significantly reduce the space complexity to $O(N_bM)$ where N_b is the block size. However, for large scale applications the number of items can reach millions or hundreds of millions so even $O(N_bM)$ can become too large. To deal with this problem we propose to selectively use only a small subset of similarity scores for each user. This is achieved by storing only the largest ρ scores for each user and zeroing out the rest.

The motivation behind using only the largest scores comes from the fact that we want to concentrate all model effort on maximizing the accuracy at the top of the ranking. Items with large scores are thus particularly important since they would appear at the top for each user. Furthermore, it is well

[4] This excludes the cost of computing **S**.

Algorithm 1 SVD block-factorization

```
Input: R
Parameters: rank r, block size N_b, sparsity factor ρ
for i = 1 to N/N_b do
  init block score matrix S_b = sparse(N_b, M)
  for u = (i − 1)N_b + 1 to iN_b do
    calculate top-ρ scores for u using Eq. 1 or 2
    store top-ρ scores in S_b(u, :)
  end for
  if i == 1 then
    compute initial factorization:
      [U_r, S_r, V_r] = SVD(S_b, r)
  else
    update current factorization:
      [U_r, S_r, V_r] = block-SVD(U_r, S_r, V_r, S_b)
  end if
end for
Output: U_r, S_r, V_r
```

known that SVD produces factorizations that are closest to the target matrix in Frobenius norm (i.e., root squared error). By zeroing out low scores we force SVD to concentrate on ordering items at the top correctly and put less emphasis on relative orderings at the bottom.

This approach allows us to further reduce the space requirement for each block to $O(N_b\rho)$ since sparse format can now be used and zeros don't need to be explicitly stored. Sparse representation also allows for more efficient matrix multiplication and the complete block-factorization can now be computed in $O(T_{mult}r + (N + M)r^2)$ where T_{mult} is the cost of matrix-vector multiplication with sparse score matrix [11]. Given that the entire score matrix now has at most $N\rho$ non-zero entries, the matrix-vector product can be computed in time proportional to $N\rho$, and for $\rho \ll M$ we get that $T_{mult} \ll NM$ [25]. Note that $O(T_{mult}r + (N + M)r^2)$ is an order of magnitude more efficient than WRMF with complexity $O(r^2\mathcal{N} + (N + M)r^3)$. The full SVD algorithm with all the enhancements is outlined in Algorithm 1.

4.3 Strong Generalization

An important problem in CF is to efficiently provide accurate recommendations to new users that were not available during model optimization. This problem is often referred to as *strong generalization* and must be addressed by any successful recommender system. Neighbor-based models can generally be applied to new users without any difficulties since similarities can be straightforwardly re-calculated to incorporate new data. Model-based approaches on the other hand, often use complicated non-convex objectives and thus require expensive gradient updates to be conducted for every new user. In this section we address the strong generalization problem in our SVD model and derive a simple update equation to efficiently produce latent factors for new users.

One way of dealing with new users/items is to run a full block SVD update to generate new latent factors and also update the rest of the model. While in a real-world application we would want run such an update after enough new users/items have been added, it is infeasible to run it for every new user. To deal with this problem we propose a simple approach to approximate latent factors by utilizing the properties of SVD factorization. First, note that the score vector for every user u is approximated by the user-item factor product:

$$\mathbf{S}(u,:) \approx \mathbf{U}_r(u,:)\mathbf{V}_r^T$$

where $\mathbf{\Sigma}_r$ is absorbed into $\mathbf{U}_r$. From this it follows that:

$$\mathbf{U}_r(u,:) \approx \mathbf{S}(u,:)\mathbf{V}_r^{T(-1)}$$

but since $\mathbf{V}_r$ is approximately orthogonal we get that $\mathbf{V}_r^{-1} \approx \mathbf{V}_r^T$ and:

$$\mathbf{U}_r(u,:) \approx \mathbf{S}(u,:)\mathbf{V}_r \quad (9)$$

Similar approach can be used to derive an equation for item factors: $\mathbf{V}_r(v,:) \approx \mathbf{S}(:,v)^T\mathbf{U}_r$. Equation 9 gives us a simple and effective way to approximate user factors for a new user u by (1) calculating top-ρ neighbor scores $\mathbf{S}(u,:)$ and (2) multiplying $\mathbf{S}(u,:)$ with $\mathbf{V}_r$ to get $\mathbf{U}_r(u,:)$.

In production-level systems we can use Equation 9 to quickly generate recommendations for each new user, then run full block update once enough new users/items have been added. Note that unlike gradient-based models, block update doesn't require any iterative optimization or parameter tuning (initialization, learning rate, weight penalty etc.) and can efficiently update the entire model.

In summary, our SVD-based model provides the following advantages:

- Low complexity and storage requirement block update that can efficiently update the entire model.
- Only two parameters to tune: rank r and sparsity factor ρ (block size N_b is typically selected to maximize RAM usage).
- Existing distributed implementations (e.g., Mahout's stochastic SVD [17]) allow this model to easily scale to very large CF problems.
- Approximate procedure to quickly incorporate new users/items into existing model with one matrix multiplication.

4.4 Relation to Existing Work

The idea of using SVD in CF is not new and a number of SVD-based methods have been proposed. One of the first uses of SVD for CF can be traced back to [6]. A number of extensions have since been proposed that incorporate additional information and control for user privacy [22, 19]. Incremental SVD updates in the context of CF have been investigated by Sarwar et al., [24], their approach however only produced latent factors for new users and did not update the existing model. This method is thus unsuitable for incrementally learning/updating the full model.

To the best of our knowledge all existing SVD methods apply factorization to the raw preference matrix $\mathbf{R}$ and are thus not suitable for binary feedback. Moreover, since SVD can't handle missing data, applying it directly to $\mathbf{R}$ is equivalent to setting all missing values to 0. The factorization then minimizes the Frobenius norm between this "filled in" matrix and the SVD approximation. Setting missing values to 0 is not ideal in most CF applications since it assumes that *all* unobserved items should have a low score. For this reason SVD has now largely been replaced by other matrix factorization approaches such as PMF [21] that only optimize the reconstruction error on observed data. Our approach avoids this problem by applying SVD to the sparse neighbor similarity score matrix instead of $\mathbf{R}$. In our model setting small

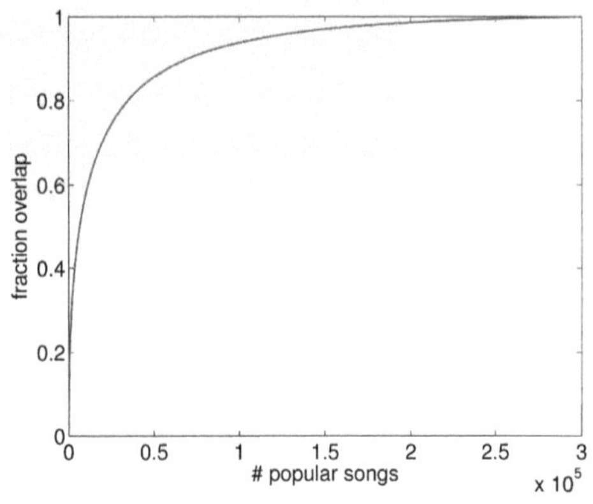

Figure 1: Fraction overlap between training data for the target 110K MSD users and popular songs sorted in the order of popularity.

scores to 0 is valid since these items are to be ranked at the bottom of the list and should have low reconstruction scores from SVD. To the best of our knowledge this approach is the first successful application of SVD to the binary CF setting.

4.5 Alternative Formulations

The idea of using neighbor similarity information to train factor models is not limited to the SVD model. By replacing the original binary matrix **R** with **S** (Equations 1 and 2) we can apply most existing model-based approaches. Below we give some examples of the objective functions that can be used to learn **U** and **V**. We begin with the more commonly used regression objectives such as the squared error and weighted squared error (used in WRMF):

$$\textbf{sq. error:} \quad \sum_{n=1}^{N}\sum_{m=1}^{M}(\mathbf{S}(u_n,v_m)-\mathbf{U}_r(u_n,:)\mathbf{V}_r(v_m,:)^T)^2$$

$$\textbf{wrmf:} \quad \sum_{n=1}^{N}\sum_{m=1}^{M}c_{nm}(1-\mathbf{U}_r(u_n,:)\mathbf{V}_r(v_m,:)^T)^2$$

$$c_{nm}=1+\alpha\mathbf{S}(u_n,v_m)$$

Note that in both cases **S** is a sparse matrix containing only the top-ρ scores for each user. Unlike the traditional CF where most effort is concentrated on rating prediction, for binary preference CF the goal is to optimize the ranking accuracy. Ranking-based objectives might thus be better suited for this problem. Since **S** provides rich ordering information over the items, we can apply virtually any objective from learning-to-rank [16] to this domain. Here we give examples of two such objectives RankNet [8] (also used in BPR-MF) and ListNet [9]:

$$\textbf{ranknet:} \quad \sum_{(u_n,v_m,v_l)}\log(1+e^{-\mathbf{U}_r(u_n,:)(\mathbf{V}_r(v_m,:)-\mathbf{V}_r(v_l,:))^T})$$

$$\text{for } \mathbf{S}(u_n,v_m)>\mathbf{S}(u_n,v_l)$$

listnet:

$$-\sum_{n=1}^{N}\sum_{m=1}^{M}\frac{\phi(\mathbf{S}(u_n,v_m))}{\sum_{l=1}^{M}\phi(\mathbf{S}(u_n,v_l))}\log\left(\frac{\phi(\mathbf{U}_r(u_n,:)\mathbf{V}_r(v_m,:)^T)}{\sum_{l=1}^{M}\phi(\mathbf{U}_r(u_n,:)\mathbf{V}_r(v_l,:)^T)}\right)$$

All of the above objectives require gradient optimization and thus lack the advantages of the SVD approach outlined in Section 4.3. In this work we thus chose to concentrate on the SVD model and leave gradient optimization for future work.

Table 1: MSD MAP@500 private leaderboard results. SVD results are reported for four different rank sizes 1K, 5K, 10K, and 20K; all models were trained on top 50,000 and 100,000 of the most popular songs. The winning team achieved a score of 0.1791 [3] using an optimized blend of user-user and item-item approaches. The best model-based approach was reported to get 0.1095.

	1K	5K	10K	20K
50,000 most popular songs				
item-item (0.1498)				
ii-SVD-1K	0.1249	0.1466	0.1492	0.1493
ii-SVD-5K	**0.1261**	**0.1472**	**0.1497**	**0.1494**
ii-SVD-full	0.1258	0.1470	0.1495	**0.1494**
100,000 most popular songs				
item-item (0.1628)				
ii-SVD-1K	0.1258	0.1539	0.1598	0.1622
ii-SVD-5K	**0.1274**	**0.1550**	**0.1606**	0.1621
ii-SVD-full	0.1272	0.1548	0.1604	**0.1623**

5. EXPERIMENTS

To validate the proposed approach we conducted extensive experiments on three large publicly available datasets: song dataset from the Kaggle's MSD challenge and two movie datasets MovieLens and Netflix. We implemented Algorithm 1 in Matlab, employing stochastic SVD library by Mark Tygert [5] and block SVD library by David Wingate [6]. For block SVD we modified the provided code by replacing the call to Matlab's `svds` routine with a much faster stochastic SVD call. This implementation was then used in all experiments. We used MyMediaLite [10] library to run the WRMF and BPR-MF baselines and extensively tuned both models on each dataset.

Across all datasets we consistently found that the accuracy of user-user and item-item approaches can be significantly improved by applying both row and column normalizations (Equations 3 and 4). We also found that the order in which these normalizations are applied is important and used validation set to determine the best combination for each dataset. Generally, we observed that applying row followed by column normalization worked best across most datasets and folds. For all SVD experiments we first validated normalization for each neighbor approach and then applied SVD to the best performing combination.

5.1 MSD Experiments

The MSD dataset was used in the Kaggle Million Song Dataset Challenge [18] and consists of listening histories for 1.2M users and 380K songs. The goal of the challenge was to use these listening histories to recommend 500 songs for a subset of 110K test users. The data for the 110K test users was partitioned into training and test sets, and only training portion was made available to the challenge participants (in addition to full listening history for the other 1.1M users). The test set was further split into two subsets with 10K and 100K users respectively. The results on the smaller 10K subset were made visible throughout the challenge ("public leaderboard"), while results on the 100K

[5]`pca.m` from `cims.nyu.edu/~tygert/software.html`
[6]`addblock_svd_update.m` from `www.mit.edu/~wingated/resources.html`

Table 2: MovieLens weak generalization results. uu-SVD and ii-SVD are SVD factorizations computed using scores from user-user and item-item neighbor approaches respectively. Number of non-zero scores ρ used to calculate each SVD factorization is shown on the right, for instance ii-SVD-100 uses 100 scores for each user and ii-SVD-full uses all M scores.

	NDCG@10 binary				NDCG@10 rating			
	10%	30%	50%	70%	10%	30%	50%	70%
user-user	0.5416	0.5324	0.4660	0.3710	**0.6354**	0.6512	0.6765	0.7227
uu-SVD-100	0.5503	0.5468	0.4690	0.3700	0.6288	0.6508	0.6751	0.7205
uu-SVD-500	0.5545	0.5434	0.4743	0.3742	0.6309	**0.6515**	**0.6769**	**0.7230**
uu-SVD-full	0.5513	0.5452	0.4744	0.3757	0.6316	0.6513	0.6768	0.7229
item-item	0.4910	0.5957	0.5330	0.4321	0.5903	0.6223	0.6564	0.7108
ii-SVD-100	0.5504	0.5910	0.5287	0.4271	0.6092	0.6243	0.6537	0.7076
ii-SVD-500	**0.5672**	**0.6113**	0.5514	0.4434	0.6107	0.6293	0.6604	0.7124
ii-SVD-full	0.5484	0.5982	0.5523	0.4479	0.6121	0.6259	0.6562	0.7115
WRMF	0.5570	0.5969	**0.5557**	**0.4857**	0.6046	0.6280	0.6511	0.7071
BPR-MF	0.4428	0.5238	0.4976	0.4213	0.6190	0.6223	0.6585	0.7131

subset were only revealed at the end of the challenge ("private leaderboard"). All submissions had to provide rankings of top-500 songs for each of the 110K test users and were evaluated using MAP@500. At the end of the challenge organizers released all the challenge data (including test data) into public domain.

Note that the MSD dataset has more than 20 times more items than both MovieLens and Netflix, and is over 100 times more sparse. This makes the problem very challenging since many user/items have very little data to build accurate representations. The sparsity problem is further illustrated in Figure 4.4, which shows fraction overlap between the training data for the 110K target users and most popular songs sorted in the order of popularity. From the figure we see that more that 93% of all the training data is contained within the first 100K most popular songs, leaving less than 7% of data for the remaining 280K songs.

We mentioned above that model-based approaches were found to perform poorly in this challenge. The best model-based submission was reported to get MAP@500 of 0.1095, while the winning solution achieved 0.1791 using a blend of user-user and item-item approaches [3]. These results indicate that neighbor methods produce over 60% relative improvement in accuracy on this data compared to model-based approaches. In the following section we show that our approach eliminates this performance gap achieving results that are comparable to neighbor methods.

In all MSD experiments we follow the same set-up that was used during the competition and tune models on the 10K public leaderboard set, then evaluate on the 100K private leaderboard set.

5.1.1 Results

MAP@500 private leaderboard results are shown in Table 1. For this dataset we found that using larger rank generally improved performance, and we report results for four different rank sizes: 1K, 5K, 10K and 20K. To reduce experiment complexity we downsampled the item space to only include most popular songs and experimented with top 50,000 and 100,000 songs. From Figure 4.4 we see that 100,000 (50,000) most popular songs contain over 93% (80%) of all training data. Consequently, selecting only the popular songs allows us to reduce the item space by a factor of 4 while keeping most of the training data.

Table 3: MSD training runtimes in hours for the SVD model with four different rank sizes 1K, 5K, 10K and 20K. For comparison, on the same hardware WRMF took 10.9 hours to complete for rank 250 and would take over a month for rank 10K.

	1K	5K	10K	20K
50,000 most popular songs				
ii-SVD-1K	0.9	1.9	4.6	17.9
100,000 most popular songs				
ii-SVD-1K	1.8	2.8	5.6	24.6

From results in Table 1 we see that the SVD model with large enough rank is able to match the performance of the corresponding item-item approach. The results for the best SVD model place it in top-3 (out of 150 teams) on Kaggle's leaderboard with a score of 0.1623. To the best of our knowledge this is by far the highest score for model-based approach in this competition. All of the top-10 teams used combinations of user-user and/or item-item approaches, and the best model-based approach was reported to only get 0.1095. We also see that SVD-1K performs comparably to SVD-full on both 50,000 and 100,000 songs suggesting that scores for only 1,000 songs per user are required to produce accurate factorizations.

5.1.2 Runtime

MSD is the largest of the three datasets that we selected with, and we use it to benchmark the runtimes for the SVD approach and the best existing model-based approach WRMF. To ensure accurate comparison all experiments were conducted on the same server with 32 Intel Xeon E5-2690 2.90GHz cores and 64GB of RAM. Runtimes in hours for the SVD model are shown in Table 3. From this table we see that full factorization with 100,000 songs can be completed in under 3 hours with rank 5,000 and under 6 hours with rank 10,000. For comparison, WRMF took over 10 hours to complete with rank 250, and using complexity bounds we estimate that for rank 10,000 it would take over a month. These results demonstrate that our approach is considerably more efficient than the existing state-of-the-art and scales well to large datasets.

Table 4: MovieLens strong generalization results. 1000 randomly chosen users were withheld during model optimization and then added into the model either via full model block update (SVD-block) or via inference procedure outlined in Section 4.3 (SVD-infer); ρ was set to 500 across all training splits. Item-item baseline was computed using all users and item-item\1000 was computed with 1000 test users removed from the training data and excluded for item similarity calculation.

	NDCG@10 binary				NDCG@10 rating			
	10%	30%	50%	70%	10%	30%	50%	70%
item-item	0.5276	0.5985	0.5320	0.4298	0.6076	0.6352	0.6730	0.7199
item-item\1000	0.5101	0.5802	0.5112	0.4119	0.6044	0.6327	0.6688	0.7167
ii-SVD-block	**0.5837**	**0.6144**	**0.5539**	**0.4414**	**0.6273**	**0.6443**	**0.6754**	**0.7217**
ii-SVD-infer	0.5533	0.6043	0.5387	0.4264	0.6214	0.6411	0.6722	0.7200

5.2 MovieLens

For MovieLens experiments we use the largest of the available datasets MovieLens-10M with 10 million ratings from 72,000 users on 10,000 movies. This dataset contains ratings on the scale of 1 to 5 with half point increments, and each users has rated at least 20 movies. To simulate binary feedback we binarized the data setting all ratings to 1. Binarization simulates implicit feedback that we would get from actions like movie purchases, plays or clicks.

To get an estimate of how each model's performance is affected by training set size we repeat all experiments 4 times with different percentages of training ratings: 10%, 30%, 50%, 70%. For each percentage θ, θ percent of ratings for each user are randomly selected for training and the rest are kept for testing. Partitioning data in this way allows us to gradually increase the training set size from 10% to 70% while keeping distributions of ratings across users consistent. All parameter selection was done using 5-fold cross validation and the best models were re-trained on the full training set and evaluated on the test set. Rank size was validated in the range 5 to 250 for each model.

We evaluate both weak and strong generalization. For weak generalization training data from all users is used to learn the models, and average NDCG is computed on the withheld test data from same users (see Section 2 for details on NDCG calculation). On the other hand, for strong generalization a subset of users is removed from training data and all model estimation is done on the remaining users. Once the models are estimated, the goal is to use the training data from withheld users to incorporate them into the model (without full re-training) and produce accurate recommendations. In SVD model we proposed two ways of dealing with new users: block update and approximate inference (see Section 4.3). We evaluate both approaches and compare their performance.

Taking advantage of the fact that we have access to explicit preferences in the form of ratings we conduct two types of evaluation. After training each model using only binary data, we evaluate the recommended rankings on both binary relevance and full ratings. For binary relevance we use the procedure outlined in Section 2 and compute NDCG using full rankings of all the items that are not in the training set for each user. For rating evaluation we only rank the rated test set items for each user and calculate NDCG using rating values (1-5) as relevance for those items. Assuming that ratings provide the ground truth preference information, rating NDCG estimates the degree to which models trained on weaker binary data generalize to ground truth. While this assumption might not be completely valid due to inherent noise in ratings, rating NDCG still gives us a more accurate metric to compare the models.

5.2.1 Weak Generalization

Table 2 shows MovieLens weak generalization results for four training set sizes 10%, 30%, 50% and 70%. For each training set size, Table 2 shows binary and rating NDCG@10 results. We apply our SVD method to both user-user (uu-SVD-ρ) and item-item (ii-SVD-ρ) scores and vary the sparsity factor ρ of the similarity score matrix. In addition to SVD, we also evaluate WRMF and BPR-MF approaches, all models were learned and tuned using binary data only.

We can observe several patterns from Table 2. First, item-item approach significantly outperforms user-user on binary NDCG for all training set sizes except 10%, while user-user significantly outperforms item-item on rating NDCG. The difference in performance is somewhat puzzling and implies that improvement on binary feedback doesn't necessarily translate to improvement on explicit preferences. This suggests an optimization approach where explicit feedback is first solicited from a subset of users and the best binary model is then chosen based on the accuracy on this explicit data.

Second, SVD model always performs at least as well as the underlying similarity approach (user-user or item-item) and in many cases beats it. This leads to the conclusion that applying low-rank compression to similarity scores is beneficial and can improve accuracy by removing/shrinking noisy dimensions. The gains from SVD model are especially significant on very sparse training sets with 10% and 30% of data where it outperforms neighbor approaches on both binary and rating NDCG. We also see that SVD-500 perform almost as well as SVD-full indicating that only 500 top scores (out of nearly 10,000 items) are required for each user to produce accurate factorizations. This reduces storage requirement for each block update by a factor of 20 and significantly speeds up runtime. Consistent performance on both binary and rating NDCG suggests that the SVD model can readily be used if explicit data approach to model selection is chosen. In this setting, explicit preferences from a subset of users would first be used to select the best neighbor method. SVD model would then be applied to the chosen neighbor method to generate latent factors for all users and items.

Third, similarly to neighbor approaches, WRMF outperforms BPR-MF on binary NDCG while BPR-MF significantly outperforms WRMF on rating NDCG. We also see that best SVD model consistently outperforms both approaches on binary and rating NDCG.

Table 5: **Netflix weak generalization results. uu-SVD and ii-SVD are SVD factorizations computed using scores form user-user and item-item neighbor approaches respectively. Number of non-zero scores ρ used to calculate each SVD factorization is shown on the right, for instance SVD-500 uses 500 scores for each user and SVD-full uses all M scores.**

	NDCG@10 binary				NDCG@10 rating			
	10%	30%	50%	70%	10%	30%	50%	70%
user-user	0.4717	0.4456	0.3844	0.2995	0.6226	0.6287	0.6489	0.6846
uu-SVD-500	0.4888	0.4602	0.3889	0.3005	0.6226	0.6299	0.6491	0.6845
uu-SVD-1000	0.4889	0.4609	0.3924	0.3043	0.6212	0.6303	0.6493	0.6850
uu-SVD-full	0.4846	0.4608	0.3939	0.3044	0.6196	0.6299	0.6498	0.6847
item-item	0.4980	0.4840	0.4297	0.3394	0.6287	0.6518	0.6698	0.7009
ii-SVD-500	**0.5172**	0.5164	0.4502	0.3487	0.6275	**0.6544**	0.6703	0.7008
ii-SVD-1000	0.5108	0.5200	0.4521	0.3500	**0.6299**	0.6519	**0.6715**	**0.7017**
ii-SVD-full	0.4994	0.5127	0.4521	0.3541	0.6203	0.6501	0.6708	0.7014
WRMF	0.5060	**0.5485**	**0.5072**	**0.4522**	0.6077	0.6376	0.6632	0.7000
BPR-MF	0.4273	0.4744	0.4447	0.3660	0.5985	0.6309	0.6606	0.6930

5.2.2 *Strong Generalization*

Strong generalization results are shown in Table 4. For strong generalization 1000 randomly chosen users were withheld during model optimization and then added into the model either by doing a full model block update (SVD-block) or via inference procedure outlined in Section 4.3 (SVD-infer). For all SVD experiments ρ was set to 500 so top-500 scores were used for each user. We only show results for item-item similarity, results with user-user similarity were similar and are omitted from this table.

From the table we see that SVD-infer generalizes well and suffers only a small drop in performance relative to block-SVD which updates the entire model. Both SVD-block and SVD-infer significantly outperform the item-item approach on binary and rating NDCG. These results support the conclusion that the approximate inference procedure can be used to quickly generate recommendations for new users with acceptable accuracy.

5.3 Netflix Experiments

For Netflix experiments we used the full Netflix dataset with 100M ratings from 480K users on 17.7K movies. Similar to the MovieLens experiments, we binarized all ratings and evaluated performance using both binary and rating NDCG@10. We partitioned the dataset using 10%, 30%, 50% and 70% of ratings from each user for training and the rest for testing. All parameter selection was done using 5-fold cross validation and the best models were re-trained on the full training set and evaluated on the test set. Rank size was validated in the range 5 to 250 for each model.

5.3.1 *Weak Generalization*

Weak generalization results are shown in Table 5. From this table we see that, unlike the results for the MovieLens data, item-item approach significantly outperforms user-user on both binary and rating NDCG. This could be attributed to the fact that Netflix dataset is considerably larger and more sparse. A number of previous studies have shown that item-item similarity tends to work better than user-user in sparse settings [12].

From the table we also see that, first, our SVD approach either performs comparably or outperforms both user-user and item-item methods on binary and rating NDCG. Second, WRMF achieves very strong performance on binary NDCG beating our approach on all splits except 10% but under-performs on rating NDCG losing by as much as 2 points. This difference in performance could be attributed to overfitting. We discussed in Section 4 that WRMF and BPR-MF treat all items with observed preferences ($\mathbf{R}(u, v) = 1$) as equally relevant. Both methods are thus susceptible to outliers that are often present in noisy CF data and can produce suboptimal user representations. In this experiment outliers correspond to items with low ratings (≤ 2). Placing such items at the top of the ranking improves binary NDCG while significantly hurting rating NDCG. Neighbor methods are able to detect such outliers and thus tend to do better on rating NDCG.

Lastly, both SVD-500 and SVD-1000 fully match the performance SVD-full leading to a conclusion that only 500 items (out of over 17,000) are needed to build accurate models for each user.

5.3.2 *Strong Generalization*

Strong generalization results for the Netflix dataset are shown in Table 6. Similarly to MovieLens, we withheld a subset of 1000 randomly chosen users during main model optimization, and then added these users to the model via block update and approximate inference procedures. Binary and rating NDCG results for both procedures are shown in Table 6.

From the table we see that SVD-infer suffers only a minor drop in performance relative to SVD-block on rating NDCG. Also, surprisingly, SVD-infer outperforms SVD-block on binary NDCG for 50% and 70% training splits. These results further validate the approximate inference procedure as a useful way to quickly generate recommendations for new users.

6. CONCLUSION AND FUTURE WORK

We presented a general approach to deal with binary preferences in CF. In our approach, observed binary matrix is first transformed into a score matrix by applying neighborhood similarity rescaling. The score matrix is then factorized to produce accurate user and item representations. We demonstrated that with this approach even simple factorization techniques like SVD produce accurate representations using only a small subset of the highest scores for each user.

Table 6: Netflix strong generalization results. 1000 randomly chosen users were withheld during model optimization and then added to the model either via full model block update (SVD-block) or via inference procedure outlined in Section 4.3 (SVD-infer); ρ was set to 500 across all training splits. Item-item baseline was computed using all users and item-item\1000 was computed with 1000 test users removed from the training data and exclude for item similarity calculation.

	NDCG@10 binary				NDCG@10 rating			
	10%	30%	50%	70%	10%	30%	50%	70%
item-item	0.4441	0.4754	0.4227	0.3364	**0.6380**	**0.6583**	0.6734	**0.7074**
item-item\1000	0.4484	0.4922	0.4391	0.3492	0.6224	0.6492	0.6688	0.7045
ii-SVD-block	**0.4897**	0.5113	0.4441	0.3449	0.6277	0.6568	**0.6741**	**0.7074**
ii-SVD-infer	0.4736	**0.5117**	**0.4624**	**0.3645**	0.6190	0.6498	0.6718	0.7044

In the future work we plan to explore more complex factorization procedures that can potentially lead to better latent representations. We also plan to investigate ways to deal with discrepancy between model performance on implicit/binary and explicit data. We have shown that improvement on implicit/binary data doesn't always lead to improvement on explicit preferences. We believe that this discrepancy must be considered in every approach designed for binary data. Finally, we plan to extend our approach beyond the binary setting and apply it to graded preferences (ratings).

Acknowledgments

We would like to thank Richard Zemel and Tomi Poutanen for many useful ideas and discussions. We also thank the anonymous reviewers for their comments and suggestions.

7. REFERENCES

[1] P.-A. Absil, C. G. Baker, and K. A. Gallivan. Trust-region methods on riemannian manifolds. *Foundations of Computational Mathematics*, 7(3), 2007.

[2] G. Adomavicius and A. Tuzhilin. Toward the next generation of recommender systems: A survey of the state-of- the-art and possible extensions. *IEEE Transactions on Knowledge and Data Engineering*, 17(6), 2005.

[3] F. Aiolli. Efficient top-n recommendation for very large scale binary rated datasets. In *ACM Recommender Systems*, 2013.

[4] R. Baeza-Yates and B. Ribeiro-Neto. *Information Retrieval.* Addison-Wesley, 1999.

[5] J. Bennet and S. Lanning. The Netflix prize. `www.cs.uic.edu/~liub/KDD-cup-2007/NetflixPrize-description.pdf`.

[6] D. Billsus and M. J. Pazzani. Learning collaborative information filters. In *International Conference on Machine Learning*, 1998.

[7] M. Brand. Fast low-rank modifications of the thin singular value decomposition. *Linear algebra and its applications*, 415(1), 2006.

[8] C. J. C. Burges, T. Shaked, E. Renshaw, A. Lazier, M. Deeds, N. Hamilton, and G. Hullender. Learning to rank using gradient descent. In *International Conference on Machine Learning*, 2005.

[9] Z. Cao, T. Qin, T.-Y. Liu, M.-F. Tsai, and H. Li. Learning to rank: From pairwise approach to listwise approach. In *International Conference on Machine Learning*, 2007.

[10] Z. Gantner, S. Rendle, C. Freudenthaler, and L. Schmidt-Thieme. MyMediaLite: A free recommender system library. In *ACM Recommender Systems*, 2011.

[11] N. Halko, P. G. Martinsson, and J. A. Tropp. Finding structure with randomness: Probabilistic algorithms for constructing approximate matrix decompositions. *SIAM Review*, 53(2), 2011.

[12] J. Herlocker, J. A. Konstan, and J. Riedl. An empirical analysis of design choices in neighborhood-based collaborative filtering algorithms. *Information Retrieval*, 5(4), 2002.

[13] Y. Hu, Y. Koren, and C. Volinsky. Collaborative filtering for implicit feedback datasets. In *International Conference on Data Engineering*, 2008.

[14] Z. Huang, D. Zeng, and H. Chen. A comparison of collaborative-filtering recommendation algorithms for e-commerce. *IEEE Intelligent Systems*, 22(5), 2007.

[15] K. Jarvelin and J. Kekalainen. IR evaluation methods for retrieving highly relevant documents. In *ACM Special Interest Group on Information Retrieval*, 2000.

[16] T.-Y. Liu. *Learning to rank for information retrieval.* Springer, 2011.

[17] Apache Software Foundation. Mahout stochastic singular value decomposition. `https://mahout.apache.org/users/dim-reduction/dimensional-reduction.html`.

[18] B. McFee, T. Bertin-Mahieux, D. P. Ellis, and G. R. Lanckriet. The Million Song Dataset Challenge. `http://www.kaggle.com/c/msdchallenge`. In *International World Wide Web Conference*, 2012.

[19] H. Polat and W. Du. SVD-based collaborative filtering with privacy. In *ACM Symposium On Applied Computing*, 2005.

[20] S. Rendle, C. Freudenthaler, Z. Gantner, and L. Schmidt-Thieme. BPR: Bayesian personalized ranking from implicit feedback. In *Conference on Uncertainty in Artificial Intelligence*, 2009.

[21] R. Salakhutdinov and A. Mnih. Probabilistic matrix factorization. In *Neural Information Processing Systems*, 2008.

[22] B. Sarwar, G. Karypis, J. Konstan, and J. Riedl. Application of dimensionality reduction in recommender system - a case study. Technical report, DTIC Document, 2000.

[23] B. Sarwar, G. Karypis, J. Konstan, and J. Riedl. Item-based collaborative filtering recommendation algorithms. In *International World Wide Web Conference*, 2001.

[24] B. Sarwar, G. Karypis, J. Konstan, and J. Riedl. Incremental singular value decomposition algorithms for highly scalable recommender systems. In *International Conference on Information Systems*, 2002.

[25] R. Yuster and U. Zwick. Fast sparse matrix multiplication. *ACM Transactions on Algorithms*, 1(1), 2005.

Personalized Recommendation via Parameter-Free Contextual Bandits

Liang Tang Yexi Jiang Lei Li Chunqiu Zeng Tao Li
School of Computing and Information Sciences, Florida International University
11200 S.W. 8th Street, Miami, FL 33199, USA
{ltang002,yjian004,lli003,czeng001,taoli}@cs.fiu.edu

ABSTRACT

Personalized recommendation services have gained increasing popularity and attention in recent years as most useful information can be accessed online in real-time. Most online recommender systems try to address the information needs of users by virtue of both user and content information. Despite extensive recent advances, the problem of personalized recommendation remains challenging for at least two reasons. First, the user and item repositories undergo frequent changes, which makes traditional recommendation algorithms ineffective. Second, the so-called *cold-start* problem is difficult to address, as the information for learning a recommendation model is limited for new items or new users. Both challenges are formed by the dilemma of exploration and exploitation.

In this paper, we formulate personalized recommendation as a contextual bandit problem to solve the exploration/exploitation dilemma. Specifically in our work, we propose a parameter-free bandit strategy, which employs a principled resampling approach called online bootstrap, to derive the distribution of estimated models in an online manner. Under the paradigm of probability matching, the proposed algorithm randomly samples a model from the derived distribution for every recommendation. Extensive empirical experiments on two real-world collections of web data (including online advertising and news recommendation) demonstrate the effectiveness of the proposed algorithm in terms of the click-through rate. The experimental results also show that this proposed algorithm is robust in the *cold-start* situation, in which there is no sufficient data or knowledge to tune the parameters.

Categories and Subject Descriptors:
H.3.5[Information Systems]: On-line Information Services;
I.2.6[Computing Methodologies]: Learning;
H.2.8[Database Applications]: Data Mining

Keywords: Recommender Systems;Personalization;Contextual Bandit;Probability Matching;Bootstrapping

SIGIR'15, August 09 - 13, 2015, Santiago, Chile.
 ISBN 978-1-4503-3621-5/15/08 ...$15.00.
DOI: http://dx.doi.org/10.1145/2766462.2767707.

1. INTRODUCTION

Personalized recommender systems promptly identify popular items and tailor the content according to users' interest. A user's interest often evolves over time. The uncertainties of information need can only be captured via collecting users' feedbacks in real time and adapting recommendation models to the interest changes. Further, a significant number of users/items might be completely new to the system, that is, they may have no consumption history at all, which is known as the *cold-start* problem [28]. Such a setting renders traditional recommendation approaches ineffective in providing reasonable recommendation results, as it is difficult to learn the match between user preferences and items in a *cold-start* situation.

The aforementioned issues are often recognized as an exploration/exploitation problem, in which we have to find a tradeoff between two competing goals: maximizing users' satisfaction in a long run, while exploring uncertainties of user interests [3]. For instance, a news recommender should prompt breaking news to users while maintaining user preferences based on aging news stories. In practice, such a dilemma is often formulated as a contextual bandit problem [35]. The problem setting consists of a series of trials. Each trial provides a context. An algorithm selects an arm to pull, and after pulling, it receives a reward. The reward is drawn from some unknown distribution determined by the selected arm with the context. The goal is to maximize the total received reward. In personalized recommendation, each trial is seen as a user visit. Every arm is an item (e.g., a news article or advertisement). Pulling an arm is recommending that item. A context is a set of user features. The reward is the user response (e.g., a click). Therefore, personalized recommendation can be seen as an instance of the contextual bandit problem.

Typical solutions of the contextual bandit problem involve unguided exploration (e.g., ϵ-greedy [34], epoch-greedy [18]) and guided exploration (e.g., LinUCB [19], EXP4 [4]). Most of the existing algorithms require an input parameter to control the importance of exploration, such as ϵ in greedy-based algorithms and α in LinUCB. In practice, however, it is often difficult to determine the optimal value for the input parameter. The EXP4 algorithm adopts the exponential weighting technique, but it is computationally expensive especially when the context is high-dimensional.

Another family of algorithms is *probability matching* [32], which randomly allocates the pulling opportunities according to the probability that an arm gives the largest expected reward[1]. Compared with other methods, the benefit of probability matching is that the tradeoff between exploration and exploitation evolves with the learning process, rather than being arbitrarily set [8]. The pulling allocation is usually implemented by random sampling from the posterior distribution of Bayesian learning models [29, 21]. This strategy is also referred to as Thompson sampling or Bayesian bandits. It provides promising performance in many empirical studies [13, 14, 29, 36]. However, an improper prior for Bayesian learning models can lead to imbalanced exploration and exploitation and jeopardize the overall performance. Moreover, in the *cold-start* situation, there is no enough data for tuning the prior or parameters.

This paper proposes a non-Bayesian implementation of the *probability matching* strategy. The key idea is to apply the online bootstrap to maintain a collection of bootstrap replications for learning model coefficients. To make each recommendation decision, the model coefficient vector is randomly drawn from these bootstrap replications, rather than the posterior distribution. One advantage of this method is that it does not require a prior or predefined parameters that can affect the tradeoff of exploration and exploitation. In summary, the contribution of our work is three-fold:

- We propose a non-Bayesian method based on the *probability matching* strategy to solve the personalized recommendation problem. This method has no input parameter affecting the tradeoff between exploration and exploitation, and is suitable for the *cold-start* situation.
- We give both theoretical and empirical analyses to show that the performance of Thompson sampling depends on the choice of the prior.
- We conduct extensive experiments on real data sets to demonstrate the efficacy of the proposed method compared with other baseline algorithms. The results show that our method is relatively stable. Other algorithms can have a poor performance if the initial parameter or prior is not appropriate.

The rest of this paper is organized as follows. In Section 2, the preliminaries of our work are introduced, and the detailed algorithmic description is presented in Section 3. Extensive empirical evaluation results are reported in Section 4. Section 5 presents a brief summary of prior work relevant to bandit problems, probability matching and bootstrapping. Finally, Section 6 concludes the paper.

2. PRELIMINARIES

In this section, we briefly describe the online learning paradigm for the contextual bandit problem in the setting of personalized recommendation, and then discuss the framework of probability matching in solving the contextual bandit problem. Table 1 lists the important notations throughout the paper.

2.1 Personalized Recommendation and Contextual Bandits

[1]The traditional probability matching is based on the probability of an arm having the largest reward, not the largest expected reward.

Personalized recommender systems recommend items (e.g., movies, news articles) to users based on the predicted users' interests on these items. The user's response helps the system improve their future interest prediction [1]. However, the response to particular items can only be available after these items are recommended. If the items are never shown to the users, the recommender systems cannot collect the response on these items. This problem can be naturally modeled as a contextual bandit problem [35].

Table 1: Important Notations

Notation	Description
$a^{(i)}$	the i-th arm.
$\mathcal{A}$	the set of arms, $\mathcal{A} = \{a^{(1)}, ..., a^{(k)}\}$.
$\mathbf{x}_t$	the context of the t-th trial, and represented by a vector.
r_{t,a_t}	the reward of pulling the arm a_t in the t-th trial, $a_t \in \mathcal{A}$.
$\hat{r}_{t,a_t}$	the expected reward of pulling the arm a_t in the t-th trial, $a_t \in \mathcal{A}$.
$\mathbf{y}_t$	the observation received in the t-th trial, $\mathbf{y}_t = (\mathbf{x}_t, a_t, r_{t,a_t})$.
$\mathcal{D}_t$	the set of received observations from the beginning to the t-th trial, i.e., $\{\mathbf{y}_1, ..., \mathbf{y}_t\}$.
$\mathcal{D}_t^{(i)}$	the set of observations in $\mathcal{D}_t$ that are received only by pulling the arm $a^{(i)}$.
$\tilde{\mathcal{D}}_t^{(i)}$	a bootstrap sample of $\mathcal{D}_t^{(i)}$.
$n_t^{(i)}$	the number of observations in $\mathcal{D}_t^{(i)}$.
$f(\mathbf{x}, \boldsymbol{\theta})$	the reward prediction function using the context $\mathbf{x}$ and the model coefficient vector $\boldsymbol{\theta}$.
$\boldsymbol{\theta}_{a^{(i)}}$	the coefficient vector of the reward prediction model for the arm $a^{(i)}$.
$\hat{\boldsymbol{\theta}}_{a^{(i)}}$	the estimation of $\boldsymbol{\theta}_{a^{(i)}}$.
$\tilde{\boldsymbol{\theta}}_{a^{(i)}}$	a bootstrap replication of $\hat{\boldsymbol{\theta}}_{a^{(i)}}$, which is the estimation of $\boldsymbol{\theta}_{a^{(i)}}$ using a bootstrap sample.
$\mathcal{L}(\boldsymbol{\theta}; \mathbf{y})$	the likelihood of $\mathbf{y}$ given $\boldsymbol{\theta}$.

Formally, given a set of independent arms $\mathcal{A}$, a contextual bandit algorithm makes a decision for each trial $t = 1, 2, ..., n$. For the t-th trial, the context is a feature vector $\mathbf{x}_t$. The algorithm selects an arm $a_t \in \mathcal{A}$ to pull. By pulling the arm a_t, the algorithm receives a reward r_{t,a_t}, which is drawn from some unknown distribution determined by the arm a_t with the context $\mathbf{x}_t$. The goal of the algorithm is to maximize the total received reward $R = \sum_{t=1}^{n} r_{t,a_t}$. Contextual bandit algorithms can make use of the past t trial data $\mathcal{D}_t = \{(\mathbf{x}_1, a_1, r_{1,a_1}), ..., (\mathbf{x}_t, a_t, r_{t,a_t})\}$ to improve the decision for future trials [18], but the past data may not be sufficient for learning. Typically, in the t-th trial the algorithm first predicts the expected reward $\hat{r}_{t,a}$ for each arm a before making the decision. The expected reward is

$$\hat{r}_{t,a} = f(\mathbf{x}_t, \boldsymbol{\theta}_a),$$

where $\boldsymbol{\theta}_a$ is a vector of the unknown coefficients with respect to the arm a and f is a predefined prediction function. For instance, $f(\mathbf{x}_t, \boldsymbol{\theta}_a) = 1/(1 + \exp(-\mathbf{x}_t^T \boldsymbol{\theta}_a))$ is the logistic regression model. By learning from the past observations $\mathcal{D}_t$, the unknown coefficients $\boldsymbol{\theta}_a$ can be estimated.

Several recommendation algorithms consider both user and item information simultaneously, and represent the data as a feature-based user-item matrix. The recommendation can be achieved by utilizing feature-based matrix factorization techniques [9], and the goal is to fill the missing values in the matrix. Our problem setting is orthogonal to theirs as we expect that the total reward is maximized by running a series of trials.

2.2 Probability Matching

Probability matching is a widely used decision strategy in k-armed bandit algorithms [8, 29]. In this strategy, the probability of pulling the arm $a, a \in \mathcal{A}$ equals to the probability that a has the largest expected reward. In the t-th trial, the probability of arm $a^{(i)}$ having the largest expected reward is

$$\begin{aligned} Q(i) &= \Pr(\hat{r}_{t,a^{(i)}} = \max\{\hat{r}_{t,a^{(1)}}, ..., \hat{r}_{t,a^{(k)}}\}), \\ &= \Pr(f(\mathbf{x}_t, \boldsymbol{\theta}_{a^{(i)}}) = \max\{f(\mathbf{x}_t, \boldsymbol{\theta}_{a^{(1)}}), ..., f(\mathbf{x}_t, \boldsymbol{\theta}_{a^{(k)}})\}), \end{aligned}$$

where $i = 1, ..., k$. The selected arm is a random sample drawn from $Q(i)$. But $Q(i)$ does not need to compute explicitly. The algorithms usually draw a vector $\hat{\boldsymbol{\theta}}_{a^{(i)}}$ from the probability distribution of $\boldsymbol{\theta}_{a^{(i)}}$, $i = 1, ..., k$, and select the arm $a^{(i^*)}$, where

$$i^* = \arg\max_{i=1,...,k} f(\mathbf{x}_t, \hat{\boldsymbol{\theta}}_{a^{(i)}}).$$

In Thompson sampling [32], the probability distribution of $\boldsymbol{\theta}_{a^{(i)}}$ in the t-th trial is the posterior distribution, denoted as $\Pr(\boldsymbol{\theta}_{a^{(i)}}|\mathcal{D}_{t-1}^{(i)})$, where $\mathcal{D}_{t-1}^{(i)}$ denotes the set of observations in $\mathcal{D}_{t-1}$ that are only obtained by pulling the arm $a^{(i)}$ [8]. It assumes that the unknown coefficient $\boldsymbol{\theta}_{a^{(i)}}$ follows a predefined probability model, e.g., a Gaussian model,

$$\boldsymbol{\theta}_{a^{(i)}} \sim \mathcal{N}(\boldsymbol{\mu}, \boldsymbol{\Sigma}),$$

where $\boldsymbol{\mu}$ and $\boldsymbol{\Sigma}$ are unknown parameters. Estimating $\Pr(\boldsymbol{\theta}_{a^{(i)}}|\mathcal{D}_t^{(i)})$ is to find $\boldsymbol{\mu}_t$, $\boldsymbol{\Sigma}_t$ such that $\mathcal{N}(\boldsymbol{\mu}_t, \boldsymbol{\Sigma}_t)$ and $\Pr(\boldsymbol{\theta}_{a^{(i)}}|\mathcal{D}_t^{(i)})$ are close to each other. Sampling from the posterior distribution is similar to sampling from $\mathcal{N}(\boldsymbol{\mu}_t, \boldsymbol{\Sigma}_t)$.

Based on Thompson sampling, in the $(t+1)$-th trial, the sampling area of $\boldsymbol{\theta}_{a^{(i)}}$ is determined by the variance of $\Pr(\boldsymbol{\theta}_{a^{(i)}}|\mathcal{D}_t^{(i)})$. When t is not sufficiently large, $\Pr(\boldsymbol{\theta}_{a^{(i)}}|\mathcal{D}_t^{(i)})$ mainly depends on the prior $\Pr(\boldsymbol{\theta}_0)$, denoted by $\mathcal{N}(\boldsymbol{\mu}_0, \boldsymbol{\Sigma}_0)$. In other words, if $\boldsymbol{\Sigma}_0$ is large, the algorithm performs more exploration; otherwise, it does less. Therefore $\boldsymbol{\Sigma}_0$ mainly controls the tradeoff between exploration and exploitation in early trials. Moreover, $\boldsymbol{\Sigma}_0^{-1}$ is the regularization weight for estimating $\boldsymbol{\mu}_t$. If $\boldsymbol{\Sigma}_0$ is too small, the sampling will only focus on a small area around $\boldsymbol{\mu}_0$, but $\boldsymbol{\mu}_0$ may not be accurate. For instance, let $f(\mathbf{x}_t, \boldsymbol{\theta}_a) = 1/(1+\exp(-\mathbf{x}_t^T\boldsymbol{\theta}_a))$, then the prediction model is a logistic regression model. Let $\mathcal{D}_t^{(i)} = \{(\mathbf{x}_1^{(i)}, a^{(i)}, r_1^{(i)}), ..., (\mathbf{x}_{t^{(i)}}^{(i)}, a^{(i)}, r_{t^{(i)}}^{(i)})\}$. By Laplace approximation [33],

$$\boldsymbol{\Sigma}_t^{-1} = \boldsymbol{\Sigma}_0^{-1} + \nabla\boldsymbol{\Sigma}^{-1},$$

where

$$\nabla\boldsymbol{\Sigma}^{-1} = \sum_{j=1}^{t^{(i)}} f(\mathbf{x}_j^{(i)}, \boldsymbol{\mu}_t)(1 - f(\mathbf{x}_j^{(i)}, \boldsymbol{\mu}_t))\mathbf{x}_j^{(i)}\mathbf{x}_j^{(i)T}.$$

$\boldsymbol{\Sigma}_0^{-1}$ is the start point of $\boldsymbol{\Sigma}_t^{-1}$. In the *cold-start* situation, since we do not know the values from the data $\mathcal{D}_t^{(i)}$ in advance, it is not easy to come up with $\boldsymbol{\Sigma}_0^{-1}$ that is balanced with $\nabla\boldsymbol{\Sigma}^{-1}$.

Therefore, the given $\Pr(\boldsymbol{\theta}_0)$ dominates the balance of exploration and exploitation in early trials. An improper estimation in earlier trials also affects later trials. "Good" arms might be underrated in earlier trials, and then would have few chances to be pulled later and be corrected. As a result, the algorithm would take a long time to converge to the optimal estimation.

3. ALGORITHM

In this section, we present a non-Bayesian algorithm to implement the probability matching strategy. The basic idea is using the sampling distribution obtained by the bootstrap instead of the posterior distribution to sample the prediction model coefficients for each item. We first discuss an offline bootstrap method for solving the contextual bandit problem. Then, we present an online implementation of the bootstrap method along with an online optimization algorithm.

3.1 Bootstrap for Contextual Bandits

The bootstrap is a method to derive the distribution of an estimator by data resampling [10]. Instead of specifying a generative model for data generating process, it only uses the information from the observed data.

In the $(t+1)$-th trial, we have the previous t pulling observations, $\mathcal{D}_t$. Let $\mathcal{D}_t^{(i)}$ denote the observations only from pulling the arm $a^{(i)}$, $i \in \{1, ..., k\}$. k is the number of arms. $\mathcal{D}_t = \mathcal{D}_t^{(i)} \cup ... \cup \mathcal{D}_t^{(k)}$. Let $n_t^{(i)}$ be the number of observations in $\mathcal{D}_t^{(i)}$. When any $\mathcal{D}_t^{(i)}$ is not sufficient large (e.g., less than 30 observations [15]), $i = 1, ..., k$, we randomly select an arm. When all $\mathcal{D}_t^{(i)}$ are sufficient large, for the $(t+1)$-th trial, given the context $\mathbf{x}_{t+1}$, the offline bootstrap based contextual bandit algorithm has the following steps:

- For each $i = 1, ...k$,
  1. Randomly sample $n_t^{(i)}$ observations from $\mathcal{D}_t^{(i)}$ with replacement, denoted by $\tilde{\mathcal{D}}_t^{(i)}$;
  2. Estimate $\boldsymbol{\theta}_{a^{(i)}}$ using $\tilde{\mathcal{D}}_t^{(i)}$ based on maximum likelihood estimation, denoted by $\tilde{\boldsymbol{\theta}}_{a^{(i)}}$;
- Pull the arm $a^{(i^*)}$, where $i^* = \arg\max_{i=1,...,k} f(\mathbf{x}_{t+1}, \tilde{\boldsymbol{\theta}}_{a^{(i)}})$;
- Receive the reward r_{t+1} of pulling the arm $a^{(i^*)}$, $\mathcal{D}_{t+1}^{(i^*)} \leftarrow \mathcal{D}_t^{(i^*)} \cup \{(\mathbf{x}_{t+1}, a^{(i^*)}, r_{t+1})\}$.

where $\tilde{\boldsymbol{\theta}}_{a^{(i)}}$ is a bootstrap replication of $\hat{\boldsymbol{\theta}}_{a^{(i)}}$. If the step 1 and step 2 are repeated for many times, we can have a collection of bootstrap replications of $\hat{\boldsymbol{\theta}}_{a^{(i)}}$, which approximately represents the sampling distribution of $\hat{\boldsymbol{\theta}}_{a^{(i)}}$. Therefore, $\tilde{\boldsymbol{\theta}}_{a^{(i)}}$ can be seen as a random sample drawn from the distribution of $\hat{\boldsymbol{\theta}}_{a^{(i)}}$.

Let $\mathcal{L}(\boldsymbol{\theta}; \mathbf{y})$ denote the likelihood of an observation $\mathbf{y}$ by given $\boldsymbol{\theta}$, where $\boldsymbol{\theta}$ is the unknown coefficient vector. Assuming the observations are i.i.d and the arms are independent, we have the following lemma.

LEMMA 1. *The offline bootstrap based contextual bandit algorithm implements the probability matching strategy.*

PROOF. In the $(t+1)$-th trial, given a context $\mathbf{x}_{t+1}$, let $\mathbf{a} = \arg\max_{a^{(i)} \in \mathcal{A}} f(\mathbf{x}_{t+1}, \hat{\boldsymbol{\theta}}_{a^{(i)}})$, where $\hat{\boldsymbol{\theta}}_{a^{(1)}}, \ldots, \hat{\boldsymbol{\theta}}_{a^{(k)}}$ are the model coefficient vectors estimations of the k arms. Since these estimations vary with different observations, $\hat{\boldsymbol{\theta}}_{a^{(1)}}, \ldots, \hat{\boldsymbol{\theta}}_{a^{(k)}}$ are random variables. Then, $\mathbf{a}$ is a random variable and randomized by the joint random variable $(\hat{\boldsymbol{\theta}}_{a^{(1)}}, \ldots, \hat{\boldsymbol{\theta}}_{a^{(k)}})$. Based on *probability matching*, the selected arm should be a sample randomly drawn from the distribution $\Pr(\mathbf{a})$.

Let $\pi_{a^{(i)}}$ denote some unknown distribution for generating the observations by pulling arm $a^{(i)}$, $i = 1, \ldots, k$. $\mathbf{Y}_1^{(i)}, \mathbf{Y}_2^{(i)}, \ldots$ are independent random variables following $\pi_{a^{(i)}}$. Let $\mathbf{D}_t^{(i)} = \{\mathbf{Y}_1^{(i)}, \ldots, \mathbf{Y}_{n_t^{(i)}}^{(i)}\}$. Obviously, $\mathcal{D}_t^{(i)}$ is the observed value of $\mathbf{D}_t^{(i)}$. $\hat{\boldsymbol{\theta}}_{a^{(i)}}$ is the maximum likelihood estimation of $\boldsymbol{\theta}_{a^{(i)}}$, so in the t-th trial,

$$\hat{\boldsymbol{\theta}}_{a^{(i)}} = \arg\max_{\boldsymbol{\theta} \in R^d} \log \mathcal{L}(\boldsymbol{\theta}; \mathbf{D}_t^{(i)}),$$

where d is the dimensionality of the context. $\hat{\boldsymbol{\theta}}_{a^{(i)}}$ is randomized by $\mathbf{D}_t^{(i)}$. Since every observation in $\tilde{\mathcal{D}}_t^{(i)}$ is drawn from $\pi_{a^{(i)}}$ and every random variable in $\mathbf{D}_t^{(i)}$ follows $\pi_{a^{(i)}}$, $\tilde{\mathcal{D}}_t^{(i)}$ is also a random sample of $\mathbf{D}_t^{(i)}$. Then, based on the bootstrap method, $\tilde{\boldsymbol{\theta}}_{a^{(i)}} = \arg\max_{\boldsymbol{\theta} \in R^d} \log \mathcal{L}(\boldsymbol{\theta}; \tilde{\mathcal{D}}_t^{(i)})$ is also a random sample of $\hat{\boldsymbol{\theta}}_{a^{(i)}}$.

To sum up all k arms, $\tilde{\boldsymbol{\theta}}_{a^{(1)}}, \ldots, \tilde{\boldsymbol{\theta}}_{a^{(k)}}$ are random samples of $\hat{\boldsymbol{\theta}}_{a^{(1)}}, \ldots, \hat{\boldsymbol{\theta}}_{a^{(k)}}$, respectively. Since the arms are independent, $(\tilde{\boldsymbol{\theta}}_{a^{(1)}}, \ldots, \tilde{\boldsymbol{\theta}}_{a^{(k)}})$ is a sample randomly drawn from $\Pr(\hat{\boldsymbol{\theta}}_{a^{(1)}}, \ldots, \hat{\boldsymbol{\theta}}_{a^{(k)}})$. Then $a^{(i^*)} = \arg\max_{a^{(i)} \in \mathcal{A}} f(\mathbf{x}_{t+1}, \tilde{\boldsymbol{\theta}}_{a^{(i)}})$ can be seen as a sample randomly drawn from $\Pr(\mathbf{a})$. □

3.2 An Online Implementation

In real recommender systems, each recommendation decision must be made in real time. The algorithm cannot go through all previous observations to generate a bootstrap sample $\tilde{\mathcal{D}}_t^{(i)}$. On the other hand, the learning algorithm cannot estimate $\tilde{\boldsymbol{\theta}}_{a^{(i)}}$ utilizing the entire $\tilde{\mathcal{D}}_t^{(i)}$. Therefore, in our problem setting, we apply the online bootstrap method to solve the contextual bandit problem [23].

3.2.1 Online Bootstrap

The basic idea of online bootstrap is to generate a random variable P_j, which is the proportion of times the j-th observation is picked to a bootstrap sample. Then in the online setting, when we receive the j-th observation, we know how many times this observation should appear in a bootstrap sample. After processing the j-th observation, we do not pick it again. Let $\mathcal{D}_t^{(i)}$ be the set of received observations by pulling the arm $a^{(i)}$. $n_t^{(i)}$ is the size of $\mathcal{D}_t^{(i)}$. $\tilde{\mathcal{D}}_t^{(i)}$ is a bootstrap sample of $\mathcal{D}_t^{(i)}$. $\mathcal{D}_t^{(i)}$ and $\tilde{\mathcal{D}}_t^{(i)}$ have the same number of elements. The elements in $\tilde{\mathcal{D}}_t^{(i)}$ are randomly resampled from $\mathcal{D}_t^{(i)}$ with replacement. For each resampling, each element in $\mathcal{D}_t^{(i)}$ has an identical probability of $1/n_t^{(i)}$ to be picked. There are $n_t^{(i)}$ independent chances of resampling. Therefore, $P_j \sim \mathrm{Binom}(n_t^{(i)}, 1/n_t^{(i)})$. When $n_t^{(i)}$ is large, this binomial distribution is approximated to a Poisson distribution $\mathrm{Pois}(n_t^{(i)} \cdot 1/n_t^{(i)}) = \mathrm{Pois}(1)$ [23]. Then,

$$P_j \sim \mathrm{Poisson}(1).$$

P_j does not depend on t.

3.2.2 Online Learning and Bootstrapping

The online learning algorithm processes every observation in a streaming manner. When a new observation is received, by online bootstrap, this observation should appear P_j times in the bootstrap sample, where $P_j \sim \mathrm{Poisson}(1)$. We invoke the online learning algorithm to learn this observation P_j times. Then, the learned model is approximated to the model that learns observations in a bootstrap sample offline.

In our proposed algorithm, we apply this idea with the stochastic gradient ascent algorithm for updating the estimation of each bootstrap replication. Let $\tilde{\boldsymbol{\theta}}_{a^{(i)}}$ be a current bootstrap replication of $\boldsymbol{\theta}_{a^{(i)}}$. η_z is the current learning rate for this bootstrap replication in the stochastic gradient ascent algorithm, where z is the number of updated times. Usually, $\eta_z = 1/\sqrt{z+1}$ [16]. $\mathbf{y}_t = (\mathbf{x}_t, a^{(i)}, r_{t,a^{(i)}})$ is the received new observation. Based on online bootstrap, we draw a random integer p_t from Poisson(1). The new bootstrap replication of $\boldsymbol{\theta}_{a^{(i)}}$ is $\tilde{\boldsymbol{\theta}}_{a^{(i)}}^{(p_t)}$, where

$$\tilde{\boldsymbol{\theta}}_{a^{(i)}}^{(l)} = \tilde{\boldsymbol{\theta}}_{a^{(i)}}^{(l-1)} + \eta_{z+l-1} \nabla \log \mathcal{L}(\tilde{\boldsymbol{\theta}}_{a^{(i)}}^{(l-1)}; \mathbf{y}_t), \tag{1}$$

$l = 1, \ldots, p_t$, $\tilde{\boldsymbol{\theta}}_{a^{(i)}}^{(0)} = \tilde{\boldsymbol{\theta}}_{a^{(i)}}$, η_{z+p_t} is the new learning rate.

If we only maintain one bootstrap sample for each arm, the decisions made for different trials may not be fully independent. Our solution is to maintain a collection of independent bootstrap samples for each arm at the same time. In every trial, we randomly select one of them to make the reward prediction. Let B be the number of bootstrap samples for each arm. There are B independent bootstrap replications of $\hat{\boldsymbol{\theta}}_{a^{(i)}}$ maintained for each $a^{(i)} \in \mathcal{A}$, denoted by $\mathcal{B}_{a^{(i)}} = \{\tilde{\boldsymbol{\theta}}_{a^{(i)},1}, \ldots, \tilde{\boldsymbol{\theta}}_{a^{(i)},B}\}$. In each trial and arm $a^{(i)}$, we randomly select a bootstrap replication from $\mathcal{B}_{a^{(i)}}$, where every bootstrap replication has an equal probability to be selected. Let $\tilde{\boldsymbol{\theta}}_{a^{(i)}}$ be the selected replication. $\Pr(\hat{\boldsymbol{\theta}}_{a^{(i)}})$ is represented by $\mathcal{B}_{a^{(i)}}$. When B and $n_t^{(i)}$ are sufficiently large, $\mathcal{B}_{a^{(i)}}$ provides an approximation of the sampling distribution of $\hat{\boldsymbol{\theta}}_{a^{(i)}}$ [23, 26]. The details of the online bootstrap algorithm for contextual bandits are stated in Algorithm 1.

Algorithm 1 *OnlineBootstrapBandit*

```
Receive the context x_t.
for i = 1, ..., k do
    Randomly select a vector from {θ̃_{a(i),1}, ..., θ̃_{a(i),B}}, denoted by θ̃_{a(i)}.
end for
Pull the arm a^(i*), where i* = argmax_{i=1,...,k} f(x_t, θ̃_{a(i)}).
Receive the reward r_t.
y_t ← {x_t, a^(i*), r_t}.
for j = 1, ..., B do
    Draw p from Pois(1)
    for z = 1, ..., p do
        η_{i,j} ← 1/sqrt(n_{i,j} + 1)
        θ̃_{a(i*),j} ← θ̃_{a(i*),j} + η ∇ log L(θ̃_{a(i*),j}; y_t)
        n_{i,j} ← n_{i,j} + 1
    end for
end for
```

In general, the time complexity of calculating a log-likelihood is $O(d)$, where d is the dimensionality of context feature vectors. Let $T(t)$ be the time cost of a trial in Algorithm 1. Generating a Poisson random variable is $O(p_t)$, where p_t is the generated value [17]. Eq.(1) has p_t iterations, and hence updating one bootstrap estimation requires $O(p_t \cdot d + p_t) = O(p_t \cdot d)$. Based on the cumulative distribution function (CDF) of Poisson(1), $\Pr(p_t \leq p) = e^{-1} \sum_{z=0}^{p} \frac{1}{z!}$. For example, the probability of $p_t \leq 3$ is 0.981. Therefore, the time cost of updating one bootstrap estimation is $O(d)$ with a high probability. There are k arms and B bootstrap replications for each arm. As a result, $T(t) = O(Bkd)$ with a high probability.

In practice, the larger the B, the better the sampling distribution approximation. However, the memory cost and time cost will become significantly large. Thus, the choice of B depends on the actual computational power of the system. As the B bootstrap replications are independent, they can be easily implemented in a parallel system, where each computing node handles a few replications independently.

4. EVALUATION

We verify the proposed algorithm on two real-world data sets, including news recommendation data (i.e., Yahoo! Today News) and online advertising data (i.e., KDD Cup 2012, Track 2). We start with an introduction to these two data sets, and then describe the implementation of the baseline algorithms. Finally, we present experimental results of the proposed algorithm with comparison to the baselines.

4.1 Data Collections

4.1.1 Yahoo! Today News

Personalized news recommendation aims to display suitable news articles on the web page for different users based on the prediction of their individual interests. The prediction model is usually built upon user feedbacks on displayed news. However, the feedbacks are only available when the news articles are displayed to the users. Therefore, the problem of personalized news recommendation can be regarded as an instance of the contextual bandit problem.

The experimental data set is collected by Yahoo! Today module and published by Yahoo! research lab[2]. The news were randomly displayed on the Yahoo! Front Page from October 2nd, 2011 to October 16th, 2011. The data set contains 28,041,015 user visit events to the Today Module on Yahoo! Front Page. Each visit event is associated with the user's information, e.g., age, gender, behavior targeting features, etc., represented by a binary feature vector of dimension 136. This data set has been used for evaluating contextual bandit algorithms in other literatures [19, 8, 20]. 2 million user visit events are used in this evaluation.

4.1.2 KDD Cup 2012 Online Advertising

Online advertising systems deliver relevant advertisements (ads) to individual users to maximize the click-though rate (CTR) of the displayed ads. Sponsored search is one typical instance of online advertising. Given a user profile and a set of search keywords, the search engine selects an ad (advertisement) to display in the search result page. In practice, a huge amount of new ads will be continually imported into the ad pool. The system has to display these new ads to users and then collects the feedbacks to improve the CTR prediction. Hence, the ad selection problem is an instance of the contextual bandit problem, where an arm is an ad, a trial is an ad impression for a search activity, the context is the user profile with the search keywords, and the reward is the click count of the user.

The experimental data set is collected by a search engine and published by KDD Cup 2012[3]. In this data set, each instance is an ad impression, which consists of the user profile, search keywords, displayed ad information and the click count. The user profile contains the user's gender and age. In our work, the context is represented as a binary feature vector, each entry of which denotes whether a query token is contained in the search query or not. The user's profile information is also appended to the context vector using the binary format. The dimension of the context feature for this data set is 1,070,866. 1 million user visit events are used in the experiments.

4.2 Experimental Setup

For evaluation purpose, we use the averaged reward as the metric, which is the total reward divided by the total number of trials, i.e., $\frac{1}{n} \sum_{t=1}^{n} r_t$, where n is the number of trials. In the aforementioned data sets, the averaged reward is the overall CTR (click-through rate) of the corresponding items (news articles or ads). The higher the CTR, the better the performance. In the experiments, to avoid the leakage of business-sensitive information, we report the relative CTR, which is the overall CTR of an algorithm divided by the overall CTR of random selection.

To demonstrate the efficacy of our proposed approach, we implement the following algorithms as baselines:

- `Random`: it randomly selects an arm to pull.
- `Exploit`: it selects the arm of the largest predicted reward and has no exploration. `Exploit` is equivalent to ϵ-`greedy`(0), `LinUCB`(0) and `TSNR`($+\infty$).
- ϵ-`greedy`(ϵ): it randomly selects an arm with probability ϵ and selects the arm of the largest predicted reward with probability $1 - \epsilon$.
- `LinUCB`(α): it is an extension of the UCB algorithm for contextual bandit problems [19]. In each trial, it pulls the arm of the largest score, which is a linear combination of the mean and standard deviation of the predicted reward. Given a context $\mathbf{x}$, the score is $\hat{\boldsymbol{\mu}}^T \mathbf{x} + \alpha \sqrt{\mathbf{x}^T \hat{\boldsymbol{\Sigma}}^{-1} \mathbf{x}}$, where $\hat{\boldsymbol{\mu}}$ and $\hat{\boldsymbol{\Sigma}}$ are the estimated mean and covariance of the posterior distribution $\Pr(\boldsymbol{\theta}|\mathcal{D}_t)$, and α is a predefined parameter. When $\alpha = 0$, it becomes the `Exploit` policy that has no exploration.
- `TS`(q_0): thompson sampling with logistic regression [8], described in Section 2.2, it randomly draws the coefficients from the posterior distribution, and selects the arm of the largest predicted reward. The priori distribution is $\mathcal{N}(\mathbf{0}, q_0^{-1}\mathbf{I})$.
- `TSNR`(q_0): it is similar to `TS`(q_0), but in the stochastic gradient ascent, there is no regularization by the prior. The priori distribution $\mathcal{N}(\mathbf{0}, q_0^{-1}\mathbf{I})$ is only used in the calculation of the posterior distribution for the coefficients sampling, but not in the stochastic gradient ascent. When q_0 is arbitrarily large, the variance approaches 0 and `TSNR` becomes `Exploit`.

[2]http://webscope.sandbox.yahoo.com/catalog.php.

[3]http://www.kddcup2012.org/c/kddcup2012-track2.

- `Bootstrap`: it is proposed in this paper and described in Algorithm 1.

In the following experiments, the reward in a single recommendation activity is the user click, which is a binary value. Therefore, logistic regression is applied as the learning model. Since the contextual bandit algorithms are online algorithms, stochastic gradient ascent is used as the learning algorithm [7]. Notice that the algorithms digest the data in an online manner, and hence all the user visits in the data sets are used for the testing purpose.

Thompson sampling with logistic regression is described in [8]. The prediction function $f(\mathbf{x}, \boldsymbol{\theta}) = (1+\exp(-\boldsymbol{\theta}^T\mathbf{x}))^{-1}$. The posterior distribution is obtained by Laplace approximation and the unknown coefficient vector $\boldsymbol{\theta}$ is assumed to be normally distributed [7]. Let $\mathcal{N}(\boldsymbol{\mu}_t, \boldsymbol{\Sigma}_t)$ denote the posterior distribution after receiving t observations. The estimated $\boldsymbol{\mu}_t$ is the *maximum a posteriori* (MAP) estimation , which is learned by the stochastic gradient ascent method. The inverse of the estimated covariance $\boldsymbol{\Sigma}_t^{-1} = \boldsymbol{\Sigma}_0^{-1} + \sum_{j=1}^{t} y_j(1-y_j)\mathbf{x}_j\mathbf{x}_j^T$, where $\boldsymbol{\Sigma}_0$ is the given priori covariance, $y_t = f(\mathbf{x}_t, \boldsymbol{\theta}_t)$, and $\mathbf{x}_1, \ldots, \mathbf{x}_t$ are the context feature vectors [8].

As we mentioned in Section 2, to decrease the exploration in Thompson sampling, we can give a small variance to the prior. But when the variance of the prior is small, the weight for the regularization in the stochastic gradient ascent will be high. As a result, the learned $\boldsymbol{\mu}_t$ would focus on a small area around the mean of the prior. To solve this conflict, we propose a variation of Thompson sampling, `TSNR`. In stochastic gradient ascent, it ignores the regularization by the prior in the learning step. The prior is only used to compute the variance of the posterior.

4.3 Evaluation Method

The experiments on the Yahoo! Today news is evaluated by the *replayer* method [20], which provides an unbiased offline evaluation by utilizing the historical logs. It shows that, for a testing algorithm, the CTR estimated by this *replayer* approaches the real CTR of the deployed online system if the items in historical user visits are random uniformly recommended. Therefore, we apply the *replayer* to evaluate the performance of various algorithms on the Yahoo! Today News data. The basic idea of *replayer* is to replay each user visit to the testing algorithm. If the recommended item is equal to displayed news in the log, this visit is regarded as a matched visit. The estimated CTR is the sum of the user clicks in the matched visits over the total number of matched visits.

However, the *replayer* only works for a small item pool. When the number of items is large, the number of matched visits for each item would be very small. As a result, the CTR estimation based on a small number of matched visits is not reliable and would have a large variance [8]. For the Yahoo! Today news, the number of recommending articles is less than 50. But for online advertising data, the number of ads is usually over 16,000. We evaluate the KDD Cup 2012 online ads data using a simulation method, which is used in [8] for the same purpose. To this end, we select 100 ads from the entire ads pool. The context data of these ads are real and given in the data, but the rewards are simulated using a weight vector $\mathbf{w}$ for each ad. Given a context $\mathbf{x}$, the click of an ad is generated with a probability $(1+\exp(-\mathbf{w}^T\mathbf{x}))^{-1}$. For each user visit and each arm, the weight vector $\mathbf{w}$ is drawn from a fixed normal distribution that is randomly generated before the testing.

4.4 Experimental Results

We consider the performances of algorithms in two situations: cold start and warm start. In cold start, there is no training data at the beginning for every algorithm. The algorithm can only learn the model by exploration. In warm start, we have 10,000 records of user activities for training. We train the logistic regression model using these data first. Tables 3 and 2 report the results of Yahoo! News data and KDD Cup 2012 online ads data, respectively. For each algorithm, we enumerate different parameter values. Except for `LinUCB` and `Exploit`, all other algorithms are randomized algorithms. For each trial, we also randomly shuffle the pool of recommending items. Thus, the performance of `LinUCB` and `Exploit` may vary in different runs. We run each algorithm with each parameter value 10 time, and keep track of the mean, standard deviation, minimum and maximum of the overall CTR. The best mean is highlighted in **bold**. The worst mean is marked with an asterisk (*).

As depicted in the tables, the baseline algorithms of ϵ-`greedy` and `LinUCB`, which take into account both exploration and exploitation, exhibit a common trend: when the controlling parameter is small, i.e., with more exploitation, the algorithms can achieve better performance in terms of the CTR, whereas the deviation is high; Comparatively, when the parameter is set to be larger, i.e., with more exploration, the CTR shrinks, but the deviation decreases. Hence, the problem of personalized recommendation requires a trade-off between exploration and exploitation. Further, the performance of ϵ-`greedy`, `LinUCB` highly depends on the parameter setting. The parameters of both algorithms explicitly or implicitly control the balance of the exploration and exploitation. If the parameter setting is perfect, the performance approaches the optimal. If the parameter setting is improper, the performance is poor. This conclusion is also mentioned in the empirical studies of [5, 31].

`TS` and `TSNR` are two types of Thompson sampling. `TS` is the straightforward implementation. It makes use of the given priori distribution and iteratively maximizes the posterior mean, where the inverse of the priori variance is the regularization weight. If the prior variance is large, e.g., `TS(0.001)`, the sampling area of `TS` will be too large, which may significantly sacrifice the exploitation part. If the prior variance is small, e.g., `TS(10)`, the regularization weight is large and the learned $\hat{\boldsymbol{\theta}}$ will be close to the given prior $\mathbf{0}$. Obviously, $\mathbf{0}$ is not a good guess of $\boldsymbol{\theta}$. Thus, for all parameter settings, the performance of `TS` is not satisfactory in terms of the CTR.

`TSNR` only maximizes the likelihood using stochastic gradient ascent and ignores the regularization from the prior. Therefore, the priori distribution only affects the sampling area of $\hat{\boldsymbol{\theta}}$ in the exploration part but not learning steps. As shown in Table 3 and 2, when the priori variance is appropriate, e.g., `TSNR(1000.0)`, it can achieve good performance. In `TSNR(1000.0)`, the variance is $q_0^{-1}\mathbf{I} = 1/1000.0\mathbf{I}$, which is quite small, meaning that we do not have to explore the areas that are far away from the estimated $\hat{\boldsymbol{\theta}}$. However, when q_0 is arbitrarily large, the variance approaches 0 and there will be no exploration at all. Consequently, `TSNR` becomes `Exploit`. As reported in the tables, the performance of `Ex-`

Table 2: **Relative CTR on KDD Cup 2012 Online Ads Data.**

Algorithm	Cold Start				Warm Start			
	mean	std	min	max	mean	std	min	max
`Bootstrap(1)`	**1.9933**	0.01291	1.9692	2.0098	**1.9990**	0.005678	1.9878	2.0083
`Bootstrap(5)`	1.9883	0.01106	1.9686	2.0012	1.9964	0.004983	1.9848	2.0022
`Bootstrap(10)`	1.9862	0.009128	1.9672	1.9977	1.9890	0.005434	1.9829	2.0003
`Bootstrap(30)`	1.9824*	0.01492	1.9566	2.0088	1.9886*	0.006086	1.9753	1.9954
ϵ`-greedy(0.01)`	**1.9941**	0.007293	1.9834	2.0060	**1.9971**	0.004908	1.9886	2.0038
ϵ`-greedy(0.1)`	1.9089	0.004887	1.8965	1.9145	1.8952	0.002741	1.8910	1.8986
ϵ`-greedy(0.3)`	1.7039	0.003797	1.6990	1.7101	1.6973	0.009368	1.6834	1.7193
ϵ`-greedy(0.5)`	1.5018*	0.004335	1.4965	1.5114	1.4983*	0.006319	1.4845	1.5067
`Exploit`	**1.8185***	0.05235	1.7228	1.8934	**1.9241***	0.007046	1.9152	1.9370
`LinUCB(0.01)`	1.8551	0.03543	1.7977	1.9059	**1.9279**	0.006951	1.9178	1.9371
`LinUCB(0.1)`	**1.9168**	0.005466	1.9070	1.9267	1.9202	0.004434	1.9112	1.9266
`LinUCB(0.3)`	1.8665	0.003644	1.8609	1.8726	1.8610	0.003271	1.8550	1.8661
`LinUCB(0.5)`	1.7808	0.007009	1.7669	1.7913	1.7903	0.0051	1.7823	1.7988
`LinUCB(1.0)`	1.6693*	0.004738	1.6634	1.6762	1.6742*	0.003179	1.6704	1.6792
`TS(0.001)`	1.3587	0.009703	1.3366	1.3736	1.3518	0.01002	1.3297	1.3673
`TS(0.01)`	1.4597	0.007215	1.4504	1.4749	1.4891	0.006421	1.4771	1.4994
`TS(0.1)`	**1.5714**	0.004855	1.5647	1.5791	**1.5905**	0.004176	1.5826	1.5967
`TS(1.0)`	1.5345	0.003435	1.5262	1.5384	1.5421	0.003741	1.5376	1.5480
`TS(10.0)`	0.9388*	0.4236	0.3064	1.5675	1.3174*	0.003157	1.3115	1.3212
`TSNR(0.01)`	1.4856*	0.01466	1.4657	1.5078	1.5700*	0.02163	1.5499	1.6298
`TSNR(0.1)`	1.7931	0.01284	1.7774	1.8167	1.8716	0.01035	1.8518	1.8870
`TSNR(1.0)`	1.9826	0.005853	1.9704	1.9921	1.9952	0.006996	1.9833	2.0047
`TSNR(10.0)`	**2.0118**	0.007808	1.9941	2.0208	2.0095	0.005107	2.0022	2.0198
`TSNR(100.0)`	2.0039	0.008942	1.9912	2.0215	**2.0097**	0.004586	2.0022	2.0187
`TSNR(1000.0)`	2.0047	0.01022	1.9894	2.0228	2.0088	0.004644	1.9966	2.0151

`ploit` is relatively poor compared with `Bootstrap`, ϵ`-greedy` and `LinUCB` in terms of the mean and deviation of the CTR.

The performance of `Bootstrap` is comparable with the ones of ϵ`-greedy` and `TSNR` in terms of the CTR, as it takes a non-Bayesian strategy based on bootstrapping without considering the prior and posterior distributions. The tradeoff between exploration and exploitation is handled in an evolving manner as the data size increases. In addition, when we use different numbers of bootstrap samples, the averaged reward varies very slightly. The reason here is straightforward: the number of bootstrap samples dominates the accuracy of the approximation towards the sampling distribution, rather than the one controlling the balance of the exploration and exploitation.

4.4.1 *On Bootstrap Sample Size*

The sample size of bootstrap determines the approximation accuracy of the bootstrap method. The sample size is larger, the approximation accuracy is higher. Therefore, it is not a parameter for the recommendation model. We argue that once the sample size is large enough, it would not affect the performance much, as it is not a dominant factor to control the exploration/exploitation or the recommendation model. To verify this claim, we set different bootstrap sample sizes from 1 to 500, and report the result in Figure 1. As depicted in this figure, the performance is still relative stable comparing to other algorithms. It is interesting to see that even if $B = 1$, in which the sampled bootstrap replications have some dependence for the same arm, the performance of

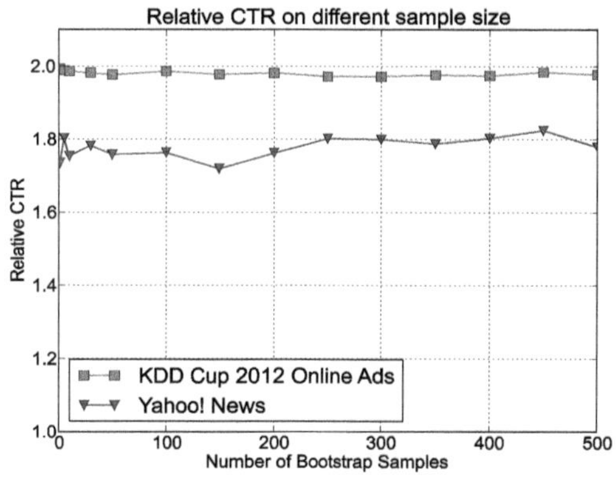

Figure 1: Relative CTR on different bootstrap sample sizes.

`Bootstrap` is not poor. Hence, `Bootstrap` provides a better and safe choice for personalized recommendation when we do not have any prior information about the data, and in this sense, we argue that our proposed method is parameter-free in terms of the exploration/exploitation tradeoff.

We also investigate the scalability of `Bootstrap` (see Figure 2). We focus on the time cost for each model update with online estimation on different bootstrap sample sizes. As presented in Figure 2, the number of bootstrap samples increases from 50 to 500 (10 times), whereas the milliseconds per update increases about 3 times. Hence, a real-

Table 3: Relative CTR on Yahoo! News Data.

Algorithm	Cold Start				Warm Start			
	mean	std	min	max	mean	std	min	max
Bootstrap(1)	1.7350*	0.08327	1.6032	1.9123	1.7029*	0.1392	1.4299	1.8358
Bootstrap(5)	**1.8025**	0.07676	1.6526	1.9127	1.8366	0.07996	1.7118	1.9514
Bootstrap(10)	1.7536	0.07772	1.6338	1.8814	**1.8403**	0.08518	1.6673	1.9296
Bootstrap(30)	1.7818	0.08857	1.6092	1.9025	1.8311	0.08699	1.7230	1.9396
ϵ-greedy(0.01)	**1.7708**	0.09383	1.6374	1.9503	**1.8466**	0.05494	1.7846	1.9755
ϵ-greedy(0.1)	1.7375	0.04992	1.6452	1.8003	1.8132	0.03502	1.7621	1.8721
ϵ-greedy(0.3)	1.5486	0.03703	1.4812	1.5930	1.5976	0.02739	1.5591	1.6491
ϵ-greedy(0.5)	1.3819*	0.02341	1.3489	1.4169	1.3753*	0.02884	1.3173	1.4020
Exploit	**1.1782***	0.2449	0.9253	1.5724	**1.1576***	0.00198	1.1554	1.1607
LinUCB(0.01)	**1.6349**	0.08967	1.4849	1.7360	**1.8103**	0	1.8103	1.8103
LinUCB(0.1)	1.2037	0.02321	1.1682	1.2577	1.2394	0	1.2394	1.2394
LinUCB(0.3)	1.1661	0.01073	1.1552	1.1926	1.1650	1.863e-08	1.1650	1.1650
LinUCB(0.5)	1.1462	0.01215	1.1136	1.1571	1.1752	1.317e-08	1.1752	1.1752
LinUCB(1.0)	1.1361*	0.01896	1.0969	1.1594	1.1594*	1.317e-08	1.1594	1.1594
TS(0.001)	**1.2203**	0.026	1.1842	1.2670	**1.2725**	0.03175	1.2301	1.3422
TS(0.01)	1.1880	0.02895	1.1585	1.2466	1.2377	0.01886	1.2132	1.2713
TS(0.1)	1.1527	0.01988	1.1289	1.1811	1.1791	0.02225	1.1437	1.2169
TS(1.0)	1.1205	0.0142	1.1009	1.1472	1.1362	0.02203	1.0971	1.1599
TS(10.0)	0.7669*	0.1072	0.5445	0.9526	0.8808*	0.01557	0.8483	0.9031
TSNR(0.01)	1.2173*	0.03369	1.1430	1.2561	1.2972*	0.02792	1.2479	1.3394
TSNR(0.1)	1.2285	0.01948	1.1915	1.2610	1.3028	0.02121	1.2701	1.3461
TSNR(1.0)	1.2801	0.02365	1.2558	1.3303	1.3250	0.03148	1.2486	1.3634
TSNR(10.0)	1.6657	0.03285	1.6025	1.7125	1.6153	0.05608	1.5210	1.7128
TSNR(100.0)	**1.7816**	0.07609	1.7093	1.9278	1.8399	0.1134	1.5240	1.9200
TSNR(1000.0)	1.7652	0.09946	1.6123	1.9346	**1.8769**	0.03731	1.8409	1.9656

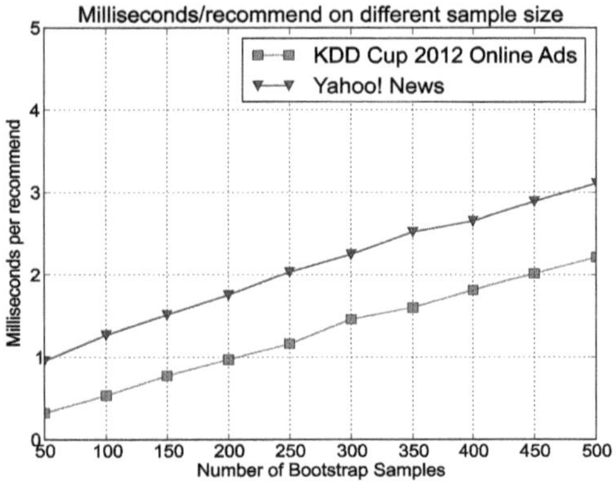

Figure 2: Time cost on different bootstrap sample sizes.

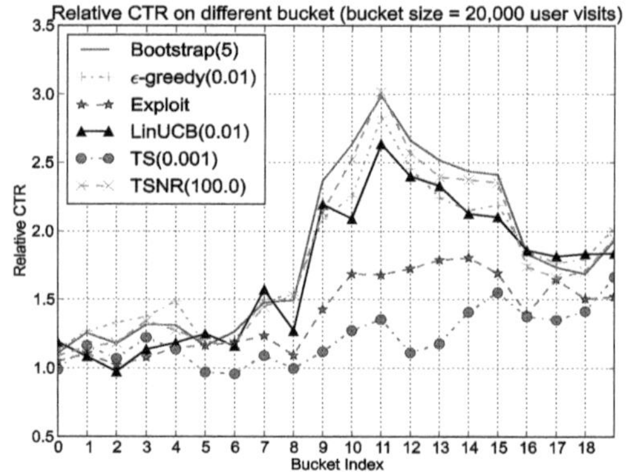

Figure 3: Relative CTR on different time buckets for Yahoo! Today News.

world production server cluster can easily handle more than 1000 bootstrap samples for personalized recommendation services, e.g., online advertising or news recommendation.

4.4.2 On Time Bucket

Besides the overall CTR of each algorithm, we also evaluate the CTR on individual time bucket. The CTR on each bucket is only calculated by the clicks collected in that bucket. The entire testing data is split into 20 time buckets. For Yahoo! Today news data, each bucket has 100,000 user visits. For KDD Cup 2012 online ad data, each bucket has 50,000 user visits. All the user visit events are order by the time. Figures 3 and 4 show the relative CTR on individual buckets. As shown in Figure 3, Bootstrap(5), TSNR(100) and ϵ-greedy are superior to other baselines starting from the 8-th bucket. Also, on different buckets the lift of each algorithm with respect to random is different. The main reason is that the user interests on these news articles may change over time. It is worthy to note that the large lifts of CTR are only in the middle buckets. In the last a few buckets, the lifts become smaller, although the prediction models have more feedback to learn. In other words, when

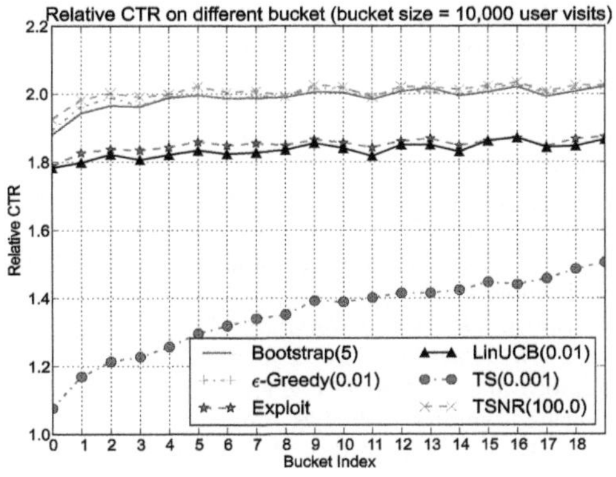

Figure 4: Relative CTR on different time buckets for KDD Cup 2012 Online Ads.

a news article becomes aging, there is no much space for a recommender system to improve its CTR. Therefore, the recommender system should be able to promptly learn the predictive model in an online manner. If it takes a long time to cumulate user feedbacks, user preferences may have changed even if the prediction model can be trained well.

The reward of the KDD Cup 2012 online ads is simulated by the logistic regression function and a fixed weight vector with some random noises. For each ad, the relation between the context and reward is much simpler than the Yahoo! Today news data. Thus, the data is easy to learn by a logistic regression model. The CTR curves in Figure 4 are very stable. `Bootstrap`(5), `TSNR`(100) and ϵ-`greedy` converge very quickly staring from the second bucket. The performance of `TS`(0.001) increases slowly. The prior variance of `TS`(0.001) is $(1/0.001)\mathbf{I} = 1000\mathbf{I}$, which is very large. The sampled coefficients are usually far away from the posterior mean in the early stage. But when it learns more data, the posterior variance becomes smaller and the performance increases gradually.

To summarize, our findings from the experiments are three-fold: (1) For solving the contextual bandit problem, the algorithms of ϵ-`greedy` and `LinUCB` can achieve the optimal performance, but the input parameters that control the exploration need to be tuned carefully; (2) The probability matching strategies, e.g., Thompson sampling, can have the optimal result, but it highly depends on the selection of the prior; and (3) Our proposed approach, `Bootstrap`, is a safe choice of building predictive models for contextual bandit problems under the scenario of *cold-start*.

5. RELATED WORK

Our work is primarily relevant to three active areas of research, namely (1) modeling multi-armed bandit problems, (2) probability matching for contextual bandit problems, and (3) bootstrapping for statistics estimation.

Multi-armed bandit problem: The primary challenge in multi-armed bandit problems is to balance the tradeoff between exploration and exploitation. In practice, for solving a *cold-start* problem, neither a pure exploitation or a pure exploration works best, as there are always uncertainties of user preferences to explore. A wide range of application-oriented problems have been modeled as the context-free multi-armed bandit problem, such as online advertising [25, 30], web search and content optimization [2, 27], network optimization [11], game playing [12], routing [6], etc. A list of computational strategies have been proposed in the past decades, including ϵ-greedy, EXP3 [4], upper confidence bound (UCB) [5, 19], etc. The basic paradigm for solving the context-free bandit problem is to run multiple trials to estimate the reward distribution. However, these solutions are either sub-optimal or require careful settings of the balancing parameters. In our work, we present a parameter-free algorithm to avoid the process of parameter tuning, i.e., without the input parameter to allocate the importance of exploration.

Probability matching for contextual bandit: A more general version of the bandit problem is called contextual bandit, which has not been well studied. Here the contextual information is related to the specific environment of pulling the arms with a learning problem; for example, in online advertising systems, the context might involve a user's query, or the web page on which an ad is placed. Several interesting approaches have been reported by following the ϵ-greedy or UCB [4, 19] paradigms.

Another family of algorithms for solving contextual bandit problems is *probability matching* [32], which pulls different arms according to the probability that the corresponding arm has the largest expected reward. Instead of requiring a controlling parameter for the balance of exploration/exploitation, the strategy of probability matching enables the learning process to automatically adjust the tradeoff [8]. Representative work along this stream involves [8, 14, 22], which follow the Bayesian paradigm to estimate the uncertainties. However in many practical scenarios, an inappropriate prior for Bayesian learning models may lead to imbalanced exploration/exploitation in the early stage of learning, and consequently jeopardize the overall performance. Comparatively in our work, we propose a non-Bayesian algorithm based on the framework of probability matching, which utilizes bootstrapping for coefficient estimation, and does not require the input of priors.

Bootstrapping for statistics estimation: Bootstrapping, in statistics, is a useful technique for estimating some statistical properties of an estimator [10]. This technique resamples the observed data with replacement, and then utilizes the resampled data sets to infer the properties of the estimator. In machine learning, it is often used in the bootstrap aggregation (bagging) to ensemble different learning algorithms. However, the traditional bootstrap method operates in an offline way in which the observations are all already given. In some situations, the observations arrive from a data stream and the bootstrapping must be made in an online manner. To handle the online setting, [23] presents an online paradigm of data resampling using a Poisson distribution. [26] makes use of this method to improve the robustness of the learning model for large data sets. In our work, we employ the idea of online bootstrapping to the scenario of estimating coefficients of contextual bandit models.

6. CONCLUSION

In personalized recommender systems, the dilemma of exploration/exploitation in the cold-start situation remains a challenging issue due to the uncertainty of user preferences. In this paper, we formulate the problem of personalized recommendation as a contextual bandit problem to balance the tradeoff between these two competing goals. We propose a parameter-free strategy for bandit problems, which employs a principled resampling approach called online bootstrap, to derive the sampling distributions of learning model estimators. The proposed algorithm is essentially an ensemble method to achieve optimal rewards without specifying exploration parameters. Extensive empirical experiments on two real-world data sets, i.e., online advertising and news recommendation, demonstrate the efficacy of our proposed approach in terms of averaged rewards.

As for the future work, the recommend items, e.g., advertisements or news articles, may have some underlying relations with each other. For example, two advertisements may belong to the same categories, or come from business competitors, or have other same features. In the future, we plan to consider the potential correlations among different items, or say, arms [24]. It is interesting to model these correlations as constraints, and incorporate them into the contextual bandit modeling process. A second direction to extend our proposed contextual model is to consider the temporal information of user preferences, as the interests of users may often evolve over time.

Acknowledgement

The work is partially supported by NSF grants CNS-1126619, IIS-1213026, and CNS-1461926, DHS grant 2010-ST-062-000039, Purdue VACCINE/DHS 4112-35822, and an FIU Dissertation Year Fellowship.

7. REFERENCES

[1] G. Adomavicius and A. Tuzhilin. Toward the next generation of recommender systems: A survey of the state-of-the-art and possible extensions. *TKDE*, 17(6):734–749, 2005.

[2] D. Agarwal, B.-C. Chen, and P. Elango. Explore/exploit schemes for web content optimization. In *ICDM*, pages 1–10. IEEE, 2009.

[3] D. Agarwal, B.-C. Chen, P. Elango, N. Motgi, S.-T. Park, R. Ramakrishnan, S. Roy, and J. Zachariah. Online models for content optimization. In *NIPS*, pages 17–24, 2008.

[4] P. Auer, N. Cesa-Bianchi, Y. Freund, and R. E. Schapire. The nonstochastic multiarmed bandit problem. *SIAM J. Comput.*, 32(1):48–77, 2002.

[5] P. Auer and N. C.-B. P. Fischer. Finite-time analysis of the multiarmed bandit problem. *Machine learning*, 47(2-3):235–256, 2002.

[6] B. Awerbuch and R. Kleinberg. Online linear optimization and adaptive routing. *Journal of Computer and System Sciences*, 74(1):97–114, 2008.

[7] C. M. Bishop. *Pattern Recognition and Machine Learning (Information Science and Statistics)*. 2006.

[8] O. Chapelle and L. Li. An empirical evaluation of thompson sampling. In *NIPS*, pages 2249–2257, 2011.

[9] T. Chen, Z. Zheng, Q. Lu, W. Zhang, and Y. Yu. Feature-based matrix factorization. *arXiv preprint arXiv:1109.2271*, 2011.

[10] B. Efron and R. J. Tibshirani. *An introduction to the bootstrap*, volume 57. 1994.

[11] Y. Gai, B. Krishnamachari, and R. Jain. Combinatorial network optimization with unknown variables: Multi-armed bandits with linear rewards and individual observations. *TON*, 20(5):1466–1478, 2012.

[12] S. Gelly, Y. Wang, R. Munos, and O. Teytaud. Modification of uct with patterns in monte-carlo go. Technical report, 2006.

[13] T. Graepel, J. Q. Candela, T. Borchert, and R. Herbrich. Web-scale bayesian click-through rate prediction for sponsored search advertising in microsoft's bing search engine. In *ICML*, pages 13–20, 2010.

[14] O.-C. Granmo. Solving two-armed bernoulli bandit problems using a bayesian learning automaton. *International Journal of Intelligent Computing and Cybernetics*, 3(2):207–234, 2010.

[15] R. V. Hogg and E. A. Tanis. *Probability and Statistical Inference*. Prentice Hall, 1996.

[16] D. Hsu, N. Karampatziakis, J. Langford, and A. J. Smola. Parallel online learning. *CoRR*, abs/1103.4204, 2011.

[17] D. E. Knuth. *The Art of Computer Programming, Volume 2 (3rd Ed.): Seminumerical Algorithms*. 1997.

[18] J. Langford and T. Zhang. The epoch-greedy algorithm for multi-armed bandits with side information. In *NIPS*, 2007.

[19] L. Li, W. Chu, J. Langford, and R. E. Schapire. A contextual-bandit approach to personalized news article recommendation. In *WWW*, pages 661–670. ACM, 2010.

[20] L. Li, W. Chu, J. Langford, and X. Wang. Unbiased offline evaluation of contextual-bandit-based news article recommendation algorithms. In *WSDM*, pages 297–306, 2011.

[21] B. C. May, N. Korda, A. Lee, and D. S. Leslie. Optimistic bayesian sampling in contextual-bandit problems. *Journal of Machine Learning Research*, 13:2069–2106, 2012.

[22] B. C. May, N. Korda, A. Lee, and D. S. Leslie. Optimistic bayesian sampling in contextual-bandit problems. *The Journal of Machine Learning Research*, 13(1):2069–2106, 2012.

[23] N. C. Oza and S. Russell. Online bagging and boosting. In *IEEE international conference on Systems, man and cybernetics*, volume 3, pages 2340–2345, 2005.

[24] S. Pandey, D. Chakrabarti, and D. Agarwal. Multi-armed bandit problems with dependent arms. In *ICML*, pages 721–728, 2007.

[25] S. Pandey and C. Olston. Handling advertisements of unknown quality in search advertising. In *NIPS*, pages 1065–1072, 2006.

[26] Z. Qin, V. Petricek, N. Karampatziakis, L. Li, and J. Langford. Efficient online bootstrapping for large scale learning. *arXiv preprint arXiv:1312.5021*, 2013.

[27] F. Radlinski, R. Kleinberg, and T. Joachims. Learning diverse rankings with multi-armed bandits. In *ICML*, pages 784–791. ACM, 2008.

[28] A. I. Schein, A. Popescul, L. H. Ungar, and D. M. Pennock. Methods and metrics for cold-start recommendations. In *SIGIR*, pages 253–260. ACM, 2002.

[29] S. L. Scott. A modern bayesian look at the multi-armed bandit. *Applied Stochastic Models in Business and Industry*, 26(6):639–658, 2010.

[30] A. Slivkins. Multi-armed bandits on implicit metric spaces. In *NIPS*, pages 1602–1610, 2011.

[31] L. Tang, R. Rosales, A. Singh, and D. Agarwal. Automatic ad format selection via contextual bandits. In *CIKM*, pages 1587–1594, 2013.

[32] W. R. Thompson. On the likelihood that one unknown probability exceeds another in view of the evidence of two samples. *Biometrika*, 25(3/4):285–294, 1933.

[33] L. Tierney and J. B. Kadane. Accurate approximations for posterior moments and marginal densities. *Journal of the American Statistical Association*, 81(393):82–86, 1986.

[34] M. Tokic. Adaptive ε-greedy exploration in reinforcement learning based on value differences. In *KI 2010: Advances in Artificial Intelligence*, pages 203–210. 2010.

[35] J. Vermorel and M. Mohri. Multi-armed bandit algorithms and empirical evaluation. In *ECML*, pages 437–448. 2005.

[36] X. Zhao, W. Zhang, and J. Wang. Interactive collaborative filtering. In *ACM CIKM*, pages 1411–1420, 2013.

Efficient and Scalable MetaFeature-based Document Classification using Massively Parallel Computing

Sérgio Canuto, and Marcos André Gonçalves
Dept. of Computer Science, Federal University of Minas Gerais
Belo Horizonte, Brazil
sergiodaniel@dcc.ufmg.br, mgoncalv@dcc.ufmg.br

Wisllay Santos, Thierson Rosa, and Wellington Martins
Instituto de Informática, Universidade Federal de Goiás
Goiânia, Brazil
wisllaysantos@inf.ufg.br, thierson@inf.ufg.br, wellington@inf.ufg.br

ABSTRACT

The unprecedented growth of available data nowadays has stimulated the development of new methods for organizing and extracting useful knowledge from this immense amount of data. Automatic Document Classification (ADC) is one of such methods, that uses machine learning techniques to build models capable of automatically associating documents to well-defined semantic classes. ADC is the basis of many important applications such as language identification, sentiment analysis, recommender systems, spam filtering, among others. Recently, the use of meta-features has been shown to substantially improve the effectiveness of ADC algorithms. In particular, the use of meta-features that make a combined use of local information (through kNN-based features) and global information (through category centroids) has produced promising results. However, the generation of these meta-features is very costly in terms of both, memory consumption and runtime since there is the need to constantly call the kNN algorithm. We take advantage of the current manycore GPU architecture and present a massively parallel version of the kNN algorithm for highly dimensional and sparse datasets (which is the case for ADC). Our experimental results show that we can obtain speedup gains of up to 15x while reducing memory consumption in more than 5000x when compared to a state-of-the-art parallel baseline. This opens up the possibility of applying meta-features based classification in large collections of documents, that would otherwise take too much time or require the use of an expensive computational platform.

Keywords

Document Classification; Meta-features; Parallelism

1. INTRODUCTION

SIGIR '15 August 09 - 13, 2015, Santiago, Chile

DOI: http://dx.doi.org/10.1145/2766462.2767743.

The processing of large amounts of data efficiently is critical for Information Retrieval (IR) and, as this amount of data grows, storing, indexing and searching costs rise up altogether with penalties in response time. Parallel computing may represent an efficient solution for enhancing modern IR systems but the requirements of designing new parallel algorithms for modern platforms such as manycore Graphical Processing Units (GPUs) have hampered the exploitation of this opportunity by the IR community.

In particular, similarity search is at the heart of many IR systems. It scores queries against documents, presenting the highest scoring documents to the user in ranked order. The kNN algorithm is commonly used for this function, retrieving the most similar k documents for each query. Another very common application domain for kNN is Automatic Document Classification (ADC). In this case, the kNN algorithm is used to automatically map (classify) a new document d to a set of predefined classes given a set of labeled (training) documents, based on the similarities between d and each of the training docoments. kNN has been shown to produce competitive results in several datasets [17]. The speedup of this type of algorithm, using some efficient parallel strategies, mainly in applications in which it is repetitively applied as the core of other applications, opens huge opportunities.

One recent application which uses kNN intensively is the generation of *meta-level features* (or simply *meta-features*) for ADC [24]. Such meta-features capture local and global information about the likelihood of a document to belong to a class, which can then be exploited by a different classifier (e.g. SVM). More specifically, meta-features capture: (i) the similarity value between a test example and the nearest neighbor in each considered class, and (2) the similarity value of the test example with the classes' centroids [1]. As shown in [24] and in our experiments, the use of meta-features can substantially improve the effectiveness of ADC algorithms.

However, the generation of meta-features is very costly in terms of both, memory consumption and runtime. In order to generate them, there is the need to constantly call the kNN algorithm. kNN, however, is known to produce poor performance (execution time) in classification tasks in comparison to other (non-lazy) supervised methods, normally being not the best choice to deal with on-the-fly classifica-

[1]Notice that this also has to be applied to all training documents in an offline procedure.

tions. Classification using kNN-based meta-features inherits this poor performance, since we need to generate meta-level features for both, all training, and each new test sample before actual classification. For textual datasets (with large vocabularies), the performance problem is hardened, since the kNN algorithm will have to run on high dimensional data. In this scenario, kNN often requires large portions of memory to represent all the training data and intensive computation to calculate the similarity between points. In fact, as we shall see the generation of meta-features is not feasible using previous meta-feature generators [7, 24] for the larger datasets we experimented with.

In this paper we present a new GPU-based implementation of kNN specially designed for high-dimensional and sparse datasets (which is the case for ADC), allowing a very fast and much more scalable meta-feature generation which allows one to apply this technique in large collections much faster. Some of the most interesting characteristics of our approach, compared to other state-of-the-art GPU-based proposals, include:

- most solutions use a brute-force approach (i.e., compare the query document to all training documents) which demands too much memory while we exploit inverted indexes along with an efficient implementation to cope with GPU memory limitations;
- in order to scale, some solutions sacrifice effectiveness using an approximated kNN solution (e.g. locality-sensitive hashing - LSH) while our proposal is an exact kNN solution which exploits state-of-the-art GPU sorting methods;
- most proposals achieve good results only when considering many queries (i.e., multiple document classification) in order to produce good speedups while our solution obtains improvements even when dealing with a single query (document); we achieve this by an effective load balacing approach within the GPU;
- some solutions require a multi-GPU approach to deal with large datasets while ours deals with large datasets using a single GPU.

Our experimental results show that we can obtain speedup gains of up to $140x$ and $15x$ while reducing memory consumption in more than $8000x$ and $5000x$ when compared to a standard sequential implementation and to a state-of-the-art parallel baseline, respectively.

This paper is organized as follows. Section 2 covers related work. Section 3 introduces the use of meta-feature in ADC. Section 4 provides a brief introduction to parallelism in GPU. Section 5 describes our GPU-based implementation, specially designed for highly dimensional, sparse data. Section 6 presents an analysis of the complexity of the proposed solution. Section 7 presents our experimental evaluation while Section 8 concludes the paper.

2. RELATED WORK

Several meta-features have been proposed to improve the effectiveness of machine learning methods. They can be based on ensemble of classifiers [3, 22], derived from clustering methods [11, 16] or from the instance-based kNN method [7, 24].

Meta-features derived from ensembles exploit the probability distribution over all classes generated by each of the individual classifiers composing the ensemble [22]. In [3] other ensemble-based meta-features were also used, including: the entropies of the class probability distributions and the maximum probability returned by each classifier. This scheme was found to perform better than using only probability distributions.

Clustering techniques may also be used to derive meta-features. In this case, the feature space is augmented using clusters derived from a previous clustering step considering both the labeled and unlabeled data [16, 11]. The idea is that clusters represent higher level "concepts" in the feature space, and the features derived from the clusters indicate the similarity of each example to these concepts. In [16] the largest n clusters are chosen as representatives of the major concepts. Each cluster c contributes with a set o meta-features like, for instance, binary feature indicating if c is the closest of the n clusters to the example, the similarity of the example to the cluster's centroid, among others. In [11] the number of clusters is chosen to be equal to the predefined number of classes and each cluster corresponds to an additional meta-feature.

Recently, [7] reported good results by designing meta-features that make a combined use of local information (through kNN-based features) and global information (through category centroids) in the training set. Despite the fact that these meta-features are not created based on an ensemble of classifiers, they differ from the previously presented meta-features derived from clusters because they explicitly capture information from the labeled set.

Although the kNN algorithm can be applied broadly, it has some shortcomings. For large datasets (n) and high dimensional space (d), its complexity $\mathcal{O}(nd)$ can easily become prohibitive. Moreover, if m successive queries are to be performed, the complexity further increases to $\mathcal{O}(mnd)$. Recently, some proposals have been presented to accelerate the kNN algorithm via a highly mutithreaded GPU-based approach. The first, and most cited, GPU-based kNN implementation was proposed by Garcia et al. [5]. They used the brute force approach and reported speedups of up to two orders of magnitude when compared to a brute force CPU-based implementation. Their implementation assumes that multiple queries are performed and computes and stores a complete distance matrix, what makes it impracticable for large data (over 65,536 documents).

Following Garcia's et al. work, Kuang and Zhao [10] implemented their own optimized matrix operations for calculating the distances, and used radix sort to find the top-k elements. Liang et al. [14] took advantage of CUDA Streams to overlap computation and communication (CPU/GPU) when dealing with several queries, and thus decrease the GPU memory requirements. The distances were computed in blocks and later merged first locally and then globally to find the top-k elements. However, such works can still be considered brute-force. Sismanis et al. [20] concentrated on the sorting phase of the brute-force kNN and provided an extensive comparison among parallel truncated sorts. They conclude that the truncated biotonic sort (TBiS) produces the best results.

Our proposal differs from the above mentioned work in many aspects. First, it exploits a very efficient GPU implementation of inverted indexes which supports an exact kNN solution without relying in brute-force. This also allows our solution to save a lot of memory space since the inverted index corresponds to a sparse representation of the data. In the distance calculation step, we resort to a smart load balancing among threads to increase the parallelism. And in the sorting step, we exploit a GPU-based sorting procedure, which was shown to be superior to other partial sorting algorithms[20], in combination with a CPU merge operation based on a priority queue.

3. USE OF META-FEATURES FOR ADC

In here, we formally introduce the meta-features whose kNN-based calculation we intend to speed up and scale with our proposed massively parallel approach.

Let $\mathcal{X}$ and $\mathcal{C}$ denote the input (feature) and output (class) spaces, respectively. Let $\mathbb{D}_{train} = \{(x_i, c_i) \in \mathcal{X} \times \mathcal{C}\}|_{i=1}^{n}$ be the training set. Recall that the main goal of supervised classification is to learn a mapping function $h : \mathcal{X} \mapsto \mathcal{C}$ which is general enough to accurately classify examples $x' \notin \mathbb{D}_{train}$.

The kNN-based meta-level features proposed in [7], are designed to replace the original input space $\mathcal{X}$ with a new informative and compact input space $\mathcal{M}$. Therefore, each vector of meta-features $m_f \in \mathcal{M}$ is expressed as the concatenation of the sub-vectors below, which are defined for each example $x_f \in \mathcal{X}$ and category $c_j \in \mathcal{C}$ for $j = 1, 2, \ldots, |\mathcal{C}|$ as:

- $\vec{v}_{\vec{x}_f}^{cos} = [\cos(\vec{x}_{ij}, \vec{x_f})]$: A k-dimensional vector produced by considering the k nearest neighbors of class c_j to the target vector x_f, i.e., , $\vec{x}_{ij}$ is the ith $(i \leq k)$ nearest neighbor to $\vec{x}_f$, and $\cos(\vec{x}_{ij}, \vec{x_f})$ is the cosine similarity between them. Thus, k meta-features are generated to represent x_f.
- $\vec{v}_{\vec{x}_f}^{L_1} = [d_1(\vec{x}_{ij}, \vec{x_f})]$: A k-dimensional vector whose elements $d_1(\vec{x}_{ij}, \vec{x}_f)$ denote the L_1 distance between $\vec{x}_f$ and the ith nearest class c_j neighbor of $\vec{x}_f$ (i.e., $d_1(\vec{x}_{ij}, \vec{x}_f) = ||\vec{x}_{ij} - \vec{x}_f||_1$).
- $\vec{v}_{\vec{x_f}}^{L_2} = [d_2(\vec{x}_{ij}, \vec{x_f})]$: A k-dimensional vector whose elements $d_2(\vec{x}_{ij}, \vec{x_f})$ denote the L_2 distance between $\vec{x}_f$ and the ith nearest class c_j neighbor of $\vec{x_f}$ (i.e., $d_2(\vec{x}_{ij}, \vec{x_f}) = ||\vec{x}_{ij} - \vec{x_f}||_2$).
- $\vec{v}_{\vec{x_f}}^{cent} = [d_2(\vec{x}_j, \vec{x_f}), cos(\vec{x}_j, \vec{x_f})]$: A 2-dimensional vector where $\vec{x}_j$ is the c_j centroid (i.e., vector average of all training examples of the class c_j).

Considering k neighbors, the number of features in vector x_f is $(3k + 2)$ per category, and the total of $(3k + 2)|\mathcal{C}|$ for all categories. The size of this meta-level feature set is much smaller than that typically found in ADC tasks, while explicitly capturing class discriminative information from the labeled set.

4. PARALLELISM AND THE GPU

In the last few years, the focus on processor architectures has moved from increasing clock rate to increasing parallelism. Rather than increasing the speed of its individual processor cores, traditional CPUs are now virtually all multicore processors. In a similar fashion, manycore architectures like GPUs have concentrated on using simpler and slower cores, but in much larger counts, in the order of thousands of cores. The general perception is that processors are not getting faster, but instead are getting wider, with an ever increasing number of cores. This has forced a renewed interest in parallelism as the only way to increase performance.

The high computational power and affordability of GPUs has led to a growing number of researchers making use of GPUs to handle massive amounts of data. While multicore CPUs are optimized for single-threaded performance, GPUs are optimized for throughput and a massive multi-threaded parallelism. As a result, the GPUs deliver much better energy efficiency and achieves higher peak performance for throughput workloads. However, GPUs have a different architecture and memory organization and to fully exploit its capabilities it is necessary considerable parallelism (tens of thousands of threads) and an adequate use of its hardware resources. This imposes some constraints in terms of designing appropriate algorithms, requiring the design of novel solutions and new implementation approaches. However, a few research groups and companies have faced this challenge with promising results in Database Scalability, Document Clustering, Learning to Rank, Big Data Analytics and Interactive Visualization [1, 21, 19, 15, 8].

The GPU consists of a M-SIMD machine, that is, a Multiple SIMD (Single Instruction Multiple Data) processor. Each SIMD unit is known as a streaming multiprocessor (SM) and contains streaming processor (SP) cores. At any given clock cycle, each SP executes the same instruction, but operates on different data. The GPU supports thousands of light-weight concurrent threads and, unlike the CPU threads, the overhead of creation and switching is negligible. The threads on each SM are organized into thread groups that share computation resources such as registers. A thread group is divided into multiple schedule units, called warps, that are dynamically scheduled on the SM. Because of the SIMD nature of the SP's execution units, if threads in a schedule unit must perform different operations, such as going through branches, these operations will be executed serially as opposed to in parallel. Additionally, if a thread stalls on a memory operation, the entire warp will be stalled until the memory access is done. In this case the SM selects another ready warp and switches to that one. The GPU global memory is typically measured in gigabytes of capacity. It is an off-chip memory and has both a high bandwidth and a high access latency. To hide the high latency of this memory, it is important to have more threads than the number of SPs and to have threads in a warp accessing consecutive memory addresses that can be easily coalesced. The GPU also provides a fast on-chip shared memory which is accessible by all SPs of a SM. The size of this memory is small but it has a low latency and it can be used as a software-controlled cache. Moving data from the CPU to the GPU and vice versa is done through a PCIExpress connection.

The GPU programming model requires that part of the application runs on the CPU while the computationally-intensive part is accelerated by the GPU. The programmer has to modify his application to take the compute-intensive kernels and map them to the GPU. A GPU program exposes parallelism through a data-parallel SPMD (Single Program Multiple Data) kernel function. During implementation, the programmer can configure the number of threads to be used. Threads execute data parallel computations of the kernel and are organized in groups called thread blocks, which in turn are organized into a grid structure. When a kernel is launched, the blocks within a grid are distributed on idle

SMs. Threads of a block are divided into warps, the schedule unit used by the SMs, leaving for the GPU to decide in which order and when to execute each warp. Threads that belong to different blocks cannot communicate explicitly and have to rely on the global memory to share their results. Threads within a thread block are executed by the SPs of a single SM and can communicate through the SM shared memory. Furthermore, each thread inside a block has its own registers and private local memory and uses a global thread block index, and a local thread index within a thread block, to uniquely identify its data.

5. GPU-BASED GENERATION OF META-FEATURES

The proposed parallel implementation, called GPU-based Textual kNN (GT-kNN), greatly improves the k nearest neighbors search in textual datasets. The solution efficiently implements an inverted index in the GPU, by using a parallel counting operation followed by a parallel prefix-sum calculation, taking advantage of Zipf's law, which states that in a textual corpus, few terms are common, while many of them are rare. This makes the inverted index a good choice for saving space and avoiding unnecessary calculations. At query time, this inverted index is used to quickly find the documents sharing terms with the query document. This is made by constructing a query index which is used for a load balancing strategy to evenly distribute the distance calculations among the GPU's threads. Finally, the k nearest neighbors are determined through the use of a truncated bitonic sort to avoid sorting all computed distances. Next we present a detailed description of these steps.

5.1 Creating the Inverted Index

The inverted index is created in the GPU memory, assuming the training dataset fits in memory and is static. Let $\mathcal{V}$ be the vocabulary of the training dataset, that is the set of distinct terms of the training set. The input data is the set $\mathcal{E}$ of distinct term-documents (t, d), pairs occurring in the original training dataset, with $t \in \mathcal{V}$ and $d \in \mathbb{D}_{train}$. Each pair $(t, d) \in \mathcal{E}$ is initially associated with a term frequency tf, which is the number of times the term t occurs in the document d. An array of size $|\mathcal{E}|$ is used to store the inverted index. Once the set $\mathcal{E}$ has been moved to the GPU memory, each pair in it is examined in parallel, so that each time a term is visited the number of documents where it appears (document frequency - *df*) is incremented and stored in the array *df* of size $|\mathcal{V}|$. A parallel prefix-sum is executed, using the CUDPP library [18], on the *df* array by mapping each element to the sum of all terms before it and storing the results in the *index* array. Thus, each element of the *index* array points to the position of the corresponding first element in the *invertedIndex*, where all (t, d) pairs will be stored ordered by term. Finally, the pairs (t, d) are processed in parallel and the *frequency-inverse document frequency* $tf\text{-}idf(t, d)$ for each pair is computed and included together with the documents identification in the *invertedIndex* array, using the pointers provided by the *index* array. Also during this parallel processing, the value of the norm for each training document, which is used in the calculus of the cosine or Euclidean distance, is computed and stored in the *norms* array. Algorithm 1 depicts the inverted index creation process.

Figure 1 illustrates each step of the inverted index creation

Algorithm 1: *CreateInvetedIndex(E)*

input : term-document pairs in $E[0..|\mathcal{E}|-1]$.
output: *df*, *index*, *norms*, *invertedIndex*.

array of integers $df[0..|\mathcal{V}|-1]$ // document-frequency array, initialized with zeros.
array of integers $index[0..|\mathcal{V}|-1]$.
array of floats $norms[0..|\mathbb{D}_{train}-1|]$.
$invertedIndex[0..|\mathcal{E}|-1]$ // the inverted index
Count the occurrences of each term in parallel on the input and accumulates in *df*.
Perform an exclusive parallel prefix sum on *df* and stores the result in *index*.
Access in parallel the pairs in E, with each processor performing the following tasks:
begin
  Compute the tf-idf value of each pair.
  Accumulate the square of the tf-idf value of a pair (t, d) in $norms[d]$.
  Store in *invertedIndex* the entries corresponding to pairs in E, according to *index*.
end
Compute in parallel the square root of the values in array *norms*.
Return the arrays: *count*, *index*, *norms* and *invertedIndex*.

for a five documents collection where only five terms are used. If we take t_2 as an example, the index array indicates that its inverted document list (d_2, d_4) starts at position 3 of the *invertedindex* array and finishes at position 4 (5 minus 1).

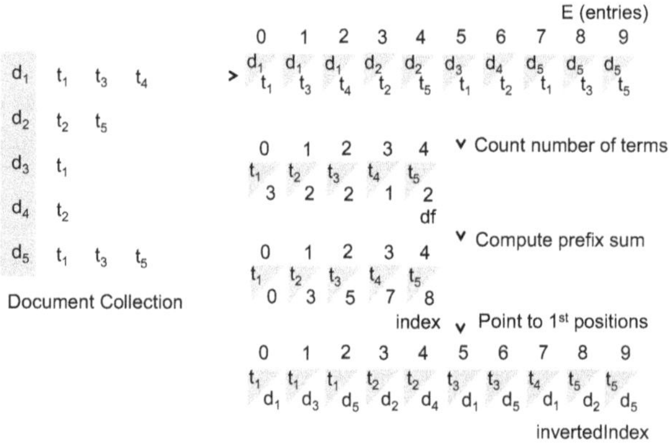

Figure 1: *Creating the inverted index*

5.2 Calculating the distances

Once the inverted index has been created, it is now possible to calculate the distances between a given query document q and the documents in $\mathbb{D}_{train}$. The distances computation can take advantage of the inverted index model, because only the distances between query q and those documents in $\mathbb{D}_{train}$ that have terms in common with q have to be computed. These documents correspond to the elements of the *invertedIndex* pointed to by the entries of the *index* array corresponding to the terms occurring in the query q.

The obvious solution to compute the distances is to distribute the terms of query q evenly among the processors and let each processor p access the inverted lists corresponding to terms allocated to it. However, the distribution of terms in documents of text collections is known to follow approximately the Zipf Law. This means that few terms occur in large amount of documents and most of terms occur in only few documents. Consequently, the sizes of the inverted list also vary according to te Zipf Law, thus distributing the work load according to the terms of q could cause a great imbalance of the work among the processors.

In this paper besides using an inverted index to boost the computation of the distances, we also propose a load balance method to distribute the documents evenly among the processors so that each processor computes approximately the same number of distances. In order to facilitate the explanation of this method, suppose that we concatenate all the inverted lists corresponding to terms in q in a logical vector $E_q = [0..|E_q|-1]$, where $|E_q|$ is the sum of the sizes of all inverted lists of terms in q. Considering the example in Fig. 1 and supposing that q is composed by the terms t_1, t_3 and t_4, the logical vector E_q would be formed by the following pairs of the inverted index: $E_q = [(t_1, d_1), (t_1, d_3), (t_1, d_5), (t_3, d_1), (t_3, d_5), (t_4, d_1)]$ and $|E_q|$ equals to six.

Given a set of processors $\mathcal{P} = \{p_0, \cdots p_{|\mathcal{P}|-1}\}$, the load balance method should allocate elements of E_q in intervals of approximately the same size, that is, each processor $p_i \in \mathcal{P}$ should process elements of E_q in the interval $[i\lceil\frac{|E_q|}{|\mathcal{P}|}\rceil, min((i+1)\lceil\frac{|E_q|}{|\mathcal{P}|}\rceil - 1, |E_q|-1)]$. Consider de example stated above, and suppose that the set of processors is $\mathcal{P} = \{p_0, p_1, p_2\}$. Thus elements of E_q with indices in the interval $[0, 1]$ would be assigned to p_0, indices in $[2, 3]$ would be processed by p_1 and indices in $[4, 5]$ would be processed by p_2.

Since each processor knows the interval of the indices of the logical vector E_q it has to process, all that is necessary to execute the load balancing is a mapping of the logical indices of E_q to the appropriate indices in the inverted index (array *invertedIndex*). In the case of the example associated to Fig. 1, the following mappings between logical indices and indices of the invertedIndex array must be performed: $0 \to 0$, $1 \to 1$, $2 \to 2$, $3 \to 5$, $4 \to 6$ and $5 \to 7$. Each processor executes the mapping for the indices in the interval corresponding to it and finds the corresponding elements in the invertedIndex array for which it has to compute the distances to the query.

Let $\mathcal{V}_q \subset \mathcal{V}$ be the vocabulary of the query document d. The mapping proposed in this paper uses three auxiliary arrays: $df_q[0..|\mathcal{V}_q|-1]$, $start_q[0..|\mathcal{V}_q|-1]]$ and $index_q[0..|\mathcal{V}_q|-1]$. The arrays df_q and $start_q$ are obtained together by copying in parallel $df[t_i]$ to $df_q[t_i]$ and $index[t_i]$ to $start_q[t_i]$, respectively, for each term t_i in the query q. Once the df_q is obtained, an inclusive parallel prefix sum on df_q is performed and the results are stored in $index_q$.

Algorithm 2 shows the pseudo-code for the parallel computation of the distances between documents in the training set and the query document. In lines 4-7 the arrays df_q and $start_q$ are obtained. In line 8 the array $index_q$ is obtained by applying a parallel prefix sum on array df_q. Next, each processor executes a mapping of each position x in the interval of indices of E_q associated to it to the appropriate position of the invertedIndex. This mapping is described in lines 10-17 of the algorithm. Then, the mapped entries of the inverted index are used to compute the distances between each document associated with these entries and the query.

Figure 2 illustrates each step of Algorithm 2 for a query containing three terms, t_1, t_3 and t_4, using the same collection presented in the example of Figure 1. Initially, the arrays df_q and $start_q$ are obtained by copying in parallel entries respectively from arrays *df* and *index*, corresponding to the three query terms. Next a parallel prefix sum is applied to array df_q and the $index_q$ array is obtained. Finally the Figure shows the mapping of each position of the logical array E_q into the corresponding positions of the invertedIndex array.

Algorithm 2: *DistanceCalculation(invertedIndex, q)*

```
input : invertedIndex, df, index, query q[0..|V_q|-1].
output: distance array dist[0..|D_train|-1] initialized
        according to the distance function used.
1  array of integers df_q[0..|V_q|-1] initialized with zeros
2  array of integers index_q[0..|V_q|-1]
3  array of integers start_q[0..|V_q|-1]
4  for each term t_i ∈ q, in parallel do
5      df_q[i] = df[t_i];
6      start_q[i] = index[t_i];
7  end
8  Perform an inclusive parallel prefix sum on df_q and stores
   the results in index_q
9  foreach processor p_i ∈ P do
10     for x ∈ [i⌈|E_q|/|P|⌉, min((i+1)⌈|E_q|/|P|⌉ - 1, |E_q|-1)] do
           // Map position x to the correct position
              indInvPos of the invertedIndex
11         pos = min(i : index_q[i] > x);
12         if pos = 0 then
13             p = 0; offset = x;
14         else
15             p = index_q[pos - 1]; offset = x - p;
16         end
17         indInvPos = start_q[pos] + offset
18         uses q[pos] and invertedIndex[indInvPos] in the
           partial computation of the distance between q and
           the document associated to
           invertedIndex[indInvPos]
19     end
20 end
```

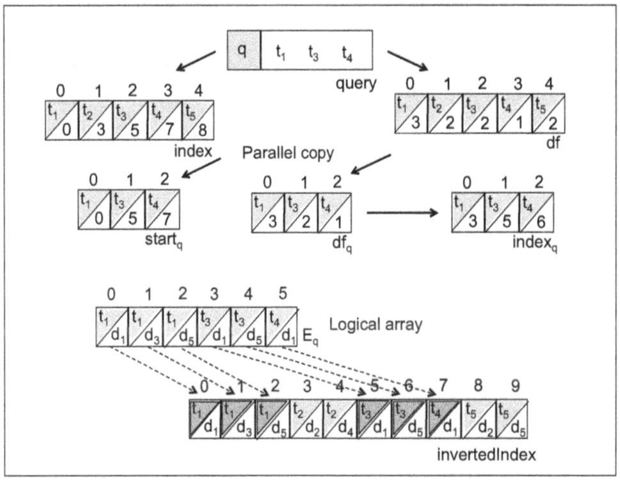

Figure 2: *Example of the execution of Algorithm 2 for a query with three terms.*

5.3 Finding the k Nearest Neighbors

With the distances computed, it is necessary to obtain the k closest documents. This can be accomplished by making use of a partial sorting algorithm on the array containing the distances, which is of size $|\mathbb{D}_{train}|$. For this, we implemented a parallel version of the Truncated Bitonic Sort (TBiS), which was shown to be superior to other partial sorting algorithms in this context [20]. One advantage of the parallel TBiS is data independence. At each step, the algorithm distributes elements equally among the GPU's threads avoiding synchronizations as well as memory access conflicts. Although the partial bitonic sort is $O(|\mathbb{D}_{train}| \log^2 k)$, worse than the best known algorithm which is $O(|\mathbb{D}_{train}| \log k)$, for a small k the ratio of $\log k$ becomes almost negligible. In the case of ADC using kNN, the value of k is usually not greater than 50. Our parallel TBiS implementation also uses a reduction strategy, allowing each GPU block to act independently from each other on a partition of array containing the computed distances. Results are then merged in the CPU using a priority queue.

6. ANALYSIS OF THE SOLUTION

In this section we analyze the amount of time and memory used to construct the index and to compute the k nearest neighbors for a given query document q. The first step of the construction of the inverted index is to obtain the *df* array (line 5 of the Algorithm 1). During this step, the set of input pairs E is read in parallel by all processors in $\mathcal{P}$ and for each term the corresponding document counter is incremented. This takes time $\mathcal{O}(\frac{|E|}{|\mathcal{P}|})$. The parallel prefix sum algorithm applied to array *df* to obtain the *index* takes time $\mathcal{O}(\frac{|\mathcal{V}|}{|\mathcal{P}|}\log|\mathcal{V}|)$ [18]. Next, the computation of *tf-idf*, the computation of accumulated square of *tf-idf* (to compose the norms of the documents), and the insertion of pairs in the invertedIndex (lines 9-11) are done by accessing elements of E in parallel, thus taking time $\mathcal{O}(\frac{|E|}{|\mathcal{P}|})$. Finally the square roots of the norms are computed in time $\mathcal{O}(\frac{|\mathbb{D}_{train}|}{|\mathcal{P}|})$. The total time of the index construction is $\mathcal{O}(\frac{|E|}{|\mathcal{P}|})+\mathcal{O}(\frac{|\mathcal{V}|}{|\mathcal{P}|}\log|\mathcal{V}|)+\mathcal{O}(\frac{|E|}{|\mathcal{P}|})+\mathcal{O}(\frac{|\mathbb{D}_{train}|}{|\mathcal{P}|})$. Since in real text collections $|E| > |\mathbb{D}_{train}| > |\mathcal{V}|$, we conclude that the time complexity of the index construction is $\mathcal{O}(\frac{|E|}{|\mathcal{P}|})$.

The computation of the distances between each training document and the query document q starts by obtaining the arrays df_q and $start_q$ (lines 4-7 of Algorithm 2). This step is executed in parallel by all processors in $\mathcal{P}$. Thus the two arrays are computed in time $\mathcal{O}(\frac{|\mathcal{V}_q|}{|\mathcal{P}|})$. The computation of array $index_q$ is the result of the use of the parallel prefix sum on array df_q, thus it is done in time $\mathcal{O}(\frac{|\mathcal{V}_q|}{|\mathcal{P}|}\log|\mathcal{V}_q|)$.

Each processor $p_i \in \mathcal{P}$ executes the mapping of $\frac{|E_q|}{|\mathcal{P}|}$ positions of the logical array E_q. It is possible to estimate the value of $|E_q|$ in terms of the sizes of $\mathcal{V}$ and $\mathcal{V}_q$. Remember that the logical array E_q represents the concatenation of all inverted lists of terms in the query document q, that is, $|\mathcal{V}_q|$ inverted lists. Considering that the training collection follows the Zipf Law, we have that the probability of the occurrence of a term t with rank k is given by $\frac{k^{-s}}{\sum_{i=1}^{|\mathcal{V}|}\frac{1}{i^s}}$, where s is the value of the exponent characterizing the distribution. The term with greatest probability is the term with rank 1. Thus the expected document frequency of this term is given by $\frac{|E|}{\sum_{i=1}^{|\mathcal{V}|}\frac{1}{i^s}}$. If we use the classic version of Zipf's law, the exponent s is 1, then the document frequency of this term is $\frac{|E|}{\sum_{i=1}^{|\mathcal{V}|}\frac{1}{i}} \approx \frac{|E|}{\ln|\mathcal{V}|}$. This value represents an upper bound for lengths of the document frequency of each term in q. Thus, in the worst case, we have that $|E_q| \approx |\mathcal{V}_q|\frac{|E|}{\ln|\mathcal{V}|}$. According to Heaps Law, the size of vocabulary is $|\mathcal{V}| = k|W|^\beta$, where k is a constant, usually in the range 10-100, W is the set formed by all occurrences of all terms in the collection, and β is another constant in the range 0.4-0.6. The size of W can be taken as an upper bound for the size of the input pairs E. Thus $|E_q| = \mathcal{O}(|\mathcal{V}_q|\frac{|W|}{\log_\beta(k|W|^\beta)}) = \mathcal{O}(|\mathcal{V}_q|\frac{|W|}{|W|\beta\log_\beta k}) = \mathcal{O}(|\mathcal{V}_q|)$. We conclude that and each processor p_i executes the mapping of $\mathcal{O}(\frac{|\mathcal{V}_q|}{|\mathcal{P}|})$ positions.

Now we analyze the time to compute the mapping of a single position (lines 11-17 of Algorithm 2). The computing of variable *pos* in line 11 can be performed in time $\mathcal{O}(\log|\mathcal{V}_q|)$ because values in array df_q are disposed in ascending order and a binary search can be used to find the minimum index required. All the remaining operations (lines 12-18) are computed in constant time ($\mathcal{O}(1)$). The processing of each mapped pair of the inverted index, as part of the computation of the distance between q and the corresponding document in the pair, is also done in constant time. Thus, the execution time of one iteration of inner loop (lines 10-18) is $\mathcal{O}(\log|\mathcal{V}_q|)+\mathcal{O}(1) = \mathcal{O}(\log|\mathcal{V}_q|)$. Finally the partial sort of the distances is computed in time $\mathcal{O}(|\mathbb{D}_{train}|\log k)$. Consequently, the overall execution time of Algorithm 2 corresponds to $\mathcal{O}(\frac{|\mathcal{V}_q|}{|\mathcal{P}|}) + \mathcal{O}(\frac{|\mathcal{V}_q|}{|\mathcal{P}|}\log|\mathcal{V}_q|) + \mathcal{O}(\frac{|\mathcal{V}_q|}{|\mathcal{P}|})(\mathcal{O}(\log|\mathcal{V}_q|)+\mathcal{O}(|\mathbb{D}_{train}|\log k) = \mathcal{O}(\frac{|\mathcal{V}_q|}{|\mathcal{P}|})(\mathcal{O}(\log|\mathcal{V}_q|)+\mathcal{O}(|\mathbb{D}_{train}|\log k)$.

The work of Garcia et al.[5] processes many query documents in parallel, however, each query q is compared to every document in the training set. Besides, the query and each document are represented as arrays of sizes $|\mathcal{V}|$. Thus, the processing time of query q is $\mathcal{O}(|\mathcal{V}||\mathbb{D}_{train}|)+\mathcal{O}(|\mathbb{D}_{train}|\log k)$.

When Comparing the speedup of our solution over the Garcia's algorithm we do not take into consideration the time to sort the array of distances, since this task ads the same computing time in both solution. As consequence the speedup achieved is $\frac{\mathcal{O}(|\mathcal{V}||\mathbb{D}_{train}|)}{\mathcal{O}(\frac{|\mathcal{V}_q|}{|\mathcal{P}|})(\mathcal{O}(\log|\mathcal{V}_q|)}$. If we take $|\mathcal{V}|$ as upper bound for $|\mathcal{V}_q|$, we have that the speedup obtained is:

$$speedup = \mathcal{O}(\frac{|\mathbb{D}_{train}||\mathcal{P}|}{\log|\mathcal{V}|})$$

If we consider that number of processors is constant (in one GPU), and that, according to Heaps Law the number of new words in vocabulary V does not grow much as the collection size increases, we have that, the speedup increases proportionally to the number of documents in the collection.

Considering memory space requirements, the proposed solution consumes $2|\mathcal{E}|$ units of memory to store arrays E and *invertedIndex*, consumes $2|\mathcal{V}|$ units to store arrays *df* and *index*, consumes $\mathcal{O}(|\mathcal{V}_q|)$ space to store the related-to-query arrays (df_q, $start_q$, and $index_q$) and $\mathcal{O}(|\mathbb{D}_{train}|)$ space to store the array containing the norms of the documents and the array containing the distances. Thus, the space complexity of the solution is $\mathcal{O}(|\mathcal{E}|)+\mathcal{O}(|\mathcal{V}|)+\mathcal{O}(|\mathcal{V}_q|)+\mathcal{O}(|\mathbb{D}_{train}|) = \mathcal{O}(|\mathcal{E}|)+\mathcal{O}(|\mathbb{D}_{train}|)$.

The solution presented by Garcia et al. [5] uses a matrix with dimensions $|\mathcal{V}||\mathbb{D}_{train}|$ to store the training set and an array of size $|\mathcal{V}|$ to store the query q. Thus the space complexity of their solution is $\mathcal{O}(|\mathcal{V}||\mathbb{D}_{train}|)+\mathcal{O}(|\mathbb{D}_{train}|)$. The ratio between the space used by Garcia's solution and ours solution is $\mathcal{O}(\frac{|\mathcal{V}||\mathbb{D}_{train}|}{(|\mathcal{E}|)})$. This corresponds to a mesure of the sparsity of the matrix storing the training set in Garcia's solution.

7. EXPERIMENTAL EVALUATION

7.1 Experimental Setup

In order to evaluate the meta-feature strategies, we consider six real-world textual datasets, namely, 20 Newsgroups, Four Universities, Reuters, ACM Digital Library, MEDLINE and RCV1 datasets. For all datasets, we performed a traditional preprocessing task: we removed stopwords, using the standard SMART list, and applied a simple feature selection by removing terms with low "document frequency (DF)"[2]. Regarding term weighting, we used TFIDF for both, SVM and kNN. All datasets are single-label. In particular, in the case of RCV1, the original dataset is multi-label with the multi-label cases needing special treatment, such as score thresholding, etc. (see [13] for details). As our current focus is on single-label tasks, to allow a fair comparison among the other datasets (which are also single-label) and all baselines (which also focus on single-label tasks), we decided to transform all multi-label cases into single-label ones. In order to do this fairly, we randomly selected, among all documents with more than one label, a single label to be attached to that document. This procedure was applied in about 20% of the documents of RCV1 which happened to be multi-label. More details about the datasets are shown in Table 1.

Dataset	Classes	# attrib	# docs	Density	Size
4UNI	7	40,194	8,274	140.325	14MB
20NG	20	61,049	18,766	130.780	30MB
ACM	11	59,990	24,897	38.805	8.5MB
REUT90	90	19,589	13,327	78.164	13MB
MED	7	803,358	861,454	31.805	327MB
RCV1Uni	103	134,932	804,427	79.133	884MB

Table 1: General information on the datasets.

All experiments were run on a Intel® i7-870, running at 2.93GHz, with 16Gb RAM. The GPU experiments were run on a NVIDIA Tesla K40, with 12Gb RAM. In order to consider the costs of all data transfers in our efficiency experiments, we report the wall times on a dedicated machine so as to rule out external factors, like high load caused by other processes. To compare the average results on our cross-validation experiments, we assess the statistical significance of our results with a paired t-test with 95% confidence and Bonferroni correction to account for multiple tests. This test assures that the best results, marked in **bold**, are statistically superior to others.

We compare the computation time to generate meta-features using three different algorithms: (1) **GT*k*NN**, our GPU-based implementation of kNN[3]; (2) **BF-CUDA**, a brute force kNN implementation using CUDA proposed by Garcia et al. [5]; and (3) **ANN**, a C++ library that supports exact and approximate nearest neighbor searching[4]. We use the ANN exact version, since it was used in the previous meta-feature works [7, 24]. We chose BF-CUDA because it is the main representative of the GPU-based brute force approach. However, the other implementations mentioned in Section 2 (some not available for download) also work with a complete distance matrix and would produce similar results.

We also conducted controlled experiments to evaluate the effectiveness of classifiers learned with three different sets of features. The names and the descriptions of each set of features are given as follows: (1) **Bag of Words**, a set containing only the original features, i.e, TF-IDF weights of the document's terms; (2) **Meta-features**, a set of meta-features proposed recently in literature (state-of-art meta-features) and described in Section 3; and (3) **Bag + Meta-features**, the combination of the above sets. The effectiveness of the features were compared using two standard text categorization measures: micro averaged F_1 (MicroF_1) and macro averaged F_1 (MacroF_1), which capture distinct aspects of the ADC task [13, 23]. To evaluate the performance of different groups of features, we adopted the LIBLINEAR [4] implementation of the SVM classifier, which received as input either the original space of features (Bag of Words), the Meta-features we generate to represent the original space, or the combination Bag + Meta-features. The regularization parameter was chosen by using 5-fold cross-validation in the training set. For the size of neighborhood used for generating the kNN-based meta-features, we adopted $k = 30$ in all experiments, since it was empirically demonstrated as the best parameter for text classification [2, 9, 23].

We would like to point out that some of the results obtained in some datasets with and without the meta-features may differ from the ones reported in other works for the same datasets (e.g., [6, 12]). Such discrepancies may be due to several factors such as differences in dataset preparation[5], the use of different splits of the datasets (e.g., some datasets have "default splits" such as REUT and RCV1[6]), the application of some score thresholding, such as SCUT and PCUT, which, besides being an important step for multi-label problems, also affects classification performance by minimizing class imbalance effects, among other factors. We would like to stress that we ran all alternatives under the same conditions in all datasets, using the best traditional feature weighting scheme, using standardized and well-accepted cross-validation procedures that optimize parameters for each of alternatives, and applying the proper statistical tools for the analysis of the results. Our datasets are available for result replication and testing of new configurations.

7.2 Experimental Results

7.2.1 *Effectiveness*

We start by demonstrating the effectiveness of the meta-features. As shown in Table 2, in most datasets, the use of the traditional bag-of-words was statistically worse than meta-features, justifying meta-features as a replacement for

[2]We removed all terms that occur in less than six documents (i.e., DF<6).
[3]Source code is available under GNU Public License (GPL) at `http://purl.oclc.org/NET/gtknn/`.
[4]`http://www.cs.umd.edu/~mount/ANN/`
[5]For instance, some works do exploit complex feature weighting schemes or feature selection mechanisms that do favor some algorithms in detriment to others.
[6]We believe that running experiments only in the default splits is not the best experimental procedure as it does not allow a proper statistical treatment of the results.

Dataset	*Meta-features*		*Bag of Words*			
			SVM		*kNN*	
	$MacF_1$	$MicF_1$	$MacF_1$	$MicF_1$	$MacF_1$	$MicF_1$
4UNI	**62.50 ± 2.27**	**76.52 ± 1.44**	54.55 ± 1.64	70.18 ± 0.77	52.34 ± 1.77	68.25 ± 1.61
20NG	**89.26 ± 0.23**	**89.59 ± 0.33**	87.08 ± 0.33	87.34 ± 0.45	83.89 ± 0.72	84.40 ± 0.96
ACM	**63.83 ± 2.05**	**76.03 ± 0.27**	53.62 ± 1.12	67.61 ± 0.53	57.11 ± 1.64	70.71 ± 0.42
REUT90	**38.96 ± 1.04**	**77.13 ± 1.04**	29.13 ± 2.03	65.92 ± 0.78	30.01 ± 1.03	65.64 ± 1.68
MED	74.33 ± 0.17	83.55 ± 0.07	**75.15 ± 0.18**	85.65 ± 0.07	58.66 ± 0.50	**86.05 ± 0.30**
RCV1Uni	**55.77 ± 0.92**	77.41 ± 0.21	**55.32 ± 0.66**	**78.28 ± 0.12**	46.32 ± 0.72	68.23 ± 0.16

Table 2: MicroF$_1$ and MacroF$_1$ of different sets of features.

Dataset	*Meta-features*		*Bag + Meta-features*	
	$MacF_1$	$MicF_1$	$MacF_1$	$MicF_1$
4UNI	**62.50 ± 2.27**	**76.52 ± 1.44**	**62.93 ± 2.03**	**75.38 ± 1.76**
20NG	89.26 ± 0.23	**89.59 ± 0.33**	**90.11 ± 0.30**	**90.36 ± 0.43**
ACM	**63.83 ± 2.05**	**76.03 ± 0.27**	**63.58 ± 1.15**	**76.77 ± 0.24**
REUT90	**38.96 ± 1.04**	**77.13 ± 1.04**	37.36 ± 1.31	74.98 ± 0.71
MED	74.33 ± 0.17	83.55 ± 0.07	**79.90 ± 0.20**	**87.43 ± 0.08**
RCV1Uni	55.77 ± 0.92	77.41 ± 0.21	**57.21 ± 0.32**	**78.92 ± 0.16**

Table 3: MicroF$_1$ and MacroF$_1$ of the meta-features and the combination of meta-features and bag-of-words.

Dataset	*Execution Time*			*Speedup*	
	GTkNN	BF-CUDA	ANN	BF-CUDA	ANN
4UNI	**40 ± 1**	259 ± 46	1590 ± 29	6.4	39.6
20NG	**187 ± 4**	2004 ± 17	10947 ± 1323	10.7	68.7
ACM	**112 ± 3**	1760 ± 91	13589 ± 1539	15.7	141.3
REUT90	**625 ± 12**	2242 ± 5	3024 ± 303	3.6	4.8
MED	4637 ± 43	*	*	*	*
RCV1Uni	33884 ± 111	*	*	*	*

Table 4: Average time in seconds (and 95% confidence interval) to generate meta-features using different kNN strategies. GTkNN is significantly better than others and makes the generation of meta-features possible to MED and RCV1Uni.

the original high dimensional feature space, as demonstrated in previous work. Most of the results of SVM on the original space (bag-of-words) are superior or tied with kNN.

The only datasets in which the effectiveness of meta-features was not better than that of bag-of-words were MED and RCV1Uni. We hypothesize that it is due to the fact that these datasets have a large training dataset, which allows the classification method (SVM) to deal better with the highly dimensional data, since there is enough training examples to learn discriminative patterns from more dimensions.

Although bag-of-words achieved good results in MED and RCV1Uni, the combination Bag + Meta-features proposed in this work achieved the best results all datasets but REUT90, as shown in Table 3. This demonstrates the complementarity between the Bag and Meta-features in these datasets. REUT90 was the only case in which bag + meta-features was worse than the meta-features alone. Since this dataset has only a few training examples per class, the inclusion of more noisy features (from the bag-of-words) only makes it more difficult to find an effective SVM model.

7.2.2 *Computational Time to Generate Meta-features*

Table 4 shows the average time to generate meta-features for a batch of test examples using ours and the baseline's kNN implementations. Since we use a 5-fold cross validation, we measure the time to generate meta-features for all the examples in the batch of examples in each test fold. Notice that the time to generate meta-features is practically the average time to classify a fold, since the time to classify the test examples with the SVM implementation is negligible.

As can be seen in Table 4, the generation of meta-features using GTkNN shows significant speedups in relation to the other kNN implementations. In particular, the speedups for the small datasets range from 4.8 to 141.3 in relation to the ANN implementation, used in previous works to generate meta-features. This high speedup was somewhat expected, since the ANN do not explore parallelism to compute the distances. However, even when compared to the parallel BF-CUDA implementation[5], GTkNN was able to achieve speedups ranging from 3.6 to 15.7. This was possible mainly because BF-CUDA does not optimize the distance calculations to deal with the low density of terms present in textual documents nor tries to balance the load among threads.

GTkNN produced the best speedups in 4UNI, 20NG and ACM, but it obtained a lower speedup in REUT90. This may be due to the fact that REUT90 has a large number of classes and only a few documents in each class. Since the meta-features are generated one class at a time, we could not explore the parallelism in its full potential. For example, if there are only 10 training documents in a class, we can only perform at most 10 simultaneous distance calculations, leaving most CUDA cores idle.

GTkNN was the only implementation able to generate meta-features for the larger datasets: MED and RCV1Uni. In fact, ANN and BF-CUDA are extremely slow in this context. Figure 3 shows the time to generate meta-features for a single test example considering a sample size of 100 up to 2000 documents in MED. Since this dataset has more

Dataset	Time to Generate meta-features			Speedup	
	GT*k*NN	BF-CUDA	ANN	BF-CUDA	ANN
4UNI	**0.012 ± 0.003**	0.316 ± 0.001	0.534 ± 0.233	26.3	45.3
20NG	**0.033 ± 0.007**	1.112 ± 0.002	1.974 ± 0.642	33.7	59.8
ACM	**0.016 ± 0.002**	1.012 ± 0.003	2.084 ± 0.769	63.2	130.2
REUT90	**0.139 ± 0.028**	1.369 ± 0.001	0.524 ± 0.156	9.8	3.8
MED	0.027 ± 0.002	*	*	*	*
RCV1Uni	0.191 ± 0.023	*	*	*	*

Table 5: **Average execution time in seconds (and standard deviations) to classify each test example.**

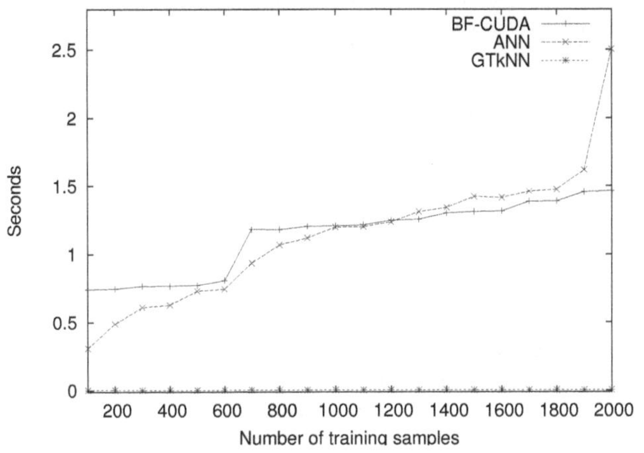

Figure 3: **Time to generate meta-features for one example with different sample sizes from the MED dataset. GT*k*NN keeps very low execution time (up to 0.005 seconds). The other two approaches slow down dramatically as the training dataset grows in size.**

than 800,000 features, even a small fraction of it (e.g. 2000 documents - 0.3%) requires a significant time (2.5 and 1.5 seconds for ANN and BF-CUDA respectively) to generate meta-features. On the contrary, GT*k*NN takes no more than 0.005 seconds to generate the meta-features. This discrepancy is expected since the calculations involved to deal with such high dimensions (greater than 800,000) are huge. The sequential nature of ANN and the lack of support for data sparsity make both ANN and BF-CUDA less competitive in this situation.

The average time to generate meta-features for a single test example is presented in Table 5. In this experiment, we use a leave-one-out methodology, where only one example is chosen as a test example, leaving all others as training examples. GT*k*NN never takes more than 0.2 seconds to generate meta-features to a test example. It makes possible to classify examples on-the-fly even using very big training datasets. The most costly examples are in REUT90 and RCV1Uni due the fact that GT*k*NN cannot fully explore the parallelism with multiple classes on the current implementation, as described before.

Although the ANN speedups are similar in Tables 5 and 4, we notice that the BF-CUDA speedups in Table 5 are much higher than the ones previously presented in Table 4. This happens because the BF-CUDA implementation is optimized to perform multiple queries in parallel, which matches the needs for generating meta-features to multiple examples. However, when a single test example has to be processed, the meta-feature generation using the BF-CUDA implementation is considerably slowed down.

7.2.3 Memory Consumption

For textual datasets, the traditional data representation using a D x V matrix with D training documents and V features (the vocabulary of the collection) is not a good choice as the density of words in each document is very low. The proposed GT*k*NN approach represents textual data in a very compact way by exploiting an efficient in-memory GPU-based implementation of an inverted index, allowing us to store only the word statistics of each document.

Table 6 shows the memory consumption figures required to generate meta-features using the three kNN implementations. The numbers correspond to the peak memory consumption during the meta-feature generation process. An estimate of memory consumption, based on the allocation of data structures, was made for the ANN and BF-CUDA implementations with MED and RCV1Uni, since these implementations are not capable of processing these large datasets.

Dataset	Memory Consumption		
	GT*k*NN	BF-CUDA	ANN
4UNI	92	1697	945
20NG	93	1257	395
ACM	90	2541	2487
REUT90	90	909	494
MED	339	1859104	2857048
RCV1Uni	120	43245	69328

Table 6: **Memory consuption in Megabytes.**

Our GT*k*NN implementation stands out way ahead of the competition when it comes to memory usage. The most impressive memory reduction occurs in MED. Although the second largest dataset, MED has only a few classes. Since our meta-feature generation strategy is performed one class at a time, a great number of documents has to be processed for each class. Thus MED consumes the largest amount of memory (339 MB) for our implementation, but the baselines ANN and BF-CUDA consume more than 5,000x and 8,000x this space respectively for the same dataset. We can also obtain a large memory demand reduction in RCV1, but not as expressive as in MED due to its large number of classes. In general, for all kNN implementations, the peak memory usage depends on the class with most training examples.

8. CONCLUSION

The use of meta-features in automatic document classification has permitted important improvements in the efficiency of classification algorithms. One of these meta-feature approaches is based on intensive use of the kNN algorithm, in order to exploit local information regarding the neighborhood of training documents. However, intensive use of kNN, combined with the high dimensionality and sparsity of textual data, make this a challenging computational task. We have presented a very fast and scalable GPU-based approach for computing kNN-based meta-feature document classification. Different from other GPU-based kNN implementations, we avoid comparing the query document with all training documents. Instead we build an inverted index in the GPU that is used to quickly find the documents sharing terms with the query document. Although the index does not allow a regular and predictable access to the data, we use a load balancing strategy to evenly distributed the computation among thousand threads in the GPU. After calculating the distances, we again use a massive number of threads to select the k smallest distance by implementing a truncated bitonic sort in the GPU followed by a merge operation in the CPU. We tested our approach in a very memory-demanding and time consuming task which requires intensive and recurrent execution of kNN. Our results show very significant gains in speedup and memory consumption when compared to our baselines. In fact, running our baselines in the largest datasets demonstrated to be unfeasible, stressing the value of our contribution. And even in scenarios where the dataset is too big for our implementation (a single GPU), our approach can easily be extended by spiting the dataset, executing the kNN in each part, and merging the partial results. Thus, meta-feature based classification can be applied in huge collections of documents, taking a reasonable time and without requiring expensive machines. As future work, we intend to approach other tasks and exploit Multi-GPU platforms to improve even further our solutions.

9. ACKNOWLEDGMENTS

This work was partially supported by CNPq, CAPES, FAPEMIG, INWEB and FAPEG. We thank NVIDIA Corporation for equipment donations.

10. REFERENCES

[1] Y.-S. Chang, R.-K. Sheu, S.-M. Yuan, and J.-J. Hsu. Scaling database performance on gpus. *Information Systems Frontiers*, 14(4):909–924, 2012.

[2] H. Chen and T. K. Ho. Evaluation of decision forests on text categorization. In *Proc. SPIE Conf. Document Recognition and Retrieval*, pages 191–199, 2000.

[3] S. Dzeroski and B. Zenko. Is combining classifiers with stacking better than selecting the best one? *Machine Learning*, 54(3):255–273, 2004.

[4] R.-E. Fan, K.-W. Chang, C.-J. Hsieh, X.-R. Wang, and C.-J. Lin. LIBLINEAR: A library for large linear classification. *JMLR*, 9:1871–1874, 2008.

[5] V. Garcia, E. Debreuve, and M. Barlaud. Fast k nearest neighbor search using gpu. In *CVPR Workshops*, pages 1–6, 2008.

[6] S. Godbole and S. Sarawagi. Discriminative methods for multi-labeled classification. In *Proc. PAKDD*, pages 22–30, 2004.

[7] S. Gopal and Y. Yang. Multilabel classification with meta-level features. In *Proc. SIGIR*, pages 315–322, 2010.

[8] T. Graham. A gpu database for real-time big data analytics and interactive visualization - (map-d). In *NVIDIA GTC-GPU Technology Conference-2014*, 2014.

[9] T. Joachims. Text categorization with suport vector machines: Learning with many relevant features. In *Proc. ECML*, pages 137–142, 1998.

[10] Q. Kuang and L. Zhao. L.: A practical gpu based knn algorithm. In *In Proc. ISCSCT)*, pages 151–155, 2009.

[11] A. Kyriakopoulou and T. Kalamboukis. Using clustering to enhance text classification. In *Proc. SIGIR*, pages 805–806, 2007.

[12] M. Lan, C.-L. Tan, and H.-B. Low. Proposing a new term weighting scheme for text categorization. In *Proc. AAAI*, pages 763–768, 2006.

[13] D. D. Lewis, Y. Yang, T. G. Rose, and F. Li. Rcv1: A new benchmark collection for text categorization research. *JMLR.*, 5:361–397, 2004.

[14] S. Liang, C. Wang, Y. Liu, and L. Jian. Cuknn: A parallel implementation of k-nearest neighbor on cuda-enabled gpu. In *IEEE YC-ICT'09.*, pages 415–418, 2009.

[15] O. Netzer. Getting big data done on a gpu-based database - (sqream). In *NVIDIA GTC-GPU Technology Conference-2014*, 2014.

[16] B. Raskutti, H. L. Ferrá, and A. Kowalczyk. Using unlabelled data for text classification through addition of cluster parameters. In *Proc ICML*, pages 514–521, 2002.

[17] F. Sebastiani. Machine learning in automated text categorization. *ACM Comput. Surv.*, 34(1):1–47, 2002.

[18] S. Sengupta, M. Harris, M. Garland, and J. D. Owens. Efficient parallel scan algorithms for many-core gpus. *Sci. Comp. with Multicore and Acc.*, pages 413–442, 2011.

[19] A. Shchekalev. Using gpus to accelerate learning to rank - (yandex). In *NVIDIA GTC-GPU Technology Conference-2014*, 2014.

[20] N. Sismanis, N. Pitsianis, and X. Sun. Parallel search of k-nearest neighbors with synchronous operations. In *HPEC*, pages 1–6. IEEE, 2012.

[21] B. E. Teitler, J. Sankaranarayanan, H. Samet, and M. D. Adelfio. Online document clustering using gpus. In *New Trends in Databases and Information Systems*, pages 245–254. Springer, 2014.

[22] K. M. Ting and I. H. Witten. Issues in stacked generalization. *J. Artif. Int. Res.*, 10(1):271–289, 1999.

[23] Y. Yang. An evaluation of statistical approaches to text categorization. *Inf. Ret.*, 1:69–90, 1999.

[24] Y. Yang and S. Gopal. Multilabel classification with meta-level features in a learning-to-rank framework. *Mach. Learn.*, 88:47–68, 2012.

Listwise Collaborative Filtering

Shanshan Huang[1*]
huangshanshansdu
@163.com

Shuaiqiang Wang[2*]
shuaiqiang.wang
@jyu.fi

Tie-Yan Liu[3]
tie-yan.liu
@microsoft.com

Jun Ma[1]
majun@sdu.edu.cn

Zhumin Chen[1]
chenzhumin@sdu.edu.cn

Jari Veijalainen[2]
jari.veijalainen@jyu.fi

[1]School of Computer Science and Technology, Shandong University, Jinan, China
[2]Department of Computer Science and Information Systems, University of Jyväskylä, Jyväskylä, Finland
[3]Microsoft Research Asia, Beijing, China

ABSTRACT

Recently, ranking-oriented collaborative filtering (CF) algorithms have achieved great success in recommender systems. They obtained state-of-the-art performances by estimating a preference ranking of items for each user rather than estimating the absolute ratings on unrated items (as conventional rating-oriented CF algorithms do). In this paper, we propose a new ranking-oriented CF algorithm, called ListCF. Following the memory-based CF framework, ListCF directly predicts a total order of items for each user based on similar users' probability distributions over permutations of the items, and thus differs from previous ranking-oriented memory-based CF algorithms that focus on predicting the pairwise preferences between items. One important advantage of ListCF lies in its ability of reducing the computational complexity of the training and prediction procedures while achieving the same or better ranking performances as compared to previous ranking-oriented memory-based CF algorithms. Extensive experiments on three benchmark datasets against several state-of-the-art baselines demonstrate the effectiveness of our proposal.

Categories and Subject Descriptors

H.3.3 [**Information Storage and Retrieval**]: Information Search and Retrieval-*Information filtering*

Keywords

Recommender systems; Collaborative filtering; Ranking-oriented collaborative filtering

1. INTRODUCTION

In recent years, recommender system has become a key technology behind e-commerce to help customers find their desirable products [14, 22]. As one of the most successful recommendation techniques, collaborative filtering (CF) avoids the necessity of collecting extensive content information about items and users by fully utilizing the user-item rating matrix to make recommendations. As a result, CF can be easily applied to different recommender systems without requiring additional domain knowledge [15]. In the literature, many CF algorithms have been proposed, which roughly fall into two categories: rating-oriented CF and ranking-oriented CF.

Rating-oriented CF, such as user-based CF [1, 5], predicts a user's potential ratings on unrated items based on the rating information from other similar users. The similarity between two users is calculated based on their rating scores on the set of commonly rated items. A popular similarity measure is the Pearson correlation coefficient [5]. Since this technique focuses on predicting each user's rating on an unrated item, we refer to it as *pointwise* CF. Please note that pointwise CF might not be able to achieve the ultimate goal of recommender systems, which is to present a ranking or recommendation list to a user rather than predict the absolute value of the ratings [25]. In fact, it has been observed that improvements in pointwise error metrics such as RMSE (Root Mean Squared Error) do not necessarily lead to improved ranking effectiveness [4].

Different from rating-oriented CF, ranking-oriented CF algorithms [18] directly generate a preference ordering of items for each user without the intermediate step of rating prediction. Related works include memory-based algorithms such as EigenRank [15] and VSRank [27, 28], and model-based algorithms such as CoFiRank [29], ListRank-MF [25] and CCF [30]. In this paper, we focus on memory-based CF algorithms since they have demonstrated many advantages such as strong robustness, interpretability, and competitive performance [6].

Existing memory-based ranking-oriented CF algorithms [15, 27, 28] can also be referred to as *pairwise* ranking-oriented CF, since they predict pairwise ordering of items based on the correlation between users' pairwise preferences of the items. A commonly used correlation measure is the Kendall's τ correlation coefficient [17]. Although pairwise ranking-oriented CF has demonstrated significant improvement over previous algorithms in terms of ranking accuracy, it suffers from high computational complexity. Suppose there are N items, and each user has rated n items on

*Indicates equal contribution.

SIGIR'15, August 09 - 13, 2015, Santiago, Chile.
© 2015 ACM. ISBN 978-1-4503-3621-5/15/08 ...$15.00.
DOI: http://dx.doi.org/10.1145/2766462.2767693.

average. The average number of commonly rated items for each pair of users is $\overline{n}$, and the number of the neighbor users is l. Then the time complexity of computing the correlation between each pair of users is $\mathcal{O}\left(n + \overline{n}^2\right)$, and the time complexity of the ranking prediction procedure is $\mathcal{O}\left(l(N-n)^2\right)$ for each user. In most cases, the majority of the items are unrated for each user, resulting in a very large value of $N - n$. As a consequence, the computations of the pairwise ranking-oriented CF algorithms are usually much more expensive than the pointwise rating-oriented CF algorithms.

Beside the computational complexity, there could be problems with the accuracy of pairwise ranking-oriented CF algorithms too. First, Kendall's τ correlation coefficient ignores the ranking positions of the items, which may lead to inaccurate similarities when discovering similar users. Second, Kendall's τ correlation coefficient cannot handle the equal preferences tie, which may cause information loss in training and prediction. Third, pairwise ranking-oriented CF algorithms attempt to predict relative preferences between pair of items rather than the total rankings, which may also result in accuracy loss due to rank aggregation.

To tackle the aforementioned problems with the pairwise CF algorithms, we propose ListCF, a *listwise* memory-based ranking-oriented CF algorithm, which can reduce the time complexity of both the training and prediction phases while maintaining or even improving the prediction accuracy as compared to conventional pairwise ranking-oriented CF algorithms. ListCF directly predicts a ranking list of items for the target user based on the probability distributions over the permutations of items and thus avoids the accuracy loss caused by the prediction and aggregation of pairwise preferences.

In particular, ListCF utilizes the Plackett-Luce model [17], a widely used permutation probability model in the literature of learning to rank, to represent each user as a probability distribution over the permutations of rated items. In this way, both the ranking positions and equal preferences can be well considered. In ListCF, the similarity between two users is measured based on the Kullback–Leibler (KL) divergence [11] between their probability distributions over the set of commonly rated items. Then for each user, those users who have higher similarity scores are selected as the set of neighborhood users. Given a target user and the neighborhood users, ListCF infers predictions by minimizing the cross entropy loss between their probability distributions over permutations of items with gradient descent. Extensive experiments on three benchmark datasets in comparison with several state-of-the-art algorithms demonstrate the advantages of our approach.

The rest of the paper is organized as follows. Section 2 reviews the related work. Section 3 formulates the listwise collaborative filtering paradigm and presents the details of our algorithm. Section 4 analyzes the relationships between our listwise CF approach and conventional memory-based CF approaches. Section 5 reports the experimental results and analysis, and Section 6 concludes the paper.

2. RELATED WORK

2.1 Recommender Systems

In recent years, many recommendation algorithms have been proposed, which fall into content-based, collaborative filtering (CF) and hybrid algorithms. Content-based algorithms make recommendations based on similarities between the vector representing the user profile and the vectors representing the items, where the vectors for user profile and items are weighted explicit features [16]. CF avoids the necessity of collecting extensive content information about items and users by fully utilizing the user-item rating matrix to make recommendations. Thus, CF can be easily adopted in different recommender systems without requiring additional domain knowledge [15]. Given the effectiveness and convenience, many CF algorithms have been proposed, which are either rating-oriented CF or ranking-oriented CF. In addition, hybrid recommendation algorithms have also been proposed to combine two or more recommendation techniques to gain better performance [2].

In this paper, we focus on CF recommendation algorithms and propose a listwise CF algorithm which demonstrates advantages in recommendation efficiency and accuracy.

2.2 Rating-oriented CF

Traditional rating-oriented CF predicts the absolute value of ratings of individual users to unrated items, thus we refer to it as *pointwise* CF. Conventionally, pointwise rating-oriented CF can be either memory-based or model-based.

In memory-based rating-oriented algorithms, two representatives are user-based CF [5] and item-based CF [14, 23], which make predictions by utilizing historical ratings associated with similar users or similar items. The commonly used similarity metrics are Pearson correlation coefficient [5] and cosine similarity [1].

Model-based rating-oriented CF learns a model based on the observed ratings to make rating predictions. Latent factor models such as matrix factorization (MF) [9] that uses dimensionality reduction techniques have become important research directions in this area. A variety of adaptations of the MF model have demonstrated promising prediction performance, such as Probabilistic Matrix Factorization (PMF) [19], Non-negative Matrix Factorization (NMF) [12], and Max-Margin Matrix Factorization (MMMF) [21].

2.3 Ranking-oriented CF

Different from rating-oriented CF, ranking-oriented CF [18] directly predicts a preference ranking of items for each user. Similarly, ranking-oriented CF algorithms can be also categorized into memory-based ranking-oriented CF [15, 27] and model-based ranking-oriented CF [10, 20, 25].

EigenRank [15] is a classic memory-based ranking-oriented CF algorithm, which measures the similarity between users based on the correlation between their pairwise rankings of the co-rated items and ranks items by the preferences of similar users. VSRank [27] adopts the vector space model in representing user pairwise preferences and makes further improvement by considering the relative importance of each pairwise preference. Resulting from the pairwise preference based representations and predictions, we refer to EigenRank and VSRank as *pairwise* memory-based ranking-oriented CF algorithms. Although they achieve better performance in recommendation accuracy than rating-oriented CF, they suffer from serious efficiency problem. In this paper, we propose a *listwise* memory-based ranking-oriented CF algorithm to reduce the computational complexity while maintaining or even improving the ranking performance.

A variety of model-based ranking-oriented CF algorithms have been presented by optimizing ranking-oriented objective functions, e.g., bayesian personalized ranking (BPR) [20], CLiMF [24], CoFiRank [29], and ListRank-MF [25]. BPR and CLiMF model the binary relevance data and optimize binary relevance metrics, i.e., Area Under the Curve (AUC) in BPR and Mean Reciprocal Rank (Mean) in CLiMF, which are not suited for graded relevance data. CoFiRank [29] minimizes a convex upper bound of the Normalized Discounted Cumulative Gain (NDCG) [7, 8] loss through matrix factorization while ListRank-MF [25] integrates the learning to rank technique into the matrix factorization model for top-N recommendation.

3. LISTWISE COLLABORATIVE FILTERING

In this section, we propose ListCF, a listwise ranking-oriented collaborative filtering (CF) algorithm based on the memory-based CF framework. Generally, memory-based CF works in two phases [28]: The similarity calculation phase (Phase I) calculates the similarities between pair of users, based on which a set of most similar neighborhood users can be discovered for each user; Then the ranking prediction phase (Phase II) predicts the preference ordering of unrated items for each target user by aggregating preferences of neighborhood users for recommendation purpose.

3.1 Phase I: Similarity Calculation

In ListCF, we utilize Plackett-Luce model [17], a widely used permutation probability model, to represent each user as a probability distribution over the permutations of rated items. It is assumed that given a ranking function on a set of items, any permutation on the item set is possible. However, different permutations may have different probabilities, and more "correct" permutations where items with larger ranking scores are ranked higher are assigned with larger probabilities.

Let I be a set of items. A permutation of I is a bijection from I to itself and it can be represented as an ordered list $\pi = \langle \pi_1, \pi_2, \ldots, \pi_n \rangle$, where $\pi_i \in I$ denotes the item at position i and $\pi_i \neq \pi_j$ if $i \neq j$. The set of all the possible permutations of I is denoted as Ω^I.

DEFINITION 1. (PROBABILITY OF PERMUTATION). *Let $\phi(\cdot)$ be an increasing and strictly positive function. Given a permutation $\pi = \langle \pi_1, \pi_2, \ldots, \pi_n \rangle$ and the rating scores of the items $\{r_{\pi_1}, r_{\pi_2}, \ldots, r_{\pi_n}\}$, the probability of π is defined as follows:*

$$P(\pi) = \prod_{i=1}^{n} \frac{\phi(r_{\pi_i})}{\sum_{k=i}^{n} \phi(r_{\pi_k})}.$$

In this paper, we use the exponential function $\phi(r) = e^r$. For a set of n items, the number of different permutations is $n!$. Thus, it is too time-consuming to calculate the probabilities of all the permutations. To cope with this problem, an alternative solution is the *top-k probability model* [3] ($1 \leq k \leq n$), which only focuses on the permutations of items within the top-k positions.

DEFINITION 2. (TOP-k PERMUTATION SET). *Given a set of items I, the top-k permutation set $\mathcal{G}_k(i_1, i_2, \ldots, i_k)$ of I is a set containing all the permutations of I which share the same top-k items, i.e., $i_1, i_2, \ldots, i_k$ where $i_1, i_2, \ldots, i_k \in I$. Formally,*

$$\mathcal{G}_k(i_1, i_2, \ldots, i_k) = \{\pi \mid \pi \in \Omega^I, \pi_j = i_j, j = 1, ..., k\}.$$

Two top-k permutation sets of I are different if the items in the top-k positions are different. Let $\mathcal{G}_k^I$ denote the set of different top-k permutation sets for I. Please note that the cardinality of $\mathcal{G}_k(i_1, i_2, \ldots, i_k)$ is $(n-k)!$, and the cardinality of $\mathcal{G}_k^I$ is $n!/(n-k)!$.

EXAMPLE 1. *Let $I = \{i_1, i_2, i_3\}$. There are totally $3! = 6$ possible permutations in Ω^I: $\langle i_1, i_2, i_3 \rangle$, $\langle i_1, i_3, i_2 \rangle$, $\langle i_2, i_1, i_3 \rangle$, $\langle i_2, i_3, i_1 \rangle$, $\langle i_3, i_1, i_2 \rangle$, and $\langle i_3, i_2, i_1 \rangle$. There are merely $3!/2! = 3$ top-1 permutation sets: $\mathcal{G}_1^I = \{\mathcal{G}_1(i_1), \mathcal{G}_1(i_2), \mathcal{G}_1(i_3)\}$, where $\mathcal{G}_1(i_1) = \{\langle \underline{i_1}, i_2, i_3 \rangle, \langle \underline{i_1}, i_3, i_2 \rangle\}$, $\mathcal{G}_1(i_2) = \{\langle \underline{i_2}, i_1, i_3 \rangle, \langle \underline{i_2}, i_3, i_1 \rangle\}$, and $\mathcal{G}_1(i_3) = \{\langle \underline{i_3}, i_1, i_2 \rangle, \langle \underline{i_3}, i_2, i_1 \rangle\}$.*

Based on the Definition 2, the probability of the top-k permutation $P(\mathcal{G}_k(i_1, i_2, \ldots, i_k))$ equals to the sum of the probabilities of permutations in which the items $i_1, i_2, \ldots, i_k$ are ranked in the top-k positions. To calculate all the probabilities of top-k permutation sets in $\mathcal{G}_k^I$, we need consider $n!/(n-k)!$ top-k permutation sets, each containing $(n-k)!$ permutations of I. Therefore we still have to calculate $n!/(n-k)! \cdot (n-k)! = n!$ probabilities of permutations in total. In [3], an efficient way to calculate the probability of the top-k permutation set $P(\mathcal{G}_k(i_1, i_2, \ldots, i_k))$ is shown in Lemma 1.

LEMMA 1. *The probability of the top-k permutation set $P(\mathcal{G}_k(i_1, i_2, \ldots, i_k))$ equals to the probability of that the items $i_1, i_2, \ldots, i_k$ are ranked in the top-k positions respectively. Formally,*

$$P(\mathcal{G}_k(i_1, i_2, \ldots, i_k)) = \prod_{j=1}^{k} \frac{\phi(r_{\pi_j})}{\sum_{l=j}^{n} \phi(r_{\pi_l})}, \ \forall j = 1, \ldots, k : \pi_j = i_j \quad (1)$$

where r_{π_l} is the rating score of the item which is ranked in position l, $l = 1, 2, ..., n$.

Obviously, the probabilities of the top-k permutation sets in $\mathcal{G}_k^I$ form a probability distribution, which can be calculated much more efficiently than the probability distribution over $\mathcal{G}^I$. In this study, we refer to the probability distribution over the top-k permutation sets as the *top-k probability model*, which uses the top-k permutation sets instead of the full permutations of all the items.

In recommender systems, for each pair of users u and v, let $I_{u,v}$ be the set of their commonly rated items. Then $\mathcal{G}_k^{I_{u,v}}$ represents the set of top-k permutation sets of $I_{u,v}$. We use P_u and P_v to denote the probability distributions of u and v over $\mathcal{G}_k^{I_{u,v}}$ according to the top-k probability model, which can be calculated with Equation (1) based on their rating scores. Thus the similarity between user u and v can be estimated as the similarity between the probability distributions of P_u and P_v.

In this study, we use Kullback-Leibler (KL) divergence [11] based metric for similarity calculation, since it is a common measure of the difference between two probability distributions in probability theory and information theory. Given two users u and v, the KL divergence of P_u from P_v

is defined as follows:

$$D_{KL}(P_v\|P_u) = \sum_{g\in\mathcal{G}_k^{I_{u,v}}} P_v(g)\log_2\left(\frac{P_v(g)}{P_u(g)}\right),$$

where $P_u(g)$ and $P_v(g)$ is the probability of the top-k permutation set $g \in \mathcal{G}_k^{I_{u,v}}$ for u and v respectively. $D_{KL}(P_u\|P_v)$ can be calculated in the similar way. Obviously, the KL divergence is asymmetric, i.e., $D_{KL}(P_v\|P_u) \neq D_{KL}(P_u\|P_v)$. In this study, we define a symmetric similarity metric based on the KL divergence, which is shown as follows:

$$s(u,v) = 1 - \frac{1}{2}\Big[D_{KL}(P_v\|P_u) + D_{KL}(P_u\|P_v)\Big]. \quad (2)$$

The similarity metric in Equation (2) suffers from computing high similarity between users with few ratings in common. Like in [5], this can be alleviated by multiplying the similarity function with $\min\{|I_{u,v}|/c, 1\}$, where c is a threshold. When the number of commonly rated items falls below this threshold, the similarity is scaled down.

Since $D_{KL}(P_v\|P_u), D_{KL}(P_u\|P_v) \geq 0$, according to Equation (2), the similarity between each pair of users is no greater than 1. Formally, $\forall u, v \in U : s(u,v) \leq 1$. The similarity between u and v reaches the maximum bound ($s(u,v) = 1$) only if their probability distributions P_u and P_v over the top-k permutation sets are the same. We also note that $s(u,v)$ may be negative and has no lower bound. However, this is not an important issue in our model because we are just interested in discovery of limited number of users with high similarities to the target user as the neighborhood users.

3.2 Phase II: Ranking Prediction

For a target user u, let N_u be the set of neighborhood users and $T_u = \{t_1, t_2, \ldots, t_p\}$ be the set of items to be predicted. The ultimate goal of ranking-oriented CF is to predict a preference ranking of items in T_u for u.

Let $\hat{P}_u$ be the probability distribution over the set of top-k permutation sets $\mathcal{G}_k^{T_u}$ to be predicted for u. In order to guarantee that the sum of the probabilities in $\hat{P}_u$ is equal to 1, for each top-k permutation set $\forall g \in \mathcal{G}_k^{T_u}$, the probability $\hat{P}_u(g)$ is denoted as follows:

$$\hat{P}_u(g) = \frac{\varphi_{u,g}}{\sum_{g'\in\mathcal{G}_k^{T_u}}\varphi_{u,g'}}, \quad (3)$$

where $\{\varphi_{u,g}|\forall g \in \mathcal{G}_k^{T_u}\}$ are unknown variables to be predicted for user u and $\sum_{g\in\mathcal{G}_k^{T_u}}\hat{P}_u(g) = 1$ holds.

In this study, following the same assumption of memory-based CF, we make predictions based on a set of neighborhood users with similar ranking preferences to the target user. If users have similar ranking preferences in the past, they are most likely to have similar ranking preferences in the future, which means that $\hat{P}_u$ should be as close as possible to the probability distributions of the neighborhood users over their sets of top-k permutation sets.

We use the cross entropy loss function to make predictions, as it is widely-used for optimizing similarity/distance between probability distributions in machine learning, and it has been successfully used in the text mining [3], multimedia retrieval [13], and pattern recognition [26] fields.

Given a target user u with a set of unrated items T_u and a neighborhood user $v \in N_u$, let I_v be the set of items that the neighborhood user v has rated, and $T_{u,v} = T_u \cap I_v$. Thus $\mathcal{G}_k^{T_{u,v}}$ is the set of top-k permutation sets of $T_{u,v}$. Let $\hat{P}'_u$ and P'_v be the respective probability distributions of u and v over $\mathcal{G}_k^{T_{u,v}}$. The cross entropy between $\hat{P}'_u$ and P'_v can be calculated as follows:

$$E(\hat{P}'_u, P'_v) = -\sum_{g\in\mathcal{G}_k^{T_{u,v}}} P'_v(g)\log_2(\hat{P}'_u(g)). \quad (4)$$

Please note that in the above equation, P'_v is different from P_v that is used in similarity calculation. As they are based on different sets of items, where P'_v is based on $T_{u,v}$ while P_v is based on the commonly rated items $I_{u,v} = I_u \cap I_v$ of user u and v. Obviously $\sum_{g\in\mathcal{G}_k^{T_{u,v}}} P'_v(g) = 1$ holds.

ListCF attempts to make predictions by minimizing the weighted sum of the cross entropy loss between the probability distributions of the target user and his neighborhood users over the set of the top-k permutation sets of $T_{u,v}$. For a target user u and the set of unrated items T_u, the cross entropy-based loss function is:

$$\begin{aligned}&\arg\min_{\varphi_u} \sum_{v\in N_u} s(u,v)\cdot E(\hat{P}'_u, P'_v)\\ &s.t. \quad \forall g \in \mathcal{G}_k^{T_u} : \varphi_{u,g} \geq 0.\end{aligned} \quad (5)$$

According to Equation (2) and Equation (4), the objective function can be specified as follows:

$$\begin{aligned}F(\varphi_u) &= \sum_{v\in N_u} s(u,v)\cdot E(\hat{P}'_u, P'_v)\\ &= -\sum_{v\in N_u} s(u,v)\sum_{g\in\mathcal{G}_k^{T_{u,v}}} P'_v(g)\log_2(\hat{P}'_u(g))\\ &= -\sum_{v\in N_u} s(u,v)\sum_{g\in\mathcal{G}_k^{T_{u,v}}} P'_v(g)\log_2\left(\frac{\varphi_{u,g}}{\sum_{g'\in\mathcal{G}_k^{T_{u,v}}}\varphi_{u,g'}}\right)\\ &= \sum_{v\in N_u} s(u,v)\sum_{g\in\mathcal{G}_k^{T_{u,v}}} P'_v(g)\left[\log_2\left(\sum_{g'\in\mathcal{G}_k^{T_{u,v}}}\varphi_{u,g'}\right) - \log_2(\varphi_{u,g})\right].\end{aligned} \quad (6)$$

We optimize Equation (6) with the gradient descent method. The derivative of F with respect to $\varphi_{u,g}$ is:

$$\begin{aligned}&\frac{\partial F}{\partial\varphi_{u,g}}\\ &= \sum_{v\in N_u}\left(\frac{s(u,v)\sum_{g\in\mathcal{G}_k^{T_{u,v}}}P'_v(g)}{\ln 2\cdot\sum_{g'\in\mathcal{G}_k^{T_{u,v}}}\varphi_{u,g'}}\right) - \frac{\sum_{v\in N_u}s(u,v)P'_v(g)}{\ln 2\cdot\varphi_{u,g}}\\ &= \sum_{v\in N_u}\frac{s(u,v)}{\ln 2\cdot\sum_{g'\in\mathcal{G}_k^{T_{u,v}}}\varphi_{u,g'}} - \frac{\sum_{v\in N_u}s(u,v)P'_v(g)}{\ln 2\cdot\varphi_{u,g}}.\end{aligned} \quad (7)$$

Given a learning rate η, the update formula of the gradient descent method is:

$$\varphi_{u,g} \leftarrow \varphi_{u,g} - \eta\frac{\partial F}{\partial\varphi_{u,g}}. \quad (8)$$

Algorithm 1: The ListCF Algorithm

Input: An item set I, a user set U, and a rating matrix $R \in \mathbb{R}^{M \times N}$. A set of rated items $I_u \subseteq I$ by each user $u \in U$. The maximal number of iterations $maxIteration$ and error threshold ϵ.

Output: A ranking $\hat{\tau}_u$ of items for each user $u \in U$.

1 **for** $u \in U$ **do**
2 | **for** $v \in U$ *and* $u \neq v$ **do**
3 | | $P_u, P_v \leftarrow$ TopKProDist(I_u, I_v, R) `/* Eq.1 */`
4 | | $sim(u, v) \leftarrow$ Similarity(P_u, P_v) `/* Eq.2 */`
5 | **end**
6 | $N_u \leftarrow$ SelectNeighbors$(\{sim(u, v)\}_{v \in U/u})$
7 **end**
8 **for** $u \in U$ **do**
9 | $t = 1$
10 | **repeat**
11 | | $\varepsilon = 0$
12 | | Initialize(φ_u^0)
13 | | **for** $g \in \mathcal{G}_k^{T_u}$ **do**
14 | | | $\varphi_{u,g}^t \leftarrow$ Update(N_u, sim, R) `/* Eq.8 */`
15 | | | $\varepsilon + = \sqrt{\sum (\varphi_{u,g}^t - \varphi_{u,g}^{t-1})^2}$
16 | | **end**
17 | | $t \leftarrow t + 1$
18 | **until** $t > maxIteration$ *or* $\varepsilon < \epsilon$;
19 | **for** $t \in T_u$ **do**
20 | | $P(t) \leftarrow$ Aggregation$(\{\varphi_{u,g}\}_{g \in \mathcal{G}_k^{T_u}})$
21 | **end**
22 | $\hat{\tau}_u \leftarrow$ Ordering$(\{P(t)\}_{t \in T_u})$
23 **end**

After updating $\varphi_{u,g}$, we can easily get the probabilities $\hat{P}_u(g)$ according to Equation (3), which meets the constraint of $\sum_{g \in \mathcal{G}_k^{T_u}} \hat{P}_u(g) = 1$.

In order to obtain an ultimate ranking of T_u for each user u, the probabilities of the top-k permutation sets need to be aggregated. One intuitive way is to get the probabilities of the top-1 permutation sets and rank the items in T_u according to the descending order of the corresponding probabilities. The probability of the top-1 permutation set $P(\mathcal{G}_1^{T_u}(t_j))$ actually equals to the sum of the probabilities of the top-k ($k > 1$) permutation sets with the item $t_j \in T_u$ ranked in the top-1 position. Here gives an example.

EXAMPLE 2. *Suppose user u has items $I = \{i_1, i_2, i_3\}$ to be recommended. We have probability distribution $\{0.2, 0.3, 0.1, 0.1, 0.1, 0.2\}$ over the set of top-2 permutation sets $\mathcal{G}_2^I = \{\mathcal{G}_2(i_1, i_2), \mathcal{G}_2(i_1, i_3), \mathcal{G}_2(i_2, i_1), \mathcal{G}_2(i_2, i_3), \mathcal{G}_2(i_3, i_1), \mathcal{G}_2(i_3, i_2)\}$. We can obtain the probabilities of that each item is ranked in the top-1 position: $P(\mathcal{G}_1(i_1)) = 0.2 + 0.3 = 0.5, P(\mathcal{G}_1(i_2)) = 0.1 + 0.1 = 0.2$, and $P(\mathcal{G}_1(i_3)) = 0.1 + 0.2 = 0.3$. Since $P(\mathcal{G}_1(i_1)) > P(\mathcal{G}_1(i_3)) > P(\mathcal{G}_1(i_2))$, the recommendation list is ordered as $\langle i_1, i_3, i_2 \rangle$.*

3.3 Pseudocode and Discussion

The pseudocode of the ListCF algorithm is shown in Algorithm 1, where lines 1-7 calculate the similarities between users and discover the neighbor users for each target user, and lines 8-23 predict the ranking of items to make recommendations. When $k > 1$ in the top-k probability model, lines 19-21 aggregate the probabilities of the top-k permutation sets to obtain the probabilities of the top-1 permutation sets, that are the probabilities of each item $t \in T_u$ ranked in the first position.

In the proposed ListCF model, we use the top-k ($k \geq 1$) probability model [3] in the similarity calculation and ranking prediction phases. ListCF with different values of k may achieve different recommendation performances. On one hand, generally the accuracy will be higher when a larger k value is used. On the other hand, the computational complexity of similarity calculation and ranking prediction procedures will be exponentially increased. In particular, for a user u associated with n items, the number of permutation sets in the top-k probability model is $n!/(n-k)!$, and specially this number is merely n when $k = 1$. Thus the time complexity of ListCF based on the top-k ($k > 1$) probability model is $(n-1)!/(n-k)!$ times higher than that of ListCF based on the top-1 probability model.

Table 1: Accuracy and efficiency comparison of ListCF with different k.

	k=1	k=2	k=3
Accuracy (NDCG@5)	0.7866	0.7953	0.8052
Runtime of Phase I	8s	71s	3463s
Runtime of Phase II	1.5s	20.2s	731.7s

For illustration purpose, we randomly selected 1000 users from the MovieLens-1M dataset and conducted experiments to compare the ranking accuracy as well as the runtime of the similarity calculation and ranking prediction phases (Phase I and II respectively) of ListCF when $k = 1, 2$ and 3. The size of neighborhood users was set to be 50, and 50 unrated items were predicted for each user in Phase II. The results are reported in Table 1.

From the table we can see that, when $k > 1$ in ListCF, the improvement in recommendation accuracy is very subtle, but the degeneration of efficiency is extremely significant. For example, ListCF with $k = 3$ achieves about 0.02 improvement in NDCG@5 over ListCF with $k = 1$, but it takes 433 and 488 times longer in Phase (I) and Phase (II) respectively. Obviously, the loss outweighs the gain. Thus we set $k = 1$ when compare ListCF with other recommendation algorithms in the experimental section.

4. COLLABORATIVE FILTERING: LISTWISE VS. POINTWISE AND PAIRWISE

4.1 Relationship

Although ListCF, as a listwise memory-based CF algorithm, is completely different from pointwise and pairwise memory-based CF algorithms in similarity calculation and ranking prediction, these three categories of algorithms inherently share similar prediction strategy.

THEOREM 1. *ListCF predicts the probability of a top-k permutation set as the weighted average of the neighbors' probabilities of the corresponding top-k permutation sets, if*

$\forall v \in N_u : T_{u,v} \equiv T_u$ *holds. Formally, for* $\forall g \in \mathcal{G}_k^{T_u}$,

$$\hat{P}_u(g) = \frac{\sum_{v \in N_u} s(u,v) P'_v(g)}{\sum_{v \in N_u} s(u,v)}.$$

PROOF. If $\forall v \in N_u : T_{u,v} \equiv T_u$, then $\forall v \in N_u : G_k^{T_{u,v}} \equiv G_k^{T_u}$. For the optimization problem in Equation (5), set the derivative of F (Equation 7) to be 0:

$$\sum_{v \in N_u} \frac{s(u,v)}{\ln 2 \cdot \sum_{g' \in \mathcal{G}_k^{T_{u,v}}} \varphi_{u,g'}} - \frac{\sum_{v \in N_u} s(u,v) P'_v(g)}{\ln 2 \cdot \varphi_{u,g}}$$

$$= \frac{\sum_{v \in N_u} s(u,v)}{\ln 2 \cdot \sum_{g' \in \mathcal{G}_k^{T_u}} \varphi_{u,g'}} - \frac{\sum_{v \in N_u} s(u,v) P'_v(g)}{\ln 2 \cdot \varphi_{u,g}} = 0.$$

Thus

$$\frac{\sum_{v \in N_u} s(u,v)}{\sum_{g' \in \mathcal{G}_k^{T_u}} \varphi_{u,g'}} = \frac{\sum_{v \in N_u} s(u,v) P'_v(g)}{\varphi_{u,g}},$$

and

$$\frac{\sum_{v \in N_u} s(u,v) P'_v(g)}{\sum_{v \in N_u} s(u,v)} = \frac{\varphi_{u,g}}{\sum_{g' \in \mathcal{G}_k^{T_u}} \varphi_{u,g'}} = \hat{P}_u(g).$$

□

Theorem 1 presents the prediction formula of ListCF in a special case when all the neighbor users have rated the items in test set T_u of user u, i.e., $\forall v \in N_u : T_{u,v} \equiv T_u$ holds. In this case, for $\forall g \in \mathcal{G}_k^{T_u}$, the probability $\hat{P}_u(g)$ can be predicted as the weighted average of the neighbors' corresponding probabilities, which is the same as the pairwise preference prediction formula in pairwise memory-based CF [15, 27, 28] as well as the rating prediction formula in the pointwise memory-based CF after performing the normalization of the ratings, i.e., the average rating of the user u has been deducted from each rating $r_{u,i}$ of u, formally $r_{u,i}^{(N)} = r_{u,i} - \overline{r}_u$.

Now we explain why we cannot obtain such a result without the constraint of $\forall v \in N_u : T_{u,v} \equiv T_u$ in ListCF while we can with the constraint. In pointwise CF and pairwise CF, the ratings and the pairwise preferences of users are constant. However, in listwise CF, the probability distributions of each pair of users u and v in the ranking prediction phase vary with respect to the set of items $T_{u,v}$: (1) Given a target user u, for any two different neighborhood users v_1 and v_2, since $T_{u,v_1} \neq T_{u,v_2}$ and $\mathcal{G}_k^{T_{u,v_1}} \neq \mathcal{G}_k^{T_{u,v_2}}$, the length of the probability distribution $\hat{P}_u$ of user u could change and the values in $\hat{P}_u$ could be different; (2) Given two different target users u_1 and u_2 who have a same neighborhood user v, the probability distribution of P'_v for user v could also be different. Thus we cannot simply make predictions with a weighted average formula as pointwise and pairwise CF do. However, with the constraint of $\forall v \in N_u : T_{u,v} \equiv T_u$, $\mathcal{G}_k^{T_{u,v}} = \mathcal{G}_k^{T_u}$, the probabilities $\hat{P}_u(g)$ and $P'_v(g)$ ($\forall g \in \mathcal{G}_k^{T_u}$) in the ranking prediction formula are invariable, which is the same as those in pointwise CF and pairwise CF. In this case, we can obtain the same result shown in Theorem 1.

4.2 Advantages of ListCF

In comparison with conventional pairwise ranking-oriented CF, listwise CF demonstrates many advantages in efficiency (when $k = 1$) and accuracy on account of the listwise representation.

On the efficiency side, let M and N be the number of users and items. Suppose each user has rated n items on average, and the number of commonly rated items for each pair of users is $\overline{n}$. In the similarity calculation phase, the time complexity of ListCF is $\mathcal{O}\left(M^2(n+\overline{n})\right)$. Recall that the complexity of pairwise CF is $\mathcal{O}\left(M^2(n+\overline{n}^2)\right)$, which is $(n + \overline{n}^2)/(n + \overline{n})$ times higher than that of ListCF. Suppose each user has l neighbor users on average, and each prediction process maximally performs d iterations for gradient descent optimization. In the ranking prediction phase, the time complexity of ListCF is $\mathcal{O}\left(M(N-n)ld\right)$, where $N - n$ is the number of items to recommend. Recall that the complexity of pairwise CF is $\mathcal{O}\left(M(N-n)^2 l\right)$, which is $(N-n)/d$ times higher than that of ListCF, and $d \ll N - n$ in our experiments. Since d is a constant, the ratio of the complexity of pairwise CF to that of ListCF increases linearly with the growth of the number of items to be predicted in the ranking prediction phase.

On the accuracy side, firstly, permutation probability based similarity metric considers the ranking position information of items, which can discover more accurate neighbor users with similar preferences. Secondly, permutation probability based representation can easily handle the the case of equal preferences on items, i.e., assigns equal probability to the permutations in which the top items have equal ranking scores. Thirdly, ListCF attempts to make top-n recommendation by optimizing listwise loss function, which is more natural and accurate. The following example demonstrates the accuracy loss of the Kendall's τ correlation coefficient because of not considering the ranking position information of items.

EXAMPLE 3. *Suppose there are three users* $U = \{u_1, u_2, u_3\}$ *and three items* $I = \{i_1, i_2, i_3\}$, *where* u_1 *assigned ratings of* $\{5, 3, 4\}$ *to items,* u_2 *assigned* $\{5, 4, 3\}$, *and* u_3 *assigned* $\{4, 3, 5\}$.

In pointwise CF, the similarity (Pearson correlation coefficient) between u_1 *and* u_2 *and the similarity between* u_1 *and* u_3 *are* $\rho(u_1, u_2) = \rho(u_1, u_3) = 0.5$.

In pairwise CF, the similarity (Kendall's τ *correlation coefficient) between* u_1 *and* u_2 *and the similarity between* u_1 *and* u_3 *are* $\tau(u_1, u_2) = \tau(u_1, u_3) = 0.333$.

In ListCF, according to Equation (1), the top-1 probability distributions of users u_1, u_2 *and* u_3 *are* $P_{u_1} = (0.665, 0.090, 0.245)$, $P_{u_2} = (0.665, 0.245, 0.090)$, *and* $P_{u_3} = (0.245, 0.090, 0.665)$. *According to Equation (2),* $s(u_1, u_2) = 0.776$ *and* $s(u_1, u_3) = 0.395$, *and thus* $s(u_1, u_2) > s(u_1, u_3)$.

Since recommender systems aim to recommend the items that users may be most interested in, we should emphasize the items with highest scores in the similarity calculation and ranking prediction phases, and thus u_2 is more similar to u_1 than u_3 in Example 3. Obviously, ListCF can successfully recognize it while pointwise CF and pairwise CF cannot.

5. EXPERIMENTS

5.1 Experimental Settings

5.1.1 Datasets

Table 2: Statistics on the three datasets.

	Movielens-1M	EachMovie	Netflix
#users	6,040	36,656	429,584
#items	3,952	1,623	17,770
#ratings	1,000,209	2,580,222	99,884,940
#ratings/user	165.6	70.4	232.5
#ratings/item	253.1	1589.8	5621.0
sparsity	93.7%	95.7%	98.7%

We conducted a series of experiments on three real-world rating datasets: Movielens-1M, EachMovie, and Netflix. All of these datasets are commonly used benchmark datasets in evaluating recommendation performance. The ratings in Movielens-1M and Netflix are on a scale from 1 to 5, while the EachMovie rating scale is from 1 to 6. In order to guarantee that there are adequate number of ratings per user for training and testing, we removed those users who have rated less than 20 items from these datasets. Several statistics on the resulting datasets are presented in Table 2, where the sparsity levels in the last row are calculated as follows [23]:

$$Sparsity = 1 - \frac{\#\text{rating scores}}{\#\text{users} \times \#\text{items}}.$$

5.1.2 Comparison Algorithms

In our experiments, we mainly compared the performance of ListCF with three memory-based CF algorithms of PointCF[1], EigenRank [15] and VSRank [27, 28], a classic pointwise rating-oriented algorithm and two state-of-the-art pairwise ranking-oriented algorithms respectively. In particular, PointCF uses the Pearson correlation coefficient to calculate the similarity between users, and ranks the items according to the predicted ratings for each user. In EigenRank and VSRank, the greedy aggregation method is used to aggregate the predicted pairwise preferences of items into total ranks. In the memory-based CF algorithms, the number of neighborhood users was set to be 100 in Movielens-1M and EachMovie, and 300 in Netflix. Since ListCF is also a memory-based CF algorithm, a direct comparison of them will provide valuable and irreplaceable insights.

Besides, we also chose CoFiRank [29] and ListRank-MF [25], two state-of-the-art model-based ranking-oriented CF algorithms for comparison to further demonstrate the promising performance of ListCF. Like [29], the dimensionality of latent features was set be to 10.

5.2 Efficiency Comparison

In order to evaluate the efficiency of our model, we chose PointCF and EigenRank as our comparison partners, as they share the same memory-based CF framework with ListCF. Since CofiRank[1] and ListRank-MF[2] are two model-based CF algorithms and the implementation of them is based on the publicly available software packages written in different program languages from us, we did not include them in this section.

We conducted experiments to compare their runtime of the similarity calculation phase and ranking prediction phase on the datasets. Due to the huge size of the Netflix data, we selected users from Netflix who had rated no more than 50 items to form an extremely sparse dataset containing about 100,000 users. As analyzed in Section 4.2, when the number of items each user has rated increases the difference between EigenRank and ListCF would be more distinct, and we omit the result here. Experiments were run on a computer with 4 core 2 GHz CPU and 64 GB RAM.

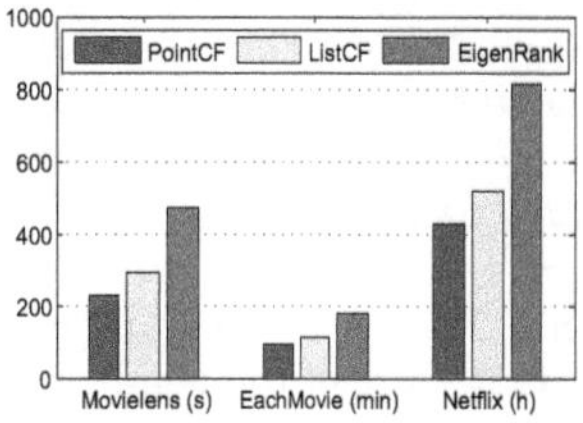

Figure 1: Runtime comparison of the similarity calculation phase.

Figure 1 demonstrates the respective runtime of the similarity calculation phase of PointCF, ListCF and EigenRank on three datasets. Note that the units of the runtime are Second (s), Minute (min) and Hour (h) for the datasets of Movielens-1M, EachMovie and Netflix respectively. From Figure 1, we can observe that in the similarity calculation phase:

- The runtime of ListCF is comparable with PointCF, where ListCF is merely around 1.2 times higher than PointCF. The slight increase of the runtime of ListCF mainly results from an extra step of computing the top-1 probability distributions for each pair of users.
- The runtime of ListCF is much lower than that of EigenRank, saving almost 40% time. This observation is consistent with our theoretical analysis in Section 4.2, which is that in the similarity calculation phase, the computational cost of pairwise CF is $(n + \overline{n}^2)/(n + \overline{n})$ higher than that of ListCF, where n is the average number of items rated by users, and $\overline{n}$ is the average number of co-rated items by each pair of users.

Figure 2 shows the runtime comparison of the ranking prediction phase of the three CF algorithms, where the horizontal axis in these four sub-figures is the number of items to be predicted for each user. The vertical axis in Figure 2(a), 2(b) and 2(c) is the runtime of the algorithms, and the vertical axis in Figure 2(d) is the runtime ratio of EigenRank to ListCF. From the figures we can see that, in the ranking prediction phase ListCF demonstrates significant improvement in prediction efficiency in comparison with EigenRank.

[1]http://www.CoFiRank.org/

[2]http://mmc.tudelft.nl/users/yue-shi

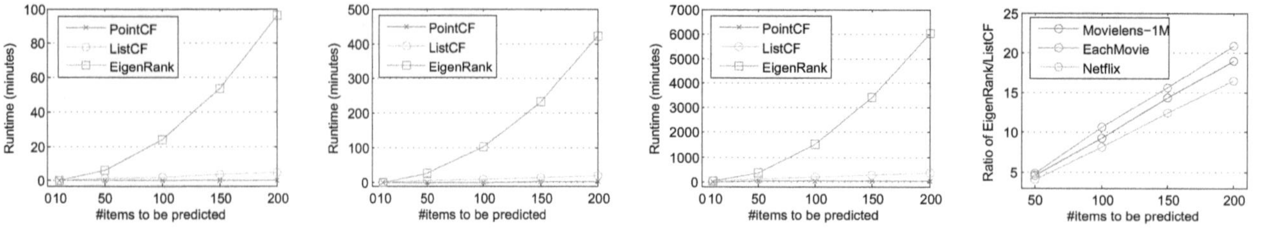

(a) Runtime on Movielens (b) Runtime on EachMovie (c) Runtime on Netflix (d) Runtime improvement

Figure 2: Runtime comparison of the ranking prediction phase.

- From Figure 2(a), 2(b) and 2(c) we can see that the runtime of both ListCF and PointCF is linearly increased with the growth of the number of items to be predicted, while the increase of EigenRank (the pairwise CF) is quadratic. This observation is consistent with our theoretical analysis in Section 4.2 that, in the ranking prediction phase, the computational costs of ListCF and pairwise CF are $\mathcal{O}(M(N-n)ld)$ and $\mathcal{O}\left(M(N-n)^2l\right)$ respectively, where M is the number of users, and $N-n$ is the number of items to be predicted. l is the size of the neighbor set, and d is the maximal number of iterations in the gradient descent based optimization method.
- From Figure 2(d) we can see that the runtime ratio of EigenRank to ListCF increases linearly with the growth of the number of items to be predicted in the ranking prediction phase. This observation is consistent with our analyzed result $(N-n)/d$ in Section 4.2, where $N-n$ is the number of items to be predicted, and d is a constant, i.e., the maximal number of iterations in the gradient descent optimization method. The gradients of the curves are slightly different because some iterative optimization processes could converge before reaching the maximal number of iterations d.
- The runtime of ListCF is significantly reduced as compared to EigenRank even when no more than 200 items are predicted. For example, for the EachMovie dataset, ListCF takes 20min to predict the total rankings of 200 items for 36656 users, while the runtime of EigenRank is 423min, which is 21 times longer. The results on Movielens-1M and Netflix are 19 times and 16 times longer respectively.

5.3 Prediction Accuracy Comparison

To demonstrate the recommendation accuracy of our model, we compare ListCF with all of the state-of-the-art recommendation algorithms mentioned in Section 5.1.2 on three datasets of Movielens-1M, EachMovie and Netflix. For each dataset, we randomly select each user's 10 rated items and their corresponding ratings to form test set, and the remaining ratings are used to form train set.

5.3.1 Evaluation Metric

For rating-based CF algorithms, the standard evaluation criteria are the Mean Absolute Error (MAE) and the Root Mean Square Error (RMSE). Both criteria measure the error between true ratings and predicted ratings. Since our study focuses on improving item rankings instead of rating prediction, we employ the Normalized Discounted Cumulative Gain (NDCG) [7, 8] as the evaluation metric, which is the most popular accuracy metric in information retrieval for evaluating ranking of retrieved documents with multi-level relevance scores.

In the context of collaborative filtering, item ratings assigned by users can naturally serve as relevance judgments. The NDCG metric is evaluated over some number of the top items on the ranked item list. Let U be the set of users and r_u^p be the rating score assigned by user u to the item at the pth position of the ranked list. The NDCG value at the nth position with respect to the given user u is defined as follows:

$$NDCG_u@n = Z_u \sum_{p=1}^{n} \frac{2^{r_u^p}-1}{\log(1+p)},$$

where Z_u is a normalization factor calculated so that the NDCG value of the optimal ranking is 1. $NDCG@n$ takes the mean of the $NDCG_u@n$ over the set of users U, which is defined as follows:

$$NDCG@n = \frac{1}{|U|}\sum_{u=1}^{|U|} NDCG_u@n,$$

where $|U|$ is the cardinality of the set of users.

5.3.2 Performance on Movielens-1M and EachMovie

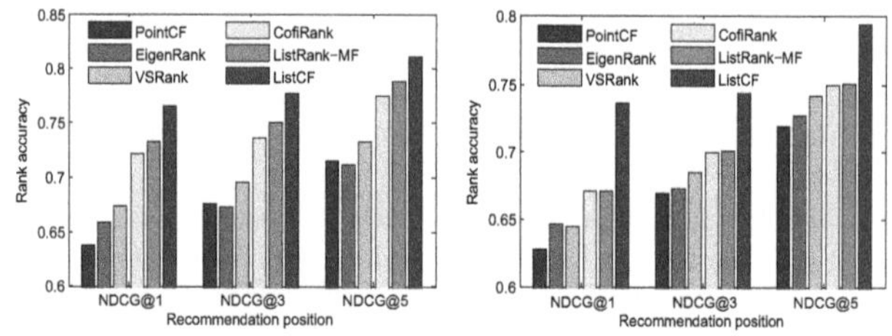

(a) Movielens-1M (b) EachMovie

Figure 3: Ranking performance comparison on Movielens-1M and EachMovie.

Figure 3 shows the performance comparison results in terms of NDCG@1, 3 and 5 on the Movielens-1M and EachMovie datasets. From the figure we can observe that:

- Ranking-oriented CF algorithms generally achieve more accurate top recommendations than the rating-oriented CF algorithm (PointCF) under most conditions except NDCG@3 and 5 on Movielens-1M.
- ListCF outperforms all of the comparison partners, including the pairwise ranking-oriented CF algorithms

Table 3: **Ranking performance comparison on Netflix with different user groups. The percentages are the improvements of ListCF over the corresponding approaches.**

User group	Metric	PointCF	EigenRank	VSRank	CoFiRank	ListRank-MF	ListCF
20-50	NDCG@1	0.6581 6.42%	0.6600 6.12%	0.6590 6.28%	0.6824 2.56%	0.6929 1.08%	**0.7004**
	NDCG@3	0.6866 4.49%	0.6791 5.64%	0.6723 6.71%	0.7106 0.96%	**0.7218** -0.61%	0.7174
	NDCG@5	0.7233 3.40%	0.7144 4.69%	0.7126 4.95%	0.7322 1.72%	**0.7570** *-0.90%*	0.7502
50-100	NDCG@1	0.6693 10.14%	0.6898 6.87%	0.6883 7.10%	0.6990 5.46%	0.7233 1.92%	**0.7372**
	NDCG@3	0.7057 7.17%	0.7085 6.75%	0.7117 6.27%	0.7153 5.73%	0.7359 2.77%	**0.7563**
	NDCG@5	0.7445 5.00%	0.7364 6.15%	0.7406 5.55%	0.7591 2.98%	0.7679 1.80%	**0.7817**
100-200	NDCG@1	0.6765 13.32%	0.6900 11.10%	0.7014 9.30%	0.6954 10.24%	0.7357 4.20%	**0.7666**
	NDCG@3	0.7093 9.11%	0.7174 7.88%	0.7228 7.07%	0.7235 6.97%	0.7494 3.27%	**0.7739**
	NDCG@5	0.7491 6.62%	0.7565 5.58%	0.7641 4.53%	0.7755 2.99%	0.7794 2.48%	**0.7987**

and also listwise model-based CF algorithms. The improvement is more distinct on EachMovie dataset. For example, ListCF achieves improvements of 9.25% over EigenRank and 5.9% over ListRank-MF on EachMovie in terms of NDCG@5.

- In comparison with all the other algorithms, the improvements of ListCF are more significant in terms of NDCG at higher positions. For example, for Movielens-1M, ListCF improves 19.88%, 14.97%, and 13.41% in terms of NDCG@1, 3 and 5 in comparison with PointCF, and these numbers are 16.29%, 15.51%, and 13.93% respectively in comparison with EigenRank. For EachMovie, we can get similar trends. This is because ListCF considers the ranking position issue in the similarity calculation phase, which is demonstrated in Example 3 in Section 4.2.

5.3.3 *Performance on Netflix*

In previous experiments, we show that ListCF can generate superior performance in top-n recommendation on Movielens-1M and EachMovie datasets compared with other recommendation algorithms. In order to compare our model with the other algorithms thoroughly, distinct from previous validations focusing on comparing global quality of recommendations over all users, here we are particularly interested in testing the performance of respective algorithms in regard to different groups of users. We first select user groups based on the number of observed ratings in the training set. We use group "20-50", "50-100" and "100-200" as experimental subjects, and each user group contains about 90 thousand users. User group "20-50" denotes users who have rated more than 20 and less than 50 items in the training set. User groups represent different datasets with different sparsities. The sparsity of user group "20-50" is 99.87%, and it is the sparsest dataset among three datasets.

The detailed experimental results are reported in Table 3. From the table we can see that:

- All of the recommendation algorithms perform worse on sparser datasets. For example, our memory-based algorithm ListCF achieves 0.7666 in NDCG@1 on group "100-200" while 0.7004 on group "20-50", and the numbers of the model-based algorithm ListRank-MF are 0.7357 on group "100-200" while 0.6929 on group "20-50".

- Our ListCF can significantly outperform other memory-based algorithms, both pointwise (PointCF) and pairwise CF (EigenRank and VSRank), in all evaluation metrics of NDCG@1, 3 and 5. In addition, similar to the results on Movielens-1M and EachMovie, ranking-oriented algorithms, both pairwise and listwise CF, achieve more accurate predictions than rating-oriented CF (PointCF).

- ListCF can outperform the model-based ranking-oriented algorithms under most conditions except NDCG@3 and NDCG@5 on group "20-50" of ListRank-MF. The reason might be that ListCF, as a memory-based algorithm, cannot find useful neighborhood users and make accurate predictions if the dataset is too sparse because of that the commonly rated items between users are too rare. However, even on this dataset with the sparsity of 99.87%, ListCF can also achieve the best performance in NDCG@1, with improvements of 2.56% and 1.08% over CoFiRank and ListRank-MF respectively.

- As a whole, the improvements of ListCF are more distinct on denser datasets in comparison with other algorithms. For example, on the densest dataset (group "100-200"), the improvements of ListCF are 13.32%, 9.11% and 6.62% in terms of NDCG@1, 3 and 5 respectively compared with PointCF, while on the sparsest dataset (group "20-50"), these numbers become 6.42%, 4.49% and 3.40%. The reason is similar to the previous observation, which is that the number of co-rated items between users are larger on a denser dataset, and thus ListCF can find more accurate neighborhood users to make predictions.

- Similar to the experimental results on Movielens-1M and Eachmovie, the improvements of ListCF over other algorithms are more significant in terms of NDCG at higher positions as a whole. We can see that the improvements of ListCF are increased with decrease of positions (n) in NDCG@n. For example, for the group "100-200", ListCF improves 13.32%, 9.11% and 6.62% over PointCF in terms of NDCG@1, 3 and 5 respectively, and similar results can be obtained as compared with other algorithms on all of the three groups. This is because the permutation probability model in ListCF consider the ranking position issue in the similarity calculation phase, which is demonstrated in Example 3 in Section 4.2.

6. CONCLUSION

In this paper, we propose ListCF, a listwise ranking-oriented model for collaborative filtering. ListCF measures the user-user similarity based on the Kullback-Leibler divergence between users' probability distributions over permutations of commonly rated items. It predicts item rankings for each user by minimizing the cross entropy loss between the target user and his neighbors with weighted similarities. Experimental results on three benchmark datasets show that ListCF demonstrates many advantages in recommendation efficiency and ranking accuracy. In addition, we prove that ListCF shares similar prediction strategy with pointwise and pairwise memory-based CF under certain constraints.

In the future, we plan to explore other possible listwise loss functions in ListCF. In addition, it is also interesting to investigate model-based listwise CF algorithms based on the top-k probability representations.

7. ACKNOWLEDGMENTS

This work was supported by the Natural Science Foundation of China (61272240, 61103151, 71402083, 71171122), Humanity and Social Science Foundation of Ministry of Education of China (12YJC630211), the Natural Science foundation of Shandong province (ZR2012FM037, BS2012DX012), Academy of Finland (268078), the Doctoral Fund of Ministry of Education of China (20110131110028).

8. REFERENCES

[1] J. S. Breese, D. Heckerman, and C. Kadie. Empirical analysis of predictive algorithms for collaborative filtering. In *UAI*, pages 43–52, 1998.

[2] R. Burke. Hybrid recommender systems: Survey and experiments. *User Model. User-Adap. Inter.*, 12:331–370, 2002.

[3] Z. Cao, T. Qin, T.-Y. Liu, M.-F. Tsai, and H. Li. Learning to rank: From pairwise approach to listwise approach. In *ICML*, pages 129–136, 2007.

[4] P. Cremonesi, Y. Koren, and R. Turrin. Performance of recommender algorithms on top-n recommendation tasks. In *RecSys*, pages 39–46, 2010.

[5] J. Herlocker, J. A. Konstan, and J. Riedl. An empirical analysis of design choices in neighborhood-based collaborative filtering algorithms. *Inform. Retr.*, 5(4):287–310, 2002.

[6] T. Hofmann. Latent semantic models for collaborative filtering. *ACM Trans. Inform. Syst.*, 22(1):89–115, 2004.

[7] K. Järvelin and J. Kekäläinen. IR evaluation methods for retrieving highly relevant documents. In *SIGIR*, pages 41–48, 2000.

[8] K. Järvelin and J. Kekäläinen. Cumulated gain-based evaluation of ir techniques. *ACM Trans. Inform. Syst.*, 20(4):422–446, 2002.

[9] Y. Koren, R. Bell, and C. Volinsky. Matrix factorization techniques for recommender systems. *Computer*, 42(8):30–37, 2009.

[10] Y. Koren and J. Sill. Ordrec: an ordinal model for predicting personalized item rating distributions. In *RecSys*, pages 117–124, 2011.

[11] S. Kullback. *Information Theory and Statistics*. Courier Dover Publications, 1997.

[12] D. D. Lee and H. S. Seung. Algorithms for non-negative matrix factorization. In *NIPS*, pages 556–562, 2001.

[13] X. Li, E. Gavves, C. G. Snoek, M. Worring, and A. W. Smeulders. Personalizing automated image annotation using cross-entropy. In *MM*, pages 233–242, 2011.

[14] G. Linden, B. Smith, and J. York. Amazon. com recommendations: Item-to-item collaborative filtering. *IEEE Internet Comput.*, 7(1):76–80, 2003.

[15] N. N. Liu and Q. Yang. Eigenrank: A ranking-oriented approach to collaborative filtering. In *SIGIR*, pages 83–90, 2008.

[16] P. Lops, M. de Gemmis, and G. Semeraro. Content-based recommender systems: State of the art and trends. In F. Ricci, L. Rokach, B. Shapira, and P. B. Kantor, editors, *Recommender Systems Handbook*, pages 73–105. Springer US, 2011.

[17] J. I. Marden. *Analyzing and modeling rank data*. CRC Press, 1996.

[18] S. M. McNee, J. Riedl, and J. A. Konstan. Being accurate is not enough: How accuracy metrics have hurt recommender systems. In *CHI*, pages 1097–1101, 2006.

[19] A. Mnih and R. Salakhutdinov. Probabilistic matrix factorization. In *NIPS*, pages 1257–1264, 2007.

[20] S. Rendle, C. Freudenthaler, Z. Gantner, and L. Schmidt-Thieme. Bpr: Bayesian personalized ranking from implicit feedback. In *UAI*, pages 452–461, 2009.

[21] J. D. Rennie and N. Srebro. Fast maximum margin matrix factorization for collaborative prediction. In *ICML*, pages 713–719, 2005.

[22] B. Sarwar, G. Karypis, J. Konstan, and J. Riedl. Analysis of recommendation algorithms for e-commerce. In *EC*, pages 158–167, 2000.

[23] B. Sarwar, G. Karypis, J. Konstan, and J. Riedl. Item-based collaborative filtering recommendation algorithms. In *WWW*, pages 285–295. ACM, 2001.

[24] Y. Shi, A. Karatzoglou, L. Baltrunas, M. Larson, N. Oliver, and A. Hanjalic. Climf: learning to maximize reciprocal rank with collaborative less-is-more filtering. In *RecSys*, pages 139–146, 2012.

[25] Y. Shi, M. Larson, and A. Hanjalic. List-wise learning to rank with matrix factorization for collaborative filtering. In *RecSys*, pages 269–272, 2010.

[26] Y. Taigman, M. Yang, M. Ranzato, and L. Wolf. DeepFace: Closing the gap to human-level performance in face verification. In *CVPR*, pages 1701–1708, 2013.

[27] S. Wang, J. Sun, B. J. Gao, and J. Ma. Adapting vector space model to ranking-based collaborative filtering. In *CIKM*, pages 1487–1491, 2012.

[28] S. Wang, J. Sun, B. J. Gao, and J. Ma. VSRank: A novel framework for ranking-based collaborative filtering. *ACM Trans. Intell. Syst. Technol.*, 5(3):No.51, 2014.

[29] M. Weimer, A. Karatzoglou, Q. V. Le, and A. Smola. Maximum margin matrix factorization for collaborative ranking. In *NIPS*, pages 1329–1336, 2007.

[30] S.-H. Yang, B. Long, A. J. Smola, H. Zha, and Z. Zheng. Collaborative competitive filtering: Learning recommender using context of user choice. In *SIGIR*, pages 295–304, 2011.

BROOF: Exploiting Out-of-Bag Errors, Boosting and Random Forests for Effective Automated Classification *

Thiago Salles Marcos Gonçalves Victor Rodrigues
Federal University of Minas Gerais
Computer Science Department
Belo Horizonte, Brazil
{tsalles, mgoncalv, victor.rodrigues}@dcc.ufmg.br

Leonardo Rocha
Federal University of São João Del-Rei
Computer Science Department
São João Del-Rei, Brazil
lcrocha@ufsj.edu.br

ABSTRACT

Random Forests (RF) and Boosting are two of the most successful supervised learning paradigms for automatic classification. In this work we propose to combine both strategies in order to exploit their strengths while simultaneously solving some of their drawbacks, especially when applied to high-dimensional and noisy classification tasks. More specifically, we propose a boosted version of the RF classifier (BROOF), which fits an additive model composed by several random forests (as weak learners). Differently from traditional boosting methods which exploit the training error estimate, we here use the stronger out-of-bag (OOB) error estimate which is an out-of-the-box estimate naturally produced by the bagging method used in RFs. The influence of each weak learner in the fitted additive model is inversely proportional to their OOB error. Moreover, the probability of selecting an out-of-bag training example is increased if misclassified by the simpler weak learners, in order to enable the boosted model to focus on complex regions of the input space. We also adopt a selective weight updating procedure, whereas only the out-of-bag examples are updated as the boosting iterations go by. This serves the purpose of slowing down the tendency to focus on just a few hard-to-classify examples. By mitigating this undesired bias known to affect boosting algorithms under high dimensional and noisy scenarios—due to both the selective weighting schema and a proper weak-learner effectiveness assessment—we greatly improve classification effectiveness. Our experiments with several datasets in three representative high-dimensional and noisy domains—topic, sentiment and microarray data classification—and up to ten state-of-the-art classifiers (covering almost 500 results), show that BROOF is the only classifier to be among the top performers in all tested datasets from the topic classification domain, and in the vast majority of cases in sentiment and microarray domains, a surprising result given the knowledge that there is no single top-notch classifier for all datasets.

*This work was partially supported by CNPq, CAPES, FINEP, FAPEMIG and INWEB.

SIGIR'15, August 09–13, 2015, Santiago, Chile
Copyright 2015 ACM 978-1-4503-3621-5/15/08...$15.00.
http://dx.doi.org/10.1145/2766462.2767747.

Categories and Subject Descriptors

I.5.4 [**Applications**]: Text processing

General Terms

Algorithms; Experimentation

Keywords

Classification; Random Forests; Boosting

1. INTRODUCTION

This paper advances the state of the art in automatic classification by "smoothly" combining, in an original way, characteristics of two learning strategies which excel in a variety of learning tasks: the Random Forest classifier and boosting. Proposed in [2], the Random Forest (RF) classifier has been surprisingly successful in a wide variety of automatic classification tasks, being considered by many [6, 14] as a top-notch supervised algorithm, comparable (sometimes superior) to Support Vector Machine (SVM) classifiers.

The RF classifier is a variation of the classic bagging (bootstrapped aggregation) procedure, where an ensemble of m decision tree classifiers are trained with sets of bootstrapped samples[1] drawn from the training set $\mathbb{D}_{train}$. The crucial aspects, as pointed out in [2], that make the RF classifier a good classifier are (i) the reduced correlation between the decision trees composing the ensemble and (ii) the better-than-random-guess predictions of each tree. In fact, to achieve reduced correlation, each tree is learned with a bootstrapped sample of $\mathbb{D}_{train}$ and each decision node is specified by a chosen attribute drawn from a randomly chosen subset of features. To achieve strong decision trees (i.e., trees with better prediction performance than random guessing), each tree is typically grown to its maximum depth. Taken together, the RF classifier averages several de-correlated (rather complex) models, ultimately reducing variance while keeping the bias unchanged [14]. This typically brings up better models, with higher generalization power, that can successfully be applied to a wide variety of datasets.

A very important aspect for the sake of our work, is that the RF classifier is able to produce robust estimates of generalization power, the so-called out-of-bag (OOB) error estimate, which comes naturally from the bagging procedure

[1]Examples randomly sampled with replacement.

this classifier exploits. As the RF classifier bootstraps the training dataset, roughly e^{-1} training examples are left out when learning a decision tree[2]. These examples, the so-called OOB samples, can be effectively used to assess generalization power of the tree. Considering the tree ensemble, an averaged estimate can be used to assess the generalization power of the RF classifier. As it is already known, the out-of-bag estimates are efficient to compute, since they can be measured when learning the classifier, with little additional effort. Moreover, it is capable of producing close approximations of the expected error rate, which is unbiased (unlike the training error rate). As we shall see, the exploitation of the OOB error is one of the core aspects of our proposal.

However, RFs are not free of drawbacks. Despite being a classifier with great generalization capabilities, when learned from *noisy* data, common in datasets based on human language or imprecise measurements, RFs have been known to cause overfitting [25], degrading classification effectiveness on unseen test data. More specifically, it has been shown that the RF classifiers whose decision trees are grown to their maximum depth are deemed to perform poorly in the presence of many noisy attributes (e.g., rare, anomalous, irrelevant, with low discriminative power and low generalization in the test sets).

In fact, [25, 27] validate the overfitting issue faced by random forest models when learning to classify high-dimensional noisy data. In both works, the authors showed that there exist some data distributions where maximal unprunned trees used in the random forests do not achieve as good performance as the trees with smaller number of splits and/or smaller node size. This has to do with the unnecessary variance [14] incurred by the model: the bagged decision trees become plagued by irrelevant or noisy attributes, which introduces unnecessary model complexity. This ultimately hampers its effectiveness when applied to new unseen data. However, if one simply prunes the RF's trees, the overall classification effectiveness may be compromised in high-dimensional classification tasks plagued by irrelevant attributes, since the probability of selecting informative attributes is reduced [18]. This is a critical issue, since in real world problems it is entirely conceivable that one can be confronted with noisy, skewed, correlated and high-dimensional data.

As we shall see in our experiments, contrasting the effectiveness of the traditional Random Forest classifier in a series of datasets—characterized by high dimensionality and noise—against the baselines we can observe that the effectiveness of such a classifier is often not satisfactory, performing poorly when compared to other classifiers in most cases. This confirms some of the posed arguments regarding the drawbacks of this algorithm in the target scenario.

Another well studied and successful classification technique is boosting. Recent studies [3, 10] have shown that boosting provides excellent predictive performance across a wide variety of tasks. It is an iterative algorithm which combines several models, called weak-learners, which influence the final decision proportionally to their accuracy. Furthermore, each successive classification model focuses on even more complex regions of the input space, by means of input data manipulation. Two aspects play a key role here: (*i*) the influence of each learner in the fitted additive model, and (*ii*) the focus on hard to classify regions of the input space. More importantly, since boosting combines the predictions of multiple weak-learners it also is able to significantly reduce unnecessary variance. Thus, the fundamental aspects that must be defined include: (*i*) how to re-weight the training examples in each subsequent iteration, and (*ii*) how to weight each single prediction in order to generate the final prediction. Such weights are usually based on the in-sample error rate. The downside is that it is an overly optimistic estimate of generalization performance.

The above discussion highlights potential opportunities to combine random forests and boosting in order to exploit their strengths while, at the same time, helping to solve some of their drawbacks, especially for automatic classification of high-dimensional noisy data. That is exactly what we do. In more details, we propose to exploit a boosting strategy to guide a sequence of random forest classifiers in specific sub-regions of the input space (those with higher uncertainty), ultimately constraining the input space search to relevant sub-regions and thus mitigating the overfitting issue by avoiding noisy and irrelevant features. This has the potential to circumvent some of the aforementioned drawbacks that may degrade the performance of the traditional RF classifier under high-dimensional noisy classification tasks. However, differently from traditional boosting methods, which uses the training error estimate as a basis to update the ensemble, we here propose to use the stronger out-of-bag (OOB) error estimate which is out-of-the-box estimate naturally produced by the bagging method used in RFs. In such way, the random forest classifier can produce much more robust estimates for generalization capability, which can be exploited by the boosting process both to re-weight training examples and to weight the sequence of predictors in order to come up with a more robust final classification model. A *second important* difference is that we employ a less aggressive selective weight update. In other words, by selectively updating only the weights associated with the out-of-bag examples, we slow down the undesired bias of the boosting strategy towards a few hard-to-classify examples, which helps to prevent overfitting, while still driving down misclassification rate of the ensemble.

In sum, the main contribution of this work is an advance in the state of the art in automatic classification by the proposition of a new, original classifier (BROOF), which smoothly combines properties of RFs and boosting. The originality of our proposal comes from two aspects: (i) we propose a new weighting scheme which is able to greatly improve the boosting strategy by means of a much more reliable measure of generalization power, offered by the RF itself: the out-of-bag error estimate, and (ii) we also propose to exploit a selective weight updating scheme, which slows down the undesired bias towards a few input points, thus preventing overfitting while boosting effectiveness. We demonstrate that both contributions, as well as their interactions, are equally important for our improvements. Moreover, our experiments (covering almost 500 results) show that, in all cases, the proposed BROOF is the only classifier to be among the top performers in all tested datasets from the topic classification domain, and in the vast majority of cases in sentiment and microarray domains, each composed

[2]The constant e denotes the base of the natural logarithm. $e^{-1} \approx 0.37$.

by a series of high-dimensional and noisy datasets and a rich set of 10 state-of-the-art representative baselines. This is a surprising result given the knowledge that there is no single top-notch classifier for all datasets. This highlights the benefits of such a synergy between both widely used strategies. Moreover, we also empirically demonstrate that our classifier is more "training-efficient", i.e., it requires less training than the baselines to produce its best results.

2. RELATED WORK

This work deals with two well known learning strategies, the RF classifier, as well as the meta-algorithm boosting. As we shall detail, we here propose to take advantage of a RF's key characteristic to provide a very accurate boosting classifier, which, as we empirically show, excels in automatic classification of high-dimensional and noisy data. In this section, we discuss some relevant work on these matters, pointing out our motivations and tying together with the literature the major contributions of this work.

2.1 Random Forests

The RF classifier was proposed in [2] as a variation of bagging of decision trees. An ensemble of low-correlated decision trees is built through a series of random procedures, such as bootstrapping of training data and random attribute selection to compose the decision nodes. A plethora of proposals aimed at improving the RF effectiveness can be found in the literature, usually characterized by reducing the correlation among the trees composing the ensemble. We review some of them here. Since our proposal is based on boosting, considering the RF classifier as weak-learner, we also discuss some important work on this matter.

The popularity of RF classifiers is highlighted by their successful application in several domains, such as object segmentation [24] and human pose recognition [26], outperforming state-of-the-art strategies, such as the SVM classifier. Thus, it is natural to expect several extensions to such classifier, in order to improve its effectiveness even more.

In this direction, in [20] two strategies were proposed to improve RF by increasing the strength of the decision trees or reducing the correlation among them. The author proposes the use of several attribute evaluation metrics to select the attributes to be used in decision nodes, and the inclusion of a sophisticated weighted voting schema which takes into account the effectiveness of decision trees when applied to the training instances most similar to the test instance. In order to introduce more randomness (and thus, reduce the correlation among the decision trees), in [21] the so-called Rotation-RF was proposed. This strategy randomly groups the attributes, building subproblems which are projected into new feature subspaces, reduced via PCA. The principal components are, then, used to learn the classifier.

Some previous work dynamically build the RF classifier, taking a closer look into the potential each decision tree in the ensemble has to increase the overall ensemble effectiveness. More specifically, in [29], the RF classifier is modified in order to keep just the most useful decision trees in the ensemble. When classifying a new example x, the decision trees with highest prediction effectiveness considering the out-of-bag examples most similar to x receive a higher vote in the final prediction average. That is, the final prediction is a weighted average of the individual decision trees, whereas each weight is proportional to the prediction performance of the trees considering the out-of-bag training examples in the neighborhood of x.

Aware of the potential overfitting issue faced by boosting strategies when confronted with noisy data, in [1] the authors propose an improved random forest classifier which exploits the adaptive re-sampling principle of boosting: the dynamic random forests classifier. Instead of boosting random forest classifiers, as we do here, the authors propose to proceed with the usual bagging approach of a traditional RF. However, when learning the decision trees composing the ensemble, an additional sample re-weighting schema (reminding boosting by re-sampling) is followed in order to build new decision trees that focus more on hard-to-classify regions of the input space. Starting with a uniform probability mass assigned to every training example, as new trees are added to the ensemble, the current misclassification rate of the out-of-bag samples are computed and used to re-weight them. When learning the next decision tree to be added in the ensemble, the weights of each training sample are used to influence both the splitting criterion and the base prediction. As stated by the authors, this serves the purpose of guiding the ensemble to hard-to-classify regions of the input space in a slower and smoother way (one only updates the weights of out-of-bag samples), thus avoiding the bias towards a few hard-to-classify examples. Thus, instead of applying boosting and then bagging (such as in the proposed BROOF classifier), the authors propose to apply bagging and then boosting. As the authors observed in the reported experimental evaluation, such strategy is not robust to the presence of many irrelevant attributes. In fact, the compromise between compensating previous errors (by means of sample re-weighting) and reinforcing correct prediction (by means of relating the weights to the accuracy of the entire ensemble on the previous iteration) may not be enough to guarantee robustness to datasets with many irrelevant attributes, since overfitted trees may lead to misleading weights due to the presence of many irrelevant paths on the decision trees, specially on the initial iterations. Since the evaluation of the entire ensemble is critical for the reweighting step on the next iteration, and the previous ensemble state may be already overfitted, the errors may be unwittingly propagated as the random forest is built, being not robust to such high dimensional noisy data.

In sum, most of the previous work has tackled issues related to improving the choice of features or the quality of the forest of trees. Here, we tackle a different issue, trying to overcome problems related to overfitting, known to happen in RFs in the presence of noisy/irrelevant data mainly in highly dimensional problems.

In the light of the peculiarities observed in high dimensional noisy classification tasks, here we focus on exploring the RF classifier in a boosting strategy in order to provide a highly effective learner for such tasks, by means of a novel approach which is able to overcome the mentioned challenges regarding both the RF classifier and the boosting strategy. We also revisit the state-of-the-art in automatic classification, providing an in-depth comparison of RF-based classifiers (including BROOF) with a series of baseline algorithms known to produce highly accurate predictions, considering three representative automatic classification domains covering a variety of high dimensional and noisy datasets.

2.2 Boosting Methods

Before delving into our proposed strategy, we briefly discuss some work regarding boosting algorithms for classification. Boosting [23] is a meta-algorithm which employs a general voting method for learning from a sequence of (simple) models. It is a sequential algorithm which learns several weak-learners (that is, classifiers able to produce predictions slightly better than random guessing) to devise very accurate predictions. For each iteration i of the boosting algorithm, let Δ^i be a probability distribution over the training set of size m. When $i = 0$, $\Delta^0(i) = \frac{1}{m}$, $\forall i|_{i=1}^{m}$. At iteration $i > 0$, for each training example x_k, if x_k is misclassified, its weight is increased so that, in the next iteration, an updated training set distribution Δ^{i+1} is considered, which puts more emphasis on the previously misclassified examples (i.e., the hardest to classify ones).

The perhaps most widely used strategy is AdaBoost, which has been shown to significantly improve the performance of base learners. Based on the traditional AdaBoost, several boosting strategies have been proposed in the literature, ranging from the updating strategy along the boosting iterations, to the choice of weak-learners. Regarding multiclass boosting, there are some variations of the AdaBoost algorithm, such as the AdaBoost.M1 and AdaBoost.M2, where the main distinctions have to do with the assumed weak-learning conditions, as detailed in [19].

Of special importance here, we cite the boosted version of the RF classifier, proposed in [13] (here called *ADARF*), further studied in [32] and successfully applied in domains such as breast cancer survivability prediction [28] and face detection [31]. As the name suggests, it explores the random forest classifier as weak-learner in a boosting algorithm based on AdaBoost. In [13] such a technique was shown to perform well in a traffic flow problem, outperforming the traditional AdaBoost algorithm. In [31], ADARF outperformed eight classifiers considering the UCI's glass dataset. Finally, in [28], ADARF outperformed ten classifiers (including AdaBoost, Decision Trees, Naïve Bayes and SVM) considering a breast cancer survivability dataset. We here inspire ourselves in the promising synergy between boosting and Random Forests in order to tackle the challenging text classification task. As we shall see, there is opportunity to leverage automatic classification quality by exploring some advantages of both algorithms. However, we performed such integration with different strategies, which we believe are more suitable to our target domains.

In fact, boosting algorithms have their limitations. Although the boosting strategy was initially considered to be immune to overfitting, it is already known that such strategy suffers from this problem, specially in the presence of noisy data [22, 30]. The overfitting problem can be observed when inconsistent data (e.g., misclassified training data) is given to the learner. It becomes even more critical if the employed weak-learner is too strong to fit the model. That is, if instead of combining predictions of simple learners, one combines several complex hypothesis, such as done in [13, 28, 31, 32], chances are that the model becomes even more overfitted to noise data. Under an overfitted situation, the boosting algorithm may focus on erroneous regions of the input space, leading to suboptimal decision boundaries. In fact, such issue presents a challenge to boosting algorithms when applied to real-world datasets [8, 12], and it can be even more challenging if one consider real-world data, such as textual data (due to not only noise but also to some aspects inherently related to natural languages, such as ambiguity and the dynamics of the language, to name a few).

We thus propose to use the RF classifier as weak-learner for a boosting algorithm. But, unlike previous work which did not deal with the challenging high dimensional and noisy automatic classification scenario, we here pay special attention to the overfitting issue. Towards this end, we take advantage of the OOB estimation, readily available when building such a classifier, as well as of a selective weight updating strategy, in order to circumvent the overfitting issue which can arise from both the stronger nature of the RF classifier and to the intrinsic characteristics of such challenging data. Next we describe in details our proposal.

3. BOOSTED RANDOM FOREST

In this section, we describe the proposed learning algorithm: the BROOF classifier, a smooth combination of boosting and random forests aimed at exploiting their strengths while simultaneously solving some of their drawbacks in noisy and high dimensional settings.

BROOF is an additive model composed of several random forest classifiers, which act as weak-learners. Each fitted model influences the final decision proportionally to its accuracy, focusing—as the boosting iterations go by—on ever more complex regions of the input space, in order to drive down the expected error. As usual in a boosting strategy, two aspects play a key role: (*i*) the influence of each learner in the fitted additive model, and (*ii*) the strategy to update the sample distribution Δ^i based on the previous boosting iteration $i - 1$. As we shall describe next, we deal with both aspects by means of the out-of-bag (OOB) error estimate computed when learning each random forest classifier.

The out-of-bag error yields an estimate of the expected error, sometimes referred to as the generalization error, and is directly computed when learning a random forest classifier. Recall that such a classifier uses bootstrapped examples to build a series of decision trees. For each decision tree, roughly $\frac{1}{e} \approx 37\%$ training examples are left out by the sampling procedure [14]. Unlike the training error estimation, which considers the same data used to learn the model to assess misclassification rate, these out-of-bag examples gets classified by the corresponding decision trees, acting as an independent set (since they were not used to learn the tree). The final classification is given by averaging all predictions for each example. In fact, it can be shown [14] that the OOB error estimate is less biased than the training error estimate usually adopted to weight the weak-learners votes in traditional boosting methods. Consequently, it leads to better approximations for the expected error rate. This is rather an expected result since the out-of-bag examples are not used to learn a classifier, similarly to cross validation procedures to assess an unbiased estimate of expected error rate. Thus, we hypothesize that a less biased combination of weak-learners (by means of a proper weight calculation through OOB, as we shall see) potentially leads to an improved boosting algorithm.

More formally, let $\mathbb{D}_{trn}$ be the training set. Initially, all training samples have the same associated probability mass w_i. Such sample probability distribution (i.e., $w_i, \forall i$) is employed to drive the ensemble towards hard to classify regions of the input space. Let h_i be a random forest classifier trained at iteration i of the boosting algorithm, considering the bootstrapped samples $\mathbb{D}_{rnd} \subset \mathbb{D}_{trn}$. The out-of-bag samples $\mathbb{O} \leftarrow \mathbb{D}_{trn} \setminus \mathbb{D}_{rnd}$ are used to assess the accuracy of h_i. Considering the samples $x \in \mathbb{O}$, those misclassified by h_i typically lie down in hard to classify regions of the input space. Thus, if the model focuses on such regions, the ensemble capability of accurately covering such complex regions increases. We do so by considering a weighted out-of-bag error estimate, denoted by OOB^w_{err}, when updating the sample distribution. In this case, the probability of correctly classifying the currently misclassified out-of-bag samples will tend to increase as the iterative process continues.

The proposed strategy to update the probability distribution Δ^i at boosting iteration i, which associates a probability mass with each training example x, is based on a weighted error estimate OOB^w_{err}. It considers not only the misclassification of x by the weak learner but also the probability mass in the previous boosting iteration, which is proportional to the complexity of classifying x. More specifically, the probabilities associated to the out-of-bag examples are updated based on the estimate $OOB^w_{err} \leftarrow \frac{\sum_{i \in \mathbb{O}} w_i \mathbb{I}(y \neq \hat{y})}{\sum_{i \in \mathbb{O}} w_i}$, where $\mathbb{I}(\cdot)$ is the indicator function. As the iterative process continues, the influence of h_i predictions are properly updated (according to h_i effectiveness when classifying the out-of-bag samples), as well as the probability mass associated with each $x \in \mathbb{O}$, by the factor $\log\left(\frac{1-OOB^w_{err}}{OOB^w_{err}}\right)$.

Recall that, as previously discussed, boosting algorithms tend to overly increase the weights of a few hard-to-classify examples, specially in the presence of noisy data. In the proposed algorithm, just the probabilities w_i related to the selected out-of-bag examples are updated at each round, minimizing the undesired bias towards these hard-to-classify examples—thus reducing the negative effect of the overfitting problem—while still driving down the misclassification rate. That is, we hope that the weak learner h_{i+1} will have better generalization power than the weak learner h_i without overfitting to hard-to-classify regions, while maintaining high classification effectiveness due to the stronger nature of the base-learners. We summarize the proposed method in Algorithm 1. The final prediction rule is then given by an additive combination of the weak-learners, weighted by α_m.

Algorithm 1 BROOF: Pseudocode

function TRAIN($\mathbb{D}_{trn}$)
  $w_i \leftarrow \frac{1}{|\mathbb{D}_{trn}|}$
  for each $m = 1$ **to** M **do**
    $\langle h^{RF}_m, (x, y, \hat{y})^{oob}_i \rangle \leftarrow$ LEARNRF($\mathbb{D}_{trn}, n_{trees}$)
    $OOB^w_{err} \leftarrow \frac{\sum_{i \in \mathbb{O}} w_i \mathbb{I}(y \neq \hat{y})}{\sum_{i \in \mathbb{O}} w_i}$, where $\mathbb{O} = (x, y, \hat{y})^{oob}_i$
    $\alpha_m \leftarrow \log\left(\frac{1-OOB^w_{err}}{OOB^w_{err}}\right)$
    $w_i \leftarrow w_i e^{\alpha_m \mathbb{I}(y \neq \hat{y})}$, where $i \in \mathbb{O}$
  end for
end function

4. EXPERIMENTAL EVALUATION

In order to evaluate the effectiveness of our proposal, we contrast BROOF against a large set of baselines covering a variety of learning paradigms, including traditional ones—SVM, KNN, Decision Trees (DT), Naïve Bayes (NB)—as well as "natural baselines": Random Forests, AdaBoost.M2, Gradient Boosted Decision Trees and the closest approach to ours: ADARF. In the following, we provide a brief description of the experimental workload (i.e., classifiers and datasets)[3]. Then, we report and discuss our results.

In our experiments, we considered six real-world textual datasets for topic classification, ten for sentiment classification, and six for microarray classification, covering overall 22 datasets. As we shall detail, we consider 11 classification algorithms and two evaluation metrics. This encompasses a set of 484 results, an extensive experimental evaluation.

4.1 Baseline Classifiers

As the traditional classifiers (SVM, KNN, DT, NB) are well known in the literature, here we only describe in details the less known ones or those more similar to our approach.

AdaBoost.M2 (ADA.M2) is an extension of the traditional AdaBoost classifier for multiclass classification problems [7]. For each boosting iteration, a bootstrap sample of the training set is picked in order to learn the weak classifier. A pseudo-loss function is then computed in order to update the weights of each training example and the weight associated to the weak-learner which reflects its influence in the final model. We here adopt as weak-learner the so-called decision stumps—decision trees with a single decision node—as it is the most common strategy. We also consider what we call AdaBoost.FGDT (ADA.FGDT), where full grown decision trees are used as weak-learners [3]. Some previous work have shown that this strategy may outperform boosted decision stumps.

AdaBoost.RF (ADARF) is an AdaBoost-based classifier in which a random forest classifier acts as a weak-learner [13, 32]. Unlike our approach, here the usual weighting strategy is adopted, where the in-sample error rate is key when updating the probability mass associated with each training example as the boosting iterations go by. Similarly to the AdaBoost algorithm, the weight of a misclassified example is increased, enabling the boosting procedure to concentrate on the hard examples in the training set in subsequent rounds. Such weighting schema, which is based on training error and updates all training instances as the boosting iterations go by is prone to overfitting in scenarios such as the observed in text classification tasks, since it tends to focus on a *few* hard-to-classify examples, as previously mentioned.

Gradient Boosted Decision Trees (GBDT). Unlike the AdaBoost variants described above, here we fit an additive model in a stage-wise manner, in the form of a typical

[3]All reference datasets can be downloaded at `http://homepages.dcc.ufmg.br/~tsalles/broof/`. Our implementation of the classifiers will be available soon under request.

functional gradient descent procedure. At each iteration a new tree that best minimizes a loss function L is added to the model, according to L's negative gradient. Since our task is classification, we optimize for the deviance loss function [9]. We also consider its stochastic counterpart (SGBDT), by fitting trees considering a random subset of training data (thus reducing the variance of the final model).

4.2 Topic Categorization

One of the challenges when categorizing textual data into topics is that textual documents are usually represented by a great amount of features (high dimensionality) and most of them could be irrelevant or noisy, due to inherent properties of natural languages, such as the presence of synonyms, ambiguities, to name a few. However, despite being a challenging application domain, it is of great importance nowadays, due to its wide applicability and demand. In order to evaluate the BROOF classifier for topic categorization, we consider here six real-world datasets, related to computer science articles (ACM), news (REUT and UniRCV1), web pages (4UNI) and medicine (MEDLINE). Due to space restrictions, a detailed description of each can be found in an online appendix[4].

For all datasets, we performed a traditional preprocessing task: we removed stopwords, using the standard SMART list, and applied a simple feature selection by removing terms with low "document frequency" (DF)[5]. In particular, in the case of the original RCV1 dataset, a multi-label one, the multi-label cases need special treatment, such as score thresholding, etc. (see [17] for details), in order to be properly consumed by unilabel classifiers. As our current focus is on unilabel tasks, to allow a fair comparison among the other datasets (which are also unilabel) and all baselines (which also focus on unilabel tasks), we decided to remove the documents assigned to more than one class from RCV1, deriving a new dataset which we call *UniRCV1*. This collection has 101 classes and about 20% less documents. Nevertheless, as we shall see, the effectiveness levels obtained by our method and the best baselines are still compatible with those of the original multilabel RCV1.

In terms of baseline implementations, for SVM we use the liblinear library [5] while for the other algorithms we developed our own implementations. In particular, for NB we adopt the Multinomial Naïve Bayes approach. The free parameters of these classifiers include the cost C for SVM, neighborhood size k for KNN and minimum number of examples δ_{min} in a leaf node for DT. For the Random Forest (RF) algorithm, we considered unprunned trees, since it is already known that unprunned trees perform better than pruned trees when applied to high dimensional noisy datasets [18]. The free parameter of this classifier has to do with the number of trees to compose the ensemble. Finally, all the training and test examples were represented by TFIDF vectors for all algorithms, except for Multinomial NB (whose optimal performance was obtained using TF).

4.2.1 Experimental Protocol

The methods were compared using two standard information retrieval measures: micro averaged F_1 (microF_1) and macro averaged F_1 (MacroF_1). While the MicroF_1 measures the classification effectiveness over all decisions (i.e., the pooled contingency tables of all classes), the MacroF_1 measures the classification effectiveness for each individual class and averages them.

All experiments were executed using a two-round 10-fold cross-validation procedure. This is a cross-validation procedure in which the free parameters of each classifier are set by means of an additional cross-validation step over the training set and the effectiveness of the algorithms are measured in the test partition[6]. Concerning the proposed BROOF classifier, we fixed the size of the weak-learners to 5 trees, setting the maximum number of iterations to 200. For the RF classifier, we learned at most 200 trees and, for all datasets, convergence was reached with at most 100 trees. We assess the statistical significance of our results by means of a paired t-test with 95% confidence. The obtained results can be found in Table 1. The top-performers, with 95% confidence, are shown in bold.

Before diving into the results, we would like to notice that some of the results obtained in some datasets may differ from the ones reported in other works for the same datasets (e.g., [11, 16]). Such discrepancies may be due to several factors such as differences in dataset preparation[7], the use of different splits of the datasets (e.g., some datasets have "default splits" such as REUT and RCV1[8]), the application of some score thresholding, such as SCUT, PCUT, etc., which, besides being an important step for multilabel problems, also affects classification performance by minimizing class imbalance effects, among other factors. We would like to stress that we ran all algorithms under the same conditions, with the best standard weighting schemes for each of them, using standardized and well-accepted cross-validation procedures that optimize parameters for each of them and apply the proper statistical tools for the analysis of the results. We consider that those decisions are in accordance with our main evaluation goal (i.e., to compare the learning algorithms), since its is fundamental to carefully isolate the important factors under study. Therefore, we believe our results are a valid comparison across datasets and algorithms. Moreover, all our datasets (and implementations in the near future) are available for others to replicate our results and test different configurations.

4.2.2 Discussion and Analyses

Briefly, regarding our experimental results, they show that, overall, BROOF outperforms or ties all the state-of-the-art topical text classifiers (SVM, NB and DT), as well as the traditional RF (that, to the best of our knowledge, had not been thoroughly investigated in this scenario). It also outperforms, by large margins, the widely used lazy classifier KNN.

In our experiments, the proposed BROOF classifier was the only classifier to produce the best results in all tested

[4] `http://homepages.dcc.ufmg.br/~tsalles/broof/`.

[5] We removed all terms with DF ≤ 5.

[6] A more reliable procedure than setting up an single "validation set", since it allows us to assess statistical significance when tuning the free parameters.

[7] For instance, some works do exploit complex feature weighting schemes or feature selection mechanisms that do favor some algorithms in detriment to others.

[8] In fact, we do believe that running experiments only in the default splits is not the best experimental procedure as it does not allow a proper statistical treatment of the results.

		20NG	4UNI	REUT	ACM	UniRCV1	MEDLINE
BROOF	micF1	**87.98 ± 0.71**	**82.03 ± 1.54**	**65.07 ± 1.44**	**72.02 ± 1.14**	**84.76 ± 0.03**	**86.84 ± 0.11**
	macF1	**88.02 ± 0.78**	**69.43 ± 1.95**	**31.98 ± 1.59**	**60.77 ± 1.54**	**63.63 ± 0.04**	**76.87 ± 0.44**
RF	micF1	70.65 ± 1.41	**82.00 ± 0.98**	61.76 ± 2.17	69.51 ± 0.92	70.96 ± 0.27	81.09 ± 0.15
	macF1	69.67 ± 1.28	**69.56 ± 1.90**	23.58 ± 2.31	55.38 ± 1.00	46.74 ± 1.00	71.78 ± 0.41
DT	micF1	44.25 ± 1.05	70.49 ± 1.25	55.20 ± 1.19	57.54 ± 0.73	65.58 ± 1.08	76.20+ = 0.10
	macF1	43.60 ± 0.89	59.22 ± 2.81	18.20+ = 1.37	45.87 ± 1.50	37.49 ± 1.27	64.87+ = 0.37
NB	micF1	86.49 ± 1.12	61.41 ± 1.38	**66.64 ± 1.77**	**73.77 ± 1.03**	66.65 ± 0.25	80.94 ± 0.12
	macF1	85.71 ± 1.02	53.18 ± 2.18	**33.58 ± 1.97**	57.21 ± 0.84	49.97 ± 0.09	64.66 ± 0.63
KNN	micF1	**89.16 ± 0.63**	71.63 ± 1.36	**65.18 ± 1.67**	71.34 ± 0.96	75.28 ± 0.13	83.01 ± 0.13
	macF1	**88.84 ± 0.59**	57.15 ± 1.91	**32.25 ± 2.60**	**60.92 ± 1.47**	62.51 ± 0.21	72.70 ± 0.42
SVM	micF1	84.51 ± 1.56	75.37 ± 1.17	**66.90 ± 2.19**	**74.55 ± 1.00**	**84.56 ± 0.09**	**86.99 ± 0.09**
	macF1	83.85 ± 1.70	65.56 ± 1.81	**33.53 ± 3.27**	**63.01 ± 1.74**	**63.55 ± 0.12**	**77.11 ± 0.56**
ADA.FGDT	micF1	76.36 ± 0.81	78.61 ± 1.78	61.45 ± 0.60	60.19 ± 0.78	68.07 ± 0.23	78.51 ± 0.03
	macF1	74.80 ± 0.75	58.18 ± 1.03	**30.02 ± 0.42**	46.08 ± 1.16	47.12 ± 0.10	64.91 ± 0.06
GBDT	micF1	80.38 ± 1.20	78.93 ± 1.42	59.23 ± 2.61	**72.70 ± 0.77**	81.42 ± 1.03	**85.05 ± 0.14**
	macF1	80.45 ± 0.75	62.88 ± 1.99	29.82 ± 2.17	**60.66 ± 2.04**	58.23 ± 1.25	**77.83 ± 0.30**
SGBDT	micF1	81.45 ± 1.10	82.96 ± 1.16	59.27 ± 1.58	**72.98 ± 0.77**	**83.37 ± 0.44**	81.79 ± 0.17
	macF1	80.63 ± 0.86	**70.33 ± 1.98**	**32.24 ± 1.60**	**61.85 ± 0.77**	61.38 ± 0.61	73.71 ± 0.35
ADA.RF	micF1	84.75 ± 0.98	78.45 ± 1.34	**62.73 ± 1.88**	70.21 ± 1.11	67.96 ± 0.14	77.19 ± 0.05
	macF1	83.98 ± 0.87	62.23 ± 1.75	**31.42 ± 1.99**	47.50 ± 0.99	48.02 ± 0.09	65.63 ± 0.02
ADA.M2	micF1	53.01 ± 0.82	73.00 ± 1.55	57.43 ± 0.98	57.98 ± 1.77	65.80 ± 0.55	63.78 ± 0.98
	macF1	54.27 ± 0.93	62.79 ± 2.14	25.02 ± 1.41	48.44 ± 1.33	45.96 ± 0.22	66.82 ± 0.04

Table 1: Experimental Evaluation—Obtained Results for Topic Categorization.

datasets considering all metrics, a surprising result given the knowledge that there is no single universal top-notch classifier for all problems. Moreover, when compared to its traditional counterpart (RF), we obtained gains of up to 24.53% in MicroF_1 (20NG) and 35.62% in MacroF_1 (REUT), being better than traditional RF in five out of six datasets (and tied in the other one). Notice also that the traditional RF does not perform so well, losing to traditional classifiers such as KNN and SVM in several datasets. These results corroborates two of our arguments: (*i*) the drawbacks of the traditional RF for classification of noisy and high dimensional data; and (*ii*) our proposal was successful in overcoming these drawbacks.

Considering the boosting baselines, our experiments show that our proposal achieves consistently higher effectiveness. Particularly, when compared to the closest approach to ours (ADARF), we can see that our proposal beats this classifier in 5 out of 6 datasets, tying only in one case. In fact, large gains of up to 24.72% in MicroF_1 (UniRCV1) and 32.5% in MacroF_1 (also UniRCV1) can be obtained. The gains against GBDT and other boosting baselines are also similar. This clearly demonstrates the benefits of using the out-of-bag estimates, along with the selective weight updates, as described in Section 3. When compared to the overall best baseline (SVM), we statistically outperformed it in 2 out of 6 datasets, with gains of up to 8.84% in MicroF_1 and 5.90% in MacroF_1 (4UNI), tying in the other four datasets. Compared to the lazy baseline classifier (i.e., KNN), we obtained statistically significant improvements in most datasets, with gains of up to 149.87% and 131.76% in Micro-F_1 and Macro-F_1 (UniRCV1).

Overall, it is now clear the benefits of taking advantage of the successful boosting strategy smoothly coupled with the RF classifier, which is able to produce rich information through the out-of-bag samples.

4.2.3 *Effects of the Weighting Strategy*

An important aspect to analyze is the extent to which the two key components of our proposed algorithm, namely: (*i*) the use of OOB weights and (*ii*) the selective weight updates, influence the final results in order to better understand the obtained improvements. For this we run a full 2^k factorial design experiment [15] in which the two factors under study are the use of OOB based weights and the use of selective updates. For each factor, we assume $k = 2$ levels: presence or absence. The response variable is the classification effectiveness, given by micro-averaged F_1.

Dataset	Explained Variation (%)			
	OOB Weights	Selective Updates	Interaction	ε
20NG	32.03	33.65	31.30	2.02
4UNI	32.55	33.54	31.24	2.67
ACM	32.99	33.99	30.00	3.02

Table 2: The explained variation of the OOB weighting and the selective weight updates on MicroF_1.

For each configuration, we run a 10-fold cross validation to assess classification effectiveness and account for experimental errors. The results of this experiment are shown in Table 2. For space reasons, in this analysis we only show results for the datasets in which we obtained the largest gains. As we can observe, not only the main factors (the use of selective updates and an OOB based weighting schema) play an important role in improving the boosting algorithm with random forests as weak-learners, but also their interactions. As reported in Table 2, each factor explains roughly 33% of the variations observed in classification effectiveness, as well as their interactions. This means that, although one can achieve some improvements in classification effectiveness by considering a single factor in isolation, it is usually better to consider both, since their interactions also provide observable variations in the response variable.

4.2.4 *Sample Size Experiments*

Finally, we discuss issues related to the convergence and the need of training samples for our proposed method and the baselines. We have empirically found that in most cases BROOF needs less training data to achieve good classification results. This has positive implications in the practical application of the algorithm, mainly regarding labeling effort in real-world scenarios, which is usually very expensive and cumbersome. For space reasons, in here we only show results for MacroF_1, but results for MicroF_1 follow somewhat similar patterns. Also for space reasons, we show results only

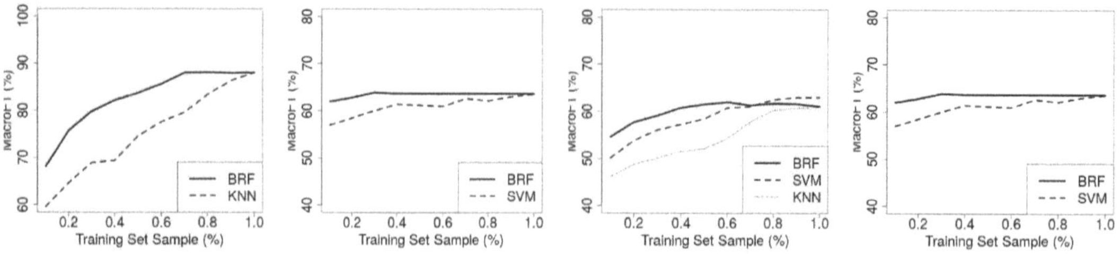

(a) 20NG (b) 4UNI (c) ACM (d) UniRCV1

Figure 1: Effect of training sample size on classification effectiveness (Macro-F_1).

for four datasets, as the patterns found in the other two datasets are similar. In our analysis, we compare BROOF with the best baselines in each dataset. Figure 1 shows the results of this analysis, when we vary the size of the training set to 10%, 20%, ···, 100%. Results correspond to the average of 10 test runs. We do not show confidence intervals for the sake of readability.

As it can be seen in Figure 1(a), for 20NG, the best baseline (KNN) is only competitive when using all the available training, while BROOF stabilizes around 70% of training data. Similarly, for 4UNI (Figure 1(b)), the best baseline in this dataset (RF) could only achieve competitive results when using the entire training data. However, differently from before, our proposed method keeps improving with more training. In any case BROOF results with around 70-80% of the training data are very competitive. For ACM, BROOF stability is achieved with about 60% of the training data, with small fluctuations for larger fractions, all within the statistical tie margins. The best baseline, SVM, becomes competitive with BROOF when it is uses about 70% of training, loosing in all cases when smaller fractions are used. The second best baseline (NB) is only competitive using 100% of training. Notice also that in this dataset the effectiveness of BROOF is much more stable, with results with about 50% of training not far away from the peak in effectiveness. Finally, in UniRCV1 (Figure 1(d)), the curves for BROOF and the best baseline (SVM) are the closest ones among those analyzed, but, as before, SVM only ties with our proposed method when using about 100% of the training data. More importantly, differently from the previous datasets, BROOF performance stabilizes around 30% of training, which means that only this fraction of the training data is enough for our solution to achieve its best effectiveness. In sum, BROOF needs much less training than the best baselines in all datasets to achieve its highest effectiveness, which usually occurs, when using around 30-80% of the original training set.

4.3 Other Application Domains

Topic categorization is not the only domain with noisy and high dimensional data where there is great benefit of providing highly accurate classifiers. Clearly, other domains do exist and we here focus on two of them: sentiment analysis and microarray data classification.

In order to evaluate BROOF over such different domains, we adopted the same experimental protocol and setup discussed in Section 4.2.1, evaluating the same set of nine classifiers described in Section 4.1. In the following we detail the performed evaluation. In particular, for space reasons, we do not delve into the specific analyses we have performed in the previous section regarding the effects of the weighting strategies and sample size, but experiments in the domains analyzed in this section indicate that results are very similar.

4.3.1 *Sentiment Analysis*

Considering sentiment analysis, we tackle the problem of automatically identifying the polarity of user provided content, which can be reviews for some topic or item (e.g., movies, products), posts on social networks (e.g., tweets), among others. The polarity of a user generated content refers to the degree to which such content express a positive or negative opinion about a topic. As with any human generated content in natural language, there is a lot of noise (due to several factors such as misspellings, the presence of ambiguity and so on) generally embedded in a high dimensional space. Clearly, accurately predicting the polarity of such noisy high dimensional data is paramount to support decision making, being of great business importance.

We evaluate the effectiveness of BROOF considering ten datasets for polarity detection, consisting of reviews (e.g., Amazon), posts on online social networks (e.g., Twitter, Debate), user comments (e.g, Youtube) and snippets of opinion news (NYT). Due to space issues, a detailed description of each can be found in the online appendix. The obtained results can be found in Table 3.

As we can observe in Table 3, BROOF is among the top performers in 8 out of 10 datasets, being the single classifier to be among the top performers in the vast majority of cases. Compared to the traditional RF classifier, BROOF achieved gains of up to 16.70% and 17.72% in MicroF_1 and MacroF_1, respectively. Compared to the ADA.RF baseline, BROOF achieved gains of up to 6.44% in MicroF_1 (Yelp) and 17.84% in MacroF_1 (MySpace). Compared to SVM classifier, our approach obtained gains of up to 2.44% and 3.89% in MicroF_1 (BBC) and MacroF_1 (Amazon), respectively. The cases in which BROOF was not the top performer were Debate and Digg datasets. Considering Debate, SVM was the best performer, achieving gains of 4.23% and 3.91% over BROOF. The situation for Digg was a bit more competitive: neither SVM nor KNN were able to outperform BROOF in both metrics, being tied to BROOF in one of them.

4.3.2 *Microarray Analysis*

Microarray analysis is a popular method in bioinformatics, allowing the investigation of thousands of genes simultaneously. Gene expression microarray data usually contains a very large number of attributes, related to the expression of several genes, but a small number of samples (due to the

		Amazon	BBC	Debate	Digg	MySpace	NYT	Tweets	Twitter	Yelp	Youtube
BROOF	micF1	**69.94**	**86.59**	72.07	73.04	**84.27**	**55.98**	**75.64**	**73.73**	**89.94**	**78.36**
	macF1	**71.02**	**62.72**	71.86	59.70	**65.27**	**56.03**	**75.36**	**70.89**	**89.87**	72.20
RF	micF1	59.93	84.80	73.01	74.38	82.83	53.43	**74.48**	68.84	87.29	77.88
	macF1	60.33	58.37	72.82	58.49	59.28	52.71	**74.14**	65.03	87.23	71.89
DT	micF1	56.70	73.29	68.66	68.01	79.67	49.97	68.45	66.19	79.88	71.19
	macF1	55.41	50.11	65.42	55.13	53.02	50.11	68.22	63.40	80.01	66.44
NB	micF1	**69.87**	**87.38**	71.34	73.54	**84.45**	54.38	**74.08**	67.45	87.49	78.00
	macF1	**70.04**	58.32	70.84	59.65	56.91	54.84	73.85	66.21	87.45	**74.07**
KNN	micF1	69.02	**86.37**	71.99	**76.29**	83.47	53.85	73.99	68.47	83.48	78.03
	macF1	**69.84**	51.49	71.53	53.27	51.40	53.28	73.52	66.17	83.30	72.34
SVM	micF1	68.73	84.53	**75.12**	74.62	82.74	**56.37**	**74.80**	72.14	**90.73**	**79.12**
	macF1	68.36	**62.95**	**74.67**	**63.09**	**65.78**	**56.38**	**74.51**	**71.02**	**90.26**	**74.61**
ADA.FGDT	micF1	**69.38**	82.78	72.81	72.50	**84.23**	51.03	73.20	68.33	85.55	77.54
	macF1	68.97	57.11	70.42	59.16	**64.97**	52.03	**75.33**	67.90	85.11	72.04
GBDT	micF1	67.68	83.07	**75.39**	73.85	83.21	53.36	71.84	70.13	**89.80**	77.43
	macF1	67.54	51.15	**75.22**	60.10	58.89	52.98	71.75	67.32	**89.79**	69.83
SGBDT	micF1	67.36	83.07	**74.51**	73.46	82.97	53.44	72.56	70.34	**90.05**	76.28
	macF1	67.08	51.68	**74.41**	58.29	60.90	53.13	72.26	67.99	**90.49**	68.49
ADA.RF	micF1	67.75	84.23	**74.98**	72.01	83.14	52.05	72.64	69.27	85.00	76.83
	macF1	67.11	58.17	72.49	58.09	55.39	**56.76**	71.22	68.30	84.96	72.88
ADA.M2	micF1	66.24	82.21	70.49	70.09	81.33	51.74	71.33	67.16	84.01	76.94
	macF1	67.93	60.22	71.44	58.99	59.56	52.60	70.44	66.07	83.88	73.02

Table 3: Experimental Evaluation—Obtained Results for Sentiment Analysis.

associated costs of producing such samples, availability, privacy issues, among others). Furthermore, such kind of data is usually plagued with both technical noise and the presence of genes weakly correlated or not correlated at all with the outcome. Such a high dimensional characteristic, along with the presence of noise, provide a real challenge to come up with accurate prediction models capable of uncovering the relationship between gene expression and outcome (e.g., presence of cancer).

Unlike topic categorization and sentiment analysis domains, which deal specifically with textual data, the microarray analysis domain deals with continuous, real-valued, gene expression measurements. Thus, for this particular domain, some of the previously adopted baselines may be suboptimal. More specifically, instead of adopting a Multinomial NB classifier, which is specifically designed (and known to perform better) for textual data, we adopt the Gaussian NB approach. Furthermore, we adopt, for the microarray domain, the libsvm implementation [4] for the SVM classifier since, unlike in textual data, non-linear class boundaries may be observed due to the much more complex relationship between gene expression and the outcome [9]. We adopt a SVM with non-linear RBF kernel, tuning both the cost parameter and the gamma parameter for the kernel function.

We evaluate the effectiveness of BROOF considering six gene expression microarray datasets. Due to space limitation, their details can be found in an online appendix. The obtained results can be found in Table 4. As it can be observed, BROOF again was the top performer in the majority of evaluated cases (4 out of 6). BROOF outperformed RF with gains of up to 13.22% in MicroF_1 and 22.53% in MacroF_1 (both in the Prostate dataset). Considering the SVM classifier, BROOF achieved gains of up to 8.10% and 12.54% in MicroF_1 and MacroF_1, also in the Prostate dataset. ADA.RF was outperformed in all but 9tumors and Brain1 datasets, in some cases by large margins. Brain2 was the only dataset in which BROOF was outperformed by another baseline (e.g., KNN) in both metrics, with a somewhat mild margin (just as observed with our previous sentiment analysis evaluation). Interestingly, in this domain, SVM was not the closest competitor as in the previous domains.

[9]In fact, linear SVM obtained poor results in this domain.

5. CONCLUSIONS AND FUTURE WORK

In this work, we propose an original classifier which exploits the synergy between the classification paradigms exploited by RF classifiers and boosting schemes, especially for classification of high dimensional noisy data. We have done that in an original way, by: (*i*) exploiting, in the boosting algorithm (which uses RFs as base learners), new weighting strategies that naturally come from the OOB sets produced by RFs, and by (*ii*) applying a less aggressive, selective weight updating strategy that mitigates overfitting, a common problem high-dimensional noisy task.

We summarize our findings regarding the behavior of all analyzed classifiers in the three explored application domains in Table 5, which counts the number of times each algorithm figured out as a top performer. As our experimental results clearly show, our proposal is in great advantage over the other explored baselines in terms of prediction accuracy, being the classifier of choice in the vast majority of cases. We also show that BROOF requires less training to achieve its best results, which is of great importance to guarantee its practical applicability.

As future work, we intend to provide theoretical bounds over our proposed setting, in order to provide some guarantees regarding misclassification rates, complementing our extensive empirical comparison.

References

[1] S. Bernard, S. Adam, and L. Heutte. Dynamic random forests. *Patt. Recog. Letters*, 33(12):1580–1586, 2012.

[2] L. Breiman. Random forests. *Mach. Learn.*, 45(1):5–32, 2001.

[3] R. Caruana and A. Niculescu-Mizil. An empirical comparison of supervised learning algorithms. In *ICML*, pages 161–168, 2006.

[4] C.-C. Chang and C.-J. Lin. LIBSVM: A library for support vector machines. *ACM Transactions on Intelligent Systems and Technology*, 2:27:1–27:27, 2011.

[5] R.-E. Fan, K.-W. Chang, C.-J. Hsieh, X.-R. Wang, and C.-J. Lin. Liblinear: A library for large linear classification. *J. Mach. Learn. Res.*, 9:1871–1874, 2008.

[6] M. Fernández-Delgado, E. Cernadas, S. Barro, and D. Amorim. Do we need hundreds of classifiers to solve real world classification problems? *JMLR*, 15:3133–3181, 2014.

		9tumors	Brain1	Brain2	DLBCL	Leukemia	Prostate
BROOF	micF1	**86.63**	72.07	73.04	**86.99**	**73.99**	**77.84**
	macF1	**77.26**	71.86	59.70	64.42	**73.52**	**79.07**
RF	micF1	**86.80**	73.01	74.38	**86.19**	72.74	68.75
	macF1	58.37	72.82	58.49	62.92	**73.27**	64.53
DT	micF1	25.76	70.42	66.24	67.93	68.83	66.35
	macF1	15.52	61.63	53.24	60.29	67.98	58.27
NB	micF1	84.28	70.94	73.22	84.45	**74.84**	69.04
	macF1	72.34	69.28	60.34	56.91	**73.85**	64.93
KNN	micF1	80.28	**77.22**	**75.50**	76.79	**73.27**	60.91
	macF1	55.38	62.91	**61.69**	**73.18**	**74.28**	56.39
SVM	micF1	83.96	74.01	71.43	**85.50**	**73.24**	72.01
	macF1	68.95	**74.10**	59.21	65.80	**74.51**	70.26
ADA.FGDT	micF1	84.33	73.42	72.60	82.02	**73.65**	67.33
	macF1	72.90	72.09	**61.77**	62.77	**74.88**	63.01
GBDT	micF1	80.11	**76.67**	**75.06**	82.75	**72.99**	72.65
	macF1	57.98	72.63	58.00	64.04	**73.62**	67.27
SGBDT	micF1	81.67	74.44	72.00	87.01	**72.71**	**78.97**
	macF1	60.28	68.86	60.00	60.71	70.52	**79.97**
ADA.RF	micF1	**86.02**	72.44	70.73	84.00	71.42	70.17
	macF1	71.14	71.17	58.25	65.22	70.69	65.54
ADA.M2	micF1	81.32	72.00	69.81	83.01	70.55	67.98
	macF1	70.98	71.22	60.30	63.24	71.10	63.79

Table 4: Experimental Evaluation—Obtained Results for Microarray Analysis.

Algorithm	Winning Counts									Sum of Totals
	Topic			Sentiment			Microarray			
	MicroF_1	MacroF_1	Total	MicroF_1	MacroF_1	Total	MicroF_1	MacroF_1	Total	
BROOF	6	6	12	8	7	15	4	3	7	34
SVM	4	4	8	5	9	14	2	2	4	26
KNN	2	3	5	2	1	3	3	3	6	14
SGBDT	2	3	5	2	2	4	2	1	3	12
GBDT	2	2	4	2	2	4	3	1	4	12
NB	2	1	3	4	2	6	1	1	2	11
ADA.FGDT	0	1	1	2	2	4	1	2	3	8
RF	1	1	2	1	1	2	2	1	3	7
ADA.RF	1	1	2	1	1	2	1	0	1	5

Table 5: Number of times each algorithm was the top performer in the performed evaluation. ADA.M2 and DT not shown since they were not top performers in any evaluated case.

[7] Y. Freund and R. E. Schapire. A decision-theoretic generalization of on-line learning and an application to boosting. *J. Comput. Syst. Sci.*, 55(1):119–139, Aug. 1997.

[8] J. Friedman, T. Hastie, and R. Tibshirani. Additive logistic regression: a statistical view of boosting, 1998.

[9] J. H. Friedman. Greedy function approximation: A gradient boosting machine. *Ann. Statist.*, 29(5):1189–1232, 2001.

[10] M. Galar, A. Fernández, E. Barrenechea, H. Bustince, and F. Herrera. A review on ensembles for the class imbalance problem: Bagging-, boosting-, and hybrid-based approaches. *IEEE Trans Syst Man Cybern C Cybern*, 42(4):463–484, 2012.

[11] S. Godbole and S. Sarawagi. Discriminative methods for multi-labeled classification. In *PAKDD*, pages 22–30, 2004.

[12] A. J. Grove and D. Schuurmans. Boosting in the limit: Maximizing the margin of learned ensembles. In *AAAI/IAAI*, pages 692–699, 1998.

[13] Y. R. Guy Leshem. Traffic flow prediction using adaboost algorithm with random forests as a weak learner. *Int. Jour. Intell. Tech.*, 2:1305–6417, 2007.

[14] T. Hastie, R. Tibshirani, and J. H. Friedman. *The Elements of Statistical Learning*. Springer, 2009.

[15] R. Jain. *The Art of Computer Systems Performance Analysis: Techniques for Experimental Design, Measurement, Simulation, and Modeling*. John Wiley, New York, NY, 1991.

[16] M. Lan, C.-L. Tan, and H.-B. Low. Proposing a new term weighting scheme for text categorization. In *AAAI*, pages 763–768, 2006.

[17] D. D. Lewis, Y. Yang, T. G. Rose, and F. Li. Rcv1: A new benchmark collection for text categorization research. *JMLR.*, 5:361–397, 2004.

[18] Z. H. Li X. Weighted random subspace method for high dimensional data classification. *Stat Interface*, 2(2):153–159, 2009.

[19] I. Mukherjee and R. E. Schapire. A theory of multiclass boosting. *JMLR*, 14(1):437–497, Feb. 2013.

[20] M. Robnik-Sikonja. Improving random forests. In *ECML*, pages 359–370, 2004.

[21] J. J. Rodriguez, L. I. Kuncheva, and C. J. Alonso. Rotation forest: A new classifier ensemble method. *IEEE Trans. Pattern Anal. Mach. Intell.*, 28(10):1619–1630, 2006.

[22] B. N. Saha, G. Kunapuli, N. Ray, J. A. Maldjian, and S. Natarajan. Ar-boost: Reducing overfitting by a robust data-driven regularization strategy. In *ECML/PKDD*, pages 1–16, 2013.

[23] R. E. Schapire and Y. Freund. *Boosting: Foundations and Algorithms*. The MIT Press, 2012.

[24] F. Schroff, A. Criminisi, and A. Zisserman. Object class segmentation using random forests. In *British Machine Vision Conf.*, pages 1–10, 2008.

[25] M. R. Segal. Machine Learning Benchmarks and Random Forest Regression. Technical report, Univ. of California, 2004.

[26] J. Shotton, A. Fitzgibbon, M. Cook, T. Sharp, M. Finocchio, R. Moore, A. Kipman, and A. Blake. Real-time human pose recognition in parts from single depth images. In *CVPR*, pages 1297–1304, 2011.

[27] A. Statnikov, L. Wang, and C. F. Aliferis. A comprehensive comparison of random forests and support vector machines for microarray-based cancer classification. *BMC bioinformatics*, 9(1):319+, 2008.

[28] J. Thongkam, G. Xu, and Y. Zhang. Adaboost algorithm with random forests for predicting breast cancer survivability. In *IJCNN*, pages 3062–3069. IEEE, 2008.

[29] A. Tsymbal, M. Pechenizkiy, and P. Cunningham. Dynamic integration with random forests. In *ICML*, pages 801–808, 2006.

[30] A. Vezhnevets and O. Barinova. Avoiding boosting overfitting by removing confusing samples. In *ECML*, pages 430–441, 2007.

[31] J.-Y. Zeng, X.-H. Cao, and J.-Y. Gan. An improvement of adaboost for face detection with random forests. In *Adv. Intell. Comp. Theor. and App.*, pages 22–29. 2010.

[32] Z. Zhang and X. Xie. Research on adaboost.m1 with random forest. In *ICCET*, pages 647–652, 2010.

Monolingual and Cross-Lingual Information Retrieval Models Based on (Bilingual) Word Embeddings

Ivan Vulić and Marie-Francine Moens
Department of Computer Science
KU Leuven, Belgium
{ivan.vulic, marie-francine.moens}@cs.kuleuven.be

ABSTRACT

We propose a new unified framework for monolingual (MoIR) and cross-lingual information retrieval (CLIR) which relies on the induction of dense real-valued word vectors known as word embeddings (WE) from comparable data. To this end, we make several important contributions: (1) We present a novel word representation learning model called Bilingual Word Embeddings Skip-Gram (BWESG) which is the first model able to learn bilingual word embeddings solely on the basis of document-aligned comparable data; (2) We demonstrate a simple yet effective approach to building document embeddings from single word embeddings by utilizing models from compositional distributional semantics. BWESG induces a shared cross-lingual embedding vector space in which both words, queries, and documents may be presented as dense real-valued vectors; (3) We build novel ad-hoc MoIR and CLIR models which rely on the induced word and document embeddings and the shared cross-lingual embedding space; (4) Experiments for English and Dutch MoIR, as well as for English-to-Dutch and Dutch-to-English CLIR using benchmarking CLEF 2001-2003 collections and queries demonstrate the utility of our WE-based MoIR and CLIR models. The best results on the CLEF collections are obtained by the combination of the WE-based approach and a unigram language model. We also report on significant improvements in ad-hoc IR tasks of our WE-based framework over the state-of-the-art framework for learning text representations from comparable data based on latent Dirichlet allocation (LDA).

Categories and Subject Descriptors

H.3.3 [**Information Storage and Retrieval**]: Information Search and Retrieval-Information filtering

Keywords

Word embeddings; cross-lingual information retrieval; text representation learning; ad-hoc retrieval; comparable data; semantic composition; multilinguality; vector space retrieval models

1. INTRODUCTION

A revolution in text representation learning ignited by the recent success of neural network architectures and their variants is yet to find its breakthrough in the fundamental IR research. The current state-of-the-art text representation learning framework learns structured word representations known as *word embeddings* (WEs), which are simply (intelligently induced) dense real-valued continuous vectors. Besides improving computational efficiency, WEs lead to better generalizations, even allowing to generalize over the vocabularies observed in labelled data, and hence partially alleviating the ubiquitous problem of data sparsity. Their utility has been validated and proven in various semantic tasks such as semantic word similarity, synonymy detection or word analogy (e.g., [26, 1, 32, 22]). Moreover, the word embeddings have been proven to serve as useful unsupervised features for plenty of standard natural language processing tasks such as named entity recognition, chunking, semantic role labeling, part-of-speech tagging, etc. [40, 7].

Knowing the long-standing and firm relationship between vector space models, semantics modeling and IR [37, 16], *one goal of this paper is to establish a new link between the recent text representation learning methodology based on word embeddings and modeling in information retrieval*, with the focus on the fundamental ad-hoc retrieval task.

Moreover, following the recent trend of multilingual word embedding induction (e.g., [14, 11]), *in this paper we also focus on the induction of bilingual word embeddings (BWEs), and show how to use BWEs in cross-lingual information retrieval tasks.* We show that WE-based monolingual ad-hoc retrieval models may be considered as special and less general cases of the cross-lingual retrieval setting (i.e., operating with only one language instead of two), which results in a unified WE-based framework for monolingual and cross-lingual IR.

When operating in multilingual settings, it is highly desirable to learn embeddings for words denoting similar concepts that are very close in the *shared inter-lingual embedding space* (e.g., the representations for the English word *school* and the Spanish word *escuela* should be very similar). All prior work critically requires sentence-aligned parallel data and readily-available translation dictionaries [14, 11] to induce bilingual word embeddings (BWEs) that are consistent and closely aligned over languages. In this paper, we alleviate this strong requirement by using comparable data.

Contributions. Summarizing all this, in this paper, we investigate three key research questions:

(Q1) *Is it possible to induce high-quality bilingual word embeddings without the need of parallel data and any other readily available translation resources such as bilingual lexicons?* If the answer is positive, we will pave a way for bilingual word representation learning from comparable data for language pairs with limited and non-structured bilingual data resources.

(Q2) *Is it possible to combine word embeddings using the estab-*

SIGIR'15, August 09 - 13, 2015, Santiago, Chile.
© 2015 ACM. ISBN 978-1-4503-3621-5/15/08$15.00
DOI: http://dx.doi.org/10.1145/2766462.2767752.

lished models of semantic composition to construct similar representations for text units beyond the word level? If the answer is positive, we will be able to build structured representations of documents and queries to be used in various IR tasks.
(Q3) *Are word embeddings useful in ad-hoc information retrieval?* If the answer is positive, we will be able to build new models for monolingual and cross-lingual information retrieval which use the additional semantic information implicitly coded in the structured real-valued representations of words, documents and queries.

By aiming at providing the answers to Q1-Q3, this paper delivers several contributions as follows:
(C1) We present a novel word representation learning model called *Bilingual Word Embeddings Skip-Gram (BWESG)* which is the first model able to learn the bilingual word embeddings solely on the basis of document-aligned comparable data. BWESG is supported by recent advances in word representation learning.
(C2) We demonstrate a simple yet effective LSI-inspired approach to building document and query embeddings from single word embeddings by utilizing additive models from compositional distributional semantics. BWESG induces a *shared cross-lingual embedding vector space* in which words, queries, and documents may be presented in a uniform way as dense real-valued vectors.
(C3) We construct a novel unified framework for ad-hoc monolingual (MoIR) and cross-lingual information retrieval (CLIR) which relies on the induced word embeddings and constructed query and document embeddings. Experiments for English and Dutch MoIR, as well as for English-to-Dutch and Dutch-to-English CLIR using benchmarking CLEF 2001-2003 collections and queries demonstrate the utility of our novel MoIR and CLIR models based on word embeddings induced by the BWESG model.

2. BWESG: MODEL ARCHITECTURE

Before we describe our architecture for learning bilingual word embeddings (BWEs) from comparable data, we provide a short overview of the underlying skip-gram word representation learning model in monolingual settings. Our new bilingual representation learning model called BWESG is an extension of skip-gram (SG) to multilingual settings with multilingual comparable training data, and serves as the basis of our novel IR/CLIR framework introduced later in sect. 3.2.

2.1 Why Embeddings and Skip-Gram?

The idea of representing words as continuous real-valued vectors dates way back to mid-80s [36]. The idea met its resurgence in [2], where a neural language model learns word embeddings as part of a neural network architecture for statistical language modeling. This work inspired other approaches that learn word embeddings within the neural-network language modeling framework [6, 7]. Word embeddings are tailored to capture semantics and encode a continuous notion of semantic similarity (as opposed to semantically poorer discrete representations), necessary to share information between words and other text units.

Recently, the skip-gram and continuous bag-of-words (CBOW) model from [24, 25] revealed that the full neural-network structure is not needed at all to learn high-quality word embeddings (with extremely decreased training times compared to the full-fledged neural network models, see [24] for the full analysis of complexity of the models). These models are in fact simple single-layered architectures, where the objective is to predict a word's context given the word itself (skip-gram) or predict a word given its context (CBOW). Similar models called vector log-bilinear models were recently proposed in [30, 32].

Due to its simplicity, as well as its efficacy and consequent popularity in various tasks [25, 21, 22], in this paper we will focus on the adaptation of the skip-gram model with negative sampling from [25]. Our new model will operate in multilingual settings and use only document-aligned comparable data for training.

2.2 Skip-Gram Model

As already hinted in sect. 2.1, our departure point is the log-linear skip-gram model from [24] trained using the negative sampling procedure [25], as implemented in the `word2vec` package.[1] The skip-gram model learns word embeddings (WEs) in a similar way to neural language models [2, 6], but without a non-linear hidden layer.

In the monolingual setting, we assume one language L with vocabulary V, and a corpus of words $w \in V$, along with their contexts $c \in V^c$, where V^c is the context vocabulary. Contexts for each word w_n are typically neighboring words in a context window of size cs (i.e., $w_{n-cs}, \dots, w_{n-1}, w_{n+1}, \dots, w_{n+cs}$), so effectively it holds $V^c \equiv V$.[2]

Each word type $w \in V$ is associated with a vector $\vec{w} \in \mathbb{R}^{dim}$ (its pivot word representation or pivot word embedding, see fig. 1), and a vector $\vec{w_c} \in \mathbb{R}^{dim}$ (its context embedding). dim is the dimensionality of WEs. The entries in these vectors are latent, and treated as parameters θ to be learned by the model.

In short, the idea of the skip-gram model is to scan through the corpus (which is typically unannotated [24]) *word by word* in turn (i.e., these are the pivot words), and learn from the pairs *(word, context)*. The learning goal is to maximize the ability of predicting context words for each pivot word in the corpus. The probability of observing the context word v given the pivot word w is defined by the softmax function:

$$P(v|w) = \frac{1}{1 + \exp(-\vec{w} \cdot \vec{v_c})} \tag{1}$$

Each word token w in the corpus is treated in turn as the pivot and all pairs of word tokens $(w, w \pm 1)$,...,$(w, w \pm t(cs))$ are appended to the training dataset D, where $t(cs)$ is an integer sampled from a uniform distribution on $\{1, \dots, cs\}$.[3] The global training objective J is then to maximize the probabilities that all pairs from D are indeed observed in the corpus:

$$J = \arg\max_{\theta} \sum_{(w,v) \in D} \log \frac{1}{1 + \exp(-\vec{w} \cdot \vec{v_c})} \tag{2}$$

where θ are the parameters of the model, that is, pivot and context word embeddings which have to be learned. One may see that this objective function has a trivial solution by setting $\vec{w} = \vec{v_c}$, and $\vec{w} \cdot \vec{v_c} = Val$, where Val is a large enough number [10]. In order to prevent this trivial training scenario, the *negative sampling* procedure comes into the picture [6, 25].

In short, the idea behind negative sampling is to present the model with a set D' of artificially created or sampled "negative pivot-context" pairs (w, v'), which by assumption serve as negative examples, that is, they do not occur as observed/positive *(word,*

[1] `https://code.google.com/p/word2vec/`

[2] Testing other options for context selection such as dependency-based contexts [19] is beyond the scope of this work, and it was recently shown that these contexts may not lead to any gains in the final WEs [13].

[3] The original skip-gram model utilizes dynamic window sizes, where cs denotes the maximum window size. Moreover, the model takes into account sentence boundaries in context selection, that is, it selects as context words only words occurring in the same sentence as the pivot word.

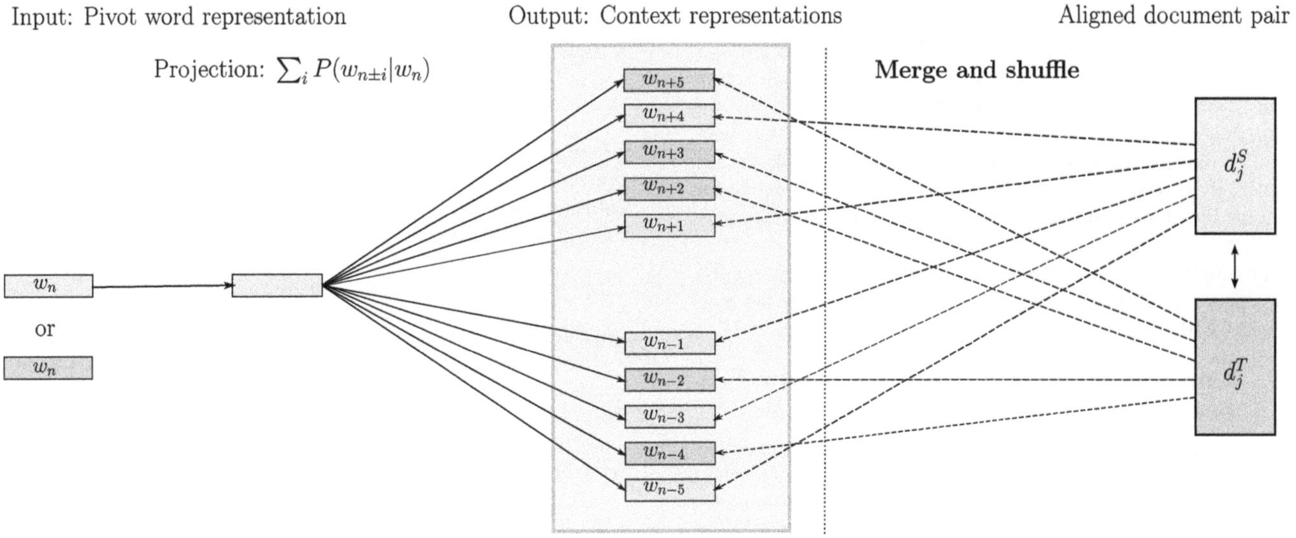

Figure 1: The architecture of our BWE Skip-Gram model for learning bilingual word embeddings from document-aligned comparable data. Source language words and documents are drawn as light gray/unshaded boxes, while target language words and documents as blue/shaded boxes. The right side of the figure (separated by a vertical dashed line) illustrates how a pseudo-bilingual document is constructed from a pair of aligned documents; two documents are first merged, and then words in the pseudo-bilingual document are randomly shuffled to ensure that both source language words and target language words occur as context words.

context) pairs in the training corpus. The model then has to adjust the parameters θ in such a way to also maximize the probability that these negative pairs will not occur in the corpus. The interested reader may found further details about the negative sampling procedure, and the new exact objective function along with its derivation in [21]. For illustrative purposes and simplicity, here we present the approximative objective function with negative sampling by Goldberg and Levy [10]:

$$J = \arg\max_{\theta} \sum_{(w,v)\in D} \log \frac{1}{1+\exp(-\vec{w}\cdot\vec{v_c})} + \sum_{(w,v')\in D'} \log \frac{1}{1+\exp(\vec{w}\cdot\vec{v_c'})} \quad (3)$$

The free parameters θ are updated using stochastic gradient descent and backpropagation, with global learning rate as defined in `word2vec` [24]. By optimizing the objective from eq. (3), the model incrementally pushes observed pivot WEs towards context WEs of their collocates in the corpus. After training, words that predict similar context words should end up having similar WEs.

2.3 Final Model: BWE Skip-Gram

In the next step, we extend the skip-gram model to work with bilingual document-aligned comparable data (e.g., Wikipedia articles in different languages aligned through inter-wiki links). An overview of our architecture for learning BWEs from comparable data is given in fig. 1.

Let us assume that we possess a document-aligned comparable corpus which is defined as $\mathcal{C} = \{d_1, d_2, \ldots, d_N\} = \{(d_1^S, d_1^T), (d_2^S, d_2^T), \ldots, (d_N^S, d_D^T)\}$, where $d_j = (d_j^S, d_j^T)$ denotes a pair of aligned documents in the source language L_S and the target language L_T, respectively, and N is the number of documents in the corpus. V^S and V^T are vocabularies associated with languages L_S and L_T. The goal is to learn word embeddings for all words in both V^S and V^T which will be semantically coherent and closely aligned over languages.

In the first step, we *merge* two documents d_j^S and d_j^T from the aligned document pair d_j into a single "pseudo-bilingual" document d_j' and remove sentence boundaries. Following that, we randomly *shuffle* the newly constructed pseudo-bilingual document. The intuition behind this pre-training shuffling step (see fig. 1) is to assure that each word w, regardless of its actual language, obtains word collocates from both vocabularies. The idea of having bilingual contexts for each pivot word in each pseudo-bilingual document will steer the final model towards constructing a shared inter-lingual embedding space. Since the model depends on the alignment at the document level, in order to ensure the bilingual contexts instead of monolingual contexts, it is intuitive to assume that larger window sizes will lead to better bilingual embeddings. We test this hypothesis and the effect of window size in sect. 5.1.

The final model called BWE Skip-gram (BWESG) then relies on the monolingual variant of the skip-gram model trained on these shuffled pseudo-bilingual documents. The model learns word embeddings for source and target language words which are aligned over the dim embedding dimensions and may be represented in the same shared inter-lingual embedding space. The BWESG-based representation of word w, regardless of its actual language, is then a dim-dimensional vector:

$$\vec{w} = [f_{w,1}, \ldots, f_{w,k}, \ldots, f_{w,dim}] \quad (4)$$

where $f_{w,k} \in \mathbb{R}$ denotes the score for the k-th inter-lingual feature associated with w within the dim-dimensional shared inter-lingual embedding space. Since all words share the embedding space, semantic similarity between words may be computed both monolingually and across languages. We will extensively use this property during the construction of our MoIR and CLIR models.

3. BWESG-BASED IR: FROM WORD EMBEDDINGS TO RETRIEVAL MODELS

The BWESG model induces structured representations from comparable data for single words only. In this section, we show how to compute similar structured representations for text units beyond the level of single words. The compositional approach will be used to construct embeddings for *documents* and *queries*, and it will be the basic building block of our MoIR and CLIR models. To this end, we rely on two key modeling assumptions: (1) We treat documents and queries as bags of words and do not impose any syntactic information to the document structure. This simplification is the standard practice in IR modeling, as in the ubiquitous unigram language model (e.g., [35, 3, 23]), relevance models (e.g., [18, 17]) or topic model based retrieval models (e.g., [44, 45, 12]; (2) We rely on the intuitions behind *semantic composition* models from the literature on distributional compositional semantics (e.g., [4, 27]).

For simplicity, we only discuss CLIR modeling in this section. The simpler MoIR models may be directly derived from the more general CLIR setting.

3.1 Constructing Document and Query Embeddings

Let us assume that a document d from a target document collection $\mathcal{DC}$ is a bag of word tokens $d = \{w_1, w_2, \ldots, w_{|N_d|}\}$, where $|N_d|$ denotes the length of the document d expressed by the number of word tokens.

In order to present the document d in the dim-dimensional embedding space induced by the BWESG model, we need to apply a model of *semantic composition* to learn its dim-dimensional vector representation $\overrightarrow{d}$. Formally, we may specify its vector representation as the dim-dimensional vector/embedding:

$$\overrightarrow{d} = \overrightarrow{w_1} \star \overrightarrow{w_2} \star \ldots \star \overrightarrow{w_{|N_d|}} \quad (5)$$

where $\overrightarrow{w_1}$,...,$\overrightarrow{w_{|N_d|}}$ are dim-dimensional WEs learned from the training data (see eq. (4)), and $\star$ is a compositional vector operator such as addition, point-wise multiplication, tensor product, matrix multiplication, etc.

A plethora of models for semantic composition have been proposed in the relevant literature, differing in their choice of vector operators, input structures and required knowledge (e.g., [29, 38, 4, 11, 27], to name only a few). In this work, driven by the observed linear linguistic regularities in the embedding spaces (e.g., [26, 20])[4], we opt for simple *addition* (denoted by +) from [29] as the compositional operator, due to its simplicity, the ease of applicability considering the bag-of-words assumption, as well as its solid performance in various compositional tasks [29, 27]. The dim-dimensional document embedding (DE) $\overrightarrow{d}$ is then a vector:

$$\overrightarrow{d} = \overrightarrow{w_1} + \overrightarrow{w_2} + \ldots + \overrightarrow{w_{|N_d|}} \quad (6)$$

We have constructed a document representation in the same embedding space where word embeddings live (see eq. (4) again):

$$\overrightarrow{d} = [f_{d,1}, \ldots, f_{d,k}, \ldots, f_{d,dim}] \quad (7)$$

We call this composition model for the DE induction *ADD-BASIC*.

In an extended approach, we may weigh the summands from eq. (6) using their *self-information* as weights. The idea is that the IDF-inspired weights will assign more importance to words bearing more information content during the compositional process. The property should then be reflected in a better document $\overrightarrow{d}$ in the dim-dimensional embedding space, and its "truer" semantics. We compute the self-information weight si_w of word w based on its occurrence in the target document collection $\mathcal{DC}$ using the standard formula [8] as follows:

$$si_w = -\ln \frac{freq(w, \mathcal{DC})}{|N_{\mathcal{DC}}|} \quad (8)$$

where $freq(w, \mathcal{DC})$ denotes the frequency of word w in the target document collection $\mathcal{DC}$, and $|N_{\mathcal{DC}}|$ is the size of the document collection measured by the total number of word tokens. A document embedding is then constructed out of its WEs as follows:

$$\overrightarrow{d} = si_{w_1} \cdot \overrightarrow{w_1} + si_{w_2} \cdot \overrightarrow{w_2} + \ldots + si_{w_{|N_d|}} \cdot \overrightarrow{w_{|N_d|}} \quad (9)$$

We call this composition model for the DE induction *ADD-SI*.

The construction of query embeddings (QEs) under the bag-of-words assumption proceeds in a completely analogous manner. As the knowledge of the target document collection may not be known from the query side, we restrict the construction of QEs to the ADD-BASIC composition model. A QE of a query $Q = \{q_1, q_2, \ldots, q_m\}$ containing m query terms in the embedding space is then:

$$\overrightarrow{Q} = \overrightarrow{q_1} + \overrightarrow{q_2} + \ldots + \overrightarrow{q_m} \quad (10)$$

$$\overrightarrow{Q} = [f_{Q,1}, \ldots, f_{Q,k}, \ldots, f_{Q,dim}] \quad (11)$$

3.2 Final MoIR and CLIR Models

In the previous section, we have demonstrated how to build embeddings for documents and queries, and how to represent them in the same embedding semantic space. This property makes the computation of semantic similarity between some document d from the target document collection and the issued query almost trivial. The similarity score $sim(d, Q)$ directly related to the relevance of d for Q is computed by applying a similarity function (SF) on their embeddings. In this paper, we use the standard cosine similarity measure as SF, the standard choice in the embedding induction literature (e.g., [25, 30, 21]):

$$sim(d, Q) = SF(d, Q) = \frac{\overrightarrow{d} \cdot \overrightarrow{Q}}{|\overrightarrow{d}| \cdot |\overrightarrow{Q}|} \quad (12)$$

The documents from $\mathcal{DC}$ are then ranked in descending order according to their similarity scores with query Q.

Since our new BWESG model learns to represent words from two different languages in the same shared cross-lingual embedding space, we may use exactly the same modeling approach to monolingual and cross-lingual information retrieval. All words in the embedding space retain their "language annotations"; although the words from two different languages are represented in the same semantic space, we still know whether a word belongs to language L_S (e.g., English) or language L_T (e.g., Dutch). We may now summarize the complete CLIR retrieval process as follows:

1. Given is a document-aligned comparable corpus in two languages L_S and L_T with vocabularies V^S and V^T. **Induce** the set of bilingual word embeddings $\mathcal{BWE}$ using the BWESG embedding learning model (see sect. 2.3). The set comprises dim-dimensional word embeddings $\overrightarrow{w}$ for each word $w \in V^S$ and each word $w \in V^T$.
2. Given is a target document collection $\mathcal{DC} = \{d'_1, \ldots, d'_{N'}\}$ in language L_T, where N' denotes the number of documents in the collection. **Compute** dim-dimensional document embeddings $\overrightarrow{d'}$ for each $d' \in \mathcal{DC}$ using the dim-dimensional WEs from the set $\mathcal{BWE}$ obtained in the previous step and a semantic composition model (ADD-BASIC or ADD-SI; see eq. (6) and eq. (9)).

[4]Recent work has shown that word embeddings are excellent at capturing semantic regularities in language, where the semantic relations are typically characterized by a relation-specific linear offset. The famous example from [26] states that the linear combination of word embeddings $\overrightarrow{king} - \overrightarrow{man} + \overrightarrow{woman}$ will result in a new vector closest to the embedding of $\overrightarrow{queen}$.

Table 1: Statistics of the experimental setup: (a) Monolingual EN→EN and NL→NL retrieval; (b) Cross-lingual EN→NL and NL→EN retrieval. In the "Query Set" column: for instance, EN'01:41-90 denotes the language of the query (EN) and the year of the campaign (2001), while 41-90 denotes the corresponding standard CLEF themes used to extract queries for that campaign.

Monolingual					Cross-lingual				
Direction	$\mathcal{DC}$	# Docs	Query Set	# Queries	*Direction*	$\mathcal{DC}$	# Docs	Query Set	# Queries
EN→EN 2001	LAT	110,861	EN'01: 41-90	47	NL→EN 2001	LAT	110,861	NL'01: 41-90	47
EN→EN 2002	LAT	110,861	EN'02: 91-140	42	NL→EN 2002	LAT	110,861	NL'01: 91-140	42
EN→EN 2003	LAT+GH	166,753	EN'03: 141-200	53	NL→EN 2003	LAT+GH	166,753	NL'03: 141-200	53
NL→NL 2001	NC+AD	190,604	NL'01: 41-90	50	EN→NL 2001	NC+AD	190,604	EN'01: 41-90	50
NL→NL 2002	NC+AD	190,604	NL'02: 91-140	50	EN→NL 2002	NC+AD	190,604	EN'02: 91-140	50
NL→NL 2003	NC+AD	190,604	NL'03: 141-200	56	EN→NL 2003	NC+AD	190,604	EN'03: 141-200	56

3. After the query $Q = \{q_1, \ldots, q_m\}$ is issued in language L_S, **compute** a dim-dimensional query embedding using the ADD-BASIC composition model (see eq. (11)).
4. **For each** $d' \in \mathcal{DC}$, **compute** the semantic similarity score $sim(d', Q)$ which quantifies each document's relevance to the query Q (see eq. (12)).
5. **Rank** all documents from $\mathcal{DC}$ according to their similarity scores from the previous step.

The only difference in the MoIR retrieval process is the fact that both the query and the target document collection are given in the same language. Strictly speaking, when performing monolingual retrieval, one does not require a comparable bilingual corpus any more, as the monolingual WEs may be simply learned on a large monolingual corpus (e.g., [25, 30]).[5] However, for the clarity of presentation, we have decided to stress the complete modeling analogy between the monolingual and cross-lingual approach to IR. In summary, we have created a unified framework for MoIR and CLIR which relies solely on word embeddings induced in an unsupervised fashion from document-aligned comparable data.

4. EXPERIMENTAL SETUP

Training Collections. We use the same training data collection as in [41, 42]. The training dataset comprises 7,612 document-aligned English-Dutch Wikipedia article pairs together with 6,206 Europarl English-Dutch document pairs [15]. We do not exploit alignments at the sentence level in Europarl and treat it as a corpus aligned only at the document level. After the stop words removal, the final vocabularies consist of 76,555 words in English and 71,168 words in Dutch [41].

Test Collections and Queries. All our experiments were performed on the standard datasets used in the cross-lingual evaluation of the CLEF 2001-2003 campaigns (e.g., [33, 34]). The target collection in Dutch (NL) comprises 190,604 Dutch news articles from the NRC Handelsblad 94-95 and the Algemeen Dagblad 94-95 newspapers (NC+AD). In English (EN), one target collection comprises 110,861 news articles from the 1994 LA times (LAT), and another target EN collection additionally includes the Glasgow Herald 1995 and comprises 166,753 news articles in total (LAT+GH).

As a standard practice [17, 44, 41], both English and Dutch queries have been extracted from the *title* and *description* fields of the CLEF themes for the years 2001-2003. Stop words were removed from queries, and queries without relevant documents were removed from the query sets in both languages.

[5]Investigating the differences in the MoIR performance when embeddings are trained on a larger monolingual corpus (as opposed to only the monolingual part from a comparable dataset) is left for future work.

We evaluate all retrieval models within the CLEF 2001-2003 evaluation campaigns in (1) *monolingual ad-hoc retrieval*: (1a) English queries and English target documents ($EN \rightarrow EN$); (1b) Dutch queries and Dutch target documents ($NL \rightarrow NL$), and (2) *cross-lingual ad-hoc retrieval*: (2a) English queries and Dutch target documents ($EN \rightarrow NL$); (2b) Dutch queries and English target documents ($NL \rightarrow EN$). Tab. 1 provides an overview of the complete experimental setup.

Mean Average Precision (MAP) scores are used as the main evaluation metric for all experiments. We have also experimented with recall-precision curves, but for brevity we omit these in the final presentation, as the main findings were in line with the analysis based on the MAP scores.

Retrieval Models in Comparison. We use the same families of models for both MoIR and CLIR.

WE-VS. Our new retrieval model which relies on the induction of word embeddings and their usage in the construction of query and document embeddings is described in sect. 3.2. We investigate the retrieval ability of our new vector space retrieval model based on (bilingual) word embeddings by comparing it to the set of standard MoIR and CLIR models. We opt for ADD-BASIC as the composition model unless noted otherwise. Later we show the comparison of ADD-BASIC and ADD-SI (see sect. 5.3).

LM-UNI. The first baseline model in comparison is the omnipresent standard query likelihood model from Ponte and Croft [35] which generates the query Q under the bag-of-words assumption that terms are independent given the documents. It is a unigram language model specified by the following formula with standard Dirichlet smoothing [46]:

$$P(Q|d) = \prod_{i=1}^{m} P(q_i|d)$$
$$= \prod_{i=1}^{m} \frac{N_d}{N_d + \mu} P(q_i|d) + (1 - \frac{N_d}{N_d + \mu}) P(q_i|\mathcal{DC}) \quad (13)$$

where N_d is the length of document d from the target collection $\mathcal{DC}$, and μ is the parameter of Dirichlet smoothing. $P(q_i|d)$ is the maximum likelihood estimate of the query term q_i in d, while $P(q_i|\mathcal{DC})$ is its maximum likelihood estimate in the entire target collection. In the actual implementation, we operate with log probabilities. It is intuitive that the LM-UNI model will lead to much better results in the monolingual setting, as the amount of shared words between different languages is typically very limited, and therefore other representations for CLIR are sought [41] (see next).

LDA-IR. Another baseline retrieval model similar to WE-VS, relies on structured semantic-representations of words and documents obtained by the latent Dirichlet allocation (LDA) model [5] for the monolingual setting, and its bilingual variant called bilingual LDA [28, 31] for the cross-lingual setting. The LDA-based MoIR model was introduced in [44], while the description of the BiLDA-based CLIR model is available in [41]. In short, query likelihood is computed as follows:

$$P(Q|d) = \prod_{i=1}^{m} P(q_i|d) = \prod_{i=1}^{m} \sum_{k=1}^{K} P(q_i|z_k)P(z_k|d) \quad (14)$$

where z_k denotes the k-th (cross-lingual) latent topic induced from training data (out of K topics), $P(q_i|z_k)$ is a probability score learned from the training data, and $P(z_k|d)$ are probability scores after running the trained LDA/BiLDA model on each document of the target collection. In the cross-lingual setting the latent topics act as a bridge over the lexical chasm between two different languages [41, 43].

LM-UNI+LDA-IR. It was shown both for the monolingual [44] and cross-lingual retrieval [41] that *combining* the basic unigram language model with a semantically aware model such as LDA-IR leads to improved retrieval models, where the combined model typically scores significantly higher than each of the single models. Since LM-UNI and LDA-IR are probabilistic models, it is straightforward to combine them using the following formula [44, 41]:

$$P(q_i|d) = \lambda P_{lda}(q_i|d) + (1 - \lambda)P_{lm}(q_i|d) \quad (15)$$

where $P_{lda}(q_i|d)$ is the probability score of the LDA-IR model acquired following eq. (14), and $P_{lm}(q_i|d)$ is the probability score of LM-UNI following eq. (13). λ is the linear interpolation parameter which assigns the weight balance between the two constituent models. The combined LM-UNI+LDA-IR is a very strong monolingual baseline [44], and is a state-of-the-art CLIR model that requires only comparable data for training [41], the same setup as for our BWESG model and the corresponding WE-VS retrieval model.

LM-UNI+WE-VS. Following the same line of thinking, we hypothesize that the combination of the unigram model with our new semantically aware WE-VS model will also lead to improved retrieval scores. While the comparison of single LDA-IR and WE-VS models will directly analyze which of the two semantic representations (LDA-based or embeddings-based) is better fit for the ad-hoc MoIR and CLIR retrieval tasks, the comparison of the combined LM-UNI+LDA-IR and LM-UNI+WE-VS will analyze whether we profit from introducing the WE-based semantic representations into the combined model. We combine the two models using a simple approach as follows: (1) separately rank the documents from $\mathcal{DC}$ using LM-UNI ($score_{lm}(d, Q)$, see eq. (13)) and WE-VS (see sect. 3.2, the score is $score_{we}(d, Q)$); (2) normalize the scores in both ranked lists to the interval $[0, 1]$; (3) linearly combine the normalized scores, with λ as the interpolation parameter:

$$score(d, Q) = \lambda score_{we}(d, Q) + (1 - \lambda)score_{lm}(d, Q) \quad (16)$$

GT+LM+LDA: An additional baseline in the CLIR setting uses an SMT system (i.e., *Google Translate* (GT)) to translate the query from the source to target language, and then the actual retrieval is performed monolingually using the LM-UNI+LDA-IR monolingual model as described in [44, 41]. Unlike the LDA-based and WE-based CLIR models, this (SMT-based) model does not construct a shared inter-lingual semantic space, and in addition it uses an external translation resource as an extra source of knowledge.

Parameters. Since each of the retrieval models comes with the burden of its own parameters, we list the parameters by model. The parameter values from the single models are also used in the combined models unless stated otherwise.
WE-VS: We have trained the BWESG model with random shuffling on 10 random corpora shuffles of our training data with all other parameters set to the default parameters for skip-gram from the `word2vec` package [25]. We have varied the number of dimensions d from 100 to 800 in steps of 100. Moreover, in order to test the effect of window size on final results, we have varied the maximum window size cs from 10 to 100 in steps of 10.
LM-UNI: The Dirichlet interpolation parameter is set to the standard suggested value: $\mu = 1000$ [46, 44].
LDA-IR: We have trained LDA and BiLDA using Gibbs sampling [39, 43] with the suggested value for the number of topics: $K = 1000$ which yielded optimal or near-optimal results in MoIR and CLIR as reported in the literature [44, 39, 41]. All other parameters of the topic models (i.e., hyper-parameters, the number of iterations of the Gibbs sampler) have also been set to the standard values reported before in the relevant literature.
LM-UNI+LDA-IR: In order to ensure the optimal performance of the baseline combined model, the grid search over λ values $\{0.0, \ldots, 1.0\}$ (in steps of 0.1) has been performed, and the results with the optimal λ value are reported.
LM-UNI+WE-VS: We have tested several typical values for the interpolation parameter λ: 0.3 (more weight is assigned to LM-UNI); 0.5 (equal importance); 0.7 (more weight is assigned to WE-VS).

5. RESULTS AND ANALYSIS

In this section, we evaluate our novel WE-based framework in the ad-hoc monolingual and cross-lingual tasks. We again stress that for CLIR we operate in a difficult setting which requires only comparable data to induce cross-lingual structured semantic representations, and does not rely on any parallel sentence-aligned data or readily available bilingual lexicons.

5.1 Experiment I: Monolingual Retrieval

Test I: Single Models. The results of the single MoIR models (WE-VS, LM-UNI and LDA-IR) are available in tab. 2. We show the results with $dim = 300$ and $dim = 600$, and the maximum window size cs set to 60. We investigate the influence of the dimensionality of representation and maximum window size later in Test III. All MAP scores for WE-VS are computed as averages over 10 different random corpora shuffles.[6] Based on the results, we may observe several interesting phenomena:

(i) Across all evaluation runs, our new WE-VS retrieval model which relies on the induction of word embeddings scores higher than LDA-IR, the other model which relies on structured semantic representations of words and documents. It is the first evidence that combining the BWESG model for inducing word embeddings plus a semantic composition model to induce document and query embeddings may be more beneficial in IR applications than previously widely used LDA- and BiLDA-based representations and approaches. All differences in scores are highly statistically significant (see the results of statistical significance tests in tab. 2).

[6]We have conducted a small experiment testing the influence of the random shuffling procedure, and have detected that the fluctuation of results for all models relying on the BWESG embeddings caused by the random shuffling procedure is typically non-significant. Moreover, the fluctuation is lesser than the fluctuation caused by the inherent randomness of the original skip-gram model (due to negative sampling and window size sampling) [25], and may be further decreased by relying on larger window sizes.

Table 2: A comparison of single and combined MoIR models. All results are given as MAP scores. LM+LDA is an abbreviation denoting the LM-UNI+LDA-IR model, while LM+WE refers to LM-UNI+WE-VS model. y and x denote statistically significant improvements ($p < 0.05$ and $p < 0.01$, respectively) of the WE-VS model over LDA-IR using a two-tailed Wilcoxon signed rank test. They also denote statistically significant improvements ($p < 0.05$ and $p < 0.01$, respectively) of the combined LM+WE model over another combined LM+LDA model (which is by design an upper bound of the LM-UNI model) using the same test.

	EN→EN			NL→NL		
Model	2001	2002	2003	2001	2002	2003
LM-UNI	.381	.360	.359	.256	.323	.357
LDA-IR	.279	.216	.241	.131	.143	.130
dim:300; *cs*:60						
WE-VS	.324x	.258x	.257y	.203x	.237x	.224x
dim:600; *cs*:60						
WE-VS	.329x	.281x	.262y	.204x	.262x	.231x
LM+LDA	.399	.360	.379	.260	.326	.357
dim:300; *cs*:60						
LM+WE (λ=0.3)	.412y	.381x	.401y	.271x	.349x	.372x
LM+WE (λ=0.5)	.429x	.394x	.407x	.279x	.370x	.382x
LM+WE (λ=0.7)	.451x	.392y	.389	.270	.364x	.373y
dim:600; *cs*:60						
LM+WE (λ=0.3)	.419y	.382x	.403y	.274x	.350x	.373x
LM+WE (λ=0.5)	.436x	.391x	.408x	.282x	.371x	.383x
LM+WE (λ=0.7)	.430x	.392y	.381	.268	.367x	.374y

Table 3: A comparison of single and combined CLIR models. All results are given as MAP scores. LM+LDA+WE denotes a combination of all three single models. y and x denote statistically significant improvements ($p < 0.05$ and $p < 0.01$, respectively) of the WE-VS model over LDA-IR using a two-tailed Wilcoxon signed rank test. They also denote statistically significant improvements ($p < 0.05$ and $p < 0.01$, respectively) of the combined LM+WE and LM+LDA+WE models over baseline LM+LDA using the same test.

	NL→EN			EN→NL		
Model	2001	2002	2003	2001	2002	2003
LM-UNI	.094	.108	.092	.078	.125	.112
LDA-IR	.197	.139	.123	.145	.137	.171
dim:300; *cs*:60						
WE-VS	.187	.204x	.120	.174	.185y	.157
dim:600; *cs*:60						
WE-VS	.222y	.230x	.127	.178y	.219x	.181
LM+LDA	.267	.225	.199	.225	.268	.278
GT+LM+LDA	.307	.275	.248	.230	.240	.244
dim:300; *cs*:60						
LM+WE (λ=0.3)	.189	.273	.197	.101	.159	.150
LM+WE (λ=0.5)	.218	.283y	.220	.113	.184	.167
LM+WE (λ=0.7)	.255	.307x	.219	.180	.209	.208
dim:600; *cs*:60						
LM+WE (λ=0.3)	.205	.281y	.198	.107	.167	.154
LM+WE (λ=0.5)	.236	.299x	.215	.123	.203	.183
LM+WE (λ=0.7)	.286	.317x	.222	.190	.249	.225
dim:600; *cs*:60						
LM+LDA+WE (λ=0.3)	.277	.263	.210	.229	.288	.283
LM+LDA+WE (λ=0.5)	.281y	.281y	.214	.240	.297y	.290
LM+LDA+WE (λ=0.7)	.302x	.302x	.227	.244y	.311x	.302y

(ii) Due to the larger number of dimensions, WE-VS with $dim = 600$ should provide more semantic expressiveness than WE-VS with $dim = 300$. The difference in results seems to be consistent across all evaluation runs. However, the difference is small and statistically insignificant for most of the evaluation runs.

(iii) As expected, LM-UNI is the best scoring single MoIR model and it scores better even then our new WE-VS model. This is consistent with previous findings (e.g., [44, 45]) for the monolingual setting, where it has been stated that structured semantic representations such as LDA-based representations (LDA-IR) (or now embeddings) are too coarse-grained to produce retrieval scores on a par with the scores obtained by a query likelihood unigram language model. However, the prior work also demonstrates that structured semantic representations are very useful when fused with the unigram language model (see next).

Test II: Combined Models. Another test aimed at detecting which of the semantic representations (i.e., LDA-based or WE-based) is more helpful when combined with the LM-UNI model. The MAP scores presented in tab. 2 reveal the following:

(i) Our new combined LM-UNI+WE-VS model which combined the semantic knowledge coded in document embeddings with a unigram language model produces the highest overall MAP scores over all evaluation runs. The MAP scores obtained by LM-UNI+WE-VS are also higher than the scores obtained by the other combined model in comparison, which fuses LM-UNI and LDA-IR (LM-UNI+LDA-IR), and the improvements are largely significant.

(ii) Since we have used the optimal value for λ when reporting the scores for LM-UNI+LDA-IR, all results of that combined model are by design higher than LM-UNI alone. It leads to this general conclusion: Including additional semantic knowledge (in the form of document embeddings composed from the previously induced word embeddings) is useful for MoIR modeling as it captures complementary pieces of information and encodes the document semantics that a simple unigram model cannot capture. The semantic knowledge is better coded in word and document embeddings than in the previously widely used LDA-based representation models for IR.

Test III: Influence of Dimensionality and Window Size. In order to test how the dimensionality of embeddings and the size of the local context cs influence the final retrieval scores, we conducted two experiments. In the first experiment, we fixed the parameter cs to 60 and then varied the number of dimensions dim from 50 to 800. The MAP scores across different settings for dim for the WE-VS and LM-UNI+WE-VS MoIR retrieval models for a selection of evaluation runs (2001 and 2002 campaigns) are presented in fig. 2(a) and fig. 2(b). In another experiment, we fixed the parameter dim to 300 and varied the number of dimensions cs from 10 to 100. The results for WE-VS and LM-UNI+WE-VS are displayed in fig. 3(a) and fig. 3(b). We may summarize the findings here:

(i) The performance of WE-VS is stable across different settings for parameter dim for larger dim-s (≥ 300). Smaller vectors ($d = 50, 100, 200$) are simply not semantically expressive, and do not capture and encode all semantic properties of words and documents. On the other hand, it is interesting to notice that the combined LM-UNI+WE-VS is fairly robust to the change of the parameter dim controling the dimensionality of representation, and all embedding models (even with $d = 50$) help boost the scores in the combined model.

(ii) The performance of WE-VS is also relatively stable across different settings for cs for larger values of the parameter (≥ 30), but comparable results are obtained even with smaller window sizes. Again, we may notice that the combined model is robust to the fluctuation of cs.

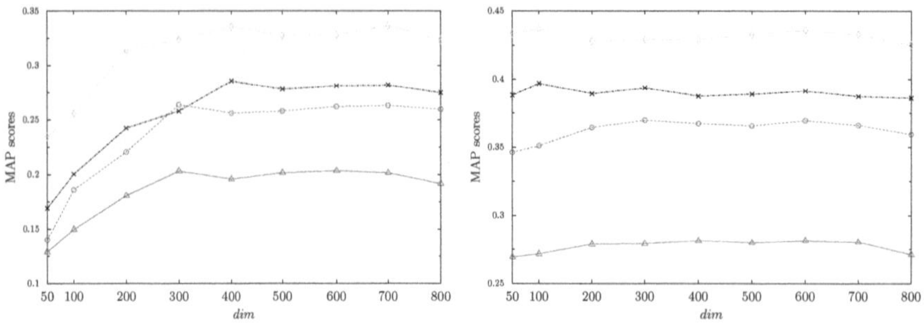

(a) WE-VS, $cs = 60$ (b) LM-UNI+WE-VS, $cs = 60$

Figure 2: An analysis of the behavior of (a) WE-VS and (b) LM-UNI+WE-VS across different parameter settings for dimensionality dim of WEs, QEs, and DEs constructed using the BWESG model. The maximum window size cs is set to 60 for all models.

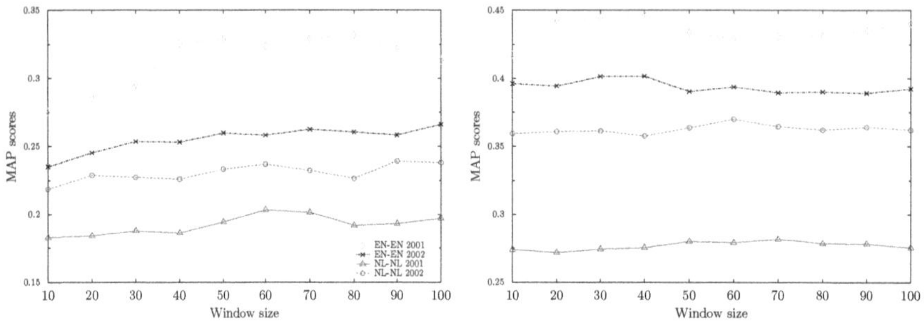

(a) WE-VS, $dim = 300$ (b) LM-UNI+WE-VS, $dim = 300$

Figure 3: An analysis of the behavior of (a) WE-VS and (b) LM-UNI+WE-VS across different settings for the maximum window size parameter cs of WEs, QEs, and DEs constructed using the BWESG model. Dimensionality of the representation dim is set to 300.

Based on these analyses, we may conclude that the inclusion of embeddings in the retrieval process is invariantly useful. The same conclusion is valid for the cross-lingual retrieval scenarios, but we do not show these results due to space constraints.

5.2 Experiment II: Cross-Lingual Retrieval

Test I: Single Models. The results of the single CLIR models (WE-VS, LM-UNI and LDA-IR) are available in tab. 3. We again show the results with $dim = 300$ and $dim = 600$, and the maximum window size cs set to 60, and all MAP scores for WE-VS are computed as averages over 10 different random corpora shuffles.

(i) WE-VS is now the best scoring single CLIR model across all evaluation runs. LM-UNI, which was the best scoring MoIR model, is now outscored by the other two models which rely on structured semantic representations. While the words shared between a query and a target document are very strong indicators for the retrieval process in the monolingual setting, their importance is heavily diminished in the cross-lingual setting, as the amount of shared words between two different languages is very limited. In the setting without any bilingual dictionaries or parallel data, the shared cross-lingual semantic representations become increasingly important. (ii) LDA-IR model which relies on the BiLDA topic model [28] is the current state-of-the-art single model for CLIR with comparable data [41]. However, we may see that our new WE-VS CLIR model outperforms LDA-IR across all evaluation runs.

Test II: Combined Models. Similar as for MoIR, the combined CLIR models are also compared. The results are available in tab. 3.

(i) The combined LM-UNI+LDA-IR model for CLIR, which was the top scoring query likelihood model in [41, 42], is outperformed by LM-UNI+WE-VS for the NL-to-EN retrieval direction. However, it is not the case for the EN-to-NL retrieval, where the LM+LDA combination significantly outperforms the new LM+WE model. Although the single WE-VS model compares favorably to LDA-IR, the advantage of WE-VS is lost in the combined model. We have investigated the causes of such behavior and the difference in results for NL-to-EN and EN-to-NL retrieval directions, and have come to the following conclusion: (1) In the NL-to-EN retrieval direction, many queries do not contain any NL terms to be found in the EN target collectiosn. Therefore, the LM-UNI model is unable to provide any ranking of the documents there, and the ranking is provided solely on the basis of the semantic models such as LDA-IR or WE-VS. Moreover, the NL terms which are found in both NL queries and EN target collections are typically very relevant to the information need (e.g., named entities such as *Alberto Tomba*, *Miguel Indurain*), so the combined model may profit from the information from both single models. However, in the EN-to-NL direction, many irrelevant and general terms from EN queries are found in the NL target collection (e.g., words like *words*, *document*, *telling*) which lead LM-UNI and the combined model astray; (2) Since WE-VS is a vector space model, while LM-UNI is a probabilistic language model, their combination is executed post-hoc, after obtaining the rankings separately and then normalizing the scores (see eq. (16) in sect. 4). This way, the errors from the LM-UNI model are assigned too much weight in the combined model. This negative effect is removed when combining LM-UNI and LDA-IR (see eq. (15) in sect. 4), since both models are probabilistic and their combination is executed at the level of single query terms. This way, the errors from LM-UNI may be immediately corrected by smoothing it with semantically aware LDA-IR.

Test III: Yet Another Combined Model. Knowing all this, in order to test whether embeddings may be useful even for the EN-to-NL retrieval direction, we have constructed a new combined model which combines the evidence from all three single models. The new combined LM-UNI+LDA-IR+WE-VS model first computes

Table 4: A comparison (MAP scores) of two different semantic composition models from sect. 3.2 (ADD-BASIC and ADD-SI) utilized to construct document embeddings from the word embeddings induced by BWESG. The retrieval model is WE-VS. dim is set to the value 300 and 600 (in brackets), while cs is 60 for all models. y and x denote statistically significant improvements ($p < 0.05$ and $p < 0.01$, respectively) of ADD-SI over ADD-BASIC using a two-tailed Wilcoxon signed rank test.

	Monolingual						Cross-lingual					
	EN→EN			NL→NL			NL→EN			EN→NL		
Composition	2001	2002	2003	2001	2002	2003	2001	2002	2003	2001	2002	2003
ADD-BASIC (300)	.324	.258	.257	.203	.237	.224	.187	.204	.120	.174	.185	.157
ADD-SI (300)	.338	.278y	.255	.212	.253y	.227	.216x	.213y	.122	.189y	.208x	.161
ADD-BASIC (600)	.329	.281	.262	.204	.262	.231	.221	.230	.127	.178	.219	.181
ADD-SI (600)	.344y	.301y	.263	.215	.275y	.234	.237y	.233	.130	.189	.229x	.184

separate retrieval scores using WE-VS and LM-UNI+LDA-IR (this way, we diminish the effect of the errors caused by using LM-UNI alone), normalizes the scores to the interval $[0, 1]$, and then computes the combined scores using eq. (16) again. The results for the new combined model are given in tab. 3.

(i) We may observe that the new combined model now significantly outperforms the LM-UNI+LDA-IR model [41] over all evaluation runs with English queries and Dutch target collections. The LDA-IR model decreases the errors from LM-UNI, and then the WE-VS model introduces additional semantic knowledge that is coded in document embeddings. Although both LDA-IR and WE-VS rely on structured semantic representations of documents and query terms, it seems that the two models capture partially complementary pieces of information, and combining them is beneficial for the complete retrieval process.

(ii) As already detected in [44, 41], fusing complementary retrieval evidence in the combined models leads to better overall models. The fusion of different retrieval clues is especially important in the minimalist CLIR setting which relies only on comparable training data for the induction of additional semantic knowledge in the form of structured text representations.

5.3 Experiment III: Composition Models

In the final experiment, we test whether better semantic composition models lead to higher-quality document embeddings, and consequently to higher overall retrieval scores. A more informed and better composition function should better reflect how the composite meaning of a document is constructed from the meanings of its constituents, that is, single words. We compare our ADD-BASIC and the ADD-SI approach to semantic composition from sect. 3.1 using the WE-VS model for MoIR and CLIR. The results are reported in tab. 4.

The results clearly reveal that ADD-SI which is an additive model with additional weighting based on self-information outperforms the simpler ADD-BASIC model. The improvements are small, but consistent across all evaluation runs both for MoIR and CLIR. Encouraged by the findings, we plan to study more elaborate composition models and their influence on the IR models in future work.

6. CONCLUSIONS AND FUTURE WORK

We have presented a novel unified framework for monolingual and cross-lingual information retrieval that relies on the induction of dense real-valued word vectors known as word embeddings. This paper is a pilot study focusing on the importance and ability of the new neural-net inspired semantically-aware text representations in the IR/CLIR setting.

We have introduced a new model for learning structured monolingual and bilingual word embeddings known from comparable data. Our Bilingual Word Embeddings Skip-Gram (BWESG) model is the first model that is able to learn the shared cross-lingual semantic embedding space without the need for parallel data or readily available bilingual dictionaries. These minimal requirements make the model easily applicable to plenty of language pairs.

Further, we have presented how to compose query and document embeddings from single word embeddings induced by the BWESG model, and how to use these embeddings in the construction of novel monolingual and cross-lingual retrieval models. The new models which rely on the semantic knowledge coming from the embeddings demonstrate better results than previous state-of-the-art models in the monolingual and cross-lingual retrieval tasks conducted on the benchmarking CLEF datasets.

We believe that the proposed framework is only a start, as it ignites a series of new research questions and perspectives. (i) A straightforward path of future research is to use the BWESG model for other language pairs, and apply to other tasks such as (cross-lingual) document classification and clustering [14, 11]. (ii) Another straightforward extension is to replace the simple pre-training shuffling procedure with a more systematic context selection method. (iii) In this paper, we have relied only on simple additive semantic composition models, but based on the results from sect. 5.3, we believe that better results may be achieved by introducing more complex composition models available in the literature (e.g., [4, 27]). (iii) Finally, we have only investigated query likelihood approaches to ad-hoc retrieval, but one path of future work leads to studying the potential of the embedding-based approaches with the pseudo-relevance feedback modeling frameworks such as [17, 9].

Acknowledgments

We would like to thank the reviewers for their comments and suggestions. This research has been carried out in the frameworks of the Smart Computer-Aided Translation Environment (SCATE) project (IWT-SBO 130041) and the Personalised AdveRtisements bullt from web Sources (PARIS) project (IWT-SBO 110067).

7. REFERENCES

[1] M. Baroni, G. Dinu, and G. Kruszewski. Don't count, predict! A systematic comparison of context-counting vs context-predicting semantic vectors. In *ACL*, pages 238–247, 2014.

[2] Y. Bengio, R. Ducharme, P. Vincent, and C. Janvin. A neural probabilistic language model. *Journal of Machine Learning Research*, 3:1137–1155, 2003.

[3] A. Berger and J. Lafferty. Information retrieval as statistical translation. In *SIGIR*, pages 222–229, 1999.

[4] W. Blacoe and M. Lapata. A comparison of vector-based representations for semantic composition. In *EMNLP-CoNLL*, pages 546–556, 2012.

[5] D. M. Blei, A. Y. Ng, and M. I. Jordan. Latent Dirichlet Allocation. *Journal of Machine Learning Research*, 3:993–1022, 2003.

[6] R. Collobert and J. Weston. A unified architecture for natural language processing: Deep neural networks with multitask learning. In *ICML*, pages 160–167, 2008.

[7] R. Collobert, J. Weston, L. Bottou, M. Karlen, K. Kavukcuoglu, and P. P. Kuksa. Natural language processing (almost) from scratch. *Journal of Machine Learning Research*, 12:2493–2537, 2011.

[8] T. M. Cover and J. A. Thomas. *Elements of Information Theory*. Wiley-Interscience, 1991.

[9] F. Diaz and D. Metzler. Improving the estimation of relevance models using large external corpora. In *SIGIR*, pages 154–161, 2006.

[10] Y. Goldberg and O. Levy. Word2vec explained: Deriving Mikolov et al.'s negative-sampling word-embedding method. *CoRR*, abs/1402.3722, 2014.

[11] K. M. Hermann and P. Blunsom. Multilingual models for compositional distributed semantics. In *ACL*, pages 58–68, 2014.

[12] J. Jagarlamudi and H. Daumé III. Extracting multilingual topics from unaligned comparable corpora. In *ECIR*, pages 444–456, 2010.

[13] D. Kiela and L. Bottou. Learning image embeddings using convolutional neural networks for improved multi-modal semantics. In *EMNLP*, pages 36–45, 2014.

[14] A. Klementiev, I. Titov, and B. Bhattarai. Inducing crosslingual distributed representations of words. In *COLING*, pages 1459–1474, 2012.

[15] P. Koehn. Europarl: A parallel corpus for statistical machine translation. In *MT SUMMIT*, pages 79–86, 2005.

[16] T. K. Landauer and S. T. Dumais. Solutions to Plato's problem: The Latent Semantic Analysis theory of acquisition, induction, and representation of knowledge. *Psychological Review*, 104(2):211–240, 1997.

[17] V. Lavrenko, M. Choquette, and W. B. Croft. Cross-lingual relevance models. In *SIGIR*, pages 175–182, 2002.

[18] V. Lavrenko and W. B. Croft. Relevance-based language models. In *SIGIR*, pages 120–127, 2001.

[19] O. Levy and Y. Goldberg. Dependency-based word embeddings. In *ACL*, pages 302–308, 2014.

[20] O. Levy and Y. Goldberg. Linguistic regularities in sparse and explicit word representations. In *CoNLL*, pages 171–180, 2014.

[21] O. Levy and Y. Goldberg. Neural word embedding as implicit matrix factorization. In *NIPS*, pages 2177–2185, 2014.

[22] O. Levy, Y. Goldberg, and I. Dagan. Improving distributional similarity with lessons learned from word embeddings. *Transactions of ACL*, to appear, 2015.

[23] C. D. Manning, P. Raghavan, and H. Schütze. *Introduction to Information Retrieval*. Cambridge University Press, 2008.

[24] T. Mikolov, K. Chen, G. S. Corrado, and J. Dean. Efficient estimation of word representations in vector space. In *ICLR Workshop Papers*, 2013.

[25] T. Mikolov, I. Sutskever, K. Chen, G. S. Corrado, and J. Dean. Distributed representations of words and phrases and their compositionality. In *NIPS*, pages 3111–3119, 2013.

[26] T. Mikolov, W. Yih, and G. Zweig. Linguistic regularities in continuous space word representations. In *NAACL-HLT*, pages 746–751, 2013.

[27] D. Milajevs, D. Kartsaklis, M. Sadrzadeh, and M. Purver. Evaluating neural word representations in tensor-based compositional settings. In *EMNLP*, pages 708–719, 2014.

[28] D. Mimno, H. Wallach, J. Naradowsky, D. A. Smith, and A. McCallum. Polylingual topic models. In *EMNLP*, pages 880–889, 2009.

[29] J. Mitchell and M. Lapata. Vector-based models of semantic composition. In *ACL*, pages 236–244, 2008.

[30] A. Mnih and K. Kavukcuoglu. Learning word embeddings efficiently with noise-contrastive estimation. In *NIPS*, pages 2265–2273, 2013.

[31] X. Ni, J.-T. Sun, J. Hu, and Z. Chen. Mining multilingual topics from Wikipedia. In *WWW*, pages 1155–1156, 2009.

[32] J. Pennington, R. Socher, and C. Manning. Glove: Global vectors for word representation. In *EMNLP*, pages 1532–1543, 2014.

[33] C. Peters, M. Braschler, J. Gonzalo, and M. Kluck, editors. *CLEF 2001, Revised Papers*, 2002.

[34] C. Peters, M. Braschler, J. Gonzalo, and M. Kluck, editors. *CLEF 2002, Revised Papers*, 2003.

[35] J. M. Ponte and W. B. Croft. A language modeling approach to information retrieval. In *SIGIR*, pages 275–281, 1998.

[36] D. E. Rumelhart, G. E. Hinton, and R. J. Williams. Learning representations by back-propagating errors. *Nature*, 323:533–536, 1986.

[37] G. Salton, A. Wong, and C. S. Yang. A vector space model for automatic indexing. *Communications of the ACM*, 18(11):613–620, 1975.

[38] R. Socher, B. Huval, C. D. Manning, and A. Y. Ng. Semantic compositionality through recursive matrix-vector spaces. In *EMNLP-CoNLL*, pages 1201–1211, 2012.

[39] M. Steyvers and T. Griffiths. Probabilistic topic models. *Handbook of Latent Semantic Analysis*, 427(7):424–440, 2007.

[40] J. P. Turian, L. Ratinov, and Y. Bengio. Word representations: A simple and general method for semi-supervised learning. In *ACL*, pages 384–394, 2010.

[41] I. Vulić, W. De Smet, and M.-F. Moens. Cross-language information retrieval models based on latent topic models trained with document-aligned comparable corpora. *Information Retrieval*, 16(3):331–368, 2013.

[42] I. Vulić and M. Moens. A unified framework for monolingual and cross-lingual relevance modeling based on probabilistic topic models. In *ECIR*, pages 98–109, 2013.

[43] I. Vulić, W. D. Smet, J. Tang, and M. Moens. Probabilistic topic modeling in multilingual settings: An overview of its methodology and applications. *Information Processing and Management*, 51(1):111–147, 2015.

[44] X. Wei and W. B. Croft. LDA-based document models for ad-hoc retrieval. In *SIGIR*, pages 178–185, 2006.

[45] X. Yi and J. Allan. A comparative study of utilizing topic models for information retrieval. In *ECIR*, pages 29–41, 2009.

[46] C. Zhai and J. Lafferty. A study of smoothing methods for language models applied to information retrieval. *ACM Transactions on Information Systems*, 22(2):179–214, 2004.

Learning to Rank Short Text Pairs with Convolutional Deep Neural Networks

Aliaksei Severyn*
Google Inc.
aseveryn@gmail.com

Alessandro Moschitti†
Qatar Computing Research Institute
amoschitti@qf.org.qa

ABSTRACT

Learning a similarity function between pairs of objects is at the core of learning to rank approaches. In information retrieval tasks we typically deal with query-document pairs, in question answering – question-answer pairs. However, before learning can take place, such pairs needs to be mapped from the original space of symbolic words into some feature space encoding various aspects of their relatedness, e.g. lexical, syntactic and semantic. Feature engineering is often a laborious task and may require external knowledge sources that are not always available or difficult to obtain. Recently, deep learning approaches have gained a lot of attention from the research community and industry for their ability to automatically learn optimal feature representation for a given task, while claiming state-of-the-art performance in many tasks in computer vision, speech recognition and natural language processing. In this paper, we present a convolutional neural network architecture for reranking pairs of short texts, where we learn the optimal representation of text pairs and a similarity function to relate them in a supervised way from the available training data. Our network takes only words in the input, thus requiring minimal preprocessing. In particular, we consider the task of reranking short text pairs where elements of the pair are sentences. We test our deep learning system on two popular retrieval tasks from TREC: Question Answering and Microblog Retrieval. Our model demonstrates strong performance on the first task beating previous state-of-the-art systems by about 3% absolute points in both MAP and MRR and shows comparable results on tweet reranking, while enjoying the benefits of no manual feature engineering and no additional syntactic parsers.

Categories and Subject Descriptors

H.3 [**Information Storage and Retrieval**]: H.3.3 Information Search and Retrieval; I.5.1 [**Pattern Recognition**]: Models—*Neural nets*

Keywords

Convolutional neural networks; learning to rank; Question Answering; Microblog search

*The work was carried out at University of Trento.
†Professor at University of Trento, DISI.

SIGIR'15, August 09 - 13, 2015, Santiago, Chile.
 ISBN 978-1-4503-3621-5/15/08 ...$15.00.
DOI: http://dx.doi.org/10.1145/2766462.2767738.

1. INTRODUCTION

Encoding query-document pairs into discriminative feature vectors that are input to a learning-to-rank algorithm is a critical step in building an accurate reranker. The core assumption is that relevant documents have high semantic similarity to the queries and, hence, the main effort lies in mapping a query and a document into a joint feature space where their similarity can be efficiently established.

The most widely used approach is to encode input text pairs using many complex lexical, syntactic and semantic features and then compute various similarity measures between the obtained representations. For example, in answer passage reranking [31] employ complex linguistic features, modelling syntactic and semantic information as bags of syntactic and semantic role dependencies and build similarity and translation models over these representations.

However, the choice of representations and features is a completely empirical process, driven by the intuition, experience and domain expertise. Moreover, although using syntactic and semantic information has been shown to improve performance, it can be computationally expensive and require a large number of external tools — syntactic parsers, lexicons, knowledge bases, etc. Furthermore, adapting to new domains requires additional effort to tune feature extraction pipelines and adding new resources that may not even exist.

Recently, it has been shown that the problem of semantic text matching can be efficiently tackled using distributional word matching, where a large number of lexical semantic resources are used for matching questions with a candidate answer [33].

Deep learning approaches generalize the distributional word matching problem to matching sentences and take it one step further by learning the optimal sentence representations for a given task. Deep neural networks are able to effectively capture the compositional process of mapping the meaning of individual words in a sentence to a continuous representation of the sentence. In particular, it has been recently shown that convolutional neural networks are able to efficiently learn to embed input sentences into low-dimensional vector space preserving important syntactic and semantic aspects of the input sentence, which leads to state-of-the-art results in many NLP tasks [18, 19, 38]. Perhaps one of the greatest advantages of deep neural networks is that they are trained in an end-to-end fashion, thus removing the need for manual feature engineering and greatly reducing the need for adapting to new tasks and domains.

In this paper, we describe a novel deep learning architecture for reranking short texts, where questions and documents are limited to a single sentence. The main building blocks of our architecture are two distributional sentence models based on convolutional neural networks. These underlying sentence models work in parallel, mapping queries and documents to their distributional vectors, which are then used to learn the semantic similarity between them.

The distinctive properties of our model are: (i) we use a state-of-the-art distributional sentence model for learning to map input sentences to vectors, which are then used to measure the similarity between them; (ii) our model encodes query-document pairs in a rich representation using not only their similarity score but also their intermediate representations; (iii) the architecture of our network makes it straightforward to include any additional similarity features to the model; and finally (iv) our model does not require manual feature engineering or external resources. We only require to initialize word embeddings from some large unsupervised corpora [1]

Our sentence model is based on a convolutional neural network architecture that has recently showed state-of-the-art results on many NLP sentence classification tasks [18, 19]. However, our model uses it only to generate intermediate representation of input sentences for computing their similarity. To compute the similarity score we use an approach used in the deep learning model of [38], which recently established new state-of-the-art results on answer sentence selection task. However, their model operates only on unigram or bigrams, while our architecture learns to extract and compose n-grams of higher degrees, thus allowing for capturing longer range dependencies. Additionally, our architecture uses not only the intermediate representations of questions and answers to compute their similarity but also includes them in the final representation, which constitutes a much richer representation of the question-answer pairs. Finally, our model is trained end-to-end, while in [38] the output of the deep learning model is used to learn a logistic regression classifier.

We test our model on two popular retrieval tasks from TREC: answer sentence selection and Microblog retrieval. Our model shows a considerable improvement on the first task beating recent state-of-the-art system. On the second task, our model demonstrates that previous state-of-the-art retrieval systems can benefit from using our deep learning model.

In the following, we give a problem formulation and provide a brief overview of learning to rank approaches. Next, we describe our deep learning model and describe our experiments.

2. LEARNING TO RANK

This section briefly describes the problem of reranking text pairs which encompasses a large set of tasks in IR, e.g., answer sentence selection in question answering, microblog retrieval, etc. We argue that deriving an efficient representation of query-document pairs required to train a learning to rank model plays an important role in training an accurate reranker.

2.1 Problem formulation

The most typical setup in supervised learning to rank tasks is as follows: we are given a set of retrieved lists, where each query $\mathbf{q}_i \in \mathbf{Q}$ comes together with its list of candidate documents $\mathbf{D}_i = \{\mathbf{d}_{i1}, \mathbf{d}_{i2}, ..., \mathbf{d}_{in}\}$. The candidate set comes with their relevancy judgements $\{y_{i1}, y_{i2}, \dots, y_{in}\}$, where documents that are relevant have labels equal to 1 (or higher) and 0 otherwise. The goal is to build a model that for each query $\mathbf{q}_i$ and its candidate list $\mathbf{D}_i$ generates an optimal ranking $\mathbf{R}$, s.t. relevant documents appear at the top of the list.

More formally, the task is to learn a ranking function:

$$h(\mathbf{w}, \psi(\mathbf{q}_i, \mathbf{D}_i)) \rightarrow \mathbf{R},$$

where function $\psi(\cdot)$ maps query-document pairs to a feature vector representation where each component reflects a certain type of similarity, e.g., lexical, syntactic, and semantic. The weight vector $\mathbf{w}$ is a parameter of the model and is learned during the training.

2.2 Learning to Rank approaches

There are three most common approaches in IR to learn the ranking function h, namely, *pointwise*, *pairwise* and *listwise*.

Pointwise approach is perhaps the most simple way to build a reranker where the training instances are triples $(\mathbf{q}_i, \mathbf{d}_{ij}, y_{ij})$ and it is enough to train a binary classifier: $h(\mathbf{w}, \psi(\mathbf{q}_i, \mathbf{d}_{ij})) \rightarrow y_{ij}$, where ψ maps query-document pair to a feature vector and $\mathbf{w}$ is a vector of model weights.

The decision function $h(\cdot)$ typically takes a linear form simply computing a dot product between the model weights $\mathbf{w}$ and a feature representation of a pair generated by $\psi(\cdot)$. At test time, the learned model is used to classify unseen pairs $(\mathbf{q}_i, \mathbf{d}_{ij})$, where the raw scores are used to establish the global rank $\mathbf{R}$ of the documents in the retrieved set. This approch is widely used in practice because of its simplicity and effectiveness.

A more advanced approaches to reranking, is *pairwise*, where the model is explicitly trained to score correct pairs higher than incorrect pairs with a certain margin:

$$h(\mathbf{w}, \psi(\mathbf{q}_i, \mathbf{d}_{ij})) \geq h(\mathbf{w}, \psi(\mathbf{q}_i, \mathbf{d}_{ik})) + \epsilon,$$

where document $\mathbf{d}_{ij}$ is relevant and $\mathbf{d}_{ik}$ is not. Conceptually similar to the *pointwise* method described above, the *pairwise* approach exploits more information about the ground truth labelling of the input candidates. However, it requires to consider a larger number of training instances (potentially quadratic in the size of the candidate document set) than the *pointwise* method, which may lead to slower training times. Still both *pointwise* and *pairwise* approaches ignore the fact that ranking is a prediction task on a list of objects.

The third method, referred to as a *listwise* approach [6], treats a query with its list of candidates as a single instance in learning, thus able to capture considerably more information about the ground truth ordering of input candidates.

While *pairwise* and *listwise* approaches claim to yield better performance, they are more complicated to implement and less effective train. Most often, producing a better representation $\psi()$ that encodes various aspects of similarity between the input query-document pairs plays a far more important role in training an accurate reranker than choosing between different ranking approaches. Hence, in this paper we adopt a simple *pointwise* method to reranking and focus on modelling a rich representation of query-document pairs using deep learning approaches which is described next.

3. OUR DEEP LEARNING MODEL

This section explains our deep learning model for reranking short text pairs. Its main building blocks are two distributional *sentence models* based on convolutional neural networks (ConvNets). These underlying sentence models work in parallel mapping queries and documents to their distributional vectors, which are then used to learn the semantic similarity between them.

In the following, we first describe our *sentence model* for mapping queries and documents to their intermediate representations and then describe how they can be used for learning semantic matching between input query-document pairs.

3.1 Sentence model

The architecture of our ConvNet for mapping sentences to feature vectors is shown on Fig. 1. It is mainly inspired by the architectures used in [18, 19] for performing various sentence classifica-

[1]Given a large training corpora our network can also optimize the embeddings directly for the task, thus omitting the need to pre-train the embeddings.

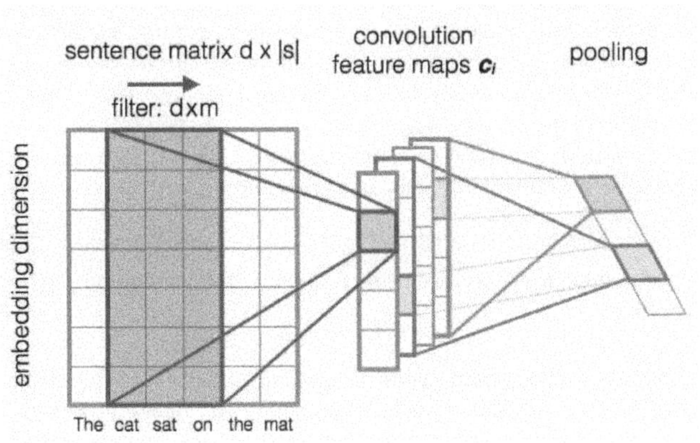

Figure 1: Our sentence model for mapping input sentences to their intermediate feature representations.

tion tasks. However, different from previous work the goal of our distributional sentence model is to learn good intermediate representations of the queries and documents, which are then used for computing their semantic matching.

Our network is composed of a single *wide* convolutional layer followed by a non-linearity and simple *max* pooling.

The input to the network are raw words that need to be translated into real-valued feature vectors to be processed by subsequent layers of the network. In the following we give a brief explanation of the main components of our convolutional neural network: sentence matrix, activations, convolutional and pooling layers.

3.1.1 Sentence matrix

The input to our sentence model is a sentence $\mathbf{s}$ treated as a sequence of words: $[w_1, .., w_{|s|}]$, where each word is drawn from a vocabulary V. Words are represented by distributional vectors $\mathbf{w} \in \mathbb{R}^d$ looked up in a word embeddings matrix $\mathbf{W} \in \mathbb{R}^{d \times |V|}$ which is formed by concatenating embeddings of all words in V. For convenience and ease of lookup operations in $\mathbf{W}$, words are mapped to integer indices $1, \ldots, |V|$.

For each input sentence $\mathbf{s}$ we build a sentence matrix $\mathbf{S} \in \mathbb{R}^{d \times |s|}$, where each column i represents a word embedding $\mathbf{w}_i$ at the corresponding position i in a sentence (see Fig. 1):

$$\mathbf{S} = \begin{bmatrix} | & & | \\ \mathbf{w}_1 & \ldots & \mathbf{w}_{|s|} \\ | & & | \end{bmatrix}$$

To learn to capture and compose features of individual words in a given sentence from low-level word embeddings into higher level semantic concepts, the neural network applies a series of transformations to the input sentence matrix $\mathbf{S}$ using convolution, non-linearity and pooling operations, which we describe next.

3.1.2 Convolution feature maps

The aim of the convolutional layer is to extract patterns, i.e., discriminative word sequences found within the input sentences that are common throughout the training instances.

More formally, the convolution operation $*$ between two vectors $\mathbf{s} \in \mathbb{R}^{|s|}$ and $\mathbf{f} \in \mathbb{R}^m$ (called a filter of size m) results in a vector $\mathbf{c} \in \mathbb{R}^{|s|+m-1}$ where each component is as follows:

$$\mathbf{c}_i = (\mathbf{s} * \mathbf{f})_i = \mathbf{s}^T_{[i-m+1:i]} \cdot \mathbf{f} = \sum_{k=i}^{i+m-1} s_k f_k \qquad (1)$$

The range of allowed values for i defines two types of convolution: *narrow* and *wide*. The *narrow* type restricts i to be in the range $[1, |s| - m + 1]$, which in turn restricts the filter width to be $\leq |s|$. To compute the *wide* type of convolution i ranges from 1 to $|s|$ and sets no restrictions on the size of m and s. The benefits of one type of convolution over the other when dealing with text are discussed in detail in [18]. In short, the *wide* convolution is able to better handle words at boundaries giving equal attention to all words in the sentence, unlike in *narrow* convolution, where words close to boundaries are seen fewer times. More importantly, *wide* convolution also guarantees to always yield valid values even when $\mathbf{s}$ is shorter than the filter size m. Hence, we use *wide* convolution in our sentence model. In practice, to compute the *wide* convolution it is enough to pad the input sequence with $m - 1$ zeros from left and right.

Given that the input to our ConvNet are sentence matrices $\mathbf{S} \in \mathbb{R}^{d \times |s|}$, the arguments of Eq. 1 are matrices and a convolution filter is also a matrix of weights: $\mathbf{F} \in \mathbb{R}^{d \times m}$. Note that the convolution filter is of the same dimensionality d as the input sentence matrix. As shown in Fig. 1, it slides along the column dimension of $\mathbf{S}$ producing a vector $\mathbf{c} \in \mathbb{R}^{|s|-m+1}$ in output. Each component c_i is the result of computing an element-wise product between a column slice of $\mathbf{S}$ and the filter matrix $\mathbf{F}$, which is then flattened and summed producing a single value.

It should be noted that an alternative way of computing a convolution was explored in [18], where a series of convolutions are computed between each row of a sentence matrix and a corresponding row of the filter matrix. Essentially, it is a vectorized form of 1d convolution applied between corresponding rows of $\mathbf{S}$ and $\mathbf{F}$. As a result, the output feature map is a matrix $\mathbf{C} \in \mathbb{R}^{d \times |s|-m+1}$ rather than a vector as above. While, intuitively, being a more general way to process the input matrix $\mathbf{S}$, where individual filters are applied to each respective dimension, it introduces more parameters to the model and requires a way to reduce the dimensionality of the resulting feature map. To address this issue, the authors apply a folding operation, which sums every two rows element-wise, thus effectively reducing the size of the representation by 2.

So far we have described a way to compute a convolution between the input sentence matrix and a single filter. In practice, deep learning models apply a set of filters that work in parallel generating muliple feature maps (also shown on Fig. 1). The resulting filter bank $\mathbf{F} \in \mathbb{R}^{n \times d \times m}$ produces a set of feature maps of dimension $n \times (|s| - m + 1)$.

In practice, we also add a bias vector[2] $\mathbf{b} \in \mathbb{R}^n$ to the result of a convolution – a single b_i value for each feature map $\mathbf{c}_i$.

3.1.3 Activation units

To allow the network learn non-linear decision boundaries, each convolutional layer is typically followed by a non-linear activation function $\alpha()$ applied element-wise to the output of the preceding layer. Among the most common choices of activation functions are the following: sigmoid (or logistic), hyperbolic tangent *tanh*, and a rectified linear (ReLU) function defined as simply $max(0, \mathbf{x})$ to ensure that feature maps are always positive. The choice of activation function has been shown to affect the convergence rate and the quality of obtained the solution. In particular, [22] shows that rectified linear unit has significant benefits over sigmoid and $tanh$ overcoming some of the their shortcomings.

3.1.4 Pooling

The output from the convolutional layer (passed through the activation function) are then passed to the pooling layer, whose goal

[2]bias is needed to allow the network learn an appropriate threshold

is to aggregate the information and reduce the representation. The result of the pooling operation is:

$$\mathbf{c}_{\text{pooled}} = \begin{bmatrix} \text{pool}(\alpha(\mathbf{c}_1 + b_1 * \mathbf{e})) \\ \cdots \\ \text{pool}(\alpha(\mathbf{c}_n + b_n * \mathbf{e})) \end{bmatrix}$$

where $\mathbf{c}_i$ is the ith convolutional feature map with added bias (the bias is added to each element of $\mathbf{c}_i$ and $\mathbf{e}$ is a unit vector of the same size as $\mathbf{c}_i$) and passed through the activation function $\alpha()$.

There are two conventional choices for the pool$(\cdot)$ operation: average and max. Both operations apply to columns of the feature map matrix, by mapping them to a single value: pool$(\mathbf{c}_i)$: $\mathbb{R}^{1\times(|s|+m-1)} \rightarrow \mathbb{R}$. This is also demonstrated in Fig. 1.

Both *average* and *max* pooling methods exhibit certain disadvantages: in average pooling, all elements of the input are considered, which may weaken strong activation values. This is especially critical with *tanh* non-linearity, where strong positive and negative activations can cancel each other out.

The *max* pooling is used more widely and does not suffer from the drawbacks of average pooling. However, as shown in [40], it can lead to strong overfitting on the training set and, hence, poor generalization on the test data. To mitigate the overfitting issue of max pooling several variants of stochastic pooling have been proposed in [40].

Recently, *max* pooling has been generalized to k-max pooling [18], where instead of a single max value, k values are extracted in their original order. This allows for extracting several largest activation values from the input sentence. As a consequence deeper architectures with several convolutional layers can be used. In [18], the authors also propose dynamic k-max pooling, where the value of k depends on the sentence size and the level in the convolution hierarchy [18].

Convolutional layer passed through the activation function together with pooling layer acts as a non-linear feature extractor. Given that multiple feature maps are used in parallel to process the input, deep learning networks are able to build rich feature representations of the input.

This ends the description of our sentence model. In the following we present our deep learning network for learning to match short text pairs.

3.2 Our architecture for matching text pairs

The architecture of our model for matching query-document pairs is presented in Fig. 2. Our sentence models based on ConvNets (described in Sec. 3.1) learn to map input sentences to vectors, which can then be used to compute their similarity. These are then used to compute a query-document similarity score, which together with the query and document vectors are joined in a single representation.

In the following we describe how the intermediate representations produced by the sentence model can be used to compute query-document similarity scores and give a brief explanation of the remaining layers, e.g. hidden and softmax, used in our network.

3.2.1 *Matching query and documents*

Given the output of our sentence ConvNets for processing queries and documents, their resulting vector representations $\mathbf{x}_q$ and $\mathbf{x}_d$, can be used to compute a query-document similarity score. We follow the approach of [2] that defines the similarity between $\mathbf{x}_q$ and $\mathbf{x}_d$ vectors as follows:

$$sim(\mathbf{x}_q, \mathbf{x}_d) = \mathbf{x}_q^T \mathbf{M} \mathbf{x}_d, \tag{2}$$

where $\mathbf{M} \in \mathbb{R}^{d\times d}$ is a similarity matrix. The Eq. 2 can be viewed as a model of the noisy channel approach from machine translation, which has been widely used as a scoring model in information retrieval and question answering [13]. In this model, we seek a transformation of the candidate document $\mathbf{x}'_d = \mathbf{M}\mathbf{x}_d$ that is the closest to the input query $\mathbf{x}_q$. The similarity matrix $\mathbf{M}$ is a parameter of the network and is optimized during the training.

3.2.2 *Hidden layers*

The hidden layer computes the following transformation:

$$\alpha(\mathbf{w}_h \cdot \mathbf{x} + b),$$

where $\mathbf{w}_h$ is the weight vector of the hidden layer and $\alpha()$ is the non-linearity. Our model includes an additional hidden layer right before the softmax layer (described next) to allow for modelling interactions between the components of the intermediate representation.

3.2.3 *Softmax*

The output of the penultimate convolutional and pooling layers is flattened to a dense vector $\mathbf{x}$, which is passed to a fully connected softmax layer. It computes the probability distribution over the labels:

$$p(y = j|\mathbf{x}) = \frac{e^{\mathbf{x}^T\theta_\mathbf{j}}}{\sum_{k=1}^{K} e^{\mathbf{x}^T\theta_\mathbf{k}}},$$

where θ_k is a weight vector of the k-th class. $\mathbf{x}$ can be thought of as a final abstract representation of the input example obtained by a series of transformations from the input layer through a series of convolutional and pooling operations.

3.2.4 *The information flow*

Here we provide a full description of our deep learning network (shown on Fig. 2) that maps input sentences to class probabilities.

The output of our sentence models (Sec. 3.1) are distributional representations of a query $\mathbf{x}_q$ and a document $\mathbf{x}_d$. These are then matched using a similarity matrix $\mathbf{M}$ according to Eq. 2. This produces a single score x_{sim} capturing various aspects of similarity (syntactic and semantic) between the input queries and documents. Note that it is also straight-forward to add additional features $\mathbf{x}_{\text{feat}}$ to the model.

The join layer concatenates all intermediate vectors, the similarity score and any additional features into a single vector:

$$\mathbf{x}_{\text{join}} = [\mathbf{x}_q^T; x_{\text{sim}}; \mathbf{x}_d^T; \mathbf{x}_{\text{feat}}^T]$$

This vector is then passed through a fully connected hidden layer, which allows for modelling interactions between the components of the joined representation vector. Finally, the output of the hidden layer is further fed to the softmax classification layer, which generates a distribution over the class labels.

3.3 Training

The model is trained to minimise the cross-entropy cost function:

$$\begin{aligned} C &= -\log \prod_{i=1}^{N} p(y_i|\mathbf{q}_i, \mathbf{d}_i) + \lambda\|\theta\|_2^2 \\ &= -\sum_{i=1}^{N} [y_i \log \mathbf{a}_i + (1 - y_i)\log(1 - \mathbf{a}_i)] + \lambda\|\theta\|_2^d, \end{aligned} \tag{3}$$

where $\mathbf{a}$ is the output from the softmax layer. θ contains all the parameters optimized by the network:

$$\theta = \{\mathbf{W}; \mathbf{F}_q; \mathbf{b}_q; \mathbf{F}_d; \mathbf{b}_d; \mathbf{M}; \mathbf{w}_h; b_h; \mathbf{w}_s; b_s\},$$

namely the word embeddings matrix $\mathbf{W}$, filter weights and biases of the convolutional layers, similarity matrix $\mathbf{M}$, weights and biases of the hidden and softmax layers.

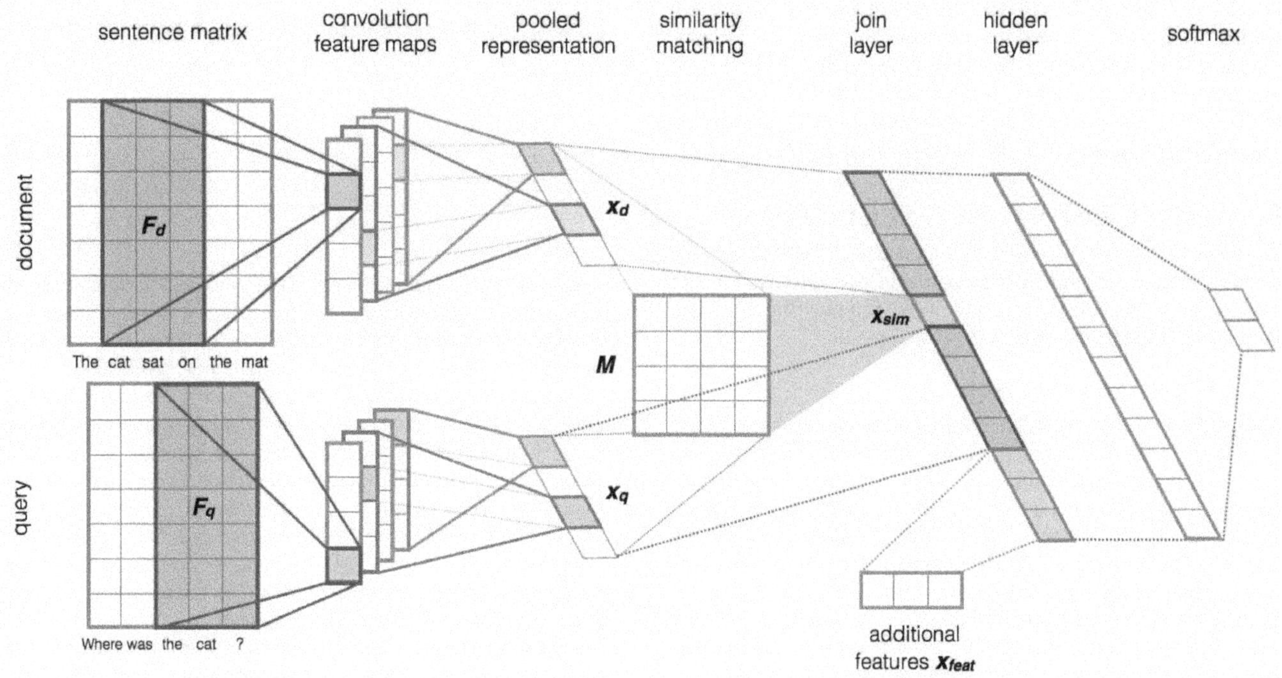

Figure 2: Our deep learning architecture for reranking short text pairs.

The parameters of the network are optimized with stochastic gradient descent (SGD) using backpropogation algorithm to compute the gradients. To speedup the convergence rate of SGD various modifications to the update rule have been proposed: *momentum*, *Adagrad* [12], *Adadelta* [39], etc. *Adagrad* scales the learning rate of SGD on each dimension based on the $l2$ norm of the history of the error gradient. *Adadelta* uses both the error gradient history like *Adagrad* and the weight update history. It has the advantage of not having to set a learning rate at all.

3.4 Regularization

While neural networks have a large capacity to learn complex decision functions they tend to easily overfit especially on small and medium sized datasets. To mitigate the overfitting issue we augment the cost function with l_2-norm regularization terms for the parameters of the network.

We also experiment with another popular and effective technique to improve regularization of the NNs — dropout [30]. Dropout prevents feature co-adaptation by setting to zero (dropping out) a portion of hidden units during the forward phase when computing the activations at the softmax output layer. As suggested in [14] dropout acts as an approximate model averaging.

4. EXPERIMENTS AND EVALUATION

We evaluate our deep learning model on two popular retrieval benchmarks from TREC: answer sentence selection and TREC microblog retrieval.

4.1 Training and hyperparameters

The parameters of our deep learning model were (chosen on a dev set of the answer sentence selection dataset) as follows: the width m of the convolution filters is set to 5 and the number of convolutional feature maps is 100. We use ReLU activation function and a simple max-pooling. The size of the hidden layer is equal to the size of the $\boldsymbol{x}_{\text{join}}$ vector obtained after concatenating query and document vectors from the distributional models, similarity score and additional features (if used).

To train the network we use stochastic gradient descent with shuffled mini-batches. We eliminate the need to tune the learning rate by using the Adadelta update rule [39]. The batch size is set to 50 examples. The network is trained for 25 epochs with early stopping, i.e., we stop the training if no update to the best accuracy on the dev set has been made for the last 5 epochs. The accuracy computed on the dev set is the MAP score. At test time we use the parameters of the network that were obtained with the best MAP score on the development (dev) set, i.e., we compute the MAP score after each 10 mini-batch updates and save the network parameters if a new best dev MAP score was obtained. In practice, the training converges after a few epochs. We set a value for L2 regularization term to $1e-5$ for the parameters of convolutional layers and $1e-4$ for all the others. The dropout rate is set to $p = 0.5$.

4.2 Word embeddings

While our model allows for learning the word embeddings directly for a given task, we keep the word matrix parameter $\boldsymbol{W}$ static. This is due to a common experience that a minimal size of the dataset required for tuning the word embeddings for a given task should be at least in the order of hundred thousands, while in our case the number of query-document pairs is one order of magnitude smaller. Hence, similar to [11, 19, 38] we keep the word embeddings fixed and initialize the word matrix $\boldsymbol{W}$ from an unsupervised neural language model. We choose the dimensionality of our word embeddings to be 50 to be on the line with the deep learning model of [38].

4.3 Size of the model

Given that the dimensionality of the word embeddings is 50, the number of parameters in the convolution layer of each sentence model is $100 \times 5 \times 50$. Hence, the total number of parameters in each of the two convolutional networks that map sentences to vectors is 25k. The similarity matrix is $\boldsymbol{M} \in \mathbb{R}^{100\times 100}$, which adds another 10k parameters to the model. The fully connected hidden layer is and a softmax add about 40k parameters. Hence the total number of parameters in the network is about 100k.

5. ANSWER SENTENCE SELECTION

Our first experiment is on answer sentence selection dataset, where answer candidates are limited to a single sentence. Given a question with its list of candidate answers the task is to rank the candidate answers based on their relatedness to the question.

5.1 Experimental setup

Data and setup. We test our model on the manually curated TREC QA dataset[3] from Wang et al. [36], which appears to be one of the most widely used benchmarks for answer reranking. The dataset contains a set of factoid questions, where candidate answers are limited to a single sentence. The set of questions are collected from TREC QA tracks 8-13. The manual judgement of candidate answer sentences is provided for the entire TREC 13 set and for the first 100 questions from TREC 8-12. The motivation behind this annotation effort is that TREC provides only the answer patterns to identify if a given passage contains a correct answer key or not. This results in many unrelated candidate answers marked as correct simply because regular expressions cannot always match the correct answer keys.

To enable direct comparison with the previous work, we use the same train, dev and test sets. Table 1 summarizes the datasets used in our experiments. An additional training set TRAIN-ALL provided by Wang et. al [36] contains 1,229 questions from the entire TREC 8-12 collection and comes with automatic judgements. This set represents a more noisy setting, nevertheless, it provides many more QA pairs for learning.

Word embeddings. We initialize the word embeddings by running `word2vec` tool [20] on the English Wikipedia dump and the AQUAINT corpus[4] containing roughly 375 million words. To train the embeddings we use the skipgram model with window size 5 and filtering words with frequency less than 5. The resulting model contains 50-dimensional vectors for about 3.5 million words. Embeddings for words not present in the `word2vec` model are randomly initialized with each component sampled from the uniform distribution $U[-0.25, 0.25]$.

We minimally preprocess the data only performing tokenization and lowercasing all words. To reduce the size of the resulting vocabulary V, we also replace all digits with 0. The size of the word vocabulary V for experiments using TRAIN set is 17,023 with approximately 95% of words initialized using `wor2vec` embeddings and the remaining 5% words are initialized at random as described in Sec. 4.2. For the TRAIN-ALL setting the $|V| = 56,953$ with 85% words found in the `word2vec` model.

Additional features. Given that a certain percentage of the words in our word embedding matrix are initialized at random (about 15% for the TRAIN-ALL) and a relatively small number of QA pairs prevents the network to directly learn them from the training data, similarity matching performed by the network will be suboptimal between many question-answer pairs.

Additionally, even for the words found in the word matrix, as noted in [38], one of the weaknesses of approaches relying on distributional word vectors is their inability to deal with numbers and proper nouns. This is especially important for factoid question answering, where most of the questions are of type *what, when, who* that are looking for answers containing numbers or proper nouns.

Table 1: Summary of TREC QA datasets for answer reranking.

Data	# Questions	# QA pairs	% Correct
TRAIN-ALL	1,229	53,417	12.0%
TRAIN	94	4,718	7.4%
DEV	82	1,148	19.3%
TEST	100	1,517	18.7%

To mitigate the above two issues, we follow the approach in [38] and include additional features establishing relatedness between question-answer pairs. In particular, we compute word overlap measures between each question-answer pair and include it as an additional feature vector $\boldsymbol{x}_{\text{feat}}$ in our model. This feature vector contains only four features: word overlap and IDF-weighted word overlap computed between all words and only non-stop words. Computing these features is straightforward and does not require additional pre-processing or external resources.

Evaluation. The two metrics used to evaluate the quality of our model are Mean Average Precision (MAP) and Mean Reciprocal Rank (MRR), which are common in Information Retrieval and Question Answering.

MRR is computed as follows: $MRR = \frac{1}{|Q|}\sum_{q=1}^{|Q|}\frac{1}{rank(q)}$, where *rank(q)* is the position of the first correct answer in the candidate list. MRR is only looking at the rank of the first correct answer, hence it is more suitable in cases where for each question there is only a single correct answer. Differently, MAP examines the ranks of all the correct answers. It is computed as the mean over the average precision scores for each query $q \in Q$: $\frac{1}{Q}\sum_{q=1}^{Q} AveP(q)$. We use the official `trec_eval` scorer to compute the above metrics.

5.2 Results and discussion

We report the results of our deep learning model on the TRAIN and TRAIN-ALL sets also when additional word overlap features are used. Additionally, we report the results from a recent deep learning system in [38] that has established the new state-of-the-art results in the same setting.

Table 2 summarises the results for the setting when the network is trained using only input question-answer pairs without using any additional features. As we can see our deep learning architecture demonstrates a much stronger performance compared to the system in [38]. The deep learning model from [38], similarly to ours, relies on a convolutional neural network to learn intermediate representations. However, their convolutional neural network operates only on unigram or bigrams, while in our architecture we use a larger width of the convolution filter, thus allowing for capturing longer range dependencies. Additionally, along with the question-answer similarity score, our architecture includes intermediate representations of the question and the answer, which together constitute a much richer representation. This results in a large improvement of about 8% absolute points in MAP for TRAIN and almost 10% when trained with more data from TRAIN-ALL. This emphasizes the importance of learning high quality sentence models.

Table 3 provides the results when additional word *overlap* features are added to the model. Simple word overlap features help to improve the question-answer matching. Our model shows an improvement of about a significant improvement over previous state-

[3]`http://cs.stanford.edu/people/mengqiu/data/qg-emnlp07-data.tgz`
[4]`https://catalog.ldc.upenn.edu/LDC2002T31`

Table 2: Results on TRAIN and TRAIN-ALL from Trec QA.

Model	MAP	MRR
TRAIN		
Yu et al. [38] (unigram)	.5387	.6284
Yu et al. [38] (bigram)	.5476	.6437
Our model	**.6258**	**.6591**
TRAIN-ALL		
Yu et al. [38] (unigram)	.5470	.6329
Yu et al. [38] (bigram)	.5693	.6613
Our model	**.6709**	**.7280**

Table 3: Results on TREC QA when augmenting the deep learning model with word overlap features.

Model	MAP	MRR
TRAIN		
Yu et al. [38] (unigram)	.6889	.7727
Yu et al. [38] (bigram)	.7058	.7800
Our model	**.7329**	**.7962**
TRAIN-ALL		
Yu et al. [38] (unigram)	.6934	.7677
Yu et al. [38] (bigram)	.7113	.7846
Our model	**.7459**	**.8078**

Table 4: Survey of the results on the QA answer selection task.

Model	MAP	MRR
Wang et al. (2007) [36]	.6029	.6852
Heilman and Smith (2010) [15]	.6091	.6917
Wang and Manning (2010) [35]	.5951	.6951
Yao et al. (2013) [37]	.6307	.7477
Severyn & Moschitti (2013) [26]	.6781	.7358
Yih et al. (2013) [33]	.7092	.7700
Yu et al. (2014) [38]	.7113	.7846
Our model (TRAIN)	**.7329**	**.7962**
Our model (TRAIN-ALL)	**.7459**	**.8078**

of-the-art in both MAP and MRR when training on TRAIN and TRAIN-ALL. Note that the results are significantly better than when no overlap features are used. This is possibly due to the fact that the distrubutional representations fail to establish the relatedness in some cases and simple word overlap matching can help to drive the model in the right direction.

Table 4 reports the results of the previously published systems on this task. Our model trained on a small TRAIN dataset beats all of the previous state-of-the-art systems. The improvement is further emphasized when the system is trained using more question-answer pairs from TRAIN-ALL showing an improvement of about 3% absolute points in both MAP and MRR. The results are very promising considering that our system requires no manual feature engineering (other than simple word overlap features), no expensive preprocessing using various NLP parsers, and no external semantic resources other than using pre-initialized word embeddings that can be easily trained provided a large amount of unsupervised text.

In the spirit, our system is most similar to a recent deep learning architecture from Yu et al. (2014) [38]. However, we employ a more expressive convolutional neural network for learning intermediate representations of the query and the answer. This allows for performing a more accurate matching between question-answer pairs. Additionally, our architecture includes intermediate question and answer representations in the model, which result in a richer representation of question-answer pairs. Finally, we train our system in an end-to-end fashion, while [38] use the output of their deep learning system as a feature in a logistic regression classifier.

Table 5: Summary of TREC Microblog datasets.

Data	# Topic	# Tweet pairs	% Correct	# Runs
TMB2011	49	60,129	5.1%	184
TMB2012	59	73,073	8.6%	120

6. TREC MICROBLOG RETRIEVAL

To assess the effectiveness and generality of our deep learning model for text matching, we apply it on tweet reranking task. We focus on the 2011 and 2012 editions of the ad-hoc retrieval task at TREC microblog tracks [23, 29]. We follow the setup in [27], where they represent query-tweet pairs with a shallow syntactic models to learn a tree kernel reranker. In contrast, our model does not rely on any syntactic parsers and requires virtually no preprocessing other than tokenizaiton and lower-casing. Our main research question is: Can our neural network that requires no manual feature engineering and expensive pre-processing steps improve on top of the state-of-the-art learning-to-rank and retrieval algorithms?

To answer this question, we test our model in the following settings: we treat the participant systems in the TREC microblog tasks as a black-box, and implement our model on top of them using only their raw scores (ranks) as a single feature in our model. This allows us to see whether our model is able to learn information complementary to the approaches used by such retrieval algorithms. Our setup replicates the experiments in [27] to allow for comparing to their model.

6.1 Experimental setup

Data and setup. Our dataset is the tweet corpus used in both TREC Microblog tracks in 2011 (TMB2011) and 2012 (TMB2012). It consists of 16M tweets spread over two weeks, and a set of 49 (TMB2011) and 59 (TMB2012) timestamped topics. We minimally preprocess the tweets—we normalize elongations (e.g., sooo → so), normalize URLs and author ids. Additionally, we use the system runs submitted at TMB2011 and TMB2012, which contain 184 and 120 models, respectively. This is summarized in Table 5.

Word embeddings. We used the `word2vec` tool to learn the word embeddings from the provided 16M tweet corpus, with the following setting: (i) we removed non-english tweets, which reduces the corpus to 8.4M tweets and (ii) we used the skipgram model with window size 5 and filtering words with frequency less than 5. The trained model contains 330k words. We use word embeddings of size 50 — same as for the previous task. To build the word embedding matrix $\boldsymbol{W}$, we extract the vocabulary from all tweets present in TMB2011 and TMB2012. The resulting vocabulary contains 150k words out of which only 60% are found in the word embeddings model. This is due to a very large number of misspellings and words occurring only once (hence they are filted by the `word2vec` tool). This has a negative impact on the performance of our deep learning model since around 40% of the word vectors are randomly initialized. At the same time it is not possible to tune the word embeddings on the training set, as it will overfit due to the small number of the query-tweet pairs available for training.

Training. We train our system on the runs submitted at TMB2011, and test it on the TMB2012 runs. We focus on one direction only to avoid training bias, since TMB2011 topics were already used for learning systems in TMB2012.
Submission run as a feature. We use the output of participant systems as follows: we use rank positions of each tweet rather than raw scores, since scores for each system are scaled differently, while ranks are uniform across systems. We apply the following transformation of the rank r: $1/\log(r+1)$. In the training phase, we take the top 30 systems from the TMB2011 track (in terms of P@30). For each query-tweet pair we compute the average transformed rank over the top systems. This score is then used as a single feature $\boldsymbol{x}_{\text{feat}}$ by our model. In the testing phase, we generate this feature as follows: for each participant system that we want to improve, we use the transformed rank of the query-tweet taken from their submission run.
Evaluation. We report on the official evaluation metric for the TREC 2012 Microblog track, i.e., precision at 30 (P@30), and also on mean average precision (MAP). Following [4, 23], we regard minimally and highly relevant documents as relevant and use the TMB2012 evaluation script. For significance testing, we use a pairwise t-test, where △ and ▲ denote significance at $\alpha = 0.05$ and $\alpha = 0.01$, respectively. Triangles point up for improvement over the baseline, and down otherwise. We also report the improvement in the absolute rank (R) in the official TMB2012 ranking.

6.2 Results and discussion

Table 6 reports the results for re-ranking runs of the best 30 systems from TMB2012 (based on their P@30 score) when we train our system using the top 30 runs from TMB2011.

First, we note that our model improves P@30 for the majority of the systems with a relative improvement ranging from several points up to 10% with about 6% on average. This is remarkable, given that the pool of participants in TMB2012 was large, and the top systems are therefore likely to be very strong baselines.

Secondly, we note that the relative improvement of our model is on the par with the STRUCT model from [27], which relies on using syntactic parsers to train a tree kernel reranker. In contrast, our model requires no manual feature engineering and virtually no preprocessing and external resources. Similar to the observation made in [27], our model has a precision-enhancing effect. In cases where MAP drops a bit it can be seen that our model sometimes lowers relevant documents in the runs. It is possible that our model favours query-tweet pairs that exhibit semantic matching of higher quality, and that it down-ranks tweets that are of lower quality but are nonetheless relevant. Another important aspect is the fact that a large portion of the word embeddings (about 40%) used by the network are initialized at random, which has a negative impact on the accuracy of our model.

Looking at the improvement in absolute position in the official ranking (R), we see that, on average, our deep learning model boosts the absolute position in the official ranking for top 30 systems by about 7.8 positions.

All in all, the results suggest that our deep learning model with no changes in its architecture is able to capture additional information and can be useful when coupled with many state-of-the-art microblog search algorithms.

While improving the top systems from 2012 represents a challenging task, it is also interesting to assess the potential improvement for lower ranking systems. We follow [27] and report our results on the 30 systems from the middle and the bottom of the official ranking. Table 7 summarizes the average improvements for three groups of systems: top-30, middle-30, and bottom-30.

Table 7: Comparison of the averaged relative improvements for the top, middle (mid), and bottom (btm) 30 systems from TMB2012.

	STRUCT [27]		Our model	
band	MAP	P@30	MAP	P@30
top	3.3%	5.3%	2.0%	6.2%
mid	12.2%	12.9%	9.8%	13.7%
btm	22.1%	25.1%	18.7%	24.3%

We find that the improvement over underperforming systems is much larger than for stronger systems. In particular, for the bottom 30 systems, our approach achieves an average relative improvement of 20% in both MAP and P@30. The performance of our model is on the par with the STRUCT model [27].

We expect that learning word embeddings on a larger corpora such that the percentage of the words present in the word embedding matrix $\boldsymbol{W}$ should help to improve the accuracy of our system. Moreover, similar to the situation observed with answer selection experiments, we expect that using more training data would improve the generalization of our model. As one possible solution to getting more training data, it could be interesting to experiment with training our model on much larger pseudo test collections similar to the ones proposed in [4]. We leave it for the future work.

7. RELATED WORK

Our learning to rank method is based on a deep learning model for advanced text representations using distributional word embeddings. Distributional representations have a long tradition in IR, e.g., Latent Semantic Analysis [10], which more recently has also been characterized by studies on distributional models based on word similarities. Their main properties is to alleviate the problem of data sparseness. In particular, such representations can be derived with several methods, e.g., by counting the frequencies of co-occurring words around a given token in large corpora. Such distributed representations can be obtained by applying neural language models that learn word embeddings, e.g., [3] and more recently using recursive autoencoders [34], and convolutional neural networks [8].

Our application of learning to rank models concerns passage reranking. For example, [17, 24] designed classifiers of question and answer passage pairs. Several approaches were devoted to reranking passages containing definition/description, e.g., [21, 28, 31]. [1] used a cascading approach, where the ranking produced by one ranker is used as input to the next stage.

Language models for reranking were applied in [7], where answer ranks were computed based on the probabilities of bigram models generating candidate answers. Language models were also applied to definitional QA in [9, 25, 32].

Our work more directly targets the task of answer sentence selection, i.e., the task of selecting a sentence that contains the information required to answer a given question from a set of candidates (for example, provided by a search engine). In particular, the state of the art in answer sentence selection is given by Wang et al., 2007 [36], who use quasi-synchronous grammar to model relations between a question and a candidate answer with the syntactic transformations. Heilman & Smith, 2010 [15] develop an improved Tree Edit Distance (TED) model for learning tree transformations in a q/a pair. They search for a good sequence of tree edit operations using complex and computationally expensive Tree Kernel-based heuristic. Wang & Manning, 2010 [35] develop a probabilistic

Table 6: System performance on the top 30 runs from TMB2012, using the top 10, 20 or 30 runs from TMB2011 for training.

	TMB2012			STRUCT [27]			Our model		
#	runs	MAP	P@30	MAP	P@30	R%	MAP	P@30	R%
1	hitURLrun3	0.3469	0.4695	0.3328 (-4.1%)▽	0.4774 (1.7%)	0	0.3326 (-4.1%)▽	0.4836 (3.0%)	0
2	kobeMHC2	0.3070	0.4689	0.3037 (-1.1%)	0.4768 (1.7%)	1	0.3052 (-0.6%)	0.4899 (4.5%)△	1
3	kobeMHC	0.2986	0.4616	0.2965 (-0.7%)	0.4718 (2.2%)	2	0.2999 (0.4%)	0.4830 (4.6%)△	2
4	uwatgclrman	0.2836	0.4571	0.2995 (5.6%)▲	0.4712 (3.1%)△	3	0.2738 (-3.5%)▽	0.4516 (-1.2%)	-1
5	kobeL2R	0.2767	0.4429	0.2744 (-0.8%)	0.4463 (0.8%)	0	0.2677 (-3.3%)▽	0.4409 (-0.5%)	-2
6	hitQryFBrun4	0.3186	0.4424	0.3118 (-2.1%)	0.4554 (2.9%)	2	0.3220 (1.1%)▲	0.4849 (9.6%)▲	5
7	hitLRrun1	0.3355	0.4379	0.3226 (-3.9%)▽	0.4525 (3.3%)	2	0.3188 (-5.0%)▽	0.4610 (5.3%)▲	3
8	FASILKOM01	0.2682	0.4367	0.2820 (5.2%)▲	0.4531 (3.8%)▲	3	0.2622 (-2.2%)▽	0.4346 (-0.5%)	-1
9	hitDELMrun2	0.3197	0.4345	0.3105 (-2.9%)	0.4424 (1.8%)	4	0.3246 (1.5%)	0.4723 (8.7%)▲	8
10	tsqe	0.2843	0.4339	0.2836 (-0.3%)	0.4441 (2.4%)	5	0.2917 (2.6%)	0.4660 (7.4%)▲	7
11	ICTWDSERUN1	0.2715	0.4299	0.2862 (5.4%)▲	0.4582 (6.6%)▲	7	0.2765 (1.8%)▲	0.4484 (4.3%)△	6
12	ICTWDSERUN2	0.2671	0.4266	0.2785 (4.3%)△	0.4475 (4.9%)▲	7	0.2786 (4.3%)△	0.4478 (5.0%)△	7
13	cmuPrfPhrE	0.3179	0.4254	0.3172 (-0.2%)	0.4469 (5.1%)▲	8	0.3321 (4.5%)△	0.4585 (7.8%)▲	9
14	cmuPrfPhrENo	0.3198	0.4249	0.3179 (-0.6%)	0.4486 (5.6%)▲	9	0.3359 (5.0%)△	0.4591 (8.1%)▲	10
15	cmuPrfPhr	0.3167	0.4198	0.3130 (-1.2%)	0.4379 (4.3%)△	8	0.3282 (3.6%)△	0.4572 (8.9%)▲	11
16	FASILKOM02	0.2454	0.4141	0.2718 (10.8%)▲	0.4508 (8.9%)▲	11	0.2489 (1.4%)	0.4201 (1.5%)△	1
17	IBMLTR	0.2630	0.4136	0.2734 (4.0%)△	0.4441 (7.4%)▲	10	0.2703 (2.8%)△	0.4346 (5.1%)▲	8
18	otM12ihe	0.2995	0.4124	0.2969 (-0.9%)	0.4322 (4.8%)▲	7	0.2900 (-3.2%)▽	0.4239 (2.8%)△	3
19	FASILKOM03	0.2716	0.4124	0.2859 (5.3%)▲	0.4452 (8.0%)▲	14	0.2740 (0.9%)	0.4270 (3.5%)▲	7
20	FASILKOM04	0.2461	0.4113	0.2575 (4.6%)▲	0.4294 (4.4%)▲	9	0.2414 (-1.9%)▽	0.4220 (2.6%)△	5
21	IBMLTRFuture	0.2731	0.4090	0.2808 (2.8%)	0.4311 (5.4%)▲	10	0.2785 (2.0%)△	0.4415 (8.0%)▲	14
22	uiucGSLIS01	0.2445	0.4073	0.2575 (5.3%)▲	0.4260 (4.6%)▲	9	0.2478 (1.4%)	0.4233 (3.9%)△	7
23	PKUICST4	0.2786	0.4062	0.2909 (4.4%)△	0.4514 (11.1%)▲	18	0.2832 (1.7%)▲	0.4491 (10.6%)▲	18
24	uogTrLsE	0.2909	0.4028	0.2977 (2.3%)	0.4282 (6.3%)▲	9	0.3131 (7.6%)▲	0.4484 (11.3%)▲	19
25	otM12ih	0.2777	0.3989	0.2810 (1.2%)	0.4175 (4.7%)▲	10	0.2752 (-0.9%)	0.4119 (3.3%)△	5
26	ICTWDSERUN4	0.1877	0.3887	0.1985 (5.8%)▲	0.4164 (7.1%)▲	10	0.2040 (8.7%)▲	0.4220 (8.6%)▲	11
27	uwatrrfall	0.2620	0.3881	0.2812 (7.3%)▲	0.4136 (6.6%)▲	9	0.2942 (12.3%)△	0.4314 (11.2%)▲	16
28	cmuPhrE	0.2731	0.3842	0.2797 (2.4%)	0.4136 (7.7%)▲	12	0.2972 (8.8%)△	0.4352 (13.3%)▲	19
29	AIrun1	0.2237	0.3842	0.2339 (4.6%)▲	0.4102 (6.8%)▲	5	0.2285 (2.2%)△	0.4157 (8.2%)▲	13
30	PKUICST3	0.2118	0.3825	0.2318 (9.4%)▲	0.4119 (7.7%)▲	14	0.2363 (11.6%)▲	0.4415 (15.4%)▲	23
	Average			3.3%	5.3%	7.3	2.0%	6.2%	7.8

model to learn tree-edit operations on dependency parse trees. They cast the problem into the framework of structured output learning with latent variables. The model of Yao et al., 2013 [37] applies linear chain CRFs with features derived from TED to automatically learn associations between questions and candidate answers. Severyn and Moschitti [26] applied SVM with tree kernels to shallow syntactic representation, which provide automatic feature engineering. Yih et al. [33] use distributional models based on lexical semantics to match semantic relations of aligned words in QA pairs.

More recently, Bordes et al. [5] used siamese networks for learning to project question and answer pairs into a joint space whereas Iyyer et al. [16] modelled semantic composition with a recursive neural network for a question answering task. The work closest to ours is [38], where they apply deep learning to learn to match question and answer sentences. However, their sentence model to map questions and answers to vectors operates only on unigrams or bigrams. Our sentence model is based on a convolutional neural network with the state-of-the-art architecture, we use a relatively large width of the convolution filter (5), thus allowing the network to capture longer range dependencies. Moreover, the architecture of deep learning model along with the question-answer similarity score also encodes question and answer vector representations in the model. Hence, our model constructs and learns a richer representation of the question-answer pairs, which results in superior results on the answer sentence selection dataset. Finally, our deep learning reranker is trained end-to-end, while in [38] they use the output of their neural network in a separate logistic scoring model.

Regarding learning to rank systems applied to TREC microblog datasets, recently [27] have shown that richer linguistic representations of tweets can improve upon state of the art systems in TMB-2011 and TMB-2012. We directly compare with their system, showing that our deep learning model without any changes to its architecture (we only pre-train word embeddings) is on the par with their reranker. This is remarkable, since different from [27], which requires additional pre-proccesing using syntactic parsers to construct syntactic trees, our model requires no expensive pre-processing and does not rely on any external resources.

8. CONCLUSIONS

In this paper, we propose a novel deep learning architecture for reranking short texts. It has the benefits of requiring no manual feature engineering or external resources, which may be expensive or not available. The model with the same architecture can be successfully applied to other domains and tasks.

Our experimental findings show that our deep learning model: (i) greatly improves on the previous state-of-the-art systems and a recent deep learning approach in [38] on answer sentence selection task showing a 3% absolute improvement in MAP and MRR; (ii) our system is able to improve even the best system runs from TREC Microblog 2012 challenge; (iii) is comparable to the syntactic reranker in [27], while our system requires no external parsers or resources.

Acknowledgments. This work has been supported by the EC project CogNet, 671625 (H2020-ICT-2014-2, Research and Innovation action). The first author was supported by the Google Europe Doctoral Fellowship Award 2013.

REFERENCES

[1] A. Agarwal, H. Raghavan, K. Subbian, P. Melville, D. Gondek, and R. Lawrence. Learning to rank for robust question answering. In *CIKM*, 2012.

[2] J. W. Antoine Bordes and N. Usunier. Open question answering with weakly supervised embedding models. In *ECML*, Nancy, France, September 2014.

[3] Y. Bengio, R. Ducharme, P. Vincent, and C. Jauvin. A neural probabilistic language model. *Journal of Machine Learning Research*, 3:1137–1155, 2003.

[4] R. Berendsen, M. Tsagkias, W. Weerkamp, and M. de Rijke. Pseudo test collections for training and tuning microblog rankers. In *SIGIR*, 2013.

[5] A. Bordes, S. Chopra, and J. Weston. Question answering with subgraph embeddings. In *Proceedings of the 2014 Conference on Empirical Methods in Natural Language Processing (EMNLP)*, pages 615–620, Doha, Qatar, October 2014. Association for Computational Linguistics.

[6] Z. Cao, T. Qin, T.-Y. Liu, M.-F. Tsai, and H. Li. Learning to rank: From pairwise approach to listwise approach. In *Proceedings of the 24th International Conference on Machine Learning*, ICML '07, pages 129–136, New York, NY, USA, 2007. ACM.

[7] Y. Chen, M. Zhou, and S. Wang. Reranking answers from definitional QA using language models. In *ACL*, 2006.

[8] R. Collobert and J. Weston. A unified architecture for natural language processing: deep neural networks with multitask learning. In *ICML*, pages 160–167, 2008.

[9] H. Cui, M. Kan, and T. Chua. Generic soft pattern models for definitional QA. In *SIGIR*, Salvador, Brazil, 2005. ACM.

[10] S. Deerwester, S. Dumais, G. Furnas, T. Landauer, and R. Harshman. Indexing by latent semantic analysis. *Journal of the American Society of Information Science*, 1990.

[11] M. Denil, A. Demiraj, N. Kalchbrenner, P. Blunsom, and N. de Freitas. Modelling, visualising and summarising documents with a single convolutional neural network. Technical report, University of Oxford, 2014.

[12] J. Duchi, E. Hazan, and Y. Singer. Adaptive subgradient methods for online learning and stochastic optimization. *J. Mach. Learn. Res.*, 12:2121–2159, 2011.

[13] A. Echihabi and D. Marcu. A noisy-channel approach to question answering. In *ACL*, 2003.

[14] I. J. Goodfellow, D. Warde-Farley, M. Mirza, A. C. Courville, and Y. Bengio. Maxout networks. In *ICML*, pages 1319–1327, 2013.

[15] M. Heilman and N. A. Smith. Tree edit models for recognizing textual entailments, paraphrases, and answers to questions. In *NAACL*, 2010.

[16] M. Iyyer, J. Boyd-Graber, L. Claudino, R. Socher, and H. Daumé III. A neural network for factoid question answering over paragraphs. In *Proceedings of the 2014 Conference on Empirical Methods in Natural Language Processing (EMNLP)*, pages 633–644, Doha, Qatar, October 2014. Association for Computational Linguistics.

[17] J. Jeon, W. B. Croft, and J. H. Lee. Finding similar questions in large question and answer archives. In *CIKM*, 2005.

[18] N. Kalchbrenner, E. Grefenstette, and P. Blunsom. A convolutional neural network for modelling sentences. *Proceedings of the 52nd Annual Meeting of the Association for Computational Linguistics*, June 2014.

[19] Y. Kim. Convolutional neural networks for sentence classification. In *EMNLP*, pages 1746–1751, Doha, Qatar, October 2014.

[20] T. Mikolov, I. Sutskever, K. Chen, G. S. Corrado, and J. Dean. Distributed representations of words and phrases and their compositionality. In *Advances in Neural Information Processing Systems 26*, pages 3111–3119, 2013.

[21] A. Moschitti, S. Quarteroni, R. Basili, and S. Manandhar. Exploiting syntactic and shallow semantic kernels for question/answer classification. In *ACL*, 2007.

[22] V. Nair and G. E. Hinton. Rectified linear units improve restricted boltzmann machines. In *Proceedings of the 27th International Conference on Machine Learning (ICML-10)*, pages 807–814, 2010.

[23] I. Ounis, C. Macdonald, J. Lin, and I. Soboroff. Overview of the TREC-2011 microblog track. In *TREC*, 2011.

[24] F. Radlinski and T. Joachims. Query chains: Learning to rank from implicit feedback. *CoRR*, 2006.

[25] Y. Sasaki. Question answering as question-biased term extraction: A new approach toward multilingual qa. In *ACL*, 2005.

[26] A. Severyn and A. Moschitti. Automatic feature engineering for answer selection and extraction. In *Proceedings of the 2013 Conference on Empirical Methods in Natural Language Processing*, pages 458–467, Seattle, Washington, USA, October 2013. Association for Computational Linguistics.

[27] A. Severyn, A. Moschitti, M. Tsagkias, R. Berendsen, and M. de Rijke. A syntax-aware re-ranker for microblog retrieval. In *SIGIR*, 2014.

[28] D. Shen and M. Lapata. Using semantic roles to improve question answering. In *EMNLP-CoNLL*, 2007.

[29] I. Soboroff, I. Ounis, J. Lin, and I. Soboroff. Overview of the TREC-2012 microblog track. In *TREC*, 2012.

[30] N. Srivastava, G. Hinton, A. Krizhevsky, I. Sutskever, and R. Salakhutdinov. Dropout: A simple way to prevent neural networks from overfitting. *Journal of Machine Learning Research*, 15:1929–1958, 2014.

[31] M. Surdeanu, M. Ciaramita, and H. Zaragoza. Learning to rank answers to non-factoid questions from web collections. *Comput. Linguist.*, 37(2):351–383, June 2011.

[32] J. Suzuki, Y. Sasaki, and E. Maeda. Svm answer selection for open-domain question answering. In *COLING*, 2002.

[33] W. tau Yih, M.-W. Chang, C. Meek, and A. Pastusiak. Question answering using enhanced lexical semantic models. In *ACL*, August 2013.

[34] P. Vincent, H. Larochelle, I. Lajoie, Y. Bengio, and P.-A. Manzagol. Stacked denoising autoencoders: Learning useful representations in a deep network with a local denoising criterion. *J. Mach. Learn. Res.*, 11:3371–3408, Dec. 2010.

[35] M. Wang and C. D. Manning. Probabilistic tree-edit models with structured latent variables for textual entailment and question answer- ing. In *ACL*, 2010.

[36] M. Wang, N. A. Smith, and T. Mitaura. What is the jeopardy model? a quasi-synchronous grammar for qa. In *EMNLP*, 2007.

[37] P. C. Xuchen Yao, Benjamin Van Durme and C. Callison-Burch. Answer extraction as sequence tagging with tree edit distance. In *NAACL*, 2013.

[38] L. Yu, K. M. Hermann, P. Blunsom, and S. Pulman. Deep learning for answer sentence selection. *CoRR*, 2014.

[39] M. D. Zeiler. Adadelta: An adaptive learning rate method. *CoRR*, 2012.

[40] M. D. Zeiler and R. Fergus. Stochastic pooling for regularization of deep convolutional neural networks. *CoRR*, abs/1301.3557, 2013.

Context- and Content-aware Embeddings for Query Rewriting in Sponsored Search

Mihajlo Grbovic[†], Nemanja Djuric[†], Vladan Radosavljevic[†],
Fabrizio Silvestri[‡], Narayan Bhamidipati[†]
{mihajlo, nemanja, vladan, silvestr, narayanb}@yahoo-inc.com
Yahoo Labs
[†]701 First Ave, Sunnyvale, CA, USA
[‡]125 Shaftesbury Ave, London, England

ABSTRACT

Search engines represent one of the most popular web services, visited by more than 85% of internet users on a daily basis. Advertisers are interested in making use of this vast business potential, as very clear intent signal communicated through an issued query allows effective targeting of users. This idea is embodied in a sponsored search model, where each advertiser maintains a list of keywords they deem indicative of increased user response rate with regards to their business. According to this targeting model, when a query is issued all advertisers with a matching keyword are entered into an auction according to the amount they bid for the query and the winner gets to show their ad. One of the main challenges is the fact that a query may not match many keywords, resulting in lower auction value, lower ad quality, and lost revenue for advertisers and publishers. Possible solution is to expand a query into a set of related queries and use them to increase the number of matched ads, called query rewriting. To this end, we propose rewriting method based on a novel query embedding algorithm, which jointly models query content as well as its context within a search session. As a result, semantically similar queries are mapped into vectors close in the embedding space, which allows expansion of a query via simple K-nearest neighbor search. The method was trained on more than 12 billion sessions, one of the largest corpus reported thus far, and evaluated on both public TREC data set and an in-house sponsored search data set. The results show that the proposed approach significantly outperformed existing state-of-the-art, strongly indicating its benefits and monetization potential.

Categories and Subject Descriptors

H.3.3 [**Information Storage and Retrieval**]: Information Search and Retrieval

General Terms

Information Retrieval; Query Rewriting; Algorithms.

Keywords

Query rewriting; word embeddings.

SIGIR '15, August 09 - 13, 2015, Santiago, Chile
Copyright 2015 ACM 978-1-4503-3621-5/15/08.
http://dx.doi.org/10.1145/2766462.2767709 ...$15.00.

1. INTRODUCTION

In recent years targeted advertising has become one of the largest and most lucrative advertising channels. Despite the fact that traditional offline advertising still accounts for the majority of advertising expenditures [34], future potential of this burgeoning field is clearly exemplified by reported ad revenue of over 20 billion dollars in the first half of 2013 in the US alone, combined with a remarkable growth of around 20% on a yearly basis [21]. The size and importance of the online advertising, as well as the interesting open questions that the scale and variety of the targeting tasks bring, has drawn attention of many researchers from both industry and academia, resulting in a number of novel methods and improvements to the flourishing field [1, 18, 32].

Due to a large diversity of the internet medium, targeted advertising has evolved to encompass many different outlets for the advertisers interested in reaching their target audience. These include behavioral targeting [12] (where users are targeted based on their general browsing behavior), e-mail retargeting [18] (targeting users based on their e-mail interaction patterns), site re-targeting (targeting users based on their historical search queries), to name a few. In this work we consider a task of sponsored search advertising [17, 22], a very popular advertising model that targets users with the most relevant ads by considering an immediate query issued by a user. It has become one of the prevalent means of advertising due to a fact that the current query carries a strong signal about an immediate intent of the user, resulting in a highly effective targeting model [15].

In the sponsored search model each advertiser maintains a list of keywords that they deem relevant to their product (e.g., Nike may maintain a keyword list containing terms such as "running shoes" and "athletics"). In addition to a list of keywords, each advertiser also specifies a monetary bid amount they are willing to pay if their ad is shown and clicked by the user. Then, when a user issues a query in a search engine, the query is compared against each advertisers' keyword list, and all advertisers with the matching keyword are entered into an auction. Finally, according to advertiser's bid amount and the estimated quality and relevance of an ad that they wish to show, one advertiser and their corresponding ad are chosen for user targeting. Value of the auction increases when number of matched advertisers and their bids are high, which directly results in a better ad quality and higher revenue for both advertisers and publishers (i.e., websites that host the ads).

Due to a large number of queries that the users could possibly issue, a common occurrence is that an exact query match cannot be found, as the advertisers usually cannot cover all relevant queries related to their product or service. However, even when the exact match does not exist, most often there does exist a non-matching keyword that is still highly related to the query. For example, query "purina one" and bidded keyword "dog food" are strongly related yet a string match would fail to make the connection, which directly translates into lost revenue. To mitigate this problem, query rewriting is used to expand the original query by providing K related ones for which ads are available, and which can be used instead to qualify advertisers for an auction [9, 23, 40]. In the above example, a query rewriting method can be used to rewrite "purina one" into related queries such as "dog food", "cat food", "purina pro plan", and others, thus increasing likelihood of retrieving more high-quality, relevant ads, likely to be clicked by a user that issued the query.

In this paper we address this critical step in sponsored search, and propose a novel query rewriting algorithm motivated by recent advances in distributed neural language models [14, 30, 31]. We explore and expand upon these approaches for the task of query rewriting, resulting in significant performance improvements over the current state-of-the-art methods. Key contributions are summarized below:

- We describe an application of distributed language models to query rewriting, where we propose to use three novel methods for learning distributed, low-dimensional query representations that compactly capture their semantic meaning;
- We propose and discuss how to add ad clicks and search result clicks to query context, which allows specialization of representations for various tasks of critical interest to search engine companies (e.g., query suggestion, query-to-ad matching, query categorization), indicating even wider applicability of the method in the advertising domain;
- We trained and evaluated the models using more than 12 billion search sessions, resulting in rewriting results of high quality. Empirical results show that the proposed approach significantly outperform the existing state-of-the-art methods.

2. RELATED WORK

In this section we describe related work in the domains of query rewriting and neural language modeling that motivated the approach proposed in this work.

2.1 Query rewriting for sponsored search

Owing to the importance of query rewriting for the success of query-ad auctions, various algorithms have been proposed in the literature to address this critical step. These include graph-based methods such as Query Flow Graph (QFG) [6, 7] that learn from users' browsing behavior, as well as methods that exploit syntactical relationships between queries [11, 23]. However, disadvantage of existing solutions is that they mostly do not take into account complex semantic relationships between queries, which may lead to suboptimal rewrites. For example, the rewrites typically result in the original queries with added or removed terms, such as "purina one" being rewritten as "purina" or "purina one pro". Thus, they are often obvious and have already been considered by the advertisers that targeted the original query, and do not add a significant value to the auction.

We note that query rewriting task is related to the problem of query suggestion, albeit the goals of the two techniques are quite different. In the case of query suggestion the objective is to provide users with queries that are important for meeting users' information needs [2, 7, 39], while in query rewriting the task is to expand query to increase both the number and quality of retrieved ads. We refer an interested reader to [36] for an overview of query log mining approaches as applied to query suggestion task.

2.2 Neural language models

In a number of natural language processing (NLP) applications, including information retrieval, part-of-speech tagging, chunking, and many others, the specific objective can be generalized to the task of assigning a probability value to a sequence of words. To this end, language models have been developed, defining a mathematical model to capture statistical properties of words and the dependancies among them [3, 27]. Traditionally, language models represent each word as a feature vector using one-hot representation, where a word vector has the same length as the size of a vocabulary, and a vector element that corresponds to the observed word is equal to 1, and 0 otherwise. However, this approach often exhibits significant limitations in practical tasks, suffering from high dimensionality of the problem and severe data sparsity, resulting in suboptimal performance.

Neural language models have been proposed to address these issues, inducing low-dimensional, distributed embeddings of words by means of neural networks [4, 13, 38]. Such approaches take advantage of the word order in text documents, explicitly modeling the assumption that closer words in the word sequence are statistically more dependent. Historically, inefficient training of the neural network-based models has been an obstacle to their wider applicability, being proportional to the size of the vocabulary which may grow to several millions in practical tasks. However, this issue has been successfully addressed with recent advances in the field, particularly with the development of highly scalable continuous bag-of-words (CBOW) and skip-gram (SG) language models [30, 31] for learning word representations. These powerful, efficient models have shown very promising results in capturing both syntactic and semantic relationships between words in large-scale text corpora, obtaining state-of-the-art results on a plethora of NLP tasks. More recently, the concept of distributed representations has been extended beyond word representations to sentences and paragraphs [14, 28], relational entities [8, 37], general text-based attributes [26], descriptive text of images [25], nodes in graph structure [33], and other applications going beyond NLP domain for which they were originally proposed.

3. PROPOSED APPROACH

To address the shortcomings of the existing state-of-the-art methods for query rewriting, we propose to take a radically new approach to this task, motivated by the recent success of distributed language models in NLP applications [31, 38]. In the context of NLP, distributed models are able to learn word representations in a low-dimensional continuous vector space using a surrounding context of the word in a sentence, where in the resulting embedding space semantically similar words are close to each other [31]. Our objective is to take advantage of this property for the task of query rewriting, and to learn query representations in a low-dimensional space where semantically similar queries would be close. As a result, and in contrast to rewriting methods commonly used in practice, related queries could have a high similarity score even if they do not have any shared terms. Clearly, such approach would allow us to reduce complex task of query rewriting to a trivial K-nearest-neighbor search in the new embedding space.

However, application of distributed language models to the task of query rewriting is not an easy endeavour. Finding distributed query representation, as opposed to finding word representations, brings very unique challenges quite different from those found in everyday NLP problems. First, there are significant differences between language used in everyday language and web searches [10, 35]. For example, web search users often use summarization when searching for content (e.g., typing "vacations Spain" instead of "vacations in Spain"), thus omitting frequent words. Further, some n-grams that rarely appear in everyday language often appear together in web search [24], and queries are characterized by more spelling mistakes. Moreover, contrary to everyday language where linguistic rules and notions of words and sentences are clearly defined, search queries are composed of terms where there is no existing notion of "sentence of queries" or the surrounding context equivalent to natural language domain.

In this paper we address these issues, and propose three query rewriting methods that bring the state-of-the-art distributed language models closer to the setting of sponsored search: 1) context2vec, where we exploit the fact that user query is recorded with a timestamp, from which we create "query sentences" and apply state-of-the-art language model [31]; 2) content2vec, where we propose to learn distributed query vector representations from its content without considering session information, which is equivalent to paragraph2vec method from [28]; and 3) context-content2vec, where we propose to use a novel two-level architecture [14] that jointly models content of queries (i.e., word tokens that form the query) along with the query context (defined as other temporally close queries within a search session). Empirical results suggest that the resulting rewrites are highly related to the original queries, while being more diverse than rewrites produced by the current state-of-the-art methods. In addition, using a large data base of query-bids collected for thousands of advertisers, we show that the rewrites produced by the proposed method match the highest percentage of bidded queries, providing a strong positive impact on the overall revenue of both publishers and advertisers.

In addition to search query logs, search engines systematically log a number of other valuable signals that can help better explain and model the user intent. For example, ad clicks and clicks on search results are also recorded, and may provide a supplementary intent signal that can be used to improve query representations. To help exploit these two valuable sources of information, we propose to incorporate both ad clicks and search result clicks into user query sessions, and show how the additional signals are seamlessly handled by the proposed models. The benefits of including the ad and search clicks for query rewriting task are clearly confirmed by the empirical results, showing increased relevance of query rewrites and higher coverage of advertisers' bid terms. Moreover, in addition to improving query representations, in this way we also learn low-dimensional representations of ad clicks and search clicks in the same embedding space, which opens doors for using the proposed methods on a number of important online tasks, such as query-to-ad matching, query suggestion, and query categorization, to name a few.

4. METHODOLOGY

In this section we describe the proposed methodology for the task of query rewriting in sponsored search. As discussed earlier, the goal is to find queries related to the issued one, which would allow us to retrieve relevant ads that were not matched by the original query. To solve this problem, we propose to learn representation of queries in low-dimensional space from historical search logs using neural language models. Query rewriting can then be performed by finding K nearest neighbors of the issued query in the learned embedding space.

More specifically, given a set $\mathcal{S}$ of S search sessions obtained from online users, where each session $s = (q_1, \ldots, q_{M_s}) \in \mathcal{S}$ is defined as an uninterupted sequence of M_s queries, and each query $q_m = (w_{m1}, w_{m2}, \ldots w_{mT_m})$ consists of T_m words, our objective is to find D-dimensional real-valued representation $\mathbf{v}_{q_m} \in \mathcal{R}^D$ of each query q_m such that semantically similar queries lie nearby in the new space.

We propose three approaches for learning query representations that address specifics of the web search environment. We first propose context2vec and content2vec methods that consider query context and query content, respectively, motivated by previous work on learning word representations from news articles [30, 31]. We then detail context-content2vec, a two-level architecture for joint modeling of both query context and query content, which results in better, more useful query representations.

4.1 Model 1: context2vec

The context2vec model involves learning low-dimensional representations of queries from search logs by using a notion of a search session as a "sentence" and queries within the session as "words", borrowing the terminology from NLP domain (see Figure 1a). More specifically, context2vec learns query representations using the skip-gram model [31] by maximizing the objective function over the entire set $\mathcal{S}$ of search sessions, defined as

$$\mathcal{L} = \sum_{s \in \mathcal{S}} \sum_{q_m \in s} \sum_{-b \leq i \leq b, i \neq 0} \log \mathbb{P}(q_{m+i}|q_m). \tag{4.1}$$

Probability $\mathbb{P}(q_{m+i}|q_m)$ of observing a neighboring query q_{m+i} given the current query q_m is defined using soft-max,

$$\mathbb{P}(q_{m+i}|q_m) = \frac{\exp(\mathbf{v}_{q_m}^\top \mathbf{v}'_{q_{m+i}})}{\sum_{q=1}^{V} \exp(\mathbf{v}_{q_m}^\top \mathbf{v}'_q)}, \tag{4.2}$$

where $\mathbf{v}_q$ and $\mathbf{v}'_q$ are the input and output vector representations of query q, b is defined as length of the context for query

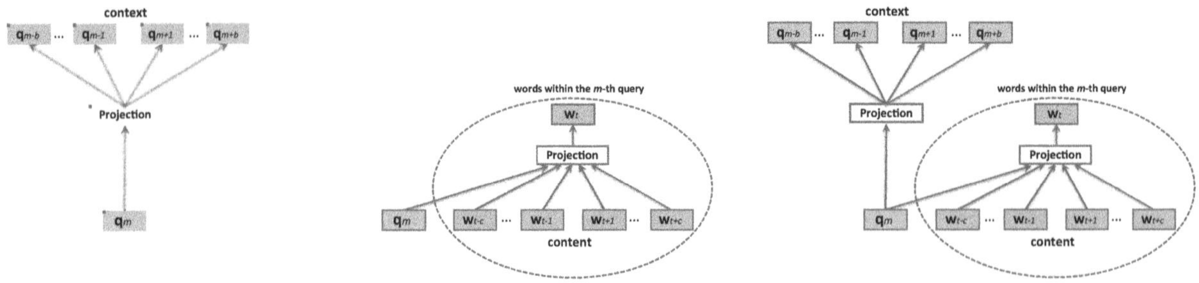

(a) context2vec (b) content2vec (c) context-content2vec

Figure 1: Query embedding models

sequences, and V is the number of unique queries in the vocabulary. From equations (4.1) and (4.2) we can see that context2vec models temporal context of query sequences, where queries with similar contexts (i.e., with similar neighboring queries) will have similar vector representations in the projected semantic space.

4.2 Model 2: content2vec

We propose content2vec method to simultaneously learn vector representations of queries and the words contained within them, motivated by the paragraph2vec algorithm [28]. The content2vec architecture is illustrated in Figure 1b. Training data set was derived from user search logs by disregarding the query timestamps, and consisted of queries q_m and their containing words $q_m = (w_{m1}, w_{m2}, \ldots w_{mT_m})$. During training, query vectors are learned so they predict the words in their content, while word vectors are learned so they predict their context words within the query. More specifically, objective of content2vec is to maximize the log-likelihood over the set $\mathcal{S}$ of all query sessions,

$$\mathcal{L} = \sum_{s \in \mathcal{S}} \Big(\sum_{q_m \in s} \log \mathbb{P}(q_m | w_{m1} : w_{mT_m}) + \sum_{w_{mt} \in q_m} \log \mathbb{P}(w_{mt} | w_{m,t-c} : w_{m,t+c}, q_m) \Big), \tag{4.3}$$

where c is length of the context for words within the query. The probability $\mathbb{P}(w_{mt} | w_{m,t-c} : w_{m,t+c}, q_m)$ is defined using a soft-max function,

$$\mathbb{P}(w_{mt} | w_{m,t-c} : w_{m,t+c}, q_m) = \frac{\exp(\bar{\mathbf{v}}^\top \mathbf{v}'_{w_{mt}})}{\sum_{w=1}^{V} \exp(\bar{\mathbf{v}}^\top \mathbf{v}'_w)}, \tag{4.4}$$

where $\mathbf{v}'_{w_{mt}}$ is the output vector representation of w_{mt}, and $\bar{\mathbf{v}}$ is averaged vector representation of the context including corresponding q_m, defined as

$$\bar{\mathbf{v}} = \frac{1}{2c+1} (\mathbf{v}_{q_m} + \sum_{-c \le j \le c, j \ne 0} \mathbf{v}_{w_{m,t+j}}), \tag{4.5}$$

where $\mathbf{v}_w$ is the input vector representation of w. Similarly, the probability $\mathbb{P}(q_m | w_{m1} : w_{mT_m})$ is defined as

$$\mathbb{P}(q_m | w_{m1} : w_{mT_m}) = \frac{\exp(\bar{\mathbf{v}}_m^\top \mathbf{v}'_{q_m})}{\sum_{w=1}^{V} \exp(\bar{\mathbf{v}}_m^\top \mathbf{v}'_w)}, \tag{4.6}$$

where $\mathbf{v}'_{q_m}$ is the output vector representation of q_m, and $\bar{\mathbf{v}}_m$ is averaged input vector representation of all the words within the query q_m, computed as

$$\bar{\mathbf{v}}_m = \frac{1}{T_m} \sum_{t=1}^{T_m} \mathbf{v}_{w_{mt}}. \tag{4.7}$$

4.3 Model 3: context-content2vec

Both context2vec and content2vec models have limited modeling power in the light of the available data. This is due to the fact that they are not capable of exploiting all the available query log information as they model only one aspect of the data at hand (i.e., either make use of the context of queries in search sessions or their content, respectively). To overcome this limitation, we propose a two-layer context-content2vec [14] specifically tailored for the purpose of modeling query logs. The two-layer architecture of the proposed model is illustrated in Figure 1c. The upper layer models the temporal context of query sequences in search sessions, based on the assumption that temporally closer queries are statistically more dependent. On the other hand, the bottom layer models the content information of word sequences found within queries.

More formally, given S sessions of queries together with their content, objective of the two-layer context-content2vec model is to maximize the log-likelihood of the training data,

$$\mathcal{L} = \sum_{s \in \mathcal{S}} \sum_{q_m \in s} \Big(\sum_{-b \le i \le b, i \ne 0} \log \mathbb{P}(q_{m+i} | q_m) + \alpha_m \log \mathbb{P}(q_m | w_{m1} : w_{mT_m}) + \sum_{w_{mt} \in q_m} \log \mathbb{P}(w_{mt} | w_{m,t-c} : w_{m,t+c}, q_m) \Big), \tag{4.8}$$

where α weights are hyperparameters that trade off between minimization of the log-likelihood of query sequences (i.e., query context) and the log-likelihood of word sequences (i.e., query content). Denoting frequency of the mth query as K_m, we set the hyperparameters as $\alpha_m = \frac{1}{\log(1+K_m)}$, such that rarely seen queries rely more on content and frequently seen queries more on context.

As can be observed, context-content2vec model combines the two earlier models, using the context2vec model in the upper layer and the content2vec model in the lower layer. Note that the probabilities from equation (4.8) are defined in equations (4.2), (4.4), and (4.6). In order to learn from both contextual and content information, the training data set is a union of context and content training data sets defined previously in sections 4.1 and 4.2.

4.4 Training and inference

The models are optimized using stochastic gradient ascent, suitable for large-scale problems. However, computation of gradients $\nabla\mathcal{L}$ in (4.1), (4.3), and (4.8) is proportional to the vocabulary size V, which is computationally expensive in practical tasks as V could easily reach hundreds of millions. As an alternative, we used negative sampling approach proposed in [31], which significantly reduces the computational complexity.

When the vector representations of all queries are found, we can perform query rewriting in a straightforward manner. For a given user query q, we generate K query rewrites using K nearest neighbors (K-NN) of query q in the low-dimensional space with respect to a cosine distance [31].

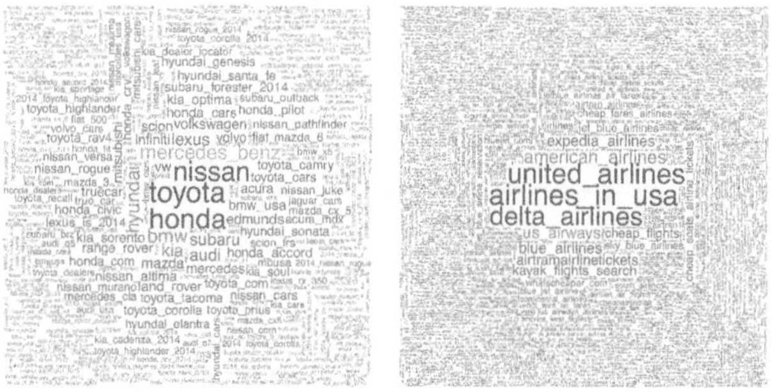

(a) automotive-related ad (b) air travel-related ad

Figure 2: Examples of most similar queries to select ads

5. EXPERIMENTS

In this section we describe the considered data set and give empirical evaluation of the proposed rewriting methods. We learned embeddings for more than 45 million queries, using one of the largest search data sets reported so far, comprising over 12 billion sessions collected on the US website of Yahoo Search. The vectors were used to produce query rewrites, evaluated in terms of relevance and ad coverage and compared to the state-of-the-art methods from the literature.

5.1 Training data sets

5.1.1 Query content data

For purposes of learning query embeddings from query content, we took 45 million most frequent queries and formed dataset $D_{content} = \{(q_m, w_{m1}, w_{m2}, \ldots, w_{mT_m})\}$, where q_m is the m-th query and $(w_{m1}, w_{m2}, \ldots w_{mT_m})$ are the words contained within q_m.

5.1.2 Search session data

Search sessions are defined as uninterrupted sequences of web search activity. Following [16], the session ends when a user is inactive for more than 30 minutes. A new session is initiated with the following search query.

To be able to learn query embeddings from interactions of queries within a search session we created dataset $D_{context} = \{s_i, i = 1, ..., S\}$, derived by sessionizing user search logs data into sessions s_i, that were in turn represented as a set of queries ordered in time, $s_i = (q_{i1}, q_{i2}, ..., q_{iM_i})$. In a case of repetitive queries, such as $s_i = (q_{i1}, q_{i2}, q_{i3} = q_{i2}, q_{i4} = q_{i2}, q_{i5})$, repetitions were de-duplicated to obtain $s_i = (q_{i1}, q_{i2}, q_{i5})$. Finally, search sessions that contained only a single search query were discarded.

5.1.3 Ad clicks and search link clicks

In a search session, queries are often accompanied by ad clicks and search link clicks. These events can be used as additional context to improve query representations and specialize them for a specific task. For example, while one of the main goals of query rewriting in sponsored search is to produce relevant alternatives to the original query, another important goal is for rewrites to match as many bid terms as possible to increase the auction value. Thus, to produce more commercial query rewrites, we use ad click events within query contexts when learning vector representations.

For this purpose we extend the session data set by adding ad click events to user sessions, where each ad click is uniquely identified by ad identification number. The data set $D_{ad} = \{s_i, i = 1, ..., S\}$ consists of sessions s_i comprising both search queries and ad clicks, $s_i = (q_{i1}, q_{i2}, a_{i3}, q_{i4}, a_{i5} ..., q_{iM_i})$, where q_{im} refers to search queries, and a_{im} refer to ad click events. Moreover, to further improve learned query representations we also considered adding search link clicks to the user sessions (i.e., clicks that a user made on links given as search results, also referred to as *organic* results), motivated by the idea behind QFG approach. To this end, we expanded data set D_{ad} to obtain data set $D_{ad+link} = \{s_i, i = 1, ..., S\}$, formed by further adding link click events l_{im} to search sessions s_i.

5.2 Training details

5.2.1 Handling "search stopwords"

Unlike in everyday language, where the most frequent tokens are articles and prepositions (e.g., *a*, *the*, *in*), in search data the most frequent tokens are navigational queries, such as *google*, *yahoo*, *facebook*, etc. Due to the fact that over a longer period they occur in a direct neighborhood of majority of other queries, there is a risk that the embedding space will shrink. We have empirically observed this phenomenon, and during training the navigational queries tend to pull all other queries towards them, preventing the vectors from spreading further away in the hyperspace.

The authors of [31] suggested to deal with the frequent tokens in news articles by downsampling. This heuristic involved discarding words with probability $\mathbb{P}(w_i) = 1 - \sqrt{\frac{\tau}{f(w_i)}}$, where $f(w_i)$ is the frequency of word w_i, and τ is a user-set parameter. However, this approach is not applicable in a context of web search which poses quite different requirements. In particular, we aim to learn good representations of navigational queries while at the same time prevent them from adversely influencing representation learning for non-navigational queries. To achieve this objective, we propose a one-direction learning rule for navigational queries. In particular, their vectors are being updated by vectors of queries appearing in the context, but are not used to update the vectors of other queries in their context. We identified navigational queries editorially by evaluating the most frequent 3,000 queries for navigational intent.

5.2.2 Training parameters

Models were trained using a cluster of 9 machines with 256GB of RAM memory and 24 cores. Dimensionality of the

Table 1: Differences in query rewrites of context2vec and context-content2vec for tail queries

Query	cx2vec	cx-cn2vec
minnesota insurance exam crossword puzzles	satellite tv otego	minnesota insurance
	satellite tv menominee	minnesota insurance license practice exams
	satellite tv west end	online insurance exam crossword puzzles
	satellite tv townsend	colorado insurance exam crossword puzzles
	satellite tv lake sara	online minnesota insurance exam crossword puzzles
microwave food safety	staphylococcal enteritis definition	microwave oven food safety
	salmonella enteritis definition	microwave baby food safety
	listeria monocytogenes prevention	microwave food safety studies
	e coli cdc	microwave food safety issues
	preventing cross contamination	foodsafety.com
what to cook in cast iron skillet	steak sauce substitute	cast iron skillet recipes
	montreal seasoning ingredients	how to cook with cast iron skillet
	ground turkey breakfast sausage	how to cook in a cast iron skillet
	how to cook steak on cast iron skillet	how to cook with a cast iron skillet
	reseason cast iron	chicken in cast iron skillet
iphone 6 repair services	mp3attic music	at&t iphone repair service
	donar ovulos en elche	iphone 5c repair service
	credit a la consommation rapide	iphone repair
	smart phone repair service	iphone service repair
	social security disability bronx ny	iphone repair services

Table 2: Examples of query rewrites with and without ad clicks in training data (bolded rewrites matched bid-terms)

makeup (no ads)	makeup (with ads)	snowboarding (no ads)	snowboarding (with ads)	seafood (no ads)	seafood (with ads)
makeup tips	lipstick	snowbaording	snowboards	sea food	**seafood restaurant**
fashion makeup	**mac makeup**	snow boarding	**snowboarding gear**	crab legs	**seafood restaurants**
make up	**makeup sets**	snowboarding information	**burton snowboarding**	best seafood	crab shack
makeup pictures	eye shadow	snowboarding jumps	**snowboard deals**	oysters	**seafood market**
makeup images	**makeup covergirl**	snowboard pics	**snowboards on sale**	lobster recipes	sea food
makeup tutorial	makeup items	shaun white snowboarding	snowboarding mountains	**seafood market**	**sea food menu**

embedding space was set to $D = 300$, context neighborhood size was set to 5 and content neighborhood size was set to 7. Finally, we used negative sampling to speed up the training, and used 10 random samples in each vector update.

5.3 Query rewriting models

We considered the following approaches in our empirical analysis, where each resulted in vector representation for 45 million most frequent queries.

1) word2vec$_{\text{news}}$ model was used as a simple baseline. Query vectors were constructed by summing publicly available word vectors for word tokens in a query (whitespace was used as a token separator), trained on Google News data set with English stopwords removed[1].

2) word2vec$_{\text{search}}$ query vectors constructed by summing word vectors for word tokens in a query, trained using $D_{content}$ data set.

3) content2vec model (cn2vec) was trained using $D_{content}$ where queries were used as a global context to the containing words, as illustrated in Figure 1b.

4) context2vec model (cx2vec) was trained using $D_{context}$, as illustrated in Figure 1a.

5) context-content2vec model (cx-cn2vec) used both $D_{content}$ and $D_{context}$ data to train query vectors, leveraging the two-layer architecture from Section 4.3. Since the model learns from both content and context, one of the motivations behind cx-cn2vec is to improve embeddings for queries that were not seen in many sessions. In Table 1 we give several illustrative examples of such tail queries. Unlike cx2vec, cx-cn2vec relies more on content in case of rare queries, and thus provides better rewrites. For example, at the time of creation of our data set the query "iphone 6 repair service" was a tail query, resulting in poor cx2vec rewrites such as "mp3attic music" or "social security disability bronx ny". On the other hand, cx-cn2vec provided more relevant rewrites.

[1]https://code.google.com/p/word2vec

6) cx-cn2vec$_{\text{ad}}$ model was trained using $D_{context}$ and D_{ad} (i.e., context data with ad clicks added). Training resulted in additional 8.5 million ad vectors.

As illustrated in Table 2, we can see that addition of D_{ad} resulted in quite different query rewrites than using a data set without ad clicks. For example, rewrites for query "makeup" mainly contain terms that are related to tips, tutorials, and pictures when no ads were used in training. Conversely, rewrites for the same query when clicks on ads are considered contain more commercial search terms.

In addition, given ad and query vectors in the same embedding space, we can easily retrieve similar queries for any given ad. This by-product is extremely useful for suggesting new bid keywords for specific categories of ads (note that in our system ads are categorized into one or more interest categories, such as "sports" or "travel"). As an example, in Figure 2 we show $K = 5{,}000$ most similar queries to ads in "automotive" and "air travel" categories. Keywords with higher cosine similarity are shown with larger font sizes. We can observe that the key concepts of the category are well captured with the most similar queries.

7) cx-cn2vec$_{\text{ad+link}}$ model was trained using $D_{content}$ and $D_{ad+link}$ (i.e., context data with ad clicks and link clicks added). Training resulted in additional 19 million search link vectors and 8.5 million ad vectors.

8) QFG$_{\text{ad+link}}$ model was trained using a click-flow graph constructed from $D_{ad+link}$ dataset, with additional 19 million search link vectors and 8.5 million ad vectors.

To produce rewrites for out-of-dictionary queries, embedding models generated their vectors by summing the existing vectors of word tokens within queries (excluding stopwords). Unlike the embedding methods, QFG could not produce rewrites for queries that were not seen in the graph.

Our evaluation did not include topic models such as LDA [5] or PLSA [19], as earlier research [20] found that these methods perform poorly on short text documents.

Table 3: Mean and standard deviation (in brackets) of query similarity (cosine distance) between pairs of editorially judged query rewrites (top: in-dictionary queries, bottom: out-of-dictionary queries)

grade	pairs	cn2vec	cx2vec	cx-cn2vec	cx-cn2vec$_{ad}$	**cx-cn2vec$_{ad+link}$**	word2vec$_{news}$	word2vec$_{search}$	QFG$_{ad+link}$
Excellent	1,518	0.630 (0.136)	0.658 (0.107)	0.669 (0.107)	0.668 (0.114)	**0.733 (0.094)**	0.818 (0.146)	0.648 (0.151)	0.329 (0.667)
Good	5,531	0.599 (0.136)	0.621 (0.125)	0.637 (0.100)	0.632 (0.104)	**0.683 (0.097)**	0.770 (0.152)	0.614 (0.155)	0.205 (0.574)
Fair	4,021	0.550 (0.167)	0.565 (0.129)	0.577 (0.124)	0.566 (0.130)	**0.605 (0.132)**	0.749 (0.190)	0.567 (0.173)	0.114 (0.366)
Bad	4,229	0.398 (0.196)	0.363 (0.170)	0.349 (0.184)	0.336 (0.187)	**0.425 (0.179)**	0.517 (0.280)	0.395 (0.201)	0.166 (0.584)
avg. p-value	-	1.39e-15	5.44e-26	8.27e-28	2.99e-30	**1e-100**	4.121e-07	1.014e-14	0.013
Excellent	2,119	0.791 (0.166)	0.623 (0.141)	0.628 (0.134)	0.623 (0.143)	**0.668 (0.147)**	0.824 (0.145)	0.790 (0.157)	-
Good	11,305	0.752 (0.155)	0.587 (0.135)	0.592 (0.130)	0.584 (0.137)	**0.612 (0.141)**	0.796 (0.145)	0.756 (0.156)	-
Fair	11,146	0.715 (0.136)	0.561 (0.145)	0.565 (0.139)	0.558 (0.146)	**0.584 (0.147)**	0.769 (0.175)	0.707 (0.141)	-
Bad	7,849	0.635 (0.199)	0.383 (0.211)	0.387 (0.209)	0.382 (0.212)	**0.410 (0.208)**	0.509 (0.311)	0.602 (0.208)	-
avg. p-value	-	4.99e-26	1.137e-27	4.0423e-32	1.196e-30	**2.926e-40**	2.038e-16	9.388e-22	-

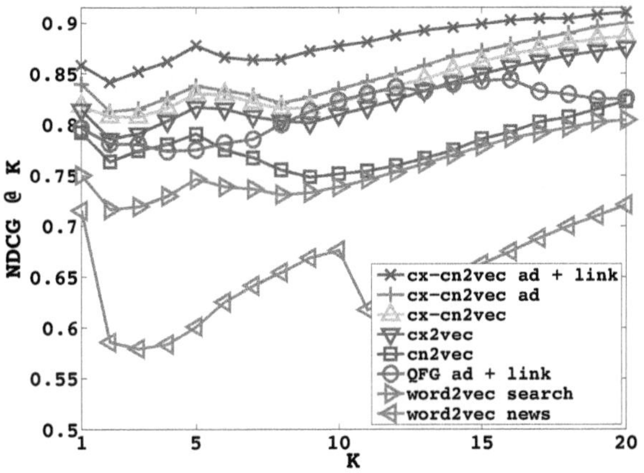

Figure 3: NDCG@K for different competing methods

5.4 Evaluation

In the following two sections we show our main experimental results, where we report performance of the competing approaches in terms of relevance and ad coverage of query rewrites. We also provide examples of rewrites by cx-cn2vec$_{ad+link}$ method in an online video[2].

5.4.1 *Relevance*

We used editorial judgments of query rewrites to compare query rewriting methods in terms of relevance.

In-house data. The first data set we used is an in-house data set consisting of the query and several rewrites produced by current production system that were graded editorially. The editors were instructed to assign the following grades: *bad*, *fair*, *good*, and *excellent*. In total, the data set includes more than 40,000 (query, rewrite, grade) tuples, such as ("nfl news", "latest nfl news", "excellent"), ("nfl news", "nfl shooting", "fair"), ("nfl news", "nfl rumor", "good"), ("metro transit", "metro pcs", "bad").

Given a query we ranked the rewrite candidates based on a model's output score and retrieved the top K candidates. Next, we computed the NDCG metric using editorial grades of rewrites as labels (0 for bad, 1 for fair, 2 for good, and 3 for excellent) at values of K ranging from 1 to 20. In Figure 3 we report the results for different models.

[2]http://youtu.be/pvfFQSCYhqI

By considering the reported results, several conclusions can be drawn. Regarding models that did not utilize search session data (i.e., word2vec$_{news}$, word2vec$_{search}$, and cn2vec), we can see that the word embeddings specifically tailored for search queries perform better than using word embeddings learned using news data. In addition, learning query vectors as global context of words using cn2vec leads to slightly better results than directly summing the words. However, all three models performed worse than the QFG$_{ad+link}$ baseline method, which made use of the co-occurrence of queries, ads, and links in search sessions. Query embeddings trained directly on search sessions, i.e. cx2vec, already outperform QFG$_{ad+link}$. Further improvements were observed when embeddings were learned from both context and content. Finally, incorporating ad and link click events showed incremental boost in relevance. The largest gain was observed when links were added as an additional context.

In addition, in Table 3 we report average similarities of (query, rewrite) pairs in each editorial grade group. It is important to note that scores are comparable only within the same method and not across methods. For conclusive comparison we calculated the level of separation between the groups by p-value of t-test, which tests the hypothesis that the means of two neighboring grades are equal. By comparing p-values reported we can quantify which method does the best job of separating the four grade groups. Findings are similar to the ones from Figure 3. Additionally, we find that QFG$_{ad+link}$ method has issues with "bad" grade group, and that without incorporating search context, the embedding models have similar average scores in "good" and "fair" grade groups. As expected, separation improves when embedding models incorporate search context, with the standard deviation between the groups reducing even further when ads and links were considered as an additional context.

In the case when one or both queries from the editorial grade list were not found in a model, we generated the vectors by summing vectors of query tokens. Bottom part of Table 3 shows results for such cases. We can observe that similar conclusion hold even for such out-of-dictionary queries.

TREC data. The second data we used was a publicly available TREC Web Track data set[3] from 2009 to 2013, containing a total of 250 queries. Using the competing methods we produced 5 rewrites for each query, and evaluated the result editorially. The editors were given instructions to rate the rewrites in the following way: grade 0 if the rewrite is irrelevant, grade 1 if relevant, and grade 2 if it is excellent.

[3]http://trec.nist.gov/

Table 4: Examples of rewrites obtained using the competing methods (bolded rewrites matched bid-terms)

Original	$QFG_{ad+link}$	cn2vec	cx-cn2vec	$cx\text{-}cn2vec_{ad}$
wedding budget calculator	wedding budget	monthly budget calculator	**wedding planning checklist**	**wedding budget worksheet**
	wedding cost calculator	online budget calculator	wedding budget template	wedding vendors
	wedding calculator	**budget wedding**	**wedding budget worksheet**	**the knot**
	wedding cost breakdown	budget calculator free	wedding checklist printable	wedding planning checklist
	wedding budget worksheet	average wedding budget	wedding costs average	**wedding wire**
gmat prep classes	gmat prep	gmat prep online	**gmat preparation courses**	**gmat study books**
	gmat classes	gmat prep courses	sample gmat tests	**gmat test prep classes**
	gmat	**gmat online prep**	**gmat prep class**	**gmat prep class**
	kaplan gmat course	online gmat prep	which is easier gre or gmat	**kaplan gre courses**
	kaplan gmat	best gmat prep courses	how much is the gmat	free gmat sample tests
how to build a fence	building a fence	how to build fence	**how to build a fence on a hill**	how to build a fence minecraft
	build your own fence	build fence	how to fence a yard	fancy fences and gates
	how to build a wood fence	build a fence	how to build a fence gate	**how to build a metal fence**
	do it yourself fence	how to build a cheap fence	how to build a brick wall fence	**home depot com fencing**
	how to build a privacy fence	build your own fence	**how to build a fence video**	**back yard fences**
solar panels	**solar panels for homes**	solar panels for your home	**solar power**	**solar power**
	solar electric panels	solar panels for residential homes	**solar energy**	**solar panels for homes**
	solar power	**solar panels for**	**solar panels for homes**	**solar panels on sale**
	ebay solar panels	solar panels on ebay	**solar power systems**	**solar panel kits**
	how to make solar panels	davis solar	solar panel	**solar panels for sale**

Editorial grades for each method as well as the Levenshtein distance [29] were averaged and reported in Table 5. We can see that the $cx\text{-}cn2vec_{ad+link}$ query embedding method, learned from query content and search session context including ad and link clicks, returned the most relevant rewrites and outperformed the baseline QFG method. Once more, learning query embeddings from content of queries on its own was not enough to outperform QFG. Interestingly, there was just a small difference between cx2vec and cx-cn2vec models. It can be explained by the fact that cx-cn2vec generally improves rewrites for tail queries, while TREC data set mostly consists of frequent queries.

In addition to providing highly relevant rewrites, $cx\text{-}cn2vec_{ad+link}$ showed the highest diversity, a favorable property for rewrite algorithms. Considering the performance in terms of Levenshtein distance, we can observe that rewrites produced by models which learned from content are less diverse than the ones produced by approaches that modeled query context during training.

Examples of query rewrites obtained by the competing methods are given in Table 4. As can be seen, there exist significant differences between the rewrites of the competing approaches. As discussed earlier, the content-based model cn2vec is sensitive to cases when the query words appeared in different contexts across the query dictionary. For example, words "budget" and "calculator" from the query "wedding budget calculator" mostly appeared in more general financial contexts. For this reason in the first 5 rewrites we have queries that are not related to wedding. The model that utilized both content and context data cx-cn2vec outputs highly relevant, interesting rewrites that capture a number of meanings and contexts of the original query. The model that considered ads during training $cx\text{-}cn2vec_{ad}$ produced more commercial rewrites, referencing stores and sales. We also bolded queries that matched the actual bidterms in the system, discussed in more detail in the following experiment. Examples of query rewrites produced by $cx\text{-}cn2vec_{ad+link}$ are shown in an online video[4]. The video mostly covers queries from TREC 2010 data set.

[4]http://youtu.be/n5kHKyKQAa8

Table 5: Comparison of query rewrite methods (TREC data)

Method	Editorial grade	Levenshtein dist.
$QFG_{ad+link}$	1.0441	11.70
$word2vec_{news}$	0.9189	10.91
$word2vec_{search}$	0.9492	11.32
cn2vec	0.9571	11.37
cx2vec	1.1273	13.79
cx-cn2vec	1.1343	13.13
$cx\text{-}cn2vec_{ad}$	1.2281	13.62
$cx\text{-}cn2vec_{ad+link}$	**1.2457**	13.25

5.4.2 Ad coverage

In the previous section we showed the advantage of proposed methods in terms of relevance. In this section we evaluate how beneficial those rewrites are from the ad matching perspective. It is of fundamental interest to sponsored search to ensure that the rewrites being provided as alternatives to the users' queries match as many additional relevant bidterms as possible. The percentage of rewrites that match bid terms is defined as *coverage*. We conducted an off-line experiment to compare query rewriting methods: 1) on an in-house dataset of 2,000 editorially selected queries which the editors deemed representative of the query set; and 2) on the TREC data set. For each query in the data sets we generated $K = 5$ rewrites and look-up bidterms in our current sponsored search demand. We report average coverage (relative improvement over QFG) over the entire set of queries for each of the two data sets. Table 6 summarizes the results of our analysis.

To estimate monetary value of each query rewriting method we used two proxy measures. First, for the query rewrites produced by each method we look-up the bid amounts for the queries that were matched in the bidterm database. We report the total sum of these amounts, and refer to this metric as "revenue potential". In addition, for each rewrite method we calculated effective cost per mille (eCPM). Given a query rewrite q, and an ad a for which q was a bidterm, we calculated eCPM value e_{qa} by multi-

Table 6: Relative improvement over the QFG method of different query rewrite methods on query-bid data

	In-house data			TREC data		
Method	Coverage	Revenue potential	eCPM	Coverage	Revenue potential	eCPM
$\text{QFG}_{\text{ad+link}}$	1.00	1.00	1.00	1.00	1.00	1.00
$\text{word2vec}_{\text{news}}$	0.76	0.39	0.46	0.32	0.66	0.73
$\text{word2vec}_{\text{search}}$	0.87	0.58	0.77	0.57	0.84	0.75
cn2vec	0.89	0.62	0.84	0.59	0.84	0.74
cx2vec	1.16	1.80	1.41	1.41	1.16	1.20
cx-cn2vec	1.18	1.86	1.38	1.44	1.21	1.19
cx-cn2vec$_{\text{ad}}$	**1.20**	**1.89**	**1.60**	**1.52**	**1.35**	**1.31**
cx-cn2vec$_{\text{ad+link}}$	1.18	1.88	1.45	1.50	1.28	1.22

plying cost per click (CPC) dollar amount and the click-through rate (CTR) of that (query, ad) pair, computed as number of ad clicks divided by number of ad impressions. Finally, we report the weighted sum of eCPM's, $\sum_q \sum_a w_q e_{qa}$, where the weight w_q is proportional to the number of times the query appeared in the search logs. Considering the results presented in Table 6, we can see that query embedding models trained using news documents and query content achieved lower average coverage than QFG method. However, QFG was in turn outperformed by the coverage of rewrites produced using query embedding approaches.

Moreover, by taking the results from both experiments into account, it can be concluded that cx-cn2vec$_{ads+links}$ is the best choice as it achieves the highest relevance while maintaining large ad coverage. When link clicks were added on top of ad clicks we observed a large improvement in relevance, with ad coverage remaining almost the same.

6. CONCLUSION

In this paper we described novel query rewriting methods based on recently proposed neural language models. The methods learn low-dimensional, distributed representations of search queries based on context (context2vec), content (content2vec), or combined context and content (context-content2vec) of the queries within search sessions. To specialize the query rewrites for sponsored search application, we further incorporated ad clicks and search link clicks into the training data. We evaluated the proposed methods using both in-house and publicly available TREC data sets. When compared to the current state-of-the-art approaches, we showed that context-content2vec generates the most relevant query rewrites, while at the same time maintains high level of ad coverage. The results clearly indicate significant advantages of context-content2vec over the state-of-the-art query rewrite algorithms, and suggest high monetization potential of the query embedding approach to the task of sponsored search advertising. In our ongoing work, we plan to experiment with more involved search sessionization algorithms and navigational query detection algorithms.

7. REFERENCES

[1] M. Aly, A. Hatch, V. Josifovski, and V. K. Narayanan. Web-scale user modeling for targeting. *WWW*, 2012.

[2] R. Baeza-Yates, C. Hurtado, and M. Mendoza. Query recommendation using query logs in search engines. In *Proceedings of the 2004 International Conference on Current Trends in Database Technology*, EDBT'04, pages 588–596, Berlin, Heidelberg, 2004. Springer-Verlag.

[3] R. Baeza-Yates, B. Ribeiro-Neto, et al. *Modern information retrieval*, volume 463. ACM press New York, 1999.

[4] Y. Bengio, H. Schwenk, J.-S. Senécal, F. Morin, and J.-L. Gauvain. Neural probabilistic language models. In *Innovations in Machine Learning*, pages 137–186. Springer, 2006.

[5] D. M. Blei, A. Y. Ng, and M. I. Jordan. Latent dirichlet allocation. *the Journal of machine Learning research*, 3:993–1022, 2003.

[6] P. Boldi, F. Bonchi, C. Castillo, D. Donato, A. Gionis, and S. Vigna. The query-flow graph: Model and applications. In *Proceedings of the 17th ACM Conference on Information and Knowledge Management*, CIKM '08, pages 609–618, New York, NY, USA, 2008. ACM.

[7] F. Bonchi, R. Perego, F. Silvestri, H. Vahabi, and R. Venturini. Efficient query recommendations in the long tail via center-piece subgraphs. In *Proceedings of the 35th International ACM SIGIR Conference on Research and Development in Information Retrieval*, SIGIR '12, pages 345–354, New York, NY, USA, 2012. ACM.

[8] A. Bordes, N. Usunier, A. Garcia-Duran, J. Weston, and O. Yakhnenko. Translating embeddings for modeling multi-relational data. In *Advances in Neural Information Processing Systems*, pages 2787–2795, 2013.

[9] D. E. Bowman, M. L. Hamrick, T. R. Kohn, R. E. Ortega, and J. R. Spiegel. Refining search queries by the suggestion of correlated terms from prior searches, Dec. 21 1999. US Patent 6,006,225.

[10] A. Broder. A taxonomy of web search. In *ACM Sigir forum*, volume 36, pages 3–10. ACM, 2002.

[11] A. Z. Broder, P. Ciccolo, M. Fontoura, E. Gabrilovich, V. Josifovski, and L. Riedel. Search advertising using web relevance feedback. In *Proceedings of the 17th ACM Conference on Information and Knowledge Management*, CIKM '08, pages 1013–1022, New York, NY, USA, 2008. ACM.

[12] Y. Chen, D. Pavlov, and J. F. Canny. Large-scale behavioral targeting. *KDD*, 2009.

[13] R. Collobert, J. Weston, L. Bottou, M. Karlen, K. Kavukcuoglu, and P. Kuksa. Natural language processing (almost) from scratch. *The Journal of Machine Learning Research*, 12:2493–2537, 2011.

[14] N. Djuric, H. Wu, V. Radosavljevic, M. Grbovic, and N. Bhamidipati. Hierarchical neural language models for joint representation of streaming documents and their content. In *International World Wide Web Conference (WWW)*, 2015.

[15] D. C. Fain and J. O. Pedersen. Sponsored search: A brief history. *Bulletin of the American Society for Information Science and Technology*, 32(2):12–13, 2006.

[16] D. Gayo-Avello. A survey on session detection methods in query logs and a proposal for future evaluation. *Inf. Sci.*, 179(12):1822–1843, May 2009.

[17] M. Grbovic, N. Djuric, V. Radosavljevic, and N. Bhamidipati. Search retargeting using directed query embeddings. In *International World Wide Web Conference (WWW)*, 2015.

[18] M. Grbovic and S. Vucetic. Generating ad targeting rules using sparse principal component analysis with constraints. *WWW*, 2014.

[19] T. Hofmann. Probabilistic latent semantic indexing. In *Proceedings of the 22nd annual international ACM SIGIR conference on Research and development in information retrieval*, pages 50–57. ACM, 1999.

[20] L. Hong and B. D. Davison. Empirical study of topic modeling in twitter. In *Proceedings of the First Workshop on Social Media Analytics*, pages 80–88. ACM, 2010.

[21] A. K. Jain, L. Hong, and S. Pankanti. Iab internet advertising revenue report: 2013 first six months' results. Technical report, Interactive Advertising Bureau, 2013.

[22] B. J. Jansen and T. Mullen. Sponsored search: An overview of the concept, history, and technology. *International Journal of Electronic Business*, 6(2):114–131, 2008.

[23] R. Jones, B. Rey, O. Madani, and W. Greiner. Generating query substitutions. In *Proceedings of the 15th international conference on World Wide Web*, pages 387–396. ACM, 2006.

[24] F. Keller and M. Lapata. Using the web to obtain frequencies for unseen bigrams. *Computational linguistics*, 29(3):459–484, 2003.

[25] R. Kiros, R. Zemel, and R. Salakhutdinov. Multimodal neural language models. In *Proceedings of the 31th International Conference on Machine Learning*, 2014.

[26] R. Kiros, R. S. Zemel, and R. Salakhutdinov. A multiplicative model for learning distributed text-based attribute representations. *arXiv preprint arXiv:1406.2710*, 2014.

[27] V. Lavrenko and W. B. Croft. Relevance based language models. In *SIGIR*, pages 120–127. ACM, 2001.

[28] Q. V. Le and T. Mikolov. Distributed representations of sentences and documents. *arXiv preprint arXiv:1405.4053*, 2014.

[29] V. Levenshtein. Binary codes capable of correcting deletions, insertions, and reversals. In *Soviet Physics-Doklady*, volume 10, 1966.

[30] T. Mikolov, K. Chen, G. Corrado, and J. Dean. Efficient estimation of word representations in vector space. *CoRR*, abs/1301.3781, 2013.

[31] T. Mikolov, I. Sutskever, K. Chen, G. S. Corrado, and J. Dean. Distributed representations of words and phrases and their compositionality. In *Advances in Neural Information Processing Systems*, pages 3111–3119, 2013.

[32] S. Pandey, M. Aly, A. Bagherjeiran, A. Hatch, P. Ciccolo, A. Ratnaparkhi, and M. Zinkevich. Learning to target: what works for behavioral targeting. *CIKM*, 2011.

[33] B. Perozzi, R. Al-Rfou, and S. Skiena. Deepwalk: Online learning of social representations. *arXiv preprint arXiv:1403.6652*, 2014.

[34] PwC. Global entertainment and media outlook: 2014-2018. Technical report, 2014.

[35] C. Silverstein, H. Marais, M. Henzinger, and M. Moricz. Analysis of a very large web search engine query log. In *ACm SIGIR Forum*, volume 33, pages 6–12. ACM, 1999.

[36] F. Silvestri. Mining query logs: Turning search usage data into knowledge. *Found. Trends Inf. Retr.*, 4:1–174, Jan. 2010.

[37] R. Socher, D. Chen, C. D. Manning, and A. Ng. Reasoning with neural tensor networks for knowledge base completion. In *Advances in Neural Information Processing Systems*, pages 926–934, 2013.

[38] J. Turian, L. Ratinov, and Y. Bengio. Word representations: a simple and general method for semi-supervised learning. In *Proceedings of the 48th Annual Meeting of the Association for Computational Linguistics*, pages 384–394. Association for Computational Linguistics, 2010.

[39] H. Vahabi, M. Ackerman, D. Loker, R. Baeza-Yates, and A. Lopez-Ortiz. Orthogonal query recommendation. In *Proceedings of the 7th ACM Conference on Recommender Systems*, RecSys '13, pages 33–40, New York, NY, USA, 2013. ACM.

[40] W. V. Zhang and R. Jones. Comparing click logs and editorial labels for training query rewriting. In *WWW 2007 Workshop on Query Log Analysis: Social And Technological Challenges*, 2007.

Retrieval of Relevant Opinion Sentences for New Products

Dae Hoon Park
Department of Computer Science
University of Illinois at Urbana-Champaign
Urbana, IL 61801, USA
dpark34@illinois.edu

Hyun Duk Kim
Twitter Inc.
1355 Market St Suite 900
San Francisco, CA 94103, USA
hkim@twitter.com

ChengXiang Zhai
Department of Computer Science
University of Illinois at Urbana-Champaign
Urbana, IL 61801, USA
czhai@cs.illinois.edu

Lifan Guo
TCL Research America
2870 Zanker Road
San Jose, CA 95134, USA
GuoLifan@tcl.com

ABSTRACT

With the rapid development of Internet and E-commerce, abundant product reviews have been written by consumers who bought the products. These reviews are very useful for consumers to optimize their purchasing decisions. However, since the reviews are all written by consumers who have bought and used a product, there are generally very few or even no reviews available for a new product or an unpopular product. We study the novel problem of retrieving relevant opinion sentences from the reviews of other products using specifications of a new or unpopular product as query. Our key idea is to leverage product specifications to assess product similarity between the query product and other products and extract relevant opinion sentences from the similar products where a consumer may find useful discussions. Then, we provide ranked opinion sentences for the query product that has no user-generated reviews. We first propose a popular summarization method and its modified version to solve the problem. Then, we propose our novel probabilistic methods. Experiment results show that the proposed methods can effectively retrieve useful opinion sentences for products that have no reviews.

Categories and Subject Descriptors

H.3.3 [**Information Storage and Retrieval**]: Information Search and Retrieval—*Retrieval models*; H.4.0 [**Information Systems Applications**]: General

General Terms

Algorithms, Design

Keywords

opinion mining, probabilistic information retrieval

SIGIR'15, August 09 - 13, 2015, Santiago, Chile.

DOI: http://dx.doi.org/10.1145/2766462.2767748.

1. INTRODUCTION

The role of product reviews has been more and more important. Reevoo, a social commerce solutions provider, surveyed 1,000 consumers on shopping habits and found that 88 percent of them sometimes or always consult customer reviews before purchase.[1] According to the survey, 60 percent of them said that they were more likely to purchase from a site that has customer reviews on. Also, they considered customer reviews more influential (48%) than advertising (24%) or recommendations from sales assistants (22%). With the development of Internet and E-commerce, people's shopping habits have changed, and we need to take a closer look at it in order to provide the best shopping environment to consumers.

Even though product reviews are considered important to consumers, the majority of the products has only a few or no reviews. Products that are not released yet or newly released generally do not have enough reviews. Also, unpopular products in the market lack reviews because they are not sold and exposed to consumers enough. How can we help consumers who are interested in buying products with no reviews? In this paper, we propose methods to automatically retrieve review text for such products based on reviews of other products. Our key insight is that opinions on similar products may be applicable to the product that lacks reviews. For example, if products X and Y have the same CPU clock rate, then people's opinion on CPU clock rate for product X may be applicable to that for product Y as well. The similarity between products can be computed based on product specifications which are often available, where an example of product specifications is shown in Figure 1. %Here is an example of review text we manually retrieved for a certain product's specification "Resolution: 12.1 megapixels" from real reviews of products that have the same resolution.

> 12.1 MP captures very minute details even at highest zoom. This 12.1 megapixel megazoom offers an awesome value as the pictures it produces are on par with some cheap DSLRs. I will not longer bring my big DSR camera on my vacations. 12MP is too much, I use it with 8MP - that's more than plenty. What I like most about the W200 is my ability to get crystal clear 4000x3000 12.1 meg photos without having to

[1]https://www.reevoo.com/news/half-of-consumers-find-social-content-useful-when-shopping-online/

Feature	*Value*
AE/AF Control	FlexiZone
Face Detection	Automatic Face Tracking technology
Digital Video Format	MOV
Image Recording Format	RAW + JPEG
Max Video Resolution	1920 x 1080
AV Interfaces	composite video/audio
Manufacturer	Canon

Figure 1: A part of product specifications in CNET.com.

> spend a couple of thousand dollars on an digital SLR camera body and then even more cash on the accessories (e.g. lens).

Even though these sentences are not necessarily coherent opinions, they are clearly very useful for users to understand the product feature and get access to relevant discussion of opinions. Since a user would hardly have a clue about opinions on a new product, such a retrieved review text can be expected to be useful. As a minimum, it can be very useful to help users prioritizing what to read in the existing reviews of other products. Not only from a consumer's perspective, but also from a manufacturer's perspective, such techniques would be beneficial to collect opinions on its new or unpopular products. From the retrieved opinions, the manufacturers would be able to predict what consumers would think even before their product release and react to the predicted feedback in advance.

This paper makes the following contributions:

1. We introduce and study a novel problem of relevant opinion retrieval for products that do not have reviews in order to provide useful information to consumers and manufacturers. To the best of our knowledge, no previous work has addressed this problem.

2. To solve the problem, we propose a new probabilistic retrieval method, Translation model, Specifications Generation model, and Review and Specifications Generation model, as well as standard summarization model MEAD, its modified version MEAD-SIM, and standard ad-hoc retrieval method. Our suggested probabilistic methods are also able to retrieve per-feature opinions for a query product.

3. We create a new data set for evaluating the new problem and conduct experiments to show that our translation model indeed retrieves useful opinions and outperforms other baseline models. We also provide an interesting way to evaluate retrieved sentences for new products.

In order to evaluate the automatically retrieved opinions for a new or unpopular product, we pretend that the query product does not have reviews and predict its review text based on similar products. Then, we compare the predicted review text with the query product's actual reviews to evaluate the performance of suggested methods. Experiment results show that our translation model effectively retrieves opinions for a product without reviews and it significantly outperforms baseline methods.

2. RELATED WORKS

Reviews are one of the most popular sources in opinion analysis. Opinion retrieval and summarization techniques attracted a lot of attentions because of its usefulness in Web 2.0 environment. There are several surveys which summarize the existing opinion mining work [9, 21, 14]. Compared to text data in other general retrieval problems, opinionated articles such as product reviews have some different characteristics. In opinion analysis, analyzing polarities of input opinions are crucial. Also, majority of the opinion retrieval works are based on product feature (aspect) analysis. They first find sub-topics (features) of a target and show positive and negative opinions for each aspect. By further segmenting the input texts into the smaller units, they showed more details in a structured way [7, 15, 16, 18, 25, 28, 10]. Meanwhile, product reviews have been also employed to predict ratings [20, 5] or sales [3] of a product. However, no existing work addressed the problem of retrieving opinion sentences for new products yet.

In this paper, we also utilize unique characteristics of product data: specifications (structured data) as well as reviews (unstructured data). Although product specifications have been provided in many e-commerce web sites, there are only a limited number of studies that utilized specifications for product review analysis. Zhou and Chaovalit [32] performed sentiment classification on reviews using domain ontology database, which may be regarded as product specifications. Bhattattacharya *et al.* [2] employed IMDb's structured data to categorize documents, and Yu *et al.* [30] built an aspect hierarchy using product specifications and reviews. Wang *et al.* [29] and Peñalver-Martínez *et al.* [23] also employed product specifications to summarize product features. Product reviews and specifications were jointly modeled using topic models by Duan et al. [4] to improve product search and by Park et al. [22] to generate augmented specifications with useful information. Park et al. [22] retrieved review sentences for each (feature, value) pair, but they did not study their model's performance on products with no reviews. In addition, their model does not consider similarity among products or specifications, which is an important factor for the problem. Likewise, there are a few studies that employed product specifications, but their goals are different from ours.

Our work is related to text summarization, which considers centrality of text. Automatic text summarization techniques have been studied for a long time due to the need of handling large amount of electronic text data [19, 11, 6]. Automatic summarization techniques can be categorized into two types, extractive summary and abstractive summary. Extractive summarization makes a summary by selecting representative text segments, usually sentences, from the original documents. Abstractive summarization does not directly reuse the existing sentences but generates sentences based on text analysis. Our work is similar to extractive summarization in that we select sentences from original documents but different in that we retrieve sentences for an entity that does not have any text. Among the previous work, MEAD [26] is one of the most popular public extractive summarization toolkits, which supports multi-document summarization in general domain. The goal of MEAD is different from ours in that we want a summary for a specific product, and also MEAD does not utilize external structured data (specifications).

Cold start problem in recommendation systems [27], where no one has rated new items yet, is also related to our problem. However, unlike rating connections between items and users, each user review carries its unique and complex meaning, which makes the problem more challenging. Moreover, our goal is to provide useful relevant opinions about a product, not recommending a product. XML retrieval [12] that utilizes structured information of documents is also related to our work, in that reviews and specifications can be represented as a special XML. However, unlike general XML retrieval, in this paper, we propose more specialized methods for product reviews using product category and specifications. In addition, because we require the retrieved sentences to be central in reviews, we consider both centrality and relevance while general retrieval methods focus on relevance only. As far as we know, none of the existing work tried to solve the same problem as ours.

3. PROBLEM DEFINITION

The product data consists of N products $\{P_1, ..., P_N\}$. Each product P_i consists of its set of reviews $R_i = \{r_1, ..., r_m\}$ and its set of specifications $S_i = \{s_{i,1}, ..., s_{i,F}\}$, where a specification $s_{i,k}$ is a feature-value pair, $(f_k, v_{i,k})$, and F is the number of features. Given a query product P_z, for which R_z is not available, our goal is to retrieve a sequence of relevant opinion sentences T in K words for P_z.

Note that our problem setup is a mixture of retrieval and summarization. On the one hand, it can be regarded as a ranking problem, similar to retrieval; on the other hand, it can also be regarded as a summarization problem since we restrict the total number of words in the retrieved opinions .

This is a new problem that has not been addressed in any previous work. The problem is challenging for several reasons. Retrieved sentences for P_z should conform to its specifications S_z while we do not know which sentences are about which specific feature-value pair. In addition, the retrieved sentences should be central across relevant reviews so that they reflect central opinions. Despite the challenges, we try to show that achieving the goal is feasible. In the next a few sections, we propose multiple methods to solve the problem.

4. OVERALL APPROACH

When reviews are not available for a product, a consumer has no way to obtain opinions on it. In order to help consumers in such situation, we believe that product specifications are the most valuable source to find similar products. We thus leverage product specifications to find similar products and choose relevant sentences from their user reviews. In this approach, we assume that if products have similar specifications, the reviews are similar as well. For example, here is an actual review sentence from the review of a digital camera that takes a picture at high resolution: "the best camera I have ever owned, takes unbelievable crisp sharp photos with it's 16.1 Megapixels." It is admitted that the consumer is very impressed with the feature-value pair, ("Resolution", "16.1 Megapixels"), and we can expect that other digital cameras with the same feature-value pair could impress their consumers as well. The assumption may not be valid in some cases, *i.e.*, same specifications may yield very different user reviews. We thus try to retrieve "central" opinions from similar products so that the retrieved sentences can become clearly useful.

5. SIMILARITY BETWEEN PRODUCTS

We assume that similar products have similar feature-value pairs (specifications). In general, there are many ways to define a similarity function. We are interested in finding how well a basic similarity function will work although our framework can obviously accommodate any other similarity functions. Therefore, we simply define the similarity function between products as

$$SIM_p(P_i, P_j) = \frac{\sum_{k=1}^{F} w_k SIM_f(s_{i,k}, s_{j,k})}{\sum_{k=1}^{F} w_k} \quad (1)$$

where w_k is a weight for the feature f_k, and the weights $\{w_1, ..., w_F\}$ are assumed identical ($w_k = 1$) in this study, so the similarity function becomes

$$SIM_p(P_i, P_j) = \frac{\sum_{k=1}^{F} SIM_f(s_{i,k}, s_{j,k})}{F} \quad (2)$$

where $SIM_f(s_{i,k}, s_{j,k})$ is a cosine similarity for feature f_k between P_i and P_j and is defined as

$$SIM_f(s_{i,k}, s_{j,k}) = \frac{\mathbf{v_{i,k}} \cdot \mathbf{v_{j,k}}}{\sqrt{\sum_{v \in \mathbf{v_{i,k}}} v^2}\sqrt{\sum_{v \in \mathbf{v_{j,k}}} v^2}} \quad (3)$$

where $\mathbf{v_{i,k}}$ and $\mathbf{v_{j,k}}$ are phrase vectors in values $v_{i,k}$ and $v_{j,k}$, respectively. Both $SIM_p(P_i, P_j)$ and $SIM_f(s_{i,k}, s_{j,k})$ range from 0 to 1.

In this paper, we define the phrases as comma-delimited feature values. $SIM_f(s_{i,k}, s_{j,k})$ is similar to cosine similarity function, which is used often for measuring document similarity in Information Retrieval (IR), but the difference is that we use a phrase as a basic unit while a word unit is usually adopted in IR. We use a phrase as a basic unit because majority of the words may overlap in two very different feature values. For example, the specification phrases "Memory Stick Duo", "Memory Stick PRO-HG Duo", "Memory Stick PRO Duo", and "Memory Stick PRO Duo Mark2" have high word cosine similarities among themselves since they at least have 3 common words while the performances of the specifications are very different. Thus, our similarity function with phrase unit counts a match only if the phrases are the same.

6. METHODS

In this section, we suggest multiple methods for relevant opinion sentences retrieval. We first suggest a standard summarization tool, MEAD [26]. In order to make up for the MEAD's weak points, we also suggest modified version of MEAD. Then, we propose our probabilistic models to solve the problem.

6.1 MEAD: Retrieval by Centroid

For our problem, text retrieval based only on query-relevance is not desirable. The retrieved sentences need to be central in other reviews in order to obtain central opinions about specifications. For example, if there are more opinions that contains a word "big" than a word "small" for a certain feature-value pair, it is desired to assign higher score to the sentences having the word "big". However, since the query contains only feature-value pair words, classic information retrieval approaches are not able to prefer such sentences. Therefore, we suggest using a method that considers centrality among sentences.

MEAD [26] is a popular centroid-based summarization tool for multiple documents, and it was shown to effectively generate summaries from a large corpus. It provides an auto-generated summary for multiple documents. For a corpus R, a score of ith sentence t in a document is computed by sum of centroid and position scores of words, which is defined as

$$score(t; R) = w_c C_t + w_o O_t \quad (4)$$

where C_t is a sum of centroid scores of words in t, which is defined as $C_t = \sum_w C_{w,t}$, and O_t is a position score, which gives higher score to the sentences appearing earlier in a document and defined as $O_t = \frac{(n-i+1)}{n} \cdot C_{max}$ where n is the number of sentences in the document and C_{max} is the maximum centroid score in the document. Centroid score of a word, $C_{w,t}$, is a TFIDF value in the corpus R, and w_c and w_o are weights for C_t and O_t, respectively. Please refer to [26] for more details.

In order to retrieve sentences that are likely to be relevant to the query product P_z, which has no reviews, we employ specifications to find products similar to P_z and use the similarity as a clue for finding relevant sentences. Since the score formula (4) utilizes only centrality and does not consider relevance to the query product, we augment it with product similarity to P_z so that we can find sentences that are query-relevant and central at the same time. In addition, MEAD employs position score that is reasonable for news articles, but it may not be appropriate for reviews; unlike news articles, it is hard to say that the sentences appearing earlier in the reviews are more important than those appearing later. Thus, we remove position score term from formula (4), and we augment it with similarity to query. The new score function is defined as

$$score(t, S_y; R, S_z) = C_t \cdot SIM_p(S_y, S_z) \tag{5}$$

where t is a sentence in a review for product P_y and SIM_p (S_y, S_z) is a product similarity between P_y and the query product P_z, which is defined in equation (2).

6.2 Probabilistic Retrieval

To solve the problem in a more principled way, we introduce our probabilistic methods. Query likelihood retrieval model [1], which assumes that a document generates a query, has been shown to work well for ad-hoc information retrieval. Similarly, we attempt to generate the query specifications S_z from a candidate sentence t via several generative scenarios.

6.2.1 Specifications Generation Model

The generative story is described as follows. Each sentence t from reviews of its product P_y first generates its specifications S_y. The specifications S_y then generates the query specifications S_z. Following the dependencies among variables, the scoring function is defined as

$$\begin{aligned} score(t, S_y; R, S_z) &\propto p(t, S_y|S_z) \\ &= \frac{p(S_z|S_y)p(S_y|t)p(t)}{p(S_z)} \end{aligned} \tag{6}$$

We can interpret $p(t, S_y|S_z)$ as the probability that t and S_y satisfy information needs of a user given S_z. $p(S_z|S_y)$ measures proximity of S_y to S_z. $p(S_y|t)$ measures proximity of t to S_y, and $p(t)$ is a general preference on t. Since we assume no preference on sentences, we ignore $p(t)$ for ranking. $p(S_z)$ is also ignored because it does not affect the ranking of sentences for S_z. Thus, the formula assigns high score to a sentence if its specifications S_y match S_z well and the sentence t matches its specifications S_y well. $p(t, S_y|S_z)$ is then defined as

$$\begin{aligned} p(t, S_y|S_z) &\propto p(S_z|S_y)p(S_y|t) \\ &= \sum_{k=1}^{F} p(s_{z,k}|s_{y,k})p(s_{y,k}|t) \end{aligned} \tag{7}$$

where a set of specifications such as S_y is decomposed into feature-value pairs $s_{y,k}$. We assume that a k'th feature-value pair of one specification set generates only the k'th feature-value pair of another specification set, not other feature-value pairs. This is to ensure that sentences not related to a specification $s_{z,k}$ are scored low even if their word score $p(s_{y,k}|t)$ is high. $p(s_{z,k}|s_{y,k})$, proximity of $s_{y,k}$ to $s_{z,k}$, is estimated as follows.

$$p(s_{z,k}|s_{y,k}) \propto \frac{SIM_f(s_{z,k}, s_{y,k})}{\sum_{s \in Distinct(k)} SIM_f(s, s_{y,k})} \tag{8}$$

where $Distinct(k)$ is a set of distinct feature-value pairs for a feature f_k. $p(s_{y,k}|t)$ is defined as

$$p(s_{y,k}|t) = \prod_{w \in s_{y,k}} p(w|t) = \prod_{w \in U} p(w|t)^{c(w, s_{y,k})} \tag{9}$$

where U is a vocabulary set in corpus R, and $c(w, s_{y,k})$ is a count of word w in the feature-value pair $s_{y,k}$. $p(w|t)$ follows t's unigram language model [24], and it means a word w's likelihood in a sentence t. One of the standard ways to estimate $p(w|t)$ is using maximum likelihood (ML) estimator, which gives $p(w|t) = \frac{c(w,t)}{|t|}$, where $c(w, t)$ is the count of w in t, and $|t|$ is the number of words in t. Thus, $p(s_{y,k}|t)$, likelihood of a feature-value pair $s_{y,k}$ in a sentence t, becomes higher if more words in the feature-value pair appear often in t. To avoid over-fitting and prevent $p(s_{y,k}|t)$ from being zero, we smooth $p(w|t)$ with Jelinek-Mercer smoothing method [8], which is shown in [31] to work reasonably well. Using Jelinek-Mercer smoothing, $p(w|t)$ is defined as:

$$p(w|t) = (1 - \lambda)p_{ml}(w|t) + \lambda p(w|R) \tag{10}$$

where $p_{ml}(w|t)$ and $p(w|R)$ follow a sentence language model and a corpus language model, respectively, estimated with ML estimator. To smooth $p(w|t)$, a reference language model $p(w|R)$ is used so that we can have general word likelihood that nicely augments $p_{ml}(w|t)$. The resulting $p(w|t)$ can be regarded as weighted average of $p_{ml}(w|t)$ and $p(w|R)$.

6.2.2 Review and Specifications Generation Model

Specifications Generation model in section 6.2.1 does not consider centrality among reviews. However, as explained in section 6.1, centrality as well as query-relevance should be considered for the task. Here, we assume that a candidate sentence t of product P_y generates the product's reviews R_y except itself t. This generation enables us to measure centrality of t among all other sentences in the reviews for P_y. Then, t and $R_y^{\setminus t}$ jointly generate its specifications S_y, where $R_y^{\setminus t}$ is a set of reviews for P_y except the sentence t. Intuitively, it makes more sense for S_y to be generated by both t and $R_y^{\setminus t}$ than by only t. S_y then generates the query specifications S_z. Following the dependencies, the score function is defined as

$$\begin{aligned} score(t, R_y^{\setminus t}, S_y; R, S_z) &\propto p(t, R_y^{\setminus t}, S_y|S_z) \\ &= \frac{p(S_z|S_y)p(S_y|t, R_y^{\setminus t})p(R_y^{\setminus t}|t)p(t)}{p(S_z)} \\ &\propto p(S_z|S_y)p(S_y|t, R_y^{\setminus t})p(R_y^{\setminus t}|t) \end{aligned} \tag{11}$$

where $p(t)$ and $p(S_z)$ are ignored for the same reason as in section 6.2.1. Now, $p(R_y^{\setminus t}|t)$, a proximity of t to the reviews $R_y^{\setminus t}$, is computed to consider centrality of t. Also, $p(S_y|t, R_y^{\setminus t})$, a proximity of t and $R_y^{\setminus t}$ to the specifications S_y, is computed to promote sentences from reviews that match its specifications well. Thus, a sentence t is preferred if (1) its specifications S_y is similar to S_z, (2) S_y represent its reviews R_y well, and (3) $R_y^{\setminus t}$ represents t well.

$p(t, R_y^{\setminus t}, S_y|S_z)$ can be re-written as

$$p(t, R_y^{\setminus t}, S_y|S_z) = p(R_y^{\setminus t}|t) \sum_{k=1}^{F} p(s_{z,k}|s_{y,k}) \prod_{w \in s_{y,k}} p(w|t, R_y^{\setminus t}) \quad (12)$$

where $p(w|t, R_y^{\setminus t})$ is smoothed to $(1-\lambda)\delta(w|t, R_y^{\setminus t})+\lambda p(w|R)$, where $\delta(w|t, R_y^{\setminus t})$ is defined as

$$\delta(w|t, R_i) = \begin{cases} 0 & \text{if } w \notin t \\ \frac{c(w,t)+c(w,R_i)}{|t|+|R_i|} & \text{if } w \in t \end{cases} \quad (13)$$

We ignore w if w is not in t in order to require the retrieved sentences to contain words in $s_{y,k}$. The proximity of t to $R_y^{\setminus t}$, $p(R_y^{\setminus t}|t)$, is estimated by TFIDF cosine similarity function $SIM(R_y^{\setminus t}, t)$, where TFIDF cosine similarity between documents d and d' is defined as

$$SIM(d, d') = \frac{\sum_{w \in d,d'} c(w, d) \cdot c(w, d') \cdot IDF(w)^2}{\sqrt{\sum_{w \in d}(c(w, d) \cdot IDF(w))^2} \cdot \sqrt{\sum_{w' \in d'}(c(w', d') \cdot IDF(w'))^2}} \quad (14)$$

where IDF of word w is defined as

$$IDF(w) = \log \frac{|R|}{1 + DF(w)} \quad (15)$$

where $|R|$ is the number of reviews in the whole corpus, and $DF(w)$ is the number of documents that contain w.

6.2.3 Translation Model

In Review and Specifications Generation model, we assumed a sentence t of product P_y generates its reviews R_y, and t and R_y jointly generate their specifications S_y. However, we can also assume that t generates reviews of an arbitrary product because there may be better reviews that can represent t and generate S_y well. In other words, there may be a product P_x that translates t and generates P_z based on the translation with a better performance.

The generative story is described as follows. A candidate sentence t of a product P_y generates each review set of all products, which will be used as translations of t. t and each of the generated review sets, R_x, jointly generates t's specifications S_y, and S_y generates specifications of R_x, S_x, and the query specifications S_z. We intend S_y to generate specifications of the translating product S_x so as to penalize the translating product if its specifications are not similar to S_y. Following the generative story, the score function is defined as

$$\begin{aligned} &score(t, S_y; R, S_z) \propto p(t, S_y|S_z) \\ &= \frac{p(S_z|S_y) \sum_{P_x \in P^{\setminus z}} p(S_x|S_y)p(S_y|t, R_x)p(R_x|t)p(t)}{p(S_z)} \\ &\propto p(S_z|S_y) \sum_{P_x \in P^{\setminus z}} p(S_x|S_y)p(S_y|t, R_x)p(R_x|t) \end{aligned} \quad (16)$$

where $p(S_z)$ and $p(t)$ are ignored for the same reason as before. As described, the score function contains a loop over all products (except P_z), instead of using only t's review set R_y, to get the votes from all translating products. The features in different specifications are paired together, which decompose $p(t, S_y|S_z)$ as follows.

$$\begin{aligned} &p(t, S_y|S_z) \\ &\propto \sum_{k=1}^{F} p(s_{z,k}|s_{y,k}) \sum_{P_x \in P^{\setminus z}} p(s_{x,k}|s_{y,k})p(s_{y,k}|t, R_x)p(R_x|t) \\ &= \sum_{k=1}^{F} p(s_{z,k}|s_{y,k}) \sum_{P_x \in P^{\setminus z}} p(s_{x,k}|s_{y,k})p(R_x|t) \prod_{w \in s_{y,k}} p(w|t, R_x) \end{aligned} \quad (17)$$

where proximity between specifications are estimated using cosine similarity function SIM_f as in specifications generation model, and the proximity of t to arbitrary reviews R_x, $p(R_x|t)$, is estimated by TFIDF cosine similarity function. In order to consider the case P_y is the same as P_x, we define $p(w|t, R_x)$ as

$$p(w|t, R_x) = \begin{cases} (1 - \lambda)\delta(w|t, R_x) + \lambda p(w|R) & \text{if } P_x \neq P_y \\ (1 - \lambda)\delta(w|t, R_x^{\setminus t}) + \lambda p(w|R) & \text{if } P_x = P_y \end{cases} \quad (18)$$

Meanwhile, looping over all non-query products is probably too expensive in terms of computational complexity. We thus choose X translating products P^X to reduce the complexity. Perhaps, the most promising translating products may be those who are similar to the query product P_z. We want the retrieved sentences to be translated well by the actual reviews of P_z, which means that those reviews of products not similar to P_z are not considered important. Since we assume that products similar to P_z are likely to have similar reviews, we exploit the similar products' reviews to approximate R_z, where we measure similarity using specifications. Therefore, we loop over only X translating products P^X that are most similar to P_z, where similarity function SIM_p is employed to measure similarity between products. Since P_x needs to be similar to P_z, we further assume that P_x generates P_z, which yields proximity of P_x to P_z, $p(P_z|P_x)$, and it is defined as

$$p(P_z|P_x) = \frac{SIM_p(P_z, P_x)}{\sum_{x' \in P^X} SIM_p(P_z, P_{x'})} \quad (19)$$

and this product-level similarity is used as a weight of P_x in formula (17).

7. EXPERIMENTAL SETUP

7.1 Data Set

Since we study a new task that has not been studied before, there is no existing test collection available to use for evaluation. We thus must solve the challenge of creating a test set. We address this problem by using products with known reviews as test cases. We pretend that we do not know their reviews and use our methods to retrieve sentences in K words; we then compare these results with the actual known review of a test product. This allows for evaluating the task without requiring manual work, and is a reasonable way to perform evaluation because it would reward a system that can retrieve review sentences that are very similar to the actual review sentences of a product.

We now describe how to build our data set in detail. First, it is required for our problem to obtain reviews and specifications for products, and this kind of data is available in several web sites such as Amazon.com, BestBuy.com, and CNET.com. Among them, we chose CNET.com because they have reasonable amount of review data and relatively well-organized specifications. There are several product categories in CNET.com, and we chose digital camera and MP3 player categories since they are reasonably popular and therefore the experiment results can yield significant impact. From CNET.com, we crawled product information for all products that were available on February 22, 2012 in both categories. For each product, we collected its user reviews and specifications.

Table 1: Statistics of the data for digital camera and MP3 player categories.

	Digital Camera	MP3 Player
Num. of products	1,153	605
Num. of reviews	12,779	14,159
Num. of sentences	137,599	291,858
Num. of word tokens	754,888	172,5192
Vocabulary size	6442	6959
Num. of features	9	8
Num. of distinct feature values	1,038	384

We pruned out products that do not contain reviews or specifications. (We found that about two thirds of the products didn't have any user reviews.) To preprocess the review text, we performed sentence segmentation, word tokenization, and lemmatization using Stanford CoreNLP [17] version 1.3.5. We lowered word tokens and removed punctuations. Then, we removed word tokens that appear in less than five reviews and stopwords. We also preprocessed specifications data. In general, specifications contain dozens or hundreds of distinct features, and many of them are not mentioned in the reviews. Therefore, we choose features that are considered important by users. In order to choose such key features, we simply adopt highlighted features provided by CNET.com assuming that they chose the features based on importance. The highlighted features are listed in Table 2. We removed feature values that appear in less than five products. Then, we tokenized the feature and feature value words, and we lowered the word tokens. The statistics of the reviews and specifications data is shown in Table 1. While digital camera category has more products, more reviews are written for mp3 player categories. Also, in general, users wrote more texts per review for mp3 players than digital cameras. The number of highlighted features used for digital cameras is similar to that for mp3 players while there are much more distinct feature values for digital cameras.

Table 2: CNET.com's highlighted features for digital camera and MP3 player categories.

Digital Camera	MP3 Player
Manufacturer	Manufacturer
Product Type	Product Type
Resolution	Digital Storage
Digital Video Format	Flash Memory Installed
Image Stabilizer	Built-in Display – Diagonal Size
Lens System – Type	Battery / Power – Battery
Memory / Storage – Supported Mem. Cards	Digital Player / Recorder – Supported Digital Audio Standards
Camera Flash – Camera Flash	Battery / Power – Mfr. Estimated Battery Life
Optical Sensor Type	

In order to evaluate the performance of our methods for retrieving review sentences for a new or unpopular product, we perform the following experiment. To choose test products, which will be regarded as products with no reviews, we selected top 50 qualified products by the number of reviews in each category in order to obtain statistically reliable gold standard data. Please note that we did not select (qualify) products that have their different versions such as colors or editions, in order to ensure that review sentences from the different version of the same product are not retrieved. For each of the top products, P_z, all sentences of other products are regarded as candidate sentences. Pretending P_z does not have any reviews, we rank those candidate sentences and generate a text of first K word tokens, and we compare it with the actual reviews of P_z. We assume that if the generated review text is similar to the actual reviews, it is a good review text for P_z. The average number of reviews in the top 50 products is 78.5 and 152.2 for digital cameras and mp3 players, respectively. For the probabilistic retrieval models, we use λ to control the amount of smoothing for language models, and we empirically set it to 0.5 for both product categories, which showed the best performance.

7.2 Evaluation Metrics

To evaluate a quality of the length-K retrieved text based on actual reviews for the query, we face another challenge: how should we measure the performance? We could consider using standard retrieval measures, but neither NDCG, nor MAP seems appropriate since we do not have multiple levels of judgments or even binary judgments. We thus decided to measure the proximity between the retrieved text and the actual reviews. Regarding the retrieved text as a summary for the query product, we can view our task as similar to multiple document summarization, whose goal is to generate a summary of multiple documents. Thus, we employ ROUGE evaluation method [13], which is a standard evaluation system for multiple document summarization. In general, ROUGE evaluates the quality of an automatically generated summary by comparing it with one or more manually generated reference summaries. Assuming the actual reviews of the query product are manually generated reference summaries, we can adopt ROUGE to evaluate the retrieved sentences. Among various ROUGE metrics, we employ ROUGE-1 and ROUGE-2, which are unigram and bigram matching metrics, respectively, and have been shown to perform well for the task. We compute precision, recall, and F1-score of each metric. For example, recall of ROUGE-n is defined as

$$\text{ROUGE-}n(r,s) = \frac{\sum_{gram_n \in S} Count_{match}(gram_n)}{\sum_{gram_n \in S} Count(gram_n)} \quad (20)$$

where r and s are reference and retrieved summaries, respectively, $gram_n$ is n-gram text, $Count_{match}(gram_n)$ is the maximum number of n-grams co-occurring in the retrieved summary and a reference summary. When there are multiple reference summaries are available, they use the following evaluation formula.

$$\text{ROUGE-}n_{multi} = max_i \text{ROUGE-}n(r_i, s) \quad (21)$$

Please note that each of the precision, recall, and F1-score takes the maximum from the reference summaries. More details about ROUGE can be found in [13].

However, the problem of ROUGE metrics is that it does not consider importance of words. All words have different level of importance; for example a word such as "of" is much less important than a word "megapixel" since "of" appears too often in documents and does not carry useful information. If a retrieved text contains many unimportant words, it may obtain a high score by ROUGE metrics, which is not desired. Therefore, we also employ TFIDF cosine similarity, which considers word importance by Inverse Document Frequency (IDF). TFIDF cosine similarity function between two documents is defined in equation (14). While the formula measures similarity based on bag of words, bigram provides important information about distance among words, so we adopt bigram-based TFIDF cosine similarity as well. Similar to ROUGE-n_{multi}, we take a maximum from $SIM(r_i, s)$ among different reference summaries because we still evaluate based on multiple reference summaries. For both ROUGE and SIM metrics, we use retrieved text length 100, 200, and 400, which reflect diverse users' information needs.

8. EXPERIMENT RESULTS

8.1 Qualitative Analysis

Table 3: Top ten sentences retrieved for Pentax *ist DS (Digital Camera) by Translation model with X=5.

(1) This was my first and my last Pentax .
(2) This pentax is a great value for money , and a nice entry level dslr , compatible with most Pentax lens .
(3) I have found the Pentax DL to be high quality , with great features .
(4) Nice job pentax .
(5) I have been a Pentax SLR user for years , beginning with the SuperProgram , ZX-50 , and ZX-5n .
(6) When I bought it , I was in bankruptcy and the cheaper Pentax came to me .
(7) Pentax have been making great lenses and cameras for a long time , and this range is no exception .
(8) Great photos , color , ease of use , compact size , compatible with Pentax mount lenses .
(9) I had owned a great 35mm Pentax camera before that took wonderful pictures , which , after 20 years went caput .
(10) Very smart Pentax .

Table 4: Specifications for Pentax *ist DS. Note that some feature values are not available.

Feature	Value
Manufacturer	Pentax
Product Type	Digital camera - SLR
Resolution	6.1 megapixels
Digital Video Format	
Image Stabilizer	
Lens System – Type	3 x x Zoom lens - 18 mm - 55 mm - F/3.5-5.6 DA Pentax KAF
Memory / Storage – Supported Mem. Cards	SD Memory Card
Camera Flash – Camera Flash	Pop-up flash
Optical Sensor Type	CCD

In order to see the usefulness of the sentences retrieved by our novel Translation model, we show the top retrieved sentences for query products and compare them with the actual review sentences for the query products. Table 3 lists top retrieved sentences for a product in each category, where the sentences are ordered by their scores, and the specifications of the product is listed in Table 4.We set the number of translating products to five, which is reasonable if we consider the computational cost of the model.

For the digital camera Pentax *ist DS, several top retrieved sentences such as (2), and (8) mention about its compatibility with Pentax lenses. Surprisingly, there were several reviews for Pentax *ist DS that praise its lens compatibility, and here are two actual examples from review sentences: "Plus the DS is backwards compatible with all old Pentax lenses, which have a well-deserved reputation among photographers." and "I can use my pile of old (and very old) Pentax lenses including the m42 lenses." Also, the retrieved sentences such as (7), (8), (9), and possibly (3) mention about Pentax's great picture quality, which is supported by the following actual review sentences: "Amazingly sharp lens." and "It has a much better lens package than the Rebel and the base 20D kit." Sentences (2) and (6) claim the product's good value, which is again supported by actual review sentences: "Better value than you think" and "The camera is also cheaper than the comparable Nikon and Canon." The retrieved sentence such as (8) mentions about ease of use for the camera, and many users actually complimented the camera on its ease of use, indeed. The supporting sentences are as follows: "Very easy to use right out of the box." and "The controls are very easy to learn and are, for the most part, very intuitive." Meanwhile, the sentence (1) carries inconsistent opinion, which shows negative sentiment on Pentax camera. Nevertheless, in a user's perspective, who does not know much about Pentax *ist DS or other Pentax cameras, the listed information would be highly informative especially if the camera has no or few reviews. Although some of the retrieved sentences do not carry useful information, it is clear that some other retrieved sentences are indeed useful.

Our probabilistic retrieval models have a capability of retrieving relevant sentences for a specific feature. For each of the probabilistic models, we can assume that the number of features F is one so that the score functions compute only for one feature. Table 5 shows top retrieved sentences for the feature "Lens System – Type" of Pentax *ist DS. As found in the top sentences for the whole product in Table 3, we can easily find that all the sentences except (2) praise the lens compatibility of Pentax, indeed. In addition, all sentences except (1) praises high quality of its lens, which is coherent with the top sentences for the whole product. From the sentences, users can learn much about the given product's lens such as other consumers' general sentiment and specific reasons why they like or dislike its lens.

Table 5: Top sentences retrieved by Translation model (X=5) specifically for the feature "Lens System – Type" of Pentax *ist DS.

(1) This pentax is a great value for money , and a nice entry level dslr , compatible with most Pentax lens .
(2) Pentax have been making great lenses and cameras for a long time , and this range is no exception .
(3) Great photos , color , ease of use , compact size , compatible with Pentax mount lenses .
(4) The kit lens is better than what ships with some competitors , and the camera is compatible with most older Pentax lenses , making it possible to save hundreds by buying used lenses rather than having to sink money into new digital lenses .
(5) Compatibility with older Pentax lenses is a real bonus too , as these are usually of very high quality and can be picked up at good prices second-hand .

Manually finding relevant opinions for a query product or its specific feature is extremely time-consuming for users; they need to find similar products by manually comparing specifications and extract relevant and central sentences from all the reviews of the similar products, which may take too much time. Here, we verified the automatically retrieved sentences can be indeed useful for users. In the next section, we quantitatively compare our Translation model with other suggested methods.

8.2 Quantitative Evaluation

To retrieve review sentences that are likely to be written for a new or unpopular product, we employ several methods. In order to see the effectiveness of a standard ad-hoc retrieval method, we employ query likelihood (QL) language model approach [24], and we define the score func-

Table 6: **Unigram and bigram TFIDF cosine similarity @ K for Digital Camera and MP3 Player categories.**

Category	Model	COS1@100	COS1@200	COS1@400	COS2@100	COS2@200	COS2@400
Digital Camera	QL	0.112	0.128	0.147	0.0185	0.0215	0.0257
	MEAD	0.131	0.124	0.141	0.0258	0.0204	0.0184
	MEAD-SIM	0.136	0.130	0.158	0.0271	0.0226	0.0223
	SpecGen	0.143	0.173	0.206	0.0230	0.0270	0.0291
	ReviewSpecGen	0.171	0.208	0.231	0.0210	0.0244	0.0298
	Translation	**0.314**†‡	**0.327**†‡	**0.333**†‡	**0.0736**†‡	**0.0743**†‡	**0.0794**†‡
	(increase %)	(+131%)	(+152%)	(+111%)	(+172%)	(+229%)	(+256%)
MP3 Player	QL	0.090	0.99	0.118	0.0147	0.0159	0.0173
	MEAD	0.089	0.078	0.091	0.0123	0.0128	0.0117
	MEAD-SIM	0.131	0.136	0.145	0.0206	0.0197	0.0178
	SpecGen	0.153	0.183	0.208	0.0225	0.0274	0.0294
	ReviewSpecGen	0.206	0.227	0.253	0.0261	0.0270	0.0327
	Translation	**0.267**†‡	**0.297**†‡	**0.316**†‡	**0.0458**†‡	**0.0567**†‡	**0.0649**†‡
	(increase %)	(+104%)	(+118%)	(+118%)	(+104%)	(+188%)	(+265%)

tion as $score(t; R, S_z) = \sum_{k=1}^{F} \prod_{w \in s_{z,k}} p(w|t)$, where $p(w|t)$ is smoothed as in equation (10). We suggested a modified version of one of the standard summarization tools, MEAD-SIM in formula (5), which considers both query-relevance and centrality. We employ MEAD-SIM as one of the baseline methods, and we also show results from the basic MEAD in formula (4) to see the effect of query-relevance addition to MEAD; we set $w_c = 1$ and $w_o = 0$ since position score is inappropriate for reviews. We also introduced several probabilistic retrieval methods for the task. Review and Specifications Generation model (ReviewSpecGen) considers both query-relevance and centrality, so we use it as another baseline method. Specifications Generation model (SpecGen) focuses on query-relevance, and we show its results to compare with ReviewSpecGen and QL. We then suggested our novel Translation model (Translation). We tuned X to be 100 for digital cameras and 10 for mp3 players, unless otherwise specified, which showed the best TFIDF cosine similarity values. The results from Translation model are mainly compared with the two baselines MEAD-SIM and ReviewSpecGen. † and ‡ are used to mark if the improvement for Translation model is statistically (paired t-test with p=0.05) significant in each measure from MEAD-SIM and ReviewSpecGen, respectively. We also record how much Translation model outperforms MEAD-SIM in parentheses.

Table 6 shows TFIDF cosine similarity evaluation results for both digital cameras and mp3 players. Both unigram (COS1) and bigram (COS2) measures are listed for the suggested methods. In general, models that exploit specifications as query (MEAD-SIM, SpecGen, ReviewSpecGen, and Translation) except QL outperform MEAD, which does not compute query-relevance. QL outperforms MEAD in mp3 player data set, but it does not outperform other models in both data sets, since does not consider specifications similarity between products. MEAD-SIM outperforms MEAD in all cosine similarity measures (12/12), which means that centrality alone cannot perform well. ReviewSpecGen adds centrality computation to SpecGen, and the results show that its centrality helps it outperform SpecGen in most measures (9/12). ReviewSpecGen outperforms MEAD-SIM in all unigram measures (6/6) and most bigram measures (5/6). Translation model significantly outperforms MEAD-SIM in all measures (12/12), and the average performance increase percentage is 162%. It also significantly outperforms ReviewSpecGen in all measures (12/12), which means that choosing products similar to the query product as translating products was more effective than choosing only one product the candidate sentence belongs. Translation model outperforms other models especially in bigram measures, which means that Translation model retrieves more connected fragments that are in the actual reviews.

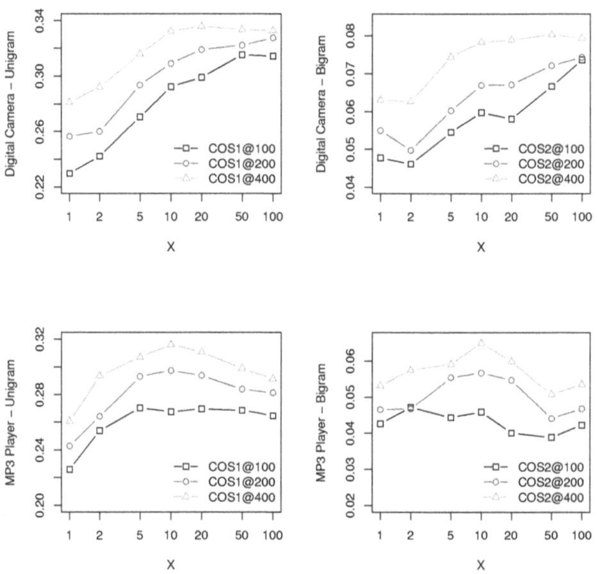

Figure 2: TFIDF cosine similarity evaluation results for Translation model with different number (X) of translating products. Upper figures are for digital cameras, and lower figures are for mp3 players. Left figures are results based on unigrams, and right figures are those base on bigrams.

We also evaluate retrieval results with ROUGE metrics. Although ROUGE does not consider importance of words, it is able to compute recall, precision, and F1 score in both unigram (ROUGE1-R, ROUGE1-P, and ROUGE1-F) and bigram (ROUGE2-R, ROUGE2-P, and ROUGE2-F) units. The ROUGE evaluation results for mp3 players are shown in Table 7. QL outperforms MEAD in all measures, but it is outperformed by MEAD-SIM in all measures since QL does not consider specifications similarity between products. SpecGen outperforms ReviewSpecGen in most measures (13/18) especially in bigram measures (9/9), which is different from the TFIDF cosine similarity results; this means that the sentences retrieved by SpecGen are more similar to ac-

Table 7: Unigram and bigram ROUGE @ K for MP3 Players category.

K	Model	ROUGE1-R	ROUGE1-P	ROUGE1-F	ROUGE2-R	ROUGE2-P	ROUGE2-F
100	QL	0.278	0.218	0.150	0.0545	0.0308	0.0297
	MEAD	0.202	0.217	0.132	0.0364	0.0242	0.0227
	MEAD-SIM	0.328	0.319	0.196	0.0615	0.0381	0.0367
	SpecGen	0.303	0.299	0.191	0.0727	0.0480	0.0406
	ReviewSpecGen	0.323	0.320	0.204	0.0650	0.0431	0.0378
	Translation	**0.369**†‡	**0.375**‡	**0.236**†‡	**0.1151**†‡	**0.0742**†‡	**0.0634**†‡
	(increase %)	(+11%)	(+12%)	(+20%)	(+87%)	(+95%)	(+73%)
200	QL	0.384	0.213	0.166	0.0812	0.0264	0.0300
	MEAD	0.266	0.171	0.127	0.0453	0.0186	0.0203
	MEAD-SIM	0.434	0.266	0.201	0.0834	0.0290	0.0333
	SpecGen	0.413	0.273	0.204	0.0913	0.0423	0.0395
	ReviewSpecGen	0.411	0.267	0.197	0.0848	0.0324	0.0344
	Translation	**0.481**†‡	**0.318**†‡	**0.239**†‡	**0.1582**†‡	**0.0664**†‡	**0.0657**†‡
	(increase %)	(+11%)	(+20%)	(+19%)	(+90%)	(+129%)	(+97%)
400	QL	0.501	0.186	0.175	0.1159	0.0205	0.0265
	MEAD	0.370	0.154	0.141	0.0517	0.0111	0.0146
	MEAD-SIM	0.560	0.224	0.210	0.1260	0.0207	0.0268
	SpecGen	0.535	0.221	0.207	0.1228	0.0293	0.0342
	ReviewSpecGen	0.546	0.221	0.204	0.1171	0.0254	0.0314
	Translation	**0.595**†‡	**0.240**†‡	**0.225**†‡	**0.2112**†‡	**0.0431**†‡	**0.0542**†‡
	(increase %)	(+6%)	(+7%)	(+7%)	(+68%)	(+108%)	(+102%)

tual reviews than those retrieved by ReviewSpecGen, but ReviewSpecGen retrieved more "important" relevant words. Translation model outperforms all other models in all measures (18/18), and the increase from MEAD-SIM and ReviewSpecGen is statistically significant in most measures (17/18 and 18/18, respectively). Similar to TFIDF cosine similarity results, the performance difference in bigram is clearer than in unigram, which means Translation model retrieves bigger fragments of actual reviews well. The increase in unigram ROUGE measures is not as big as that in unigram TFIDF cosine similarity measures, which means that the number of relevant words from Translation model is not very different from other models, but Translation model retrieves much more important relevant words.

We also evaluated retrieved sentences for digital cameras with ROUGE metrics. In general, Translation model outperforms other models in all measures. More specifically, it significantly outperforms MEAD-SIM and ReviewSpecGen in most measures (16/18 and 18/18, respectively). We do not list ROUGE evaluation results for digital cameras since the other patterns are similar to those for mp3 players.

Overall, ROUGE evaluation results are similar to cosine similarity evaluation results in general. The difference between the two metrics is that the TFIDF cosine similarity metric differentiates various models more clearly since they consider importance of word while the ROUGE metric does not; TFIDF cosine similarity metric prefers retrieved text that contains more important words, which is a desired property in such evaluation. On the other hand, ROUGE metric considers various evaluation aspects such as recall, precision, and F1 score, which can possibly help us analyze evaluation results in depth.

In order to reduce computation complexity of Translation model, we proposed to exploit X number of most promising products that are similar to the query product, instead of all products, under the assumption that similar products are likely to have similar reviews. We performed experiments with different X values to find how many translating products are needed to obtain reasonably good performance. The results are evaluated with TFIDF cosine similarity @ K for unigrams and bigrams, and the results are shown in Figure 2. Surprisingly, only a few translating products (e.g., ten) are enough to perform reasonably well especially for mp3 players. These results mean that only a few "good" translating products are enough to translate a candidate sentence well, and the "good" translating products may be selected by their similarity to the query product.

9. CONCLUSION AND FUTURE WORK

In this paper, we studied the problem of automatic relevant review text retrieval for products having no reviews. Relevant review sentences for new or unpopular products can be very useful for consumers who seek for relevant opinions, but no previous work has addressed this novel problem. We proposed several methods to solve this problem, including summarization-based methods such as MEAD and MEAD-SIM and probabilistic retrieval methods such as Specifications Generation model, Review and Specifications Generation model, and Translation model. To evaluate relevance of retrieved opinion sentences in the situation where human-labeled judgments are not available, we measured the proximity between the retrieved text and the actual reviews of a query product. Experiment results show that our novel Translation model indeed retrieves useful sentences and significantly outperforms the baseline methods.

Our work opens up a new direction in text data mining and opinion analysis. The new problem of review text retrieval for new products can be studied from multiple perspectives. First, it can be regarded as a summarization problem as the retrieved sentences need to be central across different reviews. Second, as done in this paper, it can also be regarded as a special retrieval problem with the goal of retrieving relevant opinions with product specifications as a query. Finally, it can also be studied from the perspective of collaborative filtering where we would leverage related products to recommend relevant "opinions" to new products. All these are interesting future directions that can potentially lead to even more accurate and more useful algorithms.

10. ACKNOWLEDGMENTS

This work is supported in part by a gift fund from TCL and by the National Science Foundation under Grant Number CNS-1027965.

11. REFERENCES

[1] A. Berger and J. Lafferty. Information retrieval as statistical translation. In *Proceedings of ACM SIGIR 1999*, pages 222–229, 1999.

[2] I. Bhattacharya, S. Godbole, and S. Joshi. Structured entity identification and document categorization: two tasks with one joint model. In *Proceedings of ACM KDD 2008*, pages 25–33, 2008.

[3] C. Dellarocas, X. M. Zhang, and N. F. Awad. Exploring the value of online product reviews in forecasting sales: The case of motion pictures. *Journal of Interactive marketing*, 21(4):23–45, 2007.

[4] H. Duan, C. Zhai, J. Cheng, and A. Gattani. Supporting keyword search in product database: A probabilistic approach. *Proc. VLDB Endow.*, 6(14):1786–1797, Sept. 2013.

[5] G. Ganu, N. Elhadad, and A. Marian. Beyond the stars: Improving rating predictions using review text content.

[6] E. Hovy and C.-Y. Lin. Automated text summarization in SUMMARIST. In I. Mani and M. T. Maybury, editors, *Advances in Automatic Text Summarization*. MIT Press, 1999.

[7] M. Hu and B. Liu. Mining and summarizing customer reviews. In *Proceedings of KDD '04*, pages 168–177, 2004.

[8] F. Jelinek. Interpolated estimation of markov source parameters from sparse data. *Pattern recognition in practice*, 1980.

[9] H. D. Kim, K. Ganesan, P. Sondhi, and C. Zhai. Comprehensive review of opinion summarization. *Computer Science Research and Tech Reports*, 2011.

[10] H. D. Kim and C. Zhai. Generating comparative summaries of contradictory opinions in text. In *CIKM '09: Proceeding of the 18th ACM conference on Information and knowledge management*, pages 385–394, New York, NY, USA, 2009. ACM.

[11] J. Kupiec, J. Pedersen, and F. Chen. A trainable document summarizer. In *Proceedings of ACM SIGIR '95*, pages 68–73, 1995.

[12] M. Lalmas. Xml retrieval (synthesis lectures on information concepts, retrieval, and services). *Morgan and Claypool, San Rafael, CA*, 2009.

[13] C.-Y. Lin. Rouge: A package for automatic evaluation of summaries. In *Text Summarization Branches Out: Proceedings of the ACL-04 Workshop*, pages 74–81, 2004.

[14] B. Liu. Sentiment analysis and subjectivity. In N. Indurkhya and F. J. Damerau, editors, *Handbook of Natural Language Processing, Second Edition*. CRC Press, Taylor and Francis Group, Boca Raton, FL, 2010. ISBN 978-1420085921.

[15] B. Liu, M. Hu, and J. Cheng. Opinion observer: analyzing and comparing opinions on the web. In *Proceedings of WWW '05*, pages 342–351, 2005.

[16] Y. Lu, C. Zhai, and N. Sundaresan. Rated aspect summarization of short comments. In *Proceedings of WWW '09*, pages 131–140, 2009.

[17] C. D. Manning, M. Surdeanu, J. Bauer, J. Finkel, S. J. Bethard, and D. McClosky. The Stanford CoreNLP natural language processing toolkit. In *Proceedings of 52nd Annual Meeting of the Association for Computational Linguistics: System Demonstrations*, pages 55–60, 2014.

[18] Q. Mei, X. Ling, M. Wondra, H. Su, and C. Zhai. Topic sentiment mixture: modeling facets and opinions in weblogs. In *Proceedings of WWW '07*, pages 171–180, 2007.

[19] C. D. Paice. Constructing literature abstracts by computer: techniques and prospects. *Inf. Process. Manage.*, 26(1):171–186, 1990.

[20] B. Pang and L. Lee. Seeing stars: Exploiting class relationships for sentiment categorization with respect to rating scales. In *Proceedings of the 43rd Annual Meeting on Association for Computational Linguistics*, pages 115–124. Association for Computational Linguistics, 2005.

[21] B. Pang and L. Lee. Opinion mining and sentiment analysis. *Found. Trends Inf. Retr.*, 2(1-2):1–135, 2008.

[22] D. H. Park, C. Zhai, and L. Guo. Speclda: Modeling product reviews and specifications to generate augmented specifications. In *Proceedings of the 2015 SIAM International Conference on Data Mining*. SIAM, 2015.

[23] I. Peñalver-Martínez, R. Valencia-García, and F. García-Sánchez. Ontology-guided approach to feature-based opinion mining. In *Natural Language Processing and Information Systems*, pages 193–200. Springer, 2011.

[24] J. M. Ponte and W. B. Croft. A language modeling approach to information retrieval. In *Proceedings of the 21st annual international ACM SIGIR conference on Research and development in information retrieval*, pages 275–281. ACM, 1998.

[25] A.-M. Popescu and O. Etzioni. Extracting product features and opinions from reviews. In *Proceedings of HLT-EMNLP 2005*, pages 339–346, 2005.

[26] D. R. Radev, H. Jing, and M. Budzikowska. Centroid-based summarization of multiple documents: sentence extraction, utility-based evaluation, and user studies. In *Proceedings of the 2000 NAACL-ANLP Workshop on Automatic Summarization*, pages 21–30. Association for Computational Linguistics, 2000.

[27] A. I. Schein, A. Popescul, L. H. Ungar, and D. M. Pennock. Methods and metrics for cold-start recommendations. In *Proceedings of the 25th annual international ACM SIGIR conference on Research and development in information retrieval*, pages 253–260. ACM, 2002.

[28] I. Titov and R. McDonald. Modeling online reviews with multi-grain topic models. In *Proceedings of WWW '08*, pages 111–120, 2008.

[29] T. Wang, Y. Cai, G. Zhang, Y. Liu, J. Chen, and H. Min. Product feature summarization by incorporating domain information. In *Database Systems for Advanced Applications*. Springer, 2013.

[30] J. Yu, Z.-J. Zha, M. Wang, K. Wang, and T.-S. Chua. Domain-assisted product aspect hierarchy generation: towards hierarchical organization of unstructured consumer reviews. In *Proceedings of EMNLP 2011*, pages 140–150, 2011.

[31] C. Zhai and J. Lafferty. A study of smoothing methods for language models applied to ad hoc information retrieval. In *Proceedings of the 24th annual international ACM SIGIR conference on Research and development in information retrieval*, pages 334–342. ACM, 2001.

[32] L. Zhou and P. Chaovalit. Ontology-supported polarity mining. *Journal of the American Society for Information Science and technology*, 59(1):98–110, 2008.

Learning Hierarchical Representation Model for Next Basket Recommendation

Pengfei Wang, Jiafeng Guo, Yanyan Lan, Jun Xu, Shengxian Wan, Xueqi Cheng
CAS Key Lab of Network Data Science and Technology
Institute of Computing Technology, Chinese Academy of Sciences
{wangpengfei,wanshengxian}@software.ict.ac.cn
{guojiafeng,lanyanyan,junxu,cxq}@ict.ac.cn

ABSTRACT

Next basket recommendation is a crucial task in market basket analysis. Given a user's purchase history, usually a sequence of transaction data, one attempts to build a recommender that can predict the next few items that the user most probably would like. Ideally, a good recommender should be able to explore the sequential behavior (i.e., buying one item leads to buying another next), as well as account for users' general taste (i.e., what items a user is typically interested in) for recommendation. Moreover, these two factors may interact with each other to influence users' next purchase. To tackle the above problems, in this paper, we introduce a novel recommendation approach, namely hierarchical representation model (HRM). HRM can well capture both sequential behavior and users' general taste by involving transaction and user representations in prediction. Meanwhile, the flexibility of applying different aggregation operations, especially nonlinear operations, on representations allows us to model complicated interactions among different factors. Theoretically, we show that our model subsumes several existing methods when choosing proper aggregation operations. Empirically, we demonstrate that our model can consistently outperform the state-of-the-art baselines under different evaluation metrics on real-world transaction data.

Categories and Subject Descriptors

H.2.8 [**Database Management**]: Database Applications-Data Mining

General Terms

Algorithms, Experiments, Performance, Theory

Keywords

Hierarchical Representation Model; Sequential Behavior; General Taste; Next Basket Recommendation

SIGIR 15, August 09 - 13, 2015, Santiago, Chile.

http://dx.doi.org/10.1145/2766462.2767694 .

1. INTRODUCTION

Market basket analysis helps retailers gain a better understanding of users' purchase behavior which can lead to better decisions. One of its most important tasks is next basket recommendation [7, 8, 12, 20]. In this task, usually sequential transaction data is given per user, where a transaction is a set/basket of items (e.g. shoes or bags) bought at one point of time. The target is to recommend items that the user probably want to buy in his/her next visit.

Typically, there are two modeling paradigms for this problem. One is sequential recommender [5, 25], mostly relying on Markov chains, which explores the sequential transaction data by predicting the next purchase based on the last actions. A major advantage of this model is its ability to capture sequential behavior for good recommendations, e.g. for a user who has recently bought a mobile phone, it may recommend accessories that other users have bought after buying that phone. The other is general recommender [1, 23], which discards any sequential information and learns what items a user is typically interested in. One of the most successful methods in this class is the model based collaborative filtering (i.e. matrix factorization models). Obviously, such general recommender is good at capturing the general taste of the user by learning over the user's whole purchase history.

A better solution for next basket recommendation, therefore, is to take both sequential behavior and users' general taste into consideration. One step towards this direction is the factorizing personalized Markov chains (FPMC) model proposed by Steffen Rendle et al. [23]. FPMC can model both sequential behavior (by interaction between items in the last transaction and that in the next basket) and users' general taste (by interaction between the user and the item in the next basket), thus achieves better performance than either sequential or general recommender alone. However, a major problem of FPMC is that all the components are linearly combined, indicating that it makes strong independent assumption among multiple factors (i.e. each component influence users' next purchase independently).

Unfortunately, from our analysis, we show that the independent assumption is not sufficient for good recommendations.

To tackle the above problems, we introduce a novel hierarchical representation model (HRM) for next basket recommendation. Specifically, HRM represents each user and item as a vector in continuous space, and employs a two-layer structure to construct a hybrid representation over user and items from last transaction: The first layer forms the transaction representation by aggregating item vectors from last transaction; While the second layer builds the hybrid representation by aggregating the user vector and the transaction representation. The resulting hybrid representation is then used to predict the items in the next basket. Note here the transaction representation involved in recommendation models the sequential behavior, while the user representation captures the general taste in recommendation.

HRM allows us to flexibly use different types of aggregation operations at different layers. Especially, by employing nonlinear rather than linear operations, we can model more complicated interactions among different factors beyond independent assumption. For example, by using a max pooling operation, features from each factor are compared and only those most significant are selected to form the higher level representation for future prediction. We also show that by choosing proper aggregation operations, HRM subsumes several existing methods including markov chain model, matrix factorization model as well as a variation of FPMC model. For learning the model parameters, we employ the negative sampling procedure [27] as the optimization method.

We conducted experiments over three real-world transaction datasets. The empirical results demonstrated the effectiveness of our approach as compared with the state-of-the-art baseline methods.

In total the contributions of our work are as follows:

- We introduce a general model for next basket recommendation which can capture both sequential behavior and users' general taste, and flexibly incorporate different interactions among multiple factors.
- We introduce two types of aggregation operations, i.e. average pooling and max pooling, into our hierarchical model and study the effect of different combinations of these operations.
- Theoretically we show that our model subsumes several existing recommendation methods when choosing proper aggregation operations.
- Empirically we show that our model, especially with nonlinear operations, can consistently outperform state-of-the-art baselines under different evaluation metrics on next basket recommendation.

2. RELATED WORK

Next basket recommendation is a typical application of recommender systems based on implicit feedback, where no explicit preferences (e.g. ratings) but only positive observations (e.g. purchases or clicks) are available [2, 7]. These positive observations are usually in a form of sequential data as obtained by passively tracking users' behavior over a sequence of time, e.g. a retail store records the transactions of customers. In this section, we briefly review the related work on recommendation with implicit feedback from the following three aspects, i.e. sequential recommender, general recommender, and the hybrid model.

Sequential recommender, mainly based on a Markov chain model, utilizes sequential data by predicting users' next action given the last actions [6]. For example, Zimdar et al. [3] propose a sequential recommender based on Markov chains, and investigate how to extract sequential patterns to learn the next state using probablistic decision-tree models. Mobasher et al. [18] study different sequential patterns for recommendation and find that contiguous sequential patterns are more suitable for sequential prediction task than general sequential patterns. Ghim-Eng Yap et al. [29] introduce a new Competence Score measure in personalized sequential pattern mining for next-items recommendation. Shani et al. [24] present a recommender based on Markov decision processes and show that a predictive Markov Chain model is effective for next basket prediction. Chen et al. [5] model playlists as a Markov chain, and propose logistic Markov Embedding to learn the representations of songs for playlist prediction. The main difference of our work to all the previous approaches is the inclusion of users' general taste in recommendation beyond sequential behavior. Besides, the previous sequential recommenders seldom address the interactions among items in sequential factors.

General recommender, in contrast, does not take sequential behavior into account but recommends based on users' whole purchase history. The key idea is collaborative filtering (CF) which can be further categorized into memory-based CF and model-based CF [1, 26]. The memory-based CF provides recommendations by finding k-nearest-neighbour of users or products based on certain similarity measure [16]. While the model-based CF tries to factorize the user-item correlation matrix for recommendation. For example, Lee et al. [12] treat the market basket data as a binary user-item matrix, and apply a binary logistic regression model based on principal component analysis (PCA) for recommendation. Hu et al. [10] conduct the factorization on user-item pairs with least-square optimization and use pair confidence to control the importance of observations. Pan et al. [19] also introduce the weights to user-item pairs, and optimize the factorization with both least-square and hinge-loss criteria. Rendle et al . [22] propose a different optimization criterion, namely Bayesian personalized ranking, which directly optimizes for correctly ranking over item pairs instead of scoring single items. They apply this method to matrix factorization and adaptive KNN to show its effectiveness. General recommender is good at capturing users' general taste, but can hardly adapt its recommendations directly to users' recent purchases without modeling sequential behavior.

Hybrid model, tries to integrate both sequential behavior and users' general taste for a better recommendation. A state-of-the-art method is the FPMC model proposed by Rendle et al. [23]. In their work, a transition cube is constructed where each entry of the cube gives the probability of a user buying next item given he has bought a certain item in the last transaction. By factorizing this cube, they interpret this probability by three pairwise interactions among user, items in the last transaction and items in the next basket. In this way, FPMC models sequential behavior by interaction between items in the last transaction and that in the next basket, as well as users' general taste by interaction between the user and the item in the next basket. It has been shown that such a hybrid model can achieve better performance than either a sequential or general recommender alone.

3. MOTIVATION

Next basket recommendation is the task of predicting what a user most probably would like to buy next when his/her sequential transaction data is given. When tackling this problem, both the sequential and general recommender have their own advantages. The sequential recommender can ful-

Figure 1: Next basket recommendation by linear combination of sequential and general factors. The numbers above the movie denote the recommendation scores produced by the recommender.

ly explore the sequential transaction data to discover the correlation between items in consequent purchases, leading to very responsive recommendation according to users' recent purchase. While the general recommender can leverage users' whole purchase histories to learn the taste of different users, and thus achieve better personalization in recommendation.

As shown in previous work [23], it is better to take both sequential and general factors into account for better recommendation. A simple solution is to use a linear combination over these two factors. Furthermore, when modeling the sequential factor, items in the last transaction are often linearly combined in predicting the next item [23]. Obviously, one major assumption underlying these linear combinations is the independence among multiple factors. That is, both sequential and general factor influence the next purchase independently, and each item in the last transaction influence the next purchase independently as well. Here comes the question: Is the independent assumption among multiple factors sufficient for good recommendation?

To answer the above question, we first consider the independent assumption between the general and sequential factors. Let us take a look at an example shown in Figure 1. Imagine a user in general buys science fiction movies like 'The Matrix' and 'X-men'. In contrast to his usual buying behavior, he recently has become fascinated in Scarlett Johansson and purchased 'Match Point' to watch. A sequential recommender based on recent purchase would recommend movies like 'Lost in Translation' (0.9) and 'Girl with a Pearl Earring' (0.85), which are also dramas performed by Scarlett Johansson. (Note that the number in the parentheses denotes the recommendation score). In contrast, a general recommender which mainly accounts for user's general taste would recommend 'The Dark Knight' (0.95) and 'Inception' (0.8) and other science fiction movies. By taking into account both factors, good recommendations for the user might be the movies like 'Lucy' and 'The Avengers', which are science fiction movies performed by Scarlett Johansson. However, if we linearly combine the two factors, i.e. independent in prediction, we may not obtain the right results as we expected. The reason lies in that a good recommendation under joint consideration of the two factors may not obtain a high recommendation score when calculating from each individual factor. For example, the scores of 'Lucy' (0.3) and 'The Avengers' (0.2) in sequential recommender are low since they do not match well with the genre preference (i.e. drama) based on the last purchase of the user. Their scores are also not very high in general recommender since there are many better and popular movies fitting the science fiction taste. Thus the linear combination cannot boost the good recommendations to the top.

Let us take a further look at sequential factor alone, i.e. recommending next items based on the last transaction. For example, people who have bought pumpkin will probably buy other vegetables like cucumber or tomato next, while people who have bought candy will probably buy other snacks like chocolate or chips next. However, people who have bought pumpkin and candy together will very probably buy Halloween costumes next. Again, we can see that if we simply combine the recommendation results from pumpkin and candy respectively, we may not be able to obtain the right recommendations.

From the above examples, we find that models based on linear combination do have limitations in capturing complicated influence of multiple factors on next purchase. In other words, independent assumption among different factors may not be sufficient for good recommendations. We need a model that is capable of incorporating more complicated interactions among multiple factors. This becomes the major motivation of our work.

4. OUR APPROACH

In this section, we first introduce the problem formalization of next basket recommendation. We then describe the proposed HRM in detail. After that, we talk about the learning and prediction procedure of HRM. Finally, we discuss the connections of HRM to existing methods.

4.1 Formalization

Let $U = \{u_1, u_2, \ldots, u_{|U|}\}$ be a set of users and $I = \{i_1, i_2, \ldots, i_{|I|}\}$ be a set of items, where $|U|$ and $|I|$ denote the total number of unique users and items, respectively. For each user u, a purchase history T^u of his transactions is given by $T^u := (T_1^u, T_2^u, \ldots, T_{t_u-1}^u)$, where $T_t^u \subseteq I$, $t \in [1, t_u - 1]$. The purchase history of all users is denoted as $T := \{T^{u_1}, T^{u_2}, \ldots, T^{u_{|U|}}\}$. Given this history, the task is to recommend items that user u would probably buy at the next (i.e. t_u-th) visit. The next basket recommendation task can then be formalized as creating a personalized total ranking $>_{u,t} \subset I^2$ for user u and t_u-th transaction. With this ranking, we can recommend the top n items to the user.

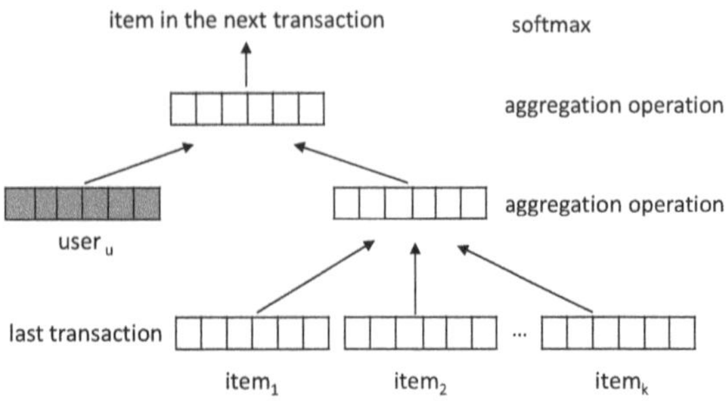

Figure 2: The HRM model architecture. A two-layer structure is employed to construct a hybrid representation over user and items from last transaction, which is used to predict the next purchased items.

4.2 HRM Model

To solve the above recommendation problem, here we present the proposed HRM in detail. The basic idea of our work is to learn a recommendation model that can involve both sequential behavior and users' general taste, and meanwhile modeling complicated interactions among these factors in prediction.

Specifically, HRM represents each user and item as a vector in a continuous space, and employs a two-layer structure to construct a hybrid representation over user and items from last transaction: The first layer forms the transaction representation by aggregating item vectors from last transaction; While the second layer builds the hybrid representation by aggregating the user vector and the transaction representation. The resulting hybrid representation is then used to predict the items in the next basket. The hierarchical structure of HRM is depicted in Figure 2. As we can see, HRM captures the sequential behavior by modeling the consecutive purchases, i.e. constructing the representation of the last transaction from its items for predicting the next purchase. At the same time, by integrating a personalized user representation in sequential recommendation, HRM also models the user's general taste.

More formally, let $V^U = \{\vec{v}_u^U \in \mathbb{R}^n | u \in U\}$ denote all the user vectors and $V^I = \{\vec{v}_i^I \in \mathbb{R}^n | i \in I\}$ denote all the item vectors. Note here V^U and V^I are model parameters to be learned by HRM. Given a user u and two consecutive transactions T_{t-1}^u and T_t^u, HRM defines the probability of buying next item i given user u and his/her last transaction T_{t-1}^u via a softmax function:

$$p(i \in T_t^u | u, T_{t-1}^u) = \frac{exp(\vec{v}_i^I \cdot \vec{v}_{u,t-1}^{Hybrid})}{\sum_{j=1}^{|I|} exp(\vec{v}_j^I \cdot \vec{v}_{u,t-1}^{Hybrid})} \qquad (1)$$

where $\vec{v}_{u,t-1}^{Hybrid}$ denotes the hybrid representation obtained from the hierarchical aggregation which is defined as follows

$$\vec{v}_{u,t-1}^{Hybrid} := f_2(\vec{v}_u^U, f_1(\vec{v}_l^I \in T_{t-1}^u))$$

where $f_1(\cdot)$ and $f_2(\cdot)$ denote the aggregation operation at the first and second layer, respectively.

One advantage of HRM is that we can introduce various aggregation operations in forming higher level representation from lower level. In this way, we can model different interactions among multiple factors at different layers, i.e. interaction among items forming the transaction representation at the first layer, as well as interaction between user and transaction representations at the second layer. In this work, we study two typical aggregation operations as follows.

- *average pooling*: To aggregate a set of vector representations, average pooling construct one vector by taking the average value of each dimension. Let $V = \{\vec{v}_l \in \mathbb{R}^n | l = 1, \ldots, |V|\}$ be a set of input vectors to be aggregated, average pooling over V can be formalized as

$$f_{avg}(V) = \frac{1}{|V|} \sum_{l=1}^{|V|} \vec{v}_l$$

  Obviously, average pooling is a linear operation, which assumes the independence among input representations in forming higher level representation.

- *max pooling*: To aggregate a set of vector representations, max pooling constructs one vector by taking the maximum value of each dimension, which can be formalized as

$$f_{max}(V) = \begin{bmatrix} max(\vec{v}_1[1],\ldots,\vec{v}_{|V|}[1]) \\ max(\vec{v}_1[2],\ldots,\vec{v}_{|V|}[2]) \\ \vdots \\ max(\vec{v}_1[n],\ldots,\vec{v}_{|V|}[n]) \end{bmatrix}$$

  where $\vec{v}_l[k]$ denotes the k-th dimension in $\vec{v}_l$. In Contrary to average pooling, max pooling is a nonlinear operation which models interactions among input representations, i.e. features from each input vector are compared and only those most significant features will be selected to the next level. Take the movie recommender mentioned in Section 3.1 for example, we suppose vector representations are used for both sequential and general factors. If there are two dimensions capturing the genre and actor/actress preference respectively, max pooling then selects the most significant feature in each dimension (e.g. science fiction and Scarlett Johansson) in aggregating the two vectors.

Note that there are other ways to define the aggregation operations, e.g. top-k average pooling or Hadamard product. We may study these operations in the future work. Besides, one may also consider to introduce nonlinear hidden layers as in deep neural network [4]. However, we resort to simple models since previous work has demonstrated that such models can learn accurate representations from very large data set due to low computational complexity [17, 27].

Since there are two-layer aggregations in HRM, we thus can obtain four versions of HRM based on different combinations of operations, namely HRM_{AvgAvg}, HRM_{MaxAvg}, HRM_{AvgMax}, and HRM_{MaxMax}, where the two abbreviations in subscript denote the first and second layer aggregation operation respectively. For example, HRM_{AvgMax} denotes the model that employs average pooling at the first layer and max pooling at second layer.

As we can see, these four versions of HRM actually assume different strength of interactions among multiple factors. By only using average pooling, HRM_{AvgAvg} assume independence among all the factors. We later show that HRM_{AvgAvg} can be viewed as some variation of FPMC.

Both HRM$_{AvgMax}$ and HRM$_{MaxAvg}$ introduce partial interactions, either among the items in last transaction or between the user and transaction representations. Finally, by using nonlinear operations at both layers, HRM$_{MaxMax}$ assumes full interactions among all the factors.

4.3 Learning and Prediction

In learning, HRM maximizes the log probability defined in Equation (1) over the transaction data of all users as follows

$$\ell_{HRM} = \sum_{u \in U} \sum_{T_t^u \in T^u} \sum_{i \in T_t^u} \log p(i \in T_t^u | u, T_{t-1}^u) - \lambda \|\Theta\|_F^2$$

where λ is the regularization constant and Θ are the model parameters (i.e. $\Theta=\{V^U,V^I\}$). As defined in Section 4.1, the goal of next basket recommendation is to derive a ranking $>_{u,t}$ over items. HRM actually defines the ranking as

$$i >_{u,t} i' :\Leftrightarrow p(i \in T_t^u | u, T_{t-1}^u) > p(i' \in T_t^u | u, T_{t-1}^u)$$

and attempts to derive such ranking by maximizing the buying probability of next items over the whole purchase history.

However, directly optimizing the above objective function is impractical because the cost of computing the full softmax is proportional to the size of items $|I|$, which is often extremely large. Therefore, we adopt the negative sampling technique [21, 27] for efficient optimization, which approximates the original objective ℓ_{HRM} with the following objective function

$$\ell_{NEG} = \sum_{u \in U} \sum_{T_t^u \in T^u} \sum_{i \in T_t^u} \Big(\log \sigma(\vec{v}_i^I \cdot \vec{v}_{u,t-1}^{Hybrid}) + k \cdot \mathbb{E}_{i' \sim P_I} [\log \sigma(-\vec{v}_{i'}^I \cdot \vec{v}_{u,t-1}^{Hybrid})] \Big) - \lambda \|\Theta\|_F^2$$

where $\sigma(x) = 1/(1+e^{-x})$, k is the number of "negative" samples, and i' is the sampled item, drawn according to the noise distribution P_I which is modeled by empirical unigram distribution over items. As we can see, the objective of HRM with negative sampling aims to derive the ranking $>_{u,t}$ in a discriminative way by maximizing the probability of observed item i and meanwhile minimizing the probability of unobserved item i's.

We then apply stochastic gradient descent algorithm to maximize the new objective function for learning the model. Moreover, when learning the nonlinear models, we also adopt Dropout technique to avoid overfitting. In our work, we simply set a fixed drop ratio (50%) for each unit.

With the learned user and item vectors, the next basket recommendation with HRM is as follows. Given a user u and his/her last transaction $T_{t_u-1}^u$, for each candidate item $i \in I$, we calculate the probability $p(i \in I | u, T_{t_u-1}^u)$ according to Equation (1). We than rank the items according to their probabilities, and select the top n results as the final recommendations to the user.

4.4 Connection to Previous Models

In this section, we discuss the connection of the proposed HRM to previous work. We show that by choosing proper aggregation operations, HRM subsumes several existing methods including Markov chain model, matrix factorization model as well as a variation of FPMC model.

4.4.1 *HRM vs. Markov Chain Model*

To show that HRM can be reduced to a certain type of Markov chain model, we first introduce a special aggregation operation, namely select-copy operation. When aggregating a set of vector representations, the select-copy operation select one of the vectors according to some criterion, and copy it as the aggregated one. Now we apply this operation to both levels of HRM. Specifically, when constructing the transaction representation from item vectors, the operation randomly selects one item vector and copies it. When combining the user and transaction representations, the operation always selects and copies the transaction vector. We refer the HRM with this model architecture as HRM$_{CopyItem}$. The new objective function of HRM$_{CopyItem}$ using negative sampling is as follows:

$$\ell_{CopyItem} = \sum_{u \in U} \sum_{T_t^u \in T^u} \sum_{i \in T_t^u} \Big(\log \sigma(\vec{v}_i^I \cdot \vec{v}_s^I) + k \cdot \mathbb{E}_{i' \sim P_I} [\log \sigma(-\vec{v}_{i'}^I \cdot \vec{v}_s^I)] \Big) - \lambda \|\Theta\|_F^2$$

where $\vec{v}_s^I$ denotes the vector of randomly selected item in last transaction.

Similar as the derivation in [21], we can show that the solution of HRM$_{CopyItem}$ follows that

$$\vec{v}_i^I \cdot \vec{v}_s^I = PMI(v_i^I, v_s^I) - \log k$$

which indicates that HRM$_{CopyItem}$ is actually a factorized Markov chain model (FMC) [23], which factorizes a transition matrix between items from two consecutive transactions with the association measured by *shifted PMI* (i.e. $PMI(x,y) - \log k$). When $k = 1$, the transition matrix becomes a PMI matrix.

In fact, if we employ noise contrastive estimation [27] for optimization, the solution then follows that:

$$\vec{v}_i^I \cdot \vec{v}_s^I = \log P(v_i^I | v_s^I) - \log k$$

which indicates the transition matrix factorized by HRM$_{CopyItem}$ become a (shifted) log-conditional-probability matrix.

4.4.2 *HRM vs. Matrix Factorization Model*

Now we only apply the select-copy operation to the second layer (i.e. aggregation over user and transaction representations), and this time we always select and copy user vector. We refer this model as HRM$_{CopyUser}$. The corresponding objective function using negative sampling is as follows:

$$\ell_{CopyUser} = \sum_{u \in U} \sum_{T_t^u \in T^u} \sum_{i \in T_t^u} \Big(\log \sigma(\vec{v}_i^I \cdot \vec{v}_u^U) + k \cdot \mathbb{E}_{i' \sim P_I} [\log \sigma(-\vec{v}_{i'}^I \cdot \vec{v}_u^U)] \Big) - \lambda \|\Theta\|_F^2$$

Again, we can show that HRM$_{CopyUser}$ has the solution in the following form:

$$\vec{v}_u^U \cdot \vec{v}_i^I = PMI(v_u^U, v_i^I) - \log k$$

In this way, HRM$_{CopyUser}$ reduces to a matrix factorization model, which factorizes a user-item matrix where the association between a user and a item is measured by shifted PMI.

4.4.3 *HRM vs. FPMC*

FPMC conducts a tensor factorization over the transition cube constructed from the transition matrices of all users. It is optimized under the Bayesian personalized ranking (BPR) criterion and the objective function using MAP-estimator is

Table 1: Statistics of the datasets used in our experiments.

dataset	users $\|U\|$	items $\|I\|$	transactions T	avg.transaction size	avg.transaction per user
Ta-Feng	9238	7982	67964	7.4	5.9
BeiRen	9321	5845	91294	9.7	5.8
T-Mall	292	191	1805	5.6	1.2

as follows [23]:

$$\ell_{FPMC} = \sum_{u\in U}\sum_{T_t^u\in T^u}\sum_{i\in T_t^u}\sum_{i'\notin T_t^u} \log\sigma(\hat{x}_{u,t,i}-\hat{x}_{u,t,i'}) - \lambda\|\Theta\|_F^2 \quad (2)$$

where $\hat{x}_{u,t,i}$ denotes the prediction model

$$\begin{aligned}\hat{x}_{u,t,i} &:= \hat{p}(i\in T_t^u | u, T_{t-1}^u)\\ &:= \vec{v}_u^U\cdot\vec{v}_i^I + \frac{1}{|T_{t-1}^u|}\sum_{l\in T_{t-1}^u}(\vec{v}_i^I\cdot\vec{v}_l^I) \quad (3)\end{aligned}$$

To see the connection between HRM and FPMC, we now set the aggregation operation as average pooling at both layers and apply negative sampling with $k=1$. We denote this model as $\text{HRM}_{AvgAvgNEG1}$ and its objective function is as follows

$$\begin{aligned}\ell_{AvgAvgNEG1} &= \sum_{u\in U}\sum_{T_t^u\in T^u}\sum_{i\in T_t^u}\Big(\log\sigma(\vec{v}_i^I\cdot\vec{v}_{u,t-1}^{Hybrid})\\ &\quad +\mathbb{E}_{i'\sim P_I}[\log\sigma(-\vec{v}_{i'}^I\cdot\vec{v}_{u,t-1}^{Hybrid})]\Big) - \lambda\|\Theta\|_F^2\\ &= \sum_{u\in U}\sum_{T_t^u\in T^u}\sum_{i\in T_t^u}\sum_{i'\notin T_t^u}\Big(\log\sigma(\vec{v}_i^I\cdot\vec{v}_{u,t-1}^{Hybrid})\\ &\quad +\log\sigma(-\vec{v}_{i'}^I\cdot\vec{v}_{u,t-1}^{Hybrid})\Big) - \lambda\|\Theta\|_F^2 \quad (4)\end{aligned}$$

where

$$\vec{v}_{u,t-1}^{Hybrid} = \frac{1}{2}(\vec{v}_u^U + \frac{1}{|T_{t-1}^u|}\sum_{l\in T_{t-1}^u}\vec{v}_l^I) \quad (5)$$

With Equation (3) and (5), we can rewrite Equation (4) as follows

$$\begin{aligned}\ell_{AvgAvgNEG1} &= \sum_{u\in U}\sum_{T_t^u\in T^u}\sum_{i\in T_t^u}\sum_{i'\notin T_t^u}\Big(\log\sigma(\hat{x}_{u,t,i})\\ &\quad +\log\sigma(-\hat{x}_{u,t,i'})\Big) - \lambda\parallel\Theta\parallel_F^2 + C\\ &= \sum_{u\in U}\sum_{T_t^u\in T^u}\sum_{i\in T_t^u}\sum_{i'\notin T_t^u}\Big(\log\sigma(\hat{x}_{u,t,i})\\ &\quad +\log(1-\sigma(\hat{x}_{u,t,i'}))\Big) - \lambda\parallel\Theta\parallel_F^2 + C \quad (6)\end{aligned}$$

Based on the above derivations, we can see that both $\text{HRM}_{AvgAvgNEG1}$ and FPMC share the same prediction model denoted by Equation (3), but optimize with slightly different criteria. FPMC tries to maximize the pairwise rank, i.e. an observed item i ranks higher than an unobserved item i', by defining the pairwise probability using a logistic function as shown in Equation (2). While $\text{HRM}_{AvgAvgNEG1}$ also optimizes this pairwise rank by maximizing the probability of item i and minimizing the probability of item i', each defined in a logistic form as shown in Equation (6). In fact, we can also adopt BPR criterion to define the objective function of HRM_{AvgAvg}, and obtain the same model as FPMC.

Based on all the above analysis, we can see that the proposed HRM is actually a very general model. By introducing different aggregation operations, we can produce multiple recommendation models well connected to existing methods. Moreover, HRM also allows us to explore other prediction functions as well as optimization criteria, showing large flexibility and promising potential.

5. EVALUATION

In this section, we conduct empirical experiments to demonstrate the effectiveness of our proposed HRM on next basket recommendation. We first introduce the dataset, baseline methods, and the evaluation metrics employed in our experiments. Then we compare the four versions of HRM to study the effect of different combinations of aggregation operations. After that, we compare our HRM to the state-of-the-art baseline methods to demonstrate its effectiveness. Finally, we conduct some analysis on our optimization procedure, i.e. negative sampling technique.

5.1 Dataset

We evaluate different recommenders based on three real-world transaction datasets, i.e. two retail datasets Ta-Feng and BeiRen, and one e-commerce dataset T-Mall.

- The Ta-Feng[1] dataset is a public dataset released by RecSys conference, which covers products from food, office supplies to furniture. It contains 817,741 transactions belonging to 32,266 users and 23,812 items.
- The BeiRen dataset comes from BeiGuoRenBai[2], a large retail enterprise in China, which records its supermarket purchase history during the period from Jan. 2013 to Sept. 2013. It contains 1,123,754 transactions belonging to 34,221 users and 17,920 items.
- The T-Mall[3] dataset is a public online e-commerce dataset released by Taobao[4], which records the online transactions in terms of brands. It contains 4298 transactions belonging to 884 users and 9,531 brands.

We first conduct some pre-process on these transaction datasets similar as [23]. For both Ta-Feng and BeiRen dataset, we remove all the items bought by less than 10 users and users that has bought in total less than 10 items. For the T-Mall dataset, which is relatively smaller, we remove all the items bought by less than 3 users and users that has bought in total less than 3 items. The statistics of the three datasets after pre-processing are shown in Table 1.

Finally, we split all the datasets into two non overlapping set, i.e. a training set and a testing set. The testing set contains only the last transaction of each user, while all the remaining transactions are put into the training set.

[1] http://recsyswiki.com/wiki/Grocery_shopping_datasets
[2] http://www.brjt.cn/
[3] http://102.alibaba.com/competition/addDiscovery/index.htm
[4] http://www.taobao.com

Table 2: Performance comparison among four versions of HRM over three datasets

(a) Performance comparison on Ta-Feng

Models	d=50			d=100			d=150			d=200		
	F1-score	Hit-ratio	NDCG	F1-score	Hit-ratio	NDCG	F1-score	Hit-ratio	NDCG	F1-score	Hit-ratio	NDCG
HRM_{AvgAvg}	0.051	0.240	0.073	0.060	0.276	0.082	0.063	0.283	0.080	0.063	0.286	0.086
HRM_{MaxAvg}	0.059	0.275	0.080	0.064	0.279	0.087	0.065	0.290	0.083	0.067	0.298	0.086
HRM_{AvgMax}	0.057	0.262	0.080	0.064	0.288	0.085	0.065	0.289	0.082	0.068	0.293	0.090
HRM_{MaxMax}	**0.062**	**0.282**	**0.089**	**0.065**	**0.293**	**0.088**	**0.068**	**0.298**	**0.085**	**0.070**	**0.312**	**0.093**

(b) Performance comparison on BeiRen

Models	d=50			d=100			d=150			d=200		
	F1-score	Hit-ratio	NDCG	F1-score	Hit-ratio	NDCG	F1-score	Hit-ratio	NDCG	F1-score	Hit-ratio	NDCG
HRM_{AvgAvg}	0.100	0.463	0.119	0.107	0.475	0.128	0.112	0.505	0.137	0.113	0.509	0.137
HRM_{MaxAvg}	0.105	0.485	0.131	0.113	0.498	0.138	0.115	0.509	0.139	0.115	0.505	0.141
HRM_{AvgMax}	0.106	0.494	0.131	0.114	0.512	0.140	0.115	0.510	0.141	0.115	0.510	0.140
HRM_{MaxMax}	**0.111**	**0.501**	**0.134**	**0.115**	**0.515**	**0.144**	**0.117**	**0.516**	**0.146**	**0.118**	**0.515**	**0.145**

(c) Performance comparison on T-Mall

Models	d=10			d=15			d=20			d=25		
	F1-score	Hit-ratio	NDCG	F1-score	Hit-ratio	NDCG	F1-score	Hit-ratio	NDCG	F1-score	Hit-ratio	NDCG
HRM_{AvgAvg}	0.052	0.154	0.119	0.055	0.139	0.146	0.061	0.180	0.146	0.063	0.186	0.151
HRM_{MaxAvg}	0.062	0.186	0.133	0.063	0.148	0.157	0.066	0.196	0.154	0.068	0.202	0.158
HRM_{AvgMax}	0.061	0.186	0.133	0.063	0.148	0.153	0.064	0.191	0.157	0.066	0.196	0.159
HRM_{MaxMax}	**0.065**	**0.191**	**0.142**	**0.066**	**0.197**	**0.163**	**0.070**	**0.207**	**0.163**	**0.071**	**0.212**	**0.168**

5.2 Baseline Methods

We evaluate our model by comparing with several state-of-the-art methods on next-basket recommendation:

- TOP: The top popular items in training set are taken as recommendations for each user.
- MC: A Markov chain model (i.e. sequential recommender) which predicts the next purchase based on the last transaction of the user. The prediction model is as follows:

$$p(i \in T^u_{t_u} | T^u_{t_u-1}) := \frac{1}{|T^u_{t_u-1}|} \sum_{l \in T^u_{t_u-1}} p(i \in T^u_{t_u} | l \in T^u_{t_u-1})$$

  The transition probability of buying an item based on the last purchase is estimated from the training set.

- NMF: A state-of-the-art model based collaborative filtering method [14]. Here Nonnegative Matrix Factorization is applied over the user-item matrix, which is constructed from the transaction dataset by discarding the sequential information. For implementation, we adopt the publicly available codes from NMF:DTU Toolbox[5].
- FPMC: A state-of-the-art hybrid model on next basket recommendation [23]. Both sequential behavior and users' general taste are taken into account for prediction.

For NMF, FPMC and our HRM[6] methods, we run several times with random initialization by setting the dimensionality $d \in \{50, 100, 150, 200\}$ on Ta-Feng and BeiRen datasets, and $d \in \{10, 15, 20, 25\}$ on T-Mall dataset. We compare the best results of different methods and demonstrate the results in the following sections.

[5]http://cogsys.imm.dtu.dk/toolbox/nmf/

[6]http://www.bigdatalab.ac.cn/benchmark/bm/bd?code=HRM

5.3 Evaluation Metrics

The performance is evaluated for each user u on the transaction $T^u_{t_u}$ in the testing dataset. For each recommendation method, we generate a list of N items (N=5) for each user u, denoted by $R(u)$, where $R_i(u)$ stands for the item recommended in the i-th position. We use the following quality measures to evaluate the recommendation lists against the actual bought items.

- F1-score: F1-score is the harmonic mean of precision and recall, which is a widely used measure in recommendation [9, 15, 23]:

$$\text{Precison}(T^u_{t_u}, R(u)) = \frac{|T^u_{t_u} \bigcap R(u)|}{|R(u)|}$$

$$\text{Recall}(T^u_{t_u}, R(u)) = \frac{|T^u_{t_u} \bigcap R(u)|}{|T^u_{t_u}|}$$

$$\text{F1-score} = \frac{2 \times \text{Precision} \times \text{Recall}}{\text{Precision} + \text{Recall}}$$

- Hit-Ratio: Hit-Ratio is a All-but-One measure used in recommendation [13, 28]. If there is at least one item in the test transaction also appears in the recommendation list, we call it a *hit*. The Hit-Ratio is calculated in the following way:

$$\text{Hit-Ratio} = \frac{\sum_{u \in U} I(T^u_{t_u} \bigcap R(u) \neq \phi)}{|U|}$$

  where $I(\cdot)$ is an indicator function and ϕ denotes the empty set. Hit-Ratio focuses on the *recall* of a recommender system, i.e. how many people can obtain at least one correct recommendation.

- NDCG@k: Normalized Discounted Cumulative Gain (NDCG) is a ranking based measure which takes into

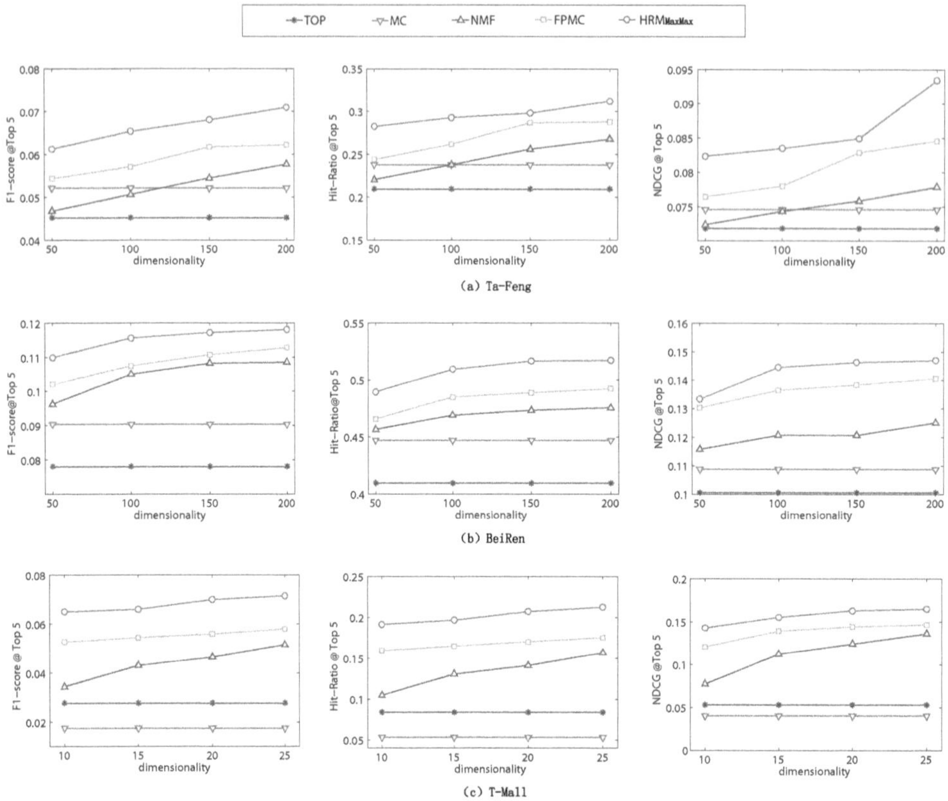

Figure 3: Performance comparison of HRM among TOP,MC,NMF, and FPMC over three datasets. The dimensionality is increased from 50 to 200 on Ta-Feng and BeiRen, and 10 to 25 on T-Mall.

account the order of recommended items in the list[11], and is formally given by:

$$NDCG@k = \frac{1}{N_k}\sum_{j=1}^{k}\frac{2^{I(R_j(u)\in T_{tu}^u)}-1}{log_2(j+1)}$$

where $I(\cdot)$ is an indicator function and N_k is a constant which denotes the maximum value of NDCG@k given $R(u)$.

5.4 Comparison among Different HRMs

We first empirically compare the performance of the four versions of HRM, referred to as HRM_{AvgAvg}, HRM_{MaxAvg}, HRM_{AvgMax}, HRM_{MaxMax}. The results over three datasets are shown in Table 2.

As we can see, HRM_{AvgAvg}, which only uses average pooling operations in aggregation, performs the worst among the four models. It indicates that by assuming independence among all the factors, we may not be able to learn a good recommendation model. Both HRM_{MaxAvg} and HRM_{AvgMax} introduce partial interactions by using max pooling either at the first or the second layer, and obtain better results than HRM_{AvgAvg}. Take the Ta-Feng dataset as an example, when compared with HRM_{AvgAvg} with dimensionality set as 50, the relative performance improvement by HRM_{MaxAvg} and HRM_{AvgMax} is around 13.6% and 9.8%, respectively. Besides, we also find that there is no consistent dominant between these two partial-interaction models, indicating that interactions at different layers may both help the recommendation in their own way. Finally, by applying max pooling at both layers (i.e. full interactions), HRM_{MaxMax} can outperform the other three variations in terms of all the three evaluation measures. The results demonstrate the advantage of modeling interactions among multiple factors in next basket recommendation.

5.5 Comparison against Baselines

We further compare our HRM model to the state-of-the-art baseline methods on next basket recommendation. Here we choose the best performed HRM_{MaxMax} as the representative for clear comparison. The performance results over Ta-Feng, BeiRen, and T-Mall are shown in Figure 3.

We have the following observations from the results. (1) Overall, the Top method is the weakest. However, we find that the Top method outperforms MC on the T-Mall dataset. This might be due to the fact that the items in T-Mall dataset are actually brands. Therefore, the distributions of top popular brands on both training and testing datasets are very close, which accords with the assumption of the Top method and leads to better performance. (2) The NMF method outperforms the MC method in most cases. A major reason might be that the transition matrix estimated in the

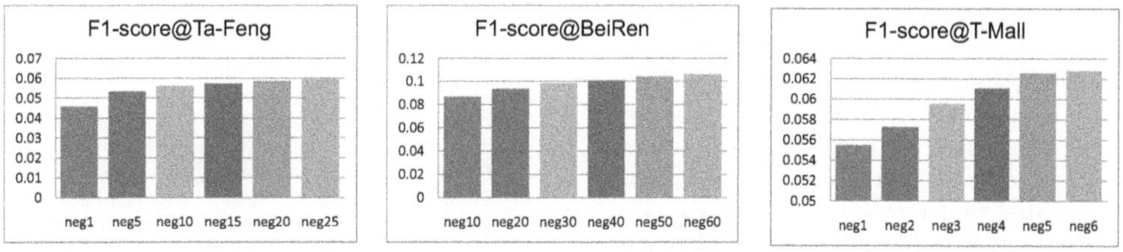

Figure 4: Performance variation in terms of F1-score against the number of negative samples over three datasets with HRM_{MaxMax}. The number of negative samples is increased from 1 to 25 on Ta-Feng, 10 to 60 on BeiRen, and from 1 to 6 on T-Mall.

Table 3: Performance comparison on Ta-Feng over different user groups with dimensionality set as 50.

user activeness	method	F1-score	Hit-Ratio	NDCG@5
Inactive	Top	0.036	0.181	0.054
	MC	0.042	0.206	0.058
	NMF	0.037	0.198	0.046
	FPMC	0.043	0.216	0.060
	HRM_{MaxMax}	**0.048**	**0.236**	**0.062**
Medium	Top	0.051	0.230	0.084
	MC	0.059	0.262	0.088
	NMF	0.052	0.234	0.072
	FPMC	0.059	0.263	0.087
	HRM_{MaxMax}	**0.068**	**0.299**	**0.097**
Active	Top	0.045	0.207	0.074
	MC	0.050	0.212	0.075
	NMF	0.056	0.223	0.075
	FPMC	0.054	0.224	0.080
	HRM_{MaxMax}	**0.062**	**0.246**	**0.087**

MC method are rather sparse, and directly using it for recommendation may not work well. One way to improve the performance of the MC method is to factorize the transition matrix to alleviate the sparse problem [23]. (3) By combining both sequential behavior and users' general taste, FPMC can obtain better results than both MC and NMF. This result is quite consistent with the previous finding in [23]. (4) By further introducing the interactions among multiple factors, the proposed HRM_{MaxMax} can consistently outperform all the baseline methods in terms of all the measures over the three datasets. Take the Ta-Feng dataset as an example, when compared with second best performed baseline method (i.e. FPMC) with dimensionality set as 200, the relative performance improvement by HRM_{MaxMax} is around 13.1%, 11.1%, and 12.5% in terms of F1-score, Hit-Ratio and NDCG@5, respectively.

To further investigate the performance of different methods, we split the users into three groups (i.e., inactive, medium and active) based on their activeness and conducted the comparisons on different user groups. Take the Ta-Feng dataset as an example, a user is taken as inactive if there are less than 5 transactions in his/her purchase history, and active if there are more than 20 transactions in the purchase history. The remaining users are taken as medium. In this way, the proportions of inactive, medium and active are 40.8%, 54.5%, and 4.7% respectively. Here we only report the comparison results on Ta-Feng dataset under one dimensionality (i.e. $d = 50$) due to the page limitation. In fact, similar conclusions can be drawn from other datasets. The results are shown in Table 3.

From the results we can see that, not surprisingly, the Top method is still the worst on all the groups. Furthermore, we find that MC works better than NMF on both inactive and medium users in terms of all the measures; While on active users, NMF can achieve better performance than MC. The results indicate that it is difficult for NMF to learn a good user representation with few transactions for recommendation. By combining both sequential behavior and users' general taste linearly, FPMC obtains better performance than MC on inactive and active users, and performs better than NMF on inactive and medium users. However, we can see the improvements are not very consistent on different user groups. Finally, HRM_{MaxMax} can achieve the best performance on all the groups in terms of all the measures. It demonstrates that modeling interactions among multiple factors can help generate better recommendations for different types of users.

5.6 The Impact of Negative Sampling

To learn the proposed HRM, we employ negative sampling procedure for optimization. One parameter in this procedure is the number of negative samples we draw each time, denoted by k. Here we investigate the impact of the sampling number k on the final performance. Since the item size is different over the three datasets, we tried different ranges of k accordingly. Specifically, we tried $k \in \{1, 5, 10, 15, 20, 25\}$ on Ta-Feng, $k \in \{10, 20, 30, 40, 50, 60\}$ on BeiRen, and $k \in \{1, 2, 3, 4, 5, 6\}$ on T-Mall, respectively. We report the test performance of HRM_{MaxMax} in terms of F1-score against the number of negative samples over the three datasets in Figure 4. Here we only show the results on one dimension over each dataset (i.e. $d = 50$ on Ta-Feng and BeiRen and $d = 10$ on T-Mall) due to the space limitation.

From the results we find that: (1) As the sampling number k increases, the test performance in terms of F1-score increases too. The trending is quite consistent over the three datasets. (2) As the sampling number k increases, the performance gain between two consecutive trials decreases. For example, on Ta-Feng dataset, when we increase k from 20 to 25, the relative performance improvement in terms of F1-score is about 0.0011%. It indicates that if we continue to sample more negative samples, there will be less performance improvement but larger computational complexity. Therefore, in our performance comparison experiments, we set k as 25, 60, 6 on Ta-Feng, BeiRen and T-Mall, respectively.

6. CONCLUSION

In this paper, we propose a novel hierarchical representation model (HRM) to predict what users will buy in next basket. Our model can well capture both sequential behavior and users' general taste in recommendation. What is more important is that HRM allows us to model complicated interactions among multiple factors by using different aggregation operations over the representations of these factors. We conducted experiments on three real-world transaction datasets, and demonstrated that our approach can outperform all the state-of-the-art baseline methods consistently under different evaluation metrics.

For the future work, we would like to try other aggregation operations in our HRM. We also want to analyze what kind of interactions are really effective in next basket prediction. Moreover, we would like to study how to integrate other types of information into our model, e.g. the transaction timestamp, which may introduce even more complicated interactions with the existing factors.

7. ACKNOWLEDGMENTS

This research work was funded by 973 Program of China under Grant No.2014CB340406, No.2012CB316303, 863 Program of China under Grant No.2014AA015204, Project supported by the National Natural Science Foundation of China under Grant No.61472401, No.61433014, No.61425016, and No.61203298. We would like to thank the anonymous reviewers for their valuable comments.

8. REFERENCES

[1] G. Adomavicius and A. Tuzhilin. Toward the next generation of recommender systems: A survey of the state-of-the-art and possible extensions. *IEEE Trans. on Knowl. and Data Eng.*, 17(6):734–749, June 2005.

[2] T. R. Andreas Mild. An improved collaborative filtering approach for predicting cross-category purchases based on binary market basket data. *Journal of Retailing and Consumer Services*, 2003.

[3] C. M. Andrew Zimdars, David Maxwell Chickering. Using temporal data for making recommendations. *The Conference on Uncertainty in Artificial Intelligence*, 2001.

[4] E. Arisoy, T. N. Sainath, B. Kingsbury, and B. Ramabhadran. Deep neural network language models. In *Proceedings of the NAACL-HLT 2012 Workshop: Will We Ever Really Replace the N-gram Model? On the Future of Language Modeling for HLT*, WLM '12, pages 20–28, Stroudsburg, PA, USA, 2012. Association for Computational Linguistics.

[5] S. Chen, J. L. Moore, D. Turnbull, and T. Joachims. Playlist prediction via metric embedding. In *Proceedings of the 18th ACM SIGKDD International Conference on Knowledge Discovery and Data Mining*, KDD '12, pages 714–722, New York, NY, USA, 2012. ACM.

[6] A. G. Chetna Chand, Amit Thakkar. Sequential pattern mining: Survey and current research challenges. *International Journal of Soft Computing and Engineering*, 2012.

[7] A. Christidis, K. Exploring customer preferences with probabilistic topics models. In *European Conference on Machine Learning and Principles and Practice of Knowledge Discovery in Databases*, 2010.

[8] M. Gatzioura, A. ;Sanchez Marre. A case-based recommendation approach for market basket data. *Intelligent Systems, IEEE*, 2014.

[9] D. Godoy and A. Amandi. User profiling in personal information agents: A survey. *Knowl. Eng. Rev.*, 20(4):329–361, Dec. 2005.

[10] Y. Hu, Y. Koren, and C. Volinsky. Collaborative filtering for implicit feedback datasets. In *Proceedings of the 2008 Eighth IEEE International Conference on Data Mining*, ICDM '08, pages 263–272, Washington, DC, USA, 2008. IEEE Computer Society.

[11] K. Järvelin and J. Kekäläinen. Ir evaluation methods for retrieving highly relevant documents. In *Proceedings of the 23rd Annual International ACM SIGIR Conference on Research and Development in Information Retrieval*, SIGIR '00, pages 41–48, New York, NY, USA, 2000. ACM.

[12] S. K. Jong-Seok Lee, Chi-Hyuck JunčňJaewook Lee. Classification-based collaborative filtering using market basket data. *Expert Systems with Applications*, 2005.

[13] G. Karypis. Evaluation of item-based top-n recommendation algorithms. In *Proceedings of the Tenth International Conference on Information and Knowledge Management*, CIKM '01, pages 247–254, New York, NY, USA, 2001. ACM.

[14] D. D. Lee and H. S. Seung. Algorithms for non-negative matrix factorization. In T. Leen, T. Dietterich, and V. Tresp, editors, *Advances in Neural Information Processing Systems 13*, pages 556–562. MIT Press, 2001.

[15] W. Lin, S. A. Alvarez, and C. Ruiz. Efficient adaptive-support association rule mining for recommender systems. *Data Min. Knowl. Discov.*, 6(1):83–105, Jan. 2002.

[16] G. Linden, B. Smith, and J. York. Amazon.com recommendations: Item-to-item collaborative filtering. *IEEE Internet Computing*, 7(1):76–80, Jan. 2003.

[17] T. Mikolov, K. Chen, G. Corrado, and J. Dean. Efficient estimation of word representations in vector space. *CoRR*, abs/1301.3781, 2013.

[18] T. Mobasher, B. ; Sch. of Comput. Sci. Using sequential and non-sequential patterns in predictive web usage mining tasks. *The IEEE International Conference on Data Mining series*, 2002.

[19] R. Pan and M. Scholz. Mind the gaps: Weighting the unknown in large-scale one-class collaborative filtering. In *Proceedings of the 15th ACM SIGKDD International Conference on Knowledge Discovery and Data Mining*, KDD '09, pages 667–676, New York, NY, USA, 2009. ACM.

[20] Y. L. Pengfei Wang, Jiafeng Guo. Modeling retail transaction data for personalized shopping recommendation. In *23rd International Conference on Information and Knowledge Management*, 2014.

[21] T. M. Quoc V. Le. distributed representations of sentences and documents. *The 31st International Conference on Machine Learning*, 2014.

[22] S. Rendle, C. Freudenthaler, Z. Gantner, and L. Schmidt-Thieme. Bpr: Bayesian personalized ranking from implicit feedback. In *Proceedings of the Twenty-Fifth Conference on Uncertainty in Artificial Intelligence*, UAI '09, pages 452–461, Arlington, Virginia, United States, 2009. AUAI Press.

[23] S. Rendle, C. Freudenthaler, and L. Schmidt-Thieme. Factorizing personalized markov chains for next-basket recommendation. In *Proceedings of the 19th International Conference on World Wide Web*, WWW '10, pages 811–820, New York, NY, USA, 2010. ACM.

[24] G. Shani, R. I. Brafman, and D. Heckerman. An mdp-based recommender system. In *Proceedings of the Eighteenth Conference on Uncertainty in Artificial Intelligence*, UAI'02, pages 453–460, San Francisco, CA, USA, 2002. Morgan Kaufmann Publishers Inc.

[25] R. Srikant and R. Agrawal. Mining sequential patterns: Generalizations and performance improvements. In *Proceedings of the 5th International Conference on Extending Database Technology: Advances in Database Technology*, EDBT '96, pages 3–17, London, UK, UK, 1996. Springer-Verlag.

[26] X. Su and T. M. Khoshgoftaar. A survey of collaborative filtering techniques. *Adv. in Artif. Intell.*, 2009:4:2–4:2, Jan. 2009.

[27] K. C. G. C. J. D. Tomas Mikolov, Ilya Sutskever. Distributed representations of words and phrases and their compositionality. *Neural Information Processing Systems Foundation*, 2013.

[28] L. Xiang, Q. Yuan, S. Zhao, L. Chen, X. Zhang, Q. Yang, and J. Sun. Temporal recommendation on graphs via long- and short-term preference fusion. In *Proceedings of the 16th ACM SIGKDD International Conference on Knowledge Discovery and Data Mining*, KDD '10, pages 723–732, New York, NY, USA, 2010. ACM.

[29] G.-E. Yap, X.-L. Li, and P. S. Yu. Effective next-items recommendation via personalized sequential pattern mining. In *Proceedings of the 17th International Conference on Database Systems for Advanced Applications - Volume Part II*, DASFAA'12, pages 48–64, Berlin, Heidelberg, 2012. Springer-Verlag.

Parametric and Non-parametric User-aware Sentiment Topic Models

Zaihan Yang Alexander Kotov Aravind Mohan Shiyong Lu
Department of Computer Science
Wayne State University
Detroit, MI 48202 USA
{zaihan.yang|kotov|aravind.mohan|shiyong}@wayne.edu

ABSTRACT

The popularity of Web 2.0 has resulted in a large number of publicly available online consumer reviews created by a demographically diverse user base. Information about the authors of these reviews, such as age, gender and location, provided by many online consumer review platforms may allow companies to better understand the preferences of different market segments and improve their product design, manufacturing processes and marketing campaigns accordingly. However, previous work in sentiment analysis has largely ignored these additional user meta-data. To address this deficiency, in this paper, we propose parametric and non-parametric User-aware Sentiment Topic Models (USTM) that incorporate demographic information of review authors into topic modeling process in order to discover associations between market segments, topical aspects and sentiments. Qualitative examination of the topics discovered using USTM framework in the two datasets collected from popular online consumer review platforms as well as quantitative evaluation of the methods utilizing those topics for the tasks of review sentiment classification and user attribute prediction both indicate the utility of accounting for demographic information of review authors in opinion mining.

Categories and Subject Descriptors

H.2.8 [**Database Applications**]: Data mining; I.2.7 [**Natural Language Processing**]: Text analysis

Keywords

Opinion Mining; Topic Models; Dirichlet Process

1. INTRODUCTION

The emergence of online consumer review platforms, such as Amazon[1], Tripadvisor[2], and MSN Autos[3], allowed consumers to publicly express their opinions about a wide variety of products and services. The popularity of such platforms has resulted in large amounts of online review content created by a demographically diverse user base. Due to popularity and public availability, online consumer reviews have become an increasingly important and valuable source of information not only for consumers, who often base their decisions about purchasing a product or using a service on opinions of other people, but also for companies and manufacturers, who are trying to understand consumer preferences in different market segments and adjust their product design, manufacturing processes and marketing campaigns accordingly. However, the large volume of on-line reviews has made manual analysis and summarization of reviews, even for a single market segment, a very labor-intensive and time-consuming task. The need to automate such analysis gives rise to a novel problem of *summarization of contrasting opinions about aspects of products or services by different demographic groups of consumers*, which we introduce and address in this work.

Previous studies in opinion mining have largely focused on three major tasks: identification and extraction of opinion aspects, when the reviews are segmented into fine-grained aspects (topics); detection of sentiment polarity (positive, negative or neutral) towards these aspects; and summarization of aspects by sentiment polarity. Although recently proposed unsupervised topic models, such as Joint Sentiment Topic Model (JST) [17], Aspect and Sentiment Unification Model (ASUM) [8] as well as its hierarchical extension (HASM) [10], allow to summarize both the major aspects as well as the sentiments towards them in collections of on-line reviews, they ignore demographic information about review authors, such as their age, gender and location. However, such information may play an important role in opinion mining and sentiment analysis, since different demographic groups of consumers may have different opinions about the same product aspect.

Meta-data about review authors (e.g. location, gender and age), often provided by on-line consumer review platforms in user profiles, can be viewed as a discrete set of textual labels (or tags) associated with individual reviews, which introduce an element of supervision into sentiment summarization using topic models. Therefore, demographic groups of consumers (or market segments) in this setting can be defined as groups of on-line review authors sharing one or several user meta-data tags. For example, if such tags are organized along the dimensions of age (e.g. "18-25", "26-35", "35-50"), gender ("male" or "female") and location (e.g "san francisco", "new york", ...), then some of the possible market segments are "females", "people aged 18-25", "26-35 year-old males", "females living in new york", etc. In the simplest case, market segments correspond to a set of all distinct user meta-data tags in a given collection of reviews, however arbitrary market segments can be dynamically created by combining two or more tags depending on the required resolution of topic summaries. The textual con-

[1]http://www.amazon.com/
[2]http://www.tripadvisor.com/
[3]http://www.msn.com/en-us/autos/

SIGIR'15, August 09 - 13, 2015, Santiago, Chile.

ACM 978-1-4503-3621-5/15/08 ...$15.00.
DOI: http://dx.doi.org/10.1145/2766462.2767758 .

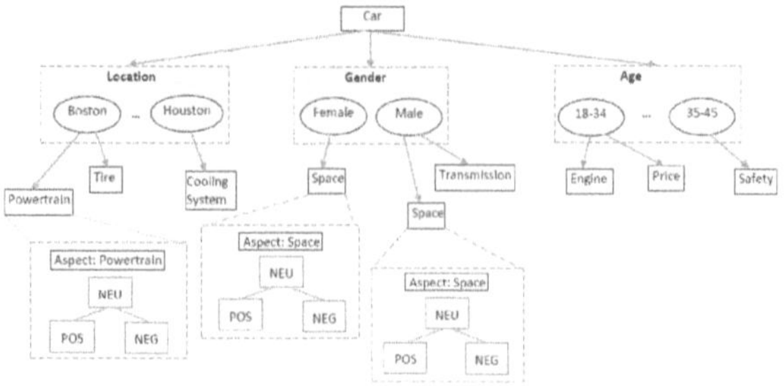

Figure 1: **Topical structure of automotive reviews with respect to market segments defined by distinct user meta-data tags.**

tent of reviews can be analyzed to identify specific product aspects, while the user meta-data can be used to jointly determine collective preferences of different market segments. We hypothesize that establishing associations between the content of reviews and demographic properties of review authors can facilitate fine-grained understanding of product adoption by different customers, from which the companies can benefit by reshaping their product development, marketing and consumer relationship strategies. Since each review may have multiple associated user meta-data tags and there can be a large number of such tags (and corresponding market segments), summarization of reviews across all market segments can be challenging.

In this work, we propose User-Aware Sentiment Topic Models (USTM for short), a framework for modeling user meta-data, topical aspects and sentiments in a unified way. Each of the topic models in the USTM framework identifies several topical aspects frequently discussed in reviews by each market segment. Each aspect is in turn a two-level topical hierarchy, the first level of which corresponds to the summary of objective comments related to this aspect and its positive and negative subtopics constitute the second level. Figure 1 provides an example of the topical structure identified by USTM in automotive reviews with respect to market segments defined by distinct user meta-data tags grouped into the demographic dimensions of location, gender and age.

The proposed USTM framework includes the following 4 topic models:

- User-aware Sentiment Topic Model with Fixed number of Topics and Sentence-based sentiment assignment (**USTM-FT(S)**) is a parametric topic model that extends the Partially Labeled Topic Model [24] to jointly model market segments defined by user meta-data tags, topical aspects and sentiment-based subtopics in reviews based on the assumption that each market segment is associated with the same pre-defined number of topical aspects. Similar to ASUM [8] and HASUM [10], USTM-FT(S) also assumes that all words within the same review sentence can be associated with different topics, but can either be neutral or assigned to the *sentiment selected for the entire sentence*;

- The User-aware Sentiment Topic Model with Fixed number of Topics and Word-based sentiment assignment (**USTM-FT(W)**) is a parametric topic model that is different from USTM-FT(S) in that it assumes that *sentiment is associated with each individual word* rather than an entire sentence;

- **USTM-DP(S)** is a non-parametric alternative to USTM-FT(S), which is based on the Dirichlet Process and allows *different number of topical aspects per each market segment*;

- **USTM-DP(W)** is a non-parametric alternative to USTM-FT(W), which is based on the Dirichlet Process and assumes that *sentiment is associated with each individual word rather than an entire sentence*.

Overall, the key contributions of this work are two-fold:

1. we propose novel parametric and non-parametric topic models for market segment-based opinion summarization, which incorporate demographic information about the authors of reviews in the form of textual user meta-data tags and linguistic information in the form of asymmetric sentiment priors;
2. we experimentally demonstrate the effectiveness of the proposed topic models for opinion mining as well as for the tasks of sentiment classification and user attribute prediction on two real world data sets.

The remainder of this paper is organized as follows. Section 2 provides a brief overview of previous relevant work. All topic models within USTM framework are presented in Section 3. Experimental results are reported in Section 4 and Section 5 concludes the paper.

2. RELATED WORK

The topic models proposed in this paper build upon the previous work along the following two research directions.

Aspect-based sentiment analysis. In the past decade, several machine learning methods [6, 23, 14] have been proposed for opinion mining and sentiment analysis at the word/phase, sentence and document levels. In recent years, there is a surging interest in aspect-based sentiment analysis, which aims at extracting aspects of entities commented on in reviews and opinions towards them. A majority of the previously proposed approaches for review aspect discovery rely on natural language processing techniques such as dependency relations [6], supervised sequence labeling [7] and centering theories [19]. However, some of these approaches are either supervised and require training data in the form of manually identified aspects or aspect terms, or they cannot group extracted terms from multiple reviews into high-level cross-user latent topics (aspects).

More recently, probabilistic topic models have become the main tool for aspect-based opinion mining due to their ability to identify and concisely represent latent topics in collections of reviews. Several topic models for opinion analysis extending the basic topic models have been proposed. The initial work in this direction is the Topic-Sentiment Model (TSM) [20] which considers each document as a mixture of topics and sentiments. However, TSM is based upon PLSA [5] and, thus, is prone to overfitting. Titov and McDonald proposed the MG-LDA [28] model and a further extended MAS [27] model both of which aim to determine the local and global topics from reviews with structured aspects and numeric rating associated with each aspects. Both MG-LDA and MAS assume that at least one aspect is rated in one review, which is impractical; Lin et al. proposed the LDA-based Joint-Sentiment/Topic model (JST) [17], which assumes that each sentiment has a multinomial distribution over topics, and that each sentiment-topic pair has a multinomial distribution over words. This model, however, cannot accurately distinguish the different sentiments of each topic. Lin et al. later proposed a Reverse JST model (R-JST) [18] by reversing the association between sentiments and topics in JST, which, however, performed poorly. Jo et al. [8] recently developed the Aspect-Sentiment Unification Model (ASUM), which is based on the assumption that all words in one sentence are associated with the same topic and sentiment. Mukherjee et al. [22] proposed a Seeded

Aspect and Sentiment Model, which discovers aspect-based sentiments given sets of seed words for aspect categories. Sauper et al. [25] developed a topic model to jointly identify properties and attributes of review snippets rather than complete reviews. Wang et al. [30] introduced Latent Aspect Rating Analysis, a new aspect-level sentiment analysis task aiming to discover both topical aspects and each individual reviewer's latent rating for each aspect. Moghaddam [21] et al. addressed the same latent rating prediction problem and proposed three different versions of topic models to solve it. Nevertheless, most of the previously proposed topic modeling approaches for aspect-level sentiment analysis largely ignore other valuable supportive information, such as the meta-data of review authors.

Several previous works [26, 4, 31, 16, 11] utilized user information in opinion mining and information retrieval, although in a different way from this work. In particular, [26] and [4] are not topic modeling-based approaches, while [31] and [16] model users as random variables and not the attributes of users in the topic modeling process. However, all these approaches are parametric and require to specify a pre-defined number of topics (aspects) per review. To overcome this limitation, USTM framework includes non-parametric topic models based on Dirichlet Process. The work that is the closest to ours is [10] Hierarchical Aspect Sentiment Unification Model (HASUM), which extends the ASUM model by integrating it with the recursive Chinese Restaurant Process [9], a modified version of the nested Chinese Restaurant Process [1], thus allowing to identify hierarchical aspect-sentiment structure. However, HASUM does not consider user meta-data. Li [15] et al. also explored the structure in on-line reviews.

Supervised/partially supervised topic models. Many researchers have recently directed their attention to incorporating supervision in the form of additional meta-data associated with textual content into topic models. Supervised LDA [2] extended the traditional Latent Dirichlet Allocation [3] by adding a response variable associated with each document. Partially Labeled Topic Model [24] is based on the assumption that if a document is associated with a set of labels (tags), then those tags play a direct role in generating its content. In particular, PLDA and PLDP introduce an additional layer of latent variables that determine associations of each word with a document tag and topic. Topic models incorporating the locations of Twitter users extracted from their profiles have been shown to improve microblog retrieval in [12] and [13]. Although these models shed some light on how to incorporate useful meta-data into topic modeling process, none of them has been applied to aspect-based sentiment analysis. Therefore, the USTM framework proposed in this paper can be viewed as an extension and unification of the previous work on supervised/partially supervised topic modeling and aspect-based sentiment analysis.

3. USTM FRAMEWORK

In this section, we introduce the four different topic models that constitute the framework for User-Aware Sentiment Topic Modeling. Table 1 provides a summary of notations used in our discussion of the topic models in the USTM framework.

Given a collection $C = \{d_1, \ldots, d_m\}$ of M reviews, in which each review consists of $\{w_1, \ldots, w_{N_{dw}}\}$ words and is associated with $\{t_1, \ldots, t_{N_{dt}}\}$ user meta-data attributes (tags), the primary goal of topic models in USTM framework is to discover associations between user meta-data attributes, topical aspects and sentiments associated with those aspects across different demographic groups of users. In the following sections, we discuss how parametric and non-parametric topic models in USTM framework achieve this goal.

Table 1: **Summary of notations used in this paper**

Symbol	Description
	Counts
M	number of reviews
W	vocabulary size
T	number of distinct user meta-data tags (attributes)
K	number of topics associated with each tag (parametric models)
S	number of sentiment polarities
K_t	number of topics associated with tag t (non-parametric models)
N_{dw}	the number of words in review d
N_{dt}	the number of tags in review d
N_{ds}	the number of sentences in review d
N^w_{di}	the number of words in the sentence i of review d
	Random Variables
ψ	proportion of review words assigned to different tags
θ	proportion of review words assigned to different tag-specific topics
ϕ	sentiment-specific topics for each user meta-data attribute (tag)
ξ	trinomial/binomial distribution of sentiments for tag-specific topics
ϑ	binomial distribution of (review, tag, topic) triples over sentiments
t_{di}	tag assigned to word i in review d
z_{di}	topic assigned to word i in review d
p_{di}	subjectivity assigned to word i in review d
s^s_{di}	sentiment assigned to sentence i of review d
s^w_{dij}	sentiment assigned to word j in sentence i of review d
	Hyper-Parameters
α	Dirichlet prior for θ
β^w_s	weight of word w in the Dirichlet prior for the topics with sentiment s
$\hat{\beta}_s$	sum of the weights of all words in the Dirichlet prior for the topics with sentiment s
β	hyper-parameter of the uniform Dirichlet prior
η	hyper-parameter of the uniform Dirichlet prior for ψ
γ	hyper-parameter of the uniform Dirichlet prior for ξ
δ	hyper-parameter of the uniform Dirichlet prior for ϑ

3.1 Parametric models

3.1.1 USTM-FT(W)

USTM-FT(W) extends the PLDA model [24] by jointly modeling user meta-data attributes and sentiments in a generative process. In particular, USTM-FT(W) associates a multinomial distribution over topics with each tag (or a combination of tags) from a set of tags $\mathbf{\Lambda_d}$ for d, a trinomial distribution over sentiments (neutral, positive or negative) with each tag-specific topic and a multinomial distribution over words with sentiment-specific topics for each tag. It generates the reviews according to the following generative process:

1. for each tag t, topic z and sentiment s, draw a distribution over words $\phi_{tzs} \sim Dir(\beta_s)$
2. for each review d:
   (a) draw a distribution over tags $\psi_d \sim Dir(\eta)$
   (b) for each tag $t \in \mathbf{\Lambda_d}$, draw a distribution over topics $\theta^t_d \sim Dir(\alpha)$
   (c) for each pair (t, z), draw a distribution over sentiments $\xi^{tz}_d \sim Dir(\gamma)$
   (d) for each word position i in d:
      i. draw a tag $t \sim \psi_d$
      ii. for the sampled tag t, draw a topic $z \sim \theta^t_d$
      iii. for the sampled tag t and topic z, draw a sentiment $s \sim \xi^{tz}_d$

iv. draw a word $w \sim \phi_{tzs}$ from the topic corresponding to the sampled tag t, topic z and sentiment s

The graphical model for USTM-FT(W) in plate notation is presented in Figure 2. Since this model is parametric, each user metadata tag is associated with a fixed number of topics, which is a parameter that needs to be specified a priori. Sentiment information is incorporated into USTM-FT(W) using asymmetric Dirichlet priors for positive and negative sentiment-specific topics, in which each word w in the corpus vocabulary is assigned a weight β_s^w ($s \in 0,1,2$), which can be pre-defined or learned off-line by bootstrapping from a set of seed words for the corresponding sentiment polarity s. In general, positive sentiment words will be assigned larger weight in the prior for positive topics than in the prior for negative topics and vice versa. Posterior inference of USTM-FT(W) model parameters is done using Gibbs sampling. At each state of the Markov chain for the Gibbs sampler, the latent tag $t_{d,i}$, topic $z_{d,i}$ and sentiment $s_{d,i}$ are sampled for each word i in review d according to the following formula:

$$P(t_{d,i}=j, z_{d,i}=k, s_{d,i}=s|t_{\neg d,i}, z_{\neg d,i}, s_{\neg d,i}, \alpha, \gamma, \beta_s^w, \hat{\beta}_s)$$
$$\propto \frac{n_{d,j,k,\cdot,\cdot}^{(\neg d,i)}+\alpha}{n_{d,\cdot,\cdot,\cdot,\cdot}^{(\neg d,i)}+N_{dt}*K*\alpha} \cdot \frac{n_{\cdot,j,k,\cdot,w}^{(\neg d,i)}+\beta}{n_{\cdot,j,k,\cdot,\cdot}^{(\neg d,i)}+V*\beta} \cdot \frac{n_{d,j,k,s,\cdot}^{(\neg d,i)}+\gamma}{n_{d,j,k,\cdot,\cdot}^{(\neg d,i)}+3*\gamma} \times$$
$$\times \frac{n_{\cdot,j,k,s,w}^{(\neg d,i)}+\beta_s^w}{n_{\cdot,j,k,s,\cdot}^{(\neg d,i)}+\hat{\beta}_s}$$

where $n_{d,j,k,\cdot,\cdot}^{(\neg d,i)}$ is the total number of words in review d that have been assigned to tag j and topic k; $n_{d,\cdot,\cdot,\cdot,\cdot}^{(\neg d,i)}$ is the total number of words in review d; $n_{\cdot,j,k,\cdot,w}^{(\neg d,i)}$ is the total number of times the word w has been assigned to tag j and topic k in the entire corpus; $n_{\cdot,j,k,\cdot,\cdot}^{(\neg d,i)}$ is the total number of words in the entire corpus that have been assigned to tag j and topic k; $n_{d,j,k,s,\cdot}^{(\neg d,i)}$ is the total number of words in review d that have been assigned to tag j, topic k and sentiment s; $n_{\cdot,j,k,s,w}^{(\neg d,i)}$ is the total number of times the word w has been assigned to tag j, topic k, and sentiment s in the entire corpus; $n_{\cdot,j,k,s,\cdot}^{(\neg d,i)}$ is the total number of words in the entire corpus that have been assigned to tag j, topic k, and sentiment s. All these counts exclude the word i for which the associated tag, topic and sentiment are being sampled.

After sampling is complete, the distributions for latent variables θ, ϕ, ξ are calculated as follows:

$$\theta_{djk} = \frac{n_{d,j,k,\cdot,\cdot}+\alpha}{n_{d,j,\cdot,\cdot,\cdot}+K*\alpha} \quad (1)$$

$$\phi_{jksw} = \frac{n_{\cdot,j,k,s,w}+\beta_s^w}{\sum_{w=1}^{V} n_{\cdot,j,k,s,w}+\hat{\beta}_s} \quad (2)$$

$$\xi_{djks} = \frac{n_{d,j,k,s,\cdot}+\gamma}{n_{d,j,k,\cdot,\cdot}+3*\gamma} \quad (3)$$

3.1.2 *USTM-FT(S)*

Previous studies [8, 10] indicate that assigning sentiment to the entire sentence rather than each individual word might be a better strategy for opinion mining. Following this idea, we propose USTM-FT(S), which is based on the assumption that all the words in a given sentence have the same sentiment, but can be associated with different tags and topics. We also distinguish the subjectivity of each word, which indicates whether a word is a topic word (e.g. "car", "hotel", "engine", "breakfast", etc.) or a sentiment word (e.g. "great", "wonderful", "awful", etc.). Therefore, given the sentiment $s_{d,m} \in \{1,2\}$ (1 = positive and 2 = negative) assigned to the sentence m in document d and the subjectivity $p_{d,m,i} \in \{0,1\}$ assigned to the word i in sentence m, the sentiment of this word $s_{d,m,i} \in \{0,1,2\}$ (0 = neutral, 1 = positive and 2 = negative) is determined as $s_{d,m} * p_{d,m,i}$. USTM-FT(S) generates each review according to the following generative process:

1. for each tag t, topic z and sentiment s, draw a distribution over words $\phi_{tzs} \sim Dir(\beta_s)$
2. for each review d:
   (a) for each tag $t \in \mathbf{\Lambda_d}$, draw a distribution over topics $\theta_d^t \sim Dir(\alpha)$
   (b) for each pair (t,z), draw subjectivity distribution over words ϑ_d^{tz}
   (c) for sentence m in review d:
      i. draw a sentiment $s \sim \xi_d^{tz}$
      ii. for each word i in sentence m of review d:
         A. draw a tag $t \sim \psi_d$
         B. for the sampled tag t, draw a topic $z \sim \theta_d^t$
         C. for the sampled tag t and topic z, draw a subjectivity $p \sim \vartheta_d^{tz}$
         D. draw a word $w \sim \phi_{tz\{s*p\}}$ from the topic corresponding to the sampled tag t, topic z and sentiment $s*p$

The graphical model for USTM-FT(S) in plate notation is presented in Figure 3. Each state of the Markov chain for the Gibbs sampler used for posterior inference of parameters of USTM-FT(S) consists of two steps. In the first step, we sample the sentiment for each sentence in a review based upon the tag, topic and subjectivity assignments to each word in the sentence in the previous iteration of the Gibbs sampler. In particular, the probability of choosing sentiment s for sentence m in review d can be computed by multiplying the probabilities of assigning every word i in sentence m to the sentiment s:

$$P(s_{d,m}^s = s) = \frac{n_{d,s,\cdot}^{(\neg d,m)}+\gamma}{n_{d,\cdot,\cdot}^{(\neg d,m)}+2*\gamma} \cdot \prod_{w \in s_{d,m}} P(w_{d,m,i}|t_{d,m,i}, z_{d,m,i}, \quad (4)$$

$$w_{d,m,i}^s) = \frac{n_{d,s,\cdot}^{(\neg d,m)}+\gamma}{n_{d,\cdot,\cdot}^{(\neg d,m)}+2*\gamma} \cdot \prod_{w \in s_{d,m}} \frac{n_{\cdot,j,k,s*p,w}+\beta_{s*p}^w}{n_{\cdot,j,k,s*p,\cdot}+\hat{\beta}_{s*p}}$$

where $n_{d,s,\cdot}^{(\neg d,m)}$ indicates the number of sentences, which have been assigned sentiment s in review d.

In the second step, based on the chosen sentiment for the entire sentence, we further sample the latent tag $t_{d,m,i}$, topic $z_{d,m,i}$ and sentiment $s_{d,m,i}$ for each word in that sentence, according to the following formula:

$$P(t_{d,m,i}=j, z_{d,m,i}=k, s_{d,m,i}=(s*p)|t_{\neg d,i}, z_{\neg d,i}, s_{\neg d,i}, \alpha, \gamma, \beta_{s*p}^w,$$
$$\hat{\beta}_{s*p}) \propto \frac{n_{d,j,k,\cdot,\cdot}^{(\neg d,i)}+\alpha}{n_{d,\cdot,\cdot,\cdot,\cdot}^{(\neg d,i)}+N_{dt}*K*\alpha} \cdot \frac{n_{d,j,k,s*p,\cdot}^{(\neg d,i)}+\delta}{n_{d,j,k,\cdot,\cdot}^{(\neg d,i)}+2*\delta} \cdot \frac{n_{\cdot,j,k,\cdot,w}^{(\neg d,i)}+\beta}{n_{\cdot,j,k,\cdot,\cdot}^{(\neg d,i)}+V*\beta} \times$$
$$\times \frac{n_{\cdot,j,k,s*p,w}^{(\neg d,i)}+\beta_{s*p}^w}{n_{\cdot,j,k,s*p,\cdot}^{(\neg d,i)}+\hat{\beta}_{s*p}}$$

After sampling is complete, the distributions for latent variables θ, ϕ, ξ are calculated similar to Equations 1, 2 and 3.

3.2 Non-parametric models

3.2.1 *Dirichlet Process*

A major limitation of parametric USTM models is that they require to specify a fixed number of topics per each market segment a priori, while such number cannot be easily estimated. Moreover, although it is possible to empirically determine the optimal setting for the number of topics by optimizing an evaluation metric (e.g., perplexity), such an approach is generally impractical. To overcome this deficiency, we propose two non-parametric topic models, USTM-DP(W) and USTM-DP(S), which build upon the Dirichlet Process (DP for short) and allow to automatically discover the latent topical structure in collections of reviews annotated with user meta-data.

In non-parametric Bayesian statistics, a Dirichlet process is a method of assigning a probability distribution over other probability distributions. Given a Dirichlet Process $DP(H, \alpha)$ which is characterized by a base distribution (or a base measure) H and a concentration parameter α, a draw $G \sim DP(H, \alpha)$ will return a random distribution over some values that can be drawn from H. If we further draw a parameter $\theta_i \sim G$ and use it as a prior for a mixture model, we get the Dirichlet Process mixture model (DPM), from which we can draw observed data points.

The Chinese Restaurant Process (CRP) metaphor is one typical representation of the Dirichlet Process, which generates partitions of variables that exhibit the same clustering structure as the one created by the Dirichlet Process. The CRP process can be described as assignment of dining tables to new customers, who enter a restaurant with an infinite number of tables. In the initial state, all the tables are empty, and the probability of the ith customer, z_i, who enters the restaurant, to choose the tth table is:

$$p(z_i = t) = \begin{cases} \frac{n_t}{\sum_t n_t + \alpha}, & \text{for an existing table} \\ \frac{\alpha}{\sum_t n_t + \alpha}, & \text{for a new table} \end{cases} \tag{5}$$

where n_t indicates the number of customers who are sitting at the table t. Following the same idea, we can assign each observed word either to a new or to an existing topic (the number of topics can be infinite).

3.2.2 USTM-DP(W) and USTM-DP(S)

USTM-DP(W) and USTM-DP(S) are the non-parametric counterparts of USTM-FT(W) and USTM-FT(S), in which the LDA-based topic inference is replaced by the Dirichlet Process. In both of these models, a word w is assigned to a user meta-data tag and one of its sentiment-specific topics in proportion to how often other words have been assigned to the given tag, topic and sentiment, or to a new sentiment-specific topic created for some tag in proportion to the concentration parameter α.

Similar to USTM-FT(W), USTM-DP(W) assigns sentiment to each individual word. The following Gibbs Sampler updating formula shows the probability of choosing the tag j, topic k and sentiment s for the ith word in review d:

$$P(t_{d,i} = j, z_{d,i} = k, s_{d,i} = s | t_{\neg d,i}, z_{\neg d,i}, s_{\neg d,i}, \alpha, \gamma, \beta_s^w, \hat{\beta}_s)$$
$$\propto \begin{cases} \frac{n_{d,j,k,\cdot,\cdot}^{(\neg d,i)}}{n_{d,\cdot,\cdot,\cdot,\cdot}^{(\neg d,i)} + \alpha} \cdot \frac{n_{d,j,k,s,\cdot}^{(\neg d,i)} + \gamma}{n_{d,j,k,\cdot,\cdot}^{(\neg d,i)} + 3*\gamma} \cdot \frac{n_{\cdot,j,k,\cdot,w}^{(\neg d,i)} + \beta}{n_{\cdot,j,k,\cdot,\cdot}^{(\neg d,i)} + V*\beta} \cdot \frac{n_{\cdot,j,k,s,w}^{(\neg d,i)} + \beta_s^w}{n_{\cdot,j,k,s,\cdot}^{(\neg d,i)} + \hat{\beta}_s}, \\ \text{for an existing topic} \\ \frac{\alpha}{n_{d,\cdot,\cdot,\cdot,\cdot}^{(\neg d,i)} + \alpha} \cdot \frac{n_{d,j,\cdot,s,\cdot}^{(\neg d,i)} + \gamma}{n_{d,j,\cdot,\cdot,\cdot}^{(\neg d,i)} + 3*\gamma} \cdot \frac{\beta}{V*\beta} \cdot \frac{\beta_s^w}{\hat{\beta}_s}, \text{ for a new topic} \end{cases}$$

USTM-DP(S) assigns sentiment on a sentence-based level. Similar to USTM-FT(S), it first samples a sentiment for the ith sentence in review d based on Equation 4 and then samples the tag $t_{d,m,i}$, topic $z_{d,m,i}$ and sentiment $s_{d,m,i}$ for each word in that sentence, according to the following formula:

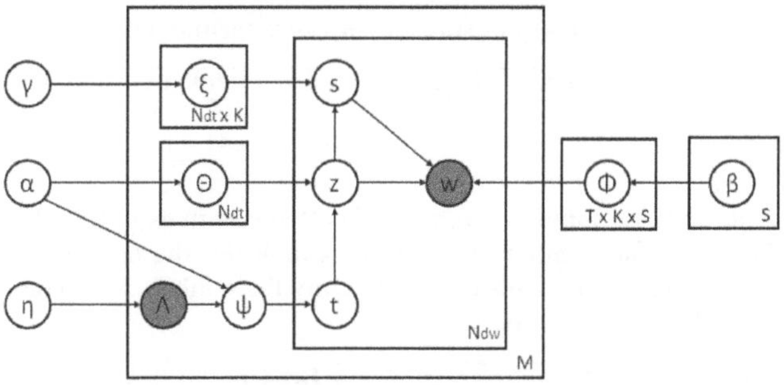

Figure 2: **Graphical model of USTM-FT(W).**

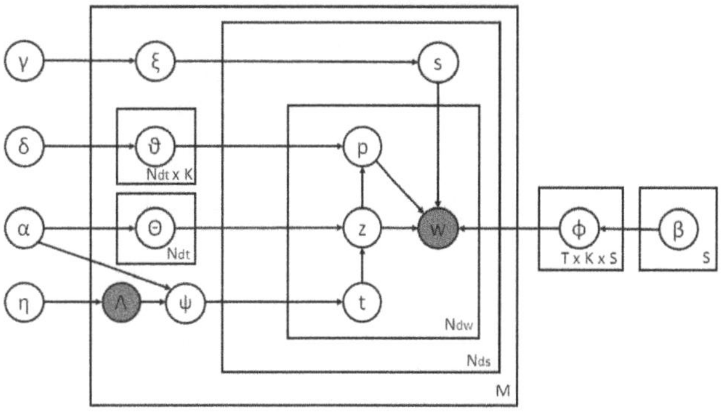

Figure 3: **Graphical model of USTM-FT(S).**

$$P(t_{d,m,i} = j, z_{d,m,i} = k, s_{d,m,i} = (s*p) | t_{\neg d,i}, z_{\neg d,i}, s_{\neg d,i}, \alpha, \gamma, \beta_s^w, \hat{\beta}_s)$$
$$\propto \begin{cases} \frac{n_{d,j,k,\cdot,\cdot}^{(\neg d,i)}}{n_{d,\cdot,\cdot,\cdot,\cdot}^{(\neg d,i)} + \alpha} \cdot \frac{n_{d,j,k,s*p,\cdot}^{(\neg d,i)} + \delta}{n_{d,j,k,\cdot,\cdot}^{(\neg d,i)} + 2*\delta} \cdot \frac{n_{\cdot,j,k,\cdot,w}^{(\neg d,i)} + \beta}{n_{\cdot,j,k,\cdot,\cdot}^{(\neg d,i)} + V*\beta} \cdot \frac{n_{\cdot,j,k,s*p,w}^{(\neg d,i)} + \beta_{s*p}^w}{n_{\cdot,j,k,s*p,\cdot}^{(\neg d,i)} + \hat{\beta}_{s*p}}, \\ \text{for an existing topic} \\ \frac{\alpha}{n_{d,\cdot,\cdot,\cdot,\cdot}^{(\neg d,i)} + \alpha} \cdot \frac{n_{d,j,\cdot,s*p,\cdot}^{(\neg d,i)} + \delta}{n_{d,j,\cdot,\cdot,\cdot}^{(\neg d,i)} + 2*\delta} \cdot \frac{\beta}{V*\beta} \cdot \frac{\beta_{s*p}^w}{\hat{\beta}_{s*p}}, \text{ for a new topic} \end{cases}$$

4. EXPERIMENTAL EVALUATION

Experimental evaluation of the proposed topic models was performed according to the following four aspects: perplexity on the test data, qualitative analysis of the discovered topics, review sentiment classification and prediction of demographic attributes of review authors. The results of an experimental evaluation for each of these aspects are provided below.

4.1 Experimental setup

4.1.1 Data sets

Experimental evaluation of the proposed models was conducted on two real world data sets. This first data set (further referred to as **Auto**) consists of reviews crawled from FordForum.com[4], a public automobile on-line review website, which provides the meta-data of review authors, such as location, gender and occupation (in this work, we are only interested in location and gender). The second data set (further referred to as **Hotel**) consists of reviews of hotels crawled from TripAdvisor[5] along with the meta-data of review authors, such as location, gender and age[6].

[4]http://www.fordforum.com/forum/

[5]http://www.tripadvisor.com

[6]both datasets are available at https://github.com/teanalab/USTM

Table 2: **Summary of statistics of experimental datasets.**

Dataset	# reviews	# tags	voc. size	# tokens	avg. len
Auto	11254	401	4952	362,225	32.19
Hotel	7266	324	6430	441,489	60.75

Table 3: **Most popular demographic attributes in experimental datasets. The number in parenthesis indicates the number of reviews associated with the label. Only these labels were considered in experiments.**

Dataset	Locations	Gender	Age groups
Hotel	london, uk (288)	female (2285)	35-49 (1788)
	new york, new york (184)	male (1853)	25-34 (1076)
	toronto, canada (119)		50-64 (1006)
	boston, massachusetts (116)		65 (145)
	sydney, australia (101)		18-24 (112)
Auto	de pere, wi (1535)	male (2335)	
	yorkshire, ny (1263)	female (183)	
	denver, colorado (577)		
	iowa (442)		
	fresno, ca (134)		

For both of these datasets, we performed pre-processing by lowercasing all words, removing stop-words and retaining only those words, which appear in the English dictionary of the spell-checking program *aspell*. Since we intend to discover sentiment topics, we kept certain stopwords like *not, don't, doesn't* and *won't*. We consider only those reviews in each data set, which are associated with at least one user label. From those reviews, we further filtered out the words that are either too rare (i.e. appear less than 5 times in the entire corpus) or too common (i.e. appear in more than 30% of the reviews). Sentences were segmented based on punctuation ('.', '?', '!' and new line). Various statistics of experimental datasets are summarized in Table 2.

All experimental results reported in this paper were obtained by considering user meta-data tags belonging to three dimensions (location, gender and age). To avoid the sparsity issue, in addition to the gender tags, we considered the top 5 location tags in both data sets as well as the top 5 age tags in the **Hotel** dataset in terms of the number of reviews associated with them (there is no age information for the review authors in the **Auto** data set). Statistics of the user meta-data tags considered in the experiments reported in this work are presented in Table 3 .

4.1.2 *Sentiment seed words and asymmetric priors*

Sentiment information is incorporated into our models via asymmetric Dirichlet priors (β) for sentiment-specific topics. For example, the words with strongly positive sentiment polarity like "good", "better" or "great" will have the higher weights in the Dirichlet prior for positive topics than for negative topics, so that these words will have a higher probability to be sampled for positive aspects of reviews.

In order to calculate the weights for words in the asymmetric priors for sentiment-specific topics, we utilized the sentiment lexicons from the previous studies as seed words with strong sentiment polarity. In particular, we used the **PARADIGMhasm** sentiment lexicon [10] consisting of 31 positive and 33 negative words, and the **MPQA** [29] sentiment lexicon consisting of 2718 positive words and 4911 negative words. After filtering out the words from the MPQA lexicon, which are not in the vocabulary of our datasets, we obtained sentiment lexicons consisting of 341 positive and 356 negative words for the **Auto** dataset, and of 671 positive and 572 negative words for the **Hotel** dataset.

Table 4: **Summary of statistics of considered bigrams.**

Datasets	# bi-grams	# pos. HASM	# neg. HASM	# pos. MPQA	# neg. MPQA
Auto	27791	785	1114	3511	3099
Hotel	7751	924	88	1596	477

We first set the neutral, positive and negative priors for all words in the corpus to 0.01. Then for each word found in the known sentiment lexicon with polarity s, we set its weight in the Dirichlet prior for the topics with the same sentiment polarity β_s^w to 2.0, and its weight in the Dirichlet prior for the topics with the opposite sentiment polarity to 0.001. For example, using this approach, the weights of a word that belongs to a positive sentiment lexicon in the Dirichlet priors for neutral, positive and negative topics will be 0.01, 2.0, 0.001, respectively. All results reported in this work were obtained by setting the hyper-parameters γ, η, and δ to 0.1, β to 0.01, α to $50/K$ and 10^{-8} for parametric and non-parametric models, respectively.

4.1.3 *Unigrams vs. Bigrams*

Bigrams are generally more informative than unigrams in expressing sentiments for topics. For example, if the fragment of a review "this hotel has a great location" is represented as a unigram bag of words {"hotel", "great", "location"}, it is hard to tell whether the hotel is great or the location is great. The bigram "great location", however, clearly indicates positive sentiment about the aspect of "location". In order to compare the different representations of topics, we replaced individual words in reviews with bigrams and ran the topic models in the USTM framework on the resulting collection. To create bigrams, we combined all pairs of consecutive words in reviews and retained only those bigrams, which appear in more than five and less than 30% of all reviews in each collection. Table 4 shows the statistics of considered bigrams in both collections. To determine the weight of each bigram in the Dirichlet priors for topics of different sentiment polarity, we assumed that if only one word in the bigram belongs to the known sentiment lexicon and it is not preceded by a negation like "not", then the weight of the entire bigram is determined based on this lexicon. If a bigram is preceded by a negation, then the weight is set based on the sentiment lexicon of the opposite sentiment polarity. If both terms in the bigram belong to the same subjectivity lexicon, then the weight is set based on the sentiment lexicon of this subjectivity and, if words in the bigram belong to different subjectivity lexicons, we considered such bigram as neutral.

4.2 Results

In this section, we evaluate the different aspects of performance of the proposed models with respect to the state-of-the-art baselines Aspect-Sentiment Unification Model (ASUM) [8] and Joint Sentiment-Topic Model (JST) [17], which jointly model aspects and sentiments but do not consider demographic attributes of review authors. ASUM associates aspect and sentiment with an entire sentence and uses asymmetric priors to incorporate sentiment information for individual words. JST associates sentiment and aspect with each word rather than an entire sentence and uses symmetric priors for sentiment-specific topics. Both ASUM and JST are parametric models and require to specify the number of topics a priori.

In all experiments, we use the following settings of parameters for ASUM and JST. For ASUM we set α to $50/K$ and γ to 1. The weights of the seed words from the sentiment lexicons were set to 1.0 in the Dirichlet priors for the topics with the same polarity and to 0 in the priors for the topics with the opposite polarity. The weights of all other words in the priors were set to 0.001. For JST, we set α to $50/K$, β to 0.01, γ for positive document-sentiment associations to 0.01 and negative document-sentiment associations to 5.0.

4.2.1 *Influence of sentiment lexicons*

In the first set of experiments, we evaluate the performance of different models in the USTM framework depending on unigram or bigram representation of reviews (Uni for Unigram and Bi for Bigram) as well as the sentiment lexicon (P for PARADIGMhasm and M for MPQA) used to create the Dirichlet priors for topics with different sentiment polarity. Performance of the model is evaluated in terms of perplexity, which is a measure derived from the likelihood of the data in the testing subset (10% of all reviews) under the model estimated on the training subset (90% of all reviews) of each dataset. The results for this set of experiments are summarized in Table 5.

Table 5: **Perplexity of parametric and non-parametric models using different lexicons for unigram and bigram review representations. Lower perplexity is better.**

Model	Auto	Hotel
Parametric models		
USTM-FT(W)+Uni+P	849.37	2146.48
USTM-FT(W)+Uni+M	959.80	2512.26
USTM-FT(S)+Uni+P	744.10	2099.34
USTM-FT(S)+Uni+M	782.93	2257.53
USTM-FT(W)+Bi+P	1324.27	3188.09
USTM-FT(W)+Bi+M	1435.38	3221.79
USTM-FT(S)+Bi+P	1236.58	2749.09
USTM-FT(S)+Bi+M	1314.75	3066.19
Non-parametric models		
USTM-DP(S)+Uni+P	704.85	1792.55
USTM-DP(W)+Uni+P	835.45	2007.32
Baselines		
ASUM+Uni+P	1190.92	2317.13
ASUM+Uni+M	1247.09	2563.96
ASUM+Bi+P	1358.87	2883.01
ASUM+Bi+M	1581.50	3160.39
JST+Uni+P	1091.01	2093.46
JST+Uni+M	1127.07	2272.31
JST+Bi+P	1297.85	2709.09
JST+Bi+M	1457.08	2982.82

As follows from Table 5, the lowest perplexity on both datasets is achieved by the non-parametric topic models using the PARADIGMhasm lexicon as a source of sentiment seed words. Second, sentence-based sentiment association consistently results in lower perplexity than word-based sentiment association across all lexicons and priors for both parametric and non-parametric topic models. Furthermore, USTM models perform consistently better on unigrams than on bigrams and when using PARADIGMhasm lexicon instead of MPQA. The proposed topic models also outperform ASUM on most combinations, except when using bigram representation of the **Hotel** dataset and have lower perplexity than JST on the **Auto** data set.

4.2.2 *Qualitative Topic Models results*

The primary goal of incorporating user meta-data into topic modeling process is to summarize the opinions of different market segments about various aspects of products and services. Therefore, we select several examples of sentiment-specific topics from the list of all topics discovered for different market segments that are designated by one or several user demographic attributes. Sample topics presented in Tables 6 and 7 were discovered by the USTM-FT(S) model in the Auto dataset using unigram-based representation of reviews. 10 terms with the highest weight are reported for each topic.

Table 6: **Sample topics discovered in the Auto dataset for the tag "male".**

#	sent.	topic words
1	NEU	new car battery engine thanks start help oil pump know
	POS	good new recommend great car thank engine oil help battery
	NEG	problem bad new car battery thanks junk help start oil
2	NEU	truck engine drive new thanks time transmission car know check
	POS	good drive recommend truck new engine driving thank vehicle right
	NEG	problem truck new bad engine issue transmission driving vehicle help
3	NEU	fuel engine help start light new pump car running truck
	POS	good fuel engine thank great start recommend help light thanks
	NEG	problem bad fuel engine start truck help light got running
4	NEU	report check cost vehicle using service free try government link
	POS	report recommend vehicle check using free service good history provides
	NEG	problem check vehicle link try time report alternative history service
5	NEU	report fuel help vehicle check thanks know new try rear
	POS	good report recommend help check engine new thank know service
	NEG	problem check help vehicle thanks sorry cost try bad report

Table 7: **Sample topics discovered in the Auto dataset for the tag "female".**

#	sent.	topic words
1	NEU	engine said light oil air driving check explorer probably knows
	POS	good engine light mechanic new power runs said oil wanted
	NEG	engine problem light coils run said know check explorer notice
2	NEU	truck coding ads heard ranger opinion work day repair second
	POS	truck having happy work great dealership heard radio funny best
	NEG	wrong problem told getting truck took cars saturn driver days
3	NEU	new don battery bought used plug right truck player wiring
	POS	new good love enjoy plug bought control code don positive
	NEG	new bad sorry free shift plug bought months mess negative
4	NEU	view allow account clicking try easiest set access email fuel
	POS	thank view says sharing fuel account controls set runs stay
	NEG	view problem account fuel pump info files says allow set
5	NEU	car drive got check went transmission know lot use focus
	POS	car thanks got miles good offer replaced mph help thought
	NEG	car went wrong focus escape auto help drive sensors miles

Several observations can be made based on examples in Tables 6 and 7. First, the proposed topic models can obtain coherent sentiment-specific topics for different aspects discussed in reviews by the corresponding market segments. For example, the first, second and third topics in Table 6 are related to battery, transmission and lights, respectively. Second, the proposed topic models can assign subjective terms to the correct sentiment-specific topics corresponding to the same aspect of reviews. Third, aspects are different between males and females. In particular, males tend to focus on mechanical aspects of the car, while females, although paying attention to some mechanical topics like Topic 1 (engine light) in Table 7, also talk about more general topics like dealerships (Topic 2) and account information (Topic 4).

Table 8 illustrates the difference between the sentiment-specific topics discovered by different age groups in the **Hotel** dataset, and Table 10 shows the example sentiment-specific topics for different combinations of gender and location.

As follows from Table 8, one major difference between the users in the age group "65" and "18-24" is that older people care more about tips as well as how quiet and comfortable their rooms are, while younger people pay more attention to the location of the hotel, breakfast and friendliness of staff. Tables 9 and 10 show sam-

Table 8: **Sample topics discovered in the Hotel dataset for the age tags "65" and "18-24".**

65	
NEU	breakfast times subway square place street tip close tips quiet
POS	new tips comfortable york floor desk excellent amazing square suite
NEG	service hotels lobby walk time little terrible bathroom breakfast place
18-24	
NEU	new night nice lobby central city floor free price time
POS	york times square check night time friendly lovely fantastic minutes
NEG	bed floor service bathroom breakfast trip disappointing beds problem night

Table 9: **Sample topics discovered in the Auto dataset for the location tag "fort worth, texas" and gender "female" and "male".**

female	
NEU	conditioner heat heater explorer turn car truck air help engine amp
POS	hot good conditioner vents heater dash air correct small blow
NEG	amp left turn signal bad explorer suggestions bulbs negative
male	
NEU	defrost heater hot vents time trying works fix fine waste
POS	battery water engine flow check truck mods thermostat deg correct
NEG	original heated happening part food bad truck works circuit care

ple topics discovered for females and males in "fort worth, texas" and "minnesota", respectively. Several interesting observations can be made based on these examples. First, both males and females in Texas are talking about the climate control systems in the car ("heater" and "conditioner"), while review authors in Minnesota are more focused on the "battery" and "starter" issues. Therefore, location appears to have a noticeable influence on the aspects people care about, since the summer temperatures in Fort Worth, TX are typically very high and therefore reviews often mention climate control systems (e.g. "conditioner"), while extremely cold winters in Minnesota seem to cause battery and starter issues. Second, gender influences preferences towards particular makes and models of cars, since "truck" and "mustang" are more frequently mentioned in reviews written by males than by females.

Table 11 presents an example of the topics discovered from the bigram-based representation of the **Auto** dataset. As follows from Table 11, bigram-based representation of reviews results in much more direct and closer associations between the topical aspects and sentiments than unigram-based representation. In this example, females in "dover, ohio" seem to be more interested in aesthetic aspects of vehicles, such as interior design (e.g. "seats"), while males tend to care more about the functional components of a car ("injector", "engine", etc.).

4.2.3 *Review sentiment classification*

Automatic detection of the overall sentiment of a review is one of the fundamental problems in opinion analysis. In this section, we report the results of using the associations between the words, user meta-data tags and sentiment aspects discovered by the topic models in USTM framework for the task of review sentiment prediction. We adopt a probabilistic approach and estimate $P(s|d)$, a distribution of predicted sentiments for a given review d. In particular, we compare the probabilities of assigning positive $P(s = pos|d)$ and negative $P(s = neg|d)$ sentiments to a review and classify the review as positive if $P(s = pos|d) > P(s = neg|d)$. Since the proposed topic models do not directly provide $P(s|d)$ as a result of posterior inference, we derive this distribution from the sentiment-based topics for each market segment, ϕ, by marginalizing out the topics, z, and user attributes (meta-data tags), t, as follows:

$$P(s|d) \propto P(d|s) = \prod_{w \in \boldsymbol{w}_d} P(w|s) = \prod_{w \in \boldsymbol{w}_d} \sum_{t=1}^{N_{dt}} \sum_{z=1}^{K_t} P(w|s, z, t) \quad (6)$$

Table 10: **Sample topics discovered in the Auto dataset for the location tag "minnesota" and gender "female" and "male".**

female	
NEU	cold new know looking work fine headers control start thanks
POS	starter remote cold lights computer battery positive snow good focus
NEG	problem engages battery truck gear half hour negative bad
male	
NEU	fuel thanks caliper gas valve drier tank start gt wiring
POS	battery wires freeze positive power engine relay large tank
NEG	fuel bad car check mustang air cowl valve defrost

Table 11: **Examples of bigram topics discovered in the Auto dataset.**

location "dover ohio" and gender "female"	
NEU	ford bronco, make sure, lincoln ls, back seat, air control, fuse box, cherry bombs, seat belt, power loss, plugs wires
POS	car club, seat belt, back seat, key goes, wheel base, bench seat, good deal, local ford, ford dealer, heard good
NEG	isn't bad, bad wire, bad wheel, gone bad, go wrong, find bad, wrong time, connection bad, negative battery, bad water
location "dover ohio" and gender "male"	
NEU	throttle body, plugs wires, position sensor, ignition parts, power steering, fuel system, timing belt, system cleaner, rough running, rear wheels
POS	dash light, nice car, back seat, battery side, fuel injector, drive truck, trans fluid, right side, high end, engine light
NEG	engine runs, automatic transmission, bad wheel, ford thunderbird, go wrong, fluid changed, correct level, started acting, bad wire, bad wheel

Since the **Auto** dataset does not provide any information based on which the sentiment polarity of each review could be automatically derived, we only used the **Hotel** dataset for this experiment. In this dataset, each review is associated with graded ratings for six different aspects: service, value, sleep quality, room, location and cleanliness. Each of these ratings is a numeric score between 0 (lowest) and 5 (highest). The overall sentiment polarity of each review in the golden standard created for this dataset was determined automatically based on the average score for these six aspects as follows. If the average score for a given review is equal or greater then 3, then the review was considered as overall positive. If the average score of a review is equal or less than 2, then the review was considered as overall negative. Reviews with the average score between 2 and 3 were considered as neutral. Out of 9411 reviews with known ratings, 8553 were labeled as positive, 351 were labeled as negative and 507 were labeled as neutral, using the above method.

For this experiment, we used unigrams as lexical units and both PARADIGMhasm and MPQA lexicons as the sets of seed words for deriving sentiment-specific priors. Since ASUM and JST only consider positive or negative sentiments, we evaluate the performance of all models based only on those reviews, for which the ground truth labels are either positive or negative and are associated with at least one user attribute label in Table 3. The reported results are macro-averaged based on 5-fold cross validation. Figure 4 illustrates the change in accuracy by varying the number of topics per tag for the USTM topic models as well as the ASUM and JST baselines.

Several interesting observations can be made based on Figure 4. First, USTM-FT(W) has a comparatively stable prediction performance as there is a small change in accuracy when the number of topics per tag changes. The accuracy of USTM-FT(S) model, however, significantly improves as the number of topics per tag increases, while the performance of both ASUM and JST gradually drops. Table 12 compares the best accuracy, precision, recall, F1 score of the topic models in the USTM framework with ASUM and JST baselines for the review sentiment classification task.

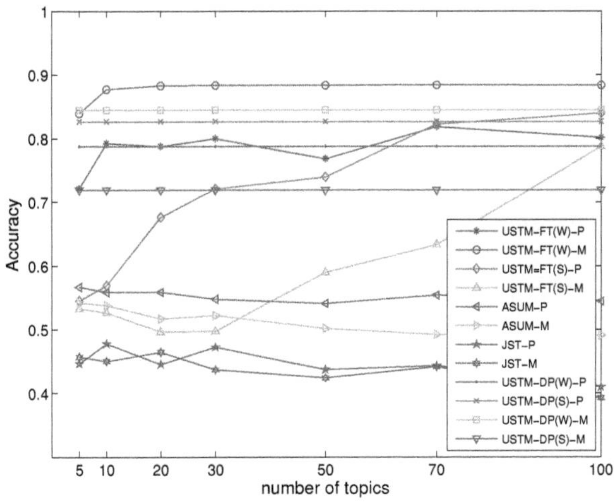

Figure 4: **Accuracy of sentiment prediction by varying the number of topics per tag (Hotel dataset)**

Table 12: **Performance the proposed models and the baselines for the task of predicting review sentiment. Best values for each performance metric on each dataset is highlighted in bold.**

Model	Precision	Recall	F1	Accuracy
USTM-FT(W)+P	**0.9651**	**0.8282**	**0.8914**	0.8194
USTM-DP(W)+P	0.9613	0.7789	0.8605	0.7878
USTM-FT(S)+P	0.9555	0.8279	0.8871	**0.8396**
USTM-DP(S)+P	0.9630	0.8193	0.8854	0.8264
ASUM + P	0.9626	0.5725	0.7180	0.5668
JST + P	0.9563	0.4812	0.6402	0.4778
USTM-FT(W)+M	**0.9685**	**0.8915**	**0.9284**	**0.8836**
USTM-DP(W)+M	0.9644	0.8294	0.8918	0.8447
USTM-FT(S)+M	0.9534	0.7658	0.8494	0.7880
USTM-DP(S)+M	0.9648	0.7217	0.8257	0.7190
ASUM + M	0.9654	0.5579	0.7071	0.5421
JST + M	0.9506	0.4588	0.6189	0.4643

Several important conclusions can be derived based on the results in Table 12. First, topic models in the proposed USTM framework significantly outperform the ASUM and JST baselines in terms of both accuracy and F1 score. Second, topic models assigning sentiment to each word individually outperform the models assigning sentiment on a per-sentence basis. Third, tuning the number of topics for parametric topic models allows to significantly improve their classification performance, ultimately outperforming the non-parametric topic models. Fourth, in most cases (except USTM-FT(W)-P and USTM-DP(W)-P), using PARADIGMhasm lexicon to derive sentiment-specific priors results in better accuracy than using MPQA lexicon. Since the experimental datasets are domain specific, larger generic lexicons may not translate into better performance. Finally, although the high precision of all models can be attributed to the small number of negative reviews in experimental dataset, USTM models still show better performance in predicting positive reviews than the baseline algorithms.

4.2.4 *User attribute prediction*

Predicting the attributes of the author of a review based on its lexical content is another interesting opinion mining task, for which the topic models in the proposed USTM framework is a natural choice. Similar to the sentiment classification task, the distribution over user attributes (or meta-data tags), $P(t|d)$, for each review, d, can also be estimated using sentiment-based topics for each market segment, ϕ, by marginalizing out the topics, z, and sentiments, s, as follows:

$$P(t|d) \propto P(d|t) = \prod_{w \in \boldsymbol{w}_d} P(w|t) = \prod_{w \in \boldsymbol{w}_d} \sum_{z=1}^{K_t} \sum_{s=1}^{S} P(w|s,z,t) \quad (7)$$

Since each review can be associated with several user attributes, we use Mean Average Precision (MAP), which takes into account the positions of the actual user attributes in the list of predicted ones, as a measure of performance of the topic models for this task. For this experiment, we used both the **Auto** and **Hotel** datasets and considered only the reviews that are associated with at least one of 100 most frequent tags in each dataset. We also used only unigrams as lexical units and PARADIGMhasm as the seed set for deriving the sentiment priors. The reported MAP is obtained using 5-fold cross validation and macro-averaged over the folds.

First, to optimize the configuration and evaluate the impact of different number of topics on the attribute prediction performance of parametric topic models (USTM-FT(W) and USTM-FT(S)), we varied the number of topics from 5 to 100 and recorded MAP for each setting. Figure 5 presents the results of this experiment along with the performance of non-parametric models (UMTM-DP(W) and UMTM-DP(S)) for comparison.

As follows from Figures 5a and 5b, the user attribute prediction accuracy reaches the maximum value when the number of topics is set to 20 for the **Auto** data set. For the **Hotel** data set, it reaches the maximum value at 70 and 100 for USTM-FT(S) and USTM-FT(W) respectively. Table 13 summarizes and compares the best results achieved by the proposed parametric and non-parametric topic models for the task of predicting the attributes of review authors on both experimental datasets.

Table 13: **Performance of the topic models in the USTM framework for the task of predicting the attributes of review authors.**

Dataset	Model	MAP
Auto	USTM-FT(W)+P	**0.7678**
Auto	USTM-DP(W)+P	0.6563
Auto	USTM-FT(S)+P	0.7630
Auto	USTM-DP(S)+P	0.6226
Hotel	USTM-FT(W)+P	**0.4516**
Hotel	USTM-DP(W)+P	0.4278
Hotel	USTM-FT(S)+P	0.4466
Hotel	USTM-DP(S)+P	0.4052

As follows from Table 13, the proposed models can be used to predict the attributes of review authors with reasonable accuracy. Furthermore, analysis of the results presented in Table 13 leads to three important conclusions. First, all proposed models consistently perform better on the **Auto** dataset than on the **Hotel** data set. Second, similar to the sentiment prediction task, topic models assigning sentiment to each word individually are more accurate than the models assigning sentiment on a per-sentence level. Third, the optimized parametric topic models achieved better accuracy than non-parametric ones for this task.

5. CONCLUSION AND FUTURE WORK

In this paper, we introduced a novel research problem of market segment-based summarization of contrasting opinions about different aspects of products or services in on-line consumer reviews, which has extensive practical applications. We also proposed two parametric extensions of LDA and two non-parametric extensions of the Dirichlet Process to address this problem. The proposed models incorporate asymmetric sentiment priors and jointly model

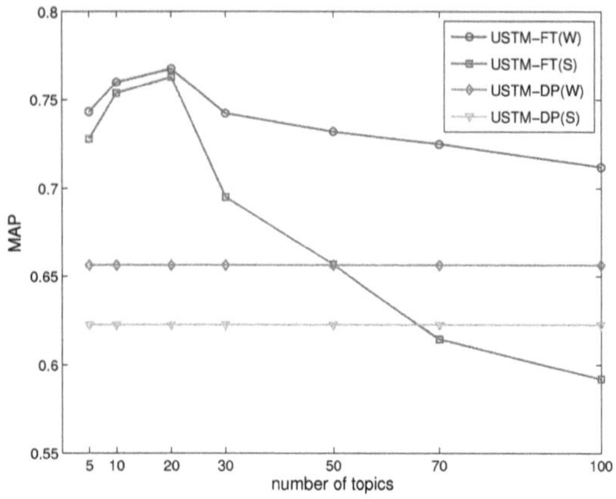

(a) **Auto dataset**

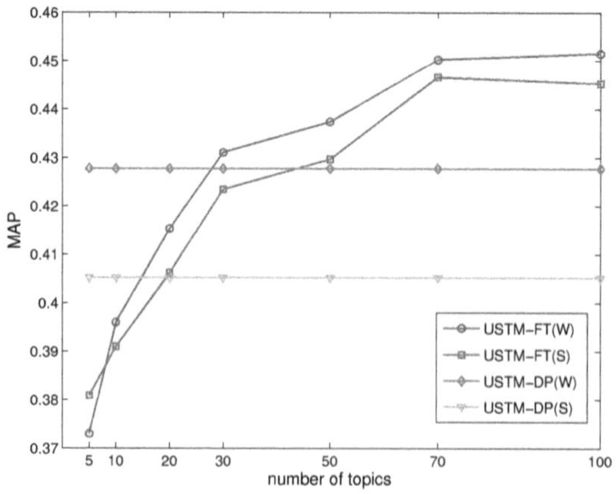

(b) **Hotel dataset**

Figure 5: **Accuracy of user attribute prediction for user-sentiment topic models by varying the number of topics**

demographic information of review authors and topical aspects of reviews. Qualitative analysis of sentiment-based topics discovered by the proposed models in two real-world collections of on-line consumer reviews using both unigrams and bigrams as lexical units indicates that incorporating user information into opinion analysis of on-line consumer reviews allows to better understand the preferences of different demographic groups of customers. We also demonstrated through quantitative evaluation that the proposed models can be used to accurately predict the overall sentiment of reviews as well as the demographic attributes of their authors.

We envision future work to proceed along the following two directions. First, machine learning techniques can be leveraged to learn the sentiment-specific priors for each individual word rather than a group of words. The second direction can focus on leveraging natural processing techniques, such as chunkers and part-of-speech taggers, to improve aspect-sentiment summaries by partitioning the text of reviews into more descriptive lexical units and better accounting for negations.

6. REFERENCES

[1] D. M. Blei, T. L. Griffiths, and M. I. Jordan. The Nested Chinese Restaurant Process and Bayesian Nonparametric Inference of Topic Hierarchies. *JACM*, 57(7), 2010.

[2] D. M. Blei and J. D. McAuliffe. Supervised Topic Models. In *Proceedings of the 20th NIPS*, pages 121–128, 2007.

[3] D. M. Blei, A. Y. Ng, and M. I. Jordan. Latent Dirichlet Allocation. *Journal of Machine Learning Research*, 3:993–1022, 2003.

[4] W. Gao, N. Yoshinaga, N. Kaji, and M. Kitsuregawa. Modeling User Leniency and Product Popularity for Sentiment Classification. In *Proceedings of the 6th IJCNLP*, pages 1107–1111, 2013.

[5] T. Hofmann. Probabilistic Latent Semantic Indexing. In *Proceedings of the 22nd SIGIR*, pages 50–57, 1999.

[6] M. Hu and B. Liu. Mining and Summarizing Customer Reviews. In *Proceedings of the 10th ACM SIGKDD*, pages 168–177, 2004.

[7] N. Jakob and I. Gurevych. Extracting Opinion Targets in a Single- and Cross-domain Setting with Conditional Random Fields. In *Proceedings of the 2010 EMNLP*, pages 1035–1045, 2010.

[8] Y. Jo and A. H. Oh. Aspect and Sentiment Unification Model for Online Review Analysis. In *Proceedings of the 4th WSDM*, pages 815–824, 2011.

[9] J. H. Kim, D. Kim, S. Kim, and A. Oh. Modeling Topic Hierarchies with the Recursive Chinese Restaurant Process. In *Proceedings of the 21st ACM CIKM*, pages 783–792, 2012.

[10] S. Kim, J. Zhang, Z. Chen, A. H. Oh, and S. Liu. A Hierarchical Aspect-Sentiment Model for Online Reviews. In *Proceedings of the 27th AAAI*, pages 526–533, 2013.

[11] A. Kotov and E. Agichtein. The Importance of Being Socially-Savvy: Quantifying the Influence of Social Networks on Microblog Retrieval. In *Proceedings of the 22nd CIKM*, pages 1905–1908, 2013.

[12] A. Kotov, V. Rakesh, E. Agichtein, and C. K. Reddy. Geographical Latent Variable Models for Microblog Retrieval. In *Proceedings of the 37th ECIR*, pages 635–647, 2015.

[13] A. Kotov, Y. Wang, and E. Agichtein. Leveraging Geographical Metadata to Improve Search over Social Media. In *Proceedings of the 22nd WWW*, pages 151–152, 2013.

[14] H. Lakkaraju, C. Bhattacharyya, I. Bhattacharya, and S. Merugu. Exploiting Coherence for the Simultaneous Discovery of Latent Facets and associated Sentiments. In *Proceedings of the 11th SDM*, pages 498–509, 2011.

[15] F. Li, C. Han, M. Huang, X. Zhu, Y.-J. Xia, S. Zhang, and H. Yu. Structure-aware Review Mining and Summarization. In *Proceedings of the 23rd COLING*, pages 653–661, 2010.

[16] F. Li, S. Wang, S. Liu, and M. Zhang. SUIT: A Supervised User-Item Based Topic Model for Sentiment Analysis. In *Proceedings of the 28th AAAI*, pages 1636–1642, 2014.

[17] C. Lin and Y. He. Joint Sentiment/Topic Model for Sentiment Analysis. In *Proceedings of the 18th CIKM*, pages 375–384, 2009.

[18] C. Lin, Y. He, R. Everson, and S. Ruger. Weakly Supervised Joint Sentiment-Topic Detection from Text. *IEEE Transactions on Knowledge and Data Engineering*, 24(6):1134–1145, 2012.

[19] T. Ma and X. Wan. Opinion Target Extraction in Chinese News Comments. In *Proceedings of the 23rd COLING*, pages 782–790, 2010.

[20] Q. Mei, X. Ling, M. Wondra, H. Su, and C. Zhai. Topic Sentiment Mixture: Modeling Facets and Opinions in Weblogs. In *Proceedings of the 16th WWW*, pages 171–180, 2007.

[21] S. Moghaddam and M. Ester. ILDA: Interdependent LDA Model for Learning Latent Aspects and Their Ratings from Online Product Reviews. In *Proceedings of the 34th SIGIR*, pages 665–674, 2011.

[22] A. Mukherjee and B. Liu. Aspect Extraction Through Semi-supervised Modeling. In *Proceedings of the 50th ACL*, pages 339–348, 2012.

[23] A.-M. Popescu and O. Etzioni. Extracting Product Features and Opinions from Reviews. In *Proceedings of the 2005 EMNLP-HLT*, pages 339–346, 2005.

[24] D. Ramage, C. D. Manning, and S. Dumais. Partially Labeled Topic Models for Interpretable Text Mining. In *Proceedings of the 17th SIGKDD*, pages 457–465, 2011.

[25] C. Sauper, A. Haghighi, and R. Barzilay. Content Models with Attitude. In *Proceedings of the 49th ACL-HLT*, pages 350–358, 2011.

[26] C. Tan, L. Lee, J. Tang, L. Jiang, M. Zhou, and P. Li. User-level Sentiment Analysis Incorporating Social Networks. In *Proceedings of the 17th ACM SIGKDD*, pages 1397–1405, 2011.

[27] I. Titov and R. Mcdonald. A Joint Model of Text and Aspect Ratings for Sentiment Summarization. In *Proceedings of 46th ACL-HLT*, pages 308–316, 2008.

[28] I. Titov and R. McDonald. Modeling Online Reviews with Multi-grain Topic Models. In *Proceedings of the 17th WWW*, pages 111–120, 2008.

[29] P. D. Turney and M. L. Littman. Measuring Praise and Criticism: Inference of Semantic Orientation from Association. *ACM TOIS*, 21(4):315–346, 2003.

[30] H. Wang, Y. Lu, and C. Zhai. Latent Aspect Rating Analysis on Review Text Data: A Rating Regression Approach. In *Proceedings of the 16th SIGKDD*, pages 783–792, 2010.

[31] T. Zhao, C. Li, Q. Ding, and L. Li. User-sentiment Topic Model: Refining User's Topics with Sentiment Information. In *Proceedings of the ACM SIGKDD Workshop on Mining Data Semantics*, 2012.

Learning to Extract Local Events from the Web

John Foley*
Center for Intelligent
Information Retrieval
University of Massachusetts
jfoley@cs.umass.edu

Michael Bendersky
Google
bemike@google.com

Vanja Josifovski*
Pinterest
vanja@pinterest.com

ABSTRACT

The goal of this work is extraction and retrieval of local events from web pages. Examples of local events include small venue concerts, theater performances, garage sales, movie screenings, etc. We collect these events in the form of retrievable calendar entries that include structured information about event name, date, time and location.

Between existing information extraction techniques and the availability of information on social media and semantic web technologies, there are numerous ways to collect commercial, high-profile events. However, most extraction techniques require domain-level supervision, which is not attainable at web scale. Similarly, while the adoption of the semantic web has grown, there will always be organizations without the resources or the expertise to add machine-readable annotations to their pages. Therefore, our approach bootstraps these explicit annotations to massively scale up local event extraction.

We propose a novel event extraction model that uses distant supervision to assign scores to individual event fields (event name, date, time and location) and a structural algorithm to optimally group these fields into event records. Our model integrates information from both the entire source document and its relevant sub-regions, and is highly scalable.

We evaluate our extraction model on all 700 million documents in a large publicly available web corpus, ClueWeb12. Using the 217,000 unique explicitly annotated events as distant supervision, we are able to double recall with 85% precision and quadruple it with 65% precision, with no additional human supervision. We also show that our model can be bootstrapped for a fully supervised approach, which can further improve the precision by 30%.

In addition, we evaluate the geographic coverage of the extracted events. We find that there is a significant increase in the geo-diversity of extracted events compared to existing explicit annotations, while maintaining high precision levels.

*Work done while at Google.

SIGIR'15, August 09-13, 2015, Santiago, Chile.
ACM 978-1-4503-3621-5/15/08.
DOI: http://dx.doi.org/10.1145/2766462.2767739 .

Categories and Subject Descriptors

H3.3 [**Information Storage And Retrieval**]: Information Search and Retrieval

Keywords

Information Retrieval; Information Extraction

1. INTRODUCTION

With the increasing trend toward personalized mobile applications and user experiences, there is a need for information systems that react to user preferences and location. In the past few years, this challenge has gathered more attention in the research community. Lagun et al. find that not only is local context useful in search, but that users are interested in explicit feedback in locality-sensitive tasks [16]. The Contextual Suggestion Track in the Text Retrieval Conference (TREC) presents the task of recommending establishments or venues to users given the preferences of a user in another city [5]. In this work, we explore a similar task, presenting users with *events* near them, rather than locations. Unlike the contextual suggestion track, we move away from whole-page relevance judgments toward extracting relevant atomic event records.

We define an event as an object having three mandatory properties, keeping in mind our goal: to recommend, display, and make searchable all events that can be extracted from the web.

Definition An event occurs at a certain location, has a start date and time, and a title or description. In other words, to be useful to a user, an event must be able to answer the questions: *What?*, *When?*, and *Where?*

Succintly, we are interested in events that users may want to add to their calendars to be reminded of and potentially attend. This is in contrast to many other definitions of an event, such as those in works discussing real-time detection of natural disasters, riots, pandemics or terrorist attacks in microblog streams [26, 36, 20], or the classic event definition in computational linguistics, which can be as broad as "a situation that occurs" [25].

Before a recommendation system for events can be created and evaluated, there is the information extraction challenge of discovering and collecting all available events in all areas. Simple approaches to this problem include:

- Mining and recommending events from social media [14].

- Leveraging semantic web annotations like `Schema.org`[1].
- Traditional wrapper induction and data mining.

Unfortunately, both semantic web and social media approaches require organizations to maintain their data in a particular format. With social media, this means an updated organization page, and with semantic web technologies, this means marking up the page with microdata (e.g., `Schema.org`). Unfortunately, smaller businesses, charities, and truly local organizations will lack the funding or the expertise required to fully and correctly adopt semantic web technologies.

Similarly, most existing approaches to information extraction require supervision at either the page or domain level, or some sort of repeated element structure [34]. As it would be infeasible and costly to annotate all such pages - or even a single page per domain, existing systems that mine for events or other structured data fall short of our goal of local event extraction from *all* web pages.

Examples of events that we consider local and that are unlikely to have existing markup, or sufficient social media presence are farmer's markets, poetry readings, library book sales, charity dinners, garage sales, community band concerts, etc. These events are of interest to a smaller, local community, and are unlikely to be selling tickets on high-profile sites or paying for advertisement.

In this work, our goal is to leverage the well-advertised, high-profile events to learn to extract a greater variety and depth of events, including the kinds of local events described above. Specifically, we leverage the existing `Schema.org` microdata annotations (there is an example of how these annotations appear in Figure 1) as a source of data for distant supervision, allowing us to learn to extract events that do not have semantic web annotations, including local events, without actually collecting judgments specifically for our task.

We introduce a model for scoring event field extractions and an algorithm that groups these fields into complete event records. We scale up our technique to the entire ClueWeb12 corpus (700 million pages), extracting 2.7 million events. We evaluate our precision at various recall-levels, and show that we can double event coverage of a system with respect to the available semantic web annotations at an 85% precision level. We briefly explore using our judgments for a supervised approach to this task and are able to improve precision by 30% on another million events with only 30 annotator-hours.

We also explore the geographic diversity of our dataset, finding that existing markup is heavily biased toward large cities (e.g. New York, Chicago, and Los Angeles) and that the results of our extraction cover a wider variety of locations. We validate this hypothesis via visual mapping, and by showing that we have good precision in a random sample of 200 cities across the world.

In the next section, we introduce related work in detail. In Section 3, we introduce our event field extraction and scoring model, and our event record grouping algorithm. In Section 4, we discuss our corpus and our judgments in more detail, and we present the results of our experiments in Section 5. We end with our conclusions in Section 6.

[1] `http://schema.org/Event`

Figure 1: Example Microdata adapted from `Schema.org`

```
<div itemscope itemtype=“http://schema.org/Event”>
  <span itemprop=“name”>
    Miami Heat at Philadelphia 76ers
  </span>
  <meta itemprop=“startDate”
        content=“2016–04–21T20:00”>
    Thu, 04/21/16 8:00 p.m.
  <div itemprop=“location” itemscope
        itemtype=“http://schema.org/Place”>
    Wells Fargo Center
    <div itemprop=“address” itemscope
          itemtype=“http://schema.org/PostalAddress”>
      <span itemprop=“addressLocality”>
        Philadelphia
      </span>,
      <span itemprop=“addressRegion”>PA</span>
    </div>
  </div>
</div>
```

2. RELATED WORK

Our work is characterized by using the explicitly annotated `Schema.org` as training data to learn to extract local events from the web. While there is work looking at events on social media, work leveraging semantic web annotations, and work on extraction in general, to our knowledge, our work is the first to leverage this data in this way, and the first to attempt this task.

2.1 Similar Tasks

The Contextual Suggestion Track [5] considers the task of a known user spending time and looking for entertainment in a new city. Evaluation is done on the snippet and page level, with users judging sites as interesting or not, effectively making the task about retrieving venues or establishments. In a similar motivation, we would like to consider the task of finding events relevant to a user in their current location, but because no large corpora of events exist, we consider first the task of extracting local events.

There are numerous works that identify the availability of semantic web information [27, 21, 3] but there is very little prior work on using this information as a source of distant supervision. Petrovski et al. use `Schema.org` annotations for products to learn regular expressions that help identify product attributes such as CPU speed, version, and product number [22]. Gentile et al. work on dictionary-based wrapper induction methods that learn interesting XPaths using linked data [7, 8]. Because Linked Data websites like DBPedia and Freebase are not typical web pages as those with `Schema.org` data, the structural features we are able to learn are not available in these works. We also attempt to learn about less structured fields, in particular, our *What?* aspect of events.

Another similar work comes from the historical domain. Smith worked on detecting, and disambiguating places and dates within historical documents in a digital libraries setting. He looked at collocations between these places and dates as events, and ranked them to identify significant date-place collocations that might merit further study by historians [32]. In a follow-up work, he looked at associating terms with these collocations and building interfaces for browsing [31].

2.2 Event Detection in other Domains

There is an entire class of work on detecting events within microblogs or real-time social media updates [26, 36, 20]. Becker describes identification of unknown events and their content in her thesis, but focuses on trending events on social media sites, and classification is used to separate event from non-event content clusters [2]. Our work, in contrast, is looking to find events in an offline manner that are explicitly described so as to present them in a search or recommendation system to users.

Kayaalp et al. discuss an event-based recommendation system integrated with a social media site, but focus on events already available through Facebook and Last.fm [14]. In this work, we consider these social media sites as two examples of the larger concept of "head domains" which are likely to have or adopt semantic web technologies, or be worthwhile candidates for supervised wrapper induction techniques.

Extraction of named events in news is another topic in which there has been work, e.g., [15]. Again, the definition of these news events is different from our local event definition.

2.3 Information Extraction

In the extraction domain, there is an immense amount of work on reducing boilerplate, whether directly, through template extraction [10, 23, 18], or through the more general idea of region extraction and classification. Sleimen and Corchuelo provide a detailed survey of region extractors in web documents, including those that leverage visual features [29]. Region extractors, in general, attempt to classify portions of a page into their purpose, i.e. navigation links, main content, and are studied in part to index only the content present on web pages. At least part of our task could be phrased within this context: an attempt to classify regions as either containing an event or not.

Work on temporal knowledge bases and extraction needed for automatic construction is similar to our task [11], except in a different domain and context. Most popular knowledge bases, have some ties to Wikipedia, which requires articles to be notable. By definition, we are seeking to extract events that do not have global relevance.

Additionally, there are a number of works that focus on repeated structure for extraction. Taking cues from HTML tables [9, 17, 4, 1, 39], or repetitive command tags or terms in general [34], these techniques do not require microdata, but require repetitive structure and make the assumption that there will always be a multitude of records to extract [35]. Recently, there has been a number of works about extracting data from web documents that were generated from the same templates [12, 30, 28]. In contrast to these works, we are interested in extracting local event records, which may or may not be generated from a pre-specified template.

3. EVENT EXTRACTION MODEL

We approach the task of extracting structured event information as a scoring or ranking method. We do this because we do not expect our target data – the listings of events on the web – to be particularly clean or perfectly aligned with any schema. Therefore, we wish to have a technique that joins several field scoring functions, which together give a multi-faceted score of how well the extracted structure fits our model of an event. The scoring functions take into account the source web page (Section 3.1), extraction sub-region (Section 3.2), and the individual extracted fields (Section 3.3).

The fact that there may be multiple extractions from overlapping regions on the page, poses an additional challenge of grouping the extracted fields into disjoint event records that contain event name, date, time and location. To this end, we propose a greedy selection and grouping algorithm that provides an efficient way to optimize the quality of extracted event records. This algorithm is described in detail in Section 3.4.

Formally, we represent each extracted event record as a set of fields ($\mathcal{F} = \{f_1, f_2 \ldots f_n\}$), their enclosing region ($\mathcal{R}$), and the source document ($\mathcal{D}$).

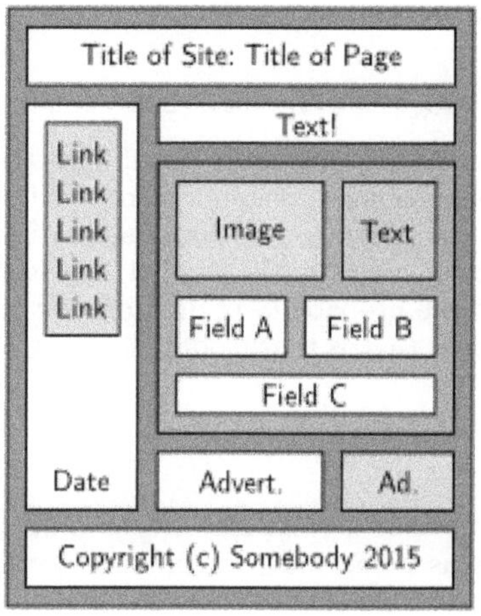

Figure 2: Example of an HTML document structure, presented visually. The boxes present represent nodes, the white boxes are the ones that are plausibly detected as fields in this example. Subsets of these fields represent possible event extractions.

An example HTML document is shown in Figure 2. If we consider the case where this document represents only one event, it is likely that Fields A,B, and C ($\mathcal{F}$) are the key fields in our event, and that the date in the navigation bar and in the copyright are false-positive fields. An event extraction only including the copyright field should get a low score, and similarly, the event containing all the fields should be considered too big and also receive a low score. We define the region of a fieldset to be the first shared parent of its fields, so for fields A and B, the $\mathcal{R}$ should be the box that contains all lettered fields, the image and the text node.

We formulate our scoring function, ϕ, which relates all our available context, as follows

$$\phi(\mathcal{F}, \mathcal{R}, \mathcal{D}) = \alpha(\mathcal{D})\beta(\mathcal{R})\gamma(\mathcal{F})$$

We discuss the scoring components in order, and note where we adapted this object-general model to our event domain. Our document scoring, $\alpha(\mathcal{D})$, our region scoring $\beta(\mathcal{R})$, and our field scoring $\gamma(\mathcal{F})$ are discussed in depth in the following sections.

3.1 Document Scoring

We want our event scoring function to take into account the page's likelihood of discussing an event, therefore we include a document-level score ($\alpha(\mathcal{D})$).

We take a naive-Bayes approach to this problem, and examine the probability of a web page discussing an event (belonging to the event class). We denote the candidate document $\mathcal{D}$ and the event class E, and consider the following ratio

$$\frac{P(E|\mathcal{D})}{P(\overline{E}|\mathcal{D})} > 1.$$

In other words, we consider a page worth investigating if the probability of it belonging to the event class (E) is higher than the probability that it does not belong to the event class ($\overline{E}$). In practice, the division of small fractions can lead to underflow, so we consider the equivalent relationship, asking whether the so-called log-odds of a page belonging to an event class is greater than zero.

$$logP(E|\mathcal{D}) - logP(\overline{E}|\mathcal{D}) > 0$$

We estimate these probabilities based upon the commonly-used language modeling framework introduced by Ponte and Croft [24]. In the language modeling framework, we estimate the probability of a word given a model X (which will be one of $\{E, \overline{E}\}$) as the probability of drawing it randomly from the bag of words that is that model.

$$P(w \in X) = \frac{tf(w, X)}{tf(*, X)}$$

The bag of words assumption means that we can treat all our terms as being independent, and we estimate the probability of a whole document by the probability of all its component terms ($w \in \mathcal{D}$) under the model.

$$P(\mathcal{D} \in X) = \prod_{w \in \mathcal{D}} \frac{tf(w, X)}{tf(*, X)}$$

Because our event class may be sparse in comparsion to any given document, we apply linear smoothing [13] to our positive class to avoid zero probabilities.

$$P(E|D) = \prod_{w \in \mathcal{D}} \lambda P(w \in E) + (1 - \lambda) P(w \in C)$$

In contrast, because we approximate our non-event class by the language model of the entire collection, $\overline{E} = C$, no smoothing is needed because all terms are present by construction.

$$P(\overline{E}|\mathcal{D}) = \prod_{w \in \mathcal{D}} P(w \in C)$$

Since we run our algorithm on millions of pages, we chose to use this page scoring mechanism as a first pass filter, restricting our calculation of other scoring components to those whose $\alpha(\mathcal{D}) > 0$, where α is defined as follows:

$$\alpha(\mathcal{D}) = \begin{cases} 1 & logP(E|\mathcal{D}) - logP(\overline{E}|\mathcal{D}) > 0 \\ 0 & \text{otherwise} \end{cases}$$

What remains now is identifying an initial set of documents that are used to construct the language model for the event class E. For this, we bootstrap existing semantic annotations on the web. Specifically, we consider all the pages that contain any `http://schema.org/Event` annotations (see Figure 1 for an example) as belonging to the event class E, since mark-up by their creators suggests that they discuss events. Overall, we have close to 150,000 such pages, which allows creating a robust event model.

3.2 Region Scoring

Region scoring ($\beta(\mathcal{R})$) is considered on the enclosing region $\mathcal{R}$ in the document. Since this region encloses all of event potential fields, it is a good unstructured representation of the extracted event. In fact, we present this enclosing region to annotators to understand our event prediction performance separately from our field prediction.

Therefore, we decided on a simple region filtering approach, which simply removed from consideration regions above certain length

$$\beta(\mathcal{R}) = \begin{cases} 1 & |\mathcal{R}| < \tau \\ 0 & \text{otherwise} \end{cases}$$

τ is set to 2^{12} in all the subsequent experiments. Our empirical evaluation have shown that this simple approach effectively removed the majority of bad regions. In fact, we considered a number of more sophisticated approaches, including learning probability distributions of the size of the region and enclosing region tags. However, in experiments not listed here due to space constraints, we found the effects of such additional information negligible, especially since region features were included on a per-field basis within our field-scoring functions (see Section 3.3).

3.3 Field Set Scoring

We explore field scoring in a way that requires at least one of each required field to be part of our extracted field set ($\mathcal{F}$). Therefore our formulation for $\gamma(\mathcal{F})$ includes both a scoring function γ_S and an indicator function that tests for required fields, γ_R.

$$\gamma(\mathcal{F}) = \begin{cases} \gamma_S(\mathcal{F}) & \gamma_R(\mathcal{F}) \\ 0 & \text{otherwise} \end{cases}$$

We will discuss the breakdown of the γ_S and γ_R functions below. Generally, we jointly score field occurrences, and this joint scoring considers the independent scores, $\delta_k(f)$, assigned to each field f of type $k \in \{\text{What}, \text{When}, \text{Where}\}$.

3.3.1 Independently Scoring Fields

In this work, we consider a number of ways to assign independent scores to fields that allows us to define $\delta_k(f)$ for any f and $k \in \{\text{What}, \text{When}, \text{Where}\}$. Formally, we define f as a tuple with a (begin, end) index range within the source document $\mathcal{D}$. Because the document itself has some HTML structure, the offsets within the field allow us to understand where in the structure of the page it occurs and leverage that as part of our scoring features.

Pattern-based approaches to tagging of dates, times and postal addresses in text yields results of reasonable accuracy, as evidenced by the approaches in HeidelTime [33], StanfordNLP [19], as well as some prior work on address detection [38]. Therefore, we consider pattern-based baselines for our extraction of event 'When' and 'Where' fields. While dates, times, and places have inherent and sometimes obvious structure, patterns do not make sense as a baseline for the 'What' of an event, so we assign an equal score to all candidates.

Table 1: Features used in Field Classification.

Category	Feature	Description
Text	Unigrams	Stopped and stemmed unigrams, hashed to 10,000 count-features.
	Bigrams	Stopped and stemmed bigrams, hashed to 10,000 count-features.
NLP	Capitalization	Ratio of terms capitalized, first term capitalized.
	Address overlap	Number of address fields that overlap the target span.
	Date overlap	Number of date fields that overlap the target span.
	Time overlap	Number of time fields that overlap the target span.
Structural	Size	Ratio of size to parent and to page.
	Location	Ratio of start and end locations to page.
	Attribute Text	Unigrams present in attributes; can capture style information.
	Parent tag	Hashed vocabulary of size 10 of lower-case parent tag.
	GrandParent tag	Hashed vocabulary of size 10 of lower-case parent's parent tag.
	Sibling tags	Hashed vocabulary of size 1000 sibling tags.
	Reverse XPath	10 features for each XPath entry going backwards toward HTML.

No classification uses baseline approaches for all fields.

$\delta_{\text{What}}(f) = 0.5$
$\delta_{\text{Where}}(f) = \text{matches}(f, \text{Address})$
$\delta_{\text{When}}(f) = \text{matches}(f, \text{Date/Time})$

What classification uses baseline approaches except for What fields.

$\delta_{\text{What}}(f) = \vec{W}^T_{\text{What}} \cdot \vec{X}_f$
$\delta_{\text{Where}}(f) = \text{matches}(f, \text{Address})$
$\delta_{\text{When}}(f) = \text{matches}(f, \text{Date/Time})$

What-When-Where classification uses multiclass classification to rescore the boolean baseline approaches for all fields.

$\delta_{\text{What}}(f) = \vec{W}^T_{\text{What}} \cdot \vec{X}_f$
$\delta_{\text{Where}}(f) = \text{matches}(f, \text{Address}) \cdot \vec{W}^T_{\text{Where}} \cdot \vec{X}_f$
$\delta_{\text{When}}(f) = \text{matches}(f, \text{Date/Time}) \cdot \vec{W}^T_{\text{When}} \cdot \vec{X}_f$

Our baseline methods are implemented by the function matches(f, r_k) where f is a field, and r is a set of regular expressions for field type k, returning 1 if a field f is considered a match for field type k, and 0 otherwise.

Our classification methods leverage features $\vec{X}_f$ extracted from the candidate field f and weights $\vec{W}_k$ learned using LIBLINEAR [6]. The features used encompass textual, natural-language, and structural features that are more fully described in Table 1. Evaluation of these prediction methods is discussed in Section 5.1. All other evaluations consider only the What-When-Where classification method for independent field scoring.

In order to train our classification methods we turn once again to the pages in the event class E, described in Section 3.1. Using these pages, we label all the HTML tags with semantic mark-up related to one of our three target fields ('What', 'When', 'Where') with their respective field type. In addition, we label all other textual HTML tags on these pages as 'Other'. We then use this bootstrapped training data to construct a multiclass classifier with label set

$$\mathcal{K} = ['What', 'When', 'Where', 'Other'],$$

and learn a weight vector $\vec{W}_k$, for each $k \in \mathcal{K}$. See Section 4.3 for more details on this process.

3.3.2 Jointly Scoring Fields

Given $\boldsymbol{\mathcal{F}}^R = \{\text{What}, \text{When}, \text{Where}\}$ as the set of required fields for an event, a field set $\boldsymbol{\mathcal{F}}$ has all its required fields if and only if $\gamma_R(\boldsymbol{\mathcal{F}})$ is true. We make the assumption that the field type k, with the maximum score $\delta_k(f)$ is the PREDICTEDTYPE of the given field f. Formally:

$$\text{PREDICTEDTYPE}(f) = \underset{k \in \boldsymbol{\mathcal{F}}^R}{\text{argmax}}\, \delta_k(f)$$

We test for the presence of all required fields by containment; the required fields should be a subset of the predicted types of the entire field set we are scoring. As an example, a set of fields may comprise an event if it has an extra date or time, but it may not if it doesn't have a date or time at all.

$$\gamma_R(\boldsymbol{\mathcal{F}}) = \boldsymbol{\mathcal{F}}^R \subseteq \{\text{PREDICTEDTYPE}(f) | f \in \boldsymbol{\mathcal{F}}\}$$

We combine the individual field scores within $\gamma_S(\boldsymbol{\mathcal{F}})$, our field set scoring function, using the same notation as before for per-field-type scorers ($\delta_k(f)$).

$$\gamma_S(\boldsymbol{\mathcal{F}}) = \prod_{f \in \boldsymbol{\mathcal{F}}} \max_{k \in \boldsymbol{\mathcal{F}}^R} \delta_k(f)$$

The individual score for each field is still labeled with a function, $\delta_k(f)$, which computes the score for the maximally-likely class for each field, reusing $\boldsymbol{\mathcal{F}}^R$ to describe the set of required classes.

In this formulation, we expect the output range of δ_k to be $[0, 1]$. Since our independent scores are all in this range, it means that our function for γ_S will tend to prefer field sets with fewer higher-scored fields, with γ_R ensuring that we do not consistently predict incomplete events.

3.4 Event Record Grouping Algorithm

We consider all HTML tags that contain any baseline (regular expression pattern-based) matches on the page to be candidates for field scoring, rather than exhaustively iterating over all the subsets of text fields on the page. Even with this relatively-smaller number of candidate fields, the prediction algorithm is computationally difficult. Recall that we have formulated our field scoring as a ranking problem. Therefore, grouping these ranked fields into complete event records is a variation of the general subset selection problem, which is known to be NP-hard in most cases [37].

To ameliorate this problem, we choose to add a constraint that no field may be used twice (predicted events should not overlap) and to use a greedy approach to assigning fields to event records, so that we at least are able to predict the best events correctly. This greedy algorithm for event record grouping is presented in Algorithm 1. We rank our predicted nodes by score, and greedily select the highest scoring events, whose enclosing regions ($\mathcal{R}$) do not overlap.

Algorithm 1 Greedy event record grouping algorithm.

```
# All tags and all regex matches on the page:
candidate_fields = {span, ...}
# All tags on the page containing candidate_fields.
candidate_tags = {span, ...}

# Score and collect candidates
possible_events = ∅
for R in each candidate_tag:
  F = set(candidate_fields inside R)
  score = φ(F, R, D)
  if score > 0:
    add (score, F, R, D) to possible_events

# Greedily select highest scoring, non−overlapping tags
output = ∅
for event in sorted(possible_events):
  if event fields do not overlap with any fields in output:
    add event to output

return output;
```

As another nod to efficiency, we implement ϕ by considering the parts independently, in terms of cost. Because $\alpha(\mathcal{D})$, $\beta(\mathcal{R})$, and $\gamma_R(\mathcal{F})$ are simple to calculate and may return zero scores, we calculate these parts first and skip the relatively-more expensive independent field calculations ($\gamma_S(\mathcal{F})$). Additionally, this reduces the number of field sets that must be considered, lowering the overall cost of the algorithm in practice.

An example HTML structure is shown in Figure 3. Nodes D,E,F, and G are textual nodes, which contain fields. D has been detected as a *What* field, E has been detected as a *When* field, F has both a *Where* and a partial *When* (only a relative date) and maybe a *What* field. Node G is an example of a date that is nearby but irrelevant to the event itself.

Running on this example, our algorithm would walk through the nodes, assigning ϕ scores to each node. Node D would receive a score of zero, because it is missing required field types (γ_R). Similarly, nodes E,F, and G would be removed from consideration due to missing fields. The *best* selection for this event would either be Node B or Node C, depending on whether Node D is required to describe the event or if Node F is considered sufficient *What* explanation. Because of our joint field scoring, even if we do not apply a *What* field classifier, Node A will receive a lower score since it has an extra date field, which will lower its γ_S score and overall score.

3.4.1 Deduplication

During development, our annotators reported seeing numerous instances of duplicate events, particularly of high-profile events that were advertised on many sites. Therefore, we

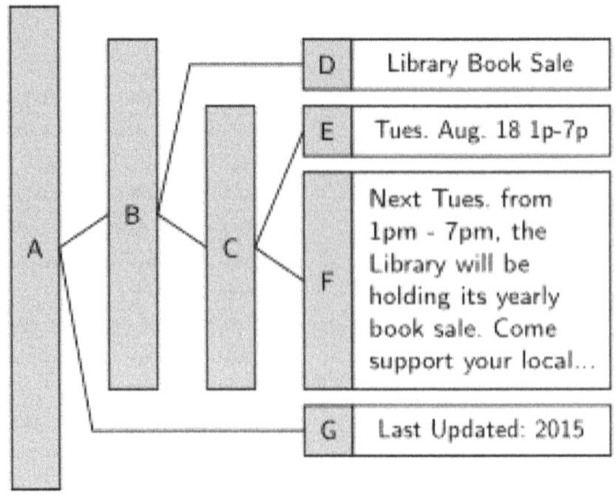

Figure 3: Example document structure handled by our algorithm. The boxes labeled with letters represent nodes in the HTML structure. Nodes D-G are textual nodes whose text is present. The lines display the parent-child relationships in the tree.

applied an exact-string matching duplicate detection method that ignored differences in capitalization, HTML tags and whitespace as a baseline and found that it was difficult to improve upon this baseline as our annotators no longer reported finding duplicates in our sampling of events. In all following analyses, we deduplicate all the extracted events using this method. We leave using extracted date/time and place information to perform a more domain-specific duplicate detection for future work.

4. EXPERIMENTAL SETUP

We evaluate our technique for extracting events on the ClueWeb12[2] corpus, which contains about 733 million pages. We extract `http://schema.org/event` records as microdata and rDFa in a first pass. This generates 145,000 unique web pages with events, and about 900,000 events on those pages. After deduplication, there are 430,000 unique events. Of these unique events, we map `Schema.org` properties to our three fields: What, Where, and When, and we are left with 217,000 complete events without any further processing.

We use incomplete events to train our field classifiers, but we will later consider recall in respect to the number of unique, complete `Schema.org` events, and we remove all pages with `Schema.org` events from our processing of the corpus moving forward, except for training data generation purposes.

4.1 Collecting Judgments

During the development of our system, we collected 2,485 binary judgments for understanding precision of event predictions. Each of these judgments contains the ClueWeb12 id, the start and end offsets of the events (in bytes after the WARC header), and a judgment: 1 if it is an event, and 0 otherwise.

For a large number of events in our best method, and in our method comparsion, we evaluate at the field level as well as at the event level, but only if the extraction actually is an event. For these judgments, as well as the agreement judgments, we turn to a crowdsourcing platform (Amazon

[2] `http://lemurproject.org/clueweb12/`

Mechanical Turk) to rapidly accumulate high-quality per-field judgments. We paid annotators $0.05 for event-level judgments and $0.10 for field-level judgments. We allowed annotators to mark *I can't tell from the available information* for any field or event, and removed these from our evaluation (Only 46 events in total out of the 2500).

For the fields, we asked annotators if they believed the selected snippet answered the given question about the event. As an example, we asked annotators to be picky about the "When" field in particular: two of our options were *No, it only includes a date* and *No, it only includes a time.*

4.2 Annotator Agreement

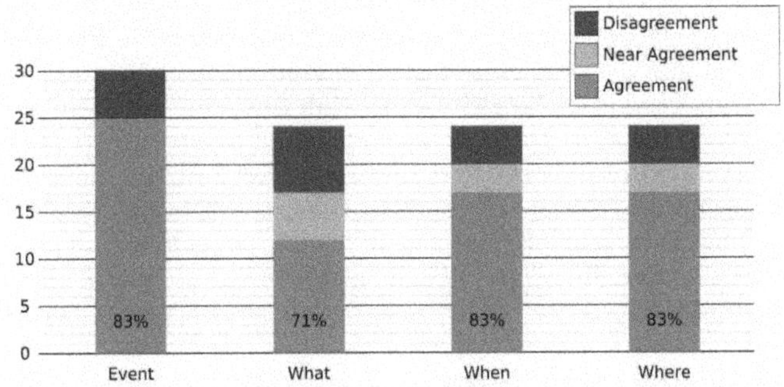

Figure 4: Agreement on Events and Fields

We calculated agreement on a set of thirty events randomly selected from our best-performing technique. Results are displayed in Figure 4. Because we asked our annotators for reasons when a field was inaccurate, we have some data on which the annotators agreed the field was incorrect, but disagreed on the reason: for example, one reviewer said the field was too short and the other said that they could not tell.

Our agreement is relatively high (>80%) on all but the "What" field, and our local reviewers found that agreement tended to be correlated with quality. The relative field performance here displays the ambiguity inherent in deciding what should describe an event in comparison to the stricter definitions of location and time.

4.3 Training Field Classifiers

Earlier, in Section 3.3.1, we discuss our approach to assigning scores to fields, and our classification methods. We list the features that we extract in Table 1, and we have already mentioned that we were able to parse 430,000 unique events from websites with `Schema.org` markup.

The question remains - how do we use this data as training for *What Classification* and *What-When-Where Classification*? Our first attempt to learn from this data involved a cross-fold evaluation setup, where we split events by domain into train, validate and test splits, extract features, and try to predict the fields in our validate and test sets. We split by domain here to better prepare ourselves for new data in our cross-validation setup, to avoid overtfitting to head domains that would have been present in all cross-validation sets.

While `Schema.org` gives us plenty of positive examples for each field, we don't necessarily have obvious negative examples. In the end, we found that taking all the tags, including other `Schema.org` properties, gave us the richest, most accurate representation of our problem space. We want our field classifiers to be able to select tags that actually correspond to an event from all the other tags on a page that has events. In early experiments, we found that using a single-class classifier was a mistake - the best negative examples for *What* include the positives for *When* and *Where*, as judged by the way our *What* field initially predicted dates and times and places. We moved to a multiclass setup, and this seemed to improve on this problem. Even for our *What Classification* setup, we emitted training, validation, and test data. We used our validation data to tune the C and ϵ parameters for LIBLINEAR and to choose between L1 and L2 normalization.

Even with the care taken to select negative examples, our cross-validation estimate of field classifier performance was still extremely high ($F_1 > 75\%$) for our three fields, which as we discuss later, is not the case when evaluated on pages without `Schema.org`.

5. RESULTS

5.1 Evaluating our Field Prediction Methods

Table 2: Fields Classified by Method. (N,W) denote significant improvements, where 99% of bootstrap samples of the target method have higher precision than 99% of samples from the None and What methods, respectively.

	None	What	What-Where-When
Event	0.54	0.51	0.76 (N,W)
What	0.09	0.30 (N)	0.36 (N)
When	0.17	0.20	0.32
Where	0.32	0.32	0.66 (N,W)

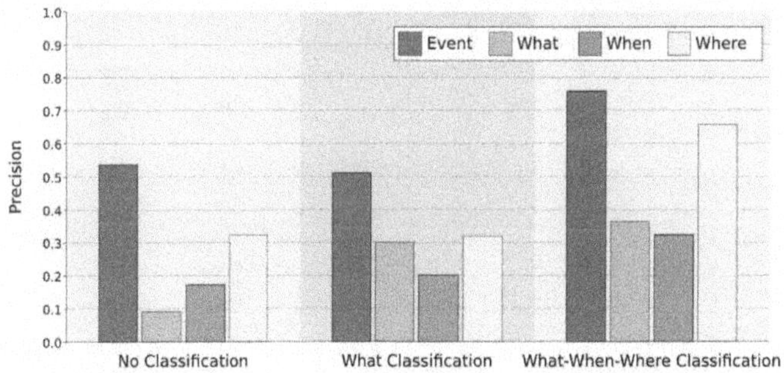

Figure 5: Comparison of Precision of Field Detection Methods

A key part of our overall event extraction system is the ability to assign meaningful independent scores to fields. We introduced three field scoring systems in Section 3.3.1 based on our baseline ability to detect Where/When aspects of events through regular expressions, and combining these baselines with classification.

In the *No Classification* system, we don't use any training data, and end up leveraging text near our Where/When fields for our What predictions. In our *What Classification* system, we use classification on only the What field, for which the baseline is weakest, and in our *What/When/Where Classification* system, we combine our baseline and classification approaches for all fields, leveraging the semi-supervision of our `Schema.org` extracted fields to learn weights for features as described earlier.

Table 3: Precision Levels used in evaluation.

	V. High	High	Medium	Low
Predicted	25,833	201,531	452,274	1,575,909
Increase	12%	93%	208%	725%
Judgments	155	567	482	491
Precision	0.92	0.85	0.65	0.55

In order to compare these methods, we first attempted to use our semi-supervised data - the `Schema.org` events and fields. Unfortunately, on such an event-focused dataset, all of our methods performed well. We believe that because of the format of microdata, and how it requires that each field be represented succinctly and separately in its own tag, these training instances were actually too simple. As a result, we were not able to leverage the `Schema.org` data to compare methods, and we had to create our own judgments.

We chose the top 30,000 pages by our document scoring method: $\alpha(\mathcal{D})$, and ran our algorithm three times on each page, once with each of our classification methods, and generated a pool of events from each. From each pool we sampled 100 random events (any attempt at a pairwise comparison would not have accurately compared the different methods).

We used bootstrap sampling with 10,000 samples to obtain 99% confidence intervals for each of our evaluations. We mark improvements where the 1% (worst-case) of the treatment is greater than the 99% (best-case) of the baseline. The improvements are marked in terms of the *None* baseline (N) and the *What* baseline (W), and the raw, mean values are presented in the Table 2.

5.2 Exploring Precision and Recall

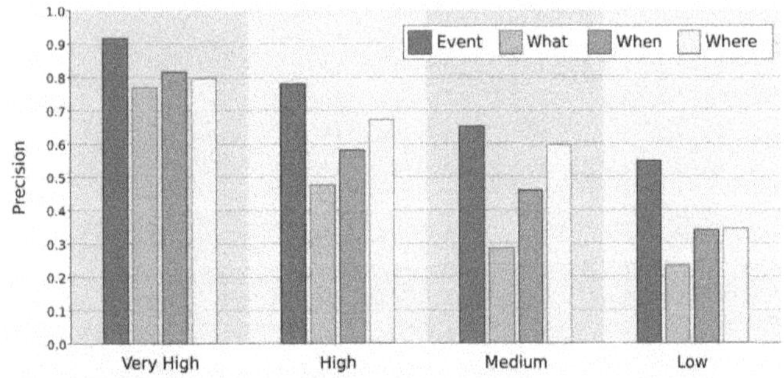

Figure 6: Precision Evaluated at Recall Levels

As we discussed earlier, there were only about 217,000 unique, complete events used in our semi-supervised approach for training. We cannot evaluate our recall perfectly because we simply do not know how many events are on the internet, or even in ClueWeb12's 700 million pages. Additionally, we think the most interesting way to evaluate recall is to consider a number of interesting recall points (precision categories) for evaluation based on the ratio of events predicted to the size of our semi-supervised input (`Schema.org`) events).

We consider a "Very High" precision category, chosen because it was a cutoff found to have over 90% precision. Our "High" precision category is chosen because it represents about a 1:1 prediction to training ratio. Our "Medium" precision category captures the case where we predict two events for each training instance, and our "Low" precision category contains the lowest score range in which we collected judgments, at about a 7:1 prediction ratio. These pseudo-recall levels are listed in Table 3.

In Figure 6, precision for each component of the event is illustrated. As overall precision drops, we can see how the weakest part of our detection is still the Event title, or the *What* field. Intuitively, this makes sense, as it is less structured and even our annotators had trouble agreeing on *What* field with respect to the other fields. Another finding that's interesting here is that even though the field precision degrades rapidly, (partly because it is conditioned on the event being correct) our event precision is significantly higher, particularly in the "Low" precision level. This suggests that even our noisy field detection has value, particularly to a selection algorithm like ours.

5.3 Supervised Evaluation

As a qualitative observation, when we had false-positives for event classification, they were often near-misses, in the form of album releases, band histories, obituaries, or biographies. They tended to be rich in field information, but from the wrong domain. In general, our technique introduced some false positives as the domain broadened from the focus on commercial music events of the `Schema.org` events.

Since we had collected a large number of judgments, we decided to briefly explore a human-supervised approach. In all other sections, we discuss distant supervision results, where we had no gold-truth human assigned labels, but only the silver-truth of the `Schema.org` data. This evaluation serves two purposes: (1) determining whether our impression of easily-detected domain mismatches is true, and (2) evaluating the amount of effort needed to apply a supervised approach to this problem.

Since we were interested in understanding annotator effort, we only used our 1100 Mechanical Turk annotations for this part, as they were automatically timed. We break our judgments into two parts, taking 800 events from medium to very-high precision, as our training and validation data, and 300 events in our low-precision bracket (original Precision of 0.55). We build a simple unigram classifier with 10,000 hashed term features as well as document, region, and individual field scores for the best field of each kind from those predictions, again using LIBLINEAR.

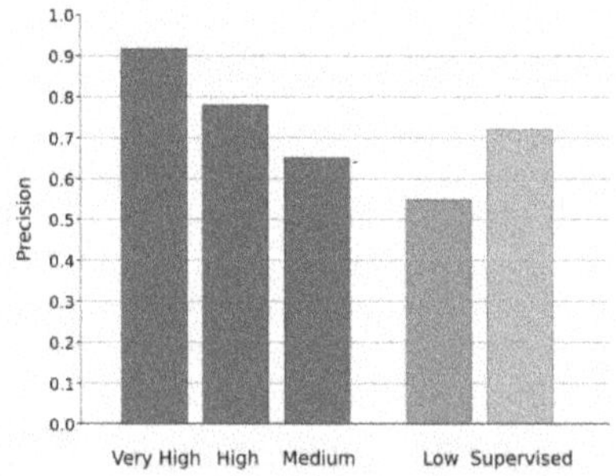

Figure 7: Supervised Event Prediction of Low-precision data based on other judgments. On the left, we have the training/validation data, and their precision represented (Very High, High, and Medium), and on the right, we have the test data, and its original precision (Low) and its new precision under supervision (Supervised).

This classifier works extremely well over our 300 evaluation events from the low range, boosting the precision from 0.55 to 0.72, with a 92% relative recall (the new classifier rejected another 8% of the 300 events). This experiment is displayed in Figure 7, where the blue bars correspond to the training data, the red bar with the original performance of the low-precision events, and the green bar with the supervised precision of the low-precision events.

This experiment supports our claim that a large amount of false-positives from our technique are simple to eliminate with minimal training data and annotation effort (~30 total hours of annotator time for the 1100 train/validate/evaluation judgments used).

5.4 Geographic Evaluation

We use a publicly-available geocoding and address API[3] to convert our extracted "Where" fields into full street addresses, and latitude/longitude information. The street addresses are used to evaluate our performance on future retrieval tasks, and the latitude and longitude pairs are used to generate maps to better understand our coverage and that of the Schema.org data.

5.4.1 City Coverage around the World

Table 4: Retrieval Metrics for 200 random cities.

MRR@5	P@1	P@2	P@3	P@4	P@5
0.78	0.71	0.70	0.69	0.70	0.70

The TREC Contextual Suggestion Track considers the task of recommending venues or destinations to users in new cities [5]. In this work, we briefly evaluate the suitability of our dataset to be applied to a similar task: the task of recommending events to users based on their location. Because the work we present is not about the recommendation task itself, but rather the extraction of events, we evaluate our ability to provide event coverage in a random city.

We group our events by city, and select events from 200 cities at random. We then judge, using Amazon Mechanical Turk, the 5 highest scoring events from each city. We evaluate as a retrieval task, where our query is the random city, and our ranking function for now is our confidence in the event prediction. The mean reciprocal rank (MRR) of finding an event is 0.78 on this data: on average there is an event at either rank 1 or rank 2. Our event precision at 1 is 0.71. Full results are listed in Table 4. The precision numbers here seem flat because there tend to be five or so valid events for each location. It is nice to see this consistency, because it suggests that our system is able to find many events for randomly selected locations.

5.4.2 Geographic Display

In Figure 8, we display a small world map where our events are plotted to understand our international coverage. Since the dataset we used, ClueWeb12 is biased toward English pages, it is understandable that the events we have extracted are mostly found in the United States, and north-western Europe. There is also some token coverage in other parts of the world, including India and Australia, but we focus on areas that we expect to have good coverage based on the ClueWeb12 English-speaking bias.

In Figure 9, you can see our events plotted on a US Map in two colors: green for high and very-high confidence $P >= 0.65$, and yellow for $0.55 < P < 0.65$. The blue dots are events parsed from Schema.org pages. The key takeaway from this

[3]https://developers.google.com/maps

Figure 8: Events across the world. Note that we have good coverage of countries where English is the dominant language, in a reflection of our corpus, ClueWeb12.

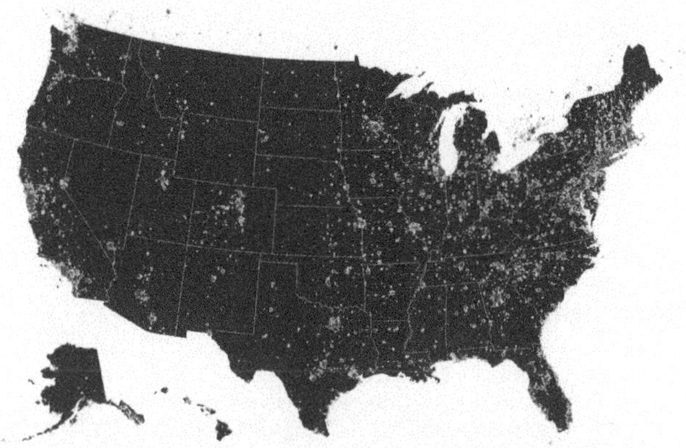

Figure 9: Events within the United States. Blue data points indicate Schema.org data, Green represents high confidence (P=0.65..0.85+), and Yellow represents low to medium confidence points (P=0.55..0.65). All points have more than 5 unique events, and are logarithmically scaled according to weight.

map is that Schema.org events are definitely more prevalent in large cities, specifically in New York, Los Angeles, and Chicago, and visually, our technique does quite a good job of expanding coverage geographically. Note that we only plot a point if there are more than five unique event occurrences at that location, and we have restricted our sampled precision to be above 0.55, and there are many more events at the larger dots, as their size is logarithmically scaled.

6. CONCLUSION

In this work, we introduce a new task inspired by the TREC Contextual Suggestion Track and the increasing population of mobile users: to retrieve and recommend events that users might want to attend. Because we are particularly interested in local events, our work focuses on the identification and extraction of events on the open internet.

We show that using semantic web technologies, and specifically Schema.org microdata to collect distant supervision data can be useful for training semi-supervised approaches to extraction problems like ours. This setup has the advantage that as more organizations adopt such technologies, the performance of our extractions will increase over time without any additional labeling effort.

We propose a novel model of event extraction based on independent field scoring and a greedy algorithm for grouping these fields into complete event records, with confidence scores assigned to them. Our features for field classification allow us to combine elements commonly seen in region extraction approaches with both information retrieval-based and linguistically-inspired features. As the proposed model depends heavily upon the ability to assign individual field scores, we evaluate a number of score assignment methods, and find that classification that learns from using the distant supervision of the `Schema.org` data is significantly beneficial.

7. ACKNOWLEDGEMENTS

This work was supported in part by the Center for Intelligent Information Retrieval. Any opinions, findings and conclusions or recommendations expressed in this material are those of the authors and do not necessarily reflect those of the sponsor.

8. REFERENCES

[1] M. D. Adelfio and H. Samet. Schema extraction for tabular data on the web. *VLDB'13*, 6(6):421–432, 2013.

[2] H. Becker. *Identification and characterization of events in social media*. PhD thesis, Columbia University, 2011.

[3] C. Bizer, K. Eckert, R. Meusel, H. Mühleisen, M. Schuhmacher, and J. Völker. Deployment of rDFa, microdata, and microformats on the web–A quantitative analysis. *ISWC*, pages 17–32, 2013.

[4] M. J. Cafarella, A. Halevy, and J. Madhavan. Structured data on the web. *CACM'11*, 54(2):72–79, 2011.

[5] A. Dean-Hall, C. L. Clarke, J. Kamps, P. Thomas, N. Simone, and E. Voorhees. Overview of the trec 2013 contextual suggestion track. Technical report, DTIC Document, 2013.

[6] R.-E. Fan, K.-W. Chang, C.-J. Hsieh, X.-R. Wang, and C.-J. Lin. Liblinear: A library for large linear classification. *The Journal of Machine Learning Research*, 9:1871–1874, 2008.

[7] A. L. Gentile, Z. Zhang, I. Augenstein, and F. Ciravegna. Unsupervised wrapper induction using linked data. In *K-CAP '13*, pages 41–48, New York, NY, USA, 2013. ACM.

[8] A. L. Gentile, Z. Zhang, and F. Ciravegna. Self training wrapper induction with linked data. In *Text, Speech and Dialogue*, pages 285–292. Springer, 2014.

[9] R. Gupta and S. Sarawagi. Answering table augmentation queries from unstructured lists on the web. *VLDB'09*, 2(1):289–300, 2009.

[10] S. Gupta, G. Kaiser, D. Neistadt, and P. Grimm. Dom-based content extraction of html documents. In *WWW'03*, pages 207–214. ACM, 2003.

[11] J. Hoffart, F. M. Suchanek, K. Berberich, and G. Weikum. Yago2: a spatially and temporally enhanced knowledge base from wikipedia. *Artificial Intelligence*, 194:28–61, 2013.

[12] J. L. Hong, E.-G. Siew, and S. Egerton. Information extraction for search engines using fast heuristic techniques. *Data & Knowledge Engineering*, 69(2):169–196, 2010.

[13] F. Jelinek and R. L. Mercer. Interpolated estimation of markov source parameters from sparse data. In *Proceedings of the Workshop on Pattern Recognition in Practice*, 1980.

[14] M. Kayaalp, T. Ozyer, and S. Ozyer. A collaborative and content based event recommendation system integrated with data collection scrapers and services at a social networking site. In *ASONAM'09*, pages 113–118. IEEE, 2009.

[15] E. Kuzey, J. Vreeken, and G. Weikum. A fresh look on knowledge bases: Distilling named events from news. In *CIKM'14*, pages 1689–1698. ACM, 2014.

[16] D. Lagun, A. Sud, R. W. White, P. Bailey, and G. Buscher. Explicit feedback in local search tasks. In *SIGIR'13*, pages 1065–1068. ACM, 2013.

[17] G. Limaye, S. Sarawagi, and S. Chakrabarti. Annotating and searching web tables using entities, types and relationships. *VLDB'10*, 3(1-2):1338–1347, 2010.

[18] R. Manjula and A. Chilambuchelvan. Extracting templates from web pages. In *Green Computing, Communication and Conservation of Energy (ICGCE), 2013 International Conference on*, pages 788–791. IEEE, 2013.

[19] C. D. Manning, M. Surdeanu, J. Bauer, J. Finkel, S. J. Bethard, and D. McClosky. The Stanford CoreNLP natural language processing toolkit. In *ACL*, pages 55–60, 2014.

[20] D. Metzler, C. Cai, and E. Hovy. Structured event retrieval over microblog archives. In *ACL'12*, pages 646–655. Association for Computational Linguistics, 2012.

[21] H. Mühleisen and C. Bizer. Web data commons-extracting structured data from two large web corpora. *LDOW*, 937, 2012.

[22] P. Petrovski, V. Bryl, and C. Bizer. Learning regular expressions for the extraction of product attributes from e-commerce microdata. 2014.

[23] J. Pomikálek. Removing boilerplate and duplicate content from web corpora. *Disertacnı práce, Masarykova univerzita, Fakulta informatiky*, 2011.

[24] J. M. Ponte and W. B. Croft. A language modeling approach to information retrieval. In *SIGIR'98*, pages 275–281. ACM, 1998.

[25] J. Pustejovsky, P. Hanks, R. Sauri, A. See, R. Gaizauskas, A. Setzer, D. Radev, B. Sundheim, D. Day, L. Ferro, et al. The timebank corpus. In *Corpus linguistics*, volume 2003, page 40, 2003.

[26] T. Sakaki, M. Okazaki, and Y. Matsuo. Earthquake shakes twitter users: real-time event detection by social sensors. In *Proceedings of the 19th international conference on World wide web*, pages 851–860. ACM, 2010.

[27] M. Schmachtenberg, C. Bizer, and H. Paulheim. Adoption of the linked data best practices in different topical domains. *ISWC*, pages 245–260, 2014.

[28] H. Sleiman and R. Corchuelo. Trinity: on using trinary trees for unsupervised web data extraction. 2013.

[29] H. A. Sleiman and R. Corchuelo. A survey on region extractors from web documents. *Knowledge and Data Engineering, IEEE*, 25(9):1960–1981, 2013.

[30] H. A. Sleiman and R. Corchuelo. Tex: An efficient and effective unsupervised web information extractor. *Knowledge-Based Systems*, 39:109–123, 2013.

[31] D. A. Smith. Detecting and browsing events in unstructured text. In *SIGIR'02*, pages 73–80. ACM, 2002.

[32] D. A. Smith. Detecting events with date and place information in unstructured text. In *Proceedings of the 2nd ACM/IEEE-CS joint conference on Digital libraries*, pages 191–196. ACM, 2002.

[33] J. Strötgen and M. Gertz. Heideltime: High quality rule-based extraction and normalization of temporal expressions. In *Workshop on Semantic Evaluation, ACL*, pages 321–324, 2010.

[34] W. Thamviset and S. Wongthanavasu. Information extraction for deep web using repetitive subject pattern. *WWW'13*, pages 1–31, 2013.

[35] W. Thamviset and S. Wongthanavasu. Bottom-up region extractor for semi-structured web pages. In *ICSEC'14*, pages 284–289. IEEE, 2014.

[36] K. Watanabe, M. Ochi, M. Okabe, and R. Onai. Jasmine: a real-time local-event detection system based on geolocation information propagated to microblogs. In *CIKM'11*, pages 2541–2544. ACM, 2011.

[37] W. J. Welch. Algorithmic complexity: three np-hard problems in computational statistics. *Journal of Statistical Computation and Simulation*, 15(1):17–25, 1982.

[38] Z. Yu. High accuracy postal address extraction from web pages. Master's thesis, Dalhousie University, Halifax, Nova Scotia, 2007.

[39] Z. Zhang. Towards efficient and effective semantic table interpretation. In *ISWC'14*, pages 487–502. Springer, 2014.

Rank-GeoFM: A Ranking based Geographical Factorization Method for Point of Interest Recommendation

Xutao Li[1] Gao Cong[1] Xiao-Li Li[2] Tuan-Anh Nguyen Pham[1] Shonali Krishnaswamy[2]
[1]School of Computer Engineering, Nanyang Technological University, Singapore.
{lixutao@, gaocong@, pham0070@e.}ntu.edu.sg
[2]Institute for Infocomm Research(I2R), A*STAR, Singapore.
{xlli, spkrishna}@i2r.a-star.edu.sg

ABSTRACT

With the rapid growth of location-based social networks, Point of Interest (POI) recommendation has become an important research problem. However, the scarcity of the check-in data, a type of implicit feedback data, poses a severe challenge for existing POI recommendation methods. Moreover, different types of context information about POIs are available and how to leverage them becomes another challenge. In this paper, we propose a ranking based geographical factorization method, called Rank-GeoFM, for POI recommendation, which addresses the two challenges. In the proposed model, we consider that the check-in frequency characterizes users' visiting preference and learn the factorization by ranking the POIs correctly. In our model, POIs both with and without check-ins will contribute to learning the ranking and thus the data sparsity problem can be alleviated. In addition, our model can easily incorporate different types of context information, such as the geographical influence and temporal influence. We propose a stochastic gradient descent based algorithm to learn the factorization. Experiments on publicly available datasets under both user-POI setting and user-time-POI setting have been conducted to test the effectiveness of the proposed method. Experimental results under both settings show that the proposed method outperforms the state-of-the-art methods significantly in terms of recommendation accuracy.

Categories and Subject Descriptors

H.3.3 [**Information Storage and Retrieval**]: Information Filtering

Keywords

Collaborative Filtering; Factorization Model; Ranking

1. INTRODUCTION

Recently, location-based social networks (LBSN) have emerged, such as Foursquare. These online systems enable people to check in and share their experiences with friends when they visit a point of interest (POI), e.g., restaurant, and shopping mall. These networks are growing at an unprecedented pace. Taking Foursquare as an example, it had attracted 45 million users with more than 5 billion check-ins until January 2014. The huge volume of data contains valuable information about POIs, and human preference, which can be exploited for POI recommendation [1].

POI recommendation aims at learning the users' visiting preferences and recommending a user the POIs *that s/he may be interested in but has never visited.* This task is important and meaningful, as it not only helps local residents or tourists to explore interesting unknown places in a city, but also creates the opportunities for POI owners to increase their revenues by finding and attracting potential visitors.

POI recommendation is challenging for two reasons. First, the check-in data in LBSN is very sparse, and thus recommendation methods suffer from the data scarcity problem. The check-in data is usually represented as a user-POI matrix, shown as in Figures 1(a) and 1(b). As we will see in the experiments, the density of check-in matrix is usually less than 0.5%. Moreover, when considering context-aware POI recommendation, the user-POI check-in data (matrix) needs to be separated and represented as a tensor, e.g., as shown in Figures 1(c) and 1(d) for time-aware POI recommendation. This will make the data more sparse, and the density of the check-in tensor in experiments is less than 0.05%, which is extremely small compared to 1.2% for Netflix data [2]. Worse still, the check-in is a type of implicit feedback [11], which makes the POI recommendation more difficult. Different from conventional movie rating data, where users explicitly denote their "like" or "dislike" to an item with different rating scores, the check-ins offer only *positive examples* that a user likes, and the POIs without check-ins, marked as "?" in Figures 1(a) and 1(c), are either unattractive or undiscovered but potentially attractive. In other words, we need to infer his/her preference and non-preference based on the check-in data. Most of the existing POI recommendation methods [22, 3, 14, 9, 7, 12] overlook data scarcity and implicit feedback facts, and adapt conventional memory or model-based collaborative filtering for POI recommendation. Therefore, these methods suffer from the data scarcity problem.

Second, in POI recommendation, different types of context information are available, e.g., geographical coordinates of POIs, time stamps of check-ins, friendship of users, categories of POIs, etc. It is important to exploit context information to improve the recommendation accuracy. For

SIGIR'15, August 09 - 13, 2015, Santiago, Chile

DOI: http://dx.doi.org/10.1145/2766462.2767722 .

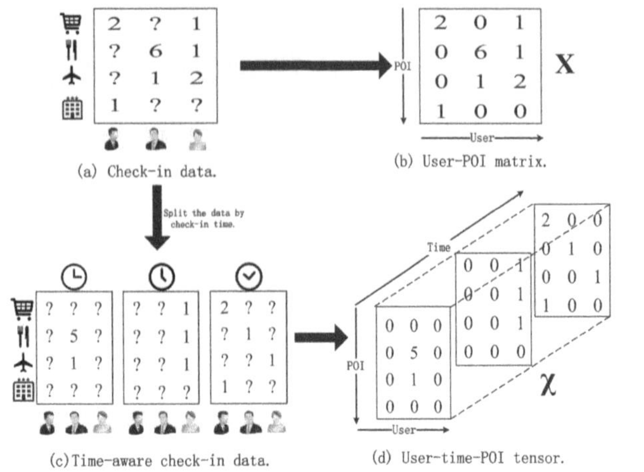

Figure 1: An example of check-in data of three users in two scenarios.

example, geographical coordinates, as an important type of context information which is not available in conventional recommendation tasks, are exploited for POI recommendation [22, 15, 3], since users have a much higher probability to visit nearby POIs [22, 15]. Previous work [22, 3, 12, 11] develops different approaches to exploiting the different types of context information. However, these approaches are usually developed for a particular type of context and it is difficult to generalize them to handle another type of context information.

In this paper, we propose a new ranking based factorization method for the POI recommendation problem. We consider obtaining factorizations in a ranking way because of two reasons: on the one hand it works better for implicit feedback data [16], and on the other hand the sparsity problem can be alleviated because both visited (positive examples) and unvisited POIs will contribute to the learning of a ranking function. Specifically, we assume that the higher the check-in frequency is, the more the POI is preferred by a user; and the unvisited POIs are less preferred than the visited ones. Instead of fitting the check-in frequency as conventional matrix factorization based methods do, we fit the users' preference rankings for POIs to learn the latent factors of users and POIs. In our proposed method, the unvisited POIs also contribute to the learning, which will help alleviate the sparsity problem.

In addition to addressing the data scarcity issue, our factorization model can easily incorporate different types of context information. In the proposed method, we compute the recommendation score of a POI by the sum of pairwise interaction scores between it and each context variable considered. This enables us to easily incorporate different types of context information by simply including more interaction scores. The pairwise prediction also unifies the way to handle matrix and tensor data. That is, the POI recommendation and context-aware POI recommendation can be handled with one unified framework.

Our contributions in this paper can be summarized as follows:

- We propose a new Ranking based Geographical Factorization Method (called Rank-GeoFM) for POI recommendation, which addresses the data scarcity problem and incorporates the geographical influence, an important type of context information.
- To optimize the objective function of the Rank-GeoFM, we use the stochastic gradient descent method. However, there are two difficulties in calculating stochastic gradient descents. First, the objective function is indifferentiable. To address this issue, we propose a continuous approximation to the objective function. Second, to calculate the stochastic gradients, we need compute the prediction scores of all POIs, which costs heavy computations. To tackle this issue, we develop a sampling based fast learning scheme to calculate the gradients.
- The proposed method can be generalized easily when other types of context information are available. We take temporal information as an example, and demonstrate how our model can be used to incorporate it for time-aware POI recommendation.
- Extensive experiments on two real-life datasets Foursquare and Gowalla demonstrate that Rank-GeoFM outperforms the state-of-the-art methods significantly for both POI recommendation and time-aware POI recommendation in terms of accuracy.

The rest of this paper is organized as follows: In Section 2, we briefly review related work. In Section 3, we introduce the proposed method. The experimental results are given in Section 4. Finally, we conclude the paper in Section 5.

2. RELATED WORK

2.1 POI Recommendation

POI Recommendation. Memory-based collaborative filtering (CF) techniques, such as user-based CF and item-based CF, are exploited for POI recommendation. Ye *et al.* [22] adopt linear interpolation to incorporate both the social and geographical influences into the user-based CF framework for POI recommendation. Their experimental results show that user-based CF outperforms item-based CF for POI recommendation, incorporating the geographical influence into the user-based CF model can significantly improve the recommendation accuracy, and the social influence has little impact on the performance. Levandoski *et al.* extend item-based CF method by considering the travel distance as penalty [9].

Memory-based CF methods easily suffer from the data sparsity problem, since the user-user or item-item similarities need to be calculated based on common check-ins. When the check-ins are scarce, two users or items will share very few common check-ins and thus the resulting similarities are unreliable for making effective recommendations.

Model-based CF techniques are also exploited for POI recommendation. Noulas *et al.* [14] find that matrix factorization (MF) performs worse than user-based CF and item-based CF for POI recommendation. In their work, conventional MF method for explicit feedback data is applied to POI recommendation, which thus is not suitable and delivers bad performance. Based on the observation that individual's check-in locations are usually around several centers, Cheng *et al.* [3] introduce a Multi-center Gaussian Model to compute the geographical influence and then combine it heuristically with MF for POI recommendation. In this approach,

MF is performed by fitting nonzero check-ins only and thus it suffers from the data sparsity issue easily. Liu *et al.* [12] propose a geographical probabilistic factor analysis framework, namely GTBNMF, which incorporates geographical influence and textual influence based on the Bayesian Nonnegative Matrix Factorization (BNMF). However, the BNMF is performed by fitting both zero and nonzero check-ins, which might not be reasonable because zero check-ins may be missing values and should not be fitted directly. All these factorization methods do not exploit the implicit feedback property of POI recommendation.

Recently, considering the check-ins as implicit feedbacks, Lian *el al.* [11] develop a model, namely GeoMF, based on Weighted Matrix Factorization (WMF), and the geographical influence is incorporated into WMF. The method fits the nonzero check-ins by using large weights and zero check-ins by using smaller weights. Although assigning large weights can highlight nonzero check-ins, directly fitting zero check-ins may not be very reasonable because zero check-ins may be missing values. Moreover, because of the limitation of WMF, it is not easy to generalize the method to other types of context information.

Context-aware POI recommendation. Most of the aforementioned methods for POI recommendation exploit the geographical influence in making recommendations. However, their approaches of handling the geographical influence cannot handle other types of context information. Time is another important type of context, and time-aware POI recommendation aims to recommend POIs for a user at a given time. Yuan *et al.* propose a method called UTE+SE, which extends the user-based CF to incorporate both the temporal and geographical effects with a linear combination framework [24]. Yuan *et al.* further present a graph based method, called BPP, for time-aware POI recommendation [25], which makes recommendations by preference propagation on a graph constructed from the check-in data. BPP [25] performs better than UTE+SE [24]. In addition, Gao *et al.* [7] study the temporal effect on the POI recommendation, but not the time-aware POI recommendation. They develop a regularized nonnegative matrix factorization method but they do not consider the geographical influence.

Other types of contexts utilized in POI recommendation include category of POI [13], text description of POI [23, 12, 10, 8, 26], and currently-visited POI [4, 6].

2.2 Ranking based Learning Criteria

Bayesian personalized ranking (BPR) [16] is a famous ranking-based objective criterion, which can produce promising performance for implicit feedback problems combining with matrix factorization model. BPR learns the ranking models based on pairwise comparison of items such that the Area Under the ROC Curves (AUC) can be maximized. It gives equal weights to each item pair [19, 21]. Ordered Weighted Pairwise Classification (OWPC) [20] is another recently proposed loss metric for ranking. The method considers ranking as a set of pairwise classification problems and emphasizes the classifications at top-N positions by assigning higher weights. OWPC has been successfully applied in text retrieval [20] and image annotation [21].

In this paper, we consider the POI recommendation based on the OWPC criterion. Our proposed method differs from the existing approaches [20, 21] in two aspects. First, existing OWPC is developed for ranking problem with binary values, i.e., relevance or irrelevance, while in this paper we extend the objective function to rank POIs with different visiting frequencies, and provide the solutions for stochastic gradient descent optimization. Second, we develop a general factorization method for POI recommendation, which is able to exploit different types of context information.

Table 1: List of notations

$\mathcal{U}$	the set of users $\{u_1, u_2, \cdots, u_{\vert\mathcal{U}\vert}\}$
$\mathcal{L}$	the set of POIs $\{\ell_1, \ell_2, \cdots, \ell_{\vert\mathcal{L}\vert}\}$
$\mathcal{T}$	the set of time slots $\{t_1, t_2, \cdots, t_{\vert\mathcal{T}\vert}\}$
$\mathcal{L}^u$	the set of POIs that user u has visited
$\mathbf{X} = [x_{u\ell}]$	a $\vert\mathcal{U}\vert \times \vert\mathcal{L}\vert$ user-POI check-in matrix
$\mathcal{X} = [x_{ut\ell}]$	a $\vert\mathcal{U}\vert \times \vert\mathcal{T}\vert \times \vert\mathcal{L}\vert$ user-time-POI tensor
$\mathcal{D}_1$	the user-POI pairs: $\{(u, \ell) \vert x_{u\ell} > 0\}$
$\mathcal{D}_2$	the user-time-POI tuples: $\{(u, t, \ell) \vert x_{ut\ell} > 0\}$
$d(\ell, \ell')$	the distance between POIs ℓ and ℓ'
$\mathcal{N}_k(\ell)$	the set of k nearest POIs of ℓ
$y_{u\ell}$	recommendation score of POI ℓ for user u

3. PROPOSED METHOD

In this section, we present the proposed ranking based factorization method for POI recommendation. We first formulate the POI recommendation problem by a ranking objective function, and then introduce how to optimize it. Finally, we generalize the model for time-aware POI recommendation.

We first summarize the notations used in this paper in Table 1. Then the POI recommendation problem is defined as follows:

DEFINITION 1. ***POI recommendation:*** *given a user u, we recommend the POIs that s/he will like to visit, and are not in $\mathcal{L}^u$.*

3.1 Ranking based Geographical Factorization

3.1.1 Preference Ranking Objective Function

In this subsection, we formulate our objective function for POI recommendation. Due to the sparsity of check-in data, we design objective function by fitting user's preference rankings for POIs, instead of fitting his/her check-in frequencies as traditional factorization methods do.

First, we need to infer a user's preference rankings for POIs based on his/her check-in data. Intuitively, we assume that the higher the check-in frequency is, the more the POI is preferred by a user; and the unvisited POIs are less preferred than the visited ones. In other words, for a given user u, POI ℓ should be ranked higher than POI ℓ' if $x_{u\ell} > x_{u\ell'}$, where $x_{u\ell}$ denotes the frequency that user u visited POI ℓ.

Based on the intuition, we develop a method to measure the incompatibility between the inferred rankings and the rankings produced by a factorization model. In particular, for a given user u and POI ℓ, the incompatibility can be measured by:

$$Incomp(y_{u\ell}, \varepsilon) = \sum_{\ell' \in \mathcal{L}} I(x_{u\ell} > x_{u\ell'}) I(y_{u\ell} < y_{u\ell'} + \varepsilon) \quad (1)$$

where $I(\cdot)$ is an indicator function, $I(a) = 1$ when a is true, and 0 otherwise; ε is a positive number; $y_{u\ell}$ denotes the recommendation score of POI ℓ for user u, which will be calculated by a factorization model in this paper. We can see Eq. (1) counts the number of POIs that are supposed to be ranked lower than ℓ for user u according to the check-in data, but ranked higher than ℓ by the factorization model. Note that ε-margin is used to compute the rankings for the factorization model, i.e., we consider that ℓ' is ranked higher than ℓ for user u only if $y_{u\ell} < y_{u\ell'} + \varepsilon$. The $Incomp(y_{u\ell}, \varepsilon)$ measures the number of POIs that are incorrectly ranked higher than ℓ for user u, and we call it "ranking incompatibility" in this paper.

Next, we design our preference ranking objective function for learning a factorization model. Specifically, a good factorization method should minimize the ranking incompatibility as much as possible, and thus we propose the following objective function for minimizing:

$$\mathcal{O} = \sum_{(u,\ell)\in\mathcal{D}_1} E\left(Incomp(y_{u\ell}, \varepsilon)\right) \tag{2}$$

where $E(\cdot)$ is a function used to convert the ranking incompatibility $Incomp(y_{u\ell}, \varepsilon)$ into a loss:

$$E(r) = \sum_{i=1}^{r} \frac{1}{i} \tag{3}$$

and we define $E(0) = 0$.

In Eq. (2), we aggregate the losses incurred for all the user-POI pairs in $\mathcal{D}_1$ to compute the overall loss. We note that $Incomp(y_{u\ell}, \varepsilon)$, according to Eq. (1), is always equal to zero for the user-POI pairs $(u, \ell) \notin \mathcal{D}_1$. Following OWPC [20, 21], we adopt a smooth weighting scheme to convert $Incomp(y_{u\ell}, \varepsilon)$ into a loss. Specifically, the function $E(r)$ in Eq. (3) embodies such a conversion. It can be seen that $E(r)$ calculates the sum over losses at each rank position (from 1 to r) for the incorrectly-ranked POIs, where each position i is assigned with a loss $1/i$. For example, assume we have $Incomp(y_{u\ell}, \varepsilon) = 3$, i.e., three POIs are incorrectly ranked higher than POI ℓ for user u. The loss for this pair (u, ℓ) is thus given by $E(3) = 1 + \frac{1}{2} + \frac{1}{3}$.

One merit of our objective function is its ability to overcome the data sparsity issue. According to Eq. (1), the ranking incompatibility of a POI ℓ for a user is determined by all the other POIs $\ell' \in \mathcal{L}$, which are mostly unvisited POIs (because a user often visits very few POIs). Therefore, the unvisited POIs also contribute to learning the model, while they are ignored in conventional MF. Hence, by leveraging the objective function, we can address the sparsity problem of check-in data, without directly fitting zero check-ins.

3.1.2 Geographical Factorization Method

In this subsection, we propose a ***geographical factorization method*** for calculating the recommendation score. Our factorization model is capable of characterizing the user's preferences over POIs. In addition, it also incorporates the influence of the geographical context for POI recommendation. On the one hand, we parameterize the latent factors of users and POIs into a K-dimensional space as matrices $\mathbf{U}^{(1)} \in \mathbb{R}^{|\mathcal{U}|\times K}$ and $\mathbf{L}^{(1)} \in \mathbb{R}^{|\mathcal{L}|\times K}$, respectively. They are used to model the user's own preference as traditional matrix factorization methods do. On the other hand, we introduce one extra latent factor matrix $\mathbf{U}^{(2)} \in \mathbb{R}^{|\mathcal{U}|\times K}$ for users, and employ $\mathbf{U}^{(2)}$ to model the interaction between users and POIs for incorporating the geographical influence. To this end, we further construct an $|\mathcal{L}| \times |\mathcal{L}|$ geographical influence matrix $\mathbf{W}$, where $w_{\ell\ell'}$ is the probability that POI ℓ is visited given that POI ℓ' has been visited. By following previous studies [22, 3, 12], we set $w_{\ell\ell'} = (0.5+d(\ell, \ell'))^{-1}$ if $\ell' \in \mathcal{N}_k(\ell)$, and 0 otherwise. Here we consider only k-nearest neighbors $\mathcal{N}_k(\ell)$ of each POI ℓ. The intuition behind the formula is that users usually tend to visit nearby POIs. We normalize each row of the matrix $\mathbf{W}$ such that $\sum_{\ell'\in\mathcal{L}} w_{\ell\ell'} = 1$, because it represents the influence probabilities.

Let $\Theta = \{\mathbf{U}^{(1)}, \mathbf{L}^{(1)}, \mathbf{U}^{(2)}\}$ denote the parameters of our geographical factorization model. We will present the proposed method of learning these parameters in Section 3.2. Suppose that these parameters are already learned. Given user u and POI ℓ, we compute recommendation score $y_{u\ell}$ as follows:

$$y_{u\ell} = \mathbf{u}_u^{(1)} \cdot \mathbf{l}_\ell^{(1)} + \mathbf{u}_u^{(2)} \cdot \sum_{\ell^*\in\mathcal{N}_k(\ell)} w_{\ell\ell^*} \mathbf{l}_{\ell^*}^{(1)} \tag{4}$$

where operator $\cdot$ denotes the inner product, and $\mathbf{u}_u^{(1)}$ represents the u-th row of matrix $\mathbf{U}^{(1)}$. Similar notations are used for other matrices. In Eq. (4), the first term models the ***user-preference score***, while the second term models the ***geographical influence score*** that a user likes a POI because of its neighbors.

To avoid the overfitting problem, we constrain the latent factors of our model into a ball, which acts as a regularizer [21]. Specifically, we have the following constraints:

$$\left\|\mathbf{u}_u^{(1)}\right\|_2 \le C, \qquad u = 1, 2, \ldots, |\mathcal{U}| \tag{5}$$

$$\left\|\mathbf{l}_\ell^{(1)}\right\|_2 \le C, \qquad \ell = 1, 2, \ldots, |\mathcal{L}| \tag{6}$$

$$\left\|\mathbf{u}_u^{(2)}\right\|_2 \le \alpha C, \qquad u = 1, 2, \ldots, |\mathcal{U}| \tag{7}$$

where $C > 0$ and $0 \le \alpha \le 1$ are hyperparameters. We constrain the latent factors from $\mathbf{U}^{(1)}$ and $\mathbf{L}^{(1)}$ into a small ball with radius C, and constrain the latent factor from $\mathbf{U}^{(2)}$ into a smaller ball with radius αC. Here, we introduce the hyperparameter α to balance the contributions of user-preference and geographical influence scores. Using basic algebra, we have $|\mathbf{a} \cdot \mathbf{b}| \le \|\mathbf{a}\|_2 \|\mathbf{b}\|_2$ for any two vectors $\mathbf{a}$ and $\mathbf{b}$. Thus, we know that the user-preference score $\mathbf{u}_u^{(1)} \cdot \mathbf{l}_\ell^{(1)}$ is always in $[-C^2, C^2]$. As we have $\left\|\sum_{\ell^*\in\mathcal{N}_k(\ell)} w_{\ell\ell^*} \mathbf{l}_{\ell^*}^{(1)}\right\|_2 \le \sum_{\ell^*\in\mathcal{N}_k(\ell)} w_{\ell\ell^*} \left\|\mathbf{l}_{\ell^*}^{(1)}\right\|_2 \le \sum_{\ell^*\in\mathcal{N}_k(\ell)} w_{\ell\ell^*} C = C$, the geographical influence score $\mathbf{u}_u^{(2)} \cdot \sum_{\ell^*\in\mathcal{N}_k(\ell)} w_{\ell\ell^*} \mathbf{l}_{\ell^*}^{(1)}$ is thus in $[-\alpha C^2, \alpha C^2]$. As a result, tuning the hyperparameter α can balance the contributions of user-preference and geographical influence scores to the final recommendation score.

3.2 Optimization and Learning Algorithm

Next we present the proposed method of learning model parameters Θ such that $\mathcal{O}$ in Eq. (2) is minimized. As $\mathcal{O}$ is computed by summing the loss for each user-POI pair, we adopt the stochastic gradient descent (SGD) method for optimization. That is, we aim to minimize $E\left(Incomp(y_{u\ell}, \varepsilon)\right)$ given each training instance $(u, \ell) \in \mathcal{D}_1$. However, there are two difficulties: (1) $E\left(Incomp(y_{u\ell}, \varepsilon)\right)$ is non-continuous and indifferentiable, which makes it hard to optimize; (2) we need to know $Incomp(y_{u\ell}, \varepsilon)$ for optimization; however, calculating it is time-consuming. Next we introduce how to address the two issues.

3.2.1 *Continuous Approximation*

In order to make $E\left(Incomp(y_{u\ell},\varepsilon)\right)$ continuous over parameters Θ, we rewrite it as follows:

$$
\begin{aligned}
& E\left(Incomp(y_{u\ell},\varepsilon)\right)\cdot 1 \qquad (8)\\
= \; & E\left(Incomp(y_{u\ell},\varepsilon)\right)\frac{\sum_{\ell'\in\mathcal{L}} I(x_{u\ell} > x_{u\ell'})I(y_{u\ell} < y_{u\ell'}+\varepsilon)}{Incomp(y_{u\ell},\varepsilon)}\\
\approx \; & E\left(Incomp(y_{u\ell},\varepsilon)\right)\frac{\sum_{\ell'\in\mathcal{L}(u,\ell)} s(y_{u\ell'}+\varepsilon-y_{u\ell})}{Incomp(y_{u\ell},\varepsilon)}
\end{aligned}
$$

where $\mathcal{L}(u,\ell) := \{\ell' | I(x_{u\ell} > x_{u\ell'})I(y_{u\ell} < y_{u\ell'}+\varepsilon) = 1\}$, and $s(a) := \frac{1}{1+\exp(-a)}$ is the sigmoid function, which is used to approximate the indicator function. Based on the rewriting, we can compute the stochastic gradient for updating Θ. Specifically, we have

$$
\begin{aligned}
& \frac{\partial E\left(Incomp(y_{u\ell},\varepsilon)\right)}{\partial\Theta} \qquad (9)\\
\approx \; & E\left(Incomp(y_{u\ell},\varepsilon)\right)\frac{\sum_{\ell'\in\mathcal{L}(u,\ell)} \frac{\partial s(y_{u\ell'}+\varepsilon-y_{u\ell})}{\partial\Theta}}{Incomp(y_{u\ell},\varepsilon)}\\
= \; & \frac{E\left(Incomp(y_{u\ell},\varepsilon)\right)}{Incomp(y_{u\ell},\varepsilon)}\sum_{\ell'\in\mathcal{L}(u,\ell)}\delta_{u\ell\ell'}\frac{\partial(y_{u\ell'}+\varepsilon-y_{u\ell})}{\partial\Theta}
\end{aligned}
$$

where $\delta_{u\ell\ell'} = s(y_{u\ell'}+\varepsilon-y_{u\ell})(1-s(y_{u\ell'}+\varepsilon-y_{u\ell}))$. We note that Eq. (9) is not a standard gradient computation, because $E\left(Incomp(y_{u\ell},\varepsilon)\right)$ and $Incomp(y_{u\ell},\varepsilon)$ are also related to Θ, but we do not consider their derivatives. Our analogous gradient calculation here follows the idea in [21]. Although the stochastic gradient can be calculated by Eq. (9), it is infeasible in practice. This is because both the summation and $Incomp(y_{u\ell},\varepsilon)$ in Eq. (9) require to compute the recommendation scores of all POIs as Eq. (4), which costs $O(K|\mathcal{L}|k)$ operations and is time-consuming.

In the next subsection, we introduce a fast learning scheme to address the issue.

3.2.2 *Fast Learning Scheme*

Our key idea of fast learning is to eliminate the summation and estimate $Incomp(y_{u\ell},\varepsilon)$ with a sampling method.

Let us first revisit Eq. (8). We can see from the first equality in Eq. (8) that only incorrectly-ranked POI, i.e., the POI ℓ' satisfying $I(x_{u\ell} > x_{u\ell'})I(y_{u\ell} < y_{u\ell'}+\varepsilon) = 1$, contributes to the loss $E\left(Incomp(y_{u\ell},\varepsilon)\right)$. Thus, Eq. (8) can be reinterpreted as an expectation of the loss incurred by a set of incorrectly-ranked POI samples, where each POI sample ℓ' incurs a loss:

$$\bar{E} = E\left(Incomp(y_{u\ell},\varepsilon)\right) s(y_{u\ell'}+\varepsilon-y_{u\ell}) \qquad (10)$$

and each POI sample has the probability $\frac{1}{Incomp(y_{u\ell},\varepsilon)}$ to be chosen. This motivates us to approximately calculate the stochastic gradient by sampling one incorrectly-ranked POI. In this case, we have

$$\frac{\partial\bar{E}}{\partial\Theta} = E\left(Incomp(y_{u\ell},\varepsilon)\right)\delta_{u\ell\ell'}\frac{\partial(y_{u\ell'}+\varepsilon-y_{u\ell})}{\partial\Theta} \qquad (11)$$

which is an approximation of Eq. (9). Apparently, the summation is eliminated.

To calculate gradients by Eq. (11), we still need to know $Incomp(y_{u\ell},\varepsilon)$. We compute its approximate value by sampling one incorrectly-ranked POI. Specifically, given a user-POI pair (u,ℓ), we repeat sampling one POI from $\mathcal{L}$ until we obtain an incorrectly-ranked POI ℓ' such that $I(x_{u\ell} > x_{u\ell'})I(y_{u\ell} < y_{u\ell'}+\varepsilon) = 1$. Let n denote the number of sampling trials before obtaining such a POI ℓ'. Apparently, n follows a geometric distribution with parameter $p = \frac{Incomp(y_{u\ell},\varepsilon)}{|\mathcal{L}|}$. Since we know the expectation of a geometrical distribution with parameter p is $\frac{1}{p}$, we have $n \approx \left\lfloor\frac{1}{p}\right\rfloor = \left\lfloor\frac{|\mathcal{L}|}{Incomp(y_{u\ell},\varepsilon)}\right\rfloor$. Thus, we can estimate $Incomp(y_{u\ell},\varepsilon) \approx \left\lfloor\frac{|\mathcal{L}|}{n}\right\rfloor$. Our idea here is similar to that used in [21] for a different problem.

Algorithm 1: Rank-GeoFM

input : check-in data $\mathcal{D}_1$, geographical influence matrix $\mathbf{W}$, hyperparameters ε, C and α, and learning rate γ
output: model parameters $\Theta = \{\mathbf{U}^{(1)}, \mathbf{L}^{(1)}, \mathbf{U}^{(2)}\}$

Initialize Θ with Normal distribution $\mathcal{N}(0, 0.01)$;
Shuffle the samples in $\mathcal{D}_1$ randomly;
repeat
  for $(u,\ell) \in \mathcal{D}_1$ **do**
    Compute $y_{u\ell}$ as Eq. (4), and set n=0;
    repeat
      Sample a POI ℓ';
      Compute $y_{u\ell'}$ as Eq. (4), and set $n = n + 1$;
    until $I(x_{u\ell} > x_{u\ell'})I(y_{u\ell} < y_{u\ell'}+\varepsilon) = 1$ *or* $n > |\mathcal{L}|$;
    if $I(x_{u\ell} > x_{u\ell'})I(y_{u\ell} < y_{u\ell'}+\varepsilon) = 1$ **then**
      $\eta = E\left(\left\lfloor\frac{|\mathcal{L}|}{n}\right\rfloor\right)\delta_{u\ell\ell'}$;
      $\mathbf{g} = \left(\sum_{\ell^*\in\mathcal{N}_k(\ell')} w_{\ell,\ell^*}\mathbf{l}^{(1)}_{\ell^*} - \sum_{\ell^+\in\mathcal{N}_k(\ell)} w_{\ell,\ell^+}\mathbf{l}^{(1)}_{\ell^+}\right)$;
      $\mathbf{u}^{(1)}_u \leftarrow \mathbf{u}^{(1)}_u - \gamma\eta(\mathbf{l}^{(1)}_{\ell'} - \mathbf{l}^{(1)}_{\ell})$;
      $\mathbf{u}^{(2)}_u \leftarrow \mathbf{u}^{(2)}_u - \gamma\eta\mathbf{g}$;
      $\mathbf{l}^{(1)}_{\ell'} \leftarrow \mathbf{l}^{(1)}_{\ell'} - \gamma\eta\mathbf{u}^{(1)}_u$;
      $\mathbf{l}^{(1)}_{\ell} \leftarrow \mathbf{l}^{(1)}_{\ell} + \gamma\eta\mathbf{u}^{(1)}_u$;
    Project the updated latent factors to enforce constraints in Eqs. (5)~(7), e.g., if $\left\|\mathbf{u}^{(1)}_u\right\|_2 > C$, then set $\mathbf{u}^{(1)}_u \leftarrow C\frac{\mathbf{u}^{(1)}_u}{\left\|\mathbf{u}^{(1)}_u\right\|_2}$;
until *convergence*;
return $\Theta = \{\mathbf{U}^{(1)}, \mathbf{L}^{(1)}, \mathbf{U}^{(2)}\}$

By using the estimation, we rewrite Eq. (11) by:

$$\frac{\partial\bar{E}}{\partial\Theta} \approx E\left(\left\lfloor\frac{|\mathcal{L}|}{n}\right\rfloor\right)\delta_{u\ell\ell'}\frac{\partial(y_{u\ell'}+\varepsilon-y_{u\ell})}{\partial\Theta} \qquad (12)$$

Here $E\left(\left\lfloor\frac{|\mathcal{L}|}{n}\right\rfloor\right)$ acts as an adaptive scaling factor for the gradient. When n is small, the gradient will have a large magnitude, which is reasonable because a small n implies that $Incomp(y_{u\ell},\varepsilon)$ is large, and in this case the parameters should be updated with large steps. Similarly, when n is large, we will obtain a reasonable gradient with a small magnitude. With Eq. (12), the SGD based optimization is performed as follows:

$$\Theta \leftarrow \Theta - \gamma\frac{\partial\bar{E}}{\partial\Theta} \qquad (13)$$

where γ is the learning rate.

Using the gradient calculation in Eq. (12) can gain significant speedups. The complexity of Eq. (9) is $O(K|\mathcal{L}|k)$ while the complexity of Eq. (12) is $O(Knk)$. In general, we have $n \ll |\mathcal{L}|$ at the start of training and $n < |\mathcal{L}|$ when the training reaches a stable phase. At the beginning, the model is not well-trained and thus $Incomp(y_{u\ell},\varepsilon)$ is often large, which leads to a very small n, i.e., $n \ll |\mathcal{L}|$; when the training reaches a stable phase, it is expected that more visited POIs are ranked correctly, and thus $Incomp(y_{u\ell}, \varepsilon)$ becomes smaller and n will become a bit larger. However, it is very unlikely that every visited POI is ranked correctly, so in general we still have $n < |\mathcal{L}|$. We find that the speedup is in orders of magnitude in our experiments.

We summarize the proposed Ranking based Geographical Factorization Method (Rank-GeoFM) in **Algorithm** 1. In the algorithm, we iterate through all the user-POI check-in pairs in $\mathcal{D}_1$ and update the latent factors until the procedure converges (lines 3∼16). In each iteration, given a user-POI pair, the sampling process is first performed so as to estimate $Incomp(y_{u\ell}, \varepsilon)$ and obtain one POI sample (lines 6∼8). Based on the estimation of $Incomp(y_{u\ell}, \varepsilon)$ and the sampled POI ℓ', we update the relevant latent factors by using SGD method (lines 9∼15). The norm constraints are checked for the updated latent factors, and the ones violating the constraints are projected (line 16).

3.3 Time-aware POI Recommendation

In this subsection, we use the temporal information as an example context to illustrate how our method can be easily generalized to incorporate other types of context. We consider time-aware POI recommendation.

DEFINITION 2. ***Time-aware POI recommendation:*** *given a user u and time slot t (e.g., 3:00pm∼4:00pm), we recommend the POIs that s/he will like to visit in this time slot, and are not in* $\mathcal{L}^u$.

The objective function in Eq. (2) can be easily extended to incorporate the temporal context. To calculate the recommendation score, we extend Eq. (4) with two additional terms capturing the temporal factor. One term is ***temporal popularity score*** which indicates whether this POI is popular in the time slot. The other term is referred to as ***temporal influence score***, which is based on the following observation made in previous work [24, 25]: the popularity of a POI at one time slot is always influenced by some close or similar time slots, i.e., popularity are correlated among close or similar time slots.

We introduce three more latent factor matrices besides $\mathbf{U}^{(1)}$, $\mathbf{U}^{(2)}$ and $\mathbf{L}^{(1)}$ for the two additional terms. Specifically, we parameterize the latent factors of time slots as a $|\mathcal{T}| \times K$ matrix $\mathbf{T}$; and parameterize another two latent factor matrices $\mathbf{L}^{(2)}$ and $\mathbf{L}^{(3)}$ for POIs, where $\mathbf{L}^{(2)}$ is to model interactions with time slot for temporal popularity score, and $\mathbf{L}^{(3)}$ is to model interactions with close or similar time slot for temporal influence score. We further construct a $|\mathcal{T}| \times |\mathcal{T}|$ matrix $\mathbf{M}$, where m_{tt^*} is the probability that the popularity scores of POIs in time slot t are influenced by those in time slot t^*. By following previous studies [24, 7], we compute m_{tt^*} as:

$$m_{tt^*} = \frac{\sum_{u \in \mathcal{U}} \sum_{\ell \in \mathcal{L}} x_{ut\ell} x_{ut^*\ell}}{\sqrt{\sum_{u \in \mathcal{U}} \sum_{\ell \in \mathcal{L}} x_{ut\ell}^2} \sqrt{\sum_{u \in \mathcal{U}} \sum_{\ell \in \mathcal{L}} x_{ut^*\ell}^2}} \quad (14)$$

and we normalize $\mathbf{M}$ into a matrix such that each row is a probability vector. Given a user u and time slot t, the recommendation score of POI ℓ is computed as follows:

$$\begin{aligned} y_{ut\ell} \quad = \quad & \mathbf{u}_u^{(1)} \cdot \mathbf{l}_\ell^{(1)} + \mathbf{t}_t \cdot \mathbf{l}_\ell^{(2)} + \qquad (15) \\ & \mathbf{u}_u^{(2)} \cdot \sum_{\ell^* \in \mathcal{N}_k(\ell)} w_{\ell\ell^*} \mathbf{l}_{\ell^*}^{(1)} + \mathbf{l}_\ell^{(3)} \cdot \sum_{t^* \in \mathcal{T}} m_{tt^*} \mathbf{t}_{t^*} \end{aligned}$$

where the four terms indicate the user-preference score, temporal popularity score, geographical influence score and temporal influence score, respectively. We denote the parameters of our factorization model in this setting as $\Theta = \{\mathbf{U}^{(1)}, \mathbf{L}^{(1)}, \mathbf{U}^{(2)}, \mathbf{T}, \mathbf{L}^{(2)}, \mathbf{L}^{(3)}\}$. Similar to POI-user setting, norm constraints are imposed to prevent overfitting:

$$\|\mathbf{t}_t\|_2 \leq C, \qquad t = 1, 2, \ldots, |\mathcal{T}| \quad (16)$$

$$\left\|\mathbf{l}_\ell^{(2)}\right\|_2 \leq C, \qquad \ell = 1, 2, \ldots, |\mathcal{L}| \quad (17)$$

$$\left\|\mathbf{l}_\ell^{(3)}\right\|_2 \leq \beta C, \qquad \ell = 1, 2, \ldots, |\mathcal{L}| \quad (18)$$

where $0 \leq \beta \leq 1$ is to control the importance of temporal influence in computing the recommendation score.

Algorithm 1 can be adapted easily for time-aware POI recommendation. Specifically, we iterate through all user-time-POI tuple in $\mathcal{D}_2$ to update the latent factors. Given each $(u, t, \ell) \in \mathcal{D}_2$, we keep sampling POIs until obtain one POI ℓ' satisfying $I(x_{ut\ell} > x_{ut\ell'}) I(y_{ut\ell} < y_{ut\ell'} + \varepsilon) = 1$, and again $Incomp(y_{ut\ell}, \varepsilon)$ is estimated as $\left\lfloor \frac{|\mathcal{L}|}{n} \right\rfloor$. The stochastic gradient can be calculated similarly by:

$$\frac{\partial \bar{E}}{\partial \Theta} \approx E\left(\left\lfloor \frac{|\mathcal{L}|}{n} \right\rfloor\right) \delta_{ut\ell\ell'} \frac{\partial (y_{ut\ell'} + \varepsilon - y_{ut\ell})}{\partial \Theta} \quad (19)$$

where $\delta_{ut\ell\ell'} = s(y_{ut\ell'} + \varepsilon - y_{ut\ell})(1 - s(y_{ut\ell'} + \varepsilon - y_{ut\ell}))$. Based on it, the relevant latent factors are updated accordingly.

4. EXPERIMENTS

We conduct comprehensive experiments to evaluate the performance of the proposed method for both POI recommendation and time-aware POI recommendation.

4.1 Experimental Setup

4.1.1 Datasets

We use two real-world datasets [24][1] in our experiments. One is the Foursquare check-in data made in Singapore between Aug. 2010 and Jul. 2011, and the other is the Gowalla check-in data made in California and Nevada between Feb. 2009 and Oct. 2010. The Foursquare data comprises 194,108 check-ins made by 2,321 users at 5,596 POIs, and the Gowalla data comprises 456,988 check-ins made by 10,162 users at 24,250 POIs. Each check-in is associated with a time stamp.

For each user, we mask off 20% of his/her most recent check-ins as *testing set* to evaluate the performance of different algorithms. The earliest 70% of check-ins are used as *training set*, and the remaining 10% check-ins are used as *validation set*. Based on the training sets, we construct a user-POI matrix $\mathbf{X}$ with 73,011 and 210,894 nonzero entries for Foursquare and Gowalla, respectively, which will be used in the POI recommendation. The densities of $\mathbf{X}$ are 0.56% and 0.085% for Foursquare and Gowalla matrices, respectively. For time-aware POI recommendation, we split the data into 24 hours (time slots), and then obtain a tensor $\mathcal{X}$ with 91,228 and 244,580 nonzero entries for Foursquare and Gowalla, respectively. The density of $\mathcal{X}$ are 0.029% and 0.0041% for the two data, respectively. We can see that both matrix $\mathbf{X}$ and tensor $\mathcal{X}$ are very sparse.

[1]Available at http://www.ntu.edu.sg/home/gaocong/data/poidata.zip

4.1.2 Metrics

We use two widely used metrics to evaluate the performance of different recommendation algorithms, namely precision@N and recall@N (denoted by Pre@N and Rec@N), where N is the number of recommended POIs.

For POI recommendation, given a user u, we compute Pre@N and Rec@N as follows [22]:

$$\text{Pre@N} = \frac{tp_u}{tp_u + fp_u} \quad \text{and} \quad \text{Rec@N} = \frac{tp_u}{tp_u + tn_u} \tag{20}$$

where tp_u is the number of POIs contained in both the ground truth and the top-N results produced by algorithms; fp_u is the number of POIs in the top-N results by algorithms but not in the ground truth; and tn_u is the number of POIs contained in ground truth but not in the top-N results by algorithms. The Pre@N (Rec@N) reported is an average of precision(recall) values of all users [22].

For time-aware POI recommendation, given a user u and a time slot t, we let tp_{ut}, fp_{ut} and tn_{ut} be a time-specific extension of tp_u, fp_u and tn_u, respectively. Then, at time t, the Pre@N(t) and Rec@N(t) are calculated as follows [24]:

$$\text{Pre@N(t)} = \frac{\sum_{u \in \mathcal{U}} tp_{ut}}{\sum_{u \in \mathcal{U}} (tp_{ut} + fp_{ut})} \tag{21}$$

$$\text{Rec@N(t)} = \frac{\sum_{u \in \mathcal{U}} tp_{ut}}{\sum_{u \in \mathcal{U}} (tp_{ut} + tn_{ut})} \tag{22}$$

As in [24, 25], the average Pre@N (Rec@N) is then reported by averaging the precision (recall) values of all time slots. For both metrics, we consider N=5, 10 and 20 in our experiments respectively (by default N=5), as top recommendations are more important.

4.1.3 Baseline methods

For POI recommendation, we compare our model with the following baseline methods.

- **UCF**: This is user-based CF method, where user-user similarity is calculated based on the check-in data.
- **UCF+G**: This method incorporates the geographical influence into user-based CF in a linear interpolation way [22], which is a representative method for POI recommendation.
- **PMF**: Probabilistical matrix factorization [18] is a well-known factorization developed for recommendation systems.
- **BPR-MF**: As our method is ranking-based factorization, we also consider BPR-MF as a baseline, which is the most popular ranking-based matrix factorization with Bayesian Personalized Ranking criterion [16]. Note that this method has not been evaluated in previous work on POI recommendation.
- **GTBNMF**: As mentioned in Section 2, GTBNMF is a recent method for POI recommendation [12], which combines Bayesian matrix factorization with the topic model. In our data, no text information is available and thus we only use the factorization part of this model to compare.
- **GeoMF**: GeoMF is the state-of-the-art method for POI recommendation [11].

For time-aware POI recommendation, the following methods are used as baselines.

- **UCF(+G)**: These are UCF and UCF+G described above. Both of them do not make use of temporal information and hence produce the same recommendations for all the time slots.
- **UTF**: UTF is a user-based temporal collaborative filtering method [5], which computes the similarity between users by weighting the check-ins with a time decay function.
- **UCLAF**: UCLAF is a PARAFAC-based tensor decomposition model, originally proposed to recommend locations and activities with user-location-activity tensor data [27], where Laplician regularization terms are imposed on decompositions to incorporate extra information. We apply this model to the tensor $\mathcal{X}$, and use the matrices $\mathbf{W}$ and $\mathbf{M}$ to construct Laplician regularization terms for incorporating geographical influence and temporal influence, respectively.
- **PITF**: This is a ranking-based tensor factorization method [17], where the Bayesian Personalized Ranking criterion is employed.
- **LRT**: This is a recently developed matrix factorization method for POI recommendation with time information [7]. LRT incorporates temporal influence by constraining the latent factors of a user to be similar in two consecutive time slots.
- **UTE+SE**: As introduced in Section 2, this method utilizes both the geographical influence and temporal influence for time-aware POI recommendation [24]. The model is denoted by UTE when considering temporal influence only, otherwise it is denoted by UTE+SE.
- **BPP**: This is the state-of-the-art method for time-aware POI recommendation [25], which incorporates both the geographical and temporal influences.

Among these methods, UTF, PITF and LRT do not exploit the geographical influence.

4.2 Experimental Results

4.2.1 Parameter Tuning

In the experiments, we set the hyperparameters $\varepsilon = 0.3$ and $C = 1.0$ for all the data sets. For the learning rate γ, we set a small value 0.0001 in our experiments to ensure the generalization accuracy. For other parameters, we tune them based on the validation set to find the optimal values, and subsequently use them in the test set.

Figure 2(a) shows the performance of Rank-GeoFM under both settings on both data sets as we vary parameter α for geographical influence. We find that Rank-GeoFM perfoms the best at $\alpha = 0.2$ for POI recommendation on both data, and performs the best at $\alpha = 0.1$ for time-aware POI recommendation on both data. Figure 2(b) shows the performance of Rank-GeoFM as we vary parameter k used in the construction of geographical influence matrix. We can see that the best performance is achieved at $k = 300$ for all cases. Figure 2(c) demonstrates the effect of parameter β,

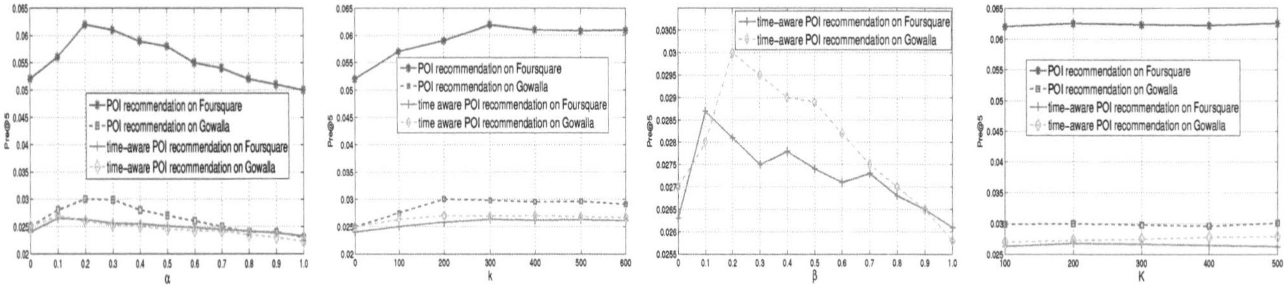

(a) Tuning α (b) Tuning k (c) Tuning β (d) Tuning K

Figure 2: Parameter tuning for Rank-GeoFM.

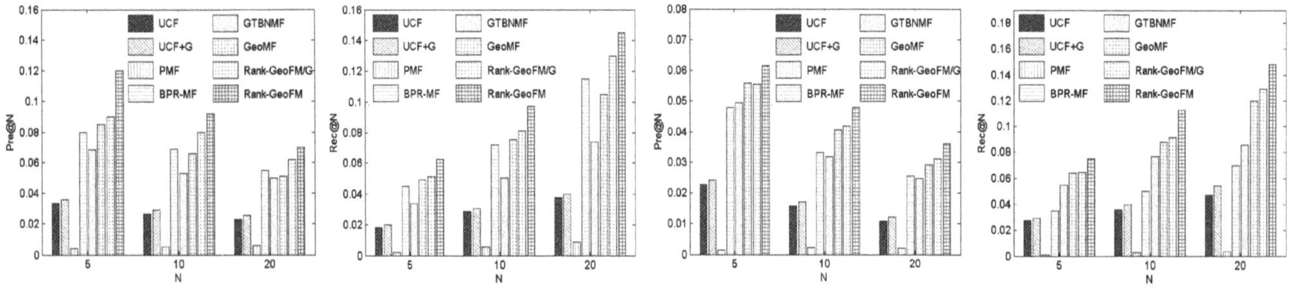

(a) Pre@N-Foursquare (b) Rec@N-Foursquare (c) Pre@N-Gowalla (d) Rec@N-Gowalla

Figure 3: Performance comparison on POI recommendation.

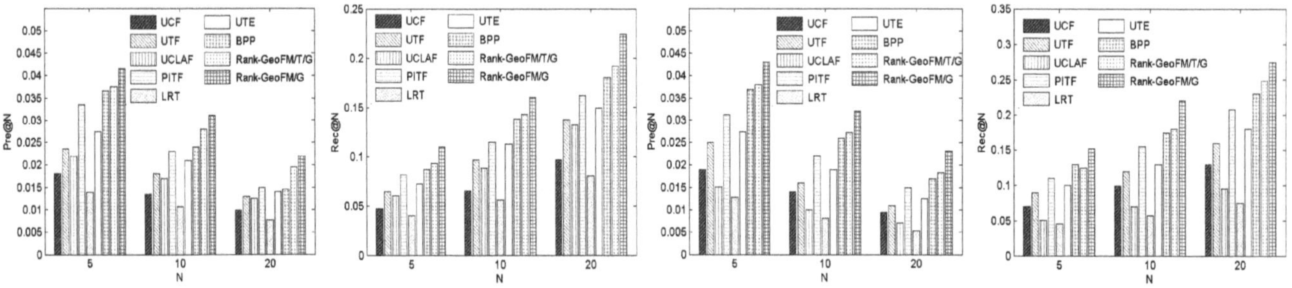

(a) Pre@N-Foursquare (b) Rec@N-Foursquare (c) Pre@N-Gowalla (d) Rec@N-Gowalla

Figure 4: Performance comparison on time-aware POI recommendation without geographical influence.

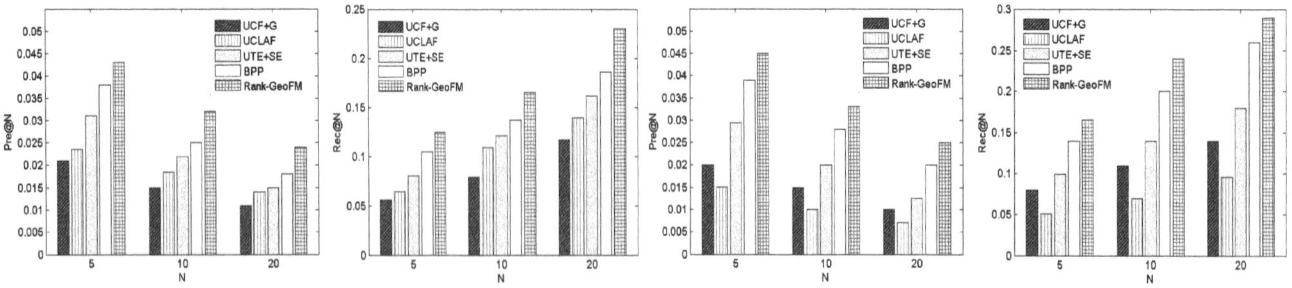

(a) Pre@N-Foursquare (b) Rec@N-Foursquare (c) Pre@N-Gowalla (d) Rec@N-Gowalla

Figure 5: Performance comparison on time-aware POI recommendation with geographical influence.

which is for temporal influence under time-aware POI recommendation. We can see that the best performance are produced at $\beta = 0.1$ and $\beta = 0.2$ on Foursquare and Gowalla, respectively. Finally, we show the effect of dimension K of latent factors on performance in Figure 2(d). We find that the performance of Rank-GeoFM is insensitive to the dimension K, and we use $K = 100$ in our experiments.

4.2.2 Results on POI Recommendation

Figures 3(a)–(d) show the performance of all the methods on both datasets for POI recommendation. First, we can see that memory-based methods UCF and UCF+G perform worse than the other methods except for PMF, which are all factorization based methods, and UCF+G improves UCF due to the consideration of geographical influence. PMF performs the worst because it is developed for explicit feedback data such as user-movie ratings. It is not suitable for POI recommendation, where check-ins are implicit feedbacks. This is in accordance with the finding in [14].

Among the other factorization based methods, the performance of BPR-MF is very promising, although this method cannot utilize the geographical influence, and has not been employed for POI recommendation in previous work. The reason is that BPR-MF, as a ranking-based factorization method, is more appropriate for handling implicit feedback data. We observe GeoMF performs better than GTBNMF. This is because GTBNMF conducts the factorization by fitting the zero and nonzero entries in $\mathbf{X}$ equally, while GeoMF solves the factorization by assigning higher weights to nonzero entries, which is more suitable for implicit data.

We can see that the proposed Rank-GeoFM consistently outperforms the state-of-the art method GeoMF. The improvements, in terms of Pre@5, are more than 41.6% and 10% on Foursquare and Gowalla datasets, respectively. The reason is that GeoMF addresses the data sparsity problem by fitting both nonzero and zero check-ins with different weights, which is less reasonable than our ranking methodology because zero check-ins may be missing values and should not be fitted directly. Rank-GeoFM/G denotes our model without considering the geographical influence. It can be seen that Rank-GeoFM/G performs better than BPR-MF, a ranking based MF method without considering geographical influence. This may be attributed to our ranking objective function. Moreover, we observe Rank-GeoFM improves Rank-GeoFM/G by 30.3% and 10.5% in terms of Pre@5 on both datasets, respectively, due to the incorporation of geographical influence.

Finally, we note that all improvements of our method over baselines are statistically significant in terms of paired t-test with p-value < 0.01.

4.2.3 Results on Time-aware POI Recommendation

Figures 4(a)–(d) show the performance of all the methods for time-aware POI recommendation when the geographical influence is not utilized. Among all memory-based methods, UCF performs worse than UTF and UTE because it does not capture the correlations between time slots. Although both UTF and UTE consider the correlations between time slots, UTF still performs worse than UTE because UTE smooths the check-in data for handling data sparsity issue.

Among the factorization methods UCLAF, PITF and LRT, LRT performs the worst because it obtains the factorization by fitting the nonzero entries in tensor $\mathcal{X}$, which suffers

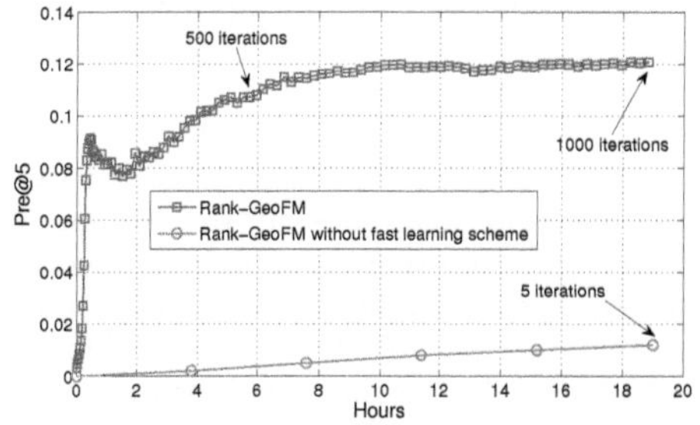

Figure 6: Learning rate comparison of Rank-GeoFM with and without fast learning. Each square denotes ten iterations and each circle denotes one. Each iteration comprises the updates for all user-POI pairs.

from the sparsity problem significantly. The performance of UCLAF is also not good because the method fits both zero and nonzero entries in $\mathcal{X}$, which is not very reasonable. PITF performs the best among the three and its performance is also very promising compared to other methods. The reason is that PITF is a ranking-based factorization method that can alleviate the sparsity problem. Moreover, we observe that the graph-based method BPP, which is the state-of-the-art method, outperforms all the memory-based and factorization based baseline methods.

Rank-GeoFM/G denotes our model with temporal influence but without geographical influence. We observe our model consistently outperforms the state-of-the-art method BPP, which is 13.7% and 16.2% better than BPP, in terms of Pre@5, on Foursquare and Gowalla, respectively. Rank-GeoFM/T/G denotes our model without considering both the temporal and geographical influences. We observe Rank-GeoFM/T/G always outperforms another ranking-based method PITF. Moreover, due to the incorporation of temporal influence, we observe Rank-GeoFM/G improves Rank-GeoFM/T/G by 10.6% and 13.1% in terms of Pre@5 on both data, respectively.

Figures 5(a)–(d) show the performance of the methods incorporating the geographical influence further. Note that we report the results only for the methods that can utilize geographical influence. It shows that Rank-GeoFM outperforms all the other methods by 13.1% and 15.3%, in terms of Pre@5, on Foursquare and Gowalla, respectively.

We note that all improvements of our method over baselines are statistically significant in terms of paired t-test with p-value < 0.01.

4.2.4 Comparison of Rank-GeoFM with and without Fast Learning Scheme

We compare the learning rate of Rank-GeoFM with and without the fast learning scheme introduced in Section 3.2.2. Figure 6 shows the result, where Foursquare data is taken as an example for the comparison. Rank-GeoFM without fast learning scheme means we use Eq. (9) to calculate gradients and perform updates in Algorithm 1. We observe Rank-GeoFM (with fast learning scheme) finishes 1000 iterations of updates in 19 hours while the counterpart without fast learning scheme finishes only 5 iterations. Rank-GeoFM obtains a well-trained model within 8 hours, which leads to the best performance, while the counterpart cannot build an acceptable model after 19 hours of training. This result demonstrates the efficiency as well as necessity of using fast learning scheme. Moreover, we find that the first 500 iterations of Rank-GeoFM take 5.5 hours, while the next 500 iterations take 13.5 hours. The reason is that at the start of training, POIs are not well-ranked by our model and thus it takes less time to sample an incorrectly-ranked POI; however, as the training process goes on, the ranking becomes better and we need more time to sample an incorrect one. Another interesting observation is that we find there is a dip in precision after around 100 iterations for Rank-GeoFM. The observation may be because our learning procedure is transiting from coarse search to fine tuning, i.e., $E\left(\left\lfloor \frac{|\mathcal{L}|}{n} \right\rfloor\right)$ (or the magnitude of gradient) is decreasing from a large value to a small one.

5. CONCLUSIONS

In this paper, we propose a ranking based factorization method, Rank-GeoFM, for POI recommendation. In the proposed model, we learn the factorization by fitting the user's preference rankings for POIs, which alleviates the data sparsity problem. Extensive experimental results on both POI recommendation and time-aware POI recommendation show that Rank-GeoFM outperforms the state-of-the-art methods significantly.

Rank-GeoFM is very flexible to incorporate context information. In the future, it would be interesting to investigate with Rank-GeoFM how the other context information impacts the performance of POI recommendation. For example, if we know the category of each POI ℓ is $cat(\ell)$, the recommendation score in Eq. (4) can be modified as follows to incorporate this information:

$$y_{u\ell} = \mathbf{u}_u^{(1)} \cdot \mathbf{l}_\ell^{(1)} + \mathbf{u}_u^{(2)} \cdot \sum_{\ell^* \in \mathcal{N}_k(\ell)} w_{\ell\ell^*} \mathbf{l}_{\ell^*}^{(1)} + \mathbf{u}_u^{(3)} \cdot \mathbf{c}_{cat(\ell)}$$

where $\mathbf{c}_i$ is the latent factor of category i and the last term in this equation denotes the interaction score between category $cat(\ell)$ and user u. We will leave this as our future work.

6. ACKNOWLEDGEMENT

This work is supported in part by a grant awarded by a Singapore MOE AcRF Tier 2 Grant (ARC30/12), a Singapore MOE AcRF Tier 1 Grant (RG66/12), and a grant awarded by Microsoft Research Asia.

7. REFERENCES

[1] J. Bao, Y. Zheng, D. Wilkie, and M. F. Mokbel. A survey on recommendations in location-based social networks. *GeoInformatica*, 2014.

[2] R. M. Bell and Y. Koren. Lessons from the Netflix prize challenge. *ACM SIGKDD Explorations Newsletter*, 9(2):75–79, 2007.

[3] C. Cheng, H. Yang, I. King, and M. R. Lyu. Fused matrix factorization with geographical and social influence in location-based social networks. In *AAAI*, 2012.

[4] C. Cheng, H. Yang, M. R. Lyu, and I. King. Where you like to go next: Successive point-of-interest recommendation. In *IJCAI*, pages 2605–2611, 2013.

[5] Y. Ding and X. Li. Time weight collaborative filtering. In *CIKM*, pages 485–492. ACM, 2005.

[6] S. Feng, X. Li, Y. Zeng, G. Cong, Y. M. Chee, and Q. Yuan. Personalized ranking metric embedding for next new POI recommendation. In *IJCAI*, 2015.

[7] H. Gao, J. Tang, X. Hu, and H. Liu. Exploring temporal effects for location recommendation on location-based social networks. In *Recsys*, pages 93–100. ACM, 2013.

[8] H. Gao, J. Tang, X. Hu, and H. Liu. Content-aware point of interest recommendation on location-based social networks. In *AAAI*, 2015.

[9] J. J. Levandoski, M. Sarwat, A. Eldawy, and M. F. Mokbel. LARS: A location-aware recommender system. In *ICDE*, pages 450–461. IEEE, 2012.

[10] Y. Li, J. Nie, Y. Zhang, B. Wang, B. Yan, and F. Weng. Contextual recommendation based on text mining. In *COLING*, pages 692–700. ACL, 2010.

[11] D. Lian, C. Zhao, X. Xie, G. Sun, E. Chen, and Y. Rui. GeoMF: joint geographical modeling and matrix factorization for point-of-interest recommendation. In *SIGKDD*, pages 831–840. ACM, 2014.

[12] B. Liu, Y. Fu, Z. Yao, and H. Xiong. Learning geographical preferences for point-of-interest recommendation. In *SIGKDD*, pages 1043–1051. ACM, 2013.

[13] X. Liu, Y. Liu, K. Aberer, and C. Miao. Personalized point-of-interest recommendation by mining users' preference transition. In *CIKM*, pages 733–738. ACM, 2013.

[14] A. Noulas, S. Scellato, N. Lathia, and C. Mascolo. A random walk around the city: New venue recommendation in location-based social networks. In *PASSAT*, pages 144–153. IEEE, 2012.

[15] A. Noulas, S. Scellato, C. Mascolo, and M. Pontil. An empirical study of geographic user activity patterns in Foursquare. *ICWSM*, 11:70–573, 2011.

[16] S. Rendle, C. Freudenthaler, Z. Gantner, and L. Schmidt-Thieme. BPR: Bayesian personalized ranking from implicit feedback. In *UAI*, pages 452–461. AUAI Press, 2009.

[17] S. Rendle and L. Schmidt-Thieme. Pairwise interaction tensor factorization for personalized tag recommendation. In *WSDM*, pages 81–90. ACM, 2010.

[18] R. Salakhutdinov and A. Mnih. Probabilistic matrix factorization. In *NIPS*, pages 1257–1264, 2007.

[19] Y. Shi, A. Karatzoglou, L. Baltrunas, M. Larson, A. Hanjalic, and N. Oliver. TFMAP: optimizing map for top-N context-aware recommendation. In *SIGIR*, pages 155–164. ACM, 2012.

[20] N. Usunier, D. Buffoni, and P. Gallinari. Ranking with ordered weighted pairwise classification. In *ICML*, pages 1057–1064. ACM, 2009.

[21] J. Weston, S. Bengio, and N. Usunier. Large scale image annotation: learning to rank with joint word-image embeddings. *Machine Learning*, 81(1):21–35, 2010.

[22] M. Ye, P. Yin, W.-C. Lee, and D.-L. Lee. Exploiting geographical influence for collaborative point-of-interest recommendation. In *SIGIR*, pages 325–334. ACM, 2011.

[23] H. Yin, Y. Sun, B. Cui, Z. Hu, and L. Chen. Lcars: A location-content-aware recommender system. In *SIGKDD*, pages 221–229. ACM, 2013.

[24] Q. Yuan, G. Cong, Z. Ma, A. Sun, and N. M. Thalmann. Time-aware point-of-interest recommendation. In *SIGIR*, pages 363–372. ACM, 2013.

[25] Q. Yuan, G. Cong, and A. Sun. Graph-based point-of-interest recommendation with geographical and temporal influences. In *CIKM*, pages 659–668. ACM, 2014.

[26] K. Zhao, G. Cong, Q. Yuan, and K. Zhu. SAR: A sentiment-aspect-region model for user preference analysis in geo-tagged reviews. In *ICDE*, 2015.

[27] V. W. Zheng, B. Cao, Y. Zheng, X. Xie, and Q. Yang. Collaborative filtering meets mobile recommendation: A user-centered approach. In *AAAI*, pages 236–241, 2010.

GeoSoCa: Exploiting Geographical, Social and Categorical Correlations for Point-of-Interest Recommendations

Jia-Dong Zhang
Department of Computer Science
City University of Hong Kong
jzhang26-c@my.cityu.edu.hk

Chi-Yin Chow
Department of Computer Science
City University of Hong Kong
chiychow@cityu.edu.hk

ABSTRACT

Recommending users with their preferred points-of-interest (POIs), e.g., museums and restaurants, has become an important feature for location-based social networks (LBSNs), which benefits people to explore new places and businesses to discover potential customers. However, because users only check in a few POIs in an LBSN, the user-POI check-in interaction is highly sparse, which renders a big challenge for POI recommendations. To tackle this challenge, in this study we propose a new POI recommendation approach called GeoSoCa through exploiting *geographical correlations*, *social correlations* and *categorical correlations* among users and POIs. The geographical, social and categorical correlations can be learned from the historical check-in data of users on POIs and utilized to predict the relevance score of a user to an unvisited POI so as to make recommendations for users. First, in GeoSoCa we propose a kernel estimation method with an adaptive bandwidth to determine a personalized check-in distribution of POIs for each user that naturally models the geographical correlations between POIs. Then, GeoSoCa aggregates the check-in frequency or rating of a user's friends on a POI and models the social check-in frequency or rating as a power-law distribution to employ the social correlations between users. Further, GeoSoCa applies the bias of a user on a POI category to weigh the popularity of a POI in the corresponding category and models the weighed popularity as a power-law distribution to leverage the categorical correlations between POIs. Finally, we conduct a comprehensive performance evaluation for GeoSoCa using two large-scale real-world check-in data sets collected from Foursquare and Yelp. Experimental results show that GeoSoCa achieves significantly superior recommendation quality compared to other state-of-the-art POI recommendation techniques.

Categories and Subject Descriptors

H.3.3 [**Information Storage and Retrieval**]: Information Search and Retrieval – Information Filtering

SIGIR'15, August 09 - 13, 2015, Santiago, Chile
 ISBN 978-1-4503-3621-5/15/08 ...$15.00
DOI: http://dx.doi.org/10.1145/2766462.2767711.

Keywords

Location-based social networks; point-of-interest recommendations; geographical correlations; social correlations; categorical correlations; popularity

1. INTRODUCTION

As an increasingly popular application of location-based services, location-based social networks (LBSNs), such as Foursquare and Yelp, have attracted millions of users to check in their preferred points-of-interest (POIs), e.g., museums, restaurants and stores, and share their experiences of visiting these POIs with friends. For example, as of December 2014, Foursquare had over 6 billion check-ins with millions more every day contributed by more than 55 million users worldwide. These historical check-in data incorporate rich information about users and POIs, and thus bring new opportunities to mine the user visiting preferences for personalized POI recommendations that not only help users explore new POIs but also benefit for businesses to discover potential customers.

In the problem of personalized POI recommendations, the key tasks are to estimate the preference or relevance scores of a user to her unvisited POIs and return the POIs with the top-k highest preference scores for the user. Most existing POI recommendation methods (e.g., [3, 5, 6, 10, 11, 14, 25, 26, 37]) apply the traditional memory-based or model-based collaborative filtering techniques with the user-POI check-in matrix to compute the preference score between a user and an unvisited POI. However, the user-POI check-in matrix is highly sparse because users have only visited a very small proportion of POIs in an LBSN. As a result, these methods usually suffer from low recommendation quality.

In this paper, we predict the preference scores of any target user to her unvisited POIs based on **three important types of correlations among the user and unvisited POIs** that can be derived from the historical check-in data of users on POIs, as depicted in Figure 1. (1) **Geographical correlations.** The first law of geography [17] states that: "Everything is related to everything else, but near things are more related than distant things." For example, in reality a person usually visits a POI, e.g., museums, and then travel to its nearby POIs, e.g., restaurants and stores. That is, the close POIs have the stronger geographical correlations than the POIs that are far from each other. Thus, we can estimate a user's relevance score for an unvisited POI based on the geographical correlations between *the user's visited POIs* and *unvisited POI.* (2) **Social correlations.** In the real world, a person may prefer POIs highly recommended

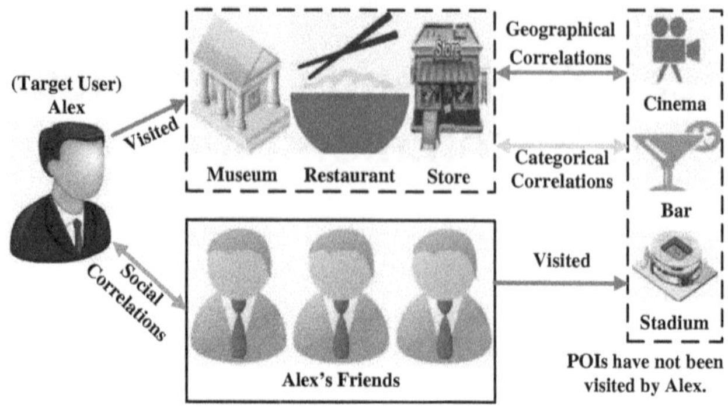

Figure 1: Three important types of correlations

by her friends. For instance, they often visit POIs, e.g., museums, restaurants or stores together. In other words, social friends are more likely to share common interests on POIs than strangers. Likewise, in LBSNs, users establish social links with each other to share their experiences of visiting POIs. Hence, we can compute the relevance score of a user for an unvisited POI in terms of the social correlations between *the user* with *her friends* who have visited the POI. (3) **Categorical correlations.** LBSNs often predefine a universal set of categories and attach each POI to a certain subset of categories. The category of a POI reflects its usual business activities and nature. In reality people have different biases on the categories of POIs: a foodie often visits restaurants to taste a variety of food, and a tourism enthusiast usually travels on tourism attractions all over the world. Accordingly, we can deduce the relevance score of a user to an unvisited POI based on the categorical correlations in the categories of *the user's visited POIs* and *the unvisited POI*.

Therefore, we are motivated to propose a new probabilistic approach for point-of-interest recommendations through exploiting and integrating **Geo**graphical, **So**cial and **Ca**tegorical correlations, called **GeoSoCa**. (1) **Geographical correlation modeling.** With the visited POIs of a user, we estimate a personalized check-in distribution over the geographical latitude and longitude coordinates for the user; the personal check-in distribution naturally models the geographical correlations between *the user's visited POIs* and *her unvisited POIs* and is able to compute the geographical relevance score of the user to any unvisited POI. (2) **Social correlation modeling.** Given an unvisited POI of a user, we first aggregate the check-in frequency or rating on the POI from her social friends; then the social check-in frequency (or rating) is transformed into a social relevance score of the user to the unvisited POI, based on the social check-in frequency (or rating) distribution that is estimated from the historical check-in data of all users. (3) **Categorical correlation modeling.** At first, we derive the bias of a user to a certain category according to her visited POIs; then the bias is used to weigh the popularity of an unvisited POI in the corresponding category. Further, the weighed popularity for the user to the unvisited POI is also mapped into a categorical relevance score based on the popularity distribution estimated from the historical check-in data of all users. The categorical correlation also takes into account the POI popularity from all users which indicates the quality of the POI and benefits for POI recommendations.

The main contributions of this study can be summarized:

- To model the geographical correlations, we extend the kernel density estimation by applying an adaptive bandwidth that is learned from the underlying check-in data. Our adaptive kernel estimation method can improve the predictive ability of the estimated check-in distribution for a user, in comparison to the kernel density estimation with a fixed bandwidth [30, 31, 34, 35] and the common distance distribution for all users [9, 13, 15, 22, 23, 28, 29]. (Section 3.2)
- To model the social correlations, we develop a method to estimate the social check-in frequency or rating by a user's friends to a POI as a power-law distribution that is learned from the historical check-in data of all users. Our method is distinct from the current works [2, 4, 20, 21, 23, 27, 30, 31, 34, 35, 36] that derive the similarities between users in terms of their social links and then integrate them into the traditional collaborative filtering techniques. (Section 3.3)
- To model the categorical correlations, we devise a method to combine the category bias of a user and the popularity of a POI into a relevance score between the user and POI in terms of the estimated popularity distribution from the historical check-in data of all users. Our method is different from the existing works [1, 8, 15, 18, 27, 36] that separately utilize the category and/or popularity information of POIs. (Section 3.4)
- To the best of our knowledge, our proposed GeoSoCa is the first study to integrate the geographical, social, categorical and popularity information for POI recommendations. (Section 3.5)
- We conduct extensive experiments to evaluate the recommendation accuracy of GeoSoCa using two large-scale real-world data sets collected from Foursquare and Yelp. Experimental results show that GeoSoCa significantly outperforms other state-of-the-art POI recommendation techniques. (Section 4)

The rest of this paper is organized as follows. We review the related work on POI recommendations in Section 2. Our proposed methods to model geographical, social and categorical correlations are presented in Section 3, followed by experimental evaluation in Section 4. Finally, Section 5 concludes this paper.

2. RELATED WORK

This section reviews existing POI recommendation techniques on how they employ the geographical, social, categorical, and popularity information.

POI recommendations using geographical information. Based on the fact that the geographical proximity significantly affects the check-in behaviors of users on the POIs, the geographical information has been intensively used in POI recommendations. One way is to simply consider the current locations of users to filter out the POIs that are far from the users [1, 4, 20, 14]. Another way is to apply the geographical latent factor or topic models to derive latent features of regions or POIs [7, 8, 12, 16, 25, 26]. The more sophisticated way is to estimate the geographical correlations of check-in POIs as a common distance distribution for all users, e.g., a multi-center Gaussian distribution [2], a power-law distribution [9, 13, 15, 22, 23, 28, 29, 32], or a personalized nonparametric distribution for each user [30, 33, 34]. In particular, the recent works [31, 35] employed the kernel density estimation method with the fixed bandwidth to model the geographical check-in distribution of POIs for each user over the latitude and longitude coordinates. Further, in this paper we develop an adaptive kernel estimation method to enhance the ability of the obtained check-in distributions to predict the relevance score between a user and an unvisited POI.

POI recommendations using social information. Social links between users have also been widely utilized to improve the quality of location-based recommender systems, since the social friends are more likely to share common interests on POIs than strangers. Most current works derive the similarities between users from social links and put them into the traditional memory-based or model-based collaborative filtering techniques. For example, some literatures [4, 20, 23, 27, 30, 31, 34, 35] seamlessly integrated the similarities of users into the user-based collaborative filtering techniques, while others [2, 21, 36] employed the user similarities as the regularization terms or weights of latent factor models. In this paper, we contrive a new method to exploit the social correlations between users by aggregating the check-in frequency or rating of friends to POIs and transforming them into relevance scores, based on the estimated social check-in frequency or rating distribution from the historical check-in data of all users.

POI recommendations using categorical information. The categories of POIs visited by a user implicitly indicate the activities of the user in the POIs. For instance, a person checking in a cinema means that she is watching a movie there. Thus, the category information of POIs is useful for modeling the specific preference of a user. However, there are only a few studies that utilize the category information for POI recommendations. Rahimi and Wang [18] simply identified the preference of a user to a POI with the bias of the user to the category of the POI. Bao et al. [1] calculated the category biases of users to compute the similarity of the users for the user-based collaborative filtering method. Besides *the category biases of users*, Ying et al. [27] also derived *the category weights of POIs* from the tags annotated on the POIs and then estimated the relevance scores between users and POIs based on the inner product of the category biases and weights. Liu et al. [15] clustered POIs into groups based on their categories, built a user-category transition matrix instead of user-POI check-in matrix from the historical check-in data of users, and applied the matrix factorization technique to discover the next top-k categories that a user would like to check in. Zhao et al. [36] clustered users into communities and represented each community as a weighted category vector, in which each dimension is the check-in counts of a particular POI category by users in the community; to apply the user-based collaborative filtering method, they further computed the similarity of users according to the category vectors of the communities of the users. Hu et al. [8] leveraged the matrix factorization technique to associate each category with a latent vector and deuced the relevance score of a user to a POI based on the latent vectors of the categories of the POI.

POI recommendations using popularity information. The popularity of a POI reflects the quality of products or services provided by the POI. For example, a restaurant receiving a lot of visits from customers indicates that the restaurant provides high-quality foods for its customers. Thus, the popularity of POIs is also helpful for POI recommendations. Most existing works regard the popularity of a POI as the universal prior preference of users to the POI. Specifically, the study [27] employed the prior preference of users to unvisited POIs as the weight of the edges between the users and POIs in the complete bipartite graph, while other studies utilize *the prior preference* to adjust *the posterior preference* that are derived from the geographical information [8, 13, 14, 28]. However, in these studies the prior preference is not personalized for users and thus in practice the benefit from the popularity is considerably limited. On the other hand, the current works [1, 8, 15, 18, 27, 36] **separately** modeled the effect of the category and popularity of POIs and may not take full advantage of them for POI recommendations. In this paper, we devise a new method to combine the category bias of a user and the popularity of a POI into a relevance score between the user and POI so as to personalize the effect of the popularity of the POI on the user.

Table 1: Key Notations in the Paper

Symbol	Meaning
U	Set of all users in an LBSN
u	Some user: $u \in U$
L	Set of POIs in an LBSN
l	Some POI with a pair of geographical latitude and longitude coordinates (x, y): $l \in L$
C	Set of categories of POIs in an LBSN
c	Some category: $c \in C$
$\mathbf{R}_{\|U\|\times\|L\|}$	Check-in matrix: $\mathbf{R}_{u,l}$ is the check-in frequency or rating of user u on POI l
$\mathbf{S}_{\|U\|\times\|U\|}$	Social link matrix: if $u, u' \in U$ have a social link, $\mathbf{S}_{u,u'} = 1$; otherwise, $\mathbf{S}_{u,u'} = 0$.
$\mathbf{B}_{\|U\|\times\|C\|}$	Categorical bias matrix: $\mathbf{B}_{u,c}$ is the frequency of user u visiting category c
$\mathbf{P}_{\|C\|\times\|L\|}$	Popularity matrix: $\mathbf{P}_{c,l}$ is the popularity of POI l in category c

3. MODELING CORRELATIONS FOR POI RECOMMENDATIONS

In this section, we introduce the research problem with the required data structures (Section 3.1), model the geographical, social, and categorical correlations (Sections 3.2, to 3.4), and integrate these three correlations to recommend POIs to users (Section 3.5).

3.1 Problem Statement

Here we define the data structures and the research problem in this paper. These data structures can be extracted from the rich information in an LBSN, incorporating the historical check-in data of users on POIs, social links between users, the categories of POIs, and the geographical latitude and longitude coordinates of POIs. Table 1 lists the key symbols used in this paper.

DEFINITION 1 **(Check-in matrix).** Given the historical check-in data of users on POIs from an LBSN, we can easily build a check-in matrix $\mathbf{R}_{|U|\times|L|}$, in which each entry

$\mathbf{R}_{u,l}$ represents the check-in frequency (e.g., Foursquare) or rating (e.g., Yelp) of user $u \in U$ on location $l \in L$, and U and L are the sets of users and POIs in the LBSN, respectively. Note that most entries in $\mathbf{R}$ are zero, since users have only visited a very small proportion of POIs in the LBSN.

DEFINITION 2 (**Social link matrix**). Given the social links between users from an LBSN, it is easy to construct a social link matrix $\mathbf{S}_{|U|\times|U|}$, in which if there exists a social link between two different users $u, u' \in U$, $\mathbf{S}_{u,u'} = 1$; otherwise, $\mathbf{S}_{u,u'} = 0$.

DEFINITION 3 (**Categorical bias matrix**). Given the historical check-in data of users on POIs and the categories of POIs from an LBSN, we construct a categorical bias matrix $\mathbf{B}_{|U|\times|C|}$, in which each entry $\mathbf{B}_{u,c}$ represents the frequency of user u visiting the POIs that belong to category $c \in C$, and C is the universal set of categories of POIs that is often predefined in the LBSN. Note that a POI could belong to multiple categories.

DEFINITION 4 (**Popularity matrix**). We build a popularity matrix $\mathbf{P}_{|C|\times|L|}$, in which each entry $\mathbf{P}_{c,l}$ represents the popularity of POI l in category c, i.e., the check-in frequency or overall rating of all users on l. Note that most entries of $\mathbf{P}$ are zero, because a POI only belongs to a certain subset of the universal category set C.

DEFINITION 5 (**Geographical coordinates**). A POI $l \in L$ is associated with a pair of geographical latitude and longitude coordinates (x, y).

Problem definition on POI recommendations. Given the geographical coordinates of POIs, check-in matrix $\mathbf{R}_{|U|\times|L|}$, social link matrix $\mathbf{S}_{|U|\times|U|}$, categorical bias matrix $\mathbf{B}_{|U|\times|C|}$, and popularity matrix $\mathbf{P}_{|C|\times|L|}$, the goal is to predict the preference score $s(u, l)$ of a user u to an unvisited POI l (i.e., $\mathbf{R}_{u,l} = 0$), and then return the top-k POIs with the highest preference score $s(u, l)$ for the user u.

3.2 Geographical Correlations

Distinctly from non-spatial items, such as books and music in conventional recommendation systems, in LBSNs users are required to physically interact with POIs to consume their offered products or services, e.g., eating food at restaurants or watching movies at cinemas. Thus, the geographical proximity of POIs plays a significant role in the check-in behaviors of users. In other words, the close POIs have the stronger geographical correlations than the far POIs. Therefore, we can exploit the geographical correlations between *a user's visited POIs* and *her unvisited POI* to estimate the relevance score of the user on the unvisited POI. To model the geographical correlations between POIs, we estimate a personalized check-in distribution over the geographical coordinates for each user based on her own visited POIs.

Due to the fact that the check-in distributions of users are different from one another, e.g., indoorsy persons like visiting venues around their living areas while outdoorsy persons prefer exploring new interesting places by traveling around the world. Accordingly, the current works [30, 31, 34, 35] learn the distribution form from the check-in POIs of a user based on a nonparametric estimation method, i.e., the kernel density estimation with a fixed bandwidth [19]. Nonetheless, the fixed bandwidth does not reflect the facts in the

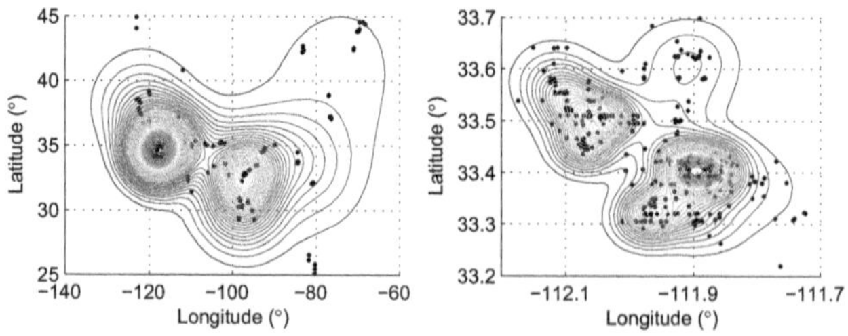

(a) A user in Foursquare (b) A user in Yelp

Figure 2: Geographical check-in distribution (contour line) of random users from the real-world data

user check-in data: dense urban areas will have high check-in density and sparsely-populated rural areas will have low check-in density. To this end, in this paper we adapt the kernel bandwidth to each check-in data point and the adaptive bandwidth itself is also learned from the underlying check-in data. In general, the adaptive kernel estimation method includes three steps: *pilot estimation*, *local bandwidth determination*, and *adaptive kernel estimation for geographical relevance score*.

Step 1: Pilot estimation. First, we find a pilot estimation based on the kernel density estimation with a fixed bandwidth [19]. Let $L_u = \{l_1, l_2, \cdots, l_n\}$ be the set of check-in POIs of user u, in which each POI l_i is associated with a pair of latitude and longitude (x_i, y_i). Specifically, we use the frequency or rating of user u on POI l_i, i.e., $\mathbf{R}_{u,l_i}$ (DEFINITION 1), as the weight of l_i because a higher frequency or rating at a POI indicates that it is more important to the user. The pilot estimation $\tilde{f}_{Geo}(l|u)$ of the check-in distribution of user u on an unvisited POI l is given by

$$\tilde{f}_{Geo}(l|u) = \frac{1}{N}\sum_{i=1}^{n}(\mathbf{R}_{u,l_i} \cdot K_H(l - l_i)) \tag{1}$$

together with

$$N = \sum_{i=1}^{n} \mathbf{R}_{u,l_i} \tag{2}$$

and

$$K_H(l - l_i) = \frac{1}{2\pi H_1 H_2} \exp\left(-\frac{(x - x_i)^2}{2H_1^2} - \frac{(y - y_i)^2}{2H_2^2}\right), \tag{3}$$

where $K_H(l - l_i)$ is the normal kernel function with the fixed bandwidth H consisting of two global bandwidths (H_1, H_2) for the latitude and longitude, given by

$$H_1 = 1.06n^{-\frac{1}{5}}\sqrt{\frac{1}{N}\sum_{i=1}^{n}\left(\mathbf{R}_{u,l_i} \cdot x_i - \frac{1}{N}\sum_{j=1}^{n}\mathbf{R}_{u,l_j} \cdot x_j\right)^2} \tag{4}$$

and

$$H_2 = 1.06n^{-\frac{1}{5}}\sqrt{\frac{1}{N}\sum_{i=1}^{n}\left(\mathbf{R}_{u,l_i} \cdot y_i - \frac{1}{N}\sum_{j=1}^{n}\mathbf{R}_{u,l_j} \cdot y_j\right)^2}, \tag{5}$$

where (H_1, H_2) are computed from the standard deviation of the latitude and longitude values in the check-in data of user u, respectively [19].

Step 2: Local bandwidth determination. Further, instead of directly using the pilot estimation $\tilde{f}_{Geo}(l|u)$ in Equation (1) to predict the relevance score of user u to POI l, we utilize the pilot estimation to determine the local bandwidth h_i for each check-in POI l_i, given by

$$h_i = \left(g^{-1} \cdot \tilde{f}_{Geo}(l_i|u)\right)^{-\alpha}, \quad (6)$$

where α is the sensitivity parameter with $0 \le \alpha \le 1$, i.e., the larger the parameter α, the more sensitive the local bandwidth h_i will be to the pilot estimation $\tilde{f}_{Geo}(l_i|u)$, and g is the geometric mean:

$$g = \sqrt[n]{\prod_{i=1}^{n} \tilde{f}_{Geo}(l_i|u)} \quad (7)$$

which imposes the constraint that the geometric mean of the h_i $(i = 1, 2, \cdots, n)$ is equal to one.

Step 3: Adaptive kernel estimation for geographical relevance score. Finally, with the global bandwidth $H = (H_1, H_2)$ in Equations (4) and (5) and the adaptive local bandwidth h_i in Equation (6), the adaptive kernel estimation $f_{Geo}(l|u)$ of the check-in distribution of user u on an unvisited POI l is computed through

$$f_{Geo}(l|u) = \frac{1}{N}\sum_{i=1}^{n}(\mathbf{R}_{u,l_i} \cdot K_{Hh_i}(l - l_i)), \quad (8)$$

where

$$K_{Hh_i}(l - l_i) = \frac{1}{2\pi H_1 H_2 h_i^2} \exp\left(-\frac{(x - x_i)^2}{2H_1^2 h_i^2} - \frac{(y - y_i)^2}{2H_2^2 h_i^2}\right). \quad (9)$$

It is important to note that: When a check-in POI l_i lies in the area with a higher check-in density, it has a larger pilot estimation $\tilde{f}_{Geo}(l_i|u)$ in Equation (1) or a smaller local bandwidth h_i in Equation (6) that will produce a peak adaptive kernel estimation $f_{Geo}(l|u)$ around l_i in Equation (8). In contrast, when a check-in POI l_i lies in the area with a lower check-in density, it has a smaller pilot estimation $\tilde{f}_{Geo}(l_i|u)$ in Equation (1) or a larger local bandwidth h_i in Equation (6) that will generate a smooth adaptive kernel estimation $f_{Geo}(l|u)$ around l_i in Equation (8). Therefore, our adaptive kernel estimation method can improve the predictive ability of the estimated check-in distribution for the geographical relevance score of user u on an unvisited POI l, i.e., $f_{Geo}(l|u)$.

Example. Figure 2 depicts the contour line of the geographical check-in distribution estimated through Equation (8) with $\alpha = 0.5$ for a user who is randomly selected from two publicly available real-world data sets: Foursquare [6] and Yelp [24], respectively. The estimated geographical distribution is able to capture the geographical preference of a specific user on POIs: the user in Foursquare visits POIs over the world, with concentration on two areas, while the user in Yelp checks in POIs only in Arizona of USA, with focus on three areas.

3.3 Social Correlations

In reality, friends often go to some places like movie theaters or restaurants together or a person may travel on spots highly recommended by her friends. In other words, the social correlations between users greatly affect the check-in behaviors of users to POIs. Likewise, in LBSNs users create social links with each other to indicate the social friendships among them. Accordingly, we can deduce the relevance score of a user and an unvisited POI through leveraging the social correlations between *the user* with *her friends* who have visited the POI. The process consists of three steps: *social aggregation, distribution estimation of social frequency or rating*, and *social relevance score computation.*

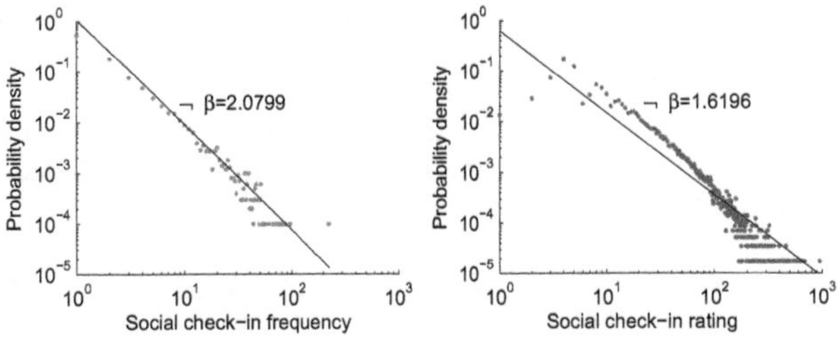

(a) Foursquare (b) Yelp

Figure 3: Social check-in frequency or rating distribution in the real-world data

Step 1: Social aggregation. Formally, given a user u and an unvisited POI l, we aggregate the check-in frequency or rating $x_{u,l}$ of the user u's friends (i.e., u' with $\mathbf{S}_{u,u'} = 1$) on the POI l, given by

$$x_{u,l} = \sum_{u' \in U} \mathbf{S}_{u,u'} \cdot \mathbf{R}_{u',l}, \quad (10)$$

where $\mathbf{R}_{u',l}$ is the check-in frequency or rating of user u' on POI l (DEFINITION 1) and $\mathbf{S}_{u,u'}$ indicates whether there exists a social link between users u and u' (DEFINITION 2).

One can naively regard the social check-in frequency or rating $x_{u,l}$ as the relevance score between user u and POI l or simply divide $x_{u,l}$ by the number of friends of u as in the traditional collaborative filtering techniques. More sophisticatedly, in this study we transform the social check-in frequency (or rating) into a normalized relevance score based on the social check-in frequency (or rating) distribution that is learned from the historical check-in data of all users.

Step 2: Distribution estimation of social frequency or rating. In real-world data sets, the social check-in frequency or rating random variable x follows a power-law distribution, the probability density function of which is defined by

$$f_{So}(x) = (\beta - 1)(1 + x)^{-\beta}, x \ge 0, \beta > 1, \quad (11)$$

where β is estimated by the check-in matrix $\mathbf{R}$ and social link matrix $\mathbf{S}$:

$$\beta = 1 + |U||L|\left[\sum_{u' \in U}\sum_{l' \in L} \ln\left(1 + \sum_{u'' \in U} \mathbf{S}_{u',u''} \cdot \mathbf{R}_{u'',l'}\right)\right]^{-1}, \quad (12)$$

in which $\sum_{u'' \in U} \mathbf{S}_{u',u''} \cdot \mathbf{R}_{u'',l'}$ is the social check-in frequency or rating of the friends u'' of user u' on POI l'.

To observe the real distribution of the social check-in frequency or rating, we conducted analysis on the two publicly available real-world data sets: Foursquare [6] and Yelp [24]. Figure 3 shows that the social check-in frequency or rating (i.e., the dots) in the two real-world data sets fits a certain power-law distribution very well (i.e., the line), estimated through Equations (11) and (12). Thus, modeling the social check-in frequency or rating as a power-law distribution is reasonable and effective.

Step 3: Social relevance score computation. The estimated probability density function f_{So} in Equation (11) is monotonically decreasing with respect to the social check-in frequency (or rating) x, but the social relevance score should be monotonically increasing with regard to the social check-in frequency (or rating) because friends share more common interests on POIs. Thus, we define the social relevance score of $x_{u,l}$ in Equation (10) based on the cumulative distribution function of f_{So}, given by

$$F_{So}(x_{u,l}) = \int_0^{x_{u,l}} f_{So}(z)dz = 1 - (1 + x_{u,l})^{1-\beta}, \quad (13)$$

where F_{So} is an increasing function respecting the social check-in frequency or rating $x_{u,l}$ because of $1-\beta < 0$. Moreover, based on the cumulative distribution function F_{So} in Equation (13), the social check-in frequency (or rating) $x_{u,l}$ is transformed into a social relevance score that reflects the relative position of $x_{u,l}$ in all social check-in frequencies (or ratings) of users on POIs.

3.4 Categorical Correlations

In LBSNs, each POI is attached to a few categories. The category of a POI has a strong indication about what activities happen in the POI and what products or services are provided by the POI. For instance, a person visiting a restaurant means that she may have a meal there and a Chinese restaurant indicates that Chinese food will be provided for customers. In practice, people have shown distinct biases on the categories of POIs, e.g., a foodie likes visiting restaurants to taste various food and a tourism enthusiast prefers traveling all over the world to view tourism attractions. Hence, we also can derive the relevance score of a user to an unvisited POI through exploiting the categorical correlations between *the visited POIs* and *the unvisited POI* of the user.

In addition, the popularity of a POI reflects the quality of products or services offered by the POI, e.g., a popular restaurant usually indicates that it supplies high-quality foods. Therefore, it is helpful to utilize the popularity for POI recommendations. Specifically, we develop a new method to combine the category bias of a user and the popularity of a POI into a relevance score between the user and POI through three steps: *weighing popularity by categorical bias*, *distribution estimation of categorical popularity*, and *categorical relevance score computation*.

Step 1: Weighing popularity by categorical bias. At first, we take the bias of a user u to a certain category c as $\mathbf{B}_{u,c}$, i.e., the frequency of user u visiting the POIs that belong to category c (DEFINITION 3). Then, the bias $\mathbf{B}_{u,c}$ is used to weigh the popularity of an unvisited POI l in category c, i.e., $\mathbf{P}_{c,l}$ (DEFINITION 4). Correspondingly, we obtain the categorical popularity $y_{u,l}$ for user u on POI l:

$$y_{u,l} = \sum_{c \in C} \mathbf{B}_{u,c} \cdot \mathbf{P}_{c,l}, \quad (14)$$

where C is the predefined universal set of categories in an LBSN. A larger value of $y_{u,l}$ indicates that the category of POI l is more satisfied with the bias of user u and the POI l is more popular to the general public.

One may naively consider the categorical popularity $y_{u,l}$ as the relevance score between user u and POI l or simply normalize the categorical bias $\mathbf{B}_{u,c}$ in advance. Nevertheless, in this research the categorical popularity of a user to an unvisited POI is sophisticatedly mapped into a relevance score based on the distribution of the categorical popularity that is learned from the historical check-in data of all users.

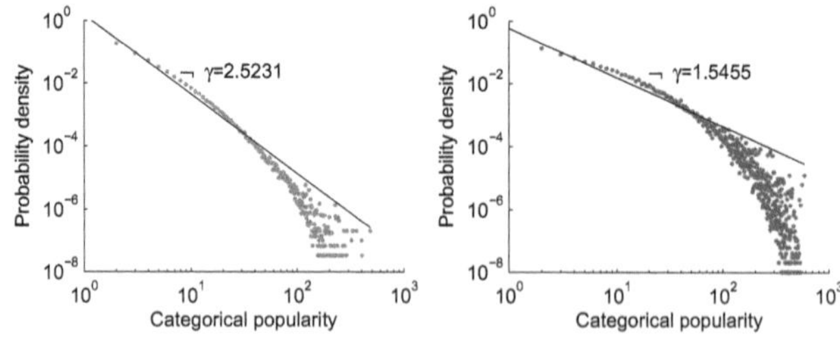

(a) Foursquare (b) Yelp

Figure 4: Categorical popularity distribution in the real-world data

Step 2: Distribution estimation of categorical popularity. As the distribution of the social check-in frequency or rating, we apply the similar process to build the distribution of the categorical popularity. Formally, we assume the probability density function of the categorical popularity random variable y, defined by

$$f_{Ca}(y) = (\gamma - 1)(1 + y)^{-\gamma}, y \geq 0, \gamma > 1, \quad (15)$$

in which γ can be learned from the categorical bias matrix $\mathbf{B}$ and popularity matrix $\mathbf{P}$:

$$\gamma = 1 + |U||L| \left[\sum_{u' \in U} \sum_{l' \in L} \ln \left(1 + \sum_{c \in C} \mathbf{B}_{u',c} \cdot \mathbf{P}_{c,l'} \right) \right]^{-1}, \quad (16)$$

where $\sum_{c \in C} \mathbf{B}_{u',c} \cdot \mathbf{P}_{c,l'}$ is the categorical popularity of user u' on POI l'.

As depicted in Figure 4, we have also observed that the categorical popularity (i.e., the dots) in the two real-world data sets approaches to the power-law distribution (i.e., the line) that is estimated in terms of Equations (15) and (16). Thus, these results have validated that the assumption of the power-law distribution is in accordance with reality.

Step 3: Categorical relevance score computation. Similarly, the estimated probability density function f_{Ca} in Equation (15) is monotonically decreasing regarding the categorical popularity y; however, the categorical relevance score is monotonically increasing respecting the categorical popularity, since people prefer the popular POIs that also meet their categorical biases. To this end, we employ the cumulative distribution function of f_{Ca} to obtain the categorical relevance score of $y_{u,l}$ in Equation (14), given by

$$F_{Ca}(y_{u,l}) = \int_0^{y_{u,l}} f_{Ca}(z)dz = 1 - (1 + y_{u,l})^{1-\gamma}, \quad (17)$$

where due to $1 - \gamma < 0$, F_{Ca} is an increasing function with respect to the categorical popularity $y_{u,l}$. Importantly, the categorical $y_{u,l}$ is also normalized into a categorical relevance score, i.e., the relative position of $y_{u,l}$ compared to other categorical popularities of users on POIs.

3.5 POI Recommendations

Finally, we integrate the geographical, social and categorical relevance scores, given by Equations (8), (13) and (17), into a unified preference score $s(u, l)$ for user u to unvisited POI l based on the product rule:

$$s(u, l) = f_{Geo}(l|u) \cdot F_{So}(x_{u,l}) \cdot F_{Ca}(y_{u,l}). \quad (18)$$

The top-k POIs l with the highest score $s(u, l)$ are recommended to user u. It is worth mentioning that the product

Table 2: Statistics of the two data sets

	Foursquare	Yelp
Number of users	4,163	70,817
Number of POIs	121,142	15,579
Number of categories	35	591
Number of check-ins or ratings	483,813	335,022
Number of social links	32,512	303,032
User-POI matrix density	2.83×10^{-4}	1.46×10^{-4}

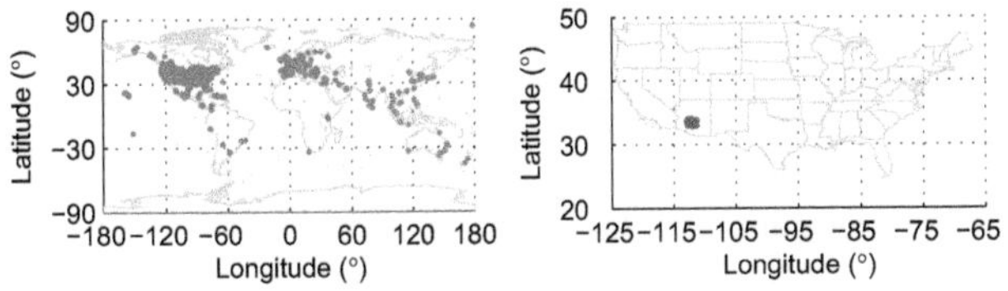

(a) Foursquare (b) Yelp

Figure 5: Distribution of POIs in the two data sets

rule has been widely used to fuse different factors for POI recommendations in the previous works [2, 13, 30, 34] and has shown high robustness.

4. EXPERIMENTS

In this section, we conduct intensive experiments to evaluate the recommendation quality of GeoSoCa, compared to state-of-the-art POI recommendation techniques. We present experimental settings in Section 4.1 and analyze experimental results in Section 4.2.

4.1 Experimental Settings

Two real data sets. We use the two publicly available large-scale real check-in data sets that have been studied in Section 3 and were crawled from Foursquare [6] and Yelp [24]. Note that the Foursquare data set provides the check-in frequencies of users to POIs and the Yelp data set offers the ratings of users on POIs. Table 2 shows the statistics of the data sets and Figure 5 depicts the distribution of POIs over the world from Foursquare while the greater Phoenix, Arizona, USA from Yelp. The half of check-in data with earlier check-in times are used as the training set and the other half of check-in data are used as the testing set, because in practice we can only utilize the past check-in data to predict the future check-in events.

Evaluated techniques. Our proposed method, i.e., GeoSoCa, is compared with the state-of-the-art POI recommendation techniques including:

- USG: This method is a unified location recommendation framework that integrates User preferences, Social and Geographical information [23].
- CoRe: This method fuses social collaborative filtering and geographical check-in distribution using kernel density estimation with a fixed bandwidth [31].
- DRW: This method is a Dynamic Random Walk model that combines social, category and popularity information [27].
- LCARS: This method builds a Location-Content-Aware Recommender System based on the well-known topic model (i.e., latent Dirichlet allocation) to infer personal interest and local preference [25, 26].
- NCPD: This method applies matrix factorization to incorporate the influence of Neighborhood, Category, Popularity and Geographical distance of POIs [8].

Performance metrics. To evaluate the quality of POI recommendations, it is important to find out how many POIs actually visited by a user **in the testing set** are discovered by the recommendation techniques. For this purpose, we employ two standard metrics:

$$\text{Precision} = \frac{\text{No. of discovered POIs}}{\text{No. of POIs recommended for the user: } k},$$

$$\text{Recall} = \frac{\text{No. of discovered POIs}}{\text{No. of POIs actually visited by the user}}.$$

Parameter settings. We examine the precision and recall with respect to various numbers of POIs recommended for users (top-k from 2 to 50) and numbers of POIs visited by users **in the training set** (n from 2 to 50). Further, we investigate the recommendation accuracy of the three components in GeoSoCa and the effect of sensitivity parameter α, by default $\alpha = 0.5$, in Equation (6). Note that β and γ are not free parameters and are learned from check-in data according to Equations (12) and (16), respectively.

4.2 Experimental Results

We compare our GeoSoCa with the state-of-the-art POI recommendation techniques in Section 4.2.1, study the recommendation quality of the three components in GeoSoCa in Section 4.2.2, and investigate the effect of sensitivity parameter α in Section 4.2.3.

4.2.1 Method Comparison

Figures 6 and 7 depict the recommendation accuracy of our GeoSoCa compared to the state-of-the-art POI recommendation techniques with respect to the number k of POIs recommended for users and the number n of POIs visited by users in the training set. The trends in the precision and recall of all evaluated methods are intuitive. For example, as k increases, the precision gets lower and the recall becomes higher, because recommending more POIs for users can discover more POIs that the users would like to check in, but some recommended POIs are less possible to be visited by the users. With the increase of n, the precision and recall gradually raise, since all methods can learn better recommendation models through using more check-in data.

The absolute accuracy of POI recommendation techniques is usually not high, because the density of user-POI check-in matrix is pretty low as shown in Table 2, but POI recommendation techniques will perform better as more check-in data are collected. This phenomenon has been repeatedly observed in previous works (e.g., [23, 31]). Instead, we concentrate on contrasting the relative accuracy of the evaluated POI recommendation techniques.

USG. This method [23] linearly integrates user preference from user-based collaborative filtering, social influence from social collaborative filtering, and geographical influence from a common distance distribution for all users, but it does not take into account the category and popularity information of POIs. Moreover, it is not advisable to apply the universal linear weights for user preference, social influence, and geographical influence, since some users are affected by social

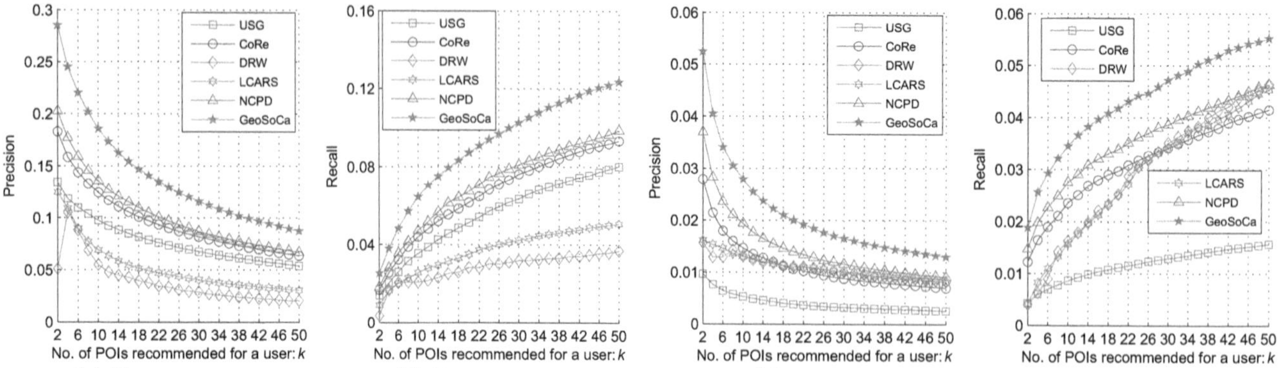

(a) Foursquare (b) Foursquare (c) Yelp (d) Yelp

Figure 6: Recommendation accuracy with respect to top-k values

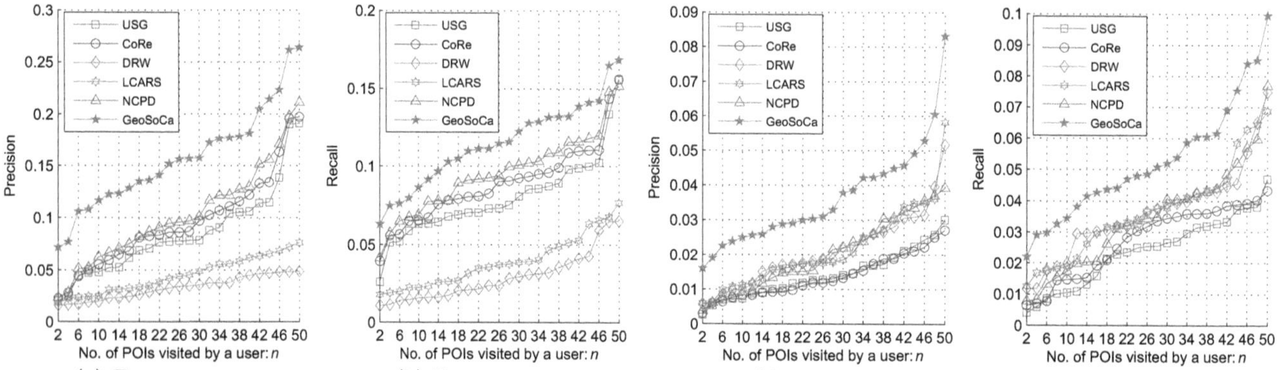

(a) Foursquare (b) Foursquare (c) Yelp (d) Yelp

Figure 7: Recommendation accuracy with respect to given-n values

friends more and other users may rely on the geographical influence more. According to Figures 6 and 7, USG subsequently gives the third worst recommendation result on the Foursquare data set and the worst recommendation accuracy on the Yelp data set that has two time lower density than the Foursquare data set, as depicted in Table 2.

CoRe. This method [31] employs the social influence in the same way as USG, but it models a personalized geographical check-in distribution for each user and combines the social and geographical influences by a more robust product rule rather than using the linear sum rule. CoRe accordingly outperforms USG to some extent as depicted in Figures 6 and 7. However, CoRe still misses the category and popularity information of POIs and estimates the geographical check-in distribution based on the kernel density estimation method with a fixed bandwidth. As a result, in general it only generates the third best recommendation precision and recall on the two data sets.

DRW. This method [27] adopts a dynamic random walk model to fuse the social links between users and the category and popularity information of POIs, but it does not consider the unique characteristic of POI recommendations for LBSNs, i.e., the influence of geographical information of POIs on the check-in behaviors of users. Consequently, DRW reports the lowest recommendation accuracy on the Foursquare data set, as shown in Figures 6(a), 6(b), 7(a), and 7(b). Interestingly, on the Yelp data set with lower density in Figures 6(c), 6(d), 7(c), and 7(d), DRW is superior to USG through taking full advantage of the popularity of POIs to deal with the sparsity of data.

LCARS. This method [25, 26] exploits the well-known topic model, i.e., latent Dirichlet allocation, to infer the personal interest of users and local preference (i.e., local specialty) of regions (e.g., a city). The personal interest or local preference is represented as a mixture of topics, in which each topic is a distribution over POIs and is learned from the check-in data and categories of POIs. Nonetheless, LCARS ignores the geographical and social characteristics in the check-in behaviors of users on POIs, so it also suffers from the low recommendation accuracy as in DRW.

NCPD. This method [8] utilizes matrix factorization to derive a latent factor vector for each user, POI and category, a geographical bias for each user, and a popularity bias for each POI. Then, NCPD computes the preference score of a user to a POI based on (1) the latent factor vectors of the user, the categories that the POI belongs to, and the neighborhoods of the POI, (2) the user's geographical bias, and (3) the POI's popularity bias. Accordingly, NCPD shows the second best recommendation result as depicted in Figures 6 and 7. However, its improvement is very limited in comparison to CoRe, because NCPD simply regards the geographical and popularity influence as a bias, instead of modeling them as a geographical or popularity distribution.

GeoSoCa. Our proposed GeoSoCa always exhibits the best recommendation quality in terms of both precision and recall. In particular, it achieves the significant improvement compared to the second best recommendation technique

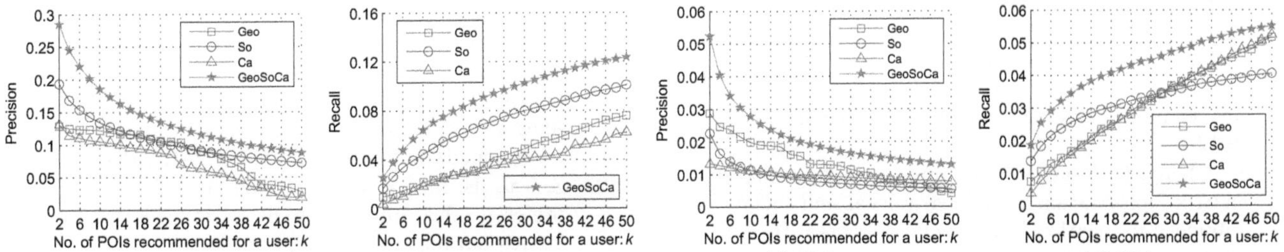

(a) Foursquare (b) Foursquare (c) Yelp (d) Yelp

Figure 8: Recommendation accuracy of the three components of GeoSoCa

NCPD. The reason is threefold: (1) GeoSoCa models the geographical check-in distribution using the adaptive kernel estimation method, in which the bandwidth is adaptive to each check-in data point rather than using a fixed bandwidth. This adaptive method can capture the real geographical check-in patterns of users on POIs, e.g., high check-in density in dense urban areas and low check-in density in sparsely-populated rural areas. (2) GeoSoCa exploits the social check-in frequency or rating of friends based on the power-law distribution which is learned from the historical check-in data of users. This method can effectively transform the social check-in frequency or rating into a reasonable relevance score and is superior to the traditional social collaborative filtering. (3) GeoSoCa takes full advantage of the category and popularity information through seamlessly combining the categorical bias of users and the popularity of POIs into a reasonable relevance score based on the estimated power-law distribution from check-in data of users.

4.2.2 *Study on Three Components in GeoSoCa*

Here we study the three components of GeoSoCa including geographical, social and categorical correlations, written as Geo, So and Ca, respectively. Figure 8 depicts the recommendation accuracy of the three components based on Equations (8), (13) and (17), respectively. We have two observations: (1) All the three components play a key role in GeoSoCa for POI recommendations and they are competitive to one another. For example, So outperforms Geo and Ca on the Foursquare data set, but reversely on the Yelp data set. And the performance of Geo and Ca is similar on the two data sets. (2) The integration of the three components is helpful for enhancing the recommendation quality, since GeoSoCa is significantly superior to each component, i.e., Geo, So and Ca. The behind reason is that in practice people are affected by the geographical, social and categorical correlations in varying degrees; it is unable to model the check-in behaviors of all users by considering only one type of correlations. Thus, POI recommendations should take full advantage of various types of useful information implied the check-in behaviors of users on POIs.

4.2.3 *Effect of Sensitivity Parameter* α

Figure 9 depicts the effect of the sensitivity parameter α in Equation (6) on the precision and recall of GeoSoCa in the two real-world data sets; note that β and γ are not free parameters and are learned from the check-in data. We have the following three observations: (1) The optimal value of α usually lies between 0.4 and 0.6 that generates the highest recommendation accuracy. (2) As the value of α varies from 0.4 to 0, the local bandwidth gets less sensitive to the pilot

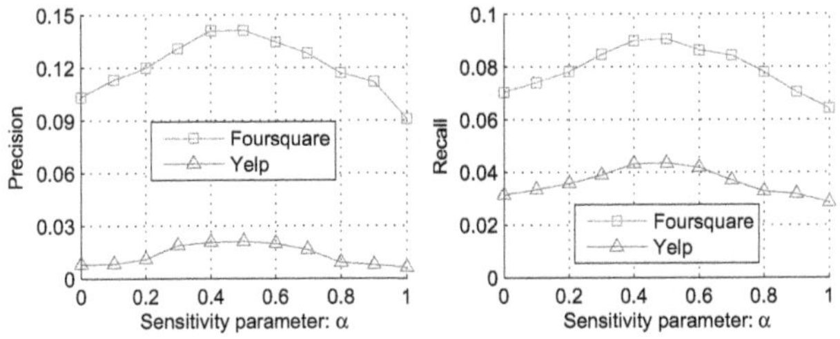

(a) GeoSoCa - Precision (b) GeoSoCa - Recall

Figure 9: Effect of sensitive parameter α on recommendation accuracy of GeoSoCa

estimation in terms of Equation (6), i.e., the local bandwidth is less related to the check-in data. Especially, when $\alpha = 0$, the adaptive local bandwidth is degraded to the fixed bandwidth that has nothing to do with the check-in data. As a result, the precision and recall decrease. (3) In contrast, when the value of α becomes higher from 0.6 to 1, the local bandwidth gets more sensitive to the pilot estimation in Equation (6), i.e., the local bandwidth is prone to overfitting the check-in data. Thus, the recommendation quality deteriorates as well.

5. CONCLUSION AND FUTURE WORK

This paper proposes a new POI recommendation approach GeoSoCa by exploiting three types of correlations that are derived from the historical check-in data of users on POIs. (1) GeoSoCa uses the kernel estimation with an adaptive bandwidth to model the geographical correlations between POIs as a personalized geographical check-in distribution of POIs for each user. (2) GeoSoCa models the social check-in frequency or rating as a power-law distribution to utilize the social correlations between users. (3) GeoSoCa models the popularity of POI categories as a power-law distribution to employ the categorical correlations between POIs. The experimental results on the two large-scale real-world data sets collected from Foursquare and Yelp show that GeoSoCa significantly improves the recommendation accuracy of the current state-of-the-art POI recommendation approaches. As a part of our future work, we plan to extend our GeoSoCa by integrating the sentiment or opinion extracted from the textual reviews of users commenting POIs to improve the recommendation quality of GeoSoCa.

6. ACKNOWLEDGEMENTS

The authors were supported by Guangdong Natural Science Foundation of China under Grant S2013010012363.

7. REFERENCES

[1] J. Bao, Y. Zheng, and M. F. Mokbel. Location-based and preference-aware recommendation using sparse geo-social networking data. In *ACM SIGSPATIAL*, 2012.

[2] C. Cheng, H. Yang, I. King, and M. R. Lyu. Fused matrix factorization with geographical and social influence in location-based social networks. In *AAAI*, 2012.

[3] C. Cheng, H. Yang, M. R. Lyu, and I. King. Where you like to go next: Successive point-of-interest recommendation. In *IJCAI*, 2013.

[4] G. Ference, M. Ye, and W.-C. Lee. Location recommendation for out-of-town users in location-based social networks. In *ACM CIKM*, 2013.

[5] H. Gao, J. Tang, X. Hu, and H. Liu. Exploring temporal effects for location recommendation on location-based social networks. In *ACM RecSys*, 2013.

[6] H. Gao, J. Tang, X. Hu, and H. Liu. Content-aware point of interest recommendation on location-based social networks. In *AAAI*, 2015.

[7] B. Hu and M. Ester. Spatial topic modeling in online social media for location recommendation. In *ACM RecSys*, 2013.

[8] L. Hu, A. Sun, and Y. Liu. Your neighbors affect your ratings: On geographical neighborhood influence to rating prediction. In *ACM SIGIR*, 2014.

[9] T. Kurashima, T. Iwata, T. Hoshide, N. Takaya, and K. Fujimura. Geo topic model: Joint modeling of user's activity area and interests for location recommendation. In *ACM WSDM*, 2013.

[10] K. W.-T. Leung, D. L. Lee, and W.-C. Lee. CLR: A collaborative location recommendation framework based on co-clustering. In *ACM SIGIR*, 2011.

[11] J. J. Levandoski, M. Sarwat, A. Eldawy, and M. F. Mokbel. LARS: A location-aware recommender system. In *IEEE ICDE*, 2012.

[12] D. Lian, C. Zhao, X. Xie, G. Sun, E. Chen, and Y. Rui. GeoMF: Joint geographical modeling and matrix factorization for point-of-interest recommendation. In *ACM KDD*, 2014.

[13] B. Liu, Y. Fu, Z. Yao, and H. Xiong. Learning geographical preferences for point-of-interest recommendation. In *ACM KDD*, 2013.

[14] B. Liu and H. Xiong. Point-of-interest recommendation in location based social networks with topic and location awareness. In *SDM*, 2013.

[15] X. Liu, Y. Liu, K. Aberer, and C. Miao. Personalized point-of-interest recommendation by mining users' preference transition. In *ACM CIKM*, 2013.

[16] Y. Liu, W. Wei, A. Sun, and C. Miao. Exploiting geographical neighborhood characteristics for location recommendation. In *ACM CIKM*, 2014.

[17] H. J. Miller. Tobler's first law and spatial analysis. *Annals of the Association of American Geographers*, 94(2):284–289, 2004.

[18] S. Rahimi and X. Wang. Location recommendation based on periodicity of human activities and location categories. In *PAKDD*, 2013.

[19] B. W. Silverman. *Density estimation for statistics and data analysis.* Chapman and Hall, 1986.

[20] H. Wang, M. Terrovitis, and N. Mamoulis. Location recommendation in location-based social networks using user check-in data. In *ACM SIGSPATIAL*, 2013.

[21] D. Yang, D. Zhang, Z. Yu, and Z. Wang. A sentiment-enhanced personalized location recommendation system. In *ACM HT*, 2013.

[22] Z. Yao, B. Liu, Y. Fu, H. Xiong, and Y. Ge. User preference learning with multiple information fusion for restaurant recommendation. In *SDM*, 2014.

[23] M. Ye, P. Yin, W.-C. Lee, and D.-L. Lee. Exploiting geographical influence for collaborative point-of-interest recommendation. In *ACM SIGIR*, 2011.

[24] Yelp. Challenge Data Set [accessed 25-april-2014]. `http://www.yelp.com/dataset_challenge`, 2014.

[25] H. Yin, B. Cui, Y. Sun, Z. Hu, and L. Chen. LCARS: A spatial item recommender system. *ACM TOIS*, 32(3):11:1–11:37, 2014.

[26] H. Yin, Y. Sun, B. Cui, Z. Hu, and L. Chen. LCARS: A location-content-aware recommender system. In *ACM KDD*, 2013.

[27] J. J.-C. Ying, W.-N. Kuo, V. S. Tseng, and E. H.-C. Lu. Mining user check-in behavior with a random walk for urban point-of-interest recommendations. *ACM TIST*, 5(3):40:1–40:26, 2014.

[28] Q. Yuan, G. Cong, Z. Ma, A. Sun, and N. Magnenat-Thalmann. Time-aware point-of-interest recommendation. In *ACM SIGIR*, 2013.

[29] Q. Yuan, G. Cong, and A. Sun. Graph-based point-of-interest recommendation with geographical and temporal influences. In *ACM CIKM*, 2014.

[30] J.-D. Zhang and C.-Y. Chow. iGSLR: Personalized geo-social location recommendation - a kernel density estimation approach. In *ACM SIGSPATIAL*, 2013.

[31] J.-D. Zhang and C.-Y. Chow. CoRe: Exploiting the personalized influence of two-dimensional geographic coordinates for location recommendations. *Information Sciences*, 293:163–181, 2015.

[32] J.-D. Zhang and C.-Y. Chow. Spatiotemporal sequential influence modeling for location recommendations: A gravity-based approach. *ACM TIST, accepted to appear*, 2015.

[33] J.-D. Zhang and C.-Y. Chow. TICRec: A probabilistic framework to utilize temporal influence correlations for time-aware location recommendations. *IEEE TSC, accepted to appear*, 2015.

[34] J.-D. Zhang, C.-Y. Chow, and Y. Li. iGeoRec: A personalized and efficient geographical location recommendation framework. *IEEE TSC, accepted to appear*, 2014.

[35] J.-D. Zhang, C.-Y. Chow, and Y. Li. LORE: Exploiting sequential influence for location recommendations. In *ACM SIGSPATIAL*, 2014.

[36] Y.-L. Zhao, L. Nie, X. Wang, and T.-S. Chua. Personalized recommendations of locally interesting venues to tourists via cross-region community matching. *ACM TIST*, 5(3):50:1–50:26, 2014.

[37] V. W. Zheng, Y. Zheng, X. Xie, and Q. Yang. Towards mobile intelligence: Learning from gps history data for collaborative recommendation. *Artificial Intelligence*, 184-185:17–37, 2012.

Optimised Scheduling of Online Experiments

Eugene Kharitonov[1,2], Craig Macdonald[2], Pavel Serdyukov[1], Iadh Ounis[2]
[1]Yandex, Russia
[2]University of Glasgow, UK
[1]{kharitonov, pavser}@yandex-team.ru
[2]{craig.macdonald, iadh.ounis}@glasgow.ac.uk

ABSTRACT

Modern search engines increasingly rely on online evaluation methods such as A/B tests and interleaving. These online evaluation methods make use of interactions by the search engine's users to test various changes in the search engine. However, since the number of the user sessions per unit of time is limited, the number of simultaneously running on-line evaluation experiments is bounded. In an extreme case, it might be impossible to deploy all experiments since they arrive faster than are proccessed. Consequently, it is very important to efficiently use the limited resource of the user's interactions. In this paper, we formulate the novel problem of schedule optimisation for the queue of the online experiments: given a limited number of the user interactions available for experimentation, we want to re-order the queue so that the number of successful experiments is maximised. In order to build a schedule optimisation algorithm, we start by formulating a model of an online experimentation pipeline. Next, we propose to reduce the task of finding the optimal schedule to a learning-to-rank problem, where we require the most promising experiments to be ranked first in the schedule. To evaluate the proposed approach, we perform an evaluation study using two datasets containing 82 interleaving and 35 A/B test experiments, performed by a commercial search engine. We measure the quality of a schedule as the number of successful experiments executed under limited user interactions. Our proposed schedulers obtain improvements of up to 342% compared to the unoptimised baseline schedule on the dataset of interleaving experiments and up to 43% on the dataset of A/B tests.

Categories and Subject Descriptors: H.3.3 [Information Storage & Retrieval]: Information Search & Retrieval

Keywords: online evaluation; interleaving; A/B tests

1. INTRODUCTION

Online experimentation methods have increasingly attracted attention from researchers and practitioners. The major search engines such as Google [22] and Bing [12] have developed large-scale online experimentation pipelines. Kohavi et al. [12] claimed that the number of A/B tests deployed by Bing grew exponentially over the years.

We define an online *experiment* as a single unit of the online evaluation that aims to test a single change in the search engine. An online experiment might span weeks and affect millions of user sessions. An experiment where the tested change proved to improve a considered metric with respect to the baseline system is further referred to as a *successful experiment*. We assume that obtaining a large number of such successful experiments per unit of time is important for the evaluation pipeline as a whole, as it allows a search engine to evolve quickly. In a typical scenario, several groups work on improving the search engine's ranking simultaneously and in different areas (e.g. ranking algorithms, ranking features). However, when tested online, the majority of their changes turn out to be useless or harmful [10].

Since the number of experiments grows with the intensity of the search engine development, after some point, these experiments need to "compete" for a limited resource of user interactions available to the search engine. These observations lead us to the idea of optimising the order of the online experiments: we need to order the schedule of the experiments so that the most promising experiments are performed first. Indeed, the earlier a successful comparison is performed, the earlier the corresponding change will be deployed. In an extreme case, when the experiments are arriving faster than they are proccessed, it is also beneficial to schedule only the promising experiments, without spending resources on the less promising ones.

In this paper, we study the problem of the online experiment schedule optimisation. We start with formally describing the model of the experimentation pipeline and the requirements for the scheduling algorithms. Further, we concentrate on the effectiveness-related experiments, where the changes that affect the ranking of the results are tested. We propose to reduce the problem of the optimal scheduling of such experiments to a learning-to-rank problem, considering pointwise and pairwise formulations. We describe a rich feature representation of the online experiments, used in the machine learning step. Finally, we perform a thorough evaluation study of the efficiency of the resulting scheduling algorithms. The contributions of this work are three-fold:

- We formulate the novel problem of the optimal scheduling of online experiments;
- We propose to reduce the problem of the optimal scheduling of the experiments to a learning-to-rank problem, and consider pointwise and pairwise formulations of this learning-to-rank problem;
- We thoroughly evaluate the proposed scheduling algorithms.

SIGIR'15, August 09 - 13, 2015, Santiago, Chile.
 ISBN 978-1-4503-3621-5/15/08 ...$15.00.
DOI: http://dx.doi.org/10.1145/2766462.2767706.

The remainder of this paper is organised as follows. After discussing the related work in Section 2, we briefly review how online experiments are typically performed and describe our experimentation pipeline in Section 3. In Section 4 we discuss how the scheduling problem can be reduced to a learning-to-rank machine learning problem. In Section 5 we discuss the datasets we use in our evaluation study. The evaluation methodology is described in Section 6. The evaluation results we obtained are discussed in Section 7. We conclude the paper and discuss future work in Section 8.

2. RELATED WORK

Our work relates to existing research in improving the efficiency of online experimentation, as discussed below.

Tang et al. [22] described the multi-layer framework of overlapping experiments used in Google. The motivation of this framework is to build a scalable online experimentation mechanism. The core idea of the framework is to use different *layers* of experiments, with each layer being associated with a set of variables influencing the user experiments. This allows each user interaction to participate in several experiments simultaneously. For instance, one of these experiments can compare two ranking algorithms, another can evaluate changes in the UI, etc. A similar framework is used by the Bing search engine [12].

Our work shares the same goal: to make the online experimentation pipeline more efficient, but extends [22] further. Even in the framework proposed by Tang et al., in some layers (e.g. the ranking layer) we might want to run the most promising experiments earlier or experiments might arrive faster than they could be processed. As a result, the problem of the optimal scheduling of these experiments is still an issue. We consider a complementary approach: assuming that only a part of the experiments can be successful, we propose to schedule the queue of the experiments so that more successful experiments are performed.

Notable efforts [9, 18, 23] have been applied to improve the sensitivity of the interleaving experiments, so that each interleaving experiment can be finished faster. Yue et al. [23] proposed a machine-learned approach to interpret click feedback from the users, so that the intrinsic noise of the clicks is reduced. Chapelle et al. [1] additionally considered some simple heuristic weighting schemes that can be used while aggregating the user's clicks in a single impression. We study a complimentary approach to increase the experimentation efficiency: under the optimising schedule, more successful experiments can be performed.

An important step in our approach is to predict how likely a particular experiment is to be successful. Hofmann et al. [4] proposed to estimate the interleaving comparison outcomes by treating historical user sessions as comparison events between tested alternatives. Kharitonov et al. [9] used the historical click data to calculate the expected difference in the number of clicks each interleaving alternative receives after an interleaving experiment is deployed. This step can be considered as a predictor of the experiment's result. In a recent work, Li et al. [14] proposed to leverage historical click data and natural variance in the search engine's result pages to predict the results of A/B tests.

In this work, we also use historical click data to predict the interleaving experiment outcome. However, there are considerable differences with the above discussed work [4, 9, 14]. Indeed, predicting an outcome of an experiment is just one of the steps of our proposed experiment scheduling approach. Moreover, the historical click data forms only a part of the features we use in our study: we additionally consider features that are based on the offline effectiveness-based evaluation, and online exploration.

Radlinski and Craswell [17] studied the agreement between the offline evaluation metrics, such as nDCG@n or Precision@n, and the results of interleaving experiments. Their work is related to our research, since they demonstrated that some metrics, such as nDCG@n, have a statistically significant correlation with the outcomes of interleaving experiments. This fact implies that offline evaluation metrics can be useful in predicting the interleaving experiment results. A similar experiment was performed by Chapelle et al. [1], who measured the correlation between DCG@5 and the absolute online metrics used in A/B tests.

However, since the agreements reported in [1, 17] are not perfect, the following question arises: Can a better prediction can be achieved by using other features apart from the search result effectiveness? In our evaluation study we address this question. Further, Radlinski and Craswell [17] performed their study on a dataset containing three experiments with major changes, and two experiments with minor improvements. However, major changes are rare in modern commercial search engines. Similarly, the analysis of the absolute online metrics used in A/B tests, performed by Chapelle et al. used a dataset of 6 comparisons. In contrast, we use two datasets, containing 82 real-life interleaving experiments and 35 A/B tests, performed by a commercial search engine as part of its development. Thus, we argue that our study uses more representative datasets.

Overall, to the best of our knowledge, our paper is the first work that studies the optimisation of the schedule of the online experiments. However, our work finds a solid foundation in the research discussed above.

3. ONLINE EXPERIMENTATION

In the next section we shortly review how online experiments are performed (Section 3.1) and the model of the experimentation pipeline we consider (Section 3.2).

3.1 Evaluation Methods

Suppose, we want to compare two different ranking algorithms, referred to as A (the current system) and B (the tested improvement). There are two popular online evaluation approaches to do that: A/B tests and interleaving.

A/B tests An intuitive way to compare two systems is to split users in two groups, the treatment and the control group. Each group of users is served by one of the algorithms (A or B). After collecting the user behaviour data in the experiment e, an online user satisfaction metric σ is calculated for A ($\sigma_A(e)$) and B ($\sigma_B(e)$). If the collected data suggests that the alternative B demonstrates statistically significant improvement in the selected user metric (i.e. $\sigma_B(e) >_{st.s} \sigma_A(e) \Rightarrow B \succ A$) then the experiment is considered as successful. We use the clickthrough rate online metric, which indicates the ratio of the clicked result pages in the query stream. The inverse of the clickthrough rate, the abandonment rate is frequently used in the literature, e.g. [1, 2, 19]. Our approach does not rely on the specific properties of the metric used, so it can be applied with any of the existing online metrics.

Interleaving In an interleaving experiment, result pages are generated by interleaving (mixing) results from both alternatives. Next, the user's click feedback is interpreted in order to derive which of the tested algorithms provides the users with a better results ranking.

While the scheduling approaches discussed in this paper can be applied to any of the existing interleaving methods [5, 8, 17, 18], in our evaluation study we use a dataset of Team Draft-based [17] interleaving experiments. The Team Draft modification we use leverages the *deduped binary* click aggregation scheme [1], which proved to be sensitive, i.e. allowing a faster convergence rate. In a user interaction, alternative A (B) is assigned with credit equal to the total number of clicks its results received in the interaction. If the top k results in A and B are identical, then the clicks on these results are ignored. After that, in each user interaction the alternative that has more credit is defined as a winner. If both alternatives have equal credits, the result of the comparison in this interaction is a tie. In an experiment e we denote the number of user interactions with ties as $ties(A, B)$, the number of interactions won by A (B) as $wins(A)$ ($wins(B)$). The outcome of the experiment e is the following quantity [1]:

$$s(e) = \frac{wins(B) + \frac{1}{2}ties(A, B)}{wins(A) + wins(B) + ties(A, B)} - \frac{1}{2} \quad (1)$$

If $s(e)$ is significantly above zero, then it is concluded that B outperforms A ($B \succ A$) and the experiment e is successful.

3.2 Experimentation pipeline

In this paper, we work under a particular case of the experimentation pipeline. We specify this model by describing three assumptions, as discussed below:

A1 *The upper bound of the user interactions available for each experiment (the experiment's budget) is pre-defined and equal to T.*

In practice, usually the part of the query stream used for a single experiment is fixed and set to several percent [12]. At the same time, the size of the query traffic of a search engine is influenced by various factors, including the time of the day, the day of the week, and the season of the year. However, we assume that the experiments are deployed long enough that the per-day variations of traffic are averaged out, while the seasonal variations are smooth enough not to influence the size of the traffic while experiments are performed. This can be achieved by fixing the duration of the experiments to be of a size of a week or two [12]. This assumption allows us to simplify the schedule planning and evaluation steps.

A2 *Once an experiment is started, it is never interrupted.*

After an experiment is started it is never stopped (such an interruption is referred to as preemption [13]) until one of the two outcomes is achieved: one of the alternatives (A or B) wins the comparison, or the experiment's budget n is entirely exhausted. In the case of interleaving experiments, where no *early stopping* scheme is available, we assume that the experiment is always performed until its budget is exhausted. On the other hand, in the case of A/B tests, an experiment might be stopped before using all interactions if an early stopping mechanism is used, such as the scheme proposed in Section 4.3 of [12].

Notably, a currently running experiment is never stopped, even if a new experiment comes to the queue and it turns out to be more promising. Although this restriction can result in a sub-optimal use of the user interactions, this assumption ensures some desired properties of the experiments. First, it is generally accepted to deploy online experiments for an integer number of weeks of continuous time, so that every week day is represented in the experimental data [12]. Thus the situation where a 7 day experiment is started on Monday, stopped on Tuesday, and continued next Monday is not desirable as not each day of the week is covered. Moreover, interrupting an A/B experiment with another experiment might result in increased variance in the observations (due to the carry-over effect [11]), and thus reduce the sensitivity of the experiments. At the same time, most of the changes at search engines are relatively small and hence are difficult to detect immediately. As a result, the metrics used in A/B tests should be measured for a relatively long and continuous period of time. Finally, this assumption makes the whole pipeline predictable and understandable, which is an important property of a production-level system.

As new experiments continually arrive in the queue, it is possible that an old experiment will not be executed for a long time, i.e. it *starves*. The question arises as how to handle this case: should we prioritise old experiments over new ones? In this paper, we work with the following assumption:

A3 *It is acceptable for some experiments to starve. The experiments should "compete equally" no matter how long ago they arrived in the queue.*

This assumption simplifies modelling the queue and makes the scheduling algorithm easy to understand and predict. To alleviate the consequences of infinite starving in a real-life production setting, the scheduling algorithm can be accompanied by a manually handled queue. Experiments that are essential to be deployed despite the predictions of the scheduler can be deployed in this manual queue, if necessary.

The task of the scheduler we study is to sort the queue of the experiments, so that the number of successful experiments performed under the limited number of the user interactions is maximised. When studying this task, the exact implementation of the experimentation pipeline does not play an important role. We only require A1-A3 to hold. For instance, two experiments can run parallel for two weeks, using 5% of the user interaction stream each, or the first experiment can be deployed for a week on 10% of the traffic, followed by the second experiment. From the scheduling point of view, we do not differentiate between these two cases.

4. OPTIMISING THE SCHEDULE

In this section, we firstly formulate the problem of optimised scheduling (Section 4.1), using the assumptions discussed in Section 3.2. Since this formulation relies on feature-based machine learning, in Section 4.2 we describe the feature representation of the online experiments we use. Finally, in Section 4.3 we describe our approach to reduce the scheduling problem to a learning-to-rank problem.

4.1 Scheduling Model

The aim of the scheduler is to maximise the number of successful experiments performed. We firstly define "the probability of success" $P(e)$ for an experiment $e \in \mathbb{E}$. This probability is equal to the frequency of the experiment's success (B winning A), if it was repeatedly deployed. Given a fixed schedule S, the expected number of successful experiments is equal to

$$O = \sum_{i=1}^{|\mathbb{E}|} P(S(i)) \mathbb{I}\left[\sum_{j=1}^{i} n_{S(j)} \leq T\right] \quad (2)$$

where T is the number of user interactions available for the experimentation, $n_{S(j)}$ is the number of interactions used for the jth experiment in the schedule ($S(j)$), and $\mathbb{I}(\cdot)$ is the indicator function. To optimise the number of successful experiments, we use a greedy, shortest job first-like, scheduling

Input: Set of sessions Q
Output: The click model parameters for each document u: a_u, s_u

$a_u^N \leftarrow 0$; $a_u^D \leftarrow 0$
$s_u^N \leftarrow 0$; $s_u^D \leftarrow 0$
Init beta priors: $\alpha_a = 1, \alpha_s = 1, \beta_a = 1, \beta_s = 1$
foreach *session* $s \in Q$ **do**
  foreach *result* u *above or on the last clicked position* **do**
    $a_u^D \leftarrow a_u^D + 1$
  end
  foreach *clicked result* u **do**
    $a_u^N \leftarrow a_u^N + 1 \quad s_u^D \leftarrow s_u^D + 1$
  end
  $u \leftarrow$ last clicked document in s
  $s_u^N \leftarrow s_u^N + 1$
end
foreach u **do**
  $a_u \leftarrow \frac{a_u^N + \alpha_a}{a_u^D + \alpha_a + \beta_a} \quad s_u \leftarrow \frac{s_u^N + \alpha_s}{s_u^D + \alpha_s + \beta_s}$
end

Algorithm 1: Training the sDBN model, as described by Chapelle et al. [3].

algorithm. This algorithm prioritises the interleaving experiments such that the experiments that are ranked higher are expected to be likely more successful. Overall, the greedy scheduling algorithm can be organised as follows. Suppose, a set of the experiments $\mathbb{E}_0$ is available in the queue, currently ordered according to schedule $S_0 = \{e_{S_0(1)}, ..., e_{S_0(|\mathbb{E}_0|)}\}$. Importantly, the queue is ordered so that if an experiment e_i is ranked earlier in the schedule than another e_j, then this necessarily implies that the first experiment e_i has a higher probability of being successful. Denoting the position of the experiment e in the queue S as $S^{-1}(e)$, this requirement can be formalised as follows:

$$S_0^{-1}(e_i) < S_0^{-1}(e_j) \Rightarrow P(e_i) \geq P(e_j) \quad (3)$$

In the next step, a set of new experiments $\mathbb{E}_{new}$ arrives in the queue: $\mathbb{E}_1 = \mathbb{E}_0 \bigcup \mathbb{E}_{new}$. After that, for each new experiment e, the estimate of its probability of success $P(e)$ is calculated. A new schedule S_1 is obtained by sorting the full set of experiments $\mathbb{E}_1$ so that Equation (3) holds. Once a currently running experiment finishes, the firstly scheduled algorithm ($S(1)$, with the highest value of $P(e)$) is deployed.

Under the assumptions A1-A3 this algorithm is optimal[1]:

FACT 1. *Assume the probability of success $P(e)$ is available for each experiment $e \in \mathbb{E}$. Then the greedy scheduling algorithm is optimal, i.e. it maximises Equation* (2).

To run this greedy algorithm, a procedure to estimate the probability of an experiment's success is required. To build such an algorithm, we propose to use a learning-to-rank approach. Further, we discuss the feature representation used in our work (Section 4.2) and the machine learning algorithms (Section 4.3).

4.2 Features

We divide our features into three groups: effectiveness-based features, click model-based features, and the online exploration features. All of these features characterise a particular pair of compared systems A and B. For this reason, most of the features (except for one, interleaving-specific, feature) can be used for scheduling A/B tests and interleaving experiments.

Effectiveness-based group (12 features) The commonly accepted way to evaluate the difference between two ranking algorithms is to assess their quality within the offline evaluation paradigm. Under this paradigm, a set of previously labelled queries are submitted to both alternatives. After retrieving the search result lists (SERPs), they are intersected with the available document labels. Finally, the quality of the ranking is represented by one of the offline metrics, such as Precision@N, ERR@N [2], DCG@N [6].

To get a fine-grained representation of the experiments, we vary the cut-off depth and the way the unlabelled documents are treated while calculating these metrics. We calculate the average values of the metrics for both alternatives, while considering non-labelled documents as irrelevant. Next, we calculate the averages of the same metrics only for queries where both alternatives (A and B) have all top-N documents labelled. This procedure was applied to Precision@1, Precision@3, ERR@3, DCG@3, ERR@5, and DCG@5 metrics. To get a feature representation for an experiment e from the averages of the metrics, we calculate the differences between the averaged values over the queries of the metrics for both alternatives tested in the experiment (e.g. the difference between the averaged values of Precision@1 of alternatives A and B is a feature). Thus each experiment is associated with (Precision@1, Precision@3, ERR@3, DCG@3, ERR@5, DCG@5) × (unlabelled documents are treated as irrelevant, or the corresponding pairs of SERPs are ignored) $= 6 \times 2 = 12$ effectiveness-based features.

Click model-based group (3 features) The relevance judges can misinterpret queries and misunderstand the user's intentions. A possible way to address this is to use implicit feedback from the real users. In this work, we use pre-trained user click models to predict how users will behave once they are presented with a result page from A or B. Specifically, we train a Simplified Dynamic Bayesian Network (sDBN) [3] click model using a separate part of the dataset. Under the sDBN click model, for a fixed query, each document u has two parameters defined: the probability of the user clicking on the document if it was examined (attractiveness) a_u, and the probability that the document will satisfy the user, if it was clicked, s_u. These parameters are calculated by Algorithm 1, proposed by Chapelle et al. [3].

After that, we use this pre-trained click model to calculate the following features. First, we calculate the difference in the probabilities of the user satisfaction (as defined by the sDBN model) by the result pages of A and B (Algorithm 2). We calculate the value of this difference for two cut-off levels, considering three and five top-ranked results from both alternatives. We use only the top-ranked results, as they are likely to have sufficient click data in the logs. Second, we calculate the expected difference in the number of clicks for alternatives A and B in the interleaving experiment (Algorithm 3). The latter feature is used only for the scheduling of the interleaving experiments, as it is designed to simulate an interleaving experiment. We use a cut-off level of five.

In Algorithms 2 & 3 we use the following notation. The set of interleaved result lists generated for the query is denoted as $\mathbb{L}$, and the probability of showing the interleaved result list L_i to the users is f_i.

Online exploration group (1 feature) A completely different approach to gain useful information about an experiment e is to perform a preliminary deployment for a short period of time. After this, we calculate a feature representing

[1]Due to space constraints, the proof is omitted here.

Input: Parameters of the click model, a_u, s_u; the result page R, the cut-off level k
Output: The probability of the user's satisfaction with R, P_{sat}

```
//P_dsat is the probability of the user's dissatisfaction
P_dsat ← 1
for r ← 1 to min(k, |R|) do
    // u is the document on the rth position
    u ← R(r)
    //update the probability of dissatisfaction
    P_dsat ← P_dsat · (1 − a_u s_u)
end
P_sat ← 1 − P_dsat
```

Algorithm 2: Calculating the probability of the user's satisfaction with the result page R.

Table 1: Descriptive statistics of the datasets.

Dataset	#Exp	B wins A	Impressions: Min	Median	Mean	Max	Total
Interleaving	82	31	178K	1M	2M	39M	174M
A/B tests	35	10	1.4M	42M	54M	196M	1899M

Input: Parameters of the click model, a_u, s_u; the set of interleaved result lists, $\mathbb{L}$, the cut-off level k.
Output: The expected difference D in the number of clicks obtained by alternatives A and B.

```
//P_e(r) denotes the probability of examining the rth position
P_e(1) ← 1
foreach L_i ∈ 𝕃 do
    for r ← 1 to min(k, |L_i|) do
        // u is the document on the rth position
        u ← L_i(r)
        //update the expected difference
        D ← D + f_i P_e(r) a_u (𝕀[r from A] − 𝕀[r from B])
        //probability of examining the next document
        P_e(r + 1) ← P_e(r) (1 − a_u s_u)
    end
end
```

Algorithm 3: Calculating the expected difference in clicks obtained by A and B in an interleaving comparison.

the outcome of this preliminary experiment (Equation (1) for interleaving, and $\sigma_B(e) - \sigma_A(e)$ for A/B tests). To calculate this feature in our model, we sample a pre-defined number of user interactions from the experiment data. As the number of interactions sampled can greatly influence the prediction quality (i.e. if we sample sufficiently enough interactions while doing exploration we might not need the experiment itself), in our empirical study we vary this number to gain additional insights into the relative usefulness of this feature. This exploration step is akin to the exploration step in the muti-armed bandit setup [21]. Indeed, given a set of experiments ("arms"), we need to identify which of them is more likely to be successful. However, the pipeline requirements we work under do not permit the use of the existing bandit algorithms, as A2 assumes that a deployed experiment cannot be interrupted.

Feature aggregation After calculating the effectiveness-based and click model-based features, we additionally aggregate them by averaging over four groups according to the query length measured by the number of space-separated terms: (1) all queries, (2) queries of length of 1, (3) queries of length of 2, (4) queries of length of 3 and longer. The exploration feature is not included in this aggregation step. Our intuition behind this feature aggregation step is that it allows the machine-learned algorithms to detect cohorts of queries where the main change in the experiment occurs. For instance, if major relevance changes are observed in the group of long queries, which are likely to be rare, the click model-based features can be less useful. As a result of this aggregation, each interleaving experiment $e \in \mathbb{E}$ is represented as a point in a space of $(12+3)\cdot 4+1 = 61$ features. Similarly, each A/B test is represented as a point in a feature space with $(12+2)\cdot 4+1 = 57$ dimensions.

Different sets of features might be useful in different scenarios. For instance, in some interleaving experiments, such as those that test changes in the personalisation algorithms, the personalised relevance labels might be unavailable. In contrast, the exploration-based feature can be valuable in this case. On the other hand, the click model-based features can be less useful for the experiments where only the ranking of the long-tail queries is affected. We argue that combining all these groups of features can improve the performance.

4.3 Learning Framework

To apply a greedy scheduling algorithm, we need to estimate the experiments' probability of success. We consider this problem as a ranking problem, and further discuss pointwise and pairwise learning-to-rank approaches to it.

Pointwise A simple approach to predict the experiment's probability of being successful is to train a classifier that discriminates successful experiments from others. We associate experiments with one of the two classes $\{0,1\}$: $y(e) = \mathbb{I}[B \succ A]$. Informally, the experiments for which B statistically significantly outperforms A are considered as instances of the positive class 1. All other experiments, including those where no statistically significant difference between A and B was found, belong to the negative class 0. In the second step, we train a machine learning algorithm to predict the class of the considered experiment. We use two popular methods to build such a binary classifier. First, we use logistic regression with L1 regularisation [16]. The regularisation parameter is tuned by a ten-fold cross-validation on the training set. Second, we use the gradient boosted trees algorithm provided in the GBM package for R [20]. The parameters (e.g. number of trees) are tuned throught cross-validation.

Pairwise In the pointwise approach all positive examples are treated equally. However, in some of the experiments, the difference between the alternatives is bigger. With everything else being equal, it is better to deploy such experiments earlier, as the corresponding search engine's improvement is larger. This idea is naturally represented by the pairwise learning-to-rank paradigm. We firstly define a set $\mathbb{P}$ of pairs of experiments $(e_i, e_j) \in \mathbb{E} \times \mathbb{E}$ such that the outcome of the first experiment in the pair is higher than that of the outcome of the second. $\mathbb{P}$ formulated as follows:

$$\mathbb{P} = \{(e_i, e_j) : \sigma(e_i) > \sigma(e_j), e_i, e_j \in \mathbb{E}\}$$

where $\sigma(e) = s(e)$ for the interleaving experiments, and $\sigma(e) = \sigma_B(e) - \sigma_A(e)$ in the case of A/B tests.

We use the GBM [20] package for R to find the function $f(r_e)$ that minimises the number of misordered pairs. As an alternative pairwise ranker we use RankingSVM [7].

5. DATASETS

Before discussing the experimental study in the next section, we briefly describe the datasets used in this paper.

The first dataset consists of the subset of the interleaving experiments performed by Yandex during a five week period in Spring 2014. The sample contains 82 interleaving experiments, 31 of which were successful (the alternative B outperformed A statistically significantly, $p < 0.05$). The experiments test changes in the non-personalised ranking of the search engine. The second dataset contains 35 A/B tests, performed over a period of two months in Winter/Spring 2014. In 10 A/B tests, B outperformed A by a statistically significant margin ($p \leq 0.05$). On average, the A/B tests and interleaving experiments were deployed for 10 days.

Salient statistics of the datasets are provided in Table 1. The number of interactions per experiment varies, as each experiment was selected to be deployed for time periods of different length, or for different shares of the query stream. The interleaving experiments were performed using the Team Draft interleaving method with the deduped binary scoring scheme, as described in Section 3. The parameters of the sDBN model [3] used for calculating the click model-based features (Section 4.2) are estimated using a separate query log sample from a two-week period. All experiments in the datasets were deployed after this period. All online experiments were deployed on the Russian market.

6. EVALUATION METHODOLOGY

Since our proposed scheduling algorithm relies on predicting the outcomes of the online experiments, we split our evaluation study in two steps: (1) evaluating the experiment outcome prediction, (2) evaluating the quality of the schedules obtained by our proposed scheduling algorithms. We formulate three research questions that we aim to address:

(**RQ1**) *Is it possible to predict the outcomes of the online experiments using the pre-experimental data only, so that the quality of the predictions is improved in comparison with the random order?*

(**RQ2**) *What are the best performing prediction algorithms? How do the proposed features compare to each other?*

(**RQ3**) *How do the learned approaches compare in terms of the quality of the schedules they generate?*

As we discuss in Section 6.4, the random order we compare to in **RQ1** is not an artificial baseline, instead it reflects the stochastic order of the experiments arriving to the experimentation pipeline if no scheduling is performed. In other words, we consider the performance of the randomised order to be similar to the performance of an unoptimised schedule. Notably, each of the groups of features, discussed in Section 5.2, can be considered as a simple predictor of the experiment outcome. Indeed, the experiments in the queue can be ordered according to their DCG scores, or the experiment outcome prediction, based on the click modelling, or based on the results of the exploration step. To obtain additional insights into the relative importance of the features, we additionally investigate the performance of the schedulers that sort experiments according to the separate features.

6.1 Prediction quality

Since our goal is to schedule the successful experiments with a higher priority, it is natural to measure the quality of the schedule ranking as the fraction of the correctly ordered pairs of the experiments. In an ideal ranking, successful experiments ($B \succ A$) are deployed first. Moreover, it is natural to require the successful experiments with higher difference between A and B to be scheduled earlier. This idea can be represented by the Area Under Curve (AUC) quality met-

Input: Number of user interactions available for an experiment n; the total number of available user interactions T; A set of experiments $\mathbb{E}$
Output: Estimated values of $AUC(S)$ and $Q(S)$.
$A \leftarrow 0$; $Q \leftarrow 0$
foreach $train, test \leftarrow RandomStratifiedSplit(\mathbb{E}, nSplits = 100)$ **do**
  Train the ranker: $C \leftarrow fit(train)$
  Greedily schedule the test experiments:
  $S \leftarrow predict(C, test)$
  Update the AUC estimate:
  $A \leftarrow A + AUC(S)$
  Initialise the estimate of Q for the current split:
  $Q_i \leftarrow 0$
  Calculate the bootstrapping estimate Q_i:
  while $i < N$ **do**
    The remaining experimentation budget:
    $\hat{T} \leftarrow T$
    Starting with the first experiment:
    $j \leftarrow 1$
    while $j < |S|$ *and* $\hat{T} > 0$ **do**
      Sample n sessions from experiment $S(j)$
      $data \leftarrow sample(S(j))$
      Check if the experiment is successful, based on $data$:
      if $B \succ A$ **then**
        $Q_i \leftarrow Q_i + 1$
      end
      Reduce the budget by the number of sampled sessions and proceed to the next experiment:
      $\hat{T} = \hat{T} - n$; $j \leftarrow j + 1$
    end
  end
  $Q \leftarrow Q + \frac{1}{N} Q_i$
end
Calculate averages of the metrics across the splits:
$Q(S) \leftarrow \frac{1}{nSplits} Q$, $AUC(S) \leftarrow \frac{1}{nSplits} A$

Algorithm 4: The bootstrap-based evaluation protocol.

ric of a classifier S separating successful experiments from unsuccessful ones [15].

We firstly define the set of pairs of experiments $\mathbb{R} = \{(e_{i,1}, e_{i,2})\}_i$ that are used in the evaluation. This set contains all the pairs of experiments such that at least one of the experiments has the alternative B winning the comparison with $p \leq 0.05$ and the relative scores of B are different when compared across experiments. We impose the first requirement as we are not interested in evaluating how good a particular scheduling algorithm is at ranking unsuccessful experiments. The AUC metric $AUC(S)$ of a schedule S can be calculated using the following expression:

$$AUC(S) = \frac{\sum_{e_1, e_2 \in \mathbb{R}} \mathbb{I}\left[\left(S^{-1}(e_1) - S^{-1}(e_2)\right)\left(\sigma(e_1) - \sigma(e_2)\right) < 0\right]}{|\mathbb{R}|} \tag{4}$$

where $\sigma(e) = \sigma_B(e) - \sigma_A(e)$ in the case of the A/B tests and $\sigma(e) = s(e)$ for the interleaving experiments.

6.2 Evaluating the Schedule

While the AUC measure as defined in the previous section is intuitive, it evaluates the quality of the predictions only, not the quality of the resulting schedule. However, there is a noteworthy difference. Indeed, the AUC metric reflects a scenario where there are enough resources (user impressions) to deploy all the required experiments, but an approach to deploy the promising experiments first is needed. Indeed, a scenario when one cannot deploy all the available experiments due to restricted resources is possible. In this case, AUC is less suitable, as it also measures the quality of the ranking of the experiments that cannot be deployed. Thus, we propose to measure the quality of the scheduling algorithm as the number of the successful experiments it can fit in the number of available user interactions.

Consider a schedule S, representing the order of the experiments to be run, $S = \{e_{S(1)}, e_{S(2)}..., e_{S(|\mathbb{E}|)}\}$. Ideally, the schedule should allow us to run and finish as many experiments where B wins, as possible. At the same time, we have a limited number of the user interactions that can be used in the experiments, denoted T. Thus, we are interested in minimising the following measure, similar to Equation (2):

$$Q(S) = \sum_{i=1..|S|} \left(\mathbb{I}[B(e) \succ A(e)] \cdot \mathbb{I}\left[\sum_{j=1}^{i} n(e_i) \leq T\right] \right) \quad (5)$$

$Q(S)$ measures the number of experiments with B winning the comparison ($\mathbb{I}[B(e) \succ A(e)]$), under the limited number of user interactions T, as only the experiments that are performed before T is reached ($\sum_{j=1}^{i} n(e_i) \leq T$) can contribute to $Q(S)$. Notably, the metric $Q(S)$ can be considered as a generalisation of *Precision@R*. Indeed, if the number of interactions available for each experiment $n(e_i) = n = const$ is large enough for any experiment to have a definite outcome, then $Q(S) \approx precision@R$, where $R = \frac{T}{n}$.

6.3 Statistical Methodology

To evaluate a quality of a schedule S, we perform a bootstrap estimation of the metric values $AUC(S)$ and $Q(S)$ using the datasets described in the previous section. This estimation is performed in several steps. First, we select the experiment that S schedules to run first, $S(1)$. After that, we compare the number of the interactions required to perform the experiment n to the available limit T. If the required number is less than T, we continue, and stop otherwise. From the available dataset of user interactions for the experiment $S(1)$, we perform a bootstrap sampling of the user interactions until the stopping criterion is met. After that, we proceed to the next scheduled experiment, $S(2)$. Again, we sample the user interactions until the stopping criterion is met. We proceed, until the limit T is reached, and calculate the value of $Q(S)$ according to Equation (5). We repeat this described procedure N times and, as a result, it provides us with the bootstrapped estimates of the performance of the tested scheduler.

Further, as the machine learning-based approaches require separated testing and training set, we repeat the described quality estimation algorithm with the train-test split varied. Each split is obtained by randomly selecting 10% of the experiments in the dataset as a test set, with the remaining experiments used for training. The splits are performed in a stratified manner, so that the distribution of the successful experiments is the same in training and test sets. The evaluation algorithm is formally described in Algorithm 4.

We ensure that the total number of user impressions used in the evaluation is equal for all evaluated schedulers. If a scheduler performs an exploration step, we subtract the number of sessions used for exploration from the overall experimentation budget T.

Table 2: Performance of the scheduling algorithms, measured by AUC on the dataset of interleaving experiments. The values in bold outperform other values in the same row, $p < 0.05$ (excluding *UB*).

#sample					
	Rnd	CM	DCG	ERR	UB
–	$0.51_{\pm0.03}$	**$0.77_{\pm0.02}$**	**$0.77_{\pm0.02}$**	$0.74_{\pm0.02}$	$1.0_{\pm0.0}$
	Explore	LR	SVM	LGBM	PGBM
0	–	$0.76_{\pm0.02}$	$0.72_{\pm0.03}$	**$0.83_{\pm0.01}$**	$0.81_{\pm0.02}$
$0.01 \cdot T$	$0.62_{\pm0.02}$	$0.76_{\pm0.02}$	$0.73_{\pm0.02}$	**$0.83_{\pm0.01}$**	$0.81_{\pm0.02}$
$0.02 \cdot T$	$0.70_{\pm0.02}$	$0.77_{\pm0.02}$	$0.74_{\pm0.02}$	**$0.83_{\pm0.01}$**	**$0.82_{\pm0.02}$**
$0.05 \cdot T$	$0.77_{\pm0.02}$	$0.77_{\pm0.02}$	$0.74_{\pm0.02}$	**$0.83_{\pm0.01}$**	**$0.82_{\pm0.02}$**
$0.10 \cdot T$	**$0.83_{\pm0.02}$**	$0.78_{\pm0.02}$	$0.75_{\pm0.03}$	**$0.85_{\pm0.01}$**	**$0.84_{\pm0.02}$**
$0.20 \cdot T$	**$0.88_{\pm0.03}$**	$0.79_{\pm0.02}$	$0.77_{\pm0.03}$	**$0.86_{\pm0.01}$**	**$0.86_{\pm0.02}$**

Table 3: Performance of the scheduling algorithms, measured by AUC on the dataset of A/B tests. The value in bold outperforms other values with the same exploration step size (excluding *UB*), $p < 0.05$.

#sample			#sample		
	Rnd	DCG		ERR	UB
–	$0.49_{\pm0.04}$	**$0.56_{\pm0.04}$**	–	**$0.59_{\pm0.03}$**	$1.00_{\pm0.00}$
	Explore	LR		Explore	LR
0	–	**$0.68_{\pm0.04}$**	$0.05 \cdot T$	$0.59_{\pm0.04}$	**$0.66_{\pm0.03}$**
$0.01 \cdot T$	$0.56_{\pm0.03}$	**$0.67_{\pm0.04}$**	$0.10 \cdot T$	$0.64_{\pm0.04}$	$0.66_{\pm0.03}$
$0.02 \cdot T$	$0.54_{\pm0.03}$	**$0.67_{\pm0.04}$**	$0.20 \cdot T$	**$0.73_{\pm0.04}$**	$0.65_{\pm0.03}$

6.4 Baselines

Random The first baseline we consider assigns a random order to the online experiments. Since experiments arrive stochastically to the queue, we believe that the performance of this baseline is a good indicator of the average performance of the un-prioritised schedule that never re-arranges the incoming experiments. In other words, this baseline is not an artificial one, but instead it reflects the performance of the real-world schedules. As this paper is the first to address the problem of the online experiment scheduling optimisation, more elaborate baselines do not exist.

UpperBound The *UpperBound* scheduler provides us with an upper bound on the possible scheduler performance. In case of the interleaving experiments, *UpperBound* sorts the experiments in the queue according to the values $s(e)$ of the experiment's outcome (Equation (1)). For the A/B tests data, *UpperBound* sorts the experiments according to the obtained value of $\sigma_B(e) - \sigma_A(e)$. This baseline uses the data produced by the experiment, which is unavailable before the experiment was performed.

7. RESULTS AND DISCUSSION

We use the following notation in this section. The *UpperBound*, and *Random* baseline schedulers are denoted as *UB* and *Rnd*, respectively. The schedulers based on the pointwise predictors, logistic regression and GBM, are referred to as *LR*, and *LGBM*, respectively. The schedulers based on pairwise RankingSVM and GBM, are denoted as *SVM* and *PGBM*, respectively. Finally, the schedulers based on the single DCG@3, ERR@3, and Explore features are referred to as *DCG*, *ERR*, and *Explore*. When calculating the effectiveness metrics used in the effectiveness-based schedulers *DCG* and *ERR*, we consider unlabelled results as non-relevant.

CM denotes the scheduler that ranks experiments according to the click model-based feature, which calculates the expected difference in the number of clicks A and B will obtain in the interleaving experiment. We include it as it

Table 4: The quality of the scheduling algorithms measured by $Q(S)$ on the dataset of the interleaving experiments. The values in bold outperform other in the same scenario (T, #sample), $p < 0.05$ (except for *UB*).

#sample	$T = 3 \cdot 10^5$					$T = 4.5 \cdot 10^5$				
	Rnd	*CM*	*DCG*	*ERR*	*UB*	*Rnd*	*CM*	*DCG*	*ERR*	*UB*
–	$0.60_{\pm 0.05}$	$\mathbf{1.99}_{\pm 0.12}$	$1.04_{\pm 0.13}$	$1.20_{\pm 0.12}$	$2.42_{\pm 0.11}$	$0.58_{\pm 0.06}$	$\mathbf{2.20}_{\pm 0.14}$	$1.37_{\pm 0.11}$	$1.42_{\pm 0.13}$	$2.70_{\pm 0.11}$
	Explore	*LR*	*SVM*	*LGBM*	*PGBM*	*Explore*	*LR*	*SVM*	*LGBM*	*PGBM*
0	–	$1.14_{\pm 0.14}$	$1.45_{\pm 0.14}$	$1.93_{\pm 0.10}$	$\mathbf{2.17}_{\pm 0.08}$	–	$1.39_{\pm 0.16}$	$1.71_{\pm 0.14}$	$2.28_{\pm 0.14}$	$\mathbf{2.56}_{\pm 0.12}$
$0.01 \cdot T$	$0.78_{\pm 0.07}$	$1.14_{\pm 0.13}$	$1.44_{\pm 0.15}$	$1.87_{\pm 0.11}$	$\mathbf{2.18}_{\pm 0.08}$	$0.85_{\pm 0.07}$	$1.37_{\pm 0.13}$	$1.73_{\pm 0.13}$	$2.35_{\pm 0.11}$	$\mathbf{2.54}_{\pm 0.11}$
$0.02 \cdot T$	$0.89_{\pm 0.12}$	$1.13_{\pm 0.10}$	$1.44_{\pm 0.14}$	$1.90_{\pm 0.10}$	$\mathbf{2.13}_{\pm 0.08}$	$1.00_{\pm 0.08}$	$1.39_{\pm 0.13}$	$1.69_{\pm 0.11}$	$2.32_{\pm 0.14}$	$\mathbf{2.54}_{\pm 0.14}$
$0.05 \cdot T$	$1.06_{\pm 0.08}$	$1.12_{\pm 0.10}$	$1.34_{\pm 0.13}$	$1.91_{\pm 0.11}$	$\mathbf{2.10}_{\pm 0.08}$	$1.26_{\pm 0.10}$	$1.44_{\pm 0.14}$	$1.69_{\pm 0.11}$	$2.30_{\pm 0.11}$	$\mathbf{2.50}_{\pm 0.11}$
$0.10 \cdot T$	$1.18_{\pm 0.09}$	$1.04_{\pm 0.10}$	$1.35_{\pm 0.13}$	$1.81_{\pm 0.11}$	$\mathbf{2.02}_{\pm 0.09}$	$1.45_{\pm 0.11}$	$1.36_{\pm 0.14}$	$1.87_{\pm 0.12}$	$2.30_{\pm 0.11}$	$\mathbf{2.50}_{\pm 0.14}$
$0.20 \cdot T$	$1.31_{\pm 0.10}$	$0.94_{\pm 0.11}$	$1.20_{\pm 0.11}$	$1.57_{\pm 0.09}$	$\mathbf{1.83}_{\pm 0.08}$	$1.68_{\pm 0.13}$	$1.26_{\pm 0.08}$	$1.71_{\pm 0.10}$	$2.19_{\pm 0.14}$	$\mathbf{2.46}_{\pm 0.12}$

Table 5: The quality of the scheduling algorithms measured by $Q(S)$ on the dataset of A/B tests. The values in bold outperform other with the same exploration step size (except for *UB*), $p < 0.05$.

#sample			#sample		
	Rnd	UB		DCG	ERR
–	$0.42_{\pm 0.03}$	$0.92_{\pm 0.06}$	–	$0.54_{\pm 0.03}$	$\mathbf{0.61}_{\pm 0.03}$
	Explore	LR		Explore	LR
0	–	$\mathbf{0.60}_{\pm 0.04}$	$0.05 \cdot T$	$0.52_{\pm 0.03}$	$\mathbf{0.57}_{\pm 0.04}$
$0.01 \cdot T$	$0.46_{\pm 0.03}$	$\mathbf{0.59}_{\pm 0.04}$	$0.10 \cdot T$	$0.56_{\pm 0.04}$	$0.56_{\pm 0.04}$
$0.02 \cdot T$	$0.48_{\pm 0.03}$	$\mathbf{0.57}_{\pm 0.06}$	$0.20 \cdot T$	$\mathbf{0.61}_{\pm 0.04}$	$0.57_{\pm 0.04}$

resembles the interleaving experiment outcome prediction feature used in [9] and thus it is interesting to compare to it. However, as it simulates an interleaving comparison, we do not include it as a scheduler for the A/B test evaluation.

As the A/B tests dataset is smaller than the interleaving dataset, and it has considerably fewer successful experiments and thus less training data (Section 5), we found that the use of more elaborated pairwise and GBRT-based techniques did not result in any improvements over a basic logistic regression-based scheduler *LR*. For this reason, in the experiments based on the A/B tests, we report only *LR*.

We use the Wilcoxon test to compare the performance of the schedulers (excluding *UpperBound*). The reported confidence intervals correspond to 95% confidence.

7.1 Prediction Quality

In Tables 2 and 3, we report the results of our evaluation of the quality of the experiment outcome prediction algorithms, measured on the datasets of the interleaving and A/B test experiments, respectively. The quality is measured by AUC, and the measurement is performed by Algorithm 4. The values in bold statistically significantly outperform other values in the same row/exploration step size ($p < 0.05$). We set the number of user interactions T available for running all experiments such that each experiment in the test parts of the datasets is deployed for 10^5 and $2 \cdot 10^6$ interactions for the interleaving experiments and A/B tests, respectively (A/B tests require more user interactions [1] due to lower sensitivity). The number of user interactions used in the exploration step is varied, we report it in the corresponding cells (#sample). We measure the size of exploration step as a fraction of the total number of available impressions T. For instance, if #sample $= 0.05 \cdot T$, then a scheduler uses $0.05 \cdot T$ interactions for exploration. These interactions are uniformly divided among the test experiments. For fairness, we ensure that the same number of impressions is used for each schedule evaluation step, whether the evaluated scheduler uses exploration or not.

From the top parts of Tables 2 & 3, we firstly notice that the baselines demonstrate their expected behaviour. Indeed, the *UB* scheduler achieves the highest performance possible (1.0), and *Rnd* has an AUC close to 0.5, indicating that under a random permutation, the probability of the correct ordering of the pair of experiments is equal to the probability of the inverse ordering. Next, we notice that the effectiveness-based experiment outcome predictors, *ERR* and *DCG*, as well as the click model-based *CM* perform better than the randomised baseline. However, the AUC scores of *DCG*, *ERR*, and *CM* schedulers (e.g. 0.77, 0.74, and 0.77, respectively, Table 2) are far from 1. This implies that there is a considerable room for improvement. Indeed, on examination of the performance of the machine-learned schedulers that do not perform exploration (bottom parts of Tables 2 & 3, #sample = 0), we observe that these schedulers (e.g. *LR* 0.76, *LGBM* 0.83, and *PGBM* 0.81 for the interleaving dataset; *LR* 0.68 for the A/B tests dataset) can achieve a performance higher than that of the *Random* scheduler and of the schedulers based on individual non-exploratory features (*DCG*, *ERR*, and *CM*). On the interleaving experiments dataset (Table 2), the AUC score of the *LGBM* scheduler is 8% better than that of the best of the schedulers that are based on a single feature (*DCG*, 0.83 vs. 0.77, $p < 0.01$), and considerably better than that of the *Random* scheduler (0.83 vs. 0.51, $p < 0.01$). Similarly, on the A/B tests dataset (Table 2), the machine-learned scheduler *LR* outperforms the best effectiveness-based scheduler *ERR* (0.68 vs. 0.59, 15% improvement, $p < 0.01$), and the *Random* scheduler (0.68 vs. 0.49, 63% improvement, $p < 0.01$).

These observations allows us to answer **RQ1**: it is possible to outperform the random scheduler in the task of predicting the experiment outcome by combining different features in the machine learned schedulers, such as *LGBM* and *LR*.

As the number of the user interactions available for exploration grows, the performance of the exploration-based scheduler *Explore* too: on the interleaving experiments dataset, its AUC score starts from 0.62 when $0.01 \cdot T$ interactions are used, and increases up to 0.88 when $0.20 \cdot T$ interactions are used. A similar behaviour is observed on the A/B tests dataset: the AUC score grows from 0.56 to 0.73.

Interestingly, the machine-learned schedulers demonstrate a comparable performance when little or no exploration is used. Indeed, on the interleaving experiments dataset, *LGBM* achieves an AUC of 0.83 when exploration is not used, which is comparable to the score of *Explore* using $0.10 \cdot T$ interactions for exploration (Table 2, 0.83). Similarly, on the A/B tests dataset, Table 3, *LR* with no exploration obtained an AUC of 0.68, close to the AUC score of *Explore* with $0.1 \cdot T$ interactions used for exploration. This indicates that the use of the machine-learned algorithms can considerably reduce the number of user interactions used in the exploration step.

On comparing the machine-learned schedulers on the interleaving dataset, we note that more advanced *LGBM* & *PGBM* schedulers achieve higher scores than *LR* and *SVM*. This relation holds for all sizes of the exploration step (#sample) we consider.

These observations allow us to answer **RQ2**. On the interleaving experiment dataset, *LGBM* outperforms other schedulers, and it improves over the best effectiveness-based scheduler *DCG* by a margin of 8%. On the A/B tests dataset, among the non-exploratory schedulers, *LR* demonstrates the highest performance with 15% improvement over the best effectiveness-based *ERR* scheduler. When all schedulers are considered on the dataset of A/B tests, *Explore* (#sample = $0.2 \cdot T$) achieves the highest performance.

7.2 Evaluating the Schedule

In Table 4, we report our results obtained when evaluating the quality $Q(S)$ of the scheduling algorithms on the interleaving experiments dataset. To get additional insights into the performance of the scheduling algorithms, we vary the total number of user interactions available for the experimentation T, $T \in \{3 \cdot 10^5, 4.5 \cdot 10^5\}$. In both cases, after the scheduler ranks the experiments in the test set, we deploy the three[2] experiments ranked first for evaluation. The user interactions left after performing the exploration step are split for these three experiments uniformly, e.g. the non-exploratory schedulers, such as *ERR*, run these three most promising experiments for 10^5 and $1.5 \cdot 10^5$ interactions. The interactions used for exploration are distributed among the test experiments uniformly.

First, we note that the performance of the *Random* scheduler is considerably lower than the upper bound (e.g. 0.60 vs. 2.42, $T = 3 \cdot 10^5$). This indicates that the quality of a random, un-scheduled queue can be markedly improved. Next, we observe that the effectiveness-based schedulers, *DCG* and *ERR*, outperform the random baseline by a considerable margin (e.g. *ERR* 1.42 vs. 0.58, 144% improvement, $p < 0.01$, $T = 4.5 \cdot 10^5$). Consequently, one can get an improved scheduling quality even by simply sorting the queue of the experiments by the effectiveness scores obtained in the offline evaluation. *DCG* performs slightly worse than *ERR* (e.g. 1.37 vs. 1.42, $T = 4.5 \cdot 10^5$). Interestingly, *CM* demonstrates the highest performance among the schedulers that do not use exploration and machine learning, and outperforms *ERR* by a considerable margin (e.g. 1.99 vs. 1.20, $T = 3 \cdot 10^5$). Notably, by performing a short exploration step where only $0.01 \cdot T$ interactions are used, up to 47% improvement might be obtained in comparison with the un-scheduled (*Random*) baseline (*Explore* 0.85 vs. *Rnd* 0.58, $T = 4.5 \cdot 10^5, p < 0.01$). This can be extremely useful in the cases where no relevance judgements are available, such as for the evaluation of the personalised ranking algorithms.

[2]We believe this is a reasonable choice, as in each cross validation split the test set contains less than 10 experiments.

The effectiveness-based schedulers are markedly outperformed by the machine-learned scheduling algorithms. The best-performing algorithm, *PGBM*, outperforms the best effectiveness-based scheduler *ERR*, by 81% (2.17 vs. 1.20, $T = 3 \cdot 10^5$, no exploration) and 80% (2.56 vs. 1.42, $T = 4.5 \cdot 10^5$, no exploration). Moreover, *PGBM* outperforms *Random* by 262% ($T = 3 \cdot 10^5$) and 342% ($T = 4.5 \cdot 10^5$).

The quality of the schedule generated by the *Explore* scheduler grows as the number of the user interactions used for exploration grows (0.78, 0.89, 1.06, 1.18, 1.31) for the exploration sample sizes of $T \cdot \{0.01, 0.02, 0.05, 0.10, 0.20\}$, left part of Table 4). The score of 1.31 corresponds to an improvement of 144% with respect to *Rnd*. However, when the machine-learned schedulers are considered (e.g., *PGBM*) the increased exploration actually harms the performance of the scheduler, as interactions are spent on exploration, instead of being spent on running the experiments. The same effect is observed on the right part of Table 4.

On comparing the results with T varied (left and right parts of Table 4, T is the total number of user interactions available for experimentation) we notice that as T increases, the values of the $Q(S)$ metric increase for all tested schedulers. In particular, the upper bound of the scheduling performance grows from 2.42 to 2.70. This result is intuitive: as we fixed the number of experiments we are attempting to deploy, more user interactions are available for running an experiment, and thus the number of experiments where no statistically significant difference between A and B is detected, is reduced. Some of the experiments "become" successful, and the metric values grow.

In Table 5 we report the $Q(S)$ metric, measured on the dataset of A/B tests. We set the number of interactions available for the experimentation pipeline T to be equal to $4 \cdot 10^6$, and deploy the two first ranked experiments. Similarly to the study performed on the interleaving dataset, we observe that the "natural" stochastic scheduler *Rnd* has a performance considerably lower than the upper bound *UB* (0.42 vs. 0.92). This indicates a possibility of improvement. Indeed, the effectiveness-based schedulers such as *DCG* and *ERR* outperform *Rnd* (e.g., *Rnd* 0.42 vs. *ERR* 0.61). On this dataset, *Explore* with #sample = $0.20 \cdot T$, *ERR*, and *LR* demonstrate similar performance, and outperform *Random* by 43%. A possible explanation for *LR* performing close to the individual features is the small size of the dataset.

To obtain an additional insight into the behaviour of the schedulers, we vary the overall number of user interactions available to the experimentation pipeline (T) in a pre-defined set $T = m \cdot 10^5, m \in \{1, ..., 6\}$, and measure the quality $Q(S)$ of the resulting schedules. At each step, we try to deploy m experiments scheduled first for evaluation. We run this study only on the interleaving dataset, as it has more experiments. We report the results in Figure 1. From Figure 1 we observe that in all situations *Rnd* is dominated by other schedulers, including the effectiveness-based scheduler *ERR*. *Explore* with #sample = $0.10 \cdot T$ demonstrates a performance similar to *ERR*. Interestingly, *CM* outperforms both *ERR* and *Explore* by a considerable margin, and is close to *PGBM* that uses exploration. In each situation *PGBM* with no exploration demonstrates the best performance.

We now can answer **RQ3**. On the interleaving experiments dataset, the machine-learned schedulers demonstrate the best performance: *LGBM* outperforms the random baseline by 342% maximum, and the closest effectiveness-based scheduler, *ERR*, by up to 81%. In turn, by using the *ERR*

Figure 1: Quality $Q(S)$ of the best schedulers as the number of the user sessions available grows, measured on the interleaving dataset. *PGBM 0.0* and *PGBM 0.10* are almost indistinguishable.

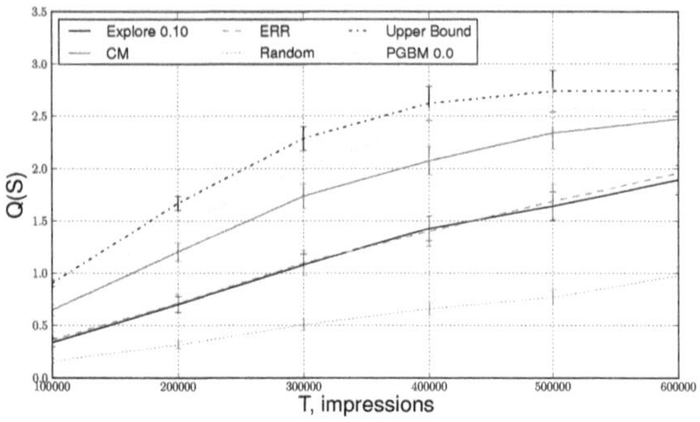

scheduler, an improvement of 144% over the un-scheduled queue can be obtained. Finally, by performing an exploration step using $0.20 \cdot T$ user interactions, *Explore* improves over the baseline by up to 190% on the interleaving dataset. When the A/B tests dataset is considered, an improvement over the baseline of 45% can be achieved by using the non-exploratory *LR*. A similar improvement can be obtained by using *Explore* that samples $0.20 \cdot T$ interactions.

Our evaluation study allowed us to answer all of the stated research questions. Our obtained results suggest that the random ("natural") order of the experiment schedule can be improved by the greedy scheduling algorithm, both for interleaving and A/B tests. A considerable improvement can be achieved when the greedy scheduling algorithm uses effectiveness measurements (*ERR* and *DCG*), or the pre-experimental click data (*CM*). A further improvement is observed on the interleaving dataset when the greedy scheduling algorithm was used with the predictions from *PGBM*. Finally, *Explore* demonstrated a good performance, which can be important for a practical application, as it does not require document labels and pre-experimental click data.

8. CONCLUSIONS

In this paper, we stated the problem of the optimal scheduling of the online experiments. We described an experimentation pipeline model and formulated the optimal scheduling problem. Next, we introduced a greedy scheduling algorithm that ranks experiments according to their predicted probability of success. This algorithm allowed us to reduce the scheduling problem to a learning-to-rank problem. We studied pointwise and pairwise formulations of this learning-to-rank problem. To obtain a feature representation of the experiments, we considered relevance-based, click model-based, and exploration features. Finally, we performed a thorough evaluation study, examining how our proposed approaches compare to each other and to the baselines in terms of the prediction quality and the quality of the resulting schedules. We used two datasets that contain interleaving and A/B test experiments.

Our findings suggest that our proposed machine-learned schedule optimisation algorithms outperform the randomised, "natural" schedule by up to 342% when the number of the successful experiments performed under a limited number of available user interactions is measured on the dataset of the interleaving experiments. We also showed that a simple scheduler that ranks experiments according to their ranking effectiveness can achieve a smaller, but still a considerable improvement over the "natural" random baseline (up to 144% on the interleaving dataset, and up to 43% on A/B tests). Our study also suggests that an exploration-based scheduler can achieve a considerable improvement over an unoptimised schedule (43% improvement on the A/B tests dataset, 118% on the dataset of interleaving experiments). Notably, this can by applied for experiments where neither relevance judgements, nor historical click data is available.

An interesting direction for future work is to develop a two-stage scheduler, which uses offline-available features to pre-select experiments for exploration.

9. REFERENCES

[1] O. Chapelle, T. Joachims, F. Radlinski, and Y. Yue. Large-scale validation and analysis of interleaved search evaluation. *ACM TOIS*, 30(1):6, 2012.

[2] O. Chapelle, D. Metlzer, Y. Zhang, and P. Grinspan. Expected reciprocal rank for graded relevance. In *CIKM 2009*.

[3] O. Chapelle and Y. Zhang. A dynamic bayesian network click model for web search ranking. In *WWW 2009*.

[4] K. Hofmann, S. Whiteson, and M. de Rijke. Estimating interleaved comparison outcomes from historical click data. In *CIKM 2012*.

[5] K. Hofmann, S. Whiteson, and M. de Rijke. A probabilistic method for inferring preferences from clicks. In *CIKM 2011*.

[6] K. Järvelin and J. Kekäläinen. Cumulated gain-based evaluation of IR techniques. *ACM Trans. Inf. Syst.*, 20(4):422–446, 2002.

[7] T. Joachims. Optimizing search engines using clickthrough data. In *KDD 2002*.

[8] T. Joachims. Evaluating retrieval performance using clickthrough data. In J. Franke, G. Nakhaeizadeh, and I. Renz, editors, *Text Mining*. Physica/Springer Verlag, 2003.

[9] E. Kharitonov, C. Macdonald, P. Serdyukov, and I. Ounis. Using historical click data to increase interleaving sensitivity. In *CIKM 2013*.

[10] R. Kohavi, T. Crook, R. Longbotham, B. Frasca, R. Henne, J. L. Ferres, and T. Melamed. Online experimentation at Microsoft. *Data Mining Case Studies*, page 11, 2009.

[11] R. Kohavi, A. Deng, B. Frasca, R. Longbotham, T. Walker, and Y. Xu. Trustworthy online controlled experiments: Five puzzling outcomes explained. In *KDD 2012*.

[12] R. Kohavi, A. Deng, B. Frasca, T. Walker, Y. Xu, and N. Pohlmann. Online controlled experiments at large scale. In *KDD 2013*.

[13] J. Y. Leung. *Handbook of scheduling: algorithms, models, and performance analysis*. CRC Press, 2004.

[14] L. Li, J. Y. Kim, and I. Zitouni. Toward predicting the outcome of an A/B experiment for search relevance. In *WSDM 2015*.

[15] C. X. Ling, J. Huang, and H. Zhang. AUC: a statistically consistent and more discriminating measure than accuracy. In *IJCAI 2003*.

[16] F. Pedregosa, G. Varoquaux, A. Gramfort, V. Michel, B. Thirion, O. Grisel, M. Blondel, P. Prettenhofer, R. Weiss, V. Dubourg, J. Vanderplas, A. Passos, D. Cournapeau, M. Brucher, M. Perrot, and E. Duchesnay. Scikit-learn: Machine learning in Python. *JMLR 2011*.

[17] F. Radlinski and N. Craswell. Comparing the sensitivity of information retrieval metrics. In *SIGIR 2010*.

[18] F. Radlinski and N. Craswell. Optimized interleaving for online retrieval evaluation. In *WSDM 2013*.

[19] F. Radlinski, M. Kurup, and T. Joachims. How does clickthrough data reflect retrieval quality? In *CIKM 2008*.

[20] G. Ridgeway. The GBM package. *R Foundation for Statistical Computing, Vienna, Austria*, 2004.

[21] R. S. Sutton and A. G. Barto. *Reinforcement Learning: An Introduction*. MIT Press, 1998.

[22] D. Tang, A. Agarwal, D. O'Brien, and M. Meyer. Overlapping experiment infrastructure: More, better, faster experimentation. In *KDD 2010*.

[23] Y. Yue, Y. Gao, O. Chapelle, Y. Zhang, and T. Joachims. Learning more powerful test statistics for click-based retrieval evaluation. In *SIGIR 2010*.

Predicting Search Satisfaction Metrics with Interleaved Comparisons

Anne Schuth*
University of Amsterdam
anne.schuth@uva.nl

Katja Hofmann
Microsoft
katja.hofmann@microsoft.com

Filip Radlinski
Microsoft
filiprad@microsoft.com

ABSTRACT

The gold standard for online retrieval evaluation is AB testing. Rooted in the idea of a controlled experiment, AB tests compare the performance of an experimental system (treatment) on one sample of the user population, to that of a baseline system (control) on another sample. Given an online evaluation metric that accurately reflects user satisfaction, these tests enjoy high validity. However, due to the high variance across users, these comparisons often have low sensitivity, requiring millions of queries to detect statistically significant differences between systems. Interleaving is an alternative online evaluation approach, where each user is presented with a combination of results from both the control and treatment systems. Compared to AB tests, interleaving has been shown to be substantially more sensitive. However, interleaving methods have so far focused on user clicks only, and lack support for more sophisticated user satisfaction metrics as used in AB testing.

In this paper we present the first method for integrating user satisfaction metrics with interleaving. We show how interleaving can be extended to (1) directly match user signals and parameters of AB metrics, and (2) how parameterized interleaving credit functions can be automatically calibrated to predict AB outcomes. We also develop a new method for estimating the relative sensitivity of interleaving and AB metrics, and show that our interleaving credit functions improve agreement with AB metrics without sacrificing sensitivity. Our results, using 38 large-scale online experiments encompassing over 3 billion clicks in a web search setting, demonstrate up to a 22% improvement in agreement with AB metrics (constituting over a 50% error reduction), while maintaining sensitivity of one to two orders of magnitude above the AB tests. This paves the way towards more sensitive and accurate online evaluation.

Categories and Subject Descriptors

H.3 [**Information Storage and Retrieval**]: H.3.3 Information Search and Retrieval

Keywords

Information retrieval; Evaluation; Interleaved comparisons

*Most of this work done during internship at Microsoft Research.

SIGIR'15, August 09 - 13, 2015, Santiago, Chile.

ACM 978-1-4503-3621-5/15/08 ...$15.00.
DOI: http://dx.doi.org/10.1145/2766462.2767695.

1. INTRODUCTION

Evaluation has long played a key role in information retrieval (IR). Most commonly, systems are evaluated following the Cranfield approach [25]. Using this approach, systems are evaluated in terms of document relevance for given queries, which is assessed by trained experts. While the Cranfield paradigm ensures high internal validity and repeatability of experiments, it has been shown that the users' search success and satisfaction with an IR system are not always accurately reflected by standard IR metrics [29, 31]. One reason is that the relevance judges typically do not assess queries and documents that reflect their own information needs, and have to make assumptions about relevance from an assumed users point of view. Because the true information need can be difficult to assess, this can cause substantial biases [10, 30, 36].

To address the gap between offline evaluation and true use of IR systems, *online* evaluation has been used to directly measure observable user behavior on alternative systems. The biggest challenge for online evaluation is to identify metrics that accurately reflect user satisfaction. This has motivated a large amount of research on online metrics. While early online evaluation focused on simple metrics such as click-through rate (CTR, the fraction of queries for which users click a result) or the ranks of clicked documents [14], more sophisticated metrics have been recently developed. These include observing which results users skip over [34], the time between search engine visits [3], and focusing on "satisfied" (long-duration) clicks (which we refer to as SAT clicks) [4].

Given an IR system and an appropriate online metric, the standard experimental procedure for comparing systems is AB testing [17]. This means that a controlled experiment is conducted on users of a running system. A random sample of users is exposed to the treatment system, a second sample is exposed to the control system. Given that the assignment to systems is random and the experimental units (e.g., users) can be assumed independent of each other, any differences in online performance measured on the two samples can be attributed to differences between treatment and control system. If the measured differences are statistically significant, we can make highly confident decisions on which system to deploy. Unfortunately, the variance in user behavior is typically high, which results in low sensitivity of such AB comparisons. This means that, to reach high confidence levels, large samples need to be collected over a long period of time (e.g., millions of samples) [1]. Considering the effects of exposing users to potentially lower quality systems over long periods of time, it can be seen that AB comparisons can be extremely expensive.

An alternative online evaluation approach, interleaving, was developed to improve on the AB design [14]. It avoids many of the sources of variance by combining results from both the treatment and control systems, for all queries. In particular, the results returned by the two systems are combined in a way that is fair to both, in the sense that neither system would be preferred in expectation if users were to click on documents at random. Observed user clicks on the combined result list are then credited to one of the systems to infer which system would be preferred by the user [24]. In comparison to AB tests, interleaved comparisons have been shown to be substantially more sensitive. For instance, in an empirical comparison of five AB tests and corresponding interleaving experiments, Chapelle et al. [1] observed that AB experiments required 145 times more data than interleaving to achieve statistical significance.

While high sensitivity makes interleaving very attractive for online evaluation, existing methods have primarily focused on observed clicks, and ignore the richer user satisfaction signals that have been incorporated into AB metrics. As a result, it was unclear to what degree interleaved comparisons agree with user satisfaction, as measured by specifically designed AB tests. This is challenging to address because by their very nature interleaving methods change rankings and attribute credit in a non straight forward way, making it far from trivial to align them with AB metrics. This paper is the first to address this limitation of interleaving methods.

In particular, we make the following contributions:

Sensitivity: Starting with existing AB and interleaving metrics (defined in Section 3), we propose a new, statistical method for assessing the sensitivity of these metrics from estimated effect sizes (Section 4). The resulting method allows a detailed comparison between metrics in terms of the power of statistical tests at varying sample sizes. Our analysis shows that AB tests typically require two orders of magnitude more data than interleaved comparisons.

Agreement: Turning to the agreement between existing metrics, we find that current interleaved comparisons achieve from random up to 76% agreement with AB user satisfaction metrics.

Credit Formulation: Motivated by the results of our analysis, we propose novel interleaving *credit functions* that are (a) designed to closely match the implementation and parameters of AB metrics, or (b) are parameterized to allow optimization towards agreement with arbitrary AB metrics (Section 5). We further propose the first approach for automatically maximizing agreement between such parameterized interleaving credit functions and AB metrics.

Optimization: We demonstrate that interleaving credit functions can be automatically optimized, and that learned parameters generalize to unseen experiments. These results demonstrate for the first time that interleaving can be augmented with user satisfaction metrics, to accurately predict the outcomes of AB comparisons that would require one to two orders of magnitude more data.

Large Scale Evaluation: Finally, our empirical results, obtained from experiments with 3 billion user impressions and 38 paired (AB and interleaving) experiments demonstrate the effectiveness of our proposed approach (Section 6). In particular, we achieve agreement of up to 87%, while maintaining high sensitivity.

2. RELATED WORK

In this section, we discuss prior work on measuring user satisfaction with online IR systems, starting with absolute relevance metrics: Metrics that measure a single number for a given ranking system (2.1). We then present existing results on online evaluation using interleaving (2.2). Finally we discuss approaches for optimizing online evaluation metrics as relevant to this paper (2.3).

2.1 Absolute User Metrics

The most common type of online evaluation today is AB testing, where online performance is estimated on two independent samples of users: One exposed to a treatment system, the other exposed to a control system [17]. Standard assumptions allow experimenters to obtain unbiased online performance estimates, and confidence estimates or hypothesis testing are available via statistical methods such as the two-sample t-test. For instance, this methodology has been effectively used to compare systems in terms of CTR (e.g., for news recommendation [20]).

While simple to measure, CTR has been shown to be a poor metric for measuring user satisfaction in search [15]. Consequently, a large body of work has developed online metrics that more accurately measure search satisfaction. An established signal is dwell time, where clicks followed by only short visits to the corresponding result document are considered “unsatisfied”, i.e., the user is unlikely to have found the document as relevant [36]. Moving beyond a single time threshold for identifying user satisfaction, sophisticated click satisfaction classifiers combine a range of user signals, and have been shown to accurately detect satisfied clicks [16].

Other proposed online metrics also consider the effect of tabbed browsing (opening several results in browser tabs in quick succession) [13]. Conversely, the lack of a click (abandonment) is often taken as a signal of a lack of relevance, but this interpretation has posed a challenge for evaluating richer search engine result pages, where relevant information may be presented directly, without the need to click. A number of papers have proposed methods to determine when abandonment indicates satisfaction [20, 28]. Follow-on queries can also be considered indicative of a lack of success [8], as can skipping results be indicative of incorrect result order [34]. Of course, to accurately interpret user clicks, we must also consider which results users examined. If a user never looked at a search result, their lack of engagement on this result cannot be indicative of low relevance. A number of studies have shown that mouse movement can be an indicator of user examination of search results, and of specific sections within search results [2, 5, 6, 9, 35]. Similarly, in a mobile setting recording how long each part of the screen is visible can be considered an indicator of relevance [18].

Finally, although the majority of online evaluation has focused on user satisfaction for individual queries, it has been argued that the correct unit of measurement is the user session, or a search task. A number of session based metrics have been proposed [7, 33].

In this paper we specifically focus on AB metrics that capture click-level search satisfaction [16] (cf., Section 3.1).

2.2 Interleaved Comparisons

While providing flexibility and control, AB comparisons typically require a large number of observations. Given typical differences in IR system performance in state of the art systems, many AB metrics have been found to require millions of users [1]. Interleaved methods, originally proposed by Joachims [14], reduce the variance of measurement by combining documents retrieved by both the control and the treatment system. Projecting user clicks on the resulting interleaved document lists back to the original document rankings is then taken as an estimate of which system would be preferred by the user. This mixing substantially reduces variance and was found to reduce required sample sizes by up to two orders of magnitude [1, 24]. A variety of interleaving approaches have been proposed (e.g. [11, 14, 23, 24, 26, 27]). The most frequently used interleaving algorithm is Team Draft Interleaving (TDI) [24]. We use TDI as our baseline. It is described in detail in Section 3.2.

2.3 Optimizing Interleaving Metrics

The interleaving approaches described above measure which ranker is more likely to attract user clicks in a fair, paired comparison. However, as described in Section 2.1, raw clicks can be misleading. Previous research has shown that with interleaving there may be biases due to highlighting in search result titles [38] and other caption effects such as title and snippet length [12]. Proposed methods to mediate these biases were shown to improve agreement

Table 1: AB metrics implemented as ground truth for comparisons with interleaving. See Section 3.1 for notation.

AB Metric	Description	Implementation $\frac{1}{Q_A}\sum_{q\in Q_A}\cdots$
AB	Number of queries that received at least one click.	$\mathbf{1}(\lvert C^q\rvert > 1)$
$AB@1$	Number of queries that received at least one click on the first position.	$\mathbf{1}((\sum_{c\in C^q}\mathbf{1}(\text{rank}(c)=1)) > 1)$
AB_S	Number of queries that received at least one SAT click.	$\mathbf{1}((\sum_{c\in C^q}\mathbf{1}(\text{is\_sat}(c))) > 1)$
$AB_S@1$	Number of queries that received at least one SAT click on the first position.	$\mathbf{1}((\sum_{c\in C^q}\mathbf{1}(\text{rank}(c)=1)\cdot\mathbf{1}(\text{is\_sat}(c))) > 1)$
AB_T	Time from the query being issued until the first click.	$\min_{c\in C^q}\text{time}(c)$
$AB_T@1$	Time to the first click on the top position.	$\min_{c\in C^q}\text{time}(c)\cdot\mathbf{1}(\text{rank}(c)=1)$
$AB_{T,S}$	Time to the first click classified as SAT.	$\min_{c\in C^q}\text{time}(c)\cdot\mathbf{1}(\text{is\_sat}(c))$
$AB_{T,S}@1$	Time to the first click on the top position classified as SAT.	$\min_{c\in C^q}\text{time}(c)\cdot\mathbf{1}(\text{rank}(c)=1)\cdot\mathbf{1}(\text{is\_sat}(c))$

with offline evaluation [12, 38], but optimizing agreement with online metrics remains an open challenge.

Also, the above approaches may improve interleaving by removing some click bias, they still aim to be *unbiased* rather than *predictive of satisfaction*. In this paper, we show how to create an interleaving evaluation that instead aims to predict the outcome of an AB experiment for any given AB metric, while maintaining the sensitivity improvements of interleaving. In particular, we take into account whether clicks are indicators of success by reimplementing the classifier learned by Kim et al. [16].

The goal of this paper is also related to prior work on optimizing the sensitivity of interleaving algorithms, where interleaving algorithms were learned to be more statistically powerful [37], or to satisfy given choices about the value of any given preference observed [23]. In contrast, our work is the first that focuses on optimizing "correctness" of an interleaving outcome as captured in terms of agreement with AB metrics, while maintaining high sensitivity. Our results show that in this way agreement between interleaving and any given AB metric can be dramatically improved.

3. BACKGROUND

In this section we describe the most commonly used AB metrics, and the interleaved evaluation approach that we build on in the remainder of this paper. We will take the presented AB metrics as the *ground truth* user satisfaction metrics we aim to predict with much smaller interleaving samples.

3.1 Common AB Metrics

As described above, a large number of AB metrics have been developed. Most have in common that clicks are the basic observed interaction with users, thus this is our focus too. We note that many common AB metrics can be categorized as taking into account particular attributes of clicking behavior. The most common attributes include (i) estimating clicks as indicative of satisfaction or not, (ii) giving particular importance to clicks at the top position of Web search results, and (iii) measuring the time spent by the user prior to clicking. Consequently, we implement the following AB metrics. An overview is given in Table 1.

3.1.1 Click-through Rate

Click-through rate (CTR) is often used as a baseline AB metric, e.g., in [1]. It can be implemented as the average number of clicks per search result page, or as the fraction of pages for which there are any clicks. We follow the second definition. We use $|C^q|$ to denote the number of clicks for query q. The indicator function $\mathbf{1}(\cdot)$ is used and evaluates to 1 when the argument is true, and 0 otherwise.

3.1.2 Click Rank

It was noted by [1] that of all the AB metrics studied in a large scale comparison of AB tests and interleaving evaluation, the AB metric that most reliably agreed with known experimental outcomes was the fraction of search results pages with a click at the top position. As such, we also use two types of metrics: Those which only consider clicks at the top position (named *@1*) and those that consider all clicks (the others). In equations we use $\text{rank}_A(c)$ to denote the rank of click c in the results returned by ranker A.

3.1.3 User Satisfaction

While clicks are often directly interpreted as a user preference, they are known to be both noisy and biased. To remedy the noise, a common approach is to only consider satisfied clicks (here: SAT clicks) with dwell time above a fixed cutoff of 30 seconds [36].

However, only using time as a threshold for satisfaction is problematic as some queries naturally require users to spend more time than others. Recently, Kim et al. [16] showed that taking more user signals into account leads to better prediction of user satisfaction. For this paper, we partially re-implement the SAT click classifier from that work.Our classifier uses the dwell time, document readability, document topic and query topic features suggested by Kim et al. [16]. In particular, the features beyond dwell time are assumed to partially explain the dwell time necessary for a given query and document. We combine these features using quantile regression forests [21]. The model is trained to predict the probability of a SAT click, given user signals. It can be turned into a classifier by selecting a decision threshold, e.g., based on the distribution over classes in the training set. With training on approximately 3,000 manually labeled clicks, our classifier obtains an accuracy of 77%, which is marginally lower than the 81% reported by Kim et al. [16]. The major difference between the implementations is that we do not represent dwell time distributions per topic. Instead, we use raw dwell time values directly as input for our classifier.

The output of this SAT click classifier is used throughout this paper. For a given click c, we define $\text{sat}(c)$ as the estimated probability that c indicates user satisfaction. For succinctness, we also define $\text{is\_sat}(c) := \mathit{true}$ whenever $sat(c) > 0.8$ (the threshold based on the class distribution). Half of the AB metrics we consider use the $\text{is\_sat}(c)$ signal to filter out clicks c that are not deemed satisfied by our classifier. These AB metrics are marked with subscript S.

3.1.4 Time To Click

Another commonly used metric is the time that the user spends on the search result page before clicking a document. As time spent is the key cost to search system users, reducing this time is considered good (e.g. [1]). Our metrics that measure time to click are marked with subscript T. In equations we use $\text{time}(c)$ to denote the time from the user issuing the query until the click c.

Combining all possible choices of AB metrics leads to the eight metrics shown in Table 1. The first four (AB, $AB@1$, AB_S, $AB_S@1$) focus on the presence of a click, while the other four capture the time to the first click of a particular type, if such a click occurred (AB_T, $AB_T@1$, $AB_{T,S}$ and $AB_{T,S}@1$).

3.2 Interleaving

In this paper, we use Team Draft Interleaving (TDI) [24] as our interleaving baseline. This algorithm is most frequently used in

Algorithm 1 Team-Draft Interleaving [24]

1: **Input**: Rankings $A = (a_1, a_2, \ldots)$ and $B = (b_1, b_2, \ldots)$
2: **Init**: $L \leftarrow (); \sim TeamA \leftarrow \emptyset; \sim TeamB \leftarrow \emptyset; i \leftarrow 1$
3: **while** $A[i] = B[i]$ **do** .... *common prefix*
4: $\quad L \leftarrow L + A[i]$ ..... *append result to L without assigning teams*
5: $\quad i \leftarrow i + 1$ .... *increment i*
6: **while** $(\exists i : A[i] \notin L) \wedge (\exists j : B[j] \notin L)$ **do** *not at end of A or B*
7: $\quad$ **if** $(|TeamA| < |TeamB|) \vee$ $((|TeamA| = |TeamB|) \wedge (RandBit() = 1))$ **then**
8: $\quad\quad k \leftarrow \min_i\{i : A[i] \notin L\}$ ...... *top result in A not yet in L*
9: $\quad\quad L \leftarrow L + A[k]$ .... *append it to L*
10: $\quad\quad TeamA \leftarrow TeamA \cup \{A[k]\}$ .... *clicks credited to A*
11: $\quad$ **else**
12: $\quad\quad k \leftarrow \min_i\{i : B[i] \notin L\}$ .... *top result in B not yet in L*
13: $\quad\quad L \leftarrow L + B[k]$ .... *append it to L*
14: $\quad\quad TeamB \leftarrow TeamB \cup \{B[k]\}$ .... *clicks credited to B*
15: **Output**: Interleaved ranking $L, TeamA, TeamB$

practice, and has been empirically shown to be equally effective as Balanced Interleaving [1, 14].

Given an incoming user query, TDI produces a result list as follows. The algorithm takes as input two ranked lists of documents for the query, $A = (a_1, a_2, \ldots)$ and $B = (b_1, b_2, \ldots)$. The goal is to produce a combined ranking $L = (l_1, l_2, \ldots)$. This is done in the same way that sports teams may be constructed in a friendly match, with two team captains taking turns picking players for their team.

The algorithm is detailed in Algorithm 1. It initializes the interleaved list L with any common prefix of A and B, if this exists. For this common prefix, no teams are assigned, as no preferences should be inferred.[1] Then, on line 6, the algorithm continues in phases by adding two documents to L: In each phase, on line 7, we first flip an unbiased coin to decide if ranker A or B is given priority. Assuming that ranker A is given priority, A appends its highest ranked result that is not already in L to L (i.e. $l_1 \leftarrow a_1$ in the first instance), and assigns it to $TeamA$. Then, B selects its first result not already present in L (in the first instance either b_1 if it differs from a_1, and b_2 otherwise) and again appends it to L and $TeamB$. This repeats until all results in A or B have been consumed or until L reaches the desired length.

The interleaved ranking L is then shown to the user. Any clicks on documents contributed by A (in $TeamA$) are credited to A. Clicks on documents in $TeamB$ are credited to B. Over an observed sample of interleaving observations, a preference for A or B is then inferred based on which ranker was credited with more clicks. The final outcome of the interleaving comparison experiment can thus be written as:

$$O_{TDI}(A, B) = \text{sign}(\frac{1}{|Q|} \sum_{q \in Q} |C_A^q| - |C_B^q|), \qquad (1)$$

where Q is the set of all query impressions (non-unique queries issued by all users during the interleaving experiment), and C_X^q denotes the set of clicks observed in $TeamX$ on q.

We use TDI as our baseline throughout this paper. In addition, all our approaches use the *interleaving* (i.e., list construction) algorithm shown in Algorithm 1 and described above. Our focus is on replacing the credit function (Eq., 1). We will introduce our methods in Section 5.

4. DATA ANALYSIS

Many of the AB user satisfaction methods that we introduced in Section 3.1 have been developed recently. Therefore, it is not clear to what degree interleaved comparisons agree with these metrics. In this section, we conduct an empirical analysis of the sensitivity and directional agreement between these AB metrics and TDI. We start by describing the data we use in this section and in the remainder of this paper (4.1). We then propose a new approach for comparing the sensitivity (in terms of statistical power) of AB and TDI comparisons, and use this method to analyze the relative power of the different approaches (4.2). This also lets us estimate the probability of agreement between approaches at varying sample sizes. The results of our analysis are presented in Section 4.3. They motivate why an improved approach is needed, as discussed in Section 4.4.

4.1 Data

For our experiments, we start with a set of 38 pairs of rankers for which both an AB comparison, and a TDI interleaving comparison were performed. All ranker comparisons reflect changes that are typical for the normal development of a commercial web search engine. They consist of changes to the ranking function used to order web search results, in terms of parameters of the ranking function, modified ranking features, and so forth. The comparisons were all run in the first 9 months of 2014, in the United States locale. The experimental unit consisted of assigning users to individual ranking conditions uniformly at random.

The AB and interleaving comparisons were run for varying durations, usually around one week for AB comparisons and around 4 days for interleaving comparisons. Additionally, AB comparisons were typically run with higher volume, resulting in about 80 times more queries for each AB comparison than each interleaving comparison. In all, this data consists of over 3 billion clicks. Depending on the experiment, between 2% and 30% of interleaved queries with clicks had at least one click on a result assigned to one of the teams.

4.2 Estimating Power and Agreement

We now propose an approach for assessing the relative power of AB measurement compared to TDI, and further show how this approach can be used to estimate agreement between approaches at varying sample sizes.

As described earlier, AB tests perform controlled experiments. Users are exposed to either treatment or control result rankings, rendering this a *between subject* experiment. In interleaving, each user is exposed to results from both rankers, rendering them *within subject* experiments. We can measure the importance of this difference using a power computation, which tells us how many independent samples we need to obtain a statistically significant outcome for each approach, as follows.

We start with AB comparisons, following the standard methodology described in [17]: Two independent samples are collected by exposing a random fraction of users to treatment A, and another to treatment B. An AB metric is used to assess each sample, and we are interested in determining whether there is a statistically significant difference between A and B in terms of this metric. This question is typically addressed using a two-sample t-test.

Power of AB comparisons. Assume that the target metric is approximately normally distributed (this is reasonable due to the central limit theorem), with means μ_A and μ_B and equal variance σ_{AB}. Formally, we have $A \sim \mathcal{N}(\mu_A, \sigma_{AB})$ and $B \sim \mathcal{N}(\mu_B, \sigma_{AB})$. We are interested in detecting whether $\mu_A \stackrel{?}{=} \mu_B$. This gives us the null hypothesis $H_0 : \mu_A = \mu_B$ and the alternative hypothesis $H_1 : \mu_A \neq \mu_B$. We also choose the probability of Type-I error we are willing to accept, e.g., $\alpha = 0.05$. The t-test then assumes that H_0 is true and assesses the probability of observing differences of at least the observed sample difference $|\hat{A} - \hat{B}|$ under H_0.

While Type-I error is controlled in the significance test, here we

[1]This was shown to substantially increase sensitivity of the simpler original TDI algorithm [1, 22].

are interested in the *power* (also called sensitivity) of the conducted test. Assuming H_1 is actually true, power quantifies the probability of correctly rejecting H_0. It is affected by the true effect size $\delta_{AB} = (\mu_A - \mu_B)/\sqrt{1/n_A + 1/n_B}\sigma$, where n_A, n_B are the respective sample sizes.

We can assess the power of a test as follows. Under H_1 (samples are drawn from normal distributions with means $\mu_A \neq \mu_B$ and shared variance σ_{AB}) we observe sample A, B and compute the test statistic [19]: $t(A,B) = \frac{(\bar{A}-\bar{B})}{\sqrt{\frac{1}{n_A}+\frac{1}{n_B}}} / \sqrt{\frac{\sum(A_i-\bar{A})^2+\sum(B_j-\bar{B})^2}{v_{AB}}}$. The test statistic $t(A,B)$ follows a non-central t distribution $\bar{A} - \bar{B} \sim nct(\delta_{AB}, v_{AB})$, with non-centrality parameter δ_{AB} (the effect size, from above) and degrees of freedom $v_{AB} = n_A + n_B - 2$.

H_0 is correctly rejected when $t(A,B) \geq C_0$. The power of the test is the probability $P(reject(H_0)|H_1) = P(t(A,B) \geq C_0)$ and can be computed (solved using linear programming[2]):

$$P(t(A,B) \geq C_0) = \int_{C_0}^{\infty} nct(\delta_{AB}, v_{AB})dy. \quad (2)$$

Power of interleaving comparisons. The analysis for interleaving is closely related, but relies on the typically more powerful (one-sample) paired t-test. Instead of independent samples, we now observe a single sample I of paired comparisons, assumed to be normally distributed with $I \sim \mathcal{N}(\mu_I, \sigma_I)$. We want to detect whether $\mu_I \stackrel{?}{=} 0$ with $H_0 : \mu_I = 0$ and $H_1 : \mu_I \neq 0$. Given μ_I and sample size n_I, the test statistic $t(I)$ follows a non-central t-distribution $t(I) \sim nct(\delta_I, v_I)$ with non-centrality parameter $\delta_I = \sqrt{n}\mu_I/\sigma_I$ and $v_I = n_I - 1$ degrees of freedom. The power calculation is[3]

$$P(t(I) \geq C_0) = \int_{C_0}^{\infty} nct(\delta_I, v_I)dy. \quad (3)$$

Probability of agreement. Given Equations (2) and (3), we can compute the probability of comparison outcomes at varying sample sizes. For example, the probability that an AB comparison with parameters $\mu_A, \mu_B, \sigma_{AB} : \mu_A - \mu_B > 0$ agrees with the true AB outcome at sample sizes n_A, n_B is computed by plugging into Equation (2) and computing $P(\bar{A} - \bar{B} > 0) = P(t(A,B) > 0)$. Correspondingly, the probability that an interleaving comparison with parameters μ_I, σ_I would agree with the same outcome is computed using Equation (3) so that $P(\bar{I} > 0) = P(t(I) > 0)$.

4.3 Data Analysis Results

We apply the analysis methodology described above to the set of 38 ranking algorithms described in Section 4.1. In Figure 1 we show the power obtained using AB comparisons and interleaving comparisons at increasing sample sizes. We see that on average across the set of 38 experiments, 80% power[4] with AB experiments is obtained with between 10^7 and 10^8 observations (queries). On the other hand, the same power is obtained with between 10^5 and 10^6 observations with TDI. This difference of approximately two orders of magnitude is also consistent with previous work [1].

Having presented the relative power of the approaches, we return to the key question: Do the metrics agree on which ranker is better? We use the method developed in the previous section to estimate agreement between AB and interleaving comparisons, and

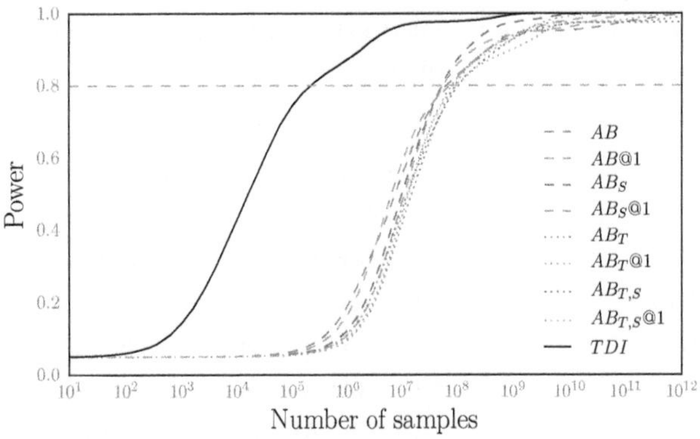

Figure 1: Power as a function of sample size, computed using the observed effect sizes for 38 interleaving and AB comparisons, averaged over all comparisons (assuming two-sided t-test with $p = 0.05$, as described in Section 4.2).

Table 2: Agreement of AB metrics on our data. We measure agreement with TDI, with a sub-sample of AB of the same size as the TDI comparison, and with a sub-sample of AB with the same size as the original AB comparison (this is an upper-bound on agreement for each AB metric). For TDI, values in bold are statically significantly different from 50%.

		self-agreement	
AB Metric	TDI	AB_{Sub}	AB_{Up}
AB	0.63	0.63	0.94
$AB@1$	**0.71**	0.62	0.95
AB_S	**0.71**	0.61	0.96
$AB_S@1$	**0.76**	0.60	0.95
AB_T	0.53	0.58	0.91
$AB_T@1$	0.45	0.59	0.90
$AB_{T,S}$	0.47	0.59	0.88
$AB_{T,S}@1$	0.42	0.60	0.87

AB comparisons at varying sample sizes. The first column in Table 2 summarizes the agreement rates of TDI and AB metrics. We see that agreement rates are generally low. This agreement of TDI with AB metrics is a *baseline* that we want to improve upon in this paper. In the results in Section 6, this baseline is referred to as TDI.

Recall that our goal is to predict the outcome of a large AB comparison given the much smaller amount of data used in interleaving comparisons. As such, another reasonable baseline is to assess how well a smaller AB comparison predicts the outcome of the full AB comparison. We can answer this question using the methodology for assessing the probability of agreement developed above (Section 4.2), by plugging in the observed effect sizes and setting the sample size to that of the corresponding interleaving comparison. This our second *baseline*, which we refer to as AB_{Sub}. Results are given in the second column of Table 2. Generally, these AB metrics computed on small subsamples have low agreement with the experiment outcome given the complete data, of around 60%.

We also compute an upper bound of agreement with AB metrics by actually measuring how well a subsample of the same size as the full AB, AB_{Up}, would agree with itself, using the same methodology. This can be seen as a measure of how predictable a metric is. The last column of Table 2 shows that the time-based metrics are much less predictable than count-based AB metrics. Given these lower and upper bounds on AB agreement with itself, we can restate our goal as follows. We aim to augment TDI to improve over the above two baselines (TDI and AB_{Sub}) and to close the gap with the upper bound AB_{Up}.

[2]We use the python implementation `statsmodels.stats.power.tt_ind_solve_power`, http://statsmodels.sourceforge.net/

[3]We use the python implementation `statsmodels.stats.power.tt_solve_power`.

[4]Controlled experiments are typically designed for 80-95% power.

Table 3: **Definitions for interleaving credit functions. The $\delta(C_A)$ functions give credit to ranker A based on attributes of the clicked documents assigned to ranker A. The last row actually computes a combination of credit functions above it.**

Credit functions designed to match AB metrics (cf., 5.2)		$\delta(C_A) =$
TDI	Number of clicks on ranker A	$\lvert C_A \rvert$
$TDI@1$	Number of clicks on documents that A ranks first	$\sum_{c \in C_A} \mathbf{1}(\text{rank}_A(c) = 1)$
TDI_S	Number of SAT clicked documents contributed by A	$\sum_{c \in C_A} \mathbf{1}(\text{is\_sat}(c))$
$TDI_S@1$	Number of SAT clicked document ranked first by A	$\sum_{c \in C_A} \mathbf{1}(\text{is\_sat}(c)) \cdot \mathbf{1}(\text{rank}_A(c) = 1)$
TDI_T	Time to clicks on documents contributed by A	$\sum_{c \in C_A} \text{time}(c)$
$TDI_T@1$	Time to clicks on documents ranked first by A	$\sum_{c \in C_A} \mathbf{1}(\text{rank}_A(c) = 1) \cdot \text{time}(c)$
$TDI_{T,S}$	Time to SAT clicks on documents contributed by A	$\sum_{c \in C_A} \mathbf{1}(\text{is\_sat}(c)) \cdot \text{time}(c)$
$TDI_{T,S}@1$	Time to SAT clicks on documents ranked first by A	$\sum_{c \in C_A} \mathbf{1}(\text{rank}_A(c) = 1) \cdot \mathbf{1}(\text{is\_sat}(c)) \cdot \text{time}(c)$
Parameterized credit functions (cf., 5.3)		$\delta(C_A) =$
$TDI_S^{t_s}, t_s \in \{0.1..0.9\}$	Number of clicks with SAT probability $\geq t_s$, on documents contributed by ranker A	$\sum_{c \in C_A} \mathbf{1}(\text{sat}(c) \geq t_s)$
$TDI_{T,S}^{t_s}, t_s \in \{0.1..0.9\}$	Time to clicks with SAT probability $\geq t_s$, on documents contributed by ranker A $\geq t_s$	$\sum_{c \in C_A} \mathbf{1}(\text{sat}(c) \geq t_s) \cdot \text{time}(c)$
Combined credit functions (cf., 5.4)		$\delta(C_A) =$
$TDI_{T,S}^{\mathbf{w}}, w_i \in \{0.1..0.9\}$	Weighted combination of the credit functions above	$\sum_{w_i \in \mathbf{w}} w_i \delta_i(C_A)$

4.4 Implications

Summarizing the results above motivates the rest of this work: AB metrics have been developed guided by real analysis of user behavior. Yet they usually have relatively low power. Interleaving has much higher power, but low agreement with most AB metrics, being blind to richer behavioral signals. Thus, we aim to optimize interleaving to increase agreement with AB metrics, while maintaining the statistical power of the technique. The AB metric is treated as the gold standard to which interleaving must compare itself.

As noted in the Section 2, this goal is similar to that addressed by [37]. However, they only focused on optimizing sensitivity, while we focus on optimizing correctness in the sense of agreeing with AB metrics. It is similar to [12, 38] in the sense that our method can reduce click bias in interleaved comparisons, however the earlier work only considered agreement with offline metrics.

5. METHOD

In this section we describe how to incorporate user signals into TDI comparisons, to increase agreement with AB metrics. We first formalize the notion of interleaving credit in a way that allows us to incorporate user signals (Section 5.1). We then design a set of credit functions that closely match user satisfaction AB metrics (Section 5.2). Because agreement between interleaving and AB metrics is not necessarily maximized by mirroring AB parameters, we then introduce parameterized credit functions (Section 5.3), and combined credit functions (Section 5.4) designed to be automatically tuned to maximize agreement. Finally, our methodology for maximizing agreement is detailed in Section 5.5.

5.1 Formalizing Interleaving Credit

Formally, for all pairs of rankers A and B, we aim to find an interleaving method that agrees with the *sign* of the differences in AB metrics that we found in an AB comparison. The sign of such a difference should be interpreted as a preference for either A, B, or neither. We denote such a preference, the comparison outcome O_{AB}, of the metric AB as:

$$O_{AB}(A, B) = \text{sign}(AB(A) - AB(B)). \tag{4}$$

Instances of AB metrics are *click through rate*, *clicks at one*, and *time to click* (see Table 1 for details).

As opposed to AB metrics, interleaving methods are directly defined on pairs of rankers. Following the same notation, the outcome of an interleaving comparison with TDI can thus be denoted as:

$$O_{TDI}(A, B) = \text{sign}(TDI(A, B)). \tag{5}$$

Interleaving preferences, when using TDI (cf., Section 3.2), come from differences between credit acquired by each ranker:

$$TDI(A, B) = \frac{1}{|Q|} \sum_{q \in Q} \delta(C_A^q) - \delta(C_B^q). \tag{6}$$

Here, Q is a set of query impressions and $\delta(C_A)$ a credit function that attributes credit to ranker A depending on user interactions with the result list. Next, we introduce a new set of credit functions that is designed to mirror the use of user signals in AB comparisons.

5.2 Matching AB Credit

We now present instantiations of credit functions $\delta(C_A)$ designed to match the AB metrics in Section 3.1. All our interleaving credit functions are defined on a set of clicks assigned to a ranker (e.g., for ranker A these are $c \in C_A$), for a query impression. Clicks are associated with user signals.

The details of our *matching* credit functions are given in the first part of Table 3. The following signals are used:

- $|C_A|$ the number of clicks for ranker A for a query impression. See Section 3.1.1.
- $\text{rank}_A(c)$ is the rank of the clicked document in the original ranking A (before interleaving: i.e., rankers A and B can have different documents at rank 1). See Section 3.1.2 for the a description of this signal as used in AB metrics.
- $\text{is\_sat}(c)$ is a binary indicator that is *true* if the SAT classifier identified the click as SAT click, see Section 3.1.3 for details on the SAT click classifier.
- $\text{sat}(c)$ is the probability of the click being a SAT click. Again, details are in Section 3.1.3.

- time(c) is the time from query submission to the observed click, in seconds. See Section 3.1.4 for the corresponding AB signal.

Previously proposed interleaved comparison methods, such as TDI, use the credit function TDI shown in the table. It can be interpreted as a close match to the AB metric AB, because it estimates whether a given ranker would have obtained a click in an AB comparison.

The credit functions $TDI@1$, TDI_S, and $TDI_S@1$ are designed to closely match the AB metrics $AB@1$, AB_S, and $AB_S@1$. For clicks at rank one, we consider whether a clicked document would have been placed first by the original ranker, as this reflects the most accurately whether the ranker would be likely to receive a click at the top rank in an AB comparison. For SAT clicks, we use the same classifier as for our AB comparisons above, as in Section 3.1.3.

The four time-based credit functions TDI_T, $TDI_T@1$, $TDI_{T,S}$, and $TDI_{T,S}@1$ are designed to match the time-based AB metrics. E.g., TDI_T reflects the AB metric AB_T, however we use the average time to click for a ranker, as it tends to be more robust than the time to the first click. The remaining three metrics implement filters on which clicks contribute, parallel to the click-based metrics described above.

5.3 Parameterized Credit Functions

Next, we propose a second set of interleaving credit functions that can be parameterized to automatically calibrate them to maximize agreement with AB metrics. Effectively calibrating these credit functions would allow users of interleaved comparisons to automatically identify credit functions that maximize agreement with arbitrary AB metrics.

For instance, we define a credit function that captures user satisfaction. We filter out clicks c that have a low satisfaction probability sat(c) by thresholding this probability using a threshold t_s. This leads to the following credit function:

$$\delta(C_A)^{t_s} = \sum_{c \in C_A} \mathbf{1}(\text{sat}(c) > t_s). \tag{7}$$

The threshold, t_s in this case, of such a parametrized credit function can be tuned to maximize agreement with AB metrics. We define two such parameterized functions, the first click-based, as shown above, the second time-based. We list our parameterized credit functions in the second part of Table 3.

5.4 Combined Credit Functions

Now that we have several credit functions, as listed in the first two sections of Table 3, we can take it a step further and start combining them. We propose to combine the interleaving credit functions in a weighted linear combination:

$$TDI^{\mathbf{w}}(A, B) = \frac{1}{|Q|} \sum_{q \in Q} \sum_{w_i \in \mathbf{w}} w_i \delta_i(C_A^q) - w_i \delta_i(C_B^q), \tag{8}$$

where $\mathbf{w}$ denotes the weights used to combine several credit functions. We thus define the interleaving preference as a weighted sum of credit functions we introduced earlier.

In the original TDI, we have a single credit function as defined in the first row of Table 3 and a weight vector of $\mathbf{w} = (1)$.

5.5 Maximizing Agreement with AB Metrics

We return to our initial goal, to optimize the agreement between interleaving metrics and AB metrics, and present a method for automatically tuning interleaving credit functions to maximize agreement with a given AB metric. Together with the parameterized

Algorithm 2 Maximizing Agreement

1: **Input**: Ranker pairs $C = ((A_1, B_1), \ldots, (A_n, B_n))$, AB
2: **Init**: test agreements $A \leftarrow []$, weights $W \leftarrow []$
3: **for all** $n \leq N$ **do** .... *N repetitions*
4: $\quad S \leftarrow sample\_with\_rep(C, |C|)$. *bootstrap sample, train set*
5: $\quad \hat{\mathbf{w}} \leftarrow \arg\max_{\mathbf{w}} \sum_{(A,B) \in S} \mathbf{1}(O^{\mathbf{w}}_{TDI}(A, B) = O_{AB}(A, B))$
6: $\quad O \leftarrow C \setminus S$ .... *'out of bag' sample, test set*
7: $\quad A \leftarrow A + \frac{1}{|O|} \sum_{(A,B) \in O} \mathbf{1}(O^{\hat{\mathbf{w}}}_{TDI}(A, B) = O_{AB}(A, B))$
8: $\quad W \leftarrow W + \hat{\mathbf{w}}$ .... *append weight vector*
9: **Output**: weights $mean(W)$, agreement $mean(A)$

and combined credit functions presented above, this allows tuning interleaving to an arbitrary AB metric. Our approach treats the AB metric as a black box presented by an experimenter who presumably selected this metric for some reason.

The weights introduced in Equation (8) can be optimized such that we maximize the agreement:

$$\hat{\mathbf{w}} = \arg\max_{\mathbf{w}} \sum_{(A,B) \in S} \mathbf{1}(O^{\mathbf{w}}_{TDI}(A, B) = O_{AB}(A, B)). \tag{9}$$

I.e., we maximize the number of times the outcome of an AB comparison agrees with the outcome of an interleaving comparison for all of ranker comparisons S.

To implement and validate the maximization step in Equation (9), we use the bootstrap procedure presented in Algorithm 2. This takes as input a set C of pairs of rankers that have been compared (such as those described in described in Section 4.1) and an AB metric such as AB. For N repetitions, a bootstrap sample S of size $|C|$ is taken from C. On this sample we compute $\hat{\mathbf{w}}$ using Equation (9) for all $\mathbf{w}$ we consider. We validate the agreement that this weight vector $\hat{\mathbf{w}}$ gives on unseen data and we report the mean $\hat{\mathbf{w}}$ and mean agreement. In our experiments $N = 100$ and we consider $\mathbf{w} = (w_i \in \{0, 0.01 \ldots 1\}, \ldots, w_n)$.

We use the same procedure to optimize the parameters t_s of the parameterized credit functions described in Section 5.3. Instead of computing the argmax on Line 5 over all $\mathbf{w}$, we compute the optimal $\hat{t_s}$:

$$\hat{t_s} = \arg\max_{t_s} \sum_{(A,B) \in S} \mathbf{1}(O^{t_s}_{TDI}(A, B) = O_{AB}(A, B)). \tag{10}$$

6. EXPERIMENTS AND RESULTS

In Section 4, we examined the agreement between TDI and AB metrics, and the sensitivity of both types of comparison methods. Depending on the AB metric, agreement ranges from random up to 75%, while sensitivity of TDI is on average two orders of magnitude higher than that of AB metrics. In this section we evaluate our new interleaving credit functions. First, we analyze what level of agreement can be reached by matching interleaving credit functions with the parameters of AB metrics. Second, we evaluate our parameterized credit functions, and our method for optimizing agreement with AB metrics.

6.1 Matching AB Credit

In our first set of experiments, we evaluate our *matching* credit functions. These are designed to match the parameters of the AB metric that we wish to optimize, as explained in Section 5.2. For instance, for the target AB metric AB_S we classify observed clicks on interleaving impressions using the same classifier used by the AB comparison, and only assign interleaving credit for satisfied clicks.

Table 4: Agreement of *matching* interleaving credit functions (designed to match AB metric parameters). Boldface indicates values significantly different from 0.5 (two-sided binomial test, p = 0.05). On the diagonal are metrics for which parameters are designed to match (gray background). Best agreement per AB metric is underlined.

	Interleaving Credit							
AB Metric	TDI	$TDI@1$	TDI_S	$TDI_S@1$	TDI_T	$TDI_T@1$	$TDI_{T,S}$	$TDI_{T,S}@1$
AB	0.63	0.66	**0.84**	0.66	0.61	0.61	0.58	0.53
$AB@1$	**0.71**	**0.68**	**0.76**	0.63	0.63	0.47	0.55	0.55
AB_S	**0.71**	**0.68**	**0.87**	**0.68**	**0.68**	0.58	0.61	0.55
$AB_S@1$	**0.76**	**0.68**	**0.82**	0.63	**0.74**	0.53	0.61	0.50
AB_T	0.53	0.55	0.47	0.55	**0.71**	0.55	**0.68**	0.58
$AB_T@1$	0.45	0.47	0.45	0.58	0.63	0.58	0.61	0.61
$AB_{T,S}$	0.47	0.55	0.53	**0.71**	0.66	0.66	0.58	0.53
$AB_{T,S}@1$	0.42	0.50	0.53	0.66	0.61	0.66	0.58	0.58

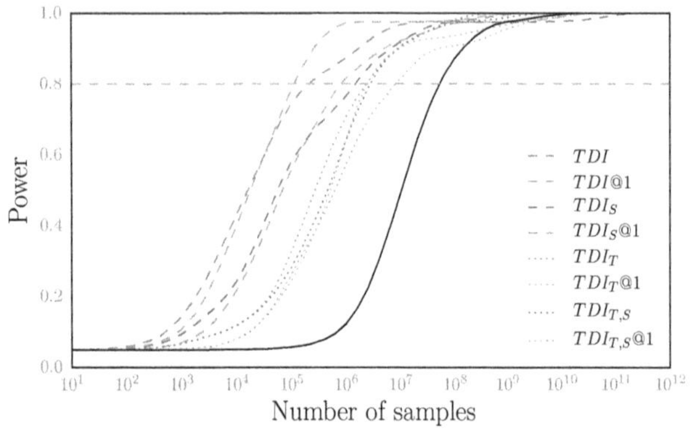

Figure 2: Power for TDI with matching credit functions (assuming two-sided t-test with $p = 0.05$, as described in Section 4.2). The black line denotes AB_S, the AB metric with most power.

As we study 8 AB metrics, this gives rise to 8 possible variants of TDI with matching credit functions.

Table 4 shows the agreement between each AB metric and each variant of TDI. In the first column, we see the agreement between baseline TDI and each AB metric, computing each as previously defined. The lowest agreement is observed between the original TDI and the AB metric $AB_{T,S}@1$, at 42%. The highest agreement is observed between TDI_S and the AB metric it is designed to optimize (AB_S), with 87%. Given the small sample of 38 comparisons, only the agreement rates above 68% are statistically significantly different from random agreement, and are shown in bold in the table. These compare favorably with typical inter-judge agreement rates in offline evaluations of around 65% [32], and with the bounds on AB self-agreement AB_{Sub}, AB_{Up} in Table 2.

We note that using different credit functions often increases agreement between AB metrics and TDI, but interestingly the maximal agreement is often not seen when the AB metric matches the credit function used for interleaving. This can be observed by comparing the metrics that match in terms of their parameters (indicated by the gray cells in Table 4), to the ones that achieved highest agreement (underlined). For example, agreement with AB_S is maximized by TDI_S, but agreement with $AB_{T,S}$ is maximized by $TDI_S@1$. A reason for this is the interplay between bias and noise. By more aggressively removing noise in the interleaving comparison (in this case, by only considering SAT clicks at the top position), we may increase agreement with related AB metrics, even those for which there is bias due to a slight mismatch between the interleaving and AB metric.

Our results show that agreement between interleaving and AB comparisons can be substantially improved by matching interleaving credit parameters to those of the target AB metrics. We also need to ensure that in doing so, we do not decrease the sensitivity of interleaving. Intuitively, removing observations (e.g., clicks beyond the first position) may reduce sensitivity. On the other hand, if the removed observations are noisy, the interleaving signal may actually become more discriminative, and sensitivity can be increased. Figure 2 shows the power for TDI with replaced scoring functions. We see that TDI with matching credit functions typically has lower power than standard TDI. In particular, sensitivity decreases for time-based metrics, which may also explain the relatively lower agreement between time-based interleaving credit functions and AB metrics. However, the power of these variants of TDI is still 1 to 2 orders of magnitude larger than the power of the AB metric with most power. Sensitivity is increased by TDI_S, the credit function that also shows highest agreement. This result indicates that focusing interleaving credit on low-noise clicks is a very promising way to achieve both high sensitivity and good agreement with user satisfaction metrics.

The results of the analysis in this section motivate the next set of questions. Given a target AB metric, what is the best credit function that should be applied to TDI? Just as the correct credit function may not be the same as the target AB metric, the parameters of the credit function may need to be tuned. And, once we automatically optimize the parameters of interleaving credit functions, to what degree do optimal values generalize to unseen ranker comparisons? We address these questions next.

6.2 Parameterized Credit Functions

One way to increase agreement of TDI with AB metrics is to take an interleaving credit function with parameters (see Section 5.3) and tune the parameters towards a given AB metric. For instance, previous work has shown that it is possible to estimate the probability that a given click indicates user satisfaction [16]. While an AB metric such as AB_S must incorporate a threshold below which clicks are not considered to indicate user satisfaction, the threshold for TDI need not be the same. Rather, we can find the optimal threshold t_s for $TDI_S^{t_s}$ at which to consider a click as satisfied. This optimization procedure might lead to reduced variance, and thereby increase agreement with AB metrics.

We use the maximization procedure described in Section 5.5 and in particular Equation (10) to find an optimal threshold for each AB metric we consider. Note that, as opposed to experiments in the previous section, here we obtain averages over $N = 100$ iterations of the maximization procedure, instead of averages over the 38 comparisons. This allows us to perform statistical significance testing using a one-sample two-sided student's t-test. In our result table we indicate statistically significant improvements over TDI by ▲ ($p < 0.01$) (losses ▼). Also, as opposed to before, we now

Table 5: Agreement for $TDI^{t_s}_S$, $TDI^{t_s}_{T,S}$, and $TDI^{\mathbf{w}}_{T,S}$. Parameters t_s and w are chosen to maximize agreement with the AB metrics on held out data. Higher agreement than TDI is bold. Stat. sig. improvements over TDI are indicated by ▲ ($p < 0.01$) (losses ▼).

		(a) $TDI^{t_s}_S$		(b) $TDI^{t_s}_{T,S}$		(c) $TDI^{\mathbf{w}}_{T,S}$		
AB Metric	TDI	Agreement	t_s	Agreement	t_s	Agreement	w_1	w_2
AB	0.63	**0.82** ▲	0.76 (0.09)	0.53 ▼	0.52 (0.40)	**0.84** ▲	1.00 (0.00)	0.00 (0.00)
AB@1	0.71	**0.79** ▲	0.74 (0.19)	0.54 ▼	0.40 (0.32)	**0.75** ▲	1.00 (0.00)	0.05 (0.22)
AB_S	0.71	**0.84** ▲	0.76 (0.09)	0.48 ▼	0.29 (0.31)	**0.85** ▲	1.00 (0.00)	0.00 (0.00)
AB_S@1	0.76	**0.84** ▲	0.68 (0.24)	0.48 ▼	0.37 (0.32)	**0.82** ▲	1.00 (0.00)	0.02 (0.14)
AB_T	0.53	0.47 ▼	0.67 (0.28)	**0.67** ▲	0.54 (0.27)	**0.68** ▲	0.99 (0.11)	0.90 (0.30)
AB_T@1	0.45	**0.49** ▲	0.57 (0.35)	**0.62** ▲	0.61 (0.34)	**0.56** ▲	0.96 (0.22)	0.79 (0.41)
$AB_{T,S}$	0.47	0.46	0.46 (0.38)	**0.61** ▲	0.41 (0.30)	**0.63** ▲	0.91 (0.30)	0.88 (0.33)
$AB_{T,S}$@1	0.42	**0.52** ▲	0.30 (0.39)	**0.62** ▲	0.42 (0.34)	**0.50** ▲	0.06 (0.65)	0.25 (0.41)

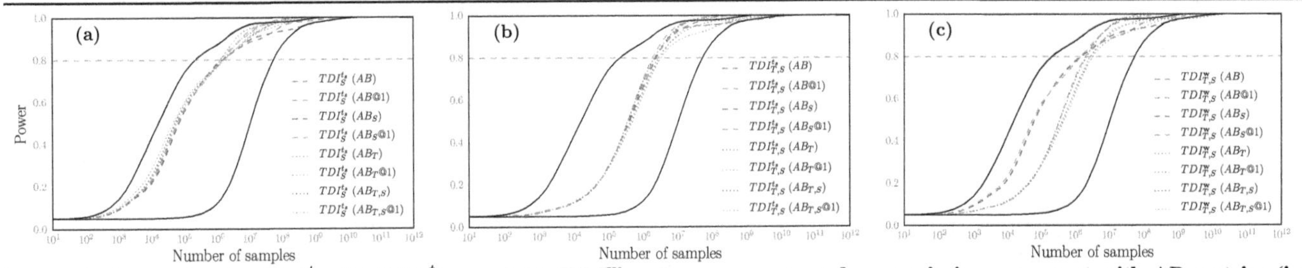

Figure 3: Power for (a) $TDI^{t_s}_S$, (b) $TDI^{t_s}_{T,S}$, and (c) $TDI^{\mathbf{w}}_{T,S}$. Parameters t_s and w maximize agreement with AB metrics (in brackets) on held out data, see Table 5. The upper black line denotes TDI, the lower AB_S, the AB metric with most power.

measure how far our optimized credit functions generalize to unseen data.

The results for maximizing agreement of $TDI^{t_s}_S$ are shown in column (a) in Table 5. In the table, we see substantially and signficantly increased agreement rates of up to 84% for the AB metrics that only depend on clicks, reducing disagreement rates by between 6% and 20%. E.g. in Table 5, for $t_s = 0.76$ in the first row means that clicks predicted to have less than a 76% chance of indicating satisfaction are ignored. This causes 58% of clicks to be ignored on average. We see that across many folds, the optimal value is between 0.67 and 0.85, and we found that the precise value does not impact the outcome significantly.

Interestingly, the optimal threshold at which clicks should be included in the score calculation are around $t_s = 0.75$, which is lower than the $t_s = 0.8$ which is used in the AB_S and AB_S@1 AB metrics. It is equally interesting that learning such a threshold changes agreement between TDI and time-based AB metrics much less but generally decreases it, and selects a t_s threshold that is much lower.

In contrast, if we take the credit function $TDI^{t_s}_{T,S}$, that does take time as well as satisfaction into account and if we learn the same threshold t_s, then in column (b) of Table 5 we see a very different result than before in column (a). Now, the agreement between TDI and AB metrics that incorporate time increases substantially and significantly (from 42-53% to 61-67%, a net disagreement error reduction of between 4% and 22%) while disagreement increases significantly with the non-time based metrics. Now, for the time based metrics we also outperform the baseline AB_{Sub} which uses as many query impressions as TDI does (see Table 2).

These changes in agreement exhibit the same pattern as seen when tuning a simpler threshold on satisfaction (as reported in column (a) in Table 5). In particular, the deterioration in agreement from tuning a feature that does not represent a measure included in the AB metric reduces agreement. We hypothesize that this is due to the maximization procedure failing to find a optimal value that generalizes well to unseen data, as the target AB metrics that are based only on clicks have low correlation with the credit function we are optimizing. These results motivate our next approach: optimize a combination of interleaving credit functions that best matches a given AB metric.

But first, we look at what happens to the power of TDI when we optimize parameters of a credit function. Results are in Figures 3 (a) and 3 (b). We see that again, the power for our adjust interleaving credit functions lies between standard TDI and the AB metric with the highest power. In other words, we increased agreement while maintaining an advantage in terms of power over AB comparisons.

6.3 Combined Credit Functions

As we saw in the previous section and in columns (a) and (b) in Table 5, for different types of AB metrics we need different interleaving credit functions to increase agreement. Optimizing a single parameter (t_s) for a single credit function proved not powerful enough. In this section we use the maximization procedure described in Section 5.5 and in particular Equation (9) to find weights $\mathbf{w}$ for a weighted combination of already optimized credit functions that maximizes agreement. That is, we take for each AB metric the threshold t_s that in the previous section maximized agreement. Note that we only optimize a weighted combination of *two* credit functions, namely, we learn w_1 for $TDI^{\hat{t_s}}_S$ and w_2 $TDI^{\hat{t_s}}_{T,S}$. The intuition behind this simple model is that it should be able to capture attributes of each of the AB metrics.

We obtain the results presented in column (c) in Table 5. Where in the previous section, in columns (a) and (b) in Table 5, we obtained average agreement of 65% and 57% respectively, now we obtain an average agreement of 70%. Agreement with all individual AB metrics increased significantly from 42-76% to 50-85%. Interestingly, we see that the weights w_1 and w_2 that are the result of the optimization procedure are mostly selecting ($w_2 \approx 0$) the $TDI^{\hat{t_s}}_S$ credit function for the click based AB metrics. While the time based AB metrics additionally put weight ($w_2 \gg 0$) on the time based credit function $TDI^{\hat{t_s}}_{T,S}$.

Lastly, turning to the sensitivity, in Figure 3 (c) we see that also for the combined credit functions sensitivity stayed 1 to 2 orders of magnitude higher compared to AB metrics.

7. CONCLUSION

In this paper, we showed how to optimize interleaving outcomes to agree better with a given target AB metric, while maintaining the sensitivity advantage of interleaved comparisons over AB tests. We started by analyzing the agreement of team draft interleaving (TDI) with a set of 8 AB metrics based on combinations of click count, click positions, satisfied clicks, and time to click signals. To enable this analysis, we introduced a method for comparing AB and interleaved comparison metrics in terms of power and agreement across varying sample sizes. We found that, while TDI is very sensitive, its agreement with user satisfaction AB metrics on realistic ranking evaluations is low, from random up to 76%.

Results of this analysis motivated our approach. We proposed to replace the default credit function of TDI with novel credit functions that take richer user signals into account. In particular, we designed sets of credit functions that (1) match the parameters of AB metrics, (2) are parameterized and (3) combine (parameterized) credit functions. To automatically tune the parameters of these last credit functions, we further introduced a bootstrapping algorithm that can automatically maximize agreement with arbitrary AB metrics.

Our empirical results, obtained on 38 paired experiments with a total of 3 billion clicks, showed that our approach can substantially and significantly increase agreement with AB metrics. In particular, learning a combination of parameterized credit functions resulted in agreement of up to 85%, improving the agreement with AB metrics by up to 22% (almost halving these disagreements). We also showed that the sensitivity for all our adapted versions of TDI is still 1 to 2 orders of magnitude higher than that of AB metrics.

The most important implication of our results is that it enables, for the first time, the integration of rich user satisfaction signals with highly sensitive interleaved comparison methods. This will dramatically reduce the required sample sizes, and therefore cost, of such online evaluations. Opportunities for future work include the development of yet more sophisticated (learned) credit functions, e.g., to take into account session-level or task-level features. Furthermore, more accurate prediction of AB outcomes may be possible by additionally taking into account the magnitude and uncertainty of AB metrics of individual experiments. Finally, it would be interesting to see where disagreements between interleaving and AB outcomes are highest; for what queries and for what kind of comparisons.

Acknowledgements. We would like to thank Ahmed Hassan Awadallah, Dan Liebling, Maarten de Rijke, Milad Shokouhi, Nick Craswell, Paul Bennett, Peter Bailey, Rich Caruana, Ryen White for helpful discussions and insights. This research was partially supported by the Dutch national program COMMIT.

REFERENCES

[1] O. Chapelle, T. Joachims, F. Radlinski, and Y. Yue. Large-scale validation and analysis of interleaved search evaluation. *ACM TOIS*, 30(1):1–41, Feb. 2012.

[2] F. Diaz, R. White, G. Buscher, and D. Liebling. Robust models of mouse movement on dynamic web search results pages. In *CIKM*, pages 1451–1460. ACM Press, Oct. 2013.

[3] G. Dupret and M. Lalmas. Absence time and user engagement: Evaluating ranking functions. In *WSDM*, pages 173–182, 2013.

[4] S. Fox, K. Karnawat, M. Mydland, S.Dumais, and T.White. Evaluating implicit measures to improve web search. *ACM TOIS*, 23: 147–168, 2005.

[5] Q. Guo and E. Agichtein. Understanding "Abandoned" Ads: Towards Personalized Commercial Intent Inference via Mouse Movement Analysis. *SIGIR-IRA*, 2008.

[6] Q. Guo and E. Agichtein. Towards predicting web searcher gaze position from mouse movements. In *CHI EA*, page 3601, Apr. 2010.

[7] A. Hassan, R. Jones, and K. Klinkner. Beyond DCG: user behavior as a predictor of a successful search. In *WSDM*, 2010.

[8] A. Hassan, X. Shi, N. Craswell, and B. Ramsey. Beyond clicks: query reformulation as a predictor of search satisfaction. In *CIKM*, 2013.

[9] Y. He and K. Wang. Inferring search behaviors using partially observable markov model with duration (POMD). In *WSDM*, 2011.

[10] W. Hersh, A. H. Turpin, S. Price, B. Chan, D. Kramer, L. Sacherek, and D. Olson. Do batch and user evaluations give the same results? In *SIGIR*, pages 17–24, 2000.

[11] K. Hofmann, S. Whiteson, and M. de Rijke. A probabilistic method for inferring preferences from clicks. In *CIKM*, page 249, 2011.

[12] K. Hofmann, F. Behr, and F. Radlinski. On Caption Bias in Interleaving Experiments. In *CIKM*, 2012.

[13] J. Huang, T. Lin, and R. White. No search result left behind. In *WSDM*, page 203, 2012.

[14] T. Joachims. Evaluating Retrieval Performance using Clickthrough Data. In J. Franke, G. Nakhaeizadeh, and I. Renz, editors, *Text Mining*, pages 79–96. Physica/Springer, 2003.

[15] T. Joachims, L. A. Granka, B. Pan, H. Hembrooke, F. Radlinski, and G. Gay. Evaluating the accuracy of implicit feedback from clicks and query reformulations in Web search. *ACM TOIS*, 25(2):7+, Apr. 2007.

[16] Y. Kim, A. Hassan, R. White, and I. Zitouni. Modeling dwell time to predict click-level satisfaction. In *WSDM*, 2014.

[17] R. Kohavi, R. Longbotham, D. Sommerfield, and R. Henne. Controlled experiments on the web: survey and practical guide. *Data Mining and Knowledge Discovery*, 18(1):140–181, 2009.

[18] D. Lagun, C. Hsieh, D. Webster, and V. Navalpakkam. Towards Better Measurement of Attention and Satisfaction in Mobile Search. In *SIGIR*, 2014.

[19] E. L. Lehmann and J. P. Romano. *Testing statistical hypotheses*. springer, 2006.

[20] J. Li, S. Huffman, and A. Tokuda. Good abandonment in mobile and pc internet search. In *SIGIR '09*, pages 43–50, 2009.

[21] N. Meinshausen. Quantile regression forests. *jmlr*, 7:983–999, 2006.

[22] F. Radlinski and N. Craswell. Comparing the sensitivity of information retrieval metrics. In *SIGIR*, pages 667–674, 2010.

[23] F. Radlinski and N. Craswell. Optimized interleaving for online retrieval evaluation. In *WSDM*, 2013.

[24] F. Radlinski, M. Kurup, and T. Joachims. How does clickthrough data reflect retrieval quality? In *CIKM*, pages 43–52. ACM Press, 2008.

[25] M. Sanderson. Test Collection Based Evaluation of Information Retrieval Systems. *Foundations and Trends in Information Retrieval*, 4(4):247–375, 2010.

[26] A. Schuth, F. Sietsma, S. Whiteson, D. Lefortier, and M. de Rijke. Multileaved Comparisons for Fast Online Evaluation. In *CIKM*, pages 71–80, 2014.

[27] A. Schuth, R.-J. Bruintjes, F. Büttner, J. van Doorn, C. Groenland, H. Oosterhuis, C.-N. Tran, B. Veeling, J. van der Velde, R. Wechsler, D. Woudenberg, and M. de Rijke. Probabilistic multileave for online retrieval evaluation. In *SIGIR*, 2015.

[28] Y. Song, X. Shi, R. White, and A. Hassan. Context-Aware Web Search Abandonment Prediction. In *SIGIR*, 2014.

[29] J. Teevan, S. Dumais, and E. Horvitz. The potential value of personalizing search. In *SIGIR*, pages 756–757, 2007.

[30] A. Turpin and W. Hersh. Why batch and user evaluations do not give the same results. In *SIGIR*, pages 225–231, 2001.

[31] A. Turpin and F. Scholar. User performance versus precision measures for simple search tasks. In *SIGIR*, pages 11–18, 2006.

[32] E. M. Voorhees. Variations in relevance judgments and the measurement of retrieval effectiveness. *IPM*, 36(5):697 – 716, 2000.

[33] H. Wang, Y. Song, M. Chang, X. He, A. Hassan, and R. White. Modeling Action-level Satisfaction for Search Task Satisfaction Prediction. In *SIGIR*, 2014.

[34] K. Wang, T. Walker, and Z. Zheng. PSkip: Estimating relevance ranking quality from web search clickthrough data. In *KDD*, pages 1355–1364, 2009.

[35] K. Wang, N. Gloy, and X. Li. Inferring search behaviors using partially observable Markov (POM) model. In *WSDM*, 2010.

[36] E. Yilmaz, M. Verma, N. Craswell, F. Radlinski, and P. Bailey. Relevance and Effort: An Analysis of Document Utility. In *CIKM*, 2014.

[37] Y. Yue, Y. Gao, O. Chapelle, Y. Zhang, and T. Joachims. Learning more powerful test statistics for click-based retrieval evaluation. In *SIGIR*, pages 507–514, 2010.

[38] Y. Yue, R. Patel, and H. Roehrig. Beyond position bias: examining result attractiveness as a source of presentation bias in clickthrough data. In *WWW*, pages 1011–1018, 2010.

Sequential Testing for Early Stopping of Online Experiments

Eugene Kharitonov[1,2], Aleksandr Vorobev[1], Craig Macdonald[2], Pavel Serdyukov[1], Iadh Ounis[2]
[1]Yandex, Russia
[2]University of Glasgow, UK
[1]{kharitonov, alvor88, pavser}@yandex-team.ru
[2]{craig.macdonald, iadh.ounis}@glasgow.ac.uk

ABSTRACT

Online evaluation methods, such as A/B and interleaving experiments, are widely used for search engine evaluation. Since they rely on noisy implicit user feedback, running each experiment takes a considerable time. Recently, the problem of reducing the duration of online experiments has received substantial attention from the research community. However, the possibility of using sequential statistical testing procedures for reducing the time required for the evaluation experiments remains less studied. Such sequential testing procedures allow an experiment to stop early, once the data collected is sufficient to make a conclusion. In this work, we study the usefulness of sequential testing procedures for both interleaving and A/B testing. We propose modified versions of the O'Brien & Fleming and MaxSPRT sequential tests that are applicable for testing in the interleaving scenario. Similarly, for A/B experiments, we assess the usefulness of the O'Brien & Fleming test, as well as that of our proposed MaxSPRT-based sequential testing procedure. In our experiments on datasets containing 115 interleaving and 41 A/B testing experiments, we observe that considerable reductions in the average experiment duration can be achieved by using our proposed tests. In particular, for A/B experiments, the average experiment durations can be reduced by up to 66% in comparison with a single step test procedure, and by up to 44% in comparison with the O'Brien & Fleming test. Similarly, a marked relative reduction of 63% in the duration of the interleaving experiments can be achieved.

Categories and Subject Descriptors: H.3.3 [Information Storage & Retrieval]: Information Search & Retrieval

Keywords: A/B experiments; interleaving; statistical testing

1. INTRODUCTION

Online evaluation methods, such as A/B and interleaving experiments, have proven to be an important tool in web search evaluation [3, 9, 11]. In contrast to a Cranfield-based evaluation method, online evaluation methods interpret the implicit feedback of the real users. As a result, the online evaluation methods can be applied in several scenarios where offline evaluation might be impractical. Examples of such scenarios include cases where the large-scale labelling of the document relevance is hard, e.g. the evaluation of personalised ranking algorithms or the ranking of fresh content. Another example is the evaluation of changes in the search engine that do not affect search result ranking, such as changes in the UI, where A/B experiments can be applied.

However, the existing online methods have some limitations. As these methods rely on noisy implicit feedback from the users, each online evaluation experiment requires a considerable number of observations to be made before a reliable experiment outcome can be obtained [11]. As a result, usually each experiment is deployed on up to several per cent of query stream for several days, e.g. A/B experiments might be deployed for a week or two on several per cent of queries [11]. Similarly, Chapelle et al. [3] used a dataset of interleaving experiments that span up to 5 days. Due to these constraints, the number of simultaneously running experiments is bounded and, consequently, the throughput of the evaluation pipeline is limited. Since this limits the applicability of the online experimentation methods, an important research problem is to improve the online experimentation methods, so that they reach a reliable outcome faster.

Once the evaluated search engine modification is worse than the baseline system, the users who participate in the corresponding evaluation experiment are exposed to a somewhat degraded search experience. On the other hand, it was reported that such online experiments with negative outcome constitute a considerable part of all experiments [11]. Again, this supports the need to improve online evaluation so that the outcomes of experiments are obtained earlier: the negative changes are quickly rejected, and improvements are deployed as soon as possible.

These concerns become even more important in initiatives such as Living Labs [1], where industrial participants are invited to share a part of their live traffic for use by academic researchers. Indeed, the ability to quickly detect and disable an erroneous experiment can be extremely useful in such a shared infrastructure.

As we will discuss in Section 2, several approaches to reduce the duration of interleaving experiments have previously been studied. However, the possibility to reduce the duration of the interleaving experiments by using *sequential testing procedures* remains less studied. Such testing procedures are capable of stopping the experiments early once the available data is sufficient to make a reliable comparison

SIGIR'15, August 09 - 13, 2015, Santiago, Chile.
 ISBN 978-1-4503-3621-5/15/08 ...$15.00.
DOI: http://dx.doi.org/10.1145/2766462.2767729.

outcome. In this work, we aim to close this gap. We demonstrate that by modifying two sequential testing procedures to make them applicable for interleaving, we obtain a considerable improvement in the average time an experiment takes.

Similarly, to the best of our knowledge, there are no studies published that quantitatively assess the usefulness of sequential testing in the context of the A/B experiment-based search evaluation. In this work, we propose a new sequential test developed to match the distribution of one of the popular absolute online metrics, namely the abandonment rate. Moreover, we perform an experimental study on a dataset of A/B experiments, where we evaluate both our proposed test and the standard O'Brien&Fleming sequential test.

Overall, the contributions of this work are two-fold:

- We propose several sequential testing methods that reflect the distributions of the data generated in A/B and interleaving experiments, and describe how to adjust their stopping thresholds based on query log data;
- We perform an extensive evaluation study of the performance of our proposed methods using real-life datasets of A/B and interleaving experiments.

The remainder of this paper is organised as follows. In Section 2 we discuss the related work. In Section 3 we briefly review how A/B test and interleaving experiments are performed. In Section 4 we introduce several methods for performing sequential statistical analysis. The datasets used in our empirical study are described in Section 5. Our evaluation methodology and the results we obtained are described in Sections 6 and 7, respectively. We conclude this paper and discuss future work in Section 8.

2. RELATED WORK

Our work is closely related to two areas of research. The first area is concentrated on developing approaches to speed up the existing online evaluation methods and we discuss these approaches in Section 2.1. The sequential analysis methods are reviewed in Section 2.2.

2.1 Improving online evaluation

The first interleaving method, Balanced Interleaving, was proposed by Joachims [7]. The method was further developed in Team Draft Interleaving [18], Probabilistic Interleaving [6], Optimised Interleaving [17], and their modifications.

A thoroughly studied approach to reduce the time required to run interleaving experiments is to reduce noise in the user feedback and thus to improve the convergence rate of the interleaving experiments. This can be achieved by modifying the way the user clicks are aggregated and the aggregated credit is assigned to the tested alternatives. Radlinski and Craswell [16] studied approaches to weight user clicks according to the ranks of the clicked results. Chapelle et al. [3] considered ten different heuristic click aggregation schemes. For instance, in one of the schemes the result of each interleaved impression is represented by the difference between clicks obtained by compared systems, divided by the total number of clicks in the corresponding impression. In another scheme, the result is binary, equal to -1 if the baseline system received more clicks than the tested, +1 in the opposite case, and equal to 0 if they receive equal number of clicks. Overall, Chapelle et al. found that some of the tested credit assignment rules improve convergence rate of the interleaving outcomes.

A more elaborated approach to interpret click feedback was considered by Yue et al. [24], who proposed to machine-learn the click aggregation scheme using a feature-based representation of the clicks. Under their proposed approach, the combination of the features is learned to maximise the confidence in the outcomes of the earlier performed experiments.

Another approach was proposed by Radlinski and Craswell in [17]. Based on a novel interleaving framework, they studied how a sensitive interleaving method (i.e. the method that quickly converges) can be built by means of maximising the uncertainty of the comparison winner within a single session. Building on their work, Kharitonov et al. [8] proposed an approach to leverage pre-experimental data to improve the interleaving sensitivity.

Deng et al. [4] studied an approach to improve the convergence rate of A/B experiments by using pre-experimental data. This reduction is achieved, for instance, by means of stratification of the users into groups, such that the between-strata variance of the observed metric is removed.

All of the above discussed approaches share the same statistical testing scenario. In this scenario, an online evaluation experiment is deployed. After running this experiment for a pre-defined period of time (e.g. a week), the experiment is stopped. Next, some form of statistical test, such as the binomial test in the case of interleaving, is performed on the collected user interaction data to infer if a statistically significant difference between the tested alternatives was observed. Importantly, in this scenario, each experiment is deployed for the period of time that is fixed before the experiment starts. However, it is likely that in some experiments highly contrasting alternatives are compared, and in that case it should be possible to stop the experiment early and still be able to reliably detect preferences between the compared alternatives. In this paper, we study how to conduct a statistical analysis which is capable of stopping such experiments early, and thus reduces the mean experiment evaluation time. In our experimental study, we demonstrate that our proposed early-stopping approach is complementary to the approaches studied before, and the online evaluation methods can benefit from combining approaches to improve sensitivity and to stop early.

2.2 Sequential testing

Sequential statistical testing appeared to address the demands of the military testing during World War II, resulting in Wald's *sequential probability ratio test* (SPRT) [20]. This test performs an analysis in steps. At each step, a new data point is considered, and the decision is taken if the observed data is enough to make a reliable conclusion about the considered hypotheses and the experiment should be finished, or more measurements are required.

Despite its simplicity, SPRT was shown [21] to be optimal when comparing two simple alternatives. Further research was conducted to improve the SPRT-based methods in a variety of directions. For instance, the 2-SPRT test was proposed to minimise the expected sample size at a specified parameter when discriminating hypotheses $H_0 : \theta = \theta_0$ against $H_1 : \theta = \theta_1 > \theta_0$ [2]. Another SPRT-based test that can be used to test against a complex hypothesis, MaxSPRT [12], was proposed for the post-approval drug safety surveillance. These tests can be applied when the specific parameters of one of the tested hypothesis are not known before running the experiment. A similar problem arises while running online experiments. Indeed, in interleaving experiments the null hypothesis can be specified (both evaluated algorithms are equally likely to win in a particular user session), but the difference between the evaluated algorithms is hard to estimate before running an experiment.

As an alternative to the SPRT-based tests, "repeated significance tests" (RST) were proposed. As conventional single-sample tests are often used in clinical trials, the motivation behind RST is to apply them repeatedly during the trial. These tests evolved into a group sequential RST [15], where the data is accumulated between tests. Further, O'Brien and Fleming [14] proposed a group sequential testing procedure that had a better performance. These methods became popular within clinical trials, as the sequential procedures reduce the time the participants are exposed to ineffective or harmful treatments.

Thereafter, the group sequential testing approach was intensively developed. Wang and Tsiatis [23] suggested a parametric family of tests, which generalises both Pocock and O'Brien&Fleming tests, and can be optimised to be nearly optimal w.r.t. a fixed expected difference between the alternatives. Another improvement was proposed by Lan and DeMets [13], which accounts for some specifics of the clinical trials: the number of subjects available between stops is not known in advance and can vary greatly.

Overall, sequential testing is a highly developed discipline, and a variety of tests that differ by their properties and assumptions was proposed. A review can be found in [2, 19]. Due to their properties, we select the O'Brien&Fleming and MaxSPRT tests as a foundation for our study. These tests are very practical, they do not require any a priori assumptions about the expected effect size or its boundaries. The O'Brien&Fleming test can be interpreted as a repeated standard Pearson's chi-square test with progressive stopping thresholds, so that the last threshold is close to the one test scenario, which is very appealing from the practical perspective. Similarly, the MaxSPRT-based tests do not require any pre-experimental knowledge, and their decisions are extremely transparent.

Finally, to the best of our knowledge, the only work that mentions the use of sequential testing procedures in online web search evaluation is [11]. In their work, Kohavi et al. reports that the O'Brien&Fleming test is used in Bing to abort A/B experiments early when a severe degradation in metrics is observed. In contrast, we propose modifications of the MaxSPRT tests for interleaving and A/B experiments, and modify the O'Brien&Fleming test for the interleaving evaluation. Moreover, we perform a thorough evaluation of the usefulness of the considered tests.

3. ONLINE EXPERIMENTATION

In this section we briefly review how the A/B and interleaving experiments are performed.

3.1 A/B tests

To perform an A/B comparison of a modified system B to the baseline system A, each of the systems is assigned to serve its own bucket of users (a bucket is a random sample of users). Usually, each experiment lasts for a week or two [11], so that the data collected contains sessions from each day of the week. After stopping the experiment, some absolute online metrics are measured on each bucket. These metrics are compared across buckets, and the statistical significance of the difference of the metrics is analysed, e.g. by means of a t-test. More formally, denoting the expected values of the metric μ on buckets A and B, as μ_A and μ_B respectively, we are interested in comparing two statistical hypotheses, H_0 and H_1:

$$H_0 : \mu_A = \mu_B, \quad H_1 : \mu_A \neq \mu_B \tag{1}$$

A variety of online absolute metrics were proposed, and, usually, a number of metrics is used in combination. For instance, when optimising for revenue one needs to ensure that there is no degradation in user satisfaction metrics [10]. Additionally, a set of diagnostic metrics might be used to automatically terminate a deployed experiment, when a severe degradation in one of the metrics is observed [11]. The early stopping procedures we study in this work are especially useful in controlling the changes in the diagnostic metrics.

In our study we use the abandonment rate metric, which is equal to the fraction of the user interactions with no results clicked on. We believe that the extension of our study to account for other metrics such as those representing user engagement [5] is a promising direction for future work.

3.2 Interleaving

All of the existing interleaving methods share the same idea. Suppose we want to compare two alternative ranking algorithms, A (baseline) and B (evaluated system). To compare them, we randomly select a sample of user sessions in the session stream and use them in the experiment. For each query submitted in the experiment, the results from A and from B are retrieved. In the next step, these results are mixed (interleaved) and then presented to the user.

While the approaches we discuss in our work can be applied for any existing interleaving methods, below we review the Team Draft [18] interleaving method, as it is used in our evaluation study. The interleaved result list is generated from the result lists of A and B by the following algorithm. The first result is selected from a random alternative. After that, from the second alternative, we take the first result that is not already included in the interleaved result list. These two steps are repeated until the required number of results is obtained.

As we discussed in Section 2, several approaches to aggregate the user clicks observed in a session into a credit obtained by A and B were proposed [3, 16, 24]. In this study, we experiment with two aggregation schemes: the *binary*, and the *deduped binary* schemes. Under the binary scheme, in each interaction, the alternative with the most results clicked receives a unit credit and is referred to as the winner. The deduped binary scheme is similar, but clicks on the top-k results which are identical both in A and B are ignored. In both schemes, interactions without clicks are ignored. If in a session both A and B obtained an equal number of clicks, the session is considered as tie.

The deduped credit assignment removes some additive zero-mean noise from the user feedback. Despite its simplicity, it was reported [3] that the deduped binary scheme is one of the top-performing schemes, markedly reducing the number of user interactions required to obtain a statistically significant experiment outcome.

Let us denote a variable S that represents the probability of B winning A in a session with a click, assuming that the ties are broken randomly. After running an experiment, S can be estimated as follows:

$$\hat{S} = \frac{w^B + \frac{1}{2}t}{w^A + t + w^B} \tag{2}$$

where w^B and w^A denote the number of sessions where B and A win, respectively; t is the number of ties.

The goal of the statistical analysis methods we discuss in Section 4 is to compare two statistical hypotheses, H_0 (A and B are equally likely to win a particular impression) and H_1 (the chances to win differ):

$$H_0 : S = \frac{1}{2}, \quad H_1 : S \neq \frac{1}{2} \tag{3}$$

4. STATISTICAL ANALYSIS

In this section, we introduce the sequential testing procedures we consider in this work. We start by describing the procedures applicable for interleaving experiments (Section 4.1): O'Brien&Fleming's sequential test, modified for interleaving (OBF-I), and the MaxSPRT test. After that, we describe two tests applicable for A/B tests: the standard O'Brien&Fleming test, and our proposed MaxSPRT-AB test, tailored for A/B test experiments. For all of these tests, we also describe algorithms to train their stopping thresholds.

4.1 Interleaving

While analysing an interleaving experiment, our goal is to compare two statistical hypotheses (Equation (3)): under the null hypothesis (H_0), A and B have equal chances to win an interleaving comparison in an interaction; under the alternative hypothesis (H_1) these chances are not equal.

OBF-I Initially, the O'Brien & Fleming's sequential test was formulated for clinical trials that compare two treatments on two different groups of participants. In contrast, in interleaving experiments only one group of users is used. Below we describe our adaptation OBF-I of the OBF test to the case of interleaving experiments.

Assume that the number of possible stops, where a sequential test is allowed to analyse accumulated data and make a decision, is set to N. Let us introduce a random variable x that is equal to 1 (-1) if B (A) wins in a comparison in an interaction, and 0 if a tie is observed. By x_j we denote the realisation of x observed in jth session. Further, we denote the number of sessions between the $(i-1)$th and ith stops as K_i. Under the null hypothesis, the probabilities of winning a comparison in a session for A and B are equal. Thus, according to the central limit theorem, the normalised mean R_i of the realisations x_j observed between the $(i-1)$th and ith stops approaches the standard normal distribution as K_i grows:

$$R_i = \frac{(x_1 + .. + x_{K_i})}{(K_i \cdot D[x])^{\frac{1}{2}}} \sim \mathbb{N}(0, 1) \tag{4}$$

where $D[x]$ is an estimate of the variance of x.

Further, we denote the total number of sessions occurred before the ith stop as T_i ($T_i = \sum_{j<i} K_j$), and the accumulated number of comparisons won by A (B) before the ith stop as w_i^A (w_i^B). Assuming that the number of the sessions occurring between the stops is approximately the same and equal to K, we define the accumulated statistic $O_i = (\frac{1}{\sqrt{i}} \sum_1^i R_j)^2$. Since $\sum_1^i R_j$ is a sum of variables that are distributed according to $\mathbb{N}(0, 1)$, their scaled sum $\frac{1}{\sqrt{i}} \sum_1^i R_j$ also has the standard normal distribution. Thus, as a square of a standard normal variable, O_i is distributed according to the chi-squared distribution with one degree of freedom:

$$O_i = \left(\frac{1}{\sqrt{i}} \sum_{j=1}^{i} R_j\right)^2 = \frac{(w_i^B - w_i^A)^2}{iK \cdot D[x]} = \frac{(w_i^B - w_i^A)^2}{T_i \cdot D[x]} \sim \chi^2(1) \tag{5}$$

The estimate of the variance $D[x]$ is:

$$D[x] = \frac{1}{T_i - 1} \sum_{j=1}^{T_i} (x_j - \bar{x})^2, \quad \bar{x} = \frac{w_i^B - w_i^A}{T_i} \tag{6}$$

O'Brien and Fleming [14] proposed to apply a progressive decision criterion where at the ith stop, O_i is compared to a threshold $\frac{1}{i}\hat{a}$ that decreases at each stop ($\hat{a}$ depends on the number of stops and required Type I error). This ensures an intuitive requirement that to terminate an experiment earlier, one needs to have a higher confidence in H_1.

In an equivalent but more convenient formulation, at each stop, a statistic $i \cdot O_i$ can be considered, and compared to a single fixed threshold a. Once it exceeds a, the experiment is terminated, and H_1 is accepted. To infer the experiment outcome, the difference between w_i^A and w_i^B is used (i.e. if $w_i^B > w_i^A$ then $B \succ A$). If at the last stop $N \cdot O_N$ still does not reach a then the hypothesis H_0 is accepted.

For the cases of small numbers of stops (less or equal to 5), the values of the threshold a can be found in [14]. Since in our experiments we use a higher number of stops, we briefly review how the threshold can be obtained from running Monte-Carlo simulations. The general idea is to replace R_i with random numbers generated from $\mathbb{N}(0, 1)$, and adjust a so that the test will detect a difference in the α (required Type I error level) fraction of the generated tests. Formally, to perform one iteration of the simulation, we sample N (N is the required number of stops) random numbers from the standard normal distribution ($U_1, ..., U_N \sim \mathbb{N}(0, 1)$), and calculate the maximum square of their partial sums $U_m^2 = \max(U_1^2, (U_1+U_2)^2, ..., (U_1+...U_N)^2)$. We collect these maximums over 10,000 simulations. Finally, we select a value that corresponds to $(1-\alpha)$ percentile of these maximums.

A possible heuristic is to replace $D[x]$ with its upper bound[1] 1. While this substitution might increase the time required for O_i to achieve the threshold a, it also makes the decision rule even simpler: at each stop i, a normalised square of the difference between the wins of A and B is multiplied by the number of the stop and compared to the threshold a. We refer to a rule with this heuristic applied as **OBF-I***.

Notably, OBF-I and OBF-I* assume that the number of sessions performed between stops is large enough so that the central limit theorem can be applied.

MaxSPRT At the core of the SPRT family of tests is the likelihood ratio statistic. Informally, this statistic equates to the likelihood of the observed data under the alternative hypothesis H_1 divided by the likelihood of the data under H_0. Once this ratio becomes big enough, H_0 can be rejected. To formalise this idea, we use the same notation as before. By T_i we denote the total number of sessions before the ith stop, w_i^A (w_i^B), and t_i are the numbers of sessions where A (B) wins, and the number of sessions with ties, respectively. Further, by m_i we denote our estimate of the number of the comparisons won by B after breaking the ties:

$$m_i = w_i^B + \frac{1}{2} t_i$$

Under this notation, the logarithm of the likelihood statistic can be specified as follows:

$$L_i = \log \frac{p_1^{m_i} (1 - p_1)^{T_i - m_i}}{p_0^{m_i} (1 - p_0)^{T_i - m_i}} \tag{7}$$

[1] A unit variance is achieved if on each tie a coin is tossed and a unit credit is assigned to a random alternative. However, this might be a good approximation since for a tie to occur at least two results must be clicked, which happens rarely.

Input: Type I error tolerance α, a set of A/A experiments Q.
Output: $\bar{L}$ threshold.

```
//the vector of the ratio values observed in experiments
Ls ← ∅
//iterate over experiments
foreach e ∈ Q do
    //iterate over sessions in e
    L_m ← 0
    foreach i ∈ 1..|e| do
        T_i ← w_i^B + t_i + w_i^A,   m_i ← w_i^B + (1/2)t_i
        //find the max. likelihood estimate p̂_1^i of p_1
        p̂_1^i ← (1/T_i) [w_i^B + (1/2)t_i]
        L_i ← log ((p̂_1^i)^{m_i} (1-p̂_1^i)^{T_i-m_i}) / (p_0^{m_i} (1-p_0)^{T_i-m_i})
        //update the maximum value of L_m for the current experiment
        L_m ← max(L_m, L_i)
    end
    Ls ← Ls ∪ {L_m}
end
Ls ← sorted(Ls)
L̄ ← Ls[|Ls| · (1 - α)]
```

Algorithm 1: Learning the $\bar{L}$ threshold for MaxSPRT from a dataset of A/A experiments.

where p_0 and p_1 are probabilities of B winning in a comparison in an interaction under H_0 and H_1, respectively. Under the null hypothesis, the alternatives are equally likely to win, so p_0 equals to $\frac{1}{2}$. However, it is hard to specify p_1 before actually running the experiment. An intuitive idea is to replace it with the maximum likelihood estimate $\hat{p}_1^i$, based on the experimental data observed before the ith stop. Informally, by estimating $\hat{p}_1^i$ we choose H_1 that is the most likely to be accepted in comparison with H_0. This idea was proposed and studied by Kulldorff et al. [12] for the Poisson and Binomial distributions, and resulted in a test called MaxSPRT. Under our notation, the maximum likelihood estimate of p_1 at the ith step is:

$$\hat{p}_1^i = \frac{1}{T_i}\left(w_i^B + \frac{1}{2}t_i\right)$$

At each stop, $\hat{p}_1^i$ is estimated, and is used as a substitute of p_1 in L_i (Equation (7)). After that, L_i is compared to a pre-defined threshold $\bar{L}$. If $L_i \geq \bar{L}$, then the experiment is stopped, and H_1 is accepted. If $\hat{p}_1^i > \frac{1}{2}$ ($\hat{p}_1^i < \frac{1}{2}$) then it is inferred that $B \succ A$ ($A \succ B$). If $L_i < \bar{L}$, the experiment is continued. H_0 is accepted if the experiment reaches a pre-defined maximum length, without achieving $\bar{L}$.

To specify the threshold $\bar{L}$, Kulldorff et al. [12] used a Monte-Carlo method, where a series of Binomial samples were generated. However, as we further discuss in Section 7, in the case of the interleaving experiments where the ties are interpreted according to Equation (2), this Monte-Carlo threshold adjustment is suboptimal, as it generates data with variance higher than observed in experiments.

Instead, we propose to train the threshold $\bar{L}$ on a set of experiments where a system is compared with itself. As we discuss further in Section 5, such experiments are referred to as A/A experiments. Intuitively, a statistical test with Type I error set to α should detect differences in A/A experiments approximately with the probability α. Using this idea, we adjust the threshold $\bar{L}$ so that $\bar{L}$ exceeds all values of L_i in $(1-\alpha)$ of the A/A experiments. A formal description of the optimisation of the threshold can be found in Algorithm 1.

Further, the MaxSPRT test with the threshold $\bar{L}$ trained using Monte-Carlo simulations is denoted as **MaxSPRT-I-MC**. The test with the threshold $\bar{L}$ trained using the A/A comparisons is referred to as **MaxSPRT-I-AA**.

Note that when the deduped binary click scoring scheme is applied, all clicks in A/A experiments are ignored, since in the results lists of the compared alternatives all their results are identical. However, we still want our test not to detect a difference between systems when the results are not identical documents, but are equally likely to be clicked, to satisfy the user. Thus, we use the thresholds trained using the binary click aggregation scheme when evaluating the test on the experiments with the binary deduped scheme applied.

The MaxSPRT test assumes that the data points arrive one-by-one, which might be impractical on modern large-scale web search engines. Indeed, an infrastructure is needed that is capable of providing a near real-time stream of individual comparisons. It can be easier to implement the data delivery in batches, e.g. each batch of data corresponding to an hour or a day of the user activity. Since the discussed tests can be applied to analyse batch data by simply considering the aggregated values of the variables such as w_i^A w_i^B, we experiment in the batch scenario.

4.2 A/B tests

The goal of the statistical analysis of the A/B tests is to compare two hypotheses (Equation (1)). Under the null hypothesis, the means of a considered metric are equal in the buckets assigned for A and B, while under the alternative hypothesis they are different.

OBF The original test proposed by O'Brien&Fleming can be directly applied to A/B tests. Below we shortly review how it is defined. By $\hat{\mu}_i^A$ and $\hat{\mu}_i^B$ we denote the sample mean values of a metric μ calculated using the data collected before the ith stop on buckets (samples of users) associated with A and B, respectively. The total number of sessions that took place before the ith stop are referred to as T_i^A and T_i^B. The number of stops is fixed to N, the number of sessions between stops is assumed to be roughly equal and large enough for the central limit theorem to be applicable.

At each stop, the following statistic is considered:

$$Z_i = i\frac{(\hat{\mu}_i^A - \hat{\mu}_i^B)^2}{D[\hat{\mu}^A - \hat{\mu}^B]} \tag{8}$$

We follow [14] and use the pooled estimate of variance $D[\hat{\mu}^A - \hat{\mu}^B]$ assuming H_0:

$$\begin{aligned} D[\hat{\mu}_i^A - \hat{\mu}_i^B] &= \left(\frac{1}{T_i^A} + \frac{1}{T_i^B}\right) D[x], \\ D[x] &= \frac{1}{T_i^A + T_i^B - 1}\left(\sum_{j=1}^{T_i^A+T_i^B}(x_j - \overline{x})^2\right) \end{aligned} \tag{9}$$

where x_j iterates over the metric values observed in all observed interactions before the ith stop.

Similarly to the interleaving case, at each stop the value of the statistic Z_i is compared to a constant threshold a. Once it reaches the threshold, the experiment is stopped and H_1 is accepted. If at the last stop Z_N is still less than a, H_0 is accepted. The threshold a is calculated using the same Monte-Carlo algorithm as in the case of interleaving.

MaxSPRT-AB The MaxSPRT rule cannot be easily applied for the case of A/B experiments, since the distribution of the considered metric is unknown both under H_0 and H_1. To address this, we propose to estimate both the distribution of the metric under the null hypothesis and under the alternative hypothesis using data from the experiment itself.

Under the null hypothesis, the distribution of the metric coincides in both buckets, but under H_1 the distributions are different. Further, by D_i^A (D_i^B) we denote the data observed in a bucket corresponding to A (B) upto the ith stop. In that case, the likelihood ratio statistic in the case of the abandonment rate metric can be represented as follows:

$$L_i = \log \frac{P(D_i^A, D_i^B | p_i^A, p_i^B)}{P(D_i^A, D_i^B | p_i^0)} \quad (10)$$

where p_i^A and p_i^B are the maximum likelihood estimates of the probabilities of a user abandoning the result page, obtained on buckets corresponding to A and B, respectively. Similarly, p_i^0 is the maximum likelihood estimate of the probabilities of a user abandoning the result page, calculated on both buckets. $P(D_i^A, D_i^B | p_i^A, p_i^B)$ is calculated according to Equation (11):

$$\begin{aligned} P(D_i^A, D_i^B | p_i^A, p_i^B) = \; & (p_i^A)^{C_i^A} (1 - p_i^A)^{T_i^A - C_i^A} \cdot \\ & \cdot (p_i^B)^{C_i^B} (1 - p_i^B)^{T_i^B - C_i^B} \end{aligned} \quad (11)$$

where C_i^A and C_i^B are the number of abandoned result pages for A and B buckets before the ith stop, respectively. Similarly, T_i^B and T_i^A are the total numbers of sessions in these buckets before the ith stop.

Under the null hypothesis, the likelihood of the observed data is calculated as follows:

$$\begin{aligned} P(D_i^A, D_i^B | p_i^0) = \; & (p_i^0)^{C_i^A} (1 - p_i^0)^{T_i^A - C_i^A} \cdot \\ & \cdot (p_i^0)^{C_i^B} (1 - p_i^0)^{T_i^B - C_i^B} \end{aligned} \quad (12)$$

The maximum likelihood estimates p_i^0, p_i^A, and p_i^B can be found as follows:

$$p_i^0 = \frac{C_i^A + C_i^B}{T_i^A + T_i^B}, \quad p_i^A = \frac{C_i^A}{T_i^A}, \quad p_i^B = \frac{C_i^B}{T_i^B} \quad (13)$$

Once L_i achieves a pre-fixed threshold $\bar{L}$, the experiment is stopped and H_1 is accepted. Otherwise, the experiment is continued. If the experiment reaches a fixed duration, H_0 is accepted. Again, the threshold is learned by finding the $(1 - \alpha)$ percentile of the distribution of L_i statistic on the dataset of A/A experiments, as in Algorithm 1.

5. DATASETS

In our evaluation study we use datasets of A/B and interleaving experiments obtained from Yandex. For diagnostic purposes, it is useful for a search engine to deploy a constantly running online experiment that compares the current production system with itself ([10], Section 2). Further, we refer to such an experiment as an A/A comparison, whether the comparison is performed by A/B test or by means of interleaving. Since we know that the alternatives are equal in this comparison, we want the statistical testing procedure to find statistical differences in this evaluation rarely (i.e. H_0 should be rejected about 1% of the time, when testing is performed on $p < 0.01$ significance level).

Another source of the experiments are the regular experiments that are deployed to evaluate new search engine improvements. In our evaluation study, we compare the sequential testing approach to a standard scenario, where experiments are deployed for an integer number of weeks. To increase the size of the dataset, we consider the case of the experiments that last for one week. However, as the experiments differ in the expected effect size (detecting smaller differences between A and B require more sessions), they also vary in their duration. For this reason, we restrict each experiment to its first 7 days. The ground-truth outcomes used in our evaluation are calculated using the full experimental data. However, the one-step baseline tests (t-test and binomial test) use the same restricted experimental data as is provided for the evaluated sequential tests.

Interleaving In our dataset of interleaving experiments, we include data from two interleaving-based A/A experiments over a period of 300 days during 2014. These two experiments were deployed in two different countries. Further, we sampled 206 real-life interleaving experiments that were deployed to evaluate changes in the ranking algorithms, and lasted for at least a week during the same 300 days. Among these experiments, a statistically significant outcome (binary credit scheme, $p < 0.001$, binomial test) is observed in 115 experiments (B outperforms A in 56 experiments).

A/B tests Similarly to the interleaving dataset, we included the query log data generated by two long-term A/A tests that compare the production system with itself. This data spans a two month period, from April to May, 2014. These two experiments were deployed in two countries. Further, we also sample 62 A/B tests that were performed as a part of the search engine's evaluation routine. From these experiments, we select 41 experiments that have a statistically significant outcome (abandonment rate metric, $p < 0.01$, t-test). In 14 experiments, B outperformed A.

6. EVALUATION METHODOLOGY

We split our discussion of the evaluation methodology in two sections. In Section 6.1 we introduce the quality metrics we use in our evaluation. In Section 6.2 we describe the evaluation procedure we use.

6.1 Metrics

Our first metric, **Type I error**, represents the probability of a statistical test rejecting the null hypothesis H_0 when it holds:

$$\alpha = P(H_1 \; accepted \; | H_0 \; holds)$$

Generally, we want Type I error to be low, as each experiment wrongly accepted as successful might result in expensive development, wastes both human and computational resources without improving the search engine.

The second metric we consider is **Type II error**, which measures the probability of accepting the null hypothesis when it does not hold:

$$\beta = P(H_0 \; accepted \; | H_1 \; holds)$$

High values of β indicate that non-equal alternatives A and B are frequently accepted as equal, and this results in ignoring opportunities to improve a search engine.

The Type II error metric defined as above does not penalise cases when the null hypothesis is correctly rejected, but the preference is inferred incorrectly (e.g. $A \succ B$ is accepted when in reality $B \succ A$)[2]. Thus we introduce two one-sided accuracy metrics, $Acc_{A \succ B}$ and $Acc_{B \succ A}$:

$$\begin{aligned} Acc_{A \succ B} &= P(accepted \; that \; A \succ B | A \succ B) \\ Acc_{B \succ A} &= P(accepted \; that \; B \succ A | B \succ A) \end{aligned}$$

These metrics are related to Type II error, however they additionally penalise the above discussed cases of the incorrectly inferred preferences.

[2]This situation arises as our tests have effectively three outcomes: $A \succ B$, $B \succ A$, and B is not different from A.

Mean deployment time, $\mathbb{E}(T)$. This metric is defined as the mean time the experiment is deployed before a sequential testing procedure stops. For the non-sequential one-step tests that we use (namely, t-test and binomial sign test), the value of this metric is set to the experiment length. For convenience, we measure this metric in days. Generally, it might be more important to stop an experiment where $A \succ B$ than an experiment where $B \succ A$, as in the former case the user experience is degraded. Thus we additionally consider two time-related metrics which measure the expected duration of the experiments where $A \succ B$ and $B \succ A$. We denote these metrics as $\mathbb{E}(T|A \succ B)$ and $\mathbb{E}(T|B \succ A)$.

Mean relative number of sessions, $\mathbb{E}(\frac{N}{N_0})$. The last metric we use represents the relative number of search interactions required until the experiment is stopped, averaged over all experiments in the dataset. In other words, if an experiment contains N_0 sessions (after restricting to its first 7 days), and the sequential testing procedure stops an experiment after observing only N sessions, the value of the metric is equal to $\frac{N}{N_0}$ on this experiment.

In our evaluation study, for each sequential testing procedure we fix the Type I error probability and the maximum deployment time to be the same. Under these constraints, the baseline one-step approach achieves the minimum Type II error level among all possible rules. Thus, *our goal is to find a sequential testing procedure that reduces the mean deployment time for the experiments in our dataset as much as possible, and has its Type II error level close to the baseline approach.*

6.2 Evaluation Protocol

The A/A experiments, which compare a system with itself, either by means of interleaving or in a A/B test, are a perfect source of the data to calculate the Type I error probability (i.e. probability of finding a difference when there is none). Indeed, in the A/A experiments the null hypothesis H_0 definitely holds. Thus, any event where a statistical test detects a difference between the tested alternatives in an A/A experiment, is a Type I error.

Using this observation, we apply the following scheme to measure the Type I error probability for a statistical test. First, we split each of the available A/A experiments in two non-overlapping parts. The first part is used for learning the stopping thresholds. The second part is used for calculating the Type I error probability. To calculate this probability, we generate a set of smaller experiments of length equal to the length of the real experiments in the dataset (7 days). This set is generated by moving a sliding window from the beginning of the A/A experiment towards its end. The length of the window is equal to 7 days for both the A/B and interleaving experiments. We measure the Type I error probability as the relative number of generated experiments where the testing procedure detects a difference between two compared systems. The initial splitting is repeated in the cross-validation process, so that each day of the experiment is included in the evaluation subset exactly once. We use 20-fold cross-validation in the case of interleaving, and 10-fold for A/B tests (due to a smaller size of the dataset).

In the evaluated tests, we set the tolerances for the Type I error to be 0.01 and 0.05 for the interleaving and the A/B experiments, respectively. Generally, we want to experiment with lower tolerance values, as this closer resembles the requirements for real experiments. These tolerance levels should be higher than the p-values we use to infer the ground-truth labels, so that the measurements are meaningful. In turn, using low p-values when obtaining the ground-truth labels significantly reduces the sizes of the datasets. Thus we believe that the selected values are reasonable.

To calculate the remaining metrics (Type II error, $Acc_{A \succ B}$, $Acc_{B \succ A}$, $\mathbb{E}(T)$, $\mathbb{E}(\frac{N}{N_0})$), we use the experiments that compare real-life changes in a search engine. As a ground-truth labels ($A \succ B$ or $B \succ A$) we use the results of the binomial test ($p < 10^{-3}$) for the interleaving experiments, and the t-test ($p < 10^{-2}$) for A/B experiments.

An alternative approach to calculate Type II errors is to use a set of experiments, where the tested alternative B is specifically degraded with respect to A. This degradation might be achieved by swapping the first and the second results, degraded snippets, using an inferior ranking algorithm, etc. However, building a big dataset of experiments, where the user experience is specifically degraded in different ways, can be unrealistic. Another concern is that such manually devised degradations cannot be considered as a representative sample of the real-life experiments, and thus measuring how they can be accelerated might be useless.

In our evaluation study, we vary the number of the stops used. In the first case, the stops are performed each day (i.e. 7 stops), and in the second case stops are performed every hour (i.e. $7 \cdot 24 = 168$ stops). While the SPRT-based tests can be applied on the per-interaction level, the gains from such a scenario cannot be more than an hour in comparison with the scenario with stops every hour.[3] On the other hand, to apply a per-interaction SPRT test, one would need to build an elaborated near real-time data delivery system.

7. RESULTS AND DISCUSSION

In this section we discuss the results of our evaluation study on the datasets of interleaving (Section 7.1) and A/B (Section 7.2) experiments. Further, we perform a visualisation of the decisions of the best-performing tests in Section 7.3.

7.1 Interleaving

By OBF-I we denote the adaptation of the O'Brien&Fleming test which we discussed in Section 4.1. By OBF-I* we denote the simplified modification of OBF-I that approximates the variance by the unity. MaxSPRT-I-MC is the MaxSPRT test with its $\bar{L}$ threshold trained by the Monte-Carlo approach. In contrast, MaxSPRT-I-AA corresponds to the MaxSPRT test with its $\bar{L}$ threshold trained on the dataset of A/A experiments by Algorithm 1.

In Tables 1 & 2 we report the results of the evaluation of the sequential testing rules on the dataset of the interleaving experiments, in the cases of the binary and deduped binary click aggregation schemes, respectively. On analysing these results we firstly notice that the Type I error levels measured for all the considered testing rules are close to the tolerance level we set in the threshold learning process, 0.01. The observed deviations might be caused by a limited size of the dataset we use.

Further, on analysing the Type II error metric reported in Table 1, we notice that the values of this metric are very close for all tests and are in the range of $0.10 - 0.13$, except for the MaxSPRT-I-MC test, which has higher error levels (e.g. Type II error probabilities are 0.23 and 0.19, for the cases with 7 and $7 \cdot 24$ stops, respectively). In the case

[3] Due to the design of the test. This observation is also supported by our preliminary experiments.

Table 1: The quality metrics of the considered tests, measured on the dataset of interleaving experiments (binary scheme). The values of the metrics in bold outperform other in the same column; the values marked with △ outperform the values of the metric among other sequential tests, $p < 0.05$, Wilcoxon paired test (across folds).

Test	# stops	Type I	Type II	$Acc_{B \succ A}$	$Acc_{A \succ B}$	$\mathbb{E}(T)$, days	$\mathbb{E}(T \mid B \succ A)$	$\mathbb{E}(T \mid A \succ B)$	$\mathbb{E}(\frac{N}{N_0})$
Binomial	1	**0.00**	0.10	**0.75**	0.90	7.00	7.00	7.00	1.00
OBF-I*	7	0.01	0.10	0.73	0.92	3.17	3.17	3.04	0.44
OBF-I	7	0.01	**0.09**$^{\triangle}$	0.73	**0.95**$^{\triangle}$	3.00	3.04	2.92	0.42
MaxSPRT-I-MC	7	**0.00**$^{\triangle}$	0.23	0.64	0.76	3.96	4.00	3.92	0.53
MaxSPRT-I-AA	7	**0.00**$^{\triangle}$	0.13	0.71	0.87	3.10	3.20	3.30	0.44
OBF-I*	$7 \cdot 24$	0.01	0.11	**0.75**$^{\triangle}$	0.88	3.58	3.54	3.67	0.45
OBF-I	$7 \cdot 24$	0.01	**0.09**$^{\triangle}$	**0.75**$^{\triangle}$	0.93	3.33	3.38	3.29	0.44
MaxSPRT-I-MC	$7 \cdot 24$	**0.00**$^{\triangle}$	0.19	0.71	0.76	3.38	3.38	3.42	0.43
MaxSPRT-I-AA	$7 \cdot 24$	**0.00**$^{\triangle}$	0.12	0.73	0.89	**2.61**$^{\triangle}$	**2.63**$^{\triangle}$	**2.58**$^{\triangle}$	**0.35**$^{\triangle}$

with the deduped binary scheme (Table 2) the Type II error probabilities are also close for all the considered tests. However, they are considerably smaller, in the $0.03 - 0.05$ range. In both Table 1 and Table 2 the lowest Type II error is achieved by the OBF-I test. Similarly, in both cases OBF-I demonstrates the highest $Acc_{A \succ B}$ and $Acc_{B \succ A}$ metrics. In particular, in Table 1, the $Acc_{B \succ A}$ metric of 0.75 is achieved when $7 \cdot 24$ stops are used, and the $Acc_{A \succ B}$ of 0.95 is achieved when 7 stops are used.

However, when considering the mean time metric $\mathbb{E}(T)$, the difference between the tests becomes marked. In the case of the binary click aggregation scheme (Table 1), all the evaluated rules achieved considerable improvements over the standard 7-day scenario. Among the tests that use 7 stops, on average, MaxSPRT-I-MC stops the experiments later than other tests (e.g. 3.96 MaxSPRT-I-MC vs 3.10 MaxSPRT-I-AA, 7 stops). The shortest mean time (3.00) is demonstrated by the OBF-I test. Somewhat higher, but a close value of 3.10 is achieved by MaxSPRT-I-AA.

On comparing the scenarios with 7 and with $7 \cdot 24$ stops, we firstly notice that the MaxSPRT-I-MC and MaxSPRT-I-AA tests greatly benefit from using additional stops. Indeed, the mean time is reduced for the MaxSPRT-I-MC test from 3.96 to 3.38. Similarly, MaxSPRT-I-AA has improved the mean experiment running time from 3.10 to 2.61, and achieved the best performance. This behaviour is intuitive: with more stops available, there is more potential to stop earlier.

In contrast, OBF-I and OBF-I* the tests demonstrate some degradation in their $\mathbb{E}(T)$ metrics when $7 \cdot 24$ stops are used. For instance, OBF-I increased the mean deployment time from 3.00 to 3.33. A possible explanation is that OBF-I and OBF-I* rely on the central limit theorem, which only holds when the sample size approaches infinity. On the other hand, as the number of stops used by a test increases, less sessions are observed between stops, and this might harm the performance of OBF-I and OBF-I*. Another possible source of the error is that the OBF-based tests assume that the number of sessions between stops is uniform, which can be violated when stops are close.

From Table 2, we observe that MaxSPRT-AA has the shortest mean deployment time both among the tests with 7 stops (1.81), and among the tests with $7 \cdot 24$ stops (1.28). When 7 stops are used, OBF-I has a relatively close performance (1.83), but underperforms in the case of $7 \cdot 24$ stops.

Again, we notice that the OBF-I and OBF-I* tests degrade when the number of stops is increased, but MaxSPRT-I-MC and MaxSPRT-I-AA both improve their performance. Moreover, MaxSPRT-I-AA achieves the shortest mean deployment time when $7 \cdot 24$ stops are used.

On comparing Tables 1&2, we observe that when the deduped click aggregation scheme is applied, the Type II error probability and the mean deployment time decrease, while the $Acc_{A \succ B}$ and $Acc_{B \succ A}$ metrics grow for all the evaluated tests. This indicates that the deduped binary click scheme leads to marked gains in the sensitivity of the interleaving experiments.

An interesting observation is that the difference in the mean deployment times for OBF-I and OBF-I* are relatively close (not more than 0.25 days or 6 hours in the scenario with 7 stops). However, the difference between MaxSPRT-I-AA and MaxSPRT-I-MC is bigger (0.86 days $\approx$ 21 hours maximum). In all scenarios MaxSPRT-I-AA outperforms MaxSPRT-I-MC, indicating that replacing the Monte-Carlo threshold estimate with the threshold learned from the A/A tests improves the test's performance.

We also observe that the relative improvements measures by the $\mathbb{E}(T)$ metric are well aligned with the improvements measured by the $\mathbb{E}(\frac{N}{N_0})$ metric (e.g. MaxSPRT-I-AA with $7 \cdot 24$ stops reduces the mean deployments time by 82%, and uses only 0.15 of the available sessions).

We conclude that the MaxSPRT-I-AA test with $7 \cdot 24$ stops and the deduped binary click aggregation scheme achieves the smallest deployment time. In comparison to the standard 7-day scenario with the binary click aggregation scheme, on our dataset of the interleaving experiments, the combination of the sequential testing approach and the improved click aggregation scheme achieves 82% increase in the efficiency (1.28 vs 7.00 days).

7.2 A/B experiments

To discuss our evaluation of the sequential tests that can be applied for the A/B experiments, we use the following notation. By OBF we denote the original O'Brien&Fleming test [14], discussed in Section 4.2. Our proposed adaptation of the MaxSPRT test to the A/B experiments is further referred to as MaxSPRT-AB.

On analysing Table 3, we notice that the Type I error probabilities are close to 0.05. Again, we believe that the deviations can be explained by a limited size of the dataset. Further, we observe that the Type II error levels vary considerably among the tests: from 0.15 for the OBF test with 7 stops to 0.03 for the MaxSPRT-AB test with $7 \cdot 24$ stops.

As earlier, we observe that in terms of the mean deployment time metric MaxSPRT-AB test considerably benefits from increasing of the number of stops: $\mathbb{E}(T)$ decreases from 3.28 to 2.38. However, OBF demonstrates virtually the same mean deployment time for these two cases (4.38 vs 4.25).

Table 2: The quality metrics of the considered tests, measured on the dataset of interleaving experiments (binary deduped scheme). The values of the metrics in bold outperform other in the same column; the values marked with $\triangle$ outperform the values of the metric among other sequential tests, $p < 0.05$, Wilcoxon paired test (across folds).

Test	# stops	Type I	Type II	$Acc_{B\succ A}$	$Acc_{A\succ B}$	$\mathbb{E}(T)$, days	$\mathbb{E}(T\|B \succ A)$	$\mathbb{E}(T\|A \succ B)$	$\mathbb{E}(\frac{N}{N_0})$
Binomial	1	**0.00**	**0.03**	**0.82**	**0.95**	7.00	7.00	7.00	1.00
OBF-I*	7	0.01	**0.03**$^\triangle$	**0.82**$^\triangle$	**0.95**$^\triangle$	1.96	1.83	2.04	0.24
OBF-I	7	0.01	**0.03**$^\triangle$	**0.82**$^\triangle$	**0.95**$^\triangle$	1.83	1.71	2.00	0.23
MaxSPRT-I-MC	7	**0.00**$^\triangle$	0.05	**0.82**$^\triangle$	0.93	2.19	2.00	2.37	0.25
MaxSPRT-I-AA	7	**0.00**$^\triangle$	0.05	**0.82**$^\triangle$	0.93	1.81	1.64	1.98	0.22
OBF-I*	$7 \cdot 24$	0.01	0.04	**0.82**$^\triangle$	**0.95**$^\triangle$	2.13	2.04	2.21	0.26
OBF-I	$7 \cdot 24$	0.01	**0.03**$^\triangle$	**0.82**$^\triangle$	**0.95**$^\triangle$	1.96	1.92	2.05	0.24
MaxSPRT-I-MC	$7 \cdot 24$	**0.00**$^\triangle$	0.05	**0.82**$^\triangle$	0.93	1.63	1.44	1.85	0.17
MaxSPRT-I-AA	$7 \cdot 24$	**0.00**$^\triangle$	0.05	**0.82**$^\triangle$	0.93	**1.28**$^\triangle$	**1.11**$^\triangle$	**1.44**$^\triangle$	**0.15**$^\triangle$

Further, we notice that for any number of stops, MaxSPRT-AB demonstrates shorter mean deployment time than OBF (e.g. 4.25 vs 2.38 in the case of $7 \cdot 24$ stops). The overall minimum of $\mathbb{E}(T)$ is achieved by MaxSPRT when $7 \cdot 24$ stops are used. This value corresponds to the 66% reduction in time in comparison to the standard one-stop scenario.

7.3 Visualisation

We illustrate the best-performing MaxSPRT-I-AA and MaxSPRT-AB tests as follows. First, we sample a random subset of experiments, including experiments with A outperforming B, B outperforming A (according to the ground-truth labels), and A/A experiments. Second, for each of these experiments, at each stop i we calculate the log-likelihood ratio L_i multiplied by the sign of the current estimate of difference between A and B. More specifically, in the case of interleaving experiments, we multiply the log-likelihood (Equation (7)) by the sign of the current estimate of $(\hat{p}_1^i - \frac{1}{2})$:

$$sign\left(\hat{p}_1^i - \frac{1}{2}\right) \cdot L_i \tag{14}$$

In the case of A/B experiments, we multiply the log-likelihood ratio L_i (Equation (10)) by the sign of the differences of the current estimates of $\hat{p}_i^B - \hat{p}_i^A$:

$$sign\left(\hat{p}_i^B - \hat{p}_i^A\right) \cdot L_i \tag{15}$$

By definition, the absolute values of Equations (14)&(15) are equal to the log-likelihood ratio L_i, and their signs indicate which system tends to be better according to the observed data[4] (e.g. if (14) is positive, then $B \succ A$, and vice-versa). As a result, whenever the values of Equations (14)&(15) leave the corresponding interval $[-\bar{L}, +\bar{L}]$ ($\bar{L}$ is different for interleaving and A/B experiments), the experiment is terminated and a decision is made (e.g. $B \succ A$ if the upper boundary is touched).

We report our obtained results in Figure 1. Figures 1a and 1b correspond to the MaxSPRT-I-AA test with the binary and the binary deduped click aggregation schemes. Figure 1c corresponds to the MaxSPRT-AB test. The green and red lines correspond to the experiments that are labelled as $B \succ A$ and $A \succ B$ according to the ground-truth labels. The black lines correspond to the sampled A/A experiments. The horizontal dashed lines indicate the boundaries of the intervals $[-\bar{L}, +\bar{L}]$.

From Figure 1 we observe that despite some fluctuations, the likelihood ratios for the sampled A/A experiments are well within the boundaries of the decision interval at each of the stops. Next, for most of the interleaving experiments with A outperforming B, the statistic (14) falls towards the lower bound ($-\bar{L}$). In contrast, several experiments with $B \succ A$ have their statistic reaching the wrong boundary. These cases result in decreasing the $Acc_{B\succ A}$ value. This observation agrees with the results reported in Tables 1 & 2. Indeed, the $Acc_{B\succ A}$ metric values are lower than $Acc_{A\succ B}$ in every row of these tables. Thus, in a random sample it is more likely to meet errors of wrongly rejecting $B \succ A$ than the opposite case of rejecting $A \succ B$. Finally, on comparing Figure 1a and Figure 1b, we observe that the experiments are terminated faster in Figure 1b that corresponds to the case of the binary deduped click aggregation scheme. Again, this observation agrees with the results discussed above.

Overall, from our experiments we observe that by using sequential testing procedures considerable gains can be obtained in the mean time experiments are deployed, without significant degradation in other metrics, such as Type I, Type II errors, $Acc_{A\succ B}$, and $Acc_{B\succ A}$. In the case of the interleaving experiments with the binary click aggregation, a reduction in the execution time of 63% can be achieved by using the MaxSPRT-I-AA test with $7 \cdot 24$ stops. Moreover, the proposed sequential tests can be combined with the previously proposed deduped click aggregation scheme, and this combination results in even bigger improvements (82%). A similar observation holds in the case of the A/B tests: a decrease in the mean execution time of 66% is achieved by the MaxSPRT-AB test.

8. CONCLUSIONS AND FUTURE WORK

In this work we address an important problem of increasing the efficiency of the online evaluation experiments. In particular, we studied how sequential testing procedures can be adapted to reduce the time online evaluation experiments require. These procedures are designed so that they can stop online experiments when the observed data is sufficient to make a reliable conclusion about the experiment's outcome.

We proposed a modification of the O'Brien&Fleming group sequential test that can be applied to interleaving evaluation. Further, we described an approach to improve the MaxSPRT test's performance by adjusting its stopping threshold on the dataset of A/A experiments. Finally, we described a MaxSPRT-based test that can be applied in the A/B experiments to assess differences in the means of the abandonment rate metric.

In our evaluation study we used two datasets, containing 115 interleaving and 41 A/B experiments. Our study

[4]In the case of MaxSPRT-AB this holds as the log-likelihood ratio (10) is non-negative.

Table 3: The quality metrics of the considered tests, measured on the dataset of A/B experiments. The values of the metrics in bold outperform other in the same column; the values marked with △ outperform the values of the metric among other sequential tests in the column, $p < 0.05$, Wilcoxon paired test (across folds).

Test	# stops	Type I	Type II	$Acc_{B \succ A}$	$Acc_{A \succ B}$	$\mathbb{E}(T)$, days	$\mathbb{E}(T \mid B \succ A)$	$\mathbb{E}(T \mid A \succ B)$	$\mathbb{E}(\frac{N}{N_0})$
T-test	1	0.03	**0.03**	**1.00**	**0.93**	7.00	7.00	7.00	1.00
OBF	7	0.03	0.15	0.93$^{\triangle}$	0.70	4.38	3.90	4.65	0.60
MaxSPRT-AB	7	**0.00**$^{\triangle}$	0.11	0.87	0.78	3.28	3.48	3.17	0.43
OBF	$7 \cdot 24$	0.03	0.05	**1.00**$^{\triangle}$	0.89$^{\triangle}$	4.25	3.80	4.80	0.57
MaxSPRT-AB	$7 \cdot 24$	0.03	**0.03**$^{\triangle}$	0.93$^{\triangle}$	0.85$^{\triangle}$	**2.38**$^{\triangle}$	**2.54**$^{\triangle}$	**2.33**$^{\triangle}$	**0.31**$^{\triangle}$

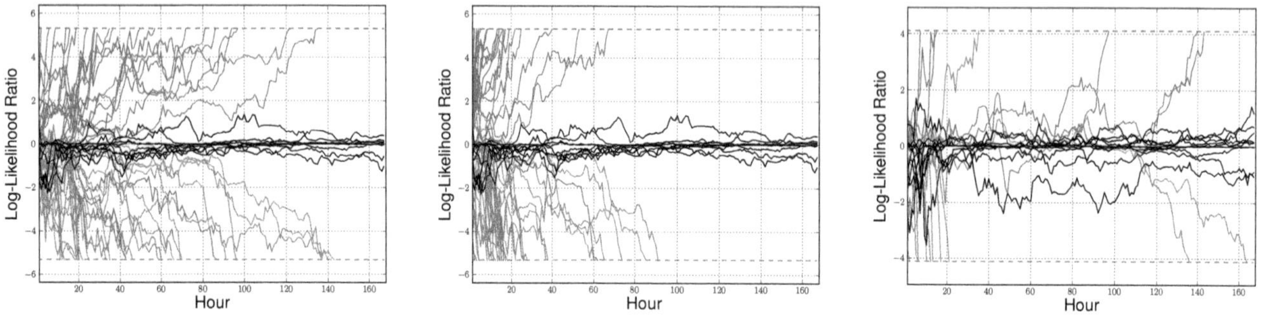

(a) MaxSPRT-I-AA, binary scheme. (b) MaxSPRT-I-AA, binary deduped scheme. (c) MaxSPRT-AB, abandonment rate.

Figure 1: Illustrating the MaxSPRT tests. Green and red lines correspond to the experiments with $B \succ A$ and $A \succ B$ ground-truth labels, respectively. Black lines correspond to A/A experiments. The horizontal dashed lines denote the threshold values for accepting $B \succ A$ (green) and $A \succ B$ (red).

demonstrates that by using the sequential testing procedures, a marked reduction in the duration of the experiments can be achieved, without significant losses in other metrics, such as Type I and Type II error probabilities. The maximal improvement over a standard 7 day one-stop scenario on the dataset of interleaving experiments reaches 63% by using the MaxSPRT-I-AA test, which examines the experiment data every hour. Further improvement can be obtained by additionally using an improved deduped binary click aggregation scheme, and it reaches 82%. This supports the idea that the sequential testing approach is complimentary to the previous research, which concentrated on reducing noise in the user feedback. On the dataset of A/B experiments, the MaxSPRT-AB test obtains an improvement of 66% over the same standard evaluation scenario. An interesting direction of future work is to devise a MaxSPRT-based test for the non-binomial A/B metrics (e.g., absence time [5]).

9. REFERENCES

[1] K. Balog, L. Kelly, and A. Schuth. Head first: Living labs for ad-hoc search evaluation. In *CIKM 2014*.

[2] J. Bartroff, T. L. Lai, and M.-C. Shih. *Sequential Experimentation in Clinical Trials: Design and Analysis*, volume 298. Springer, 2012.

[3] O. Chapelle, T. Joachims, F. Radlinski, and Y. Yue. Large-scale validation and analysis of interleaved search evaluation. *ACM TOIS*, 30(1):6, 2012.

[4] A. Deng, Y. Xu, R. Kohavi, and T. Walker. Improving the sensitivity of online controlled experiments by utilizing pre-experiment data. In *WSDM 2013*.

[5] G. Dupret and M. Lalmas. Absence time and user engagement: evaluating ranking functions. In *WSDM 2013*.

[6] K. Hofmann, S. Whiteson, and M. de Rijke. A probabilistic method for inferring preferences from clicks. In *CIKM 2011*.

[7] T. Joachims. Optimizing search engines using clickthrough data. In *KDD 2002*.

[8] E. Kharitonov, C. Macdonald, P. Serdyukov, and I. Ounis. Using historical click data to increase interleaving sensitivity. In *CIKM 2013*.

[9] R. Kohavi, T. Crook, R. Longbotham, B. Frasca, R. Henne, J. L. Ferres, and T. Melamed. Online experimentation at microsoft. *Data Mining Case Studies*, page 11, 2009.

[10] R. Kohavi, A. Deng, B. Frasca, R. Longbotham, T. Walker, and Y. Xu. Trustworthy online controlled experiments: Five puzzling outcomes explained. In *KDD 2012*.

[11] R. Kohavi, A. Deng, B. Frasca, T. Walker, Y. Xu, and N. Pohlmann. Online controlled experiments at large scale. In *KDD 2013*.

[12] M. Kulldorff, R. L. Davis, M. Kolczak, E. Lewis, T. Lieu, and R. Platt. A maximized sequential probability ratio test for drug and vaccine safety surveillance. *Sequential Analysis*, 30(1):58–78, 2011.

[13] K. G. Lan and D. L. DeMets. Discrete sequential boundaries for clinical trials. *Biometrika*, 70(3):659–663, 1983.

[14] P. C. O'Brien and T. R. Fleming. A multiple testing procedure for clinical trials. *Biometrics*, 1979.

[15] S. J. Pocock. Group sequential methods in the design and analysis of clinical trials. *Biometrika*, 64(2):191–199, 1977.

[16] F. Radlinski and N. Craswell. Comparing the sensitivity of information retrieval metrics. In *SIGIR 2010*.

[17] F. Radlinski and N. Craswell. Optimized interleaving for online retrieval evaluation. In *WSDM 2013*.

[18] F. Radlinski, M. Kurup, and T. Joachims. How does clickthrough data reflect retrieval quality? In *CIKM 2008*.

[19] D. Siegmund. *Sequential analysis: tests and confidence intervals*. Springer, 1985.

[20] A. Wald. Sequential tests of statistical hypotheses. *Ann. Math. Statist.*, 16(2):117–186, 06 1945.

[21] A. Wald and J. Wolfowitz. Optimum character of the sequential probability ratio test. *The Annals of Mathematical Statistics*, pages 326–339, 1948.

[22] K. Wang, T. Walker, and Z. Zheng. Pskip: estimating relevance ranking quality from web search clickthrough data. In *SIGKDD 2009*.

[23] S. K. Wang and A. A. Tsiatis. Approximately optimal one-parameter boundaries for group sequential trials. *Biometrics*, 1987.

[24] Y. Yue, Y. Gao, O. Chapelle, Y. Zhang, and T. Joachims. Learning more powerful test statistics for click-based retrieval evaluation. In *SIGIR 2010*.

Inferring Searcher Attention by Jointly Modeling User Interactions and Content Salience

Dmitry Lagun*
Google
dlagun@google.com

Eugene Agichtein†
Emory University and Yahoo Labs
eugene@mathcs.emory.edu

ABSTRACT

Modeling and predicting user attention is crucial for interpreting search behavior. Current applications include quantifying web search satisfaction, estimating search quality, and measuring and predicting online user engagement. The most direct way to measure attention is through eye gaze tracking, which is not yet widely available. While prior research has demonstrated the value of mouse cursor data and other interactions as a rough proxy of user attention, accurately predicting where a user is looking on a page remains a challenge. This problem is exacerbated when moving beyond the traditional search result pages to other domains, where high diversity of content and visual presentation often affect how users examine a page. We posit that in order to accurately model user attention online, interaction signals should be grounded to the underlying content. To this end, we introduce a principled model to connect interaction signals with page content features, which we call Mixture of Interactions and Content Salience (MICS). To our knowledge, our model is the first to effectively combine user interaction data with visual prominence, or salience, of the page content elements. Extensive experiments on multiple popular types of Web content demonstrate that our model significantly outperforms previous approaches to searcher gaze prediction, which use only the interaction information. Grounding the observed interactions to the underlying page content provides a general and robust approach to user attention modeling, which could enable more powerful tools for search behavior interpretation, and ultimately search quality improvements.

Keywords

searcher attention; search behavior; content salience

1. INTRODUCTION

Inferring searcher attention in Web search, and more general online settings, has been recognized as a key aspect of relevance evaluation, search quality, and user interface design. More generally, inferring and measuring user attention is key for diverse areas such as online advertising, education, and crowdsourcing. The availability of accurate user attention data at scale could potentially enable vast opportunities for search quality evaluation and richer models of user interaction with generic Web page content. The challenge is how to infer attention robustly and for diverse kinds of content - the problem we aim to address in this paper.

Inferred attention has already been used in a variety of applications ranging from improvements of web site usability [24, 28], to search relevance estimation[15, 16], and automatic generation of attention-biased summaries [1]. User attention data gains even greater importance as Web search shifts towards addressing user information needs directly on the search result page, which does not require a click on the result, making click-based evaluation of search quality more challenging (e.g., [13, 19, 32, 26]).

Previous work on attention modeling from cursor interactions on the Web has mostly focused on Web search and E-learning settings, where a user's eye gaze, and mouse cursor positions, are somewhat coordinated[34, 14, 18].

When extending the attention prediction task to other Web page types, prediction becomes more challenging. For example, as search over social media gains popularity, attention models must be adapted to take into account more complicated page layouts, with some content static (not query-specific), whereas other, related content in fact might answer the search intent directly. Figure 1 (b), based on the data reported by [25], illustrates searcher attention heatmap for a popular social media site. Note that attention is shifted to

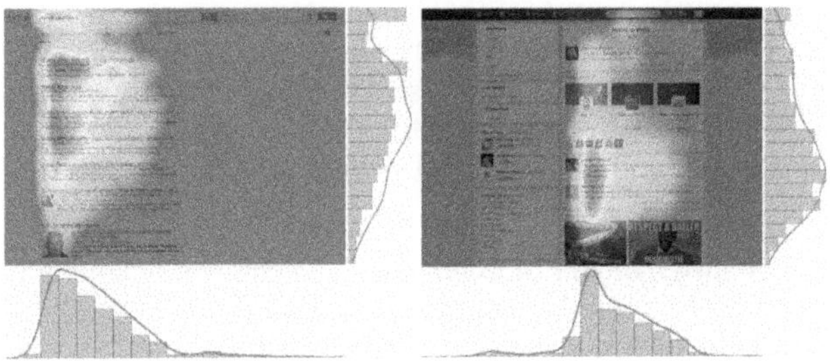

(a) (b)

Figure 1: User attention on a Web search result page (a) vs. on a social network Web site (b). The color indicates the time spent viewing a region of the page, ranging from red (high concentration of attention) to blue (low attention). The marginal distributions are projected onto the horizontal and vertical axes.

*Work done as student at Emory University.

†Work done at Emory University.

SIGIR'15, August 09 - 13, 2015, Santiago, Chile.

ACM 978-1-4503-3621-5/15/08 ...$15.00.
DOI: http://dx.doi.org/10.1145/2766462.2767745.

the right and towards the bottom of the page – contrasting it with the more well known "golden triangle" examination pattern for a traditional Web search result page, illustrated in Figure 1 (a). As search spans increasingly diverse domains, such differences abound. Furthermore, as search engines increasingly incorporate images and other visually attractive elements into the search result, models of searcher attention have to be revisited accordingly.

Our aim is to develop a robust, yet principled model of searcher attention that combines both content and interaction signals. For this, we adapt techniques and ideas from computational neuroscience of *visual saliency* to develop a Mixture of Interaction and Content Salience (*MICS*) model, that is able to integrate content-based static signals, together with the user's interaction data, in order to predict where on a page a searcher is paying attention. We show that our model achieves significantly lower error compared to previously reported state-of-the-art techniques using interaction-only signals. Specifically, our contributions are:

- A novel model of combining content and behavioral signals to predict searcher attention (Section 3).
- Significant accuracy improvements in predicting eye gaze position for a given user, in multiple popular search domains (Section 6).

Next, we review previous work on predicting searcher attention. Then, in Section 3 we present out general *MICS* model for inferring user attention on Web pages, and describe the specific reference implementation for popular search domains (Section 4). In Sections 5 and 6 we present empirical results on using our *MICS* model to predict user attention. Finally, we outline the implications and directions for future work in Section 7, which concludes the paper.

2. BACKGROUND AND RELATED WORK

Our work bridges three main areas of research: computational modeling of visual attention, primarily developed in the fields of computational neuroscience and computer vision, user engagement and attention modeling on the Web, and searcher interaction modeling, primarily focused on the web search domain, from the fields of human computer interaction and information retrieval.

2.1 Computational Visual Salience

There has been extensive research on automatically identifying the most important, or *salient* regions in a given image, where a person examining the image is likely to attend. As we build on the ideas explored in computational visual salience research for Web search tasks, we briefly introduce the underlying ideas and techniques.

Different formulations of salience have been proposed, e.g., focusing on identifying the image regions which initially attracts attention, or the aggregate attention distribution after a longer period of examination. In order to model salience computationally, three major factors were identified that affect human attention during visual examination of an image (or a Web page): (i) the visual importance, or salience of areas in the scene, (ii) memory and expectations about where to find the information, and (iii) the task and information need at hand. Depending on the modeling choices, the resulting models can be either task-agnostic (i.e., only consider the salience of the image regions based on content alone) or task-driven (i.e., that consider salient regions for a given task). These models are typically categorized as either bottom-up models or top-down models.

In bottom-up models the salience of image areas is typically computed based on low-level image characteristics, particularly contrast, color, intensity, edge density, and edge orientation (see [20]). One well known (*bottom-up*) salience model was introduced by Itti [20]. As do other *bottom-up* approaches, this framework attempts to simulate human attention as a feed-forward neural network. That is, it takes various features of the stimulus, such as the color contrast, gradient and motion maps, as input, and produces a single salience map that highlights the locations where the human gaze is mostly likely to attend. According to at least some neuroscience theories[20], a representation similar to the described salience map may be used by the human brain to control the human oculomotor system and to direct eye gaze to explore the stimulus, such as an image or a web page.

While it is thought that the human eye is initially attracted by the most salient regions of the image, theories about subsequent examination differ. For example, some have argued that the subsequent examination points are planned in order to maximize the resulting *information gain* [20, 21, 39]. While low level visual salience may direct the first gaze position, or fixation, it is believed that ultimately memory and expectations (e.g., about what is shown in the image and where to find specific objects) begin to also play important roles in subsequent examination positions. To take advantage of this insight, *top-down* (task specific) models which account for these effects were introduced [20, 30, 31].

2.2 User Attention and Engagement on the Web

Modeling searcher attention on the Web introduces additional challenges as content can be more varied semantically (e.g., combining both images and text), dynamic, and interactive. Stone and Dennis [38] used latent semantic analysis of topics to predict eye movement fixations on a generic Web page given position of text elements and hyperlinks. Our work is different in that we incorporate much richer information about elements semantics. In addition, we aim to combine Web page content salience with user interactions on the page. More recently, reference[35] predicted aggregated salience of Web pages based on visual content alone. As in most visual salience approaches, the authors used pixel based information to construct variety of salience maps (based on pixel level contrast, color, orientation) that are combined to produce a single map that approximates distribution of eye gaze fixations on a Web page. Our method builds on some of the ideas in these papers, but takes a different approach by modeling user attention with a parametric distribution derived on a relatively small number of prominent Web page elements. It allows us to avoid dealing with pixel level salience (and high computational complexity associated with it) and develop a unified model of user attention on Web pages that takes advantage of Web page element importance and user interaction with the page.

More closely related to our work, Buscher el al. [4] analyzed the factors determining fixation time, i.e., the time a user spends carefully examining, or fixating on, individual elements of a Web page. They found that the size of an HTML element and its proximity to the top left corner of the Web page play a major role in amount of attention this element receives. Instead of implicitly modeling scrolling activity like in [4], our work focuses on modeling user attention on a visible portion of the page (i.e., *viewport*).

In the Web search domain, studies of user attention using eye tracking provided numerous insights about typical content examination strategies, such as top to bottom scanning of Web search results [11, 29]. Other studies have investigated the effect of caption length and quality on searcher attention, identifying relevant page regions, and for many other tasks. Perhaps the most well known outcome of this line of work is the "golden triangle" of attention on Web search results, often present in the traditional search result layouts. A more comprehensive overview of classical models of searcher attention is available in [17]. More recently, a line of research on user engagement with online content has emerged[27]. For example, the users' engagement with news examination is often influenced by affect, sentiment, and visual clues[2] – which in turn can be used to better predict attention.

2.3 Searcher Attention Prediction

Perhaps the most practical application of attention modeling is to predict searcher attention – which could be applied for tasks such as search evaluation, improving search quality, and search advertising. Due to the high cost and the necessarily small scale of eye tracking studies (due to requiring specialized eye tracking equipment), a considerable amount of research has been devoted to finding more scalable methods of attention measurement. In particular, mouse cursor tracking was proposed as a cheap alternative to eye tracking by inferring searcher gaze position from mouse cursor position. The relationship between cursor and gaze has been studied empirically[8, 34, 14, 18, 32]. Chen et al. [8] was one of the first to study coordination patterns between mouse cursor and gaze. They classified mouse cursor movement into five classes: "Stay Nowhere", "Go Nowhere", "Stay the Same Region" and "Go to New Region". They found that the distance between mouse cursor and gaze position was smallest when the user moved mouse cursor in order to perform an action, e.g., pointing or clicking. However, when the cursor remained inactive, the reported accuracy of attention measurement degraded.

In the context of Web search, the coordination between mouse cursor and eye movements was first reported by Rodden et al. [34]. They reported the alignment between the user's eye movements and mouse movements when scanning a web search results page, and identified three patterns of active mouse usage: *following the eye position vertically, following the eye position horizontally,* and *using the mouse to mark a relevant result.* Guo and Agichtein [14] proposed a natural extension Rodden's work - to predict eye-mouse coordination (i.e., whether the mouse cursor is in close proximity to eye gaze at any given point in time). These works were further extended by Huang et al. [18] to directly predict the gaze position from mouse cursor movement, showing that the cursor and eye gaze are best aligned when the user is performing click action, and have the largest average distance in periods of cursor inactivity. Navalpakkam et al. [32] studied the coordination of cursor and gaze on non linear search result page layouts, e.g., in the presence of rich information panel on the right side. They showed that a non-linear regression model offers more accurate predictions of gaze position, and outperforms previous approaches. Also related to our work is the research of Diaz et al.[9], which proposed a two-dimensional attention transition model based on mouse cursor movement over grid layouts.

In this work, we build upon these ideas[18, 32, 9] and instead of predicting gaze position in isolation (without spatial constraints) we develop the first model that combines the evidence provided by interaction data with the information about Web page elements visible to the user through the browser's visible part of the page, or viewport. Furthermore, unlike in previous work in gaze prediction, we extend our model to predict attention on pages in other domains, moving beyond web search result pages.

3. MICS: COMBINING CONTENT AND INTERACTION SIGNALS

In this section we present our *MICS* model that allows us to more effectively infer user attention on Web pages by combining content and interaction signals. This is an even more challenging problem than predicting attention in images, as is done in computational visual salience research: Web pages contain extensive layout structure and multiple layers of meaning encoded in the text, layout, and metadata about a page.

To address this challenge, we exploit the observation that web pages, more so than image-only stimuli, can be effectively annotated with areas of interests (i.e., potential targets in the *top-down* models terminology), that can enable more accurate modeling of user gaze during web browsing or information seeking activities. Such annotations can be based on set of rules or rely on an automatic classifier to segment page elements that take part in the model. While the ultimate accuracy of the model is likely to depend on the quality of the page segmentation, for now let us assume that for popular types of Web pages (e.g., Search Engine Result pages or social media news feeds) such segmentation is available. The details of the particular page segmentation algorithm used in this work are provided in Section 4.1. Assuming a page segmentation is given to us, we can now define our Mixture of Interactions and Content Salience (MICS) model.

3.1 MICS: Definition

Our approach to modeling the allocation of user attention on a page is derived from the general idea of the *mixture of experts* model in machine learning [22]. Our goal is estimating the task-specific (top-down) element importance on the page, and then *refine* the prediction based on how long each element on a page was displayed to the user, and where it was in the viewport[1] and what interactions the user performed.

MICS operates by sub-dividing the visual space into regions - each corresponding to a particular Web page element. While the distribution of gaze positions within each element is determined only by the features of the element, the probability of attending a page element depends on relative attractiveness of *all the elements* displayed in the visible portion of the Web page. Intuitively, in our model each element "competes" for user attention against other visible elements on the page. Unlike previous approaches, which mainly use the visual stimuli information on pixel level (i.e., visual salience) to predict attention, our model takes advantage of the information about page element rendering (how elements are displayed by an Web browser to a user) and constructs compact, yet expressive, distribution of user attention in the browser viewport.

More formally, our model defines a probability distribution of gaze position over the visual space (browser viewport)

[1]We use the term *viewport* to denote the portion of a Web page visible to the user at given point of time.

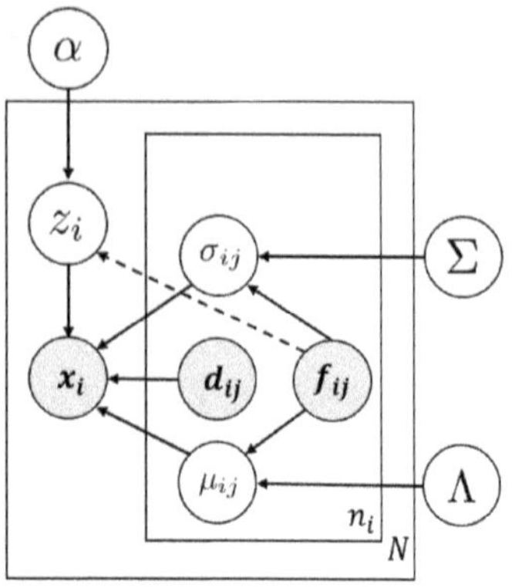

Figure 2: The *MICS* model for search attention modeling.

Variable	Description
N	number of gaze data points
n_i	number of Web page elements at i-th viewport
$\mathbf{x_i} \in \mathbb{R}^2$	i-th gaze position
$z_i \in \{1, .., n_i\}$	index of the Web page element being viewed at i-th viewport
$\mu_{ij} \in \mathbb{R}^2$	mean of the j-th element Normal distribution
$\sigma_{ij} \in \mathbb{R}^2$	variance of the j-th element Normal distribution
$d_{ij} \in \mathbb{R}^2$	position of the j-th element
p	dimensionality of element's feature space
$\alpha \in \mathbb{R}^p$	feature weights for the element importance distribution (z_i)
$\Lambda \in \mathbb{R}^{(p\times 2)}$	feature weights for the element means μ_{ij}
$\Sigma \in \mathbb{R}^{(p\times 2)}$	feature weights for the element variances (σ_{ij})
$\mathbf{f_j} \in \mathbb{R}^p$	feature vector of j-th page element.

Table 1: Summary of the notation used in the *MICS* model.

which is represented as a mixture of distributions - each corresponding to a particular web page element. This can be viewed as a particular type of a mixture of experts model (MoE, [22]), where each expert corresponds to a distribution representing the individual Web page elements. The reason MoE formulation is particularly well-suited to this setting is that it naturally manages uncertainty about the "attractiveness" of each element, which can be refined using additional features of the content element itself, or, later on, with interaction data.

MICS can also be viewed as a generative model. Figure 2 presents the *MICS* model diagram in plate notation. Table 1 defines the notation used in Figure 2. In the diagram, i stands for each data point, which consists of the set of elements and their locations on a page, visible at that time on the page, and the corresponding gaze position coordinates x_i. *MICS* states that the $i-th$ gaze position is generated from the observed element positions d_{ij} with their corresponding features $\mathbf{f_{ij}}$. The element's μ_{ij} parameters are defined as:

$$\mu_{ij}^{(x)} = d_{ij}^{(x)} + width_{ij} \cdot sigmoid(\Lambda^{(x)} \cdot \mathbf{f_{ij}})$$

where $\mu_{ij}^{(x)}$ is the horizontal component of element's Normal distribution mean parameter, $d_{ij}^{(x)}$ is the element's top left coordinate x, $width_{ij}$ is the width of the element, Λ is a free parameter estimated during training, and $\mathbf{f_{ij}}$ is vector of element's features. The element's variance parameter σ_{ij} is computed as:

$$\sigma_{ij} = exp(\Sigma \cdot \mathbf{f_{ij}})$$

where Σ is free parameter estimated during training. The probabilities of viewing an element are parametrized using the softmax function with the free parameter α:

$$P(z_i = j|\alpha, \mathbf{f}) = \frac{exp(\alpha \cdot \mathbf{f_{ij}})}{\sum_{j=1}^{n_i} exp(\alpha \cdot \mathbf{f_{ij}})}$$

3.2 MICS Training

To make the model training more tractable, we make a simplifying assumption that all gaze positions are generated independently from each other. This allows us to derive an efficient inference and learning algorithm. Our algorithm learns the element importance weights α for the *MICS* model as follows. Let the dataset $D = \{\mathbf{x_i}\}_{i=1}^{N_k}$ collection of N_k gaze positions for k-th page view. Note that depending on the scroll position of the browser, there could be a different number of elements visible in the viewport, we denote this number as n_i. We assume that information about position of page elements (d_{ij}) and their features f_{ij} is available.

In order to find plausible values for model parameters $\Theta = \{\alpha, \Sigma, \Lambda\}$ we perform maximum likelihood estimation That is we optimize log-likelihood of gaze observations given the model parameters:

$$\mathcal{L}(\mathbf{x_i}|\Sigma, \Delta, \alpha) = \sum_{k=1}^{K}\sum_{i=1}^{N_k}\sum_{j=1}^{n_i} P(z_i = j) \log \mathcal{N}(\mathbf{x_i}|d_{ij} + \mu_{ij}, \sigma_{ij}^2)$$

In order to optimize the log-likelihood we use Stochastic Gradient Ascent (SGA) method with learning rate annealing. The model is implemented using symbolic differentiation tool Theano[3] that automatically generates code for gradient computation.

3.3 MICS Inference

Once the *MICS* model is trained, gaze prediction distribution is computed as:

$$P(\mathbf{x_i}|\Sigma, \Delta, \alpha) = \sum_{j=1}^{n_i} P(z_i = j|\alpha, \mathbf{f_{ij}})\mathcal{N}(d_{ij} + \mu_{ij}, \sigma_{ij}^2)$$

Note that $P(z_{ij} = j)$ gives us an importance weight (from 0 to 1) for each of page element d_{ij}. Thus, we could view it as a mixture distribution of n_i Normal distributions associated with the attractiveness and uncertainty predicted for each element, respectively. Computing the density of this distribution over a fixed grid of 2-dimensional points is tractable, as we demonstrate in the experiments section. Given the predicted density, the expected gaze position can be obtained by computing the maximum likelihood estimate of the x and y values under the predicted density distribution.

Since *MICS* is a generative model, for completeness we describe the generative process of how gaze positions could be generated by our trained model. The following generative process can be used to generate an i-th sample from our model:

1. Generate z_i with probability $P(z_i = j|\alpha, \mathbf{f_{ij}})$
2. Generate gaze position $\mathbf{x_i} \sim \mathcal{N}(d_{ij} + \mu_{ij}, \sigma_{ij}^2)$, where d_{ij} is position of j-th element on the screen,

In practice, in order to avoid computationally costly sampling procedure, we could obtain estimates of gaze positions by numerically computing expectation over the predictive density:

$$\bar{\mathbf{x}_\mathbf{i}} = \sum_{l=1}^{L} \sum_{m=1}^{M} \mathbf{x}_{\mathbf{lm}} P(\mathbf{x}_{\mathbf{lm}} | \Sigma, \Delta, \alpha, \mathbf{f}_{\mathbf{ij}}, \mathbf{d}_{\mathbf{ij}})$$

where L and M are number if integration points in $\mathbf{x}_{\mathbf{lm}}$ are nodes in two dimensional grid used for computing the expectation.

Having defined the general *MICS* model, we now turn to the specific implementations of *MICS* to be validated on two increasingly difficult tasks, as described next.

4. MODEL IMPLEMENTATION

We now describe the specific implementation of the *MICS* model including Web page segmentation and content features that were used in this work.

4.1 Extracting Prominent Web Page Elements

Identifying most prominent Web page elements is not always a trivial task. Often, Web pages contain thousands of HTML elements, many of which are not even displayed to the user. As our goal is to model attention in presence of significant (visible and important) page elements, it is desirable to eliminate page elements that are unlikely to attract user attention, thus, considerably simplifying modeling complexity. To this end, our web page content analysis consists of first segmenting a web page into HTML DOM elements, then selecting a subset of the elements to consider, and finally extracting content features just from that subset. To take advantage of all Web pages in our dataset we employ both rule based segmentation, applied for frequent page types, and classifier based segmentation, applied for less frequent page types in our dataset. We would like to emphasize that this is just one of many ways to implement content element segmentation and other variations could be explored in future work to further improve performance.

For web pages that occur relatively frequently in our data, such Google search result pages or Twitter pages, we implement manually engineered segmentation. This is a common approach taken in previous work, and is applicable to a large and important subset of web pages which tend to share the same layout and page template.

For less frequent pages, we apply a supervised automatic classifier that for each web page *layout* element outputs a binary decision - whether this needs to be segmented or not. This makes our approach potentially applicable to a wider range of web pages. To perform this classification we use Gradient Boosting Decision Tree classifier (GBDT) [10]. The classifier uses page element's features to determine if element needs to be included or not. In order to train the this classifier we manually annotated page segmentation for 20 pages. Table 2 shows features used by our classifier. We utilized several types of information including the element's DOM Tree features (e.g. amount of links), the element's position information and size (e.g., width and height), as rendered by the browser at the time of page visit, and the element's style (e.g. visibility and text font size).

Figure 3 shows example of the page segmentation output for a Google search result page. While the granularity of the segmented elements varies for different page types, we see that the elements carrying most important content information are captured. The fact that such segmentation only eliminates page elements that are not displayed in the browser or used only for layout or formatting, simplifies the salience modeling in a sense that we do not need to account for thousands of elements in our model.

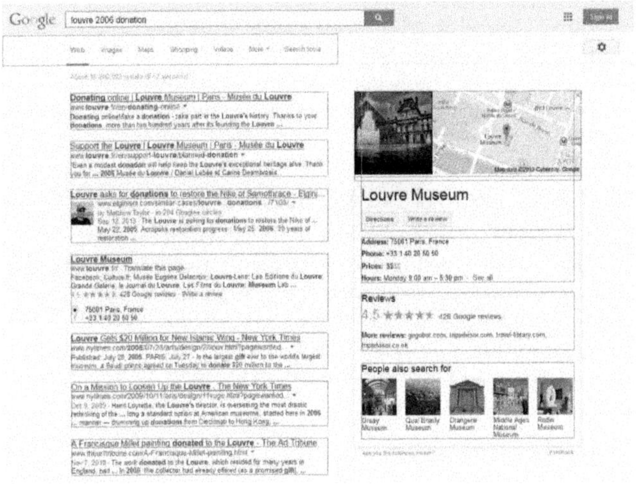

Figure 3: Example of page segmentation for a search result page (bottom of screen shot is cropped to fit).

4.2 Content and Interaction Features

We re-use content features employed by page segmentation algorithm (shown in Table 2, Content feature group). Our features encode information about element size, position on the page, style and font size, and simple information content measures such as number of words normalized by area. As discussed, additional more sophisticated content representation features could be invented, but in this reference implementation we opted for simplicity and generality. Despite the simplistic representation, the *MICS* model is able to use these features effectively, as shown in the experiments below.

MICS naturally allows to enrich the previously proposed regression models by allowing the features to be *element-specific*. For example, how *MICS* can exploit the information on how close is the mouse cursor to the particular element or whether a mouse cursor will hover over the element in the next few seconds. Such features allow the *MICS* model to learn cursor gaze coordination patterns not only on the overall behavior level, but on the element level as well. For example, if the mouse cursor hovers over the search box element, it is very likely that the user is going to reformulate the query terms, which implies the attention is focused on the search box. In contrast, if the cursor hovers over the elements located on the right side the search result page, it is less likely that the user's attention is following the cursor. Thus, to capture user interaction with the given element we include features that encode relative position of the cursor the element, cursor velocity, binary features indicating whether cursor is currently hovering the element or user is clicking on the element. Table 2 lists both Content and Interaction features used in our model. To account for a potential lag between interaction and eye gaze movement we concatenate features in the Interaction group at adjacent time d steps. The offsets for the adjacent time steps are $\{\pm 1, \pm 2, \pm 4, \pm 8, \pm 16\}$.

We train the *MICS* model using Stochastic Gradient Ascent algorithm with minibatch size = 100 and learning rate 0.001. To improve convergence speed we randomly shuffle training examples before start of the training.

To obtain the predicted gaze position using the *MICS* model the we use expected $\bar{\mathbf{x}}$ under the predicted attention distribution as described in Section 3.3 with number of integration steps $L = M = 100$.

5. EXPERIMENTAL SETUP

In order to compare the effectiveness of different approaches for attention modeling, we performed a realistic user study, with eye tracking to collect the eye gaze data as ground truth. In the rest of the section we provide the details on data collection, the baseline models that were proposed in prior work, and the evaluation metrics used for the experiments in the next section.

5.1 User Study

In order to investigate the effects of domain and task on searcher attention, we systematically varied the *scope* of the search task, and the search *domain*. The tasks were modeled on the studies in [12, 33] to be representative of the common search tasks in common search domains. Specifically, the task (*scope*) was designated as either *Focused* or *Broad*. The *Focused* information need required the users to find specific information, e.g., "How many megapixels does Nexus 5 camera have?" in *Web Search* domain, while *Broad* information tasks had no specific answer, but rather asked the users to learn about a particular topic, e.g., "Learn what people on Twitter are saying about gay marriage" in the *Social Network* domain. Two focused and two broad tasks were performed by each user in each of the five common search domains: *Web Search* (Google), *Shopping* (Amazon), *Social Network* (Twitter), *News* (CNN) and *Wikipedia*, for a total of 20 tasks per user. We randomized the presentation order of the tasks to eliminate possible learning effects. To reduce the biases in the training data, we balanced the study design by ensuring that the same amount of data was collected for each (*domain, scope*) pair.

For the user study, we recruited 20 undergraduate and graduate students (11 of them males) from a major university. Each user was asked to perform four "warm-up" practice tasks to become familiar with the study flow, followed by the 20 tasks that we use in our analysis. All user actions, including query input, page navigation, clicks and mouse cursor movements were recorded using a custom extension to the Firefox internet browser. To capture the user's eye movements we used the Tobii T60 eye tracker system built into a 17" monitor with 1280×1024 screen resolution, recording eye gaze positions with frequency of 60 Hz. The Tobii system is head-free, where the participant could sit and interact with the computer naturally without being locked into a specific head position or body posture, making the collected interaction data more realistic. The eye movement data was pre-processed using Tobii Studio software to segment the data points into eye fixations (i.e., times of slow and detailed examination) and saccades (i.e., times of fast movement when the eye jumps to examine a new position).

5.2 Data

Overall, the data includes eye movement and interactions data for 2,890 page views, with 673 page views corresponding to the search pages. The eye gaze data contains 93,290 fixations. As in prior work [18, 32] we interpolated the gaze and cursor data every 100ms using nearest neighbor interpolation method, which resulted in 233,225 aligned eye gaze and cursor data points. Discretizing gaze data with fixed sample rate greatly simplifies prediction task by eliminating need to infer fixation duration [18, 32]. The dataset size is comparable to previously reported studies, and was primarily limited by the effort required to recruit and supervise the user study participants.

5.3 Baseline Models

Several works have attempted to infer the user's gaze position from cursor interactions. Most of the prior approaches trained a regression model to estimate the gaze position from cursor interaction features. We describe the two recent well known models that we use as state-of-the-art baselines for the subsequent experiments.

Linear Regression (LR). Huang et al. [18] proposed to directly predict a searcher's eye gaze position from mouse cursor movements on search result pages. They used a linear regression model to learn the relationship between eye gaze and cursor movement features. Their model can be formulated as:

$$\mathbf{x}_i = \langle \mathbf{w}, \mathbf{v}_i \rangle$$

where $\mathbf{w}$ is the vector of feature weights, $\mathbf{v}_i$ is vector of features for the i-th data point. During training the model computes an optimal vector of weights $\mathbf{w}$, such that the discrepancy between model predictions and the actual gaze positions is minimized. Specifically, the optimization minimizes the *squared error* between the actual eye gaze positions and the predicted positions.

Non-Linear Regression with Kernels (KR). Recently, a more sophisticated model of attention prediction from was introduced by Navalpakkam et al. [32]. Unlike the LR model, which assumes a linear relationship between cursor features and gaze position, the KR model is able to capture nonlinearities of the data, but adding an additional transformation ϕ over the feature vector. The KR model is defined as:

$$f(\mathbf{v}_i) = \langle \mathbf{w}, \phi(\mathbf{v}_i) \rangle$$

where $\mathbf{w}$ is the vector of feature weights, $\mathbf{v}_i$ is vector of features for the i-th datapoint, and $\phi(\mathbf{v}_i)$ is the Nystrom approximation of the Gaussian Radial Basis Function kernel matrix [36] with $n = 500$ basis vectors. This transformation is known as a "kernel trick" that helps capture non-linear dependencies between cursor features and gaze, while maintaining relatively easy training procedure. During model training we find the optimal set of vectors $\mathbf{w}$ so that it minimizes the discrepancy between the model predictions and gaze positions in the training data.

Baseline Interaction Features In our experiments we use the same basic cursor movement features for all models for a fair comparison. This set of features include and extend the published features used in prior work [18, 32]. These feature vectors are computed to represent each data point (mouse cursor position):

- Mouse cursor x and y positions
- The time since the page load
- The absolute values of cursor speed (vertical and horizontal), and movement direction (angle)
- The cursor distance traveled in the page up to this point
- The time and position of the most recent click on the page, if any

Group	Feature Name	Description
Content	Num{Links, Images,P }	Number of {a, img, p} tags in the given element
	IsTagName	Collection of binary features which equal 1 if the element's tag matches particular type (otherwise feature value is zero). The tags are $\langle a \rangle$, $\langle img \rangle$, $\langle p \rangle$, $\langle div \rangle$, $\langle span \rangle$, $\langle h1 - h3 \rangle$, $\langle em \rangle$, $\langle b \rangle$, $\langle li \rangle$, $\langle ol \rangle$, $\langle ul \rangle$
	Left, Top, Width, Height	Position and size information (in pixels)
	TimeOnPage	Time since the page load
	NumChildren	Number of child elements
	{Text, Image}Area	Total area of all {Text, Image} elements inside of the given element
	FontSize	Font size of the element's text
	TextToAreaRatio	Number of words (tokenized by white spaces) in the element divided by the element's area
Interaction	Cursor{X, Y}	Cursor position in pixels
	Speed{X, Y, Abs}	Horizontal, vertical and absolute speed of cursor movement
	Cursor{On, L, R, T, B}	Binary features indicating cursor position with respect to the element position (OnElement, Left, Right, Top, Bottom)
	CursorSame{Vert, Horiz}	Binary features indicating whether cursor position overlaps with the element vertically or horizontally
	DistX, DistY, DistEuclidean	Distance from the cursor to the element's center
	ClickOn	Non-zero if cursor click occurs on the element at given time step
	ClickDistX, ClickDistY, ClickDistEuclidean	Distance from the click position to the element center (zero if there is no click)
	TimeToScroll, TimeSinceScroll	Time since last scroll and time to the next scroll.
	OffsetFromScreenCenter{X, Y}	Vertical and horizontal offset of the element with respect to center of the viewport

Table 2: Content and interaction features used by MICS.

- The vertical scroll position, in pixels
- The time since the last scroll event, if any.

To account for longer range dependencies between the gaze and cursor movement for each time step we include features from previous time steps, logarithmically spaced, following the approach of [32]. The time step offsets were chosen as $\{\pm 1, \pm 2, \pm 4, \pm 8, \pm 16\}$, capturing the 100ms to 1.6 second "history" of the mouse movements. While this is a minor extension compared to previously proposed approaches, all the compared methods benefited from this additional contextual information.

5.4 Evaluation Metrics

For comparing the performance of the *MICS* model against the baseline LR and KR models, we use the root mean squared error (RMSE) and mean absolute error (MAE) metrics, used in prior work for this task.

More formally, given a sequence of true and predicted gaze positions $\mathbf{x}^{(i)}_{\mathbf{gaze}}$ and $\mathbf{x}^{(i)}_{\mathbf{pred}}$, RMSE is computed as:

$$RMSE = \sqrt{\frac{1}{N} \sum_{i=1}^{N} |\mathbf{x}^{(i)}_{\mathbf{gaze}} - \mathbf{x}^{(i)}_{\mathbf{pred}}|^2}$$

where N is the number of gaze data points, $\mathbf{x}^{(i)}_{\mathbf{gaze}}$ is the actual gaze position at step i, and $\mathbf{x}^{(i)}_{\mathbf{pred}}$ is the predicted position, and the difference is the square of the Eucledian distance between the two. While RMSE is convenient from the optimization perspective (both LR and KR minimize the mean squared error, or MSE, on the training data), it dis-proportionally weights large errors. Therefore, we also consider mean absolute error, also used in prior work, which does not introduce this bias. The MAE is computed as:

$$MAE = \frac{1}{N} \sum_{i=1}^{N} |\mathbf{x}^{(i)}_{\mathbf{gaze}} - \mathbf{x}^{(i)}_{\mathbf{pred}}|$$

where the sum is over the Euclidean distance between the actual and the predicted gaze positions.

To achieve more robust estimates of models' performance, all the experiments were performed with 3-fold cross validation (CV). Each of the metrics is computed as the average across the hold-out (test) folds.

6. RESULTS AND DISCUSSION

Table 3 summarizes prediction performance for the baseline models LR and KR and our *MICS* model, averaged across the hold-out samples, in the cross validation setting. *MICS* performs significantly better than LR and KR in all of the domains ($p < 0.001$, two tailed t-test). Reduction in error varies from 7% in *Shopping* domain to 35% in *Social Network* domain $RMSE$=237.8 px. The lowest prediction error was obtained in the *Social Network* domain ($RMSE$=237.8px, MAE=206.3px), while the *Shopping* domain appeared to be the most difficult to predict resulting in the highest error ($RMSE$=335.7 px, MAE=298.6px). We believe that the reason for the large performance improvements lie in the additional power available to the *MICS* model. Both LR and KR models make strong assumptions about the relationship between gaze and cursor interactions, relying on a constant bias term independent of the actual content shown to the user. Since user attention distribution heavily depends on what is shown the screen (e.g, see Figure 1), a constant bias that works for different types of pages may not exist. In contrast, *MICS* , by design, follows the content, and is able to supply a multi-modal predictive distribution dictated by the Web page elements visible to the user.

Interestingly, on the Web search domain, *MICS* also exhibits substantial reduction in error on the horizontal dimension ($RMSE_x$ and MAE_x), making it even more appealing for evaluation – when search results may be shown to the right of the organic search results [32]. Such results attempt to provide users with direct answers to their information needs without requiring users to click. Previously, it has been proposed [32, 26] to utilize user attention for evaluation, providing a natural application of *MICS* for this task.

Our results demonstrate that it is possible to learn Web page element salience or attractiveness that is generalizable across different page types. This is even more encouraging

Web Page Domain	Method	$RMSE_x$	$RMSE_y$	RMSE	MAE_x	MAE_y	MAE
Web Search	LR	234.0	236.6	332.7 (N/A)	181.9	194.1	294.8 (N/A)
	KR	207.4	220.6	302.8 (-8%)	172.3	181.3	273.4 (-7%)
	MICS	156.1	202.6	**255.8 (-23%)**	128.8	160.1	**225.7 (-23%)**
News	LR	262.2	279.1	383.0 (N/A)	209.7	229.5	340.6 (N/A)
	KR	176.4	247.8	304.2 (-21%)	144.5	204.7	272.4 (-20%)
	MICS	174.5	208.3	**271.7 (-29%)**	138.1	167.0	**237.3 (-30%)**
Wikipedia	LR	219.7	242.0	326.8 (N/A)	173.6	195.5	288.1 (N/A)
	KR	290.0	272.5	398.0 (+22%)	242.5	223.9	360.8 (25%)
	MICS	87.2	277.4	**290.8 (-11%)**	70.2	210.9	**235.7 (-18%)**
Shopping	LR	249.1	259.2	359.5 (N/A)	196.3	211.2	319.5 (N/A)
	KR	281.5	285.9	401.2 (+12%)	225.6	231.1	359.3 (+12%)
	MICS	257.6	215.3	**335.7 (-7%)**	201.4	179.6	**298.6 (-7%)**
Social Network	LR	260.4	256.2	365.3 (N/A)	206.5	207.0	322.1 (N/A)
	KR	205.6	263.0	333.9 (-9%)	162.2	210.0	293.3 (-9%)
	MICS	146.9	187.0	**237.8 (-35%)**	113.3	146.7	**206.3 (-36%)**

Table 3: Predictions results for LR, KR and *MICS* , for different Web page domains. The *MICS* model consistently outperforms prior methods in all domains (differences in RMSE and MAE are significant $p<0.001$ with two tailed t-test).

since the Web search engines are constantly experimenting with various ways to improve user interface of search results and maintaining an attention model that can only work for a certain page configuration would severely impact its use cases. While *MICS* outperforms prior approaches in the gaze prediction task, it provides a general and principled way to integrate page content information into the attention model. The behavioral features allow MICS to make more sensible, time dependent predictions and capturing cursor-gaze coordination patterns.

6.1 Discussion

We have shown that *MICS* is able MICS to learn salience of Web page elements and to combine it with information about user interaction. In this section we highlight implications of this work, provide more intuition on why *MICS* is able to outperform previous models and discuss potential limitations of our approach.

We first analyze the contributions of the content-based vs. interaction-based signals to better understand the performance improvements of the *MICS* model. To this end, we performed a feature ablation experiment, where we compare the model variants while removing the corresponding feature groups (Table 4). We find that certain page types benefit from *Content* and *Interaction* to different extent. In *Web Search* and *Wikipedia* domains we find that both Content and Interaction feature groups are not particularly helpful independently of each other. *Interaction* features appear to be more important for *News*, *Shopping* and *Social Network* domains, where model performance drops substantially, compared to the model with ablated *Content* features. In all cases, the combination of both content and interaction features performs better than either signal alone.

To further understand *which* Web page elements *MICS* finds important we examined element importance weights given by $P(z_i)$. Figure 4a shows an example prediction for a part of a Social Network Web page. Red boxes boxes indicate the segmented Web page elements. Line width of the bounding boxes reflects the element's relative importance weight given by the *MICS* model. Hence, only a few elements stand out as important in Figure 4a. We see that the Twitter message displayed in the center of the page draws most of the attention. The next most prominent element on the page is another message, displayed towards the bottom of the page. In contrast, the "recommended users" feature elements receive much smaller weights - an indication that *MICS* is able to find elements which are likely to attract user attention. Another example is shown on Figure 4b. It visualizes the relative importance weights for a Wikipedia page. We see that text paragraphs near the center of the screen (on the right column) are the most prominent. Menu items and contents navigation blocks receive smaller weights. This is in agreement with prior work of Buscher et al. [5] that analyzed aggregated pattern of user attention on the screen. These examples illustrate that *MICS* identifies task-specific, salient page elements across different page layouts. These elements (as described in Section 3) are then used to construct a mixture distribution that helps predict user attention on any given viewport.

Weight	Feature
-0.821	DistEuclidean(dt=+16)
0.763	Height
0.720	CursorOn(dt=+8)
0.615	IsH3
0.483	NumP
-0.414	SpeedAbs(dt=0)
0.405	CursorSameVert(dt=+2)
0.402	CursorOn(dt=0)
0.383	SpeedY(dt=-4)
0.372	IsP

Table 5: Features with largest weights learned by the *MICS* model.

To further understand which element and interaction features *MICS* considers important with respect to "attracting" attention, we report the weights α assigned to the element features (Table 5). For interaction features we include the time step offset modifier. The DistEuclidean feature has largest negative weight, which reduces element importance when cursor moves further away (DistEuclidean increases) from the element in next 16 time steps which in our data translates to 1.6 seconds. Height is positively related with element importance and has weight of 0.763. Interestingly, CursorOn(dt+=8) has almost two times higher weight than 0.402 CursorOn(dt=0) – which capture element hover interaction. This is consistent with findings of Huang et al. [18] who reported a positive lag of 700ms between gaze and cursor positions. *MICS* assigns relatively high weights

MICS Features	Web Search		News		Wikipedia		Shopping		Social Network	
	RMSE	MAE	RMSE	MAE	RMSE	MAE	RMSE	MAE	RMSE	MAE
All	**290.8**	**235.7**	**271.7**	**237.3**	**290.8**	**235.7**	**335.7**	**298.6**	**237.8**	**206.3**
– ContentSalience	331.8	284.2	275.3	244.0	331.8	284.2	338.6	302.8	240.8	209.9
– Interactions	333.3	283.8	305.8	269.2	333.3	283.8	363.1	327.4	267.8	236.0

Table 4: Regression performance of the *MICS* model when ablating *Content* and *Interaction* feature groups in MICS.

to features related to the element's tag (IsH3–header and IsP–paragraph). Regardless of the element importance, the weights decrease when the cursor starts moving (SpeedAbs has negative weight -0.414), indicating the attention is no longer on the element. Finally, *MICS* finds CursorSameVert to be positively related with the element importance.

This work can be potentially improved or extended in an number of ways. In particular, web page segmentation approaches (rule based and classifier based) used in the current implementation can be improved. That is, rule-based segmentation may only capture a limited set of pages with pre-defined HTML template or layout. Alternatives include other popular Web page segmentation approaches, such as [7], or using semantic relationship between Web page blocks [37], or a combination of visual, text and link information [6]. These more powerful segmentation mechanisms can be naturally incorporated into the *MICS* implementation with operates over whatever page elements are provided by the segmentation step. Another area of improvement is efficiency of the implementation. More accurate prediction performance comes at a price of higher computational complexity during training, compared to the baseline models. While LR and KR models enjoy the benefits of convex optimization and even allow closed form solutions (in a matrix form), optimization problem that comes with *MICS* model is inherently non-convex and requires application of iterative methods. In our experiments, *MICS* converged in about 10-20 iterations, which translate to 1-2 hours of run time using Theano [3] generated code on Tesla K20 GPU. At inference time, *MICS* incurs the additional cost of computing the expected gaze position through a numerical integration described in Section 3.3. Our results demonstrate that our optimization method (Stochastic Gradient Ascent) is able to successfully train a model that performs well on the evaluation metrics. As another promising future direction, Navalpakkam et al.[32] showed that gaze prediction error may be further reduced by personalization – i.e., by additionally tuning the set of vectors $\mathbf{w}$ for each user. While personalization is orthogonal to the ideas proposed in this paper, further personalizing the *MICS* model can be explored in future work.

7. CONCLUSIONS

We have introduced *MICS* , a robust and principled method for connecting interaction data with the underlying page content for predicting user attention. Results validated against eye gaze tracking data show that *MICS* is more accurate than previous state of the art models that consider interactions alone. We have shown that the cursor interaction features allow *MICS* to make more sensible predictions that capture cursor-gaze coordination patterns on specific Web page content. Importantly, *MICS* forces the most likely gaze position to be within, or in close proximity to, the prominent web page elements. This feature could potentially offer better gaze prediction performance for users who do not use the mouse pointer actively, or only to perform necessary actions. This could be particularly important for attention prediction in mobile phones and tablets [16, 26]. The *MICS* implementation as well as the user study data, including the eye gaze ground truth, will be made available to the research community[2].

Our work can be expanded in multiple directions. First, other complementary content features could be designed, capturing visual attractiveness, semantic concepts embedded in the text, or readability. Similarly, more complex behavior or mouse cursor movement features could be incorporated into the model, including cursor patterns discovered automatically, e.g., as in [23]. These richer features can be naturally incorporated into the *MICS* model to further improve prediction performance. In turn, accurately inferring search attention prediction from observable user behavior data, obtained at Web scale, could enable numerous improvements to the user experience in search and other online settings.

ACKNOWLEDGMENTS: This work was supported by the National Science Foundation grant IIS-1018321, the National Institutes of Health grant R01EB014266, the DARPA grant D11AP00269, and the Yahoo FREP program.

8. REFERENCES

[1] Mikhail Ageev, Dmitry Lagun, and Eugene Agichtein. Improving search result summaries by using searcher behavior data. In *Proc. of SIGIR*, 2013.

[2] Ioannis Arapakis, Mounia Lalmas, B Barla Cambazoglu, Mari-Carmen Marcos, and Joemon M Jose. User engagement in online news: Under the scope of sentiment, interest, affect, and gaze. *JASIST*, 2014.

[3] James Bergstra, Olivier Breuleux, Frédéric Bastien, Pascal Lamblin, Razvan Pascanu, Guillaume Desjardins, Joseph Turian, David Warde-Farley, and Yoshua Bengio. Theano: a cpu and gpu math expression compiler. In *Proceedings of SciPy*, volume 4, 2010.

[4] Georg Buscher, Edward Cutrell, and Meredith Ringel Morris. What do you see when you're surfing?: using eye tracking to predict salient regions of web pages. In *Proc. of CHI*, pages 21–30, 2009.

[5] Georg Buscher, Andreas Dengel, and Ludger van Elst. Eye movements as implicit relevance feedback. In *CHI Extended Abstracts*, pages 2991–2996, 2008.

[6] Deng Cai, Xiaofei He, Zhiwei Li, Wei-Ying Ma, and Ji-Rong Wen. Hierarchical clustering of www image search results using visual, textual and link information. In *Proceedings of the ACM Int. Conf. on Multimedia*, pages 952–959. ACM, 2004.

[7] Deng Cai, Shipeng Yu, Ji-Rong Wen, and Wei-Ying Ma. Vips: A vision-based page segmentation algorithm. Technical report, Microsoft technical report, MSR-TR-2003-79, 2003.

[8] Mon Chu Chen, John R Anderson, and Myeong Ho Sohn. What can a mouse cursor tell us more?: correlation of eye/mouse movements on web browsing. In *CHI extended abstracts*, pages 281–282, 2001.

[9] Fernando Diaz, Ryen White, Georg Buscher, and Dan Liebling. Robust models of mouse movement on dynamic

[2]See `http://ir.mathcs.emory.edu/software-data/`

(a) Social Network Web Page

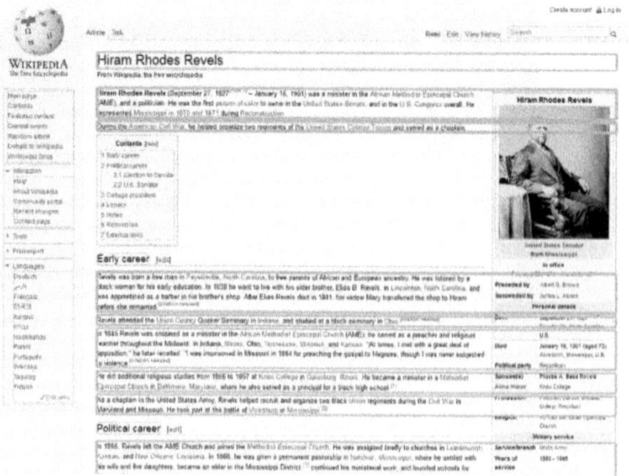

(b) Wikipedia Web Page

Figure 4: Example of element importance for user examination of different Web pages. Line thickness indicates the element's relative importance compared to all other elements within the viewport.

web search results pages. In *Proceedings of CIKM*, pages 1451–1460, 2013.

[10] Jerome H Friedman. Greedy function approximation: a gradient boosting machine. *Annals of Statistics*, pages 1189–1232, 2001.

[11] Laura A. Granka, Thorsten Joachims, and Geri Gay. Eye-tracking analysis of user behavior in www search. In *Proc. of SIGIR*, pages 478–479, 2004.

[12] Laura A Granka, Thorsten Joachims, and Geri Gay. Eye-tracking analysis of user behavior in www search. In *Proc. of SIGIR*, 2004.

[13] Qi Guo and Eugene Agichtein. Ready to buy or just browsing?: detecting web searcher goals from interaction data. In *Proceedings of SIGIR*, pages 130–137, 2010.

[14] Qi Guo and Eugene Agichtein. Towards predicting web searcher gaze position from mouse movements. In *CHI Extended Abstracts*, pages 3601–3606, 2010.

[15] Qi Guo and Eugene Agichtein. Beyond dwell time: estimating document relevance from cursor movements and other post-click searcher behavior. In *Proc. of WWW*, pages 569–578. ACM, 2012.

[16] Qi Guo, Haojian Jin, Dmitry Lagun, Shuai Yuan, and Eugene Agichtein. Mining touch interaction data on mobile devices to predict web search result relevance. In *Proc. of SIGIR*, pages 153–162, 2013.

[17] Marti Hearst. *Search user interfaces.* Cambridge University Press, 2009.

[18] Jeff Huang, Ryen White, and Georg Buscher. User see, user point: gaze and cursor alignment in web search. In *Proc. of CHI*, pages 1341–1350, 2012.

[19] Jeff Huang, Ryen W White, and Susan Dumais. No clicks, no problem: using cursor movements to understand and improve search. In *Proc. of CHI*, pages 1225–1234, 2011.

[20] Laurent Itti and Christof Koch. Computational modelling of visual attention. *Nature Reviews Neuroscience*, 2(3):194–203, 2001.

[21] Laurent Itti, G Rees, and J Tsotsos. Models of bottom-up attention and saliency. *Neurobiology of Attention*, 582, 2005.

[22] Robert A Jacobs, Michael I Jordan, Steven J Nowlan, and Geoffrey E Hinton. Adaptive mixtures of local experts. *Neural computation*, 3(1):79–87, 1991.

[23] Dmitry Lagun, Mikhail Ageev, Qi Guo, and Eugene Agichtein. Discovering common motifs in cursor movement data for improving web search. In *Proc. of WSDM*, 2014.

[24] Dmitry Lagun and Eugene Agichtein. Viewser: enabling large-scale remote user studies of web search examination and interaction. In *Proc. of SIGIR*, 2011.

[25] Dmitry Lagun and Eugene Agichtein. Effects of task and domain on searcher attention. In *Proc. of SIGIR*, 2014.

[26] Dmitry Lagun, Chih-Hung Hsieh, Dale Webster, and Vidhya Navalpakkam. Towards better measurement of attention and satisfaction in mobile search. In *Proc. of SIGIR*, pages 113–122, 2014.

[27] Janette Lehmann, Mounia Lalmas, Elad Yom-Tov, and Georges Dupret. Models of user engagement. In *User Modeling, Adaptation, and Personalization*, pages 164–175. Springer, 2012.

[28] Luis Leiva. Automatic web design refinements based on collective user behavior. In *CHI Extended Abstracts*, pages 1607–1612, 2012.

[29] Lori Lorigo, Maya Haridasan, Hrönn Brynjarsdóttir, Ling Xia, Thorsten Joachims, Geri Gay, Laura Granka, Fabio Pellacini, and Bing Pan. Eye tracking and online search: Lessons learned and challenges ahead. *Proc. of JASIST*, 59(7):1041–1052, 2008.

[30] Vidhya Navalpakkam and Laurent Itti. A goal oriented attention guidance model. In *Biologically Motivated Computer Vision*, pages 453–461. Springer, 2002.

[31] Vidhya Navalpakkam and Laurent Itti. Modeling the influence of task on attention. *Vision research*, 45(2):205–231, 2005.

[32] Vidhya Navalpakkam, LaDawn Jentzsch, Rory Sayres, Sujith Ravi, Amr Ahmed, and Alex Smola. Measurement and modeling of eye-mouse behavior in the presence of nonlinear page layouts. In *Proc. of WWW*, 2013.

[33] Bing Pan, Helene A Hembrooke, Geri K Gay, Laura A Granka, Matthew K Feusner, and Jill K Newman. The determinants of web page viewing behavior: an eye-tracking study. In *Procc. of ETRA*, pages 147–154. ACM, 2004.

[34] Kerry Rodden, Xin Fu, Anne Aula, and Ian Spiro. Eye-mouse coordination patterns on web search results pages. In *CHI Extended Abstracts*, pages 2997–3002, 2008.

[35] Chengyao Shen and Qi Zhao. Webpage saliency. In *ECCV 2014*, pages 33–46. Springer, 2014.

[36] Alex J Smola and Bernhard Schölkopf. Sparse greedy matrix approximation for machine learning. 2000.

[37] Ruihua Song, Haifeng Liu, Ji-Rong Wen, and Wei-Ying Ma. Learning block importance models for web pages. In *Proc. of WWW*, pages 203–211, 2004.

[38] Benjamin Stone and Simon Dennis. Using lsa semantic fields to predict eye movement on web pages. In *Proc. CSS*, pages 665–670, 2007.

[39] Yuan-Chi Tseng and Andrew Howes. The adaptation of visual search strategy to expected information gain. In *Proc. of CHI*, pages 1075–1084, 2008.

Different Users, Different Opinions: Predicting Search Satisfaction with Mouse Movement Information

Yiqun Liu†, Ye Chen†, Jinhui Tang‡, Jiashen Sun⋆, Min Zhang†, Shaoping Ma†, Xuan Zhu⋆
†Tsinghua National Laboratory for Information Science and Technology, Department of Computer Science & Technology, Tsinghua University, Beijing, China
‡School of Computer Science & Engineering, Nanjing University of Science and Technology
⋆Samsung R&D Institute China - Beijing
yiqunliu@tsinghua.edu.cn

ABSTRACT

Satisfaction prediction is one of the prime concerns in search performance evaluation. It is a non-trivial task for two major reasons: (1) The definition of satisfaction is rather subjective and different users may have different opinions in satisfaction judgement. (2) Most existing studies on satisfaction prediction mainly rely on users' click-through or query reformulation behaviors but there are many sessions without such kind of interactions. To shed light on these research questions, we construct an experimental search engine that could collect users' satisfaction feedback as well as mouse click-through/movement data. Different from existing studies, we compare for the first time search users' and external assessors' opinions on satisfaction. We find that search users pay more attention to the utility of results while external assessors emphasize on the efforts spent in search sessions. Inspired by recent studies in predicting result relevance based on mouse movement patterns (namely motifs), we propose to estimate the utilities of search results and the efforts in search sessions with motifs extracted from mouse movement data on search result pages (SERPs). Besides the existing frequency-based motif selection method, two novel selection strategies (distance-based and distribution-based) are also adopted to extract high quality motifs for satisfaction prediction. Experimental results on over 1,000 user sessions show that the proposed strategies outperform existing methods and also have promising generalization capability for different users and queries.

Categories and Subject Descriptors

H.3.3 [**Information Storage and Retrieval**]: Information Search and Retrieval

Keywords

Search satisfaction; User behavior; Mouse movement

SIGIR'15, August 09 - 13, 2015, Santiago, Chile.
© 2015 ACM. ISBN 978-1-4503-3621-5/15/08 ...$15.00.
DOI: http://dx.doi.org/10.1145/2766462.2767721.

1. INTRODUCTION

Search satisfaction prediction is essential in Web search performance evaluation researches. Although there are plenty of existing studies [18, 4, 8, 17, 16] on this research topic, it is still a challenging task for two major reasons: (1) The definition of satisfaction is rather subjective and different users may have different opinions in satisfaction. Therefore, satisfaction feedback from different users for the same result ranking list may be very different (see Section 4). (2) There usually lacks enough explicit feedback information to infer users' opinions in satisfaction for practical search engines. Different from relevance prediction researches in which result clicks can be regarded as strong signals of user preference, the feedback information of satisfaction is related with a number of different interaction behaviors. Many existing approaches on satisfaction prediction rely on users' click-through or query reformulation behaviors [23, 4]. However, for many search sessions neither mouse clicks nor query reformulations are available [13, 20] and these solutions are therefore not applicable.

For the first problem (subjectivity in satisfaction judgment), some researchers design systems to collect users' explicit feedback as the ground truth for satisfaction [8, 4]. However, the quality of data cannot always be ensured because collecting feedback information explicitly usually affects users' search processes. Other researchers choose not to interrupt users' search process. Instead, they employ external assessors to review the original searchers' behavior logs and make judgments according to their own experiences [16]. According to recent studies on query intent labelling and relevance annotations [13, 28], external assessments may be very different from users' self-annotations. However, the question of whether there exist such differences in search satisfaction evaluation remains uninvestigated (*RQ1*).

For the second problem (lack of explicit feedback information), although click-through and query reformulation behaviors are not always available for all search sessions, there are other interactions that can be collected in most cases. Among these interaction behaviors, mouse movement has recently been paid much attention to. It can be adopted as a proxy of eye fixation behavior [6, 22] and can easily be collected at large scale as well. Existing studies indicate that mouse movement behaviors can provide insights into result examination [22] and result relevance estimation [1, 7, 9, 12]. Guo et al. [8] are among the first to predict search satisfaction (namely search success in their work) with fine-grained mouse interactions (e.g., hovers, scrolls, etc.) in addition

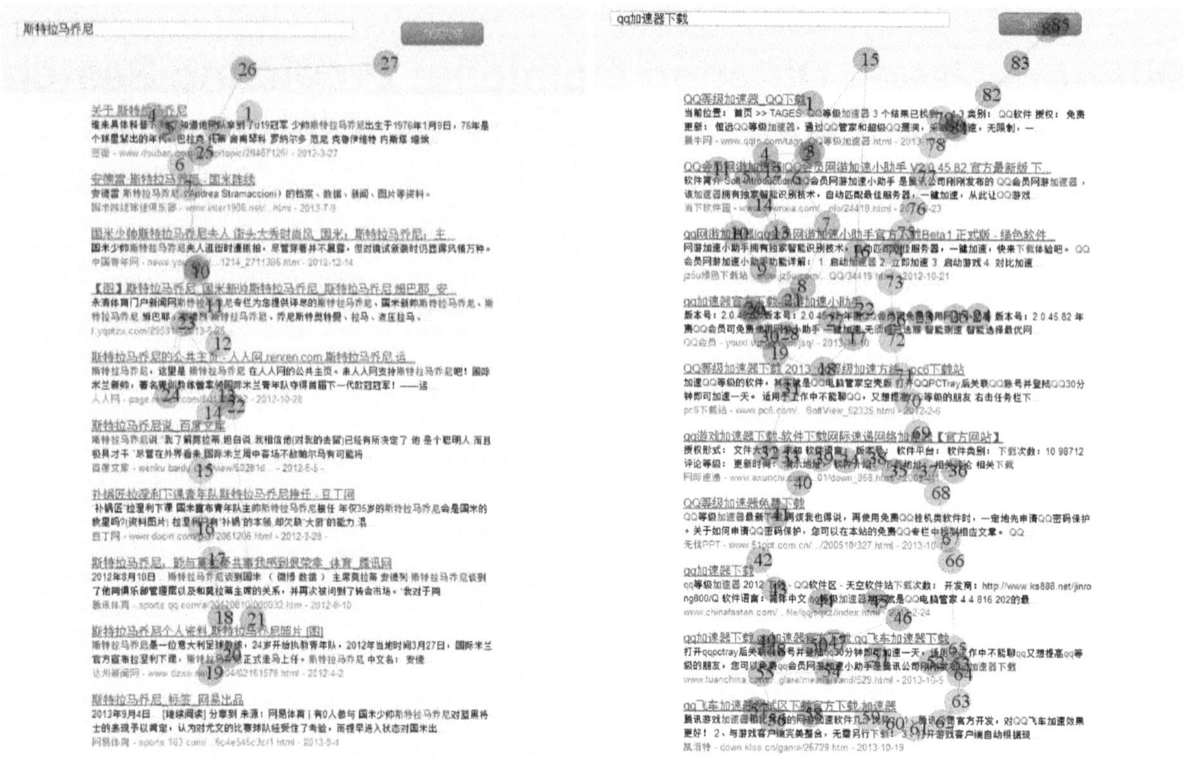

(a) Example of a satisfied(SAT) search session (b) Example of a dissatisfied(DSAT) search sessioin

Figure 1: Examples of Users' Mouse Movement Trails on SERPs

to clicks. However, mouse movement data contains much richer interaction information between users and search engine result pages (SERPs) than these behavior signals. Recent studies [19] already show that automatically discovered mouse movement subsequences (namely motifs) can be utilized to infer result relevance. Therefore, the question of whether satisfaction prediction can benefit from the rich interaction information stored in mouse movement logs needs to be investigated (*RQ2*).

To shed light on these research questions, we construct an experimental search engine system which can collect users' click-through and mouse movement information simultaneously. The explicit feedback of users on search satisfaction and external assessors' opinions are collected as well. Figure 1 shows two examples of users' mouse movement process on SERPs with the constructed experimental search engine (see Section 3), where Figure 1(a) shows an example of SAT (self-reported satisfactory) case and Figure 1(b) shows a DSAT (self-reported dissatisfactory) case. Mouse movement trail is shown in circles and the numbers in them correspond to the sequence of mouse movement positions. The red circles in both figures are movement patterns (namely motifs, which means frequently appeared subsequences in mouse movement data) extracted and selected by the algorithms described in Section 5. In Figure 1(a), the user appears to examine the first result (which is a key resource to the corresponding query) carefully and just take a quick look at other results before ending the search session. This sequence means that he/she succeeds in finding necessary information with relatively little effort. In contrast, most results on the SERP in Figure 1(b) seem not to meet the user's information need. We can see from the mouse trail that the user examines almost all results on the SERP carefully during the session, which means he/she may take much effort without obtaining much information. Therefore, mouse movement information can help us infer that the user in search session shown in Figure 1(a) is likely to be satisfied while the one in Figure 1(b) is not.

The examples in Figure 1 indicate that mouse movement data records richer information in the sequence of examining, reading relevant/irrelevant results and so on. Our work focuses on extracting these movement patterns from the sequence of cursors on SERPs to help predict search satisfaction. To avoid too much subjectivity in satisfaction judgment, we adopt and compare two different sources of satisfaction labels from both search users and external assessors and introduce manipulated SERPs to control annotation qualities. Following recent efforts in understanding users' judgments of satisfaction [17, 16], we compare the different roles of result utility (benefit) and user effort (cost) in different satisfaction labels as well.

The major difference between our work and existing studies in search satisfaction prediction lies in that we adopt rich interaction patterns (or motifs) in mouse movement data. Although previous studies such as [8] already introduce mouse behavior features in addition to result clicks, motifs are not among their investigated features. According to the cases in Figure 1, motifs may contain important feedback information and should not be ignored. Our work also differs from the motif extraction method proposed by Lagun et al. [19] in that they focused on the problem of relevance estimation instead of search satisfaction prediction. We also propose two specific strategies (distance-based and distribution-based) in the motif extraction process to efficiently select effective patterns. Compared with the frequency-based strategy proposed in [19], they are more suitable for the task of satisfaction prediction by achieving better prediction performance with fewer motifs.

Our contributions in this paper are three-fold: (1) To our best knowledge, this is the first attempt to predict search satisfaction with mouse movement patterns (or motifs) on SERPs. (2) We propose to use distance-based and distribution-based strategies in the selection of motifs, which outperforms existing frequency-based strategy in choosing the most effective motifs to separate SAT sessions from DSAT ones. (3) With an experimental search system, we compare satisfaction labels collected from both search users and external assessors and observe for the first time that users and assessors have different criteria in search satisfaction judgments.

The rest of this paper is organized as follows: Related studies are discussed in Section 2. The experimental system and corresponding data collection process are presented in Section 3. The differences in satisfaction judgments from users and external assessors are investigated in Section 4. Motif extraction method and corresponding selection strategies are proposed in Section 5. Experimental results in satisfaction prediction are introduced and discussed in Section 6. Finally come the conclusions and future work directions.

2. RELATED WORK

Two lines of researches are related to the work we describe in this article: (1) User satisfaction understanding and prediction. (2) Search performance evaluation with mouse movement information.

The concept of satisfaction was first introduced in IR researches in 1970s according to Su et al. [27]. A recent definition states that "satisfaction can be understood as the fulfillment of a specified desire or goal" [18]. However, search satisfaction itself is a subjective construct and is difficult to measure. Some existing studies tried to collect satisfaction feedback from users directly. For example, Guo et al.'s work [8] on predicting Web search success and Feild et al.'s work [4] on predicting searcher frustration were both based on searchers' self-reported explicit judgements. Differently, other researchers employed external assessors to restore the users' search experience and make annotations according to their own opinions. For example, Guo et al.'s work [10] on predicting query performance and Huffman et al.'s work [14] on predicting result relevance were based on this kind of annotations. Recent research [28] showed that annotations on result relevances from external assessors may not be a good estimator of users' own judgements. However, the relationship between searchers' and external assessors' opinions in search satisfaction remains uninvestigated.

A number of different interaction behaviors have been taken into consideration in the prediction of search user satisfactions including both coarse-grained features (e.g. click-through based features in [10]) and fine-grained ones (e.g. cursor position and scrolling speed in [8]). Recently, a number of studies (e.g. [17, 16]) chose to use the cost-benefit framework to analyze users satisfaction judgment in search process. In this framework, both document relevance (or attractiveness, or utility) and the efforts users spend on examining SERPs and browsing landing pages are considered. In this work, we also follow the same framework and try to predict result utilities and user efforts with mouse movement features. We also want to investigate the differences in search satisfaction annotations collected from user side and external assessor side.

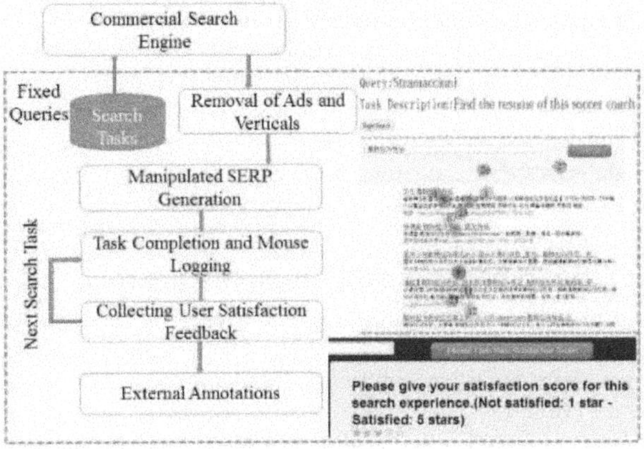

Figure 2: Data Collection Procedure

In the second line of related studies, mouse movement information like scroll and hover have proven to be valuable signals in inferring user behavior and preferences [6, 7, 12, 25], search intent [5], search examination [22] and predicting result relevance [13]. However, none of these studies tried to extract mouse movement patterns and adopt them to predict search satisfaction.

With the advancement of technology, more detailed and scalable mouse information can be collected. Arapakis et al. extracted mouse gestures to measure within-content engagement [2]. Lagun et al. [19] introduced the concept of frequent cursor subsequences (namely motifs) in the estimation of result relevance. Different from their work, we focus on how to extract and select effective mouse movement patterns from SERPs to help predict search result utility, searcher effort, and satisfaction at a search task level instead of result level. We also propose different motif selection strategies to improve the prediction performance.

3. DATA COLLECTION PROCESS

3.1 Experiment Procedure

To collect user behavior data during search process and corresponding satisfaction annotation data, we construct an experimental search engine. With the system, users' interaction process while completing search tasks were recorded, including click-through, mouse movement and satisfaction annotations. During the experimental procedure, satisfaction feedback as well as a variety of mouse movement information, including mouse coordinates, clicks, hovers and scrolls are logged by injected Javascript on SERPs.

We recruited 40 participants (among which 16 are female and 24 are male) for the data collecting process. All participants are first-year undergraduate students from our university with a variety of self-reported search engine utilization experiences. Their majors include life science, economic and social science. We didn't invite computer science or electrical engineering students because they may be too familiar with the use of search engines and cannot represent ordinary search engine users.

The procedure of the experiment is shown in Figure 2. In the experiment, each participant was asked to complete 30 search tasks within about 1 hour. Before each task, the participant was shown the search query and corresponding explanations to avoid ambiguity. After that, he/she would be guided to a pre-designed search result page where the query is not allowed to change. The participant was asked to examine the results provided by our system and end the search session either if the search goal was completed or he/she was disappointed with the results. Each time they end a search session, they were required to label a 5-point satisfaction score to the session where 5 means the most satisfactory and 1 means the least. Then they would be guided to continue to the next search task.

3.2 Search Tasks and Quality Control

To predict search satisfaction at a search task level, we selected 30 search tasks from NTCIR IMine task [21], among which there are 10 navigational tasks and 20 informational tasks. All these queries were collected from a commercial search engine and were neither long-tailed nor hot ones. Different from the IMine task, we provided detailed task explanations to the participants to avoid unnecessary ambiguity.

For each search task, we fix the query and results to ensure the consistency of our data. The search results were collected from a popular commercial search engine and only top 10 organic results are retained. Vertical results and advertisements were not included because they may affect users' search behaviors [29]. The investigation on SERPs involving verticals and advertisement will be left to future research.

Considering the fact that users may have different criteria or even be distracted during the satisfaction annotation process, we manipulate the SERPs to make a quality control of the data collection process. We invite three professional assessors from a commercial search engine to label the relevance scores for all query-result pairs. The KAPPA coefficient of the their annotation is 0.70, which can be characterized as a substantial agreement according to Cohen [3]. We then design two different types of SERPS for each query based on the relevance annotations. For each query, the results on two SERPs are the same but in different ranking orders. On the first page, the results were ranked in the order of relevance and on the second one they were ranked in the reverse order of relevance. We call these two pages ordered-page and reversed-page, which should entail different levels of satisfaction. The pages are used to determine if an annotator is reliable by observing how these pages are annotated.

For the data collection process, we had 90 (30 queries * 3 different SERPs) search conditions in total. Each participant needs to complete 30 queries using our search engine system, which contain 10 SERPs from each kind of conditions. We adopted a Graeco-Latin square design and randomized sequence order to ensure that each task condition had the same opportunity to be shown to users. It is reasonable to believe that searchers tend to be more satisfied with ordered-pages and less satisfied with reversed-pages. Therefore, we can determine whether a participant is reliable based on his/her satisfaction annotation on these SERPs.

3.3 External Annotations

To compare the satisfaction annotations from actual users and external assessors, we recruited three assessors to annotate the satisfaction scores of the collected search sessions. The assessors are different from the ones in the query-result relevance annotation process and had worked in the commercial search engine company for at least one year. They can be regarded as professionals who have deep understanding in search engine's opinions of search satisfaction.

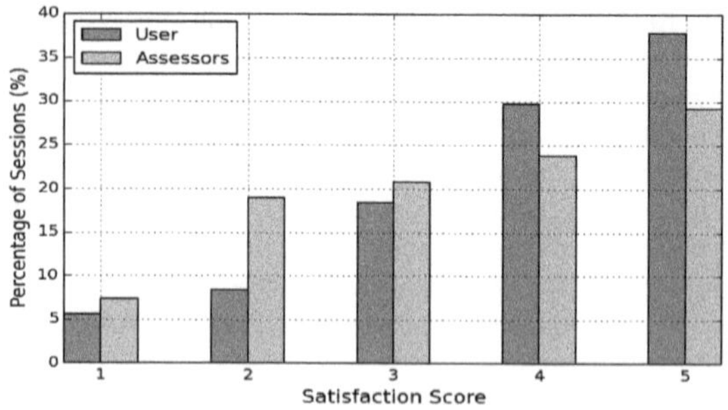

Figure 3: Distribution of Satisfaction Annotations from Users and External Assessors

In the satisfaction annotation process, we follow the settings in existing studies [16] and extract key information from users' search behavior logs. The assessors were shown a list of behavior items of users including search dwell time, mouse click action and click dwell time, mouse hover action and hover time, and the action of cursor movement from one search result to another. We used such detailed information to help our assessors maximally restore the original searchers' search experience and make as reasonable annotations as possible. The assessors were also asked to give a 5-point satisfaction score so that the satisfaction scores from two resources would be comparable. The KAPPA coefficient of assessors' annotations is 0.41, which can be characterized as a moderate agreement.

All the collected data is available for download through the first author's Web site[1].

4. USERS V.S. EXTERNAL ASSESSORS

With the data collected in the experiment process, we want to compare the satisfaction annotations from actual users and external assessors. Figure 3 shows the distribution of satisfaction scores from users and assessors.

From the figure we can see that both users and assessors tend to give a high satisfaction score for the search tasks, which shows that the commercial search engine generally provides promising results for these non-long-tailed queries. We can also see from the figure that assessors annotated much more sessions with scores of 1 or 2 (26.3% v.s. 14.0%), which indicates that assessors may be stricter than users and tend to regard search session as DSAT ones.

To verify the reliability of satisfaction annotations from users and assessors, we use the two kinds of pre-defined SERPs (ordered-page and reversed-page) in the experiment process. Figure 4 shows the distribution of the satisfaction scores from two different resources on the pre-defined SERPs.

Results in Figure 4(a) show that users tend to feel more satisfied with ordered-pages and less satisfied with reversed-pages, which is in line with our expectations. It indicates that users' satisfaction scores will be affected by the relevance of search results but the impact is not as large as we have imagined. Figure 4(b) shows a similar distribution tendency in assessors' annotations. We notice that the percentages of reversed-pages with scores of 4 or 5 in assessors' annotations are much lower than those in users' annotations. This observation is consistent with our finding from Figure 3 that assessors may be stricter than users. It may also indicate that assessors examine the results more carefully and

[1]http://www.thuir.cn/group/~yqliu

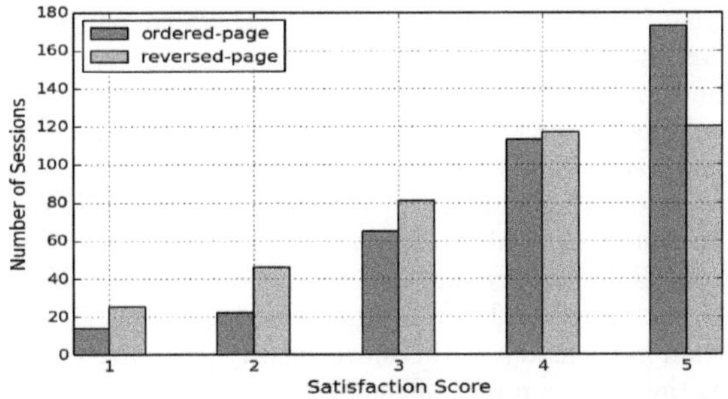

(a) Users' Annotations

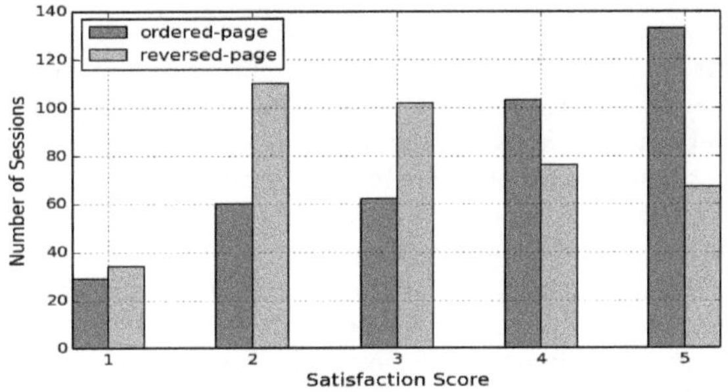

(b) Assessors' Annotations

Figure 4: Distribution of Satisfaction Scores on Three Types of Manipulated SERPs

their annotations are more reliable because reverse-pages are not supposed to provide satisfactory results.

Inspired by existing researches on the understanding of search satisfactions [17, 28], we also analyze the different roles of utilities and efforts in the satisfaction annotation process. This cost-benefit framework may help us better understand the differences in satisfaction annotations from users and assessors.

As for search result utility, we choose to measure it with session cumulated gain (sCG) and normalized discounted cumulative gain (nDCG@N, N=3, 5, 10) [15] based on the relevance annotations from professional assessors. Three different metrics were adopted to measure search effort, including search dwell time, maximum clicked rank and number of clicks. These effort-based metrics are widely adopted in search satisfaction related studies [4, 8].

In Tables 1 and 2, we show the Pearson correlation coefficients between satisfaction annotations and the utility/efforts metrics including sCG (U1), NDCG@3 (U2), NDCG@5 (U3), NDCG@10 (U4), search duration (E1), maximum clicked rank (E2) and number of clicks (E3). We can see that all measurements of result utility have a positive correlation with both user satisfaction and assessors' annotations. Meanwhile all measurements of user effort have a negative correlation with those annotations. All correlations are statistically significant except that between assessors' annotation and sCG. We also find that NDCG@3, search dwell time and number of clicks may have a comparatively large effect on satisfaction judgement. Such correlation between these metrics and satisfaction will be used for predicting satisfaction in later sections.

From the statistics shown in Tables 1 and 2, we see an interesting phenomenon that users and assessors may have different criteria in the annotation of search satisfaction. We can see that the correlations between users' annotations and utility-based metrics (U1-U4) are higher than those between

Table 1: Correlations between Satisfaction and Utilities (*indicates statistical significance at $p<0.01$)

	sCG (U1)	NDCG@3 (U2)	NDCG@5 (U3)	NDCG@10 (U4)
User	0.22*	**0.24***	0.25*	0.27*
Assessors	0.03	**0.22***	0.20*	0.14*

Table 2: Correlations between Satisfaction and Effort (All results are statistically significant, $p < 0.01$)

	Session duration (E1)	Maximum clicked rank(E2)	Number of clicks (E3)
User	-0.14	-0.10	**-0.15**
Assessors	**-0.59**	-0.35	-0.39

assessors and U1-U4. Meanwhile, the correlations between assessors' annotations and effort-based metrics (E1-E3) are much higher. It means that users tend to pay more attention to the utility of search results while assessors emphasize on the effect of search effort. Such result is reasonable since users may be satisfied as long as their search need is met in not a very long time (The average search dwell time of all users in our research is 37 seconds). Meanwhile, assessors tend to require search engines to help users locate necessary information within short time periods. They may not be able to judge how much information is enough for search users, but if the search task can be completed promptly, they are usually sure that it is a successful session and user should be satisfied.

We also expand the work in [28] to measure the consistency of the satisfaction scores from users and assessors. We calculate the correlation coefficient between the satisfaction annotations from assessors and users. Inspired by the above findings, we also divide users' satisfaction scores by three different measurements of effort since assessors tend to care more about search effort. Results are shown in Table 3. We can see that there is a fair agreement between the two resources of satisfaction annotations, which is comparable with the findings in [28]. However, if we divide users' satisfaction annotations by search efforts, we achieve a moderate agreement, which further validates the assumption that assessors pay more attention to search efforts.

These results show that utility and effort play a quite different role in users' and assessors' satisfaction judgement. Original users pay more attention to search utilities and external assessors care more about search effort. It indicates that the annotations from professional assessors may be more reliable (considering the results shown in Figure 4) but not always consistent with users' opinions. Although the explicit feedback process during search sessions may interrupt users and information collected may be noisy, we cannot simply replace the annotations with professional assessors' because they emphasize on different factors. It also means that a better satisfaction feedback strategy which collects users' opinions implicitly (e.g. the one proposed in our work which predicts satisfaction based on motifs) is necessary for the evaluation of search performances.

5. MOTIF EXTRACTION AND SELECTION

5.1 Motif Candidate Extraction

The concept of motif is first introduced by Lagun et al. [19] and defined as frequent subsequences in mouse cursor movement data. They proposed to automatically extract

Table 3: Correlation between Satisfaction Annotations from Users and External Assessors (All values are statistically significant, $p < 0.01$)

	User	User\E1	User\E2	User\E3
Assessors	0.27	**0.49**	0.33	**0.54**

motifs from web search examination data and used it for document relevance prediction and search result ranking. Although the method can be adopted to all kinds of Web pages, they focused on extracting motifs from landing pages so that users implicit preference feedback could be inferred. Different from their work, we try to extract motifs from mouse cursor movement logs on SERPs because we believe that whether users are satisfied can be predicted by their interaction behaviors on SERPs. We first introduce the definition of motif in our work and explain the extraction process from cursor movement data to motifs.

Definition: A motif is a frequently-appeared sequence of mouse positions, which can be represented by $T = \{(x_i, y_i)\}_{i=1}^{N}$, where (x_i, y_i) is the coordinates of the cursor at time t_i.

To extract motifs from cursor data, we first use a sliding window to perform data pre-processing and generate candidates from raw data. In the generation of motifs, we also use DTW(Dynamic Time Warping)[26] for distance measurement as in [19] but try both Euclidean and Manhattan distances in calculation. Euclidean distance which is not selected by [19] is also used in our method because we believe that motif extraction on SERPs and ordinary Web pages are different. The size and number of components on SERPs are generally fixed and the direct distances between points are mostly comparable across different search sessions.

During the process of clustering similar motifs, we adopted a similar early abandonment and lower bounding strategy as in [19] and a number of time series mining studies such as [24]. The difference is that we just remove the candidate motifs which have overlapping subsequences instead of using a range parameter R to distinguish good motifs from candidates. By this means, we are able to get more candidate motifs and adopt specific strategies to select out motifs with high quality for satisfaction predicting.

5.2 Motif Selection Strategies

A major difference between our motif extraction method and the one in [19] is that we use a number of selection strategies to find the most predictive motifs from candidates. Different from the frequency-based strategy in [19] which selects motifs with the most appearances in training set, we make use of the data distribution information to locate the motifs which can separate SAT sessions from DSAT ones. We believe that frequently-appeared motifs may not always be predictive ones because they may appear in both SAT and DSAT sessions. Therefore, a better selection strategy should use both frequency information and the differences between different kinds of sessions.

We firstly define $SAT\_DATA/DSAT\_DATA$ as the search sessions which are labelled as satisfactory/unsatisfactory ones annotated by users/assessors. M_SAT and M_DSAT are then defined as the sets of motifs extracted from SAT_DATA and $DSAT\_DATA$. When we select proper motifs with high predictive power from M_SAT and M_DSAT, they could be adopted to generate features for each search session. If we get a series of predictive motifs $C_1, C_2, ..., C_N$, we can obtain N distance features for a certain search session S: $Dist(C_1, S), Dist(C_2, S)...Dist(C_N, S)$, which will then be used as the N features in the prediction method.

One should note that although the motif selection strategies adopted in our method is different from that in [19], the efficiency of online satisfaction prediction process is similar with the existing method if the same number (N) of motifs are selected. This is because in the prediction process, both methods require the calculation of similarity between predictive motifs and motifs from search sessions. The computation complexity is therefore mostly unchanged if both adopt the same number of motifs.

5.2.1 Distance-based Selection

This strategy is based on a **Difference Hypothesis**: predictive motifs in M_SAT should be quite different from the ones in M_DSAT and vice versa. This hypothesis probably holds because it is reasonable to assume that users have different mouse movement patterns when they are satisfied / unsatisfied with the search results. The examples in Figure 1 also validates this assumption.

To select the motifs that are significantly different, we use the average distance between motifs in different sets to measure the difference. For example, for a motif candidate C_SAT_i in M_SAT, we have:

$$S_{dist}(C\_SAT_i) = \frac{\sum_{C_j \in M\_DSAT} DTW(C\_SAT_i, C_j)}{|M\_DSAT|} \quad (1)$$

$DTW(C\_SAT_i, C_j)$ represents the DTW distance of two candidate motifs, C_SAT_i and C_j. Intuitively, this equation represents the average DTW distance between C_SAT_i and all motifs in M_DSAT. Similarly, for motifs in M_DSAT, we have:

$$S_{dist}(C\_DSAT_i) = \frac{\sum_{C_j \in M\_SAT} DTW(C\_DSAT_i, C_j)}{|M\_SAT|} \quad (2)$$

With equations (1) and (2), we can select motifs with large difference from the motifs in the other kind of sessions, which have large chances to be predictive ones.

5.2.2 Distribution-based Selection

This strategy is based on a **Covering Hypothesis**: predictive motifs in M_SAT/M_DSAT should cover sufficient sessions in $SAT\_DATA/DSAT\_DATA$. We introduce this hypothesis because when a certain motif can only cover a small number of sessions, it is not reasonable to select it even if it is quite different from the motifs in the other set. We want to focus on the general behavior patterns in satisfied/unsatisfied sessions. Therefore, it is necessary to use the distribution information to filter possible noises and retain the ones with large coverage.

We define the distance of a motif C and a session S first to determine whether a motif covers a specific session.

$$Dist(C, S) = min\{DTW(C_i, C) | C_i \in S\} \quad (3)$$

As shown in (3), we use a sliding window to capture several motif candidates (C_i) from session S and calculate the distance between C and these motifs. The smallest distance is defined as the distance between C and S. We then define the coverage rate of a motif C on a dataset D:

$$CR(C, D) = \frac{|\{\frac{|D| Dist(C, S_i)}{\sum_{S_i \in D} Dist(C, S_i)} < r | S_i \in D\}|}{|D|} \quad (4)$$

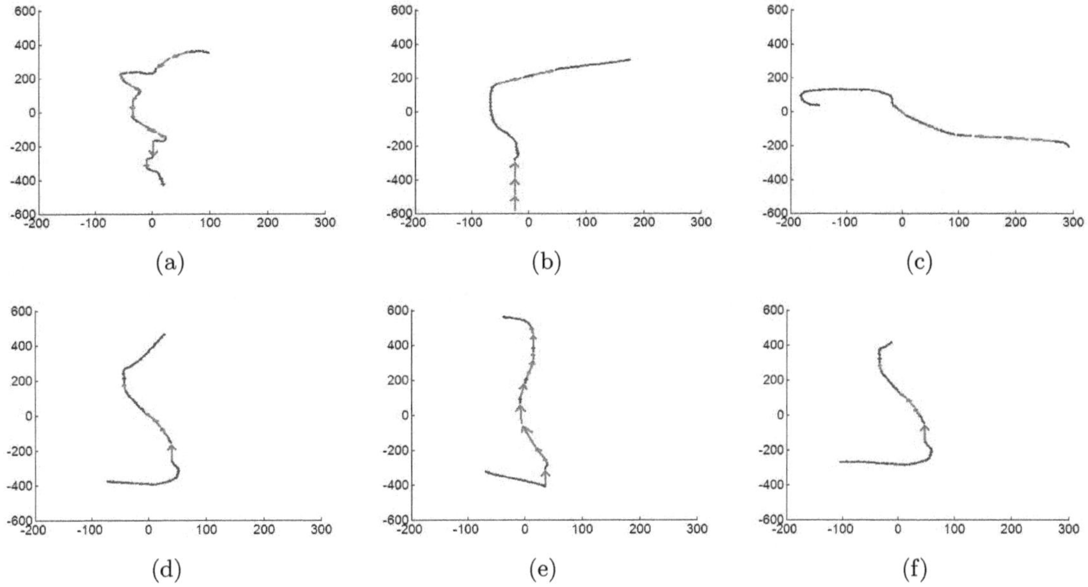

Figure 5: Predictive motifs discovered from SAT_DATA (a-c) and $DSAT\_DATA$ (d-f)

In (4), r is the parameter to ensure we can select enough motifs, which we set as $\frac{1}{30}$ in our experiment. With the concept of coverage rate, we can define the score for each motif based on distribution difference as follows:

$$S_{distri}(C\_SAT_i) = \frac{CR(C\_SAT_i, SAT\_DATA)}{CR(C\_SAT_i, DSAT\_DATA)} \quad (5)$$

$$S_{distri}(C\_DSAT_i) = \frac{CR(C\_DSAT_i, DSAT\_DATA)}{CR(C\_DSAT_i, SAT\_DATA)} \quad (6)$$

Similar to the method in 5.2.1, we select motifs with high scores since they tend to have a large distribution difference.

5.3 Example of Predictive Motifs

The distance-based and distribution-based strategies can help discover predictive motifs from mouse movement data and a few examples are shown in Figure 5. Figure 5(a), 5(b) and 5(c) show 3 of the 10 most predictive motifs extracted from SAT_DATA while Figure 5(d), 5(e) and 5(f) show 3 of the 10 most predictive motifs extracted from $DSAT\_DATA$. The motifs are selected based on distribution-based strategy while distance-based strategy produce similar results according to our experiments. The movement directions are annotated by arrows and the coordinate axis is in pixels.

We can see that the motif in Figure 5(a) shows a process that user examines the top results carefully and then take a quick look at the lower-ranked results and Figure 1(a) can be regarded a practical example. Figure 5(b) probably shows the process of re-visiting a previous checked result while Figure 5(c) mainly indicates the behavior of using the mouse as a reading aid or the action of moving mouse to click. In contrast, the three motifs show in Figure 5(d), 5(e) and 5(f) are similar and all reflect the process of moving the mouse from bottom to the top after carefully examining a result at a lower position. This is reasonable since we can infer that a searcher may not be satisfied if he has to re-examine a number of results after examining a lower-ranked one. These motifs extracted automatically from mouse data will play an important role in satisfaction predicting, as will be discussed in the next section.

6. EXPERIMENTAL RESULTS

6.1 Experiment Setups

In this section, we demonstrate the value of our method by predicting the satisfaction annotation results of users and assessors. After the motif extraction and selection process described in Section 5, the motifs from the data sets collected in Section 3 are adopted as features in the prediction process. There are two parameters in the motif extracting algorithm we discussed in section 6.1, namely the length of sliding window and the distance measurement method for two basic points. Based on the result of quite a number of experiments, we find that a sliding window of 3 seconds can make the model perform best. We also found that the Euclidean distance measurement can help the model achieve a promising accuracy with just a small number of motifs. It is extremely important considering the fact that the procedure of extracting motifs may be time-consuming. Such findings are different from that in [19], where a sliding window of 5 seconds and the Manhattan distance measurement is used. This difference may come from the fact that we focus on discovering motifs from SERPs while Lagun et al. mainly try to discover motifs from landing pages. A time period of 3 seconds may be enough for a mouse action on SERPs because there are mainly ten blue links without many other components. The Euclidean distance measurement may better reflect the distance of two points in a two-dimensional space on SERPs because the sizes of components on SERPs are similar with each other.

We compare the performance of the proposed model in predicting satisfaction scores from users and external assessors. We exclude sessions with a satisfaction score of 3 since we consider that users or assessors do not have a satisfaction tendency in such sessions. Thus we use 951 search sessions from users and 923 search sessions with assessors' annotations for satisfaction predicting, where sessions with a score of 4 or 5 are regarded as SAT cases and those with a score of 1 or 2 are regarded as DSAT ones.

The learning algorithm in the prediction process is logistic regression, which is widely used in satisfaction prediction

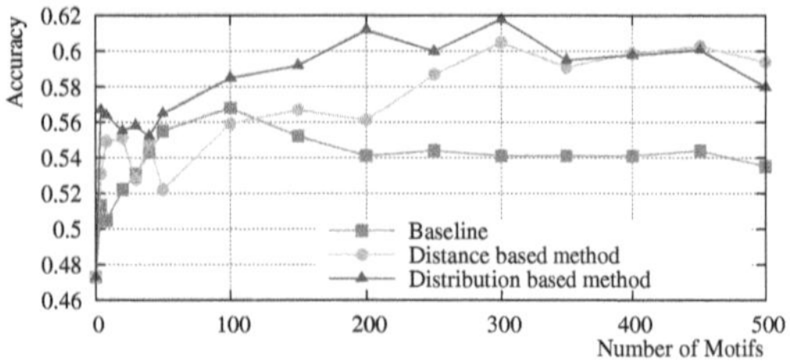

(a) Users' Annotations

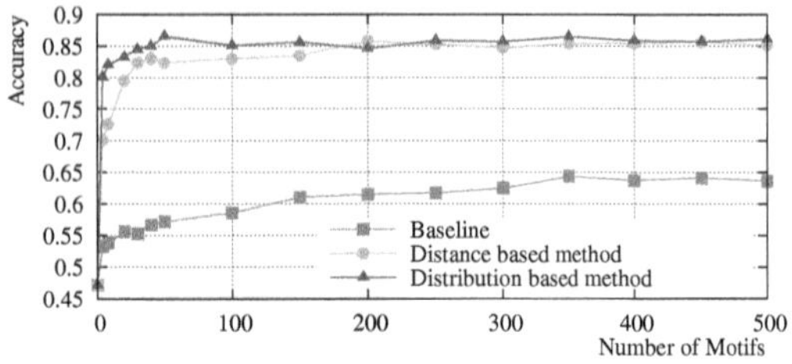

(b) Assessors' Annotations

Figure 6: Prediction Performance with Different Motif Selection Strategies

tasks [8]. All results are based on 5-fold cross-validation on the data collections unless specified otherwise.

6.2 Comparison of Motif Selection Strategies

To compare the different strategies for selecting motifs, we use the method used in [19] as a baseline, which selects motifs based on frequency in training set. Experimental results on the prediction of both users' and assessors' annotations are shown in Figures 6.

Results on both datasets shown in Figure 6 indicates that the proposed selection strategies based on distance and distribution outperform the selecting strategy based on frequency. The performance of the proposed prediction model performs better as the number of motifs increases. Between the two selecting methods we proposed in section 6.2, we consider the one based on distribution better since it can reach a high accuracy with comparatively a small number of motifs on both two datasets. We want to predict satisfaction with a small number of motifs so that the motif extraction process can be efficient. Therefore, prediction models used in the following sections all adopt the distribution-based selection strategy.

Another important finding from Figure 6 is that our predict model can reach an accuracy of more than 0.85 on assessors' annotations while that on users' satisfaction annotations is only around 0.60. This indicates that users' self-annotations may be quite subjective and may be more difficult to be predicted, which validates the necessity of investigating results based on these two different satisfaction annotations as we did in Section 4.

6.3 Comparison of Quality Control Strategies

Considering the fact that different users may have different opinions in satisfaction judgement, satisfaction annotations collected from users may be subjective and sometime even unreliable. To obtain reliable satisfaction annotations from users, we introduce a number of quality control strategies with the manipulated SERPs described in Section 3.3. Specifically, we test the performance of our prediction model on the following three different datasets:

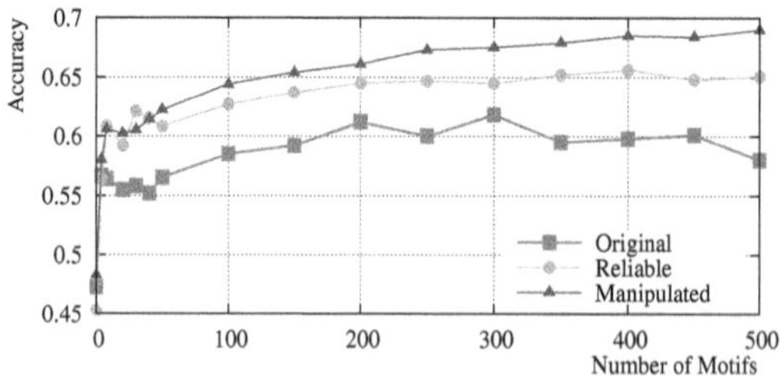

Figure 7: Comparison of Prediction Accuracies with Different Quality Control Methods

The original dataset. This dataset is the one we use in Figure 7(a), which includes all search sessions with satisfaction scores of 1, 2, 4 or 5 from users.

The reliable dataset. We use the manipulated SERPs as a information source for quality control and remove data from unreliable users. For each participant, we define x_1 to represent the number of ordered-pages which he/she gave a satisfaction score of 1 and y_1 to represent the number of reversed-pages which he gave a satisfaction score of 1. Similarly, we get $x_i, y_i (i = 2, 3, 4, 5)$. We can then use a combination of x_i, y_i to calculate a score for each participant to measure his/her reliability.

$$\mathbf{S}(participant) = f(x_1, x_2...x_5, y_1, y_2...y_5) \qquad (7)$$

We think that users tend to be more satisfied with ordered-pages and less satisfied with reversed-pages. If a searcher gives high satisfaction scores for ordered-pages and low scores for reverse pages, we consider him/her as a reliable source of annotation information. Based on this assumption, we define the reliability score as:

$$\mathbf{S}(participant) = x_5 + y_1 + y_2 - x_1 - x_2 - y_5 \qquad (8)$$

It is reasonable to think that the lower the score is, the participant tends to be less reliable. We remove annotations coming from participants with the five lowest reliability scores and the remaining 827 search sessions are regarded as the reliable dataset.

The manipulated dataset. We define the sessions with ordered-pages as satisfied cases and those with reversed-pages as unsatisfied ones. It should be noticed that this dataset is objective since it has nothing to do with users' original satisfaction feedback. The only information we use is the mouse movement information collected during users' search process.

Performance of our predict model on these three datasets are shown in Figure 8. We can see that the proposed model performs best on the manipulated dataset and also gain promising results on the reliable dataset. Prediction performance on the original dataset is the worst because the annotations from unreliable users are not removed and the subjectivity of annotations are also expected. We also notice that the accuracies on manipulated and reliable datasets are still lower than that on the external assessors' annotations in Figure 6(b). It indicates that users' annotations on search satisfaction are rather subjective. Although we can reduce possible noises with certain quality control strategies, it is still difficult for prediction models to provide high-quality predictions.

6.4 Predicting Utility and Effort

We try to estimate utility and effort with motifs in this section since some metrics like NDCG@3, search dwell time

Table 4: NRMSE of Proposed Method for Predicting Utility and Effort

Number of Motifs	NDCG@3	Dwell time	Number of Clicks
5	0.287	0.134	0.158
10	**0.287**	**0.133**	0.151
50	0.288	0.137	0.127
100	0.299	0.142	**0.126**
300	0.383	0.181	0.147
500	0.583	0.259	0.223

and number of clicks have a remarkable correlation with satisfaction annotations according to Section 4. If we could predict these factors in user sessions, it also helps us better understand why users are satisfied or unsatisfied with certain result lists.

We use Normalized Root Mean Square Error (NRMSE, smaller value means better estimation) to evaluate the model performance as in most regression-based methods. The experimental results are shown in Table 4.

From the results shown in Table 4 we see that motifs can moderately estimate NDCG@3, session dwell time and number of clicks since the NRMSE value is considerably small. We also notice that motifs can probably better estimate search effort since the NRMSE value is much smaller for session dwell time and number of clicks. Another important finding is that we gain best performance when the number of motifs used is around 50, which indicates that the estimation model may overfit if too much motifs are incorporated.

6.5 Prediction across Users and Queries

According to Section 5, the motif selection strategy relies on data distributions on training sets to locate the most predictive motifs. Therefore, it is important to investigate the generalization power of the proposed predict model across different users and queries. According to previous studies on predicting examination sequence with mouse movement information [11], different users may have rather different mouse movement patterns and this may lead to poor generalization power of proposed prediction models.

To verify the prediction performance of the proposed models while dealing with new users or queries, we adopted three different training strategies. **random sampling**: the segmentation of training and testing data in cross validation is completely random. **sampling by user**: in the segmentation of training and testing data in cross validation, sessions from a same user can only be grouped into either the training set or the testing set. **sampling by query**: in the segmentation of training and testing data in cross validation, sessions for a same query can only be grouped into either the training set or the testing set. With the latter two strategies, we can ensure that data from the same user/query cannot be adopted for both training and testing.

We also implement a satisfaction prediction method proposed in [8] (with both coarse-grained features such as number of clicks and fine-grained features such as scroll speed) and adopted it as the baseline method. We choose the method because it is also based on mouse behavior data (although without motifs) and is one of the most closely related studies. The baseline method and our proposed method are both tested with the three different training strategies and results are shown in Table 5.

Table 5: Comparison of Accuracy with the baseline method in [8] across different users and queries(* indicates statistical significance at $p < 0.1$ level)

Annotation & Sampling strategy	Features in [8]	Motif Features	All Features
User annotation & random sample	0.570	0.580 (+1.75%)	0.598 (+4.91%)
User annotation & sample by user	0.523	0.578 (+10.5%*)	0.552 (+5.54%*)
User annotation & sample by query	0.602	0.631 (+4.82%)	0.638 (+5.98%)
Assessor annotation & random sample	0.920	0.861 (-6.41%*)	0.922 (+0.217%)
Assessor annotation & sample by user	0.921	0.859 (-6.73%)	0.930 (+0.977%)
Assessor annotation & sample by query	0.924	0.886 (-4.11%*)	0.938 (+1.52%)

Results in Table 5 reveal a number of interesting findings: 1) The prediction performance of the proposed method with motif features doesn't change much with different training strategies. It means that the method can be adopted to deal with previously-unseen queries and users, which is important for practical Web search applications. 2) Compared with the "fine-grained" interaction features (e.g. scroll speed, y-axis maximum coordinate, etc) proposed in [8], the proposed motif-based method performs better in predicting users' annotations but worse in predicting assessors' annotations. When we investigate the differences between two sets of features, we found that the features related with y-axis maximum coordinates in [8] are quite predictive. It probably accords with our findings in Section 4 that assessors emphasize on search effort in satisfaction annotations because the maximum coordinates in y-axis is a strong signal for the efforts of users. As for the prediction of users' annotations, the motif-based method studies better, especially in predicting the opinions of unseen users (with a significant improvement of 10.5%). This means that the proposed method makes use of more details in users' interaction process and is probably more suitable for practical applications (in which predicting previous-unseen users' opinion is important). 3) With all the features proposed in baseline method and our proposed method, we gain best prediction performance for both users' and assessors' annotations. It shows that the motif features can be used to improve state-of-the-art technologies and they can be extremely useful for the satisfaction prediction of previous-unseen users.

7. CONCLUSIONS AND FUTURE WORK

Search satisfaction prediction is a non-trivial task in search performance researches. The definition of satisfaction is subjective, which makes the consistency of feedback from users can't be ensured. External assessors are employed to annotate the satisfaction scores but such annotations may be different from those of users. In this work, we collect data from both users and assessors to make a deep analysis. We find that there is a moderate agreement between satisfaction annotations from those two resources. Users pay more attention to the utility of results while external assessors also emphasize on the search effort.

We further propose a motif based learning framework to predict result utility, search effort as well as satisfaction annotations for both users and assessors. We introduce specific methods for extracting high quality motifs directly from SERPs and demonstrate that our proposed distance-based and distribution-based strategies outperforms existing solutions. The proposed method is shown to be more effective than state-of-the-art satisfaction prediction methods in predicting previously-unseen users' opinions, which makes it applicable for practical Web search environment.

For future work, we would like to further improve the efficiency of mining motifs and try to incorporate other features into satisfaction predicting models. Besides, we also want to research how motifs can be used in a heterogeneous Web search environment and also other web search applications.

8. ACKNOWLEDGMENTS

This work is supported by Tsinghua University Initiative Scientific Research Program(2014Z21032), National Key Basic Research Program (2015CB358700) and Natural Science Foundation (61472206, 61073071) of China. Part of the work has been done at the Tsinghua-NUS NExT Search Centre, which is supported by the Singapore National Search Foundation & Interactive Digital Media R&D Program Office, MDA under research grant (WBS:R-252-300-001-490).

9. REFERENCES

[1] M. Ageev, D. Lagun, and E. Agichtein. Improving search result summaries by using searcher behavior data. In *SIGIR'13*, pages 13–22. ACM, 2013.

[2] I. Arapakis, M. Lalmas, and G. Valkanas. Understanding within-content engagement through pattern analysis of mouse gestures. In *CIKM'14*, pages 1439–1448. ACM, 2014.

[3] J. Cohen. Weighted kappa: Nominal scale agreement provision for scaled disagreement or partial credit. *Psychological bulletin*, 70(4):213, 1968.

[4] H. A. Feild, J. Allan, and R. Jones. Predicting searcher frustration. In *SIGIR'10*, pages 34–41. ACM, 2010.

[5] Q. Guo and E. Agichtein. Exploring mouse movements for inferring query intent. In *SIGIR'08*, pages 707–708. ACM, 2008.

[6] Q. Guo and E. Agichtein. Towards predicting web searcher gaze position from mouse movements. In *CHI'10*, pages 3601–3606. ACM, 2010.

[7] Q. Guo and E. Agichtein. Beyond dwell time: estimating document relevance from cursor movements and other post-click searcher behavior. In *WWW'12*, pages 569–578. ACM, 2012.

[8] Q. Guo, D. Lagun, and E. Agichtein. Predicting web search success with fine-grained interaction data. In *CIKM'12*, pages 2050–2054. ACM, 2012.

[9] Q. Guo, D. Lagun, D. Savenkov, and Q. Liu. Improving relevance prediction by addressing biases and sparsity in web search click data. In *WSCD'12*, pages 71–75, 2012.

[10] Q. Guo, R. W. White, S. T. Dumais, J. Wang, and B. Anderson. Predicting query performance using query, result, and user interaction features. In *Adaptivity, Personalization and Fusion of Heterogeneous Information*, pages 198–201, 2010.

[11] J. Huang, R. White, and G. Buscher. User see, user point: gaze and cursor alignment in web search. In *SIGCHI'12*, pages 1341–1350. ACM, 2012.

[12] J. Huang, R. W. White, G. Buscher, and K. Wang. Improving searcher models using mouse cursor activity. In *SIGIR'12*, pages 195–204. ACM, 2012.

[13] J. Huang, R. W. White, and S. Dumais. No clicks, no problem: using cursor movements to understand and improve search. In *SIGCHI'11*, pages 1225–1234. ACM, 2011.

[14] S. B. Huffman and M. Hochster. How well does result relevance predict session satisfaction? In *SIGIR'07*, pages 567–574. ACM, 2007.

[15] K. Järvelin, S. L. Price, L. M. Delcambre, and M. L. Nielsen. Discounted cumulated gain based evaluation of multiple-query ir sessions. In *Advances in Information Retrieval*, pages 4–15. Springer, 2008.

[16] J. Jiang, A. H. Awadallah, X. Shi, and R. W. White. Understanding and predicting graded search satisfaction. In *WSDM'15*, 2015.

[17] J. Jiang, D. He, and J. Allan. Searching, browsing, and clicking in a search session: Changes in user behavior by task and over time. 2014.

[18] D. Kelly. Methods for evaluating interactive information retrieval systems with users. *Foundations and Trends in Information Retrieval*, 3(1-2):1–224, 2009.

[19] D. Lagun, M. Ageev, Q. Guo, and E. Agichtein. Discovering common motifs in cursor movement data for improving web search. In *WSDM'14*, 2014.

[20] J. Li, S. Huffman, and A. Tokuda. Good abandonment in mobile and pc internet search. In *SIGIR'09*, pages 43–50. ACM, 2009.

[21] Y. Liu, R. Song, M. Zhang, Z. Dou, T. Yamamoto, M. Kato, H. Ohshima, and K. Zhou. Overview of the ntcir-11 imine task. In *NTCIR*, volume 14, 2014.

[22] Y. Liu, C. Wang, K. Zhou, J. Nie, M. Zhang, and S. Ma. From skimming to reading: A two-stage examination model for web search. In *CIKM'14*, 2014.

[23] M.Ageev, Q.Guo, D.Lagun, and E.Agichtein. Find it if you can: A game for modeling different types of web search success using interaction data. In *SIGIR'11*, 2011.

[24] T. Rakthanmanon, B. Campana, A. Mueen, G. Batista, B. Westover, Q. Zhu, J. Zakaria, and E. Keogh. Searching and mining trillions of time series subsequences under dynamic time warping. In *SIGKDD'12*, 2012.

[25] K. Rodden, X. Fu, A. Aula, and I. Spiro. Eye-mouse coordination patterns on web search results pages. In *CHI'08*, pages 2997–3002. ACM, 2008.

[26] H. Sakoe and S. Chiba. Dynamic programming algorithm optimization for spoken word recognition. 1978.

[27] L. T. Su. Evaluation measures for interactive information retrieval. *Information Processing & Management*, 28(4):503–516, 1992.

[28] S. Verberne, M. Heijden, M. Hinne, M. Sappelli, S. Koldijk, E. Hoenkamp, and W. Kraaij. Reliability and validity of query intent assessments. *JASIST*, 64(11):2224–2237, 2013.

[29] C. Wang, Y. Liu, M. Zhang, S. Ma, M. Zheng, J. Qian, and K. Zhang. Incorporating vertical results into search click models. In *SIGIR'13*, pages 503–512. ACM, 2013.

Predicting Search Intent Based on Pre-Search Context

Weize Kong[1], Rui Li[2], Luo Jie[2], Aston Zhang[3], Yi Chang[2], James Allan[1]
[1]Center for Intelligent Information Retrieval, University of Massachusetts Amherst, Amherst, MA 01003
[2]Yahoo! Labs, 701 First Ave, Sunnyvale, CA 94089
[3]Department of Computer Science, University of Illinois at Urbana-Champaign, Urbana, IL 61801
{wkong,allan}@cs.umass.edu, {ruililab,luojie,yichang}@yahoo-inc.com, lzhang74@illinois.edu

ABSTRACT

While many studies have been conducted on query understanding, there is limited understanding on why users start searches and how to predict search intent. In this paper, we propose to study this important but less explored problem. Our key intuition is that searches are triggered by different pre-search contexts, but the triggering relations are often hidden. For example, a user may search "bitcoin" because of a news article or an email the user just read, but the system does not know which of the pre-search contexts (the news article or the email) is the triggering source. Following this intuition, we conduct an in-depth analysis of pre-search context on a large-scale user log, which not only verifies the hidden triggering relations in the real world but also identifies a set of important characteristics of pre-search context and their triggered queries. Since the hidden triggering relations make it challenging to directly use pre-search context for intent prediction, we develop a mixture generative model to learn without any supervision how queries are triggered by different types of pre-search context. Further, we discuss how to apply our model to improve query prediction and query auto-completion. Our experiments on a large-scale of real-world data show that our model could accurately predict user search intent with pre-search context and improve upon the state-of-the-art methods significantly.

Categories and Subject Descriptors: H.3.3 [Information Search and Retrieval]: Search Process

Keywords: Search Context; Pre-Search Context; Search Intent; Query Auto-Completion; Query Prediction

1. INTRODUCTION

To improve user search experience, many studies have been proposed to understand user search intent given issued queries (*e.g.*, query suggestion and query disambiguation) via exploring clickthrough data, user search history, and search session context. However, there is very limited work on search intent prediction – *predicting what a user is going to search even before the search task starts.*

SIGIR'15, August 09 - 13, 2015, Santiago, Chile.

ACM 978-1-4503-3621-5/15/08 ...$15.00.
DOI: http://dx.doi.org/10.1145/2766462.2767757.

Search intent prediction is an important problem, as it will largely improve search experience. First, it could enable "query-less" search (*e.g.*, Google Now) to greatly save user efforts. For example, if we could predict that a user is looking for Philippine Peso's value, we could directly recommend related queries (*e.g.*, "Philippine Peso") or their results once the user opens a mobile search app, without any user input. In addition, it could also improve existing applications such as query auto-completion and query disambiguation. For example, when the user types "P" in a search box, we can accurately suggest query "Peso" or "Philippine Peso" instead of "Pinterest" or "Paypal", which are more likely to be suggested by current search engines. When the user searches "Peso" as his query, we could correctly interpret the intent as Philippine Peso instead of Mexico Peso.

Recently Cheng et al. [7] found that many searches are triggered by webpages users browsed, and proposed a model to predict queries triggered by a given browsed webpage. While this work provides a good start for search intent prediction, it has critical limitations in reality. In the real-world setting, searches could also be triggered by factors other than browsing, and systems often do not know if the current search will be triggered by the browsed webpage or other factors. Therefore, blindly predicting search intent solely based on browsed webpage is inadequate in practice. In this paper, we study this important problem of predicting search intent in this more realistic setting.

A Key Insight We hypothesize that searches are triggered by different contexts prior to the search activities, which we call *pre-search contexts.* For example, a user searches "peso", because she reads a news article about "Devaluation of Philippine peso" and she is interested in its current value; a user searches "restaurants nearby" as she is visiting a new place and want to taste local food; and a user searches "Lady Gaga tour" as she hears about Lady Gaga's coming concert and wants to book tickets. In these examples, the news article, the new location, and the coming event are the pre-search contexts that trigger users to search. It is clear that pre-search context is very different from user search history or search session context, which are explored by many previous studies for understanding search intent.

We emphasize that a pre-search context, by definition, is just prior to the search but does not necessarily trigger it. This definition reflects the hidden nature of triggering relations between pre-search context and searches in *a real-world setting.* That is, while many types of pre-search context (*e.g.*, news articles, new locations, events) could trigger searches, the system does not observe which particular pre-search context triggers the current search. Ideally, if we can capture various types of pre-search context, and identify the particular one that triggers searches each time, we could predict search intent based on the identified pre-search context.

An In-depth Analysis In Section 3 we conduct an in-depth analysis to understand how pre-search context triggers queries. We focus on a specific type of pre-search context – the news article a user browsed before the search, because: 1) a large number of search queries are triggered by news pre-search context daily, as we will show in the analysis; 2) it is easier to log browsing activity than other off-line activities in practice; 3) studying news pre-search context will provide guidelines for exploring other pre-search context in the future.

In the analysis, we use large-scale real-world data by joining user browsing logs (*i.e.*, what news articles users have read) and search logs (*i.e.*, what queries users have searched after reading news) from Yahoo!. We first find that a significant amount of queries are triggered by news pre-search context (*i.e.*, tens of millions queries per day), which verifies the assumption of queries being triggered by pre-search context. More importantly, we discover insightful characteristics of news pre-search context and their triggered queries. Some of our interesting observations are: 1) news articles often trigger *new* queries (*i.e.*, 96% of triggered queries have never been searched by their users before), which are often difficult to predict or understand if only using history data; 2) most of the triggered queries are related to named entities mentioned in the news articles; 3) triggered queries are more likely to appear in the beginning part of those articles; 4) triggered queries could diverge from the main topics of the news articles, which are quite different from queries that lead clicks to the articles.

While this analysis shows the great potential of using news pre-search context for predicting search intent, it also validates the hidden nature of triggering relations in the real-world setting as mentioned previously. Based on the data, we estimate a large percent of queries are triggered by other pre-search context instead of news articles. The system does not know if current search will be triggered from the browsed news articles or other pre-search context. This hidden nature poses two challenges in reality that, to the best of our knowledge, have not been addressed before: 1) how to predict search intent with hidden triggering relations; 2) if/how can we learn prediction models and avoid using expensive labels for uncovering the hidden triggering relations (*i.e.*, identify which pre-search context is the triggering factor).

An Intent Prediction Model To address these real-world challenges, in Section 4, we develop a pre-context aware search intent model that learns how queries are triggered by different pre-search context with hidden triggering relations without any supervision. More specifically, we first introduce the model as a general generative mixture model to principally captures that a search intent could be triggered by different pre-search context with unknown triggering source. We then customize the expectation-maximization (EM) algorithm to learn the parameters of our model, so that we can take advantage of large-size browsing and search logs that are directly available, avoiding relying on expensive manually labeled data. In addition, we discuss how to instantiate our model for query prediction and query auto-completion tasks as concrete examples to validate the generality of our proposed model. We also identify a set of effective features for our model based on our analysis in Section 3.

Comprehensive Experiments Finally, in Section 5, we carry out a comprehensive set of experiments to evaluate our model on query prediction and query suggestion tasks. We show that: 1) pre-search context is very useful in predicting queries compared to other types of data (*e.g.*, user search history and clickthrough data); 2) the state-of-the-art method [7] is inadequate in a real-world setting; 3) instead, our model captures pre-search context with hidden triggering relations effectively and outperforms the state-of-the-art method (*i.e.*, 25% improvement) under the real-world setting; 4) our model also *consistently* improves over other methods in query auto-completion, and achieves larger improvement in the most challenging cases, in which users have only typed one or two letters.

2. RELATED WORK

We divide information used for modeling user search intents into two categories – long-term history and short-term context.

The *long-term history* contains user behavior information, such as queries, clickthrough and browsed webpages, over a long period. It is often used to build user profiles and capture users' general search interest. For example, in query auto-completion, many search engines suggest the completions that have been most popular among users in the past history [1]. For personalized search, Gauch et al. [12] learn user profiles from browsing history, Speretta and Gauch [25] build profiles using search history. The *short-term context* instead provides a more direct information for inferring users' current search intent. We believe there exist two types of short-term contexts – pre-search context and in-search context. The *pre-search context*, as we defined, is the search context that is prior to a search task and could trigger the search; in-search context is the search context during a search task, such as query reformulation and user clickthrough during a search session.

In-Search context. There is a large body of work studying in-search context. In almost all of the work, in-search context is essentially used as additional information for understanding search intent during a search task. Different models have been proposed for utilizing in-session context to improve various aspects of search, including query classification [28, 27], query suggestions and auto-completion [5, 6, 4, 1, 11], document ranking [23, 29, 17], modeling search satisfaction [14, 13, 24, 22], search evaluation at session or task level [16, 15], and search personalization [26, 18, 2]. Despite the rich types of contexts and applications covered by these studies, the kind of context that could trigger a search task (*i.e.*, pre-seach context) is still relatively unexplored.

Pre-Search context. There is limited work studying pre-search context. Dumais et al. [10] have a demonstration that automatically suggests queries while users are reading emails. However, details of the model used for the system are not provided, and no evaluation is performed for the system. Rahurkar et al. [20] detect if a query searched right after browsing is relevant to the browsed webpage, and achieve nearly perfect classification performance with 0.96 precision and 0.90 recall. But they do not consider modeling intent based on context. The same authors also carry out a preliminary study [21] that uses the browsed webpage to improve search relevance. The work aims to find webpages similar to the browsed webpage, which may not be what the user needs: as we will show that triggered search intent may diverge from the original browsed webpage in Section 3.3.1. Liebling et al. [19] try to predict what webpages users are likely to look for after browsing a webpage, based on the popularity of webpages that have been searched under the same browsing context. However, their approach is difficult to be generalized for fresh or less-popular webpages that do not have enough browsing history.

There are two recent studies [7, 3] that are similar to our work. Both of them try to predict/suggest what users are likely to search about a browsed webpage. Cheng et al. [7] collect searches after users browse a webpage in the search history, and then rank them as suggestions for that webpage using a learning to rank framework. Instead of relying on historic browsing and search information, Bordino et al. [3] focus on using webpage content, so that their approach can be generalized for previous unseen webpages. Our work significantly differs from the two studies in that: 1) we study a different problem. Motivated by the hidden nature of triggering relations in the real-world setting, we target at predicting search intent based on pre-search context, which may or may not trigger the current search, while they target at predicting search intent for a given *known* triggering factor, which is normally unrealistic; 2) we perform an in-depth analysis. It verifies the hidden nature of triggering relations and discovers insightful characteristics of pre-search context, some of which have important implications on feature design. Previous analysis [7] is limited to verifying triggering relations ; 3) our model captures hidden triggering relations and learns from large-size "free" unlabeled data, while their models require expensive human labels to identify triggering sources for learning.

3. ANALYSIS OF PRE-SEARCH CONTEXT

In this section, we present an in-depth analysis of how pre-search context triggers users to search, focusing on browsed news articles (as explained in Section 1). Particularly, we first verify the triggering relations and their hidden nature in a real-world setting, and then explore the characteristics of news pre-search context and its triggered queries.

3.1 Dataset

To understand how pre-search context triggers queries in real world, we join *browsing logs*, which record user "browsing events" on Yahoo! news sites (*e.g.*, News, Sports, Finance), and *search logs*, which record user "search events" on Yahoo! Search, and then focus on "browsing-search pairs" in the joined logs. All the logs are from the English/US market and are anonymized. Formally, we can abstract our logs as follows.

- A **browsing event** contains three fields {*userID*, *timestamp*, *URL*}, which records the event that a user browses a URL at a specific time;
- A **search event** contains three fields {*userID*, *timestamp*, *query*}, which records the event that a user issues a query at a specific time.
- A **browsing-search pair** is a pair of a browsing event and a subsequent search event within a predefined time window (*e.g.*, 30 mins) in the logs.

In the rest of the paper, we refer to the webpage and the query in a browsing-search pair as **browsed webpage** and **following query** respectively. As not all the following queries are indeed triggered by the browsed webpages, we name the following queries that are triggered by the browsed webpages as **triggered queries** and the other following queries as **non-triggered queries**.

We process 25 successive days of browsing and search logs in February 2014. In the following studies and experiments, we use the logs from the first 24 days as *history data*, from which we extract statistics such as user search history and the queries that lead clicks to a certain webpage, and the logs from the last day as *experiment data*, which we use for our analysis and experiments. We have 1,796,313 browsing-search pairs after pre-processing and filtering (*e.g.*, filtering out browsing-search pairs whose webpages are not accessible due to outdated links or technical issues). We randomly sample 6,000 pairs for annotators to label. The annotators are asked to label whether or not the following query is triggered by the browsed webpage or whether they cannot decide. Those labeled pairs are further split into 3 different sets randomly, namely STUDY, TRAIN and EVALUATE. We use both STUDY and TRAIN for our analysis, TRAIN for model training, and EVALUATE for testing. Table 1 shows the statistics of annotated pairs in the three sets.

Table 1: Label distributions of three datasets.

	STUDY	TRAIN	EVALUATE
triggered	126 (6.3%)	114 (5.7%)	106 (5.3%)
non-triggered	1,849 (92.5%)	1,878 (93.9%)	1,891 (94.6%)
cannot decide	25 (1.3%)	8 (0.4%)	3 (0.2%)

3.2 Verifying Hidden Triggering Relations

To empirically justify our key insight, we first need to verify the triggering relations (*i.e.*, whether queries are triggered by news pre-search context) in our user logs. Particularly, by investigating the logs in our dataset, we first find that 3.6% of all the webpage browsing events are followed by immediate search events (no other events in between browsing and search) within 30 minutes. These "following" queries consist of 10% of all search traffic. Further, from the human-annotated browsing-search pairs, shown in Table 1, we see that around 6% of these "following" queries are triggered by their browsed webpages. Thus, we estimate at least 0.6% all search queries are triggered by news pre-search context (*i.e.*, browsed news articles). This actually underestimates the significance of news triggered searches due to that users may search in other search engines after browsing, which is not logged in our data. If we consider that there are many billions of queries everyday [1], tens of millions of queries are triggered by news pre-search context. As an illustration, Table 2 shows some following queries, comprising triggered queries (queries triggered by the browsed webpages) and non-triggered queries for three webpages. We can clearly see that some following queries (*e.g.*, "what is a bitcoin") indeed are triggered by the corresponding browsed webpages (*e.g.*, Bitcoin exchange Mt. Gox goes dark in blow to virtual currency).

[1]Google processes 3.5 billion searches daily `http://www.statisticbrain.com/google-searches/`

Table 2: Examples for the triggered, non-triggered and leading queries from three popular news articles.

Webpage A: Bitcoin exchange Mt. Gox goes dark in blow to virtual currency	
`http://finance.yahoo.com/news/bitcoin-exchange-mt-goxs-website-062314988.html`	
triggered	bitcoin, what is bitcoin, bitcoin heist
non-triggered	facebook, amanda knox, galaxy s5 launch
Webpage B: Harold Ramis Star of Ghostbusters Director of Caddyshack Dies at 69	
`https://movies.yahoo.com/blogs/yahoo-movies/-ghostbusters--actor-harold-ramis-dies-at-69-173530161.html`	
triggered	harold ramis, animal house movie, autoimmune inflammatory vasculitis, cast of ghostbusters
non-triggered	craigslist, amanda bynes, ali fedotowsky, ebay
leading	harold ramis death, harold ramis died, ghostbuster movie actor dies, what star of ghostbuster movie dies
Webpage C: 6 Stars Who Have Returned to Regular Jobs	
`https://celebrity.yahoo.com/blogs/yahoo-celebrity/6-stars-returned-regular-jobs-194630934.html`	
triggered	susan boyle, susan boyle bio, susan boyle movie, steven seaga
non-triggered	facebook, free credit score
leading	regular jobs for celebrities, stars that returned back to regular jobs

The analysis above verifies the triggering relations between news pre-search context and searches. However, the triggering relations are hidden: the system does not directly observe whether queries will be triggered by news pre-search context or other pre-search context (*e.g.*, locations, events). Based on Table 1, we estimate that around 94% of following queries are triggered by pre-search context other than browsed news articles, and the system does not know which pre-search context triggers the current search. This hidden nature poses two real-world challenges that are not addressed in previous studies [7, 3]: 1) how to predict searches with systems not knowing when/if searches will be triggered by the browsed webpages; 2) if/how can we learn prediction models and avoid using expensive labels for identifying which queries are triggered by the browsed webpages. We will propose a generative mixture model to principally address them in Section 4.

3.3 Characterizing Triggered Queries

Next, to predict user search intent based on pre-search context, we need to characterize how pre-search context triggers searches. Particularly, we derive characteristics of triggered queries, which distinguish them from other following queries, from two main aspects: 1) relevance between browsed webpages and following queries and 2) types of following queries themselves.

3.3.1 *Relevance between Following Queries and Pre-Search Context*

As it is natural to expect that triggered queries are relevant to the content of their browsed webpages (the page that triggered the query), we first focus on whether triggered/non-triggered queries are actually relevant to the browsed webpages.

Text Matching We start with a basic question – *can we distinguish triggered queries and non-triggered queries by how well they match the text content of browsed webpages?*

To answer this question, we compare triggered queries with non-triggered queries according to two text matching metrics: 1) *exactly matching*, which measures whether a query appears in a webpage; 2) *overlapping*, which measures whether a query has at least one word overlapping with the webpage, ignoring stopwords in the query. In Table 3, we show the percentages of the matched queries and the overlapped queries among the triggered/non-triggered queries, as well as the percentages of the triggered/non-triggered queries belong to the matched and overlapped queries. We have two important observations from the results.

First, the results confirm our expectation that triggered queries are more relevant to browsed webpages than the non-triggered ones. Particularly, 48.41% (96.03%) of triggered queries match (overlap) with browsed webpages, while only 0.49% (8.22%) of non-triggered queries do. In fact, by examining queries in detail, we find that 1) less than 4% of triggered queries that do not overlap browsed webpages are semantically related to them (*e.g.*, after browsing a webpage about Ford, a user searches a specific automobile store, whose name does not appear in the webpage) and the 0.5% of the non-triggered queries which exactly match browsed webpages, are mostly popular navigational queries (*e.g.*, "facebook", "google" and "espn").

Second, the results suggest that, unfortunately, we cannot distinguish triggered from non-triggered queries very well with text matching only. Specifically, we can only obtain a high precision (87.14%) but low recall (48.41%) classifier or a high recall (96.03%) but low precision (44.32%) classifier for predicting triggered/non-triggered queries with the matching or overlapping measures respectively. This implies that we should also consider other features for modeling triggering relations.

Table 3: Matching and overlapping of triggered and non-triggered queries.

	% exactly matching	% overlapping
triggered	48.41%	96.03%
non-triggered	0.49%	8.22%
	% triggered	**% non-triggered**
exactly matching	87.14%	12.86%
overlapping	44.32%	56.68%

Matching Positions Due to the limitations of matching and overlapping in distinguishing triggered and non-triggered queries, we next investigate whether *where the matched queries of triggered/non triggered queries appear in the webpages* can distinguish the classes. Our intuition is that because users read from top to bottom and news articles often position important/interesting information at the top, triggered queries are likely to come from the beginning of browsed webpages.

To answer the question, we plot distributions of the document positions where triggered/non-triggered queries first appear in Figure 1. In the figure, document positions from top to bottom are normalized to a value between 0 and 1 by word number. Triggered/non-triggered queries that do not appear in the news articles have no valid document positions, and are thus not included in this plot. Figure 1 shows that most triggered queries appear in the beginning part of the news articles, and the non-triggered queries randomly appear in the beginning and the end of browsed webpages. The results here verify our intuition above, which could be an effective feature for distinguishing triggered and non-triggered queries.

Figure 1: Distributions of triggered & non-triggered queries' first occurrences in their browsed webpages.

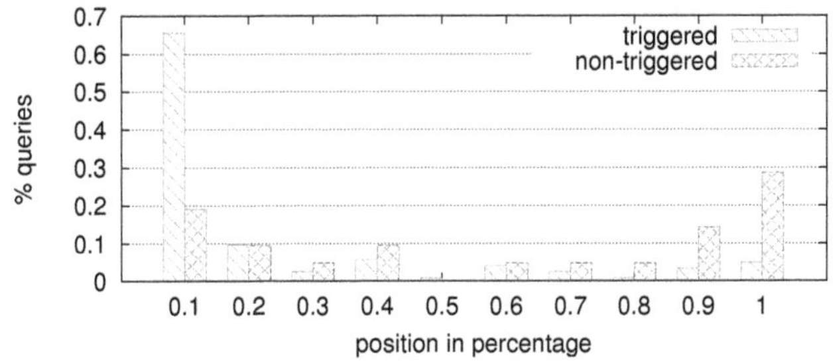

Topic Relevance After measuring text similarity, we further measure *how relevant the triggered and non-triggered queries of a webpage are to its main topic.*

To answer this question, we compare triggered and non-triggered queries with the title of a webpage, which is a good representation of the main topic of the webpage. Specifically, we measure the cosine similarity between queries and news article titles based on their term-frequency vectors. In addition, we compute the similarity between "leading" queries of a webpage and the title of the webpage, as a baseline. Here, leading queries of a webpage are queries after which people click on the webpage, known to be relevant to the main topic of the webpage [8, 30]. Table 2 also shows some leading queries of two of the webpages.

Table 4 shows that, as we expected, triggered queries are more relevant to the topic of a browsed webpage than the non-triggered ones. However, interestingly, both triggered and non-triggered queries are much less relevant to the main topics of browsed webpages than the leading queries. This can also be illustrated by the examples in Table 2. For Webpage B, which is about the death of a film director, the leading queries all focus on the death of Harold Ramis, while triggered queries might be about his movies, "animal house movie". It can be explained as users may be interested in any specific information in a webpage.

Table 4: Cosine similarity between triggered/non-triggered/leading queries and news titles.

Triggered	Non-Triggerd	Leading
0.1641	0.0274	0.4782

While the above results suggest relevance to the main topic could be a marginally effective feature, the results are still valuable to us because: 1) they reveal an important fact that the triggered queries of a webpage could diverge from its main topic; and 2) they show clear differences between leading queries and triggered queries, which motivate of our study of triggered queries from a new aspect.

3.3.2 *Types of Following Queries*

We would like to understand if some particular types of queries are more likely to be triggered by a *news* pre-search context. Intuitively, we assume that if users issue queries because of reading articles (*e.g.*, Bitcoin exchange Mt. Gox goes dark in blow to virtual currency), they are likely to look for explanations of some unknown concepts (*e.g.*, "what is bitcoin") or related information for some entities (*e.g.*, "bitcoin value"). Thus we expect the triggered queries are *new* to the user and *entity oriented.* Next, we empirically verify these two assumptions.

New assumption We verify that triggered queries are more likely to be new to the users (who issued the queries) than non-triggered ones by checking if triggered queries have been searched by the users before. We assume that a query never searched by a user before is likely to be a "new" concept to the user. We find almost all (95.4%) of news-triggered queries have never been searched by their users (the particular user who issued the triggered query) in their personal history data (previous 24 days), while this percentage is much lower for non-triggered queries (78.64%) and for all queries issued by the same set of users in the same day (77.2%). This assumption can also be illustrated from the examples in Table 2, where in the first example some query prefixes start with "what is", suggesting users are searching concepts new to them.

This result not only reveals another important characteristic of news triggered queries, but also implies that they will be much more difficult to predict than other queries if we solely depend on user search history.

Entity oriented assumption To verify that triggered queries are more likely to be about entities mentioned in browsed webpages than are non-triggered ones, we apply an in-house named entity extractor on browsed webpages, and compare triggered/non-triggered queries with the recognized named entities. We find that over half (55.8%) of the triggered queries contain at least one named entity recognized in the browsed webpages, and the percentage goes down to 1% for the non-triggered queries. Among the triggered queries with entities, 61.2% are exactly named entities without any other modifiers: for example, after reading Webpage C in Table 2, many users search query "susan boyle", who is a celebrity mentioned in the webpage. Another 38.8% of these queries are named entity with some modifiers: for example, users also issue the query "susan boyle bio" and "susan boyle movie" after reading that news page. This observation clearly suggests that the named entities mentioned in the browsed webpages will be useful in predicting search intent triggered by the webpages.

We note that there could be more named entity related queries than these estimations, because 1) many named entities in the news articles are not recognized by our entity extractor, e.g. "bitcoin", and 2) queries may use different variations of the named entity: *e.g.*, "bit coin" and "bitcoin", "the walking dead" and "walking dead".

4. PRE-SEARCH CONTEXT AWARE SEARCH INTENT MODELING

Though our analysis shows news pre-search context provides useful information for search intent prediction, it also recognizes the hidden triggering relation challenge in real systems, that has not been addressed previously (Section 3.2). To address that challenge, we propose a Pre-search Context-aware Intent Model (PCIM) based on a generative mixture model to effectively learn from a large amount of unlabeled data. This model differs from a previous model [7] in that 1) it captures multiple types of pre-search context with *unknown* triggering source; and 2) it takes advantage of a large amount of unlabeled data to learn without supervision.

With the hope to improve different search related tasks, we first describe PCIM as a general search intent model. Then we illustrate how this general model can be applied to two specific applications, query prediction and query auto-completion.

4.1 Pre-Search Context Aware Intent Model

4.1.1 Search Intent

We define a search intent model as a probability distribution over a set of intents, $P(I), \forall I \in \mathcal{I}$, where the set of intents $\mathcal{I}$ can be composed of words, phrases, or even ODP categories, depending on the specific application. For example, in query prediction and query auto-completion, the set of intents contains all the query candidates that the user may search. Instead, if we use ODP categories as intents, then the search intent model can also be applied to classify search intent. We use this general definition for our search intent model, so that the model can be applied to different search related tasks. We will apply this general model to query prediction and query auto-completion as examples in Section 4.2.

4.1.2 A Generative Mixture Model

As discussed in Section 1, search intents can be triggered by different types of pre-search contexts C, such as browsed webpages ("Devaluation of Philippine Peso"), locations (new place visited) and events (Lady Gaga's coming concert). We also denote the set of all the pre-search context as $\mathcal{C}$. Based on this, we assume that search intents are generated from different pre-search contexts according to the following generative process:

1. A pre-search context C is selected as the triggering source from an unknown multinomial distribution, $C \sim \mathit{Multinomial}(\boldsymbol{\lambda})$, where $C \in \mathcal{C}$.

2. The search intent I is generated by the given pre-search context C according to another unknown distribution $I \sim P(I|C)$.

According to this generative process, the mixture generative model for I can be written as

$$P(I) = \sum_{C \in \mathcal{C}} P(I|C)P(C), \tag{1}$$

where $P(C) = \lambda_C$ is the prior for each pre-search context following the multinomial distribution, $\mathit{Multinomial}(\boldsymbol{\lambda})$. While there are many different ways to model the intent distribution $P(I|C)$, we choose a standard log-linear model as the hypothesis function. Its function can be written as

$$P(I|C) = \frac{1}{Z} \exp\left(\boldsymbol{w}_C^T \boldsymbol{f}(I, C)\right), \tag{2}$$

where $Z = \sum_{I \in \mathcal{I}} \exp\left(\boldsymbol{w}_C^T \boldsymbol{f}(I, C)\right)$ is the normalizer, $\boldsymbol{f}(I, C)$ is a vector of features characterizing how likely will intent I be triggered by pre-search context C, and $\boldsymbol{w}_C$ are the corresponding feature weights. The details of used features are described in Section 4.2.3.

4.1.3 Parameter Estimation

The PCIM model defined in Equation 1 contains parameters $\boldsymbol{\theta} = \{\boldsymbol{\lambda}, \boldsymbol{W}\}$, where $\boldsymbol{\lambda} = \{\lambda_C\}$ is the prior probabilities for each type of pre-search context; $\boldsymbol{W} = \{\boldsymbol{w}_C\}$ are the feature weights for each type of pre-search context in calculating $P(I|C)$. To estimate $\boldsymbol{\theta}$, a straightforward way is to maximize the likelihood value of $P(\{I_i\}_i)$ on a given training data set $\{I_i\}_{i=1,\cdots,N}$, where N is the total number of training instances. Assuming independence between different search intent examples I_i, the log-likehood of the example collection is

$$l(\boldsymbol{\theta}) = \log \prod_i P(I_i; \boldsymbol{\theta}) = \sum_i \log \sum_{C \in \mathcal{C}} P(I_i|C; \boldsymbol{w}_C) P(C; \lambda_C). \tag{3}$$

Unfortunately, since log-likelihood in Equation 3 involves logarithm of a summation, there is no exact analytical solution for $\boldsymbol{\theta}$. Therefore, we propose to use the EM algorithm for estimating $\boldsymbol{\theta}$ instead.

In the E-step, we evaluate the posterior probability of a search intent being generated from a particular pre-search context given the previous model parameter estimation $\boldsymbol{\theta}' = \{\boldsymbol{\lambda}', \boldsymbol{W}'\}$:

$$P(C|I_i; \boldsymbol{\theta}') \propto P(I_i|C; \boldsymbol{w}'_C) P(C; \lambda'_C). \tag{4}$$

In the M-Step, based on posterior estimates from the E-step, we maximize the lower bound of the log-likelihood:

$$l(\boldsymbol{\theta}) \geqslant l'(\boldsymbol{\theta}) = \sum_i \sum_{C \in \mathcal{C}} P(C|I_i; \boldsymbol{\theta}') \log \frac{P(I_i|C; \boldsymbol{w}_C) P(C; \boldsymbol{\lambda}_C)}{P(C|I_i; \boldsymbol{\theta}')}. \tag{5}$$

By taking derivative of $l'(\boldsymbol{\theta})$ w.r.t. $\boldsymbol{\lambda}$ and setting the derivative to zero, we can easily update $\boldsymbol{\lambda}$ by $\lambda_C = \frac{P(C|I_i;\boldsymbol{\theta}')}{N}$. For $\boldsymbol{W}$, we calculate the derivative according to the following function, and use gradient ascent to maximize $l'(\theta)$,

$$\nabla_{\boldsymbol{w}_C} l'(\boldsymbol{\theta}) = \sum_i P(C|I_i; \boldsymbol{\theta}') \left(\boldsymbol{f}(I_i, C) - \frac{\sum_{I' \in \mathcal{I}_i} \exp\left(\boldsymbol{w}_C^T \boldsymbol{f}(I', C)\right) \boldsymbol{f}(I_i, C)}{\sum_{I' \in \mathcal{I}_i} \exp\left(\boldsymbol{w}_C^T \boldsymbol{f}(I', C)\right)} \right), \tag{6}$$

where $\mathcal{I}_i$ is the set of candidate search intents for the current search intent I_i.

4.2 Applications

The PCIM described above is a general model that could be applied to different search related tasks. Now we show how to apply it to query prediction and query auto-completion as examples. In the query prediction task, our goal is to suggest a ranked list of queries that a user is likely to search (after the user browses a webpage, which may or may not trigger the search in the real-world setting). The query auto-completion task is similar to query prediction, except that it predicts (auto-complete) the query after the user has typed some initial characters of the query, which restrict the set of possible suggested queries to those that begin with the initial letters as prefix.

To apply PCIM to the two applications, we need to 1) specify search intent and pre-search context representations, 2) adapt the model for the chosen representation, and 3) design specialized features for the specific applications. Next, we describe each of these issues in detail.

4.2.1 Representation

In both query prediction and query auto-completion tasks, the basic unit of the search intent set $\mathcal{I}$ is a query. Hence we will use query Q instead of intent I in our specific models. The candidate queries can be pooled from search logs and the browsed webpages. For query auto-completion, those candidate queries need to begin with the initial letters the user has typed. As an illustration, we consider only two types of pre-search context C in both tasks for the sake of feasibility and simplicity: 1) the webpage D the user just browsed before search; 2) a special background pre-search context G based on long-term search history, which we assume summarizes all other uncaptured pre-search context. We use this background pre-search context, because many other types of pre-search context could trigger searches, but are not accessible to the system (*e.g.*, locations, events). We believe it is easy to extend our model for more types of pre-search context when they are accessible, which we leave as future work.

4.2.2 Model

Given the representation, PCIM in Equation 1 can be rewritten as

$$P(Q) = \lambda \cdot P(Q|D) + (1 - \lambda) \cdot P(Q|G), \quad (7)$$

where, similar to Equation 2, $P(Q|D)$ is the probability that webpage D triggers query Q, and λ is the prior for the query being triggered from D. $P(Q|G)$ is the probability of the query being triggered by the background context. In our study, we will estimate $P(Q|G)$ using the user's search history H_u and general search history H_g for all the users:

$$P(Q|G) = \gamma P(Q|H_u) + (1 - \gamma)P(Q|H_g), \quad (8)$$

where $P(Q|H_u) \propto |Q \in H_u|$, and $P(Q|H_g) \propto |Q \in H_g|$ with $|Q \in H|$ denoting the frequency of query Q in H.

The model parameters can be estimated using the EM algorithm proposed in Section 4.1.3. After parameter estimation, we rank query candidates according to their probability $P(Q)$ as predictions/suggestions. Note that if we set $\lambda = 0$ and $\gamma = 0$, Equation 7 will only contain the $P(Q|H_g)$ part, which ranks queries based only on query frequency in the search logs. This special case is the same as the MPC model [1] used in query auto-completion task. If we only set $\lambda = 0$, the model becomes a personalized version of MPC, in which it jointly considers both search history from all users and the current user.

4.2.3 Features

To characterize how likely it is that D will trigger query Q for $P(Q|D)$, we use query-document matching and browsing-search history features as in previous work [7]. In addition, we design new features based on named entities, document position, and query freshness to the user, inspired by our in-depth analysis. All the proposed features are listed in Table 5.

Query-document matching features measure if the query is relevant to the document according to some pre-defined similarity measures. Here we check if the query appears in different parts of the document by *dMatch, hMatch.* We also measure word overlap between query and document, calculated as $\frac{|Q \cap D|}{|Q|}$, where Q, D are represented by the words after removing stopwords. In addition, we use features based on history browsing-search pairs. The intuition is that if many users issue the same query after browsing a certain webpage, then the webpage is very likely to trigger the particular query. Based on this, we use *qf* to count the frequency of a query being searched after users browse a webpage in the search history. Many popular navigational queries, such as "facebook", "google" are searched regardless of what webpages user have just browsed. In order to demote these non-triggered queries, we use *idf*, which represents the inverse frequency of different documents being browsed before users issue the query, in the same fashion as the conventional *idf* definition.

Table 5: Pre-search context features for a webpage D triggering a search query Q.

Feature	Description
	Query-document matching features
dMatch	if Q appears in D
dOverlap	word overlap between Q and D
hMatch	if Q appears in the headline of D
hOverlap	word overlap between Q and the headline of D
	Browsing-search history features
qf	tf of Q in history browsing-search patterns
idf	idf of Q in history browsing-search patterns
qf.idf	$qf \times idf$
	Newly designed features
eMatch	if Q appears as a named entity in D
eContain	if Q contains a named entity mentioned in D
eOverlap	word overlap between Q and named entities in D
eFreq	entity frequency of Q in D
ehFreq	entity frequency of Q in the headline of D
pos	position of Q's first occurrence in D
freshness	if Q has been searched by the user before

As we find named entities are important in our analysis, we use many entity-based features. We check if the query is or contains a named entity mentioned in the document by *eMatch* and *eContain.* We also use entity frequency to count the times of the query appearing as a named entity in the document by *eFreq* and *ehFreq.* Our analysis shows that users tend to search about 1) the beginning part of the a document and 2) new concepts that are fresh to the users. Therefore we use feature *pos* and *freshness* accordingly. Position in *pos* is normalized to 0 to 1 by word counts as described in Section 3.3.1, and set to 1 if the query does not appear in the news article.

5. EXPERIMENTS

In this section, we carry out a comprehensive set of experiments to evaluate our model on query prediction and query auto-completion. Particularly, we aim to empirically demonstrate that 1) pre-search context is useful for predicting user search intent and 2) our proposed model can effectively capture how queries are triggered with the hidden triggering relations in the real-world setting.

5.1 Experimental Settings

Dataset In order to evaluate our model in real-world scenarios, we continue to use the browsing and search logs described in Section 3.1. Here, we give a brief summary. We have two datasets: the first one is *history data*, which consists of 24 days of search and browsing logs. We only use it to extract user search history and click history. The second one is *experiment data*, which consists of 6,000 browsing-search pairs. We use it to train and test models. Specifically, we split the experiment data set into three subsets: STUDY (S), TRAIN (T), and EVALUATE (E). We use TRAIN to train models and set aside STUDY and EVALUATE for testing.

Tasks We evaluate our model in two search tasks to demonstrate its effectiveness for search intent prediction: 1) *query prediction* aims to predict what a user is going to search (*i.e.*, her query) with the awareness of the pre-search context (*i.e.*, after browsing a webpage); 2) *query auto-completion* aims to suggest queries after a user browses a webpage and enters several prefix characters of a new query.

For both tasks, we use browsing-search pairs to evaluate. Specifically, for each browsing-search pair, we use the browsed webpage as the news pre-search context and the query issued after (within a limited time) as the correct answer. We emphasize that our research problem is predicting searches in this real-world setting, where the query may not actually be triggered by the browsed webpage – that is, it may be triggered by other uncaptured pre-search context such as locations and events.

To collect the candidate queries for both tasks, we pool the 100 most popular queries from the user's search history, the 100 most popular queries from search history across all users, and named entities appearing in the browsed webpage. To ensure there is an correct answer for comparing different models, we also include the following query in the candidate set. We believe this is a fair setting for comparison, which would reflect prediction effectiveness within the collected candidate set. The candidates for query auto-completion are almost the same as those for query prediction, except that now the query candidates are restricted to begin with the prefix characters.

Methods To demonstrate the usefulness of pre-search context and the effectiveness of our model, we compare against a wide range of baseline models as listed below.

- *Global Query Frequency* (GQF). This method estimates the probability $P(Q)$ that a query Q will be searched based on global search history, which is $P(Q|H_g)$ used in our model in Section 4.2.2. It is a widely used method [1] in query auto-completion. We use it as a baseline to compare the usefulness of the pre-search context and general search logs.
- *Global and User Query Frequency* (GUQF). This method estimates the probability $P(Q)$ that a user searches a query Q based on both global search history and user search history, which is $P(Q|G)$ used in our model in Section 4.2.2. We use it as a baseline to compare the usefulness of the pre-search context and user search history.
- *Leading Query Frequency* (LQF). This method estimates the probability $P(Q)$ that a user searches a query Q (with awareness of pre-search context) based on the frequency of Q in the leading queries of the browsed webpage in history. Particularly, $P(Q) \propto LQF(Q, D)$, where $LQF(Q, D)$ is the frequency of Q being a leading query for D in history. We use this method to demonstrate the difference between the triggering relationship and the clicking relationship, which is widely studied in the literature [8, 30].
- *Ranking SVM* (RSVM). Recent work [7] uses Ranking SVM to rank queries that are likely to be triggered by a browsed webpage as predictions for user searches. As mentioned before, in the real-world setting, searches may also be triggered by pre-search context other than browsed webpages. Therefore, using this model to blindly predict searches solely based on browsed webpage could be inadequate in the real-world setting. To test this hypothesis, we include this model as a baseline. In contrast to our model, this model requires expensive labeled triggered queries of each browsed webpages for training. In the experiments, we train the model with both the "real" triggered queries annotated by a human, denoted as RSVM-T, and pseudo triggered queries by assuming queries that appear in the browsed webpage are triggered by the webpage, denoted as RSVM-P. We use the same set of features as described in Table 5 for RSVM models.
- *Pre-search Context aware Intent Model* (PCIM). This is our proposed model described in Section 4.2.2. The model does not need labels for trigger/non-triggered queries for training, and aims to predict search intent in real-world settings where queries may be triggered by the browsed webpages *or* other pre-search context.

The parameters of all the models (*e.g.*, λ, γ and $\boldsymbol{w}$) are trained and tuned using the TRAIN dataset.

Metrics We use the following metrics to evaluate the effectiveness of different models.

- *Mean Reciprocal Rank (MRR)*. As both tasks aim to predict correct queries (only one for each evaluation case), we use the standard mean reciprocal rank [9] as our main measure.
- *Log-Likelihood*. In addition, we report how well a model "explains" the browsing-search pairs by the average of the log-likelihood of the queries in training and test data. For LQF, GQF and GUQF, when the query frequency is zero, we smooth the probability simply by assigning probability 1^{-10}. For RSVM, since Ranking SVM only produces scores $\boldsymbol{w}^T\boldsymbol{x}+b$ for ranking and does not provide probabilities, to calculate its log-likelihood we estimate its query probability based on the score as $P(Q) \propto \exp\{\boldsymbol{w}^T\boldsymbol{x}+b\}$.

For all the experiments, we also perform significance tests using paired t-test with 0.05 as the p-value threshold.

5.2 Experimental Results

5.2.1 Results for Query Prediction

We first evaluate different models for query prediction. Table 6 shows MRR of each method on STUDY and EVALUATE testing dataset. Table 7 shows the average log-likelihood of each model on both testing and training datasets (*i.e.*, STUDY, EVALUATE and TRAIN). Generally speaking, our model performs much better than all the baselines in terms of both MRR and log-likelihood on both test sets. The differences between our model and the baselines are statistically significant. We note that the log-likelihood of our model in training and testing data is close, which suggests that our model is not over-tuned. Next, we analyze the results in detail.

To begin with, we compare PCIM with the baselines that explore different data (*i.e.*, GQF, GUQF, and LQF). First, GQF performs worst in terms of MRR and the second worst in terms of log-likelihood, which clearly shows that the query frequency in general search history is not enough for query

Table 6: **MRR for query prediction on STUDY(S) and EVALUATE(E).**

	GQF	GUQF	LQF	RSVM-P	RSVM-T	PCIM
S	0.0426	0.1350	0.0498	0.0616	0.1206	**0.1705**
E	0.0429	0.1187	0.0447	0.0666	0.1242	**0.1556**

Table 7: Log-likelihood of different models on STUDY(S), EVALUATE(E) and TRAIN(T).

	GQF	GUQF	LQF	RSVM-P	RSVM-T	PCIM
S	-11.29	-10.62	-22.97	-4.95	-4.95	**-4.74**
E	-11.40	-10.83	-22.96	-4.94	-4.93	**-4.78**
T	-11.15	-10.49	-22.99	-4.95	-4.93	**-4.73**

prediction. Second, LQF performs worst in terms of log-likelihood and second worst in terms of MRR, which validates that clicking relationships between queries and webpages are different from the triggering relationships between webpages and queries and are not effective for query prediction. Third, GUQF largely improves over GQF and LQF in both metrics, which suggests that user personal search history provides valuable personal preference information for query prediction. PCIM, which captures the browsing pre-search context in additional to general and personal search history, performs the best and improves over the best baseline (GUQF) on MRR by 31% (on EVALUATE). It clearly demonstrates the effectiveness of pre-search context in query prediction.

Then, we compare PCIM with the state-of-the-art methods for triggered query prediction (*i.e.*, RSVM-P and RSVM-T). RSVM-P, trained on pseudo triggered queries, performs much worse than PCIM. Even though RSVM-T largely improves over RSVM-P due to the manually labeled triggered queries used in training, PCIM still largely improves over it on MRR by 25% (on Evaluate). These observations verify that RSVM models are inadequate or less effective than PCIM under the real-world setting where queries can be triggered from different types of pre-search context (*i.e.*, not only the browsed webpages) with the triggering source being hidden. The experiment results also demonstrate that PCIM can effectively learn from the unlabeled data to predict queries based on both the browsing pre-search context and background pre-search context that summarizes other un-captured pre-search context.

To justify our assumptions, we further break down the overall results by triggered (T) and non-triggered (N) cases (by manually labeling) in Table 8. We only report MRR on EVALUATE in these experiments because of space limitations, noting that MRR is consistant with other measures and the best aligned with our task. We have some interesting findings. First, GUQF largely improves GQF for non-triggered queries and has limited improvement for triggered queries, which shows the need for exploring pre-search context. This also validates our analysis in Section 3 that triggered queries are new and cannot be effectively predicted via exploring personal search history. Second, RSVM-P and RSVM-T perform better than PCIM for triggered queries but perform much worse than PCIM for non-triggered queries. The superior performance of RSVM models over PCIM on triggered queries implies that in the normally unrealistic setting of knowing searches are triggered from a specific pre-search context, supervised models that focus on learning queries triggered from a *single* type of pre-search context is a better choice than our unsupervised mixture model that tries to capture multiple types of pre-search context. However, we emphasize that the triggering relations are usually hidden in a real-world setting (Section 3.2). The system could not know if the current search will be triggered by the browsed webpage, and therefore could not apply RSVM models only on these triggered cases. The evaluation that combines both triggered and non-triggered queries in Table 6 and 7 reflects a realistic setting, in which we have shown that PCIM largely outperforms RSVM models.

Table 8: MRR for triggered(T) and non-triggered(N) queries.

	GQF	GUQF	LQF	RSVM-P	RSVM-T	PCIM
T	0.0090	0.0295	0.0699	0.425	**0.6169**	0.2807
N	0.0445	0.1228	0.0433	0.0463	0.0967	**0.1478**

Finally, we demonstrate the usefulness of our newly proposed features. Specifically, we compare the performance with and without the new features (eMatch, eContain, eOverlap, eFreq, ehFreq, pos, freshness, described in Table 5) on RSVM-P, RSVM-T and PCIM. The results are reported in Figure 2. We can see that for almost all the cases, excluding the proposed features results in large decreases in performance, clearly demonstrating the utility of our proposed features.

Figure 2: MRR for models with and without our proposed features. "full" and "part" stand for with and without proposed features respectively. "A", "T" and "N" stand for all cases, triggered cases and non-triggered cases, respectively.

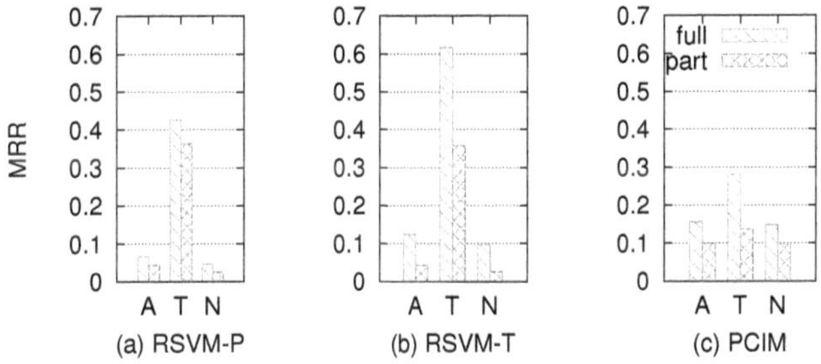

5.2.2 Results for Query Auto-Completion

In this section, we report results of different models on the query auto-completion task. In Table 9, we report MRR of different models evaluated for different initial lengths (the number of characters that a user has typed in).

Table 9: MRR for query auto-completion on varying length of prefix characters.

	Len=1	Len=2	Len=3	Len=4	Len=5
RSVM-T	0.1129	0.1671	0.2318	0.2533	0.2618
GQF	0.0926	0.1647	0.2848	0.3640	0.4165
GUQF	0.1810	0.2441	0.3512	0.4213	0.4676
PCIM	**0.2675**	**0.3077**	**0.3797**	**0.4395**	**0.4779**

Generally speaking, the results confirm our findings from the previous experiment. GUQF improves over GQF, and PCIM further improves over GUQF and RSVM-T in query auto-completion. Most importantly, the improvements of our model are consistent for any length of query prefix, and the differences are all statistically significant. The results again suggest that our model can effectively model pre-search context, and consistently outperforms baseline models. Further, we have some specific findings from this task. First, MRR for each model increases as prefix length increases, suggesting that the problem of query auto-completion become easier as the user types more letters. Second, the improvement for both GUQF over GQF and PCIM over GUQF decreases as initial length increases. This is because as a user types more and more letters, the additional information personal search history and pre-search context can provide becomes less and less helpful. However, from another point of view, this observation also suggests that pre-search context is particularly useful for the most challenging cases, in which the user has only typed one or two letters.

6. CONCLUSIONS

In this paper, we study the problem of predicting search intent based on pre-search context with hidden triggering relations, which advances the research of search intent prediction into a realistic setting. We make the following contributions to the problem.

- We provide a key insight that searches could be triggered by different types of pre-search context, and search systems often do not observe which particular one triggers each search (*i.e.*, hidden triggering relations).
- We conduct an in-depth analysis of how news pre-search context triggers searches based on real-world browsing and search logs. The analysis verifies the hidden nature of triggering relations between pre-search context and triggered queries, identifies interesting characteristics of them that lead to informative features, and provides guidelines for studying other pre-search context in the future.
- To address the challenge of hidden triggering relations, we developed an unsupervised generative mixture model to learn how queries are triggered by different types of pre-search context by taking advantage of large-size unlabeled data. We also identify a set of effective features which can be used in future work.
- Our experiment results show that: 1) pre-search context is useful in predicting search intent; 2) in the normally unrealistic case of knowing searches are triggered from a specific pre-search context, supervised models that focus on learning queries triggered from that specific pre-search context is more effective than our proposed unsupervised mixture model; but 3) in the realistic setting of hidden triggering relations, our proposed unsupervised model could learn effectively without expensive labels that are required in the supervised models, and predict search intents more accurately than them.

7. ACKNOWLEDGMENTS

This work was done during the first author's internship at Yahoo! Labs. It was also supported in part by the Center for Intelligent Information Retrieval. Any opinions, findings and conclusions or recommendations expressed in this material are those of the authors and do not necessarily reflect those of the sponsor.

8. REFERENCES

[1] Z. Bar-Yossef and N. Kraus. Context-sensitive query auto-completion. In *WWW'11*.

[2] P. N. Bennett, R. W. White, W. Chu, S. T. Dumais, P. Bailey, F. Borisyuk, and X. Cui. Modeling the impact of short-and long-term behavior on search personalization. In *SIGIR'12*.

[3] I. Bordino, G. De Francisci Morales, I. Weber, and F. Bonchi. From machu_picchu to rafting the urubamba river: anticipating information needs via the entity-query graph. In *WSDM'13*.

[4] H. Cao, D. H. Hu, D. Shen, D. Jiang, J.-T. Sun, E. Chen, and Q. Yang. Context-aware query classification. In *SIGIR'09*.

[5] H. Cao, D. Jiang, J. Pei, E. Chen, and H. Li. Towards context-aware search by learning a very large variable length hidden markov model from search logs. In *WWW'09*.

[6] H. Cao, D. Jiang, J. Pei, Q. He, Z. Liao, E. Chen, and H. Li. Context-aware query suggestion by mining click-through and session data. In *KDD'08*.

[7] Z. Cheng, B. Gao, and T.-Y. Liu. Actively predicting diverse search intent from user browsing behaviors. In *WWW'10*.

[8] N. Craswell and M. Szummer. Random walks on the click graph. In *SIGIR'07*.

[9] W. B. Croft, D. Metzler, and T. Strohman. *Search engines: Information retrieval in practice*. Addison-Wesley Reading, 2010.

[10] S. Dumais, E. Cutrell, R. Sarin, and E. Horvitz. Implicit queries (iq) for contextualized search. In *SIGIR'04*.

[11] H. Feild and J. Allan. Task-aware query recommendation. In *SIGIR'13*.

[12] S. Gauch, J. Chaffee, and A. Pretschner. Ontology-based user profiles for search and browsing. *Journal of Personalization Research, Special*, pages 1–3, 2002.

[13] A. Hassan, R. Jones, and K. L. Klinkner. Beyond dcg: user behavior as a predictor of a successful search. In *WSDM'10*.

[14] A. Hassan, Y. Song, and L.-w. He. A task level metric for measuring web search satisfaction and its application on improving relevance estimation. In *CIKM'11*.

[15] K. Järvelin, S. L. Price, L. M. Delcambre, and M. L. Nielsen. Discounted cumulated gain based evaluation of multiple-query ir sessions. In *Advances in Information Retrieval*, pages 4–15. 2008.

[16] E. Kanoulas, B. Carterette, P. D. Clough, and M. Sanderson. Evaluating multi-query sessions. In *SIGIR'11*.

[17] E. Kanoulas, M. M. Hall, P. Clough, B. Carterette, and M. Sanderson. Overview of the trec 2011 session track. In *TREC'11*.

[18] L. Li, Z. Yang, B. Wang, and M. Kitsuregawa. Dynamic adaptation strategies for long-term and short-term user profile to personalize search. In *Advances in Data and Web Management*, pages 228–240. 2007.

[19] D. J. Liebling, P. N. Bennett, and R. W. White. Anticipatory search: using context to initiate search. In *SIGIR'12*.

[20] M. Rahurkar and S. Cucerzan. Predicting when browsing context is relevant to search. In *SIGIR'08*.

[21] M. A. Rahurkar and S. Cucerzan. Using the current browsing context to improve search relevance. In *CIKM'08*.

[22] K. Raman, P. N. Bennett, and K. Collins-Thompson. Toward whole-session relevance: exploring intrinsic diversity in web search. In *SIGIR'13*.

[23] X. Shen, B. Tan, and C. Zhai. Context-sensitive information retrieval using implicit feedback. In *SIGIR'05*.

[24] Y. Song, X. Shi, R. White, and A. H. Awadallah. Context-aware web search abandonment prediction. In *SIGIR'14*.

[25] M. Speretta and S. Gauch. Personalized search based on user search histories. In *WI'05*.

[26] K. Sugiyama, K. Hatano, and M. Yoshikawa. Adaptive web search based on user profile constructed without any effort from users. In *WWW'04*.

[27] R. W. White, P. Bailey, and L. Chen. Predicting user interests from contextual information. In *SIGIR'09*.

[28] R. W. White, P. N. Bennett, and S. T. Dumais. Predicting short-term interests using activity-based search context. In *CIKM'10*.

[29] B. Xiang, D. Jiang, J. Pei, X. Sun, E. Chen, and H. Li. Context-aware ranking in web search. In *SIGIR'10*.

[30] J. Yi and F. Maghoul. Query clustering using click-through graph. In *WWW'09*.

Leveraging Procedural Knowledge for Task-oriented Search

Zi Yang
Language Technologies Institute
Carnegie Mellon University
5000 Forbes Ave
Pittsburgh, PA 15213
ziy@cs.cmu.edu

Eric Nyberg
Language Technologies Institute
Carnegie Mellon University
5000 Forbes Ave
Pittsburgh, PA 15213
ehn@cs.cmu.edu

ABSTRACT

Many search engine users attempt to satisfy an information need by issuing multiple queries, with the expectation that each result will contribute some portion of the required information. Previous research has shown that structured or semi-structured descriptive knowledge bases (such as Wikipedia) can be used to improve search quality and experience for general or entity-centric queries. However, such resources do not have sufficient coverage of procedural knowledge, i.e. what actions should be performed and what factors should be considered to achieve some goal; such procedural knowledge is crucial when responding to task-oriented search queries. This paper provides a first attempt to bridge the gap between two evolving research areas: development of procedural knowledge bases (such as wikiHow) and task-oriented search. We investigate whether task-oriented search can benefit from existing procedural knowledge (*search task suggestion*) and whether automatic procedural knowledge construction can benefit from users' search activities (*automatic procedural knowledge base construction*). We propose to create a three-way parallel corpus of queries, query contexts, and task descriptions, and reduce both problems to sequence labeling tasks. We propose a set of textual features and structural features to identify key search phrases from task descriptions, and then adapt similar features to extract wikiHow-style procedural knowledge descriptions from search queries and relevant text snippets. We compare our proposed solution with baseline algorithms, commercial search engines, and the (manually-curated) wikiHow procedural knowledge; experimental results show an improvement of +0.28 to +0.41 in terms of Precision@8 and mean average precision (MAP).

Categories and Subject Descriptors

H.3.3 [**Information Storage and Retrieval**]: Information Search and Retrieval

Keywords

procedural knowledge base; search log; query suggestion; wikihow; search intent

SIGIR'15, August 09–13, 2015, Santiago, Chile.

ACM 978-1-4503-3621-5/15/08...$15.00
DOI: http://dx.doi.org/10.1145/2766462.2767744 .

1. INTRODUCTION

Many search engine users attempt to satisfy an information need by issuing multiple queries, with the expectation that each subtask will contribute some portion of the required information[1]. For example, to organize a conference (task), the organizer needs to look for information related to choosing a hotel, identifying and deciding among banquet options, recruiting volunteers, selecting and contacting publishers, etc (subtasks). For each specific task, users must gather more detailed information. For example, when choosing a hotel, the organizer must consider the number and size of conference rooms, potential arrangements for meal catering and menu planning, whether or not a discounted rate will be available, etc. There is a huge demand for search engines to better assist their users in achieving their intended goals for such *ad hoc* tasks.

Researchers have studied problems related to search intent analysis for general queries; for example, how to identify search intents [13, 11, 37, 25, 9, 19, 24, 28], how to suggest search queries to the user [3, 12, 32, 22, 41], how to rank results that cover diverse aspects of the task, etc. Most studies have so far mostly relied on queries and search logs, search result texts, behavioral information, etc. to improve search quality for entity-centric queries [15]. Recently, research has shown that structured knowledge bases (such as Wikidata or formerly FreeBase[2]) or semi-structured knowledge bases (such as Wikipedia[3]) can be used to improve search quality and experience [14, 6, 26, 43]. However, such knowledge bases focus on representing *descriptive knowledge* (also known as *declarative* or *propositional* knowledge), i.e. the knowledge of the attributes and features of things, and do not have sufficient coverage of *procedural knowledge* used for task-based problem solving [2, 18]. In the past decade, hundreds of thousands of how-to guides have been created by the community and/or professional editors on sites such as wikiHow[4] or eHow[5], which provide procedural knowledge in a semi-structured text format. There have also been attempts to define ontologies [7] to represent procedural knowledge, and algorithms have been proposed to automatically construct structured procedural knowledge bases such as PAA [1] from semi-structured procedural knowledge [34, 23, 1, 36]. However, to the best of our knowledge, structured or semi-structured procedural knowledge has not been studied in the context of task-oriented search as a means to improve search quality and experience.

[1] *(Sub)task* in this paper refers to an action that is performed to achieve a goal in a general context [29], which differs from the notion of *task* in the search scenario [20, 21]. We use *(sub) search task* to denote the latter case.
[2] `http://wikidata.org/`
[3] `http://wikipedia.org/`
[4] `http://wikihow.com/`
[5] `http://ehow.com/`

This paper provides a first attempt to bridge the gap between the two evolving research areas: procedural knowledge base and task-oriented search. We investigate whether task-oriented search can benefit from an existing procedural knowledge base and whether automatic procedural knowledge construction can benefit from users' search activities.

- In particular, we first study how to define features that capture the procedural knowledge writing style, in order to extract queryable phrases from descriptions of the tasks related to the user's information need. We use these features to design a supervised framework and to automatically build a three-way parallel corpus without manual annotation.

- We also study how to construct a procedural knowledge base from users' raw search data (e.g. search logs) as well as data aggregated from multiple users (e.g. suggested queries), based on the hypothesis that the overall goal of task-oriented search is accomplished through a series of searches using multiple queries, which are either reformulated by users or suggested by search engines and accepted by users.

We attempt to leverage the style guidelines for writing semi-structured procedural knowledge, such as the wikiHow guide[6], which indicates that an action-oriented instruction beginning with a verb is required at the beginning of each procedural step, but we also attempt to process articles that do not fully comply with the guide. We accordingly propose a set of textual features and structural features to identify query spans from each task description, and then adapt similar features to extract wikiHow-style procedural knowledge descriptions from search queries and relevant text snippets. We compare our proposed solution with baseline algorithms as well as commercial search engines and the manually-curated procedural knowledge base wikiHow for both problems; experimental results show an improvement of +0.28 to +0.41 in terms of Precision@8 and mean average precision (MAP). Our work can directly benefit search task mining problems such as the NTCIR-11 IMine TaskMine task[7] [29]; automatically extracted procedural knowledge can also provide decision processes for retrieval-based decision support systems such as QUADS [42].

2. RELATED WORK

In this section, we review related work in search intent analysis and task-oriented search, for which we summarize applications focusing on query suggestion. We then survey prior work on procedural knowledge acquisition and its application, focusing on ontology definition for procedural knowledge and algorithms to automatically extract semi-structured procedural knowledge from text.

2.1 Search intent & task-oriented search

Broder [8] and Rose and Levinson [38] propose to categorize search queries into *informational*, *navigational*, and *transactional* and relate them to a more fine-grained *goal hierarchy*. Marchionini [30] analyzed the user's high-level "need to know" and introduced the concept of *exploratory search* as an extension of the traditional *lookup*. Researchers have also proposed to predict both high-level and specific search intents from textual and behavioral information such as Web page contents [13], search queries [11], click logs [37, 25, 9], mouse movements and scrolling [19], and results of individual user questionnaires [24, 28]. Identifying searchers' intents and incorporating them into the search process can contribute to search query suggestion and prediction [3, 12, 32, 22, 41] and selection of exact responses (such as various Google search special features) [40]. The suggested query type depends on the original search query and the predicted intent. E.g., when a user searches for an entity, search engines may suggest other relevant entities [6, 5], actions paired with the entity [27], or attributes [14], mostly using declarative knowledge bases such as Freebase or Wikipedia. However, whether a task-oriented search can achieve an analogous benefit from a procedural knowledge base has not been studied.

In the area of search intent analysis, Hassan et al. [20, 21] studied the *complex search task*, a search behavior that is usually applied to task-oriented search, using search queries. In comparison, our work focuses specifically on task-oriented search, and ignores other types of search (such as browsing different attributes of an object), which allows us to take the advantage of existing procedural knowledge to more reliably support search tasks (when compared to the use of general search logs). We also study to how to build a procedural knowledge base with a full text representation of task-oriented knowledge. The work by Weber et al. [40] on extracting tips from Yahoo! Answers to address how-to Web queries also incorporates task-oriented question and tip extraction from unstructured question-answer texts, whereas our work deals with only complex task-related queries and focuses on identifying queryable snippets from more structured procedural knowledge. Moreover, we also study how to construct procedural knowledge bases from search queries and result snippets, which can be extended to facilitate automatic question answering for community-based QA.

More recently, the IMine Subtopic Mining subtask [29] and the pilot subtask TaskMine at NTCIR focuses on identifying subtasks for a given complex task, and is highly relevant to our work. For a given task (e.g. "lose weight"), possible outputs are expected to be subtask steps (e.g., "do physical exercise", "measure calorie intake"). We make a similar assumption that the given queries are focused on seeking information (subtasks) for complex tasks.

2.2 Procedural knowledge acquisition

Cognitive psychology defines "procedural knowledge" (or imperative knowledge) as the knowledge exercised in the performance of some task [2, 18]. The Semantic Web community has attempted to formally define ontologies to represent procedural knowledge [7], which usually include an *instruction* (or *action* sequence) and a *purpose* (or *goal*). Also defined in such ontologies are the relations between procedural knowledge elements, at different levels of granularity, such as *has-step*, *has-goal* [34] or *is-achieved-by* [17].

Several automatic procedural knowledge base construction approaches have also been proposed to extract instructions from semi-structured texts, e.g. eHow or wikiHow articles [34, 23, 1, 36], recipes [36], community-based QA [4], etc. Most approaches take advantage of structural information (e.g. HTML tags [4], enumeration indicators [16, 23]), and define rules or templates to extract textual content. In a separate step, NLP tools are applied to extract relations and normalize each goal and action to its ontological form, to support linking to other ontological resources. Researchers have also studied how to identify script knowledge [39] which focuses on the temporal ordering of events [10].

In contrast, our approach takes advantage of the writing style of semi-structured procedural texts and proposes a set of structural and textual features for identifying procedural knowledge; the implemented approach can be optimized with a supervised learning method. Moreover, beyond the conventional use of small-scale procedural knowledge in AI planning [33] or NLP [4], this paper studies the problem of how to apply an online large-scale procedural knowledge base to complex task search problems.

[6] http://wikihow.com/wikiHow:Writer's-Guide

[7] http://dl.kuis.kyoto-u.ac.jp/ntcir-11/taskmine/

3. PROBLEM DEFINITION

In this section, we first give our formal definition of *procedural knowledge base*, and then introduce the two main problems we will study in this paper: *search task suggestion using procedural knowledge base (STS)* and *automatic procedural knowledge base construction from search activities (APKBC)*.

Many knowledge bases such as Wikipedia or Wikidata that have been widely utilized contain a huge amount of *descriptive knowledge*. Procedural knowledge [2, 18], also known as *know-how*, is the knowledge exercised in the accomplishment of a task, i.e. how to do things, which is usually acquired by experience and considered *tacit* and not easily shared, compared to *descriptive knowledge*. However, shared explicit procedural knowledge lays a foundation for efficiently coordinated action, which is often referred to as *best practices* or *business rules* within communities or organizations. As wikiHow and many similar how-to Web sites allow users to easily share procedural knowledge, semi-structured large-scale procedural knowledge bases have become available. People have also attempted to construct structured procedural knowledge bases by defining ontologies or incorporating other existing representations such as PDDL[8] [34, 23, 1, 36]. Since we notice that many of the proposed definitions use different terminologies, e.g. *goal* vs. *target* vs. *purpose*, *instruction* vs. *action sequence*, *step* vs. *action*, etc, although their meanings are identical, we first formally define the terminology related to procedural knowledge base.

Definition 1 (Task)**.** *A **task** t is represented by a short and concise **summary** and a detailed **explanation** for clarification.*

Definition 2 (Is-achieved-by relation)**.** *A task is connected with an ordered list of n tasks $s_1, \ldots, s_n$ (referred to as **subtasks**) that contribute to the task t by **is-achieved-by** relations $r(t, s)$. A* weight *$w(t, s)$ may also associate with each relation $r(t, s)$. We assume the weights associated with the outgoing relations should sum to one, i.e. $\sum_i r(t, s_i) = 1$.*

Definition 3 (Procedural knowledge graph)**.** ***Procedural knowledge graph** $G = (T, R)$ is the set of all tasks T and all is-achieved-by relations R.*

Definition 4 (Plan, goal, and primitive tasks)**.** *A **plan** is a subgraph of G, which is a tree with root being the **goal** and the leaves being the **primitive tasks**.*

A *semi-structured procedural knowledge base* such as wikiHow has an identical structure, but it allows users to more easily view and edit; each article corresponds to a task, whose summary is given in the title and whose explanation is detailed in the introduction section. Each step (or substep) also corresponds to a task. The is-achieved-by relations have three representation forms: numbered *steps* in each article page (first-level subtasks), bulleted substeps under each step description (second-level subtasks), and free links[9] directed from a step to another task page. Steps that have no substeps or outgoing free links are considered *primitive tasks*. Current semi-structured procedural knowledge bases do not allow editors to explicitly specify the the relation strength between tasks, or the importance of each subtask[10]. Therefore, we assume each relation shares an equal weight with all other outgoing relations, i.e. $w(t, s) = 1/\text{od}(t)$, where od is the out-degree of the task t.

Procedural knowledge captures how people decompose a complex task into a mixture of several mental actions (e.g. "choose", "determine", etc.) and/or physical actions (e.g. "visit", "store", etc.). When users turn to search engines for information seeking and problem solving, we investigate how existing procedural knowledge can be leveraged to help understand a user's search intent and suggest sub search tasks to users.

Problem 1 (Search task suggestion using procedural knowledge, STS). *Given a procedural knowledge graph G and a task-oriented search task q, we aim to (a) identify the task $t \in T$ the user intends to accomplish, and then (b) retrieve a list of k subtasks $s_1, \ldots, s_k \in T$ and also (c) suggest the corresponding sub search tasks $p_1, \ldots, p_k$.*

A search task is usually represented by a search query or a key phrase [29, 20, 21]. Similarly, we assume both the input search task q and the suggested search tasks $p_1, \ldots, p_k$ are queryable phrases. As a result, the problem can be straightforwardly solved by suggesting relevant (sub)queries for task-oriented queries. In contrast to the entities and attributes in a descriptive knowledge base, which are usually words or phrases and can used directly in query suggestion, summaries and explanations in a procedural knowledge usually contain richer action and condition information. Therefore, the problem poses three challenges. First, we need to identify the task $t \in T$ the user intends to accomplish. If the query corresponding to the search task exactly matches the summary of a task t (exact string match or after lexical transformations), then we can directly return t. However, in most cases when an exact match does not exist, we need to incorporate additional information such as the search result page of the query and the full description of each task, and rank candidate tasks using a retrieval method. Second, we need to choose the tasks $s_1, \ldots, s_k \in T$ to suggest and then prioritize them based on the knowledge G containing relations V. Intuitively, we can choose the task t's top-k subtasks ordered by the weight of the is-achieved-by relation. Finally, we need to extract queryable phrases from each task description, and the algorithm should thus learn how searchers have been trained to formulate queries.

Although community-centric procedural knowledge bases may have collected hundreds of thousands of task descriptions, users still face *ad hoc* situations (tasks) that are not covered by an existing procedural knowledge base. However, we hypothesize that other searchers may have faced similar situations in the past and have already interacted with search engines to attempt a solution, which means we may discover implicitly expressed procedural knowledge from users' raw search activities (e.g. search logs) as well as those aggregated from many searchers (e.g. suggested queries). Therefore, we investigate whether we can automatically construct a procedural knowledge base like wikiHow using search queries and relevant documents returned from search engines.

Problem 2 (Automatic procedural knowledge base construction from search activities, APKBC). *Given a task t, we aim to (a) identify a search task q, and (b) collect k related search tasks $p_1, \ldots, p_k$, and then (c) identify n $(\leq k)$ search tasks $p_{i_1}, \ldots, p_{i_n}$ to generate n tasks $s_1, \ldots, s_n$ that can be performed to accomplish the task t with text description.*

Related search tasks can be identified from users' search activities [37, 25, 9] and/or suggested by search engines [3, 12, 32, 22, 41]. Depending on the search intent, related actions, attributes, entities, or any form of reformulation of the original search task may be considered related, which however do not necessarily embed

[8] http://www.plg.inf.uc3m.es/ipc2011-deterministic/attachments/Resources/kovacs-pddl-3.1-2011.pdf

[9] http://en.wikipedia.org/wiki/Help:Wiki_markup#Free_links

[10] As users may verbally express their confidence and/or their attitude toward the importance in the task explanation section, we can hence incorporate richer linguistic features such as modality particles, verbal auxiliaries, etc. to identify verbal expression of weight.

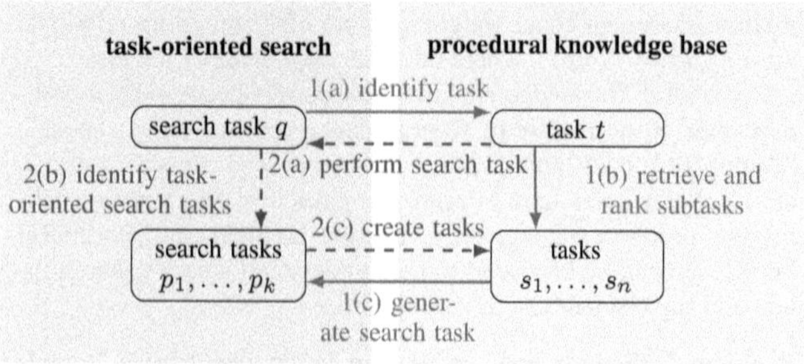

Figure 1: Subproblems in *search task suggestion using procedural knowledge* problem (brown solid arrows and brown labels) and *automatic procedural knowledge base construction from search activities* problem (purple dashed arrows and purple labels)

procedural knowledge. Therefore, the first challenge in extracting procedural knowledge is to identify the is-achieved-by relations, i.e., which of them correspond to the tasks that can achieve the goal. A textual description is a less ambiguous representation of a task in a procedural knowledge base, which can be accessed both by humans and by automatic decision support systems that require predefined natural language decision processes as input (e.g. QUADS [42]). Our second challenge is therefore to automatically generate text descriptions for procedural knowledge which attempt to conform to a common writing style. We summarize the interactions between task-oriented search and procedural knowledge base construction in Figure 1.

4. PROPOSED APPROACH

In this section, we propose a supervised learning framework, which requires zero extra manual annotation, and instead takes advantage of available artifacts; users' search activities and manually curated procedural knowledge are used to train models for both STS and APKBC problems. In particular, existing search logs can reveal how searchers have been trained to formulate queries, but they don't necessarily or sufficiently cover how to search for procedural knowledge. On the other hand, existing procedural knowledge bases indicate how to accomplish tasks in a very comprehensive manner, but are not necessarily optimized for interactive search. We first describe how to build a *three-way parallel corpus* for training, and then define linguistic and structural features for training sequence labeling models for both problems. Then, we present detailed procedures for suggesting search tasks using procedural knowledge and constructing procedural knowledge bases from search logs.

4.1 Three-way parallel corpus construction

We create a three-way parallel corpus that contains triples $\{\langle q, t, c\rangle\}$ with a query q, a matching task t, and a context c of q and t, which is a passage of text that describes the task. We build the three-way parallel corpus in an iterative manner.

We first identify the exact matching pairs of searchers' issued search tasks and task summaries in the procedural knowledge base, which guarantees precision in the first step, although we expect that many lexically distinct but semantically identical pairs may exist that will not be extracted. To achieve this, we may scan through the entire search query log to find each query q that matches the description of the task t. We then retrieve the context c by extracting the textual content from the top documents relevant to the description of the task t. We add the triple $\langle q, t, c\rangle$ to the parallel corpus. In addition, we collect related queries by combining the user-issued queries from the same session and the list of queries suggested by the search engine for the next iteration.

If we have no large query log, we may also manually create task-oriented search tasks for the tasks in the procedural knowledge base. Specifically, we use the summary of the task t to form a search query q and issue it to the search engine to extract the context c. Since these search queries are "artificially" created, and do not necessarily represent how searchers normally formulate queries for these tasks in similar situations, we exclude the triple $\langle q, t, c\rangle$ that contains the original query q from the parallel corpus, which is only used for search engines to suggest real queries for the next iteration.

Once we collect a list of related queries for q, we compare them with the known subtasks of t, i.e. the tasks connected by is-achieved-by relations in the procedural knowledge base. For each related query p, we first find the subtasks $s_1, \ldots, s_n$ that contain p in either its summary or explanation, and retrieve its context d. We then add all $\{\langle p, s_i, d\rangle\}_{i\in[1,n]}$ to the parallel corpus. As we assume that all necessary subtasks have been detailed in the procedural knowledge base, we consider a related query irrelevant to accomplishing the task if it is not mentioned in any of the subtasks, and it is excluded in the parallel corpus and discarded for future iterations, which solves Problem 2(b). We also ignore subtasks that are not matched to any related query, a situation that may arise from a lack of evidence from query logs, or truncation due to limited space for displaying suggested queries on a result page. We continue the iterative process.

Furthermore, we annotate the occurrence of the query q in the task t's description. We also similarly annotate the occurrence of the summary and explanation of the task t in the context c by finding the contiguous sequence of words (a passage) from the context that is most relevant to the task summary or explanation. An example is shown in Figure 2. For training a sequence labeling model, we employ the `BIO` encoding, i.e., each token in the task description (or context) that begins each occurrence of the query phrase (or the task summary or explanation) is labeled as $\mathtt{B}^{\mathtt{Q}}$ (or $\mathtt{B}^{\mathtt{TS}}$, $\mathtt{B}^{\mathtt{TE}}$), the tokens that continue in the query phrase (or the task summary or explanation) are labeled as $\mathtt{I}^{\mathtt{Q}}$ (or $\mathtt{I}^{\mathtt{TS}}$, $\mathtt{I}^{\mathtt{TE}}$), and all other tokens in the task (or the context) are labeled as `O`.

4.2 Feature definition and model construction

We use the constructed parallel corpus, which contains triples of queries, task representations, and contexts, to train supervised models that can automatically create task-oriented queries for tasks, as well as task descriptions for task-oriented search tasks. We view both problems as a word sequence extraction problem, which is usually reduced to a sequence labeling task. Therefore, we define the features by taking advantage of the writing style prevalent in semi-structured procedural knowledge bases, and then apply a common statistical model for sequence labeling (such as Conditional Random Fields (CRF)), which also enables us to process articles that do not fully comply with a style guide.

We define both syntactic features and structural (positional) features that are motivated by the writing guide as follows:

Location (LOC). As suggested in the wikiHow writing guide, a task should provide both "skimmable information that readers can quickly understand" in the title of the article and in the beginning sentence of each step, and "rich informative articles for more patient users" in the article's introduction and in the sentences which follow in the detailed explanation of each step. Therefore, we define features to capture the location of each word.

Part of speech (POS). Since both the article title and the first sentence in each step are required to begin with a verb in bare in-

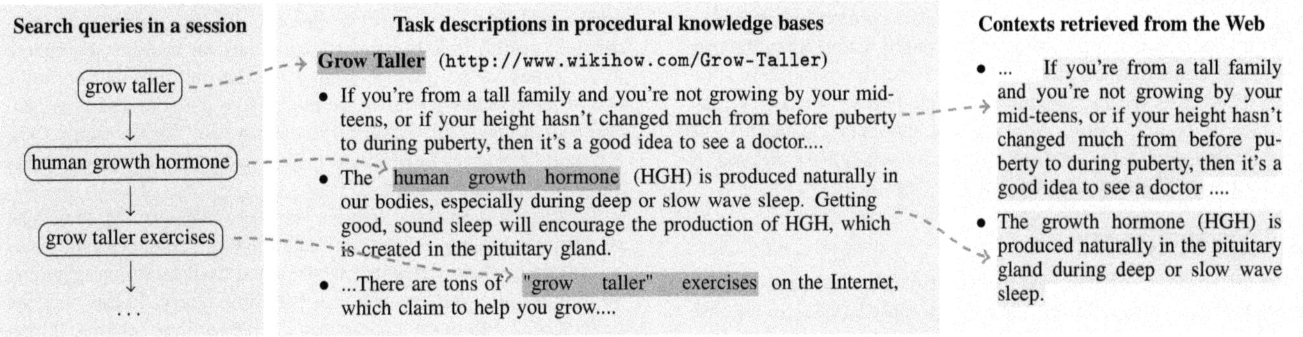

Figure 2: An example of the parallel corpus construction process

finitive form, we also extract the fine-grained part-of-speech value for each token.

Parsing (PAR). To further understand the *task facets* such as occurrences of subsidiary resources (e.g. a target object) or constraints (e.g. a duration), we include features extracted from dependency parsing, named entity extraction, and chunking.

Word and context. As in other natural language sequence labeling tasks, we also define features including the token's surface form, its stem form, its TF-IDF score, as well as the word features and the part-of-speech tags of the previous and the next words in the task summary or explanation.

We extract the same set of features (except the location feature) from both the context c (X^c) and task description t (X^t) for each triple in the parallel corpus, which together with the corresponding annotated BIO label (Y^c and Y^t) comprises a training instance for sequence labeling. We train a query construction model $M^{\mathtt{Q}}$ using the training sets (X^t, Y^t), a task summary construction model $M^{\mathtt{TS}}$ and a task explanation construction model $M^{\mathtt{TE}}$ using (X^c, Y^c).

To construct search queries for an unseen task t, we first extract the features x^t from the task description, and then apply the query construction model $M^{\mathtt{Q}}$ to extract each search query candidate q_i, i.e. to identify each word sequence $\mathbf{w}_i = w_{i1} \dots w_{il_i}$ from t with the corresponding $\mathbf{y}_i^{t*}$ labeled as $\mathtt{B}^{\mathtt{Q}}\mathtt{I}^{\mathtt{Q}} \dots \mathtt{I}^{\mathtt{Q}}$, where l_i represents the length of $\mathbf{w}_i$, and $\mathbf{y}^{t*}$ is the optimal label sequence, i.e.,

$$\mathbf{y}^{t*} = \operatorname*{argmax}_{\mathbf{y}^t \in \{\mathtt{B}^{\mathtt{Q}}, \mathtt{I}^{\mathtt{Q}}, \mathtt{O}\}^{|t|}} p(\mathbf{y}^t | \mathbf{x}^t; M^{\mathtt{Q}}) \quad (1)$$

where $|t|$ represents the length of the task t's description. Similarly, to construct task descriptions for an unseen query q, we first retrieve the context c and extract the features x^c from the context, and then apply the task description construction model M^c to extract each word sequence labeled as $\mathtt{B}^{\mathtt{TS}}\mathtt{I}^{\mathtt{TS}} \dots \mathtt{I}^{\mathtt{TS}}$ and $\mathtt{B}^{\mathtt{TE}}\mathtt{I}^{\mathtt{TE}} \dots \mathtt{I}^{\mathtt{TE}}$ as the summary and the explanation of a task t_i respectively from optimizing the following equation:

$$\mathbf{y}^{c*} = \operatorname*{argmax}_{\mathbf{y}^c \in \{\mathtt{B}^{\mathtt{T}\cdot}, \mathtt{I}^{\mathtt{T}\cdot}, \mathtt{O}\}^{|c|}} p(\mathbf{y}^c | \mathbf{x}^c; M^{\mathtt{T}\cdot}) \quad (2)$$

4.3 Search task suggestion

Given a task-oriented search task represented by query q, we first retrieve a list of candidate tasks from the procedural knowledge base that mention the query q in either the summary or the explanation. When more than one task is returned from the procedural knowledge base, we need to determine which task is the best fit for the user's search intent. Therefore, we leverage the query construction model $M^{\mathtt{Q}}$ to estimate the likelihood of the j-th occurrence of the query q in a retrieved task t_i's description (i.e. a word sequence $\mathbf{w}_{ij} = w_{ij1} \dots w_{ijl}$, where l is the length of query q). We select the i^*-th task that contains the j^*-th word sequence which maximizes the conditional probability, i.e.

$$i^*, j^* = \operatorname*{argmax}_{i,j} p(\mathbf{y}_{ij}^{t_i} = \mathtt{B}^{\mathtt{Q}}\mathtt{I}^{\mathtt{Q}} \dots \mathtt{I}^{\mathtt{Q}} | \mathbf{x}^{t_i}; M^{\mathtt{Q}}) \quad (3)$$

Once we have identified the task t, we identify the tasks in the procedural knowledge base for future query suggestion using a few heuristic strategies. First, we may select only the first-level subtasks and order the weight of the is-achieved-by relation in descending order. We may also select both the first-level and second-level subtasks and use the weight of each first-level subtask or the weight of each second-level subtask multiplied by the weight of its corresponding first-level subtask.

When a list of subtask candidates $s_1, \dots, s_n$ are retrieved from the existing procedural knowledge base, we apply the query construction model $M^{\mathtt{Q}}$ again, for each subtask s_i's summary and explanation to identify each word sequence $\mathbf{w}_{ij}$ labeled as $\mathtt{B}^{\mathtt{Q}}\mathtt{I}^{\mathtt{Q}} \dots \mathtt{I}^{\mathtt{Q}}$ using Eq. 1. Among the extracted query candidates $\{\mathbf{w}_{ij}\}_j$ for each subtask s_i, we choose the query p_i that maximizes the likelihood $p(\mathbf{y}_{ij}^{s_i} = \mathtt{B}^{\mathtt{Q}}\mathtt{I}^{\mathtt{Q}} \dots \mathtt{I}^{\mathtt{Q}} | \mathbf{x}^{s_i}; M^t)$. The "winning" query candidates $p_1, \dots, p_n$ corresponding to the subtask candidates are globally ranked by multiplying the weight obtained from subtask retrieval with the likelihood estimation; finally, we select the top-k queries. This process guarantees that the queries are extracted from distinct subtask candidates, which can lead to the most coverage of all necessary subtasks. Alternatively, a diversity-aware ranking approach can also be applied to global rank all query candidates $\{\mathbf{w}_{ij}\}_j$. A *plan* can be gradually implemented and detailed when we iteratively apply this approach.

4.4 Automatic procedural knowledge base construction

Given a task description t, we directly apply the query construction model $M^{\mathtt{Q}}$ to extract a task-oriented search query q using Eq. 1, and then (similar to the process in building the parallel corpus) we identify the the queries related to q in both search logs and suggested queries. The entire search session (reformulation of queries, click activities, etc.) can be analyzed to determine how a specific user works to accomplish a task; therefore, by mining the search session data, we should be able to model how users typically accomplish tasks. As a result, the search engine should be able to correctly suggest to the user related tasks, rather than related entities or attributes. Although this assumption may not always hold in real-world search scenarios, it allows us to consider how related tasks can be further explored to extract subtasks for t, as long as the task description construction model can identify any passage that can be used for the task summary or explanation. In Section 5, we observe whether or to what extent this assumption holds for actual search scenarios.

For each related query p_i, we collect its context by extracting relevant document snippets from search engines, and apply the task description construction model $M^{T\cdot}$ to extract the most likely summary candidate $\mathbf{w}_l$ and explanation candidate $\mathbf{v}_l$ for task s_i, according to Eq. 2, among all extracted summary candidates and explanation candidates for s_i. We select the top-n tasks ordered by the estimated likelihood for their summaries.

5. EXPERIMENT

In this section, we describe the experiments conducted to evaluate the effectiveness of the approach proposed in Section 4. We first introduce the data sets for the experiments, and then we describe the experiment settings. The experimental results are presented in three subsections for the constructed three-way parallel corpus and the two problems we introduced in Section 3; we also analyze the limitations of the current query suggestion approaches for task-oriented search, and the coverage and quality of current procedural knowledge bases for search suggestion. The data and code used in this section are available to download[11].

5.1 Data Preparation

We used two publicly available data sets (an English wikiHow data dump and the AOL search log) and public search engines (Google and Bing) to collect the suggested queries and contexts.

English wikiHow data dump. We crawled an English wikiHow data dump using a modified version of the WikiTeam tool[12], which contains 198,163 non-redirect articles within namespace "0" (Main)[13]. We also filtered out the articles that are marked as `stub` (incomplete and need more information) or have no "Introduction" or "Steps", which results in a collection of 149,975 valid articles. We performed minimal pre-processing to reformat the articles to the MediaWiki format[14], without changing any textual content.

In particular, we first extracted the top-level task summary and explanation after identifying the title and the introduction of each article. We then located the "Steps" section and extracted the enumerated or bulleted items to build a local subtask hierarchy. Next, we built a procedural knowledge graph by creating nodes representing all the top-level tasks and their subtasks and establishing relations based on both the task-subtask relation as well as internal links. Applying this approach, the constructed procedural knowledge graph contains a total of 1,488,587 tasks and 1,439,217 relations, where 265,509 of the tasks are non-primitive, and 100,605 relations come from internal links. We built a Lucene[15] index for all task descriptions, which supports retrieval of candidate tasks for the search task suggestion problem described in Section 4.3.

AOL search query log. We also used the publicly available AOL search query log, which consists of over 21M Web queries (over 10M unique queries) collected over three months in 2006 from AOL [35]. We downcased the query strings and task summaries, and removed all non-alphanumeric characters. We identified that 867 unique queries (corresponding to 9,847 new queries from 23,099 lines) match some task summary in our constructed procedural knowledge base. In the experiment, we identified 639 unique queries that have at least two tokens (corresponding to 3,086 new queries from 7,019 lines), which tend to be less ambiguous and more likely task-oriented. We could estimate that each task-oriented search task is repeated 4.8 times on average, compared to 2.1 times for all queries, supporting the intuition that common task-oriented searches tasks are more often encountered than general search tasks, providing further motivation for our study. The 639 unique queries correspond to 619 tasks if punctuation marks and whitespaces are ignored.

To retrieve the related queries issued by users in the same session from the query log, we first identified related query candidates by collecting the queries that were issued by the same user within 30 minutes after they issued each matching query. In this way, we collected 33,548 query candidates (31,955 unique queries, 50 per query). We did not use other commonly adopted session detection heuristics such as edit distance or cosine similarity between query pairs, since a task-oriented search query may not share words in common with related search queries. For example, we identified a case where "visit niagara falls"[16] is followed by another query "map of northeast" in the AOL search log, "design a living room"[17] is followed by another query "choosing colors", etc. We instead counted on the three-way parallel corpus construction process to correctly identify which of the query candidates are relevant to accomplishing the task.

Queries suggested by search engines. To create "artificial" search tasks, we randomly sampled 1,000 non-primitive tasks from the constructed procedural knowledge that do not appear in the query log. We limited the total number of tasks in building the parallel corpus partly due to our limited access to commercial search engines, and also because in a preliminary experiment we found that performance of the sequence labeling model on the test set had become stable. We merged them with the 639 identified queries from AOL search query log, using commercial search engines (Google and Bing) to build the parallel corpus, which correspond to 1,619 tasks. We constructed each query without using additional operators such as quotes, plus signs, minus sign, etc., unless quotes appear in the summary. Google may suggest up to eight queries at the bottom of the search page for each search task and Bing may suggest up to sixteen queries within the search result column and on the right side of the results page. We collected a total of 9,906 queries suggested by Google (6.11 per query on average, 8 maximum) and 9,715 suggested queries by Bing (5.99 per query on average, 13 maximum).

We notice that both Google and Bing are able to display procedures directly on the result page from wikiHow (only Bing) or other procedural data sources (Google), which allows users to grasp the knowledge without an extra click, but hardly helps users or automatic decision support systems identify how to explore more related information from the Web. We also found that both commercial search engines tend to suggest and display related queries for short queries, as they are more likely topically broad and semantically ambiguous. However, for task-oriented search, the complexity of describing the task does not necessarily reflect the difficulty of accomplishing the task, in terms of which aspects to consider and the steps to perform. In Section 5.4, we further evaluate whether commercial search engines are effective for task suggestion.

Context extracted from search engines. We used Goolge to collect the contexts of the queries both in the parallel corpus (used for model training and testing) and those that are potentially useful for new procedural knowledge discard auxiliary words such as pronouns, articles, etc. when they formulate queries, retaining only nouns, verbs, adjectives, etc., we also plan to study whether we can

[11] `http://github.com/ziy/pkb`

[12] `http://github.com/WikiTeam/wikiteam/`. Unlike most MediaWiki sites, each article on wikiHow has a URL which is formed by concatenating the words in its title using a hyphen ("-") rather than an underscore ("_"), so we modified the code accordingly.

[13] `http://www.mediawiki.org/wiki/Manual:Namespace`

[14] `http://www.mediawiki.org/wiki/Help:Formatting`

[15] `http://lucene.apache.org/`, Ver. 4.10.1

[16] Also on wikiHow: `http://www.wikihow.com/Visit-Niagara-Falls`

[17] Also on wikiHow: `http://www.wikihow.com/Design-a-Living-Room`

extract queryable key words from non-continuous text spans.overy (used for end-to-end APKBC evaluation). We first extracted URLs for context candidates from their first search result pages, and excluded Web documents from the `wikihow.com` domain to increase the reliability and generalizability of the trained model, and also excluded `google.com` domains and URLs that have only domain names without subpaths, which are usually navigational search results. Then, we used the Boilerpipe[18] to extract textual content from the HTML documents. For queries in the parallel corpus, we finally downloaded 7,440 context documents and successfully processed 7,437 documents using Boilerpipe, and for end-to-end evaluation, we downloaded and extracted 3,512 context documents.

5.2 Experiment Settings

We describe the experiment settings, including the tools we used to extract features and learn the sequence labeling models, the evaluation methods, and baseline methods.

Evaluation methods. We conducted two types of evaluation for both problems. We first evaluate the performance of proposed sequence labeling approach on the query construction and task description construction tasks using the automatically labeled parallel corpus. Then, based on manual judgment, we evaluate our proposed end-to-end solution for both STS and APKBC problems, and compare with commercial search engine suggestions and the current wikiHow knowledge base, respectively.

We performed 10-fold cross validation on the constructed parallel corpus, and report average performance results. We extracted text spans from the predicted labels and used precision, recall and F-1, averaged over the performance on all test instances (macro-averaged) and averaged on each task then across all tasksalso (micro-averaged), to compare the proposed approach with baseline methods. We also employed two ROUGE scores (F-1 based ROUGE-2 and ROUGE-S4[19]), after we removed common English stop words[20] and constructed an array of words in lemma forms.

In the end-to-end comparison, we randomly sampled 50 triples from the parallel corpus and we applied both our approach for search task suggestion and commercial search engine services to produce up to eight related queries. We manually judged whether each search query can obtain a search result that can help achieve the user's goal. Similarly, we applied our procedural knowledge base construction approach to generate up to eight procedural descriptions and merged it with the wikiHow "steps". We manually judged whether each subtask summary and explanation that the system produced can be considered a valid "step" description for wikiHow. Given that this judgment is binary, we report the macro-averaged and micro-averaged Precision@8, and MAP averaged over all 50 test instances.

Baseline methods. For the query construction and task description construction tasks, we compare the proposed approach **CRF** with other supervised and unsupervised approaches. We varied the classifier to evaluate **HMM**, a Hidden Markov Model based sequence labeling approach based on surface forms, **LR**, a logistic regression classifier, and an **SVM** classifier. The latter two are trained on the same set of features to classify `B`, `I`, and `O` without the sequence labeling assumption. We also compared performance with models that use only one category of the proposed features (**W/**), all but one category (**W/O**), and only local or context features. Finally, we compare with a key word extraction method based on TF-IDF (**TFIDF**), where we try to maximize the macro-averaged F-1 score by tuning the TF-IDF score threshold when determining whether a word is selected as a key word.

Feature extractors and learners. We used Stanford CoreNLP[21] to extract sentences, tokens, stems, POS tags, dependency labels, chunks (noun phrases and verb phrases), and named entities using the default configuration. We used MALLET[22] [31] to learn and test the sequence labeling models (CRF and HMM) with `sparse` weighting method, LibLinear[23] for training and testing LR and SVM models. As the Web documents tend to be noisy, we preprocessed the texts by inserting periods at certain places to improve the parsing performance. Details can be found in the source code.

Table 1: Averaged number and percentage of related queries suggested by Google or Bing or issued by the users subsequently in the same session that are mentioned by a task description in wikiHow

	Averaged number			Percentage (%)		
	Google	Bing	Log	Google	Bing	Log
Full phrase	0.070	0.046	0.050	1.162	0.727	1.131
New words	0.473	0.592	0.164	8.487	9.522	4.639

5.3 Parallel corpus construction result

Including the 639 queries that have already been associated with some tasks in the procedural knowledge base, we identified that a total of 1,182 query-task description pairs (from 1,146 distinct descriptions) among the suggested queries can be found in the subtask descriptions of the task corresponding to the original query. We annotated the context with each corresponding task summary and explanation. Specifically, we segmented the context into sentences and selected those that contain all the tokens in the task summary or at least 70% of the tokens in the task explanation as task description embedding sentences, and annotated the minimal span that contains all overlapping tokens.

To further understand how many of the related queries are aligned to a task description, we show in Table 1 the averaged number and percentage of related queries suggested by Google or Bing or issued by users subsequently in the same session that are mentioned within a task description. "New words" refer to the subset of words that are in the suggested queries but not in the original queries. First, we can see that the queries identified in the same session do not have a higher quality (1.131% – 4.639%) in related task suggestion, which may be due to an over-simplified session detection algorithm. In comparison, related queries collected from commercial search engines tend to be more relevant (0.727% – 9.522%). Moreover, if we focus on the new words, we identify many more (from 0.727% – 1.162% to 8.487% – 9.522%) tasks that are aligned with the queries suggested by the search engines.

We note that if a query cannot be aligned with a task description using our proposed construction method, this does not guarantee that the query is not semantically identical (e.g. a paraphrase) of any task description. In fact, as motivated in Section 4.1, the surface form matching approach can simplify the parallel corpus construction process while still guarantee the parallelity.

5.4 Search task suggestion result

We first compare the query construction result between the proposed approach and the baseline methods in Table 2. We also con-

[18] `http://code.google.com/p/boilerpipe/`, Ver. 1.2.0

[19] We did not use any unigram based metric (such as ROUGE-1 or ROUGE-SU) or recall based metric because we did not set a limit for either the number of chunks or the total length of the text returned for each task.

[20] We used `/resources/stopwords-rouge-default.txt` from ROUGE 2.0 tool. `http://kavita-ganesan.com/content/rouge-2.0.`

[21] `http://nlp.stanford.edu/software/corenlp.shtml`, Ver. 3.5.2

[22] `http://mallet.cs.umass.edu/`, Ver. 2.0.7

[23] `http://www.csie.ntu.edu.tw/~cjlin/liblinear/`, Ver. 1.8

Table 2: Evaluation results for search task suggestion (STS) and automatic procedural knowledge base construction (APKBC). A dagger (†) and one to three stars ($\star$) represent significance levels of $p \leq 0.1$, 0.05, 0.01, and 0.001 respectively, and ns represents not significant.

	Classifiers					W/ subsets of features (+context)				W/O subsets of features (+context)				Local	Context
	CRF	HMM	SVM	LR	TFIDF	POS	PAR	LOC	WORD	POS	PAR	LOC	WORD		
STS															
Macro P	.8691	.5281***	.7589***	.8461^{ns}	.0087***	.8346†	.6846***	.2476***	.8164**	**.8811**†	.8689^{ns}	.8431**	.8699^{ns}	.7808**	.8155**
Macro R	**.6563**	.1984***	.6428†	.5728***	.0072***	.4720***	.3245***	.0900***	.5849***	.6493^{ns}	.6519^{ns}	.6470*	.5133***	.5935**	.6248**
Macro F1	**.7471**	.2870***	.6955**	.6826***	.0079***	.6015***	.4390***	.1241***	.6803***	.7466^{ns}	.7442^{ns}	.7311**	.6444***	.6737**	.7068**
Micro P	.9359	.9160†	.8641***	.9142*	.4431***	.9248^{ns}	.8811**	.5980*	.9105**	.9400^{ns}	.9357^{ns}	.9153**	**.9411**^{ns}	.8935**	.8983**
Micro R	**.6934**	.3113***	.6674*	.6078***	.0262***	.5487***	.3973***	.1671***	.6185***	.6856†	.6864^{ns}	.6800*	.5867***	.6449**	.6538**
Micro F1	**.6930**	.3161***	.6612**	.6144***	.0244***	.5541***	.4018***	.1678***	.6175***	.6870†	.6861†	.6785*	.5911***	.6447**	.6535**
ROUGE-2	**.8112**	.5200***	.7922*	.7476**	.2279***	.7108***	.6020***	.3488***	.7713**	.8113^{ns}	.8069†	.8104^{ns}	.7322**	.7807**	.7907*
ROUGE-S4	**.8087**	.5147***	.7892*	.7446**	.2041***	.7079***	.5954***	.3420***	.7657**	.8082^{ns}	.8044†	.8065^{ns}	.7299**	.7746**	.7857**
APKBC: summary															
Macro P	.7576	.0042***	.1464***	.1131***	.0160***	.5325*	.3175**	-	**.7738**^{ns}	.7489^{ns}	.7723^{ns}	-	.5359*	.7590^{ns}	.7736†
Macro R	**.3260**	.0008**	.1116**	.0489**	.1254*	.2881^{ns}	.0641**	-	.2464**	.2651**	.3167^{ns}	-	.2945^{ns}	.2757*	.3113†
Macro F1	**.4207**	.0014**	.1175***	.0668**	.0271**	.3556^{ns}	.0988**	-	.3279**	.3460**	.4129^{ns}	-	.3632^{ns}	.3755*	.4081^{ns}
Micro P	.8524	.1213***	.4585***	.4210**	.0556***	.7093**	.7893†	-	**.9061***	.8813^{ns}	.8749†	-	.7084**	.8439^{ns}	.8604^{ns}
Micro R	**.3344**	.0010**	.1041**	.0476**	.1347*	.2923^{ns}	.0838**	-	.2433**	.2576**	.3088†	-	.3185^{ns}	.2734*	.3159^{ns}
Micro F1	**.3455**	.0015**	.1119***	.0511**	.0683**	.3153^{ns}	.1996**	-	.2526**	.2695**	.3198†	-	.3408^{ns}	.2902*	.3260^{ns}
ROUGE-2	**.4463**	.1017**	.2425**	.1734**	.1583**	.3822^{ns}	.1996*	-	.3435**	.3678**	.4170*	-	.3787^{ns}	.4053*	.4069*
ROUGE-S4	**.4392**	.0660**	.2301**	.1692**	.1026**	.3788^{ns}	.1968*	-	.3412**	.3645**	.4118*	-	.3704^{ns}	.4006*	.4022*
APKBC: explanation															
Macro P	.4984	.0000***	.0053***	.0000***	.0002***	.1904**	**.7000**^{ns}	-	.4901^{ns}	.4722†	.4837^{ns}	-	.2546**	.1337***	.4534^{ns}
Macro R	**.3310**	.0000**	.0026**	.0000**	.0015**	.0463**	.0000**	-	.3056†	.3198^{ns}	.3169†	-	.0247**	.0355**	.2879*
Macro F1	**.3853**	.0000***	.0034***	.0000***	.0003***	.0687**	.0000***	-	.3639†	.3695^{ns}	.3718^{ns}	-	.0410**	.0521***	.3359*
Micro P	.7180	.4724*	.4911**	.6978^{ns}	.0062***	.7588^{ns}	**.9909*****	-	.7292^{ns}	.7206^{ns}	.7274^{ns}	-	.7575^{ns}	.6105^{ns}	.6823^{ns}
Micro R	.3342	.0050**	.0012**	.0000**	.0363**	.0704**	.0000**	-	.2961^{ns}	**.3411**^{ns}	.3208^{ns}	-	.0194**	.0370**	.2723^{ns}
Micro F1	**.3577**	.0050**	.0018**	.0000**	.0103**	.0889**	.0000**	-	.3176^{ns}	.3554^{ns}	.3468^{ns}	-	.0292**	.0474**	.2922^{ns}
ROUGE-2	.3698	.2450*	.1737**	.1470**	.2657†	.1647**	.1325**	-	.3489^{ns}	.3580^{ns}	**.3804**^{ns}	-	.1614**	.1858**	.3532^{ns}
ROUGE-S4	.3686	.2324*	.1659**	.1408**	.2498*	.1637**	.1325**	-	.3472^{ns}	.3554^{ns}	**.3793**^{ns}	-	.1614*	.1828**	.3500^{ns}

ducted a t-test to calculate the significance level of each baseline method compared against the proposed approach (CRF). We can see the proposed CRF-based sequence labeling approach can significantly outperform other baseline classifiers (at a significance level of ≤ 0.05 in terms of F-1 and ≤ 0.1 in terms of ROUGE).

The performance gap between the sequence labeling approaches and the independent classification-based approaches such as LR and SVM suggests that the query construction problem is similar to other sequence labeling problems such as named entity detection or supervised key word extraction. With only surface form features, HMM performs worse than CRF. All the supervised approaches, which take advantage of the constructed parallel corpus, can outperform the unsupervised approach (TF-IDF).

When we test each feature category (POS, Parsing, Location, Word, Local, and Context) independently, we can see none of them can beat the proposed approach with a confidence level of ≥ 0.99. We also see that word features contribute the most to performance, which can achieve around 90% of the performance in terms of F-1 and 95% in terms of ROUGE when all the features are used. Both F-1 and ROUGE scores drop when we remove any feature category from the feature list, and they drop the most when Word features are removed, which implies that all the features have positively contributed to the query construction task.

To better understand what non-Word features most likely promote a word to become a $\mathtt{B}^{\mathtt{Q}}$ or $\mathtt{I}^{\mathtt{Q}}$, we shows the top-5 features for $\mathtt{O} \rightarrow \mathtt{I}^{\mathtt{Q}}$, $\mathtt{B}^{\mathtt{Q}} \rightarrow \mathtt{I}^{\mathtt{Q}}$, $\mathtt{I}^{\mathtt{Q}} \rightarrow \mathtt{I}^{\mathtt{Q}}$ transitions in Table 3. We see that the whole query phrase is very likely extracted from the summary part of a description (sum) due to its clarity and conciseness. We also see that both singular nouns (NN or NNP) and verbs in either VB or VBP forms are selected as indicators for beginning a query, and verb phase (VP) is a useful feature when deciding whether to continue a query.

Table 4: End-to-end evaluation results for search task suggestion (STS) and title (TI) and explanation (EX) generation for automatic procedural knowledge base construction (APKBC). PROP/P. corresponds to the proposed approach and WH corresponds to the wikiHow knowledge.

	STS				APKBC		
	PROP	GOOG	BING	LOG	P. TI	P. EX	WH
Macro P	**.4457**	.0972	.0333	.0676	**.0997**	.2046	**.9677**
Micro P	**.4457**	.0973	.0313	.0612	**.0995**	.2041	**.9515**
MAP	**.3361**	.0553	.0120	.0549	**.0527**	.1331	**.9404**

We then evaluated the end-to-end performance of the proposed STS solution using the query construction model. We present the results in Table 4 and show examples in Table 5. We see the proposed solution can outperform the commercial search engines by +0.35 to +0.41 in terms of Precision@8 and +0.28 to +0.32 in terms of MAP. We see that our proposed method, which is tailored for task-oriented search, can provide unique insights when suggesting tasks, compared to current general-purpose commercial search engines, which have been designed for entity-centric search and tend to suggest queries by appending keywords such as "product", "image", "logo", "online", "free", etc. We discovered three types of errors from our system: (1) Some suggested queries are ambiguous when presented by themselves (e.g. "fix it", "install"). (2) duplicated queries are suggested from different subtasks. (3) the manually created knowledge sometimes still contains a few non-instructional "steps". We could further improve the proposed approach by conducting a co-reference analysis or other approaches to incorporate original queries and contexts in the suggested queries. We could also collectively rank the candidates to avoid suggesting duplicated tasks.

Table 3: The non-Word features that contribute the most to each label in both search task suggestion (STS) and automatic procedural knowledge base construction (APKBC) problems. "+1"/"-1" presents the feature of the next/previous word, "sum" refers to summary, "VP"/"NP" represents if the word is inside a verb/noun phrase, "Begin" refers to the beginning of the text.

	STS (M^Q)			APKBC: summary (M^{TS})			APKBC: explanation (M^{TE})		
	$O \to B^Q$	$B^Q \to I^Q$	$I^Q \to I^Q$	$O \to B^{TS}$	$B^{TS} \to I^{TS}$	$I^{TS} \to I^{TS}$	$O \to B^{TE}$	$B^{TE} \to I^{TE}$	$I^{TE} \to I^{TE}$
1	*POS*: NNP	POS^{-1}: VB	*LOC*: sum	*POS*: VB	POS^{-1}: VB	POS^{-1}: VBP	Begin	VP	POS^{-1}: NN
2	*LOC*: sum	*LOC*: sum	POS^{-1}: IN	*POS*: VBP	POS^{-1}: VBP	*POS*: NNP	*POS*: VBG	POS^{-1}: NN	VP
3	*DEP*: ccomp	POS^{-1}: VBP	VP	*POS*: NN	POS^{-1}: NNP	POS^{-1}: IN	*POS*: NN	POS^{-1}: DT	POS^{-1}: NNS
4	*POS*: VB	POS^{-1}: NNP	*DEP*: dobj	*DEP*: appos	POS^{-1}: NN	*DEP*: xcomp	*DEP*: compound	NP	POS^{-1}: ,
5	*DEP*: nsubjpass	POS^{-1}: NN	POS^{+1}: JJ	*POS*: NNP	*DEP*: case	*POS*: JJR	*DEP*: nsubj	POS^{-1}: VB	POS^{-1}: NNP

Table 5: Comparison of top 4 suggested queries produced by the proposed STS system and commercial search engines for example tasks.

PROPOSED	GOOGLE	BING
Task: make blueberry banana bread		
blend the mixture	vegan blueberry banana bread	best blueberry banana bread
mix flour	buttermilk blueberry banana bread	bisquick banana blueberry bread
add 1 egg	great blueberry banana bread recipe	banana blueberry cake
vanilla extract	blueberry banana bread with yogurt	healthy banana blueberry bread
Task: slim down		
weight loss	slim down diet	the slim down club
heavy food	7 day slim down	how to slim down fast
junk food	weight loss	slim down challenge
keep up the mood	slim down thighs	how to slim down legs
Task: play red alert2		
build a barracks	red alert 2 complete (iso) original 2 disc	play red alert 2 game
build a war factory	play red alert 2 free	play ra2 online
radar chould	play red alert 2 online free	red alert 2 download
build a power plant/tesla reactor	play red alert 3	free red alert 3

Table 6: Partial suggested tasks from the top 8 outputs produced by the proposed APKBC system for example tasks.

Task: sign up for airbnb
Airbnb is no longer running the $50 OFF $200 promo but you can still save $25 OFF Your First Airbnb Stay of $75 or more by copying and pasting this link into your browser: ...
Task: make blueberry banana bread
Please don't use regular whole wheat in this recipe – the loaf will turn out very dense
Add the wet ingredients - the egg mixture to the flour mixture and stir with a rubber spatula until just combined
If you're in need of a quick, easy and delicious way to use up the ripe bananas in your house... definitely
Task: become a cell phone dealer
However, the cell phone provider may place restrictions on the manner in which you can use its company name, phone brands and images
Visit the state's business licensing agency's website and your city's occupational/business licensing department's website to determine if you need a license for your prepaid cell phone business

5.5 Automatic procedural knowledge base construction result

We compare the results of our proposed approach with the baseline methods for task description (title and explanation) construction in Table 2. We first see that all the methods produce much lower F-1 and ROUGE scores for APKBC than those for STS, which suggests that task description generation is a difficult task, esp. explanation construction. Nevertheless, we can see that the proposed approach significantly outperforms all other classifiers in terms of F-1 and ROUGE metrics (at a significance level of ≤ 0.1).

When comparing with the results from using each feature category, we see that not a single category can reach the same performance level as the proposed approach, which again implies that all the feature categories have contributed to the overall performance in task description construction problem. Comparing with using all but one feature categories, we can find that Word features are crucial for summary generation but not explanation generation, whereas POS and Parsing features are crucial for explanation generation but not summary generation. We also observe the non-Word features that contribute the most in Table 3. Although the performance does not match that of the query construction approach, we can still find interesting patterns in the results. First, we can see that nouns and verbs are still crucial in constructing task descriptions, and verbs (VB and VBP) rather than nouns are more likely selected as the beginning of a summary. To begin the task explanation, the word is expected to have a "Begin" indicator and/or a dependency type of nsubj, meaning the nominal subject of a sentence. Verb phrases are also important in identifying a task description.

Finally, we evaluated our proposed end-to-end APKBC solution, and compared it with wikiHow articles in Table 4. Due to the difficulty of the task description construction problem and lack of high-quality task-oriented search query candidates, we find that the automatic approach performs much worse than manual curation in building a brand new procedural knowledge base from scratch; nevertheless, we still find that the proposed approach is able to discover relevant subtasks that are not covered in the current wikiHow article, i.e. it can be used to improve the coverage and quality of existing procedural knowledge bases. Some examples are shown in Table 6. For example, for the task "sign up for airbnb", one of the suggested queries "sign up for airbnb coupon" implies a coupon may be an important subsidiary resource of a task that the current wikiHow article does not know. For this particular task, a statement with the detailed coupon info is able to be extracted to describe the concrete task related to the resource. Even though this result may be from an advertisement Web page, it still delivers the freshest information that can hardly be added and updated instantly in manually created procedural knowledge bases.

We also summarize the errors into three major categories: (1) ambiguous task representations. For example, the "find a match" article on wikiHow[24] describes how to "look for a partner", whereas search engines try to disambiguate the search intent by also suggesting queries in the context of data analysis such as "find a match in excel", "find a match spreadsheet", etc., (2) duplicated descriptions, and (3) quality of the text extracted from noisy Web documents. Moreover, as we note that not all wikiHow articles exactly follow the writing guide, the proposed approach can be used estimate the quality of each existing task description, similar to Eq. 3, and report potentially suspicious low-quality articles or spurious steps such as "You're done.", which violate the writing guidelines.

[24] `http://www.wikihow.com/Find-a-Match`

6. CONCLUSION

This paper provides a first attempt to bridge the gap between the two evolving research areas: construction of procedural knowledge bases and task-oriented search. We investigated two problems: *search task suggestion using procedural knowledge* and *automatic procedural knowledge base construction from search activities*. We proposed the creation of a three-way parallel corpus of queries, query contexts, and task descriptions, and reduced both problems to sequence labeling tasks. We proposed a supervised framework to identify the queryable phrases from task descriptions and extract procedural knowledge from search queries and relevant text snippets. We compared our proposed solution with baseline algorithms, and used commercial search engines and manually-curated procedural knowledge for both problems; experimental results show an improvement of +0.28 to +0.41 in terms of Precision@8 and MAP.

As a next step, we intend to conduct a user study to estimate to what extent the users can find good tips for real-world information needs. We also plan to further study how to properly rank the candidate queries and task descriptions, and also study the APKBC problem by leveraging a supervised natural language generation framework in addition to the proposed sequence labeling approach.

7. REFERENCES

[1] A. Addis and D. Borrajo. From unstructured web knowledge to plan descriptions. In *DART'2009*, volume 324, pages 41–59, 2011.

[2] J. R. Anderson. *Cognitive psychology and its implications*. WH Freeman/Times Books/Henry Holt & Co, 1990.

[3] R. Baeza-Yates, C. Hurtado, and M. Mendoza. Query recommendation using query logs in search engines. In *Proceedings of EDBT'2004*, pages 588–596, 2005.

[4] S. Banerjee and S. Bandyopadhyay. Question classification and answering from procedural text in english. In *Proceedings of QACD'2012*, pages 11–26, 2012.

[5] I. Bordino, G. De Francisci Morales, I. Weber, and F. Bonchi. From machu_picchu to rafting the urubamba river: anticipating information needs via the entity-query graph. In *Proceedings of WSDM'2013*, pages 275–284, 2013.

[6] I. Bordino, Y. Mejova, and M. Lalmas. Penguins in sweaters, or serendipitous entity search on user-generated content. In *Proceedings of CIKM'2013*, pages 109–118, 2013.

[7] C. Brewster, K. O'Hara, S. Fuller, Y. Wilks, E. Franconi, M. A. Musen, J. Ellman, and S. Buckingham Shum. Knowledge representation with ontologies: the present and future. *IEEE Intell. Syst.*, pages 72–81, 2004.

[8] A. Broder. A taxonomy of web search. In *ACM SIGIR forum*, volume 36, pages 3–10, 2002.

[9] H. Cao, D. Jiang, J. Pei, Q. He, Z. Liao, E. Chen, and H. Li. Context-aware query suggestion by mining click-through and session data. In *Proceedings of SIGKDD'2008*, pages 875–883, 2008.

[10] N. Chambers and D. Jurafsky. Unsupervised learning of narrative event chains. In *Proceedings of ACL-08: HLT*, pages 789–797, 2008.

[11] Z. Cheng, B. Gao, and T.-Y. Liu. Actively predicting diverse search intent from user browsing behaviors. In *Proceedings of WWW'2010*, pages 221–230, 2010.

[12] N. Craswell and M. Szummer. Random walks on the click graph. In *Proceedings of SIGIR'2007*, pages 239–246, 2007.

[13] H. K. Dai, L. Zhao, Z. Nie, J.-R. Wen, L. Wang, and Y. Li. Detecting online commercial intention (oci). In *Proceedings of WWW'2006*, pages 829–837, 2006.

[14] J. Dalton, L. Dietz, and J. Allan. Entity query feature expansion using knowledge base links. In *Proceedings of SIGIR'2014*, pages 365–374, 2014.

[15] N. Dalvi, R. Kumar, B. Pang, R. Ramakrishnan, A. Tomkins, P. Bohannon, S. Keerthi, and S. Merugu. A web of concepts. In *Proceedings of PODS'2009*, pages 1–12, 2009.

[16] E. Delpech and P. Saint-Dizier. Investigating the structure of procedural texts for answering how-to questions. In *Proceedings of LREC'2008*, pages 46–51, 2008.

[17] Y. Fukazawa and J. Ota. Automatic modeling of user's real world activities from the web for semantic ir. In *Proceedings of SemSearch'2011*, pages 5:1–5:9, 2010.

[18] M. P. Georgeff and A. L. Lansky. Procedural knowledge. *Proceedings of the IEEE*, 74(10):1383–1398, 1986.

[19] Q. Guo and E. Agichtein. Ready to buy or just browsing?: detecting web searcher goals from interaction data. In *Proceedings of SIGIR'2010*, pages 130–137, 2010.

[20] A. Hassan and R. W. White. Task tours: helping users tackle complex search tasks. In *Proceedings of CIKM'2012*, pages 1885–1889, 2012.

[21] A. Hassan Awadallah, R. W. White, P. Pantel, S. T. Dumais, and Y.-M. Wang. Supporting complex search tasks. In *Proceedings of CIKM'2014*, pages 829–838, 2014.

[22] R. Jones, B. Rey, O. Madani, and W. Greiner. Generating query substitutions. In *Proceedings of WWW'2006*, pages 387–396, 2006.

[23] Y. Jung, J. Ryu, K.-m. Kim, and S.-H. Myaeng. Automatic construction of a large-scale situation ontology by mining how-to instructions from the web. *Web Semant.*, 8(2–3):110–124, 2010.

[24] M. P. Kato, T. Yamamoto, H. Ohshima, and K. Tanaka. Investigating users' query formulations for cognitive search intents. In *Proceedings of SIGIR'2014*, pages 577–586, 2014.

[25] U. Lee, Z. Liu, and J. Cho. Automatic identification of user goals in web search. In *Proceedings of WWW'2005*, pages 391–400, 2005.

[26] Y. Li, B.-J. P. Hsu, and C. Zhai. Unsupervised identification of synonymous query intent templates for attribute intents. In *Proceedings of CIKM'2013*, pages 2029–2038, 2013.

[27] T. Lin, P. Pantel, M. Gamon, A. Kannan, and A. Fuxman. Active objects: Actions for entity-centric search. In *Proceedings of WWW'2012*, pages 589–598, 2012.

[28] J. Liu, M. J. Cole, C. Liu, R. Bierig, J. Gwizdka, N. J. Belkin, J. Zhang, and X. Zhang. Search behaviors in different task types. In *Proceedings of JCDL'2010*, pages 69–78, 2010.

[29] Y. Liu, R. Song, M. Zhang, Z. Dou, T. Yamamoto, M. Kato, H. Ohshima, and K. Zhou. Overview of the ntcir-11 imine task. In *Proceedings of NTCIR-11*, pages 8–23, 2014.

[30] G. Marchionini. Exploratory search: from finding to understanding. *Commun. ACM*, 49(4):41–46, 2006.

[31] A. K. McCallum. Mallet: A machine learning for language toolkit. 2002.

[32] Q. Mei, D. Zhou, and K. Church. Query suggestion using hitting time. In *Proceedings of CIKM'2008*, pages 469–478, 2008.

[33] K. L. Myers. A procedural knowledge approach to task-level control. In *AIPS'1996*, pages 158–165, 1996.

[34] P. Pareti, E. Klein, and A. Barker. A semantic web of know-how: Linked data for community-centric tasks. In *Proceedings of WIC'2014*, pages 1011–1016, 2014.

[35] G. Pass, A. Chowdhury, and C. Torgeson. A picture of search. In *InfoScale*, volume 152, page 1, 2006.

[36] M. Perkowitz, M. Philipose, K. Fishkin, and D. J. Patterson. Mining models of human activities from the web. In *Proceedings of WWW'2004*, pages 573–582, 2004.

[37] F. Radlinski, M. Szummer, and N. Craswell. Inferring query intent from reformulations and clicks. In *Proceedings of WWW'2010*, pages 1171–1172, 2010.

[38] D. E. Rose and D. Levinson. Understanding user goals in web search. In *Proceedings of WWW'2004*, pages 13–19, 2004.

[39] R. C. Schank and R. P. Abelson. *Scripts, plans, goals, and understanding: An inquiry into human knowledge structures.* Psychology Press, 2013.

[40] I. Weber, A. Ukkonen, and A. Gionis. Answers, not links: Extracting tips from yahoo! answers to address how-to web queries. In *Proceedings of WSDM'2012*, pages 613–622, 2012.

[41] R. W. White and J. Huang. Assessing the scenic route: measuring the value of search trails in web logs. In *Proceedings of SIGIR'2010*, pages 587–594, 2010.

[42] Z. Yang, Y. Li, J. Cai, and E. Nyberg. Quads: Question answering for decision support. In *Proceedings of SIGIR'2014*, pages 375–384, 2014.

[43] X. Yu, H. Ma, B.-J. P. Hsu, and J. Han. On building entity recommender systems using user click log and freebase knowledge. In *Proceedings of WSDM'2014*, pages 263–272, 2014.

Personalizing Search on Shared Devices

Ryen W. White
Microsoft Research
Redmond, WA 98052 USA
ryenw@microsoft.com

Ahmed Hassan Awadallah
Microsoft Research
Redmond, WA 98052 USA
hassanam@microsoft.com

ABSTRACT

Search personalization tailors the search experience to individual searchers. To do this, search engines construct interest models comprising signals from observed behavior associated with machines, often via Web browser cookies or other user identifiers. However, shared device usage is common, meaning that the activities of multiple searchers may be interwoven in the interest models generated. Recent research on activity attribution has led to methods to automatically disentangle the histories of multiple searchers and correctly ascribe newly-observed search activity to the correct person. Building on this, we introduce *attribution-based personalization* (ABP), a procedure that extends traditional personalization to target individual searchers on shared devices. Activity attribution may improve personalization, but its benefits are not yet fully understood. We present an oracle study (with perfect knowledge of which searchers perform each action on each machine) to understand the effectiveness of ABP in predicting searchers' future interests. We utilize a large Web search log dataset containing both person identifiers and machine identifiers to quantify the gain in personalization performance from ABP, identify the circumstances under which ABP is most effective, and develop a classifier to determine when to apply it that yields sizable gains in personalization performance. ABP allows search providers to personalize experiences for individuals rather than targeting all users of a device collectively.

Categories and Subject Descriptors

H.3.3 [**Information Storage and Retrieval**]: Information Search and Retrieval—*search process*; *selection process*.

Keywords

Attribution-based personalization; Interest model; Personalization.

1. INTRODUCTION

Personalization can be a powerful mechanism to individualize the search experience [5][19][35][38][39]. The application of personalization at scale relies on unique identifiers assigned to machines based on browser cookies or client-side software such as browser toolbars. Individualizing the search experience relies on a one-to-one correspondence between machine identifiers and individuals. Previous work has shown that machine identifiers are frequently associated with the search activity of multiple people (e.g., on over half of devices [47]), potentially impacting personalization effectiveness. We conjecture that by attributing observed search behavior to the correct *person* during the construction of interest models (profiles) and when processing received queries, the performance of personalization algorithms for applications such as predicting future interests or re-ranking search results will improve. We refer to this new approach as *attribution-based personalization*, defined as:

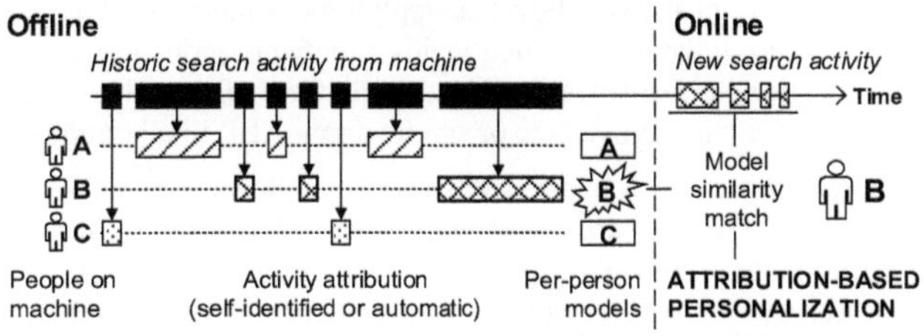

Figure 1. Activity attribution and search personalization. Interest model construction happens offline (e.g., as part of a periodic process) and matching of new activity happens online (i.e., at query time). Historic and new data assigned to people using activity attribution (oracle or [47]). Models are built per person not per machine. New activity is assigned to searcher *B*.

DEFINITION: Attribution-based personalization (ABP) is a procedure to tailor search experiences to individuals. The three phases are (1) activity attribution and interest model construction for individual searchers from historic machine activity, (2) attribution of newly-observed activity to the correct searcher, and (3) application of that searcher's specific interest model for personalization.

Figure 1 illustrates the ABP process. Methods exist for phases 1 and 2 [47]. We focus herein on the value of attribution for phase 3.

Studies of personalization have examined its performance in controlled settings, given a clear mapping between people and profiles [39]. For the application of personalization in practice, e.g., at large scale in Web search engines, such mappings cannot be guaranteed. Shared used of a single machine is common and we have shown in previous work that we can build models to accurately attribute observed search activity to the correct person [47]. However, little is known about the value of attribution for personalization. To estimate this we perform an oracle study. The study compares interest models constructed given perfect (oracle) assignment of activity to people against models built from all machine activity, the standard practice in personalization [5][35]. The development of new methods for ABP is an exciting new frontier for Information Retrieval research. Our goal is to frame the ABP challenge and estimate the gains attainable from applying ABP in practice. To estimate its utility, we target future interest prediction, an important task in settings such as search, advertising, and recommendation [26][30][45].

We make the following contributions with this paper:

- Introduce attribution-based personalization as an important new area of personalization research and estimate its value for personalizing search experiences for people who share devices.
- Characterize differences in the searcher interest models constructed from person- and machine-based activity. We do so via a search log containing machine and person identifiers for each query. We demonstrate differences in the interest models built by attributing activity to specific people rather than machines.
- Show that these differences between identifier type (machine or person) are meaningful for an important application: predicting

SIGIR '15, August 09 - 13, 2015, Santiago, Chile
© 2015 ACM. ISBN 978-1-4503-3621-5/15/08…$15.00
DOI: http://dx.doi.org/10.1145/2766462.2767736

searchers' future interests. We experiment with using different sources for interest model construction (i.e., all historic activity linked to the identifier versus only activity for related queries).
- Controlling for search task effects, we identify properties of interest models (e.g., the number of searchers on machine) and queries (e.g., popularity, topic) for which ABP performs best.
- Learn a model from properties of the query and the constructed interest models to accurately predict *when* to apply ABP on a per-query basis. We show that applying this model for our task of future interest prediction yields significant gains in personalization performance over models that use all search activity from the current machine or simply apply ABP to all queries.

The remainder of this paper is structured as follows. Section 2 presents related work in areas such as personalization, activity attribution, and interest modeling. Section 3 describes our study, including research questions and methods. Section 4 characterizes multi-person searching. Section 5 describes a comparison of machine- and person-based interest models for future interest prediction. Section 6 explores the effect of query and model properties on ABP performance, as well as introducing a classifier to enable the selective application of ABP on a per-query basis. We discuss our findings and their implications in Section 7, and conclude in Section 8.

2. RELATED WORK

Research in a number of areas relates to our work here: (1) improving search using behavioral data, (2) search personalization, (3) attribution of search activity to individuals, (4) the construction of interest models, and (5) applications of these models for tasks such as recommending resources or predicting future searcher interests.

Improving Search using Behavioral Data: Behavioral data from search engines has been mined extensively to improve search relevance [1][21]. Radlinski and Joachims [28] proposed the use of query chains comprising connected sequences of queries to learn richer models of relevance that can capitalize on session behavior. Moving beyond individual queries, Radlinski et al. [29] model intent from queries and clicks for direct consumption by Web search engines. Similarly, Downey et al. [15] examined relationships between search queries and search goals estimated from the terminal page within the search session. Bilenko and White [7] used signals from aggregate post-query navigation trails to learn result rankings.

Search Personalization: The personalization of the search experience has received significant attention [5][19][23][33][39]. The potential for personalization [41] quantifies the improvement in retrieval performance that is attainable via personalization versus the performance that is obtained from trying to meet many searchers' needs. Long-term behavior has been applied to personalize search [35], focused on previous queries associated with the similar tasks over multiple search sessions [38]. Teevan et al. [39] showed that personalization improves as more data is available about the current searcher. Other signals such as short-term activity (e.g., in the same session) are also effective personalization signals [8][44][46]. Backing off from the activity of individual searchers, other signals such as physical location [4], the search activity of those engaged in similar tasks [48], or searchers similar along one or more other dimensions [43][50] have also been shown to be useful for personalization, especially when addressing "cold-start" scenarios where limited data can affect system performance [31].

Attribution of Search Activity: Truly personalizing the search experience relies on assigning observed search activity to an individual. At scale in search settings this is usually performed via an automatically-assigned unique identifier based on Web browser cookies, or to a toolbar or browser instance. Dasgupta et al. [13] studied the challenge of connecting different cookies to track the same user over time. This is important since cookie based identifiers are subject to cookie churn. Similarly, there may also be user variations within the machine identifier. White et al. [47] used the same dataset as employed in this study and showed that observing multiple people searching on the same machine is common (i.e., 56% of machine identifiers comprised activity from multiple searchers). They presented models to accurately estimate the number of searchers on a machine and attribute new search activity to specific searchers. The search activity attribution challenge that White et al. identified shares characteristics with other related domains such as fraud detection (to detect anomalous behaviors) [16] and signal processing (e.g., in blind signal separation, used to distinguish interleaved signal sources) [2][9]. However, there has been little attention (including in [47]) on the *application* of attribution for personalization. To our knowledge, the only exception is an early study by Singla et al. [34], who experimented with attribution methods for personalization, yielding some promising results. Since that study used a specific attribution method for a specific task (re-ranking results), the findings offer limited general insight about the potential utility of ABP. We address that shortcoming with the research in this paper.

Building Interest Models: To personalize the search experience, systems need to build and apply models that represent searcher interests. Interest models are common in user modeling and recommendation. Models can be constructed based on online activity only (as is the case with the personalization that we target in this paper), or based on client-side data, which can provide more complete insight into searcher preferences than is available from remote monitoring alone [24][39]. Interest models can assume a number of forms, including the text of search queries [33][36], specific URLs or Web domains visited in search [20][42] or browsing [24][44], or topical representations [19][35] (including topics specified explicitly [11][23]). Searcher interest models are often stored remotely, although client-side storage has been adopted if there is a need to access local data [39] or to address privacy concerns [6].

To reduce noise, personalization methods can target on-task activity only [5][38]. One extreme example is revisitation to the same URL for the same query. So called *personal navigation* [42], is also a powerful signal for search personalization and requires models comprising query-URL pairs mined from historic data. Personalization methods traditionally use overlap between queries to detect activity on the same task [38]. Such on-task interest models can be constructed from activity at different timeframes (short-term or long-term), and there are noteworthy tradeoffs in personalization performance given these timeframes (e.g., long-term models typically perform better for the first query in a session, where there is no session history) [5]. Other factors, such as the click entropy of the query, can also impact personalization performance [14].

Recommendation and Prediction: Once searcher interest models have been constructed, there are different ways in which they can be applied for personalization purposes. The traditional application is to adjust the ranking of search results, either through generating a new result set tailored to the searcher [27] or through re-ranking the initial results returned by a search engine [5][35][39]. Other applications of interest models include predicting which search results searchers will click [26], which display advertisements they will select [30], or which Web pages or topics they will focus on next [45][46]. For this study, we target the challenge of predicting future interests given historic interest models. The log data used in our study only contained data about queries and clicks (i.e., no result lists). Therefore, we could not reliably reconstruct the top-ranked search results presented at query time, as has been possible in prior personalization studies, where top retrieved results appeared in the logs used [4][5]. We therefore focus on future interest prediction.

Table 1. Descriptive statistics of dataset. Model building based on six months of logs. Evaluation uses one month of logs.

Statistic	*Dataset*	
	Model building	*Evaluation*
Total # machines	28,003 (of 490,754*)	
Total # searchers	68,908	49,869
Total # queries	19,145,916	3,619,913
Total # clicks	9,339,421	1,778,824
Avg. # queries/machine	683.3 (stdev=756.2)	129.2 (stdev=157.9)
Avg. # clicks/machine	333.3 (stdev=350.8)	63.5 (stdev=73.3)

*Number of machines with queries in train/test period for number of clicks ≥ 0.

Contributions: We extend prior work in many ways. First, through ABP, we focus on personalization at the sub-machine level, rather than assuming an exact correspondence between machine and individual, as has traditionally been the case in personalization. Second, we perform an *oracle* study highlighting differences in interest models depending the identifier type (machine or person) associated with search activity. This differs from the work of Singla et al. [34], where the focus was on applying a particular automatic attribution method, limiting the generalizability of derived claims about the effectiveness of ABP. Third, we show that observed differences between machine- and person-based models are meaningful, in our case for the task of future interest prediction. Fourth, we identify scenarios where ABP is most effective. As part of that analysis, we built a classifier to accurately determine when to apply ABP for each query, yielding strong gains in personalization performance.

3. EVALUATING ABP PERFORMANCE

We now describe our oracle study to understand the potential value from ABP. We describe our research questions, the data used, the models created, and their application in predicting future interests.

3.1 Research Questions

We answer the following four questions with our research:

RQ1 (Characterize interest models): What are some salient differences in interest models constructed based on the search activity from different identifier types (machine and person)?

RQ2 (Predict future interests): How accurately can we predict searchers' future interests by applying interest models based on search activity associated with the different identifier types?

RQ3 (Effect of interest model and query properties): What is the impact of properties of queries and interest models on the performance of models built from historic person or machine activity?

RQ4 (Automatically determine model source): Can we automatically determine which model source to apply per query? If so, what is the impact of taking this action on future interest prediction?

Answers to these questions help understand the value of ABP and useful scenarios for it. The answers can help search providers decide whether to invest in ABP and when to apply it in practice.

3.2 Data

The data that we used for our study was provided under contract by the Internet analytics company comScore. They recruited an opt-in consumer panel that has been validated to be representative of the online population and projectable to the United States population [18]. Millions of panelists provide comScore with explicit permission to passively measure all of their online activities using monitoring software installed on their computers. In exchange for joining the panel and providing search data, participants are offered a variety of benefits, including computer security software, Internet data storage, virus scanning, and chances to win cash or prizes.

The full dataset comprised unfiltered search queries on major Web search engines such as Google, Bing, and Yahoo!, collected over a two-year period from mid-2011 to mid-2013. The logs contained the text of queries, search result clicks, and the time that the events occurred (in the searcher's local time). Importantly for our study, the comScore search logs also contained a machine identifier (assigned to the machine) and a person identifier (assigned to each person who used the machine). An application is installed on the machine to record search activity and searchers are required to indicate to the logging software that they are searching at any given time. Machine-based identifiers are used in a range of online applications, either through Web browser cookies or other mechanisms such as search-provider toolbars; so their use in this study reflects the current state of the art. To remove variability caused by cultural and linguistic variation in search behavior, we only include log entries from the English-speaking United States locale. An advantage of using these data beyond the availability of both person and machine identifiers, is that they can be purchased from comScore to replicate and extend many of our findings (although the costs of data access may be prohibitive to some). The use of these logs is an important distinction from many log-based studies reported in the research literature, which rely on proprietary search logs, analyzed only by employees of commercial search providers. A disadvantage of using these data is that it limits the applications that can be studied to those not requiring result lists, e.g., we target interest prediction and not re-ranking since result lists are not available in this set.

For our study, we divided our dataset into two subsets: (1) *model building*: six months of comScore search logs for use in model construction (January 2013 to June 2013 inclusive)[1], and (2) *evaluation*: one month immediately following for use in evaluating the performance of the interest models at predicting future interests (July 2013). Activity (result clicks) from each person is used to construct the person-based models. All individuals associated with a machine are used in building the machine models. To ensure that we had sufficient data for our analysis, we required that there were at least 100 clicks from the machine during the model building period and at least 15 clicks from the same machine during the evaluation period. Note that searchers in our dataset only used a single machine; there was no movement of searchers between machines.

Summary statistics on the two datasets are shown in Table 1. These include some basic descriptive statistics such as the total number of queries and clicks in each set. As part of the data cleaning process, we removed machine identifiers that exhibited signs of being automated traffic by issuing more than 1000 queries on any given day.

3.3 Building Interest Models

We constructed interest models for each of the identifier types (machine and person) based on topical categorization of the clicked URLs in the *model building* dataset. We represented interest models as a distribution across categories in the Open Directory Project (ODP, dmoz.org) topical hierarchy (as in [45]). This provides a consistent topical representation of page visits from which to build models. ODP categories can also be effective for reflecting topical differences in the search results for a query [3] or a search context [46]. Given the large number of pages in our log data, we used automatic classification techniques to assign an ODP category label to each page. Our classifier assigned one or more labels to the pages based on a lookup into the ODP hierarchy using a similar approach

[1] Although logs spanned two years, we only used six months of log data for this task since (i) it captures searchers' recent interests, and (ii) we wanted to retain sufficient data for the set of prediction experiments described in Section 6.3.

Table 2. ODP-category-based interest models from all historic activity from the machine identifier and for each individual (*A*, *B*, *C*) whose activity comprises the machine history. Highlighting denotes top category in each model (column).

ODP Category	*Machine*	*Individual searchers*		
		A	*B*	*C*
Sports/Football	0.25	**0.75**	–	–
Sports/Tennis	**0.33**	–	**0.70**	0.30
Shopping/Clothing	0.07	–	0.10	0.10
Arts/Movies	0.18	0.25	0.10	0.20
Society/Issues	0.17	–	0.10	**0.40**

to [32]. In this approach, classification begins with URLs in the ODP and incrementally prunes non-present URLs until a match is found or miss declared. Similar to [32], we excluded pages labeled with the *Regional* and *World* top-level ODP categories, since they are location-based and are typically uninformative for constructing models of searcher interests. Since a Web page can appear in multiple categories in ODP, there may be more than one category assigned for each page. For URLs that were not present via direct lookup into the ODP, we instead used the output of a content-based ODP classifier [3] applied by the Microsoft Bing search engine during indexing. This combined approach resulted in coverage of 88% of all distinct clicked URLs in our dataset. The remaining 12% of URLs were not indexed by the search engine. Focusing on topics rather than URLs allowed us to build models with better coverage and were more semantically meaningful than might have been possible for models constructed from URLs or Web domains alone.

Table 2 presents fictitious but representative interest models comprising ODP categories, based on patterns observed in our dataset. The search activity on this machine comprised the queries and clicks from three searchers: *A*, *B*, and *C*. The table presents the normalized distributions for ODP categories for each individual. The table shows that the category distributions can be quite different between individual searchers and the machine, as well as between searchers. For example, *Sports/Tennis* receives most weight in the machine model, but is only highest weighted for one searcher (*B*) and is not an interest of searcher *A*. Some topics receive broad interest, e.g., all searchers are interested in movies. Although this is only one example, it is representative of the types of differences that we observe in our data and provides motivation for targeting interest models to specific searchers. Such individualized models may more accurately capture searchers' interests than combining all search activity associated with the machine into a single model.

3.4 Applying Interest Models

In this study, our chosen application of the interest models constructed during model building is in predicting future interests of searchers. Future interest prediction is employed in a variety of scenarios, including advertising [30], the development of relevance models [10], and recommending future content [45]. Given each of the queries in the one-month *evaluation* dataset, we focus on predicting the assigned ODP topic of the clicked URL given the interest models as described in the previous section. We use the ODP category label (pl_1) with the highest weight as the model prediction. For example, returning to Table 2, highlighted in bold are the predicted ODP labels for all activity in the models associated with the machine identifier and with each of the three individuals.

Task-relevant search activity: In addition to varying the *identifier type* (machine or person), we also varied the mechanism used for matching evaluation queries with those in interest model construction (i.e., the *match type*). We either used all historic activity or on-

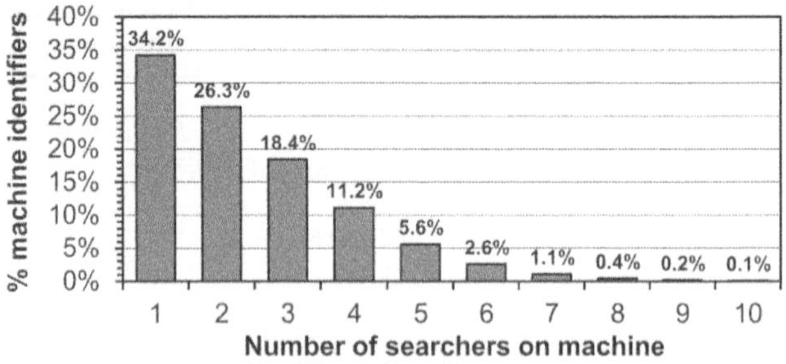

Figure 2. Fraction of machine identifiers in model building phase (6 months) with different numbers of searchers (k).

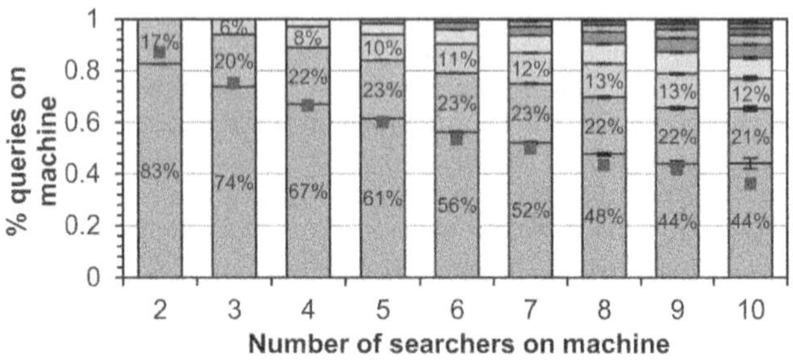

Figure 3. Distributions of queries per person across machines with different numbers of searchers (k) (±SEM).

task activity only. Given a query, we define the *on-task* historic activity as clicks associated with queries with at least one non-stopword term in common with the provided query. Such a query matching methodology has been used in personalization to build focused, relevant models of searchers' historic interests [5][38].

Prior to analyzing the predictive performance of the models constructed by grouping based on the four combinations of identifier type and match type, we characterize shared device searching.

4. SHARED DEVICE SEARCHING

For the task of characterizing shared device searching we analyze data in the *model building* set. We examine the prevalence of shared device searching, how queries are distributed within machines, and the impact of multi-person searching on the general diversity of topical interests captured in models constructed from these data.

4.1 Prevalence

Figure 2 shows the fraction of machine identifiers that comprised different numbers of searchers. To construct this plot, we use data from the *model building* dataset (i.e., with at least 100 search-result clicks from the machine identifier over the six-month duration of that set). The figure shows that a significant fraction (65.8%) of machine identifiers comprise the search queries of more than one person. To understand the sensitivity of these trends to the duration of the activity used in model building, we also computed the distribution over one and three months of historic activity. In that data, 44.3% and 56.7% of machine identifiers comprised the search activity of multiple people for one and three months respectively. A core assumption in personalization is that all historic activity is associated with one person (the individual consumer of the service). The prevalence of shared device searching underscores the need to attribute search activity during model building and query handling.

4.2 Distribution between Individuals

Another important question relates to the distribution of queries between the individuals using a machine. For shared machines with more than one searcher (i.e., $k \geq 2$), we ranked searchers by the fraction of clicks and computed the average fraction of the total

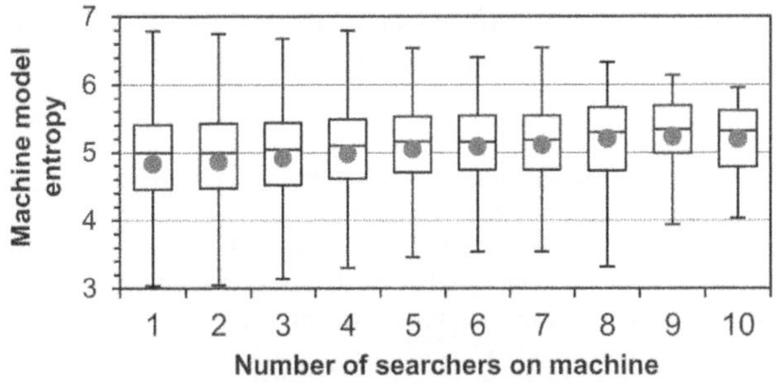

Figure 4. Box-and-whisker plot of machine model entropy for machines with diff. *k*. Mean is dot. Median is horizontal line.

query volume associated with each person. Figure 3 reports the distribution of queries per person across machines with different numbers of searchers. Each individual is allotted a region on the stacked bar (searcher #1 is first in blue, searcher #2 is second in orange, etc.). Percentage values are shown for the three most active searchers for each k. Other percentage values are excluded given space constraints and to simplify the graph. Also shown in the figure are error bars denoting the standard error of the mean (SEM). Given concerns about data skew, we also report the median percentages for the dominant searcher (squares in Figure 3), with similar trends.

The results show that for all values of $k \geq 2$ there is clearly a dominant searcher on each machine. For example, when k=2, there is usually an 80/20 division between click volumes on the machine between the primary and the secondary searcher. Although these are shared machines, the sharing is clearly not happening evenly. As the value of k increases, the query volume attributed to the dominant individual decreases in relation to the others (decreasing to around 40% at k=9). It is interesting to note that we only observe large changes in the search query volume associated with the primary/dominant searcher; the contributions of all other searchers on the machine remains largely unchanged and in some cases even increase with changes in k. The decrease in the contribution for the dominant searcher is also observed, even more markedly in fact, when we consider the median percentage of the query volume rather than the mean. These trends have implications for the effectiveness of ABP. At lower k, much of the activity associated with a machine identifier is already connected to an individual, meaning that ABP may be less effective. Also, since query volumes for non-dominant searchers are static or increase with k, there may be sufficient activity from at least some non-dominant searchers, irrespective of k, to build reliable interest models. We study the impact of k in the future interest prediction experiments reported later.

4.3 Diversity of Topical Interests

We were also interested in how k affected the breadth of resources accessed. Personalization performance would largely be unaffected by activity attribution, perhaps even hindered given sparser profiling data, if search intents were the same across different people. We computed the model entropies of the machine-based interest models, defined as $-\sum_{c \in C} p(c|m) \log(p(c|m))$, where c is a category drawn from the set of all ODP categories (C) assigned to result URLs clicked on machine m. Figure 4 presents a box-and-whisker plot for of this value across different k values. The horizontal segments inside the boxes represent the median, the top and bottom of the boxes denote the first and third quartiles, and the whiskers denote the maximum and minimum. The mean is denoted as a circle.

Figure 4 shows that there is an increasing trend in the topical diversity of interest models as the number of individuals associated with the machine increases (mean entropy = 4.83 at k=1 and 5.20 at k=10, Pearson's r = 0.981, $p < 0.001$). Interest models built based

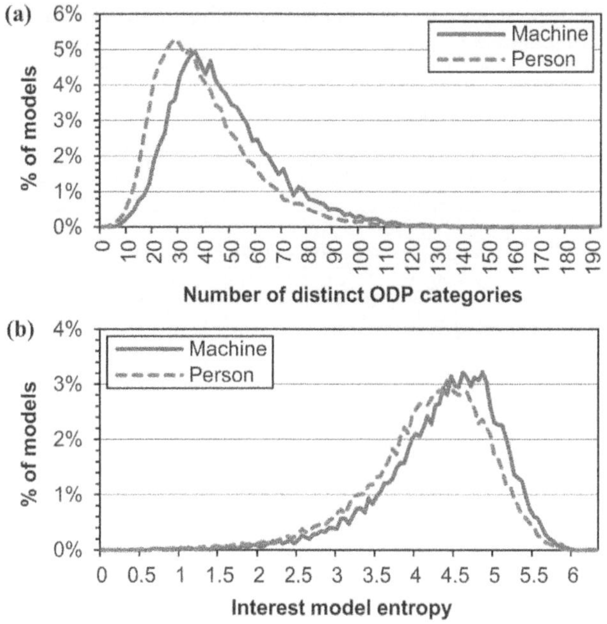

Figure 5. Comparison of person- and machine-based interest models in terms of: (a) number of distinct ODP categories comprising interest models, and (b) entropy of the models.

on historic data associated with the machine could therefore be more diverse and noisier if multiple people search on the machine.

Turning our attention to comparing the person- and machine-based models, we examine the number of unique ODP categories and the interest model entropy. Figure 5 shows the distributions for each model type and highlights the differences between interest models constructed from machines or individuals. Models built from machine activity are generally more diverse, both in terms of the number of ODP categories assigned to clicks and the entropy of the normalized distribution of ODP categories. The differences are apparent visually and statistically (independent measures t-tests, both $p < 0.001$). We now explore whether the model differences are meaningful for an important application: predicting future interests.

5. PREDICTING FUTURE INTERESTS

We now describe the prediction task, the method, and the results.

5.1 Prediction Task

The prediction task was to predict the ODP categories of the clicked results for queries in our evaluation set. For each query, a distribution of ODP categories was computed, at the same hierarchy level as used for model construction (see Section 5.4.1). The analysis is performed at the query level, with the clicks from the person issuing the query as ground truth to evaluate the model. To avoid skewing our metrics toward highly-active searchers, we filtered the evaluation dataset to a maximum of 10 queries with result clicks per person. The exact number of queries per person in the evaluation set varies based on additional filters described at the end of Section 5.3, including the requirement that result clicks be classifiable in ODP.

5.2 Methodology

Given our evaluation set of queries and clicks (Q) comprising one month of logs, we generate tuples comprising {timestamp, machine identifier, person identifier, query, {result clicks}} for each query (q) in Q. Given this set of test queries and associated result clicks, we then took the following steps:

For each *identifier type* in {*machine*, *person*}:

- For each *match type* in {*all*, *on-task*}:

Table 3. Avg. metric values and percentage change for each combination of *match type* and *identifier type*. Bold = best.

Match type	*Identifier type*	*Metric* P	R	F1	RR
All activity	*Machine*	0.179	**0.820**	0.294	0.307
	Person	**0.206**	0.781	**0.326**	**0.343**
	% Δ	+15.1	–4.8	+10.9	+11.6
On-task activity	*Machine*	0.625	**0.736**	0.676	0.695
	Person	**0.892**	0.732	**0.804**	**0.865**
	% Δ	+42.7	–0.5	+19.0	+24.5

- For each $q \in Q$:
  - If *identifier type* == *machine*:
    - If *match type* == *all*: Obtain all historic queries from the machine from the model building dataset.
    - Else if *match type* == *on-task*: Find all historic queries from the machine with ≥ 1 non-stopword terms in common with q in the model building dataset.
  - Else if *identifier type* == *person*:
    - If *match type* == *all*: Obtain all historic queries from the searcher from the model building dataset.
    - Else if *match type* == *on-task*: Find all historic queries from the searcher with ≥ 1 non-stopword terms in common with q in the model building dataset.
  - Obtain the clicked results for each of the queries.
  - Assign ODP categories to the clicked results using the methods described in Section 3.3.
  - Build an interest model (u) comprising the normalized distribution of ODP categories from the assignment.
  - Select top-weighted predicted label in u, denoted pl_1.
  - Compute the effectiveness of the method in relation to the ground truth (the normalized distribution of ODP categories across the URLs selected by the searcher).
- Average metric values for matchtype across all $q \in Q$ to compute the overall performance metrics for each of the four combinations of *identifier type* and *match type*.

Since we focus on shared device usage, we study devices with $k \geq 2$ in the rest of our analysis. This is a reasonable assumption practically. ABP will only apply when $k \geq 2$ and prior work has shown that shared device searching can be predicted with high accuracy (86%) given access to long-term search activity on a machine [47].

5.3 Metrics

We computed a number of metrics to assess the nature of the interest models that were created and their performance in predicting future activity in the form of a normalized distribution over ODP categories of the results that were accessed. Specifically, the metrics were associated with prediction correctness (i.e., the match between the predicted and actual category label(s)), measured as:

Precision (*P*): Precision was computed based on whether the top predicted label pl_1 equaled the actual label l_1 (1 or 0). For pages with multiple categories or queries with multiple clicks, a match was determined if pl_1 equaled *any* of the true categories. This strategy was adopted for the computation of the other metrics described in this section. Precision was averaged over all queries in the evaluation set to compute the final average precision value.

Recall (*R*): Recall is 1 or 0 depending on whether l_1 appears in the model, i.e., $\{pl_1, \ldots, pl_p\}$, where the recall depth (p) is computed based on the number of predicted categories in the model or 10 (the median number of predicted categories across all queries and interest models), whichever is smaller. Limiting the depth of p is important in ensuring that obtaining a recall of 1 is a non-trivial task.

F1 score: This is the harmonic mean of P and R (i.e., $2 \times (P \times R) / (P + R)$). F1 has been used in a range of similar settings including the KDD Cup [22], as well as in related studies on the efficacy of models to predict future interests in search and browsing [45][46].

Reciprocal rank (*RR*): This is a commonly-used measure in Web search evaluation tasks, e.g., [12]. To compute this measure, the l_1 for the actual category label was compared progressively down the ranked list of category label predictions. If l_1 matched pl_i, the score assigned was the reciprocal of the prediction rank position $1/i$, and 0 otherwise. This was averaged across all queries evaluation dataset to compute the mean reciprocal rank (MRR) score.

Many of these metrics have been used previously in the assessment of search interest models [45]. They are computed for queries in the evaluation set for which we have: (1) clicks that can be classified in ODP, (2) a machine-based interest model from the search history, and (3) a person-based interest model from the search history. For the on-task variant, for (2) and (3) there needed to be at least one matching query in the search history from which to create interest models. There were a total of 442,690 queries that met all of these criteria for the all-activity analysis and 135,075 queries for the on-task portion of the analysis. The queries in both sets were used to evaluate predictive performance, although the on-task set is used for more analysis since it allows us to control for task effects, which have been shown to significantly affect search behavior [15].

5.4 Results: Person vs. Machine Models

We computed the range of metrics described in the previous section to compare the person and machine models. Table 3 reports the average metric scores for this comparison, for models built from all activity and on-task activity. The on-task models more accurately reflect the state-of-the-art in personalization [5][42]. The results reported suggest that there is a large benefit from ABP. We observe significant gains in precision, F1, and RR for person-based models over machine-based models of 11-15% for all activity and 19-43% for on-task search activity (two-way multivariate analysis of variance (MANOVA) over the four metrics, with *match type* and *identifier type* as factors: $F(4{,}2311056) = 10.22$, $p < 0.001$). All paired differences between machine and person were significant at $p < 0.001$ using Tukey post-hoc tests, with the exception of the recall comparison for on-task. Overall, the gain is higher from on-task activity. This reflects interests related to the current task, resulting in more focused interest models and better quality predictions. Recall is slightly higher for machine-based models for both match types, likely because these models are a superset of person-based models. Given the similar trends in our findings with the different metrics, we elect to focus on F1 for the remainder of our analysis. Focusing on F1 is useful since it considers both precision and recall, which are both important depending on the application.

5.4.1 *Handling Near Misses*

Since we rely on the structure of the ODP for our models, the metrics are sensitive to the match granularity. In particular, the metrics presented thus far rely on matching the full ODP labels in the interest models with the full label in the ground truth. We penalize the interest models for *any* mismatch between the predicted and actual label. However, small differences in estimates of search interests may be unimportant to search and recommendation systems. For example, interests represented by the ODP category *Sports/Football/NFL* could also be represented by *Sports/Football* with only a slight loss in precision. Using the matching approach described thus far, this would be regarded as a total miss, whereas it is actually a *near* miss. An amelioration strategy involves backing-off on all labels in the ground truth and the predictions to a specified level. One-level back-off means convert all ODP category labels to their

Table 4. Percentage change in F1-score at different hierarchy levels for person-based versus machine-based models (e.g., 1 = top level in ODP). Paired *t*-tests: ** $p < 0.001$, *** $p < 0.0001$.

ODP hierarchy level	*Match type*	
	All activity	*On-task activity*
1	+6.71%**	+10.25%***
2	+8.02%***	+13.48%***
3	+9.56%***	+17.87%***
All	+10.92%***	+19.02%***

top level (e.g., *Sports*), and two-level back-off means convert all labels to their top two levels (e.g., *Sports/Football*).

To understand the impact of such near misses on our experimental findings, we analyzed the percentage gain in F1 over the machine-based models from restricting the ODP category labels in both model building and evaluation to the top one, two, or three levels in the ODP hierarchy. The results are shown in Table 4. The table show that the gains still persist across all levels of category back-off, but the gains reduce in magnitude as we move up the hierarchy. As noted in the table, all differences remain significantly different (at $p < 0.001$) at all levels of back-off. The reduction in performance with higher ODP levels is interesting, and suggests that nuances in searchers' topical interests are important. These subtleties may be lost by backing off to higher levels in the hierarchy. This is also evident in Table 2, where the category *Sports* is insufficient to distinguish the preferences of person A for football from those of persons B and C, who favor tennis. For this reason, we utilize all hierarchy levels for the experiments in the remainder of the paper.

The results presented in this section are promising. They show that ABP can improve the performance of search personalization. We hypothesized that there may be other characteristics of the models and queries that may contribute to the performance of ABP.

6. IMPACT OF ADDITIONAL FACTORS

We now present additional analysis of the performance of the interest models for predicting future interests, conditioned on characteristics of the machine-based models and queries. To control for task effects, which influences behavior and hence experimental outcomes, we focus on the on-task variant of the models. We report comparative performance against the machine-based baseline, the state-of-the-art in model construction for personalization.

6.1 Effect of Model Properties

We study the effect of model properties on the performance of the person-based models. We focus on three aspects: (1) the entropy of the machine models, (2) the relative size of the person-based models as a fraction of the machine-based models, and (3) the number of searchers on the machine. We consider each property in turn.

6.1.1 Model Entropy

We were interested in whether there were any effects from the entropy of the machine models (defined in Section 4.3) on the relative performance of ABP. We hypothesized that if machine-based interests were diverse, then ABP would improve performance. We split machine entropy values into three equally-sized buckets (high, medium, low) and computed the average percentage gain in performance for each of the entropy groups. The results are reported in Figure 6a. The performance across all queries is shown with a dotted line in the figure. Error bars denote standard error of the mean (SEM). Given the large sample sizes, the error bars in this and other figures in this section are frequently small. The results show clear differences in the predictive performance as a function of the entropy of the machine model (one-way ANOVA, $F(2{,}135072)$ =

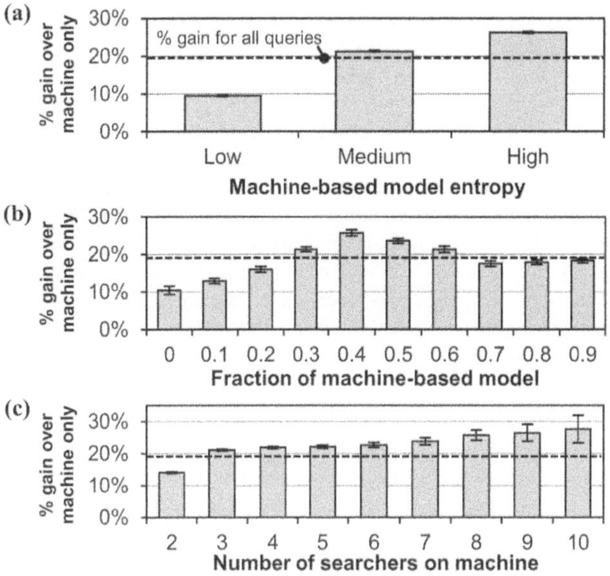

Figure 6. Effect of *model properties* on relative performance of machine-based vs. person-based models (±SEM). Effect of: (a) machine model entropy, (b) fraction of machine model, and (c) number of searchers. Dotted line denotes the predictive performance across all queries (i.e., % gain: 19.02).

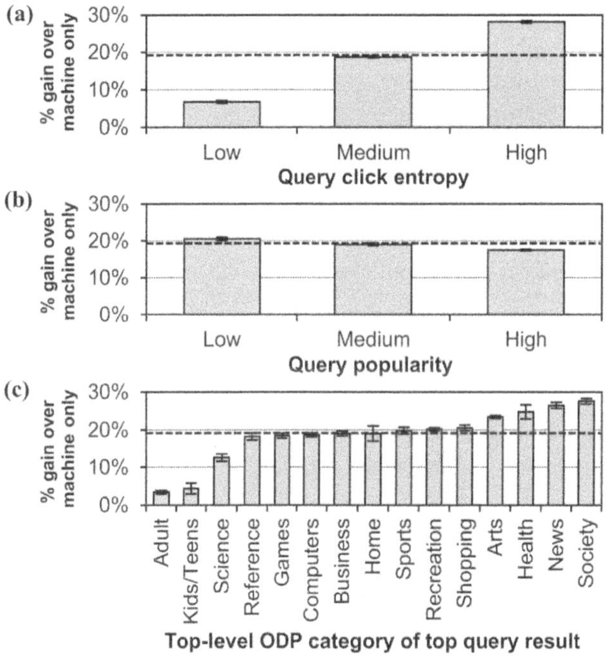

Figure 7. Impact of *query properties* on relative performance of machine- vs. person-based models (±SEM). Effect of: (a) query click entropy, (b) query popularity, (c) ODP category. Dotted line denotes the gain across all queries (i.e., 19.02%).

8.53, $p < 0.001$). When the entropy is high, it is more likely that multiple searchers' interests are reflected in the machine activity (as seen in Figure 4), and applying ABP will be more beneficial.

6.1.2 Relative Model Size

Another factor that may contribute to the relative differences in the performance of the person-based models is the relative model size. That is, the fraction of the number of clicks used to compute the person-based models compared to the total number of clicks for the machine models. Since we focus on machines with multiple searchers and all searchers contribute clicks, this fraction is always in the range (0,1). We bucket these fractions by rounding down to the nearest decile and compute the percentage gain over the machine-based models for each fraction. Figure 6b reports the percentage gain over the machine-based models for each of {0.0,...,0.9}. There are clear differences in the gains depending on the fraction of machine-based model that the person occupies ($F(9, 135072) = 3.55$, $p < 0.001$). The gains from ABP are most apparent when there is no highly dominant searcher (in the range 0.4-0.6). In this region there may be sufficient data on each searcher's interests—which may not be the case when there is a highly-dominant searcher and one or more non-dominant counterparts with less data. The performance at 0.8 or above is similar to the baseline, likely because the machine and person models are more similar at high fractions.

6.1.3 Number of Searchers

Also related to the relative model size is the number of searchers on the machine, and in turn the number of searchers represented in the interest model. We speculated that more searchers lead to noisier and more diverse machine models, and greater benefit from ABP. To estimate the impact of the number of searchers, we computed the percentage gain in prediction performance of the person-based model across the range of different numbers of searchers on the machine, from 2-10. Figure 6c visualizes the performance across this range. The findings show an increase of predictive performance with a growth in the number of searchers (Pearson's $r = 0.913$, $p < 0.01$). The more searchers there are on the machine, the more likely the interests represented in the machine-based models are to be diverse, and the greater the benefit obtained from ABP.

6.2 Effect of Query Properties

In addition to properties of the interest models, we also examined the effect of query properties, namely: (1) click entropy, (2) popularity, and (3) topic. We consider each of these properties in turn.

6.2.1 Click Entropy

We examine the predictive performance of the machine and person models by considering the click entropy for the query. Click entropy measures the diversity in the clicks for the query [14]. To compute that statistic for the queries in our dataset, we used a separate set of query-click logs from the Microsoft Bing Web search engine, collected over a time period of two years overlapping fully the timeframe from the comScore logs. We did this since the search engine logs were much larger, enabling more reliable computations of click entropy and better query coverage than if we had used comScore logs alone. Indeed, 89% of the queries in our evaluation set appeared in the Bing logs, while only 65% appeared in comScore. Click entropy (CE) was divided into three buckets: (1) *high* ($CE \geq 2$), (2) *medium* ($1 \leq CE < 2$), and (3) *low* ($CE < 1$), based on the click entropy thresholds used in a prior personalization study [40]. The average percentage gains over the machine-based models for each of the three query-click entropy buckets are shown in Figure 7a. There are differences in click prediction performance between the three buckets (higher entropy is associated with higher gains for the person-based models, $F(2,120079) = 9.21$, $p < 0.001$). Higher click entropy queries represent more diverse interests are more amenable to personalization [40]. For these high CE queries, ABP is over 20% more effective than the machine-based baseline.

6.2.2 Popularity

To obtain information about query popularity, we used the same set of queries from the Bing search engine used in the calculation of click entropy. The queries in this dataset were grouped into three popularity buckets: (1) *low popularity-queries* that occur fewer than 10 times, (2) *medium popularity-queries* that occur 10-10,000 times, and (3) *high popularity-queries* that occur more than 10,000 times. The average percentage gains over the machine-based models for each of the three query popularity buckets are shown in Figure 7b. Although there are significant differences between the groups ($F(2, 120079) = 4.62$, $p = 0.01$), perhaps expected given the sample size), the effect size was small (partial eta squared (η^2) = 0.01) suggesting that differences are less meaningful. One explanation is the bucketing criteria (although our experiments with variations in the thresholds did not dramatically affect the results), or that raw popularity is not a good discriminator of queries for which person-based models may help (e.g., there may still be individual preferences for search results even within popular queries [42]).

6.2.3 Topic

As a final aspect of the analysis of query properties, we also examined the effect of the query topic on the performance of person-based models vs. machine-based models. For our analysis, the topic of the query was taken from the ODP category assigned to the top result returned for that query by the search engine whose logs were used to obtain entropy and popularity estimates. To simplify the analysis, we focus on the 15 top-level categories (again *World* and *Regional* were removed). Figure 7c shows the percentage gain for each of the topics. The topics are ordered on the x-axis in ascending order of gain with respect to the machine-based model. We see that although performance for many of topics was similar to the baseline, there were some topics that performed much better or worse than the machine-based baseline ($F(14,1004008) = 3.20$, $p < 0.001$). In the cases where the benefit was lowest (*Adult* and *Kids & Teens*) it is likely that only a subset of the household is interested in that content, so the machine-based approach is sufficient. For topics where the gain from ABP was highest (*News* and *Society*), there may be more general interest across searchers, and also more diversity in searcher preferences.

Although we examined the properties separately, there are likely to be *interactions* between these and other factors that influence the effectiveness of ABP. One way to understand this is to learn and inspect a classifier to predict when to use ABP on a per-query basis.

6.3 Applying Model and Query Properties

We used a separate set of 132,887 evaluation queries from 2,549 people (1,000 machines) taken from one month of comScore logs. We constructed on-task interest models from the six months prior (as before). These sets did not overlap in machines or time with the sets used in Sections 4 and 5. We featurized each model and query property described in the previous two subsections, namely:

- *MachineModelEntropy*: Entropy of the interest model constructed from activity on the current machine.
- *RelativeModelSize*: Fraction of machine interest model occupied by classified historic clicks from the current searcher.
- *NumberOfSearchers*: Number of distinct searchers whose activity is used in building the machine-based interest model.
- *QueryClickEntropy*: Click entropy for the query, computed based on the held-out Bing search log data (see Section 6.2.1).
- *QueryPopularity*: Popularity of the query, computed based on the number of instances in the same held-out search log.
- *QueryTopic*: Top-level ODP category of the top result for the query from the same search engine for the held-out data.

In practice, these features could be computed automatically for the query. Individual interest models for each searcher and the number of searchers can already be estimated from search histories [47].

For each of the queries in the 1000-machine dataset, we compared the F1 score of predictions using the machine- and person-based models. The prediction task is defined as predicting when to apply

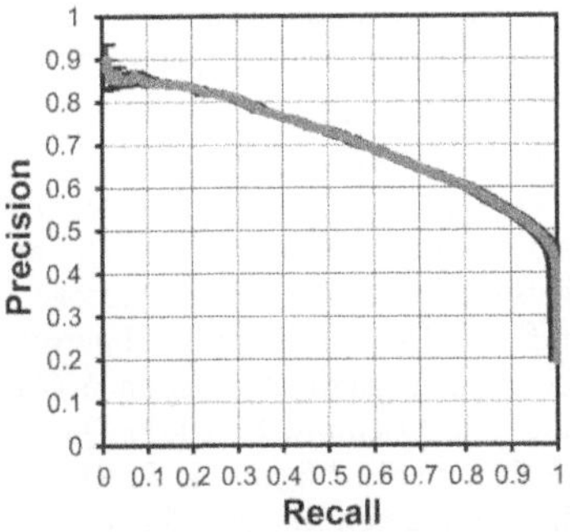

Figure 8. Precision-recall curve for the prediction of when to selectively apply attribution-based personalization. Values in the curve are averaged across ten folds for one run (±SEM).

ABP (vs. sticking with the machine-based model). In the dataset used for training (six months) and testing (one month), if the prediction based on the person-based model was more accurate (higher F1), then that was a positive example; if the prediction based on the machine-based model was more accurate, then it constituted a negative. Ties were treated as negative examples since in practice this would mean that ABP would not be applied by the search engine.

We used the featurized properties and these positive and negative labels to learn a binary classifier to determine when to apply ABP on a per-query basis. We applied a Multiple Additive Regression Trees (MART) [17] classifier to perform the prediction. MART uses gradient tree boosting methods for regression and classification. Advantages of MART include model interpretability (e.g., a ranked list of features is generated), facility for rapid training and testing, and robustness against noisy labels and missing values.

We employed ten-fold cross validation, stratified on the person identifier, so that queries from a person were either in train or test, but not both at the same time. We ran the experiment 100 times, each with a random assignment of searchers to folds, and compute the average F1 across all 100 runs. The findings of our experiments show that we can predict when to apply ABP with good accuracy. The average accuracy of the classifier (0.9179) exceeds the marginal baseline (0.7912) of always predicting the application of the machine-based interest models (the dominant class since in only 20.88% of queries ABP performs best; in 8.78% of queries the machine-based interest models perform best, and in the remaining 70.34% of queries the performance is tied). The gains over the marginal model are significant using a paired t-test ($t(999) = 4.73$, $p < 0.001$). Figure 8 shows the precision-recall curve generated by the model averaged across 10 folds for one experimental run. Examining the model in more detail, the most important features ranked based on their evidential weight are *MachineModelEntropy* (max), *RelativeModelSize* (0.699 of max), and *QueryTopic* (0.441 of max). The breadth of the topical interests on the machine, the contribution of the individual to the overall machine activity using in interest model construction, and the search topic of the query most affects the reliability of predictions about when to apply ABP.

While the strong classification performance is welcome, the test of true utility lies whether this will lead to gains in the accuracy of future interest prediction when the classifier is applied. To test this, we re-ran the prediction experiment described in Section 5, using the output of our classifier to determine whether we should apply ABP for each query. The results are reported in Table 5. The table shows clear gains from selective application over both models for all activity and on-task activity (all gains significant, $p < 0.001$). To help frame the magnitude of the observed gains, Table 5 also reports the performance of an oracle model (upper bound) that selects the best model source (machine or person) for each query in the evaluation set based on F1. We see that applying our classifier leads to ABP performance that is 88-96% of the oracle, a significant increase over always applying the person-based model and demonstrating the benefits of intelligently applying ABP for each query.

Table 5. Percentage change in F1 for selectively applying ABP models vs. always applying the machine-based model (all diffs sig. at $p < 0.001$, using paired t-tests).

Attribution Method	***Match type*** *All activity*	*On-task activity*
Always ABP	+10.90%	+19.02%
Learned	+14.13%	+23.00%
Oracle	+18.64%	+26.11%

7. DISCUSSION AND IMPLICATIONS

Shared searching on devices is common. Our oracle study, with perfect knowledge of the identifier (machines and people) to which actions were attributed, demonstrated clear utility from ABP. Conditioning on query and interest model properties showed that there are particular attributes that can help determine when to apply ABP for each query. We used the insights from our analysis to learn a model to accurately predict this type, and from its application, strong gains in personalization were realized. The effectiveness of ABP has significant implications for personalization, and heralds a new frontier for research in individualizing the search experience.

Before proceeding, we should discuss some limitations of the work as presented. This is a log-based analysis, meaning that we had limited insight into the intentions and interests of the searchers whose activity was examined. Interest prediction has been the focus of this and previous studies [45][46], but other applications such as re-ranking need to be studied (but could not be studied here given the lack of results lists in our logs). Although our study demonstrated the potential of attribution-based personalization, we only explored one implementation (via distributions of ODP categories). Experiments with other representations (e.g., page URLs or domains) and sources (e.g., query text or browsing behavior) are also needed. Finally, our focus is on long-term personalization and for queries with non-empty historic models for machine and person (i.e., only queries with some related history, a limitation of personalization generally [5]). Prior work has also employed within-session activity [8][44]. However, within session usage by multiple individuals is much less common: 97% of the search sessions in our logs are from one person. The remaining 3% are related to noise in using an inactivity timeout (30 mins, as in [46]) to demarcate search sessions.

Performing this oracle study required ground truth with both person and machine identifiers. This was needed to measure the value of ABP independent of the specific attribution method. Previous work has shown that the accurate automatic attribution to individuals is quite feasible [47]. We need to understand how ABP performance changes with such automated attribution. In addition, self-identification approaches (e.g., sign-in) need to be explored in this context, as do trends toward closer associations between people and their devices, which affects the prevalence of shared device usage.

8. CONCLUSIONS

We introduced attribution-based personalization and performed an oracle study to quantify the potential benefit of using it for future interest prediction. We show that there are significant opportunities to enhance search personalization via models tailored to individuals. We observe an increased accuracy in future interest predictions (11-19% in F1-score, depending on the match type) by applying this approach. The gains vary when we study particular properties of the interest models and the queries. We also show that further gains are obtainable by selectively applying ABP. Our findings show that ABP has strong potential, and we hope that they will inspire future work in this area. Our own future work will explore the application of automated attribution methods (building on [47]) to develop individualized interest models and combine these methods with our models to selectively apply ABP. Overall, it is clear that ABP could facilitate the delivery of more personalized results and recommendations to those searching on shared devices.

REFERENCES

[1] Agichtein, E., Brill, E., and Dumais, S. (2006). Improving web search ranking by incorporating user behavior information. *SIGIR*, 19–26.

[2] Amari, S.I., Cichocki, A., and Yang, H.H. (1996). A new learning algorithm for blind signal separation. *NIPS*, 757–763.

[3] Bennett, P., Svore, K., and Dumais, S. (2010). Classification-enhanced ranking. *WWW*, 111–120.

[4] Bennett, P.N. *et al.* (2011). Inferring and using location metadata to personalize web search. *SIGIR*, 135–144.

[5] Bennett, P.N. *et al.* (2012). Modeling the impact of short and long-term behavior on search personalization. *SIGIR*, 185–194.

[6] Bilenko, M. and Richardson, M. (2011). Predictive client-side models for personalized advertising. *SIGKDD*, 413–421.

[7] Bilenko, M. and White, R.W. (2008). Mining the search trails of surfing crowds: Identifying relevant websites from user activity. *WWW*, 51–60.

[8] Cao, H. *et al.* (2009). Context-aware query classification. *SIGIR*, 3–10.

[9] Cardoso, J.F. (1998). Blind signal separation: Statistical principles. *IEEE*, 86(10): 2009–2025.

[10] Chapelle, O. and Zhang, Y. (2009). A dynamic bayesian network click model for web search ranking. *WWW*, 1–10.

[11] Chirita, P. *et al.* (2005). Using ODP metadata to personalize search. *SIGIR*, 178–185.

[12] Chowdhury, A. and Soboroff, I. (2002). Automatic evaluation of World Wide Web search services. *SIGIR*, 421–422.

[13] Dasgupta, A. *et al.* (2012). Overcoming browser cookie churn with clustering. *WSDM*, 83–92.

[14] Dou, Z., Song, R., and Wen, J.R. (2007). A large-scale evaluation and analysis of personalized search strategies. *WWW*, 581–590.

[15] Downey, D., Dumais, S., Liebling, D., and Horvitz, E. (2008). Understanding the relationship between searchers' queries and information goals. *CIKM*, 449–458.

[16] Fawcett, T. and Provost, F. (1997). Adaptive fraud detection. *Data Mining and Knowledge Discovery*, 1(3): 291–316.

[17] Friedman, J.H., Hastie, T., and Tibshirani, R. (1998). Additive logistic regression: a statistical view of boosting. Technical Report, Department of Statistics, Stanford University.

[18] Fulgoni, G.M. (2005). The "Professional Respondent" Problem in Online Survey Panels Today. Slides online at: http://www.sigmavalidation.com/tips/05_06_02_Online_Survey_Panels.ppt (Downloaded on May 15, 2015).

[19] Gauch, S., Chaffee, J. and Pretschner, A. (2003). Ontology-based interest models for search and browsing. *WIAS*, 219.

[20] Ieong, S., Mishra, N., Sadikov, E., and Zhang, L. (2012). Domain bias in web search. *WSDM*, 413–422.

[21] Joachims, T. (2002). Optimizing search engines using click-through data. *KDD*, 133–142.

[22] Li, Y., Zheng, Z., and Dai, H.K. (2005). KDD CUP-2005 report: facing a great challenge. *SIGKDD Expl.*, 7(2): 91–99.

[23] Ma, Z., Pant, G., and Sheng, O. (2007). Interest-based personalized search. *ACM TOIS*, 25(1): 5.

[24] Matthijs, N. and Radlinski, F. (2011). Personalizing web search using long term browsing history. *WSDM*, 25–34.

[25] Pitkow, J. *et al.* (2002). Personalized search. *CACM*, 45(9).

[26] Piwowarski, B. and Zaragoza, H. (2007). Predictive user click models based on click-through history. *CIKM*, 175–182

[27] Radlinski, F. and Dumais, S. (2006). Improving personalized web search using result diversification. *SIGIR*, 691–692.

[28] Radlinski, F. and Joachims, T. (2005). Query chains: Learning to rank from implicit feedback. *KDD*, 239–248.

[29] Radlinski, F., Szummer, M., and Craswell, N. (2010). Inferring query intent from reformulations and clicks. *WWW*, 1171–1172.

[30] Richardson, M., Dominowska, E., and Ragno, R. (2007). Predicting clicks: Estimating the click-through rate for new ads. *WWW*, 521–530.

[31] Schein, A.I. *et al.* (2002). Methods and metrics for cold-start recommendations. *SIGIR*, 253–260.

[32] Shen, X., Dumais, S.T., and Horvitz, E. (2005). Analysis of topic dynamics in web search. *WWW*, 1102–1103.

[33] Shen, X., Tan, B., and Zhai, C.X. (2005). Implicit user modeling for personalized search. *CIKM*, 824–831

[34] Singla, A. *et al.* (2014). Enhancing personalization via activity attribution. *SIGIR*, 1063–1066.

[35] Sontag, D. *et al.* (2012). Probabilistic models for personalizing web search. *WSDM*, 433–442.

[36] Speretta, M. and Gauch, S. (2005). Personalizing search based on user search histories. *WI*, 622–628.

[37] Sugiyama, K., Hatano, K., and Yoshikawa, M. (2004). Adaptive web search based on interest model constructed without any effort from users. *WWW*, 675–684.

[38] Tan, B., Shen, X., and Zhai, C. (2006). Mining long-term search history to improve search accuracy. *KDD*, 718–723.

[39] Teevan, J., Dumais, S.T., and Horvitz, E. (2005). Personalizing search via automated analysis of interests and activities. *SIGIR*, 449–456.

[40] Teevan, J., Dumais, S.T., and Liebling, D.J. (2008). To personalize or not to personalize: Modeling queries with variation in user intent. *SIGIR*, 163–170.

[41] Teevan, J., Dumais, S.T., and Horvitz, E. (2010). Potential for personalization. *TOCHI*, 17(1): 4.

[42] Teevan, J., Liebling, D.J., and Ravichandran, G.G. (2011). Understanding and predicting personal navigation. *WSDM*, 85–94.

[43] Teevan, J., Morris, M.R., and Bush, S. (2009). Discovering and using groups to improve personalized search. *WSDM*, 15–24.

[44] Ustinovskiy, Y. and Serdyukov, P. (2013). Personalization of web-search using short-term browsing context. *CIKM*, 1979–1988.

[45] White, R.W., Bailey, P., and He, L. (2009). Predicting user interests from contextual information. *SIGIR*, 363–370.

[46] White, R.W., Bennett, P.N., and Dumais, S.T. (2010). Predicting short-term interests using activity-based search context. *CIKM*, 1009–1018.

[47] White, R.W. *et al.* (2014). From devices to people: Attribution of search activity in multi-user settings. *WWW*, 431–442.

[48] White, R.W. *et al.* (2013). Enhancing personalized search by mining and modeling task behavior. *WWW*, 1411–1420.

[49] Xiang, B. *et al.* (2010). Context-aware ranking in web search. *SIGIR*, 451–458.

[50] Yan, J., Chu, W., and White, R.W. (2014). Cohort modeling for enhanced personalized search. *SIGIR*, 505–514.

Leveraging User Reviews to Improve Accuracy for Mobile App Retrieval

Dae Hoon Park
Department of Computer Science
University of Illinois at Urbana-Champaign
Urbana, IL 61801, USA
dpark34@illinois.edu

Mengwen Liu
College of Computing and Informatics
Drexel University
Philadelphia, PA 19104, USA
ml943@drexel.edu

ChengXiang Zhai
Department of Computer Science
University of Illinois at Urbana-Champaign
Urbana, IL 61801, USA
czhai@cs.illinois.edu

Haohong Wang
TCL Research America
2870 Zanker Road
San Jose, CA 95134, USA
haohong.wang@tcl.com

ABSTRACT

Smartphones and tablets with their apps pervaded our everyday life, leading to a new demand for search tools to help users find the right apps to satisfy their immediate needs. While there are a few commercial mobile app search engines available, the new task of mobile app retrieval has not yet been rigorously studied. Indeed, there does not yet exist a test collection for quantitatively evaluating this new retrieval task. In this paper, we first study the effectiveness of the state-of-the-art retrieval models for the app retrieval task using a new app retrieval test data we created. We then propose and study a novel approach that generates a new representation for each app. Our key idea is to leverage user reviews to find out important features of apps and bridge vocabulary gap between app developers and users. Specifically, we jointly model app descriptions and user reviews using topic model in order to generate app representations while excluding noise in reviews. Experiment results indicate that the proposed approach is effective and outperforms the state-of-the-art retrieval models for app retrieval.

Categories and Subject Descriptors

H.3.3 [**Information Storage and Retrieval**]: Information Search and Retrieval—*Retrieval models*

General Terms

Algorithms, Design

1. INTRODUCTION

Nowadays, mobile apps occupy a large share of our everyday life. According to a recent analysis by Flurry, average American consumers spend about three hours (177 minutes) per day on mobile devices,[1] which is more than the average time spent on TVs (168 minutes). An analysis in 2013 shows that 80% of the time spent on mobile devices is inside apps and 20% is spent on the mobile web.[2] The time spent on the mobile web remained flat in 2014 while the time spent inside apps increased. While consumers spend much of their time inside apps, they constantly download new mobile apps.[3] This means that the role of app search and recommendation system remains important.

Meanwhile, the number of mobile apps in app store is explosively increasing so that search function in app store becomes essential. As of July 2014, there are about 1.3 million apps in Google Play app store and 1.2 million apps in Apple App Store.[4] The myriad apps made consumers extremely hard to find apps without search or recommendation functions. For example, Google Play does not list all of the apps. Instead, it lists only recommended or popular apps because finding an app through the long list does not make sense any more. Moreover, in an app developer's view, new or unpopular apps are barely discovered by consumers if they are not recommended by the app stores. Therefore, app search engine is definitely essential for both consumers and developers.

Thus, it is our goal to find apps based on a query given by a user. Specifically, given a user query that describes an aspect of an app, the desired search result would show a ranked list of apps where higher ranked apps are more likely to have the described aspect. For example, for a query "book a flight", we expect the search result to include apps such as "Expedia Hotels & Flights" and "Orbitz – Flights, Hotels, Cars" in high ranks since these apps meet the user's need quite well. However, if an app description is not written well, *e.g.*, too short or hardly useful, the retrieval system would not rank the app high even though the app is actually relevant to a query. In addition, app descriptions are written by app developers while search queries are made by

SIGIR'15, August 09 - 13, 2015, Santiago, Chile.

ACM 978-1-4503-3621-5/15/08 ...$15.00.
DOI: http://dx.doi.org/10.1145/2766462.2767759 .

[1]http://www.flurry.com/blog/flurry-insights/mobile-television-we-interrupt-broadcast-again
[2]http://www.flurry.com/bid/95723/Flurry-Five-Year-Report-It-s-an-App-World-The-Web-Just-Lives-in-It
[3]http://www.flurry.com/blog/flurry-insights/app-install-addiction-shows-no-signs-stopping
[4]http://www.statista.com/statistics/276623/number-of-apps-available-in-leading-app-stores/

users, and this may result in vocabulary gap between them. Therefore, to improve accuracy for mobile app retrieval, we propose to leverage user reviews, which provide more information about an app in a user's vocabulary.

As an interesting new retrieval task, app retrieval has not yet been rigorously studied in the literature. Indeed, no test collection has ever been created yet for quantitatively evaluating this task. To address this problem, we conduct the first systematic study of effectiveness of both existing retrieval models and new retrieval models for this task, and we create the very first test collection for evaluating this new retrieval problem.

This paper makes the following contributions:

1. We introduce and study a novel research problem of mobile app retrieval leveraging user reviews. To the best of our knowledge, this is the first effort in this area, and no other research work studied the same problem as ours.

2. We propose a novel probabilistic topic model that jointly models user reviews and unstructured product information (product description) in order to obtain representation of apps. The model captures topics jointly from reviews and descriptions so that the topics reflect vocabulary of both users (user reviews) and developers (app descriptions). The model is unsupervised and general, so it can be applied to other domains where there are unstructured text about an entity and an associated set of unstructured text.

3. We create a new data set for evaluating the task and conduct experiments to show that the proposed method outperforms baseline approaches for mobile app retrieval. The mobile app data set is crawled from a major app store, Google Play. We let domain experts generate queries based on android forums. Then, we collect query relevance data via crowdsourcing service. The test collection is available at `http://timan.cs.uiuc.edu/downloads.html`. As far as we know, no previous research for mobile app retrieval has performed quantitative evaluations.

2. RELATED WORK

Recommendation systems are highly related to retrieval systems in that they rank objects to fulfill needs of users, and the recommendation systems are surveyed well in [10]. App recommendation systems have been studied by a few researchers [32, 30]. For example, Lin *et al.* [15] addressed cold start problem in app recommendation system by leveraging social network data. However, retrieval systems are different from recommendation systems mainly because a user explicitly expresses his or her needs in retrieval systems while the recommendation systems suggest items based on user profile without asking for the user's needs. Recommendation systems may be more convenient for users since a user does not have to input his or her needs, but they are likely to be less accurate than retrieval systems since they barely know the user's current needs. In addition, recommendation systems encounter a cold start problem when a user does not have his or her profile yet or when the system does not have enough transaction data yet. On the other hand, retrieval systems do not require such data, so there is no cold start problem for them.

There have been extensive studies for XML retrieval, which is related to our work since app data consist of elements such as app descriptions and user reviews. Some of the XML retrieval studies also support simple keyword queries [16] while some other XML retrieval studies support only structured queries [26]. However, our goal is to augment app descriptions with user reviews to obtain a better representation for an app, while XML retrieval focuses more on document structure in general. In addition, while retrieval unit in our task is clearly defined as a mobile app, in XML retrieval, every element is a retrievable unit [12], which makes XML retrieval different from our task.

Entity ranking and entity search is closely related to our problem [4]. While entity ranking usually focuses on exploiting rich structures [24, 19], Ganesan and Zhai [8] studied opinion-based entity ranking leveraging review text. In their work, a query is structured with preferences on different aspects of an entity. The known-type entities are then ranked based on aspect-based sentiment from user reviews, while we rank unknown-type apps based solely on query relevance. Product search is highly related to our work. Duan *et al.* [5] leveraged product specifications and user reviews to improve performance on keyword search in product database. However, while products usually have such structured specifications that characterize products, mobile apps usually have no structured specifications since there is no standardized features of apps, which makes the problem harder. Meanwhile, there has been some efforts to build commercial app search engines such as [3]. However, mobile app retrieval problem has not yet been studied rigorously with systematic experiments.

3. PROBLEM DEFINITION

In order to find an app, a user constructs a text query q, where we assume q represents the search intent of the user, and q is input to an app retrieval system. Then, the app retrieval system searches for apps that satisfy the user intent and shows the user a list of apps that are ranked according to their relevance to q, which conforms to the probability ranking principle [22]. Formally, we are given M apps $\boldsymbol{A} = \{a_1, ..., a_M\}$. For each app a_i, there is an unstructured app description d_i and user reviews that are concatenated to a single review document, r_i. Our goal is to retrieve a list of apps for each q based on their descriptions and/or reviews and rank them in order of the probability of relevance.

To the best of our knowledge, retrieval of entities exploiting opinionated content as well as entity description is a new problem that has not been well addressed yet in previous work. Kavita and Zhai [8] ranked entities leveraging user reviews but no associated descriptions. In [7] and [5], the researchers exploited user reviews and associated structured data to rank entities while we do not use structured data but unstructured description data about entities.

User reviews are good extra sources to find apps especially when an app description is too short or is poorly described. However, leveraging both app descriptions and user reviews is challenging because the two types of unstructured text are written by different authors in different views. Consequently, different topics are stressed and different vocabulary sets are used in the two types of data, which make them hard to combine. In addition, user reviews often contain content that does not address the entity's features; indeed, a huge portion of reviews is about installation problems or general sentiment on the whole app. Therefore, careful unification of the two different types of data is desired.

The main research questions we would like to answer in our study are:

1. *How can we create a test collection for evaluating this new retrieval task?* When query log data is not available, obtaining realistic queries is challenging and important for research.

2. *How effective are the existing general retrieval models for this task?* Since there is no previous work studied on this task, we do not know how well existing models will work for app retrieval.

3. *Can reviews help?* User reviews can be easily obtained at app stores, but it is unknown whether app retrieval systems can be improved leveraging them.

4. *Can topic models be used to more effectively combine descriptions and reviews?* Given two different types of text data, how can we effectively generate unified representation of descriptions and reviews?

4. TEST SET CREATION

4.1 Collecting Apps from App Stores

App descriptions and user reviews are available at multiple app stores such as Google Play, Apple App Store, and Amazon Appstore. Among them, we chose Google Play because it is one of the largest app stores with abundant reviews. In Google Play app store, there are 41 categories of apps, where each app is assigned with only one category. From each category, we crawled about one thousand popular apps on average, which are somehow ranked by Google, resulting in about 43 thousand apps in total. For each app, we crawled up to the first 50 user reviews, which are ranked by their helpfulness votes. To compare our methods with the search engine in Google Play, we also crawled top 20 retrieved apps and their reviews from Google Play for each search query. After all, we crawled 43,041 app descriptions (one description per app) and 1,385,607 user reviews in total (32.2 reviews per app on average). We pre-processed text in the descriptions and reviews in the following way. We first tokenized text into word tokens and lemmatized them using Stanford CoreNLP [17] version 1.3.5. We lowered word tokens and removed punctuation. Then, stopwords and word tokens that appear in less than five descriptions and five reviews were removed. Also, word tokens that appear in more than 30 percent of descriptions or reviews were removed since they do not carry important meanings. We finally have 18,559 unique word tokens (V), and the statistics of the resulting text data is shown in Table 1.

Table 1: Statistics of text data in app descriptions (D) and user reviews (R).

	D	R
Average number of tokens	94.1	176.4
Total number of tokens	4,051,366	7,592,779

4.2 Where Can We Obtain Realistic Queries?

In order to quantitatively evaluate how well the suggested methods perform, we need a query set and a query relevance data set. Unfortunately, there does not yet exist such test collection. We thus create our own test collection. However, collecting realistic queries that embed the needs of users for app search is not easy. Researchers who do not work for companies that provide an app search engine generally do not have access to the query log data, hence it is hard for them to know which apps users want to find and which apps are difficult to find. To collect such real queries, we propose to leverage an app forum.

There is an Android forum[5] where users frequently ask various kinds of questions about Android including Android apps. We employ Google search engine to find threads containing an exact phrase "looking for an app" in the forum in order to find posts about app search. This can be done by giving the following query to the Google search engine: *"looking for an app" site:forums.androidcentral.com.* Then, for each search result, we systematically determined to collect the post or not. We retained a post only if the user looks for an app and the thread includes one or more answers that recommend relevant apps because there are users who look for non-existing apps. The first sixty such posts were saved, and one of them with title "walkie talkie app" is shown below.

> I'm looking for an app that if I push a button and choose either of my kids android phones. I want it to just play on their phone without having to click on a voice file or do something interactive. Kind of like an intercom. Does anything like this exist?

Next, we asked domain experts to write a short search query (usually a couple of keywords) for each post, by pretending they were the authors who wrote those posts and want to search for the app at app stores. Examples of such generated queries are: "locate cell tower", "podcast streamer", "nightstand clock", "auto text while driving", and "music player for church". Please note that the collected queries may not precisely reflect representative queries in actual app stores, and collecting such queries is left as our future work. Meanwhile, one may be concerned that the queries are biased towards difficult ones since we obtain them from forum posts, where users post questions when they do not know the answers. The relevance data in the next section show that the queries are not "very" difficult.

4.3 Collecting Query Relevance Data

To judge whether a retrieved app is relevant to a query, we need human-labeled relevance data. However, labeling all the retrieved apps by humans is too expensive. We thus created a pool, which consists of top retrieved apps from different retrieval systems, and we employed a crowdsourcing service, CrowdFlower[6], to label them at affordable prices. Specifically, for each query, we pooled together the top 20 retrieved apps from each of the suggested methods with multiple parameter combinations. Then, for each of the (query, retrieved app) pairs, we made a question providing the short query, the entire post, and the link of the retrieved app, and we asked three annotators to label it. Each annotator was asked to read the query and entire question post, follow the link to the app store, read the app description, and then judge if the app satisfies the search intent on three relevance levels (no satisfaction at all (0), partial satisfaction (1), and perfect satisfaction (2)).

Collecting a high-quality gold standard data set through crowdsourcing is often difficult since there are lots of abusers. To control quality of the relevance judgments, we manually judged relevance of 120 (query, app) pairs and used them as quiz questions. Each annotator was allowed to start labeling the data set only if the annotator passes our quiz session with at least 75% of accuracy, where the quiz session consists of eight randomly selected quiz questions. We also inserted a random quiz question for every four (query, app) pairs in a random order, without telling which one is a quiz question. If the annotator's accuracy goes below 75% at any point of time, we removed all the answers from the annotator and asked other annotators to judge them. We paid five cents for each judgment, and each annotator was limited to judge up to 250 questions. When all the needed judgments were made, we verified the given links to the app store, and if the links are no longer valid, we removed the (query, app) pairs since the annotators may have made random answers when

[5]http://forums.androidcentral.com/

[6]http://www.crowdflower.com/

they encountered the broken links. The three resulting judgments for each (query, app) pair were averaged to be used as a relevance score. From the 60 queries, we discarded four queries that Google Play search engine could not retrieve relevant apps in top 10 apps.

Table 2: Statistics of relevance data for 56 queries. Some statistics include standard deviations followed by "±".

Avg. # of words in each query	4.04 ± 1.43
# of distinct (query, app) pairs judged	4,534
# of all judgments	13,602
Avg. # of (query, app) pairs for each query	81.0 ± 17.5
# of all annotators	272
Avg. # of judgments for each annotator	50.0 ± 48.1
Fleiss' kappa	0.39
Perfect agreement rate	0.71

The statistics of relevance data for the resultant 56 queries are shown in Table 2. To measure inter-annotator agreement, we employed Fleiss' kappa. The kappa value is 0.39, which can be interpreted as between "Fair agreement" and "Moderate agreement" according to [13]. Perfect agreement rate, the proportion of (query, app) pairs where all three annotators agree on judgment, is 0.71. To see how difficult each query is, we counted the number of judgments where at least two annotators judged as perfect relevant. For each query, there are 13.6 such relevant apps on average with standard deviation being 7.87, which means that the queries are not very difficult considering the size of the data set. This may be due to the fact that the forum post was uploaded a while ago so that the non-existing apps could have been released before we crawled the data set.

5. METHODS

In order to retrieve apps that best match a query q, we first try existing standard retrieval models based only on app descriptions, which is a typical information retrieval problem. Then, we add user reviews to the data set to see if they are useful for the task. To combine app descriptions with user reviews, we propose a topic model-based method as well as traditional methods.

5.1 Standard Text Retrieval

Despite the importance of app retrieval problem, it has not been answered how well standard text retrieval methods perform. We, therefore, employ existing state-of-the-art methods here.

5.1.1 Okapi BM25

The Okapi BM25 method has been one of the state-of-the-art methods for ad-hoc retrieval. As presented in [6], BM25 scores a document d with respect to q as follows:

$$score(q,d) = \sum_{w \in q \cap d} [\frac{(k_3+1)c(w,q)}{k_3+c(w,q)} \times \frac{(k_1+1)c'(w,d)}{k_1+c'(w,d)} \times \log \frac{N+1}{df(w)+0.5}] \quad (1)$$

where $c(w,q)$ is w's count in q, $df(w)$ is a document frequency of w in a corpus, N is the number of all documents in a corpus, and k_1, k_3, and b are parameters. A normalized count of w in d, $c'(w,d)$, is defined as

$$c'(w,d) = \frac{c(w,d)}{1-b+b\frac{N_d}{avl(d)}} \quad (2)$$

where $c(w,d)$ is w's count in d. N_d is the length of d, $avl(d)$ is the average length of d in a corpus. We use this model as one of the most popular text retrieval methods.

5.1.2 Query Likelihood Language Model (QL)

Query Likelihood retrieval model was introduced by Ponte and Croft in [21] using multiple Bernoulli to model documents. Instead of multiple Bernoulli, most researchers have focused on using multinomial to model documents since it was shown to perform better than multiple Bernoulli model [23]. Therefore, we use Query Likelihood method with multinomial model (unigram language model) in this paper. Query Likelihood scores a document d with respect to q as follows:

$$score(q,d) = \prod_{w \in q} p(w|d) \quad (3)$$

where $p(w|d)$ is a probability of w being in d. In order to avoid over-fitting and keep $p(w|d)$ from being zero, $p(w|d)$ is smoothed by Dirichlet smoothing technique and defined as

$$p(w|d) = \frac{N_d}{N_d+\mu} p_{ml}(w|d) + \frac{\mu}{N_d+\mu} p(w|\boldsymbol{D}) \quad (4)$$

where $\boldsymbol{D}$ is a set of all documents, and $p_{ml}(w|d)$ and $p(w|\boldsymbol{D})$ are estimated by maximum likelihood estimator (MLE), yielding $p_{ml}(w|d) = \frac{c(w,d)}{\sum_{w'} c(w',d)}$ and $p(w|\boldsymbol{D}) = \frac{c(w,\boldsymbol{D})}{\sum_{w'} c(w',\boldsymbol{D})}$. Smoothing parameter μ enables the system to dynamically smooth $p_{ml}(w|d)$ based on the length of d, N_d. Consequently, Query Likelihood Language Model with Dirichlet smoothing is regarded as one of the state-of-the-art retrieval models, and we call it QL in this paper. Please refer to [31] for more information on smoothing language models.

5.1.3 Topic Model-based Approach

Traditional retrieval models such as BM25 and QL do not consider association among words, which makes the system unable to retrieve documents that do not contain a query word. If there exists a vocabulary gap between queries and documents, the retrieval system is not supposed to work well. To solve the problem, we focus on enriching document representation with topic models. Please note that techniques such as query expansion can be combined with our suggested methods.

A topic model is a probabilistic model that can find latent themes and their distributions in a document from a text collection, where a theme (topic) is a cluster of words whose occurrence in documents overlap frequently. Thus, even if a document d does not contains a certain word w, $p(w|d)$ can be high enough if d contains many words that are in the same topic as w. For example, even if a word "bistro" is not contained in a description for a restaurant finder app, the app can be retrieved if the description contains a word "restaurant" since the two words are likely to be in the same topic(s). The two most popular topic models are Probabilistic Latent Semantic Analysis (PLSA) [9] and Latent Dirichlet Allocation (LDA) [1]. PLSA has two main problems: (1) the number of parameters grows as the data set size grows, and (2) it does not generate a new document, which has not been seen in training data. Those problems are solved in LDA by utilizing Dirichlet allocation, and thus, we employ LDA in this work.

For app retrieval problem, we suggest to exploit LDA-based document model (LBDM) [27], which has been shown to effectively model documents. The LBDM-based retrieval system was shown in [28] to generally outperform a retrieval system with a more sophisticated topic model, Pachinko Allocation Model (PAM) [14], which captures correlations among topics. Thus, we employ LBDM as one of the baselines in this study. We still use the same scoring formula as in (3), where the document language model $p(w|d)$ is replaced with LBDM. As presented in [27], $p(w|d)$ of LBDM involves a linear interpolation of MLE-estimated language model and LDA document model, which is defined as

$$p(w|d) = \lambda\left[\frac{N_d}{N_d+\mu}p_{ml}(w|d) + \frac{\mu}{N_d+\mu}p(w|\boldsymbol{D})\right] + (1-\lambda)p_{lda}(w|d) \quad (5)$$

where the LDA document model, $p_{lda}(w|d)$, is described in [27] in detail. As in equation (4), MLE-estimated document model, $p_{ml}(w|d)$, is smoothed with MLE-estimated corpus model, $p(w|\boldsymbol{D})$.

5.2 Retrieval with Descriptions and Reviews

App descriptions are not written perfectly by app developers. For example, some descriptions are too short, and some others may contain too much useless information for search. Luckily, abundant user reviews are available, which may be a good source to complement such descriptions. Another important reason to leverage user reviews is that both search queries and user reviews are written from a user's perspective while descriptions are written from a developer's perspective. Due to the nature of apps, app descriptions are usually written mainly about their features. However, app developers may not exactly know what terms users would like to use to describe the features. For example, an app description may contain a phrase "find nearby restaurants" to describe its feature. If a user searches for "food near me", which does not have any common terms with the description, the app will not be retrieved by simple keyword matching even though the two phrases are about the same feature. In such case, user reviews may play an important role to bridge vocabulary gap between app developers and users. If there is a user review containing a phrase such as "good app for locating food near me" and the retrieval system indexes the review as well, the app would be retrieved even when the description does not have such terms.

To leverage user reviews, we need to somehow combine representations of a description d and a concatenated user review r. Combining representations of two different data sets by simply adding words in them together may not be a good idea if the data sets have different characteristics. In this section, we describe how to combine them using our novel method as well as traditional methods.

5.2.1 BM25F

BM25F has been known as state-of-the-art for structured information retrieval. Regarding descriptions and reviews as different fields of a document, we can apply BM25F to our problem. Similar to [20], we replace $c'(w,d)$ in equation (1) with $c''(w,a)$, which is defined as

$$c''(w,a) = \frac{boost_d \cdot c(w,d)}{1 - b_d + b_d\frac{|d|}{avl(d)}} + \frac{boost_r \cdot c(w,r)}{1 - b_r + b_r\frac{|r|}{avl(r)}} \quad (6)$$

where $boost_d$ and $boost_r$ are weights for d and r, respectively, and b_d and b_r play the same role as b does for BM25. $|r|$ is a length of review r, and $avl(r)$ is the average length of r in a review corpus.

5.2.2 Combined Query Likelihood

To combine two different types of text data, it may be better to assign some portion of an app representation to description data and some other portion of it to user review data. Thus, the unigram language model for a description and a review, $p(w|d)$ and $p(w|r)$, respectively, can be combined as in [18] to build a unified language model for an app, $p(w|a)$, which is defined as

$$p(w|a) = (1-\eta)p(w|d) + \eta p(w|r) \quad (7)$$

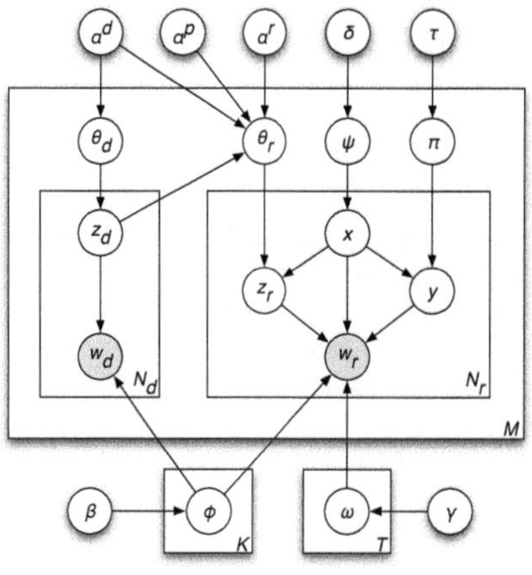

Figure 1: Graphical representation of AppLDA.

where η is a parameter to determine the proportion of review language model for $p(w|a)$. To score apps with respect to q, we follow the score function of QL. $p(w|d)$ and $p(w|r)$ are estimated by MLE and smoothed as in QL, and the resulting score function for q and a is defined as

$$score(q,a) = \prod_{w\in q} p(w|a) = \prod_{w\in q}\left[(1-\eta)p(w|d) + \eta p(w|r)\right]$$
$$= \prod_{w\in q}\left[(1-\eta)\left(\frac{N_d}{N_d+\mu_d}p_{ml}(w|d) + \frac{\mu_d}{N_d+\mu_d}p(w|\boldsymbol{D})\right)\right. \quad (8)$$
$$\left. + \eta\left(\frac{N_r}{N_r+\mu_r}p_{ml}(w|r) + \frac{\mu_r}{N_r+\mu_r}p(w|\boldsymbol{R})\right)\right]$$

where $p(w|\boldsymbol{R})$ is a review corpus language model, N_r is the number of words in r, and μ_d and μ_r are Dirichlet smoothing parameters for d and r, respectively.

5.2.3 AppLDA: a topic model for app descriptions and user reviews

In our task, the role of topic model is similar to that of user reviews in that they both provide augmentation of vocabulary. In addition to bridging vocabulary gap, we design a topic model that can also remove noise in reviews. The key idea is to simultaneously model app descriptions and user reviews by sharing topics between the two different types of text and discarding parts of reviews if they don't share topics with app descriptions. Intuitively, when a user writes a review, the user would decide if he or she writes about a topic in app description or some other topics such as installation problems. Assuming that those other topics (review-only topics) do not help us retrieve relevant apps, we remove review texts that are about review-only topics in order to have a better estimation of app representations. We thus form review-only topics as well as shared topics to filter out review texts that are not useful for retrieval.

The graphical representation of AppLDA is depicted in Figure 1, and its generative process is described in Algorithm 1. The generation of app description by an app developer can be regarded as a typical topic modeling process that is explained for regular LDA in earlier this section. After an app description is generated, each word $w_{r,i}$ of review r with length N_r for an app a is written by a user. The user first chooses whether to write about topics that are shared with descriptions or some other topics that are far from the shared topics using switch $x_{r,i}$ according to a Bernoulli distribution $\boldsymbol{\psi}_a$, which is drawn from a Beta distribution with a symmetric tuple $\boldsymbol{\delta}$. If shared topics are chosen ($x_{r,i}=0$), the

Algorithm 1 Generative Process of AppLDA

for each shared topic z do
  draw $\boldsymbol{\phi}_z \sim Dirichlet(\boldsymbol{\beta})$
end for
for each review topic y do
  draw $\boldsymbol{\omega}_y \sim Dirichlet(\boldsymbol{\gamma})$
end for
for each app a with a description d and a review r do
  draw $\boldsymbol{\theta}_d \sim Dirichlet(\boldsymbol{\alpha}^d)$
  for each $i \in \{1, \ldots, N_d\}$ do
    draw $z_{d,i} \sim Multi(\boldsymbol{\theta}_d)$
    draw $w_{d,i} \sim Multi(\boldsymbol{\phi}_{z_{d,i}})$
  end for
  draw $\boldsymbol{\psi}_r \sim Beta(\boldsymbol{\delta})$
  draw $\boldsymbol{\theta}_r \sim Dirichlet(K \cdot \boldsymbol{\alpha}^p \cdot prior(\boldsymbol{\alpha}^d, \boldsymbol{z}_d) + \boldsymbol{\alpha}^r)$
  draw $\boldsymbol{\pi}_r \sim Dirichlet(\boldsymbol{\tau})$
  for each $i \in \{1, \ldots, N_r\}$ do
    draw $x_{r,i} \sim Bernoulli(\boldsymbol{\psi}_r)$
    if $x_{r,i} = 0$ then
      draw $z_{r,i} \sim Multi(\boldsymbol{\theta}_r)$
      draw $w_{r,i} \sim Multi(\boldsymbol{\phi}_{z_{r,i}})$
    else
      draw $y_{r,i} \sim Multi(\boldsymbol{\pi}_r)$
      draw $w_{r,i} \sim Multi(\boldsymbol{\omega}_{y_{r,i}})$
    end if
  end for
end for

user further specifies a shared topic $z_{r,i}$ from the topic distribution in r, $\boldsymbol{\theta}_r$, which is drawn from a Dirichlet distribution with an asymmetric vector $K \cdot \boldsymbol{\alpha}^p \cdot prior(\boldsymbol{\alpha}^d, \boldsymbol{z}_d) + \boldsymbol{\alpha}^r$. Here, K is the number of all shared topics, and $\boldsymbol{\alpha}^p$ is a symmetric vector. $prior(\boldsymbol{\alpha}^d, \boldsymbol{z}_d)$ is a distribution generated from topics in d, which is estimated by $\frac{N_{z,d}+\alpha^d}{N_d+K\alpha^d}$, where N with subscription and/or superscription means the number of words satisfying subscription/superscription conditions. For example, $N_{z,d}$ means the number of words assigned with z in d, and N_d is the number of words in d. Then, the user writes a word $w_{r,i}$ about the chosen shared topic according to a multinomial word distribution $\boldsymbol{\phi}_{z_{r,i}}$, which is drawn from a Dirichlet distribution with a symmetric vector $\boldsymbol{\beta}$. On the other hand, if the user chooses to write about topics that are far from shared topics ($x_{r,i} = 1$), the user further chooses a review topic $y_{r,i}$ according to a multinomial topic distribution $\boldsymbol{\pi}_r$, which is drawn from a Dirichlet distribution with a symmetric vector $\boldsymbol{\tau}$. Then, $w_{r,i}$ is chosen according to a word distribution $\boldsymbol{\omega}_{y_{r,i}}$, which is drawn from a Dirichlet distribution with a symmetric vector $\boldsymbol{\gamma}$. This process is repeated for all words in all app descriptions and user reviews for I iterations. Please note that all values in a symmetric vector are the same; *e.g.*, $\boldsymbol{\alpha} = \{\alpha, ..., \alpha\}$.

In order to guide the model to learn hidden topics in reviews, we use prior knowledge from topic distribution in app descriptions by $prior(\boldsymbol{\alpha}^d, \boldsymbol{z}_d)$. Intuitively, when a user writes a review about shared topics, the distribution of shared topics in reviews is likely to be at least somewhat similar to that in app descriptions. For example, if an app description is about finding nearby restaurants, the reviews are more likely to contain topics regarding restaurants than other topics such as finance or game topics. The prior knowledge in app descriptions is thus passed to reviews in the form of asymmetric prior distribution, $prior(\boldsymbol{\alpha}^d, \boldsymbol{z}_d)$, and this distribution is referred to draw topics in reviews. Here, the strength of the prior knowledge is controlled by the symmetric vector $K \cdot \boldsymbol{\alpha}^p$, and the prior knowledge is smoothed with the symmetric vector $\boldsymbol{\alpha}^r$. In other words, we can view this process as follows. A user is given a set of topics in an app description, and the user writes a review about the app referring to the topics in the description. Such prior knowledge can be employed via imposing asymmetric priors on the topic distributions of reviews. More information on applying asymmetric priors in a topic model can be found in [25].

The collapsed Gibbs sampling formulas to learn latent variables z_d, z_r, x, and y for an app a are as follows. Learning a topic of the ith word in d, $z_{d,i}$, is defined as

$$\begin{aligned} & p(z_{d,i}|\boldsymbol{W}^d, \boldsymbol{Z}^d_{\backslash d,i}, \boldsymbol{\alpha}^d, \boldsymbol{\beta}) \\ & \propto p(w_{d,i}|z_{d,i}, \boldsymbol{W}^d_{\backslash d,i}, \boldsymbol{Z}^d_{\backslash d,i}, \boldsymbol{\beta}) p(z_{d,i}|\boldsymbol{Z}^d_{\backslash d,i}, \boldsymbol{\alpha}^d) \\ & \propto \frac{N^{\backslash d,i}_{w_{d,i}|z_{d,i}} + \beta}{N^{\backslash d,i}_{z_{d,i}} + V\beta} \times \frac{N^{\backslash d,i}_{z_{d,i}|d} + \alpha^d}{N_d - 1 + K\alpha^d} \end{aligned} \tag{9}$$

where $\boldsymbol{W}^d$ is a set of all words in the description corpus, $\boldsymbol{Z}^d$ is all shared-topic assignments for those words in all descriptions, V is the size of vocabulary $\boldsymbol{V}$, and K is the number of all shared topics. Again, N with subscription and/or superscription means the number of words satisfying subscription/superscription conditions, and "$\backslash d, i$" means excluding d's ith data. To learn a shared topic ($x_{r,i} = 0$) for the ith word in r, $z_{r,i}$, we define the Gibbs sampling formula as

$$\begin{aligned} & p(x_{r,i} = 0, z_{r,i}|\boldsymbol{W}^r, \boldsymbol{Z}^r_{\backslash r,i}, \boldsymbol{Z}^d, \boldsymbol{X}_{\backslash r,i}, \boldsymbol{\alpha}^d, \boldsymbol{\alpha}^r, \boldsymbol{\alpha}^p, \boldsymbol{\delta}, \boldsymbol{\beta}) \\ & \propto p(x_{r,i} = 0|\boldsymbol{X}_{\backslash r,i}, \boldsymbol{\delta}) \times p(w_{r,i}|z_{r,i}, \boldsymbol{W}^r_{\backslash r,i}, \boldsymbol{Z}^r_{\backslash r,i}, \boldsymbol{\beta}) \\ & \times p(z_{r,i}|\boldsymbol{Z}^r_{\backslash r,i}, \boldsymbol{Z}^d, \boldsymbol{\alpha}^d, \boldsymbol{\alpha}^r, \boldsymbol{\alpha}^p) \\ & \propto \frac{N^{\backslash r,i}_{x=0|r} + \delta}{N_r - 1 + 2\delta} \times \frac{N^{\backslash r,i}_{w_{r,i}|z_{r,i}} + \beta}{N^{\backslash r,i}_{z_{r,i}} + V\beta} \times \frac{N^{\backslash r,i}_{z_{r,i}|r} + K\alpha^p \frac{N_{z_{r,i}|d}+\alpha^d}{N_d+K\alpha^d} + \alpha^r}{(\sum_z N^{\backslash r,i}_{z|r}) + K(\alpha^p + \alpha^r)} \end{aligned} \tag{10}$$

where $\boldsymbol{W}^r$ is all words in the review corpus, and $\boldsymbol{Z}^r$ is all shared-topic assignments for those words in all reviews. On the other hand, to learn a review-only topic ($x_{r,i} = 1$) for the ith word in r, $y_{r,i}$, we define the Gibbs sampling formula as

$$\begin{aligned} & p(x_{r,i} = 1, y_{r,i}|\boldsymbol{W}^r, \boldsymbol{Y}_{\backslash r,i}, \boldsymbol{X}_{\backslash r,i}, \boldsymbol{\tau}, \boldsymbol{\delta}, \boldsymbol{\gamma}) \\ & \propto p(x_{r,i} = 1|\boldsymbol{X}_{\backslash r,i}, \boldsymbol{\delta}) \times p(w_{r,i}|y_{r,i}, \boldsymbol{W}^r_{\backslash r,i}, \boldsymbol{Y}_{\backslash r,i}, \boldsymbol{\gamma}) \\ & \times p(y_{r,i}|\boldsymbol{Y}_{\backslash r,i}, \boldsymbol{\tau}) \\ & \propto \frac{N^{\backslash r,i}_{x=1|r} + \delta}{N_r - 1 + 2\delta} \times \frac{N^{\backslash r,i}_{w_{r,i}|y_{r,i}} + \gamma}{N^{\backslash r,i}_{y_{r,i}} + V\gamma} \times \frac{N^{\backslash r,i}_{y_{r,i}|r} + \tau}{(\sum_y N^{\backslash r,i}_{y|r}) + T\tau} \end{aligned} \tag{11}$$

where $\boldsymbol{Y}$ is a set of review-only topic assignments for all words in all reviews, and T is the number of all review-only topics.

Retrieval with AppLDA.

In order to retrieve apps relevant to a query q, we need document representations for apps, so we create a unigram language model for each a, $p_{lda}(w|a)$, which is defined as

$$\begin{aligned} p_{lda}(w|a) &= \sum_{z=1}^{K} p(w|z, \boldsymbol{W}^d, \hat{\boldsymbol{Z}}^d, \boldsymbol{\beta}) p(z|a, \hat{\boldsymbol{Z}}^d, \hat{\boldsymbol{Z}}^r, \boldsymbol{\alpha}^d, \boldsymbol{\alpha}^r, \boldsymbol{\alpha}^p) \\ & \propto \sum_{z=1}^{K} \frac{\hat{N}_{w|z} + \beta}{\hat{N}_z + V\beta} \times \frac{\hat{N}_{z|d} + \alpha^d + \hat{N}_{z|r} + K\alpha^p \frac{\hat{N}_{z|d}+\alpha^d}{N_d+K\alpha^d} + \alpha^r}{N_d + K\alpha^d + (\sum_z \hat{N}_{z|r}) + K(\alpha^p + \alpha^r)} \end{aligned} \tag{12}$$

where $\hat{\boldsymbol{Z}}^d$ and $\hat{\boldsymbol{Z}}^r$ are topics for descriptions and reviews estimated from AppLDA, respectively, and $\hat{N}$ with subscription is the estimated number of words satisfying the subscription condition. The formula can be interpreted as the unification of LDA-estimated language models for descriptions and reviews, where the words that are not assigned with the shared topics are removed. In other words, the description and the cleaned review form a single unified document for each app, and the unified language model is used for retrieval. The AppLDA-estimated language model is combined with the MLE-estimated language models to define the score function for q and a as follows:

$$score(q,a) = \prod_{w \in q} p(w|a) = \prod_{w \in q} \Big((1-\lambda) p_{lda}(w|a) + \lambda \big[\frac{N_d + N_{x=0|r}}{N_d + N_{x=0|r} + \mu} p_{ml}(w|a) + \frac{\mu}{N_d + N_{x=0|r} + \mu} p(w|\boldsymbol{A}) \big] \Big) \quad (13)$$

where $N_{x=0|r}$ is the number of words assigned with shared topics in reviews, and $p_{ml}(w|a)$ is MLE-estimated language model for a's description and cleaned review, which is defined as

$$p_{ml}(w|a) = p(w|a, \boldsymbol{W}^d, \boldsymbol{W}^r, \hat{\boldsymbol{X}}) \propto \frac{N_{w|d} + N_{x=0,w|r}}{N_d + N_{x=0|r}} \quad (14)$$

and $p(w|\boldsymbol{A})$ is estimated by MLE for descriptions and cleaned reviews of all apps $\boldsymbol{A}$, and it is defined as

$$p(w|\boldsymbol{A}) = p(w|\boldsymbol{A}, \boldsymbol{W}^d, \boldsymbol{W}^r, \hat{\boldsymbol{X}}) \propto \frac{N_{w|\boldsymbol{D}} + N_{x=0,w|\boldsymbol{R}}}{N_{\boldsymbol{D}} + N_{x=0|\boldsymbol{R}}} \quad (15)$$

and μ is a Dirichlet smoothing parameter for MLE-estimated language models, and λ is a weight for MLE-estimated language models against the topic model-estimated language model. In order to estimate reliable values for LDA estimated language models, it is recommended to use multiple Markov chains in [27]. Similar to the results in [27], we found that three Markov chains with 100 Gibbs sampling iterations each show reasonably reliable performance, so we follow this setting.

6. EXPERIMENTS

In this section, we first describe how we set parameters for the experiments. Then, we qualitatively analyze the search results from the suggested methods, and we quantitatively evaluate the results using our test collection.

6.1 Parameter Setting

The following parameter values are used in the experiments unless otherwise specified. The parameters are tuned from our data set based on average of four NDCG measures specified in section 6.3. For BM25, we use the standard value k_3=1,000, and we set the parameters k_1=4.0 and b=0.4, which showed the best performance. For BM25F, we tune the parameters at our best, and we consider the following values: k_3=1,000, k_1=3.5, b_d=0.4, b_r=0.3, $boost_d$=0.6, and $boost_r$=0.4. For Query Likelihood Language Model (QL), μ is tuned to be 1,000. For Combined Query Likelihood (CombQL), the same μ is used, and we set μ_r=300 and η=0.4, which showed the best performance. For LBDM, K is tuned to be 300, and we set topic model parameters $\alpha=\frac{50}{K}$ and β=0.01, which is the common setting in the literature. Its retrieval parameters λ and μ are tuned to be 0.5 and 1,000, respectively. To see how well regular QL and LBDM perform with both data sets $\boldsymbol{D}$ and $\boldsymbol{R}$, we simply add words in reviews to the corresponding descriptions and used the merged documents as an input to QL and LBDM; we call these methods as QL($\boldsymbol{D},\boldsymbol{R}$) and LBDM($\boldsymbol{D},\boldsymbol{R}$). μ for QL($\boldsymbol{D},\boldsymbol{R}$) is tuned to be 800. For LBDM($\boldsymbol{D},\boldsymbol{R}$), K is tuned to be 300, and the same α and β values are used as for regular LBDM, and retriever parameters λ and μ are tuned to be 0.5 and 800, respectively. For our proposed model AppLDA, we set K=300 and T=30, which showed the best performance. We use the standard values for other topic model parameters: $\alpha^d=\alpha^r=\frac{50}{K}$, $\tau=\frac{50}{T}$, and $\beta=\gamma$=0.01. If one believes that the reviews have a specific amount of shared-topic proportion, then δ can be used as asymmetric prior. However, we let the model fully figure out the proportions, so we set δ=0.5 for symmetric vector $\boldsymbol{\delta}$, which is a small value. A larger value of $alpha^p$ lets the distribution of shared-topics in reviews be more similar to that in app descriptions; α^p is tuned to be 0.05. For retrieval parameters of AppLDA, we set λ=0.5 and μ=800, which showed the best performance.

6.2 Qualitative Analysis

Table 3: Top shared topics by AppLDA.

slot	check	photo	news
bonus	deposit	picture	article
win	mobile	pic	story
machine	account	gallery	break
spin	bank	image	read
casino	balance	effect	local
coin	banking	editing	latest
payout	credit	editor	content
slots	transfer	filter	fox
jackpot	transaction	edit	live

Table 4: Top review-only topics by AppLDA.

log	interface	ad	addictive
account	uus (ui)	pop	pass
login	design	annoying	addicting
sign	function	remove	enjoy
error	miss	advert	addict
password	lack	advertisement	challenge
website	user	rid	kill
connect	functionality	full	entertaining
server	improvement	seconds	interesting
access	clean	click	challenging

Table 5: Top topics in the reviews by LDA.

log	upgrade	purchase	note
account	battle	refund	support
check	spend	upgrade	pro
mobile	character	reinstall	developer
login	gold	bug	sync
password	rpg	force	program
sign	gameplay	year	tool
deposit	attack	month	dev
service	level	lose	tablet
bank	fight	block	draw

Table 3 and 4 show the biggest shared topics and review-only topics (measured by $\hat{N}_z$), respectively, estimated by AppLDA. At Google Play, 18 of 41 categories are game-related categories, so they are reflected in the topics; for example, the biggest shared topic is about "casino game", and the fourth review-only topic is about "sentiment towards games". The other biggest shared topics are about "mobile banking", "photo editor", and "news article", and each of them represents a feature of an app well. Review-only topics seem reasonable since the words in them are likely to appear more often in reviews than in descriptions. We also compare top review-only topics from AppLDA with top topics from regular LDA when we use only user reviews, which is shown in Table 5. Comparing the biggest topics of them, which are both about "account", it is shown that the topic in

Table 6: **Top retrieved apps for a query "locate cell tower". Strikethrough indicates irrelevant apps.**

QL	LBDM	CombQL	AppLDA
~~GPS Tracker Pro~~	zBoost Signal Finder	Cell Map	Cell Map
Tower Collector	3G 4G WiFi Map & Speedtest	zBoost Signal Finder	Map My Cell Tower
3G 4G WiFi Map & Speedtest	~~GPS Tracker Pro~~	Signal Finder	zBoost Signal Finder
~~Locate -Find Friends & Family~~	Tower Collector	Network Signal Info Pro	Signal Finder
~~Find My Phone~~	Map My Cell Tower	Tower Collector	Network Signal Info Pro
inViu OpenCellID	~~Locate -Find Friends & Family~~	Map My Cell Tower	Tower Collector
~~Signal Booster Reloaded~~	inViu OpenCellID	3G 4G WiFi Map & Speedtest	Cell Info Display
~~Signal Booster for Android~~	Signal Finder	~~Family Tracker: Locate Phones~~	3G 4G WiFi Map & Speedtest
~~Family Tracker: Locate Phones~~	~~Find My Phone~~	inViu OpenCellID	~~Sprint Family Locator~~
~~Digital Leash Locate~~	~~Family Tracker: Locate Phones~~	~~GPS Tracker Pro~~	~~GPS Tracker Pro~~

LDA is corrupted with "bank"-related words such as "bank" and "deposit" while the topic in AppLDA is about general accounts of apps. An "account problem" topic is more likely to appear in review-only topics while a "mobile banking" topic is more likely to appear in shared topics. AppLDA is able to separate such topics well by forming two different types of topics. Interestingly, AppLDA's shared-topics consist of words that do not carry sentiment while review-only topics often contains words carrying sentiment such as "miss", "lack", "annoying", and "addicting". This means that AppLDA separated the two different types of topics reasonably well; since regular LDA does not explicitly separate them, top topics in reviews contain few sentiment words, but several words of them are likely to appear often in app descriptions.

To show the difference of retrieved apps from different models, we retrieve apps for a query "locate cell tower" using the suggested methods. The top retrieved apps are showed in Table 6. According to the question post, the query looks for an app that locates a cell tower the phone is currently attached to. By comparing methods that do not leverage user reviews (QL and LBDM) with methods that do leverage user reviews (CombQL and AppLDA), we can see the effect of adding more review text. The relevant apps such as "Map My Cell Tower" and "zBoost Signal Finder" do not contain the query word "locate", which makes them hard to find. However, since the reviews of those apps contain phrases such as "Won't even locate my cell tower" and "Handy app to locate towers", CombQL and AppLDA could rank them high. While the reviews help bridge vocabulary gap by adding absent words from review text, topic model-based method also bridges vocabulary gap by connecting associated words. LBDM gave high scores to relevant apps such as "zBoost Signal Finder", "Map My Cell Tower", and "Signal Finder", which do not contain the word "locate" in their reviews, even though it does not leverage user reviews. Since the descriptions of those apps contain words such as "gps" and "map" that are in the same topics as "locate" is, they could be ranked high.

6.3 Quantitative Analysis

Since we average relevance judgments of three annotators, the aggregated relevance is defined as a real number in [0,2]. Hence, evaluation metrics such as Mean Average Precision (MAP), which requires binary relevance, cannot be employed. We instead employ Normalized Discounted Cumulative Gain (NDCG) [11] as the evaluation metric because NDCG is able to measure ranking performance on multiple-level relevance data. Specifically, we measure NDCG at 3, 5, 10, and 20 top retrieved apps to reflect diverse users' information needs. Unlike traditional web search, NDCG@3 might be quite important; it is common for app stores to show only one or a couple of retrieved apps on a smartphone screen. On the other hand, obtaining judgments for top 20 retrieved apps of retrieval systems with all combinations of

Table 7: NDCG evaluation results for mobile app retrieval. The first three methods exploit only app descriptions, *D*, while the next five methods leverage user reviews, *R*, as well as app descriptions, *D*.

	N@3	N@5	N@10	N@20
BM25	0.578	0.550	0.527	0.537
QL	0.541	0.517	0.511	0.515
LBDM	0.584	0.563	0.543	0.565
BM25F	0.597	0.596	0.583	0.597
QL (*D*,*R*)	0.613	0.618	0.585	0.586
CombQL	0.637	0.624	0.602	0.593
LBDM(*D*,*R*)	0.610	0.625	0.613	0.626
AppLDA	**0.651**†§	**0.656**†‡	**0.627**†	**0.634**†‡
Google Play	0.589	0.575	0.568	0.566

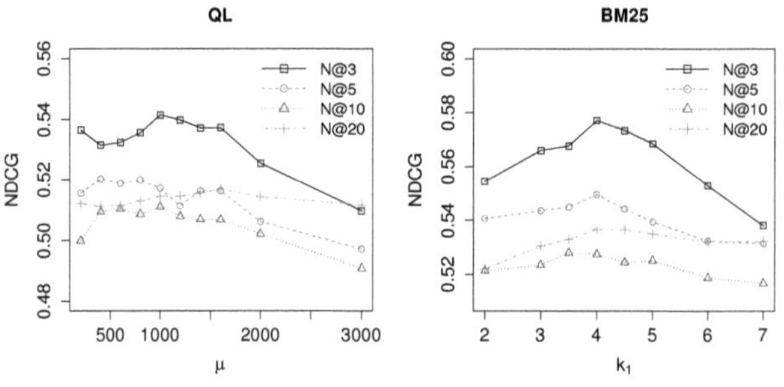

Figure 2: NDCG measures for different μ values of QL (left) and for different k_1 values of BM25.

parameter values is too expensive and not realistic in practice. We judged top 20 retrieved apps of the suggested retrieval systems with 22 parameter value combinations. The relevance data may be thus incomplete. However, it is shown in [29, 2] that ignoring unjudged documents is effective in such situations. Therefore, we alternatively employ induced NDCG at k judged apps, which shares the same philosophy as induced MAP in [29]. Induced NDCG ignores unjudged apps from the ranked list and is calculated in the same way as regular NDCG. We simply call it NDCG in this paper.

We compare the performance of the suggested methods as well as Google Play's app search engine. Table 7 shows the evaluation results. †, ‡, and § are used to mark if the improvement for AppLDA is statistically (paired t-test with $p \leq 0.05$) significant in each measure over LBDM, CombQL, and LBDM($\boldsymbol{D}$,$\boldsymbol{R}$), respectively. As expected, LBDM outperforms BM25 and QL in all measures when only app descriptions are available because LBDM is able to recognize semantically related words. When only app descriptions are used, BM25 outperforms QL in all measures, and their performance on different parameter values is shown in Figure 2. However, when both descriptions and reviews are used, QL($\boldsymbol{D}$,$\boldsymbol{R}$) and CombQL outperform BM25F in all measures except NDCG@20, which means QL and CombQL are more suitable to combine different data types for app retrieval than BM25F. It is clear to see that the models that leverage user reviews perform better than the models that use only descriptions. For example, BM25F outperforms BM25, and CombQL and QL($\boldsymbol{D}$,$\boldsymbol{R}$) outperform QL with a relatively big performance difference. In addition, AppLDA and LBDM($\boldsymbol{D}$,$\boldsymbol{R}$) outperform LBDM, which means that topic model's capability of bridging vocabulary is even amplified when user reviews are added. QL($\boldsymbol{D}$,$\boldsymbol{R}$) exploits user reviews by concatenating descriptions and user reviews, and it is outperformed by CombQL that combines description model and user review model with linear interpolation. This means that the review data set and description data set have their own characteristics, so they need to be combined without losing them. AppLDA outperforms CombQL and LBDM($\boldsymbol{D}$,$\boldsymbol{R}$), and the improvement is statistically significant in two measures and one measure, respectively. While CombQL does not score high in NDCG@10 and NDCG@20, LBDM($\boldsymbol{D}$,$\boldsymbol{R}$) does not score high in NDCG@3. AppLDA seems to complement such drawbacks of CombQL and LBDM($\boldsymbol{D}$, $\boldsymbol{R}$) by effectively modeling app descriptions and user reviews.

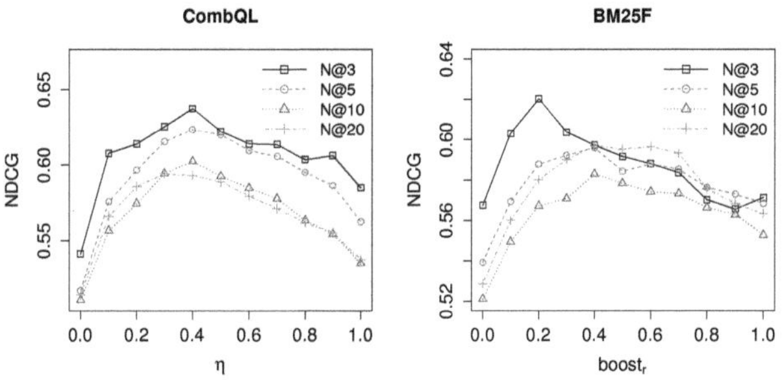

Figure 3: NDCG measures for different review weights (η) of CombQL (left) and for different review weights ($boost_r$) of BM25F when $boost_d = 1.0 - boost_r$ (right).

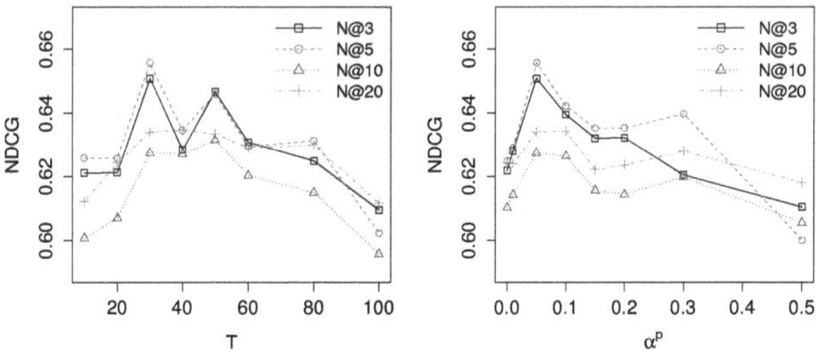

Figure 4: NDCG measures for AppLDA when different numbers of review-only topics (T) are used (left) and different prior weights (α^p) are used (right).

In order to understand the effects of leveraging reviews, we further investigate performance when different proportions of review representations are used. NDCG measures for different η values of CombQL and different $boosts_r$ values of BM25F are shown in Figure 3. η is a weight of review language model in CombQL, and $boost_r$ is a weight of normalized count of word in reviews. Here, we set $boost_d = 1.0 - boost_r$ for BM25F. When $\eta = 1.0$ or $boost_r = 1.0$, the models exploit only reviews while they exploit only descriptions when $\eta = 0.0$ or $boost_r = 0.0$. Surprisingly, for both models, using only reviews gives a better performance than using only descriptions; which means that review data set may be a better resource for app search than description data set. Since both reviews and queries are written by users, there may be less vocabulary gap between them, resulting in reviews being more useful for app retrieval than descriptions. Combining app descriptions and user reviews yields even better performance, which peaks when $\eta = 0.4$ and $boost_r$ is around 0.4. This means that descriptions and reviews supplement each other well.

Figure 4 shows AppLDA's performance when different numbers of review-only topics T are used and different values of α^p priors are used. It seems that about 30 to 50 review-only topics exist in the review data set, and setting too few or too many review topics harm the performance. The number of review-only topics is much smaller than that of shared topics (300). This is because there are various available features for each category of apps while the topics users mention other than app features converge to a small set of topics such as "installation problems" and "user interface". Meanwhile, α^p controls the amount of topic distribution priors for user reviews, and it is obtained from topic distribution of app descriptions. The priors are used to give clues when identifying topics in reviews under the assumption that the distribution of shared topics in reviews is likely to be similar to that of app descriptions. Indeed, it is shown in Figure 4 that adding priors is helpful while adding too much priors is rather harmful. The performance peaks at $\alpha^p = 0.05$ when $K = 300$, which means that giving about fifteen guiding words to a noise-removed review is generally desired, in other words.

7. CONCLUSION

In this paper, we conducted the first study of a new retrieval task, *i.e.*, mobile app retrieval. Since no test collection exists yet, we created the first one to evaluate this task. We used this test collection to systematically study the effectiveness of both existing retrieval models and a new model that we proposed to effectively leverage the companion review data with apps. Specifically, in order to combine different vocabulary sets in app descriptions and user reviews and to filter out noise in reviews, we proposed a topic model (AppLDA) that jointly models reviews and app descriptions and extracts aligned topics between reviews and descriptions. Evaluation results show that (1) BM25 outperforms QL when only descriptions are used while QL and CombQL generally outperforms BM25F when reviews are added, (2) leveraging reviews indeed helps app retrieval, (3) AppLDA significantly outperforms traditional retrieval models, and (4) adding priors in AppLDA helps align topics between app descriptions and user reviews.

Our work can be further extended in several ways: (1) collecting representative queries when query log data is not available can be further studied, (2) one can explore other directions such as query expansion and feedback-based models for app retrieval problem, and (3) one can identify other characteristics of mobile apps to design a better retrieval model. Our created test collection is made publicly available and thus enables further study of this new problem.

8. ACKNOWLEDGMENTS

This work is supported in part by a gift fund from TCL and by the National Science Foundation under Grant Number CNS-1027965.

9. REFERENCES

[1] D. M. Blei, A. Y. Ng, and M. I. Jordan. Latent dirichlet allocation. *the Journal of machine Learning research*, 3:993–1022, 2003.

[2] C. Buckley and E. M. Voorhees. Retrieval evaluation with incomplete information. In *Proceedings of the 27th annual international ACM SIGIR conference on Research and development in information retrieval*, pages 25–32. ACM, 2004.

[3] A. Datta, K. Dutta, S. Kajanan, and N. Pervin. Mobilewalla: A mobile application search engine. In *Mobile Computing, Applications, and Services*, pages 172–187. Springer, 2012.

[4] A. P. De Vries, A.-M. Vercoustre, J. A. Thom, N. Craswell, and M. Lalmas. Overview of the inex 2007 entity ranking track. In *Focused Access to XML Documents*, pages 245–251. Springer, 2008.

[5] H. Duan, C. Zhai, J. Cheng, and A. Gattani. Supporting keyword search in product database: A probabilistic approach. *Proc. VLDB Endow.*, 6(14):1786–1797, Sept. 2013.

[6] H. Fang, T. Tao, and C. Zhai. A formal study of information retrieval heuristics. In *Proceedings of the 27th annual international ACM SIGIR conference on Research and development in information retrieval*, pages 49–56. ACM, 2004.

[7] K. Ganesan and C. Zhai. Findilike: preference driven entity search. In *Proceedings of the 21st international conference companion on World Wide Web*, pages 345–348. ACM, 2012.

[8] K. Ganesan and C. Zhai. Opinion-based entity ranking. *Information retrieval*, 15(2):116–150, 2012.

[9] T. Hofmann. Probabilistic latent semantic indexing. In *Proceedings of the 22nd annual international ACM SIGIR conference on Research and development in information retrieval*, pages 50–57. ACM, 1999.

[10] D. Jannach, M. Zanker, A. Felfernig, and G. Friedrich. *Recommender systems: an introduction.* Cambridge University Press, 2010.

[11] K. Järvelin and J. Kekäläinen. Cumulated gain-based evaluation of ir techniques. *ACM Transactions on Information Systems (TOIS)*, 20(4):422–446, 2002.

[12] J. Kamps, M. Marx, M. De Rijke, and B. Sigurbjörnsson. Xml retrieval: What to retrieve? In *Proceedings of the 26th annual international ACM SIGIR conference on Research and development in informaion retrieval*, pages 409–410. ACM, 2003.

[13] J. R. Landis and G. G. Koch. The measurement of observer agreement for categorical data. *biometrics*, pages 159–174, 1977.

[14] W. Li and A. McCallum. Pachinko allocation: Dag-structured mixture models of topic correlations. In *Proceedings of the 23rd international conference on Machine learning*, pages 577–584. ACM, 2006.

[15] J. Lin, K. Sugiyama, M.-Y. Kan, and T.-S. Chua. Addressing cold-start in app recommendation: latent user models constructed from twitter followers. In *Proceedings of the 36th international ACM SIGIR conference on Research and development in information retrieval*, pages 283–292. ACM, 2013.

[16] Z. Liu, J. Walker, and Y. Chen. Xseek: a semantic xml search engine using keywords. In *Proceedings of the 33rd international conference on Very large data bases*, pages 1330–1333. VLDB Endowment, 2007.

[17] C. D. Manning, M. Surdeanu, J. Bauer, J. Finkel, S. J. Bethard, and D. McClosky. The stanford corenlp natural language processing toolkit. In *Proceedings of 52nd Annual Meeting of the Association for Computational Linguistics: System Demonstrations*, pages 55–60, 2014.

[18] P. Ogilvie and J. Callan. Combining document representations for known-item search. In *Proceedings of the 26th annual international ACM SIGIR conference on Research and development in informaion retrieval*, pages 143–150. ACM, 2003.

[19] J. Pehcevski, A.-M. Vercoustre, and J. A. Thom. Exploiting locality of wikipedia links in entity ranking. In *Advances in Information Retrieval*, pages 258–269. Springer, 2008.

[20] J. Pérez-Iglesias, J. R. Pérez-Agüera, V. Fresno, and Y. Z. Feinstein. Integrating the probabilistic models bm25/bm25f into lucene. *arXiv preprint arXiv:0911.5046*, 2009.

[21] J. M. Ponte and W. B. Croft. A language modeling approach to information retrieval. In *Proceedings of the 21st annual international ACM SIGIR conference on Research and development in information retrieval*, pages 275–281. ACM, 1998.

[22] S. E. Robertson. The probability ranking principle in ir. *Readings in information retrieval*, pages 281–286, 1997.

[23] F. Song and W. B. Croft. A general language model for information retrieval. In *Proceedings of the eighth international conference on Information and knowledge management*, pages 316–321. ACM, 1999.

[24] A.-M. Vercoustre, J. A. Thom, and J. Pehcevski. Entity ranking in wikipedia. In *Proceedings of the 2008 ACM symposium on Applied computing*, pages 1101–1106. ACM, 2008.

[25] H. M. Wallach, D. Minmo, and A. McCallum. Rethinking lda: Why priors matter. 2009.

[26] N. Walsh, M. Fernández, A. Malhotra, M. Nagy, and J. Marsh. Xquery 1.0 and xpath 2.0 data model (xdm). *W3C recommendation, W3C (January 2007)*, 2007.

[27] X. Wei and W. B. Croft. Lda-based document models for ad-hoc retrieval. In *Proceedings of the 29th annual international ACM SIGIR conference on Research and development in information retrieval*, pages 178–185. ACM, 2006.

[28] X. Yi and J. Allan. A comparative study of utilizing topic models for information retrieval. In *Advances in Information Retrieval*, pages 29–41. Springer, 2009.

[29] E. Yilmaz and J. A. Aslam. Estimating average precision with incomplete and imperfect judgments. In *Proceedings of the 15th ACM international conference on Information and knowledge management*, pages 102–111. ACM, 2006.

[30] P. Yin, P. Luo, W.-C. Lee, and M. Wang. App recommendation: a contest between satisfaction and temptation. In *Proceedings of the sixth ACM international conference on Web search and data mining*, pages 395–404. ACM, 2013.

[31] C. Zhai and J. Lafferty. A study of smoothing methods for language models applied to ad hoc information retrieval. In *Proceedings of the 24th annual international ACM SIGIR conference on Research and development in information retrieval*, pages 334–342. ACM, 2001.

[32] H. Zhu, H. Xiong, Y. Ge, and E. Chen. Mobile app recommendations with security and privacy awareness. In *Proceedings of the 20th ACM SIGKDD international conference on Knowledge discovery and data mining*, pages 951–960. ACM, 2014.

Towards a Game-Theoretic Framework for Information Retrieval

ChengXiang Zhai
University of Illinois, Urbana-Champaign
czhai@illinois.edu

Abstract

The task of information retrieval (IR) has traditionally been defined as to rank a collection of documents in response to a query. While this definition has enabled most research progress in IR so far, it does not model accurately the actual retrieval task in a real IR application, where users tend to be engaged in an interactive process with multipe queries, and optimizing the overall performance of an IR system on an entire search session is far more important than its performance on an individual query.

In this talk, I will present a new game-theoretic formulation of the IR problem where the key idea is to model information retrieval as a process of a search engine and a user playing a cooperative game, with a shared goal of satisfying the user's information need (or more generally helping the user complete a task) while minimizing the user's effort and the resource overhead on the retrieval system. Such a game-theoretic framework offers several benefits. First, it naturally suggests optimization of the overall utility of an interactive retrieval system over a whole search session, thus breaking the limitation of the traditional formulation that optimizes ranking of documents for a single query. Second, it models the interactions between users and a search engine, and thus can optimize the collaboration of a search engine and its users, maximizing the "combined intelligence" of a system and users. Finally, it can serve as a unified framework for optimizing both interactive information retrieval and active relevance judgment acquisition through crowdsourcing. I will discuss how the new framework can not only cover several emerging directions in current IR research as special cases, but also open up many interesting new research directions in IR.

Categories and Subject Descriptors

H.3.3 [Information Search and Retrieval]: Retrieval models

General Terms

Algorithms

Keywords

interactive information retrieval; search engines; game theory; retrieval models

SIGIR'15, August 09-13, 2015, Santiago, Chile.
ACM 978-1-4503-3621-5/15/08.
http://dx.doi.org/10.1145/2766462.2767853

BIO

ChengXiang Zhai is a Professor of Computer Science and Willett Faculty Scholar at the University of Illinois at Urbana-Champaign, where he is also affiliated with the Graduate School of Library and Information Science, Institute for Genomic Biology, and Department of Statistics. He received a Ph.D. in Computer Science from Nanjing University in 1990, and a Ph.D. in Language and Information Technologies from Carnegie Mellon University in 2002. He worked at Clairvoyance Corp. as a Research Scientist and a Senior Research Scientist from 1997 to 2000. His research interests include information retrieval, text mining, natural language processing, machine learning, biomedical and health informatics, and intelligent education information systems. He has published over 200 research papers in major conferences and journals. He is an Associate Editor for Information Processing and Management and previously served as an Associate Editor of ACM Transactions on Information Systems, and on the editorial board of Information Retrieval Journal. He is a conference program co-chair of ACM CIKM 2004, NAACL HLT 2007, ACM SIGIR 2009, ECIR 2014, ICTIR 2015, and WWW 2015, and conference general co-chair for ACM CIKM 2016. He is an ACM Distinguished Scientist and a recipient of multiple awards, including the ACM SIGIR 2004 Best Paper Award, the ACM SIGIR 2014 Test of Time Paper Award, Alfred P. Sloan Research Fellowship, IBM Faculty Award, HP Innovation Research Program Award, Microsoft Beyond Search Research Award, and the Presidential Early Career Award for Scientists and Engineers (PECASE).

Representative & Informative Query Selection for Learning to Rank using Submodular Functions

Rishabh Mehrotra
Dept of Computer Science
University College London, UK
r.mehrotra@cs.ucl.ac.uk

Emine Yilmaz
Dept of Computer Science
University College London, UK
emine.yilmaz@ucl.ac.uk

ABSTRACT

The performance of Learning to Rank algorithms strongly depend on the number of labelled queries in the training set, while the cost incurred in annotating a large number of queries with relevance judgements is prohibitively high. As a result, constructing such a training dataset involves selecting a set of candidate queries for labelling. In this work, we investigate query selection strategies for learning to rank aimed at actively selecting unlabelled queries to be labelled so as to minimize the data annotation cost. In particular, we characterize query selection based on two aspects of *informativeness* and *representativeness* and propose two novel query selection strategies (i) Permutation Probability based query selection and (ii) Topic Model based query selection which capture the two aspects, respectively. We further argue that an ideal query selection strategy should take into account both these aspects and as our final contribution, we present a submodular objective that couples both these aspects while selecting query subsets. We evaluate the quality of the proposed strategies on three real world learning to rank datasets and show that the proposed query selection methods results in significant performance gains compared to the existing state-of-the-art approaches.

Categories and Subject Descriptors

H.3.3 [**Information Storage And Retrieval**]: Information Search and Retrieval—*Learning to Rank*

Keywords

Learning to Rank, Query Selection, Active Learning, Submodularity

1. INTRODUCTION

Most modern search technologies are based on machine learning algorithms that learn to rank documents given a query, an approach that is commonly referred to as "learning to rank". Learning to Rank algorithms aim to learn ranking functions that achieve good ranking objectives on test data.

SIGIR'15, August 09 - 13, 2015, Santiago, Chile.

DOI: http://dx.doi.org/10.1145/2766462.2767753.

Such learning methods require labelled data for training. As is the case with many supervised learning algorithms, the performance of Learning to Rank algorithms are often highly correlated with the amount of labelled training data available[1][17][7].

Constructing such labelled training data for learning-to-rank tasks incurs prohibitive costs since it requires selecting candidate queries, extracting features from query-document pairs and annotating documents in terms of their relevance to these queries (annotations are used as labels for training). The major bottleneck in constructing learning-to-rank collections is annotating documents with query specific relevance grades. It is essential therefore, both for the efficiency of the construction methodology and for the efficiency of the training algorithm, that only a small subset of queries be selected. The query selection, though, should be done in a way that does not harm the effectiveness of learning.

Active Learning algorithms help reduce the annotation costs by selecting a subset of informative instances to be labelled. Unlike traditional algorithms, active learning strategies for ranking algorithms are more complex because of the inherent query-document pair structure embodied in ranking datasets, non-smooth cost functions, etc., hence these cannot be applied directly in ranking setting.

Existing approaches for active learning for ranking have focused on selecting documents [1], selecting queries [17] or balancing number of queries with depth of documents judged using random query selection [27].

In this work, we focus on selecting subset of queries to be labelled so as to minimize the data annotation cost. Prior work on selecting queries made use of expected loss optimization [17] to estimate which queries should be selected but their approach is limited to rankers that predict absolute graded relevance which is not the case with modern Learning to Rank algorithms since many of them induce a ranking and not absolute labels [4]. Apart from the learning to rank setting, query selection has also received significant attention for evaluation setting [13] wherein the goal was to find a subset of queries that most closely approximates the system evaluation results that would be obtained if instead documents for the full set of queries was judged instead. However, it was shown by Aslam *et a.l*[1] that learning to rank and evaluation of retrieval systems are quite different from each other and that datasets constructed for evaluating quality of retrieval systems are not necessarily good for training and vice versa. Therefore, query selection strategies that are directly devised for learning to rank purposes are needed.

Intuitively, an optimal subset of queries constructed for learning to rank should have two characteristics: (i) *informativeness*, which measures the ability of an instance (query) in reducing the uncertainty of a statistical model (ranking model) and (ii) *representativeness*, which measures if an instance (query) well represents the possible input patterns of unlabelled data (unlabelled queries) [22]. Most existing active learning for ranking algorithms solely focus on the informativeness aspect of queries without considering the representativeness aspect which can lead to possible selection of *noisy* queries, not quite representative of the whole population of queries; thus, significantly limiting the performance of query selection.

In this work, we focus on query selection strategies for learning to rank and propose novel query selection algorithms aimed at finding an optimal subset of queries to be labelled. Since problems associated with subset selection are generally NP-Hard or NP-Complete[12], we approximate the solution by an iterative query selection process so as to minimize the data annotation cost without severely degrading the performance of the ranking model.

We describe two paradigms of query selection strategies based on the aspects of *informativeness* and *representativeness* described above and propose novel query selection techniques: Permutation Probability based query selection and query selection based on topic models which capture these two aspects, respectively. We further present a new algorithm based on defining a submodular objective that combines the powers of the two paradigms. Submodular functions have the characteristic of diminishing returns [19], which is an important attribute of any query-subset selection technique since the value-addition from individual queries should ideally decrease as more and more queries are selected. Thus, not only are submodular functions natural for query subset selection, they can also be optimized efficiently and scalably such that the result has mathematical performance guarantees.

We show that our proposed algorithms result in significant improvements compared to state-of-the-art query selection algorithms thereby helping in reducing data annotation costs.

2. RELATED WORK

Active Learning for Labelling Cost Reduction:
A number of active learning strategies have been proposed for the traditional supervised learning setting, a common one being *uncertainty sampling* which selects the unlabelled example about which the model is most uncertain how to label. Some of the others adopt the idea of reducing the generalization error and select the unlabelled example that has the highest effect on the test error, i.e. points in the maximally uncertain and highly dense regions of the underlying data distribution[9]. A comprehensive active learning survey can be found in [22].

Reducing judgment effort for learning to rank has received significant amount of attention from the research community. Learning to rank methods are quite different than approaches used for classification as they require optimizing nonsmooth cost functions such as NDCG and AP [24]. Moreover, owing to the unique *query-document* structure which inherent to the learning to rank setting, it is not straightforward to extend the models devised for traditional supervised learning settings to ranking problems. In recent years, active learning has been actively extended to rank learning and can be classified into two classes of approaches: document level and query level active learning.

Document Selection for Learning to Rank:
Based on uncertainty sampling, Yu *et al*[28] selected the most ambiguous document pairs, in which two documents received close scores predicted by the current model, as informative examples. Donmez *et al.*[8] chose those document pairs, which if labelled could change the current model parameters significantly. Silva *et al* [23] proposed a novel document level active sampling algorithm based on association rules, which does not rely on any initial training seed.

Query Selection for Learning to Rank:
For query level active learning, Yilmaz *et al.* [27] empirically showed that having more queries but shallow documents performed better than having less queries but deep documents. They balance number of queries with depth of documents judged using random query selection. Cai *et al.* [5] propose the use of Query-By-Committee (QBC) based method to select queries for ranking adaptation but omit the evaluation of the query selection part and focussed on the ranking adaptation results instead. Long *et al.* [17] introduced an expected loss optimization (ELO) framework for ranking, where the selection of query and documents were integrated in a principled 2 staged active learning framework and most informative queries selected by optimizing the expected DCG loss but the proposed approach is limited to rankers that predict absolute graded relevance and hence not generalizable to all rankers. Authors in [2] adapt ELO to work with any ranker by introducing a calibration phase where a classification model is trained over in the validation data. Moreover, they show that estimating expected loss in DCG is more robust than NDCG even when the final performance measure is NDCG.

Thus, QBC attempts to capture the informativeness aspect of queries by selecting queries which minimize the disagreement among a committee of rankers while the Expected loss optimization based approach formulates informativeness in terms of expected DCG loss; both these approaches fail to capture the representativeness aspect of queries which we show outperforms both these approaches.

Submodular Maximization:
Submodularity is a property of set functions with deep theoretical and practical consequences. Submodular maximization generalizes to many well-known problems, e.g., maximum weighted matching, max coverage, and finds numerous applications in machine learning and social networks. In Information Retrieval, submodular objectives have been majorly employed for diversified retrieval[29] & learning from implicit feedback[21]. A seminal result of Nemhauser *et al.* [19] states that a simple greedy algorithm, based on a submodular objective, produces solutions competitive with the optimal (intractable) solution. In fact, if assuming nothing but submodularity, no efficient algorithm produces better solutions in general [10].

3. QUERY SELECTION STRATEGIES

Our aim is to *actively* select the optimal subset of unlabelled queries for obtaining relevance judgements so as to reduce data annotation costs. Intuitively, the selected queries should have two major properties: informativeness & representativeness. We describe both these properties below and provide intuitions motivating each.

3.1 Informativeness

Informativeness measures the ability of an instance in reducing the uncertainty of a statistical model[22]. Ideally, the selected queries should be maximally informative to the ranking model. In learning to rank setting, Informativeness based query selection focusses on greedily selecting queries which are most informative to the current version of the ranking model.

Different notions of informativeness can be encapsulated by different techniques depending on how query-level informativeness is quantified. Two possible measures of capturing a query's informativeness include: (i) *Uncertainty* based informativeness & (ii) *Disagreement* based informativeness.

Uncertainty based informativeness quantifies the query-level information as the uncertainty associated with the optimal document ranking order for that query. Query selection strategies focusing on uncertainty reduction would greedily select the query instance about which the current ranking model is most uncertain about, thereby trying to reduce the overall uncertainty associated with the ranking model.

Disagreement based informativeness, on the other hand, quantifies the query-level informativeness as the disagreement in this query's document rankings among a committee of ranking models. The key idea here is that the maximally informative query is one about whose document rankings, the committee of ranking models maximally disagree; hence obtaining relevance labels for such a query would provide the maximum information. Among the existing approaches for query selection for ranking models, the Query-by-Committee [5] attempts to capture the Informativeness aspect of queries based on a disagreement measure.

3.2 Representativeness

Representativeness measures if an instance well represents the overall input patterns of unlabelled data [22]. Web search queries can span a multitude of topics and information needs, with even a small dataset containing a broad set of queries ranging from simple navigational queries to very specific domain-dependent queries. In learning to rank settings, this implies that selected queries should have strong correlation with the remaining queries, as without this correlation there is no generalizability and predictive capability. Different notions of representativeness can be defined covering different characteristics of individual queries. Improving the representativeness of the selected query subset improves the coverage aspect of the query collection - the more representative selected queries are, the more they cover the entire query collection.

3.3 Informativeness vs Representativeness

Selecting queries solely based on their informativeness aspects could possibly lead to selection of *noisy* queries. In line with the Meta-Search Hypothesis [14][15], rankers tend to agree on relevant documents and disagree about nonrelevant docs. Hence, the queries that a ranker is unsure about or there is big disagreements across rankers are likely to be the ones that contain a lot of nonrelevant documents. Such noisy, *outlier* queries which majorly have non-relevant documents would lead to maximal disagreement and uncertainty among ranking models, and thus would be wrongly labelled maximally informative. Also, the set of informative queries might not necessarily represent the set of all possible queries, which lead to less coverage of the unlabelled query set.

On the other hand, selecting queries based on representativeness aspects could lead to the selection of a query that is very similar to the a query already in the labelled set and hence, does not provide much information to the ranking model. Despite being representative, such queries possibly offer redundant information to the ranking models. Ideally, a query selection algorithm should take into account both these aspects while selecting queries. Existing work has majorly looked into selecting queries by considering informativeness based on disagreement among rankers (Query-by-Committee) or informativeness in terms of expected DCG loss (Expected loss optimization). Both these approaches fail to capture the representativeness aspect of queries. In addition to a novel informativeness approach based on uncertainty reduction, we present a representativeness based approach and finally couple both these aspects for query selection via a joint submodular objective which jointly incorporates informativeness & representativeness.

As our first contribution, we present a novel informativeness based query selection scheme (§ 4) based on permutation probabilities of document rankings which tries to reduce uncertainty among rankers. While no existing query selection scheme for learning to rank incorporates the representativeness aspect of queries, we propose a LDA topic model based query selection scheme (§ 5) which captures the representative aspect of queries while constructing the query subset. An ideal query subset would have both informative & representative queries. As our third contribution, we combine the two paradigms of representativeness & informativeness by proposing a coupled model based on submodular functions(§ 6).

4. CAPTURING INFORMATIVENESS VIA PERMUTATION PROBABILITIES

Our first novel query selection scheme is aimed at capturing the informative-aspect of queries. We maintain a committee of ranking models $C = \{\theta^1, \theta^2, ..., \theta^C\}$ which are trained on a randomly selected subset from the current labelled set, and thus contain different aspects of the training data depending on the queries in their subset. It is to be noted that these ranking models could be generated using any learning to rank algorithm. Given the set of currently labelled query instances, our goal is to pick the next query (q^*) from the set of unlabelled queries by selecting the maximally informative query instance. The query-level informativeness is defined in terms of the uncertainty associated with the optimal document ranking orders among the $|C|$ ranking models. We follow a similar approach as outlined by Cai *et al.*[5] to maintain a committee of rankers. However, unlike Query-By-Committee [5] which encapsulates informativeness via ranker disagreements, our approach presents an alternate view of informativeness based on uncertainty reduction wherein a ranking model's uncertainty for the query's document ranking order is defined based on the concept of permutation probabilities.

More specifically, each committee ranking model is allowed to score the documents associated with each query following which a permutation probability is calculated on the ranking obtained on sorting these document scores. Thus, each query gets a permutation probability score by each committee member. The most informative query is considered to be the query instance which minimizes the maximum permutation probability of document scores given by each ranking model committee member.

We postulate that a query which has the minimum permutation probability score from among the maximum scores assigned between the different ranking models is maximally informative in the sense that even the best ranker among the committee is highly uncertain about its document rankings and hence this query obtained the least permutation probability score among the set of unlabelled candidate queries. We select a query for which the probability with respect to the most certain (maximum permutation probability) model is minimal, i.e., a query for which even the most certain committee member has minimum confidence.

To define permutation probabilities, we make use of the Plackett-Luce model [20]. The Plackett-Luce (P-L) model is a distribution over rankings of items (documents) which is described in terms of the associated ordering of these items (documents). We define $P(\pi|\upsilon)$ as the probability of obtaining the ranking order (π) based on the score (υ_k) assigned to each document (k) by the ranking model learnt thus far. For each query, we rank the documents based on the scores assigned by model learnt so far and calculate the probability of the ranking order obtained (π) using the permutation probability defined as follows:

$$P(\pi|\upsilon) = \prod_{i=1,\ldots,K} \frac{\upsilon_{\omega_i}}{\upsilon_{\omega_i} + \cdots + \upsilon_{\omega_K}} \tag{1}$$

where each ranking π has an associated ordering of document scores $\omega = (\omega_1, \cdots, \omega_K)$ and an ordering is defined as a permutation the K document indices with υ_{ω_i} representing the score assigned to document i (at rank ω_i) by the ranking model. We make use of a committee of ranking models and select the maximally informative query based on a greedy min-max algorithm described next.

4.1 Min-Max PL Probability Algorithm

Building a Min-Max PL Probability based selection system involves two components: (i) building a committee of ranking models that are well diversified and compatible with the currently labelled data and (ii) computing permutation probabilities by each committee member for each query in the unlabelled set of queries & selecting maximally informative query as per the min-max score.

Committee Construction:
Following the work of [5], we use query-by-bagging approach to construct the members. Given the set of currently labelled instances, bagging generates C partitions of sub samples by sampling uniformly with replacement, and then the committee can be constructed by training each of its members on one portion of the sub-sample partitions. We randomly initialize the initial set of labelled queries with a small base set of queries and their labelled documents. We sample with replacement for C times in the set of labelled queries and train a ranking model on each subset of queries. Such a sampling procedure allows us to create various different training datasets that each represent a subset of the data possibly having very different characteristics than each other. These C models represents our C committee members. We set the size of each subset to be 50 % of the current labelled subset size at each step. The maximally informative query q^* is selected for annotation which obtains the lowest min-max score, the calculation of which is described below.

Calculating min-max score:
For each query q in the candidate set of unlabelled queries, the C committee members return C ranked lists. Following the construction of $|C|$ ranking models, for each ranking model per query, we sort the documents based on the scores given by the ranking model and compute the permutation probability of obtaining this ranking order.

Thus, each query has $|C|$ permutation probability scores. In order to minimize the overall uncertainty associated with the ranking models, we select the maximally informative query q^*, i.e., the query that has the minimum value of the permutation probability assigned by its *most certain* committee member, i.e., the committee member that has the highest permutation probability score associated with the query's document ranking order. Thus,

$$q^* = argmin_{q \in D_u} \left[max_{c \in C} \left\{ P(\pi_q^c | \upsilon_q^c) \triangleq \prod_{k=1,\ldots,K} \frac{\upsilon_{\omega_k}^c}{\upsilon_{\omega_k}^c + \cdots + \upsilon_{\omega_K}^c} \right\} \right] \tag{2}$$

where each ranking π_q^c has an associated ordering $\omega = (\omega_1^c, \cdots, \omega_K^c)$ and an ordering is defined as a permutation the K document indices with $\upsilon_{\omega_k}^c$ representing the score assigned to document k by the ranking model c.

5. CAPTURING REPRESENTATIVENESS VIA LDA TOPICS

A major drawback associated with pure-Informativeness based models is that often they tend to select outlier queries. As is confirmed by the Meta-Search Hypothesis [14][15], rankers tend to agree on relevant documents but disagree on non-relevant documents. In such a scenario, an outlier query which majorly has non-relevant documents would lead to maximal disagreement and uncertainty in the ranking model, and thus will be wrongly labelled maximally informative. This motivates the need for considering the representativeness aspect of queries.

The information-seeking behaviour of users tend to vary based on the search task at hand [25] which suggests that the importance of feature weights for queries belonging to different tasks or topics are likely to be very different. The relative importance of different features are likely to be very different for different tasks. For example, queries belonging to a topic such as news would warrant high authority websites to be ranked higher (i.e., larger weight on the pagerank score) while queries belonging to (say) educational informational content would prefer the documents better matched with their query terms be ranked higher (i.e., larger weight on the relevance features such as BM25). To capture these diverse variations in the feature weights, the training set should ideally be composed of representative queries from different tasks. This makes it necessary that the labelled set of queries have representative queries spanning the entire array of different topics. We propose a Latent Dirichlet Allocation (LDA) [3] topic model based query selection scheme which tries to capture this insight by selecting representative queries which are most *topically* similar to the set of unlabelled queries.

Based on this intuition, we conjecture that representative queries would be those that are most similar to the set of unlabelled queries in terms of their topical distribution. To capture the heterogeneity among all queries in the search logs, we make use of the concept of latent topics. We learn these latent topics from the collection of queries and represent each query as a probability distribution over these latent topics. We train an LDA model, a generative model which posits that each document (query in our case) is a mixture of a small number of topics and that each word's (query term's) creation is attributable to one of the document's (query's) topics. Each query is represented as a feature vector corresponding to its distribution over the LDA topics. To find representative queries, we select the query with the maximum average similarity from among the unlabelled set of queries, i.e.,

$$q^* = argmax_q \frac{1}{|D_u|} \sum_{q_i \in D_u} sim(T_q, T_{q_i}) \tag{3}$$

where $|D_u|$ represents the number of queries in the unlabelled set D_u; T_q represents the query q's feature vector in the LDA topic space and $sim(T_q, T_{q_i})$ can be any similarity score between queries; we use the cosine similarity between the topic-space representations of queries q and q_i.

6. COMBINING REPRESENTATIVENESS & INFORMATIVENESS

The approaches discussed so far have looked at either the *informativeness* of queries and selected queries which are most informative in terms of their ability reduce the uncertainty of the ranking model or they have focussed on *representativeness* of queries and selected representative queries spanning the entire array of different topics. As we discussed earlier in subsection 3.3, optimizing for only one of the two criteria for query selection could significantly limit the performance of query selection by selecting suboptimal query subsets. In this section we present a way of combining the two objectives by means of submodular functions and propose a submodular objective which jointly captures the notions of representativeness and informativeness.

6.1 Submodular Functions

Submodular functions are discrete functions that model laws of diminishing returns and can be defined as follows:[19]: Given a finite set of objects (samples) $Q = \{q_1, ..., q_n\}$ and a function $f : 2^S \rightarrow \Re^+$ that returns a real value for any subset $S \subseteq Q$, f is submodular if given $S \subseteq S'$, and $q \notin S'$

$$f(S+q) - f(S) \geq f(S'+q) - f(S') \tag{4}$$

That is, the incremental "value" of q decreases when the set in which q is considered grows from S to S'. A function is *monotone submodular* if $\forall S \subseteq S'$, $f(S) \leq f(S')$. Powerful guarantees exist for such subtypes of monotone submodular function maximization. Though NP-hard, the problem of maximizing a monotone submodular function subject to a cardinality constraint can be approximately solved by a simple greedy algorithm [19] with a worst-case approximation factor $(1-e^{-1})$. This is also the best solution obtainable in polynomial time unless P=NP [10].

6.2 Problem Formulation

Submodularity is a natural model for query subset selection in Learning to Rank setting. Indeed, an important characteristic of any query-subset selection technique would be to decrease the value-addition of a query $q \in Q$ based on how much of that query has in common with the subset of queries already selected (S). The value $f(q|S)$ of a query in the context of previously selected subset of queries S further diminishes as the subset grows $S' \supseteq S$. In our setting, each $q \in Q$ is a distinct query, Q corresponds to the entire collection of queries and S corresponds to the subset of queries already selected from Q.

Mathematically, the query subset selection problem can be formulated as selecting the subset of queries S which maximizes the value of $f(S)$ where $f(S)$ captures both the representativeness aspect as well as the informativeness aspects of queries. We next describe in detail the construction of such a monotone submodular function and later present a greedy algorithm to approximately solve the problem of query subset selection.

6.3 Submodular Query Selection

We model the quality of the query subset in terms of both the representativeness & informativeness. To capture both these traits, we model the quality of the query subset as:

$$F(S) = \beta\Phi(S) + (1-\beta)\Psi(S) \tag{5}$$

where $\Phi(S)$ captures the representativeness aspect of the query subset (S) with respect to the entire query set Q while $\Psi(S)$ rewards selecting informative queries. The parameter β controls the trade-off between the importance of representativeness & informativeness while selecting queries. A single weighting scheme would not be suitable for all problems since depending on the constituent queries, size of the overall dataset and the size of the subset that needs to be selected, different weighting schemes would produce different results. The function $F(S)$ will be monotone submodular if each of $\Phi(S)$ and $\Psi(S)$ are individually monotone submodular. We defer an in-depth analysis of the trade-off between representativeness & informativeness aspects to subsection 8.1 and next describe the details of both these functions.

6.3.1 Representativeness: $\Phi(S)$

$\Phi(S)$ can be interpreted either as a set function that measures the similarity of query subset S to the overall query set Q, or as a function representing some form of "representation" of Q by S. Most naturally, $\Phi(S)$ should be monotone, as representativeness improves with a larger subset. $\Phi(S)$ should also be submodular: consider adding a new query to two query subsets, one a subset of the other. Intuitively, the increment when adding a new query to the small subset should be larger than the increment when adding it to the larger subset, as the information carried by the new query might have already been covered by those queries that are in the larger subset but not in the smaller subset. Indeed, this is the property of diminishing returns.

We employ the same functional form of $\Phi(S)$ as was adopted by Lin *et al.*[16]. Specifically, a saturated coverage function is defined as follows:

$$\Phi(S) = \sum_{q \in Q} min \{C_q(S), \alpha C_q(Q)\} \tag{6}$$

where $C_q(S)$ is a set based function defined as $C_q(S) : 2^S \rightarrow \Re$ and $0 \leq \alpha \leq 1$ is a threshold co-efficient. Intuitively, $C_q(S)$ measures how *topically* similar S is to query q or how much of the query q is covered by the subset S. Building on top of the earlier proposed LDA topic model based query selection, we define the coverage function $C_q(S)$ in terms of the *topical coverage* of queries. More specifically,

$$C_q(S) = \sum_{q' \in S} w_{q,q'} \tag{7}$$

where $w_{q,q'} \geq 0$ measures the topical similarity between queries q and q'. Since $C_q(S)$ measures how *topically* similar S is to query q, summing $C_q(S)$ $\forall q \in Q$ would measure how similar the current subset S is to the overall set of queries Q. It is important to note that $C_q(Q)$ is just the largest value $C_q(S)$ can ever obtain because Q is the set of all the queries we have and it maximally represents all the information we have. We call a query q *saturated* by the subset of queries S when $min \{C_q(S), \alpha C_q(Q)\} = \alpha C_q(Q)$. When q is saturated in this way, any new query cannot further improve the coverage even if it is very similar to the query q. Thus, this gives other queries which are not yet saturated a higher chance of being better covered and hence the resulting subset tends to better cover the entire set of queries Q.

6.3.2 *Informativeness:* $\Psi(S)$

The $\Phi(S)$ function described above intuitively captures the notion of coverage or representativeness by selecting subset of queries S which are topically most representative of the entire set of queries Q. While representativeness is an important trait, we also wish to capture the informativeness aspect of queries and select queries which are most informative to the current version of the ranking model. We formulate the functional form of $\Psi(S)$ based on top of the earlier proposed ways of encapsulating query-level informativeness in terms of either ranker disagreements or model uncertainity, or both. As a precursor, it is worth mentioning that to define the function $\Phi(S)$ we make use of LDA topic model which gives us k-topics and we associate each query to one of these k-topics. Formally, we define the $\Psi(S)$ function as follows:

$$\Psi(S) = \sum_{i=1}^{K} \sqrt{\sum_{q \in P_i \cap S} \Upsilon_q} \tag{8}$$

where $P_i, i = 1, ..., K$ is the topical-partition of the set of queries Q into K-topics and Υ_q captures the informativeness carried by the query q based on the current ranking model. The function $\Psi(S)$ rewards topical-diversity along with valuing informativeness since there is usually more benefit to selecting a query from a topic not yet having one of its query already chosen. As soon as a query is selected from a topic, other queries from the same topic start having diminishing gain owing to the square root function ($\sqrt{2}+\sqrt{1} > \sqrt{3}+\sqrt{0}$). It is easy to show that $\Psi(S)$ is submodular by the composition rule. The square root is non-decreasing concave function. Inside each square root lies a modular function with non-negative weights (and thus is monotone). Applying the square root to such a monotone submodular function yields a submodular function, and summing them all together retains submodularity.

The informativeness of a query Υ_q can be defined based on the metrics proposed earlier. To incorporate the informativeness aspects of queries, we experiment with various different formulations of the singleton-query rewards (Υ_q) include the following::

- Disagreement Score for a query - this allows us to capture information about the disagreement about the document rankings for a query among a committee of ranking models [5]
- Uncertainty associated with the query - this allows us to capture the ranking model's uncertainty about the query's document rankings 4
- Combination of uncertainty & disagreement.

Based on empirical analysis, we find that the disagreement based reward functions perform better than the rest of the formulations across all datasets, so we skip the performance comparisons among these.

6.4 Greedy Optimization

Having defined the individual functions based on the different paradigms, we formulate the overall query subset selection problem as the selection of the subset S of queries which maximizes the following function:

$$\begin{aligned} F(S) &= \beta \sum_{q \in Q} min \left\{ \sum_{q' \in S} w_{q,q'}, \alpha \sum_{q' \in Q} w_{q,q'} \right\} \\ &+ (1-\beta) \sum_{i=1}^{K} \sqrt{\sum_{q \in P_i \cap S} \Upsilon_q} \end{aligned} \tag{9}$$

Modelling the query selection problem in such an objective provides many advantages. Firstly, the submodular formulation provides a natural way of coupling the different aspects of query selection. Secondly, the above formulation can be optimized efficiently and scalably given the monotone submodular form of the function $F(S)$. Assuming we wish to select a subset of N queries from the total unlabelled set of Q queries, the problem reduces to solving the following optimization problem:

$$S^* = \underset{S \subseteq Q, |S| \leq N}{\text{argmax}} \; F(S) \tag{10}$$

While solving this problem exactly is NP-complete [10], techniques like ILP [18] can be used but scaling it to bigger datasets becomes prohibitive. Since the function $F(S)$ is submodular, it can be shown that a simple greedy algorithm will have a worst-case guarantee of $f(S^*) \geq (1-\frac{1}{e})F(S_{opt}) \approx 0.63F(S_{opt})$ where S_{opt} is the optimal and S^* is the greedy solution [10]. This constant factor guarantee has practical importance. First, a constant factor guarantee stays the same as N grows, so the relative worst-case quality of the solution is the same for small and for big problem instances. Second, the worst-case result is achieved only by very contrived and unrealistic function instances - the typical case is almost always much better. The greedy solution works by starting with an empty set and repeatedly augmenting the set as

$$S \leftarrow S \cup \underset{q \in Q \setminus S}{\text{argmax}} \, F(q|S) \tag{11}$$

	MQ2007 Dataset					
nQueries	SF	LDA	PL	ELO	QBC	RDM
30	**0.496**$^{*\&}$	0.495	0.493	0.493	0.493	0.482
50	**0.502**$^{*\&}$	0.501	0.496	0.494	0.490	0.485
100	0.509	0.504	**0.510**$^{*\&}$	0.506	0.500	0.501
150	**0.518**$^{*\&}$	0.517	0.510	0.511	0.506	0.507
250	**0.528**$^{*\&}$	0.527	0.519	0.517	0.513	0.516
350	0.527	**0.528***	0.523	0.520	0.525	0.523
400	**0.531**$^{*\&}$	**0.531**$^{*\&}$	0.526	0.523	0.526	0.524
500	**0.535**$^{*\&}$	0.531	0.530	0.528	0.527	0.526

	MQ2008 Dataset					
nQueries	SF	LDA	PL	ELO	QBC	RDM
30	**0.730***	0.728	0.722	0.716	0.728	0.714
50	**0.735***	0.731	0.731	0.720	0.734	0.721
100	**0.741**$^{*\&}$	0.740	0.739	0.724	0.735	0.733
150	**0.743***	0.742	0.740	0.729	0.742	0.734
250	0.745	0.745	**0.748**$^{*\&}$	0.735	0.746	0.740
350	**0.751**$^{\&}$	0.749	0.745	0.749	0.747	0.744
400	**0.753**$^{*\&}$	0.750	0.748	0.746	0.747	0.745

	OHSUMED Dataset					
nQueries	SF	LDA	PL	ELO	QBC	RDM
25	**0.466***	0.459	0.463	0.463	0.465	0.432
30	0.464	0.466	**0.473**$^{*\&}$	0.454	0.455	0.462
35	0.463	**0.478**$^{*\&}$	0.476	0.467	0.458	0.463
40	**0.478**$^{*\&}$	0.460	0.468	0.455	0.469	0.460
45	**0.481**$^{*\&}$	0.473	0.456	0.455	0.464	0.473
50	**0.484**$^{*\&}$	0.466	0.467	0.467	0.472	0.464

Figure 1: Performance evaluation based on NDCG@10 scores for the different algorithms; SF: Submodular function based query selection, LDA: LDA Topic Model based query selection, PL: Permutation Probability Based Query Selection, ELO: expected loss minimization baseline, QBC: Query-By-Committee baseline, RDM: Random query selection baseline. nQueries is the number of queries in the labelled set = base set + actively labelled queries. * and & indicates a statistically significant result (t-test, $p \leq 0.05$) when compared to ELO & QBC respectively.

until we select the N number of queries in the subset we intended.

Overall, we select query subsets based on the aforementioned formulations; we next describe in detail the experimental evaluation performed to compare the performances of the three proposed approaches against state-of-the-art baselines.

7. EXPERIMENTAL EVALUATION

We evaluate the proposed query selection strategies on web search ranking and show that the proposed techniques can result in good performance with much fewer labelled queries. We next describe our experimental settings along with the baselines, dataset and evaluation metrics used.

7.1 Compared Approaches

We compare the performance of the proposed query selection strategies against existing state-of-the-art approaches. The compared approaches include:

- **Query-By-Committee (QBC)**: The Query-By-Committee (QBC) approach involves maintaining a committee of models wherein each member is then allowed to vote on the labellings of query candidates. The most informative query is considered to be the instance about which the committee members most disagree. QBC based query selection strategy was used in [5] for ranking adaptation.
- **Expected Loss Optimization (ELO)**: Based on the ELO framework described by Long et al [17], we implemented the query-selection phase of the originally proposed 2-phase active learning framework to select queries wherein the most informative queries are selected by optimizing the expected DCG loss. As is mentioned in the original paper, we use score-range normalization to calculate the gain function. For details, please refer to [17].
- **Random Query Selection (RDM)**: Queries are selected randomly for labelling from among the set of unlabelled queries. It is to be noted that random query selection is the primary method used in most settings [6].
- **Permutation Probability Model (PL)**: Our first proposed approach (§ 4) based on capturing informativeness of queries via the uncertainty reduction principle.
- **Topic Model (LDA)**: Our second proposed approach (§ 5) based on selecting *representative* queries which are most *topically* similar to the set of unlabelled queries.
- **Submodular Model (SF)**: Our final proposed approach (§ 6) based on the coupled submodular objective which incorporates both the aspects of query informativeness & representativeness.

7.2 Dataset

We use three commonlyused real-world learning to rank datasets: (i) MQ2007; (ii) MQ2008 from LETOR 4.0 which uses query sets from Million Query track of TREC 2007, TREC 2008 and (iii) the OHSUMED test collection, a subset of the MEDLINE database, which is a bibliographic database of important, peer-reviewed medical literature maintained by the National Library of Medicine. It is worth mentioning that the proposed approaches make use of query term information which is not available in many other ranking datasets, hence we restrict our evaluation to these three datasets having query term information. There are ~1700 queries in MQ2007, ~800 queries in MQ2008 and ~100 queries in the OHSUMED dataset. The MQ2007 & MQ2008 datasets are of notable size and query selection indeed makes sense in the such datasets; the OHSUMED dataset, on the other hand, has too few queries to select from which isn't ideal for a query selection scenario. Nevertheless, we compare performances across all datasets.

We adopt a 5-fold cross validation scheme with each fold divided into three parts, one each for training, validation and testing in the ratio 3:1:1. Each query-document pair is represented using 46 features [45 in case of the OHSUMED dataset) along with the relevance score from among {0,1,2}. The test set is used to evaluate the different query selection strategies while active learning is performed on queries from the training set.

7.3 Experimental Setting

We start with a base set of 40 labelled queries randomly sampled from the entire query set; the rest of the queries form the candidate set. We make use of $C = 4$ committee members (where applicable) each of which is constructed based on the procedure described earlier (subsection 4.1). To learn the initial ranking models for each of the committee members, we randomly select a sample of 20 queries from the base set of 40 queries and build a ranking model based

	MQ2008 Dataset						MQ2007 Dataset					
% Queries	SF	LDA	PL	ELO	QBC	RDM	SF	LDA	PL	ELO	QBC	RDM
~5%	0.726	**0.731***	0.721	0.729	0.730	0.728	**0.514**$^{*\&}$	0.505	0.486	0.501	0.498	0.498
~10%	0.735	**0.737**$^{*\&}$	0.733	0.734	0.734	0.726	**0.508***	0.498	0.501	0.503	0.507	0.496
~25%	**0.738**$^{*\&}$	0.732	0.733	0.731	0.730	0.727	**0.513**$^{*\&}$	0.509	0.511	0.507	0.511	0.504
~50%	**0.745**$^{*\&}$	0.731	0.734	0.735	0.734	0.728	**0.516**$^{*\&}$	0.510	0.505	0.509	0.514	0.505

Table 1: Generalizability across different Learning to Rank algorithm: NDCG performance based on ADARANK algorithm. Performance evaluation based on NDCG@10 scores for the different algorithms; SF: Submodular function based query selection, LDA: LDA Topic Model based query selection, PL: min-max Plackett-Luce Based Query Selection, ELO: expected loss minimization baseline, QBC: Query-By-Committee baseline, RDM: Random query selection baseline. % Queries is the % of queries in the labelled set = base set + actively labelled queries. * and & indicates a statistically significant result (t-test, p≤0.05) when compared to ELO & QBC respectively.

on these queries as training data. We first focus on LambdaMART [11], (a state-of-the-art learning to rank algorithm that was the winner of the Yahoo! Learning to Rank challenge [4]) to build ranking models used in the initial part of our experiments. We later show (subsection 8.2) that the queries selected by this method could also be used by other Learning to Rank algorithms.

The entire experiment is repeated multiple times over the 5 folds on each dataset. We perform batch mode Active Learning for queries by selecting a batch of top 10 queries from the candidate set of queries based on the query selection criterion at each round and iteratively add them to our base set. Queries having no relevant documents were ignored while calculating the different metrics. Based on empirical estimation, the threshold parameter in equation 6 was initialized as $\alpha = 0.8$. For our initial results, we evaluate the performance of the proposed query selection strategies based on their NDCG@10 values in the test set. We later analyse the generalizability of our approach on a different metric (MAP).

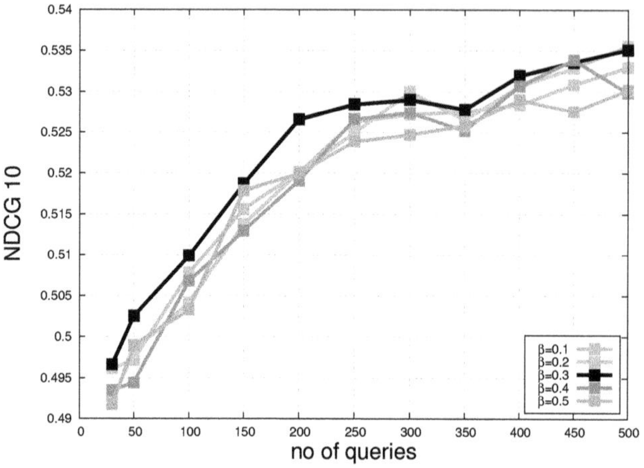

Figure 2: Tradeoff analysis between Informativeness & Representativeness for the MQ2007 datasets. The β coefficient in equation 5 controls the relative importance of the two aspects.

8. RESULTS

We compare the NDCG@10 performance of the test set against the number of queries in training set (base queries plus actively selected) in Figure 1 for the different datasets and compare the performance of the proposed query selection schemes against the QBC, ELO and Random baselines (statistically significant results are highlighted in the respective tables). For all the methods, the NDCG@10 values tends to increase with the number of iterations which is in line with the intuition that the quality of the ranking model is positively correlated with the number of examples in the training set.

While min-max PL based query selection stems from the same class of approaches (informativeness based) like the two baselines ELO & QBC, it performs better than both these baselines in most cases; this is in line with our initial claim of capturing informative queries from an alternate view of informativeness based on uncertainty reduction. We observe that LDA Topic Model based query selection performs better than existing baselines as well as the PL model which suggests that the quality of the queries selected by this scheme is better than those selected by other strategies which are mostly based on the informativeness aspect. Perhaps selecting queries based on the informativeness results in some noisy *outlier* queries getting selected, a case which LDA topic model based query selection avoids by selecting representative queries. The minor fluctuations and occasional dip in the NDCG values on adding more queries to the labelled set could be explained by the fact that some queries are indeed noisy and selecting such queries induces noise in the ranking models, which results in a slightly worse ranker performance.

Finally, we observe from the results that the submodular objective (SF) outperforms the baselines as well as (in most cases) our own proposed purely informativeness & purely representativeness based query selection schemes across the different datasets. While purely informativeness based methods tend to select noisy queries, purely representativeness based methods might possibly select queries which are representative but add redundant information. Hence, selecting queries based on the coupled aspects selects queries which are not only representative of other unselected queries, but are also informative to the ranking model.

8.1 Trade-Off between Informativeness & Representativeness

Our main motivation behind introducing the submodular objective was to couple the notions of informativeness and representativeness in a joint coherent manner. Indeed, an ideal subset of queries would be a fine blend of queries which convey the maximal amount of *information* to the ranking model while at the same time, be characteristic of the unselected set of queries. In Figure 2, we present a example analysis on one of the datasets of the relative importance of the two aspects and how they contribute to the overall ranking performance. As can be seen in the figure, a relative weight-

	MQ2008 Dataset						MQ2007 Dataset					
% Queries	SF	LDA	PL	ELO	QBC	RDM	SF	LDA	PL	ELO	QBC	RDM
~5%	**0.354***$^{*\&}$	**0.354***$^{*\&}$	0.344	0.341	0.340	0.342	**0.164****	0.147	0.147	0.154	0.163	0.149
~10%	**0.371***$^{*\&}$	0.328	0.354	0.362	0.361	0.352	**0.164***$^{*\&}$	0.146	0.155	0.148	0.160	0.159
~25%	0.362	**0.369***$^{*\&}$	0.357	0.357	0.362	0.361	**0.165***$^{*\&}$	0.158	0.161	0.157	0.161	0.160
~50%	0.360	**0.371***$^{*\&}$	0.367	0.369	0.346	0.365	**0.166***$^{*\&}$	**0.166***$^{*\&}$	0.160	0.153	0.135	0.159

Table 2: Generalizability across different Learning to Rank algorithm: AP performance based on Adarank algorithm. Performance evaluation based on NDCG@10 scores for the different algorithms; SF: Submodular function based query selection, LDA: LDA Topic Model based query selection, PL: min-max Plackett-Luce Based Query Selection, ELO: expected loss minimization baseline, QBC: Query-By-Committee baseline, RDM: Random query selection baseline. % Queries is the % of queries in the labelled set = base set + actively labelled queries. * and & indicates a statistically significant result (t-test, p≤0.05) when compared to ELO & QBC respectively.

ing scheme of $\beta = 0.3$ (which weighs representativeness-vs-informativeness in 3:7 proportions) works best for query selection. This highlights that while representativeness is important, selecting informative queries from the different topics indeed helps. Also, it must be noted that the informativeness term in Equation 9 not only contains contributions from query's singleton informativeness reward, but also has contributions from the topical segregation of queries into partitions. Overall, we chose the coefficient $\beta = 0.3$ to weigh the contributions from the two aspects while reporting results. It is to be noted that domain knowledge about the dataset in consideration can be used to vary β accordingly, depending on the desired proportion of representativeness & informativeness.

For a milder sized dataset (MQ2008), putting more weight on informativeness helps initially while the relative contributions tend toequal out once a certain threshold of queries have been selected. Overall, the general weighting factor or $\beta = 0.3$ works well consistently across different datasets.

8.2 Generalizability Across Learning Algorithms & Metrics

For initial results shown before, the query selection method uses LambdaMART as the learning to rank algorithms optimized for the NDCG metric. Since the labelled learning to rank dataset generated as a result of the query selection process could potentially be used in any future ranking systems, the selected queries should ideally be usable by any learning to rank algorithm, optimized for any metric. We analyze such generalization performance in these sets of experiments. While the initial set of results presented above were NDCG values based on LambdaMART ranking algorithm optimizing for NDCG metric, we divert from our original setting and present results on a different ranker: AdaRank [26] in table 1. Similar results for the OHSUMED dataset can be seen in Fig 3. Additionally, we demonstrate the performance of the proposed query selection strategies on a different metric (MAP) and report results in Table 2. Overall, we can see that the proposed query selection methodologies consistently perform better than the baselines across different ranking algorithms and metrics.

8.3 Labelling Cost Reduction

We next analyse the reduction in labelling cost achieved as compared to the case where the entire set of unlabelled queries were labelled. The performance of the ranking function trained with the whole labelled data set is referred to as the optimal performance. When the performance of the active learning model obtained with the proposed algorithms is comparable to the optimal performance, we call the size of training data as the saturated size (SS). Table 3 highlights the *approximate* labelling cost reduction (LCR) results obtained via the proposed query selection techniques. The %-ages were calculated based on the average number of queries in the training set. The corresponding values were calculated using the LambdaMART implementation with NDCG metric. Experimental evaluation shows the proposed query selection algorithms indeed require less number of queries to be labelled than baseline methods to achieve comparable ranking performance. It is worth mentioning that at some point, adding more queries to the labelled training set doesn't help improve ranking performance, as can be seen by the results of the RDM algorithm in the table: with about 720 labelled queries out of 1015 queries, the algorithm is able to demonstrate comparable ranking performance.

	MQ2007		MQ2008		OHSUMED	
Algorithm	SS	LCR	SS	LCR	SS	LCR
SF	~ 370	63%	~ 330	57%	~ 45	29%
LDA	~ 390	61%	~ 400	48%	~ 55	14%
PL	~ 490	51%	~ 510	35%	~ 55	14%
ELO	~ 560	44%	~ 520	34%	~ 60	6%
QBC	~ 620	39%	~ 540	31%	~ 60	6%
RDM	~ 720	29%	~ 570	27%	~ 60	6%

Table 3: The performance in terms of the Labelling Cost Reduction (LCR) and the Saturated Size (SS) for the various compared approaches.

	OHSUMED Dataset					
nQueries	SF	LDA	PL	ELO	QBC	RDM
30	0.473	0.469	**0.478**	0.477	**0.478**	0.466
40	**0.478**	**0.478**	0.475	0.472	0.477	0.467
50	**0.478**	0.466	0.469	0.477	0.477	0.473

Figure 3: Results on the OHSUMED dataset with LamdaMART Learning to Rank algorithm. * and & indicates a statistically significant result (t-test, p≤0.05) when compared to ELO & QBC respectively.

9. CONCLUSION & FUTURE WORK

We formulated approaches to the query selection problem into two classes: *informativeness* based and *representativeness* based strategies and proposed two novel query selection strategies, one from each class respectively: permutation probability based and LDA Topic Model based query selection. Additionally, we argued that an ideal query selection scheme should incorporate insights from both the aspects and presented a principled way of coupling information from the two aspects. Based on rigorous experiments we demonstrated the efficacy of the proposed query selection schemes. A possible line of future work could look at enriching the representativeness aspect by adding document level information to the topic model.

10. REFERENCES

[1] J. A. Aslam, E. Kanoulas, V. Pavlu, S. Savev, and E. Yilmaz. Document selection methodologies for efficient and effective learning-to-rank. In *Proceedings of the 32nd international ACM SIGIR conference on Research and development in information retrieval*, pages 468–475. ACM, 2009.

[2] M. Bilgic and P. N. Bennett. Active query selection for learning rankers. In *Proceedings of the 35th international ACM SIGIR conference on Research and development in information retrieval*, pages 1033–1034. ACM, 2012.

[3] D. M. Blei, A. Y. Ng, and M. I. Jordan. Latent dirichlet allocation. *the Journal of machine Learning research*, 3:993–1022, 2003.

[4] C. J. Burges, K. M. Svore, P. N. Bennett, A. Pastusiak, and Q. Wu. Learning to rank using an ensemble of lambda-gradient models. In *Yahoo! Learning to Rank Challenge*, 2011.

[5] P. Cai, W. Gao, A. Zhou, and K.-F. Wong. Relevant knowledge helps in choosing right teacher: active query selection for ranking adaptation. In *Proceedings of the 34th international ACM SIGIR conference on Research and development in Information Retrieval*, pages 115–124. ACM, 2011.

[6] O. Chapelle and Y. Chang. Yahoo! learning to rank challenge overview. In *Yahoo! Learning to Rank Challenge*, 2011.

[7] O. Chapelle, Y. Chang, and T.-Y. Liu. Future directions in learning to rank. In *Yahoo! Learning to Rank Challenge*, 2011.

[8] P. Donmez and J. G. Carbonell. Optimizing estimated loss reduction for active sampling in rank learning. In *Proceedings of the 25th international conference on Machine learning*, pages 248–255. ACM, 2008.

[9] P. Donmez, J. G. Carbonell, and P. N. Bennett. Dual strategy active learning. In *Machine Learning: ECML 2007*, pages 116–127. Springer, 2007.

[10] U. Feige. A threshold of ln n for approximating set cover. *Journal of the ACM*, 1998.

[11] Y. Ganjisaffar, R. Caruana, and C. V. Lopes. Bagging gradient-boosted trees for high precision, low variance ranking models. In *Proceedings of the 34th international ACM SIGIR conference on Research and development in Information Retrieval*, pages 85–94. ACM, 2011.

[12] Y. Hamo and S. Markovitch. The compset algorithm for subset selection. In *IJCAI*, pages 728–733, 2005.

[13] M. Hosseini, I. J. Cox, N. Milic-Frayling, M. Shokouhi, and E. Yilmaz. An uncertainty-aware query selection model for evaluation of ir systems. In *Proceedings of the 35th international ACM SIGIR conference on Research and development in information retrieval*, pages 901–910. ACM, 2012.

[14] J. H. Lee. Combining multiple evidence from different properties of weighting schemes. In *Proceedings of the 18th annual international ACM SIGIR conference on Research and development in information retrieval*, pages 180–188. ACM, 1995.

[15] J. H. Lee. Analyses of multiple evidence combination. In *ACM SIGIR Forum*. ACM, 1997.

[16] H. Lin and J. Bilmes. Multi-document summarization via budgeted maximization of submodular functions. In *Human Language Technologies: The 2010 Annual Conference of the North American Chapter of the Association for Computational Linguistics*. Association for Computational Linguistics, 2010.

[17] B. Long, O. Chapelle, Y. Zhang, Y. Chang, Z. Zheng, and B. Tseng. Active learning for ranking through expected loss optimization. In *Proceedings of the 33rd international ACM SIGIR conference on Research and development in information retrieval*, pages 267–274. ACM, 2010.

[18] G. L. Nemhauser and L. A. Wolsey. *Integer and combinatorial optimization*, volume 18. Wiley New York, 1988.

[19] G. L. Nemhauser, L. A. Wolsey, and M. L. Fisher. An analysis of approximations for maximizing submodular set functions-i. *Mathematical Programming*, 1978.

[20] R. L. Plackett. The analysis of permutations. *Applied Statistics*, pages 193–202, 1975.

[21] K. Raman, P. Shivaswamy, and T. Joachims. Online learning to diversify from implicit feedback. In *Proceedings of the 18th ACM SIGKDD international conference on Knowledge discovery and data mining*. ACM, 2012.

[22] B. Settles. Active learning literature survey. *University of Wisconsin, Madison*, 52:55–66, 2010.

[23] R. Silva, M. A. Gonçalves, and A. Veloso. Rule-based active sampling for learning to rank. In *Machine Learning and Knowledge Discovery in Databases*, pages 240–255. Springer, 2011.

[24] M. Taylor, J. Guiver, S. Robertson, and T. Minka. Softrank: optimizing non-smooth rank metrics. In *Proceedings of the 2008 International Conference on Web Search and Data Mining*. ACM, 2008.

[25] R. W. White and D. Kelly. A study on the effects of personalization and task information on implicit feedback performance. In *Proceedings of the 15th ACM international conference on Information and knowledge management*, pages 297–306. ACM, 2006.

[26] J. Xu and H. Li. Adarank: a boosting algorithm for information retrieval. In *Proceedings of the 30th annual international ACM SIGIR conference on Research and development in information retrieval*. ACM, 2007.

[27] E. Yilmaz and S. Robertson. Deep versus shallow judgments in learning to rank. In *Proceedings of the 32nd international ACM SIGIR conference on Research and development in information retrieval*, pages 662–663. ACM, 2009.

[28] H. Yu. Svm selective sampling for ranking with application to data retrieval. In *Proceedings of the eleventh ACM SIGKDD international conference on Knowledge discovery in data mining*, pages 354–363. ACM, 2005.

[29] Y. Yue and C. Guestrin. Linear submodular bandits and their application to diversified retrieval. In *Advances in Neural Information Processing Systems*, 2011.

Impact of Surrogate Assessments on High-Recall Retrieval

Adam Roegiest
University of Waterloo

Gordon V. Cormack
University of Waterloo

Charles L.A. Clarke
University of Waterloo

Maura R. Grossman*
Wachtell, Lipton, Rosen & Katz

ABSTRACT

We are concerned with the effect of using a surrogate assessor to train a passive (i.e., batch) supervised-learning method to rank documents for subsequent review, where the effectiveness of the ranking will be evaluated using a different assessor deemed to be authoritative. Previous studies suggest that surrogate assessments may be a reasonable proxy for authoritative assessments for this task. Nonetheless, concern persists in some application domains—such as electronic discovery—that errors in surrogate training assessments will be amplified by the learning method, materially degrading performance. We demonstrate, through a re-analysis of data used in previous studies, that, with passive supervised-learning methods, using surrogate assessments for training can substantially impair classifier performance, relative to using the same deemed-authoritative assessor for both training and assessment. In particular, using a single surrogate to replace the authoritative assessor for training often yields a ranking that must be traversed much lower to achieve the same level of recall as the ranking that would have resulted had the authoritative assessor been used for training. We also show that steps can be taken to mitigate, and sometimes overcome, the impact of surrogate assessments for training: relevance assessments may be diversified through the use of multiple surrogates; and, a more liberal view of relevance can be adopted by having the surrogate label borderline documents as relevant. By taking these steps, rankings derived from surrogate assessments can match, and sometimes exceed, the performance of the ranking that would have been achieved, had the authority been used for training. Finally, we show that our results still hold when the role of surrogate and authority are interchanged, indicating that the results may simply reflect differing conceptions of relevance between surrogate and authority, as opposed to the authority having special skill or knowledge lacked by the surrogate.

*The views expressed herein are solely those of the author and should not be attributed to her firm or its clients.

SIGIR'15, August 09-13, 2015, Santiago, Chile.
ACM 978-1-4503-3621-5/15/08.
http://dx.doi.org/10.1145/2766462.2767754.

Categories and Subject Descriptors: H.3.4 Systems and Software Performance evaluation (efficiency and effectiveness).

Keywords: recall; assessor error; evaluation; eDiscovery; electronic discovery; relevance ranking; supervised learning.

1. INTRODUCTION

In high-recall information retrieval tasks—such as electronic discovery ("eDiscovery") in civil litigation [11], systematic review in evidence-based medicine [24], and preparation of test collections for information retrieval research [14]—supervised learning is often used to separate relevant from non-relevant documents [37]. In supervised learning, each of a pre-selected set of documents (the "training set") is labeled as relevant or not by a human assessor, and used to train a machine-learning algorithm, which then classifies or ranks the documents in a corpus (the "evaluation set") according to their likelihood of relevance. We focus here on a type of supervised learning, which, in eDiscovery is referred to as "simple passive learning" [12], to distinguish it from active learning, where the training set is selected incrementally, using feedback from the learning algorithm [38, 11].

To measure the effectiveness of a high-recall retrieval effort, it is necessary to estimate the number r of relevant documents from the evaluation set that are retrieved, as well as the number m that are missed. If r and m were known with certainty, it would be a simple matter to compute an effectiveness measure: For example, recall = $\frac{r}{r+m}$. However, the very notion of relevance is subjective [31, 32, 33], and necessarily relies on imperfect human judgement to determine m and r, and hence recall.

For many high-recall tasks, the opinion of a single subject-matter expert ("the authority") provides the ultimate determination of relevance. In the eDiscovery domain, the authority might be a senior lawyer representing the responding party; in the intellectual property domain, the authority might be a patent examiner; in the medical domain, the authority might be a senior researcher. In all cases, obtaining authoritative opinions for even a small set of documents may be impossible, or may incur unacceptable costs and delays.

Previous studies have investigated the impact of replacing the opinion of the authority with that of a surrogate assessor [41, 46, 28]. The results of those studies suggest that, at least under certain experimental conditions, a surrogate can reasonably replace the authority, thereby increasing the allure of using cheaper, more readily available surrogates as proxies for authorities. On the other hand, some practitioners claim that the use of authoritative assessors is of critical importance in training the machine-learning algorithms used for eDiscovery tasks. One commentator [19], writing in a trade magazine, expressed the concern that errors in relevance assessments will be amplified by a chosen learning method to an irrecoverable extent. Others, including one court [2], have referred to this training issue more generally as "garbage in, garbage out."

1.1 Overview of experiments

After a review of related work in Section 2, and a discussion of our general experimental methodology in Section 3, in Section 4, we describe our studies using the TREC-4 test collection and supplementary assessments described by Voorhees [41]. Using the official and supplementary sets of assessments, we trained a support vector machine ("SVM") on each set and ranked the entire corpus through the use of ten-fold cross validation. From these rankings, we determined the depth in the ranking required (i.e., the number of documents reviewed) to achieve a particular level of recall, when each of the three assessors was deemed to be the authority, while the others were treated as surrogates.

Extending these experiments, we explored whether the inclusion of training assessments that reflected greater diversity in the interpretation of relevance would improve ranking performance. We implemented this diversification strategy in two different ways. First, we created three new surrogate-assessment sets, each corresponding to a pair of the three original assessors, which we imagined as working together to judge the training set. We generated the merged set for a surrogate pair by randomly dividing the documents 50/50 between the two surrogates, with each determining relevance for their half. An SVM was then trained on each of these merged surrogates, and the results evaluated using cross-validation, treating the third assessor's opinion as authoritative.

As an alternate means of diversification, we took the union of each surrogate pair, such that a document was deemed relevant if either constituent had designated it as relevant. Again, an SVM was trained on each of these union surrogates and evaluated using cross-validation, treating the third assessor's opinion as authoritative.

In Section 5, we directly explore the impact of a more liberal interpretation of relevance on passive supervised learning. The University of Waterloo, in the course of participating in the TREC-6 adhoc task, created an independent set of relevance assessments that included a third relevance category —"iffy"—denoting documents which they believed to be of borderline relevance. The availability of three relevance categories (i.e., relevant, non-relevant, and iffy) allowed us to take two views of relevance: a "conservative" view, which considered only those documents actually labeled as "relevant" to be relevant; and a "liberal" view, which considered documents labeled as "iffy" to be relevant, in addition to documents actually labeled as "relevant."

We continue in Section 6 with an experiment investigating the applicability of liberal and diverse interpretations of relevance in the legal domain. The TREC 2009 Legal interactive task used initial assessments generated by volunteer law students and contract attorneys, that were subsequently adjudicated by senior lawyers ("topic authorities"). In addition, the University of Waterloo generated sets of assessments using a high-recall retrieval system. An SVM was trained using each of: the assessments generated by Waterloo; the initial TREC assessments; a combination of Waterloo and the initial TREC assessments; and the final assessments. All classifiers were evaluated with respect to the final assessments. After this, we conducted a brief follow-up experiment to test the hypothesis that adding judgments from a third assessor for documents not originally included in the training set could reduce recall depth.

In Section 7, we discuss our findings and the limitations of our results, and in Section 8, we offer our conclusions.

2. RELATED WORK

Voorhees observed that the retired professional analysts who assessed the TREC-4 adhoc task agreed on relevance, as measured by the Jaccard index, less than 50% of the time [41]. As a consequence, when one assessor's judgements were assumed to be correct and used to evaluate the other's, the other's judgements were found to have both recall and precision on the order of 65%, leading Voorhees to opine, "a practical upper bound on retrieval system performance is 65% precision at 65% recall since that is the level at which humans agree with one another." While Voorhees' primary measure, mean average precision ("MAP"), is a reasonable choice for ad hoc retrieval, it provides little insight into the performance of high-recall retrieval due to the focus on early precision present in the measure. We know of no study that has investigated the applicability of Voorhees' results to a measure suitable for evaluating high-recall retrieval.

Voorhees is not alone in noting that relevance judgements differ for different assessors, and for the same assessor at different times [34, 30, 16, 45, 20, 21], or that differences in assessors, while resulting in different estimates of effectiveness measures, have little impact on determining the relative effectiveness of retrieval methods [3, 26, 7, 9, 40].

Webber and Pickens [46], using the same relevance assessments as Voorhees, deemed Voorhees' "primary" assessor for each topic to be "authoritative." Webber and Pickens reported that, on average, using a non-authoritative assessor for training resulted in a 14% decrease in F_1 and a 24% increase in the number of top-ranked documents that must be retrieved to achieve a recall of 75%.

Cheng et al. [8] and Scholtes et al. [35] have similarly observed that non-authoritative training assessments have a significant but moderate negative impact on high-recall effectiveness. In contrast, Pickens [28] has suggested that non-authoritative training assessments may improve high-recall effectiveness when active (instead of passive) supervised-learning methods are used.

The issue of mitigating training and evaluation error is one of general interest in machine learning [47]. None of these studies specifically considered the interaction between assessor judgements for training and evaluation. A different source of interaction—inclusion bias introduced by the pooling method—is also a subject of current interest [6].

The TREC routing task [29, 44] bears substantial resemblance to high-recall retrieval, but differs by focusing on disjoint training and test collections, and evaluation using precision, rather than recall. Voorhees has suggested that examining the effect of differing relevance assessments on routing-like tasks is an important area of study [41]. To the best of our knowledge, this has yet to be investigated.

The effect of label noise (i.e., incorrect relevance assessments) is an ongoing topic of investigation within the IR

Corpus	Documents	Min. Prevalence	Avg. Prevalence	Max. Prevalence
TREC 4	713,049	0.002%	0.017%	0.028%
TREC 6	556,077	0.0002%	0.0097%	0.057%
Legal 2009	723,386	0.58%	0.72%	0.94%

Table 1: Summary statistics of all three corpora. The official NIST assessor was deemed as the gold standard for these statistics.

community [25, 13, 36], as well as in other communities [5, 17]. A comprehensive study by Frénay and Verleysen [17] outlined research on various facets of label noise (e.g., sources of label noise, its effects on classification, etc). Brodley and Friedl found that removing labels identified as incorrect, primarily by majority or consensus voting filters, improved overall classifier performance [5]. The e-mail spam filtering community has also noticed that label noise can drastically affect spam-filter performance [25, 36, 13].

3. EXPERIMENTAL METHODOLOGY

Our experiments follow the Cranfield paradigm [42], using test collections consisting of documents, topics, and relevance assessments from several TREC tracks. Table 1 offers summary statistics, including the number of documents and the average prevalence of topics, for each of the test collections used in this work; further details on each collection are provided in subsequent sections. In this section, we provide an overview of the general experimental methodology used in all of our experiments.

In these experiments, we used assessments generated by several independent assessors to train our classifiers and evaluate their performance. For the experiments described in Sections 4 and 5, we used assessments only for documents that were assessed by all of the assessors for the particular collection; any document for which there was not a complete set of assessments was treated as non-relevant. This choice was made to control for the fact that some assessors rendered (many) more assessments than others, and using the extra assessments would confound comparison. In addition, using the additional assessments would change the number of training examples and would result in testing a different hypothesis than the one in which we were interested (i.e., the effect of quantity versus quality of assessments).

In contrast, for the experiments reported in Section 6, we used assessments for all documents in the TREC judging pool, while maintaining the roles (initial assessor, topic authority, and independent assessor) established in the original experiment. In cases where there was no independent assessment for a document in the pool, we evaluated two different methods: (i) deeming the assessment to be "not relevant," and (ii) deeming the assessment to be the same as the initial assessment.

The TREC judging pools used for training form convenience samples of the full collections since they are composed of the top-ranked documents from participant submissions. To mitigate any effects from training on a narrowly selected set of documents (i.e., those that appeared relevant to some participant system), we augmented each training set with 1,000 randomly selected documents that were treated as non-relevant. This step broadened the representativeness of documents in each training set, to ensure that the resultant classifier was not focused exclusively on fine-grained distinctions between relevant and non-relevant documents in the judging pool, to the exclusion of non-relevant documents outside the pool.

To rank the documents, we used SVM^{light}[18], with default parameters. The features supplied were tf-idf term scores for all alphabetic words. Scores were generated after the Porter stemmer and case folding were applied.

Because our training and evaluation sets were not disjoint, we used ten-fold cross validation to approximate the effect of an independent evaluation set. Documents appearing in both sets were evenly distributed among 10 splits, as were documents appearing only in the evaluation set. The documents in each split were scored by a classifier whose training set was the union of the other nine splits, and a ranking was formed by sorting documents in the evaluation set according to score. We first tested our experimental methodology by replicating the Webber and Pickens study [46], successfully reproducing their results.

Our primary evaluation measure was *Recall Depth*, which is the size of the shortest prefix of the ranking that achieved a particular level of recall, expressed as percentage of the size of the corpus.

Our graphical results show, for each method, the average over all topics of (log transformed) recall depth, as a function of recall. In addition, for direct comparison, we show the average of (log transformed) relative recall depth—the ratio of recall depths between pairs of interest. Our tabular results show the same recall depth for 75% recall—a previously reported recall target [12]. We computed the significance of the surrogate-trained classifiers relative to the authority-trained classifier, applying a t-test to the log-transformed difference. In our tables, † denotes $p < 0.05$; ‡ denotes $p < 0.0001$.

4. INDEPENDENT JUDGMENTS

In this section, we describe our experiments using documents, topics, and relevance assessments from the TREC-4 adhoc task [22]. For this test collection, the official relevance assessments were augmented by two independent sets of relevance assessments rendered by different assessors within the course of Voorhees' experiments [41]. We labeled these assessment sets as J1, J2, and J3. While the assessments in J1 were (a subset of) those used for the official TREC evaluation, our experiments treated J1, J2, and J3 equally, treating each in turn as the "authority," and the others as surrogates. We restricted our experiments to topics where all three assessors found at least eight relevant documents, with the intent of reducing variance created by very low prevalence topics, consistent with previous work [46].

J1, J2, and J3 each reflect a single interpretation of relevance. To explore our hypothesis that a more diverse interpretation of relevance derived from several assessors would result in better training, we took each pair of surrogates and merged their assessments by randomly splitting the training set in half and assigning each half to one of the surrogates. The resulting merged-surrogate sets, which we denote J1|J2, J1|J3, and J2|J3, might then be viewed as the result of the two surrogate assessors working together to assess a single set of documents. Classifiers trained using each of the merged-surrogate sets were evaluated using J3, J2, and J1, respectively, as the authoritative assessor. Each merged-surrogate set contains the same documents as the single-surrogate set, reflecting the same amount of training effort.

To explore our hypothesis that a more liberal interpretation of relevance would result in better training, we evaluated training using the union of each pair of surrogates, denoted J1+J2, J1+J3, and J2+J3, in which a document was considered relevant if either of two surrogates considered it relevant. The classifiers constructed using these union surrogates were evaluated using J3, J2, and J1, respectively, as the authoritative assessor. Each of the union-surrogate sets contained the same documents as the single-surrogate and merged-surrogate sets, but reflected twice as much assessment effort. We do not believe that such a practice would necessarily be cost prohibitive, given the assumption that surrogate assessments are substantially less expensive than authoritative assessments.

4.1 Results

Figure 1 shows that the single-surrogate-trained classifiers are generally inferior to the corresponding authority-trained classifiers, requiring greater recall depth to achieve any particular level of recall. This result is reiterated in the relative recall depth plots in Figure 2, and the 75% recall depth values presented in Table 2. The differences among surrogates are most apparent at high levels of recall; as Figure 2 illustrates, some individual surrogates are substantially better than others.

Table 2 shows that with J1 and J3 as the authority, the authority-trained classifiers significantly outperform classifiers trained by individual surrogates. However, with J2 as the authority, the difference is not significant, particularly with respect to the case in which J1 is used as the surrogate assessor. While this reduced difference may be due to chance, it may also be an artifact of the assessment process. J1 corresponds to the official NIST assessments, for which the assessor reviewed the entire TREC-4 pool. This pool was much larger and had a lower prevalence of relevant documents than the pool reviewed by J2. An inverse relationship between prevalence and recall [39] might account for J1's assessments being more liberal than they would have been had J1 assessed only the documents that were assessed by J2.

Figures 1 and 2, as well as Table 2, show that the merged surrogates achieve effectiveness close to the better of the individual surrogates, occasionally exceeding both.

The union surrogates trained substantially and significantly ($p<0.01$) superior classifiers compared to the individual surrogates, as is evident in Figures 1 and 2, as well as Table 2.

Authority	Training J1	Training J2	Training J3
J1	0.082% (0.058 - 0.115)	0.542%‡ (0.254 - 1.156)	0.284%‡ (0.139 - 0.584)
J2	0.103% (0.061 - 0.174)	0.087% (0.051 - 0.149)	0.161% (0.083 - 0.312)
J3	0.146%† (0.077 - 0.278)	0.359%‡ (0.162 - 0.797)	0.066% (0.044 - 0.101)
	J1|J2	J1|J3	J2|J3
J1	-	-	0.321%‡ (0.162 - 0.636)
J2	-	0.092% (0.059 - 0.143)	-
J3	0.182%† (0.096 - 0.346)	-	-
	J1+J2	J1+J3	J2+J3
J1	-	-	0.094%† (0.054 - 0.164)
J2	-	0.062%† (0.043 - 0.091)	-
J3	0.094% (0.054 - 0.164)	-	-

Table 2: 75% recall depth values for the TREC-4 experiments, with 95% confidence intervals. Significance is determined by comparing surrogate-trained classifiers to the authority-trained classifier. († denotes $p < 0.05$; ‡ denotes $p < 0.0001$.)

5. LIBERAL ASSESSMENT

In this section, we describe our experiments using documents, topics, and relevance assessments from the TREC-6 adhoc task [43], augmented by assessments rendered independently by the University of Waterloo in the course of their participation in TREC-6, using a process of interactive search and judging [10]. While TREC-6 used binary assessments, Waterloo used three categories of relevance: relevant, not relevant, and "iffy." This "iffy" label was used to identify documents for which the Waterloo assessors were unsure of the true relevance (i.e., they were of borderline relevance).

In Voorhees' study, these "iffy" assessments were treated as non-relevant. One of our hypotheses was that a more liberal interpretation of relevance would result in better classifier performance with respect to an independent third party (i.e., in this case, NIST). To this end, we compared the two classifiers trained by treating these "iffy" documents, alternatively, as non-relevant and as relevant. These different sets of assessments are labeled WaterlooRel and WaterlooRel+Iffy, respectively. In this experiment, WaterlooRel+Iffy represents a "liberal" assessor, while WaterlooRel represents a "conservative" assessor.

We used the NIST assessments to evaluate classifiers trained using each of: the NIST assessments, the WaterlooRel assessments, and the WaterlooRel+Iffy assessments. While our primary interest was in the relative effectiveness of using the liberal versus conservative Waterloo assessments for training, we also reversed the roles of surrogate and authority, as for our previous experiment. We did not investigate the use of the conservative Waterloo assessments as the surrogate and the liberal Waterloo assessments as the authority, or vice versa, as these sets of assessments were not independent.

5.1 Results

Our hypothesis—that surrogate assessors taking a more liberal view of relevance would produce better classifiers—is supported by the results presented in Figures 3a and 4a, where training using the liberal assessor is seen to achieve significantly better recall depth than both the conservative assessor and the NIST assessor. Table 3 shows the difference at 75% recall depth, with 95% confidence intervals. Across all recall levels, the liberally-trained classifier generally performs as well as, or better than, the authority, while the conservatively-trained classifier performs significantly worse.

Table 3, as well as panels (b) and (c) of Figures 3 and 4, show that, consistent with our previous results, classifiers trained using the NIST assessments fall short when evaluated using either the liberal or conservative Waterloo assessments as the authority. It is no surprise that the shortfall is greater with respect to the liberal assessments.

Authority \ Training	NIST	WaterlooRel	WaterlooRel+Iffy
NIST	0.110% (0.065 - 0.185)	0.261%† (0.142 - 0.481)	0.072% (0.049 - 0.105)
WaterlooRel	0.244% (0.130 - 0.458)	0.152% (0.094 - 0.246)	-
WaterlooRel+Iffy	0.882%‡ (0.515 - 1.511)	-	0.129% (0.094 - 0.177)

Table 3: 75% recall depth values for the TREC-6 experiments for Waterloo and NIST-trained classifiers, evaluated using NIST assessments, with 95% confidence intervals. Significance is shown relative to the NIST-trained classifier. († denotes $p < 0.05$; ‡ denotes $p < 0.0001$.)

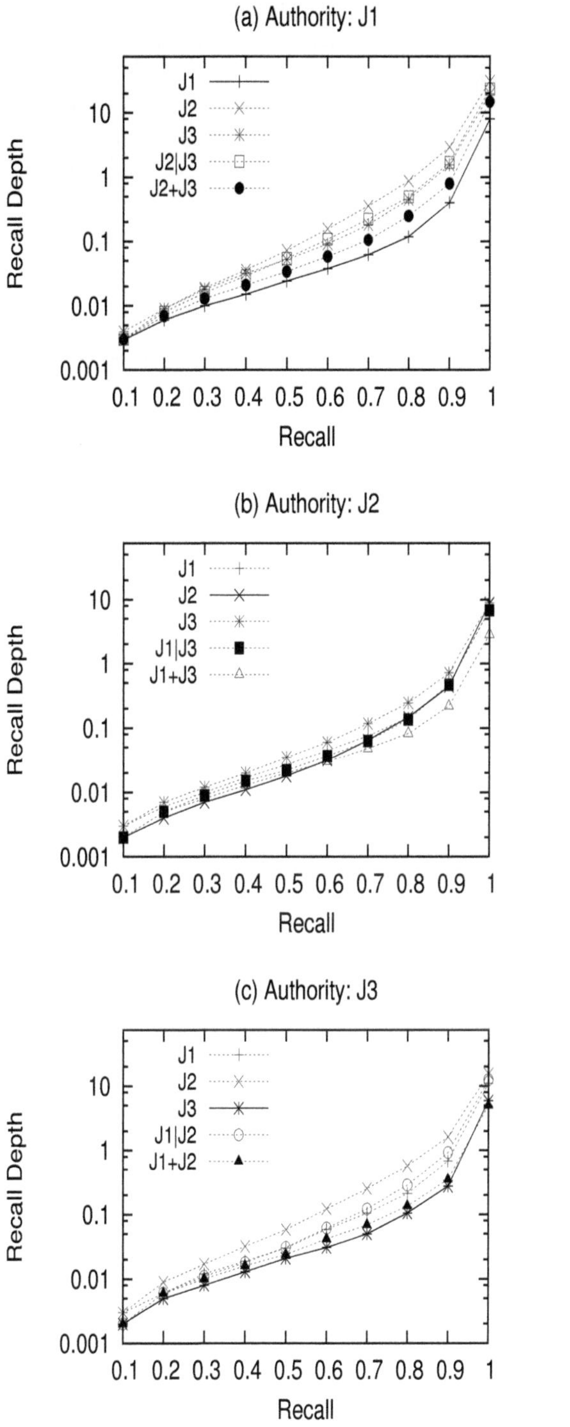

Figure 1: Recall depth plots for the TREC-4 experiments, using (a) JI, (b) J2, and (c) J3 as the authority.

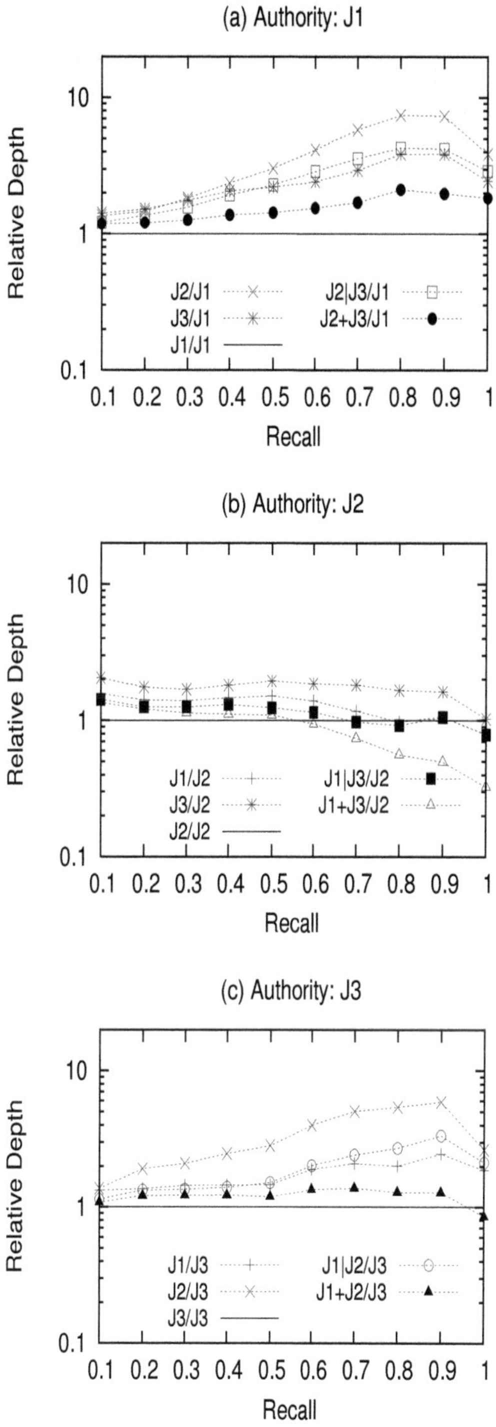

Figure 2: Relative recall depth plots for the TREC-4 experiments, using (a) J1, (b) J2, and (c) J3, as the authority.

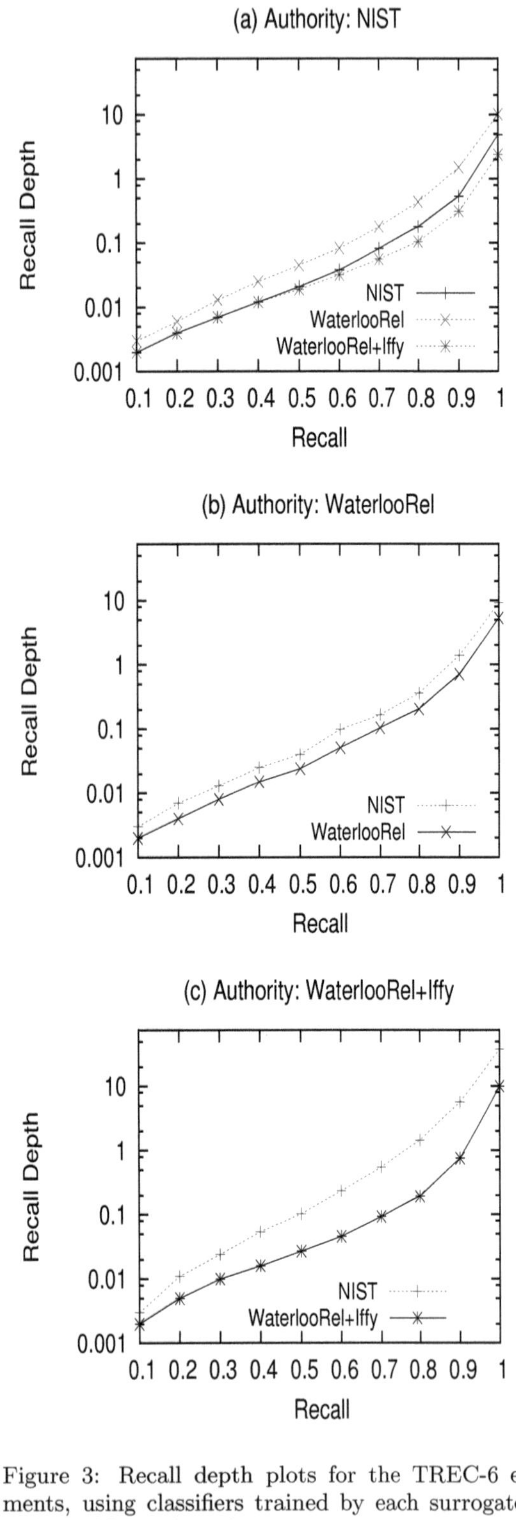

Figure 3: Recall depth plots for the TREC-6 experiments, using classifiers trained by each surrogate, and evaluated by each authority.

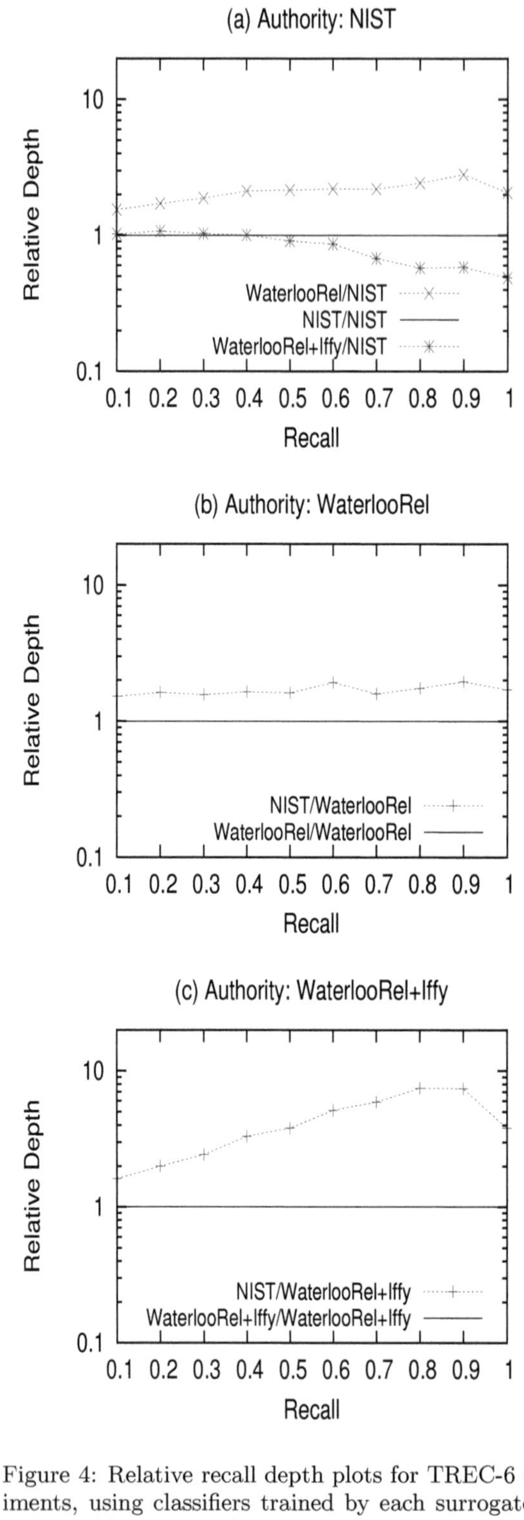

Figure 4: Relative recall depth plots for TREC-6 experiments, using classifiers trained by each surrogate, and evaluated by each authority.

Topic	Initial	Waterloo	Waterloo w/ Initial	Final
201	1.056%	0.214%	0.254%	0.215%
202	1.005%	0.977%	0.993%	0.936%
203	6.542%	0.955%	0.816%	0.456%
207	1.314%	1.401%	1.324%	1.236%

Table 4: 75% recall depth values for the TREC 2009 Legal experiments, using classifiers trained by Waterloo and initial assessments, and evaluated using final assessments.

	Judging Pool		Full Corpus	
Topic	Precision	Recall	Precision	Recall
201	0.40	0.70	0.05	0.76
202	0.93	0.93	0.27	0.80
203	0.47	0.25	0.13	0.25
207	0.98	0.88	0.89	0.79

Table 5: Recall and Precision of initial assessments in the TREC 2009 Legal Track judging pool versus the full corpus.

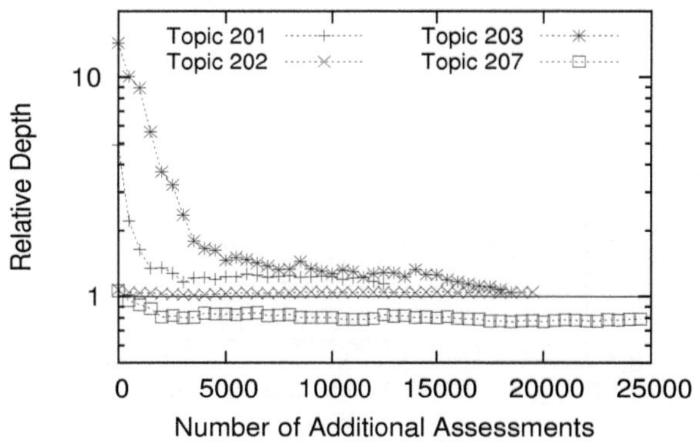

Figure 6: Per-topic 75% relative recall depth plots for the retrospective TREC 2009 Legal experiment, using classifiers trained on initial assessments, progressively augmented by Waterloo assessments, and evaluated using final assessments.

6. TREC 2009 LEGAL TRACK

The TREC 2009 Legal interactive task [23], simulated a high-recall eDiscovery task. For each topic in this task, the judging pool was a stratified sample of the document collection. An initial assessment of the judging pool was rendered using volunteer law students or contract attorneys. The initial assessments were provided to participating teams, who were invited to appeal assessments with which they disagreed. The appealed assessments were adjudicated by a TREC-designated *Topic Authority*, a senior lawyer who rendered the final, authoritative relevance assessments that were used to evaluate submissions. During the course of their participation in TREC 2009, the University of Waterloo developed an independent set of assessments using their own interactive, high-recall retrieval system for four of the task topics (Topics 201, 202, 203, and 207) [15].

Because the TREC judging pool included a large random sample of the document population, only a relatively small fraction (17.7%) of the documents in the pool were included in the Waterloo assessments; the rest were excluded by Waterloo's search method, as unlikely to be relevant. We investigated two approaches to determine the relevance of these documents for training purposes. The "Waterloo" surrogate assessments deemed the excluded documents to be "not relevant" for the purpose of training, and used the final TREC assessments as the sole authority for evaluation. The "Waterloo w/Initial" surrogate assessments used the initial NIST assessment for each excluded document. Thus, the "Waterloo" assessments were fully independent of the initial assessments, whereas the "Waterloo w/Initial" assessments, while not fully independent, might better model the situation in which the excluded documents had been manually assessed.

We evaluated the effect of training using the two sets of Waterloo surrogate assessments, as well as the initial and final assessments, using the final assessments as authoritative.

6.1 Results

Figure 5 shows relative recall depth plots, with respect to the final assessments, for each of the four topics. Table 4 shows 75% recall depth values for the same four topics. Overall, the surrogate-trained results appear inferior for high recall, but substantially so only when using the initial assessments as surrogate, and only for Topics 202 and 207. We note that Topics 202 and 207 have much higher prevalence than Topics 201 and 203, and due to the stratified sampling used to select the judging pool, the initial assessments achieved much higher precision and recall within the pool than in the collection at large, as illustrated in Table 5.

Figure 5 and Table 4 further indicate that the combination of assessments generally yields results as good as, and often superior to, the better of the individual surrogates.

6.2 Interactive Training

Retrospectively, we conducted one final supplemental experiment in an effort to shed some light on the applicability of our results to a more interactive, high-recall retrieval effort. Our supplemental experiment tracked improvement in relative recall depth as the initial assessments were supplemented incrementally with batches of 500 Waterloo assessments.

Figure 6 shows 75% relative recall depth, as a function of the number of Waterloo assessments. For Topics 201, 203, and 207, we see a dramatic gain from supplementing the assessments with a small fraction of the Waterloo assessments. For Topic 202, we see little improvement over the near-perfect initial assessments. The result suggests that having an independent assessor judge a fairly small fraction of the documents can result in a dramatic improvement in effectiveness, but further study is needed.

7. DISCUSSION

Our results show that it matters who assesses relevance; in particular, it matters whether the assessors whose judgements are used to train the system are the same as those whose judgements are used to evaluate the result. A statistic like "75% recall" conveys little meaning without considering, "according to whom?"

In one of the first cases where a court ruled in favor of the responding party's use of machine learning for eDiscovery, over the requesting party's objection, the responding party's brief [1] asserts:

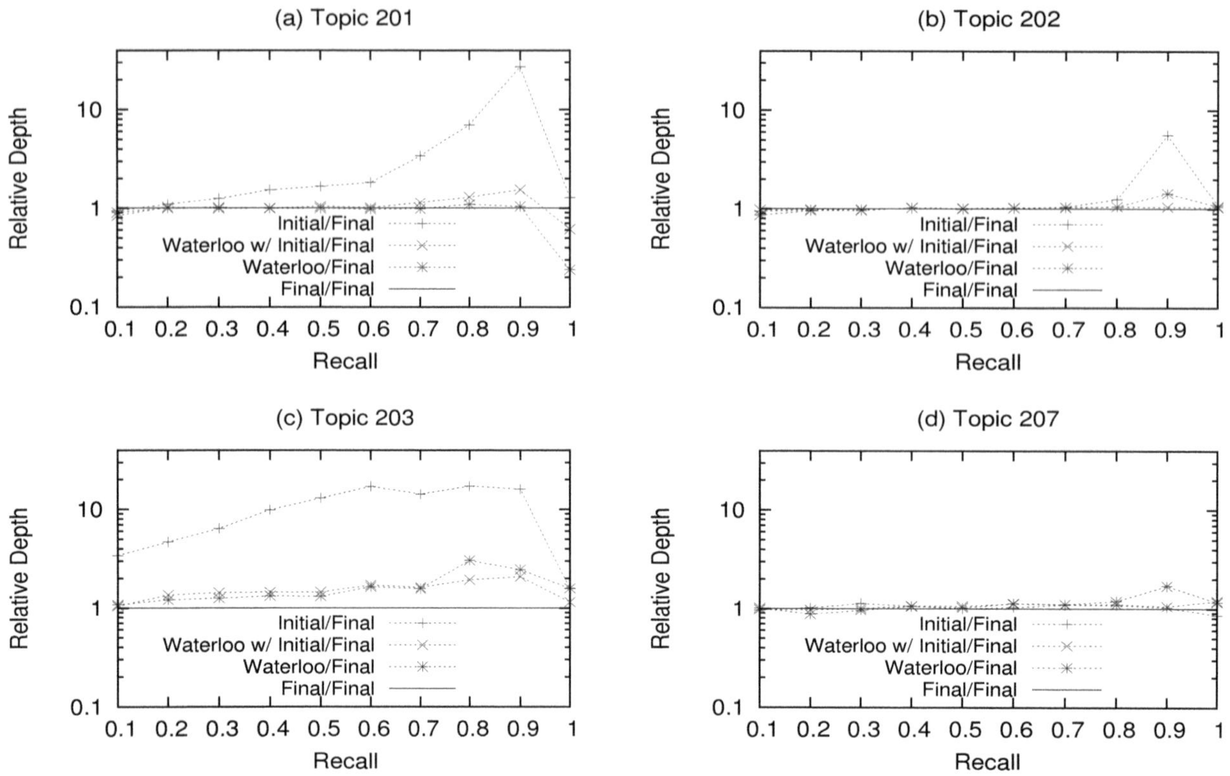

Figure 5: Relative recall depth plots for the TREC 2009 Legal experiments, using classifiers trained by each surrogate, and evaluated by the final assessments.

> Given that recall for linear review averages only 59.3%, [the responding party] proposes an acceptable recall criterion of 75%. In other words, predictive coding will conclude once the sampling program establishes that at least 75% of the relevant documents have been retrieved from the [responding party's electronically stored information] and are available to [them] for discovery purposes.

The 59.3% recall average was derived from Grossman and Cormack's analysis of the TREC 2009 Legal Track results [20], calculating the precision and recall of the initial assessments, evaluated with respect to the final (i.e., independent) authoritative assessments. The acceptance criterion of 75% recall, however, was established using the responding party's own reviewers, who were, we presume, also involved in training the system. Our results suggest that, had recall been evaluated using an independent assessor, the calculated recall value might have been considerably lower.

The designation of a particular assessor to be "authoritative" is, in many ways, an artificial construct designed to sidestep well-known uncertainties in the definition of relevance, and hence recall (see Webber et al. [45]). While some assessors may be more knowledgeable or skillfull than others, it is well known that even expert assessors will disagree on a substantial number of assessments [3]. The IR literature suggests than an exhaustive assessment effort by one such expert would be unlikely to achieve more than 65% recall and 65% precision in the eyes of another, equally skilled and knowledgeable expert [41]. The surrogates used for our TREC-4 and TREC-6 experiments achieved comparable recall and precision levels: When assessed by J1, J2 achieved recall of 52.9% and precision of 80.8%, and J3 achieved recall of 63.1% and precision of 78.1%; when assessed by NIST, the conservative Waterloo surrogate achieved recall of 62.8% and precision of 65.2%, while the liberal Waterloo surrogate achieved recall of 86.6% and precision of 50.0%.

Our results do not support the proposition that the use of machine learning "amplifies" inconsistencies between the surrogate and authority. The classifier trained using a surrogate's assessments achieves higher recall—at a recall depth corresponding to a fraction of the corpus—than the surrogate would achieve by assessing the entire corpus. For example, Figure 1 shows that a classifier trained using J2's assessments achieves 55% recall at a recall depth corresponding to 0.1% of the corpus, while a classifier trained using J2's assessments achieves 75% recall at a recall depth corresponding to 0.542% of the corpus.

Notwithstanding the discussion above, it is a worthwhile objective to try to maximize recall with respect to an authoritative assessor, either because that assessor has been stipulated to be the purveyor of true relevance, or because that assessor acts as a proxy for an as-yet-unavailable authority, such as a judge or regulator. Presumably, if a system achieves high recall at low recall depth with respect to one reasonable independent assessor, it is likely to achieve similar results with respect to another.

The results from our three experiments indicate that using a surrogate assessor instead of the authoritative assessor for training can dramatically increase recall depth. While the effect is not universally large, the instances in which it is, cannot be attributed to chance ($p<0.05$, corrected for multiple hypothesis testing). On the other hand, there are several instances where surrogate training appears to be as good as, or better than, authoritative training. The same general effect is observed, regardless of which assessor is deemed to be authoritative.

Our TREC-4 experiments suggest that randomly intermingling the assessments of two surrogates achieves recall depth similar to that of the better surrogate, while using the union of the two surrogates' assessments improves on both, approaching the effectiveness of using the authority's assessments.

Our TREC-6 experiments show that, when the surrogate assessor makes the deliberate choice to label marginally relevant documents as relevant, recall depth is substantially and significantly reduced, relative to the case in which such documents are labeled as non-relevant. Furthermore, training using this liberal assessment strategy yields a materially lower 75% recall depth than authoritative training. While caution must be exercised in extrapolating this result to other assessors' efforts, it strongly suggests that a surrogate can, at least in this instance, train a classifier as effectively as the authority, even when the authority's assessments are deemed to be the gold standard.

Our TREC 2009 Legal experiments show the same pattern as the others: For two topics, training using the initial assessor yields substantially inferior results to training using the authority; for the other two topics, the difference was small and not significant. This apparent dissonance might be explained by the fact that, for the latter two topics, the recall and precision of the surrogate—with respect to the judging pool—were exceptionally high. For the former two topics, they were substantially inferior.

7.1 Limitations

Our experiments study only the case of simple passive learning, where a fixed training set is to used to train a learning method to rank the entire corpus, and the top-ranked documents are reviewed until high recall is achieved. Although this practice appears to be widely employed in eDiscovery today, the state of the art is perhaps better represented by interactive, active-learning approaches [12, 27]. Accordingly, our results are applicable only to the former method; their utility in guiding individual stages of an interactive or active approach has not been established.

Our "convenience sample" of available assessments and collections may not be representative of a typical application of passive supervised machine learning. In our experiments, the judging pool was far from a random sample of the collection, as evidenced in Table 5. Nor was it the result of uncertainty sampling as commonly used in active learning. The judging pools for the TREC-4 and TREC-6 experiments might be construed to be representative of relevance feedback, because the documents were those ranked highly by TREC submissions. The judging pool for the TREC 2009 Legal experiments might be construed to represent query-by-committee, as it was constructed using strata to illuminate disagreements among the TREC submissions.

While our findings indicate quite strongly that some combinations of surrogates and authorities fare poorly, while others fare very well, more research is needed—with a larger population of assessors—to gain a thorough understanding of the causal factors. That said, our results clearly suggest that, when other factors are held constant, increasing the diversity or liberality of training assessments increases the quality of ranking, relative to that produced by a single surrogate.

8. CONCLUSIONS

Situations where assessments from a single authoritative assessor are unavailable, expensive, or limited, may occasion the use of a surrogate assessor to train a passive supervised-learning method to rank documents. In many situations, the resulting ranking is significantly and substantially inferior to that which would have occurred, had the authoritative assessor been used for training. Our experiments indicate that this effect can be mitigated, and sometimes overcome, by merging the assessments of multiple surrogates, or by instructing the surrogate to use a more liberal interpretation of relevance.

We question whether it is possible to sweep away uncertainties in relevance determination simply by arbitrarily deeming relevance to be the judgment of a single authoritative assessor. It is well known that informed, qualified assessors disagree, and even the same assessor will disagree with him or herself, at different times and in different circumstances. We wonder whether it is useful to expend heroic efforts to anticipate the judgments of one particular assessor, and posit, instead, that it might be better to target a hypothetical "reasonable authority," selected from a pool of equally competent choices. In any event, it is important when evaluating the recall of a retrieval effort, to ask, "according to whom?" 75% recall measured through independent assessment is a formidable achievement, but the same 75% recall measured through self-assessment is unremarkable.

9. REFERENCES

[1] Memorandum in Support of Motion for Protective Order Approving the Use of Predictive Coding, *Global Aerospace v. Landow Aviation*, No. CL 61040, 2012 WL 1419842 (Va. Cir. Ct., Loudoun Cnty., Apr. 9, 2012).

[2] *Da Silva Moore v. Publicis Groupe*, 287 F.R.D. 182 (S.D.N.Y., 2012).

[3] P. Bailey, N. Craswell, I. Soboroff, P. Thomas, A. P. de Vries, and E. Yilmaz. Relevance assessment: are judges exchangeable and does it matter? In *Proc. SIGIR*, 2008.

[4] T. Barnett, S. Godjevac, J.-M. Renders, C. Privault, J. Schneider, and R. Wickstrom. Machine learning classification for document review. In *ICAIL DESI III Workshop*, 2009.

[5] C. E. Brodley and M. A. Friedl. Identifying mislabeled training data. *J. of A.I. Research*, 11, 2011.

[6] C. Buckley, D. Dimmick, I. Soboroff, and E. Voorhees. Bias and the limits of pooling for large collections. *Information Retrieval*, 10(6), 2007.

[7] R. Burgin. Variations in relevance judgments and the evaluation of retrieval performance. *Information Processing & Management*, 28(5), 1992.

[8] J. Cheng, A. Jones, C. Privault, and J.-M. Renders. Soft labeling for multi-pass document review. In *ICAIL DESI V Workshop*, 2013.
[9] C. W. Cleverdon. *The Effect of Variations in Relevance Assessments in Comparative Experimental Tests of Index Languages.* Cranfield Library, 3, 1970.
[10] G. V. Cormack, C. L. A. Clarke, C. R. Palmer, and S. S. L. To. passage-based refinement (MultiText experiments for TREC-6). In *Proc. TREC-6*, 1997.
[11] G. V. Cormack and M. R. Grossman. The Grossman-Cormack glossary of technology-assisted review with foreword by John M. Facciola, Magistrate Judge. *Fed. Courts Law Rev.*, 7(1), 2013.
[12] G. V. Cormack and M. R. Grossman. Evaluation of machine-learning protocols for technology-assisted review in electronic discovery. In *Proc. SIGIR*, 2014.
[13] G. V. Cormack and A. Kolcz. Spam filter evaluation with imprecise ground truth. In *Proc. SIGIR*, 2009.
[14] G. V. Cormack and T. R. Lynam. Spam corpus creation for TREC. In *Proc. 2nd CEAS*, 2005.
[15] G. V. Cormack and M. Mojdeh. Machine learning for information retrieval: TREC 2009 Web, Relevance Feedback and Legal Tracks. In *Proc. TREC-18*, 2009.
[16] G. V. Cormack, M. D. Smucker, and C. L. A. Clarke. Efficient and effective spam filtering and re-ranking for large web datasets. *Information Retrieval*, 14(5), 2011.
[17] B. Frénay and M. Verleysen. Classification in the presence of label noise: a survey. *IEEE Trans. Neural Networks and Learning Systems*, 25(5), 2013.
[18] T. Joachims. Making large-scale SVM learning practical. In *Advances in Kernel Methods - Support Vector Learning.* MIT Press, 1999.
[19] D. Gonsowski. A look into the e-discovery crystal ball. *Inside Counsel*, Dec. 2, 2011.
[20] M. R. Grossman and G. V. Cormack. Technology-assisted review in e-discovery can be more effective and more efficient than exhaustive manual review. *Rich. J. Law & Tech.*, 17, 2011.
[21] M. R. Grossman and G. V. Cormack. Inconsistent responsiveness determination in document review: Difference of opinion or human error? *Pace Law Rev.*, 32, 2012.
[22] D. Harman. Overview of the Fourth Text REtrieval Conference (TREC-4). In *Proc. TREC-4*, 1995.
[23] B. Hedin, S. Tomlinson, J. R. Baron, and D. W. Oard. Overview of the TREC 2009 Legal Track. In *Proc. TREC-18*, 2009.
[24] J. P. Higgins, S. Green, eds. *Cochrane Handbook for Systematic Reviews of Interventions*, Wiley Online Library, 2008.
[25] A. Kolcz and G. V. Cormack. Genre-based decomposition of email class noise. In *Proc. KDD*, 2009.
[26] M. E. Lesk and G. Salton. Relevance assessments and retrieval system evaluation. *Information Storage and Retrieval*, 4(4), 1968.
[27] C. Li, Y. Wang, P. Resnick, and Q. Mei. ReQ-ReC: High Recall Retrieval with Query Pooling and Interactive Classification. In *Proc. SIGIR*, 2014.
[28] J. Pickens. In TAR, wrong decisions can lead to the right documents (a response to Ralph Losey). http://web.archive.org/save/http://www.catalystsecure.com/blog/2014/02/in-tar-wrong-decisions-can-lead-to-the-right-documents-a-response-to-ralph-losey/.
[29] S. Robertson and I. Soboroff. The TREC 2002 Filtering Track report. In *Proc. TREC-11*, 2002.
[30] H. L. Roitblat, A. Kershaw, and P. Oot. Document categorization in legal electronic discovery: Computer classification vs. manual review. *J. Am. Soc. for Info. Sci. and Tech.*, 61(1), 2010.
[31] T. Saracevic. Relevance: A review of the literature and a framework for thinking on the notion in information science. *J. Am. Soc. Info. Sci.*, 26(6), 1975.
[32] T. Saracevic. Relevance: A review of the literature and a framework for thinking on the notion in information science. Part II: Nature and manifestations of relevance. *J. Am. Soc. for Info. Sci. and Tech.*, 58(13), 2007.
[33] T. Saracevic. Relevance: A review of the literature and a framework for thinking on the notion in information science. Part III: Behavior and effects of relevance. *J. Am. Soc. for Info. Sci. and Tech.*, 58(13), 2007.
[34] L. Schamber. Relevance and information behavior. *Annual Rev. Info. Sci. and Tech. (ARIST)*, 29, 1994.
[35] J. C. Scholtes, T. van Cann, and M. Mack. The impact of incorrect training sets and rolling collection on technology assisted review. In *ICAIL DESI V Workshop*, 2013.
[36] D. Sculley and G. V. Cormack. Filtering email spam in the presence of noisy user feedback. In *Proc. CEAS*, 2008.
[37] F. Sebastiani. Machine learning in automated text categorization. *ACM Comput. Surv.*, 34(1), 2002.
[38] B. Settles. *Active learning literature survey.* TR 1648, University of Wisconsin, Madison, 2010.
[39] M. D. Smucker and C. P. Jethani. Human performance and retrieval precision revisited. In *Proc. SIGIR*, 2010.
[40] A. Trotman and D. Jenkinson. IR evaluation using multiple assessors per topic. In *Proc. ADCS*, 2007.
[41] E. M. Voorhees. Variations in relevance judgments and the measurement of retrieval effectiveness. *Information Processing & Management*, 36(5), 2000.
[42] E. M. Voorhees. The philosophy of information retrieval evaluation. In *Evaluation of Cross-Language Information Retrieval Systems.* Springer, 2002.
[43] E. M. Voorhees and D. Harman. Overview of the Sixth Text REtrieval Conference (TREC-6). In *Proc. TREC-6*, 1997.
[44] E. M. Voorhees and D. K. Harman, eds. *TREC: Experiment and Evaluation in Information Retrieval.* MIT Press, 2005.
[45] W. Webber, D. W. Oard, F. Scholer, and B. Hedin. Assessor error in stratified evaluation. In *Proc. CIKM*, 2010.
[46] W. Webber and J. Pickens. Assessor disagreement and text classifier accuracy. In *Proc. SIGIR*, 2013.
[47] X. Zhu and X. Wu. Class noise vs. attribute noise: A quantitative study. *A. I. Rev.*, 22(3), 2004.

The Benefits of Magnitude Estimation Relevance Assessments for Information Retrieval Evaluation

Andrew Turpin
University of Melbourne, Australia
aturpin@unimelb.edu.au

Falk Scholer
RMIT University, Australia
falk.scholer@rmit.edu.au

Stefano Mizzaro
University of Udine, Italy
mizzaro@uniud.it

Eddy Maddalena
University of Udine, Italy
eddy.maddalena@uniud.it

ABSTRACT

Magnitude estimation is a psychophysical scaling technique for the measurement of sensation, where observers assign numbers to stimuli in response to their perceived intensity. We investigate the use of magnitude estimation for judging the relevance of documents in the context of information retrieval evaluation, carrying out a large-scale user study across 18 TREC topics and collecting more than 50,000 magnitude estimation judgments. Our analysis shows that on average magnitude estimation judgments are rank-aligned with ordinal judgments made by expert relevance assessors. An advantage of magnitude estimation is that users can chose their own scale for judgments, allowing deeper investigations of user perceptions than when categorical scales are used.

We explore the application of magnitude estimation for IR evaluation, calibrating two gain-based effectiveness metrics, nDCG and ERR, directly from user-reported perceptions of relevance. A comparison of TREC system effectiveness rankings based on binary, ordinal, and magnitude estimation relevance shows substantial variation; in particular, the top systems ranked using magnitude estimation and ordinal judgments differ substantially. Analysis of the magnitude estimation scores shows that this effect is due in part to varying perceptions of relevance, in terms of how impactful relative differences in document relevance are perceived to be. We further use magnitude estimation to investigate gain profiles, comparing the currently assumed linear and exponential approaches with actual user-reported relevance perceptions. This indicates that the currently used exponential gain profiles in nDCG and ERR are mismatched with an average user, but perhaps more importantly that individual perceptions are highly variable. These results have direct implications for IR evaluation, suggesting that current assumptions about a single view of relevance being sufficient to represent a population of users are unlikely to hold. Finally, we demonstrate that magnitude estimation judgments can be reliably collected using crowdsourcing, and are competitive in terms of assessor cost.

SIGIR '15, August 09–13, 2015, Santiago, Chile

ACM 978-1-4503-3621-5/15/08 ... $15.00.
DOI: http://dx.doi.org/10.1145/2766462.2767760.

Categories and Subject Descriptors

H.3.4 [**Information Storage and Retrieval**]: Systems and software—*performance evaluation.*

Keywords

Magnitude estimation; evaluation; relevance assessments; relevance

General Terms

Measurement, performance, experimentation

1. INTRODUCTION

Relevance is an important concept in information retrieval (IR), and relevance judgments form the backbone of test collections, the most widely-used approach for the evaluation of IR system effectiveness. Document relevance judgments are typically made using ordinal scales, historically at a binary level, and more recently with multiple levels [28]. However, despite its importance, operationalizing relevance for the evaluation of IR systems remains a complicated issue; for example, when using an ordinal scale it is unclear how many relevance categories should be chosen [26].

Magnitude estimation is psychophysical technique for measuring the sensation of a stimulus. Observers assign numbers to a series of stimuli, such that the numbers reflect the perceived difference in intensity of each item. The outcome is a ratio scale of the subjective perception of the stimulus; if a magnitude of 50 is assigned to one stimulus, and 10 to another, then it can be concluded that the two items are perceived in a 5:1 ratio of sensation [18]. While initially developed for the measurement of the sensation of physical stimuli such as the intensity of a light source, magnitude estimation has been successfully applied to the measurement of non-physical stimuli including the usability of interfaces [17].

Being able to derive ratio scales of subjective perceptions of the intensity of stimuli, magnitude estimation may be a useful tool for measuring and better understanding document relevance judgments. The application of magnitude estimation in the IR field has been limited to the consideration of the relevance of carefully curated abstracts returned from bibliographic databases [10], and our own small-scale pilot study [15, 21]. While suggestive, these studies have been limited in terms of demonstrating the broader utility of the approach, or its direct application to IR evaluation. In this work, we investigate the larger-scale application of magnitude estimation to document relevance scaling, reporting on a user study over 18 TREC topics and obtaining judgments for 4,269 documents. This is also the first work to consider the direct application of magnitude estimation to the evaluation of IR systems. Specifically, we consider three research questions.

RQ1. Is the magnitude estimation technique suitable for gathering document-level relevance judgments, and are the resulting relevance scales reasonable with respect to our current knowledge of relevance judgments?

RQ2. How does IR system evaluation change when ratio scale magnitude estimation relevance judgments are used to calibrate the gain levels of the widely-used nDCG and ERR evaluation metrics, compared to using arbitrarily set gain values for a pre-chosen number of ordinal levels?

RQ3. Can magnitude estimation relevance scores provide additional insight into user perceptions of relevance, into actual gain values, and into individual gain profiles?

In the next section, background material and related work are presented. Details of our user study and experimental methodology are provided in Section 3, and the analysis and discussion of our results, corresponding to the three research questions, is presented in Sections 4 to 6. Our conclusions and directions for future work are included in the final section of the paper.

2. BACKGROUND

Relevance: Relevance is an important concept in information science and information retrieval [19]. IR system effectiveness is most often measured with reference to a test collection, consisting of a set of search topics, a static set of documents over which to search, and human-generated assessments that indicate, for an answer document returned by a search system in response to a topic, whether the document is relevant [28]. Typically, these assessments are made based on "topical" relevance, that is, a judgment of whether the document contains any information that is "about" the material that the search topic is asking for. Other aspects of relevance, such as novelty or contextual factors, are not considered [19]. Based on the relevance judgments, each ranked answer list returned by a system is aggregated into a number that reflects the system's performance, using a chosen effectiveness metric. The metrics themselves reflect either implicit or explicit assumptions about searcher behavior, for example that a relevant document that is returned by a system lower down a ranked list is of less value than if the same document had been returned earlier.

Historically, relevance judgments were often made using a *binary* scale, where a document is classed as either being relevant to the search topic or not, and many effectiveness metrics use this notion of relevance, including *precision*, *recall*, *mean average precision* (MAP), and *precision at a specified cutoff* [28]. More recently, based on the observation that searchers can generally distinguish between more than two levels of relevance, evaluation metrics that incorporate *multi-level* relevance have been proposed [12]. Here, relevance is typically measured on an ordinal scale; metrics that include this more fine-grained notion of relevance include *normalized discounted cumulative gain* (nDCG) [12] and *expected reciprocal rank* (ERR) [5]. Some examples of previous choices for the number of levels in ordinal relevance scales include 3 (TREC Terabyte Track [6]), 4 (TREC newswire re-assessments by Sormunen [23]), and 6 (TREC Web Track [7]). Tang et al. [26] studied the self-reported confidence of psychology students when assessing the relevance of bibliographic records on ordinal scales from 2 to 11 levels, and observed that for this specific task, confidence is maximized with a 7-point scale. However, the issue is far from settled: in a broader survey of the optimal number of levels in an ordinal response scale, Cox [8] concludes that there is no single number of response alternatives that is appropriate for all situations.

Magnitude estimation: Magnitude estimation is a psychophysical technique for the construction of measurement scales for the intensity of sensations. An observer is asked to assign numbers to a series of presented stimuli. The first number can be any value that seems appropriate, with successive numbers then being assigned so that their relative differences reflect the observer's subjective perceptions of differences in stimulus intensity [9]. A key advantage of using magnitude estimation is that the responses are on a ratio scale of measurement [11], meaning that all mathematical operations may be applied to such data, and parametric statistical analysis can be carried out. In contrast, for ordinal (or ranked category) scales certain operations are not defined; for example, the median can be used as a measure of central tendency for ordinal data, but the mean is not meaningful since the distance between the ranked categories is not defined [22].

Proposed by Stanley Stevens in the 1950s, magnitude estimation has a long history, and is the most widely-used psychophysical ratio scaling technique [11]. Initially developed to measure perceptions of physical stimuli, such as the brightness of a light or the loudness of a sound, magnitude estimation has also been successfully applied to a wide range of non-physical stimuli in the social sciences (including occupational preferences, political attitudes, the pleasantness of odors, and the appropriateness of punishments for crimes [25]), in medical applications (such as levels of pain, severity of mental disorders, and emotional stress from life events [11]), in user experience research (for example, as a measure of usability in HCI [17], and for healthcare applications [13]), and in linguistics (including judging the grammaticality of sentences [2]).

In information retrieval research, Eisenberg [10] investigated magnitude estimation in the context of judging the relevance of document citations from a library database (including fields such as author, title, keywords and abstract), and concluded that participants are able to effectively use magnitude estimation in such a scenario. A related technique was used by Spink and Greisdorf [24], where participants in a user study were required to fill in a worksheet with information about the relevance of resources that were retrieved from a library database for personal research projects; this included indicating the level of relevance on a 4-level ordinal scale, providing feedback about other levels of relevance such as utility and motivation, and marking the level of relevance on a 77mm line. The line was then decoded into numbers at a 1mm resolution so was in effect a 78-level ordinal scale.

To the best of our knowledge, the only previous investigation of magnitude estimation for document-level relevance judging in the context of IR evaluation was our own small pilot study [15, 21]. That study indicated that magnitude estimation could be useful for measuring document-level relevance, but used only 3 information need statements and 33 documents.

3. EXPERIMENTAL METHODOLOGY

In this section we describe the details of the experiments that were carried out to gather the needed relevance judgments.

3.1 Topics and Documents

Document-level relevance assessments have traditionally been made using binary or multi-level ordinal scales. To compare magnitude estimation judgments to these approaches, we selected a set of search tasks and documents from the TREC-8 ad hoc collection, which studies informational search over newswire documents. The TREC-8 collection includes binary relevance judgments made by

Topic #	# docs	# units	$\mathtt{H}_k$	$\mathtt{N}_k$	Back 0	Back 1	Back 2^+	Fail 0	Fail 1	Fail 2^+
402	278	460	LA111689-0162	FBIS3-10954	452	8	0	426	18	16
403	111	182	LA092890-0067	LA071290-0133	178	4	0	120	19	43
405	214	354	LA061490-0072	FBIS3-13680	347	6	1	322	20	12
407	212	350	FT921-6003	FR940407-2-00084	346	3	1	324	9	17
408	188	310	FT923-6110	LA062290-0070	306	4	0	266	16	28
410	212	350	FBIS4-64577	FBIS4-44440	346	4	0	326	10	14
415	179	295	FBIS3-60025	FBIS4-10862	289	4	2	255	23	17
416	174	287	FBIS4-49091	LA112590-0107	286	1	0	267	12	8
418	243	402	LA102189-0167	FT924-6324	394	8	0	372	15	15
420	164	270	LA121590-0108	LA112690-0001	266	4	0	256	4	10
421	342	567	FT941-428	LA073189-0033	554	11	2	537	16	14
427	195	322	FT943-5736	LA080590-0077	315	7	0	214	52	56
428	253	419	FT943-9226	FBIS3-20994	412	6	1	396	13	10
431	203	335	FBIS3-46247	FT944-5962	333	2	0	296	27	12
440	264	437	FT942-3471	LA020589-0074	427	10	0	397	19	21
442	408	677	LA011390-0057	FT923-4524	672	5	0	629	25	23
445	210	347	FT924-8156	LA031989-0092	334	11	2	334	10	3
448	419	695	LA080190-0139	FBIS3-16837	687	8	0	652	21	22
Sum:	4269	7059			6944	106	9	6389	329	341
Percentage:					98	2	0	90	5	5

Table 1: Topics, number of documents, number of units, $\mathtt{H}_k$, $\mathtt{N}_k$, number of back buttons usage, number of failures in the (c) and (d) checks, as detailed in the text.

NIST assessors [27]. Subsequently, Sormunen [23] carried out a re-judging exercise where a subset of topics and documents were judged by a group of six Master's students of information studies, fluent in English although not native speakers, on a 4-level ordinal relevance scale: N–not relevant (0); M–marginally relevant (1); R–relevant (2); H–highly relevant (3).

The 18 *search topics* used in our study are the subset of TREC-8 topics which also have Sormunen ordinal judgments available. They are listed in the first column of Table 1. The *documents* for which we collected magnitude estimation judgments are the set of the top-10 items returned by systems that participated in TREC-8. This gives a total of 4,269 topic-document pairs, of which 3881 have binary TREC relevance judgments available, and 805 of which have Sormunen ordinal judgments available. The number of documents for each topic is shown in Table 1 (2nd column).

3.2 User Study

We carried out a user study through the CrowdFlower crowdsourcing platform during December 2014 and January 2015. The experimental design was reviewed and approved by the RMIT University ethics review board. Participants were paid $0.2 for each task *unit*, defined as a group of magnitude estimation judgments for 8 documents in relation to one topic. The number of units for each topic is shown in Table 1 (3rd column).

Practice task: After agreeing to take part in the study, a participant was shown a first set of task instructions, including a brief introduction to the experiment and explanation of the magnitude estimation process. Since magnitude estimation may not be familiar to participants, they were first asked to complete a practice task, making magnitude estimations of three lines of different lengths, shown one at a time. If they successfully completed this practice task (success was defined as assigning magnitudes such that the numbers were in ascending order when the lines were sorted from shortest to longest), participants were able to move on to the main part of the experiment.

Main task: The main task of the experiment required making magnitude estimations of the relevance of documents. Participants were informed, by means of a second set of instructions, that they would be shown an information need statement, and then a sequence of eight documents that had been returned by a search system in response to the information need statement, presented in an arbitrary order, and that: *Your task is to indicate how relevant these documents appear to you, in relation to the information need.*

For the main task, the title, description and narrative of a TREC topic were first displayed at the top of the screen. After reading the information need, participants had to respond to a 4-way multiple-choice question, to test their understanding of the topic. The test questions focused on the main information concepts presented in the topic statements, and were intended to check that participants were engaging with the task, and as a mechanism to remove spammers. Participants who were unable to answer the test question correctly were unable to continue with the task.

Next, participants were presented with eight documents, one at a time. For each document, the participant was required to enter a magnitude estimation number in a text box displayed directly below the document, and a brief justification of why they entered their number into a larger text field. They were then able to proceed to the next document. A back button was available in the interface, with participants being advised that this should only be used if they wish to correct a mistake; under 3% of submitted jobs included use of this feature (details on the occurrences of clicks on the back button are shown in Table 1, where the number of units with zero, one, or two or more back button clicks are shown).

After entering responses for eight documents, the task was complete. Participants were able to complete further tasks for other topics, up to a maximum of 18 tasks, as they were not able to re-assess the same topic.

Magnitude estimation assignments: Regarding the assignment of ME scores, participants were instructed that: *You may use any numbers that seem appropriate to you – whole numbers, fractions, or decimals. However, you may not use negative numbers, or zero. Don't worry about running out of numbers – there will always be a larger number than the largest you use, and a smaller number than the smallest you use. Try to judge each document in relation to the previous one. For example, if the current document seems half as relevant as the previous one, then assign a score that is half of your previously assigned score.* (The complete instructions that were shown to participants are available at `http://cs.rmit.edu.au/~fscholer/ME/SIGIR15`.) While some applications of magnitude estimation use a fixed modulus (specifying a particular number that is to be assigned to the first stimulus that is presented), this has been found to promote clustering of responses and the potential over-representation of some numbers [18]; we therefore allowed participants to freely choose their own values.

Document ordering: As explained above, each participant task *unit* required the judging of a set of eight documents for a particular search topic statement. The experiments used a randomized design, with documents presented in random order, to avoid potential ordering effects and first sample bias [18]. The document sets were constructed such that two of the documents in each set were a known ordinal H and N document for the topic; these documents (henceforth $\mathtt{H}_k$ and $\mathtt{N}_k$) were the same for all the participants working on the same topic (the TREC document identifiers for each topic are shown in Table 1). This was to ensure that each participant saw at least one document from the high and low ends of the relevance continuum. Ensuring that stimuli of different intensity levels are included in a task has been found to be important for the magnitude estimation process [11], and also has an impact on the score normalization process, described below. Moreover, including the two $\mathtt{N}_k$ and $\mathtt{H}_k$ documents with "known" ordinal relevance values enabled a further data collection quality control check: after judging all eight documents, participants who had assigned magnitude estimation scores for the N_k document that were larger than for the H_k document were not able to complete the task. In total, at least 10 ME scores were gathered for each topic-document pair.

Quality checks: Three quality checks were included in the data gathering phase of our experiments:

(a) a practice task requiring magnitude estimation of line lengths;

(b) a multiple-choice test question to check a participant's understanding of the topic; and

(c) a check that the magnitude estimations score for H_k was greater than that assigned to N_k.

In addition, a time-based quality check was also used:

(d) each participant had to spend at least 20 seconds on each of the 8 documents.

If any of (a) or (b) was unsuccessful, the participant could not continue with the task (they were allowed to restart from scratch, on a different unit and therefore on a randomly selected topic, if willing to do so; the same quality checks were applied again). If checks (c) or (d) were unsuccessful, the participant received the message "*Your job is not accurate enough. You can revise your work to finish the task*", and was allowed to use the back button and revise their previously assigned scores if they wished (the same two checks (c) and (d) were performed again in such a case); however, participants were not made aware which documents or scores were the "offending" responses. Less than 10% of units resulted in conditions (c) or (d) being triggered (see details in Table 1, where the number of eventually successful units with 0, 1, or two or more failed checks are shown), and as already mentioned the back button was used in less than 3% of units. Finally, there was a syntax check that the numeric scores input by the participants were in the $(0, +\infty)$ range. If any of the checks were not successfully completed, no data for that unit was retained. As such, we did not do any further filtering once the data had been collected.

Crowd Judging: As detailed in Table 1, with 7,059 units comprised of 8 documents each, we collected more than 50,000 judgments in total, at a cost of around \$1,700 (CrowdFlower fees included). This is in the order of magnitude of \$0.4 for each document, which is broadly competitive when compared with the cost of TREC assessors or other similar crowdsourcing initiatives; for example, according to Alonso and Mizzaro [1, Footnote 2], gathering ordinal scale judgments cost around \$0.1 per document. However, the comparison is more favorable when considering that in our experiments 10 redundant judgments per document are collected, and the N_k and H_k documents receive multiple judgments, whereas in Alonso and Mizzaro's work only 5 redundant judgments were collected, and there was nothing similar to our N_k vs. H_k check.

3.3 Score Normalization

Magnitude estimation is a highly flexible process, with observers being free to assign any positive number, including fractions, as a rating of the intensity of a presented stimulus. The key requirement is that the ratio of the numbers should reflect the ratio of the differences in perception between stimulus intensities. As the stimuli are presented in a randomized order, and observers are free to assign a number of their choice to the first presented item, it is natural that different participants may make use of different parts of the positive number space. Magnitude estimation scores are therefore normalized, to adjust for these differences. Geometric averaging is the recommended approach for the normalization of magnitude estimation scores [11, 17], and was applied in our data analysis.

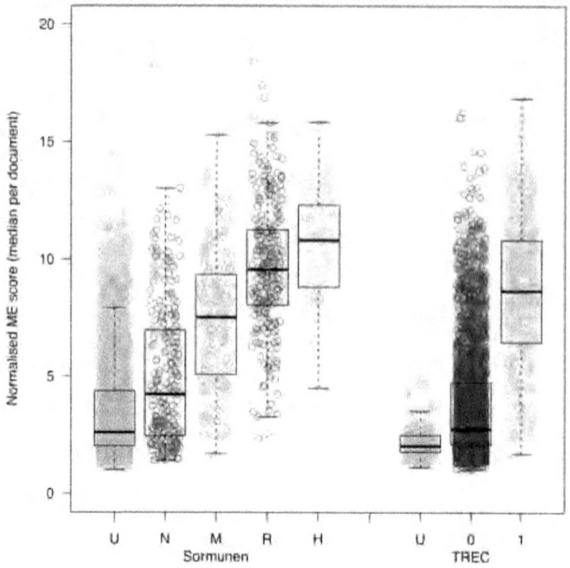

Figure 1: ME score distribution by Sormunen and TREC levels.

Recall that for a given search topic, participants made magnitude estimation judgments for groups of eight documents (a unit). To normalize the scores, first the log of each raw score is taken. Next, the arithmetic mean of these log scores is calculated for each unit (μ_u), and for the topic as a whole (μ). Each individual log score is then adjusted by the unit and topic means, and the exponent is taken of the resulting quantity, giving the final normalized score:

$$s'_i = \exp(\log(s_i) - \mu_u + \mu)$$

Intuitively, normalization by geometric averaging means that the raw magnitude estimation scores are moved along the number line, both in terms of location and spread. The log transformation is theoretically motivated by the fact that magnitude estimation scores of perceived stimulus intensities have been found to be approximately log-normal [16]. Importantly, normalization through geometric averaging has the property of preserving the ratios of the original scores, the essential feature of the magnitude estimation process. Unless otherwise noted, all analysis reported in this paper uses normalized magnitude estimation scores.

4. MAGNITUDE ESTIMATION RELEVANCE JUDGMENTS

Having obtained magnitude estimation scores for 4,269 topic-document pairs, we analyze the user-perceived relevance to answer the first research question, whether the magnitude estimation technique is suitable for gathering document level relevance judgments, and whether the resulting relevance scales are reasonable with respect to our current knowledge of relevance judgments.

4.1 Consistency of Magnitude Estimation and Ordinal Relevance

The distribution of the median normalized magnitude estimation scores for each document are shown in Figure 1, aggregated across all 18 topics, and split by Sormunen ordinal relevance levels (left side of figure, levels are N, M, R, H, and U, the group of docu-

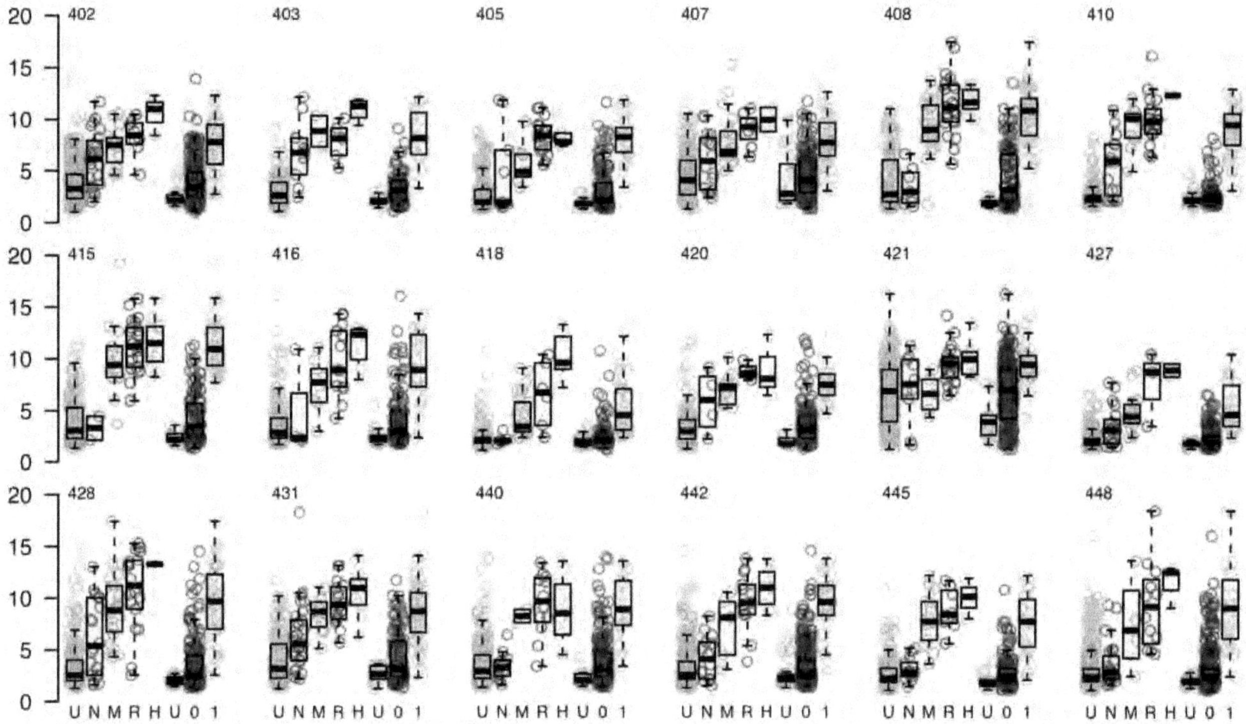

Figure 2: ME score distribution by Sormunen (U, N, M, R, H) and TREC (U, 0, 1) levels: breakdown for individual topics.

ments that were not judged by Sormunen), and by TREC binary levels (right side of figure, levels are 0, 1, and U, the documents that were not judged by TREC, as not all participating runs were included in the judging pool). This boxplot (and subsequent boxplots) show the median as a solid black line; boxes show the 25th to 75th percentile; and whiskers show the range, up to 1.5 times the inter-quartile range. There is a clear distinction between each of the four adjacent Sormunen levels, (two-tailed t-test, $p < 0.002$), with the magnitude estimation scores on average following the ordinal scale rank ordering. The differences between the two TREC levels are also significant ($p < 0.001$), with the magnitude estimation scores on average again being aligned with the binary levels. This is strong evidence for the overall validity of the magnitude estimation approach.

Figure 2 shows the magnitude estimation score distributions for each of the 18 individual topics. Although there is some variability across topics, overall the figure confirms that the magnitude estimation scores are usually aligned with ordinal categories even when considering individual topics: the medians of the median magnitude estimation scores (the solid black lines) generally follow the ordinal categories, for all categories and for all topics (there are some exceptions for some of the Sormunen adjacent categories in topics 403, 405, 410, 420, 421, and 440; there are no exceptions for non-adjacent categories, nor for TREC categories). Since for each topic there could potentially be 3 exceptions for adjacent categories, and 6 exceptions in general, plus one exception for the two TREC categories, the 6 exceptions found are out of $3*18+18 = 72$ possible cases when considering only adjacent categories, or out of $6*18+18 = 126$ cases when considering also non-adjacent categories. Such a limited fraction of exceptions (in the 5%-8% range) is further strong evidence for the validity of our approach, even at the single topic level.

Regarding the set of documents that were not judged by Sormunen (left-most boxes in Figure 1 and sub-plots in Figure 2), based on the magnitude estimation scores it can be inferred that the bulk of this class are likely to be non-relevant; however there are also instances that occur across the central parts of the marginal to highly relevant score distributions. There were also a handful of documents unjudged by TREC that seemed to be rated highly by our judges. It can also be observed that while the overall distributions of magnitude estimation scores are strongly consistent with the ordinal and binary categories, there are also documents in each class where the ME scores fall into the central region of a different class. We therefore next investigate judge agreement.

4.2 Judge Agreement

It is well-known that relevance is subjective, even when focusing on "topical" relevance as is typically done in evaluation campaigns such as TREC, and that judges will therefore not perfectly agree. To investigate the level of agreement when using different scales for judging relevance, we compare the pairwise orderings between binary, ordinal and magnitude estimation relevance judgments. Figure 3 shows the proportion of document pairs that agree on the order of relevance. For example, when comparing ordinal and magnitude estimation ratings, if two documents are rated N and M, and the corresponding magnitude estimation score of the first is lower than or equal to the score for the second, this would be an agreement, while if the magnitude estimation score was higher for the second document, it would indicate disagreement. The figure shows the pairwise agreement proportions between magnitude estimation (ME), Sormunen (S) and TREC (T), for each of the six possible combinations of ordinal relevance levels. Red circles indicate the mean score for each group. It can be seen that the rates of agreement are highly consistent when comparing any of the three relevance scales. In particular, ME leads to a higher average agree-

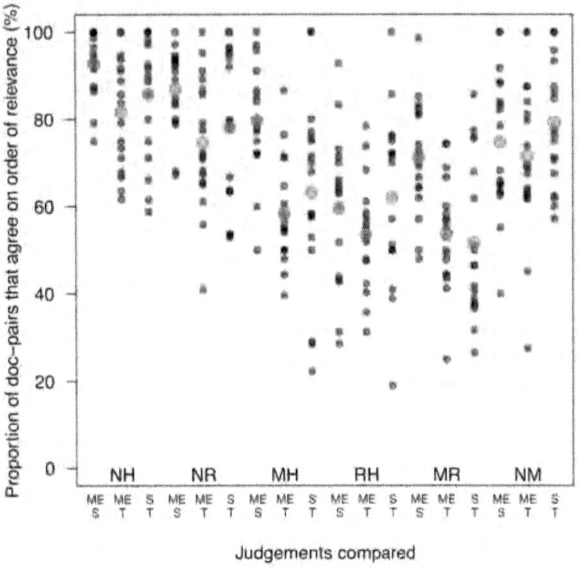

Figure 3: Agreement on the ordering of relevance of all document pairs (one small dot per topic) between judges as indicated on the x-axis (ME: magnitude estimation, S: Sormunen and T: TREC). The large (red) dot is the mean over all topics.

ment with Sormunen than TREC with Sormunen for documents in the NH, NR, MH, and MR pairs, and slightly lower for RH and NM: it can be said that normalized ME scores agree, in terms of ranks, with Sormunen at least as well as TREC agrees with Sormunen. Across all groups, the overall average agreement rates are 77% between magnitude estimation and Sormunen, 64% between magnitude estimation and TREC, and 65% between Sormunen and TREC. This further supports the validity of the magnitude estimation approach for gathering relevance judgments.

4.3 Failure Analysis

Despite the similar overall levels of agreement between the magnitude estimation method and ordinal relevance, Figures 1 and 2 show that some individual documents appear to be "misjudged". We therefore conducted a failure analysis, manually examining a subset of documents for which the Sormunen relevance level and the median magnitude estimation scores were substantially different (for example, where a particular document was assigned an ordinal Sormunen relevance level of N, but the median magnitude estimation score for the document was closer to the magnitude estimation scores assigned to H documents for the same topic, and substantially higher than the magnitude estimation scores assigned to other N documents for the same topic). Based on the manual examination of 34 documents where there appeared to be a significant flip between the ordinal and magnitude estimation scores, we found two broad classes of disagreements: those where one group of assessors appeared to be clearly wrong; and a class where the topic statement itself is so unclear as to be open to interpretation.

Of 34 documents that were examined, we found 14 cases (41.2%) where the Sormunen ordinal judgments appeared clearly wrong, and 9 (26.5%) of cases where the crowd-based magnitude estimation assessments appeared clearly wrong. For this class of clear disagreements, where some assessors appear to be clearly wrong in the assignment of relevance (whether ordinal or magnitude estimation), the cause mostly appears to be that the assessors have missed or ignored a specific restriction included as part of the TREC topic. For example, the narrative of topic 410, *"Schengen agreement"*, includes the statement that: *"Relevant documents will contain any information about the actions of signatories of the Schengen agreement such as: measures to eliminate border controls..."*. Document FT932-17156 makes clear reference to nine signatories of Schengen, and the process of removing passport checks. As such, it seems implausible that the document should be classed as N, or completely non-relevant. The original TREC binary judgment supports this view, having assigned a rating of 1 (indicating that the document is at least marginally relevant).

For the remaining 11 (32.4%) of cases, it was not possible to determine that one assessment was clearly correct and the other wrong. Here, the original TREC topic statement itself was ambiguous, preventing a clear conclusion to be drawn based on the limited information that the topic statement provided. For example, a number of topics list several concepts in the narrative about what is or is not deemed relevant. However, they introduce ambiguity about whether the document must meet all of the listed criteria, or whether a subset is sufficient. For example, topic 407, *"poaching, wildlife preserves"*, states that *"A relevant document must discuss poaching in wildlife preserves, not in the wild itself. Also deemed relevant is evidence of preventive measures being taken by local authorities."* This raises the ambiguity of whether preventative measures by authorities against poaching, but not specifically in wildlife preserves, should be considered as being at least somewhat relevant, or completely non-relevant. We note that further ambiguity is introduced due to the temporal mismatch between the time when the documents and topics were written (1990s), and when the magnitude estimation judgments are being made (2010s). This is particularly the case for topics that include terms such as "current".

The above failure analysis must also be interpreted in the context that it is known that assessors make mistakes when judging, perhaps due to fatigue or other lapses in attention, leading to self-inconsistencies [4, 20]; or they may display systematic errors due to a misunderstanding of the relevance criteria, or relevance drift [29]. Clearly, assessor errors will lower overall agreement rates when comparing assessments. Determining whether magnitude estimation relevance assessments lead to higher or lower error rates compared to using ordinal or binary scales is left for future work.

Overall, the examination of a set of clear disagreements demonstrates that there are cases where both groups of assessors (ordinal or magnitude estimation) are at odds with certain details of the TREC topic statements, and that these appear to occur at broadly similar rates. Moreover, the topic statements themselves are sometimes a cause of ambiguity, placing a practical upper-limit on the agreement that can be achieved. We conclude therefore that the magnitude estimation relevance judgments are sound and sensible, having similar agreement rates with the ordinal Sormunen judgments as the Sormunen judgments have with TREC assessments.

5. MAGNITUDE ESTIMATION FOR SYSTEM-LEVEL EVALUATION

The second research question concerns the direct application of magnitude estimation relevance judgments for the evaluation of IR systems, by considering their use for calibrating gain levels in two widely used gain-based IR evaluation metrics, nDCG and ERR.

5.1 Gain in the nDCG and ERR Metrics

Magnitude estimation provides scores that reflect ratios of human perceptions of the intensity of relevance of different documents in relation to a topic. This is directly related to the notion of gain in effectiveness metrics such as normalized discounted cumulative gain (nDCG). For example, Järvelin and Kekäläinen [12] describe "cumulative relevance gain" that a user receives by examining a search results list, and discuss setting "relevance weights at different relevance levels". That is, weights are applied to each level of an ordinal relevance scale, and can be chosen to reflect different assumptions about searcher relevance behavior. However, the "standard" approach that has been adopted when using nDCG is to simply assign ascending integer values to the ordinal levels, starting with 0 for the lowest (non-relevant) level; for a 3-level ordinal scale, the default gains would be 0, 1 and 2, as for example implemented in `trec_eval`.[1]

In addition to modeling different levels of gain, or relevance, the discounted cumulative gain metric also includes a discounting function, so that documents that are retrieved further down in a ranked search results list contribute smaller amounts of gain, reflective of factors such as the effort or time that a user must invest while working their way through the list [12]. Using a logarithmic discount, discounted cumulative gain at cutoff N is calculated as

$$\text{DCG@N} = G_1 + \sum_{i=2}^{N} \frac{G_i}{\log_2(i)},$$

where G_i is the gain value for the document at position i in the ranked list. To enable fair comparisons across topics with different numbers of relevant documents, the DCG@N score is divided by an *ideal* gain vector, a ranking of documents in decreasing relevance order, to obtain normalized discounted cumulative gain, nDCG@N.

Expected reciprocal rank is a metric based on a cascade model of searcher behavior, where the probability of continuing on to the next position in the ranked results list is influenced by the relevance of previous items. The metric calculates the expected reciprocal rank at which the searcher will stop [5], and is defined as

$$\text{ERR@N} = \sum_{i=1}^{N} \frac{R(G_i)}{i} \prod_{j=1}^{i-1} (1 - R(G_i)),$$

where $R(G) = (2^{G_i} - 1)/2^{G_{max}}$. In the analysis that follows, we calculate both nDCG and ERR up to a depth of $N = 10$.

For both nDCG and ERR, gain is based on the relevance of a document, which has previously been measured on an ordinal scale, typically with 3 [14] or 4 [12] levels, depending on the test collection being used. Since magnitude estimation relevance judgments are continuous rather than ordinal in nature, and reflect the perceived level of relevance for individual topic-document combinations, it is possible to assign more fine-grained gain values, potentially reflecting different gains for individual documents, or even for individual searchers.

5.2 Comparative System Rankings

Given that the agreement between our magnitude scores, TREC judgments and Sormunen's judgments is not perfect, it is reasonable to expect that relative system effectiveness orderings computed with each of these as a basis may differ. We first examine the correlation between system orderings using magnitude estimation scores and TREC relevance as gain values, as for both these judgment sets we have nearly complete coverage of the top 10 documents of all runs submitted to TREC-8, for our 18 judged topics. Figure 4 shows the system scores obtained using median magnitude estimation scores per document (x-axis), and binary TREC categories (y-axis). It can be seen that there are definite changes in system rankings when using the different relevance scales. When using the nDCG@10 metric, there is only small movement of the top ranked systems (cluster of points towards the top right), but when using the ERR@10 metric there is a large perturbation of the top ranked systems using the different judgments.

As the aim of system evaluation is to identify top-performing systems, we also consider changes in the *top set*, defined as the group of systems that are statistically indistinguishable from the system with the highest mean effectiveness, using a paired Wilcoxon signed-rank test with $p < 0.05$. The overlap of the top set, based on the TREC and magnitude estimation relevance judgments is 44% for nDCG@10 and 76% for ERR@10, confirming that the perturbation in system ordering has an impact on which systems are identified as being the best performers.

Since the Sormunen judgments only cover around 19% of the documents that occur in the top 10 of all TREC-8 ad hoc runs, evaluating the original runs using these relevance judgments is problematic, due to the large number of unjudged documents. However, the judgment coverage of individual ranked lists (that is, for particular topics within a run) varies substantially. Therefore, to enable a comparison between the ordinal judgment and magnitude estimation judgments on system orderings, we simulate runs that only include ranked lists for topics that are fully judged by Sormunen.

For each topic, we identify all ranked lists within the full set of runs that have Sormunen judgments for all top 10 documents for that topic; we call each of these a *complete sub-run*. There are 12 topics where there are at least two complete sub-runs out of all of the TREC-8 ad hoc runs for that topic. To form a simulated retrieval system, we then randomly choose one complete sub-run for each of the 12 topics to give a "full run" over all 12 topics. Using this method, we construct 100 simulated system runs that are random merges of complete sub-runs from real runs. While these simulated systems are not actual TREC submissions, they are plausible in that each individual topic ranking is from a real TREC run.

Figure 5 shows that there is also a large discordance between the system rankings using the Sormunen categories and median magnitudes as gain values. However, note that the scale is different in this figure than in Figure 4, as the simulated systems all have relevant documents in the top 10, and so are high scoring. The overlaps in top sets are 51% for nDCG@10 and 81% for ERR@10. The relatively high performance of systems on this simulated collection is to be expected, as only complete sub-runs were selected, and around half of the Sormunen judgments are for documents that were originally rated as relevant by TREC, and so the runs in the simulated systems have a high number of relevant documents. It is interesting that there is still a sizable change in the top set using both metrics, however.

5.3 Judgment Variability

There is substantial variation in the magnitudes assigned to documents by our judges. As we have at least 10 judgments per topic-document pair, rather than using the median score per document as in the previous section, we can resample individual scores many times, recompute system orderings, and get a distribution of τ values. The results are shown in Figure 6: the correlations between system orderings using sampled magnitudes as gains are generally lower than when using the median magnitudes. This reflects the wide range of individual variation – differences in perceptions of relevance – that in turn leads to a wide range of τ values.

An alternate explanation for the low τ values is that gains set as magnitudes are generally much higher than the gains set by Sormunen's categories. From Figure 1 it is apparent that magnitudes are generally in the range of 2 to 15 (although some are as large as

[1]`http://trec.nist.gov/trec_eval`

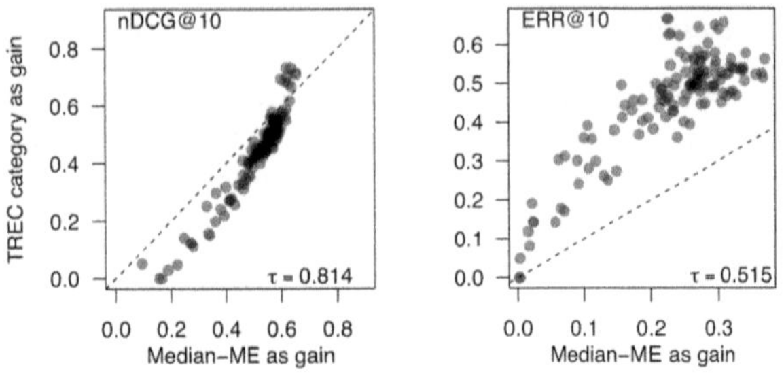

Figure 4: System scores using TREC categories (y-axis) and magnitudes (x-axis) as gains in the nDCG@10 and ERR@10 metrics. There is one dot per system participating in the TREC-8 ad hoc track. Kendall's τ is shown.

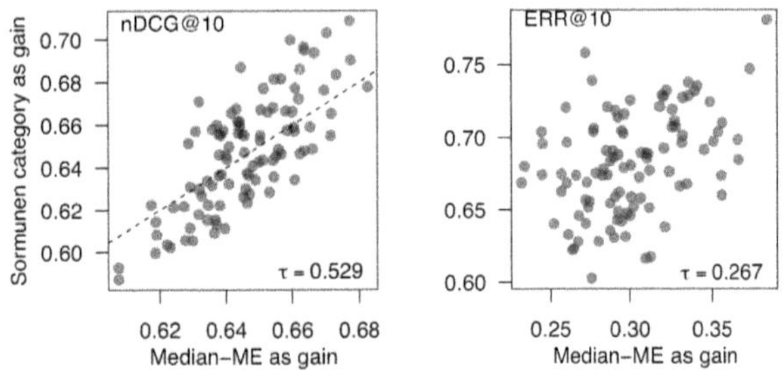

Figure 5: System scores using Sormunen categories (y-axis) and magnitudes (x-axis) as gains in the nDCG@10 and ERR@10 metrics. There is one dot per simulated system (see text). Kendall's τ is shown.

100 or 1000), whereas using categories as gains the values are 0, 1, 2 or 3. However, because both nDCG and ERR are normalized, this scale effect is nullified to a degree. For example, multiplying gains by a constant has no effect on nDCG, and even altering the category scores using a small exponential or additive constant has little effect. Table 2 shows this for our 12 topics on the simulated systems. The final row hints that using magnitudes that are gathered on a wide scale may alter system rankings using nDCG@10 compared with simply using the category values as gains. Similarly, the first row suggests that using gains gathered on a wide scale may alter rankings using ERR@10. One way to examine this further is to split our data into *narrow* units, those whose $\mathrm{H}_k/\mathrm{N}_k$ ratios are less

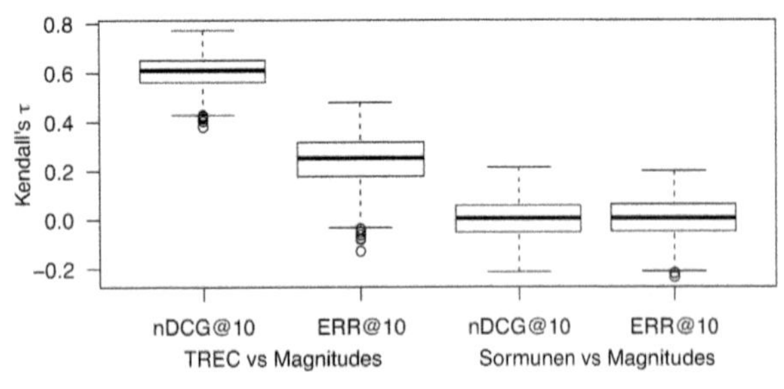

Figure 6: Kendall's τ between system rankings obtained using gains from the judgments and metrics indicated on the x-axis, where magnitudes are randomly sampled for each document 1000 times. Compare with τ in Figures 4 and 5.

Mapping	nDCG@10	ERR@10
$G_i = 100 \times C_i$	1.0000	0.8719
$G_i = 1 + C_i$	0.9994	0.9985
$G_i = 10 + C_i$	0.9950	0.9949
$G_i = 2^{1+C_i}$	0.9568	0.8738
$G_i = 10^{1+C_i}$	0.7833	0.8719

Table 2: Correlation (Kendall's τ) between system orderings when using Sormunen categories as gain ($G_i = C_i$), and other mappings on the simulated systems, when using the nDCG@10 and ERR@10 metrics.

Source of gains	Narrow	All	Wide
TREC, τ			
nDCG@10	0.780	0.814	0.765
ERR@10	0.537	0.515	0.434
TREC, top set			
nDCG@10	89%	44%	100%
ERR@10	56%	76%	95%
Sormunen-Simulated, τ			
nDCG@10	0.491	0.529	0.361
ERR@10	0.179	0.267	-0.010
Sormunen-Simulated, top set			
nDCG@10	67%	51%	82%
ERR@10	100%	81%	100%

Table 3: Correlation (Kendall's τ) and overlap of the top set between system orderings when median document magnitude scores are based on narrow, wide or all units.

than 5 (the median value), and *wide* units, where the ratios $\mathrm{H}_k/\mathrm{N}_k$ are 5 or more.

Table 3 shows the correlation (Kendall's τ) between system orderings, and overlap of runs in the top set, when using TREC and Sormunen judgments, and magnitude estimation scores when the median is obtained from units that used a narrow scale, a wide scale, or from all units (note that the τ values in the All column match those in Figures 4 and 5). When there was no narrow or wide judgment for a topic-document pair (all units containing that topic-document pair had $\mathrm{H}_k/\mathrm{N}_k$ above or below the median), the minimum or maximum magnitude over all units was taken, respectively. System orderings based on narrow or wide units show greater differences (lower τ values) than when considering the full data set. This is consistent with the results in Table 2. The overlap of the top set is generally less than 100% for the narrow/wide data sets, indicating that some perturbation of the set of "equivalent" top systems is occurring, but the pattern is not as clear as for τ values. This may be due to the relatively small number of topics that is being considered, especially for the simulated systems, and more topics are required before a definitive conclusion about the effect of narrow and wide units on the top set can be made.

Overall, there are clear differences in system effectiveness orderings as measured using Kendall's τ, when using narrow and wide units. In particular, it appears that using the median of narrow units, or of all units, leads to higher correlations with existing measurement techniques, compared to when using wide units. We

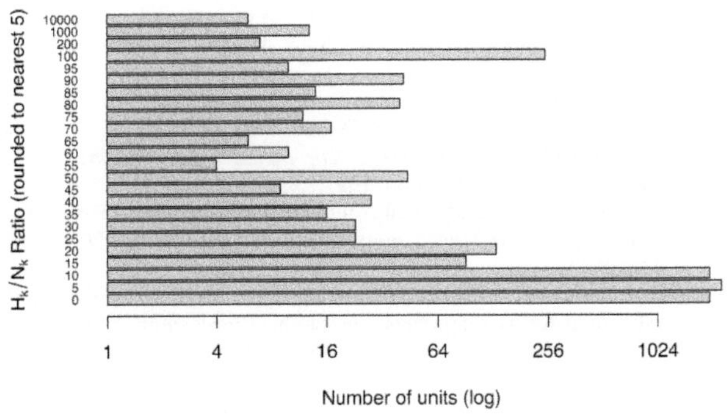

Figure 7: Number of units with a particular H_k/N_k ratio over all topics. There were a total of 7,059 units. 37 units with frequency less than 4 are not shown.

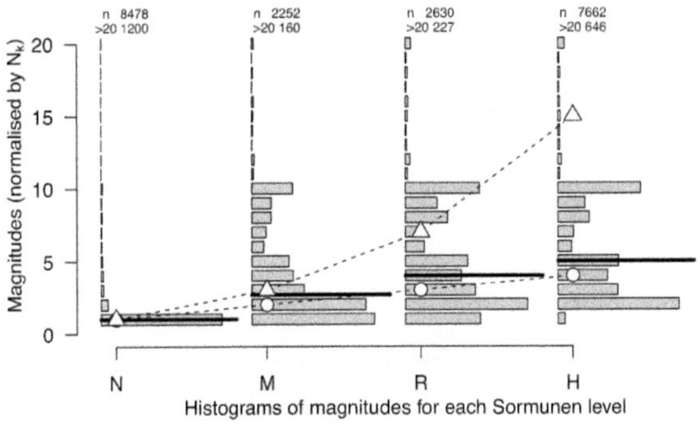

Figure 8: Distribution of magnitudes (normalized by N_k) for each Sormunen level. Circles are linear gain values, $\{1, 2, 3, 4\}$, while triangles represent exponential gain values, $\{2^1, 2^2, 2^3, 2^4\}$. Black lines are medians; the text "n" gives the total number of magnitudes in the level, and "> 20" shows the count of scores above 20.

can therefore infer that current evaluations using nDCG@10 and ERR@10 do not assume wide units as their underlying user model. This is important because it shows that nearly half of our participants are not behaving according to the user model assumed by current evaluation techniques. Figure 7 shows the full distribution of the "width" (H_k/N_k ratio) of units rounded to the nearest 5 (with bars containing less than 4 units omitted).

6. INVESTIGATING GAIN USING MAGNITUDE ESTIMATION

The previous section used perturbations in system orderings to examine the difference between using magnitude estimate relevance scores and the usually employed ordinal relevance levels as gains. This section directly considers gain profiles, answering our third research question by considering what additional insights magnitude estimation can provide into user perceptions of relevance.

The gain weights of the nDCG metric allow for the modeling of different user relevance preferences. However, in practice gains are usually set to one of two profiles: a *linear* setting (as defined in Section 5); or an *exponential* setting, where the ordinal relevance level forms a power of 2 [3], placing more emphasis on highly relevant documents. Figure 8 shows the distribution of magnitude estimation scores, normalized by the N_k score in each unit (intuitively, a measure of relevance standardized for each user). Black lines show the median magnitudes for each group. Superimposed are the two default profiles, linear (white circles), and exponential (white triangles). It can be seen that, compared to actual user perceptions of the relevance space, the linear gain profile is fairly close to the gain that should be allocated at each level to satisfy the (mythical) median user. The exponential profile is further from the median, overestimating the gain for the R and H levels, but catering for some judgments.

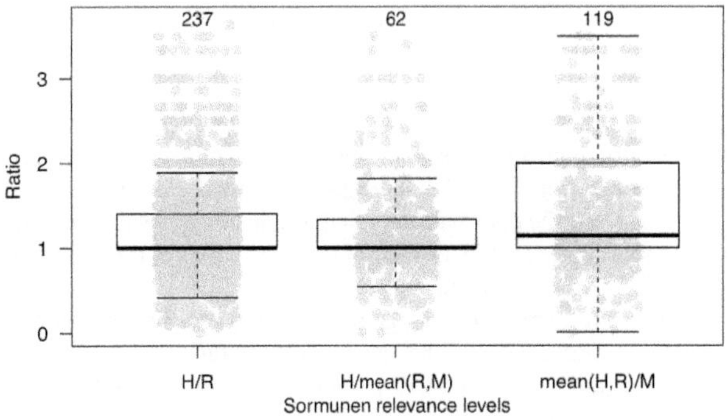

Figure 9: Ratio of the magnitude scores assigned to the Sormunen categories highly relevant (H) to relevant (R) and marginally relevant (M) over all pairs of documents. Numbers indicate the count of document pairs that are greater than 3.5 for each box.

It is readily apparent, however, that the large spread of the distributions of magnitudes cannot be captured in a single gain formulation. There is simply too much individual variation to warrant the simplification of relevance perceptions to a single profile.

Our final piece of analysis is given in Figure 9, which shows the ratio of magnitudes for document pairs in the Sormunen levels highly relevant and partially relevant. We combine the three relevance levels into two to allow comparison with Kanoulas and Aslam [14]. They recommend a ratio of 1.1 for relevant to highly relevant, which is supported by the medians in Figure 9. However, again, we see a wide variation from this median.

7. DISCUSSION AND CONCLUSIONS

This is the first study to have collected large scale, real user data about relevance perceptions using magnitude estimation. Our first research question investigated the suitability of using magnitude estimation for gathering relevance judgments. As shown in Section 4, magnitude estimation scores are consistent with classical ordinal scores, both on single topics and overall on the 18 aggregated topics; ordering agreement between magnitude estimation judgments and ordinal judgments is higher than between ordinal and binary judgments; and failure analysis demonstrated that disagreement is often due not to problems with magnitude estimation per se but rather to different judging context. It is likely that using a classical scale one would get a similar agreement level.

Considering the impact of magnitude estimation relevance judgments on IR system evaluation, the second research question, our analysis showed that system orderings vary substantially when different relevance scales are used, with a τ of 0.81 for nDCG@10 when comparing magnitude estimation scores with binary relevance across TREC runs, and 0.53 when comparing with ordinal relevance on simulated runs. When individual variability is considered, these correlations are even lower. The analysis suggests that it is important to incorporate different judging scales – users who have wider or thinner perceptions of the differences in relevance.

We also employed magnitude estimation to directly investigate gain profiles, the third research question. Typically, gains are set as linear or exponential profiles. Our analysis of user-reported relevance perception showed that the linear profile is close to the "average" user, but the distribution of magnitudes suggests that attempting to fit a single profile, or view of relevance, for system evaluation is unlikely to be sufficient.

While on average our magnitudes were broadly equivalent to previous ordinal scales, the outstanding feature of our data was the wide range of scores that participants chose to employ in the judging task. In particular, at least half of the participants chose gain values that are not consistent with currently used values. Section 5.2 shows that using judgments made on a wide scale leads to different system rankings than judgments collected on a narrow scale. Recall that these scales are not imposed on the judge, as they are in all previous relevance judgment tasks in the literature, but are chosen by the participants themselves.

This is another key contribution of this study: when a priori categorical scales are used for relevance judgment tasks, there is no possible way to capture variance in human perception of the scale of relevance. In turn, this limits our understanding of how gain should be set in DCG-like metrics, and hence our ability to accurately evaluate systems.

Throughout the paper we have assumed that topical relevance collected using magnitude estimation can be used directly as gain in DCG-like measures. While perhaps being more representative of user perceptions than other relevance scales, this still makes many assumptions about the user's search process which are probably untrue: for example, ignoring the interdependence of documents and other aspects of relevance. In future work, we plan to investigate whether magnitude estimation can be used to reliably scale other aspects of relevance such as novelty, as well as search outcome measures such as satisfaction, and to examine whether this can lead to more meaningful gain representations.

Acknowledgments This work was supported by the Australian Research Council (*Discovery Project* DP130104007).

References

[1] O. Alonso and S. Mizzaro. Using crowdsourcing for TREC relevance assessment. *Information Processing and Management*, 48(6):1053–1066, 2012.

[2] E. G. Bard, D. Robertson, and A. Sorace. Magnitude estimation of linguistic acceptability. *Language*, 72(1):32–68, 1996.

[3] C. Burges, T. Shaked, E. Renshaw, A. Lazier, M. Deeds, N. Hamilton, and G. Hullender. Learning to rank using gradient descent. In *Proceedings of the 22nd international conference on Machine learning*, pages 89–96, Bonn, Germany, 2005.

[4] B. Carterette and I. Soboroff. The effect of assessor error on IR system evaluation. In *Proceedings of the ACM SIGIR International Conference on Research and Development in Information Retrieval*, pages 539–546, Geneva, Switzerland, 2010.

[5] O. Chapelle, D. Metlzer, Y. Zhang, and P. Grinspan. Expected reciprocal rank for graded relevance. In *Proceedings of the ACM CIKM International Conference on Information and Knowledge Management*, pages 621–630, Hong Kong, 2009.

[6] C. Clarke, N. Craswell, and I. Soboroff. Overview of the TREC 2004 terabyte track. In *The Fourteenth Text REtrieval Conference (TREC 2005)*, Gaithersburg, MD, 2005. NIST.

[7] K. Collins-Thompson, P. Bennett, F. Diaz, C. L. Clarke, and E. M. Voorhees. TREC 2013 Web Track Overview. In *22nd Text REtrieval Conference (TREC 2013)*, Gaithersburg, MD, 2014.

[8] E. P. Cox,III. The optimal number of response alternatives for a scale: A review. *Journal of marketing research*, 17(4):407–422, 1980.

[9] W. H. Ehrenstein and A. Ehrenstein. Psychophysical methods. In U. Windhorst and H. Johansson, editors, *Modern techniques in neuroscience research*, pages 1211–1241. Springer, 1999.

[10] M. Eisenberg. Measuring relevance judgements. *Information Processing and Management*, 24:373–389, 1988.

[11] G. Gescheider. *Psychophysics: The Fundamentals*. Lawrence Erlbaum Associates, 3rd edition, 1997.

[12] K. Järvelin and J. Kekäläinen. Cumulated gain-based evaluation of IR techniques. *ACM Transactions on Information Systems*, 20(4):422–446, 2002.

[13] K. Johnson and A. Bojko. How much is too much? Using magnitude estimation for user experience research. *Proceedings of the Human Factors and Ergonomics Society Annual Meeting*, 54(12):942–946, 2010.

[14] E. Kanoulas and J. A. Aslam. Empirical justification of the gain and discount function for nDCG. In *Proceedings of the ACM CIKM International Conference on Information and Knowledge Management*, pages 611–620, Hong Kong, 2009.

[15] E. Maddalena, S. Mizzaro, F. Scholer, and A. Turpin. Judging relevance using magnitude estimation. In *Advances in Information Retrieval - Proceedings of 37th ECIR*, volume 9022 of *LNCS*, pages 215–220, Vienna, Austria, 2015.

[16] L. Marks. *Sensory Processes: The new Psychophysics*. Academic Press, 1974.

[17] M. McGee. Usability magnitude estimation. *Proceedings of the Human Factors and Ergonomics Society Annual Meeting*, 47(4):691–695, 2003.

[18] H. R. Moskowitz. Magnitude estimation: notes on what, how, when, and why to use it. *Journal of Food Quality*, 1(3):195–227, 1977.

[19] T. Saracevic. Relevance: A review of the literature and a framework for thinking on the notion in information science. Part II: nature and manifestations of relevance. *JASIST*, 58(13):1915–1933, 2007.

[20] F. Scholer, A. Turpin, and M. Sanderson. Quantifying test collection quality based on the consistency of relevance judgements. In *Proceedings of the ACM SIGIR International Conference on Research and Development in Information Retrieval*, pages 1063–1072, Beijing, China, 2011.

[21] F. Scholer, E. Maddalena, S. Mizzaro, and A. Turpin. Magnitudes of relevance: Relevance judgements, magnitude estimation, and crowdsourcing. In *The Sixth International Workshop on Evaluating Information Access (EVIA 2014)*, Tokyo, Japan, 2014.

[22] D. Sheskin. *Handbook of parametric and nonparametric statistical procedures, 4th ed.* CRC Press, 2007.

[23] E. Sormunen. Liberal relevance criteria of TREC: Counting on negligible documents? In *Proceedings of the ACM SIGIR International Conference on Research and Development in Information Retrieval*, pages 324–330, Tampere, Finland, 2002.

[24] A. Spink and H. Greisdorf. Regions and levels: Measuring and mapping users' relevance judgments. *JASIST*, 52(2):161–173, 2001.

[25] S. S. Stevens. A metric for the social consensus. *Science (New York, NY)*, 151(3710):530–541, 1966.

[26] R. Tang, W. M. Shaw, and J. L. Vevea. Towards the identification of the optimal number of relevance categories. *JASIS*, 50(3):254–264, 1999.

[27] E. M. Voorhees and D. K. Harman. Overview of the Eighth Text REtrieval Conference (TREC-8). In *The Eighth Text REtrieval Conference (TREC-8)*, pages 1–24, Gaithersburg, MD, 1999.

[28] E. M. Voorhees and D. K. Harman. *TREC: experiment and evaluation in information retrieval*. MIT Press, 2005.

[29] W. Webber and J. Pickens. Assessor disagreement and text classifier accuracy. In *Proceedings of the ACM SIGIR International Conference on Research and Development in Information Retrieval*, pages 929–932, Dublin, Ireland, 2013.

Learning to Reweight Terms with Distributed Representations

Guoqing Zheng
School of Computer Science
Carnegie Mellon University
5000 Forbes Avenue
Pittsburgh, PA 15213, USA
gzheng@cs.cmu.edu

Jamie Callan
School of Computer Science
Carnegie Mellon University
5000 Forbes Avenue
Pittsburgh, PA 15213, USA
callan@cs.cmu.edu

ABSTRACT

Term weighting is a fundamental problem in IR research and numerous weighting models have been proposed. Proper term weighting can greatly improve retrieval accuracies, which essentially involves two types of query understanding: interpreting the query and judging the relative contribution of the terms to the query. These two steps are often dealt with separately, and complicated yet not so effective weighting strategies are proposed. In this paper, we propose to address query interpretation and term weighting in a unified framework built upon *distributed representations* of words from recent advances in neural network language modeling. Specifically, we represent term and query as vectors in the same latent space, construct features for terms using their word vectors and learn a model to map the features onto the defined target term weights. The proposed method is simple yet effective. Experiments using four collections and two retrieval models demonstrates significantly higher retrieval accuracies than baseline models.

Categories and Subject Descriptors

H.3.3 [**Information Search and Retrieval**]: Retrieval models

General Terms

Algorithms, Experimentation

Keywords

Query term weighting, distributed representations, word vectors

1. INTRODUCTION

Performance of text search engines relies heavily on query understanding, of which one important problem is how to weight the contribution of each individual term to the retrieval score[1]. When proper weights (such as ground truth *term recall* weights [22]) are used, they can boost retrieval accuracies by up to 30% given relevance judgments. Properly setting the query term weights requires accurately interpreting and properly representing the query first. This is no easy task as query intent understanding itself is a diffcult problem in IR research [7].

In this paper, we attempt to address query interpretation and term weighing from a different angle, with a unified framework built upon recent advances in neural network language modeling [13, 3]. Recent research in the application of neural network to text problems exploits the co-occurrence of words to represent words by multidimensional vectors. Distributed representations learned from neural network based models [13, 3] are designed and shown to be effective for measuring semantic similarity among words and identifying similar neighbors for a given word. The mapping from words to vectors gives the ability to not only measure word-word similarity but also ways to represent the query in the same vector space from word vectors from its terms (such as taking the average of the word vectors of all terms as the vector representation for the query).

As proper query term weights reflects the relative importance of the term with respect to the query, specifically we propose to construct features from word vectors representations of terms and the query and to learn the relationship between the feature vectors and target term weight (such as the term recall weight [22] estimated from relevance judgments). A regularized linear regression problem from the feature vectors onto term weights is formulated and the predicted term weights are used for both bag-of-words queries and term dependency queries. We demonstrate the effectiveness of our method using two popular retrieval models, four standard test collections, word vectors developed from a variety of sources, and three baseline methods.

The contributions of our work are three fold. First, we join the work of distributed word vectors to the prediction of query term weights in IR, and propose a simple yet effective framework to predict effective term weights. Second, we observe significant improvement over the baseline mod-

[1]People use "term weight" to describe two different settings: one is the matching score a retrieval function assigns to a term and a document pair; the other is the relative importance of the term to the query. The first setting is handled by the retrieval model while the query model deals with the second one; in this paper, we refer "term weight" or "term reweighting" to that in the second setting.

SIGIR'15, August 09 - 13, 2015, Santiago, Chile.
© 2015 ACM. ISBN 978-1-4503-3621-5/15/08 ...$15.00.
DOI: http://dx.doi.org/10.1145/2766462.2767700.

els with two retrieval models over four standard collections when using predicted term recall as term weights. Third, the proposed method is much more efficient than previous work on query term weight prediction, i.e., term recall weight, which requires an initial retrieval and a local SVD for every new incoming query to obtain features for predicting term recall [22]. The proposed framework derives feature vectors directly from precomputed distributed word vectors; simple computations are sufficient for predicting term weights for new queries.

The remainder of this paper is organized as follows: Section 2 introduces prior research related to query term weighting and term recall weight. Section 3 discusses the preliminaries for term recall prediction and distributed word vectors. Section 4 formally presents our approach in term weight modeling and estimation. Section 5 describes the data sets and the experimental settings. Experimental results as well as data analysis are presented in Section 6. At last, we conclude the paper and discuss some future work in Section 7.

2. RELATED WORK

Query term weighting has been extensively studied in IR literature and a retrieval model reflects its choice of query term weights used. Conceptually, any retrieval model can be abstracted as the following scoring function:

$$Score(q, D) = \sum_{t \in q \cap D} w(t) f(t, D) \qquad (1)$$

where $f(t, D)$ is the *matching score* of term t and document D (for example, term frequency), and $w(t)$, the query term weight, which doesn't specifically depend on D (for example, inverse term frequency), is the quantity we are interested in this paper. By formulating this way, existing retrieval models make different choices about term weight. The most commonly used query term weights in the literature is idf, for example, the vector space model, language model [21], BM25, etc.

Another well known term weight, the term recall weight, is closely related to idf and also attracts broad attention. It is originally captured by the Binary Independence Model (BIM)[16] to emphasize the importance of query term weights, as shown below:

$$Score(q, D) \propto \sum_{t_i \in q \cap D} \log \left(\frac{\mathbb{P}(t_i|R_q)}{1 - \mathbb{P}(t_i|R_q)} \times \frac{1 - \mathbb{P}(t_i|\bar{R}_q)}{\mathbb{P}(t_i|\bar{R}_q)} \right) \quad (2)$$

where R_q is the set of relevant documents, $\bar{R}_q$ is the set of non-relevant documents, d is a document to be ranked, q is the query, and t_i is a query term. The probability $\mathbb{P}(t|R_q)$ provides one way to weight query terms, known as the RSJ term weight, to improve retrieval performance. However, due to involvement of the relevant set of documents of query q, it is hard to give a reliable estimation of $\mathbb{P}(t|R_q)$ when relevance information is unavailable. Indeed, researchers recognized that the use of term recall weight could lead to huge retrieval gain as $\mathbb{P}(t|R_q)$ is actually the only term about relevance in the ranking function [22], and proposed several ways to predict it.

Croft and Harper [5] modeled the query term weight as a tuned constant (the Croft/Harper Combination Match model). Greiff [6] tried to predict term weight and $\mathbb{P}(t|\bar{R}_q)$ with a linear function of idf. His experiments showed some improvement over the BIM model. More recently, Metzler [12] modeled term weight as a linear function of document frequency. The above modeling of term weight only used df or idf features. The predictions were inadequate as they did not reflect the insight that $\mathbb{P}(t|R_q)$ is a query dependent quantity and that query dependent features are needed to estimate term weight. Recently, Zhao et al. [22] proposed a framework to construct features for query terms from pseudo relevance feedback [20] and use them to predict term weight.

Retrieval models that capture term dependencies have attracted research attention and also demonstrated their retrieval effectiveness compared to unigram query models. One widely used model is the sequential dependency model (SD) [10], which features three types of *query concepts*: terms, bigrams and proximity expression. An example of a sequential dependency query in the Indri query language for the bag-of-words query `apple pie recipe` is:

```
#weight( 0.8 #combine( apple pie recipe )
         0.1 #combine( #1(apple pie)
                       #1(pie recipe) )
         0.1 #combine( #uw8(apple pie)
                       #uw8(pie recipe) )
)
```

#1(apple pie) matches when `apple` and `pie` form a bigram. #uw8(apple pie) matches when `apple` and `pie` occur in any order within a window of 8 words. And #combine is a probabilistic AND operator.

The sequential dependence model provides basic weighting for different types of query concepts. Broad empirical results have validated the effectiveness of SD over the unweighted bag-of-words query model [1, 2, 10]. However, concepts of the same type share the same weight, which is not optimal. Recent research proposed to predict term weights for each concept using features computed from collection statistics, an adaptive model, and an optimization goal of maximizing an evaluation metric such as Mean Average Precision (MAP) [1, 2]. Term weighting strategy emphasizing query aspects is also proposed [23].

Our approach differs from the above methods in that we represent terms and queries using distributed word vectors in a semantic vector space learnt from a global corpus and we construct novel feature vectors from the distributed representations to automatically learn term weights for efficient retrieval.

3. PRELIMINARIES

In this section, we briefly introduce recent work on distributed representations learning from neural network language models and also defines the target term weights we use in our framework.

3.1 Distributed word vectors

Neural network based language models aim to learn the word vector representations and a statistical language model for the underlying text. These models can be mainly attributed to two categories. Models from the first category try to learn the word vector representations and the language model jointly. One example is the neural network language model (NNLM) [3], where a linear projection layer and a non-linear hidden layer are adopted to form a feedforward neural network. Models in the second category learn the word vector representations first and then train the language model with the word vectors. For example, Mikolov, et al. [14] used one neural network with a single hidden layer to learn word vector representations and then trained an N-gram language model on the word vectors. Typically the simple structure of the neural networks used by the second approach makes it less computationally expensive, thus we confine the discussion to this type of system.

Recently, Mikolov et al. [13] proposed two new models, the Continuous Bag-of-Words model (CBOW) and the Continuous Skip-gram model, that have greater training efficiency. CBOW tries to maximize classification of a word by building a log-linear classifier with word vectors of several history words and future words around that location as input, while the Continuous Skip-gram model tries to predict words within a range before and after the current word given the word vector of the current word. Both CBOW and the Continuous Skip-gram model have only one projection layer between the input and output layer without any hidden layer, which significantly reduces the computational cost caused by the non-linear hidden layers in prior neural network based language models. Negative sampling is used to learn the CBOW and the Continuous Skip-gram models [15]. Word vector representations on a Google News corpus with 100 billion words for a vocabulary of 3 million words can be learned in less than one day using modest hardware.

Word vectors learned by both models have performed well in several semantic related task evaluations [13]. Mikolov et al. released the software for training CBOW and Continuous Skip-gram models and a set of pre-trained 300-dimensional word vector representations on the above mentioned Google News corpus[2]. Table 1 presents an example of the 10 closest words to '`Chinese river`' in terms of cosine similarity in the word vector representation space.

Table 1: Example of closest n-gram terms to the phrase '`Chinese river`'.

Word	Cosine similarity
`Yangtze_River`	0.667376
`Yangtze`	0.644091
`Qiantang_River`	0.632979
`Yangtze_tributary`	0.623527
`Xiangjiang_River`	0.615482
`Huangpu_River`	0.604726
`Hanjiang_River`	0.598110
`Yangtze_river`	0.597621
`Hongze_Lake`	0.594108
`Yangtse`	0.593442

It can be seen that the neighbors given by word vectors are indeed semantically related to the input. Also, in this example, unlike `Yangtze_River`, the phrase `Chinese_river` does not belong to the vocabulary of the model; there is no word vector representation for `Chinese_river`. Instead, word vectors for both `Chinese` and `river` are fetched and **averaged** to represent `Chinese_river` in the search for the closest neighbors, which yields meaningful results. A recent analysis [8] justifies the above results by showing that the learning of distributed representations is essentially factorizing a word-context matrix which ensures that words sharing similar context (thus similar meaning) will have similar vector representations.

*This **word vector addition property** is the key motivation to represent query and terms as word vectors and thus to derive term features from them to predict target term weights.* See [15] for more examples of word vector addition property. In this paper, we adopt the CBOW framework to learn word vectors and use them to build a term weight prediction framework. The proposed framework can also be applied to word vectors learned by the Continuous Skip-gram model, which we leave as future work.

[2]`https://code.google.com/p/word2vec/`

3.2 Target term weights

As discussed in Section 1, proper query term weights reflects the relative importance of a term to a query and should also help improve retrieval performance. We choose *term recall* weight as our target term weight to predict in our framework for its simplicity to compute and also great potential to improve retrieval performance [22]. Given relevance judgments, it can be estimated as $\mathbb{P}(t|R_q) = \frac{|R_{q,t}|}{|R_q|}$, where R_q is the set of relevant documents to q and $R_{q,t} \subseteq R_q$ is the subset of relevant documents that contain term t.

3.3 Term weights and retrieval models

In this section, we present how true or estimated target term weights can be integrated into different retrieval models.

3.3.1 *Probabilistic language model*

One commonly used retrieval model in IR is the language model, often together with Dirichlet smoothing as shown in Eq. (3),

$$Score(q, D) = \sum_{t \in q \cap D} \log \frac{tf_{t,D} + \mu \frac{cf_t}{|C|}}{|D| + \mu} \quad (3)$$

where tf_t is the term frequency of term t in document D, cf_t is the collection frequency of t, $|D|$ is the length of document D, $|C|$ is the total length of the collection and μ is the smoothing parameter.

True term recall weight or term recall weight estimates can used by a language model in similar fashion as [9], as shwon in Eq. (4).

$$Score(q, D) = \sum_{t \in q \cap D} \left(\mathbb{P}(t|R) \cdot \log \frac{tf_{t,D} + \mu \frac{cf_t}{|C|}}{|D| + \mu} \right) \quad (4)$$

The term recall weighted language model shown above is equivalent to the relevance model under the assumption of binary term occurrences and uniform document length [22].

3.3.2 *BM25*

Another widely adopted retrieval model is BM25, as shown in Eq. (5)

$$Score(q, D) = \sum_{t \in q \cap D} \log \left(\frac{N - df_t + 0.5}{df_t + 0.5} \right) \cdot \frac{tf_{t,D} \cdot (k_1 + 1)}{tf_{t,D} + k_1 (1 - b + b \frac{|D|}{avgdl})} \quad (5)$$

where df_t is the document frequency of term t, $avgdl$ is the average document length over the collection and k_1 and b are free parameters. BM25 is actually more directly connected to term recall weight, as the above original BM25 model is an extension of the BIM [16]. By inserting the recall weight estimates to BM25, we get the recall-enhanced BM25 as shown in Eq. (6).

$$Score(q, D) = \sum_{t \in q \cap D} \log \left(\frac{\mathbb{P}(t|R)}{1 - \mathbb{P}(t|R)} \cdot \frac{N - df_t + 0.5}{df_t + 0.5} \right) \cdot \frac{tf_{t,D} \cdot (k_1 + 1)}{tf_{t,D} + k_1 (1 - b + b \frac{|D|}{avgdl})}. \quad (6)$$

4. TERM WEIGHTS LEARNING WITH DISTRIBUTED WORD VECTORS

In this section, we present our model for estimating term weights with distributed word vectors.

Table 2: Notations

M	number of queries
N	total number of terms in all M queries
n_i	number of terms in the ith query
q_i	the ith query
t_{ij}	the jth term of the ith query
r_{ij}	true term weight for t_{ij}
p	dimension of distributed word vector
$\boldsymbol{w}_{ij}$	distributed word vector for t_{ij}
$\boldsymbol{x}_{ij}$	feature vector for t_{ij}
$\boldsymbol{X}$	feature matrix
$\boldsymbol{y}$	regression labels vector
λ	regularization parameter
$\boldsymbol{\beta}$	feature weights vector

Suppose we have a set of M queries $Q = \{q_1, q_2, ..., q_M\}$ and each query q_i has n_i terms for $i = 1, 2, ..., M$. Let t_{ij} represent the jth term of query q_i for $j = 1, 2, ..., n_i$, r_{ij} denote the true term weight estimated from relevance judgments for t_{ij}, hence $r_{ij} \in [0, 1]$ and $N = \sum_{i=1}^{M} n_i$ denote the total number of query terms. (Refer to Table 2 for a summary of notations.)

Let $\boldsymbol{w}_{ij} \in \mathbb{R}^p$ denote the continuous distributed word vector representation for term t_{ij}, where p is the dimension of the word vector. In this paper, we propose to directly construct the feature vector $\boldsymbol{x}_{ij}$ for term t_{ij} from the distributed word vector representations of term t_{ij} and other terms in the same query q_i as

$$\boldsymbol{x}_{ij} = \boldsymbol{w}_{ij} - \overline{\boldsymbol{w}}_{q_i} \tag{7}$$

where

$$\overline{\boldsymbol{w}}_{q_i} = \frac{1}{n_i} \sum_{k}^{n_i} \boldsymbol{w}_{ik} \tag{8}$$

is the mean of all word vectors of terms in q_i. Hence, the feature vectors have the same dimension as the word vectors. An naive example of feature vector construction with $p = 2$ is illustrated in Figure 1.

Intuitively, proper term weights measures the relative importance of a term w.r.t. the whole query (hence w.r.t. the other terms in the same query). In other words, a term with a higher term weight means that it's more important for the term to represent the meaning of the query. Meanwhile, the feature vector of a term defined above is the difference of the term to the center of distributed representations for all terms in the query, which also serves as the vector representation for the entire query (by applying the word vector addition properties). Hence, *the feature vector measures the semantic difference of a term to the whole query.* Believing that the above two measures are somewhat related, we propose to construct features above and learn a model to map from the feature vectors to term weight labels.

As a side note, we can see that the above constructed feature vectors are hence query dependent, which is also necessary in that term weight, from its definition, is also query dependent. As we will see in the experiments, the above construction is simple and yet effective.

Having defined the features, we now turn to formulate the model to map from feature to term weight labels. As the

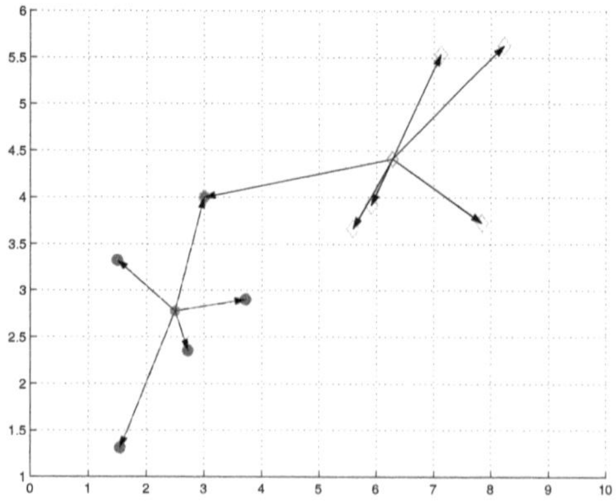

Figure 1: Demonstration of transforming global 2-dimensional word vectors into feature vectors local to the query. In the graph, blue solid circles represent terms in one query and green diamonds represent terms in another query. Note that the two queries share one common term located at (3, 4). The red solid circle represents the center for the circles, and the red diamond represents the center for the diamonds. The dashed and solid arrows are then the transformed feature vectors for all the terms.

adopted target term weight is a probability, we first map it from (0, 1) onto the real line $\mathbb{R}$ with a logit function to avoid numerical issues, as shown below.

$$y_{ij} = \text{logit}(r_{ij}) = \log \frac{r_{ij}}{1 - r_{ij}} \tag{9}$$

We then formulate the "transformed" term weight y as a linear function of the term feature vectors defined above, that is $y = \boldsymbol{\beta}^\top \boldsymbol{x}$, and employ ℓ_1-norm regularization to learn the feature weights $\boldsymbol{\beta}$ (We also tried ℓ_2-norm regularization and ℓ_1-norm regularization works a little better). Formally, the optimization problem is

$$\hat{\boldsymbol{\beta}} = \arg \min_{\boldsymbol{\beta} \in \mathbb{R}^p} \frac{1}{2} \sum_{i=1}^{M} \sum_{j=1}^{n_i} (y_{ij} - \boldsymbol{\beta}^\top \boldsymbol{x}_{ij})^2 + \lambda \|\boldsymbol{\beta}\|_1 \tag{10}$$

where $\lambda \geq 0$ is the regularization parameter controlling the balance between prediction error on training data and model complexity, and needs to be tuned by cross validation. In matrix form, the above optimization problem can be expressed as

$$\hat{\boldsymbol{\beta}} = \arg \min_{\boldsymbol{\beta} \in \mathbb{R}^p} \frac{1}{2} \|\boldsymbol{y} - \boldsymbol{X}\boldsymbol{\beta}\|_2^2 + \lambda \|\boldsymbol{\beta}\|_1 \tag{11}$$

where $\boldsymbol{y} \in \mathbb{R}^N$ is

$$\boldsymbol{y} = (y_{11}, y_{12}, ..., y_{1n_1}, y_{21}, y_{22}, ...y_{2n_2}, ..., y_{M1}, y_{M2}, ..., y_{Mn_M})^\top \tag{12}$$

is target term weight vector with term weights of all terms in the training queries stacked, and $\boldsymbol{X} \in \mathbb{R}^{N \times p}$ is

$$\boldsymbol{X} = (\boldsymbol{x}_{11}, \boldsymbol{x}_{12}, ..., \boldsymbol{x}_{1n_1}, \boldsymbol{x}_{21}, \boldsymbol{x}_{22}, ...\boldsymbol{x}_{2n_2}, ..., \boldsymbol{x}_{M1}, \boldsymbol{x}_{M2}, ..., \boldsymbol{x}_{Mn_M})^\top \tag{13}$$

It is easy to verify that optimization problem (11) is equivalent to (10) and is of standard form of LASSO regression [19].

Specifically, the subgradient of the objective function w.r.t $\boldsymbol{\beta}$ in problem (11) is

$$\frac{\partial f(\boldsymbol{\beta})}{\partial \boldsymbol{\beta}} = \boldsymbol{X}^\top(\boldsymbol{X}\boldsymbol{\beta} - \boldsymbol{y}) + \lambda \boldsymbol{s} \tag{14}$$

where

$$s_i \in \begin{cases} \text{sign}(\beta_i) & \text{if } \beta_i \neq 0 \\ [-1, 1] & \text{if } \beta_i = 0 \end{cases} \tag{15}$$

Efficient gradient based methods can be applied to solve the above problem and after we get the optimum $\hat{\boldsymbol{\beta}}$, when a new query term t_* with feature vector $\boldsymbol{x}_*$ arrives, we predict its term weight as

$$\widehat{\mathbb{P}(t_*|R)} = \text{sigmoid}\left(\hat{\boldsymbol{\beta}}^\top \boldsymbol{x}_*\right) = \frac{\exp\left(\hat{\boldsymbol{\beta}}^\top \boldsymbol{x}_*\right)}{1 + \exp\left(\hat{\boldsymbol{\beta}}^\top \boldsymbol{x}_*\right)} \tag{16}$$

We refer to the above proposed method as `DeepTR` for it using distributed representations of words to model term weights.

`DeepTR` is a very efficient method of predicting term weights, which enables it to be used in online services where latency (the time required to respond to a query) must be kept low. The word vectors and the regression model are trained offline. Predicting $\mathbb{P}(t_{ij}|R)$ for a new query involves loading the word vectors for the query terms, transforming them into feature vectors (averaging and subtraction), an inner product with the learned feature weights, and a sigmoid function. This is far more efficient than some prior methods that were effective but computationally complex (e.g., [22]).

After we gain estimates of the term weights, we construct the following query model variations in Indri query language (with the above `apple pie recipe` keyword query as an example):

- `DeepTR-BOW`:

```
#weight( P̂(apple|R) apple
         P̂(pie|R) pie
         P̂(recipe|R) recipe )
)
```

- `DeepTR-SD`:

```
#weight(
0.8 #weight( P̂(apple|R) apple
             P̂(pie|R) pie
             P̂(recipe|R) recipe
0.1 #combine(#1(apple pie)
             #1(pie recipe) )
0.1 #combine(
             #uw8(apple pie)
             #uw8(pie recipe) )
)
```

Note that in `DeepTR-SD`, we mainly focus on reweighting the unigrams, as unigram reweighting plays a much more significant role than bigrams and proximity expressions in improving retrieval accuracies, which is also confirmed by previous studies [22, 1, 2]. The proposed framework can be directly extended to bigrams, proximity expressions and other query concepts that can be represented by a standard inverted list containing positions, however the training data are more sparse for more complex concepts, thus we leave that for future study.

The two query model variations proposed above can be used with language modeling and BM25 retrieval models; in the next section, we present experiments with both types of retrieval model.

5. EXPERIMENTAL METHODOLOGY

This section describes how we evaluated our work experimentally. We conduct experiments on 4 TREC test collections consisting of one Robust track dataset and three Web Track datasets. The document collections differ in size, from a small and traditional TREC Robust Track collection to large Web Track collections of web documents. The dataset sizes and the queries used with each dataset are shown in Table 3. The first three datasets are standard datasets used without change. The ClueWeb09B dataset is the standard ClueWeb09 Category B dataset after spam documents are removed. The Waterloo Fusion spam scores[3] were used, and the filtering threshold was set to 70%.

Table 3: Collections and topics. Spam documents were removed from the ClueWeb09 Category B dataset (Waterloo Fusion spam scores, 70% threshold).

Collection	# Docs	# Words	TREC Topics
ROBUST04	528K	253M	351-450, 601-700
WT10g	1,692K	1,076M	451-550
GOV2	25,205K	24,007M	701-850
ClueWeb09B	29,038K	23,890M	1-200

We use the Indri search engine[4] to index the corpus. The Krovetz stemmer was used on queries and documents. A standard list of English stop words is maintained for query processing. Additionally, for thee web track datasets, anchor texts from in-links is treated as part of the document and hence is indexed. We use descriptions of the TREC topics as queries stopped by a list of standard stop words and several *stop phrases* such as "find information".

We use `DeepTR-BOW` to denote the re-weighted keyword queries and `DeepTR-SD` to denote the re-weighted sequential dependency queries. All of the above query models can be expressed in the Indri query language. When constructing the sequential dependency model queries, we use weights 0.8, 0.1 and 0.1 for terms, bigrams and unordered windows, respectively as they have shown to be effective in prior research and practical applications [10, 11].

For retrieval, we use a language model with Dirichlet smoothing [21] and BM25 to test both types of weighted queries. Although sequential dependency model queries are not typically used with the BM25 retrieval model, they are not incompatible with BM25. It is straightforward to calculate the *tf* and *df* statistics that BM25 needs in order to calculate scores for bigrams (`#1(apple pie)`) and proximity expressions (`#uw8(apple pie)`) [2]. We show the results for these query concepts with BM25 to demonstrate the effectiveness of our method. A minor change is made to Indri to allow for the insertion of term weight estimates to the BM25 retrieval model, as shown in Eqn. (6). Retrieval parameters are all set to Indri default values, which is $\mu = 2500$ for language model and $k_1 = 1.2, b = 0.75$ for BM25.

[3]`http://plg.uwaterloo.ca/~gvcormac/clueweb09spam`
[4]`http://lemurproject.org/indri/`

For DeepTR, we use several sets of distributed word vector representations. The first one is the pre-trained 300-dimensional vectors released by Google, which is trained on a Google News corpus of about 100 billion words.[5] The second set of word vectors was trained on a subset of the ClueWeb09 Category B corpus.[6] Spam documents were removed, as described above; the remaining documents were processed by Boilerpipe[7] to remove the "unimportant" parts of each page. Mikolov's Continuous Bag-of-Words Model software [13, 15] was used to learn the word vectors with 100, 300, 500 dimensions, repectively. We also trained word vectors on the ROBUST04 and WT10g collections with 300 dimensions to enable comparison of corpus-specific word vectors trained from small datasets with corpus-independent word vectors trained on larger web datasets.

We train DeepTR on the set of queries with 5-fold cross validation and report the averaged performance. That is, we divide the queries to 5 folds and on each fold, we train the model using three of them, validates the performance on one fold of them as development set to pick the regularization parameter λ from $\{0, 0.0001, 0.001, 0.01, 0.1, 1, 10, 100\}$ and report the performance on the rest fold as testing data. After the model is trained on each fold, term weights for queries in the testing fold are predicted and retrieval performances for the reweighted queries are reported.

We use the **trec_eval**[8] tool provided by TREC to assess the retrieval results. We focus mainly on the Mean Average Precision (MAP) and Precision at 10 (P@10) metrics. For web collections such as GOV2 and ClueWeb09B, where graded relavence judgments are available, we also report Normalized Discounted Cumulative Gain (NDCG) at 20 and Expected Reciprocal Rank (ERR)[4] at 20 values using the **gdeval.pl**[9] tool provided by TREC. Statistical significance of model differences in terms of retrieval performance is judged by a two-sided paired randomization test with $\alpha < 0.05$ rather than the Wilcoxon signed rank test that was used in prior research [1], which is prone to type I errors and considered not reliable for ad hoc IR [17, 18].

We compare the retrieval performance of DeepTR to three baseline query models. The first is the unstructured bag-of-words query model (BOW). The second is the original sequential dependency model (SD) [10]. The third is the weighted sequential dependence model (WSD) [1], which is the state of the art model for query reweighting. For WSD, we implemented the model with coordinate ascent [11] to directly optimize MAP on the training queries for WSD. However, we got slightly worse results than reported in [1, 2], possibly due to that we didn't have the MSN query log feature used in the original paper. As we use an overlapping set of collections and set of queries, and our BOW and SD baseline results are very close to the ones reported in the WSD paper, we decide to show and compare with the performance numbers of WSD reported in the original paper [1, 2]. We also implemented the method proposed by Zhao et al. [22] to predict term recall, but the experimental results on our datasets were worse than our unweighted bag-of-words query baselines, thus we omit the comparison from this paper.

[5]https://code.google.com/p/word2vec/

[6]http://lemurproject.org/clueweb09/

[7]https://code.google.com/p/boilerpipe/

[8]http://trec.nist.gov/trec_eval/trec_eval_latest.tar.gz

[9]http://trec.nist.gov/data/web/10/gdeval.pl

6. EXPERIMENTAL RESULTS

This section presents the results of experiments that compare the DeepTR method of setting term weights in two retrieval models (language models, BM25) to three baseline methods (unweighted queries, sequential dependency models, weighted sequential dependency models); the effects of word vectors of varying dimensionality; and the effects of word vectors trained from different types of data.

6.1 Retrieval results with Language Model

The first experiment compared query term weights provided by DeepTR in the language model retrieval model to three baseline methods (unweighted queries, sequential dependency models, weighted sequential dependency models). Experimental results are shown in Table 4 for both DeepTR-BOW and DeepTR-SD. In this experiment, we fix the dimension of word vectors to be 300 and compare the performances of the proposed models with different sources of word vectors.

DeepTR-BOW term weights perform better than the unweighted bag-of-words query model (BOW) over all collections, significantly outperforming BOW on ROBUST04 and GOV2 in terms of MAP and on ROBUST 04 in terms of P@10. DeepTR-BOW even achieves higher MAP than the sequential dependency model (SD) on WT10g, however the results are not statistically significant. DeepTR-BOW gains comparable MAPs to WSD in ROBUST04, WT10g and ClueWeb09B. This suggests that DeepTR-BOW which models no bigrams and proximity expressions is able to achieve comparable retrieval performances with the sequential dependency models (both unweighted and weighted).

The DeepTR-SD query model performs better than the standard sequential dependency model over all collections with all sources of word vectors. Particularly, significant differences are observed on ROBUST04, WT10g and GOV2 with all sets of word vectors; DeepTR-SD with word vectors trained on the Google News corpus achieves significantly higher MAPs over BOW and SD on all four collections. The significant gains of DeepTR-SD with respect to SD range from 4.2% to 12.1% in MAP. Similar significant improvements for P@10 are also observed. While we cannot draw statistical significance conclusions as we have no performance on individual query of WSD, on ROBUST04 and WT10g, DeepTR-SD attains better MAPs than WSD. This validates the effectiveness of using distributed representations of words as feature sources to predict term weights in improving both overall retrieval performance and top-rank results over the baseline models.

6.2 Retrieval results with BM25

We also show the retrieval results with BM25 in Table 5 for bothDeepTR-BOW and DeepTR-SD to demonstrate the boost in retrieval performance with different retrieval models. Prior research on weighted sequential dependency models [1] did not publish results for BM25, so we are unable to compare against that baseline in this experiment.

DeepTR-BOW term weights perform better than the unweighted bag-of-words query model (BOW) over all collections, significantly outperforming BOW for MAP over all data sets and all word vector variations except for ClueWeb09B with the Google word vectors; although not statistically significant, DeepTR-BOW also performs better than SD with all word vectors settings on ROBUST04, WT10g and GOV2.

Table 4: Retrieval performance of DeepTR-BOW using language model retrieval. In the first column, the parenthesis indicates the word vector source. Other parentheses show improvements over BOW and SD, respectively. (For WSD, there were no P@10 values reported and no results on ClueWeb09B were reported in [2])

Query Model	ROBUST04		WT10g		GOV2		ClueWeb09B	
	P@10	MAP	P@10	MAP	P@10	MAP	P@10	MAP
BOW	0.4245	0.2512	0.3290	0.1943	0.5054	0.2488	0.2667	0.0702
SD	0.4414	0.2643	0.3400	0.2032	0.5342	0.2688	0.2798	0.0745
WSD (Table 7 in [2])	-	0.2749	-	0.2260	-	0.2946	-	-
DeepTR-BOW (Corpus-specific 300)	0.4430^b	0.2591^b *(+3.2/-1.9)*	0.3280	0.2103 *(+8.2/+3.5)*	0.5208	0.2646^b *(+6.3/-1.6)*	0.2682	0.0718 *(+2.2/-3.6)*
DeepTR-BOW (GOV2 300)	0.4430^b	0.2650^b *(+5.5/+0.3)*	0.3330	0.2111^b *(+8.7/+3.9)*	0.5208	0.2646^b *(+6.3/-1.6)*	0.2667	0.0741 *(+5.6/-0.5)*
DeepTR-BOW (ClueWeb09B 300)	0.4454^b	0.2657^b *(+5.8/+0.5)*	0.3270	0.2129 *(+9.6/+4.8)*	0.5121	0.2685^b *(+7.9/-0.1)*	0.2682	0.0718 *(+2.2/-3.6)*
DeepTR-BOW (Google 300)	0.4450^b	0.2673^b *(+6.4/+1.2)*	0.3380	0.2122^b *(+9.3/+4.5)*	0.5221	0.2630^b *(+5.7/-2.2)*	0.2667	0.0732 *(+4.2/-1.8)*
DeepTR-SD (Corpus-specific 300)	0.4558^b_s	0.2754^b_s *(+9.6/+4.2)*	0.3510	0.2182^b_s *(+12.3/+7.4)*	0.5490^b	0.2831^b_s *(+13.8/+5.3)*	0.2879^b	0.0748 *(+6.5/+0.5)*
DeepTR-SD (GOV2 300)	0.4610^b_s	0.2781^b_s *(+10.7/+5.2)*	0.3700^b_s	0.2223^b_s *(+14.4/+9.4)*	0.5490^b	0.2831^b_s *(+13.8/+5.3)*	0.2854	0.0806^b_s *(+14.8/+8.2)*
DeepTR-SD (ClueWeb09B 300)	0.4659^b_s	0.2810^b_s *(+11.9/+6.3)*	0.3610^b_s	0.2279^b_s *(+17.3/+12.1)*	0.5597^b_s	0.2890^b_s *(+16.2/+7.5)*	0.2879^b	0.0748 *(+6.5/+0.5)*
DeepTR-SD (Google 300)	0.4627^b_s	0.2842^b_s *(+13.1/+7.5)*	0.3560	0.2256^b_s *(+16.1/+11.0)*	0.5497^b	0.2814^b_s *(+13.1/+4.7)*	0.2869	0.0780^b_s *(+11.0/+4.7)*

b : Statistically significant difference with BOW
s : Statistically significant difference with SD

The DeepTR-SD query model performs better than unweighted queries and the standard sequential dependency model, delivering significantly higher MAPs over all collections and all sources of word vectors except for ClueWeb09B with the Google word vectors. The significant gains of DeepTR-SD over SD range from 1.9% to 7.3%. Similar trends over P@10 are also observed. DeepTR-SD with word vectors trained on ClueWeb09B achieves significantly higher P@10 than SD on ROBUST04, WT10g and GOV2.

6.3 Word vector dimensionality

Word vectors of different dimensionality provide different levels of granularity that may or may not be useful for setting term weights; they may also require different amounts of training data. Our third experiment investigates the effects of word vectors containing 100, 300, and 500 dimensions on term weights produced for language models. The ClueWeb09B corpus is used for these experiments due to its size, availability, and strong performance in the experiments above. Experimental results for DeepTR-BOW and DeepTR-SD are shown d together in Table 6.

Word vectors of 100 dimensions work best for unstructured BOW queries on ROBUST04, WT10g and ClueWeb09B, while the best MAP for GOV2 is achieved with word vectors of 300 dimensions. Similar trends are observed for the DeepTR-SD query model. Notably, DeepTR-SD with word vectors of 100 dimensions attains a significant 7.9% MAP improvement over SD on ROBUST04, and a significant 16.8% MAP improvement over SD on WT10g. On GOV2, word vectors of 300 dimensions help DeepTR-SD significantly improve over SD by 7.5%; last on ClueWeb09B, word vectors of 500 dimensions achieve the best result over all three dimensions, by a 4.9% over SD. We also observe similar results on P@10 when varying the dimensionality of word vectors. We also evaluated the effects of word vector dimensionality on term weights for BM25 retrieval and trends are similar to those for language model retrieval; the results are omitted due to space constraints.

Our results suggest that 100 dimensions is sufficient for estimating very effective term weights.

6.4 Corpus effects

We turn back to Tables 4 and 5 to compare retrieval results obtained with corpus-specific word vectors and word vectors trained from larger, more general, and external corpora (GOV2, ClueWeb09B, and Google News).

DeepTR-BOW performed about equally well with all three external corpora; the differences among them were too small and inconsistent to support any conclusion about which is best. However, although no external corpus was best for all datasets, the language model and BM25 retrieval models agreed on which source of word vectors was best for a particular corpus. This agreement suggests that the learned term weights are independent of a particular retrieval model, which was the purpose of training with term weight values.

The corpus-specific word vectors were never best in these experiments, even for GOV2 and ClueWeb09, which are large and provided 'best' performance for other datasets. However, given the wide range of training data sizes – varying from 250 million words to 100 billion words – it is striking how little correlation there is between search accuracy and the amount of training data.

Similar trends are observed for the DeepTR-SD query models.

6.5 Robustness analysis

Figure 2 presents the detailed number of queries improved or hurt by proposed method using word vectors trained from various sources compared to the LM baseline. It's clear that for all methods using the predicted term weights, the numbers of improved queries are significantly larger than that of hurt queries. Moreover, when compared to sequential dependency model (SD), all the methods using the estimated weights help more and hurt fewer queries than sequential dependency model (SD), especially in the [-20%, 0) range as shown in the figure.

Table 5: Retrieval performance of DeepTR-BOW and DeepTR-SD using BM25 retrieval. In the first column, the parenthesis indicates the word vector source. (No WSD results are reported as no BM25 experiments are conducted in [2])

Query Model	ROBUST04		WT10g		GOV2		ClueWeb09B	
	P@10	MAP	P@10	MAP	P@10	MAP	P@10	MAP
BOW	0.4189	0.2460	0.3330	0.1783	0.4926	0.2334	0.2030	0.0566
SD	0.4394	0.2546	0.3350	0.1817	0.5215	0.2409	0.2030	0.0600
DeepTR-BOW (Corpus-specific 300)	0.4341^{b}	0.2566^{b} *(+4.3/+0.8)*	0.3280	0.1903^{b} *(+6.7/+4.7)*	0.5107	0.2430^{b} *(+4.1/+0.9)*	0.2086	0.0593^{b} *(+4.7/-1.2)*
DeepTR-BOW (GOV2 300)	0.4390^{b}	0.2561^{b} *(+4.1/+0.6)*	0.3340	0.1910^{b} *(+7.1/+5.1)*	0.5107	0.2430^{b} *(+4.1/+0.9)*	0.2136^{b}	0.0596^{b} *(+5.3/-0.7)*
DeepTR-BOW (ClueWeb09B 300)	0.4426^{b}	0.2590^{b} *(+5.3/+1.8)*	0.3390	0.1932^{b} *(+8.3/+6.3)*	0.5081	0.2462^{b} *(+5.5/+2.2)*	0.2086	0.0593^{b} *(+4.7/-1.2)*
DeepTR-BOW (Google 300)	0.4382^{b}	0.2600^{b} *(+5.7/+2.1)*	0.3450	0.1922^{b} *(+7.8/+5.7)*	0.5181^{b}	0.2449^{b} *(+4.9/+1.7)*	0.2091	0.0584 *(+3.1/-2.7)*
DeepTR-SD (Corpus-specific 300)	0.4406^{b}	0.2595^{b}_{s} *(+5.5/+1.9)*	0.3470_{s}	0.1944^{b}_{s} *(+9.0/+7.0)*	0.5356^{b}_{s}	0.2478^{b}_{s} *(+6.1/+2.9)*	0.2066	0.0613^{b}_{s} *(+8.2/+2.1)*
DeepTR-SD (GOV2 300)	0.4450^{b}	0.2609^{b}_{s} *(+6.1/+2.5)*	0.3500_{s}	0.1941_{s} *(+8.8/+6.8)*	0.5356^{b}_{s}	0.2478^{b}_{s} *(+6.1/+2.9)*	0.2091	0.0616^{b}_{s} *(+8.8/+2.6)*
DeepTR-SD (ClueWeb09B 300)	0.4486^{b}_{s}	0.2630^{b}_{s} *(+6.9/+3.3)*	0.3510_{s}	0.1951^{b}_{s} *(+9.4/+7.3)*	0.5349^{b}_{s}	0.2502^{b}_{s} *(+7.2/+3.9)*	0.2066	0.0613^{b}_{s} *(+8.2/+2.1)*
DeepTR-SD (Google 300)	0.4458^{b}	0.2627^{b}_{s} *(+6.8/+3.2)*	0.3510_{s}	0.1938_{s} *(+8.7/+6.7)*	0.5322^{b}	0.2461^{b} *(+5.4/+2.2)*	0.2030	0.0604 *(+6.8/+0.7)*

b : Statistically significant difference with BOW
s : Statistically significant difference with SD

Table 6: Retrieval performance of DeepTR-BOW and DeepTR-SD using language model retrieval. In the first column, the parenthesis indicates the word vector source. (For WSD, there were no P@10 values reported and no results on ClueWeb09B were reported in [2])

Query Model	ROBUST04		WT10g		GOV2		ClueWeb09B	
	P@10	MAP	P@10	MAP	P@10	MAP	P@10	MAP
BOW	0.4245	0.2512	0.3290	0.1943	0.5054	0.2488	0.2667	0.0702
SD	0.4414	0.2643	0.3400	0.2032	0.5342	0.2688	0.2798	0.0745
WSD (Table 7 in [2])	-	0.2749	-	0.2260	-	0.2946	-	-
DeepTR-BOW (ClueWeb09B 100)	0.4410^{b}	0.2681^{b} *(+6.7/+1.4)*	0.3440	0.2239^{b} *(+15.3/+10.2)*	0.5228	0.2667^{b} *(+7.2/-0.8)*	0.2727	0.0727 *(+3.6/-2.4)*
DeepTR-BOW (ClueWeb09B 300)	0.4454^{b}	0.2657^{b} *(+5.8/+0.5)*	0.3270	0.2129 *(+9.6/+4.8)*	0.5121	0.2685^{b} *(+7.9/-0.1)*	0.2682	0.0718 *(+2.2/-3.6)*
DeepTR-BOW (ClueWeb09B 500)	0.4398^{b}	0.2679^{b} *(+6.6/+1.4)*	0.3480	0.2179^{b} *(+12.1/+7.2)*	0.5054	0.2655^{b} *(+6.7/-1.2)*	0.2707	0.0726 *(+3.4/-2.5)*
DeepTR-SD (ClueWeb09B 100)	0.4711^{b}_{s}	0.2851^{b}_{s} *(+13.5/+7.9)*	0.3700^{b}_{s}	0.2373^{b}_{s} *(+22.1/+16.8)*	0.5557^{b}_{s}	0.2848^{b}_{s} *(+14.4/+5.9)*	0.2874^{b}	0.0778^{b}_{s} *(+10.8/+4.5)*
DeepTR-SD (ClueWeb09B 300)	0.4659^{b}_{s}	0.2810^{b}_{s} *(+11.9/+6.3)*	0.3610^{b}_{s}	0.2279^{b}_{s} *(+17.3/+12.1)*	0.5597^{b}_{s}	0.2890^{b}_{s} *(+16.2/+7.5)*	0.2879^{b}	0.0748 *(+6.5/+0.5)*
DeepTR-SD (ClueWeb09B 500)	0.4606^{b}_{s}	0.2817^{b}_{s} *(+12.2/+6.6)*	0.3660^{b}_{s}	0.2306^{b}_{s} *(+18.7/+13.5)*	0.5550^{b}	0.2860^{b}_{s} *(+14.9/+6.4)*	0.2894^{b}	0.0781^{b}_{s} *(+11.3/+4.9)*

b : Statistically significant difference with BOW
s : Statistically significant difference with SD

6.6 Query length

We investigate how DeepTR-SD performs on queries with different lengths. We divide the queries into three groups: with no more than 3 terms (Len -3), 4 to 5 terms (Len 4-5) and 6 terms or more (Len 6+). Figure 3 shows the relative gains of SD and DeepTR-SD (using vectors pre-trained from Google News) over BOW. It's clear that DeepTR-SD works significantly better than SD on mid-range and long queries (Len 4-5 and Len 6+) on all collections. It's worth noting that SD performs worse than BOW for long queries on WT10g, while in contrast DeepTR-SD improves BOW by 14%. For short queries (Len -3), DeepTR-SD outperforms SD over 3 out of 4 collections, which also renders DeepTR-SD a better alternative for SD.

6.7 Graded relevance

Our final experiment investigates retrieval quality using the graded relevance judgments that are available for web collections such as GOV2 and ClueWeb09B. Table 7 presents the experimental results using the NDCG@20 and ERR@20 metrics that have been widely used in web search scenarios. Similar to prior experiments, we see that DeepTR-SD produces more accurate rankings than BOW and SD on both GOV2 and ClueWeb09.

7. CONCLUSIONS AND FUTURE WORK

In this paper, we present a novel framework for learning term weights using distributed representations of words from the deep learning literature. We motivate the framework by adopting the word vectors to represent terms and further to represent the query due to the ability to represent things semantically of word vectors. Therefore we propose to construct features for terms directly from the word vectors and model the target term weight as a regression problem.

We conducted experiments with two retrieval models, the language model and BM25, over four text collections of vary-

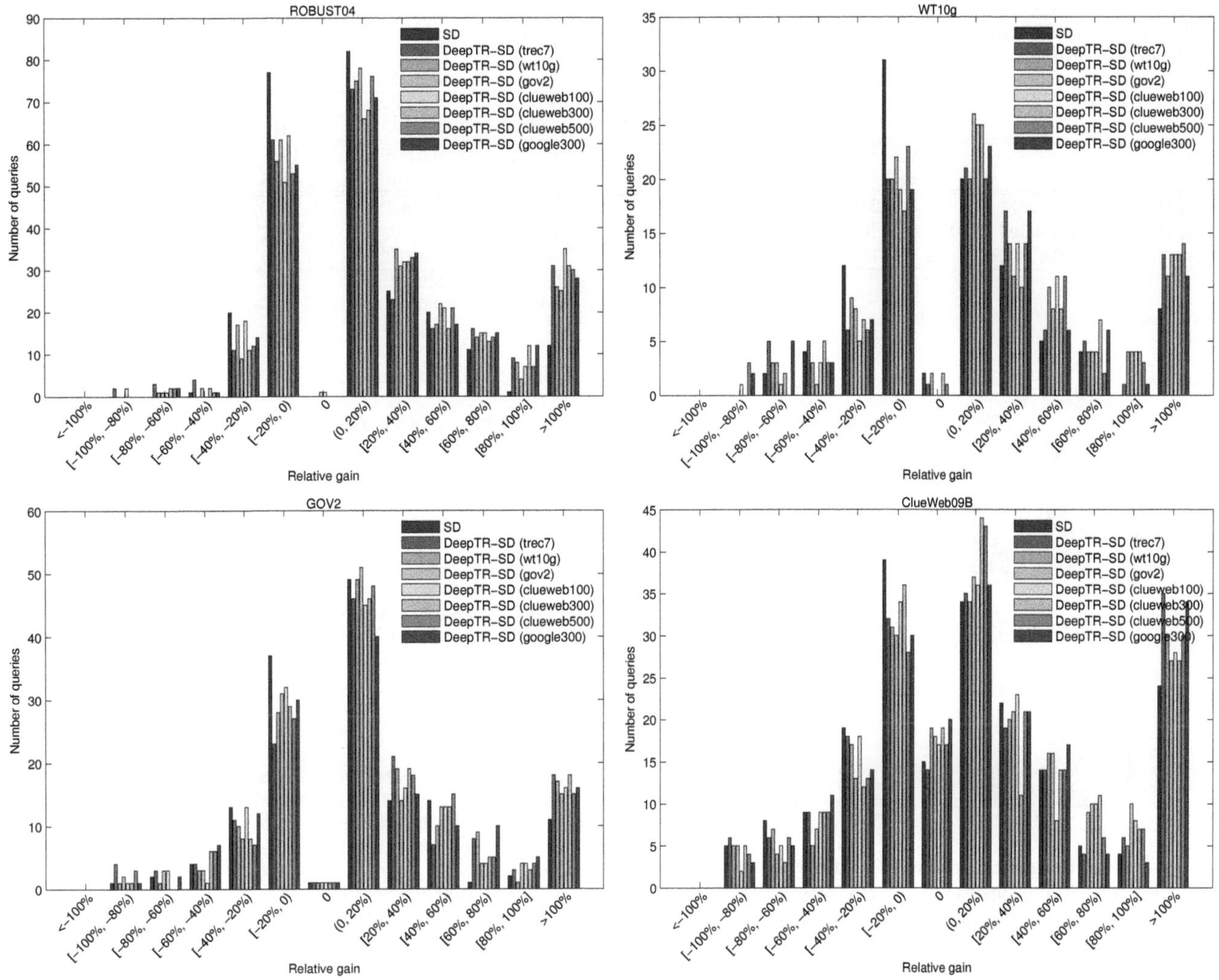

Figure 2: Robustness analysis over all data sets in terms of MAP over LM (best viewed in color)

ing sizes to demonstrate the effectiveness of the proposed framework. Specifically, the proposed framework predicts term weight for query terms that can be used to weight unstructured bag-of-words queries and queries that are a slight variant of the sequential dependency model. We observed significant improvements at high precision and throughout the rankings over the unweighted bag-of-words queries and the original unweighted sequential dependency model queries.

The proposed method is time efficient. Once the word vectors are trained in an offline step (that is itself relatively efficient), online prediction of term weight for new query terms involves only a simple inner product with the learned feature weights.

There are several promising directions for further research. One can extend the method from creating vectors for bigrams and proximity terms by averaging the word vectors of their constituents to a direct modeling of bigrams and proximity terms; although one might expect sparse training data for these query terms to be a problem, our results with small corpora suggest that it may not be necessary to have massive amounts of information for each term. Word vectors may also be useful for identifying terms that should be the focus of query expansion or terms that would be good expansion terms.

Acknowledgements

This work is supported by National Science Foundation under grant IIS-1018317. We thank the anonymous reviewers for their helpful comments.

8. REFERENCES

[1] M. Bendersky, D. Metzler, and W. B. Croft. Learning concept importance using a weighted dependence model. In *Proceedings of the third ACM international conference on Web search and data mining*, pages 31–40. ACM, 2010.

[2] M. Bendersky, D. Metzler, and W. B. Croft. Parameterized concept weighting in verbose queries. In *SIGIR*, pages 605–614, 2011.

[3] Y. Bengio, R. Ducharme, P. Vincent, and C. Janvin. A neural probabilistic language model. *Journal of Machine Learning Research*, 3:1137–1155, 2003.

[4] O. Chapelle, D. Metlzer, Y. Zhang, and P. Grinspan. Expected reciprocal rank for graded relevance. In *CIKM*, pages 621–630, 2009.

Table 7: Retrieval performance of DeepTR-SD using graded relevance judgments. Parenthesis indicates the word vector source.

Query Model	Language Model Retrieval				BM25 Retrieval			
	GOV2		ClueWeb09B		GOV2		ClueWeb09B	
	NDCG@20	ERR@20	NDCG@20	ERR@20	NDCG@20	ERR@20	NDCG@20	ERR@20
BOW	0.3732	0.1493	0.1597	0.1253	0.3789	0.1487	0.1188	0.1075
SD	0.4059	0.1607	0.1694	0.1243	0.3940	0.1554	0.1294	0.1059
DeepTR-SD (GOV2 300)	0.4121^b	0.1626^b	0.1743^b	0.1312_s	0.4008^b_s	0.1590^b_s	0.1307	0.1068
DeepTR-SD (ClueWeb09B 300)	0.4146^b	0.1614^b	0.1663	0.1255	0.4033^b_s	0.1587^b_s	0.1305	0.1067
DeepTR-SD (Google 300)	0.4112^b	0.1600	0.1698	0.1302	0.4010^b_s	0.1586_s	0.1298	0.1050

b : Statistically significant difference with BOW
s : Statistically significant difference with SD

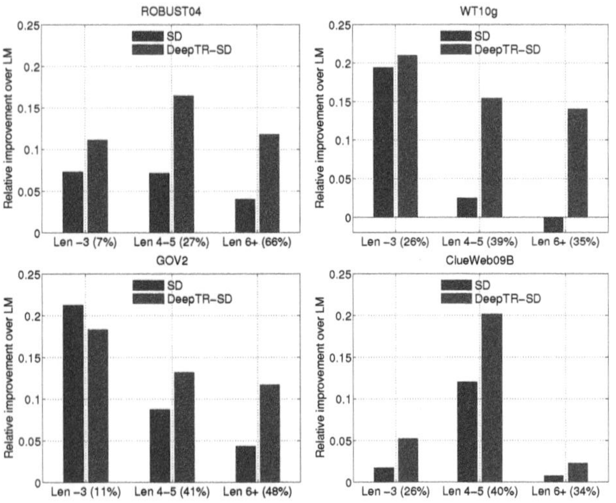

Figure 3: Performance gains of SD and DeepTR-SD over BOW w.r.t to query length. Y-axis shows the relative gain in MAP over BOW and parentheses in X-axis present the percentage of queries in each group. All retrievals are performed using LM. (best viewed in color)

[5] W. B. Croft and D. J. Harper. Using probabilistic models of document retrieval without relevance information. *Journal of Documentation*, 35:285–295, 1979.

[6] W. R. Greiff. A theory of term weighting based on exploratory data analysis. In *Proceedings of the 21st Annual International ACM SIGIR Conference on Research and Development in Information Retrieval*, pages 11–19. ACM Press, 1998.

[7] B. J. Jansen, D. L. Booth, and A. Spink. Determining the user intent of web search engine queries. In *Proceedings of the 16th International Conference on World Wide Web, Banff, Alberta, Canada, May 8-12, 2007*, pages 1149–1150, 2007.

[8] O. Levy and Y. Goldberg. Neural word embedding as implicit matrix factorization. In *Advances in Neural Information Processing Systems 27: Annual Conference on Neural Information Processing Systems 2014, December 8-13 2014, Montreal, Quebec, Canada*, pages 2177–2185, 2014.

[9] D. Metzler and W. B. Croft. Combining the language model and inference network approaches to retrieval. *Inf. Process. Manage.*, 40(5):735–750, 2004.

[10] D. Metzler and W. B. Croft. A markov random field model for term dependencies. In *Proceedings of the 28th annual international ACM SIGIR conference on Research and development in information retrieval*, pages 472–479. ACM, 2005.

[11] D. Metzler and W. B. Croft. Linear feature-based models for information retrieval. *Information Retrieval*, 10(3):257–274, 2007.

[12] D. Metzler, V. Lavrenko, and W. B. Croft. Formal multiple-bernoulli models for language modeling. In *Proceedings of the 27th annual international ACM SIGIR conference on Research and development in information retrieval*, pages 540–541. ACM, 2004.

[13] T. Mikolov, K. Chen, G. Corrado, and J. Dean. Efficient estimation of word representations in vector space. *CoRR*, abs/1301.3781, 2013.

[14] T. Mikolov, J. Kopecký, L. Burget, O. Glembek, and J. Cernocký. Neural network based language models for highly inflective languages. In *ICASSP*, pages 4725–4728, 2009.

[15] T. Mikolov, I. Sutskever, K. Chen, G. S. Corrado, and J. Dean. Distributed representations of words and phrases and their compositionality. In *NIPS*, pages 3111–3119, 2013.

[16] S. E. Robertson and K. S. Jones. Relevance weighting of search terms. *Journal of the American Society for Information science*, 27(3):129–146, 1976.

[17] M. Sanderson and J. Zobel. Information retrieval system evaluation: Effort, sensitivity, and reliability. In *Proceedings of the 28th Annual International ACM SIGIR Conference on Research and Development in Information Retrieval*, SIGIR '05, pages 162–169, New York, NY, USA, 2005. ACM.

[18] M. D. Smucker, J. Allan, and B. Carterette. A comparison of statistical significance tests for information retrieval evaluation. In *Proceedings of the Sixteenth ACM Conference on Conference on Information and Knowledge Management*, CIKM '07, pages 623–632, New York, NY, USA, 2007. ACM.

[19] R. Tibshirani. Regression shrinkage and selection via the lasso. *Journal of the Royal Statistical Society, Series B*, 58:267–288, 1994.

[20] J. Xu and W. B. Croft. Query expansion using local and global document analysis. In *In Proceedings of the 19th Annual International ACM SIGIR Conference on Research and Development in Information Retrieval*, pages 4–11, 1996.

[21] C. Zhai and J. Lafferty. A study of smoothing methods for language models applied to ad hoc information retrieval. In *Proceedings of SIGIR*, pages 334–342. ACM, 2001.

[22] L. Zhao and J. Callan. Term necessity prediction. In *Proceedings of the 19th ACM International Conference on Information and Knowledge Management*, pages 259–268. ACM, 2010.

[23] W. Zheng and H. Fang. Query aspect based term weighting regularization in information retrieval. In *Advances in Information Retrieval, 32nd European Conference on IR Research, ECIR 2010, Milton Keynes, UK, March 28-31, 2010. Proceedings*, pages 344–356, 2010.

A Probabilistic Model for Information Retrieval Based on Maximum Value Distribution

Jiaul H. Paik
University of Maryland, College Park, USA
jia.paik@gmail.com

ABSTRACT

The main goal of a retrieval model is to measure the degree of relevance of a document with respect to the given query. Probabilistic models are widely used to measure the likelihood of relevance of a document by combining within document term frequency and term specificity in a formal way. Recent research shows that tf normalization that factors in multiple aspects of term salience is an effective scheme. However, existing models do not fully utilize these tf normalization components in a principled way. Moreover, most state of the art models ignore the distribution of a term in the part of the collection that contains the term. In this article, we introduce a new probabilistic model of ranking that addresses the above issues. We argue that, since the relevance of a document increases with the frequency of the query term, this assumption can be used to measure the likelihood that the normalized frequency of a term in a particular document will be maximum with respect to its distribution in the elite set. Thus, the weight of a term in a document is proportional to the probability that the normalized frequency of that term is maximum under the hypothesis that the frequencies are generated randomly. To that end, we introduce a ranking function based on maximum value distribution that uses two aspects of tf normalization. The merit of the proposed model is demonstrated on a number of recent large web collections. Results show that the proposed model outperforms the state of the art models by significantly large margin.

Categories and Subject Descriptors

H.3.3 [**Information Systems**]: Information Search and Retrieval: Retrieval Models

General Terms

Algorithm; Experimentation; Performance

SIGIR'15, August 09 - 13, 2015, Santiago, Chile.
 ISBN 978-1-4503-3621-5/15/08 ...$15.00.
DOI: http://dx.doi.org/10.1145/2766462.2767762.

Keywords

Document ranking; Retrieval model; Extreme value theory

1. INTRODUCTION

To measure the weight of a term in a document, most well known functions combine three major components - the term frequency, the inverse document frequency and the document length. The term frequency factor is a key evidence for determining a term's salience in a document, while inverse document frequency is used for attenuating the effect of terms that occur too often in the collection to be meaningful for relevance determination. On the other hand, term frequency is closely related with document length, since long documents tend to use a term repeatedly. Thus, term frequency normalization, in accordance with the document length, is necessary to remove the advantage that the long documents have in retrieval over the short documents.

Given these three major components, the key question is then how these components can be integrated to produce a composite weight for each query term in each document and that is where one model differs from the other. Most well known weighting functions under the vector space model compute the composite weight by taking the product of the tf factor and the *idf* factor, where the tf factor is some combination of tf and the document length. Classical probabilistic models (for example BM25 [24]), adopt somewhat the same strategy. Although, they have the same objective, the two models have very different ways of determining the functional form of the tf factor. The nature of the tf functions under the vector space framework are generally constructed empirically, which are primarily guided by the experimental results, while BM25 formula is derived by approximating the logarithm of odds ratio of two Poisson distributions- one for relevant documents and the other for non-relevant documents. On the other hand, language models (LM) [21] differ from the above models in a fundamental way in the sense that the documents are ranked based on the likelihood that the query has been generated from the document in consideration. In addition, unlike tf.idf models, language models do not use explicit length normalization. The length of the document is an integral part of the probability estimation. Non-parametric probabilistic models are also known to be very effective in information retrieval. One of the widely used non-parametric probabilistic model is divergence from randomness (DFR) [1] based approaches, where the term weight is computed by measuring the divergence between a term distribution produced by a random process and the actual term distribution. One major deficiency with these models is that they consider only the document length normalized tf and ignore within document relative tf distributions. Recent research [20] shows that integration of within document relative tf into scoring model improves performance significantly. However, it is yet not clear how this variable can be added into the existing models formally.

This article describes a probabilistic retrieval model that obviates empirical way of determining a ranking function, unlike existing tf-idf models [29, 20]. The model introduces a tf factor based on the distribution of maximum values of normalized tf. The model achieves a number of important goals. First, it integrates the recent multi-aspect tf normalization schemes into a probabilistic framework. Second, the model automatically factors in the distribution of normalized tf in a term specific way, unlike many standard models. Third, it uses a mixture of two maximum value distribution to better model distributions of terms having varying heaviness of tails. To the best of our knowledge, this work is the first to address the ranking problem using the distribution of maximum values.

The effectiveness of the proposed model is evaluated on a number of recent web test collections containing millions of documents. We compare the performance of the proposed method to the state of the art representative baselines from tf-idf model, classical probabilistic model, language model and divergence from randomness model. Our primary experimental results show that the proposed model almost always outperforms the state of the art baselines by a significantly large margin. We carry out additional set of experiments to compare the performance of the proposed model against a log-logistic (LL) based model that uses multi-aspect tf normalization. Once again, the results suggest that the proposed model is often significantly better than LL model. Moreover, the results demonstrate that our model is more precise than the state of the art models, thereby making it a potential choice for web search.

We organize the article as follows. Section 2 reviews the state of the art. The proposed approach is described in Section 3. The experimental setup is detailed in Section 4. In Section 5, we present the experimental results. Finally, we conclude in Section 6.

2. PRIOR WORK

Modeling term weight is the central issue in an information retrieval system. Three widely used models in IR are the probabilistic models [23], the vector space model [28, 27], and the inference network based model [31]. Furthermore, probabilistic models can be broadly classified into three groups, namely the classical probabilistic model, language model and a non-parametric divergence from randomness model. A large number of instances of these models exist in the literature. In this section we mainly review the state of the art representatives from each of these categories.

2.1 Classical Probabilistic Model

The key part of the probabilistic models is to estimate the probability of relevance of the documents for a query. This is where most probabilistic models differ from one another. Since the introduction of full text search, a large number of weighting formulae have been developed that attempt to measure document relevance probabilistically and BM25 [22] seems to be the most effective weighting function from among them. BM25 model approximates the two Poisson model of relevance. The approximation is done using a increasing asymptotic tf function. Although, structurally, BM25 and tf-idf functions are very similar (in the sense that they both use tf and *idf* factor), they differ in many respects. First, BM25 has a well grounded theory, while most of the tf-idf models have an empirical background. Second, anatomically, IDF factor of BM25 discounts the collection size by the document frequency of the term, which is different from the standard IDF factor. Third, BM25 uses a different query term frequency function, unlike tf-idf models where that function is linear. The length normalization factor uses the average document length and a parameter has been introduced to control the relative length effect.

2.2 Language Model

Probabilistic language modeling approaches [21, 15] follow a different principle in estimating the relevance of a document, unlike classical probabilistic models. Typically, language modeling approaches compute the probability of generating a query from a document, assuming that the query terms are chosen independently. Unlike TF-IDF models, language modeling approaches do not explicitly use document length factor and the *idf* component. It seems that the length of the document is an integral part of this formula and that automatically takes care of the length normalization issue. However, smoothing is crucial and it has very similar effect as the parameter that controls the length normalization factor and term specificity in pivoted normalization or BM25 model. Three major smoothing techniques (Dirichlet, Jelinek-Mercer and Two-stage) are commonly used in this model [32].

Although, query likelihood model is reasonably effective, one major deficiency with using a multinomial distribution as a language model is that all term occurrences are treated independently. The term-independence assumption in information retrieval is often adopted in theory and practice, as it renders the retrieval problem tractable. It is well known that once a term occurs in a document, it is more likely to reappear in the same document. This phenomenon is known as word burstiness [18] and is a type of dependency that is not modelled in the multinomial language model. Cummins et al. [8] present a Smoothed Polya Urn Document language model, which incorporates word burstiness only into the document model. They use the Dirichlet compound multinomial (DCM) to model documents in place of the standard multinomial distribution, whereas the standard multinomial is used to model query generation.

2.3 Divergence from Randomness Model

Amati and Rijsbergen [1] proposed a class of non-parametric probabilistic approaches to term weighting called divergence from randomness (DFR) model. The weight of a term in DFR models is the amount of divergence between a term distribution produced by a random process and the actual term distribution. The anatomy of the weighting function of DFR is defined as follows

$$w(t,d) = -log_2(Prob_1) \cdot (1 - Prob_2). \quad (1)$$

The left factor measures the information content of the term in a document based on its distribution in the entire collection, while the right factor measures the information gain of the term with respect to its occurrence in the elite set (set of documents that contains the term). $Prob_1$ is computed using various well known distributions (such as Bose-Einstein statistics, Poisson distributions etc), while $Prob_2$ is measured using Laplace law of succession or the ratio of two Binomial distributions. Like other models, DFR models use the same basic components. However, the integration of various component are derived theoretically. DFR models use explicit length normalization and following standard practice, average document length is considered as the ideal document length.

2.4 Vector Space Models

In vector space model, the search problem is viewed in a different way. Queries and documents are represented as the vectors of terms. To compute a score between a document and a query, the model measures the similarity between the query and document vector using cosine function. The central part of the vector space model is to determine the weight of the terms that are present in the query and the documents. Salton and Buckley [26] summarize a number of term weighting approaches which use various types of normalization. It is evident that document length is an important component in effective term weighting. Singhal et al. [29] identify a number of weaknesses of cosine and maximum tf normalization and they observe that a weighting formula that retrieves documents with chances similar to their probability of relevance performs better. Following this observation, they propose a pivoted normalization scheme that acts as a correction factor of old normalization and is one of the most effective term weighting schemes in the vector space framework. Typically, the term weighting functions in vector space model are constructed empirically. Several work tried to go beyond purely empirical approaches and use the data instead to learn the patterns that satisfy the data. For example, Greiff [12] uses exploratory data analysis to uncover some important relationship between the document frequency and the relevance of a document.

Most of the earlier work on vector space model normalizes the term frequency in accordance with the length of the documents. Paik [20] argued that the length based normalization alone is not sufficient to capture the different aspects of term salience and that within document distribution of the terms plays an important role. He then proposed a two-aspect normalization scheme. An asymptotic bounded increasing function (much in spirit with BM tf function) is then used to transform the normalized tf values. Two tf components are then combined using query length information. However, the main weakness of the model is its highly empirical nature and that is where the model proposed in this article differs from [20]. The proposed model has a formal probabilistic foundation that directly produces the weighting function.

2.5 Other Models

In inference network, document retrieval is modeled as an inference process [31]. A document instantiates a term with a certain strength and given a query, the credit from multiple terms is accumulated to compute a relevance, which is very much equivalent to the similarity score of vector space model. From an operational angle, the strength of instantiation of a term for a document can be considered as weight of the term in a document. The strength of instantiation of a term can be computed using any reasonable formula.

Some models go beyond the use of bag of words features only and incorporates the proximity/phrases of query terms in the documents [6, 9]. Metzler and Croft [19] develop a general formal framework for modeling term dependencies via Markov Random Fields. The model allows arbitrary text features, such as occurrence of single term, ordered phrases and unordered phrases to be incorporated as the potential evidences of relevance. They explore full independence (bag of words) , full dependence (between every pair of query terms) and sequential dependence (between consecutive query terms) in the language modeling framework. Since, the model has to compute the positional information during query processing time, it is more computationally complex than our model.

Fang et al. [10] give a comprehensive analysis of four retrieval models by defining a set of constraints that needs to be satisfied for effective retrieval. Using these constraints the strengths and weaknesses of some well known models are analyzed and some of the models are modified. There are also a number of recent works that focus on the constraint based analysis of the retrieval models [4, 7].

3. PROPOSED WORK

In this section we describe the proposed ranking model. We first revisit the key variables used in a typical ranking model and describe the roles they play. We then describe how maximum value can be used for ranking. Finally, we turn on to present the maximum value based models and their parameter estimation.

3.1 TF-IDF Model: A Probabilistic View

Within document Term frequency and inverse document frequency (idf) are the two main building blocks of information retrieval models that measure query-document similarity. These two variables play a complementary role in ranking documents in response to a query. The idf factor of a term t ($idf(t)$) measures the information gain of randomly picking a document that will fall in the elite set for t (the set of document that contains t and henceforth we denote it as $E(t)$). On the other hand, tf factor of t for a document d, ($tff(t,d)$) measures the relative weights of documents within $E(t)$. Thus, from an operational perspective, $idf(t)$ balances the weight between different $E(t)$, while $tff(t,d)$ adjusts the relative weights of documents within the same elite set. Term frequency hypothesis suggests that $tff(t,d)$ is an increasing function of normalized term frequency. Intuitively, this means, if the rank of a document d having $ntf(t,d)$ (normalized tf of t in d) is relatively high in $E(t)$, the contribution made by $tff(t,d)$ is also high. Hence, given the distribution of normalized tf of a term in $E(t)$, a natural way to measure $tff(t,d)$ is to take the percentage of documents in $E(t)$ having normalized tf not higher than $ntf(t,d)$. Thus, $tff(t,d)$ can be defined as follows:

$$tff(t,d) \propto P(X \leq ntf(t,d)) \qquad (2)$$

where X is the random variable on normalized tf values in $E(t)$.

Lv and Zhai [17] argued that straightforward non-parametric (plain percentile based) way of estimating this probability does not fully factor in the main objective of tf hypothesis, since it ignores the quantum of differences of normalized tf values. Thus, they advocate the use of parametric probability distribution functions to circumvent this limitation.

They use log-logistic distribution for computing $tff(t,d)$ as follows

$$tff(t,d) = P(X \leq ntf(t,d)|c,\alpha) = F(ntf(t,d)|c,\alpha) = \frac{ntf(t,d)^{\alpha}}{c^{\alpha} + ntf(t,d)^{\alpha}} \quad (3)$$

where $c > 0$ and $\alpha > 0$ are the model parameters which can be estimated from the normalized tf values in $E(t)$. The main issue in this approach is to choose the right distribution function that captures the distribution of normalized values properly. We use maximum value distribution of two aspect normalized tf values in the above framework to measure the $tff(t,d)$. In the next two sections, we describe multi-aspect tf normalization scheme followed by the maximum value based model.

3.2 Term Frequency Normalization

Raw term frequencies are known to be less effective because of its correlation with the document length. Thus, a long document enjoys preference over a short document if the term frequency is used as is. A document becomes longer if it contains many unrelated contents together. Therefore, although the frequency of a term may not increase in this case, the document uses many distinct terms. Since, the chance of a random match of a term between a query and a document is approximately proportional to the number of distinct terms in the document, long documents get an additional advantage over shorter documents. On the other hand, documents also become longer if they repeat the same content, thereby resulting in higher term frequencies without giving any additional useful information.

Therefore, to enhance retrieval accuracy, it is imperative to regularize the term frequency in accordance with the document length. A standard and successful approach for doing this is to compare the length of the concerned document to the length of an ideal document (pivotal document). Both, pivoted tf-idf and BM25 effectively use this strategy where the length of the pivotal document is the average document length of the retrieval collection. Thus, the tf of an average length document remain unchanged, while tf of the documents longer (shorter) than average length document are punished (rewarded).

Recently, Paik [20] argued that the traditional length based normalization alone is not sufficient to capture the different aspects of term importance and proposed two normalization formulae- one is based on within document average term frequency, while the other makes use of the traditional length based approach. These two normalized tfs are then combined. We use the same normalization schemes as described in [20], since it gives state of the art results. For convenience, the normalization factors are called $ritf(t,d)$ (relative intra-document frequency of term t in the document d) and $lrtf(t,d)$ (length normalized frequency of term t in the document d). The following equations formally define the normalization schemes.

$$ritf(t,d) = \frac{log(1 + tf(t,d))}{log(k + mtf(d))} \quad (4)$$

$$lrtf(t,d) = tf(t,d)\, log(1 + \frac{adl}{l(d)}) \quad (5)$$

The terms mtf, adl and $l(d)$ denote the mean term frequency of the document that contains t, the average document length of the collection and the length of the document d, and k (≥ 1) is a smoothing parameter. The proposed model combines these frequency normalizations in a probabilistic framework.

3.3 Limitations of Existing Models

In the last section we have described multi-aspect tf normalization scheme. In this section we discuss the potential limitations of existing methods and the major difficulties in integrating multi-aspect tf normalization into the state of the art probabilistic models.

We start our discussion with the MATF model. We reiterate that, although, *idf* function does not vary much from one model to the other, it is the tf function that often makes the main difference. In [20], the function $\frac{x}{1+x}$ is used to transform the normalized tf values to enforce term coverage. However, the function has a number of notable shortcomings. First, the choice of the function is purely empirical in nature. Second, the function does not have the knowledge of the distribution of tf in the elite set. Third, since the function operates on the tf values having incompatible range (range of $ritf$ is much smaller than that of $lrtf$), one component overpowers the other component, thereby compromising the ultimate effectiveness.

BM25 model is a nice bridge between tf.idf and probabilistic model. Anatomically, BM25 is clearly separable into tf and *idf* component, where the tf function is a special case of log-logistic model and is guided by 2-Poisson model. BM25 normalizes tf in accordance with the document length where average document length is used as an ideal (or pivotal) document. However, it is not clear how to integrate relative intra-document tf into this model, since the notion of pivot for relative intra-document tf is hard to define. Moreover, BM25's tf function is also distribution independent.

Unlike the previous two models, divergence from randomness model (DFR) takes a more principled approach in terms of factoring in the term distribution. Once again, it is yet unknown how relative intra document tf ($ritf(t)$) can be added to this model that will be theoretically consistent with DFR's basic principle. Moreover, normalized tf values are continuous valued random variable and thus, an attempt to integrate it into DRF will give rise to theoretical anomaly, since DFR uses discrete distributions to measure information gain.

Language model is very different from all the models discussed above primarily because it neither uses *idf* explicitly nor it uses length normalization. Thus we confine our discussion on the models that have explicit tf and *idf* factors. In the next section we describe the maximum value based model and how it can be used to circumvent some of the problems outlined above, followed by the development of a model that uses two aspect tf normalization in a probabilistic framework.

3.4 Maximum Value Model

Unlike existing ranking models, we attempt to measure $tff(t,d)$ based on the nature of some of the largest values of normalized tf for that term. A natural consequence of using maximum value based ranking is that it makes the weight of a term in a document dependent upon the distribution of normalized tfs in $E(t)$.

To that direction, the simplest possible approach could be to take the maximum value of normalized tf for a term t

and then measure $tff(t,d)$ relative to the maximum value. Clearly, this scoring is perfectly consistent with tf hypothesis, where the document having highest normalized tf gets highest weight. We can easily think of two naive approaches to measure $tff(t,d)$ that are based on maximum values. One potentially feasible approach can be percentile based scoring that we have outlined before, while the other simple approach can be to measure $tff(t,d)$ as a ratio of $ntf(t,d)$ (or some increasing function of ratio) and the maximum normalized tf for that term in the collection. To understand the limitations of these two approaches, let us consider the following examples.

Let $x_1, x_2, \ldots, x_{n-1}, x_n$ be the normalized tf values for a term t in ascending order. As our first case, let us assume that $(x_n - x_{n-1}) \approx 0$. The percentile based method may give higher weight for x_n compared to x_{n-1} even if they are nearly the same. This happens because percentile based method does not factor in the magnitude of difference, which consequently violates the tf hypothesis. As a second case, if it happens that $x_n \gg x_{n-1}$, scoring based on ratio gives too much priority on the maximum value alone, which results in sharp discount of scores of other documents. As a consequence, a document even if genuinely relevant, is undesirably punished.

These problems are addressed using a sampling based technique which exclusively focuses on maximum values of samples. Rather than relying on a single value, we attempt to measure the distribution of values at the right tail where some of the largest values fall. Hence, our main goal is to model the nature of the right tail of $ntf(t,d)$. We hypothesize that the most potentially relevant documents for a term fall on that part of the distribution. Quite clearly, this hypothesis is consistent with the standard tf hypothesis. Thus, the main challenge is to model the nature of the right most tail as accurately as possible. In other words, this model measures the likelihood that $ntf(t,d)$ will fall on the right most tail. Thus, if the probability is higher, likelihood of d being relevant will also be higher.

We now focus on the models for maximum values. We reiterate that in order to avoid the influence of a single quantity (maximum value), the following sampling based approach is taken to derive maximum value distributions. Let us assume that N samples, each of size n are drawn from the same population. From each sample we can get the largest value. Thus in nN observations we have N largest values corresponding to each random sample. The distribution of the largest values in nN observations will tend to follow the same asymptotic expression as the distribution of the largest value in samples of size n. Consequently, the asymptote must be such that the largest value of a sample of size n taken from it must have the same asymptotic distribution. Formally, the maximum value distribution is defined as follows. Let $X_1, X_2, \ldots, X_n$ be independent and identically distributed random variable with distribution F.
Let $M_n = max(X_1, X_2, \ldots X_n)$. Then,

$$\begin{aligned} Pr(M_n \leq x) &= Pr(X_1 \leq x, X_2 \leq x \ldots X_n \leq x) \quad (6) \\ &= F^n(x) \quad (7) \end{aligned}$$

Since a linear transformation does not change the form of the distribution, the probability that the largest value is less than x should be equal to the probability of a linear function

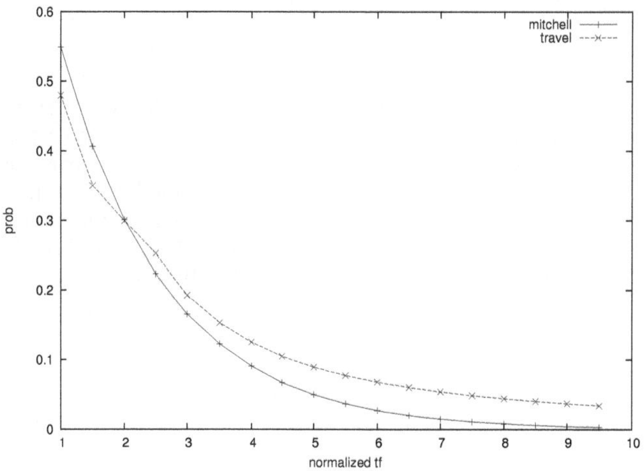

Figure 1: Distributions of random samples of normalized elite set term frequency of *mitchell* and *travel*.

of x. Thus, the above equation is equivalent to

$$Pr(\frac{M_n - b_n}{a_n} \leq x) = F^n(a_n x + b_n). \quad (8)$$

Fisher-Tippett-Gnedenko theorem [11] states that if a pairs of real numbers (a_n, b_n) (a_n and b_n must be functions of n) exist such that $a_n > 0$ and

$$\lim_{n \to \infty} F^n(a_n x + b_n) \to D(x) \quad (9)$$

for a distribution F, then $D(x)$ can be Type I or Type II distribution defined below.

The type I distribution [13] (known as Gumbel distribution) is defined as

$$F_g(x) = \exp(-\exp(-\frac{x-\mu}{\alpha})), \ \mu \in R; \ \alpha > 0. \quad (10)$$

while type II distribution [13] (Frechet distribution) for positive random variable is defined as

$$F_f(x) = \exp(-\left(\frac{\mu}{x}\right)^{\alpha}), \ x \geq 0; \ \mu > 0; \ \alpha > 0. \quad (11)$$

Having defined the maximum value distribution, our next major goal is to verify that the maximum value distributions satisfy the mandatory preconditions in order to be applicable in our task. Specifically, the data must be coming from a distribution F that satisfies **Fisher-Tippett-Gnedenko theorem**. Thus, our primary goal is to fix the underlying distribution function from which the data have been supposedly generated. In order to guess F, we first examine the distributions of normalized frequencies for a few randomly chosen terms. We noticed that the density graphs near the extreme right tail are not monotonically decreasing and it happens primarily because of the presence of random noise or extreme outliers. We empirically (by plotting) identify the points at which the density graphs violate this smoothness for the first time and ignore all the data larger than this particular point. On Clueweb collections, our analysis suggests that normalized tf values between 70-80 seem to be a reasonable cut-off point and thus, in our experiments we set it to 75 empirically (but that value may depend on the nature of the collection). We then plot the distributions of the truncated data. As an example, Figure 1 shows distributions for two selected terms. To better understand the relationship between the pattern of distributions and term's collection level occurrence, we choose two terms (*"mitchell"* and *"travel"*) of varying specificity. Figure 1 clearly shows that both the terms seem to be following long tail distributions with monotonically decreasing density functions. We consider two such long tail distributions – namely, exponential distribution and Pareto distribution. Note that the nature of the tails are different in these two cases.

Case 1.
Suppose the data have been distributed from exponential distribution. Thus, $F(x) = 1 - \exp(-x/\alpha)$, $\alpha > 0$. If we choose $a_n = 1$ and $b_n = \ln n$, Then

$$F^n(a_n x + b_n) = \left(1 - \exp(-\frac{-x - \ln n}{\alpha})\right)^n \quad (12)$$

$$= \lim_{n \to \infty} \left(1 - \frac{\exp(-x/\alpha)}{n}\right)^n \quad (13)$$

$$= \exp(-\exp(-x/\alpha)). \quad (14)$$

Thus, if the data is generated from exponential distribution, for $a_n = 1$ and $b_n = \ln n$, maximum value distribution converges to Gumbel distribution.

Case 2.
Suppose now the data have Pareto tail. Thus, $1 - F(x) = cx^{-\alpha}$ as $x \to \infty$, with $c > 0$ and $\alpha > 0$. Again if we set $a_n = n^{\frac{1}{\alpha}}$ and $b_n = 0$, then for $x > 0$ we have

$$F^n(a_n x) = (1 - c(a_n x)^{-\alpha})^n \quad (15)$$

$$= \lim_{n \to \infty} \left(1 - c\frac{x^{-\alpha}}{n}\right)^n \quad (16)$$

$$= \exp(-(\frac{\mu}{x})^\alpha)\ (\text{setting}\ c = \mu^\alpha) \quad (17)$$

which turned out to be Frechet distribution. Hence, the above results provide us the necessary evidence that the maximum value distributions can be applied on our data.

Mixture Model.
Although, F_g and F_f are the asymptotic approximations to maximum value models, the shapes of their distributions are not identical. Frechet distribution has longer right tail (Pareto tail) than Gumbel. This has some interesting corelation with the distribution of term frequencies in a large collection. If a term is more general (but not really stopwords), the frequency distribution for that term likely to have a longer tail than that of more specific term. Figure 1 illustrates this point clearly: the density curve of "*mitchell*" (which is a rare term) touches the x-axis much before that of "*travel*" (which is a more general term). Thus, an attempt to model the distribution of a term using only one of Gumbel and Frechet may lead to lower accuracy. Any real query contains terms having varying collection frequency and this motivates us to use a weighted mixture of the two distributions. Thus, our resulting distribution is defined as

$$G(x) = p \cdot F_g(x) + (1-p) \cdot F_f(x), \quad 0 < p < 1 \quad (18)$$

where p can be considered as prior of $F_g(x)$. A straightforward way to estimate p is to use a standard method such as gradient ascent method that directly optimizes a target retrieval metric (such as NDCG@20). Indeed, we adopt such an approach, but not directly on p. As we have discussed earlier, F_g (Gumbel) distribution seems better in modeling the distribution of a term having relatively smaller *df* values (more specific). Thus, instead of optimizing the value of p independently, we make the value of p dependent on *df*. Specifically, if a term has low *df* (high *idf*) we give higher weight to $F_g(x)$. In other words, p should be higher for high *idf* terms. We formalize this intuition using the following well known linear model

$$\frac{p}{1-p} = \beta \cdot idf \quad (19)$$

which gives the following solution for p

$$p = \frac{\beta \cdot idf}{1 + \beta \cdot idf}. \quad (20)$$

where β (> 0) is a free parameter.

3.5 Scoring Function

We are now ready to define our final scoring function. Our scoring function uses two aspect tf normalization in maximum value distribution framework. Formally, if X and Y be the random variables corresponding to $ritf(t)$ and $lrtf(t)$ in $E(t)$ respectively, then $tff(t,d)$ is defined as

$$tff(t,d) = \alpha \cdot P(X \le ritf(t,d)) + (1-\alpha) \cdot P(Y \le lrtf(t,d))$$
$$= \alpha \cdot G(ritf(t,d)) + (1-\alpha) \cdot G(lrtf(t,d)) \quad (21)$$

where $0 < \alpha < 1$, is the interpolation parameter. Consequently, the final scoring function for a query $Q = q_1 q_2 \ldots q_n$ and a document d is defined as

$$S(Q,d) = \sum_{q \in Q} tff(t,q) \cdot idf(q) \quad (22)$$

where $idf(t) = \log(N/df(t))$. The parameter $\alpha \in (0,1)$ in Equation 21 is set empirically.

3.6 Model Parameter Estimation

In this section we detail our method for estimating the parameters of the two maximum value distribution models described in the last section. These parameters play important role in determining the actual shape of the distributions which in turn make them term dependent. There are many methods for parameter estimation including maximum likelihood estimation (MLE), which perhaps is an obvious choice. However, in our case, MLE does not seem to be a good choice for the reason we detail next.

We explain the difficulty with Gumbel distribution only (similar argument holds for Frechet). The log-likelihood function of Gumbel based on random sample $x_1, x_2, \ldots, x_n$ is given by

$$L(\alpha,\mu) = -\sum_{i=1}^{n} \frac{x_i - \mu}{\alpha} - n \ln \alpha - \sum_{i=1}^{n} exp(-\frac{x_i - \mu}{\alpha}). \quad (23)$$

The system of differential equations (used for MLE)

$$\frac{\partial L}{\partial \mu} = \frac{\partial L}{\partial \alpha} = 0 \quad (24)$$

yields the following estimates for μ and α

$$\mu = \alpha(\ln n - ln \sum_{i=1}^{n} exp(-\frac{x_i}{\alpha})) \quad (25)$$

and

$$\bar{x} = \alpha + \frac{\sum_{i=1}^{n} x_i exp(-\frac{x_i}{\alpha})}{\sum_{i=1}^{n} exp(-\frac{x_i}{\alpha})}. \quad (26)$$

Clearly, Equation 26 shows that α does not have closed form expression. Thus, we need to apply iterative numerical methods to find value of α. Iterative methods may take substantial amount of time for very large collection such as Clueweb, since it needs to iterate over the set of maximum values from each random sample for each distinct term in the collection. This is precisely the reason we use point estimates (with a somewhat empirical transformation) of central tendencies for these models.

3.6.1 *Parameter Estimation for Gumbel*

The mean of Gumbel distribution is

$$\mu + 0.57 \cdot \alpha \quad (27)$$

while the standard deviation is

$$\frac{\pi}{\sqrt{6}}\alpha. \quad (28)$$

To estimate the values of α and μ we equate them with corresponding sample mean and standard deviation, which finally gives the following estimates.

$$\alpha = \frac{\sqrt{6}}{\pi}s \quad \text{and} \quad \mu = \bar{x} - 0.58 \cdot \frac{\sqrt{6}}{\pi}s \quad (29)$$

where $\bar{x}$ and s are sample mean and standard deviation respectively. Since our data is positive random variable and originates from exponential distribution we use Equation 14 for final ranking. Thus, we do not need to worry about the parameter μ. Our only concern is the parameter α. Surprisingly, point estimate of α as is does not perform well in practice. Thus, in practice, we use a linear transformation, $\alpha = z_1 + z_2 \cdot s$, where z_1 and z_2 are set empirically to 2.5 and 0.04 respectively.

3.6.2 *Parameter Estimation for Frechet*

Mean and variance for Frechet are defined respectively as

$$\mu\Gamma(1 - 1/\alpha), \quad \alpha > 1 \quad (30)$$

and

$$\mu^2(\Gamma(1 - 2/\alpha) - \Gamma^2(1 - 1/\alpha)), \quad \alpha > 2. \quad (31)$$

Once again, the above two expressions are not very convenient to use since the improper integral $\Gamma(.)$ needs to be evaluated in order to compute the parameter. Fortunately, median and mode of Frechet distribution have much manageable expressions. Median is defined as

$$\mu 0.69^{-1/\alpha} \quad (32)$$

and mode is defined as

$$\mu(1 + \frac{1}{\alpha})^{-1/\alpha}. \quad (33)$$

As in Gumbel, we can equate these two expressions to sample median and mode to estimate the model parameters. However, unlike Gumbel, the parameters do not have closed form solution, which can be achieved by using any standard numerical method. Note that, in this case we do not need to iterate over the sample of maximum values, instead mode and median computed once for a term is enough. It is also important to note that although median for a sample is easy to determine, we need to do a little processing to compute mode from a set of real numbers. To compute mode of a sample, we create non-overlapping bins of numbers having 0.5 as the interval. We then take the median of the bin having highest frequency as our sample mode. We have adopted computationally efficient parameter estimation methods. However, a large number of other methods exist in the literature. Thus, it may be interesting to see whether other estimation strategies can improve the retrieval results without sacrificing efficiency too much.

4. EXPERIMENT SETUP

In this section, we describe the experiment setup used to evaluate the proposed model. Our experiments have the following two major objectives.

1. To compare the performance of the model against the state of the art probabilistic models (Section 5.1).

2. To compare against a recently proposed multi-aspect tf-idf weighting scheme [20] (Section 5.2).

Table 1: Summary of the test collections and topics used in our experiments. 'M' stands for million.

Collection	# doc	topics	# topics
Clueweb.B-09 & 10	50M	1-100	100
Clueweb.B-11 & 12	50M	101-200	100
MQ-2009	50M	20001-30000	684
Clueweb.A-09 & 10	500M	1-100	100
Clueweb.A-11 & 12	500M	101-200	100

We summarize the test collections used in our experiments in Table 4. The test collections are taken from TREC web tasks of recent years (2009-2012) as well as from million query 2009 (MQ-2009). The collections contain web documents and real web queries sampled from a search engine log. The documents are crawled from web and hence they have variety of content quality. Clueweb.B collection contains nearly 50 million documents, while ClueWeb.A collection contains approximately 500 million web pages. In MQ-2009 collection, although many queries available, not all queries have been judged. Thus, we use 684 queries for which judgments are available. All the collections have graded relevance assessment. It is important to note that, MQ-2009 queries have incomplete relevance assessment. Therefore, our evaluation methodology skips the unjudged documents from the ranked lists in order to compute the values of well known metrics following the recommendation made in [25].

Documents and queries are stemmed via Porter stemmer. Stopwords are removed from documents and queries. Statistically significant performance differences are determined using a paired t-test at 95% confidence level ($p < 0.05$). All our experiments are done using *title* field of the topics.

Table 2: Retrieval effectiveness of the proposed method (MVD) compared to probabilistic models. Statistically significant improvements are indicated using the first letter of the less effective method. The highest value per column is boldfaced. The numbers in parenthesis indicate relative improvement over LM, PL2 and BM25, respectively.

		Clueweb.B-09 & 10	Clueweb.B-11 & 12	MQ-2009	Clueweb.A-09 & 10	Clueweb.A-11 & 12
ERR@20	LM	0.309	0.264	0.367	0.254	0.219
	PL2	0.312	0.263	0.373	0.256	0.219
	BM25	0.306	0.253	0.372	0.248	0.221
	MVD	**0.337**^{lpb}	**0.286**^{lpb}	**0.408**^{lpb}	**0.286**^{lpb}	**0.257**^{lpb}
		(8.9, 7.9, 9.9)	(8.2, 8.8, 12.9)	(11.2, 9.5, 9.8)	(12.7, 11.4, 15.0)	(17.8, 17.5, 16.4)
NDCG@10	LM	0.282	0.228	0.395	0.200	0.194
	PL2	0.285	0.231	0.393	0.205	0.196
	BM25	0.284	0.222	0.391	0.208	0.191
	MVD	**0.332**^{lpb}	**0.268**^{lpb}	**0.422**^{lpb}	**0.261**^{lpb}	**0.231**^{lpb}
		(17.9, 16.5, 16.8)	(17.3, 16.1, 20.4)	(7.0, 7.4, 7.9)	(30.7, 27.0, 25.3)	(19.0, 17.8, 21.3)
NDCG@20	LM	0.275	0.228	0.459	0.193	0.196
	PL2	0.278	0.228	0.458	0.195	0.198
	BM25	0.280	0.225	0.453	0.208	0.186
	MVD	**0.325**^{lpb}	**0.265**^{lpb}	**0.479**^{b}	**0.248**^{lpb}	**0.228**^{lpb}
		(18.4, 17.0, 16.4)	(15.9, 16.2, 17.8)	(4.5, 4.5, 5.8)	(28.7, 27.4, 19.0)	(16.4, 15.2, 22.7)

4.1 Baselines

The performance of the proposed model is compared to a number of state of the art retrieval models from different families. BM25 [24] is chosen as the representative baseline from the classical probabilistic model. From language model, we choose Dirichlet smooth version [32], since it is known to be the most effective among the language models [10]. From divergence from randomness family, we choose PL2 [1] as the baseline, following recent work [10, 14].

Pivoted document length normalization is chosen as a basic TF-IDF baseline. MATF [20] is chosen as another state of the art tf-idf model. Note that, MATF is a highly effective empirical tf-idf model and one of the major objectives of the proposed model is to advance the multi-aspect TF model using a probabilistic foundation. Finally, since our model attempts to capture the distribution of normalized tf, we also compare to multi-aspect TF normalization with a log-logistic distribution which has similar purpose. Thus, our set of baselines contains members from all state of the art families.

4.2 Free parameters and evaluation metrics

All the baseline models (except MATF) and the proposed model contain one or more free parameters. It is important to note that the parameters of these models often influence the performance to a statistically significant degree. Hence, for the sake of reliable and competitive comparison, the parameters are optimized using 5-fold cross validation with the corresponding evaluation measure (ERR@20 [2], NDCG@10 [16] or NDCG@20) as the target metric.

We choose expected reciprocal rank (ERR), NDCG@10, and NDCG@20 as our evaluation measures. ERR has been the primary evaluation metric for recent TREC web tracks [3]. NDCG@k leverages graded relevance and also has a position wise discounting. Thus, it reflects the overall quality of the documents at top k. On the other hand, ERR@k is a precision bias metric that leverages graded relevance assessment. Thus, ERR is more suitable metric for web search.

Clueweb collections contain substantial number of spam documents. Thus, following previous work [5], we have filtered out spam documents from the collections. Specifically, documents assigned by Waterloo's spam classifier [5] with a score below 70 were filtered out from the initial corpus. The score indicates the percentage of all documents in ClueWeb that are presumably "spammier" than the document at hand. The models are then run on the residual corpus to produce final ranked lists.

5. RESULTS

In this section we summarize retrieval performance of the proposed method and the baseline methods. Throughout the result section MVD denotes the proposed model.

5.1 Comparison to Probabilistic Models

Table 2 compares the performance of MVD to that of the three probabilistic models, namely, language model with Dirichlet prior, BM25 and PL2. First, we compare the performances measured by ERR@20. Table 2 shows that, on two Clueweb.B collections, MVD outperforms LM, PL2 and BM25 by a margin of 8% to 12% and all the differences are statistically significant. On MQ-2009 collection, MVD is once again always statistically significant compared to all the baselines with a margin more than 9%. Similarly, on two Clueweb.A datasets, MVD is unequivocally superior to the baselines and quite clearly the performance differences are even larger than that on Clueweb.B and MQ-2009. The baseline methods seem to be performing nearly equally and in none of the cases, the performance differences among the baselines found to be statistically significant.

Our next goal is to analyze the results measured in terms of NDCG@10. Once again, MVD gives consistent performance improvement over LM, BM25 and PL2 on Clueweb.B collections. The performance differences are always statistically significant with more than 15% relative improvements. Results on MQ-2009 collection also show that MVD is significantly more effective than all the baselines, however the relative differences are smaller compared to Clueweb collec-

Table 3: Retrieval effectiveness of the proposed method (MVD) compared to tf-idf models. Statistically significant improvements are indicated using the first letter of the less effective method. The highest value per column is boldfaced. The numbers in parenthesis indicate relative improvement over PIVOT, MATF and LL, respectively.

		Clueweb.B-09 & 10	Clueweb.B-11 & 12	MQ-2009	Clueweb.A-09 & 10	Clueweb.A-11 & 12
ERR@20	PIVOT	0.263	0.234	0.367	0.169	0.196
	MATF	0.283	0.282	0.388	0.227	0.251
	LL	0.290	0.275	0.391	0.244	0.240
	MVD	$\mathbf{0.337}^{pml}$	$\mathbf{0.286}^{pl}$	$\mathbf{0.408}^{pml}$	$\mathbf{0.286}^{pml}$	$\mathbf{0.257}^{pl}$
		(27.9, 18.8, 16.0)	(22.0, 1.5, 3.9)	(11.2, 5.1, 4.4)	(69.6, 26.1, 16.9)	(31.2, 2.7, 7.1)
NDCG@10	PIVOT	0.219	0.196	0.381	0.177	0.175
	MATF	0.276	0.240	0.402	0.197	0.213
	LL	0.287	0.234	0.418	0.207	0.206
	MVD	$\mathbf{0.332}^{pml}$	$\mathbf{0.268}^{pml}$	$\mathbf{0.422}^{pm}$	$\mathbf{0.261}^{pml}$	$\mathbf{0.231}^{pml}$
		(51.6, 20.5, 15.8)	(36.6, 11.4, 14.5)	(10.8, 5.0, 1.0)	(47.5, 32.3, 25.8)	(32.5, 8.7, 12.5)
NDCG@20	PIVOT	0.212	0.200	0.442	0.181	0.171
	MATF	0.286	0.243	0.466	0.202	0.209
	LL	0.284	0.235	0.477	0.201	0.198
	MVD	$\mathbf{0.325}^{pml}$	$\mathbf{0.265}^{pml}$	$\mathbf{0.479}^{pm}$	$\mathbf{0.248}^{pml}$	$\mathbf{0.228}^{pml}$
		(53.5, 13.5, 14.4)	(32.0, 9.0, 12.7)	(8.3, 2.8, 0.4)	(37.2, 22.7, 23.0)	(33.2, 9.4, 15.0)

tions. One reason for smaller difference is that the baseline NDCG@10 numbers are very high, which makes the relative improvements smaller. The effectiveness of MVD on Clueweb.A collections is even more encouraging. MVD surpasses the baselines on Clueweb.A-09 & 10 collection by more than 20% margin which is clearly highly significant. We observe similar trend on the other Clueweb.A collection. As in ERR@20, the baselines seem to be performing with equal effectiveness.

We notice very similar (as in ERR@20 and NDCG@20) behavior of MVD on Clueweb.B collections measured by NDCG@20. Once again, MVD is consistently and significantly better than all the baselines with noticeably large margin of relative improvement. The picture is slightly different on MQ-2009 collection. Although, MVD is better than all the baselines, difference against BM25 only found to be significant. We suspect that sparser relevance judgements of MQ-2009 collection is a possible reason behind smaller differences. Finally, MVD beats the baselines by a convincingly large margin thereby maintaining its consistency as in the previous cases.

Overall, the results indicate that the proposed model based on distribution of maximum values yields consistent and significant retrieval performance improvement over the three state of the art probabilistic baselines from different categories measured by NDCG measures. We conclude that the proposed model is significantly more precise than the baselines on all the collections, thereby making it a very suitable for web search. The experiments also reveal that the performance of the baselines are very similar to each other, irrespective of the collection, which corroborates earlier findings that if parameters of the models are properly optimized, language model, BM25 and divergence from randomness model are closely comparable.

5.2 Comparison to TF-IDF Models

The experiments in this section are designed to compare the proposed method to a number of tf-idf models. By this set of experiments, we intend to achieve the following major goals.

1. How does the proposed model perform compare to a basic tf-idf model that uses only pivoted document length normalization?

2. Since MVD is based on multi-aspect term frequency normalization in a new probabilistic framework, how does it compare against a recent tf-idf model (MATF) that introduced multi-aspect tf normalization? We reiterate that this is the main issue we sought to address using maximum value based model.

3. We mentioned before that MATF combines the two normalized tf using an empirical tf function that transforms normalized tf values. Moreover, it does not factor in the distribution of normalized tf in the elite set for the particular term. Thus, in this section we compare the performance of MVD to a method that uses log-logistic probability distribution of two normalized tfs. The method is denoted as LL in the table. The parameters of this model is estimated using the method detailed in [17].

Table 5.2 compares the performance of tf-idf methods and MVD. First, it is clear from the table that MVD is highly significantly better than PIVOT. This holds for all collection and measured by all three evaluation measures. The performance differences are unequivocally statistically significant. On Clueweb (both A and B) collections, MVD gives upto 50% relative improvement over PIVOT. Second, MATF, which is based on relative intra-document tf normalization and length based normalization (which we call multi-aspect tf normalization), is always poorer than MVD and the differences are almost always statistically significant. More importantly, the margin of improvement by MVD is often noticeably high.

Thus, we conclude that maximum value distribution has large impact on retrieval performance. Finally, we compare the proposed method to log-logistic distribution based method denoted as LL in the table. Note that LL uses distribution of multi-aspect tf normalization for estimating relevance and thus has probabilistic interpretation. Table 5.2 once again shows that MVD often significantly surpasses LL.

6. CONCLUSION

In this paper we introduce a probabilistic information retrieval model. The proposed model is guided by the principle that given the normalized frequency of a term in a document, the score is proportional to the likelihood that the normalized tf is maximum with respect to its distribution in the elite set for the corresponding term. We use a mixture of two maximum value distribution, that factors in varying specificity of query terms. The proposed model, integrates multi-aspect tf normalization scheme proposed recently in a probabilistic framework. Unlike many existing models, the proposed model takes into account the term specific distribution in the elite set. However, the unique contribution is that the model measures the likelihood of relevance focussing on the maximum values of the distribution, which we believe the first such effort to view ranking problem from this perspective. An empirical evaluation on large web collections containing millions of documents and hundreds of real world web queries demonstrates that the model significantly outperforms the state of the art probabilistic models from different families. As a future work, we plan to incorporate term proximity (ordered and un-ordered bigram) information into our model.

Acknowledgments

I thank Doug Oard for useful discussions and suggestions. Without his support and advice this work would not have been possible. This research was supported in part by DARPA contract HR0011-12-C-0015 and NSF award 1065250.

7. REFERENCES

[1] G. Amati and C. J. Van Rijsbergen. Probabilistic models of information retrieval based on measuring the divergence from randomness. *ACM Trans. Inf. Syst.*, 2002.

[2] O. Chapelle, D. Metlzer, Y. Zhang, and P. Grinspan. Expected reciprocal rank for graded relevance. In *ACM CIKM, 2009.*

[3] C. L. A. Clarke, N. Craswell, I. Soboroff, and E. M. Voorhees. Overview of the trec 2011 web track. In *TREC*, 2011.

[4] S. Clinchant and E. Gaussier. Retrieval constraints and word frequency distributions a log-logistic model for ir. *Inf. Retr.*, 2011.

[5] G. V. Cormack, M. D. Smucker, and C. L. Clarke. Efficient and effective spam filtering and re-ranking for large web datasets. *Information retrieval*, 2011.

[6] W. B. Croft, H. R. Turtle, and D. D. Lewis. The use of phrases and structured queries in information retrieval. In *ACM SIGIR, 1991.*

[7] R. Cummins and C. O'Riordan. A constraint to automatically regulate document-length normalisation. In *ACM CIKM, 2012*

[8] R. Cummins, J. H. Paik, and Y. Lv. A polya urn document language model for improved information retrieval. *ACM Trans. Inf. Syst.*, 2015.

[9] J. Fagan. Automatic phrase indexing for document retrieval. In *ACM SIGIR, 1987.*

[10] H. Fang, T. Tao, and C. Zhai. Diagnostic evaluation of information retrieval models. *ACM Trans. Inf. Syst.*, 2011.

[11] R. A. Fisher and L. H. C. Tippett. Limiting forms of the frequency distribution of the largest or smallest member of a sample. In *Mathematical Proceedings of the Cambridge Philosophical Society*, 1928.

[12] W. R. Greiff. A theory of term weighting based on exploratory data analysis. In *ACM SIGIR, 1998.*

[13] E. J. Gumbel. *Statistics of extremes.* Courier Dover Publications, 2012.

[14] B. He and I. Ounis. A study of the dirichlet priors for term frequency normalisation. In *ACM SIGIR, 2005.*

[15] D. Hiemstra, S. Robertson, and H. Zaragoza. Parsimonious language models for information retrieval. In *ACM SIGIR, 2004.*

[16] K. Järvelin and J. Kekäläinen. Cumulated gain-based evaluation of ir techniques. *ACM Trans. Inf. Syst.*, 20(4), Oct. 2002.

[17] Y. Lv and C. Zhai. A log-logistic model-based interpretation of tf normalization of bm25. In *ECIR, 2012*

[18] R. E. Madsen, D. Kauchak, and C. Elkan. Modeling word burstiness using the dirichlet distribution. In *ICML, 2005.*

[19] D. Metzler and W. B. Croft. A markov random field model for term dependencies. In *ACM SIGIR, 2005.*

[20] J. H. Paik. A novel tf-idf weighting scheme for effective ranking. In *ACM SIGIR, 2013.*

[21] J. M. Ponte and W. B. Croft. A language modeling approach to information retrieval. In *ACM SIGIR, 1998.*

[22] S. Robertson and H. Zaragoza. The probabilistic relevance framework: Bm25 and beyond. *Found. Trends Inf. Retr.*, 3(4), Apr. 2009.

[23] S. E. Robertson. Readings in information retrieval. chapter The probability ranking principle in IR. 1997.

[24] S. E. Robertson and S. Walker. Some simple effective approximations to the 2-poisson model for probabilistic weighted retrieval. In *ACM SIGIR, 1994.*

[25] T. Sakai. Alternatives to bpref. In *ACM SIGIR, 2007.*

[26] G. Salton and C. Buckley. Term-weighting approaches in automatic text retrieval. *Inf. Process. Manage.*, 24(5), Aug. 1988.

[27] G. Salton and M. J. McGill. *Introduction to Modern Information Retrieval.* McGraw-Hill, Inc., 1986.

[28] G. Salton, A. Wong, and C. S. Yang. A vector space model for automatic indexing. *Commun. ACM*, 18(11), Nov. 1975.

[29] A. Singhal, C. Buckley, and M. Mitra. Pivoted document length normalization. In *ACM SIGIR, 1996.*

[30] K. Sparck Jones. Document retrieval systems. chapter A statistical interpretation of term specificity and its application in retrieval. 1988.

[31] H. Turtle and W. B. Croft. Evaluation of an inference network-based retrieval model. *ACM Trans. Inf. Syst.*, 9(3), July 1991.

[32] C. Zhai and J. Lafferty. A study of smoothing methods for language models applied to information retrieval. *ACM Trans. Inf. Syst.*, 22(2), Apr. 2004.

Non-Compositional Term Dependence for Information Retrieval

Christina Lioma
Department of Computer Science
University of Copenhagen, Denmark
c.lioma@di.ku.dk

Jakob Grue Simonsen
Department of Computer Science
University of Copenhagen, Denmark
simonsen@di.ku.dk

Birger Larsen
Department of Communication
Aalborg University Copenhagen, Denmark
birger@hum.aau.dk

Niels Dalum Hansen
Department of Computer Science
University of Copenhagen, Denmark
nhansen@di.ku.dk

ABSTRACT

Modelling term dependence in IR aims to identify co-occurring terms that are too heavily dependent on each other to be treated as a bag of words, and to adapt the indexing and ranking accordingly. Dependent terms are predominantly identified using lexical frequency statistics, assuming that (a) if terms co-occur often enough in some corpus, they are semantically dependent; (b) the more often they co-occur, the more semantically dependent they are. This assumption is not always correct: the frequency of co-occurring terms can be separate from the strength of their semantic dependence. E.g. `red tape` might be overall less frequent than `tape measure` in some corpus, but this does not mean that `red+tape` are less dependent than `tape+measure`. This is especially the case for *non-compositional phrases*, i.e. phrases whose meaning cannot be composed from the individual meanings of their terms (such as the phrase `red tape` meaning bureaucracy).

Motivated by this lack of distinction between the frequency and strength of term dependence in IR, we present a principled approach for handling term dependence in queries, using both lexical frequency and semantic evidence. We focus on non-compositional phrases, extending a recent unsupervised model for their detection [21] to IR. Our approach, integrated into ranking using Markov Random Fields [31], yields effectiveness gains over competitive TREC baselines, showing that there is still room for improvement in the very well-studied area of term dependence in IR.

Categories and Subject Descriptors

H.4 [**Information Systems Applications**]: Miscellaneous; H.3.3 [**Information Search and Retrieval**]

SIGIR'15, August 09 - 13, 2015, Santiago, Chile.
 ISBN 978-1-4503-3621-5/15/08 ...$15.00.
DOI: http://dx.doi.org/10.1145/2766462.2767717.

General Terms

Theory, Experimentation

1. INTRODUCTION

Frege's *principle of compositionality* posits that the meaning of an expression is a function of the meanings of its constituent expressions and the ways they combine [59]. Applied to linguistics by Montague, this principle implies that the meaning of some text is not just the collective meaning of its words, but also a function of how these words are arranged. Whereas this holds most of the times, occasionally language is *non-compositional*, i.e. the meaning and arrangement of words alone is not enough to convey the overall semantics. E.g. the phrase `red tape` (meaning bureaucracy) is not a `tape` of type `red`. This linguistic phenomenon is known as *non-compositionality.*

The challenges posed by non-compositionality have spurred Natural Language Processing (NLP) research in automatic non-compositionality detection, e.g. in nouns [1, 47], verb-noun [20] and verb-particle [30] combinations, using techniques such as latent semantic analysis [20], compositional translations to multiple languages [44], sense induction [22] and word space models [23, 42]. An active line of research focuses on distributional and vector-based models of word and phrase meaning leading to vector-space models for compositionality [8, 35, 41]. These advances have not penetrated IR research notably (with the exception of [33], discussed in Section 2), despite long and persistent IR interest in term dependence. A resulting risk is that the strength of term dependence may be consistently miscalculated in IR. We explain this next.

In IR, dependent terms are predominantly identified using lexical frequency statistics: if terms co-occur often enough in some typically large dataset, they are assumed to be dependent, and the strength of their dependence is typically assumed proportional to their frequency of co-occurrence, e.g. see [10, 34]. Simply stated, the more frequently two terms co-occur, the more dependent we assume they are. This assumption is not always correct. In linguistics, the frequency of term co-occurrence can be somewhat separate from the strength of semantic dependence. Even though the former can be indicative to some extent of the latter, their relation is not symmetric. E.g. `red tape` might be overall less frequent than `tape measure` in some corpus, but this does not mean that red+tape are semantically less dependent than tape+measure; quite the contrary. Non-compositionality lies at the heart of this because non-compositional terms are maximally dependent, *regardless* of their frequency of co-occurrence. So, whereas the strength of term dependence within compositional phrases, e.g., tape measure, white horse, can be reasonably approximated by their frequency of co-occurrence in a corpus, this is *not* true for non-compositional phrases, like red tape, dark horse.

Motivated by this lack of distinction in IR between frequency of term co-occurrence and strength of term dependence, we present a principled approach for treating term dependence in queries. This approach extends a recent unsupervised model for detecting non-compositional phrases using lexical frequency and semantic evidence [21]. The main idea consists of (a) substituting a term in a phrase by a synonym (e.g. red tape would become scarlet tape) and (b) measuring the semantic divergence of the replacement phrase from the original phrase. If their meanings diverge, the original phrase is more likely to be non-compositional. If however their meanings do not diverge much (e.g. tax office would become tax bureau), then the original phrase is less likely to be non-compositional. We extend the vector space model proposed for measuring this divergence in [21] with a probabilistic model that measures the Kullback-Leibler divergence between the language models of the original and replacement phrase (Sections 3-4). We apply both approaches to detect strongly dependent query terms, which we then treat in a non-bag of words fashion during ranking (Section 6). Experiments with 350 TREC queries show that our approaches consistently outperform competitive baselines, and are particularly effective for 2-, 3-, and 4-term queries in the web search task.

2. RELATED WORK

Broadly speaking, efforts to model term dependence, also known as *term co-occurrence, adjacency* and *lexical affinities*[1] in IR, typically model phrases found in queries and/or documents, motivated by the intuition to consider as *more* relevant those documents in which terms appear in the same order and patterns as they appear in the query, and as *less* relevant those documents in which terms are separated [51]. These efforts were initiated mainly in the 1980s, and intensified in the 1990s, reporting retrieval benefits. Later, efforts decreased: baseline performance improved, and the cost associated with linguistic processing was not worth the small benefits over the already improved baselines [54].

Generally, term dependence is detected using either statistical or linguistic information. Research began with the early work on statistical term associations [6, 14, 24, 56] and syntax-based approaches [3, 7, 45], continuing with work on probabilistic term dependence models [15, 46, 60, 61, 63], syntactic methods [5, 32, 49, 50] and statistical approaches [10, 25, 26]. From the mid-1990s onwards, research focused on hybrid methods combining syntactic and statistical approaches of phrase processing [9], phrase-based enhancement of the indexed term representations [64], and phrase-based term weighting [37, 39, 57]. More recent research has focused on statistical methods, primarily using language modelling [31, 34, 36, 52, 55] but not exclusively [28, 40], while attention has also been given to term dependence and efficient large-scale indexing [12, 27]. The Markov Random Field (MRF) model of term dependence [31] reported significant improvements in retrieval effectiveness.

Several more recent studies address term dependence, for instance using heuristics [58], formalising the term position in the document [29], or extending the MRF model to concepts [4], all reporting positive findings. This continued interest in term dependence may indicate that it is still an open problem. However, to our knowledge, none of these approaches addresses non-compositionality, except Michelbacher et al. [33], who focus primarily on the automatic detection of the head modifier inside non-compositional phrases and use IR as a task illustrating that the information they detect can be useful. They experiment with a small non-TREC dataset and report statistically significant gains in retrieval precision.

3. NON-COMPOSITIONALITY DETECTION (NCD)

Non-Compositionality Detection (NCD) aims to identify the presence and strength of non-compositional phrases in language. This is typically realised as a measurement, i.e. through some function that outputs a compositionality score for a phrase. Given a scale of such scores, the minimum and maximum reflect the total absence of compositionality (non-compositionality), e.g. red tape, and complete compositionality, e.g. tax office, respectively. Sliding along such a scale corresponds to moving across phrases of various levels of compositionality, practically facilitating the comparison of phrases on the grounds of their term dependence. We reason that such a comparison may be useful to IR, where systems need to process differently queries at different positions of this scale, i.e. keyword-based (= compositional) queries such as London transportation, and queries containing heavily dependent terms (=non-compositional) such as red tape AL register car.

This section presents how we use non-compositionality to model term dependence in IR. Among the various NCD approaches outlined in Section 1, we use the recent approach of [21] because it is unsupervised, resource-efficient, and performs competitively on benchmark tests. We extend this NCD approach, which uses vector spaces, by adding a second estimation of non-compositionality, this time probabilistic. In addition, we formally express the methodological description of [21] as a model of query perturbation, and we model non-compositional term dependence specifically for IR queries, not general phrases like [21], with considerations to data constraints in an IR context.

3.1 Non-compositionality in queries

Given a query, we aim to detect the presence and strength of non-compositionality in it. Kiela and Clark [21] posit that non-compositional phrases can be identified by substituting each of the original words in them, one at a time, by some other relevant/synonymous term, and comparing the meaning of each phrase resulting from the substitution to the meaning of the original phrase. The more they diverge, the less compositional the original phrase is. E.g. replacing car by vehicle in import car gives import vehicle, which is semantically similar to the original, but replacing red by

[1] *Dependence, co-occurrence, adjacency* and *lexical affinities* are not synonyms [16], but in IR they are used interchangeably.

`scarlet` in **`red tape`** gives `scarlet tape`, which is semantically different from the original. Hence, **`red tape`** is less compositional than **`import car`**. The core idea is that such substitutions are likely to have a low impact on the semantics of compositional phrases, but a high impact on the semantics of non-compositional phrases. The resulting *semantic divergence* is then approximately inversely proportional to compositionality.

Conceptually, we see this approach as applying perturbations over some signal in order to study the resulting effects upon the signal. In our case, the signal is the query and the perturbation is the replacement of a query term by another term. We express this perturbation as follows: Let $S_q(I;T)$ be the semantic space S of query q containing the ordered set of terms T, where I is the information conveyed by T. Let $\bar{T}$ denote the ordered set of query terms where one of them has been replaced by another term (e.g., a synonym). I.e., $\bar{T}$ is the perturbation of T. Then, the non-compositionality N_q, and the compositionality C_q of query q, can be expressed as a function of the divergence ψ of the resulting semantic spaces $\psi(S_q(I;T), S_q(I;\bar{T}))$, for all $m = |T|$ divergences resulting from all substitutions:

$$N_q = f\{\psi(S_q(I;T), S_q(I;\bar{T}) : \bar{T} \in \{T_1, \dots, T_m\})\} \quad (1)$$

$$C_q = g(N_q) \quad (2)$$

where f is typically some summation or averaging function over the set of divergences, and g is some decreasing function, e.g. $g(x) \mapsto 1/x$. Thus, non-compositionality increases with semantic divergence, but compositionality *de*creases with semantic divergence.

Unless constrained, such perturbations risk drifting semantically further away than intended, e.g., if two out of all three terms in a query are replaced simultaneously. Kiela & Clarke address this using two constraints, which we also adopt: (a) only one term is replaced at a time, and (b) a term is replaced by its synonym or a closely related term such as a hyper- or hyponym[2]. We identify a further risk of degrading performance by considering too many synonyms: The set of perturbations for query q consisting of terms $t_1 \cdots t_m$, where s_j is a synonym of t_j, is:

$$\{p_1, \dots, p_m\} = \left\{ \begin{array}{c} s_1 t_2 \cdots t_m \\ t_1 s_2 \cdots t_m \\ \vdots \\ t_1 \cdots t_{j-1} s_j t_{j+1} \cdots t_m \\ \vdots \\ t_1 \cdots t_{m-1} s_m \end{array} \right\}$$

where p_m denotes the mth perturbation. As a term may have more than one synonym, of various grades of synonymity, the set of perturbations can grow to include all synonyms of the query terms. A selection process must control the perturbations so that: (a) "best possible" synonyms (as opposed to near-synonyms) are used, and (b) the number of perturbations is minimised, i.e. we perturb the queries no more than necessary for computing their compositionality. We thus use one perturbation per query term and experimentally show (in Section 6) that this suffices for IR. Other tasks, including NCD *per se*, may require more perturbations per term.

[2]We henceforth refer to all forms of closely related terms as synonyms.

3.2 Semantic divergence

Computing the divergence in Equation 1 requires that both the query and perturbations be represented in some semantic space that is tractable and amenable to measurement. Kiela & Clarke propose vector spaces (Section 3.2.1). We propose probability spaces as a complementary representation (Section 3.2.2). We present and experiment with both.

3.2.1 Vector Space

We re-express the vector space representation of Kiela & Clarke for queries and their perturbations as follows. Let $\vec{v}(q)$ and $\vec{v}(p_j)$ be the vector of query q and its perturbation p_j respectively. The semantic divergence ψ between the query and its perturbation can be modelled as the distance d between their vectors ($\psi \approx d$), where d is some appropriate distance function. This d can be chosen as any vector distance function, e.g. Euclidean, Chebychev, or the better-known Cosine we use here. Then, assuming a summation function f in Equation 1, the non-compositionality of a query containing terms $t_1 \cdots t_m$ of k synonyms is:

$$\frac{1}{mk} \sum_{j=1}^{m} \sum_{i=1}^{k} d(\vec{v}(q), \vec{v}(p_{ij})) \quad (3)$$

where p_{ij} is the perturbation $t_1 \cdots t_{j-1} s_{ij} t_{j+1} \cdots t_m$ and s_{ij} is the ith synonym of term t_j. Using one synonym per term only (as we do) reduces this to:

$$\frac{1}{m} \sum_{j=1}^{m} d(\vec{v}(q), \vec{v}(p_j)) \quad (4)$$

The main idea is to represent a query and its perturbation as vectors, so that we can interpret their distance as semantic divergence. Practically this means mapping ψ from Equation (1) to d above. Dating back to Salton, the IR and NLP literature abounds with variations of how the above vector representation can be implemented and interpreted, any of which can be used here. We describe how we build the vectors and how we compare their distance in Section 4.

3.2.2 Kullback-Leibler Divergence

We now present our probabilistic representation of queries and their perturbations. The high-level difference from the previous representation is that instead of representing a query as a vector of terms, we represent it as a distribution of events, where the events correspond to terms. Such representations are called probabilistic because they allow computing the probability of an event occurring, i.e. the probability of a term occurring in the query. When these probabilities are interpreted in a frequentist way, they are approximated by relative frequencies (i.e. normalised word counts). In text processing, this is known as language modelling.

We reason that, if queries and their perturbations are represented as event distributions, then their divergence can be computed using standard methods, one of the better known being their Kullback-Leibler divergence (KLD). Even though KLD is not a distance metric (it is not symmetric), it is widely used in IR to approximate the semantic distance between texts, where higher KLD values indicate more divergence. We apply this to compute the semantic divergence ψ in Equation 1, by building a language model for the query and each perturbation. Then, their KLD should be proportional to the semantic divergence ψ in Equation (1), i.e.

($\psi \approx KLD$). Let LM_q and LM_p denote the language models of query q and perturbation p respectively. Their KLD is:

$$KLD(LM_q||LM_p) = LM_q \log \frac{LM_q}{LM_p} \quad (5)$$

We next describe how we build LM_q, LM_p and how we operationalise Equation (5).

4. MODEL INDUCTION

Both vector and probability space representations presented above approximate how different a perturbation is from the original query, albeit in different ways. This section describes their exact mechanics.

We start by describing what the above vectors and language models actually consist of. As the approach is the same for both queries and their perturbations, we henceforth refer to their union as Q. For each term $t \in Q$, we build a *context window* as follows: we extract bags of terms occurring within a window of maximum n terms away from t in some large document corpus, so that the window consists of $2n + 1$ terms. E.g., if n=5, then we consider 11 terms in total: 5 (immediately preceeding t) + t + 5 (immediately succeeding t). The underlying assumption is that all the terms in a document have some relationship to all other terms in the document, modulo window size, outside of which the relationship is not taken into consideration. In statistical NLP this is a standard way of inducing word semantics from "the company they keep", a.k.a. distributional semantics [11]. These context windows provide the ingredients of the vector and probabilistic representation of our queries and perturbations, explained next.

4.1 Vector representation

After all context windows of a term $t \in Q$ are extracted, we compute a term weight vector w_t for t with the aim of capturing the salience of term t. Kiela & Clarke show that such weights can function in a discriminative way for the task of NCD. For each query, we generate a term weight vector by combining the term weight vectors of the terms in the query. Next we explain how we compute the weights of the individual query terms and the weight of the whole query or perturbation.

4.1.1 *Individual Term Weights*

Kiela & Clarke experiment with these five well-known weighting schemes, adapted to the context window scenario, (even though they only report results from LTU), which we also use:

ATC [43]:

$$w_{it} = \frac{\left(0.5 + 0.5 \times \frac{f_{it}}{max_f}\right) \log\left(\frac{N}{n(t)}\right)}{\sqrt{\sum_{i=1}^{N}\left(\left(0.5 + 0.5 \times \frac{f_{it}}{max_f}\right) \log\left(\frac{N}{n(t)}\right)\right)^2}} \quad (6)$$

LTU [48]:

$$w_{it} = \frac{(\log(f_{it}) + 1.0) \log \frac{N}{n(t)}}{0.8 + 0.2\frac{M_i}{av.M}} \quad (7)$$

Mutual Information (MI) [38]:

$$w_{it} = \log \frac{\frac{f_{jt}}{N}}{\frac{\sum_{j=1}^{N} f_{jt}}{N} \times \frac{\sum_{k=1}^{M_i} f_{ik}}{N}} \quad (8)$$

Okapi [18]:

$$w_{it} = \left(\frac{f_{it}}{0.5 + 1.5 \times \frac{M_i}{av.M} + f_{it}}\right) \times \log\left(\frac{N - n(t) + 0.5}{f_{it} + 0.5}\right) \quad (9)$$

TFxIDF [53]:

$$w_{it} = \log(f_{it}) \times \log\left(\frac{N}{n(t)}\right) \quad (10)$$

where w_{it} is the weight of term t in context window i; f_{it} is the frequency of t in context window i; N is the total number of context windows; $n(t)$ is the number of context windows containing t; M_i is the number of terms in context window i; $av.M$ is the average number of terms in all context windows; and max_f is the maximum frequency of any term in any context window.

To construct a vector $\vec{v}(t)$ for each $t \in Q$, we extract the context windows for t, which we denote cw_t. For each term, t', represented by an entry in $\vec{v}(t)$, the corresponding weight is computed as the average of $w_{it'}$ for $i \in cw_t$.

4.1.2 *Query/Perturbation Weights*

Having built such a vector for each $t \in Q$, the vector of the entire query or perturbation can be constructed in several ways, for instance as the element-wise sum of the vectors of its terms, or as their dilation, or as their pointwise multiplication. We choose the latter because it has been shown more effective for semantic vector representations in NLP [21, 35]. The final query vector $\vec{q}$ for query q consisting of terms $t_1 \cdots t_m$ is:

$$\vec{v}(q) = \vec{v}(t_1) \odot \cdots \odot \vec{v}(t_m) \quad (11)$$

where $\odot$ is the binary operator on equal-length vectors of real numbers defined by $(x_1, \ldots, x_n) \odot (y_1, \ldots, y_n) = (x_1 \times y_1, \ldots, x_n \times y_n)$. The perturbation vectors are built identically to this. Note that as $\odot$ is associative and commutative, the jth component of $\vec{v}(q)$ is simply the product of all the jth components of the vectors $\vec{v}(t_1), \ldots, \vec{v}(t_m)$.

As Kiela & Clarke point out, using pointwise multiplication has a somewhat 'reverse' effect on the semantic distance: overlapping components (i.e. terms appearing in common contexts) are stressed; since their vectors have little overlap outside the non-compositional meaning, their perturbations also have little overlap, resulting in a smaller change in distance when perturbed. Another effect of pointwise multiplication is that the frequency of terms occurring in the context windows of a query term will be strengthened: if a term t has a high weight in both $\vec{v}(t)$ and $\vec{v}(t')$, it will have a high weight in $\vec{v}(t) \odot \vec{v}(t')$; however, low weight in either one of $\vec{v}(t)$ or $\vec{v}(t')$ will correspond to low weight in $\vec{v}(t) \odot \vec{v}(t')$. This means that the vectors of the terms of non-compositional queries, which will in general occur in very different contexts, will have entries with fairly low absolute values. In contrast, for compositional queries, substituting a term by its synonym may yield constructions that can be expected to occur in a number of contexts wildly different from the original, hence will have markedly different contextual statistics and thus greater distance d.

4.2 Language modelling representation

The alternative representation we propose for queries and perturbations is to use the set of all context windows of the terms in a query or perturbation to build a respective language model LM_q, LM_p (introduced in Equation 5). There exist various ways of building language models from term counts, involving some sort of smoothing of the counts; we use two among the best known, *Laplace* and *Simple Good-Turing*.

Laplace (or add-one) estimates the probability of a term t in the language model of query q, $P_{LP}(q,t)$, as:

$$P_{LP}(q,t) = \frac{c_{q,t}+1}{C_q+V} \quad (12)$$

where $c_{q,t}$ is the count of t in q, C_q is the count of all terms in the context windows of q, and V is the number of terms in the language model of q. We compute it identically for perturbations (replacing $_q$ by $_p$ above).

For sparse data over large vocabularies, Laplace tends to make a very big change to the counts and resulting probabilities because it moves too much probability mass to all unseen events (zero counts). We could move a bit less mass by adding a fractional count rather than 1 (e.g. add "δ-smoothing" [17]), but that would require choosing δ dynamically, risking inappropriate discounting for many counts, and producing overall counts with poor variances [19]. For these reasons, we also apply *Simple Good-Turing* [13] smoothing, which uses (i) the counts of *hapax legomena* (events occurring once) to estimate the counts of unseen events, and (ii) *double counts*, i.e. the frequency of a frequency. Simple Good-Turing estimates the probability of a term t with frequency r in the language model of query q, $P_{GT}(q,t)$, as:

$$P_{GT}(q,t) = \frac{(r+1)\cdot S(ff_{r+1})}{C_q \cdot S(ff_r)} \quad \text{for } r>0 \quad (13)$$

where ff is a vector with frequencies for term frequencies, C_q is as defined as in Equation 12, and S is a function fitted through the observed values of ff to get the *expected* count of these values (see [13] for more). For zero count values the probability is calculated as follows:

$$P_{GT}(q,t) = \frac{ff_1}{C_q} \quad \text{for } r=0 \quad (14)$$

where ff_1 is the frequency of frequency of *hapax legomena*. We normalise the resulting language model to sum to 1. Simple Good-Turing is known to perform well, especially for large numbers of observations drawn from large vocabularies.

The above two smoothing methods produce a language model for *each term* per query or perturbation. To produce one language model for the whole query or perturbation, we sort the language models of their terms and combine them in four different ways: (1) summing their values in quantiles 2 & 3[3]; (2) averaging their values in quantiles 2 & 3; (3) multiplying their values; (4) using the median of their values. Overall, the above 2 smoothing methods × 4 combinations produce 8 language modelling variations of NCD.

[3]We use quantiles 2 & 3 to avoid outliers.

5. DISCUSSION OF OUR NCD APPROACH

Both representations (vector and probability space) of the NCD approach we present are parameterised over the notion of semantic divergence, which we operationalise with different weightings, each corresponding to some variation of computing this divergence. Our use of semantic divergence, measured typically as a real number in the model, corresponds to the observation that compositionality is not dichotomous: phrases in general are not only compositional or non-compositional; rather, a fine-grained range of compositionality exists, a fact corroborated by human raters asked to score degrees of compositionality [2, 30]. Suitable divergence functions that could mimic the scores of human raters may exist, but we have not attempted to do so.

We have also not attempted to estimate the semantic 'accuracy' of the phrases resulting from each perturbation, i.e. the extent to which they are non-sensical, even though Kiela & Clarke state that this is possible with their approach [21]. We estimate solely the divergence between the query and a perturbation, and not how much sense the perturbed phrase makes, for two reasons: (a) we reason that the semantic divergence should in principle suffice for indicating compositionality as we intend to use it in IR; (b) to our knowledge, no scalable automatic approach can adequately approximate such a semantic assessment for query logs.

Another point of departure from Kiela & Clarke is our treatment of query terms as a list, i.e. a set endowed with a strict order. In principle, all computations presented, both by Kiela & Clarke and by us, can be used with ordinary (i.e., unordered) sets of terms too, as has also been done with term dependence models in IR [31]. We use strictly ordered sets because non-compositionality is never manifested in language in any other way, for instance by mixing the order of non-compositional terms, or by interrupting them by another term. E.g., `red tape` can function non-compositonally (and mean bureaucracy) only when the terms `red` and `tape` appear adjacent and in that specific order. Ergo, no variation of `red .+ tape` or `tape .+ red` (in RegEx notation) can have the non-compositional meaning of bureaucracy.

Finally, perturbations are common in science, and the practice of perturbing queries has even been used in IR before, albeit for different reasons. For instance Vinay et al. [62] employ different query (and document) perturbations for query performance prediction: by altering the query term weights, they observe the documents retrieved, and study the relationship between the amount, or *sensitivity of perturbation* and the quality of the ranking. Our approach, apart from having a different overall scope, namely term dependence as opposed to query performance prediction, also differs from [62] in that it applies a linguistically informed selection process for each perturbation: we replace query terms by their synonyms, not by varying their respective term weights within some range.

6. EVALUATION

6.1 Using NCD for selective term dependence

This section presents experiments aiming to quantify the effectiveness of processing query term dependence, not as a bag of words, but as a 'set phrase' of strict ordered adjacency, i.e. matching documents that contain an identical (ordered & uninterrupted) sequence of terms. The main idea is to use NCD to select which among a batch or stream of queries contain dependent terms, and process only those queries as a 'set phrase'; the rest of the queries can be processed as a bag of words. For this initial study, we focus on the non-compositionality of the *whole query*, not of phrases *within* queries.

We use the non-compositionality score of each query (computed with any of the 5 vector space or 8 language modelling variants presented in Section 4) as a proxy of term dependence. This allows to detect queries *more likely to be non-compositional*, hence more likely to contain highly dependent terms, rather than those queries that are *strictly non-compositional*. We do this by ranking queries by their non-compositionality and selecting the θ least compositional. These θ queries are processed with the MRF model of fully dependent query terms; the rest of the queries in the batch are treated as a bag of words.

6.2 Experimental Setup

6.2.1 Baselines & Our Methods

We use three baselines: (1) bag of words for all queries, which allows for no term dependence; (2) the MRF model of sequentially dependent query terms [31], which treats as a 'set phrase' only adjacent query terms; (3) the MRF model of fully dependent query terms [31], which treats as a 'set phrase' the whole query. We compare these baselines against our selective term dependence approach that treats as a 'set phrase' the whole query iff the NCD score of this query indicates that it is likely to be non-compositional; this is controlled by the threshold θ presented above.

All three baselines and our 13 NCD variants use a unigram, query likelihood, Dirichlet-smoothed language model for ranking. Note that we use 'language model' in two different ways in this work, for two entirely different computations: (a) to estimate the semantic divergence between queries and perturbations (in Section 3.2.2), and (b) to rank documents with respect to queries.

6.2.2 Data & Tuning

We use the TREC 6-8 queries (301-450, title only) of the AdHoc track with Disks 4-5 (minus the Congressional Records for TREC7-8), and queries 1-200 of the Web AdHoc tracks of TREC 2009-2012 with ClueWeb09B[4] (see Table 1). We extract the distributional semantics of the NCD model (i.e. build the context windows) from Disks4-5 for queries 301-450, and from ClueWeb09B for queries 1-200. We use no stemming and remove stop words from the queries only (as in [31]). We use Indri 5.8[5] for indexing and retrieval of at most 1000 documents per query. We evaluate retrieval effectiveness using standard measures of early and deep precision (MAP, NDCG@10, P@10).

The Dirichlet ranking model includes a parameter μ that we tune as follows: $\mu \in \{100, 500, 800, 1000, 2000, 3000, 4000, 5000, 8000, 10000\}$. We also vary the number θ of least compositional queries selected each time: $\theta \in 1 \ldots 45$ per TREC batch of 50 queries. All tuning is done per evaluation measure using 3-fold cross validation. We report the average of the three test folds. For NCD we extract the first synonym suggested by WordNet[6] (to be used for perturbing the query). For these initial experiments, we do not vary the value of the window of co-occurrence described in Section 4: we set $n = 5$, i.e. the context window size is 11.

[4]http://lemurproject.org/clueweb09.php/
[5]http://www.lemurproject.org/
[6]http://wordnet.princeton.edu

Table 1: Datasets

	Disks4-5	ClueWeb09B
# Documents	556077	50220423
# Queries	301-450	1-200
TREC track	TREC6-8 AdHoc	Web09-12 AdHoc

Table 2: Query length (without stopwords)

	#1	#2	#3	#4	#5
DISKS4-5	11	56	76	7	-
CWEB09B	57	65	63	13	2

6.3 Findings

Table 3 shows the retrieval precision of our baselines and NCD approaches. Each cell also displays the % of queries that are treated as a 'set phrase'. For the MRF models, 100% means that all queries are treated as a 'set phrase', including single-term queries, for which this treatment makes no difference over a bag of words treatment. Overall, our NCD approaches outperform all baselines at all times. The improvement over the strongest baseline is modest (up to >+3.5% for MAP with ATC, >+3.3% for NDCG@10 with MI, and >+4.5% for P@10 with MI), however it is consistent for both datasets and for all evaluation measures (deep and early precision). This means that the performance gain spans across the range of relevant documents (those retrieved in the top ranks, but also those retrieved further down). Unlike earlier findings that the use of co-occurrence information tends to reduce retrieval effectiveness [46], possibly due to the fact that the term relationships modelled may have little discriminating power [31], we notice an overall modest but clear gain in effectiveness.

Breaking this down to a per-query basis (cf. the two top plots in Fig. 1), the following two findings emerge. (I) The scale of improvement is higher than that of deterioration: between $\sim$+0.13 and -0.07 for MAP; and between +0.68 and -0.4 for NDCG@10, for our Laplace sum approach (chosen illustritatively) from the strongest baseline (MRF with full dependence). (II) More queries improve than deteriorate by our approach. Hence, the improvements in Table 3 are not artificially inflated by outliers that might affect the means of the evaluation measures, but are rather representative of the whole body of queries.

Furthermore, we show examples of queries yielding the highest and lowest precision difference from the strongest baseline in Table 5. The best queries are *not* strictly non-compositional; however they do have strongly contextualised semantics and term co-dependence. E.g. `french lick resort casino` does not denote some other meaning than a particular casino, but it is presumably irrelevant to the semantics of the verb `to lick` and `french` as a language or nationality. Most of the best queries in Table 5 are web queries, which often tend to include abbreviations and acronyms, e.g. `vbart sf`. These are not non-compositional either, but rather idiomatic or colloquial phrases of strong term dependence, and are selected by our NCD approach because they are likely to diverge in meaning if perturbed (i.e. it is not possible to express their meaning alternatively, for instance by near-synonyms). Hence, using NCD to approximate strong term dependence is effective in these

Table 3: Retrieval precision of the 3 baselines (in grey rows) vs. our 13 non-compositionality approaches. Bold marks >highest baseline. The star * marks best overall per measure & collection. %DQ is the % of queries processed as dependent (the rest of the queries in the batch are processed as bags of words).

	METHOD	DISKS4-5		CWEB09B		DISKS4-5		CWEB09B		DISKS4-5		CWEB09B	
		MAP	%DQ	MAP	%DQ	NDCG@10	%DQ	NDCG10	%DQ	P@10	%DQ	P@10	%DQ
	Bag of words	.1905	-	.1151	-	.4276	-	.3502	-	.3907	-	.4167	-
	Sequential Dependence [31]	.1814	100%	.1077	100%	.3983	100%	.3463	100%	.3687	100%	.4120	100%
	Full Dependence [31]	.1933	100%	.1151	100%	.4341	100%	.3514	100%	.4007	100%	.4176	100%
LANG. MODEL	Laplace sum	**.1948**	63%	**.1188**	34%	**.4406**	70%	**.3596**	18%	**.4047**	67%	**.4317**	30%
	Laplace average	**.1948**	63%	**.1186**	34%	**.4406**	70%	**.3596**	18%	**.4047**	67%	**.4307**	36%
	Laplace median	**.1947**	67%	**.1176**	51%	**.4390**	48%	**.3585**	18%	**.4060**	67%	**.4278**	31%
	Laplace multiplication	**.1948**	48%	**.1182**	46%	**.4388**	36%	**.3617**	22%	**.4040**	59%	**.4303**	22%
	GoodTuring sum	**.1940**	81%	**.1168**	50%	**.4402**	57%	**.3618**	31%	**.4040**	79%	**.4288**	28%
	GoodTuring average	**.1940**	81%	**.1167**	50%	**.4402**	57%	**.3618**	29%	**.4040**	79%	**.4288**	26%
	GoodTuring median	**.1949**	73%	**.1168**	56%	**.4422**	51%	**.3583**	15%	**.4067***	51%	**.4283**	32%
	GoodTuring multiplication	**.1943**	71%	**.1171**	29%	**.4390**	59%	**.3623**	28%	**.4053**	72%	**.4302**	22%
VECTOR	ATC	**.1950***	77%	**.1191***	47%	**.4446***	55%	**.3604**	31%	**.4053**	56%	**.4308**	53%
	LTU	**.1948**	75%	**.1184**	40%	**.4444**	51%	**.3592**	29%	**.4053**	52%	**.4278**	33%
	MI	**.1946**	81%	**.1188**	51%	**.4445**	59%	**.3631***	32%	**.4053**	52%	**.4364***	52%
	Okapi	**.1948**	73%	**.1180**	48%	**.4427**	57%	**.3597**	20%	**.4040**	57%	**.4293**	21%
	TFIDF	**.1941**	56%	**.1175**	30%	**.4422**	61%	**.3605**	39%	**.4053**	53%	**.4294**	30%

Table 4: Retrieval precision for 2/3/4-term queries with our three best non-compositionality approaches. (± %): difference from the strongest baseline. Rest of notation as in Table 3.

METHOD	DISKS4-5 2 terms (56 queries) MAP		%DQ	3 terms (76 queries) MAP		%DQ	4 terms (7 queries) MAP		%DQ
Bag of words	.1994		-	.1985		-	.1181		-
Sequential Dependence [31]	.1953		100%	.1722		100%	.1120		100%
Full Dependence [31]	.2022		100%	.1976		100%	.1143		100%
GoodTuring median	**.2115***	(+4.6%)	48%	**.2046***	(+3.1%)	45%	**.1245***	(+5.4%)	29%
ATC	**.2114**	(+4.5%)	48%	**.2046***	(+3.1%)	46%	**.1245***	(+5.4%)	29%
MI	**.2114**	(+4.5%)	48%	**.2046***	(+3.1%)	46%	**.1245***	(+5.4%)	29%

METHOD	DISKS4-5 2 terms (56 queries) NDCG@10		%DQ	3 terms (76 queries) NDCG@10		%DQ	4 terms (7 queries) NDCG@10		%DQ
Bag of words	.4331		-	.4699		-	.3549		-
Sequential Dependence [31]	.4183		100%	.3685		100%	.3394		100%
Full Dependence [31]	.4174		100%	.4421		100%	.3768		100%
GoodTuring median	**.4855***	(+12.1%)	32%	**.4968***	(+5.7%)	33%	**.3902***	(+3.6%)	29%
ATC	**.4855***	(+12.1%)	32%	**.4968***	(+5.7%)	33%	**.3902***	(+3.6%)	29%
MI	**.4855***	(+12.1%)	32%	**.4968***	(+5.7%)	33%	**.3902***	(+3.6%)	29%

METHOD	DISKS4-5 2 terms (56 queries) P@10		%DQ	3 terms (76 queries) P@10		%DQ	4 terms (7 queries) P@10		%DQ
Bag of words	.4018		-	.4286		-	.3000		-
Sequential Dependence [31]	.3909		100%	.3429		100%	.3000		100%
Full Dependence [31]	.3873		100%	.4208		100%	**.3400***		100%
GoodTuring median	**.4545***	(+13.1%)	20%	**.4649***	(+8.5%)	30%	**.3400***	(±0.0%)	29%
ATC	**.4527**	(+12.7%)	20%	**.4649***	(+8.5%)	30%	**.3400***	(±0.0%)	29%
MI	**.4527**	(+12.7%)	20%	**.4649***	(+8.5%)	30%	**.3400***	(±0.0%)	29%

METHOD	CWEB09B 2 terms (65 queries) MAP		%DQ	3 terms (63 queries) MAP		%DQ	4 terms (13 queries) MAP		%DQ
Bag of words	.1290		-	.1391		-	.1046		-
Sequential Dependence [31]	.1126		100%	.1235		100%	.0949		100%
Full Dependence [31]	.1234		100%	.1377		100%	.0982		100%
GoodTuring median	**.1371**	(+6.3%)	43%	**.1480**	(+6.4%)	43%	**.1120**	(+7.1%)	15%
ATC	**.1368**	(+6.0%)	48%	**.1519**	(+9.2%)	46%	**.1128***	(+7.8%)	23%
MI	**.1368**	(+6.0%)	48%	**.1520***	(+9.3%)	46%	**.1128***	(+7.8%)	23%

METHOD	CWEB09B 2 terms (65 queries) NDCG@10		%DQ	3 terms (63 queries) NDCG@10		%DQ	4 terms (13 queries) NDCG@10		%DQ
Bag of words	.4003		-	.2907		-	.3552		-
Sequential Dependence [31]	.3671		100%	.2902		100%	.2409		100%
Full Dependence [31]	.3412		100%	.2958		100%	.3213		100%
GoodTuring median	**.4142**	(+3.5%)	32%	**.3267**	(+10.4%)	33%	**.3873***	(+9.8%)	31%
ATC	**.4143**	(+3.5%)	34%	**.3291***	(+11.3%)	35%	**.3838**	(+8.1%)	31%
MI	**.4142**	(+3.5%)	34%	**.3291***	(+11.3%)	35%	**.3838**	(+8.1%)	31%

METHOD	CWEB09B 2 terms (65 queries) P@10		%DQ	3 terms (63 queries) P@10		%DQ	4 terms (13 queries) P@10		%DQ
Bag of words	.4894		-	.3600		-	.3538		-
Sequential Dependence [31]	.4318		100%	.3550		100%	.2692		100%
Full Dependence [31]	.4167		100%	.3617		100%	.3615		100%
GoodTuring median	**.5152**	(+5.3%)	20%	**.4067**	(+12.4%)	21%	**.4154***	(+14.9%)	38%
ATC	**.5167***	(+5.6%)	25%	**.4100***	(+13.4%)	19%	**.4154***	(+14.9%)	38%
MI	**.5167***	(+5.6%)	25%	**.4100***	(+13.4%)	19%	**.4154***	(+14.9%)	38%

cases. Our worst performing queries consist of phrases for which many more variants that denote the same meaning exist. E.g. `tv show, television programme/broadcast, signs/symptoms/indications heart attack/failure`, etc. Restricting this type of queries to strict 'set phrase' matching limits the retrieval scope significantly with resulting drops in performance.

Next we focus the analysis on two pertinent aspects of our approach: the number of strongly term dependent queries selected and retrieval performance for 2-4 term queries.

6.3.1 *Number of least compositional queries*

The number of queries treated as a 'set phrase' is lower for our approach than for MRF by ~1/3 for Disks4-5 and ~2/3 for ClueWeb09B, or by ~1/4 for Disks4-5 and ~1/3 for ClueWeb09B if we ignore 1-term queries (statistics in Table 2). Compositionality and term dependence in general cannot be measured for single terms, hence 1-term queries are ignored.

Since we treat the number θ of least compositional queries as a tuneable parameter, one may wonder to what extent the gains we report are due to tuning as opposed to the inherent strength of our approach in detecting term dependence. To answer this, Fig. 2 shows the MAP and NDCG@10 of our MI approach across the range of θ values for ClueWeb09B (we can confirm similar trends for P@10 and Disks4-5, and our other NCD approaches). We see that our approach outperforms the strongest baseline (marked by a horizontal line) consistently across the range of θ, peaking when roughly θ =80 least compositional queries (out of 200, or 143 if one excludes 1-term queries) are treated as strongly term dependent. Practically this means that our approach can be used without necessarily tuning θ and is likely not to give large fluctuations in both early and deep precision.

6.3.2 *Queries of 2-4 terms*

Finally, we focus on queries of 2, 3 and 4 terms because these are the most likely to include strong term dependence, hence they are ideal for comparing our approaches to the MRF models.

Table 4 shows the retrieval precision of our baselines and our three best NCD approaches (marked by * in Table 3) specifically for queries of these lengths. Again all our approaches outperform all baselines at all times. The only exception is for 4-term queries in Disks4-5 and P@10, where our methods perform equally to the strongest baseline (no gain, no loss). Overall, our NCD approaches outperform the strongest baseline by up to ~>+5% for MAP, ~>+6% for NDCG@10, and ~>+8% for P@10, on average. The two middle and lower plots in Fig. 1 show that these improvements are not due to outliers, but are instead spread over the queries. Fig. 1 illustrates this for 2- and 3-term queries w.r.t. MAP and NDCG@10, but we confirm that the same trend applies to 4-term queries and P@10. Hence, for queries of length 2-4, i.e. predominantly phrasal queries, our approaches outperform all baselines notably. This finding, combined with the relative robustness of the threshold θ discussed above, mean that our approach could be used as part of the IR pipeline, e.g. for ~80% of the incoming queries of length 2-4. Note that these types of queries form the majority of all queries, at least in our TREC data (see Table 2), hence they are not a negligible sample.

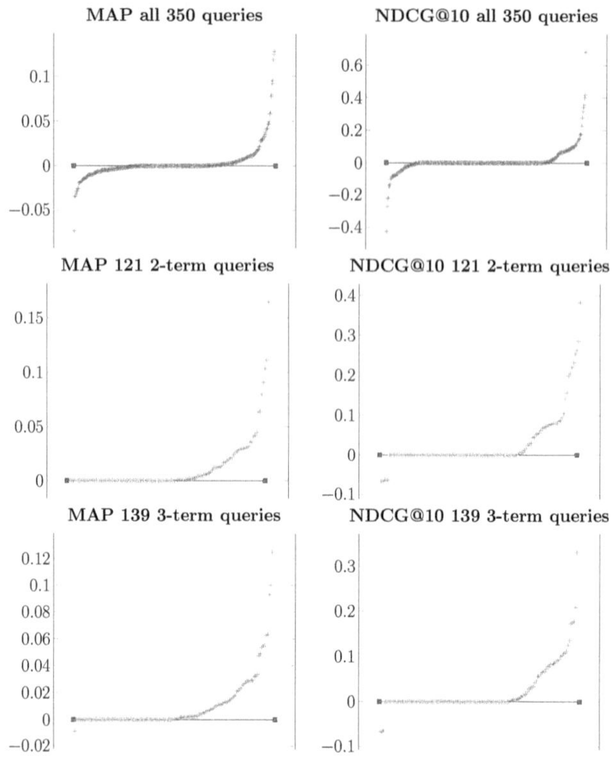

Figure 1: Sorted per-query difference (y-axis) in MAP/NDCG@10 between the strongest baseline (*Full Dependence*) and our *Laplace sum* method, for all, 2-term, & 3-term queries in DISKS4-5 & CWEB09B. The horizontal line marks the baseline (points above are gains). Each point is a query.

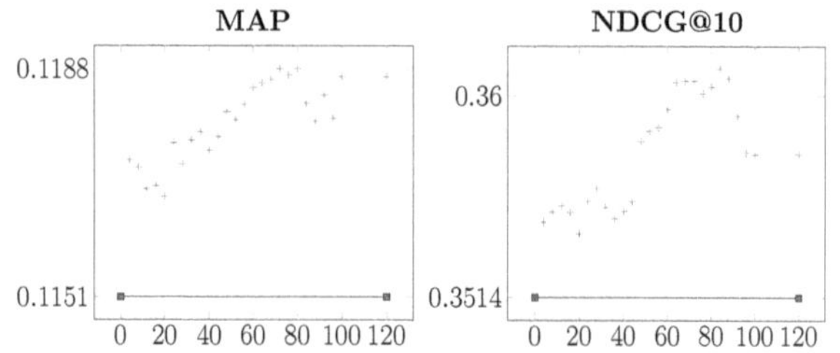

Figure 2: MAP & NDCG@10 (y-axis) vs. θ most non-compositional queries in CWEB09B according to MI (x-axis). The horizontal line marks the baseline. Each point is a query.

Table 5: Queries with most gain/loss from NCD.

Best	Worst
bart sf	*tv show*
ct jobs	*industrial espionage*
french lick resort casino	*export controls cryptography*
civil right movement	*signs heartattack*

7. DISCUSSION

The relative gains in retrieval precision reported above should not be considered as indications of accurate non-compositionality detection. The suitability of our proposed probabilistic representation of queries and their perturbations in particular remains to be evaluated for NCD accuracy. Moreover, several of our choices of NCD settings can be further explored, e.g. synonymy selection or smoothing choices. In this initial study we opted for default or popular settings, where possible. For these reasons, we have refrained from making a quantitative comparison between the vector space and probability space NCD variations, other than reporting the retrieval precision they yield. This means that the NCD variations we present are not necessarily calibrated to this domain or task. Calibrating them could potentially improve performance even more, but would incur some computational cost, the major bulk of which would likely lie in the extraction of context windows from some large dataset. In an IR scenario, this can be done offline, and is perhaps not too distant from the query analytics widely used.

Regarding our data, the query sets we use are 'curated' by TREC, in the sense that those queries that are perhaps not understood by human assessors, or for which no relevant documents are easily found during pooling, may have been omitted. This selection may have affected non- or low-compositionality queries. This agrees with the finding that the number of IR benchmark queries that contain strongly dependent terms in general is small [65]. Unfiltered query logs may contain more such queries, making our approach potentially even more useful in such a practical setting.

8. CONCLUSIONS

We presented an approach for detecting strongly dependent query terms using the linguistic property of non-compositionality. Non-compositional meaning cannot be induced from the meanings of individual words or their arrangement in a query. E.g., `hot dog` is not a type of `dog` that is `hot`, but rather a type of food. We used unsupervised measurement of non-compositionality to approximate the detection of strongly dependent query terms. Such queries are challenging to IR because they cannot be processed to some reasonable accuracy by bag of words approaches. Motivated by this, we focussed not on how these queries can be treated during ranking (there is a lot of literature in this area generally for term dependence, which can be applied here), but on how these queries can be selected from a batch or stream of incoming queries. This specific question has so far been addressed by assuming that the more frequently terms co-occur in a query, the more dependent they are. This assumption is however not always true, because frequency is not always proportional to the strength of semantic association. The unsupervised method for measuring non-compositionality that we used is recent and uses vector spaces [21]. We extended it by adding a probabilistic representation that uses Kullback-Leibler divergence. We experimentally showed that all variants of our approach were effective in selecting which queries to treat as term dependent and resulted in gains for both early and deep precision ($> 5\%$) with respect to a range of baselines (standard bag of words and competitive MRF with sequential and full dependence [31]).

In the future we plan to analyse the amount of non- or low-compositionality queries in real-life query logs, as opposed to TREC data. As discussed in Section 7, there may be more low-compositionality queries in those samples. We also intend to investigate optimal ways of measuring non-compositionality *within* a query, as opposed to considering the non-compositionality of a query as a whole as we did here. Another interesting direction is the direct mapping of the non-compositionality score of a query into the strength of its term dependence used during ranking. In this initial study we treated all queries selected as least-compositional in the same way as fixed phrases processing them identically; in doing so, we ignored their grades of non-compositionality. Modelling this may yield further improvements and is an interesting research question in its own right.

Acknowledgments.

Partially funded by the first author's *FREJA research excellence* fellowship (grant no. 790095).

9. REFERENCES

[1] T. Baldwin, C. Bannard, T. Tanaka, and D. Widdows. An empirical model of multiword expression decomposability. In *ACL Multiword Expressions Wksh.*, pages 89–96. 2003.
[2] C. Bannard, T. Baldwin, and A. Lascarides. A statistical approach to the semantics of verb-particles. In *ACL Multiword Expressions Wksh.*, pages 65–72, 2003.
[3] P. B. Baxendale. Machine-made index for technical literature. *IBM Journal for R&D*, 2:354–361, 1958.
[4] M. Bendersky, D. Metzler, and W. B. Croft. Learning concept importance using a weighted dependence model. In *WSDM*, pages 31–40, 2010.
[5] M. Dillon and A. Gray. FASIT - a fully automatic syntactically based indexing system. *JASIS*, 34:99–108, 1983.
[6] L. B. Doyle. Indexing and abstracting by association. Part I. *Am. Doc.*, 13:378–390, 1962.
[7] L. L. Earl. The resolution of syntactic ambiguity in automatic language processing. *Information Storage and Retrieval*, 8:277–308, 1972.
[8] K. Erk. Vector space models of word meaning and phrase meaning: A survey. *Language and Linguistics Compass*, 6(10):635–653, 2012.
[9] D. A. Evans and C. Zhai. Noun-phrase analysis in unrestricted text for IR. In *ACL*, pages 17–24, 1996.
[10] J. L. Fagan. The effectiveness of a non syntactic approach to automatic phrase inducing for document retrieval. *JASIS*, 40:115–132, 1989.
[11] J. R. Firth. A synopsis of linguistic theory. *Selected papers of J.R. Firth 1952-1959*, pages 168–205, 1968.
[12] S. Fujita. More reflections on aboutness TREC-2001 evaluation experiments at Justsystem. In *TREC*, pages 331 – 338, 2001.
[13] W. Gale and G. Sampson. Good-Turing frequency estimation without tears. *J. of Quant. Ling.*, 2(3):217–237, 1995.
[14] V. E. Giuliano and P. E. Jones. Linear associative IR. *Vistas in Information Handling: The Augmentation of Man's Intellect by Machine*, 1:30–54, 1963.
[15] D. J. Harper and C. J. K. van Rijsbergen. An evaluation of feedback in document retrieval using concurrence data. *J. of Doc.*, 34:189–216, 1978.
[16] F. Heylighen and J. Dewaele. Variation in the contextuality of language. *F. of Sci.*, 7(3):293–340, 2002.
[17] H. Jeffreys. *Theory of Probability.* Clarendon, 1948.
[18] R. Jin, C. Falusos, and A. G. Hauptmann. Meta-scoring: Automatically evaluating term weighting schemes in IR without precision-recall. In *SIGIR*, pages 83–89, 2001.

[19] D. Jurafsky and J. Martin. *Speech and Language Processing*. Pearson, 2009.
[20] G. Katz and E. Giesbrecht. Automatic identification of non-compositional multi-word expressions using LSA. In *ACL Multiword Expressions Wksh.*, pages 12–19. 2006.
[21] D. Kiela and S. Clark. Detecting compositionality of multi-word expressions using nearest neighbours in vector space models. In *EMNLP*, pages 1427–1432, 2013.
[22] I. Korkontzelos and S. Manandhar. Detecting compositionality in multi-word expressions. In *ACL-IJCNLP*, pages 65–68, 2009.
[23] L. Krčmář, K. Ježek, and P. Pecina. Determining compositionality of expresssions using various word space models and methods. In *Continuous Vector Space Models and their Compositionality Wksh.*, pages 64–73, 2013.
[24] M. E. Lesk. Word-word associations in document retrieval systems. *Am. Doc.*, 20:27–38, 1969.
[25] D. D. Lewis. An evaluation of phrasal and clustered representations on a text categorization task. In *SIGIR*, pages 37–50, 1992.
[26] D. D. Lewis and W. B. Croft. Term clustering of syntactic phrases. In *SIGIR*, pages 385–404, 1990.
[27] J. Lin. Indexing & Retrieving Natural Language Using Ternary Expressions. Master's thesis, U. of Maryland, USA, 2001.
[28] R. Losee. Term dependence: Truncating the Bahadur Lazarsfeld expansion. *IPM*, 30(2):293–303, 1994.
[29] Y. Lv and C. Zhai. Positional language models for information retrieval. In *SIGIR*, pages 299–306, 2009.
[30] D. McCarthy, B. Keller, and J. Caroll. Detecting a continuum of compositionality in phrasal verbs. In *ACL Multiword Expressions Wksh.*, pages 73–80. 2003.
[31] D. Metzler and B. Croft. A MRF model for term dependencies. In *SIGIR*, pages 472–479, 2005.
[32] D. P. Metzler, T. Noreault, L. Richey, and P. B. Heidorn. Dependency parsing for information retrieval. In *SIGIR*, pages 313–324, 1984.
[33] L. Michelbacher, A. Kothari, M. Forst, C. Lioma, and H. Schütze. A cascaded classification approach to semantic head recognition. In *EMNLP*, pages 793–803, 2011.
[34] G. Mishne and M. de Rijke. Boosting web retrieval through query operations. In *ECIR*, pages 502–516, 2005.
[35] J. Mitchell and M. Lapata. Composition in distributional models of semantics. *Cognitive Science*, 34(8):1388–1429, 2010.
[36] R. Nallapati and J. Allan. Capturing term dependencies using a language model based on sentence trees. In *CIKM*, pages 383–390, 2002.
[37] M. Narita and Y. Ogawa. The use of phrases from query texts in IR. In *SIGIR*, pages 318–320, 2000.
[38] P. Pantel and D. Lin. Document clustering with committees. In *SIGIR*, pages 199–206. ACM, 2002.
[39] J. Pederson, C. Silverstein, and C. Vogt. Verity at TREC-6: out-of-the-box and beyond. In *TREC-6*, pages 259 – 274, 1997.
[40] V. Plachouras and I. Ounis. Multinomial randomness models for retrieval with document fields. In *ECIR*, pages 28–39, 2007.
[41] S. Reddy, I. Klapaftis, D. McCarthy, and S. Manandhar. Dynamic & static prototype vectors for semantic composition. In *IJCNLP*, pages 705–713, 2011.
[42] S. Reddy, D. McCarthy, S. Manandhar, and S. Gella. Exemplar-based word-space model for compositionality detection: shared task system description. In *DiSCo*, pages 54–60. 2003.
[43] J. W. Reed, Y. Jiao, T. E. Potok, B. A. Klump, M. T. Elmore, and A. R. Hurson. TF-ICF: A new term weighting scheme for clustering dynamic data streams. In *ICMLA*, pages 258–263, 2006.
[44] B. Salehi and P. Cook. Predicting the compositionality of multiword expressions using translations in multiple languages. In *SEM*, pages 266–275. 2013.
[45] G. Salton. Automatic phrase matching. *Readings in Automatic Language Processing*, pages 169–188, 1966.
[46] G. Salton, C. Buckley, and C. T. Yu. An evaluation of term dependence models in information retrieval. In *SIGIR*, pages 151–173, 1982.
[47] S. Schulte im Walde, S. Müller, and S. Roller. Exploring vector space models to predict the compositionality of German noun-noun compounds. In *SEM*, pages 255–265. 2013.
[48] A. Singhal. AT&T at TREC-6. In *TREC-6*, pages 215–225, 1997.
[49] A. Smeaton and K. van Rijsbergen. Experiment on incorporation syntactic processing of user queries into a document retrieval strategy. In *SIGIR*, pages 31–51, 1988.
[50] A. F. Smeaton. Incorporating syntactic information into a document retrieval strategy: An investigation. In *SIGIR*, pages 103–113, 1986.
[51] F. J. Smith and K. Devine. Storing and retrieving word phrases. *IPM*, 21(3):215–224, 1985.
[52] F. Song and W. B. Croft. A general language model for IR. In *CIKM*, pages 316–321, 1999.
[53] K. Spärck-Jones. A statistical interpretation of term specificity and its application in retrieval. *J. of Doc.*, 28(1):132–142, 1972.
[54] K. Spärck-Jones and J. Tait. *Charting a New Course: MLP and IR: Essays in Honour of Karen Spärck Jones*. Springer, 2005.
[55] M. Srikanth and R. K. Srihari. Incorporating query term dependencies in language models for document retrieval. In *SIGIR*, pages 405–406. ACM, 2003.
[56] H. E. Stiles. The association factor in information retrieval. *Journal of the ACM*, 8:271–279, 1961.
[57] T. Strzalkowski and F. Lin. Natural language IR TREC-6 report. In *TREC*, pages 347 - 366, 1997.
[58] T. Tao and C. Zhai. An exploration of proximity measures in ir. *SIGIR*, pages 295–302. ACM, 2007.
[59] R. H. Thomason. *Formal Philosophy. Selected Papers of Richard Montague*. Yale University Press, 1974.
[60] H. Turtle and B. Croft. Evaluation of an inference network-based retrieval model. *TOIS*, 9(3):187–222, 1991.
[61] C. J. K. van Rijsbergen. A theoretical basis for the use of co-occurrence data in information retrieval. *J. Doc.*, 33:106–119, 1977.
[62] V. Vinay, I. J. Cox, N. Milic-Frayling, and K. R. Wood. On ranking the effectiveness of searches. In *SIGIR*, pages 398–404, 2006.
[63] C. T. Yu, C. Buckley, K. Lam, and G. Salton. A generalised term dependence model in IR. *Information Technology: R&D*, 2:129–154, 1983.
[64] C. Zhai, X. Tong, N. Milic-Frayling, and D. A. Evans. Evaluation of syntactic phrase indexing - CLARIT NLP track report. In *TREC-5*, pages 347–358, 1997.
[65] J. Zobel and A. Moffat. Inverted files for text search engines. *ACM Comput. Surv.*, 38(2):6, 2006.

On the Relation Between Assessor's Agreement and Accuracy in Gamified Relevance Assessment

Olga Megorskaya Vladimir Kukushkin Pavel Serdyukov

Yandex
Moscow, Russia
{omegorskaya, wowone, pavser}@yandex-team.ru

ABSTRACT

Expert judgments (labels) are widely used in Information Retrieval for the purposes of search quality evaluation and machine learning. Setting up the process of collecting such judgments is a challenge of its own, and the maintenance of judgments quality is an extremely important part of the process. One of the possible ways of controlling the quality is monitoring inter-assessor agreement level. But does the agreement level really reflect the quality of assessor's judgments? Indeed, if a group of assessors comes to a consensus, to what extent should we trust their collective opinion? In this paper, we investigate, whether the agreement level can be used as a metric for estimating the quality of assessor's judgments, and provide recommendations for the design of judgments collection workflow. Namely, we estimate the correlation between assessors' accuracy and agreement in the scope of several workflow designs and investigate which specific workflow features influence the accuracy of judgments the most.

Keywords

Relevance labels; agreement vs. accuracy; judgments collection workflow.

1. INTRODUCTION

Expert judgments is an important resource used by search engines for the purposes of machine learning and search quality evaluation. Creating an environment for collecting assessors' judgments is a nontrivial task that faces the challenges of managing the quality of judgments and providing scalability and flexibility of the labeling system. However, expert judgments are subjective by their nature, and hence it is not obvious how their quality should be estimated.

One might calculate an assessor's *accuracy*: the share of documents judged by the assessor correctly, i.e. by assigning the correct relevance label. A label might be considered correct if it matches the one from the *golden set* (a set of documents assessed by a reliable and knowledgeable expert). However, creating a high quality golden set is a costly process, because such a set needs to be comprehensive and representative (i.e. proportional to the number of assessors and the assessments they generate) to fairly and realistically evaluate assessors' accuracy. The reason is that, in the case of professional assessors (opposed to crowd workers), we need to constantly monitor if the assessors are keeping the quality of their judgments on a high level, and hence filtering plain cheaters with a small and trivial golden set is usually not enough. Apart for the high costs of maintenance of the golden set, such approach also implies a risk of systematically biasing judgments by accepting opinions of just one or several persons as the ground truth.

Another metric - *agreement level* - is also often used to estimate the quality of judgments. Measuring agreement level is practically convenient and cheap, as it does not require any additional efforts/costs. But does agreement level really correlate with the overall quality of judgments (i.e. with their accuracy)? If it is so, one would be able to create an effective infrastructure for collecting judgments where the quality control is maintained by only monitoring inter-assessor agreement level, which makes the whole system more scalable and agile.

In our study, we propose a new gamified workflow of collecting judgments with some varied parameters in order to study different aspects that might influence the relation between the agreement and accuracy. The idea of the workflow is that assessors are able to make their judgments collectively, so, for each assessor, the evaluation process splits in two parts: making a single judgment and arrival to the final decision during a discussion within a group. In the case of the absence of a consensus, an additional assessor - *a referee* - is assigned to be responsible for the final judgment. The varied parameters of the workflow are: assessors' motivation, communication ability, the size of discussion groups (*overlap*) and the strategy of choosing a referee. We investigate how certain parameters of the proposed workflow affect the quality of judgments in terms of accuracy, agreement level and correlation between them. We assume that the most optimal parameters should provide us with the most accurate judgments by ensuring a strong correlation between the agreement and accuracy. Also, we are interested in some additional aspects of assessors' behaviour which could affect the system, such as how often assessors call for a referee, how productive discussions are, how quickly the experience spreads through a group of assessors.

SIGIR'15, August 09 - 13, 2015, Santiago, Chile.
 ISBN 978-1-4503-3621-5/15/08 ...$15.00.
DOI: http://dx.doi.org/10.1145/2766462.2767727.

We begin our study with the estimation of the baseline correlation between agreement and accuracy keeping all the parameters unadjusted. Then we search for the answers to the following research questions that are induced by a number of intuitions that we wanted to verify:

- **RQ1**: Is monitoring of agreement level a sufficient measure of quality control? **Intuition**: Supposedly, if assessors are only motivated to maximize their agreement level regardless of the actual quality of their judgments then, in the ultimate case, all assessors can agree on always making the same judgment, and the workflow will collapse, if no additional mechanisms of quality control are introduced;

- **RQ2**: Does communication between assessors help to increase the quality of judgments? **Intuition**: We expect that if assessors do not discuss disagreement cases between each other, it is harder for them to gain experience and to learn, so the quality of these judgments is expected to be lower;

- **RQ3**: Does a larger overlap provide better correlation between agreement level and accuracy? **Intuition**: We suppose that increasing of the overlap leads to increasing of the speed of information propagation, so that the accuracy, the agreement and the correlation between them will also increase.

- **RQ4**: Are moderators better than "common" referees? We tested two strategies of choosing a referee: a referee could be chosen among the regular assessors or among highly experienced assessors (*moderators*). **Intuition**: We expect that the cases when all assessors make different judgments are more difficult than others, and to define the final judgment one needs to have a higher level of expertise in evaluation.

In this paper, we observed that agreement level, under certain circumstances, can be used as a substitute for accuracy for measuring the quality of assessor's judgments. Based on the lessons learned from our study, we provide recommendations towards a design of a workflow that sets agreement level as the target for assessors and provides high quality of collected judgments.

The next section describes the related work. The default workflow design and the dataset are presented in Section 3. The experimental setup is presented in Section 3.4. Section 4 describes the set of metrics used in this study. The experimental results are presented in Section 5. Section 6 concludes the paper and describes a few directions for the future work.

2. RELATED WORK

Many studies refer to metrics of assessors' agreement and accuracy, analyze them independently of each other and investigate how these metrics are affected by various parameters, such as HIT design, task difficulty, assessors' motivation and qualification, etc [5, 2, 1, 8]. Some of the studies investigate similar aspects of evaluation workflows, but address them with a different purpose. For example, Kazai et al. in [5] show that the quality control is necessary for obtaining consistent judgments. They compared two groups of assessors: the first group was under severe judgment control conditions and the assessors from the second group were exposed to a smaller number of quality control mechanisms. It was shown that the quality of judgments of the second group was substantially lower. Other studies [4, 7] compared professional trained assessors with crowd workers in traditional relevance assessment tasks and showed that professional assessors have higher level of both accuracy and agreement. The studies of Alonso and Baeza-Yates [1], as well as of Kosinski et al. [8] show that a collective judges opinion is better than a single vote, and the accuracy of a consolidated output can be increased by increasing the number of participants per task. Finally, Kazai et al. introduced a gamified HIT design for collecting judgments for book search purposes on a crowdsourcing platform, where crowd workers were allowed to communicate with each other before they make the final decision [6]. They showed that the initial judgments made by the assessors could change as the result of a dialogue, but neither measured how these dialogues influenced the quality of judgments, nor provided any other details on how communication affected the evaluation workflow and its participants in general.

While our study continues the research on the optimal evaluation workflow designs, it focuses on a number of novel aspects. First, we investigate the correlation between the assessors' accuracy and agreement, and how it depends on specific parameters of a workflow. Second, we focus on the impact of discussions on assessors' accuracy, agreement, experience and the overall effectiveness of a workflow. Besides, we study such parameters of communication as the size of a discussion group and analyze how it affects the quality of judgments when they are produced collectively.

3. WORKFLOW DESIGN AND DATA

In this section, we describe the design of our set of experiments: its participants, the evaluation set preparation and the default workflow design. In order to not only get quantitative data, but also to observe the real process of assessors communication, as well as its evolution in time, we have organized a series of experiments in a form of an offline game. During each of 6 games, participants had to evaluate a given set of documents in the scope of a respective workflow.

3.1 Participants

98 participants took part in the experiments described in this paper. They were randomly assigned to one of 6 groups: one *control* group and five *experimental* groups. The control group took part in a "pure" default experiment: participants evaluated documents according to the general rules (see Section 3.3). For all experimental groups, the evaluation rules and conditions were modified in different ways (see Section 4). None of the participants knew ahead to which group they would be assigned.

All the participants have passed a standard job entrance exam that all assessors have to pass to get hired (at the search engine under study). Out of them, 16 were randomly selected from professional assessors who had already been working on their position for several years, and all of them were assigned to the same experimental group. All the others did not have any reported experience in being an assessor before.

3.2 Evaluation sets

We prepared a special dataset for evaluation. Several volunteers among our colleagues who reported to have expertise in some topic were asked to generate keywords which related to the topic of their expertise. We did not limit our volunteers in choosing the topics of their expertise, so, finally, we obtained a very diverse list of keywords related to one of the following topics: *antiviruses, table tennis, guitar, athletics, hiking, management, football, medicine, linguistics, alpine skiing, Internet-memes, chess* and *repair.* Then we extracted real user queries that contained the above-mentioned keywords from the logs of a commercial search engine, hence obtaining a set of real user queries related to the topics of our volunteers' expertise. We randomly selected 3 documents out of the top 10 search results generated by the commercial search engine for every query and asked our volunteers to evaluate them according to a standard 6-grade relevance scale similar to the one used at TREC (Web search track)[1]. Thus, we have collected 64 queries corresponding to 192 documents evaluated by the experts on the topics of those queries, and used this set as the golden set for estimating the accuracy of the judgments produced by other assessors. As far as our experiment was conducted completely offline, all the documents were printed out on a color printer, so that all the participants evaluated the same instances of the web documents.

3.3 Workflow design

The default evaluation game that we organized has the following description and consists of 8 rounds. In every round each assessor receives one task. Each task is assigned to two assessors. Each task consists of a query and 3 related documents. None of the tasks is evaluated twice during the game. Assessors evaluate each document according to the same 6-graded relevance scale as the topic experts used when they created the golden set (see Section 3.2). Right before the start of a game, assessors were provided with a short 1-page description of the relevance grades with examples.

The workflow is based on the idea of communication between assessors. After receiving a task, assessors read the documents related to the task and make judgments on their own. Afterwards, they meet their partner, the assessor who were assigned with the same task, discuss their judgments and make the final collective decision. By design, two particular assessors cannot be paired in more than one round during the same game.

Depending on what judgments assessors made before and after the discussion, they can receive cards of different colors: green, blue, red, black or gold. Each of them stands for a special score which we calculate for each assessor. There are 3 possible outcomes of a discussion:

- Assessors make the same judgment initially, i.e. before the discussion. In this case, each of them receives one green card.

- Assessors make different judgments initially, but come to a consensus after the discussion. The assessor who initially made the judgment which is approved by the consensus gains a blue card. Another assessor gains a red card. If they decide that the correct judgment differs from both their initial judgments, they both receive red cards.

- Assessors make different judgments initially, but do not come to a consensus after discussion. The absence of the consensus might mean that at least two approaches are equally possible in evaluation of that document. For the purposes of machine learning and search quality evaluation, every document must have only one label, so, in order to choose the only judgment we need to make an additional decision. One of the possible strategies is to create and maintain an assessors' rating list, which could inform us about who of the two assessors is more reliable. This approach has a sufficient disadvantage: if both assessors have a low rating level, we might accept a wrong judgment. We propose another approach. In case of the absence of the consensus, the third assessor - a *referee* - is invited. At the first round, the referee is chosen randomly from all the assessors: at every following round, the referee is chosen among vacant assessors (i.e. who are not occupied with a dispute) with the largest number of green cards by that moment, thus, we are sure that a referee is a definitely reliable person. The referee evaluates the same document by taking the assessors' opinions and arguments into account. The referee's opinion is considered as final and cannot be appealed. Both assessors who called for the referee receive a black card, the referee receives nothing. If a pair of assessors has more than one unresolved dispute in the scope of the same task (each task consists of 3 documents to assess), still only one referee is called to make the final decisions in all unresolved cases[2].

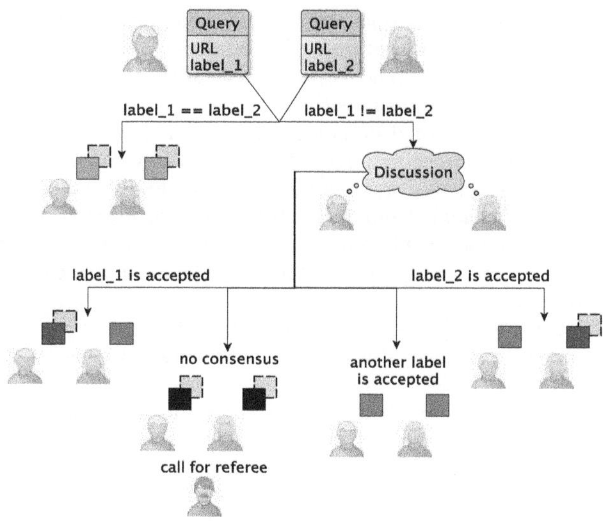

Figure 1: The workflow design. Dashed gold cards mean that the assessor can receive them if his/her label matches the corresponding golden set label.

[1]http://trec.nist.gov

[2]Of course, in these experiments we could choose a referee with the highest number of gold cards, but since the agreement metric is aimed to substitute the accuracy, we use it advisedly for this purpose.

As a result, every document receives one final judgment: either the judgment that both of the assigned assessors agreed on or the judgment made by a referee. After that, we compare the final judgment with the corresponding golden set judgment. If the final judgment matches the judgment from the golden set, the assessor who had initially made it additionally receives a gold card, even if she had to call for a referee to defend her judgment. If the assessor initially made the correct judgment, but was convinced by the opponent that the opponent's opinion is correct, she did not receive a gold card.

Once the cards are given to assessors, the next round begins. Figure 1 illustrates the described workflow. The game stops after the 8th round.

Green and gold cards might be considered as gamified metrics of the agreement and the accuracy correspondingly. Other cards: blue, red and black indicate an assessor's productivity during discussions. Blue cards show how successfully an assessor insists on her judgments during discussions. On the contrary, red cards show how often an assessor agrees with the opponent's judgment. Finally, black cards show how inflexible an assessor is in disputes.

After all, we are able to compose a portrait of each assessor in terms of her cards. From the point of view of judgments collection system we are interested in assessors who make precise judgments and capable of convincing their opponents of correctness of own opinion. Thus, a successful assessor should have many gold, some blue, and as few as possible red and black cards. As for green cards, we do not know how many of them a good assessor should have. Ideally, if we have perfect judges, they should have as many green cards as gold, but, practically, we do not know if it is possible for one person to have many green but only a few gold cards, and vice versa.

There are two possible winners in a game: the assessor who gains the most number of green cards (i.e. the most predictable assessor), and the assessor who gains the most number of gold cards (the most accurate assessor), however, there could be one person who get both prizes. The other types of cards did not determine the winners, they were used only for our post-analysis and the participants were informed about that.

The described workflow was the default one. Depending on a specific experiment, this workflow was changed in the ways which are described below.

3.4 Experiment setup

Experiment 1: Control. The control experiment had the default workflow. We are highlighting the most important points to compare them with the other experiments. 16 inexperienced assessors took part in our control experiment. They did not have any reported experience of working as an assessor before and were not familiar with the detailed evaluation guidelines (see Section 3.1). Each task was evaluated by 2 assessors, the referees were selected among the participants. The game lasted 8 rounds and each assessor evaluated 24 documents. Two targets were set for the participants: to gain as many green and/or gold cards as possible. The purpose of this experiment was in the baseline estimation of the assessors agreement level and the accuracy, calculating the correlation coefficient between them and comparing these metrics across all experiments.

Experiment 2: With Instigators. The difference of this experiment comparing with the control experiment was in the assessors' target. The participants were only told that they need to gain as many green cards as possible, and they were not told that their judgments are also compared with the golden set. We expected that if assessors knew that their only target is to maximize their agreement with other assessors, sooner or later they would start to agree with each other more often, and, in the ultimate case, they would start making one and the same judgment for every document, thus obtaining a very high agreement level, but a very low quality of judgments. In order to model such extreme situation during our experiment, we invited two *instigators* to take part in this experiment. One of the instigators was selected from our professional assessors, another was selected from the participants and had no assessor experience. They were asked to indirectly and informally (during coffee breaks or discussions of disagreement cases) hint to other participants to follow that "optimal" strategy. Thus, we assumed that the average agreement level should be high opposed to the average accuracy which should be low. Besides, we expected to see no correlation between these variables.

Experiment 3: With No Communication. We expected that discussing disagreement cases helps assessors share and gain useful experience, as well as synchronize their approaches towards evaluation. In Experiment 3 we did not let assessors discuss disagreement cases. At every round in this experiment, two assessors compared their judgments for the same document; if the judgments matched, assessors received green cards, if the judgments did not match, they received nothing and proceeded to the next round of the game. Consequently, as there were no discussions, there were no referees to arbitrate cases when assessors could not come to a conclusion, and there were no blue, red and black cards. In the case when two assessors made different judgments, the final judgment for the document was chosen randomly among these two. All other parameters of the workflow were the same as in the control experiment. Since the conditions of this experiment are considered as the degradation in respect to the control, we expected both the average agreement level and the average accuracy to be lower in comparison with the control group. As for the correlation, we did not have any expectation how strong it should be in this case.

Experiment 4: With Experienced Assessors. We expected that trained assessors have higher consistency of judgments and wanted to make sure that both our metrics - agreement level and accuracy reflect it. Unlike in the other experiments whose participants never worked as assessors before, all participants of Experiment 4 were experienced assessors who had already been working as assessors for a long time. All other parameters of the workflow were the same as in the control experiment. Obviously, since the participants were more experienced in relevance assessment than the other assessors, we expected to see higher levels of both accuracy and agreement than in the control group.

Experiment 5: With Overlap 3. In this experiment, each task was evaluated by 3 assessors at every round. Since the total number of participants should have been divisible by three, 18 assessors (instead of 16 as in the previous experiments) took part in this game. As far as three judgments per document are compared with each other, the agreement notion should be adjusted here. An assessor received a green card if her initial judgment matched the majority vote (e.g.

Experiment	Description	# of participants	Experience	Accuracy Control	Communication	Overlap
1	Control	16 assessors	no	yes	yes	2
2	With instigators	14 assessors 2 instigators	no	**no**	yes	2
3	With no communication	16 assessors	no	yes	**no**	2
4	With experienced assessors	16 assessors	**yes**	yes	yes	2
5	With overlap 3	18 assessors	no	yes	yes	**3**
6	With moderators	16 assessors **4 moderators**	no	yes	yes	2

Table 1: Experimental design. Modified parameters are marked in bold.

at least two assessors out of three independently made the same choice). A referee was called only if all three assessors made different judgments. All other parameters of the workflow were the same as in the control experiment. Apparently, increasing the overlap parameter should increase the intensity of information propagation between the participants and, consequently, assist assessors in learning rules-of-thumb of relevance assessment. Thus, we expected to see all three statistics: the agreement level, the accuracy and the correlation to be higher than in the control experiment.

Experiment 6: With Moderators. We assumed that in the cases when all assessors, first, independently make different judgments, and then cannot come to a common decision even after a discussion are specifically difficult. We hypothesized that such extra-difficult cases cannot be fairly resolved by regular assessors, and we should ask for an opinion of some specific highly-trusted referees. In order to test this idea, we have introduced an additional role to our game: *moderator*. In all other experiments, a referee was chosen among the assessors with the highest agreement level, and any assessor could become a referee during a game. In Experiment 6, in addition to 16 inexperienced assessors, we invited 4 *moderators*: highly-trusted experienced assessors. In those cases when two assessors had initially made different judgments and could not come to a conclusion during the discussion, they called for a moderator to arbitrate their dispute. All other parameters of the workflow were the same as in the control experiment. As far as moderators are much more experienced than "common" referees, the final judgments in the cases of disputes were expected to be more accurate than in the other experiments. Moreover, the moderators could share their knowledge during the discussions, so this could affect not only the final judgments, but both the accuracy and agreement levels, which we expected to be higher than in the control group.

All the specifics of each game performed are summarized in Table 1. The modified parameter in every experiment is highlighted.

4. METHODOLOGY

To search for an answer for our Research Questions (see Section 1), we calculated a number of metrics for every experiment. These metrics are based on the numbers of cards received by each assessor during a game. The following 4 metrics describe the agreement level:

- Assessor's agreement level I (Agr. I): the percentage of the cases in which the assessor's initial judgment matched the judgment made by another assessor responsible for the same task, i.e. the number of green cards gained by the assessor divided by the number of documents she evaluated. We could not use just the number of green cards as an agreement level metric, since in Experiment 5, assessors evaluated less documents than in the others, and hence they could gain less green cards than assessors from the other groups. In order to eliminate this problem, we applied this normalization (division by the number of evaluated documents).
- Assessor's agreement level II (Agr. II): Cohen's kappa calculated for the assessor's judgments with respect to the judgments which were made by all her partners assigned to the same documents. Agr. I metric was convenient to discuss with assessors, because it is transparent and clear for understanding. However, in our analysis we used both Agr. I and Agr. II metrics.
- Average agreement levels for all assessors participating in the experiment (avgAgr I, avgAgr II).

In the further analysis we will show that Agr I and Agr II strongly correlate with each other, and, consequently, avgAgr I and avgAgr II have a high correlation level too.

The following 3 metrics relate to the notion of accuracy:

- Assessor's accuracy (Acc.): the percentage of the cases in which the assessor's initial judgment matched the corresponding golden set judgment (and was defended during the discussion if that occurred), i.e. the number of gold cards gained by the assessor divided by the number of documents she evaluated. We compared each assessor's judgments with the corresponding golden set judgments and calculated the fraction of correct answers;
- Average accuracy of assessors per experiment (avgAcc).
- Accuracy of the final set of judgments generated during an experiment (FA). A final judgment is a judgment either made by the majority of assessors, or as a result decision after a discussion, or as a referee's judgment. These judgments were compared with the golden set

Exp. No.	Description	avgAcc	avgAgr I	Corr. I	avgAgr II	Corr. II	FA	Corr. III
1	Control	0.378	0.479	0.417	0.315	0.381	0.534	0.979
2	With instigators	0.388	0.531	0.232	0.342	0.367	0.492	0.846
3	With no communication	0.318($\star$)	0.391($\star$)	0.638	0.193($\star$)	0.71	0.433($\star$)	0.969
4	With experienced assessors	0.448	0.615($\star$)	0.465	0.462($\star$)	0.521	0.543	0.987
5	With overlap 3	0.369	0.459	0.72	0.227	0.705	0.53	0.888
6	With moderators	0.344	0.422($\star$)	0.358	0.232	0.324	0.515	0.96

Table 2: The Results of the experiments. Average values of agreement levels I and II, average accuracy, final accuracy for every experiment; correlation between agreement level I and accuracy, correlation between agreement level II and accuracy, correlation between agreement I and agreement II. Values that differ significantly from the results of the control experiment are marked with $\star$ ($\alpha = 0.05$).

judgments and the fraction of correct answers was calculated.

We normalize the number of gold cards in the same way as we normalized green cards. The final judgments accuracy reflects the overall quality of judgments that can be collected within a given workflow.

The following 2 metrics show the correlation between the accuracy and the agreement.

- Pearson correlation coefficient between Agr. I and Acc. (Corr. I);
- Pearson correlation coefficient between Agr. II and Acc. (Corr. II).

It is the target group of statistics. If a workflow provides a strong correlation between the accuracy and the agreement, and keeps the accuracy on a high level, this allows us to consider it as a successful workflow, because such a workflow allows us to monitor the quality using the agreement level.

Finally, the following 2 metrics relate to the black cards:

- Normalized number of calls for a referee (CR): the number of the assessor's black cards divided by the number of documents she evaluated (i.e. maximum possible number of disputes);
- Average number of calls for a referee per experiment (avgCR):

For each experiment we also estimated the statistical significance of the differences between the experimental and the control group for each of the described metrics except Corr. I and Corr. II. The significance of the differences was measured by using the bootstrap method with resampling and estimating 95% confidence interval. The cases where the difference is significant are marked with an asterisk sign in Table 2. Pearson correlation coefficients were interpreted according to the widely accepted rule-of-thumb. Namely, the correlation between 0.2 and 0.4 was considered as weak, between 0.4 and 0.6 – moderate and between 0.6 and 1 – strong.

As far as there were no discussions in Experiment 3, its final judgments were sampled randomly from the two judgments of the assessors who disagreed on them. In order to reduce random effects in our analysis we perform this selection 1000 times and then average the accuracy and both agreement levels I and II.

Additionally, in order to estimate the relation between two agreement metrics, we calculated Pearson correlation coefficient between Agr. I and Agr. II (Corr. III).

We also collected some subjective reports. After each experiment, we had a discussion with the participants in which we asked them to tell us about their impressions, discovered winning strategies and other thoughts on the pros and cons of the game.

5. RESULTS

In this section we present the results of our experiments in terms of accuracy, agreement level, correlation between them and effectiveness of disputes between assessors. The results are provided in Tables 2 and 3, and illustrated in Figures 2 and 3.

5.1 Accuracy

In this section we analyze the average accuracy per experimental group (avgAcc) and the accuracy of the final set of judgments generated (FA). Both these values differ significantly from the values in Experiment 1 only in Experiment 3. We see that the communication capability has a significant influence on the quality of judgments: if assessors do not discuss disagreement cases with each other, they do not get any feedback on the quality of their judgments and cannot improve it, and, as the result, the accuracy of the judgments produced within this experiment was significantly lower than in the others. In all other experiments we do not observe statistically significant differences in accuracy levels, but some trends are interesting to analyze.

First of all, despite our expectations, we do not observe significantly higher accuracy of judgments provided by the experienced assessors in Experiment 4, though the accuracy of its judgments was the highest among others. In fact, we estimated that p-value of that difference is bounded between 0.05 and 0.06. The absence of significance might be related to the nature of the particular set of documents assessors had to evaluate.

In the experiment with instigators, while the average accuracy is the second best among all experiments (which means that assessors were generally making reasonable judgments at the stage of individual evaluation), the final accuracy is the second worst among all. Since the final accuracy depends on the judgments assessors agreed on after the discussions, this fact shows that assessors were not motivated to search for the correct judgment during the discussions. In subjective reports some of the participants admitted that they were really influenced by the instigators and tried to predict their opponent's thoughts and make a judgment that would rather match their opponent's judgment than the judgment that they believed it had to be, and, particularly, they had no motivation to come to the correct answer during discussions. However, not all assessors were affected by this temptation, some of them blamed the cheaters for this dishonest strategy and ignored such behavior.

In fact, the average accuracy in Experiment 2 is slightly higher than in the control group because of the influence of one of the instigators. As it was mentioned in Section 3.4, one of the instigators was selected from the professional assessors. He played his role of an instigator perfectly, but, at the same time, he made very accurate judgments. As a result, he received the most number of gold cards and became one of the winners in this experiment. If we do not take him into account while calculating the average accuracy (avgAcc), it decreases from 0.388 to 0.372.

Experiment 6 demonstrates a mirrored situation: the rank of this experiment according to the final accuracy is relatively higher than according to the average assessors' accuracy. This difference shows the impact of moderators who joined the discussions and generated accurate judgments, while the quality of judgments produced by the assessors themselves was not high. This effect will be considered later in detail in Section 5.4.

5.2 Agreement level

We observe that Experiment 4 shows the highest level of agreement both in terms of green cards gained by assessors (avgAgr I) and in terms of Cohen's kappa (avgAgr II). This observation matches with our expectations: experienced assessors who were trained to follow the same guideline are expected to have a high agreement level. At the same time, Experiment 3 (with no communication) has the lowest agreement level according to both metrics. Indeed, if assessors do not communicate, do not get any feedback and do not share their experience with each other, it is difficult for them to synchronize their approach towards evaluation. Although, the agreement level in Experiment 6 is significantly lower only according to avgAgr I, but not according to avgAgr II, it is one of the lowest among all other experiments. We think that it reflects the fact that assessors in this experiment were not motivated to learn from each other: instead they were waiting for the moderator to come and present the correct answer. The difference in the agreement level between other experiments is insignificant.

As it was expected, assessors in Experiment 2 have the highest agreement level among the inexperienced assessors, which confirms that the instigators' target has been hit. At the same time, the absence of the significance in this case could mean that their efforts were not enough. Anyway, we estimated the corresponding p-value and it is bounded between 0.07 and 0.08. On the other hand, we see from the subjective reports that some assessors were not affected by the instigators even after their attempts to incline them to cheating. Thus, we can optimistically suppose that there should be always fundamentally honest persons who never follow a cheating strategy, and such assessors make the difference insignificant. However, we think that the time period of the experiment was too short, and we would see the significant difference between the agreement levels if we extended the number of rounds. Of course, in this case, participants from other experiments could also realize "benefits" of cheating, but we suppose that the speed of information propagation with instigators is much higher than without them, so we still would see the significant difference.

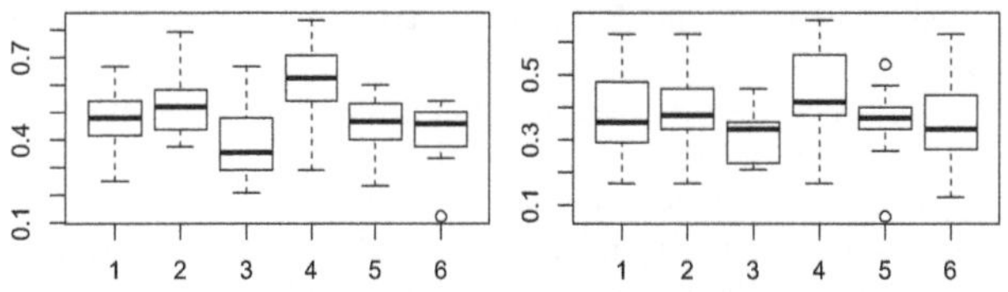

Figure 2: Accuracy (left) and agreement level I (right) per experiment.

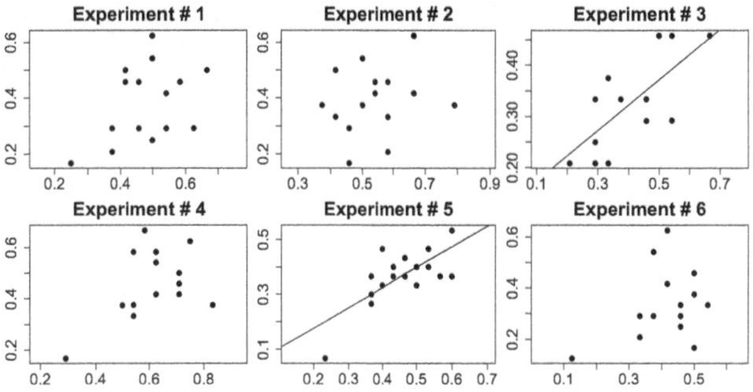

Figure 3: Correlation between accuracy and agreement per experiment. We plot the regression lines on the scatterplots if the corresponding correlation coefficients are greater than 0.6.

Finally, there is a very strong correlation Corr. III in all experiments, which confirms that both agreement metrics Agr. I and Agr. II are applicable. We may also note that in Experiments 2 and 5, Corr. III is not so large than in the others. In Experiment 5, such differences are really possible here, because in the case when overlap is 3 (opposed to the other experiments where overlap is 2), Agr I is calculated as the number of cases when an assessor's opinion matches the majority's opinion, but Agr II is still calculated as Cohen's kappa, i.e. as the number of cases when an assessor's opinion matches all partners' opinions she met. Anyway, since both avgAgr I and avgAgr II values in Experiment 5 are large (0.72 and 0.705 correspondingly), there are no contradictions with overlap 3 here. As for Experiment 2, the reason of a comparably low correlation is one of the assessors who adopted cheating strategy and made a lot of identical judgments. According to a property of Cohen's kappa, if one of the assessors always makes the same judgment, the kappa equals to zero [3]. Thus, the kappa of this cheater was very low, while the number of green cards was normal since she made one of the most frequent judgments, and hence, this slightly decreased the correlation. If we remove her, the correlation increases up to 0.97.

5.3 Correlation between accuracy and agreement

Next, we analyze the correlation between two metrics discussed above: the accuracy and the agreement level of assessors in each experiment. All the conclusions within this subsection are based on Corr I metric. Conclusions based on Corr II are the same. Two of six experiments - 2 and 6 - have a weak correlation (0.232 and 0.358), two experiments - 1 and 4 - have moderate correlation (0.417 and 0.465) and the other two - 3 and 5 - have a strong correlation (0.638 and 0.72).

Changing assessors' target to maximization of green cards in Experiment 2 led to the expected results: the agreement level in this experiment is one of the highest, while the accuracy is not so high and is near to the control group. In other words, in Experiment 2, assessors made approximately the same number of mistakes, but there were more "agreed" mistakes. As a result, this led to a strong decrease of the correlation between these statistics in comparison with the control group.

In Experiment 6, we observe a low correlation level too. This result could be associated with the specific behavior of the participants which will be described later in Section 5.4.

As we have already mentioned in Section 5.1, the accuracy of judgments produced by the experienced assessors (Experiment 4) was not significantly higher comparing to the control experiment, while the agreement level of experienced assessors was very high. Consequently, we observe a moderate correlation between accuracy and agreement level in this experiment.

Interestingly, in Experiment 3, we observe a strong correlation, but, as discussed above, both the accuracy and the agreement level are the lowest among all experiments. So, when assessors work completely on their own, do not communicate with each other and do not get any feedback on their work, their agreement level may well predict the accuracy of their judgments. However, there appears to be no benefit of such correlation, as though the accuracy can be predicted by the agreement in this experiment, its value stays way below the level that we expect from a high-quality evaluation workflow design.

Our control Experiment 1 shows a moderate correlation between accuracy and agreement, but we see how increasing the parameter of overlap in Experiment 5 may lead to an increase of this correlation. At the same time, the average accuracy in Experiment 5 is by 0.009 less than in the control experiment, which is not too much, and the difference is not statistically significant. So, strong correlation allows us to use the agreement as a quality metric, but only in the scope of this workflow out of all six we experimented with.

This means that assessors' quality monitoring should be based not only on the agreement metric, but on the accuracy metric too. So, we cannot abandon golden sets completely, but we can reduce the size of the golden set. Indeed, if we use only the accuracy as an assessor's quality metric, the size of the golden set for one assessor could be calculated according to a well-known formula related to finding confidence interval for a single proportion [9]:

$$n \simeq p(1-p)\left(\frac{z_{\alpha/2}}{\delta}\right)^2,$$

where n is the sample size (i.e. the size of the golden set), p is the expected assessor's accuracy (e.g. the accuracy for the previous period of time), δ is a margin error, α is a significance level, $z_{\alpha/2}$ is a $\alpha/2$ quantile of the normal distribution. Obviously, we use the same golden set for all assessors, but still there are too many documents. As a matter of fact, commercial web search engines need to collect a huge amount of judgments, and the number of the documents to be checked may be equal to several thousands of documents per month. Now, in the scope of the proposed workflow, we are allowed to check the same volume of judgments using the agreement level (i.e. without the golden set), and the golden set judgments will be used just to make assessors feel that they are watched. We do not have a specific recommendation for the size of a golden set to be used for such sanity checks only, but, obviously, it should be essentially less than in the case when accuracy is the only means of control.

5.4 Efficiency of disputes

This section is devoted to the efficiency of disputes between assessors. The efficiency might be considered from two points of view. The first one relates to the accuracy. Indeed, if several assessors independently make the same judgment of the given document intuitively, this judgment is likely to be correct. However, if assessors independently make different judgments, may one expect that their discussion will help them choose the correct judgment? In general, are the judgments made after a discussion more accurate than the judgments that were initially made by the assessors? Moreover, if one of the assessors initially made the correct judgment, which did not match the judgment of her partner, would the correct judgment be chosen as the result of the discussion with that partner? In order to obtain an answer we need to calculate the average accuracy before and after the disputes.

So far, we measured the assessor's accuracy as the number of gold cards divided by the number of total documents the assessor evaluated, but, according to our workflow, an assessor does not gain a gold card if she cannot defend her judgment in the dispute. Now, we calculate "pure" assessors' accuracy as the proportion of cases where their initial judgment matches the corresponding judgment from the golden set, this is what we call *assessor's accuracy before a dispute*. *Assessor's accuracy after disputes* is the proportion of correct final judgments, no matter whether they are obtained with or without a dispute, with or without a referee. Obviously, referees affect the accuracy after disputes, but still we want to take them into account, because we are interested in the cases when one of the assessors knows the correct judgment and finally this judgment is accepted, even if a referee is called for that. Afterwards, we calculate delta of the difference between the accuracy before and after disputes and their statistical significance using paired t-test for two population means. The results are provided in Table 3.

The efficiency might be also related to the frequency of calls for a referee. Obviously, in our workflow, calling for a referee (or a moderator as in Experiment 6) means additional costs, so given that all major metrics (accuracy, agreement and correlation between the two) are comparable, the workflow that produces less calls for referees is more effective. The frequency of calls for a referee (avgCR) is also presented in Table 3.

Experiments 2 and 5 have a significantly lower number of calls for a referee comparing to other experiments. In Experiment 2 assessors were only motivated to gain as many green cards as possible, i.e. to match with a counterpart at the stage of independent evaluation. So, after they did not match, they were not motivated to fight for the correct judgment and preferred to agree on something rather than call for a referee. We also do not see any significant increase of average accuracy after the discussions in this experiment. When assessors are only motivated to maximize their default (pre-dispute) agreement level, disputes mean nothing to them and do not help increase accuracy of final judg-

Exp.	avgAcc before	avgAcc after	p-value	delta	avgCR
1	0.435	0.536	0.0003	0.102	0.208
2	0.453	0.49	0.199	0.036	0.062($\star$)
3	0.424	0.424	NA	NA	NA
4	0.516	0.542	0.283	0.026	0.146
5	0.454	0.533	0.002	0.08	0.033($\star$)
6	0.419	0.516	0.002	0.096	0.359($\star$)

Table 3: Average accuracy in groups before and after discussion, their delta, t-test p-value and the average number of calls for referee. avgCR values that differ significantly from the control experiment are marked with $\star$ ($\alpha = 0.05$). NA values relate to Experiment 3 with no communication.

ments. This conclusion fits the previous conclusion about the motivation of this group of assessors made in Section 5.1.

However, we observe a different case in Experiment 5: even though the number of calls for referees was also low, the efficiency of disputes here was very high. Evidently, if three people participate in the discussion, they are more likely to come to a consistent decision which will be supported by at least two of them, that is why they did not need to call for a referee often within this workflow.

Experiment 6 demonstrates a significantly higher number of calls for a referee (a moderator) comparing to other experiments. It means that the number of cases when assessors could not come to an agreement was very high. We tend to explain it by a psychological effect: in a game where any of assessors may become a referee, participants of the discussion try to come to a conclusion and learn by themselves, because they believe that there is no any person with a principally higher level of expertise to help them. But, in the experiment with moderators, assessors' motivation to learn by themselves was shifted to the motivation to be taught by a more knowledgeable person: instead of thinking "We both do not know the answer, so let us think together and find a solution", assessors' way of thinking changed into "We both do not know the answer, so let us go and ask someone who will provide us with an explanation". On the other hand, the deltas of accuracy before and after disputes in both experiments 1 and 6 are approximately the same, almost 0.1, so experienced moderators gave almost the same profit as regular referees who were chosen from among the participants. So, since the final accuracy in these experiments is comparable (0.534 and 0.515 correspondingly) and the difference between them is not significant, there is no need to assign a special role of moderator, because it is more expensive and because it makes assessors lazier.

Despite that both Experiments 1 and 4 had a moderate frequency of calls for a referee, in Experiment 1, disputes helped to significantly increase the accuracy of judgments, while in Experiment 4 disputes did not affect the final accuracy significantly. It may be explained by the fact that the experienced assessors in Experiment 4 initially had a very high accuracy, and it could not go much higher than their common level of expertise in given topics. At the same time, for untrained assessors in Experiment 1 these discussions were very useful, which emphasizes the value of communication specifically for new assessors at the stage of learning.

6. CONCLUSIONS

In our study we proposed a new gamified workflow of collecting judgments. In order to investigate how certain parameters of the proposed workflow affect the quality of judgments in terms of accuracy, agreement level and the correlation between these two metrics, we have conducted a set of offline experiments in a form of a game. Based on the results of these experiments we obtain the following answers to our research questions.

RQ1. Agreement level may be used as one of the targets for assessors in our workflow. However, it is not sufficient: once assessors are told that their only target is maximizing agreement level, they often lose motivation to care about the accuracy of their judgments; a high agreement level of an assessor in such circumstances does not predict high accuracy of her judgments and cannot serve as the only measure of quality control. The workflow of collecting judgments should necessarily contain some additional quality control mechanism that would not allow assessors to always make one and the same judgment, thus artificially maximizing their agreement level. Assessors should always know that some of their judgments may be checked in order to estimate their accuracy. This conclusion allows practitioners to essentially reduce the size of the golden set, and use it only for maintaining assessors' feeling that they are watched.

RQ2. Communication between assessors plays a great role in the process of learning and sharing experience between assessors: they are likely to choose the correct judgment during the disputes. Also, we see that the absence of communication in our workflow affects the accuracy of judgments negatively, and discussing disputable cases by assessors helps increase both the accuracy of judgments and the inter-assessor agreement level, and its effect is even more significant for inexperienced assessors.

RQ3. Increasing the number of assessors performing the same task indeed leads to a stronger correlation between the accuracy and the agreement.

RQ4. Difficult evaluation cases in which assessors cannot come to a common conclusion even after a discussion should not be solved by any specially chosen highly-trusted experts. Despite our expectations, the institute of moderators introduced into our workflow led neither to an increase in accuracy, nor to an increase in agreement level, demotivated the assessors to learn by themselves and increased the costs of the whole workflow, because the assessors tended to call for a referee to arbitrate their disputes much more often.

Based on these results, we formulate our recommendations towards the collecting judgments workflow. Agreement level may serve as the main metric of assessor's quality, but assessors should know that the accuracy of their judgments is also observed. Assessors should have the opportunity to discuss disagreement cases with each other, and the process of training of a new assessor may be reduced to simply performing a set of tasks and discussing them with other assessors. Difficult disagreement cases can be solved by adding one more assessor to the discussion, and no specific roles are needed. Finally, we assume that the overlap in a real production workflow should be from 3 to 5 assessors performing the same task (participation of more than five assessors may make discussions less transparent). In our experiments, Experiment 5 adopted all the recommendations given above, and it provided the best correlation between the accuracy and agreement, keeping all other measures high, such as accuracy, agreement, final accuracy and efficiency of discussions.

To sum up, the workflow we propose does not require significant managerial efforts towards the preparation of comprehensive detailed guidelines (assessors mainly learn from each other), spending time on training the assessors and checking samples of assessors' judgments (first of all one monitors the agreement level, which is calculated automatically, and the accuracy checking may be reduced to a minimum needed to maintain assessors' motivation to make reasonable judgments), which makes the whole process of collecting judgments more agile.

7. FURTHER WORK

In the future, we plan to create and test an online interface which would allow assessors to evaluate real web documents online and discuss disagreement cases with their colleagues in an anonymous chat. Once we get a more convenient instrument for producing further experiments, we aim to experiment with larger overlaps and provide a deeper investigation of the role of overlap in the effectiveness of an evaluation workflow.

Another interesting question is what size of the golden set in the proposed workflow is enough for stimulating assessors to do their work properly and do not follow a cheating strategy.

Also, for the workflows with high overlaps we plan to explore in which cases an assessor should receive a green card. In the current version of Experiment 5, an assessor received a green card when she matched with the decision of the majority. However, another possible approach is to give a green card to an assessor when her judgment matches with the median of the set of all assessors' opinions. On the one hand, if all assessors make different judgments, median judgment can always be obtained, while the majority vote decision will not exist and we will have to call for a referee. On the other hand, encouraging assessors to match with the median judgment may discourage them from making extreme judgments: when they are in doubt, assessors may tend to choose judgments from the middle of the evaluation scale because they will more likely match with a median one.

Finally, it is interesting to take a closer look at the psychological aspects of communication in the evaluation process. Does the communication strategy which assessor decides to follow depend on the features of the characteristics of assessor's personality? Does it depend on the difficulty of certain tasks? Is there a relation with the design of evaluation workflows in general? It seems that there is a relation between the communication strategy and assessor's personal characteristics, because judgment discussions are similar to conflict situations, which are investigated by psychologists in conflict theories. Next, we suppose that assessors' can behave in different ways depending on the difficulty of the task. For example, they could lose their motivation to come up with the correct judgment if the task is hard to assess. And if it is true, how can we motivate them in such cases?

8. REFERENCES

[1] O. Alonso and R. Baeza-Yates. Design and implementation of relevance assessments using crowdsourcing. In *Advances in Information Retrieval. 33rd European Conference on IR Research, ECIR 2011, Dublin, Ireland, April 18-21, 2011. Proceedings*, pages 153–164. Springer, 2011.

[2] P. Bailey, N. Craswell, I. Soboroff, P. Thomas, A. P. de Vries, and E. Yilmaz. Relevance assessment: Are judges exchangeable and does it matter. In *Proceedings of the 31st Annual International ACM SIGIR Conference on Research and Development in Information Retrieval*, SIGIR '08, pages 667–674, New York, NY, USA, 2008. ACM.

[3] K. Gwet. Inter-rater reliability: dependency on trait prevalence and marginal homogeneity. *Statistical Methods for Inter-Rater Reliability Assessment Series*, 2:1–9, 2002.

[4] G. Kazai, N. Craswell, E. Yilmaz, and S. Tahaghoghi. An analysis of systematic judging errors in information retrieval. In *Proceedings of the 21st ACM International Conference on Information and Knowledge Management*, CIKM '12, pages 105–114, New York, NY, USA, 2012. ACM.

[5] G. Kazai, J. Kamps, M. Koolen, and N. Milic-Frayling. Crowdsourcing for book search evaluation: Impact of hit design on comparative system ranking. In *Proceedings of the 34th International ACM SIGIR Conference on Research and Development in Information Retrieval*, SIGIR '11, pages 205–214, New York, NY, USA, 2011. ACM.

[6] G. Kazai, N. Milic-Frayling, and J. Costello. Towards methods for the collective gathering and quality control of relevance assessments. In *Proceedings of the 32Nd International ACM SIGIR Conference on Research and Development in Information Retrieval*, SIGIR '09, pages 452–459, New York, NY, USA, 2009. ACM.

[7] G. Kazai, E. Yilmaz, N. Craswell, and S. Tahaghoghi. User intent and assessor disagreement in web search evaluation. In *Proceedings of the 22Nd ACM International Conference on Conference on Information & Knowledge Management*, CIKM '13, pages 699–708, New York, NY, USA, 2013. ACM.

[8] M. Kosinski, Y. Bachrach, G. Kasneci, J. Van-Gael, and T. Graepel. Crowd iq: Measuring the intelligence of crowdsourcing platforms. In *Proceedings of the 4th Annual ACM Web Science Conference*, WebSci '12, pages 151–160, New York, NY, USA, 2012. ACM.

[9] P. Mathews. *Sample Size Calculations: Practical Methods for Engineers and Scientists.* Mathews Malnar and Bailey, Incorporated, 2010.

Assessor Differences and User Preferences in Tweet Timeline Generation

Yulu Wang[1], Garrick Sherman[2], Jimmy Lin[1], and Miles Efron[2]
[1] University of Maryland, College Park
[2] University of Illinois, Urbana-Champaign
{ylwang,jimmylin}@umd.edu, {gsherma2,mefron}@illinois.edu

ABSTRACT

In information retrieval evaluation, when presented with an effectiveness difference between two systems, there are three relevant questions one might ask. First, are the differences statistically significant? Second, is the comparison stable with respect to assessor differences? Finally, is the difference actually meaningful to a user? This paper tackles the last two questions about assessor differences and user preferences in the context of the newly-introduced tweet timeline generation task in the TREC 2014 Microblog track, where the system's goal is to construct an informative summary of non-redundant tweets that addresses the user's information need. Central to the evaluation methodology is human-generated semantic clusters of tweets that contain substantively similar information. We show that the evaluation is stable with respect to assessor differences in clustering and that user preferences generally correlate with effectiveness metrics even though users are not explicitly aware of the semantic clustering being performed by the systems. Although our analyses are limited to this particular task, we believe that lessons learned could generalize to other evaluations based on establishing semantic equivalence between information units, such as nugget-based evaluations in question answering and temporal summarization.

Categories and Subject Descriptors: H.3.4 [Information Storage and Retrieval]: Systems and Software—Performance evaluation

Keywords: TREC evaluation; microblog search; user study

1. INTRODUCTION

In response to information needs, search systems should strive to return as much relevant content as possible. However, there are other factors that systems might consider beyond topical relevance: often, users may not wish to see multiple pieces of text that "say the same thing"; frequently, users desire diverse results that cover multiple aspects of the topic they are interested in. These considerations are particularly important in the context of searching tweets on Twitter. Due to the nature of the medium, there are frequently duplicate, near-duplicate, and highly-similar posts—for example, a breaking news event may be reported by multiple outlets at roughly the same time, each using slightly different language. In turn, these posts are retweeted, sometimes with additional commentary, copy-and-pasted, and discussed as part of a global conversation. This creates a cacophony of voices that obscures the underlying information content.

SIGIR'15, August 09 - 13, 2015, Santiago, Chile.

ACM 978-1-4503-3621-5/15/08 ...$15.00.
DOI: http://dx.doi.org/10.1145/2766462.2767699.

The Microblog track at TREC began in 2011 to explore information retrieval challenges in the context of social media services such as Twitter. The main task since 2011 has been temporally-anchored ad hoc retrieval ("At time T, give me the most relevant tweets about an information need expressed as query Q"). In response to the considerations above, the tweet timeline generation (TTG) task was introduced in 2014, where the goal is to construct a "timeline" of relevant and non-redundant tweets that best addresses the user's information need.

This paper presents a meta-evaluation of the TTG task from two perspectives: First, do assessor differences affect evaluation stability? Ultimately, TTG evaluation boils down to judgments about the semantic content of tweets, for which we would expect inter-assessor disagreements. Do these differences prevent us from drawing conclusions about the relative effectiveness of systems? Second, do user preferences correlate with our evaluation metrics? That is, are our metrics meaningful in being able to capture aspects of what users care about in timelines for making system comparisons? Our major findings are summarized as follows:

- We find that assessors do exhibit substantial differences in semantic clustering. However, these differences do not impact the stability of system comparisons.
- We find that user preferences correlate with metric differences, and for precision and unweighted F_1, agreement increases as the magnitude of the difference increases.

Although this work focuses on a specific TREC task, tweet timeline generation is representative of a class of information retrieval evaluations based on identifying atomic units of information and establishing semantic equivalences between these units. Thus, we believe that lessons learned from our study can be applied to similar types of evaluations.

2. BACKGROUND AND RELATED WORK

At a high level, the tweet timeline generation task bears a family resemblance to topic detection and tracking (TDT)

[33, 3], "other" nuggets in question answering [32, 9, 8], nugget-based evaluations in DARPA's BOLT program,[1] and temporal summarization at TREC [12, 5]. These tasks all share the insight that atomic units of information should be grouped together into semantic equivalence classes to provide more useful responses to users (we refer to this generically as "clustering"). In TDT the atomic units were documents, which were grouped into those discussing the same event. For question answering, nuggets were short phrases that provided interesting information about a target entity. In temporal summarization, sentences formed the atomic units that conveyed essential information about a particular event. These notions are also reflected in variants of ad hoc retrieval such as aspect retrieval [21] (or, alternatively, facet or sub-topic retrieval [34]) and result diversification [1, 28], although less explicitly.

The two biggest challenges of formulating such an evaluation are (1) defining the atomic unit of information and (2) defining semantic equivalence between those units. Once these two issues are resolved, computing a metric is reasonably straightforward, although variations abound. The first issue is more difficult than it initially seems if the atomic unit does not correspond to a logical entity such as a document. Experience from question answering evaluations has shown that users disagree about the granularity of nuggets—for example, whether a piece of text encodes one or more nuggets and how to treat partial semantic overlap between two pieces of text [20]. The solution that most evaluations adopt today is to simply declare the atomic information unit *by fiat*: in tweet timeline generation, tweets form the atomic units, and in temporal summarization [5], they are sentences. This sweeps many nuances under the rug, but yields workable evaluations in practice.

The second issue—semantic equivalence between atomic information units—is challenging because making such judgments requires taking into account context and fine-grained distinctions in meaning. In the same way that assessors disagree over relevance judgments (see [6] for a nice summary), humans also disagree about whether two pieces of text have the same semantic content. This issue is typically resolved by acknowledging these assessor differences and simply accepting the opinion of a *single* assessor. In the same way that Voorhees [31] demonstrated the stability of system rankings with respect to assessors' divergent document-level relevance judgments, the implicit assumption is that for these semantic clustering tasks, assessor differences don't matter if our goal is to induce a set of system comparisons.

To our knowledge, however, this assumption has never been validated at scale. For example, "ground truth" nuggets for question answering evaluations were generated by a single assessor (for each entity) [32, 9].[2] Thus, it is unclear if an alternative set of nuggets (i.e., generated by another assessor) would have altered system rankings. A more recent iteration of the nugget-based evaluation methodology [22] has not to our knowledge examined assessor differences in the "nuggetization" process either. One of the major contributions of this paper is that, for tweet timeline generation, we devoted the resources necessary to answer this question by procuring two independent sets of semantic clusters for all topics in the test collection. Our results verify that system rankings are stable with respect to assessor differences in the TTG task, which gives us some confidence that the same results will carry over to similar tasks as well.

With respect to the second part of our paper—an exploration of user preferences in tweet timeline generation—there is a long history of research that examines the correlation between effectiveness metrics from system-oriented evaluations with task-based metrics from user-oriented evaluations [13, 29, 4, 30, 14, 2, 26, 25, 27]. The broader goal of this thread of work is to understand when system effectiveness improvements are meaningful or useful in improving users' information seeking abilities in practice. Early studies suggest that "better" systems (as measured by system-oriented metrics) don't necessarily translate into better task performance [13, 29, 30]. Smith and Kantor [26] explained that users "do well" with poor search engines because they reformulate queries. Along these lines, Lin and Smucker [19] suggested that browsing can compensate for poor search results. However, more recent work has been able to detect a correlation between various system effectiveness metrics and human preferences [2, 25] (by using larger sample sizes) and between precision and user performance [27] (by more carefully controlling the experimental setup). These results give the community some degree of confidence that system-oriented evaluations can guide progress in producing more useful systems.

Our study follows the general setup of Sanderson et al. [25], i.e., asking users which of two system outputs they prefer. There are, however, a few important differences. Whereas their work examined ad hoc retrieval, we explore the more complex task of tweet timeline generation. Whereas they restricted system comparisons to those with "large" differences and "small" differences in effectiveness, we sampled our comparison conditions and analyzed the results in a way that allows us to characterize user sensitivity to different magnitudes of differences. Finally, whereas Sanderson et al. used judgments from Amazon's Mechanical Turk service, we took the route of training local assessors,

3. TWEET TIMELINE GENERATION

3.1 Task Definition

Tweet timeline generation (TTG) was introduced at the TREC 2014 Microblog track to supplement the existing ad hoc retrieval task. The putative user model is as follows: "At time T, I have an information need expressed by query Q, and I would like a summary that captures relevant information." The system's task is to produce a "summary" timeline, operationalized as a list of non-redundant, chronologically ordered tweets. It is imagined that the user would consume the entire summary (unlike a ranked list, where the user might stop reading at any time).

We conceived of a reference architecture in which a TTG module processes the output of an ad hoc retrieval system to generate the timeline. Thus, tweet timeline generation introduces two additional challenges beyond ad hoc retrieval:

- Systems must detect (and eliminate) redundant tweets. This is equivalent to saying that systems must detect if a tweet contains novel information.

[1] http://www.nist.gov/itl/iad/mig/bolt_p1.cfm

[2] Subsequent "nugget pyramid" extensions [17, 9, 8] had multiple assessors assigning importance *weights*, but the underlying nuggets were still the same; similarly, researchers have studied how assessors identify nuggets in a piece of text [20], but the analyses were restricted to a *single* set of nuggets.

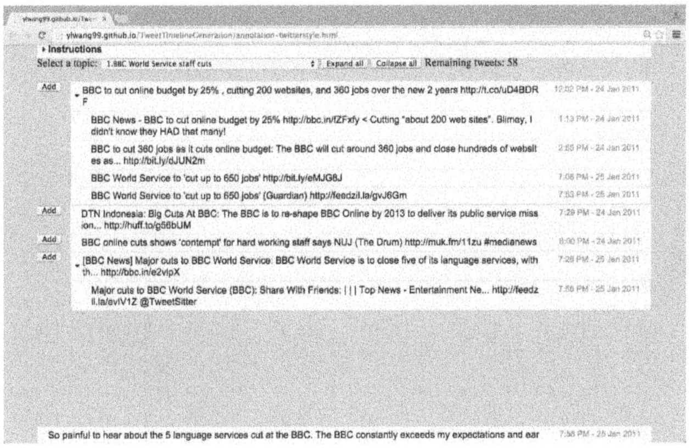

Figure 1: Screenshot of the annotation interface. Tweets are presented one at a time in chronological order (bottom). For each tweet, the assessor can add it to an existing cluster or create a new cluster.

- Systems must determine how many tweets to return. Some topics have more relevant and non-redundant tweets than others and a system must be able to automatically infer this. Systems can make different precision/recall tradeoffs along these lines.

We operationalized redundancy as follows: for every pair of tweets, if the chronologically later tweet contains substantive information that is not present in the earlier tweet, the later tweet is considered novel; otherwise, the later tweet is redundant with respect to the earlier one. In our definition, redundancy and novelty are antonyms, and so we use them interchangeably, but in opposite contexts.

Due to the temporal constraint, redundancy is *not* symmetric. If tweet A precedes tweet B and tweet B contains substantively similar information found in tweet A, then B is redundant with respect to A, but not the other way around. We also assume transitivity. Suppose A precedes B and B precedes C: if B is redundant with respect to A and C is redundant with respect to B, then by definition C is redundant with respect to A. In this task setup, redundancy boils down to the definition of "contains substantively similar information", which is more precisely defined below.

3.2 Annotation Methodology

The TTG definition of redundancy and the assumption of transitivity means that the task can be viewed as semantic clustering—that is, we wish to group relevant tweets into clusters in which all tweets share substantively similar information. Within each cluster, the earliest tweet is novel; all other tweets in the cluster are redundant with respect to all earlier tweets.

Our annotation methodology builds exactly on this idea. We begin with a list of all relevant tweets, ordered chronologically, from earliest to latest. These tweets are presented, one at a time, to a human assessor. For each tweet, the assessor can add it to an existing cluster if she thinks the tweet contains substantively similar information with respect to tweets in the existing cluster, or she can create a new cluster for the tweet. We have developed a JavaScript-based annotation interface to help assessors accomplish this task. A screenshot is shown in Figure 1.

In the interface, the next tweet to be clustered is shown at the bottom of the screen. The assessor can either add the tweet to an existing cluster by clicking the "Add" button next to the cluster or create a new cluster by hitting the space bar. At any time, the assessor can expand a cluster to show all tweets contained in it, or collapse the cluster to show only the first tweet. The interface also implements an undo feature that allows the assessor to reverse the action taken and go back to the previous tweet.

The TTG evaluation methodology boils down to this central question: what exactly does "substantively similar information" mean? Like document relevance in ad hoc retrieval, assessors make the final determination and we expect natural variations among humans. However, pilot studies helped us devise a set of guidelines, which were provided as instructions to the assessors. We told them: a good rule of thumb is that if two tweets "say the same thing", then they're substantively similar. To speed up the clustering process, the annotators were asked not to consider external content (e.g., follow links in the tweets).

To provide further guidance, we devised a few questions that the assessors might consider in determining whether two tweets should be in the same cluster:

- If I had already seen the first tweet, would I have missed out on some information if I didn't see the second tweet?
- If two tweets are similar but the second contains an addition to or endorsement of the first, is the addition or endorsement important enough that I would be interested in seeing both tweets?
- Sometimes two tweets look similar but actually narrate the development of an event. Are the tweets different enough from each other that I would want to see both tweets to understand how an event develops or unfolds?

Since TTG was originally conceived as a stage following ad hoc retrieval, the track guidelines asked TTG participants to also submit ad hoc runs. For the evaluation, NIST assessors developed 55 topics and used a standard pooling methodology to generate tweet-level relevance judgments; see the track overview for more details [18]. Tweets in the pool were assigned one of three judgments: not relevant, relevant, and highly relevant. In the cluster annotation process, assessors at UMD and UIUC worked on the relevant and highly-relevant tweets from the NIST judgment pools. Due to resource constraints, NIST assessors were not able to perform the clustering, and thus a weakness of our setup is that the individual with the information need was not the one who created the clusters. The two assessors at UMD were graduate students in computer science (both male). The two assessors at UIUC were graduate students in library and information science (one male, one female). All were familiar with Twitter.

Assessors were first trained in the laboratory: the session included an introduction to the task and an overview of the annotation interface. After that, assessors were free to perform annotations at their own pace on their own machines, at any location of their choosing. This was possible because the annotation interface was implemented in JavaScript and hence accessible over the web. All assessors began with a throwaway "practice topic" (although they were not aware of the throwaway nature) and then proceeded to annotate topics in batches (roughly ten topics per batch). Topics were

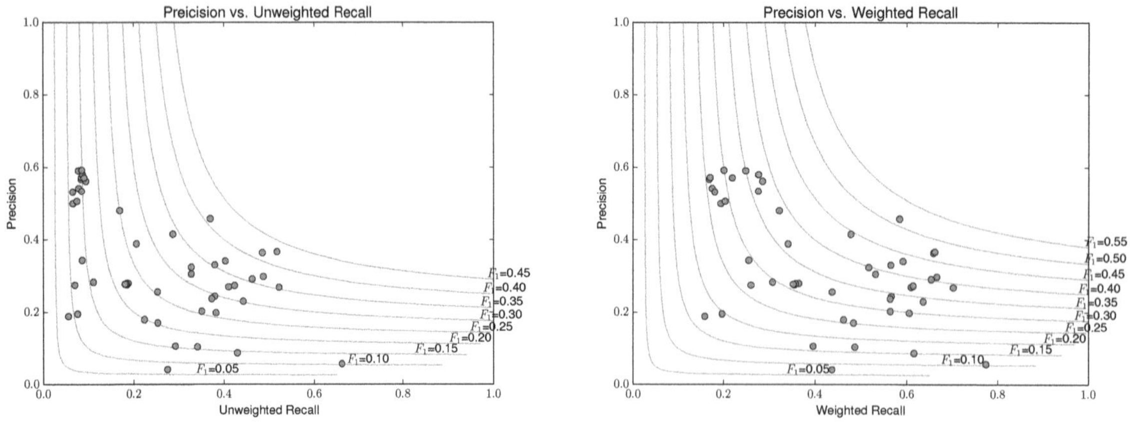

Figure 2: Scatter plots showing precision vs. unweighted recall (left) and precision vs. weighted recall (right) for all submitted runs in the TREC 2014 TTG task, overlaid with iso-F_1 contours.

grouped into batches of roughly equal size (in terms of the number of relevant tweets) prior to the beginning of the annotation process. When an assessor completed a batch, he or she could request another batch to work on.

Each site annotated the topic batches in the opposite order, and when a covering set for all topics had been obtained, we designated those clusters to be the "official" judgments. However, the annotation process continued until both sites had processed all topics, giving us alternate judgments. Thus, both the official and alternate clusters contained annotations generated from both sites.

3.3 Metrics and Results

The output of the human annotation process is an ordered list of tweet clusters. Within each cluster, the tweets are sorted by temporal order (earliest to latest). The clusters themselves are sorted by the temporal order of their earliest tweet. Following the heuristic of using the most straightforward metric when defining a new task (and then subsequently refining the metric as needed), we decided to measure cluster-based precision and recall. The measure is cluster-based in the sense that systems only receive credit for returning one tweet from each cluster—that is, once a tweet is retrieved, all other tweets in the cluster are automatically considered not relevant. From this, we can compute precision, recall, and F-score in the usual way (lacking any basis for setting the β parameter, we simply computed F_1). Since the user model assumes that the user will consume the entire summary, set-based metrics seemed appropriate.

The only additional refinement is that we computed both weighted and unweighted variants of recall. In weighted recall, each cluster is assigned a weight proportional to the sum of relevance grades from every tweet in the cluster (relevant tweets receive a weight of one and highly-relevant tweets receive a weight of two). This weighting scheme implements the heuristic that larger clusters and those containing more highly-relevant tweets are more important, and the denominator in the weighted recall computation is the sum of all cluster weights. In unweighted recall, all clusters are considered equally important, and the denominator is simply the total number of clusters.

Note that this setup gives equal credit to retrieving *any* tweet from a cluster. Intuitively, however, this seems overly simplistic—users would certainly prefer seeing certain tweets over others, even if they contain substantively similar information [15]. For example, users might prefer the earliest tweet, a tweet from the most "authoritative" user (e.g., a verified news account), or a tweet from someone close by in their network (e.g., a tweet from someone they follow). We currently do not have sufficient understanding to accurately model such preferences, and thus explicitly made the decision not to tackle this challenge.

The evaluation metrics for TTG represent straightforward extensions of previous work: aspect recall [21], sub-topic recall [34], and the "nugget pyramid" approach from the TREC question answering evaluations [17]. Alternative metrics we had considered include those based on gain [7, 5] and the extension of mean average precision to graded relevance judgments [24]. The challenge with gain-based approaches is the complex parameterization necessary to fully instantiate a particular model; we lacked the empirical data to properly develop such a model. The graded extension to mean average precision is elegant, but our underlying user model is better captured by set-based metrics.

In total, 13 groups submitted 50 runs to the tweet timeline generation task at TREC 2014. Recognizing that systems make different choices with respect to balancing precision and recall, it is illustrative to visualize the tradeoffs in a scatter plot. Figure 2 shows precision vs. unweighted recall (left) and precision vs. weighted recall (right) for all runs. Iso-F_1 contours are plotted in blue; points on the same contour line have the same F_1 score, but with different precision/recall tradeoffs. Note that the effectiveness of individual runs is not relevant for the purposes of our meta-analysis, so we refer readers to the track overview for additional details [18].

4. ASSESSOR DIFFERENCES

Our first research question revolves around assessor differences in the semantic clustering task for tweet timeline generation and their impact on evaluation stability. For the TREC 2014 evaluation, we devoted the necessary resources to generate two independent sets of reference clusters, which we refer to as the "official" and "alternate" judgments. Note that the official judgments were simply the ones obtained first and used to report evaluation results at TREC; there is no implication that they are somehow more "authoritative".

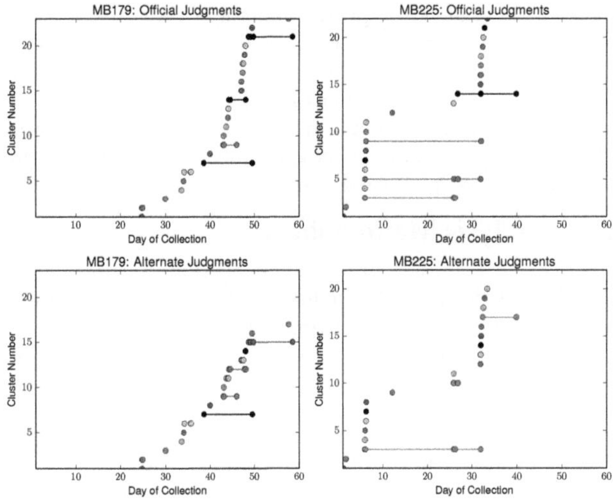

Figure 3: Visualization of the clusters for two topics.

4.1 Descriptive Characterization

We begin with a descriptive characterization of the semantic clusters generated by the assessors. In this and subsequent analyses, relevant and highly-relevant tweets are both considered "relevant". Each topic (55 in total) contains 194 relevant tweets on average: the official judgments averaged 89 clusters per topic, while the alternate judgments averaged 73 clusters per topic. These differences suggest that humans perform the semantic clustering task at different levels of granularity.

In Figure 3 we attempt to visualize these differences. In each plot, a point represents a tweet, and its x-axis position denotes the time when it was posted. Tweets that were assigned to the same cluster are at the same y-axis position and connected by horizontal lines. Thus, each horizontal "level" represents a semantic cluster, ordered by the first tweet; each cluster is assigned a different color for clarity. On the left, we show topic 179 "care of Iditarod dogs" and on the right, we show topic 225 "Barbara Walters, chicken pox". The top row shows the official judgments and the bottom row shows the alternate judgments. These topics were selected primarily for visual clarity: enough relevant tweets to show interesting clusters, but not too many relevant tweets as to be overly cluttered. From these visualizations, it is apparent that there are substantial assessor differences in the formation of the clusters. For example, the alternate assessor created fewer clusters for topic 179, and in topic 225, the alternate assessor did not seem to agree with two early clusters found by the official assessor.

To quantitatively characterize the differences between the official and alternate clusters, we computed the Adjusted Rand Index [23], which is a measure of similarity between two clusterings that is corrected for chance groupings (ranging from -1 to $+1$.). This metric has two other desirable properties: first, it is symmetric, which is appropriate since the official judgments aren't any more "correct" than the alternate judgments; second, it ignores permutations in that the similarity values don't depend on the "cluster labels" (which, in our case, are just arbitrary numeric identifiers). We computed the Adjusted Rand Index on a per topic basis ($N = 55$) between the official and alternate judgments and obtained a mean of 0.445, a median of 0.492, and a standard deviation of 0.225. As a point of reference, for topic 179 (left, Figure 3), the Adjusted Rand Index is 0.687, and for topic 225 (right, Figure 3), the Adjusted Rand Index is 0.305. We observe that the topics exhibit a wide range of similarity values, ranging from a minimum of 0.007 to a maximum of 0.977, which suggests that agreement is to a large extent dependent on the nature of the information need. However, it would be fair to say that there is substantial disagreement between assessors overall.

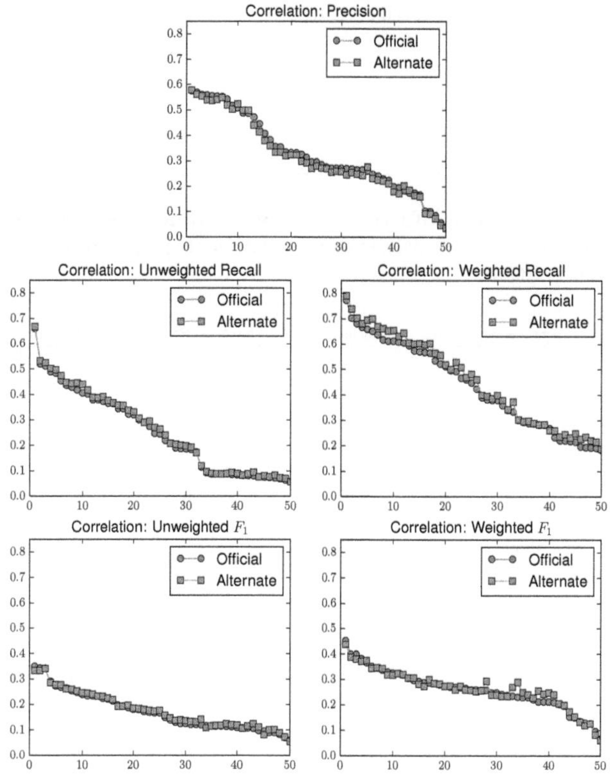

Figure 4: Comparison between scores based on the official judgments and the alternate judgments for various metrics. Runs are sorted by score based on the official judgments in descending order.

4.2 Stability Analysis

With the two independent sets of judgments, we can conduct a stability analysis of the evaluation to determine the extent to which assessor differences impact our ability to make system comparisons, i.e., that system X is more effective than system Y. An evaluation is considered stable if system rankings and pairwise system comparisons are insensitive to assessor differences. Here, we follow the well-established methodology of Voorhees [31], who examined assessor differences in document-level relevance judgments for ad hoc retrieval.

Figure 4 shows scores for all runs based on the official judgments and the alternate judgments for each of the five metrics. Results are sorted by scores based on the official judgments. We see that the rankings produced by both sets of judgments are highly correlated, with the exception of a few cases in weighted F_1. Furthermore, the absolute values of the metrics are also quite similar (particularly the unweighted metrics).

Metric	Rank Swaps	Kendall's τ
precision	30	0.951
unweighted recall	27	0.956
weighted recall	22	0.964
unweighted F_1	46	0.925
weighted F_1	90	0.853

Table 1: Count of rank swaps and Kendall's τ correlation based the official and alternate judgments for each metric.

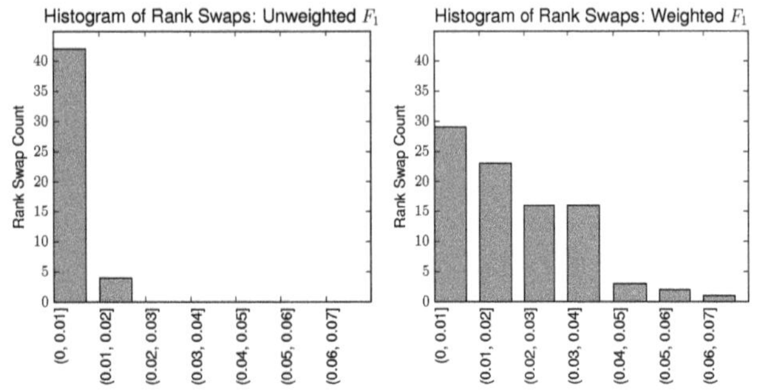

Figure 5: Histogram of rank swaps for unweighted F_1 and weighted F_1, binned by score differences.

In Table 1, we show the Kendall's τ correlation between rankings induced by the two different sets of judgments. These values are in the same range as those reported by Voorhees [31] for ad hoc retrieval, which is generally regarded by the IR community to be stable with respect to assessor differences in document-level relevance judgments. Table 1 also shows the number of rank swaps for each metric. A rank swap is a pairwise comparison where, according to one set of judgments, run A scores higher than run B, but according to the other set of judgments, run B scores higher than run A. There are a total of $(50 \times 49)/2 = 1225$ pairwise comparisons, so the numbers of rank swaps observed in Table 1 are quite small.

A tally of the rank swaps does not tell the complete story because rank swaps do not capture the magnitude of the score differences. In particular, we are less concerned with rank swaps in which the absolute score differences between the two conditions are small. Histograms of the rank swaps for unweighted F_1 and weighted F_1 binned by absolute score differences are shown in Figure 5. We see that, indeed, most of the rank swaps are small. For space considerations, we only show the histograms for these two metrics, which have the lowest Kendall's τ correlations. The histograms for the other metrics show even larger fractions of rank swaps where the score differences are small.

The conclusion from these analyses is fairly clear: assessor differences do not appear to impact the stability of the evaluation, at least in terms of the metrics we have examined. Although our findings are limited to tweet timeline generation, there is no reason to believe that these results would not carry over to other types of evaluations built around the notion of semantic clustering.

5. USER PREFERENCES

The second major research question we tackle in this paper concerns user preferences: when comparing TTG systems, do our metrics capture differences that are actually meaningful to users? Following previous work, we operationalize the notion of "meaningful" in terms of user preferences [2, 25]. If the evaluation tells us that system X is better than system Y, and a human can actually detect this difference (better than chance), we might reasonably claim that the improvement is meaningful from a user perspective.

5.1 Analysis Methodology

Unlike most studies discussed in Section 2, which focus on ad hoc retrieval (and variants), our analyses have a more complex setup because tweet timelines are variable in length. We are specifically interested in three distinct types of effectiveness differences:

- For two systems that exhibit roughly the same recall, how sensitive are users to differences in precision?
- For two systems that exhibit roughly the same precision, how sensitive are users to differences in recall?
- For two systems that exhibit similar precision-recall tradeoffs, how sensitive are users to differences in F_1?

Our general strategy was to sample system output from the submitted TREC 2014 TTG runs and to generate system comparisons on a per-topic basis for user preference assessment. Unlike some previous work that artificially manipulated system output to generate results of a particular level of effectiveness (e.g., [4, 30]), our procedure yields more realistic comparisons.

The sampling process proceeded as follows: First, we selected a set of 30 topics, biased toward "typical" topics that have neither too many nor too few relevant tweets. Let $x_i = r_i - \bar{r}$ be the difference between r_i, the number of relevant tweets for topic i, and $\bar{r}$, the median number of relevant tweets over all topics: the probability of "drawing" topic i is proportional to the density at x_i of a normal distribution with $\mu = 0$ and $\sigma = 20$ (chosen heuristically).

Next, we performed some filtering of the submitted runs: we discarded all runs that contained unjudged tweets to eliminate the effects of missing relevance judgments. We also discarded all runs longer than 41 tweets, which is the median length of submitted runs (after the first filter). A pilot study indicated that long runs are very difficult to judge, and this is roughly the point after which the judgments become too onerous to make.

After filtering, we randomly (i.e., uniformly) selected 20 "base" runs, and for each, sampled up to 20 different "comparison" runs per metric based on the following criteria:

- For what we call *precision sampling*, we selected runs that differed by less than 0.1 in recall, but more than 0.1 in precision. Previous work suggests that users have a hard time distinguishing small differences in effectiveness metrics, so we did not want to waste assessor effort.
- For what we call *recall sampling*, we selected runs that differed by less than 0.1 in precision, but more than 0.1 in recall. This is the opposite of precision sampling.
- For what we call F_1 *sampling*, we want the two comparison runs to make approximately the same tradeoff in terms of precision and recall. We selected runs where the value of $T = |P - R|$ for the base run is within 0.1 of the T for the comparison run, as long as the difference in *either* precision or recall between the two runs exceeds 0.1.

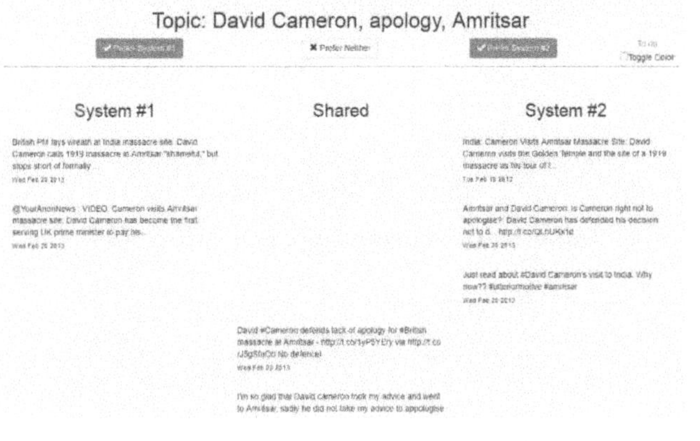

Figure 6: A screenshot of the web-based assessment interface for eliciting preference judgments. System outputs are presented in the left and right columns, with shared content in the middle column.

Note that all sampling was performed on the cluster-based TTG metrics, i.e., taking into account redundancy. We used the unweighted variants of the metrics for simplicity. Finally, we discarded all pairs where the two sampled runs differ in length by more than 20 tweets. Based on the pilot study, we found that assessors struggled to compare runs that differed significantly in length.

Each trial of the above sampling procedure yields a large number of comparisons, from which we further sampled 180 pairs comprised of roughly an equal number of pairs from precision, recall, and F_1 sampling. This represents a single batch that we gave to assessors to judge; assessors could request additional batches if they desired after completing a batch. The first batch for each assessor contained a shared set of 30 comparisons (i.e., all assessors judged the same pairs), but for the remaining pairs in the first batch (and all subsequent batches), each assessor worked on unique pairs, which we ensured in the batch preparation process.

For eliciting user preference judgments, we designed a web-based assessment interface (see screenshot in Figure 6). The comparison screen displays the sampled TTG outputs for a given topic side by side: System #1 on the left and System #2 on the right. Sampled pairs were mapped to the two positions randomly to avoid introducing any systematic biases. The topic is shown at the top. The output of each system is ordered chronologically, and each tweet is displayed with its timestamp. To help the assessor compare the two timelines, tweets returned by both systems are displayed in the middle "Shared" column. This means that an output might have gaps, indicating that one system returned more tweets than the other prior to the shared tweets (as is the case in Figure 6). We converged on this design after trying various display alternatives in a pilot study—we learned that assessors wanted an easy way to compare the two systems in terms of the tweets they *both* returned, so we designed the interface to facilitate this comparison.

In the assessment instructions, we asked the assessors which of the two system outputs they thought was better. They were reminded to evaluate system outputs as timelines, rather than as ranked lists. To be consistent with the clustering task, assessors were told to evaluate tweets based solely on their contents, ignoring any links they may contain. The assessor could click "Prefer System #1" or "Prefer System #2" above each of the two conditions, to indicate a preference, or a button labeled "Prefer Neither" in the middle if the assessor could not decide.

We avoided prescriptively dictating what it meant for a timeline to be "good". Specifically, the instructions made no reference to precision, recall, or redundancy. This is an important feature in our evaluation design to mitigate the effects of demand characteristics.[3] However, we tried to help the assessors frame their task with a few neutral reminders:

- We are asking you about relative quality. Even if you feel that both systems do a bad job, do your best to determine which does a better job.
- The tweets are presented in chronological order (earliest first), so you should keep in mind the timeframe covered by each result.
- The timelines are displayed with a "shared" column in the middle. This column contains all tweets that were returned by both systems, and should help you more quickly determine how similar the results are. Since the timelines are aligned by their shared tweets, this middle column will also help you compare the results according to chronological blocks.

Assessors were first trained in the laboratory. They were given an introduction to the task and an explanation of the web interface, which included time spent with practice topics that were discarded for analysis. After this training session, the assessors could proceed at their own pace anywhere they had an internet connection. The server that hosted the web assessment interface recorded all interactions: both the preference judgments and their timestamps.

Evaluation proceeded concurrently at UMD and UIUC. Judgments at UMD were performed by two male computer science graduate students. One of these assessors completed two batches of comparisons, while the other completed one. The assessors at UIUC were two graduate students in library and information science (one male, one female) and one former library and information science graduate student (male) who was working nearby. One of the assessors completed two batches, while the remaining assessors completed one each. These assessors were not the same as the annotators who created the clusters (at both sites).

5.2 Results

After the assessments were completed, the user preferences were correlated against the preferences implied by the sampled metric, using Cohen's κ as the agreement metric. Cohen's κ ranges from -1 to $+1$, where 0 indicates that any agreement is attributable to chance. To compute κ, we first discarded "prefer neither" judgments. In the precision sampling case, we correlated the human preferences against the implied preference based on the precision scores. In the recall sampling case, we correlated the human preferences against the implied preference based on both unweighted recall and weighted recall. In the F_1 sampling case, we correlated the human preferences against the implied preference based on unweighted F_1 and weighted F_1.

Figure 7 shows these correlations binned by differences in the sampled metric, aggregated across all assessors. The

[3]An experimental artifact where participants form an interpretation of the experiment's purpose and unconsciously change their behavior to fit that interpretation.

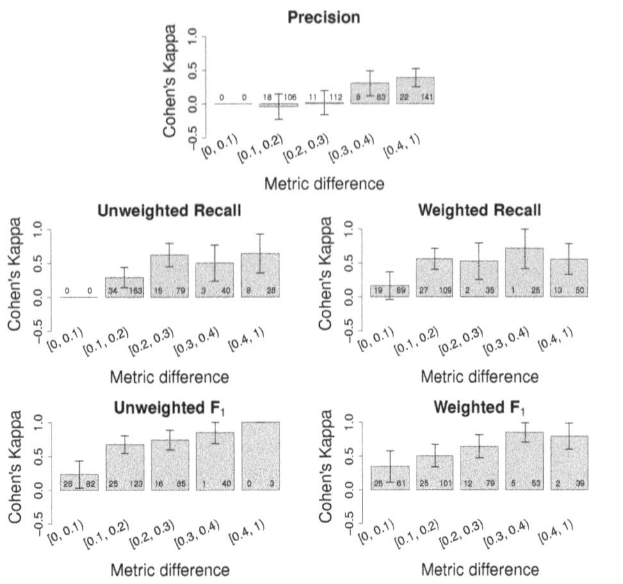

Figure 7: Cohen's κ for each metric binned by differences in the sampled metric. Error bars show 95% confidence intervals. The numbers in the bottom left of each bar show the number of "prefer neither" while those in the bottom right show the number of preference judgments in that condition.

κ	Strength of Agreement
<0.00	Poor
0.00-0.20	Slight
0.21-0.40	Fair
0.41-0.60	Moderate
0.61-0.80	Substantial
0.81-1.00	Almost perfect

Table 2: Interpretations of κ from [16].

Metric	F-value	p-value
precision	$F(3, 16) = 3.397$	0.0437
unweighted recall	$F(3, 16) = 1.749$	0.1970
weighted recall	$F(4, 20) = 1.475$	0.2470
unweighted F_1	$F(3, 16) = 5.093$	0.0115
weighted F_1	$F(4, 20) = 1.322$	0.2960

Table 3: ANOVA results for each metric. Metrics displayed in bold show a statistically significant difference ($p < 0.05$) in mean κ across bins.

error bars show the 95% confidence intervals, computed following Fleiss et al. [11]. The numbers in the bottom of each bar show the number of "prefer neither" (on the left) and the number of preference judgments, i.e., users preferred one system over the other (on the right). Note that by the design of the sampling procedure, no comparisons fell into the $[0, 0.1)$ bucket for precision and unweighted recall, although some samples did fall into that bucket for the other metrics.

In Figure 8, we show agreement broken down by each individual assessor in a "small multiples" visualization scheme. Each row shows a particular metric, and each column shows the agreement for an individual assessor for that metric. For clarity, the bar charts are shown without labels, but they are organized in exactly the same manner as in Figure 7. Note that confidence intervals here are much larger because fewer samples fall into each bin.

In both Figures 7 and 8, the bars are arranged by putative difficulty of the preference judgments, from left to right. Since there were generally fewer samples in which the metric differed by more than 0.4, all difference greater than 0.4 were placed in the same bin. The leftmost bar represents those runs where the metric difference is less than 0.1, for which we would expect humans to have the most difficulty distinguishing differences in output quality. Similarly, the rightmost bar should represent the "easiest" comparisons, in that the metric differences are the largest. We can intuitively think of these charts as quantifying how "sensitive" users are to differences in the underlying system-oriented metrics. Put another way, they tell us how much "better" or "worse" a system would have to be in order for users to notice.

Overall, we do see a general trend of the agreement increasing from left to right, both at the aggregate and at the individual level. At the aggregate level, we see that there tend to be more "prefer neither" judgments in cases where the metric difference is small, which makes sense. However, there are clearly individual differences that buck the overall trend, as shown in Figure 8. For example, assessor 4 (fourth column from the left) does not appear to be sensitive to precision at all—agreement remains near and sometimes worse than chance, even for very large differences in precision.

One of the downsides of κ is that it lacks an intuitive interpretation. To address this, Landis and Koch [16] proposed a guide, which we replicate in Table 2. Under this rubric, the minimum κ values we observe per metric range from "poor" (for precision) to "fair" (for weighted F_1), whereas the maximum κ values we observe for each metric range from "fair" (for precision) to "almost perfect" (for unweighted and weighted F_1). The differences between maximum and minimum κ values per metric support the apparent relationship between metric differences and annotator preferences.

It is worth emphasizing here that all our metrics already take into account redundancy (i.e., they are cluster-based). Since we *did not* explicitly ask the assessors to consider redundancy in the assessment instructions, these results show that humans are nevertheless sensitive to the redundancy removal performed by the systems.

To add statistical rigor to our analyses about the relationship between agreement and metric differences, we performed analysis of variance (ANOVA) comparing the κ values across bins. That is, we treat the κ of each individual assessor for a particular bin as a point estimate of the "true" κ for that bin (magnitude of metric difference), and want to know if the mean κ values across the bins are significantly different. The results are shown in Table 3. We found statistically significant differences in mean κ across bins for precision and unweighted F_1 at $p < 0.05$. From this, we can conclude that increases in metric differences are associated with better agreement for those metrics.

A surprising result is the lack of statistical significance for both unweighted and weighted recall. What does this mean? The recall bar charts in Figure 7 show that differences in recall between pairs of runs *are* detectable by annotators; however, the *magnitude* of the difference does not appear to affect the agreement, i.e., the κ values are not significantly different across the bins. We believe that this is due to the nature of evaluating recall, which requires knowledge of the

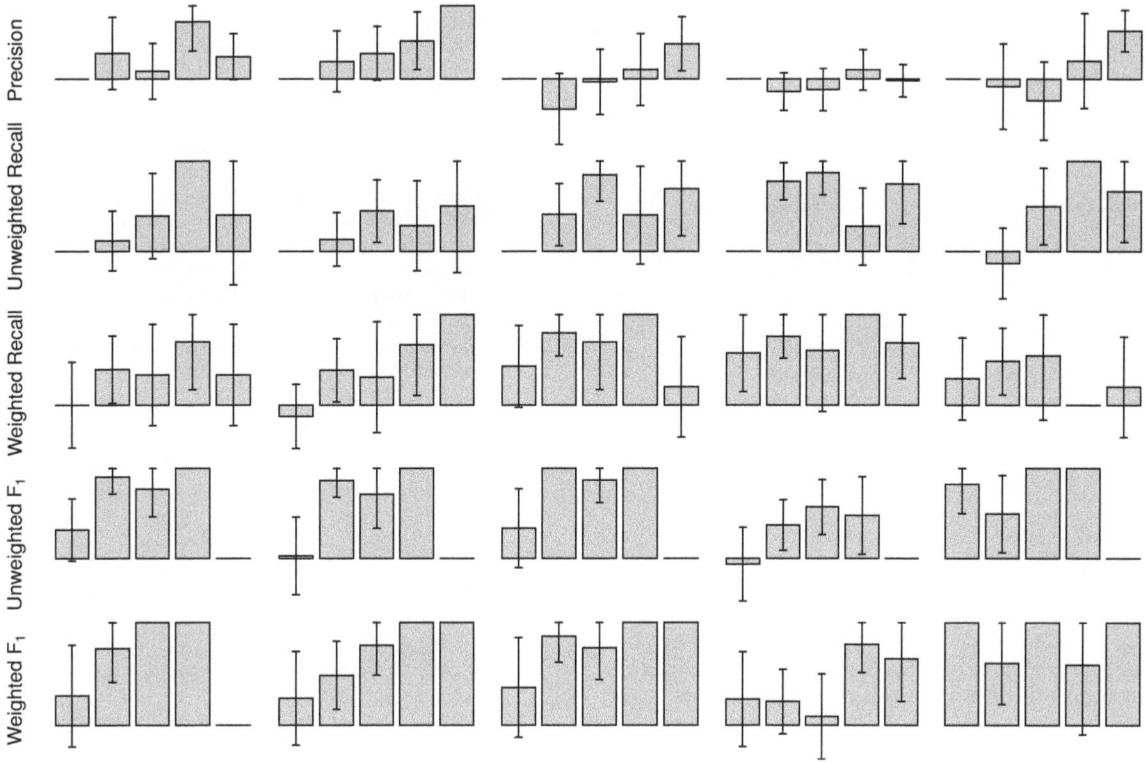

Figure 8: Cohen's κ for each metric (row), for each individual assessor (column) arranged in "small multiples". Each bar chart is organized in the same manner as those in Figure 7.

complete relevance judgments. When comparing two runs, it is relatively easy to detect recall differences (i.e., if one system returned a relevant tweet that was absent from the other system), but without access to all the relevance judgments, it is difficult to tell *how much* better one is than the other (i.e., the marginal recall increase from returning one more relevant tweet is dependent on the number of relevant tweets for that topic). Note that in contrast, for precision, annotators *do* appear capable of detecting the magnitude of the difference. This is again unsurprising since precision can be assessed directly from the displayed tweets.

We were surprised at the high p-value for weighted F_1, particularly in comparison to unweighted F_1. This result indicates that although assessors consistently achieved better than chance agreement, they either had difficulty assessing the importance of individual tweets or our weighting scheme does not accurately capture users' notion of importance. The second possibility points to future work in developing more meaningful metrics for modeling importance.

Figure 7 shows another surprising result: we observe relatively low agreement for precision (compared to the other metrics). We believe that this may be an artifact of our sampling strategy, where we discarded overly verbose runs. This choice was made out of necessity, as our pilot study suggested that it was not feasible to ask assessors to compare timelines with, say, hundreds of tweets. The problem is this: while it is certainly possible to obtain low precision in a short timeline, the amount of "pain" associated with such low precision timelines is relatively low (bounded by the total number of returned tweets). However, if a timeline were an order of magnitude longer, say, the burden imposed by poor precision would be much heavier. In other words, our sampling procedure selected only those runs where differences in precision were "not a big deal" from the assessor's point of view because the timelines were relatively short.

We also analyzed the relationship between the time assessors spent on each comparison (reconstructed from our logs) and the observed agreement. This is shown in Figure 9, binned in intervals of 30 seconds for each metric. The numbers at the top of each bar show the number of "prefer neither" and preference judgments. "Prefer neither" judgments were not included in the agreement calculation. Missing bars indicate an undefined κ while dashes indicate a κ of zero. We see no clear relationship between κ and the amount of time it takes to make a judgment; this is somewhat surprising as we would have expected "easy judgments" to result in higher agreement.

Finally, we analyzed agreement on the set of 30 shared comparisons provided to each of the five annotators at the beginning of the first batch. We calculated Fleiss' κ [10], a variant of Cohen's κ intended for more than two raters, and found a value of 0.294 for this shared set. Under Landis and Koch's scheme, this represents only a fair level of agreement among annotators. This finding is noteworthy because it indicates that user preferences correlate with metric differences, *despite* the fact that humans only achieve "fair" agreement among themselves.

Summarizing these results, our user study suggests that user preferences do agree with system preferences as measured by the TTG metrics—that users are sensitive to differences in precision, recall, and F_1, although to different degrees. We can therefore conclude that system-oriented metrics are meaningful in being able to capture aspects of what users care about in timeline summaries.

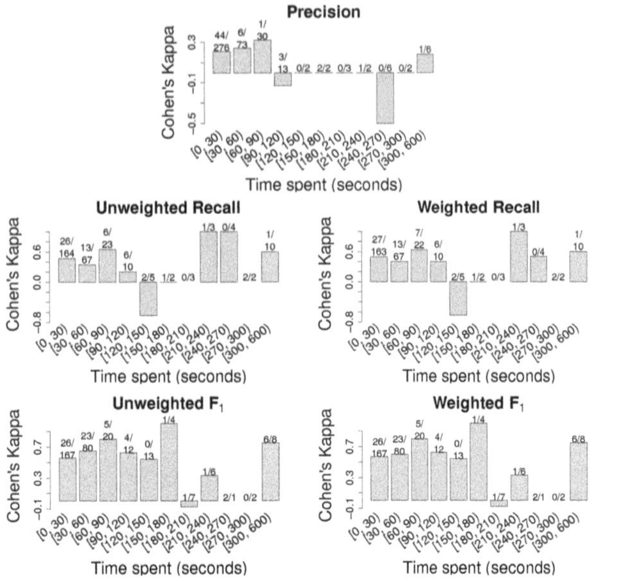

Figure 9: Cohen's κ binned by time spent on each comparison (at 30 second intervals). Numbers at the top of each bar show the number of "prefer neither" and preference judgments. Missing bars indicate an undefined κ while dashes indicate a κ of zero.

6. CONCLUSIONS

As primarily an empirical discipline, progress in information retrieval is built on system comparisons. This paper explores assessor differences and user preferences in the context of the tweet timeline generation task in the TREC 2014 Microblog track. Analyses show that the evaluation methodology appears to be sound, which strengthens our confidence in existing and future results. Although our findings are limited to this particular task, we believe that lessons learned could generalize to other "cluster-based" evaluations, informing related tasks such as question answering and temporal summarization.

7. ACKNOWLEDGMENTS

This work was supported in part by the National Science Foundation under IIS-1217279 and IIS-1218043. Any opinions, findings, conclusions, or recommendations expressed are those of the authors and do not necessarily reflect the views of the sponsor. We are grateful to Ellen Voorhees and the assessors at NIST for making TREC possible.

8. REFERENCES

[1] R. Agrawal, S. Gollapudi, A. Halverson, and S. Ieong. Diversifying search results. *WSDM*, 2009.

[2] A. Al-Maskari, M. Sanderson, P. Clough, and E. Airio. The good and the bad system: Does the test collection predict users' effectiveness? *SIGIR*, 2008.

[3] J. Allan. *Topic Detection and Tracking: Event-Based Information Organization.* Kluwer, 2002.

[4] J. Allan, B. Carterette, and J. Lewis. When will information retrieval be "good enough"? User effectiveness as a function of retrieval accuracy. *SIGIR*, 2005.

[5] J. Aslam, M. Ekstrand-Abueg, V. Pavlu, R. McCreadie, F. Diaz, and T. Sakai. TREC 2014 temporal summarization track overview. *TREC*, 2014.

[6] P. Bailey, N. Craswell, I. Soboroff, P. Thomas, A. de Vries, and E. Yilmaz. Relevance assessment: Are judges exchangeable and does it matter? *SIGIR*, 2008.

[7] C. Clarke, M. Kolla, G. Cormack, O. Vechtomova, A. Ashkan, S. Büttcher, and I. MacKinnon. Novelty and diversity in information retrieval evaluation. *SIGIR*, 2008.

[8] H. Dang and J. Lin. Different structures for evaluating answers to complex questions: Pyramids won't topple, and neither will human assessors. *ACL*, 2007.

[9] H. Dang, J. Lin, and D. Kelly. Overview of the TREC 2006 question answering track. *TREC*, 2006.

[10] J. Fleiss. Measuring nominal scale agreement among many raters. *Psychological Bulletin*, 76(5):378–382, 1971.

[11] J. Fleiss, J. Cohen, and B. Everitt. Large sample standard errors of kappa and weighted kappa. *Psychological Bulletin*, 72(5):323–327, 1969.

[12] Q. Guo, F. Diaz, and E. Yom-Tov. Updating users about time critical events. *ECIR*, 2013.

[13] W. Hersh, A. Turpin, S. Price, B. Chan, D. Kramer, L. Sacherek, and D. Olson. Do batch and user evaluations give the same results? *SIGIR*, 2000.

[14] S. Huffman and M. Hochster. How well does result relevance predict session satisfaction? *SIGIR*, 2007.

[15] J. Hurlock and M. Wilson. Searching Twitter: Separating the tweet from the chaff. *ICWSM*, 2011.

[16] J. Landis and G. Koch. The measurement of observer agreement for categorical data. *Biometrics*, 33(1):159–174, 1977.

[17] J. Lin and D. Demner-Fushman. Will pyramids built of nuggets topple over? *NAACL*, 2006.

[18] J. Lin, M. Efron, Y. Wang, and G. Sherman. Overview of the TREC-2014 Microblog track. *TREC*, 2004.

[19] J. Lin and M. Smucker. How do users find things with PubMed? Towards automatic utility evaluation with user simulations. *SIGIR*, 2008.

[20] J. Lin and P. Zhang. Deconstructing nuggets: The stability and reliability of complex question answering evaluation. *SIGIR*, 2007.

[21] P. Over. TREC-6 interactive report. *TREC*, 1997.

[22] V. Pavlu, S. Rajput, P. Golbus, and J. Aslam. IR system evaluation using nugget-based test collections. *WSDM*, 2012.

[23] W. Rand. Objective criteria for the evaluation of clustering methods. *JASA*, 66(336):846–850, 1971.

[24] S. Robertson, E. Kanoulas, and E. Yilmaz. Extending average precision to graded relevance judgments. *SIGIR*, 2010.

[25] M. Sanderson, M. Paramita, P. Clough, and E. Kanoulas. Do user preferences and evaluation measures line up? *SIGIR*, 2010.

[26] C. Smith and P. Kantor. User adaptation: Good results from poor systems. *SIGIR*, 2008.

[27] M. Smucker and C. Jethani. Human performance and retrieval precision revisited. *SIGIR*, 2010.

[28] K. Tao, C. Hauff, and G.-J. Houben. Building a microblog corpus for search result diversification. *AIRS*, 2013.

[29] A. Turpin and W. R. Hersh. Why batch and user evaluations do not give the same results. *SIGIR*, 2001.

[30] A. Turpin and F. Scholer. User performance versus precision measures for simple search tasks. *SIGIR*, 2006.

[31] E. Voorhees. Variations in relevance judgments and the measurement of retrieval effectiveness. *SIGIR*, 1998.

[32] E. Voorhees. Overview of the TREC 2004 question answering track. *TREC*, 2004.

[33] C. Wayne. Multilingual topic detection and tracking: Successful research enabled by corpora and evaluation. *LREC*, 2000.

[34] C. Zhai, W. Cohen, and J. Lafferty. Beyond independent relevance: Methods and evaluation metrics for subtopic retrieval. *SIGIR*, 2003.

User Variability and IR System Evaluation

Peter Bailey
Microsoft,
Australia
pbailey@microsoft.com

Alistair Moffat
The University of Melbourne,
Australia
ammoffat@unimelb.edu.au

Falk Scholer
RMIT University,
Australia
falk.scholer@rmit.edu.au

Paul Thomas
CSIRO,
Australia
paul.thomas@csiro.au

ABSTRACT

Test collection design eliminates sources of user variability to make statistical comparisons among information retrieval (IR) systems more affordable. Does this choice unnecessarily limit generalizability of the outcomes to real usage scenarios? We explore two aspects of user variability with regard to evaluating the relative performance of IR systems, assessing effectiveness in the context of a subset of topics from three TREC collections, with the embodied information needs categorized against three levels of increasing task complexity. First, we explore the impact of widely differing queries that searchers construct for the same information need description. By executing those queries, we demonstrate that query formulation is critical to query effectiveness. The results also show that the range of scores characterizing effectiveness for a single system arising from these queries is comparable or greater than the range of scores arising from variation among systems using only a single query per topic. Second, our experiments reveal that searchers display substantial individual variation in the numbers of documents and queries they anticipate needing to issue, and there are underlying significant differences in these numbers in line with increasing task complexity levels. Our conclusion is that test collection design would be improved by the use of multiple query variations per topic, and could be further improved by the use of metrics which are sensitive to the expected numbers of useful documents.

Categories and Subject Descriptors

H.3.3 [**Information Storage and Retrieval**]: Information Search and Retrieval—*performance evaluation.*

Keywords

User behavior, test collections, relevance measures

1. INTRODUCTION AND BACKGROUND

In the Cranfield and TREC paradigm, information retrieval test collections (consisting of a corpus, topics, relevance judgments, and a relevance measure – collectively representing a sample of some population of a real-world information retrieval task) allow *comparative* system performance experiments to be carried out. This approach, sometimes referred to as *batch evaluation*, assesses the *system or algorithmic aspect* of relevance, as defined by Saracevic [26]. Almost all sources of variability are removed in this classical design of test collections, including users and tasks, leaving topics as the primary source of variability within the collection. The relevance measure encodes (either explicitly or implicitly) an abstracted model of user behavior, and rewards systems which deliver relevant material more efficiently or comprehensively according to the model. Statistical assessments of comparative effectiveness as determined by the relevance measure can be used to determine improvements in algorithm design. Statistical power analysis calculations can be used to determine the number of topics needed to quantify the probabilities of making type I and type II errors.

An important aspect of test collection use that has perhaps been under-investigated is the degree to which they have *external validity*. Crudely put, external validity characterizes the extent to which an experiment (typically relative system effectiveness according to the relevance measure in the case of test collections) generalizes to other real world circumstances. Such circumstances might encompass use by different users (stay-at-home parents vs retired intelligence analysts) or over different document sets (a subset of the Web vs a collection of news articles) or for different interaction tasks (factoid question answering vs ad hoc topical information discovery). We propose some potential properties of a test collection that relate to the degree to which they have external validity. These include: *fidelity* – whether the relative effectiveness of systems is consistent when a population of users/topics/documents/task (of which the test collection is a sample) uses the systems; *corpus-generalizability* – whether outcomes from this test collection are consistent across other test collections modeling the same task, as investigated by Robertson and Kanoulas [24]; *task-generalizability* – whether outcomes from this test collection are consistent across other test collections with different tasks (i.e., generalizability across situations); and *user-generalizability* – whether outcomes are consistent in the presence of different user behaviors for the same task and topics (i.e., generalizability across people). We provide brief definitions for some other key concepts in Figure 1.

In this work, we are motivated to improve the *user-generalizability* property of test collections. In particular, we seek to understand how introducing some simple sources of variability in users, namely individual query formulation and expectations of the quantities of relevant information needing to be found, might affect how test collections are constructed, and how batch evaluations are carried

SIGIR '15, August 09–13, 2015, Santiago, Chile

ACM 978-1-4503-3621-5/15/08 ... $15.00.
http://dx.doi.org/10.1145/2766462.2767728.

Task	An information seeking activity.
Topic	A description of information content or subject matter required for some task.
Task complexity	A categorized model of cognitive information processing for some task.
T	Expected number of useful documents required to satisfy a task for some topic.
Q	Expected number of queries required to satisfy a task for some topic.
Q02, R03, T04	Our subsets of the topics and judgments from TREC test collections corresponding to Question Answering 2002, Robust 2003, Terabyte 2004 tracks.
AP, ERR, NDCG, RBP p, Qβ	Various relevance measures: Average Precision, Expected Reciprocal Rank, Normalized Discounted Cumulative Gain, Rank-Biased Precision, and the Q-Measure.

Figure 1: Definitions of significant terms and abbreviations used.

out. We use the lens of *task complexity* (discussed below) to help assess these issues across a range of information seeking scenarios.

To examine *user-generalizability* in a batch evaluation setting, we pose a series of research questions assessed in the sections below.

RQ1 Does the existence of individual variation in initial query formulation for a single information need alter the evaluation of system performance? (Section 4)

RQ2 Is there significant variation among users of the anticipated effort in terms of the number of documents viewed and queries to be issued, and is there a relationship between a user's anticipated effort and the information task complexity? (Section 5)

RQ3 Does incorporating anticipated effort within adaptive metrics lead to changes in relative system performance assessments? (Section 6)

The overarching issue we consider is: to what extent do measures of system effectiveness depend on (lack of) variation in user behavior and thus do test collections have insufficient *user-generalizability*?

We are not the first to consider this issue. In a 1977 report on the design for an ideal test collection, Spärck Jones and Bates [29] recommend that:

> *The effects on the retrieval of relevant documents of such variations over requests should be counteracted by the use of additional queries specifically designed to exhaust the relevant document set.*

The 1999 TREC Query Track examined sets of queries for topics, and the coordinators Buckley and Walz [8] similarly conclude that:

> *We've reaffirmed the tremendous variation that sometimes gets hidden underneath the averages of a typical IR experiment. Topics are extremely variable; queries dealing with the same topic are extremely variable...; and systems were only somewhat variable.*

In a comprehensive study examining different types and sets of judges as the source of user variability, Voorhees [32] found that the TREC-4 and TREC-6 collections were reasonably stable in relative outcomes for participating systems, both for similar users' judgments and different users' judgments. She also observed that inter-system comparisons required more substantial differences in measure scores than for intra-system comparisons. More recently, Bailey et al. [4] examined consequences of using relevance labels originating from judges of differing task and topic expertise. They found that variation in expertise levels led to consistent differences in relevance outcomes and also to questions about the robustness of relative system performance measures over the TREC Enterprise 2007 test collection. Kazai et al. [16] confirmed that such systematic bias between different kinds of judge may exist.

The project described here encompasses exploration of just two (among many) aspects of user variability, thereby to connect user experiences more closely with batch evaluation outcomes.

2. RELATED WORK

Task complexity In information science, the complexity of a search task has long been recognized as having an important impact on information seeking behavior and use, including for example the type and complexity of information needed, and the number and diversity of sources consulted [31].

Byström and Järvelin [9] proposed a five-level task complexity taxonomy, ranging from automatic information processing tasks (tasks that are completely determinable so that they could in theory be automated) to genuine decision tasks (unexpected, unstructured tasks). This taxonomy was refined into three levels by Bell and Ruthven [7], with the distinction between levels being based primarily on the initial determinability and clarity of the task.

Focusing more directly on task complexity in the context of interactive information retrieval, Wu et al. [35] proposed a hierarchy based on the Cognitive Process Dimension of Krathwohl's Taxonomy of Learning Objectives [17], which is itself a refinement of Bloom's Taxonomy of educational objectives. Through a user study, Wu et al. demonstrated a tendency for participants to spend more time, issue a greater number of queries, and click on more search results for tasks with greater cognitive complexity. We use three levels of this taxonomy for our experiments, explained below.

Factors that influence searcher behavior Wu et al. [36] investigated the relationship between information scent (signals of relevance on a search results page) and search behavior such as query reformulation, search depth and stopping, demonstrating that a higher density of relevant items on the first page increases the probability of query reformulation, and decreases that of pagination.

The relationship between constraints and searcher behavior was studied by Fujikawa et al. [13], who showed that when the number of queries that a searcher can enter is restricted, greater attention is given to query formulation and more time is invested in viewing search results pages. Similar effects were observed when constraints were placed on the number of documents that can be viewed.

Azzopardi et al. [3] studied the effect of query cost on the behavior of searchers, examining the influence of different interfaces, designed to require differing amounts of effort. Users of the "structured" (highest cost) interface displayed different behavior, submitting fewer queries and spending longer when examining search result pages. A strong relationship between searcher behavior and task type and structure was also reported by Toms et al. [30], with users showing different rates of query reformulation and page views.

In a focused study, White and Kelly [34] varied the threshold acquired from individual document examination times as an input to an implicit relevance feedback algorithm, across a number of individuals and search tasks. They found that there was substantial variation in individual examination times, and that it was possible to improve relevance performance by using task information to determine the threshold. Attempts to tailor the threshold on a per-individual basis led to degraded performance however, suggesting intra-task-consistency was higher than intra-individual-consistency.

Gwizdka and Spence [14] examined observable measures of information seeking activities (such as documents viewed, time spent etc.) of a set of psychology students within a laboratory setting. They characterized relationships between the objective operationalized task complexity (in a manner influenced by [7]) and subjective searcher assessments of task difficulty with respect to these observable measures, and analyzed which measures were more important in predicting the difficulty experienced by the searcher. They found that task complexity affected both the relative importance of these predictors and the subjective assessment of difficulty. They also observed that individual variation (in factors like experience, verbal ability, other cognitive abilities etc.) played an important part in affecting performance and relative assessment of difficulty. We use individual variation in query formulation and expected goals of search to examine how batch evaluation outcomes change, and use task complexity as an analysis factor.

Query variability Searchers use an IR system to resolve an information need. To do so they need to translate their internal information requirement into an explicit query that is submitted to the search system. Multiple queries can represent a single information need, and indeed a single user may issue multiple queries within a single search session. Finally, interactive query (re-)formulation systems are increasingly common and have been demonstrated to assist in improving retrieval performance by (among others) Kumaran and Allan [18]. In that work, the authors also demonstrate how programmatic query expansion or relaxation can lead to significant increases in performance, across a selection of TREC test collections.

The 1999 TREC Query Track [8] investigated the issue of query variability through the creation of 23 query "sets", alternative query statements corresponding to 50 TREC topics. Analysis confirmed previous research showing that differences between topics introduces substantial variability into IR experimental results, and further showed that the variability of queries dealing with the same topic also introduced significant variability, typically greater than differences between retrieval systems. However, Buckley and Walz note that formal conclusions cannot be drawn from the full data set, due to the presence of "blundered queries" and the presence of multiple versions of the same basic system [8]. Other investigations of query variability in the TREC setting were shown to improve query performance through data fusion [5, 6].

Modave et al. [20] carried out a study of the quality of health-related information related for people seeking information about weight-loss using Google. While measuring query variability was not a focus of the study, this effect was accounted for by generating a range of queries about the weight-loss topic, eliciting specific queries from 20 study participants as well as the Google auto-complete feature.

Evaluation metrics Batch evaluations rely on objective scoring of search response listings. Long-standing mechanisms include Reciprocal Rank (RR); Precision at depth *k*; and Average Precision (AP), the average of the precisions achieved at the depths in the ranking of the relevant documents. A wide range of further alternatives have been developed over the last decade, including Normalized Discounted Cumulative Gain (NDCG) [15]; Rank-Biased Precision (RBP) [22]; Expected Reciprocal Rank (ERR) [10]; and the Q-Measure [25]. Per-query scores from one or more of these metrics are then averaged in some way, and paired statistical tests applied in order to draw experimental conclusions.

Metrics are sensitive to system performance in different ways. Precision at 10 and RBP with parameters less than about $p = 0.8$ are "shallow" metrics, and hence better match the behavior of a typical web search user than do "deep" metrics such as AP, NDCG, and the Q-Measure. In terms of judgment effort, shallow metrics are also cheaper to evaluate than deep metrics. On the other hand, deep metrics tend to lead to a higher fraction of statistically significant system differences being identified (the discrimination ratio), and to be just as predictive of the behavior of shallow metrics as are the shallow metrics themselves [33]. Moffat [21] provides further commentary on ways effectiveness metrics can be categorized.

User goals and persistence Users vary in the way they process search response pages, and hence if a metric is to reflect the user's perception of their experience, should be sensitive to that variation. Moffat and Zobel [22] argued that a metric should match a *user model*, a description of the behavior of the presumed user; and parameterized their RBP metric with a persistence parameter p. Rather than quantifying persistence in terms of documents, Smucker and Clarke [28] used time as the primary persistence factor in the model, and make use of data from a user study to calibrate their gain calculations. Moffat et al. [23] note that users may have differing goals, even for the same query or same information need, and introduce the notion of an "expected goal of search", their parameter T, and use it to shape predictions about what happens when that user is viewing a page, thereby creating a more refined user model that in turn leads to further alternative effectiveness metrics. A user study provided evidence to support that hypothesis, bringing user and batch evaluations a step closer. We build on their work by examining how user variation in queries and expected goals can be combined. Next we describe our overall experimental framework.

3. EXPERIMENTAL FRAMEWORK

Search can be viewed as a process that starts with an information need, out of which a particular query is formulated by a user and submitted to a retrieval system. However, batch evaluations typically start with a single query per information need and regard the system as being the primary variable that impacts on effectiveness. Our experimental framework attempts to reintroduce two aspects of user variability into the batch evaluation process. We start by describing the process we adopted for formulating information need statements that could then be used to investigate user-generalizability.

Information needs To investigate user generalizability, several aspects of searcher behavior were studied through a crowd-sourced experiment. We first required a set of labeled search tasks for the experimental participants to carry out. To obtain a broad cross-section of information-seeking tasks, a set of 180 TREC topics was selected:

- **Q02** Question Answering Track 2002, 70 topics (1824–1893)
- **R03** Robust Track 2003, 60 topics (selected from 303–610)[1]
- **T04** Terabyte Track 2004, 50 topics (701–750)

For each topic, a *backstory* was created; this was a short information need statement that was intended to motivate and contextualize the search request, making the topic statements less abstract and more engaging. Four annotators created the backstories, based on the full original TREC title, description and narrative fields. They were also free to explore related background information using online resources. An example topic from each of the three TREC tracks is shown in Figure 2. To encourage our eventual experimental participants to engage more fully with these search tasks, and to treat them as personal searches rather than abstract impersonal ones,

[1] The topic numbers are non-contiguous because half of the topics selected for the Robust Track 2003 were chosen as they were known to be difficult from previous Ad-Hoc tracks.

Q02.1828, Remember*; "What was Thailand's original name?"*

While visiting Thailand for a beach holiday last year, you decided to visit some local museums to learn more about Thailand's history. You learned many interesting things about the country, including that it was not always called Thailand. What was it called originally?

R03.356, Understand*; "postmenopausal estrogen Britain"*

A friend, who lives in Britain, has started estrogen treatment. This surprises you as you thought it's no longer recommended. You want to find out more about the use of hormone replacement therapy or estrogen treatment in the U.K.

T04.734, Analyze*; "Recycling successes"*

Your city has recently embarked on an ambitious zero-waste policy for household and industrial garbage. Recycling is going to be a big component of the program. You wish to find out what recycling projects have been successful, including the places or product programs that have worked, and what they understood success to mean.

Figure 2: Backstory associated with three TREC topics from different tasks in different years, together with the task type.

Number: 734

Recycling successes

Description: What recycling projects have been successful?

Narrative: Guidelines by themselves are not relevant. Titles in a table of contents are relevant if they identify places or product programs which have had success. Must be declared successful or success should be clearly assumed from the description. Name of state identified as successful recycler is relevant. Listing of recycled products for sale are relevant.

Figure 3: Topic 734 from the TREC 2004 Terabyte Track.

the backstories were written to speak directly to the reader, and to include hypothetical family members or friends. Figure 3 shows the original TREC presentation of one of the topics shown in Figure 2.

The original topic statements from the Terabyte and Robust tracks contain substantial detail about what information a document should or should not contain to be considered relevant, and the created backstories aimed to reflect the bulk of these requirements. Nevertheless, we acknowledge that there is potential for drift between the interpretations of the backstory and the original TREC topic description that led to relevance judgments being created. Topics from the QA Track were more difficult as they are typically presented simply as question statements, such as "*How much gravity exists on mars?*" (Q02.1871). Simply posing the question statement to the experimental participants might lead to these being entered directly as a search query, rather than then being read as an information need statement, so the QA topics are also presented with a backstory. When possible, pronouns or other indirect references to the query subject were used, to reduce the likelihood that participants would simply copy and paste the final question as their query.

Task complexity Different information-seeking tasks have different characteristics, and task complexity is a key feature that may influence searcher behavior. For our experiments we adapt three levels from the cognitive complexity hierarchy proposed by Wu et al. [35], derived from a taxonomy of learning objectives presented by Anderson and Krathwohl [2]. This hierarchy considers a spectrum of information needs, with the lowest level consisting of searches that involve *"retrieving, recognizing, and recalling relevant knowledge"*. Such *Remember* queries therefore involve finding a fact in response to a simple "when", "where" or "what" question, such as "*How did Eva Peron die?*". The next level in the hierarchy, *Understand*, involves *"constructing meaning from oral, written, and graphic messages through interpreting, exemplifying, classifying, summarizing, inferring, comparing, and explaining"*. We also use a third level, *Analyze*; tasks at this level of the hierarchy involve *"breaking material into constituent parts, determining how the parts relate to one another and to an overall structure or purpose through differentiating, organizing, and attributing"*. Each of the example tasks in Figure 2 indicates the corresponding complexity category.

Based on the created backstories, each of the 180 selected TREC topics were assigned to one of the task complexity types. Four annotators independently rated each topic: broadly speaking, topics that required a simple factoid answer tended to be assigned to the *Remember* category; where topics required the production of list of things, even if relatively complex and sourced from different pages, they tended to be assigned as *Understand*; and, where topics required synthesis of disparate information, and eventual summary, or balancing of competing viewpoints and opinions, they were allocated to the *Analyze* category.[2] The overall inter-annotator agreement among the four judges for the initial ratings was 0.664, measured by Fleiss' κ [12], a statistic that measures agreement across multiple raters and corrects for agreement by chance. It is interesting to note that the per-category agreement varied substantially, from 0.456 for the highest of the three hierarchy levels (*Analyze*) to 0.907 for the lowest level (*Remember*), indicating that *Remember* tasks are relatively easy to identify and agree on, while differentiating between *Remember* and *Analyze* tasks is more difficult. For all cases where there was no majority rating among the four annotators, the tasks were carefully discussed until agreement was reached, resulting in a single confirmed type for each.

Gathering data To investigate user variability in a test collection setting, an experiment was carried out using the CrowdFlower crowd-sourcing platform.[3] The experiment was reviewed and approved by the <anonymous institution> ethics board.

On signing up for the experiment, a participant was first presented with an information need statement, one of the created backstories. They were then required to answer three questions. First, participants were asked: *How many useful web pages do you think you would need to complete the search task?*. Responses were selected from the following: 0 useful pages (I'd expect to find the answer in the search results listing, without reading any of the pages); 1 useful page (I'd expect to find the answer in the first useful page I found); 2 useful pages; 3-5 useful pages; 6-10 useful pages; 11-100 useful pages; 101+ useful pages. Second, they were asked: *In total, how many different queries do you think you would need to enter to find that many useful pages?* with answers selectable from the following: 1 query (I'd expect to be able to complete the search task after the first query); 2 queries; 3-5 queries; 6-10 queries; 11+ queries. Third, participants were asked: *What would your first query be?*; answers to this question were entered in a textbox. Participants were free to complete as many topics as they liked, from one to a maximum of 180. The resulting data set had 10,800 responses from 115 workers,

Cleaning crowd data It cannot be expected that all anonymous

[2]To promote reproducibility, the full set of 180 topic backstories and corresponding task complexity labels will be available on request.

[3]`http://www.crowdflower.com`

	Task complexity		
	Remem.	Under.	Analyze
number of topics	70	81	29
average queries per topic	44.3	44.4	44.0
average query length (chars)	25.9	32.9	37.1
average query length (words)	5.6	6.0	6.5
average query entropy (bits)	19.9	26.0	30.5

Table 1: Query properties after normalization: average query length in characters, not counting white-space characters; average query length in words; and average query entropy in bits. To calculate the last, the frequency distribution of words appearing in the queries for each topic was computed, and then the average information cost of representing the queries for that topic computed using that frequency distribution, and averaged over task complexities.

workers took their task seriously, and where it was possible to identify clearly inappropriate responses, those workers were removed from further analysis (but still paid). First, if any worker suggested the same first query for two or more tasks, they were considered unreliable and all their responses were removed – recall that no worker got the same task twice, so it is extremely unlikely that two tasks would attract identical queries. This rule removed 15 of 115 workers. Two further workers who had copy/pasted apparently nonsensical parts of the topic statement as their first query were also identified and removed. This left 7,971 responses from 98 workers, covering all 180 topics with 41–48 responses per topic (median 44).

4. VARIATION IN FIRST QUERIES

Having described the data collection process, we first examine the sets of queries suggested by the experimental subjects.

Normalization One of the components in each interaction pane asked *"What would your first query be?"* Workers then entered text in to a textbox. As with all web queries, the resultant strings are noisy, with a wide range of spelling and grammatical errors. In this regard, the behavior of the crowd workers probably corresponds closely to other users. To ameliorate this type of behavior, web search systems include a "did you mean?" query modification feature. To faithfully reflect that behavior, the query strings typed by the crowd-sourced subjects were converted to US English, and corrections applied whenever they could be unambiguously identified. For example, "theropy" was changed to "therapy" in the context of topic R03.356 (Figure 2). In some cases the correction was not clearcut, or the erroneous word was actually a correct spelling of something different. Manual interactions with a major search engine were used to decide whether to alter these queries. For example, "cheapskate bay" was altered to "chesapeake bay", because that is what happened at a web search interface. On the other hand, "calgary provicence" was altered to "calgary providence" rather than "calgary province", which would have better fitted the topic in question, because the first alteration was what was suggested at the same search interface. As a further part of the normalization process all punctuation characters were removed, including periods. Finally, two queries ("zdvfdzfvg" and "fxghfsdg") not caught by the earlier quality-control mechanisms were removed. The resulting query set contained 7,969 queries, of which 5,046 were unique.

Query diversity Table 1 lists some properties of the queries received, averaged over the three query classes after quality control and normalization mechanisms were applied. The table shows a clear trend to longer queries as the information need becomes more complex, both in terms of characters typed and in terms of words typed. The final row of the table represents the average diversity of the terms across the pool of queries generated for each topic, by computing the term frequencies of all terms used in queries for that topic, then calculating the entropy of each query relative to that distribution, and finally averaging those average entropies. The entropy of a query increases as the length of the query increases, and is also high if a broad set of term is being used across the pool of queries for that topic – if queries are less predictable. This measure confirms that the more complex the information need, the more expressive are the queries posed to resolve it.

city recycling projects (2)
city recycling scheme progress
council website
most successful recycling programs
recycling policy update
recycling projects (2)
recycling projects for household and industrial garbage
recycling projects program
recycling projects successes and effects
recycling projects that have been successful
recycling successes
reducing waste to zero success stories
successful city recycling policies
successful municipal recycling projects
successful recycling programs (2)
successful recycling projects (11)
successful recycling projects place product programs
successful zero waste
what are the recycling projects that have been successful
what does it take to make a successful recycling program
what recycling projects have been successful (6)
where have recycling projects been successful and
how do they define success
zero waste policy (2)
zero waste policy for household and industrial garbage
zero waste policy for household and industrial garbage programs

Figure 4: The 44 user-generated queries for Topic 734 (Figure 3). Numbers in parentheses indicate multiplicity.

As a single example, Figure 4 lists the complete set of queries generated for one of the 180 information need statements (see Figure 2). One query dominates – an extended version of the TREC title-only query for this topic, "recycling successes" – but nearly half of the queries generated by the subjects occur only once.

Query effectiveness – In the small Two different retrieval systems were then used to execute each query against the corresponding document collection: Indri[4] with an Okapi similarity computation, and Indri with a sequential dependency computation [19]. Using Indri for both ranking algorithms ensures the system effects are due to fundamental differences in the retrieval algorithms, rather than other factors related to query or document processing. Rankings of length 200 documents were generated and scored; with documents for which no judgment was available deemed to be not relevant.

Figure 5 shows the range of scores that resulted when four standard relevance measures were applied to the rankings for the set of 44 queries generated in response to Topic 734 (Figures 2 and 4), with the Indri Okapi BM25 and SDM ranking functions. The blue diamonds show the corresponding scores for the canonical TREC

[4]http://www.lemurproject.org/indri/.

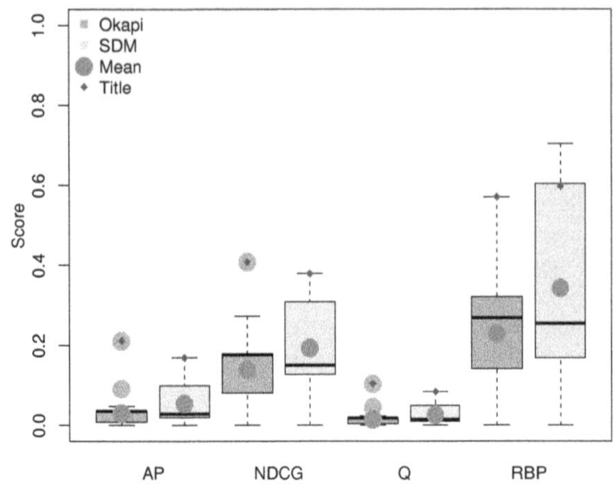

Figure 5: Retrieval effectiveness measured by AP, NDCG, Q1 and RBP0.85 for Topic 734. Green and blue boxes show scores obtained from running the different user queries using BM25 and SDM, respectively. Grey points indicate the mean for each column, black bars the median, and the blue diamonds show the effectiveness of the corresponding TREC title-only query.

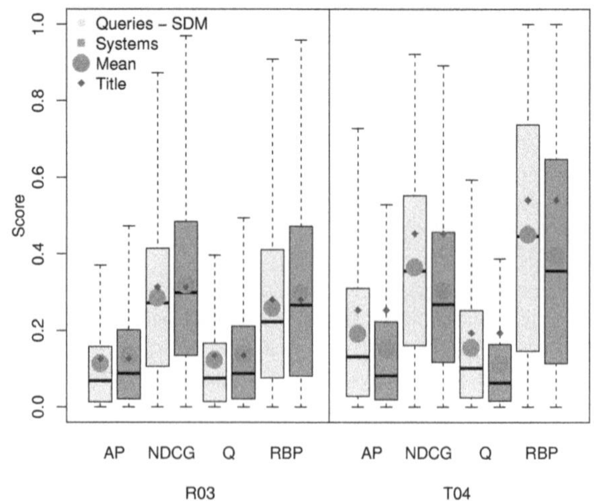

Figure 6: Retrieval effectiveness as measured by AP, NDCG, Q1 and RBP0.85, for two subcollections R03 and T04. Blue boxes show scores obtained from running different user queries with SDM retrieval, while red boxes show scores achieved by different TREC contributing system runs. Grey points indicate the mean for each column, black bars the median, and the blue diamonds show the effectiveness of an Indri SDM run using the corresponding TREC title-only query. The average residuals for the four RBP measurements were (left to right) 0.153, 0.038, 0.235, and 0.059. The Indri SDM runs had RBP residuals of 0.017 for R03, and 0.056 for T04.

title-only query (again, see Figure 2) when evaluated using the same two retrieval mechanisms. The results for this one query reflect a trend that we also saw more widely – that for typical user queries the mean performance of SDM is superior to that of Okapi. That difference is consistent, but not absolute, and for most combinations of metric and topic there are also queries for which Okapi out-scored SDM. On Topic 734 the title-only query was the highest-scoring query (of the 44) for AP, NDCG, and Q1 for both Okapi and SDM models, and also the highest-scoring for RBP0.85 for Okapi (the query "successful recycling projects place product programs" scored 0.703 when the SDM similarity model is used), but this topic was unusual in that regard. For example, for Topic 356 (Figure 2), more than half of the user-generated queries outperformed the canonical title-only query. The omission from the corresponding backstory of the word "postmenopausal", which appears in the TREC topic description ("identify documents discussing the use of estrogen by postmenopausal women in Britain"), may have had an effect. Some level of unintentional topic drift is always possible in our process.

A risk factor in any experimentation in which judgments are re-used is the extent to which they provide coverage of the documents retrieved by the systems being compared. For Topic 736, the RBP *residuals* when $p = 0.85$ are 0.518 and 0.469 for Okapi and SDM, respectively. These represent the assessment weight of the unjudged documents in RBP [22], with 0.0 representing a situation with all required judgments available, and larger values indicating that the RBP score would increase by that much if all unjudged documents were in fact relevant. For Topic 734 the average residual for the user-generated queries was in excess of 0.25, and the available judgments covered less than 75% of the RBP probability mass. That is, the relativities shown in Figure 5 need to be taken cautiously. With more complete judgment coverage, the RBP scores for this topic (and hence the scores for other metrics) might change considerably. Similar situations were encountered for several other topics. On the other hand, the title-only queries have consistently low residuals, because they were used by some of the systems that contributed to the pools from which the judgments were created.

Query effectiveness – In the large The Q02 queries were especially prone to the problems arising from sparse judgments, with RBP0.85 residuals that averaged around 0.5 over that set of 70 topics. One reason may be that QA relevance was focused on answer fragments, not document-level relevance. Coverage was somewhat better on the R03 and T04 queries (but with considerable variation, as already noted).

Figure 6 incorporates score information derived from all of the TREC participating systems that contributed runs for the Robust-03 and Terabyte-04 tracks. The boxes show variation over the corresponding R03 and T04 topics of score responses to user-generated queries (blue) and score responses across the set of contributed TREC runs for that year (red), factoring in all of the user-generated queries when evaluated using the Indri SDM model. The average of the Indri scores for the title-only queries for those topics is also marked on each bar. It is clear that query-derived variations are just as broad as are the variations caused by system diversity, and hence that improved performance relative to the Indri SDM title-only runs is thus equally likely to be derived from query reformulation as it is from system improvement. Note also that for the user-generated queries (blue boxes) there is a considerable amount of metric weight still sitting in the residuals, which might be released with further judgments, and result in higher scores.

Variability analyzed The effect of query choice is illustrated further in an analysis of variance for each metric, modeling score as a response to topic, system, and query. In this analysis "topic" is a nominal variable, one level per TREC topic; "system" has one level for each TREC system, plus two levels for our Indri runs; and "query" has one level for all TREC systems plus one for each query processed by Indri. (We do not know the exact query used by each TREC system, but by assuming it is always the same we will underestimate the variability due to query phrasing and overestimate that due to system.) Q02 looks very different, as discussed above, and those runs are not included in this analysis since these measures are document-relevance centric.

Metric		η^2	SS	df	F
AP	query	0.55	158.40	4977	4.58
	system	0.20	32.61	147	31.90
	topic	0.14	22.05	179	17.72
NDCG	query	0.59	279.02	4977	5.38
	system	0.28	75.64	147	49.35
	topic	0.16	36.56	179	19.59
Q1	query	0.57	145.79	4977	5.05
	system	0.19	24.83	147	29.12
	topic	0.18	23.63	179	22.76
RBP0.85	query	0.53	341.80	4977	4.23
	system	0.20	77.12	147	32.33
	topic	0.11	38.90	179	13.39

Table 2: ANOVA for four metrics, modeled as a response to system, topic, and query string. Partial η^2 values reported; all F statistics significant at $p \ll .001$. In each case, the effect due to query phrasing is substantially larger than that due to topic or system.

Table 2 summarizes the results. Each of query, system, and topic has a statistically significant effect ($p \ll .001$ in all cases, Wald test) and the effect of each factor is medium/large, with the possible exception of topic for RBP, but the effects are of very different scales. The variation due to system is slightly larger than that due to topic (e.g. partial η^2 of 0.20 and 0.14 for AP), so slightly more variation in final score is explained by changes to system than by changes to topic. The variation due to query phrasing, however, dwarfs other effects and over 50% of variation in final score can be attributed to phrasing *even after system and topic are taken into account* (partial η^2 in the range 0.53–0.59).

Observations Particular choices of query clearly can lead to widely different scores, independent of the topic, the system, or the metric. We commonly want to use variation in scores to say something about differences between systems (i.e., "system B is better"); less commonly, we want to use variation in scores to say something about topics (i.e., "topic 734 is hard"). In either case we need to be aware of query wording as a confound, and an extra source of variation which in fact dominates system and topic.

Two macro implications can be drawn from this analysis regarding test collection design and development. First, since this approach supplies between one and two orders of magnitude more queries for a given set of topics within a collection, even given some cross-query document overlap when judging pools on a per topic basis, this would sharply increase the required judging budgets. Given finite budgets, this implies that measures that accommodate missing judgments such as RBP or the suite of inferred AP and NDCG measures developed by Yilmaz and Aslam [37] are required and/or more cost-effective judgment acquisition methods such as crowd-sourcing approaches (e.g., as discussed by Alonso et al. [1]) should be employed. Second, systems could be provided with each topic's collection of queries, and can then make use of any methods desired to create a single top-K ranking for the topic. Document pools would be formed in the usual way, but on the scale of number of topics, not number of queries. In the absence of search engine logs, this might provide some partial subset of the data that is available to commercial search providers about variant phrasing, and hence techniques such as pseudo relevance feedback or query reformulation merging [27] could be employed.

Factor	Effect (mult. odds) T	Q
Worker	0.005–7520.3	10^{-9}–22316.9
Author	0.8–1.3	0.9–1.5
Remember (baseline)	1.0	1.0
Understand	14.1	11.2
Analyze	21.9	18.9

Table 3: Significant factors in fitted models for estimates of T and Q. Effect sizes > 1 correspond to higher values of T or Q being more likely. All effects significant at $p < 0.05$, Wald test.

5. VARIATION IN EXPECTATIONS

As well as differing in their behavior (issuing different queries, in our example), users may have different expectations of a search system and of a task and it would be appropriate to consider this when evaluating search systems. For example, if one user expects to issue a query then read three or four documents – perhaps to compare information from different sources – then it would not be appropriate to evaluate based on the rank of only the first relevant result. If another expects to issue several queries in succession, then it may be appropriate to evaluate a session rather than a single question. Other, similar, scenarios are easy to imagine. Two questions in our instrument aimed to understand some of these varied expectations.

Expected number of documents Cooper [11] noted that (p.31) "most measures do not take into account a crucial variable: the amount of material relevant ... which the user actually needs". Following Moffat et al. [23], we denote this quantity by T. Cooper further observes (p.33):

> *A search request is therefore to be conceived in the abstract as involving two parts: a relevance description (normally a subject specification) and a quantity specification. To put it another way, every search request has a definite quantification.*

To understand this quantification and how it varies, we asked: "how many useful web pages do you think you would need to complete the search task?". We plot the responses for each task complexity category in Figure 7. The distribution of responses across the three types of task are significantly different ($\chi^2 = 2067.0, df = 12, p \ll .001$), and it seems that descriptions of more complex tasks prompt people to expect more reading.

Clearly estimates of T vary with task complexity, and they may vary with other factors as well. Some of these factors are captured in our instrument, and some are external and not captured. To clarify some of the instrument-captured factors, we used cumulative logistic regression (also called ordinal regression) to model T as a response to a number of potential explanatory variables: complexity (three levels), worker (98 levels, or one per worker), topic author (four levels), and CrowdFlower run (two levels). Model selection was performed to minimize the Akaike information criterion (AIC), which measures likelihood but with a penalty for complex models.[5]

The model is summarized in Table 3, where effects are given as multipliers to odds ratios. Effects greater than 1 represent a higher probability of answers higher up the scale. For example, a multiplier of 2 would mean the odds of estimating T as 1 vs estimating T as 0 are twice as high as the baseline; likewise, the odds of estimating T as 2 vs either 1 or 0 would be twice the baseline, and so on.

The largest effects are due to the CrowdFlower workers. Our workers varied substantially, with a worker at one extreme claiming

[5]Modeling used R's `ordinal::clm` and `ordinal::step.clm` functions.

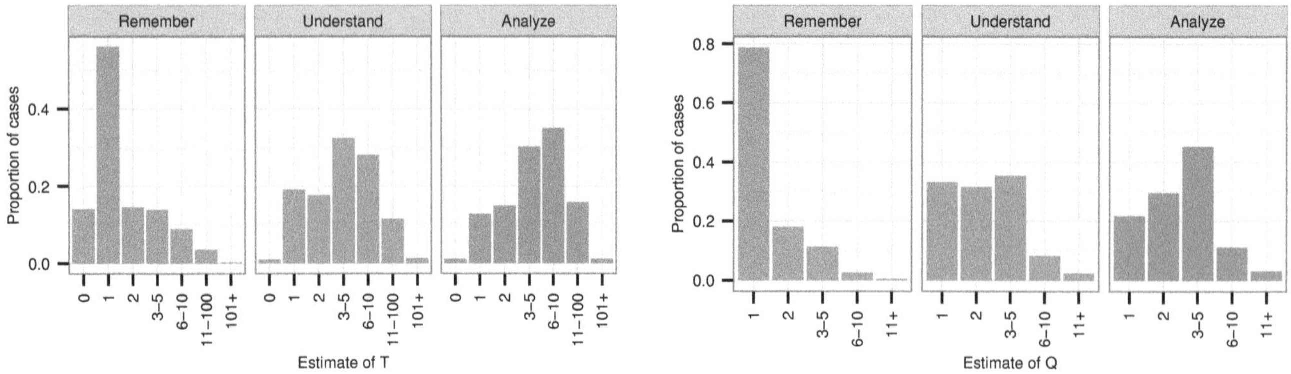

Figure 7: Judges' estimates of T, the number of relevant documents they expect to read, vary with task complexity (left); as do their estimates of Q, the number of queries they expect to issue (right). Judges expect to need more interactions for more complex tasks.

they expected to read documents for only five out of 65 topics and one worker at the other extreme expecting to read 11 or more documents in every case. This is reflected in the model, where per-worker effects are highly variable and again dominate all other effects – odds ratios change by six orders of magnitude for T.

There is a smaller but still notable effect due to task complexity, with *Understand* tasks more likely to prompt higher estimates of T and *Analyze* more likely still – the difference between *Remember* and *Understand* being larger than that between *Understand* and *Analyze*. Finally, there is an effect due to topic author: even after controlling for task complexity and worker, some authors provoked higher T estimates, an effect that was statistically significant, but practically negligible. We also checked for batch effects (the tasks were released to workers in two rounds), but they were not evident.

Expected number of queries Users may also vary in the number of queries they expect to issue – be it a single query, if they think a task is simple or well-supported, or very many in succession, if they think the task is more complex. We denote this expected number of queries Q and plot it in the right-hand side of Figure 7. As before, per-judge effects dominate – the variability here is even more pronounced than for T, with odds ratios varying across thirteen orders of magnitude. Clearly different users have very different expectations of their search engine interactions, even for the same topic. There are again significant differences across complexity levels, with similar effects to those seen for T. Again the difference between a *Remember* and an *Understand* task is larger than the difference between *Understand* and *Analyze*. We also note a significant but small effect due to topic author, and no significant batch effect.

Observations Just as with individual variation in query formation, we observed significant individual variation in expectations of documents and queries to satisfy that need. Given that T is correlated with task complexity and is strongly influenced by user-specific expectations, a natural question to ask is whether it is possible to include T – and progress made towards attaining T as a ranked list is consumed – into an relevance measure in a meaningful way. In the next section, we develop this possibility using the data we collected.

6. SENSITIVE EVALUATION

Current effectiveness metrics are insensitive to both T, the initial expectation of the user, and to the evolving expectation of T as the search is prosecuted. For example, while the p parameter of RBP [22] provides adjustment for user persistence and can be adjusted so as to influence the expected depth in the ranking that the user will examine, the user model associated with RBP requires that the user proceeds to the next document with fixed probability, regardless of how much information has already been accumulated, or what depth has been reached. We believe that as more relevance is accumulated, the user becomes less likely to continue their search.

Expected search length Cooper's definition of ESL [11] is simple: it is the total number of documents inspected before T relevant ones have been found. As such, it is always greater than or equal to T, with larger values representing inferior performance. To obtain a metric with the usual behavior (bounded by zero and one, with larger values indicating better performance) we scale by T and invert, to obtain an ESL- and RR-inspired metric:

$$\mathrm{RRT}(T) = \frac{T}{\text{rank of } T \text{ th relevant document}} . \quad (1)$$

As is the case with RBP, Prec, and RR, the score returned by this metric corresponds to the average rate at which utility (relevance) is acquired per document inspected, with a user model defined by a person who seeks exactly T relevant documents, and stops their search immediately upon finding a T th answer in the ranking. Queries that have fewer than T answers in a system's ranking are scored as zero. There is a clear connection between RRT and precision – RRT is equal to precision at the T th relevant document. Note also that $\mathrm{RRT}(1)$ is exactly reciprocal rank, RR.

Probabilistic users A second option is to form a probabilistic composite of RBP and ERR [10]. Suppose that the user makes a biased decision after encountering each relevant document, continuing to scan with probability $p = (T-1)/T$, and ending their search with probability $(1-p) = 1/T$. In this user model the expected utility per document inspected is given by:

$$\mathrm{ERRT}(T) = \frac{1}{T}\sum_{t=1}^{\infty}\left[\left(\frac{T-1}{T}\right)^{t-1} \cdot \mathrm{RRT}(t)\right] . \quad (2)$$

The geometric distribution means that the average number of relevant documents identified by the time the user stops scanning is $1/(1-p) = T$, and that the value of ERRT is non-zero even if fewer than T relevant documents appear in the run. There is also a clear relationship between ERRT and AP, the latter being an unweighted sum of all R precision scores: $\mathrm{AP} = (1/R)\sum_{t=1}^{R}\mathrm{RRT}(t)$, where R is the number of relevant documents for that topic. A key difference between AP and ERRT is that computation of the latter does not require knowledge of R. Nor is AP sensitive to T, of course.

Moffat et al. [23] have also considered effectiveness metrics that are sensitive to T. Their INSQ and INSQ′ functions are weighted precision metrics defined in terms of the conditional probability $C(i)$

T	Upper	Lower		
		INSQ	INSQ′	INST
1	2.58	2.58	1.64	1.33
3	6.53	6.53	4.36	3.27
10	20.51	20.51	13.93	10.26
30	60.50	60.50	41.29	30.25

Table 4: Expected search length for INSQ-based metrics for different values of T, when no documents in the ranking are relevant (column "upper"); and when every document is (columns "lower").

of the user continuing from the document at depth i in the ranking to the document at depth $i+1$. They define INSQ and INSQ′ via

$$C(i) = \left(\frac{i+2T-1}{i+2T}\right)^2 \quad \text{and} \quad C'(i) = \left(\frac{i+T+T_i-1}{i+T+T_i}\right)^2,$$

respectively, where T_i is the amount of relevance (or gain) that has not yet been accumulated by depth i, $T_i = T - \sum_{j=1}^{i} r_i$, and where $0 \leq r_i \leq 1$ is the relevance of the ith document in the ranking. Both versions of INSQ are sensitive, in that higher values of T lead to more patient search behavior and a greater expected depth in the ranking. In addition, INSQ′ is *adaptive* – as relevant documents are identified, the expected remaining search cost decreases.

INST: An improved INSQ′ In the formulation of Moffat et al. [23], T_i is required to be positive. We remove that restriction, and allow T_i to be negative too, covering situations in which more gain has been accrued than was initially anticipated. The altered metric, still using the continuation function $C'(i)$, is denoted as INST. Table 4 shows why we prefer this change: it lists expected search depth for INSQ, INSQ′ and INST in two extreme situations – when no documents in the ranking are relevant, and when every document in the ranking is relevant. As is evident in the table, INSQ is not adaptive, and has the same behavior in both extreme situations, examining an average of $2T+0.5$ documents. On the other hand, the expected search length in INSQ′ and INST decreases if relevant documents are encountered. Our preference for INST over INSQ′ is based on its expected search length of approximately $T+0.25$ when all documents are relevant, intuitively a better fit than the approximately $1.4T$ expectation of INSQ′. That is, INST anticipates that a user seeking T relevant documents will examine, on average, between T and $2T$ documents before leaving the ranking, with the actual exit depth depending on the number (and locations) of the relevant documents. In addition, INST retains the other features that made INSQ a more representative model for user behavior [23]. Compared to the INSQ/INST variants, RRT and ERRT give rise to models in which the user may only exit the ranking as they encounter each relevant document. On rankings that do not contain any relevant documents at all, the models associated with RRT and ERRT (like RR and AP before them) have the user scanning the full collection.

Retrieval effectiveness We use RRT(T), ERRT(T), INSQ(T), and INST(T) in our experimentation. To set the parameter T, the distribution of T-bands indicated by the crowd-workers for each topic is employed, and the mapping $0 \to 1$, $1 \to 1$, $2 \to 2$, 3–5 $\to 3$, 6–10 $\to 6$, 11–100 $\to 11$, and 101+ $\to 101$. That is, each score computed for RRT, ERRT, INSQ, and INST is a weighted average of up to six different T-based scores.

Table 5 lists scores for the 110 R03 and T04 queries topics and the user-generated queries, as measured by the four T-sensitive metrics; together with the expected depth at which users exit the result ranking. All of these metrics allow residuals to be computed;

Metric	Score	Residual	Depth
RRT	0.421±0.267	0.195±0.188	48.98
ERRT	0.453±0.267	0.114±0.113	44.17
INSQ	0.310±0.213	0.251±0.185	10.46
INST	0.366±0.249	0.206±0.186	8.57

Table 5: Averages and standard deviations of topic means for 4,871 user-generated queries over 110 R03 and T04 topics, using Indri SDM retrieval, and weighted distributions of T for each query. The final column lists the expected retrieval depth in the corresponding user models, also as a weighted average.

the variation in queries means that these are again relatively high compared to title-only queries. Note that the residuals associated with INST are smaller than those of INSQ, a consequence of the shallower expected depth; and the relatively implausible evaluation depths associated with RRT(T) and ERRT(T) (these would be even higher if the rankings were extended beyond 200 documents).

Kendall's τ for TREC systems Table 6 lists Kendall's τ-b coefficients, computed by scoring TREC systems using a total of nine metrics, and ordering the 70 Terabyte 2004 systems (the coefficients above the diagonal) and the 78 Robust 2003 systems (below the diagonal) according to the average metric score across topics, using the R03 and T04 topic sets, and the same weighted-by-user-T computation as was employed for Table 5. The four T-aware metrics have relatively high similarity to each other in terms of the system orderings they induce, and fit in to the middle of the spectrum, in terms of being neither deep metrics (like NDCG) nor shallow (like RRT 1, which is equivalent to RR). They also yield system orderings that are similar to the ordering generated by RBP0.85, for which the corresponding user model has an expected search depth of 6.7.

7. CONCLUSIONS

We have demonstrated that query variability among individuals leads to substantial changes across a range of standard relevance measures, and the effect of this source of variability is substantially more than that arising from topic or system effects. We also found that variation in expected goals of search in the number of documents (and number of queries) arises substantially from user-based factors, and is broadly correlated with increasing task complexity. Finally, we found that relevance measures that capture expectations of relevant documents and are adaptive to individual behavior are more similar to each other in terms of system orderings, and sharply dissimilar from deep metrics like AP and shallow metrics like RR.

We conclude that the aspects of variability among users regarding individual query formulation and expected goals of search can be incorporated within a batch evaluation process. The use of multiple queries per topic arising from different searchers provides a more representative characterization of the mapping from information need than just one. Systems which can perform well across such a range of queries per topic are more likely to exhibit user-generalizability. Incorporating estimates of variance due to user query-factors in a statistical power calculator would help determine the number of topics needed to reliably detect certain effect sizes.

We also suggest that the adaptive and expectation-sensitive measures we presented (especially INST) display potential in having more user-generalizability *and* more task-generalizability than existing measures, which tend to overemphasize either shallow or deep recall user behaviors. We hope to build a test collection in future to carry out more conclusive experiments on this matter.

	NDCG	AP	Q1	INSQ	RBP 0.85	INST	RRT	ERRT	RRT 1
NDCG	–	**0.95**	**0.93**	0.83	0.81	0.79	0.79	0.78	0.68
AP	0.84	–	**0.93**	0.83	0.80	0.79	0.78	0.77	0.66
Q1	0.80	0.81	–	0.84	0.82	0.81	0.81	0.78	0.67
INSQ	0.79	0.69	0.75	–	**0.96**	**0.96**	**0.94**	**0.92**	0.79
RBP 0.85	0.78	0.71	0.68	0.87	–	**0.95**	**0.95**	**0.92**	0.79
INST	0.77	0.67	0.74	**0.97**	0.85	–	**0.96**	**0.95**	0.82
RRT	0.78	0.67	0.76	**0.94**	0.86	**0.95**	–	**0.94**	0.81
ERRT	0.71	0.61	0.64	0.87	0.79	0.89	0.85	–	0.86
RRT 1	0.52	0.49	0.38	0.59	0.59	0.60	0.57	0.71	–

Table 6: Kendall's τ-b coefficients for the 70 Terabyte 2004 system runs ordered by the scores computed for the T04 queryset (above the lead diagonal); and for the 78 Robust 2003 system runs ordered according to the scores computed for the R03 queryset (below the diagonal). Metrics are ordered according to their τ-b coefficients relative to NDCG in the T04 comparison. Bold is for scores ≥ 0.9.

Acknowledgment This work was supported by the Australian Research Council's *Discovery Projects* Scheme (projects DP110101934 and DP140102655). We thank Alec Zwart and Xiaolu Lu.

References

[1] O. Alonso, D. E. Rose, and B. Stewart. Crowdsourcing for relevance evaluation. In *SIGIR Forum*, volume 42, pages 9–15, 2008.

[2] L. W. Anderson and D. A. Krathwohl. *A Taxonomy for Learning, Teaching and Assessing: A Revision of Bloom's Taxonomy of Educational Objectives*. Longman, New York, 2001.

[3] L. Azzopardi, D. Kelly, and K. Brennan. How query cost affects search behavior. In *Proc. SIGIR*, pages 23–32, 2013.

[4] P. Bailey, N. Craswell, I. Soboroff, P. Thomas, A. P. de Vries, and E. Yilmaz. Relevance assessment: are judges exchangeable and does it matter? In *Proc. SIGIR*, pages 667–674, 2008.

[5] N. J. Belkin, C. Cool, W. B. Croft, and J. P. Callan. Effect of multiple query representations on information retrieval system performance. In *Proc. SIGIR*, pages 339–346, 1993.

[6] N. J. Belkin, P. Kantor, E. A. Fox, and J. A. Shaw. Combining the evidence of multiple query representations for information retrieval. *Inf. Proc. Man.*, 31(3):431–448, 1995.

[7] D. J. Bell and I. Ruthven. Searchers' assessments of task complexity for web searching. In *Proc. ECIR*, pages 57–71, 2004.

[8] C. Buckley and J. Walz. The TREC-8 query track. In *Proc. TREC*, 1999. NIST Special Publication 500-246.

[9] K. Byström and K. Järvelin. Task complexity affects information seeking and use. *Inf. Proc. Man.*, 31(2):191–213, 1995.

[10] O. Chapelle, D. Metzler, Y. Zhang, and P. Grinspan. Expected reciprocal rank for graded relevance. In *Proc. CIKM*, pages 621–630, 2009.

[11] W. S. Cooper. Expected search length: A single measure of retrieval effectiveness based on the weak ordering action of retrieval systems. *Amer. Doc.*, 19(1):30–41, 1968.

[12] J. L. Fleiss. Measuring nominal scale agreement among many raters. *Psych. Bull.*, 76(5):378, 1971.

[13] K. Fujikawa, H. Joho, and S. Nakayama. Constraint can affect human perception, behaviour, and performance of search. In *Proc. Int. Conf. Asia-Pacific Digital Libraries*, pages 39–48. 2012.

[14] J. Gwizdka and I. Spence. What can searching behavior tell us about the difficulty of information tasks? A study of Web navigation. *Proc. Amer. Soc. Inf. Sc. Tech.*, 43(1):1–22, 2006.

[15] K. Järvelin and J. Kekäläinen. Cumulated gain-based evaluation of IR techniques. *ACM Trans. Inf. Sys.*, 20(4):422–446, 2002.

[16] G. Kazai, N. Craswell, E. Yilmaz, and S. Tahaghoghi. An analysis of systematic judging errors in information retrieval. In *Proc. CIKM*, pages 105–114, 2012.

[17] D. R. Krathwohl. A revision of Bloom's taxonomy: An overview. *Theory Into Practice*, 41(4):212–218, 2002.

[18] G. Kumaran and J. Allan. Adapting information retrieval systems to user queries. *Inf. Proc. Man.*, 44(6):1838–1862, 2008.

[19] D. Metzler and W. B. Croft. A Markov random field model for term dependencies. In *Proc. SIGIR*, pages 472–479, 2005.

[20] F. Modave, N. K. Shokar, E. Peñaranda, and N. Nguyen. Analysis of the accuracy of weight loss information search engine results on the internet. *Amer. J. Public Health*, 104(10):1971–1978, 2014.

[21] A. Moffat. Seven numeric properties of effectiveness metrics. In *Proc. AIRS*, pages 1–12, 2013.

[22] A. Moffat and J. Zobel. Rank-biased precision for measurement of retrieval effectiveness. *ACM Trans. Inf. Sys.*, 27(1):2:1–2:27, 2008.

[23] A. Moffat, P. Thomas, and F. Scholer. Users versus models: What observation tells us about effectiveness metrics. In *Proc. CIKM*, pages 659–668, 2013.

[24] S. E. Robertson and E. Kanoulas. On per-topic variance in IR evaluation. In *Proc. SIGIR*, pages 891–900, 2012.

[25] T. Sakai and N. Kando. On information retrieval metrics designed for evaluation with incomplete relevance assessments. *J. Inf. Ret.*, 11(5): 447–470, 2008.

[26] T. Saracevic. Relevance reconsidered. In *Proc. Conf. Conceptions of Library and Inf. Sc.*, pages 201–218, 1996.

[27] D. Sheldon, M. Shokouhi, M. Szummer, and N. Craswell. Lambdamerge: merging the results of query reformulations. In *Proc. WSDM*, pages 795–804, 2011.

[28] M. D. Smucker and C. L. A. Clarke. Time-based calibration of effectiveness measures. In *Proc. SIGIR*, pages 95–104, 2012.

[29] K. Spärck Jones and R. Bates. Report on the Design Study for the "Ideal" Information Retrieval Test Collection. *British Library Research and Development Report*, 5428, 1977.

[30] E. G. Toms, H. O'Brien, T. Mackenzie, C. Jordan, L. Freund, S. Toze, E. Dawe, and A. Macnutt. Task effects on interactive search: The query factor. In *Focused Access to XML Documents*, pages 359–372. Springer, 2008.

[31] P. Vakkari. Task complexity, problem structure and information actions: Integrating studies on information seeking and retrieval. *Inf. Proc. Man.*, 35(6):819 – 837, 1999.

[32] E. M. Voorhees. Variations in relevance judgments and the measurement of retrieval effectiveness. *Inf. Proc. Man.*, 36(5):697–716, 2000.

[33] W. Webber, A. Moffat, J. Zobel, and T. Sakai. Precision-at-ten considered redundant. In *Proc. SIGIR*, pages 695–696, 2008.

[34] R. W. White and D. Kelly. A study on the effects of personalization and task information on implicit feedback performance. In *Proc. CIKM*, pages 297–306, 2006.

[35] W.-C. Wu, D. Kelly, A. Edwards, and J. Arguello. Grannies, tanning beds, tattoos and NASCAR: Evaluation of search tasks with varying levels of cognitive complexity. In *Proc. IIiX*, pages 254–257, 2012.

[36] W.-C. Wu, D. Kelly, and A. Sud. Using information scent and need for cognition to understand online search behavior. In *Proc. SIGIR*, pages 557–566, 2014.

[37] E. Yilmaz and J. A. Aslam. Estimating average precision with incomplete and imperfect judgments. In *Proc. CIKM*, pages 102–111, 2006.

An Entity Class-Dependent Discriminative Mixture Model for Cumulative Citation Recommendation*

Jingang Wang
School of Computer Science
Beijing Institute of Technology
bitwjg@bit.edu.cn

Dandan Song†
School of Computer Science
Beijing Institute of Technology
sdd@bit.edu.cn

Qifan Wang
Dept. of Computer Science
Purdue University
wang868@purdue.edu

Zhiwei Zhang
Dept. of Computer Science
Purdue University
zhan1187@purdue.edu

Luo Si
Dept. of Computer Science
Purdue University
lsi@purdue.edu

Lejian Liao
School of Computer Science
Beijing Institute of Technology
liaolj@bit.edu.cn

Chin-Yew Lin
Knowledge Mining Group
Microsoft Research
cyl@microsoft.com

ABSTRACT

This paper studies Cumulative Citation Recommendation (CCR) for Knowledge Base Acceleration (KBA). The CCR task aims to detect potential citations of a set of target entities with priorities from a volume of temporally-ordered stream corpus. Previous approaches for CCR that build an individual relevance model for each entity fail to handle unseen entities without annotation. A baseline solution is to build a global entity-unspecific model for all entities regardless of the relationship information among entities, which cannot guarantee to achieve satisfactory result for each entity. In this paper, we propose a novel entity class-dependent discriminative mixture model by introducing a latent entity class layer to model the correlations between entities and latent entity classes. The model can better adjust to different types of entities and achieve better performance when dealing with a broad range of entities. An extensive set of experiments has been conducted on TREC-KBA-2013 dataset, and the experimental results demonstrate that the proposed model can achieve the state-of-the-art performance.

Categories and Subject Descriptors

H.3.3 [**Information Search and Retrieval**]: Retrieval Models

*This work was partially done when the first author was visiting Purdue University and Microsoft Research Asia.
†Corresponding Author

SIGIR'15, August 09-13, 2015, Santiago, Chile.

DOI: http://dx.doi.org/10.1145/2766462.2767698.

Keywords

Cumulative Citation Recommendation; Knowledge Base Acceleration; Mixture Model; Information Filtering

1. INTRODUCTION

In recent years, we have witnessed a proliferation of open domain Knowledge Bases (KBs) such as Freebase[1] and Yago[2]. They have been used in many applications such as query answering, entity search and entity linking and have shown great promises. These KBs are usually organized around entities such as persons, organizations, locations, and so on. Currently, the maintenance of a KB mainly relies on human editors. However, with the explosion of information, large-scale KBs are hard to be kept up-to-date solely by human editors. Taking English Wikipedia for example, there are approximately 4.7 million entities but merely 132,938 active editors[3]. The less popular entities cannot be updated in time because they are not spotlighted. As reported in [14], the median time delay between a cited document's publishing and its citation in Wikipedia is almost one year. An outdated KB severely limits the effectiveness of applications depending on it. This gap could be bridged if relevant documents of KB entries can be automatically detected as soon as they emerge online and then be recommended to the editors with various levels of relevance. This is called the Cumulative Citation Recommendation (CCR). Formally, given a KB entity, CCR is a task to filter highly relevant documents from a chronological stream corpus and evaluate their citation-worthiness to the target entity.

Most previous approaches (e.g., [2, 25]) for CCR are highly supervised and require sufficient training data to build an individual relevance model for each entity. These approaches are infeasible when dealing with a large-scale KB, since the

[1] https://www.freebase.com/
[2] http://www.mpi-inf.mpg.de/departments/databases-and-information-systems/research/yago-naga/yago/
[3] http://meta.wikimedia.org/wiki/List_of_Wikipedias#1_000_000.2B_articles

labeling work is labor intensive. One solution is to build a global entity-unspecific discriminative model and optimize it to achieve an overall optimal performance for all entities [29, 36]. However, these models ignore the distinctions between different entities and learn a set of fixed model parameters for all entities, which leads unsatisfactory performance when dealing with a diverse entity set. For instance, it is not intuitve to apply the same discriminative model for *Geoffery Hinton* and *Appleton Museum of Art*. The former entity is a computer scientist, while the latter one is a museum. Nevertheless, the global model treats them equally without considering the prior entity class knowledge. We assume that entities from a same class have similar tastes and preferences when citing relevant documents, which means they have similar combination weights in the discriminative model. Therefore, for an entity with little training data, the training data of its similar entities from the same class can be utilized to learn the combination weights. In comparison to the global model, more accurate combination weights are learned for each entity by this manner.

Based on this observation, we build an adaptive discriminative model for different types of entities by utilizing the underlying entity class information, i.e. entity class dependent discriminative mixture model. We introduce an intermediate latent entity class layer and define a joint distribution over the entity-document pairs and latent classes conditioned on the observations. The aim is to achieve relevance estimation through learning a mixture model which is expected to outperform the global model, while maintaining the capability to reveal the hidden correlations between entities and entity classes. The model can be viewed as a hierarchical combination of a discriminative component and a mixing component, so two types of features are required: entity-document features for the discriminative component and entity-class features for the mixing component.

For the discriminative component, we develop a set of bursty features as temporal features in addition to semantic features. The bursty features are detected from two independent data sources: the stream corpus (internal) and certain third-party data (external) like Google Trends.

For the mixing component, we explore two types of entity-class features to model the correlations between entities and hidden classes, including profile-based features and category-based features. Profile-based features are constructed from the entity's profile in KB, while category-based features rely on the existing category labels for the entity in KB.

To the best of our knowledge, this is the first research work that focuses on modeling correlations between entities and hidden entity classes in discriminative model for CCR. Our model is capable of tackling less popular entities with little training data and unseen entities that do not exist in the training set, which is indispensable in a practical CCR system. Empirical studies have been conducted on TREC-KBA-2013 dataset to show the effectiveness and robustness of the proposed mixture model. Experimental results demonstrate that our model achieves the state-of-the-art performance on TREC-KBA-2013 dataset.

The rest of this paper is organized as follows. Section 2 summarizes related works. Section 3 introduces an entity class-dependent discriminative mixture model for CCR. Section 4 describes features required in our model, especially the temporally bursty features and their detection methods. Section 5 presents the detailed experimental results and provides some discussion. Section 6 concludes this paper and points out possible future work.

2. RELATED WORK

Although CCR was first proposed in TREC-KBA tracks, the similar research problem has been studied in several topics of information retrieval.

Topic/Event Detection and Tracking.

Topic Detection and Tracking (TDT) is a track hosted by TREC from 1997 to 2004 [1]. A similar research topic in recent years is event detection. Both TDT and event detection are concerned with the development of techniques for finding and following events in broadcast news or social media. The techniques adopted for TDT and event detection can be broadly classified into two categories: (1) clustering documents based on the semantic distance between them [34], or (2) grouping the frequent words together to represent events [22]. In [22], a finite automaton model is proposed to detect events in stream by modeling events as state transitions. This method has been validated widely by lots of other studies [18, 17, 35]. We also adopt this model to detect KB entities' bursts in the stream corpus and then extract bursty features for them. Different from above works, we model entities' occurrences to capture bursty activities instead of words' occurrences. Another difference between CCR and TDT is that CCR needs to make fine-grained citation-worthiness distinctions between relevant documents further.

Cumulative Citation Recommendation.

TREC has launched the KBA-CCR track since 2012. Participants treat CCR as either a ranking problem [3, 2, 4] or a classification problem [3, 5, 29]. Classification and Learning to Rank methods have been compared and evaluated [2, 15], and both of them can achieve the state-of-art performance with a powerful feature set. Several supervised learning techniques, such as SVM [21], language models [26, 10], Markov Random Fields [7], and Random Forests [4, 5, 29] are utilized. Meanwhile, a variety of relevance scoring methods have been tried, including standard Lucene scoring [6], and custom ranking functions based on entity co-occurrences [25]. A time-aware evaluation paradigm is developed to study time-dependent characteristics of CCR [9].

However, some highly supervised methods require training instances for each entity to build a relevance model, limiting their scalabilities. Entity-unspecific methods, regardless of entity distinctions, are employed to address this problem [29, 28]. Nevertheless, characteristics of different entities are lost in the entity-unspecific methods. Some other researchers employ transfer learning techniques to learn across entities by using entity-unspecific meta-features [36], or utilize a semi-supervised approach to profile an entity by leveraging its related entities and weighting them with the training data [23]. These methods have demonstrated that the correlations between entities are useful for CCR. Nevertheless, all these methods are empirically designed and the performance can be improved further.

What's more, query expansion is often employed because the name of the target entity is too sparse to be a good query. Other name variants and contextual information of terms or related entities from Wikipedia or from the document stream

[7, 6] are used to enrich the semantic features of entities. In addition to semantic features, temporal features have been proved especially helpful in CCR [2, 5, 29].

Mixture Model.
Mixture model has been proved effective to address the problem of data insufficiency in several information retrieval tasks, including expert search [11], federated search [19], collaborative filtering [20] and image retrieval [30]. By introducing latent layers to learn flexible combination weights for different feature vectors, mixture model can always outperform simple discriminative models with fixed combination weights. Hence, we propose an entity class-dependent discriminative mixture model to deal with the entities with little training data, which will be described in next section.

3. DISCRIMINATIVE MODEL FOR CCR

This section proposes a novel learning framework by modeling each entity's distribution across hidden entity classes and combining it with a logistic regression model to form a final discriminative model. First we provide a formal definition of the research problem and model it as a classification task, and then present two discriminative models: a global model and an entity class-dependent mixture model.

3.1 Problem Statement

We consider CCR as a binary classification problem that treats the relevant entity-document pairs as positive instances and irrelevant ones as negative instances. Many probabilistic classification techniques in the literature generally fall into two categories: generative models and discriminative models. Discriminative models have attractive theoretical properties [24] and generally perform better than their generative counterparts in the field of information retrieval [16, 32]. Therefore, we adopt discriminative probabilistic models in this paper.

Given a set of KB entities $\mathcal{E} = \{e_u\}(u = 1, \cdots, M)$ and a document collection $\mathcal{D} = \{d_v\}(v = 1, \cdots, N)$, our objective is to estimate the relevance of a document d to a given entity e. In other words, we need estimate the conditional probability of relevance $P(r|e, d)$ with respect to an entity-document pair (e, d). Each entity-document pair (e, d) is represented as a feature vector $\mathbf{f}(e, d) = (f_1(e, d), \cdots, f_K(e, d))$, where K indicates the number of entity-document features. Moreover, to model the hidden entity class information, each entity can be represented as an entity-class feature vector $\mathbf{g}(\mathbf{e}) = (g_1(e), \cdots, g_L(e))$, where L indicates the number of entity-class features. The entity-document features and entity-class features will be introduced in Section 4 later.

3.2 Global Discriminative Model

This paper utilizes logistic regression, a traditional discriminative model, to estimate the conditional probability $P(r|e, d)$, in which $r(r \in \{1, -1\})$ is a binary label to indicate the relevance of the entity-document pair (e, d). The value of r is 1 if the document d is relevant to the entity e, otherwise $r = -1$. Formally, the parametric form of $P(r = 1|e, d)$ can be expressed as follows in terms of logistic functions over a linear combination of features,

$$P(r = 1|e, d) = \delta(\sum_{i=1}^{K} \omega_i f_i(e, d)) \quad (1)$$

where $\delta(x) = 1/(1 + \exp(-x))$ is the standard logistic function, and ω_i is the combination parameter for the ith entry of the feature vector. For the irrelevant class, we have

$$P(r = -1|e, d) = 1 - P(r = 1|e, d) = \delta(-\sum_{i=1}^{K} \omega_i f_i(e, d)) \quad (2)$$

It is worth noting that for different values of r, the only difference in $P(r|e, d)$ is the sign within the logistic function. Therefore, we adopt the general representation of $P(r|e, d) = \delta(r \sum_{i=1}^{K} \omega_i f_i(e, d))$ in the following sections. The conditional probability of relevance $P(r|e, d)$ represents the extent to which the document d is relevant to the entity e. The entity-documents pairs are then classified as positive or negative according to the value of $P(r = 1|e, q)$. Since the learned weights are identical for all entity-document pairs and regardless of specific entities, this model is also denoted as global discriminative model (GDM) in this paper.

Several other approaches for CCR [5, 29] can be deemed as global discriminative models adopting different classification functions such as decision trees and Support Vector Machine (SVM).

3.3 Entity Class-Dependent Mixture Model

In the GDM introduced in Subsection 3.2, a fixed set of combination weights (i.e., ω) are learned to optimize the overall performance for all entities. However, the best combination strategy for a given entity is not always the best for others. The entities stored in KBs are extremely diverse, including persons, organizations, locations, events, etc. Different entities have personalized criteria to detect relevant documents.

We propose an entity class-dependent discriminative mixture model (ECDMM) by introducing an intermediate latent class layer to capture the entity class information in the learning framework. A latent variable z is utilized to indicate which entity class the combination weights $\omega_{z\cdot} = (\omega_{z1}, \cdots, \omega_{zK})$ are drawn from. The choice of z depends on the target entity e in the entity-document pair (e, d). The joint probability of relevance r and the latent variable z is represented as

$$P(r, z|e, d; \alpha, \omega) = P(z|e; \alpha)P(r|e, d, z; \omega) \quad (3)$$

where $P(z|e; \alpha)$ is the mixing coefficient, representing the probability of choosing hidden entity class z given entity e, and α is the corresponding parameter. $P(e, d, z; \omega)$ denotes the mixture component which takes a logistic functions for $r = 1$ (or $r = -1$). $\omega = \{\omega_{zi}\}$ is the set of combination parameters where ω_{zi} is the weight for the *ith* feature vector entry for the given training instance (e, d) under the hidden class z. By marginalizing out the latent variable z, the corresponding mixture model can be written as

$$P(r|e, d; \alpha, \omega) = \sum_{z}^{N_z} P(z|e; \alpha)\delta\left(r \sum_{i=1}^{K} \omega_{zi} f_i(e, d)\right) \quad (4)$$

where N_z is the number of latent entity classes. If $P(z|e; \alpha)$ follows the multinomial distribution, the model cannot easily generalize the combination weights to unseen entities beyond the training set since each parameter in multinomial distribution specifically corresponding to a training entity. To address this problem, we adopt a soft-max function $\frac{1}{Z_e} \exp(\sum_{j=1}^{L_z} \alpha_{zj} g_j(e))$ to model $P(z|e; \alpha)$ instead. α_{zj} is the weight parameter associated with the *jth* entity feature in the latent entity class z and Z_e is the normalization factor that scales the exponential function to be a proper probability distribution. In this representation, each entity e is denoted by a bag of entity-class features $(g_1(e), \cdots, g_{L_z}(e))$ where L_z is the number of entity features. By plugging the soft-max function into Eq. 4, we can get

$$P(r|e,d;\alpha,\omega) = \frac{1}{Z_e}\sum_{z=1}^{N_z}\exp\left(\sum_{j=1}^{L_z}\alpha_{zj}g_j(e)\right)\delta\left(r\sum_{i=1}^{K}\omega_{zi}f_i(e,d)\right) \quad (5)$$

Because α_{zj} is associated with each entity feature instead of each entity, the above model allows the estimated α_{zj} to be applied to less popular entities and even unseen entities.

Suppose entity-document pairs in training set are represented as $\mathcal{T} = \{(e_u, d_v)\}$, and $\mathcal{R} = \{r_{uv}\}$ denotes the corresponding relevance judgment (i.e., $+1$ or -1) of (e_u, d_v), where $u = 1, \cdots, M$ and $v = 1, \cdots, N$. Assume training instances in $\mathcal{T}$ are independently generated, the conditional likelihood of the training data is written as follows.

$$P(\mathcal{R}|\mathcal{T}) = \prod_{u=1}^{M}\prod_{v=1}^{N}P(r_{uv}|e_u,d_v) =$$

$$\prod_{u=1}^{M}\prod_{v=1}^{N}\left(\frac{1}{Z_{e_u}}\sum_{z=1}^{N_z}\exp(\sum_{j=1}^{L_z}\alpha_{zj}g_j(e_u))\delta(r_{uv}\sum_{i=1}^{K}\omega_{zi}f_i(e_u,d_v))\right) \quad (6)$$

3.4 Parameter Estimation

The parameters (i.e. ω and α) in Eq. 6 can be estimated by maximizing the following data log-likelihood function,

$$\mathcal{L}(\omega,\alpha) = \sum_{u=1}^{M}\sum_{v=1}^{N}\log\left(\sum_{z=1}^{N_z}(\frac{1}{Z_{e_u}}\exp(\sum_{j=1}^{L_z}\alpha_{zj}g_j(e_u))) \delta(r_{uv}\sum_{i=1}^{K}\omega_{zi}f_i(e_u,d_v))\right) \quad (7)$$

where M is the number of the entities and N is the number of the documents in training set. $g_j(e_u)$ denotes the jth feature for the uth entity and r_{uv} denotes the relevance judgment for the pair (e_u, d_v). A typical approach to maximize Eq. 7 is to use Expectation-Maximization (EM) algorithm [8].

E-Step.

The E-step can be derived as follows by computing the posterior probability of z given entity e_u and document d_v.

$$P(z|e_u,d_v) = \frac{\exp(\sum_{j=1}^{L_z}\alpha_{zj}g_j(e_u))\delta(r_{uv}\sum_{i=1}^{K}\omega_{zi}f_i(e_u,d_v))}{\sum_z\exp(\sum_{j=1}^{L_z}\alpha_{zj}g_j(e_u))\delta(r_{uv}\sum_{i=1}^{K}\omega_{zi}f_i(e_u,d_v))} \quad (8)$$

M-Step.

By optimize the auxiliary Q function, we can derive the following parameter update rules.

$$\omega_z^* = \arg\max_{\omega_z}\sum_{uv}P(z|e_u,d_v)\log\left(\delta(r_{uv}\sum_{i=1}^{K}\omega_{zi}f_i(e_u,d_v))\right) \quad (9)$$

$$\alpha_z^* = \arg\max_{\alpha_z}\sum_u\left(\sum_v P(z|e_u,d_v)\right)\log\left(\frac{1}{Z_{e_u}}\exp(\sum_{j=1}^{L_z}\alpha_{zj}g_j(e_u))\right) \quad (10)$$

The M-step can be optimized by any gradient descent method. To optimize Eq. 9 and Eq. 10, we employ the **minFunc** toolkit[4], a collection of Matlab functions for solving optimization problems using Quasi-Newton strategy. When the value of $\mathcal{L}(\omega,\alpha)$ converges to a local optima, the estimated parameters can be plugged back into the model to compute the probability of relevance for entity-document pairs. Since EM is only guaranteed to converge to local optima given different starting points, we try several starting points and choose the model that leads to the greatest log-likelihood.

3.5 Discussion

The ECDMM can exploit the following two advantages over the GDM: (1) the combination weights are able to change across entities and hence lead to a gain of flexibility. (2) it offers probabilistic semantics for the latent entity classes and thus each entity can be associated with multiple classes.

Determining the number of latent Variables.

The number of hidden entity classes can be determined by some model selection criterion. We choose Akaike Information Criteria (AIC), which has been shown suitable in determining the number of latent classes in mixture models. As a measure of the goodness of fit of an estimated statistical model, AIC is defined as

$$2m - 2\mathcal{L}(\omega,\alpha) \quad (11)$$

where m is the total number of parameters in the model. AIC offers a relative estimation of the information loss when a given model is used to represent the process that generates the data. Given a set of models, the preferred model is the one with the minimum AIC value.

4. FEATURES

In this section, we present the two types of features used in the discriminative models. Entity-document features $\mathbf{f}(e,d)$ are used in the discriminative components of GDM and ECDMM. In addition, ECDMM requires entity-class features $\mathbf{g}(e)$ to learn the mixing coefficients in the mixture component.

4.1 Entity-Document Features

Entity-document features (i.e., $\mathbf{f}(e,d)$) are composed of semantic and temporal features.

4.1.1 *Semantic Features*

We adopt the semantic features listed in Table 1, which have been proved effective in CCR [28, 29]. Semantic features can model semantic characteristics of document-entity pairs.

4.1.2 *Temporal Features*

Entities are evolving in the stream corpus as time goes by, yet semantic features are not capable of portraying the

[4]http://www.cs.ubc.ca/~schmidtm/Software/minFunc.html

Table 1: **Semantic features.**

Feature	Description
$N(e_{rel})$	# of entity e's related entities found in its profile page
$N(d, e)$	# of occurrences of e in document d
$N(d, e_{rel})$	# of occurrences of the related entities in document d
$FPOS(d, e)$	First occurrence position of e in d
$FPOS_n(d, e)$	$FPOS(d, e)$ normalized by the document length
$LPOS(d, e)$	Last occurrence position of e in d
$LPOS_n(d, e)$	$LPOS(d, e)$ normalized by the document length
$Spread(d, e)$	$LPOS(d, e) - FPOS(d, e)$
$Spread_n(d, e)$	$Spread(d, e)$ normalized by document length
$Sim_{cos}(d, s_i(e))$	Cosine similarity between d and the ith section of e's profile
$Sim_{jac}(d, s_i(e))$	Jaccard similarity between d and the ith section of e's profile
$Sim_{cos}(d, c_i)$	Cosine similarity between d and the ith citation of e in the KB
$Sim_{jac}(d, c_i)$	Jaccard similarity between d and the ith citation of e in the KB

dynamic characteristics of entities. So we resort temporal features to make up this deficiency. Previous work [2, 5, 29] considering temporal features can be summarized as a straightforward strategy that counts the daily (or hourly) occurrences of target entities in the stream corpus and calculates some statistical indicators as temporal features. To exploit the effectiveness of temporal features, novel bursty features are introduced in this paper. The underlying intuition is that the occurrences of entities in the stream do not distribute uniformly. If the amount of documents referring to an entity increases sharply in a short time period when something important is happening around the entity, this time period is detected as one bursty period of this entity. We make an assumption that documents occur in a bursty period of an entity are more likely to be related to it than those not.

The bursty periods of an entity can be detected either from stream corpus or from third-party data sources, denoted as internal bursty periods and external bursty periods respectively. Due to the heterogeneity of data sources, we use different burst detection methods to identify internal bursty periods and external bursty periods for entities.

Internal Burst Detection.

Burst detection from a stream of documents have been thoroughly investigated in TDT and event detection [22, 17, 31].

Since our goal is not to develop a new burst detection algorithm, we simply adopt Kleinberg's 2-state finite automaton model [22] to identify bursty periods of entities. There are two states q_0 and q_1 in the finite automaton $\mathcal{A}$. For every target entity e, when $\mathcal{A}$ in state q_0, it has low emission rate $\beta_0 = \frac{|R_d(e)|}{T}$, where $R_d(e)$ is the number of all documents referring to e over the whole time range T. When $\mathcal{A}$ in state q_1, the rate is increased to $\beta_1 = s \cdot \frac{|R_d(e)|}{T}$, where $\beta_1 > \beta_0$ because s is a scaling factor larger than 1.0 and s is empirically set as 2.0 in our work. The larger the number of documents referring to entity e at time t, the higher the likelihood of e being identified as a bursty entity at t.

After performing the burst detection algorithm, if the automaton of entity e is in the state q_1 during a time period $[t_{start}, t_{end}]$, $[t_{start}, t_{end}]$ is a burtsy period of e with a bursty weight $bw_{(t_{start}, t_{end})}(e)$. The bursty weight is defined as the cost improvement incurred by assigning state q_1 over the bursty period instead of q_0, and can be found in [22].

External Burst Detection.

External resources, such as daily view statistics of entities' profile pages, are utilized as temporal features in previous work [2, 29]. Since some KBs do not provide page view statistics for entities as Wikipedia, we also include Google Trends[5] to detect external bursts. Akin to Wikipedia statistics, Google Trends can provide a numeric sequence $\mathbf{v} = (v_1, \cdots, v_T)$ for each entity e, where v_i denotes the normalized search volume of e in the ith day.

We detect external bursts of entity e from $\mathbf{v}$ with a tailored moving average (MA) method [27]. More concretely, for each v_i in $\mathbf{v}$,

1. Calculate a moving average sequence of length w as
$$MA_w(i) = \frac{v_i + v_{i-1} + \cdots + v_{i-w+1}}{w}$$
2. Calculate a cutoff $c(i)$ based on previous MA sequences $Pre_{MA} = (MA_w(1), \cdots, MA_w(i))$ as
$$c(i) = mean(Pre_{MA}) + \beta \cdot std(Pre_{MA})$$
3. Detect bursty day sequence $\mathbf{d}$, where $\mathbf{d} = \{i | MA_w(i) \geq c(i)\}$
4. Calculate the bursty weight sequence $\mathbf{w} = (w_1, \cdots, w_T)$ for e as follows.
$$w_i = \begin{cases} 0, i \notin \mathbf{d} \\ \dfrac{MA_w(i)}{c(i)}, i \in \mathbf{d} \end{cases}$$
5. Compact each segment of consecutive days in $\mathbf{d}$ into a bursty period $[t_{start}, t_{end}]$ of entity e, and the bursty weight $bw_{(t_{start}, t_{end})}$ is calculated as the average weight of all the bursts in this period.

The moving average length can be varied to detect long-term or short-term bursts. We set the moving average length as 7 days (i.e., $w = 7$). The cutoff value is empirically set as 2 times the standard deviation of the MA (i.e., $\beta = 2$).

Bursty Feature Representation.

Given an entity-document pair (e, d), we define a bursty value $b(e, d)$ to represent the temporal correlation between d and e. Let t be the timestamp of d. If t falls in one of e's bursty periods, say $[t_{start}, t_{end}]$, then $b(d, e)$ is calculated as Eq. 12 shows. If t is not in any bursty period of e, $b(d, e)$ is set as 0.

$$b(d, e) = (1 - \frac{t - t_{start}}{t_{end} - t_{start}}) \cdot bw_{(t_{start}, t_{end})}(e), \quad t \in [t_{start}, t_{end}] \tag{12}$$

In Eq. 12, $1 - \frac{t - t_{start}}{t_{end} - t_{start}}$ is a decaying coefficient reflecting the intuition that the documents appear at the beginning of a bursty period are more informative than those appear

[5]http://www.google.com/trends/

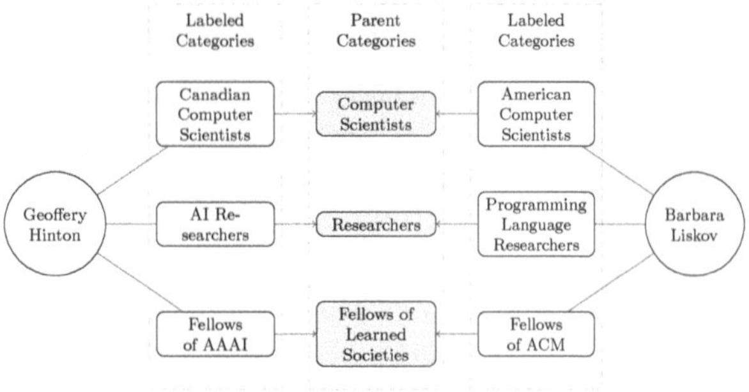

Figure 1: Two entities without common labeled categories but with shared parent categories.

at the end. Please note that $b(d, e)$ can be calculated based on external bursts and internal bursts respectively. To avoid using future information during burst detection, we carefully perform burst detection algorithm (either internal or external) in a daily incremental manner. When dealing with an entity-document pair, the bursty periods are determined by the data before the timestamp of this document.

4.2 Entity-Class Features

In ECDMM, besides entity-document features, entity-class features (i.e., $g(e)$ in Eq. 5) are required to learn the mixing coefficients. Here we consider two types of prior knowledge to design entity-class features.

4.2.1 *Profile-based features*

Each entity in KBs is uniquely identified by its profile page, which contains the basic information of this entity, such as name, address and experiences. We crawl the profile pages of all the entities as a profile collection. After removing stop words, we represent each entity as a feature vector with the bag-of-words model, where term weights are determined by the TF-IDF scheme.

4.2.2 *Category-based features*

Some KBs like Wikipedia organize entities with hierarchical categories. For example, `Geoffrey Hinton` in Wikipedia, is labeled with categories such as `Canadian computer scientists`, `Artificial intelligence researchers`, and `Fellows of AAAI`. Besides these labeled categories, we take the parent categories of the labeled categories into consideration to deal with the circumstance in Figure 1. The two alike entities can not be correlated if we only consider labeled categories.

Similar to profile-based feature vector, we leverage a "bag-of-categories" model to represent each entity as a category-based feature vector. Given an entity without category information, we manually assign a meta-category for it according to its profile. We supplement three meta-categories: **person**, **facility** and **organization**, which can cover all the entities in our dataset. The category-based feature vector of entity e is denoted as $g^c(e) = (c_1(e), \cdots, c_N(e))$, where N is the total number of categories. $c_i(e)$ equals to 1 if e is labeled with category c_i, otherwise $c_i(e)$ is 0.

Therefore, given a target entity set $\mathcal{E}$, we can generate two feature vectors for each $e \in \mathcal{E}$: profile-based vector $\mathbf{g}^p(e)$ and category-based vector $\mathbf{g}^c(e)$ respectively.

5. EXPERIMENTS

In this section, we first introduce the dataset for experiments. After that, we report an extensive set of experimental results of our proposed models and baselines in two scenarios of CCR. At last, analysis and discussion are presented based on the experimental results.

5.1 Dataset

We conduct our experiments on TREC-KBA-2013 dataset[6], a standard test bed provided by TREC. The data set is composed of a target entity set and a document collection called stream corpus.

Entity Set.

The target entity set includes 121 Wikipedia entities and 20 Twitter entities, more specifically, 98 people, 19 organizations, and 24 facilities from 14 inter-related communities such as small towns like `Danville, KY` and academic communities like `Turing award winners`.

Stream Corpus.

The temporally-ordered stream corpus, containing approximately 1 billion documents crawled from October 2011 to the end of February 2013. Each document is associated with a timestamp indicating its time of crawling. The corpus have been split with documents from October 2011 to February 2012 as training instances and the remainder for evaluation. We adopt the same training/test range setting in our experiments.

Annotation.

The relevance of entity-document pairs are labeled following a four-point scale relevance setting, including *vital*, *useful*, *neural* and *garbage*. The definitions are listed in Table 2.

Table 2: Four-point scale relevance estimation in TREC-KBA-2013.

Vital	timely info about the entity's current state, actions, or situation. This would motivate a change to an already up-to-date KB article.
Useful	possibly citable but not timely, e.g., background biography, secondary source information.
Neutral	informative but not citable, e.g., tertiary source like Wikipedia article itself.
Garbage	no information about the target entity could be learned from the document, e.g., spam.

The details of the annotations for Wikipedia and Twitter entities are demonstrated in Table 3.

5.2 Evaluation Scenarios

According to different granularity settings, we evaluate the proposed models in two classification scenarios respectively.

[6]http://trec-kba.org/kba-stream-corpus-2013.shtml

Table 3: The number of training and test instances (entity-document pairs) for Wikipedia and Twitter entities respectively.

	Training				Test			
	Vital	Useful	Neutral	Garbage	Vital	Useful	Neutral	Garbage
Wikipedia	2096	2257	1162	1756	8639	16053	5649	18694
Twitter	182	326	72	569	1808	2953	1491	4103
Total	2278	2583	1234	2325	10447	19006	7140	22797

Vital Only.

Only *vital* entity-document pairs are treated as positive instances, and the others are negative instances. This scenario is the essential task of CCR.

Vital + Useful.

Both *vital* and *useful* entity-document pairs are treated as positive instances, and the others are negative ones.

5.3 Experimental Methodology

Experiments in this section investigate the effectiveness of our proposed mixture model and baseline methods in the two scenarios. The following methods are compared:

- Global Discriminative Model (**GDM**). As presented in Subsection 3.2, this approach learns a set of fixed weights for all entity-documents pairs.

- Naïve Entity Class-Dependent Discriminative Mixture Model (**Naïve_ECDMM**). This approach uses entity-document features instead of entity-class features for the mixing component (i.e., $\mathbf{g}(e) := \mathbf{f}(e, d)$ in Eq. 5) of ECDMM.

- Profile-based Entity Class-Dependent Discriminative Mixture Model (**profile_ECDMM**). This approach utilizes profile-based features as entity-class features for the mixing component of ECDMM.

- Category-based Entity Class-Dependent Discriminative Mixture Model (**category_ECDMM**). This approach utilizes category-based features as entity-class features for the mixing component of ECDMM.

- Combination Entity Class-Dependent Discriminative Mixture Model (**combine_ECDMM**). This approach utilizes profile-based and category-based features together as entity-class features for the mixing component of ECDMM. In our experimental setting, we simply union the two feature vectors together into an integral feature vector.

For reference, we also include three top-ranked approaches in the TREC-KBA-2013 track as baselines.

- **Official Baseline** [13]. A string matching approach implemented by TREC-KBA organizers. For each target entity, they split the entity's name into different tokens and manually composite them into reliable aliases of the entity. These alias are utilized to filter relevant documents from the stream corpus with the strategy that documents referring to any alias are rated as *vital* to the target entity. A relevance score is estimated according to the length of matched string.

- **BIT-MSRA** [29]. An entity-unspecific random forests classification model, which is the first place approach in TREC-KBA-2013 track. This approach can be considered as a variant of GDM utilizing a different kernel.

- **UDEL** [23]. An entity-centric query expansion approach that achieves the second best performance in TREC-KBA-2013 track. Given a target entity, the approach first detect related entities from the profile page of the entity. Then, these related entities are utilized as expansion terms and combine with the target entity as a new query to detect and rank the relevant documents. The optimal weights of query terms are learned from the training data. The relevance score of a document is estimated according to its position in the ranking list.

5.4 Hidden Classes Analysis

For all mixture models, the number of hidden classes are determined according to AIC value. The optimal numbers of latent classes of all variants of ECDMM are reported in Table 4. The number of optimal classes of category_ECDMM is obviously larger than the optimal numbers of the other mixture models, which possibly caused by the hierarchical structures of categories in our category-based feature set. Although the incorporation of parent categories can build the correlation between two similar entities without common labeled categories, it brings some noisy correlations in the meantime. For instance, a politician and a business man both living in Florida share a common parent category "`Living people from Ocala, FLorida`", this correlation will mislead the model and come to an non-optimal fit to the data.

Table 4: Number of hidden classes determined by AIC for each mixture model.

Model	Vital	Vital + Useful
naïve_ECDMM	9	10
profile_ECDMM	7	6
category_ECDMM	13	12
combine_ECDMM	9	8

5.5 Overall Results

This section presents the overall performance of all experimental methods. We adopt F_1 (harmonic mean between precision and recall), accuracy and AUC (Area Under Curve) [12] as the evaluation measurements. All the measurements are computed in an entity-insensitive manner. In other words, the measurements are computed based on the test pool of all entity-document pairs regardless of specific entities. The results are reported in Table 5.

Table 5: Overall classification results of evaluated models.

Methods	Vital Only					Vital + Useful				
	P	R	F_1	Accu	AUC	P	R	F_1	Accu	AUC
Official Baseline	.171	**.942**	.290	.175	.475	.540	**.972**	.694	.532	.488
BIT-MSRA	.214	.790	.337	.445	.580	.589	.974	.734	.615	.578
UDEL	.169	.806	.280	.259	.473	.573	.893	.698	.579	.547
GDM	.218	.507	.304	.587	.556	.604	.913	.727	.565	.588
naïve_ECDMM	.223	.400	.286	.644	.548	.627	.912	.744	.656	.631
profile_ECDMM	.332	.376	.353	.754	.606	.669	.866	.755	.692	.675
category_ECDMM	.316	.422	.362	..734	.612	.672	.894	.767	.704	.685
combine_ECDMM	**.397**	.418	**.407**	**.783**	**.640**	**.703**	.877	**.780**	**.731**	**.716**

We notice that combine_ECDMM achieves best on all measurements except recall. The official baseline achieve the best recall of all methods, which is not surprising since the official baseline is a manual method to detect as many relevant documents as possible by manually selecting reliable aliases of an entity in advance.

Compared with GDM regardless of entity class information, all the mixture models employing entity-class features explicitly (i.e., profile_ECDMM, category_ECDMM and combine_ECDMM) achieve better classification performance in both scenarios. Even Naïve_ECDMM which does not employ entity-class features explicitly can outperform GDM and other three baselines. This reveals that the mixture model is an effective strategy to enhance the straightforward discriminative model. Naïve_ECDMM is not robust in two scenarios. Although it outperforms GDM in *vital + useful* scenario, it cannot beat GDM in *vital only* scenario. This is possibly caused by its implicitly employment of entity-class features. The entity-document features are noisy, because the document-related counterpart contributes nothing to capture hidden entity classes.

Both profile_ECDMM and category_ECDMM outperform naïve_ECDMM remarkably, revealing that profile-based features and category-based features are effective in modeling hidden entity classes. Category-based features are more promising than profile-based features, which is reasonable because the category labels in KBs contain prior human knowledge on entity class and taxonomy information. Even though combine_ECDMM combines profile-based features and category-based features in a straightforward manner, it achieves the best performance. In comparison to GDM, combine_ECDMM improve F_1 more than 10 percent and AUC approximately 10 percent. We believe that the performance can be enhanced further with more comprehensive entity class information and combination strategy.

5.6 Fine-grained Results

This section compares the methods in a fine-grained level. We need guarantee our mixture models not only achieve remarkable overall performance, but also perform well in entity-level. Hence, we recomputed the measurements in an entity-sensitive manner.

Based on the classification results for each entity e_i ($i = 1, \cdots, M$) in the test set, precision and recall of each model are first calculated as $P(e_i)$ and $R(e_i)$. Then, we compute the macro-averaged precision and recall over all entities, denoted as $macro\_P = \frac{\sum_1^M P(e_i)}{M}$ and $macro\_R = \frac{\sum_1^M R(e_i)}{M}$ respectively. At last, macro-averaged F_1 is computed according to $macro\_P$ and $macro\_R$.

The macro-averaged measurements in two scenarios are reported in 2(a) and 2(b) respectively. The three baselines are labeled with red color, and the blue dots represent our proposed methods. The best method is labeled with pentagram in both figures. The parallel solid curves are contour lines of F_1 value, which means the dots in the same curve achieve same F_1 values. The dots lying in upper right achieve higher F_1 than the lower left ones. Obviously, combine_ECDMM achieves the best F_1 in both scenarios. We also find our mixture models (i.e., blue dots) achieve higher precision in *vital only* scenario, demonstrating our models can detect vital documents more accurately than the baselines.

5.7 Performance on Unseen Entities

This section evaluates the generalization ability of our proposed models to handle unseen entities in the training set. A robust model is able to handle unseen entities as well as training entities. As listed in Table 6, there are 10 unseen entities in the TREC-KBA-2013 dataset. We evaluate the performance of our models on the unseen entity set composed of these 10 entities. We choose macro-averaged accuracy as the evaluation measurement. Due to the sparse positive instances for some unseen entities, it is improper to adopt precision, recall and F_1 for evaluation because they possibly become 0, in which case these measurements cannot reflect the performance suitably. The results are reported in Table 7.

Table 7: The averages of accuracies over 10 unseen entities.

Methods	accu@(vital)	accu@(vital + useful)
Official Baseline	.175	.532
BIT-MSRA	.445	.614
UDEL	.259	.579
GDM	.552	.565
naïve_ECDMM	.587	.608
profile_ECDMM	**.623**	**.647**
category_ECDMM	.565	.431
combine_ECDMM	.580	.582

In both scenarios, the best classification results are achieved by profile_ECDMM, which outperforms category_ECDMM and combine_ECDMM. A possible explanation for the unsatisfactory performance of category_ECDMM is that the category information of unseen entities are not covered well in the training set, especially the Twitter entities. For these entities, there is too little category information to model their hidden classes accurately.

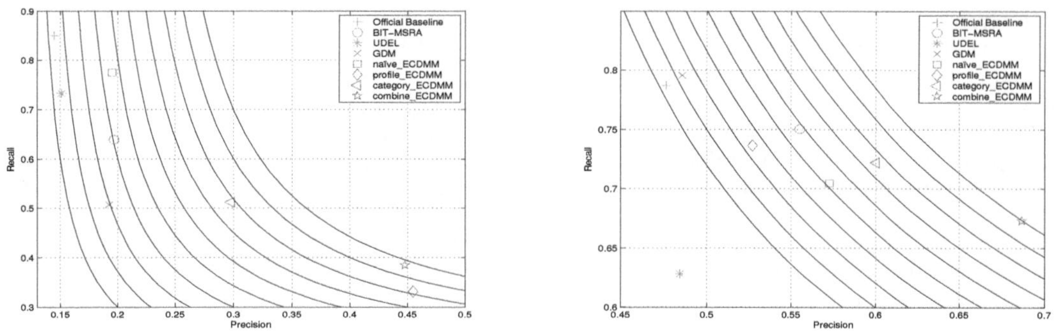

(a) *Vital Only* (b) *Vital + Useful*

Figure 2: Macro-averaged recall VS. macro-averaged precision over all test entities. The best approach is dotted as pentagram.

Table 6: The statistics of test instances for 10 unseen entities.

Entity	KB	vital	useful	neutral/garbage	total
The Ritz Apartment (Ocala,Florida)	Wiki	4	1	5	10
Keri Hehn	Wiki	3	0	0	3
Chiara Nappi	Wiki	2	3	55	60
Chuck Pankow	Wiki	7	0	10	17
John H. Lang	Wiki	2	0	1	3
Joshua Boschee	Wiki	191	23	5	219
MissMarcel	Twitter	52	13	3	68
evvnt	Twitter	1	3	40	44
GandBcoffee	Twitter	0	2	2	4
BartowMcDonald	Twitter	1	18	9	28

In *vital only* scenario, all the variants of our mixture model can achieve better classification performance than GDM and the other baselines. The results validate the flexibility of our mixture model as expectation, which is essential for a practical CCR system. Our mixture model is not only good at handling existing entities in the training set, but also capable of dealing with unseen entities.

5.8 Bursty Feature Analysis

To further validate the effectiveness of the proposed bursty features, we evaluate them with the help of Information Gain (IG). Table 8 reports the IGs of the proposed features in two scenarios. All the IGs are computed following the method proposed in [33]. The higher of the IG achieved by a feature, the more powerful role it plays in the classification. The *maximum*, *mean* and *median* IGs of semantic features are also presented for reference. Since the bursty features are only used in the discriminative counterpart of ECDMM, we evaluate them with GDM.

In Table 8, external bursty features perform best out of all features in both scenarios, conforming that external bursts of an entity are accompanied with occurrences of its relevant documents. However, internal bursts are not so helpful in *vital + useful* scenario as in *vital only* scenario. This is possibly caused by the incompleteness of the stream corpus. As we know, the stream corpus are crawled from the web, so it is possibly a biased snapshot of the true web. In addition, we only utilize the occurrences of a target entity itself in the stream corpus to detect its internal bursts currently. We can include more evidences to improve the accuracy of internal burst detection. For instance, contextual related entities can be resorted to enhance the detection accuracy of internal burst.

Table 8: Information gain values of features.

	Information Gain	
Feature	Vital Only	Vital + Useful
external bursty feature	**0.130**	**0.286**
internal bursty feature	0.020	0.008
max[1]	0.121	0.175
mean[2]	0.046	0.081
median[3]	0.039	0.067

[1] maximum IG of all semantic features
[2] mean IG of all semantic features
[3] median IG of all semantic features

6. CONCLUSIONS AND FUTURE WORK

The objective of Cumulative Citation Recommendation (CCR) is to detect citation-worthy documents for a set of KB entities from a chronological stream corpus. To address the problem of training data insufficiency for less popular entities, we propose an entity class-dependent discriminative mixture model (ECDMM) by introducing a latent entity class layer to model the hidden entity class information. The model can be adjusted to different types of entities by learning flexible combination parameters according to underlying entity classes. Experimental results demonstrate that ECDMM can improve the performance of CCR. Entity-document features and entity-class features are developed for the discriminative and mixing components of ECDMM respectively. In terms of entity-class features, profile-based and category-based features are validated separately and in a combination strategy. The novel bursty features developed as entity-document features are proved rewarding. Our ECDMM with proposed semantic and temporal features can achieve the state-of-the-art performance on TREC-KBA-2013 dataset.

For future work, we wish to explore more useful entity-class features and apply more proper combination strategies to improve the entity class-dependent mixture model.

Acknowledgement

The authors would like to thank Jing Liu and Ning Zhang for their valuable suggestions and the anonymous reviewers for their helpful comments. This work is funded by the National Program on Key Basic Research Project (973 Program, Grant No. 2013CB329600), National Natural Science Foundation of China (NSFC, Grant Nos. 61472040 and 60873237), and Beijing Higher Education Young Elite Teacher Project (Grant No. YETP1198).

7. REFERENCES

[1] J. Allan. Introduction to topic detection and tracking. In *Topic Detection and Tracking*, volume 12 of *The Information Retrieval Series*, pages 1–16. Springer US, 2002.

[2] K. Balog and H. Ramampiaro. Cumulative citation recommendation: classification vs. ranking. In *SIGIR*, pages 941–944. ACM, 2013.

[3] K. Balog, H. Ramampiaro, N. Takhirov, and K. Nørvåg. Multi-step classification approaches to cumulative citation recommendation. In *OAIR*, pages 121–128. ACM, 2013.

[4] R. Berendsen, E. Meij, D. Odijk, M. d. Rijke, and W. Weerkamp. The university of amsterdam at trec 2012. In *TREC*. NIST, 2012.

[5] L. Bonnefoy, V. Bouvier, and P. Bellot. A weakly-supervised detection of entity central documents in a stream. In *SIGIR*, pages 769–772. ACM, 2013.

[6] Z. W. C. Tompkins and S. G. Small. Sawus: Siena's automatic wikipedia update system. In *TREC*. NIST, 2012.

[7] J. Dalton and L. Dietz. Bi-directional linkability from wikipedia to documents and back again: Umass at trec 2012 knowledge base acceleration track. In *TREC*. NIST, 2012.

[8] A. P. Dempster, N. M. Laird, and D. B. Rubin. Maximum likelihood from incomplete data via the em algorithm. *Journal of the Royal Statistical Society. Series B (Methodological)*, pages 1–38, 1977.

[9] L. Dietz and J. Dalton. Time-aware evaluation of cumulative citation recommendation systems. In *SIGIR 2013 Workshop on Time-aware Information Access (TAIA2013)*, 2013.

[10] L. Dietz, J. Dalton, and K. Balog. Umass at trec 2013 knowledge base acceleration track. In *TREC*. NIST, 2013.

[11] Y. Fang, L. Si, and A. Mathur. Discriminative probabilistic models for expert search in heterogeneous information sources. *Information Retrieval*, 14(2):158–177, 2011.

[12] T. Fawcett. An introduction to roc analysis. *Pattern Recogn. Lett.*, 27(8):861–874, June 2006.

[13] J. Frank, S. J. Bauer, M. Kleiman-Weiner, D. A. Roberts, N. Triouraneni, C. Zhang, and C. Rè. Evaluating stream filtering for entity profile updates for trec 2013. In *TREC*. NIST, 2013.

[14] J. R. Frank, M. Kleiman-Weiner, D. A. Roberts, F. Niu, C. Zhang, C. Re, and I. Soboroff. Building an Entity-Centric Stream Filtering Test Collection for TREC 2012. In *TREC*. NIST, 2012.

[15] G. G. Gebremeskel, J. He, A. P. d. Vries, and J. Lin. Cumulative citation recommendation: A feature-aware comparison of approaches. In *Database and Expert Systems Applications (DEXA)*, pages 193–197. IEEE, 2014.

[16] A. Genkin, D. D. Lewis, and D. Madigan. Large-scale bayesian logistic regression for text categorization. *Technometrics*, 2007.

[17] Q. He, K. Chang, and E.-P. Lim. Using burstiness to improve clustering of topics in news streams. In *ICDM*, pages 493–498. IEEE, 2007.

[18] Q. He, K. Chang, E.-P. Lim, and J. Zhang. Bursty feature representation for clustering text streams. In *SDM*, pages 491–496. SIAM, 2007.

[19] D. Hong and L. Si. Mixture model with multiple centralized retrieval algorithms for result merging in federated search. In *SIGIR*, pages 821–830. ACM, 2012.

[20] R. Jin, L. Si, and C. Zhai. A study of mixture models for collaborative filtering. *Information Retrieval*, 9(3):357–382, 2006.

[21] B. Kjersten and P. McNamee. The hltcoe approach to the trec 2012 kba track. In *TREC*. NIST, 2012.

[22] J. Kleinberg. Bursty and hierarchical structure in streams. In *KDD*, pages 91–101. ACM, 2002.

[23] X. Liu, J. Darko, and H. Fang. A related entity based approach for knowledge base acceleration. In *TREC*. NIST, 2013.

[24] A. Y. Ng and M. I. Jordan. On discriminative vs. generative classifiers: A comparison of logistic regression and naive bayes. In T. Dietterich, S. Becker, and Z. Ghahramani, editors, *Advances in Neural Information Processing Systems 14*, pages 841–848. MIT Press, 2002.

[25] A. D. O. Gross and H. Toivonen. Term association analysis for named entity filtering. In *TREC*. NIST, 2012.

[26] J. H. C. B. S. Araujo, G. Gebremeskel and A. de Vries. Cwi at trec 2012 kba track and session track. In *TREC*. NIST, 2012.

[27] M. Vlachos, C. Meek, Z. Vagena, and D. Gunopulos. Identifying similarities, periodicities and bursts for online search queries. In *SIGMOD*, pages 131–142. ACM, 2004.

[28] J. Wang, L. Liao, D. Song, L. Ma, C.-Y. Lin, and Y. Rui. Resorting relevance evidences to cumulative citation recommendation for knowledge base acceleration. In *WAIM*, 2015.

[29] J. Wang, D. Song, C.-Y. Lin, and L. Liao. Bit and msra at trec kba ccr track 2013. In *TREC*. NIST, 2013.

[30] Q. Wang, L. Si, and D. Zhang. A discriminative data-dependent mixture-model approach for multiple instance learning in image classification. In *ECCV*, pages 660–673. 2012.

[31] J. Weng and B.-S. Lee. Event detection in twitter. In *ICWSM*, volume 11, pages 401–408. AAAI, 2011.

[32] Y. Yang and X. Liu. A re-examination of text categorization methods. In *SIGIR*, pages 42–49. ACM, 1999.

[33] Y. Yang and J. O. Pedersen. A comparative study on feature selection in text categorization. In *ICML*, pages 412–420, 1997.

[34] Y. Yang, T. Pierce, and J. Carbonell. A study of retrospective and on-line event detection. In *SIGIR*, pages 28–36. ACM, 1998.

[35] W. X. Zhao, R. Chen, K. Fan, H. Yan, and X. Li. A novel burst-based text representation model for scalable event detection. In *ACL*, pages 43–47. ACL, 2012.

[36] M. Zhou and K. C.-C. Chang. Entity-centric document filtering: boosting feature mapping through meta-features. In *CIKM*, pages 119–128. ACM, 2013.

Scientific Information Understanding via Open Educational Resources (OER)

Xiaozhong Liu
School of Informatics and Computing
Indiana University Bloomington
Bloomington, IN, USA, 47405
liu237@indiana.edu

Zhuoren Jiang
College of Transportation Management
Dalian Maritime University
Dalian, China, 116026
jzr_dlmu@hotmail.com

Liangcai Gao
Institute of Computer Science and Technology
Peking University
Beijing, China, 100871
glc@pku.edu.cn

ABSTRACT

Scientific publication retrieval/recommendation has been investigated in the past decade. However, to the best of our knowledge, few efforts have been made to help junior scholars and graduate students to understand and consume the essence of those scientific readings. This paper proposes a novel learning/reading environment, OER-based Collaborative PDF Reader (OCPR), that incorporates innovative scaffolding methods that can: 1. auto-characterize student emerging information need while reading a paper; and 2. enable students to readily access open educational resources (OER) based on their information need. By using meta-search methods, we pre-indexed 1,112,718 OERs, including presentation videos, slides, algorithm source code, or Wikipedia pages, for 41,378 STEM publications. Based on the computational information need, we use text mining and heterogeneous graph mining algorithms to recommend high quality OERs to help students better understand the scientific content in the paper. Evaluation results and exit surveys for an information retrieval course show that the OCPR system alone with the recommended OERs can effectively assist graduate students better understand the complex STEM publications. For instance, 78.42% of participants believe the OCPR system and recommended OERs can provide precise and useful information they need, while 78.43% of them believe the recommended OERs are close to exactly what they need when reading the paper. From OER ranking viewpoint, MRR, MAP and NDCG results prove that learning to rank and cold start solutions can efficiently integrate different text and graph ranking features.

Categories and Subject Descriptors

H.3.3 [**Information Storage and Retrieval**]: Information Search and Retrieval

General Terms

System, Algorithms, Experimentation, Measurement

SIGIR'15, August 09 - 13, 2015, Santiago, Chile.
 ISBN 978-1-4503-3621-5/15/08 ...$15.00.
DOI: http://dx.doi.org/10.1145/2766462.2767750.

Keywords

Scaffolding; Information Need Characterization; Education; Heterogeneous Graph Mining; Evaluation; Information Understanding

1. INTRODUCTION AND MOTIVATION

"I don't think I need those books... I cannot understand them anyway..." This was a student's response when I suggested that she should find some statistics methods books in the university library. Actually, her response is quite representative when students face STEM (Science, Technology, Engineering, and Mathematics) readings. In the last decade, while the volume of STEM publications has increased dramatically in university and digital libraries, few efforts have been made to help students/junior scholars understand them. From an educational viewpoint, understanding the content of scientific publications in STEM course environments remains daunting [**?**], i.e., **Information Access $\neq$ Information Understanding**. For instance, a number of search/recommendation algorithms ensure Google Scholar and Microsoft Academic give users access to the high quality scientific readings, but junior scholars/graduate students may not necessarily understand them. In a recent study of STEM [**?**], PhD students (in computer science domain) claimed that the complex models, formulas, and methods in the readings were deemed too difficult to understand because of the students' limited knowledge in computer science and mathematics. Students need innovative scaffolding methods/systems to better assist in understanding scientific publications[1].

While the content of scientific publications is challenging and difficult for students, a large number of open educational resources (OERs) are increasingly available and have great potential to assist students better understand the essence of these publications. For example, scholars, organizations and institutions commonly share conference slides, video lectures, tutorials, Wikipedia pages, datasets and source codes generated from research. As these OERs are often seamlessly blended or integrated with other scholarly publications or research topics, students can, we surmise, better understand the papers by leveraging those OERs. In this paper, we define it as OER-based Scaffolding. In a study by Liu [**?**], for example, students expect that a blend of OER-based learning objects could significantly improve learning. Unfortunately, not all OERs exist in a publication as cited references; some may be scattered across different social media (e.g., *TED, SlideShare, authorStream, GitHub, SourceForge, YouTube, Google Code, VideoLecture*, and

[1]In education, scaffolding refers to a variety of instructional techniques used to move students progressively toward stronger understanding and, ultimately, greater independence in the learning process. http://edglossary.org/scaffolding/

Wikipedia). While the cost of manually locating those OERs for large-scale STEM topics or publications is prohibitive, as another challenge, the existing system cannot use those innovative OERs to address students' emerging information needs, i.e., using or recommending OER(s) to address students' questions on a particular section/paragraph/sentence/formula of a scientific publication.

Motivated by these observations, we propose a new solution and an innovative system framework to help students and scholars better understand and learn from scientific publications in a course environment by leveraging OERs, i.e., OER-based scaffolding. A new learning system, called the **OER-based Collaborative PDF Reader (OCPR)**, is to be implemented as a first step towards this effort. Theoretically speaking, the system is also designed to accommodate the needs of students in MOOCs (massive open online courses) in addition to students from varied backgrounds. As Figure **??** shows, the system can auto-characterize student's emerging information need while reading a paper, while recommending high quality OERs to help them understand the publication.

With the exception of using text mining for OER recommendation (i.e., using highlighted text to find relevant OERs), OCPR also employs heterogeneous graph mining to enhance scaffolding performance by investigating the weighted relations between OER pair; OER and paper; OER-topic association; paper-topic association; and the topic-topic relationships, which help to prioritize important OERs and filter out the noisy resources. The meta-path and supervised random-walk-based graph algorithms [?] will be used to explore the important OERs (vertices) given student's implicit and explicit information needs (topic and paper seed vertices). For example, we can assume that when a student is reading a paper, she can be interested in finding OERs relevant to the paper, specific sentences in the paper, the paper's topics, or weekly teaching topics. From an information need perspective, for link-based recommendations, student information need is characterized by some seed vertices on the heterogeneous networks, i.e. the paper or topics that the student is currently reading, and supervised random walk algorithms can be used to recommend candidate OERs.

Evaluation result shows that, first, auto-recommended OERs can provide important and useful information to help students better understand the content of the scientific publications, i.e., MRR (mean reciprocal rank) score is 0.8609 (students find the useful OERs in the 1st or 2nd position in the result ranking list). This assumption is also confirmed in the exit survey, where 78.42% of participants believe the OCPR system along with recommended OERs can provide precise and useful information they need, while 78.43% of them believe the recommended OERs are close to exactly what they need. From system perspective, 80.39% of participates believe the OCPR system and real-time OER recommendation function is easy to use. Second, based on the students' judgments, we found all the OER recommendation can be potentially useful, and the learning to rank method can be quite useful to enhance the recommendation performance. As Table **??** shows, learning to rank and cold start methods significantly ($p < 0.0001$) outperform other methods.

The contribution of this paper is fourfold. First, we propose a novel auto-scaffolding method to help students better understand the scientific readings in a course environment by leveraging various kinds of OERs. Second, a new system, OCPR, is employed to capture student reading behavior while enabling them to ask questions or highlight the confusing part of the readings. Third, novel algorithms are proposed to characterize students' information need and recommend OERs to them while reading a paper. Last but not least, an experiment (with 51 participates) is employed to validate the usefulness of the system and to evaluate the OER recommendation algorithms.

2. RELATED WORK

Scaffolding is defined as a "process that enables a child or novice to solve a problem, carry out a task, or achieve a goal which would be beyond his unassisted efforts" [?]. Since 1976, the term scaffolding has been widely used in educational research [?], and the scaffolding construct is being applied more broadly [?]. In particular, the concept of scaffolding is applied to the studies of computer-assisted learning environments, i.e. computer-mediated scaffolding [?]. Naturally, the focus of scaffolding research is on system design and usage. One of the most recent efforts is to utilize existing social tagging and annotation tools. Social tagging and annotation have produced positive results in a number of tasks, including promoting student learning [?, ?, ?]. For example, students were found to have positive perceptions of usefulness, ease of use, learning satisfaction, and willingness for future use towards the Personalized Annotation Management Software (PAMS) 2.0 system [?]. In Johnson's et al. study [?], students achieved better reading comprehension and metacognitive skills when using a social annotation approach within the context of small team collaboration. Such tools have the advantage of allowing users to highlight learning materials in context, comment on part of a document, share ideas, and provide feedback among a group of users.

However, prior studies also found those scaffolding approaches, by leveraging social tagging or annotation, can be quite limited [?], and students cannot essentially benefit from such systems when reading a challenging text. Not until recently did researchers begin to focus on the usefulness of OER. For instance, Dennis, et al. [?] found that an additional link to video presentation had significantly positive impacts on students' learning based on quiz scores. More recently, Liu [?, ?] found OERs, like YouTube video, dataset, and Wikipedia page, can assist students better understand the scientific readings. Meanwhile, he found information retrieval methods, i.e., language model and BM25, can help to build OER index for a large number of publications automatically. However, this research cannot address students' emerging information need while reading a paper. For instance, existing method cannot help students to understand a specific sentence or paragraph. Meanwhile, existing methods generate a large number of noisy OERs [?]. For instance, Liu found a large number of YouTube videos do not have high quality text descriptions, and methods based on text similarity may be not accurate.

For this study, we use text retrieval and heterogeneous graph mining plus random walk [?] to recommend OERs while filtering our the noisy data. Similar approaches have been used to recommend YouTube video. For instance, Baluja et al., [?] used user-video graph plus random walk to provide personalized video suggestions for users. A heterogeneous network is defined as a directed graph $G = (\mathcal{V}, \mathcal{E})$ with an object type mapping function $\tau : \mathcal{V} \to \mathcal{A}$ and a link type mapping function $\phi : \mathcal{E} \to \mathcal{R}$, where each object $v \in \mathcal{V}$ belongs to one particular object type $\tau(v) \in \mathcal{A}$, each link $e \in \mathcal{E}$ belongs to a particular relation $\phi(e) \in \mathcal{R}$, and if two links belong to the same relation type, the two links share the same starting object type as well as the ending object type. The network schema, denoted as $T_G = (\mathcal{A}, \mathcal{R})$, is a meta template for the heterogeneous network $G = (\mathcal{V}, \mathcal{E})$ with the object type mapping $\tau : \mathcal{V} \to \mathcal{A}$ and the link mapping $\phi : \mathcal{E} \to \mathcal{R}$, which is a directed graph defined over object types $\mathcal{A}$, with edges as relations from $\mathcal{R}$ [?].

The concept of meta-path was first proposed in [?], which can systematically capture the semantic relationships between objects in a heterogeneous information network scenario. A meta-path $\mathcal{P}$ is a path defined on the graph of network schema $T_G = (\mathcal{A}, \mathcal{R})$, and

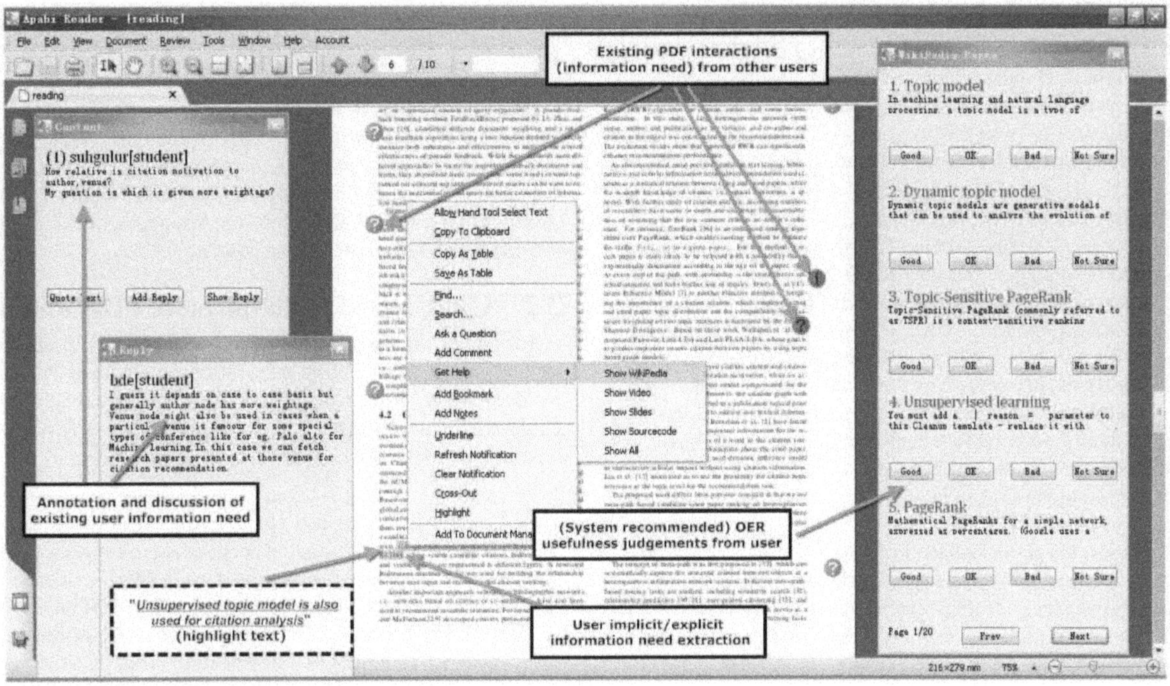

Figure 1: OER-based Collaborative PDF Reader System.

is denoted in the form of $\dot{A}_1 \xrightarrow{R_1} \dot{A}_2 \xrightarrow{R_2} \ldots \xrightarrow{R_l} \dot{A}_{l+1}$, which defines a composite relation $R = R_1 \circ R_2 \circ \ldots \circ R_l$ between types $\dot{A}_1$ and $\dot{A}_{l+1}$, where $\circ$ denotes the composition operator on relations. Different meta-path-based mining tasks are studied, including similarity search [?], relationship prediction [?, ?], user-guided clustering [?], and recommendation [?, ?, ?]. It turns out that meta-path serves as a very critical feature extraction tool for most of the mining tasks in a heterogeneous information network. In this paper, we also employed the supervised random walk methods which have been investigated in [?, ?] and prior studies show that the supervised random walk can significantly enhance the classical unsupervised graph mining methods.

3. RESEARCH METHODS

In this section we discuss the research method in detail which includes: to collect different kinds of candidate OERs for scientific publications (**??**), to design OCPR system (**??**), and to design the text- and graph-based OER recommendation algorithms (**??**).

3.1 OER Collection Indexation via Meta-Search

In order to recommend high-quality OERs to help students better understand scientific readings, we need to index different kinds of OERs. In this study, we collect four kinds of OERs, presentation video, slides, source code, and Wikipedia pages. For OER collection, the most straightforward method is to search for the paper title (exact match) in different search engines. However, this method has two major limitations. First, given a relatively long publication title, if we use exact string match, search engines can hardly find any results. On average, based on our experiment with some random sampled publications, only 0.35 resources were retrieved (for each testing publication). We also found that the quality of resources was not good. A large portion consisted of publisher or digital library access pages for the target publication, which are not helpful for scholars and students to understand the paper. Second, the computational cost of this method is quite high. Given the very large potential publication collection, we needed to send multiple queries for each publication. However, most search engines, i.e., Google and YouTube, restrict the number of automated visits, which makes this method inefficient.

Table 1: Meta-search for OER collection generation.

Resource type	**Search engines**	**Query**
Wikipedia page	Wikipedia dump (local database)	[Keyword]
Slides	Google, Slideshare	Google: [Keyword] AND (filetype:ppt OR slides); Slideshare: [Keyword]
Video	YouTube, TED, Videolecture	[Keyword]
Source code	GitHub, SourceForge	[Keyword]

In this research, we used a more economical method to cope with this problem. We assumed each publication was composed of a list of topics with each topic represented by an author-assigned keyword. For each resource type, we first aggregated all resources retrieved using the publication keywords (topics) and then used a ranking algorithm to identify the most important resources based on publication content. By using this method, we can significantly reduce the amount of queries sent to different search engines. For instance, take ACM DL corpus as an example, for 41,378 publications, we only need to collect OERs for 9,263 popular author assigned keywords (appear at least 5 times in the corpus). Such resources are highly likely to be relevant to the publication content and could help students or scholars understand the essence of the publication. For this method, we assumed that helping scholars or students understand the topics (keywords) of the paper will eventually help them to understand the paper itself.

In order to effectively generate OERs for each topic, we use meta-search approaches where a Boolean query was sent to one or more search engines for each scientific keyword and OER type. The detailed query list for each resource type is listed in the Table **??**. The first column is the OER type. The target query for each type was sent to one or more search engines or web services.

For example, in order to get the slides OERs for a topic (keyword), the query *"[Keyword] AND (filetype:ppt OR slides)"* (column 3) was sent to Google (column 2), where [Keyword] was replaced with the target keyword content. Similarly, for video OERs, the query *"[Keyword]"* was sent to YouTube, TED, and Videolecture. For slides and source code, different queries were sent to different search engines. For performance reasons, we indexed the Wikipedia page dump (2014 May) locally.

In this experiment, we used the top 15 retrieved results from each search engine to aggregate the final result collection for each resource category. Each retrieved result is a triple of title, URL, and snippet, and we use the result URL to download the HTML page content. We then used a list of pre-defined rules (regular expressions) to identify the key content on the HTML page. For example, for each YouTube or Videolecture video, we extract the video description and tags to represent the content of the video. However, if the pre-defined rules don't work for a specific page, we just use the HTML (after removing HTML tags and script code) as the content of the target resource.

In most cases, the result collection was a combination of informative resources and noisy results. Experience in information retrieval reveals that since different search engines return very diverse and erratic results for the same or similar query, irrelevant data may pollute the search results and mislead users. To address this problem, we used an information retrieval ranking algorithm, language model[2] [?, ?], to prioritize those informative resources for the target scientific keywords while filtering out the irrelevant information. In other words, we want to use ranking fusion to find out the most important resources from multiple ranking lists. Because the OERs will be used to help scholars and students better understand the essence of the readings, most retrieval resources (low ranked), at this stage, will be filtered out. We also use the paper abstract as query to search the OER content to find the candidate OERs for a publication. So, for each keyword K_i, we will index top m OERs with similarity score $S(K_i, R_j) = P_{LM}(K_i|R_j)$, where $P_{LM}(K_i|R_j)$ is the language model ranking score for keyword probability given a OER, R_j, content. Similarly, we also index the publication-OER similarity score, $P_{LM}(P_i|R_j)$ (P_i is a paper, represented by title and abstract content). So, for topic, K_i, we index triples $\{K_i, R_j, P_{LM}(K_i|R_j)\}$, and for paper, P_i, we index triples $\{P_i, R_j, P_{LM}(P_i|R_j)\}$.

The performance of this method is highly dependent on the quality of the OER text description. However, different kinds of OERs have varying text quality. Wikipedia pages (extracted from Wikipedia dump) have very high text quality, but a large number of YouTube/Videolecture videos and Google/Slideshare slides do not associate with high quality text description. Consequently, a text search may generate some noisy OER data which may pollute the recommendation results. In order to solve this problem, we will use heterogeneous graph mining method to recommend OERs to students (introduced in Section 3.3). The connections between OERs, then, can be important. For instance, Wikipedia pages are interlinked via incoming/outgoing links, and each YouTube, Slideshare, Videolecture, TED, GitHub, and SourceForge OER has "related" OERs. The related resources are provided by the target online service. While the algorithm behind that is a black box, most related resources come from 1. resource content similarity, 2. the ownership of these resources (i.e., if two resources uploaded by the same user), and 3. user co-visitation (or co-watched) probability [?].

[2]In this paper, we use language model with Dirichlet smoothing for all the text match tasks.

We index the relationships between OERs in a graph database, i.e., $R_1 \xrightarrow{r} R_2$.

Note that, unlike other meta-search problems, the ranking lists of some OER types in this research were totally disjoint. For example, for videos, we sent queries to YouTube, TED, and Videolecture. Their indexes are almost disjoint (i.e. TED videos may not exist in YouTube video libraries), and some sophisticated meta-search ranking fusion algorithms are not appreciate, e.g., Borda's method [?] and Markov chain methods [?].

3.2 OER-based Collaborative PDF Reader

To validate the new scaffolding hypothesis and help students better understand the scientific publications in a course environment, we design and implement the novel learning and reading system, OER-based Collaborative PDF Reader (OCPR). The new system has three main functionalities:

- Capture evidence and characterize students' emerging implicit/explicit information needs when reading a scientific paper. For instance, students can ask a specific question given a piece of text, which serves as evidence of an explicit information need, or highlight part of a text in the paper, as evidence of an implicit information need. In either case, the OCPR is able to capture the student reading behavior and the reading context from the target PDF document.
- Automatically recommend high quality OERs, such as videos, slides, source code, or Wikipedia pages, to resolve students' information needs, while helping them understand a publication more effectively.
- Other students (classmates) can find their colleagues' interaction in the PDF system and actively contribute to this auto-learning process by recommending, changing, annotating, or removing certain resources given an information need. They can also provide additional comments and suggestions to help others.

The first two functions focus on OER-based scaffolding, and the third one mainly addresses user incentive. For instance, students, when reading the paper, can find her colleagues' interactions with the system (by clicking the question marks on the side of PDF reading), i.e., the questions or highlights with the target paper. Meanwhile, students could discuss for an existing interaction by using OCPR. We will investigate the third function in the future study, and in this study, we focus on the first two.

At the backend, the Collaborative PDF Reader has access to the OER index (created in last section), the list of assigned class readings, and the algorithm package, which guarantees efficient OER recommendations and different scaffolding methods.

OCPR is designed for course usage, and it can manage class readings and student information.By using the OCPR, the class instructor can easily manage the class reading list by uploading the class syllabus (in a pre-defined format). In this syllabus, the instructor needs to identify the weekly reading schedule and weekly teaching topic; he or she can then upload the readings for each week to the server. For instance, the following is an exemplar OCPR syllabus snippet, which is corresponding a one week teaching schedule. The exemplar snippet has two topics (for teaching), and students will need to read two papers for this week. Based on the paper IDs, the system can locate the readings (in PDF format) from the database. Each reading in the database has title, abstract, full content, associated topics, citation information, and associated OERs (described in the last section).

```
<week_5>
    <topic> Information Extraction </topic>
    <topic> Maximum Entropy Markov Model </topic>
    <reading_ID> 5323544 </reading_ID>
    <reading_ID> 2742755 </reading_ID>
</week_5>
```

Additionally, the instructor can also upload the student roster to the system, which will automatically register each student while sending student email invitation to download the OCPR reading system. By logging into the reading system, students can access the class weekly readings and use the new scaffolding functions.

The main function of OCPR is OER based scaffolding, which captures evidence of students' emerging implicit or explicit information needs when reading a scientific paper and recommends high quality OERs to address their information needs. As Figure 1 shows, by using OCPR, students could ask a specific question given a piece of text, which serves as evidence of an explicit information need, or highlight part of a text in the paper, as evidence of an implicit information need. In either case, the OCPR is able to capture the selected or input question and its reading context from a student in the PDF document. The evidence of students' information needs will then be sent to the backend recommendation and ranking algorithms for information need characterization. For instance, as Figure 1 shows, user highlighted text is focusing on *"unsupervised topic modeling for citation analysis"*, and the paper content mainly addresses *"dynamic topic modeling and PageRank-based citation recommendation"*. The recommended Wikipedia pages (on the right) are focusing on those topics.

The algorithms presented in the next section recommend the optimized OERs given the information need, which will be able to help students better understand the essence of the targeted reading. A student can also select the specific type of OERs in the "right click menu", you may want use "context menu" instead, i.e., Mac is ctrl + click that he or she prefers and the system will capture and log the selected OERs. Meanwhile, students can also provide relevance and usefulness feedback for system recommended OERs. For instance, as Figure 1 shows, students can click *"Good", "OK", "Bad"* or *"Not Sure"* for each recommended OER given their information need. The judgments and student click information will be saved as system logs, which will be important for OER recommendation algorithms, i.e., training learning to rank model, and algorithm evaluation.

Unlike the common practice of accessing PDF documents locally on one's personal computer, OCPR gives students and their instructor cloud access on the server, i.e., everyone works on the same document. All users' asynchronous interactions with the PDFs will be saved in a central database along with their user IDs, and the interactions - i.e., PDF highlighting, proposing questions, recommending OERs, OER judgments to an existing information need - will be useful to characterize computational user information need and to train OER recommendation model.

3.3 OER Recommendation and Ranking

As aforementioned, student's emerging information needs while reading a paper can be very complex. For instance, when a student highlights a paragraph in a paper, it's challenging to understand the reason and motivation. We employ multiple recommendation features to characterize students' information need, $\Phi(f_1(\chi), f_2(\chi) \ldots f_k(\chi))$, where each feature, f_i, is a OER ranking function given input space χ. We propose three OER ranking assumptions: *1)*, straightforwardly, student' information needs can be related to the OCPR interactions while reading, i.e., explicit questions and highlight content of the paper; *2)* students' information may be related to the target paper and paper's associated topics; *3)* in a course environment, student's information need may address the weekly teaching schedule (in the syllabus). Because, even a single paper can cover multiple topics, the weekly topics from the course syllabus can be important. Each assumption will be represented by a number of OER ranking features, and the input space χ includes 1) user question or highlight text, 2) paper and paper's topic, and 3) weekly topic. While we can hardly estimate the importance of each feature, in this paper, we use learning to rank to weight each of those, Φ_{L2R}. The training data come from the OCPR collected OER relevance judgments. However, we also need to address the cold start problem. When training data is sparse, we assume information need is a linear function, Φ_{cold}, and the online features (assumption 1) should be more important than other offline ones.

From a performance viewpoint, the first assumption is based on **online** text ranking features. Since it cannot host any complex algorithms, we used text information retrieval algorithm to cope with this problem. The second and third assumptions are **offline**, and we can pre-index a number of OERs closely related to paper, paper's topic and syllabus topics with higher computational cost. We use heterogeneous graph mining to implement it.

Figure **??** illustrates the graphical OER recommendation problem, where the OER recommendation is conceptualized as a random walk problem on a heterogeneous graph. Four kinds of vertices, paper, topic, weekly topic and OER, are interconnected by using different kinds of edges. More detailed information is depicted in Table **??**.

The links and paths between the vertices can be important to enhance the OER recommendation performance. As section **??** shows, we use meta-search and crawler to index the OER by using keyword search. However, this method generates noisy data which may pollute the recommendation results. For instance, given the keyword (topic), *"Question Answering"*, the system may find a Wikipedia page or YouTube video *"Question the Answers"* (content relevant), which is a pop song. Simply using content match, this noisy resource may pollute the OER recommendation result. However, from a random walk viewpoint, via meta-path $K^* \xrightarrow{s} R \xleftarrow{r} R^?$, the OER, $R^?$, useful probability equals the random walk probability from the seed (query) topic K^* to the candidate OER $R^?$ (via all the related interim OERs). Given the earlier example, even though *"Question the Answers"* is related to the keyword with text match, but, all its related resources are about the related music and artists (not related to the topic), and, then, the random walk probability from the seed topic to this noisy OER will be very low. Comparing with that, the correct Wikipedia page's interlinked pages are more likely to be relevant to the target topic or paper, and the random walk probability (following this meta-path) can be high. Similarly, because a large number of YouTube videos or Slideshare slides do not associate with high quality textual descriptions, we cannot totally trust the video/slide-topic or video/slide-paper similarly, and the relationship between videos/slides can be important. For instance, if two YouTube videos' co-watched probability is high, they can be related [**?**], and this information may not totally depend on the video text description. For this experiment, we collected video, slide or source code relationships by using YouTube, Videolecture, GitHub or Slideshare API. We find, in most cases, useful OER's related OERs can be also relevant to the target topic/paper, and noisy video's related ones are not likely to be relevant to the target keyword. Random walk can be important to filter those noisy OERs.

Explained it in another way, from the random walk perspective, user information needs are represented by different kinds of seed vertices (as input space χ), i.e., the paper/topic/weekly syllabus topic that student is reading with, on the graph, and different kinds of meta-paths can navigate the seeds vertices to the target OER vertices, instead of the noisy OER vertices. On the navigation tour, text or topical relevance is characterized as the transitioning probability between vertices, while the physical links, i.e., OER relationship and citation links, can be important to calculate the random walk probabilities.

Figure 2: Heterogeneous graph for OER recommendation

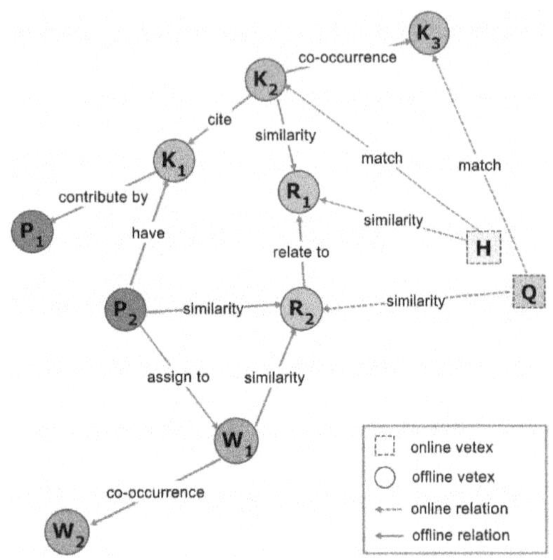

Table 2: Vertices and edges in the constructed heterogeneous graph

Vertex	Description
R	Open Education Resource
P	Paper
K	Keyword
W	Weekly Topic (from Syllabus)
$^*H$	User highlight text
$^*Q$	User additional question
Edge	**Description**
$P \xrightarrow{h} K$	Paper is related to keyword (using LLDA)
$P \xrightarrow{a} W$	Paper is assigned to weekly topic
$P \xrightarrow{s} R$	Paper-resource relationship based on similarity
$K \xrightarrow{cite} K$	Keyword cites keyword (probability)
$K \xrightarrow{co} K$	Keyword-keyword co-occurrence (probability)
$K \xrightarrow{cont} P$	Keyword is contributed by paper (PageRank with prior)
$K \xrightarrow{s} R$	Keyword-resource relationship based on similarity
$W \xrightarrow{co} W$	Weekly topic-weekly topic co-occurrence
$W \xrightarrow{s} R$	Weekly topic-resource relationship based on similarity
$R \xrightarrow{r} R$	OER is related to OER (collected from service sites)
$^*H \xrightarrow{s} R$	Highlight text-OER content similarity
$^*H \xrightarrow{m} K$	Highlight text related to keyword (greedy match algorithm)
$^*Q \xrightarrow{s} R$	User question-OER content similarity
$^*Q \xrightarrow{m} K$	User question related to keyword (greedy match algorithm)

$*$ Dynamically created by user when reading a paper

For any vertex on the graph, the sum of the same type of outgoing links equals 1. For instance, The weight of $P_i \xrightarrow{h} K_j$ is the normalized LLDA (Labeled LDA) [?] probability of topic K_j given the content of P_i, $P(Z_{K_j}|P_i)$, and K_j is the keyword provided by the author of the paper P_i, and the topic probability is generated by the paper title plus abstract content. All the similarity edges are calculated by using language model with Dirichlet smoothing [?]. Similarly, we also generate the edges $K \xrightarrow{co} K$ and $K \xrightarrow{cite} K$ to connect keyword pair via co-occur and citation probability. Weekly topic, W, is a special kind of topic, and all the readings from that week connected to the target topic(s), $P \xrightarrow{a} W$.

The weight of $K \xrightarrow{cont} P$ is the normalized topic authority score, which characterize the importance (or contribution) of each paper. Note that $topic_j$ is contributed by $paper_i$ ($K_j \xrightarrow{cont} P_i$) doesn't necessarily mean $paper_i$ is relevant to $topic_j$ ($P_i \xrightarrow{r} K_j$). For example, some *"natural language processing"* papers can contribute to, but not related to, *"information retrieval"* topic, which is similar to the OER links, i.e., Wikipedia page *"natural language processing"* is linked to *"information retrieval"* and *"question answering"*. As a result, the contribution link may be able to help to find the correct OER. In order to estimate the contribution of each paper to a topic, we calculated the paper importance given a topic K by using a PageRank with Prior algorithm [?]. The normalized topical PageRank authority score is used for the weights of $K \xrightarrow{cont} P$. For this step, we used homogeneous graphs where, on each graph, the vertex is a paper and each vertex is also characterized by a topic prior vector, i.e., on the paper graph, the paper topical prior distribution is $P(Z_{K_i}|paper)$. The result of PageRank (with prior) is the paper topic authority vector, $Authority(paper_i|Z_{k_j})$ (weight of $K_j \xrightarrow{cont} P_i$). This link can help students to investigate the background or foundation of a topic. For instance, the feature $K^* \xrightarrow{cont} P \xrightarrow{s} R \xleftarrow{r} R^?$ explores the publications make essential contribution to topic K^*, and the OERs related to those publications can be helpful to assist students understand the target topic.

All the meta-path based OER ranking features are listed in Table **??**. Each feature start from a kind of seed vertex(s) $\in \chi$, and the $R^?$ is the candidate OER. The first 4 features are online or semi-online ranking, which is based on the student input highlight text or question content, also $\in \chi$. For performance reason, we cannot use LLDA to infer the topic of input text. Instead, greedy match is employed to extract the keyword information from the input string, i.e., $H \xrightarrow{m} K$ or $Q \xrightarrow{m} K$. For example, if *"music information retrieval"* existed in the user question, we won't use the keyword *"information retrieval"* as the interim topic K in the meta-path.

We use meta-path plus random walk from the seed vertices to candidate OER, the random walk probability can be estimated by:

$$r(v_i^{(1)}, v_j^{(l+1)}) = \sum_{t=v_i^{(1)} \rightsquigarrow v_j^{(l+1)}} RW(t)$$

where t is a tour from $v_i^{(1)}$ to $v_j^{(l+1)}$ following the meta-path, and $RW(t)$ is the simulated random walk probability of the tour t. Suppose $t = (v_{i1}^{(1)}, v_{i2}^{(2)}, \ldots, v_{il+1}^{(l+1)})$, the random walk probability is then,

$$RW(t) = \prod_j w(v_{ij}^{(j)}, v_{i,j+1}^{(j+1)})$$

where $w(v_{ij}^{(j)}, v_{i,j+1}^{(j+1)})$ is the weight of edge $v_{ij}^{(j)} \rightarrow v_{i,j+1}^{(j+1)}$.

For example, given meta-path $K^* \xrightarrow{s} R^?$, the relevance score from $K_k{}^*$ to $R_r{}^?$ can be calculated by $w(K_k{}^* \xrightarrow{s} R_r{}^?)$, where $w(K_k{}^* \xrightarrow{s} R_r{}^?)$ is the weight of edge which is the similarity of K_k between $R_r{}^?$.

The total ranking score from a set of starting vertices to a candidate OER vertex can be defined as:

$$r(Q, v_j^{(l+1)}) = \sum_{v_i^{(1)} \in Q} r(v_i^{(1)}, v_j^{(l+1)})$$

We can also consider two or multiple parallel meta-paths leading to the same type of query nodes, for example, $\dot{A}_1 \xrightarrow{R_1} \dot{A}_2 \xrightarrow{R_2}$

$\ldots \xrightarrow{R_l} \dot{A}_{l+1}$ and $(A'_1) \xrightarrow{R'_1} (A'_2) \xrightarrow{R'_2} \ldots \xrightarrow{R'_l} (A'_{t+1})$, where $A_{l+1} = A'_{t+1}$. In this case, we can define similarity from different sets of objects to a result node from different meta-paths:

$$s(Q_1 \cup Q_2, r) = s_{MP_1}(Q_1, r)^{\alpha} \cdot s_{MP_2}(Q_2, r)^{1-\alpha}$$

For instance, $K^* \overset{cont}{\rightarrow} P \overset{s}{\rightarrow} R \overset{r}{\leftarrow} R^? \overset{s}{\leftarrow} K^*$ is a combined restricted meta-path, which combines two meta-paths: $K^* \overset{cont}{\rightarrow} P \overset{s}{\rightarrow} R \overset{r}{\leftarrow} R^?$ and $K^* \overset{s}{\rightarrow} R^?$. So, based on the above formula, the ranking score of candidate OER, $R^?$, is the combination of two random walk scores for both sub-meta-paths. Theoretically, we need to tune parameter α for each meta-path to optimize the weight of each sub-meta-path. For this study, because of the sparseness of the training data, we set $\alpha = 0.5$. More sophisticated parameter tuning will be addressed in future work.

Based on text mining methods and meta-path based methods, we proposed 21 ranking features for OER recommendation. All the features investigated in this study are listed in table ??. Please note that, we doesn't consider the edge direction, as long as the two vertices are connected, the meta-path can be created. There are three types of features: online feature, semi-online feature, offline feature. Online features can only be calculated online, offline features are pre-calculated, while semi-online features combine online calculation and offline calculation results.

After we calculate all the ranking features, we need to integrate them as a OER recommendation mode, $\Phi(f_1(\chi), f_2(\chi)...f_k(\chi))$. In this study, we use two methods. First, without user judgments, we generate $\Phi_{cold}(f_1(\chi), f_2(\chi)...f_k(\chi))$ based on a low-cost linear function (cold start). We assume the online or semi-online features (No. 1-4), based on user OCPR interactions, are more important then offline features. So, the online features' weights are 3 times higher than the offline features.

When OER usefulness judgments are available (collected by OCPR system), we use learning to rank to statistically combine different ranking features, $\Phi_{L2R}(f_1(\chi), f_2(\chi)...f_k(\chi))$, while avoiding manual parameter tuning. As this study is not focusing on learning to rank, we used a relative simple algorithm, Coordinate Ascent [?], which iteratively optimizes a multivariate objective ranking function, for OER ranking feature integration and algorithm evaluation.

4. EXPERIMENT

In this section, we describe the experimental setting, results and exit survey.

4.1 Dataset

We tested this reading system and the associated OER ranking algorithms in a real learning environment. A graduate-level information retrieval course at Indiana University is used for this experiment. 51 students (masters and PhDs) voluntarily participated this experiment (33 male and 18 female), and they were required to use the OCPR system for 8 weeks (with 8 required readings) [3]. They could use OCPR functions to get access to the system recommended OERs. Meanwhile, we asked each participant to provide OER relevance judgments for the top 5 system-recommended OERs (they can rate more). There are totally valid 5,132 judgments we collected (for 1,051 student requests). We use those judgments to train the learning to rank model and to evaluate the algorithm performance. For all the requests, there are 77 explicit questions from students (each question is also associated with a piece of highlight text). On average, each paper got 9.36 questions, and the average character length for a question is 42.25 (with highlight character length 64.08). Based on students' feedback, averagely, they use the system about 3 hours per week when reading the paper.

At the backend of OCPR, we created a heterogeneous graph for OER recommendation. As aforementioned, there are 4 kinds of vertices and 10 kinds of relations in this heterogeneous graph, for paper vertices, we used 41,370 publications from 1,553 venues (mainly from the ACM digital library). The paper vertices are connected to 9,263 keyword labeled topics. For this course, based on course syllabus, there are a total of 34 weekly topics. By using meta-search, we collected a total of 1,112,718 OERs. More detailed information can be found in Table ??. Note that even though we only used a small number of readings in this experiment, the keyword co-occur, keyword-paper contribution, and citation relationships on the large graph will help to enhance the OER recommendation performance. Theoretical, user could use OCPR to read any paper in this collection.

Table 4: Vertices and edges in the heterogeneous graph

Vertex	
Type	Count
Paper	41,378
Keyword	9,263
Weekly Topic	34
Open Education Resource(wiki)	128,772
Open Education Resource(sourcecode)	45,775
Open Education Resource(slides)	151,616
Open Education Resource(video)	786,555
Open Education Resource(total)	1,112,718
Edge	
Type	Count
paper has keywords	587,252
paper is assigned to weekly topic (for 8 required readings)	34
paper-wiki relationship based on similarity	8,068,451
paper-slides relationship based on similarity	8,039,382
paper-sourcecode relationship based on similarity	7,973,611
paper-video relationship based on similarity	8,112,065
paper-OER relationship based on similarity (total)	32,193,509
keyword cites keyword	206,522
keyword-keyword co-occurrence	1,250,910
keyword is contributed by paper	3,577,111
keyword-wiki relationship based on similarity	2,196,341
keyword-slides relationship based on similarity	2,684,119
keyword-sourcecode relationship based on similarity	557,426
keyword-video relationship based on similarity	2,094,405
keyword-OER relationship based on similarity (total)	7,532,291
weekly topic-weekly topic co-occurrence	114
weekly topic-OER relationship based on similarity	68,000
OER is related to OER	1,963,866

4.2 Experiment results

For all the OER judgments, participants rated 21.63% of the recommended OERs as *"Good"*, 29.36% as *"OK"*, 40.10% as *"Bad"* and 8.9% as *"Not Sure"*. For this experiment, we use the cold start solution to recommend OERs to students. From an NDCG viewpoint, we score $Good = 2, OK = 1$, and $Bad = 0$. The OER recommendation performance can be found in Table ??. As the OER recommendation is more like a QA problem, and students are more interested to find the first useful resource, we use MRR as the indicator to train the learning to rank model. For evaluation, 10-folder cross-validation was used.

The ranking feature 3, 14, and 17 are the most important features (highest feature weights in Coordinate Ascent model). Ranking feature 14 and ranking feature 17 were offline feature. Feature 14 ($K^* \overset{cite}{\rightarrow} K \overset{s}{\rightarrow} R \overset{r}{\leftarrow} R^? \overset{s}{\leftarrow} K^*$) carried the keyword citation, keyword-OER similarity, keyword-OER related and OER-OER related information. Similarly, feature 17 ($K^* \overset{cont}{\rightarrow} P \overset{s}{\rightarrow}$

[3]The dataset can be download in the project website http://scholarwiki.indiana.edu/OCPR

Table 3: Graphic representation for all the ranking features

No.				Ranking feature	Description(hypothesis)
1				$H^* \overset{s}{\rightarrow} R^?$	The OER can be useful if OER content is similar as the user highlight text (language model)
2				$H^* \overset{m}{\rightarrow} K \overset{s}{\rightarrow} R^?$	The OER can be useful if OER content is similar as the keywords (topics) extracted from the user highlight content (greedy match keyword extraction)
3				$Q^* \overset{s}{\rightarrow} R^?$	The OER can be useful if OER content is similar as the question content from user (language model)
4				$Q^* \overset{m}{\rightarrow} K \overset{s}{\rightarrow} R^?$	The OER can be useful if OER content is similar as the keywords (topics) extracted from the user query content (greedy match keyword extraction)
5				$P^* \overset{s}{\rightarrow} R^?$	The candidate OER should related to the target paper
6				$K^* \overset{s}{\rightarrow} R^?$	The candidate OER should related to the target keywords (topics)
7				$W^* \overset{s}{\rightarrow} R^?$	The candidate OER should related to the weekly topics (extracted from syllabus)
8				$P^* \overset{s}{\rightarrow} R \overset{r}{\leftarrow} R^?$	The candidate OER should related to the paper's related OER
9				$P^* \overset{s}{\rightarrow} R \overset{r}{\leftarrow} R^? \overset{s}{\leftarrow} P^*$	1. The candidate OER should related to the paper's related OER; 2. the candidate OER should related to the paper
10				$K^* \overset{s}{\rightarrow} R \overset{r}{\leftarrow} R^?$	The candidate OER should related to the important keyword's related OER
11				$K^* \overset{cite}{\rightarrow} K \overset{s}{\rightarrow} R \overset{r}{\leftarrow} R^?$	The OER can be useful is it is related to the OER related to the keyword cited by the important keyword
12				$K^* \overset{co}{\rightarrow} K \overset{s}{\rightarrow} R \overset{r}{\leftarrow} R^?$	The OER can be useful is it is related to the OER related to the keyword co-occurred with the important keyword
13				$K^* \overset{s}{\rightarrow} R \overset{r}{\leftarrow} R^? \overset{s}{\leftarrow} K^*$	1. The candidate OER should related to the important keyword's related OER; 2. The candidate OER should related to the important keyword
14				$K^* \overset{cite}{\rightarrow} K \overset{s}{\rightarrow} R \overset{r}{\leftarrow} R^? \overset{s}{\leftarrow} K^*$	1.The OER can be useful is it is related to the OER related to the keyword cited by the important keyword; 2.the candidate OER should related to the important keyword
15				$K^* \overset{co}{\rightarrow} K \overset{s}{\rightarrow} R \overset{r}{\leftarrow} R^? \overset{s}{\leftarrow} K^*$	1.The OER can be useful is it is related to the OER related to the keyword co-occurred with the important keyword; 2. the candidate OER should related to the important keyword
16				$K^* \overset{cont}{\rightarrow} P \overset{s}{\rightarrow} R \overset{r}{\leftarrow} R^?$	The OER can be useful is it is related to the OER related to the paper contributes the important keyword
17				$K^* \overset{cont}{\rightarrow} P \overset{s}{\rightarrow} R \overset{r}{\leftarrow} R^? \overset{s}{\leftarrow} K^*$	1. The OER can be useful is it is related to the OER related to the paper contributes the important keyword; 2. the candidate OER should related to the important keyword
18				$W^* \overset{s}{\rightarrow} R \overset{r}{\leftarrow} R^?$	The candidate OER should related to the weekly topic's related OER
19				$W^* \overset{s}{\rightarrow} R \overset{r}{\leftarrow} R^? \overset{s}{\leftarrow} W^*$	1.The candidate OER should related to the corresponding weekly topic's related OER; 2.the candidate OER should related to the corresponding weekly topic
20				$W^* \overset{co}{\rightarrow} W \overset{s}{\rightarrow} R \overset{r}{\leftarrow} R^?$	The OER can be useful is it is related to the OER related to the weekly topic co-occurred with the corresponding weekly topic
21				$W^* \overset{co}{\rightarrow} W \overset{s}{\rightarrow} R \overset{r}{\leftarrow} R^? \overset{s}{\leftarrow} W^*$	1.The OER can be useful is it is related to the OER related to the weekly topic co-occurred with the corresponding weekly topic; 2. the candidate OER should related to the corresponding weekly topic

online feature semi-online feature offline feature

Table 5: Measures of different OER ranking algorithms (*significant test: 1. cold start vs. other features; 2. L2R vs. cold start; * p < 0.01, ** p < 0.001, *** p < 0.0001*)

Ranking	MAP@3	MAP@5	MAP@all	NDCG@3	NDCG@5	NDCG@all	P@1	P@3	MRR(OK)	MRR(Good)
Feature1	0.6375	0.8146	0.8222	0.7504	0.8093	0.8140	0.7412	0.6000	0.8257	0.7872
Feature2	0.5317	0.7222	0.7306	0.6430	0.7321	0.7379	0.5765	0.4890	0.6992	0.6249
Feature3	0.3014	0.4894	0.4974	0.4287	0.5448	0.5507	0.0682	0.1286	0.2885	0.2868
Feature 4	0.2970	0.4860	0.494	0.4233	0.5415	0.5474	0.0624	0.1239	0.2838	0.2768
Feature 5	0.4586	0.6372	0.6452	0.5756	0.6599	0.6650	0.4012	0.3871	0.5524	0.4707
Feature 6	0.6436	0.8188	0.8258	0.7446	0.8045	0.8076	0.7635	0.6322	0.8393	0.7085
Feature 7	0.6398	0.8123	0.8188	0.7421	0.8013	0.8042	0.7624	0.6086	0.8315	0.732
Feature 8	0.5556	0.732	0.7382	0.6602	0.7358	0.7386	0.6329	0.4980	0.7384	0.5857
Feature 9	0.5827	0.7545	0.7615	0.6913	0.7601	0.7633	0.6847	0.5196	0.7775	0.6427
Feature 10	0.6196	0.7926	0.7994	0.7144	0.7814	0.7839	0.7318	0.5965	0.8227	0.6493
Feature 11	0.376	0.5625	0.5705	0.4942	0.6041	0.6093	0.2459	0.2294	0.4307	0.3819
Feature 12	0.3778	0.5651	0.5732	0.4967	0.6067	0.6120	0.2518	0.2322	0.4355	0.3881
Feature 13	0.5926	0.7682	0.7739	0.6940	0.7648	0.7663	0.6871	0.5604	0.7871	0.6307
Feature 14	0.3577	0.5461	0.5542	0.4801	0.5916	0.5969	0.2118	0.2035	0.4013	0.3535
Feature 15	0.3591	0.5474	0.5555	0.4809	0.5923	0.5977	0.2141	0.2059	0.4027	0.3543
Feature 16	0.3495	0.5376	0.5459	0.4748	0.5861	0.5917	0.2071	0.1933	0.3986	0.354
Feature 17	0.3556	0.545	0.5531	0.4768	0.5903	0.5956	0.2071	0.2024	0.3976	0.3479
Feature 18	0.6089	0.7787	0.7848	0.7069	0.7708	0.7733	0.7047	0.5729	0.8010	0.6414
Feature 19	0.608	0.7772	0.7834	0.7153	0.7764	0.7791	0.7212	0.5533	0.8038	0.6729
Feature 20	0.5937	0.765	0.7714	0.6956	0.7628	0.7653	0.6894	0.5475	0.7866	0.6379
Feature 21	0.5997	0.7694	0.7754	0.7045	0.7694	0.7717	0.7047	0.5388	0.7907	0.6625
Cold Start	***0.7114****	***0.8856****	***0.8946****	***0.8079****	***0.8559****	***0.8613****	***0.8600****	***0.7208****	***0.9140****	***0.8179***
L2R	***0.7409****	***0.9090****	***0.9161***	***0.8426****	***0.8789****	***0.8811****	***0.8871**	***0.7373****	***0.9329**	***0.8609****

$R \overset{r}{\leftarrow} R^? \overset{s}{\leftarrow} K^*$) carries keyword-paper contribution, paper-OER similarity, keyword-OER similarity and OER-OER related information, in which, the keyword-paper contribution information is also calculated from citation information and key-paper related information (via LLDA). Question-OER (feature 3) is an online feature, and this indicates the question content from the student can improve the recommendation performance. From a performance viewpoint, evaluation results show that, first, auto-recommended OERs can provide important and useful information to help students better understand the content of the scientific publications, i.e., both learning to rank and cold start methods' MRR (Good) score is higher than 0.8 (which means students are finding the useful OERs in the 1st or 2nd position in the result ranking list). In this table, MRR (OK) investigated the multiplicative inverse of the rank of the first OER user rated *"OK"*, and MRR (Good) used first user rated *"Good"* OER in the ranking list. This finding is also confirmed in the exit survey where 78.42% of participants believe the OCPR system along with recommended OERs can provide precise and useful information.

Second, based on the student judgments, we found that a number of OER recommendation features, including online and offline, can be potentially useful, and the learning to rank method can be useful to enhance the recommendation performance comparing with cold start model ($p < 0.01$). When training instances are sparse or not available, manual parameter setup (cold start) can be a effective solution. Cold start significantly outperforms other ranking features ($p < 0.0001$), except for MRR(Good) ($p = 0.014$). From a ranking perspective, both MAP and NDCG proved that the cold start solution and learning to rank can be efficient for OER recommendation. Third, we find that different kinds of seed vertices can be useful. Weekly topic, W^*, is especially useful. For instance, features 18-21 performed well in this experiment, which means class teaching schedule can be important in helping the system better understand student information needs. The evaluation results prove that cold start solution and learning to rank significantly outperform the classic text-based or graph-based approachs.

From performance viewpoint, as the online or semi-online features are implemented via language model and greedy match and the offline features are pre-computed, the system performance is acceptable. In most cases, after students highlight text or ask a question, system can give students OER results within 5 seconds.

4.3 Exit Survey

From a usability perspective, we used an exit survey to investigate the usefulness of the new reading environment and the effectiveness of the new OER-based scaffolding method. In the survey, we asked 13 questions for each participate. More detailed information can be found in the project website [4]. Based on students' feedback, 78.42% of participants believe the OCPR system along with recommended OERs can provide precise and useful information, while 78.43% believe the recommended OERs are close to what they need when reading the target paper. From a system perspective, 80.39% of participates believe the OCPR (prototype) system, i.e., highlight and ask question function, is easy to use.

Meanwhile, based on students' feedback, we found Wikipedia page and video presentation (or video lecture) are more helpful for them to understand the publication, compared with slides and source code. In this experiment, very few students actually read the source code to understand the paper content. Overall, 49.02% of students found the system can effectively help them better understand the target publication, while 33.33% found the system and OERs somewhat helpful. Only 1.96% of the participants described the recommended OERs as useless.

5. ANALYSIS AND CONCLUSION

In this study, we propose a novel task to assist students to better understand scientific publications by leveraging high-quality OERs. By using the OCPR system, a number of reading behaviors are captured to characterize students' information needs. Text and graph mining algorithms are used as ranking features to recommend high-quality OERs. Experiment results show that both text mining and graph mining algorithms can potentially contribute to the OER recommendation. Meanwhile, different seed vertices on the heterogeneous graph, i.e., paper, topic, weekly topic, highlights, and questions, are important to characterize student information need. Learning to rank is efficient to integrate different OER ranking features, when training data is available. However, when training data is sparse or unavailable, human generated ranking rules can be useful to cope with the cold start problem. We also find heterogeneous graph mining can be useful to solve this proposed problem. When OER text quality is not high (e.g. some YouTube videos have low quality descriptions), relations between the OERs become very important to filter out the noisy resources. For instance, we find the relations between OERs and keyword relations are useful to enhance the OER recommendation performance which is difficult for classical text mining methods.

From statistical analysis of student survey responses, we found only a handful of them like to propose an explicit question when using the OCPR system: only 77 questions out of the 1,051 requests are found to be explicit, although proposing explicit questions can help them locate the useful OERs. Instead, most students prefer to highlight some text and ask for system help. Evaluation shows that highlighted text provides important information to find the correct OER (features 1 and 2). However, noisy OER can pollute the quality of the recommendation result. In this case, graph mining methods help to enhance the OER ranking accuracy as well as filtering out the noisy OERs. For instance, features 13, 18, 20, and 21 based on paper topic or weekly topic achieve good recommendation and ranking performance.

One major limitation of this study is the lack of personalization. Intuitively, different students may have different kinds of information needs even though they pose the same question or select the same part of a text in a paper. For example, given the same piece of text in a target paper that students want to understand, some students may prefer to watch a video, while others may want to read a Wikipedia page or access the source code of the scaffolding. In order to tailor the recommendation results for each student, we need to generate a computational profile for each of them. However, we will also need to address the challenge of data spareness problem for personalization model training.

We also hope to have a chance to use the user comment function to enhance the OER ranking and scaffolding performance in the future. Supported by OCPR, other students (classmates) and instructors can actively contribute to the auto-learning process by recommending, changing, annotating, or removing certain resources given an information need. Users can easily click the question marks on the side of PDF reading for viewing or commenting on their colleagues' interactions with the system, which provide important incentives for using the OER-scaffolding functions. In the future, we will enhance the OER recommendation by using this function and motivate students participation.

Finally, this system can serve other purposes in addition to student learning. For instance, by using OCPR, a system can help journal readers better understand the scientific content within the articles. Different experiments and ranking features need to be designed to achieve this goal.

6. REFERENCES

[1] Javed A Aslam and Mark Montague. Models for metasearch. In *Proceedings of the 24th annual international ACM SIGIR conference on Research and development in information retrieval*, pages 276–284. ACM, 2001.

[2] Shumeet Baluja, Rohan Seth, D Sivakumar, Yushi Jing, Jay Yagnik, Shankar Kumar, Deepak Ravichandran, and

[4] Project URL is http://scholarwiki.indiana.edu/OCPR

Mohamed Aly. Video suggestion and discovery for youtube: taking random walks through the view graph. In *Proceedings of the 17th international conference on World Wide Web*, pages 895–904. ACM, 2008.

[3] James Davidson, Benjamin Liebald, Junning Liu, Palash Nandy, Taylor Van Vleet, Ullas Gargi, Sujoy Gupta, Yu He, Mike Lambert, Blake Livingston, et al. The youtube video recommendation system. In *Proceedings of the fourth ACM conference on Recommender systems*, pages 293–296. ACM, 2010.

[4] Alan R Dennis, Kelly O McNamara, Stacy Morrone, and Joshua Plaskoff. Improving learning with etextbooks. In *Proceedings of the 48th Hawaii International Conference on System Sciences*, pages 5253–5259, 2015.

[5] Cynthia Dwork, Ravi Kumar, Moni Naor, and Dandapani Sivakumar. Rank aggregation methods for the web. In *Proceedings of the 10th international conference on World Wide Web*, pages 613–622. ACM, 2001.

[6] Tristan E Johnson, Thomas N Archibald, and Gershon Tenenbaum. Individual and team annotation effects on students' reading comprehension, critical thinking, and meta-cognitive skills. *Computers in human behavior*, 26(6):1496–1507, 2010.

[7] Ni Lao and William W Cohen. Relational retrieval using a combination of path-constrained random walks. *Machine learning*, 81(1):53–67, 2010.

[8] Xiaozhong Liu. Generating metadata for cyberlearning resources through information retrieval and meta-search. *Journal of the American Society for Information Science and Technology*, 64(4):771–786, 2013.

[9] Xiaozhong Liu and Han Jia. Answering academic questions for education by recommending cyberlearning resources. *Journal of the American Society for Information Science and Technology*, 64(8):1707–1722, 2013.

[10] Xiaozhong Liu and Jian Qin. An interactive metadata model for structural, descriptive, and referential representation of scholarly output. *Journal of the Association for Information Science and Technology*, 65(5):964–983, 2014.

[11] Xiaozhong Liu, Yingying Yu, Chun Guo, and Yizhou Sun. Meta-path-based ranking with pseudo relevance feedback on heterogeneous graph for citation recommendation. In *Proceedings of the 23rd ACM International Conference on Conference on Information and Knowledge Management*, pages 121–130. ACM, 2014.

[12] Donald Metzler and W Bruce Croft. Linear feature-based models for information retrieval. *Information Retrieval*, 10(3):257–274, 2007.

[13] Elena Novak, Rim Razzouk, and Tristan E Johnson. The educational use of social annotation tools in higher education: A literature review. *The Internet and Higher Education*, 15(1):39–49, 2012.

[14] Roy D Pea. The social and technological dimensions of scaffolding and related theoretical concepts for learning, education, and human activity. *The journal of the learning sciences*, 13(3):423–451, 2004.

[15] Jay M Ponte and W Bruce Croft. A language modeling approach to information retrieval. In *Proceedings of the 21st annual international ACM SIGIR conference on Research and development in information retrieval*, pages 275–281. ACM, 1998.

[16] Sadhana Puntambekar and Roland Hubscher. Tools for scaffolding students in a complex learning environment: What have we gained and what have we missed? *Educational psychologist*, 40(1):1–12, 2005.

[17] Daniel Ramage, David Hall, Ramesh Nallapati, and Christopher D Manning. Labeled lda: A supervised topic model for credit attribution in multi-labeled corpora. In *Proceedings of the 2009 Conference on Empirical Methods in Natural Language Processing: Volume 1-Volume 1*, pages 248–256. Association for Computational Linguistics, 2009.

[18] Addison Su, Stephen JH Yang, Wu-Yuin Hwang, and Jia Zhang. A web 2.0-based collaborative annotation system for enhancing knowledge sharing in collaborative learning environments. *Computers & Education*, 55(2):752–766, 2010.

[19] Y. Sun, R. Barber, M. Gupta, C. Aggarwal, and J. Han. Co-author relationship prediction in heterogeneous bibliographic networks. In *Proc. 2011 Int. Conf. Advances in Social Network Analysis and Mining (ASONAM'11)*, Kaohsiung, Taiwan, 2011.

[20] Y. Sun, J. Han, C. C. Aggarwal, and N. Chawla. When will it happen? relationship prediction in heterogeneous information networks. In *Proc. 2012 ACM Int. Conf. on Web Search and Data Mining (WSDM'12)*, Seattle, WA, 2012.

[21] Y. Sun, J. Han, X. Yan, P. S. Yu, and T. Wu. PathSim: Meta path-based top-k similarity search in heterogeneous information networks. In *Proc. 2011 Int. Conf. Very Large Data Bases (VLDB'11)*, Seattle, WA, 2011.

[22] Y. Sun, B. Norick, J. Han, X. Yan, P. S. Yu, and X. Yu. Integrating meta-path selection with user guided object clustering in heterogeneous information networks. In *Proc. of 2012 ACM SIGKDD Int. Conf. on Knowledge Discovery and Data Mining (KDD'12)*, Beijing, China, 2012.

[23] Scott White and Padhraic Smyth. Algorithms for estimating relative importance in networks. In *Proceedings of the ninth ACM SIGKDD international conference on Knowledge discovery and data mining*, pages 266–275. ACM, 2003.

[24] Joanna Wolfe. Annotations and the collaborative digital library: Effects of an aligned annotation interface on student argumentation and reading strategies. *International Journal of Computer-Supported Collaborative Learning*, 3(2):141–164, 2008.

[25] David Wood, Jerome S Bruner, and Gail Ross. The role of tutoring in problem solving*. *Journal of child psychology and psychiatry*, 17(2):89–100, 1976.

[26] X. Yu, X. Ren, Y. Sun, B. Sturt, U. Khandelwal, Q. Gu, B. Norick, and J. Han. Heterec: Entity recommendation in heterogeneous information networks with implicit user feedback. In *Proc. of 2013 ACM Int. Conf. Series on Recommendation Systems (RecSys'13)*, Hong Kong, 2013.

[27] Xiao Yu, Xiang Ren, Yizhou Sun, Quanquan Gu, Bradley Sturt, Urvashi Khandelwal, Brandon Norick, and Jiawei Han. Personalized entity recommendation: A heterogeneous information network approach. In *Proc. 2014 ACM Int. Conf. on Web Search and Data Mining (WSDM'14)*, New York, 2014.

[28] Chengxiang Zhai and John Lafferty. A study of smoothing methods for language models applied to ad hoc information retrieval. In *Proceedings of the 24th annual international ACM SIGIR conference on Research and development in information retrieval*, pages 334–342. ACM, 2001.

In Situ Insights

Yuanhua Lv
Microsoft Research
Redmond, WA 98052, USA
yuanhual@microsoft.com

Ariel Fuxman *
Google Inc.
Mountain View, CA 94043, USA
afuxman@gmail.com

ABSTRACT

When consuming content in applications such as e-readers, word processors, and Web browsers, users often see mentions to topics (or concepts) that attract their attention. In a scenario of significant practical interest, topics are explored *in situ*, without leaving the context of the application: The user selects a mention of a topic (in the form of continuous text), and the system subsequently recommends references (e.g., Wikipedia concepts) that are relevant in the context of the application. In order to realize this experience, it is necessary to tackle challenges that include: users may select any continuous text, even potentially noisy text for which there is no corresponding reference in the knowledge base; references must be relevant to both the user selection and the text around it; and the real estate available on the application may be constrained, thus limiting the number of results that can be shown.

In this paper, we study this novel recommendation task, that we call *in situ insights*: recommending reference concepts in response to a text selection and its context in-situ of a document consumption application. We first propose a selection-centric context language model and a selection-centric context semantic model to capture user interest. Based on these models, we then measure the quality of a reference concept across three aspects: *selection clarity*, *context coherence*, and *concept relevance*. By leveraging all these aspects, we put forward a machine learning approach to simultaneously decide if a selection is noisy, and filter out low-quality candidate references. In order to quantitatively evaluate our proposed techniques, we construct a test collection based on the simulation of the in situ insights scenario using crowdsourcing in the context of a real-word e-reader application. Our experimental evaluation demonstrates the effectiveness of the proposed techniques.

Categories and Subject Descriptors

H.3.3 [**Information Search and Retrieval**]: Information Filtering

*This work was done while the author was at Microsoft Research.

SIGIR'15, August 09 - 13, 2015, Santiago, Chile.
 ISBN 978-1-4503-3621-5/15/08 ...$15.00.
DOI: http://dx.doi.org/10.1145/2766462.2767696.

General Terms

Algorithms

Keywords

In situ insights, entity recommendation

1. INTRODUCTION

When consuming content in applications such as e-readers, word processors, and Web browsers, users often see mentions to topics (or concepts) that attract their attention. In a scenario of significant practical interest, topics are explored *in situ*, without leaving the context of the application: The user selects a mention of a topic (in the form of continuous text), and the system subsequently recommends references (e.g., Wikipedia concepts) that are relevant in the context of the application.[1] We call this capability *in situ insights*.

As an example, consider a user who is reading an article on Health Hazard. At some point, the user may select the term "antibiotics". Figure 1 shows a screenshot of the resulting in situ insights experience. Recommended references include the Wikipedia concepts "Antibacterial" [2] and "Antibiotic misuse" [3].

In order to realize the in situ insights experience, a number of challenges must be faced. First, users may select any continuous text, even potentially noisy text for which there is no corresponding reference in the knowledge base. (See [20] for a discussion on users selecting text "unconsciously"). In such cases, the in situ insights system should generally avoid recommending any result. Back to the screenshot in Figure 1, suppose the user unconsciously selects "conjunction" in the third line. It is unclear what result would be relevant to the selection, and it is probably best not to show any result.

Second, the in situ insights system should understand not only the text selection but also the context of the document that the user is reading. For instance, consider a user who is reading an article on History of Antibiotics and selects the term "antibiotics". It would now make sense to recommend the reference "Alexander Fleming" [4] instead of the "Antibiotic misuse" reference recommended in Figure 1. However, context may not always be useful, and may even be harmful if it is *incoherent* with the text selection [30]. Moreover, although the reading context is critical in the in situ insights experience, revealing it to an external recommender system may raise privacy concerns or even legal problems, as the

[1] Previous work [20] has shown that "text selection", by dragging the mouse pointer, double clicking the text, etc., is one of the most precise indicators of user interest.

[2] http://en.wikipedia.org/wiki/Antibacterial

[3] http://en.wikipedia.org/wiki/Antibiotic_misuse

[4] http://en.wikipedia.org/wiki/Alexander_Fleming

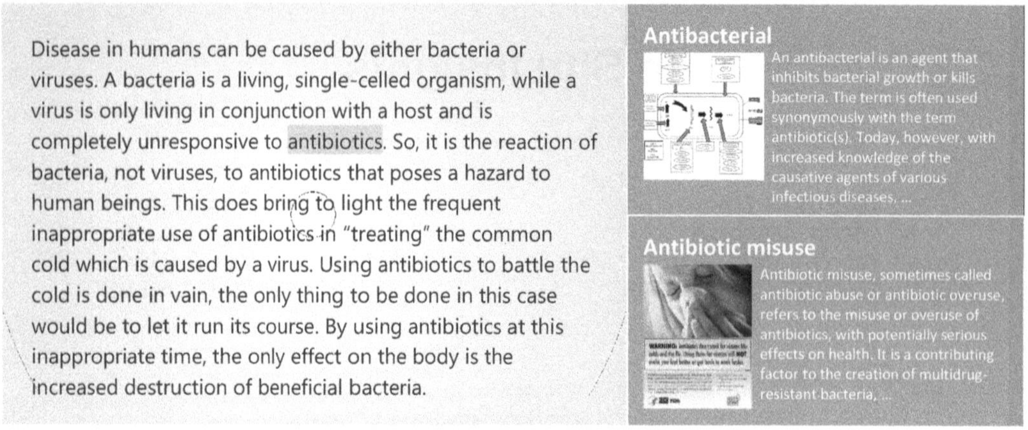

Figure 1: In situ insights experience.

document may be a private email or enterprise confidential documentation. In this paper, we address both issues.

Finally, since the problem is defined in situ of a document consumption application, the "real estate" (display space) available for the recommendation results may be constrained. As a result, it is acceptable, and occasionally even desirable, to limit the number of results shown for a given text selection. This is in contrast to conventional information retrieval systems which always return results if the corpus contains documents lexically related to the query (e.g., some query terms appear in the document).

In this paper, we study this novel recommendation task, that we call *in situ insights*: recommending reference concepts in response to a text selection and its context in-situ of a document consumption application. Our contributions include:

- We explore the in situ insights problem, frame it as the task of automatically predicting whether or not a candidate reference is contextually relevant, and motivate a client-side solution to relax the privacy concerns.
- We conduct a user study using crowdsourcing by simulating the environment of a reader consuming content in an application that has in situ insights capabilities, and construct a dataset[5] for training and evaluating in situ insights techniques.
- We present a selection-centric context language model and a selection-centric context semantic model for modeling and understanding context.
- We propose three aspects (*context coherence, selection clarity* and *reference relevance*) for measuring context quality, detecting noisy selections, and computing the relevance of a reference concept, respectively. We then take these three aspects as a roadmap, and design and compare a set of features. Finally, we develop a filtering algorithm to leverage the complementary relative strengths of various features, by employing a state-of-the-art machine learning algorithm.
- We conduct a thorough experimental evaluation, which shows the effectiveness of the proposed technique. We also show that regression plus filtering works more effectively than ranking for in situ insights.

[5]research.microsoft.com/en-us/people/yuanhual/insights.aspx

2. RELATED WORK

2.1 Content Recommendation

Recommendation has been studied extensively in the past. Content-based filtering and collaborative filtering are the two main types of recommendation techniques that have been considered [1]. In situ insights is a new instance of content-based filtering. Content-based filtering, e.g., [34, 42], typically focuses on recommending documents that reflect users' long-term interests (e.g., a user might generally like sports). In contrast, our work recommends content related to users' *ad hoc* interests implied by the text selection when reading a document.

Related content recommendation (e.g., [28]), cumulative citation recommendation (e.g., [4, 44]), contextual citation recommendation(e.g., [19]), and contextual advertising (e.g., [33]) are also in the direction of ad hoc content-based filtering. They recommend related content, such as news articles, Wikipedia articles, academic papers, Web documents or ads, to a target document. Of particular interest is entity-centric document filtering [44], where, given an entity represented by its Wikipedia page, the task is to find relevant documents with respect to the input entity. These works are based on a problem formulation that is insufficient for in situ insights, as they do not allow for a text selection as part of its input.

There are other applications that also attempt to enhance the reading experience by bringing to bear other content, e.g., enriching Web tables with entities [26] and enriching textbooks with images [2]. They also differ with in situ insights in that they do not take user interaction into account.

Inline citation recommendation proposed by Livne et al. [27] is arguably the most related work to ours. Their setting can be regarded as a special case of in-situ recommendation that focuses on recommending reference papers to an academic paper being authored by a user. In contrast, in situ insights is an open domain problem, in which there are no restrictions on the type of user selections or references to be retrieved.

Our recent poster paper [15] gives a high-level overview of a recommendation system, called Leibniz, that was powered by the situ insights algorithm that we present and evaluate in this work. In another recent work, we have further explored in situ insights by exploiting the Wikipedia graphs [25].

2.2 Information Retrieval

Our work is related to context-sensitive search, such as IntelliZap [12], Y!Q [24, 23], UCAIR [38], and the recent work by Sun and Lou [40]. All these context-sensitive search systems and our system leverage general-purpose search engines, and exploit contextual information to postprocess the search results. However, a significant difference is that the problem at hand involves dealing with entity recommendation, while these related works are in the scope of Web search. Moreover, conventional information retrieval in general, and context-sensitive search [12, 24, 23, 38] in particular, always return results if the corpus contains documents lexically related to the query. In contrast, our problem is defined in-situ of a document consumption application, and thus it is acceptable, and occasionally even desirable, not to show any results (or to limit the number of results) for a given text selection. This need to decide "whether to swing" has been observed in many other application domains; an eloquent argument in the online advertising domain can be found in [6]. In any case, as a point of comparison throughout our paper, we use as a baseline a context-sensitive search (re-ranking) system as done in [12, 24, 23, 38], in order to highlight the need for our proposed methods.

Entity search [32, 5] and related entity finding [3] are also related to our work. Entity search aims to answer a query with direct entity answers extracted from documents or entity records in a knowledge base; related entity finding takes as input a query entity, the type of the target entity, and the nature of their relation, and outputs a ranked list of related entities. Besides, another two related problems are named entity linking (e.g., [11]) and Wikipedia cross-reference (e.g., [31]), where the goal is to disambiguate the mention of an entity in unstructured text to the entity's record in some knowledge base. However the task at hand is principally different: recommending related entities (often more than one) that are related to (beyond the notion of "linking") *any* text selection (which can be any continuous text, including but not limited to entity mentions) in the context of the document being consumed.

3. PROBLEM FORMULATION

We next define the problem of in situ insights.

Selection or Text Selection. A selection s is a mention to a topic or concept that attracts a user's attention, and for which the user would like to explore more and gain insights about. It can be a word, phrase or any span of continuous text in the article that the user is reading. In our example in Figure 1, the selection is "antibiotics". Table 1 shows more examples of selections chosen by crowd annotators.

When reading an article, a user can focus his/her attention in various ways, such as text tracing, link pointing, text selection, and text highlighting [20, 8]. In situ insights can potentially take any of these actions as input. Without loss of generality, we mainly employ "text selection" to describe the scenarios, as it is one of the most precise indicators of user interest [20].

Context. The context c represents the content that the user is consuming. In Figure 1, the context consists of the article on Health Hazard. In this paper, we will evaluate an *ad hoc* context – the text around the text selection. We leave long-term context, such as all the text that the user has read so far, as future work.

Reference, Concept, or Document. A reference d can be any concept, entity, or topic. In this paper, we use Wikipedia concepts/documents. In Figure 1, there are two references recommended: the Wikipedia concepts 'Antibacterial" and "Antibiotic misuse".

In situ insights. Given a selection s and a context c, the problem of in situ insights consists of the following 3 steps:

First, identify a set of candidate references $D(s,c)$. This is a typical information retrieval task; and the retrieval system must be scalable and fast. Moreover, our goal is to recommend relevant *reference concepts* for a selection from a knowledge source, in a way similar to recommending citations for a research paper, so we choose Wikipedia as our target corpus, which provides a reasonably large number of concepts with high quality. We thus leverage a major commercial search engine to obtain candidate results, where each query is appropriately site-restricted by adding an operator site:en.wikipedia.org.

Second, design a prediction function to score each candidate as $h(d|s,c,D(s,c))$, where $d \in D(s,c)$. This is the focus of this paper, and will be discussed in detail later.

Third, recommend d, if $h(d|s,c,D(s,c)) \geq \tau$, where τ is a pre-defined threshold; discard d otherwise. By setting the threshold τ very high, we will only show references in a small number of cases where the reference quality is very high. On the other hand, if the threshold is set very low, then references will be shown for many text selections, although the quality of the references would not be as good. Therefore, the threshold should be considered a parameter that can be used in conjunction with a well-accepted evaluation metric to determine whether or not to show a reference.

There is another important issue regarding the in situ insights experience: *privacy*. When retrieving candidate references, if we send much context to an external search engine, it may raise privacy concerns or even legal problems, since the context may be a private email or enterprise confidential documentation. To relax this issue in our insights system, inspired by the idea of client-side personalized search [38], we only send to the search engine a query purely based on the text selection, while *leaving all the context-related computation at the client-side* to postprocess the search results.

4. DATASET CONSTRUCTION

In this section, we first present a crowdsourcing exercise that we conducted in order to collect text selections and contexts by simulating the environment of a reader consuming content in an application that has in situ insights capabilities. We then describe the construction of our evaluation dataset.

4.1 Crowdsourcing Text Selections

We employed a corpus consisting of all English textbooks from the Wikibooks site (2600 books in total). The textbooks cover a broad spectrum of topics, such as engineering, humanities, health sciences, and social sciences. We randomly sampled 500 books from the corpus, and one paragraph from each book. The 500 paragraphs were then shown to each of the 100 annotators via crowdsourcing, using a UI that shows the paragraph in the context of the page of the book where it appears. To acquire the text selections, the annotators were asked to select from the paragraph any mentions of topics or concepts for which they would like to see additional references from an external knowledge source (such as Wikipedia), and they could choose not to make any selection if they did not find anything interesting. Table 1 shows some representative examples of the user selections we collected.

As a result of the crowdsourcing exercise, each paragraph was assigned 13.3 selections on average (we kept the selections made by at least two annotators); 2.2 out of these

Creators of Java or C#
antibiotics
Byzantine literature
zeroed out
Punya Mishra
Sir Martin Evans
ISO
Python and C++ don't need interfaces

Table 1: Examples of user selections.

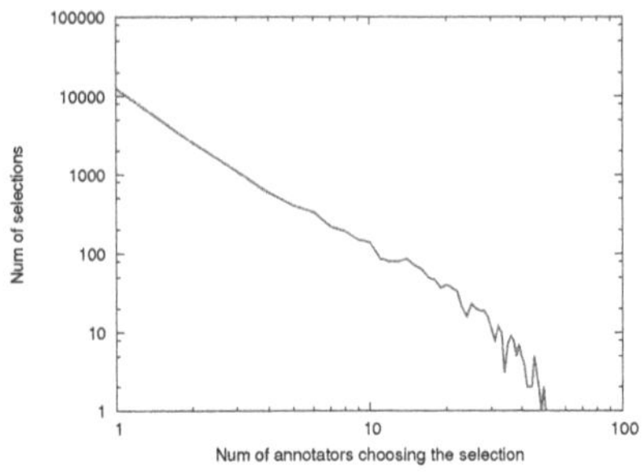

Figure 2: Power-Law distribution of selections.

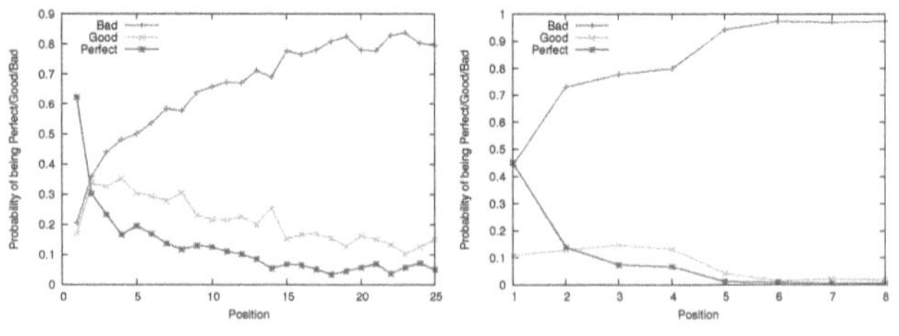

Figure 4: Relevance label distributions for regular (left) and random (right) selections respectively.

	Regular Selections	Random Selections
#selections	490	299
avg(#words)	3.02	1
stdev(#words)	10.22	0
#perfect	1353	219
#good	2165	177
#bad	6477	1923

Table 2: Dataset characteristics.

13.3 selections were chosen by at least 10 annotators. For 78.8% of the paragraphs, there is at least one selection that was chosen by at least 10 annotators. On the one hand, this indicates a reasonable level of agreement, given that the annotators can choose any continuous text from the entire paragraph (and they can also choose not to select anything). On the other hand, there is still a large number of long-tail selections, which is evidenced by the power-law distribution of the selection frequency in Figure 2.

We sampled 500 distinct selections proportional to frequency. We refer to them as "regular selections". In addition, we create another set to account for the fact that in actual reading environments users may select text "unconsciously" [20] (i.e., random text selections for which they may not necessarily expect a reasonable result). When selections are made by clicking with a mouse or tapping with a finger, it is reasonable to assume that these selections will tend to be single words. To simulate these selections, we randomly sampled another 300 words as "selections" from the 500 paragraphs proportional to word frequency. We refer to this set as "random selections". Finally, we combined the two sets and constructed a dataset with 800 selections in total.

4.2 Dataset Construction

After running each selection as a query through a commercial search engine, we obtained a set of (selection, document) pairs. A document is comprised of three components: title, url and snippet, as shown in Figure 3.

Figure 3: A sample document (i.e., search result).

Overall, we retrieved Wikipedia documents for 490/500 regular selections and 299/300 random selections. There were a few selections for which the search engine did not return any result. In the following sections, we only considered these 490 regular selections and 299 random mentions.

For each regular selection, we sent the top-25 documents, if any, to crowd labelers for relevance labeling. An analysis of the crowsourced results showed that there on average 7.2 perfect/good results in the top-25 documents. For each random selection, we only sent the top-8 documents for relevance labeling, since based on our analysis in Figure 4, we can safely assume any result after the eighth position has a negligible probability of being relevant.

We had each <selection, document> pair labeled by ten crowd labelers using a user interface that we designed for that purpose: on the left hand side, a page with the selected text; and on the right hand side, the corresponding Wikipedia document. The labelers were provided with appropriate guidelines and asked to answer a succession of questions, such as:

- Is this the result that you expected?
- Do you see a connection between this result and the selected text?
- Would you like to explore the article in the right hand side?

The questions were then mapped to three relevance labels: "Perfect"; "Good" and "Bad". If the result was what the labeler expected, then it was labeled as "Perfect"; if the labeler could find a connection, and she was willing to explore the result, then it was labeled as "Good"; otherwise, it was labeled as "Bad".

We followed the majority voting method [22] to aggregate labels from multiple crowd labelers, but adjusted it empirically to the characteristics of our task: (1) if the majority of the labels is "Bad" we consider the result to be "Bad"; (2) otherwise, if the number of "Perfect" labels is larger than the number of "Good" labels, we consider the result to be "Perfect"; (3) otherwise, we consider the result to be "Good". We plot the label distribution in Figure 4, which shows that, although the search engine has done a good job to rank documents, it is not satisfactory for in situ insights due to the existence of many "Bad" results on top.

We summarize the dataset characteristics in Table 2, including the number of selections with relevance judgments, the average and standard deviation of the length of selections, and the total numbers of "Perfect", "Good" and "Bad" judgments in each dataset.

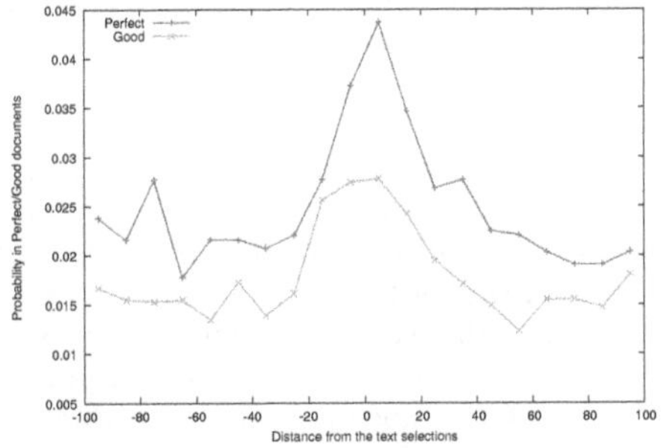

Figure 5: Relevance of a context term against its proximity to the text selection.

5. MODELING CONTEXT

Context may not be always useful, and at times may even be harmful if it is *incoherent* to the text selection [30]. Thus, one key to the in situ insights problem is properly modeling the context around a text selection. In this section, we present a selection-centric context language model and a selection-centric context semantic model, which will be used to compute several important features in Section 6.

5.1 Selection-Centric Context Language Model

It has been shown in the information retrieval literature (e.g., [30]) that terms closer to the occurrences of the query (in analogy to the text selection) in a document are more likely to be related to the query. To examine this heuristic in the in situ insights problem, we compute the probability of every context term occurring in Perfect/Good documents[6], and plot the average probability of terms with the same distance to their corresponding text selections with respect to the distance in Figure 5. As we can see, this verifies the proximity heuristic that the relevance of a context term decreases with the distance to the text selection.

This motivates us to factor in the selection s in the estimation of the context language model. Specifically, we estimate the conditional probability $p(w|s,c)$ in terms of the joint probability of observing a term w with the selection s at every position given the context c. Formally,

$$p(w|s,c) \propto p(w,s|c) = \sum_{i=1}^{|c|} p(w,s,i|c) \tag{1}$$

where i is a random variable which indicates a "term" position in context c, and $|c|$ is the total number of positions in c. We then factor the probability $p(w,s,i|c)$ in a way similar to [30]. Formally, $p(w,s,i|c) = p(i|c) \cdot p(s|c,i) \cdot p(w|c,i)$, where we assume that every position is equally likely, i.e., $p(i|c) = \frac{1}{|c|}$. Then, we obtain the following estimate:

$$p(w|s,c) \propto \sum_{i=1}^{|c|} p(s|c,i) \cdot p(w|c,i) \tag{2}$$

where $p(w|c,i)$ is the probability of sampling term w at position i in context c. For efficiency reasons, $p(w|c,i)$ is simply calculated using an indicator function $\mathbf{1}\{c[i] = w\}$, which is 1 if w occurs at position i in c, and 0 otherwise.

The other term $p(s|c,i)$ is the key component to model the term proximity and position information, which can be estimated using the positional language model [29]. However, different from the conventional keyword queries, *the selection s as a whole often represents a single semantic unit in which there is strong dependency among the words.* Considering this, when computing $p(s|c,i)$, we take the selection s (which may consist of multiple words) as a single "term", rather than assuming word independency and computing $\prod_{w \in s} p(w|c,i)$ instead. This was also shown to work better than the bag-of-words representation of s in our task.

We choose the Gaussian kernel to implement the context language model, as it is consistent to the curves observed in Figure 5 and was also shown to be effective in [29, 30]:

$$p(s|c,i) = \frac{\sum_{j=1}^{|c|} \mathbf{1}\{c[j] = s\} \exp\left[\frac{-(i-j)^2}{2\sigma^2}\right]}{\sqrt{2\pi\sigma^2}} \tag{3}$$

where the standard deviation σ in the Gaussian kernel is set to 60 empirically.

5.2 Selection-Centric Context Semantic Model

One potential problem to apply this context language model to score each reference document is that a document is very short (see the snippet in Figure 3), which may make the score sub-optimal due to the word mis-matching problem. To address this problem, we adopt a state-of-the-art semantic analysis technique, namely Explicit Semantic Analysis (ESA) [16, 17], to map the context (as well as the text selection and the document) into the semantic space. ESA represents a word w as a weighted vector of actual (explicit) Wikipedia concepts $\mathbf{V}(w)$. That is, the meaning of a word is given by a vector of concepts paired with the relevance score of each concept to the word. And then, a text fragment can be represented as the centroid of the vectors representing its words. So the relatedness of any pair of texts can be computed as the cosine similarity between their concept vectors.

We build an ESA index using a Wikipedia dump (English) from March 2014, which contains 700,514 Wikipedia concepts after preprocessing and pruning the noise from the total 10,836,201 concepts using the heuristic rules proposed in [17]. Note that the ESA index can be regarded as a highly compressed inverted index, but it is not appropriate for directly computing the relevance score of every candidate reference (which can be any Wikipedia article), due to the low coverage (6.5%) of the index, in particular for fresh Wikipedia articles. To assess the quality of our ESA index, we apply it to compute word relatedness on the widely-accepted WS-353 benchmark dataset [12], which contains 353 word pairs, and our experiments show a Spearman's rank correlation of 0.735, which is consistent to the previously reported numbers [16, 17].

With both the ESA index and the proposed selection-centric context language model $p(w|s,c)$, we can compute a selection-centric context semantic vector $\mathbf{V}(s,c)$ based on the centroid of the semantic vector of each term. Formally,

$$\mathbf{V}(s,c) = \sum_{w \in c} p(w|s,c) \cdot \mathbf{V}(w) \tag{4}$$

Although using ESA for semantic matching is not entirely novel, we are the first to leverage the term proximity evidence when computing the ESA vector.

6. PREDICTING REFERENCE QUALITY

We model reference quality from three aspects: the coherence of the context, the clarity of the selection, and the relevance of the reference with respect to the selection and the context.

[6]That is, the ratio of the number of Perfect/Good documents containing the term to the total number of Perfect/Good documents

6.1 Context Coherence

Intuitively, if the context is more coherent, it tends to be more consistent with the text selection. Therefore, a more coherent context may be trusted more than a less coherent one.

One classic method to measure text coherence is using the entropy of its language model. If context c is about a clear and coherent topic, the language model is usually characterized by large probabilities for a small number of topical terms, while if c is non-coherent (e.g., only consisting of uncorrelated words), the language model would be smoother. Since the classic entropy may be dominated by common terms (e.g., 'the', 'and', ...), we instead compute a relative entropy [10], which essentially measures the language usage associated with c as compared to the background language model $p(w|B)$ of the whole collection. With the selection-centric context language model $p(w|s,c)$ proposed in Section 5.1 (Equation 2), we can now compute the relative entropy of context, which we denote as **ContextClarity**:

$$clarity(c) = \sum_{w \in V} p(w|s,c) \log \frac{p(w|s,c)}{P(w|B)} \quad (5)$$

where generally the higher the coherence, the larger the ContextClarity score.

Arguably, if the selected text s repeats in many sentences in the context, the context is more likely to be coherent with the selected text. We thus propose another feature using the number of the sentences that contain the selected text.

Yet in some cases, even if the selected text s occurs in many sentences, it is still unclear whether or not the remaining sentences that do not contain s are also coherent with s, since it might be the case that the first half of the context contains s and is more coherent, whereas the second half does not contain s and is about a different topic. To capture this intuition, we propose another feature, namely **TopicDominanceInContext**, as the cosine similarity (Equation 8) between the set of sentences that contain s and the set of sentences that do not, where the $tf \cdot idf$ weight of each term w in both vectors is calculated in the same way as D_w in Section 6.3.1.

6.2 Selection Clarity

The motivation of modeling the clarity of the selection s is that, if s is unclear/ambiguous/noisy, we may rely more on the context, or decide not to show any results for this s.

We present one feature by exploiting the anchor texts. Specifically, we calculate the entropy of the distribution of the links for which s is the anchor text, and denote it as **SelectionEntropy**:

$$\text{Entropy(s)} = -\sum_{p} \frac{L(s,p)}{\sum_{p'} L(s,p')} \log_2 \frac{L(s,p)}{\sum_{p'} L(s,p')} \quad (6)$$

where $L(s,p)$ denotes the frequency that a web page p is linked with an anchor text s. A smaller entropy means that s is used as an anchor text to mostly link to a single web page, suggesting that s is more likely to be a specific topic/concept; a larger entropy indicates that s is used as the anchor text to link to different web pages, and thus s might be a too general or ambiguous topic/concept.

SelectionEntropy measures the selection clarity at the "topic" level. We also introduce a set of features to measure the clarity at the term level based on the IDF distribution – if s contains high-IDF terms, it is more likely to be a clear topic. Indeed, Scholer et al. [37] have shown that the query term IDF is a useful signal for predicting query performance. We use maximum IDF, average IDF and the standard deviation of IDF.

The above features are all pre-retrieval features without using the results from the search engine. After receiving the search results, we can also explore post-retrieval features. One well-known post-retrieval query performance predictor is the relative entropy of the language model estimated on the search results to the background language model $p(w|B)$, namely query clarity [10]. We employ this idea to measure the clarity of the document set D. Specifically, we first estimate a standard multinomial language model based on the maximum likelihood estimator and Formula 9, formally $p(w|D) = \frac{f(w,D)}{\sum_{w' \in D} f(w',D)}$. Then a new feature **DocumentSetClarity** can be computed as follows:

$$clarity(D) = \sum_{w \in V} p(w|D) \log \frac{p(w|D)}{P(w|B)} \quad (7)$$

6.3 Reference Relevance

6.3.1 *Syntactic Similarity*

We first present several features that use a standard retrieval function, i.e., cosine similarity, to compute how a document is syntactically relevant to the text selection and the context. The cosine similarity $sim(Q,D)$ between a "query" Q and a "document" D is computed as follows:

$$sim(Q,D) = \frac{\sum_{w \in Q \cap D} Q_w \cdot D_w}{\sqrt{\sum_{w \in Q} Q_w^2} \cdot \sqrt{\sum_{w \in D} D_w^2}} \quad (8)$$

where Q_w and D_w are the $tf \cdot idf$ weights of term w in Q and in D, respectively. Following the term frequency normalization formulas in BM25 [35, 39], the $tf \cdot idf$ weight in the "query" is as $Q_w = f(w,Q) \log \frac{N+1}{DF(w)+0.5}$, while the $tf \cdot idf$ weight in the "document" is as $D_w = \frac{f(w,D) \cdot (k_1+1)}{f(w,D)+k_1} \log \frac{N+1}{DF(w)+0.5}$, where N is the total number of (Wikipedia) documents, $DF(w)$ is the number of documents that contain w, and k_1 is a free parameter in BM25 that is empirically set to 1.5.

Our query consists of two parts: the text selection s and the context c. Note that the term frequency $f(w,c)$ for the context is special, as we would like to assign more weights to terms closer to the text selection based on the proximity heuristic [30]. To this end, we use the selection-centric context language model developed in Section 5.1 as the context term frequency, i.e., $f(w,c) = p(w|s,c)$.

Our "document" consists of two fields, as shown in Figure 3: (1) the title field d_t; (2) the snippet field d_s. Besides, we represent the whole document using a weighted linear combination of the term frequencies from both fields, similar to the idea of BM25F [36], which is denoted as "document" d, with empirically tuned weights 3 and 1 for title and snippet respectively: $f(w,d) = 3 \cdot f(w,d_t) + f(w,d_s)$.

Therefore, we generate six features by combining two types of "queries" and three types of "documents" in different ways.

In addition, we introduce another feature that attempts to capture the topical consistency of the entire set of documents as a whole to the context. Intuitively, the relevance of an individual document should be promoted if all the documents in the set are likely to share the same topic with the context. We denote this feature as **DocumentSetRelatedness**, which measures the similarity between the context c and the document set D. The key step is to calculate the term frequency for D, i.e., $f(w,D)$. We follow the idea of BM25F [36], and use a weighted linear combination of the term frequencies from all documents $d \in D$ with an appropriate weight $w(d)$ for each document. We borrow the idea of DCG [21], and set $w(d) = \log_2^{-1}(R(d)+1)$, where $R(d)$ is the ranking position of d. Then, the frequency of w in D is computed as:

$$f(w, D) = \sum_{d \in D} w(d) \cdot (3 \cdot f(w, d_t) + f(w, d_s)) \quad (9)$$

where d_t and d_s are the title and snippet fields of d, respectively. Finally, we can compute DocumentSetRelatedness using the cosine similarity between the context vector and the document set vector.

6.3.2 *Semantic Similarity*

The syntactic similarity would often suffer from the word-mismatching problem, since we are dealing with short "documents". To relax this problem, as discussed in Section 5.2, we map each text fragment into the semantic space using ESA [16]. We have presented how to build a selection-centric context semantic vector. Similarly, following the notation in Section 5.2, we can also build a semantic vector for the selection s: $\mathbf{V}(s) = \sum_{w \in s} \frac{f(w,s)}{\sum_{w' \in s} f(w',s)} \mathbf{V}(w)$, as well as a semantic vector for each of the three types of "document" and the document set: $\mathbf{V}(d) = \sum_{w \in d} \frac{f'(w,d)}{\sum_{w' \in d} f'(w',d)} \mathbf{V}(w)$, where $f'(w,d) = \frac{f(w,d) \cdot (k_1+1)}{f(w,d)+k_1}$.

Finally, we generate a set of 7 semantic-similarity based features by comparing the corresponding pairs of semantic vectors.

6.3.3 *Surface Matching*

Inspired by the entity linking works (e.g., [43]), we also include several features to measure the surface/string similarity between the selection s and the document title d_t, including the edit distance between s and d_t, and abbreviation matching that indicates if s is an abbreviation of d_t or d_t is an abbreviation of s. Moreover, the length of the selections often varies a lot as shown in Table 2, which motivates us to propose another two normalized matching features, e.g., the normalized edit distance, which divides the edit distance by the length of the longer one between s and d_t (to avoid overly penalizing long selections).

6.4 Learning a Prediction Function

We have proposed 27 features from three aspects. Given the proposed features and the constructed dataset, we use a state-of-the-art regression algorithm, namely MART (Multiple Additive Regression Trees) [41], to develop a prediction function. MART is based on the stochastic gradient boosting approach described in [13, 14] which performs gradient descent optimization in the functional space. In our experiments, we used the log-likelihood as the loss function, steepest-descent (gradient descent) as the optimization technique, and binary decision trees as the fitting function.

We construct a training instance for each (selection, context, reference, reference set) quadruple that consists of a set of features and a relevance label. The training data is fed into MART to build a regression model, which we use to score each document in the test data.

7. EXPERIMENTS

7.1 Experimental Setting

In Situ Insights is in the line of content-based filtering. It makes a set of binary decisions to accept or reject each candidate reference concept. We first evaluated our system based on the metrics widely used in the TREC filtering task [34], including precision, recall and F_β.

Precision, recall and F_β are all binary metrics. Hence, we employed two strategies to map the trinary label (i.e., "Perfect", "Good" and "Bad") to a binary label:

- **Aggressive Recommendation**: we map labels "Perfect" and "Good" to "Correct", and "Bad" to "Incorrect". In this way, the system is encouraged to recommend not only perfect results that users expect but also good results that can help users explore the topic.
- **Conservative Recommendation**: we map labels "Perfect" to "Correct", and both "Good" and "Bad" to "Incorrect". In this way, the system is encouraged to only recommend perfect results.

Precision is then computed by averaging the precision of all selections for which the system shows results. Recall is computed by averaging the recall of all selections that have at least one correct label in the judgment set. With precision and recall ready, F_β is computed as follows:

$$F_\beta = (1+\beta^2)\frac{\text{precision} \cdot \text{recall}}{\beta^2 \cdot \text{precision} + \text{recall}}$$

where we follow the TREC filtering task [34] to set $\beta = 0.5$.

Next, in order to account for the multiple-graded relevance labels, we also report DCG [21] at different positions:

$$DCG@k = \sum_{i=1}^{k} \frac{r(i)}{\log_2^{(i+1)}}$$

where k is the cutoff position.

The in situ insights problem differs from conventional information retrieval in that it is acceptable, and occasionally even desirable, not to show any results for a given selection. As a result, the "additive" nature of DCG (and other Web search metrics) is not suitable in this application. To see why, look at two scenarios: (1) algorithm A returns exclusively a "Perfect" result, while algorithm B returns a "Perfect" result followed by a "Bad" one; (2) algorithm A returns nothing, while algorithm B returns a set of "Bad" results. In both scenarios, DCG will produce the same score for both algorithms, although algorithm A is more desirable in both cases. This is mainly caused by the always non-negative relevance labels in DCG, which does not penalize *false positives* results appropriately. To overcome this limitation, in our work, we map "Bad" to a negative value -1, and "Perfect" and "Good" to 2 and 1 respectively. DCG is then computed as the average DCG of all selections.[7]

Our algorithm is labeled as **Insights**. We employed a 3-fold cross-validation for training and evaluating different methods. We randomly split the dataset (including 490 regular selections and 299 random selections) into 3 folds, and then fixed the folds in the experiments. Each time we trained the algorithm on two folds, and then ran the algorithms on the remaining test fold. Since there was a threshold τ that required tuning, we ran another process of cross-validation, in which we tuned τ to optimize the F_β score on two folds, and evaluated it on the remaining fold.

In situ insights is a novel problem, and there is no state-of-the-art system readily available to be used as a baseline. For this reason, we resorted to the two following baselines:

[7] Note that we do not use NDCG because the DCG of a selection may be negative in our setting, for which the "normalization" in NDCG does not make sense.

Scenario	Metric	All Selections		Regular Selections		Random Selections	
		Baseline	Insights	Baseline	Insights	Baseline	Insights
Aggressive	F_β	0.521	**0.606**	0.567	**0.612**	0.362	**0.561**
	Precision	0.509	**0.651**	0.629	**0.707**	0.314	**0.544**
	Recall	0.576	0.474	0.408	0.398	0.942	0.638
	Coverage	-	93.3%	-	98.6%	-	84.6%
Conservative	F_β	0.316	**0.575**	0.365	**0.567**	0.221	**0.606**
	Precision	0.279	**0.709**	0.336	**0.695**	0.185	**0.764**
	Recall	0.673	0.328	0.550	0.326	0.972	0.331
	Coverage	-	51.2%	-	65.9%	-	27.1%

Table 3: Performance comparison. "Coverage" shows the percentage of selections with any results shown. All improvements in F_β and precision pass the Wilcoxon non-directional significant test at the 0.001 level.

- The first baseline consists of straightforward querying of the commercial search engine without applying the proposed filtering algorithm, labeled as **Baseline**. In fact, we also evaluated several query expansion methods which extracted a few keywords from the context and sent them to the search engine together with the "query". In particular, we tried a modified IntelliZap method [12] (where we used explicit semantic analysis [16] to compute word relatedness), a positional relevance model [30, 18], and a machine learning approach [9]. All these query expansion methods improved the precision slightly, but significantly decreased the recall and the result coverage. For example, the search engine returned candidate references for 490/500 regular selections using pure text selections as queries, but only returned results for at most 415/500 selections using these query expansion methods. As a result, these query expansion methods performed worse than this simple "Baseline" on both F_β and DCG.

- We also compare Insights with a machine-learned ranker using a state-of-the-art learning to rank algorithm, LambdaMART [7]. This baseline is labeled as **CtxRank**. It was trained on the same feature set to re-rank the candidate documents using the same 3-fold cross-validation by optimizing DCG. We include CtxRank mainly to investigate if filtering/classification works better than ranking, since a recent work has shown that ranking is better than classification for a related problem, namely cumulative reference recommendation [4].

7.2 Performance Comparison

We first compare Insights with Baseline for aggressive recommendation. Note that the problem at hand is defined in-situ of a document consumption application, in which the display space for the recommendation results is constrained and only allows to show a few results. In this work, the comparison is done at the fourth position, by assuming that at most four references can be shown.

The results are summarized in Table 3. We can see that, for all selections, Insights outperforms the Baseline significantly by 16.3% and 27.9% in terms of F_β and precision, respectively. Furthermore, we inspect the regular and random selections separately. The results show that Insights works effectively on both types of selections. In particular, Insights even improves precision significantly (+12.4%) with only a slight decrease (-2.5%) in recall on the regular selections, while on the random selections, Insights achieves an F_β improvement as high as 55.0%. In addition, Insights can produce reference recommendation for over 93.3% selections.

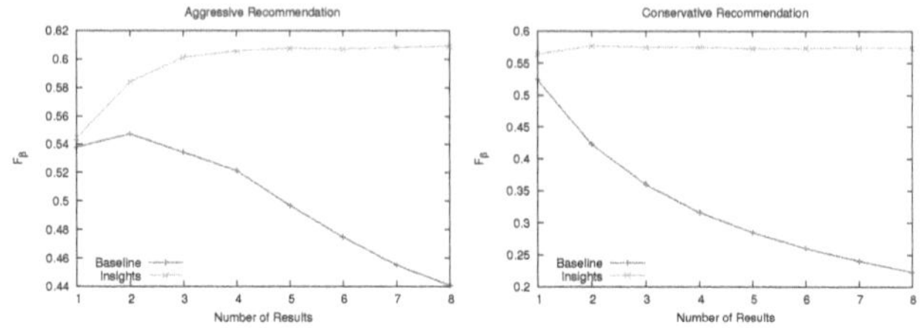

Figure 7: Comparison of F_β w.r.t. the maximum number of references to show.

Next, we compare the conservative recommendation performance in Table 3. Conservative recommendation is harder than aggressive recommendation, because there are often no "Perfect" references for many selections; this is also reflected by the numbers: we can see that the F_β of Baseline drops dramatically for conservative recommendation as compared with aggressive recommendation. In contrast, the F_β of Insights only decreases slightly, or even increases for random selections. As a result, over all selections, Insights outperforms Baseline by 82.0% in terms of F_β. Here, we would like to highlight the "coverage" numbers: Insights can cover more regular selections (65.9%) than random selections (27.1%), and automatically discards 72.9% random selections; this is highly valuable for improving user experience.

We also compare the precision-recall curves of Insights and Baseline in Figure 6. We can see that Insights can improve the precision significantly with a reasonable degradation of recall for both aggressive and conservative recommendation.

We fixed the maximum number of references to four in the previous experiments. And now we examine if our Insights algorithm can still do well when the system allows to display more or fewer references. We plot the F_β w.r.t. the maximum number of references allowed in Figure 7. It clearly shows that Insights consistently outperforms Baseline in all cases, and the improvement of Insights becomes even larger when we show more results.

So far, the experiments are mainly based on binary evaluation metrics. Next, we evaluate Insights using a graded-relevance metric, i.e., DCG@k, with different length cutoff k. Besides the "Baseline", we also compare Insights with a contextual ranking model, CtxRank, as described in Section 7.1. CtxRank serves as a strong representative of the contextual search systems [12, 24, 23, 38]. The comparison is presented in Table 4. We can see that: (1) Insights improves over Baseline significantly, especially for larger k; (2) CtxRank also performs better than Baseline, confirming the observation in previous work [12, 24, 23, 38]; (3) Insights outperforms CtxRank significantly, suggesting that the proposed filtering technique is desirable, and that filtering works better than ranking for in situ insights; (4) the DCG scores

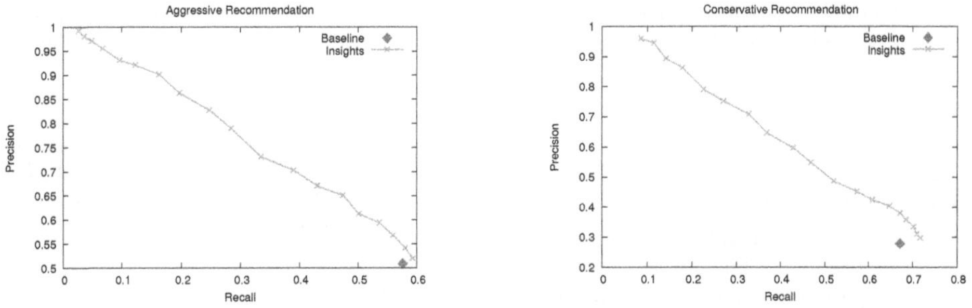

Figure 6: Comparison of the precision-recall curves

Metric	Baseline	CtxRank	Insights	Insights+
DCG@1	0.951	0.972	0.997^{1}	1.018^{1}
DCG@2	1.080	1.145^{1}	1.267^{1}	1.306^{12}
DCG@3	1.096	1.185^{1}	1.435^{12}	1.478^{12}
DCG@4	1.045	1.138^{1}	1.534^{12}	1.575^{12}
DCG@5	0.952	1.063^{1}	1.605^{12}	1.663^{123}

Table 4: DCG Comparison. Superscripts 1, 2 and 3 indicate significant improvements over Baseline, CtxRank and Insights at the 0.01 level using the Wilcoxon non-directional test.

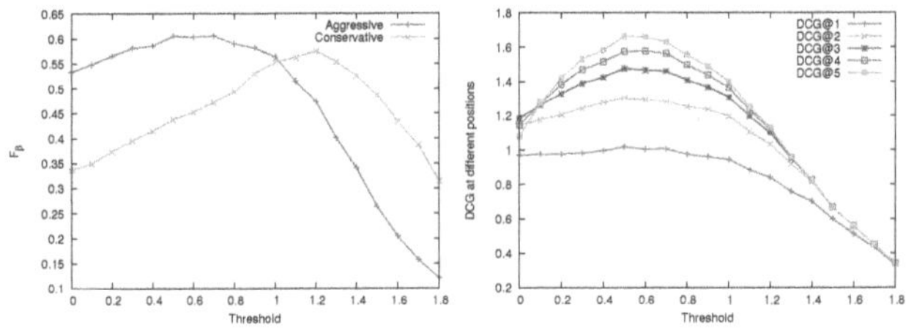

Figure 8: Sensitivity of F_β/DCG to the threshold.

of Baseline and CtxRank decrease when we increase k to some value, but in contrast, Insights increases steadily.

Can we combine Insights and CtxRank to further improve the performance? To answer this question, we introduce "Insights+", which does both filtering and ranking. We report its DCG numbers in Table 4. We observe that Insights+ only improves over Insights slightly, i.e., re-ranking does not help much after result filtering. This is probably because the search engine already does a good job at ranking "Perfect" results relatively higher than "Good" results, though it might not work well for recognizing "Bad" results without the contextual information. This suggests that Insights alone already works very well, and that it may not be necessary to maintain an additional ranking model.

The setting of the threshold is important for a filtering task. We now examine the sensitivity of the F_β and DCG scores against the threshold in Figure 8. We can see that in both aggressive and conservative recommendation scenarios, F_β is sensitive to the threshold value, and the optimal threshold value for the aggressive and conservative recommendation is within $[0.5, 0.7]$ and $[1.0, 1.3]$, respectively. DCG is also sensitive to the threshold value, but DCG at different positions appears to largely share the optimal threshold, which is usually in $[0.5, 0.7]$.

7.3 Feature Analysis

We go in depth to analyze what the relative contributions of each category of features are (see Section 6). We remove each category of features one by one, and examine how much

Ablated Features	Aggressive F_β		Conservative F_β	
	Regular	Random	Regular	Random
-	0.612	0.561	0.567	0.606
Selection Clarity	0.611	0.554	0.560	0.576
Context Coherence	0.610	0.550	0.562	0.599
Syntactic & Semantic Similarity	0.579	0.548	0.563	0.516
Surface Matching	0.607	0.547	0.559	0.537

Table 5: Feature ablation analysis.

the F_β score decreases after excluding one category.[8] The results are presented in Table 5.

The proposed features all work well. Features based on syntactic and semantic similarity contribute the most. And for regular selections, these similarity based features play a more significant role in aggressive recommendation than in conservative recommendation, suggesting that they are better at excluding "Bad" results rather than identifying "Perfect" results, probably because "Perfect" and "Good" results are easily mixed up for regular selections. For random selections, however, these similarity features work more effectively in conservative recommendation (i.e., identifying "Perfect" results) than in aggressive recommendation (i.e., excluding "Bad" results), probably because "Good" and "Bad" results are easily mixed up for random selections.

The other three categories of features, i.e., surface matching, selection clarity, and context coherence, also contribute to Insights, especially for random selections.

8. CONCLUSIONS

In this paper, we proposed a novel recommendation task, In Situ Insights, which adaptively recommends reference concepts in response to a text selection in-situ of a document consumption application. We developed a selection-centric context language model and a selection-centric context semantic model to measure user interest. We then proposed different aspects for characterizing reference quality, including context coherence, selection clarity, and reference relevance with respect to the selection and the context. We also constructed a dataset using crowdsourcing by simulating the environment of a reader consuming content in an application that has in situ insights capabilities. Finally, we developed a prediction model based on the proposed features using machine learning, and conducted a thorough experimental evaluation to show the effectiveness of the proposed techniques.

As a new class of content recommendation, in situ insights opens up many interesting future directions. One of the most interesting directions is to conduct online evaluation

[8] We combine syntactic similarity and semantic similarity together since they highly correlate to each other.

for measuring insights experience in real applications. Another interesting direction is to leverage rich user reading history (such as other documents a user has consumed/created, history insights experience, etc.) to improve the recommendation performance.

9. ACKNOWLEDGMENTS

We thank Ashok Chandra, Bernhard Kohlmeier, Bo Zhao, Dhyanesh Narayanan, and Pradeep Chilakamarri for their invaluable comments in many discussions about this project. We also thank the anonymous reviewers for their helpful feedback.

10. REFERENCES

[1] G. Adomavicius and A. Tuzhilin. Toward the next generation of recommender systems: A survey of the state-of-the-art and possible extensions. *IEEE TKDE*, 17(6):734–749, June 2005.

[2] R. Agrawal, S. Gollapudi, A. Kannan, and K. Kenthapadi. Enriching textbooks with images. In *CIKM '11*, pages 1847–1856, 2011.

[3] K. Balog, A. P. de Vries, P. Serdyukov, P. Thomas, and T. Westerveld. Overview of the trec 2009 entity track. In *TREC '09*. NIST, November 2009.

[4] K. Balog and H. Ramampiaro. Cumulative citation recommendation: Classification vs. ranking. In *SIGIR '13*, pages 941–944, 2013.

[5] I. Bordino, Y. Mejova, and M. Lalmas. Penguins in sweaters, or serendipitous entity search on user-generated content. In *CIKM '13*, pages 109–118, 2013.

[6] A. Broder, M. Ciaramita, M. Fontoura, E. Gabrilovich, V. Josifovski, D. Metzler, V. Murdock, and V. Plachouras. To swing or not to swing: learning when (not) to advertise. In *CIKM '08*, pages 1003–1012, 2008.

[7] C. J. Burges. From ranknet to lambdarank to lambdamart: An overview. Technical Report MSR-TR-2010-82, Microsoft Research, 2010.

[8] G. Buscher, R. W. White, S. Dumais, and J. Huang. Large-scale analysis of individual and task differences in search result page examination strategies. In *WSDM '12*, pages 373–382, 2012.

[9] G. Cao, J.-Y. Nie, J. Gao, and S. Robertson. Selecting good expansion terms for pseudo-relevance feedback. In *SIGIR '08*, pages 243–250, 2008.

[10] S. Cronen-Townsend, Y. Zhou, and W. B. Croft. Predicting query performance. In *SIGIR '02*, pages 299–306, 2002.

[11] S. Cucerzan. Large-scale named entity disambiguation based on Wikipedia data. In *EMNLP-CoNLL '07*, pages 708–716, 2007.

[12] L. Finkelstein, E. Gabrilovich, Y. Matias, E. Rivlin, Z. Solan, G. Wolfman, and E. Ruppin. Placing search in context: The concept revisited. *ACM Trans. Inf. Syst.*, 20(1):116–131, Jan. 2002.

[13] J. H. Friedman. Greedy function approximation: A gradient boosting machine. *Annals of Statistics*, 29:1189–1232, 2000.

[14] J. H. Friedman. Stochastic gradient boosting. *Comput. Stat. Data Anal.*, 38:367–378, February 2002.

[15] A. Fuxman, P. Pantel, Y. Lv, A. Chandra, P. Chilakamarri, M. Gamon, D. Hamilton, B. Kohlmeier, D. Narayanan, E. Papalexakis, and B. Zhao. Contextual insights. In *WWW Companion '14*, pages 265–266, 2014.

[16] E. Gabrilovich and S. Markovitch. Computing semantic relatedness using wikipedia-based explicit semantic analysis. In *IJCAI '07*, pages 1606–1611, 2007.

[17] E. Gabrilovich and S. Markovitch. Wikipedia-based semantic interpretation for natural language processing. *J. Artif. Int. Res.*, 34(1):443–498, Mar. 2009.

[18] S. Gottipati and J. Jiang. Linking entities to a knowledge base with query expansion. In *EMNLP '11*, pages 804–813, 2011.

[19] Q. He, J. Pei, D. Kifer, P. Mitra, and L. Giles. Context-aware citation recommendation. In *WWW '10*, pages 421–430, 2010.

[20] Y. Hijikata. Implicit user profiling for on demand relevance feedback. In *IUI '04*, pages 198–205, 2004.

[21] K. Järvelin and J. Kekäläinen. Cumulated gain-based evaluation of ir techniques. In *ACM Trans. Inf. Syst.*, volume 20, pages 422–446, 2002.

[22] G. Kazai, J. Kamps, M. Koolen, and N. Milic-Frayling. Crowdsourcing for book search evaluation: Impact of hit design on comparative system ranking. In *SIGIR '11*, pages 205–214, 2011.

[23] R. Kraft, C. C. Chang, F. Maghoul, and R. Kumar. Searching with context. In *WWW '06*, pages 477–486, 2006.

[24] R. Kraft, F. Maghoul, and C. C. Chang. Y!q: Contextual search at the point of inspiration. In *CIKM '05*, pages 816–823, 2005.

[25] J. Lee, A. Fuxman, B. Zhao, and Y. Lv. Leveraging Knowledge Bases for Contextual Entity Exploration. To appear in *KDD '15*, 2015.

[26] G. Limaye, S. Sarawagi, and S. Chakrabarti. Annotating and searching web tables using entities, types and relationships. *Proc. VLDB Endow.*, 3(1-2):1338–1347, Sept. 2010.

[27] A. Livne, V. Gokuladas, J. Teevan, S. T. Dumais, and E. Adar. Citesight: Supporting contextual citation recommendation using differential search. In *SIGIR '14*, pages 807–816, 2014.

[28] Y. Lv, T. Moon, P. Kolari, Z. Zheng, X. Wang, and Y. Chang. Learning to model relatedness for news recommendation. In *WWW '11*, pages 57–66, 2011.

[29] Y. Lv and C. Zhai. Positional language models for information retrieval. In *SIGIR '09*, pages 299–306, 2009.

[30] Y. Lv and C. Zhai. Positional relevance model for pseudo-relevance feedback. In *SIGIR '10*, pages 579–586, 2010.

[31] D. Milne and I. H. Witten. Learning to link with wikipedia. In *CIKM '08*, pages 509–518, 2008.

[32] D. Petkova and W. B. Croft. Proximity-based document representation for named entity retrieval. In *CIKM '07*, pages 731–740, 2007.

[33] B. Ribeiro-Neto, M. Cristo, P. B. Golgher, and E. Silva de Moura. Impedance coupling in content-targeted advertising. In *SIGIR '05*, pages 496–503, 2005.

[34] S. Robertson and I. Soboroff. The trec 2002 filtering track report. In *TREC '02*, 2002.

[35] S. Robertson, S. Walker, S. Jones, M. Hancock-Beaulieu, and M. Gatford. Okapi at trec-3. In *TREC '96*, pages 109–126, 1996.

[36] S. Robertson, H. Zaragoza, and M. Taylor. Simple bm25 extension to multiple weighted fields. In *CIKM '04*, pages 42–49, 2004.

[37] F. Scholer, H. E. Williams, and A. Turpin. Query association surrogates for web search: Research articles. *J. Am. Soc. Inf. Sci. Technol.*, 55(7):637–650, May 2004.

[38] X. Shen, B. Tan, and C. Zhai. Implicit user modeling for personalized search. In *CIKM '05*, pages 824–831, 2005.

[39] A. Singhal. Modern information retrieval: A brief overview. *IEEE Data Eng. Bull.*, 24(4):35–43, 2001.

[40] A. Sun and C. Lou. Towards Context-aware Search with Right Click. In *SIGIR '14*, pages 847–850, 2014.

[41] Q. Wu, C. J. Burges, K. M. Svore, and J. Gao. Adapting boosting for information retrieval measures. *Inf. Retr.*, 13(3):254–270, June 2010.

[42] Y. Zhang, J. Callan, and T. Minka. Novelty and redundancy detection in adaptive filtering. In *SIGIR '02*, pages 81–88, 2002.

[43] Z. Zheng, F. Li, M. Huang, and X. Zhu. Learning to link entities with knowledge base. In *HLT '10*, pages 483–491, 2010.

[44] M. Zhou and K. C.-C. Chang. Entity-centric document filtering: Boosting feature mapping through meta-features. In *CIKM '13*, 2013.

Islands in the Stream: A Study of Item Recommendation within an Enterprise Social Stream

Ido Guy*, Roy Levin**, Tal Daniel**, and Ella Bolshinsky***

*Yahoo Labs, Haifa, Israel idoguy@acm.org[1]

**IBM Research-Haifa, Israel {royl, taldan}@il.ibm.com

***Department of Computer Science, Technion, Haifa, Israel ellabo@cs.technion.ac.il

ABSTRACT

Social streams allow users to receive updates from their network by syndicating social media activity. These streams have become a popular way to share and consume information both on the web and in the enterprise. With so much activity going on, filtering and personalizing the stream for individual users is a key challenge. In this work, we study the recommendation of enterprise social stream items through a user survey with 510 participants, conducted within a globally distributed organization. In the survey, participants rated their level of interest and surprise for different items from the stream and could also indicate whether they were already familiar with the item. Thus, our evaluation goes beyond the common accuracy measure and examines aspects of serendipity and novelty. We also inspect how various features of the recommended item, its author, and reader, influence its ratings. Our results shed light on the key factors that make a stream item valuable to its reader within the enterprise.

Categories and Subject Descriptors: H.3.3 [Information Search and Retrieval]: Information filtering

Keywords: Beyond accuracy; enterprise; novelty; recommender systems; serendipity; social media; social streams; surprise.

1. INTRODUCTION

Social streams are becoming one of the most prevalent ways to consume information on the web. From the Twitter firehose to the Facebook news feed, social streams allow users to keep track of others' activity, typically within a social media website or a group of sites. Social streams have also recently emerged within enterprises [18,21,28], allowing employees to track updates from their colleagues and peers. For example, the enterprise activity stream within IBM was reported to include over 13,000 items per business day [22]. With this number of items on the rise, the need for effective filtering techniques becomes more acute, so individual employees can keep track of the portion of the stream most useful to them.

The task of effectively filtering a social stream is challenging, both within the enterprise and on the web. Twitter, the leading microblogging service, filters a user's stream of messages based on the people that user chooses to follow. This model is often insufficient, since there may be relevant messages from outside the user's list of "followees". On the other hand, some of the messages from the user's followees might not be relevant. Facebook, whose feed is based on the user's network of friends, recently stated that "*Our ranking isn't perfect, but in our tests, when we stop ranking and instead show posts in chronological order, the number of stories people read and the likes and comments they make decrease*" [14]. Yet, little is known about the algorithms Facebook applies to score news feed items.

Enterprise social streams pose a unique filtering challenge of their own. In a global organization, employees use the enterprise stream to keep track of relevant activity from colleagues, groups, projects, or topics they are involved with or are interested in. They also use it to share and promote ideas, get to know new people in the organization, and increase their awareness of themes and projects that take place across the organization [12,22]. The usefulness of an item to employees may also be affected by organizational characteristics, such as their business unit or work location.

In this work, we study recommendation of items within an enterprise social stream. We employ a comprehensive personalization model, which extends a previous work that compared the personalization of an enterprise stream using three types of user profiles, based on the user's related people, terms, and entities (blog posts, wiki pages, etc.), respectively [20]. In that work, filtering was based on a binary check of whether the item was related to a person (or term, or entity) in the user profile. As noted, this approach might be inadequate, since the user may be interested in more (or fewer) items than the profile can produce, which makes a finer-grained ranking of the stream's items necessary. Our extended model builds a profile that combines all three elements – people, terms, and entities – and assigns a personalized recommendation score to an item by issuing the profile objects as a query to a unified search index [3]. In addition, we experimented with two non-personalized popularity-based techniques, which generate items based on popular authors and popular entities, and compared their results with those of the personalized model.

Our evaluation is based on a user survey, in which 510 active users of an enterprise social media platform rated items from the platform's activity stream. In our survey, participants were asked to provide ratings not only of their interest in an item, but also of their surprise from it. We did not explicitly define interest or surprise, but let participants form their own interpretation. Surprise is commonly associated with the measure of *serendipity* in recommender systems (RS). There is an agreement within the RS community that accuracy on its own is insufficient for measuring user satisfaction; serendipity is one of the key

[1] Part of the research was conducted while working at IBM Research

SIGIR '15, August 09 - 13, 2015, Santiago, Chile.
 ISBN 978-1-4503-3621-5/15/08…$15.00.
DOI: http://dx.doi.org/10.1145/2766462.2767746

supplementary measures [19,24,30]. Nevertheless, most RS studies focus on recommendation accuracy as the sole evaluation measure and overlook serendipity [33], partly because it is hard to evaluate through A/B testing or offline experiments [24]. In some of the studies that do examine serendipity, it is measured as the pure portion of surprising or unexpected items [32,38], while in other studies serendipitous items are considered as items that are both surprising and accurate [1,19,24].

In the survey, we also asked participants if they were already familiar with the presented item. With this question, we wanted to assess *novelty*, which is another measure commonly mentioned as complimentary to interest [1,7,30,38]. In stream recommendation, however, novelty is likely to be less of an issue, due to the short relevancy period of items and the high appearance rate of new items, compared to traditional taste domains, such as movies, hotels, or music. As in previous studies, we identified the following link between novelty and serendipity: an item already known to the user cannot be surprising [1,26]. We thus asked for the surprise rating only when the item was not marked as already known. To the best of our knowledge, this is the first study to directly evaluate the recommendation of social stream items using beyond-accuracy measurements.

As part of our analysis, we examined the effect on ratings of different non-personalized characteristics of the recommended item, including its type and the activity rate of its author and entity. We also analyzed the ratings of recommended items based on the organizational characteristics – work location, business unit, and managerial status – of the item's reader as well as its author. The main contribution of this work is twofold: (1) we use a unique beyond-accuracy evaluation to analyze interest versus surprise ratings for personalized versus popular items; (2) our findings help understand what makes a valuable recommendation of a social stream item in the workplace.

In our evaluation, we found that most of the items that were rated surprising were also rated interesting, indicating that users mostly associate surprise with interest and interpret it in a positive way. While personalized items were found to have significantly higher interest ratings, popular items were found significantly more serendipitous and novel, with significantly higher portion of items rated as both interesting and surprising. Additionally, based on the set of inspected measurements, we report a list of factors that are likely to make an item more valuable to its reader within the organization. For example, items that originate from an active entity (e.g., an active blog), but a less active author, are likely to be more valuable; items that originate from the same country or business unit are likely to be more interesting, but less surprising; and items that originate from a manger in an internal (corporate) unit are likely to be more valuable, especially when read by an employee from a non-technical (sales or corporate) unit.

2. RELATED WORK

Much of the social stream research has been conducted over Twitter, the leading microblogging service, which is a homogenous stream of short messages ("tweets"). For example, several studies suggested extending the Twitter personalization model by taking into account topical context [5,13]) and others focused on personalized tweet ranking and recommendation [8,17]. In this work, we study a heterogeneous social stream that includes different types of items. The most prominent example for a heterogeneous stream is the Facebook news feed, which provides a summary of friends' activity, such as posting a photo, writing a message, sharing a link, or organizing an event. Paek et al. [34] used machine learning to predict the importance of both friends and posts on the Facebook news feed. Their evaluation was based on a survey of 24 Facebook users. Cui et al. [9] proposed a matrix factorization approach for predicting item-level social influence in a stream. Their experiments were conducted over a Facebook-style Chinese social network site (SNS) based on user-post sharing interactions and showed their method increased the prediction's precision.

Another prominent example of a heterogeneous social stream is the LinkedIn stream, which enables users to receive updates from their professional network. Hong et al. [25] proposed a probabilistic latent factor model that combined information retrieval and collaborative filtering techniques to rank updates in the LinkedIn stream and evaluated it based on clickthrough data. In a recent study, Agrawal et al. [2] described the machine-learning system used for ranking the LinkedIn's stream items. They included online bucket evaluation based on click-through data and found that a personalized model often achieves a large performance enhancement. Berkovsky et al. [4] developed a predictive model for items in a heterogeneous stream of an eHealth portal; the model was based on user-to-user and user-to-action scores. Evaluation used click-through data and showed that their personalization method achieved better accuracy than non-personalized baselines. The focus of all of these studies was on improving the accuracy of the items in the stream.

The literature on enterprise social streams is rather sparse. Freyne et al. [18] suggested a method for narrowing the stream of an enterprise SNS based on person and action relevance inferred from users' browsing behavior; they provided an initial evaluation based on clickthrough data. Daly et al. [10] proposed a user experience with multiple sharable user profiles, called "lenses", to support better filtering of the enterprise stream. Lunze et al. [28] ran a small experiment with 9 users over the Communote enterprise social stream and found that analyzing the item's text is essential for identifying important items. Guy et al. [20] compared the use of people, terms, and entities in a user's profile for personalizing an enterprise activity stream. They showed that building the user's profile based on data from the stream itself is effective for the personalization task. Our own personalization method builds on that model and further generalizes it to combine people, terms, and entities in one profile. Despite being held within an enterprise, none of these studies explored the effect of enterprise-specific user characteristics, such as business unit, work location, or managerial status, on personalization quality.

In our survey, aside from rating the interest level in an item, participants were asked to indicate if they already knew it and how surprised they were by it. McNee et al. [30] mentioned that evaluating recommender systems by accuracy alone is insufficient and suggested other measures, including novelty and serendipity, to complement RS evaluation. Novelty refers to the quality of a recommended item being unknown to the user [1,7,30]. Zhang et al. [37] defined it as the ability to introduce users to items they have not previously experienced in real life. Often times, novelty is enhanced by increasing the diversity among recommendations, with respect to different features [38].

Serendipity is the quality most related to an item being surprising. There have been several attempts to define serendipity. McNee et al. [30] defined it as the experience of getting an unexpected and fortuitous item recommendation. Desrosiers and Karypis [11] defined it as the extension of novelty by helping users find an interesting item they might not have otherwise discovered. Herlocker et al. [24] defined serendipity as the extent to which the items are both attractive and surprising to users. Zhang et al. [37] stated that serendipity represents the "unusualness" or "surprise" of recommendations and noted that in taste domains, a serendipitous recommendation challenges users to expand their tastes, in addition to potentially increasing user satisfaction.

Serendipity is not only hard to define, but also hard to evaluate, due to its subjective characteristics [19,24,26]. Murakami et al. [32] proposed a measure of unexpectedness based on the distance from a basic prediction method's results (for a whole recommendation list). Ge et al. [19] built on this unexpectedness measure and suggested intersecting it with a usefulness measure to evaluate serendipity. Iaquinta et al. [26] enhanced serendipity by promoting items that have both a strong positive and a strong negative prediction scores. Onuma et al. [33] proposed a graph-based approach, which gives high scores to nodes that are well connected both to the user's preferred items and to unrelated items. Zhang et al. [37] suggested a measure of "un-serendipity" based on the average similarity between items in the user's history and a new recommendation. These studies were all conducted in taste domains, such as television shows and music. In this work, we bring the serendipity notion to social stream recommendation and measure it directly through user feedback.

3. EXPERIMENTAL SETUP

In this section, we describe our research settings, including the platform used for our experiments, the recommendation algorithms, and the user survey we conducted.

3.1 Research Platform

For our research, we used a deployment of IBM Connections (IC) [27] within a large global enterprise, in which social media has been widely used for several years. IC is a social media application suite for the enterprise. It consists of different types of social media applications that allow employees to share and interact behind an organization's firewall: an enterprise SNS that enables employees to tag and connect to each other; a blogging application that facilitates the creation of blogs; a social bookmarking application that allows employees to store, share, and tag intranet and internet pages; a file sharing system; a forum application for creating and replying to forum topics; a microblogging service that allows posting messages of up to 500 characters; a collaborative task management service that allows employees to create, assign, and mark tasks as complete; and a wiki system that allows co-editing of pages.

IC publishes an activity stream that includes all public actions taking place within its applications [22]. Each item in the stream includes a textual description with the activity, author, entity(ies) involved, and a short excerpt of the text. The author and entities are linked to their unique IC identifier. For example, an item can tell that "Alice Oh liked the blog post '10 most useful Eclipse tips' in the Eclipse Development blog." Table 1 describes the different types of items in the stream, including the involved entity and possible activities. Each of these items may be performed as part of a community [35] or as a "standalone" activity by the individual user. Previous research has found that the vast majority of the enterprise stream's items focus on workplace-related activity, such as discussing projects, products, ideas, potential customers, organizational tools and processes, and similar topics [12,22,28]. The stream is also composed of network activities, which include connecting to and tagging another person on the enterprise SNS. We did not include these items in our recommendations since they were previously found of particularly low interest [20].

Table 1. Items included in the IC's activity stream

Entity	Activity
Blog post	create, edit, comment, like
Bookmark	create, edit
File	create, edit, share, comment, like
Forum topic	create, edit, reply, like
Microblog message	create, edit, share, comment, like
Task	create, edit, assign, complete
Wiki page	create, edit, comment, like

IC includes various mechanisms to update users about relevant activity in the stream. Users can follow other individuals and entities to get email notifications whenever a related item occurs. IC also sends weekly and/or daily digests summarizing activity related to friends and followed individuals or entities.

3.2 Recommendation Algorithms

Our experiments included recommendations of both personalized and popular items. In this section, we describe the algorithms used for both types of recommendation.

3.2.1 Personalized Items

Our user profile is based on data originating from the stream itself, which was shown to be advantageous in a previous study [20]. That study separately explored the use of people, terms, and entities (e.g., blog posts, wiki pages; referred to as 'places' in that work) for recommending stream items and found that all three are effective. Entities produced the most accurate recommendations (79%), followed by people (58.1%), and then terms (44.8%). On the other hand, terms were shown to produce items more frequently (528 items per term per month) than people (104.3) and entities (only 12.2). Based on these results, we extended the model and built a profile that jointly contains people, terms, and entities, with entities boosted by a factor of 5 over people and people boosted by a factor of 5 over terms. We experimented with three profile sizes: for each user u, a profile $Pr_s(u)=\{T_s(u),P_s(u),E_s(u)\}$, $s \in \{5,10,15\}$ was created. The user profile included a set of s related terms $T_s(u)$, s related people $P_s(u)$, and s related entities $E_s(u)$, all with their relationship score to the user u[1]. The value of s for each user was selected in a round-robin order.

For the profile, we considered a stream that included all items in the year that preceded our experiment. We define the *user's stream* as the set of all items authored by that user. We next describe how we generated the profile for a given user.

Related entities were extracted by considering all the entities in which the user was active, i.e., all entities that appear on the user's stream. These may include blog posts the user authored, commented on, or liked; wiki pages s/he created and edited; files s/he edited and shared; and so forth. These entities were scored by the number of items in the user's stream that related to them.

[1] In practice, we did not expect the "ideal" profile to include an identical number of terms, people, and entities. But as we had no prior knowledge about the desired ratio, we opted to experiment with three configurations with equal number of each, to fairly inspect the effect of the overall profile size. Our goal was to examine the profile size as one of many factors we experimented with, rather than find the optimal profile configuration, which is left beyond the scope of this paper.

Thus, if a user performed more activity over an entity, its relationship score to that user would grow.

Related people were extracted by considering both direct and indirect relations. Direct relations considered other people who appear on items from the user's stream (e.g., connecting on the enterprise SNS or tagging one another). Indirect relations were inferred by considering users who have common entities with the user, i.e., entities that appear both on the user's stream and their stream. For example, people who commented on the same blog post as the user or people who liked a file the user created. The overall relationship score with a person was determined by considering all direct and indirect relations between the user and that person (see full details in [20]).

Related terms were extracted by detecting the most representative keywords in the user's stream. To this end, we used the KL+TB method [6], which has been shown effective for term extraction in social streams [21]. The method uses the Kullback-Leibler divergence (KL), which is a non-symmetric distance measure between two given distributions. In our case, we sought out terms that maximize the KL divergence between the language model of the user's stream and the language model of the entire stream. Intuitively, a term would receive a higher KL score if it appeared more often on the user's stream and less frequently on the rest of the stream. On top of the KL measure, a tag boost (TB) was applied, promoting keywords that are likely to appear as tags when appearing in the content. This "likelihood" is determined based on a well-tagged folksonomy, in our case based on the IC's bookmarking application. The weighted list of a user's related terms was generated by applying KL+TB on that user's stream, after filtering out people's names and reserved keywords (such as 'blog', or 'like') and stemming.

Given a user profile $Pr_s(u)=\{T_s(u),P_s(u),E_s(u)\}$, we generated the personalized items by issuing an OR query containing all the profile objects (people, terms, entities) to a social search system [21]. The social search system, which is built on top of Lucene [29], indexes all the items in the stream, as detailed in Table 1. It takes advantage of Lucene's real-time indexing capabilities to keep the index fresh with the most recent items, up to a one-minute delay between an item's publishing time and its inclusion in the index [21]. The system uses a unified approach, which maps the relationships among the stream's items, related people, related entities, and related terms, in a way that makes all four (items, people, terms, entities) both searchable and retrievable [3]. For the task of producing recommendations, the query to the social search system included a combination of people, terms, and entities, while the results were stream items that matched the query, ordered by their recommendation score. The recommendation score of an item i to user u was calculated according to the following formula:

$$RSc(u,i) = e^{-\alpha\tau(i)} \cdot [\beta \sum_{e \in E(u)} w(u,e) \cdot w(e,i) + \gamma \sum_{p \in P(u)} w(u,p) \cdot w(p,i)$$

$$+(1-\beta-\gamma) \sum_{t \in T(u)} w(u,t) \cdot w(t,i)]$$

where $\tau(i)$ is the number of days passed since the occurrence of i; α is a decay factor (set in our experiments to 0.05); β and γ are parameters that control the relative weight among entities, people, and terms. According to our boosting mentioned previously, we set $\beta = {}^{25}/_{31}$ and $\gamma = {}^{5}/_{31}$; $w(u,e)$, $w(u,p)$, and $w(u,t)$ are the scores of an entity e, person p, or term t, given as part of $Pr_s(u)$ and reflecting their relationship strength to the user u, as explained before; and $w(e,i)$, $w(p,i)$, and $w(t,i)$ denote the relevance score of item i to e, p, or t, respectively, as determined by the social search system.

After retrieving the top 100 items with their recommendation scores, the list was traversed from top to bottom and two types of items were filtered out: (1) items that the user authored, and (2) items that belong to a thread of which another item has already been recommended. To this end, we define a *thread* of items as a set of items in the stream that includes all activities that relate to the same entity (see Table 1 for a list of entities). For example, a thread can include all items (creation, comments, likes) that relate to a certain microblog message. This way, we only recommended the top-scored item of a thread and avoided recommending multiple items from the same thread.

3.2.2 Popular Items

We experimented with two different methods for generating popular items. The first, denoted *pop-auth*, was based on popular authors and the second, *pop-ent*, was based on popular entities. We selected popular authors based on the number of people who tagged them within the IC enterprise SNS [16]. Popular entities were identified based on the number of distinct users who performed any type of activity over them during the month that preceded the survey. We identified the 50 most popular authors and 50 most popular entities. For each, we retrieved the most recent related item that occurred during the month preceding the survey (if such existed, in the case of popular authors). This produced a list of (at most) 50 items, of which we selected the popularity-based recommendations at random for each user.

3.3 User Survey

Our evaluation was based on a user survey, in which employees were asked to rate (up to) 15 items originating from the IC activity stream. Of these 15 items, 11 were generated based on the personalization algorithm and 4 were based on popularity: 2 *pop-auth* and 2 *pop-ent*. After generating all 15 recommendations, we randomized their presentation order. In the (rare) cases of an identical item among the three groups (personalized, *pop-auth*, *pop-ent*), such item was presented once and analyzed as part of each of the groups it belonged to.

In the survey, participants were asked to rate each item with regard to their interest in it, their surprise from it, and whether they were already familiar with it. As in previous studies, we asserted that an item marked as already known cannot be surprising and therefore only asked for the surprise rating if the item was not marked as known [1,26]. The different questions allowed us to evaluate the recommendations by aspects that go beyond the common accuracy metric [19].

Figure 1 illustrates an item in our survey. The upper part shows the item itself, including a photo of the author and an icon representing the originating IC application. The item's text includes a description and an excerpt from the content, when relevant. Each underlined element in the item's description is a link to its corresponding IC page. Below the text is an indication of the item's freshness, e.g., "3 days ago".

The lower part asks for the user's feedback: the interest level (not interesting, interesting, very interesting), whether the item is already known (yes/no by a checkbox, which is unselected by default) and the surprise level (not surprising, surprising, very surprising). If the user selected the "already know" box, the surprise rating would gray out.

The survey participants were active users of IC, for whom we could extract at least 15 related terms, 15 related people, and 15

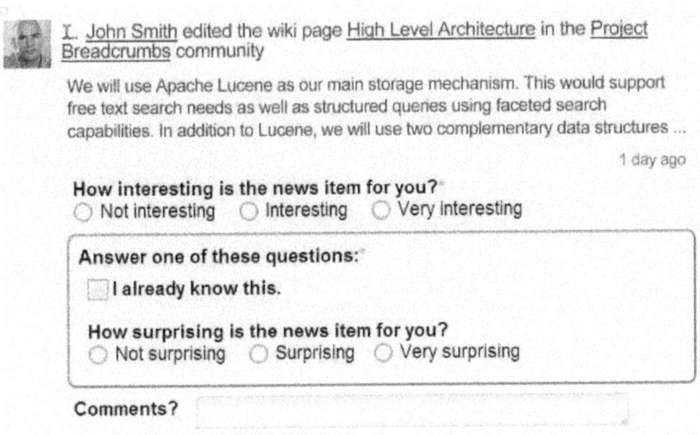

Figure 1. Item recommendation as presented in the survey.

related entities. We identified 1715 such users and sent them an invitation to participate in the survey by email. We note that this sample does not represent the entire organization's employee population, but rather active enterprise social media users, who are the target population for our recommendations. We received a response from 510 users who fully completed the survey (29.7%), rating a total of over 7600 items. More demographic information about our participants is provided in Section 4.4.

4. EXPERIMENTAL RESULTS

Overall in our survey, 59.1% of the items were rated as either interesting or very interesting (15.4% were rated very interesting). Figure 2 shows the interest ratings of personalized versus popular items. Personalized items were significantly more interesting, with 65.1% of the items vs. 42.5% for popular items (p<.001)[2].

25.8% of the items were marked "I already know this". This relatively high portion is likely due to the existing mechanisms for updating IC users, including email notifications and periodic digests according to user preferences, as explained in the previous section. For personalized items, 32.6% were marked as already known, compared to only 7.1% for popular items (p<.001). This fits the intuition that popular items are more exploratory than items that were tailored for the users, and are thus more likely to be novel.

Comparing the ratings for the two types of popular items, *pop-auth* and *pop-ent*, reveals that they were very similar to each other. For interest ratings, 43.8% of the *pop-auth* items were rated [very] interesting (i.e., interesting or very interesting) vs. 41.3% of the *pop-ent* items (p>.05). For surprise ratings, 31.3% of the *pop-auth* items were rated [very] surprising vs. 30.8% of the *pop-ent* items (p>.05). Already-know (AK) portions were also similar:

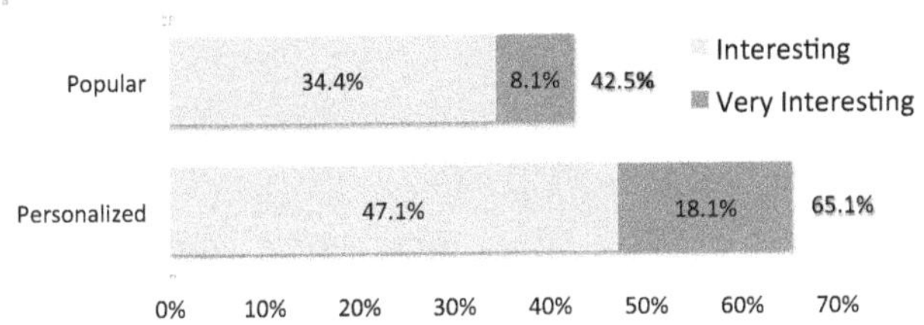

Figure 2. Interest ratings for personalized vs. popular items.

[2] Our tests for statistical significance were performed using a two-tailed unpaired t-test when comparing two groups and a one-way ANOVA with Games-Howell post-hoc analysis when comparing three or more groups.

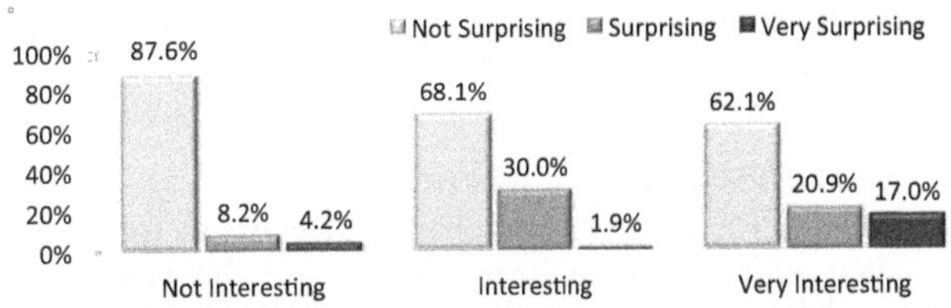

Figure 3. Surprise ratings by interest ratings.

7.1% for *pop-auth* vs. 7.2% for *pop-ent* (p>.05). We therefore jointly refer to both types of popular items from this point onward.

4.1 Surprise Ratings

Overall, 24.8% of the items were rated surprising, of which 5.2% were rated very surprising. Figure 3 presents the distribution of surprise ratings according to the item's interest ratings. It can be seen that less than 13% of the non-interesting items were marked [very] surprising. In contrast, over 30% of the interesting items and almost 40% of the very interesting items were found [very] surprising. The differences among the three interest groups were significant, $F(2,7650)=243.42$, $p<.001$. The portion of very surprising items is especially high for very interesting items at 17%. Overall, it seems that most participants interpret "surprising" as a positive surprise that is joined with interest in the item itself. In total, **79.6%** of the items rated surprising were also rated interesting.

Table 2 (upper part) shows the surprise ratings for personalized versus popular items. Popular items had a significantly higher portion of items rated surprising (p<.001). The lower part of Table 2 shows the surprise ratings for personalized versus popular, focusing only on items that were rated [very] interesting. It can be seen that given that an item is interesting, it has a significantly higher chance of being surprising if it is a popular item (over 50%) rather than a personalized item (less than 30%, p<.001).

As we have seen, most items that were rated surprising were also rated interesting. Ultimately, it is desirable to recommend an item that is both interesting and surprising to the user, in order to achieve a "good surprise" [19,24]. As we have also witnessed, personalized items had a higher portion of interesting items, while popular items had a higher portion of surprising items. But which of them had a higher portion of items rated as **both** interesting and surprising? We found that popular items had a significantly higher portion than personalized items at **22%** vs. **18.9%** (p<.01).

Table 3 summarizes the results mentioned throughout this section comparing personalized and popular items[3]. It can be seen that while personalized items have a clear advantage in terms of

Table 2. Surprise ratings for personalized vs. popular items

	Not Surp.	Surp.	Very Surp.
Personalized	77.5%	18.3%	4.2%
Popular	69%	23.3%	7.7%
Personalized & [Very] Interesting	70.9%	24.2%	4.9%
Popular & [Very] Interesting	48.2%	41.9%	9.9%

Table 3. Summary comparison of personalized vs. popular items

	Int	V. Int	AK	Surp	V. Surp	Int & Surp
Personalized	65.1%$^{\wedge}$	18.1%$^{\wedge}$	32.6%$^{\wedge}$	22.5%	4.2%	18.9%
Popular	42.5%	8.1%	7.1%	31%$^{\wedge}$	7.7%*	22%*

[3] t-test significant differences: $^{+}$p<.05, *p<.01, $^{\wedge}$p<.001

accuracy, in all other beyond-accuracy aspects – AK, surprising, very surprising, and interesting+surprising rates – popular items have the advantage (all differences are statistically significant).

4.2 Personalization Characteristics

In the following analysis, we examine the effect of two factors on the ratings of personalized items: the size of the profile, as determined by *s*, and the recommendation score, calculated as explained in Section 3. We refer to *interest (surprise) rates* as the portions of items rated [very] interesting (surprising) and *AK rates* as the portion of items marked as already known.

4.2.1 Profile Size

Figure 4 shows the rating results for the three types of profile size *s* we used in our experiments[4]. As explained in Section 3, a profile size *s* indicates that the profile includes *s* related people, *s* related terms, and *s* related entities. While we speculated that a smaller profile size would yield higher accuracy, results indicate that the larger the profile, the higher the ratings. Interest rates for $s=5$ were significantly lower than for $s=10$ and $s=15$, $F(2,5610)=9.853$, $p<.001$. It could be that a smaller profile produces a smaller amount of accurate items. It is also likely that a larger profile produces more diverse items, while items for the smaller profile may sometimes be perceived as similar to those that previously appeared and therefore yield less interest. For example, with a smaller profile it is more likely that many items originate from the same author. The mid-size profile (s=10) yielded significantly higher surprise rates than the two others ($F(2,5610)=15.034$, $p<.001$) and also lower AK rates ($F(2,5610)=5.433$, $p<.01$). Overall, we see that a profile of $s=15$ yielded the highest interest rates, while a profile of $s=10$ yielded the highest surprise rates. From this point onward, the analysis for personalized items is performed across all three profile sizes.

4.2.2 Recommendation Score

Figure 5 shows the AK, interest, and surprise rates of personalized items as a factor of the recommendation score, RSc, as described in Section 3 (based on 8 equally-sized bins). As expected, a higher RSc leads to higher interest rates, up to 76.7% at the top bin. The more substantial rise starts right after the median point (fourth bin). Also, starting at that point, the AK rates noticeably increase with the RSc, up to 49.2% for the top bin. In parallel, the surprise rates start decreasing. Overall, a high recommendation score produces items with a higher likelihood of being interesting, but also already known and less surprising.

4.3 Recommended Item Characteristics

In this sub-section, we examine the effect of various features of the recommended item on its ratings. The analysis usually presents the results separately for personalized and popular items, since their distributions across the feature values were different.

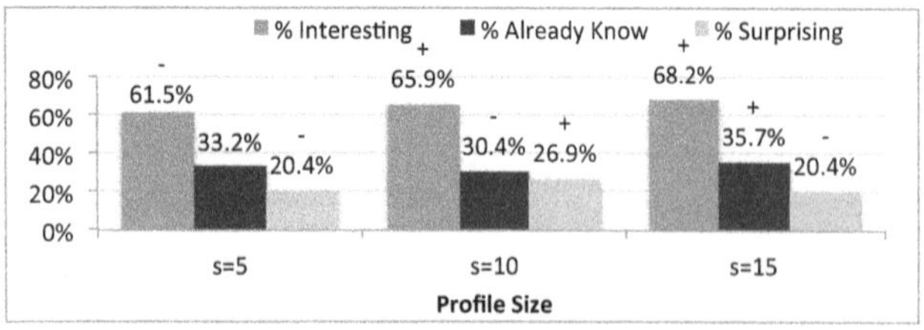

Figure 4. Ratings by profile size (s).

[4] ANOVA Results: values marked by '+' are significantly higher than values marked by '-'; in addition, values marked by '>' are significantly higher than values marked by '<'.

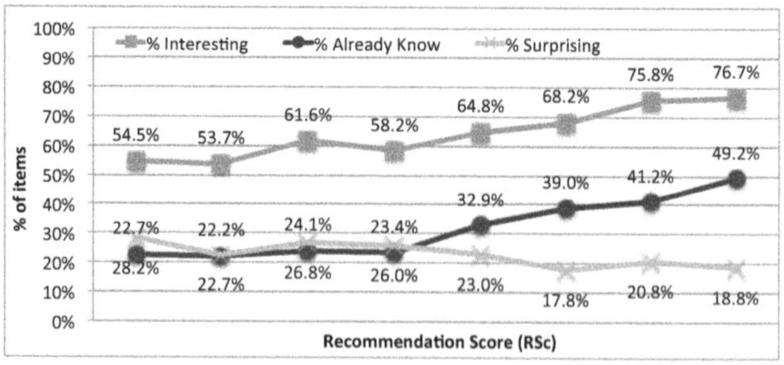

Figure 5. Personalized item ratings by recommendation score.

4.3.1 Application Source

As Table 1 indicates, items in the stream can originate from seven different applications. Figure 6 (upper part) shows the interest ($F(6,5610)=35.635$, $p<.001$) and surprise ($F(6,5610)=3.561$, $p<.01$) rates for personalized items for each of these applications. In brackets is the occurrence of the source, i.e., the portion of items that belonged to it out of all personalized items in our survey. Wikis and blogs were the most common, accounting for 36.1% and 28% of the items, respectively. However, while blogs yielded items with the highest interest rates among all sources (76.9%), wikis had the lowest interest rates (54%). Microblogs and forums also had high interest rates, while tasks had low interest rates. For surprise rates, bookmarks and microblogs, followed by blogs, had the highest surprise rates, while file items were the least surprising. Overall, blogs and microblogs produced the best combination of high interest and high surprise rates, while wikis and tasks had both low interest and low surprise rates. Blogs and microblogs present a more personal type of updates, while wikis and tasks are "dryer" and typically consist of many incremental edits.

The lower part of Figure 6 shows the same statistics for popular items. The occurrence of the sources is quite different than for personalized items. In general, it can be seen that popular items tend to be of the sources that also receive higher ratings. Therefore, the portion of blogs (almost 50% of all items) and microblogs substantially increases and that of wiki substantially decreases, as compared to personalized items. As for interest ($F(6,2040)=10.394$, $p<.001$) and surprise ($F(6,2040)=2.385$, $p<.05$) rates, the results are rather similar to the case of personalized items, with blogs, microblogs, and bookmarks having the highest interest and surprise rates, while tasks and wikis yielding low interest and surprise.

As mentioned in Section 3, an item can be performed in the context of a community [35]. For 5 of the 7 applications, their content type can be associated with a community. These include

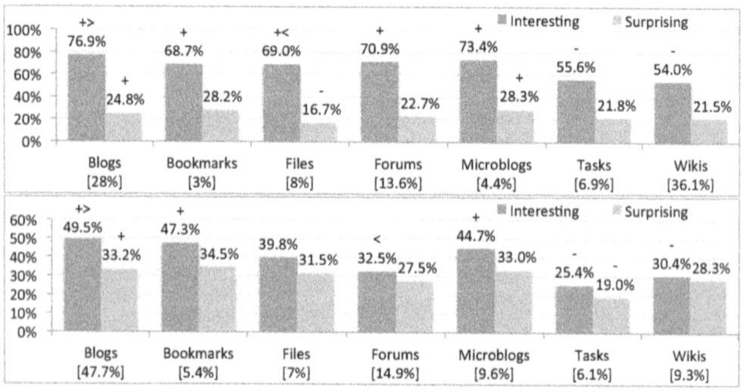

Figure 6. Ratings by application source for (top:) personalized and (bottom:) popular items.

Table 4. Ratings based on association with a community

Community Related?	Personalized				Popular			
	%	Int	AK	Surp	%	Int	AK	Surp
No	23	61.7	33.6	20.6	26.2	40.7	5.8	33
Yes	77	66.8^{*}	32.8	23.1	73.8	44.3^{+}	7.4	31.1

blogs, bookmarks, files, forums, and wikis. For these sources, we compared the ratings received for items associated with a community to items that were not related to a community. Overall, 77% of the personalized items and 73.8% of the popular items of these 5 types were associated with a community. Table 4 presents this comparison's results. It can be seen, for both personalized and popular items, that those associated with a community were significantly more interesting, while similarly surprising. Belonging to a community may scope the item in a clearer way and therefore make it more interesting. An item performed as part of a community may also have an initial audience who is more likely to notice it and is more committed to give feedback, helping it become more interesting.

4.3.2 Activity Type

Table 5 presents the ratings per each of the four most common activity types (across all applications): create, edit, comment, and like. Together these accounted for 94.3% of the personalized items and 99.4% of the popular items in our survey. As can be seen in the occurrence columns (marked by '%'), edits were most commonly recommended for personalized items, but much less commonly as popular items, for which liking activities were the most common.

Inspecting the interest rates, it is evident that edit activities, which incrementally change a document's content and include many wiki-page edits, are the least interesting for both personalized and popular items. For personalized items, liking and commenting were the most interesting with over 70%. Curiously, creation activities came only third, behind the two feedback activities. AK rates for personalized items were highest for commenting and liking, and lowest for editing. For popular items, AK rates were low in general, but lowest for comments and edits. Finally, inspecting the surprise rates reveals they were highest for create activities. Likes also received high surprise rates, while comments and edits were less surprising. These findings are similar for both personalized and popular items. Overall, among the four activity types, liking yielded the highest interest, while creation yielded the most surprise. On the other hand, editing triggered both low interest and low surprise.

4.3.3 Entity and Author's Activity

In this sub-section, we examine the activity frequency of the item's entity and author and their effect on the item's ratings. We focus on personalized items, since popular items have an inherent bias towards active entities and authors. For the analysis, we inspected the number of items produced by the author or entity in the six months preceding our survey. Table 6 compares the ratings for the top half, which includes the more active entities, with the bottom half, which includes the less active entities (median was 7

Table 5. Ratings by activity type

Activity Type	Personalized				Popular			
	%	Int	AK	Surp	%	Int	AK	Surp
Create	17.8	$68.9^{+<}$	31.7^{-}	26.6^{+}	21.2	44.7^{+}	9.2^{+}	32.7
Edit	44.9	56.3^{-}	27.6^{-}	22.2^{-}	15.6	33.2^{-}	5.3	25.1
Comment	10.9	72.5^{+}	$44.3^{+>}$	18.7^{-}	19.7	40.7	4.7^{-}	30.5
Like	20.7	$76.9^{+>}$	$37.6^{+<}$	22.9	42.9	45.8^{+}	7.8	32.4

Table 6. Ratings of personalized items by entity and author's activity frequency

	Entity Activity				Author Activity			
	%	Int	AK	Surp	%	Int	AK	Surp
Top	50	$69.2^{\wedge}$	$36.7^{\wedge}$	22.4	50	64.1	32.2	21.7
Bottom	50	60.5	28.1	22.8	50	66.2	33.1	23.4

activities) and analogously for authors (median was 20). It can be seen that items originating from entities that were more active were significantly more interesting, with significantly higher AK rates. Despite the higher AK rates, the surprise rates were similar to items from less active entities. Intuitively, active entities are likely to represent popular or trendy posts, pages, or topics, whose items yield more interest.

For authors, interestingly, the situation is different. Less active authors produce slightly higher interest (p=.07). The AK rates are similar for more active and less active authors, while the surprise rates are also slightly higher for the less active authors (p=.05). Inspecting the two extreme deciles based on author activity reveals a stronger trend: 65.1% interest for the bottom decile (authored 2 items or less) vs. 60.8 for the top decile (272 items or more, p<.05), and 24.6% vs. 19.1% for surprise rates (p<.05). One could have thought that the more active authors are more experienced in producing interesting items and commonly arouse a lot of interest, which also encourages them to keep active. Our results, however, indicate that originating from a less active user increases an item's likelihood of being interesting and surprising. It could be that very active authors often produce repetitive or noisy items, while infrequent authors may arouse more curiosity since it is less common to see them on the stream.

4.4 Reader-Author Relationship

In this section, we examine the effect of different organizational characteristics of an item's reader and author on its ratings.

4.4.1 Work Location

We examine work location in two granularities: country and office address. Our survey participants (readers) originated from 37 countries, while the authors of items presented in the survey originated from 54 countries. The upper part of Table 7 compares the ratings of items whose authors were from the same country and items from different countries. In general, almost half of the personalized items (49.2%) originated from the same country, compared to only 17.8% of the popular items. This indicates that our personalization method is biased towards the same country, even though it does not directly consider it. Inspecting the rating results, we see that interest rates of items from the same country were significantly higher for both personalized and popular items. For personalized items, AK rates were significantly higher for items from the same country, leading to significantly lower surprise rates . For popular items, these differences did not exist.

Survey participants came from 186 different office addresses and items' authors came from 414 different addresses. 15.7% of the personalized items and only 1.6% of the popular items had the same office address for both the reader and the author. Due to the very low number for popular items, we only conducted the comparison of similar versus different office address for personalized items. The lower part of Table 7 presents these results. Interest and AK rates were significantly higher for items originating from the same office address. In spite of the large difference in AK rates, surprise rates were insignificantly higher for items originating from a different office address. One explanation for this can be the reader's expectation of knowing

Table 7. Ratings by reader and author work location

		%	Int	AK	Surp
Country - Personalized	Same	49.2	$69.2^{\wedge}$	$37.8^{\wedge}$	20.2
	Different	50.8	59.3	26.9	24.5^{*}
Country - Popular	Same	17.8	45.7^{+}	7	31.4
	Different	82.2	40.9	6.8	31.4
Office Address - Personalized	Same	15.7	$72.7^{\wedge}$	$43.6^{\wedge}$	21
	Different	84.3	63.7	30.6	22.8

"everything going on in their office". Overall, items originating from authors in the same office location were more interesting, but also more likely to be already known.

4.4.2 Manager vs. Employee

In our survey, 16.3% of the participants and 18.6% of the items' authors were managers (the general portion of managers within the organization is about 13% [23]). Table 8 shows the ratings for each of the four employee-manager reader-author combinations. For personalized items, interest rates were lowest when both reader and author were employees, and significantly higher when both were managers. For popular items, the highest interest rates were for an employee reading a manager's item. In general, for personalized items, when the author was a manager, interest rates were higher compared to an employee author (regardless of the reader) at 72.7% vs. 63.5% (p<.001). For popular items, this difference was similar at 48.5% vs. 40.8% (p<.01). It is plausible that managers' greater involvement in business decisions and their often-broader business perspective make their items more likely to be interesting.

Inspecting the AK rates, for personalized items, they were significantly higher when the reader was a manager as compared to an employee reader at 39.3% vs. 31.3% (p<.001). They were highest when both author and reader were managers, at 43.4%. For popular items, there was also a slight difference in AK rates for a manager reader compared to an employee reader, at 8.1% vs. 6.9% (p>.05); in addition, there was a significant difference when the author was a manager as compared to an employee author at 10.1% vs. 6.2% (p<.01). Overall, managers marked more items as already known, probably as they are more connected in the organization. For popular items, an item authored by a manager was more likely to be known by others within the organization.

It can be clearly seen that managers were less surprised than employees. For personalized items, the surprise rates for a manager reader were 17.3%, compared to 23.6% for an employee reader (p<.001), and for popular items, they were 26.2% compared to 31.9%, respectively (p<.05). It could be that managers have more years of tenure within the organization and are also better connected, so they are less likely to be surprised. Overall, the analysis in this section reveals that managers are likely to produce more interesting items, while they also tend to be familiar with and less surprised by the items they read.

Table 8. Ratings by managerial role of author and reader

Manager	Personalized				Popular			
	%	Int	AK	Surp	%	Int	AK	Surp
None	70.6	$62.9^{-<}$	31.5^{-}	23.1^{+}	66.3	41.2^{-}	6	31.3
Reader	11.7	$67.3^{<}$	37.7^{+}	17.4^{-}	12.3	38.7^{-}	7.5	26.1^{-}
Author	13.1	$69.5^{+<}$	30.5^{-}	$26^{+>}$	17.5	50^{+}	10.1	34.4^{+}
Both	4.6	$81.8^{+>}$	43.4^{+}	$17.1^{<}$	3.9	41.8	10.1	26.6

4.4.3 Business Unit

The studied organization consists of four main business units (divisions): Sales, Services, R&D (including Software, Systems, and Research), and Corporate (CIO's office, HR, Finance, Legal, etc.). Our analysis mostly focuses on the personalized items, due to data sparsity for popular items. Overall, 19.8% of our participants were from Sales, 29.8% from Services, 25.6% from R&D, and 24.8% from Corporate. The distribution of authors for personalized items in our experiment was very similar, but for popular items, R&D authors accounted for only 10.3% of all items, while Corporate and Sales authors had a higher proportion.

Overall, 63.9% of all personalized items originated from the same division as the reader's. As we observed for location, our personalization method favors similar people without directly taking the similarity attributes into account. In contrast, only 24.9% of the popular items were from the same division, indicating no bias. For personalized items, those from the same division were significantly more interesting than those from a different division (69.8% vs. 54%, p<.001) and had significantly higher already-know rates (37.8% vs. 22.7%, p<.001). For popular items, these differences were insignificant at 44.4% vs. 40.6% for interest rates (p=.167) and 8.9% vs. 6.2% for AK rates (p=.075). For personalized items, surprise rates within the same division were significantly lower than across different divisions at 21.1% vs. 25% (p<.01). For popular items, surprise rates were almost identical at 31.2% versus 31.5%, respectively (p>.05).

Table 9 shows the ratings for each reader-author pair across the different divisions, for personalized items. ANOVA-based significance marks are shown only for the Total-Reader and Total-Author comparisons. It can be seen that for interest rates, Sales were interested in Corporate and R&D, in addition to their own items, but much less interested in Services; Services were also interested in Corporate; R&D were also interested in Corporate and Sales; and Corporate were most interested in Sales, in addition to their own items. Overall, Corporate authors yielded the most interesting items, while Services attracted less interest (see Total-Author column). It is reasonable that Corporate employees write more about internal programs and processes that are of broad interest to the entire employee population. Corporate and Sales were generally more interested in items than Services and R&D (Total-Reader row). This can be explained by the fact that both of these divisions require deeper knowledge of the

Table 9. Ratings by reader and author's business unit

Reader / Author	Sales	Services	R&D	Corporate	Total-Author
% Interest					
Sales	74.1	46.3	55.6	62.1	$64.9^{+<}$
Services	42.7	64.8	39.1	50.5	57.8^{-}
R&D	65.4	53.7	67.8	54.1	$64.2^{+<}$
Corporate	69.6	63.3	61.1	75.5	$72.2^{+>}$
Total-reader	66.2^{+}	61.5^{-}	61.7^{-}	68^{+}	
% Already Know					
Sales	40.2	16.3	17.4	35.6	31.5
Services	21.9	38.3	18.6	23.3	32.5
R&D	29.6	20.7	34.3	18	30.2^{-}
Corporate	28.4	22	28.3	39.1	35.3^{+}
Total-reader	33.7^{+}	32.8	29.3^{-}	34^{+}	
% Surprise					
Sales	20.7	23.8	21.3	20.7	21.3^{-}
Services	21.3	21.4	18.6	24.8	21.6^{-}
R&D	22.8	29.9	19.4	28.7	22.2
Corporate	30.4	31.2	31.9	22.5	25.1^{+}
Total-reader	22.2	23.4^{+}	20.7^{-}	23.4^{+}	

organization to successfully carry out their tasks, compared to the more technical divisions.

For AK rates, items from Corporate employees were slightly more known, while items from R&D people were the least known. More noticeably, R&D readers marked fewer items as already known, perhaps indicating they are less aware of what is going on across the organization. Corporate authors yielded the highest portion of surprise rates, even though their items also had higher already-know rates. For readers, R&D employees were the least surprised by items they read.

5. CONCLUSIONS AND FUTURE WORK

5.1 Result Summary and Discussion

Our results indicate a trade-off between accuracy, reflected in interest ratings, to serendipity and novelty, reflected in surprise and already-know ratings. In terms of accuracy, personalized items achieved 65% interest rates across all recommended items, while popular items only reached 42.5%. The accuracy for personalized items went beyond 75% under certain conditions, such as for items with a very high recommendation score, items that originate from the blog application, or involve a 'liking' activity.

In contrast, personalized items were less effective than popular items in terms of novelty and serendipity. This was reflected in significantly higher already-know rates and significantly lower surprise rates, ultimately leading to a significantly lower portion of personalized items that were both interesting and surprising. These results suggest that popular items pose their own value with respect to novelty and serendipity, at the expense of accuracy. This stands in contrast to previous literature in traditional RS domains, where popular items were suggested as a baseline for non-serendipitous and non-novel recommendations [7,38]. The reason for this difference is the unique character of popular items in the social stream domain, due to their short life span: while movies or books, for example, usually remain popular for years, a popular stream item normally lasts only a few days, after which other trendy items take its place. Stream filtering applications should therefore consider combining popularity-based recommendations within a personalized stream. This could be done, for example, by a popularity boost or by interleaving pure popularity-based items in the recommended stream. Users can also be involved in this process, by indicating their desired level of surprise, as has been previously suggested for other RS [36].

We experimented with two different types of popular items, generated based on popular entities and popular authors. The two methods yielded very similar rating results for interest, already-know, and surprise ratings, granting more validity to our findings about their superiority over personalized items in terms of serendipity. The RS literature proposes various methods to enhance the serendipity of recommendations [26,32,33]. Future research should examine the adaptation of such methods to the social stream domain.

We experimented with three types of profile size. Our results show that the two larger profiles produced better combinations of interest and surprise rates. The largest profile produced the highest interest rates, while the mid-size profile produced the highest surprise rates. We believe that the diversity supported by a larger profile size contributes to its overall recommendation quality. Future work should further examine different size configurations, with different number of people, terms, and entities.

Our study examined various organizational aspects that influence an item's ratings. We found that items from the same work location and business unit are rated more interesting, but less surprising. This indicates that homophily ("love of the same") [31] plays an important role in stream personalization: users tend to be more interested in activity from people who are similar to them, but such activity is also less likely to surprise them. Our analysis also indicated that managers author more interesting items and tend to be more familiar with and less surprised by the items they read. Further analysis revealed that items originating from an internal (Corporate) unit produce higher interest and surprise. Additionally, employees who belong to a technical (R&D) unit are more indifferent to items they read, reflected in lower interest, surprise, and already-know ratings.

Overall, we examined different factors that may influence the value of an item to its reader within the enterprise, in terms of accuracy, novelty, and serendipity. We discovered that an item is more likely to be valuable when it has the following characteristics:

- Originates from the blog, microblog, or bookmark applications, which typically include more appealing content.
- Is carried out in the context of a community, which may provide more focus and scope.
- Is about a create, comment, or 'like' activity, rather than an 'edit' activity, which is typically of smaller value.
- Involves an active entity, but a less active author. Active entities may represent trendy posts, while infrequent authors may sometimes arouse more curiosity when they finally take action.
- Its author is a manger from an internal (Corporate) unit, who is more likely to discuss a topic of relevance to broader parts of the company.
- Its reader belongs to a Corporate or Sales unit (rather than a technical unit), who may have a stronger need to understand the organizational environment.

Understanding the characteristics of valuable items in the enterprise stream can help enhance the adoption and use of enterprise social media in general and enterprise social streams in particular within organizations. This is becoming a key challenge as social media continues to gain popularity and as younger populations, more accustomed to consuming information through social streams and news feeds, are joining the workforce.

5.2 Addressing Limitations

The experiments in this work were based on a user survey and do not include analysis of user behavior in a live system. A/B testing is often used by the industry to analyze usage, such as click-through, on a large scale. In social streams, however, interest is not necessarily reflected by click-through data, as users often read a valuable item and continue scrolling through the stream, without any click. Moreover, novelty and serendipity are particularly difficult to evaluate by analyzing user behavior [24]. The survey enabled us to directly ask for user feedback regarding these qualities. Facebook has recently conducted a user survey to gain an in-depth understanding of what factors give posts on the news feed higher quality [15]. As far as we are aware, the results have not been published. Our survey was relatively short, to allow broad participation with feedback on many items. Future research may use additional questions to expand the understanding of user satisfaction, for instance by directly asking how much an item is "useful" or "valuable".

We used a personalization technique that extends a previous method used for stream personalization in the enterprise and includes all three elements in the user profile: related people (as currently done in leading social media sites such as Twitter), related terms (as suggested in previous studies [5,13]), and related entities (found productive in [20]). Additionally, we segmented the results based on various factors that may affect the personalization performance, including the item's personalization score, application source, activity type, and profile size. Other personalization techniques can be applied, which may perform differently than our own method. Yet, we believe that the comprehensive user model and the segmentation analysis help make our results broadly relevant for stream recommendation in the enterprise.

The results of our study are influenced by the characteristics of the studied organization and its use of enterprise social media. We hope to see further research on the topic in the future, but note that the basic concepts discussed (related people/terms/entities, popular authors/entities, work location and managerial status, sales, technical, and internal business units) are generally relevant to enterprise social streams and can therefore be valid for other organizations. Moreover, we experimented with applications that represent common social media both within the enterprise and outside the firewall. We therefore believe that some of our findings may also apply for social streams on the web.

6. REFERENCES

[1] Adamopoulos, P. & Tuzhilin, A. 2011. On unexpectedness in recommender systems: or how to expect the unexpected. *RecSys '11 Workshop on Novelty and Diversity in RS*, 11-18.

[2] Agarwal, D. et al. 2014. Activity ranking in LinkedIn feed. *Proc. KDD '14*, 1603-1612.

[3] Amitay, E., Carmel, D., Har'El, N., Ofek-Koifman, S., Soffer, A., Yogev, S., & Golbandi, N. 2009. Social search and discovery using a unified approach. *Proc. HT '09*, 199-208.

[4] Berkovsky, S., Freyne, J., & Smith, G. 2012. Personalized network updates: increasing social interactions and contributions in social networks. *Proc. UMAP '12*, 1-13.

[5] Bernstein, M.S., Suh, B., Hong, L., Chen, J., Kairam, S., & Chi, E.H. 2010. Eddi: interactive topic-based browsing of social status streams. *Proc. UIST '10*, 303-312.

[6] Carmel, D., Uziel, E., Guy, I., Mass, Y., & Roitman, H. 2012. Folksonomy-based term extraction for word cloud generation. *ACM TIST*, *3*(4), 60.

[7] Celma, Ò. & Herrera, P. 2008. A new approach to evaluating novel recommendations. *Proc. RecSys '08*, 179-186.

[8] Chen, K., Chen, T., Zheng, G., Jin, O., Yao, E., & Yu, Y. 2012. Collaborative personalized tweet recommendation. *Proc. SIGIR '12*, 661-670.

[9] Cui, P., Wang, F., Liu, S., Ou, M., Yang, S., & Sun, L. 2011. Who should share what?: item-level social influence prediction for users and posts ranking. *Proc. SIGIR '11*, 185-194.

[10] Daly, E.M., Muller, M.J., Gou, L., & Millen, D.R. 2011. Social lens: personalization around user defined collections for filtering enterprise message streams. *Proc. ICWSM '11*.

[11] Desrosiers, C. & Karypis, G. 2011. A comprehensive survey of neighborhood-based recommendation methods. *Recommender systems handbook*, 107-144.

[12] DiMicco, J., Millen, D.R., Geyer, W., Dugan, C., Brownholtz, B., & Muller, M. 2008. Motivations for social networking at work. Proc. CSCW '08, 711-720.

[13] Esparza, S.G., O'Mahony, M.P., & Smyth, B. 2013. Catstream: categorising tweets for user profiling and stream filtering. *Proc. IUI '13*, 25-36.

[14] Facebook for Business – A Window into News Feed: https://www.facebook.com/business/news/News-Feed-FYI-A-Window-Into-News-Feed

[15] Facebook for Business – Showing More High Quality Content: https://www.facebook.com/business/news/News-Feed-FYI-Showing-More-High-Quality-Content

[16] Farrell, S., Lau, T., Nusser, S., Wilcox, E., & Muller, M. 2007. Socially augmenting employee profiles with people-tagging. *Proc. UIST '07*, 91-100.

[17] Feng, W. & Wang, J. 2013. Retweet or not?: personalized tweet re-ranking. *Proc. WSDM '13*, 577-586.

[18] Freyne, J., Berkovsky, S., Daly, E.M., & Geyer, W. 2010. Social networking feeds: recommending items of interest. *Proc. RecSys '10*, 277-280.

[19] Ge, M., Delgado-Battenfeld, C., & Jannach, D. 2010. Beyond accuracy: evaluating recommender systems by coverage and serendipity. *Proc. RecSys '10*, 257-260.

[20] Guy, I., Ronen, I., & Raviv, A. 2011. Personalized activity streams: sifting through the river of news. *Proc. RecSys '11*, 181-188.

[21] Guy, I., Steier, T., Barnea, M., Ronen, I., & Daniel, T. 2012. Swimming against the Streamz: search and analytics over the enterprise activity stream. *Proc. CIKM '12*, 1587-1591.

[22] Guy, I., Steier, T., Barnea, M., Ronen, I., & Daniel, T. 2013. Finger on the pulse: the value of the activity stream in the enterprise. *Proc. Interact '13*, 411-428.

[23] Guy, I., Ur, S., Ronen, I., Weber, S., & Oral, T. Best faces forward: a large-scale people search in the enterprise. *Proc. CHI '12*, 1775-1784.

[24] Herlocker, J.L., Konstan, J.A., Terveen, L.G., & Riedl, J.T. 2004. Evaluating collaborative filtering recommender systems. *ACM TOIS*, *22*(1), 5-53.

[25] Hong, L., Bekkerman, R., Adler, J., & Davison, B. D. 2012. Learning to rank social update streams. *Proc. SIGIR '12*, 651-660.

[26] Iaquinta, L., De Gemmis, M., Lops, P., Semeraro, G., Filannino, M., & Molino, P. 2008. Introducing serendipity in a content-based recommender system. *Proc. HIS '08*, 168-173.

[27] IBM Connections – Enterprise Social Software: http://www.ibm.com/software/products/conn

[28] Lunze, T., Katz, P., Röhrborn, D., & Schill, A. 2013. Stream-based recommendation for enterprise social media streams. *Proc. BIS '13*, 175-186.

[29] McCandless, M., Hatcher, E., & Gospodneti, O. 2010. Lucene in action, 2nd edition. *Manning Publications Co.*

[30] McNee, S.M., Riedl, J., & Konstan, J.A. 2006. Being accurate is not enough: how accuracy metrics have hurt recommender systems. Proc. *CHI EA '06*, 1097-1101.

[31] McPherson, M., Smith-Lovin, L., & Cook, J.M. 2001. Birds of a feather: Homophily in social networks. *Annual review of sociology*, 415-444.

[32] Murakami, T., Mori, K., & Orihara, R. 2007. Metrics for evaluating the serendipity of recommendation lists. *Proc. JSAI '07*, 40-46.

[33] Onuma, K., Tong, H., & Faloutsos, C. 2009. TANGENT: a novel, 'surprise me', recommendation algorithm. *Proc. KDD '09*, 657-666.

[34] Paek, T., Gamon, M., Counts, S., Chickering, D. M., & Dhesi, A. 2010. Predicting the importance of newsfeed posts and social network friends. *Proc. AAAI '10*, 1419-1424.

[35] Ronen, I., Guy, I., Kravi, E., & Barnea, M. Recommending social media items to community owners. *Proc. SIGIR '14*, 243-252.

[36] Tintarev, N. & Masthoff, J. 2007. A survey of explanations in recommender systems. *3rd WPRSIUI Workshop, Proc. ICED '07*, 801-810.

[37] Zhang, Y.C., Séaghdha, D.Ó., Quercia, D., & Jambor, T. 2012. Auralist: introducing serendipity into music recommendation. *Proc. WSDM '12*, 13-22.

[38] Ziegler, C.N., McNee, S.M., Konstan, J.A., & Lausen, G. 2005. Improving recommendation lists through topic diversification. *Proc. WWW '05*, 22-32.

Evaluating Streams of Evolving News Events

Gaurav Baruah
Computer Science
University of Waterloo
gbaruah@uwaterloo.ca

Mark D. Smucker
Management Sciences
University of Waterloo
mark.smucker@uwaterloo.ca

Charles L. A. Clarke
Computer Science
University of Waterloo
claclark@plg.uwaterloo.ca

ABSTRACT

People track news events according to their interests and available time. For a major event of great personal interest, they might check for updates several times an hour, taking time to keep abreast of all aspects of the evolving event. For minor events of more marginal interest, they might check back once or twice a day for a few minutes to learn about the most significant developments. Systems generating streams of updates about evolving events can improve user performance by appropriately filtering these updates, making it easy for users to track events in a timely manner without undue information overload. Unfortunately, predicting user performance on these systems poses a significant challenge. Standard evaluation methodology, designed for Web search and other adhoc retrieval tasks, adapts poorly to this context. In this paper, we develop a simple model that simulates users checking the system from time to time to read updates. For each simulated user, we generate a trace of their activities alternating between away times and reading times. These traces are then applied to measure system effectiveness. We test our model using data from the TREC 2013 Temporal Summarization Track (TST) comparing it to the effectiveness measures used in that track. The primary TST measure corresponds most closely with a modeled user that checks back once a day on average for an average of one minute. Users checking more frequently for longer times may view the relative performance of participating systems quite differently. In light of this sensitivity to user behavior, we recommend that future experiments be built around clearly stated assumptions regarding user interfaces and access patterns, with effectiveness measures reflecting these assumptions.

Categories and Subject Descriptors: H.3.4 [Information Storage and Retrieval]: Systems and Software — *Performance evaluation (efficiency and effectiveness)*

Keywords: search; streams; evaluation

SIGIR'15, August 09 - 13, 2015, Santiago, Chile.

ACM 978-1-4503-3621-5/15/08 ...$15.00.
DOI: http://dx.doi.org/10.1145/2766462.2767751.

1. INTRODUCTION

On December 4, 2012, Typhoon Bopha made landfall on the eastern coast of the Philippine island of Mindanao. The strongest typhoon in the island's recorded history, the storm system had formed in the Pacific in late November, growing into a tropical storm by November 28th, and into a severe tropical storm by November 30th. On December 1st, as the storm moved west towards the island, it rapidly intensified into a category 4 typhoon. Two days later, only miles from shore, it reached category 5, a super typhoon, with winds up to 150 mph. At 4:45AM it hit. Heavy rains and waves exceeding 25 feet washed across villages and towns, destroying homes, flooding roads, and cutting communications. Initial reports limited the death toll to one, but by the next day it had increased to over 200, mostly killed by flooding and debris. Over the next week, the number of fatalities grew to a final total of over 600, with more than 200,000 people displaced or otherwise impacted.

In this paper we consider how to evaluate a search engine that aggregates a stream of information and provides a means for people to obtain the latest, most relevant information regarding an event of interest. As time permits, a user of such a search engine will check back multiple times in order to find out new information about the event.

We envision that there will be a wide variety of users of such a search engine. Government and health care workers, as well as people in the immediate vicinity, would likely need to learn of new information soon after it becomes available. People interested in the event, but not directly affected, would likely have a less urgent need for new information. Some people would be willing to consume a large amount of content in the hope of not missing any relevant information, while others may desire a minimal amount of content.

One way of designing an information retrieval system for streams of evolving events would be to allow users to visit and query the system whenever they want the latest information. In this type of system, the user *pulls* information. An alternative approach would be to create a system that *pushes* select pieces of information to users that have set up a search query or profile. In either case, users would want to control the frequency and duration of their interaction with the system. In the pull scenario, the user controls the frequency by how often they visit and controls the duration by how long they consume content during a visit's session. In the push scenario, the user would need to specify up front how often content should be sent to them as well as the amount of content to be sent.

In this paper, we propose a new effectiveness measure for the evaluation of retrieval systems that produce streams of content for evolving events. We call this measure *modeled stream utility* (MSU). This new effectiveness measure models users in terms of the time spent away from the system and the time spent with the system. In effect, we model users in terms of their frequency and duration of interaction with the system, which is a model applicable to either push or pull variants of this type of retrieval system. We measure utility in the number of relevant information nuggets the user is likely to find. Search users naturally vary, and we model this variation as well by modeling a population of users and simulating many different users' interaction with the retrieval system. A significant advantage of MSU as an effectiveness measure is that by making it user-centered, the measure has the potential to be easily calibrated using recorded user behavior.

We demonstrate MSU using the TREC 2013 Temporal Summarization Track [4]. Participating groups in the temporal summarization track (TST) take a large stream of content and attempt to produce a filtered stream of content relevant to a given search topic. For each topic, the track has determined a set of relevant nuggets of information and has judged a pool of content and determined which nuggets are present in the content.

To evaluate the runs submitted to TST, we use MSU in a scenario where users pull information from the retrieval system. MSU simulates user interaction with the retrieval system. When a simulated user visits the retrieval system and queries it for a given search topic, the user is shown the most recently filtered content in reverse chronological order. In TST, filtered content consists of sentence length material extracted from a stream of larger documents. After a simulated user has read an element of content, we measure the user's gain in terms of the number of nuggets the user is likely to have found relevant in the content. If a user has read a nugget earlier, MSU assumes that a repeated nugget will not be found relevant and has a gain value of zero. The temporal summarization track has estimated when nuggets are first known in the aggregate stream, and in the MSU simulation, nuggets delivered late to a user are less likely to be found relevant.

In addition to demonstrating MSU applied to the TREC 2013 temporal summarization track, we compare MSU to the track's existing primary measure, ELG, as well as conduct a parameter sweep over a range of the MSU user model's parameters to better understand how the measure behaves. We find that:

- When we set MSU's parameters to that of a reasonably interested user who visits the system for 2 minutes every 3 hours on average, MSU's ranking of TST submitted runs is significantly different from TST's primary measure, ELG (Kendall's $\tau = 0.47$).

- Of the parameter settings included in our sweep, ELG correlates best with a model of users who visit for only 1 minute per day (Kendall's $\tau = 0.62$). In terms of content consumed, a minute-long visit amounts to a user reading approximately 4-5 sentences.

- The ranking of systems produced by the MSU effectiveness measure appears to be most sensitive to the amount of content consumed by the simulated users.

Given that the amount of content consumed appears to affect system rankings the most, this result has implications for the design of retrieval systems that generate streams of information updates. The temporal summarization track gave participating groups the task of filtering a stream, but different users are going to be interested in different amounts of material. Rather than filter a stream, retrieval systems for evolving events may be better designed as best-match rankers that must balance recency and relevancy. No matter how such systems are designed, MSU provides a user-centered measure that allows for calibration with actual measured user behavior.

2. BACKGROUND

The news about an event, such as Typhoon Bopha, has an impact on large sections of society. The sudden onset of such events can generate related information needs among governments, aid agencies, observer groups, as well as those affected and their families. Usually such events are unexpected and can be dynamic and evolve over time.

A large number of documents will be authored in connection with significant events and made available for consumption via the Internet in near real time. Publishers of this content include social networking services such as Twitter and Facebook as well as newspapers, news feeds, and blogs. Authors can range from journalists to government agencies to persons experiencing the event first hand. We consider all newly created content in aggregate as a stream of material from which a person might want to find relevant information.

The closest analogues to this type of retrieval are microblog search [12] and temporal summarization [2, 4]. The TREC 2011 Microblog track [12] included a single adhoc retrieval task where the retrieval system receives a query at time t and must retrieve the most relevant and recent Twitter postings prior to time t. The track organizers used precision at rank 30 to evaluate submissions, but found that the task was under-specified with respect to how results should be ranked in terms of relevance and recency, making comparisons between participating groups difficult.

In the TREC 2012 Microblog track [14], the adhoc retrieval task remained and was adjusted so that participants were simply to score the microblog posts for ranking purposes. The only notion of recency was that the postings had to have occurred before the time of the query. Relevance of a posting was formulated with respect to the informativeness of the posting without considerations of recency or novelty. To evaluate a ranking, the organizers computed its precision at 30 and its receiver operating characteristic (ROC). For TREC 2013, the microblog track continued to use precision at 30 as its primary retrieval measure [11].

Temporal summarization systems attempt to extract relevant information from an aggregate stream and relay this information to the user as soon as possible. In contrast to a microblog search task, a temporal summarization task extends over a period that roughly corresponds to the period that an event is in the news. Being a summarization task, the evaluation of temporal summarization systems has focused on determining the overall quality of the resulting summary even though the nature of temporal summarization means that the summary grows over time and is likely being consumed by an end user at regular intervals, e.g. for a multi-day event, we would expect a user to seek new information daily.

The temporal summarization work of Allan, Gupta, and Khandelwal [2] defined new precision and recall measures that incorporate notions of usefulness and novelty. A useful sentence is one that would be helpful for use in a summary and a novel sentence is one that is new and contains information not previously seen. In addition, they examine the importance of summary size and recency of information.

Guo et al. [10] primarily focus on finding updates for rapidly evolving news events for which the information need is urgent (or time-critical). They consider an event to be composed of a number of subtopics. Each update may contain one or more subtopics as well. Accordingly, the precision for an update is the fraction of the update's subtopics that are also subtopics for the event, and, the recall for an update is the the fraction of the event's subtopics contained in the update. They define measures *expected precision* and *expected recall* to be the average precision (and recall respectively) over the complete set of updates.

The TREC 2013 Temporal Summarization Track (TST) [4] follows the temporal summarization framework defined by Allan et al. [2] with two significant changes. The first change is that while Allan et al. required that summarization happen on-the-fly as each news story was received, in TST, systems are only restricted to be certain that summaries produced at time t only use content available at t or earlier. For example, if a system wanted to, it could wait to process several days of content before producing a single result. The TST directly evaluates the recency of information and thus does not have to restrict systems in when or how they produce summaries. The second change is that the TST uses a web-scale aggregate stream of world wide web content as opposed to the comparatively small collection available to Allan et al. in 2001.

The TST uses sentences (*updates* in TST terminology) as the primary retrieval unit. Groups participating in TST had the task of filtering the aggregate stream and emitting sentences containing timely and novel information regarding a news event. The TST judges the relevance of sentences by noting the presence of individual nuggets of information. Sentences are annotated such that it is known what pieces (nuggets) of relevant information the sentences contain.

The TST assessors identified nuggets about an event from Wikipedia. For example, Typhoon Bopha has its own detailed Wikipedia page[1]. TST attached a timestamp to every nugget as determined by the first occurrence of the nugget in the Wikipedia edit history for the topic's article.

The TST organizers crafted effectiveness measures that are nugget-based variants of precision and recall that incorporate several key criteria for the updates produced by a system. In addition to an update needing to contain novel nuggets, the nuggets should be emitted as early as possible (latency) and shorter updates are better than longer updates (verbosity). Each update is assigned a score based on these criteria and the track's set-based effectiveness measures are computed as averages over all updates.

Participating groups produced runs consisting of emitted updates. When an update is emitted, it is given a timestamp equal to the most recent material consumed by the system from the aggregate stream of material. Thus, a system that delayed emitting any updates until it had consumed all of the material in the period of interest, would have all of its updates given a timestamp equal to the very end of the period. If an update contains a nugget, the nugget's *latency* is the difference between the update's timestamp and the nugget's Wikipedia assigned time. The gain for a reported nugget is discounted as a function of its latency, such that, with increasing latency, the gain for a nugget drops substantially within the first 24 hours, after which its discounted gain stays under 20%. It is possible for an update to be "earlier" than the nugget's timestamp, in which case the latency discount function awards the update a bonus for reporting the nugget early. Reflecting novelty, repeated nuggets have no value, providing zero gain.

Finally, sentences are penalized for being overly verbose. To incorporate verbosity into the track's measures, an update may count as more than a single update in the computation of the average. The *verbosity* of an update is based on the extra number of nuggets the update could have contained. For example, if an update contains zero nuggets and is 60 words long, and if the average number of words per nugget is 15, then this update has a verbosity penalty of 60 / 15 = 4 and when averaged counts as 5 updates, i.e. itself (1) plus its verbosity penalty (4). If the number of words in an update equals the sum of the words in the nuggets in the update, then the update counts as a single update.

TST's evaluation has two primary metrics, expected latency gain (ELG), which measures the gain per update while discounting latency and penalizing verbosity, and latency comprehensiveness (LC), which measures coverage of nuggets relating to the topic. ELG and LC are analogous to precision and recall respectively. While both ELG and LC are important to be considered together, we consider the ELG measure to be the primary measure of the track given that runs were presented from best to worst ELG in the track overview [4]. ELG for a set $\mathcal{D}$ of system generated updates is formulated as,

$$\mathbf{ELG_V}(\mathcal{D}) = \frac{1}{\sum_{d\in\mathcal{D}} \mathbf{V}(d)} \sum_{d\in\mathcal{D}} \mathbf{G}(d,\mathcal{D}) \qquad (1)$$

where, $\mathbf{V}(d)$ is the verbosity normalization of update d, $\mathbf{G}(d,\mathcal{D})$ is the latency discounted gain for update d, and $\mathbf{G}(d,\mathcal{D})$ is non zero when d is the earliest update from the set $\mathcal{D}$ to report one or more nuggets for the topic. Once a nugget is reported, it does not contribute to gain if it appears again in later updates. The LC metric replaces the denominator in equation (1), with $\sum_{n\in\mathcal{N}} \mathbf{R}(n)$, where $\mathcal{N}$ is the set of nuggets identified by the assessors and $\mathbf{R}(n)$ is the relevance for n based on its importance ($\mathbf{R}(n) = 1$ for binary relevance). Essentially LC computes the recall of relevant material by the system. Unjudged sentences are elided from run submissions.

It is clear that users are kept in mind in the formulation of effectiveness measures for temporal summarization. For example, an update should be timely and contain relevant, novel information without extraneous material. In addition to these qualities, we believe that it important to also consider the user's desired frequency and duration of interaction with the system. A government agency may well assemble a team of people to monitor a stream of updates 24 hours a day for the duration of a crisis. An individual in the midst of a crisis may be limited by extrinsic circumstances to only having a few moments each day to check for updates.

[1] http://en.wikipedia.org/wiki/Typhoon_Bopha

ID	Time	Nugget
n_9	12/05/12 15:13:56	The typhoon destroyed 70-80% of plantations, mostly bananas for export.
n_{10}	12/06/12 17:45:12	Damage to agriculture and infrastructure in Compostela Valley province could reach at least 4 billion pesos, equivalent to 75 million or $98 million U.S.
n_{11}	12/04/12 18:31:18	About 40 people were killed or missing in flash floods and landslides near a mining area on Mindanao.
n_{12}	12/04/12 03:17:18	Typhoon Bopha made landfall on Mindanao early on December 4 as a category 4.
n_{13}	12/05/12 10:31:21	Late on December 3, Bopha made landfall over Baganga, Mindanao, as a category 5 super typhoon.
n_{14}	12/05/12 13:55:42	As of 5 December, 238 deaths had been reported on Mindana with hundreds missing.

Table 1: Nuggets reported to user (read by user) in the example session (Table 2). Times for each nugget are their time of first occurrence in Wikipedia's edit history.

3. MODELED STREAM UTILITY

We have designed our new effectiveness measure, modeled stream utility (MSU), to be an easily calibrated user-centered effectiveness measure. A user-centered effectiveness measure must take into consideration both the user interface of the retrieval system and user behavior with the user interface. For an effectiveness measures to be easily calibrated to user behavior, the measure's user model must be designed such that the model's parameters can be set based on actual measurements of user behavior.

3.1 User Interface and User Behavior

Our hypothetical user interface provides a means for the user to query the system and receive a ranked list of results (i.e. updates about an event). Each result is a short piece of text. The retrieval system produces a stream of information that is consumed by the user in the order produced. In other words, after issuing a query and receiving the ranked list of results, the user reads the results in rank order. No other interaction with the retrieval system is possible.

Our simulated user is not limited to one visit with the retrieval system. Our simulated user will repeatedly visit the search engine with a frequency reflective of their interest in the evolving event or reflective of their availability to visit. On each visit, the simulated user enters the same query, and expects to receive the most recent and relevant updates concerning their event of interest. As with their frequency of visits, the simulated user will read during a visit for an amount of time reflective of their interest or time available. We will call visits *sessions*, with each having a duration.

No two users are the same. Each user will visit the search engine with different frequencies and durations. Each user will have their own reading speed. We model frequency and duration by modeling the time a user spends away from the system and by separately modeling the time a user spends with the system. We model each user with three parameters:

- A: Average time away.
- D: Average session duration.
- V: Reading speed, e.g. words per minute.

To estimate user performance with the retrieval system, we draw multiple simulated users from population distributions and average user performance over all simulated users. We model the user population's time away and their session duration with two separate log-normal distributions. Log-normal distributions are such that when one takes the natural log of the data, a normal distribution fits the resulting distribution. Usually one describes a log-normal distribution in terms of the mean, μ, and standard deviation, σ, of the normal distribution fit to the log of the data.

For both the time-away and the session-duration distributions, we will describe them in this paper in terms of the underlying distribution's mean and standard deviation. If the underlying data has mean M and standard deviation S, then, for the log-normal distribution, the variance is $\sigma^2 = log(1 + S^2/M^2)$, and the mean is $\mu = log(M) - 0.5\sigma^2$. As we describe later in the paper, we consider a wide range of user behavior by varying the time away and session duration population distributions. To model the population's reading speed, we use the log-normal parameters from Clarke and Smucker [8] wherein, the distribution of reading speed across users is described by a log-normal distribution with $\mu = 1.29$ and $\sigma = 0.558$.

Given these three population distributions, we can generate as many simulated users as needed for numerical precision in our estimate of average user performance. For example, a possible *reasonable* setting of the population parameters is:

- Time away mean, $M_A = 3$ hours, and standard deviation, $S_A = 1.5$ hours.
- Session duration mean, $M_D = 2$ minutes, and standard deviation, $S_D = 1$ minute.
- Reading speed log-normal (words per second): $\mu = 1.29$ and $\sigma = 0.558$, i.e. a mean reading speed of 255 words per minute.

A random user drawn from this distribution will spend more or less time away, have longer or shorter session durations, and read faster or slower than the above population averages. Overall, the population of simulated users will have average behavior equal to the population means. To simulate a single user's interaction with the search engine over a given period of time, we construct a *user-trace* (Figure 1d) consisting of alternating sessions with the search engine and time intervals spent away from the search engine.

It would be unusual for a user to visit on a fixed frequency and visit for the exact same amount of time on each visit. To model variation in a user's time away and session duration, we use their mean time away and mean session duration as parameters to two separate exponential distributions. An exponential distribution is commonly used to model phenomena such as the time between radioactive decay of nuclei or the time between events in a Poisson process. For example, to simulate random session duration times with a mean of D, we draw random deviates from an exponential distribution [9] with a rate parameter of $\lambda = 1/D$.

3.2 Gain

A simulated user will repeatedly visit the search engine. During a visit, the user will read the search results in rank order. Each search result has an amount of gain (possibly zero) associated with it. The simulated user will accumulate

Time	Conf.	Update Sentence Produced by System at Time Shown in Column 1	TtR	CTtR	Nuggets
9:52	0.95	Typhoon Bopha , with central winds of 75 mph and gusts of up to 93 mph, battered beach resorts and dive spots in northern Palawan on Wednesday, but there was little damage as the storm began to weaken.	10.1 s	10.1 s	
9:52	0.95	Hardest hit were the coastal, farming and mining towns in the southern Mindanao region, where Bopha made landfall on Tuesday, destroying homes, causing landslides and flash flooding and killing at least 230 people.	8.8 s	18.9 s	n_{11}, n_{12}, n_{13}, n_{14}
9:52	0.95	About 60 people died in the municipality of New Bataan alone and around 245 were still missing, Uy said, adding the area was initially cut off by road blocks.	7.7 s	26.7 s	
9:52	0.91	Damage to agriculture and infrastructure in Compostela Valley province could reach at least 4 billion pesos ($98 million), with the typhoon destroying 70-80 percentof plantations, mostly bananas for export, Uy said.	8.5 s	35.2 s	n_9, n_{10}
9:50	0.87	A man looks at the dead bodies of relatives killed by landslides after Typhoon Bopha hit Compostela town. / Getty Disaster-response agencies reported 13 other typhoon-related deaths elsewhere.	7.5 s	42.7 s	
9:15	0.91	Typhoon Bopha : Philippines Storm Kills 238 - Yahoo!	2.4 s	45.1 s	n_{14}
7:45	0.87	Most Popular Today's five most popular stories World's oldest person dies at age 116 Snake on a plane forces emergency landing What city has world's best quality of life?	7.7 s	52.8 s	
7:31	0.87	(AP Photo)</em&gt ; May 1960 A magnitude 9.5 earthquake in southern Chile and ensuing tsunami kill at least 1,716 people.< br> <em&gt ;Caption: A soldier stands guard nearrubble strewn around an electrical shop which was shattered by an earthquake in Concepcion , Chile , on May 24, 1960.	13.1 s	65.9 s	

Table 2: Example user session: User reads at 225 words per minute, spending 60 seconds reading, starting at 9:55, on Dec 06, 2012. The column heading "Time" indicates the time at which the update was emitted, "Conf." is short for "Confidence", "TtR" means "Time to Read" and "CTtR" means "Cumulative Time to Read".

gain at the end of each search result. If the simulated user does not finish reading a search result during a session, the result is considered unread and no gain is recorded. We consider unjudged updates as non-relevant, and we do not elide them.

We measure the gain of a search result as the number of nuggets of relevant information contained in the result. A nugget can be considered an atomic piece of information. Example nuggets from the TST 2013 qrels are shown in Table 1. Our simulated users consider only novel nuggets to be relevant. Previously seen nuggets provide no gain.

Users interested in evolving events want the update produced by the search engine to be recent as well as relevant. Nuggets delivered late to a user are less likely to be considered relevant by the user. Given that different users will visit the search engine at different times, our notion of nugget timeliness must be relative to the simulated user. To make nugget timeliness relative to the user, we define a nugget as being *late* if it existed in the aggregate stream at a time equal to or before the start of the previous visit. In other words, if a user reads a result that contains a nugget that the search engine could have delivered during a previous visit, the nugget is late. To measure how late a nugget is, we define a function $\alpha(n)$ that returns how many sessions ago the nugget could have been reported (Figure 1f). A nugget that is reported on time has an $\alpha(n)$ of zero.

While we do not know how the probability that a user will consider a nugget relevant changes with its lateness, an exponential decay seems reasonable. Therefore we compute the gain for every read nugget n as:

$$g(n) = 1 \times L^{\alpha(n)} \quad (2)$$

where, L is the decay parameter for late reporting of nuggets and can vary between 0 and 1. L is a pre-determined value representing how much less a user is likely to consider the nugget to be relevant if it is reported late. For our experiments, we vary L from 0 to 1, where 0 indicates that a nugget loses all value if it is reported late, and 1 indicates that the nugget does not lose any value ever regardless of how late the reporting.

The gain from each read nugget is summed to get the cumulative gain for a user over the user trace (Figure 1d). Thus a simulated user's MSU for a search topic is given by:

$$MSU = \sum_{n} g(n) \quad (3)$$

where n is the set of nuggets read by the user. We compute the MSU for a system by computing for each simulated user their mean MSU over all topics and then averaging all users' mean MSU to produce a system mean MSU. To increase the numerical precision of our system's MSU estimate, we only need to increase the number of simulated users.

3.3 MSU and TST

To demonstrate modeled stream utility (MSU), we use the TST 2013 test collection. The TST is a close but imperfect fit for MSU. The primary issue with using TST to demonstrate MSU is that the runs submitted by the participating groups were guided by the set-based effectiveness measures of TST.

As described in section 2, each participating group submitted runs to the TST that consisted of a set of updates. Each update has both a timestamp and a confidence associated with it. The timestamp is when the system emitted the update and the confidence is a system generated score indicating how relevant the update is.

For MSU, the simulated users check the retrieval system as per their user-trace to read the system's updates. At the start of every session in the user-trace, the updates emitted between the end of the last session and the start of the current session are presented to the user in a reverse chronological order, so that most recent information is read first.

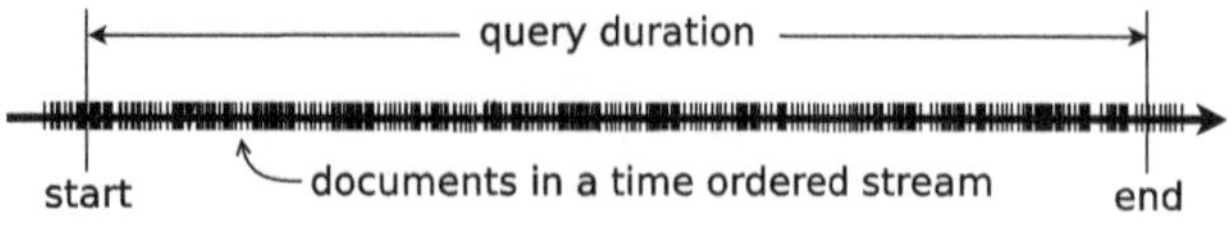

(a) Input: A time ordered document stream.

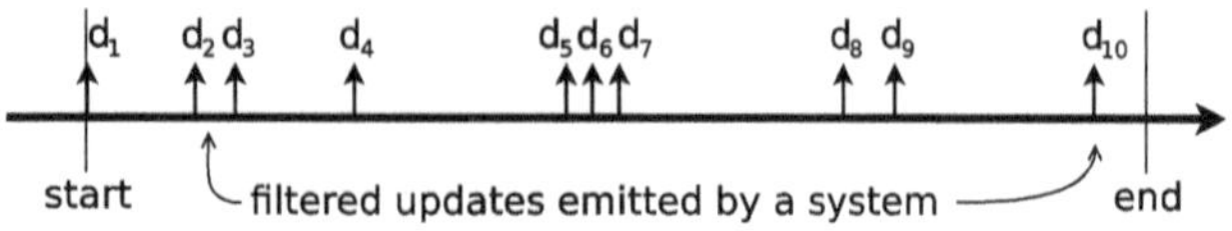

(b) Output: Stream of updates $d_1..d_{10}$ emitted at various times by a system.

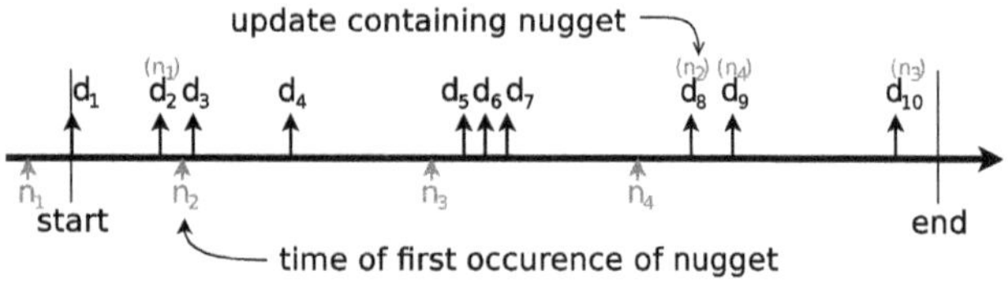

(c) Update-trace: Times of first occurrence of nuggets are identified. Updates containing nuggets are noted.

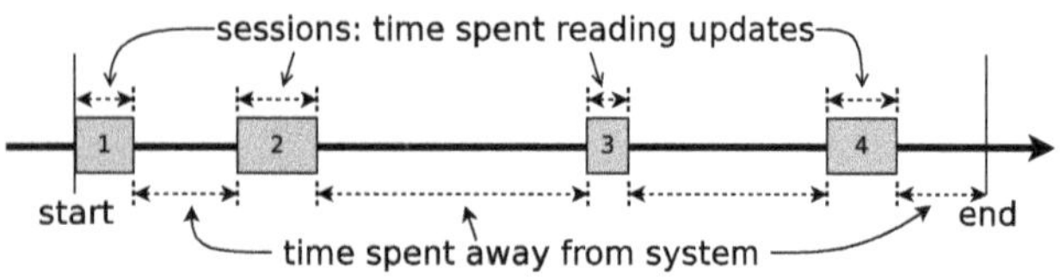

(d) User-trace: Simulated behavior of a user who reads updates from the stream from time to time.

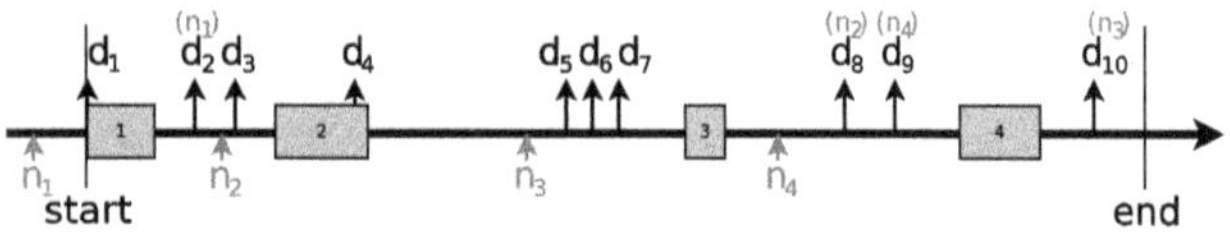

(e) Reading-trace: Determines which updates are available to read for every session. e.g. d_3, d_2 are available to read at the start of session 2. The user's reading speed V determines which nuggets are actually read. Reading updates that contain nuggets adds to gain.

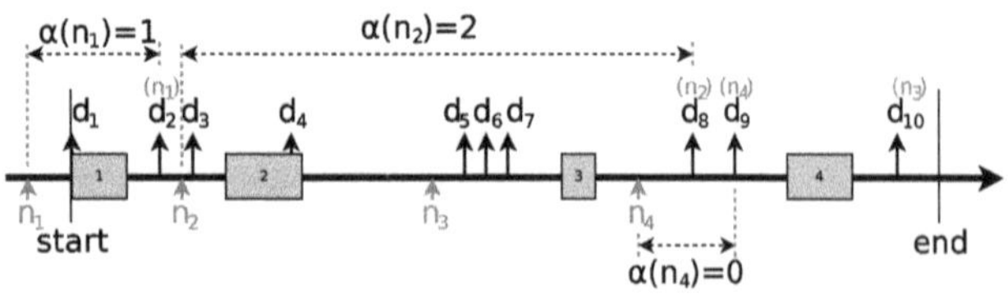

(f) $\alpha(n)$: Gain is discounted by $L^{\alpha(n)}$. $\alpha(n)$ is the number of sessions between the first occurrence of nugget n and the current session within which an update reporting n is read by the user. α is computed only if the update containing n is read by the user.

Figure 1: Evaluation Model

Updates with the same timestamp are shown in descending order given their confidence. The simulated user starts reading the latest update and then reads the next older update, and so on, until the user runs out of time or encounters an already read update and stops reading further. In case the session ends, the last update that is partially read in the session, is considered as unread. The first user session always begins at the start of the query duration. To determine if a nugget is late, we use the TST assigned Wikipedia times as described in section 2. As with the TST, the gain of a novel, on-time nugget is 1.

3.4 MSU Example for User Gain in a Session

Figure 1 illustrates the MSU model of evaluation. Figures 1a and 1b show the input to and output of a system that generates a stream of updates. The evaluation process begins at Figure 1c, where the nuggets, their time of first occurrence and the updates containing the nuggets are identified. The user-trace in Figure 1d is generated for a modeled user by alternatively sampling the exponential distributions for the session duration and the away time respectively. With the user-trace overlaid over the update-trace we get a reading-trace (Figure 1e). The reading-trace identifies updates available to read at each user session, and by incorporating the reading speed of the user it determines which updates are actually read. Thus the reading-trace determines if any relevant updates were read by the user or not, for every user session.

For a more concrete example, consider a modeled user with A of 1 day, D of 60 seconds and a reading speed V, of 225 words per minutes. Let us also assume that this user considers late information to be half as likely to be relevant, for every session where it is unreported ($L = 0.5$). Suppose that this user checks for updates at about 10:00 am every day and had previously checked for updates at 10:02 am on Dec 4, at 10:11 am on Dec 5, and at 9:50 am on Dec 6, 2012.

On Dec 7, 2012, the user starts a session at 9:55 am. The user finds the updates listed in Table 2 at the start of the session. The times at which the updates were emitted by the system are listed in the first column. In this case, all updates were emitted on the morning of Dec 7 before the user started the session. The updates are presented to the user in reverse chronological order. In case multiple updates are emitted at the same time, the updates are ordered by their system assigned confidence (as for the 4 updates emitted at 9:52).

The user starts by reading the most recent update (delivered at 9:52 am). The user continues on to read the second update and finds 4 nuggets n_{11}, n_{12}, n_{13}, n_{14}. Table 1 lists the nuggets found in the session. These are nuggets that the user had not seen before and therefore experiences an increase in gain.

However, as per each nugget's Wikipedia time, n_{11} first occurred at 6:31 p.m. on Dec 4, 2012. It should ideally have been reported to the user at the session starting at 10:11 am on Dec 5. The system further missed reporting the nugget at the session at 9:50 on Dec 6. Therefore $\alpha(n_{11})$ is 2. By similar calculation $\alpha(n_{12}) = 3$, as it should have been reported for the user session at 10:02 on Dec 4. For nuggets n_{13} and n_{14}, $\alpha(n_{13})$ and $\alpha(n_{14})$ are 1.

As the user reads further down the list, more nuggets (n_9, n_{10}) are read and gain increases accordingly. n_{10} is reported in time at the current session and $\alpha(n_{10}) = 0$. The user gets no gain from reading the update emitted at 9:15 as

RunID (GroupID)	#Upd. / topic	ELG	Reason. MSU	ELG Rank	Reason. MSU Rank	Best Ranks achieved by Systems						
						Best Rank	MSU @Best	Parameter values for Best Rank				
								M_A	S_A	M_D	S_D	L
cluster5 (PRIS)	21.9	0.136	4.35	1	17	8	4.06	1 d	12 h	30 s	30 s	0.9
run2 (ICTNET)	93.8	0.127	9.45	2	4	1	9.27	1 d	12 h	5 m	2.5 m	0.1
run1 (ICTNET)	97.8	0.125	9.46	3	3	1	14.65	1 d	12 h	30 m	15 m	0.9
TuneExternal2 (hltcoe)	799.4	0.118	5.34	4	16	13	9.77	3 h	1.5 h	30 m	15 m	0.9
TuneBasePred2 (hltcoe)	2,696.1	0.114	5.49	5	15	11	9.89	1 h	30 m	15 m	7.5 m	0.9
cluster3 (PRIS)	42.3	0.103	5.99	6	11	5	5.83	1 d	12 h	30 s	15 s	1.0
cluster2 (PRIS)	122.1	0.074	9.31	7	5	1	12.02	3 h	1.5 h	30 s	30 s	1.0
uogTrNMTm1MM3	358.8	0.069	7.28	8	7	6	12.79	1 h	30 m	30 s	15 s	1.0
cluster1 (PRIS)	164.8	0.067	9.57	9	1	1	16.45	5 m	10 m	30 s	30 s	1.0
cluster4 (hltcoe)	163.0	0.067	9.55	10	2	1	16.15	10 m	20 m	30 s	30 s	1.0
BasePred (PRIS)	8,790.7	0.067	5.84	11	13	1	14.17	6 h	6 h	30 m	15 m	0.9
Baseline (hltcoe)	12,743.0	0.063	5.87	12	12	1	15.02	30 m	15 m	30 m	15 m	0.9
uogTrNSQ1	139.0	0.060	6.85	13	9	4	11.35	3 h	3 h	30 s	15 s	1.0
EXTERNAL (hltcoe)	22,476.1	0.055	5.60	14	14	1	20.38	30 m	1 h	30 m	15 m	1.0
uogTrNMTm3FMM4	168.3	0.049	6.33	15	10	5	10.52	3 h	1.5 h	30 s	15 s	1.0
uogTrNMM	954.7	0.045	7.63	16	6	1	19.07	30 m	15 m	15 m	7.5 m	1.0
uogTrEMMQ2	2,077.8	0.040	6.88	17	8	2	18.55	30 m	15 m	15 m	15 m	1.0
SUS1 (wim_GY_2013)	2,338.7	0.036	3.62	18	18	17	7.44	1 h	1 h	2 m	60 s	1.0
rg4 (UWaterlooMDS)	41,863.3	0.028	1.44	19	20	1	22.11	5 m	10 m	30 m	15 m	1.0
rg3 (UWaterlooMDS)	42,534.1	0.026	1.45	20	19	2	21.54	5 m	5 m	30 m	15 m	1.0
rg2 (UWaterlooMDS)	299,559.6	0.022	0.32	21	25	18	14.02	5 m	10 m	30 m	15 m	1.0
rg1 (UWaterlooMDS)	312,863.3	0.021	0.30	22	26	19	13.39	5 m	10 m	30 m	15 m	1.0
UWMDSqlec4t50	213,735.7	0.018	1.02	23	21	6	12.20	5 m	5 m	30 m	15 m	0.9
UWMDSqlec2t25	230,056.0	0.017	0.61	24	23	14	15.87	5 m	10 m	30 m	15 m	1.0
CosineEgrep (UWMDS)	11.9	0.010	0.55	25	24	19	0.30	1 d	12 h	60 s	30 s	0.3
NormEgrep (UWMDS)	151.3	0.001	0.73	26	22	19	0.52	3 h	1.5 h	30 s	15 s	0.5

Table 3: Main results. The 26 runs submitted to the TREC 2013 Temporal Summarization Track (TST) are ordered by the TST primary measure, ELG. The column "#Upd./topic" shows the average number of updates produced by the run per topic. The "Reason. MSU" column shows the score for modeled stream utility (MSU) with a reasonable set of parameters as described in section 4.2. On the right side of the table we report an experiment where we selected parameter settings from our parameter sweep that give a run the best rank possible relative to the other runs (section 4.3).

nugget n_{14} was read earlier. Since the session duration was 60 seconds, the last update was partially read and the user gets no gain on reading it. Thus the total gain (MSU) for this user, from this session on Dec 7, is 2.875.

4. EXPERIMENTS

We explore the parameter space of MSU by applying it to evaluate the runs submitted to the TST 2013. We compare MSU's ranking of the TST runs to the TST's track's primary measure, ELG. The ELG measure is described in section 2.

The 2013 TST evaluated 26 runs from 6 groups over 9 topics. Topics in the track are instances of event types from the set {accident, bombing, earthquake, shooting, storm}. Each topic had a time period (query duration) of 10 days. In other words, a run must summarize 10 days of material from the TREC KBA stream corpus [1] for each topic.

The KBA corpus is essentially a time ordered document stream spanning from October 2011 to January 2013, containing over 1 billion documents crawled from the web. The corpus contains documents with 3 categories, i.e. the documents were crawled from URLs of public newswires (news), blogs and forums (social), and the URLs submitted for shortening at `www.bitly.com`. Documents are segmented into sentences and some documents are tagged with named entities using NLP tools. There are on average 93,037 documents per hour [5] in the corpus.

4.1 Parameter Sweep

Keeping the user population's reading speed distribution the same across all parameter sets, we sweep the parameter space by setting MSU's parameters to the following values:

- User population mean session duration, M_D = {0.5, 1, 2, 5, 15, 30} minutes.
- User population mean time away, M_A = {5, 10, 30 minutes, 1, 3, 6, 24 hours}).
- Lateness decay parameter, L = {0, 0.1, 0.25, 0.5, 0.75, 0.9, 1}.

For the standard deviations of the session duration, S_D, and the time away, S_A, we multiplied the mean by the values 0.5, 1, 2. For example, a mean session duration of 30 seconds, was associated with standard deviations of 15, 30 and 60 seconds. In total we generated 7 (M_A) x 3 (S_A) x 6 (M_D) x 3 (S_D) x 7 (L) = 2646 parameter-tuples (points in the parameter space). For instance, the parameter tuple (M_A= 6 hours, S_A= 3 hours, M_D= 5 minutes,S_D= 5 minutes, L = 1), is a point in the parameter space that represents users who spend an average of 5 minutes every 6 hours reading updates, unaffected by late reporting of nuggets.

For each tuple (selected point from the parameter space) in the parameter sweep, we simulated 1000 users. For each simulated user, we generated their user-trace, determined which updates they read, and computed their average MSU across the topics for every run submitted to TST 2013.

4.2 Reasonable Parameters

We believe that a *reasonable* setting of MSU's parameters is a user population where the users visit on average for 2 minutes every 3 hours and for whom late material quickly

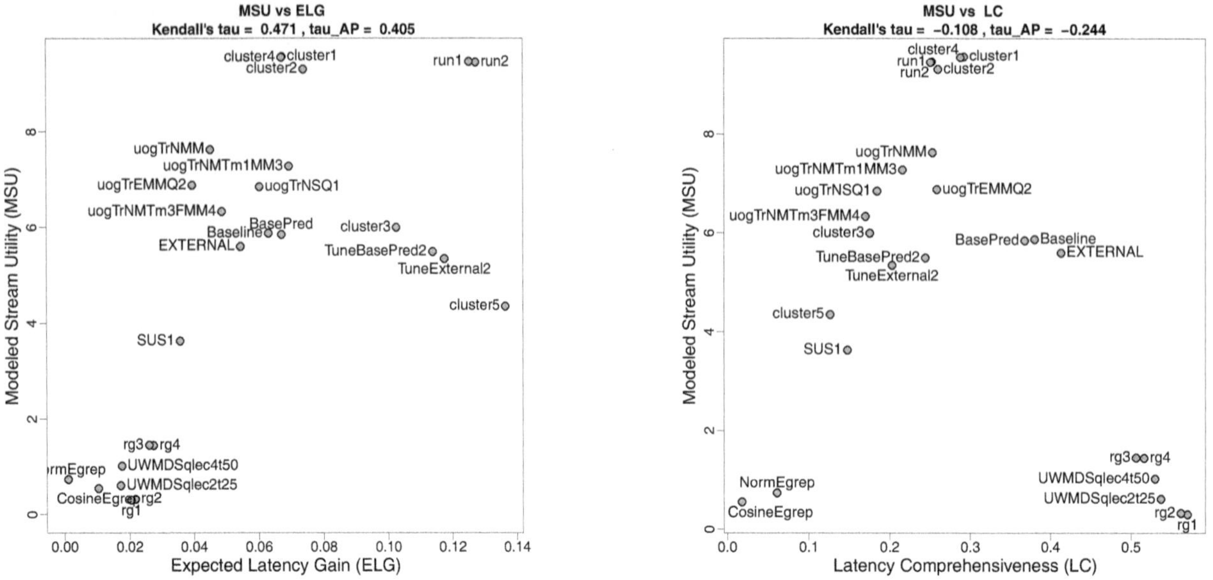

(a) Reasonable Users, MSU vs ELG Correlation.

(b) Reasonable Users, MSU vs LC Correlation.

Figure 2: MSU with reasonable parameter settings (M_A= 3 hours, S_A= 1.5 hours, M_D= 2 minutes, S_D= 1 minute, L= 0.5), compared to TST 2013 measures, ELG and LC.

becomes less likely to be considered relevant. This corresponds to the parameter tuple (M_D = 2 minutes, S_D = 1 minute, M_A = 3 hours, S_A = 1.5 hours, L = 0.5).

Both Figure 2a and Table 3 show the results of MSU vs. the TST measure ELG, given these reasonable parameter settings. For both MSU and ELG, larger values indicate better runs. At these parameter settings, MSU and ELG do not rank systems the same (Kendall's τ = 0.471). As Figure 2a shows, the runs in the middle-lower positions of the ELG ranking jump to the top positions. A similar observation can be made in Figure 2b for MSU vs. the LC measure. Here as well, MSU and LC rank systems differently (Kendall's $\tau = -0.108$). ELG and LC are themselves negatively correlated (Kendall's $\tau = -0.28$). The AP correlation coefficient (τ_{AP}) [16, 13], which is more sensitive to changes in higher ranks is also reported in Figure 2.

Across the entire set of swept parameter settings, the maximum Kendall's τ correlation was found to be 0.625 for the parameters: M_A= 24 hours, S_A= 12 hours, M_D= 1 minute, S_D= 2 minutes, L = 0.1. These results are shown in Figure 3. While not a high correlation, this result shows us that ELG best correlates with a simulated user population where users on average visit once a day for 1 minute. In other words, over the 10 days of the query period, an average user reads about 10 minutes of material. If we were to understand ELG in terms of the users that would prefer its top ranked runs, then ELG is tuned for highly time constrained and selective users with low tolerance for late reporting.

A correlation of 0.625 correlation is not high, and MSU and ELG are behaving quite differently. We believe that there are likely two main reasons for the different rank order of the runs. The first reason is that run performance with MSU is affected by the amount of material that the simulated user reads. If a run does not supply enough material for a session visit, then the simulated user will stop reading and also stop accumulating gain.

For example, Table 3 shows that the top ELG run `cluster5` averages only 21.9 updates per topic over a 10 day query duration. With the reasonable parameter settings, MSU simulated users spend about 2 minutes every 3 hours, i.e. about 160 minutes reading, on average, over a 10 day query duration. With an average length of each TST update being 63 words, and the average reading speed being 4.3 words per second, it takes on average just 319 seconds to read all the 21.9 updates of `cluster5`. A simulated user, who is willing to read for 160 minutes in total over 10 days, thus derives very low gain from `cluster5` because such a user's visit is cut short from a lack of material to read.

Figure 4 shows the user performance at the point (M_A= 5 minutes, S_A= 10 minutes, M_D= 30 minutes, S_D= 15 minutes, L = 1) that has the minimum correlation of MSU with ELG (Kendall's τ = -0.04), in our parameter set. This set of users seem inclined to spend almost all their time with the system reading updates taking a 5 minute break every 30 minutes on average, without any dissatisfaction for late reporting of information. Unsurprisingly, these users achieve the highest amount of MSU (22.11) with run `rg4`. While seemingly an unreasonable parameter setting for MSU, such user behavior could be achieved by a team interested in constant monitoring of a stream of updates.

This result also shows that MSU scores are related to the amount of material read by the simulated users. MSU measures gain as the number of relevant nuggets read in the total content consumed by a user, while discounting for lateness if required. The amount of material read depends on the characteristic behavior of the user (or user population) as well as the number of updates emitted by the system. MSU for a system is simply the average over all simulated users.

A second reason for differences between ELG and MSU is likely that ELG is a set-based measure that measures av-

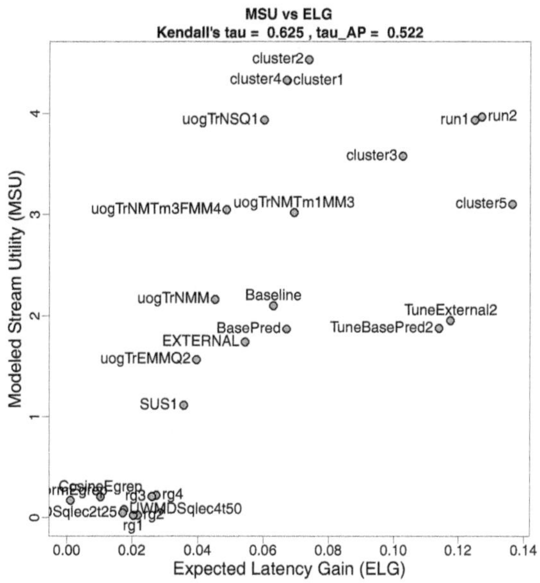

Figure 3: Maximum correlation of MSU with ELG is obtained with parameters (M_A= 24 hours, S_A= 12 hours, M_D= 1 minute, S_D= 2 minutes, L= 0.1).

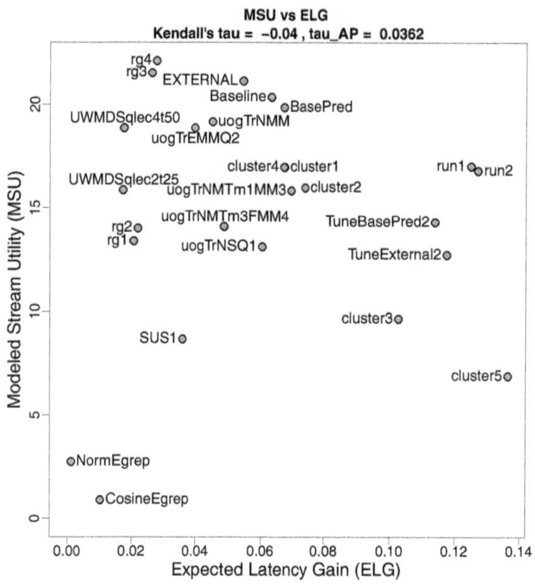

Figure 4: Minimum correlation of MSU with ELG is obtained with parameters (M_A= 5 minutes, S_A= 10 minutes, M_D= 30 minutes, S_D= 15 minutes, L= 1).

erage quality of an update. In contrast, MSU is estimating the total number of nuggets read and considered by the simulated user to be relevant. To see how much the set-based nature of ELG is causing it to be different than MSU, we transformed MSU into a similar measure by taking MSU and dividing it by the time the simulated user spent reading (MSU/second).

In our experiments, MSU/second has the highest correlation (Kendall's $\tau = 0.754$) with ELG (Figure 5), with parameters (M_A= 24 hours, S_A= 12 hours, M_D= 1 minute,S_D= 1 minutes, L = 0.1). The correlation between MSU/second and ELG is greater than the maximum correlation between MSU and ELG. Of note, the top ranked run for MSU/second is now the same as for ELG: `cluster5`. The MSU/second top 4 runs in Figure 5 are 4 of the 5 runs with the lowest number of updates submitted (Table 3).

4.3 Everyone's a Winner (Almost)

Noting how the ranking of systems can change greatly based on the wide range of parameter settings in our sweep, we decided to find the instances in our parameter sweep for which a particular system was ranked the highest across all parameter sets. Table 3 shows the results of this analysis on its right side. Some systems achieved their best rank for multiple parameter sets. In such cases, we chose the parameter set for which the system had the highest MSU.

The relationship between time spent and user performance can be seen as we look at the parameter settings from top to bottom of Table 3. Systems that had very few updates submitted, performed well for users who might visit a system about once a day for 30 seconds to 30 minutes on average. The run `cluster2` seems to be the best performing system for users who return to the system about every 3 hours for 30 seconds on average. As we go lower in the table, we see that spending more time reading (larger M_D) and taking shorter breaks (smaller M_A) improves performance of systems that ranked lower on ELG. These systems are typically those that submitted a large number of updates.

As Table 3 shows, almost all groups have at least one run that is able to achieve a rank 1 performance under some setting of MSU's parameters. If we want to know which system is the best, we must calibrate MSU given actual user behavior. This result may also show that submitted TST systems had very different notions of the appropriate amount of material to make available to users. TST's ELG measure is set-based, but the decision of how large of a set to return to users is left to system designers. In contrast, MSU guides system designers to return a suitable amount of material based on the model of user behavior.

5. OTHER RELATED WORK

Our work builds directly on recent research in modeling user behavior for improved evaluation of information retrieval systems [7]. Of these new effectiveness measures, Clarke and Smucker's [8] Time Well Spent (TWS) measure is the most similar. Like modeled stream utility (MSU), TWS provides a means to evaluate systems that produce a stream of content. Unlike TWS, MSU models multiple visits to the same system, and MSU models variation in each simulated user's behavior. MSU should be amenable to the same statistical analyses that TWS enables.

Other researchers have also evaluated systems by defining a hypothetical user interface and then simulating user behavior with the interface. Of the more recent work that goes beyond a single query and results list is that of Baskaya, Keskustalo, and Järvelin [6] who conducted an experiment that considered many different parameter settings for their model and investigated various query reformulation strategies that could be utilized by a user. Yang and Lad [15] also employ a user model based evaluation for information distillation systems and it would be interesting to compare MSU with their method in future work.

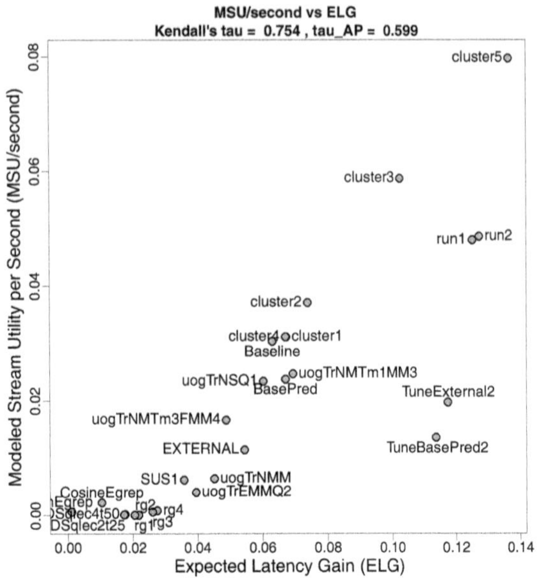

Figure 5: Maximum correlation of MSU/second with ELG is obtained with parameters (M_A= 24 hours, S_A= 12 hours, M_D= 1 minute, S_D= 1 minutes, L= 0.1).

6. DISCUSSION

ELG has aspects that try to capture characteristics of good updates, i.e. updates should be on time, not long, and have relevant material. ELG seems to be a measure oriented towards measuring the performance of systems that push highly relevant updates with low frequency to the user. ELG does not provide an easy means to be calibrated to known user behavior.

Our experiments and analysis show that it matters how much material is read. By specifying the amount of material in user terms, we have a way of then calibrating a measure once we know actual user behavior. Observing actual user behavior while evolving events are actually taking place would involve monitoring users' browsing histories. The sudden nature of news events makes a live user study difficult to organize. Search log-analysis may provide some indirect insight into user behavior when such events are running. Our analysis also shows that there may be a case for personalization of stream filtering systems for different user behaviors. As other future work, we hope to extend our understanding of MSU, both in terms of its formal properties and in terms of empirical meta-evaluation criteria, including robustness to noise, discriminativeness between systems, and strictness [3].

7. CONCLUSION

We introduced an effectiveness measure that utilizes a model of user behavior for evaluating systems producing streams of information about evolving events. Our measure is designed to be calibrated based on actual usage data. Our user model simulates a user checking back with the system to read the most recent information from time to time. Users can check back with different frequencies and for different amounts of time depending on various factors. By modeling user behavior, our effectiveness measure produces a score that is easily interpretable as the number of relevant nuggets of information read by the user. As would be expected, we found that for streams of updates, the gain is sensitive to the amount of time a user spends for reading updates. While temporal summarization systems have traditionally been evaluated in term of their precision and recall, we believe that it is important to consider both the user interface and the user behavior with this interface when evaluating such systems. Given the degree to which the rankings of systems changed as we modified the behavior of the user population, we believe that an effectiveness measure such as ours when calibrated with user data will allow system developers and researchers to build better performing systems tuned to user behavior.

8. ACKNOWLEDGMENTS

This work was made possible by the facilities of SHARCNET (www.sharcnet.ca) and Compute/Calcul Canada, and was supported in part by GRAND NCE, in part by an Amazon AWS in Education Research Grant, in part by NSERC, in part by a Google Founders Grant, and in part by the University of Waterloo.

9. REFERENCES

[1] KBA Stream Corpus 2013. http://trec-kba.org/kba-stream-corpus-2013.shtml.

[2] J. Allan, R. Gupta, and V. Khandelwal. Temporal Summaries of New Topics. In *SIGIR*, pp. 10–18, 2001.

[3] E. Amigó, J. Gonzalo, and S. Mizzaro. A Formal Approach to Effectiveness Metrics for Information Access: Retrieval, Filtering, and Clustering. In *ECIR*, pp. 817–821. 2015.

[4] J. Aslam, F. Diaz, M. Ekstrand-Abueg, V. Pavlu, and T. Sakai. TREC 2013 Temporal Summarization. In *TREC*, 2013.

[5] G. Baruah, A. Roegiest, and M. D. Smucker. The Effect of Expanding Relevance Judgements with Duplicates. In *SIGIR*, pp. 1159–1162, 2014.

[6] F. Baskaya, H. Keskustalo, and K. Järvelin. Modeling Behavioral Factors in Interactive Information Retrieval. In *CIKM*, pp. 2297–2302, 2013.

[7] C. L. Clarke, L. Freund, M. D. Smucker, and E. Yilmaz. Report on the SIGIR 2013 workshop on Modeling User Behavior for Information Retrieval Evaluation (MUBE 2013). *SIGIR Forum*, 47(2):84–95, Jan. 2013.

[8] C. L. A. Clarke and M. D. Smucker. Time Well Spent. In *IIiX*, pp. 205–214, 2014.

[9] B. P. Flannery, W. H. Press, S. A. Teukolsky, and W. T. Vetterling. Numerical Recipes in C, pp. 214–215, Cambridge University Press, 1988.

[10] Q. Guo, F. Diaz, and E. Yom-Tov. Updating Users About Time Critical Events. In *ECIR*, pp. 483–494, 2013.

[11] J. Lin and M. Efron. Overview of the TREC-2013 Microblog Track. In *TREC*, 2013.

[12] I. Ounis, C. Macdonald, J. Lin, and I. Soboroff. Overview of the TREC-2011 Microblog Track. In *TREC*, 2011.

[13] M. D. Smucker, G. Kazai, and M. Lease. Overview of the TREC 2013 Crowdsourcing Track. In *TREC*, 2013.

[14] I. Soboroff, I. Ounis, J. Lin, and I. Soboroff. Overview of the TREC-2012 Microblog Track. In *TREC*, 2012.

[15] Y. Yang and A. Lad. Modeling Expected Utility of Multi-Session Information Distillation. In *ICTIR*, pp. 164–175, 2009.

[16] E. Yilmaz, J. A. Aslam, and S. Robertson. A new Rank Correlation Coefficient for Information Retrieval. In *SIGIR*, pp. 587–594, 2008.

Information Retrieval as Card Playing: A Formal Model for Optimizing Interactive Retrieval Interface

Yinan Zhang
Department of Computer Science
University of Illinois at Urbana-Champaign
Urbana, IL 61801
yzhng103@illinois.edu

Chengxiang Zhai
Department of Computer Science
University of Illinois at Urbana-Champaign
Urbana, IL 61801
czhai@illinois.edu

ABSTRACT

We propose a novel formal model for optimizing interactive information retrieval interfaces. To model interactive retrieval in a general way, we frame the task of an interactive retrieval system as to choose a sequence of interface cards to present to the user. At each interaction lap, the system's goal is to choose an interface card that can maximize the expected gain of relevant information for the user while minimizing the effort of the user with consideration of the user's action model and any desired constraints on the interface card. We show that such a formal interface card model can not only cover the Probability Ranking Principle for Interactive Information Retrieval as a special case by making multiple simplification assumptions, but also be used to derive a novel formal interface model for adaptively optimizing navigational interfaces in a retrieval system. Experimental results show that the proposed model is effective in automatically generating adaptive navigational interfaces, which outperform the baseline pre-designed static interfaces.

1. INTRODUCTION

Developing formal models for information retrieval (IR) has always been an important fundamental challenge. For example, the Probability Ranking Principle (PRP) [18] proposed more than three decades ago has laid out a solid foundation and provided a theoretical justification for framing the retrieval task as a ranking problem, leading to the development of many effective retrieval functions for ranking documents that are used in current search engines (e.g., [20, 19, 17, 10, 1, 21, 6]). Despite the great success of PRP, however, it is also known that it is based on two problematic assumptions, i.e., sequential browsing and independent relevance (utility) of documents, which are generally not true in practice. As a result, e.g., the traditional retrieval models developed based on PRP cannot handle redundancy among documents directly (and must rely on post-processing of search results), an immediate consequence of the independence assumption of document relevance. The sequential browsing assumption implies limitations on the interface also, and in particular ignores the actions that a user can take when interacting with an interface displaying search results (e.g., faceted browsing).

Recognizing these limitations and attempting to generalize the PRP for interactive IR, Fuhr[8] has recently proposed a novel formal framework for optimizing interactive retrieval and derived a PRP for interactive IR (IIR-PRP) where a user's effort and benefit are captured when optimizing the ranking of documents. This work effectively addressed the independence assumption made in the PRP and provides a theoretical foundation for optimizing document ranking when a user is assumed to interactively browse a list of search results. Unfortunately, it has not addressed the sequential browsing assumption, which remains an assumption made for optimizing ranking in interactive retrieval. In this work, we relax this assumption and propose a more general formal model than IIR-PRP for optimizing interactive retrieval.

The sequential browsing assumption touches a much larger problem of how to model a user's reactions to a retrieval result interface, which further depends on what the interface looks like, raising the interesting question "how can we formally model the problem of interface design for an interactive IR system?" Interestingly, in contrast with a large body of work on formal methods for optimizing ranking, there has been little work on formal methods for optimizing the interface of a system, despite that the dynamic and interactive nature of information seeking process has long been recognized and studied from information science perspective (see, e.g., [4, 11]). While optimizing ranking is clearly very important for optimizing a retrieval system, when we consider optimizing an *interactive* retrieval system, we must also optimize the interface part of the system so as to optimize the *whole* system, which is the goal of our study.

The study of interface optimization is especially important in the current era of ever faster technology advancement, leading to the emergence of smart phones and various kinds of wearable devices with very small screens, which generally require a different interface than the popular interface designed for desktops. For example, while showing a document list on a relatively large screen is popular and appropriate, it may not be appropriate to do so on a very small screen where an interface with navigational tags might be more useful as it enables a user to more efficiently navigate into the relevant information. Even if we consider the current interface of a Web search engine such as Google or Bing on a large screen, which typically shows a list of fixed number of snippets on each page, there are still many interesting questions

SIGIR'15, August 09 - 13, 2015, Santiago, Chile.
© 2015 ACM. ISBN 978-1-4503-3621-5/15/08 ...$15.00.
DOI: http://dx.doi.org/10.1145/2766462.2767761 .

related to the optimization of the interface. For example, how many snippets should we display on each page? The commonly used number, 10, is not necessarily always the best choice. Also, what about shortening some snippets to make room for more results or vice versa? These questions have been tackled by Human-Computer Interaction (HCI) researchers with many empirical findings. Unfortunately, it is still unclear how we can leverage these findings to build an intelligent IR system that can automatically optimize its interaction interface adaptively both to the screen size and to the user's information need.

In this paper, we study the novel problem of *automatic* interface optimization formally, and propose a new general formal model, called the *Interface Card* model, for optimizing interactive retrieval interface. The basic idea behind this model is to view an interactive retrieval process as a process of the retrieval system playing a cooperative card game[1] with the user in the following way: at each interaction lap, facing a current retrieval *context*, the system would choose an optimal "interface card" to present to the user. The user can then perform any action from a set of possible actions associated with the interface card presented. Depending on the user's action on the interface card (e.g., selecting a particular facet value), the system would then transition to a new context, and have to choose another (generally new) interface card to show to the user. The game would continue in such a way until the user decides to stop (either due to satisfaction of the information need or abandoning the search). At each interaction lap, the system's goal is to choose an interface card that can maximize the expected gain of relevant information for the user while minimizing the effort of the user with consideration of a user action model and any desired constraints on the interface card.

We show that such a general formal interface card model can not only cover IIR-PRP as a special case by making multiple simplification assumptions, including the sequential browsing assumption, but also be used to derive a novel formal interface model for adaptively optimizing navigational interfaces in a retrieval system by assuming that an interface card is composed of one or more information blocks to support interactive navigation and a user's action is mainly to select one of the presented blocks. The derived model enables, for the first time, automatic generation of optimal navigational interfaces that can be adaptive to screen sizes and user interactions. Experimental results show that the proposed model is effective in automatically generating adaptive navigational interfaces, which outperform the baseline pre-designed static interfaces.

2. RELATED WORK

The majority work on formal models for IR has been based on the Probability Ranking Principle (PRP) [18] and all attempt to optimize a ranking function defined on a query-document pair; they include all kinds of traditional retrieval models such as vector space models [20], classic probabilistic models [19], language models [17, 10, 22], divergence from randomness [1], inference networks [21], axiomatic approaches [6], and recent extensions in the direction of learning to rank [7, 14]. These works generally do not model user interactions, thus providing no guidance for interface design.

[1]http://en.wikipedia.org/wiki/Card_game

The PRP for interactive IR (IIR-PRP) [8] generalizes the PRP to optimize ranking in an interactive IR setting, where a number of important concepts for modeling user interaction from the perspective of decision making were introduced, including situation, effort and benefit, and an optimal ordering principle is derived for ranking items when a user is assumed to sequentially browse the list. Our model shares a similar high-level goal with the IIR-PRP in that both attempt to establish a formal model for interactive retrieval, but it is more general than the IIR-PRP, which can be shown as a special case of our model under a set of simplification assumptions. Due to its generality, our model does not make the sequential browsing assumption and can be directly used to optimize the interaction interface; as a result, our model can suggest interfaces that would dynamically adapt to the assumed screen sizes, which cannot be achieved in any existing work on formal models.

The dynamic and interactive nature of information seeking process has long been recognized and studied from information science perspective (see, e.g., [4, 11]). Our work can be regarded as an attempt to formalize some of the theoretical arguments in these literature with an operational mathematical model that can be used for building an intelligent IR system with an adaptive interface for navigation.

Our model of dynamic information need is related to the ostensive model (OM) [5], which provides a framework for modeling the evolution of information needs over time. Our model is sufficiently general to allow us to refine it with the ostensive model or any other model of evolving information needs. Our proposed framework enables any such model to be adopted for optimizing navigational interface.

The model we derived for optimizing navigational interface uses an objective function to maximize the difference between a user's benefit and cost for finding a relevant information item. Such a decision criterion is related to some recent works that have explored economic models for IR (e.g., [2]). Furthermore, optimizing the ranking of documents with consideration of user actions has also been studied in the context of feedback to optimize the session-level utility [12] and using a POMDP framework in [15], where a dual-agent POMDP was proposed to model both user actions and system actions. However, none of these studies has proposed a model to optimize navigational interface, a primary goal of this paper.

Optimizing search engine interface has been extensively studied in the Human-Computer Interaction community (see, e.g., the survey in the book [9]), including designing and evaluating faceted browsing systems and coming up with various ad hoc ways to optimize such systems (e.g. [3] and [13]). However, no existing work can optimize a navigational interface with an explicitly defined objective function, which our model attempts to achieve.

3. INTERFACE CARD MODEL

In general, any interaction between a user and an interactive information retrieval system can be partitioned into a series of interaction laps, in each of which the user issues an action and the system then reacts to the user's action by selecting an optimized interface instance to show to the user. For example, in a traditional search engine, the first interaction lap consists of the user issuing a query and the search engine responding with 10 most relevant items as the first result page. After this interaction lap, the user may issue a second action by either clicking an item or "next page," and the interface reacts by displaying a second interface instance optimized for the perceived user action.

The interaction laps may be defined in various levels of granularity and the set of user actions would change accordingly. The previous example can be regarded as modeling the interaction at the page level. If, however, the 10 search results could not simultaneously fit into the screen of the interface as in the case of searching with a smart phone, then the interaction can be modeled at a finer granularity - the current screen shown to the user, and the user actions would additionally include scrolling up/down, to which the interface reacts by "sliding" the screen up/down by one position. In this scenario, when the user scrolls down, the interface in theory could have a chance to decide again according to the user's action about the item to be shown next, which may be different from the one originally ranked at this position. Such "drilling down" of the interaction granularity could continue, if we consider a user's every eye movement as an action and the interface may dynamically change the displayed content accordingly, assuming the availability of an eye-tracker device[2].

How do we model an arbitrary interactive retrieval system formally at any given interaction granularity level? To address this question, we propose to view any user-interface interaction as a card game, in which the "interface player" determines the optimal card to play in each lap, and we present a novel interface card model to formally model the interactive retrieval task. Unlike a real card game where players maximize their own benefits, however, the interface card model assumes a cooperative game in which the "interface player" always maximizes the user's benefit by taking into consideration the user's current action, the interaction history, the reward and cost of the user's next possible actions and any constraints posed onto the card the "interface player" plays at the current lap. We now formally introduce the model by first defining all these components and then the core mathematical optimization problem.

Definition 3.1 (Lap). A *lap* is the interaction unit between the user and the interface in which the user issues an action and the interface then reacts by generating an optimized interface instance: $t = 1, 2, \ldots$

The laps serve as the timestamps for the user-system interactions and will always be shown as superscripts.

Definition 3.2 (Card). A *card* is an interface instance generated by the interface system in reaction to the user action in each lap: q^t.

The notion of card generalizes a wide range of interface instances including a result page or a screen of a partial result page in a search engine, a question in a conversational retrieval interface the system uses to clarify the user's information need, etc.

Definition 3.3 (Constraint). The *constraint* is a possible set of restrictions a card needs to satisfy in a lap, and for simplicity is assumed to have the form of a single constraint function: $f_c^t(q^t) \leq 0$.

[2] In theory, we could go even deeper: imagine that we might some day have sensors installed for everyone to track every neuron excitement in their brain and consider that as an interaction unit.

The constraint is typically associated with the design and restrictions of the interface. For instance, a result page of a traditional search engine may display at most 10 items at a time. If screens are considered as a finer unit for the interaction, when the user scrolls down, all the items on the next screen except the bottom one are restricted to be the ones sliding from the previous screen. In more complicated interface designs like faceted browsing interfaces, there might be panels of facet values and items regulating how much space they could respectively occupy.

In many cases, the constraint could not be captured within a single constraint function. The notion of the single constraint function is only meant for the purpose of notational simplicity, and more complicated forms of constraint do not change the model in any fundamental way.

Definition 3.4 (Action). An *action* is a move the user chooses to take next from a set of possible moves that may depend on the current card: $a^{t+1} \in \mathcal{A}(q^t)$.

The interaction is initiated either by the user or the system, and we allow both situations in this model. Most of the time, the user is the initiator, and the interaction starts with a^1 (followed by the interface playing the first card q^1, then the user issuing the second action a^2, etc.). For example, when a user queries a search engine, a^1 would be the very first query the user enters. Alternatively, if the search engine attempts to display a possibly personalized search homepage to each user and at each time, then we could define a^1 to be the user's action of entering the website. In both cases, the first card the interface plays is designated to be the first interface instance that needs to be optimized according to the user's action. Typically, we are not interested in the set of possible actions for the very first user action a^1 because a^1 is always regarded as given to the model and there isn't any uncertainty in it.

There are occasionally situations where the interface system is the initiator of the interaction, e.g. if a smart phone is set to alert the user whenever some interesting news events happen by popping up a screen of news event snippets. In such a scenario, we set q^1 to be this first screen and set a^1 to be a "null" action.

For the sake of simplicity, from now on we always assume that the action set $\mathcal{A}(q^t)$ is either finite or countably infinite, so that we could use the summation sign "$\sum$" for summing over all possible actions in a particular lap. In cases where the action set is not countable (e.g. if a touch-screen smart phone measures how much force the user uses when touching the screen), we could replace the "$\sum$" signs with the "$\int$" sign and the core model is not affected in any fundamental way.

Definition 3.5 (Context). The *context* is all the information the interface system has accumulated till a particular lap about the user for estimating the user's choice on the next card: c^t. Such information includes (a) a priori information about the user, i, if any, (b) interactions in all previous laps, if any, between the user and the interface (i.e. the sequence of previous actions issued by the user and previous cards played by the interface), and (c) the action the user just issued in the current lap. The context is expressed as a vector starting with $c^1 = (i, a^1)$ and iteratively updated by $c^{t+1} = (c^t, q^t, a^{t+1})$.

Typically, the a priori information about the user may capture any prior belief about the user, e.g. any available personalization information.

Definition 3.6 (Action Model). The *action model* specifies the system's estimated probability distribution of the user's actions in the next lap given the current card and under the current context: $p(a^{t+1}|c^t, q^t)$.

Here we are assuming a probabilistic model for user actions, which provides a general solid framework for formally modeling most real world scenarios.

Definition 3.7 (Reward). The *reward* is the system's estimated expected benefit to the user for issuing an action given the current card and under the current context: $r(a^{t+1}|c^t, q^t)$.

The reward may capture the short-term benefit to the user from a relevant item, as well as any long-term benefit, e.g., if the action serves to navigate the user to a new information subspace (as in the case of answering a clarification question in a conversational retrieval system or clicking a facet value in a faceted browsing system). The reward may depend on future laps if the system decides to perform the estimation computation in such a way, but here for notational simplicity, we only put c^t and q^t into $r(a^{t+1}|c^t, q^t)$ and hide any possible dependency of the reward on future laps in the reward function r.

Definition 3.8 (Cost). The *cost* is the system's estimated expected effort the user spends for issuing an action given the current card and under the current context: $s(a^{t+1}|c^t, q^t)$.

For example, the cost function typically captures any possible effort the user needs to take for scanning through a result page of a search engine, for the decision-making process to determine whether to click or skip a particular item, etc.

Definition 3.9 (Surplus). The *surplus* is the difference between the reward and the cost to the user for issuing an action given the current card and under the current context: $u(a^{t+1}|c^t, q^t) = r(a^{t+1}|c^t, q^t) - s(a^{t+1}|c^t, q^t)$.

Here we borrow the concept of surplus from economics studies to designate the net benefit to the user for issuing an action. From the user's perspective, they would typically tend to choose actions leading to higher surplus, and there have been well established economics theories, e.g. the discrete choice model [16], for modeling such behaviours. In this study, however, we do not go deeper in such directions and stop at the level of the action model in formalizing the user's behavior from the interface system's perspective.

With all the necessary components defined, we formally introduce the core mathematical optimization problem:

Definition 3.10 (Interface Card Optimization). In each lap t, the interface system should play a card q^t that maximizes the expected surplus u^t given the current context and under the current constraint, where the expectation is taken with respect to the user action model:

$$\begin{aligned} \underset{q^t}{\text{maximize}} \quad & E(u^t|c^t, q^t) \\ & = \sum_{a^{t+1} \in \mathcal{A}(q^t)} p(a^{t+1}|c^t, q^t)\, u(a^{t+1}|c^t, q^t) \quad (1) \\ \text{subject to} \quad & f_c^t(q^t) \leq 0 \end{aligned}$$

A possible source of confusion is that there are in total two levels of expectations in this formalism: the inner one being encapsulated within the notion of surplus that deals with the uncertainty in the reward and cost for individual actions (recall that the reward and cost are both defined as expectations), and the outer one that deals with the uncertainty in the user's decision on which action to issue. Such an encapsulation generally holds in reality and lays down a convenient formalism framework for multiple ways of instantiating the interface card model as we will further discuss in the following sections.

The proposed interface card model is very general and does not make the "sequential browsing" assumption that is underlying all other existing theoretical IR models. Rather, we only adopts a "sequential interaction" scheme where the interaction laps between the user and the interface system take place sequentially, which is a much broader notion than "sequential browsing". The reason is that "sequential browsing" is *positional* - it assumes that the user follows a strict sequential order when scanning the positions on a list. In contrast, "sequential interaction" is *temporal* - it only assumes that the interaction flows in a sequential manner, and if we think more deeply, as interaction always flows in the same direction as time passes, the "sequential interaction" notion is essentially stating that time passes uni-directionally, which is universally and always true. In such a sense, we are effectively adopting the broadest possible "assumption" underlying any human-computer interaction process. We will show in the following section that we can make simplification assumptions to reduce our "sequential interaction" scheme to the traditional "sequential browsing" scheme and derive the IIR-PRP model proposed in [8].

4. PLAIN CARD

As our first instantiation of the interface card model, we will show that the interface card model can cover the IIR-PRP model as a special case under a set of simplification assumptions including particularly the sequential browsing assumption. Consider the problem setting of a generalized interactive information retrieval (IIR) system as introduced in [8], where the system's task is to present a sequential list of binary choices to the user, and the system needs to determine the optimal order of the list so as to maximize the user's expected benefit. Such a problem formulation generalizes a wide range of IIR tasks. (Please refer to [8] for more in-depth explanations.)

In order to instantiate the IIR-PRP model, we first need to incorporate the "sequential browsing" assumption into our model, and we do so by reducing "sequential interaction" to "sequential browsing" using the following pair of assumptions, which is essentially stating the "sequential browsing" assumption in the language of our model:

Assumption 4.1 (Plain Card). Each card is defined to be a choice in the ranked list. The choices are sequentially denoted by $e^t, t = 1, 2, \ldots$, and we define $q^t = e^t$.

Assumption 4.2 (Binary Action). There are two possible user actions in each lap: $\mathcal{A}(e^t) = \{a_0^{t+1}, a_1^{t+1}\}$, where a_0^{t+1} and a_1^{t+1} respectively represent the actions of accepting e^t and rejecting e^t (to examine the next choice e^{t+1}).

The interface card optimization problem is now equivalent to determining which choice to place on each position of the list. We are implicitly modeling the interaction at the level of the user's eye movement: imagine that the interface system is accompanied with an eye-tracking device that could sense the user's eye movement and automatically scroll the page whenever it detects that the user intends to skip to the next choice; in such a way we get rid of the necessity of the scrolling action and the action of clicking "next page."

Since a card is simply assumed to be a choice on the list, there is no interesting constraint defined on the interface. Further, we adopt the independence assumption in [8] and assume that the probability of the user accepting a choice is independent of the choices they have rejected, so that the action model does not depend on any previous cards or user actions until an accept action takes place. We also follow [8] to focus on the optimization problem before the user's first accept action (the optimization problem afterwards is regarded as a new round of optimization), so the context is simply collapsed to the a priori information about the user (if any). We thus omit the notion of context in the following writing, and define the shorthand notation $p(e^t)$ for specifying the action model: $p(e^t) = p(a_0^{t+1}|e^t) = 1 - p(a_1^{t+1}|e^t)$. (Please refer to [8] for the notion of "situations" to understand the details and rationales of these assumptions.)

Assumption 4.3 (Rejection reward). The reward for a reject action is the expected surplus in the next lap:

$$r(a_1^{t+1}|e^t) = E(u^{t+1}|e^{t+1}) \tag{2}$$

Here we choose to explicitly model the dependency of the reward in the current lap on the future laps, so in order to optimize the first card, we would need to simultaneously optimize all the following cards (i.e. all choices in the list).

We define another shorthand notation $r(e^t)$ for the reward of accepting choice e^t: $r(e^t) = r(a_0^{t+1}|e^t)$. In [8], this reward is further decomposed into the expectation of two cases - (a) the accept action is right and (b) the accept action is wrong. We do not go further along this direction; the main line of the derivation would not be affected in any fundamental way.

Assumption 4.4 (Decision cost). The costs for the accept and reject actions are the same in each lap, which equal the amount of effort the user spends to examine the current choice for deciding whether they should accept or reject it:

$$s(a_0^{t+1}|e^t) = s(a_1^{t+1}|e^t) = s(e^t) \tag{3}$$

Now, with all the necessary assumptions introduced, we plug Equation (2) and (3) into Equation (1), extract the common decision cost out of the summation, and come to:

$$E(u^t|e^t) = -s(e^t)+p(e^t)r(e^t)+(1-p(e^t))E(u^{t+1}|e^{t+1}) \tag{4}$$

We recursively apply Equation (4) starting from the first lap and obtain:

$$E(u^1|\mathbf{e}) = \sum_{t=1}^{\infty}\left(\prod_{j=1}^{t-1}(1-p(e^j))\right)(-s(e^t)+p(e^t)\,r(e^t)) \tag{5}$$

where $\mathbf{e}$ denotes the vector of all choices on the list. (The summation could alternatively be defined as a finite one if we assume a finite list but the derivation stays the same.)

Since the surplus captures all long-term benefits (via its reward part), u^1 in Equation (5) captures the surplus of the entire list. We explicitly wrote out the dependency of u^1 on all future cards (i.e. all following choices) by expanding "$E(u^1|e^1)$" to "$E(u^1|\mathbf{e})$" for the purpose of clarity.

Finally, from Equation (5), we follow the approach used in [8] by considering optimizing the order of each consecutive choice pair and obtain the IIR-PRP model: assuming that all $p(e^t)$ are greater than 0, $E(u^1|\mathbf{e})$ is maximized when the choices are ranked in decreasing order of:

$$\rho(e^t) \stackrel{\text{def}}{=} r(e^t) - \frac{s(e^t)}{p(e^t)} \tag{6}$$

We have thus mathematically demonstrated that the interface card model is a generalization of the IIR-PRP model. As a remark, although we stated earlier that we would typically need an eye-tracking device to model user interactions at the granularity level of eye movement, it turns out that there's no need for the eye-tracking device under the set of assumptions in this example: the ranking could be pre-generated from the "ρ" values of the choices and never needs to dynamically change according to the user's eye movement.

5. NAVIGATIONAL CARD

We now come to the second instantiation example of the interface card model, where we demonstrate that without assuming "sequential browsing" and given the availability of a richer set of navigational elements, the interface card model can lead to very powerful optimization results that could not be achieved by any existing formal frameworks.

We go back to the classic IR setting where the user is looking for some items using the search engine, but we consider a new popular set of real world scenarios where we have some navigational elements to show on the interface in addition to the items themselves, which we collectively refer to as *tags*. For example, when we are searching for books in an online library catalog, we may use subject headings to quickly narrow down the set of books we need to examine. In a news browsing website, as another example, the news keywords could serve as navigational tags following which the user is able to identify an interesting news article much faster than they could if they are only given an article list, even a well optimized one. In general, these navigational tags themselves are not what the user is looking for, but they are linked to (possibly overlapping) subsets of items into which the user could quickly zoom by selecting the tags.

One key challenge in this setting is that, since the user is now faced with both a list of tags and a list of items, there is no longer a single list of choices which is assumed by [8], and the sequential browsing assumption no longer holds. As a result, many interesting questions regarding how to optimally generate a navigational interface in such cases cannot be answered in a theoretically rigorous way: e.g., (a) how many tags and items should we present in each interface instance, and how do we optimally partition the interface into the tag panel and the item panel? (b) should we allocate a larger proportion of the screen space to tags in smaller screens, and if so, how do we make such adjustment optimally? (c) along the interaction process, do we start by showing tags and then switch to the items when the system becomes more certain about the user's information need, and if so, what would be the optimal time for the switch?

We address all these questions in a novel principled approach by establishing another instantiation of the interface card model that only assumes a "sequential interaction" scheme without going further towards "sequential browsing". We first present a set of assumptions and notations and then demonstrate the effectiveness of our approach.

Definition 5.1 (Block). A *block* b is a display unit on a card representing either a tag or an item that could be selected by the user. A block representing a tag / item is referred to as a *tag / item block*.

Assumption 5.1 (Navigational Card)**.** Each card is a subset of blocks along with their presentation strategy.

The presentation strategy of the blocks on the card is a generalized notion that typically incorporates any ordering and/or panel layout of the blocks. Note that the user may or may not follow any order in examining the blocks (as is assumed in the traditional sequential browsing scheme).

Assumption 5.2 (Selection Action)**.** In each lap t, the user could either select a block on the card q^t or select "next card": $\mathcal{A}(q^t) = q^t \cup \{a_N^{t+1}\}$, where a_N^{t+1} denotes the "next card" action.

From now on, we will directly use q^t to designate the set of blocks on q^t, and we use e to represent items (which we used to represent choices in the previous section). The "next card" action is a generalization of many real world user actions to skip everything shown in the current interaction lap and see more options, e.g. clicking "next page", scrolling down, shifting eye focus one position down, etc.

Definition 5.2 (Preference)**.** The *preference* is the system's estimated probability distribution characterizing the user's interest in each item e. The system relies on the context to progressively update the preference along the interaction process and we designate the preference at lap t by $p(e|c^t)$.

Definition 5.3 (Item Action Model)**.** The *item action model* for item e is the user's action model on the current card given their interest in item e: $p(a^{t+1}|e, q^t)$.

In practice, the item action model serves as the main linkage between our interface model and the item-tag relations. The intuition is that a user interested in a particular item would generally be more likely to select a tag related to the item. Of course, if the item block corresponding to the item itself is displayed on the card, the user would almost always select the item block rather than any tag block. But if neither the item block nor any related tag block is displayed, the user would most likely issue the "next card" action. We will come back to this in more detail later.

The original action model could now be written as the expected item action model, where the expectation is taken with respect to the preference:

$$\begin{aligned} p(a^{t+1}|c^t, q^t) &= \sum_e p(e|c^t, q^t)\, p(a^{t+1}|e, c^t, q^t) \\ &= \sum_e p(e|c^t)\, p(a^{t+1}|e, q^t) \end{aligned} \tag{7}$$

where we assume that (a) the preference is independent of the next card given the context and (b) the item action model is independent of the context given the item of interest to the user, both of which are very reasonable in general.

The rationale underlying such a decomposition of the original action model into two probabilistic models, the preference and the item action model, is two folds. Firstly, by dividing the action model at the item level, we allow for more flexibility in user modeling efforts in practice. Secondly, the decomposition naturally leads to a principled way of updating the preference via Bayes' theorem:

$$\begin{aligned} &p(e|c^{t+1}) = p(e|c^t, q^t, a^{t+1}) \\ &= \frac{p(e|c^t, q^t)\, p(a^{t+1}|e, c^t, q^t)}{p(a^{t+1}|c^t, q^t)} = \frac{p(e|c^t)\, p(a^{t+1}|e, q^t)}{p(a^{t+1}|c^t, q^t)} \end{aligned} \tag{8}$$

where $p(a^{t+1}|c^t, q^t)$ comes from Equation (7) and we adopted the same two assumptions we made in deriving Equation (7).

To make the optimization problem more tractable, we make the following assumption about the reward function to prevent the optimization from depending on future laps:

Assumption 5.3 (Information Gain Reward)**.** The reward of an action is the information gain in the preference distribution estimated in the next lap over the current lap:

$$\begin{aligned} r(a^{t+1}|c^t, q^t) &= \mathit{InfoGain}(\mathbf{p}(e|c^{t+1}), \mathbf{p}(e|c^t)) \\ &= H(\mathbf{p}(e|c^t)) - H(\mathbf{p}(e|c^{t+1})) \end{aligned} \tag{9}$$

where $p(e|c^{t+1})$ comes from (8) and H is the information or entropy function: $H(\mathbf{p}) = -\sum_p p \log p$.

Intuitively, at a high level, the interactive retrieval process resembles an encoding of the user preference: the lower the entropy of the preference, the more the system knows about the user's information need, and the easier it would be for the system to help the user find some interesting items. Therefore, the amount of reduction in the entropy of the preference becomes a natural choice for approximating the reward. (We could have explicitly written out the dependency of the reward on future laps just as what we did in the previous section, but it would make the computation overly complicated and intractable.)

Now, we come to address the problem that the user may not always follow the sequential browsing scheme while examining a card due to the fact that the card may often be more complicated than a simple list. Ideally, we want a "browsing model" to characterize the browsing behavior of users, which may be obtained through user studies or estimated based on interaction logs, but as an initial step along such a generalization direction, we choose to focus on interfaces with a *relatively small capacity* with respect to humans' attention, and we make the following two assumptions:

Assumption 5.4 (Capacity Constraint)**.** The only constraint on the blocks shown on a card is that the total space the blocks occupy does not exceed the capacity of the card:

$$f_c^t(q^t) = \sum_{b \in q^t} w(b) - 1 \tag{10}$$

where $w(b)$ is the space block b occupies relative to the card.

Assumption 5.5 (Uniform Cost)**.** The cost is assumed to be uniform across any action the user issues on a card:

$$s(a^{t+1}|c^t, q^t) = s, \ \forall a^{t+1} \in \mathcal{A}(q^t) \tag{11}$$

A key implication behind the capacity constraint is that, since it serves as the only constraint on the cards, we do not further impose any requirement regarding (a) what proportion of the card should be allocated to tag blocks and item blocks, (b) how many tag blocks and item blocks should be shown on the card, and (c) whether the card should be completely devoted to tag blocks or item blocks. Essentially, there is no presentation strategy - we are setting a completely "flexible" interface layout that our interface card model could freely optimize. (We implicitly assumed that the blocks are all of regular shapes, so that a block could always be packed into the card as long as the amount of space left on the card is no less than the space the block occupies.)

Meanwhile, the uniform cost assumption also has a key implication: we assume the user could browse the blocks on the card in *any* order and, due to the relatively small capacity of the card, it always takes the user a constant, very small amount of attention to browse the blocks and make a decision on what action to issue next no matter what order the user follows in browsing the blocks. In such a way we are effectively relaxing the sequential browsing assumption.

With all the necessary assumptions and definitions laid down, we plug Equation (9), (10) and (11) into Equation (1). It is easily observed that two terms could be extracted out of the summation: (a) the entropy of the current preference, $H(\mathbf{p}(e|c^t))$, and (b) the constant cost, s, and since these two terms do not involve q^t, we could simply remove them from the objective function without affecting the optimization result. Eventually, the final optimization problem for our navigational card becomes:

$$\begin{aligned} \underset{q^t}{\text{minimize}} \quad & \sum_{a^{t+1} \in \mathcal{A}(q^t)} p(a^{t+1}|c^t, q^t)\, H(\mathbf{p}(e|c^{t+1})) \\ \text{subject to} \quad & \sum_{b \in q^t} w(b) - 1 \leq 0 \end{aligned} \tag{12}$$

where $p(a^{t+1}|c^t, q^t)$ and $p(e|c^{t+1})$ respectively come from Equation (7) and (8).

Now, we continue with analytical and real user experiments to demonstrate that Equation (12) leads to very interesting and powerful interface optimization results not achievable by any other existing method in principled ways.

Before we go into real computations, we first need to have (a) an initial preference model as the starting point for the series of context updates along the interaction, and (b) a working item action model. Since this study is not meant to be a user modeling study, from now on we simply assume a flat initial preference distribution:

Assumption 5.6 (Uniform Initial Preference)**.** The initial user preference is uniform across a set of n items, i.e. $p(e_i|c^1) = 1/n, \forall i = 1, 2, \ldots, n$.

In reality, the system usually has a better estimate of the user preference in the initial lap. For example, the a priori information may suggest to the system that the user is generally more interested in certain categories of items. Additionally, in cases of search engines, the system may have estimates of the probability of relevance for each item with respect to the user's query, so that the probability of the user's interest in each item along the ranked list returned by the system should be decreasing. The assumption of uniform initial preference we make here is for the sake of computational convenience; it is solely meant to reduce some distracting details not relevant to the core model.

Definition 5.4 (Item-Tag Map)**.** An *item-tag map* is a weighted bipartite network composed of (a) item nodes and tag nodes respectively corresponding to the set of all items and tags, (b) weighted edges between item and tag nodes if the item and tag they represent are related, with the edge weight quantifying the strength of their relation. A *uniform item-tag map* is an item-tag map in which all edges are of uniform weights. For nomenclature purpose, we say that a tag *covers* an item if there's an edge linking their corresponding nodes in the item-tag map.

Definition 5.5 (Simple Item Action Model)**.** Under the *simple item action model*, given the user's interest in item e and the set of blocks shown on card q^t, the user would issue an action based on the following three rules:

1. If the item block corresponding to e, b_e, is on the card, the user always selects it: if $b_e \in q^t$, then $p(b_e|e, q^t) = 1$; $p(b|e, q^t) = 0, \forall b \neq b_e$; and $p(a_N^{t+1}|e, q^t) = 0$.
2. Otherwise, if the card contains at least one tag block covering e, the user will either select one of these tag block(s) or "next card" with probabilities proportional to the corresponding edge weight(s) in the item-tag map and a predefined parameter ε, respectively:

$$\begin{cases} p(b|e, q^t) = \dfrac{v(e, b)}{\sum_{b' \in q^t} v(e, b') + \varepsilon} & (13) \\ p(a_N^{t+1}|e, q^t) = \dfrac{\varepsilon}{\sum_{b' \in q^t} v(e, b') + \varepsilon} & (14) \end{cases}$$

   where $v(e, b)$ denotes the weight of the edge between the nodes in the item-tag map representing e and b.

3. Otherwise, the user will always select "next card", i.e. $p(a_N^{t+1}|e, q^t) = 1$ and $p(b|e, q^t) = 0, \forall b \in q^t$.

The *simple uniform item action model* denotes the simple item action model on top of a uniform item-tag map, and the *perfect uniform item action model* is the simple uniform item action model with ε set to 0.

We implicitly assumed in the second rule that, in cases of "competing" blocks, i.e. multiple blocks covering the same item simultaneously appearing on the card, the relative tendencies of the user selecting these blocks are kept constant, and equal the relative weights of the corresponding edges in the item-tag map. Such a simplification may not always hold in reality, since the relative tendencies of block selections might depend on the user, the lap, and other blocks on the card; however, it is in general a valid approximation and could greatly simplify the computation.

The user might sometimes accidentally miss a related tag and select "next card", which could be captured using the ε parameter, though we assume that the user would never miss the items they are interested in.

5.1 Analytical Experiments

We apply our result for optimizing navigational cards in some simple example scenarios to analytically demonstrate the effectiveness of the interface card model in generating optimal interactive interfaces. Although it might be possible to develop alternative ad hoc approaches that could result in the very same analytical solutions we derive here, our approach adopts a principled way that is solidly rooted in a theoretical IR model, which no existing approaches could achieve. In this section, we mainly focus on mathematically deriving the optimal conditions for the blocks on the card, and in particular the tag blocks (since the cases for item blocks are generally simpler); we leave the demonstration of our model's effectiveness in automatically generating optimal interface layout in reality to the user study experiment.

To make the presentation cleaner, we omit the lap and context notions in all places: we assume that all the discussion here is about the optimization in the initial lap, and we adopt the *uniform initial preference assumption*. We also adopt the *perfect uniform item action model* for the sake of mathematical convenience. Furthermore, in order to better focus on the most crucial line of the calculation without worrying about any trivial technical details, we assume a "perfect world" of tag navigation:

Assumption 5.1.1 (Complete Tag Set). There always exists some tag that precisely covers any given item subset.

As a consequence, we could entirely focus on deriving the mathematical conditions for the optimal tag(s) we should pick onto the card without worrying about whether such tag(s) actually exist or not in reality.

5.1.1 One Tag Per Card

In this example, we assume that the card only has space for a single tag block:

Assumption 5.1.1.1 (One Tag Per Card). $w(b) = 1, \forall b$.

The optimization question now becomes: what is the optimal number of items the picked tag should cover? If the user is interested in some item covered by the picked tag, then the user will select the tag; otherwise, the user will select "next card". Based on Equation (8), in the first case, the preference is updated to narrow down towards the subset of items covered by the picked tag, and in the second case, the preference narrows down towards the subset of items not covered by the picked tag. Suppose the picked tag covers x items, $x \in \{1, 2, \ldots, n\}$. We plug the entropies of the two updated preference distributions into Equation (12) and after some straightforward algebraic simplifications, the optimization problem becomes:

$$\underset{x}{\text{minimize}} \quad \frac{1}{n}\left(x \log x + (n - x) \log (n - x)\right) \tag{15}$$

We consider Equation (15) as a function of x and extend its domain to real numbers in $[1, n]$. By taking the derivative, we conclude that the minimization solution is:

$$x = \frac{n}{2} \tag{16}$$

Therefore, selecting a tag block covering around half of the items leads to an optimal card. This result shows the model tends to create a balanced partition of the item preference distribution, which coincides with our intuition.

5.1.2 Two Tags Per Card

In this example, we "expand" the card and assume it has space for two tag blocks:

Assumption 5.1.2.1 (Two Tags Per Card). $w(b) = 1/2, \forall b$.

Now, the optimization problem becomes two-folds: (a) how many items should each of the two picked tags cover? and (b) how many items should the two tags' coverages overlap? To answer these two questions, let the number of items covered by the two tags respectively be x and y, $x, y \in \{1, 2, \ldots, n\}$, and let the number of common items covered by the two tags be t, $t \in \{0, 1, \ldots, n\}$, $t \le x$, $t \le y$, $x + y - t \le n$. A crucial difference between this example and the last one is that if the user is interested in some item in the two tags' overlap, the user may select either one of them with equal probabilities, which affects the calculation of the action model and the updated preferences. After some tedious algebraic simplifications, the optimization problem in Equation (12) eventually comes to:

$$\begin{aligned}\underset{x,y,t}{\text{minimize}} \quad \frac{1}{n}\Big(&t \log 2 + (x - \frac{t}{2}) \log (x - \frac{t}{2}) \\ &+ (y - \frac{t}{2}) \log (y - \frac{t}{2}) \\ &+ (n - x - y + t) \log (n - x - y + t)\Big)\end{aligned} \tag{17}$$

Again, we consider Equation (17) to be a function of x, y and t, and we relax the integer constraint. By taking the partial derivatives, without going much into the technical details, we conclude that the final minimization solution is:

$$x = y = \frac{n}{3}, \ t = 0 \tag{18}$$

There are two implications from this result: (a) it reassures that the model would favor a balanced partition of the preference distribution, and (b) it additionally suggests that the model would minimize the partitions' overlaps, coinciding again with our intuition.

5.2 User Study Experiments

To further demonstrate the effectiveness of our interface card model, we built real prototype interface systems based on the navigational card model to show that our model could lead to automatic interface layout adjustment, which no existing method could achieve in a principled way, and we validate the superiority of our automatic interface layout results by comparing them with baseline pre-designed static interfaces in user studies.

The prototype interfaces were built on top of the set of most popular news articles and their associated keywords returned from the New York Times Most Popular API[3], in which the articles and the keywords respectively correspond to the items and the tags in our model. We developed two interfaces with different sizes, a medium sized one[4] and a very small one[5]. We assumed in our implementation that the user would follow the simple uniform item action model, and we heuristically set $\varepsilon = 0.5$.

Though the optimization problem in Equation (12) was shown to have closed form solutions in our two analytical experiments, it is generally difficult to solve for real world scenarios. For building the prototype interfaces, we implemented a straightforward randomized algorithm to tackle the problem. The algorithm heuristically generates multiple candidate cards at each lap, and chooses the one minimizing Equation (12). To obtain each candidate card, the algorithm picks blocks to add to the card one at a time that (a) do not violate the capacity constraint and (b) have a minimal overlap with all blocks that are already picked onto the card (as in line with what we observed in the analytical experiments). Since algorithmic designs are not the focus of this paper, we don't go into all the technical details of our algorithm due to space limitations. However, we point out that the algorithm is very efficient - its time complexity is linear with respect to the input size, i.e. the total number of items and the total number of tags of all items.

5.2.1 Sample Cards

In Figure 1, the left and top-right images are screenshots of an initial interface layout on the medium sized screen and the very small screen, respectively, as automatically determined by the interface card model based on the popular news articles in New York Times and their keywords some time in late January 2015. We see that the algorithm intelligently decided to include only tag blocks on the small

[3]http://developer.nytimes.com/

[4]http://timan102.cs.illinois.edu/yzhng103/fomalhaut/m-times-navigation.php

[5]http://timan102.cs.illinois.edu/yzhng103/fomalhaut/s-times-navigation.php

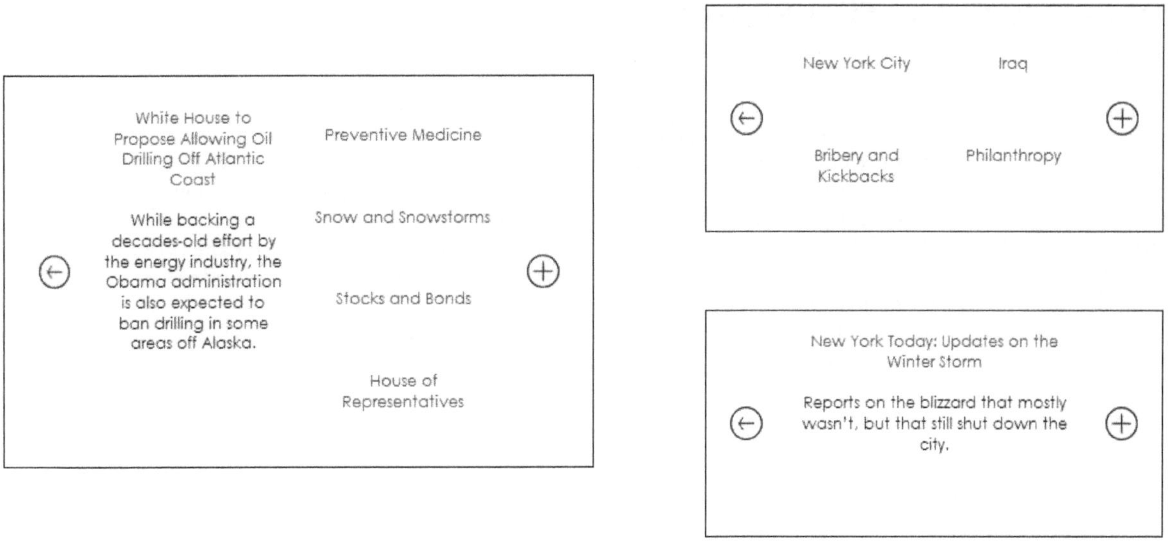

Figure 1: Screen shots of example cards.

screen, but include both tag blocks and item blocks on the medium sized screen. Such a decision makes sense since unless we are relatively sure about what item the user is looking for (which unlikely happens in the initial interaction lap), it would likely be a waste of screen space if specific items are displayed; in contrast, tags are potentially more useful. The bottom-right screenshot in Figure 1 shows an automatic layout adjustment in response to the user's action of selecting the "New York City" tag in the top-right interface. Despite its limited capacity, the screen is entirely filled with an item block because the estimated user preference is narrowed down to only a few items and the system determined that directly showing an item is more beneficial. These results demonstrate that our model can effectively achieve automatic layout adjustment according to both the screen size and the user interaction.

5.2.2 User Studies

We built two baseline interfaces for comparison purpose: one is for the medium sized screen, where we put a separate static tag panel on the right side of the main item panel[6]; for the very small screen, we have either a tag panel or an item panel on the screen at each time, and put a switch button to allow users to switch between the two panels[7]. These two baselines represent popular layouts seen on many mobile interfaces with medium and small screen sizes[8]. We conducted real user experiments on Amazon Mechanical Turk[9] to compare the two baselines with our interfaces (on both medium and small screens) for a task of navigating into the most interesting article that was pre-identified by the user, and we measure the number of interaction laps for the users to reach their target article and compute p-values based on a one-side Wilcoxon sign-ranked test. We also varied the size of the item set to see its impact. The results in Table 1 show that our interface outperforms the baseline interface in all the cases, though with varying significance levels (p-values less than 0.05 are highlighted). It is clearly observed that the superiority of our interface over the baseline interface is higher when the screen is smaller, and is also higher when there are more items.

Table 1: Significance levels of comparison results.

Card size	Item set size	Valid sample size	P-value
Small	20	19	**0.004753**
Small	50	23	**0.0003546**
Medium	20	18	0.09183
Medium	50	20	**0.01097**

We also asked the users survey questions for their opinions on the two types of interfaces to obtain some qualitative comparisons, and a majority of the users indicated that our interface was both quicker and easier to use. For example, one user wrote: "*the interface seemed to intuitively know what article I wanted from just selecting two keywords.*" Many users noted that the baseline interface felt familiar and thus was straightforward to use, but they also pointed out that it did not take much effort to lean how to use our interface: "*at first I was unsure of how I would find my target article but followed my instincts and found it right away.*" The difference in navigational efficiency between the two interfaces was more exaggerated in the very small screen, even in the search space of 20 articles. Since the baseline interface layout does not automatically switch between the keywords and the articles, a lot of users were not able to take full advantage of the keywords and simply ended up being scrolling through the entire article list: "*it seemed like I had to search longer and scroll through almost every article to find the one I wanted.*" In the medium sized screen, even though the baseline interface shows both the tag panel and the article panel, quite a few users noticed the ability of our interface to dynamically change the layout and applauded it: "*I liked that the interface gave such large amount of results when you clicked on a tag.*"

[6]http://timan102.cs.illinois.edu/yzhng103/fomalhaut/m-times-duplex.php
[7]http://timan102.cs.illinois.edu/yzhng103/fomalhaut/s-times-simplex.php
[8]http://itunes.apple.com/app/amazon-mobile/id297606951
[9]http://www.mturk.com/

6. CONCLUSIONS AND FUTURE WORK

We proposed a novel general formal model for optimizing interactive information retrieval interfaces by viewing the interactive retrieval process as a process of a system playing a cooperative card game with a user with the goal of minimizing the user's effort and maximizing the user's gain of relevant information. At each interaction lap, the system would choose an optimal interface card (i.e., an interface instance) to present to the user based on the current context, a model of the user's possible actions on the interface, and a model of the user's gain and effort. The user can then choose an action to take on the prompted interface, which would lead to a new context for the system to choose the next optimal interface card.

We showed that this general interface card model can cover the PRP for Interactive IR as a special case under a set of simplification assumptions, particularly the sequential browsing assumption (thus also easily cover the classic PRP as a more special case). We further derived a novel model for optimizing navigational interfaces that are adaptive to both the screen size and the user's information need. Experimental results with real users show that the proposed model can effectively optimize a navigational interface and is significantly better than baseline static interfaces that are heuristically customized for different screen sizes.

The interface card model is very general and can model interactions at any meaningful granularity level as long as we can define meaningful interface cards and user actions; thus we can model both "micro" interactions at the level of actions such as scrolling up/down inside a page, and "macro" interactions at the level of page navigation. The new model opens up many interesting new directions in optimizing the whole interactive retrieval system through incorporating machine learning and HCI study results. Specifically, the proposed formal framework naturally fits a wide variety of state-of-the-art machine learning techniques, and can easily adopt learning to rank methods [7, 14] and models such as the ostensive model [5] for evolving information needs to further improve the estimate of user preferences. With abundant interaction log data that can be recorded automatically, such learning techniques would provide more accurate estimate of multiple components in the framework. Also, findings from HCI research could be directly incorporated into the constraint part in our optimization problem, providing our model guidance in certain domains that currently could not be formalized in a straightforward way, e.g. learnability concerns, error tolerance, etc. With the general trend in IR pushing researchers to focus more on the interface part and formalize interactive IR, we hope this paper can stimulate alternative and more advanced formalisms for interactive IR to be developed in the coming years (e.g., those in line of economic models for IR [2] and POMDP [15]).

7. REFERENCES

[1] G. Amati and C. J. Van Rijsbergen. Probabilistic models of information retrieval based on measuring the divergence from randomness. *ACM Trans. Inf. Syst.*, 20(4):357–389, Oct. 2002.

[2] L. Azzopardi. Modelling interaction with economic models of search. In *SIGIR '14*, pages 3–12, 2014.

[3] S. Basu Roy, H. Wang, G. Das, U. Nambiar, and M. Mohania. Minimum-effort driven dynamic faceted search in structured databases. In *CIKM '08*, pages 13–22, 2008.

[4] N. J. Belkin, R. N. Oddy, and H. M. Brooks. Ask for information retrieval: Part I.: Background and theory. *Journal of Documentation*, 38(2):61–71, 1982.

[5] I. Campbell and K. V. Rijsbergen. The ostensive model of developing information needs. In *CoLIS 2*, pages 251–268, 1996.

[6] H. Fang and C. Zhai. An exploration of axiomatic approaches to information retrieval. In *SIGIR '05*, pages 480–487, 2005.

[7] N. Fuhr. Optimum polynomial retrieval functions based on the probability ranking principle. *ACM Trans. Inf. Syst.*, 7(3):183–204, July 1989.

[8] N. Fuhr. A probability ranking principle for interactive information retrieval. *Information Retrieval*, 11(3):251–265, 2008.

[9] M. A. Hearst. *Search User Interfaces.* Cambridge University Press, 2009.

[10] D. Hiemstra and W. Kraaij. Twenty-one at TREC-7: ad-hoc and cross-language track. In *TREC-7*, volume 500-242, pages 227–238, 1999.

[11] P. Ingwersen. Cognitive perspectives of information retrieval interaction: elements of a cognitive IR theory. *Journal of Documentation*, 52:3–50, 1996.

[12] X. Jin, M. Sloan, and J. Wang. Interactive exploratory search for multi page search results. In *WWW '13*, pages 655–666, 2013.

[13] A. Kashyap, V. Hristidis, and M. Petropoulos. FACeTOR: Cost-driven exploration of faceted query results. In *CIKM '10*, pages 719–728, 2010.

[14] T.-Y. Liu. Learning to rank for information retrieval. *Found. Trends Inf. Retr.*, 3(3):225–331, Mar. 2009.

[15] J. Luo, S. Zhang, and H. Yang. Win-win search: Dual-agent stochastic game in session search. In *SIGIR '14*, pages 587–596, 2014.

[16] D. McFadden and K. Train. Mixed MNL models for discrete response. *Journal of Applied Econometrics*, 15(5):447–470, 2000.

[17] J. M. Ponte and W. B. Croft. A language modeling approach to information retrieval. In *SIGIR '98*, pages 275–281, 1998.

[18] S. E. Robertson. The probability ranking principle in IR. *Journal of Documentation*, 33(4):294–304, 1977.

[19] S. E. Robertson and K. S. Jones. Relevance weighting of search terms. *Journal of the American Society for Information Science*, 27(3):129–146, 1976.

[20] G. Salton, A. Wong, and C. S. Yang. A vector space model for automatic indexing. *Commun. ACM*, 18(11):613–620, Nov. 1975.

[21] H. Turtle and W. B. Croft. Evaluation of an inference network-based retrieval model. *ACM Trans. Inf. Syst.*, 9(3):187–222, July 1991.

[22] C. Zhai. Statistical language models for information retrieval a critical review. *Found. Trends Inf. Retr.*, 2(3):137–213, Mar. 2008.

From Queries to Cards

Re-ranking Proactive Card Recommendations Based on Reactive Search History

Milad Shokouhi
Microsoft
Cambridge, United Kingdom
milads@microsoft.com

Qi Guo
Microsoft
Bellevue, Washington
qiguo@microsoft.com

General Terms

The growing accessibility of mobile devices has substantially reformed the way users access information. While the *reactive* search by query remains as common as before, recent years have witnessed the emergence of various *proactive* systems such as Google Now and Microsoft Cortana. In these systems, relevant content is presented to users based on their context without a query. Interestingly, despite the increasing popularity of such services, there is very little known about how users interact with them.

In this paper, we present the first study on user interactions with information cards. We demonstrate that the usage patterns of these cards vary depending on time and location. We also show that while overall different topics are clicked by users on proactive and reactive *platforms*, the topics of the clicked documents by the same user tend to be consistent cross-platform. Furthermore, we propose a supervised framework for re-ranking proactive cards based on the user's context and past history. To train our models, we use the viewport duration and clicks to infer pseudo-relevance labels for the cards. Our results suggest that the quality of card ranking can be significantly improved particularly when the user's reactive search history is matched against the proactive data about the cards.

Categories and Subject Descriptors

Information Systems [**Information Retrieval**]: Users and interactive retrieval—*Personalization*

Keywords

Proactive ranking; zero query; Information cards

1. INTRODUCTION

Mobile devices account for a significant fraction of online search and browsing traffic. The number of mobile queries has grown fivefold in the past three years [6]. In fact, the number of mobile queries has recently exceeded the number of those submitted from desktop devices in the United States and many other countries [1].

SIGIR'15, August 09 - 13, 2015, Santiago, Chile.
 ISBN 978-1-4503-3621-5/15/08 ...$15.00.
DOI: http://dx.doi.org/10.1145/2766462.2767705.

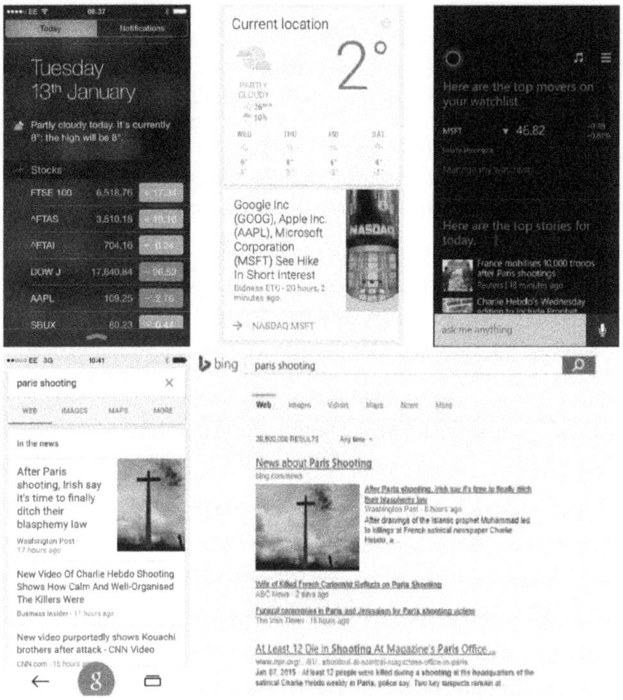

Figure 1: Examples of interfaces with *proactive* "cards" presented respectively in Apple Siri, Google Now and Microsoft Cortana (top). Examples of *reactive* search queries submitted to Google on mobile and Bing on desktop (bottom) for query `paris shooting`.

Consequently, information retrieval systems are constantly evolving into more contextual and mobile-friendly services.

Among recent enhancements, the introduction of *zero-query* systems [8] is arguably one of the most significant breakthroughs. In 2012 at a workshop, a group of 45 leading experts in the field acknowledged zero-query search to be one of the six most interesting research directions in information retrieval (IR).

> "Future information retrieval systems must anticipate user needs and respond with information appropriate to the current context without the user having to enter a query." [8]

The major players in the search industry have embraced the new trends by releasing systems such as Google Now [4], Apple Siri [5] and Microsoft Cortana [2]. In all these systems, in addition to the typical *reactive search* by a query, *proactive information cards* are presented to users based on their context. Proactive systems are typically implemented in form of *apps* that once triggered by the user, present several information cards. Each card is particularly designed to satisfy a domain-specific set of information needs. Many of these apps can also run in the background and pop up certain cards proactively depending on the user's context. The top screenshots in Figure 1 include a few examples of proactive cards from Apple Siri (weather, stocks), Google Now (weather, news) and Microsoft Cortana (stock, news) respectively from left to right. It is worth pointing out that there are no explicit queries associated with these cards. In comparison, the screenshots at the bottom of Figure 1 depict two typical reactive searches on – Google – mobile (left), and – Bing – desktop (right) for query `paris shooting`.

Despite the growing importance and popularity of proactive systems, not much have been published on how users interact with them. In this paper, we present the first study of such kind. We start by investigating various aspects of user engagement with different types of cards. For instance, we show that users are likely to interact with different types of cards depending on the time of the day, and to a lesser degree based on their location. In addition, we demonstrate that while the overall topical distributions of clicked documents differ in reactive and proactive logs, the topics of documents that are clicked by the same user tend to be similar between proactive and reactive interactions.

In the light of observations made in the first part of the paper, we focus on improving the quality of proactive ranking in the second part. We propose Carré, a card reranking model that deploys several features based on the user's context and history to improve the ranking of proactive recommendations. Our experimental results conducted over large-scale logs of a commercial search engine confirm that the reactive search history of users – along with several other contextual features – can be used to improve the ranking of proactive recommendations.

The key research contributions of this paper are fourfold,

- Present the first study of user engagement with proactive cards. In particular, we explore how presentation position, local and temporal aspects can affect the user engagement with cards (Section 4).
- Characterize the cross-platform clicks of users and explore the topical similarity of clicked documents across platforms (Section 5).
- Propose Carré, a card reranking model based on context and past history. Inspired by previous work on search personalization [13, 22], we devise an offline optimization framework for reranking proactive cards based on context (Section 6).
- Evaluate card reranking models by inferring pseudo-relevance labels not only based on clicks, but also by viewport tracking of their mobile screens (Section 7).

The remainder of this paper is structured as follows. We continue by summarizing the most related work in the next section. In Section 3, we define our terminology and explain the user logs that are used in our experiments. We study the card usage patterns with respect to presentation position, time and location in Section 4. We characterize the cross-platform clicks in Section 5 and show that the topics of interest for a user are typically consistent across platforms. We then introduce a supervised model for reranking cards based on the user's context and past history in Section 6, and evaluate its performance in Section 7. We summarize our findings and discuss their limitations in Section 8, and conclude in Section 9.

2. RELATED WORK

While the study of proactive systems, as introduced in this paper, is a new research area, it has roots in earlier research. A proactive system *aggregates* information from multiple sources (e.g., weather, news, sports) as *recommendations* in the form of *cards*, according to *personal* preferences. Hence, our work is related to the areas of aggregated search, information cards, personalization, and recommendations. In this paper, we also focus on predicting future interactions with the cards for this new modality, which is also related to prior work on click prediction. Next, we will discuss the related research in each of the aforementioned areas.

Proactive information retrieval. Rhodes and Maes [37] introduced just in-time information retrieval (JITIR) agents as softwares that proactively retrieve and present relevant information based on the user's context. The context could be inferred based on the content of documents viewed by the user, or physical attributes such as time and location. As in earlier systems [14, 31], Rhodes and Maes [37] focused on textual recommendations such as keywords, emails and documents. However, the content presented in modern information cards is substantially more heterogeneous. The authors nonetheless listed three key features for JITIR namely, (1) proactive (2) non-intrusive, and (3) contextual. that are all still critical in the context of modern proactive systems.

Aggregated search. The proactive system is an aggregator of various types of information that are valuable to the user, such as calendar, weather, news, stocks, and places. Its counterpart for the reactive scenario is the aggregated search, where contents from specialized verticals are blended into organic web search results. Diaz [21] studied the integration of news vertical into web search, and proposed modeling the collection and query dynamics to detect queries with the news intent. Arguello et al. [9] later extended this line of research to integrate various types of verticals, such as news, travel, images, and videos. Ponnuswami et al. [34] proposed a randomized online audition framework for optimizing the aggregated ranking based on clicks.

Information cards. The cards presented proactively do not always need to be clicked to be useful. Sometimes, the displayed content of the card is sufficient to satisfy the user's information need. This is analogous to *good abandonment* [30] in aggregated search, where the aggregated content from verticals do not always need to be clicked to satisfy the user's intent. Recent research by Guo et al. [24] shed some light on this problem on mobile devices. The authors modeled viewing behavior based on touch interactions, and demonstrated the correlation of document relevance and viewport changing patterns on touch-enabled mobile devices. Lagun et al. [29] extended this line of research to model the viewports for inferring user attention and satisfaction on the reactive search engine result pages. In this paper, we incorporate the viewport-based dwell time as card (pseudo) relevance labels to address this long-standing challenge of "good abandonment".

Personalization. Proactive recommendations are highly personalized based on the user interests and context, thus making personalization an integral part the system. In reactive web search, personalization has been well studied for tailoring search results by modeling individual user preferences from history interactions. One of earlier works on leveraging user interaction to infer document relevance is by Fox et al. [22], who showed that the user behavior such as dwell time, has strong association with explicit judgments of satisfaction and can be served as implicit feedback to improve the search experience. Following this research, Xu et al. [48], proposed a method to estimate personalized word-level dwell time from the user's search and browse history. The proposed model can be used to estimate personalized dwell time on new documents to customize search result ranking. More recently, White et al. [46] proposed to model cohorts of users who conduct similar tasks to improve the search personalization.

Recommender systems. The proactive system also shares many properties of typical recommender systems [36]. Similar to such systems, we aim to present the most relevant content to the user in the absence of an explicit query. However, the recommendations in the proactive system are for a smaller set of items that are highly repeatable and heterogeneous, and need to be personalized and contextualized in its ranking. Furthermore, we do not compare preferences across users and items as is common in collaborative filtering systems [40].

Click prediction. Different models have been proposed in previous research to address various biases in presentation which affect the prediction of future click-through. One example is by Chapelle and Zhang [19], in which the authors proposed a Dynamic Bayesian Network model, aiming to recover actual relevance from clicks by separating the modeling of presentation bias in result attractiveness. Our task are similar in that we aim to predict future interactions with cards presented by the proactive system. However, the major differences lie in the lack of explicit queries, leading to heavier contextualized modeling of the user interests, and alleviating the lack of clicks by utilizing viewport-based metrics.

We will revisit this list in the following sections and provide more details about the most relevant studies when appropriate.

3. TERMINOLOGY & DATA

In this section, we introduce the data and the terminology that we use in the rest of of this paper.

Terminology. We follow the common IR terminology when referring to reactive searches. Each reactive search *impression* consists of a query submitted by a user at a given time and location, together with all clicks and interaction signals that were collected on those results. Clicks followed by a dwell time of 30 seconds or longer are considered as satisfied (SAT) clicks.[1] As in previous work [17, 35, 45], a *session* is defined as a sequence of impressions with no interval of inactivity longer than 30 minutes.

For proactive scenarios we borrow the same terminology and apply similar constraints. A proactive impression consists of a ranking of cards presented to the user together with corresponding interaction logs recorded such as clicks, viewports and scrolling. Viewport tracking is enabled through JavasScript embedded in the proactive impressions, and the viewport data is buffered and then sent back to the server through HTTP requests. We record the screen size, the positions and sizes of the cards rendered on the proactive impressions in pixels, as well as the viewport changing events with timestamps, allowing us to reconstruct the viewing behavior of the users and calculate the time users spent dwelling on each card.

While reactive impressions start with a query, a proactive impression is triggered when the user launches the app (e.g. clicking on Google Now, or Cortana icons). Consistent with the proactive scenario, a session is comprised of all user interactions with the cards with no interval of inactivity longer than half an hour. In our *cross-platform* analysis, we monitor the behavior of the same users in reactive and proactive sessions.

[1]In this paper, clicks always mean SAT clicks regardless of whether they are on card or on a document.

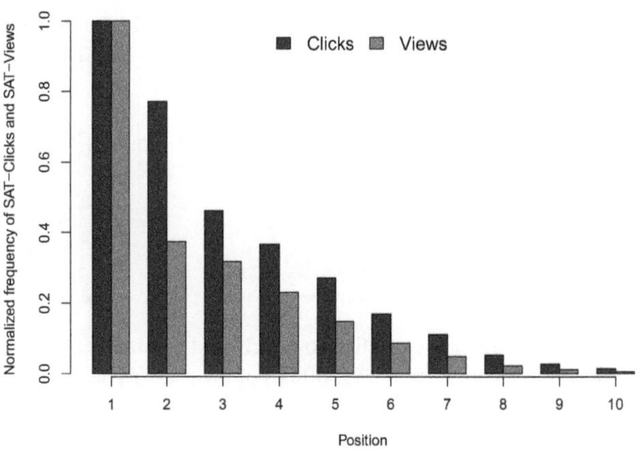

Figure 2: The relative SAT-click and SAT-view frequency recorded across different positions. The numbers are re-scaled with respect to frequency at the first position.

User logs. For our experiments we first sampled 365,612 unique users randomly from the proactive logs of Microsoft Cortana [2]. We then collected all proactive history of these users between 08 Nov 2014 – 7 Dec 2014 (1 month). In total, there are 2,663,472 proactive impressions in our dataset. We use the first week of data to study the general card usage patterns (Section 4). The remaining impressions from the last three weeks (811,681 impressions in total after removing impressions with no engagement[2]) are used to train and evaluate our card reranking models (Section 6).

We also extracted the reactive history of this set of users from the query logs of Bing search engine between 1 Sep 2014 – 31 Oct 2014. We deliberately chose an earlier non-overlapping period to avoid any potential patterns that might be caused by general temporal trends rather than user related factors. Each user is distinguished by a unique and anonymized identifier (based on Microsoft Live ID) which is common across Bing and Cortana platforms. This *user-ID* is persistent across both sets of logs and can be used to join all related information about a user. Therefore, the reactive search history of users can be easily compared against their proactive activities. In total, there are 4,113,977 reactive (search) impressions in our dataset.

4. PROACTIVE INTERACTIONS

In order to learn effective models for ranking cards, it is essential to understand how users interact with them. While reactive query logs have been extensively studied [10, 27, 28], to the best of our knowledge, there is no previous published work on proactive cards. This section aims to analyze the user interaction with proactive cards and verify if similar patterns hold in general. We later use the insights obtained from these analyses to generate effective features for ranking cards.

For the experiments in this section, we only report the results for seven types of cards namely: sports, places, calendar, finance, news, traffic, and weather. These are the most popular cards in terms of user interactions, and represent more than 80% of proactive *engagement* (clicks, views) in our dataset. The *sports* card, shows

[2]SAT click or long dwell on viewport.

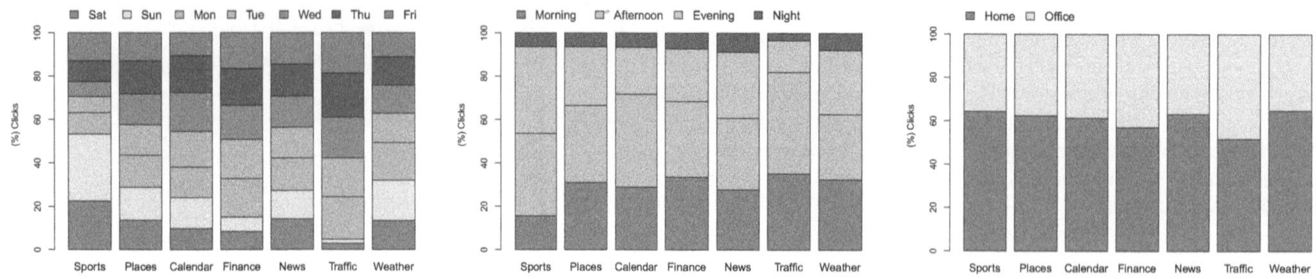

Figure 3: The percentage of clicks on each card given the day of the week (left) and time of day (middle). The percentage of clicks on each card given the location (home vs. office) of the user (right).

the latest scores and fixtures for the team(s) specified by the user. The *places* card recommends restaurants and points of interests nearby based on the user's current location as identified by GPS. The *calendar* card lists the upcoming events and appointments, while the *finance* card tracks the latest stock values for the corporation(s) pre-specified by the user. The *news* card presents the most recent headlines, while the *weather* and *traffic* cards provide forecasts and updates based on the user's current location and most frequently visited destinations (e.g. home and work).

The effect of card position. The click distributions on different positions of search results have been well-studied in the past. Agichtein et al. [7] showed that the click distribution on search results is significantly *top-heavy* where the top-ranked documents account for most of the clicks. Joachims et al. [28] explained the skewed distribution by associating it to both relevance and *position bias*. Similar trends have been reported on other ranking platforms such as auto-completion [26] and mobile search results [29]. In the latter case, it is worth pointing out that the authors mostly focused on gaze and viewport rather than clicks. Interestingly, they reported trends that, contrary to previous studies, were not monotonically decreasing by position.

In Figure 2 we repeat a similar analysis on cards. For now, please focus on the blue bars and ignore the red ones as we will come back to them later. Here, the x-axis corresponds to the card position (in the ranking of cards presented to the user), and the y-axis shows the relative click frequency on that position. The frequencies are normalized so that the click frequency at the top position is equal to 1. The trends are consistent with those reported in the past for search queries [7, 28]. Most of the clicks are recorded on the top positions and cards presented at lower ranks get relatively little engagement. However, further investigation would be needed to distinguish the impact of position bias from relevance.

Temporal & local trends. The user interests and engagement are affected by various factors. For instance, Beitzel et al. [10] showed that users are likely to query for different topics depending on the time of the day. Similarly, Halvey et al. [25] reported that users web surfing patterns and browsed documents vary depending on time. We verify if the same patterns exist for proactive cards. Figure 3 (left) depicts the percentage of clicks on each card on different days of the week. The boxes in each column are color coded according to the day of the week and their total value sums to one. It is immediately apparent that the card usage varies depending on the day. For example, the traffic card is used on weekdays most often, while the sports card is more likely to be used during weekends. The news and weather cards have roughly uniform usage throughout the week, while the finance card has relatively little engagement during the weekends. This is consistent with findings of Mei and Church [32] on reactive logs that suggested users issue more entertainment-related and fewer business-related queries during weekends.

The middle plot in Figure 3 provides a similar breakdown but for time of the day. We divide the day into four parts based on the time as follows: Morning (6-12], Afternoon (12-18], Evening (18-24], and Night (24-6]. It turns out that users are more likely to click on traffic and finance cards in the morning. The latter is consistent with the observations of Beitzel et al. [10] on search logs, that suggested users are more likely to issue finance-related queries in the morning. Among the cards, news and sports have highest engagement during evening hours whereas the calendar and traffic cards are used more often in the afternoon. Note that the ranking of cards presented to each user does not vary significantly over time in our datasets. On average, more than 82% of cards presented in two consecutive impressions are the same (usually with updated content). The position of a card in the ranking is also fairly stable. On average, the rank of a card changes by *half* a position in two consecutive proactive impressions. The overall trends do not substantially vary either. For instance, the finance and sport cards respectively appear in 2.5%–2.6% and 2.5%–4.9% of daily impressions, although as we observed, their click likelihood could be very different on each day. Therefore, we are confident that the trends observed here are mostly due to temporal factors.

Similar to time, the impact of user location on search behavior has been the subject of extensive research [12, 38, 44]. Cho et al. [20] reported that the mobility of users is mostly centered around two locations: home and work. Therefore, we devote our focus to card usage patterns at work and at home. We infer the centroid of the GPS data from the user in the evening as home, and the centroid of the GPS data during the day as office. Further details of our location inference models are beyond the scope of this paper, but similar approaches can be found elsewhere [20]. We consider the area within 1*km* radius of the user's home location as home area. The office area is defined similarly based on the inferred work location of the user. The right plot in Figure 3 illustrates the percentage of card usage split between home and work. The results suggest that – ignoring clicks from miscellaneous locations – two-third of card clicks take place at home and one-third at the office. Overall, there seems to be very little difference between cards in terms of their usage patterns with respect to the user's location. The only exceptions are the finance and traffic cards, that are split roughly 50-50 between home and office.

The left and middle plots in Figure 3 reveal strong temporal changes in card usage. However, they provide no details about temporal dynamics of engagement by the same user. In Figure 4 we investigate the distribution of temporal gaps between two consecutive clicked proactive impressions from the same user. On the

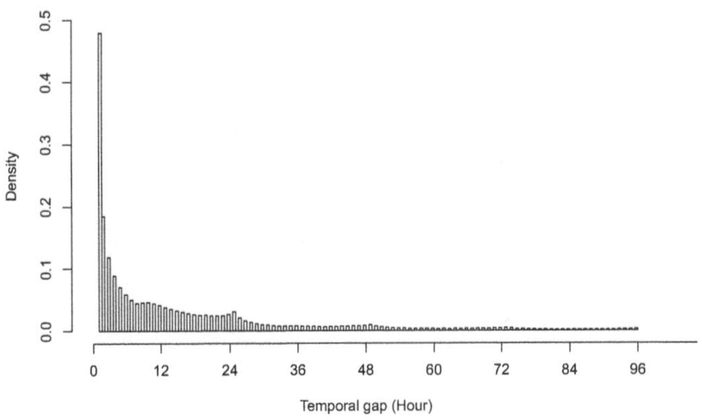

Figure 4: The temporal gap between the last click and the next click on cards. The x-axis is in hours and the y-axis shows the density of clicks that fall in hourly interval.

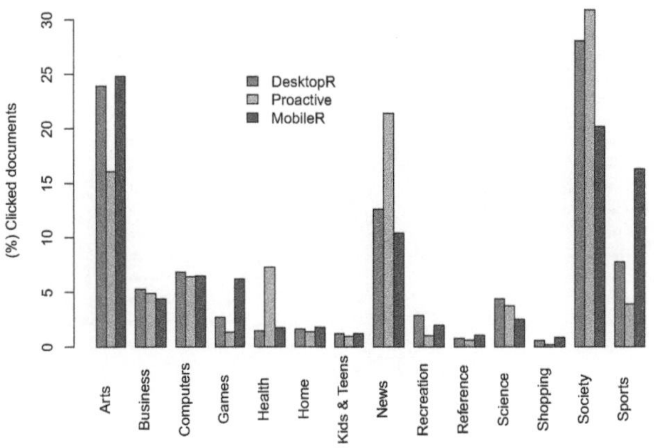

Figure 5: The distribution of ODP categories for documents clicked across different platforms.

x-axis we have the temporal gap (in hours), and on the y-axis we show the density of consecutive impressions that fall in that bucket. The results show that once the user clicks on a card, the next clicked impression is most likely to appear within an hour. It is also interesting to note the spikes around 24, 48, and 72 hours, suggesting that many users engage with the cards at the same time of the day.[3]

Overall, the results summarized in this section suggest that the dynamics of user interactions with the cards, follow similar patterns to those observed previously in reactive search logs.

5. CROSS-PLATFORM CLICKS

Thus far we have shown that the user engagement with the cards varies depending on the time and to a less extent based on location. Next, we investigate the topics of documents that users click on in their proactive impressions and compare them against their reactive history. It is important to note that not all the cards direct the user to a document. For instance, the traffic and finance cards direct the user to an app. Therefore, for this part of study, we limit ourselves to clicks from sports, news and places cards. We use the top level categories from the Open Directory Project (ODP) [3] to represent the document topics. To train topic classifiers, we followed the approach suggested by Bennett et al. [11] and used a 2008 crawl of ODP that was split into a 70%–30% train/validation set. We too discarded the `Regional` class as it is not topical which leaves us with 14 categories overall. For each topic, we train a logistic regression classifier with L2 regularization. We then run each clicked document in proactive and reactive impressions against all these classifiers and assign it to the topic that receives the highest score.

To distinguish between patterns that can be attributed to using different devices (Mobile vs. Desktop), rather than different platforms (reactive vs. proactive), we further divide the reactive user history based on the device on which the document was clicked. We respectively use DesktopR and MobileR to refer to documents that were clicked on desktop and mobile devices in reactive impressions. Figure 5 compares the topical categories of documents clicked on different platforms. It is evident that the overall distribution is different across platforms, although it is more similar between reactive impressions from mobile and desktop. There are certain categories such as `Health` and `News` that appear relatively more often among the documents clicked in proactive impressions. In contrast, categories such as `Art`, `Games` and `Sports` are relatively under-represented. The comparison between MobileR and DesktopR impressions confirm that users click on different types of documents on different devices. Similar argument can be made about the proactive-reactive differences although it should be noted that distribution of proactive clicks is also affected by what was presented to users in the cards.

Figure 5 illustrates the overall topical distribution of clicked documents aggregated over all users. However, it does not inform us about how the same user accesses information on different devices and platforms. Wang et al. [43] and Montanez et al. [33] studied the topics of documents that users click on cross-device. Here, we perform the same comparison cross-platform; that is, between proactive and reactive impressions. On each platform we discard all but the strongest ODP category associated with each user. For each pair (M_p, M_q) of the three modalities, (Proactive, MobileR and DesktopR), we calculate the Normalized Point-wise Mutual Information (NPMI), to measure the association of a pair of ODP categories (o_i, o_j) conditioned on the pair of modalities. The NPMI value is denoted as the output of function N, using the following formula:

$$N(o_i, o_j \mid M_p, M_q) = \frac{\log \frac{P(o_i, o_j \mid M_p, M_q)}{P(o_i \mid M_p, M_q) P(o_j \mid M_p, M_q)}}{-\log P(o_i, o_j \mid M_p, M_q)} \qquad (1)$$

The value of N ranges between -1 and 1, where 1 indicates that the two categories completely co-occur given the two modalities, -1 indicates that the two categories occur separately but not together, and 0 indicates that the two categories are independent. We visualize the cross-platform NPMI values for each pair of platforms and across all topics as heatmaps in Figure 6. The right diagonals of the three heatmaps have the darkest colors, indicating that, overall, the same category is clicked by the user across all pairs of modalities.

The consistency of the topics viewed cross-platform by the user suggests that the users' reactive history might provide useful signals for ranking their proactive recommendations. In the next sections, we put this assumption to the test.

[3]The data gets sparser and skewed towards 'heavy' users for longer periods. Therefore, we left the study of longer intervals (e.g. weekly/monthly) for future work.

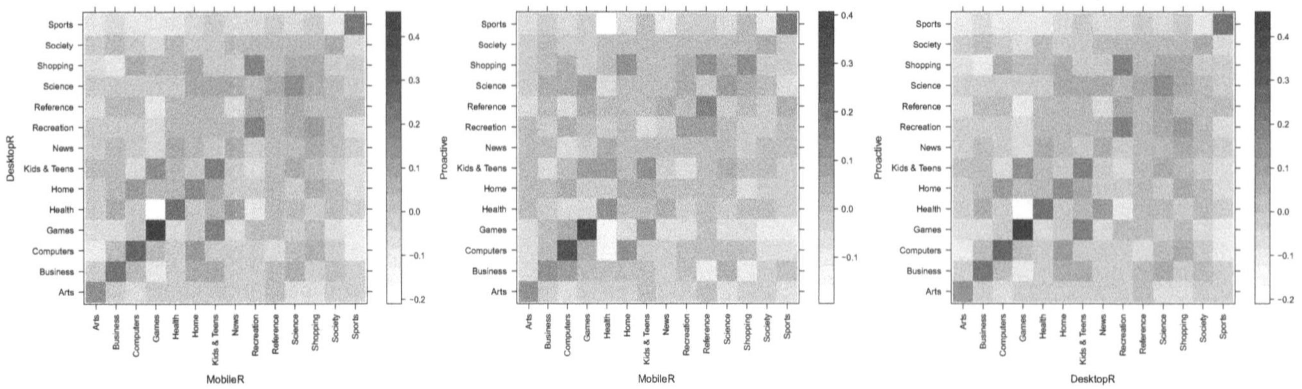

Figure 6: The ODP categories of documents clicked by the same user across different platforms. The colors in the heatmaps represent the normalized point-wise mutual information (NPMI) gains, where darker means higher.

Table 1: Offline labeling of proactive cards based on clicks (left). The ranking produced by Carré for the same impression (right). The reciprocal rank of each ranking is computed based on clicks and presented in the last row.

Position	Baseline (π)	Clicked	Carré (π^*)
1	Weather	(✗)	Weather
2	Finance	(✗)	News
3	News	(✓)	Calendar
4	Calendar	(✗)	Finance
5	Places	(✗)	Places
RR (E)	0.33		0.5

6. RERANKING PROACTIVE CARDS

The results described so far suggest that the user's engagement with the cards is subject to various factors such as time, location, and position. They also reveal that the documents that are clicked by a user across proactive and reactive platforms tend to be consistent in terms of topicality. In this section, we use these insights to develop features that can be used to train a supervised model for reranking cards. We will refer to our trained model for card reranking as Carré.

Formal definition. Given a set of proactive cards $\mathcal{C}$, and the ranking produced over them by a default ranker $\pi(\mathcal{C})$, our task is to learn a reranking model F (a.k.a. Carré) that reorders this list – if necessary – based on available features Θ. The reranker is optimized towards a pre-defined metric E, so that its produced ranking $\pi^*(\mathcal{C})$ outperforms the original order with respect to that metric. That is,

$$\pi^*(\mathcal{C}) = F(\pi(\mathcal{C}), \Theta) \quad \textit{where,} \quad E(\pi^*(\mathcal{C})) > E(\pi(\mathcal{C})) \qquad (2)$$

Therefore, to optimize Carré (F), the first question that needs to be addressed is the choice of optimization metric E and labels.

Pseudo-relevance labels. Collecting context sensitive labels for training personalized rankers is not trivial. Different users in similar context (or even the same user in different contexts) may prefer different cards. The previous work in reactive search personalization addresses this problem by relying on clicks and inferring pseudo-relevance labels [12, 13, 38, 42]. Fox et al. [22] showed if a user dwells on a clicked document for longer than 30(s), that document is likely to be relevant. Inferring implicit labels for proactive cards is an open question. We apply the following three strategies in our experiments:

- **SAT-Clicks ($\mathcal{R}_c$):** We adopt the common click-based strategy for labeling cards. For each proactive impression in our logs, we consider clicked cards with $\geq$ 30(s) dwell time as relevant and others as non-relevant.

- **SAT-Views ($\mathcal{R}_v$):** The main problem with SAT-clicks is that there are many type of cards that do not require a click to satisfy the user's information need. For instance, although clicking on the weather card provides more details about the upcoming forecast, the current temperature is often what the user is looking for and it is always available on the card. This is analogous to the *good abandonment* phenomenon [30] in aggregated search, where the results of some verticals may not require a click to satisfy users. To remedy this issue, we rely on the viewport information to measure how long the user had the card visible on the screen during a proactive impression. Lagun et al. [29] demonstrated that viewport duration and gaze duration are highly correlated. While the authors did not specify a particular threshold for mapping viewport duration to relevance, previous work suggests that for short text segments – roughly the size of a paragraph – display time of $\geq$ 30(s) is a good indicator of relevance and is potentially more accurate than gaze for that purpose [16]. Therefore, we generate a second set of labels based on the viewport time. Cards with viewport duration $\geq$ 30(s) are considered as (pseudo) relevant and the others as non-relevant.[4] The red bars in Figure 2 depict the distributions of SAT-Views generated from viewport duration for cards presented at different positions. The trends are similar to what we observed for SAT-Clicks (blue bars) although the drop at position two is more substantial.

- **SAT-Hybrid ($\mathcal{R}_h$):** This approach combines the two options above and considers all cards with a SAT-Click or a SAT-view as (pseudo) relevant.

[4]Experiments using a tighter threshold ($\geq$ 15 seconds) produced similar results, and hence are excluded.

Table 2: The features used for reranking cards by Carré. The suits in brackets specify the experimental group that each feature belongs to. Note that the textual and topical features are only available to cards that recommend web documents and are left blank otherwise.

Feature	Group	Description
ReactiveImpressionCount	(♣)	No. previous reactive search impressions by the user.
DesktiopImpressionCount	(♣)	No. previous reactive search impressions by the user issued from desktop.
MobileImpressionCount	(♣)	No. previous reactive search impressions by the user issued from a mobile device.
ReactiveDomainMatches	(♣)	No. domains (e.g. cnn.com) that appear in the card and have been clicked by the user in reactive logs.
PrevCardClicks	(♠)	Number of previous clicks by the user on this type of card.
ProactiveImpressionCount	(♠)	No. previous proactive impressions by the user.
ProactiveDomainMatches	(♠)	No. domains (e.g. cnn.com) that appear in the card and have been clicked by the user in proactive logs.
HuDist	(♥)	2 features indicating the distance from the user's home, and office (in kilometers).
IsTimeOfDay	(♥)	4 binary features indicating the time of day ∈{morning, afternoon, evening, night}.
IsDayOfWeek	(♥)	7 binary features indicating the day of week ∈{Sat, Sun, ···, Fri}.
TemporalGap	(♥)	Time elapsed since the last proactive impression by the user (in hours).
Position	(■)	The position of card in the impression presented to the user.
CardCount	(■)	The number of cards presented to the user in the proactive impression.
IsCardType	(■)	12 binary features generated for the most popular cards (e.g. IsSports).
IsOtherType	(■)	A binary feature that is set to one only if none of the IsCardType features is 1.
NumActiveDays	(■)	No. days with at least one impression in user's proactive and reactive history.
ImpressionNo	(■)	No. previous proactive impressions in the same session.
StaticRank	(■)	Computed based on number of SAT-Clicks and SAT-Views recorded on that type of card during the training period.
ReactiveTermMatch	(♦, ♣)	No. overlapping terms in URL-titles presented in the card and clicked URLs in reactive history (weighted by freq).
ProactiveTermMatch	(♦, ♠)	No. overlapping terms in URL-titles presented in the card and clicked URLs in proactive history (weighted by freq).
ReactiveCatMatch	(♦, ♣)	Similar to ReactiveTermMatch but computed based on the ODP categories assigned to URLs.
ProactiveCatMatch	(♦, ♠)	Similar to ProactiveTermMatch but computed based on the ODP categories assigned to URLs.

While admittedly none of these approaches are ideal, we believe that they provide a reasonable benchmark for first step experimentation in this direction. We leave further investigation of the right labeling strategy as future work.

Given that than 2/3 of proactive impressions in our logs have only one card with a positive label (Hybrid-SAT = *true*), we decided to pick mean reciprocal rank (MRR) as our evaluation metric E. RR is defined as the reciprocal rank of the highest-ranked relevant card in an impression, and is considered as 0 in the absence of positive labels. MRR is computed by averaging RR over the test impressions. Our choice is in line with several previous works on search personalization that also used MRR as their evaluation metric [12, 38, 39, 42].

Training. To train Carré, we sampled proactive impressions from the logs of a commercial search engine as described in Section 3. Each impression consists of a unique and persistent user identifier that can be matched against reactive logs, a set of cards that were presented to the user, and the related click statistics and time-stamps. The relevance labels are assigned to the cards based on clicks and viewport duration as explained above. We then train a model that learns to rank the (pseudo) relevant cards on top based on available features and penalizes their demotion. Table 1 illustrates our labeling and evaluation process in a toy example. Here, the sampled impression contains 5 cards that were presented to a user. Among them, the user had a SAT-Click (or a SAT-View) on the news card which was shown at the third position (Hence, RR = $1/3 = 0.33$). Suppose that Carré has taken this impression along with the available features and reranked it as it is displayed on the right column of the table. Here, since the news card is placed higher at the second position we consider the ranking to be more effective than the original order (RR = $1/2 = 0.50$).

We chose LambdaMART [47] as our preference learning model. LambdaMART is a learning to rank approach based on gradient boosted decision trees and is an extension to LambdaRank [15]. It has been shown to be one of the most effective models for learning to rank [18], and has been a common choice among previous work on personalized ranking [12, 13, 38, 39, 42]. We performed a parameter sweep over the number of trees {20,100,500}, number of leaves per tree {2,4,8,···,128}, the learning rate {0.02,0.05,0.1,0.4} and the minimum number of instances per leaf {1,10,50} over our validation datasets to tune the parameters. We split the proactive logs explained in Section 3 based on time-stamps into three sets for training, validation and testing. Impressions collected between 15 Nov 2014 – 21 Nov 2014 were used for training (291,039 in total), those collected between 22 Nov 2014 – 28 Nov 2014 (248,353 in total) were used for validation, and the remainder of impressions logged between 29 Nov 2014 – 7 Dec 2014 (272,289 in total) were used for testing and generating the reported results.

Features. Our experiments in the previous sections highlighted various factors that can affect the user engagement with the cards. Inspired by those observations we develop several features that can be used for card reranking in Carré. The comprehensive list of features is provided in Table 2, although in general they can be all summarized in five overlapping groups:

- Reactive history (♣): These are features that are generated based on the reactive search history of the user collected separately as described in Section 3.
- Proactive history (♠): These are features that are generated based on the last two weeks proactive history of the user.
- Lexical/Topical features (♦): These features are generated based on lexical and topical similarity between the URLs presented in the card, and documents clicked by the same user in previous proactive and reactive impressions. They are only available for cards that contain URL links and are set to zero elsewhere.
- Local/Temporal features (♥): These features are generated based on the time and the location of user when the proactive impression was presented.
- Constant features (■): Features that do not belong to any of the categories above (e.g. card position).

We can draw connection between many of the features used in our model to those deployed previously in the search personalization literature. For instance, the ProactiveCatMatch and ReactiveCatMatch features are similar to category-query features used by Bennett et al. [11]. The ReactiveDomainMatches and ProactiveDomainMatches features are related to the personal navigation models [41] but here we compute them at the domain level. Moreover, Position and ImpressionNo are both commonly used for reranking search results [11, 12, 38, 39, 42]

Baselines. We compare our results against two baselines. Our first baseline which we refer to as the *Default-ranker* is the original ranking of cards before ordering (middle column in Table 1). The Default-ranker is the production ranker of a commercial system (Cortana) that is already trained to produce the best ranking of cards at each impression. As our second baseline we use a static ranking of cards which produces the same ordering across all impressions. We count the number of times that each type of card receives SAT-Clicks or SAT-Views in our training period, and then rank the cards in all our testing impressions accordingly. We refer to this baseline as *Static-ranker* in our experiments. The effectiveness of Static-ranker highlights how well such non-personalized usage-based rankers can perform in the absence of other contextual signals.

7. EXPERIMENTS

We now focus on evaluating the effectiveness of our card reranking models. We begin our analysis by comparing Carré against our baselines. Given the proprietary nature of the Default-ranker, we do not disclose its absolute MRR, but instead compare the performance of other models against it in terms of relative changes in MRR. The results in Table 3 show that regardless of how the (pseudo) relevance labels are assigned, Carré outperforms the Default-ranker. The gains range between 6%-10% in terms of MRR and are all statistically significant according to the t-test ($p < 0.01$). The Static-ranker is significantly outperformed by the Default-ranker on all metrics ($p < 0.01$) which confirms the quality of the original rankings produced by the production system.

To verify if the gains and losses are distributed uniformly across users we decided to group users based on their *loyalty*. We ranked users in terms of the number of their proactive impressions in our logs. We then assigned the users in the top 15% and the bottom 15% of this ranking to separate groups that we respectively refer to as *Head* and *Tail*. Table 4 compares the performance of different approaches on Head and Tail user groups. Once again, the results are presented in terms of relative changes in MRR with respect to Default-ranker and all differences are statically significant except for one case (Carré, Tail users, $\mathcal{R}_v$). Carré consistently outperforms the Default-ranker on both sets of users. The gains are more substantial on the Head set across all metrics. This is expected as most of the proactive/reactive history (♣, ♠) and lexical/topical features (♦) are set to their default values for the Tail users due to lack of enough historical data. In addition, it can be noted that the gains are higher on the click-based evaluations ($\mathcal{R}_c$). Given that clicks can be considered as a more direct feedback from the user compared to the relatively more noisy labels inferred from viewport, perhaps it is not surprising to see the click-based models to be most effective. The performance of the Static-ranker is less affected by the user group, although the overall numbers follow similar trends.

Feature analysis. We demonstrated that the rankings produced by Carré consistently outperform both baselines on all metrics and user groups. Next we investigate which feature groups contribute most to these gains.

Table 3: The effectiveness of card re-ranking models against the Default-ranker. The gains and losses are only reported in relative delta values (ΔMRR%) to respect the proprietary nature of the baseline ranker. The MRR values computed based on SAT-Clicks, SAT-Views and SAT-Hybrid label sets ($\mathcal{R}_c$, $\mathcal{R}_h$, $\mathcal{R}_h$) are grouped separately. All differences are statistically significance ($p < 0.01$) according to the pair t-test.

	ΔMRR ($\mathcal{R}_c$)	ΔMRR ($\mathcal{R}_v$)	ΔMRR ($\mathcal{R}_h$)
Static-Ranker	▼ -0.72%	▼-13.24%	▼-1.59%
Carré	▲10.85%	▲ 6.88%	▲ 8.71%

Table 4: The effectiveness of Carré against the baseline ranker for different groups of users (Head vs. Tail). The gains and losses are only reported in relative delta values (ΔMRR). Statistically significance gains and losses according to the pair t-test ($p < 0.01$) are respectively denoted by ▲ and ▼.

	ΔMRR ($\mathcal{R}_c$)	ΔMRR ($\mathcal{R}_v$)	ΔMRR ($\mathcal{R}_h$)
Head users			
Static-Ranker	▲ 2.12%	▼ -2.82%	▲ 1.52%
Carré	▲19.69%	▲16.35%	▲17.69%
Tail users			
Static-Ranker	▼-1.57%	▼-8.86%	▼-3.47%
Carré	▲ 3.96%	0.22%	▲ 0.79%

We train separate rankers by excluding all features from each feature group and compare them with a Carré model trained over the complete feature set. The results are summarized in Table 5. As before, statistically significant differences (losses) according to the t-test ($p < 0.01$) are distinguished by ▼. Dropping the features from the constant group (■) hurts the performance more than any other subset regardless of the choice of labels. In particular, Position (original rank) is the most influential feature which is consistent with prior work on search personalization [12, 13, 38, 42]. The temporal/local (♥) features have the least impact on performance which is expected as none of them are card-specific. Features based on reactive history of the user (♣) are at least as effective as those generated based on the proactive history (♠). This is notable as it suggests that the previous search history of the users can be used for reranking cards, and is particularly useful for the first time users of proactive recommendations. Dropping all lexical/topical features (♦) computed over the reactive and proactive search history of users, substantially degrades the performance on all metrics. This confirms that the fact that the same user browses similar topics across platforms (Figure 6) can be used to improve their proactive recommendations.

8. DISCUSSION

The results presented so far, confirm the effectiveness of Carré for reranking proactive cards across all metrics. However, as we noted in Section 6, the click-based (pseudo) relevance labels may not be appropriate for evaluating all types of cards, and while the viewport-based measures partially address this problem, they are yet to be carefully tested on proactive scenarios. The threshold we picked was based on previous work on short segments of text [16], however different values might be discovered to be more suitable in proactive mobile settings.

Table 5: The effectiveness of card re-ranking models trained excluding the specified features against the Carré ranker trained with all features. The gains and losses are only reported in relative delta values (ΔMRR) against the Carré model trained with all features. Statistically significant differences ($p < 0.01$) according to the pair t-test are denoted by ▼.

	ΔMRR ($\mathcal{R}_c$)	ΔMRR ($\mathcal{R}_v$)	ΔMRR ($\mathcal{R}_h$)
Carré (−♠)	▼-1.04%	-0.04%	▼-0.69%
Carré (−♣)	▼-0.99%	-0.25%	▼-0.94%
Carré (−♦)	▼-7.15%	▼ -5.71%	▼-6.58%
Carré (−♥)	▼-0.28%	0.23%	▼-0.13%
Carré (−■)	▼-7.85%	▼-10.06%	▼-7.90%

Table 6: The accuracy of news click prediction models trained excluding the specified features against the classifier trained with all features (bottom row). All differences are statistically significant according to the McNemar's Chi-Square (χ^2) test.

	Accuracy	ΔAccuracy
Carré (−♠)	0.7980	▼-0.86%
Carré (−♣)	0.7988	▼-0.77%
Carré (−♦)	0.7932	▼-1.46%
Carré (−♥)	0.7997	▼-0.65%
Carré (−■)	0.7829	▼-2.74%
The accuracy when trained with all features: 0.8050		

To remedy this issue, we decided to conduct another experiment in which we exclusively focus on predicting clicks on news cards. Focusing solely on news would allow us to simplify the problem to a binary classification task. We also would not need to worry about the viewport-based metrics, as our news cards are clickable[5] and take the users directly to documents for which we know SAT-click signals can be used reliably to infer relevance [11–13, 22, 39, 46]. Therefore, we updated our experimental datasets described in Section 3 to form new sets that only include data for the news cards. The details of training/validation/testing split remain unchanged and the list of features stays identical. Instead of training a ranker based on boosted decision trees (LambdaMART [47]), we train a binary classifier based on gradient boosted decision trees [23]. The parameter sweep is performed over the same set of ranges that was specified in Section 6.

The motivation here is that if clicks on news cards can be predicted accurately, one can use this information to demote/promote their positions accordingly. The results in Table 6 show the click prediction accuracy of multiple Carré classifiers trained over different subsets of features. Accuracy is defined as the ratio of cards that were correctly classified ($\frac{\textit{True positives}+\textit{True negatives}}{\textit{All}}$) and the bottom row contains the accuracy of Carré when trained with all features. McNemar's Chi-Square (χ^2) confirms that all differences are statistically significant ($p < 0.01$) against this full model that we consider as our baseline.[6]

Overall, the results are consistent with our previous experiments. Excluding the constant (■) and lexical/topical (♦) features degrades the accuracy more than any other feature group. The temporal/local (♥) features have the lowest impact while proactive (♠) and reactive (♣) features make similar contributions to accuracy. Using AUC as metric instead of accuracy led to similar conclusions. For instance, AUC dropped from 0.6909 to 0.6660 (▼-3.60%) in the absence of lexical/topical features (♦), and dropped to as low as 0.5987 (▼-13.34%) when constant features were excluded. We skip more details for brevity.

[5]We ignore the potential *headline glance* interactions here.

[6]We used the t-test previously for measuring the statistical significance of differences in our ranking experiments. However, it is not applicable to this classification task.

9. CONCLUSIONS

In this paper, we presented the first analysis on user interactions with proactive cards. We found several resemblances between the user interaction patterns with proactive cards and those recorded from reactive search logs. We demonstrated that similar to reactive search results, proactive card rankings also have a top-heavy click distribution. We also showed that similar to search queries, the card usage patterns are affected by temporal and local dynamics. For instance, there are certain cards (e.g. finance) that are likely to be clicked by the user in the morning, or at work. Furthermore, we investigated the topics of documents clicked by the user in different platforms and discovered that users are consistent across platforms in terms of the topics they interact with.

In the second half of our study, we used the insights obtained in the first half to develop features that can be used for reranking cards. We proposed a new approach for inferring the relevance of a presented card based on the user's click and viewport duration. We then deployed these implicit labels in a supervised framework for reranking cards. Our experimental results confirmed the effectiveness of our method (Carré) and showed that it consistently produces better results than the original ranker (and a static baseline). They also confirmed that features generated based on the reactive search history of users can be used to improve their proactive card recommendations.

There are several directions for future work. Inferring implicit relevance labels for proactive cards is still an open question. We tried to address that by adopting common techniques and thresholds based on previous studies on text, and also focusing exclusively on the news cards for some parts of this work. However, further investigations would be needed to better understand the user's interaction with the cards in order to derive realistic user models and metrics. While all our experiments were based on synthetic inferred labels, it would be important to assess our findings with real users in a user study or on live user traffic. In addition it would be useful to collect the proactive and reactive history of users over an extended and consistent range of dates to measure the impact of short-term and long-term history in each of these platforms. Last but not least, we demonstrated that the reactive history of users can be used to improve their proactive ranking; it would be interesting to investigate if the reverse holds true as well.

Acknowledgments. The authors are grateful to Peter Bailey, Sebastian Blohm, and Zeynab Raeesy for their thoughtful feedback on the first draft of this paper.

References

[1] Google, Inside AdWords. http://bit.ly/1JrajCg/. Accessed: 2015-05-14.

[2] Cortana - Microsoft - USA. http://www.microsoft.com/en-us/mobile/campaign-cortana/. Accessed: 2015-05-14.

[3] DMOZ - the Open Directory Project. http://www.dmoz.org/. Accessed: 2015-05-14.

[4] Google now. https://www.google.com/landing/now/. Accessed: 2015-05-14.

[5] Apple - iOS 8 - Siri. https://www.apple.com/ios/siri/. Accessed: 2015-05-14.

[6] 2013 Strategic Imperative: Marketing as Applied Science | RKG Blog. http://bit.ly/1AnYMNZ, 2013. Accessed: 2015-05-14.

[7] E. Agichtein, E. Brill, S. Dumais, and R. Ragno. Learning user interaction models for predicting web search result preferences. In *Proc. SIGIR*, pages 3–10, Seattle, WA, 2006.

[8] J. Allan, B. Croft, A. Moffat, and M. Sanderson. Frontiers, challenges, and opportunities for information retrieval: Report from swirl 2012 the second strategic workshop on information retrieval in lorne. *SIGIR Forum*, 46(1):2–32, May 2012.

[9] J. Arguello, J. Callan, and F. Diaz. Classification-based resource selection. In *Proc. CIKM*, Hong Kong, China, 2009.

[10] S. M. Beitzel, E. C. Jensen, A. Chowdhury, D. Grossman, and O. Frieder. Hourly analysis of a very large topically categorized web query log. In *Proc. SIGIR*, pages 321–328, Sheffield, UK, 2004.

[11] P. N. Bennett, K. Svore, and S. T. Dumais. Classification-enhanced ranking. In *Proc. WWW*, pages 111–120, Raleigh, NC, 2010.

[12] P. N. Bennett, F. Radlinski, R. W. White, and E. Yilmaz. Inferring and using location metadata to personalize web search. In *Proc. SIGIR*, pages 135–144, Beijing, China, 2011.

[13] P. N. Bennett, R. W. White, W. Chu, S. T. Dumais, P. Bailey, F. Borisyuk, and X. Cui. Modeling the impact of short- and long-term behavior on search personalization. In *Proc. SIGIR*, pages 185–194, Portland, OR, 2012.

[14] J. Budzik and K. Hammond. Watson: Anticipating and contextualizing information needs. In *Proc. ASIS*, volume 36, pages 727–740, 1999.

[15] C. Burges, R. Ragno, and Q. Le. Learning to rank with non-smooth cost functions. In *Advances in Neural Information Processing Systems 19*. MIT Press, Cambridge, MA, January 2007.

[16] G. Buscher, L. van Elst, and A. Dengel. Segment-level display time as implicit feedback: A comparison to eye tracking. In *Proc. SIGIR*, pages 67–74, 2009.

[17] L. D. Catledge and J. E. Pitkow. Characterizing browsing strategies in the world-wide web. *Comput. Netw. ISDN Syst.*, 27(6):1065–1073, Apr. 1995.

[18] O. Chapelle and Y. Chang. Yahoo! Learning to Rank Challenge Overview. In *Proceedings of the Yahoo! Learning to Rank Challenge*, pages 1–24, Haifa, Israel, 2011.

[19] O. Chapelle and Y. Zhang. A dynamic bayesian network click model for web search ranking. In *Proc. WWW*, pages 1–10, Madrid, Spain, 2009.

[20] E. Cho, S. A. Myers, and J. Leskovec. Friendship and mobility: User movement in location-based social networks. In *Proc. KDD*, pages 1082–1090, San Diego, CA, 2011.

[21] F. Diaz. Integration of news content into web results. In *Proc. WSDM*, pages 182–191, Barcelona, Spain, 2009.

[22] S. Fox, K. Karnawat, M. Mydland, S. Dumais, and T. White. Evaluating implicit measures to improve web search. *ACM Trans. Inf. Syst.*, 23(2), Apr. 2005.

[23] J. H. Friedman. Greedy function approximation: a gradient boosting machine. *Annals of Statistics*, pages 1189–1232, 2001.

[24] Q. Guo, H. Jin, D. Lagun, S. Yuan, and E. Agichtein. Mining touch interaction data on mobile devices to predict web search result relevance. In *Proc. SIGIR*, pages 153–162, Dublin, Ireland, 2013.

[25] M. Halvey, M. T. Keane, and B. Smyth. Time based patterns in mobile-internet surfing. In *Proc. CHI*, pages 31–34. ACM, 2006.

[26] K. Hofmann, B. Mitra, F. Radlinski, and M. Shokouhi. An eye-tracking study of user interactions with query auto completion. In *Proc. CIKM*, pages 549–558, Shanghai, China, 2014.

[27] B. J. Jansen, A. Spink, and T. Saracevic. Real life, real users, and real needs: A study and analysis of user queries on the web. *Inf. Process. Manage.*, 36(2):207–227, Jan. 2000.

[28] T. Joachims, L. Granka, B. Pan, H. Hembrooke, F. Radlinski, and G. Gay. Evaluating the accuracy of implicit feedback from clicks and query reformulations in web search. *ACM Trans. Inf. Syst.*, 25(2), Apr. 2007.

[29] D. Lagun, C.-H. Hsieh, D. Webster, and V. Navalpakkam. Towards better measurement of attention and satisfaction in mobile search. In *Proc. SIGIR*, pages 113–122, Gold Coast, Queensland, Australia, 2014.

[30] J. Li, S. Huffman, and A. Tokuda. Good abandonment in mobile and pc internet search. In *Proc. SIGIR*, pages 43–50, 2009.

[31] H. Lieberman. Autonomous interface agents. In *Proc. CHI*, pages 67–74. ACM, 1997.

[32] Q. Mei and K. Church. Entropy of search logs: How hard is search? with personalization? with backoff? In *Proc. WSDM*, pages 45–54, Palo Alto, CA, 2008.

[33] G. D. Montanez, R. W. White, and X. Huang. Cross-device search. In *Proc. CIKM*, pages 1669–1678, Shanghai, China, 2014.

[34] A. K. Ponnuswami, K. Pattabiraman, Q. Wu, R. Gilad-Bachrach, and T. Kanungo. On composition of a federated web search result page: Using online users to provide pairwise preference for heterogeneous verticals. In *Proc. WSDM*, Hong Kong, China, 2011.

[35] F. Radlinski and T. Joachims. Query chains: Learning to rank from implicit feedback. In *Proc. KDD*, pages 239–248, Chicago, Illinois, USA, 2005.

[36] P. Resnick and H. R. Varian. Recommender systems. *Commun. ACM*, 40(3):56–58, Mar. 1997.

[37] B. J. Rhodes and P. Maes. Just-in-time information retrieval agents. *IBM Syst. J.*, 39(3-4):685–704, July 2000.

[38] M. Shokouhi. Learning to personalize query auto-completion. In *Proc. SIGIR*, pages 103–112, Dublin, Ireland, 2013.

[39] M. Shokouhi, R. W. White, P. Bennett, and F. Radlinski. Fighting search engine amnesia: Reranking repeated results. In *Proc. SIGIR*, Dublin, Ireland, 2013.

[40] X. Su and T. M. Khoshgoftaar. A survey of collaborative filtering techniques. *Adv. in Artif. Intell.*, 2009:4:2–4:2, Jan. 2009.

[41] J. Teevan, D. J. Liebling, and G. Ravichandran Geetha. Understanding and predicting personal navigation. In *Proc. WSDM*, pages 85–94, Hong Kong, China, 2011.

[42] L. Wang, P. N. Bennett, and K. Collins-Thompson. Robust ranking models via risk-sensitive optimization. In *Proc. SIGIR*, Portland, OR, 2012.

[43] Y. Wang, X. Huang, and R. W. White. Characterizing and supporting cross-device search tasks. In *Proc. WSDM*, pages 707–716, Rome, Italy, 2013.

[44] I. Weber and C. Castillo. The demographics of web search. In *Proc. SIGIR*, pages 523–530, Geneva, Switzerland, 2010.

[45] R. W. White and S. M. Drucker. Investigating behavioral variability in web search. In *Proc. WWW*, pages 21–30, Banff, Alberta, Canada, 2007.

[46] R. W. White, W. Chu, A. Hassan, X. He, Y. Song, and H. Wang. Enhancing personalized search by mining and modeling task behavior. In *Proc. WWW*, pages 1411–1420, Rio de Janeiro, Brazil, 2013.

[47] Q. Wu, C. J. Burges, K. M. Svore, and J. Gao. Adapting boosting for information retrieval measures. *Inf. Retr.*, 13(3):254–270, June 2010.

[48] S. Xu, H. Jiang, and F. C. M. Lau. Mining user dwell time for personalized web search re-ranking. In *Proc. IJCAI*, pages 2367–2372, Barcelona, Catalonia, Spain, 2011.

Author Index

Aberer, Karl 1037
Agichtein, Eugene ... 483, 855, 1143
Aiello, Luca Maria 173
Akbari, Mohammad 213
Albakour, M-Dyaa 711
Al-Dhelaan, Mohammed 715
Allan, James 503
Allegretti, Marco 719
Alonso, Omar 1089, 1145
Altingovde, Ismail Sengor 739
An, Xiangdong 883
Arapakis, Ioannis 203
Arguello, Jaime 23, 1147
Arkhipova, Olga 723
Arkoudas, Konstantine 1075
Arora, Piyush 1051
Awadallah, Ahmed Hassan 523
Azarbonyad, Hosein 727
Azzopardi, Leif 183, 293, 767, 903, 1107
Badache, Ismail 731
Baeza-Yates, Ricardo 123, 1093
Bagdouri, Mossaab 1053
Bah, Ashraf 735
Bai, Xiao 203
Bailey, Peter 655
Baillie, Lynne 843
Bakkal, Emre 739
Ballatore, Andrea 1101
Barreda-Ángeles, Miguel 203
Baruah, Gaurav 675
Barzegar, Siamak 1027
Bast, Hannah 243
Batko, Michal 1039
Belkin, Nicholas J. 1
Bendersky, Michael 423, 1121
Bennett, Paul N. 787
Berberich, Klaus 1149
Bernardi, Lucas 1097
Bhamidipati, Narayan 383
Blanco, Roi 173, 1047
Boldi, Paolo 173
Bolshinsky, Ella 665
Bouadjenek, Mohamed Reda 803
Boughanem, Mohand 731
Bravo-Marquez, Felipe 743
Bron, Marc 293
Bruintjes, Robert-Jan 955
Brusilovsky, Peter 1155
Buchhold, Björn 243
Büttner, Fritjof 955
Callan, Jamie 605, 771
Cambazoglu, B. Barla 153, 203
Canuto, Sérgio 333
Capra, Robert 23
Carmel, David 1143
Carterette, Ben 735, 747
Cataldi, Mario 1101
Catena, Matteo 751
Cavedon, Lawrence 991
Caverlee, James 233, 1149
Chakraborty, Anirban 755
Chandar, Praveen 735
Chang, Yi 123, 143, 503, 1073
Chen, Chao 303
Chen, Hsin-Hsi 759
Chen, Ye 493
Chen, Yu-Ren 759
Chen, Zhumin 343
Cheng, Jian 1019
Cheng, Xueqi 113, 403
Cheng, Zhiyong 1029
Chow, Chi-Yin 443
Chua, Tat-Seng 213
Chuklin, Aleksandr 1111, 1113
Clarke, Charles L. A. ...555, 675, 827, 1117, 1143
Cocks, Bernadine 967
Cohl, Howard S. 951
Cong, Gao 433
Cormack, Gordon V. 555, 763
Craswell, Nick 863
Crescenzi, Anita 23, 767, 1055
Croft, W. Bruce 927, 1035
Dai, Zhuyun 771
Daniel, Tal 665
Davis, Brian 1027, 1045
Davis, Chad 1097
de Rijke, Maarten 33, 93, 263, 273, 293, 955, 975, 995, 1111, 1113
de Vries, Arjen 293, 783, 1047
Dean-Hall, Adriel 827
Dehghani, Mostafa 727
Deng, Hongbo 123, 143
Di Nunzio, Giorgio Maria 1031
Di Santo, Giovanni 775
Dias, Gaël 823, 911
Diaz, Fernando 1141, 1147
Djuric, Nemanja 383
Dong, Anlei 123, 143
Dorando, Jonathan J. 1075
Dori-Hacohen, Shiri 1057
Drutsa, Alexey 779
Du, Jia Tina 967
Du, Xiaoyong 879
Dungs, Sebastian 13
Efron, Miles 645, 1149
Eickhoff, Carsten 13, 783
Elnikety, Sameh 63
Elsweiler, David 133
Engels, Gregor 831
Eswaran, Dhivya 787
Eugster, Manuel J. A. 1043
Fang, Anjie 791
Fayazi, Amir 233
Ferrari, Stéphane 823
Ferraro, Gabriela 803
Foley, John 423
Frank, Eibe 743
Freitas, Andre 1027, 1045
Fu, Yun 875
Fukumizu, Kenji 815
Fuxman, Ariel 595
Ganguly, Debasis 795
Gao, Liangcai 585
Gao, Ning 799
Gao, Wei 1003
Ghosh, Kripabandhu 755
Gionis, Aristides 851
Głowacka, Dorota 1043
Golestan Far, Mona 803
Goncálves, Marcos André 333, 353
Goyal, Amit 143
Grauer, Lidia 723
Grbovic, Mihajlo 383

Groenland, Carla 955
Grossman, Maura R. 555, 763
Grotov, Artem 273
Guan, Chu 983
Gunter, Carl A. 143
Guo, Chun 807
Guo, Jiafeng 113, 403
Guo, Lifan 393
Guo, Qi 695
Gupta, Manish 1033, 1121
Guy, Ido 665, 855
Gwizdka, Jacek 811, 1151
Habel, Philip 791
Hadjigeorgieva, Maria 719
Halvey, Martin 843
Han, Jiawei 143
Hanbury, Allan 103
Handschuh, Siegfried 1027, 1045
Hansen, Niels Dalum 625
Hara, Kazuo 815
Harel, Maayan 819
Harman, Craig 919
Harvey, Morgan 133
Hasanuzzaman, Mohammed 823
Hashemi, Seyyed Hadi 827
Hauff, Claudia 133, 1023, 1149
Hauger, David 947
Haussmann, Elmar 243
Hawking, David 803, 1077
He, Jiyin 293
He, Qi 1007
He, Yuxiong 63
Hearst, Marti A. 1145
Heindorf, Stefan 831
Helmer, Sven 163
Hiemstra, Djoerd 1097
Hoenkamp, Eduard 835
Hofmann, Katja 463
Hofmann, Thomas 783
Hsieh, Hsun-Ping 839
Htun, Nyi Nyi 843
Huang, Jimmy Xiangji 883
Huang, Shanshan 343
Hung, Nguyen Quoc Viet 1037
Izhutov, Pavel 979
Jacucci, Giulio 1043
Jansen, Aren 919
Järvelin, Kalervo 903
Jiang, Yexi 323
Jiang, Zhuoren 585
Jones, Gareth J. F. 795
Jones, Timothy 847
Jose, Joemon M. 7191151
Josifovski, Vanja 423
Kamps, Jaap ...727, 827, 1097, 1145
Kanhabua, Nattiya 915
Kantor, Paul B. 1125
Kanza, Yaron 855
Kaski, Samuel 1043
Kawale, Jaya 875
Kazantsev, Gary 1075
Kelly, Diane 183, 767, 1141
Keskustalo, Heikki 903
Kharitonov, Eugene 453, 473
Kim, Hyun Duk 393
Kim, Jin Young 1129
Kim, Yubin 771
Kiseleva, Julia 827, 979
1059, 1097
Knees, Peter 1133
Kobayashi, Kei 815
Kong, Weize 143, 503
Kostakis, Orestis 851
Kotov, Alexander 253, 413
Kovacek, Ivan 1097
Kravi, Elad 855
Krishnaswamy, Shonali 433
Krstovski, Kriste 859
Kukushkin, Vladimir 635
Kuralenok, Igor 723
Kurtz, Michael J. 859
Kuznetsov, Mikhail 979
Lagun, Dmitry 483
Lan, Weiyu 879
Lan, Yanyan 113, 403
Larsen, Birger 625
Lavrenko, Victor 907
Lee, Chia-Jung 863
Lee, Kyumin 233
Levin, Roy 665
Li, Cheng-Te 839
Li, Dongsheng 303
Li, Hang 1071
Li, Houqiang 53
Li, Jingfei 871
Li, Jiyi 867
Li, Lei 323
Li, Liangda 123
Li, Pengfei 1061
Li, Qiuchi 871
Li, Rui 503
Li, Sheng 875
Li, Tao 323
Li, Xiao-Li 433
Li, Xirong 879
Li, Xutao 433
Liao, Lejian 575
Liao, Shuai 879
Limsopatham, Nut 791
Lin, Chin-Yew 575
Lin, Jimmy 645, 1147
Lin, Xuemin 999
Lioma, Christina 625
Lipani, Aldo 103
Lipka, Nedim 1035
Líška, Martin 1063
Liu, Baiyan 883
Liu, Chao 1079
Liu, Junming 983
Liu, Mengwen 533
Liu, Tie-Yan 343
Liu, Xiaoguang 1015, 585, 807
Liu, Xin 887
Liu, Yiqun 193, 283, 493
Liu, Zeyang 193
Lu, Hanqing 1019
Lu, Kai 891
Lu, Shiyong 413
Lu, Xiaolu 1065
Lucchese, Claudio 73, 895
Luo, Jie 503
Luo, Jiyun 1049
Lupu, Mihai 103
Lv, Qin 303
Lv, Yuanhua 595
Ma, Jun 343
Ma, Shaoping 193, 283, 493
Maarek, Yoelle 1105
Macdonald, Craig 453, 473, 711
751, 775, 791
Maddalena, Eddy 565

Maiya, Arun S. 899
Makarenkov, Victor 1137
Makhani, Asif 1081
Malherbe, Emmanuel 1101
Mann, Gideon 1075
Marinho, Leandro 1155
Markl, Volker 951
Markov, Ilya 1111, 1113
Martins, Wellington 333
Marx, Maarten 727
Maxwell, David 903
McAuley, Julian 43
McCann, Julie A. 83
McCreadie, Richard 775
Megorskaya, Olga 635
Mehrotra, Rishabh 545
Mei, Tao 53
Meij, Edgar 33, 263
Mejer, Avihai 855
Mika, Peter 1047
Mitra, Bhaskar 3
Mitra, Mandar 795
Mizzaro, Stefano 565
Moens, Marie-Francine 363
Moffat, Alistair 655, 931
Mohan, Aravind 413
Moradi, Pooya 1011
Moran, Sean 907
Moreno, Jose G. 911
Moschitti, Alessandro 373, 959
Moshfeghi, Yashar 719
Mostafa, Javed 1151
Mueller, Melanie J.I. 1097
Murdock, Vanessa .. 863, 1083, 1149
Myllymäki, Petri 1043
Nandagopal, D (Nanda) 967
Nardini, Franco Maria 73, 895
Nejdl, Wolfgang 153
Ngo, Chong-Wah 53
Ngo, Vuong M. 163
Nguyen, Tu Ngoc 915
Nie, Jian-yun 283
Nie, Liqiang 213
Niederée, Claudia 915
Nikolaev, Fedor 253
Novak, David 1039
Nyberg, Eric 513
Oard, Douglas W. 799, 919
Odijk, Daan 33
Ofek, Nir 1137
Oosterhuis, Harrie 955
Orlando, Salvatore 73, 895
Ounis, Iadh 453, 473, 711
775, 791
Paik, Jiaul H. 615
Pal, Aditya 923
Pan, Yingwei 53
Paritosh, Praveen 1143
Park, Dae Hoon 393, 533
Park, Jae Hyun 927
Parra, Denis 1155
Parui, Swapan Kumar 755
Pasi, Gabriella 719
Peetz, Maria-Hendrike 975
Pelleg, Dan 855, 1143
Peltonen, Jaakko 1043
Peña-Araya, Vanessa 935, 1041
Pereda-Baños, Alexandre 203
Perego, Raffaele 73, 895
Petri, Matthias 931
Pfahringer, Bernhard 743
Pfeiffer III, Joseph J. 787
Pham, Tuan-Anh Nguyen 433
Poblete, Barbara 935, 1041
Pollick, Frank E. 719
Potthast, Martin 831
Qin, Yongrui 1007
Qiu, Shuang 1019
Quezada, Mauricio 935, 1041
Radlinski, Filip 463
Radosavljevic, Vladan 383
Rahman, M. Ataur 939
Reijonen, Aki 1043
Reinanda, Ridho 263
Ren, Shaolei 63
Ren, Zhaochun 93
Riezler, Stefan 943
Rocha, Leonardo 353
Rodrigues, Victor 353
Roegiest, Adam 555
Rosa, Thierson 333
Roy, Dwaipayan 795
Ruotsalo, Tuukka 1043
Saha, Sriparna 823
Sales, Juliano Efson 1027, 1045
Salles, Thiago 353
Sanderson, Mark 847, 991
Sankepally, Rashmi 919
Sanne, Scott 803
Santos, Wisllay 333
Schamoni, Shigehiko 943
Schedl, Markus 947, 1133
Scholer, Falk 565, 655, 847
Schubotz, Moritz 951
Schuth, Anne 463, 955
Sedhai, Surendra 223
Serdyukov, Pavel 453, 473, 635
723, 1085
Severyn, Aliaksei 373, 959
Shakery, Azadeh 1011
Shang, Li 303
Shapira, Bracha 1137
Shemshadi, Ali 1007
Shen, Dou 1087
Shen, Jialie 1029
Sheng, Quan Z. 1007
Sherman, Garrick 645
Shi, Qinfeng ('Javen') 43
Shokouhi, Milad 695
Shokouhi, Milad 963, 1149
Shovon, Md. Hedayetul Islam 967
Si, Luo 575
Sijaranamual, Isaac 33
Silvestri, Fabrizio 383
Simonsen, Jakob Grue 625
Smith, David A. 859
Smucker, Mark D. 675, 1117
Soboroff, Ian 1157
Song, Dandan 575
Song, Dawei 871
Song, Xuemeng 213
Spina, Damiano 975, 991
Spirin, Nikita 979
Spirin, Yaroslav V. 979
Squicciarini, Anna 233
Stafseng Einarsen, Mats 1097
Stein, Benno 831
Stones, Rebecca J. 1015
Sun, Aixin 223
Sun, Jiashen 493
Sun, Jing 983

Sun, Pengyu 1015
Suzuki, Ikumi 815
Szpektor, Idan 1143
Tan, Jiwei 987
Tang, Jinhui 493
Tang, Liang 323
Targett, Christopher 43
Teevan, Jaime 1071
Thang, Duong Chi 1037
Thomas, Paul 655, 847
Thomee, Bart 1149
Tonellotto, Nicola 73, 751, 895
Tong, Jiancong 1015
Toroslu, Ismail Hakki 739
Tran, Cong-Nguyen 955
Tran, Giang 153
Tran, Vu 13
Trattner, Christoph 1155
Trevisiol, Michele 173
Trippas, Johanne R. 991, 1067
Trotman, Andrew 1147
Tsagkias, Manos 995
Turk, Ata 153
Turpin, Andrew 565
Tuzhilin, Alexander 1097
van den Hengel, Anton 43
van der Velde, Jos 955
van Dijk, David 995
van Doorn, Joost 955
Vardell, Emily 23
Vasa, Parth 1075
Veeling, Bas 955
Veijalainen, Jari 343
Venturini, Rossano 73
Vijayalakshmi, Ramasamy 967
Visser, Dale 899
Volkovs, Maksims N. 313
Vorobev, Aleksandr 473
Vulić, Ivan 363
Vuurens, Jeroen B. P. 1047
Wan, Andrew 899
Wan, Shengxian 403
Wan, Xiaojun 987
Wang, Chao 283
Wang, Gang 1015
Wang, Haohong 533
Wang, Jingang 575
Wang, Liang 971
Wang, Meng 283
Wang, Pengfei 403
Wang, Qifan 575
Wang, Shuaiqiang 343
Wang, Shuxin 891
Wang, Xianzhi 1007
Wang, Yang 999
Wang, Yulu 645
Wechsler, Roger 955
Wei, Zhongyu 1003
Weidlich, Matthias 1037
White, Jerome 919
White, Ryen W. 523, 963
Whiteson, Shimon 273
Wilson, Max L. 939, 1151
Woudenberg, David 955
Wu, Lin 999
Wu, Shu 971
Wu, Wei 887
Xia, Long 113
Xiao, Jianguo 987
Xiong, Hui 983
Xiong, Yun 983
Xu, Jun 113, 403
Xu, Song 971
Yan, Rui 839
Yang, Gang 879
Yang, Hui 1049, 1157
Yang, Zaihan 413
Yang, Zi 513
Yao, Lina 1007
Yao, Ting 53
Yilmaz, Emine 545, 963, 1117,1129
Yom-Tov, Elad 819
Youssef, Abdou 951
Yu, Guang Wei 313
Yu, Weiren 83
Yulianti, Evi 1069
Yun, Jeong-Min 63
Zamani, Hamed 1011
Zeng, Chunqiu 323
Zezula, Pavel 1039
Zha, Hongyuan 123
Zhai, ChengXiang 393, 533, 543, 685
Zhang, Aston 143, 503
Zhang, Jia-Dong 443
Zhang, Lanbo 891
Zhang, Luming 213
Zhang, Min 193, 493
Zhang, Peng 871
Zhang, Qing 999
Zhang, Rui 1015
Zhang, Wenjie 999
Zhang, Xi 1019
Zhang, Yi 891
Zhang, Yinan 685
Zhang, Yinglong 811
Zhang, Zhiwei 575
Zhao, Yingying 303
Zhao, Yue 1023
Zheng, Guoqing 605
Zhiltsov, Nikita 253
Zhou, Andrew Jie 1049
Zhou, Ke 193, 283
Zhu, Xiaofei 915
Zhu, Xuan 493
Zhu, Yangyong 983
Zhu, Zhenfeng 1019
Zuccon, Guido 1107

www.ingramcontent.com/pod-product-compliance
Ingram Content Group UK Ltd.
Pitfield, Milton Keynes, MK11 3LW, UK
UKHW051420290926
15471UKWH00009B/1704

9 781450 338882